ELLINGER'S MODERN BANKING LAW

Ellinger's Modern Banking Law

Fifth Edition

E.P. ELLINGER, EVA LOMNICKA,

AND

C.V.M. HARE

OXFORD

UNIVERSITY PRESS

Great Clarendon Street, Oxford OX2 6DP

Oxford University Press is a department of the University of Oxford.
It furthers the University's objective of excellence in research, scholarship,
and education by publishing worldwide in

Oxford New York

Auckland Cape Town Dar es Salaam Hong Kong Karachi
Kuala Lumpur Madrid Melbourne Mexico City Nairobi
New Delhi Shanghai Taipei Toronto

With offices in

Argentina Austria Brazil Chile Czech Republic France Greece
Guatemala Hungary Italy Japan Poland Portugal Singapore
South Korea Switzerland Thailand Turkey Ukraine Vietnam

Oxford is a registered trade mark of Oxford University Press
in the UK and in certain other countries

Published in the United States
by Oxford University Press Inc., New York

Database right Oxford University Press (maker)

Second edition 1995
Third edition 2002
Fourth edition 2006

British Library Cataloguing in Publication Data
Data available

Library of Congress Cataloging in Publication Data
Data available

Typeset by Newgen Imaging Systems (P) Ltd, Chennai, India
Printed in Great Britain
on acid-free paper by
Ashford Colour Press Limited, Gosport, Hampshire

ISBN 978-0-19-923209-3

1 3 5 7 9 10 8 6 4 2

Contents

Part I Banks and Banking Business

Anti money Laundey

Part III The Bank as Financier and Lender in Domestic Transactions

Preface to the Fifth Edition

Since Professor Peter Ellinger first published this text in 1987, various chapters of the book have passed through the hands of different co-authors, yet the overall structure of the book and much of the detailed discussion remains true to the original text. It is for this reason that the fifth edition continues to bear Professor Ellinger's name, despite him having handed over the overall responsibility for the book to his co-authors. Professor Eva Lomnicka has taken over the helm as the guiding force behind the text and has assumed responsibility for the chapters dealing with bank regulation and money laundering (Chapters 2 and 4), payment cards (Chapter 14) and security (Chapters 18–21). Professor Lomnicka has also dealt with the issues of consumer credit arising in Chapters 10 and 17. The remaining chapters (Chapters 1, 3, 5–13 and 15–17)—essentially those for which Professor Ellinger himself and Professor Richard Hooley assumed responsibility in the fourth edition—have been handed over to Christopher Hare for this edition. Responsibility for Chapter 22, dealing with the law relating to guarantees, has again been assumed by Professor John Phillips, one of the foremost authorities on this particular subject. Although the fifth edition adopts the same structure as the fourth edition, every chapter of the book has required either revision or a thorough update.

Chapter 1 has been updated to reflect changes in the structure of UK banking following the global financial crisis, including the collapse of Northern Rock and the subsequent raft of bank mergers and acquisitions. The text also considers the advent of the UK Payments Council and the UK Payments Administration and builds on the discussion in the fourth edition on the level of competition within the UK banking industry. In relation to investment banking, the book considers the decision of the Australian Federal Court in *Australian Securities and Investments Commission v. Citigroup Global Markets Australia Pty Ltd (No.4)*.

Chapter 2 has been revised primarily to reflect changes to the banking regulatory regime, in the wake of the global financial crisis. The Banking Act 2009 and the Financial Services Act 2010 are noted (as well as international (especially EU) developments) and the proposed overhaul of the UK's regulatory regime has been anticipated to the extent possible at the time of going to press. The new 'Banking and Payment Services' ('BPS') conduct of business regulatory regime operated by the FSA, which (amongst other things) resulted in the replacement of the Banking Code by the BCOBS Module of the FSA Handbook and the Lending Code, is also considered. The discussion of the regulation of consumer credit (amended by the implementation of the Consumer Credit Directive in February 2011) has been moved to this chapter from Chapter 3.

Although Chapter 3 is now somewhat shorter than in the fourth edition as a result of consumer credit regulation now being considered in Chapter 2, it still covers a number of important developments regarding the meaning of 'bank', 'banker' and 'banking business' at common law and under statute. Important developments include the Canadian Supreme Court decision in *Canadian Western Bank v. Alberta* and the full Australian Federal Court decision in *Siminton v. Australian Prudential Regulation Authority*.

Chapter 4 has been up-dated (in particular by noting the amendments introduced by the Serious Organized Crime and Police Act 2005 and those required by the implementation of the Third Money Laundering Directive) and continues to pay particular attention to the dilemmas posed to banks when seeking to give effect to their obligations under the legislation, as illustrated by *Squirrell Ltd v National Westminster Bank plc* and *HM Customs & Excise* [2005] EWHC 664 *K v National Westminster Bank* [2006] EWCA 1039. As well as considering developments in other jurisdiction, new English cases covered in Chapter 5 include the Court of Appeal's re-affirmation of the general absence of fiduciary duties owed by a bank to a customer in *Tamimi* v. *Khodari* and the numerous decisions that have continued to probe the elements of the House of Lords' seminal decision in *Royal Bank of Scotland* v. *Etridge (No 2)* on the nature of undue influence. Most significant have been the developments in relation to the duty of skill and care that a bank owes to its customers: not only has the important decision in *Customs and Excise Commissioners v. Barclays Bank plc* (on the bank's duty of care to prevent the disposal of customer funds in breach of a freezing injunction) made it to the House of Lords since the fourth edition, but there has also been detailed consideration of the bank's duties of care when comply-ing with the Proceeds of Crime Act 2002 (*Shah v HSBC Private Bank (UK) Ltd*) and in relation to the selling of complex financial products (*JP Morgan Chase Bank* v. *Springwell Navigation Corporation, Titan Steel Wheels Ltd* v. *Royal Bank of Scotland plc* and *Raiffeisen Zentralbank Osterreich AG* v. *Royal Bank of Scotland plc*). Also new to this edition in rela-tion to the bank's duty of confidentiality is a detailed consideration of Council Regulation (EC) 1206/2001 on the Co-operation between Member States in the Taking of Evidence in Civil or Commercial Matters and *Masri* v. *Consolidated Contractors International Company SAL*. Consideration is also given to the Privy Council's decision in *National Commercial Bank of Jamaica Ltd* v. *Olint Corporation Ltd* in relation to the termination of the banker-customer contract.

If the most significant development in the fourth edition's Chapter 7 was the House of Lord's decision in *Twinsectra Ltd* v. *Yardley* on the meaning of 'dishonesty' for the purposes of dishonest assistance liability, the most significant change for the fifth edition would be the retreat from *Twinsectra* in *Barlow Clowes International Ltd* v. *Eurotrust International Ltd* and *Abou-Rahmah* v. *Abacha*. Besides the significant impact of the FSA's BPS regime and the Payment Services Regulations 2009 on current accounts, nota-ble case law developments include *Morrell* v. *Workers Savings & Loan Bank* (on verifi-cation clauses), *Fraser* v. *Oystertec plc* (on combination of accounts), *Charter plc* v. *City Index Ltd* and *Farah Construction Pty Ltd* v. *Say-Dee Pty Ltd* (on knowing receipt), and *BMP Global Distribution Inc* v. *Bank of Nova Scotia, Re BA Peters plc, Cooper v. PRG Powerhouse Ltd* and *Serious Fraud Office* v. *Lexi Holdings plc* (on tracing). Chapters 8 and 9 consider other types of account besides current accounts. Important additions to the fifth edition include *Fielding* v. *Royal Bank of Scotland plc* and *Pecore* v. *Pecore* (on joint accounts), *Brazzill* v. *Willoughby* (on solicitor clients' accounts), *Re Global Trader Europe Ltd* (on investment business' accounts), *Haugesund Kommune* v. *Depfa ACS Bank* (on local authority accounts), *Gorjat* v. *Gorjat* (on mentally incapacitated person's accounts), and *European Bank Ltd* v. *Citibank Ltd* (on foreign-currency deposits).

The fifth edition contains three chapters dealing with payment by cheques: Chapter 10 considers bills of exchange and cheques generally, whilst Chapters 11 and 15 deal respec-tively with the paying and collecting bank. One of the most significant developments in this regard are the development of the '2-4-6' time-frame relating to the collection of cheques. Significant case-law developments include *Lomax Leisure Ltd* v. *Miller* (on consideration supporting a cheque), *Fiorentino Comm Giuseppe Srl* v. *Farnesi* (on present-ment of cheques), *Fourie* v. *Le Roux* (on freezing injunctions), *Pettit* v. *Novakovic* (on the effect of bankruptcy orders on accounts), and *OBG Ltd* v. *Allan* and *Architects of Wine Ltd* v. *Barclays Bank plc* (on the conversion of cheques). As regards electronic payments, Chapter 13 discusses the recent structural changes to the BACS and CHAPS payment systems and the recent introduction of the 'Faster Payments Service'. Although there are some notable case-law developments (*PT Berlian Laju Tanker TBK* v. *Nuse Shipping Ltd*), by far the most significant development is the implementation of the Payment Services Directive by the Payment Services Regulations 2009. Chapter 14 is updated to take account of developments in the payment card sector, in particular the significant impact of the Payment Services Regulations 2009.

As well as considering the House of Lords' decision in *Deutsche Morgan Grenfell Group Inc.* v. *Inland Revenue Commissioner* and *Sempra Metals Ltd* v. *Inland Revenue Commissioner* in relation to mistaken payments, Chapter 12 also considers recent refinements to the defence of change of position and payment over in *Jones v Churcher*. In relation to the incidental services performed by banks, Chapter 16 considers recent case law relating to Lord Tenterden's Act, such as *Contex Drouzhba Ltd* v. *Wiseman*, and safety-deposit boxes, such as *Schwarzschild* v. *Harrods Ltd*. There have been a number of changes made to Chapter 17 in the light of significant case law developments. New cases include *Office of Fair Trading* v. *Abbey National plc* (on the validity of current account overdraft charges), *Sempra Metals Ltd* v. *Inland Revenue Commissioner* and *Halliday* v. *HBOS plc* (on compound interest), and *IFE Fund SA* v. *Goldman Sachs* and *Raiffeisen Zentralbank Osterreich AG* v. *Royal Bank of Scotland plc* (on syndication).

Chapters 18–22 have been thoroughly updated and the changes effected by the Companies Act 2006 and amendments to the consumer credit and financial services regulation regimes noted.

All the authors wish to record their thanks to the various industry bodies that have provided them with information and materials, especially the British Banking Association and the Association for Payment Clearing Services. Christopher Hare also wishes to acknowledge the assistance of Lester Su and Sean Donovan, both students at the University of Auckland, in locating materials and references.

Our thanks are also due to Oxford University Press and its personnel for their cooperation and assistance. The law is stated as on [**January 1, 2011**].

E. P. Ellinger   Eva Lomnicka   Christopher Hare
Singapore   *London*   *Auckland*

List of Abbreviations

A. Bus LR	*Australian Business Law Review*
AFB	Association of Foreign Bankers
ALJ	*Australian Law Journal*
BEQB	*Bank of England Quarterly Bulletin*
CCA	Consumer Credit Act 1974
CLJ	*Cambridge Law Journal*
FSA	Financial Services Authority
FSMA	Financial Services and Markets Act 2000
Harv. Int.	*Harvard International Law Journal*
HC	*House of Commons Reports*
JBL	*Journal of Business Law*
JIB	*Journal of the Institute of Bankers*
LMCLQ	*Lloyd's Maritime and Commercial Law Quarterly*
LQR	*Law Quarterly Review*
MLR	*Modern Law Review*
OFT	*Office of Fair Trading*
POCA	Proceeds of Crime Act 2002
PSR 2009	Payment Services Regulations 2009, S.I. 2009/209

List of Abbreviations

Table of Cases

Table of Statutes

Table of Statutory Instruments

Table of European Directives, Regulations and Decisions

Table of European and International Treaties and Conventions

PART I
Banks and Banking Business

1

The Structure of the British Banking World

1 The problem in context

The public tends to regard banks as comprising a single group. Usually, banks are contrasted with rival institutions, such as building societies, finance companies, and credit unions. In reality, the banks themselves can be divided into a number of groups on the basis of different criteria. A discussion of the classification of the different types or categories of bank operating in the United Kingdom, and of their respective organizations, is of considerable importance, as it provides the background to the analysis of the general legal principles governing the activities of banks in the United Kingdom in subsequent chapters. In classifying the different types of bank, however, the criteria that one might use tend to change over time and new criteria tend to emerge. For example, it was once possible to differentiate between banks operating within the United Kingdom by reference to their geographical location, separating the banks of England and Wales from those of Scotland and Northern Ireland. Nowadays, this division seems increasingly inappropriate, especially given the acquisition of the National Westminster Bank by the Royal Bank of Scotland and the merger of Halifax plc and the Bank of Scotland to form Halifax Bank of Scotland plc (or HBOS plc), which in turn was acquired by Lloyds TSB Bank plc in 2009 to form Lloyds Banking Group plc. Given the inability of geographical location to provide a satisfactory framework for classification, an alternative might be to adopt a functional classification according to the respective business activities undertaken by the different banks. The increasing overlap in the business activities of banks that traditionally specialised in different aspects of banking business, however, creates certain difficulties in the way of this providing a sound conceptual basis for classifying British banks. Nowadays, many banks are multifunctional institutions engaged in a wide range of business activities extending well beyond their traditional core activities of deposit-taking and lending.[1] Indeed, many modern banks commonly engage in activities as diverse as securities dealing, investment management, insurance, and estate agency, usually through different subsidiary companies within the same banking group. One possible way of overcoming this increasing overlap in the business activities of banks traditionally operating in different areas of banking business, however, may be to have regard to the umbrella organizations to which the particular bank belongs. Each of these organizations represents the interests of its members and is in turn represented on the British Bankers' Association (BBA). Generally, the members of each umbrella organization follow a

---

[1] Nowadays, the provision of payment services should also be regarded as an aspect of 'core' banking activity as a result of the Payment Services Regulations 2009, S.I. 2009/209 (PSR 2009), implementing Directive 2007/64/EC on Payment Services in the Internal Market [2007] OJ L319: Ch. 2, Sect. 6 & Ch. 13, Sect. 5 below.

defined general pattern in their business activities, although naturally there remain certain variations in business practice even among the members of a given organization.

Subject to these observations, it appears possible to divide virtually all the banks with a presence in the United Kingdom into six broad groups. First and foremost is the group comprising 'the clearing banks' or the 'clearers', which term encompasses not only the major retail banks, but also any retail bank or institution whose activities include an involvement in the clearing procedures. The largest clearing banks are Barclays Bank, Lloyds Banking Group plc (formed as a result of the acquisition of HBOS plc by Lloyds TSB Bank plc in 2009), HSBC Bank (formerly Midland Bank), and National Westminster Bank (part of the Royal Bank of Scotland Group since March 2000). These four banks, together with Williams and Glyn's Bank, were the traditional members of the Committee of London Clearing Banks (CLCB). The operational responsibilities of the CLCB for the clearings were taken over in 1985 by the Association for Payment Clearing Services (APACS), which was in turn replaced by the UK Payments Administration Ltd (UKPA) on 6 July 2009. In addition, the four major clearing banks are members of the three clearing companies that operate under the aegis of UKPA (although other banks, including some foreign banks and one building society, are represented as well)[2] and continue to play their traditionally major role in the activities of the BBA.[3]

The second group of banks comprises the 'merchant banks', which are nowadays more commonly referred to as 'investment banks'.[4] Originally, the banks in this group had two umbrella organizations, the members of which were, respectively, the accepting houses and the issuing houses. In 1988, the two organizations merged into the London Investment Banking Association (LIBA), formerly the British Merchant Banking and Securities Houses Association. Its members, who do not maintain branch networks, are engaged in the traditional activities of merchant or investment banking, which comprises the financing of international trade and all types of transaction related to capital issues. The third group is made up of those banks operating in the wholesale money markets. The London Money Market Association (LMMA) represents the interests of those banks and other financial institutions that operate in the sterling money market. Discount houses used to operate in the short-term money markets, but changes in Bank of England practices, in particular the sanction of the gilt repo as an approved instrument for Open Market Operations and the widening of the Bank of England's list of approved counterparties, resulted in the disappearance of these houses and their representative body, the London Discount Market Association. The fourth group comprises the foreign banks. Until 1996, this group could be divided between those banks that were members of the British Overseas and Commonwealth Banks Association (BOCBA) and those that were members of the Foreign Banks and Securities Houses Association (FBSA). The BOCBA banks carried out their main activities in Commonwealth countries and former British protectorates and included the Standard Chartered Bank, the major Australian banks, and certain South East Asian and Far Eastern banks. Other foreign banks were members

---

[2] For example, the Nationwide Building Society is a member of the Cheque and Credit Clearing Co. Ltd and BACS Payment Schemes Ltd, and Citigroup is a member of the CHAPS Clearing Co. Ltd. Even certain non-United Kingdom-based banks have become members of UKPA organizations, such as Danske Bank, which is a member of BACS Payment Schemes Ltd and CHAPS Clearing Co. Ltd, and Deutsche Bank AG and UBS AG, which are both members of CHAPS Clearing Co. Ltd.

[3] In 1988, the British Bankers' Association replaced the Committee of London and Scottish Banks (CLSB), which was formed as a trade association for the clearing banks in 1986.

[4] The global credit crisis has had a significant impact on the investment-banking model in the United Kingdom and the United States: Ch. 2, Sect. 1 below.

of the FBSA. In 1996, the BOCBA was absorbed into the FBSA to form the Association of Foreign Banks (AFB). The AFB represents the interest of over 180 member banks and securities houses whose ultimate ownership is outside the United Kingdom, or whose activities are principally international in focus. The fifth and sixth groups are respectively the United States banks, whose organization is the American Financial Services Association (formerly the American Banking and Securities Association in London) and the Japanese banks, whose organization is the Japanese Bankers Association.[5] This sixfold classification informs the structure of the discussion below.

In addition to the banking organizations considered above, there are a number of other organizations, trade associations, or statutory bodies that are relevant to banks. Probably the most important is the Financial Services Authority (FSA), which, as discussed subsequently,[6] is responsible for the regulation and prudential supervision of United Kingdom banks. Next in terms of importance is probably the BBA, which, as discussed below,[7] is a trade association the membership of which is open to all banks with a presence in the United Kingdom and which is designed to promote the interests of, and represent, the United Kingdom banking industry. In addition, there are a number of bodies representing entities that engage in different types of banking activity, such as the Council of Mortgage Lenders, the UKPA, the Payments Council, and the UK Cards Association to name but a few. These bodies *inter alia* will be discussed in subsequent chapters where relevant.

2 The clearing banks[8]

(i) The London scene

Historically, the clearing banks—the institutions generally regarded by the public as 'the banks'—are the successors of the joint-stock banks. The development of the major clearing banks can be traced back to the late eighteenth century, although their influence and financial strength became paramount during the last three decades of the nineteenth century. It was around this time that they became known as the 'clearing banks' or 'clearers'. Nowadays, apart from the (now) four major clearing banks—Barclays Bank plc, Lloyds Banking Group plc (formed after Lloyds TSB Bank plc acquired the fifth major clearing bank, HBOS plc, in 2009), HSBC Bank, and National Westminster Bank plc—there are a number of smaller clearing banks operating in England and Wales. These include Abbey National plc (part of Grupo Santander since July 2004 and rebranded 'Santander' on 11 January 2010),[9] Clydesdale Bank (which acquired Yorkshire Bank in 2001), Co-operative Bank plc, (which absorbed the Britannia Building Society in August 2009) Alliance & Leicester Commercial Bank (part of Grupo Santander since October

---

[5] In addition to these groups, which are concerned with the activities of banks centred in London, there are the Committee of Scottish Clearing Bankers and the Northern Ireland Bankers' Association, which are represented as groups on the BBA.

[6] Ch. 2, Sect. 4 below.   [7] Sect. 6 below.

[8] For the position up to 1970, see The London Clearing Banks, *Evidence Submitted by the Committee of London Clearing Bankers to the Committee to Review the Functioning of Financial Institutions* (November 1970).

[9] In September 2008, Abbey National plc acquired the savings business and branches of Bradford & Bingley plc, which were similarly rebranded 'Santander' in January 2010. The remainder of the bank was nationalized and merged on 1 October 2010 with Northern Rock (Asset Management) plc under a single holding company, UK Asset Resolution Ltd.

2008),[10] and Northern Rock plc.[11] Special mention must also be made of the Royal Bank of Scotland Group, which acquired the National Westminster Bank and its wholly-owned subsidiary, Coutts, in March 2000.[12] As the Royal Bank of Scotland had previously amalgamated with Williams and Glyn's Bank (an established member of the CLCB),[13] its role as a clearer is as well entrenched as that of any of the (now) four major clearing banks.

The major clearing banks of London used to number more than the current four. In the early 1960s, there were in fact ten,[14] but their number decreased with the mergers that took place in the late 1960s and early 1970s. Prior to that time, banks were dissuaded from attempts to merge by the Report of the Colwyn Committee on Bank Amalgamations, which had expressed concern in 1918 about the concentration of banks in the hands of a limited number of powerful houses. Following this report, a bank merger would only generally obtain the required approval of the Treasury and Bank of England if the banks involved were not in direct competition with one another. For example, under this regime, the first significant merger was proposed because the District Bank had its main network of branches in North-west England, whereas the National Provincial Bank was relatively inactive. The scene was cleared for further mergers in 1967, however, when the Report on Bank Charges, prepared by the National Board for Prices and Incomes, advised that the Bank of England and the Treasury had made it plain that they would not obstruct some further amalgamations if the banks chose this course.[15] This policy statement initiated a number of mergers,[16] at the conclusion of which the City was left with the four current

---

[10] Alliance & Leicester Commercial Bank, formerly known as Girobank, was a founding member of APACS, the functions of which were taken over by UKPA on 6 July 2009. It was also a member of the three associated clearing companies, but left the Clearing House Automated Payments System (CHAPS) in June 1999. In view of its restricted activities—principally the acceptance of deposits from corporate customers—Alliance & Leicester Commercial Bank is not generally regarded as a typical clearer, but as it remains a member of two of the clearing companies operating under the UKPA umbrella—the Cheque and Credit Clearing Co. Ltd and BACS Payment Schemes Ltd—and plays a role in the clearing systems, it has the status of a clearing bank. As a result of its acquisition by the Spanish banking group, Grupo Santander, the bank transferred its business to Santander UK in May 2010 and has been rebranded accordingly.

[11] Northern Rock plc was one of the biggest United Kingdom casualties of the global credit crisis that started in 2007. Following an agreement on 3 September 2007 by the FSA, Bank of England, and the Treasury to provide financial support to Northern Rock plc so that it could maintain its liquidity, there was a 'run' on the bank between 14 and 17 September 2007. On 22 February 2008, the Northern Rock plc was temporarily nationalized by the British Government pursuant to the terms of the Banking (Special Provisions) Act 2008 and the Northern Rock plc Transfer Order 2008, S.I. 2008/432. Compensation to former shareholders in Northern Rock plc was to be determined according to the terms of the Northern Bank plc Compensation Scheme Order 2008, S.I. 2008/718: see generally *R (on the application of SRM Global Master Fund LP)* v. *Treasury Commissioner* [2009] EWHC 227 (Admin), affd. [2009] EWCA Civ 788. The bank was subsequently managed at arm's length through UK Financial Investments Ltd and, on 1 January 2010, was split into a 'good bank' (Northern Rock plc) with responsibility for deposit-taking and new lending and a 'bad bank' (Northern Rock (Asset Management) plc) with responsibility for existing mortgages and the repayment of government lending. On 1 October 2010, this 'bad bank' was merged with the nationalized part of the Bradford & Bingley plc under a single holding company, UK Asset Resolution Ltd. See generally D. Singh, 'Northern Rock, Depositors and Deposit Insurance Coverage: Some Critical Reflections' [2010] *JBL* 55. See further Ch. 2, Sect. 1 below.

[12] The British Government was forced to take a controlling stake in the Royal Bank of Scotland Group in November 2008 when the bank's attempt to raise fresh capital from the public was undersubscribed. The Government's stake in the bank was increased in January 2009 and then increased even further in November 2009.

[13] Glyn, Mills & Co., which merged to form Williams and Glyn's Bank in the 1960s, was one of the oldest commercial and clearing banks in England.

[14] The London Clearing Banks, n.8 above, 21.   [15] Ibid., 20 ff.

[16] Mergers took place between Barclays Bank and Martins Bank; National Provincial Bank (which had already amalgamated with the District Bank) and Westminster Bank; and Williams Deacon & Co., Glyn Mills & Co., and the National Bank.

major clearing banks, plus Williams and Glyn's Bank. A merger of Barclays and Lloyds was, however, opposed by the Monopolies Commission, which was concerned about the effect that such a development was bound to have on competitiveness in the banking world. When Williams and Glyn's Bank became fully amalgamated with the Royal Bank of Scotland, the latter acquired the former's seat on the CLCB. Seats on the CLCB were offered also to the Bank of Scotland and, subsequently, to the Standard Chartered Bank.

The clearing banks used to be the only active participants in the clearing-house activities. The position changed in the 1980s when three additional banks—the Trustee Savings Bank of England and Wales (subsequently part of Lloyds TSB Bank, which in turn became part of Lloyds Banking Group plc in January 2009), the Co-operative Bank, and the National Girobank (now Alliance & Leicester Commercial Bank, which has in turn been part of Grupo Santander since October 2008)—became functional members of the clearing house, although they were not offered seats on the CLCB. Basically, this meant that the functional clearers acquired direct access to the clearing house through their own clearing departments, but they were denied a direct role in the formulation of the relevant policies and in the periodic reviews of the Clearing House Rules,[17] both of which were the domain of the CLCB.

The scene changed altogether following the recommendations of the Child Report in December 1984,[18] which reviewed the organization, membership, and control of the clearing system's various elements. Three independent systems were at that time in existence. The first was the clearing house itself, which was responsible for the 'general clearing' of cheques and paper-generated giro credits issued in England and Wales and for the 'town clearing', which was used solely for the same-day clearing of effects of not less than £10,000 (raised to £500,000 by 1992) drawn on a branch within the boundaries of the City of London and collected by another City branch.[19] The clearing house was under the CLCB's direct control, although ownership was vested in a company, in which the major clearing banks were the principal shareholders. The remaining two clearing systems were under the CLCB's indirect control and were owned by separate companies: the Bankers Automated Clearing Services (BACS),[20] which cleared all types of electronically generated payment, such as periodic payments and direct debits; and the Clearing House Automated Payment System (CHAPS), which effected the electronic transfer of substantial amounts[21] on a same-day clearing basis throughout the United Kingdom. The Child Report's main recommendation was that these three clearing systems, each of which should be under the control of a separate company, should be brought

---

[17] For the legal implications of the Clearing House Rules, see Ch. 10, Sect. 2 & Ch. 13, Sect. 1(v) below.

[18] *Payment Clearing Systems, Review of Organisation, Membership and Control*, Report of a Working Party appointed by the Ten Member Banks of the Bankers Clearing House (Banking Information Services, 1984; 2nd reprint by APACS, 1990).

[19] The 'town clearing' was abolished in February 1995.

[20] In 1986, the company was renamed 'BACS Ltd' and, in December 2003, BACS was divided into two separate companies: BACS Payment Schemes Ltd manages the scheme, whilst VocaLink Ltd (formerly BACS Ltd and then Voca Ltd) physically processes payments and maintains the network. The BACS clearing system operates under the UKPA umbrella: www.ukpayments.org.uk. See further Ch. 13, Sect. 3(iii) below.

[21] Although the CHAPS clearing was initially used for payments over £10,000, the last financial restriction on the value of CHAPS Sterling transfers was removed in January 1993. Nevertheless, the system is still mainly used for high-value transactions, although there is increasingly evidence of low-value payments (for less than £10,000) passing through the CHAPS Sterling system: APACS, *In Brief—Payments Market Briefing 2000*, 11. In 2004, the average value of a CHAPS transfer was £1.86 million, which was down from £1.9 million in 2003, 'indicating that the growth in volume is derived from the lower-value non-financial customer sector': APACS, *CHAPS Sterling and CHAPS Euro Volumes and Values (www.apacs.org.uk)*. As a result of this trend, and in order to speed up low-value transfers, APACS (now UKPA) launched the 'Faster Payment Service' in May 2008. This new service appears to be having a significant impact on traditional CHAPS Sterling transfers, with volumes declining at an annual rate of 2.6 per cent and values at an annual rate of 12 per cent: UK Payments Administration, *Statistical Release—9 September 2010*, (London, 2010), 7. See further Ch. 13, Sects. 1 & 3(iv) below.

within the framework and control of an 'umbrella organization', membership of which was to be liberalized by being open to all settlement members and individual clearing companies. Other recommendations were that membership of the three clearing systems should be liberalized and that other appropriately regulated institutions using the clearing facilities through agent banks should be offered associate membership. These recommendations were implemented in full in 1985 with the formation of a single umbrella body, APACS, which acquired control of the various clearing systems and accordingly took over one of the CLCB's major functions. One of the results of these structural changes was that access to the clearing house was no longer confined to banks, and membership of APACS was widened to include any bank or building society operating in the United Kingdom, as well as any credit institution based in other European Union, European Economic Area, or G10 countries.[22] Until 1997, every APACS member had also to be a member of one or more of the clearing companies, but membership was subsequently opened to any institution that was a principal member of a payment scheme that was widely used or otherwise significant in the United Kingdom (i.e. a payment scheme that handled more than one per cent of the United Kingdom's payment volumes and/or more than 0.1 per cent of the United Kingdom's payment values).[23] APACS also had a number of affiliate members that provided payment services to their customers through at least one of the APACS clearing systems via agency arrangements with a full member, or that otherwise issued payment cards in the United Kingdom.[24]

APACS ceased to exist on 6 July 2009, at which time it had 28 full members. APACS' functions have now been taken over by a private company, UKPA, which 'is not itself a membership body but the service company providing people, facilities and expertise to the UK payments industry'.[25] As the clearing banks, including two of the three former 'functional clearers', are members of all three companies,[26] the nature and activities of the clearing banks is very closely related to UKPA's role in the clearing of cheques and other payment orders. Although UKPA services a significant part of the United Kingdom payments industry, its remit does not extend to Visa, MasterCard, LINK, or SWITCH Maestro. Its functions do, however, include operating as an umbrella body for four payment industry groups (Financial Fraud Action UK, the Payments Council, the UK Cards Association, and SWIFT UK) and for the three companies that are responsible for the various clearing systems. First, the Cheque and Credit Clearing Co. Ltd has taken over control of the general clearing, which comprises the clearing of cheques and paper-generated giro credits issued in England and Wales and which has since been extended to Scotland.[27] The company's shareholders are the Bank of England, the clearing banks, and one building society.[28] Secondly, the CHAPS Clearing Co. Ltd is in charge of CHAPS Sterling, the United Kingdom's real-time gross settlement, same-day value, electronic sterling credit transfer system, frequently used for high-value transfers.[29] Its members are all banks.[30] Previously, CHAPS also operated a Euro-denominated credit transfer system, but this was decommissioned on 16 May 2008.[31]

---

[22] Additionally, APACS published certain membership criteria.
[23] APACS, *Annual Report 2003* (London, 2004), 46. See also *APACS Constitution* (July 2005), [6.1] & Appendix 1.
[24] There were 26 APACS Affiliate Members at APACS' dissolution in July 2009.
[25] For this description, see www.ukpayments.org.uk.
[26] Alliance & Leicester Commercial Bank (now part of Grupo Santander) is not a member of CHAPS Sterling and was not a member of CHAPS Euro. All the clearers, large or small, are also members of the BBA, which represents the general interests of banks in the United Kingdom: Sect. 6 below.
[27] Ch. 10, Sect. 2 & Ch. 13, Sect. 3(i)–(ii) below.
[28] As at October 2010 (www.chequeandcredit.co.uk).
[29] For evidence of increasing use of CHAPS Sterling for lower-value payments, see n.21 above, although the 'Faster Payments Service' may now lead to some slowdown in this trend.
[30] As at October 2010 (www.chapsco.co.uk).   [31] Ch. 13, Sect. 3(iv) below.

In the same month, however, CHAPS introduced the 'Faster Payments Service', which was designed to extend the benefits of the CHAPS payment system to lower-value transactions, namely internet and phone payments for less than £10,000 and standing orders for less than £100,000. The principal advantages of this new system are that transfers can occur within minutes (or sometimes hours), rather than on the previous three-day cycle, and that such transfers can be made all day, every day. Apart from one building society, all 13 founding members are banks.[32] Thirdly, BACS Payment Services Ltd, has simply taken over the activities of the existing body, BACS Ltd. Its members comprise the Bank of England, 13 banks, and one building society.[33]

A significant number of payments are nowadays cleared by these three companies through their various settlement systems. In the year ending June 2009, the total number of items cleared through the various clearing systems exceeded 6.8 billion. Out of these, approximately 1.02 billion were cheques and giro credits, approximately 5.6 billion items were cleared by BACS, approximately 32.7 million items were cleared by CHAPS Sterling, and over 207 million items were cleared through the 'Faster Payments Service', launched in May 2008.[34] The importance of the clearing banks' role in achieving these figures cannot be overstated. In 2004, it was estimated that 95 per cent of the adult population in the United Kingdom had some form of bank or building society account that could be used to effect payment,[35] and, as considered further below, this is likely to increase further as a result of the 'universal banking services' initiative following the Cruickshank Report. Furthermore, the ease with which funds in an account can be accessed, and payments can thereby be effected, has increased significantly in recent years. Traditionally, customers gained access to their accounts through the bank's network of branches throughout the country. Although the branch network remains extensive, its size has reduced in recent years.[36] Indeed, many customers seldom visit a branch at all, nowadays preferring to access their accounts remotely via the bank's telephone banking service, a personal computer connected to the internet, WAP-enabled mobile telephone,[37] or digital television. Most clearing banks now offer their customers telephone and internet banking services, and some newly established banks have no branches at all, operating only via the internet.[38]

The integrity of the clearing system is protected by additional membership criteria. A bank or other financial institution that applies for membership of the Cheque and

---

[32] For a list of founding members, see APACS' Press Release, *Phased Roll Out for New Faster Payments Service* (28 April 2008).

[33] As at October 2010 (www.bacs.co.uk).

[34] UK Payments Administration, *Clearing Statistics—June 2009* (London, 2009), 1. According to these statistics, the amount by value cleared through CHAPS Sterling far exceeds the others: Cheques and Credit Clearing—£1.03 trillion; BACS—£3.91 trillion; CHAPS Sterling—£70.6 trillion; 'Faster Payments Service'—£76.2 billion. For a forecast of payment volumes and values between 2007 and 2017, see Payments Council, *Annual Review 2008—Driving Change in UK Payments* (London, 2008), 10–15.

[35] APACS, *Yearbook of Payment Statistics 2004* (2004), 6.

[36] Ibid., 36, which states that the number of United Kingdom branches for APACS members reduced from 15,709 in 1990 to 11,241 in 2003.

[37] Although the Payments Council investigated the feasibility of an industry-wide payments service allowing spontaneous account-to-account payments by mobile phone (Payments Council, *National Payments Plan—Setting the Strategic Vision for UK Payments* (London, 14 May 2008), 41–42; Payments Council, *Progress Report—Delivering the National Payments Plan* (London, March 2009), 4–5), it has concluded that 'due to the rapid evolution of the mobile market and competitive developments' the initiative would be temporarily shelved (Payments Council, *Progress Report: Delivering the National Payments Plan* (June 2010), 4).

[38] Frequently, the 'internet banks' are subsidiaries of established banks, such as Cahoot (the internet division of Santander UK plc), Smile (a division of the Co-operative Bank), and Egg Banking plc (a division of Citigroup), which transferred its credit card business to Barclays Bank in 2011.

Credit Clearing Co. Ltd and its clearing house has to undertake to maintain its own clearing department,[39] to which all cheques payable to the bank's customers are sent by the branches charged with their collection. Such cheques are largely processed at the bank's own clearing centre and are thereafter delivered to the 'clearing house'— located, since October 2003, in Milton Keynes—where the bank also picks up any cheques drawn on itself.[40] As the processing at the clearing centres involves a costly automated procedure, an institution is most unlikely to establish one unless it is of a certain size and has sufficient business to justify the expenditure involved. Even where an institution is prepared to meet this requirement, however, it still has to demonstrate its ability to meet the remaining criteria laid down for membership, including certain requirements respecting the applicant's financial standing.[41] Unsurprisingly, many banks in England and Wales consider it unprofitable to maintain their own clearing department. As a general rule, the same can be said for the foreign banks,[42] most of which are situated in London, and the merchant or investment banks, although some of these latter banks do have customers who open current accounts with them. This means that cheques drawn by customers of these banks, as well as cheques payable to them, need to be cleared.

From the eighteenth century until the end of the Second World War, banks that were not members of the cheque clearing house presented cheques for payment and received cheques drawn on themselves by an inefficient and time-consuming procedure known as the 'walks',[43] which involved the handling of the cheques by messengers several times each day. Gradually, the 'walks' was entirely replaced by the system of 'agency banks', under which a non-clearing bank uses one of the clearing banks as its agent to present cheques for payment and collect their proceeds. Each cheque payable to a customer of the respective non-clearing bank is sent to the agent's clearing department for collection. Cheques drawn on an account maintained with the non-clearing bank are delivered by the relevant payee's bank to the agent bank at the clearing house. This process is facilitated by a simple device—the non-clearing bank is given a sorting number that identifies the bank and its particular branch,[44] that is printed on any cheques that the bank issues to its customers, and that is also encoded on cheques collected for its customers. Since the agent bank's own branches have a similar identifying number, the non-clearing bank is treated for the purposes of the clearing process as if it were a branch of its agent bank. The resulting network of agency banks is formidable, covering many banks of considerable size.

The clearing banks' role in the payment and collection of cheques and other payment orders is directly related to one of their main activities—the maintenance of current

---

[39] There is now provision for the outsourcing of cheque processing to other non-bank companies.

[40] In fact, many cheques are exchanged directly between major banks themselves. For procedural innovations, including the exchange of code line information over a secure telecommunication link (IBDE) operated by BACS, and cheque truncation generally, see Ch. 10, Sect. 2 below.

[41] For the membership criteria of the main United Kingdom payment schemes, see D. Cruickshank, *Competition in UK Banking—A Report to the Chancellor of the Exchequer* (London, March 2000) (available at www.bankreview.org.uk), Table 3.2. See further Sect. 2(iii) below. The membership criteria of the Cheque and Credit Clearing Co. Ltd include 'financial strength and stability': www.chequeandcredit.co.uk.

[42] Although no foreign bank is a member of the Cheque and Credit Clearing Co. Ltd, the majority of foreign banks involved with clearing payments in the United Kingdom are members of the CHAPS Clearing Co. Ltd (www.chapsco.co.uk), and Danske Bank has been a member of BACS Payment Schemes Ltd since 2006 (www.bacs.co.uk).

[43] Ch. 10, Sect. 2 below.

[44] A sorting number is either a printed or an imprinted message readable by the 'reader-sorter' computer facility.

accounts. In this regard, the clearing banks are fairly liberal in accepting persons, whether individuals or companies, as customers. Not only is this liberal approach mandated by law, given that there is a specific prohibition on racial discrimination in the furnishing of banking services,[45] but further liberalization has also resulted from government initiatives that encourage banks to offer 'basic bank accounts' in order to combat financial exclusion.[46] That said, clearing banks are at least required by legal considerations to request that every new customer furnish proof of identity.[47] One consequence of the clearing banks maintaining current accounts is that those banks have control of substantial amounts of money repayable on demand. Accommodation can be provided to customers on such an account by way of an overdraft that is, conceptually, also repayable on demand.[48] The interest chargeable on an overdraft varies between banks, and it can no longer be said with certainty that interest on an overdraft will be lower than that charged on a loan.[49] New internet-only banks, with lower transaction-processing costs, have tried to attract customers by offering higher interest rates on savings and lower rates on borrowings. In recent years, however, customers have become increasingly aware of their money's earning capacity and, given the extremely modest rates of interest payable on some (but not all) current account balances, they have tended to place their savings in interest-bearing accounts, such as fixed deposits. This has enabled the clearing banks to make even more medium- and long-term loans available to customers at lower rates of interest than would be payable on an overdraft facility.[50]

Apart from their typical branch banking activities, the clearing banks engage in all other types of banking business. Each of the (now) four largest clearing banks have international divisions and offices in foreign countries. Furthermore, many of the clearing banks' major local branches offer international banking facilities, including the financing of exports and imports, dealings in foreign currency and gold, and the furnishing of guarantees, performance bonds, and letters of credit. In addition, most of the clearing banks underwrite new issues of commercial paper and, like the merchant or investment banks, provide lines of credit to commercial customers. From about the end of the Second World War, the clearing banks have also been willing to provide customers with financial advice and portfolio services. These services are quite separate from the furnishing of bankers' references, which has been a traditional activity of the clearing banks.[51] The clearing banks are thus engaged in a wide range of banking business.

Before concluding this discussion of the clearing banks, it is necessary to say something about each of the three institutions that operated as 'functional clearers' prior to the clearing system's restructuring in 1985. First, the Co-operative Bank plc maintains branches in all parts of the United Kingdom. Originally, these were located in the department stores of its owner, the Co-operative Wholesale Society, with the result that most of its customers came from among the regular clients of these stores. The bank has grown substantially in recent years, however, and it had already established a Corporate Business Department as early as 1985. Currently, it offers most of the services provided by the older clearing banks. Since 2002, the Co-operative Bank plc has been controlled by a new holding company, the Co-operative Financial Services Ltd, which absorbed the Britannia Building Society in August 2009.

---

[45] Race Relations Act 1976, s.20.   [46] Sect. 2(iii) below.

[47] For the 'customer due diligence' requirements of the Money Laundering Regulations 2007, S.I. 2007/2157, (as amended by S.I. 2007/3299 & S.I. 2009/209), see Ch. 4, Sect. 3(iv) below. For the statutory defence available to a collecting bank that has converted a cheque, see Ch. 15, Sect. 4(iv) below).

[48] For the nature of overdrafts, see Ch. 17, Sects. 1–2 below.

[49] Ch. 17, Sect. 1 below.   [50] Id.   [51] Ch. 16, Sect. 2 below.

Secondly, Girobank was originally founded as a body offering certain banking services on behalf of the Post Office. Girobank's establishment was sanctioned by legislation[52] that authorized the Post Office to provide such banking services as it saw fit and that deemed it 'for all practical purposes to be a banker and carrying on the business of banking'.[53] In 1978, the Girobank was renamed the National Girobank and subsequently became an authorized institution under the Banking Act 1987. When the Alliance and Leicester Building Society acquired Girobank in 1990, the close connection with the Post Office was not entirely severed and Girobank continued to use the Post Office as a branch network. Pursuant to the Alliance and Leicester (Girobank) Act 1993, the personal accounts of Girobank were transferred to Alliance and Leicester plc, and, in July 2003, Girobank was renamed Alliance & Leicester Commercial Bank, which subsequently became authorized and regulated by the FSA under the Financial Services and Markets Act 2000 (FSMA 2000).[54] In October 2008, the Alliance & Leicester Commercial Bank became part of Grupo Santander and, in May 2010, the bank transferred its business to Santander UK and has been rebranded accordingly. In terms of activities, Girobank (in its various subsequent incarnations) has specialized since 1994 in the provision of cash-handling facilities for, *inter alia*, major retailers—cash that it uses to supply the needs of the Post Office and other banking customers, such as filling ATMs. Girobank (in its various subsequent incarnations) also provides bill payment services through its relationship with the Post Office,[55] has become a merchant acquirer,[56] and engages in some lending activity to businesses.

Thirdly, the TSB Bank originated with the establishment of the trustee savings banks, which were initially sanctioned by the Trustee Savings Banks Act 1817.[57] At that time, their object was to provide a savings facility for the 'working classes', who had no access to the trading banks. Until 1985, trustee savings banks were established on a local basis and were constituted as friendly societies, supervised by the Trustee Savings Banks Central Board. Accordingly, they were outside the regime of the Banking Act 1979, being listed in its Schedule 1. Their traditional business was the acceptance of money on deposit, but they were empowered to engage in banking business generally in 1981.[58] Within a short period, the trustee savings banks were offering their customers a variety of banking services, including overdrafts, current accounts, and money-transfer facilities, and this encouraged small businesses to shift their accounts to these banks. By 1985, the trustee savings banks' business had diversified and increased to such an extent that a reorganization under a corporate structure was considered timely. Sections 3(1)–(3) of the Trustee Savings Banks Act 1985 accordingly made provision for the transfer of all the individual trustee savings banks' assets and liabilities (whether transferable or not)[59] to a new company, the Trustee Savings Bank of England plc (or 'TSB Bank'), on 21 July 1986.[60]

---

[52] Post Office Act 1969, s.7(1)(b) (replaced by the British Telecommunications Act 1981, s.58(1), which has in turn since been repealed by the Postal Services Act 2000, s.127(6) & Sched. 9). Pursuant to the Postal Services Act 2000, s.62, all the property, rights, and liabilities of the Post Office were transferred to Consignia plc (now Royal Mail Holdings plc) on 26 March 2001. See also the Post Office Company (Nomination and Appointed Day) Order 2001, S.I. 2001/8.

[53] Ibid., s.40 (as amended by the Banking Act 1979, Sched. 4, para. 7). As a consequence, Girobank acquired the protection conferred on collecting banks by the Cheques Act 1957, s.4: Ch. 15, Sect. 4 below.

[54] Ch. 2, Sect. 4 below.

[55] Other banks have developed a relationship with the Post Office through their 'basic bank accounts' that can be accessed through the Post Office: British Bankers' Association, '7.3 Million Basic Bank Accounts at the End of the First Quarter' (18 July 2008). See further Sect. 2(iii) below.

[56] See generally Ch. 14 below.   [57] E.P. Ellinger, *Modern Banking Law* (Oxford, 1987), 11–13.

[58] Trustee Savings Banks Act 1981, s.18(1).   [59] Trustee Savings Banks Act 1985, s.3(6).

[60] Ibid., s.3(3). See also Trustee Savings Banks Act 1985 (Appointed Day) (No. 3) Order 1986, S.I. 1986/1222, art. 2. See generally *Ross v. Lord Advocate* [1986] 1 WLR 1077 (HL).

Similarly named banks were also established in Scotland and Northern Ireland. The TSB Bank offered a full range of banking services to its customers and was authorized under the Banking Act 1987. In 1995, the TSB Bank merged with Lloyds Bank to form Lloyds TSB Bank plc, one of the United Kingdom's main clearers. In January 2009, Lloyds TSB Bank plc acquired HBOS plc to avert the latter's failure as a result of the global credit crisis that began in 2007, and the resulting combined entity became the Lloyds Banking Group plc, in which the Treasury holds a significant minority shareholding.

(ii) The clearing banks of Scotland and Northern Ireland

The business of the Scottish and Northern Irish clearers is comparable to that of the London clearers, and some of the former group similarly have overseas offices. The clearing procedure used by the clearing banks in London, Scotland, and Northern Ireland is also the same. The four members of the Committee of Scottish Clearing Banks—the Bank of Scotland,[61] the Clydesdale Bank,[62] the Royal Bank of Scotland, and Lloyds TSB Scotland[63]—maintain a clearing centre in Edinburgh.[64] The Northern Irish clearing banks—the Bank of Ireland,[65] the First Trust Bank,[66] Northern Bank Ltd (owned by Danske Bank since March 2005), and Ulster Bank Ltd (part of the Royal Bank of Scotland Group since 2000)—have their own clearing house in Belfast, which is managed by the Belfast Bankers' Clearing Committee. All the Scottish banks are settlement members of BACS and CHAPS, whereas the Northern Irish banks only have indirect access through agency arrangements with members.

(iii) The Cruickshank Report

In recent years, the provision of banking and financial services to personal and business customers has become increasingly competitive. Traditional United Kingdom clearing banks must now compete for business with a range of other financial institutions. First, there are the building societies that have converted from mutual associations to public limited companies and have become banks. Examples include the Abbey National plc (part of Grupo Santander since July 2004 and rebranded 'Santander' on 11 January 2010),[67] Alliance and Leicester plc (part of Grupo Santander since October 2008),[68] Halifax plc (initially part of HBOS plc, and subsequently part of Lloyds Banking Group plc since January 2009), Northern Rock plc (now split into two parts),[69] and Woolwich plc (part of the Barclays Bank Group since 2000, and now the Barclays mortgage brand in the United Kingdom). Secondly, there is an increasing number of foreign banks operating in the United Kingdom. For example, Deutsche Bank, National Australia Bank, Wachovia Corporation,[70] DnB NOR ASA, and

---

[61] In 2001, the Bank of Scotland and Halifax merged to form HBOS plc, which was subsequently reorganized by the HBOS Group Reorganization Act 2006. In January 2009, Lloyds TSB Bank plc acquired HBOS plc to form the Lloyds Banking Group plc. The 'Bank of Scotland' brand is used for the Scottish branches of the merged entity.

[62] In 2001, Clydesdale Bank acquired the Yorkshire Bank.

[63] In January 2009, Lloyds TSB Scotland became part of the Lloyds Banking Group plc. The 'Bank of Scotland' brand is used for the Scottish branches of the merged entity.

[64] Since 1996, this has been operated by the Cheque and Credit Clearing Co. Ltd under the APACS (now UKPA) umbrella.

[65] The bank was the object of a substantial 'rescue package' by the Irish Government in February 2009.

[66] The bank is part of the AIB Group, which was the object of a significant 'rescue package' by the Irish Government in February 2009 and was effectively nationalized by the Irish Government in September 2010.

[67] N.9 above.   [68] N.10 above.

[69] N.11 above.   [70] In December 2008, Wachovia Corporation was acquired by Wells Fargo.

Bank of Tokyo-Mitsubishi UFJ Ltd are members of some of the companies operating under the UKPA umbrella with responsibility for payment clearing in the United Kingdom. In other cases, some foreign banks have acquired ownership of United Kingdom banks. For example, in October 2008, Grupo Santander acquired Abbey National plc and Alliance and Leicester Commercial Bank. Thirdly, a range of supermarkets and retail chains now provide banking and other financial services, such as Tesco, Sainsbury's, Marks and Spencer, and Virgin. Often this was done through a joint venture with an established clearer or other financial institution. For example, Sainsbury's Bank (now Sainsbury's Finance) is the result of a joint venture between Sainsbury's supermarket and the Bank of Scotland (now part of the Lloyds Banking Group), Tesco was initially partnered with the Royal Bank of Scotland (although Tesco acquired the Royal Bank of Scotland's share in the joint venture company in 2008, and Tesco Personal Finance became Tesco bank in October 2009), and Virgin Money was originally formed as a joint venture between Virgin and the Norwich Union, although the Virgin Group has since acquired its entire shareholding. Fourthly, there are the internet banks, which usually operate as a subsidiary of an established bank.[71] Despite this competitive environment, however, the British Government commissioned in November 1998 a review of the level of competition within the United Kingdom banking industry, excluding investment banking. Following the publication of an interim report in 1999, the review committee, chaired by Don Cruickshank, published its final report in March 2000.[72] The review committee concentrated on levels of competition in three key areas: money transmission (namely, the flow of money through payment systems), the provision of banking services to personal customers, and the provision of banking services to small and medium-sized enterprises (SMEs).[73] It found competition problems in all three areas and made 55 recommendations to the British Government, which accepted the majority of those recommendations.[74]

Two particular issues, however, merit closer examination. The first issue relates to money transmission services supplied in the United Kingdom. The Cruickshank Committee found that these were run through a series of unregulated networks, mostly controlled by the same few large banks—the (now) four major clearers and the two largest Scottish banks—which in turn dominated the market for services to individuals and

---

[71] N.38 above.   [72] D. Cruickshank, n.41 above.

[73] Following the Cruickshank recommendations concerning the supply of banking services to SMEs, the Competition Commission published its own report: *The Supply of Banking Services by Clearing Banks to Small and Medium-sized Enterprises* (London, Cm. 5319, March 2002). This report found that the main clearing groups were charging excessive prices and making excessive profits, and identified other adverse effects on choice and the level of information available to SME customers. The Competition Commission's recommendations were implemented by means of undertakings agreed between the Office of Fair Trading (OFT) and the banks. The OFT conducted a review of compliance with these undertakings during 2006 and reported its conclusions to the Competition Commission in January 2007, having found that banks had complied with their undertakings and recommending that the four main banks be released from their undertakings to pay interest on business accounts and to offer free core money transmission services. According to the OFT, there was sufficient competition to ensure these practices would continue without the need for formal undertakings, but the undertakings in other areas should continue as the SME banking services market was still not functioning properly: www.oft.gov.uk/news/press/2007/122-07. In August 2007, the Competition Commission provisionally decided to lift price controls on the four main business banks, but retained 11 of their other undertakings relating to SME banking services. After wide consultation, the Competition Commission confirmed its provisional decision in December 2007: www.competition-commission.org.uk.

[74] HM Treasury, *Competition in UK Banking: The Cruickshank Report—Government Response* (London, August 2000) (www.hm-treasury.gov.uk). The Government declined to follow the review committee's recommendation that all mergers between financial institutions should be referred to the Competition Commission for investigation if the merging entities have material shares of the relevant market: ibid., Response to Recommendation 12.

SMEs.[75] The Committee also examined the entry restrictions on membership of these schemes, including those restrictions on membership of APACS (now UKPA) clearings, and concluded that the membership criteria of the main United Kingdom payment schemes distorted competition by restricting full access to banks and other deposit-taking institutions.[76] The Committee's response recommended the establishment of a licensing regime for payment systems.[77] Under the new regime, all payment system participants would be subject to a class licence that would require non-discriminatory access to the payment system.[78] Most importantly, the Committee recommended the establishment of an independent payment systems commission ('PayCom') to supervise the new licensing regime.[79] The British Government was attracted by the Cruickshank Report's recommendations, although it reserved its final decision until completion of a widespread consultation exercise.[80] Initially, responsibility for regulating and reforming United Kingdom payment systems was conferred upon the Office of Fair Trading (OFT),[81] which set up the Payment Systems Task Force in 2004. This was itself wound-up in November 2006 and, after producing its final report,[82] was replaced in 2007 by the Payments Council, a self-regulated body supported by the Treasury and the OFT.[83] In May 2008, the Payments Council published the *National Payments Plan*, its strategic framework for innovation and change in the area of payment services over the following decade,[84] and highlighted a number of priority areas for longer-term reform. Of more immediate significance in this context, however, is the advent of the Payment Services Directive,[85] which will significantly increase competition by allowing any entity to seek authorization[86] as a 'payment

---

[75] D. Cruickshank, n.41 above, Executive Summary, [11].   [76] Ibid., [3.94].

[77] Ibid., [3.186].   [78] Ibid., [3.197].

[79] Ibid., [3.204].   [80] HM Treasury, n.74 above, Response to Recommendations 21, 22, & 23.

[81] HM Treasury Consultation Document (London, December 2000); HM Treasury Press Release, 21 December 2000. In May 2003, the OFT published a report containing a market study covering the United Kingdom's money transmission clearing systems and a review of its work on debit, credit, and ATM card networks since 2000: *UK Payment Systems* (London, 2003).

[82] Payment Systems Task Force, *Final Report of the Payment Systems Task Force* (February 2007), Sect. 3, which makes clear that the Task Force has had a significant impact, contributing *inter alia* to the development of the 'Faster Payments Service' (Ch. 13, Sects. 1(iv) & 3(iv)(b) below), to streamlining the governance structure of the LINK scheme, and to the introduction of the uniform '2-4-6' time-limits for cheque clearance (Ch. 10, Sect. 2 below).

[83] The Payments Council board consists of four independent directors and 11 directors representing the main banks involved in processing payments. The Payments Council has produced its first annual report (*Annual Review 2008—Driving Change in UK Payments* (2008)) and progress reports (Payments Council, *Progress Report—Delivering the National Payments Plan* (London, March 2009); Payments Council, *Progress Report: Delivering the National Payments Plan* (London, June 2010)). The OFT has conducted a review of the Payments Council's first two years and, whilst concluding that the Payments Council had been 'largely successful' in meeting two of its objectives, considered that the Payments Council's work on the 'cross-scheme integrity of payment systems has been disappointing' and that it should make more effort to follow up initiatives, to be proactive, and to address the impression that it is 'dominated by banking interests': OFT, *Review of the Operations of the Payments Council* (London, March 2009). The Payments Council's response in August 2009 highlighted a number of areas in which it would seek to improve performance. Recently, the Payments Council has launched a consultation on updating the National Payments Plan: Payments Council, *Updating the National Payments Plan—A Consultation for the 2011 Review of the NPP* (April 2011).

[84] Payments Council, *National Payments Plan—Setting the Strategic Vision for UK Payments* (14 May 2008).

[85] Directive 2007/64/EC on Payment Services in the Internal Market, [2007] OJ L 319.

[86] Ibid., art. 10(1).

institution'[87] so that it can provide 'payment services'[88] within the European Union, provided that such an entity complies with requirements relating to initial capital and own funds.[89] This effectively brings into force something similar to the licensing regime originally proposed in the Cruickshank Report. The 'Payment Services Directive' was implemented in the United Kingdom by the Payment Services Regulations 2009 (PSR 2009),[90] and the prudential supervision of 'payment institutions' was conferred upon the FSA.[91]

The second issue relates to consumer access to banking services, since between 2.5 and 3.5 million of the adult population in the United Kingdom are estimated to be without any form of bank account. Many of these will be on low incomes and may have been refused a current account because of the risk that the account could become overdrawn.[92] This is a real problem, given that a current account is usually required to gain access to a number of money transmission systems, whether these involve the use of cheques, debit cards, or electronic funds tranfers. The Cruickshank Committee considered that it should be made easier for those without a current account to get access to basic banking services.[93] The Government has echoed the Committee's concern and expressed support for the idea of a universal bank to be run through the Post Office network.[94] Part of the Government's response was to establish the Financial Inclusion Taskforce, which works with the Payments Council[95] and advises the Treasury about increasing participation in the banking system. Alongside these initiatives, the major clearing banks and other retail banks have introduced 'universal banking services', which include 'basic bank accounts' that can usually be accessed either at the Post Office or through branches and ATMs, but that do not allow for overdrafts.[96] According to the BBA, the 'universal banking' initiative and the emphasis on 'basic bank accounts' has markedly reduced financial exclusion.[97]

---

[87] Ibid., arts. 1(1)(d), 4(4), 10(1). This does not include 'credit institutions' and 'electronic money institutions' as these are already subject to home state authorization pursuant to Directive 2006/48/EC, [2006] OJ L 177/1: Ch. 2, Sect. 7(i) & (iii) below.

[88] Ibid., arts. 4(3) & Annex. These include cash deposits, cash withdrawals and execution of payment instructions on a 'payment account' (defined: ibid, art. 4(14)), the 'execution of payment transactions where the funds are covered by a credit line', issuing and acquiring payment instruments, money remittance, and execution of orders given by electronic means.

[89] Ibid., arts. 6–8.   [90] S.I. 2009/209.

[91] Ibid, reg. 4. For the PSR 2009, see Ch. 2, Sect. 6(iii) & Ch. 13, Sects. 5(iv)–(vi) below.

[92] D. Cruickshank, n.41 above, [7.5], which noted that OFT research indicates that up to a quarter of applications for a current account may be refused. Nevertheless, the issue remains controversial with the BBA pointing to an independent report by Kempson and Whyley (University of Bristol) suggesting that the main reason for the lack of bank accounts in the adult population was the absence of any need or desire to use an account, rather than banks' refusal of accounts. In recent years, the BBA has heralded the increase in basic bank accounts amongst the adult population in the United Kingdom: British Bankers' Association, n.55 above. This figure had risen to 7.8 million basic bank accounts by 26 June 2009.

[93] Ibid., [7.20]–[7.28].   [94] HM Treasury, n.74 above, Response to Recommendation 54.

[95] Payments Council, *Progress Report: Delivering the National Payments Plan* (June 2010), 3.

[96] The usual features of basic bank accounts are that wages, benefits, pensions, and tax credits can be paid in directly; sterling cheques can be paid in for free; cash can be withdrawn from ATMs and at Post Office counters; bills can be paid by direct debit; most accounts also permit over-the-counter bank transactions; and some accounts include a debit card or the ability to make payments by standing order: FSA, *Moneymadeclear: Just the Facts about Basic Bank Accounts* (November 2009), 2. For a similar, earlier definition, see *Banking Code* (March 2008), 30, which also highlights that overdrafts are usually unavailable on such accounts. See also *Office of Fair Trading* v. *Abbey National plc* [2008] EWHC 875 (Comm.), [37]; [2008] EWHC 2325 (Comm.), [66]–[76]. , rev'd on a different point: [2010] 2 All ER (Comm.) 945 (UKSC). See further *Lending Code* (March 2011), *Glossary*.

[97] British Bankers' Association, n.55 above, which indicates that, since April 2003, '3.2 million post-office accessible accounts have been opened, half for customers with no previous banking relationship'. See also Financial Inclusion Taskforce, *Fourth Annual Report* (London, October 2009).

3 The merchant or investment banks[98]

During the 1970s and early 1980s, the merchant (now investment) banks were divided into two groups: the acceptance houses and the issuing houses. To appreciate the nature of these two types of bank and their differences, it is necessary to consider their background. The acceptance houses originated in the late eighteenth and early nineteenth centuries,[99] and comprised the seven members of the Accepting Houses Committee. Although most of them became incorporated in the twentieth century, they usually commenced their operations either as individual merchants or partnerships. In their early days, the acceptance houses were 'merchants' in the true sense of the word, as they traded on their own capital, primarily in the import and export of goods. Some even had their own fleets of ships. Later on, their ships were also used by other merchants engaged in current transactions; and, in due course, the acceptance houses began to finance such smaller traders. The facility used by the acceptance houses in the nineteenth century to finance other traders was the acceptance credit,[100] which provided for bills of exchange to be drawn by the trader on the house. The house's acceptance of the bills facilitated their discount, usually with another acceptance house, and reimbursement for any amounts paid upon the maturity of any acceptance was usually made out of the proceeds of the mercantile transaction in question. The acceptance house usually charged an acceptance fee, which constituted its direct profit from the transaction. As a result of their activity in the export trade, the acceptance houses played an important role in the development of such commercial facilities as the cif and fob contract and the documentary letter of credit.[101] Over time, the acceptance houses broadened their activities to include foreign-exchange dealings, money-management dealings (including portfolio investments for customers), the financing of current and capital transactions by means of short-term, medium-term, and even long-term loans, and eventually even capital ventures. In modern times, they became involved also in capital issues and in underwriting their clients' issues of shares and bonds.[102]

The issuing houses constituted a very different group. First, the issuing houses' origin differed from that of the acceptance houses, since many of the former were new faces in the City. Secondly, as indicated by their name, the issuing houses' main business was in the field of capital issues. Some of the issuing houses were not involved with current transactions and those that engaged in this type of business regarded it as incidental or secondary to their main underwriting and capital-issues business. Thus, the issuing houses specialized in one specific type of merchant-banking business. Thirdly, a bank could qualify for membership of the issuing houses' organization—the Issuing Houses Association—even if it was not under British control, whereas this was not the case as regards the acceptance houses' organization.

The structure of merchant (now investment) banking changed radically following the general increase in global financial activity during the 1980s, which made specialization unattractive. Many banking institutions, including some issuing houses and some

---

[98] J.J. Clay & B.S. Wheble, *Modern Merchant Banking* (3rd edn., London, 1990).

[99] V. Cowles, *The Rothschilds: A Family of Fortune* (revd. edn., London, 1979); J. Ellis, *Heir to Adventure: The Story of Brown & Co.* (London, 1960).

[100] Ch. 10, Sects. 1 & 10 below.

[101] E.P. Ellinger, *Documentary Letters of Credit: A Comparative Study* (Singapore, 1970), ch. 2; E.P. Ellinger & D. Neo, *The Law and Practice of Documentary Letters of Credit* (Oxford, 2010), ch. 1.

[102] Additionally, most of the acceptance houses engaged in bullion transactions, but not generally the factoring of accounts: see generally N. Ruddy, S. Mills, & N. Davidson, *Salinger on Factoring* (4th edn., London, 2006).

acceptance houses, started to work in close association with firms engaged in investment services, such as substantial stockbrokers and bond dealers. The formation of these links led to the replacement in 1988 of the two older organizations with the British Merchant Banking and Securities Houses Association. This subsequently became the London Investment Banking Association (LIBA), which is now the principal United Kingdom trade association for firms that are active in the investment banking and securities industry. Not all of its members are banks, but most of them operate under an authorization granted pursuant to the FSMA 2000.[103] This means that the members of LIBA engage in a diverse range of business activities from the traditional activities of the acceptance houses in international trade, on the one hand, to all types of capital issues and financial and investment services business, such as fund management and the arrangement of transactions respecting equities and bonds, on the other. This diversity is evident in Jacobson J's description of modern investment banking business in *Australian Securities and Investments Commission* v. *Citigroup Global Markets Australia Pty Ltd (No. 4):*[104]

> ...the term 'investment bank' is not capable of precise definition but the influence and importance of investment banks in the financial system is vast; they are integral to the efficient operation of the system... [m]ajor investment banks are listed public companies which operate internationally. They describe themselves, and are referred to, as global financial services firms and financial services conglomerates. They provide a diverse range of services including financial advisory services to corporations on mergers and acquisitions, issuing, buying and selling securities, investment research and transactions financing. This is not an exhaustive list...

As this statement also makes clear, what unites the members of LIBA is not so much the business activities they have in common, but rather the type of business in which they do not engage, namely the provision of those personal banking services that are most closely associated with retail banking. A consequence of this is that, unlike the clearing banks, the merchant (now investment) banks do not maintain chains of branches and are not generally members of the clearing companies that fall under the UKPA umbrella. Instead, many of the LIBA members operate from a single office in the City, although some have up to three or four branches or offices in the City or in major industrial towns. Furthermore, the merchant (now investment) banks cater mainly to the needs of corporations and large unincorporated enterprises, and do not seek out individual customers. Thus, although nowadays more commonly referred to as 'investment banks', LIBA members have remained true to their original description as 'merchant banks', engaged in mercantile transactions.[105]

4 Discount houses and the wholesale money markets

Until the late 1990s, discount houses formed a specialist group of banks that operated in London's short-term money markets. Originally, they were discounters of bills of exchange drawn under acceptance credits issued by banks,[106] but they subsequently expanded their

---

[103] Ch. 2, Sect. 4 below. For LIBA members, see www.liba.org.uk.

[104] (2007) 241 ALR 705, [255]–[256] (FCA). For a statutory definition of the term, 'investment bank', see Banking Act 2009, s.232.

[105] The global credit crisis has radically changed the investment banking landscape in the United States, with the largest investment banks either being taken over by, or converting to, commercial banks, which are now precluded from engaging in proprietary trading and related activities: Dodd-Frank Wall Street Reform and Consumer Protection Act 2010 (US), s.619. See further Ch. 2, Sect. 1 below.

[106] Gillett Bros., *The Bill on London* (London, 1976). See further Ch. 10, Sect. 10 below.

business by discounting other obligations, such as Treasury bills, and further specialized in the placing of money on the short-term markets. To this end, the discount houses accepted deposits from banks and other financial institutions and invested these in marketable securities and bonds issued by government departments, local authorities, and commercial firms. Discount houses have now disappeared, however, together with the association representing those houses that operated in the City—the London Discount Market Association. This resulted from the Bank of England's decision to sanction the use of gilt repos as an approved instrument for 'Open Market Operations', and to widen its list of approved counterparties, which meant that the discount houses no longer occupied a unique position in money market operations. Since 1997, the London Money Market Association has represented the interests of those banks and other financial institutions that operate in the sterling money market.[107] The Bank of England, through daily money market operations, supplies the settlement banks operating in the wholesale clearing systems with funds that enable them to settle accounts *inter se*. By setting the interest rate for these operations, the Bank of England influences the general level of interest rates throughout the financial system. In these operations, the Bank of England buys high quality assets in exchange for cash, either outright or through a repo transaction. Eligible collateral for 'Open Market Operations' include Treasury bills, gilt-edged stock, eligible bank bills, and securities issued by European Union governments and supranational institutions.

5 Foreign banks

(i) Overview

London is a major centre of international banking, and unsurprisingly most major banks in the Western world have a presence in the City. There are three organizations for such foreign banks: the Association of Foreign Banks, the American Financial Services Association, and the Japanese Bankers Association.[108] A number of foreign banks have now changed form or disappeared entirely following the global credit crisis, which affected banks in the United States[109] and Iceland[110] particularly severely.

(ii) The Association of Foreign Banks

The Association of Foreign Banks (AFB)[111] has one of the largest memberships of financial institutions in the City—currently around 160 members,[112] which are all foreign banks or securities houses that have their ultimate ownership in countries outside the United Kingdom. The AFB is organized along the lines of a typical international banking operation. Business committees cover business continuity, corporate and institutional

---

[107] There are other money markets, such as the foreign exchange and bullion markets. For the LMMA members, see www.lmma.org.uk.

[108] There are also Europe-wide banking associations and bodies, such as the Euro Banking Association, the European Payments Council, and the European System of Central Banks.

[109] N.105 above.

[110] See generally *R v. HM Treasury, ex parte Kaupthing Bank hf* [2009] EWHC 2542 (Admin.). See also *Rawlinson & Hunter Trustees SA v. Kaupthing Bank hf* [2011] EWHC 566 (Comm.), [10]–[34].

[111] Formerly, the Foreign Banks & Securities Houses Association, which was established in 1947 and which absorbed the British Overseas and Commonwealth Banks Association in 1996: A. Gleeson, *London Enriched* (London, 1997).

[112] For current members, see www.foreignbanks.org.uk.

banking, markets, and trade finance. Technical committees cover, *inter alia*, human resources, operations, legal and regulatory issues, taxation, and risk management. The AFB also supervises the needs of foreign banks' representative offices with a special purpose committee. The AFB is governed by a board of directors, but also maintains an advisory council comprising members' representatives from general management as well as the chairmen of some of the business and operational committees. The business activities of the banks organized under the AFB umbrella vary a great deal. It is natural that each bank in the group has a special interest in customers from its home country, and in the promotion of the business links of firms in its country with correspondents in the United Kingdom. Nevertheless, member banks are involved in a wide range of international banking transactions. Their business is concerned mainly with wholesale rather than retail activities, although some member banks do provide current accounts for their customers.

(iii) **The American and Japanese banks**

The American and Japanese banks have established a presence of such significance in the City that it was reasonable for them to found their own respective organizations in London. Each of the two organizations is concerned solely with the respective interests of its members.

6 The British Bankers' Association

The existence in the banking world of so many groups of banks and banking associations resulted in the need for an additional organization to act as co-ordinator. This led to the establishment of the British Bankers' Association (BBA), which is a trade association made up of over 200 member banks and other financial services firms operating in the United Kingdom, as well 45 'professional associate' member firms.[113] Eighty-five per cent of its members provide wholesale banking services and three-quarters of its members are of non-United Kingdom origin, representing 60 different countries. BBA Membership is open to two types of institution. The first type is an institution authorized by the FSA under the FSMA 2000 with permission to carry on one or more of the following regulated activities:[114] (a) accepting deposits; (b) dealing in investments as principal; (c) dealing in investments as agent; (d) managing investments; and (e) arranging deals in investments. The second type is an institution that is not so authorized by the FSA, but is authorized by another European Union regulator to carry on the same regulated activities as just mentioned and that also has an establishment in the United Kingdom. Subject to the approval of the BBA Council, membership is also open to other organizations that do not fulfil the normal BBA membership criteria, but that nevertheless serve the financial services industry.

The BBA's main objects are to promote the interests of the United Kingdom banking industry and to represent the views of, and where necessary negotiate on behalf of, members in dealings with official bodies in the United Kingdom, the European Union, and elsewhere. In addition, the BBA provides members with a forum for agreeing policy on matters of common interest and providing information and other services to members. Other

---

[113] Figures as at October 2010: see www.bba.org.uk.
[114] On the term 'regulated activity' (including its extension to cover retail mortgage business and payment services), see Ch. 2, Sect. 4 below.

important objectives of the BBA include upholding London's position as an international financial centre and (until the advent of the FSA's new 'Banking and Payment Services Regime' in November 2009 covering the regulation of both deposit-taking and the provision of payment services)[115] sponsoring the *Banking Code* and *Business Banking Code*. The BBA has continued to perform the latter function, at least in the areas of bank lending and credit card finance to consumers, micro-enterprises, and smaller charities, by promulgating the *Lending Code* and *A Statement of Principles: Banks and Micro-enterprises—Working Together* in November 2009. These two publications were replaced by a new edition of the *Lending Code* and the *Guide to the Lending Code for Micro-Enterprises* in March 2011.

7 Comparison with building societies[116]

Building societies originated in the early nineteenth century as friendly societies and have been the subject of statutory regulation since the Building Societies Act 1836. At present, they are governed by the Building Societies Act 1986,[117] which has brought under its regime all the pre-existing societies regardless of their type.[118] Building societies' traditional business was the acceptance of deposits from members and mortgage lending to members. Over the years, however, building societies have been empowered to widen their activities. In particular, during the last two decades, the gap has narrowed between the activities of building societies and those of the clearing banks. Indeed, even under the previous regime in the Building Societies Act 1962, there was already an overlap between these two types of institution in respect of their acceptance of deposits and their mortgage lending. Although it is true that building societies dealt primarily with members, whilst clearing banks borrowed from and lent to the public at large, in practice, virtually any individual could become a member of a building society. The distinction was, therefore, largely illusory. Another similarity between the clearing banks and building societies was that both traditionally operated through branches, although the branch networks of the larger clearers were (and still are) more extensive than those of the building societies.

Accordingly, the main difference between the clearing banks and building societies prior to the enactment of the Building Societies Act 1986 lay in the narrower range of services provided by the building societies, including the range of transactions financed by them. Whilst the clearing banks have always provided credit facilities for general purposes, the building societies' lending remained predominantly related to transactions involving the acquisition of land. Two additional important distinctions were, first, that

---

[115] Ch. 2, Sect. 6 below. One aspect of the BBA's role in representing the interests of banks is to participate in litigation on behalf of its members generally; see, for a recent example, *R (on the application of the British Bankers Association)* v. *Financial Services Authority* [2011] EWHC 999 (Admin.), [2]–[11].

[116] E.A. Wurtzburg & J. Mills, *Building Society Law* (15th edn., by T. Lloyd, M. Water, & E. Ovey, London, 1989).

[117] The Building Societies Act 1986 has been in force *in toto* since 1 January 1988, and it repealed and replaced the Building Societies Act 1962, which in turn had consolidated earlier legislation: E.A. Wurtzburg & J. Mills, n.116 above, [1.04]. For amendments to the Building Societies Act 1986, see in particular the Building Societies Act 1997 and the Banking (Special Provisions) Act 2008, s.11.

[118] Building societies used to be either incorporated or unincorporated. Before the Building Societies Act 1986, the former were regulated by the Building Societies Act 1962, and the latter by the Benefit Building Societies Act 1836. In the twentieth century, the unincorporated building society ceased to exist and the incorporated form became predominant. Although most incorporated building societies were 'permanent', some were 'terminating' and ceased to exist on a given date or event. The Building Societies Act 1986 rendered all these distinctions obsolete and now deems all building societies to be permanent.

building societies were restricted to dealings with individuals and, secondly, that a build-ing society could not provide members with current account facilities involving draw-ing cheques on the society itself.[119] The building societies regime changed considerably, however, with the Building Societies Act 1986,[120] which had two aims: first, to relax the tight statutory controls on building societies' commercial powers, so as to allow them to compete more effectively with banks in the more deregulated financial and mortgage markets of the 1980s; and, secondly, to introduce a modern system of prudential regu-lation and supervision and to improve the protection of societies' investing members. Despite these changes, building societies could still only provide those services that were explicitly permitted by the Building Societies Act 1986. Further deregulation took place in 1988,[121] although a number of the restrictions that remained were only removed with the permissive regime of the Building Societies Act 1997, which allowed societies to carry out any type of business activity within their objects, unless it was explicitly prohibited.

This regime has not, however, escaped the sweeping changes to the regulation of the financial services industry introduced by the FSMA 2000. First, under the Building Societies Act 1986, the Building Societies Commission was constituted the supervisory body for all existing and future building societies.[122] The Commission has now ceased to function, as, under section 336(1) of the FSMA 2000, the Treasury was given power to order that its functions be transferred primarily to the FSA, with any remaining func-tions being exercised by the Treasury itself. This transfer was effected by the Financial Services and Markets Act 2000 (Mutual Societies) Order 2001.[123] Accordingly, depos-it-taking by both banks and building societies became regulated by the FSA under the FSMA 2000 regime,[124] and (together with the regulation of payment services) now falls within the FSA's 'Banking and Payment Services' regime that has been effective since 1 November 2009.[125] The second important consequence of the FSMA 2000 was the aboli-tion of the Building Societies Investor Protection Board, which administered the scheme to protect investors in an insolvent building society,[126] as a result of the Financial Services and Markets Act 2000 (Mutual Societies) Order 2001.[127] Investors are now protected by the Financial Services Compensation Scheme established under Part 15 of the FSMA 2000, as recently amended by Part 4 of the Banking Act 2009.[128]

The changes brought about by the Building Societies Act 1986, together with the amendments in 1988 and 1997, allow building societies to provide a whole host of banking and other financial services to their members. For example, building socie-ties nowadays offer their members current accounts that are operable by cheque and

---

[119] This problem was exacerbated by building societies not having direct access to the cheque clearing house, although some tried to overcome this obstacle by making arrangements for the payment of their customers' accounts by issuing the society's own cheques. An ingenious scheme, introduced in the 1980s in collaboration with some of the clearers, enabled the building societies' members to draw cheques, bearing the name of the building society, on the bank that supported the scheme. In essence, the building society was the drawer, the bank was the drawee, and the building society member, whose account details were set out in the instrument's magnetic ink line, completed the instrument and signed it. These cheques could be cleared through the respective bank by means of a direct-debit entry in the customer's account. Conceptually, the customer drew the cheque on the bank under the building society's authority.

[120] Building Society Commission, *Annual Report 1999–2000*, ch. 3.

[121] Building Societies (Commercial Assets and Services) Order 1988, S.I. 1988/1141, as amended by S.I. 1989/839 (now lapsed).

[122] Building Societies Act 1986, s.1. For the Building Societies Commission's powers of control, see ibid., ss.36–57, Sched. 3, Pts. III, IV & Scheds. 7A, 8A.

[123] S.I. 2001/2617, art. 4.   [124] Ch. 2, Sect. 4 below.

[125] Ch. 2, Sect. 6 below.   [126] Building Societies Act 1986, ss.24–29A & Scheds. 5–6.

[127] S.I. 2001/2617, art. 11. See also FSMA 2000, s.337.   [128] Ch. 2, Sect. 4(viii) below.

electronic means, as well as offering money-transfer services.[129] To facilitate this, the defences available to banks in respect of the payment and the collection of cheques have also been conferred on building societies.[130] The success of the building societies in this field is evidenced by some of them having taken up membership of APACS,[131] and, since APACS' dissolution, by them continuing to be members of the companies responsible for clearing payments in the United Kingdom that operate under the UKPA umbrella.[132] Accordingly, the Building Societies Act 1986, as amended, has generally narrowed the gap between the clearing banks and building societies. Indeed, a building society can now opt to transfer its entire business to a commercial company,[133] thereby ceasing to be a statutory corporation and becoming an entity regulated by the companies' legislation. Nevertheless, a society that converts to corporate status and becomes a bank continues to be protected from being made the subject of a take-over bid for a period of five years following conversion.[134]

This route from mutual society to bank has proved attractive to a number of former building societies, for example, Abbey National plc (part of Grupo Santander since July 2004 and rebranded 'Santander' on 11 January 2010),[135] Alliance and Leicester plc (part of Grupo Santander since October 2008),[136] Halifax plc (initially part of HBOS plc, and subsequently part of Lloyds Banking Group plc since January 2009), and Woolwich plc (part of the Barclays Bank Group since 2000, and now the Barclays United Kingdom mortgage brand). The number of authorized societies has fallen from 137 in 1986 to 68 in 2000,[137] and eight of the ten largest societies have become banks, halving the sector's market share.[138] Despite the significant deregulation that subsequently took place in 1988 and 1997, the Building Societies Act 1986 was still mentioned by a number of building societies as one of the factors motivating their decision to convert.[139] The global credit crisis that began in 2007 has further impacted on the number of United Kingdom building societies that remain in existence: since 1 December 2008, the Derbyshire Building Society and the Cheshire Building Society have been trading divisions of the Nationwide Building Society, which also acquired the assets of the Dunfermline Building Society on 30 March 2009; since 31 December 2008, the Barnsley Building Society has been a trading name of the Yorkshire Building Society following its acquisition; since 31 December 2008, the Skipton Building Society and the Scarborough Building Society have merged to form an enlarged society; and, during 2008, the Bradford & Bingley plc, was partly nationalized[140] and partly acquired by the Abbey National plc, which is itself now owned by Grupo Santander. Accordingly, whilst in 2008 there were 59 members of the Building Societies

---

[129] From 1 November 2009, the provision of 'payment services' has been regulated by the PSR 2009, implementing Directive 2007/64/EC on Payment Services in the Internal Market, [2007] OJ L 319: Ch. 2, Sect. 6(iii) & Ch. 13, Sects. 5(iv)–(vi) below.

[130] Building Societies Act 1997, s.12(3).

[131] As at July 2009, only the Nationwide Building Society was an APACS member, although a number of demutualized societies continued with their membership as banks. For example, the Halifax Building Society was a full APACS member (even before becoming part of HBOS plc and then the Lloyds Banking Group plc, which were themselves APACS members), and the Woolwich Building Society was an APACS associate member (before becoming part of the Barclays Bank Group, which was itself a full APACS member).

[132] For example, the Nationwide Building Society is a member of the Cheque and Credit Clearing Co. Ltd and BACS Payment Schemes Ltd.

[133] Building Societies Act 1986, ss.97–100.   [134] Ibid., s.101.

[135] N.9 above.   [136] N.10 above.

[137] Building Society Commission, n.120 above, [3.7].   [138] Id.

[139] Ibid., [3.3].

[140] The nationalized part of the bank was merged with Northern Rock (Asset Management) plc under a single holding company, UK Asset Resolution Ltd, on 1 October 2010.

Association—the trade association for all building societies in the United Kingdom—this had dropped further to only 52 members by August 2009.[141]

That said, whatever amount of deregulation may have occurred, building societies remain subject to a number of key restrictions under the Building Societies Act 1986. First, the legislation affirms that a building society's principal purpose is to make loans for the purchase of residential property by its members.[142] Secondly, a building society must ensure that loans fully secured on residential property make up at least 75 per cent of its total assets, or group assets if applicable, less fixed and liquid assets and any long-term insurance fund.[143] Thirdly, a society must raise at least half of its funding from its members in the form of shares.[144] Fourthly, there are restrictions on building societies engaging in transactions, such as trading in commodities or currencies or transactions involving derivatives.[145] Finally, a building society is prohibited from creating a floating charge on the whole or part of its undertaking or property.[146]

8 Other financial institutions

The banks and building societies are the major financial institutions in the United Kingdom. In addition, there are some entities with a specialized type of business that do not fall under either umbrella. Thus, the finance companies, such as Lombard Tricity Finance Ltd (now part of the Royal Bank of Scotland Group), specialize in what used to be hire-purchase business, but which has now become the general provision of consumer finance. These have grown rapidly since the end of the Second World War, and nowadays provide finance not only to consumers, but also to industry and commerce, and also engage in the leasing of equipment to business firms.[147] Nowadays, a number of banks have substantial shareholdings in finance companies.

Additionally, there are some other bodies that carry on borrowing and lending activities but that are not involved in full-scale banking, such as the Crown Agents, the credit unions, and the National Savings Bank.[148] Finally, and of increasing importance in the United Kingdom, are entities that provide specialized banking services to the Islamic community.[149] Whilst some of the major banks have recognized the demand for Sharia'a-compliant banking products and have accordingly positioned themselves to enter this novel and lucrative market,[150] there are also entities that specialize in such products

---

[141] For a list of members, see www.bsa.org.uk.

[142] Building Societies Act 1986, s.5(1) (as amended). A building society's rules must provide that no person will be a member of the society unless he is a shareholder, borrower or both: ibid., Sched. 2, para. 5(1) (as substituted by the Building Societies Act 1997, s.2(1)). A 'shareholding member' is a person who holds a share in the society: ibid., Sched. 2, para. 5(2), as substituted. A 'borrowing member' is an individual who is indebted to the society (1) in respect of a loan that is fully secured on land, or (2) if the rules of the society so provide, in respect of a loan that is (within the meaning of the rules) substantially secured on land: ibid., Sched. 2, para. 5(2), as substituted.

[143] Ibid., ss.6–6B.   [144] Ibid., s.7.

[145] Ibid., s.9A.   [146] Ibid., s.9B.

[147] Before accepting deposits from the public, finance companies must obtain authorization under the FSMA 2000: Ch. 2, Sect. 4 below.

[148] Originally established under the Post Office Savings Bank Act 1969, s.94(1) and currently regulated by the National Savings Bank Act 1971. Its business is to accept deposits from the public, which can be as little as £20, but cannot exceed £100,000. This bank is outside the regime of the FSMA 2000: Ch. 2, Sect. 4 below.

[149] See generally M. Kabir Hassan & M.K. Lewis, *Islamic Finance* (Cheltenham, 2007).

[150] The association for institutions providing Islamic banking products and services is the Institute of Islamic Banking and Insurance: www.islamic-banking.com.

and that operate alongside the traditional banking sector (for example, hawaladars).[151] The growing importance of such banking products in the United Kingdom is reflected by the extent to which they have featured in recent litigation.[152]

9 Review of the system

The City of London's banking community is split into a number of groups that have frequently developed on historical rather than functional lines. Some organizations are regional in character, such as the American Financial Services Association and the Japanese Bankers Association, whilst others comprise institutions that have similar interests, such as the old discount houses and their umbrella organization. Up to a point, the same is also true for the merchant (now investment) banks. It is clear, however, that there are overlaps between the different groupings. Accordingly, where an organization's rules do not include a restriction, a given entity may belong to two associations. In particular, many banks are members of their own specific organization and the BBA. From a functional point of view, it is probably best to classify both the banks and their organizations into specialist and general providers of banking services. The clearing banks constitute the generalists; all other organizations tend to represent specialized banks. The emergence of multifunctional banking groups, however, means that both generalist and specialist banking services are now provided by associated companies within the same commercial group. In contrast, from the public's viewpoint, the clearing banks tend to be regarded as 'the banks'. This is a realistic approach, as only the clearers from amongst the banks cater for all the needs of the public and are capable of accommodating the individual, the small business, and the multinational corporation.

---

[151] *Azam v. Iqbal* [2007] EWHC 2025 (Admin.), [20]–[22].
[152] *Shamil Bank of Bahrain EC v. Beximco Pharmaceuticals Ltd* [2004] 2 Lloyd's Rep 1 (CA); *Azam v. Iqbal*, n.151 above; *Musawi v. RE International (UK) Ltd* [2008] 1 Lloyd's Rep 326. See also *Latifah Bte Mat Zin v. Rosmawati Bte Sharibun* [2006] 4 MLJ 705, [30]–[31] (MCA); *Arab-Malaysian Merchant Bank Bhd v. Silver Concept Sdn Bhd* [2010] 3 MLJ 702.

2

The Control of Banking Activities in the United Kingdom

1 The need for controls

(i) Introduction

The global financial turmoil that began in the summer of 2007 demonstrated that the business of banking is fraught with dangers, arising principally from the instability in the world economy and from human error or misjudgement. Like any other enterprise, a bank may be overtaken by events or may be managed unwisely. Bank failures are, therefore, no novelty. Indeed, the Bank of England itself faced serious financial problems within two years of its foundation in 1694.[1] More modern examples are not hard to find. The most serious, before the recent crisis, was the financial upheaval during the Depression between the two World Wars,[2] which led to the collapse of numerous banks. A secondary banking crisis occurred in the United Kingdom in 1973–6 and there were further banking collapses in the 1980s (Johnson Matthey Bank), in the 1990s (the Bank of Credit and Commerce International (BCCI) and Barings), and since 2007 the turmoil in the global financial sector. Lack of liquidity (the 'credit crunch') in the wholesale money markets as a result of fears that fellow banks were overly exposed to the US sub-prime mortgage market, initially led to the near-collapse of those UK banks, such as Northern Rock and HBOS, that were heavily dependent on those markets for funding. Northern Rock was temporarily nationalized and HBOS was taken over by Lloyds TSB. Other banks had to recapitalize, with the Government taking a temporary shareholding in RBS and in the merged Lloyds TSB/HBOS, through a specially formed holding company UKFI Ltd. The seismic events in the US financial markets during 2008, with the collapse or take-over of most of its investments banks[3] and the bail-out of its largest insurer AIG as well as its largest mortgage lenders Fannie Mae and Freddie Mac, compounded the loss of confidence in the global financial system.

Banks face many pitfalls in their daily operations. The better-known examples[4] are unsound lending practices (whether this is lending to countries with unstable economies or to uncreditworthy customers), hazardous dealings in foreign currencies, and liquidity crises caused by the investment of money received on short-term loans (such as deposits

---

[1] Sir John Clapham, *The Bank of England—A History* (Cambridge, 1944), ii. 30–1. A shortage of funds resulted—just two decades later—in the widening of the Bank's borrowing powers: Bank of England Act 1716.

[2] Particularly the crash of 1929–33.   [3] Most spectacularly, the insolvency of Lehman Bros.

[4] Note also the collapse of the Icelandic banking system in 2008 as a result of a combination of an inappropriate monetary policy and over-sized banking sector that government funds were insufficient to rescue.

or wholesale loans) in long-term transactions.[5] As mentioned above, this last practice was the initial cause (the 'credit crunch') of the banking crisis in the United Kingdom and elsewhere in 2007/8. Turbulence in the banking system has a disadvantageous effect on the real economy. To start with, banks invest funds deposited with them by the public. The collapse of a bank has a disastrous effect on the position of its customers, be they individual account-holders or business enterprises. In addition, the collapse of a medium-sized bank or even of a small one—to say nothing of a major bank—can induce financial panic. As recent events have shown, a run on any bank by its customers affects confidence in the banking system generally. Thus, fears about the solvency of Northern Rock in 2007 and the consequent run on that bank saw the beginning of the financial turmoil in the UK economy. A particular low was reached in October 2008 with the plummeting of bank shares prices and the announcement by the Treasury of an unprecedented 'rescue package' to improve liquidity, including an offer of more capital to banks in exchange for a government shareholding.

(ii) **The general position in the United Kingdom**

In order to safeguard the stability of the banking system, a degree of regulation and supervision[6] needs to be imposed on banks themselves. Entry into the banking sector is controlled by restricting who may accept deposits from the public. Hence, to engage in this type of business in the United Kingdom, an institution must be authorized by the Financial Services Authority (FSA)[7] to undertake it. The maintenance of adequate capital reserves and liquidity, and other matters of banking prudence, is a precondition to obtaining and maintaining such authorization. The collapse of the Northern Rock bank was partly due to inadequate application of the regulatory regime, that is, to failures in prudential supervision by the FSA.[8] But as the 2007/8 crisis demonstrated, regulation and supervision is just one part of the measures that need to be taken to ensure financial stability. However, these wider issues are beyond the scope a legal text.

The regulation of banking in the United Kingdom began with informal controls by the Bank of England and was eventually placed on a statutory basis by the Banking Act 1979. The 1970s also saw initiatives being taken in the sphere of banking regulation at the 'supranational' level by the European Economic Community (as it then was[9]) and the Basle Committee on Banking Supervision.[10] The former sought to create a 'single market' in (*inter alia*) financial services whilst the latter was concerned with the stability of the banking sector worldwide in response to its increasing interdependence. These initiatives have had a significant impact on domestic policy. The following decades saw the passing of the Banking Act 1987 which increased the Bank of England's regulatory and supervisory powers and the implementation of those international initiatives through related legislation. These international dimensions of banking regulation are considered at Sections 7 and 8, below.

---

[5] This practice was also one of the factors that triggered the secondary banking crisis: 'The Secondary Banking Crisis', *BEQB* (June 1978), n.[*3].

[6] 'Regulation' is the term usually reserved for rule-making, whilst 'supervision' is the term for ensuring that the rules are complied with.

[7] Or, corresponding regulators in other EEA Member States. See further, Sect. 7 below.

[8] See the FSA's own internal audit report of 28 March 2008, into its supervision of that bank.

[9] Established by the Treaty of Rome: see further, Sect. 7(i).

[10] See further, Sect. 8.

The election of a Labour Government in 1997 resulted in two significant changes in banking regulation. First, the Bank of England Act 1998, as well as giving the Bank independence in determining monetary policy, also transferred the Bank's responsibility for banking regulation and supervision to the FSA. The FSA—the old Securities and Investments Board (SIB) renamed[11]—became a 'super regulator', having responsibility for the regulation and supervision of the whole financial services sector: banking, insurance, and investment business and markets. This was achieved by the Financial Services and Markets Act 2000 (FSMA 2000).[12] The interconnecting roles of the so-called 'Tripartite Authorities' or 'TPA' (the Bank of England (monetary policy),[13] the FSA (the banking regulator and supervisor),[14] and the Treasury (the ultimate paymaster through fiscal policy)), were set out in a 'Tripartite Memorandum of Understanding'. This, together with the whole UK financial regulatory system, was put to the test and found wanting during the 2007/8 financial upheaval.

(iii) **The Banking Act 2009**

As the United Kingdom did not have any special regime for dealing with banks in financial difficulties, in the midst of the 2007/8 crisis, a (temporary) Banking (Special Provisions) Act 2008 was passed to enable the resolution of problems caused by Northern Rock and (later) the UK branches and subsidiaries of collapsed Icelandic banks. That Act was replaced by the Banking Act 2009,[15] which provided for a 'Special Resolution Regime' (SRR) for dealing with 'distressed' banks. The SSR is in two main parts, the first dealing with pre-insolvency 'stabilization' and the second with banking insolvency and administration. The two-part SRR places saving the viable parts of a bank to the forefront and then deals with any insolvent part under existing insolvency or administration procedures, duly modified for banks so as to accommodate the public interest as well as creditors' rights.

As to the first 'pre-insolvency' part, the SRR comprises three stabilization options:[16] the transfer of all or part of a bank to a private sector purchaser[17] or to a 'bridge bank' set up, wholly-owned and run by the Bank of England[18] or the temporary nationalization of the bank.[19] These options are listed in order of desirability. They are triggered if the bank fails to satisfy its 'threshold conditions' for FSA-authorization (in particular, its capital adequacy and suitability requirements)[20] and hence may come into play even if the bank is still solvent. The stabilization options are to be achieved through the exercise of wide 'stabilisation powers' enabling the transfer of shares or other property.[21] The market risks

---

[11] The SIB, a private company limited by guarantee, was formed (by the Bank of England) in 1985 in anticipation of becoming the 'delegated authority'—the regulator —under the Financial Services Act 1986. It was renamed the FSA in October 1997.

[12] See further, Sect. 4.   [13] See further, Sect. 2.

[14] See further, Sect. 4(i).

[15] Preceded by three consultation documents: (i) *'Financial Stability and depositor protection: strengthening the framework'* (Jan 2008), (ii) *'Financial Stability and depositor protection: further consultation'* (July 2008), (iii) *'Financial Stability and depositor protection; special resolution regime'* (July 2008).

[16] Banking Act 2009 s.1(2)(a). In addition, the Government may use its existing power to provide financial support to the bank, for example through the provisions of guarantees.

[17] Ibid., ss.1(3)(a), 11.

[18] Ibid., ss.1(3)(b), 12. The aim is to facilitate onward sale to a private sector purchaser, but if this is not possible the bridge bank will be wound up or taken into temporary public ownership.

[19] Ibid., ss.1(3)(c), 13.   [20] See Sect. 4(iv) below.

[21] Banking Act 2009, s.1(4) referring to ss.15, 16, 26–31, 85 (share transfer powers), and ss.33, 42–46 (property transfer powers).

created by the width of these powers (especially in the context of partial transfers) and hence the uncertainty as to their exercise prompted much concern and criticism, which the legislature attempts to address. The exercise of similar powers under the Banking (Special Provisions) Act 2008 promoted challenge (primarily on the basis of the Human Rights Act 1998) by shareholders in Northern Rock who obtained no compensation when the bank was nationalized.[22] In so far as all or part of the distressed bank cannot be saved, the second part of the SRR comprises two new insolvency procedures: a special banking insolvency procedure (BIP)[23] and a bank administration procedure.[24] Both procedures are a modified version[25] of the ordinary insolvency and administration procedures in the Insolvency Act 1986.

As regards insolvency, the view was taken that the lengthy existing procedure, in particular in not enabling depositors to access their funds quickly, would exacerbate the loss of confidence already caused by a failing bank. Therefore, the existing procedure has been modified, but only to the extent necessary to ensure that depositors receive their FSCS payments promptly.[26] As regards bank administration, the special bank procedure will only be used in relation to the residual insolvent part of a failing bank where the rest has been 'saved' by a partial transfer to a private sector bank or bridge bank and where special provisions are necessary to ensure a smooth transfer. These special provisions enable the residual insolvent bank to continue operations, for example providing facilities to depositors, until the transferor bank can take them over.[27] This would not be possible under the ordinary administration (or insolvency) procedure, which would also introduce the possibility of disputes between the transferee bank and the residual bank.

There are intricate provisions on the respective roles and powers of each of the TPA under the SSR, with overarching obligations to consult the other two.[28] The expectation is that the TPA Standing Committee will be at the centre of any discussion and decision-making but it is clearly desirable that ultimate responsibility for decisions made be clearly placed on one or other of the TPA. This addresses one of the problems with the pre-Act regime: lack of clarity as to which authority should take the lead in orchestrating the response. In essence the FSA, as regulator of the banks, is given the decision whether the bank has 'failed'. The Bank of England is then given the lead role in operating the SRR, overseen by the new Financial Stability Committee (FSC) of the court of the Bank of England. The Treasury is responsible for decisions involving public finances.

(iv) **The future**

A Financial Services Act 2010 was passed just before the May 2010 election which amended FSMA 2000 by strengthening the powers of the FSA and giving it a 'financial stability' objective. However, the incoming Coalition Government announced a drastic overhaul of the regulatory architecture by the dismantling of the FSA, with prudential regulation going to a subsidiary of the Bank of England (the Prudential Regulation Authority, PRA), a new Financial Policy Committee (FPC) in the Bank of England being responsible for macro-prudential regulation and most other functions being vested

---

[22] *R (on the application of SRM Global Masters Fund)* v. *The Commissioners of Her Majesty's Treasury* [2009] EWCA 788.

[23] Banking Act 2009, s.1(2)(b) and Pt. 2.   [24] Ibid., s.1(2)(c) and Pt. 3.

[25] See the tables of modifications in s.103 (BIP) and s.145 (bank administration).

[26] For the FSCS, see Sect. 4(viii). And note the role of the FSCS, including the power 'to participate in proceedings': s.123.

[27] See Banking Act 2009, s.136(2)(c).   [28] Ibid., ss.7(5), 8(3), 9(4).

in a Financial Conduct Authority (FCA). At the time of writing, a Financial Services Regulation Bill, giving effect to these reforms, is expected.

2 The Bank of England

The regulation and supervision of banking in the United Kingdom was, until June 1998,[29] in the hands of the Bank of England.[30] The Bank was incorporated by the Bank of England Act 1694 and its original objective was to raise the money required for the war with Louis XIV. Right from its inception, and for many generations to follow, the Bank of England was a joint stock corporation. Apart from its dealings in bills of exchange and in the issuing of banknotes, the Bank further effected remittances of money to Flanders for the purposes of the war with France. The resultant engagement in foreign currency dealings remained one of its activities for a long period afterwards. The Bank also started to maintain accounts opened by private bankers-goldsmiths of the period.

The maintenance of the bankers-goldsmiths' accounts can, possibly, be regarded as the origin of another function of the Bank of England, namely its role in the settlement of the daily-accrued balances between individual banks. Where two banks maintained accounts with the Bank of England, it was natural for one bank to pay a balance due to the other by effecting a direct transfer of funds. This function became firmly entrenched with the development of the clearing house in the eighteenth century.[31]

The Bank's regulatory and supervisory function, as well as its role as a central bank, developed at a later date. The idea of conferring some regulatory and supervisory powers on the Bank was first mooted during the second half of the nineteenth century. Before then, the Bank's indirect control of the banking system was based on its ability to influence interest rates by applying them to the accounts maintained with it. In 1873 Bagehot[32] emphasized the Bank's duties in its role as lender of last resort and asserted that the Bank therefore required suitable supervisory powers. Although the Bank Charter Act 1844 imposed no such duty and, accordingly, did not confer the proposed powers, the Bank nevertheless acted promptly in the Baring failure.[33] Joining forces with some 16 banking institutions, the Bank guaranteed Baring's debts.[34]

The next development in the Bank's role as a central bank occurred during 1913–14. The need to confer on the Bank the power to determine the margins to be maintained with it by the banks was one of the main topics of the general debate on the regulation of the banking system in the United Kingdom. The maintenance of substantial margins by the banking institutions of the country had the object of providing the funds required by the Bank of England in order to maintain and even increase its gold reserves, which, of course, were essential in an age in which the currency was tied to the gold standard.[35] However, the decisive step in the direction of developing the Bank's function as a central bank took place after the end of the First World War.

---

[29] On the implementation of the Bank of England Act 1998 see Sect. 1 above.

[30] Previous editions of this work summarized the Bank's history. For more detail, see Sir John Clapham, *The Bank of England—A History* (Cambridge, 1944); W. M. Acres, *The Bank of England from Within* (Oxford, 1931); J. Giuseppi, *The Bank of England* (London, 1966).

[31] R.M. Holland, 'The London Bankers' Clearing House' and 'The English Banking System', *US Monetary Commission*, 1910, 269, 280. And see Clapham, n.1 above, i. 222, ii. 250–1.

[32] W. Bagehot, *Lombard Street* (London, 1873).

[33] Not to be confused with the complete collapse of Barings in 1995.

[34] H.S. Sayers, *The Bank of England 1891–1944* (Cambridge, 1976), i. 1–3.

[35] Ibid.

In terms of structure, the Bank remained largely unchanged until 1946 when it was nationalized by the new Labour Government. Under the Bank of England Act of that year, the Bank's stock was transferred from the then owners to the Treasury Solicitor. The previous stockholders were, of course, compensated. The Bank is now a government institution but operates independently of government. Changes to its governance were made by the Bank of England Act 1998.[36]

The Bank of England Act 1946 gave the Bank general powers to make requests or recommendations to banks and, if authorized by the Treasury, to issue directions.[37] These first statutory regulatory powers were augmented by the more specific provisions of the Banking Act 1979 and, later on, under the more elaborate provisions of the Banking Act 1987. The factors that led to the passing of these two Acts are briefly discussed below.[38]

The Banking Acts of 1979 and 1987 imposed on the Bank not only the power but also the duty to supervise the banks authorized by it to carry on a deposit-taking business in the United Kingdom. An innovative measure of the 1987 Act (although one had already been included a year earlier in the Financial Services Act 1986 in relation to the Securities and Investments Board), was the conferment on the Bank of statutory immunity against damages claims. Under section 1(4), in the absence of bad faith, neither the Bank nor any of its directors, officers, or employees could be liable in damages for anything done or omitted in the discharge of the functions or purported functions of the Bank under the 1987 Act. Practically, this provision removed any doubts left as regards the position at common law.[39] However, on the collapse of BCCI, an attempt was made to hold the Bank of England responsible.[40] The FSA, which has taken over the regulatory and supervisory responsibilities of the Bank, has a similar statutory protection under the Financial Services and Markets Act 2000.[41]

3 The Banking Acts 1979 and 1987

The Banking Act 1979 was the first Act to deal comprehensively with the licensing of institutions accepting deposits from the public. It was superseded by the Banking Act 1987. Two main factors led to the passing of this earlier measure. The first was the secondary banking crisis, noted above.[42] The second factor was the European Communities' First Banking Directive. As noted below,[43] this Directive required Members States to authorize 'credit institutions', that is, banks. However, the criteria to be employed for the granting of such an authorization were not spelt out but were left to be settled by

---

[36] See especially, Bank of England Act 1998, ss.1–5 and Sched. 1.

[37] Bank of England Act 1946, s.4(3).   [38] See Sect. 3.

[39] See *Johnson Matthey plc* v. *Arthur Young and Bank of England* [1989] 2 All ER 105; *Yuen* v. *Att. Gen. of Hong Kong* [1988] AC 175 (PC) (recognizing the immunity of the Commissioner of Banking of Hong Kong, whose powers are, however, considerably more restricted than the Bank's were) and *Davis* v. *Radcliffe* [1990] 1 WLR 821 (PC) (following *Yuen* in relation to Isle of Man banking regulators).

[40] See *Three Rivers District Council and others* v. *Governor and Company of the Bank of England (No. 3)* [2000] 2 WLR 15 (HL). The depositors with BCCI subsequently brought an action against the Bank for, *inter alia*, misfeasance in public office but the case collapsed for lack of evidence.

[41] Sched. 1, para. 19. For a case seeking to hold the SIB (the predecessor to the FSA) liable, see *Melton Medes Ltd* v. *SIB* [1995] Ch. 137.

[42] And see the White Paper preceding the enactment of the 1979 Act: *The Licensing and Supervision of Deposit Taking Institutions* (Cmnd. 6584, London, 1976).

[43] See Sect. 7(i).

individual Member States. The 1979 Act lay down the standards applicable in the United Kingdom.

The cornerstone of the 1979 Act was the prohibition, in section 1, of the acceptance in the United Kingdom of deposits from the public by any person carrying on a deposit-taking business except certain bodies empowered to do so or exempted from the prohibition under the Act. But the Act did not apply a uniform criterion for the authorization of all the institutions covered by it. Instead, it divided deposit-taking institutions into four groups: (a) the Bank of England, (b) 'recognized banks', (c) licensed institutions described as 'licensed deposit-takers', and (d) institutions listed in Schedule 1 to the Act, such as building societies and the central banks of EC Member States, which were entitled to accept deposits from the public without securing a licence or an authorization. The administration of the Act was in the hands of the Bank of England, which had the power to determine the list of 'recognized banks' and of 'licensed deposit-takers', basing its decisions on the criteria laid down in the Act.[44] By and large, the recognized banks were treated as the more established and hence the weightier financial institutions. The Bank of England tended to supervise them less strictly than the licensed deposit-takers, relying to a certain extent on goodwill and co-operation.

Many of the inadequacies of the 1979 Act regime surfaced after the collapse of Johnson Matthey Bank (JMB) in 1984. JMB, which enjoyed the status of a 'recognized bank', went into insolvency mainly due to a substantial number of imprudent loans granted to certain customers. It became clear that if JMB had been subjected to the more stringent supervision applied to 'licensed deposit-takers', its financial difficulties would have been discovered earlier. Following the JMB affair, the question of bank supervision was reviewed and resulted in the White Paper on Banking Supervision,[45] which was given effect by the Banking Act 1987. The principal new measures introduced by it can be summarized as follows.

First was the appointment of the new Bank of England Board of Banking Supervision Division. The Board consisted of three *ex officio* members from the Bank and six independent members appointed jointly by the Treasury and the governor. In practical terms this meant that the City, through the independent members, was given a role to play in bank supervision.

Secondly, section 1(1) of the 1987 Act, clarified the Bank's role by conferring on it 'the duty generally to supervise the institutions authorized by it in the exercise of those powers'. Moreover, it gave the Bank powers (similar to but more detailed than those it previously only had over licensed institutions) to demand information required for the exercise of the its supervisory function and powers to appoint inspectors. Thirdly, the 1987 Act abolished the two-tier system, which separated licensed deposit-takers from recognized banks. Quite apart from these specific new measures, the 1987 Act was considerably more detailed than the 1979 Act. Its complexity increased substantially when the EC Second Banking Co-ordination Directive (2BCD) was brought into effect.[46]

As mentioned above, the incoming Labour Government of 1997 undertook a major overhaul of the regulation of the whole financial services sector, including banking. The cornerstone of the new system was the creation of a single, 'super' regulator—the FSA—to regulate and supervise the entire financial services sector. The Financial Services and Markets Act 2000 put the new regime in place. In anticipation of that Act,

---

[44] Banking Act 1979, s.3.   [45] Cmnd. 9695 (London, Dec. 1985), preceded by Cmnd. 9550.

[46] by the Banking Co-ordination (Second Council Directive) Regulations 1992, S.I. 1992/3218, made under the European Communities Act 1972. For a discussion of the 2BCD (now consolidated in the BCD) see below, Sect. 7(i).

the Government took the early legislative opportunity presented by the Bank of England Act 1998—which gave operational independence to the Bank of England in respect of monetary policy—to transfer the Bank's supervisory function to the Financial Services Authority (FSA).

A detailed analysis of the provisions of the FSMA 2000 is outside the scope of a general work on banking law. Nevertheless, an outline of the regime as it affects banking, will now be given.

4 The Financial Services and Markets Act 2000[47]

(i) Background

The FSMA 2000,[48] confers extensive regulatory and supervisory powers over the whole financial services sector on the FSA. The Treasury is left with residual responsibility, primarily to define the scope of the regime by Order.[49] The regulatory and supervisory functions themselves are conferred directly on the FSA, which has been given four statutory 'regulatory objectives'[50] and seven regulatory principles[51] to guide it in discharging its 'general functions'.[52] The FSA has been described as 'one of the most powerful financial regulators in the world in terms of scope, powers and discretion'.[53] Its scope is broad in three respects. First, it is cross-sectoral, covering the whole financial sector: banking, insurance, and investment business and markets. Secondly, it regulates and supervises both the prudential and conduct of business (including market conduct) aspects of those businesses. Finally, it has enormous powers: authorizing firms, legislating (in the sense of drawing up a rulebook (the 'FSA Handbook')[54]), monitoring, investigating, and enforcing the regime. It is also responsible for establishing one compensation scheme[55] and one Ombudsman scheme,[56] covering the whole financial sector. Such 'one-stop' regulation and supervision clearly has significant advantages in terms of efficiency[57] although

---

[47] Note the proposed Bill, mentioned at Sect. 1(iv), above, which will completely overhaul the regulatory regime.

[48] For detailed analyses, see M. Blair, *Blackstone's Guide to the Financial Services and Markets Act 2000* (London, 2009), J. Perry (ed.), *The Financial Services and Markets Act: A Practical Legal Guide*, (London, 2001), Lomnicka, *The Financial Services and Markets Act: An Annotated Guide*, (London, 2002), D. Sabalot & R. Everett, *The Financial Services and Markets Act 2000; Butterworths New Law Guides* (London, 2004) and E. Lomnicka & J. Powell, *Encyclopedia of Financial Services Law* (loose-leaf, London, 1987), Part 2A. For specialist banking regulation texts, see W. Blair (ed.), *Banking and Financial Services Regulation*, (Looseleaf).

[49] Thus, it makes the RAO and the Exemption Order (see below) defining the scope of regulation and the FPO (see Sect. (iii), below) defining the scope of the financial promotion regime. The Treasury also has functions (in relation to the new SRR) under the Banking Act 2009, see Sect. 1(iii), above.

[50] FSMA 2000, s.2(2): (a) market confidence, (b) consumer protection, (c) the reduction of financial crime and (d) financial stability (added by the Financial Services Act 2009, which essentially replaced the original 'public awareness' objective with the Consumer Financial Education Body).

[51] Ibid., s.2(3).

[52] Defined in ibid., s.2(4) to include its legislative and policy-making functions. The definition is deliberately kept at a general level and thus these objectives and principles are unlikely to be helpful in challenging individual FSA decisions.

[53] See the first report of the Joint Parliamentary Scrutiny Committee: *Draft Financial Services and Markets Bill: First Report* (1999 HL, 50 I–II); (1999 HL, 328 I–II) (27 Apr. 1999).

[54] See Sect 4(vi) below.   [55] See Sect. 4(viii) below.   [56] See Sect. 4(ix) below.

[57] See C. Briault, 'The Rationale for a Single National Financial Services Regulator' (FSA Occasional Paper, London, May 1999) and E. Lomnicka, 'Reforming UK Financial Service Regulation: The Creation of

the extent of the changes should not be overstated. This regime carries forward many of the features of the old regimes it consolidated[58] and is careful to differentiate—so far as is still appropriate—between the regulatory demands of the different sectors. Thus, the regime presents a further step in the evolution of—rather than a revolution in—banking regulation. But there have been extensions of regulation as far as banks are concerned. First, their retail mortgage business became regulated for the first time as a 'regulated activity.' Later that regulation was extended to so-called 'Islamic mortgages' and similar home-purchase products.[59] Moreover, the implementation of the EC Electronic Money Directive[60] has resulted in the extension of regulation to 'issuers of electronic money' whilst the EC Payment Services Directive[61] has resulted in the FSA regulating 'payment services' undertaken by banks.[62]

(ii) **The need for authorization**

The FSMA 2000 carries forward the need for institutions to be authorized in order to carry on banking in the United Kingdom in the sense of 'accepting deposits'. It does so by imposing the so-called 'general prohibition' on anyone carrying on 'regulated activity in the United Kingdom'.[63] Only 'authorised persons'[64] or 'exempt persons'[65] may undertake such activity.[66] 'Regulated activity'—defined in the 'Regulated Activities Order' (RAO) made by the Treasury[67]—covers the whole range of financial sector activity, including 'accepting deposits' by way of business.[68] Initially, the scope of 'regulated activity' was generally coextensive with that of the statutes which the FSMA 2000 replaced, but it has been extended to cover retail mortgage (including so-called 'Islamic mortgage') business, the issuing of electronic money, and payment services. Being contained in a statutory instrument, the scope of regulation may be further refined without primary legislation.[69]

The sanctions for breach of the 'general prohibition' are extensive. First, such a breach is a criminal offence[70] of strict liability, albeit with a due diligence defence.[71] Secondly, if the deposit is not returnable on demand, the depositor may apply to court, which has

---

a Single Regulator' [1999] *JBL* 480. See also C. Briault, 'Revisiting the rationale for a single national financial services regulator' (FSA Occasional Paper, OP16, London, Feb. 2002).

[58] It replaces the Financial Services Act 1986 and most of the Banking Act 1987, the Insurance Companies Act 1982 together with the legislation regulating the mutuals sector.

[59] See the Regulation of Financial Services (Land Transactions) Act 2005 and the RAO (see below), arts. 63A–63I (added by the Financial Services and Markets Act 2000 (Regulated Activities) (Amendment No. 2) Order 2006, SI 2006/2383.

[60] Directive 2000/46/EC [2000] OJ L275/39 replaced by a new Directive (prompted by the Payment Services Directive): 2009/110/EC. For the EU Dimension, see Sect. 7 below.

[61] Directive 2007/64/EC. See Sect. 7(vi) below.   [62] See further, Sect. 6(iii) below.

[63] FSMA 2000, s.19 and see *Financial Services Authority* v. *Anderson* [2010] EWHC 599 (Ch).

[64] See Sect. 4(v) below.   [65] See Sect. 4(iv) below.   [66] See Sect. 4(iii) below.

[67] Under FSMA 2000, s.22, and see Sched. 2. For the RAO see S.I. 2001/544, as extensively amended.

[68] See ibid., Sched. 2, para. 4 and RAO, art. 5 and see *Financial Services Authority* v. *Anderson* [2010] EWHC 599 (Ch).

[69] For example, the implementation of the Electronic Money Directive (see n.60) was largely effected by amending the RAO (by adding arts. 9B–9L) and bringing the issuing of electronic money within its scope. However, the bringing of so-called 'Islamic mortgages' within the scope of regulation (by adding arts. 63A–63I) was preceded by primary legislation: see n.59 above.

[70] FSMA 2000, s.23: the 'authorisation offence'. As far as banking is concerned, it replaces s.3 of the 1987 Act.

[71] Ibid., s.23(2).

discretion to order its return.[72] Finally, the FSA has power to apply to court for injunctions and 'disgorgement' orders against both the person acting in breach of the general prohibition and anyone else 'knowingly concerned' in the breach.[73] The latter is a very useful power which enables the FSA to pursue and recover money from persons taking deposits whilst unauthorized.[74]

The general scope of the prohibition against taking deposits should be noted. First, it is territorially limited in applying only to accepting deposits 'in the United Kingdom'. There is no guidance on the core meaning of this phrase and thus the notoriously difficult task of deciding when activity is 'in' the United Kingdom remains. However, the Act extends the natural meaning of 'in the United Kingdom'—and thus the Act's territorial scope—to cover the activities of institutions with a base in the United Kingdom even if their activities affect those outside it.[75] This gives effect to current international thinking on the regulation of cross-border financial services activity, which recommends the allocation of primary regulatory responsibility to the 'home' state.[76] The implementation of the Electronic Commerce Directive[77] has further modified the allocation of regulatory responsibility between European Economic Area (EEA) Member States. In essence, a bank providing services by electronic means from another EEA Member State need only comply with the regulatory regime of its 'country of origin', although there are limited 'derogations' from this country of origin principle permitting some of the consumer protection measures of the 'country of destination' (i.e. the consumer's State) to be imposed.

Secondly, only the accepting of deposits 'by way of business' is covered. Again, the core meaning of 'business' is not clarified,[78] but the Treasury provides some guidance by Order,[79] which essentially repeats the old provisions.[80] Thus, a person is not to be regarded as accepting deposits 'by way of business' if he *both* does not hold himself out as accepting deposits on a 'day to day basis' *and* any deposits he accepts 'are accepted only on particular occasions'. In applying this second condition, 'regard is to be had to the frequency of those occasions and to any characteristics distinguishing them from each other'.[81] This amplification of the second condition was added by the 1987 Act[82] and is repeated in the Order.

---

[72] Ibid., s.29. The court 'need not make the order' if satisfied it would not be 'just and equitable' on the basis of a reasonable belief by the contravenor that he was not in breach of the general prohibition: subss. (3), (4).

[73] Ibid., ss.380, 382. See *FSA* v. *Anderson* [2010] EWHC 1547. For a discussion of the meaning of 'knowingly concerned', see E. Lomnicka, '"Knowingly Concerned"? Participatory Liability to Regulators' (2000) 21 *Company Lawyer* 210.

[74] The FSA (previously the Bank of England) had a similar power under ss.48, 49 of the 1987 Act.

[75] See the detailed provisions in FSMA 2000, s.418, as amended.

[76] In relation to the EEA single market see, generally, Sect. 7 below.

[77] Directive 2000/31/EC [2000] OJ L178/1, noted further in Sect. 7(vi) below. It was generally implemented by the Electronic Commerce Directive (Financial Services and Markets) Regulations 2002, S.I. 2002/1775.

[78] The word was famously called an 'etymological chameleon' by Lord Diplock in *Town Investments Ltd* v. *Department of the Environment* [1978] AC 359, 383C. A broad meaning was given to the term when used in the Financial Services Act 1986: *Morgan Grenfell & Co.* v. *Welwyn Hatfield DC; Islington LBC* [1995] 1 All ER 1. See further, Lomnicka and Powell, n.48 above, para. 2A–851.

[79] Made under FSMA 2000, s.419. The Order is the Financial Services and Markets Act 2000 (Carrying on Regulated Activities by Way of Business) Order 2001, S.I. 2001/1177; art. 2 deals with deposit taking. See *Financial Services Authority* v. *Anderson* [2010] EWHC 599.

[80] Banking Act 1979, s.1(3); Banking Act 1987, s.6(2).   [81] S.I. 2001/1177, art. 2(2).

[82] Banking Act 1987, s.6(4).

Some guidance on the construction of this 'by way of business' provision may be found in the Court of Appeal's decision in *SCF Finance Co. Ltd* v. *Masri (No. 2)*.[83] This was decided under section 1(3) of the 1979 Act, which did not contain the amplification of 'particular occasion'. A firm of futures brokers accepted from its customers deposits which were commingled with the firm's general funds and, occasionally, lent to other clients. Most of the deposits in question constituted margin payments, obtained by the brokers as security for orders placed on behalf of the customers on the futures markets. Occasionally, though, the brokers also invested sums of money at the request of specific clients. It was held that the brokers had not acted by way of business. Slade LJ said that 'a person "holds himself out to accept deposits on a day to day basis" only if (by way of an express or implicit invitation) he holds himself out as generally willing on any normal working day to accept such deposits from those persons to whom the invitation is addressed who may wish to place moneys with him by way of deposit'.[84] No such invitation had ever been extended by the brokers. Turning to the second branch of the definition, Slade LJ held that 'particular occasions will be those occasions on which the [brokers] find it necessary or advisable for their own protection to demand deposits, having regard to the course of trading carried out and to be carried out by them in accordance with their clients' instructions. The mere fact that these occasions may be numerous does not render them any less "particular"'.[85] He further concluded that the remaining deposits, received from select customers for investment, were also received on particular occasions. Whilst Slade LJ's construction of the first branch of the provision—concerning the 'holding out' element—is still of relevance, care should be taken in applying his interpretation of 'particular occasions' in the light of the subsequent statutory amplification noted above. The amplification gives considerably greater weight to the frequency at which deposits are received than Slade LJ's interpretation. At the same time, the amplification makes it possible to treat deposits as falling within different groups if there are characteristics distinguishing them from each other. When seeking to establish whether deposits are accepted on 'particular occasions', the two criteria—frequency and distinguishing characteristics—have to be considered in combination. It follows that the greater the distinguishing characteristics the more often deposits can be accepted and not be by way of business. Thus, it would appear that the decision in *Masri* could have been reached under the new provision.

(iii) 'Accepting deposits'

As mentioned above,[86] the RAO made by the Treasury defines the activities that need authorization. It includes a detailed definition of 'accepting deposits' which largely reflects the old provisions.[87] As also mentioned above, this definition may be relatively easily altered in the future by amendments to the RAO.

Article 5(1) of the RAO defines 'accepting deposits' in terms of two alternative categories of activity.[88] The first is where 'money received by way of deposit is lent to others'. The second is where 'any other activity of the person accepting the deposit is financed wholly or to any material extent, out of the capital or of interest on money received on deposit'. Thus, essentially, banking is receiving money in order to lend to others or to finance activity.

---

[83] [1987] QB 1007, followed in *Financial Services Authority* v. *Anderson* [2010] EWHC 599.
[84] Ibid., at 1022.   [85] Ibid., at 1022–3.
[86] Sect. 4(ii).   [87] Banking Act 1979, s.1; Banking Act 1987, ss.5–7.
[88] Reflecting s.6(1) of the 1987 Act, applied in *Financial Services Authority* v. *Anderson* [2010] EWHC 599. See Sect. 4(vii), below where it is noted that the definition of 'accepting deposits' for the purposes of regulating the *promotion* of deposit-taking is very similar.

The core concept, 'deposit', is itself defined in Article 5(2)–(3) of the RAO, which again reflects the old definitions.[89] Broadly speaking, it means a sum of money paid on the basis that it will be repaid with or without interest or premium either on demand or as agreed. Moreover, it does not include an arrangement for the payment of money on terms that are 'referable to the provision of property (other than currency) or services or the giving of security'. This phrase is given an elaborate definition in Article 5(3). In practical terms, the definition excludes from the definition of 'deposit' any advances made on account of sales or similar contracts, and any sums furnished as a security for the performance of a contractual undertaking or, effectively, as a sum obtained to secure losses. Notably, in *SCF Finance Co. Ltd* v. *Masri (No. 2),*[90] Slade LJ held that the deposits received by brokers as margins in respect of orders placed by clients constituted payments for the provision of services within the meaning of the predecessor to this provision.

Articles 6 to 9AB of the RAO then list sums that are excluded from this general definition of 'deposit'. Again, these exclusions reflect, to a large extent, those in previous legislation. Article 6 excludes sums *paid* (i.e. lent) by certain institutions. These named institutions include the Bank of England and other EEA central banks, the IMF, and similar bodies. Notably, they also include authorized banks, insurance companies, and money-lending institutions. In addition, loans between companies in the same group or transactions between relatives or in the context of a partnership are also excluded. Articles 7 to 9 then exclude from the definition of 'deposit' sums *received* by certain persons. Thus, Article 7 excludes sums received by practising solicitors in the course of their profession, Article 8 excludes sums received by certain authorized and exempt persons and Article 9 excludes sums received in consideration for the issue of debt securities. Article 9A[91] excludes a sum 'if it is immediately exchanged for electronic money' because the issuing of electronic money is a 'regulated activity' in its own right.[92] Moreover, Article 9AA[93] implements the EC Electronic Commerce Directive[94] by excluding the accepting of deposits by electronic means by a credit institution established in another EEA Member State. Article 9AB implements the Payment Services Directive[95] by excluding funds received for 'payment services' by authorized payment institutions as such institutions are regulated under the Payment Services Regulations.[96]

(iv) **Exempt persons**

Although persons 'accepting deposits' 'in the United Kingdom' 'by way of business' generally require authorization, the FSMA 2000 enables the Treasury—by Order[97]—to exempt institutions from this requirement. Such persons are termed 'exempt persons' and again the list, being in a statutory instrument, may be relatively easily altered in the future.

---

[89] See s.1(4) of the 1979 Act and s.5 of the 1987 Act. Again, see Sect. 4(vii), below where it is noted that the definition of 'deposit' for the purposes of regulating the *promotion* of deposit-taking is that in the RAO.

[90] Above n.83, at 1020–1.

[91] Added by the Financial Services and Markets Act 2000 (Regulated Activities) (Amendment) Order 2002, S.I. 2002/682, art. 3(2), implementing the Electronic Money Directive 2000/46/EC [2000] OJ L275/39.

[92] RAO, art. 9B, added by ibid., art. 4. 'Small issuers' (certified as such by the FSA) are excluded: RAO, arts. 9C–9K.

[93] Added by the Financial Services and Markets Act 2000 (Regulated Activities) (Amendment) (No. 2) Order 2002, S.I. 2002/1776, art. 3(2).

[94] Directive 2000/31/EC [2000] OJ L 178/1, noted further in Sect. 7(vi) below.

[95] Directive 2007/64/EC, noted further in Sect. 7(vi) below.

[96] S.I. 2009/209. See also Sect. 6(iii) n.472.

[97] FSMA 2000, s.38. See the Financial Services and Markets Act 2000 (Exemption) Order 2001, S.I. 2001/1201, as amended, (the 'Exemption Order').

First, the Bank of England, other EEA central banks, the EU and related international institutions, as well as certain development banks, are 'exempt persons'.[98] Clearly, it would be inappropriate for the FSA to regulate these bodies. Secondly, bodies that are affiliated to government or to local authorities are exempt.[99] These institutions, which may be regarded as being effectively supervised by bodies other than the FSA, include: (a) municipal banks, which are bodies corporate transacting aspects of banking business in conjunction with a local authority,[100] (b) school banks certified for this purpose by the National Savings Bank or any authorized person, (c) local authorities, (d) any other body that has the power to issue a precept to a local authority in England or Wales or to issue a requisition to a local authority in Scotland, and (e) charities in certain circumstances.

It should be noted that banks that are authorized in other EEA Member States and thus are entitled to exercise their 'single European passport'[101] are not 'exempt persons' under the FSMA 2000, although they are 'exempt' from having to obtain authorization from the FSA.[102] As will be explained in the next section, they are granted automatic authorization and treated—with the requisite qualifications—as 'authorised persons' for the purposes of regulation by the FSA. 'Exempt persons', in the strict sense of persons exempted by Treasury Order, are completely outside the regulatory regime operated by the FSA.[103]

(v) **Authorized persons**

Unless enjoying the status of 'exempt person', anyone 'accepting deposits' 'in the United Kingdom' 'by way of business' must be an 'authorised person'.[104] There are two main categories of 'authorised person'. The first are persons obtaining authorization from the FSA. The second are persons authorized in other EEA Member States and entitled to exercise their 'single European passport' in establishing branches in or providing cross-border services into the United Kingdom. This second category is, in accordance with the United Kingdom's EU obligations, granted automatic authorization for the purposes of the FSMA 2000. Persons within it are, in principle, subject to regulation by the FSA in so far as they operate in the United Kingdom, but in a manner that is consistent with EU law. Each category will now be considered in turn.

The first category of 'authorised persons'—domestic institutions—obtains authorization by applying to the FSA for 'permission' to carry on regulated activity. Part IV of the FSMA 2000 contains elaborate provisions about such 'permission' (termed 'Part IV permission'), which enable the FSA to establish and operate the 'permission' regime. Of particular importance are the so-called 'threshold conditions', set out in Schedule 6 to the Act, which determine a firm's eligibility for permission.[105] They carry forward the criteria that already applied under the old legislation and reflect EU law.[106] First, a bank

---

[98] Exemption Order, art. 3 and Sched. 1.

[99] Exemption Order, art. 4 and Sched. 2. These bodies are exempt only in respect of banking.

[100] Defined in Banking Act 1987, s.103; note that under subs.(1)(c) an institution falls within the definition only if its deposits are guaranteed by the local authority.

[101] See Sect. 7(ii) below.   [102] See Sect. 4(v) & Sect. 7(ii).

[103] They are also largely outside the financial promotion restriction: see Sect. 4(vii) and FPO, art. 16.

[104] See the 'general prohibition' in s.19, considered in Sect. 4(ii), above. This also applies to persons 'issuing electronic money', unless they are 'certified' (by the FSA) small issuers: see RAO, arts. 9B–9K, noted above.

[105] These replace the criteria in Sched. 2 to the 1979 Act and Sched. 3 to the 1987 Act. See also the COND Module of the FSA Handbook (see Sect. (vi), below) which amplifies these 'Threshold' requirements.

[106] See Sect. 7 below. Thus, EEA firms (see below) will have satisfied similar conditions in their home Member State.

must be either a body corporate or a partnership.[107] Further 'governance' requirements are set out in the FSA Handbook, which carries forward the so-called 'four eyes' principle required by EU law: that at least two individuals direct the business. Also in accordance with EU law, which requires banks to be authorized (and regulated) where they genuinely carry on business, banks applying for Part IV permission must have their head offices in the United Kingdom.[108] And in compliance with the so-called 'post-BCCI directive',[109] the FSA must be satisfied that it can supervise the bank effectively, taking into account the structure of the group to which it belongs (or other firms with which it has defined links) and the laws of any non-EEA country to which it may be subject.[110] This requirement seeks to avoid a repetition of the BCCI fiasco where its complex group structure resulted in ineffective regulation. Of central importance is the requirement that banks have 'adequate resources'.[111] This is the capital adequacy requirement that is set out in very general terms in the Act. However the FSA has articulated its approach in much greater detail in its 'Prudential Sourcebook' which forms part ('Block 2: Business Standards') of its Handbook.[112] Equally important is the 'suitability' or 'fit and proper' requirement,[113] which is again elaborated in the FSA's Handbook. Finally, provision is made enabling the FSA to have regard to persons in a 'relevant relationship' with the applicant for permission.[114] No definition is given of 'relevant relationship'—a deliberate omission in order to give the FSA freedom of action.[115]

In granting Part IV permission, the FSA is given a very wide discretion, especially as to the scope and terms of any permission it grants.[116] It may determine the precise scope of permission by imposing limitations.[117] It may also impose 'requirements' on how a person is, or is not, to act.[118] Positive requirements could thus take the form of obliging the firm to submit frequent returns and negative requirements could take the form of precluding the firm from undertaking business beyond a certain volume or of a certain kind. Special provision is made for a so-called 'assets requirement' by which the FSA may require the freezing of assets or require them to be transferred to a trustee.[119] This is a particularly useful regulatory power where misuse of assets is suspected. There is the usual right of appeal to the Upper Tribunal by those aggrieved by the exercise of the FSA of its powers in relation to permission.[120]

The second category of authorized person is banks authorized in other EEA countries. As noted above, in accordance with EU law, these are granted automatic authorization, provided they comply with the requisite formalities.[121] They are termed 'EEA firms' and are subject to regulation as 'authorised persons' by the FSA, but in a manner that is consistent with EU law which provides for a division of responsibility between 'home' (i.e. other EEA Member States) and 'host' (UK) regulators.[122]

---

[107] FSMA 2000, Sched. 6, para. 1(2).

[108] Ibid., para. 2. A corporation with a registered office must also have that in the UK and a partnership must also carry on business in the UK.

[109] Directive 95/26/EC, [1995] OJ L168/7 (since consolidated into Directive 2000/12/EC, itself replaced by Directive 2006/48/EC), see further, Sect. 7(i) below.

[110] FSMA 2000, Sched. 6, para. 3.   [111] Ibid., para. 4.

[112] See Sect. 4(vi) below. See especially the 'BIPRU' Module (applicable to banks and similar institutions).

[113] Ibid., para. 5.   [114] Ibid., s.49(1).

[115] Admitted in the Explanatory Notes to the Act, published with the Act, para. 119.

[116] FSMA 2000, s.42.   [117] Ibid., subs.(7).

[118] FSMA 2000, s.43(1). These 'requirements' may also extend to non-regulated activities.

[119] Ibid., s.48.   [120] FSMA 2000, s.55; see further, Sect. 4(vi) below.

[121] Ibid., s.31(1)(b) and see Sched. 3. Note also s.35 (ending of authorization).

[122] See further, Sect. 7(ii) below.

Naturally, UK authorized banks are also able to exercise their single European passport throughout the EEA and special provision is made for this in the FSMA 2000.[123]

(vi) **Authorized persons: powers of the FSA**

Authorized person status brings with it regulatory and supervisory control by the FSA. As well as the power to authorize by granting Part IV permission, the FSA also has extensive delegated 'legislative' powers in the sense of being able to make rules and issue requirements as to the financial standing and conduct of authorized persons. To ensure these are being adhered to, the FSA has been given wide powers of investigation and discipline. All these powers are conferred on the FSA by the FSMA 2000 but the detail is to be found in the FSA's Handbook.

The FSA Handbook is an enormous publication in which the FSA sets out its regulatory and supervisory approach in all its aspects. The Handbook is divided into eight main parts or 'Blocks', together with an extensive 'Glossary'. Block One is entitled 'High Level Standards'. It contains the general 'Principles for Businesses' (PRIN) to which all authorized persons, including banks,[124] are subject. These are intended to articulate the fundamental obligations of authorized persons such as acting 'with integrity' and paying 'due regard to the interests of its customers and treat[ing] them fairly'.[125] The final principle requires firms to deal with the FSA 'in an open and co-operative way'. This Block also contains the 'Threshold Conditions' (COND) for authorization. Block Two (the 'Prudential Standards' Block) contains the prudential requirements. Block Three (the 'Business Standards' Block') contains specific 'conduct of business' modules applicable to the various types of financial activity. The deposit-taking activity of banks is subject to the 'BCOBS' Module[126] and their regulated mortgage activities are subject to the 'MCOB' Module. 'Regulatory processes' is the name of Block Four and it now contains 'SUP', the 'Supervision' manual and 'DEPP', the Decision Procedure and Penalty manual. Block Five is entitled 'Redress' and has a number of important components, some of which are considered in more detail in Section 4, (viii) and (ix) below. Thus, it contains details of the Financial Services Compensation Scheme[127] and the Financial Ombudsman Scheme.[128] The only other Block of particular relevance to banks is that entitled 'Regulatory Guides'. It contains the FSA's 'Enforcement Guide' (EG) and the important 'Perimeter Guidance' Manual (PERG) that sets out the FSA's approach to determining the scope (the 'perimeter') of activities it regulates and supervises.[129] Part XI of the FSMA 2000 confers extensive investigation powers on the FSA. These powers, to a large extent, carry forward those that were already available under the 1987 Act, although there has been some rationalization so that the FSA has the same powers in relation to all categories of financial firms. First, the FSA has a wide *ad hoc* power to obtain information or documents, to enable it to discharge its functions, from any authorized person (or certain 'connected

---

[123] FSMA 2000, Sched. 3, Pt. III.

[124] Originally, PRIN only applied to banks in the prudential context but since the introduction of BPS in November 2009 (see Sect. 6(iii), esp. n.494, below), they apply in full.

[125] This principle is the basis of the FSA's 'TCF' ('treating customers fairly') initiative, which requires firms to demonstrate that they were adhering to this principle. See the RPPD Module of the FSA Handbook.

[126] Standing for 'Banking Conduct of Business'. See further, Sect. 6(iii).

[127] See Sect. 4(viii) below.   [128] See Sect. 4(ix) below.

[129] See especially PERG2 (on regulated activities), PERG8 (on financial promotion, see Sect. (vii), below) and PERG14 (on the scope of the PSR 2009, see Sect. 6(iii) below).

persons') by notice.[130] This supplements the obligations on authorized persons, imposed in the Handbook,[131] to provide the FSA with information periodically or on the occurrence of specified events. Secondly, instead of just relying on the authorized person producing the information, the FSA may require the authorized person to commission a report by a person nominated or approved by the FSA.[132] Thirdly, the FSA may appoint investigators either into the affairs of an authorized person[133] or into specific suspected contraventions.[134] There are further detailed provisions on the conduct of these investigations.[135] There is an important provision,[136] reflecting the European Convention on Human Rights,[137] which limits the admissibility of statements made under compulsion to investigators. Finally, the FSA has powers to apply to the court for entry and search warrants in specified circumstances.[138]

Wide disciplinary powers are conferred on the FSA in respect of authorized persons. First, it may vary, suspend, or cancel Part IV permission[139] or, in the case of an EEA firm, impose requirements under Part XIII of the FSMA 2000.[140] Secondly, it may publicly censure.[141] Thirdly, it may impose a financial penalty.[142] Finally, it may require restitution.[143] These powers are much wider than those that were available under the old Banking Acts. When it decides to exercise these powers, the FSA must follow a formal procedure[144] involving a 'warning notice' followed by an opportunity to make representations[145] and then a 'decision notice',[146] with a right of reference to the Upper Tribunal.[147]

In addition to these extra-judicial powers, the FSA has a more general power—not limited to authorized persons—to apply to the court for injunctions and restitution (or 'disgorgement') orders.[148] It will apply to the court if it feels the added weight of judicial intervention is needed, especially if unauthorized persons (over whom it does not have disciplinary powers) are involved. The FSA may also petition for the winding up of an authorized person and may take part in any insolvency proceeding it has not initiated.[149]

---

[130] FSMA 2000, s.165 and ss.165A–165C (added by the Financial Services Act 2010, s.18). This power is also exercisable in support of certain overseas regulators: s.169 and s.169A (added by the Financial Services Act 2010, s.18).

[131] Permitted by the rule-making power in ibid., s.138. See the 'SUP' FSA Handbook Module, mentioned above.

[132] Ibid., s.166.

[133] Ibid., s.167. This power is also exercisable in support of certain overseas regulators: s.169. There was a similar power in the 1987 Act, s.41.

[134] Ibid., s.168. This power is also exercisable in support of certain overseas regulators: s.169.

[135] Ibid., ss.170–173. And note s.177 (criminal offences for non-compliance with requirements to provide information).

[136] Ibid., s.174.　　　[137] And see *Saunders* v. *UK* (1996) 28 EHRR 818.　　　[138] FSMA 2000, s.176.

[139] Ibid., s.45. This power is also exercisable in support of certain overseas regulators: s.47. For suspension of permission, see s.205A, added by the Financial Services Act 2010, s.9.

[140] This reflects the limited powers that 'host' regulators have over firms authorized in other EEA Member States. See further, Sect. 7(ii) below.

[141] FSMA 2000, s.205. It may also give private warnings.　　　[142] Ibid., s.206.

[143] Ibid., s.384.

[144] Ibid., ss.53–55 (for Pt. IV permission variation or cancellation), ss.207–209 (public censure, suspension, and penalty), ss.385–386 (for restitution). See generally, FSMA 2000, Pt. XXVI for more detail about the FSA's procedures and the DEPP Module of its Handbook .

[145] Ibid., s.387.　　　[146] Ibid., s.388.

[147] Ibid., Pt. IX (previously, the Financial Services and Markets Tribunal).

[148] Ibid., ss.380, 382, see *FSA* v. *Anderson* [2010] EWHC 1547.

[149] See, generally, FSMA 2000, Pt. XXIV.

(vii) **Financial promotion**

The Banking Act 1987 contained provisions regulating advertisements soliciting deposits.[150] The FSMA 2000—which it will be recalled covers the whole financial services area—adopts a more comprehensive approach to the whole area of 'financial promotion'. Thus the soliciting of deposits is now regulated as 'financial promotion'. Essentially, the FSMA 2000 seeks to control 'financial promotion' by ensuring this is only done by or with the approval of an authorized person (who is, of course, subject to regulation and supervision). However, there are a number of significant exemptions from regulation. To understand the method of regulation, the meaning of 'financial promotion' needs to be grasped.

'Financial promotion' is defined in outline in the FSMA 2000, section 21, but its detailed scope is determined by Treasury Order: the Financial Promotions Order, the 'FPO'.[151] The term may be broken down into four components. It means (a) 'in the course of business', (b) 'communicat[ing]', (c) 'an invitation or inducement', (d) 'to engage in investment activity'. Each of these components needs to be considered in turn. It should be noted that there is no mention of 'advertisement' or communications 'to the public'. Thus, 'one-off' communications are *prima facie* covered.[152]

First, there is the 'business' component: financial promotion must occur 'in the course of business'. The problems associated with the term 'business'—which is not defined—have already been noted.[153] The Treasury has power by Order to clarify its meaning[154] but the FPO does not contain any such clarification. However, it is clear that the phrase used in section 21 ('in the course of business') has a wider connotation than the phrase ('by way of business') used in the definition of the regulated activity of deposit-taking.[155]

Secondly, financial promotion entails 'communication'. Again there is no definition of this term but it will no doubt be construed widely to cover any form of conveying or making known to another. The term is stated[156] to include 'causing a communication to be made' and thus extends to initiating the sequence of events which results in the communication as well as actually communicating. However, the FPO provides an exemption for so-called 'mere conduits', that is, persons who merely—without controlling the content of the communication—transmit material provided by others.[157] The FPO contains some amplification of the meaning of 'communication' for the purposes of its provisions.[158] It also defines and makes special provision for various kinds of communication, for example 'real time' (or 'interactive')[159] and 'non-real time'[160] communications,

---

[150] Banking Act 1987, s.32 and the Banking Act (Advertisements) Regulations 1988, S.I. 1988/645, made thereunder, replacing earlier regulations, made under s.34 of the 1979 Act.

[151] Made under FSMA 2000, s.21. Its full name is: the Financial Services and Markets Act 2000 (Financial Promotion) Order 2005, S.I. 2005/1529, as amended, replacing the original FPO (S.I. 2001/1335). The FSA has issued extensive Guidance on Financial Promotion in its Handbook (see Sect. 4(vi), above) in PERG8.

[152] Although the FPO exempts certain 'one-off' communications in relation to investment businesses (see arts. 32 and 33), this exemption does not extend to the promotion of banking.

[153] See Sect. 4(ii), above. And note that the Treasury Order under s.419 does not apply to s.21. But see next note.

[154] FSMA 2000, s.21(4).   [155] See Sect. 4(ii) above. This is made clear in PERG8 (see n.151).

[156] In ibid., s.21(13).

[157] FPO, art. 18. Art. 18A makes special provision for 'mere conduits', 'caching', and 'hosting' in relation to electronic commerce communications.

[158] FPO, art. 6.

[159] Ibid., art. 7(1): 'a communication made in the course of a personal visit, telephone conversation or other interactive dialogue'.

[160] Ibid., art. 7(2)–(5). It includes 'communications made by letter or e-mail or contained in a publication'.

'solicited and unsolicited real time' communications.[161] As noted below, 'real time communications'[162] and certain 'non-real time communications'[163] relating to deposit-taking are exempted from regulation.

Thirdly, there must be an 'invitation or inducement'. Once more there is no definition but these words are regarded as connoting a promotional element.[164] Thus, 'neutral' information about deposits or exhortations *not* to hand over deposits is not covered unless the context of the communication implies that in fact promotion is taking place.

Finally, it is the promotion of 'engag[ing] in investment activity' that is covered. The definition of 'investment activity'—which should not be confused with 'regulated activity'[165] although in fact it is, to some extent, coextensive with it—is very complex. The definition will be considered only in so far as it relates to banking. 'Investment activity' is defined[166] in terms of 'controlled activity' and 'controlled investment'. What is 'controlled' is specified in the FPO. And the FPO specifies 'accepting deposits' as a 'controlled activity'[167] and a 'deposit' as a 'controlled investment'.[168] Although the definition of 'deposit' is the same in both the RAO and FPO,[169] the definition of 'accepting deposits' is slightly different. The core of both definitions is the same in covering the two categories of activity of taking money for lending or for financing activity. But the FPO adds the qualification that the person accepting the deposit must hold himself out as doing so 'on a day to day basis'.[170] It will be recalled that this qualification is identical to the first part of the definition of accepting deposits 'by way of business' for the purposes of the general prohibition.[171] Having established the meaning of 'controlled activity' and 'controlled investment' as far as banking is concerned, the meaning of 'engaging in investment activity' may now be determined. There are two categories of such activity.[172] The first is 'entering or offering to enter into an agreement the making or performance of which ... constitutes a controlled activity'.[173] Thus accepting or offering to accept deposits (as defined) by persons who hold themselves out as doing so on a day-to-day basis is covered. The second category is 'exercising any right conferred by a controlled investment to acquire, dispose of ... a controlled investment'.[174] This category is more relevant to other types of 'controlled investment' such as securities, but it would cover the exercise of any rights conferred in the contract of deposit to deal with the deposit.

Mention should be made of the territorial scope of 'financial promotion'. This is a thorny topic, especially in the light of modern forms of communication.[175] The position is again complex and to some extent dependant on the FPO which may refine the scope of

---

[161] Ibid., art. 8.   [162] Ibid., art. 23.   [163] Ibid., art. 22.

[164] The marginal note to s.21 is 'financial promotion' (and see s.145: 'financial promotion rules', considered in the text to n.191 below), the various *travaux préparatoires* (especially the Ministerial Statements in the Parliamentary debates) and PERG8 (see n.155) all indicate this.

[165] Which determines the scope of the 'general prohibition' and thus who needs authorization (or exemption): see Sect. 4(ii), above.

[166] In FSMA 2000, s.21(8)–(12), (14)–(15).   [167] FPO, art. 4 and Sched. 1, para. 1.

[168] FPO, art. 4 and Sched. 1, para. 12.

[169] The FPO defines 'deposit' in art. 2 as 'a sum of money which is a deposit for the purposes of article 5' of the RAO. See Sect. 4(iii) above.

[170] FPO, art. 4 and Sched. 1, para. 1.

[171] See Sect. 4(ii) above. Thus to qualify as 'financial promotion', the promotion must be done 'in the course of business' (see above) and it must relate to the acceptance of deposits by persons who hold themselves out as taking deposits on a day-to-day basis.

[172] FSMA 2000, s.21(8).   [173] Ibid., s.21(8)(a).   [174] Ibid., s.21(8)(b).

[175] IOSCO, the International Organization of Securities Commissions has issued guidance on the assertion of regulatory authority over Internet activity. See also the FSA Handbook, PERG8. 8.22 ('The Internet').

regulation in any way.[176] Unlike the definition of 'regulated activity', which talks of activity 'in the United Kingdom',[177] the general definition of 'financial promotion' in section 21 has no territorial limitation, although section 21(3) does state that so-called 'inward' communications—communication 'originating outside' the United Kingdom—are covered only if they are 'capable of having effect in the United Kingdom'. In the age of electronic communication, this is hardly a significant limitation as, for example, communications accessible via the internet in the United Kingdom would be covered. The Treasury is therefore given power, by Order, to provide further as to 'inward' communications.[178] Broadly speaking, the FPO exempts communications from outside the United Kingdom[179] as long as they are 'directed only at' persons outside the United Kingdom.[180] Moreover, in compliance with the EC Electronic Commerce Directive,[181] which generally imposes the regulatory regime of the 'country of origin' on services provided by electronic means, so-called 'incoming electronic commerce communications'[182] from other EEA Member States are also excluded from the FSMA 2000 promotions regime.[183] As for 'outward' communications—those originating from the United Kingdom—these are all *prima facie* covered, although again the FPO may provide otherwise.[184] Thus, the FPO generally exempts communications received by or 'directed only at persons outside the United Kingdom', although if such communications are 'unsolicited real time' then they are only exempt if made from a place outside, and for the purposes of a business only carried on outside, the United Kingdom.[185] It follows that unsolicited calling from the United Kingdom, even if entirely 'outward', is subject to the FSMA 2000 promotions regime. Moreover, again in compliance with the EC Electronic Commerce Directive,[186] so-called 'outgoing electronic commerce communications' from the United Kingdom to another EEA Member State[187] are not exempted and remain subject to the FSMA 2000 promotions regime.[188]

Having established the meaning of 'financial promotion' in the context of banking, how it is regulated may now be discussed. Section 21(1) of the FSMA 2000 contains the so-called 'financial promotion restriction'.[189] It imposes a blanket prohibition on 'financial promotion' (as defined and discussed above). However, the rest of section 21 then creates a number of exceptions.

First, the restriction does not apply to authorized persons, nor does it apply if the content of the communication is 'approved for the purposes of' section 21 by an authorized person.[190] This is because the FSA is given specific power to make rules regulating and supervising financial promotion by authorized persons, including provisions

---

[176] FSMA 2000, s.21(5).   [177] Ibid., s.19, see Sect. 4(ii) above.

[178] Thus it may repeal section 21(3) (see subs. (7)) and it may make other provision for such communications (subss. (5), (6)(b)–(d)).

[179] And solicited real-time or non-real time 'outward' communications, see below.

[180] FPO, art. 12(1)(b). Detailed provision is made to determine if a communication is 'directed at' non-UK persons.

[181] Directive 2000/31/EC [2000] OJ L 178/1, noted further in Sect. 7(vi) below.

[182] Defined in FPO, art. 6(g).

[183] FPO, art. 20B—unless they are unsolicited (i.e. not made in response to an express request from the recipient) and made by electronic mail.

[184] Ibid., s.21(5). See FPO, art. 12.   [185] FPO, art. 12(1), (2).

[186] Directive 2000/31/EC [2000] OJ L 178/1, noted further in Sect. 7(vi) below.

[187] Defined in FPO, art. 6(h).   [188] FPO, art. 12(7).

[189] This is how it is described in the FPO, art. 5.   [190] FSMA 2000, s.21(2).

as to the form and content of communications.[191] Thus, the mechanism of regulation is clear: authorized persons must be involved and they must act in accordance with the financial promotion rules in the Handbook.[192]

Secondly, the Treasury is given unlimited power to create exemptions from the financial promotion restriction.[193] These exemptions—which are termed 'exempt communications'—are contained in the FPO. As far as banking is concerned there are two specific exemptions. Thus, a 'non-real time communication',[194] which is accompanied by detailed information about the identity and status of the deposit-taker, is exempt.[195] This information must include whether or not the bank is regulated, whether any dispute resolution procedure or deposit protection scheme applies, and details of the bank's assets. This exempts mail (and e-mail) 'shots' as long as the requisite information is also communicated. A blanket exemption is provided for 'real-time communications',[196] whether solicited or unsolicited.[197] Thus, cold-calling which invites deposits is presently permitted—as it has always been.[198] In addition, banks may take advantage of the general exemptions that apply to communications in relation to all 'controlled activities'.[199] Those applicable to 'incoming electronic commerce communications'[200] and 'outward'[201] communications as well as the 'mere conduits'[202] exemptions have already been mentioned. Further, so-called 'generic' communications, which do not identify individual banks but promote deposit-taking by banks in general,[203] are exempt as are introductions to authorized or exempt persons[204] or to certain 'investment professionals'.[205]

Breach of the financial promotion restriction has similar consequences to breach of the general prohibition.[206] Thus, breach is a criminal offence of strict liability, with a 'due diligence' defence.[207] Agreements resulting from 'unlawful communications' are unenforceable.[208] Finally, the FSA has power to apply to court for injunctions and 'disgorgement' orders against both the person acting in breach of the financial promotion restriction and anyone else 'knowingly concerned' in the breach.[209] Authorized persons cannot be in breach of the restriction,[210] but if they act in breach of the FSA's financial promotion rules[211] applicable to them, the usual disciplinary consequence may follow.

(viii) Deposit guarantee scheme

The United Kingdom has had an industry-funded banking deposit guarantee scheme—a scheme that compensates depositors to some extent should their bank be unable to repay their deposits—since the establishment of the Deposit Protection Scheme under the Banking Act 1979. Similar compensation schemes existed in relation to investment

---

[191] Ibid., s.145. The Treasury may limit this power: subs.(5). There was power under the Banking Act 1987, s.33 to make such regulations.

[192] For the FSA Handbook, see Sect. 4(vi), above. The financial promotion rules are in BCOBS2, see also Sect. 6(iii) below.

[193] FSMA 2000, s.21(5).   [194] Defined in FPO, art. 7(1); see the text to n.160 above.

[195] FPO, art. 22.   [196] Defined in FPO, art. 7(2); see the text to n.159 above.

[197] FPO, art. 23.

[198] There was power in the 1987 Act, s.34 to proscribe unsolicited calls but it was never exercised.

[199] FPO, Pt. IV.   [200] FPO, art. 20B.   [201] FPO, art. 12.

[202] FPO, art. 18.   [203] FPO, art. 17.   [204] FPO, art. 16.   [205] FPO, art. 19.

[206] See Sect. 4(ii), above.   [207] FSMA 2000, s.25.

[208] Ibid., s.30.   [209] Ibid., ss.380, 382, see n.73 above.

[210] As it does not apply to financial promotion by authorized persons: s.21(2); see the text to n.190 above.

[211] Made under FSMA 2000, s.145; see the text to n.191 above.

businesses[212] and insurance.[213] And, as noted below,[214] the EU's DGS Directive requires Member States to have a deposit guarantee scheme. Consistently with its policy of consolidating financial services regulation and related matters, the FSMA 2000 provides for the creation of a single Financial Services Compensation Scheme (FSCS) under Part XV of that Act, covering most regulated activities,[215] including banking, undertaken by authorized persons. The FSA is given responsibility for devising the scheme and establishing the body to run it. The relevant rules are in Block Five ('Redress') of its Handbook.[216] The Act lays down requirements for ensuring the scheme's independence from the FSA and the scheme is given the same immunity from damages claims as the FSA.[217]

Such compensation schemes are justified on the basis that they enhance depositor confidence. This is especially important in banking to discourage 'runs' on banks in trouble: if depositors are assured of being compensated should their bank fail, in theory they will not rush to withdraw their deposits. On the other hand, compensation distorts competition in requiring successful (and scrupulous) enterprises to pay for the failings of less successful (or unscrupulous) ones. In addition, compensation gives rise to 'moral hazard': there is no incentive for depositors to take care in their choice of bank.[218] A stark illustration of the importance of such schemes occurred during the financial turmoil that started in 2007. The 'guaranteeing' of retail deposits was one of the first steps taken by governments in an attempt to inject confidence into that aspect of banking.[219]

Although operating as one scheme, there is differentiation between the different financial sectors covered[220] in relation to the maximum overall amount and the maximum proportion of claim payable. And each component is 'stand alone' from the point of view of funding. Thus, only the banking sector has to pay for compensation arising from failures in that sector. For bank deposits the maximum compensation originally payable was £31,700 (comprising 100 per cent of the first £2,000 and 90 per cent of the next £33,000[221]). This more than met the minimum limits set by the (then) EU DGS Directive.[222] However, in the wake of the 'run' on Northern Rock in September 2007, this was initially increased to £35,000[223] and in October 2008 to £50,000. The whole question of the level of protection is, at the time of writing, under review by the FSA and will need to be brought in line with

---

[212] The Investors Compensation Scheme (ICS) under the Financial Services Act 1986, s.54. There were also schemes covering building societies and friendly societies.

[213] The Policyholders Protection Scheme (under the Policyholders Protection Act 1975).

[214] See Sect. 7(v) below.

[215] See Sect. 4(ii) above. It does not cover (i) mortgage lending or administration or (ii) reinsurance or certain insurance activity.

[216] See Sect. 4(vi) above. The rules are in the COMP Module.

[217] See Sect. 2 above. The immunity is lost if it can be shown to have acted in 'bad faith' or in breach of the Human Rights Act 1998. However, it can be challenged by judicial review and there is case law where the ICS was so challenged: see *R.* v. *ICS, ex p. Weyell* [1994] QB 749; *R.* v. *ICS, ex p. Bowden* [1996] 1 AC 261 and, on the validity of the compensation rules themselves, *R.* v. *SIB, ex p. Sun Life Assurance plc* [1996] 2 BCLC 150 and *ICS* v. *West Bromwich BS* [1998] 1 WLR 896. See also *FSCS Ltd* v. *Abbey National Treasury Services Plc* [2008] EWHC 1897 (on the validity of COMP rules in relation to the assignments of rights of action to the FSCS).

[218] See P. Cartwright and A. Campbell, 'Deposit Insurance: Consumer Protection, Bank Safety and Moral Hazard' [1999] *EBLR* 96. Hence the introduction of a degree of 'co-insurance' with the depositor bearing a proportion of the loss.

[219] Some countries (Ireland and Denmark, in 2008) gave unlimited guarantees, whilst others (the UK, see below) increased existing protection.

[220] This is envisaged by FSMA 2000, s.214(1)(b).

[221] Hence there was a degree of 'co-insurance', see n.218 above.   [222] See Sect. 7(v) below.

[223] To calm that 'run', the deposits in Northern Rock itself were initially guaranteed to an unlimited extent and then up to £100,000.

expected amendments to the EC DGS Directive.[224] Moreover, the Banking Act 2009 and the Financial Services Act 2010 made changes to the scheme, in particular as to its funding and timeliness of payouts.[225]

(ix) **The Financial Ombudsman Service**

A voluntary Banking Ombudsman Scheme was established in 1986 on the initiative of the clearing banks to deal with complaints about banking services. It was one of a number of ombudsman schemes that existed in the financial services sector[226] providing extra-judicial, alternative disputes resolution (ADR) procedures in relation to specific complaints, through the medium of independent adjudicators. The Banking Ombudsman Scheme was entirely voluntary and moves to place the scheme on a statutory footing were resisted[227] until the advent of the FSMA 2000. Again, in accordance with the underlying policy of consolidating regulatory provision across the whole financial services sector, the Act provides for the creation of a single, 'one-stop' ombudsman scheme providing alternative dispute resolution for customers of FSA-authorized firms 'quickly and with minimum formality'.[228] This new scheme, called the Financial Ombudsman Service (FOS), is said to be the largest ombudsman scheme in the world.[229] It has recently been the subject of a review, which may result in changes to the scheme.[230]

The provisions in FSMA 2000 are detailed and complex and, as usual, are supplemented by even more detailed rules which may be found in Block Five of the FSA's Handbook.[231]

The Act provides for three types of jurisdiction: 'compulsory jurisdiction',[232] 'consumer credit jurisdiction',[233] and 'voluntary jurisdiction'.[234] Authorized persons must submit to the first two jurisdictions—although (like all ombudsman schemes) they are voluntary as far as the complainants are concerned. The third is a voluntary scheme as far as banks are concerned, although in practice commercial pressure operates to encourage firms to submit to it. The jurisdictions essentially give rise to different schemes with different

---

[224] Directive 2009/14/EC, see Sect. 7(v), below which required the limit to the raised to EUR 100,000 on 31 December 2010. See the FSA's Consultation Paper 08/15: *Financial Services Compensation Scheme: Review of limits* (October 2008). See also its Consultation Papers 08/23: *Financial Stability and Depositor Protection: FSA responsibilities* (December 2008) and 09/3: *FSCS Reform: Fast payouts for depositors and raising consumer awareness* (January 2009).

[225] See Banking Act 2009, Pt. 4 and i the Financial Services Act 2010, ss.16–17.

[226] For example, there also exist the insurance ombudsman, the (statutory) building societies ombudsmen, the unit trust ombudsman, the pensions ombudsman, and other analogous institutions in the investment-business context such as the IMRO referee. The original 'ombudsman' was the Parliamentary Commissioner for Administration established by the Parliamentary Commissioner for Administration Act 1967 to investigate maladministration in government departments.

[227] The recommendations of the Jack Report (*Report of the Review Committee on Banking Services Law and Practice* (Feb. 1989), London, Cmnd. 622) to this effect were rejected.

[228] FSMA 2000, s.225(1).

[229] With a staff of over 800 and a budget of £55 million. See R. Jones & P. Morris, 'A brave new world in ombudsmanry?' [2002] *PL* 640.

[230] The Hunt Review (2008), see P. Morris, 'The FOS and the Hunt review: Continuing Evolution in Dispute Resolution' [2008] *JBL* 785.

[231] See Sect. 4(vi), above. The rules are in the DISP Module. See also the FOS website: www.financialombudsman.org.uk.

[232] FSMA 2000, ss.226, 228–229 and Sched. 17, Pt. III.

[233] Ibid., s.226A and Sched. 17, Pt. 3A, added by the Consumer Credit Act 2006, s.59.

[234] Ibid., s.227 and Sched. 17, Pt. IV.

rules[235] and funding arrangements. However, in all other respects the FOS administers them on a similar basis. Thus, the customers who are eligible to use the schemes are similar: private individuals, small businesses with a turnover of less than £1million, and some third parties. The powers of the FOS to require disclosure of information[236]—enforceable by the possibility of contempt of court proceedings[237]—are the same. As noted below, the Act makes more precise provision for the compulsory and consumer credit jurisdiction but the voluntary jurisdiction rules generally replicate the compulsory jurisdiction provisions as far as procedure and similar matters are concerned.

In general, the 'compulsory' jurisdiction applies to authorized firms in so far as they undertake regulated activities.[238] However, it does not extend to those regulated activities involving customers who are not eligible to invoke the ombudsman jurisdiction.[239] The 'consumer credit jurisdiction' covers activities by institutions (including banks) that are licensed by the Office of Fair Trading under the Consumer Credit Act 1974 (as amended by the 2006 Act to make provision for the FOS's consumer credit jurisdiction) to carry on consumer credit and related businesses.[240] The 'voluntary' jurisdiction extends to unauthorized (as well as authorized[241]) firms and may extend to any activity that could be regulated under the FSMA 2000.[242] Essentially, the FOS has power, subject to FSA approval, to determine the scope of the voluntary scheme and it may even delegate the jurisdiction to other organizations.[243] For example, until the consumer credit jurisdiction came into force, the voluntary scheme extended to the activities of banks' subsidiaries that issued credit cards.[244] The FSMA 2000 includes three provisions regarding the determination of complaints by the FOS. They give the FOS greater freedom than a court of law would have in determining cases before it and give the complainant (but not the respondent) the choice of whether to accept the result or not. First, the Act requires the complaint to be 'determined by reference to what [the ombudsman considers is] fair and reasonable'.[245] This enables the FOS to be more flexible than a court of law, although giving effect to the parties' legal rights clearly is at the core of what is 'fair and reasonable'. Nevertheless, other factors such as the conduct of the parties (for example, whether the bank adhered to any industry guidance[246]) and legitimate expectations can be given more weight. Case law has confirmed that the FOS may reach a decision that is at variance with the parties' strict legal position.[247] The complainant has the choice whether to accept the FOS's determination or not.[248] If he does accept it, then it becomes 'binding' and 'final'.[249] Thus, there is no appeal from a determination, although the complainant (but not the respondent) may, of course, refuse to accept it and pursue other avenues of redress. Any challenge by

---

[235] See n.232.   [236] FSMA 2000, s.231.   [237] Ibid., s.232.

[238] Ibid., s.226(2),(4). For 'regulated activities', see Sect. 4(ii) above.

[239] For example, corporate finance, reinsurance.   [240] See Sect. 5(iii) below.

[241] In so far as the complaint does not fall within the compulsory or consumer credit jurisdiction.

[242] FSMA 2000, s.227(2), (4), (10).   [243] Ibid., Sched. 17, para. 19.

[244] These subsidiaries are not 'authorised' by the FSA but hold licences from the Office of Fair Trading under the Consumer Credit Act 1974 (as amended by the 2006 Act).

[245] FSMA 2000, s.228(2).

[246] The Banking Code (see Sect. 6(i), below) was often taken into account by FOS and its predecessors: see Sect. 6(ii) below.

[247] See *IFG Financial Services Ltd* v. *FOS Ltd* [2005] EWHC 1153 (Admin); *R (on the application of Heather Moor and Edgecomb Ltd* v. *Financial Ombudsman Service Ltd* [2008] EWCA 642; *The Queen on the Application of Keith Williams* v. *FOS Ltd* [2008] EWHC 2142 (Admin); *R (on the application of Bamber & BP Financial Services)* v. *Financial Ombudsman Services* [2009] EWCA 593.

[248] Ibid., s.228(4)(c), (5), (6).   [249] Ibid., s.228(5).

the respondent must be brought by judicial review[250] or by way of defence to an action to enforce a FOS decision.[251] Some of the FOS's decisions have proved controversial with respondents, accusations being made that the FOS dispenses 'palm tree justice' without accountability or consultation.[252] Its decisions requiring the 'fair' (interpreted to mean similar) treatment of both old (in particular 'captured'[253]) customers and new customers as regards interest rates[254] caused consternation to banks who, had used lower rates to attract new debtor-customers whilst not using their discretion to lower the rates of 'captured' customers.

Secondly, provision is made regarding the orders the FOS may make. It may make a 'money award'—an award 'of such amount as the ombudsman considers fair compensation for loss or damage'.[255] As well as covering 'financial loss' the FSA's compulsory jurisdiction rules may specify other types of loss or damage to which the award may extend.[256] Again, this means that the FOS need not be constrained by what would be recoverable in a court of law. The rules set a maximum amount for monetary awards (the old limit under most of the previous schemes: £100,000), but the FOS may recommend a further ex gratia payment, if greater loss has been caused.[257] Monetary awards are enforceable as county court orders.[258] The FOS may also issue a direction to the respondent to take such action 'as the ombudsman considers just and appropriate' and, again, that action need not necessarily be one that a court of law has power to order.[259] Nevertheless, such a direction is enforceable as if it were a court injunction.[260] Finally, provision is made for the award of costs.[261] In conclusion, the Banking Ombudsman Scheme has been subsumed into a much larger, statutory ADR scheme: the FOS. Being statutory, a number of new features have been imposed: the scheme has become divorced from the banking industry, there are increased powers of investigation and its determinations are enforceable through the courts. However, being an 'ombudsman' scheme it retains some of the previous features: complainants have a choice whether to invoke it and whether to accept its findings (which then become binding and final), the procedure is relatively informal, inquisitorial (not adversarial) and swift, and determinations need not necessarily follow what a court of law would decide. These aspects have, as noted above, caused controversy

---

[250] For unsuccessful challenges, see *R* v. *Financial Ombudsman Service ex p Norwich and Peterborough BS* [2002] EWHC 2379, [2003] 1 All ER (Comm) 65, Ouseley J (noted Gray (2003) JFRC 269, considered further in Sect. 6(ii), below) (FOS challenged for requiring the same treatment for old and new customers); *R* v. *Financial Ombudsman Service ex p Green Denman & Co* [2003] EWHC 338, Burnton J (allegations against the FOS of (a) procedural unfairness and (b) mistake of fact) and the cases in n.247). For a successful challenge, see *Garrison Investment Analysis* v. *FOS* [2006] EWHC 2466 (Admin) (decision 'irrational').

[251] *Bunney* v. *Burns Anderson Plc* [2007] EWHC 1240 (Ch).

[252] Some of these concerns were met by an amendment to the MoU between the FOS and the FSA (the 'wider implications process') that now requires the FOS to notify the FSA of issues with 'significant regulatory implications'.

[253] Meaning customers who had to pay a penalty charge to refinance their mortgage.

[254] See *R* v. *Financial Ombudsman Service ex p Norwich and Peterborough BS* [2002] EWHC 2379, [2003] 1 All ER (Comm) 65, considered further in Sect. 6(ii), below, which concerned the differential interest rates of old TESSA and new ISA customers. The FOS also decided that dual mortgage rates—higher ones for 'captured' customers than for new customers—were 'unfair'.

[255] Ibid., s.229(2)(a). S.229(3)–(7) makes further provision for money awards.

[256] Ibid., s.229(3)(b), (4).   [257] Ibid., s.229(5).   [258] Ibid., s.229(8)(b) and Sched. 17, para. 16.

[259] Ibid., s.229(2)(b). The direction may be made only against the respondent and not against a third party. If the 'direction' entails the payment of money, it is subject to the £100,000 cap: *Bunney* v. *Burns Anderson Plc* [2007] EWHC 1240 (Ch).

[260] Ibid., s.229(9)—or, in Scotland, by an order under s.45 of the Court of Session Act 1988. Only the complainant may bring enforcement proceedings.

[261] Ibid., s.230.

as FOS decisions inevitably have an impact on how regulated firms, including banks, operate and yet there is little of the usual safeguards associated with changing the legal framework within which firms operate. Steps have been taken to give the FSA a role in ensuring that any major policy changes that FOS decisions might give rise to are properly scrutinized.[262]

5 The Consumer Credit Act 1974

(i) Background

The object of this Act is to protect 'consumers'—a term that comprises individuals, small partnerships,[263] and unincorporated bodies—in respect of credit and hire transactions.[264] Originally, the Act imposed a financial limit, but the Consumer Credit Act 2006 abolished the then limit of £25,000 for all agreements apart from those made for business purposes.[265] The 1974 Act introduced a licensing regime for persons engaged in the type of business covered and, in addition, made provision as to the form and content of credit and hire agreements and the way in which consumer credit and hire businesses were carried on. The Act further regulates credit brokerage, debt-adjusting, debt-counselling, debt-collecting, debt administration, the provision of credit information services, and the operations of credit reference agencies.[266] These, however, are of only marginal concern to banks.

The 1974 Act was passed to give effect to the recommendations made in the Report of the Crowther Committee,[267] whose main concern was to stamp out abuses common in the consumer credit and hire industry. Banks were not among the financial institutions whose practices were then the cause for alarm but it was thought that the reforms introduced by the Act ought to apply across the board. However, banks obtained some concessions under the Act, especially in relation to overdraft agreements.[268]

After a review of the 1974 Act, the Consumer Credit Act 2006 was passed. As mentioned above, it removed the £25,000 financial limit for non-business agreements.[269] It also strengthened the licensing system and the powers of the regulator (the Office of Fair Trading), required more information and warning notices to be given to debtors and hirers and made it possible for debtors to challenge 'unfair credit relationships'. The

---

[262] Note the 'wider implications process' noted at n.251 above.

[263] i.e. partnerships of two or three persons not all of whom are bodies corporate.

[264] See the definition of 'individual' in the Consumer Credit Act 1974 (CCA 1974), s.189(1), as amended by the Consumer Credit Act 2006 (CCA 2006), s.1. The definition does not require a non-business context, hence the (financially) limited exemption for business credit in s.16B, noted below.

[265] Initially, CCA 1974, s.8 defined a 'consumer credit agreement' as a personal credit agreement for an amount not exceeding £5,000. This ceiling was increased to £15,000 from 20 May 1985 (by S.I. 1983/1878) and to £25,000 from 1 May 1998 (by S.I. 1998/996). CCA 2006, s.2 abolished the limit in s.8 but introduced a new category of exempt agreement: 'business' agreement over £25,000 (CCA 1974, s.16B). See further, Sect. 5(ii), below.

[266] CCA 1974, s.145, as amended by CCA 2006, ss.24 and 25, adding debt administration and the provision of credit information services.

[267] Cmnd. 4596, London, 1971.

[268] CCA 1974, s.74(1)(b), (3), and (3A) (inserted by the Banking Act 1979, s.38(1)). See A.G. Guest and M. Lloyd, *Encyclopaedia of Consumer Credit Law* (loose-leaf, London, 1974), para. 2–075. See also Ch. 17, Sect. 2(v) below.

[269] It also removed protection from partnerships except those with only two or three members, see n.263 above.

implementation of the Payment Services Directive[270] required further amendments,[271] although, in general, its requirements were not imposed on agreements already regulated under the 1974 Act. Most recently, the new Consumer Credit Directive,[272] required yet more amendments to the 1974 Act for agreements within its scope.[273] In June 2010 a further review of consumer credit law, partly with a view to simplifying its provisions, was announced and consideration is being given to moving the regulation of consumer credit from the Office of Fair Trading to the proposed new Financial Conduct Authority.[274] Although the 1974 Act is relevant to bankers, a detailed review of it would be out of place in this work.[275] Nevertheless, it will be useful to include a brief discussion of those aspects which concern banks. Specific sections, applicable to given types of banking business such as overdrafts, bank loans, and the issuing of payment cards, are discussed elsewhere.[276]

(ii) Agreements covered

The 1974 Act uses a specialized terminology. Basically, it extends protection to persons who enter into 'regulated agreements'.[277] These transactions cover 'regulated credit agreements'[278] and 'regulated hire agreements'.[279] In both types of contract, the debtor or hirer has to be an 'individual'[280] but the financier may be 'any person'. Banks mainly enter into credit agreements; therefore hire agreements will not be considered further here.

The 1974 Act treats certain transactions as 'exempt agreements'.[281] Exempt agreements are generally unaffected by the Act's provisions, apart from the 'unfair credit relationship' provisions.[282] Exempt agreements may also give rise to certain 'ancillary' credit businesses regulated by the 1974 Act.[283] Exempt agreements presently include certain

---

[270] Directive 2007/64/EC, see Sect. 7(vi) below.

[271] By the Payments Services Regulations 2009, S.I. 2009/209.

[272] Directive 2008/48/EC, see Sect. 7(vi) below.

[273] i.e. credit agreements other than land mortgages, 'business' credit and credit above £60,620 (i.e. Euro 100,000). However, creditors may generally 'opt-into' the Directive requirements as to form of agreements by complying with the Consumer Credit (Disclosure of Information) Regulations 2010, S.I. 2010/1013 (as amended by S.I. 2010/1969).

[274] See Sect. 1(iv) above.

[275] The leading works are R.M. Goode, *Consumer Credit Law and Practice* (loose-leaf, London, 1977); Guest and Lloyd, n.268 above.

[276] See further Ch. 17, Sect. 2(v) (overdrafts), Ch. 17, Sect. 3(iii) (bank loans) and .Ch. 14, Sect. 8 (payment cards).

[277] CCA 1974, ss.8(3), 15(2), 189(1), as amended especially by the CCA 2006.

[278] Ibid., s.8, as amended by the CCA 2006, s.2. Note that 'credit' is widely defined in s.9; it includes a 'cash loan, and any other form of financial accommodation', see further *Dimond* v. *Lovell* [2002] 1 AC 384, *McMillan Williams* v. *Range* [2004] EWCA 294; [2004] 1 WLR 1858 and *Maple Leaf Macro Volatility Master Fund* v. *Rouvroy* [2009] EWHC 257.

[279] Ibid., s.15, as amended by CCA 2006, s.2.

[280] Defined in ibid., s.189(1), as replaced by the CCA 2006, s.1 to include (i) small partnerships (see n.263) and (ii) unincorporated bodies not consisting entirely of bodies corporate.

[281] For 'exempt agreements', see CCA 1974, ss.16 (and the Consumer Credit (Exempt Agreements) Order 1989, S.I. 1989/869 (as amended), made thereunder), 16A, 16B, and 16C. Ss.16A–16B were added by the CCA 2006, ss.3 and 4 and s.16C by the Legislative Reform (Consumer Credit) Order 2008, S.I. 2008/2826 (and see S.I. 2008/831).

[282] Ibid, ss.140A–140D, added by the CCA 2006, ss.19–22, replacing ss.137–140 (the 'extortionate bargain provisions'), see further Sect. (xiii), below. The provisions do not apply to s.16(6C) exempt agreements (which are regulated by the FSA), see below.

[283] See Sects. (ix) & (x) below.

agreements secured over land, provided they are effected by specified[284] lenders. These lenders include institutions authorized by the Financial Services Authority and their subsidiaries. In consequence, many bank and finance house loans secured by land mortgages are exempt from the controls of the Act but are covered by the Financial Services and Markets Act 2000.[285] Other exempt agreements[286] are interest-free, short-term trade credit involving a limited number of repayments, certain low-interest credit agreements and credit agreements made in the course of the regular financing of export and import transactions, including those in which the UK party acts as a merchant in a sale involving parties residing overseas. Many loans extended by banks fall within the ambit of the last category. The 2006 reforms introduced three new categories of exempt agreements: agreements with 'high net worth' debtors (or hirers),[287] agreements over £25,000 made by the debtor (or hirer) 'wholly or predominantly for business purposes'[288] and 'buy-to-let' secured loans.[289]

The Act applies both to agreements involving the extension of 'fixed-sum credit'[290] and to 'running-account credit'.[291] The former type is best illustrated by a loan that is paid off either in instalments or at the end of its term. The latter type covers revolving credit agreements, under which the debtor is allowed to borrow amounts up to a given ceiling. The amount available to the debtor is automatically reduced whenever he makes a withdrawal but is increased when he pays any amount to the credit of his account. Examples are overdrafts granted on bankers' current accounts and credit card agreements.

A running-account credit agreement for business purposes is within the ambit of the 1974 Act in any one of the following cases: (a) if the credit limit is £25,000 or less or (b) if, regardless of the credit limit, the debtor is precluded from drawing out at any one time an amount exceeding £25,000, or (c) if the credit charge, or any other provision favouring the creditor, is increased when the amount drawn exceeds £25,000.[292] Furthermore, the arrangement is 'regulated' if it is probable, from the surrounding circumstances, that the debit balance will not exceed £25,000 at any one time.[293]

(iii) Provisions to be complied with: licensing

One of the cardinal principles of the Act is that creditors can engage in consumer lending only if they obtain a licence from the Office of Fair Trading (OFT).[294] The OFT, which administers both the 1974 Act and the Enterprise Act 2002, has a wide discretion to grant,

---

[284] See CCA 1974, s.16 and S.I. 1989/869 (both, as amended).   [285] See further, Sect. 4.

[286] See S.I. 1989/869 (as amended, most recently as a consequence of the Consumer Credit Directive, see S.I. 2010/1010, as amended by S.I. 2010/1969).

[287] CCA 1974, s.16A, added by the CCA 2006, s.3. And see S.I. 2007/1168 (form of declaration and statement to be included in agreement). As this exemption is incompatible with the new Consumer Credit Directive, it only applies to agreements outside the scope of the Directive, viz: those secured on land or providing credit in excess of £60,260.

[288] CCA 1974, s.16B, added by the CCA 2006, s.4. And see S.I. 2007/1168 (form of declaration which may be included in agreement).

[289] CCA 1974, s.16C, added by the Legislative Reform (Consumer Credit) Order 2008, S.I. 2008/2826 (and see S.I. 2008/831).

[290] Defined in s.10(1)(b) of the 1974 Act as anything that is not 'running-account credit': see next note.

[291] Defined in s.10(1)(a) of the 1974 Act.

[292] CCA 1974, s.10(3)(a), (b)(i), (ii), as amended (to apply to 'business' credit within s.16B) by the CCA 2006, s.5(2).

[293] Ibid., s.10(3)(b)(iii), and see s.171(1) (onus of proof). This is an anti-avoidance provision.

[294] Ibid., s.21, as amended by the CCA 2006, s.33.

vary, suspend, or revoke the required licence.[295] As well as overhauling this licensing regime, the Consumer Credit Act 2006 also conferred powers on the OFT to impose 'requirements' (backed by a new power to impose 'civil penalties' for breach),[296] to obtain information and access to premises, and to wind up a licensee's business.[297] Anybody who engages in consumer credit business without a licence commits an offence.[298] A more effective sanction is that agreements made by an offending creditor are enforceable only with the OFT's consent.[299] Two of the matters that the OFT takes into consideration in such cases are, first, the extent to which the consumer has been prejudiced by the creditor's behaviour and, secondly, whether a licence would have been granted if applied for.[300]

Generally, the licensing scheme affects banks in two ways. First, they have to hold a licence if they wish to enter into consumer credit business or to engage in 'ancillary credit business' covered by the Act.[301] Secondly, a bank has to be wary when it finances another financial institution that engages in regulated transactions or carries on an 'ancillary credit business'. If the institution concerned is not duly licensed it may end up in financial difficulties—with unenforceable agreements—which are bound to affect the bank's ability to obtain reimbursement for advances made.

(iv) **Contractual disclosure and withdrawal/cancellation rights**

The licensing regime is not the only protective measure introduced by the 1974 Act. Certain formalities have to be observed when a regulated agreement is executed. Basically, the Act now requires the full disclosure of the terms of the contract both before contracting and at the time of contracting. Moreover, section 20 empowers the Secretary of State to make regulations for the calculation of the 'true cost of credit' incurred by the consumer. The regulations so made lay down a formula for the calculation of the total cost of credit and of an annual percentage rate, known as the 'APR' (annual percentage rate).[302]

The APR calculation is based on the so-called 'present value' method and also includes some charges in addition to interest. It is an attempt to convey the 'true cost' of borrowing. However, there are some banking transactions, in particular the overdraft or credit card agreements, where the actual cost of the credit will depend on how the facility is used. In such cases, the regulations lay down the assumptions which creditors have to adopt in calculating the APR. Although the APR in such cases will only give the actual cost of the credit in those (rare) transactions where the assumptions turn out to reflect exactly how the credit is actually used, the APR does provide a 'comparator' or benchmark (as all

---

[295] Ibid., ss.25, 31–33, as extensively amended by the CCA 2006. An appeal lies to the General Regulatory Chamber (GRC), part of the First-tier Tribunal established under the Tribunal, Courts and Enforcement Act 2007: s.41, as amended by the CCA 2006 to create the Consumer Credit Appeals Tribunal which was replaced by the GRC.

[296] Ibid., ss.33A–33E (requirements) and ss.39A–39C (civil penalties), added by the CCA 2006, ss.38–42 and ss.52–54, respectively.

[297] Ibid., ss.34A, 36A–36F, added by CCA 2006, ss.32, 45–50.   [298] Ibid., s.39.

[299] Ibid., s.40, as amended by the CCA 2006, s.26.   [300] Ibid.

[301] These are defined in ibid., ss.145–146, as amended (to add two new categories of ancillary credit business, see n.266 above) by the CCA 2006. The consequences of being unlicensed are similar to those noted above: ss.147–150. See Sect. (ix) below.

[302] As a result of the implementation of the Consumer Credit Directive, there are now two sets of regulations: (a) the (old) Consumer Credit (Total Charge for Credit) Regulations 1980, S.I. 1980/51, (as amended), applicable only to land mortgages, unless the creditor has 'opted into' the 'Directive' regime and (b) the Consumer Credit (Total Charge for Credit) Regulations 2010, S.I. 2010/1011, applicable to all other regulated agreements.

creditors will have adopted the same statutory assumptions) for assessing the relative cost of credit under similar transactions.[303]

Before a regulated agreement is concluded, the debtor must now be given 'pre-contract' information in the prescribed form. The rationale is to provide a debtor with a document that he may take away and use to make comparisons between credit agreements that may be on offer from other creditors before committing himself to a particular agreement. For agreements within the scope of the Directive,[304] the information must generally be given in the form of the 'SECCI' (Standard European Consumer Credit Information)[305] whilst the older requirements apply in other cases.[306] Creditors covered by the Directive must also provide explanations of the agreement,[307] a copy of the draft agreement itself on request[308] and must assess the creditworthiness of the debtor.[309] The express terms of the agreement itself have to be embodied in a signed and legible document complying with the detailed requirements of the Agreements Regulations.[310] Again, there are two sets of Agreements Regulations, one for agreements within the scope of the Directive[311] and the older one for those outside.[312] These regulations lay down, in considerable detail, what the document needs to disclose.[313] The consumer must be given a copy of this document.[314] An agreement that is not properly executed in compliance with these provisions is unenforceable except by a court order.[315] Under the 1974 Act, in some cases the agreement was

---

[303] In practice, there is much dispute as to how these assumptions are to be interpreted and hence applied.

[304] And, for agreements outside the Directive, if the creditor chooses to comply with this regime rather than the (old) regime, see n.273.

[305] The Consumer Credit (Disclosure of Information) Regulations 2010, S.I. 2010/1013 (as amended by S.I. 2010/1969). There are special requirements for overdrafts (reg. 10) and for contracts concluded by telephone.

[306] The Consumer Credit (Disclosure of Information) Regulations 2004, S.I. 2004/1481, In the case of 'distance' contracts', these regulations do not apply as a similar requirement is imposed by the Financial Services (Distance Marketing) Regulations 2004, S.I. 2004/2095.

[307] CCA 1974, s.55A. added on 1 February 2011 by S.I. 2010/1010, reg. 3 (as amended by S.I. 2010/1969). There is no explicit sanction but (a) the OFT has the normal disciplinary powers and (b) the consequent agreement could be regarded as giving rise to an 'unfair relationship', see Sect. (xii) below.

[308] In addition to the pre-contract information, CCA 1974, s.55C. added on 1 February 2011 by S.I. 2010/1010, reg. 6. The sanction is a breach of statutory duty action (s.55C(3)).

[309] CCA 1974, s.55B. added on 1 February 2011 by S.I. 2010/1010, reg. 5. There is no explicit sanction but (a) the OFT has the normal disciplinary powers and (b) the consequent agreement could be regarded as giving rise to an 'unfair relationship', see Sect. (xii) below.

[310] CCA 1974, s.61. In the case of current accounts, information about the consequences of 'over-running' must also be given (and also given annually): s.74A, added on 1 February 2011 by S.I. 2010/1010, reg. 21 (as amended by S.I. 2010/1969).

[311] Consumer Credit (Agreements) Regulations 2010, S.I. 2010/1014 (as amended by S.I. 2010/1969). Again, for agreements outside the Directive, the creditor may choose to comply with the 'Directive' regime by complying with the Consumer Credit (Disclosure of Information) Regulations 2010, S.I. 2010/1013 (as amended by S.I. 2010/1969), see n.273.

[312] Consumer Credit (Agreements) Regulations 1983, S.I. 1983/1553 (as amended, especially by the Consumer Credit (Agreements) (Amendment) Regulations 2004, S.I. 2004/1482 and the Consumer Credit (Agreements) Regulations 2010, S.I. 2010/1014 (as amended by S.I. 2010/1969)). But see the previous note for the possibility of opting into the 'Directive' regime.

[313] For example, the amount of credit or credit limit, how and when the credit and charges are to be repaid, the total amount of credit (and its constituent parts), the annual rate of interest and the APR all need to be disclosed.

[314] CCA 1974, ss.61A–63. Again the 'copy' requirements differ depending on whether the agreement is within or outside the scope of the Directive regime.

[315] Ibid., s.65. Note s.113 (effect on security). See further Sect. (xiii) below.

completely (or 'irredeemably'[316]) unenforceable, but the CCA 2006 repealed the relevant provisions.[317]

The original statutory requirements were drafted before electronic communications were possible and therefore their terms (e.g. the use of words such as 'colour of the paper') precluded credit agreements being concluded electronically and requisite notices and documents being sent electronically. Moreover, it was sometimes unclear if some of the statutory requirements as to service of notices could be fulfilled by newer electronic methods. To facilitate the use of electronic communications in consumer credit, the 1974 Act and relevant regulations were amended[318] so that it is now possible to conclude credit agreements using electronic methods and, if the consumer consents, to serve most notices—but not default notices[319]—electronically.

As a result of the implementation of the Consumer Credit Directive,[320] debtors under credit agreements within its scope[321] now have an unconditional 14-day right to cancel the agreement, or, in the terminology of the Directive, a 'right of withdrawal'.[322] This is far more extensive than the old right to cancel regulated agreements under the 1974 Act. This old right is still available for other regulated agreements,[323] and it essentially applies only where the debtor has been subjected to 'face-to-face' persuasion and has signed the agreement other than at trade premises.[324] This 'old' right to cancel must be exercised within five days of the debtor receiving the required notice.[325] Neither the new right to 'withdraw' nor the old right to 'cancel' is available where the agreement is a 'restricted-use credit agreement' made to finance the acquisition of land, or is a bridging loan made in connection with the purchase of land.[326] In addition, contracts secured over land are not within the Directive (so no right of withdrawal arises) and are excluded from the old right to cancel.[327] However, in the case of some contracts[328] secured over land, the debtor must be given a chance to withdraw before the execution of the agreement.[329] To this end, he must be given, together with a copy of the draft agreement, a notice advising him of his right to withdraw from the transaction within one week.[330] Where the creditor fails to

---

[316] A term coined by Lord Hoffman in *Dimond* v. *Lovell* [2002] 1 AC 384. In *Wilson* v. *Secretary of State for Trade and Industry* [2003] UKHL 40 the House of Lords held that these provisions were compatible (in so far as they only related to agreements within the (then) £25,000 limit) with the European Convention on Human Rights (it being argued that the provision was a disproportionate restriction on the rights of a creditor, in contravention of art. 6(1) and/or the First Protocol to the Convention).

[317] CCA 1974, s.127(3)–(5) (if the consumer had not signed a document with certain minimum information or if notice of cancellation rights were not given), repealed by CCA 2006, s.15 as regards agreements made on or after 6 April 2007.

[318] By the Consumer Credit Act 1974 (Electronic Communications) Order 2004, S.I. 2004/3236, made under the Electronic Communications Act 2000, ss.8, 9.

[319] See Sect. (v) below.   [320] Directive 2008/48/EC, Art. 14.

[321] But also including business creditors under regulated agreements (see Sect. (ii), above).

[322] CCA 1974, s.66A, added on 1 February 2011 by S.I. 2010/1010, reg. 13 (as amended by S.I. 2010/1969).

[323] Essentially those for credit above £60,260.   [324] CCA, s.67(a).   [325] Ibid., s.68.

[326] Ibid., ss.67A(12)(c), (d) and s.67. And see Guest and Lloyd, n.268 above, para. 2-068. A 'restricted-use' agreement is defined in s.11.

[327] S.67(a).

[328] But not 'restricted-use credit agreements' (defined in CCA, s.11) made to finance the acquisition of the mortgaged land nor bridging loans made in respect of the purchase of land: CCA, s.58(2).

[329] CCA 1974, s.58.

[330] Consumer Credit (Agreements) Regulations 1983, S.I. 1983/1553 (as amended, especially by the Consumer Credit (Agreements) (Amendment) Regulations 2004, S.I. 2004/1482) and Consumer Credit (Agreements) Regulations 2010, S.I. 2010/1014 (as amended by S.I. 2010/1969). See also the Consumer Credit (Cancellation Notices and Copies of Documents) Regulations 1983, S.I. 1983/1557, reg. 4 (as amended by S.I. 2010/1969) and Sched. 1, Pt. 1; and the amendment in S.I. 1985/660.

comply with these requirements, the agreement is 'improperly executed' with the consequences noted above.[331]

The creditor's duty to supply information does not end when the agreement is executed.
As well as having to respond to a request by the debtor (sometimes[332] if accompanied by
the prescribed fee) for a copy of the agreement and a statement of account,[333] the creditor
must automatically (and without making a charge[334]) send such a statement periodically.[335] A creditor who fails to respond to the debtor's request, generally[336] cannot enforce
the agreement whilst the obligation remains unfulfilled.[337] Curiously, no explicit sanctions are imposed for failure to supply the automatic periodic statements in relation to
running-account credit[338] whilst, in relation to fixed-sum credit the agreement is stated to
be unenforceable and no interest or default sum may be charged during the period of non-
compliance.[339] The 2006 Act introduced two new types of notice that a creditor must send,
backed with the same sanctions for non-compliance. Thus, if the debtor is in arrears with
his payments, then a notice of sums in arrears must be sent to him[340] whilst if a default
sum is to be imposed, then a notice to this effect must also be given.[341] The implementation of the Consumer Credit Directive[342] resulted in two further notice requirements: in
the case of current accounts if the debtor overdraws significantly without prior arrangement[343] and in the case of certain changes in interest rate.[344] In addition, the debtor must

---

[331] Ibid., s.61(2) and see s.65 & s.113 (effect on security).

[332] No fee is allowed in relation to the obligation under s.77B (certain fixed-sum agreements of fixed duration repayable by instalments): s.77B(7). And see n.334.

[333] CCA, ss.77, 77B (fixed-sum), s.78(1)–(3) (running-account). See *McGuffick* v. *RBS Plc* [2009] EWHC
2386 (s.77) and *Carey* v. *HSBC Bank Plc* [2009] EWHC 3417 (s.78).

[334] As regards running account credit, s.78(4)–(7) (as amended by the CCA 2006, s.7) makes no mention
of a fee, and hence it would seem that the creditor is unable to charge one. As regards fixed-sum credit, s.77A
(added by the CCA 2006, s.6 and amended by the Legislative Reform (Consumer Credit) Order 2008, S.I.
2008/2826) makes this explicit: s.77A(3).

[335] Ibid., s.78(4)–(7) (as amended by the CCA 2006, s.7): running-account credit. Ibid., s.77A (added by
CCA 2006, s.6): fixed-sum credit.

[336] But a breach of s.77B (certain fixed-sum agreements of fixed duration repayable by instalments) is
actionable as a breach of statutory duty: s.77B(8).

[337] CCA, s. 77(4) (fixed-sum), 78(6) (running-account). There was also a criminal sanction until its repeal
by the Consumer Protection from Unfair Trading Regulations 2008, S.I. 2008/1277 (implementing the
Unfair Commercial Practices Directive (Directive 2005/29/EC) from 26 May 2008.

[338] Although, persistent breach may cause the OFT to discipline the creditor, see Sect. (iii) above. And
note the sanction for breach of s.77B, n.336 above.

[339] CCA, s.77A(6) (added by the CCA 2006, s.6 and amended by the Legislative Reform (Consumer
Credit) Order 2008, S.I. 2008/2826.)—the difference arising as the obligations were imposed by different
legislation.

[340] CCA 1974, s.86B (fixed-sum credit) and s.86C (running-account credit), added by the CCA 2006,
ss.10 and 11. For the prescribed form, see the Consumer Credit (Information Requirements and Duration
of Licences and Charges) Regulations 2007, S.I. 2007/1167. See also s.86A (added by CCA 1006, s.8) enabling
the OFT to prepare 'information sheets' to be included with these notices and s.86D (added by CCA 2006,
11) for the sanction.

[341] CCA 1974, s.86E, added by the CCA 2006, s.12. For the prescribed form, see the Consumer Credit
(Information Requirements and Duration of Licences and Charges) Regulations 2007, S.I. 2007/1167. See
also s.86A (added by CCA 1006, s.8) enabling the OFT to prepare 'information sheets' to be included with
this notice and s.86F (added by CCA 2006, 13) providing that only simple interest may be charged on default
sums. 'Default sum' is defined in s.187A (added by the CCA 2006, s.18).

[342] Directive 2008/48/EC, Arts. 18.2 and 11. S.77B (see nn.332, 333, and 336) is also derived from the
Directive.

[343] CCA, s.74B, added on 1 February 2011 by S.I. 2010/1010, reg. 22 (as amended by S.I. 2010/1969).

[344] CCA, s.78A, added on 1 February 2011 by S.I. 2010/1010, reg. 27. This provision is inapplicable to agreements secured on land or where s.74B (see previous note) applies.

be notified if the creditor seeks to vary or modify the agreement under a power conferred on him in the contract.[345] If a credit agreement is modified bilaterally, the onerous formal requirements applicable to 'modifying agreements' come into play.[346] As the requirements are so cumbersome, it is usually advisable to terminate the old agreement and enter into a completely new one.

(v) Default and termination

As well as requiring the creditor to notify the debtor when he falls in arrears, a default sum is to be imposed or a current account holder 'over-runs',[347] the Act seriously restricts the creditor's right to resort to contractual remedies available upon the debtor's default. Thus, the creditor has to serve on the debtor a 'default notice' before he seeks to terminate the contract, to demand early repayment of the outstanding balance, to utilize a security, or to restrict or defer the debtor's rights under the contract.[348] The debtor's right to any unused balance available to him may, however, be suspended. The default notice must state the nature of the breach and the method for remedying it or, if this is precluded, the amount to be paid as compensation. The debtor has to be given at least 14 days[349] in order to remedy the breach or pay the amount due. The consequences of the breach must also be spelt out to him.[350] Although most notices under the 1974 Act may now,[351] if the debtor consents, be sent electronically, an exception has been made for default notices which still have to be given in paper form.[352] The 1974 Act prohibits the charging of default interest, which means that the interest rate may not be increased on the debtor's breach.[353]

By way of contrast, the Act gives the debtor the right to terminate a credit agreement early or (as a result of the implementation of the Consumer Credit Directive) to repay part of the amounts owing early.[354] Moreover, early settlement—whether by virtue of this right or in any other case[355]—generally entitles the debtor to a rebate of credit charge[356] and the

---

[345] CCA 1974, s.82(1). Note the special provisions as to the variation of interest rates in s.78A referred to in the previous note. The Unfair Terms in Consumer Contracts Regulations 1999, S.I. 1999/2083 also have provisions regulating unilateral variation terms: see E. Lomnicka, 'Unilateral Variation in Banking Contracts: An "Unfair Term"?', in P. Cartwright (ed.), *Consumer Protection in Financial Services* (London, 1999).

[346] CCA1974, s.82(2)—but temporarily exceeding an overdraft credit limit is exempted (s.82(4) and see s.82(1E)).

[347] See Sect. (iv) above.

[348] Ibid., s.87. Note that s.87(1)(d) does not apply if s.98A(4) (see n.364 below) does: s.87(5).

[349] Increased from seven days by the CCA 2006, s.14 which also made other amendments to s.88.

[350] CCA, s.88. But the non-compliance with a clause, such as one calling for repayment of the outstanding balance, which becomes effective on the initial default, is not an operative breach for the purpose of s.87(3).

[351] Especially since the amendments introduced by the Consumer Credit Act 1974 (Electronic Communications) Order 2004, S.I. 2004/3236, Sect. (iv) above.

[352] See the Consumer Credit (Enforcement, Default and Termination Notices) (Amendment) Regulations 2004, S.I. 2004/3237. This is also the case for non-breach enforcement and termination notices to be given under ss.76 & 98.

[353] CCA, s.93. It is thought that this provision can be avoided by a clause under which the 'penalty' interest is stated as that ordinarily payable, but the debtor is granted a reduction in respect of each instalment paid promptly.

[354] Ibid., s.94, as amended on 1 February 2011 by S.I. 2010/1010, reg. 30. Part-payment is not available for agreements secured on land (as they are outside the scope of the Directive).

[355] For example, when calculating damages for breach, or a settlement figure on refinancing.

[356] CCA 1974, s.95. And see the Consumer Credit (Early Settlement) Regulations 2004, S.I. 2004/1483, replacing S.I. 1983/1562 and amended on 1 February 2011 (on the implementation of the Directive, Art.16.1) by S.I. 2010/1010, regs. 77–84 (as amended by S.I. 2010/1969).

creditor to a 'compensatory amount'.[357] Under the Act, any linked transaction is then also discharged.[358] The creditor is under a duty to inform the debtor of the amount to be paid upon the early discharge of the debt[359] and, (on request) if there has been part-payment, to clarify various matters arising.[360] There is no doubt that this provision gives preferential treatment to the debtor. The policy involved is based on the consideration that the creditor is able to reinvest his money at the market rate. The debtor, on the other hand, could find it difficult to obtain finance from another source if the creditor were allowed to demand early repayment.

For this reason, the Act restricts the creditor's right to terminate the contract, even in cases where his decision is not motivated by the debtor's default but is based on a specific termination clause in the agreement. In such a case the creditor has to give the debtor seven days' notice, so as to enable him to search for another source of finance.[361] The provision applies, however, only where the agreement is for a specific contractual period which has not ended by the time the creditor seeks to enforce his right.[362] Therefore it does not apply to bank overdrafts which are repayable on demand rather than available for a determined period.[363] The implementation of the Directive resulted in a further provision governing the termination of agreements without a fixed duration, for reasons other than breach, both by debtors (they may terminate, free of charge, by notice of not more than one month) and by creditors (they must give at least two months' notice).[364] However, overdrafts are excluded from this provision.[365]

(vi) Control of advertisements

The Act controls the content of certain credit advertisements. Under section 43, the relevant provisions apply to any advertisement in which a financial institution carrying on a consumer credit business or lending on mortgage to individuals states that it is prepared to provide credit.[366] The issuing of advertisements which do not include the required information, constitutes an offence.[367] The details to be included in advertisements covered by the Act are set out in the Consumer Credit (Advertisements) Regulations, which do not apply to advertisements of 'business credit'.[368] The implementation of the Consumer

---

[357] To cover its costs of early settlement: CCA 1974, s.95A added on 1 February 2011 by S.I. 2010/1010, reg. 32 (but again, inapplicable to agreements secured on land).

[358] CCA, s.96. For 'linked transactions', see Sect. (xii) below.   [359] Ibid., s.97.

[360] CCA, s.97A added on 1 February 2011 by S.I. 2010/1010, reg. 34. Those matters are: the amount of rebate (if any), any changes to the repayments, duration of agreement and amount still owing.

[361] Ibid., s.98. This notice must be in paper form: see n.352 above.

[362] Ibid., subs.(2).   [363] See Ch. 17, Sect. 2(v) below.

[364] CCA, s.98A added on 1 February 2011 by S.I. 2010/1010, reg. 38. There are also controls on the creditor's ability to exercise a contractual power to terminate or suspend the right to draw on credit, whether for breach or not: s.98A(4)–(6) and see s.87(5) (s.98A(4) applies).

[365] Ibid., s.98A(8)(a)–(c)—as are agreements secured on land (s.98A(8)(d)—as these are outside the scope of the Directive).

[366] Under subs.(2)(c), advertisements referring to contracts governed by a foreign applicable law are not covered. Note also the exclusion in subs.(3).

[367] CCA 1974, s.47. Originally, it was also a criminal offence under s.46 of the 1974 Act to issue 'false or misleading' advertisements, but this provision has been repealed and replaced by the more general provisions in the Consumer Protection from Unfair Trading Regulations 2008, S.I. 2008/1277 (implementing the Unfair Commercial Practices Directive (Directive 2005/29/EC)).

[368] The regulations are made under CCA 1974, s.44. For the 'business' exclusions, see S.I. 2004/1484, reg. 10 and S.I. 2010/1970, reg. 11.

Credit Directive[369] has again resulted in two sets of regulations; the older set[370] now only applies to credit agreements secured on land (as these agreements are outside the scope of the Directive) and new regulations[371] apply to all other credit advertisements.

The older regulations require the inclusion of a minimum amount of information (set out in Schedule 2 to the regulations) should the advertisement include certain 'trigger' amounts.[372] This minimum information must be 'given equal prominence and … be shown together as a whole'.[373] Moreover, the credit advertisement must specify the 'typical APR' if it contains certain other 'trigger' information.[374] The 'typical APR' is defined as the APR[375] at or below which it is reasonably expected that credit will be provided under at least 66 per cent of the agreements generated by the advertisement.[376] It must be designated 'typical', presented 'together with' the Schedule 2 information, and given greater prominence than any other rate of charge and that Schedule 2 information.[377] Special provision is made as to the assumptions which need to be made when calculating the APR in running-account credit, for the purposes of advertising.[378] However, there is a concession in relation to the citation of interest rates for banking overdrafts.[379] Thus, instead of the 'typical APR', banks may cite the interest rate (calculated on the same basis as the APR, but as if interest were the only charge for credit) and then specify the amounts of any specific charges such as commitment fees. Agreements must contain certain 'wealth warnings' which are subject to prominence requirements.[380] There are restrictions on the use of certain expressions in credit advertisements[381] including the term 'overdraft' which may refer only to proper current accounts operable by cheques 'or similar orders'.

The new 'Directive' advertisements regulations are generally rather simpler[382] and use the concept of 'representative APR', rather than 'typical APR', although similar provision is made as to the assumptions which need to be made when calculating the APR.[383] The 'representative APR' is the APR[384] at or below which it is reasonably expected that credit will be provided under at least 51 per cent of the agreements generated by the advertisement.[385] In general (although again there is a concession for

---

[369] Directive 2008/48/EC, Art. 4.

[370] The Consumer Credit (Advertisements) Regulations 2004, S.I. 2004/1484, as amended, replacing S.I. 1989/1125, as amended.

[371] The Consumer Credit (Advertisements) Regulations 2010, S.I. 2010/1970.

[372] Reg. 4. The 'trigger' amounts are (i) the amount of repayments of credit, (ii) the amount of other payments or charges, (iii) the total amount payable. This approach was not compatible with the Consumer Credit Directive.

[373] Reg. 4(2). The Consumer Credit Directive does not permit differences in 'prominence' of its prescribed information.

[374] Reg. 8. The 'trigger' information is (i) any other rate of charge, (ii) certain items of information listed in Sched.1 information, (iii) indications that credit is available to those with restricted access to credit, (iv) indications that the terms of the credit are particularly favourable and (v) the availability of incentives. Again, this approach was not compatible with the Consumer Credit Directive; the Directive uses the concept of 'representative' rather than 'typical' APR.

[375] For the 'APR' see Sect. (iv) above.

[376] Reg. 1(2). There is much dispute as to which agreements need to be taken into account in calculating the 'typical APR', in particular, whether agreements not covered by the terms of the advertisement but nevertheless factually generated by it, are to be taken into account.

[377] Reg. 8(5).   [378] Reg. 1(2) & Sched. 1.

[379] Reg. 8(6).   [380] Reg. 7.

[381] Such as 'no deposit' or '0% interest': reg. 9.

[382] There are no 'together as a whole' requirements or (except in the case of reg.6), see n.387 below 'prominence' requirements—although there is the usual clarity and legibility requirement (reg. 3).

[383] Reg. 1(2).   [384] For the 'APR' see Sect. (iv), above and see previous note.

[385] Reg. 1(2).

overdrafts), the 'representative APR' must be included as part of standard information in a 'representative example' if an advertisement includes any reference to the cost of credit[386] and it must be included (and given greater prominence) in certain potentially problematic advertisements.[387] The restrictions on the use of certain expressions in credit advertisements[388] including the term 'overdraft', are replicated in the new regulations.[389]

(vii) **Canvassing**

The canvassing of 'debtor-creditor' agreements,[390] such as personal loans, at premises other than the business premises of the would-be creditor, canvasser, or debtor is prohibited by section 49 of the Act. Canvassing is defined by section 48 to mean visiting the debtor without invitation, in order to persuade him to enter into the agreement. To avoid committing the offence, any invitation must be written and signed.[391]

The prohibition of canvassing applies only if the object of the visit was the soliciting of the agreement. Thus, a bank manager who, for example, at a golf club suggests to a client that the client should enter into a regulated agreement will not be canvassing unless he went to the club for that purpose, and the same applies to a visit made to the client's home.[392]

Section 49(3) creates a special exemption respecting overdrafts. It may be asked why such an exemption is needed. Banks do not usually proffer their overdrafts. However, banks encourage the opening of current accounts by stating that customers are granted overdraft facilities on application. Canvassing of this type is permitted provided, first, that the person approached already has some account with the bank and, secondly, that the canvassing relates to a current account of a type covered by a Determination of the Office of Fair Trading. The Determination so made applies to accounts operable by cheques 'or similar orders', and permits canvassing only if effected by the creditor or his employees.[393]

(viii) **Quotations**

Under section 52 of the Act, a quotation is a document in which the creditor gives 'prospective customers information about the terms on which he is prepared to do business'. Previously, extensive provision was made concerning the contents of quotations by the Quotations Regulations 1989,[394] made under that section, but these regulations were revoked in 1997. Instead, more narrowly focused regulations were made in 1999[395]

---

[386] Reg. 4, and see reg. 5 (reg. 5(5): concession for overdrafts).
[387] Reg. 6—again there is a concession for overdrafts in reg. 6(3).
[388] Such as 'no deposit' or '0% interest': reg. 9.   [389] Reg. 10.
[390] The Act divides regulated credit agreements into 'debtor-creditor' and 'debtor-creditor-supplier' agreements: ss.12, 13. The latter are, essentially, so-called 'connected loans', see Sect. (xii) below.
[391] S.48(2) & s.48(1)(b).
[392] CCA 1974, s.48, especially, subs.(1)(a). See Guest & Lloyd, n.268 above, para. 2-049. Note that canvassing for 'debtor-creditor-supplier' agreements, such as credit sales, is allowed provided the creditor holds a specially endorsed licence under s.23(3): ibid., para. 2-050.
[393] Determination of June 1977; Guest & Lloyd, n.268 above, para. 4-4800.
[394] S.I. 1989/1126, replacing S.I. 1980/55. They were revoked by S.I. 1997/211.
[395] Consumer Credit (Content of Quotations) and Consumer Credit (Advertisements) (Amendment) Regulations 1999, S.I. 1999/2725.

requiring quotations for home mortgages of any amount to contain certain 'wealth warnings'.[396]

(ix) **Credit brokers and credit intermediaries**

Credit brokerage involves the introduction, in the course of business, of a would-be borrower to a credit provider.[397] Banks are affected by the credit-brokerage provisions of the Act where they refer a customer to another finance house, provided the introduction is not effected as a mere courtesy.

A credit brokerage business needs to be licensed,[398] and an unlicensed credit broker may not recover his fee except on an order of the Office of Fair Trading.[399] A regulated agreement where the debtor is introduced by an unlicensed credit broker is also unenforceable except by order of the OFT,[400] and thus banks need to ensure that persons introducing regulated credit business to them are licensed. Personal introductions, which are not made in the course of a person's business, (for example of a new customer to a bank by an existing client) do not constitute brokerage within the meaning of the Act.

The Consumer Credit Directive[401] contains provisions regarding 'credit intermediaries', a term covering persons who, for financial consideration, deal with or for individuals entering into credit agreements.[402] Many 'credit brokers' will therefore also be 'credit intermediaries'. Three obligations are imposed on such persons, the sanction being criminal liability.[403] First, the intermediary is obliged to disclose, in his advertisements and documentation, the extent to which he is acting independently.[404] Second, if he acts for a debtor and charges him a fee, he must 'ensure' that the fee is disclosed to the debtor and then agreed to *in writing* before the agreement is concluded.[405] Third, he must also disclose such a fee to the creditor if the APR[406] is to be ascertained by the creditor, so that the creditor can take account of it in that calculation.[407]

(x) **Other 'Ancillary Credit Businesses'**

The Act covers other businesses related to consumer credit agreements: debt-adjusting, debt-counselling, debt collection, debt administration, and the provision of credit information services.[408] Debt-adjusting means, on behalf of the debtor, the negotiation of the discharge of debts due or the taking over of debt obligations or the liquidation of a debt under those types of agreements.[409] Credit-counselling is the giving of advice to a

---

[396] That 'your home is at risk' if repayments are not maintained and that, in the case of foreign currency agreements secured on land, 'the sterling equivalent of your liability...may be increased by exchange rate movements': ibid., regs. 3, 4, 6.

[397] CCA 1974, s.145(2)–(4), and see s.146 (exceptions).

[398] Ibid., s.21, as amended by the CCA 2006, s.33.   [399] Ibid., s.148.

[400] Ibid., s.149 (and see s.148(2): unlicensed trader may apply for order that he be treated as if licensed). Note also s.155 (limits on credit brokers' fees).

[401] Directive 2008/48/EC, Arts. 3(f), 21.

[402] CCA 1974, s.160A(1), (2)—almost a 'copy out' of the Directive, Art. 3. Credit agreements secured on land (as these are outside the Directive) are not covered.

[403] S.160A(6), (7).

[404] S.160A(3). In particular he must disclose whether he works exclusively with a creditor.

[405] S.169A(4).   [406] For the 'APR' see Sect. (iv) above.   [407] S.160A(5).

[408] S.145(1)(b)–(db), as amended by the CCA 2006, ss.24 & 25 (adding the last two categories). The ancillary credit business of operating a credit reference agency, is considered in Sect. (xi) below.

[409] Ibid., s.145(5), and see s.146 (exceptions). Note that the definition extends beyond regulated agreements to consumer agreements (i.e. exempt agreements are covered: see Sect. (ii) above).

consumer who has incurred debts under consumer credit agreements.[410] Debt collection is the taking of steps to procure the payment of debts under consumer credit agreements.[411] Debt administration is the performance of the credit agreement or the enforcement of rights under it, on behalf of the creditor.[412] The provision of credit information services is assisting debtors to correct their credit reference agency records.[413] A person who engages in these types of business requires a licence, and an unlicensed trader may not recover his fee except on an order of the OFT.[414]

The types of business which are primarily affected by these provisions are those of finance brokers and advisers, accountants, solicitors, mortgage and insurance brokers, and other financial consultants. Neither the clearing banks nor the investment banks engage in these types of business.

(xi) **Credit reference agencies**

A credit reference agency is an organization engaged in the business of collecting and furnishing information on the financial standing of 'individuals' as defined in the Act.[415] A business that keeps credit information for its own purposes and not for the purpose of furnishing it to others, such as a bank, is outside the definition. This is so despite the fact that banks sometimes give references on the standing of their customers at the request of other banks. Such references are given as a matter of courtesy, and are based on information available to the banks from their own records. The organizations covered by the Act are credit reference offices, detective agencies, and similar types of bodies.[416]

(xii) **Connected transactions**

A regulated consumer credit agreement is not always one involving solely the debtor and the creditor. Sometimes it is a 'debtor-creditor-supplier' agreement, in which the creditor agrees to finance a transaction between the debtor and the supplier. An example is the supply of goods or services financed by a credit card.[417] Here the supplier of the goods or services provides them on the basis of his reimbursement arrangement with the issuer of the credit card (the 'creditor').

In cases of this type section 75 of the Act imposes wide-ranging (so-called 'connected lender') liability on the creditor. Thus, if the debtor has any claim against the supplier, which is based on breach of contract or on misrepresentation, he has a 'like claim' against the creditor.[418] In practice this means that the debtor may use his claim

---

[410] Ibid., s.145(6), and see s.146 (exceptions). Again, note that the definition extends beyond regulated agreements to consumer agreements (i.e. exempt agreements are covered: see Sect. (ii) above).

[411] Ibid., s.145(7) and see s.146 (exceptions).

[412] Ibid, s.145(7A) (so far as this is not debt-collecting), inserted by the CCA 2006, s.24. And see s.146(7) (exceptions), as inserted by CCA 2006, s.24.

[413] Ibid, s.145(7B)–(7D), inserted by the CCA 2006, s.25.   [414] Ibid., ss.147 & 148.

[415] Ibid., s.145(8). For the definition of 'individual' (replaced by the CCA 2006, s.1), see n.264.

[416] Where the Act is applicable, the consumer is entitled to copies of the information pertaining to him: ss.157–159. The Data Protection Act 1998 limited these provisions to partnerships and unincorporated associations as that Act itself provides similar rights to other categories of consumers.

[417] CCA 1974, s.12. See further, Ch. 14, Sect. 8(v) below. In essence there must be 'pre-existing arrangements' between the creditor and supplier, a term defined in s.187. Arrangements for the electronic transfer of funds are not covered: s.187(3A).

[418] Ibid., s.75(1). The creditor has a right of indemnity against the supplier: s.75(2). See further, Guest and Lloyd, n.268 above, para. 2-076. See also Lomnicka, 'Connected Lender Liability' in E. Lomnicka & C.G. Morse (eds.), *Contemporary Issues in Commercial Law* (London, 1997).

to extinguish his liability under the credit agreement[419] and, if his loss exceeds his liability to the creditor, to recover such loss from the creditor. The provision applies to transactions involving an item the cash price of which is less than £30,000 and more than £100.[420] The scope of this so-called connected lender liability has been a matter of controversy, in particular between the OFT and credit card issuers. The House of Lords considered the issue in *Office of Fair Trading* v. *Lloyds TSB Bank plc*[421] where it was held that the liability extended to transactions effected by a credit card used outside the jurisdiction.

The Consumer Credit Directive[422] contains provisions on 'connected liability' that do not correspond (especially as to scope) to those in section 75. Hence a new section 75A has been added to the 1974 Act that essentially applies to cases within the scope of the Directive[423] that are not already covered by section 75. However, section 75A only applies to 'linked credit agreements'[424]—a similar but by no means identical concept to a 'debtor-creditor-supplier' agreement—and it only applies if the debtor cannot obtain satisfaction against the supplier.

The Act uses an additional, extremely wide concept, which is that of 'linked transaction'.[425] It covers certain transactions made between the debtor and a party other than the creditor. In essence, a linked transaction is either one into which the debtor enters in compliance with his regulated agreement, or is the transaction financed by a 'debtor-creditor-supplier' agreement. An ancillary agreement made in order to effect a security is, however, excluded from the definition of a linked transaction. It will be shown that the concept of linked transactions is relevant also in the case of credit cards.[426]

Under the Act, the validity of a linked transaction depends on that of the main contract.[427] A linked transaction entered into before the making of the principal agreement has no effect until this main contract is concluded.[428] Furthermore, the consumer's withdrawal or cancellation of the main credit contract operates also as his withdrawal from or cancellation of the linked transaction.[429] Sums paid under the linked transaction are, then, recoverable by the consumer.[430] Finally, on early settlement of a credit agreement,[431] any future liability under a linked transaction is discharged.[432]

---

[419] If sued by the creditor the debtor may counterclaim under s.75 and plead a set-off of his counterclaim in diminution or extinction of the creditor's claim.

[420] Ibid., s.75(3), as amended by the Consumer Credit (Increase of Monetary Limits) (Amendment) Order 1983, S.I. 1983/1878. The provision is also confined to 'regulated' credit agreements: see Sect. (ii), above.

[421] [2007] UKHL 48, considered further in Ch. 14, Sect. 8(v).

[422] Directive 2008/48/EC, Art. 15.2.

[423] So 'business credit' and credit in excess of £60,260 are excluded (as both are outside the scope of the Directive). S.75A was added on 1 February 2011 by S.I. 2010/1010, reg. 25 (as amended by S.I. 2010/1969).

[424] Defined in s.75A(5) (in words taken almost verbatim from the Directive, Art. 3(n)) to mean a credit agreement that (*inter alia*) '*exclusively*' finances an agreement for the supply of *specific* goods or the provision of a specific service.

[425] Not to be confused with the 'Directive' (and hence s.75A) term, 'linked credit agreement'. See CCA 1974, s.19 and see Guest & Lloyd, n.268 above, para. 2-020.

[426] Ch. 14, Sect. 8(v) below. The transaction financed by the card is the 'linked transaction'; s.19(1)(b).

[427] But see the Consumer Credit (Linked Transactions) (Exemptions) Regulations 1983, S.I. 1983/1560 (as amended) exempting certain linked transactions (for example, insurance and guarantee contracts) from these invalidating provisions.

[428] CCA 1974, s.19(3).

[429] Ibid., ss.57(1), 69(1). See the similar position, in the case of 'withdrawal' under s.66A (see Sect. (iv), above), provided for in s.66A(7).

[430] Ibid., s.70.   [431] See Sect. (v) above.   [432] CCA 1974, s.96.

(xiii) **Powers of the court**

As has already been mentioned,[433] certain agreements are only enforceable on an order of court, in particular those which have not been preceded by the requisite pre-contract information or those not complying with the Agreements Regulations. The court is required to dismiss the application for an enforcement order only if 'it considers it just to do so' and it must have regard to any prejudice caused by the contravention and the degree of culpability for it.[434] As also mentioned, until the Consumer Credit Act 2006 repealed the relevant provisions, some agreements which did not contain certain minimum information, were 'irredeemably unenforceable'.[435]

The CCA 1974 contains wide-ranging provisions which enable the court to re-open credit agreements that are part of 'unfair credit relationships'.[436] Unlike the position under the Unfair Terms in Consumer Contracts Regulations 1999,[437] the test of 'unfairness' may take into account both the interest rates and the behaviour of the creditor after the agreement is concluded.[438]

(xiv) **Summary**

Banks have to reckon with the hazards put in their way by the Consumer Credit Act 1974, as amended by the 2006 Act, and as a consequence of the implementation of the new Consumer Credit Directive.[439] In the first place, they are bound by the Act where they enter into any 'regulated agreement' or engage in a business requiring a licence. In the second place, banks have to keep a watchful eye on customers financed by them who are engaged in any business covered by the Act.

In addition, certain provisions of the Act have a direct bearing on specific types of banking business. Examples are bank loans made to consumers, the issuing of payment cards, and the taking of security in respect of consumer transactions. These provisions of the Act will be discussed where relevant. It is fortunate for the banks that certain provisions of the Act have been relaxed in respect of overdrafts and certain land mortgages. The new Consumer Credit Directive similarly contains concessions for overdrafts and excludes land mortgages entirely from its scope.

To protect themselves, most banks hold a licence issued by the Office of Fair Trading. Their legal departments also devote a great deal of effort in determining the implications of the Act on their activities.

---

[433] See Sect. (iv).

[434] CCA 1974, s.127(1). It must also have regard to the extensive powers it has to alter the rights of the parties under the agreement under CCA 1974, ss.134 & 135.

[435] See Sect. (iv), above. The term is that used by Lord Hoffmann in *Dimond* v. *Lovell* [2002] 1 AC 384.

[436] CCA 1974, ss.140A–140D, added by the CCA 2006, ss.19–22, replacing the previous 'extortionate credit bargain' provisions, CCA 1974, ss. 137–140 in relation to agreements made on or after 6 April 2007. For unsuccessful challenges see *Tamini* v. *Khodari* [2009] EWCA Civ 1109; *Maple Leaf Macro Volatility Master Fund* v. *Rouvoy* [2009] EWHC 257; *McGuffick* v. *RBS Plc* [2009] EWHC 2386; *Carey* v. *HSBC Bank Plc* [2009] EWHC 3417; *Shaw* v. *Nine Regions Ltd* [2009] EWHC 3514. For a successful challenge, see *Patel* v. *Patel* [2009] EWHC 3264.

[437] S.I. 1999/2083.

[438] See CCA 1974, s.140A(1) which refers to (a) 'any' of the terms of the credit agreement or 'related agreement' (as defined in s.140C(4)), (b) 'the way in which the creditor has exercised or enforced any of his rights' and (c) 'any other thing done (or not done) by, or on behalf of the creditor'.

[439] Directive 2008/48/EC.

6 Conduct of business regulation in retail banking

(i) Background: the Banking Codes

In January 1992, the banking industry produced a 'Banking Code'[440] with the aim of setting minimum standards of good practice to be followed by banks (and similar institutions[441]) in their relations with 'personal customers'. It was a voluntary code, to which the main banks (and similar institutions) subscribed. An independent[442] Banking Code Standards Board (BCSB) monitored compliance with it. There was also a 'Business Banking Code' that covered small businesses and was very similar to the Banking Code both in status (it was again a voluntary code) and in its terms and layout. The BCSB periodically reviewed the Codes, which went through a number of editions responding to developments in (and concerns with) banking practice. The last editions were issued in March 2008. The Codes were only partially successful in setting appropriate consumer protection standards and there were persistent doubts whether all of their provisions—for example those as to variation of interest rates and charges and as to customer liability for unauthorized use of accounts and cards—were consistent with consumer protection legislation.[443] When criticisms of the banks surfaced—for example in their dealings with 'superseded accounts'[444] and when they unilaterally imposed charges for the use of ATMs—appropriate changes were made to the Codes to meet these concerns, with a view to deflecting threats to impose tighter, statutory regulation. Historically, these pre-emptive moves were successful but the need to implement the conduct of business aspects of the Payment Services Directive[445] in November 2009 prompted a further reconsideration of the future of the Codes. The Payment Services Regulations 2009 (PSR 2009)[446] that implement the Directive set out detailed conduct of business rules applicable to 'payment services' effected by banks (and other 'payment service providers')[447] and it was decided that as a complement to these rules, the FSA would introduce a new Banking Conduct of Business source-book (BCOBS) to regulate deposit-taking so as to create a new 'Banking and Payment Services' (BPS) regime.[448]

Those aspects of the Codes not covered by the BPS, in particular the lending aspects, were reissued as 'the Lending Code'. Like the old Banking Code, this has a 'self-regulatory' status and is monitored and enforced by a new 'Lending Standards Board'.

---

[440] The Code was produced by the British Bankers' Association (BBA), the Building Societies' Association, and the Association for Payment Clearing Services (APACS).

[441] Building societies, credit card issuers, National Savings and Investments, the Post Office, and a number of credit unions also subscribed to it.

[442] The directors included a majority of independent members as well as representatives from the banks and building societies.

[443] Especially the Unfair Terms in Consumer Contracts Regulations 1999, S.I. 1999/2083 and the Consumer Credit Act 1974 (especially ss.83, 84). See E. Lomnicka, 'Unilateral Variation in Banking Contracts: An "Unfair Term"?' in P. Cartwright (ed.), *Consumer Protection in Financial Services* (London, 1999).

[444] See Sect. 6(ii) below.   [445] Directive 2007/64/EC, see Sect. 7 below.

[446] S.I.2008/209, in force on 1 November 2009.   [447] See further, Sect. 6(iii) & Ch. 13 below.

[448] See the FSA's Policy Statement 09/6, *Regulating retail banking conduct of business* (April 2009). See Sect. 6(iii) below.

(ii) **The legal status of the Lending Code**

Nothing is said in the Lending Code about its legal status[449] and there is no suggestion that it automatically confers any *legal* rights on customers. The fact that it is expressly stated to be 'self-regulatory' may suggest that it has no legal effect at all. Yet, as subscribing banks advertise the fact that they adhere to the Code and make it available to customers, its provisions may well be treated as implied terms in the banking contract. However, in accordance with general contractual principles, any such implied contractual provisions will yield to any inconsistent express terms that the bank may insert. Moreover, if they become contractual terms, the Code's provisions will be subject to consumer protection legislation: if they are 'unfair' under the Unfair Terms in Consumer Contracts Regulations 1999[450] or inconsistent with the Consumer Credit Act 1974,[451] they will be inoperative.

More generally, in so far as the Code seeks to articulate minimum standards of good practice, the FOS[452] is likely to take into account the extent to which a respondent bank has complied with it in deciding what is a 'fair and reasonable' result.[453] In the case of the Banking Code, this occurred when existing savers with variable rate TESSAs (a tax-efficient savings product) complained to the (Building Society) Ombudsman that they were being treated 'unfairly' as regards interest rates in comparison with new savers with ISAs (the savings product that replaced TESSAs). The Ombudsman referred to the Code's 'key commitment' that members 'act fairly and reasonably' in dealings with customers[454] and held that it required the payment of at least as much interest on superseded accounts as on current accounts. On a judicial review of his decision in *R* v. *Financial Ombudsman Service, on the application of Norwich and Peterborough Building Society*[455] he was held to have misinterpreted the Code. Nevertheless, the court upheld the Ombudsman's decision on the more general ground that he had jurisdiction to consider what was 'fair in all the circumstances' and hence reach the conclusion he did. Although the relevant statutory framework in the TESSA case was the predecessor to that under which the FOS now operates and although it specifically required the (Building Society) Ombudsman to have regard to 'any code of conduct'[456]—it being conceded that the Banking Code was the relevant Code—there seems no doubt that the Lending Code will be very relevant to the FOS's decisions. But this decision shows that the Code is merely the starting point in relation to the FOS's wide jurisdiction to determine what is 'fair'.

The FSA's 'Principles for Businesses'[457] require authorized firms to comply with standards of good practice and it would seem that the Lending Code would also be relevant in setting these. However, curiously the Code states that it 'has not been reviewed by the FSA and the FSA will not have regard to this Code when exercising its regulatory function'.[458]

---

[449]   The Introduction to the old Banking Code stated: 'As a voluntary code, it allows competition and market forces to work to encourage higher standards for the benefit of customers.' For some discussions of that Code's legal status, see P. Cartwright, *Banks, Consumer and Regulation* (Oxford, 2004), 125–6; R. Cranston, *Principles of Banking Law* (Oxford, 2002), 202.

[450]   S.I. 1999/2083. See n.443, above.   [451]   See especially ss.83, 84.

[452]   See Sect. 4(ix) above.   [453]   Ibid., especially FSMA 2000, s.228(2).

[454]   This particular 'key commitment' was subsequently deleted and is not repeated in the new Lending Code.

[455]   [2002] EWHC 2379 (Admin), [2003] 1 All ER (Comm.) 65; noted Gray (2003) JFRC 269.

[456]   See the Building Societies Act 1986, ss.83, 83A and esp. Sched. 12, para. 4(2)(c).

[457]   See Sect. 4(vi). See n.124 above: they now apply in full to the deposit-taking by banks.

[458]   Compare the consequences of breach of the FSA's BPS regime, noted in the next section.

(iii) **Retail banking regulation and the FSA's Banking and Payment Services (BPS) regime**

As mentioned above, the PSR 2009[459] implement the Payment Services Directive[460] and, as far as banks are concerned,[461] impose mandatory[462] conduct of business requirements in relation to the electronic 'payment services' they provide to certain 'retail' customers[463] within the EEA.[464] The scope of regulation turns on the meaning of 'payment service', a term that essentially covers: the operation of 'payment accounts'[465] such as current accounts and flexible savings accounts, the execution of payment transactions such as direct debits and payment card transactions, card issuing, merchant acquiring and money remittance.[466]

The PSR 2009 conduct of business requirements are considered in more detail elsewhere.[467] They comprise various information requirements that differ depending on whether the service is for a one-off transaction or whether it concerns an ongoing relationship (a 'framework contact') such as a current or (flexible) savings account.[468] There are further consumer protection provisions,[469] for example as to liability for unauthorized payments.[470]

The PSR 2009 also establish a self-standing regulatory regime for monitoring and enforcing compliance with the obligations they impose, a regime that is analogous to that under FSMA 2000,[471] with the FSA as the regulator.[472] Moreover, as is the case for breach of most of the FSA's conduct of business rules,[473] breach of these PSR 2009 obligations is actionable (as if it were an actionable breach of statutory duty) by 'private persons'[474] suffering loss.[475] Finally, the FOS[476] has jurisdiction in relation to payment service complaints.[477]

---

[459] S.I. 2009/209.   [460] Directive 2007/64/EC, see Sect. 6(i) above and Sect. 7(i) below.

[461] The Directive also requires 'payment service providers' that are not already FSA-authorized (so-called 'payment institutions') to become FSA-authorized: implemented by PSR 2009, Pts. 2–4. Hence it extends the 'single market passport' concept (see Sect. 7(ii), below) to payment service providers so as to create 'SEPA' (a Single European Payments Area).

[462] Customers who are not 'consumers' (see next note) may generally contract out of these provisions: regs. 33(4) & 51(3).

[463] *Viz.*, 'consumers' (defined in PSR 2009, reg. 2(1) to mean 'an individual…acting for purposes other than a trade, business or profession'), 'micro-enterprises' and charities. See PSR 2009, regs. 33, 51.

[464] It only applies where both payer and payee are within the EEA and where the currency is in Euro or another member state currency (such as sterling).

[465] The definitions are somewhat circular. 'Payment account' is defined in PSR 2009, reg. 2(1) as 'an account held in the name of one or more payment service users which is used for the execution of payment transactions', with 'payment service user' being defined to cover either a payee or payer who makes use of a 'payment service'.

[466] i.e. activities specified in PSR 2009, Sched. 1, Pt. 1. They must be 'carried out as a regular occupation or business activity'—a condition that will clearly be satisfied by banks. See also the long list of exclusions in PSR 2009, Sched. 1, Pt. 2. The FSA has issued guidance on the scope of the PSR 2009: see its Handbook (Sect. 4(vi), above), PERG15.

[467] See Chs. 13 & 14 below.   [468] PSR 2009, Pt. 5.   [469] PSR 2009, Pt. 6.

[470] Their application to payment cards is considered in Ch. 14 below.   [471] See Sect. 4 above.

[472] See, generally, PSR 2009, Pts. 7 and 9. For the FSMA 2000 regime, see Sect. 4(vi) above.

[473] i.e. those in COBS (see Sect. 4(vi) above) and BCOBS (see below). The right of action is conferred by FSMA 2000, s.150.

[474] As defined in PSR 2009, reg. 120(3) to mean, essentially, an individual receiving the service or any other person not acting in the course of business. A fiduciary or representative may also, generally, bring the action on behalf of a 'private person': reg. 120(2).

[475] PSR 2009, reg. 120.   [476] See Sect. 4(ix) above.

[477] PSR 2009, reg. 91.

As also mentioned above,[478] the need to establish this detailed conduct of business regime in relation to the retail payment services activities of banks once more called into question the appropriateness of the self-regulatory Banking Codes being applicable to the other retail activities of banks. As the FSA was already the banking regulator in relation to deposit-taking,[479] it was decided that it should also regulate the conduct of retail deposit-taking in the same manner as it regulates the conduct of business of other regulated activities.[480] Hence the FSA issued a new banking conduct of business rule-book (BCOBS),[481] applicable in relation to the same banking customers as the PSR 2009,[482] and added it to the 'Business Standards' part of its Handbook.[483] Consistently with the FSA's approach to other conduct of business modules in its handbook, BCOBS is drafted at a rather general, 'outcome-focused' level, in contrast to the more detailed provisions of the PSR 2009 (the detail being necessitated by the Payment Services Directive from which they are derived). BCOBS contains such 'high level' provisions regulating communications and financial promotions,[484] pre- and post-contractual information,[485] services during the contract[486] and cancellation.[487]

As BCOBS is made under FSMA 2000, this enables the FSA to invoke the extensive powers it has under that Act in securing compliance with it,[488] including the power to impose financial penalties,[489] with the FOS[490] having compulsory jurisdiction in relation to complaints. Moreover, breach of BCOBS (as is the case for breach of the other FSA conduct of business rules and the corresponding provisions of the PSR 2009[491]) is actionable, as if it were an actionable breach of statutory duty, by 'private persons' suffering loss.[492] This is in stark contrast to the consequences for breach of the Lending Code.[493] A further difference is that although very few UK branches of banks authorized in other EEA countries subscribed to the Banking Codes, BCOBS is applicable to such branches.

In consequence, there is now a new retail BPS conduct of business regulatory regime operated by the FSA.[494] The conduct of business rules are in two places: the PSR 2009 contain the rules for payment services whilst BCOBS contains the rules for deposit-taking. However, the consequences of breach of both categories of rules (enforcement by the FSA and civil actionability) are the same and hence it is possible to regard the BPS regime as one, coherent regime. Indeed, as is evident from its designation by the FSA as its 'BPS regime', it is operated as a single, integrated regime.

---

[478] See Sect. 6(i) above.   [479] See Sect. 4(ii)–(v) above.   [480] See, Sect. 4(vi) above.

[481] See the FSA's Policy Statement 09/6, *Regulating retail banking conduct of business* (April 2009). The (few) provisions in COBS that applied to banks were moved over to BCOBS and the Principles of Business (PRIN) are now fully applicable to deposit-taking (whereas they were originally only applicable to banks in the prudential context).

[482] See n.463 above.   [483] For a discussion of the Handbook, see Sect. 4(vi) above.

[484] BCOBS 2 and (for distance communications, BCOBS 3). See also Sect. 4(vii) above.

[485] BCOBS 4.   [486] BCOBS 5.   [487] BCOBS 6.

[488] See Sect. 4(vi) above.   [489] Ibid.

[490] See Sect. 4(ix) above.   [491] See n.473 above and PSR 2009, reg. 120.

[492] FSMA 2000, s.150. The definition of 'private person' (which corresponds to that in PSR 2009, reg. 120(3)) is in FSMA 2000 (Rights of Action) Regulations 2001 S.I. 2001/2256, as amended.

[493] See Sect. 6(ii) above.

[494] See FSA's Policy Statement 09/6, *Regulating retail banking conduct of business* (April 2009), esp. Annex 2. The FSA intends to issue 'information for consumers that clearly outlines their rights under BCOBS and the PSR 2009' but this is not available at the time of writing.

Nevertheless, that still leaves various aspects of retail banking activity outside that regime, in particular consumer credit activities which are still regulated by the Office of Fair Trading[495] and subject to the Lending Code.[496]

This patchwork of regulation (the BPS comprising the PSR 2009 and BCOBS, the Consumer Credit Act 1974, and the Lending Code), not to mention the complications caused by the piecemeal amendments to the existing legislation,[497] necessitated by the implementation of the Payment Services Directive and the Consumer Credit Directive, has left the retail banking regulatory landscape difficult to navigate both by banks and their customers. It is to be hoped that consolidation and rationalization will not be too long in coming.

7 The EU dimension

(i) Introduction[498]

The United Kingdom's membership of the European Community (now Union) has resulted in its banking law being significantly affected by the EU's initiatives aimed at facilitating a single market for financial services, including banking services.[499] In EU terminology, a bank is a 'credit institution' which is defined[500] as an undertaking whose business is receiving deposits from the public and granting credit. As such, banks are subject to the various EU legislative measures, mainly directives, concerned with such bodies. In 2000 most of these were consolidated into the Banking Consolidation Directive (BCD)[501] and in 2006 this Directive as recast, together with the capital adequacy requirements, in the Capital Requirements Directive (CRD).[502] However, the general provisions of the EU Treaties that provide for various 'freedoms',[503] should not be forgotten and are the backdrop to the more precise harmonization measures.[504] Thus, the European Court of Justice upheld a challenge by the French subsidiary of a Spanish bank to domestic French law that precluded the paying of interest on current bank accounts, on the basis that this was a restriction on the freedom of establishment within the (then) Treaty's Article 43.[505]

---

[495] See Sect. 5.   [496] See above and note Sect. (ii) on the Code's limited legal status.

[497] In particular FSMA 2000 (see Sect. 4) and the Consumer Credit Act 1974 (see Sect. 5).

[498] For a fuller (albeit rather dated) discussion see M. Dassesse, S. Isaacs, and G. Penn, *EC Banking Law* (2nd edn., London, 1994) (hereafter Dassesse, Isaacs, Penn).

[499] 'Financial services' in the EC context is taken to cover banking, insurance, and investment services. Note also the 'SEPA', the single European Payments Area, introduced by the Payment Services Directive (see Sect. 7(vi) below and Sect. 6(iii) above).

[500] Directive 2006/48/EC, [2006] OJ L77/1, the Capital Requirements Directive (CRD), Art. 4(1).

[501] Directive 2000/12/EC, replacing, *inter alia*, Directive 77/780/EEC (the First Banking Directive), Directive 86/635/EEC (annual and consolidated accounts), Directive 89/229/ EEC (Own Funds Directive), Directive 89/646/EEC (the Second Banking Directive), Directive 89/647/EEC (Solvency Ratio Directive), Directive 95/26/EC (Supervision on Consolidated Basis), Directive 92/121/EEC (Large Exposures Directive).

[502] Although called 'the' CRD, it in fact comprises two directives: Directive 2006/48/EC (recasting the BCD) and Directive 2006/49 (revising the capital adequacy rules, see Sects. 7(iii) & (iv) below).

[503] Of particular relevance here are those provisions of the Treaty regarding (i) the freedom of establishment and (ii) the freedom to provide services.

[504] For example, the Preamble to the CRD, n.500 above), Recital 17, confirms that matters not covered by the Directive enjoy the freedoms conferred by the Treaty.

[505] *Caixa-Bank France* v. *Ministere de l'Economie, des Finances et de l'Industrie* 2004, Case C-442/02. The BCD (see n.501 above) did not apply as the case concerned a subsidiary, not a branch or the provision of cross-border services.

The first significant measure was the First Banking Directive[506] in 1977. This enabled banks to establish branches[507] in other Member States, thus implementing one of the cardinal aims of the original Treaty of Rome—freedom of establishment. However, the 'host' Member State could still insist that the branch obtained local authorization and complied with local requirements, although certain common standards for the granting of banking authorization were laid down. In the United Kingdom the authorization requirements were imposed by the Banking Act 1979.[508] The need to adhere to host state authorization and regulation, meant that the First Banking Directive did not in practice result in banks readily operating across the state borders in the EC. However, the Directive was significant in initiating the harmonization of regulatory standards and co-operation between Member State banking regulators.

In 1985 there was a new milestone along the path towards the creation of the single market in financial services. The EC Commission issued a White Paper entitled *Completing the Internal Market*[509] which, by settling the deadline of 1992[510] for the completion of the 'Internal Market', provided a new impetus to the process of establishing a single market in financial services. In addition, it articulated a change in approach[511] to the harmonization of the regulation of financial services. It advocated the replacement of attempts at very detailed harmonization with harmonization of minimum or 'key' standards only, together with the introduction of the concept of 'home-country control' and its corollary, the 'single European passport'.[512] This new approach was influenced by the European Court of Justice's attitude to regulation in the sphere of freedom of movement of goods, as illustrated by the *Cassis de Dijon* case,[513] and of services, as illustrated by the *Coditel* case.[514] These decisions were very significant because they recognized the concept of the supremacy of home state regulation. The host state has to recognize and cannot duplicate the home state regulation, unless it can justify its regulation on the basis of limited grounds.

This approach was adopted in the Second Banking Co-ordination Directive (2BCD).[515] As noted above, the Banking Consolidation Directive (BCD) of 2000 replaced the 2BCD, together with related directives.[516] That measure, however, was merely consolidatory and did not change the substance of the directives it replaced. As also noted above, the BCD was replaced in 2006 by the first part of the CRD. Two further developments should be mentioned. First, in 1999 the European Commission issued a 'Financial Services Action

---

[506]   Directive 77/780/EEC [1977] OJ L322/30 (as amended).

[507]   But it did not expressly enable the provision of cross-border services. Some host states insisted that non-local enterprises establish a branch, thus precluding cross-border supply of services without the establishment of a branch. However, in the *German Insurance Case* (Case 20S/84 *Commission* v. *Germany* [1986] ECR 3755) the European Court of Justice held this practice contrary to the Treaty of Rome.

[508]   See Sect. 3 above.

[509]   White Paper from the Commission to the European Council, EUR–PARL–Doc. (COM(85)310 of 14 June 1985).

[510]   In fact 1 January 1993.   [511]   See especially paras. 102–103 of the White Paper.

[512]   Considered further, at Sect. 7(ii) below.

[513]   Case 120/78 *Rewe-Zentral AG* v. *Bundesmonopolverwaltung für Branntwein* [1979] ECR 649. The ECJ held that French drink (which was subject to French regulation) could be marketed in Germany without having to comply with the, largely duplicatory (but nevertheless different), German regulation.

[514]   Case 262/81 *Coditel and Others* v. *Ciné-Vog Films and Others* [1982] ECR 3381.

[515]   Directive 89/646/EEC [1989] OJ L386/1, implemented by the Banking Coordination (Second Council Directive) Regulations 1992, S.I. 1992/3218.

[516]   See n.501 above.

Plan' (FSAP) which listed 42 measures[517] that needed to be adopted in order to complete the single market by 2005. Most of these measures were adopted and the following 10 years were characterized by less EU legislation[518] and by more attention being paid to proper implementation of the FSAP measures by the Member States—whose number was increased significantly in May 2004 by the accession of ten smaller, less economically developed, countries. Secondly, dissatisfaction with the EU legislative process and the implementation of EU legislative measures (particularly in the securities field) lead to the appointment of the 'Lamfalussy' Committee—named after its chairman Baron Lamfalussy—which recommended a new, four-tiered approach (the 'Lamfalussy arrangements') to EU legislation. Whilst initially applied in the securities context, the Lamfalussy arrangements have been extended to the banking (and insurance, pensions, and asset management) fields. The first tier or 'Level 1' comprises the Directive or Regulation, which is a 'framework' measure, to be fleshed out at 'Level 2' by provisions proposed by a committee made up of regulators, after extensive consultation. In the banking context, the European Banking Committee (EBC) was established with effect from January 2004 to undertake this task. 'Level 3' entails another committee—the Committee of European Banking Supervisors (CEBS—located in London)—which is concerned with ensuring the consistent implementation of Level 1 and Level 2 legislation and the adoption of best supervisory practice across the Member States, whilst 'Level 4' involves the Commission, Member States, and financial regulators ensuring the proper implementation and enforcement of EC law. From a day-to-day practical perspective, the importance of the CEBS and the opportunities it presents for co-operation between Member State banking supervisors should not be under-estimated and it has been said[519] that 'it may be possible for effective activity at Lamfalussy Level 3 to achieve the same results more quickly and more consistently, than would previously have been secured through the introduction of new EC legislation'.

The financial turmoil of 2007/8 prompted a reconsideration of the regulatory structure in Europe and proposals for more centralization.[520] However, at the time of writing it is unclear what final form the reforms will take.

(ii) **The 'European passport'**

The 'European passport' or 'single licence' concept, which is the basis of the EC approach to the harmonization of regulatory measures in the financial services sphere, has three interrelated characteristics.[521]

---

[517] Including the Second Money Laundering Directive (considered in Ch. 4) and the Electronic Money Directive (noted in Sect. 4(ii) above).

[518] An exception being the CRD which, as well as recasting the BCD, implemented Basel II (see Sect. 8). See also the Payment Services Directive, Directive 2007/64/EC, extending the 'European passport' to payment service providers. Note also the amendments to the Deposit Guarantee Directive and those proposed to the CRD, in the wake of the 2007/8 financial turmoil, referred to in Sects. (iv) & (v) below.

[519] See the document issued jointly by the Bank of England, HM Treasury, and the FSA: *After the EU Financial Services Action Plan: A new strategic approach*, May 2004, para. 3.14.

[520] See the *De Larosiere Report* from the High Level Groups on Financial Supervision in the EU (February 2009) and subsequent Commission Communications culminating in the September 2009 proposals for reform, including the establishment of a European Systemic Risk Board (ESRB) and (instead of CEBS) a new European Banking Authority (EBA).

[521] As the Preamble to the CRD, Recital (7) (replacing BCD, Recital (7), replacing Second Banking Directive, Recital (4)) states: 'it is appropriate to effect only the essential harmonisation necessary and sufficient to secure the mutual recognition of authorisation and of prudential supervision systems, making

First, an authorization (or licence or passport) to carry on certain activities from their 'home' state regulator,[522] enables defined enterprises either to establish a branch[523] or to provide cross-border services in the 'host' state, in relation to listed activities, without the need for further authorization.

Secondly, and as a corollary, the EEA Member States have harmonized certain minimum or 'key' standards, the application of which (both initially on authorization and subsequently through supervision and monitoring) they agree are the province of the 'home' state. The Directive harmonizes minimum standards, for example, as to capital adequacy and fitness of directors, but expressly permits a Member State to impose tougher standards on its home-authorized and regulated enterprises.[524] However, as that State has to permit firms established and authorized in other EEA States complying with those minimum standards to operate within its territory, the disincentives to apply higher standards to its home enterprises are obvious. In so far as regulation inevitably imposes costs and restraints, those home enterprises will be placed at a competitive disadvantage.[525] However, more recent financial services Directives[526] (but not the CRD) have adopted a 'maximum harmonization' approach, which precludes Member States from imposing more onerous local requirements.

Thirdly, there is the principle of 'home-country control'.[527] The new approach recognizes the sole competence of the home state to authorize its home enterprises and to exercise supervisory control wherever in the EEA they operate. The host state has (to quote the White Paper) merely a 'complementary' role in relation to liquidity and conduct of business. However, problems have arisen concerning the extent to which the host country can regulate activity within its borders. Thus, the drawing of the demarcation line between the matters that are within the competence of the home and those within the competence of the host state is potentially a very difficult task.[528]

---

possible the granting of a single licence recognised throughout the Community and the application of the principle of home Member State prudential supervision'.

[522] As noted below (and as articulated in the CRD, Recital (10)), only the home state is competent to grant authorization, and thus 'regulatory arbitrage' is hampered.

[523] But if the enterprise wishes to establish a subsidiary, the CRD is inapplicable. This (longstanding) distinction between branches and subsidiaries has been criticized: see W. van Gerven, 'The Second Banking Directive and the Case-Law of the Court of Justice' (1990) 10 *Yearbook of European Law* 57, 59 ff. But the general 'Treaty' freedoms will apply: see *Caixa-Bank France* v. *Ministère de l'Économie, des Finances et de l'Industrie*, n.505 above.

[524] See the CRD, Recital (15) (replacing BCD, Recital (13), replacing Second Banking Co-ordination Directive, Recital (10)).

[525] It may be that it is unconstitutional in some Member States so to discriminate against their home enterprises: see Dassesse, Isaacs, Penn, n.498 above.

[526] For example the Payment Services Directive 2007/64/EC (see Sect. 7(vi) below and Sect. 6(iii) above) and the Consumer Credit Directive, Directive 2008/48/EC (see Sect. 7(vi) below and Sect. 5(i) above).

[527] See E. Lomnicka, 'The Home Country Control Principle in the Financial Services Directives and the Case Law', ch.11 in M. Andenas & W.-H. Roth (eds.), *Services and Free Movement in EU Law* (Oxford, 2002).

[528] Anticipated by van Gerven, n.523 above, 64 ff. The Commission has issued an Interpretative Communication (97/C 209/6) which seeks to clarify some of the issues. And note the controversy over the powers of 'host' states which surfaced when the Icelandic banks (Iceland being a member of the EEA, which is the relevant area in this context) were unable to repay the UK deposits they took in exercise of their 'passport' and the Iceland Government was unable to honour the deposit guarantee.

(iii) The Capital Requirements Directive (CRD), Part 1

This Directive is in two parts. The first[529] recasts the BCD and is still referred to as the BCD in United Kingdom Legislation.[530] It applies to 'credit institutions' (as defined[531]) and certain subsidiaries owned by one or more credit institutions and complying with other stringent conditions including the need for a guarantee from the parent(s).[532] It provides that authorization in the home state confers a passport on the institution to operate throughout the EEA[533] without the need for further authorizations.[534] Indeed, banks[535] are obliged to obtain their authorization in their home state (as defined) and cannot obtain authorization elsewhere in the EEA. As well as the initial authorization, the subsequent supervision (even when operating in another 'host' Member State) of the bank is the primary responsibility of the 'home' regulator.[536]

The activities that may be covered by the passport (sometimes called the 'passported activities') are listed in Annex I to the Directive.[537] These are not limited to the activities that characterize UK banks, such as the taking of deposits, the granting of loans, and money-transmission services. The Directive is based on the German model of the so-called 'Universal Bank', and therefore the activities extend to certain activities in relation to securities, i.e. trading in securities, participation in securities issues, advice as to mergers and acquisitions, and portfolio management and advice. Once a bank has obtained from its 'home' State regulator authorization for any of the activities listed in the Annex,[538] the 'host' State cannot preclude the pursuit of such activities by that bank in its territory even if its own local banks are not permitted to pursue these activities. This had important consequences for non-credit institutions, including the ordinary subsidiaries of UK banks, which were investment and insurance firms. They could not acquire a passport under the (then applicable) Second Banking Co-ordination Directive,[539] yet they were in competition, in relation to those investment activities, with universal banks that could. These institutions eventually acquired their 'passports' under the Investment Services Directive (for investment firms)[540] and the 'Framework Directives' (for insurance firms).[541] Until these were implemented, the universal banks had a competitive advantage: their passports under the Second Banking Co-ordination Directive.

---

[529] Directive 2006/48/EC.

[530] See the Capital Requirements Regulations 2006, S.I. 2006/3221 which implement the CRD but retain the term 'banking consolidation directive' for the first part of the CRD (i.e. Directive 2006/48/EC).

[531] In Directive 2006/48/EC, Art.4(1): see Sect. 7(i) above.

[532] See Art. 24. This provision caters for those Member States where credit institutions are obliged to form special subsidiaries in order to carry on certain banking activities such as leasing or credit card operations.

[533] Ibid., Arts. 23 (credit institutions) and 24 (their subsidiaries).

[534] Ibid., Art. 16 forbids host Member States from requiring authorization (cf. the original position, as regards branches, under the First Banking Directive, n.523 above).

[535] But not their subsidiaries.   [536] Note the limited powers of the host state in Arts. 29–37.

[537] Ibid., Art. 150(1)(f), enables the list to be amended relatively easily, without the need to amend the Directive itself.

[538] In the case of activities not on the list, ordinary principles of EC law apply; in particular, the home state may limit penetration by banks from other Member States on the basis of 'the general good' (an EC concept developed by the ECJ).

[539] Because they were not 'credit institutions' or their 'subsidiaries', as defined: see above.

[540] Directive 93/22/EEC, now replaced by the Markets in Financial Instruments Directive (MIFID), 2004/39/EC.

[541] Directive 92/49 (Third Non-life Insurance Directive) and Directive 92/96 (Third Life Insurance Directive).

A bank may operate in other ('host') EEA States either by establishing a branch[542] or by providing cross-border services,[543] but before doing so must notify its home regulator, who in turn must notify the regulator in the host state. It seems that a bank may provide cross-border services in a host state even if it has a branch undertaking the same activities there.[544]

The provisions of the FSMA 2000 (as amended) give effect to the CRD[545] and enable banks from other EEA States to carry on those 'passported' activities in the United Kingdom without the need for FSA authorization.[546] As provided by the Directive, the FSMA 2000 requires such banks (termed 'EEA firms'[547]) to notify their home regulator before they can so operate in the United Kingdom.[548] Moreover, again in accordance with the Directive, the FSA is given a limited supervisory role over EEA firms, which involves close liaison with that bank's home-banking regulators.[549] Similarly, a UK bank, by obtaining authorization under the FSMA 2000, acquires a passport enabling it to 'export' its banking services to other EEA States, assuming that the other relevant Member States have similarly implemented the CRD (or its predecessors). Before it can do so, it must notify the FSA.[550]

(iv) **Capital adequacy: the CRD, Part 2**

The EC has also been active in imposing capital adequacy requirements on banks.[551] In doing so, it has reflected the approaches of the Basle Committee, considered in the next section. In accordance with 'Basle II', it developed a universal capital adequacy framework, which covered not only banks but also investment firms.[552] Amendments are expected in the wake of the financial turmoil of 2007/8.[553]

---

[542] See Directive 2006/48/EC, n.529 above, Arts. 23 (credit institutions) and 24 (their subsidiaries). See also Arts. 25–7.

[543] See ibid. See also Art. 28.

[544] See the Commission's Interpretative Communication, n.528 above, at 12.

[545] In fact it gave effect to the (then effective) Second Banking Co-ordination Directive, n.515 above, and was amended (by S.I. 2000/2952—substituting references to the BCD) when the BCD was adopted. The regulations implementing the CRD (S.I. 2006/3221) retain the term 'banking consolidation directive' for the first part of the CRD and hence the references to the BCD in FSMA 2000 did not have to be changed in order to implement the CRD.

[546] They are 'authorised persons' without having to obtain Pt. IV permission from the FSA: FSMA 2000, s.31(b); see, further, the discussion of this Act, in Sect. 4, especially 4(v) above.

[547] FSMA 2000, Sched. 3, para. 5.   [548] Ibid., Sched. 3, Pt. II.

[549] See especially FSMA 2000, Pt. XIII, noted above in Sect. 4(vi).

[550] FSMA 2000, Sched. 3, Pt. III.

[551] See especially the Own Funds Directive, Directive 89/299 and the Solvency Ratio Directive, Directive 89/647, which followed the 1988 Basle Accord, and the Large Exposures Directive (LED), Directive 92/121, which followed the Basle Committee's 1991 recommendations on large exposures. See also the Capital Adequacy Directive (CAD), Directive 93/6 on market risk, as amended by Directive 98/31—again responding to Basle's amendments to its 1988 Accord. The present provisions are now in the second part of the CRD, implementing Basle II, see next note. For the Basle Committee see Sect. 8.

[552] See the second part of the CRD, Directive 2006/49/EC (called the 'capital adequacy directive' in UK legislation, see S.I. 2006/3221, implementing the CRD).

[553] See the Commission Proposal of October 2009 and the technical amendments made in Directive 2009/27/EC.

(v) **The Deposit Guarantee Scheme Directive**

In 1994 the EC adopted a Deposit Guarantee Scheme (DGS) Directive,[554] requiring Member States to establish a 'minimum standards' compensation scheme should banks fail and depositors lose their money. The DGS Directive follows the 'home' country control principle[555] on the basis that the (home) state regulator primarily responsible for regulation and supervision is in a better position to assess the risks and thus should also be responsible for devising the scheme for compensating depositors.[556]

The DGS Directive originally required[557] Member States to establish a minimum standards deposit guarantee scheme[558] covering at least 90 per cent of any claim up to EUR 20,000.[559] This cover is provided by the home state and applies to firms wherever within the single market they establish branches.[560] Being a 'minimum standards' directive, considerable disparity between schemes in different Member States arose. The DGS Directive makes elaborate and controversial[561] provision for this. First, if the host state's scheme is *less* generous than the home state's scheme, rather than allow banks (and their depositors) to take advantage of the more generous home state scheme, the Directive provides that the host state's scheme is the *maximum* a depositor is entitled to.[562] This is the so-called 'levelling-down' or 'export prohibition' provision. Thus, the host state can, in effect, determine the maximum cover its domestic depositors are entitled to. Secondly, if the host state's scheme is *more* generous than the home state's scheme, the host state must ensure that non-host state regulated firms are given the opportunity[563] to 'top up' their home state cover.[564] This is the so-called 'topping-up' or 'supplementary guarantee' provision. This detracts from the rationale behind the home state control principle in that the host state providing the 'top-up' is not in such a good position as the home state in assessing the bank's prudential risks and in seeking to minimize them. Such sharing of responsibility for compensation inevitably means complex mechanisms for allocating liability between home and (top-up) host schemes and provision is made in the Directive to facilitate co-operation between the two schemes.[565]

---

[554] Directive 94/19/EEC. There is a similar directive in the investment business (but not insurance) sector: the Investor Compensation Scheme Directive, 97/9/EEC. For a general discussion, see Misita, 'Depositor protection: An EC Law Perspective' [2003] JIBR 254.

[555] See Sect. 7(ii) above.

[556] See DGS Directive, n.554 above, Recital (7). The Commission examined this issue in its 'Final Report on Risk-based contributions' (June 2008).

[557] Ibid., Art. 3. But see the proposals to increase these, noted below.

[558] The means whereby the scheme is delivered are left to the Member States: ibid., Recital (23).

[559] Ibid., Art. 7. Requiring the depositor to bear some of the loss (so-called 'co-insurance') was intended to meet the 'moral hazard' objection to compensation schemes: ibid., Recital (19).

[560] Ibid., Art. 4.1, para. 1.

[561] Germany, with its generous scheme for customers of its universal banks, voted against and then (unsuccessfully) challenged the DGS Directive in the ECJ on the basis that these provisions were inconsistent with the home country control principle: Case C-233/94 *Germany* v. *European Parliament and Council* [1995] ECR 1-1141.

[562] DGS Directive, Art. 4(1).

[563] There is no obligation to 'top up', as this would be a restriction on freedom of establishment and probably disproportionate.

[564] DGS Directive, Art. 4(2).

[565] Ibid., Art. 4(3). There is a European Forum of Deposit Insurers (EFDI).

A review of the Directive[566] initially resulted in the postponement of proposals for legislative reform.[567] However, the disparities between the coverage of the various Member State schemes, including *ad hoc* extensions, became a contentious issue during the financial turmoil of 2007/8 and an amendment to the DGS Directive was hastily issued.[568] This requires Member States (a) to increase the minimum coverage level, by stages, to at least EUR 100,000 by December 2010, (b) to reduce the time it takes to pay out claims and (c) to abolish the requirement that the deposit protection only extend to 90 per cent of the amount. A thorough revision of the DGS Directive is proposed.[569]

(vi) **Other EC initiatives**

A number of other EC legislative measures have had an impact on UK banking practice. As will be discussed in Chapter 4, the EC has issued three Directives on combating money laundering,[570] which the United Kingdom has implemented. Its Electronic Commerce Directive[571] has resulted in the 'country of origin'[572] of services provided electronically having primary regulatory control over them and, as has been noted earlier in this chapter,[573] this has resulted in some modifications to the United Kingdom's regulatory regime as it applies to banking services provided electronically. The Distance Marketing Directive,[574] which seeks to harmonize domestic laws protecting consumers contracting 'at a distance' (i.e. by telephone, internet, fax, or post—without any face to face interaction), has introduced various consumer protection measures in relation to banking services marketed in such a way, including a 14-day 'cooling off' period.[575] The UK legislators have taken the view[576] that the Distance Marketing Directive is intended to operate on a 'country of origin' basis. As a consequence they have purported[577] to apply the relevant domestic UK provisions to all firms operating from a UK establishment whether they target the United Kingdom or another EEA Member State market and have provided that

---

[566] COM (2006) 729.

[567] But two reports were forthcoming: (i) The Report of DGS Efficiency (May 2008) and (ii) Final Report on Risk-based contributions (June 2008).

[568] Directive 2009/14/EC. It makes provision for further amendments, after consultation.

[569] See COM(2010) 369 (12 July 2010).

[570] 91/208/EC (implemented on 1 Jan 1993); 2001/97/EC (implemented on 15 June 2003); 2005/60/EC (implemented on 15 December 2007).

[571] 2000/31/EC, (the 'ECD').

[572] This term is not used in the text of the Directive itself, although it has been adopted by official Community explanatory documents—as has the term 'country of destination'. 'Country of origin' is the place from which the services originate and may differ from the 'home' country for the purposes of the CRD, Pt. 1. Thus in the case of a service provider with a registered and head office in Member State A, providing services from a branch in Member State B to customers in Member State C accessing its internet site, will have State A as its 'home' State (for the purposes of the CRD, Pt. 1), State B as its 'host' State (for the purposes of the CRD, Pt. 1) and 'country of origin' (for the purposes of the ECD) and State C as its 'country of destination' (for the purposes of the ECD).

[573] By amendment of the RAO (see Sect. 4(ii)) and the FPO (see Sect. 4(vii)). See also the FSA's specialist E-Commerce Directive Sourcebook (the 'ECO' Module) in its Handbook.

[574] 2002/65/EC OJ L271/16.

[575] See the Financial Services (Distance Marketing) Regulations 2004, S.I. 2004/2095, implementing that Directive in the UK.

[576] Although this is not explicitly stated in the Directive. See FSA Consultation Paper No. 196, *Implementation of the Distance Marketing Directive: proposed rules and guidance*, September 2003, para. 3.21 and HM Treasury Consultation Document, *Implementation of the Distance Marketing of Consumer Financial Services Directive*, para. 21–5.

[577] Whether they have been successful will depend on whether other member States will subordinate their private international law rules in order to give primacy to the English 'country of origin' law.

UK rules will not apply to firms operating into the United Kingdom from elsewhere in the EEA—in the expectation that that Member State's corresponding rules will apply.[578]

Although, with the completion of the FSAP,[579] the stream of substantive EC legislation of relevance to banking was expected to diminish, there have been further developments. The Payment Services Directive[580] aims to create a harmonized legal framework for payment services (so-called 'SEPA', the single market payments area) and hence extends the 'European passport'[581] to payment services providers. Its implementation has resulted in considerable changes to the regulation of the conduct of retail banking.[582] Further, a new Consumer Credit Directive[583] that aims to harmonize still further[584] the terms under which credit is offered to consumers in the EEA has been adopted and has required changes to UK consumer credit law.[585]

8 The Basle Committee on Banking Supervision

The Basle Committee on Banking Supervision, comprising the banking regulators of the major financial centres, was established in 1975 by the central bank governors of the G-10 countries in response to the increased interdependence or 'globalization' of banking activity. Its name derives from the place where it has its permanent secretariat.[586] It aims to reduce the risk posed to the global financial system by banking failure, through encouraging dialogue and co-operation between regulators and through agreeing capital adequacy standards. It has neither formal legal status nor authority, but its recommendations (so-called 'soft law') are enormously influential and are followed by banking regulators throughout the world. As will be noted below, the EU—which, as discussed above, has the different agenda of creating a single market in financial services—has adopted most of the Basle Committee's recommendations in framing its Directives.[587]

The Basle Committee began its work with the '1975 Concordat'. This recommended both regulatory co-operation through the sharing of information and the division of regulatory responsibility between home and host country over branches and subsidiaries.[588] The second significant development was the '1983 Agreement'. This focused on consolidated supervision, recommending that capital adequacy be assessed on a consolidated basis.[589] It was followed by the important '1988 Capital Accord', recommending a basis for calculating capital adequacy, which was adopted by the EC in two directives.[590] 1992

---

[578] See HM Treasury Consultation Document, *Implementation of the Distance Marketing of Consumer Financial Services Directive*, para. 22.

[579] See Sect. 7(i) above.

[580] Directive 2007/56/EC, implemented on 1 November 2009 by the Payment Services Regulations 2009, S.I. 2009/209, see Sect. 6(iii) above.

[581] See Sect. 7(ii) above.   [582] See Sect. 6(iii) above.

[583] Directive 2008/48/EC, replacing the first Directive (see next note).

[584] There was already the Consumer Credit Directive of 1987 (87/102/EEC), as amended.

[585] See Sect. 5 above, *passim*.

[586] At the Bank for International Settlements in Basle. Its documents are on the BIS website: www.bis.org.

[587] See Sect. 7(iv), esp. n.551 above. Many of the Member State banking regulators are members of the Basle Committee.

[588] The home state was to be responsible for solvency but the host state for liquidity.

[589] Simultaneously, the EC issued its first directive on consolidated supervision: Directive 83/350 [1983] OJ L193/18, since consolidated. See now the CRD, Pt. 2, Sect. 7(iv), above.

[590] The Own Funds Directive and the Solvency Ratio Directive, both n.501 above.

saw the Basle Committee (and the EC[591]) responding to the BCCI débâcle by making recommendations concerning the regulation of banking groups. A previous Basle initiative in 1991—on monitoring and controlling large exposures—was also reflected in an EC Directive.[592] The 1988 Capital Accord was amended in 1996, giving banks more freedom in assessing risk, but the EC was slow in making the requisite changes to its Capital Adequacy Directive.[593]

June 1999 saw the launch of another major revision which culminated in 'Basle II',[594] a new capital adequacy framework built on three 'pillars': minimum capital requirements (the rules for calculating credit and operational risk capital requirements), a supervisory review process (how the domestic regulator is to review and approve the rules) and effective use of market discipline (requiring banks to disclose information about their capital to the market place). The EC eventually implemented 'Basle II' in the Capital Requirements Directive, mentioned above.[595]

Basle II came under fire during the financial turmoil of 2007/8, particularly in not adequately providing for liquidity risks and the Basle Committee lost no time in responding to Basle II's shortcomings.[596] Although at the time of writing it is unclear what form the final reforms of Basle II will take (to become 'Basle III'), it is clear that significant changes will be forthcoming.

---

[591] The 'post-BCCI' or Second Directive on Consolidated Supervision: Directive 95/26/EC, n.501.

[592] The LED (Large Exposures Directive): 92/121, n.501 above.

[593] Directive 93/6, amended by Directive 98/31, since consolidated. See now the CRD, Pt. 2, Sect. 7(iv) above.

[594] Dated June 2004. It was updated in November 2005, incorporating the July 2005 guidance in the Basle Committee's paper *The Application of Basel II to Trading Activities and the Treatment of Double Default Effects*. In July 2006 a comprehensive version (including the elements of the 1988 Accord not revised during the Basel II process, the 1996 Amendment to the Capital Accord to Incorporate Market Risks, and the November 2005 paper) was issued.

[595] Directive 2006/49/EC, see Sect. 7(iv) above.

[596] See its July 2008 documents proposing amendments to the first 'pillar': (a) *Guidelines for Computing Capital for Incremental Risk in the Trading Book* and (b) *Proposed Revisions to the Basel II Market Risk Framework*.

3

Legal Definition and Privileges of Banks

1 Banks at common law

(i) Problem of defining a bank

As already discussed,[1] the United Kingdom banking industry is divided into a number of sectors, each with its own distinctive characteristics. Despite this proliferation, Parliament has not found it necessary to provide a generally applicable functional definition that distinguishes banks from other types of financial institution.[2] Different pieces of legislation do, however, define the term 'bank' for their own specific purposes.[3] Accordingly, an institution that is a 'bank' in one statutory context may not be so regarded in other contexts.[4] In attempting to define the concept of a 'bank', the following discussion has two principal parts. This first part considers the common law definition, which is based on treating a 'bank' as an institution engaged in 'banking business'. As Parliament has not determined the nature of this type of business, its construction has remained in the hands of the courts. The second part reviews the statutory definitions of 'bank' found in particular pieces of legislation, and the policy and rationale underlying these definitions. Between 1979 and 2001, much of the legislation containing a statutory definition of a 'bank' defined that concept in terms of institutions authorized under the Banking Act 1979 and then the Banking Act 1987. Such legislation has been amended or drafted to reflect the advent of the Financial Services and Markets Act 2000 (FSMA 2000).[5]

---

[1] Ch. 1, Sect. 1 above.

[2] A United Kingdom entity does not require a licence in order to engage in banking business, although it has been recommended that all payment system participants be subject to a class licence: D. Cruickshank, *Competition in UK Banking—A Report to the Chancellor of the Exchequer* (London, March 2000), [3.186]. The 20-partner limit that would otherwise have applied to banking partnerships has been abolished: Regulatory Reform (Removal of 20 Member Limit in Partnerships, etc) Order 2002, S.I. 2002/3203. Currently, the principal restriction is that an entity must be authorized under the Financial Services and Markets Act 2000 (FSMA 2000) before it accepts deposits from the public (Ch. 2, Sect. 4(ii)–(iii) above) or engages in other 'regulated activities' covered by the Financial Services and Markets Act 2000 (Regulated Activities) Order 2001, S.I. 2001/544, as amended (Ch. 2, Sect. 4(ii) above).

[3] See, for example, Banking Act 2009, s.2.

[4] Increasingly, United Kingdom and European legislation use statutory terms that avoid the necessity of distinguishing so closely between 'banks' and other types of financial institution. Examples include 'authorised UK deposit-taker' (Banking (Special Provisions) Act 2008, s.1) and 'credit institution' (Directive 2006/48/EC Relating to the Taking Up and Pursuit of the Business of Credit Institution, [2006] OJ L 177/1, Art. 4(1)). European Union legislation has also introduced other categories of financial institution that engage in traditional banking activities, such as 'electronic money institutions' and 'payment institutions': Sect. 5 below. See further Ch. 2, Sect. 7 above.

[5] See, for example, Banking Act 2009, s.2. See further Ch. 2, Sect. 4 above.

(ii) **Banking business at common law**

Under section 2 of the Bills of Exchange Act 1882 (BEA 1882), '"banker" includes a body of persons whether incorporated or not who carry on the business of banking'. Despite its patent circularity, this definition is not as unhelpful as may at first appear, as it makes clear that the determination of whether an institution is a 'bank' requires a court to review the business of the institution in question and to compare this with the types of business generally transacted by banks. Accordingly, the definition in the BEA 1882 does furnish a useful and flexible guideline for the courts when determining the common law definition of 'bank', although that guidance has one disturbing feature—it treats the 'business of banking' as being carried on by 'banks' in a uniform manner. As already indicated,[6] this approach is misguided, as a clearing bank's activities traditionally differ in nature and scope from those of a merchant (or investment) bank.[7] The relevant case law and some commentators[8] have sidestepped this inherent difficulty, however, by assuming that some types of business are conceptually those carried on by a generic group of 'banks'.[9]

In constructing the common law definition, the courts have established three cardinal principles. First, the meaning of 'banking business' can change from time to time. In *Woods* v. *Martins Bank Ltd*,[10] where Salmon J held that the giving of advice on financial matters constituted 'banking business' because, *inter alia*, the bank in that case had held itself out as being in a position to advise its customers on their investments, his Lordship observed:[11]

> ...the limits of a banker's business cannot be laid down as a matter of law. The nature of such a business must in each case be a matter of fact and, accordingly, cannot be treated as if it were a matter of pure law. What may have been true of the Bank of Montreal in 1918[12] is not necessarily true of Martins Bank in 1958.

This principle has become particularly important in recent years, as banks have become multifunctional institutions engaged in a wide range of business activity beyond their traditional core activities of deposit-taking, lending and providing payment services in connection with the operation of current accounts.[13] Nowadays, banks commonly engage

---

[6] Ch. 1 above.

[7] For the impact of the global credit crisis on investment banking in the United States, see Dodd-Frank Wall Street Reform and Consumer Protection Act 2010 (US). See further Ch. 2, Sect. 1 above.

[8] H.L. Hart, *Law of Banking* (4th edn., London, 1931), 1; Lord Chorley, *Law of Banking* (6th edn., London, 1974), 32–3; M. Hapgood (ed.), *Paget's Law of Banking* (13th edn., London, 2007), 138–140.

[9] *Argo Fund Ltd* v. *Essar Steel Ltd* [2005] 2 Lloyd's Rep. 203, [32], [38]–[39], revsd. on a different issue [2006] 2 Lloyd's Rep 134, [29]–[32], [49] (CA) recognized that the key characteristics that determine whether a particular financial institution is a 'bank' can alter according to the particular context.

[10] [1959] 1 QB 55.

[11] Ibid., 70. See also *Davies* v. *Kennedy* (1869) IR 3 Eq. 668 (Ch. App.); *Re Shields' Estate* [1901] 1 Ir.R 173, 179 (Ch. App.); *Bank of Chettinad Ltd* v. *Commissioners of Income Tax, Colombo* [1948] AC 378, 383 (PC); *United Dominions Trust Ltd* v. *Kirkwood* [1966] 2 QB 431, 445–446, 459 (CA); *Central Computer Services Ltd* v. *Toronto Dominion Bank* (1979) 1 Man R (2d) 402, [51]–[53] (MBCA).

[12] *Banbury* v. *Bank of Montreal* [1918] AC 626 (PC), in which the Privy Council held that the giving of advice on investments did not constitute 'banking business'.

[13] Payment Services Regulations 2009, S.I. 2009/209 (PSR 2009). See further Ch. 2, Sect. 6(iii) above, Ch. 7, Sect. 2 below & Ch. 13, Sects. 5(iv)–(vi) below. This expansion beyond banks' 'core' activities is partly in response to increased competition from other financial institutions that have branched out into areas that were traditionally the preserve of banks: *Canadian Pioneer Management Ltd* v. *Labour Relations Board of Saskatchewan* (1979) 2 Sask R 217, [24], [63] (SCC); *Bank of Montreal* v. *Hall* [1990] 1 SCR 121, 149 (SCC). Most notably, the Building Societies Act 1986 permitted building societies to compete with banks in retail

in activities as diverse as securities and derivatives trading, investment management, insurance,[14] and pensions usually through different subsidiary companies within the same banking group, rather than through the principal banking entity itself. Secondly, a financial institution that is regarded as engaging in 'banking business' in one jurisdiction is not necessarily so considered elsewhere.[15] For example, according to Irish[16] and Australian[17] authority, an institution that accepts money on deposit from the public for the purpose of relending it carries on banking business, even if it does not open current accounts operable by cheque. In contrast, the operation of current accounts on behalf of customers is the touchstone of a 'bank' according to authorities in the United Kingdom[18] and other common law jurisdictions.[19] These different approaches to the concept of a 'bank' are explicable, however, by reference to the differently structured banking industries in the various jurisdictions. Thirdly, an institution's reputation may be important when determining whether it is a 'bank'—an institution that is widely considered to be a 'bank' will usually be treated by the courts as engaged in banking business.[20]

Although the meaning of 'banking business' is subject to change, it is important to ascertain the types of transaction that nowadays characterize such activity. Traditionally, the hallmark of 'banking business' involved the acceptance of money on deposit from members of the public,[21] who thereby became customers of the bank,[22] and the relending or reinvesting of those funds by the bank in order to make a profit. Support for this traditional view in Ireland can be found in *Re Shields' Estate*,[23] where FitzGibbon LJ explained that

financial products, such as current accounts, and some have even demutualized and become authorized under the FSMA 2000: Ch. 1, Sect. 7 above.

[14] In Canada, 'when a bank takes insurance as security for a loan, it is engaged in the business of banking' (*Turgeon v. Dominion Bank* [1930] SCR 67, 71–72 (SCC)), but the promoting of optional insurance to customers is not considered an activity that is vital or essential to banking (*Canadian Western Bank v. Alberta* [2007] 2 SCR 3, [86], [120] (SCC)). In *ANZ National Bank Ltd v. Tower Insurance Ltd* [2010] NZCA 267, [1], [149], the New Zealand Court of Appeal expressed the view that the cross-selling of 'bank-branded insurance policies' would be considered by bank customers in general to be a 'normal function' of a bank.

[15] In *Hafton Properties Ltd v. McHugh (Inspector of Taxes)* [1987] STC 16, 25, 28–29, a financial institution that was 'a bank officially recognized as such in the Isle of Man' did not meet the English definition of 'bank' as it did not also carry out the requisite activities within the United Kingdom. See also *Commissioners of the State Savings Bank of Victoria v. Permewan, Wright & Co. Ltd* (1914) 19 CLR 457 (HCA); *Bank of Chettinad Ltd v. Commissioners of Income Tax, Colombo*, n.11 above, 383; *Woods v. Martins Bank Ltd*, n.10 above, 70.

[16] *Davies v. Kennedy*, n.11 above; *Re Shields' Estate*, n.11 above; *Commercial Banking Co. Ltd v. Hartigan* (1952) 86 Ir. LTR 109.

[17] *Commissioners of the State Savings Bank of Victoria v. Permewan, Wright & Co. Ltd*, n.15 above; *Mason v. Savings Bank of South Australia* [1925] SASR 198, 204; *Melbourne Corporation v. Commonwealth of Australia* (1947) 74 CLR 31, 64–65 (HCA); *Australian Independent Distributors Ltd v. Winter* (1964) 112 CLR 443, 455 (HCA); *PP Consultants Pty. Ltd v. Finance Sector Union of Australia* (2000) 176 ALR 205 (HCA). Although the Australian Banking Act 1959 (Cth), s.5 has contained a definition of 'banking business' since 1 July 1998, the statutory definition 'merely re-states the meaning which the courts had earlier given to it': *R v. Jost* (VCA, 1 November 2002). See also *Siminton v. Australian Prudential Regulation Authority* [2008] FCAFC 88, [50]–[60].

[18] *United Dominions Trust Ltd v. Kirkwood*, n.11 above.   [19] N.34 below.

[20] *Stafford v. Henry* (1850) 12 Ir. Eq. 400; *ex p. Coe* (1861) 3 De GF & J 335; *Re Shields' Estate*, n.11 above, 197; *Re Birkbeck Permanent Benefit Building Society* [1912] 2 Ch. 183, 208 (CA); *Commercial Banking Co. Ltd v. Hartigan*, n.16 above; *United Dominions Trust Ltd v. Kirkwood*, n.11 above. See also *Canadian Pioneer Management Ltd v. Labour Relations Board of Saskatchewan*, n.13 above, [44]–[49].

[21] This feature distinguishes a 'bank' from financial institutions, such as co-operative societies, that tend to borrow from, and lend to, a limited group of persons. In *Australian Independent Distributors Ltd v. Winter*, n.17 above, 455, a co-operative society was not considered a 'bank' as it did not accept deposits from the public, but from its members alone. The actual conclusion in *Winter* may be questioned, however, as it was just as easy to join the society in that case, as it was to become the customer of a bank. See also *Siminton v. Australian Prudential Regulation Authority*, n.17 above, [58]–[61].

[22] Ch. 5, Sect. 2 below.   [23] N.11 above, 198.

'[t]he business of banking, from the banker's point of view, is to traffic with the money of others for the purpose of making profit'. Similarly, in Australia, Isaacs J in *Commissioners of the State Savings Bank of Victoria* v. *Permewan, Wright & Co. Ltd.*[24] described the essence of banking business as 'the collection of money by receiving deposits upon loan, repayable when and as expressly or impliedly agreed upon, and the utilisation of money so collected by lending it again in such sums as are required'.[25] Finally, after initially appearing to adopt a different approach,[26] the Supreme Court of Canada in *Canadian Western Bank* v. *Alberta*[27] recently held that 'banking' certainly includes 'the securing of loans by appropriate collateral'[28] and further held that 'the lending of money, the taking of deposits, the extension of credit in the form of granting loans, as well as the taking of security for those loans, were core elements of banking'.[29] This traditional approach no longer represents the position in the United Kingdom, however, following the Court of Appeal's landmark decision in *United Dominions Trust* v. *Kirkwood*.[30] Their Lordships held that engaging in lending does not by itself make an institution a 'bank'.[31] Moreover, whilst it is implicit in *Kirkwood* that the acceptance of deposits from the public remains a *necessary* condition of an institution qualifying as a 'bank' in the United Kingdom, such activity is certainly no longer a *sufficient* condition, otherwise a building society would be a 'bank'.[32] Nowadays, according to *Kirkwood*, an entity cannot qualify as a 'bank' at common law in the United Kingdom unless it opens, on behalf of customers, current accounts operable by cheque and into which customers can pay cheques and other effects for collection.

In *Kirkwood*, a finance company brought an action to recover a loan made to a dealer, who raised as a defence the fact that the company was an unregistered moneylender, and that the loan contract was accordingly illegal as contravening the Moneylenders Act 1900.[33] The finance company claimed that it was exempt from any registration requirements by virtue of section 6(d) of that enactment because it carried on, *bona fide*, the business of banking. To this end, the finance company proved that the City regarded it as

---

[24] N.15 above, 471. For an historical background to Australian banking, see *Victorian Workcover Authority* v. *Andrews* [2005] FCA 94, [38]–[51].

[25] A single loan may be enough to establish that a financial institution has engaged in the 'business of banking' under the Banking Act 1959 (Cth), s.5 and the *Permewan* 'definition': *Siminton* v. *Australian Prudential Regulation Authority*, n.17 above, [56]–[59].

[26] In *Canadian Pioneer Management Ltd* v. *Labour Relations Board of Saskatchewan*, n.13 above, [28]–[29], [37]–[49], [78], the Supreme Court of Canada appeared to provide some support for the approach in *United Dominions Trust Ltd* v. *Kirkwood*, n.11 above.

[27] N.14 above. For criticism of *Canadian Western*, see M.H. Ogilvie, '*Canadian Western Bank* v. *Alberta*: Cooperative Federalism and the End of "Banking"' (2008) 47 *Can. Bus. LJ* 75, 85.

[28] Ibid., [85].   [29] Ibid., [118].

[30] N.11 above. See also *Joachimson* v. *Swiss Bank Corporation* [1921] 3 KB 110, 127 (CA); *Bank of Chettinad Ltd* v. *Commissioners of Income Tax, Colombo*, n.11 above, 383–384 (although the Privy Council's decision was based on a statutory definition applicable in Sri Lanka).

[31] Ibid., 451, 466. See also *Brown* v. *Commissioners of Inland Revenue* (1963) 42 ATC 244 (SC); *Hafton Properties Ltd* v. *McHugh*, n.15 above; *Argo Fund Ltd* v. *Essar Steel Ltd*, n.9 above, where Auld LJ referred to lending as a 'bank-like activity'. On the issue of whether secured lending involves 'banking' activity, see *Tennant* v. *Union Bank of Canada* [1894] AC 31, 46 (PC); *Attorney-General for Alberta* v. *Attorney-General for Canada* [1947] AC 503, 517–518 (PC); *Bank of Montreal* v. *Hall* [1990], n.13 above, 148–150; *Canadian Western Bank* v. *Alberta*, n.14 above, [120].

[32] Ibid., 446. Although money transmission has long been viewed as an important aspect of banking practice (D. Cruickshank, n.2 above, [1.14]–[1.16])—a view reinforced when the PSR 2009 came into force on 1 November 2009—the provision of such services alone will not constitute a financial institution a 'bank': *Azam* v. *Iqbal* [2007] EWHC 2025 (Admin.), [29].

[33] The Moneylenders Act 1900 was repealed by the Consumer Credit Act 1974, s.192(4) & Sched. 5, Pt. 1. Given the similarity between the definition of a 'banker' in the Moneylenders Act 1900 and the Bills of Exchange Act 1882 (BEA 1882), *Kirkwood* remains of topical importance.

a bank, that it enjoyed certain privileges given solely to banks, and that it had a clearing number. It was further established that on occasion the company had opened a 'current account' in a borrower's name and credited this with the sums that it had lent to that borrower, and that the company received 'deposits' from the public that were invariably repayable on agreed maturity dates rather than on demand. There was no evidence suggesting that the company collected cheques payable to its customers. On these facts, Lord Denning MR doubted that the company carried on the business of banking. His Lordship described the 'usual characteristics of a banker' as follows:[34]

> There are, therefore, two characteristics usually found in banks today: (i) They accept money from, and collect cheques for, their customers and place them to their credit; (ii) They honour cheques or orders drawn on them by their customers when presented for payment and debit their customers accordingly. These two characteristics carry with them also a third, namely: (iii) They keep current accounts, or something of that nature, in their books in which the credits and debits are entered.

Diplock and Harman LJJ similarly agreed that these activities formed the 'essential' characteristics of 'banking business', so that an entity could not be regarded as a 'bank' at common law if it did not engage in any of these activities. Diplock LJ further held, however, that even an institution that engaged in these three activities would not be regarded as a 'bank' if its banking business was negligible in size, or if its current accounts were opened as a mere cloak for lending transactions. This dictum was subsequently explained in *Re Roe's Legal Charge*,[35] which similarly concerned the interpretation of the term 'banking business' in the Moneylenders Act 1900. In *Roe*, the finance company had opened current accounts for some customers, collected cheques on their behalf, and provided other banking services, such as the sale of travellers' cheques, foreign-currency dealings, and facilities for the payment of customers' accounts by means of money-transfer orders. The company also obtained daily printouts that showed the state of each customer's account and sent periodic statements to customers. There were, however, four main differences between that company's business and that of a regular bank. First, the company's entire banking service was furnished through an agency bank, rather than at premises maintained in its own name. Secondly, the number of current and deposit accounts opened for customers by the company was less than 200, and only 58 cheques had been cleared for customers during 1974. Thirdly, about 75 per cent of the company's deposits were maintained by its shareholders and by its subsidiary and associated companies. Fourthly, the company did not solicit deposits from the public by means of advertisements. In holding that the company was engaged in banking business, Lawton LJ considered it immaterial that the number of items cleared through the company was very limited and that the company's banking

---

[34] N.11 above, 447. Support for *Kirkwood* can be found in Canada (*Canadian Pioneer Management Ltd* v. *Labour Relations Board of Saskatchewan*, n.13 above, [28]–[29], [37]–[43], [78], doubting *Attorney-General for Canada* v. *Attorney-General for the Province of Quebec* [1947] AC 33, 44 (PC); but compare the absence of any reference to the need for cheque facilities in *Canadian Western Bank* v. *Alberta*, n.14 above, [85], [120]) and New Zealand (*Re Securitibank Ltd* [1978] 1 NZLR 97, 148–149; *Rupa* v. *Bank of New Zealand* (NZHC, 31 January 2008), [50]). The Malaysian courts have similarly applied *Kirkwood* (*Yeep Mooi* v. *Chu Chin Chua* [1981] 1 MLJ 14, 16 (MFCA); *Re Haji Yahya Lampong, ex p. Sabah Development Bank Bhd* [1987] 2 MLJ 488, 491; *Sabah Development Bank Bhd* v. *SKBS* [1992] 1 MLJ 454, 460) and have held that this position is unaffected by the Malaysian Banking and Financial Institutions Act 1989, s.2, which introduced a statutory definition of 'banking business' (*Banque Nationale de Paris* v. *Ting Kai Hoon* [2002] 7 MLJ 703, [47]–[49]; *Light Style Sdn Bhd* v. *KFH Ijarah House (Malaysia) Sdn Bhd* [2009] MLJU 220, [22]–[24]). The Singaporean courts have applied *Kirkwood* in interpreting the term 'banking business' in Banking Act (Cap 19), s.2(1): *Vernes Asia Ltd* v. *Trendale Investment Pte Ltd* [1988] 1 SLR 202, 207–209.

[35] [1982] 2 Lloyd's Rep. 370 (CA).

business could be considered negligible in size when compared to that of a clearing bank. It was also immaterial that the company did not carry on all facets of banking business, and that its main business was in a different field.[36] The only relevant consideration was whether the company's banking business was *real* in terms of its entire business.

The characteristics listed by Lord Denning above are not the only relevant ones, however, as a 'bank' should also normally possess the qualities of 'stability, soundness, and probity'.[37] Moreover, evidence of an entity's reputation as a bank may also be relevant. Indeed, Lord Denning in *Kirkwood* thought that, in cases of doubt, it was 'permissible to look at the reputation of the firm amongst ordinary intelligent commercial men. If they recognized it as carrying on the business of banking, that should turn the scale'.[38] Accordingly, despite the company in *Kirkwood* not possessing the usual (objective) characteristics of a banker, his Lordship nevertheless held that its reputation as a 'bank' exempted it from the Moneylenders Act 1900. This conclusion was based on overt policy grounds, namely the need to avoid unwinding numerous transactions that were otherwise considered to be valid by the commercial community,[39] and the unwillingness to put a major financial institution in jeopardy simply because it failed to comply with the technicalities of the Moneylenders Act 1900.[40] Like Lord Denning, Diplock LJ considered that he was dealing with a borderline case and concurred with Lord Denning's conclusions, albeit for slightly different reasons. According to Diplock LJ, the finance company in *Kirkwood* had a marginal banking business, which by itself might not have been enough to constitute that company a 'bank', but the fact that the City considered the firm to be a bank established that it enjoyed the reputation of carrying on banking business. In contrast to Lord Denning's policy-based justification for considering evidence of a financial institution's reputation, however, Diplock LJ treated such reputation as *prima facie* evidence of the nature of the transactions that the financial institution had undertaken.[41] Accordingly, for Diplock LJ, the finance company's reputation, when coupled with its marginal banking business, sufficed to make it a 'bank'.

In his dissenting judgment, Harman LJ concluded that 'reputation alone is not enough' for an entity to be 'bank' and accordingly concluded that, as the finance company was not (objectively) carrying on the business of banking, it was a mere unregistered moneylender. Unlike the majority, his Lordship had no qualms about unwinding the finance company's many transactions. Although it is possible to find judicial support for the majority's approach and for a definition of 'bank' that is based on subjective criteria,[42] it is submitted that Harman LJ's view as to the relevance of reputation is to be preferred. If the definition of a 'bank' is to have any useful function in distinguishing between 'banks' and non-bank financial institutions, it should only encompass those entities that actually engage in activities that are characteristically banking business and not those that merely have a reputation for doing so. Moreover, a purely objective approach to the definition of a 'bank' is not only more consistent with the legislative intent underlying the Moneylenders Act 1900, but also avoids the uncertainty inherent in determining a particular entity's reputation and the difficult question of whose views should count for this purpose.

Whilst the effect of *Kirkwood* is that the 'usual' or 'essential' characteristics of banking are the collection and honouring of cheques and the entry of credits and debits in bank ledgers, this decision is based upon how banks operated in 1966. Yet in *Kirkwood*

---

[36] *Re Birkbeck Permanent Benefit Building Society*, n.20 above.   [37] N.11 above, 453.

[38] Ibid., 454.   [39] Ibid., 455.

[40] Id. See also Lord Chorley, n.8 above, 34; Lord Chorley, *Gilbart Lectures* (London, 1967); H. Megrah, 'Banks and Moneylenders' (1967) 30 *MLR* 86.

[41] N.11 above, 462, 474.   [42] N.20 above.

itself Lord Denning said that '[t]he march of time has taken us far beyond those cases of 50 years ago',[43] and this observation remains true today. Nowadays, cheques are used less and less—the annual volume of personal cheques is less than half of what it was 10 years ago[44]—and money is more frequently transferred into and out of accounts by plastic and electronic means, particularly through the use of ATMs, EFTPOS debit cards, and mobile and internet banking.[45] Indeed, the UK Payments Council has described cheque use as being 'in long-term decline'[46] and, more recently, as being 'in terminal decline'.[47] Moreover, bank accounts themselves are no longer recorded in ledgers, but on computer databases.[48] Accordingly, the definition of 'bank' and 'banking' in *Kirkwood* should probably now be updated in the light of these modern banking practices. This could be achieved by releasing the common law definitions of 'bank' and 'banking' from the shackles of an overly restrictive requirement that focuses too much on the precise mechanisms by which money is paid into and out of bank accounts.[49]

(iii) The significance of the common law definition of 'banker'

There are a number of legal consequences that result from characterising a particular entity as a 'bank' at common law. Such a financial institution becomes subject to particular duties towards those who qualify as its customers,[50] and may avail itself of certain rights, privileges, and defences that would not otherwise be available.[51] For example, such a financial institution may rely upon the banker's lien[52] or exercise the banker's right of set-off or combination conferred by the general law.[53] Furthermore, there are certain defences contained in the BEA 1882 and the Cheques Act 1957 with respect to the payment, discount, and collection of cheques.[54] Of relevance to the present discussion is the fact that these defences are subject to two limitations. First, only 'banks' (as defined at common law) are entitled to rely upon them.[55] Secondly, they do not apply to banks' dealings in negotiable instruments such as promissory notes and commercial bills of

---

[43] Ibid., 446, distinguishing *Re Bottomsgate Industrial Co-operative Society* (1891) 65 LT 712, which suggested that a company may be a 'bank' although it does not carry on all the facets of banking business. The definition of 'banker' must keep pace with modern banking practice: *Central Computer Services Ltd* v. *Toronto Dominion Bank*, n.11 above, [20]–[21], [31], [51]–[57]; *Retail Parks Investments Ltd* v. *Royal Bank of Scotland plc (No.2)* 1996 SLT 52, 58 (OH).

[44] For the relevant statistics, see Ch. 10, Sect. 2 below.   [45] Chs. 13 & 14 below.

[46] Payments Council, *National Payments Plan—Setting the Strategic Vision for UK Payments* (14 May 2008), 6. See also UK Payments Administration, *The Way We Pay 2009: UK Cheques* (London, 2009).

[47] Payments Council, *Progress Report: Delivering the National Payments Plan* (June 2010), 1.

[48] In *Central Computer Services Ltd* v. *Toronto Dominion Bank*, n.11 above, [4]–[7], [54], [57], the Manitoba Court of Appeal recognized that the keeping of computerized ledgers should be viewed as part of the 'business of banking' within the applicable legislation.

[49] In *Commissioners of the State Savings Bank of Victoria* v. *Permewan, Wright & Co. Ltd*, n.15 above, 471, Isaacs J recognized that '[t]he methods by which the functions of a bank are affected . . . are merely accidental and auxiliary circumstances any of which may or may not exist in any particular case'. No reference was made to the need for accounts to be operated by cheque in *Argo Fund Ltd* v. *Essar Steel Ltd*, n.9 above, [32], [38]–[39], revsd. on a different issue, n.9 above, [29]–[32], [49].

[50] Ch. 5, Sects. 4–5 below.   [51] *United Dominions Trust Ltd* v. *Kirkwood*, n.11 above, 442–445.

[52] Ch. 20, Sect. 2 below.   [53] Ch. 7, Sect. 4 below.

[54] Ch. 11, Sect. 4 & Ch. 15, Sect. 4 below. The statutory defences conferred on 'banks' (as defined at common law) that honour and collect cheques may be of little relevance to an entity that is engaged exclusively in investment banking rather than retail banking activity. For the common law defences conferred on paying banks, see further Ch. 11, Sect. 3 below.

[55] Building Societies Act 1997, s.12(3) also provides that, insofar as a building society is carrying on any activity comprised in the provision of a banking service, it is to be treated for all purposes as a 'bank' and as carrying on the 'business of banking'.

exchange, but only to dealings in 'cheques' and some other analogous instruments.[56] A 'cheque' is, however, defined as a bill of exchange that is payable on demand and drawn on a 'bank',[57] and the bill's drawee will be a 'bank' only if it engages in 'banking business', an essential feature of which (as indicated in *Kirkwood*) is the opening of current accounts operable by cheque. Thus, one must determine that the drawee is a 'bank' in order to conclude that a particular instrument drawn on it is a 'cheque'; but one must equally establish that the instruments drawn on a particular institution are 'cheques' before that institution can qualify as a 'bank'. To date this circularity of definition has not been the subject of judicial comment.[58] A court that is confronted with this problem would probably concentrate on the regularity in drawings and the formal appearance of the instruments, so that if the drawee regularly honoured instruments that appeared on their face to be 'cheques', the court would be inclined to regard that financial institution as a 'bank', and to deem the instruments 'cheques', provided of course that the drawee also engaged in the other essential types of banking business.

2 Rights and privileges conferred on banks by statutes utilizing other definitions

(i) The right to receive deposits from protected customers

The depositor protection legislation purports to safeguard the interests of specific groups by restricting the manner in which funds belonging to them may be invested or deposited by those acting on their behalf. Organizations with whom such funds may be invested are, obviously, assured of having a certain cash-flow. 'Banks' are invariably among the bodies with whom such funds may be invested. Originally, depositor protection legislation in the United Kingdom either utilized the common law definition of a 'bank' or introduced a regime under which certain institutions were specifically authorized to transact the type of business prescribed.[59] Most of the relevant statutory definitions were amended originally by the Banking Act 1979, then by the Banking Act 1987, and most recently by the FSMA 2000, which repealed and replaced the Banking Act 1987.[60]

An important example of the type of legislation currently under discussion is the Solicitors Act 1974, which confers on the Council of the Law Society the power to make rules requiring solicitors to deposit clients' funds with 'banks' (or now also 'building societies').[61] The definition of a 'bank' in the Solicitors Act 1974 is based on FSMA 2000, which covers the Bank of England, a person (other than a building society) who has permission under Part IV of FSMA 2000 to accept deposits, or an EEA firm that has

---

[56]   Ch. 11, Sect. 4(v) & Ch. 15, Sect. 4(i) below.

[57]   BEA 1882, s.73; Cheques Act 1957, s.6(1). See also *Aspinall's Club Ltd* v. *Fouad Al-Zayat* [2007] EWHC 362 (Comm), [10].

[58]   By not providing any definition of 'cheque' or 'bank', this circularity was avoided in the Stamp Act 1853, s.19, which preceded the BEA 1882, s.60 (Ch. 11, Sect. 4(iii) below) and which continues to confer the only defence available to banks that pay in-house drafts bearing a forged indorsement. Originally, this provision applied to given types of instrument that were functionally defined in the legislation itself.

[59]   Protection of Depositors Act 1963 (subsequently replaced by the more sophisticated conceptual regime in the Banking Act 1979).

[60]   Financial Services and Markets Act 2000 (Consequential Amendments and Repeals) Order 2001, S.I. 2001/3649.

[61]   Solicitors Act 1974, s.32 (as amended by the Access to Justice Act 1999, Sched. 15 and the Legal Services Act 2007, ss.177, 210 & Sched. 16). For the Solicitors' Accounts Rules 1998, see further Ch. 8, Sect. 6 below.

permission under FSMA 2000 to accept deposits.[62] A similar regime is applicable to insurance brokers, who were originally regulated by the Insurance Brokers Registration Council,[63] then by the self-regulatory General Insurance Standards Council,[64] and now by the Financial Services Authority, which took over responsibility for the regulation of general insurance business in the United Kingdom on 14 January 2005. The rules governing the regulation of insurance intermediaries are found in the *FSA Handbook*.[65] These require the intermediary to place client money in a 'client bank account' held at an 'approved bank'.[66] Where the account in question is opened with a United Kingdom branch, the *Glossary* of the *FSA Handbook* defines an 'approved bank' to mean the Bank of England, the central bank of an OECD Member State, a bank, a building society, or a bank supervised by the central bank or other banking regulator of an OECD Member State. The *Glossary* in turn defines a 'bank' as: (a) a firm with a permission under Part IV of FSMA 2000 that includes accepting deposits, and which is a credit institution, or whose Part IV permission requires it to comply with the General Prudential Sourcebook ('GENPRU') and the Prudential Sourcebook for Banks, Building Societies and Investment Firms ('BIPRU'), but which is not a building society, friendly society, or credit union; or (b) an EEA bank (defined as an incoming EEA firm that is a Banking Consolidation Directive credit institution) that is a full credit institution.[67]

(ii) **The right to invest in protected or supervised transactions**

In the past, banks have been given the freedom to engage in certain types of centrally controlled business transaction and given preferential treatment in respect of the relevant investments.[68] In addition, banks are empowered to lend money to certain groups that are given wide-reaching statutory protections. Two examples will suffice. First, the Agricultural Credits Act 1928 restricts the power of farmers to grant mortgages or charges over farming assets. The object of this legislation is to protect farmers against foolhardy borrowings. Mortgages and charges over their assets may, however, be given to 'banks',[69] which are defined as the Bank of England, institutions authorized to accept deposits under Part IV of FSMA 2000, or EEA firms authorized under FSMA 2000 to accept deposits.[70] Secondly, under the Housing Act 1985, the Secretary of State may advance money to 'recognized lending institutions' to enable them to grant loans to first-home purchasers.[71] The institutions listed for this purpose include institutions authorized to

---

[62] Ch. 2, Sect. 4 above.   [63] Insurance Brokers (Registration) Act 1977.

[64] FSMA 2000, Sched. 22 (effective 30 April 2001).

[65] *FSA Handbook*, Client Asset Sourcebook, Ch. 5 ('CASS 5') (www.fsahandbook.info/FSA/html/handbook/CASS/5). See also *FSA Handbook*, Insurance: Conduct of Business Sourcebook (ICOBS). For the *FSA Handbook* generally, see further Ch. 2, Sect. 4(vi) above.

[66] CASS 5.5.37.   [67] Ch. 2, Sects. 4(i) & (v) above.

[68] Until 1986, banks enjoyed an important privilege to deal in securities without having to qualify under the Prevention of Fraud (Investments) Act 1958, not by virtue of their status as banks, but by reason of their being entities carrying on some business other than the business of dealing in securities: Prevention of Fraud (Investments) Act 1958, s.16, as amended by the Banking Act 1979, Sched. 6, Pt. 1, para. 5. Under the Financial Services Act 1986 Act, s.3 (in force on 29 April 1988: Financial Services Act 1986 (Commencement) (No. 8) Order, S.I. 1988/740), the position was changed and banks had to seek the same authorization as other financial institutions. That position has been maintained under the new regulatory regime established by the FSMA 2000: Ch. 2, Sect. 4 above.

[69] Agricultural Credits Act 1928, s.5(1).

[70] Financial Services and Markets Act 2000 (Consequential Amendments and Repeals) Order 2001, S.I. 2001/3649, art. 267(1). For the FSMA 2000 generally, see further Ch. 2, Sect. 4 above.

[71] Housing Act 1985, ss.445, 447.

accept deposits under Part IV of FSMA 2000 or EEA firms authorized under FSMA 2000 to accept deposits.[72]

(iii) The Bankers' Books Evidence Act 1879

Frequently, a bank's ledgers or record books include information that is required as evidence in legal proceedings—a statement of a customer's account may be important in an action for breach of contract or in respect of income tax matters. At common law, as bankers' books would ordinarily be classified as private rather than public documents, the information that they contained could only as a general rule be received if the originals were produced in court. Furthermore, the bank's employees had to attend court in order to submit the books or other information and to give evidence about their source.[73] Such a course could potentially seriously disrupt the business of the bank concerned. Accordingly, the Bankers' Books Evidence Act 1879 was passed in order to overcome the problems involved, and to permit copies of a banker's book to be received as prima facie evidence of its entries.

Originally, this legislation applied mainly to 'banks' as defined at common law.[74] This position was originally altered by the Banking Act 1979, then by the Banking Act 1987, and most recently by the FSMA 2000.[75] Section 9(1)(a)–(1A) of the Bankers' Books Evidence Act 1879 accordingly now provides that the expressions 'bank' and 'banker' mean a 'deposit-taker' which is defined as: (a) a person who has permission under Part IV of the FSMA 2000 to accept deposits; or (b) an EEA firm of the kind mentioned in para. 5(b) of Schedule 3 to the FSMA 2000 that has permission under para. 15 of that Schedule (as a result of qualifying for authorization under para. 12(1) of that Schedule) to accept deposits or other repayable funds from the public; but it does not include a person who has permission to accept deposits only for the purpose of carrying on another regulated activity in accordance with that permission. Accordingly, a stockbroker, who may accept deposits as part of other regulated activities, would not fall within the definition of 'bank' or 'banker'. The provisions of the Bankers' Books Evidence Act 1879 are discussed subsequently.[76]

3 The meaning of 'bank' where the term is undefined

As already indicated above, not all statutes conferring rights on, or regulating the position of, banks attempt to define the institutions affected.[77] Until the passing of the Banking Act 1979, it was safe to assume that, where undefined, the term 'bank' or 'banker' had to

---

[72] Ibid., s.622.

[73] C. Tapper, *Cross and Tapper on Evidence* (12th edn., Oxford, 2010), 263, 673–674.

[74] The legislation has now been extended to other finance houses: Halsbury, *Statutes of England* (4th edn., London, 2005 reissue), vol. 18, [130].

[75] Financial Services and Markets Act 2000 (Consequential Amendments and Repeals) Order 2001, S.I. 2001/3649.

[76] Ch. 5, Sect. 5(iii) below.

[77] See, for example, Race Relations Act 1976, s.20, which prohibits any discrimination in relation to 'facilities by way of banking', a term that is not defined. The Banking and Financial Dealing Act 1971 also fails to define the word 'bank', as does the Income and Corporation Taxes Act 1988 (ICTA 1988), s.765(2) with respect to the terms 'bankers' and 'business as bankers'; but contrast ICTA 1988, s.840A (inserted by the Finance Act 1986, s.198, Sched. 37, para. 1(1)), which defines the term 'bank' when used in any provision that makes specific reference to that section (for example, as in ICTA 1988, s.349), *inter alia*, as a person who has permission under FSMA 2000, Pt. IV to accept deposits (exceptions apply). Section 284 of the FSMA

be given its common law rendering. This definition was prevalent and could, therefore, be regarded as the most accurate legal description of a 'bank'. The position changed in the 1980s when the word 'bank' became associated with the regime of the Banking Act 1979, which was replaced in turn by the Banking Act 1987 and, most recently, by the FSMA 2000.[78] At present, Acts of Parliament tend, in general, to utilize the concepts of FSMA 2000 as the basis for their definition of 'bank', rather than the common law definition. A recent example of legislation adopting such an approach is section 2 of the Banking Act 2009.

In circumstances where legislation is silent as to the meaning of the terms 'bank' or 'banker', it is not easy to decide whether the common law or a statutory definition should be employed and, if the latter course is chosen, which statute's definition would be the most appropriate one. An attractive argument is that the date of the legislation that has failed to define the term 'bank' should be determinative of that definition. According to this approach, when legislation is contemporaneous with the BEA 1882, the common law definition ought to apply. In the case of more modern legislation, especially legislation passed in the 1980s or later, a court should refer to whichever of the Banking Act 1979, the Banking Act 1987, or the FSMA 2000 as was in force at the time that the legislation in question was passed. Naturally, such an approach would have the advantage of construing particular legislation on the basis of the intention attributable to Parliament at the time of its enactment. This particular solution, however, ignores the cardinal principle that regards banking business as being of a transient nature. As discussed above, *United Dominions Trust* v. *Kirkwood*[79] expressly recognized in relation to the common law definition of a 'bank' that the courts should determine each case in the light of the practice prevailing at the relevant time. Notably, the Banking Act 1979 took a further step in this direction, as it provided guidelines for construing 'bank' and 'banker' in the light of the position then prevailing. The same is true of the Banking Act 1987 and the FSMA 2000. On this basis, it is possible to treat the statutory and common law definitions as complementary—the common law definition proclaims that a 'bank' is a body engaged in 'banking business', whilst the 1979, 1987, and 2000 legislation describes the nature of 'banking business' as transacted at present. According to this solution, the meaning of 'bank' or 'banker' in legislation that failed to define those terms would be determined by reference to banking business as envisaged in the regulatory regime in force at the time that the relevant issue falls to be decided.

4 The right to use the term 'bank' in a name

Before its repeal, section 67 of the Banking Act 1987 provided that only an 'authorised institution', which was defined as either a United Kingdom-incorporated company with paid-up share capital or undistributable reserves amounting to not less that £5 million, or a United Kingdom partnership with similar amounts of fixed capital, could use a name indicating that it was a 'bank'. Nowadays, the FSMA 2000 does not contain an equivalent provision. The omission appears to have been deliberate.[80] The Government determined

2000 refers to the 'business of banking' (without defining the term) in relation to investigations and whether the bankers' duty of confidentiality continues to apply. Schedule 15 of the FSMA 2000 also uses the term 'banker' (without further definition) in relation to persons who may be required to provide information in respect of a person under investigation by the FSA under its statutory powers.

[78] Ch. 2, Sect. 4 above.   [79] N.11 above.
[80] D.A. Sabalot, 'The bank is dead. Long live the credit institution…language games' [2002] *JIBFL* 332, 333.

early in the reform process that it was no longer necessary to protect the use of the term 'bank', but decided instead to rely on the general principles of misrepresentation and section 24 of the FSMA 2000, which makes it a criminal offence for an entity that is neither an 'authorised person' nor an 'exempt person' in relation to the regulated activity in question to describe himself as either authorized or exempt under FSMA 2000. Section 24 of the FSMA 2000 would probably still catch an institution that called itself a 'bank' without proper authorization, as this term implies such authorization.

5 Assessment of the statutory treatment of 'banking'

The treatment of banks in United Kingdom legislation lacks uniformity and harmony. Some statutes apply to 'banks' as defined at common law, others to 'banks' defined as those authorized to accept deposits under Part IV of the FSMA 2000,[81] and others still fail to define the meaning of this term at all. This means that a financial institution may be treated as a 'bank' for certain purposes, but not for others. A financial institution may, for example, be considered to be a 'bank' for the purposes of the *FSA Handbook*,[82] which is concerned with the regulation of the financial sector, because it has Part IV permission to accept deposits and is a credit institution, but it may not be considered to 'carry on the business of banking' under the BEA 1882, which governs a bank's dealings in cheques.[83] This is not surprising, and it is not undesirable. The precise meaning of the terms 'bank', 'banker', or 'banking' turns on the particular context in which they are used. The most common contexts in which the issue becomes important are the areas of bank regulation, situations where rights and duties are conferred on banks, and situations where there is an attempt to avoid a payment obligation on the ground that it arises under a contract that is void or unenforceable because it is owed by, or to, an unlicensed bank.[84] In each case, the terms 'bank, 'banker' or 'banking' may mean something different.

Not only does the context impact upon the definition of 'bank' for domestic law purposes, but European legislation has introduced new categories of financial institution that do not necessarily coincide with the domestic definitions of 'bank'. For example, in the European financial regulation context, the definitional net is often cast widely. The key term for the purposes of European legislation is 'credit institution', which is defined, *inter alia*, as 'an undertaking whose business is to receive deposits or other repayable funds from the public and to grant credits for its own account'.[85] This definition is wider than the definition of a 'bank' under English common law and includes other financial institutions such as building societies and some industrial and provident societies.[86] Moreover, European legislation has introduced other categories of financial institution besides the 'credit institution', such as 'electronic money institutions' (defined as 'an undertaking or any legal person, other than a credit institution...which issues means of payment in the form of electronic money')[87] and 'payment institutions' (defined as

---

[81] Ch. 2, Sect. 4(iii) above.   [82] Ch. 2, Sect. 4(vi) above.

[83] Bills of Exchange Act 1882, s.2, discussed in Sect. 1(ii) above.

[84] R. Cranston, *Principles of Banking Law* (2nd edn., Oxford, 2002), 5.

[85] Directive 2006/48/EC Relating to the Taking Up and Pursuit of the Business of Credit Institution, [2006] OJ L 177/1, Art. 4(1)(a). See further Ch. 2, Sect. 7(i) above. The definition of 'credit institution' also includes an 'electronic money institution'.

[86] D.A. Sabalot, n.80 above.

[87] Directive 2000/46/EC on the Taking Up, Pursuit of and Prudential Supervision of the Business of Electronic Money Institutions, [2000] OJ L 275, Art. 1(3)(a).

'a legal person that has been granted authorization…to provide and execute payment services throughout the Community').[88] Institutions that fall within the scope of these categories are likely to engage in activities that would generally be considered part of banking business, even if those institutions would not actually be considered 'banks' for domestic law purposes.

It is tempting to argue that the existing legal position could be rationalized by providing a uniform functional definition of a 'bank', and by subjecting all the financial institutions covered to a single regime. A closer look at the City demonstrates that such a reform is unattainable.[89] The term 'bank' has traditionally been used to describe a wide-ranging group of financial institutions that are not necessarily united by a common thread. A clearing giant differs in its structure, business activities, and orientation from a traditional savings or co-operative bank or from a merchant (now investment) bank.[90] Undoubtedly, for certain purposes, all three types of institution can be treated in the same manner. The soliciting of deposits from the public is a case in point.[91] Equally, it is not realistic to draw any distinction between such institutions for the purposes of the Consumer Credit Act 1974.[92] For other purposes, however, the different institutions have to be divided into separate groups. The defences conferred on banks by the BEA 1882 with respect to the payment and collection of cheques are relevant to the clearing banks,[93] but are of extremely limited importance to merchant (now investment) banks and the traditional savings and co-operative banks.[94] It is thus clear that banks are treated as composing separate groups in view of the current structure of United Kingdom banking. The law rightly recognizes the existing diversification.

---

[88] Directive 2007/64/EC on Payment Services in the Internal Market, [2007] OJ L 319, Art. 4(4). See further Ch. 2, Sect. 6(iii) above, Ch. 13, Sect. 5(iv)–(vi) below & Ch .14, Sect. 9 below.

[89] Ch. 1, Sect. 1 above.   [90] Ch. 1, Sects. 2–3 above.   [91] Ch. 2, Sect. 4(iii) above.

[92] Ch. 2, Sect. 5 above.

[93] BEA 1882, ss.60, 80, 82. The last of these has been repealed and replaced by Cheques Act 1957, s.4.

[94] Ch. 11, Sect. 4 & Ch. 15, Sect. 4 below.

4

Money Laundering and the Financing of Terrorism

1 Introduction

The sudden acquisition, without explanation, of a large sum of money—especially in cash—invites suspicion that its source is some illegitimate activity. Generally speaking, 'money laundering' is the term used to describe the process that disguises the (usually criminal) source of money. The origin of the term is disputed: some point to the literal meaning of the expression ('laundering' or 'washing' money free from its criminal associations) whilst others point to the use of laundries (or rather, laundromats) and other cash businesses (e.g. slot machine gambling) by organized crime in the US during the Prohibition Era to integrate proceeds of their crimes into the legitimate economy.[1] But it was the rise in worldwide drug trafficking in the 1980s, and the money laundering of the proceeds of that activity, that prompted law enforcers to focus on the money laundering process itself, and on those involved in it, in an attempt both to stop criminals profiting from their crimes and to trace back those proceeds in order to catch the original wrongdoers.

It is traditional to analyse the process of money laundering into three stages.[2] The first is the 'placement' stage when the proceeds of the crime, often in cash, are 'placed' into the financial system, for example, by being deposited in a bank. The second is the 'layering' stage whereby the proceeds are moved, usually through a series of transactions perhaps involving different entities, different assets, and different jurisdictions, in order to sever any audit trail and hence make tracing their origins harder. The third stage is 'integration' when the criminal resumes control of the proceeds, free from any link to their criminal source. Without the network of banks and other financial institutions to facilitate the three stages of money laundering and to lend an air of respectability to the proceeds when they eventually reappear, money laundering would be largely impossible. Therefore, the financial and related sectors have always been positioned at the forefront of the drive to combat money laundering.

As well as 'taking the profit out of crime' and hence reducing both the incentives for criminal activity and further finance to fund it, curbing money laundering has other beneficial consequences. Its detection, especially at the 'placement' stage, may lead to the identification of the perpetrators of the so-called 'predicate offence'—the offence

---

[1] But this had the unintended consequence of rendering those apparently legitimate profits taxable—and it was for tax evasion that Al Capone was eventually convicted.

[2] See, for example, the FATF Annual Report (1990) (for FATF, see Sect. 2 below); William C. Gilmore, *Dirty Money: The Evolution of International Measures to Counter Money Laundering and the Financing of Terrorism* (3rd edn., Council of Europe Publishing, 2004); HMT's *Anti-Money Laundering Strategy*, Oct. 2004, paras. 1.4–1.7.

that generated the proceeds—and to the confiscation of the proceeds. Moreover, there are pragmatic economic arguments for seeking to combat money laundering in any particular financial centre. Depriving potential money launderers of access to financial markets helps those markets maintain a reputation for 'integrity' which enhances their stability and hence attractiveness. In addition, institutions used by money launderers face a number of risks[3] whilst other legitimate businesses are prejudiced by distortions in competition caused by unlawfully financed enterprises for whom money laundering and not commercial profit is the prime objective.

Drug trafficking and dealing—with the vast sums they generate that need to be 'laundered'—were the initial focus of steps to combat money laundering.[4] The focus was then widened to encompass the proceeds of other, especially organized, criminal activity[5] and more recently attention has turned to trying to thwart the financing of terrorism.[6] Although money laundering presupposes an illegitimate *source* of funds whilst the financing of terrorism entails the illegitimate *use* of funds, both adopt similar techniques in using financial institutions to 'layer' (i.e. disguise the origin and destination of) money. Given these common features and the importance of combating both, they are now treated as similar phenomena to be dealt with in a similar manner. Hence this chapter will consider how banks are affected by measures adopted in the UK to combat both money laundering (so-called 'AML'[7] measures) and the financing of terrorism (so-called 'CTF'[8] measures).[9]

2 An international response

The ease with which money may be transmitted from jurisdiction to jurisdiction means that money laundering and the financing of terrorism usually involve a number of financial centres. Indeed, cross-border transactions—in particular using offshore centres with laws protecting the secrecy of financial transactions—are a common feature of the 'layering' process. It follows that money laundering and the financing of terrorism will only be effectively disrupted if all jurisdictions play their part in the fight against both activities. Thus an international response—in setting standards and enforcing them—is required. The first jurisdiction to tackle money laundering was the US, through its Bank

---

[3] In particular, 'reputation, operational, legal and concentration risks': see the Basle Committee's Report on *Customer Due Diligence* (2001). For the Basle Committee, see Ch. 2, Sect. 8.

[4] In the UK the first legislative response was the Drug Trafficking Offences Act 1986, s.24 (now replaced by the Proceeds of Crime Act 2002, s.328, see Sect. 3(ii)(a) below). The UN's 1988 Vienna Convention (see n.13) and the EC's First Money Laundering Directive (see Sect. 2) only covered the proceeds of drug trafficking.

[5] In the UK, see the (now repealed) Criminal Justice Act 1988. The UN's 2000 Palermo Convention (see n.13) and the EC's Second Money Laundering Directive (see Sect. 2) covered proceeds of other crimes.

[6] In the UK, see the Terrorism Act 2000 (TACT 2000). The EC's Third Money Laundering Directive (see Sect. 2) extends to the financing of terrorism.

[7] Anti-money laundering.   [8] Counter-terrorism financing.

[9] For more detailed discussions, see S. Farrell QC, R. Booth, G. Bastable, N. Yeo, *Money Laundering Law and Regulation: Practical Guide* (Oxford, 2008); C. Howard, *Butterworths Money Laundering Manual* (London, Loose-leaf); G. Stessens, *Money Laundering* (Cambridge, 2008); P. Aldridge, *Money Laundering Law* (Oxford, 2003); and, for an international perspective, T. Graham, *Butterworths International Guide to Money Laundering Law and Practice*, (2nd edn., London, 2003). See also, *passim, The Journal of Money Laundering Control* and J. Ulph, *Commercial Fraud, Civil Liability for Fraud, Human Rights and Money Laundering* (Oxford, 2006).

Secrecy Act 1970, which required the reporting of cash and similar transactions over $10,000. However, the late 1980s saw a number of international initiatives.[10]

Although a number of international organizations,[11] for example, the Basle Committee,[12] began to respond to money laundering, the most influential initial measure was the UN's 1988 Vienna Convention on Drug Trafficking.[13] It adopted the now familiar three-pronged approach to combating money laundering (although that term was not used in the Convention): requiring the criminalization of those involved in money laundering,[14] the confiscation of the proceeds of the crime (including the need to identify and trace proceeds),[15] and international co-operation between law enforcers.[16] But although the UN and other international bodies continued to develop measures to prevent and detect money laundering (and later, terrorist financing[17]), the lead institution for international initiatives to combat these activities is now the Financial Action Task Force on money laundering (FATF).[18]

The FATF is an intergovernmental body established by the G-7 Summit in July 1989 to take the lead and to develop a co-ordinated international response to impede the use of the financial system for money laundering. Its secretariat is housed at the OECD and it presently has 34 Member Countries.[19] A number of FATF-type regional bodies have also been formed, which have observer[20] or 'associate'[21] status. Building on the UN and Basle initiatives, in 1990 FATF drew up 'The 40 Recommendations' on combating money laundering which set standards that governments are expected to meet,[22] with special emphasis on the critical role that the financial sector has to play. Although initially, as was the case in all anti-money laundering measures, its focus was on the proceeds of drug offences, in

---

[10] See E. Jurith, 'International co-operation in the fight against money laundering' (2002) 9 *JFC* 212; 'The Evolution of Money Laundering Control', ch. 3 in S. Ali, *Money Laundering Control in the Caribbean* (London, 2002).

[11] One of the earliest was the Commonwealth, see Brown, 'Money laundering: international law and the Commonwealth' [1994] *Commonwealth Judicial Journal* 24. The Commonwealth Secretariat continues to play a significant part in assisting Commonwealth States to implement AML (and now CTF) measures. See its publication: *Combating Money Laundering and Terrorist Financing: The Model of Best Practice for the Financial Sector, the Professions and Other Designated Businesses*, 2005.

[12] See Ch. 2, Sect. 8. In December 1988 it issued a 'Statement of Principles' (its full name being 'Statement on Prevention of Criminal Use of the Banking System for the Purposes of Money Laundering') urging national banking regulators to encourage their banks to adopt identification procedures for customers.

[13] Convention Against Illicit Traffic in Narcotic Drugs and Psychotropic Substances. It was implemented in the UK by the Criminal Justice (International Co-operation) Act 1990. See also the UN's 2000 Palermo Convention against Trans-national Organized Crime and its associated protocols.

[14] Art. 3. Its description of the money laundering process forms the basis of most domestic (including UK) definitions of the relevant offences.

[15] Art. 5.   [16] Arts. 6 & 7.

[17] See the UN International Convention for the Suppression of the Financing of Terrorism (1999) and its Security Council Resolutions Nos. 1267, 1333, 1373, and 1390 on terrorist financing.

[18] Its website is at www.oecd.org/.

[19] Including the UK, US, Switzerland, the Russian Federation, Luxembourg, Japan, and Australia. The European Commission and the Gulf Co-operation Council are also members of FATF. At the time of writing, there are two countries with observer status: India and the Republic of Korea.

[20] EAG (Eurasia Group), ESAAMLG (Eastern and South Africa AML Group), GIABA (Intergovernmental Action Group against Money Laundering in Africa).

[21] APG (the Asia/Pacific Group on Money Laundering), CFATF (Caribbean FATF), MONEYVAL (the Council of Europe Committee of Experts on the Evaluation of AML measures and the Financing of Terrorism), GAFISUD (FATF on Money Laundering in South America), MENAFATF (Middle East and N. Africa FATF).

[22] Unlike the UN's measures, FATF's measures do not have any legal force but are nevertheless very influential in setting standards, as explained below.

1996 the FATF extended its Recommendations to cover the proceeds of all serious crime. Moreover, as money transmission mechanisms (in particular electronic transfers) and hence money laundering have become ever more sophisticated, these Recommendations are revised periodically[23] and in October 2001—in the wake of the Twin Towers terrorist attack in New York—the FATF expanded its efforts to cover the combating of the financing of terrorism. In furtherance of that expanded mission, it has also issued nine[24] 'Special Recommendations' on denying terrorists access to the international financial system. To encourage its members to meet the standards set by the Recommendations, FATF undertakes periodic 'mutual evaluations' of members' compliance with them.[25] Originally, it identified jurisdictions that were regarded as seriously falling short of these standards and publicly designated these Non-co-operative Countries and Territories (NCCTs). This 'blacklist' no longer exists but instead FATF issues periodic 'warning statements' listing countries with 'deficient' AML and CTF systems. In the UK the Treasury has power to direct anyone subject to the Money Laundering Regulations 2007[26] not to deal with anyone within a non-EEA State to which FATF 'has decided to apply counter-measures'.[27]

FATF is the acknowledged leader in tracking trends in and then developing polices against money laundering and the financing of terrorism. Its Recommendations are used by the IMF and World Bank as benchmarks in so far as their 'financial assessments' of various countries cover those issues, leading to the imposition of conditions that AML and CTF systems must be adequate.[28]

Moreover, the EU has issued a series of Money Laundering Directives and a Regulation,[29] reflecting the FATF Recommendations, which Member States must implement with the result that the EU (at least in theory) comprises an area where anti-money laundering measures are harmonized.[30] To meet these EU obligations, the UK implemented the first such Directive[31] primarily[32] by passing the Criminal Justice Act 1993 and the Money Laundering Regulations[33] of that year. It implemented the second Directive[34] primarily by passing the Proceeds of Crime Act 2002 (POCA 2002) and the Money Laundering Regulations 2003.[35] It implemented the third Directive[36] primarily by amending POCA 2002 and the Terrorism Act 2000 (TACT 2000) and by issuing the Money Laundering

---

[23] At the time of writing, the latest version is dated 20 June 2003.

[24] Originally there were eight, but a ninth (on cash couriers) was added in October 2004.

[25] See the *FATF AML/CTF Evaluations and Assessments: A Handbook for countries and assessors.*

[26] See Sect. 3(iv) below. The sanction is criminal or regulatory: see ibid.   [27] S.I. 2007/2157, reg. 18.

[28] Combating money laundering has become an IMF 'core responsibility': see its Policy Paper (April 2001): 'Enhancing Contributions to Combating Money Laundering'.

[29] The EC Regulation on Wire Transfers: Regulation 1781/2006/EC, OJ No L 345, 8.12.2006. It has issued other Regulations, for example Regulation 881/2002, [2002] OJ L 139/9, considered in *R (on the application of M) v. HM Treasury* [2008] UKHL 26, [2008] 2 All ER 1097. See also *R (on the application of Melli Bank plc) v. HM Treasury* (Admin Court), 9 July 2008.

[30] See R.C.H. Alexander, *Insider Dealing and Money Laundering in the EU: Law and Regulation* (Aldershot, 2007).

[31] Directive 91/308/EEC [1991] OJ L 166/77, following the Council of Europe Convention on Laundering, Tracing, Seizure and Confiscation of Proceeds of Crime.

[32] See also the JMLSG Guidance Notes, considered below in Sect. 3(i).   [33] S.I. 1993/1933.

[34] Directive 2001/97/EC, amending the first and extending it to all serious crimes (not just drug trafficking) and beyond the financial sector (to, for example, estate agents, accountants, and lawyers).

[35] S.I. 2003/3075. They replaced the 1993 Regulations.

[36] Directive 2005/60/EC, consolidating and updating (in line with new FAFT initiatives, especially in relation to the financing of terrorism) the previous directives. See HMT, *Implementing the Third Money Laundering Directive: a consultation document* (July 2006).

Regulations 2007.[37] The EU Regulation, reflecting FAFT's Special Recommendation VII[38] on electronic funds transfers, has been implemented partly by regulations.[39] These and related measures in the UK are considered further in the next section of this chapter.

3 The control of money laundering and the financing of terrorism in the UK

(i) General

The UK regime—which implements the EU Money Laundering Directives and hence the FATF international standards as well as UN anti-terrorist financing measures[40]—comprises three main components as far as banks are concerned.

First, there is the primary (and in relation to terrorist financing some secondary) legislation which creates a number of 'money laundering' and related offences. The main primary legislation is the TACT 2000 and POCA 2002, as amended. The so-called 'regulated sector'[41]—which includes the banks as well as the rest of the financial sector regulated by the FSA and certain other businesses and professions[42] which are attractive to money launderers—is subject to additional offences to encourage its co-operation in reporting suspicious activities and transactions. Secondly, there are the Money Laundering Regulations 2007,[43] which require 'relevant persons'[44]—a term essentially synonymous with those in the 'regulated sector' and thus again including banks—to operate their business in accordance with specified systems and procedures designed to combat money laundering and the financing of terrorism. Each of these components is considered further below.[45]

Thirdly, there are the (lengthy) Joint Money Laundering Steering Group (JMLSG) Guidance. This sets out comprehensive guidance for the UK financial sector on detecting and combating money laundering and the financing of terrorism. The JMLSG comprises the leading UK trade associations in the financial services industry, including the British Bankers' Association, and was established in 1990 to provide guidance to its members (and their members) on both the legal and regulatory requirements and good industry practice (sometimes going beyond strict legal requirements) in relation to tackling money laundering. Although beginning as a self-regulatory exercise, the Guidance achieved an enhanced status when the original Money Laundering Regulations 1993[46] stated that a court could take account of the JMLSG Guidance[47] in determining if a

---

[37] S.I. 2007/2157 (as amended by S.I. 2007/3299 and S.I. 2009/209), in force on 15 December 2007 and replacing the 2003 Regulations.

[38] On the financing of terrorism, which imposes obligations on financial firms to provide 'originator information' in relation to wire transfers.

[39] The Transfer of Funds (Information on the Payer) Regulations 2007, S.I. 2007/3298.

[40] See Sect. 2, above.

[41] Defined in POCA 2002, Sched. 9, Pt. 1, as amended by the POCA 2002 (Business in the Regulated Sector and Supervisory Authorities) Order, S.I. 2003/3074 and then as replaced by the POCA 2002 (Business in the Regulated Sector and Supervisory Authorities) Order, S.I. 2007/3278.

[42] Including accountants, lawyers, estate agents, traders in high value goods, casino operators.

[43] S.I. 2007/2157, as amended by S.I. 2007/3299 and S.I. 2009/209.   [44] Regs. 3 & 4 (exclusions).

[45] Sect. (3)(ii)–(iii).   [46] S.I. 1993/1933.

[47] Or rather 'any relevant guidance' issued by a body representative of the business at issue. The JMLSG Guidance was the only such relevant guidance.

firm had complied with those regulations. As will be noted below,[48] this approach has been carried through into the 2007 Money Laundering Regulations, although the status of the JMLSG Guidance has been strengthened by enabling it to be approved by the Treasury and then obliging the regulators and courts to take account of it.[49] Moreover, under POCA 2002 and TACT 2000, in deciding if a person in the regulated sector has committed the 'failure to report' offences,[50] again the court must consider whether that person followed the JMLSG Guidance.[51] Thus it can be said that the JMLSG Guidance constitutes the third tier of money laundering control in the UK in that compliance with them is likely to provide a bank with a 'safe harbour'. Moreover, the significance of the Guidance was recognized by Colman J in *Hosni Tayeb* v. *HSBC Bank plc*[52] where he said that 'a customer who opens an account at a bank in this country must be taken to accept and be entitled to assume that the bank, if it forms a suspicion covered by [POCA 2002] will act in accordance with that Act and the Guidelines'.

Before considering these three tiers of the regime in more detail, the crucial role played by the Serious Organised Crime Agency (SOCA),[53] should be noted. The FATF Recommendations[54] require countries to establish a central 'Financial Intelligence Unit' (a 'FIU')[55] to receive, analyse, and pass on to law enforcers, information regarding suspected money laundering or terrorist financing activity. SOCA[56] is now[57] the UK's FIU and, as will be noted below, it is the agency to which 'suspicious activity reports' (SARs—sometimes called 'suspicious transaction reports' (STRs)) in relation to money laundering or terrorist financing must eventually be made.

(ii) The Proceeds of Crime Act 2002

The Proceeds of Crime Act 2002 (POCA 2002) consolidates and extends earlier primary legislation which both penalized those involved in money laundering and gave power to the criminal courts to confiscate the profits of crime. Previous legislation, beginning with the Drug Trafficking Offences Act 1986, was characterized by piecemeal responses to UN, FATF, and EU initiatives which, as noted above,[58] began by focusing on the proceeds of drug trafficking and then extended to the proceeds of serious crime in general. As well as rationalizing previous legislation and creating a single set of money laundering and

---

[48] Sect. 3(iv).

[49] S.I. 2007/2157, regs. 42(3) & 45(2), previously S.I. 2003/3075, reg. 3. See also the Transfer of Funds (Information on the Payer) Regulations 2007, S.I. 2007/3298 (see n.39), regs. 11(3) & 14(3) for similar provisions in relation to breaches of those regulations.

[50] Under ss.330(8), 331, & s.21A(6), respectively, see Sect. 3(ii)(b) & (iii), below, respectively.

[51] Or rather, 'any relevant guidance...approved by the Treasury'. At the time of writing, the JMLSG Guidance is the only such relevant guidance.

[52] [2004] EWHC 1529 (QB), [2004] 4 All ER 1024.

[53] Its website is: www.soca.gov.uk/. For a judicial review challenge to SOCA's refusal of consent to dealing after an 'authorised disclosure' (see Sect. (ii)(a), below), see: *R (on the application of UMBS Online Ltd* v. *SOCA* [2007] EWCA Civ. 406.

[54] Recommendation 26, see Sect. 2 above.

[55] FIUs from 105 countries are members of the Egmont Group—a network formed in 1995 (at the Egmont-Arenburg Palace in Brussels) promoting co-operation between FIUs. Its website is www.egmontgroup.org.

[56] Which includes a dedicated Terrorist Finance Team.

[57] Originally, NCIS (National Criminal Intelligence Service) was the UK's FIU but SOCA was established by the Serious Organised Crime and Police Act 2005 (SOCPA) as a result of a merger of NCIS with related agencies (the National Crime Squad) and departments of the Home Office (those with responsibilities for organized immigration crime) and HM Customs and Excise (those dealing with drug trafficking).

[58] See Sect. 2.

related offences, a major innovation of the Act was the conferring of extensive powers to take civil recovery action in relation to the proceeds of crime.[59]

Part 7 of POCA 2002 consolidated[60] and considerably extended previous legislation on money laundering.[61] In addition to creating a number of criminal offences, it also renders financial and other (so-called 'regulated') institutions potentially criminally liable unless they make 'suspicious activity reports' (SARs) to SOCA when they have reasonable grounds to suspect money laundering. These provisions have since been amended.[62]

(a) The money laundering offences

POCA 2002, Part 7 creates three, widely drawn, substantive 'money laundering' offences, with severe maximum penalties.[63]

The term 'money laundering'—when used in Part 7—is stated to cover the three substantive offences and also the related offences of an attempt, conspiracy, or incitement[64] to commit any of those three offences as well as aiding, abetting, counselling, and procuring the commission of those offences, wherever in the world the relevant act occurs.[65]

The three substantive 'money laundering' offences are wide in a number of respects. First, they must be related to 'criminal property' which is very broadly defined[66] as *any* 'benefit'[67] from *any* 'criminal conduct', being conduct that either constitutes a criminal offence in any part of the UK or 'would constitute an offence in a part of the UK if it occurred there'.[68] No restrictions are placed on the 'predicate offence'[69]—as long as the conduct generating the property is regarded as an offence in any part of the UK.[70] This goes wider than the UK's strict obligations under the Third Money Laundering Directive[71] in not confining the offences to certain serious offences and in not adopting the 'double

---

[59] Originally, an agency ('ARA': the Asset Recovery Agency) was established by POCA 2002 for this purpose, but its functions were transferred to (*inter alia*) SOCA on 1 April 2008 by the Serious Crime Act 2007.

[60] In particular, in applying to proceeds of *all* crimes, it eliminated previous distinctions between proceeds of drug trafficking and proceeds of criminal conduct in general.

[61] In particular, the Drug Trafficking Act 1994 and the Criminal Justice Act 1993.

[62] By (i) SOCPA 2005 which narrowed the offences to some extent and (ii) POCA 2002 (Business in the Regulated Sector and Supervisory Authorities) Order, S.I. 2007/3278 (replacing Sched. 9) and TACT 2000 and POCA 2002 (Amendment) Regulations, S.I. 2007/3398, which implemented the EC's Third Money Laundering Directive (see Sect. 2 above).

[63] 14 years in prison. For previous Criminal Court of Appeal guidance on sentencing for money laundering, see *R* v. *Monfries* [2004] 2 Cr. App. R (S) 3.

[64] See the Serious Crime Act 2007, s.63 which provides that the reference to incitement (abolished by s.59 of that Act) has effect as a reference to (or to conduct amounting to) the offence under Pt. 2 of that Act.

[65] POCA 2002, s.340(11). For activity outside the UK the wording is 'an act which…would constitute [such an offence] if done in the UK'.

[66] POCA 2002, s.340(3). See *R* v. *Loizou* [2005] EWCA Crim. 1579, [2005] 2 Cr. App. R 37, noted [2005] CLR 885; *R* v. *Afolabi* [2009] EWCA Crim. 2879.

[67] Or anything that 'represents such benefit (in whole or part and whether directly or indirectly)'. And see provisions extending the meaning of 'benefit' in s.340(5)–(8) (including 'pecuniary advantage') and those as to 'property' (s.340(9)).

[68] POCA 2002, s.340(2). The considerable difficulties inherent in this 'single criminality' provision were considered by the Financial Markets Law Committee in their Paper 69, October 2004.

[69] See *P* v. *P* [2003] EWHC 2260 (Fam) above: tax evasion. Moreover, s.340(4) expressly provides that it is 'immaterial' who the predicate offender was, who benefited, and whether the conduct occurred before or after the passing of the Act.

[70] Thus it does not need to be an offence in the country in which it is committed.

[71] See Sect. 2 above. This is permitted by Art. 5 of the Directive.

criminality' requirement for crimes outside the UK.[72] However, as regards activity generating the property that is not criminal in the jurisdiction in which it occurs, it is now[73] a defence for the accused to prove that he knew or believed on reasonable grounds (an objective test) that the conduct occurred in that particular jurisdiction.[74] Thus, if the accused has no positive information about the location of the predicate activity, he is unable to take advantage of this defence and it will be immaterial that in fact the activity was not criminal where it occurred (as long as it is regarded as criminal in any part of the UK). Secondly, liability arises not only if the alleged money launderer 'knows' that the property is 'criminal property' but also if he 'suspects'[75] that it is—although the Act stops short of imposing liability on a person who merely should have (on an objective basis) realized that the property was 'criminal property'. However, as noted below, certain persons in the 'regulated sector' are obliged to make a SAR to SOCA in such a case—or risk criminal prosecution under the 'failure to report' offence.[76] Thirdly, the three offences are drafted so as to cover every conceivable activity that facilitates money laundering, including activities by the predicate offender himself.[77]

The first 'concealing' offence in section 327[78] covers concealing, disguising,[79] converting,[80] transferring, or removing criminal property from a part of the UK.[81] The second 'arrangements' offence in section 328[82] covers involvement[83] in an arrangement which the alleged launderer 'knows or suspects' facilitates the acquisition, retention, use,

---

[72] The original Money Laundering Regulations 1993 (see n.33) contained a 'double criminality' test.

[73] By amendments to ss.327–332 (noted below) introduced by SOCPA 2005, s.102.

[74] But the Secretary of State may, by Order, prescribe certain conduct to which, even if not criminal where it occurred, this defence does not apply. See the Proceeds of Crime Act 2002 (Money Laundering: Exceptions to Overseas Conduct Defence) Order 2006, S.I. 2006/1070: defence does not apply to 'conduct which would constitute an offence punishable by imprisonment for a maximum term in excess of 12 months in any part of the UK if it occurred there', but the Order *excludes* (*inter alia*) an offence under ss.23 or 25 of FSMA 2000 (i.e. the defence *does* apply to these FSMA offences). For those offences, see Ch. 2, Sect. 4 (ii) & (vii), above.

[75] For a discussion of this concept, see *R* v. *Da Silva* [2006] EWCA Crim. 1654, applied in *K* v. *National Westminster Bank* [2006] EWCA 1039: 'he or she must think that there is a possibility, which is more than fanciful, that the relevant facts exist'. This is subject, in an appropriate case, to the further requirement that the suspicion so formed should be of a settled nature. See also, Fisher and Bewsey, 'Laundering the Proceeds of Fiscal Crime' [2001] *JIBL* 11.

[76] POCA 2002, s.330, see Sect. 3(ii)(b) below.   [77] *R.* v. *Linegar* [2009] EWCA Crim. 648.

[78] As amended by SOCPA 2005, ss.102(2) & 103(2). It replaces (but imposes a subjective test) CJA 1988, s.93C(2) (inserted by CJA 1993, s.31) and DTA 1994, s.49—thus eliminating distinctions between the proceeds of drug trafficking and other crimes. See Stokes and Arora, 'The duty to report under the money laundering legislation within the UK' [2004] JBL 332.

[79] And s.327(3) (adopting the wording of the UN's 1988 Vienna Convention Against Illicit Traffic in Narcotic Drugs and Psychotropic Substances, see n.13 above) provides that 'concealing and disguising...includes concealing or disguising its nature, source, location, disposition, movement or ownership or any rights with respect to it.'

[80] See *R* v. *Burden* [2007] EWCA Crim. 863 on the meaning of 'converting'.

[81] Although there is no 'or' in the text, it is clear that these activities are alternatives (although they clearly, in practice, will overlap).

[82] As amended by SOCPA 2005, ss.102(3) and 103(3). It replaces CJA 1988, s.93A (inserted by CJA 1993, s.29) and DTA 1994, s.50—thus eliminating distinctions between the proceeds of drug trafficking and other crimes. See *R* v. *Tarsemval Lal Sabharwal* (2001) 2 *Cr App R* (S) 81 (on the similarly worded Drug Trafficking Act 1994, s.50) and (on s.338) *Squirrell Ltd* v. *National Westminster Bank plc; HM Customs & Excise* [2005] EWHC 664. For the suggestion that CJA 1988, s.93A was in breach of the ECHR, see T. Otty, 'Money Laundering and Human Rights' (2001) *New LJ* 634.

[83] 'enter[ing] into or becom[ing] concerned in'.

or control of criminal property[84] by or on behalf of another person. The third 'acquisition, use, and possession' offence in section 329[85] covers the acquisition, use, and possession of criminal property without providing adequate consideration.[86]

Finally, the only '*mens rea*' requirement common to all three offences is that they all relate to 'criminal property' which, as noted above, is defined so as to require the alleged money launderer to 'know or suspect' that it is such, although there is now the defence of knowing or believing on reasonable grounds that the activity generating the property occurred in a particular country where the activity is not criminal.[87] However, the second (very wide) 'arrangements' offence under section 328 requires the money launderer additionally to 'know or suspect' that the arrangement he is involved in facilitates the acquisition, retention, use, or control of criminal property by or on behalf of another person. There are no further '*mens rea*' requirements for the other two substantive money laundering offences. Thus, in essence, as soon as someone 'knows or suspects' that something represents the proceeds of activity (wherever it occurred) which would be a crime in a part of the UK, then further involvement risks being 'money laundering' under one or more of the three 'money laundering' offences unless the predicate activity was not criminal where it occurred[88] and the accused knew or believed on reasonable grounds that it occurred in that jurisdiction.

Although generally these offences may be committed irrespective of the amounts involved, a special qualification to all three money laundering offences has now been included[89] for banks and other 'deposit-taking bodies'[90] so that, in operating an account maintained with them, they will not commit the offences[91] if 'criminal property' of an amount below £250[92] is involved.

As the location of the immediate proceeds of crime often leads to the detection of the crime generating the 'criminal property' and hence to the apprehension of the perpetrator and confiscation of those proceeds, an incentive is provided to those who are at risk of criminal liability for money laundering to inform the relevant authorities. Thus it is a defence to each of the three money laundering offences if the alleged money launderer makes an 'authorised disclosure' to the relevant authorities and obtains 'the appropriate consent' to continue acting.[93] Authorized disclosures may be made before,[94] during,[95]

---

[84] As noted above, for the proceeds to be 'criminal property', the alleged launderer must also 'know or suspect' that it is such: s.340(3).

[85] As amended by SOCPA 2005, ss.102(4) & 103(4). It replaces CJA 1988, s.93B (inserted by CJA 1993, s.30) and DTA, s.51—thus eliminating distinctions between the proceeds of drug trafficking and other crimes.

[86] Defined in s.329(3)—see POCA 2002, s.329(2)(c) providing a defence for anyone providing such consideration.

[87] See n.73 above—subject to any Order made in relation to non-criminal activity of a prescribed description.

[88] And is not prescribed by Order made by the Secretary of State, see n.74.

[89] Added by the SOCPA 2005, s.103.

[90] Defined in s.340(13) (added by SOCPA 2005, s.103(6)) as a business engaging in the activity of deposit-taking or the National Savings Bank.

[91] But this concession does not apply to 'concealing' or 'disguising' criminal property within s.327(1)(a) and (b).

[92] The £250 'threshold amount' may be increased by Order made by the Secretary of State. An amount higher than the 'threshold amount' may be specified by a law enforcer in certain circumstances: see POCA 2002, s.339A, added by SOCPA, s.103(5).

[93] Ss.327(2)(a), 328(2)(a), 329(2)(a). For judicial review proceedings for refusal of consent, see n.104 below and accompanying text.

[94] S.338(2).   [95] S.338(2A), added by SOCPA, s.106(5).

or after[96] the activity that falls within one of the three money laundering substantive offences. However, disclosure during or after the activity only provides a defence if certain conditions are fulfilled. In both cases, the disclosure must be made by the defendant 'on his own initiative' and 'as soon as it is practicable'.[97] If it is made after the activity, the alleged money launderer must also have had 'good reason' for failing to disclose before acting.[98] If the disclosure is made during the activity, then at the time he embarked on the activity, he must not have known or suspected that the property represented 'benefit' from criminal conduct.[99] 'Authorised disclosures' need to be made to a constable, a customs officer, or a person nominated by the alleged offender's employer to receive such disclosures[100]—usually a Money Laundering Reporting Officer (an MLRO)[101]—and they need to be made in the prescribed form.[102] Finally, provision is made to ensure that an authorized disclosure overrides any countervailing obligations of confidentiality or the like.[103]

As well as making an 'authorised disclosure', to avoid committing the money laundering offences the informer must also obtain 'the appropriate consent' to continue acting.[104] This is consent from the person to whom the disclosure was made and, in essence, the relevant authorities have seven working days to respond. If disclosure is made directly to a customs officer or constable, then if the informer does not hear that he has been refused consent before the end of that period, he is taken to have the requisite consent.[105] If the disclosure is to an employer's 'nominated officer' such as an MLRO, he cannot give consent himself[106] but must inform SOCA who again has seven days to respond. If a refusal is forthcoming but then no further action is taken by the authorities within a further so-called 'moratorium period' of 31 days, then the activity may be undertaken at the expiry of that period.

Further defences are provided for those who 'intended to' make a disclosure 'but had a reasonable excuse not to do so'[107] and for law enforcers.[108]

(b) The 'failure to report' offences

Rendering disclosure a defence to the crime of money laundering goes some way towards encouraging the provision of information to the authorities. However, as noted above, it is of crucial importance to obtain the co-operation of those institutions who are essential for money laundering to occur at all. So, to encourage the financial (or 'regulated') sector, including banks, to be part of the information-gathering process needed to tackle money

---

[96] S.338(3), as amended by SOCPA, s.106(6) and TACT 2000 and Proceeds of Crime Act 2002 (Amendment) Regulations 2007, S.I. 2007/3398.

[97] S.338(2A)(c); (3)(c).　　　[98] S.338(3)(b).　　　[99] S.338(2A)(b).　　　[100] S.338(1)(a); (5)(a).

[101] That person will himself generally be criminally liable under either s.331 (if in the 'regulated sector') or s.332 (otherwise) if he does not pass the information on to SOCA.

[102] Under s.339. SOCPA amended s.339 to render it (generally) a criminal offence to make a disclosure otherwise than in the prescribed form.

[103] S.338(4): it 'is not to be taken to breach any restriction on the disclosure...(however imposed)'. Note the similar protection given to 'protected disclosures' by s.337, noted below.

[104] Ss.327(2)(a), 328(2)(a), 329(2)(a). For a judicial review challenge to SOCA's decision to refuse consent, see *R (on the application of UMBS Online Ltd)* v. *SOCA* [2007] EWCA Civ. 406. And see *Amalgamated Metal Trading Ltd* v. *City of London Police Financial Investigation Unit* [2003] EWHC 703, [2003] 1 WLR 2711, [2003] 4 All ER 1225 on (*inter alia*) a challenge to the withholding of consent by the (then) FIU.

[105] S.335.　　　[106] And commits a criminal offence if he does: s.336.

[107] Ss.327(2)(b), 328(2)(b), 329(2)(b).　　　[108] Ss.327(2)(c), 328(2)(c), 329(2)(d).

laundering, sections 330 and 331[109] of POCA 2002 create two new offences[110] of failing to make a 'required disclosure as soon as practicable' after suspicion of money laundering' is or ought to have been aroused. The term 'required' rather than 'authorised' is used to qualify this type of 'disclosure' in order to distinguish it from the 'authorised disclosure' which provides a defence to the three substantive money-laundering offences[111] and to emphasize that failure to report is a criminal offence. However, the concept is very similar,[112] the differences relating to the persons to whom disclosure must be made and the detail of what must be disclosed.[113]

The offences may be committed by—and hence the obligation to disclosure is imposed on—both any person acting 'in the course of a business in the regulated sector'[114] and any MLRO in the regulated sector.[115] In the former case, the disclosure must be made to the MLRO[116] or any person that SOCA has authorized for this purpose.[117] The MLRO himself must report to any person that SOCA has authorized for this purpose.[118] This potential criminal liability—together with the regulatory requirements under the Money Laundering Regulations 2007 discussed below[119]—has caused the financial sector to introduce wide-ranging 'systems' and procedures to ensure that its officers and employees fulfil these disclosure (more usually called 'reporting') obligations and hence that they do not fall foul of the criminal sanctions. These 'systems' are influenced by the JMLSG Guidance[120] as the court is required, in deciding whether a person is guilty of the offences, to consider whether he followed relevant guidance issued either by a 'supervisory authority'[121] or 'other appropriate body'[122] and approved by the Treasury.[123] The

---

[109] Ss.330 & 331 were heavily amended by SOCPA 2005, ss.102,104. Further amendments were made by the POCA 2002 and Money Laundering Regulations 2003 (Amendment) Order 2006, S.I. 2006/308 and the TACT 2000 and POCA 2002 (Amendment) Regulations, S.I. 2007/3398. See R. Stokes, 'The bank's duty of confidentiality, money laundering and the Human Rights Act' [2007] *JBL* 502 (arguing that s.330 may be incompatible with the Human Rights Act).

[110] There were more limited obligations in relation to drug dealing proceeds under the Drug Trafficking Offences Act 1986, s.26B (inserted by CJA 1993, s.18) and the Drug Trafficking Act 1994, s.52. Note the similar offences under TACT 2000, ss.19, 21A, Sect. (3)(iii), below. The maximum penalty is 5 years' imprisonment: s.334(2). There is a third 'failure to report' offence under s.332 applicable to MLROs or other employer-nominated officers to receive 'authorised' (i.e. those providing a defence to money laundering offences, see above) or 'protected' (see below) disclosures, but this is not discussed here as banks are subject to the more specific 'regulated sector' offences in ss.330 & 331.

[111] See Sect. (3)(a) above.

[112] Thus, like an 'authorised disclosure', it must be made 'as soon as practicable' and s.339 applies to enable the Secretary of State to prescribe the form and manner of disclosure and creates the offence of disclosing otherwise than in the prescribed form.

[113] Thus, as the obligation only arises if the identity of the money launderer or the whereabouts of the laundered property may be discovered (see below), such information, if known, must be disclosed as well as the general information which gives rise to the suspicious circumstances.

[114] S.330, as amended (see n.109 above). For 'regulated sector', see Sect. 3(i), above. It includes banks.

[115] S.331, as amended (see n.109 above). The section talks of 'nominated officer in the regulated sector' and the Money Laundering Regulations 2007, S.I. 2007/ 2157, reg. 20(2)(d) require the appointment of an MLRO, see Sect.(iv) below.

[116] See the elaboration of what constitutes 'disclosure to' an MLRO in s.330(9).

[117] S.330(4)(b)—as substituted by SOCPA, s.104(3).

[118] S.331(4)—as substituted by SOCPA, s.104(4).

[119] S.I. 2007/2157, as amended by S.I. 2007/3299, see Sect. (3)(iv) below.   [120] See Sect. 3(i) above.

[121] Defined in Sched. 9 (as substituted by the POCA 2002 (Business in the Regulated Sector and Supervisory Authorities) Order, S.I. 2007/3278) to include the FSA: see ss.330(12)(a) & 331(8).

[122] Defined in ss.330(13) & 331(9) to include regulators and trade bodies of professions and businesses.

[123] S.330(8); s.331(7).

JMLSG Guidance, having been approved by the Treasury, is therefore very relevant in deciding the contours of the offences.

In contrast to the substantive money laundering offences[124] and the 'tipping off' offences,[125] the *'mens rea'* requirement of these two 'failure to report' offences has an objective element.[126] First, the alleged offender must either 'know or suspect', or have 'reasonable grounds for knowing or suspecting' that another is engaging in 'money laundering'—a term which, it will be recalled,[127] includes not only the three substantive offences considered above but also aiding, abetting, counseling, and procuring the commission of those offences, wherever in the world the relevant act occurs.[128] In practice, no doubt, given the difficulties of proving actual knowledge or suspicion, most convictions are likely to be based on this objective alternative. Thus those working in banks that are used by money launderers are potentially criminally liable if they ought to have known that money laundering was occurring. This provides another[129] clear incentive on banks to adopt procedures that identify factors that provide 'reasonable grounds' for suspicion of money laundering and require employees (and ultimately their MLRO) to react to suspicions and inform the authorities. As noted above, as regards activity generating the property that is not criminal in the jurisdiction in which it occurs, it has now[130] been made a defence for the defendant to prove that he knew or believed on reasonable grounds (an objective test) that the conduct occurred in that particular jurisdiction.[131] Otherwise, it is immaterial that in fact the activity was not criminal where it occurred (as long as it is regarded as criminal in any part of the UK). However, as well as generally knowing or suspecting or having reasonable grounds to know or suspect that money laundering is occurring, the defendant must satisfy a further condition that was introduced[132] to narrow the circumstances when disclosure need be made to those circumstances when disclosure might actually help apprehend the wrongdoers. Thus, either he must be able to identify the money launderer or the whereabouts of the laundered property[133] or he must 'believe', or it must be 'reasonable to expect him to believe' (an objective test again), that the information may assist in identifying the money launderer or laundered property.

Three defences are provided but the only one that is likely to be of relevance to banks[134] is that the alleged offender 'has a reasonable excuse' for not disclosing.[135]

Finally, to cater for those situations where the common law imposes restrictions on disclosure (obvious examples being the duty of confidentiality owed by banks to

---

[124] See Sect. 3(ii)(a) above.   [125] See Sect. 3(ii)(c) below.   [126] S.330(2),(3A); s.331(2), (3A).

[127] See Sect. 3(ii)(a) above.   [128] S.340(1).

[129] In addition to having to comply with the Money Laundering Regulations 2007, see Sect. (3)(iv) below.

[130] By amendments to ss.330–331 (noted below) introduced by SOCPA 2005, s.102, see s.330(7A) & s.331(6A).

[131] But the Secretary of State may, by order, prescribe certain conduct to which, even if not criminal where it occurred, this defence does not apply. See n.74 above.

[132] By SOCPA, s.104, adding POCA 2002, s.330(3A) & s.331(3A).

[133] Tortuously defined as 'the property forming the subject-matter of the money laundering that he knows or suspects or has reasonable grounds for knowing or suspecting, that other person is engaged in': ss.330(5A), 331(5A), added by SOCPA, s.104.

[134] The others—which are only relevant to the first (s.330) offence committed by the officer or employee—are (i) the lawyers' 'legal privilege' defence (s.330(6)(b)) and (ii) that the employee did not 'know or suspect' (and hence the 'reasonable grounds' requirement is the only one that can apply) and was not provided with such training as is prescribed as to spotting money laundering (s.330(b), (c), (7)—a requirement of the Money Laundering Regulations 2007, S.I. 2007/2157, reg. 21).

[135] S.330(6)(a); s.331(6).

customers[136] or employees to employers) immunity from civil liability is provided.[137] This is part of a wider immunity enjoyed by anyone who, in the course of their trade, profession, business, or employment,[138] acquires information which causes them to know or suspect or have reasonable grounds for knowing or suspecting that someone else is engaged in money laundering.[139] Such disclosures—whether by those in the regulated sector or by those outside it who enjoy this immunity—are known as 'protected disclosures'. Such immunity is clearly desirable not only to clarify the position of those in the regulated sector when they fulfil their obligations to disclose but also to encourage voluntary disclosure by those outside that sector.

The circumstances in which a person is obliged to report suspicions of money laundering may also potentially give rise to criminal liability under the substantive money laundering offences, in particular the 'arrangements' category in section 329.[140] Thus, once someone reports that he knows or suspects that another is 'engaged in money laundering', he will be guilty of the substantive money laundering offence itself if he 'enters into or becomes concerned in an arrangement which he knows or suspects facilitates (by whatever means) the acquisition, retention, use or control of criminal property'. The word 'arrangement' is of very wide import[141] and would seem to cover any aspect of the money laundering process, for example, banking transactions. It is true that the definition of 'criminal property' requires the alleged offender to 'know or suspect' that it constitutes the proceeds of crime,[142] but once anyone 'knows or suspects' money laundering is occurring,[143] then it must follow that he 'knows or suspects' that the 'arrangement' or transaction facilitates the retention etc. of criminal property. Of course the 'required disclosure' may well satisfy the characteristics of 'authorised disclosure' and provide a defence, but this will not necessarily be the case. The 'required disclosure' has to be made 'as soon as practicable after the information...comes to him' and nothing is said about obtaining consent to continue acting. On the other hand an 'authorised disclosure' must (unless there is 'good reason' for the delay) be made before or during any involvement in the 'arrangement' and, moreover, 'appropriate consent' must be obtained to act. There is also the curiosity that SOCA is not stated to be a possible recipient of an 'authorised disclosure'[144] whereas it will be the ultimate—if not direct[145]—recipient of a 'required disclosure'.[146] A bank employee reporting suspicions to his MLRO before acting and obtaining consent from him to act is likely to be relieved of liability, but the MLRO will not give such consent until he has reported the matter to SOCA and seven days have passed. Thus in practice banks will 'freeze' transactions and wait for consent from their

---

[136] See Ch. 5, Sect. 5. And see R. Stokes, 'The bank's duty of confidentiality, money laundering and the Human Rights Act' [2007] *JBL* 502.

[137] S.337, as amended by SOCPA, ss.104(7), 105(2), & 106(3). The similar immunity for 'authorised disclosure' in s.338(4)—disclosures made to provide a defence to a money laundering offence—is noted above (see n.103).

[138] As it is only in these contexts that there may be a countervailing duty not to inform.

[139] Meaning, one of the three substantive money laundering offences considered above and also the related offences of an attempt, conspiracy, or incitement to commit any of those three offences as well as aiding, abetting, counseling, and procuring the commission of those offences, wherever in the world the relevant act occurs: s.340(11).

[140] See Sect. (3)(ii)(a) above.

[141] See, in the competition context, *Re British Basic Slag's Application* [1962] 1 WLR 986, affd. [1963] 1 WLR 727.

[142] S.340(3)(b).   [143] The prerequisite to having to make a SAR: ss.330, 331.

[144] Only a constable, a customs officer, or an MLRO is: s.338(1)(a).

[145] An MLRO must report directly to SOCA: s.331(5)(a).   [146] S.330(5)(a); s.331(5)(a).

MLRO after he has reported to SOCA. The difficulties such a course of action may create for banks are noted further below.[147]

(c) Tipping off

Investigations prompted by disclosures may be thwarted if the original criminal or any money laundering associates are 'tipped off' that suspicions of money laundering have been reported. Therefore, two so-called 'tipping off' offences are created by section 333A of POCA 2002.[148] The first offence[149] catches a 'tip off' (or 'disclosure'[150]) that someone[151] has made a disclosure under POCA 2002, Part 7[152] of information that came to that person 'in the course of a business in the regulated sector'. The second offence[153] catches a 'tip off' (or 'disclosure') that an investigation into an offence under POCA 2000, Part 7 is either being contemplated or actually being carried out. In both cases, the offence is limited in scope to tip offs by persons in the regulated sector,[154] and both offences require the tip off to be 'likely to prejudice' either 'any investigation that might be conducted following' the (initial) disclosure (in case of the first offence)[155] or the investigation envisaged or occurring (in the case of the second offence).[156] A series of defences are provided in sections 333B–333D of the Act in relation to both offences, the most general being that the defendant did not 'know or suspect' (a subjective test) that the tip off was likely to have the requisite prejudicial effect.[157] There are other defences for tip offs within an undertaking or group,[158] for tip offs between certain institutions (including between banks and lawyers) for the prevention of money laundering offences,[159] for tip offs to a 'supervisory authority',[160] and for tip offs by lawyers or accountants to their clients to dissuade those clients from criminal activity.[161] Thus banks who make SARs and employees who report

---

[147] See Sect. (4).

[148] Ss.333A–333E were inserted by the TACT 2000 and POCA 2002 (Amendment) Regulations, S.I. 2007/3398, in implementation of Art. 28 of the EC's Third Money Laundering Directive (see Sect. 2 above). The old (wider) 'tipping off' offence in s.333 (which replaced the Criminal Justice Act 1988, s.93D (inserted by CJA 1993, s.32) and the Drug Trafficking Act 1994, s.53) was repealed by *ibid.* (but see the offence of prejudicing an investigation in s.342 (as amended by the TACT 2000 and POCA 2002 (Amendment) Regulations, S.I. 2007/3398 so that it does not overlap with the offences in s.333A). The maximum custodial sentence was reduced from 5 years to 2 years (s.333A(4)(b)).

[149] S.333A(1), (2).

[150] Not to be confused with an 'authorised' disclosure (the disclosure which forms the basis of the defence to one of the three substantive money laundering offences, noted above in Sect. 3(ii)(a), see s.338) or a 'required' disclosure (required to be made under ss.330–333, noted above in Sect. 3(ii)(b)) or a 'protected' disclosure (which is subject to the civil immunity provided by s.337, noted above in Sect. 3(ii)(b)).

[151] Whether the person giving the tip off or 'another person'.

[152] See n.150, i.e. an 'authorised', 'required', or 'protected' disclosure.   [153] S.333A(3).

[154] As the information on which the tip off is based must have come to the defendant 'in the course of a business in the regulated sector': s.333A(1)(c); s.333A(3)(c). For the meaning of 'regulated sector', see Sect. 3(i), above. And note that the first offence is confined to a tip off that a disclosure has been made of information that came to the person disclosing, 'in the course of a business in the regulated sector'. The now repealed (see n.148) s.333 was not so limited.

[155] S.333A(1)(b).   [156] S.333(3)(b).

[157] S.333D(3), (4). Hence, as was the case under the now repealed (see n.148) s.333, it is not enough to have 'reasonable grounds' for knowing or suspecting (cf. the failure to disclose offences, ss.330(2)(b), 331(3)(b)).

[158] S.333B.   [159] S.333C—there are other conditions, see s.333C(2)(a), (c), (d).

[160] Of the person making the tip off: s.333D(1)(a). 'Supervisory authority' is defined in the Money Laundering Regulations 2007, S.I. 2007/2157, see Sect. 3(iv) below.

[161] S.333C(2). This is in marked contrast to the old lawyers' 'legal privilege' defence (s.333(2)(c), (3),(4)), considered in *P* v. *P*, n.69 above.

up to their MLRO[162] (as well as those in the regulated sector who 'know or suspect' that such a report has been made) must take great care in not alerting their customers that this has occurred.

Case law concerning the old 'tipping off' offences demonstrated that these offences may cause considerable difficulties to banks when faced with customers whom they suspect[163] or know[164] have criminal property in their accounts, as any freezing of the account after reporting suspicions to SOCA may 'tip off' the customer that this has occurred. The courts, whilst obviously available to give directions to the bank if it is uncertain how it should act, have encouraged the banks to try and seek a way forward with the help of SOCA before resorting to litigation.[165] The case law is considered in Section 4 of this chapter below.

(iii) The Terrorism Act 2000 and related provisions

As noted above, although efforts to prevent the financing of terrorism focus primarily on the illegitimate *use* of funds whilst those concerned with money laundering focus on the illegitimate *source* of funds, both activities have many common features, in particular the use of financial institutions to move and 'layer' their funds. Therefore the mechanisms developed in seeking to combat money laundering have been adapted and applied to combating the financing of terrorism. But, whilst money laundering detection pays particular attention to the 'placement' stage, combating the financing of terrorism relies primarily on monitoring transactions that lead up to the unlawful use of the funds. In the UK,[166] the relevant measures are now primarily found in TACT 2000[167] and in the Terrorism (United Nations Measures) Order 2006.[168]

Of particular concern to banks are the offences created by Part III of TACT 2000 Act. This defines 'terrorist property' widely as property that is either likely to be used for the purposes of terrorism or that is the proceeds of terrorism.[169] An offence (which is termed 'money laundering') is created by section 18[170] in relation to 'terrorist property' which essentially combines the features of the first two substantive money laundering

---

[162] As a 'required disclosure' covers such internal reporting.

[163] See *Governor & Company of the Bank of Scotland* v. *A Ltd* [2001] EWCA Civ 52, [2001] 1 WLR 751, [2001] All ER (D) 81, *Squirrell Ltd* v. *National Westminster Bank plc; HM Customs & Excise* [2005] EWHC 664; *K* v. *National Westminster Bank* [2006] EWCA 1039. See further, Sect. 4 below.

[164] See *C* v. *S (Money laundering: Discovery of Documents) (Practice Note)* [1999] 1 WLR 1551, [1999] 2 All ER 343. See, further, Sect. 4 below.

[165] As well as the cases in the two previous notes, see (in a family financial relief context): *P* v. *P*, n.69 above (applying them).

[166] See generally, *Combating the Financing of Terrorism: A Report on UK Action* (HMT and the Home Office, October 2002); *The financial challenge to crime and terrorism* (HMT, Home Office, SOCA, Foreign and Commonwealth Office, February 2007).

[167] Replacing, in this respect, the Prevention of Terrorism (Temporary Provisions) Act 1989 (PTTPA). That legislation was driven primarily by the IRA threat to the UK and hence preceded the New York 9/11 attacks. The relevant provisions of the 2000 Act have been amended by (i) the Anti-terrorism, Crime and Security Act 2001, (ii) SOCPA 2005, and (iii) the TACT 2000 and POCA 2002 (Amendment) Regulations, S.I. 2007/3398, implementing the EC's Third Money Laundering Directive (see Sect. 2 above).

[168] S.I. 2006/2657, replacing S.I. 2001/3365, as amended. But see *A* v. *HM Treasury* [2010] UKSC 2 where this order was held '*ultra vires*'.

[169] S.14. There is no '*mens rea*' requirement, as there is in relation to the definition of 'criminal property' in POCA 2002, s.340(3), see Sect. (3)(ii)(b) above.

[170] S.18 replaced the PTTPA, s.11. No offence is committed if the person acts in co-operation with the police, with their express consent: s.21(1).

offences in the Proceeds of Crime Act 2002[171] in relation to 'terrorist property' and similarly absolves persons who report their suspicions to the police.[172] Thus, a person commits an offence if he becomes involved in[173] an arrangement that facilitates the retention or control by another of 'terrorist property' by concealment, removal from the jurisdiction, by transfer, or 'in any other way'. Although there is no *mens rea* requirement as such, it is a defence for the accused to prove that he neither 'knew' nor had 'reasonable cause to suspect' (an objective test) that terrorist property was involved.[174] There is a more wide-ranging offence termed 'funding arrangements' that prohibits involvement in[175] arrangements 'as a result of which' money or property is made available to another in the knowledge, or with 'reasonable cause to suspect' (again an objective test), that it will or may be used for the purposes of terrorism.[176] It is conceivable that banks might commit these offences in taking part in 'arrangements' enabling a customer to move funds. In particular, as a result of the procedures and systems that they must have in place in order to detect and prevent money laundering,[177] they might be regarded as having 'reasonable cause to suspect' that terrorism is the source or purpose of the funds. There are two other offences that banks need to be aware of—fund-raising for terrorism[178] and using or possessing money to be used for terrorism[179]—not because they are particularly likely to commit them, but because these offences give rise to the 'reporting' offences noted below which do concern banks.

The Terrorism (United Nations Measures) Order 2006[180] gives effect to UN Resolutions[181] on restricting the use of funds and financial services by terrorists and it provides for the enforcement of the related EC Regulation.[182] It enables the identification of suspected terrorists and their organizations (so called 'designated persons')[183] and then provides for the freezing of their funds and economic resources[184] and the denial of financial services

---

[171] i.e. POCA 2002, ss.327 and 328, see Sect. (3)(ii)(b) above. The maximum penalty is the same: 14 years' imprisonment (s.22).

[172] Or, if an employee, reporting in accordance with procedures established by their employer for this purpose: s.21(2)–(7). See also ss.21ZA–21ZC (inserted by the TACT 2000 and POCA 2002 (Amendment) Regulations, S.I. 2007/3398, implementing the EC's Third Money Laundering Directive (see Sect. 2 above)) which provide defences to a person making disclosure to SOCA either before or after the arrangement or having a reasonable excuse not to.

[173] 'enters into or becomes concerned in'.   [174] S.18(2).

[175] 'enters into or becomes concerned in'.

[176] S.17, replacing the similar PTTPA, s.9(2). Again the maximum penalty is 14 years' imprisonment (s.22). No offence is committed if the person acts in co-operation with the police, with their express consent or if he discloses his suspicions to the police (or in accordance with an employer's procedure for that purpose): s.21. And the defences in ss.21ZA–21ZC (see n.172 above) are also applicable.

[177] See Sect. (3)(iv) below.

[178] S.15, replacing PTTPA, ss.9, 10, in part. Again the maximum penalty is 14 years' imprisonment (s.22). Again, no offence is committed if the person acts in co-operation with the police, with their express consent or if he discloses his suspicions to the police (or in accordance with an employer's procedure for that purpose): s.21. And the defences in ss.21ZA–21ZC (see n.172 above) are also applicable.

[179] S.16, replacing PTTPA, ss.9, 10, in part. Again the maximum penalty is 14 years' imprisonment (s.22). Again, no offence is committed if the person acts in co-operation with the police, with their express consent or if he discloses his suspicions to the police (or in accordance with an employer's procedure for that purpose): s.21. And the defences in ss.21ZA–21ZC (see n.172 above) are also applicable.

[180] S.I. 2006/2657, replacing S.I. 2001/3365, as amended. For a successful challenge to freezing orders made under this Order, see *A v. HM Treasury* [2010] UKSC 2.

[181] Resolution 1373 (2001) and 1453 (2002).   [182] EC Regulation 2580/2001 on CTF measures.

[183] S.I. 2006/2657, arts. 3–6. Designated persons are either those identified in the EC Council Decision 2006/379/EC (made under the EC Regulation) or in an Treasury 'direction' under art. 4: art. 3.

[184] Ibid., art. 7.

to them.[185] Thus, it is a criminal offence to deal with such funds or economic resources or provide such services[186] without a licence from the Treasury, and to intentionally enable or faciliate those offences.[187] This counter-terrorist financing legislation also imposes disclosure or reporting obligations on banks by imposing criminal sanctions for not doing so in the context of the financing of terrorism. These offences preceded those imposed by POCA 2002 and are in slightly different terms. Thus section 19 of TACT 2000[188] makes it an offence for anyone who 'believes or suspects' (a subjective test)[189] that another has committed any of the offences created by that Act in relation to terrorist financing,[190] on the basis of information encountered in the course of a trade, profession, business, or employment, not to report this 'as soon as is reasonably practicable' (rather than 'as soon as practicable')[191] to a constable,[192] irrespective of any restrictions on disclosure.[193] This provision may clearly be applicable to banks but section 21A[194] makes special provision for persons in the 'regulated sector',[195] which includes banks. In essence, an almost identical 'failure to report' offence to that in section 330 of POCA 2002[196]—but in relation to offences under TACT 2000[197]—is created covering persons in the 'regulated sector'. Thus 'reasonable grounds' for knowing or suspecting such an offence has been committed are sufficient to trigger the offence in that context[198] and disclosure must be made 'as soon as practicable'. There is also a more general offence[199] of failing to report (as soon as reasonably practicable) to a constable information which the accused 'knows or believes' (a subjective test) might assist in preventing terrorism or apprehending terrorists.[200] On the other hand, the 'failure to report' offence under the Terrorism (United Nations Measures) Order 2006 is confined to banks. Thus, they are criminally liable if they fail to inform

---

[185] Ibid., art. 8.

[186] Ibid., arts. 7(3) and 8(2)—and note the defences for those with no knowledge or 'reasonable cause to suspect' that they were committing the offence. The maximum sentence is 7 years: art. 13(1).

[187] Ibid., art. 10. The maximum sentence is again 7 years: art. 13(1).

[188] Replacing PTTPA, s.18A. S.19 was amended by the Anti-terrorism, Crime and Security Act 2001 and SOCPA 2005. It is a defence to prove that disclosure was made in accordance with an employer's procedures for this purpose (e.g. to a MLRO): s.19(4)). There is also the usual defence of 'reasonable excuse' (s.19(3)) and the usual legal privilege provisions (s.19(5), (6)). The maximum penalty is 5 years' imprisonment (s.19(8)). See 'Confidentiality and the Duty of Disclosure' [2003] JMLC 248.

[189] Compare the wording in ss.330–332 of POCA 2002: 'knows or suspects or has reasonable grounds for knowing or suspecting'. But see s.21A, noted below.

[190] i.e. 'fund-raising' for terrorism (s.15), 'use and possession' of funds for terrorism (s.16), 'funding arrangements' for terrorism (s.17), and 'money laundering' terrorist property (s.18)—all noted above. See the extraterritoriality provision in s.19(7).

[191] As is the case under POCA 2002, ss.330–332.

[192] The reference to 'constable' includes a reference to a member of SOCA: s.19(7B), added by the Anti-terrorism, Crime and Security Act 2001 and amended by SOCPA 2005.

[193] 'imposed by statute or otherwise': s.20, as amended by SOCPA 2005.

[194] Inserted by the Anti-terrorism, Crime and Security Act 2001, Sched. 2, para. 5 and amended by the SOCPA 2005 and the TACT 2000 and POCA 2002 (Amendment) Regulations, S.I. 2007/3398, implementing the EC's Third Money Laundering Directive (see Sect. 2 above). See 'Knowledge and Suspicion under the Terrorism Act' [2003] JMLC 255.

[195] Defined in Sched. 3A (also added by the 2001 Act, Sched. 2, para. 5), as amended.

[196] See Sect. (3)(ii)(b) above.   [197] i.e. under ss.15–18 of the 2000 Act, see n.190.

[198] Compliance with the JSMLG Guidance is also relevant in deciding if an offence has been committed: s.21A(6).

[199] Not even confined to information obtained in the course of trade, profession, business, or employment, as is s.19 of TACT 2000, see above.

[200] S.38B, added by s.117 of the 2001 Act, reflecting PTTPA, s.18.

(the Treasury this time), as soon as practicable, knowledge or suspicion that a customer[201] is connected to terrorism[202] or has committed certain offences under that Order.[203] Moreover, the Order gives the Treasury a wide power, backed by criminal sanction,[204] to obtain information and documents from anyone (including, of course, banks) for securing compliance with or detecting evasion of the Order.[205]

Finally, TACT 2000 contains 'tipping off' provisions that essentially correspond to those in POCA 2002.[206]

(iv) The Money Laundering Regulations 2007

Not only must banks and other institutions in the 'regulated sector'[207] take care not to commit the criminal offences created by POCA 2002 and the counter-terrorism legislation, but they[208] are subject to significant obligations to operate their business in compliance with the Money Laundering Regulations 2007.[209] Thus these regulations comprise a second layer of legislation that affects banks in the context of money laundering and terrorist financing. As noted above,[210] these regulations—as did their predecessors—implement the EC Money Laundering Directives in part and require firms to adopt 'systems' and 'procedures' to reduce the opportunities for and help detect money laundering and terrorist financing.[211] A novel feature of the 2007 Regulations is that they adopt a 'risk-sensitive' approach[212] and that they contain additional enforcement provisions, including 'regulatory'[213] as well as criminal[214] sanctions. Otherwise, the specific requirements of the regulations fall into the following familiar categories.

The first category comprises the 'customer due diligence' (CDD)[215] measures.[216] These are defined to mean measures that both identify the customer (and verify that identity)

---

[201] 'or a person with whom [the bank] has had dealings': see the definition of 'relevant person' in Sched. 1, para. 2(4).

[202] As defined in Sched. 1, para. 2(2)(a) (and hence para. 2(1)).   [203] Sched. 1, para. 2(2)(b).

[204] Sched. 1, para. 4—and the court may order the information to be given (para. 5).

[205] Sched. 1, para. 3—but see the limits on disclosure of these imposed on the Treasury by para. 6.

[206] See Sect. 3(ii)(c) above. Thus ss.21D–21H are (*mutatis mutandis*) in almost identical terms to POCA 2002, ss.333A–333E, both being inserted in the relevant Acts by the TACT 2000 and POCA 2002 (Amendment) Regulations, S.I. 2007/3398, implementing the EC's Third Money Laundering Directive (see Sect. 2 above). And see the offences of prejudicing an investigation in s.39, replacing PTTPA, s.17, (as amended by the TACT 2000 and POCA 2002 (Amendment) Regulations, S.I. 2007/3398 so that the s.39 offences do not overlap with those in s.21D).

[207] For the meaning of 'regulated sector', see Sect. 3(i) above.

[208] As 'relevant persons' for the purposes of the Regulations, see regs. 2(1), 3, and 4.

[209] S.I. 2007/2157 (as amended by S.I. 2007/3299 and S.I. 2009/209), replacing previous regulations, see Sect. 3(i) above.

[210] Sect. 3(i). And see HMT, *Implementing the Third Money Laundering Directive: a consultation document* (July 2006).

[211] See reg. 20.

[212] See, for example, reg. 20(1) and, in relation to the CDD measures, regs. 5(b), 7(3), 14(1), 13, and 14 (simplified and enhanced due diligence), 17 (reliance on others).

[213] See Pt. 5, especially the power to impose civil penalties in reg. 42 (and reg. 48: penalty recoverable as a debt).

[214] Regs. 45–47.

[215] Previously known as the 'KYC' (know your customer) procedures. Their extent must now be determined on a 'risk-sensitive' basis: reg. 7(3).

[216] Regs. 5–18. Note the absolute prohibition on dealing with 'shell' banks or establishing anonymous accounts in reg. 16. Note also the obligations under the Transfer of Funds (Information on the Payer) Regulations 2007, S.I. 2007/3298 requiring electronic transfers of funds to be accompanied by verified information about the payer.

and discover 'the purpose and intended nature' of the business relationship.[217] The CDD measures must be adopted when the bank (a) establishes an ongoing 'business relationship' (for example, the usual banker–customer relationship),[218] or (b) carries out an 'occasional transaction' above 15,000 Euros,[219] or (c) suspects money laundering or terrorist financing,[220] or (d) doubts the veracity of verifying information.[221] The measures must[222] usually be adopted before acting for the customer[223] and, on a 'risk-sensitive' basis, at other appropriate times.[224] The 2007 Regulations introduced new provisions (in line with the 'risk-sensitive' approach) enabling banks to rely on certain third parties to undertake the CCD measures[225] and differentiating between situations which only require 'simplified' due diligence[226] and those higher-risk situations which require 'enhanced' due diligence.[227] In an attempt to extend the requirements in the Regulations beyond the EEA, banks are obliged to require their branches and subsidiaries located in non-EEA States to apply ('to the extent permitted' by local law) measures at least equivalent to those in the Regulations.[228]

These CDD requirements, in focusing on the 'placement' stage of the process, are a key feature of any anti-money laundering policy. Not only is money laundering most easily detected at this stage,[229] but it is during 'placement' that the proceeds are the closest to the crime and hence detecting money laundering at this stage could lead to the apprehension of the perpetrators of the crime and the confiscation of the proceeds.

Secondly, the bank must keep detailed records, especially of the CDD procedures and of all subsequent transactions for at least five years.[230] This requirement to retain records of transactions should facilitate the establishment of an audit trail and help unravel the 'layering' stage of any money laundering or terrorist financing process.

Thirdly, banks are required to have 'risk-sensitive policies and procedures', not only as to CDD and record-keeping but also as to reporting, internal control, and risk assessment and management.[231] In particular, they must appoint an MLRO to receive reports

---

[217]   Reg. 5. The verification must be on the basis of information 'from a reliable and independent source'. And see reg. 5(b) on the need to identify the 'beneficial owner' of the customer.

[218]   Reg. 7(1)(a), 'business relationship' being defined in reg. 2(1) to mean one expected 'to have an element of duration'.

[219]   Reg. 7(1)(b), 'occasion transaction' being defined in reg. 2(1) to mean one above that financial threshold that is not part of a 'business relationship' and 'whether the transaction is carried out in a single operation or several operations which appear linked'. The technique of breaking proceeds down into smaller amounts beneath the threshold to avoid detection is called 'smurfing'.

[220]   Reg. 7(1)(c), For the meaning of 'suspects', see the discussion at Sect. 3(ii)(a), n.75 above.

[221]   Reg. 7(1)(d).   [222]   Reg. 11: requirement to cease transactions etc.

[223]   See reg. 9, which sometimes permits verification to be completed during the establishment of the relationship. In particular (reg. 9(5)), banks may open an account before verification provided that no transactions are carried out before verification has been completed.

[224]   Reg. 7(2). See also reg. 8 (ongoing monitoring of a business relationship).

[225]   Reg. 17. This reliance does not absolve the bank from liability for any failure to apply the CCD measures. Those third parties must fall within the 'reliable' categories in reg. 17(2) (e.g. other authorized banks) and must consent to being relied on.

[226]   See reg. 13, for example if the customer is another supervised bank or institution that is itself subject to the Third Money Laundering Directive.

[227]   See reg. 14, for example if the customer is not physically present or is a 'politically exposed person' (a 'PEP', as defined in reg. 14(5) and Sched. 2), with opportunities for corruption.

[228]   Reg. 15. Where local law does not permit this, the bank must inform the FSA and 'take additional measures'.

[229]   See HMT's *Anti-Money Laundering Strategy*, October 2004, para. 1.5.

[230]   Reg. 19. As regards records of identification the period is 5 years since the end of the relationship (or occasional transaction) and as regards transactions, it is 5 years from the end of the transactions.

[231]   Reg. 20.

of possible money laundering activity from other employees and officers in the organization.[232] It will be recalled that any person working in the 'regulated sector' commits a criminal offence under POCA 2002, section 330[233] or TACT 2000, section 21A,[234] if they do not report suspicions (or reasonable grounds for suspicions) to their MLRO or SOCA. The regulations reinforce this reporting obligation by requiring a bank to appoint an MLRO and to have internal procedures positively requiring such disclosures which, if not made, would give rise to that criminal offence.[235] Again reflecting the criminal liability imposed on the MLRO under POCA 2002, section 331,[236] if he does not pass on suspicions to SOCA, the bank's internal procedures must require the MLRO to consider if a report to SOCA should be made.[237]

Finally, the regulations require banks to train their workforce so that it is aware of AML and CTF law and knows how to recognize and deal with transactions that may involve money laundering or terrorist financing.[238]

These organizational obligations imposed on banks by the Money Laundering Regulations 2007 are backed both by a criminal sanction[239] and a (new) 'regulatory' sanction of the imposition of 'civil penalties',[240] both with a due diligence defence.[241] It should be noted that for breach there is no requirement that money laundering has actually taken place; it is enough if the bank's 'systems' fail to comply with the Regulations. Given the open-ended and imprecise nature of the obligations imposed, provision is made for the issuing of 'relevant Guidance' by supervisory or similar bodies, to be approved by the Treasury.[242] Acting in accordance with such Guidance is then of relevance if a court or regulator is called upon to decide if a bank has fallen short of its obligations under these Regulations.[243] For banks, the Guidance produced by the Joint Money Laundering Steering Group (JMLSG) is the 'relevant Guidance'.[244]

Finally, provision is also made to enable the Treasury to direct banks not to deal with persons based in countries to which the FATF has decided to apply countermeasures.[245] Failure to comply with such a Treasury direction has the same sanction as other breaches of the regulations.

(v) The FSA Handbook

The role of the FSA as banking regulator has been outlined in Chapter 2.[246] Originally, as part of that function, the FSA included a 'Money Laundering' Sourcebook in its Handbook, which imposed requirements on banks reflecting their obligations under the Money Laundering Regulations. Hence discipline by the FSA for breach of this Module was an added sanction for non-compliance.[247] Indeed, the FSA imposed heavy 'penalties'

---

[232] Reg. 20(2)(d).   [233] See Sect. (3)(ii)(b) above.   [234] See Sect. 3(iii) above.

[235] Reg. 20(d)(ii).   [236] See Sect. (3)(ii)(b) above.   [237] Reg. 20(2)(d)(iii).   [238] Reg. 21.

[239] Reg. 45: the maximum penalty is 2 years' imprisonment. See reg. 46 (prosecution of offences) and reg. 47 (offences by bodies corporate). The FSA is a prosecuting authority (see FSMA 2000, s.402(1)(b)).

[240] Reg. 42. There is an appeals procedure: reg. 44. The sanctions are alternative and cannot be cumulative (reg. 45(5)).

[241] i.e. the exercise of 'all reasonable steps and…all due diligence' to avoid the breach, see regs. 42(2) and 45(4).

[242] Reg. 42(3), (4) and reg. 45(2), (3).

[243] Ibid. The court or regulator 'must consider' whether relevant Guidance was followed.

[244] See Sect. 3(i) above.   [245] Reg. 18. For FATF, see Sect. (2) above.   [246] Sect. 4.

[247] See Ch. 2, Sect. 4(vi). Breach of the rules was also actionable by anyone suffering loss as a result of breach: see FSMA 2000, s.150.

on a number of banks for non-compliance with that Module.[248] However, that Module did not impose obligations over and above those arising under the AML and CTF legislation considered above and therefore it was decided to withdraw the Module and to rely on the general obligations to comply with the law elsewhere in the Handbook.

4 Some problems posed to banks by money laundering control

Before leaving this topic, mention should be made of how it has made life particularly difficult for banks, over and above the need (prompted primarily by the Money Laundering Regulations[249]) to make significant changes to the way they deal with customers and their accounts. One difficulty—the conflict between their duty of confidentiality and their obligation to report suspicions of money laundering or terrorist financing—has been addressed by the legislation.[250] However, this is but one of many dilemmas faced by banks when seeking to give effect to their obligations under the legislation.

A bank that becomes suspicious that proceeds of crime are in a customer's account faces a number of difficulties. If it does nothing and allows the customer access to the account, it risks being criminally liable for money laundering, most probably by committing the 'arranging' offence.[251] In addition, it commits an offence in not reporting its suspicions.[252] Moreover, it risks civil liability, on the basis that it has assisted in a breach of trust by the customer,[253] if it permits the payment out of funds. Indeed, the CDD obligations in the legislation[254] increase the likelihood of such civil liability, if proper inquiry would have given rise to suspicions.[255] Of course, if its suspicions are aroused, the bank is obliged to report them to SOCA.[256] As noted above, such a 'required disclosure' is likely to qualify as an 'authorised disclosure' and hence to provide a defence to any potential money laundering offences, but the bank will have to wait for 'appropriate consent' from SOCA before permitting any payment out, meanwhile freezing the account. However, it then has a customer who might wish to use his account. And if the bank refuses the customer access to the funds, the customer is likely to become suspicious that he is under investigation and therefore the bank risks criminal liability for 'tipping off',[257] especially if the customer presses for an explanation. As one judge, (with some incredulity)[258] put it: '[the bank] may commit a criminal offence if it pays or if it refuses to pay'.[259]

---

[248] For example, RBS was fined £0.75m (Dec. 2002), Abbey National £2.3m (Dec. 2003), and HBOS £1.25m (Jan. 2004).

[249] See Sect. 3(iv) above.

[250] See POCA 2002, s.337 (protected disclosures) and s.338(4) (authorized disclosures) and the corresponding provisions in TACT 2000, ss.20(3) and 21B.

[251] See Sect. 3(ii)(a) (money laundering) and Sect. 3(iii) (terrorist financing) above.

[252] See Sect. 3(ii)(b) (money laundering) and Sect. 3(iii)(terrorist financing) above.

[253] See Ch. 7(5)(iii) below.   [254] See Sect. 3(iv) above.

[255] See C. Nakajima, 'Money Laundering and Constructive Liability' in B. Rider (ed.), *The Corporate Dimension* (Bristol, 1998); *passim*, P. Birks (ed.), *Laundering and Tracing* (Oxford, 1995); *passim* F. Rose (ed.), *Restitution and Banking Law* (Oxford, 1998).

[256] See Sect. 3(ii)(b) (money laundering) and Sect. 3(iii) (terrorist financing) above.

[257] See Sect. 3(ii)(c) (money laundering) and Sect. 3(iii) (terrorist financing) above.

[258] '[it is] unthinkable that our law should put an honest institution in such a position'.

[259] Per Laddie J in *Governor & Company of the Bank of Scotland* v. *A Ltd* [2000] Lloyd's Rep. Bank 271, 287, considered further below.

Such dilemmas have already given rise to litigation and this has resulted in some limited guidance to banks.[260] The case law is considered more fully elsewhere in this work, but it is useful to draw attention to it here also. In *C* v. *S*,[261] a bank was faced with a court order requiring it to disclose certain information in the context of litigation between its customer and a defendant accused of defrauding him. The bank had already reported its suspicions to NCIS[262] and was concerned that it risked committing the 'tipping off' offence if it obeyed the court's disclosure order, a concern which was heightened when NCIS confirmed that, in its view, disclosure would constitute 'tipping off'. Thus the bank faced the dilemma of risking being in contempt of court if it did not disclose or being criminally liable for tipping off if it did. When the matter eventually came before the Court of Appeal, Lord Woolf MR gave some guidance, basically exhorting NCIS to engage in constructive negotiations with a bank, in particular as to what information could be disclosed, in order to resolve the bank's predicament. If this dialogue did not result in an acceptable solution, the court would rule on the matter, holding the balance between the interests of the individual seeking redress through the courts and the State in fighting crime. As regards the latter, Lord Woolf went so far as to say that it would normally be an abuse of process to prosecute a bank that was doing no more than obeying a court order for disclosure.

A partial solution to the more usual dilemma outlined above, when a bank is faced with a customer whom it suspects of money laundering and who demands his funds, is provided by the guidance given by Lord Woolf MR in *Governor & Company of the Bank of Scotland* v. *A Ltd*.[263] The claimant bank was informed by the Serious Fraud Office (SFO) that the defendant bank customer was under investigation and the bank therefore became concerned that, on the one hand it might become civilly liable as accessory for 'dishonest assistance'[264] if it allowed the customer access to the funds but, on the other hand, that if it froze the account it might become criminally liable for 'tipping off'. (The further dilemma posed by the money laundering offences arising if the bank permitted the customer to use the account[265] only became apparent during subsequent proceedings.) In an action where the bank tried to recover its costs in seeking an injunction to freeze the account (which was later discharged when no wrongdoing by the customer was established) the Court of Appeal gave limited guidance on how banks should approach such a dilemma in the future.[266] Lord Woolf MR again stressed the need for the authorities (the SFO in this case) to co-operate with the bank to try and find a sensible solution as to what could be revealed to the customer, but again if a bank was dissatisfied it should apply to the court for interim declaratory relief.[267] The bank should make the SFO—not the customer—the defendant (each party bearing its own costs unless acting unreasonably) and therefore any court order would protect the bank from criminal prosecution.

It has further been held that a bank that freezes a customer's account and refuses to release funds, pending the obtaining of permission to do so, is not in breach of contract

---

[260] See J. Wadsley, 'Banks in a Bind: The Implications of the Money Laundering Legislation' (2001) 16(5) *JIBL* 125.

[261] [1999] 1 WLR 1551, [1999] 2 All ER 343. Its full name is: *C* v. *S* (*Money laundering: Discovery of Documents*) (*Practice Note*).

[262] The predecessor to SOCA, see Sect. 3(i) above.

[263] [2001] EWCA Civ 52, [2001] 1 WLR 751, [2001] All ER (D) 81. See M. Chan, 'Banks Caught in the Middle' (2001) *Co Lawyer* 245–6. See further, Ch. 7(5)(iii)(c).

[264] See Ch. 7(5)(iii).

[265] See Sect. 3(ii)(a) (money laundering) and Sect. (iii) (terrorist financing) above.

[266] See also *Hosni Tayeb* v. *HSBC Bank PLC* [2004] EWHC 1529 (QB), [2004] 4 All ER 1024.

[267] Under CPR 25.

to obey its customer mandate.[268] As releasing the funds without permission would be a criminal offence, the contract is either suspended pending the giving of consent or frustrated should consent not be forthcoming. As for potential criminal liability for 'tipping off', the court[269] agreed that the bank could utilize the (then existing) 'lawyer's defence' to the tipping off offence and hence procure its solicitors to reveal to the lawyers of the customer, the reason for the freezing of the account.[270]

---

[268] *K v. National Westminster Bank* [2006] EWCA 1039; *Squirrell Ltd v. National Westminster Bank plc; HM Customs & Excise* [2005] EWHC 664, Laddie J. Both cases concerned the seeking of an injunction by the customer ordering the bank to obey its mandate to release funds. The former case also held that such limited interference with the customer's rights was not a breach of the European Human Rights Convention.

[269] *K v. National Westminster Bank* [2006] EWCA 1039.

[270] See now s.333C(2) and (1)(c),(d). The case was decided in relation to the (now repealed) POCA 2002, s.333 (see n.148 above), which provided a 'lawyer's defence' in different terms.

5

The Bank and its Customers

1 The legal nature of the problem

Presently, being the customer of a bank has no magical effect on a person's standing in everyday life. Over 90 per cent of the United Kingdom's adult population maintains a bank account and accordingly counts as a 'customer'.[1] The position differed in the nineteenth century, when the maintenance of a bank account enhanced a person's financial standing and creditworthiness, as banks were particular in their selection of customers. Indeed, until the end of the First World War, banks generally acted only for businessmen, the professions, and the landed classes, and the bank-customer relationship was a particularly close one. Nowadays, holding an account with a bank leads to three prosaic legal consequences. First, and probably of more concern to the bank than the customer, where a bank collects in good faith and without negligence a cheque for its 'customer', it is entitled to a statutory defence against the 'true owner'.[2] Secondly, a bank owes a duty to honour its customer's cheques and other payment instructions,[3] and to obey its customer's instruction as regards the collection of cheques and other effects payable to him. Thirdly, a bank owes certain incidental duties to its customer,[4] such as a common law and equitable duty of care, a duty of confidentiality and sometimes fiduciary duties similar to those owed by a trustee. These are analysed further below, once it has been established who qualifies as a 'customer' of a bank.

2 Who is a customer?

There is no comprehensive statutory definition of the term 'customer', nor is it specifically defined in the Bills of Exchange Act 1882 (BEA 1882) or the Cheques Act 1957. At one time, a person was thought to become a bank's customer only when banking services were habitually performed for him by that bank; merely opening an account in that customer's name was insufficient to confer that status.[5] This view was questioned in *Lacave*

---

[1] *Banking Services: Law and Practice*, Report by the Review Committee Chaired by Professor R.B. Jack CBE (London, 1989, Cm. 622), [2.20]. In 2004, it was estimated that around 95 per cent of the adult population in the United Kingdom had some form of bank or building society account: Association for Payment Clearing Services (APACS), *Yearbook of Payment Statistics 2004*, 6. This trend towards greater financial inclusion is likely to continue as government initiatives, such as the Financial Inclusion Taskforce, encourage banks to offer 'basic accounts' to those unable to open a standard account: Ch. 1, Sect. 2(iii) above.

[2] Cheques Act 1957, s.4, as amended by the Cheques Act 1992, s.3.   [3] Ch. 11, Sect. 1 below.

[4] A bank is more likely to owe a common law duty of care to a customer than a non-customer: *Abou-Rahmah* v. *Abacha* [2005] EWHC 2662 (QB), [68], affd. on a different point: [2007] 1 Lloyd's Rep 115 (CA).

[5] *Matthews* v. *Williams, Brown & Co.* (1894) 10 TLR 386.

& Co. v. Crédit Lyonnais,[6] and discarded in Ladbroke & Co. v. Todd,[7] in which a thief stole a cheque that he then paid into an account opened with the defendant bank in the name of the instrument's ostensible payee, before disappearing with the proceeds. The drawer of the cheque sued for its conversion. As a defence, the bank relied on section 82 of the BEA 1882 (since replaced by section 4 of the Cheques Act 1957),[8] but it was argued that this provision was inapplicable, as the thief did not become the defendant bank's customer simply by opening an account. Bailhache J held that the thief had become a customer when the bank agreed to open the account, and that the advice to the thief that the proceeds could not be withdrawn before clearance was irrelevant in this regard.

A similar conclusion was reached in Commissioners of Taxation v. English, Scottish and Australian Bank Ltd,[9] where a thief stole a cheque payable to the Commissioners of Taxation from its premises and paid it into an account opened by him with the defendant bank, which then collected the proceeds of the cheque on his behalf. Just as in Ladbroke, the success of the defendant bank's statutory defence to the Commissioners' claim for the cheque's conversion depended upon whether the thief had become that bank's customer by reason of the single transaction involved. Lord Dunedin observed:[10]

> ...the word 'customer' signifies a relationship in which duration is not of the essence. A person whose money has been accepted by a bank on the footing that they undertake to honour cheques up to the amount standing to his credit is...a customer of the bank...irrespective of whether his connection is of short or long standing. The contrast is not between an habitué and a newcomer, but between a person for whom the bank performs a casual service, such as, for instance, cashing a cheque for a person introduced by one of their customers, and a person who has an account of his own at the bank.

Where a bank performs a casual service for someone, that person does not become a customer even if the service is performed on a regular basis. In Great Western Railway Co. v. London and County Banking Co. Ltd,[11] a rate collector habitually cashed cheques at the defendant bank where his employer maintained its account. On each occasion, the rate collector retained part of the amount and asked that the balance be credited to his employer's account. In one instance, where the rate collector cashed a cheque that had been fraudulently obtained from ratepayers, the employer sued the bank in conversion. The availability of the bank's statutory defence depended upon whether the cheque had been collected by the bank for a 'customer'. The House of Lords held that, although the bank had regularly cashed cheques at the rate collector's request over the years, he was not a customer as he maintained no account with the bank.

Accordingly, the existence of an account is the touchstone of whether a person is a 'customer' of a particular bank.[12] It is irrelevant whether the account is overdrawn or in credit,[13] and whether the account is a current account, savings account, deposit account, or even a credit card account. Increasingly, however, there are suggestions that a 'customer' might include persons who receive services from a bank without necessarily holding an

---

[6] [1897] 1 QB 148, 154; Great Western Railway v. London and County Banking Co. [1901] AC 414, 420, 422–423 (HL).

[7] (1914) 30 TLR 433. Cf. Tate v. Wilts and Dorset Bank (1899) 1 LDAB 286.   [8] Ch. 15, Sect. 4 below.

[9] [1920] AC 683 (PC).

[10] Ibid., 687. See also Oriental Bank of Malaya v. Rubber Industry (Replanting) Board [1957] 1 MLJ 153, 155–156 (MCA).

[11] N.6 above, 425. Consider Brazill v. Willoughby [2009] EWHC 1633 (Ch), [54]–[58], [113]–[116].

[12] Iskandar v. Bank of America National Trust & Savings Association [1998] 1 SLR 37, [33]; Y-LL v. W-HC [2008] NZFLR 432, [34].

[13] Clarke v. London and County Banking Co. [1897] 1 QB 552, 554.

account. There are certainly judicial indications to this effect in Canada,[14] New Zealand,[15] and Malaysia.[16] In the United Kingdom, section 59(11) of the Financial Services and Markets Act 2000 (FSMA 2000) provides some support for this suggestion by defining a 'customer', in relation to an authorized person, as a person 'who is using, or who is or may be contemplating using, any of the services provided by the authorised person'. Moreover, since the introduction of the FSA's *Banking: Conduct of Business Sourcebook* (BCOBS) on 1 November 2009,[17] the *FSA Handbook* has contained the term 'banking customer', which the *Glossary* defines as a consumer, a micro-enterprise, or a charity with an annual income of less than £1 million, without there being any further requirement that those persons hold any form of account before qualifying as a 'customer'.[18] These developments have yet to have any impact on the definition utilized by the United Kingdom courts. Even on the traditional view that a 'customer' equates to an account holder, however, there remains one exceptional situation in which a person may be a 'customer' without a relevant account, namely where a clearing bank regularly collects cheques remitted by a non-clearing bank on behalf of the latter bank's customers. In *Importers Co. Ltd* v. *Westminster Bank Ltd*,[19] where an English clearing bank regularly collected cheques on behalf of a foreign bank that maintained only a 'drawing account' with the English bank, Bankes LJ stated: '[i]n this case this class of business of collecting cheques was done between bank and bank, and it seems to me impossible to contend, as a matter of law, that the bank for which the [clearing bankers] were doing business were not, in reference to that business, their customer'. Although Atkin LJ agreed with this conclusion, adopting a more traditional stance, he considered the maintenance of the 'drawing account' to be the critical feature.

Occasionally, it is important to determine the precise moment at which the banker–customer relationship comes into existence. *Ladbroke & Co.* v. *Todd*[20] suggests that this occurs when the bank agrees to open the relevant account. This view is supported by *Woods* v. *Martins Bank Ltd*,[21] in which the claimant, who had little business experience and who had inherited a considerable amount of money, received negligent investment advice from one of the defendant bank's branch managers. When the claimant sought to recover damages for his lost investments, the issue arose as to whether a banker–customer relationship existed at the time that the negligent advice was given. Although the claimant had no account with the defendant bank at the time of receiving that advice, when the claimant subsequently decided to act upon that advice, he asked the defendant bank to collect the balance of an account that he maintained with another financial institution;

---

[14] *Central Computer Services Ltd* v. *Toronto Dominion Bank* (1979) 1 Man R (2d) 402, [27] (MBCA). A wider statutory definition of 'customer' now exists in Canada after the Bank Act 2001, S.C. 2001, c. 9: M.H. Ogilvie, 'Banker and Customer: The Five-Year Review 2000–2005' (2007–2008) 23 *BFLR* 107, 110–111.

[15] *Warren Metals Ltd* v. *Colonial Catering Co. Ltd* [1975] 1 NZLR 273, 276.

[16] *Formosa Resort Properties Sdn Bhd* v. *Bank Bumiputra Malaysia Bhd* [2009] MLJU 243 (MCA).

[17] Ch. 2, Sect. 6 above.

[18] Similarly, there is no reference to account-holding in the definition of 'customer' in the *Lending Code* (November 2009), [10]; the *Lending Code* (March 2011), [12]. See also *Banking Code* (March 2008), *Glossary*; cf. *Business Banking Code* (March 2008), *Glossary*.

[19] [1927] 2 KB 297, 305 (CA). See also *Hon. Soc. of the Middle Temple* v. *Lloyd's Bank plc* [1999] 1 All ER (Comm.) 193; *Linklaters (a firm)* v. *HSBC Bank plc* [2003] 2 Lloyd's Rep. 545. See further Ch. 10, Sect. 2 below. The foreign bank's customer, on whose behalf the cheque is being collected, is not the English clearer's customer: *Aschkenasy* v. *Midland Bank Ltd* (1934) 50 TLR 209, affd. 51 TLR 34; *Kahler* v. *Midland Bank Ltd* [1948] 1 All ER 811, affd. [1950] AC 24 (HL).

[20] N.7 above.

[21] [1959] 1 QB 55. See also *Hamid* v. *Perdana Merchant Bankers Bhd* [2006] MLJ 1, [24] (MCA); cf. *Balmoral Supermarkets Ltd* v. *Bank of New Zealand* [1974] 2 NZLR 155, 157 (banker–customer relationship arises upon the actual deposit of funds).

to use the bulk of those funds to make the investments suggested by the branch manager; and to credit any remaining sums to a new account to be opened with the defendant bank. Salmon J held that the banker–customer relationship came into existence when the branch manager accepted the claimant's instruction to open an account in his name. As the investment advice had been reiterated on that occasion, his Lordship held that the defendant bank had failed to observe the contractual duty of care implied into every banker–customer relationship.[22]

Even when an account has been opened, identifying the bank's customer is not always straightforward. In *Marfani & Co. Ltd* v. *Midland Bank Ltd*,[23] a fraudster opened an account with the defendant bank in the name of 'Eliaszade', who was a client of the fraudster's employer, and paid a cheque drawn on his employer and payable to 'Eliaszade' into that account. In considering whether the bank might rely upon section 4 of the Cheques Act 1957 as a defence to the employer's conversion claim,[24] the Court of Appeal held that the bank's customer was the fraudster and not the genuine 'Eliaszade', who had never intended to create a banker–customer relationship with the defendant bank. Similarly, in *Stoney Stanton Supplies (Coventry) Ltd* v. *Midland Bank Ltd*,[25] in which A forged the signatures of B Ltd's directors in order to open an account in the company's name, no banker–customer relationship arose between B Ltd and the bank,[26] with the result that the bank did not owe the company any contractual duty of care with respect to the monies fraudulently withdrawn from that account. Accordingly, the mere opening of an account in another's name, without their authority, does not establish a banker–customer relationship between the nominal account holder and the relevant bank. There must be a meeting of their minds. Exceptionally, however, the court may find that the person named on the account implicitly consented to its opening either before or after the event.[27] One example is where a domestic bank opens a foreign-currency account with a foreign bank in the name of a British customer who will be travelling abroad. In such a case, the customer gives his tacit prior consent to the opening of the foreign-currency account when he first instructs his own bank to remit his money overseas, although the customer may also be required to sign a formal application for the account upon his arrival overseas. Other examples include situations where a director or promoter opens an account in their company's name,[28] or where a parent opens an account in his child's name. In these situations, the company or the child may only give their consent some time after the relevant account has been opened, such as upon the company's incorporation or the child reaching majority. An illustration of this last situation is *Rowlandson* v. *National Westminster*

---

[22] Ibid., 63. Salmon J could only rest his decision on a duty of care implied into the banker–customer contract, since *Woods* pre-dated the recognition of a general common law duty of care for negligent advice causing pure economic loss: *Hedley Byrne & Co. Ltd* v. *Heller and Partners Ltd* [1964] AC 465 (HL). See also *Warren Metals Ltd* v. *Colonial Catering Co. Ltd*, n.15 above; *Morgan* v. *Lloyds Bank plc* (EWCA Civ, 3 March 1998).

[23] [1968] 1 WLR 956.   [24] Ch. 15, Sect. 4 below.   [25] [1966] 2 Lloyd's Rep. 373.

[26] The forged signature was a nullity and could not be ratified: *Brook* v. *Hook* (1871) LR 6 Exch. 89.

[27] A bank's failure to identify its 'real' customer in this context could lead to potential criminal liability under the Money Laundering Regulations 2007, S.I. 2007/2157, regs.5, 7, 45 (Ch. 4, Sect. 3(iv) above) and civil liability for the conversion of cheques wrongly collected into the account, as negligence in or about the opening of an account can preclude the bank's reliance on the Cheques Act 1957, s.4 (Ch. 15, Sect. 4(iv) below). See also Financial Services Authority (FSA), *Moneymadeclear: Just the Facts about Proving your Identity* (November 2009), 2–3. See formerly *Banking Code* (March 2008), [3.1]; *Business Banking Code* (March 2008), [3.1]. See further Ch. 2, Sect. 6 above.

[28] *Diamantides* v. *JP Morgan Chase Bank* [2005] EWHC 263 (Comm.), [27]–[28], affd. on other grounds [2005] EWCA Civ 1612.

Bank Ltd,[29] in which a grandmother approached a bank, at which she was known but with which she held no account, and deposited a cheque as a gift into an account opened in her grandchildren's joint names. The grandchildren's guardians were given the right to draw on the account, even though they were never specifically notified of the account's opening nor ever expressly consented to it. After the guardians eventually learned of the account's existence, one of them deposited a cheque drawn on the grandchildren's account into his personal account. John Mills QC held that the bank had committed a breach of its fiduciary duty to the grandchildren by permitting a guardian to act in this way. Presumably, a banker–customer contract came into existence between the defendant bank and the grandchildren as a result of the guardians' subsequent tacit approval of the account's opening. *Rowlandson* probably rests, however, on its exceptional facts.

Three main conclusions follow from the above analysis of the term 'customer'. First, the banker–customer relationship comes into existence when the bank agrees to open an account in the customer's name. Habitual dealings are not a prerequisite. The fact that a bank agrees to open an account in a person's name signifies its consent to having a regular business relationship with that person, which includes honouring his cheques and executing other types of payment instruction and collecting cheques or other effects payable to him.[30] Secondly, by virtue of the banker–customer relationship, the bank agrees to act as the customer's agent in banking transactions and to exercise the same degree of care and skill in this regard as can be expected of a reasonable banker. The scope of these duties, and any additional fiduciary duties, are discussed subsequently. Thirdly, a bank acquires certain defences *vis-à-vis* third parties in situations where the bank's operations on behalf of its customer, such as the honouring and collection of cheques,[31] would otherwise expose the bank to claims, such as for the conversion of a cheque.

3 The nature of the relationship between banker and customer

The banker–customer relationship is a contractual one, but what sort of a contract is involved? Bankers developed from goldsmiths acting as depositories for their clients' plate and gold, which essentially involved a bailor–bailee relationship. Such a contractual relationship does not, however, explain the nature of money deposited to the credit of a customer's account with his bank. Money does not easily lend itself to being the subject of a bailment,[32] and, even where a specific amount of money (such as a bag of coins) is deposited for safe custody, the bailee is expected to maintain the coins *in specie*[33] and, if he uses them as his own, the 'owner' is entitled to an account for any profits made by the bailee.[34]

---

[29] [1978] 1 WLR 798. If A opens an account in the name of his nominee, B, then A remains the customer: *Thavorn* v. *BCCI SA* [1985] 2 Lloyd's Rep. 259, 263.

[30] In *Libyan Arab Foreign Bank* v. *Bankers Trust* [1989] QB 728, 749, Staughton J hinted that the services that a bank is *bound* to provide to its customers by virtue of the core account relationship include 'the delivery of cash in legal tender over the bank's counter and the honouring of cheques drawn by the customer'. Services that are optional, and dependent upon specific agreement, include 'standing orders, direct debits, banker's drafts, letters of credit, automated cash tills and foreign currency for travel abroad'.

[31] Chs. 11 & 15 below.   [32] *Akbar Khan* v. *Attar Singh* [1936] 2 All ER 545, 548 (PC).

[33] *Balmoral Supermarkets Ltd* v. *Bank of New Zealand*, n.21 above, 158 (bailment relationship existed between cash being handed to bank cashier and the bank accepting that cash for customer's account).

[34] A bailor–bailee relationship can arise out of banks' safe-deposit services: *Canadian Pioneer Management Ltd* v. *Labour Relations Board of Saskatchewan* (1979) 2 Sask R 217, [29] (SCC); *Cuvelier* v. *Bank*

Such a classification of the banker–customer relationship would accordingly defeat the main reason for banks offering account services to customers in the first place. Likewise, this relationship cannot readily be explained on the basis of trust law principles given that any deposited monies are not specifically segregated, but commingled with the bank's other funds.[35] If the banker were a trustee of his customer's money, he would again be accountable for profits,[36] and the customer would be entitled to assert a proprietary claim if the bank failed. Indeed, it is now well established that the property in the customer's money passes to the bank following its deposit and that '[m]oney paid into a bank account belongs legally and beneficially to the bank and not to the account holder'.[37] That said, this fundamental principle might become subject to a potentially significant statutory exception if a proposal to introduce 'safety deposit current accounts', which means 'a deposit account in which legal and equitable title to any money is fully vested in the customer for whom the money is held',[38] were ever to become law.

The banker–customer relationship is most easily understood when one examines the nature of the agreement between the parties, namely that an amount, equal to that deposited, has to be repaid by the bank. In the case of a current account, the amount is repayable, without interest or with minimal interest, against the customer's demand,[39] and the customer retains the right to draw on his funds by means of a cheque or other payment instruction. In the case of a fixed deposit or savings account, the amount is repayable (usually with interest) either at a determined date or at call. In all these cases, the bank is entitled to commingle its customers' deposits with its general funds and is, therefore, entitled to use the amount accumulated. Accordingly, the essence of the banker–customer contract is the bank's right to use deposits for its own purposes and its undertaking to repay an amount equal to that deposited, with or without interest, either at call or at a fixed time. Adopting this analysis, the House of Lords in *Foley* v. *Hill*[40] held that the banker–customer contract was fundamentally a contract between debtor/borrower and creditor. In that case, a customer paid money to the credit of his bank account on the understanding that it would earn interest at an annual rate of three per cent. As no interest was credited to the account for approximately six years, the customer sought an account of profits from the chancery courts on the ground that, as a customer, he was either the beneficiary of a trust or the bank's principal. The customer also argued that the fiduciary nature of the banker–customer relationship meant that his claim was not statute-barred. The House of Lords denied an account of profits on the ground that the correct course would have been to commence a debt action for the amount owing before

---

of Montreal (2000) 189 NSR (2d) 26, [29] (NSSC); *Mohtadi* v. *Canada Trust* (2002) 6 BCLR (4th) 25, [8]–[9] (BCCA); *Jefferson* v. *Toronto Dominion Bank* [2004] BCPC 152, [14]. See further Ch. 16, Sect. 4 below.

[35] *Azam* v. *Iqbal* [2007] EWHC 2025 (Admin), [15]–[17], [27]–[29]. See also *Akbar Khan* v. *Attar Singh*, n.32 above, 548; *Ung Eng Huat* v. *Arab Malaysian Bank Bhd* [2003] 6 MLJ 1, [19]; *Leong Yew Chin* v. *Hock Hua Bank Bhd* [2008] 3 MLJ 340, [70]. See further Ch. 6, Sects. 1–2 below.

[36] *Evans & Associates* v. *Citibank Ltd* [2003] NSWSC 204 ('... how the bank invests the money deposited with it in order to earn a profit for itself is no concern of the depositor'). See also *In re Belfast Empire Theatre of Varieties Ltd* [1963] IR 41, 49–50.

[37] *Foskett* v. *McKeown* [2001] 1 AC 102, 127–128 (HL). See also *Re Global Trader Europe Ltd* [2009] EWHC 602 (Ch), [63]; *Dex Asia Ltd* v. *DBS Bank (HK) Ltd* [2009] 5 HKC 289, [69]–[70].

[38] Safety Deposit Current Accounts Bill 2008, cl. 1(2). Given the requirement that funds in such an account be segregated from the bank's general assets (ibid., cl. 1(5)), the banker–customer relationship in relation to a 'safety deposit current account' is would be explicable in bailment terms.

[39] Current accounts are considered further in Ch. 7 below.

[40] (1848) 2 HLC 28 (HL). See also *Attorney-General for Canada* v. *Attorney-General for the Province of Quebec* [1947] AC 33, 44 (PC); *Canadian Pioneer Management Ltd* v. *Labour Relations Board of Saskatchewan*, n.34 above, [26].

the common law courts. Emphasizing the debtor–creditor nature of the parties' relationship, Lord Cottenham said:[41]

> The money paid into the banker's, is money known by the principal to be placed there for the purpose of being under the control of the banker; it is then the banker's money; he is known to deal with it as his own; he makes what profit he can, which profit he retains to himself....

His Lordship added that, when the account was in credit, the bank's duty was to 'repay to the principal, when demanded, a sum equivalent to that paid into [his] hands'.[42] His Lordship's reference to the need for a 'demand' is important, since, if the banker–customer relationship were an *ordinary* debtor–creditor contract, the bank (as debtor) would have to seek out its customer (as creditor) in order to arrange repayment of the money.[43] Furthermore, *Foley* recognized that the limitation period would start to run against the customer from the date of any unmet demand, rather than from the date of the deposit.[44] Obviously, when the customer's account is overdrawn (whether as a result of a specific arrangement or the bank's tacit consent to the customer exceeding the account's credit balance), this does not alter the debtor–creditor nature of the bank-customer relationship, but simply reverses the bank's and customer's respective roles as debtor and creditor. As such an overdraft is generally repayable on demand,[45] the bank's claim against its customer for recovery of any unpaid amount should be statute-barred six years after the bank's repayment demand,[46] although there is authority suggesting that the limitation period runs from the date when the bank grants the overdraft.[47]

The principle in *Foley* was further illuminated in *Joachimson* v. *Swiss Bank Corporation*,[48] in which a partnership of English and German nationals maintained an

---

[41] Ibid., 36. See also *Libyan Arab Foreign Bank* v. *Bankers Trust*, n.30 above, 748; *Duggan* v. *Governor of Full Sutton Prison* [2004] 1 WLR 1010, [30], [35] (CA); *Azam* v. *Iqbal*, n.35 above, [16], [23]–[25]; *Uzinterimpex JSC* v. *Standard Bank plc* [2008] EWCA Civ 819, [39]. The same principle applies where a bank, acting as trustee, makes an authorized deposit of trust funds with itself as banker: *Space Investments Ltd* v. *Canadian Imperial Bank of Commerce Trust Co. (Bahamas) Ltd* [1986] 3 All ER 75 (PC); *Ross* v. *Lord Advocate* [1986] 1 WLR 1077, 1094 (HL).

[42] Ibid., 36–37.

[43] *Walton* v. *Mascall* (1844) 13 M & W 452, 457, 458; *Bradford Old Bank Ltd* v. *Sutcliffe* [1918] 2 KB 833, 848.

[44] *National Bank of Commerce* v. *National Westminster Bank* [1990] 2 Lloyd's Rep. 514; *Bank of Baroda* v. *A.S.A.A. Mahomed* [1999] Lloyd's Rep. Bank. 14 (CA) (discussed in Sect. 6 below); cf. *Pott* v. *Clegg* (1847) 16 M & W 321; *Re Tidd, Tidd* v. *Overell* [1893] 3 Ch. 154.

[45] Ch. 17, Sect. 2(ii) below.

[46] Limitation Act 1980, ss.5–6; *Bradford Old Bank Ltd* v. *Sutcliffe*, n.43 above. See also *Ogilvie* v. *Adams* [1981]/VR 1041, 1051; *DFC New Zealand Ltd* v. *McKenzie* [1993] 2 NZLR 576, 583; *The Royal Bank of Scotland* v. *Home*, 2001 SC 224, [8]–[9]. Where the overdraft is secured by a mortgage or charge over real property, the limitation period is 12 years both in respect of the overdraft itself and the mortgage: Limitation Act 1980, ss.15–17, 20. See also *National Westminster Bank* v. *Ashe* [2008] BPIR 1, [90] (CA). No statutory limitation period applies to charging orders: *Yorkshire Bank Finance Ltd* v. *Mulhall* [2008] EWCA Civ 1156. Under the Limitation Act 1980, ss.29–31, the limitation period can be extended by a borrower acknowledging his indebtedness to the bank: *Bradford & Bingley plc* v. *Rashid* [2006] 4 All ER 705 (HL); *Lia Oil SA* v. *Erg Petroli SpA* [2007] 2 Lloyd's Rep 509.

[47] *Parr's Banking Co. Ltd* v. *Yates* [1898] 2 QB 468. See also *The Canton Trust & Commercial Bank Ltd* v. *Fui Men Tak* [1973–1976] 1 HKC 121.

[48] [1921] 3 KB 110 (CA). The principle in *Foley* has been adopted in Australia (*Daley* v. *Sydney Stock Exchange Ltd* (1986) 65 ALR 193, 198, 201 (HCA); *National Commercial Banking Corporation of Australia Ltd* v. *Batty* (1986) 65 ALR 385, 392, 400 (HCA)), Canada (*Corporation Agencies Ltd* v. *Home Bank of Canada* [1925] SCR 706, 721; *Canadian Pioneer Management Ltd* v. *Labour Relations Board of Saskatchewan*, n.34 above, [26]), Hong Kong (*Root* v. *Nanyang Commercial Bank Ltd* [1982] 1 HKC 417, 420–421), Ireland (*In re Ashmark Ltd* [1994] 3 IR

account with the defendant bank. Upon the outbreak of the First World War, the account's credit balance was £2,312, but the partnership was prohibited as an enemy alien from operating the account. At the end of the war, an English partner sought to wind up the partnership's affairs and brought proceedings in the partnership's name for repayment of the account balance. As these proceedings had not been preceded by a formal demand for repayment, the Court of Appeal dismissed the action as premature.[49] Atkin LJ described the banker–customer contract as follows:[50]

> The bank undertakes to receive money and to collect bills for its customer's account. The proceeds so received are not to be held in trust for the customer, but the bank borrows the proceeds and undertakes to repay them. The promise to repay is to repay at the branch of the bank where the account is kept, and during banking hours. It includes a promise to repay any part of the amount due against the written order of the customer addressed to the bank at the branch, and as such written orders may be outstanding in the ordinary course of business for two or three days, it is a term of the contract that the bank will not cease to do business with the customer except upon reasonable notice. The customer on his part undertakes to exercise reasonable care in executing his written orders so as not to mislead the bank or to facilitate forgery.[51]

On this basis, his Lordship concluded that 'the bank is not liable to pay the customer ... until he demands payment ...' Six observations can be made about the general principle derived from *Foley* and *Joachimson*.

First, a customer's demand is only necessary in the case of a current account or a savings account providing for payment at call. In the case of a fixed deposit, maturing at a predetermined time, the amount involved becomes payable on the designated day without the need for any demand.[52] If the bank has not received any instructions with respect to the renewal or otherwise of the deposit once it has reached maturity, then it is acceptable banking

---

460), Malaysia (*Bumiputra-Commerce Bank Bhd* v. *Top-A Plastic Sdn Bhd* [2008] 5 MLJ 34, [10]), New Zealand (*Westpac Banking Corporation* v. *Savin* [1985] 2 NZLR 41, 48–49, 50–51, 59; *Westpac Banking Corporation* v. *Ancell* (1993) 4 NZBLC 103,259), Northern Ireland (*Jeffers* v. *Northern Bank Ltd* [2004] NIQB 81, [21], [25]; *JJ MacMahon (Building Contractor) Ltd* v. *Ulster Bank Ltd* [2007] NIQB 32, [6]), Scotland (*Style Financial Services Ltd* v. *The Governor and Company of the Bank of Scotland (No. 2)* 1998 SLT 851, 863 (OH)), and Singapore (*Bank of America National Trust and Savings Association* v. *Herman Iskandar* [1998] 2 SLR 265, [30] (SGCA); *Damayanti Kantilal Doshi* v. *Indian Bank* [1999] 2 SLR 306, [54], revsd. in part: [1999] 4 SLR 1 (SGCA)).

⁴⁹ *Commissioner of Inland Revenue* v. *Thomas Cook (New Zealand) Ltd* [2005] 2 NZLR 722, [13] (PC) ('... no cause of action arises in respect of money standing on current account until the customer demands payment by the bank'). See also *Bank of America National Trust and Savings Association* v. *Herman Iskandar*, n.48 above, [66]; *Re French Caledonia Travel Service Pty Ltd* (2003) 48 ACSR 97, [31]–[32].

⁵⁰ N.48 above, 127. Whilst Atkin LJ stressed that the banker–customer relationship was made up of a single debtor–creditor contract, Bankes LJ (at 119) considered that the relationship was that of debtor and creditor supplemented by a 'number of implied superadded obligations'. Atkin LJ's approach is more convincing: *Tai Hing Cotton Mill Ltd* v. *Liu Chong Hing Bank Ltd* [1985] 2 All ER 947, 956 (PC). The law applicable to banking operations is *prima facie* 'the place where the branch ... is located': Regulation (EC) 593/2008 on the Law Applicable to Contractual Obligations ('the Rome I Regulation') (in force 17 December 2009), Arts. 4(1) (b), 19(2). This remains the applicable principle even though bank records are nowadays kept on centralized computers rather than in bank ledgers at individual branches: *Walsh* v. *National Irish Bank Ltd* [2007] IEHC 325, [26]–[34]. Where the customer has several accounts with the same bank in different jurisdictions, the applicable law will *prima facie* be the law of the jurisdiction where the bank's head office is situated: Rome I Regulation, Art. 4(2). See further Ch. 9, Sect. 5 below.

⁵¹ *London Joint Stock Bank* v. *Macmillan* [1918] AC 777 (HL), discussed in Ch. 11, Sect. 3(ii) below.

⁵² *Standard Chartered Bank* v. *Tiong Ngit Ting* [1998] 5 MLJ 220, 228; *Damayanti Kantilal Doshi* v. *Indian Bank*, n.48 above, [44]–[45]. A demand is insufficient for savings accounts operated by passbook: *Atkinson* v. *The Bradford Third Equitable Benefit Building Society* (1890) 25 QBD 377, 378; *Bagley* v. *Winsome and National Provincial Bank Ltd* [1952] 2 QB 236, 239 (CA); *Haythorpe* v. *Ray* [1972] VR 633, 637–638 (VSC);

practice to pay the amount involved to the credit of the customer's current account or alternatively to transfer the funds to a holding or suspense account.[53] Where the bank instead retains the money on fixed deposit, it must pay interest as if the account holder had renewed the deposit.[54] Principal and interest are then repayable on demand.[55] Secondly, the requirement that a demand for repayment must be made at the branch where the account is held is often overridden by contrary agreement.[56] This occurs when a bank permits its customers to withdraw cash from the ATMs of other branches or banks or enables customers to pay for purchases electronically at the point of sale by debit card.[57] Indeed, in *Damayanti Kantilal Doshi* v. *Indian Bank*,[58] the Singapore Court of Appeal went so far as to suggest that the principle requiring demand at the customer's own branch was nowadays obsolete as a matter of law in the light of technological developments. The English courts are yet to take this logical final step. The further issue of whether the customer's demand must also be in writing was, however, left open by Atkin LJ in *Joachimson*. In modern banking practice, banks are frequently prepared to dispense with any such writing, relying instead on other security devices, such as passwords and codes, to allow customers to access their accounts securely by such remote means as the internet or mobile phone.[59] This modern banking practice of acting upon a customer's oral instructions received some judicial support recently in *Morrell* v. *Workers Savings & Loan Bank*.[60] Thirdly, even in the case of a current account, the customer's credit balance becomes repayable without a demand if the bank is wound up,[61] or the account is closed. Fourthly, the limitation period runs from the day on which the customer makes demand and is refused.[62] Fifthly, whilst the analysis in *Foley* and *Joachimson* concentrates on the banker–customer relationship as reflected in the maintenance of an account, banks also provide other services to their customers that cannot be described in debtor–creditor terms. Thus, where valuables are left for safe custody,

---

Re Australia and New Zealand Savings Bank Ltd [1972] VR 690, 700 (VSC); cf *Root* v. *Nanyang Commercial Bank Ltd*, n.48 above, 420–422. See further Ch. 9, Sect. 4(ii) below.

[53] *Bank of America National Trust and Savings Association* v. *Herman Iskandar*, n.48 above, [61]. For the United Kingdom approach, see *Suriya & Douglas* v. *Midland Bank plc* [1999] 1 All ER (Comm.) 612 (CA).

[54] Id. See further Sect. 4(iii) below & Ch. 9, Sect. 1 below. [55] Id.

[56] *Bank of Scotland* v. *Seitz* 1990 SLT 584, 590 (Scot. 1st Div.).   [57] Ch. 14, Sect. 5 below.

[58] N.48 above, [28]. See further Ch. 11, Sect. 1(ii) below.

[59] Whilst sound banking practice probably requires written confirmation of a customer's instructions, a bank may act upon a customer's oral instructions: *Hill Street Services Co Ltd* v. *National Westminster Bank plc* [2007] EWHC 2379 (Ch), [14]–[16]. Even when the account mandate requires a customer's instructions to be in writing, a customer's subsequent oral instructions constitutes a variation of the earlier requirement: *Morrell* v. *Workers Savings & Loan Bank* [2007] UKPC 3, [10]. See also *Earles* v. *Barclays Bank plc* [2009] EWHC 2500 (QB), [17].

[60] N.59 above, [10] ('… the fact that a bank impliedly promises to repay any amount against the written order from the customer addressed to the bank at the branch does not exclude … the possibility of an oral order'). See also *Earles* v. *Barclays Bank plc*, n.59 above, [17].

[61] *Re Russian Commercial and Industrial Bank* [1955] 1 Ch. 148. See also *Proven Development Sdn Bhd* v. *Hong Kong and Shanghai Banking Corp.* [1998] 6 MLJ 150, 155.

[62] *Proven Development Sdn Bhd* v. *Hong Kong and Shanghai Banking Corporation*, n.61 above, 154–155; cf *Re Footman Bower & Co. Ltd* [1961] Ch. 443; *Bank of Baroda* v. *A.S.A.A. Mahomed*, n.44 above (considered further in Sect. 6 below). The Scottish courts have refused to apply *Joachimson* in the prescription context, so that time runs against the customer not from the date of demand, but 'from the date when the balance first appeared in the accounts and relative passbook': *MacDonald* v. *North of Scotland Bank*, 1942 SC 369, 375–376, 378–379, 382–383 (IH). At common law, an account is treated as repaid when it has been dormant for an excessive period of time: *Douglass* v. *Lloyds Bank Ltd* (1924) 34 Com. Cas. 263; *Standard Chartered Bank* v. *Tiong Ngit Ting*, n.52 above, 230–231. Under the Dormant Bank and Building Society Accounts Act 2008, s.1, a bank or building society that transfers the credit balance of an account that has remained dormant for 15 years or more to an 'authorised reclaim fund' is protected from the customer's claim for repayment of that balance.

the bank may become a bailee,[63] and, where a bank manages its customer's investment portfolio, the relationship is a complex mix of agency and a contract for services.[64] Even in the current account relationship, the basic debtor–creditor contract is augmented by an agent–principal relationship,[65] pursuant to which the bank undertakes to honour its customer's cheques and other payment instructions and to collect effects due to him.[66] Accordingly, it is erroneous to describe the banker–customer relationship *solely* in debtor–creditor terms. Whilst it would be misguided to attempt to define the banker–customer relationship in terms of status rather than contract, it is realistic to concede that it constitutes a *sui generis* contract incorporating elements of a number of specific, well-defined contracts, including elements of the debtor–creditor contract.

Sixthly, whilst *Joachimson* tends to suggest that the banker–customer and account relationships are largely regulated by *implied* contractual terms,[67] modern banking practice nowadays usually requires a customer to sign an account mandate that contains detailed *express* terms governing the account's operation.[68] Similarly, the provision of other account services by banks, such as the availability of telephone, internet, or mobile phone banking or the provision of account-linked credit and debit cards, are usually regulated by separate written agreements between the bank and its customer. Increasingly, these agreements are based upon the particular bank's own standard terms and conditions, which will usually be drafted with the best interests of the bank, but not necessarily its customers, in mind. In light of this trend, the Jack Committee recognized the need to 'achieve fairness and transparency in the banker–customer relationship', and recommended that this be achieved by means of a voluntary code of best practice, rather than through a model banking contract that might reduce flexibility and damage competition.[69] In March 1992, the banking industry implemented this recommendation by introducing *The Banking Code*, which has done much over the years to equalize the imbalance in commercial strength between banks and their 'personal customers'.[70] In 2002, in

---

[63] Ch. 16, Sect. 4 below.   [64] Ch. 16, Sect. 3 below.

[65] Ch. 7, Sect. 1 below. See also *Ung Eng Huat* v. *Arab Malaysian Bank Bhd*, n.35 above, [18].

[66] Chs. 11 & 15 below.

[67] Modern courts have been reluctant to imply terms beyond those recognized in *Joachimson* (whether in fact or law) if this would impose significant duties upon the customer: Ch. 11, Sect. 3(ii) below. Customers have also struggled to persuade the courts to supplement the banking relationship in this way: *Dovey* v. *Bank of New Zealand* [2000] 3 NZLR 641, [37]–[40]; *Jeffers* v. *Northern Bank Ltd*, n.48 above, [20]–[21]; *Halliday* v. *HBOS plc* [2007] EWHC 1780 (QB), [8]–[10]; cf. *Hill* v. *National Bank of New Zealand Ltd* [1985] 1 NZLR 736, 745. In particular, the courts have been reluctant to imply terms into the banker–customer relationship on the basis of banking practices that are not sufficiently well known to customers generally and/or that deprive them of substantive rights: *Turner* v. *Royal Bank of Scotland plc* [1999] 2 All ER (Comm.) 664 (CA) (considered in Sect. 5(vi) below); *Kitchen* v. *HSBC Bank plc* [2000] 1 All ER (Comm.) 787, 795 (Ch. 17, Sect. 2(iii)). It remains to be seen whether the reluctance to imply terms in fact in the banking context continues following *Attorney-General of Belize* v. *Belize Telecom Ltd* [2009] UKPC 10, [2009] 1 WLR 1988. Consider, in this regard, *Lancore Services Ltd* v. *Barclays Bank plc* [2009] EWCA Civ 752, [2010] 1 All ER 763; *Do-Buy 925 Ltd* v. *National Westminster Bank plc* [2010] EWHC 2862 (QB).

[68] *Fried* v. *National Australia Bank Ltd* [2001] FCA 907; *BMP Global Distribution Inc* v. *Bank of Nova Scotia* [2009] 1 SCR 504, [47]–[48] (SCC).

[69] *Banking Services: Law and Practice*, n.1 above, [4.04], [6.23], [16.10]–[16.12].

[70] N.18 above. See also FSA, *Moneymadeclear: Just the Facts about Your Bank Account* (October 2009), 3, 7, reflecting the requirements of EC Directive 2002/65, which was implemented in the United Kingdom on 31 October 2004 by the Financial Services (Distance Marketing) Regulations 2004, S.I. 2004/2095 (as subsequently amended by the Consumer Protection From Unfair Trading Regulations 2008, S.I. 2008/1277). EC Directive 2002/65 requires a bank that engages in the 'distance marketing' (such as by telephone or internet) of their financial services to consumers to follow good banking practice, such as providing customers with

response to the Cruickshank Report[71] and to head off anticipated criticism in a follow-up report of the Competition Commission,[72] the banking industry introduced the *Business Banking Code*, containing standards of best banking practice when dealing with (small) 'business customers'.[73] Despite their recent revision in March 2008, these codes have now been effectively superseded by a combination of the *Lending Code*, which is promulgated by the British Bankers' Association, and the FSA's BCOBS and *Moneymadeclear Guides*, which have been developed as part of the new 'Banking and Payment Services' (BPS) regime.[74] In addition, a customer may nowadays also rely on a variety of general common law[75] and statutory[76] techniques to police the banking contract. In this respect, the personal customer who also qualifies as a 'consumer' is better protected than the business customer.[77]

details of an account's terms and conditions before it is opened (EC Directive 2002/65, Art. 5) and providing customers with a 14-day cooling off period when opening a current or savings account (but not a fixed-rate account) (EC Directive 2002/65, Art. 6). Where the relevant 'distance contract' also constitutes a contract for a 'payment service', the distance marketing requirements in EC Directive 2002/65 have been replaced by those in EC Directive 2007/64 on Payment Services in the Internal Market (as implemented by the Payment Services Regulations 2009, S.I. 2009/209 ('PSR 2009')). See further Ch. 7, Sect. 2 & Ch. 14, Sect. 10 below. See formerly *Banking Code* (March 2008), [6.1], [7.1].

   [71] D. Cruickshank, *Competition in UK Banking—A Report to the Chancellor of the Exchequer* (London, March 2000). See further Ch. 1, Sect. 2(iii) above.

   [72] Competition Commission, *The Supply of Banking Services by Clearing Banks to Small and Medium-sized Enterprises* (London, Cm. 5319, March 2002).

   [73] N.18 above.   [74] Ch. 2, Sect. 6 above.

   [75] For example, the *contra proferentem* principle (*Tai Hing Cotton Mill Ltd* v. *Liu Chong Hing Bank Ltd*, n.50 above, 110; *Bank of Scotland* v. *Ladjadi* [2000] 2 All ER (Comm.) 583, 589 (CA); *Financial Institutions Services Ltd* v. *Negril Negril Holdings Ltd* [2004] UKPC 40, [43]; *Morrell* v. *Workers Savings & Loan Bank*, n.59 above, [33]; *Office of Fair Trading* v. *Abbey National plc* [2008] EWHC 875 (Comm), [323], revsd. on a different point: [2010] 1 All ER 667 (UKSC); *Office of Fair Trading* v. *Abbey National plc* [2008] EWHC 2325 (Comm), [21]), or the rule against penalty clauses (*Lordsvale Finance Ltd* v. *Bank of Zambia* [1996] QB 752, 767; *Frost* v. *James Finlay Bank Ltd* [2002] Lloyd's Rep IR 429, [73]; *Jeancharm Ltd* v. *Barnet Football Club Ltd* [2003] EWCA Civ 58, [15]–[18], [22], [27]–[29]; *Petromec Inc.* v. *Petroleo Brasileiro SA Petrobras* [2004] EWHC 127 (Comm), [182]–[184]; *Donegal International Ltd* v. *Zambia* [2007] 1 Lloyd's Rep 397, [509]–[519]). For the limits of the penalty clause jurisdiction, see *Office of Fair Trading* v. *Abbey National plc* [2008] EWHC 875 (Comm), [295]–[324], revsd. on a different point: [2010] 1 All ER 667 (UKSC) (validity of bank overdraft charges).

   [76] Provisions of the banker–customer contract may be invalid to the extent that they fail 'the requirement of reasonableness' if they purport to limit or exclude liability for negligence (other than negligence resulting in personal injury); or (where the customer is a 'consumer' or deals on the bank's 'written standard terms of business') purport to exclude or limit liability for breach of contract (including a clause that permits the bank to render substantially different or no performance at all): Unfair Contract Terms Act 1977 (UCTA 1977), ss.2(2), 3(2), 11. A 'consumer' can include a business customer: *Feldarol Foundry plc* v. *Hermes Leasing (London) Ltd* [2004] EWCA Civ 747. For the controls in the Consumer Credit Act 1974, see Ch. 2, Sect. 5 above & Ch. 17, Sects. 2(v) and 3(iii) below.

   [77] The Unfair Terms in Consumer Contracts Regulations 1999, S.I. 1999/2083 (UTCCR 1999) invalidates any 'unfair term' (not just exclusion or limitation clauses) in a bank's contract with a 'consumer' (limited to natural persons). Business customers are not protected. An 'unfair term' is one that has not been individually negotiated and that, contrary to the requirement of good faith, causes a significant imbalance in the parties' rights and obligations under the contract to the detriment of the consumer: UTCCR 1999, reg. 5(1). A contract term will not be individually negotiated where it has been drafted in advance, without the consumer being able to influence its substance: UTCCR 1999, reg. 5(2). For unsuccessful challenges to banking terms, see *Director-General of Fair Trading* v. *First National Bank plc* [2002] 1 AC 481 (HL) (term imposing post-judgment interest at the contractual interest rate); *Office of Fair Trading* v. *Abbey National plc* [2010] 1 All ER 667 (UKSC) (term imposing bank overdraft charges). See further Ch. 17, Sects. 2(ii) & 3(ii) below.

4 The bank's responsibility as fiduciary, for the exercise of undue influence, and for breach of its duty of care

As its customer's agent, a bank has a duty to adhere strictly to its customer's mandate.[78] In turn, a customer owes his bank a duty (as in any agent-principal relationship) to issue clear and unambiguous instructions,[79] to draw cheques with reasonable care, and to inform the bank of his knowledge relating to fraud on the account.[80] Beyond the bank's core duty to obey its customer's instructions, however, the execution of its customer's payment instructions or the performance of other incidental banking services for him may lead to the imposition of other duties or forms of liability on the bank, three of which will be considered in this section.

First, in special and narrow circumstances, a bank may become a fiduciary, owing its customer the core fiduciary duties of loyalty and fidelity. Conceptually, a bank attracts fiduciary duties as a result of its proximate relationship with a given customer, whether by actually assuming the role of a fiduciary or by knowingly dealing with a customer in circumstances that have induced the customer to regard the bank as having assumed such a role. The bank's liability for breach of fiduciary duty must be distinguished, however, from those circumstances in which a bank is 'personally liable to account as a constructive trustee'. Rather than resulting from its proximity to its customer, such liability results from the bank's nexus with a trustee or agent who has committed a breach of trust or other fiduciary duty, or its proximity to property that was originally in the hands of a fiduciary. Indeed, a bank may be personally liable to account as a constructive trustee regardless of whether its customer also happens to be a beneficiary of the trust in question. Essentially, the bank is treated as a 'stranger' who has intermeddled with trust property. Provided the bank is shown to have the requisite degree of fault, liability may arise in two situations[81]—where the bank has acted as an accessory by dishonestly assisting in the fiduciary's breach of trust and where the bank has unconscionably received trust property. Nevertheless, there are circumstances where a customer may wish to establish that the bank is *both* liable as a fiduciary and personally liable to account as a constructive trustee. For example, where the bank's customer is the victim of a fraudulent design perpetrated by the customer's agent with the 'dishonest assistance' of the bank and the bank fails to warn the customer (with whom it happens to have a proximate relationship) of the fraud, then the customer may bring claims not only in relation to the bank's dishonest assistance in a breach of trust, but also for the bank's breach of fiduciary duty in failing to speak out. Accordingly, the two forms of liability can be complementary. Nevertheless, the clear conceptual distinction between them means that they require separate discussion: the first part of the discussion below deals with the bank's position as a fiduciary,[82] whilst its personal liability to account, not being incidental to the relationship with its customers, is discussed subsequently.[83]

Secondly, whilst the courts previously tried to afford sureties dealing with banks a degree of protection by treating those banks as fiduciaries, this technique was limited

---

[78] Chs. 11 & 15 below.   [79] Ch. 11, Sect. 3(iv) below.   [80] Ch. 11, Sect. 3(ii) below.
[81] Ch. 7, Sects. 5(ii)–(iv) below.   [82] Sect. 4(i) below.   [83] Ch. 7, Sects. 5(i)–(iv) below.

to the circumstances where the surety also happened to be the bank's customer, and has accordingly become somewhat outmoded in recent years. Nowadays, the validity of mortgages or guarantees granted in a non-commercial setting is determined by asking whether the bank exercised undue influence or committed some other legal or equitable wrong against the surety or, more usually, whether the bank had notice of such wrong-doing by a third party *vis-à-vis* the surety. The second part of the discussion below deals with this issue.[84]

Thirdly, a bank owes its customer concurrent common law and contractual duties to exercise reasonable care when providing banking services or products. Whilst this general duty of care will be considered in the third part of the discussion below,[85] subsequent chapters will also deal with the more specific duties of care that may arise where a bank provides its customer with financial advice,[86] accepts its customer's valuables for safe custody,[87] or is involved with providing or obtaining a banker's reference.[88] In addition, in those rare circumstances where a bank becomes a fiduciary, the bank will owe its customer an equitable duty to take care. In *Bristol and West Building Society* v. *Mothew,*[89] Millett LJ clearly distinguished this duty from the so-called 'fiduciary duties' proper: '[i]t is essential to bear in mind that the existence of a fiduciary relationship does not mean that every duty owed by a fiduciary to the beneficiary is a fiduciary duty. In particular, a trustee's duty to exercise reasonable care, though equitable, is not specifically a fiduciary duty.'[90] Unlike the equitable duty of care,[91] *fiduciary* duties are proscriptive in nature in that they tell the fiduciary what he must not do, not what he ought to do,[92] and they attract remedies that are primarily restitutionary or restorative, rather than compensatory.[93] In this regard, Millett LJ in *Mothew* added:[94]

> The expression 'fiduciary duty' is properly confined to those duties which are peculiar to fiduciaries and the breach of which attracts legal consequences differing from those consequent upon the breach of other duties.[95] Unless the expression is so limited it is lacking in practical utility. In this sense it is obvious that not every breach of a duty by a fiduciary is a breach of a fiduciary duty . . . It is similarly inappropriate to apply the expression to the obligation of a trustee or other fiduciary to use proper skill and care in the discharge of his duties . . . The distinguishing obligation of a fiduciary is the obligation of loyalty . . . Breach of fiduciary obligation, therefore, connotes disloyalty or infidelity. Mere incompetence is not enough.

---

[84] Sect. 4(ii) below.   [85] Sect. 4(iii) below.   [86] Ch. 16, Sect. 3 below.

[87] Ch. 16, Sect. 4 below.   [88] Ch. 16, Sect. 2(ii) below.

[89] [1998] Ch. 1 (CA). See also *Henderson* v. *Merrett Syndicates Ltd* [1995] 2 AC 145, 205 (HL); *White* v. *Jones* [1995] 2 AC 207, 271 (HL).

[90] *Permanent Building Society* v. *Wheeler* (1994) 14 ACSR 109, 157 (WASC). See also *Gwembe Valley Development Co Ltd* v. *Koshy (No. 3)* [2004] 1 BCLC 131, [85] (CA); *Sherman* v. *Orenstein* [2004] OJ No 782, [6] (OSC).

[91] Sect. 4(iv) below.

[92] *Att.-Gen.* v. *Blake* [1998] 1 All ER 833, 843 (CA), affd. on other grounds: [2001] 1 AC 268 (HL); *Breen* v. *Williams* (1996) 186 CLR 71 (HCA).

[93] Sect. 4(iv) below.   [94] N.89 above, 16. See also *Grant* v. *Canada* (2005) 77 OR (3d) 481, [44] (OSC).

[95] Sect. 4(iv) below.

(i) The banker–customer relationship as a fiduciary relationship[96]

Bristol and West Building Society v. *Mothew*,[97] is also arguably the leading decision concerning the definition of the term 'fiduciary' in English law, and involved a claim by a building society against a solicitor who had been engaged to report whether a purchaser, to whom the society had advanced monies for the acquisition of a property, had incurred further borrowings to acquire the house. The solicitor acted for both the building society and the borrower and inadvertently failed to tell the society that the purchaser had borrowed a further sum secured by a second mortgage on the property. When the borrower defaulted on the loan, the society enforced its mortgage, but suffered a shortfall that it sought to recover from its solicitor, *inter alia*, on the grounds of breach of fiduciary duty. The Court of Appeal held that, whilst the solicitor's negligent oversight of the transaction rendered him liable to the society for breach of contract, there was no breach of fiduciary duty or any breach of what Millett LJ termed the 'double employment rule'[98]—the society had authorized the solicitor to act for both itself and the purchaser despite their *potentially* conflicting interests, and the solicitor had served each principal loyally and faithfully and avoided any *actual* conflict between the duties owed to each principal. In identifying those who qualify as 'fiduciaries', Millet LJ stated:[99]

> A fiduciary is someone who has undertaken to act for or on behalf of another in a particular matter in circumstances, which give rise to a relationship of trust and confidence. The distinguishing obligation of a fiduciary is the obligation of loyalty. The principal is entitled to the single-minded loyalty of the fiduciary. This core liability has several facets. A fiduciary must act in good faith; he must not make a profit out of his trust; he must not place himself in a position where his duty and his interest may conflict; he may not act for his own benefit or the benefit of a third person without the informed consent of his principal. This is not intended to be an exhaustive list, but it is sufficient to indicate the nature of fiduciary obligations. They are the defining characteristics of the fiduciary.

As the concept of 'selflessness' lies at the heart of the fiduciary relationship, a fiduciary is expected to promote his principal's interests above his own. As banks can normally be

---

[96] M.H. Ogilvie, 'Banks, Advice-Giving and Fiduciary Obligations' (1985) 17 *Ottawa L Rev.* 263; D. Waters, 'Banks, Fiduciary Obligations and Unconscionable Transactions' (1986) 65 *Can. Bar Rev.* 37; K. Curtis, 'The Fiduciary Controversy: Injection of Fiduciary Principles into the Bank-Depositor and Bank-Borrower Relationships' (1987) 20 *Loyola LR* 795; P. Finn, 'Fiduciary Law and the Modern Commercial World' in E. McKendrick (ed.), *Commercial Aspects of Trusts and Fiduciary Obligations* (Oxford, 1992); J. Glover, 'Banks and Fiduciary Relationships' (1995) 7 *Bond LR* 50; J. Breslin, 'Banks as Fiduciaries' (1998) 5 *Comm. LP* 47; M.H Ogilvie, 'Judicial Intuition and Bank Fiduciary Obligation: *Scaravelli* v. *Bank of Montreal*' (2005) 21 *BFLR* 89; R. Plato-Shinar, 'The Bank's Fiduciary Duty: An Israeli-Canadian Comparison' (2006) 22 *BFLR* 1; J. Getzler, 'Excluding Fiduciary Duties: The Problems of Investment Banks' (2008) 124 *LQR* 15.

[97] N.89 above.   [98] Ibid., 19.

[99] Ibid., 18, applied in *Arklow Investments Ltd* v. *Maclean* [2000] 1 WLR 594, 599 (PC); *Deacons* v. *White & Case Ltd* [2003] HKCU 1184, [110] (HKHC); *Woolworths Ltd* v. *Olson* [2004] NSWSC 849, [214]; *SM Trading Services* v. *Intersanctuary Ltd* [2006] 3 SLR 397, [74] (SGHC); *Sinclair Investment Holdings SA* v. *Versailles Trade Finance Ltd* [2006] 1 BCLC 60, [13] (CA); *Ratiu* v. *Conway* [2006] 1 All ER 571, [57] (CA); *Brilliant (Man Sau) Engineering Ltd* v. *Wong Chat Choor Samuel* [2006] HKCU 714, [21] (HKHC); *Saleh* v. *Abdullah* [2007] 6 MLJ 293, [80] (MCA); *Australian Securities and Investments Commission* v. *Citigroup Global Markets Australia Pty Ltd (No. 4)* (2007) 241 ALR 705, [289]–[292] (FCA); *Chirnside* v. *Fay* [2007] 1 NZLR 433, [15] (NZSC); *Amaltal Corporation Ltd* v. *Maruha Corporation* [2007] 1 NZLR 608, [138] (NZCA); *Mcleod* v. *Harnett* [2008] OJ No 1039, [45] (OSC); *The Board of Trustees of the Sabah Foundation* v. *Mohamed* [2008] 5 MLJ 469, [30] (MFC); *Premium Real Estate Ltd* v. *Stevens* [2009] 2 NZLR 384, [67] (NZSC). See also *White* v. *Jones*, n.89 above, 271. Millett LJ went on to deal separately with the position where a fiduciary deals with his principal, when the fiduciary must prove affirmatively that the transaction is fair and that full disclosure has been made.

expected to further their own commercial interests ahead of their customers', the courts have consistently stressed that banks' deposit-taking and lending activities are not generally fiduciary in character;[100] that 'on the face of it the relationship between a bank and its customer is not a fiduciary relationship';[101] and that banks 'are not charitable institutions'.[102] Accordingly, beyond the duties usually implied into the banker–customer contract, such as the duty of skill and care, banks do not generally owe their customers the fiduciary duties of loyalty and fidelity. Whilst it is certainly understandable why the courts are so hostile to imposing fiduciary duties on banks towards their *commercial* customers,[103] this reluctance has even extended to personal customers who might be considered more vulnerable when dealing with a bank. A recent example is *Wright* v. *HSBC plc*,[104] in which the claimant was a recently widowed customer, who was at risk of losing her home due to the significant business and personal liabilities that she and her husband had incurred before his death. After her husband's death, the claimant reluctantly agreed to compromise her various claims against the bank in return for continued banking facilities. Subsequently, the customer tried to resurrect those compromised claims by challenging the compromise's validity, *inter alia*, on the ground that the bank had breached its fiduciary duties by advising her to enter into that arrangement. Despite her potential vulnerability,[105] Jack J rejected this argument, since the bank had suggested that the claimant take independent legal advice[106] and had not advised her to enter into the compromise agreement, but rather had left her to make her own decision.[107] The court's starting point was that 'in the normal case...there would generally be no question of any fiduciary relationship'[108] and that customers will face an uphill struggle persuading a court otherwise.

[100] *Foley* v. *Hill*, n.40 above, 36 (discussed in Sect. 3 above). See also *Toronto Dominion Bank* v. *Forsythe* (2000) 47 OR (3d) 321, 327 (OCA); *Gowanlock* v. *Bank of Nova Scotia* (2001) 157 Man R (2d) 124, [60]–[67]; *Popek* v. *National Westminster Bank plc* [2002] EWCA Civ 42, [33]; *Scavarelli* v. *Bank of Montreal* (2004) 69 OR (3d) 295, [27]–[40], [47] (OSC); *Jeffers* v. *Northern Bank Ltd*, n.48 above, [25]; *Baldwin* v. *Daubney* (2006) 83 OR (3d) 308, [38] (OCA); *Bank of Montreal* v. *1480863 Ontario Inc.* [2007] OJ No 1494, [37]–[39]; *JJ MacMahon (Building Contractor) Ltd* v. *Ulster Bank Ltd*, n.48 above, [6]; *Tamimi* v. *Khodari* [2009] EWCA Civ 1042, [42]; *Studer* v. *Conexus Credit Union* [2010] SKQB 352, [23]–[24]. Some common activities of a multifunction bank more readily give rise to fiduciary duties than others, such as acting as the trustee of an estate or investment fund (*Bartlett* v. *Barclays Trust Co. Ltd* [1980] Ch. 515, which should now be viewed in the light of the Trustee Act 2000); managing its customer's investment portfolio under the terms of a discretionary management agreement (*Ata* v. *American Express Bank Ltd*, *The Times*, 26 June 1998, Rix J, affd. by CA; *Diamantides* v. *JP Morgan Chase Bank* [2005] EWCA Civ 1612, [42]); or acting as custodian of its customer's securities (*JP Morgan Chase Bank* v. *Springwell Navigation Corp.* [2008] EWHC 1186 (Comm), [573], aff'd [2010] EWCA Civ 1221). Where a bank is appointed as its customer's agent for a specific task, it will generally be a fiduciary in relation to that task: *Al Khudairi* v. *Abbey Brokers Ltd* [2010] EWHC 1486 (Ch), [114]–[118]. As the bank acts as agent in paying its customer's cheques (*Hollicourt (Contracts) Ltd (in liq.)* v. *Bank of Ireland* [2001] Ch 555, 563 (CA); *Ung Eng Huat* v. *Arab Malaysian Bank Bhd*, n.35 above, [18]), there have been suggestions that a bank acts as a fiduciary in such circumstances (*Nimmo* v. *Westpac Banking Corporation* [1993] 3 NZLR 218, 237). See generally *Snell's Equity* (32nd edn., London, 2010), [7-005]–[7-006], [7-008].

[101] *Governor & Company of the Bank of Scotland* v. *A Ltd* [2001] 1 WLR 751, [25] (CA); *Bournemouth & Boscombe Athletic Football Club Ltd* v. *Lloyds TSB Bank plc* [2003] EWHC 834 (Ch), [28]; *Murphy* v. *HSBC Bank plc* [2004] EWHC 467 (Ch.), [101]; *Tamimi* v. *Khodari*, n.100 above, [42].

[102] *National Westminster Bank plc* v. *Morgan* [1983] 3 All ER 85, 91 (CA).

[103] *JP Morgan Chase Bank* v. *Springwell Navigation Corp.*, n.100 above, [571]–[577], [724]–[737]; *Spencer* v. *Barclays Bank plc* [2009] All ER (D) 61 (Nov). See also *Rodaro* v. *Royal Bank of Canada* [2000] OTC 85, [304]–[312]; *Canada Trustco Mortgage Co* v. *Renard* [2006] BCSC 1609, [77]–[82], revsd. on other grounds: [2008] BCCA 343. A bank may be a fiduciary if it has undertaken to provide advice to a customer, even a commercial one: *Australian Securities and Investments Commission* v. *Citigroup Global Markets Australia Pty Ltd (No. 4)*, n.99 above, [265].

[104] [2006] EWHC 930 (QB).   [105] Ibid., [61].   [106] Ibid., [63].

[107] Ibid., [42], [47]. See also *Ung Eng Huat* v. *Arab Malaysian Bank Bhd*, n.35 above, [19].

[108] *Cornish* v. *Midland Bank plc* [1985] 3 All ER 513, 522 (CA).

Nevertheless, as indicated in *Tamimi* v. *Khodari*,[109] the courts have not entirely ruled out the possibility of a bank being its customer's fiduciary. Other than highlighting that there must be 'a special relationship or exceptional circumstances',[110] however, the courts have provided little clear or consistent guidance as to when such rare instances might arise. Indeed, even the Canadian courts, which have considered the issue of when a bank should be treated as a fiduciary far more extensively than the English courts, have similarly been criticized for trusting to intuition rather than applying legal principle.[111] This is unsurprising given the range of tests for identifying fiduciaries that have been proposed by the Canadian courts. The point is highlighted by *Scavarelli* v. *Bank of Montreal*,[112] which involved the defendant bank agreeing to finance the acquisition of a video rental franchise by the claimants' company. The bank did not consider that the company qualified for particularly favourable funding terms and, as a condition of the loan, required the claimants to give personal guarantees and security over their home. Both claimants were life-long customers of the bank, neither had any prior experience negotiating this type of deal, and the wife did not receive any independent legal advice. When the business failed, the bank sought to enforce its security and the customers argued that the bank had breached its fiduciary duties by failing to alert them to the full consequences of their increased personal liabilities and by failing to suggest alternative sources of funding on more favourable terms. Following the general retreat in Canada from classifying banks as fiduciaries,[113] Smith J rejected the customers' argument, but in doing so articulated three different legal tests as to when a fiduciary relationship might exist. The first test was based on there being 'a mutual understanding that one party has relinquished its own self-interest and agreed to act solely on behalf of the other party'.[114] Smith J's alternative test was that:[115]

> ...relationships in which a fiduciary obligation has been imposed are marked by the following three characteristics: (1) scope for the exercise of some discretion or power; (2) that power or discretion can be exercised unilaterally so as to effect the beneficiary's legal or practical interests; and (3) a peculiar vulnerability to the exercise of that discretion or power.

---

[109] N.100 above, [42].

[110] *Bank of Montreal* v. *Witkin* [2005] OJ No 3221, [59] (OSC); *Pierce* v. *Canada Trustco Mortgage Co* [2005] 254 DLR (4th) 79, [27] (OCA); *Baldwin* v. *Daubney*, n.100 above, [12]–[13]; *Toronto-Dominion Bank* v. *Solferino Café Inc* [2009] OJ No. 3928, [23] (OSC). See also *Susilawati* v. *American Express Bank Ltd* [2008] 1 SLR 237, [63] (SGHC), affd. on different grounds: [2009] 2 SLR 737 (SGCA).

[111] M.H Ogilvie, n.96 above. See also *Bank of Montreal* v. *Tseshaht Indian Band* [2003] BCSC 1095, [37]–[40]; *Baldwin* v. *Daubney*, n.100 above, [12]–[13]; *Isaacs* v. *Royal Bank of Canada* [2010] OJ No. 2620, [38]–[39].

[112] N.100 above.

[113] M.H. Ogilvie, 'Banker and Customer: The Five Year Review, 1995–2000' (2000–2001) 16 *BFLR* 231, 260–270; M.H. Ogilvie, n.14 above, 144–147; cf. *Kovacs* v. *TD Financial Group* [2010] OJ No. 2598, [39]–[51].

[114] N.100 above, [33], citing *Hodgkinson* v. *Simms* [1994] 3 SCR 377, 408–410 (SCC) (investment advice given to client by investment adviser); *Galambos* v. *Perez* [2009] 3 SCR 247, 278–282 (SCC) ('... fiduciary duties will only be imposed on those who have expressly or impliedly undertaken them'). See also *Australian Securities and Investments Commission* v. *Citigroup Global Markets Australia Pty Ltd (No. 4)*, n.99 above, [272]; *Royal Bank of Canada* v. *Achieve Medical Inc.* [2008] OJ No. 705, [16]–[19] (OSC). For a slightly different formulation, see *Bank of Montreal* v. *Witkin*, n.110 above, [60]. See also P.J. Millett, 'Equity's Place in the Law of Commerce' (1998) 114 *LQR* 214, 219. Some cases have stressed that it is not enough that a bank have a discretion to exercise (*Piper* v. *ANZ National Bank Ltd* (NZHC, 18 September 2005), [80]–[83]), but that there must be some form of 'overreaching' by the bank (*Susilawati* v. *American Express Bank Ltd*, n.110 above, [60]–[65]).

[115] Ibid. [32], citing *Frame* v. *Smith* [1987] 2 SCR 99, 136 (SCC). See also *Kian Lup Construction* v. *HongKong Bank Malaysia Bhd* [2002] 7 MLJ 283, [56] (MHC); *Canada Trustco Mortgage Co* v. *Renard*, n.103 above, [77]; *Susilawati* v. *American Express Bank Ltd* [2009] 2 SLR 737, [41] (SGCA); *HSBC Bank Malaysia Bhd* v. *Innovation Wood Sdn Bhd* [2009] MLJU 327, [60]–[69].

The third possible test suggested in *Scavarelli* was that:[116]

> …a plaintiff must demonstrate that the following four conditions exist: firstly, that advice was provided and that advice was relied upon; second, that the defendant was aware of this reliance; third, that the defendant derived a benefit from the transaction; and fourth, that the relationship was one of a confidential nature.

Given that the first of these tests closely resembles that proposed by Millett LJ in *Bristol and West Building Society* v. *Mothew*[117] and that the third test (as discussed below) is based on Sir Eric Sachs' approach in *Lloyds Bank Ltd* v. *Bundy*,[118] the English courts may have the same difficulty in articulating the relevant legal principles. That the English courts may accordingly adopt the same intuitive approach as in Canada is evidenced by the summary way in which the allegations of fiduciary relationship were dismissed in *Wright* v. *HSBC plc*,[119] *Tamimi* v. *Khodari*,[120] and *Kotonou* v. *National Westminster Bank plc*.[121]

Although the fact-sensitive nature of the enquiry makes it rather difficult to predict when a bank may be treated as a fiduciary in the future, some guidance may be derived from the two main situations in which the English courts have to date imposed such obligations on banks.[122] The first type of situation occurs when a customer is asked to execute a guarantee, charge, or other security in respect of a loan to another customer. Frequently, the surety is the debtor's spouse, an aged parent, or some other close relative and the debtor may extract the security by means of a misrepresentation or the exercise of undue influence over the surety. When the bank or other creditor eventually enforces its rights, the surety may seek to resist this by arguing that the bank has breached its fiduciary duty to him, or, more commonly, on the ground that the bank has actual or constructive notice of the debtor's wrongdoing. This latter, more recent solution to this type of problem will be discussed later.[123] The leading modern example of fiduciary-based reasoning in this context is *Lloyds Bank Ltd* v. *Bundy*,[124] in which the claimant bank obtained a guarantee secured over the house of its customer, who was aged, commercially naïve, and without any other substantial assets besides his home, in support of an overdraft granted to that customer's son. The branch manager, who took the security documents to the father's home for signature, did not disclose the extent of the son's financial problems, and failed to suggest that the father seek independent legal advice before executing the security documents. The transaction was advantageous to the bank, as the charge that the father had previously executed over his home did not adequately secure the overdraft incurred by the

---

[116] Ibid., [37]. See also *Bank of Montreal* v. *Witkin*, n.110 above, [65].   [117] N.89 above, 18.

[118] [1975] QB 326 (CA).

[119] N.104 above. See also *Solitaire Land Sdn Bhd* v. *Hong Leong Bank Bhd* [2007] 3 MLJ 756, [77] (MHC); *Bournemouth & Boscombe Athletic Football Club Ltd* v. *Lloyds TSB Bank plc*, n.101 above, [28].

[120] N.100 above, [42].   [121] [2010] EWHC 1659 (Ch), [136].

[122] Consider Ch. 17, Sect. 4(iv) below.   [123] Sect. 4(ii) below.

[124] N.118 above. See also *National Westminster Bank plc* v. *Waite* [2006] EWHC 1287 (QB), [45]; *Noor* v. *Baiduri Bank Berhad* [2009] MLJU 1621 (MCA). *Bundy* has been followed in Canada: *Royal Bank of Canada* v. *Hinds* (1978) 88 DLR (3d) 428 (OHC); *Hayward* v. *Bank of Nova Scotia* (1985) 19 DLR (4th) 154 (OCA); *Standard Investments Ltd* v. *Canadian Imperial Bank of Commerce* (1985) 22 DLR (4th) 410, 432–434 (OCA), leave to appeal refused: 53 OR (2d) 663. As in the United Kingdom, the recent Canadian trend is to assess the validity of security arrangements by reference to undue influence principles, rather than fiduciary principles: M.H. Ogilvie, *Canadian Banking Law* (2nd edn., Scarborough, Ont., 1998), 481–483; M.H. Ogilvie, n.14 above, 151. See also *Bertolo* v. *Bank of Montreal* (1986) 18 OAC 262 (OCA). Nowadays, the reluctance of the Canadian courts to impose fiduciary duties is evident not only at the point in time when the surety executes the security documents (*Gowanlock* v. *Bank of Nova Scotia*, n.100 above, [60]–[66]; *Bank of Montreal* v. *Tseshaht Indian Band*, n.111 above, [37]–[40], [52], [63]; *Toronto Dominion Bank* v. *Femia* [2008] OJ No. 3042, [18]–[21] (OSC)), but also when the bank enforces its security (*Royal Bank of Canada* v. *Achieve Medical Inc.*, n.114 above, [16]–[23]).

son at the time of the new arrangement. The Court of Appeal set aside the guarantee, as the bank had breached its duty of fiduciary care to the surety. Conceding that such a duty did not usually exist when a customer agreed with his bank to guarantee another's debts, Sir Eric Sachs emphasized that, as a customer of long standing, the guarantor in *Bundy* had relied on the bank's advice, and that the bank's failure to disclose the full facts was akin to the exercise of undue influence. His Lordship considered that a fiduciary relationship could arise in the following circumstances:[125]

> ... whilst disclaiming any intention of seeking to catalogue the elements of such a special relationship, it is perhaps of a little assistance to note some of the elements which have in the past frequently been found to exist where the court has been led to decide that this relationship existed between adults of sound mind. Such cases tend to arise where someone relies on the guidance or advice of another, where the other is aware of that reliance and where the person upon whom reliance is placed obtains, or may well obtain, a benefit from the transaction or has some other interest in it being concluded. In addition, there must, of course, be shown to exist a vital element ... referred to as confidentiality.

Accordingly, the bank's mere failure to volunteer advice does not render it a fiduciary, as the vital element of 'confidentiality' is usually absent.[126] In this context, 'confidentiality' clearly does not refer to the bank's duty of secrecy to its customer, which is present in every banker–customer relationship.[127] According to Sir Eric Sachs, 'confidentiality' means that the bank has '*vis-à-vis* a customer attained a special relationship akin to that of a "man of affairs" ' and that one of the features of 'confidentiality' is that 'once it exists, influence naturally grows out of it'.[128] In other words, a fiduciary relationship arises only in those rare cases (like *Bundy*) where the customer-surety has placed such trust and confidence in the bank, giving it influence over him.

For a number of reasons, however, courts in future are likely to exercise caution over the fiduciary duty reasoning in *Bundy*. First, in *Bundy* itself, the Court of Appeal considered the case to be 'very unusual'[129] and to involve 'special facts',[130] and accordingly subsequent courts have treated *Bundy* as an exceptional decision.[131] Secondly, whilst the conclusion in *Bundy* was unanimous, Sir Eric Sachs alone decided the case on the ground of breach of fiduciary duty. Cairns LJ considered that the bank's 'special relationship' with the father gave rise to a duty to advise, which, if breached, avoided the guarantee 'on the ground of undue influence'.[132] Lord Denning similarly agreed, preferring to explain his conclusion on other doctrinal grounds, including undue influence. Thirdly, Sir Eric Sachs considered the conflict of interests between the bank, the debtor, and the surety in *Bundy* to be an important consideration in classifying the bank as a fiduciary. On its face, this suggestion should significantly increase the potential for fiduciary duties in the surety context, since the parties' commercial interests will almost invariably conflict. In *Susilawati* v. *American Express Bank Ltd*,[133] however, the Singaporean High Court has diminished the significance of this factor to the imposition of fiduciary duties on banks to customer-sureties. *Susilawati* concerned a customer who had executed a charge over her account's credit balance as security for her son-in-law's foreign exchange trading liabilities. Shortly

---

[125] N.118 above, 341. See also *Commonwealth Bank of Australia* v. *Smith* (1991) 102 ALR 453 (FCA); *Scavarelli* v. *Bank of Montreal*, n.100 above, [37].

[126] *Union Bank of Finland* v. *Lelakis* [1995] CLC 27, 49 (third-party guarantor's undue influence claim against the creditor failed as no relationship of 'confidentiality').

[127] Sect. 5 below.   [128] N.118 above, 341, 347.   [129] Ibid., 340.   [130] Ibid., 347.

[131] *National Westminster Bank plc* v. *Morgan*, n.102 above, 689 ('very special facts'); *Cornish* v. *Midland Bank plc*, n.108 above, 522 (a 'notorious case'); *Wright* v. *HSBC plc*, n.104 above, [62].

[132] N.118 above, 340.   [133] N.110 above.

after the charge's execution, the son-in-law's indebtedness increased dramatically and the bank sought to enforce its security. In addition to challenging the charge on the ground of undue influence,[134] the claimant alleged that the bank had breached its fiduciary duty to advise her fully of the commercial risks of executing the charge and to update her as to her son-in-law's increasing liabilities. Lai Siu Chai J rejected this argument on two bases: the claimant was aware of the potential for conflict between her own interests and those of the bank and her son-in-law;[135] and imposing a duty to disclose the son-in-law's liabilities would conflict with the bank's duty to maintain his confidences.[136] Giving precedence to the bank's duty of confidentiality in this way, leaves little scope for imposing fiduciary duties upon banks that require them to divulge information to sureties.

Finally, *Bundy* will in future have to be reinterpreted in light of *National Westminster Bank plc* v. *Morgan*.[137] A customer, who had defaulted on an earlier loan from a building society that was secured upon the matrimonial home, which the customer owned jointly with his wife (who was also the bank's customer), sought to refinance the loan with his bank to prevent the building society from selling his home. As the bank required security over the matrimonial home, the branch manager visited the customer's home so that the wife could execute the necessary security documents. Despite the wife expressing her unwillingness to secure her husband's business ventures on her home, the branch manager failed to explain the wide-ranging nature of the security; reassured her erroneously (albeit in good faith) that the new charge only secured the amount advanced to refinance the original mortgage; and failed to advise the wife to seek independent legal advice. The bank sought to sell the property to recover the balance outstanding under the refinancing arrangement. Concluding that the charge should not be set aside, Lord Scarman revisited *Bundy*. Whilst doubting Lord Denning's suggestion in *Bundy* that contracting parties' 'inequality of bargaining power' provided a general ground for setting aside transactions, Lord Scarman nevertheless endorsed the result in *Bundy* and stated that Sir Eric Sachs 'got it absolutely right' in that case.[138] Unlike Sir Eric, however, Lord Scarman preferred to avoid the term 'confidentiality' when determining the availability of relief in surety cases, and used the language of 'undue influence' rather than that of 'breach of fiduciary duty' when describing the nature of the bank's liability.[139] Warning against attempts to define exhaustively the circumstances when a bank might be taken to have exercised undue influence over its customer, Lord Scarman indicated that the key question was whether, on a 'meticulous examination of the facts', the bank had 'crossed the line'.[140] Accordingly, his Lordship held that the parties' relationship in *Morgan* had remained that of banker and customer, that the branch manager had not exercised undue influence over the wife to execute the charge, and that accordingly the bank was not obliged to suggest that the wife seek independent legal advice. There were three grounds for this conclusion: first, the bank did not derive any hidden or undue benefit from the transaction, and the wife was anxious to enter the refinancing arrangement that would save her home from being sold; secondly, the branch manager's explanation of the charge was only technically inaccurate, since the bank's intention was only ever to enforce the charge in respect of the liability under the refinancing arrangement, but not in respect of the husband's general business liabilities, despite the charge being formally wide enough to cover those

---

[134] Sect. 4(ii) below.   [135] N.110 above, [72].

[136] Ibid., [81]–[82], [88]–[92]. See also *Hamilton* v. *Watson* (1845) 12 Cl&Fin 109, 119; *Scotland* v. *Greenshields*, 1914 SC 259, 266–267; *Lloyds Bank Ltd* v. *Harrison* (1925) 4 LDAB 12, 16; *Shivas* v. *Bank of New Zealand* [1990] 2 NZLR 327, 363–364.

[137] [1985] AC 686 (HL), revsg. [1983] 3 All ER 85 (CA).   [138] Ibid., 708.   [139] Ibid., 707–709.

[140] Ibid., 709. See also *Shotter* v. *Westpac Banking Corp.* [1988] 2 NZLR 316, 333–334.

debts; and, thirdly, the wife understood the general nature of the charge and was aware that, without it, the building society would sell her home. Accordingly, following *Morgan*, cases like *Bundy* have been argued and decided on the basis of the bank's notice of the undue influence (or other legal or equitable wrong) exercised by the debtor over the surety.[141] These principles are considered more fully in the following section.[142]

The second situation in which the English courts have applied the fiduciary label to banks is when they have assumed the role of their customer's adviser, as occurs when giving 'investment advice'.[143] Even in this situation, however, the starting point must still be that acting as its customer's adviser does not generally make a bank its customer's fiduciary, as most people would realize that banks will put their own interests first. Fiduciary obligations may, however, be imposed where the bank can reasonably be considered to have undertaken to act in its customer's best interests when giving the advice. In *Klein* v. *First Edina National Bank*,[144] the Supreme Court of Minnesota stated:

> We believe the correct rule to be that when a bank transacts business with a depositor or other customer, it has no special duty to counsel the customer and inform him of every material fact relating to the transaction—including the bank's motive, if material, for the transaction—unless special circumstances exist, such as where the bank knows or has reason to know that the customer is placing his trust and confidence in the bank and is relying on the bank.

The leading English example of this second type of case is *Woods* v. *Martins Bank*.[145] In advising his commercially inexperienced client to invest substantial sums in the shares of a particular company, the defendant bank's branch manager failed to disclose that that company had an excessive overdraft with the bank that was of significant concern to the bank's head office. Following the loss of his entire investment, the claimant sued the bank on a number of grounds. As discussed previously,[146] the principal argument concerned whether the claimant was the bank's customer to whom the bank owed an implied contractual duty to exercise reasonable care when tendering financial advice. Although Salmon J concluded that the claimant had indeed become the bank's customer, as an alternative line of reasoning,[147] his Lordship held that the bank had nevertheless become

---

[141] *Barclays Bank plc* v. *O'Brien* [1994] 1 AC 180 (HL); *Royal Bank of Scotland* v. *Etridge (No. 2)* [2002] 2 AC 773 (HL).

[142] Sect. 4(ii) below.

[143] *JP Morgan Chase Bank* v. *Springwell Navigation Corp.*, n.100 above, [571]–[573]; *Kian Lup Construction* v. *Hong Kong Bank Malaysia Bhd*, n.115 above, [57]–[62]; *HSBC Bank Malaysia Bhd* v. *Innovation Wood Sdn Bhd*, n.115 above, [64]. A similar view has been expressed in New Zealand (*Shotter* v. *Westpac Banking Corp.*, n.140 above, 334; *Dungey* v. *ANZ Banking Group (NZ) Ltd* [1997] NZFLR 404, 411; *Wilkins* v. *Bank of New Zealand* [1998] DCR 520, 536) and Australia (*Australian Securities and Investments Commission* v. *Citigroup Global Markets Australia Pty Ltd (No. 4)*, n.99 above, [282]–[285]; *Re Brown & Australian Securities and Investments Commission* [2009] AATA 286, [151]).

[144] 196 NW 2d 619 (1972), 623, *per curiam*. In the United States, fiduciary duties have been imposed when the banker–customer relationship is a 'confidential' one: *Bear Stearns & Co* v. *Daisy Systems Corp.*, 97 F.3d 1171 (9th Cir., 1996); *McCormack* v. *Citibank NA*, 100 F.3d 532 (8th Cir., 1996); *Ballard* v. *Royal Trust Bank*, US App. Lexis 31595 (9th Cir., 1999); *American Model Home Corp.* v. *Resource Mortgage Capital Inc*, US App. Lexis 2849 (4th Cir., 1999); *Pavlovich* v. *National City Bank*, 435 F.3d 560 (6th Cir., 2006); *Giles* v. *GMAC*, 494 F.3d 865 (9th Cir., 2007); *Interactive Intelligence Inc* v. *Keycorp*, US App. Lexis 22279 (7th Cir., 2008). A fiduciary duty can arise between commercial parties: *EBC I Inc.* v. *Goldman Sachs & Co.*, 5 NY 3d 11, 19–22 (NYCA, 2005).

[145] N.21 above, 72. See further Sect. 2 above.   [146] Sect. 2 above.

[147] As *Woods* pre-dates the recognition of a common law duty of care for negligent statements causing pure economic loss in *Hedley Byrne & Co. Ltd* v. *Heller & Partners Ltd*, n.22 above, the only orthodox basis upon which Salmon J could have imposed liability on the defendant bank for pre-contractual advice (in the absence of a banker–customer contract) was by recognizing the existence of a fiduciary duty: L.S. Sealy, 'Fiduciary Obligations, Forty Years On' (1995) 9 *JCL* 37, 42, n.45. Nowadays, *Woods* would probably be

the claimant's fiduciary as a result of the branch manager agreeing to act as financial adviser. His Lordship based this conclusion on a number of factors: first, the branch manager's conversations with the claimant had emphasized the defendant bank's financial expertise, and the manager had effectively agreed to act as the claimant's general business adviser; secondly, the bank crucially furnished its potential customers with a leaflet holding itself out as an expert in providing business and financial advice; thirdly, the branch manager advised the claimant to invest in the relevant company's shares without disclosing the conflict of interests arising from the fact that the claimant's investment would in fact go towards reducing that company's overdraft with the bank. Although his Lordship absolved the branch manager of any fraud, he considered that the manager's conduct involved a breach of a fiduciary duty of care, which arose from the trust that the claimant placed in the manager's business judgement. Fiduciary duties have similarly been imposed on banks in Canada. In *Standard Investments Ltd* v. *Canadian Imperial Bank of Commerce*,[148] where the claimants (who were customers of the defendant bank) were seeking to acquire a controlling interest in another of the bank's customers and had been promised (in good faith) the necessary guidance and assistance by one of the defendant bank's officers, the bank was held liable for breach of fiduciary duty when it failed to disclose the fact that another bank officer had already agreed that the bank would assist in blocking the claimants' takeover and failed to disclose the fact that the bank had sold its shareholding in the target company, thereby assisting another company to acquire the target. Goodman JA stressed that, as the defendant bank had never withdrawn the bank's offer of assistance with respect to the takeover[149] or informed the claimants of the conflict of interest between its two customers, the bank had effectively encouraged the claimants 'to proceed with a course of action to achieve a purpose which [the bank] had already decided to thwart'.[150] In addition, Goodman JA rejected the proposition that the defendant bank could rely upon its duty of confidentiality to one customer to justify not informing the claimants of the true state of affairs, in circumstances where the bank 'in a direct conflict with the interests of other customers who were relying on it for advice and assistance' purchased shares for its own account and benefit and with the likelihood of making a gain from those transactions.[151] Indeed, Goodman JA stressed that, even if

decided by applying *Hedley Byrne* without having resort to the device of a fiduciary relationship: *Verity & Spindler* v. *Lloyds Bank plc* [1995] CLC 1557, 1571–1572. See also *Morgan* v. *Lloyds Bank plc*, n.22 above; *Frost* v. *James Finlay Bank Ltd*, n.75 above, [29]. See further Sect. 4(iii) below.

[148] N.124 above, cited with approval in *Hodgkinson* v. *Simms*, n.114 above, [28]–[29]. See also *Hong Kong Bank of Canada* v. *Phillips* [1998] 2 WWR 606, 630 (MBQB); *Gowanlock* v. *Bank of Nova Scotia*, n.100 above, [61]–[62]; *Canada Trustco Mortgage Co* v. *Menard* [2002] Man. R. 2d Lexis 14, [29] (MBQB); *430707 BC Ltd* v. *Royal Bank of Canada* [2004] BCJ No. 558, [39] (BCSC); *Giles* v. *Westminster Savings Credit Union* [2007] BCCA 411, [34]–[48]; *Canada Trustco Mortgage Co* v. *Pierce Estate* [2007] OJ No. 525, [16]–[18] (OSC); *Toronto Dominion Bank* v. *Femia*, n.124 above, [19]. For the current Canadian trend against imposing fiduciary duties on banks, see n.124 above.

[149] Compare *Arklow Investments Ltd* v. *Maclean*, n.99 above, where a merchant bank did withdraw its offer of assistance, and the Privy Council held that, in the absence of any informal arrangement or continuing course of conduct between the bank and the claimants, there was insufficient mutuality between the parties to justify imposing a fiduciary duty of loyalty on the bank; cf. *United Pan-Europe Communications NV* v. *Deutsche Bank AG* [2000] 2 BCLC 461 (CA), where the Court of Appeal held that the defendant bank's earlier undertaking of tasks for the claimants gave rise to fiduciary duties that might arguably extend beyond those tasks. The different conclusions probably arise from the fact that in *Arklow* 'there was no relationship at all' between the parties: *JD Wetherspoon plc* v. *Van de Berg & Co Ltd* [2007] EWHC 1044 (Ch), [25].

[150] N.124 above, 431.

[151] Ibid., 437; cf. *Susilawati* v. *American Express Bank Ltd*, n.110 above, [92]. The conflicting approaches in these two cases are reconcileable—a court should be unwilling to allow a bank to shelter behind its duty of confidentiality to other customers (and thereby deny the existence of a fiduciary duty) when (as in *Standard*

the defendant bank could not disclose to the claimants any information that was confidential to its other customer, it nevertheless remained at least 'under an obligation to tell the [claimants] that it had a position adverse to their plans or that it had a conflict of interests'.[152]

In those rare instances where a bank risks being classified as a fiduciary, it may nevertheless avoid liability by making full and frank disclosure to the customer that there is an actual or potential conflict of interests and by obtaining the customer's fully informed consent to the bank continuing to act in those circumstances.[153] Whilst general advanced disclosure may be enough for some purposes, it may not be sufficiently precise to cover every situation. Express disclosure of specific circumstances will be more reliable. Ultimately, what information must be supplied to the customer before their consent will be treated as fully informed is a question that depends on all the circumstances. Where it is not possible or practical to obtain the customer's fully informed consent to the bank continuing to act in a situation of conflict, the bank must cease acting. As considered in *Standard Investments*, such a situation might arise when the bank's duty of confidentiality to another customer precludes the bank from disclosing certain information relevant to a particular conflict of interest. This situation arose in *Commonwealth Bank of Australia* v. *Smith*,[154] where the bank's branch manager introduced the claimants, who were customers, to other customers who were selling a hotel business, which the claimants were keen to acquire. The branch manager informed the claimants that, as the vendors were also customers, information concerning the vendors' account and general affairs would have to be treated as confidential. Instead of then advising the purchasers to seek independent professional advice, the branch manager assured the claimants that the proposed terms of acquisition were favourable and that it would be futile to bargain for a lower price. Moreover, when the bank received an independent valuation of the business in connection with the claimants' mortgage application, the bank failed to disclose to the claimants that the valuation was lower than the agreed purchase price. The business' real value was approximately half of what the claimants had paid. The Australian Federal Court held that, whilst a bank would generally be expected to act in its own best interests when obtaining an independent mortgage valuation for security purposes, there might nevertheless be circumstances where a customer would expect to receive advice on the wisdom of the proposed investment. Their Honours considered that the bank in *Smith* had effectively assumed the position of 'investment adviser' and had accordingly become a fiduciary.[155] As the claimants were commercially unsophisticated, and as there was a conflict

---

Investments) the bank has specifically undertaken to provide assistance, guidance, or advice in respect of a matter covered by that duty, but need not be so solicitous when (as in *Susilawati*) there is no such express undertaking.

[152] Ibid. Rejecting the bank's argument that the alleged breach of duty was based upon the respective knowledge of two separate bank officers, Goodman JA had no difficulty aggregating the knowledge of the various bank officers and attributing this to the bank itself to hold it liable: ibid., 430–431.

[153] *Australian Securities and Investments Commission* v. *Citigroup Global Markets Australia Pty Ltd (No. 4)*, n.99 above, [293]–[296]. See also *Ratiu* v. *Conway*, n.99 above, [99]–[102]; *Forsyth-Grant* v. *Allen* [2008] EWCA Civ 505, [40].

[154] N.125 above, citing *McBean* v. *Bank of Nova Scotia* (1981) 15 BLR 296, affd. (1982) ACWS (2d) 154 (OCA); *Hayward* v. *Bank of Nova Scotia* (1984) 45 OR (2d) 542, affd. (1985) 51 OR (2d) 193 (OCA); *Daly* v. *Sydney Stock Exchange Ltd* (1986) 160 CLR 371, 384–385 (HCA). See also *Grubic* v. *Commonwealth Bank of Australia* (1993) ACR 90–033 (SASC); *Australian Securities and Investments Commission* v. *Citigroup Global Markets Australia Pty Ltd (No.4)*, n.99 above, [285]; *Re Brown & Australian Securities and Investments Commission*, n.143 above, [151]–[152].

[155] Ibid, 476. A bank that merely acts as lender and not as an adviser will not owe fiduciary duties: *NMFM Property Pty Ltd* v. *Citibank Ltd (No. 10)* (2002) 186 ALR 442 (FCA); *Commonwealth Bank of Australia* v. *Finding* [2001] 1 Qd R 168, [13] (QCA); *Karam* v. *Australia & New Zealand Banking Group* [2001] NSWSC

of interests between the bank's two 'sets of customers', the bank's failure to disclose the valuation breached its fiduciary duties, even though the bank had not derived any direct benefit or financial gain from the relevant transaction. Of particular relevance to the present discussion is the fact that their Honours did not consider that the bank had discharged its fiduciary duty by simply alerting the claimants to the existence of a conflict of interest. As this conflict and the bank's duty of confidentiality to the vendors precluded the bank from disclosing certain information to the claimants, the bank should have impressed on them the importance of obtaining independent advice, and should have refrained from advising them at all.

Instead of seeking a customer's fully informed consent, a bank may include terms in the underlying banker–customer contract that purport to exclude or modify any fiduciary obligations that it might otherwise owe to a customer.[156] This technique has been endorsed by the Privy Council[157] and the House of Lords.[158] The commercial importance of multifunction banks being able to exclude liability for breaches of fiduciary duty is evident from the Australian Federal Court's decision in *Australian Securities and Investments Commission* v. *Citigroup Global Markets Australia Pty Ltd (No. 4)*.[159] The defendant bank's investment banking division was advising a customer on a takeover bid for another company and, in ignorance of the proposed bid, the bank's equities division purchased a significant shareholding in the target company on the final trading day before the bid was announced. The claimant regulatory body brought proceedings against the defendant bank for breaching the Corporations Act 2001 (Cth), *inter alia*, the requirement that a financial services licensee have adequate arrangements for the management of conflicts of interest, and the prohibition on insider trading.[160] Key to liability was showing that the bank owed its customer fiduciary obligations when advising on its takeover bid, and showing that the bank accordingly was obliged to avoid any actual or potential conflict between its duty of loyalty to its customer and its desire to profit from proprietary trading, without first obtaining that customer's fully informed consent. Despite the fact that the customer in *Citigroup* was far more commercially sophisticated than those in *Smith*, as discussed above, Jacobson J held that *prima facie* the defendant bank's relationship with its customer had 'all of the indicia of a fiduciary relationship' as the bank had undertaken to provide financial advice on the

709; *Australian Competition and Consumer Commission* v. *Oceana Commercial Pty Ltd* [2003] FCA 1516, affd. [2004] FCAFC 174; *Advanced Switching Services Pty Ltd* v. *State Bank of New South Wales* [2007] FCA 954, [20]–[42]; *JP Morgan Chase Bank* v. *Springwell Navigation Corp.*, n.100 above, [571]–[573].

[156] *Esquire (Electronics) Ltd* v. *The Hong Kong and Shanghai Banking Corp.* [2006] HKCU 1705, [103] (HKCA).

[157] *Kelly* v. *Cooper* [1993] AC 205, 214–215 (PC).

[158] *Henderson* v. *Merrett Syndicates Ltd*, n.89 above, 206. See also *JP Morgan Chase Bank* v. *Springwell Navigation Corp.*, n.100 above, [734]; *Susilawati* v. *American Express Bank Ltd*, n.110 above, [67]. Although initially supporting such an approach (*Fiduciary Duties and Regulatory Rules* (Report No. 236, London, 1995)), the Law Commission subsequently recommended that professional trustees should not be able to rely on clauses excluding their liability for breach of trust arising from negligence (Consultation Paper No. 171, *Trustee Exemption Clauses* (LCCP No. 171, London, 2002)). This particular proposal was, however, criticized for being out of touch with the needs of the wholesale financial markets, where the use of professional trustees is common practice in international bond issues: Financial Markets Law Committee Paper No. 62, *Trustee Exemption Clauses* (London, 2004). Following a consultation process, the Law Commission's latest position requires trustees 'to ensure that the settlors are aware of any trustee exemption clauses in their trust deeds': *Trustee Exemption Clauses* (Report No. 301, London, 2006), [1.13]–[1.27]. Rather than a statutory obligation, this would take the form of a 'rule of practice' to be imposed, monitored, and enforced by professional and trust bodies.

[159] N.99 above, approved in *Premium Real Estate Ltd* v. *Stevens* [2009] 1 NZLR 148, [66] (NZCA). No appeal is planned in *Citigroup*: J. Getzler, n.96 above, 21.

[160] Ibid., [13]–[33].

wisdom and merits of the takeover bid.[161] This *prima facie* conclusion had to be assessed, however, in light of the mandate letter engaging the bank to act as joint financial adviser, as this stated that the bank acted 'as an independent contractor and not in any other capacity including as a fiduciary' and made the customer aware that the bank 'may in the future provide financial or other services to other parties with conflicting interests'.[162] Jacobson J accepted as a matter of principle that, with the exception of liability for fraud and 'deliberate dereliction of duty', it was open to a fiduciary to exclude or modify the operation of fiduciary duties,[163] and concluded that the mandate letter in *Citigroup* had precisely this effect.[164]

There are, however, potential limits to this approach. First, contractual terms excluding or modifying fiduciary obligations may be held 'unreasonable' under the Unfair Contract Terms Act 1977 and/or 'unfair' under the Unfair Terms in Consumer Contracts Regulations 1999.[165] Such a term is more likely to survive legislative attack when raised against a financially sophisticated customer than an unsophisticated one.[166] Secondly, such terms will be construed *contra proferentem*. Thirdly, where the parties have a pre-existing fiduciary relationship, the fiduciary will not be able to exclude or modify its obligations without the principal's fully informed consent to the inclusion of the relevant clause.[167] In *Australian Securities and Investments Commission* v. *Citigroup Global Markets Australia Pty Ltd (No. 4)*,[168] the claimant tried unsuccessfully to invoke this principle in order to avoid the effect of a clause in the bank's mandate letter that clearly excluded the existence of any fiduciary duties. Jacobson J cast doubt upon whether the requirement to obtain the principal's prior informed consent to such an exclusion clause was one of general application,[169] and, even if it were, whether that principle would ever really apply in the general banking or investment banking contexts, since it would have no application 'unless the fiduciary is within an established category or is subject to fiduciary obligations before entering into the contract'.[170] This description is not generally apt to cover banks.[171] Fourthly, it is unlikely that contractual terms could give a bank an unrestricted general right to act for opposing parties in the *same* transaction, where the customers' respective

---

[161] Ibid., [325]–[330]. See also *Re Brown & Australian Securities and Investments Commission*, n.143 above, [151]–[152].

[162] Ibid., [145].   [163] Ibid., [278]–[281].   [164] Ibid., [324]–[325], [337].

[165] Nn.76–77 above. An exemption clause in a trust instrument is not a 'contract term or...a notice' within UCTA 1977, s.2(1): *Baker* v. *JE Clark & Co* [2006] EWCA Civ 464, [20]–[21], citing Law Commission Consultation Paper No. 171, n.158 above, [2.60]–[2.62]). The Law Commission has also tentatively expressed the view (at [2.63]) that the UTCCR 1999 would similarly be inapplicable. Cf. M. Hughes, 'More good news than bad for bond trustees' [2004] *JIBFL* 310, 311.

[166] As many clauses in commercial contracts 'define the terms upon which the parties are conducting their business' and 'prevent an obligation from arising in the first place', they are outside the scope of UCTA 1977: *JP Morgan Chase Bank* v. *Springwell Navigation Corp.*, n.100 above, [603]–[606], affd. n.372 below, [179]–[180]. See also *Titan Steel Wheels Ltd* v. *Royal Bank of Scotland plc* [2010] EWHC 211 (Comm), [98]–[100]; *Raiffeisen Zentralbank Österreich AG* v. *Royal Bank of Scotland plc* [2010] EWHC 1392 (Comm.), [313]–[315].

[167] D. Hayton, 'Fiduciaries in Context: An Overview', in P.B.H. Birks (ed.), *Privacy and Loyalty* (Oxford, 1997), 300.

[168] N.99 above.

[169] Ibid., [302]–[307], [340]–[348] (limiting the principle to 'time charging by solicitors').

[170] Ibid., [345]–[346]. Consider *JP Morgan Chase Bank* v. *Springwell Navigation Corp.*, n.100 above, [597], [606].

[171] In *Citigroup*, Jacobson J (at [359]–[360]) would not have been prepared to infer the relevant consent on the customer's part from the fact that it should have realized that an investment bank would trade in the shares of a target company. Nevertheless, on the particular facts (at [361]), the customer 'had sufficient knowledge of the real possibility of proprietary trading' by the bank.

interests conflict, or could exclude liability where the deliberate suppression of information has deceived the customer.[172]

As an alternative to using *ad hoc* contractual techniques, a bank may employ more permanent, structural mechanisms to manage its conflicts of interest. For example, a multifunction bank that provides a range of financial services to its customers may rely on a contractual term allowing it to use 'Chinese walls' (nowadays termed 'information barriers')[173] to restrict the flow of information between departments within the bank and to limit the information provided to particular customers. The defendant bank in *Citigroup* relied upon such an 'information barrier' between its investment banking and equities divisions in order to escape liability. Adopting Lord Millett's comments in *Prince Jefri Bolkiah* v. *KPMG*,[174] Jacobson J rejected any blanket rule of law that 'information barriers' were always ineffective to eliminate the risk of disclosure within a bank, but indicated that the effectiveness of a particular 'information barrier' would depend upon the particular facts.[175] An 'information barrier's' effectiveness will depend upon whether it is 'an established part of the organizational structure' of the bank, rather than being created on an *ad hoc* basis,[176] and will usually involve the physical separation of departments, educational programmes for staff, defined procedures as to when an information barrier will be treated as having been breached, internal monitoring of the barrier's effectiveness, and disciplinary sanctions for breaching the barrier.[177] On the facts of *Citigroup*, the 'information barriers' at least sufficed to satisfy the defendant bank's statutory obligations.[178]

(ii) **Undue influence**

The preceding section demonstrated that courts have occasionally sought to protect vulnerable sureties from exploitation by treating a bank as fiduciarily obliged to safeguard the surety's interests. Whilst Sir Eric Sachs in *Bundy*[179] treated the notion of 'confidentiality' as the touchstone for such fiduciary liability, Lord Scarman in *Morgan* shifted the analytical focus away from whether the bank was a fiduciary and onto whether undue influence had been exercised,[180] and accordingly onto whether one party had exercised a

---

[172] *Clark Boyce* v. *Mouat* [1994] 1 AC 428 (PC).

[173] *Asia Pacific Telecommunications Ltd* v. *Optus Networks Pty Ltd* [2007] NSWSC 350, [4].

[174] [1999] AC 222 (HL). See further C. Hollander & S. Salzedo, *Conflicts of Interest* (3rd edn., 2008), chs. 1 & 7.

[175] N.99 above, [317]–[318]. Jacobson J did warn (at [321]) that 'Chinese walls may sometimes be porous'.

[176] *Marks & Spencer plc* v. *Freshfields Bruckhaus Deringer* [2004] EWHC 1337 (Ch), [18].

[177] N.99 above, [318]–[319], [449].   [178] Ibid., [452], [593].   [179] N.118 above.

[180] N.137 above, 707–709. The juridical nature of undue influence has engendered considerable debate. One view is that the equitable doctrine of undue influence looks to the lack of good conscience on the part of the person exercising the influence and the wrongful exploitation of his counterparty: *National Commercial Bank (Jamaica) Ltd* v. *Hew* [2003] UKPC 51; *R.* v. *Attorney-General for England and Wales* [2003] UKPC 22; *Lawrence* v. *Poorah* [2008] UKPC 21, [20]. See also P.J. Millett, n.114 above, 219. The alternative view is that the undue influence doctrine may be explained in terms of the impaired consent of the person subject to undue influence: *Hammond* v. *Osborn* [2002] EWCA Civ. 885, [1], [25], [32]; *Niersmans* v. *Pesticcio* [2004] EWCA Civ 372, [20]–[23]; *Macklin* v. *Dowsett* [2004] EWCA Civ 904, [10]; *Randall* v. *Randall* [2004] EWHC 2258 (Ch), [35]–[42]; *Wright* v. *Hodgkinson* [2004] EWHC 3091 (Ch), [117]–[120]; *Daniel* v. *Drew* [2005] EWCA Civ 507, [36]; *Cattermole* v. *Prisk* [2006] 1 FLR 693, [14]; *Green* v. *Green* [2006] EWHC 2010 (Fam), [94]; *Birmingham City Council* v. *Forde* [2009] EWHC 12 (QB), [101]–[103]. See also P. Birks and C.N. Yin, 'On the Nature of Undue Influence' in J. Beatson and D. Friedmann (eds.), *Good Faith and Fault in Contract Law* (Oxford, 1995) ch.3; P. Birks, 'Undue Influence as Wrongful Exploitation' (2004) 120 LQR 34. It has been suggested that the current debate has 'ossified in bipolar form' and that there is scope for a 'multi-dimensional relational theory of undue influence': M. Chen-Wishart, 'Undue Influence: *Beyond* Impaired Consent and Wrongdoing Towards a Relational Analysis' in A. Burrows & A. Rodger,

'dominating influence' over the other,[181] rather than on whether there was a relationship of 'confidentiality'.[182] Since this analytical shift in *Morgan*, the substantive principles applicable in undue influence cases have developed apace. In *Bank of Credit and Commerce International SA* v. *Aboody*,[183] the Court of Appeal classified the different categories of undue influence. In cases of actual undue influence ('Class 1'), the claimant had to prove affirmatively that the wrongdoer had exerted undue influence over the complainant to enter into the impugned transaction. In cases of presumed undue influence ('Class 2'), the complainant had only to show a 'confidential relationship' with the wrongdoer, which in turn raised a presumption of undue influence; the burden then shifted to the wrongdoer to prove that the complainant entered into the impugned transaction freely. *Aboody* further subdivided presumed undue influence into two categories—certain relationships were deemed to be 'confidential', such as solicitor and client, medical advisor and patient, but not husband and wife, nor banker and customer ('Class 2(A)'), while, in other relationships, the complainant had to establish that she actually reposed trust and confidence in the particular wrongdoer ('Class 2(B)'). This classification was adopted in *Barclays Bank plc* v. *O'Brien*,[184] which involved the relationship between a husband and wife. Lord Browne-Wilkinson concluded that, although this relationship did not fall within Class 2(A), a wife could always prove that, in her particular case, she left decisions on financial affairs to her husband and accordingly 'reposed confidence and trust in her husband in relation to their financial affairs and therefore undue influence [was] to be presumed'.[185]

Subsequently, in *Royal Bank of Scotland* v. *Etridge (No. 2)*,[186] however, the House of Lords criticized the distinction between actual and presumed undue influence and stressed that the 'presumption' of undue influence merely provides evidential assistance in establishing whether or not undue influence has been applied.[187] Accordingly, a claimant can either adduce direct evidence of the wrongdoer's undue influence—including threats or overt acts of coercion at one end of the scale[188] or a situation where a husband 'fails to discharge the obligation of candour and fairness' that he owes to his wife who 'has reposed trust and confidence for the management of their financial affairs' at the other end[189]—or can

Mapping the Law: Essays in Memory of Peter Birks (Oxford, 2006), ch. 11. Indeed, the courts often still struggle to articulate a clear and precise rationale for undue influence: *Walker* v. *Walker* [2007] EWHC 597 (Ch), [190]–[191], [196]; *Hogg* v. *Hogg* [2007] EWHC 2240 (Ch), [42]; *Wallbank* v. *Price* [2008] 3 FCR 444, [35]. See also generally R. Bigwood, 'Undue Influence: Impaired Consent or Wicked Exploitation' (1996) 16 *OJLS* 503; D. Capper, 'Undue Influence and Unconscionability: A Rationalisation' (1998) 114 *LQR* 479; R. Bigwood, 'Contracts by Unfair Advantage: From Exploitation to Transactional Neglect' (2005) 25 *OJLS* 65; J. Devenney & A. Chandler, 'Unconscionability and the Taxonomy of Undue Influence' [2007] *JBL* 541.

[181] Cf. *Goldsworthy* v. *Brickell* [1987] Ch. 378, 401, 404 (CA).

[182] *Barclays Bank plc* v. *O'Brien*, n.141 above, 189 ('confidential relationship' arises where one person reposes 'trust and confidence', generating a presumption of undue influence). See also *Goldsworthy* v. *Brickell*, n.181 above, 401, 404; *Turner* v. *Barclays Bank plc* [1997] 2 FCR 151, 159; *Bank of Scotland* v. *Bennett* [1997] 1 FLR 801, revsd. on other grounds: [1999] 1 FLR 1115.

[183] [1990] 1 QB 923, 953–954 (CA).

[184] N.141 above, 189–191. See also *Pang Siu Hing* v. *Tsang Kwok Man* [2004] HKCU 30, [17]–[18]; *DBS Bank (Hong Kong) Ltd* v. *Hui So Yuk* [2009] HKCU 913, [30]–[31].

[185] Ibid., 190.   [186] N.141 above.

[187] Ibid., [17], [92], [98], [105]–[107], [157], [161]. See also *Ying* v. *Bank of China (Hong Kong) Ltd* [2004] HKCU 1481, [29]–[30], [33]–[34] (HKCFA).

[188] *Karsten* v. *Markham* [2009] EWHC 3658 (Ch), [130]–[131].

[189] Ibid., [32]–[33], [36]. A husband's inadvertent or deliberate failure to disclose facts material to the wife's decision to stand surety (for example, an extra-marital affair) might breach his obligation of candour and fairness: *First Plus Financial Group* v. *Hewett* [2010] EWCA Civ 312, [29]–[37]; cf. *Royal Bank of Scotland plc* v. *Chandra* [2010] EWHC 105 (Ch), [125]–[140], limiting undue influence to the husband's deliberate concealment. On appeal, Patten LJ similarly viewed undue influence as requiring 'unconscionable' conduct

rely upon the presumption of undue influence to shift the evidential burden of disproving undue influence onto the defendant. In recasting the modern presumption of undue influence,[190] Lord Nicholls stressed that two prerequisites had to be established.[191] First, a claimant must demonstrate that they 'placed trust and confidence in the other party in relation to the management of [their] financial affairs'.[192] Whilst there are certain relationships in which it is irrebuttably presumed that one party exerts *influence* over another,[193] and in which it is consequently unnecessary to prove that one party reposed trust and confidence in the other,[194] Lord Nicholls confirmed in *Etridge* that the relationship between spouses is not of such a type.[195] Secondly, the relevant transaction must be one that 'calls for an explanation', which would not ordinarily include a wife standing surety for her husband's debts or those of a company in which they are jointly interested.[196] As Lord Scott emphasized in *Etridge*,[197] this is the modern reformulation of the requirement in *Morgan* that the transaction be 'manifestly disadvantageous' to the person influenced.[198] This is a label that is now best discarded.[199] The presumption of undue influence may be rebutted by evidence that the claimant was free of undue influence and understood the implications of the proposed transaction.[200] As Lord Nicholls stated in *Etridge*,[201] this is most commonly demonstrated by evidence that the claimant received advice from an independent third party. Although the rebuttal of the presumption will depend on the nature and quality of

---

(which would include 'conscious deception' or an 'abuse of confidence') or 'some conscious act of wrongdoing' on the part of the husband: *Royal Bank of Scotland plc* v. *Chandra* [2011] EWCA Civ 192, [26]–[32], [39]. On this approach, an innocent misrepresentation (let alone an inadvertent non-disclosure) will not constitute 'undue influence', although an innocent misrepresentation (but not an innocent failure to disclose) can give rise to relief in its own right: ibid., [32].

[190] See further *Randall* v. *Randall*, n.180 above, [35]; *Hansen* v. *Barker-Benfield* [2006] EWHC 1119 (Ch), [59]; *Sanders* v. *Buckley* [2006] All ER (D) 307, [66]; *Shaw* v. *Finnimore* [2009] EWHC 367 (Ch), [71]–[73]; *Birmingham City Council* v. *Forde*, n.180 above, [98]–[110]; *Curtis* v. *Pulbrook* [2009] EWHC 782 (Ch), [138]–[139]; *Karsten* v. *Markham*, n.188 above, [130]–[131].

[191] N.141 above, [20]. Undue influence will not operate in testamentary dispositions: *Re Cooper* [2005] EWHC 2389 (Ch), [50]; *Cattermole* v. *Prisk*, n.180 above, [13]–[14]; *Edwards* v. *Edwards* [2007] All ER (D) 46, [47]. See also *Gill* v. *Woodall* [2009] EWHC 3491 (Ch), [485]–[499]; *Ark* v. *Kaur* [2010] EWHC 2314 (Ch), [18]–[20].

[192] Ibid., [14]. For a slightly wider formulation, see *Thompson* v. *Foy* [2009] EWHC 1076 (Ch), [100]; *First Plus Financial Group* v. *Hewett*, n.189 above, [27]. Whilst 'trust and confidence' usually arises from the parties' historical relationship, it can arise out of the impugned transaction itself: *Turkey* v. *Awadh* [2005] EWCA Civ. 382, [8]–[12].

[193] Recent cases have suggested that it is the *undue* nature of any influence that is irrebuttably presumed: *Niersmans* v. *Pesticcio*, n.180 above, [3]; *Randall* v. *Randall*, n.180 above, [45]; *Walker* v. *Walker*, n.180 above, [194]; *de Wind* v. *Wedge* [2008] EWHC 514 (Ch), [10]). The presumption properly relates, however, to whether *influence* exists in the first place: N. Enonchong, 'Presumed Undue Influence: Continuing Misconceptions' (2005) 121 *LQR* 29.

[194] *Royal Bank of Scotland* v. *Etridge (No. 2)*, n.141 above, [18]. Examples include parent–child, guardian–ward, trustee–beneficiary, doctor–patient, and solicitor–client relationships: *Markham* v. *Karsten* [2007] BPIR 1109, [30]–[44]. The fiancé–fiancée relationship (and the 'modern equivalent' of that relationship) also triggers the irrebuttable presumption of influence: *Stevens* v. *Newey* [2005] EWCA Civ 50, [18], criticized by N. Enonchong, 'The Irrebuttable Presumption of Influence and the Relationship Between Fiancé and Fiancée' (2005) 121 *LQR* 567.

[195] Ibid., [19].   [196] Ibid., [30]–[31].   [197] Ibid., [220].

[198] N.137 above, 704. See also *National Westminster Bank plc* v. *Waite*, n.124 above, [37]–[38]; *Smith* v. *Cooper* [2010] EWCA Civ. 722, [59]–[66].

[199] *Macklin* v. *Dowsett*, n.180 above, [17]; cf. *Radley* v. *Bruno* [2006] EWHC 2888 (Ch), [29].

[200] *Goodchild* v. *Bradbury* [2006] EWCA Civ. 1868, [27]; *Gorjat* v. *Gorjat* [2010] EWHC 1537 (Ch), [141]–[147].

[201] N.141 above, [20].

that advice, as well as the surrounding circumstances,[202] the total absence of independent advice will make any such rebuttal difficult.[203]

Since *Bundy* and *Morgan*, it has been comparatively unusual for a surety to rely upon the above principles to show that the *bank itself* exercised undue influence over the surety (or committed some other form of legal or equitable wrong against the surety) to secure the execution of a guarantee or mortgage.[204] *National Westminster Bank plc* v. *Waite* is a rare example of just such an allegation.[205] The defendants, who were husband and wife, were directors of a company that operated a care home. Although the claimant bank only agreed to provide the company with an overdraft facility on condition that the defendants guaranteed that liability, the bank made the overdraft available before the guarantee was in place. The company's bank manager chased the defendants for their guarantees and, after the defendants indicated that they did not intend to seek independent legal advice, the bank manager eventually arranged for another bank officer to visit the defendants' home to arrange the execution of the guarantees.[206] Although the defendants were advised to reconsider their decision not to obtain independent legal advice and to read the guarantee document, both signed without raising further queries.[207] The husband subsequently signed a further guarantee for increased liabilities at a meeting with the company's bank manager at the bank and the wife executed her further guarantee shortly thereafter when the manager brought the document to her home. On each occasion, the defendants signed confirmations that the guarantees had been executed freely, despite receiving oral and written warnings to seek independent legal advice.[208] When the bank sought to enforce the guarantees, the defendants alleged that the bank manager had exercised undue influence by encouraging them to give the guarantees, by failing to advise them that their company would inevitably fail, and by thereby preferring the bank's interests to those of the defendants. Despite concluding that the bank manager 'was more enthusiastic and took a greater personal interest than was usually warranted for a bank manager' and that he 'undoubtedly gave the directors advice on their business strategy', Judge Havelock-Allan QC concluded that these factors did not influence either the bank's or the defendants' behaviour, and accordingly rejected the suggestion that there had been any actual exercise of undue influence by the bank over the defendants.[209] This conclusion was bolstered by there being insufficient evidence to even raise the presumption of undue influence in the first place. Although the bank manager's conduct did cause the relationship between the bank and defendants to 'cross the line' and become one of trust and confidence[210] (as in *Bundy*),[211] the guarantee was not a transaction that called for an explanation, as the company was not doomed to failure at the time of the guarantee's execution.[212] As *Bundy* demonstrates, exceptional facts are usually required.

Although few cases have alleged that the bank *directly* exercised undue influence over a surety, there have been many cases since *Morgan* where the enforcement of a charge or guarantee has been resisted on the ground that undue influence has been exercised (or some other wrong committed)[213] against the surety by a third party, usually the principal debtor—frequently, it is a wife alleging undue influence by her husband, or elderly

---

[202] *Wright* v. *Hodgkinson*, n.180 above, [145]–[148]; *Radley* v. *Bruno*, n.199 above, [30]; *Walker* v. *Walker*, n.180 above, [210]–[215]; *de Wind* v. *Wedge*, n.193 above, [54]–[55].

[203] *Abbey National Bank plc* v. *Stringer* [2006] EWCA Civ 338, [44]–[46]; *Smith* v. *Cooper*, n.198 above, [63]–[71].

[204] *Lloyds Bank plc* v. *Waterhouse* (1993) 2 FLR 97 (CA) (surety's successful plea of *non est factum*); *Wright* v. *HSBC plc*, n.104 above, [61] (customer's unsuccessful plea of duress).

[205] N.124 above.   [206] Ibid., [14].   [207] Ibid., [43].   [208] Ibid., [21]–[22].

[209] Ibid., [45].   [210] Ibid., [45], [50].   [211] N.118 above.   [212] N.124 above, [50].

[213] Such wrongs usually involve a misrepresentation (*Royal Bank of Scotland* v. *Etridge (No. 2)*, n.141 above, [279]; *Annulment Funding Co. Ltd* v. *Cowey* [2010] EWCA Civ. 711, [62]–[65]; *Royal Bank of Scotland*

parents making a similar allegation against their son. Before 1993,[214] the authorities were difficult to reconcile and, in addition to proving that he had suffered some relevant legal or equitable wrong (usually at the debtor's hands), some cases also required the surety to demonstrate that he had acted to his detriment[215] and/or that the wrongdoing debtor's actions could be imputed to the bank before the security could be set aside.[216] This latter requirement could be satisfied by showing that the debtor obtained the execution of the charge as the bank's agent,[217] or by pointing to other specific facts that might convince the court to hold the bank liable for the wrongdoer's actions.[218] In 1993, however, the applicable principles were twice considered by the House of Lords.

In *Barclays Bank plc* v. *O'Brien*,[219] a wife was persuaded by her accountant husband to execute a charge over the matrimonial home to secure a guarantee that the husband had given to the bank in respect of his company's debts. The wife executed the relevant mortgage documents at a meeting with a bank clerk at the bank's premises, but was neither given the opportunity to read those documents nor (contrary to the branch manager's instructions to the clerk) given an explanation of the transaction's nature. Furthermore, the bank clerk failed to draw the wife's attention to a side-letter, in which she purportedly acknowledged her understanding of the transaction's nature and the bank's recommendation that she take independent legal advice. When the bank sought to enforce its security, the trial judge upheld its validity. On appeal, Scott LJ concluded that both as a matter of policy and precedent (although not all the relevant authorities supported his view) certain types of surety, such as married women and aged relatives, were treated as a 'protected class'.[220] Securities furnished by such sureties would be unenforceable by the creditor, provided (i) he was aware of the nature of the relationship between debtor and surety and the consequent likelihood of influence and reliance, (ii) the surety's consent was procured by the debtor's undue influence or misrepresentation, and (iii) the creditor had failed to take reasonable steps to ensure that the surety entered the transaction with an adequate understanding of its nature so that their ultimate consent thereto was free and informed. On this basis, the Court of Appeal set the bank's charge aside. Whilst the House of Lords affirmed this conclusion, its reasoning differed. Lord Browne-Wilkinson emphasized as a starting-point that any law designed to protect vulnerable sureties, such as wives and cohabitees, should not render the matrimonial home unacceptable to banks as security. Nevertheless, his Lordship considered that there should be circumstances where equity should be prepared to set aside a security granted by a surety (usually a wife) to a bank as a result of a

---

plc v. *Chandra*, n.189 above, [34]–[40]) or unconscionable conduct (*Portman Building Society* v. *Dusangh* [2000] Lloyd's Rep 197 (CA)).

[214] *Turnbull* v. *Duval* [1902] AC 302; *Chaplin & Co. Ltd* v. *Brammall* [1908] 1 KB 233; *Howes* v. *Bishop* [1909] 2 KB 390; *Talbot* v. *von Boris* [1911] 1 KB 854; *Bank of Montreal* v. *Stuart* [1911] AC 120; *Shears & Sons Ltd* v. *Jones* (1922) 128 LT 218.

[215] *Bank of Credit and Commerce International SA* v. *Aboody*, n.183 above, 961. See also *Goldsworthy* v. *Brickell*, n.181 above, 405; *Barclays Bank* v. *Khaira* [1992] 1 WLR 623 (CA).

[216] Cf. *Kings North Trust Ltd* v. *Bell* [1986] 1 WLR 119 (CA).

[217] *Avon Finance Co. Ltd* v. *Bridger* [1985] 2 All ER 281, 286–287 (CA); *Coldunell Ltd* v. *Gallon* [1986] QB 1184, 1196, 1200, 1206 (CA); *Midland Bank Ltd* v. *Shephard* [1988] 3 All ER 17 (CA); *Midland Bank* v. *Perry* (1988) 56 P&CR 202, 207–209 (CA); *Barclays Bank* v. *Khaira*, n.215 above. For the recent use of agency principles in the New Zealand surety context, see *Nathan* v. *Dollars & Sense Ltd* [2008] 2 NZLR 557, [23]–[26], [49] (NZSC); *Burmeister* v. *O'Brien* [2008] 3 NZLR 842, [67], [84]. These decisions are unlikely, however, to represent a fundamental shift away from the use of notice principles in New Zealand, back towards the use of agency-based reasoning: *ANZ National Bank Ltd* v. *Smith* (2009) 10 NZCPR 898, [21]–[28]; *Public Trust* v. *Ottow* (2009) 10 NZCPR 879, [60]–[67]. See further C. Hare, 'Banking Law' [2011] NZ L Rev 121.

[218] *Bank of Baroda* v. *Shah* [1988] 3 All ER 24 (CA); *Deutsche Bank AG* v. *Ibrahim* [1992] 1 Bank. LR 267.

[219] N.141 above.   [220] [1993] QB 109, 139–141 (CA).

third party debtor's undue influence (usually her husband). Naturally, this would occur if the husband/debtor acted as the bank's agent in obtaining the security from his wife,[221] with the result that the bank would be fixed with the husband's wrongdoing.

In addition to agency cases, Lord Browne-Wilkinson also held that 'if the creditor bank has notice, actual or constructive, of undue influence exercised by the husband (and consequently of the wife's equity to set aside the transaction) the creditor will take subject to that equity and the wife can set aside the transaction against the creditor... as well as against the husband'.[222] According to his Lordship, the key lay in identifying those circumstances in which the bank would be treated as having such notice. Indeed, his Lordship stressed that a proper application of the notice doctrine would eliminate the need for a special equitable doctrine applicable only to charges executed by a 'protected class' of sureties, as postulated by the Court of Appeal. Generally, a bank has the requisite constructive notice when it has knowledge of facts that should put it on enquiry as to the possibility of wrongdoing by the debtor against the surety. According to Lord Browne-Wilkinson:[223]

> A creditor is put on enquiry when a wife offers to stand surety for her husband's debts by the combination of two factors: (a) the transaction is on its face not to the financial advantage of the wife; and (b) there is a substantial risk in transactions of that kind that, in procuring the wife to act as surety, the husband has committed a legal or equitable wrong that entitles the wife to set aside the transaction.

As long as the transaction is not on its face to the surety's financial advantage, this same principle is equally applicable outside the spousal context, provided the creditor is *aware* that (a) the surety and debtor are cohabitees or (b) the surety reposes trust and confidence in the debtor in relation to his or her financial affairs.[224] His Lordship recognized, however, that banks could not be expected to conduct a detailed examination every time a wife stood surety or in every other case when it might have constructive notice of a debtor's potential wrongdoing. Accordingly, a bank could avoid being fixed with constructive notice by taking reasonable steps to satisfy itself that the wife had freely given her consent, usually by insisting 'that the wife attend a private meeting (in the absence of the husband) with a representative of the creditor at which she is told of the extent of her liability as surety, warned of the risk she is running, and urged to take independent legal advice'.[225]

---

[221] *Barclays Bank plc* v. *O'Brien*, n.141 above, 195, where Lord Browne-Wilkinson noted that, whilst it is sometimes possible 'without artificiality' to treat the husband/debtor as the bank's agent in procuring his wife's guarantee, 'such cases will be of very rare occurrence'. See also *Bank of Montreal* v. *Duguid* (2000) 185 DLR (4th) 458, [13] (OCA). In *Royal Bank of Scotland* v. *Etridge (No. 2)* [1998] 4 All ER 705, 717 (CA), Stuart-Smith LJ went further, doubting 'that it will ever be possible to treat [the husband] as the creditor's agent where he or his company is the principal debtor'. In *Nathan* v. *Dollars & Sense Ltd*, n.217 above, [23]–[26], [49], the New Zealand Supreme Court considered that Stuart-Smith LJ had probably gone too far in this respect. See also *Burmeister* v. *O'Brien*, n.217 above, [67], [84] ; *ANZ National Bank Ltd* v. *Smith*, n.217 above, [21]–[28]; *Public Trust* v. *Ottow*, n.217 above, [60]–[67].

[222] Ibid., 191.   [223] Ibid., 196.

[224] Ibid., 198. Relief has been afforded outside the spousal context: *Avon Finance Co. Ltd* v. *Bridger*, n.217 above (bank knew that parents trusted son in financial dealings); *Massey* v. *Midland Bank plc* [1995] 1 All ER 929 (CA) (surety had a longstanding sexual and emotional relationship with debtor, although neither married nor cohabiting); *Crédit Lyonnais Bank Nederland NV* v. *Burch* [1997] 1 All ER 144 (CA) (surety was young employee with no sexual, emotional, or cohabitation relationship with the debtor who was her employer); *Murphy* v. *Rayner* [2011] EWHC (Ch) 1, [304]–[329] (validity of assurances by disabled patient concerning future financial provision for his carer). See also *Barclays Bank plc* v. *Rivett* [1998] 3 FCR 304 (CA) (husband who placed trust and confidence in wife regarding financial affairs).

[225] Ibid., n.141 above, 196. See also *Wright* v. *Cherrytree Finance Ltd* [2001] EWCA Civ. 449, [32]–[34]. Lord Browne-Wilkinson in *O'Brien* added that, where the bank's knowledge of specific facts makes the exercise of

The House of Lords further clarified the applicable principles in *CIBC Mortgages plc* v. *Pitt*,[226] where a husband influenced his wife to redeem an existing mortgage over their home and enter into a refinancing agreement, which the spouses falsely described in their joint loan application as required for purchasing a holiday home. Following the mortgage's execution and the bank's disbursement of the funds, the husband used those funds to purchase shares, which had always been his real motivation for the borrowings. The wife had only reluctantly acquiesced. When the spouses fell into arrears with their loan repayments and the bank sought to enforce its security, the wife raised her husband's undue influence and the fact that she had signed the security documents unread, despite being given ample opportunity to do so before they were executed at the lender's premises. Affirming the lower courts' decision against the wife, the House of Lords nevertheless rejected the Court of Appeal's suggestion that a charge could only be set aside for undue influence if the transaction was disadvantageous, or of no benefit, to the influenced party.[227] According to Lord Browne-Wilkinson, although undue influence would not be *presumed* in the absence of such disadvantage, a charge could nevertheless be set aside, even where the element of disadvantage was absent, if *actual* undue influence was positively established on the facts. Whilst the charge in *Pitt* could have been set aside against the *husband* on this basis, Lord Browne-Wilkinson concluded that the bank was not affected by his undue influence, since the husband was not the lender's agent and the lender had not otherwise been put on enquiry:[228]

> [To the lender's knowledge], the transaction consisted of a joint loan to the husband and wife to finance the discharge of an existing mortgage on [the family's home] and, as to the balance, to be applied in buying a holiday home. The loan was advanced to both husband and wife jointly. There was nothing to indicate to the [lenders] that this was anything other than a normal advance to a husband and wife for their joint benefit.... If third parties were to be fixed with constructive notice of undue influence in relation to every transaction between husband and wife, such transactions would become almost impossible. On every purchase of a home in joint names, the building society or bank financing the purchase would have to insist on meeting the wife separately from her husband, advise her as to the nature of the transaction and recommend her to take legal advice separate from that of her husband.

His Lordship accordingly emphasized the distinction between a loan made to spouses *jointly* and the situation where a wife provides security for her husband's borrowings. Lord Browne-Wilkinson considered that requiring lenders to follow the procedures established in *O'Brien* in the former type of case would ultimately be detrimental to the interests of the average married couple requiring mortgage financing. With respect to the latter type of case, however, his Lordship stated that 'there is not only the possibility of undue influence having been exercised but also the increased risk of its having in fact been exercised because, at least on its face, the guarantee by a wife of her husband's debts is not to her financial benefit. It is the combination of these two factors which puts the creditor on enquiry.'[229]

---

undue influence a probability rather than a mere possibility, it should *insist*, rather than just suggest, that the surety obtain independent legal advice.

[226] [1994] 1 AC 200 (HL).

[227] *Bank of Credit and Commerce International SA* v. *Aboody*, n.183 above, 961; *Goldsworthy* v. *Brickell*, n.181 above, 405; *ABN Amro Bank NV* v. *Mody* [2002] HKCU 1339, [20]–[22].

[228] N.226 above, 211, applied in *Britannia Building Society* v. *Pugh* [1997] 2 FLR 7 (CA) (joint loan to spouses to finance jointly operated property development business); cf. *UCB Group Ltd* v. *Hedworth* [2003] EWCA Civ 1717, [119]–[124] (no absolute rule regarding joint advances).

[229] Ibid. Lord Browne-Wilkinson considered (ibid., 210) that a lender might nevertheless be put on enquiry if it knew that a joint advance was in reality only for the benefit, or only to discharge the liabilities,

Besides reinforcing the analytical shift away from fiduciary principles to undue influence principles to protect sureties, as discussed previously, *O'Brien* and *Pitt* have two other significant aspects. First, the House of Lords used the doctrine of notice in a novel way.[230] Traditionally, the notice doctrine is used to determine priority between successive rights over property. This does not neatly cover the *O'Brien*-type scenario where, instead of there being successive competing transactions, there is usually only one transaction, namely, that between the surety and the lender.[231] In *Barclays Bank plc* v. *Boulter*,[232] the Court of Appeal explained the *O'Brien* defence as an example of the doctrine of *bona fide* purchaser without notice, but this is unconvincing given that the *bona fide* purchaser defence protects one who innocently purchases from another with a defective title, whereas there was nothing defective about the wife's title in either *O'Brien* or *Boulter*.[233] Unsurprisingly, the *bona fide* purchaser explanation of *O'Brien* was unequivocally rejected when *Boulter* was appealed to the House of Lords,[234] Lord Hoffmann emphasizing that the bank took its charge directly from the wife, who had the necessary title to grant it. That said, Lord Hoffmann's analogy of a purchaser of a chattel whose vendor's title is vitiated by fraud may actually be little more than another example of the *bona fide* purchaser defence.[235] Subsequently, in *Royal Bank of Scotland* v. *Etridge (No. 2)*,[236] the House of Lords recognized that Lord Browne-Wilkinson in *O'Brien* had not used the equitable concept of constructive notice in a conventional manner. Their Lordships in *Etridge* preferred instead the notion of a creditor being 'put on inquiry', although Lord Nicholls accepted that even this phrase was a misnomer as a creditor was not required to make any inquiries at all.[237] This leaves the *O'Brien* principle without any satisfactory conceptual underpinning.[238] Secondly, despite the suggestion in *O'Brien*

---

of a single borrower: *Goode Durrant Administration* v. *Biddulph* [1994] 2 FLR 551 (joint loan to spouses in substance a loan to the company); *Allied Irish Bank* v. *Byrne* [1995] 1 FCR 430 (spouse's joint account used exclusively for husband's benefit); *Dunbar Bank plc* v. *Nadeem* [1998] 3 All ER 876 (CA) (part of joint loan to spouses used for husband's personal debts).

[230] C. Harpum & M. Dixon, 'Fraud, Undue Influence, and Mortgages of Registered Land' [1994] *Conv.* 421, 423; G. Battersby, 'Equitable Fraud Committed by Third Parties' (1995) 15 *LS* 35; J. O'Sullivan, 'Undue Influence and Misrepresentation after *O'Brien*: Making Security Secure', in F.D. Rose (ed.), *Restitution and Banking Law* (Oxford, 1998), 43–46. See also *Hogan* v. *Commercial Factors Ltd* [2006] 3 NZLR 618, [33]–[34] (NZCA); *Sinclair Investments (UK) Ltd* v. *Versailles Trade Finance Ltd* [2011] EWCA Civ 347, [97]–[112].

[231] For a rare case involving a two-party transaction, see *Dunbar Bank plc* v. *Nadeem*, n.229 above.

[232] [1997] 2 All ER 1002 (CA).

[233] *Royal Bank of Scotland* v. *Etridge (No. 2)*, n.221 above, 717–718. The Court of Appeal also doubted that *O'Brien* could be explained in terms of the bank's notice precluding it from raising a change of position defence to the wife's restitutionary claim.

[234] *Barclays Bank plc* v. *Boulter* [1999] 1 WLR 1919, 1925–1926 (HL).

[235] K. Barker, 'Lost in the Umbrian Hills: Seeking Direction for *O'Brien*' [2000] *RLR* 114.

[236] N.141 above, [39], [108], [145].   [237] Ibid., [44].

[238] The High Court of Australia has rejected the notice doctrine in favour of the 'special equity theory', which affords special protection to a guarantor who is the debtor's wife in circumstances where it would be unconscionable for the bank to enforce the security: *Yerkey* v. *Jones* (1939) 63 CLR 649 (HCA); *Garcia* v. *National Australia Bank Ltd* (1998) 194 CLR 395 (HCA); *Kranz* v. *National Australia Bank Ltd* [2003] VSCA 92, [29]–[31]. Doubt exists as to how far this 'special equity' extends beyond wives who voluntarily act as surety: *King Mortgages* v. *Satchithanantham* [2006] NSWSC 1303, [124]–[127]; *Satchithanantham* v. *National Australia Bank Ltd* [2009] NSWCA 268, [45]–[46]; *Narain* v. *Euroasia (Pacific) Pty Ltd* [2009] VSCA 290, [45]; *Siwicki* v. *National Australia Bank Ltd* [2010] VSC 547, [23]. See also *Willis & Bowring Mortgage Investments Ltd* v. *Ziade Investments (No. 2) Pty Ltd* [2005] NSWSC 952, [96]; *Wenczel* v. *Commonwealth Bank of Australia* [2006] VSC 324, [119]. The 'married woman's equity' theory was, however, expressly rejected in *O'Brien*. Whilst *O'Brien* has been accepted in Scotland, it has been explained in terms of the lender's good faith (*Smith & Mumford* v. *Bank of Scotland* [1997] SC 111 (HL)), although (as in *Pitt*) the creditor's obligation of good faith will not apply to a joint advance to spouses (*Royal Bank of Scotland* v. *Wilson* [2004] SC 153, [24], [59]–[60] (IH)). The position

that banks could avoid being fixed with constructive notice of wrongdoing by holding a private meeting with the wife (in the absence of her husband) at which the bank officer would explain the extent of her potential liability, warn of the risks being run, and urge her to take independent legal advice, banks have preferred not to adopt this course.[239] This was probably to avoid the risk of a surety subsequently asserting that the bank had assumed the role of advising on the wisdom of the transaction and that a presumption of undue influence had arisen directly between them.[240] Instead, standard banking practice was to insist both that the surety obtain independent legal advice and that the surety or her adviser confirm that such advice had been given and received.[241] Although this practice falls short of the *O'Brien* procedures in some regards, it also goes further in other respects, since Lord Browne-Wilkinson considered that it would only be in exceptional circumstances that a bank should not only *advise* the surety to obtain independent legal advice, but actually *insist* that this be done.[242] Nevertheless, in *Royal Bank of Scotland v. Etridge (No. 2)*,[243] the House of Lords approved of the general banking practice that had developed, subject to certain safeguards, and dropped the requirement that banks should hold a private meeting with sureties.[244]

The House of Lords in *Etridge* heard eight consolidated appeals, each involving a wife who had agreed to charge her property, usually the matrimonial home, in favour of a bank as security for her husband's personal debts, or the debts of her husband's company. In

in Scotland has not altered post-*Etridge* (*Clydesdale Bank Public Ltd Co.* v. *Black* [2002] SC 555, [31] (IH); *Royal Bank of Scotland* v. *Wilson* [2004] SC 153, [34]–[35], [52]–[55], [73]–[78] (IH)). Despite accepting that the 'jurisprudential basis of *O'Brien* remains uncertain', the New Zealand courts have applied that decision (*Wilkinson* v. *ASB Bank Ltd* [1998] 1 NZLR 674, 689–690 (NZCA)), and accepted that it is 'highly likely that the *Etridge* approach as to when creditors are on inquiry will be applied [in New Zealand], at least in banking cases' (*Hogan* v. *Commercial Factors Ltd*, n.230 above, [44], [50]; *UDC Finance Ltd* v. *Down* [2009] NZCA 192, [36]). The Land Transfer Act 1952 (NZ), s.182, however, may compel the New Zealand courts in future to deal with some *O'Brien*-type problems by applying agency rather than notice principles: *Nathan* v. *Dollars & Sense Ltd*, n.217 above, [23]–[25], [49]; but consider *Burmeister* v. *O'Brien*, n.217 above, [67], [84]. These decisions are unlikely, however, to represent a fundamental shift away from the use of notice principles in New Zealand, back towards the use of agency-based reasoning: see n.217 above. *O'Brien* has also been adopted in Ireland (*Bank of Nova Scotia* v. *Hogan* [1996] 3 IR 239 (IESC)) and *Etridge* has been applied in Hong Kong (*Ying* v. *Bank of China (Hong Kong) Ltd*, n.187 above, [28]–[30], [35]–[39]; *Bank of China (Hong Kong) Ltd* v. *Hang* [2006] HKCU 78, [13], [16]–[17] (HKCA); *Wing Hang Bank Ltd* v. *Kwok Lai Sim* [2009] HKCU 655, [10]–[58] (HKCA)), Singapore (*Bank of East Asia Ltd* v. *Mody Sonal M* [2004] 2 SLR 113, [4]–[8]; *Susilawati* v. *American Express Bank Ltd*, n.110 above, [26]), and Canada (*Gold* v. *Rosenberg* [1997] 3 SCR 767, [78]–[79] (SCC); *CIBC Mortgage Corp.* v. *Rowatt* (2002) 220 DLR (4th) 139, [11]–[21] (OCA); *Collum* v. *Bank of Montreal* (2004) 242 DLR (4th) 510, [38]–[40] (BCCA); *Faris* v. *Eftimovski* [2004] OJ No. 3407, [83]–[84]; cf. *Bank of Montreal* v. *Courtney* (2005) 261 DLR (4th) 665, [42] (NSCA)). Recent Canadian jurisprudence does not appear to attach the same significance to independent legal advice as in *Etridge*: M.H. Ogilvie, n.14 above, 147–151; M.H. Ogilvie, 'The Reception of *Etridge (No. 2)* in Canada' [2008] *JBL* 191, 200–201.

[239] According to the *Lending Code* (November 2009), [119]–[127], subscribing banks should encourage (as far as possible) any surety to take independent legal advice, and require a surety who refuses such advice to sign a declaration to that effect. Any documentation signed by the surety should reiterate the recommendation to take legal advice and the consequences of not doing so. Subscribing banks must also inform any surety that they may become liable to pay instead of (or as well as) the debtor, and inform the surety what their liability will be, including interest and charges, but banks may rely on solicitors to explain the nature of 'all monies' or continuing security. Subscribing banks are generally prohibited from taking unlimited guarantees from individuals, but may take these from companies. See also BBA, *A Statement of Principles: Banks and Micro-enterprises—Working Together* (2009), 6–7. For the current (similar) position, see the *Lending Code* (March 2011), [67]–[75]. See formerly *Banking Code* (March 2008), [13.4]; *Business Banking Code* (March 2008), [13.8].

[240] *Royal Bank of Scotland* v. *Etridge (No. 2)*, n.141 above, [51]. See also *Lloyds Bank Ltd* v. *Bundy*, n.118 above; *Wilkinson* v. *ASB Bank Ltd*, n.238 above, 689; *Nathan* v. *Dollars & Sense Ltd*, n.217 above, [23]–[25].

[241] Ibid., [51].   [242] *Crédit Lyonnais Bank Nederland NV* v. *Burch*, n.224 above.

[243] N.141 above, [51].   [244] Ibid., [55].

seven of the appeals,[245] the wife resisted the bank's claim for possession of the mortgaged property on the ground that she executed the charge as a result of her husband's undue influence or misrepresentation, which rendered the bank's charge voidable. Each appeal primarily concerned the issue of the bank's notice of the husband's alleged impropriety. As the bank in each appeal reasonably believed that a solicitor had acted for the wife in the relevant transaction, their Lordships had to determine the extent to which the solicitor's participation, or believed participation, absolved the bank of the need to make further inquiries about the circumstances surrounding the wife's execution of the charge, or to take any further steps to confirm that the wife had given true and informed consent. According to Lord Nicholls (whose opinion was said by Lord Bingham to command their Lordships' unqualified support),[246] where actual notice on the bank's part cannot be proved, two factors demonstrate that the bank has nevertheless been 'put on inquiry'[247] first, there must be a 'non-commercial relationship' between the surety and debtor;[248] and, secondly, the transaction must, on its face, be to the surety's disadvantage. Whilst the burden of proving these elements rests on the surety,[249] it is not a particularly high threshold for the surety to satisfy, with the result that a bank will be 'put on inquiry' whenever a wife stands surety for her husband's debts and the bank is aware of their relationship.[250] Similarly, applying this two-limb test, a bank would be put on inquiry where a husband guaranteed his wife's debts, where the surety and debtor were in a heterosexual or homosexual relationship (regardless of cohabitation), or where the debtor and surety were parent and child,[251] provided the bank was aware of the relevant relationship.[252] Similarly, a bank would be 'put on inquiry' where the debtor-surety relationship was one of 'trust and confidence', even if not sexual.[253] It was precisely in order to avoid drawing such arbitrary distinctions between certain relationships that would put a bank on inquiry and those that would not, that Lord Nicholls held that, in future, banks would simply be put on inquiry whenever the debtor-surety relationship was 'non-commercial'.[254] Nevertheless, there will still be cases where a bank will not be 'put on inquiry', such as a joint advance to husband and wife, unless the bank is actually aware that the loan is being made for the husband's purposes, rather than joint purposes.[255] By contrast, Lord Nicholls considered that a bank would be 'put on inquiry' where the wife stood surety for the debts of a company, in which she held shares jointly with her husband, even where the wife was the company's director or secretary—the shareholding interests, and the identity of the directors, was not a reliable guide to who actually controlled the conduct of the company's business.[256]

Once the surety has demonstrated that the bank has been 'put on inquiry', the burden then shifts to the bank to prove that it took all reasonable steps to bring home to the surety

---

[245] The eighth appeal, *Kenyon-Brown* v. *Desmond Banks & Co*, which involved a wife suing her solicitor, concerned the extent of a solicitor's duties when acting for and advising a wife executing security for her husband's debts.

[246] N.141 above, [3].   [247] Ibid., [44].

[248] The 'non-commercial' nature of the relationship is assessed from the bank's perspective, although the bank has no positive obligation 'to make enquiries about the [nature of the] relationship between its principal debtor and the proposed surety/mortgagor': *Ying* v. *Bank of China (Hong Kong) Ltd*, n.187 above, [41].

[249] *Barclays Bank plc* v. *Boulter*, n.234 above, 1925–1926. See also *Liu Chong Hing Bank Ltd* v. *Ocean Importers & Exporters Co. Ltd* [2001] HKCU 478, [43].

[250] N.141 above, [44], [84].

[251] Ibid., [84]. See also *Abbey National Bank plc* v. *Stringer*, n.203 above, [15].   [252] Ibid., [47].

[253] Ibid., [83], citing *Crédit Lyonnais Bank Nederland NV* v. *Burch*, n.224 above.

[254] Ibid., [87]–[89]. *Etridge* has no application in a commercial setting: *Donegal International Ltd* v. *Zambia*, n.75 above, [464]; *UDC Finance Ltd* v. *Down*, n.238 above, [37]; *Bank of Scotland plc* v. *Makris* (15 May 2009, Ch. D), [45]–[52] (parties to joint venture).

[255] *CIBC Mortgages plc* v. *Pitt*, n.226 above.   [256] N.141 above, [49].

the risks involved in entering into the transaction.[257] The bank's failure to take such steps does not *per se* invalidate the security, however, as the surety must also establish either that the transaction was procured by undue influence (or other wrongdoing), or that the 'evidential presumption' that the transaction was procured by undue influence applies and has not otherwise been rebutted.[258] In terms of what might constitute reasonable steps, Lord Nicholls in *Etridge* held that, as regards *past* transactions, a bank that had been 'put on inquiry' should not be expected to have discovered for itself whether a wife's consent had been procured by undue influence, nor should the bank be expected to have insisted on a solicitor's certificate confirming that he was satisfied that the wife was standing surety freely.[259] Nor should the bank be expected to have held a personal meeting with the surety.[260] According to Lord Nicholls,[261] '[t]he furthest a bank can be expected to go is to take reasonable steps to satisfy itself that the wife has had brought home to her, in a meaningful way, the practical implications of the proposed transaction. This does not wholly eliminate the risk of undue influence or misrepresentation. But it does mean that a wife enters into a transaction with her eyes open so far as the basic elements of the transaction are concerned.' Accordingly, in an *ordinary* case, it would be reasonable for a bank to have relied upon a confirmation from a solicitor,[262] acting for the wife,[263] that he had advised the wife appropriately. In an *extraordinary* case, however, where the bank either knew that the solicitor had not duly advised the wife or knew facts from which it should have realized that the wife had not received the appropriate advice, the bank would be treated as having proceeded with the transaction at its own risk.[264]

As regards *future* transactions,[265] Lord Nicholls gave detailed guidance as to the steps a bank should take 'when it has been put on inquiry and for its protection is looking to the fact that the wife had been [or reasonably appears to have been] advised independently by a solicitor'.[266] His Lordship declared that the following guidance was not optional:[267]

(a) The bank should contact the wife directly, and—

   (i) explain to her why it requires a solicitor, who is acting for her, to provide a written confirmation that he has fully explained the nature of the documents to her and their practical implications; and

   (ii) ask her to nominate a solicitor to act for her and provide the necessary confirmation, even if this is the same solicitor as is acting for her husband, although she can

---

[257] *Barclays Bank plc* v. *Boulter*, n.234 above.

[258] *Royal Bank of Scotland* v. *Etridge (No. 2)*, n.141 above, [14].   [259] Ibid., [53].

[260] Ibid., [53], [94]–[95], [148].   [261] Ibid., [54].

[262] A legal executive can provide the necessary confirmation as long as any advice tendered was independent and authorized by his principal: *Barclays Bank plc* v. *Coleman* [2001] QB 20, [78] (CA), affd. [2002] 2 AC 773, [292] (HL). A bank requires confirmation not just that the surety has seen a solicitor, but that she has also received independent advice: *Lloyds TSB Bank plc* v. *Holgate* [2003] HLR 25 (CA); *First National Bank plc* v. *Achampong* [2004] 1 FCR 18 (CA); cf. *Gov. and Co. of the Bank of Scotland* v. *Hill* [2002] 29 EGCS 152 (CA). See also *UCB Corporate Services Ltd* v. *Williams* [2002] 3 FCR 448 (CA) (bank unaware that wife had seen a solicitor).

[263] It is unclear whether this occurred in *National Westminster Bank plc* v. *Amin* [2002] 1 FLR 735 (HL).

[264] N.141 above, [56]–[57], [175].

[265] *Re Spectrum Plus Ltd* [2005] 2 AC 680, [15]–[17] (HL). It may sometimes be difficult to distinguish 'past transactions' and 'future transactions': *Royal Bank of Scotland plc* v. *Chandra*, n.189 above, [173]–[176], aff'd [2011] EWCA Civ 192, [14]–[15], [40].

[266] *Royal Bank of Scotland* v. *Etridge (No. 2)*, n.141 above, [79].

[267] Ibid., [50]–[57]. Lord Hobhouse thought that this guidance should be applied to both past and future transactions equally: ibid., [100]. For recent failures by banks to follow the *Etridge* guidelines, see *Royal Bank of Scotland plc* v. *Chandra*, n.189 above, [247]–[252], aff'd [2011] EWCA Civ 192, [40]; *First Plus Financial Group* v. *Hewett*, n.189 above, [15].

choose another solicitor if there is already a solicitor acting for her and her husband. The bank should not proceed with the transaction until it has received an
appropriate response directly from the wife.

(b) It should be routine banking practice for banks to provide the wife's solicitor with such
financial information as he needs to explain the nature of the documents and their practical implications to the wife. What information is required depends on the facts of the
particular case, but ordinarily this will include information on the purpose behind the
husband's proposed borrowing, the husband's current indebtedness, the amount of his
current overdraft facility, and the amount and terms of any new facility. The bank should
send the solicitor a copy of the husband's written application for any facility. Banks will
have to obtain the husband's consent before disclosing any confidential information,[268]
and, without such consent, the transaction should not be allowed to proceed.

(c) In exceptional cases where the bank believes or suspects that the wife has been misled
by her husband or is not entering into the transaction of her own free will, the bank
must inform the wife's solicitors of the grounds for that belief or suspicion.

(d) The bank must in every case obtain from the wife's solicitor a written confirmation to
the effect mentioned above.

Lord Nicholls also considered whether a solicitor could be treated as giving a wife independent advice when he also acted for her husband and/or the bank, or whether the solicitor was
required to act for the wife alone. On balance,[269] his Lordship concluded that the advantages
of requiring a solicitor to act solely for the wife did not justify the additional expense that this
would create for the husband. Accordingly, it is for each solicitor to exercise their judgement
whether he can serve the wife's best interests or whether there is a conflict of duty or interest.[270] Fundamental to Lord Nicholls' reasoning was the understanding that, when advising the wife, the solicitor owes his duties, both legally and professionally, to her alone, and
accordingly acts for the wife alone.[271] Accordingly, such a solicitor is not the bank's agent,
even when it is the bank that, for its own purposes, requests the relevant solicitor to advise
the wife. Should the solicitor fail to perform his role properly, the bank will not be fixed with
the solicitor's knowledge of that fact, especially when the solicitor has formally confirmed
that the wife was fully and properly advised.[272] In the ordinary case, any deficiencies in the
solicitor's advice given is a matter solely between the wife and her solicitor, and a bank is
entitled to proceed on the assumption that a solicitor has advised the wife properly, especially if the solicitor has signed a confirmation to this effect. Lord Nicholls held that the
position would be different, however, where the bank knew that the solicitor had not done
his job properly, or if it knew facts from which it ought to have deduced this.[273]

The effect of *Etridge* is essentially to shift the responsibility for protecting wives or other
vulnerable sureties from the bank to the surety's solicitor.[274] In the absence of exceptional

---

[268] Ibid., [190], where Lord Scott considered that a husband impliedly consented to his bank disclosing
any necessary information for such a purpose. The courts are, however, increasingly reluctant to imply a
customer's consent to the disclosure of confidential information: Sect. 5(v) below. Accordingly, best practice
nowadays is to obtain the debtor's express consent to disclosure: *Lending Code* (November 2009), [120]. This
position has not been altered under the *Lending Code* (March 2011), [67]–[68].

[269] Ibid., [72]–[73].

[270] Ibid., [74], [96], [173]. A solicitor advising a husband and wife jointly should ensure that advice is given
to the wife 'from her own separate point of view and for her own separate benefit': *Smith* v. *Cooper*, n.198
above, [56].

[271] Ibid.   [272] Ibid., [77]–[78], [122].

[273] *National Westminster Bank plc* v. *Breeds* (2001) 151 NLJ 170, [66]–[75].

[274] *Rawleigh* v. *Tait* [2009] NZFLR 802, [29] (NZCA).

circumstances, a bank that follows Lord Nicholls' guidance, and obtains a certificate from the surety's solicitor confirming that she has been properly advised as to the nature and effect of the transaction before it was executed, can be sure of enforcing its security. Accordingly, after *Etridge*, wives who ultimately lose their home after standing surety are more likely to sue their legal advisor and question the quality of the advice received. Indeed, there has been an increase in the number of negligence actions brought by sureties against their solicitors as banks find it easier to sidestep the *O'Brien/Etridge* defence. Whilst this is not the place to review the nature and extent of a solicitor's duties in the surety context,[275] *Etridge* may result in solicitors charging more for their services and taking a more cautious approach when tendering advice. Whilst this may increase the time necessary to complete a suretyship transaction, this may well be beneficial in terms of the quality of the advice that sureties receive. Unfortunately, there will probably still remain cases where a vulnerable surety will proceed with the transaction whatever the nature or quality of the advice given. In some such cases, the surety may simply be unable to appreciate the significance of the solicitor's advice.[276] In other cases, such as *O'Brien*, the wife may be likely to disregard any advice and execute the security documents anyway, despite comprehending the consequences of her actions, since she desires to avoid the emotional scenes that might follow her refusal to stand surety. In light of such situations, there have been suggestions that a better way of protecting vulnerable sureties would be to introduce legislative restrictions on the ability to grant security over a family home for purposes other than its acquisition.[277] Such a statutory restriction would have to be carefully tailored, since small businesses frequently rely on the availability of finance secured on the family home as start-up capital, and ring-fencing this asset could accordingly inhibit entrepreneurial activity that might otherwise benefit the particular family and society in general.

Where a surety successfully raises the *O'Brien/Etridge* defence, they are entitled to rescind the transaction with the lender, unless the lender can establish laches, acquiescence, or affirmation.[278] If the wife has received any benefits under that transaction, rescission will only be permitted if she makes counter-restitution to the lender of the value of those benefits 'to do what is practically just' between the parties.[279] There is no question of the equitable remedy of rescission being subjected to terms, however, where the wife obtained no personal benefit from the transaction. In *TSB Bank plc v. Camfield*,[280] a wife was induced to stand surety by her husband's innocent misrepresentation that her maximum liability in respect of the loan for his business was £15,000, when in fact it was unlimited. As the bank had constructive notice of the husband's misrepresentation, the issue was whether the security could be partially enforced up to £15,000. Setting the security aside in full, Nourse LJ said, '[t]he wife's right to have the transaction set aside in toto

[275] *Royal Bank of Scotland plc v. Etridge (No. 2)*, n.141 above, [64]–[67].

[276] *Goldsworthy v. Brickell*, n.181 above, 405; *Bank of Credit and Commerce International SA v. Aboody*, n.183 above, 961 (wife's lack of education prevented her appreciating the advice received).

[277] E.P Ellinger & E. Lomnicka, *Modern Banking Law* (2nd edn., Oxford, 1995), 124.

[278] *Goldsworthy v. Brickell*, n.181 above, 409–411; *Habib Bank Ltd v. Tufail* [2006] EWCA Civ. 374, [15]–[20].

[279] *Halpern v. Halpern (Nos. 1 & 2)* [2008] QB 195, [61], [76] (CA). See also *Cheese v. Thomas* [1994] 1 WLR 129, 135–136 (CA); *Dunbar Bank plc v. Nadeem*, n.229 above; *Ruttle Plant Ltd v. Secretary of State for Environment, Food & Rural Affairs* [2007] EWHC 2870 (TCC), [87]–[90]; *Smith v. Cooper*, n.198 above, [89]–[110]. Where the benefit to the surety is by nature non-returnable, rescission will be denied: *Society of Lloyds v. Khan* [1998] 3 FCR 93.

[280] [1995] 1 WLR 430 (CA). See also *Bank Melli Iran v. Samadi-Rad* [1995] 2 FLR 367, 369 (CA); *De Molestina v. Ponton* [2002] 1 Lloyd's Rep 271, [6.2], [6.7].

as against her husband is no less enforceable against the mortgagee'.[281] *Camfield* may be criticized, however, as the wife was at least prepared to guarantee payment of £15,000 and so the security should have remained enforceable up to that amount by the court making rescission subject to such a term.[282] Whilst *Camfield* has recently been approved in Hong Kong,[283] rescission on terms and partial rescission have been accepted in Australia and New Zealand.[284] Although *Camfield* may be difficult to justify in the misrepresentation context in which it was decided, it is probably correct that the security be set aside in full in undue influence cases, since the surety's consent to the transaction is totally vitiated.[285] Even in a case of undue influence, however, it may be possible to sever the tainted part of an instrument from the untainted part, and to set aside only the former, provided this does not amount to rewriting the contract.[286] Furthermore, even though a charge over a jointly owned property may be unenforceable against the wife, it may remain enforceable against the husband, so that the bank can seek an order of sale under section 14 of the Trusts of Land and Appointment of Trustees Act 1996 to realize the husband's share.[287]

Whilst it is now necessary, according to *Etridge*, for a bank to take certain steps in its own interests in order to preserve its security, a bank ordinarily owes no *positive* enforceable duty to the surety to take such steps.[288] A duty of care may arise in special cases, however, where the bank is clearly being relied upon for advice or where there is such proximity between the bank and the prospective surety that a fiduciary relationship arises between them.[289] The existence of such a duty depends upon all the circumstances of the case,

---

[281] Ibid., 437. See also *Barclays Bank plc* v. *O'Brien*, n.141 above, 199, although the wife appears only to have challenged the validity of her charge beyond £60,000, which the husband had represented was the limit of the wife's liabilities.

[282] Cf. J. Poole & A. Keyser, 'Justifying Partial Rescission in English Law' (2005) 121 *LQR* 273, 274, 284–289, suggesting such cases would involve an 'auxiliary equitable jurisdiction' permitting 'partial rescission', rather than 'rescission on terms'.

[283] *Wing Hang Bank Ltd* v. *Kwok Lai Sim*, n.238 above, [60]–[67].

[284] *Vadasz* v. *Pioneer Concrete (SA) Pty. Ltd* (1995) 184 CLR 102, 110–116 (HCA); *Maguire* v. *Makaronis* (1996) 188 CLR 449, 467–478 (HCA); *Scales Trading Ltd* v. *Far Eastern Shipping Co. Public Ltd* [1999] 3 NZLR 26 (NZCA), revsd. without reference to this point: [2001] 1 NZLR 513 (PC); *Westpac Banking Corp.* v. *Paterson* (2001) 187 ALR 168, [39]–[41] (FCA); *Emhill Pty Ltd* v. *Bonsoc Pty Ltd (No. 2)* [2007] VSCA 108, [35]–[38]. See also P. Watts, 'Rescission of Guarantees for Misrepresentation and Actionable Non-Disclosure' (2002) 61 *CLJ* 301, 309–310.

[285] M. Chen-Wishart, 'Unjust Factors and the Restitutionary Response' (2000) 20 *OJLS* 557, 576; cf. *Johnson* v. *EBS Pensioner Trustees Ltd* [2002] EWCA Civ 164, [56]–[58], [78]–[82]; *Birmingham City Council* v. *Forde*, n.180 above, [111]. The effect of setting aside the charge in full may be mitigated by subrogating the creditor to an earlier valid charge: *Castle Phillips Finance* v. *Piddington* (1994) 70 P & CR 59 (CA); *UCB Group Ltd* v. *Hedworth*, n.228 above. Where a wife executes a charge in order to replace a prior charge that is voidable for undue influence against the bank, the new charge will be similarly voidable even if there was no undue influence operating at the time of its execution: *Yorkshire Bank plc* v. *Tinsley* [2004] 3 All ER 463 (approved by N.P. Gravells, 'Undue Influence and Substitute Mortgages' (2005) 64 *CLJ* 42); *Samuel* v. *Wadlow* [2007] EWCA Civ 155, [47]–[63].

[286] *Barclays Bank plc* v. *Caplan* [1998] 1 FLR 532, 546–547 (CA); *Sanders* v. *Buckley*, n.190 above, [96]; *Annulment Funding Co. Ltd* v. *Cowey*, n.213 above, [74]–[80].

[287] *First National Bank plc* v. *Achampong*, n.262 above, [55]–[66]; *Edwards* v. *Lloyds TSB Bank plc* [2005] 1 FCR 139, [30]; *Edwards* v. *Edwards* [2010] EWHC 652 (Ch), [24]–[39].

[288] *Chetwynd-Talbot* v. *Midland Bank Ltd* (1982) 132 NLJ 901; *O'Hara* v. *Allied Irish Banks Ltd* [1985] BCLC 52; *Westpac Banking Corp.* v. *McCreanor* [1990] 1 NZLR 580; *Shivas* v. *Bank of New Zealand*, n.136 above; *Barclays Bank plc* v. *Khaira*, n.215 above; *Union Bank of Finland* v. *Lelakis*, n.126 above; *Murphy* v. *HSBC Bank plc*, n.101 above, [87]–[96]; *Bank of New Zealand* v. *Geddes* (NZHC, 28 May 2009), [21]–[25]. Cf. *Cornish* v. *Midland Bank plc*, n.108 above, 522–523; *Shotter* v. *Westpac Banking Corp.*, n.140 above; *Bank of Ireland* v. *Smith* [1996] 1 IRLM 241 (IESC). A bank does, however, owe a surety a limited duty to disclose 'any unusual features of the contract between the creditor and debtor': *Royal Bank of Scotland* v. *Etridge (No. 2)*, n.141 above, [81], [185]–[188]; *North Shore Ventures Ltd* v. *Anstead Holdings Inc* [2011] EWCA Civ 230, [7]–[37].

[289] *Barclays Bank plc* v. *Khaira*, n.215 above, 637. See also *Cain & Solicitors Nominee Co Ltd* v. *Thompson* [1996] DCR 25, 29–31; *Bank of New Zealand* v. *Geddes*, n. 288 above, [25]–[26].

including relevant banking practice.[290] Although a bank generally owes no duty to advise or explain matters to a surety who is *not* a customer, some uncertainty exists over whether the position is different when the surety happens to be an existing customer of the bank. In *Cornish* v. *Midland Bank plc*,[291] where the defendant bank had provided negligent advice to a surety, who was also a customer, Kerr LJ considered *inter alia* whether banks owed any general duty of care to their customer-sureties. His Lordship reached the tentative (and obiter) conclusion that banks owe their own customers a duty to proffer an adequate explanation about the nature and effect of any security documents before they sign. Kerr LJ's dictum has been considered subsequently on a number of occasions, and has been rejected nearly every time.[292] There are three reasons why customers and non-customers should probably be treated alike when it comes to denying any duty on the bank's part to explain or tender advice about the security documents.[293] First, it is entirely fortuitous whether the prospective surety is a customer or not, and the branch officers dealing with the transaction may not know whether the surety is a customer of another branch.[294] Secondly, any duty to proffer an explanation or advice to its customer-surety would most likely take the form of a term implied into the banker–customer contract,[295] but the alleged duty would probably fail the test of strict necessity, on business grounds,[296] that is required for the implication of a term.[297] This conclusion will also make a court reluctant to impose an equivalent common law duty on a bank.[298] Thirdly, the banker–customer relationship is not ordinarily a fiduciary one,[299] and imposing a duty to proffer an explanation or advice would undermine the arm's length nature of that relationship. Despite the absence of any duty to do so, an issue arises as to the bank's potential liability where it elects to explain the nature and extent of the security documents to the surety, but fails to do so properly. In *Barclays Bank plc* v. *O'Brien*,[300] Scott LJ drew a distinction between the situation where the bank only provides such explanation as is required to avoid the security being set aside in equity and the situation where the bank is not fulfilling that role, or goes beyond it, and accordingly voluntarily assumes the role of adviser to a surety who also happens to be a customer. In the former situation, no duty of care arises, but, in the latter situation, the bank may owe a duty to advise the surety carefully.[301] Nevertheless, a bank remains in an invidious position—by proffering an explanation or advice as to the security documents, the bank runs the risk of crossing the line and being held to have assumed an advisory role voluntarily. To avoid this risk, banks have adopted a practice of saying as little as possible themselves, but advising the surety to take independent legal advice.[302]

---

[290] *Union Bank of Finland* v. *Lelakis*, n.126 above, 47.

[291] N.108 above, 522–523.

[292] *Westpac Banking Corp.* v. *McCreanor*, n.288 above; *Shivas* v. *Bank of New Zealand*, n.136 above; *Barclays Bank plc* v. *Khaira*, n.215 above; *Union Bank of Finland* v. *Lelakis*, n.126 above. Cf. *Shotter* v. *Westpac Banking Corp.*, n.140 above.

[293] G. Andrews and R. Millett, *Law of Guarantees* (5th edn., London, 2008), [14-006]–[14-007].

[294] *Barclays Bank plc* v. *Khaira*, n.215 above, 636.

[295] *Governor and Company of the Bank of Ireland* v. *Lennon* (IEHC, 17 February 1998).

[296] *Bank of New Zealand* v. *Geddes*, n. 288 above, [18]–[21].

[297] *Liverpool City Council* v. *Irwin* [1977] AC 239, 254 (HL); *Attorney-General for Belize* v. *Belize Telecom Ltd*, n.67 above, [22].

[298] *Bank of New Zealand* v. *Geddes*, n. 288 above, [22]–[23].

[299] Ibid., [24]. See further Sect. 4(i) above.

[300] N.220 above, 140–141, 156. This issue was not considered by the House of Lords.

[301] *Midland Bank plc* v. *Perry* [1987] FLR 237 (no appeal on this point); *Cornish* v. *Midland Bank plc*, n.108 above; *Barclays Bank plc* v. *Khaira*, n.215 above, 634.

[302] *Royal Bank of Scotland plc* v. *Etridge (No. 2)*, n.141 above, [51].

(iii) Duty of care in contract and tort[303]

A customer may try to recover his losses from the bank by pleading the breach of an implied term in the banker–customer contract to exercise reasonable care and skill. Such implication can arise either at common law or by virtue of section 13 of the Supply of Goods and Services Act 1982, which implies into contracts for the supply of a service in the course of a business, a term that 'the supplier will carry out the service with reasonable care and skill'. Just as in other common law jurisdictions,[304] such as Australia[305] and New Zealand,[306] the English courts have recognized that the bank's duty may arise concurrently in tort.[307] A claimant may pursue claims concurrently in order to take advantage of differences relating to limitation periods, remoteness of damage,[308] and contributory negligence. Whilst the contractual and tortious duties are usually coextensive, there is no principled reason why a tortious duty might not be wider in scope than its contractual counterpart,[309] although the contractual relationship will often be important in defining the scope of any common law duty of care and a court will not impose any such tortious duty at all if it would be *inconsistent* with the contractual terms.[310] Accordingly, the courts will generally respect a contractual framework designed to prevent legal liability arising between two parties (particularly if they are financially sophisticated),[311] and (although not an absolute rule)[312] will ordinarily refuse to 'short-circuit' a chain of contractual relations by recognizing a duty of care between remote parties.

---

[303] There is no distinct tort of 'negligent banking' (*Toronto-Dominion Bank* v. *Solferino Café Inc.*, n.110 above, [24]–[28]) or 'negligent enablement of imposter fraud' (*Huggins* v. *Citibank NA*, 355 SC 329, 334 (So. Car. SC, 2003)).

[304] *Central Trust Co.* v. *Rafuse* (1986) 31 DLR (4th) 481, 522 (SCC); *The Jian He* [2000] 1 SLR 8, [24]–[27] (SGCA); *Royal Scottish Assurance plc* v. *Scottish Equitable plc* 2006 SCLR 300, [71] (OH); *Rickshaw Investments Ltd* v. *Von Uexkull* [2007] 1 SLR 377, [47] (SGCA); *Kensland Realty Ltd* v. *Tai, Tang & Chong* [2008] 3 HKC 90, [49] (HKCFA).

[305] *Astley* v. *Austrust Ltd* (1999) 161 ALR 155, 169–170 (HCA); *Coventry* v. *Charter Pacific Corporation Ltd* [2005] HCA 67, [143]. Consider *Central Trust Co.* v. *Rafuse*, n.304 above, 522 (SCC).

[306] *Frost & Sutcliffe* v. *Tuiara* [2004] 1 NZLR 782, [15]–[22] (NZCA); *Rolls-Royce New Zealand Ltd* v. *Carter Holt Harvey Ltd* [2005] 1 NZLR 324, [68] (NZCA).

[307] *Henderson* v. *Merrett Syndicates Ltd*, n.89 above, 193–194; *Customs & Excise Commissioners* v. *Barclays Bank plc* [2007] 1 AC 181, [19] (HL); *FFSB Ltd* v. *Seward & Kissel LLP* [2007] UKPC 16, [24]. See generally *Kleinwort Benson Ltd* v. *Lincoln City Council* [1999] 2 AC 349, 387 (HL); *Johnson* v. *Unisys Ltd* [2003] 1 AC 518, 522 (HL); *Eastwood* v. *Magnox Electric plc* [2005] 1 AC 503, 520 (HL); *Deutsche Morgan Grenfell Group plc* v. *Inland Revenue Commissioners* [2007] 1 AC 558, [50]–[51], [132], [136] (HL). For concurrent contractual and tortious claims in the banking context specifically, see *Barclays Bank plc* v. *Quincecare* [1992] 4 All ER 363, 376; *Kennedy* v. *Allied Irish Banks plc* [1998] 2 IR 48, 53–56 (IESC); *Jeffers* v. *Northern Bank Ltd*, n.48 above, [15]–[17]; *FFSB Ltd* v. *Seward & Kissel LLP*, above, [24]; *Bank Utama (Malaysia) Berhad* v. *Insan Budi Sdn Bhd* [2008] MLJU 463, [59]–[62] (MCA); *Shah* v. *HSBC Private Bank (UK) Ltd* [2009] EWHC 79 (QB), [56]–[57], affd. [2010] EWCA Civ. 31; cf. *National Australia Bank Ltd* v. *Nemur Varity Pty Ltd* (VCA, 1 March 2002).

[308] Consider *Sunny Metal and Engineering Pty Ltd* v. *Ng Khim Ming Eric* [2007] 1 SLR 853, [140], revsd. [2007] 3 SLR 782, [59] (SGCA).

[309] *Holt* v. *Payne Skillington and De Groot Collis* (1995) 77 BLR 51, 73 (CA); *Sumitomo Bank Ltd* v. *Banque Bruxelles Lambert SA* [1997] 1 Lloyd's Rep. 487, 513; *Weldon* v. *GRE Linked Life Ass. Ltd* [2000] 2 All ER (Comm.) 914, [63]; *Frost & Sutcliffe* v. *Tuiara*, n.306 above, [22].

[310] *Tai Hing Cotton Mill Ltd* v. *Liu Chong Hing Bank Ltd*, n.50 above; *IFE Fund* v. *Goldman Sachs International* [2007] 1 Lloyd's Rep 264, [71], affd. on this point: [2007] 2 Lloyd's Rep 449, [28] (CA); *JP Morgan Chase Bank* v. *Springwell Navigation Corp.*, n.100 above, [474]–[475], [479]; *Titan Steel Wheels Ltd* v. *Royal Bank of Scotland plc*, n.166 above, [85]–[92]. See also *Biffa Waste Services Ltd* v. *Maschinenfabrik Ernst Hese GmbH* [2008] EWHC 6 (TCC), [169].

[311] *IFE Fund* v. *Goldman Sachs International*, n.310 above, [63].

[312] *Riyad Bank* v. *Ahli United Bank plc* [2006] 2 Lloyd's Rep 292, [27]–[33], [37]–[50], [137] (CA). See also *Realstone Ltd* v. *J&E Shepherd* [2008] PNLR 21, [11]–[12] (OH).

Actions for breach of the bank's contractual duty of care to its customer have had a chequered history. In *Selangor United Rubber Estates Ltd* v. *Cradock (No. 3),*[313] the arrangements for the take-over of a company involved the balance of the target company's current account being loaned to a middleman, who in turn undertook to lend a similar amount to those making the take-over bid, so that they could acquire the target company's shares. This arrangement contravened the prohibition on a company giving financial assistance for the acquisition of its own shares.[314] As part of those arrangements, a large cheque drawn on the target company's account was to be exchanged for a bankers' draft issued by the target company's bank, the District Bank. The bank attended a meeting with the company's existing and future directors at which the take-over arrangements were implemented. The bank's only concern at that meeting, however, was to ensure that the company cheque was regularly signed and indorsed before it handed over the bankers' draft. Whilst the District Bank knew that its customer was the target of a take-over bid, it was unaware of the illegal nature of the transaction in which it had become involved. When the target company went into liquidation, the Official Receiver sought to recover the amount of the cheque from the bank on the ground that it was a constructive trustee or, alternatively, on the ground that the bank had breached its duty of care to the target company, as its customer. Ungoed-Thomas J held that the District Bank was liable as a constructive trustee, as discussed subsequently.[315] His Lordship also held that the bank had breached its duty to observe due care and skill. This conclusion is, however, questionable. Commercial reality militates against any doctrine that puts a bank on enquiry simply because its customer's entire account balance is subsequently lent to, or deposited with, another financial institution. Moreover, it is not clear why the bank was imputed with knowledge of the complex take-over scheme's details as a result of the mere presence of a bank employee in the room where the composite meetings had taken place, particularly when that employee's primary role involved carrying out the essentially administrative task of delivering the bank's draft against the target company's cheque. Despite these objections to the actual conclusion in *Selangor*, Ungoed-Thomas J nevertheless propounded an important statement of general principle concerning a bank's duty of care to its customers:[316]

> To my mind…a bank has a duty under its contract with its customer to exercise 'reasonable care and skill' in carrying out its part with regard to operations within its contract with its customer. The standard of that reasonable care and skill is an objective standard applicable to bankers. Whether or not it has been attained in any particular case has to be decided in the light of all the relevant facts, which can vary almost infinitely. The relevant considerations include the *prima facie* assumption that men are honest, the practice of bankers, the very limited time in which banks have to decide what course to take with regard to a cheque presented for payment without risking liability for delay, and the extent to which an operation is unusual or out of the ordinary course of business. An operation which is reasonably consonant with the normal conduct of business (such as payment by a stockbroker into his account of proceeds of sale of his client's shares) of necessity does not suggest that it is out of the ordinary course of business. If 'reasonable care and skill' is brought to the consideration of such an operation, it clearly does not call for any intervention by the bank. What intervention is appropriate in that exercise of reasonable care and skill again depends on circumstances. Where it is to inquire, then failure to make inquiry is not excused by the conviction that the inquiry would be futile, or that the answer would be false.

---

[313] [1968] 1 WLR 1555.   [314] See now Companies Act 2006, ss.678–679.
[315] Ch. 7, Sects. 5(ii)–(iv) below.   [316] N.313 above, 1608.

Ungoed-Thomas J's comments have found a certain degree of support in subsequent cases,[317] and the relevant principles were authoritatively restated by the Court of Appeal in *Lipkin Gorman* v. *Karpnale & Co.*,[318] which like *Selangor* involved claims that a bank was liable as a constructive trustee or, alternatively, had been negligent. Cass, who was a junior partner in a solicitors' firm, misused his authority to draw cheques on the firm's client account in order to finance his gambling activities. Sometimes, Cass arranged for another employee of the firm to cash over the defendant bank's counters the firm's cheques that Cass had made payable to 'cash'; at other times, Cass paid the firm's cheques into building society accounts that he had opened in the firm's name and subsequently withdrew their proceeds. On one particular occasion, Cass drew a cheque on the firm's client account payable to the defendant bank itself and used that cheque to purchase a banker's draft that Cass subsequently appropriated. Although the defendant's branch manager was concerned about Cass' own account, knew of Cass' gambling activities, and was aware that the method used for drawing the relevant cheques was unusual, he failed to inform the claimant firm's senior partners.

Reversing Alliott J, the Court of Appeal held that the bank was not liable on either suggested basis. As regards the bank's alleged breach of its duty of care, May LJ said that, conceptually, the reasonable banker test propounded in *Selangor*, imposed too stringent a duty on banks—courts should not be too ready to hold that a bank had acted in breach of its duty of care when it has honoured without question a cheque drawn within the authority of its customer's agent. Accordingly, a bank will only have acted negligently in paying a cheque if any reasonable cashier would hesitate to pay the cheque without first referring it to a superior, who in turn would hesitate to honour the instrument without making further enquiry. Indeed, if the cheque appears to be signed by the account holder and there is no reason to question the genuineness of the signature, then there will be nothing on the face of the instrument indicating fraud.[319] In contrast, where the cheque's signatory is not the account holder (such as where a director draws a cheque on a corporate account),[320] or not the only account holder (such as in the case of a joint account[321] or the partnership account in *Lipkin Gorman*),[322] then the possibility of fraud is more likely to be present.[323] Despite the existence of this indication of fraud in *Lipkin Gorman*, May LJ concluded that, given the substantial number of cheques handled daily by the particular branch, the amounts of the cheques drawn by Cass, and Cass' position as a partner in a respectable solicitors' firm, the branch manager had not been put on enquiry. Moreover, May LJ considered that any disclosure to the claimant firm of the branch manager's suspicions concerning Cass' personal account might have breached the bank's duty of confidentiality to Cass, as a customer. Parker LJ (with whom Nicholls LJ concurred on this issue) agreed with May LJ that a bank was not entitled to ignore clear evidence of fraud being perpetrated on a customer, and held that there are certain unusual cases when a bank would be put on inquiry and when its failure to investigate circumstances further would constitute a breach of its duty of care. Certainly, on the facts of *Lipkin Gorman* itself, Parker LJ was in agreement that the bank had not been put on inquiry, given the absence of any direct

---

[317] *Karak Rubber Co. Ltd* v. *Burden* [1972] 1 WLR 602; *Rowlandson* v. *National Westminster Bank Ltd*, n.29 above.

[318] [1989] 1 WLR 1340 (CA), revsd. on another point: [1991] 2 AC 548 (HL).

[319] *Verjee* v. *CIBC Bank and Trust Company (Channel Islands) Ltd* [2001] Lloyd's Rep. Bank 279. See also *Esmail* v. *Bank of Scotland* 1999 SLT 1289, 1291 (OH); *The Bank of East Asia Ltd* v. *Labour Buildings Ltd*, [2008] HKCU 127, [300].

[320] *Barclays Bank plc* v. *Quincecare*, n.307 above.

[321] *Royal Bank of Scotland plc* v. *Fielding* [2004] EWCA Civ. 64, [107]–[108], discussed in Ch. 8, Sect. 2(ii) below.

[322] See further Ch. 8, Sects. 2–3 below.

[323] *Verjee* v. *CIBC Bank and Trust Company (Channel Islands) Ltd*, n.319 above.

transfer of funds from the law firm's account to Cass' personal account. Unlike May LJ, however, Parker LJ did not expressly distance himself from *Selangor* and the test he formulated as to when a bank owes a duty to ignore its customer's payment instruction bears some resemblance to the test in that case, namely 'whether, if a reasonable and honest banker knew of the relevant facts, he would have considered that there was a serious or real possibility albeit not amounting to a probability that its customer was being defrauded'.[324] That said, his Lordship stressed that banks could neither be expected to review individual accounts on a continuing or periodic basis, nor to assume a suspicious attitude towards customers, in particular a solicitor who had been introduced and recommended by the firm whose account he was operating. Indeed, as Steyn J stated in *Barclays Bank plc* v. *Quincecare*,[325] 'in the absence of telling indications to the contrary, a banker will usually approach a suggestion that a director of a corporate customer is trying to defraud the company with an initial reaction of instinctive disbelief'. Ultimately, therefore, there may be little difference between the approaches of May and Parker LJJ. Whichever is preferred, their Lordships' approach is justifiable both in terms of protecting banks from potentially endless litigation, given the number of transactions with which they are involved, and also requiring customers to safeguard their own interests, rather than relying upon the bank to do so, at least when undertaking straightforward banking transactions.

Whilst *Lipkin Gorman* is certainly authority for the proposition that a bank does not owe its customer any particular duty of care in respect of ordinary payment transactions carried out by the authorized signatory on the customer's account,[326] this blanket proposition may nowadays need some modification in light of banks' extensive obligations under the anti-money laundering legislation.[327] In *Shah* v. *HSBC Private Bank (UK) Ltd*,[328] the defendant bank froze the claimants' account without explanation due to its suspicions that the funds therein were criminal property, and accordingly the bank made an 'authorised disclosure' under the Proceeds of Crime Act 2002 (POCA 2002). As a result, the bank delayed honouring its customers' payment instructions. This allegedly created rumours in Zimbabwe that the claimants were being investigated for money laundering in the United Kingdom and the Zimbabwean authorities consequently seized the claimants' investments in that jurisdiction. The claimants asserted that the bank had breached its duty to obey their instructions, which aspect of the case will be discussed subsequently.[329] Additionally, the claimants alleged that the bank had breached its duty to take reasonable care. Hamblen J suggested that in the context of POCA 2002 such an allegation might succeed in two situations: first, if a bank sought appropriate consent to make a bank transfer from the relevant authority under the POCA 2002 and, having obtained such consent, delayed unreasonably in carrying out the relevant payment

---

[324] N.318 above, 1378.

[325] N.307 above, 376–377. See also *National Westminster Bank plc* v. *Rabobank Nederland* [2007] EWHC 1056 (Comm), [379]; *JP Morgan Chase Bank* v. *Springwell Navigation Corp.*, n.100 above, [573]; *Sinclair Investments (UK) Ltd* v. *Versailles Trade Finance Ltd* [2010] EWHC 1614 (Ch), [90], aff'd [2011] EWCA Civ 347. The principles in *Quincecare* and *Lipkin Gorman* have been approved in Canada (*Semac Industries Ltd* v. *1131426 Ontario Ltd* [2001] OTC 649, [53] (OSC); *Vitilaire* v. *Bank of Nova Scotia* [2002] OJ No. 4902, [15], [26] (OSC)), Jersey (*Izodia* v. *Royal Bank of Scotland International Ltd* (1 August 2006, Royal Ct of Jersey)), Hong Kong (*Oriental Pearl South Africa Project* v. *Bank of Taiwan* [2006] HKCU 1670, [70]–[72], [81]; *The Bank of East Asia Ltd* v. *Labour Buildings Ltd*, n.319 above, [294]–[300]), Malaysia (*Pillai* v. *Standard Chartered Bank Malaysia Berhad* [2006] MLJU 576, [12]; *Hamid* v. *Perdana Merchant Bankers Bhd*, n.21 above, [28]), and New Zealand (*Nimmo* v. *Westpac Banking Corp.*, n.100 above, 234).

[326] *Verjee* v. *CIBC Bank and Trust Company (Channel Islands) Ltd*, n.319 above.

[327] Ch. 4, Sect. 3 above.

[328] N.307 above, [58]–[60]. See also *Burns* v. *Governor & Co. of the Bank of Ireland* [2007] IEHC 318.

[329] Ch. 11, Sect. 1(v) below.

instruction; and, secondly, if the bank decided to make an 'authorised disclosure' under the POCA 2002, but delayed unreasonably in doing so. There was insufficient evidence in *Shah*, however, to support the allegation that the defendant bank had breached the latter duty by negligently failing to make disclosure under the POCA 2002 'as soon as it was practicable to do so', as the 'authorised disclosures' had in fact been made within two days of the customer's payment instruction.[330] This view has since been confirmed on appeal.[331] There were two particular duties, however, that Hamblen J was not prepared to countenance in this context. First, his Lordship rejected a 'duty that the bank's suspicion must be formed on reasonable or rational grounds or reasonably assembled grounds',[332] as this would have been inconsistent with the scheme of the POCA 2002, which simply requires that a bank have subjective suspicions about the existence of money-laundering activity, without those suspicions needing to be based upon reasonable grounds.[333] Secondly, his Lordship rejected a duty that a bank must provide its customer with information relating to its communications with the Serious Organized Crime Agency (SOCA),[334] as such a duty might involve a bank in committing the 'tipping off' offence.[335] As regards this second duty, however, Longmore LJ appears to have adopted a different approach on appeal, accepting that it was at least sufficiently arguable that there might come a point during a bank's investigation when a customer is entitled to receive, and a bank under a duty to provide, information.[336]

Putting *Shah* to one side, however, the basic proposition in *Lipkin Gorman*—that engaging in ordinary types of banking transaction or providing everyday banking or account services to customers, such as honouring payment instructions,[337] will not usually involve a bank in a breach of its duty of care to those customers—remains good law. For example, as considered subsequently,[338] banks do not generally owe any duty to advise customers who borrow money as to the advisability of taking out the particular loan or the soundness of the transaction that they propose to finance.[339] Nor, as considered above,[340] should the courts recognize any similar duty upon banks to advise customers as to the wisdom of providing security or as to the nature and effect of such a transaction. Similarly, a bank does not generally owe a duty of care regarding *how* it enforces its security.[341] Moreover, although banks often require some form of insurance as a precondition of mortgage lending, this is usually done in the banks' own commercial best interests and should not translate into any general duty to advise borrowers to take out insurance or to take any particular step to safeguard their position in the event of death, incapacity, or unemployment. This position was

---

[330] N.307, [60]–[61].   [331] *Shah* v. *HSBC Private Bank (UK) Ltd* [2010] EWCA Civ. 31, [35]–[36].

[332] N.307 above, [62]–[63], [67].

[333] Ibid., [45], [52]. See also *K Ltd* v. *National Westminster Bank plc* [2006] 2 Lloyd's Rep 569, [20]–[22] (CA).

[334] Ibid., [72].   [335] POCA 2002, s.333. See further Ch. 4, Sect. 3(ii)(c) above.

[336] *Shah* v. *HSBC Private Bank (UK) Ltd*, n.331 above, [37]–[39].

[337] A bank does, however, owe its customer a duty of care when collecting his cheques: *JJ MacMahon (Building Contractor) Ltd* v. *Ulster Bank Ltd*, n.48 above, [7], [15]. See further Ch. 15, Sect. 9 below.

[338] Ch. 17, Sect. 5(i) below.

[339] *Williams & Glyn's Bank Ltd* v. *Barnes* [1981] Com. LR 205, 207; *Lloyds Bank plc* v. *Cobb* (CA, 18 December 1991); *National Commercial Bank (Jamaica) Ltd* v. *Hew*, n.180 above, [22]. A bank may owe a duty of care when providing borrowers with the early redemption figure for a loan: *Henderson* v. *Royal Bank of Scotland plc*, 2008 SCLR 823, [32] (OH).

[340] Sect. 4(ii) above. A bank does not owe a surety a duty of care in relation to its dealings with the borrower: *Jeffers* v. *Northern Bank Ltd*, n.48 above, [40], [42].

[341] Although a mortgagee owes a duty of 'good faith' when exercising its powers pursuant to the mortgage: Ch. 19, Sect. 2(viii) below. See also *Kotonou* v. *National Westminster Bank plc*, n.121 above, [133]–[135].

accepted in *Wilkins* v. *Bank of New Zealand*,[342] where the defendant bank escaped liability for failing to advise the claimants to insure the life of the primary breadwinner, despite its advertisements offering loans tailored to particular customer's needs, including appropriate insurance cover. Recent Canadian jurisprudence has similarly refused to hold banks liable for failing to insist that customers have appropriate insurance cover or for failing to advise as to its desirability in particular circumstances.[343] Similarly, banks owe no general duty to advise customers as to the tax efficiency of particular transactions or to have regard to the tax implications of a proposed course of action. In *Schioler* v. *Westminster Bank Ltd*,[344] the defendant bank's Guernsey branch received a dividend payment from a Malaysian company on behalf of its Dutch customer, who was not generally liable to United Kingdom tax, by means of a dividend voucher and warrant expressed in Malaysian dollars. As the Guernsey branch had no facilities for negotiating foreign currency drafts, the instrument was collected through the bank's English head office, whereupon the customer became subject to United Kingdom tax, which the bank duly deducted. Dismissing the customer's breach of contract claim, Mocatta J held that, in not seeking the customer's specific instructions regarding the foreign currency instrument, the bank had acted in accordance with standard banking practice[345] and accordingly was not liable for failing to consider the tax consequences of its actions. Finally, banks owe no implied contractual duty to keep existing customers informed of alternative, more favourable bank accounts or financing options to which they might switch,[346] and probably do not owe customers any duty to inform them that their fixed-term deposits have matured or any duty to seek the customer's instructions regarding how to deal with the matured deposit.[347]

Obviously, it is not the case that a bank can *never* be in breach of a duty of care when carrying out ordinary banking transactions for its customers. Indeed, there are two notable examples where such liability was recognized. First, in *Cornish* v. *Midland Bank plc*,[348] Kerr LJ stated obiter that banks owe their customers a duty to explain adequately the

---

[342] N.143 above. See also *Bank of New Zealand* v. *Geddes*, n.288 above, [26].

[343] *Burrows* v. *Bank of Nova Scotia* [2002] OTC 20, [15] (OSC); *Mino* v. *Pacific Coast Credit Union* [2002] BCCA 519, [9]–[13]. A duty of care has been conceded where the bank failed to forward to the insurance company life insurance policy premiums received from its customer: *Gooderham* v. *The Bank of Nova Scotia* (2000) 47 OR (3d) 554, [45]. Similarly, a bank may owe a duty to advise a customer that a change of principal borrower might invalidate his existing insurance arrangements (*Gowanlock* v. *Bank of Nova Scotia*, n.100 above, [89]) and a duty to notify a customer of the bank's intention to demand a loan's repayment when this would detrimentally effect his insurance position (*The Toronto-Dominion Bank* v. *Valentine* (2002) 61 OR (3d) 161, [48] (OCA)). See further M.H. Ogilvie, n.14 above, 156–161.

[344] [1970] 2 QB 719. See also *Australian Mutual Provident Society* v. *Derham* (1979) 25 ACTR 3 (ACTSC); *Redmond* v. *Allied Irish Banks* [1987] FLR 307 (considered in Ch. 15, Sect. 9 below); *Kaid* v. *Barclays Bank plc* (QBD, 17 October 1990).

[345] What is expected of the reasonably careful banker may change over time, as banking practice changes: *Marfani & Co. Ltd* v. *Midland Bank Ltd*, n.23 above, 972 (considered in Ch. 15, Sect. 4(iii) below). In complex cases, courts will require expert evidence on banking practice: *Barings plc* v. *Coopers & Lybrand (No. 2)* [2001] Lloyd's Rep. Bank. 83; *JP Morgan Chase Bank* v. *Springwell Navigation Corp.*, n.100 above, [469]–[470]. See generally E.P. Ellinger, 'Expert Evidence in Banking Law' (2008) 23 *JIBLR* 557.

[346] *Suriya & Douglas* v. *Midland Bank plc*, n.53 above (considered in Ch. 9, Sect. 2(iii) below); *Bournemouth & Boscombe Athletic Football Club Ltd* v. *Lloyds TSB Bank plc*, n.101 above, [28]. Banks should inform customers of their full range of banking services before an account is opened (FSA, n.70 above, 6), and, where a customer is disadvantaged by a material change in interest rates, the bank must inform the customer of comparable banking products for which the customer is eligible (FSA, *Banking: Conduct of Business Sourcebook*, 4.1.2(4)).

[347] Ibid. A bank's obligations upon the maturity of a fixed-term deposit appear different in Singapore: *Bank of America National Trust and Savings Association* v. *Herman Iskandar*, n.48 above, 280 (considered in Ch. 9, Sect. 2(iii) below), although the bank in *Iskandar* had actually received express instructions to renew a deposit at maturity.

[348] N.108 above.

nature and effect of any security documents that they intend to execute. As discussed already,[349] this conclusion has little judicial support and has been subjected to criticism. Secondly, in *Verity & Spindler* v. *Lloyd's Bank plc*,[350] the claimants approached the defendant bank for advice with respect to buying and renovating properties in accordance with its advertised financial advisory service. As one of the potential properties had major structural defects, the bank manager persuaded the claimants to purchase a different property and accordingly agreed the loan. The claimants lost money in the subsequent property slump. When the bank demanded the loan's repayment, the claimants counterclaimed for damages on the ground that the bank's negligent advice constituted a breach of its contractual and tortious duties of care. Judge Taylor held that, on the particular facts, the bank had assumed a duty to exercise reasonable care in advising the borrowers. A number of key factors influenced the Judge's decision, including: (a) the borrowers' financial inexperience; (b) the branch manager's inspection of the properties (contrary to usual lending practice) and encouragement to purchase one property over another; and (c) the wording of the bank's advertisements, which led the borrowers to expect 'tailor-made' advice for business ventures,[351] which included helping customers to decide how much they could readily afford to invest. *Verity* cannot provide any more general guide to banks' liability, however, as it was clearly decided on its own special and unusual facts.

The courts' understandable reluctance to impose a contractual or common law duty of care on banks is not, however, limited to the provision of ordinary banking services or products. A similar tendency is discernible in relation to banking products that are particularly risky, sophisticated, or unusual,[352] and is discernible in circumstances where a bank provides its customer with financing that he uses for speculative dealings or to enter risky transactions (such as currency futures or commodities), and the customer subsequently complains that its losses result from the bank's failure to warn him of a particular risk or particular market conditions. The justification for this stance in relation to speculative or high-risk transactions is slightly different from that for ordinary banking transactions. First, the speculative or risky nature of such transactions usually makes it difficult to predict whether they are likely to have a positive outcome for the investor. This accordingly militates against requiring banks to provide advice in relation to such investments and against allowing a customer to argue that he was reasonably entitled to rely on the bank's guidance.[353] Indeed, in *Stafford* v. *Conti Commodity Services*,[354] which concerned a stockbroker's potential liability for advice regarding his customer's futures trading, Mocatta J stressed the difficulty of allocating risks in a volatile market of that type. Secondly, the manner in which the customer conducts his trading activities in the relevant market, and the arrange-

---

[349] Sect. 4(ii) above.   [350] N.147 above; cf. *Murphy* v. *HSBC Bank plc*, n.101 above.

[351] Cf. *Wilkins* v. *Bank of New Zealand*, n.143 above, where the bank was not liable for failing to provide appropriate advice, despite similarly advertising 'tailor-made' loans.

[352] *Bankers Trust International plc* v. *PT Dharmala Sakti Sejahtera* [1995] Bank LR 381 (no duty of care in relation to swap transactions); *Peekay Intermark Ltd* v. *Australia & New Zealand Banking Group Ltd* [2006] 2 Lloyd's Rep 511 (CA) (no liability for misrepresentation as to the legal effects of 'structured US dollar hedged Russian treasury bill deposit'); *JP Morgan Chase Bank* v. *Springwell Navigation Corporation*, n.100 above (no duty to advise as to appropriateness of investing in 'GKO-linked notes' or as to the structure of the customer's investment portfolio). See also P. Wood, *Regulation of International Finance* (London, 2007), [14]–[16].

[353] A bank may, however, be liable for misrepresentations regarding the nature of the banking facilities provided to a customer or regarding the risks associated with a particular banking product sold to him: *Peekay Intermark Ltd* v. *Australia & New Zealand Banking Group Ltd*, n.352 above, [46]–[47]. See also *Cassa di Risparmio della Repubblica di San Marino SpA* v. *Barclays Bank Ltd* [2011] EWHC 484 (Comm), [234] ff; *Bank Leumi (UK) plc* v. *Wachner* [2011] EWHC 656 (Comm.), [168]–[184].

[354] [1981] 1 All ER 691, 696–697, applied in *Merrill Lynch Futures Inc.* v. *York House Trading Ltd* (1984) 81 Law Soc. Gaz. 2554 (CA).

ments that he makes in that connection, often indicate (as in *Stafford*) that a customer has made his own independent decision regarding a specific investment and its associated risks. This again militates against imposing liability on banks that become involved in their customers' activities of this kind. In *Valse Holdings SA* v. *Merrill Lynch International Bank Ltd*,[355] the claimant opened banking and trading accounts with the defendant bank and retained the bank to provide financial advice regarding his investment portfolio. As the accounts were under advisory rather than discretionary management, the defendant bank was not authorized to trade without the claimant's express instructions, which the bank was obliged to carry out no matter how inadvisable it considered the particular course of conduct to be. Morison J held that the bank had not breached its implied contractual duty of care by failing to stop the claimant from engaging in a high-risk investment strategy that was beyond his stated investment objectives and that significantly reduced his portfolio's value.[356] According to his Lordship, not only was the claimant sufficiently financially sophisticated to understand the risks associated with his investment decisions,[357] but the account terms also meant that 'the client is the master of the account' and accordingly took ultimate responsibility for accepting or rejecting any advice tendered.[358]

The Australian 'forex loans' debacle—a 'sad chapter in Australia's history'[359]—probably provides the leading modern instance of the courts applying the above policies in order to reject allegations that a bank should be liable for failing to advise a customer against using his banking facilities to make high-risk investments. A typical case is *Lloyd* v. *Citicorp Australia Ltd*,[360] in which the bank provided a loan facility that could be drawn down in a number of currencies to a customer with considerable experience in land development and business generally. When the customer suffered losses as a result of using the facility without hedging against currency fluctuations, he alleged that the bank had breached its duty by failing to advise him generally regarding the management of the loan and, in particular, by failing to advise him to hedge his currency dealings. Rogers J dismissed the claim, as the customer had significant business experience and the bank had never offered to monitor the customer's investments. In particular, his Honour stressed that 'in a market as volatile as the one for the Australian dollar' the exercise of skill and diligence by the investor or his advisers may make little difference as to whether the investor avoids losses or not, so that, even if a duty were to be imposed on the bank, its content would not be particularly onerous.[361] Like *Citicorp*, the

---

[355] [2004] EWHC 2471 (Comm), applied in *JP Morgan Chase Bank* v. *Springwell Navigation Corp.*, n.100 above, [483]–[486].

[356] Ibid., [22]. According to Morison J, the defendant bank did owe a more limited duty to keep the customer's investment objectives in mind when advising on particular investments: ibid., [71].

[357] Ibid., [71].   [358] Ibid., [69].

[359] A. Tyree & P. Weaver, *Weerasooria's Banking Law and the Financial System in Australia* (6th edn., Chatswood, NSW, 2006), [19.1]. See generally S. Tulloch, 'Lender Liability and Negligence: The Swiss Franc Saga' (1992) 7 *Auck. Univ. LR* 27; B.A. Hocking, 'Does Lender Liability Loom?' (1998) 14 *PN* 28; P. Nankivell, 'The Liability of Australian Banks for Swiss Franc Loans' in W. Blair (ed.), *Banks, Liability and Risk* (3rd edn., London, 2001), ch. 11.

[360] (1986) 11 NSWLR 286. For the principal decisions arising out of the Australian 'forex loans' debacle, see A. Tyree & P. Weaver, n.359 above, [19.1]–[19.8]. The authors suggest that customers probably failed far more frequently than they succeeded, despite the potential for liability under the Trade Practices Act 1974 (Cth), ss.51AB, 52: ibid., [19.6]. See also *Copping* v. *ANZ McCaughan Ltd* (SASC, 20 May 1994); *ANZ Banking Group Ltd* v. *Dunstan's Hotel* (VSC, 17 October 1995); *Drambo Pty Ltd* v. *Westpac Banking Corporation Ltd* (FCA, 1 August 1996). The relative absence (until recently at least) of English authority on the bank's duty of care in relation to complex financial products, such as 'forex loans', may be explained by the English courts accepting concurrent contractual and tortious liability later than their Australian counterparts: *Henderson* v. *Merrett Syndicates Ltd*, n.89 above, 193–194. The same may apply in New Zealand: *Eadie* v. *National Bank of New Zealand Ltd* (NZHC, 12 December 2001).

[361] Ibid., 288.

thrust of the Australian 'forex loans' decisions generally is that a bank will not readily be treated as having assumed any special duty of care regarding the management of its customer's investment account,[362] nor will any view expressed by a bank in that regard generally be treated as anything more than an expression of opinion.[363] Nevertheless, there are rare instances that fall on the other side of the line. In *Foti* v. *Banque Nationale de Paris*,[364] the claimants, two Italian labourers, borrowed funds denominated in Swiss Francs in order to reduce the financing costs for their acquisition of a shopping centre. Despite its familiarity with the claimants' background, the bank tendered no advice about the risk of adverse currency fluctuations. Holding the bank liable, Legoe J accepted expert evidence that a prudent banker would have advised a customer with no prior experience of 'forex loans' to hedge their losses.[365] Accordingly, the bank's failure to abide by this practice constituted a breach of its common law (rather than contractual) duty of care, rendering it liable to compensate the claimants for their substantial losses following the Swiss Franc's appreciation against the Australian dollar. His Honour considered other factors important to his conclusion, including the disparity in the parties' business experience; the emphasis placed by the bank's officers upon its standing and expertise; the impression given by the bank that it would monitor the transaction's foreign-currency implications, as well as monitoring the loan itself at the relevant rollover times; and the customers' consequent reliance on the bank. An important point of distinction between *Foti* and other 'forex loans' decisions, however, is that the transaction in *Foti* was not speculative in nature, nor could the claimants be described as speculators entering a hazardous market, but were simply seeking to finance a genuine business transaction. Accordingly, neither of the policies (discussed above) that usually militate against the imposition of duties on banks in this context operated in *Foti*. Like *Verity*, however, *Foti* was primarily decided on its own special facts.

As with the case of fiduciary duties considered above,[366] the general principle to be drawn from the preceding discussion is that a bank does not ordinarily owe its customers any general duty to furnish careful advice on business or banking transactions, unless such advice is specifically requested and the bank specifically undertakes to provide it.[367] The difficulty lies, however, in identifying those circumstances in which a bank may be taken to have 'crossed the line' and assumed an advisory role with the attendant duties. This was precisely the task that faced Gloster J in *JP Morgan Chase Bank* v. *Springwell Navigation Corporation*.[368] The claimant was an investment vehicle for a wealthy Greek family and held trading accounts with the defendant bank that it used to develop its investment portfolio. The claimant invested in high-risk, sophisticated instruments, such as 'GKO-Linked Notes', which were 'short-term structured (i.e. derivative) instruments... referenced to underlying short-term, non-interest bearing bonds, denominated

---

[362] A. Tyree & P. Weaver, n.359 above, [19.7].

[363] *Capers Holdings Pty. Ltd* v. *Deutsche Bank Capital Markets Australia Ltd* [1991] ACL Rep. 45 NSW 13; *Westpac Banking Corporation* v. *Potter* [1992] ACL Rep. 45 Qld. 1.

[364] (1989) 54 SASR 354, 423–427, affd. [1990] Aust. Torts Rep. 81,025 (SASC). See also *Davkot Pty. Ltd* v. *Custom Credit Corporation Ltd* (NSWSC, 27 May 1988); *Fernyhough* v. *Westpac Banking Corporation* [1992] ACL Rep. 45 FC 4.

[365] A bank could escape liability by drawing its customer's attention to the currency-exchange risks involved in a 'forex loan' and by advising him to discuss the transaction with an accountant: *David Securities Pty. Ltd* v. *Commonwealth Bank of Australia* (1990) 93 Aust. LR 271 (FCA), revsd. on a different point: (1992) 175 CLR 353 (HCA).

[366] Sect. 4(i) above.

[367] *Lloyds Bank plc* v. *Cobb*, n.339 above; *Murphy* v. *HSBC Bank plc*, n.101 above, [88]–[100]; *JP Morgan Chase Bank* v. *Springwell Navigation Corporation*, n.100 above, [441]; *Titan Steel Wheels Ltd* v. *Royal Bank of Scotland plc*, n.166 above, [93]–[97]. See further Ch. 17, Sect. 5(i) below.

[368] N.100 above.

in roubles'.[369] Following the Russian crisis, these instruments dropped dramatically in value, and the claimant sought to recover its losses by alleging, *inter alia*, that the defendant bank owed the claimant a contractual and common law duty to tender advice as to the suitability of these particular instruments for the claimant and as to their appropriateness given the overall balance of risk in the claimant's investment portfolio. As the defendant bank had never specifically undertaken to provide advisory services to the claimant,[370] the issue arose as to whether the bank nevertheless owed a common law duty to provide the claimant with whatever advice was necessary to ensure that his investment portfolio was suitably diversified. Unsurprisingly, Gloster J rejected any such duty.[371] The real significance of *Springwell* may lie, however, in her Ladyship's indication of the types of factor that a court should consider in future when determining the existence of a bank's duty to advise customers regarding the suitability of, or risks associated with, sophisticated banking products. Having been recently upheld by the Court of Appeal,[372] the assistance to be derived from Gloster J's judgment in identifying the relevant considerations in this context remains undiminished. Although clearly not the only factors that a court might give weight to when determining the existence of a duty to advise, four factors appear to be of particular importance in this regard.

First, a court should assess the customer's degree of commercial sophistication and financial acumen.[373] In *Springwell*, the fact that Gloster J considered the customer to be 'a highly sophisticated investor' was a material factor in denying the existence of any duty to advise.[374] A similar point was made in *Bankers Trust International plc* v. *P. T. Dharmala Sakti Sejahtera*,[375] in which the claimant bank sold two interest rate swaps to the defendant, an Indonesian company. When the bank sought to recover the sums due under those swaps, the defendant counterclaimed for misrepresentation and for breach of a duty to 'explain fully and properly to [the defendant] the operation, terms, meaning and effect of the proposed [swap transactions] and the risks and potential financial consequences to [the defendant] of accepting them'.[376] The alleged duty was principally based on each swap sale being preceded by various written and oral statements and representations describing the advantages and essential features of the proposed transactions. According to Mance J, the claimant bank certainly owed two narrower duties. The first duty was 'to take reasonable care not to misstate facts' or, in other words, a duty to represent fairly and accurately any facts and matters in relation to which representations had been made. According to his Lordship, this duty obliged the claimant 'to present the financial implications of the proposed swap by properly constructed graph and letter. The downside and upside of the proposal should have been presented in a balanced fashion'.[377] The second duty, which arose upon a bank undertaking to advise a customer, was to 'tender that advice fully, accurately, and properly', with particular care being taken in that regard when the bank is offering a financial product that is novel and complex. Mance J was not, however, prepared to recognize any general duty on the bank to tender advice in the first place (in the absence of any express undertaking to that effect) and rejected the wider duty for which the defendant contended. According to his Lordship the parties' relationship was not a conventional banker–customer one, but rather a commercial relationship involving the sale of novel and complex financial products,[378] with the result that a court should not be too ready to read into that relationship duties of an advisory nature.[379] Central to his Lordship's rejection of any wider duty of care, however, was the buyer having held itself out as being experienced in such swap transactions and as having

---

[369] Ibid., [3].   [370] Ibid., [434].   [371] Ibid., [94], [429], [608].
[372] *JP Morgan Chase Bank* v. *Springwell Navigation Corporation* [2010] EWCA Civ 1221.
[373] N.100 above, [431]–[433].   [374] Ibid., [264], [432], [448], [455].   [375] N.352 above.
[376] Ibid., 394.   [377] Ibid., 419, cols. 1–2.   [378] Ibid., 392.   [379] Ibid., 419.

'sufficient expertise' to understand the implications of such transactions without the benefit of unsolicited advice. Similarly, in *Titan Steel Wheels Ltd* v. *Royal Bank of Scotland plc*,[380] David Steel J rejected a claim that a bank had breached its duty to advise the claimant, who had purchased two currency swaps from the bank, that those financial products were not in fact suitable for its needs. One of his Lordship's reasons for this conclusion was the fact that it was unrealistic to categorize the claimant company's representative 'as an ingénue in the field of financial products'; rather he 'determine[d] for himself whether the products were worth purchasing'.[381] In contrast, in *Verity* and *Foti*, the defendant banks were held to owe a duty to advise customers who were relatively financially inexperienced.

Secondly, a court should examine the extent to which a bank has held itself out as offering advisory services or as a financial expert, whether orally, in its contractual documentation or in promotional literature.[382] In *Springwell*, the absence of a formal agreement for the provision of advisory services, of any formalized fee structure relating to the provision of advice, and of any reference to advisory services in the contemporaneous documents all militated against the existence of a common law duty to advise. Similarly, no duty to advise a customer was found in *Dharmala*,[383] where the documents made clear that the bank was 'not obliged to warn [the customer] of the nature of any risk involved in any transaction' and that the bank assumed the customer was 'in a position to judge the suitability of any advice'. Equally, in *Titan Wheels*,[384] the documentation made clear that no 'advisory services' would be provided without the bank's express agreement. In contrast, when imposing a duty to advise, the court in *Foti* relied upon the fact that bank officers had assured the customers of the bank's expertise and, in *Verity*, the court highlighted the offer of 'tailor-made' advice in the bank's advertisements.[385]

Thirdly, a court should treat as relevant the status and role within the bank of any individual with whom the customer deals, and the capacity in which that person tenders any alleged advice. In *Springwell*,[386] Gloster J drew a distinction between an investment adviser, properly so-called, and a bonds salesman.[387] As the individual with whom the claimant dealt in *Springwell* was only 'a salesman of a limited asset class',[388] his enthusiasm for the product he was selling and his recommendations as to which products to purchase did not by themselves make him a financial adviser any more than it would make a car salesman an adviser.[389] Similarly, in *Titan Wheels*,[390] where the claimant dealt with the defendant's 'corporate treasury manager' with a front-office role for forex business, David Steel J concluded that any advice that the manageress tendered was 'merely as a saleswoman' rather than as a financial adviser. Where the customer is particularly inexperienced, however, the fact that the claimant deals with a senior bank employee, like the experienced branch manager in *Verity*,

---

[380] N.166 above.   [381] Ibid., [94]–[96].

[382] N.100 above, [434]–[444]. Gloster J (at [472]) rejected as inconsistent with the contractual documentation internal bank documents describing it as a 'trusted financial adviser'. See also *Bankers Trust International plc* v. *P.T. Dharmala Sakti Sejahtera*, n.352 above, 419–420. Where the claimant has a personal relationship with the defendant bank's representative, with the result that the relevant discussions take place informally, the courts will be more reluctant to impose an advisory duty on the bank: *Camarata Property Inc* v. *Credit Suisse Securities (Europe) Ltd* [2011] EWHC 479 (Comm.), [143]–[150].

[383] N.352 above, 408.   [384] N.166 above, [30], [94].

[385] In *Woods* v. *Martins Bank*, n.21 above, considerable weight was given to the bank's promotional leaflets. The existence of promotional literature advertising advisory services does not always oblige the bank to volunteer unsolicited advice: *Wilkins* v. *Bank of New Zealand*, n.143 above; *James* v. *Barclays Bank plc* [1995] Bank. LR 131 (CA).

[386] N.100 above, [445]–[459].   [387] Ibid., [101]–[105], [373]–[374], [452].   [388] Ibid., [453].

[389] Gloster J (at [454]) did not suggest that a salesman could never 'cross the line' to become a financial adviser: *NMFM Property Pty Ltd* v. *Citibank Ltd (No. 10)*, n.155 above.

[390] N.166 above, [93]–[94].

may be highly relevant to establishing a duty of care, although, as *Foti* demonstrates, a bank employee's lack of seniority does not necessarily preclude the bank from being liable.

Fourthly, even in circumstances where the bank might otherwise have 'crossed the line' to become a financial adviser, a court must consider the possibility that the terms of the parties' contractual relationship may operate to negate the existence of any implied or concurrent duty of care.[391] In some cases, the contract will define the parties' obligations in such a narrow way as to prevent a duty to advise arising from the outset. An example of this technique can be found in *Springwell*,[392] where Gloster J held that the contractual documentation 'showed that the parties specifically contracted upon the basis of a trading and banking relationship which negated any possibility of a general or specific advisory duty coming into existence'.[393] As described above, the contracts in both *Dharmala* and *Titan Wheels* contained similar obligation-defining clauses, as did the contract in *Peekay International Ltd* v. *Australia & New Zealand Banking Group Ltd*,[394] where the customer had signed a 'risk disclosure statement' indicating that he had satisfied himself that the complex derivative products in that case were suitable for him. In other cases, the contract may contain a clause that seeks to exclude or limit the bank's liability for a proven breach of a duty to advise. Such a technique was also used in *Titan Wheels*.[395] The principal difference between these two types of clause relates to the fact that UCTA 1977 applies only to the second type,[396] but even then reliance on UCTA 1977 will only occasionally succeed as between commercial parties.[397]

The discussion so far has concerned the bank's duty of care to its customer, but exceptionally that duty may also extend to third parties. Such a duty is most likely to be tortious in nature, given that there may well be no direct contractual relationship between the bank and the relevant third party, and given that it is only rarely that a bank will have intended to confer a benefit on a third party that can be enforced pursuant to section 1 of the Contracts (Rights of Third Parties) Act 1999.[398] Whether a bank owes a tortious duty of care to a third party will depend broadly upon whether there is a sufficient relationship of proximity between the parties. Most recently, in *Customs & Excise Commissioners* v. *Barclays Bank plc*,[399] the House of Lords considered that there were three established approaches or tests for ascertaining whether one party owed another a duty of care in respect of pure economic loss.[400] First, a duty of care could be established by applying the 'incremental test', whereby the law of negligence develops incrementally and by analogy

---

[391] *Raiffeisen Zentralbank Österreich AG* v. *Royal Bank of Scotland plc*, n.166 above, [97], [230]–[256]; *Bank Leumi (UK) plc* v. *Wachner*, n.353 above, [185]–[210].

[392] N.100 above, [236], [263], [474]–[490]. See also *Valse Holdings SA* v. *Merrill Lynch International Bank Ltd*, n.355 above, [69]; *Peekay Intermark Ltd* v. *Australia & New Zealand Banking Group Ltd*, n.352 above, [43]; *IFE Fund* v. *Goldman Sachs International*, n.310 above, [71], affd. on this point: [2007] 2 Lloyd's Rep 449, [28] (CA).

[393] Ibid., [475], affd. n.372 above, [141]–[171], [186].   [394] N.352 above, [60].

[395] N.166 above, [30], [98].

[396] *JP Morgan Chase Bank* v. *Springwell Navigation Corp.*, n.100 above, [603]–[606]; *Titan Steel Wheels Ltd* v. *Royal Bank of Scotland plc*, n.166 above, [98]–[108]; *Raiffeisen Zentralbank Österreich AG* v. *Royal Bank of Scotland plc*, n.166 above, [313]–[315]; *Camarata Property Inc* v. *Credit Suisse Securities (Europe) Ltd*, n.382 above, [151]–[187].

[397] *IFE Fund SA* v. *Goldman Sachs International* [2007] 2 Lloyd's Rep 449, [28] (CA); *JP Morgan Chase Bank* v. *Springwell Navigation Corporation*, n.100 above, [603]–[606], affd. n.372 above, [183]; *Titan Steel Wheels Ltd* v. *Royal Bank of Scotland plc*, n.166 above, [108].

[398] E. Peel, *Treitel's The Law of Contract* (12th edn., London, 2007), [14-095]–[14-104].

[399] N.307 above, [4], [82].

[400] Ibid., [83], where Lord Mance stated that '[a]ll three approaches may often (though not inevitably) lead to the same result'. See also *Bank of Credit and Commerce International (Overseas) Ltd* v. *Price Waterhouse (No. 2)* [1998] BCC 617, 634 (CA), where Neill LJ considered that the correct approach was to look at any new set of facts by using each of the three approaches in turn and 'if the facts are properly analysed and the policy considerations are correctly evaluated the several approaches will yield the same result'.

with established areas of recovery for pure economic loss.[401] In *Barclays Bank*, however, Lord Bingham considered that the 'incremental test' was 'of little value as a test in itself' and was only helpful when used in conjunction with another test or principle capable of identifying the legally significant features of a situation.[402] Lord Mance similarly cast doubt upon the utility of incrementalism as a free-standing test,[403] and viewed that test as 'an important cross-check on any other approach'.[404] Secondly, a bank may owe a duty of care to a third party where it can be shown that there exists a 'special relationship' between them as a result of the bank 'voluntarily assuming responsibility' to that third party. This test originates from *Hedley Byrne & Co. Ltd* v. *Heller & Partners Ltd*,[405] where the House of Lords held that, but for an express disclaimer of responsibility that prevented any liability arising, the defendant bank had breached its duty of care to the enquirer by providing an erroneous banker's reference. Whilst the 'voluntary assumption of responsibility' test was originally limited to cases involving negligent advice and misstatements, the House of Lords in *Henderson* v. *Merrett Syndicates Ltd* 'extended' the principle to economic loss caused by the negligent provision of services.[406] Lord Goff also confirmed that the governing principle of '*Hedley Byrne* liability' was an assumption of responsibility by the defendant together with reliance by the claimant.[407] In some circumstances, however, the defendant can be liable where their act or omission causes economic loss to the claimant, even where there is no reliance by the latter. Thus, in *White* v. *Jones*,[408] a majority of the House of Lords held that a solicitor, who accepted instructions to draft a will, could owe a duty of care to the intended beneficiary, even where that person was not aware that the solicitor had been engaged on such a task.[409] The 'assumption of responsibility' test has now arguably become the leading one. In *Williams* v. *Natural Life Health Foods Ltd*,[410] reaffirming the test of assumption of responsibility and the element of reliance, Lord Steyn stated that 'there was, and is, no better rationalization for the relevant head of tort liability than assumption of responsibility'. Most recently, in *Barclays Bank* itself, Lord Bingham regarded an assumption of responsibility 'as a sufficient but not necessary condition of liability, a first test which, if answered positively, may obviate the need for further inquiry',[411] and Lord Mance considered assumption of responsibility to be 'on any view a core area of liability for economic loss'.[412] Thirdly, a duty of care may exist where a claimant satisfies the 'threefold test', which requires foreseeability of damage, a 'relationship of proximity', and that it be 'fair, just, and reasonable' to impose the duty.[413]

---

[401] *Caparo Industries plc* v. *Dickman* [1990] 2 AC 605, 618 (HL); *Mitchell* v. *Glasgow City Council* [2009] 1 AC 874, [21]–[25] (HL). See generally *Stone & Rolls Ltd* v. *Moore Stephens* [2009] 1 AC 1391 (HL).

[402] N.307 above, [7].   [403] Ibid., [84], [111], [113].   [404] Ibid., [93].

[405] N.22 above (considered in Ch. 16, Sect. 2(ii) below). When dealing with banker's liability for negligent misstatements, the Canadian courts, applying *Hercules Management Ltd* v. *Ernst & Young* [1997] 2 SCR 165, [41] (SCC), have preferred a test based upon the reasonable foreseeability of the claimant's reasonable reliance, rather than a test based upon a 'voluntary assumption of responsibility': *Keith Plumbing & Heating Co* v. *Newport City Club Ltd* [2000] 6 WWR 65, [83]–[89] (BCCA); *Menard* v. *Toronto-Dominion Bank* [2005] MBQB 27, [11]. This test results in 'an increased likelihood of more findings of negligent misrepresentation against banks': M.H. Ogilvie, n.14 above, 146; but consider *F&F Hudon Farms Ltd* v. *Vanguard Credit Union Ltd* [2008] MBQB 209, [57].

[406] N.89 above.   [407] Ibid, 180.   [408] N.89 above.   [409] Ibid., 262.

[410] [1998] 2 All ER 577, 583 (HL).   [411] N.307 above, [4].

[412] Ibid., [83]. Lord Rodger (at [52]) considered that the assumption of responsibility test 'may be decisive in many situations', but 'does not necessarily provide the answer in all cases'. Contrast *Phelps* v. *Hillingdon London Borough Council* [2001] 2 AC 619, 654 (HL), where Lord Slynn failed to see much of an independent role for an 'assumption of responsibility' test. See also *Merrett* v. *Babb* [2001] QB 1174, [37].

[413] *Caparo Industries plc* v. *Dickman*, n.401 above.

Despite some high-level support recently for this test,[414] their Lordships in *Barclays Bank* were somewhat equivocal about its utility. According to Lord Walker, the threefold test provides 'only a set of fairly blunt tools' and its 'usefulness is limited',[415] and Lord Mance considered that the test 'provides a convenient general framework, although it operates at a high level of abstraction'.[416]

These high-level tests (and earlier versions of them) have been used to determine the duties of banks to third parties in a variety of banking contexts, such as when responding to a request for a banker's reference.[417] The clear trend has been against imposing such liability on banks. Accordingly, a drawee bank does not generally owe a common law duty of care to the payee of a cheque that is in proper form and bears a genuine signature when deciding whether or not to honour the instrument,[418] although such a bank does owe a duty to act carefully and honestly when advising the payee of a cheque of the reasons for its dishonour.[419] Similarly, a bank that accepts an irrevocable payment order from his customer to transfer funds to a named payee will not generally owe that payee a common law duty of care to execute the order in accordance with those instructions,[420] since the payee will generally have adequate alternative recourse against the payer,[421] although such a duty might arise if there had been some form of direct communication between the payer's bank and the payee so as to give rise to a voluntary assumption of responsibility by the former to the latter.[422] Presumably, this might occur if the payer's bank sends the payee a confirmation that the funds transfer has been made or is being processed, or if the payee solicits and receives information from that bank relating to the transfer. Equally, in the converse situation, a payee bank does not generally owe a common law duty of care to the payer when effecting a funds transfer,[423] although such a duty may arise if the payee bank has communicated to the payer its intention to carry out the funds transfer properly.[424] Furthermore, absent a clear finding that the bank voluntarily assumed responsibility to the claimant, a bank will not generally owe a duty of care to a third party simply because there exists some legal or economic link between that third party and one of the bank's existing customers. Accordingly, a bank will not automatically owe any duty to the directors or shareholders of a corporate customer,[425] even where the company in question is a

---

[414] In *Van Colle* v. *Chief Constable of Hertfordshire Police* [2008] 3 All ER 977, [42] (HL), Lord Bingham stated that 'the most favoured test of liability is the three-fold test laid down by the House in *Caparo*'.

[415] N.307 above, [71]–[72].   [416] Ibid., [93].   [417] Ch. 16, Sects. 2(i)–(ii) below.

[418] *National Westminster Bank Ltd* v. *Barclays Bank International Ltd* [1975] QB 654, 662; *Dublin Port & Docks Board* v. *Governor & Company of the Bank of Ireland* [1976] IR 118, 139, 141 (IESC).

[419] *T.E. Potterton Ltd* v. *Northern Bank Ltd* [1995] Bank. LR 179 (IEHC), although *Potterton* has subsequently been limited to situations where the drawee bank has voluntarily assumed responsibility to the payee: *Kennedy* v. *Allied Irish Banks plc*, n.307 above, 56; *Carrickowen Ltd* v. *Bank of Ireland* [2006] 1 IR 570, [67] (IESC).

[420] *Wells* v. *First National Commercial Bank* [1998] PNLR 552 (CA) (discussed in Ch. 13, Sect. 5(iv)(b) below), approved in a different context in *Jeffers* v. *Northern Bank Ltd*, n.48 above, [28], [39].

[421] Ibid., 562. On this basis, the Court of Appeal in *Wells* distinguished *White* v. *Jones*, n.89 above, where the disappointed beneficiary had no alternative claim to the one against the solicitor: *Carr-Glynn* v. *Frearsons (a firm)* [1999] Ch. 326, 333–335 (CA); *Gorham* v. *British Telecommunications plc* [2000] 4 All ER 867, 876–877, 883 (CA); *Corbett* v. *Bond Pearce* [2001] 3 All ER 769, [26] (CA); *Hughes* v. *Richards* [2004] EWCA Civ 266, [24]; *Rind* v. *Theodore Goddard* [2008] EWHC 459 (Ch), [36]–[37]. See also *B. Cusano Contracting Inc.* v. *Bank of Montreal* [2006] BCCA 52, [14]. See further Ch. 13, Sect. 5(iv)(b) below.

[422] Ibid., 563.

[423] *Abou-Rahmah* v. *Abacha*, n.4 above, [68]; *So* v. *HSBC Bank plc* [2009] EWCA Civ 296, [95]–[102].

[424] *So* v. *HSBC Bank plc*, n.423 above, [42]–[51], [89]–[94]. See further C. Witting, 'Banks, Dangerous Documents and Other People's Money' (2010) 126 *LQR* 39.

[425] *Chapman* v. *Barclays Bank plc* [1997] Bank. LR 315 (CA).

'one-man' company and its sole director is not only a personal customer of the bank,[426] but has also guaranteed the company's outstanding liabilities to the bank.[427] Similarly, no duty of care will generally be owed to the sole owner of an investment vehicle that is the bank's customer.[428] In contrast, where a third party acts as 'an agent for a disclosed principal who, under a power of attorney for his principal, is the sole signatory on the account', the bank may owe that customer's agent a duty of care to detect and report any forgeries of the agent's signature upon cheques drawn on the customer's account.[429]

As presaged in the previous discussion, however, the leading modern example of the courts considering the extent of a bank's duties to a third party is *Customs & Excise Commissioners* v. *Barclays Bank plc*,[430] in which the claimant Commissioners obtained freezing injunctions against two debtor companies in support of their claim for unpaid VAT. The defendant bank was given notice of the injunctions, which specifically prohibited the disposal of assets from identified accounts that the bank held for the debtor companies. Subsequently, the bank allowed both companies to withdraw large sums from their accounts in breach of the injunction's terms. The Commissioners argued that these wrongful transfers prevented them from being able to satisfy their judgments fully from the remaining assets of the debtor companies and that the bank's negligence should render it liable for any shortfall. As a preliminary issue, the courts had to decide whether the defendant bank owed the Commissioners a common law duty of care. At first instance, Colman J rejected such a duty on the ground that the bank was in a similar position to a party in litigation who did not owe any duty of care to the adverse party, unless he had actually assumed responsibility to them.[431] This decision was subsequently reversed by the Court of Appeal,[432] but was reinstated on different grounds by the House of Lords.[433] Their Lordships considered that, whichever of the three tests considered above that they applied, the bank owed no duty of care to the Commissioners.

Applying the 'incremental test', Lord Mance considered that the recognition of a duty of care on the facts before him would not have been closely incremental upon any existing duty in an analogous situation.[434] Similarly, their Lordships concluded that no duty of care could be based upon the bank's 'voluntary assumption of responsibility' to the Commissioners, as the bank had no choice but to comply with the freezing injunction and was legally bound to do so. Accordingly, 'nothing crossed the line between the Commissioners and the bank' to communicate the fact that the bank was assuming legal responsibility towards them.[435] Without some form of direct communication between the parties, no liability could arise on this basis.[436] Moreover, their Lordships did not believe that the Commissioners had relied upon the bank in any meaningful sense, as they had simply availed themselves of the only legal remedy available and, irrespective of

---

[426] Similarly, in *Weir* v. *National Westminster Bank* [1995] Bank. LR 249, 256 (IH), Lord Hope did not consider it to be a relevant factor, when imposing a duty of care on a bank to a third party who was acting as agent in the operation of another customer's account, that the third party in question also happened to be a personal customer of the bank.

[427] *Jeffers* v. *Northern Bank Ltd*, n.48 above, [29]–[43].

[428] *Diamantides* v. *JP Morgan Chase Bank*, n.100 above, [42].

[429] *Weir* v. *National Westminster Bank*, n.426 above, 256.　　　[430] N.307 above.

[431] [2004] 1 Lloyd's Rep. 572. In the House of Lords, Lord Bingham (n.307 above, [13]) stated that the parties' relationship was not akin to 'hostile litigating parties', but was 'adverse'. Moreover, Lord Hoffman (ibid., [40]) preferred to give 'no particular weight' to this issue, Lord Walker (ibid., [76]) was 'rather disinclined to put much weight on the litigation context', and Lord Rodger (ibid., [47]) 'did not find the analogy compelling'. See further: *Trent Strategic Health Authority* v. *Jain* [2009] UKHL 4, [31].

[432] [2005] 1 Lloyd's Rep. 165 (CA).　　　[433] N.307 above.　　　[434] Ibid., [111], [113].

[435] Ibid., [14], [65], [74], [94], [109].　　　[436] *Wells* v. *First National Commercial Bank*, n.420 above, 563.

the bank's actions, would not have acted any differently.[437] In essence, there could be no voluntary assumption of responsibility when the bank found itself in a position that was 'wholly involuntary'.[438] Nor did the Commissioners fare any better applying the 'threefold test'. Whilst it was common ground between the parties that the bank could reasonably foresee that the Commissioners would suffer damage if the injunction were not obeyed, and that there was at least some degree of proximity between the parties,[439] a majority of their Lordships did not consider that the imposition of a duty of care on the bank was 'fair, just, and reasonable'.[440] A number of reasons were given: (a) the terms of the freezing injunction only referred to contempt of court as a possible remedy against a notified party who had ignored the order, indicating that such a party owes their duties to the court alone;[441] (b) as the customer whose account had been frozen did not owe a duty of care to the party holding the freezing injunction, it would have been 'strange and anomalous' for a third party with notice of the injunction to owe such a duty;[442] (c) the recognition of a duty of care owed by third parties in the context of freezing injunctions would be a 'radical innovation' leading to a similar result in respect of other court orders, such as search orders, *Norwich Pharmacal* orders, and witness summonses;[443] (d) no comparative jurisprudence recognized the civil liability of a third party notified of a freezing injunction or other court order;[444] (e) the solicitors' negligence cases cited in support of a duty of care in *Barclays Bank* had involved a 'voluntary assumption of responsibility';[445] and (f) the bank had had no opportunity to resist the freezing injunction and received limited protection from the Commissioners' undertaking in damages.[446] Their Lordships' reasons are convincing and *Barclays Bank* achieves the correct result.[447]

(iv) **Remedies**

The only remaining issue concerns the customer's remedies when a bank breaches the various duties considered above. When a bank breaches its contractual and/or tortious duty of care, the ordinary contractual and tortious remedies apply, the most usual of which is an award of compensatory damages.[448] In contrast, breach of fiduciary duty

---

[437] N.307 above, [14], [65], [112]. See also M. Stiggelbout, '"I'm Banking on You"—Rethinking Reliance' [2008] *LMCLQ* 258.

[438] Ibid., [14], [65], [74], [94], [109]. Similarly, Lord Hoffmann (ibid., [38]–[39]) stressed that a voluntary assumption of responsibility arises from 'something which the defendant has decided to do', and analogized the refusal to impose a duty of care on a bank that had been served with a freezing injunction with the law's reluctance to impose a duty of care in respect of a defendant's omissions or breach of statutory duty.

[439] Ibid., [15], [99]. Some of their Lordships differed as to the degree of proximity that was present in *Barclays Bank*—Lord Bingham considered the level of proximity to be relatively low, whereas Lord Mance considered the parties to be in a 'most proximate relationship'.

[440] Lord Walker (n.307 above, [75]–[77]) did consider it 'fair, just, and reasonable' to impose liability on banks for negligently disobeying a freezing injunction, but declined to impose a duty of care as it could not realistically be confined to the banking context.

[441] N.307 above, [17], [64]. See also *R (on the application of Revenue & Customs Prosecution Office) v. R* [2007] EWHC 2393 (Admin.), [17]–[24], [31].

[442] Ibid., [18].   [443] Ibid., [19]. See further Sect. 5(iii) below.   [444] Ibid. [20].

[445] Ibid., [21]–[22], considering *Al-Kandari* v. *JR Brown & Co* [1988] QB 665 (CA); *Dean* v. *Allin & Watts* [2001] 2 Lloyd's Rep 249 (CA).

[446] Ibid., [23]. Lord Mance (ibid., [102]) also considered that, as parties other than banks would be unlikely to have insurance cover, no duty of care should be imposed.

[447] D. Capper, 'No Tort Liability for Breaching Freezing Orders' (2006) 65 *CLJ* 484; S. Gee, 'The Remedies Carried by a Freezing Injunction' (2006) 122 *LQR* 535; M. Stiggelbout, n.437 above.

[448] E. Peel, n.398 above, chs. 18 & 20–21; *Clerk & Lindsell on Torts* (20th edn., London, 2010), chs. 28–29. See also *Mehta* v. *Commonwealth Bank of Australia* [1990] Aust. Torts Rep. 81,046, revsd. on another

attracts remedies that are primarily restitutionary or restorative in nature,[449] which can include rescission, specific restitution, or equitable compensation *in lieu*.[450] A court may also order the bank to account for, and hand over to the customer, any improper profits that it has made,[451] although a bank may be entitled to an appropriate allowance for work or expenditure when the breach of fiduciary duty is technical and in good faith.[452] As indicated above,[453] however, not every duty owed by a fiduciary is a 'fiduciary duty',[454] and the fiduciary's obligation to act with proper skill and care, in particular, is an equitable (but not fiduciary) duty. Accordingly, the remedy for breaching this duty is compensatory, not restitutionary. Equitable compensation for breach of the fiduciary's duty of skill and care is akin to an award of common law damages, and accordingly differs from equitable compensation for breach of 'fiduciary duty', which may be awarded *in lieu* of rescission or specific restitution.[455] As Millett LJ explained in *Bristol and West Building Society* v. *Mothew*:[456]

> Although the remedy which equity makes available for breach of the equitable duty of skill and care is equitable compensation rather than damages, this is merely the product of history and in this context is in my opinion a distinction without a difference. Equitable compensation for the breach of the duty of skill and care resembles common law damages in that it is awarded by way of compensation to the [claimant] for his loss. There is no reason in principle why the common law rules of causation, remoteness of damage and measure of damages should not be applied by way of analogy in such a case.

Where a bank is ordered to repay any sum received by it in breach of its fiduciary duty, a court has a long-recognized equitable jurisdiction to award compound interest.[457] In

---

point: (1991) 23 NSWLR 84 (FCA), where Rogers J concluded that the most suitable remedy in respect of a bank's mis-selling of a 'forex loan' would be to restructure the loan as if it had been originally denominated in Australian dollars, and to assess the customer's damages on that basis

[449] *Bristol and West Building Society* v. *Mothew*, n.89 above, 18; *Cia de Seguros Imperio* v. *Heath (REBX) Ltd* [2001] 1 WLR 112, 119 (CA); *Chirnside* v. *Fay*, n.99 above, [16]; *P&O Nedlloyd BV* v. *Arab Metals Co* [2007] 2 Lloyd's Rep 231, [39] (CA).

[450] Ibid., 17.

[451] *Regal (Hastings) Ltd* v. *Gulliver* [1967] 2 AC 134 (HL); *Phipps* v. *Boardman* [1967] 2 AC 46 (HL); *Hospital Products Ltd* v. *United States Surgical Corporation* (1984) 156 CLR 41 (HCA); *O'Sullivan* v. *Management Agency and Music Ltd* [1985] QB 428 (CA); *Mahoney* v. *Purnell* [1996] 3 All ER 61 (CA) (compensation awarded); *Gwembe Valley Development Co Ltd* v. *Koshy (No. 3)*, n.90 above, [43]–[45].

[452] *O'Sullivan* v. *Management Agency and Music Ltd*, n.451 above. Cf. *Guinness* v. *Saunders* [1990] 2 AC 663 (HL); but consider *Murad* v. *Al-Saraj* [2005] EWCA Civ 959. See also *Estate Realties Ltd* v. *Wignall* [1992] 2 NZLR 615; *Collier* v. *Creighton* [1993] 2 NZLR 534 (NZCA); *Chirnside* v. *Fay*, n.99 above, [38], [45], [128], [135], [138].

[453] Sect. 4 above.   [454] *Bristol and West Building Society* v. *Mothew*, n.89 above, 16.

[455] Ibid., 17. See also *Swindle* v. *Harrison* [1997] 4 All ER 705 (CA); *Youyang Pty Ltd* v. *Minter Ellison Morris Fletcher* [2003] HCA 15.

[456] Id.

[457] *President Of India* v. *La Pintada Navigacion SA* [1985] AC 104, 116 (HL); *Westdeutsche Landesbank Girozentrale* v. *Islington LBC* [1996] AC 669, 700–702, 718, 737 (HL). A majority of their Lordships in *Westdeutsche* (Lords Browne-Wilkinson, Slynn, and Lloyd; Lords Goff and Woolf dissenting) decided, however, that a claimant was only entitled to simple interest when pursuing a personal common law claim for restitution of monies paid pursuant to a void contract. This has since been overruled in *Sempra Metals Ltd* v. *Inland Revenue Commissioners* [2008] 1 AC 561 (HL), where the House of Lords held that a claimant could recover compound interest on monies paid to the defendant by mistake either to ensure full restitution (ibid., [26], [33]–[35], [111]–[114], [178], [184]), to compensate the claimant (ibid., [132]), or as part of the courts' equitable jurisdiction (ibid., [240]).

The 'Golden Med',[458] the bank's liability for failing to repay sums deposited with it, either on the basis of money had and received following a total failure of consideration or as a constructive trustee, was no longer in issue. Accordingly, the only question before Hirst J was whether the claimants were entitled to compound interest 'having regard to the defendant's breach of fiduciary duty' or only statutory interest under section 35A of the Senior Courts Act 1981. Awarding compound interest against the bank, Hirst J emphasized that the bank must be presumed to have invested the deposited funds in the course of its normal banking business, and thereby to have earned compound interest on those sums. From a commercial perspective, it is difficult to imagine how Hirst J could have reached any other conclusion, given that banks have a legally enshrined right to charge customers compound interest on overdrafts and other loan facilities.[459] Moreover, in legal terms, a modern court faced with the issue in 'The Golden Med' is likely to reach the same conclusion as Hirst J in light of the recent liberalization of claims for compound interest in *Sempra Metals Ltd* v. *Inland Revenue Commissioners*,[460] and the House of Lords' recognition of a general common law right to recover such interest.

5 The confidential nature of the contract

(i) General scope

The confidential nature of the banker–customer contract stems from the fact that that relationship comprises elements of an agency relationship.[461] As a general rule, an agent owes a duty of loyalty and confidentiality to his principal,[462] although the scope of that duty will alter according to the type of agent involved.[463] This connection between the bank's duty of confidentiality, on the one hand, and other types of agency relationship

---

[458] [1992] 2 Lloyd's Rep. 193, revsd. [1994] 2 Lloyd's Rep. 152 (CA). Although the Court of Appeal reversed Hirst J's decision to award compound interest by only awarding simple interest, this was because the higher court could not find any trust relationship between the parties arising out of their transaction. Accordingly, Hirst J's decision remains good law where a fiduciary relationship can be established between a bank and its customer. See also *Wallersteiner* v. *Moir (No. 2)* [1975] QB 373, 388; *O'Sullivan* v. *Management Agency and Music Ltd*, n.451 above, 461.

[459] Ch. 17, Sect. 2(iii) below. For the limits of this 'reciprocity' argument, see *Halliday* v. *HBOS plc*, n.67 above, [7].

[460] N.457 above. See also *Hungerfords* v. *Walker* (1989) 171 CLR 125, 142–144 (HCA); *Bank of America Canada* v. *Mutual Trust Co.* [2002] 2 SCR 601, [44]–[46] (SCC); *Clarkson* v. *Whangamata Metal Supplies Ltd* [2008] 3 NZLR 31, [22]–[36] (NZCA).

[461] Sect. 3 above.

[462] *Regal (Hastings) Ltd* v. *Gulliver*, n.451 above; *Boardman* v. *Phipps*, n.451 above. See also R. Powell, *Law of Agency* (2nd edn., London, 1961), 25–26. For the agent's liability to his principal for misusing confidential information, see P. Watts (ed.), *Bowstead and Reynolds on Agency* (19th edn., London, 2010), [6-076].

[463] For example, the confidentiality expected of the solicitor–client relationship, in which the solicitor may not even testify in court about dealings with his client (*O'Rourke* v. *Darbishire* [1920] AC 581 (HL); *Minter* v. *Priest* [1930] AC 558 (HL); *Three Rivers District Council* v. *Governor and Company of the Bank of England (No. 6)* [2005] 1 AC 610 (HL)) is much higher than that expected in other relationships, such as that between a director and his company. Where a solicitor's silence may give rise to liability as a constructive trustee, he may apply for court directions as to how to deal with funds under his control notwithstanding the confidentiality doctrine: *Finers* v. *Miro* [1991] 1 WLR 35 (CA), applied *Hakendorf* v. *Countess of Rosenborg* [2004] EWHC 2821 (QB), [79]–[80].

or relationships involving the provision of highly personal services, on the other, was emphasized by Diplock LJ in *Parry Jones* v. *Law Society*:[464]

> Such a duty [of secrecy] exists not only between solicitor and client, but, for example, between banker and customer, doctor and patient and accountant and client. Such a duty of confidence is subject to, and overridden by, the duty of any party to that contract to comply with the law of the land. If it is the duty of such a party to a contract...to disclose in defined circumstances confidential information, then he must do so, and any express contract to the contrary would be illegal and void.

The imposition of a duty of confidentiality in any particular circumstance usually has an economic imperative and operates to facilitate the particular relationship. From the principal's perspective, the imposition of a duty of confidentiality encourages him to engage others in his affairs, safe in the knowledge that such a duty will protect him from unwarranted outside attempts to enquire into his affairs or acquire his trade secrets, and accordingly may facilitate him entering a particularly competitive area of business in which he might not otherwise have engaged. Similarly, from the agent's perspective, there are certain professions that could not be conducted at all, or at least not carried out as successfully, if the person undertaking the confidential work were not able to reassure those instructing him not only of his own personal discretion, but also that he cannot in general be legally compelled to disclose confidential information. An obvious example would be a solicitor, who could hardly represent his client's interests properly unless the client was able to discuss his affairs openly. Both these economic rationales justify the duty of confidentiality in the banker–customer relationship—a person is encouraged to enter into a banking relationship by the fact that he may conduct his financial dealings with the bank hidden from the gaze of family or commercial competitors; and the services that the bank provides are facilitated by the fact that the customer is more willing to provide the bank with detailed information of his financial affairs if this is done on a confidential basis. That said, the bank's duty of confidentiality may sometimes have to give way to the interests of the state when these are considered to be of greater importance. The scope of these 'exceptions' to the duty of confidentiality are shaped not only by the importance of the state interest in question, but also by the desirability of the customer being able to place his full trust in the bank.

Before turning to consider the scope and duration of, and qualifications to, the bank's duty of confidentiality, it is necessary to consider the extent to which this duty has been bolstered by other initiatives. At present, the bank's duty of confidentiality takes the form of a term implied into the banker–customer contract. There have been suggestions, however, that the principle should be strengthened by statutory codification. This was the view of the Jack Committee, which clearly recognized that the principle of confidentiality lay at the heart of the banker–customer relationship and warned that any uncertainty on the part of consumers about the extent to which the principle of confidentiality continued to apply in the light of modern banking practices might undermine their confidence in the banking system.[465] Although a course adopted in a number of jurisdictions,[466]

---

[464] [1969] 1 Ch. 1, 9, considered in *R (on the application of Morgan Grenfell & Co Ltd)* v. *Special Commissioner of Income Tax* [2003] 1 AC 563, [26]–[33] (HL).

[465] *Banking Services: Law and Practice*, n.1 above.

[466] Federal Law on Banks and Savings Banks 1934 (Switz.), Art. 47; Banking Act 1993 (Austria), s.38 (discussed by B. Koeck (2008) 23 *JIBLR* 392); Banking Act (Cap. 19, 2003 rev. edn.) (Sing.), s.47, as amended by the Banking (Amendment) Act 2001 (noted by E.P. Ellinger (2004) 20 *BFLR* 137). In *Susilawati* v. *American Express Bank Ltd*, n.115 above, [65]–[67], the Singaporean legislation was described

the United Kingdom Government rejected the option of statutory codification as being unnecessary and as being likely to introduce new difficulties and confusion.[467] Instead, the *Banking Code* introduced, *inter alia*, voluntary standards of best practice when dealing with customer information,[468] and confirmed the existence of the bank's duty of confidentiality, subject to qualifications.[469] The *Banking Code* has now been replaced by, *inter alia*, the *Lending Code*, which is similarly a guide to best banking practice, and provides as one of its key commitments that 'personal information will be treated as private and confidential'.[470] As discussed further below,[471] the *Lending Code* also specifically prohibits the exchange of customers' information for marketing purposes with other entities in the same banking group without the customer's specific permission,[472] and similarly prohibits the disclosure of general customer information to credit reference agencies, unless the information relates to the customer's defaults, in which case it may be disclosed upon giving the customer 28 days' notice.[473] Nevertheless, despite the rejection of the Jack Committee's proposal to put the bank's duty of confidentiality itself on a statutory footing, there is nowadays legislation that impacts upon banks' storage and use of customer information. Two pieces of legislation in particular are of primary importance: the Data Protection Act 1998 (DPA 1998) and the Human Rights Act 1998 (HRA 1998).[474]

The DPA 1998, which replaced the Data Protection Act 1984, gives effect to European Council Directive 95/46 on the Protection of Individuals with regard to the Processing of Personal Data and the Free Movement of such Data.[475] Part of the impetus for this legislation was computerization and the advent of the internet, which allowed for large amounts of personal information to be stored, accessed, processed, and transmitted with relative ease by public and private institutions. The potentially sensitive nature of personal information, and the risk that an institution's computers might be 'hacked' or an electronic

---

as providing a 'more comprehensive regime' in relation to bank confidentiality than the previous common law principles.

[467] *White Paper on Banking Services: Law and Practice* (1990, London, Cm. 1026), 4.

[468] Ch. 2, Sect. 6(i) above.

[469] *Banking Code* (March 2008), [11.1]. See also Data Protection Act 1998 (DPA 1998), s.11. The *Banking Code* allowed for disclosure in the 'four exceptional cases' permitted by law: *Tournier* v. *National Provincial and Union Bank of England* [1924] 1 KB 461 (CA) (considered in Sect. 5(ii) below). Earlier versions of the *Banking Code* contained a similar provision. See also *Business Banking Code* (March 2008), [11.1], which extended the bank's duty of confidentiality to business, as well as personal, information.

[470] *Lending Code* (November 2009), [13]; *Lending Code* (March 2011), [15].　　　[471] Sect. 5(v) below.

[472] *Lending Code* (November 2009), [22]–[24]; *Lending Code* (March 2011), [23]–[27]. See formerly *Banking Code* (March 2008), [11.1].

[473] Ibid., [34]–[41]; *Lending Code* (March 2011), [40]–[42].

[474] Consider the Computer Misuse Act 1990, as amended by the Police and Justice Act 2006 (unauthorized access to, or modification of, computer material is illegal where the offender acted intentionally and with knowledge that he was unauthorized: *R.* v. *Governor of Brixton Prison, ex p. Levin* [1997] QB 65; *DPP* v. *Lennon* [2006] EWHC 1201 (Admin.)); the Regulation of Investigatory Powers Act 2000 (offence for person intentionally and without lawful authority to intercept a communication in the course of its transmission by means of a public postal service or by a public or private telecommunications system); the Telecommunications (Lawful Business Practice) (Interception of Communications) Regulations 2000, S.I. 2000/2699 (interception of communications permitted in certain limited circumstances, for example, where an employer is checking for employee e-mail abuse). As the Freedom of Information Act 2000 (FIA 2000), s.3 covers information held by 'public authorities', but not by private institutions, it has only marginal relevance for banks. Moreover, under FIA 2000, ss.23, 41, 44, information disclosed by a bank to a public authority such as the FSA (for regulatory purposes) or SOCA (to prevent money laundering) remains exempt from disclosure.

[475] [1995] OJ L281/31. See generally *S* v. *United Kingdom* [2008] 25 BHRC 557, [30]–[32] (ECtHR). See further Ch. 13, Sect. 7 below.

communication intercepted, meant that there was a need for further clarity as to how institutions, such as banks, should handle, store, and transmit such information and a need for additional protection for those about whom such information was kept, such as customers. According to section 1(1) of the DPA 1998, its protection extends to 'personal data', which is defined as data that relate to a living individual (but not a company or limited liability partnership) who can be identified either from those data alone, or when they are combined with other information in the possession of (or likely future possession of) the data controller.[476] To qualify as 'data' within this definition, the individual's information must also either be processed by computer or other automated means,[477] be recorded with the intention of it being so processed, be recorded in manual records held within 'relevant filing systems',[478] or form part of an 'accessible record'.[479] Whilst this last concept will have little application in the banking context, a 'relevant filing system' will include data held on a bank's computer database or any manual filing system that is 'sufficiently structured to allow easy access to information specific to the data subject', such as handwritten customer information cards.[480]

Before processing such personal data, an entity must be registered as a 'data controller',[481] and such processing must comply with the eight 'data protection principles',[482] which require that personal data be used fairly and lawfully; be used only for the specified purposes for which it was obtained; be adequate, relevant, and not excessive in relation to the purpose for which the data are processed; and be accurate and, where necessary, kept up to date. Additionally, appropriate measures must be taken against unauthorized or unlawful use of data and their accidental loss or damage. Personal data will only be processed 'fairly and lawfully' if one of a number of conditions is satisfied,[483] *inter alia*, that the 'data subject' (in other words, the individual who is the subject of the personal data) consents to the processing; that the processing is needed to perform or enter into a contract, to comply with a non-contractual obligation, or to fulfil certain public purposes, such as the administration of justice; or that the processing is 'neces-

---

[476] The concept of 'personal data' requires a narrow interpretation, and does not necessarily include all information retrieved by a computer search against an individual's name: *Durant* v. *Financial Services Authority* [2004] FSR 28, [27]–[29] (CA). Similarly, a document does not necessarily contain a particular individual's 'personal data' simply because he is mentioned therein, unless the information is 'biographical in a significant sense' and has the data subject as its focus. Accordingly, information concerning complaints made by an individual is not 'personal data', unless it involves an opinion expressed about that individual personally: *Ezsias* v. *Welsh Ministers* [2007] All ER (D) 65, [59]–[66], [72], [75], [80], [88], [104]. Anonymized information that was originally derived from personal data, such as banking statistics, is outside the scope of the DPA 1998: *Common Services Agency* v. *Scottish Information Commissioner* [2008] 4 All ER 851, [26]–[27], [79]–[83], [92] (HL). See further Ch. 13, Sect. 7 below. In contrast, the DPA 1998 gives 'processing' a wide meaning, which includes the basic word processing of documents that contain personal data, but not the selection of personal data from amongst other information by the exercise of human judgement alone without the assistance of a computer or other automated means: *Johnson* v. *Medical Defence Union* [2007] EWCA Civ 262, [23]–[25], [48].

[477] The mere fact that information is contained in a document that can be scanned into a computer system is insufficient to make it 'data': *Smith* v. *Lloyds TSB Bank plc* [2005] EWHC 246 (Ch), [20]–[23].

[478] DPA 1998, s.1(1). See further Ch. 13, Sect. 7 below.   [479] Ibid., s.68 & Sched. 12.

[480] *Smith* v. *Lloyds TSB Bank plc*, n.477 above, [10]–[11], [13] (unstructured bundles of documents kept in boxes are not covered). Whether information falls within the scope of the DPA 1998 is to be determined at the time of the data request: ibid., [12], [17]. See also *Durant* v. *Financial Services Authority*, n.476 above, [45]–[50].

[481] DPA 1998, s.17(1). See further Ch. 13, Sect. 7 below.

[482] Ibid., s.4(4) & Sched. 1, Pt. I. See further Ch. 13, Sect. 7 below.

[483] Certain information must be provided, or made readily available, to the individual concerned, such as the purposes for which the data are intended to be processed: DPA 1998, Sched. 1, Pt. II, para. 2.

sary for the purposes of legitimate interests pursued by the data controller or by a third party...to whom the data are disclosed'.[484] Where the relevant information includes 'sensitive personal data', namely data concerned with such matters as racial or ethnic origin, political opinions, or religious beliefs, any processing must satisfy certain alternative conditions.[485] Additionally, a 'data subject' is also given certain rights under the DPA 1998 with respect to his personal data.[486] These include the right to access personal data,[487] to prevent processing of personal data for the purposes of direct marketing,[488] to prevent any processing likely to cause damage and distress,[489] to receive compensation where damage results from a breach of the DPA 1998,[490] and to apply to the courts for correction, blocking, erasure, or destruction of inaccurate or excessive data.[491]

The HRA 1998 incorporates the European Convention for the Protection of Human Rights and Fundamental Freedoms 1950 (ECHR) into English law in three ways: first, by requiring the English courts to construe all legislation 'so far as it is possible to do so...in a way which is compatible with the [ECHR] rights';[492] secondly, by making it unlawful for a 'public authority' to act in a way that is incompatible with ECHR rights;[493] thirdly, by introducing a procedure whereby the courts can declare legislation incompatible with ECHR rights, leaving it to Parliament to amend the legislation should it wish to do so.[494] As the concept of 'public authority' in the HRA 1998 includes 'a court or tribunal',[495] the ECHR will inevitably affect such matters as the exercise of judicial discretion, and the development of the common law. The HRA 1998 does not give private citizens a direct 'horizontal' right of action against each other based on breaches of ECHR rights, but it is inevitable that the ECHR will have an indirect horizontal effect in the manner in which courts and tribunals deal with proceedings between private parties.[496] Indeed, there is already evidence that Article 8 of the ECHR, which provides that '[e]veryone has the right to respect for his private and family life, his home and his correspondence', is influencing

---

[484] DPA 1998, Sched. 2. See generally *Stone* v. *South East Coast Strategic Health Authority* [2006] EWHC 1668 (Admin.); *Grow with US Ltd* v. *Green Thumb (UK) Ltd* [2006] EWCA Civ 1201.

[485] Ibid., s.2 & Sched. 3.

[486] Ibid., s.55, which makes it an offence knowingly or recklessly to disclose personal data without the consent of the data controller: *Attorney-General's Reference (No. 140 of 2004)* [2004] EWCA Crim 3525; *R* v. *Rooney* [2006] All ER (D) 158 (CA).

[487] Ibid., s.7. This right of access is 'to enable [the 'data subject'] to check whether the data controller's processing of [the data] unlawfully infringes his privacy', but it is not an 'automatic key to any information', and does not exist to assist in the 'discovery of documents that may assist him in litigation or complaints against third parties': *Durant* v. *Financial Services Authority*, n.476 above, [27]. A 'data subject' has the right to be informed of his personal data's processing and to be given 'in an intelligible and permanent form' a description of the data, the purpose of the processing, and the information's recipients, but this does not give a right of access to documents or copies thereof at all: ibid., [26], [40]. See also *Ezsias* v. *Welsh Ministers*, n.476 above, [51]–[57]. The 'data controller' need only take reasonable and proportionate steps to identify and disclose the information it is bound to disclose: ibid., [94]. See formerly the *Banking Code* (March 2008), [11.3]; the *Business Banking Code* (March 2008), [11.3].

[488] Ibid., s.11.   [489] Ibid., s 10.   [490] Ibid., s.13.   [491] Ibid., s.14.

[492] Human Rights Act 1998 (HRA 1998), s.3.   [493] Ibid., s.6(1).   [494] Ibid., s.4.

[495] Ibid., s.6(3).

[496] A. Lester and D. Pannick, 'The Impact of the Human Rights Act on Private Law: The Knight's Move' (2000) 116 *LQR* 280, replying to H.W.R. Wade, 'Horizons of Horizontality' (2000) 116 *LQR* 217. See also M. Hunt, 'The "Horizontal Effect" of the Human Rights Act' [1998] *PL* 423; R. Buxton, 'The Human Rights Act and Private Law' (2000) 116 *LQR* 48; N. Bamforth, 'The True "Horizontal Effect" of the Human Rights Act 1998' (2001) 117 *LQR* 34; J. Morgan, 'Privacy in the House of Lords, Again' (2004) 120 *LQR* 563; F. Klug & K. Starmer, 'Standing Back from the Human Rights Act: How Effective is it Five Years On' [2005] *PL* 716, 723–726; J. Howell, 'The Human Rights Act 1998: Land, Private Citizens, and the Common Law' (2007) 123 *LQR* 618, 625.

the development of the general law protecting confidences,[497] and there seems to be no reason why this should not also be the case with the duty of confidentiality that arises in the banking context.[498]

(ii) **Duration and scope of the duty of confidentiality**[499]

Although a bank can owe a duty of confidentiality to a non-customer by giving an express undertaking to that effect, such as when a business plan is presented to the bank to secure finance, a bank usually owes a duty of confidentiality to its customers as a result of a term implied in law into the banker–customer contract.[500] The necessity of implying such a term was recognized (and its scope was authoritatively considered) in the leading decision of *Tournier* v. *National Provincial and Union Bank of England*,[501] where Bankes LJ stated that 'the credit of the customer depends very largely upon the strict observance of that confidence'.[502] In *Tournier*, the claimant, who was heavily overdrawn with the defendant bank, failed to meet the relevant branch manager's repayment demands. When the branch manager noticed that a cheque, drawn on the account of another customer at a different branch and payable to the claimant's order, had been indorsed to a bookmaker by the claimant and was being collected for that person's account, he telephoned the claimant's employers, ostensibly to ascertain the claimant's private address. During the course of that conversation, the manager disclosed that the claimant's account was overdrawn and that he had had dealings with bookmakers. The claimant's employer subsequently declined to renew the claimant's contract upon its expiration. The Court of Appeal held that the bank had breached its duty of confidentiality and awarded damages to the customer.[503] In reaching this conclusion, it was critical for the Court of Appeal to decide whether the bank's duty of confidentiality extended to information received by the bank from sources other than the customer himself or his account, since the information that the bank manager disclosed

---

[497] Its impact will depend largely upon the extent to which the HRA 1998 has 'horizontal effect', if at all. This issue remains to be finally settled (*Doherty* v. *Birmingham City Council* [2008] 3 WLR 636, [99] (HL); *White* v. *Withers LLP* [2009] EWCA Civ. 1122, [66]), although there is authority that is at least consistent with the view that the HRA 1998 has 'horizontal effect': *Douglas* v. *Hello! Ltd* [2001] QB 967 (CA); *A* v. *B plc* [2003] QB 195 (CA); *Campbell* v. *MGN* [2004] 2 AC 457 (HL). For stronger support for 'horizontal effect', see *Wilson* v. *First County Trust Ltd (No. 2)* [2004] 1 AC 816, [174] (HL); *Douglas* v. *Hello! Ltd (No. 3)* [2006] QB 125, [53] (CA), revsd., n.512 below; *Murray* v. *Express Newspapers plc* [2007] EWHC 1908 (Ch), [18]; *HRH Prince of Wales* v. *Associated Newspapers Ltd* [2008] Ch 57, [25] (CA).

[498] Art. 8 of the ECHR should guide the courts in balancing bank confidentiality against any relevant public interest that favours disclosure: R. Stokes, 'The Banker's Duty of Confidentiality, Money Laundering, and the Human Rights Act' [2007] *JBL* 502, 509–511, 526.

[499] R.M. Goode, 'The Banker's Duty of Confidentiality' [1989] *JBL* 269.

[500] Sects. 2–3 above. See also *Bodnar* v. *Townsend* [2003] TASSC 148, [3]–[6] (duty of confidentiality not limited to banks, but extends to credit unions and other financial institutions providing similar services).

[501] N.469 above.   [502] Ibid., 474.

[503] General damages may be awarded for breach of confidence: *Shah* v. *HSBC Private Bank (UK) Ltd*, n.307 above, [105]. Provided the losses were within the parties' reasonable contemplation at the time of the contract's conclusion, special damages may be awarded to cover the lost chance of repeat business when the bank's unauthorized disclosure has soured relations between the bank's customer and his trading partner: *Jackson* v. *Royal Bank of Scotland* [2005] 1 WLR 377 (HL). See also C. Hare, 'Transferable Letters of Credit: Responsibility, Remoteness and Loss of a Chance' [2005] *LMCLQ* 350. Consider now *Transfield Shipping Inc of Panama* v. *Mercator Shipping Inc of Monrovia (The Achilleas)* [2009] AC 61 (HL), [10]–[22]. Outside the banking law context, breach of confidence may give rise to proprietary relief: D. Sheehan, 'Information, Tracing Remedies and the Remedial Constructive Trust' [2005] *RLR* 82. There is no room for punitive damages: *Guertin* v. *Royal Bank of Canada* (1983) 43 OR (2d) 363, affd. 47 OR (2d) 799 (OCA); *BMP Global Distribution Inc.* v. *Bank of Nova Scotia* [2005] BCSC 1091, [433].

in *Tournier* was not acquired from operating the claimant's account, but rather from the chequing operations conducted on the drawer's account. Bankes LJ rejected the view that 'the duty of non-disclosure is confined to information derived from the customer himself or from his account', but extended to any information, regardless of its source, that was acquired 'in the character of banker'.[504] Similarly, Atkin LJ held that the bank's duty of confidentiality was not restricted to information about the actual state of the customer's account (such as the amount of the debit or credit balance) or information derived from the account itself (such as the transactions passing through the account or the security given in respect of it), but also encompassed 'information obtained from other sources than the customer's actual account, if the occasion upon which the information was obtained arose out of the banking relations of the bank and its customers'.[505] Scrutton LJ expressed the contrary view, holding that the bank's duty to respect its customers' confidences did not apply 'to knowledge derived from other sources during the continuance of the relation'.[506] On this point, the courts have subsequently preferred the majority view in *Tournier*.[507] As Lord Donaldson MR stated more recently in *Barclays Bank plc v. Taylor*,[508] '[t]he banker–customer relationship imposes upon the bank a duty of confidentiality in relation to information concerning its customer and his affairs which it acquires in the character of his banker'.

This recognition that information is only covered by the bank's duty of confidentiality when acquired by it in its capacity as banker would suggest that information acquired before the commencement of the banker–customer relationship, namely before the bank agreed to open an account for the customer,[509] would fall outside the scope of the duty (as suggested by Scrutton LJ in *Tournier*),[510] and that information received after its termination would similarly be excluded (as suggested by both Scrutton and Atkin LJJ in *Tournier*).[511] Nevertheless, there are good reasons why banks still need to exercise caution in these circumstances. First, information received by the bank before the banker–customer relationship's commencement may subsequently be repeated by the customer and accordingly may fall within the duty. Secondly, information may be passed to the bank at any time in circumstances that subject it to the general law of confidence.[512] Thirdly, the bank may have given an express undertaking to the customer to keep particular information secret, even if it technically falls outside the scope of the bank's implied duty of confidentiality. Indeed, the undertaking given by banks in the *Lending Code* that 'personal information will be treated as private and confidential' is extremely broad and includes no limitation relating to when the bank acquired the information in question.[513] Fourthly, as Atkin LJ indicated in *Tournier*, the bank's duty of confidentiality in respect of information acquired during the course of the banker–customer relationship does not cease when that relationship is terminated, but rather 'extend[s] beyond the period when the account is closed, or ceases to be an active account'.[514] Similarly, Bankes LJ considered that 'the [bank's duty of confidentiality] does not cease the moment a customer closes

---

[504] N.469 above, 473–474. See also *Jeffers v. Northern Bank Ltd*, n.48 above, [13]; *Walsh v. National Irish Bank Ltd*, n.50 above, [23].

[505] Ibid., 485.   [506] Ibid., 481.

[507] *Lipkin Gorman v. Karpnale Ltd*, n.318 above, 1357; *Asia Pacific Telecommunications Ltd v. Optus Networks Pty Ltd*, n.173 above, [82].

[508] [1989] 1 WLR 1066, 1070 (CA).   [509] Sect. 2 above.   [510] N.469 above, 481, 485.

[511] Ibid.

[512] *Attorney-General v. Guardian Newspapers Ltd (No. 2)* [1990] 1 AC 109, 281–282 (HL); *Douglas v. Hello! Ltd (No. 3)* [2008] 1 AC 1, [272]–[275], [292], [307] (HL).

[513] *Lending Code* (November 2009), [13]; *Lending Code* (March 2011), [15]. See formerly *Banking Code* (March 2008), [11.1]; *Business Banking Code* (March 2008), [11.1].

[514] N.469 above, 485.

his account', but that '[i]nformation gained during the currency of the account remains confidential unless released under circumstances bringing the case within one of the classes of qualification I have already referred to'.[515] Indeed, this duty probably even continues after the customer's death.[516]

Although the bank's duty of confidentiality *prima facie* covers all information acquired by a bank in that capacity, the courts nevertheless temper this broad rule with a degree of commonsense by excluding certain types of information that would otherwise be caught by the duty. A good illustration is *Christofi* v. *Barclays Bank plc*,[517] where the customer's husband had transferred the matrimonial home into her name before he was adjudicated bankrupt. The husband's trustee in bankruptcy registered a caution against the property, but this was subsequently cancelled. Despite the husband, who was acting as his wife's agent, specifically instructing the bank not to disclose that the caution had been cancelled, the bank nevertheless informed the husband's trustee in bankruptcy of that fact in response to the trustee's request for information. The trustee accordingly re-registered its caution. The customer claimed that the defendant bank had breached its duty of confidentiality, but the Court of Appeal, affirming the decision of L. Collins QC (as he then was), struck out the claim as disclosing no cause of action. The principal reason for this conclusion related to the statutory regime for registration and cancellation of cautions, pursuant to which cancellation of a caution would only occur once the cautioner had received notice from the Land Registry. As the trustee in bankruptcy must have been informed previously of the caution's cancellation, the bank could not have breached its implied duty of confidentiality by revealing information to someone deemed to have that information already under the statutory scheme. The situation in *Christofi* would have been different, and there would have been a breach of the bank's duty of confidentiality, if the bank had expressly undertaken not to reveal the information to the trustee in bankruptcy,[518] or had revealed the information in that case to a person who did not have a statutory right to receive it.

Nevertheless, there is one particular difficulty with the principle as formulated in *Tournier*, namely that the implied duty of confidentiality has traditionally only arisen where there exists an account relationship between the bank and its customer. Modern multifunction banks, however, provide their clients with a wide range of financial services going well beyond the traditional functions of deposit-taking and lending, and frequently there may be no account relationship between a bank and a particular client. In the absence of any express undertaking of confidentiality, the issue arises as to whether the bank's implied duty of confidentiality covers information that it acquires when acting outside its traditional deposit-taking role. This is particularly relevant where the information is acquired by the arm of a bank that does not operate its non-banking business through a separately incorporated company. It may be that this issue can only be resolved by locating the banker's duty of confidentiality within the general principles governing breach of confidence, rather than by treating bank confidentiality as a discrete area of law.[519] The general principles relating to breach of confidence were

[515] Ibid., 473. See also *Walsh* v. *National Irish Bank Ltd*, n.50 above, [25].

[516] M. Hapgood, *Paget's Law of Banking* (13th edn., London, 2007), [8.2].

[517] [1998] 2 All ER 484, 489, affd. [1999] 2 All ER (Comm.) 417 (CA).   [518] Ibid., 426.

[519] R. Cranston, *Principles of Banking Law* (2nd edn., Oxford, 2002), 171–174. See also M.H. Ogilvie, 'From Secrecy to Confidence to the Demise of the Banker–Customer Relationship: *Rodaro* v. *Royal Bank of Canada*' (2004) 19 *BFLR* 103, 112–113.

considered in *Attorney-General* v. *Guardian Newspapers Ltd (No. 2)*, where Lord Goff stated:[520]

> [A] duty of confidence arises when confidential information comes to the knowledge of a person (the confidant) in circumstances where he has notice, or is held to have agreed, that the information is confidential, with the effect that it would be just in all the circumstances that he should be precluded from disclosing the information to others…To this broad general principle there are three limiting principles…The first…is that the principle of confidentiality only applies to information to the extent that it is confidential…The second limiting principle is that the duty of confidence applies neither to useless information, nor to trivia…The third limiting principle…is that, although the basis of the law's protection of confidence is that there is a public interest that confidences should be preserved and protected by the law, nevertheless the public interest may be outweighed by some countervailing public interest which favours disclosure…

Applying this more general approach to the context of bank confidentiality does have advantages. As liability for breach of confidence arises by virtue of a general equitable obligation imposed by the law on the confidant towards the confider, rather than by means of a term implied into the banker–customer contract, it provides a legal basis for protecting confidential information revealed to a bank by a customer in a non-banking context (such as when a bank provides investment advice or asset management services) or by a non-customer (such as when presenting a business plan to secure bank finance). The general principles concerning breach of confidence do not, however, sit easily with the scope of the implied duty recognized in *Tournier*, since each recognizes different circumstances in which confidential information may nevertheless be disclosed. As indicated above, *Guardian Newspapers* generally only permits disclosure of confidential information when it is in the public interest, whereas *Tournier* recognizes that this can occur in other types of situation, such as when it is in the bank's own interests to do so. In *Tournier*, Bankes LJ identified four situations in which the bank owed no duty of confidentiality at all,[521] and in which the scope of the implied term to that effect was qualified by the circumstances:[522]

> On principle…the qualifications can be classified under four heads: (a) where disclosure is under compulsion of law; (b) where there is a duty to the public to disclose; (c) where the interests of the bank require disclosure; (d) where the disclosure is made by the express or implied consent of the customer.

These qualifications will each be considered in turn.

(iii) **Compulsion of law**

Over recent years, the amount of legislation permitting courts to order the inspection and disclosure of bank documents or otherwise requiring bank disclosure in specific

---

[520] N.512 above, 281–282. See also *Douglas* v. *Hello! Ltd (No. 3)*, n.512 above, [272]–[275], [292], [307].

[521] See also *Barclays Bank plc* v. *Taylor*, n.508 above, 1074; *El Jawhary* v. *Bank of Credit and Commerce International SA* [1993] BCLC 396, 400 (CA).

[522] N.469 above, 473. The *Tournier* duty and its qualifications have been endorsed in Canada (*Canadian Imperial Bank of Commerce* v. *Sayani* (1993) 83 BCLR (2d) 167, 172 (BCCA); '*The Golden Trinity*' (2001) FTR 1, [7]–[11] (CFC); *BMP Global Distribution Inc.* v. *Bank of Nova Scotia*, n.503 above, [153]), Ireland (*National Irish Bank Ltd* v. *Radio Telefis Eireann* [1998] 2 IR 465, 494; *Walsh* v. *National Irish Bank Ltd*, n.50 above, [23]–[24]), and Northern Ireland (*Jeffers* v. *Northern Bank Ltd*, n.48 above, [13]).

circumstances has burgeoned, making major inroads into the bank's duty of confidentiality.[523] Although it is not possible to consider all the legislation of this type, the most common examples usually involve regulatory or investigatory authorities being allowed to access the confidential information held by a bank about its customer. Thus, the police can sometimes access a suspect's banking records,[524] and a bank can sometimes be ordered by the tax authorities to supply information concerning its customers' affairs.[525] Similarly, as considered previously,[526] the Financial Services Authority (FSA) has the power to require a bank who owes a duty of confidentiality to a customer to disclose certain information if one of four conditions are satisfied: the person required to make disclosure is the person under investigation or a member of the same group as the person under investigation; the person to whom the confidence is owed is the person under investigation or a member of that person's group; the person to whom the confidence is owed consents; or there has been special authorization by the investigating authority.[527] In the company law field, a bank, as an agent of its corporate customer, may be required by the Department for Business, Innovation, and Skills, as part of its investigations, to produce books relevant to the prosecution of the customer's directors or managers.[528] Similarly, where a bank is believed to have information concerning the affairs of its insolvent corporate customer, it may be ordered by the court to submit an affidavit detailing its dealings with its customer or to 'produce any books, papers or other records' in its possession.[529] In making such an order, a court will balance the importance of the information to the relevant proceedings against the degree of oppression caused by ordering disclosure.[530] Probably the most significant example of legislation curtailing

---

[523] M.H. Ogilvie, n.14 above, 144.

[524] Police and Criminal Evidence Act 1984 (PACE 1984), s.9. See also *Re Central Criminal Court, ex p. Adegbesan* [1986] 1 WLR 1292; *R. v. Crown Court at Leicester, ex p. DPP* [1987] 1 WLR 1371; *Barclays Bank plc v. Taylor*, n.508 above; *Marcel v. Metropolitan Police Commissioners* [1992] Ch. 225 (CA); *R. v. Crown Court at Southwark, ex p. Bowles* [1998] AC 641 (HL); *R v. Manchester Stipendiary Magistrate, ex p. Granada Television Ltd* [2001] 1 AC 300 (HL); *R (on the application of Faisaltex Ltd) v. Preston Crown Court* [2008] EWHC 2832 (Admin.). See further Police and Criminal Evidence Act 1984 (Application to Revenue and Customs) Order 2007, S.I. 2007/3175. Under the Criminal Justice Act 1987, s.2, the Serious Fraud Office can obtain disclosure of bank documents when investigating serious complex fraud: *R v. Director of SFO, ex p. Smith* [1993] AC 1 (HL); *Re Arrows Ltd (No. 4)* [1995] 2 AC 75 (HL); *Marlwood Commercial Inc. v. Kozeny* [2004] 3 All ER 648 (CA); *R (on the application of Energy Financing Team Ltd) v. Bow Street Magistrates' Court* [2005] 4 All ER 285.

[525] Taxes Management Act 1970, ss.13, 17, 24; Income Tax Act 2007, s.771. See generally *R v. IRC, ex p. Taylor (No. 2)* [1990] STC 379 (CA); *T. C. Coombs & Co. v. IRC* [1991] 3 All ER 623 (HL); *R (on the application of Morgan Grenfell & Co Ltd v. Special Commissioner of Income Tax*, n.464 above; *Revenue & Customs Commissioners' Application (Section 20 Notice: Financial Institution)* [2006] STC 360; *Walsh v. National Irish Bank Ltd*, n.50 above, [8], [12]. For the courts' powers of intervention where a demand exceeds what is necessary, see *Clinch v. IRC* [1974] QB 76; *Essex v. IRC* [1980] STC 378 (CA).

[526] Ch. 2, Sect. 4(vi) above. See generally FSMA 2000, Pt. XI.

[527] FSMA 2000, ss.165, 175(5). For assistance to a foreign regulator in obtaining documents, see *Financial Services Authority v. Amro International* [2010] EWCA Civ. 123.

[528] Companies Act 1985, ss.434(2), 452(1A).

[529] Insolvency Act 1986, s.236. See also *Re Pantmaenog Timber Co. Ltd* [2004] 1 AC 158 (HL) (disqualification proceedings).

[530] *Cloverbay Ltd (Joint Administrator) v. Bank of Credit and Commerce International SA* [1991] Ch. 90 (CA); *B & C Holdings plc (Joint Administrators) v. Spicer & Oppenheim* [1993] AC 426; *Re Mid East Trading Ltd, Phillips v. Lehman Brothers* [1998] BCC 726 (documents situated abroad); *Re RBG Resources plc* [2002] BCC 1005, [23], [26], [39], [43]–[50], [56]–[62] (CA); *Daltel Europe Ltd v. Makki* [2005] 1 BCLC 594, [24]–[35]. For the relationship between Insolvency Act, s.236 and the Banking Act 1987, s.82 (since repealed and replaced by the Financial Services and Markets Act 2000 (FSMA 2000), s.348), see *Re Galileo Group Ltd* [1999] Ch. 100. See also *Real Estate Opportunities Ltd v. Aberdeen Asset Managers Jersey Ltd* [2008] 2 BCLC 116 (CA).

the bank's duty of confidentiality, however, is the recent anti-terrorist and anti-money laundering legislation, which compel banks, under pain of being criminally liable under either the Terrorism Act 2000 or the POCA 2002, to disclose to the relevant authorities their knowledge or suspicion that a customer may be involved with money launder- ing, whether the proceeds of drug offences or other criminal activity, or with terrorist activity.[531] As this will constitute a 'protected disclosure',[532] the bank is protected from liability for breach of its duty of confidentiality and may escape any liability for breach of mandate.[533]

Beyond these context-specific statutes, there exist more general legal bases upon which a bank may be legally compelled to disclose confidential information, such as the state of its customer's account, during the course of legal proceedings against its customer.[534] A bank (unlike a solicitor) cannot refuse to answer questions concerning its relationship with a customer on the ground of privilege. For example, pursuant to the jurisdiction recognized in *Norwich Pharmacal Co.* v. *Customs & Excise Comrs*,[535] a bank may be com- pelled to make pre-action disclosure of its customer's confidential information to a third party who requires that information in order to be able to commence proceedings against the customer.[536] A court will not grant a *Norwich Pharmacal* order unless three condi- tions are satisfied:[537] (i) it must at least be arguable that a wrong (whether involving civil or criminal liability)[538] has been committed; (ii) there must be the need for an order to enable action to be brought against that wrongdoer; (iii) the person against whom the *Norwich Pharmacal* order is sought must be so 'mixed up' in the acts of the wrongdoer as to have facilitated the wrongdoing and be able or likely to provide the information necessary for that wrongdoer to be sued. As regards this last requirement, banks are particularly likely to become innocently 'mixed up' in their customer's wrongdoing, given that the proceeds of the customer's fraud or other wrongdoing will frequently pass through his account, and accordingly banks are particularly susceptible to the *Norwich Pharmacal* jurisdic- tion. Indeed, in *Koo Golden East Mongolia* v. *Bank of Nova Scotia*,[539] Sir Anthony Clarke MR described the situation where a bank account holds the proceeds of wrongful activity as being the 'classic case' for *Norwich Pharmacal* relief against a bank. It is not the case, however, that relief will automatically be available once the three conditions above are

[531]   Ch. 4, Sects. 3(ii)–(iii) above. See also Money Laundering Regulations 2007, S.I. 2007/2157 (discussed in Ch. 4, Sects. 3(i) & (iv) above). See further Joint Money Laundering Steering Group, *Guidance Notes on Money Laundering for the Financial Sector* (www.jmlsg.org.uk) (discussed in Ch. 4, Sect. 3(i) above). A cus- tomer who opens an account with a United Kingdom bank is taken to accept, and is entitled to assume, that the bank will act in accordance with applicable anti-money laundering and anti-terrorism legislation: *Tayeb* v. *HSBC Bank plc* [2004] EWHC 1529 (Comm.), [2004] 4 All ER 1024, [57].

[532]   POCA 2002, s.337(1); Terrorism Act 2000, s.21B(1). See further Ch. 4, Sect. 3(ii)(b) above.

[533]   *Shah* v. *HSBC Private Bank (UK) Ltd*, n.331 above, [68]–[70]. See further Ch. 4, Sect. 4 above & Ch. 11, Sect. 1(v) below.

[534]   *Bucknell* v. *Bucknell* [1969] 1 WLR 1204; *Eckman* v. *Midland Bank Ltd* [1973] QB 519 (considering also writs of sequestration against a customer); *Messenger Newspaper Group Ltd* v. *National Graphical Association* [1984] 1 All ER 298 (CA).

[535]   [1974] AC 133, 175 (HL).

[536]   The *Norwich Pharmacal* jurisdiction continues to exist alongside the Civil Procedure Rules 1998 (CPR 1998), as neither the pre-action disclosure regime in CPR 1998, r.31.16, nor the third party disclosure regime in CPR 1998, r.31.17, applies to pre-action disclosure against non-parties to the relevant proceedings: C. Hollander, *Documentary Evidence* (10th edn., London, 2009), [5–15].

[537]   *Mitsui & Co Ltd* v. *Nexen Petroleum UK Ltd* [2005] 2 All ER 511, [21].

[538]   *Ashworth Hospital Authority* v. *MGN Ltd* [2002] 1 WLR 2033, [34], [35], [53] (HL).

[539]   [2007] EWCA Civ 1443, [37]. See also *A Co.* v. *B Co.* [2002] 2 HKC 497, [11]; *State Bank of India* v. *Fleet National Bank* [2006] HKCU 1399, [31]–[37]; *Isofoton SA* v. *Toronto Dominion Bank* (2007) OR (3d) 780, [34]–[37] (OSC); *AB* v. *CD* [2008] ABCA 51, [14]–[17].

satisfied, since *Norwich Pharmacal* relief is discretionary and has generally been viewed as an exceptional form of relief that should only be exercised when a court is satisfied that it is 'necessary'.[540] In particular, in *Koo Golden East Mongolia*,[541] the Court of Appeal recently emphasized that '[a] court should be very reluctant to make a *Norwich Pharmacal* order which involves a breach of confidence as between a bank and its customer'. Whilst the *Norwich Pharmacal* jurisdiction originally appeared limited to circumstances where the third party's disclosure was necessary to identify the potential wrongdoers so that they could be sued,[542] it now also covers situations where the claimant requires 'a missing piece of the jigsaw' to sue an identified wrongdoer.[543] As the obligation of the bank or other *Norwich Pharmacal* defendant is to provide 'full information' in relation to these matters, the bank will potentially disclose its customer's personal details and any information relating to his involvement in the commission of the relevant wrong.[544]

As confirmed by *Koo Golden East Mongolia*—where the claimant sought an order against the bank with which the proposed defendant held an unallocated gold account for disclosure of the information needed to locate the whereabouts of the gold's proceeds and to identify any third party recipients of the gold—the *Norwich Pharmacal* jurisdiction is likely to be particularly useful against banks when seeking information to assist in tracing the proceeds of fraudulent or criminal activity. A similar application of the *Norwich Pharmacal* jurisdiction to the banking context can be found in *Bankers Trust Co. v. Shapira*,[545] although this case has also been explained as involving the exercise of a distinct, but related, jurisdiction.[546] Two fraudsters obtained substantial sums by presenting to the claimant bank in New York cheques purportedly drawn on it by a Saudi Arabian bank. At the fraudsters' request, the claimant bank credited a substantial part of the proceeds to an account opened in the fraudsters' names by the defendant bank in London. As the cheques were forgeries, the claimant bank reversed the debit to the Saudi Arabian bank's account with a view to bringing proceedings against the fraudsters. In an attempt to locate them, the claimant bank applied for an order against the defendant bank, allowing the former to inspect and take copies of all correspondence between the fraudsters

---

[540] Ibid., [57]. It has been suggested that information is only 'necessary' for the purposes of the *Norwich Pharmacal* jurisdiction when it is unavailable from the proposed defendant to the substantive claim, so that the third party is the 'only practicable source of information': *Mitsui & Co Ltd v. Nexen Petroleum UK Ltd*, n.537 above, [24]; *Nikitin v. Richards Butler LLP* [2007] EWHC 173 (QB), [21]–[24]. This approach has, however, been criticized as overly restrictive: *R (on the application of Mohamed) v. Secretary of State for Foreign & Commonwealth Affairs* [2008] EWHC 2048 (Admin.), [93]–[94]. See also C. Hollander, n.536 above, [5-12]–[5-13], approved in *United Company Rusal plc v. HSBC Bank plc* [2011] EWHC 404 (QB), [110]–[137].

[541] N.539 above, [49].

[542] *Norwich Pharmacal Co. v. Customs & Excise Comrs.*, n.535 above, 175; *Koo Golden East Mongolia v. Bank of Nova Scotia*, n.539 above.

[543] *Axa Equity & Law Life v. National Westminster Bank* [1998] PNLR 433 (CA) (order sought for documents in banks' possession relating to preparation of customer's accounts in support of professional negligence claim against accountants). See also *Carlton Film Distributors Ltd v. VCI* [2003] FSR 47 (CA); *Mitsui & Co Ltd v. Nexen Petroleum UK Ltd*, n.537 above, [18]; *R (on the application of Mohamed) v. Secretary of State for Foreign & Commonwealth Affairs*, n.540 above, [133].

[544] C. Hollander, n.536 above, [5.11]–[5.12], citing *RCA v. Reddingtons Rare Records* [1974] 1 WLR 1445. See also *Arab Monetary Fund v. Hashim (No. 5)* [1992] 2 All ER 911, 914; *R (on the application of Mohamed) v. Secretary of State for Foreign & Commonwealth Affairs*, n.540 above, [128]–[132].

[545] [1980] 1 WLR 1274 (CA). A *Bankers Trust* order may often be ancillary to a freezing injunction or a search order.

[546] A *Bankers Trust* order may be justified solely by reference to equitable principles: *Murphy v. Murphy* [1998] 3 All ER 1. See also C. Hollander, n.536 above, [5–18]. Interestingly, although cited to the court, no reference was made to *Bankers Trust* in *Koo Golden East Mongolia v. Bank of Nova Scotia*, n.539 above, which also concerned attempts to locate the whereabouts of assets allegedly belonging to the claimant.

and the defendant bank, and also to photocopy all cheques drawn on their account. Reversing Mustill J, the Court of Appeal stressed that courts should not lightly use their powers to compel disclosure of information arising in the confidential banker–customer relationship, as it was 'a strong thing to order a bank to disclose the state of its customer's account and the documents and correspondence relating to it'.[547] Nevertheless, an order would be granted, even in interlocutory proceedings, where the claimant sought to trace funds and there was strong evidence that the claimant had been fraudulently deprived of those funds and that delay might result in the dissipation of any assets before trial.[548] *Arab Monetary Fund* v. *Hashim (No. 5)*[549] Hoffmann J stressed two further factors that a court should take into account before making a *Bankers Trust* order: first, unlike a request for general discovery, a bank is entitled to some specificity in the documents or information that it is required to produce; and secondly, the balance of convenience must favour the making of such an order, in that the potential advantages to the claimant must be balanced against any detriment to the bank, not merely in terms of cost, for which the bank is usually compensated on an indemnity basis by the terms of the order, but also in terms of the invasion of privacy and breach of confidentiality obligations owed to others.[550] Should an order be made, then in addition to paying the defendant bank's expenses and giving an undertaking in damages, the claimant will be required to undertake that any information be utilized solely for the purposes of the tracing exercise.[551] From the bank's perspective, whilst any disclosure pursuant to the terms of a *Bankers Trust* order will be protected from liability for breach of confidence in this jurisdiction, a bank may not necessarily enjoy a similar immunity abroad in respect of such a disclosure.[552]

As discussed previously,[553] however, a bank that is served with some form of disclosure order may face a dilemma, as shown by *C* v. *S.*[554] In the context of a claim against various defendants concerning the misappropriation of its funds, C obtained a freezing injunction against the defendants in the main action and a *Norwich Pharmacal* order that the defendants' bank disclose the information required for C to trace its funds. Unknown to C, the bank had already made money-laundering reports concerning one of the defendants to the National Criminal Intelligence Service (NCIS), now replaced by the SOCA.[555] This put the bank in a difficult situation: on the one hand, the bank was bound to obey the disclosure order and might be guilty of contempt of court if it failed to do so; on the other hand, by obeying the order, the bank risked prosecution under section 93D of the Criminal Justice

---

[547] N.545 above, 1282. See also *R (on the application of Mohamed)* v. *Secretary of State for Foreign & Commonwealth Affairs*, n.540 above, [129]–[131].

[548] Additionally, in *Arab Monetary Fund* v. *Hashim (No. 5)*, n.544 above, 918, Hoffmann J held that a *Bankers Trust* order depended upon the claimant demonstrating a 'real prospect' that the information sought might lead to the location and preservation of assets to which the claimant might make a proprietary claim. On the facts, the delay was such that there was no real prospect that the order would locate or preserve assets. See also *Wharf Ltd* v. *Lau Yuen How (No. 2)* [2009] 1 HKC 479, [10].

[549] N.544 above.   [550] Ibid., 919. See also *Wharf Ltd* v. *Lau Yuen How (No. 2)*, n. 548 above, [10].

[551] Although information disclosed pursuant to a *Bankers Trust* order may only generally be used to bring a proprietary claim to recover any funds or a related personal claim against those who have misapplied those funds (*Omar* v. *Omar* [1995] 3 All ER 571), exceptionally a court may allow a claimant to disclose such information to a third party, such as where a foreign law compels the claimant to make such disclosure (*Bank of Crete SA* v. *Koskotas (No. 2)* [1993] 1 All ER 748).

[552] *Arab Monetary Fund* v. *Hashim (No 5)*, n.544 above, 920.   [553] Ch. 4, Sect. 4 above.

[554] [1999] Lloyd's Rep. Bank. 26. For a similar dilemma regarding dishonest assistance liability, see *Governor & Company of the Bank of Scotland* v. *A Ltd*, n.101 above (discussed in Ch. 4, Sect. 4 above & Ch. 7, Sect. 5(iii)(d) below). For the bank's potential liability for refusing to comply with the instructions of a customer suspected of a money laundering offence, see Ch. 4, Sect. 4 above & Ch. 11, Sect. 1(v) below.

[555] Ch. 4, Sect. 3(i) above.

Act 1988 (now repealed and replaced by POCA 2002),[556] which established the offence of 'tipping off'—an offence committed when a person, who knows or suspects that the police are conducting, or are about to conduct, an investigation into money laundering activity relating to the proceeds of serious crime, discloses to another information that is likely to prejudice any investigation. The NCIS would not give the bank any assurance that it would not be prosecuted for 'tipping off' if it complied with the disclosure order. Accordingly, the bank applied to the court for directions. Although, by the time the case reached the Court of Appeal, it was accepted that disclosure would not prejudice any investigation, the Court nevertheless took the opportunity to provide guidelines for similar cases in the future. First, as soon as a bank is aware of a court order that may involve the disclosure of information that is potentially prejudicial to an investigation, it should notify the NCIS of this fact and the information being sought. Where the disclosure order has already been made, the existence of a 'gagging order' that generally prevents a bank from disclosing the fact that a disclosure order has been made will not preclude the bank from being able to approach the NCIS. Secondly, the NCIS bears the burden of identifying the material it does not wish to be disclosed and of indicating its preference as to how the disclosure order should be handled. In some cases, the NCIS will not be concerned about the applicant for the disclosure order knowing of the NCIS' investigation, in which case it will be enough to make disclosure by the bank conditional upon an undertaking by the applicant for the disclosure order that he will keep the relevant information confidential. In other cases, where the NCIS prefers to keep the investigation secret, it may agree to some form of partial disclosure and the applicant for the disclosure order may be satisfied with this. Thirdly, in the event that the applicant for the disclosure order is not prepared to accept partial or restricted disclosure, then the parties will need to obtain court directions by some 'stratagem' or another. Fourthly, the NCIS bears the burden of persuading the court that there is a real likelihood that disclosure would prejudice its investigations. Where the NCIS does not co-operate with the bank or comply with the court's requirements, the court may draw the inference that no prejudice would result from the bank making disclosure. Similarly, as the court has a responsibility to protect the interests of the applicant for the disclosure order, particularly when he cannot be heard, the NCIS must provide the court with 'material on which to act if it is to deprive an applicant of his normal rights'.[557]

In addition to the judicially created disclosure mechanisms discussed above, Part 34 of the Civil Procedure Rules 1998 (CPR 1998),[558] which came into force in April 1999, replaced witness subpoenas and subpoenas *duces tecum* with a new unified procedure whereby a court can issue a 'witness summons' requiring a witness to attend court to give evidence or to produce documents.[559] Moreover, the CPR 1998 introduced a new procedure whereby a claimant, who has already commenced the substantive proceedings, may obtain disclosure from non-parties.[560] Where the substantive proceedings have not been commenced, the claimant must still invoke the *Norwich Pharmacal* or *Bankers Trust* jurisdictions to obtain disclosure from a non-party. The principal difference between the witness summons procedure under CPR 34.2 and disclosure under CPR 1998, r.31.17 lies

---

[556] POCA 2002, ss.333A, 342. See further Ch. 4, Sect. 3(ii)(c) above.   [557] *C* v. *S*, n.554 above, 30.

[558] D. Baker & N. Anstey, 'Disclosure of Documents' in W. Blair (ed.), *Banks and Remedies* (2nd edn., London, 1999), ch. 4.

[559] CPR 1998, r.34.2(1). See also *Assistant Deputy Coroner for Inner West London* v. *Channel 4 Television Corporation* [2007] EWHC 2513 (QB), [3]–[4].

[560] Ibid., r.31.17. See generally *American Home Products* v. *Novartis* [2001] EWCA Civ 165; *Three Rivers District Council* v. *Bank of England (No. 4)* [2002] 4 All ER 881 (CA); *Fanmailuk.com Ltd* v. *Cooper* [2010] EWHC 2647 (Ch). See also *498410 Alberta Ltd* v. *Canadian Pacific Railway* [2006] ABQB 433, [23]–[24].

in the courts' willingness to use its coercive powers to ensure compliance with its orders under the former.[561] As an order under CPR 1998, r.31.17 usually directs a person to carry out a reasonable search for broadly defined classes of documents in his or her possession and to make those documents available to the other party, a failure to comply is unlikely to be a contempt of court, absent a contumacious refusal to obey. In contrast, a witness summons requires a person to bring to court the documents stipulated in the summons. As there is no exercise of judgement required in selecting the documents under a witness summons, a failure to comply can more readily attract penal sanctions. Furthermore, although the witness summons procedure has the potential drawback for the claimant of having to identify any documents specifically,[562] it also has other advantages, such as being available in aid of arbitral proceedings and small-track claims,[563] and having a witness attest formally to the authenticity of the particular documents.[564] The cost implications of using the witness summons procedure, however, may mean that CPR 1998, r.31.17 may ultimately prove a more effective and straightforward procedure when seeking disclosure from a bank that is not party to proceedings.[565] In either case, a court will give weight to confidentiality and privacy issues when exercising its discretion,[566] particularly when the confidence belongs to a third party as opposed to a litigant,[567] such as when a bank is summoned to produce the bank statements of a customer, who is not party to the proceedings.[568] Article 8 of the ECHR, which has been incorporated by the HRA 1998[569] and which protects a person's privacy, is likely to affect the court's exercise of its discretion in future.

More specifically to the banking context, the Bankers' Books Evidence Act 1879 (BBEA 1879)[570] establishes a special procedure for producing evidence of a person's bank account. As explained previously,[571] the BBEA 1879 was originally passed to avoid the inconvenience caused to banks by the common law rule that the *originals* of bank ledgers and books had to be physically produced to the court by a bank employee.[572] Accordingly, the BBEA 1879 renders *copies* of any entry in a 'banker's book' admissible as evidence 'in all legal proceedings'[573] against any party to the proceedings (including the party who has called for the copies),[574] and provides that such copies are to be received as *prima facie* evidence of the relevant entry and any matters recorded therein.[575] For such a copy to be admissible, however, a

---

[561] *Tajik Aluminium Plant* v. *Hydro Aluminium AS* [2006] 1 Lloyd's Rep 155, [25] (CA), criticized by C. Hollander, n.536 above, [4-12], [4-29].

[562] Ibid., [27]–[29]. See also *Financial Services Authority* v. *Amro International*, n.527 above, [55]–[58].

[563] C. Hollander, n.536 above, [4-31].   [564] Id.

[565] Ibid., [4-05]. See also *Re Howglen Ltd* [2001] 1 All ER 376.

[566] *Assistant Deputy Coroner for Inner West London* v. *Channel 4 Television Corporation*, n.559 above, [3].

[567] *Anselm* v. *Anselm* (15 December 1999, Neuberger J).

[568] *Robertson* v. *Canadian Imperial Bank of Commerce* [1994] 1 WLR 1493 (PC).

[569] HRA 1998, ss.1(1), 6(1), 6(3).

[570] As extended by the Banking Act 1979, Sched. 6, Pt. 1. See further Sect. 5(vii) below.

[571] Ch. 3, Sect. 2(iii) above. Once produced, bankers' books were treated like any other evidence: C. Tapper, *Cross and Tapper on Evidence* (12th edn., Oxford, 2010), 263, 673–674.

[572] *Wheatley* v. *Commissioner of Police of the British Virgin Islands* [2006] Cr. App. Rep. 328, [14] (PC).

[573] This includes 'any civil or criminal proceeding or inquiry in which evidence is or may be given' and arbitration (BBEA 1879, s.10), but not a commission of inquiry (*Douglas* v. *Pindling* [1996] AC 890, 901 (PC)).

[574] *Harding* v. *Williams* (1880) 14 Ch. D 197.

[575] BBEA 1879, s.3. The admissibility of an entry in a bank's book does not depend upon the court having previously made an order under the BBEA 1879, s.7: *Wheatley* v. *Commissioner of Police of the British Virgin Islands*, n.572 above, [15].

bank officer must prove, either orally or by way of affidavit, that the relevant entry forms part of the bank's ordinary books, that it was made in the usual and ordinary course of business, and that the book is in the bank's custody or control.[576] The bank officer must also confirm that the copy agrees with the original.[577] Where a bank is not party to the proceedings, it may not be compelled to produce a 'banker's book' or give oral evidence, except with a court order 'made for special cause'.[578] Furthermore, the BBEA 1879 was also passed to provide a means whereby a party could apply to the court for an order permitting them to inspect and take copies of 'banker's books'.[579] Before considering the requirements that must be satisfied before a court will order such inspection, however, it is worth noting that the practical importance of that legislation has been diminished somewhat by the general relaxation that has occurred recently in relation to the principles governing the proof and use of secondary evidence in civil and criminal proceedings.[580] Nowadays, in civil proceedings, not only do *Norwich Pharmacal* orders, *Bankers Trust* orders, and orders under CPR 1998, r.31.17 allow for expeditious access to customer records held by non-party banks both before and after proceedings have been commenced,[581] but also the Civil Evidence Act 1995[582] and Part 33 of the CPR 1998 both allow for the admission of hearsay evidence, including bank records. In criminal proceedings, the Criminal Justice Act 2003 similarly allows for hearsay documentation 'created or received by a person in the course of a trade, business, profession [etc.]' to be admitted in evidence.[583] In this regard, a bank officer will usually produce to the court a short *pro forma* statement referring to the relevant banking documents and exhibiting copy documents,[584] allowing the original documents to be retained by the bank. Until its repeal, however, the BBEA 1879 is likely to retain at least some importance in relation to the admissibility and disclosure of bank documents.

Whatever its future role, there are currently limits upon the scope and operation of the BBEA 1879.[585] In particular, it is not every bank document that falls within the scope of the legislation, but only those that qualify as 'bankers' books',[586] which include 'ledgers, day-books, cash-books, account books and other records used in the ordinary business of the bank'.[587] The concept of 'bankers' books' also includes not only a book used by the bank for reference, rather than for the purpose of making daily entries,[588] but even a casual record, such as a page from the bank's official day-book,[589] or a branch manager's diary.[590] In contrast, documents that are not part of the bank's records, such as its correspondence with its customers,[591] a deposit slip given to a customer,[592] or cancelled cheques and credit slips,[593] are not 'bankers' books'. The principal difficulty with the

---

[576] Ibid., s.4.   [577] Ibid., s.5.   [578] Ibid., s.6.   [579] Ibid., s.7.

[580] C. Hollander, n.536 above, [5–19].

[581] For the relationship between the Bankers' Books Evidence Act 1879 (BBEA 1879) and CPR 1998, r. 31.17, see *Re Howglen Ltd*, n.565 above.

[582] Civil Evidence Act 1995, ss.8–9.

[583] Criminal Justice Act 2003, ss.114(2), 117. See further C. Tapper, n.571 above, 610–611, 617.

[584] Ibid., s.133.   [585] Ch. 3, Sect. 2(iii) above.   [586] BBEA 1879, ss.3, 7.

[587] Ibid., s.9(2). See also *Re Lord Advocate's Reference (No. 1 of 1996)* 1996 SLT 740 (bank statements).

[588] *Asylum for Idiots* v. *Handysides* (1906) 22 TLR 573.   [589] *Re L. G. Batten Pty. Ltd* [1962] QWN 2.

[590] *Elsey* v. *Federal Commissioner of Taxation* (1969) 121 CLR 99 (HCA).

[591] *Re Dadson* (1983) 77 Crim. App. Rep. 91 (CA). See also *Re Howglen Ltd*, n.565 above, 381–382 (notes of meetings between a branch manager and a director of bank's customer outside the BBEA 1879); but contrast *Wee Soon Kim* v. *UBS AG* [2003] 2 SLR 91, [36] (SGCA) (correspondence between bank and customer recording a transaction on an account). Consider also *James* v. *Minister of National Revenue* (2000) 266 NR 104 (CFCA); *R* v. *Heinze* [2005] VSCA 124, [64].

[592] *Lever* v. *Maguire* [1928] VLR 262.

[593] *Williams* v. *Williams* [1988] QB 161 (CA). See also *Wee Soon Kim* v. *UBS AG*, n.591 above, [31]–[36]; *Volkering* v. *District Judge Haughton* [2005] IEHC 240, [7.3].

concept of 'bankers' books', however, is that the BBEA 1879 was enacted at a time when all banking business entries were contained in some form of written record, whether typed or handwritten. With advances in technology, banks started keeping their records on magnetic tapes and nowadays store their customers' data on computerized databases and make entries into those databases by electronic means. In *Barker* v. *Wilson*,[594] Bridge LJ held that the definition of 'bankers' books' included microfilms of a bank's records and any permanent record made by means furnished by modern technology. Any remaining doubts on this point were removed by a statutory amendment providing that 'bankers' books' included records 'kept on microfilm, magnetic tape, or any other form of mechanical or electronic data retrieval mechanism'.[595] Accordingly, printed copies of records kept in such a form are admissible as evidence and entries made on a bank's computer database may be subject to court-ordered disclosure under the BBEA 1879. In such a case, a bank will be obliged to furnish the equipment required to facilitate the inspection of its computer records at its premises.

Where a party to proceedings wishes to inspect and take copies of a 'banker's books' for the purpose of those proceedings, he may apply to the court under the BBEA 1879 for an order to that effect.[596] According to the Privy Council in *Wheatley* v. *Commissioner of Police of the British Virgin Islands*,[597] the entire purpose of this procedure is to enable the bank to make disclosure without being liable to its customer for breach of its duty of confidentiality. In deciding whether to make an inspection order under the BBEA 1879, the courts have a discretion to exercise and will be guided by the principles relating to the inspection and disclosure of documents in other contexts.[598] Giving due weight to issues of privacy and confidentiality, the courts will exercise their discretion sparingly,[599] and usually only make an order for inspection of documents that relate to a defined and limited period.[600] In particular, the courts will refuse an inspection order where the applicant is using the procedure under the BBEA 1879 'on a kind of searching enquiry or fishing expedition beyond the usual rules of discovery'.[601] Accordingly, a court will likely refuse an application to investigate the bank records where there exist only unsubstantiated suspicions about the account in question, but

---

[594] [1980] 1 WLR 884. See also *R* v. *Lemay* (2004) 247 DLR (4th) 470 (BCCA) (microfiche records of cheques admissible despite being held by separate cheque-clearing centre); *Wheatley* v. *Commissioner of Police of the British Virgin Islands*, n.572 above, [13] (microfilm records of cheques kept by bank were 'bankers' books').

[595] Banking Act 1979, s.51, Sched. 6, Pt. 1, para. 1 & Pt. 11, para. 13.

[596] BBEA 1879, s.7. The courts will apply the same principles to the granting of an inspection order, regardless of whether the application is made pre-trial or post-judgment: *DB Deniz Nakliyati TAS* v. *Yugopetrol* [1992] 1 WLR 437, 443 (CA); cf. *Sommers* v. *Sturdy* (1957) 10 DLR (2d) 269. Where a bank is unable to produce the relevant entries in its records for inspection, a court may draw certain conclusions from this fact: *Douglass* v. *Lloyds Bank Ltd*, n.62 above (absence of any reference in the bank's records to an alleged deposit led court to conclude that the deposit had not been effected at all). See further Ch. 9, Sect. 3(v) below.

[597] N.572 above, [14].

[598] *South Staffordshire Tramways Co.* v. *Ebbsmith* [1895] 2 QB 669, 674 (CA). Similarly, documents obtained under the BBEA 1879 are covered by an implied undertaking not to use them except for the purposes of the relevant proceedings: *Bhimji* v. *Chatwani* [1992] 1 WLR 1158, 1164.

[599] *Emmott* v. *Star Newspaper Co.* (1892) 62 LJQB 77; *Ironmonger & Co.* v. *Dyne* (1928) 44 TLR 579, 579–580 (CA).

[600] *Owen* v. *Sambrook* [1981] Crim. LR 329; *R.* v. *Nottingham Justices, ex p. Lynn* (1984) 79 Crim. App. Rep. 234 (DC).

[601] *Williams* v. *Summerfield* [1972] 2 QB 512, 518 (DC). See also *R* v. *Bono* (1913) 29 TLR 635, 636; 'The Golden Trinity', n.522 above, [8], [16]; *Wee Soon Kim* v. *UBS AG*, n.591 above, [24]–[25]; *Chung Oi Sim* v. *Apleichau Maxicab Service Co Ltd* [2005] HKCU 1612, [9]; *R (on the application of Energy Financing Team Ltd)* v. *Director of the Serious Fraud Office* [2005] EWHC 1626 (Admin.), [8]; *Wharf Ltd* v. *Lau Yuen How (No. 2)*, n.548 above, [8]; cf. *Sommers* v. *Sturdy*, n.596 above.

may well grant the order where there is *prima facie* evidence of unlawful activity and an examination of the account in question is likely to confirm that fact. For example, in *Williams v. Summerfield*,[602] the Divisional Court granted the police an order to inspect the accounts of the defendants, who were accused of stealing money from their employer, because there was already independent evidence of the defendants' misappropriation and the only purpose of the order was to determine the amount involved. Similarly, although inspection orders under the BBEA 1879 are available in both civil and criminal proceedings,[603] the courts appear more cautious when making such an order in the criminal context,[604] and will only exercise their discretion against non-parties to the proceedings 'with great caution'.[605] An order will only generally be made against a non-party's account where there is a close nexus between the defendant and that party, such as where the account is held by the defendant's nominee[606] or by the company of which the defendant is the director.[607] Although a court may make such an order without notice to the bank, the order must be served on the bank three clear days before it has to be obeyed so that the bank has the opportunity to object to the order.[608] Similarly, although it is best practice to give notice to the person whose account is to be inspected,[609] it is possible to grant the order in his absence.[610]

Whenever a third party applies for information from a bank about his customer using one of the above procedures, the bank does not owe its customer a duty to oppose the application or inform him that such an application has been, or is going to be, made. This was certainly the view expressed by Lord Donaldson, in *Barclays Bank plc v. Taylor*,[611] in relation to an application by the police for an 'access order' under the Police and Criminal Evidence Act 1984. Moreover, in *El Jawhary v. Bank of Credit and Commerce International SA*,[612] Sir Donald Nicholls concluded that a bank did not owe a duty to inform its customer that information concerning their banking relationship, but falling within one of the *Tournier* qualifications, had been disclosed to the bank's liquidators who sought the information in pursuance of their statutory functions. A different position appears to have been adopted, however, in *Robertson v. Canadian Imperial Bank of Commerce*,[613] where a bank was served with a subpoena *duces tecum* (nowadays a witness summons)[614] and, even though its customer was not party to the proceedings in question, the bank was ordered to produce to the court its customer's bank statements. Despite holding that the bank's disclosure fell within the first *Tournier* qualification, the Privy Council refused to exclude the possibility that, in the context of a particular banker–customer relationship, a bank might owe its customer a duty to inform the court of the fact that it had been unable to contact its customer or that

---

[602] Ibid., 519. See also *Wharf Ltd v. Lau Yuen How (No. 2)*, n.548 above, [8].

[603] *R v. Kinghorn* [1908] 2 KB 949, 950.   [604] *Williams v. Summerfield*, n.601 above, 518.

[605] *South Staffordshire Tramways Co. v. Ebbsmith*, n.598 above, 674–675, 677–678; *DB Deniz Nakliyati TAS v. Yugopetrol*, n.596 above, 442; *Chung Oi Sim v. Apleichau Maxicab Service Co Ltd*, n.601 above, [10].

[606] *Ironmonger & Co. v. Dyne*, n.599 above, 579–580. See also *Howard v. Beall* (1889) 23 QBD 1, 2.

[607] *South Staffordshire Tramways Co. v. Ebbsmith*, n.598 above, 677–678.

[608] BBEA 1879, s.7.

[609] *Arnott v. Hayes* (1887) 36 Ch. D 731; cf. *R. v. Marlborough Street Metropolitan Stipendiary Magistrate, ex p. Simpson* (1980) 70 Cr. App. Rep. 291. For the court's discretion, see *Pollock v. Garle* [1898] 1 Ch. 1; *L'Amie v. Wilson* [1907] 2 IR 130; *Staunton v. Counihan* (1957) 92 ILT 32.

[610] BBEA 1879, s.7.

[611] N.508 above, 1074–1075. See also *Fennoscandia Ltd v. Clarke* [1999] 1 All ER (Comm.) 365, 371 (CA). See further *Park v. Bank of Montreal* [1997] BCTC 456, [123]–[130].

[612] N.521 above, 400. See also *Fennoscandia Ltd v. Clarke*, n.611 above, 371.   [613] N.568 above.

[614] CPR 1998, r.34.2(1).

the bank statements in question contained material irrelevant to the proceedings.[615] Their Lordships also left open the question of whether the bank owed an implied contractual duty to inform its customer that the subpoena had been served,[616] although they did opine that any such duty could not extend beyond using best endeavours to contact the customer. Whilst it may be courteous and good banking practice for a bank to inform its customer of the service of a witness summons, the better view is that there should be no implied contractual obligation to that effect, as such a term would not satisfy the threshold of strict necessity required for the implication of terms into the banker–customer contract.[617] Furthermore, as there seems to be no logical reason why this conclusion should alter according to whether the bank has actually been served with an order or only has notice that such an order is likely to be made, or according to the different types of disclosure order available, the reasoning in *Taylor* and *El Jawhary* should be preferred to that in *Robertson*.

(iv) **Duty to the public**

Although Bankes LJ in *Tournier* clearly recognized that there was a second qualification to the bank's duty of confidentiality in circumstances 'where there is a duty to the public to disclose' the relevant information,[618] this has been described as 'the least easily comprehended of the *Tournier* exceptions'.[619] There are two potential causes of this difficulty. First, the circumstances in which the public interest requires a person to disclose confidential information, and the nature of the information that may be justifiably disclosed, are not static or immutable. What the public interest requires might alter according to the prevailing circumstances, so that disclosure of confidential information might be justified when there is some 'danger to the state',[620] such as war or a national state of emergency, but might be once again prohibited after the prevailing circumstances change. Similarly, the public interest may differ according to the character of the parties involved, so that the expectations of banks in terms of disclosure may differ from other institutions or professionals and disclosure may be more likely to be in the public interest when a bank's customer is an enemy alien or a proven criminal or terrorist. Further, the public interest may simply change over time, according to the prevailing *mores*. For example, Bankes LJ in *Tournier* doubted that a bank was entitled to disclose information concerning its customer to police officers who were investigating that person for a series of frauds,[621] whereas more recently it has been recognized that the 'duty to investigate and deal with criminal conduct…is a higher duty in the public interest than bank/customer confidentiality'[622] and that, even in

---

[615] In any event, their Lordships would have declined (on the facts) to impose liability on the bank, as the customer had failed to prove any loss suffered as a result of the bank's omission: n.568 above, 1500.

[616] Although both *Barclays Bank plc* v. *Taylor*, n.508 above, and *El Jawhary* v. *Bank of Credit and Commerce International SA*, n.521 above, were cited to the Privy Council in argument, neither authority was referred to by Lord Nolan in *Robertson*.

[617] *Liverpool City Council* v. *Irwin*, n.297 above, 254; *Attorney-General for Belize* v. *Belize Telecom Ltd*, n.67 above. See also *Park* v. *Bank of Montreal*, n.611 above, [123]–[130]. For the reluctance to imply terms into the banker–customer contract, see n.67 above.

[618] N.469 above, 473.

[619] *R* v. *Curtis* (NZCA, 3 December 1993). See also M. Hapgood, n.516 above, [8.4].

[620] N.469 above, 473, citing *Weld Blundell* v. *Stephens* [1920] AC 956, 965 (HL).   [621] Ibid., 474.

[622] *R* v. *Curtis*, n.619 above. See also *Walsh* v. *National Irish Bank Ltd*, n.50 above, [24]. Whilst a court may nowadays have little sympathy for a customer who sues his bank for breaching its duty of confidentiality by revealing the customer's criminal activity to the police, a bank may be liable for breaching its duty of skill and care to an innocent customer if the bank failed to conduct a proper internal investigation before referring the matter to the police. For possible defamation liability and the operation of the justification defence, see *Shah* v. *Standard Chartered Bank* [1998] 4 All ER 155 (CA).

the absence of relevant legislation, 'there would be a power and perhaps even a duty [on a bank] to consider and respond to police questions about [money laundering]'.[623] Secondly, in the vast majority of cases where disclosure might be considered desirable in the public interest, such as requiring banks to disclose their customer's money-laundering or terrorist-financing activities, there usually nowadays already exists legislation that compels disclosure.[624] At first sight, therefore, it appears difficult to identify a clear and distinct role for the second *Tournier* qualification beyond that of the first *Tournier* qualification. Whilst this was certainly the view of the Jack Committee, which accordingly recommended abolishing the second qualification,[625] the Government suggested that the first and second *Tournier* qualifications differed in that the former covered situations where the bank was *compelled* or *required* to provide the relevant information, whereas the latter applied to situations where the bank was *permitted* to disclose, even in the absence of compulsion.[626]

The difficulty in clearly defining the scope of the second *Tournier* qualification also arises from the fact that, until recently, it has not been subject to particularly extensive judicial analysis.[627] In *Price Waterhouse* v. *BCCI Holdings (Luxembourg) SA*,[628] however, Millett J confirmed that the second *Tournier* qualification provided an independent ground for justifying disclosure of confidential information. *Price Waterhouse* concerned disclosure by accountants (although the court's analysis applies equally to the equivalent duty owed by a bank) of confidential information concerning their client, the BCCI group, to the Bingham Inquiry—a non-statutory inquiry established by the Chancellor of the Exchequer and the Governor of the Bank of England to investigate the Bank of England's performance of its statutory supervisory functions in relation to the BCCI group.[629] As the Bingham Inquiry had no statutory power to order disclosure, Price Waterhouse sought a declaration as to whether it was nevertheless able to co-operate with the Inquiry by providing information concerning its client. In concluding that disclosure was permitted, Millett J stressed that a duty of confidentiality might sometimes be outweighed by a higher public interest in favour of disclosure, in which circumstances there would be a right, not merely a duty, to disclose information.[630] According to his Lordship, such countervailing public interest was not limited to the interest in detecting or preventing wrongdoing,[631] but included the interest that exists in ensuring the effective regulation and supervision of authorized banking institutions, as well as the protection of depositors. Millett J concluded that, just as the public interest required confidential information to be disclosed to the Bank of England (now replaced by the FSA) to enable

---

[623] *R* v. *Harris* [2000] 2 NZLR 524, 527 (NZCA).

[624] Sect. 5(iii) above. See further Ch. 4, Sects.3(ii)–(iii) above.

[625] *Banking Services: Law and Practice*, n.1 above, [5.30], [5.41].

[626] *White Paper on Banking Services: Law and Practice*, n.467 above, 15.

[627] In *Libyan Arab Foreign Bank* v. *Bankers Trust Co.*, n.30 above, 771, Staughton J tentatively suggested that a New York bank could rely, *inter alia*, on the second *Tournier* qualification to justify its discussions with the Federal Reserve Board about the claimant's accounts. Indeed, there should be a public duty to disclose confidential information to a financial regulator: *Brandeaux Advisers UK Ltd* v. *Chadwick* [2010] EWHC 3241 (QB), [23]. Similarly, *Bank of China* v. *Fan* (2003) 22 BCLR (4th) 152 has been explained as an example of the 'duty to the public qualification': M.H. Ogilvie, n.14 above, 141–142.

[628] [1992] BCLC 583. See also *Douglas* v. *Pindling*, n.573 above.

[629] For the FSA's current banking supervision regime pursuant to the FSMA 2000, see Ch. 2, Sects. 3 & 4 above.

[630] N.628 above, 601, although any right of disclosure must now be balanced against the right to privacy in the European Convention for the Protection of Human Rights and Fundamental Freedoms 1950 (ECHR), Art. 8, incorporated into English law by the HRA 1998.

[631] Ibid., 596, citing *Att.-Gen.* v. *Guardian Newspapers Ltd (No. 2)*, n.512 above, 214, 268, 282.

it to carry out its statutory functions,[632] there was at least as great a public interest in the disclosure of such information as part of the investigation into the Bank of England's past performance of its statutory functions, provided the dissemination of such information was no wider in the latter case than would have been authorized in the former case. The second *Tournier* qualification is not, however, limited to circumstances such as those in *Price Waterhouse*, where disclosure is made to a public or regulatory body, but may also occasionally cover disclosure to private persons. In *Pharaon v. Bank of Credit and Commerce International SA (in liquidation)*,[633] for example, Rattee J held that an international bank's duty of confidentiality could be overridden by the greater public interest in making confidential documents, relating to that bank's alleged fraud, available to parties to private foreign proceedings who were seeking to uncover that fraud.

(v) **The bank's own interest**

According to Bankes LJ in *Tournier*, the bank's duty of confidentiality is also qualified 'where the interests of the bank require disclosure'.[634] This qualification will most obviously cover the situation where a bank commences proceedings against its customer to recover an unpaid loan or overdraft facility and the bank has to disclose in the pleadings the extent of the customer's liabilities, although the qualification will not necessarily cover such disclosure where the proceedings are commenced by a different member of the same banking group[635] or, in other contexts, where the bank reveals confidential information in circumstances where its interests conflict with those of its customer.[636] Similarly, when a bank is a defendant to proceedings brought by its customer or a third party, a bank may be entitled to justify any 'defensive disclosures' as being in its best interests.[637] A less obvious example of a 'defensive disclosure' arose in *Sunderland v. Barclays Bank Ltd*,[638] where the defendant bank dishonoured the claimant's cheques primarily due to the account having insufficient funds, but also due to the bank's knowledge that the cheques were drawn in respect of gambling debts. During a telephone conversation between the branch manager and the claimant, the claimant's husband interceded at her request and was informed that most of his wife's cheques were drawn in favour of bookmakers. Dismissing the claim against the bank for breaching its duty of confidentiality, Du Parq LJ held that the bank's disclosure was not only justified in its own interest, but was also justified by the wife's implied consent to disclosure to her husband. Whilst it may be doubted whether the wife's complaint to the bank about it dishonouring her cheques indicated her implied consent to disclosure being made to her husband, the unjustified nature of that complaint meant that the bank had an interest in defending its reputation by informing the husband that it had valid reasons, namely the insufficiency of

---

[632] Banking Act 1987, s.39, replaced by FSMA 2000, Pt. XI. See also *Brandeaux Advisers UK Ltd* v. *Chadwick*, n. 627 above, [23].

[633] [1998] 4 All ER 455, restricted to its facts in *Travel Compensation Fund* v. *Blair* [2004] NSWSC 501, [34]–[36]. See also *BMP Global Distribution Inc.* v. *Bank of Nova Scotia*, n.503 above, [327] (no duty to the public in respect of disclosure for the purpose of discovering the counterfeiters of a cheque, when the bank was not entitled to recover the amount of the cheque and the customer was not under investigation for fraud).

[634] N.469 above, 473. Consider B. Koeck, 'Bank Confidentiality and the Sale of Loans under Austrian Law' (2008) 23 *JIBLR* 392.

[635] *Bank of Tokyo* v. *Karoon* [1987] AC 45, 53–54 (CA).

[636] *Guertin* v. *Royal Bank of Canada* (1983) 43 OR (2d) 363.

[637] *Nam Tai Electronics Inc* v. *PricewaterhouseCoopers* [2008] 1 HKC 427, [49], [53], [54] (HKCFA).

[638] (1938) 5 LDAB 163. See also *Rodaro* v. *Royal Bank of Canada* (2002) 59 OR (3d) 74, [42] (OCA) (described as a 'lost opportunity' to consider the qualification in detail: M.H. Ogilvie, n.14 above, 143); *Nam Tai Electronics Inc* v. *PricewaterhouseCoopers*, n.637 above, [63].

funds in his wife's account, for refusing to honour her cheques. Given that disclosure of the account's inadequate funds was sufficient to defend the bank's reputation, however, it is more difficult to understand why it was also justified in revealing the wife's gambling activities. Accordingly, to the extent that *Sunderland* permits a bank to disclose more information than is strictly necessary to protect its interests or reputation, the decision may be questionable. Indeed, there is no suggestion in *Tournier* that the branch manager was in any way justified in revealing the customer's gambling activities to his employer.

Despite the above criticisms of *Sunderland*, and despite the suggestion of a leading commentator (and now judge) that, once the banker's duty of confidentiality is located within the general law relating to breach of confidence, disclosure should only ever be justified in the public interest and never in the bank's own private interests,[639] the existence of the third *Tournier* qualification has been confirmed in subsequent authority.[640] Nevertheless, there seems to be a general recognition of the importance of keeping the scope of this qualification within a fairly narrow confine,[641] given its potential for abuse. In this regard, the Jack Committee noted two main areas of concern. First, concern was expressed about the sharing of confidential customer information between different entities of the same banking group, particularly if this were done for marketing purposes. It is clear that such disclosures would be *prima facie* breaches of the duty of confidentiality, since each company has a separate corporate personality,[642] but there is a danger that banks might justify all such disclosures as being 'in their interests'. In some situations, disclosure 'in the bank's interests' might be perfectly acceptable, such as where it enables banks to meet their statutory obligations to report large exposures within the banking group, whereas, in other situations, it may be more objectionable, such as where the sharing of marketing information would enable the banking group to be run in a more cost-effective and efficient manner. Accordingly, the Jack Committee recommended that banking companies within the same group should be allowed to exchange confidential information, without customer consent, provided such disclosure is reasonably necessary for the specific purpose of protecting the bank and its subsidiaries from losses that it might suffer in providing normal banking services, but not if the disclosure is for marketing purposes.[643] Moreover, the Jack Committee saw no justification for allowing the exchange of any customer information with non-banking companies in the same group,

---

[639] R. Cranston, n.519 above, 174–176.

[640] *El Jawhary* v. *Bank of Credit and Commerce International SA*, n.521 above, 398–399; *Christofi* v. *Barclays Bank plc* [1999] 2 All ER (Comm.) 417, 425–426 (CA) (disclosure of the fact that a trustee in bankruptcy's caution had been cancelled was necessary to protect the bank's commercial reputation, as the bank would otherwise have been open to the criticism that it had dealt with the property, over which the bank had a charge, behind the trustee's back and knowing of his mistake). There is an analogous qualification to the duty of confidentiality in arbitration proceedings: *Hassneh Insurance Co. of Israel* v. *Mew* [1993] 2 Lloyd's Rep 243, 248–249; *Ali Shipping Corp.* v. *Shipyard Trogir* [1998] 2 All ER 136, 147 (CA); *Associated Electric and Gas Insurance Services Ltd* v. *European Reinsurance Co. of Zurich* [2003] 1 WLR 1041, [20] (PC); *Emmott* v. *Michael Wilson & Partners Ltd* [2008] 1 Lloyd's Rep 616, [101] (CA); *Brandeaux Advisers UK Ltd* v. *Chadwick*, n.627 above, [19]–[23].

[641] *BMP Global Distribution Inc.* v. *Bank of Nova Scotia*, n.503 above, [326] (disclosure to other financial institutions by means of a 'grid warning' that a counterfeit cheque had been paid into the claimant's account was not in the defendant bank's own interests, as the fraud did not cause it any loss); cf. *Nam Tai Electronics Inc* v. *PricewaterhouseCoopers*, n.637 above, [37], [45]–[48], [66], involving an accountancy firm's confidentiality undertaking, where Ribeiro PJ accepted that confidential information may be disclosed 'where such disclosure is fairly required for the protection...of either party's legitimate interests' and considered that 'the self-interest qualification is now more liberally applied' than suggested in *Tournier* (namely, when suing on an overdraft facility or giving reasons for the dishonour of a cheque).

[642] *Bank of Tokyo* v. *Karoon*, n.635 above, 53–54; *Bhogal* v. *Punjab National Bank* [1988] 2 All ER 296, 305 (CA).

[643] N.1 above, [5.31]. See also *White Paper on Banking Services: Law and Practice*, n.467 above, [2.16]–[2.17].

unless a customer's consent was first obtained. The *Banking Code* fell somewhat short of the Jack Committee's proposals, as does its replacement, the *Lending Code*. According to the latter, banks must obtain a customer's 'specific permission' before passing on his name and address to a third party for marketing purposes, even where that third party is a member of the same corporate group as the bank in question.[644] Such consent may be given by the customer signing a form containing a clause to that effect, by signifying consent by clicking on a box in an internet form, or by giving consent over the phone.[645] Whilst the *Lending Code* also contains more general prohibitions that would cover the disclosure of confidential information for non-marketing purposes,[646] it is not explicitly stated whether this would also preclude intra-group disclosure. Accordingly, it may remain possible for banks to justify such disclosures by reference to the third *Tournier* qualification (and even possibly the fourth, if the bank can show the customer's implied consent). Furthermore, the *Lending Code* does not prevent banks using confidential customer information for its non-banking business, even for marketing purposes, provided that business is conducted through a branch and not a separate legal entity.[647]

Secondly, the Jack Committee raised concerns about the uncertainty surrounding the banking practice of disclosing customer information to credit reference agencies and whether this could be justified by reference to the third (or some other) *Tournier* qualification.[648] In its response to the Jack Committee, the Government recognized the banking practice of passing 'black' information (namely, information concerning the customer's defaults) to credit reference agencies, but considered that 'white' information (namely, information concerning customers who are not in default) should only be disclosed with the customer's express consent.[649] Although the *Banking Code* was initially silent on this issue, subsequent editions adopted the Government's position.[650] The *Lending Code* largely follows suit, providing that banks must generally inform customers who apply for lending facilities that their details may be passed to credit reference agencies.[651] If a customer has fallen behind on their payments to the bank in relation to an undisputed liability and the customer has not made any satisfactory proposal with respect to the repayment of that liability, the bank may disclose that information to a credit reference agency without that customer's consent, but must give the customer 28 days' notice of its intention to disclose such information so that the customer has the opportunity to regularize their position.[652] Other information about the day-to-day running of the account, including positive data, can only be shared with credit reference agencies with the customer's permission.[653] The *Lending Code* does not, however, explain the legal justification for disclosure to credit reference agencies. Whilst the bank's own interests might be served by disclosing such information, since this would maintain the integrity of the credit reference system so that the bank can rely upon it with confidence when it next seeks information concerning a

---

[644] *Lending Code* (November 2009), [22]; *Lending Code* (March 2011), [23]. See formerly *Banking Code* (March 2008), [8.3], [11.1]; *Business Banking Code* (March 2008), [8.3], [11.1].

[645] Ibid., [23]; *Lending Code* (March 2011), [24]. [646] Ibid., [13], [24]; *Lending Code* (March 2011), [15], [25].

[647] DPA 1998, s.11, however, provides individuals, as 'data subjects', with a specific right to prevent processing for the purpose of direct marketing.

[648] N.1 above, [5.34]–[5.37].

[649] *White Paper on Banking Services: Law and Practice*, n.467 above, [2.16]–[2.17].

[650] *Banking Code* (March 2008), [13.5]–[13.9]; *Business Banking Code* (March 2008), [13.9]–[13.12]. See further Ch. 2, Sect. 6(i) above.

[651] *Lending Code* (November 2009), [34]; *Lending Code* (March 2011), [34].

[652] Ibid., [35]–[37]; *Lending Code* (March 2011), [41], [44]. Disclosure may also be made to debt-collection agencies: ibid., [151]; *Lending Code* (March 2011), [228]–[233].

[653] Ibid., [39], [41]; *Lending Code* (March 2011), [48].

potential customer or borrower (and the Government certainly considered this whole issue in the course of discussing the third *Tournier* qualification),[654] such an approach would involve interpreting the concept of the 'bank's interests' more broadly than has hitherto been the case, so that it includes the bank's commercial convenience and advantage.[655] Equally problematic would be any justification based on a customer's implied consent.[656] In *Turner* v. *Royal Bank of Scotland plc*,[657] however, HH Judge Rudd preferred to justify the disclosure to credit reference agencies by reference to the existence of a public duty on the bank, rather than by reference to the bank's own interests. Indeed, as the recent 'global credit crisis' has demonstrated, modern consumer society is so dependent upon the availability of credit that it is in the general public interest that such credit be provided responsibly.[658]

(vi) Information disclosed with customer's authority

Finally, Bankes LJ in *Tournier* recognized that disclosure of confidential information by a bank was permitted 'where the disclosure is made by the express or implied consent of the customer'.[659] Establishing the existence of a customer's express consent is largely a factual question and its scope depends upon whether the customer consented to disclosure generally or whether the consent was limited to a particular occasion or particular information.[660] Obviously, customers do not consent to the bank providing inaccurate information about them,[661] and a bank should decline to disclose its customer's information if it has reason to believe that the customer's apparent consent was the result of compulsion, such as when disclosure is compelled by the order of a foreign court.[662] More difficulty, however, lies in identifying the circumstances when the customer's consent will be implied. In *Tournier*, Bankes LJ gave as an example of a situation falling within his third qualification 'the familiar instance...where the customer authorizes a reference to his banker',[663] and Atkin LJ similarly considered that the justification for disclosing confidential information in a banker's reference 'must be upon the basis of an implied consent of the customer'.[664] Adopting this approach, banks for many years relied upon the existence of a general banking usage whereby customers impliedly consented upon the opening of their accounts to any disclosures necessary to respond to a status enquiry.[665] Indeed, it is maybe not unreasonable to assume, when a customer is asked to supply the name of a referee or his bank when applying for such facilities as a credit card, that he is impliedly consenting to the disclosure of any necessary information by his bank.[666] Whilst the Younger Committee on Privacy supported the banks' general position on the basis that banks and their business

---

[654] *White Paper on Banking Services: Law and Practice*, n.467 above, [16].

[655] G. Howells, 'Data Protection, Confidentiality, Unfair Contract Terms, Consumer Protection and Credit Reference Agencies' [1995] *JBL* 343, 349.

[656] Ibid., 349–350; R.M. Goode, n.499 above, 271.   [657] [2001] 1 All ER (Comm.) 1057, [31] (CA).

[658] *McGuffick* v. *Royal Bank of Scotland plc* [2009] EWHC 2386 (Comm), [36]. For the importance of individual credit ratings, see *Kpohraror* v. *Woolwich Building Society* [1996] 4 All ER 119, 124 (CA).

[659] N.469 above, 473.

[660] *Murano* v. *Bank of Montreal* (1998) 41 OR (3d) 222, 228–229 (OCA). See also *Lending Code* (November 2009), [23]; *Lending Code* (March 2011), [24].

[661] Id.   [662] *Re ABC Ltd* [1985] FLR 159 (Grand Ct. of the Cayman Islands).

[663] N.469 above, 473.   [664] Ibid., 486.

[665] *Hedley Byrne & Co. Ltd* v. *Heller & Partners Ltd*, n.22 above, 503, 540, although Lord Reid (ibid., 489) retained doubts as to the existence of such a general banking usage.

[666] M. Hapgood, *Paget's Law of Banking* (11th edn., London, 1996), 124, although this view is not repeated in recent editions: M. Hapgood, n.516 above, [8.11]–[8.16]. For rejection of the 'implied consent theory', see Lord Chorley, *Law of Banking* (6th edn., London, 1974), 24. See also A. Tyree & P. Weaver, n.359 above, [30.2].

customers were aware of the practice,[667] it recognized that personal customers were largely ignorant of the practice and accordingly should be approached for consent before responding to a particular reference request. Similarly, the Jack Committee recommended the introduction of legislation requiring banks to give their customers 'a clear explanation of how the system of bankers' opinions works, and to invite them to give or withhold a general consent for the bank to supply opinions on them in response to enquiries'.[668] The Government, however, rejected the idea of legislation in favour of dealing with the matter as part of a voluntary code of banking practice.[669] Whilst initially the *Banking Code* only required banks to explain the nature of the bankers' reference system to their customers,[670] since March 1994, it has required banks to seek their customers' express consent in writing before responding to a request for a reference[671] or a status enquiry.[672] As discussed above,[673] the *Lending Code* deals with the related issue of bank disclosures to credit reference agencies and, subject to a limited exception relating to negative information,[674] provides that disclosure is only generally permitted with a customer's consent,[675] but makes no explicit reference to the practice of giving bankers' references.[676]

This omission in the *Lending Code* may be the result of the clarification provided by *Turner* v. *Royal Bank of Scotland*,[677] in which the defendant bank responded in unfavourable terms to a number of status enquiries from another bank about the creditworthiness of the claimant, who held both personal and business accounts with the defendant. On each occasion, the defendant used confidential information concerning the state of the claimant's account when formulating its response. As these disclosures took place before the changes to the *Banking Code* in March 1994, the defendant bank had not sought the claimant's express consent before responding to the status enquiries. Accordingly, the claimant alleged that the bank had breached its duty of confidentiality. Whilst the bank did not dispute the existence of that duty, it contended that 'at the relevant time...it was the general practice of banks in the ordinary course of business to respond to status enquiries made by other banks by giving information about the creditworthiness of customers'. The bank contended that the claimant (like every other customer) must be taken to have agreed to this general practice upon opening his account, irrespective of whether he actually knew of its existence or not, and accordingly that the claimant had impliedly authorized the bank to respond to status enquiries by third parties by disclosing confidential information. Rejecting this contention, Sir Richard Scott V-C (with whom Thorpe and Judge LJJ agreed) distinguished between a banking practice that operates as 'no more than a private agreement between banks' and one that constitutes an established banking usage or custom and that can accordingly form the basis of an implied term in the banker–customer contract even if the customer is unaware of it.[678] To fall within this

---

For its statutory rejection in Singapore, see *Susilawati* v. *American Express Bank Ltd*, n.110 above, [94]–[95], affd. on this point: [2009] 2 SLR 737, [65]–[67] (SGCA).

[667] (Cmnd. 5012, London, 1972). See also *White Paper on Computer and Privacy* (Cmnd. 6353 and supp. 6354, London).

[668] N.1 above, [6.39]. Alternatively, a bank could include in its banking contracts a general term permitting disclosure of a customer's credit information: *Royal Bank of Canada* v. *Compain* (1999) 178 Sask. R. 257, [10].

[669] *White Paper on Computer and Privacy*, n.667 above, [2.21].

[670] *Good Banking—Code of Practice* (London, 1991), [7.1]. See further Ch. 2, Sect. 6(i) above.

[671] *Banking Code* (March 2008), [11.2].   [672] *Business Banking Code* (March 2008), [11.2].

[673] Sect. 5(v) above.

[674] *Lending Code* (November 2009), [36]; Lending Code (March 2011), [41].

[675] Ibid., [39]; Lending Code (March 2011), [48].

[676] Equally silent is the FSA's consumer guidance: FSA, n.70 above.   [677] N.67 above.

[678] Ibid., 671.

second category, however, the banking practice had to be 'notorious, certain and reasonable and not contrary to law'.[679] In *Turner*, there was no evidence to indicate that the practice of providing bankers' references was sufficiently well known amongst customers opening accounts to be considered 'notorious' and there was even evidence that the particular bank in *Turner* operated a policy of concealing this banking practice from customers. Moreover, Sir Richard Scott V-C held that a bank could only rely upon a banking practice that deprived a customer of his substantive rights, such as his right to confidentiality, if the customer was aware of, or assented to, that practice.[680] In this regard, it was the unreasonableness of the practice, rather than its lack of notoriety, that was important. Ultimately, therefore, there was no established banking custom or usage in *Turner* that could form the basis of an implied term.

Whilst the Court of Appeal has provided some much needed clarity in the area of bankers' references, there are potentially three limitations upon the scope of *Turner*. First, the Court of Appeal in *Turner* ignored the fact that the customer held a business account with the defendant bank and accordingly limited its judgment to the relatively straightforward situation of a banker's reference given in respect of a personal customer[681]—in the case of personal customers, it is particularly difficult to accept the proposition that they are aware of the practice of answering status enquiries and have accordingly given their implied consent.[682] It is, therefore, unclear whether *Turner* applies to business customers. Whilst it might be more compelling, in the case of a business customer, to imply its consent to a banker's reference, in reality many business customers are probably just as ignorant as personal customers about the practice of providing bankers' references.[683] Some recognition of this fact was found in the *Business Banking Code*, which required banks to secure their business customers' written permission before responding to a status enquiry.[684] Although the *Business Banking Code* was replaced in November 2009,[685] the courts should probably follow its lead and extend the reasoning in *Turner* to business customers. Secondly, *Turner* does not finally determine whether a bank can rely on its customer's general consent in responding to status enquiries, or whether the customer's specific consent is required. Whilst the Jack Committee preferred the former option, the *Banking Code* generally opted for the latter approach.[686] Although the *Banking Code* has now been replaced by the *Lending Code*, which does not deal with this particular issue, Sir Richard Scott V-C stated obiter in *Turner* that the requirement for specific consent in the *Banking Code* merely reflected banks' existing common law obligations and did not set new standards.[687] It is submitted, however, that the Jack Committee's view on this point is preferable and that requiring a customer's express consent every time a banker's reference is given or a status enquiry made goes too far. Bankers' references serve a useful commercial function that could be undermined if customer consent were required in each case, since the customer, having been put on notice of the enquiry, may seek to influence the

[679] *Cunliffe-Owen* v. *Teather and Greenwood* [1967] 1 WLR 1421, 1438–1439.

[680] *Turner* v. *Royal Bank of Scotland plc*, n.67 above, 670, citing *Barclays Bank plc* v. *Bank of England* [1985] 1 All ER 385, 391.

[681] R. Hooley, 'Bankers' References and the Bank's Duty of Confidentiality: When Practice Does Not Make Perfect' [2000] *CLJ* 21, 22.

[682] Younger Committee on Privacy (Cmnd. 5012, London, 1972).

[683] Cf. Younger Committee on Privacy (Cmnd. 5012, London, 1972), although the small business culture since the 1980s probably means that the business landscape is significantly different to that in 1972.

[684] *Business Banking Code* (March 2008), [11.2].   [685] Ch. 2, Sects. 6(i)–(iii) above.

[686] *Banking Code* (March 2008), [11.2].

[687] *Turner* v. *Royal Bank of Scotland plc*, n.67 above, 671, referring to *Banking Code* (3rd edn., London, 1994), [4.5]. See also *Banking Code* (March 2008), [11.2].

terms of the reference.[688] The corollary of allowing a bank to rely on a customer's general consent, however, must be that the bank bears the burden (as recommended by the Jack Committee) of ensuring that the customer is aware of the way in which the bankers' reference system operates. Finally, although *Turner* certainly improves a customer's chances of establishing liability against a bank for breaching its duty of confidentiality by responding to a reference request without first obtaining that customer's consent, such a customer may continue to experience difficulty recovering substantial damages in respect of that breach. Whilst general damages will usually be available,[689] special damages may sometimes be difficult to recover. If the bank discloses accurate information that is favourable to the customer, the customer is unlikely to suffer any adverse consequences resulting in loss, although this is not an absolute rule;[690] if the information is accurate, but unfavourable, the customer may have difficulty showing that the bank's failure to obtain his consent *caused* his losses.[691] The only situation where special damages are likely to be readily recoverable is where the information supplied by the customer's bank proves to be inaccurate, although in such a case the customer will also have a concurrent claim based upon the breach of the bank's duty of skill and care.[692]

(vii) **Bank confidentiality and the intervention of foreign courts**

A conflict of laws problem concerning bank confidentiality can arise when a customer holds two or more accounts at a bank's branches located in different jurisdictions. Frequently, proceedings to which the customer is party in one jurisdiction may give rise to issues concerning that customer's banking operations in another jurisdiction, and the bank may then be required to produce evidence concerning its dealings with the customer in one jurisdiction to a foreign court. Such cases create difficulties because the relevant information may be privileged according to the local law of the place where it is held. Nevertheless, there are two methods by which a claimant can obtain information or evidence held by a bank abroad. First, if the relevant bank does not have any presence in the jurisdiction where the proceedings in question are taking place, or if the bank does have a branch in that jurisdiction, but the evidence is held abroad at the bank's head office or relates to banking operations taking place abroad, then the claimant may apply for 'letters of request' or 'letters rogatory'. This procedure involves the court that is hearing the proceedings ('the requesting court') sending a request to the foreign court where the relevant banking records are maintained ('the requested court') for the production of those records. As the 'letters of request' procedure depends upon the requested court's assistance, it enables the requesting court to obtain the relevant information without committing, directly or indirectly, any infringement of the other jurisdiction's sovereignty, and is accordingly largely unobjectionable. Secondly, and much more problematically, if the foreign bank that holds the relevant information has a branch within the jurisdiction where the proceedings are taking place, then the claimant may apply to the court that is hearing the proceedings for a witness summons that can then be served on the bank officers at

[688]   R. Hooley, n.681 above, 23.

[689]   *Turner* v. *Royal Bank of Scotland plc* [2000] BPIR 683, [40] (CA); *Shah* v. *HSBC Private Bank (UK) Ltd*, n.307 above, [105].

[690]   *Jackson* v. *Royal Bank of Scotland*, n.503 above.

[691]   *Turner* v. *Royal Bank of Scotland plc*, n.689 above, [39].

[692]   R.G. Toulson & C.M. Phipps, *Confidentiality* (2nd edn., London, 2006), [3-092]–[3-097]. See further Ch. 16, Sect. 2(i) below.

a branch within the jurisdiction.[693] The witness summons effectively orders those bank officers to testify in court or produce documents to the court. This type of order is frequently problematic, however, as the bank may face the unenviable choice between being held in contempt of court if it defies the witness summons, or being liable to its customer if obeying the witness summons would infringe bank confidentiality in the jurisdiction where the information is held. Each of these methods will be considered, first, in relation to the situation where the information or evidence is sought from an English bank in support of proceedings abroad, and, secondly, where an English court seeks equivalent information from a foreign bank in support of English proceedings.

(a) Evidence sought in England in support of foreign proceedings

Where a requesting court located in another EU Member State (except Denmark) issues a letter of request to obtain evidence in the United Kingdom in relation to a 'civil or commercial matter', then the position is governed by Council Regulation (EC) 1206/2001 on the Co-operation between Member States in the Taking of Evidence in Civil or Commercial Matters ('Regulation 1206/2001').[694] The request must relate to evidence that is intended for use in judicial proceedings,[695] must be transmitted directly to the competent court in the United Kingdom,[696] and must be in the prescribed form.[697] The requested court in the United Kingdom must acknowledge receipt of the request within seven days,[698] unless the request is incomplete or in an incorrect form,[699] and must execute the request in accordance with its own laws within 90 days of its receipt.[700] The requested court in the United Kingdom can decline a request that a particular person give evidence if that person is entitled to refuse to give evidence by virtue of either English law or the law of the requesting court.[701] It is arguable that this provision could entitle an English bank to resist a request for evidence on the ground that compliance would infringe the duty of confidentiality owed to one of its customers. In contrast, where the requesting court is not located in another Member State, any letter of request is governed by the Hague Convention on the Taking of Evidence Abroad in Civil or Commercial Matters 1970,[702] and, where the requested court is in the United Kingdom, the position is governed by the Evidence (Proceedings in Other Jurisdictions) Act 1975.[703] Indeed, this legislation provides the only basis upon which an English court can deal with such a letter of request from a foreign requesting court,[704] and establishes a number of limitations upon an English court's ability to respond to such a request. First, an English court will not require any particular steps to be taken in response to the letter of request unless 'they

---

[693] CPR 1998, r.34.2(1).

[694] 2001 OJ L 174, Art. 1(1) (applicable from 1 January 2004). See also CPR 1998, r.34.24. See further Dicey, Morris & Collins, *The Conflict of Laws* (14th edn., London, 2006), [8-063]–[8-067].

[695] Ibid., Art. 1(2).

[696] Ibid., Art. 2(1). A requesting court can take evidence directly without the assistance of the requested court, but this procedure is not available where coercive measures are necessary: ibid., Art. 17.

[697] Ibid., Art. 4.   [698] Ibid., Art. 7(1).

[699] Ibid., Art. 8(1). The requested court must inform the requesting court of the incompleteness within 30 days.

[700] Ibid., Art. 10. The foreign litigants and/or their representatives can request to be present when the evidence is taken in the United Kingdom: ibid., Arts. 11–12.

[701] Ibid., Art. 14(1).   [702] Cmnds. 3991, 6272.

[703] Dicey, Morris & Collins, n.694 above, [8-078]–[8-089]. The Evidence (Proceedings in Other Jurisdictions) Act 1975 only applies to requests by foreign courts, but not foreign arbitral tribunals: *Viking Insurance Co.* v. *Rossdale* [2002] 1 Lloyd's Rep. 219, [8]–[10].

[704] *Re Pan American Airways Inc.'s Application* [1992] QB 854 (CA); *Smith* v. *Phillip Morris Companies Inc.* [2006] EWHC 916 (QB), [30].

are steps which can be required to be taken by way of obtaining evidence for the purposes of civil proceedings in the court making the order'.[705] Secondly, an English court will not make a general order requiring the global production of any documents that might potentially be relevant to the foreign proceedings, but instead will only order the production of documents specified by the requesting court.[706] Accordingly, a general request for all bank statements received by a particular person during a given period is unacceptable, whilst a request for all the statements given to that person during that period by a single, nominated bank may be granted.[707] 'Fishing trips' for relevant documents are impermissible.[708] In *Land Rover North America Inc* v. *Windh*,[709] Treacy J stated that a court should apply the following two-stage test in deciding these matters:

> In summary, in considering the letters of request . . . the court should, in my opinion, ask first whether the intended witnesses can reasonably be expected to have relevant evidence to give on the topics mentioned in the amended schedule of requested testimony, and second whether the intention underlying the formulation of those topics is an intention to obtain evidence for use at the trial or is some other investigatory, and therefore impermissible intention.

Even where these limitations do not apply, an English court nevertheless exercises a discretion as to whether to accede to the foreign court's request,[710] and is unlikely to do so if this would involve the infringement of a privilege recognized by English law or the law of the requesting court,[711] such as a bank's duty of confidentiality.[712] A court also exercises a discretion as to the most appropriate manner in which the evidence can be furnished.[713]

The leading decision dealing with the Evidence (Proceedings in Other Jurisdictions) Act 1975 is *Re Westinghouse Uranium Contract*,[714] which arose out of proceedings in Virginia concerning breaches of a contract to construct nuclear power stations. By way of defence, the construction company argued that the contract had been rendered impossible

---

[705] Evidence (Proceedings in Other Jurisdictions) Act 1975, s.2(3). See also *Smith* v. *Phillip Morris Companies Inc.*, n.704 above, [30].

[706] Ibid., s.2(4). See also *Genira Trade & Finance Inc.* v. *Refco Capital Markets Ltd* [2001] EWCA Civ 1733, [32], [35].

[707] *Re Asbestos Insurance Coverage Cases* [1985] 1 WLR 331 (HL).

[708] An application for a witness' oral examination cannot be described as 'fishing' if there are sufficient grounds for believing that the intended witness might have evidence relevant to the trial (*First American Corp.* v. *Zayed* [1998] 4 All ER 439 (CA)), although the letter of request must not 'oppress' the witness, which would be the case if the witness was at risk of subsequently being joined as a party to litigation (ibid., 449). An English court should give the requesting court the benefit of the doubt where possible (*Smith* v. *Phillip Morris Companies Inc.*, n.704 above, [30], [36]), but a statement in a letter of request that evidence is to be used at trial is not necessarily conclusive of the purpose for which the evidence will be used (*United States of America* v. *Phillip Morris* [2003] EWHC 3028 (Comm), [76]). See also *Genira Trade & Finance Inc.* v. *Refco Capital Markets Ltd*, n.706 above, [28]–[32]; *Land Rover North America Inc.* v. *Windh* [2005] EWHC 432 (QB), [13], [17]–[18], [26].

[709] N.708 above, [11], [18], [19], citing *First American Corp.* v. *Zayed*, n.708 above.

[710] *Smith* v. *Phillip Morris Companies Inc.*, n.704 above, [30].

[711] Evidence (Proceedings in Other Jurisdictions) Act 1975, s.3(1). See also CPR 1998, r.34.20.

[712] Dicey, Morris & Collins, n.694 above, [8-087].

[713] Evidence (Proceedings in Other Jurisdictions) Act 1975, ss.2(1)–(2). Although an English court can only order the taking of 'evidence' under this legislation, this term does not necessarily include all information or material that is capable of being gathered by a party, even if relevant to proceedings: Dicey, Morris & Collins, n.694 above, [8-082]. 'Evidence' does not include points of claim and skeleton arguments from an earlier London arbitration that are required to demonstrate that a party to that arbitration is running inconsistent arguments in subsequent foreign proceedings: *Emmott* v. *Michael Wilson & Partners Ltd*, n.640 above, [109], [122].

[714] [1978] AC 547 (HL).

to perform, and accordingly has been frustrated, by reason of the shortage of uranium and consequent steeply rising prices. It was alleged that this situation resulted from the activities of an international cartel of uranium producers, which allegedly included two English companies. To establish the validity of this defence, the United States District Court issued letters rogatory, requesting the English High Court to order the officers of the relevant English companies, who were not in fact parties to the Virginian proceedings, to produce certain documents to, and give evidence before, the United States consulate in London. The House of Lords refused to give effect to the Virginian court's letters rogatory for a number of reasons. First, as ordering the production of the requested evidence would expose the English companies to fines for breaching European competition law, they were entitled to claim the privilege against self-incrimination available under English law. Secondly, a United States grand jury had been established to investigate whether the uranium cartel had breached United States antitrust legislation and it had issued a subpoena requiring the production to it of any evidence discovered in the Virginian proceedings.[715] As any evidence supplied pursuant to the letters rogatory could, therefore, be used in any subsequent criminal antitrust proceedings, the English companies were entitled to resist giving the evidence or producing the documents by relying on the privilege against self-incrimination contained in the Fifth Amendment to the United States Constitution. Thirdly, Lord Wilberforce gave significant weight to an intervention by the United Kingdom Attorney-General, who considered that the wide investigatory procedures available against foreign citizens under United States antitrust legislation constituted an infringement of the United Kingdom's jurisdiction and sovereignty. His Lordship considered that the courts should 'speak with the same voice as the executive', and treat as an infringement of United Kingdom sovereignty any attempt to exercise 'United States investigatory jurisdiction extraterritorially against United Kingdom companies', particularly in penal matters.[716] In *Westinghouse* itself, it was considered that responding to the United States District Court's letters rogatory would expose British subjects to proceedings conducted in the United States in respect of acts performed outside that jurisdiction, and that such an exercise of extraterritorial jurisdiction was simply 'not in accordance with international law'.[717] It is likely that an English court would give similar weight, and adopt a similar approach, to other matters considered to be in the national interest.

Their Lordships' reference in *Westinghouse* to the privilege against self-incrimination as a reason for refusing to give effect to the letters rogatory suggests that courts may be similarly reluctant to order a party, such as a bank, to disclose confidential information. Indeed, in *Re State of Norway's Application*,[718] where, at the request of the Norwegian tax authorities, the Norwegian courts issued letters rogatory seeking the oral examination of two bank officers in relation to the affairs of a trust, the Court of Appeal declined to assist the foreign court on the ground, *inter alia*, that ordering the witnesses to give evidence would involve the bank in a breach of its duty of confidentiality owed to its customer. As considered previously,[719] however, the bank's duty of confidentiality is qualified. Accordingly, the existence of such a duty does not *automatically* preclude an English court from assisting a foreign court. There may be circumstances where disclosure is justified. According to Kerr LJ in *State of Norway*, the court 'must carry out a balancing exercise' between 'the

---

[715] *Re Westinghouse Electric Corporation Uranium Contracts Litigation*, 563 F 2d. 992 (1977); *Re Uranium Antitrust Litigation*, 480 F Supp. 1238 (1979).

[716] N.714 above, 617.   [717] Ibid., 610, 631.

[718] [1987] QB 433 (CA), affd. [1990] 1 AC 723 (HL). See also *Honda Giken Kogyou Kabushiki Kaisha* v. *KJM Superbikes* [2007] EWCA Civ 313.

[719] Sects. 5(iii)–(vi) above.

desirable policy of assisting a foreign court' and the 'great weight' to be given 'to the desirability of upholding the duty of confidence'.[720] His Lordship also indicated that, where the circumstances justify giving assistance to the foreign court, the necessary disclosure can be justified under the first *Tournier* qualification, namely that disclosure is compelled by law.[721] Whilst Glidewell and Gibson LJJ agreed that the court had to balance the competing interests in favour of ordering disclosure and respecting confidentiality, Glidewell LJ preferred to justify any disclosure under the second *Tournier* qualification, namely that there is a public interest in the English courts assisting foreign courts.[722] Nevertheless, where possible, the English courts have expressed their general willingness to accede to foreign courts' letters of request, particularly where the foreign proceedings arise out of an international banking fraud.[723]

Given the difficulties associated with obtaining evidence abroad by means of the letter of request or letter rogatory procedure, as discussed above, United States courts have frequently adopted the alternative means of obtaining information concerning a bank's international and overseas operations, namely by ordering bank officers based at *local* branches in the United States to disclose the relevant information. The relevant bank officer in the United States may be ordered by the local court either to give oral testimony or to produce documents to the court and, if he refuses to obey the order, he may face contempt-of-court proceedings. Thus, in *United States* v. *Field*[724] the manager of a bank in the Cayman Islands, who was also a Canadian citizen, was served with a subpoena whilst fleetingly present in the United States and was compelled by the threat of contempt proceedings to answer questions about a customer's account maintained in the Cayman Islands before a grand jury that was investigating that customer's possible tax evasion. Although the bank manager sought to resist disclosure on the grounds that this would breach bank secrecy laws in the Cayman Islands, the Court of Appeal for the Fifth Circuit considered that disclosure was necessary in order to protect the grand jury as an institution and that disclosure did not breach foreign secrecy laws, as the Cayman Islands banking authorities could compel disclosure of the relevant information in comparable circumstances.[725] In contrast, in circumstances where equivalent disclosure would not be ordered in the foreign jurisdiction, so that compelling disclosure in the United States by local bank officers would indeed involve the bank in a breach of those foreign secrecy laws, a United States court is more likely to give weight to those foreign laws. Indeed, some United States decisions have treated a prohibition under the law of the place where the information is located as a sufficient reason in itself for refusing to make a disclosure order.[726] Since the United States Supreme Court decision in *Société Nationale Industrielle Aérospatiale* v. *US*

---

[720] N.718 above, 486–487.   [721] Ibid., 485.

[722] Ibid., 489–490. In *Pharaon* v. *Bank of Credit and Commerce International SA (in liquidation)*, n.633 above, Rattee J emphasized that such disclosure should be limited to what was reasonably necessary to satisfy the public interest in disclosure.

[723] *First American Corp.* v. *Sheikh Zayed Al-Nahyan*, n.708 above, 448–449 (although the letters of request were considered to be oppressive). An English court will assist a foreign court by remedying any defects in a letter of request, but will not re-write the letter of request so that it is 'going too far away from the original': *Smith* v. *Phillip Morris Companies Inc.*, n.704 above, [30], [41]–[45]. See also *State of Minnesota* v. *Phillip Morris Inc.* [1998] ILPr 170, [69] (CA) discussed above.

[724] 532 F 2d. 404 (1976), cert denied: 429 US 940 (1976).

[725] Accordingly, a foreign bank secrecy law that contains an absolute prohibition on disclosure will be accorded more respect than laws that are subject to qualifications: *United States* v. *First National City Bank* 396 F 2d. 897, 903 (2nd Cir., 1968).

[726] *First National City Bank of New York* v. *IRS*, 271 F 2d. 616 (1959), cert. denied: 361 U.S. 948 (1960); *Ings* v. *Ferguson*, 282 F 2d. 149 (1960); *Application of Chase Manhattan Bank*, 297 F 2d. 611 (1962); *United States* v. *Rubin*, 836 F 2d 1096, 1102 (8th Cir., 1998).

District Court for the Southern District of Iowa,[727] however, the modern trend is to balance a number of factors before compelling disclosure that might breach such foreign laws,[728] namely the importance of the documents concerned to the United States proceedings; the degree of specificity in identifying relevant documents; the location of the relevant information; the availability of alternative means for securing the information; the extent to which non-disclosure would undermine United States interests and disclosure would undermine the interests of the jurisdiction where the information is located; any hardship that might be caused to the party compelled to disclose; and the good faith or otherwise of that party.[729] This last factor in particular has often proved to be determinative. Thus, in *Société Internationale pour Participations Industrielles et Commerciales SA* v. *Rogers*,[730] where the issue concerned whether a Swiss bank's action should be dismissed for failure to comply with a United States production order, the United States Supreme Court refused to impose sanctions against the bank as there was no evidence that it had 'deliberately courted legal impediments' under Swiss law to avoid making disclosure and accordingly had not acted in bad faith by deliberately using the foreign law to evade compliance with United States law. In contrast, in *SEC* v. *Banca della Svizzera Italiana*,[731] where there was evidence that a Swiss bank had participated in, and profited from, insider trading activity and had deposited funds in a United States bank account 'fully expecting to use foreign law to shield it from the reach of [United States] laws', the District Court ordered the bank to respond to certain interrogatories despite the risk of breaching Swiss bank secrecy laws. Similarly, where the evidence indicates that a bank has not taken any *bona fide* steps in the foreign jurisdiction to obtain permission to disclose the relevant information, assuming such steps are available, a United States court is unlikely to allow a bank to rely on foreign bank secrecy laws to resist disclosure of confidential information.[732] In contrast, where a foreign bank has made a genuine, albeit unsuccessful, attempt to seek the permission of relevant foreign authorities to obtain the relevant information, a subpoena against the bank will generally be refused,[733] or, if the order has already been granted, the court will refuse to impose sanctions against the bank for non-compliance.[734]

However much restraint the United States courts purport to exercise when granting disclosure orders in such circumstances, those orders are invariably resented by the

---

[727] 482 US 522 (1987).   [728] *Strauss* v. *Crédit Lyonnais SA*, 249 FRD 429, 438–439 (SDNY, 2008).

[729] *Restatement (Second) of Foreign Relations Law of the United States* (St. Paul, Minn., 1965), s.40; *Restatement (Third) of Foreign Relations Law of the United States* (St. Paul, Minn., 1986), s.442.

[730] 357 US 197, 208–209 (1958).

[731] 92 FRD 111, 118–119 (SDNY, 1981). See also *United States* v. *Field*, n.724 above; *Arthur Andersen & Co.* v. *Finesilver*, 546 F 2d. 338 (1976); *United States* v. *Vetco*, 644 F 2d. 1324, 1331 (9th Cir., 1981); *In re Grand Jury Subpoena*, 218 F.Supp 2d 544, 554 (2000).

[732] *United States* v. *First National City Bank*, n.725 above. See also *United States* v. *Bank of Nova Scotia*, 691 F 2d 1384, 1389 (11th Cir., 1982); *United States* v. *Bank of Nova Scotia*, 740 F 2d 817, 825–826 (11th Cir., 1984); *United States* v. *Davis*, 767 F.2d 1025, 1035 (2nd Cir., 1985); *Cochran Consulting Inc.* v. *Uwatec USA Inc.*, 102 F 3d 1224, 1227 (FCA, 1996); *Weiss* v. *National Westminster Bank plc*, 242 FRD 33, 56 (2007). The United States courts do not regard the Hague Convention as precluding the making of a direct order, the principle of comity notwithstanding: *Murphy* v. *Reifenhauser KG Maschinenfabrik*, 101 FRD 360 (1984). The procedure takes place under 28 USC §1782 and provides a speedy and efficient way of obtaining information by applying directly to the United States courts. Some United States circuits allow for potentially unlimited jurisdiction; others will not grant disclosure to an extent greater than would be ordered in the foreign jurisdiction itself. See generally M. Jarrett, 'Assistance from the United States for litigants abroad' (2001) 151 *NLJ* 390.

[733] *Trade Development Bank* v. *Continental Insurance Co.*, 469 F 2d 35 (1972); *United States* v. *Bank of Nova Scotia*, n.732 above; *Minpeco SA* v. *Conticommodity Services Inc.*, 116 FRD 517 (1987).

[734] A party in breach of a United States court's disclosure order may raise a defence of 'substantial justification': United States Federal Civil Judicial Procedure Rules, r.37(b)(5)(g)(3). See also *Pharaon* v. *Bank of Credit and Commerce International SA*, n.633 above, 460.

courts of the foreign jurisdiction where the relevant information is located and subjected to obligations of confidentiality. Not only is the foreign court likely to regard the United States disclosure order as infringing its sovereignty and jurisdiction, but it is also likely to view the United States court as subordinating foreign state interests to those of its own state.[735] Accordingly, when asked to recognize or enforce such an extraterritorial order of a United States court, the English courts will usually give priority to their own domestic interests. In *X AG* v. *A Bank*,[736] the United States Department of Justice, which was conducting an investigation into the crude oil industry, served a subpoena on the head office of a United States bank for the production in the United States of documents relating to accounts held with the bank's London branch by a group of companies, one of which had had dealings on the United States crude oil market. As the bank intended to comply with the subpoena, the corporate group obtained an interim injunction restraining the bank from disclosing the relevant records. Subsequently, Leggatt J had to decide whether to continue or vacate the injunction. Despite the fact that the United States District Court had, since the granting of the English interim injunction, ordered the bank to obey the subpoena, Leggatt J continued the injunction restraining the bank from passing information concerning the corporate group's affairs either to the bank's head office in the United States or to any other person or branch. Although his Lordship had to weigh up all the relevant factors in determining whether the balance of convenience favoured the vacation or continuation of the injunction, he considered that two factors in particular favoured its continuation. First, his Lordship considered that compliance with the United States order would potentially render the bank liable to its customers for breach of its duty of confidentiality, the scope of which was to be determined by English law given that the relevant accounts were maintained in London. According to his Lordship not only would the United States District Court's order involve a 'breach of what might be termed a private interest in the sense that what is directly involved is a contract between banker and customer'; but it would also involve 'a matter of public interest, because it raises issues of wider concern than those peculiar to the parties'.[737] Secondly, his Lordship did not consider it likely that the United States District Court would commence contempt proceedings if a court of competent jurisdiction at the place where the relevant records were maintained had enjoined the bank from making disclosure. In this regard, Leggatt J concluded:[738]

> I can summarise in a sentence the balance of convenience as I see it. On the one hand, there is involved in the continuation of the injunction impeding the exercise by the United States court in London of powers which, by English standards, would be regarded as excessive, without in so doing causing detriment to the bank: on the other hand, the refusal of the injunctions, or the non-continuation of them, would cause potentially very considerable commercial harm to the [group], which cannot be disputed, by suffering the bank to act for its own purposes in breach of the duty of confidentiality admittedly owed to its customers.

Similarly, in *FDC Co. Ltd* v. *Chase Manhattan Bank*,[739] during the course of an investigation into income tax statements filed in the United States, the United States revenue authorities demanded information from the defendant bank's head office in New York about the claimants' accounts that were held with the bank's Hong Kong branch. On the

---

[735] Consider the conflicting state interests in *Re Westinghouse Uranium Contract*, n.714 above.
[736] [1983] 2 All ER 464.   [737] Ibid., 477.   [738] Ibid., 480.
[739] [1985] 2 HKC 470 (HKCA), cited with approval in *Nam Tai Electronics Inc* v. *Pricewaterhouse-Coopers*, n.637 above, [47].

claimants' application, the Hong Kong Court of Appeal enjoined disclosure. There were two aspects to the injunction. First, the defendant bank was enjoined from disclosing the claimants' account details to the United States revenue authorities in compliance with the United States court order, as such disclosure would constitute a breach of the bank's duty of confidentiality. According to Huggins VP, '[t]he Hong Kong courts could enjoin the [b]ank against disclosing the information to the United States Government in Hong Kong', since '[a]ll persons opening accounts with banks in Hong Kong, whether local or foreign banks, are entitled to look to the Hong Kong courts to enforce any obligation of secrecy that is, by Hong Kong law, implied by virtue of the relationship of banker and customer'.[740] His Honour did not consider that conclusion to be affected by the fact that the unlawful disclosure would occur in the United States, rather than within the Hong Kong jurisdiction, as 'the obligation of secrecy is not subject to territorial limits'.[741] Nor did his Honour consider that disclosure pursuant to a foreign court order was justifiable under the 'compulsion of law' qualification as recognized in *Tournier*.[742] Yang JA similarly considered that the bank's breach of confidentiality justified the injunction, since 'all the banks carrying on their business in Hong Kong owe the same obligations to customers irrespective of where their head offices happen to be'.[743] Indeed, his Honour considered that, as a customer may have opened a Hong Kong bank account in order to obtain the advantages conferred by Hong Kong bank secrecy laws, the Hong Kong courts should be slow to undermine that protection.[744] Accordingly, despite recognizing that the defendant bank faced the Hobson's choice of being prosecuted for contempt of court either in Hong Kong or New York, the Hong Kong Court of Appeal felt obliged to give effect to Hong Kong law and declined to assess the likelihood of the defendant actually being held in contempt under United States law, treating this matter as irrelevant to its decision and outside its competence. In this latter regard, the approach in *FDC* differs from Leggatt J's approach in *X AG*.

Secondly, the defendant bank was enjoined from transferring the relevant information concerning the claimants' accounts to its head office in the United States. Although it was argued that there was no basis for an injunction, since the transfer of information between a branch and its head office was simply an internal transfer between different parts of the same entity, so that there was no 'disclosure' of confidential information to third parties. Huggins VP concluded, however, that 'the Hong Kong branch of the bank should for present purposes be considered as a different entity separate from the head office in New York'. Although his Honour held that there might be circumstances (such as an internal investigation into a suspected fraud) where the ordinary course of business would require the exchange of customer information between bank offices, the transfer of information to New York in *FDC* was 'solely for the purpose of its being disclosed to the United States Government'.[745] Huggins VP considered that '[i]t would be closing our eyes to the reality of the situation to allow the [b]ank to make an internal transfer of information which it would not make in the ordinary course of business when that transfer is designed for no other purpose than to bring the information within the jurisdiction of the foreign court'.[746] Accordingly, despite the United States court order being on its face directed at the bank's head office in that jurisdiction, his Honour considered that that court order had extraterritorial effect, was 'aimed unashamedly' at information within the Hong Kong jurisdiction, and was 'nothing more nor less than a device to avoid the enforcement in Hong Kong of the orders of a foreign court'.[747]

---

[740] Ibid., 477.   [741] Ibid., 476, 485.   [742] Ibid., 476.   [743] Ibid, 478–479.   [744] Id.

[745] Ibid., 476.   [746] Ibid., 476–477.   [747] Id.

Whilst *X AG* and *FDC* demonstrate that both the English and Hong Kong courts will resist attempts by foreign courts to infringe their local bank secrecy laws, *FDC* suggests that the latter courts may do so more robustly than the former.[748] Nevertheless, in cases of international fraud, the English courts have shown less reluctance to act. In *Pharaon* v. *Bank of Credit and Commerce International SA (in liquidation)*,[749] the victim of an alleged fraudulent conspiracy involving the defendant bank, BCCI, started proceedings in New York and obtained a subpoena from the United States District Court against BCCI's auditor for the production of documents relating to BCCI. BCCI's auditors applied to the English courts for leave to comply with the United States subpoena, since there was a risk that such compliance could breach a subsisting injunction obtained by one of BCCI's customers from the English courts restraining BCCI from disclosing account information to third parties. As stated previously, Rattee J applied the second *Tournier* qualification and held that the bank's duty of confidentiality was overridden by the greater public interest in making confidential documents relating to an international bank's alleged fraud available to parties to private foreign proceedings for the purpose of uncovering that fraud.[750] His Lordship added, however, that the disclosure must not go beyond what is reasonably necessary to achieve the public interest that justifies disclosure.[751] BCCI's auditors were given leave to comply with the United States subpoena, but subject to the disclosed documents being suitably redacted to avoid disclosure of information concerning customers who were not alleged to have been involved in the conspiracy.

(b) Evidence sought abroad in support of English proceedings

An English court can assist a party to obtain evidence from a bank located abroad or from the foreign branch of an English bank for the purpose of proceedings before the English courts. Where the documents are maintained or the witnesses are located in another EU Member State, the English courts can make a request for assistance from the foreign court under the procedure in Regulation 1206/2001, which was discussed above.[752] Regulation 1206/2001 also governs the situation where the English courts wish to take evidence directly in another Member State without court assistance. Where the foreign court is located outside another Member State then neither Regulation 1206/2001 nor the Evidence (Proceedings in Other Jurisdictions) Act 1975 governs the English court's letter of request. Originally, the English courts relied upon their inherent jurisdiction to issue a letter of request in such circumstances,[753] but the CPR 1998 now expressly confers jurisdiction on the English courts.[754] Where relevant information is held abroad by a foreign bank or by the foreign branch of an English bank, litigants have sometimes requested that an English court make an order for disclosure *directly* against the bank's officers within the jurisdiction, requiring those officers to obtain the relevant information from the bank's foreign office and to disclose it to the applicant. In such cases, the English courts have generally been unwilling to interfere with the foreign court's jurisdiction. Thus, in *R. v. Grossman*,[755] the Court of Appeal discharged an order under section 7 of the BBEA 1879, which had

---

[748] Cf. *Jim Beam Brands Co.* v. *Kentucky Importers Pty. Ltd* [1994] 1 HKLR 1, 9.   [749] N.633 above.

[750] Ibid., 465, citing *First American Corp.* v. *Sheikh Zayed Al-Nahyan*, n.708 above, 448–449.

[751] Id.

[752] 2001 OJ L 174. Regulation 1206/2001 does not apply to an English court's order that an English judgment debtor identify the location of his assets wherever situated: *Masri* v. *Consolidated Contractors International Co. SAL* [2008] EWCA Civ 876, [39]–[45], [53]–[54], revsd. on a different issue: [2009] UKHL 43. See also *Re MMR and MR Vaccine Litigation (No. 10)* [2004] All ER (D) 67 (request to Irish courts granted).

[753] *Panayiotou* v. *Sony Music Entertainment (UK) Ltd* [1994] Ch. 142.   [754] CPR 1998, r.34.13(2).

[755] (1981) 73 Cr. App. Rep. 302 (CA). *Grossman* does not, however, govern the issue of jurisdiction over substantive proceedings brought against an English bank's foreign branch, as this is governed by the

been granted to the Inland Revenue authorities for the purpose of prosecuting tax offences. The order directed Barclays Bank's head office in London to obtain the bank records of a particular corporate account held with its Isle of Man branch and to enable the Inland Revenue to inspect those records. Lord Denning MR's vacation of the order was motivated by the conflict of jurisdictions that would arise if it were allowed to stand, and by the fact that the appropriate course for inspecting the bank records of the Isle of Man branch was to make an application to the Manx courts in accordance with their legislation.[756]

A similar approach was adopted in *MacKinnon* v. *Donaldson Lufkin & Jenrette Securities Corporation*,[757] which arose out of frauds allegedly committed by a defunct Bahamian company in relation to a number of international loans. The claimant, who was a victim of the fraud, obtained an order under section 7 of the BBEA 1879, which enabled him to inspect certain documents concerning the Bahamian company's account with the London branch of a New York bank and which was directed at, and served upon, that bank's London branch. The claimant also obtained a subpoena *duces tecum* (now a witness summons)[758] requiring an officer at the bank's London branch to attend the trial in order to produce all the relevant documents. Discharging the master's order, Hoffmann J emphasized that, as both the disclosure order and the subpoena were to take effect in New York, they infringed United States sovereignty and stated that it was particularly important in the case of banks to take care that the court does not exercise its jurisdiction in breach of other states' sovereignty.[759] This was because bank documents normally contain details not only of the bank's own business, but also those of the bank's customers, and bank secrecy laws in different jurisdictions protect customer confidentiality to different degrees and may be reinforced by penal sanctions and 'blocking statutes'. Hoffmann J considered that the bank's duty of confidentiality should be regulated by the jurisdiction where the particular account was kept, otherwise '[i]f every country where a bank happened to carry on business asserted a right to require the bank to produce documents relating to accounts kept in any other such country, banks would be in the unhappy position of being forced to submit to whichever sovereign was able to apply the greatest pressure.'[760] In *Masri* v. *Consolidated Contractors International Company SAL (No.2)*,[761] however, Lawrence Collins LJ recently stressed that there is no absolute rule that 'the court will never have jurisdiction to make orders under the BBEA 1879 against the London branch of a foreign bank in relation to papers held by head office, nor that it will never be possible to issue a witness summons against the bank's London branch officer in respect of head office transactions'. According to his Lordship, such disclosure orders or witness summonses would only be made when the circumstances of the particular case demonstrated 'a sufficient connection with England to justify an order'. In particular, his Lordship suggested that *Donaldson Lufkin* might have been decided differently if the papers that

Brussels I Regulation or Lugano Convention: *Mahme Trust Reg* v. *Lloyds TSB Bank plc* [2004] 2 Lloyd's Rep. 637, [32].

[756] Ibid., 307–308. See also *Walsh* v. *National Irish Bank Ltd*, n.50 above, [44]–[48] (refusal of revenue authority's application against Irish bank for information concerning accounts held with its Manx branch). See further *Chemical Bank* v. *McCormack* [1983] ILRM 350, 354.

[757] [1986] Ch. 482. Cf. *Re Mid East Trading Ltd* [1998] 1 All ER 577 (CA) (liquidator's application under Insolvency Act 1986, s.236, for disclosure of documents situated abroad). See further *United Company Rusal plc* v. *HSBC Bank plc*, n.540 above, [60]–[73].

[758] CPR 1998, Pt. 34.

[759] *Société Eram Shipping Co. Ltd* v. *Compagnie Internationale de Navigacion* [2003] 3 WLR 21, [22]–[23], [67] (HL), applying similar principles when refusing a third party debt order over a foreign account's credit balance.

[760] N.757 above, 494.   [761] [2008] EWCA Civ 303, [32]–[35].

were held by the foreign bank's head office had related to English transactions.[762] Some doubt has subsequently been cast upon these views by *Masri* v. *Consolidated Contractors International Company SAL (No.4)*,[763] when Sir Anthony Clarke MR stated that Lawrence Collins LJ may have 'somewhat understated' the current relevance of the presumption against extraterritoriality, a view with which Lawrence Collins LJ himself also agreed.[764] Indeed, Lord Mance appears to have echoed this more conservative approach when *Masri* was subsequently appealed.[765] Such uncertainty of approach is hardly welcome, given that the expansion of the international banking network and the increase in the number of multinational companies as customers is only likely to exacerbate the potential for conflicts of jurisdiction in the future. A possible solution would be an international convention along the lines of Regulation 1206/2001.

6 Termination of the relationship

As the banker–customer relationship generally, or a particular banking contract, may be terminated in accordance with its express terms, it is important to have regard to the particular terms or nature of the contract that a party is seeking to bring to an end. In situations where the contract fixes the contractual period, such as a fixed deposit maturing on an appointed date[766] or the hire of a bank safe-deposit box for a fixed period, the contract may not be terminated early, unless both parties agree. In contrast, in the case of an account that contemplates payments on demand, such as a current account or ordinary savings account, the customer may at common law terminate the relationship at any time by withdrawing the credit balance and closing the account. Where the account now falls within the scope of the Payment Services Regulations 2009 (PSR 2009),[767] as is the case with a current account, the customer's right to terminate the account relationship at any time without notice has been expressly recognized.[768] A bank may insert a provision into the current account contract requiring the customer to give notice before closing the account, but this period cannot exceed one month.[769] Furthermore, a bank can charge a customer for closing his or her current account, but this must 'reasonably correspond to the actual costs' incurred by the bank as a result of the account's closure.[770] No account closure charges may be imposed, however, if the account has been opened for at least 12 months before being closed.[771] Following the closure of a customer's current account, a bank must refund the customer a proportionate share of any charges that it imposed in advance for the services that it undertook to provide.[772] Moreover, the bank will not be obliged to pay any cheques presented after the account has been closed.

Irrespective of whether a customer's right of immediate closure arises at common law or under the PSR 2009, any proceedings for the recovery of an account credit balance

---

[762] Ibid., [34]. There might also be a 'sufficient connection' with England if the foreign bank has registered as a foreign company in the United Kingdom: *Mitsui & Co Ltd* v. *Nexen Petroleum UK Ltd*, n.537 above, [30]–[32].

[763] N.752 above, [15]–[16].   [764] Ibid., [80].

[765] *Masri* v. *Consolidated Contractors International (UK) Ltd (No. 4)* [2010] AC 90, [19], [26] (HL).

[766] Ch. 9, Sects. 1 & 2 below.

[767] This will be the case for any account falling within the definition of a 'framework contract' contained in the PSR 2009, reg. 2(1): Ch. 2, Sect. 6(iii) above , Ch. 7, Sect. 2 below & Ch. 13, Sects. 5 (iv)–(vi) below.

[768] PSR 2009, reg. 43(1). This right is without prejudice to other rights that the payer might have to treat the 'framework contract' as unenforceable or void: ibid., reg. 43(7).

[769] Id.   [770] Ibid., reg. 43(2).   [771] Ibid., reg. 43(3).   [772] Ibid., reg. 43(6).

must be commenced within the six-year limitation period that runs from the date of the customer's demand.[773] A novel issue arose in *Bank of Baroda* v. *ASAA Mahomed*,[774] where the customer demanded the closure of his deposit account and repayment of the balance. As the bank ignored the demand and continued to operate the account as normal, the customer's solicitor made a further written demand for repayment some months later, but this was again ignored. Subsequently, the issue arose as to when the customer's cause of action against the bank accrued for limitation purposes, namely whether time ran from the customer's first demand (which was outside the relevant limitation period) or the second demand (which was within the limitation period). The Court of Appeal chose the latter option, so that the customer's claim was not statute-barred. According to Simon Brown LJ, 'if a customer, having demanded closure and repayment of his account, then changes his mind, he can notify the bank accordingly and, assuming always that the bank is content to continue holding the account, the [banker–customer] contract will in effect start afresh. The cause of action arising from the original demand will have ended and a fresh one will arise upon the making of the demand.'[775] Applying this principle, his Lordship interpreted the customer's second demand as implicitly withdrawing the first demand and as making a fresh demand that commenced time running again. Agreeing with Simon Brown LJ's conclusion, Mummery LJ reasoned that neither the customer's first demand, nor the bank's subsequent actions, resulted in the account being closed or the banker–customer contract being terminated, so that, as there was no express or implied term preventing the customer from making further demands, he was free to make a fresh demand and create a new cause of action.[776] To the extent that the customer's first demand was simply a *demand for repayment*, Mantell LJ agreed with Mummery LJ and, focusing on whether the customer's first demand had the effect of terminating the banker–customer contract, concluded that neither a customer's demand for repayment (not closure) of his account, nor the bank's failure to comply with that demand, without more brought the banker–customer contract to an end.[777] His Lordship held, however, that to the extent that the customer's first demand constituted a *demand for the closure of the account*, he would adopt Simon Brown LJ's reasoning.

The position is different when the bank wishes to terminate its relationship with a customer. The position at common law was confirmed recently by Lord Hoffmann in *National Commercial Bank of Jamaica Ltd* v. *Olint Corporation Ltd*,[778] namely that 'in the absence of express contrary agreement or statutory impediment, a contract by a bank to provide banking services to a customer is terminable upon reasonable notice'.[779] The reference to any 'statutory impediment' is important, however, as current accounts and (flexible) savings accounts will nowadays constitute 'framework contracts' within the PSR 2009, which provide that a bank may only close an account opened for an indefinite period by giving at least two months' notice, provided the account contract contains a provision to that effect.[780] The reason for requiring a longer notice period on the part of the bank is so that any cheques or other effects payable to the customer and deposited into his account have time to clear before the account is closed. This was recognized in

---

[773] Sect. 3 above.
[774] N.44 above. See also *Das* v. *Barclays Bank plc* [2006] EWHC 817 (QB), [37]–[41].   [775] Ibid., 19.
[776] Ibid., 24. This reasoning may be criticized on the ground that a customer will never be time-barred after he makes a demand for repayment, so long as the account is not closed and there is no term of the contract preventing further demands from being made.
[777] Ibid., 25.   [778] [2009] UKPC 16. See also *Joachimson* v. *Swiss Bank Corp.*, n.48 above, 125, 127.
[779] Ibid., [1].
[780] PSR 2009, reg. 43(4). See also FSA, n.70 above, 12. See formerly the *Banking Code* (March 2008), [7.6] and the *Business Banking Code* (March 2008), [7.8].

Prosperity Ltd v. *Lloyds Bank Ltd*,[781] where a bank and its customer, an insurance company, had a course of dealing, whereby insurance premiums were paid by third parties directly to the credit of the customer's account. The bank gave the customer one month's notice before closing his account. McCardie J held that an account could only be closed at common law upon the giving of reasonable notice and that one month was inadequate notice given the course of dealing between the parties. Furthermore, his Lordship refused to grant a mandatory injunction ordering the bank to reopen the account, as this would have involved ordering the bank to perform personal services.[782] Accordingly, subject to proof of loss, damages were available to the customer. These principles have now received some support (albeit implicit) from Lord Hoffmann in *Olint*,[783] where the defendant bank gave its customer 32 days' notice of the closure of its account as a result of press speculation that the customer operated a pyramid selling scheme. After negotiating an extension of time before the account's closure, and without giving notice to the bank, the customer applied for an interlocutory injunction restraining the bank from closing the account. Interestingly, the customer's injunction application never suggested that the notice period provided by the bank was unreasonably short.[784] In determining whether to grant the injunction, Lord Hoffmann appears to have endorsed the suggestion in *Prosperity* that, when a customer disputes the closure of his account, damages will usually be an adequate remedy, so that an injunction (whether mandatory or prohibitory)[785] will not ordinarily be granted.[786] Indeed, Lord Hoffmann strongly disapproved of the practice of customers in such circumstances applying for injunctions without notice to the bank so as to obtain a tactical or litigation advantage.[787]

In addition, at common law, the banker–customer contract, being of a personal nature, terminates automatically when the customer dies or the contract is dissolved.[788] When the customer is insolvent, the presentation of a petition for the adjudication of an individual customer or for the winding-up of a corporate customer does not automatically revoke the bank's mandate to make payments from his customer's account,[789] but this probably occurs upon the bank receiving notice of the petition.[790] The banker–customer relationship and its associated duties are not, however, terminated until the making of

---

[781] (1923) 39 TLR 372.

[782] *Impact Traders Pty Ltd* v. *Australia and New Zealand Banking Group Ltd* [2003] NSWSC 964, [36]–[38]; *B-Filer Inc.* v. *Bank of Nova Scotia* [2005] AQBQ 704, [32].

[783] *National Commercial Bank of Jamaica Ltd* v. *Olint Corporation Ltd*, n.778 above.

[784] Ibid., [6]. The injunction was based, *inter alia*, upon allegations of abuse of dominant market position, conspiracy to restrain or injure competition, and inducing breach of contract: ibid., [7]–[11].

[785] Ibid., [19]–[20].

[786] Ibid., [16]–[21]. Lord Hoffmann indicated a number of factors pointing away from the grant of injunctions in such circumstances, including the bank being compelled to provide confidential services against its will; the bank being exposed to reputational risks or legal liability by continuing the account; the customer often being unable to satisfy any cross-undertaking in damages; and the customer usually being able to obtain alternative banking services elsewhere: ibid., [21].

[787] Ibid., [13]–[15].

[788] *Re Russian Commercial and Industrial Bank*, n.61 above. BEA 1882, s.75(2), however, provides that *notice* of the customer's death determines the bank's duty and authority to pay cheques drawn by his customer, and the same rule probably applies in the case of the customer's insanity.

[789] *Hollicourt (Contracts) Ltd (in liq.)* v. *Bank of Ireland*, n.100 above, [33].

[790] *Pettit* v. *Novakovic* [2007] BPIR 1643, [7]. In the case of a voluntary winding-up, the bank's mandate terminates upon the passing of the resolution: *Re London and Mediterranean Bank, Bolognesi's case* (1870) LR 5 Ch. App. 567 (CA); *National Westminster Bank Ltd* v. *Halesowen Presswork Assemblies Ltd* [1972] AC 785 (HL).

the winding-up order and the appointment of a liquidator over the customer's assets.[791] The same applies when it is the bank that is wound-up,[792] and the account's credit balance becomes payable to the customer or his representative. In the absence of agreement to the contrary, however, the termination of the banker–customer contract or relationship does not affect the validity of the customer's claims in respect of unauthorized debits made by the bank.[793]

---

[791] The bank's duty of confidentiality extends beyond the account's closure: *Tournier* v. *National Provincial and Union Bank of England*, n.469 above, 473.

[792] Although Wynn-Parry J in *Re Russian Commercial and Industrial Bank*, n.61 above, appears to suggest that the banker–customer relationship does not terminate until the bank's subsequent dissolution; cf. *Bank of Credit and Commerce International SA* v. *Malik* [1996] BCC 15. See also *Re London and Mediterranean Bank, Bolognesi's case*, n.790 above.

[793] *Limpgrange Ltd* v. *Bank of Credit and Commerce International SA* [1986] FLR 36.

PART II

The Bank as a Monetary Agency in Domestic Transactions

6

The Bank's Role as a Depository

1 Economic function and legal concept

Banks serve two main functions in domestic transactions. First, banks discharge their customers' liabilities by honouring their cheques and other payment orders and generally enabling customers to deposit their money in current accounts or interest-bearing accounts, such as savings accounts and fixed deposits. This first function is discussed in this Part (Chapters 6–16). Secondly, banks act as lenders. This second function is discussed in Part III (Chapters 17–22). To appreciate fully the bank's role as paymaster and as a recipient of its customer's funds, it is necessary to consider both the legal aspects of the subject and the basic economic concepts of banking. The present chapter attempts to do this, and also introduces the problems to be discussed in the remainder of this Part. It is convenient, however, to commence the analysis by reflecting on the nature of a bank's operations.

In a modern industrialized society, most transactions involving the payment of money on a regular basis are effected through banking channels with the bank acting as its customer's paymaster. In this context, 'payment' must be understood in its widest sense. 'Payment' is certainly not restricted to payments made in cash, although banks do handle cash on behalf of their customers, such as when a customer makes a cash deposit into his account, the bank pays out cash over the counter against a personal cheque drawn to 'cash',[1] or the customer withdraws cash from an ATM machine.[2] Indeed, the significance of cash in settling customers' liabilities to third parties should not be underestimated as it often remains the only way in which many smaller one-off transactions, such as payments to stall-holders, newsagents, and launderettes, can be settled. Even in the area of consumer sales and services, however, payments of more substantial one-off amounts are frequently settled by other payment means, such as by cheque supported by a cheque guarantee card, by credit card, or by debit card.[3] Indeed, the increasing number of card terminals, even in the case of relatively modest suppliers, and the overwhelming success of the 'Faster Payments Service'[4] means that banks are increasingly used for the settlement of even very small amounts due under consumer transactions or transferred for other personal reasons. Moreover, payments for the purchase of goods and services can increasingly be settled by 'electronic money' or 'digital cash', which involve the transfer of digital information representing monetary value loaded onto a 'smart card' (a plastic card with an integrated microchip), or onto the memory of a personal computer, by the consumer's bank in return for a debit to his account.[5] Whilst these e-money schemes have

---

[1] Previously, a bank could also pay cash over the counter to the payee or transferee of an uncrossed cheque, but most cheques are nowadays pre-printed with the crossing 'a/c payee only' or its equivalent. See further Ch. 10, Sect. 4 below.

[2] Ch. 14, Sect. 6 below.   [3] Ch. 14, Sect. 1 below.   [4] Ch. 13, Sect. 3(iv)(b) below.

[5] Ch. 14, Sect. 7 below.

had a considerable amount of success in some jurisdictions,[6] the market in the United Kingdom was slow to develop, but (after something of a false start)[7] there are indications that the demand for prepaid debit and credit cards is set to rise.[8] Where the customer wishes to make regular periodic payments of fixed amounts, such as employee salaries or wages, payment could be made by drawing a cheque for each employee or, more conveniently, could be remitted through the payer's bank by means of an electronic credit transfer, such as a standing order. Moreover, even where the amount varies on each date of payment, as with utility bills, payment can be effected by means of a 'direct debit',[9] in which the payee is authorized by the payer to demand and collect payment for the relevant amount from the payer's bank.

Where a customer uses its bank to effect payment in this way, no cash actually passes from the payer to the payee. In the case of payment by cheque or paper-based credit transfer, there is a piece of paper that passes between the parties via the relevant clearing system,[10] but otherwise payment is effected by the drawer's (customer's) account being debited with the amount involved and the payee's account being credited with the equivalent amount. In the case of electronic funds transfers, the transfer is effected entirely by means of such debit and credit entries.[11] The reference to credit and debit entries highlights the flipside of the bank's role as paymaster, namely to act as a depository for the customer's own funds and as an agent for the receipt of funds payable to its customer by third parties. This is because a customer would be unable to discharge his liabilities through his bank without either maintaining an adequate account balance or arranging for a suitable overdraft or loan facility. The availability of such a credit balance or such borrowing facilities depends, however, on the regular flow of funds into the customer's account with the bank. For example, an individual's ability to draw cheques, or make direct debit transfers, in order to pay his bills may depend upon whether his salary or other earnings are paid into his bank account. Similarly, a corporation may be unable to pay its employees' wages through its bank account unless its trade profits are paid into it.[12] Accordingly, it is the bank's role to collect cheques deposited by his customer into his account[13] or to credit its customer's account with sums remitted through the paper-based giro system[14] or by means of an electronic funds transfer.[15] It follows that, in addition to any roles that a bank undertakes as financier,[16] financial adviser, or bailor, the bank's main business involves acting both as the customer's paymaster and as the depository of the customer's own funds and recipient of funds from third parties.

Having examined the actual nature of banking activity, it becomes necessary to examine the economic and legal conceptualizations of the nature of banking. In economic

---

[6] Bank for International Settlements, *Survey of Developments in Electronic Money and Internet and Mobile Payments* (Basel, March 2004), [2.2.1] (www.bis.org). There are some notable success stories in other jurisdictions, such as the 'Octopus card' in Hong Kong, the 'FeliCa card' in Singapore, and the 'Chipknip card' in the Netherlands.

[7] According to the Bank for International Settlements, n.6 above, '[o]verall the UK market for both card- and network-based e-money schemes has been quiet' and '[a]ll major card-based e-money trials in the United Kingdom had been discontinued by end-2000'. This includes the 'Mondex' and 'Visa Cash' pilot schemes.

[8] Payments Council, *Progress Report: Delivering the National Payments Plan* (June 2010), 4.

[9] Ch. 13, Sect. 2(iii) below.   [10] Ch. 10, Sect. 2 below.

[11] *R v. Preddy* [1996] AC 815, 841 (HL). See further Ch. 13, Sect. 5(iii) below.

[12] Banks owe no duty to monitor the customer's account to ensure there are sufficient funds to cover any payments: *Whitehead v. National Westminster Bank Ltd*, The Times, 9 June 1982. See further Ch. 7, Sect. 4(vi) below.

[13] Ch. 10, Sect. 2 & Ch. 15, Sects. 2 & 4 below.   [14] Ch. 13, Sect. 3(i)–(ii) below.

[15] Ch. 13, Sect. 3(iii)–(iv) below.   [16] Ch. 17, Sects. 2–3 below.

terms, the constant flow of money into and out of each bank, as described above, forms the basis of the economic conceptualization of banking activity—a bank is a reservoir of money. This also provides an apt description of the banking network as a whole. This particular conceptualization highlights the fact that money flowing into the bank becomes part of a generic fund held for all the customers, and that money paid out by the bank flows not from an individualized fund held in the customer's name, but from this generic bank fund. Essentially, the 'reservoir' is that of the bank itself, not a reservoir comprising earmarked amounts owned by separate account holders. This economic conception finds echoes in the legal explanations of the banker–customer relationship. As considered previously,[17] money paid by the customer to the credit of his bank account is treated as being lent by him to the bank, and such deposited funds are not earmarked or held in trust for the customer, but become the property of the bank. Essentially, the banker–customer relationship is a debtor-creditor relationship, not one of trust, bailment or agency.[18] This conception of banking activity reflects another well-known legal doctrine, namely, that money cannot be owned in the same way as corporeal property.[19] Instead, any amount paid to the credit of a customer's account gives rise to a mere chose in action in favour of the customer that is enforceable against the bank. It is a debt that, in the case of a current account or a savings account, is payable to the customer on demand, whilst in the case of a fixed deposit it is repayable at an agreed future date.

Moreover, in *Commissioners of the State Savings Bank of Victoria* v. *Permewan, Wright & Co.*,[20] the Australian High Court explicitly recognized the validity of the economic definition of a bank. In the words of Isaacs J, '[a bank] is, in effect, a financial reservoir receiving streams of currency in every direction, and from which there issues outflowing streams where and as required to sustain and fructify or assist commercial, industrial or other enterprises or adventures'.[21] *Permewan* emphasizes two other aspects of traditional banking activity. First, a bank is an institution prepared to deal with the public.[22] In other words, any member of the public whose character is established to the bank's satisfaction should be entitled to open an account and, in appropriate circumstances, obtain a loan or overdraft facility. In contrast, a person traditionally had to be a shareholder or member in order to be entitled to deal with a building society or credit union. This situation still persists in the case of credit unions,[23] which have a 'common bond' determining who may join. The 'common bond' may limit membership to persons living in a particular geographical area, belonging to a particular profession, or answering to some other description. In practice, however, the distinction between banks and building societies has been eroded significantly, as most members of the public can become a shareholder in a building society without having to satisfy any particular qualification.[24] Indeed, building societies actively encourage the public at large to join. Secondly, as recognized in *Permewan*,[25] banks' activities in the fields of lending and deposit-taking are generic in nature. Any amount may be paid into an account, and loans may be granted by the bank for almost any purpose. In contrast, a building society or a friendly society has set guidelines on the purposes for which it can lend. Even this distinction between banks and building societies

---

[17] Ch. 5, Sect. 3 above.   [18] *Foley* v. *Hill* (1848) 2 HLC 28, 36 (HL).
[19] *Miller* v. *Race* (1758) 1 Burr. 452.
[20] (1914) 19 CLR 457, 471 (HCA). See further Ch. 3, Sect. 1(ii) above.   [21] Ibid., 471.
[22] Ibid., 479.
[23] According to the Financial Services Authority, there were 554 credit unions in England, Wales, and Scotland on 30 September 2006 and 532 on 30 September 2007: see www.fsa.gov.uk. In 2007, 71.1 per cent of registered credit unions were in England, 22.9 per cent in Scotland, and 6.0 per cent in Wales. Of the credit unions registered in England almost one quarter are found in the North West.
[24] Ch. 1, Sect. 7 above.   [25] N.20 above, 471.

may be somewhat questionable nowadays, as banks similarly have policies concerning the nature of their lending activities, even if these policies are not expressly spelt out in the bank's constitutional documents or advertising material. Accordingly, from a purely economic point of view there is no magic distinction between the activities of banks and those of other financial or lending institutions and, as considered previously,[26] the legal definition of a 'bank' is often so difficult to apply sensibly that it simply becomes a matter of examining whether the particular institution has a reputation as a bank or not.[27]

2 Practical implications of the economic and legal concept

The main legal consequence of an economic conception that treats a bank as a reservoir of money is that the customer is deemed to have lent to the bank the amounts standing to the credit of his account. Three practical consequences flow from this analysis. First, where a bank becomes insolvent, a customer is neither entitled to assert any proprietary claim to the funds paid into his account nor to recover those funds *in specie*.[28] Accordingly, customers are regarded as unsecured general creditors whose claims are subordinate to those of preferential and secured creditors.[29] As a general creditor, the customer is only entitled to a dividend that is equivalent to a *pro rata* share of any surplus remaining after secured and preferential claims have been paid. Secondly, the balance due to the customer constitutes a mere chose in action giving the customer a debt claim against his bank for the sums deposited, whilst the property in the money itself passes to the bank. Accordingly, the bank is free to use the deposited money for its own purposes and dealings and does not have to account to the customer for profits made with his particular deposits. The customer is only entitled to demand the return of a sum equivalent to his deposits, and any interest payable according to the terms governing the account. Nowadays, customers can earn modest rates of interest on current accounts, although they may also be subject to bank charges,[30] particularly in the case of an unauthorized overdraft.[31] Thirdly, as a result of the economic analysis of a bank as a reservoir of money, the bank is not a trustee of its customer, but a mere creditor. Accordingly, except in rare circumstances,[32] banks do not owe their customers any fiduciary duties.

In view of these points, one might wonder why members of the public are still prepared to invest their funds with banks. The answer is again an economic rather than a legal one. Since the eighteenth century, banks have attained a high reputation for their creditworthiness and honesty in dealings. It is this trust engendered by the high standing of banks that induces the public to deposit funds with them, even if the yield is marginally lower than that obtainable from other financial institutions. Another factor is the size of the major banks and the large, albeit reducing, number of branches throughout the United Kingdom.[33] Members of the public are naturally more inclined to invest with a branch of a financial giant than with a small concern that may not have the same economic

---

[26] Ch. 3, Sect. 1(ii) above.   [27] *United Dominions Trust* v. *Kirkwood* [1966] 2 QB 431 (CA).

[28] *Foley* v. *Hill*, n.18 above.   [29] Ch. 18, Sect. 2 below.

[30] Banks often waive bank charges for personal customers where an account is kept in credit, but may charge business customers irrespective of the state of the account.

[31] *Office of Fair Trading* v. *Abbey National plc* [2010] 1 All ER 667 (UKSC), discussed in Ch. 17, Sect. 2(ii) below.

[32] Ch. 5, Sect. 4(i) below.

[33] Despite some opposition from the rural community, banks have reduced their branches over the years as they develop alternative ways of providing banking services, such as telephone banking and internet banking.

power, standing, or creditworthiness. Moreover, the public trust has traditionally been enhanced by the fact that banks are strictly controlled and supervised by the Financial Services Authority,[34] and the fact that the Bank of England has previously shown itself willing to intervene in order to 'rescue' banks in financial difficulty, especially where a particular bank's collapse could result in the loss of public confidence in the banking system as a whole.[35] Indeed, the United Kingdom Government has recently stepped in to save a number of banks from collapse by either temporarily or partially nationalizing them, as in the cases of Northern Rock plc and Bradford & Bingley plc, or boosting capital reserves by injecting further equity into them, as in the case of the merger between HBOS plc and Lloyds TSB Bank plc. Although the willingness of the Government and the Bank of England to rescue banks may be seen as promoting confidence in the United Kingdom banking sector, there must come a point where the frequency of such steps merely serves to highlight the weakness of financial institutions and ultimately to undermine confidence in the banking sector as a whole. A case in point is the 'bailout' culture that developed over the course of 2008 following the 'global credit crunch'. This has had such a profound impact on confidence in the United Kingdom banking sector that it is unlikely to be fully restored for a number of years to come.[36]

3 The bank as a depository of its customer's funds and as paymaster of his accounts

The maintenance of an account with a bank confers on the customer two main benefits. First, in the case of any account except certain current accounts, the customer gains interest on sums standing to the credit of his account. Interest-bearing accounts, such as savings and deposit accounts are discussed in detail in Chapter 9. Principally, the consideration for the bank's agreement to pay interest is having the use of its customer's money. The rate of interest depends on different factors. Thus, for fixed deposits maturing at an agreed date, the rate is usually higher in long-term deposits than in short-term deposits or deposits payable 'at call' or 'on demand'. Furthermore, the rate may depend on the amount deposited. Thus, certain types of account that yield a higher rate of interest are only available in respect of certain minimum amounts deposited with the bank. Ordinary savings accounts, which carry the lowest rate, can of course be opened for any amount.[37] Current accounts, which are discussed in Chapter 7, are of particular importance to banks, as the sums regularly credited to these accounts are often available to the bank without its having to pay any substantial interest on the accrued balance. As there is a certain regularity in the cash-flow of current accounts, especially given the number of automated payments nowadays, banks can usually predict with reasonable certainty the amounts

---

[34] Ch. 2, Sect. 4 above.

[35] In 1984, the Bank of England organized a rescue package or 'lifeboat' for Johnson Matthey Bank, but declined to intervene in 1992 to prevent the collapse of the fraudulent Bank of Credit and Commerce International: *Three Rivers District Council* v. *Bank of England (No. 3)* [2003] 2 AC 1 (HL). A deposit guarantee scheme designed to give depositors limited compensation in the event of bank failure was first established under the Banking Act 1979, continued under the Banking Act 1987, and now exists in the Financial Services and Markets Act 2000 (FSMA 2000). As a result of the 'global credit crunch', the level of depositor protection was increased in September 2007, following the 'Northern Rock debacle', and again in October 2008, in order to bolster confidence in the United Kingdom banking sector. The depositor protection scheme in FSMA 2000 has been amended by Banking Act 2009, ss.169–180. See further Ch. 2, Sect. 4(viii) above.

[36] For the responses to the 'global credit crunch', see generally Ch. 2 above.

[37] Ch. 9, Sects. 1–2 below.

that are likely to be standing to their credit from time to time. For example, the amounts standing to the credit of business accounts tend to vary on a cyclical basis, showing a particular decrease when taxes are paid. The bank's ability to predict the fluctuations in the amounts standing to the credit of its customers' current accounts, and indeed other types of account, enables it to plan its own investments. In practical terms, therefore, a bank's profits from providing accounts to its customers is the difference between the interest that it pays to its customers and the amount that it earns by investing the amounts deposited by customers. In the past, the bank's own capital often constituted a small fraction of the money available for business purposes, but it is unlikely following the Basle III Accord that banks will be permitted to revert to this funding model following the events of the global credit crisis that began in 2007.

Secondly, in the case of any account, but most particularly current accounts, the customer can give instructions to his bank, such as an instruction to pay sums to a third party, and the bank is obliged as agent to obey these.[38] The customer may order payment by three basic means. The first method is payment by cheque. Although cheques were once the predominant method of payment, the volume and overall value of cheque transactions has dropped steadily over the years.[39] Indeed, the UK Payments Council has described cheque use as being 'in long-term decline'[40] and, more recently, 'in terminal decline',[41] and has set 31 October 2018 as the target date for the closure of cheque clearing in the United Kingdom.[42] More payments are now made by debit, credit, and charge card, and automated money-transfer methods, such as BACS, CHAPS Sterling, and the 'Faster Payments Service', than by cheque. Nevertheless, during the second quarter of 2010 some 196 million cheques were still drawn.[43] Usually, the payee remits the cheque to the credit of his account with his own bank, which then 'clears' the cheque by acquiring payment from the drawer's bank. The clearing process is discussed in Chapter 10. It is clear that the drawer's bank acts as agent in paying the cheque,[44] as does the payee's bank in collecting the instrument, except that the latter's mandate is to seek, rather than make, payment.[45] By undertaking to pay a cheque, the drawer's bank faces the risk that the cheque may have been tampered with, stolen from its genuine payee, or subject to a stop order. The bank's defences in such circumstances are discussed in Chapter 11. The payee's bank faces a different danger—if the payee is not entitled to obtain payment of the cheque, as is the case where he is a thief or a rogue who has forged his employer's signature, a bank that handles the instrument exposes itself to a common law action in conversion. The bank's position in such cases is discussed in Chapter 15.

The second method for paying the customer's accounts is the money-transfer order, which is discussed in Chapter 13. As with cheque payments, both the payer's bank and the payee's bank act in a representative capacity. The former acts as a paying agent; the latter receives payment on the payee's behalf. One of the three main differences between the settlement of debts by the use of a cheque and by the use of a money-transfer order

---

[38] Ch. 11, Sect. 1 below.   [39] For statistics on cheque use, see Ch. 10, Sect. 2 below.

[40] Payments Council, *National Payments Plan—Setting the Strategic Vision for UK Payments* (14 May 2008), 6. See also UK Payments Administration, *The Way We Pay 2009: UK Cheques* (London, 2009).

[41] Payments Council, n.8 above, 1.

[42] Payments Council, n.40 above, 6; Payments Council, n.8 above, 1. The Payments Council has predicted that by 2018 cheques will account for only two per cent of personal non-cash payments: *Annual Review 2008—Driving Change in UK Payments* (London, 2008), 11. As part of managing the reduction in cheque use, the Payments Council has announced its intention to close the cheque guarantee card scheme (discussed in Ch. 14, Sect. 4) by 30 June 2011: Payments Council, n.8 above, 2–3.

[43] UK Payments Administration, *Statistical Release—9 September 2010* (London, 2010), 6.

[44] Ch. 11, Sect. 1(i) below.   [45] Ch. 15, Sect. 3 below.

is procedural. A cheque is sent by the drawer (the debtor) to the payee (the creditor). The presentment of the cheque for payment depends accordingly on the initiative of the payee. In the case of a money-transfer order, however, the payer's bank pays the amount involved directly to the payee's bank. This is so even in the case of direct debits, where the periodic money-transfer order is executed by an authorized payee on behalf of the payer. The second major difference—perhaps now more theoretical than real—between payment by cheque and money-transfer order is that a cheque is a negotiable instrument, whilst the money-transfer order is not.[46] The significance of this distinction, which is basically related to the fact that a cheque, unlike a money-transfer order, is transferable, is discussed in Chapters 10 and 13. Nowadays, however, relatively few cheques drawn on United Kingdom banks are transferable. Since the Cheques Act 1992 introduced section 81A into the Bills of Exchange Act 1882 ('BEA 1882')—to the effect that crossed cheques marked 'account payee' or 'a/c payee', with or without the word 'only', are not transferable—United Kingdom banks now almost invariably supply their customers with cheque forms that are crossed and pre-printed with the words 'account payee', so that the cheque is only valid as between the immediate parties to it. Accordingly, the vast majority of cheques issued in the United Kingdom are not negotiable instruments, but merely payment orders directing a bank to pay the amount of the cheque to the named payee. The final point of distinction to note is that while a cheque is a paper-based payment instrument, money-transfer orders are increasingly entirely electronic, and customers may give instructions by means of telephone, internet or mobile banking services. In addition, some business customers may have direct access to the BACS or CHAPS systems allowing them to access the bank's computer and give instructions, by electronic messages, for the settlement of accounts. Even where the customer's money-transfer order to his bank is in paper form, execution of the transfer by the bank may be entirely electronic, as occurs with the BACS and CHAPS systems.[47]

The third method of payment is through the use of a debit card, often at a point of sale terminal in a retail outlet.[48] Payment using a debit card has become extremely popular with consumer customers, who can even use their debit card to obtain cash from ATMs by the use of a PIN[49] or from certain retail outlets under the 'cashback' scheme. There are now more debit card transactions each year than cheque transactions.[50] While a few debit card transactions are manual, using paper vouchers, the vast majority are by electronic means using an EFTPOS ('electronic funds transfer at point of sale') system. The instruction to pay a given amount to the supplier of goods is executed by means of a plastic card, and a payment message is transmitted electronically via one of the independent EFTPOS networks to the customer's bank and the retailer's bank.[51] Debit cards and other types of payment card are discussed in Chapter 14. Both the remitting bank and the receiving bank face certain hazards. The paying bank may remit the amount to the credit of the wrong account; the receiving bank may find that the wrong customer has been credited. In practice, the two situations arise simultaneously by virtue of the electronic operation that leads to both the crediting of the payee's account and the debiting of the payer's. The problems that such transmission errors can give rise to in the funds transfer context, as well as the question of the countermand of a money-transfer order, are discussed in Chapter 13.

---

[46] Ch. 13, Sect. 5(ii) below.   [47] Ch. 13, Sects. 3(iii)–(iv) below.

[48] Debit card use is extending beyond the traditional high street outlets into other services, such as plumbing, dentistry, utilities, and financial services.

[49] Ch. 14, Sect. 6 below.

[50] APACS, *Yearbook of Payment Statistics 2004* (London, 2004), 43; UK Payments Administration, n.43 above, 2.

[51] Ch. 14, Sect. 5 below.

4 The bank as its customer's agent for collection

Apart from paying cash to the credit of their bank accounts, customers are able to use the available banking facilities to effect the collection of items remitted to them by other parties. In many cases, the item collected is a cheque payable to the customer or a similar type of document, such as a dividend warrant. In addition, a bank receives on behalf of its customers amounts remitted to their credit by means of the money-transfer system. The funds so collected are automatically lent by the customer to the bank and, therefore, form part of the reservoir of money available to the bank itself. The bank's role in collecting cheques is discussed in detail in Chapter 15. Acting as a collecting bank raises the risk of liability *vis-à-vis* both the bank's own customer and certain interested third parties, such as the 'true owner' of a cheque.

As regards its customer, a collecting bank must ensure that it complies with two key obligations in order to avoid liability. First, the collecting bank must ensure that cheques, and any other instruments remitted by the customer to the bank for collection, are collected in a timely fashion. If the bank does not, then there will be a delay in the presentment of the cheque to the payer's bank (the 'drawee' or 'paying' bank). If the drawer closes the account upon which the cheque is drawn in the meantime, then the cheque will be dishonoured. As this will have been caused by the collecting bank's dilatoriness, its customer will be entitled to damages on account of the bank's failure to execute its instructions promptly. Moreover, the collecting bank's failure to process the cheque payable to its customer on time may lead to a situation in which the customer's balance appears, on its face, inadequate for meeting cheques subsequently drawn on that customer's account. The collecting bank may then wrongfully dishonour its own customer's cheques, in which case the customer may have an action for the wrongful dishonour of his cheque and, in certain cases, a concurrent action for defamation.[52] Secondly, the collecting bank must ensure that it collects the cheque or other instrument for the credit of its customer's account. If the bank credits the proceeds of the cheque to the wrong account, then it may be liable to its customer in the tort of conversion. A common example of such a situation occurs when an employee converts a cheque payable to his employer by paying the instrument into his own account or where a thief opens an account in the name of the cheque's payee and pays the cheque into that account. Where the 'true owner' of the cheque is not its customer, the collecting bank will similarly be liable for the cheque's conversion to whichever third party is the instrument's 'true owner'. The bank's potential defences to such a conversion claim are discussed in Chapter 15.

Where payment is effected by funds transfer, rather than by cheque, then no liability in conversion on the part of the collecting bank arises. In the case of a paper-based credit transfer, the documents involved in such a transaction are not considered 'property', and there is accordingly no suggestion that their misappropriation involves conversion.[53] The position is *a fortiori* where the credit transfer occurs electronically.[54] Moreover, until recently, it appeared that where the collecting bank had 'received' funds for its customer and paid this away to the wrong account, it could not have been sued for money had and received, since, as already pointed out, the bank would have paid out its own money rather than its customer's, thereby barring the customer's claim. Nowadays, however,

---

[52] Ch. 11, Sect. 5 below.   [53] Ch. 13, Sects. 5(ii)–(iii) below.
[54] The tort of conversion does not operate to protect intangible property: *OBG Ltd* v. *Allan* [2008] AC 1 (HL).

for the purposes of an action of this type, the money is to be treated as the customer's money,[55] removing the technical barrier to the customer's claim. That said, the collecting bank would potentially have a change of position defence depending upon its dealings with the funds following their 'receipt'.[56] There is, however, no doubt that mistakes can occur where money is remitted by means of a money-transfer order. If the transfer is to be made by direct debit, then it will be effected electronically through BACS which, it is believed, acts on behalf of the remitting bank and the receiving bank at different stages of the transaction. At common law, each bank will, therefore, be vicariously liable for its agent's negligence.[57] Alternatively, the transfer can be made by standing order through the new 'Faster Payments Service'. A specific, non-recurrent, transfer of funds may be made through the paper-based giro credit system or, more commonly nowadays, electronically through either CHAPS Sterling for larger sums or the 'Faster Payments Service' for smaller amounts. The collection of a paper-based giro credit is executed and cleared in a similar manner to a cheque. Where the collecting bank credits the proceeds of such a transfer to the wrong account, the customer is entitled to claim that his own account be credited with the amount of the transfer. Additionally, the customer may be entitled to an action for breach of contract if the collecting bank's error leads to an apparent shortage of funds in his own account resulting in the dishonour of his own cheques or other payment instructions. This question is similarly discussed in Chapter 15. Finally, the collecting bank may also be liable where it accepts a transfer to its customer's account, despite its customer's express instructions to the contrary. A customer will often give such an instruction when the funds transfer is to be made pursuant to the terms of a contract (such as a charterparty or a sale of land) that stipulates payment by a particular date. Accordingly, a customer may instruct his bank not to accept any late payments, as this might otherwise affect the customer's rights against the payer. The bank's liability if it does accept payment is discussed in Chapter 13. In practice, it is difficult for the bank to act upon a 'stop receipt' order, as this would require a significant amount of monitoring of a particular customer's account, and to date there is no adequate machinery for giving effect to such a request in an effective manner.

5 Conclusion

As has been mentioned at the outset, this chapter is basically an introduction to Part II. Chapters 7–16 will demonstrate that the legal principles defining the bank's liability as a paymaster, as a depository of funds, and as a collector of its customer's effects are closely related to the fundamental concepts underlying the banker-customer relationship. The bank, as a reservoir of funds, borrows amounts deposited with it by its customers and pays those funds out as their agent. Many of the legal principles discussed in the forthcoming chapters are, therefore, anchored in the basic rules of the law of agency. There is only one important rider to this fundamental principle. In its activities on behalf of its customer, the bank is involved both in paying the customer's cheques and in collecting cheques and other items payable to him. This brings the law relating to negotiable instruments into play. As noted above, however, most cheques drawn on United Kingdom banks are pre-printed with the words 'account payee' rendering them non-transferable

---

[55] *Agip (Africa) Ltd* v. *Jackson* [1990] Ch. 265, affd. [1991] Ch. 547 (CA); *Lipkin Gorman* v. *Karpnale* [1991] 2 AC 548 (HL).

[56] Ch. 12, Sect. 3(iii)(a) below.   [57] Ch. 13, Sects. 5(iv)–(vi) below.

and, therefore, depriving them of the characteristics of a negotiable instrument.[58] This has led one distinguished commentator (now judge) to conclude that much of the 'old learning' relating to the negotiability and indorsement of cheques should be jettisoned; that cheques should now be analysed along with other payment methods in the context of the ordinary law governing the banker–customer relationship; and that, at least in the context of the typical account-payee cheque, bills of exchange law should no longer be allowed to dominate the discussion.[59] There is much truth in this statement, but it is submitted that it would be premature to ditch all the 'old learning' on negotiability, indorsement, and the BEA 1882, not least because it remains possible for the drawer, before or at the time of issuing a cheque, to delete, and so cancel, the words 'account payee' printed on the cheque, so that the instrument becomes transferable and payable to order or bearer as the case may be. Those payees without bank accounts may well ask the drawer to do this to enable them to transfer the cheque to a friend who has a bank account, so that the cheque may be collected through that account.[60] There can be no doubt, however, that modern banking law and practice make it high time for the law of cheques to be severed from the BEA 1882 and dealt with in separate legislation.[61]

---

[58] Sect. 3 above.   [59] R. Cranston, *Principles of Banking Law* (2nd edn., Oxford, 2002), 258.

[60] For the particular problems facing the 'unbanked' payee of an 'account payee' cheque, see J.K. Macleod, 'The Plight of the Unbanked Payee' (1997) 113 *LQR* 133.

[61] This has occurred in Australia, when the Australian Cheques and Payment Orders Act 1986 was amended in 1998 and renamed the Cheques Act 1986. Moreover, the UNCITRAL Convention on Bills of Exchange and Promissory Notes (Geneva, 1988) specifically excludes cheques.

7

The Current Account

1 Special nature of the current account

Current accounts are used by a bank's customers for their regular financial transactions. Cheques payable to a customer are usually remitted by him to the credit of his current account. Some customers even ask their debtors to pay the amounts due to them directly to the credit of their accounts. A giro operation is used in such an instance.[1] In addition, the customer uses his current account for the purpose of discharging his liabilities. This can be done either by drawing cheques that he dispatches to his creditors, by using a debit card that operates directly on his current account, or by using some other form of giro transfer, such as a 'standing order' or 'direct debit'.[2] It follows that the customer's current account can be loosely described as a reservoir of his money, that the customer pays funds into and draws funds upon. At law, though, this description is inaccurate. When an amount is paid into the customer's current account, be it by means of cash, a cheque payable to him, or a giro transfer, the sum in question is forthwith regarded as being lent by the customer to the bank.[3] In this manner, the amounts paid to the credit of the customer's account are converted into debts owed to him by the bank. In reality, the indebtedness of the payor of the amount remitted is substituted with a debt incurred by the bank.

This analysis is of importance in two respects. First, it is wrong to describe the amount standing to the customer's credit as *his* cash. It is an unsecured debt that, in the bank's insolvency, will rank as subordinate to preferential claims[4] and to secured debts.[5] The customer is thus in the position of a general creditor.[6] Secondly, when the customer

---

[1] Ch. 13, Sects. 1–2 below.   [2] Ch. 13, Sect. 2 below.

[3] *Foley* v. *Hill* (1848) 2 HLC 28 (HL); *Re Charge Card Services Ltd* [1987] Ch. 150, affd. [1989] Ch. 497 (CA). Accordingly, a bank is not usually obliged to enquire about the source of the money paid to the customer's credit: *Thomson* v. *Clydesdale Bank Ltd* [1893] AC 282 (HL); *Clark* v. *Ulster Bank Ltd* [1950] NI 132, 136–137; *Selangor United Rubber Estates Ltd* v. *Cradock (No. 3)* [1968] 1 WLR 1555, 1588–1589; *Eagle Trust plc* v. *SBC Securities Ltd* [1992] 4 All ER 488, 507–508; *Cowan de Groot Properties Ltd* v. *Eagle Trust plc* [1992] 4 All ER 700, 756–757. See also *MA Hanna Co.* v. *Provincial Bank of Canada* [1935] SCR 144, 182–183 (SCC); *Banque Romande* v. *Mercantile Bank of Canada* [1971] 3 OR 433, 444–445 (OCA); *Carl B Potter Ltd* v. *Mercantile Bank of Canada* (1979) 31 NSR (2d) 402, [67]–[69] (NSSC); *Re Dover Pty Ltd* (1981) 6 ACLR 307 (NSWSC); *Koorootang Nominees Pty Ltd* v. *ANZ Banking Group Ltd* (VSC, 23 June 1997); *Glenko Enterprises Ltd* v. *Keller* (2000) 150 Man R (2d) 1, [87] (MBCA); *Provincial Drywall Supply Ltd* v. *Toronto-Dominion Bank* (2001) 153 Man R (2d) 161, [23]–[26] (MBCA); *Devron Potatoes Ltd* v. *Gordon & Innes Ltd*, 2003 SCLR 103, [16]–[17] (OH); *Evans* v. *European Bank Ltd* [2004] NSWCA 82, [160]–[161]. Furthermore, third parties cannot usually claim the account funds as their own: *Gray* v. *Johnston* (1868) LR 3 HL 1; cf. *John Shaw (Rayner's Lane) Ltd* v. *Lloyds Bank Ltd* (1945) 5 LDAB 396. See also Sect. 5(v) below.

[4] For employees' claims for wages, see Insolvency Act 1986, s.175(1) and Sched. 6, paras. 9–12. The Inland Revenue and Customs and Excise were removed from the list of preferential creditors by the Enterprise Act 2002, s.251. See further Ch. 19, Sect. 4(v) below.

[5] Such as a loan secured by a floating charge over the bank's assets, although such a charge can be avoided in certain circumstances: Ch. 19, Sect. 4 below.

[6] If the proposal for the introduction of 'safety deposit current accounts' ever became law, a customer holding such an account would be a secured creditor in the bank's insolvency: Safety Deposit Current Accounts Bill 2008, cls. 1(2), 1(5).

orders his bank to pay an amount of money to a third party, the bank discharges the instruction by paying out its own money.[7] It then reimburses itself by debiting the customer's account. It follows that, if the amount involved is paid to the wrong person, the bank is entitled to institute an action for its recovery as money paid under a mistake of fact.[8] It is true that it has been recently recognized that the customer is also entitled to institute such an action.[9] In practice, though, if payment is effected by means of a cheque that is paid to the wrong party, the customer can attempt to recover his loss by suing the collecting bank in conversion.[10] Accordingly, an action for restitution of sums paid is likely to be most useful in cases involving errors or improper payments effected by means of electronic funds transfer.

It has been shown earlier that an amount standing to the credit of the customer's current account is recoverable on demand.[11] Traditionally, this demand is made by drawing a cheque. In modern banking practice, it can also be effected by other means, such as the use of a cashpoint card and personal identification number at an automated teller machine, the use of a debit card at a point of sale terminal, or the use of telephone or internet banking facilities.[12] When the bank pays a cheque, or executes its customer's instruction to make an electronic funds transfer, for example, by making a standing order payment, it acts as its customer's agent.[13]

The bank's duty to carry out its customer's instructions is subject to a number of basic limitations and there are a number of situations in which the bank's duty to honour its customer's instructions is abrogated by law. Whilst a number of these latter situations are discussed in more detail in other chapters,[14] an analysis of the basic limitations on the bank's mandate is topical at this point to assist in defining the scope of the bank's duty. The first limitation on the bank's duty is that the bank is not obliged to honour a cheque, or meet some other form of demand, if the customer's account balance is inadequate.[15] An exception to this principle is that the bank has to meet its customer's cheque or other demand, despite the inadequacy of the credit balance, if the bank has agreed to grant the customer an overdraft and the amount of the cheque does not exceed the prescribed ceiling.[16] The balance of a current account is calculated on the basis of the amounts actually standing to its credit at the time that the customer's demand is made. The bank has a reasonable time for crediting amounts paid to the credit of a customer's account.[17] If the funds remitted by the customer are drawn upon before the bank has had a reasonable time to credit them to the account, the bank is not liable if it dishonours a cheque drawn by the customer.[18] Obviously, if the customer instructs the bank to collect cheques payable to him, he is not entitled to draw on them until the items have been cleared. There is, however, a telling difference between theory and practice in this regard. In effect, the proceeds are credited to the customer's account before the instruments are cleared. There

---

[7] *Halesowen Presswork and Assemblies Ltd* v. *National Westminster Bank Ltd* [1971] 1 QB 1, 33–34, 46 (CA), revsd. on a different point: [1972] AC 785 (HL).

[8] Money paid under a mistake of law is also recoverable through a restitutionary claim: Ch. 12, Sect. 1 below.

[9] Ch. 12, Sect. 1 below.   [10] Ch. 15, Sects. 2 & 4–5 below.   [11] Ch. 5, Sect. 3 above.

[12] See generally Chs. 13–14 below.

[13] Ch. 11, Sect. 2 below. For countermand of payment, see Ch. 11, Sect. 1(vii) below.

[14] Ch. 5, Sect. 4(iii) above, Sects. 5(i)–(iv) below & Ch. 11, Sects. 1(ii)–(viii) below.

[15] *Marzetti* v. *Williams* (1830) 1 B & Ad. 415, 424; *Bank of New South Wales* v. *Laing* [1954] AC 135, 154 (PC); *Office of Fair Trading* v. *Abbey National plc* [2008] EWHC 875 (Comm), [45], aff'd [2009] EWCA Civ116, revsd. on a different point: [2010] 1 All ER 667 (UKSC). See also *National Trust Co.* v. *Harold's Demolition Inc.* (2001) 43 RPR (3d) 212 (OSC). See further Ch. 11, Sect. 1(ii) below.

[16] Ch. 17, Sect. 2 below. See also *Fleming* v. *Bank of New Zealand* [1900] AC 577.

[17] Ch. 10, Sect. 2 & Ch. 11, Sect. 1(ii) below.   [18] Ch. 11, Sect. 1(ii) below.

is authority for the view (although its validity is rejected elsewhere in this work) that, in the absence of agreement to the contrary, the very crediting of the account evidences the bank's readiness to permit the customer to draw against the balance as shown.[19] If modern courts were to express a preference for this view, however, then it might arguably be possible to establish a usage under which it is permissible to draw against uncleared proceeds in the absence of express stipulation to the contrary. Such an argument is unlikely to have much impact in practice, however, as many banks include just such a stipulation in their standard terms and conditions for the opening of current accounts.

The second limitation to the bank's duty to honour the customer's cheques or other instructions is that the demand must be made at the branch with which the account is maintained. The customer is not legally entitled to demand payment at another branch.[20] In modern banking practice, however, this principle has effectively been abrogated by the supply of cashpoint cards and debit cards that can be used by the customer at any automated teller machine or authorized terminal.[21] Moreover, banks operating over the internet and those with telephone banking operations may have no branches at all.[22] It is, further, the practice of many banks to cash cheques presented by a customer to a branch other than that with which he maintains his account. Conceptually, though, where a cheque is cashed at such other branch, the bank is initially considered to have discounted rather than paid the cheque.[23]

The third limitation is that cheques should be paid only if presented during ordinary business hours. However, a bank does not commit a breach of its mandate by paying the cheque shortly after closure time.[24] Finally, as a matter of practice, banks dishonour cheques that have been outstanding for a long period of time. Usually, a cheque is dishonoured if presented after the lapse of more than six months from the date of its issue.[25] Likewise, although an undated cheque is not invalid,[26] it is a practice not to pay such instruments.[27]

---

[19] *Capital and Counties Bank Ltd* v. *Gordon* [1903] AC 240, 249 (HL); cf. Ch. 11, Sect. 1(ii) below. See also *Akrokerri (Atlantic) Mines Ltd* v. *Economic Bank* [1904–1907] All ER Rep 1054; *Bank of China* v. *Synn Lee & Co. Ltd* [1962] 1 MLJ 91.

[20] *Woodland* v. *Fear* (1857) 7 El. & Bl. 519; *Henry Prince* v. *Oriental Bank Corporation* (1877–1878) LR 3 App. Cas. 325, 332 (PC); *King* v. *Irvine A Lovitt* [1912] AC 212, 219 (PC); *EB Savory & Co* v. *Lloyds Bank Ltd* [1932] 2 KB 122, 141 (CA); *Maude* v. *Commissioners of Inland Revenue* [1940] 1 KB 548, 552–553; *Arab Bank Ltd* v. *Barclays Bank (DCO)* [1954] AC 495; *Canada Life Assurance Co.* v. *CIBC* [1979] 2 SCR 669, 679 (SCC). See also *Clare & Co.* v. *Dresdner Bank* [1914–1915] All ER Rep 617; *Governor & Company of the Bank of Ireland* v. *Hussey* [1965] IR 46.

[21] *Bank of Scotland* v. *Seitz* 1990 SLT 584, 590 (Scot. 1st Div.).

[22] *Damayanti Kantilal Doshi* v. *Indian Bank* [1999] 4 SLR 1, 11 (SGCA), endorsing a passage from the 2nd edition of this work and expressing doubts whether, in the light of modern technology and business practices, the principle that a demand for payment must be made at the branch where the account is kept in order to found a cause of action is still good law. See further Ch. 5, Sect. 3 above.

[23] Ch. 15, Sect. 8 below.

[24] *Baines* v. *National Provincial Bank Ltd* (1927) 32 Com. Cas. 216; (1927) 96 LJKB 801.

[25] *Commissioner of Inland Revenue* v. *Thomas Cook (NZ) Ltd* [2003] 2 NZLR 296, [38] (NZCA), affd. without reference to this point: [2005] 2 NZLR 722 (PC) ('. . . there is in New Zealand a term implied by custom and usage that banks are not bound to pay a cheque, presentment of which takes place more than six months after its date'). For further support for such a custom in New Zealand, see *Code of Banking Practice* (July 2007), [4.1(f)]. A similar banking custom probably exists in the United Kingdom: A.G. Guest, *Chalmers and Guest on Bills of Exchange, Cheques and Promissory Notes* (17th edn., London, 2009), [13-065]. Although the *Banking Code* (March 2008) is not as explicit as its New Zealand equivalent, it nevertheless provided ([9.10]), that banks must provide their personal customers with information about how they will deal with out-of-date cheques.

[26] Bills of Exchange Act 1882, s.3(4)(a). See *Aspinall's Club Ltd* v. *Al-Zayat* [2007] EWHC 362 (Comm), [10]: '. . . the absence of a date had no impact on the cheque's validity'.

[27] *Griffiths* v. *Dalton* [1940] 2 KB 264.

An important feature of the current account is that the roles of the bank and the customer can be reversed in given situations. If the account is overdrawn, the bank becomes the creditor and the customer becomes the debtor. Whether or not the overdraft—like the credit balance standing to a customer's account—is repayable on demand is a delicate question that is discussed subsequently.[28] The agency relationship existing between the customer and his bank is not altered by the existence of the overdraft. The customer continues to be the principal and the bank remains the agent.[29] It follows that no fiduciary duties of the type discussed in Chapter 5 are owed by the customer to the bank. At best, the customer owes the bank a duty of care (albeit one of a limited nature),[30] but this duty is in existence regardless of whether the account is in credit or overdrawn.

The object of the current account is to enable the customer to pay by cheque, debit card, or other funds transfer, amounts due from him, and to arrange for the collection of cheques payable to him and other receivables. The account represents the customer's 'liquid funds' available for everyday expenditure. Traditionally, the balance standing to the credit of a current account did not earn interest.[31] The main reason for this was to be found in the notion that the customer remained free to draw against the account at any time. However, if a customer maintained his balance at a given minimum amount, many banks waived their regular charges. More recently, many banks have introduced the practice of paying interest, albeit at a modest rate, on balances maintained in current accounts. Although the calculation of interest will depend upon the terms of the individual account, interest is usually calculated on a daily basis and added to the balance of the account at monthly intervals.

2 The opening and general operation of the current account

When opening a current account on behalf of a customer, banks must increasingly satisfy a number of statutory requirements. As discussed already,[32] a bank must satisfy certain 'customer due diligence' requirements contained in the Money Laundering Regulations 2007 before it 'establishes a business relationship' with its customer,[33] such as the opening of a current account, or 'carries out an occasional transaction' on behalf of its customer.[34] In this regard, the bank is required to take steps to establish and verify the customer's identity 'on the basis of documents, date or information obtained from a reliable and independent source',[35] and to obtain information from the customer concerning 'the purpose and intended nature of the business relationship'.[36] Those steps should be determined on a 'risk-sensitive basis depending on the type of customer, business relationship, product or transaction'.[37] In addition, a bank is also under an ongoing obligation to monitor the operation of the current account to scrutinize transactions occurring on the account and to keep documents, data,

---

[28] Ch. 17, Sect. 2(ii) below.

[29] *Coutts & Co.* v. *Stock* [2000] 1 WLR 906, 909; *Hollicourt (Contracts) Ltd* v. *Bank of Ireland* [2001] 2 WLR 290, 296, 300 (CA).

[30] Ch. 11, Sect. 3(ii) below.

[31] The practice has been well known in Scotland for a considerable period of time.

[32] Ch. 4, Sect. 3(iv) above. For consumer guidance on this issue, see Financial Services Authority, *Moneymadeclear: Just the Facts about Proving your Identity* (November 2009), 2–7.

[33] Money Laundering Regulations 2007, S.I. 2007/2157 (as amended by S.I. 2007/3299 & S.I. 2009/209), regs. 7(1)(a), 9(2). There are also certain circumstances when the 'customer due diligence' can be carried out during or after the opening of the current account: ibid., regs. 9(3)–(5).

[34] Ibid., regs. 7(1)(b), 9(2).

[35] Ibid., reg. 5(a). Where a third party has an interest in the account, a bank must take steps to determine the identity of those beneficially interested: ibid., regs. 5(b), 6.

[36] Ibid., reg. 5(c).　　　[37] Ibid., reg. 7(3)(a).

or information in order to keep the 'customer due diligence' up to date.[38] Where a bank is unable to carry out the 'customer due diligence' measures, it must either refuse to open the current account in the first place or, if already open, must close it.[39] Not only must banks comply with these requirements in order to avoid the criminal and civil penalties imposed by the regulations themselves,[40] but compliance is also likely to be an important factor when determining a collecting bank's potential liability for the conversion of a cheque.[41]

As well as complying with the Money Laundering Regulations 2007, since 1 November 2009, a bank that opens a current account on behalf of a customer must also normally satisfy the requirements of the new 'Banking and Payment Services' (BPS) regime,[42] which comprises two elements: the FSA's *Banking: Conduct of Business Sourcebook* (BCOBS)[43] and the Payment Services Regulations 2009 (PSR 2009).[44] The application of this regime results from the fact that a current account serves two primary functions. First, the account can be used by the customer as the means of satisfying any payment instructions that it gives to his bank and is, therefore, the means whereby a bank can provide 'payment services'[45] to its customer. Secondly, a current account enables a bank to receive deposits made by, or on behalf of, its customer. In this regard, the date on which a customer's deposits are credited to his current account will depend upon the form that the deposit takes.[46] Where a customer deposits cash into his current account,[47] and the customer in question is a 'consumer, micro-enterprise or charity',[48] those funds must be credited to the account and made available to the customer immediately after the receipt of the cash deposit by the bank.[49] In the case of other types of customer, the bank must credit the cash deposit to the customer's account and make it available to him 'no later than the end of the business day after the receipt of the funds'.[50] Where a cheque is deposited into a customer's account, the crediting of the account will depend upon the '2-4-6 commitments',[51] which require funds to be credited to an account for interest purposes on the second working day following the cheque being paid into the account, with the customer being able to withdraw the funds from the account on the fourth working day following the cheque being paid into the account. Where funds are transferred to a current account by means of a credit transfer, the payor's bank must generally ensure that the amount of the payment transaction is credited to the account of the payee's bank by the end of the business day following its receipt of the payment instruction from the payor.[52] Following its receipt of the funds, the payee's bank must credit the funds to the payee's account and make those funds available to the payee.[53] In this regard, the proceeds of the credit transfer must be at the payee's disposal immediately after the funds are credited to his account by the payee's bank[54] and must be credited to the payee's account by the end of that business day.[55]

As regards 'the activity of accepting deposits from banking customers',[56] BCOBS contains 'high level' principles regulating financial promotions and distance marketing, which require the bank to comply with certain 'distance marketing disclosure rules'

---

[38] Ibid., reg. 8(1)–(2).   [39] Ibid., reg. 11(1).   [40] Ibid., regs. 42, 45–47.

[41] Ch. 15. Sect. 4 below.   [42] Ch. 2, Sect. 6(iii) above.   [43] Ch. 2, Sect. 6 above.

[44] Ch. 2, Sect. 6 above & Ch. 13, Sect. 5 below.

[45] Payment Services Regulations 2009, S.I. 2009/209 (PSR 2009), Sched. 1.   [46] Ch. 11, Sect. 1(ii).

[47] Such an account will normally fall within the definition of a 'payment account' for the purposes of the PSR 2009, reg. 2(1).

[48] PSR 2009, reg. 2(1).   [49] Ibid., reg. 72(a).   [50] Ibid., reg. 72(b).   [51] Ch. 10, Sect. 2 below.

[52] PSR 2009, reg. 70(1). There are exceptions to this general position: ibid., regs. 70(2)–(4). See further Ch. 13, Sect. 5(iv) below.

[53] Ibid., reg. 70(5).   [54] Ibid., reg. 73(2). See further Ch. 13, Sect. 5(iv) below.

[55] Ibid., reg. 73(1).

[56] Financial Services Authority, *Banking: Conduct of Business Sourcebook* (BCOBS) 1.1.1.

before a customer can be bound by signalling his acceptance of any distance offer.[57] In addition, when opening a current account on behalf of a customer, a bank must satisfy BCOBS' 'appropriate information rule',[58] which requires the bank to make available to the prospective customer appropriate information about the account 'in good time', 'in an appropriate medium',[59] and 'in easily understandable language and in a clear and comprehensible form' so that the customer can make a decision about the account on an informed basis.[60] In determining how best to satisfy these requirements, the bank must have regard to the importance of the information to the customer's decision-making process and the time at which the information might be most useful to the customer.[61] In the context of opening a current account, the requirement that the information be provided 'in good time' means that the bank must supply the customer with the terms and conditions of the account contract before the customer becomes bound by them.[62] The type of information that must be supplied to the customer at that time should includes[63] information relating to: the bank; the different accounts that share similar features to the account about which the customer has inquired; the terms and conditions of the account contract; the interest rates applicable to any deposits and the intervals at which the interest is calculated and applied to the account; any charges payable by the customer in relation to the account; the redress available to the customer, including details of any compensation scheme;[64] any 'basic bank accounts' available;[65] and the timescales for the different stages of the cheque clearing process.[66] Furthermore, the bank must disclose to the customer his rights to terminate the account contract,[67] including the customer's right to cancel that contract within an initial 14-day period,[68] the duration of that initial right of cancellation, and the conditions for exercising it.[69] What the bank must do in order to comply with these information requirements may vary according to a number of factors, including the customer's actual or likely commitment (such as where the current account has an agreed overdraft facility); the information needs of a reasonable recipient having regard to the 'overall complexity, main benefits, risks, limitations, conditions and duration' of the account in question; whether the information is being provided by means of distance communication; and whether the information has already been supplied to the customer and when

---

[57] Ibid., 3.1.2, 3.1.8. The information must include certain details about the bank, the financial service or product that is being marketed, the contract that is being proposed and the redress available to the prospective customer: BCOBS 3, Annex 1. The 'distance marketing information' must be provided 'in a clear and comprehensible manner' (ibid., 3.1.3) and 'in a durable medium available and accessible' to the customer 'in good time' before the customer is bound by any distance offer (ibid., 3.1.6). Where the distance offer is made pursuant to an initial service contract, the 'distance marketing information' need only be provided in respect of the initial contract (ibid., 3.1.9). Where the prospective customer is contacted by telephone, the bank must explicitly identify itself and the purpose of the call at the outset (ibid., 3.1.4) and may initially provide the abbreviated 'distance marketing information' set out in BCOBS 3, Annex 2 (ibid., 3.1.11). When it is not possible to provide the 'distance marketing information' before the opening of the account because of the means of the communication requested by the customer, then the information can be provided once the account is open (ibid., 3.1.12). The customer has the right to request details of the contractual terms and conditions on paper at any time during the account relationship (ibid., 3.1.14). A bank is precluded from enforcing the obligations under any account contract that has not been requested by the customer (ibid., 3.1.15) and may not accept any attempt by the customer to waive the 'distance marketing disclosure rules' (ibid., 3.1.16). See further Ch. 2, Sects. 5(iv) & 7(vi) above & Ch. 14, Sect. 10 below.

[58] Ibid., 4.1.

[59] This should usually be on paper or 'in another durable medium' (BCOBS 4.1.2(2), 4.1.3), but where the information is given by electronic means the bank must satisfy the distance communication requirements (ibid., 3.1).

[60] BCOBS 4.1.1.   [61] Ibid., 4.1.2.   [62] Ibid., 4.1.2(2).   [63] Ibid., 4.1.4.
[64] Ch. 2, Sects. 4(viii)–(ix) above.   [65] Ch. 1, Sect. 2(iii) above.   [66] Ch. 10, Sect. 2 below.
[67] BCOBS 4.1.4(6).   [68] Ibid., 6.1.1., discussed further in Sect. 6 below.   [69] Ibid., 6.1.5.

that occurred.[70] The fact that a customer has the option of cancelling the account contract in the initial 14-day period, however, should not be a factor that the bank takes into account when determining what information to disclose to its customers.[71]

Broadly similar information requirements are imposed on banks when opening a current account for a customer by the PSR 2009, since most current accounts nowadays are likely to constitute a 'framework contract',[72] as they are normally used by a bank to provide its customers with 'payment services' (defined as including, *inter alia*, credit transfers and direct debits).[73] The information that must be disclosed in such circumstances is set out in detail in Schedule 4 of the PSR 2009 and (broadly) includes information relating to the bank, its contact details, and its regulator; the service being undertaken by the bank, including the means by which the customer must give any payment instruction and the maximum execution time for such instructions; the bank charges, interest charges, and exchange rates that might be employed in connection with the execution of a payment service; the manner of communication between the bank and its customers and any security measures applicable to 'payment services'; the duration of the account contract and the manner in which it may be terminated; and finally the redress available to the customer. This information must be disclosed to the customer[74] either 'in good time', before the customer is bound by the account contract, or, where the account contract is concluded by the payor using 'a means of distance communication', immediately after the conclusion of that contract.[75] The PSR 2009 also establish certain minimum standards concerning the manner in which any disclosure must take place—it must be made available in an easily accessible manner, in easily understandable language, in a clear and comprehensible form, and in English or some other agreed language.[76] Arguably, the most straightforward manner in which the bank can satisfy these various initial disclosure requirements is by sending the customer a copy of the draft account contract before the account is opened.[77]

Not only must the bank satisfy the above requirements on or before the opening of the current account, but it is also required to disclose the information initially required by the 'BPS Regime'[78] on a continuing basis.[79] Furthermore, the PSR 2009 impose certain information requirements that must be satisfied when actually *operating* the current account, namely whenever a customer requests the bank to provide a 'payment service' (such as making a credit transfer or making a payment by direct debit)[80] pursuant to the terms of

---

[70] Ibid., 4.1.5.   [71] Ibid., 4.1.6.

[72] PSR 2009, reg. 2(1): '…a contract for payment services which governs the future execution of individual and successive payment transactions and which may contain the obligation and conditions for setting up a payment account'.

[73] Ibid., Sched. 1, para. 1(c). A 'payment service' must also be provided from an establishment maintained by a bank or their agent in the United Kingdom; the payor's and payee's banks must be located within the European Economic Area (EEA); and the transfer must be carried out in Euros or the currency of an EEA State that has not adopted the single currency: ibid., regs. 33(1), 51(1). See further Ch. 14, Sect. 9 below.

[74] The requisite disclosure differs when the framework contract involves the use of a 'payment instrument' (such as a payment card) that can only be used to execute low-value transactions: PSR 2009, reg. 35. See further Ch. 14, Sect. 9 below.

[75] PSR 2009, reg. 40(1).

[76] Ibid, reg. 47(1). The requirement as to the form of disclosure is subject to the parties' contrary agreement: ibid., reg. 47(2).

[77] Ibid., reg. 40(2).   [78] Ch. 2, Sect. 6(iii) above.

[79] BCOBS 4.1.4 and PSR 2009, reg. 41, although the latter provision only applies if the customer specifically requests the information.

[80] PSR 2009, Sched. 1, para. 1(c). A 'payment service' must also be provided from an establishment maintained by a bank or their agent in the United Kingdom; the payor's and payee's banks must be located within the EEA; and the transfer must be carried out in Euros or the currency of an EEA State that has not adopted the single currency: ibid., regs. 33(1), 51(1). See further Ch. 13, Sect. 5 & Ch. 14, Sect. 9 below.

a 'framework contract' (in other words, the contract governing the operation of a current account).[81] Before executing a customer's payment instruction, a bank must inform the customer of the maximum execution time for the transaction, indicate the charges payable for the service, and provide a breakdown of the charges.[82] After debiting a customer's current account,[83] a bank must provide its customer with a reference number to identify the payment transaction and the payee; information about the amount of the payment transaction; information about the amount and breakdown of any charges (including any additional charges);[84] information concerning any exchange rate applied to the payment and the amount of that payment after the currency conversion;[85] and finally information about when the payment will be debited from the payor's account for the purposes of calculating account or overdraft interest.[86] As an alternative, this information can be provided to the customer by means of a periodic monthly statement.[87] The customer has the right, however, to request a hard copy of any information that his bank is required to disclose pursuant to the PSR 2009,[88] and is entitled not to be charged for any information provided, unless it is not required by the regulations or is provided more frequently than required.[89] There are also certain high-level 'conduct of business' principles contained in BCOBS that a bank must comply with when actually operating a current account, such as the need 'to pay due regard to the interests of its customers and treat them fairly',[90] 'to pay due regard to the information needs of its [customers] and communicate information to them in a way which is clear, fair and not misleading',[91] and to 'provide a service...which is prompt, efficient and fair to a banking customer'.[92] Although these principles apply to all of a bank's dealings with its customers, BCOBS makes clear that a bank must be particularly solicitous about complying with these principles when it has reason to believe that the customer in question is in financial difficulty.[93]

Whilst these information requirements and conduct of business rules will certainly go some way to redressing the inequality of information and economic power that is

---

[81] Ibid., reg. 2(1): '...a contract for payment services which governs the future execution of individual and successive payment transactions and which may contain the obligation and conditions for setting up a payment account'. Where a customer makes payment by means of a payment card that has been issued in connection with an account, a bank need only comply with the information requirements applicable to a 'single payment service contract' (ibid., reg. 2(1)) to the extent that these are not duplicated by the information already required to be provided under the 'framework contract' (ibid., reg. 2(1)): ibid, reg. 39. For the information requirements for 'single payment service contracts', see Ch. 13, Sects. 5(iv)–(vi) below. See further Ch. 14, Sect. 9 below.

[82] Ibid., reg. 44.

[83] Ibid., reg. 45(1)(a). If the payor does not use a payment account, disclosure must be made after the receipt of the payment instruction: ibid., reg. 45(1)(b).

[84] Ibid., reg. 50(1).   [85] Ibid., reg. 49(2).

[86] Ibid., reg. 45(2). Where the payment is received by a bank into its customer's account, (broadly) the same information requirements apply: ibid., reg. 46.

[87] Ibid., reg. 45(3). See further Sect. 3 below.   [88] Ibid., reg. 48(1).

[89] Ibid., reg. 48(2). Any charges imposed must reasonably correspond to the bank's actual costs: ibid., reg. 48(3).

[90] BCOBS 2.1.1.

[91] Id. BCOBS 2.2 contains 'the fair, clear and not misleading rule', which applies generally to a bank's communications with its customers and must be applied in a way that is 'appropriate and proportionate taking into account the means of communication and the information that it is intended to convey'. There are also detailed provisions concerning the content and form of bank communications generally (ibid., 2.3) and distance communications in particular (ibid., 3.1).

[92] Ibid., 5.1.1. The obligation to treat customers fairly extends to determining the order in which to process payment instructions: ibid., 5.1.2.

[93] Ibid., 5.1.4.

inherent in the banking relationship,[94] it remains possible for banks to impose terms as part of the current account relationship that operate to the detriment of their customers. Three such clauses that are frequently incorporated into contracts governing the operation of current accounts are clauses that impose charges for unauthorized overdrafts;[95] 'verification clauses' that require a customer to verify the accuracy of any bank statement and to dispute any unauthorized entries;[96] and 'unilateral variation clauses' that permit the bank to alter the terms of the current account contract at will or upon giving a certain period of notice. Such clauses may be subject to various common law controls, three of which have received specific attention in the context of the current account contract.[97] First, any ambiguity in a term of the current account contract will be construed against the bank that is relying upon that term.[98] This principle has proved particularly useful in limiting the impact of 'verification clauses', and the Privy Council has stressed on several occasions that the courts should be particularly demanding when applying the *contra proferentem* principle in this particular context.[99] Secondly, a court may imply limits upon the manner in which a bank can exercise particular powers conferred by the account contract. In the case of 'unilateral variation clauses', for example, a particular exercise of the power to vary the account contract may be invalid if 'exercised dishonestly, for an improper purpose, capriciously, or arbitrarily',[100] or in an unreasonable manner.[101] Thirdly, it may be possible to strike out clauses in the current account contract on the ground that they constitute a penalty, although the limits of that jurisdiction were recently highlighted in the current account context in *Office of Fair Trading* v. *Abbey National plc*,[102] where Peter Smith J held that charges imposed by the major UK banks upon their customers in respect of unauthorized overdraft facilities on current accounts did not constitute penalties.[103] Alternatively, it may be possible to invalidate these three types of account term by reference to the Unfair Contract Terms Act 1977 (UCTA 1977) or the Unfair Terms in Consumer Contracts Regulations 1999 (UTCCR 1999).[104]

---

[94] *Banking Services: Law and Practice*, Report by the Review Committee Chaired by Professor R.B. Jack CBE (1989, London, Cm. 622), [4.04], [6.23] & [16.10]–[16.12].

[95] Ch. 17, Sect. 2(ii) below.   [96] Sect. 3(iii) below.

[97] There is one common law control in particular that is discussed in more detail elsewhere (Ch. 11, Sect. 1(i)), namely that the clause in question should be properly incorporated into the account contract in order to be effective: *Burnett* v. *Westminster Bank Ltd* [1966] 1 QB 742. For the application of this principle to 'verification clauses', see Sect. 3(iii) below.

[98] E. Peel, *Treitel's Law of Contract* (12th edn., London, 2007), [7–015].

[99] *Tai Hing Cotton Mill Ltd* v. *Liu Chong Hing Bank Ltd* [1986] AC 80, 110 (PC); *Financial Institutions Services Ltd* v. *Negril Negril Holdings Ltd* [2004] UKPC 40, [43]; *Morrell* v. *Workers Savings & Loan Bank* [2007] UKPC 3, [33] ('...the rigorous standard of clarity and unambiguity necessary for a valid conclusive evidence clause').

[100] *Paragon Finance plc* v. *Staunton* [2002] 1 WLR 685, [36] (CA); but compare *Sterling Credit Ltd* v. *Rahman* [2002] EWHC 3008 (Ch.). See further Ch. 17, Sect. 3(ii) below. See also *Lymington Marina Ltd* v. *Macnamara* [2007] EWCA Civ 151, [39]–[41], [44]–[45], [67]–[69]; *Socimer International Bank Ltd* v. *Standard Bank London Ltd* [2008] 1 Lloyd's Rep. 558, [66] (CA); *Office of Fair Trading* v. *Abbey National plc*, n.15 above, [79].

[101] Ibid., [37]–[42].

[102] N.15 above, (Comm), [295]–[324]; [2008] EWHC 2325 (Comm), [16]–[22]. For the declarations relating to the penalty jurisdiction, see *Office of Fair Trading* v. *Abbey National plc* [2009] EWHC 36 (Comm). There was no appeal against the conclusions relating to the penalty jurisdiction: *Office of Fair Trading* v. *Abbey National plc* [2009] EWCA Civ 116, [11]; [2010] 1 All ER 667, [114] (UKSC). See also *Lansat Shipping Co.* v. *Glencore Grain BV* [2009] EWHC 551 (Comm), [17]–[19].

[103] Ch. 17, Sect. 2(ii) below.   [104] S.I. 1999/2083.

Whilst there may be some difficulty in bringing 'unilateral variation clauses'[105] and clauses imposing unauthorized overdraft charges on customers within the scope of UCTA 1977,[106] there should be no similar problem bringing 'verification clauses' within the scope of UCTA 1977,[107] or indeed in bringing 'verification clauses' and 'unilateral variation clauses' within the scope of the UTCCR 1999.[108]

Given the potential for abuse of 'unilateral variation clauses' by banks, however, such clauses have been subjected to specific controls above and beyond the general common law and statutory controls just considered. Provided the account contract constitutes a 'framework contract',[109] the PSR 2009 expressly recognizes a bank's right to insert a 'unilateral variation clause' into its account contracts,[110] subject to the customer's right to object to any changes made to the contract pursuant to such a clause before they actually take effect.[111] For a 'unilateral variation clause' to be effective, a bank must inform its customer that he will be deemed to have accepted any unilateral changes made to the account contract and that the customer has a right to terminate the contract before any changes pursuant to that clause take effect.[112] Moreover, there are certain notice requirements that a bank must comply with before exercising its right to vary an account contract unilaterally. In the case of changes to the interest or exchange rates that are applicable to an account, a bank may apply the rates immediately and without notice if they are more favourable to the customer, or if the bank has reserved such a right and has provided reference material about rates to the customer beforehand.[113] When such a rate change is made, however, the bank must notify the customer as soon as possible afterwards, unless the contract stipulates a different position.[114] With respect to any other changes, those besides interest and exchange rate changes mentioned above, a bank must give its customer at least two months' notice before they are intended to take effect.[115] Although somewhat less specific in terms of detail, BCOBS adopts a similar position with respect to changes to the current account contract: where the variation is to the disadvantage of the customer, the bank should give the customer 'reasonable notice' before the change takes effect.[116] In determining the reasonableness of the notice, a court will take into account the amount of notice that a customer must give in order to close the account,[117] and presumably will also have regard to the more precise notice periods contained in the PSR

---

[105] *Paragon Finance plc* v. *Staunton*, n.100 above, [71]–[77], where Dyson LJ held that the unilateral variation clause in that case did not fall within the Unfair Contract Terms Act 1977 (UCTA 1977), s.3(2)(b)(i).

[106] Implicit support for this may be derived from the absence of any argument relating to UCTA 1977 in *Office of Fair Trading* v. *Abbey National plc*, n.15 above; [2008] EWHC 2325 (Comm).

[107] 'Verification clauses' would potentially fall within UCTA 1977, s.13(1)(c): Sect. 3(iii) below.

[108] As a 'verification clause' arguably 'unduly [restricts] the evidence available', it would be presumptively unfair within the Unfair Terms in Consumer Contracts Regulations 1999, S.I. 1999/2083 (UTCCR 1999), Sched. 2, para. 1(q): Sect. 3(iii) below. Arguably, a 'unilateral variation clause' might be similarly treated (ibid., Sched. 2, para. 1(j)–(k)), but this provision has a more limited scope in the banking context (ibid., Sched. 2, para. 2(b)). A clause permitting a bank to impose charges in respect of an unauthorized overdraft facility will not fall within the scope of the UTCCR 1999: *Office of Fair Trading* v. *Abbey National plc* [2010] 1 All ER 667 (UKSC). See further Ch. 17, Sect. 2(ii) below.

[109] PSR 2009, reg. 2(1): '... a contract for payment services which governs the future execution of individual and successive payment transactions and which may contain the obligation and conditions for setting up a payment account'.

[110] Ibid., reg. 42(2).   [111] Id.   [112] Ibid., reg. 42(3).

[113] Ibid., reg. 42(4). Any interest or exchange rate changes must also be calculated and applied 'in a neutral manner that does not discriminate' against the customer: ibid., reg. 42(6).

[114] Ibid., reg. 42(5).   [115] Ibid., reg. 42(1).   [116] BCOBS 4.1.2(3).   [117] Id.

2009 when these also apply.[118] Moreover, as discussed previously,[119] a bank may need to satisfy the additional notice requirements in section 82 of the Consumer Credit Act 1974, where it seeks to modify the terms on which a current account overdraft is extended.[120]

3 The statement of account

(i) The nature of the problem

The initial practice was to provide the customer with a pass-book in which the bank recorded from time to time all the transactions concerning the account. To enable the bank to effect these entries, the customer occasionally left his pass-book with the bank for a few days. During the last 50 years pass-books have ceased to be used for current accounts and have been replaced by periodic statements. Banks are nowadays obliged to provide paper-based bank statements by BCOBS,[121] unless the account is covered by a pass-book, the account is operated electronically, the customer declines to receive such statements, or the bank has reasonable grounds to believe that the customer is no longer resident at their address.[122] As banks encourage customers to dispense with paper statements in favour of simply checking accounts online, paper-based current account statements will soon become as unusual as pass-books. It is obvious, however, that both pass-books and periodic statements (whether paper-based or electronic) may contain inaccuracies, resulting from errors in arithmetic or from wrong entries. The question arises whether the pass-book or the periodic statement can be used as evidence either against a customer who disputes an entry, or against the bank that wishes to rectify errors made to its disadvantage. By and large, the courts have tended to treat the pass-book and the periodic statement on one and the same basis (and presumably electronic records of the account would be treated in a similar fashion). There are, however, distinctions between a customer's right to dispute the entries in the account statement or pass-book and a bank's right to rectify errors that it has made.

(ii) The bank's right to rectify errors

A person who pays another money without any reason for that payment usually acts under a mistake. The payor, accordingly, is entitled to recover the amount involved by bringing

---

[118] In assessing 'reasonableness' for these purposes, one might also have regard to the terms of the voluntary codes that BCOBS replaced in part from 1 November 2009. According to the *Banking Code* (March 2008), para. [6.4], a bank was required to provide a customer with at least 30 days' notice of any proposed change to the terms of the account contract that operated to the customer's disadvantage, and was required to allow the customer up to 60 days from the date of the notice to switch account or close it, without incurring additional charges or interest and without having to give notice to the bank. Where the change did not operate to the customer's disadvantage, the bank could make the change immediately, but was required to inform the customer of the changes within 30 days of their taking effect: ibid., [6.5]. The *Business Banking Code* (March 2008), [6.4]–[6.5] was to similar effect. Since 1 November 2009, this same position has been reflected in the *Lending Code* (November 2009), [134]–[136] and the *Lending Code* (March 2011), [175]–[177].

[119] Ch. 2, Sect. 5(iv) above.

[120] Consumer Credit (Notice of Variation of Agreements) Regulations 1977, S.I. 1977/328 (as amended).

[121] BCOBS 4.2.1(1). The bank may not generally charge for providing account statements: ibid., 4.2.1(2).

[122] See, for example, *Boltrun Investments Inc.* v. *Bank of Montreal* (1998) 86 OTC 211, [51] (OCJ) ('There is a duty on the bank to render accounts to a customer periodically'). See also M.H. Ogilvie, 'Banker and Customer: The Five-Year Review 2000–2005' (2007) 23 *BFLR* 107, 138, referring to the 'common law duty of rendering accounts to the customer periodically or on request'.

a restitutionary claim, or by applying for a declaration that the amount involved was not due.[123] The procedure differs where a bank makes an error of the type under discussion here. In such a case, the bank credits the customer's account with the wrong amount or with a sum not due to him. When the bank discovers the mistake, it reverses the credit entry. If the customer disputes the bank's right to do so, he has to institute proceedings. Two pleas are open to him. The first is that the bank is estopped from disputing the correctness of the balance shown in the pass-book or periodic statement. The other is based on a claim that the stated balance constitutes an 'account settled' or an 'account stated'. This last plea is also relevant in respect of corrections demanded by the customer.

The success of the plea of estoppel depends on the effect that the wrongful payment has had on the customer's position. If the customer has changed his position to his detriment, the bank may find itself precluded from reversing the credit entry. This is the current position, although the early decision of the Court of Chancery in *Clayton's Case*[124] suggests that a customer can be expected to examine the entries in his pass-book and to return it for correction where an error is discovered. As considered below, however, *Clayton's Case* appears at odds with more recent authority on this point.[125] *Skyring* v. *Greenwood and Cox*[126] shows that estoppel can be invoked where an error has lulled the customer into a false belief about his financial position. In that case, the paymaster of a military corps credited an officer's account with money to which he was not entitled. The erroneous credits stretched over a period of five years, and the officer, who was unaware of the mistake, drew the money out regularly. When the paymaster discovered his error he continued to pay the officer's wages, failing to inform him of the need to rectify the position. When the officer died, the paymaster purported to set off the amounts so overpaid against the balance standing to the credit of the officer's account. The estate's action, disputing the right of the paymaster to effect such a set-off, was successful. It was held that the erroneous entries constituted representations to the effect that the amounts involved had been received for the officer's credit. As the officer had changed his position in reliance on the statements by spending more money than he would have otherwise done, the paymaster lost his right to reclaim the amounts credited. Abbott CJ observed:[127]

> It is of great importance to any man, and certainly not less to military men than others, that they should not be led to suppose that their annual income is greater than it really is. Every prudent man accommodates his mode of living to what he supposes to be his income; it therefore works a great prejudice to any man, if after having had credit given him in account for certain sums, and having been allowed to draw on his agent on the faith that these sums belonged to him, he may be called upon to pay them back.

Similarly, in *Holland* v. *Manchester and Liverpool District Banking Co.*,[128] the customer's pass-book showed a credit balance of £70 instead of the true amount of £60. In reliance on this entry, the customer drew a cheque for £67, which was dishonoured when presented. The customer's action in breach of contract succeeded. Lord Alverstone CJ held that the

---

[123] See generally Ch. 12 below.

[124] *Devaynes* v. *Noble (Clayton's Case)* (1816) 1 Mer. 529, 535–536. See also *Bank of Toronto* v. *Hamilton* (1896) 28 OR 51 (HCJ). See, generally, J.M. Holden, 'Bank Pass Books and Statements' (1954) 17 *MLR* 41.

[125] See, in particular, *Tai Hing Cotton Mill Ltd* v. *Liu Chong Hing Bank Ltd*, n.99 above.

[126] (1825) 4 B & C 281. See also *Holt* v. *Markham* [1923] 1 KB 504; *Lloyds Bank Ltd* v. *Brooks* (1950) 6 LDAB 161; *United Overseas Bank* v. *Jiwani* [1976] 1 WLR 964, 968; *Hollidge* v. *Bank of New Zealand* (NZHC, 29 March 1982); *Bank of Montreal* v. *Norman* (OSC, 15 September 1999).

[127] Ibid., 289.

[128] (1909) 14 Com. Cas. 241. See also *Equitable Eastern Banking Corporation* v. *Choa Po Sien* [1931] HKCU 7.

bank was entitled to debit the customer's account with the amount erroneously credited, but did not have the right to dishonour cheques drawn for sums within the balance conveyed to the customer 'until, at any rate, they [gave] him some notice'.[129]

The bank is always entitled to rectify the error within a reasonable time.[130] Furthermore, the customer can plead the estoppel in question only if he was misled, or had reason to be misled, by the erroneous balance. This principle was established in *British and North European Bank Ltd* v. *Zalzstein*,[131] where the customer did not discover the wrong credit entry made in his favour until it had been reversed. It was, accordingly, held that he could not dispute the respective debit entries. At present, the principle is best illustrated by *United Overseas Bank* v. *Jiwani*.[132] A bank erroneously credited its customer's account twice with the amount of a single remittance. The amount involved was substantial, and the customer was not expecting any payment additional to the one genuinely received for the credit of his account. Despite this, he drew on the balance accrued as a result of this windfall, and thereafter disputed the bank's right to reverse the undue credit entry. It was held that the customer ought to have known that the unduly high balance shown in his account was incorrect. He was not expecting any additional payment of a substantial amount to the credit of his account, and he was not entitled to shut his eyes to facts staring him in the face. *A fortiori*, the bank is entitled to rectify an error in the account records if the error is induced by the customer.[133]

(iii) **The customer's right to demand corrections**

In certain cases, the customer, rather than the bank, is interested in having the wrong entry corrected. Thus, the customer's account may have been credited with an amount smaller than that of an item payable to him or debited with an amount larger than that for which he drew a cheque. In the majority of cases, this occurs where the amount of the customer's cheque has been fraudulently raised. The customer's position in such situations is governed by the decisions discussed subsequently. In other cases, such an error in the account entries will usually arise through a computer fault.

In most cases in which the customer demands the correction of an incorrect account entry, the bank is prepared to accede to his wishes. First, the bank's reputation is at stake. If customers cannot trust their banks, they are unlikely to deposit the bulk of their liquid assets with them. Secondly, unless the amount involved is substantial, the bank will usually prefer to shoulder the loss rather than to get involved in litigation. There are, however, cases in which the amount involved is large, or in which the error is notified to the bank after the lapse of a substantial time. In addition, there are cases in which the bank suspects collusion between the customer and the payee of the erroneously debited amount. In such situations, litigation will usually ensue. One of the questions then arising is whether the customer is entitled to demand rectification of entries in his account after the lapse of a reasonable time from the date of receiving the

---

[129] Ibid., 245.

[130] *Commercial Bank of Scotland* v. *Rhind* (1860) 3 Macq. HL 643 (HL); *British and North European Bank Ltd* v. *Zalzstein* [1927] 2 KB 92.

[131] N.130 above, approved in *Simonovski* v. *Bendigo Bank Ltd* [2005] VSCA 125, [51]. See also, in Canada, *Collins* v. *Dominion Bank* (1915) 8 OWN 432; *Imperial Bank* v. *Kean* (1916) 10 OWN 80; *Hudson* v. *Royal Bank of Canada* (1920) 19 OWN 93; *Canadian Imperial Bank of Commerce* v. *Lowenberg* [2003] SKQB, [40].

[132] N.126 above. It has been held that the withdrawal of the funds by a customer does not constitute 'stealing' within the meaning of the Criminal Code (Tas.) s.234, even if the customer is aware of those funds having been credited to his account in error: *Marshall* v. *Szommer* [1989] Aust. Crim. R 198.

[133] *Saskatchewan and Western Elevator* v. *Bank of Hamilton* (1914) 18 DLR 411.

bank statement or the date of the pass-book entry. The basic answer in English law is that, in the absence of fraud, the customer is not precluded by the bank statement or the pass-book from disputing an error or an incorrect debit made by the bank or from insisting upon its correction.

The principle involved is based on the construction of the banker-customer contract. It has been held that this contract does not place the customer under a duty to peruse his account statement or the entries in a pass-book.[134] Even though he returns his pass-book or the counterfoil of his statement to the bank without referring to the error, he is able to dispute the entry subsequently.[135] This principle, assailed in an action brought before the Supreme Court of Hong Kong, was affirmed in 1985 by the Privy Council in *Tai Hing Cotton Mill Ltd* v. *Liu Chong Hing Bank Ltd.*[136] Over a number of years, a clerk, who had the custody of his employers' cheque-books, forged the general manager's signature on a substantial number of cheques, all of which were paid by the three banks with which the firm had its current accounts. As the firm did not maintain any regular audits, the clerk's defalcations remained undetected for a long time. Finding that the firm's system of internal accounts was deficient and had facilitated the fraud, Mantell J gave judgment for the bank. His decision was affirmed by the Hong Kong Court of Appeal, which held that the firm had been in breach of a duty of care owed to the bank both in contract and tort. The Privy Council reversed the Hong Kong Court of Appeal. As regards the claim in contract, Lord Scarman held that, in the absence of express agreement to the contrary, the risk of wrongful payments was borne by each of the three banks. Banks 'offer a service, which is to honour their customer's cheques when drawn upon an account in credit or within an agreed overdraft limit. If they pay out upon cheques which are not [the customer's], they are acting outside their mandate and cannot plead his authority in justification of their debit to his account. The risk is a risk of service which it is their business to offer.'[137] His Lordship emphasized that the customer's duty to refrain from facilitating a fraud applied only as regards the drawing of his cheques.[138] The customer was not under a wider duty to adhere to business practices aimed at combatting the perpetration of fraud, or a narrower

---

[134] *Lewes Sanitary Steam Laundry Co. Ltd* v. *Barclay & Co. Ltd* (1906) 95 LT 444; *Kepitigalla Rubber Estates Ltd* v. *National Bank of India Ltd* [1909] 2 KB 1010, 1027–1029; *Walker* v. *Manchester and Liverpool District Banking Co. Ltd* (1913) 108 LT 728; *Lloyds Bank Ltd* v. *Brooks*, n.126 above; *Brewer* v. *Westminster Bank Ltd* [1952] 2 All ER 650, 656; *Wealdon Woodlands (Kent) Ltd* v. *National Westminster Bank Ltd* (1983) 133 NLJ 719; *Royal Bank of Scotland plc* v. *Fielding* [2003] EWHC 986 (Ch.), affd., [2004] EWCA Civ. 64. See also *National Australia Bank Ltd* v. *Hokit Pty. Ltd* [1997] 6 Bank. LR 177 (NSWCA).

[135] *Kepitigalla Rubber Estates Ltd* v. *National Bank of India Ltd*, n.134 above.

[136] N.99 above, reversing [1984] 1 Lloyd's Rep. 555. Applied in *Yorkshire Bank plc* v. *Lloyds Bank plc* [1999] Lloyd's Rep. Bank. 191, where HHJ Pitchers applied *Tai Hing* and held that the holder of a cheque was under no duty to the paying bank to manage its affairs so as not to lose the cheque or allow it to be stolen. This applied even if the holder was itself a bank. See also *Price Meats Ltd* v. *Barclays Bank plc* [2000] 2 All ER (Comm.) 346.

[137] Ibid., 106.

[138] Ch. 11, Sect. 3(ii) below. Whilst it remains true, on the basis of *Tai Hing*, that a customer only bears the loss of facilitating a fraud when this results from his negligent drawing of a cheque, but not when this results from other types of dealing with a cheque, statutory developments have resulted in a potentially greater risk of liability for customers who pay by card or electronic funds transfers: Ch. 13, Sect. 5(iv) below & Ch. 14, Sects. 8(ii) & 9(ii) below. In particular, PSR 2009, reg. 62(2)(a) makes a payor liable for all losses resulting from his fraud, which presumably could include the fraud of employees and agents that is properly attributable to the payor. Furthermore, PSR 2009, reg. 57(2) imposes on customers an obligation to 'take all reasonable steps to keep [safe the] personalised safety features' of a payment card or device for making electronic funds transfers. The extent of the customer's liability depends upon whether he acted negligently, with gross negligence, or intentionally in failing to safeguard the personalised safety features associated with his payment cards or with the mechanisms for making electronic funds transfers.

duty to check periodic bank statements.[139] Referring to the claim in tort, Lord Scarman said:[140] '[t]heir Lordships do not believe that there is anything to the advantage of the law's development in searching for a liability in tort where the parties are in a contractual relationship. This is particularly so in commercial relationships.'

In *Henderson* v. *Merrett Syndicates Ltd*,[141] the House of Lords held that English law does not prevent a claimant from suing in contract and in tort where the substantive rights support such 'concurrence' of claims, especially if the claimant's motive is to take advantage of the practical differences that exist between contractual and tortious claims. It was held that Names at Lloyd's might sue members' agents (with whom they had a contract) for negligence, as well as for breach of contract, in the management of underwriting business, so as to gain the advantage of the longer limitation period under the Latent Damage Act 1986. Following *Henderson* v. *Merrett Syndicates*, it is clear that Lord Scarman was mistaken in *Tai Hing*,[142] when he said that there was no advantage in searching for liability in tort where the parties are already in a contractual relationship. As well as different limitation periods, there are other practical differences between contract and tort claims including, for example, the measure of recovery (rules about remoteness of damage in tort are less restrictive than those in contract),[143] the relevance of the claimant's contributory negligence (it is generally irrelevant in contract, but relevant in tort), and assignability, since only a contractual claim can generally be assigned.[144] Where there is a contract between the parties there is no reason in principle why, in particular circumstances, a tortious duty of care could not impose wider obligations than those arising under the contract.[145] However, a court will not impose a duty of care in tort (imposed by the general law) that is *inconsistent* with the terms of the contract (representing the common intention of the parties),[146] including where no implied term can be established to the same effect as the proposed tortious duty. *Tai Hing* can be justified as an example of this principle.

It follows that, by rejecting the arguments raised by the banks in *Tai Hing* both as regards liability in contract and in tort, the Privy Council has reaffirmed the principle in earlier cases placing the risk of the payment of forged cheques on the bank. Accordingly, an employer is not to be made responsible for agents or employees who forge cheques, even though the employer is probably in the best position to control fraud within his own

---

[139] *Duncan* v. *American Express Services Europe Ltd* [2009] SLT 112, [22].

[140] *Tai Hing Cotton Mill Ltd* v. *Liu Chong Hing Bank Ltd*, n.99 above, 107. See also *National Bank of Greece SA* v. *Pinios Shipping Co. (No. 1)* [1988] 2 Lloyd's Rep. 126; *Greater Nottingham Co-operative Society Ltd* v. *Cementation Pilings & Foundations Ltd* [1989] QB 71.

[141] [1995] 2 AC 145 (HL). For cases applying *Henderson*, see Ch. 5, Sect. 4(iii), n.307 above.

[142] For judicial recognition that *Tai Hing* is out of line with current thinking about concurrent liability, see *Tesco Stores Ltd* v. *Costain Construction Ltd* [2003] EWHC 1487 (TCC), [212]–[217]; *Riyad Bank* v. *Ahli United Bank (UK) plc* [2006] EWCA Civ 780, [41]–[43]; *Biffa Waste Services Ltd* v. *Maschinenfabrik Ernst Hese GmbH* [2008] EWHC 6 (TCC), [173]; *Galliford Try Infrastructure Ltd* v. *Mott MacDonald Ltd* [2008] EWHC 1570 (TCC), [189]; *Shah* v. *HSBC Private Bank (UK) Ltd* [2009] EWHC 79 (QB), [56]–[57], affd. [2010] EWCA Civ. 31.

[143] *Transfield Shipping Inc of Panama* v. *Mercator Shipping Inc of Monrovia (The Achilleas)* [2009] AC 61 (HL), [31], [52], [93]. Consider *Sunny Metal and Engineering Pty Ltd* v. *Ng Khim Ming Eric* [2007] 1 SLR 853, [140], revsd. [2007] 3 SLR 782, [59] (SGCA).

[144] E. Peel, n.98 above, [15–09].

[145] *Holt* v. *Payne Skillington and De Groot Collis* (1995) 77 BLR 51, 73 (CA), applied in *Sumitomo Bank Ltd* v. *Banque Bruxelles Lambert SA* [1997] 1 Lloyd's Rep. 487, 513; *Weldon* v. *GRE Linked Life Ass. Ltd* [2000] 2 All ER (Comm.) 914, [63]; *Frost & Sutcliffe* v. *Tuiara* [2004] 1 NZLR 782, [22] (NZCA).

[146] Ch. 5, Sect. 4(iii), n.310 above. Courts will ordinarily refuse to 'short-circuit' contractual relations by recognizing a duty of care between remote parties, but this is not an absolute rule: Ch. 5, Sect. 4(iii), n.312 above.

organization and may well carry fidelity insurance to cover any losses.[147] Nevertheless, two arguments may remain open to the bank. The first argument is that the bank might be entitled to rely on the customer's contributory negligence in order to reduce the share of the losses resulting from the fraud that it must bear. This argument is unlikely to convince a court, however, as contributory negligence cannot usually be raised as a defence to breach of a strict contractual duty[148] (such as the bank's duty to obey its customers' mandate), and this defence has in fact been specifically rejected in this context by the New Zealand Court of Appeal in *National Bank of New Zealand Ltd* v. *Walpole and Patterson Ltd*.[149] As considered further below, the Law Commission has adopted the same stance. The second argument is stronger, namely that the customer, as employer, should be held vicariously liable for the fraud of his agent or employee.[150] The defence was pleaded, but not pursued in *Tai Hing*. It gains support from dicta of Richmond J in *Walpole and Patterson Ltd*,[151] and the dissenting judgments of La Forest and McLachlin JJ in *Boma Manufacturing Ltd* v. *Canadian Imperial Bank of Commerce*.[152] It does not matter for these purposes that the agent or employee is acting in furtherance of his own interests and not those of the employer, so long as he is acting within the scope of his actual or apparent authority or in the course of his employment, which, in the case of intentional wrongdoing, is determined by examining the closeness of connection between the wrongdoing on the one hand and the agency or employment relationship on the other.[153]

---

[147] *Tai Hing* has also been followed in New Zealand (*National Bank of New Zealand Ltd* v. *Walpole and Patterson Ltd* [1975] 2 NZLR 7 (NZCA); *ASB Securities Ltd* v. *Geurts* [2005] 1 NZLR 484, [36]–[40]), India (*Canara Bank* v. *Canara Sales Corp.* [1988] LRC (Comm.) 5 (ISC)), Australia (*National Australia Bank Ltd* v. *Hokit Pty. Ltd*, n.134 above; *Fried* v. *National Australia Bank Ltd* [2001] FCA 907), and Malaysia (*UAB Bhd* v. *Tai Soon Heng Construction Sdn Bhd* [1993] 1 MLJ 182, 192–194 (MSC); *Proven Development Sdn Bhd* v. *HongKong and Shanghai Banking Corporation* [1998] 6 MLJ 150, 156–157; *OCBC Bank* v. *Omega Horizon Sdn Bhd* [2005] 1 MLJ 183, [21]–[24]; *Melewar Apex Sdn Bhd* v. *Malayan Banking Bhd* [2007] 3 MLJ 687, [16]–[18]). The position is similar in Canada: *Canadian Pacific Hotels Ltd* v. *Bank of Montreal* [1987] 1 SCR 711, 773–778 (SCC), departing from Laskin J in *Arrow Transfer Co.* v. *Royal Bank of Canada* [1972] SCR 845, 873 (SCC). See also, for example, *Ambico Ltd* v. *Loeb Inc.* (1993) 63 OAC 249, [9]–[11] (OCA); *Newell* v. *Royal Bank of Canada* (1996) 151 NSR (2d) 186, [35] (NSSC); *Don Bodkin Leasing Ltd* v. *Toronto-Dominion Bank* (1998) 40 OR (3d) 262, 269 (OCA); *Boltrun Investments Inc.* v. *Bank of Montreal*, n.122 above, [51] (OCJ); *Nesbitt Burns Inc.* v. *Canada Trustco Mortgage* (2000) 131 OAC 85, [23]–[28] (OCA); *Exceptional Resources Inc.* v. *Alberta Treasury Branches* (2001) 298 AR 187, [19]; *Royal Bank of Canada* v. *Société Générale* [2005] OJ No. 4950, [76]–[78] (OSC), [2006] OJ No. 749, [25] (OSC). See further *Boma Manufacturing Ltd* v. *Canadian Imperial Bank of Commerce* (1996) 140 DLR (4th) 463 (SCC) (but note the dissenting judgments of La Forest and McLachlin JJ (especially at 495–496)); *373409 Alberta Ltd* v. *Bank of Montreal* [2002] 4 SCR 312 (SCC). In Singapore, there has been a conflict of authority between *Consmat Singapore (Pte.) Ltd* v. *Bank of America National Trust & Savings Association* [1992] 2 SLR 828, 831 (SGHC), rejecting any extension of customers' duties, and *Khoo Tian Hock* v. *Oversea-Chinese Banking Corporation Ltd* [2000] 4 SLR 673, 720 (SGHC), suggesting that the banker–customer contract contains an implied term that a customer is under a general duty not to facilitate fraud by his negligence, quite apart from the drawing of cheques. In *Pertamina Energy Trading Ltd* v. *Crédit Suisse* [2006] 4 SLR 273, [51]–[54] (SGCA), the Singapore Court of Appeal formally declined to resolve this conflict, but did indicate that 'reconsideration of [*Tai Hing*] is unnecessary and perhaps even undesirable' and that 'a court should be slow to intervene and imply a term in a [banking] contract as a matter of law'.

[148] E. Peel, n.98 above, [20-108]–[20-110].

[149] N.147 above, 19.

[150] For the suggestion that similar principles are applicable in cases of vicarious liability and attribution in the agency context, see *Dubai Aluminium Co. Ltd* v. *Salaam* [2003] 2 AC 366, [21]–[26] (HL); *Dollars & Sense Ltd* v. *Nathan* [2008] 2 NZLR 557, [37] (NZSC).

[151] N.147 above, 14.   [152] N.147 above, 499.

[153] See, for example, *Lloyd* v. *Grace, Smith & Co.* [1912] AC 716 (HL); *Bazley* v. *Curry* (1999) 174 DLR (4th) 45 (SCC); *Jacobi* v. *Griffiths* (1999) 174 DLR (4th) 71 (SCC); *Crédit Lyonnais Bank Nederland NV* v. *Export Credit Guarantee Department* [2000] 1 AC 486 (HL); *Lister* v. *Hesley Hall Ltd* [2001] IRLR 472 (HL);

It is, perhaps, regrettable that, in reaching its conclusion, the Privy Council gave no consideration to certain well-known arguments criticizing the principle applied in that case on the ground that both common sense and good business practice require the bank's customer to verify the entries made in his account.[154] If such a perusal is not required, what is the object of the bank dispatching a statement or making detailed entries in a pass-book? If the object is merely to inform the customer of the amount standing to the credit of his account, it would be sufficient to provide him periodically with a bare statement of his balance. It may be retorted that such a statement would be meaningless, as it would not acquaint the customer with the cashflow immediately preceding the date on which the balance is struck. In other words, such a bare statement would not inform the customer which of the cheques drawn by him had been presented and paid, and which of the items payable to him had been honoured by the drawee. This reply, however, presupposes that the customer is interested in this further information. If this is so, then surely the customer can be expected to peruse the statement submitted to him with a view to detecting errors or shortfalls![155]

The Uniform Commercial Code has, indeed, taken this view. Under section 4-406, 'the customer must exercise reasonable promptness in examining the statement or the items to determine whether any payment was not authorized because of an alteration of an item or because a purported signature by or on behalf of the customer was not authorized. If, based on the statement or items provided, the customer should reasonably have discovered the unauthorized payment, the customer must promptly notify the bank of the relevant facts.' This provision imposes on the customer a duty to peruse the account statements sent to him by the bank and to notify the bank of errors. It was a duty recognized under the common law of a number of State jurisdictions prior to the promulgation of the Code.[156] Under section 4–406, if the customer fails to comply with this duty and the bank suffers loss as a result, he is precluded from disputing the regularity of the payments made. This estoppel does not apply, however, if the customer establishes lack of 'ordinary care' on the bank's part. Even in such a case, however, the customer's right to dispute payment becomes barred after the lapse of one year from the time when the statement or items are made available to him.[157]

A similar provision is unlikely to be enacted in the United Kingdom.[158] This is largely due to the difference between the banking practice in this country and in the United States.[159] In the United States, when the bank sends a statement to the customer, it attaches to it all items drawn by him and debited to his account. The verification by the customer

---

Dubai Aluminium Co Ltd v. *Salaam*, n.150 above, [39], [114]; *Bernard* v. *Attorney-General of Jamaica* [2005] IRLR 398, [18]–[19], [23] (PC); *EB* v. *Order of the Oblates of Mary Immaculate in the Province of British Columbia* [2005] 3 SCR 45 (SCC); *Strother* v. *3464920 Canada Inc.* [2007] 2 SCR 177 (SCC); *Dollars & Sense Ltd* v. *Nathan*, n.150 above, [35]–[41], [48]; *Gravil* v. *Carroll* [2008] EWCA Civ 689, [11]–[22]; *Brink's Global Services Inc* v. *Igrox Ltd* [2010] EWCA Civ 1207, [15]–[26]; *Quinn v. CC Automotive Group Ltd* [2010] EWCA Civ 1412, [17]–[23]. See further Ch. 11, Sect. 3(ii) below.

[154] F. Pollock, (1910) 26 *LQR* 4; J.M. Holden, n.124 above; Lord Chorley, *Gilbart Lectures* (London, 1954); cf. more recently, the powerful minority judgment of Laskin J in *Arrow Transfer Co. Ltd* v. *Royal Bank of Canada* (1972) 27 DLR (3d.) 81, 97–103 (SCC); the dicta of Monnin JA in *No. 10 Management* v. *Royal Bank* (1976) 69 DLR (3d.) 99, 103–104; and the dissenting judgments of La Forest and McLachlin JJ in *Boma Manufacturing Ltd* v. *Canadian Imperial Bank of Commerce*, n.147 above, 495–496.

[155] This passage was cited with approval in *Pertamina Energy Trading Ltd* v. *Crédit Suisse*, n.147 above, [62].

[156] See, for example, *Leather Manufacturers' Bank* v. *Morgan* (1886) 117 US 96 (USSC).

[157] Uniform Commercial Code, s.4–406(f).

[158] The courts have also explicitly refused to adopt the approach in UCC, s.4–406: *Wealdon Woodlands (Kent) Ltd* v. *National Westminster Bank Ltd*, n.134 above.

[159] *Pertamina Energy Trading Ltd* v. *Crédit Suisse*, n.147 above, [62].

of his signature and the discovery of any tampering with an instrument becomes an easy task. In the United Kingdom, the standard practice is that cleared effects are retained by the paying bank and are returned to the customer only if a specific request is made.[160] It follows that checking the correctness of a bank statement is a more arduous task in the United Kingdom than in the United States. In the United Kingdom, the customer's only sources for verification are, usually, the counterfoils in his cheque-book, receipts produced by point-of-sale terminals after use of his debit card, and giro forms.

When reporting in 1989, the Jack Committee accepted that there was a case for reform of the law, but rejected the idea that customers should be placed under a statutory duty to examine their bank statements.[161] However, in an effort to protect a bank against 'the most reprehensible negligence on its customer's part', the Jack Committee recommended 'a statutory provision whereby, in an action against a bank in debt or for damages, arising from an unauthorized payment, contributory negligence may be raised as a defence, but only if the court is satisfied that the degree of negligence shown by the [claimant] is sufficiently serious for it to be inequitable that the bank should be liable for the whole amount of the debt or damages'.[162]

Responding to the Jack Committee's report, the Government agreed that the law was unfair to banks and stated that it was disposed to make it more evenly balanced between banks and their customers.[163] However, before proposing any changes in the law in this area, the Government stated its intention to await a forthcoming Law Commission Report on contributory negligence as a defence in contract. The Law Commission produced its report in December 1993.[164] It recommended that 'apportionment of the [claimant's] damages on the ground of contributory negligence should be available in actions in contract where the defendant is in breach of an express or implied contractual duty to take reasonable care or exercise reasonable skill or both, but not where he is in breach of a contractual term which imposes a higher level of duty'.[165] The Law Commission accepted that this recommendation did not deal with the problem of customers sharing in the responsibility for payment under a forged mandate, as the duty of a bank to adhere to the terms of its mandate is strict and apportionment would not be available.[166] The Law Commission, like the Privy Council in *Tai Hing*, believed that banks were best placed to protect themselves against the consequences of paying on a forged mandate through the use of contract terms, such as verification clauses. Accordingly, if banks in the United Kingdom wish to tip the scales in their favour, they will have to do so by including a suitable term in their contract with the customer. This has been the practice of the Canadian banks for over 60 years. The clause in question should impose on the customer a duty to peruse his account statements promptly and to notify the bank of any errors or irregularities within a specified

---

[160] Some firms require the return of all items drawn on the account for the purpose of their annual audit, since under Cheques Act 1957, s.3, a retired cheque constitutes a receipt of payment. Should the United Kingdom ever introduce a fully truncated cheque clearing system, cheques would be retained by the collecting bank and presentation to the paying bank would be made entirely electronically. Currently, United Kingdom clearing banks operate a partially truncated system with the electronic exchange of cheque magnetic codeline information between collecting and paying banks still being followed by transfer of the actual instrument to the paying bank. See further Ch. 10, Sect. 2 below.

[161] *Banking Services: Law and Practice*, Report by the Review Committee Chaired by Professor R.B. Jack CBE (1989, London, Cm. 622), [6.13].

[162] Ibid., [6.14].

[163] *White Paper on Banking Services: Law and Practice* (Cm. 1026, London, 1990), 30.

[164] Law Commission, *Contributory Negligence as a Defence in Contract* (No. 219, London, 1993).

[165] Ibid., [4.1].   [166] Ibid., [5.20].

time. Failure so to notify the bank should be deemed to constitute a verification by the customer of the balance struck.

Canadian courts have upheld the validity of such clauses.[167] Thus, in *Columbia Graphophone Co.* v. *Union Bank of Canada*,[168] the customer completed a form in which he undertook to examine the statement and 'vouchers' accompanying it within 10 days and to sign periodic receipts confirming the correctness of the balance. He did so for a time, but then stopped. Forged cheques had been debited to his account throughout the entire period. It was held that the customer was precluded from disputing entries in account statements certified by him as correct; but he was free to refute entries in the statements he had not verified. He was able to challenge the later statements as his contract with his bank did not state that, upon his failure to notify an error, the entries were deemed to be correct.[169]

In a more modern case decided by the Supreme Court of Canada, *Arrow Transfer Co. Ltd* v. *Royal Bank of Canada*,[170] the customer had agreed, in a form executed when he opened his account, to verify all account statements sent to him and to notify the bank of any errors and inaccuracies within a given period. Thereafter, the account as kept by the bank was to constitute conclusive evidence of the entries' correctness. A clerk, who occupied a responsible position in the customer's service, forged a number of cheques. The majority of the Supreme Court held that the customer was bound by the clause in question. As the customer had failed to notify the bank about the discrepancies, he was unable to contest the genuineness of the cheques. Laskin J's concurring judgment for the bank was based on a different ground. His Honour held that the customer's persistent failure to peruse the statements and to verify the state of his account precluded him from disputing the entries based on the forged cheques. Laskin J considered, however, that the verification clause was inapplicable as it had to be construed narrowly and against the bank. Accordingly, the clause, which did not make any reference to the customer's duty to verify the genuineness of cheques forming the basis of the bank's debit entries, did not exempt the bank from its liability for the payment of forged cheques, even where the customer had failed to peruse the statements rendered to him. Laskin J's narrow construction of the verification clause is in line with the general approach to the interpretation of

---

[167] *Consmat Singapore Pte Ltd* v. *Bank of America National Trust & Savings Association*, n.147 above; *Stephan Machinery Singapore Pte Ltd* v. *Overseas-Chinese Banking Corporation* [2000] 2 SLR 191; *Elis Tjoa* v. *United Overseas Bank* [2003] 1 SLR 747; *Pertamina Energy Trading Ltd* v. *Crédit Suisse*, n.147 above, [57]–[60]. See also *Westpac Bank* v. *Metlej* (1987) Aust. Torts Rep. 80–102 (NSWCA).

[168] (1917) 34 DLR 743, followed in *Rutherford* v. *Royal Bank of Canada* [1932] 2 DLR 332 (verification by agent bank's principal); *Mackenzie* v. *Imperial Bank* [1938] 2 DLR 764. Cf. *Ewing* v. *Dominion Bank* (1904) 35 SCR 133 (SCC) (case involved a specific notification of payment by the bank of a bill alleged to be drawn by customer, but in reality it was forged); *Abbott* v. *Bank of Toronto* [1934] 3 DLR 256 (customer held not to be bound by statement in the absence of a verification agreement); *Resort Village of Shields* v. *Toronto-Dominion Bank* (1988) 64 Sask. R. 253, [16] (verification clause complete defence to statutory, tortious, and contractual claims). But the authorities emphasize the element of loss resulting from the delay. *Columbia Graphophone* also formed the basis of the modern leading decisions in this area: *Arrow Transfer Co. Ltd* v. *Royal Bank of Canada* (1972) 27 DLR (3d.) 81, 87 (SCC); *Canadian Pacific Hotels Ltd* v. *Bank of Montreal*, n.147 above, 724, 754–756.

[169] *B & G Construction Co. Ltd* v. *Bank of Montreal* [1954] 2 DLR 753, in which the customer was, surprisingly, held bound, although the bank knew informally of the forgeries: *Syndicat des Camionneurs Artisans du Québec Métropolitain* v. *Banque Provinciale du Canada* (1969) 11 DLR (3d.) 610 (clause incorporated in contract at the time of opening the account); *Booth Fisheries Canadian Co. Ltd* v. *Banque Provinciale du Canada* (1972) 7 NBR (2d.) 138 (same incorporation of clause); *Bad Boy Appliances and Furniture Ltd* v. *Toronto Dominion Bank* (1972) 25 DLR (3d.) 257 (where a letter mentioning fears of forgery was held to be inadequate notification). See also *Bank of Nova Scotia* v. *Equation* (1983) 45 AR 99, 106–107.

[170] (1972) 27 DLR (3d.) 81 (SCC) (Laskin J dissenting on this point).

exemption clauses,[171] but the common law doctrine postulated by him, and under which customers are to be precluded from disputing the correctness of statements they have failed to peruse, remains without support. It was expressly rejected by the Supreme Court of Canada in *Canadian Pacific Hotels Ltd* v. *Bank of Montreal*.[172] In that case, Le Dain J held that the existence of a duty to peruse bank statements was not established even in the case of 'sophisticated customers' such as business corporations.[173] The existence of such a duty would have to depend upon the proof of a commercial usage and 'the evidence of the practice constituting such a custom or usage would have to be such as to support an inference of an understanding between the bank and the customer that the customer would examine his bank statements with reasonable care and report any discrepancies within a reasonable time, failing which he would be precluded from setting up the discrepancies against the bank'.[174]

Le Dain J's reasoning is similar to Lord Scarman's approach in *Tai Hing Cotton Mill Ltd* v. *Liu Chong Hing Bank*, discussed above. In respect of the effectiveness of verification clauses, however, Laskin J's view in *Arrow Transfer* is the one closer to the reasoning in English cases, but this does not mean that such clauses are altogether ineffective. Although the Canadian decisions are merely of persuasive authority, they should not be ignored. That the type of clause involved is in conformity with the spirit of English law is clear from cases concerning performance bonds and first demand guarantees. It has been held, in the context of cases concerning such facilities, that the conclusive evidence clause, which is similar to the clause here proposed, is not contrary to public policy.[175] One reservation that needs to be expressed in respect of the proposed clause is that, to be effective, it has to be made an integral term of the contract between banker and customer. This cannot be done by adding such a clause at the foot of the bank statement, as this document does not evidence the terms of the contract between the parties.[176] Just as in Canada, the clause should be incorporated, as a cohesive term, in the contractual documents signed by the customer at the time the account is opened. If such a clause was not agreed upon when the customer opened his account, its incorporation can subsequently be effected only by

---

[171] The Eastern Canadian courts have tended to enforce the provisions of verification clauses in accordance with a 'plain meaning' approach adopted by the majority in *Arrow Transfer*: *Le Cercle Universitaire d'Ottawa* v. *National Bank of Canada* (1987) 61 OR (2d.) 456 (OCJ); *Kelly Funeral Homes Ltd* v. *CIBC* (1990) 72 DLR (4th) 276 (OCJ); *Don Bodkin Leasing Ltd* v. *Toronto-Dominion Bank* (1993) 14 OR (3d.) 571 (OGD), affd., n.147 above, 267–269; cf. *Farrugia* v. *Toronto-Dominion Bank* [2005] OJ No. 3912, [13]–[19], preferring the approach of Laskin J. In contrast, Western Canadian courts have tended to adopt Laskin J's narrow construction approach: *Royal Bank of Canada* v. *Larry Creighton Pro. Corp.* [1989] 3 WWR 561 (ACA); *Cavell Developments Ltd* v. *Royal Bank of Canada* (1991) 78 DLR (4th) 512 (BCCA); *239199 Alberta Ltd* v. *Patel* [1993] 8 WWR 199 (ACA); *Mirtia Holdings Ltd* v. *Toronto-Dominion Bank* (1995) 171 AR 105, [43]–[44] (AQB). See further N. Rafferty, 'Account Verification Agreements: When Can a Bank Protect Itself Against Its Own Negligence?' (1993) 8 *BFLR* 403; K.W. Perrett, 'Account Verification Clauses: Should Bank Customers be Forced to Mind Their Own Business' (1999) 14 *BFLR* 245.

[172] N.147 above.

[173] *Pertamina Energy Trading Ltd* v. *Crédit Suisse*, n.147 above, [61], where Rajah J left open the question of whether conclusive evidence clauses should be given the same effect *vis-à-vis* individual and non-corporate customers as they were against corporate customers.

[174] N.147 above, 430.

[175] *Bache & Co. (London) Ltd* v. *Banque Vernes et Commerciale de Paris SA* [1973] 2 Lloyd's Rep. 437; *R. D. Harbottle (Mercantile) Ltd* v. *National Westminster Bank Ltd* [1978] QB 146; *Edward Owen Engineering Ltd* v. *Barclays Bank International Ltd* [1978] QB 159; *Howe Richardson Scale Co. Ltd* v. *Polimex-Cekop* [1978] 1 Lloyd's Rep. 161; *Bolivinter Oil SA* v. *Chase Manhattan Bank* [1984] 1 Lloyd's Rep. 251; *ILG Capital Llc* v. *Van Der Merwe* [2008] EWCA Civ 542, [10]–[16].

[176] Cf. *Burnett* v. *Westminster Bank Ltd*, n.97 above, which concerned a clause printed on the folder of a cheque-book.

means of a valid variation of the banker-customer contract.[177] The Privy Council's decision in *Tai Hing Cotton Mill Ltd* v. *Liu Chong Hing Bank Ltd*,[178] discussed earlier, shows, further, that it is not enough to include in the document signed by the customer when the account is opened an informal or precative verification clause that falls short of imposing on the customer a definite duty to check his statements. To preclude the customer from disputing entries that he has not queried within the time prescribed for verification, the clause must be sufficiently carefully drafted to convey to the customer that the entries will be conclusively binding on him if he fails to demand their rectification within the agreed period.[179] It is clear that any ambiguities in the clause will be construed against the bank and that such a provision must be 'clear and unambiguous' in order to be effective.[180] It is clear that the courts will be quite demanding when applying this standard, as the Privy Council stressed recently in *Morrell* v. *Workers Savings & Loan Bank*[181] when it referred to 'the rigorous standard of clarity and unambiguity necessary for a valid conclusive evidence clause'.

Verification clauses must also be carefully drafted to ensure that they do not fall foul of those statutes that police exclusion and limitation clauses in standard-form business contracts and that control unfair terms in consumer contracts. Where the bank's customer is a consumer, or a non-consumer dealing on the bank's written standard terms of business, a verification clause runs the risk of being held unreasonable and, therefore, ineffective under the UCTA 1977.[182] Under section 13(1)(c) of UCTA 1977, clauses that exclude or restrict rules of evidence or procedure are treated in the same way as those that exclude or restrict liability. Where the customer is a consumer, the clause is also at risk of being held to be unfair and, therefore, unenforceable under the UTCCR 1999.[183] Schedule 2, paragraph 1(q) of the Regulations indicates that a term may be unfair where it has the object and effect of unduly restricting the evidence available to a customer against his bank or imposes a burden of proof on the customer that should, by law, be on the bank.

It is hoped that the courts will be slow to strike down a verification clause as being unreasonable[184] or unfair. By relying on such a term, the bank is, after all, doing no more than taking matters into its own hands as directed by the Privy Council in *Tai Hing*. However, three points should be kept in mind. First, the position of the consumer

[177] The existing contract between the bank and its customer may allow for the unilateral variation of its terms by the bank. For the control of 'unilateral variation clauses', see Sect. 2 above. The Canadian courts have shown some reluctance to allow a bank to vary the terms of an existing contract with its customer in order to introduce a new verification clause that is more severe than the existing clause: see, for example, *Armstrong Baum Plumbing & Heating* v. *Toronto Dominion Bank* (1994) 15 BLR (2d.) 84 (OCA) (bank made payment contrary to its customer's instructions and could not rely on exemption clause). See also *Rancan Fertilizer Systems Inc.* v. *Lavergne* (1999) 134 Man R. (2d) 73, [15] (MBCA).

[178] N.99 above, 109–110, following [1984] 1 Lloyd's Rep. 555 (HKCA). See further Ch. 11, Sect. 3(ii) below.

[179] *Lam Yin-fei* v. *Hang Lung Bank Ltd* [1982] HKLR 215; *Asien-Pazifik Merchant Finance Ltd* v. *Shanghai Commercial Bank Ltd* [1982] HKLR 273; *Sun Hung Kai Forex & Bullion Co Ltd* v. *Yick Ming Kit* [1995] HKCU 175. See also *Consmat Singapore Pte. Ltd* v. *Bank of America*, n.147 above; *Pertamina Energy Trading Ltd* v. *Crédit Suisse*, n.147 above, [56], [60].

[180] *Tai Hing Cotton Mill Ltd* v. *Liu Chong Hing Bank Ltd*, n.99 above, 110; *Financial Institutions Services Ltd* v. *Negril Negril Holdings Ltd*, n.99 above, [43]. See also *Office of Fair Trading* v. *Abbey National plc*, n.15 above, [323], [2008] EWHC 2325 (Comm), [21].

[181] N.99 above, [33].

[182] UCTA 1977, s.3. See *Pertamina Energy Trading Ltd* v. *Crédit Suisse*, n.147 above, [57], [59].

[183] S.I. 1999/2083.

[184] A court will certainly be reluctant to strike down a verification clause as unreasonable when the customer is commercially sophisticated: *Pertamina Energy Trading Ltd* v. *Crédit Suisse*, n.147 above, [63].

customer is stronger than that of the business customer. The consumer can rely on the protection of both the UCTA 1977 and the UTCCR 1999, whereas the non-consumer can rely only on the former. Secondly, a verification clause is more likely to be struck down as unreasonable under the UCTA 1977 when the customer is a consumer as opposed to a commercial entity.[185] Thirdly, a verification clause is more likely to be considered either reasonable or fair when the bank sends the relevant cheques back to the customer after they have been cleared and paid, so that the customer can check them against his bank statements.[186] This is not, however, the current banking practice in the United Kingdom.

(iv) **Bank statements and pass-book entries as accounts stated**

The plea that a periodic account statement or a pass-book constitutes an 'account stated' may be raised either by the bank or by the customer. Naturally, the argument is pressed by the party that seeks to deny the other the right to have an error or a wrong entry rectified. The significance of the plea is that, in equity, an 'account stated' has to be settled by the debtor without further regard to the individual items involved. The right has been described as a 'convenient legal fiction which avoids the necessity, if recourse has to be had to legal proceedings, of suing upon the individual items in the account'.[187] From a practical point of view, when an account is stated it becomes similar to a confirmation by a debtor that his creditor is claiming the correct amount. In the case of a current account, the customer and the bank would lose the right to query the correctness of given items once the bank statement or the pass-book became an 'account stated'.

English law has generally refused to regard a customer's pass-book or his bank statement as constituting an 'account stated'. It is true that, in *Blackburn Building Society* v. *Cunliffe, Brooks and Co.*,[188] Lord Selborne suggested that, in appropriate circumstances, a pass-book could be so regarded. This proposition was doubted, however, by the Court of Appeal in *Vagliano Bros.* v. *Bank of England*,[189] where Bowen LJ observed that there was no evidence to show that, as between a customer and his banker, the customer was under a duty to peruse his statements with a view to pointing out errors. Although Lord Halsbury, in the House of Lords, suggested that entries in a pass-book ought to have some legal effect, he did not hold that a pass-book would constitute an 'account stated' where an error was not promptly discovered and notified.[190]

---

[185] *Pertamina Energy Trading Ltd* v. *Crédit Suisse*, n.147 above, [61], [63].

[186] See, for example, *Consmat Singapore Pte. Ltd* v. *Bank of America National Trust & Savings Association*, n.147 above, where the bank had adopted a practice of returning cheques and the verification clause was held to pass the test of reasonableness in the Singapore equivalent of the UCTA 1977. The weight to be attached to this banking practice when determining the validity of a verification clause has, however, been significantly reduced following *Pertamina Energy Trading Ltd* v. *Crédit Suisse*, n.147 above, [56]. See also *Ri Jong Son* v. *Development Bank of Singapore Ltd* [1998] 3 SLR 64, where Kan J held an exemption clause, excluding the bank's liability in negligence for paying against a forged cheque, to be reasonable under the same legislation. Given that the customer was a financially sophisticated individual, being a bank manager, an English court might well reach the same conclusion. See also *Clansmen Resources Ltd* v. *T.D. Bank* (1990) 43 BCLR (2d.) 273 (BCCA).

[187] Chorley, *Law of Banking* (6th edn., London, 1974), 175.

[188] (1882) 22 Ch. D 61, 71–2, affd. *sub. nom. Brooks & Co.* v. *Blackburn and District Benefit Building Society* (1884) 9 App. Cas. 857, cited with seeming approval by Brennan J in *Bank of New South Wales* v. *Brown* (1982–1983) 45 ALR 225, 242 (HCA). See also *Bishun Chand Firm* v. *Seth Girdhari Lal* (1934) 50 TLR 465 (PC).

[189] (1889) 23 QBD 243, 263 (CA).

[190] *Bank of England* v. *Vagliano Bros.* [1891] AC 107, 115–116 (HL), rev'g (1889) 23 QBD 243 (CA) on other grounds.

The view of the Court of Appeal in *Vagliano* was, however, adopted in *Kepitigalla Rubber Estates Ltd* v. *National Bank of India Ltd*, where Bray J observed that it would be absurd to hold that the taking of a pass-book by a bank and its return to the customer established a 'settled account'.[191] Bray J added that, if the pass-book or statement of account were deemed an 'account stated', then the mere delivery of the document to an authorised representative of its corporate customer, who might in fact be the very person defrauding the customer, would preclude the company from contesting the bank's right to debit its account with amounts paid against forged instruments. In the same vein, Lord Esher MR, in *Chatterton* v. *London and County Bank*,[192] considered that the pass-book would not constitute an 'account stated' even if it was updated at regular intervals and returned to the customer accompanied by the paid effects, and even though the customer had ticked off all entries. His Lordship said that it was 'a hundred to one that [the bankers] never looked at the pass-book'. He thought, therefore, that a bank was unlikely to note that a customer had ticked off the entries made from time to time. A similar stance has recently been adopted by the Victorian Court of Appeal in *Simonovski* v. *Bendigo Bank Ltd*,[193] which involved a claim by a 'customer' to recover the sums that a pass-book indicated were standing to the credit of a building society account. One of the issues before the Court related to the evidential weight to be given to these pass-book entries. Nettle JA rejected the suggestion that the pass-book constituted an 'account stated' and accordingly conclusive evidence of the matters stated therein.[194] His Honour was of the view that 'there is no special body of law applicable to entries in passbooks', but rather that the same principles apply as would govern entries in any book.[195] According to his Honour, the correct approach when determining the evidential weight to be attached to a pass-book entry is as follows: 'If a passbook is shown to be genuine and it appears that an entry in it has been made by an officer of the bank having actual or ostensible authority to make entries of that kind, the entry will constitute an admission against the interest of the bank and therefore prima facie or rebuttable evidence of the truth of its contents.'[196]

It is submitted that the law in point is unexceptional. If either the bank or the customer is to be precluded from denying the validity of an entry made in the account statements, it is best to base the decision on all the circumstances of the case in question.[197] The doctrine of estoppel, which could be invoked as a result of the inclusion of the type of verification clause used in Canada, comes closer to this position than a principle that treats the bank statement or the pass-book as an 'account stated'.

(v) **Customer's silence with knowledge of wrong entry**

If the customer knows that an entry made in his pass-book or statement of account is wrong, but keeps silent, he will be precluded from asserting the error once the bank has

---

[191] [1909] 2 KB 1010, 1029. See also *Brewer* v. *Westminster Bank Ltd*, n.134 above; *Kok* v. *Biang Chiang Bank Ltd* [1972] 2 MLJ 134.

[192] *The Times*, 21 January 1891.

[193] N.131 above; but note Brennan J's dictum to the contrary in *Bank of New South Wales* v. *Brown*, n.188 above, 242.

[194] Ibid., [50]–[51], citing *Commercial Bank of Scotland* v. *Rhind*, n.130 above, 648; *Gaden* v. *Newfoundland Savings Bank* [1899] AC 281, 286 (PC); *British and North European Bank Ltd* v. *Zalzstein*, n.130 above, 97.

[195] Ibid., [50].

[196] Ibid., [52]. Although framed in terms of a common law exception to the rule against hearsay evidence, the test proposed in *Simonovski* has equal validity under Civil Evidence Act 1995, ss.1, 7(1).

[197] Id.

changed its position.[198] The typical case in which the point arises is where a customer knows that a cheque, paid by the bank, was issued by a forger, but for reasons of misguided loyalty or affection refrains from informing the bank. However, there is no reason in principle for limiting the customer's duty to forged cheques, and it has been held in New Zealand that the duty equally applies in circumstances where unauthorized direct credit instructions have been given to the bank by the customer's employee.[199]

A question of some difficulty is whether such an estoppel would, likewise, be operative where the customer did not have actual knowledge of the irregularity involved, but on the basis of any reasonable practice or common sense ought to have known about it or to have suspected it. The issue was addressed by Arden J in *Price Meats Ltd* v. *Barclays Bank plc*.[200] The claimant company sued the defendant bank for the sum of £172,229.21, which represented the sum of cheques drawn on the claimant's account, the signatures on which were allegedly forged. In its defence, the bank argued that the claimant had failed in its duty to inform the bank of forgeries of which it had constructive knowledge. The cheques were paid between 1993 and 1996. In 1992, the claimant had discovered that its accounts clerk had misapplied petty cash and, independently of this, the bank had warned the claimant to investigate the size of its overdraft. The bank alleged that this gave the claimant the means of discovering the forgeries and that this was enough to raise an estoppel against the claimant. The case came before Arden J on the claimant's application to strike out the bank's defence as disclosing no reasonable grounds of defence. Assuming for the purposes of the application that the signatures on the cheques had been forged, Arden J had to decide whether an estoppel would operate against a customer who had the means of knowledge, but not actual knowledge, of a forgery. Her Ladyship held that constructive knowledge, in the sense that the customer had the means of knowledge, was not enough.[201] Actual knowledge of the forgery was required, or at least evidence of shutting one's eyes to an obvious means of knowledge, which amounted to the same thing.[202] In

---

[198] *Greenwood* v. *Martins Bank Ltd* [1933] AC 51 (HL). The estoppel only operates against a person who qualifies as the bank's customer: *Royal Bank of Scotland plc* v. *Wallace International Ltd* (CA, 27 January 2000), [42]. It is not necessary that the customer know about the possible fraudulent nature of the transactions behind the erroneous entry, but simply that the entry relates to a transaction that was never authorized: *Geniki Investments International Ltd* v. *Ellis Stockbrokers Ltd* [2008] 1 BCLC 662, [45]. See further Ch. 11, Sect. 3(ii) below. In Canada, see *Ewing* v. *Dominion Bank*, n.168 above, showing that silence in the face of a written notification can result in an estoppel. See also *Abbott* v. *Bank of Toronto*, n.168 above; *Canadian Pacific Hotels Ltd* v. *Bank of Montreal*, n.147 above; *Don Bodkin Leasing Ltd* v. *Toronto-Dominion Bank* (1993) 14 OR (3d.) 571 (OGD), affd. (1998) 40 OR (3d) 262 (OCA). In Australia, see *West* v. *Commercial Bank of Australia* (1935) 55 CLR 315 (customer did not inform bank that his son was drawing cheques on his account). See also *Tina Motors Pty Ltd* v. *ANZ Banking Group Ltd* [1977] VR 205 (VSC); *National Australia Bank Ltd* v. *Hokit Pty. Ltd*, n.134 above; *Fried* v. *National Australia Bank Ltd*, n.147 above. In Hong Kong, see *Chuen* v. *Nanyang Commercial Bank Ltd* [1986] HKCU 58 (HKSC). In Singapore, see *Consmat Singapore Pte Ltd* v. *Bank of America National Trust & Savings Association*, n.147 above; *Khoo Tian Hock* v. *Oversea-Chinese Banking Corporation Ltd*, n.147 above; *Pertamina Energy Trading Ltd* v. *Crédit Suisse*, n.147 above.

[199] *Bank of New Zealand* v. *Auckland Information Bureau (Inc.)* [1996] 1 NZLR 420 (NZCA). See also *Geniki Investments International Ltd* v. *Ellis Stockbrokers Ltd*, n.198 above, [44]–[46], where the *Greenwood* principle was extended to the context of a client failing to inform its stockbroker that one of the brokers was conducting unauthorized share trading upon his account. Contrast *Banque Nationale de Paris* v. *Hew Keong Chan Gary* [2001] 1 SLR 300, where the High Court of Singapore found a 'conceptual difficulty' in implying a customer's duty of care outside money transmission operations and into contracts involving private banking activities such as share transactions and forex deals. [200] N.136 above.

[201] The bank relied on *McKenzie* v. *British Linen Co.* (1881) 6 App. Cas. 82 and *Morison* v. *London County and Westminster Bank Ltd* [1914] 3 KB 356 as supporting its proposition that constructive knowledge was enough to raise an estoppel, but Arden J, after careful examination of these cases, held that they did not stand as authority for that proposition: N.136 above, 348, 350.

[202] N.136 above, 351, adopting the different degrees of knowledge identified by Devlin J in *Roper* v. *Taylor's Central Garages (Exeter) Ltd* [1951] 2 TLR 284, 288–289. See also *Patel* v. *Standard Chartered Bank* [2001]

any event, her Ladyship also held that the evidence did not support an allegation that the claimant had reasonable grounds to believe that there had been a forgery, even if that were a good defence in law. Accordingly, the defence was struck out.

It is respectfully submitted that Arden J's decision can be supported on three grounds. First, it is clear from what Lord Tomlin said in *Greenwood* v. *Martins Bank Ltd*[203] that for there to be a representation, which is needed to get an estoppel off the ground, there has to be a deliberate silence. As Arden J rightly observed in *Price Meats*, 'that is a silence with knowledge of material facts'.[204] Secondly, to allow an estoppel to arise where the customer is merely negligent in failing to take up the means of knowledge available to him would be entirely inconsistent with the Privy Council's refusal in *Tai Hing* to subject bank customers to any wider duty of care.[205] In a case of breach of mandate, if a customer is not to be penalized for his carelessness in failing to check his bank statements, or failing to check up on his employees, he should not be penalized for his carelessness in other respects. Finally, if a customer who has received a mistaken payment from his bank is not to be denied a defence of change of position to the bank's restitutionary claim merely because he has been careless,[206] why should a customer be denied recovery of a payment made in breach of mandate when his carelessness has prevented the bank from taking steps to protect itself from further forgery? Consistency of approach would suggest that both cases should be treated in the same way.

In some cases, however, the line between constructive knowledge and actual knowledge, especially in the sense of shutting one's eyes to the obvious, may be fine.[207] Much depends on the circumstances of each case. In *Morison* v. *London County and Westminster Bank Ltd*,[208] Phillimore LJ hinted that, when a principal knows so much that it is 'a policy of an ostrich to know no more', the means of knowledge may be equated with actual knowledge. *Tina Motors Pty. Ltd* v. *Australia and New Zealand Banking Group Ltd*,[209] in which the customer assured the bank that any cheque signed by a specific agent could be taken to have been validly drawn, is an illustration in point. In this case, the bank's enquiry should have put the customer, as principal, on notice. A further illustration is *Brown* v. *Westminster Bank Ltd*.[210] Here, the servants of the customer, an old woman who was too frail to look after her own affairs, forged her signature on cheques drawn on her account. The branch manager called on the customer on several occasions to ask whether the instruments were regular. Although the customer did not expressly verify the genuineness of the cheques, she likewise refrained from questioning their payment. She was, accordingly, held to be estopped from denying the bank's right to debit her account. It is to be doubted whether conduct falling short of that in *Brown*, which

---

Lloyd's Rep. Bank. 229, [63], where Toulson J held that 'wilful blindness' is tantamount to knowledge for these purposes, but that 'it is an unacceptable leap to equate means of knowledge with actual knowledge'. See also *Nasrin Karim Professional Corp* v. *Bank of Nova Scotia* [2004] ABQB 404, [23].

[203] N.198 above, 58–59.   [204] N.136 above, 350.

[205] [1986] AC 519 (PC). In *Patel* v. *Standard Chartered Bank*, n.202 above, [63], Toulson J gave this as his main reason for rejecting the bank's argument that a customer should report fraud about which he ought, as a reasonable person, to have been put on enquiry. His Lordship also reasoned that, given the variation in characteristics and circumstances of the millions of people who hold bank accounts, any 'reasonable customer' test would be imprecise in definition and uncertain in application: ibid., [53]. This reasoning is much less convincing.

[206] Ch. 12, Sect. 3(iii)(a) below.

[207] This point is considered further in a different context in Sect. 5(iv)(b) below.

[208] N.201 above, 385. See also the more liberal principle in *Ewing* v. *Dominion Bank*, n.168 above; *Abbott* v. *Bank of Toronto*, n.168 above.

[209] N.198 above. See also *UAB Bhd* v. *Tai Soon Heng Construction Sdn Bhd*, n.147 above, 191.

[210] [1964] 2 Lloyd's Rep. 187.

operated to lull the bank into a false sense of security about the cheque, will be enough to found an estoppel.

4 Combination of accounts

(i) Problem in practice

In many cases a customer maintains more than one account with his bank. Thus, a customer may use one account for strictly personal purposes and another one for his business. Similarly, a customer who has several enterprises may decide to maintain a separate account for each of them. In other cases, a customer may open some special type of account, such as a loan account or a savings account, in addition to his current account. Furthermore, some professional men are required to open special accounts for their businesses. Thus, solicitors are required to maintain clients' accounts.[211]

There are two situations in which the bank may wish to treat all the accounts maintained by a given customer as if they were one. The first is where the customer is unable or unwilling to repay an overdraft incurred on one account, even though another account is in credit. Predominant in this group are cases arising out of a customer's insolvency. The second type of situation in which the bank may wish to combine accounts is where the customer draws a cheque for an amount exceeding the balance standing to the credit of the account in question, but the deficiency can be met out of funds deposited in another account. The two types of situation give rise to distinct problems.

In the first type of situation, the bank seeks to combine the customer's accounts for its own purposes. If the customer is unwilling to pay an amount due in respect of an overdraft or a loan, the bank can, of course, sue him for the debt. If, however, the bank is able to set off against the overdraft in 'account A' a credit balance in 'account B', it obviates the inconvenience and expense involved in legal proceedings. Furthermore, it avoids the risk of the customer's financial affairs deteriorating during the period of litigation. The bank gains an even more substantial advantage from combining the accounts of an insolvent customer. By way of illustration, take a case in which the customer's 'account A' has an overdraft of £1,000 and his 'account B' has a credit balance of £2,000. If the bank were unable to effect a set-off by combining the two accounts, its position in the customer's bankruptcy would be unfavourable. The bank would be obliged to pay the sum of £2,000 standing to the credit of 'account B' to the customer's trustee in bankruptcy and would have to lodge a proof for £1,000 in respect of the overdraft. Being an unsecured creditor, the bank would be paid a dividend together with the other general creditors. If, for example, the customer's assets yielded a dividend of 30p in the pound, the bank would recover only £300. The bank's position would be superior if it *were entitled* to combine the accounts. The bank would then set off the £1,000 owed by the customer on 'account A' against its own liability to the customer for £2,000 in respect of 'account B', and would pay the balance of £1,000 over to the trustee in bankruptcy. The bank would, accordingly, receive repayment of the overdraft in full, in priority to the claims of the other general creditors.[212] In the second type of situation, where the bank seeks to combine its customer's accounts in order to meet a cheque drawn in excess of the available balance of the account on which it is drawn, the bank is essentially acting in the customer's interest.

---

[211] Ch. 8, Sect. 6 below.
[212] The bank's right of combination can be used as a 'sword' as much as a 'shield': *Barclays Bank Ltd* v. *Okenarhe* [1966] 2 Lloyd's Rep 87, 97.

If the cheque is dishonoured, the main loss is to the customer's reputation. The bank is, basically, not obliged to meet an excessive demand.[213] It is, nevertheless, important to consider the bank's position in this type of situation.

Unsurprisingly, the analysis of the legal nature of the combination of accounts is based on authorities concerning the first type of situation. The main problems involved are the bank's right to combine accounts where there is an agreement, or the manifestation of an intention, to the contrary; the question of whether the bank is obliged to give notice before it resolves to combine the accounts; and the special issues arising out of the law of insolvency. These problems are discussed in this chapter in the light of the general common law principles. Specific contractual arrangements for a set-off are discussed subsequently.[214] The second type of situation that gives rise to the possibility of combination has not been a frequent subject of litigation. The main problem is whether the bank either is under a duty, or has the authority, to combine the accounts in the customer's interest.

(ii) **Legal meaning of 'combination of accounts'**

One basic principle supports the doctrine that in certain situations the bank is entitled to combine the accounts of a customer—it is that the customer's underlying contractual relationship is with the bank and not with the branch at which the account is maintained.[215] Moreover, the basic relationship of banker and customer governs all the accounts of a customer regardless of their type. This is so despite the slight variations in the rights of the parties in different types of account. As there is only one contract of banker and customer, there is room for the argument that, when the bank becomes the customer's creditor, it can exercise a right of set-off as regards mutual dealings with him.

The significance of the doctrine involved is demonstrated by one of the first decisions in point. In *Re European Bank, Agra Bank Claims*,[216] the OC Bank maintained three accounts with the A & M Bank: a loan account; a discount account; and a general account. The OC Bank gave the A & M Bank securities to cover acceptances of bills of exchange that were debited to the loan account. Shortly thereafter, both banks failed. The dividend paid by the OC Bank to its creditors discharged its indebtedness on the loan and the discount account, but was inadequate for meeting the overdraft incurred on the general account. The question was whether the securities given by the OC Bank to the A & M Bank could be utilized to discharge this remaining indebtedness or, having been appropriated to the loan account, were to be returned to the OC Bank's liquidator. Malins V-C held that the securities *were* available to cover the indebtedness in the general account. Affirming his decision, James LJ in the Court of Appeal in Chancery emphasized that it would be wrong to treat the three accounts as 'distinct matters'. His Lordship said:[217]

> It was only for convenience that the loan account was kept separately...In truth, as between banker and customer, whatever number of accounts are kept in books, the whole is really but one account, and it is not open to the customer, in the absence of some special contract, to say that the securities which he deposits are only applicable to one account.

---

[213] Sect. 1 above.   [214] Ch. 21, Sect. 3 below.   [215] Ch. 5, Sect. 3 above.
[216] (1872) LR 8 Ch. App. 41.
[217] Ibid., 44, approved in *Good Property Land Development Pte Ltd* v. *Société Genérale* [1996] 2 SLR 239, 249–250 (SGCA); *Pertamina Energy Trading Ltd* v. *Crédit Suisse*, n.147 above, [43].

This view has become well-established.[218] Whilst it is indisputable that there is only one basic relationship between the banker and his customer, it has to be emphasized that its details vary from account to account. Thus, a current account is operable by cheque, whilst a savings account cannot be utilized in this way. Funds deposited in an ordinary savings account are usually repayable on demand; but amounts standing to the credit of an 'extra interest account' fall due at one month's notice. In reality, it is possible to treat the contracts involved in separate types of account as distinct arrangements between the bank and its customer. *Re European Bank* and the cases following it do not overlook this point. All they suggest is that the parties to the contractual relationship effected in respect of each account are the customer and the bank. For this reason, debts accrued to the customer are due from the bank and not from an individual branch. Equally, debts due from the customer are recoverable by the bank and not by its branches. There is, thus, room for a set-off.[219]

On this basis, it is clear that in certain circumstances the bank is entitled to combine a customer's accounts. What is the legal nature of the bank's right? Some authorities have suggested that when a bank combines distinct accounts of a single customer it exercises a lien.[220] This view has, however, been questioned in English, Canadian, Malaysian, and Singaporean authorities,[221] and was rejected by the House of Lords in the leading case of *National Westminster Bank Ltd* v. *Halesowen Presswork and Assemblies Ltd.*[222] The decision is relevant as regards most questions concerning the combination of accounts and is, therefore, discussed in full at this point. In *Halesowen*, the claimants maintained a current account with the defendant bank. In April 1968, when this account showed a substantial debit balance, an 'account no. 2' was opened for the claimants' trading operations. The bank agreed that, in the absence of a material change of circumstances, 'account no. 1' would remain frozen for a period of four months. On 20 May, the claimants convened a meeting of their creditors. The bank received a notice of the meeting and resolved to leave the April arrangement in effect. On 12 June, the claimants passed a resolution to wind up voluntarily. On 19 June, the bank informed the liquidator that it had decided to set off the credit balance in 'account no. 2' against the debit balance in the frozen 'account no. 1'. The liquidator objected, as in his view the bank was bound by the April arrangement. Roskill J gave judgment for the bank. His Lordship thought that the bank had a right of set-off, which he treated as a lien. The bank's agreement to keep the two accounts separate was determined by the changed circumstances resulting from the claimants' decision to wind up. Roskill J's decision was reversed by the Court of Appeal.[223] All three judges were of the view that a bank's right to combine its customers' accounts constituted a right of set-off, and was not to be regarded as based on the exercise of a lien. The amounts deposited by a

---

[218] *Garnett* v. *M'Kewan* (1872) LR 8 Ex. 10, 13, 14; *James Kirkwood & Sons* v. *Clydesdale Bank Ltd*, 1908 SC 20, 24; *Re Sutcliffe & Sons Ltd, ex p. Royal Bank* [1933] 1 DLR 562; *Barclays Bank Ltd* v. *Okenarhe*, n.212 above, 95; *Hearn* v. *Bank of N.S.* [1970] SCR 341; *Mossman* v. *Chilcott* (NZCA, 23 July 1992); *Cinema Plus Ltd* v. *ANZ Banking Group Ltd* (2000) 35 ACSR 1 (NSWCA).

[219] *Contra*, S. McCracken, *The Banker's Remedy of Set-Off* (3rd edn., London, 2010), ch. 1; R. Derham, *Set-Off* (4th edn., Oxford, 2010), ch. 15, who see combination as a matter of account rather than of set-off.

[220] *Re Keever (a bankrupt)* [1967] Ch. 182. This was also the view of Roskill J in *Halesowen Presswork and Assemblies Ltd* v. *Westminster Bank Ltd*, n.7 above, 20–21, but this was subsequently rejected by the House of Lords (n.222 below)).

[221] *Royal Trust Co.* v. *Molsons Bank* (1912) 8 DLR 478; *Re the Firm of Tsn* [1935] 1 MLJ 139, 141; *The Chartered Bank of India, Australia & China* v. *Public Trustee* [1957] 1 MLJ 211, 219–220 (SGCA). See also *Re Sutcliffe & Sons Ltd, ex p. Royal Bank*, n.218 above; *Re E. J. Morel (1934) Ltd* [1962] Ch. 21; *Re Kim San Engineers Pte Ltd* [1992] 2 SLR 749, 758 (all three cases describe the account balance as the bank's money and the combination of accounts as involving a right of set-off).

[222] [1972] AC 785 (HL).   [223] N.7 above.

customer became the bank's money. All the customer had was the right to claim repayment of the debt by drawing a cheque on the account or by making a demand in some other manner. The bank could not, therefore, have a lien over its own money or property. A majority of the Court of Appeal (Lord Denning MR and Winn LJ) further held that in the case in question the bank was not entitled to combine the accounts. The bank had agreed to keep the accounts separate, and if it wished to cancel this arrangement in view of the changed circumstances, it had to give notice to the customer. Buckley LJ dissented, as in his view the bank was entitled to combine the accounts under section 31 of the Bankruptcy Act 1914, the predecessor to section 323 of the Insolvency Act 1986. The House of Lords restored Roskill J's decision. Their Lordships were, however, unanimous in adopting the view of the Court of Appeal to the effect that the bank's right to combine its customers' accounts was to be distinguished from a lien. Lord Cross observed that 'to describe the right to consolidate several accounts as an example of the banker's lien is…a misuse of language'.[224] The House of Lords held that, on the facts, the defendant bank had the right to combine the accounts both in view of the nature of the April arrangements and under section 31 of the Bankruptcy Act 1914. These aspects are discussed in further detail below.

The distinction drawn in *Halesowen* between the banker's lien and its right to combine a customer's accounts appears to be well-founded. Ordinarily, a person cannot have a lien over his own property. This is especially so where the property is also in his possession. Obviously, in the type of case being discussed here, the bank both owns the money and has its use. How then can it exercise a lien in respect of it? There is room for only one argument to the contrary. A bank balance is not merely an amount of money forming part of a bank's general funds. It also constitutes a debt due from the bank to the customer.[225] It is clear that a third party, such as the customer's creditor, can seek recourse to this asset by such means as a third party debt order.[226] Whilst a customer's bank cannot exercise a lien over the money as such, can it possibly exercise a lien against the asset represented by the balance? It is true that the asset is a debt due from the bank. However, in the sale of goods context, an owner may in certain cases exercise a lien over his own property. By way of illustration, take a dealer who has disposed of a car under a hire-purchase agreement. If the dealer subsequently repairs the car at the purchaser's request and for his account, he can exercise a workman's lien over the property.[227] It is perhaps arguable that the bank should have an analogous right over a balance standing in its books to the credit of a particular customer, provided it relied on this balance when it granted the customer an overdraft on another account or some special business loan.[228] It will be considered subsequently whether such a right can be acquired by the bank by means of a charge over the balance in question.[229]

The question of whether the bank's right to combine accounts constitutes a set-off or may also be based on a lien is of practical significance. If the right of combination constitutes a lien, it could be exercised over a balance standing to the credit of any of the

---

[224] N.222 above, 810. [225] Ch. 5, Sect. 3 above. [226] Ch. 11, Sect. 1(iii) below.

[227] See, generally, *Tappenden* v. *Artus* [1964] 2 QB 185 (repairer's lien); *Jarl Tra AB* v. *Convoys Ltd* [2003] 2 Lloyd's Rep 459 (carrier's lien); *Marcq* v. *Christie, Manson & Woods Ltd* [2004] QB 286 (CA) (auctioneer's lien); *Heath Lambert Ltd* v. *Sociedad de Corretaje de Seguros* [2006] 2 Lloyd's Rep 551 (insurance broker's lien).

[228] A banker does have a lien over its customer's property to secure general advances, but this is generally limited to the customer's 'securities' and the better view is that this term does not encompass the credit balance of an account: Ch. 20, Sect. 2 below.

[229] Ch. 21, Sect. 3(iv) below, considering *Re Charge Card Services Ltd*, n.3 above; and *Re Bank of Credit and Commerce International SA (No. 8)* [1998] AC 214 (HL).

customer's accounts. It would be immaterial whether the amount due was payable by the bank on demand or at some future time. Thus, where a customer was insolvent, a lien could be exercised by the bank over funds standing to the credit of his fixed deposit account. The opposite would be true if the bank's right to combine accounts were regarded as a set-off. It would then be arguable that a debt due in the future, such as a fixed deposit, could not be set off against an immediate liability. The trend of authority, admittedly, is to this effect.[230]

On the present state of the leading authorities, the bank's right to combine the balances of all the accounts of a single customer is best regarded as a right of set-off.[231] It is true that in *Re K (Restraint Order)*[232] Otton J sought to distinguish a bank's right to combine accounts from a right of set-off on the ground that the combination of accounts constituted an exercise involving the determination of the final balance due by the customer to the bank or vice versa. In essence, though, a set-off involves the very same exercise. Practically, it too is carried out by an accounting exercise in which the mutual debts between the two parties are set off against each other so as to determine the available balance.

The bank's right to combine its customers' accounts is a common law right that, as will be shown, may be abrogated by agreement.[233] In *Garnett* v. *M'Kewan*,[234] Kelly CB thought that an important ground for recognizing the bank's ordinary right to combine accounts was the mutuality in the dealings of banker and customer. As the customer had the power to order his bank to transfer amounts from one of his accounts to another, the bank had a corresponding right to set off the balances of those separate accounts. This dictum overlooks the fact, however, that when the customer gives an instruction to his bank, such as an order to transfer funds from one account to another, he acts as principal. The bank, as agent, does not have a similar right to issue instructions for the transfer of amounts from one account of its principal to another.

The right to set off, or to combine accounts, is available only in respect of dealings between a bank and a person who is involved in the relevant transactions as a customer.

---

[230] *Jeffryes* v. *Agra and Masterman's Bank* (1866) LR 2 Eq. 674, 680–681 (concerning set-off against amounts due on unretired bills); *Bower* v. *Foreign and Colonial Gas Co. Ltd* (1874) 22 WR 740; *Liverpool Freeport Electronics Ltd* v. *Habib Bank Ltd* [2007] EWHC 1149 (QB), [136]. Cf. *Business Computers Ltd* v. *Anglo-African Leasing Ltd* [1977] 1 WLR 578, 585–586 (set-off in assignment situations). So accounts with different maturity dates cannot be combined: P.R. Wood, *English and International Set-Off* (London, 1989), [3–22]. By contrast, statutory set-off on insolvency requires actual and contingent debts to be taken into account, at least where the contingent debt is owed by the insolvent: *MS Fashions Ltd* v. *Bank of Credit and Commerce International SA (No. 2)* [1993] Ch. 425, 435; *Stein* v. *Blake* [1996] AC 243, 251ff. (HL). See also *Re West End Networks Ltd* [2003] 2 BCLC 284, [13], affd. [2004] 2 All ER 1042, [6], [10], [19] (HL); *Swissport (UK) Ltd* v. *Aer Lingus Ltd* [2007] EWHC 1089 (Ch), [48]–[52]. This is now made clear in the liquidation context (Insolvency Rules 1986, S.I. 1986/1925, r.4.90(4) (as substituted by S.I. 2005/527, reg. 23)) and the administration context (Insolvency Rules 1986, S.I. 1986/1925, r.2.85(4) (as substituted by S.I. 2005/527, reg. 9)).

[231] *Pertamina Energy Trading Ltd* v. *Crédit Suisse*, n.147 above, [43], referring to 'the bank's common law right of set-off'.

[232] [1990] 2 QB 298. The main issue in the case was whether the bank's right was affected by the provisions of the Drug Trafficking Offences Act 1986. Otton J held that the bank's right to combine remained intact unless it had knowledge of the source of the funds. See also *Re Unit 2 Windows (in liq.)* [1985] 1 WLR 1383, in which Walton J regarded the Bankruptcy Act 1914, s.31 as providing the means for conducting an accounting exercise, but not as enabling a creditor to obtain an advantage by seeking to appropriate any given debt against a specific credit. Consider *Re A* [2002] 2 FCR 481, [120], where Munby J distinguished between 'a bank seeking to exercise its right to combine accounts and a contractual right of set-off or lien'.

[233] Ch. 21, Sect. 3(iii) below.

[234] N.218 above, 13, but contrast the judgment of Bramwell B (at 14–15).

In a Canadian case, *Rouxel* v. *Royal Bank of Canada*,[235] the claimant, who was owed an amount of $436 by the A Co., sent this firm an order to pay $80 to the M Co. Instead of obeying this simple instruction, the A Co. sent to the M Co. a cheque for $436 payable to the claimant. M Co. remitted this cheque to its own bankers, who in turn forwarded it to the defendant bank with an instruction that the cheque be released to the claimant against payment of the $80 that he owed to the M Co. The defendant bank asked the claimant to pay the $80 with disbursements and agreed to 'cash' the cheque for $436 on his behalf. To facilitate the clearing of the instrument the claimant was asked to indorse it. The bank subsequently decided to treat the indorsement as an implied request that the cheque be collected for the credit of a new account to be opened in the claimant's name. The defendant bank set off against the credit balance accrued in this account, following the clearing of the cheque, a debit balance in another of the claimant's accounts. It was held that the right of set-off could only be exercised by the bank in the context of the relationship of banker and customer. On the facts, the cheque in question was given to the bank merely to facilitate its presentment to the drawee bank. This was not a remittance of the cheque in the ordinary way, where a customer requests his bank to collect a cheque payable to him and to credit his account with the proceeds. The right to combine was, therefore, unavailable.

(iii) When may accounts be combined?

The general principle is well explained in *Greenwood Teale* v. *William, Williams, Brown & Co.*[236] The senior partner of a firm of solicitors opened three accounts: an office account, a deposit account, and a private account. The bank was initially told that clients' money would be paid to the credit of the deposit account. This account was subsequently closed, and thereafter both the firm's money and clients' funds were credited to the office account. As the private account was overdrawn for an amount far exceeding the credit balance of the office account, the bank resolved to combine the two accounts. Holding that the bank had acted properly, Wright J said that a bank had the right to combine a customer's separate accounts subject to three exceptions.[237] First, the right to combine could be abrogated by a special agreement. Secondly, the right to combine would be inapplicable where a special item of property was remitted to the bank and appropriated for a given purpose.[238] Thirdly, a bank could not combine a customer's private account with one known to the bank to be a trust account or one utilized for operations conducted by the customer as trustee. The bank's knowledge had to be express. The mere fact that an account was described as an office account was immaterial, as usually funds utilized by a firm through its 'office account' are not trust property. This analysis is unaffected by the decision of the House of Lords in *National Westminster Bank Ltd* v. *Halesowen Presswork and Assemblies Ltd.*[239] Moreover, the decision of the Court of Session in *James Kirkwood*

---

[235] [1918] 2 WWR 791.   [236] (1894) 11 TLR 56.

[237] *Good Property Land Development Pte Ltd* v. *Société Genérale*, n.217 above, 250; *Pertamina Energy Trading Ltd* v. *Crédit Suisse*, n.147 above, [44]. See also *Barclays Bank Ltd* v. *Okenarhe*, n.212 above, 95; *Chanyumbu Transport & Chanyumbu Trading* v. *Standard Bank Ltd* [2008] MWHC 181. The *Lending Code* (March 2011) also now recognises a number of practical limitations upon a bank's ability to set-off loan accounts, including the fact that the customer 'must be left with sufficient money to meet their reasonable day-to-day living expenses and priority debts' (ibid., [196]); set-off should not generally be used where the customer is being cooperative or the set-off will 'cause or exacerbate the customer's financial difficulties' (ibid., [196]); and set-off 'should normally only be used to make up the most recent missed payment' (ibid., [197]).

[238] *Rouxel* v. *Royal Bank of Canada*, n.235 above.   [239] N.222 above.

& *Sons* v. *Clydesdale Bank Ltd*[240] shows that the bank has the same right of combination in circumstances where its customer is not insolvent, but becomes unable to discharge a liability to the bank for other reasons.[241]

It is clear that a bank can combine the current accounts of a customer even though they are maintained with different branches. In *Garnett* v. *M'Kewan*,[242] a customer's account, maintained with the 'B branch' of the defendant bank, was overdrawn and, when he failed to discharge his liability, the account was frozen by the bank. Subsequently, the customer opened an account with the 'L branch' of the same bank in order to facilitate the collection of cheques payable to him. The bank set off the credit balance in the account with the 'L branch' against the overdraft in the account with the 'B branch'. As the bank did not give notice to the customer, he continued to draw cheques on the 'L branch' that were dishonoured by the bank. The customer sued the bank for breach of contract and defamation. Entering judgment for the bank, the Court of Exchequer held that, although there might be many accounts opened in a customer's name, there was only one contract between him and the bank.[243] The bank was entitled to combine these accounts for its own purposes, unless there was an agreement to keep them separate. Some doubts were, however, raised by Bramwell B, who observed:[244] '[t]he bank is not liable to be called on to pay at one branch just because there is a balance at another. Why, then, may the bank without notice debit the customer's account at one branch with his deficiency on another?' His Lordship resolved his doubts, however, by pointing out that it was unrealistic to allow a customer whose total balance was in debit to draw up to the credit balance maintained by the bank at any one branch. It was no hardship for the customer to be restricted to drawings within the net balance due to him from the bank. The customer was bound to know that he had a number of accounts with the bank, and was not entitled to ignore the overdrawn state of one of his accounts when drawing on another.

The assumption that a customer is, at any given time, familiar with the detailed state of all his accounts was probably questionable at the time of *Garrett*. A customer could not have been expected to know which cheques drawn by him, and which cheques paid to the credit of one of his accounts, had been cleared; at best, the customer could only have had a rough expectation concerning the state of his accounts. With the increasing popularity of internet banking, however, Bramwell B's justification for the bank's right of combination may have more currency nowadays, as there is probably a stronger expectation that a customer would have a clear understanding of the state of their accounts. Nevertheless, as discussed above, it seems advisable to rest the bank's right to combine accounts on the basic principles enunciated in *Re European Bank, Agra Bank Claim*,[245] and in *Greenwood Teale* v. *William, Williams, Brown & Co.*,[246] given that the House of Lords in *National Westminster Bank Ltd* v. *Halesowen Presswork and Assemblies Ltd*[247] relied on the very same reasoning.

Of the three exceptions to the doctrine recognizing a bank's right to combine accounts, it will be convenient to consider first the situations in which the bank has agreed to keep the accounts apart. The decision of the Privy Council in *British Guiana Bank* v. *OR*[248] suggests that an agreement that the bank keep two accounts separate is usually

---

[240] N.218 above.

[241] In *Kirkwood*, the problems arose due to the customer's death and ensuing difficulties pertaining to his estate.

[242] N.218 above. See also *Re Shaw* (1977) 17 ALR 32, 36–37 (FCA).

[243] See also *Good Property Land Development Pte Ltd* v. *Société Genérale*, n.217 above, 249–250; *Pertamina Energy Trading Ltd* v. *Crédit Suisse*, n.147 above, [43].

[244] N.218 above, 14.   [245] N.216 above.   [246] N.236 above.

[247] N.222 above.   [248] (1911) 104 LT 754 (PC).

determined if there are changed circumstances, such as the customer's insolvency. As the accounts are no longer 'current' (in the sense of 'active') the bank is entitled to revert to its original position. An Australian decision, *Direct Acceptance Corporation* v. *Bank of NSW*,[249] casts doubt on this point. The account of a company that was heavily indebted to the bank was frozen, and the bank agreed to open an 'account no. 2' for current banking operations. Shortly thereafter, a debenture holder appointed a receiver over the assets of the company. The bank thereupon sought to combine the company's two accounts so as to set off the credit balance in 'account no. 2' against the substantial debit balance in the frozen account. The liquidator disputed the bank's right to combine, and demanded the payment over of the balance standing to the credit of 'account no. 2'. Giving judgment against the bank, Macfarlan J said:[250]

> The agreement...was that the main account should be frozen and there should not be a right to set off the credit balance of the working account against the debit balance of the main account. I cannot deduce or infer from the facts...any indication that it was also agreed that this agreement was to continue in operation only so long as the accounts...were current. Also I cannot accept that when a receiver and manager is appointed, a current account necessarily ceases to be a current account and operation upon it is void.

His Honour based this decision on two factors. First, he thought that an agreement to keep the accounts separate remained in effect despite the customer's insolvency. The position depended on the intention of the parties. Secondly, he held that the appointment of a receiver did not change the nature of the company's current account. This point is well taken, as the appointment of a receiver does not necessarily mean that the company's business operations are to be suspended, as the receiver may decide that the enterprise should continue operating. A very different conclusion was reached, however, in *National Westminster Bank Ltd* v. *Halesowen Presswork and Assemblies Ltd*.[251] It was there held that a resolution to wind up the customer constituted a material change of circumstances, and that the bank's right to combine revived forthwith. Their Lordships were unanimous in holding that the words of the agreement for the opening of the working account in *Halesowen* made it clear that the arrangement would come to an end if there were materially altered circumstances.

The decisions in *Direct Acceptance* and *Halesowen* can be distinguished in two ways. First, the arrangement in *Halesowen* was of both a temporary and a contingent nature, as it was to determine at the end of four months, and even earlier than that if circumstances changed materially. In *Direct Acceptance*, however, there was no restriction of this type. Secondly, in *Direct Acceptance*, the company remained a going concern despite the appointment of a receiver. In *Halesowen*, however, the company was to cease operations for any purpose except its liquidation. The accounts, therefore, could be described as being no longer current. It is believed that the first distinction is the more important one. It will be recalled that in *Halesowen* the decision to wind up, passed on 12 June, was preceded by the calling of a meeting of creditors on 20 May. It was common ground that the calling of this meeting entitled the bank to treat the April agreement as at an end in view of the altered circumstances. The bank would have been justified in combining the accounts, although, the company's business was still a going concern at that time. The language of the clause used in *Halesowen* was wide enough to confer on the bank such a power.

Does the mere fact that an account is designated as being something other than a current account imply that its balance may not be set off in the ordinary way? The point arose in *Re E. J. Morel (1934) Ltd*.[252] A company encountering financial difficulties arranged to

---

[249] (1968) 88 WN (NSW) (Pt. 1) 498. [250] Ibid., 504. [251] N.222 above.
[252] N.221 above.

maintain three accounts with its bank: 'account no. 1' was a frozen account representing the company's outstanding liabilities; 'account no. 2' was a normal business account that the company was to use without regard to 'account no. 1'; and 'account no. 3' was a wages account. It was agreed that cheques for wages would be drawn on 'account no. 2', but that after four months the debit would be transferred to the wages account. When the company went into liquidation, 'account no. 1' had a debit balance of £1,839, 'account no. 2' had a credit balance of £1,544, and 'account no. 3' had a debit balance of £1,623. In the company's liquidation, the bank lodged a proof for £1,917, which was the net debit balance left after the combination of all three accounts. It was claimed that £910 out of this outstanding balance constituted a preferential claim, as it represented advances on wages. The liquidator disputed the claim for priority, as, in his opinion, it was necessary first to combine 'accounts nos. 2 and 3'. This would have left a preferential claim of £78 only. Adopting the liquidator's determination, Buckley J held that the doctrine of combination of accounts applied principally in respect of different current or general accounts of a given customer. Referring to *Bradford Old Bank Ltd* v. *Sutcliffe*,[253] Buckley J observed:[254]

> ...there is an important difference between a case where a customer has several current accounts, and a case where a customer has an account which is not a current account, and one or more current accounts in the bank. In the first case where all the accounts are current, the banker can combine those accounts in whatever way he chooses, treating them all as being one account of his relationship with his customer. In the other case the accounts are of a different character, and the banker is not free to combine them in that way.

It is clear that *Morel* differs on this point from *Halesowen*. The distinction is, again, based on the facts. In *Halesowen*, the bank reserved the right to combine the accounts in the event of a material change in the circumstances, whilst *Morel* defines the position where the bank does not safeguard itself in this manner.[255] The specific designation of the account as something different from a current account may, in such a case, support the argument that the account is meant to be kept apart.[256] The significance attributable to the name of an account, in a situation of this type, is further demonstrated by *Re Gross, ex p. Kingston*,[257] where it was held that an account opened by a customer as a 'police account' could not be combined with the customer's personal account.

The significance of an account's designation is evident where the question of combination arises in respect of a loan account. The circumstances leading to the opening of a loan account usually indicate that the parties have agreed that the loan account will not be combined with other accounts as long as the customer is able to carry on his business. Indeed, the customer could not engage in everyday transactions if he had to fear that a cheque, drawn by him on his current account, could be dishonoured following the bank's decision to set off the balance in his current account against the amount due under the loan agreement. Thus, in *Bradford Old Bank Ltd* v. *Sutcliffe*,[258] Pickford LJ held that the fact that one of the accounts was designated a loan account clearly showed 'that the accounts were to be kept distinct by arrangement' between the customer and the bank. This view is supported

---

[253] [1918] 2 KB 833 (CA).   [254] N.221 above, 31–32.

[255] *Fraser* v. *Oystertec plc* [2006] 1 BCLC 491, [16]–[17].

[256] *Re Johnson & Co. Ltd* [1902] 1 IR 439 supports the view that in such a case the accounts have to be kept apart even after the customer's insolvency.

[257] (1871) LR 6 Ch. App. 632.

[258] N.253 above, 839, approved in *Cinema Plus Ltd* v. *ANZ Banking Group Ltd*, n.218 above (no combination of current account and lease finance facility). See also *Barclays Bank Ltd* v. *Okenarhe*, n.212 above, 96–97. See also *Uttamchandani* v. *Central Bank of India*, The Times, 8 January 1989 (CA).

by Buckley J's decision in *Re E. J. Morel (1934) Ltd*,[259] by Lord Cross in *Halesowen*,[260] and most recently by *Fraser* v. *Oystertec plc*,[261] where Terence Mowschenson QC stated that '[i]t is well established that absent an express agreement a banker has no implied right to combine or set off the amount due under a [loan] facility (during its currency) with amounts standing to the credit of a debtor's account'.[262] Accordingly, it is clear that a loan account and a current account are usually not meant to be combined.[263] It would be unusual for the bank to exercise a right of set-off in respect of such an account whilst the customer's business was a going concern. The right may revive upon the customer's insolvency. When this happens, it is necessary to consider the precise arrangements between the parties.

There is some uncertainty whether a bank may combine accounts held within the same jurisdiction but in different currencies, or accounts held at branches in different jurisdictions. There seems no reason why accounts held in different currencies should not be combined. The mere fact that the customer has elected to hold accounts in different currencies does not evidence an implied intention to keep those accounts separate and immune from combination. The position where accounts are held in different jurisdictions is more difficult. Are the accounts governed by different contracts or by one contract? If governed by one contract, is it governed by different applicable laws, or by one applicable law? If governed by one applicable law, which one? Does the law applicable to an overseas account prohibit combination?[264] Above all, where accounts are held in different jurisdictions there seems a stronger case for arguing that there is an implied agreement not to combine. This reflects the fact that, for many purposes, overseas branches of a bank are regarded as separate entities.[265] Nevertheless, where a customer places deposits with an overseas branch, and that branch fails to repay them, it may be possible for the customer to hold the bank's head office liable for repayment.[266] In such cases the bank's head office should be able to argue that any implied agreement not to combine has been determined.

According to *Greenwood Teale* v. *William, Williams, Brown & Co.*,[267] the second exception to the bank's general right to combine accounts occurs in cases of 'specific appropriation'. It will be recalled that the point arose in this very case. However, the Court of Appeal in Chancery held that there was insufficient evidence to show that the customer had appropriated the relevant securities for some specific purpose. The question came up again in *W.P. Greenhalgh & Sons* v. *Union Bank of Manchester*.[268] The claimants, cotton brokers of Liverpool, sold a quantity of cotton to W. & Sons. The cotton was resold to spinners who issued to W. & Sons a bill of exchange for the price. W. & Sons remitted this bill to the defendant bank, with which they had their business account. That bank credited the proceeds of the bill to W. & Sons' account where the funds reduced an

---

[259] N.221 above.   [260] N.222 above, 809.   [261] N.255 above.   [262] Ibid., [16].

[263] But a bank may be able to rely on an express contractual right of combination between current and loan accounts: see, for example, *Cinema Plus Ltd* v. *ANZ Banking Group Ltd*, n.218 above; *Magill* v. *National Australia Bank* [2001] NSWCA 221.

[264] For the law applicable to the banking contract, see Ch. 5, Sect. 3, fn.50 above.

[265] See, for example, *MacKinnon* v. *Donaldson, Lufkin & Jenrette* [1986] Ch. 482, considered in Ch. 5, Sect. 5(vii) above. See also *Canada Life Assurance Co* v. *CIBC*, n.20 above, 684 ('…it is recognized that a bank may have many residences'); *Power Curber* v. *National Bank of Kuwait* [1981] 1 WLR 1233, 1241 (CA).

[266] W. Blair, 'Liability for Foreign Branch Deposits in English Law' in R. Cranston (ed.), *Making Commercial Law: Essays in Honour of Roy Goode* (Oxford, 1997). This assumes the overseas branch is not a subsidiary incorporated in the foreign country.

[267] N.236 above. See also *Mutton* v. *Peat* [1900] 2 Ch. 79.

[268] [1924] 2 KB 153. See also *Royal Bank of Canada* v. *Bender* (1994) 159 AR 303, [15].

existing overdraft. The claimants claimed that the bills had been appropriated to their contract with W. & Sons, and were meant to secure payment of the price due to themselves. The claimants further argued that notice of the appropriation of the bills had been given to the defendant bank. Entering judgment for the claimants, Swift J said:[269]

> If a person making a payment of money...to another, states definitely that such payment is to be used for a particular purpose, and the person to whom it is made does not dissent, he accepts it for the purpose and must use it... only for the purpose for which he receives it...

His Lordship added that if the purpose was to arrange for payment to a third party and that person came to know of the appropriation of the funds, he was entitled to claim the amount involved. Presumably his rights would be those of an assignee.

Greenhalgh concerned primarily the rights of third parties, but the case is also important where a bank wishes to combine a number of accounts maintained in the name of a single customer. If the bank knows that a given sum or item has been appropriated for a specific purpose, the right of set-off cannot be exercised in respect of it. The principle involved has been approved by the House of Lords in *Barclays Bank Ltd* v. *Quistclose Investments Ltd*.[270] A company facing financial difficulties obtained a loan from the respondents in order to arrange for the payment of dividends declared by the company's general meeting. The amount of the loan was paid into a special account, opened for this purpose by the company with the appellant bank. Before paying out the dividends, the company went into liquidation. The appellant bank thereupon sought to set off the balance in the special account against the overdraft incurred on the company's general account. The respondents instituted an action to establish that, as the object for which the money had been lent to the company had failed, it was held by the company as a resulting trustee for the respondents' benefit. Lord Wilberforce held that, to succeed, the respondents had to establish two points. First, they had to show that the relevant loan monies could be utilized for a specific purpose only.[271] Secondly, it was necessary to show that the bank had knowledge of the appropriation involved. His Lordship emphasized that the bank knew that the funds had been provided on the clear understanding that they could not be used for any purpose other than the payment of the dividends. Although the mere

---

[269] Ibid., 161.   [270] [1970] AC 567 (HL).

[271] In fact, 'something rather more than a specific purpose is required before a proprietary claim for return of money can be upheld so as to defeat any right of set-off that might otherwise exist. What is required is the creation of a trust': *Anglo Corporation Ltd* v. *Peacock AG* (CA, 12 February 1997). Brooke LJ held that there was no trust because there was no agreement about the purpose for which the funds were held and also because the funds were not sufficiently identifiable as they had been mixed with other funds. A considerable body of case law has built up on the question of when a *Quistclose* trust comes into existence, including *Re Kayford Ltd* [1975] 1 WLR 279; *Re Northern Developments (Holdings) Ltd* (CA, 6 October 1978); *Carreras Rothmans Ltd* v. *Freeman Mathews Treasure Ltd* [1985] Ch. 207; *Re Multi-Guarantee Co. Ltd* [1987] BCLC 257 (CA); *Re Branston & Gotthard Ltd* [1999] Lloyd's Rep. Bank. 251 (money in 'Client Money Requirement' account held on trust and was not subject to bank's right of combination); *Twinsectra Ltd* v. *Yardley* [2002] 2 AC 164 (HL); *Cooper* v. *Official Receiver* [2003] BPIR 55; *Re Crown Forestry Rental Trust* [2004] 4 All ER 558 (PC); *Re Margaretta Ltd* [2005] STC 610; *Templeton Insurance Ltd* v. *Penningtons Solicitors LLP* [2006] EWHC 685 (Ch); *Abou-Rahmah* v. *Abacha* [2006] 1 Lloyd's Rep 484, affd. on a different point: [2007] 1 Lloyd's Rep 115 (CA); *Re Farepak Foods and Gifts Ltd* [2006] EWHC 3272 (Ch); *Cooper* v. *PRG Powerhouse Ltd* [2008] EWHC 498 (Ch), [24]; Soutzos v. Asombang [2010] BPIR 960, [142]–[144]. See generally R. Chambers, *Resulting Trusts* (Oxford, 1997), ch. 3; W. Swadling (ed.), *The Quistclose Trust* (Oxford, 2004); J. Glister, 'The Nature of Quistclose Trusts: Classification and Reconciliation' (2004) 63 *CLJ* 632. See also, for example, *Salvo* v. *New Tel Ltd* [2005] NSWCA 281; *Giles* v. *Westminster Savings Credit Union* [2006] BCSC 141; *Hiranand* v. *Harilela* [2007] HKCU 1073 (HKCA); *Singapore Tourism Board* v. *Children's Media Ltd* [2008] 3 SLR 981.

request to credit an amount to a special account would not have been fatal to the bank's right to combine, the bank here had been informed of the details of the transaction. The judgment of the Court of Appeal[272] for the respondents was affirmed.

The third type of case in which, according to *Greenwood Teale* v. *William, Williams, Brown & Co.*,[273] the bank does not enjoy the right to combine a customer's accounts is where the bank knows that the account in credit is a trust account. The reason for this is plain: the bank cannot set off against the customer's personal debt an amount that is due—either legally or beneficially—to a third party, such as the beneficiary of a trust. The leading case in point is *Union Bank of Australia* v. *Murray-Aynsley*.[274] A corporation maintained three accounts with its bank: a general account; a stock account; and an 'account no. 3' used for investments made by the corporation in the administration of a certain estate. The ledger of the 'account no. 3', though, made no reference to the estate's interest. When the corporation had to be wound up, the bank sought to combine all three accounts. Dismissing the liquidator's objection, Lord Watson said that there was no evidence to show that the bank had been aware of the true nature of the 'account no. 3'. Unless the bank knew that the account was the subject of a trust, it retained the right of set-off in respect of the balance standing to its credit.[275] Although Lord Watson's decision derives support from other authorities,[276] it is open to criticism. In *Murray-Aynsley*, there was no evidence to suggest that the bank had relied on the credit balance in 'account no. 3' in order to approve overdrafts granted to the corporation in respect of other accounts. Even if the corporation had held out that the funds in 'account no. 3' belonged to it, the bank could not rely on the misrepresentation involved unless it acted on it. It is difficult to see why an amount of money, due in equity to the beneficiaries of an estate, should be used to satisfy the personal debts owed by the administrator or trustee to the bank.

A case where the bank had knowledge that the account in credit was a trust account is *Royal Bank of Scotland plc* v. *Wallace International Ltd*.[277] D plc took over WI Ltd., D plc banked with RBS, the defendant bank, and WI Ltd banked with Midland Bank, where it held £2.7 million on credit. As part of the banking rearrangements within the new 'D Group', RBS opened an account in the name of 'D plc—WI' and credited it with £2.7 million representing the monies previously held with the Midland Bank. Some months later, RBS purported to set off the credit balance on the 'D plc—WI' account against the larger debit balances on other accounts for which D plc was liable. WI Ltd commenced proceedings for declarations that D plc held the monies standing to the credit of the 'D plc—WI' account on trust for WI Ltd, and that RBS knew that such monies belonged beneficially to WI Ltd and were therefore not available for set-off against the liabilities of D plc to RBS. Upholding the trial judge, the Court of Appeal gave judgment in favour of WI Ltd. It was

---

[272] [1968] Ch. 540 (CA).   [273] N.236 above.

[274] [1898] AC 693 (PC). As regards solicitors' accounts, see the Solicitors' Act 1974, s.85(b). For the common law, see *Clark* v. *Ulster Bank Ltd*, n.3 above (right to combine monies in solicitors' account in the absence of express or implied notice about the nature of monies).

[275] *Barclays Bank Ltd* v. *Okenarhe*, n.212 above, 96. See also *Devron Potatoes Ltd* v. *Gordon & Innes Ltd*, n.3 above, [27]–[29]. The bank is not fixed with knowledge simply because the customer is likely to hold monies on behalf of others: *Clark* v. *Ulster Bank Ltd*, n.3 above, 134–135; *Banque Romande* v. *Mercantile Bank of Canada* n.3 above, 444; *Halifax Insurance Co.* v. *Canadian Imperial Bank of Commerce* (1985) 153 APR 107, 122 (NSC).

[276] *Greenwood Teale* v. *William, Williams, Brown & Co.*, n.236 above; *Bank of New South Wales* v. *Goulburn Valley Butter Co. Pty. Ltd* [1902] AC 543 (PC).

[277] [2000] All ER (D) 78 (CA). See also *Devron Potatoes Ltd* v. *Gordon & Innes Ltd*, n.3 above, [27]: '…as from the point in time when a bank becomes aware that the funds paid into the client's account…are only held by the payer in a fiduciary capacity, they have no right to set off funds against sums due to them by their customer under other accounts'.

clear on the evidence that the account in question was a trust account held by D plc for WI Ltd from the moment that it was opened, and that the bank knew this from that time onwards. The monies held in the account belonged beneficially to WI Ltd, and not D plc, and were accordingly not available to set off against D plc's liabilities.

Where a bank knows that an account is the subject of a trust, it cannot exercise a right of set-off against a balance standing to its credit to satisfy the personal debts of the trustee.[278] But can the bank set off against a credit balance in the trustee's personal account a debit balance in a trust account maintained by him? A Canadian authority, *Daniels* v. *Imperial Bank of Canada*,[279] suggests a positive answer. It was there held that, as the trustee had the right to draw on the trust account, he was to be regarded as having its control. On this basis, he was personally answerable with his own funds for any deficiency in the trust funds. The point may be questioned, however, as the trustee does not purport to transact trust business as a principal. Furthermore, if the bank requires his assurance, it can always request him to furnish a personal guarantee. In the absence of such a facility, it is difficult to see why the trustee's personal account should be utilized to cover a shortage in the trust account.

Usually, the question of a set-off arises in respect of individual accounts maintained by a customer, but is there room for a combination of accounts if one is a personal account and the other a joint account? A Canadian authority suggests that a right of set-off may be available. In *Hill* v. *Bank of Hochelaga*,[280] a joint account was opened in the name of a married couple. The husband made the initial deposit and drew the bulk of the cheques on the account. The wife subsequently notified the bank that the initial deposit had come from the proceeds of the sale of some of her own property. The question for decision was whether the bank could set off the husband's liability, incurred in respect of guarantees securing advances made at his request to a certain corporation, against the credit balance of the joint account. It was held that a set-off could be exercised in respect of the entire balance of the joint account for any advances guaranteed by the husband *before* the bank was informed of the true source of the funds initially deposited. In respect of any later advances, the set-off could be exercised only against the husband's equal share of the funds in the joint account.[281]

---

[278] However, the bank may be able to exercise a right of set-off between a personal account and a 'nominee' account where there is clear and undisputed evidence that the customer entitled to the funds in both accounts was one and the same person: *Uttamchandani* v. *Central Bank of India*, n.258 above; *Bhogal* v. *Punjab National Bank* [1988] 2 All ER 296 (CA). A similar principle applies in cases of statutory set-off on insolvency: *Bank of Credit and Commerce International SA* v. *Al-Saud* [1997] 1 BCLC 457 (CA).

In *Saudi Arabian Monetary Agency* v. *Dresdner Bank AG* [2005] 1 Lloyd's Rep 12 (CA), the Court of Appeal stressed that the critical element in cases where a bank seeks to rely on a right of equitable set off against its customer (i.e. against the person in whose name the account is held), is that their relationship is governed by the underlying banking contract to which they (and they alone) are party. There could be cases where the contract provides that there are no circumstances in which the bank can set off a third party's debt against the balance on the customer's account. Conversely, the contract could provide that the bank can set off a third party's debt against the credit balance of its customer's account whenever the bank has reasonable grounds for believing that the third party is beneficially interested in the money in that account. However, their Lordships held that, in a case where the contract is silent on the issue, the rule is that a bank is not entitled to refuse payment of money deposited with it on the basis merely of an arguable case that some other debtor of the bank has an equitable interest in the money.

[279] (1914) 19 DLR 166.   [280] [1921] 3 WWR 430 (ASC).

[281] Cf. *Re Willis, Percival & Co. Ltd, ex p. Morier* (1879) 12 Ch. D 491 (considered in *Saudi Arabian Monetary Agency* v. *Dresdner Bank AG*, n.278 above), where it was held that an executor's indebtedness on his personal account could not be set off against the credit balance in the joint account maintained with his fellow executors. The decision, however, is largely based on the trust element of the joint account. See also *Bailey* v. *Finch* (1871) LR 7 QB 34, where, in similar circumstances, combination of accounts was allowed as the executor was, in effect, also the beneficiary of the estate. See also *Abbey National plc* v. *McCann* [1997]

Attractive as this decision may appear, it is open to criticism. An amount standing to the credit of a joint account constitutes a debt owed by the bank to the depositors jointly and severally. It is true that if the bank pays the amount standing to the credit of the joint account in violation of its mandate, as is the case where it honours a cheque that does not bear all the required signatures, the bank has to compensate the depositor who loses out.[282] The bank, therefore, has to pay an amount equal to the innocent party's share of the account funds. In contrast, a bank that pays a cheque bearing the necessary signatures is not answerable to any of the depositors. This is so even if the depositors, who validly signed the cheque, issued it for improper purposes. This same principle can be applied by analogy to the bank's right to combine a joint account with the personal account of one of the joint depositors. If the depositor in question has the right to draw cheques on the account by means of his signature alone, it can be assumed that he also has the power to transfer money from the joint account to his own overdrawn account. In doing so, he would treat the money standing to the credit of the joint account as funds available for his own purposes. The bank would have no cause to question such a transfer. The bank, therefore, may justifiably assume that the amount standing to the credit of the joint account is available to either depositor, and that it is subject to a right of set-off in respect of such a depositor's personal account.

A point that has not been the subject of decision concerns the converse of the situation in *Hill*. Can a bank set off against the credit balance in a customer's personal account an overdraft or loan incurred in respect of a joint account?[283] It is believed that the bank is entitled to do so. The debts incurred in respect of the joint account are due jointly and severally from all parties. As the banks could, accordingly, sue any depositor for the full amount of an overdraft on the joint account, it stands to reason that the bank also has a corresponding right of set-off.

(iv) **Is notice required?**

Is the bank under an obligation to give notice to the customer before it combines his accounts in order to effect a set-off? This question was considered in *Garnett* v. *M'Kewan*,[284] where the Court of Exchequer answered it unanimously in the negative. In the words of Kelly CB:[285] '[i]n general it might be proper or considerate to give a notice to that effect, but there is no legal obligation on the bankers to do so, arising either from express contract or the course of dealing between the parties'. An opposite conclusion was reached in *Buckingham Co.* v. *London and Midland Bank*.[286] A customer maintained with his bank a current account and a loan account, the debit balance of which was secured by a charge over his land. When property prices dropped sharply, the bank feared that its security had

---

NIJB 158, 173 (NICA), where it was held to be arguable that a right of combination extended to a discrete part of a joint account held in the name of others which could be shown with sufficient clarity to have been in the beneficial ownership of the debtor.

[282] Ch. 8, Sect. 2 below.

[283] Cf. *Watts* v. *Christie* (1849) 11 Beav. 546, which concerned the customer's right to request a set-off. In the course of the judgment it was held that the bank did not have a 'lien' over the personal account in respect of the overdraft on the joint account.

[284] N.218 above. See also *National Australia Bank Ltd* v. *Magill* [2000] NSWSC 598.

[285] Ibid., 13.

[286] (1895) 12 TLR 70. *Buckingham* has been criticized as 'an extreme example of high-handed conduct on the part of a bank' (*Barclays Bank Ltd* v. *Okenarhe*, n.212 above, 96–97) and as 'nothing but a decision about the facts of that particular case' (*Ilawong Village Pty Ltd* v. *State Bank of New South Wales* [2004] NSWSC 18, [250], affd. without reference to the point: [2005] NSWCA 382).

lost its value. It therefore set off without notice the credit balance of the current account against the sum due under the loan account. Consequently, some of the customer's cheques were dishonoured. Mathew J asked the jury to decide whether there was a course of dealing between the parties that permitted the customer to draw cheques on his current account without having regard to the state of the loan account and, further, whether he was entitled to reasonable notice if the bank decided to cancel this arrangement. The jury answered both questions positively and awarded damages of £500 against the bank.

Buckingham is easily reconcilable with *Garnett* v. *M'Kewan*,[287] in which there was no agreement between the bank and its customer that the accounts be kept separate.[288] The bank could, therefore, exercise its right of set-off without notice. In *Buckingham*, the right was abrogated by an agreement based on a course of dealings between the parties, which could only be displaced by reasonable notice. Even in such cases, however, notice is not always required. An agreement to keep the accounts separate may be abrogated by subsequent developments. The classic case in point is where the customer becomes insolvent. His bankruptcy or winding-up usually abrogates the agreement, and may restore to the bank its right to combine the accounts without notice. Thus, in *British Guiana Bank* v. *OR*,[289] Lord Macnaghten held that an agreement to keep accounts apart remained in effect only whilst the accounts were current and that it came to an end when the accounts were frozen by the customer's insolvency.

The point was considered in detail in *National Westminster Bank Ltd* v. *Halesowen Presswork and Assemblies Ltd*.[290] As considered above, the bank agreed to keep the current account and the frozen account apart for four months, provided there was no material alteration in the customer's circumstances. Two changes took place. Initially, the customer convened a meeting of creditors, and, subsequently, it decided to wind up voluntarily. The bank had resolved not to combine the accounts after the first event, but exercised its right of combination without notice after the second event. Their Lordships were unanimous that the words of the agreement indicated that it was *automatically* terminated when the company decided to wind up. Notice by the bank of its decision to combine the accounts was, therefore, not required. Their Lordships indicated, however, that in the absence of clear language dispensing with the need for notice, notice would probably be required. Viscount Dilhorne[291] said that, if the bank had decided to combine the accounts in the wake of the customer's decision to convene a meeting of creditors, the bank would have been required to give reasonable notice. Lord Cross of Chelsea[292] said that, ordinarily, a bank would at the very least have to honour cheques drawn by the customer up to the time he was given notice of the combination of his accounts. In contrast, in *Good Property Land Development Pte Ltd* v. *Société Genérale*,[293] the Singaporean Court of Appeal was clear that '[t]here is no doubt that a bank may combine two current accounts at any time without giving notice to the customer, even if the accounts are held at different branches', but indicated that the position might be different where the bank was seeking to combine a current account and a loan account. Lai Kew Chai J viewed Lord Cross' comments in *Halesowen* as relating to the second of these situations.

It follows that the question may still be open, although some further support for the requirement that a bank should give a customer notice before combining accounts can

---

[287] N.218 above.
[288] See also *Irwin* v. *Bank of Montreal* (1876) 38 UCQB 375, 393; *Wallinder* v. *Imperial Bank of Canada* [1925] 3 DLR 390.
[289] N.248 above.   [290] N.222 above.   [291] Ibid., 807.   [292] Ibid., 810.
[293] N.217 above, 250.

be derived from the latest version of the *Lending Code* promulgated in March 2011. According to paragraph 195, 'when the lender is actively considering or is likely to exercise set-off', it should 'contact the customer to inform them in clear and simple language the generic circumstances in which set-off would be used and when'. Whether the courts should transform this statement of best practice in the Lending Code into a binding legal obligation, however, depends upon two conflicting commercial considerations. On the one hand, the need to serve notice can do irreparable harm to the bank. Notice would enable the customer either to draw on his account until the 'reasonable time' given to him had expired or to divert cheques payable to him to some other bank accounts. On the other hand, it has been shown that the bank cannot close its customer's account, and thus terminate the contract between them, without first giving reasonable notice.[294] In practice, the combination of accounts has the same effect as their closure. In both cases, the customer is precluded from utilizing his account for ordinary trading purposes. Why, then, should the bank be required to give him notice of the closure of his account, but not of its combination with other accounts? Still, it is believed that the solution proposed by Lord Cross of Chelsea presents an acceptable compromise.

(v) Special problems in insolvency situations

The most common situation in which a bank seeks to exercise its right of set-off is where an individual customer is adjudicated bankrupt or a corporate customer is being wound up. In such cases, the bank's set-off is sanctioned not only by common law principles, but also by section 323 of the Insolvency Act 1986, which replaced section 31 of the Bankruptcy Act 1914.[295] Section 323 provides for a set-off between amounts due to the creditor from an individual bankrupt and vice versa, provided 'there have been mutual credits, mutual debts or other mutual dealings' between the two parties. A similar rule applies to the liquidation of companies.[296] The requirement of mutuality means that the claim and cross-claim must be between the same parties in the same right.[297] The

---

[294] Ch. 5, Sect. 6 above.

[295] Bankruptcy Act 1914, s.31 applied to the winding up of companies under the Companies Act 1948, s.317, which was replaced by the Companies Act 1985, s.612 (in turn, repealed by the Insolvency Act 1986, s.438).

[296] Insolvency Rules 1986, S.I. 1986/1925, r.4.90(1) (as substituted by S.I. 2005/527, reg. 23). See *BCCI (Overseas) Ltd* v. *Habib Bank Ltd* [1999] Ch 340 (CA). The new administration regime introduced into the Insolvency Act 1986 by the Enterprise Act 2002 includes a mandatory set-off rule in similar form to r.4.90: Insolvency Rules 1986, S.I. 1986/1925, r.2.85 (as substituted by S.I. 2005/527, reg. 9). See further Ch. 21, Sect. 3(ii) below.

[297] In *Re West End Networks Ltd* [2004] 2 All ER 1042, [26], [38] (HL), Lord Hoffmann stated: 'Mutuality requires that each party should be debtor and creditor in the same capacity.' Thus, in *MS Fashions Ltd* v. *BCCI*, n.230 above, where a surety deposited money with a bank to secure the borrowings of his company, and by the terms of the security documentation agreed that his liability should be that of a principal debtor (and not merely that of a guarantor), Hoffmann LJ (at first instance) and the Court of Appeal held that, on the bank's subsequent liquidation, automatic mandatory insolvency set-off of the deposit against the surety's obligation to the bank operated so as to repay the principal debtor's indebtedness to the bank. It made no difference that the bank had not made a demand on the surety as he was himself severally liable for the debt. See also *TS&S Global Ltd* v. *Fithian-Franks* [2008] 1 BCLC 277, [19]–[27]. By contrast, in *Re BCCI (No. 8)* [1996] Ch. 245 (CA), affd. on other grounds: [1998] AC 214 (HL), where the surety deposited money and granted the bank a charge over it, but did not give any express covenant or personal guarantee to repay, the Court of Appeal held there was no sum due from the surety before demand and accordingly there could be no set-off on the bank's subsequent liquidation.

party relying on set-off must establish mutuality clearly on the evidence.[298] Where the conditions of the rule are satisfied, a set-off is treated as having taken place automatically on the bankruptcy date,[299] and the original claims are extinguished and only the net balance remains owing one way or the other.[300]

The scope of the original provision (Bankruptcy Act 1914, s.31) was explained in *National Westminster Bank Ltd* v. *Halesowen Presswork and Assemblies Ltd*.[301] One question that arose was whether the dealings between the defendant bank and the claimants were 'mutual'. There was no doubt that any dealings between banker and customer on an account that is current would be so regarded. *Halesowen*, however, involved one active account ('account no. 2') and one frozen account ('account no. 1'). Their Lordships agreed with the view expressed in earlier cases[302] to the effect that dealings would cease to be 'mutual' within the meaning of the section where payments were made for specific or specially designated purposes. The mere mention of a purpose, however, was inadequate. Had it been sufficient, then any 'dealings' of a customer with his bank would cease to be mutual if their purpose was mentioned. Their Lordships considered this to be an unacceptable conclusion. Lord Simon defined the meaning of 'mutual' as follows:[303] 'money is paid for a special (or specific) purpose so as to exclude mutuality of dealing within section 31 if the money is paid in such circumstances that it would be a misappropriation to use it for any other purpose than that for which it is paid'. In *Halesowen*, the dealings were mutual, as the agreement not to combine the accounts was made for a limited period and only in so far as the customer's circumstances remained materially unchanged.[304] The position has remained largely unchanged under the regime of section 323 of the Insolvency Act 1986. However, subsection (3) of this new provision clarifies one important point. Sums due from the bankrupt to the party seeking to effect the set-off are not to be included in the account taken 'if that other party had notice at the time they became due that a bankruptcy petition relating to the bankrupt was pending'. An equivalent provision also exists in relation to company liquidations.[305]

A further question raised in *Halesowen* was whether the parties could contract out of the provisions of section 31 of the Bankruptcy Act 1914. Their Lordships were unanimous that, on the facts, the parties had not intended to exclude the section. Viscount Dilhorne and Lords Simon and Kilbrandon thought, in addition, that the section was of

---

[298] In *Bank of Credit and Commerce International SA (in liq.)* v. *Al-Saud*, n.278 above, the Court of Appeal denied set-off under the Insolvency Rules, S.I. 1986/1925, r.4.90, to guarantor X whose beneficial interest in accounts in the name of Y with an insolvent bank was not shown to be clear and free from doubt. See also *Re A Company* [2004] 1 BCLC 210, [26].

[299] *Stein* v. *Blake*, n.230 above; *Re BCCI (No. 8)* [1998] AC 214, (HL); *Re West End Networks Ltd*, n.297 above, [6]. This contrasts with the common law right of combination, as it would be commercially impracticable if this operated automatically: P.R. Wood, *English and International Set-Off* (London, 1989), 47.

[300] Ibid. See also *Swissport (UK) Ltd* v. *Aer Lingus Ltd*, n.230 above, [43] ('Insolvency set-off is not just a matter of procedure; it affects the substantive rights of the parties').

[301] N.222 above.

[302] *Re Pollitt* [1893] 1 QB 455; *Re Mid-Kent Fruit Factory Ltd* [1896] 1 Ch. 567; *Re City Equitable Fire Insurance Co. Ltd* [1930] 2 Ch. 293.

[303] N.222 above, 808.

[304] In *Re West End Networks Ltd*, n.297 above, [22]–[24], Lord Hoffmann gave a broad definition to the words 'other mutual dealings' in Insolvency Rules, S.I. 1986/1925, r.4.90: 'All that is necessary therefore is that there should have been "dealings" (in an extended sense which includes the commission of a tort or the imposition of a statutory obligation) which gives rise to commensurable cross-claims.' See also *Haine* v. *Day* [2008] 2 BCLC 626, [35] (CA).

[305] Insolvency Rules 1986, S.I. 1986/1925, r.4.90(1) (as substituted by S.I. 2005/527, reg. 23).

an imperative nature.[306] They based their conclusion on the mandatory language of the section, which provided that the creditor 'shall' have the right of set-off. Lord Cross of Chelsea reached the opposite conclusion. In his Lordship's opinion, the word 'shall' was used in section 31 in order to confer a definite right of set-off on the creditor. His Lordship thought it incorrect to suggest that this right could not be abrogated by agreement.

Nowadays, section 323 of the Insolvency Act 1986 effectively supports Viscount Dilhorne's view. Subsection (2) does not confer the right to exercise a set-off on a creditor, but enacts that 'an account shall be taken of what is due from each party to the other' and that the two amounts be set off against each other.[307] It follows that the set-off in question is to be effected by the trustee in bankruptcy as a matter of course and quite regardless of the agreement between the parties.[308] It is believed that this principle is undesirable and that Lord Cross' view is preferable. In many cases, the bank's agreement to keep the accounts apart is motivated by the need to inject confidence into the customer's business standing. When the bank seeks to abrogate its agreement and to combine the accounts upon the customer's insolvency, its interests do not conflict with the customer's but with the claims of his general creditors. The creditors involved are usually the very persons who have continued to trade with the customer as a result of the bank's agreement to keep him going by separating his accounts.[309] It is unfair that these creditors be prejudiced further by the bank's set-off in an insolvency context being mandatory in nature.

One question that did not arise in *Halesowen* was whether the remittance of amounts to the credit of an account, the balance of which could be the subject of a set-off, constitutes a 'preference' within the meaning of the Insolvency Act 1986. By and large, under section 239 (applicable to the winding-up of companies) and section 340 (applicable to the bankruptcy of individuals), a debtor gives one of his creditors a preference if the debtor does anything (or suffers anything to be done) that has the effect of putting the relevant creditor in a better position in the debtor's insolvency than he would otherwise have been if the relevant act had not been done. If such a preference is given to the creditor within the specified 'relevant time' (which in most cases is six months before the commencement of the winding-up or the bankruptcy), a court has the power to make an order restoring the position to what it would have been if the debtor had not given that preference. These provisions originated, respectively, from section 44 of the Bankruptcy Act 1914 and from section 615 of the Companies Act 1985.[310] Section 44 was subject to a proviso—contained in section 45 of the Bankruptcy Act 1914—under which a transaction could not be set aside in certain cases, one of which was where the creditor had furnished valuable consideration. In *Re Keever (a Bankrupt)*,[311] it was held that where a cheque payable to a customer

---

[306] *Coca-Cola Financial Corporation* v. *Finsat International Ltd* [1998] QB 43, 52 (CA); *Re West End Networks Ltd*, n.297 above, [6] (referring to the Insolvency Rules 1986, S.I. 1986/1925, r.4.90 as 'mandatory').

[307] For the equivalent provision applicable to corporate liquidations, see Insolvency Rules 1986, S.I. 1986/1925, r.4.90(3) (as substituted by S.I. 2005/527, reg. 23).

[308] For a similar argument under Insolvency Rules 1986, S.I. 1986/1925, r.4.90, see *Re West End Networks Ltd*, n.297 above, [6]. Nor can the rules of insolvency set-off be disapplied by the court in the exercise of its discretion: *Re Bank of Credit and Commerce International SA (No. 10)* [1997] Ch. 213; *Re HIH Casualty and General Insurance Ltd* [2008] 3 All ER 869, [15]–[17], [67], [72] (HL).

[309] The Cork Committee recommended that the legislation be amended to allow such contracting out: 'Insolvency Law and Practice: Report of the Review Committee' (Cmnd. 8558, London, 1982), [1341]–[1342]. No steps have been taken to implement this recommendation.

[310] Previously, Companies Act 1948, s.320.

[311] N.220 above. Cf. *George Parker (Transport) Ltd* v. *Eynon* [1973] 1 WLR 1461, revsd. [1974] 1 All ER 900 (CA).

was remitted by him to his bank for the credit of his overdrawn account, the transaction was saved by this proviso because the customer's pre-existing debt constituted good consideration under section 27 of the Bills of Exchange Act 1882. The Insolvency Act 1986 does not have a similar proviso, but both in the winding-up of a company and the bankruptcy of an individual an order restoring the original position is available only in so far as the debtor is influenced at the time he gives the preference by a desire to confer a benefit on the relevant creditor.[312] The effect of this rule is that, where the amount is paid to the credit of the insolvent customer's account without his having the intention of conferring a preference on the bank, an order avoiding the payment ought to be refused. Where, for example, the customer arranges for a sum to be remitted, or pays it in, under pressure, the preference rule is inapplicable. This outcome is in harmony with views expressed in some cases decided in common law jurisdictions other than the United Kingdom. Thus, some early Canadian cases support the view that payment to the credit of an account in respect of which the bank is entitled to exercise a right of set-off does not constitute an undue preference.[313] However, an Australian authority,[314] decided under a statutory provision *in pari materia* with section 45 of the Bankruptcy Act 1914,[315] suggests that there are exceptions to this position. A payment of the type discussed may constitute an undue preference if obtained under pressure, and with the bank's knowledge that the customer's general creditors are likely to suffer a disadvantage as a result of it.

(vi) Combination of accounts in customer's interest

The possibility that a bank might choose to combine a particular customer's accounts in that customer's own best interests arises where the customer in question draws a cheque for a sum that exceeds the particular account balance against which it is drawn, but that is less than the total amount deposited by that customer with the bank. Two separate questions arise. The first is whether the bank has a *duty* to combine the accounts in order to meet the cheque; the second is whether, if the bank is not under such a duty, whether it does at the very least have the *right* to effect the necessary set-off.

It will be recalled that, although the customer's contract is with the bank as a whole, a demand for the repayment of amounts deposited by him must be made at the branch at which the relevant account is maintained.[316] It follows that the bank is not obliged to meet a demand made by the customer at another branch. Consequently, the bank cannot be called upon to combine accounts maintained by the customer at different branches in order to meet a cheque that is uncovered at the branch on which it is drawn. This conclusion derives support from an observation of Lord Denning in the Court of Appeal's judgment in *National Westminster Bank Ltd* v. *Halesowen Presswork and Assemblies Ltd*[317]

---

[312] Insolvency Act 1986, s.239(6) (companies' winding up); ibid., s.340(4) (individual bankruptcies). See also *Re M. C. Bacon Ltd* [1990] BCLC 324; *Re Hawkes Hill Publishing Co. Ltd* [2007] EWHC 3073 (Ch), [26].

[313] *Re Sutcliffe & Sons Ltd, ex p. Royal Bank*, n.218 above; *Ross* v. *Royal Bank of Canada* (1965) 52 DLR (2d) 578; *Re TC Marines Ltd* [1973] 2 OR 537; but compare *Re Tenwolde Construction Ltd* (1981) 48 NSR (2d) 587, [77] (NSSC); *Re Shibou* (1984) 28 Man. R. (2d) 147, [6] (MBCA). The earlier cases were decided under the Canadian Bankruptcy Act, RCS 1952, s.64, which is *in pari materia* with the Bankruptcy Act 1914, s.45.

[314] *Richardson* v. *Commercial Banking Co. of Sydney Ltd* (1952) 85 CLR 110.

[315] Bankruptcy Acts 1924–1950 (Cth), s.95. See now Bankruptcy Act 1966 (Cth), s.122.

[316] Ch. 5, Sect. 3 & Ch. 7, Sect. 1 above, See also *Joachimson* v. *Swiss Bank Corporation* [1921] 3 KB 110, 127 (CA); cf. *Damayanti Kantilal Doshi* v. *Indian Bank*, n.22 above.

[317] N.7 above, 34. See also *Bank of New South Wales* v. *Goulburn Valley Butter Co. Pty. Ltd*, n.276 above; *Houben* v. *Bank of Nova Scotia* (1970) 3 NBR (2d) 366.

and the view of Bramwell B in *Garnett* v. *M'Kewan*.[318] Bramwell B did observe, however, that in practice branch managers usually have a clear picture of their customers' dealings with the bank as a whole and were normally aware of accounts maintained by them with other branches. This statement is probably even more accurate nowadays, as the availability of computer searches and printouts enables employees at one branch to inform themselves of the particular customer's total dealings with the bank. Nevertheless, the legal position—that a bank is under no duty to combine accounts in its customer's own interests—has remained unaltered. A question on which there is no authority to date is whether or not the bank is obliged to combine different accounts maintained by a customer at the *same* branch in order to avoid having to dishonour the customer's cheque. By way of illustration, take the case in which a customer draws a cheque for £100 when his current account has a credit balance of £50 and his savings account has a balance of £150. Is the bank obliged to transfer £50 from the savings account to the current account in order to meet the cheque? It is believed that, as the customer does not expressly order the combination of his accounts, the bank is not obliged to effect a set-off. In theory, the branch manager may even resolve to dishonour the cheque. The justification for such a decision would be that the maintenance of different types of account by a customer manifests his intention that they be kept apart. In practice, the branch manager will permit his customer to overdraw his current account, leaving the savings account intact. The balance in the savings account serves as a security.[319]

The bank is thus not under an obligation to combine accounts in the customer's interests, but does the bank nevertheless have the option of effecting such a set-off? Two authorities suggest that the bank has such a right.[320] This view derives support from a fundamental principle: where a principal gives his agent an ambiguous instruction, the agent is entitled to reimbursement as long as he gives the instruction a reasonable construction which he believes to accord with the principal's genuine intention.[321] At first glance, the drawing of a cheque that exceeds the credit standing to the customer's account appears to be unambiguous. It is a request that a certain amount be paid by the bank, regardless of the state of the customer's account. A closer look suggests that this is an oversimplification. A customer is aware of the fact that his bank is not obliged to meet a cheque drawn for an amount exceeding the available balance. He is, further, expected to be familiar with the state of his accounts.[322] If he draws an excessive cheque, he may be taken to be requesting that the amount of it be paid out of any funds deposited with the bank. By effecting a set-off between the balances of the different accounts, the bank obeys the spirit of this instruction.

Although the bank is not under a duty to effect a set-off in its customer's interest, it may have to do so, in the event of his bankruptcy, for the benefit of the general creditors. In *Mutton* v. *Peat*,[323] a stockbroker maintained with his bank a current account and a loan account. To secure the debit balance in the loan account, he gave the bank some shares and bonds belonging to his clients as security. When the stockbroker was adjudicated a bankrupt, there was a credit balance in his current account. The question was whether

---

[318] N.218 above, 14. See also *Barclays Bank Ltd* v. *Okenarhe*, n.212 above, 95.

[319] Ch. 21, Sect. 3 below.

[320] *Bank of New South Wales* v. *Goulburn Valley Butter Co. Pty. Ltd.*, n.276 above; *Houben* v. *Bank of Nova Scotia*, n.317 above.

[321] Ch. 11, Sect. 3(iv) below.

[322] Although he may in certain cases be unaware whether a certain cheque has been cleared.

[323] N.267 above. See also *Goldstar Finance Ltd* v. *Singh* [2005] EWCA Civ. 1544, [51].

the bank was entitled to utilize the securities to recoup the full amount due under the loan account, or whether it had to set off against the indebtedness of the loan account the credit balance accrued in the current account. If the latter were the case, the proceeds of the securities would have to be paid to the clients after the discharge of the net debt due. The Court of Appeal held that, as the securities were not specifically appropriated to cover the debit balance in the loan account, they could be utilized only for the satisfaction of the stockbroker's net indebtedness to the bank. It is important to emphasize that, in *Mutton* v. *Peat*, the bank was unaware that the securities were not the customer's property. Furthermore, the bank's lien over the securities was not in issue. The decision that the lien was applicable only in respect of the net indebtedness of the customer to the bank is, it is submitted, unexceptional.

5 Third-party claims

(i) Definition of the problem

A bank's primary concern is its customer's interests.[324] Usually, a bank need not concern itself with the rights of 'third parties', in other words persons with whom it does not have a contractual relationship. There are, however, certain exceptional situations in which a bank receiving instructions from a customer has to take into account the feasibility of claims that might be made by third parties in order to decide whether those claims should be satisfied and whether they oblige or entitle the bank to ignore its customer's payment instructions.[325] This type of case arises mainly where the third party, whether the customer's employer, the customer's heir with an interest in his estate, or the customer's spouse, asserts a right over a customer's account on the basis that an instruction given by the customer and carried out by the bank amounts to a breach of trust by the customer to that third party. The cases in question can be divided into three categories.

The first type of case arises where an employee, an agent, a company director, or a trustee misuses his authority to his own benefit. One such case is where an employee or agent fraudulently remits a substantial amount of money from the employer's or principal's account to the credit of his personal bank account. A more unusual case might be where, at the instigation of a director, a company utilizes its funds for an inappropriate purpose that ultimately confers some benefit on the director concerned. Notably, in some of the cases of this type, the defrauded party may seek to hold the bank liable for breaching of its contractual, common law, or equitable duty of care. Such an action may be available if the fraudster uses the same bank as his employer or principal to perpetrate his fraud—for instance, where the cheque drawn by the fraudster on the employer's account is paid to the credit of an account maintained by the fraudster with the same bank. As discussed

---

[324] Ch. 5, Sect. 4 above.

[325] See, for example, *US International Marketing Ltd* v. *National Bank of New Zealand Ltd* [2004] 1 NZLR 589, [4] (NZCA): 'The law has nevertheless come to recognize that banks may be entitled, indeed obliged, in some circumstances to decline to meet the customer's demand, if to do so would, in earlier terminology, amount to giving the customer knowing assistance to commit a breach of trust.... It is now clear that a bank is entitled to decline to meet a customer's demand if to do so would, in all the circumstances, provide dishonest assistance.' See also *Westpac New Zealand Ltd* v. *MAP & Associates Ltd* [2011] 2 NZLR 90, [35]–[44] (NZCA) ('. . . a bank may also be liable to non-customers in certain circumstances, including where it acts as a dishonest assister').

previously, *Selangor United Rubber Estates Ltd* v. *Cradock (No. 3)*[326] is a case in point. If, however, the fraudster maintains his account with another bank, the victim—who would have no contractual relationship with the fraudster's bank—can succeed only if he is able to establish an appropriate cause of action available to a third party. Where the fraudster has perpetrated the fraud by drawing cheques on the customer's account, as discussed in Chapter 15, the victim's cause of action is usually for the conversion of those cheques. Where no cheques are used—for instance, where the fraudster misappropriates the funds by means of a payment card or an electronic funds transfer—the victim may have an action for money had and received or an action that the bank be liable to account as a constructive trustee. As the restitutionary action for money had and received may be defeated where the bank has changed its position following the receipt of the funds,[327] the general trend is to opt for the latter type of claim.[328]

The second type of case in which a third party may make a claim respecting funds standing to the credit of a customer's account arises where the bank wishes to set off a debit balance on the customer's personal account against a credit balance on a special account maintained by him. Occasionally, a third party steps forward and claims title to the relevant funds, either on the basis of a special appropriation or because the funds are the subject of a trust of which he is the beneficiary. Cases of this type have already been considered above[329] and arise mainly in respect of trust accounts, which are discussed subsequently.[330]

The third type of situation in which a third party is likely to demand that sums credited to a customer's account be paid over to himself is where the third party claims to have equitable title to those funds. Such a plea by a third party may be based on the argument that the sums in question were obtained from him by fraud or by means of a trick.[331] Alternatively, the third party's claim may be based on the assertion that the funds were paid to the customer's credit for the third party's use.[332] There is, obviously, a certain overlap between this type of case and the two previous ones. Indeed, in many cases of this type the third party will actually be seeking to hold the bank liable to account as a constructive trustee. In other instances, however, the third party may attempt to assert a proprietary claim to a substitute asset following a successful tracing exercise.[333]

The common thread that runs through the three types of case just outlined is that in all of them the third party's action is attempting to invoke the court's equitable jurisdiction. His action may be based upon the bank's liability to account as a constructive trustee or upon the assertion of an equitable proprietary claim to a substitute asset following a successful tracing exercise. Another feature common to these cases is that, in most of

---

[326] N.3 above, discussed in Ch. 5, Sect. 4(iii) above.

[327] Ch. 12, Sect. 3(iii)(a) below.

[328] As money is generic and, hence, cannot be identified, there is no room for an action for its conversion: *Miller* v. *Race* (1785) 1 Burr. 452; *Moss* v. *Hancock* [1899] 2 QB 111, 118; *Banque Belge pour l'Étranger* v. *Hambrouck* [1921] 1 KB 321, 326–327; *Lipkin Gorman* v. *Karpnale Ltd* [1991] 2 AC 548, 563 (HL).

[329] Sect. 4(iii) above.   [330] Ch. 8, Sect. 5 below.

[331] *Commerzbank AG* v. *IMG Morgan plc* [2005] 1 Lloyd's Rep. 298, [36] (citing *Westdeutsche Landesbank Girozentrale* v. *Islington London BC* [1996] AC 669, 716 (HL)); *Governor & Co of the Bank of Ireland* v. *Pexxnet Ltd* [2010] EWHC 1872 (Comm.), [55]–[57].

[332] Ibid. See also, for example, *Cooper* v. *PRG Powerhouse Ltd*, n.271 above (third party payment into company's account to discharge purchase price on vehicle); *Re BA Peters plc* [2008] EWHC 2205 (Ch), [18], affd. [2008] EWCA Civ 1604, [9].

[333] Tracing merely serves an evidential purpose, identifying the path of value, but does not in itself give rise to a cause of action or remedy: *Boscawen* v. *Bajwa* [1996] 1 WLR 328, 334 (CA); *Foskett* v. *McKeown* [2001] 1 AC 102, 128 (HL). See further Sect. 5(v) below.

them, the dispute arises as a result of the customer's insolvency. Thus, where the customer is a fraudster, the third party may have an action against him in deceit. Commercially, though, it will be impossible to recover any money from an impecunious or untraceable rogue, so that the only possibility of recovery is from the bank. Similarly, the bank's attempt to effect a set-off is a course it would not generally adopt unless its customer, as legal owner of the funds, was solvent. Where the bank exercises a set-off, it is, effectively, attempting to acquire priority over its customer's general creditors by combining his different accounts. Equally, in the last type of case under consideration, a third party would not attempt to sue the bank, or conduct a tracing exercise, if the customer himself had the financial means to make good the loss.

(ii) Nature and elements of constructive trust actions[334]

The difficulties faced by a third party who seeks to hold a bank liable as a constructive trustee were stated by Lord Cairns in *Gray* v. *Johnston*.[335] A substantial amount of money was left by a testator to his wife for her lifetime and upon her death to their children. The wife, as executrix, drew a cheque on the bank account opened for the purposes of the estate and paid it to the credit of her personal account with the same bank. The children, suing as beneficiaries of the trust, attempted to recover the amount involved from the bank. Giving judgment against the children, and emphasizing that the banker in the case before him did not stand to make a gain, Lord Cairns said:[336]

> . . . to hold a banker justified in refusing to pay a demand of his customer, the customer being an executor, and drawing a cheque as an executor, there must, in the first place, be some misapplication, some breach of trust intended by the executor, and there must in the second place . . . be proof that the bankers are privy to the intent to make this misapplication of the trust funds.

Another mid-nineteenth-century decision showing that banks need not be unduly concerned with third party claims is *Tassell* v. *Cooper*.[337] The bank's customer paid to

---

[334] The term 'constructive trust' is used as a shorthand, but it was explained by Lord Millett in *Dubai Aluminium Co. Ltd* v. *Salaam*, n.150 above, [141]–[142] (HL) that there is no actual trust involved in these types of case, the reference to 'constructive trust' being 'nothing more than a formula for equitable relief'. See also *Paragon Finance plc* v. *Thimbleby & Co (a firm)* [1999] 1 All ER 400, 409 (CA); *Sinclair Investment Holdings SA* v. *Versailles Trade Finance Ltd* [2007] EWHC 915 (Ch), [122]; *Sinclair Investments (UK) Ltd* v. *Versailles Trade Finance Ltd* [2010] EWHC 1614 (Ch), [67]–[68], aff'd [2011] EWCA Civ 347, [43]–[45].

[335] N.3 above, approved recently on this point in *Saudi Arabian Monetary Agency* v. *Dresdner Bank AG*, n.278 above, [13]. See also *Bodenham* v. *Hoskyns* (1852) 2 De G M & G 903; *Gray* v. *Lewis* (1869) LR 8 Eq. 526 (further proceedings (1873) LR 8 Ch. App. 1035); *Backhouse* v. *Charlton* (1878) 8 Ch. D 444; *Thomson* v. *Clydesdale Bank*, n.3 above; *Coleman* v. *Bucks and Oxon Union Bank* [1897] 2 Ch. 243; *Bank of New South Wales* v. *Goulburn Valley Butter Co. Pty. Ltd*, n.276 above. See also *Lawson* v. *Commercial Bank of South Australia* (1888) 22 SALR 74; *Dixon* v. *Bank of NSW* (1896) 17 LR (NSW) Eq. 355; *McMahon* v. *Brewer* (1897) 18 LR (NSW) Eq. 88. See further R.P. Austin, 'Constructive Trusts' in P. D. Finn (ed.), *Essays in Equity* (Sydney, 1985), 196 ff.; C. Harpum 'The Stranger as a Constructive Trustee' (1986) 102 *LQR* 114 and 267, and in P. Birks (ed.), *The Frontiers of Liability* (Oxford, 1994), i, 9; S. Gardner, 'Knowing Assistance and Knowing Receipt: Taking Stock' (1996) 112 *LQR* 56; Lord Nicholls of Birkenhead, 'Knowing Receipt: the Need for a New Landmark' in W. Cornish *et al.* (eds.), *Restitution—Past, Present and Future* (Oxford, 1998), 231; W. Blair QC, 'Secondary Liability of Financial Institutions for the Fraud of Third Parties' (2000) 30 *HKLJ* 74.

[336] Ibid., 11. These elements are also emphasized in *Coleman* v. *Bucks and Oxon Union Bank*, n.335 above, and *Thomson* v. *Clydesdale Bank*, n.3 above.

[337] (1850) 9 CB 509.

the credit of his current account a cheque received as payment for merchandise sold on behalf of his employers. Although no fraud was involved, the employer requested the bank to freeze the amount involved. As the employer furnished an indemnity, the bank consented and, subsequently, dishonoured one of the customer's cheques. Maule J held that the bank was not entitled to dishonour its customer's cheque at the request of a third party.[338]

Despite the negative signal implicit in the passage cited from Lord Cairns' decision in *Gray* and in the ruling in *Tassell*, there have been numerous cases, in the nineteenth century as well as in modern times, in which third parties have sought to hold banks liable as constructive trustees. The doctrine usually invoked is based on *Barnes* v. *Addy*,[339] decided some seven years after *Gray*. Notably, the defendant in *Barnes* v. *Addy* was not a banker, but a solicitor, who had prepared a document on the instruction of a trustee, who subsequently used the document for the purpose of a fraudulent conveyance. On the facts, it was clear that the solicitor had had no knowledge of any design and that he was not in receipt of any trust property. He was therefore held not to be liable. Lord Selborne's dictum—describing situations in which a person like the defendant in the case before him could be liable—has, however, become a *modicum classicum*. His Lordship said:[340]

> ... strangers are not to be made constructive trustees merely because they act as the agents of trustees in transactions within their legal powers, transactions perhaps of which a Court of Equity may disapprove, unless (i) those agents receive and become chargeable with some part of the trust property, or (ii) unless they assist with knowledge in a dishonest and fraudulent design on the part of the trustees.

Furthermore, to ensure that 'the transactions of mankind' can be conducted with safety, it is necessary that 'persons dealing honestly as agents [be] at liberty to rely on the legal power of the trustees, and are not to have the character of trustees constructively imposed upon them'.[341] This savings or qualification is pertinent in respect of both branches of the doctrine in *Barnes*. Undoubtedly, a third party, such as an agent, can be ordered to pay over misappropriated trust funds that are still in his control, even if he has been blameless. In such a case the remedy is proprietary and is dependent on the beneficiary being able to trace the misappropriated funds into property remaining in the agent's hands. It has no adverse effect on the agent's own financial position. But if the agent has paid out the amount received at the trustee's request, he can be held liable according to *Barnes* v. *Addy* only in the two situations mentioned.

The first type of liability in *Barnes* v. *Addy* is generally known as liability for 'knowing receipt'; the second type of liability was known as liability for 'knowing assistance', until the Privy Council in *Royal Brunei Airlines* v. *Tan*[342] considered it more appropriate to refer to it as liability for 'dishonest assistance'.[343] In both cases, liability is personal and not

---

[338] The employer's correct course was to apply for an injunction to restrain the employee from drawing against the funds involved: *Fontaine-Besson* v. *Parr's Banking Co.* (1985) 12 TLR 121.

[339] (1874) LR 9 Ch.App. 244.

[340] Ibid., 251–252.   [341] Ibid., 252.   [342] [1995] 2 AC 378 (PC).

[343] *Ultraframe (UK) Ltd* v. *Fielding* [2005] EWHC 1638 (Ch), [1476]–[1477]; *Sinclair Investment Holdings SA* v. *Versailles Trade Finance Ltd*, n.334 above, [115].

proprietary.[344] There are, however, fundamental differences between the two types of liability. As Lord Nicholls observed in *Tan*:[345]

> The first limb of Lord Selborne L.C.'s formulation is concerned with the liability of a person as a *recipient* of trust property or its traceable proceeds. The second limb is concerned with what, for want of a better compendious description, can be called the liability of an *accessory* to a trustee's breach of trust. Liability as an accessory is not dependent upon receipt of trust property. It arises even though no trust property has reached the hands of the accessory. It is a form of secondary liability in the sense that it only arises where there has been a breach of trust.

Lord Nicholls went on to opine that whereas 'recipient liability is restitution-based; accessory liability is not'.[346] The same point was made by the Court of Appeal in *Grupo Torras SA* v. *Al-Sabah*:[347]

> The basis of liability in a case of knowing receipt is quite different from that in a case of dishonest assistance. One is a receipt-based liability which may on examination prove to be either a vindication of persistent property rights or a personal restitutionary claim based on unjust enrichment by subtraction; the other is a fault-based liability as an accessory to a breach of fiduciary duty.

However, as we shall see in section (iv) below, until the issue is authoritatively decided upon by the House of Lords, the precise relationship between liability under the receipt

---

[344] *Dubai Aluminium Co. Ltd* v. *Salaam*, n.150 above, [141]–[142], where Lord Millett explained the reference to 'constructive trust' in these types of claim as being 'nothing more than a formula for equitable relief'. For the personal nature of 'knowing receipt' liability, see *Re Montagu's S.T.* [1987] Ch. 264, 276; *Ultraframe (UK) Ltd* v. *Fielding*, n.343 above, [1484]–[1486]; *Pulvers* v. *Chan* [2007] EWHC 2406 (Ch), [379]; *Charter plc* v. *City Index Ltd* [2008] Ch 313, [7] (CA); *Aerostar Maintenance International Ltd* v. *Wilson* [2010] EWHC 2032 (Ch), [192]–[196]; *Sinclair Investments (UK) Ltd* v. *Versailles Trade Finance Ltd*, n.334 above, [86], aff'd [2011] EWCA Civ 347; but consider *Sinclair Investment Holdings SA* v. *Versailles Trade Finance Ltd*, n.334 above; *Independent Trustee Service Ltd* v. *GP Noble Trustees Ltd* [2010] EWHC 1653 (Ch), [50]–[51], [122]. For the personal nature of 'dishonest assistance' liability, see *Royal Brunei Airlines Ltd* v. *Tan*, n.342 above, 387; *Twinsectra Ltd* v. *Yardley*, n.496 below, 467, affd. on this issue: [2002] 2 AC 164, 194; *Sinclair Investment Holdings SA* v. *Versailles Trade Finance Ltd*, n.334 above, [120], [129]; *Yugraneft* v. *Abramovich* [2008] EWHC 2613 (Comm.), [337]. Although equitable compensation will be the usual form of relief (*Sinclair Investment Holdings SA* v. *Cushnie* [2006] EWHC 219 (Ch), [52]; *AG of Zambia* v. *Meer Care & Desai* [2007] EWHC 1540 (Ch), [9], [27], rev'd [2008] EWCA Civ 875; *Pulvers* v. *Chan* [2007] EWHC 2406 (Ch), [382]; *Al Khudairi* v. *Abbey Brokers Ltd* [2010] EWHC 1486 (Ch), [129], [138]; *Fiona Trust & Holding Corporation* v. *Privalov* [2010] EWHC 3199 (Comm.), [1519]), it has been suggested that a party liable for 'dishonest assistance' may be under a personal liability to account for any profits made: *Ultraframe (UK) Ltd* v. *Fielding*, n.343 above, [1594] (noted by D. Prentice & J. Payne, 'Director's Fiduciary Duties' (2006) 122 *LQR* 558, 563–564); *Yugraneft* v. *Abramovich* [2008] EWHC 2613 (Comm.), [392]; *Aerostar Maintenance International Ltd* v. *Wilson* [2010] EWHC 2032 (Ch), [206]; *Fiona Trust & Holding Corp* v. *Privalov* [2010] EWHC 3199 (Comm.), [63]–[67]; but consider *Twinsectra* v. *Yardley*, n.271 above, [107] (HL) (where Lord Millett refers only to 'compensation for wrongdoing'); *Sinclair Investment Holdings SA* v. *Versailles Trade Finance Ltd*, n.334 above, [128] (doubting the availability of an account of profits). For the suggestion that an account of profits, and even proprietary relief, should be available in respect of liability for dishonest assistance, see P. Ridge, 'Justifying the Remedies for Dishonest Assistance' (2008) 124 *LQR* 445.

[345] N.342 above, 382.

[346] Ibid., 386. See also *Gold* v. *Primary Developments Ltd* (1997) 152 DLR (4th) 385, 396 (SCC); *Citadel General Assurance Co.* v. *Lloyds Bank Canada* (1997) 152 DLR (4th) 411, 433 (SCC); *Mackinnon* v. *Ontario Municipal Employees Retirement Board* (2007) 88 OR (3d) 269, [68] (OCA) ('Liability for [knowing receipt] is restitution based').

[347] [2001] Lloyd's Rep. Bank. 36 [122]. The receipt-based nature of liability for 'knowing receipt', and the fault-based nature of the accessory's liability for 'dishonest assistance', was also stressed by Lord Millett in *Twinsectra Ltd* v. *Yardley*, n.271 above, [105], [107].

category of constructive trusteeship and the law of restitution remains unclear and uncertain under English law. Crucially, if knowing receipt is located within the law of restitution does liability become strict, but subject to defences, or does it remain, as it is at present, fault-based and, if so, what is the standard of fault?[348] By contrast, following the Privy Council's landmark decision in *Royal Brunei Airlines* v. *Tan*, the requirements for accessory liability can now be stated with more certainty. Accessory liability is 'fault-based'; the 'touchstone of liability' is the accessory's dishonesty,[349] although, as discussed in the next section, there has been a degree of confusion as to what exactly constitutes 'dishonesty' in this context.

(iii) Dishonest assistance[350]

Liability for dishonest assistance will be imposed on anyone who has dishonestly been accessory to, or assisted in, a disposition of property in breach of trust.[351] In such a case, the accessory or assister is traditionally described as a 'constructive trustee' and said to be 'liable to account as a constructive trustee'.[352] However, as the accessory or assister does not have to receive any trust property for this type of liability to arise, it seems misleading to describe him as a trustee at all.[353] In fact, the expressions 'constructive trust' and 'constructive trustee' are really 'nothing more than a formula for equitable relief'.[354] The language of constructive trusteeship is merely used to mean that a dishonest accessory or assister is accountable in equity *as if* he were a trustee, which he is not.[355]

The question remains, however: what is to be gained by praying in aid a trust concept that distorts ordinary principles of trusteeship and risks causing confusion? For this reason, there seems considerable merit in the argument that it is time to take a more

---

[348] The Supreme Court of Canada, for example, has recast knowing receipt in the language of unjust enrichment while retaining a fault-based standard: *Gold* v. *Primary Developments Ltd*, n.346 above; *Citadel General Assurance Co.* v. *Lloyds Bank Canada*, n.346 above. See also *Provincial Drywall Supply Ltd* v. *Toronto Dominion Bank*, n.3 above, [33]; ('...constructive knowledge is sufficient'); *Mackinnon* v. *Ontario Municipal Employees Retirement Board*, n.346 above, [68] ('...recipient [must have] knowledge of facts sufficient to put a reasonable person on notice or enquiry'); *Holmes* v. *Amlez International Inc* [2009] OJ No. 4513, [11]. See generally *Giles* v. *Westminster Savings Credit Union*, n.271 above, [460]–[468].

[349] N.342 above, 387, 392.

[350] *Law Society of England & Wales* v. *Isaac* [2010] EWHC (Ch) 1670, [7].

[351] As discussed below, it is a moot point whether liability should extend to cases of 'dishonest assistance' in any breach of fiduciary duty and not just to assistance in a breach of trust.

[352] See, for example, *Westdeutsche Landesbank Girozentrale* v. *Islington London Borough Council*, n.331 above, 705.

[353] *Agip (Africa) Ltd* v. *Jackson* [1990] Ch. 265, 292; *Paragon Finance plc* v. *D. B. Thakerar & Co. (a firm)*, n.334 above, 409; *Governor & Company of the Bank of Scotland* v. *A Ltd* [2001] 1 WLR 751, [27] (CA); *Dubai Aluminium Co. Ltd* v. *Salaam*, n.150 above, [141]; *Sinclair Investment Holdings SA* v. *Versailles Trade Finance Ltd*, n.334 above, [122].

[354] *Dubai Aluminium Co. Ltd* v. *Salaam*, n.150 above, [141]–[142]. See also *Selangor United Rubber Ltd* v. *Cradock (No. 3)*, n.3 above, 1582; *Paragon Finance plc* v. *D. B. Thakerar & Co. (a firm)*, n.334 above, 408-409; *Coulthard* v. *Disco Mix Club Ltd* [2000] 1 WLR 707, 731; *Ultraframe (UK) Ltd* v. *Fielding*, n.343 above, [1287]; *Cattley* v. *Pollard* [2007] Ch 353, [60]; *Sinclair Investment Holdings SA* v. *Versailles Trade Finance Ltd*, n.334 above, [117], [121], [123]; *Sinclair Investments (UK) Ltd* v. *Versailles Trade Finance Ltd*, n.334 above, [67]–[68], aff'd [2011] EWCA Civ 347, [43]–[45]; *Independent Trustee Service Ltd* v. *GP Noble Trustees Ltd*, n.344 above, [50]–[51].

[355] Id. The nature of the accountability of the accessory or assister in equity, and the remedies available against him, are usefully examined by S.B. Elliott and C. Mitchell in 'Remedies for Dishonest Assistance' (2004) 67 *MLR* 16 (arguing that the assister is jointly and severally liable along with the trustee whom he has assisted). See also cases cited in n.344 above.

direct approach and dispense with the notion of constructive trusteeship altogether in this context, and to recognize dishonest participation in a breach of trust as a species of equitable wrong, rendering the participant liable to compensate the claimant, or possibly to account in equity.[356] This was the approach taken by Chadwick J in *Arab Monetary Fund* v. *Hashim*,[357] when he said:

> The defendant is held liable in equity not because he is, or has been, a trustee of trust property, but because his conduct in relation to trust property has been such that he ought to be liable in damages for its loss as if he were a trustee who had disposed of the trust property in breach of trust. The claim is a claim for monetary compensation based on fault...

This passage was cited with evident approval by the Court of Appeal in *Grupo Torras SA* v. *Al-Sabah*,[358] which concluded that '[d]ishonest assistance can therefore be described as equitable wrongdoing'. In *Twinsectra Ltd* v. *Yardley*,[359] Lord Millett made a general reference to the claimant seeking 'compensation for wrongdoing' and, later in his speech, added that 'the claim for "knowing assistance" is the equitable counterpart of the economic torts'.[360] More recently, Rix LJ in *Abou-Rahmah* v. *Abacha*[361] referred to dishonest assistance as an 'equitable tort', and in *Yugraneft* v. *Abramovich*,[362] Clarke J referred to it simply as an 'equitable wrong'.

There are four requirements for accessory liability to be imposed:[363] (a) there must have been a trust or other fiduciary relationship; (b) there must have been misfeasance involving a breach of fiduciary duty, or some other breach of trust, though *Royal Brunei Airlines* v. *Tan*[364] established that such misfeasance or breach of trust need not itself be dishonest or fraudulent; (c) the person upon whom liability is to be imposed must, as a matter of

---

[356] Lord Nicholls of Birkenhead, n.335 above, 244. On the issue of whether dishonest assistance gives rise to an account of profits, see n.344 above.

[357] *The Times*, 11 October 1994.

[358] N.347 above, [123]. See also *Casio Computer Co. Ltd* v. *Sayo* [2001] EWCA Civ 661, [14].

[359] N.271 above, [107], [127]. It should be noted that Lord Millett, dissenting in this part of his opinion, preferred to base liability on the level of the assister's knowledge and not on his subjective dishonesty.

[360] There have been suggestions that liability for dishonest assistance should be abolished in favour of other forms of liability, including the economic torts, such as inducing breach of contract, intentionally causing loss by unlawful means, deceit, or conspiracy (but not the tort of assisting a breach of trust, which does not exist: *Metall und Rohstoff* v. *Donaldson Lufkin & Jenrette* [1990] 1 QB 391, 481 (CA)): L. Hoffmann, 'The Redundancy of Knowing Assistance' in P. Birks (ed.), *The Frontiers of Liability* (Oxford, 1994) vol. I, ch. 2, 27–29; G. Andrews, 'The Redundancy of Dishonest Assistance' [2003] *Conv*. 398, 408–410. For a recent examination of the differences between accessory liability at common law and equity, following *Crédit Lyonnais Bank Nederland NV* v. *Exports Credits Guarantee Department*, n.153 above, *Dubai Aluminium* v. *Salaam*, n.150 above, and *OBG Ltd* v. *Allan* [2008] AC 1 (HL), see S. Baughen, 'Accessory Liability at Common Law and in Equity—"The Redundancy of Knowing Assistance" Revisited' [2007] *LMCLQ* 545.

[361] [2007] 1 Lloyd's Rep. 115, [2], [20], [37] (CA).

[362] N.344 above, [153]. Clarke J also referred to 'dishonest assistance' as being 'analogous to a tort': ibid., [194]. On this basis, his Lordship applied the choice of law principles for tort: ibid., [217], [223], [236]. The analogy with a tort claim also extends to the limitation period of six years applicable to dishonest assistance claims: *Cattley* v. *Pollard*, n.354 above, [93]; but compare *Statek Corporation* v. *Alford* [2008] EWHC 32 (Ch), [125]. See also C. Mitchell, 'Dishonest Assistance, Knowing Receipt, and the Law of Limitation' [2008] *Conv* 226.

[363] The essential elements of liability were identified by Peter Gibson J in *Baden, Delvaux and Lecuit* v. *Société Générale pour Favoriser le Développement du Commerce et de l'Industrie en France SA* [1993] 1 WLR 509n, 573, and later modified by the Privy Council in *Royal Brunei Airlines* v. *Tan*, n.342 above. The requirements are neatly, and accurately, summarized by Cresswell J in *Bankgesellschaft Berlin AG* v. *Makris* (QBD, 22 January 1999).

[364] N.342 above.

fact, have been accessory to, or assisted in, the misfeasance or breach of trust; and (d) the accessory must have been dishonest.

(a) There must have been a trust or other fiduciary relationship

First, there must have been a trust or other fiduciary relationship in existence.[365] Although the *Barnes* v. *Addy* doctrine started life as a response to the misapplication of trust funds by express trustees, its coverage appears to have been extended subsequently to include the breach of fiduciary duties by other types of fiduciary. The form of liability now commonly arises in the corporate context where directors and other senior officers of the company are deemed to owe fiduciary duties to the company.[366] In *Agip (Africa) Ltd* v. *Jackson*,[367] for example, a senior officer of the claimant company, its chief accountant, was held to be in breach of fiduciary duty when he misappropriated funds from the company's bank account by fraudulently altering the name of the payee on a payment order addressed to the bank after it had been signed by an authorized signatory of the company. The defendants, a group of accountants based in the Isle of Man, assisted in laundering the misapplied funds and were held liable for knowingly assisting in the breach of fiduciary duty by the company's chief accountant. Millett J noted that 'the embezzlement of a company's funds almost inevitably involves a breach of fiduciary duty on the part of one of the company's employees or agents'.[368]

However, the view that liability may arise out of dishonestly assisting a breach of fiduciary duty that does not involve a breach of trust has begun to be questioned more recently. In *Brown* v. *Bennett*,[369] the claimants were shareholders in P Ltd. They claimed that the directors of P Ltd had breached their fiduciary duties owed to the company by deliberately running down P Ltd so as to enable the business of the company to be acquired by O Ltd, a company in which the directors also had an interest. The claimants alleged that the directors' deliberate or reckless management of the company's affairs put P Ltd under unnecessary financial pressure to the point where it was forced into administrative receivership. The receivers then sold off P Ltd's business to O Ltd, the directors of P Ltd had acquired as an 'off the shelf' company after they had completed negotiations with the receivers, and which was intended to operate as the vehicle for making the purchase. The claimants commenced proceedings against O Ltd, amongst others, claiming that, by purchasing P Ltd's business, O Ltd had dishonestly assisted P Ltd's directors in their breach of trust. Rattee J struck out the claim for two reasons:[370] first, his Lordship considered that liability for dishonest assistance 'presupposes a breach of trust' and that it 'would represent an extension of that head of constructive trusteeship beyond the limits so far recognized' if liability also covered acts that assisted a director to breach his fiduciary duties to his company; secondly, as O Ltd was acquired only after the sale and purchase of P Ltd had been agreed with the receivers, it did not exist at the date of the directors' mismanagement and so could not have assisted in their alleged breach of trust. The Court of Appeal upheld Rattee J's decision on the second ground, and in so doing did not have to decide on the correctness of the first ground. However, Morritt LJ, delivering the only reasoned

---

[365] *Twinsectra* v. *Yardley*, n.271 above, [2], [13], [25], [103], [136]. See also *Transamerica Occidental Life Insurance Co* v. *Toronto-Dominion Bank* (1999) 44 OR (3d) 97, 104 (OCA); *New Cap Reinsurance Corporation Ltd* v. *General Cologne Re Industrial Ltd* [2004] NSWSC 781, [26]–[27].

[366] See, for example, *Regal (Hastings) Ltd* v. *Gulliver* [1967] 2 AC 134n (HL); *Canadian Aero Services Ltd* v. *O'Malley* (1973) 40 DLR 371 (SCC); *Sybron Corporation* v. *Rochem* [1984] Ch. 112, 127 (CA).

[367] N.353 above, affd. [1991] Ch. 547 (CA).

[368] Ibid., 290.   [369] [1999] 1 BCLC 649 (CA).   [370] [1998] 2 BCLC 97, 104–105.

judgment, stated that he could see force in the argument that liability to account as a constructive trustee should be extended to a case of dishonest assistance in any breach of fiduciary duty, and should not be limited simply to breaches of trust involving the misapplication of trust property.[371]

Since then the Court of Appeal has given further consideration to the issue. In *Satnam Investments Ltd* v. *Dunlop Heywood & Co. Ltd*,[372] after referring to *Tan*, Nourse LJ said that 'before a case can fall in either category [knowing receipt or dishonest assistance] there must be trust property or traceable proceeds of trust property'. Yet, in *Goose* v. *Wilson Sandiford & Co. (a firm)*,[373] Morritt LJ, delivering the judgment of the Court of Appeal, said that the court did not regard the statement of Nourse LJ in *Satnam* as binding on the point, but nevertheless left the issue open. Morritt LJ stated that:

> The issue is whether the dishonest breach of trust in which the defendant assisted must have involved the misapplication of trust property or its proceeds of sale. The formulation of the principle by Lord Nicholls of Birkenhead...does not embrace such a requirement. Whether or not such a requirement is an essential feature of this head of liability is not a point we have to decide and, like the Court of Appeal in that case, we should not like to shut out the possibility of such a claim in its absence.

Although subsequent cases have also tended to sidestep the issue,[374] there are scattered dicta suggesting that the House of Lords has always operated on the assumption that there can be liability for dishonestly assisting in a breach of fiduciary duty that does not involve a breach of trust.[375] This broader approach is to be commended.[376] If accessory liability is to develop as a species of equitable wrongdoing, analogous to the tort of inducing a breach of contract, there seems little reason to restrict its application to a breach of trust involving the misappropriation of trust property.[377] Dishonest assistance in the breach of any equitable obligation, including an obligation not to misapply trust property, should be enough to attract liability.

---

[371] N.369 above, 657.

[372] [1999] 3 All ER 652, 671 (CA). See also *Petrotrade Inc.* v. *Smith* [2000] 1 Lloyd's Rep. 486, 491–492.

[373] [2000] EWCA Civ. 73, [2001] Lloyd's Rep. P.N. 189, [88].

[374] *Gencor ACP Ltd* v. *Dalby* [2000] 2 BCLC 734, 758 (where Rimer J saw the point as 'a difficult one'); *Rockbrook Ltd* v. *Khan* [2006] EWHC 101 (Ch), [37]–[40] (where Roger Wyand QC stated that '[w]ith the greatest respect to Nourse LJ [in *Satnam*], I do not find this passage easy'). Cf. *Banque Nationale de Paris* v. *Hew Keong Chan Gary*, n.199 above, 336 (SGHC) (for dishonest assistance to apply there need not be a misapplication of trust property, so long as the assistance caused the loss in question).

[375] *Twinsectra Ltd* v. *Yardley*, n.271 above, [107] ('Liability is not restricted to the person whose breach of trust or fiduciary duty caused the original diversion...nor is it limited to those who assist him in the original breach...'); *Dubai Aluminium Co Ltd* v. *Salaam*, n.150 above, [9] ('the equitable wrong of dishonest participation in a breach of trust or fiduciary duty'); *Revenue & Customs Commissioners* v. *Total Network SL* [2008] AC 1174, [97] (HL) ('a claim for dishonest assistance in breach of fiduciary duty').

[376] *Sphere Drake Insurance Ltd* v. *Euro International Underwriting Ltd* [2003] EWHC 1636 (Comm.), [40]; *JD Wetherspoon plc* v. *Van de Berg & Co Ltd* [2009] EWHC 639 (Ch), [518]; *Aerostar Maintenance International Ltd* v. *Wilson* [2010] EWHC 2032 (Ch), [178]–[179]; *Fiona Trust & Holding Corp* v. *Privalov* [2010] EWHC 3199 (Comm.), [61]. There are indications that the broader formulation encompassing breach of fiduciary duty may apply in Canada: *Waxman* v. *Waxman* (2004) 44 BLR (3d) 165, [544]–[549] (OCA); *Ruwenzori Enterprises Ltd* v. *Walji* [2004] BCSC 741, [199]–[200]; *Giles* v. *Westminster Savings Credit Union*, n.271 above, [466]–[467]. On the 'broader approach', see R. Stevens, 'The Proper Scope of Knowing Receipt' [2004] *LMCLQ* 421, 424 ('There is no logical difficulty in finding someone liable for dishonestly assisting a breach of fiduciary duty where the fiduciary is not also a trustee'); S. Baughen, n.360 above.

[377] n.360 above. *Royal Brunei Airlines* v. *Tan*, n.342 above, 387. See also Lord Nicholls of Birkenhead, n.335 above..

(b) **There must have been a misfeasance or breach of trust**

There must be a breach of trust or, if the argument in the preceding section is accepted, a breach of fiduciary duty. In *Barnes* v. *Addy*, Lord Selborne LC specifically referred to assistance 'in a dishonest and fraudulent design on the part of the trustees'.[378] This statement is not surprising when read against the background of the facts in that case, given that the trustee in *Barnes* was clearly engaged in a dishonest and fraudulent design. Lord Selborne LC's dicta were subsequently interpreted, however, as laying down a steadfast rule that the trustee's breach of trust had to be a dishonest and fraudulent breach for the accessory to be held liable for 'knowing assistance'. Most notably, an attempt by Ungoed-Thomas J, in *Selangor United Rubber Estates Ltd* v. *Cradock (No. 3)*,[379] to jettison the requirement was emphatically rejected by the Court of Appeal in *Belmont Finance Corporation Ltd* v. *Williams*,[380] on the ground that to depart from it would introduce an undesirable degree of uncertainty over the level of unethical conduct that would suffice if dishonesty were not to be the criterion.[381] It was not until 1995, when the Privy Council delivered its advice in *Royal Brunei Airlines* v. *Tan*,[382] that the need to establish dishonesty or fraud on the part of the trustee or other fiduciary was finally abandoned as a prerequisite to accessory liability. Indeed, this was the main point at issue in *Tan*. The claimants, Royal Brunei Airlines, appointed a company ('BLT') to act as their general travel agent for the sale of passenger and cargo transportation. Under the terms of their agreement, BLT was required to account to the airline for all amounts received from ticket sales. In fact, BLT was afforded a 30-day credit period before it was required to pay the airline. However, the agreement expressly provided that all amounts received from ticket sales were to be held by BLT on trust for the airline. In practice, money received by BLT was not paid into a separate account but credited to BLT's current account, where it was used to meet the company's normal business expenditure. All this was done to the knowledge, and with the assistance, of the defendant, who was the managing director and principal shareholder of BLT. When BLT defaulted on its payments to the airline and became insolvent, the claimants sought to make the defendant personally liable on the basis that he assisted the admitted breach of trust.

The Court of Appeal of Brunei found for the defendant on the ground that accessory liability was dependent on the breach of trust being dishonest, whereas here the admitted breach of trust was the result of bad management and not dishonesty. Lord Nicholls, delivering the advice of the Privy Council, took the opposite view of the law.[383] Liability under the accessory category of constructive trusteeship required a breach of trust or other fiduciary duty, but it did not have to be a dishonest one. His Lordship considered that Lord Selborne LC's dictum (the '*Barnes* v. *Addy* straight-jacket') had too often been interpreted as though it were a statute, and that this had inhibited a proper analysis of underlying concepts.[384] Furthermore, Lord Nicholls could point to authority pre-dating *Barnes* where there had been no requirement that the breach of trust be dishonest and fraudulent.[385] Lord Nicholls preferred to regard the dishonesty of the accessory, not of the

---

[378] (1874) LR 9 Ch. App. 244, 252.

[379] N.3 above, 1591.   [380] [1979] Ch. 250.

[381] Ibid., 267, 274. It was conceded by counsel for the claimant that mere innocence on the part of the trustee, or other fiduciary, was not enough.

[382] N.342 above.

[383] Ibid., 385, 392. The Judicial Committee also considered that the breach of trust in this case had been dishonest; that the defendant was the directing mind of the company; and that his own dishonesty could be imputed to the company (ibid., 393B).

[384] Ibid., 386.

[385] Ibid., 385, citing *Fyler* v. *Fyler* (1841) 3 Beav. 550; *Att.-Gen.* v. *Corporation of Leicester* (1844) 7 Beav. 176; *Eaves* v. *Hickson* (1861) 30 Beav. 136. See also C. Harpum, 'The Basis of Equitable Liability' in

trustee, as the touchstone of liability. If the accessory was dishonest, it did not matter that the trustee was innocent: '[t]he alternative view would mean that a dishonest third party is liable if the trustee is dishonest, but if the trustee did not act dishonestly that of itself would excuse a dishonest third party from liability. That would make no sense'.[386] On this issue, however, there may be an increasing divergence between the approaches in the United Kingdom and Australia. Although there are dicta of the High Court of Australia approving *Tan*,[387] in *Farah Construction Pty Ltd v. Say-Dee Pty Ltd*[388] the High Court recently left open the issue of whether Australia should finally adopt *Tan* or continue with the traditional requirement that accessory liability in this context depends upon the 'defendant participating with knowledge in a dishonest and fraudulent design'[389] as originally formulated in *Barnes*. Their Honours were at such pains to emphasize how radical a departure it would be for the Australian courts to accept *Tan* that it appears unlikely that the two jurisdictions will come into line any time soon. Similarly, the Supreme Court of Canada in *Citadel General Assurance Co. v. Lloyds Bank Canada*[390] has continued to view the requirement of 'a fraudulent and dishonest design on the part of the trustees' as a necessary requirement of accessory liability.

(c) The person upon whom liability is to be imposed must as a matter of fact have been an accessory or assisted in the misfeasance or breach of trust[391]

This is essentially 'a simple question of fact'.[392] The notion of 'assistance' encompasses not only persons who assist with the original breach of trust, but also those who assist

---

P. Birks (ed.), *The Frontiers of Liability* (Oxford, 1994), i, 9, 12 ff.; C. Harpum, 'The Stranger as Constructive Trustee' (1986) 102 *LQR* 114 & 267.

[386] N.342 above, 385.

[387] *Forestview Nominees Pty Ltd v. Perpetual Trustees WA Ltd* (1998) 193 CLR 154, 165 (HCA); *Giumelli v. Giumelli* (1999) 196 CLR 101, 112 (HCA); *Pilmer v. The Duke Group Ltd* (2001) 207 CLR 165, 174 (HCA). For other Australian cases endorsing *Tan*, see *Farrow Finance Co. Ltd v. Farrow Properties Pty Ltd* [1999] 1 VR 584, 626–627 (VSC); *Beach Petroleum NL v. Abbott Tout Russell Kennedy* (1999) 33 ACSR 1, [405] (NSWSC); *Lurgi (Aust) Pty Ltd v. Ritzer Gallagher Morgan Pty Ltd* (VSC, 4 August 2000); *National Australia Bank Ltd v. Rusu* [2001] NSWSC 32; *Aeqitas Ltd v. AEFC* [2001] NSWSC 14; *Re-Engine Pty Ltd v. Fergusson* [2007] VSC 57, [113]–[116].

[388] (2007) 236 ALR 209, [159]–[164] (HCA). See also *Chameleon Mining NL v. Murchison Metals Ltd* [2010] FCA 1129, [123]–[128]. In Australia, it may not be necessary to show 'a dishonest and fraudulent design' on the part of the fiduciary, where the third party is liable as principal for knowingly inducing or immediately procuring breaches of the fiduciary's duties, rather than merely liable as an accessory for assisting in those breaches: *Kation Pty Ltd v. Lamru Pty Ltd* [2009] NSWCA 145, [114]–[118].

[389] Ibid., [163]. For the traditional Australian position, see *Consul Developments Pty Ltd v. DPC Estates Pty Ltd* (1975) 132 CLR 373 (HCA). Not only do *Farah* and *Consul* continue to require dishonesty on the part of the fiduciary, but the level of knowledge required of the accessory differs from that in *Tan*: Sect. 5(iii)(d) below. See also *Gertsch v. Atsas* [1999] NSWSC 898; *Esanda Finance Corporation Ltd v. Reyes* [2001] NSWSC 234; *NCR Australia v. Credit Connection Pty Ltd* [2004] NSWSC 1, [164]–[167]; *Lewis v. Nortex Pty Ltd* [2004] NSWSC 1143, [178]–[181]; *Yeshiva Properties No 1 Pty Ltd v. Marshall* [2005] NSWCA 23, [20]–[22].

[390] N.346 above, [19]. See also *Air Canada v. M&L Travel Ltd* [1993] 3 SCR 787, [37] (SCC); *Gold v. Rosenberg* [1997] 3 SCR 767, [31]–[32] (SCC); *Commercial Union Life Assurance Co of Canada v. John Ingle Insurance Group Inc.* (2002) 61 OR (3d) 296, [2] (OCA); *Glenko Enterprises Ltd v. Keller* [2006] MBQB 191, [26]. Consider *Giles v. Westminster Savings Credit Union*, n.271 above, [470] ('[t]here is a debate in the law as to whether dishonest conduct on the part of the trustee is required'). The Canadian courts have equally left open the issue of whether the 'dishonesty' standard in *Tan* applies: *3464920 Canada Inc. v. Strother* [2005] BCCA 385, [25].

[391] C. Mitchell, 'Assistance' in P. Birks & A. Pretto (eds.), *Breach of Trust* (Oxford, 2002), ch. 6.

[392] *Baden, Delvaux and Lecuit v. Société Générale pour Favoriser le Développement du Commerce et de l'Industrie en France SA*, n.363 above, 574–575.

in the continued diversion of the trust funds or who help launder the proceeds.[393] There are, however, limits to this broad concept. In *Brinks Ltd* v. *Abu-Saleh (No. 3)*,[394] a gang of robbers was able to steal a large quantity of gold bullion because a security guard at the warehouse where the gold was stored provided the gang with a key and other assistance. An associate of the gang then made several trips to Switzerland to launder the proceeds of the crime. His wife accompanied him on these trips. When the claimants brought civil proceedings against the wife for 'dishonest assistance', Rimer J held that, although the security guard had dishonestly breached the fiduciary obligations of honesty and loyalty owed to the claimants as his employers, the wife had not provided any assistance in furtherance of his breach of trust. His Lordship held that she went on the trips to Switzerland in her spousal capacity, and that her presence did not constitute 'assistance' in furtherance of the breach of trust. Accordingly, acts will not qualify as 'assistance' for these purposes unless they 'have some causative significance'[395] in relation to the breach of trust or other fiduciary duty. The causative link need not be direct (in the sense that the acts of assistance need not be a 'but for' cause of the breach),[396] but the acts or omissions complained of must at least have made the commission of the breach easier than it would otherwise have been,[397] or have facilitated the disposal or concealment of the funds.

On this approach, banks will not find it so easy to avoid the charge that they were accessory to, or assisted in, a breach of trust, especially one that involves the fraudulent misapplication of trust funds. Although it has been suggested that 'the mere passive receipt of trust property does not count as assistance',[398] a bank is something more than a passive repository for funds, as it will normally provide some form of positive banking service to the persons behaving in a fraudulent or improper manner.[399] For example, a bank may be required to take active steps to collect the proceeds deposited with it (if the funds are deposited by cheque) or may comply with a request to move funds between different bank accounts held with it. More obviously, a bank may comply with a request (for example, by a company's directors) to transfer funds from its customer (in this example, the company)

---

[393] *Twinsectra* v. *Yardley*, n.271 above, [107]; *Ultraframe (UK) Ltd* v. *Fielding*, n.343 above, [1497] ('The assistance may be given after the event as part of a cover up'). See also *PBM (Hong Kong) Ltd* v. *Allan* [2002] HKCU 632, [13]; *Courtney Polymers Pty Ltd* v. *Deang* [2005] VSC 318; *Re-Engine Pty Ltd* v. *Fergusson*, n.387 above, [126]–[129].

[394] [1996] CLC 133, approved in *Ultraframe (UK) Ltd* v. *Fielding*, n.343 above, [1510]; *Re-Engine Pty Ltd* v. *Fergusson*, n.387 above, [122]. See also *Yugraneft* v. *Abramovich*, n.344 above, [391]–[392] (sale of shares did not amount to dishonest assistance as it had 'no causative effect in relation to any breach of trust').

[395] *Yugraneft* v. *Abramovich*, n.344 above, [388]–[392]. See also *Re-Engine Pty Ltd* v. *Fergusson*, n.387 above, [124].

[396] S. Baughen, 'Accessory Liability at Common Law and in Equity—"The Redundancy of Knowing Assistance" Revisited' [2007] *LMCLQ* 545, 553 ('The claimant need not show the contribution made by the assistance to its loss. As long as it can show that the secondary party dishonestly rendered some assistance, which made the breach of trust easier, the necessary participation link will have been made out to make the secondary party liable in respect of losses flowing from the breach of trust or fiduciary duty').

[397] S.B. Elliott and C. Mitchell, n.355 above, 20, citing *Grupo Torras SA* v. *Al-Sabah (No 5)* (QBD, 24 June 1999). See also *Casio Computer Co. Ltd* v. *Sayo*, n.358 above, [15]; *Yugraneft* v. *Abramovich*, n.344 above, [388]–[392]. In *Re-Engine Pty Ltd* v. *Fergusson*, n.387 above, [117], [120]–[123], Dodds-Streeton J held that 'assistance or participation must be facilitative conduct or activity which is more than mere knowledge or notice of the breach of duty', in other words the assistance should 'make a difference'. Consider *Adelaide Partnerships Ltd* v. *Danison* [2011] All ER (D) 01 (Mar).

[398] *Ultraframe (UK) Ltd* v. *Fielding*, n.343 above, [1509]. See also *Re-Engine Pty Ltd* v. *Fergusson*, n.387 above, [120] ('[m]ere passive acquiescence' is not assistance).

[399] *Re-Engine Pty Ltd* v. *Fergusson*, n.387 above, [117] indicating that 'the use of bank accounts as a conduit for funds without beneficial receipt' does amount to relevant 'assistance'.

to a third party account held with another bank or even located abroad.[400] In such cases, the banks that hold the relevant accounts, as well as any other bank involved as an intermediary in the funds transfer process, run the risk of providing 'assistance' to the dishonest fiduciary.[401] More worrying still, at least from the bank's point of view, is that the mere provision of advisory services to the fiduciary can be deemed 'assistance' where there is a sufficient causative link between that advice and the breach of trust,[402] even though the bank itself never comes into contact with the misapplied funds.

It is precisely because the 'assistance' net can be cast so widely that attention has focused so crucially on the mental state required of the person giving assistance for him to be held liable under this head of constructive trusteeship. Banks and other financial institutions that are involved in millions of money transmission activities on a daily basis are particularly vulnerable to the charge of 'assistance', and accordingly have always argued that the level of mental intent should be high.

(d) The accessory must have been dishonest

It is the presence of the necessary mental state, which, following *Royal Brunei Airlines* v. *Tan*, is dishonesty, that is the fourth requirement for accessory liability to be imposed. *Tan* has finally settled an issue that has plagued the English courts for many years, namely the level of knowledge that the accessory or assister had to possess concerning the breach of trust before liability for 'knowing assistance' could be imposed. The question was whether liability was to be imposed only on those who had actual knowledge of the breach of trust, including those who turned a blind eye to the truth, or whether it should also extend to those deemed to have constructive notice of the breach, i.e., knowledge of circumstances that would indicate the facts to an honest and reasonable man or would put such a man on enquiry. In other words, was negligence enough or did the accessory have to be dishonest for liability to be imposed on him?

The conflicting case law is summarized by Lord Nicholls in *Tan*.[403] It is now mainly of historical interest in the United Kingdom,[404] although it may have continuing relevance in Australia[405] and Canada.[406] The first modern decision on the point was *Selangor United Rubber Estates Ltd* v. *Cradock (No. 3)*.[407] Ungoed-Thomas J held that liability extended to a bank that had constructive notice of the improper application of its customer's funds (in other words, knowledge of circumstances that would indicate to 'an honest, reasonable

---

[400] See, for example, *Selangor United Rubber Estates Ltd* v. *Cradock (No. 3)*, n.3 above; *Karak Rubber Co. Ltd* v. *Burden (No. 2)* [1972] 1 WLR 602; *Papamichael* v. *National Westminster Bank plc* [2003] 1 Lloyd's Rep. 341; *Re-Engine Pty Ltd* v. *Fergusson*, n.387 above, [118].

[401] Money laundering frequently involves the transfer of misappropriated funds overseas and intermediary banks are commonly used in international fund transfer operations. See further Ch. 13, Sect. 1(vi) below.

[402] *Brown* v. *Bennett*, n.369 above. See also A. Hudson, 'Current Legal Problems Concerning Trusts, Fiduciaries and Finance' (2006) 21 *JIBLR* 149, 149; T. Petch, 'The Investment Adviser as Constructive Trustee' (2006) 21 *JIBLR* 377, 384–386.

[403] N.342 above. For a thorough review of the authorities preceding *Tan*, reference should be made to E.P Ellinger & E. Lomnicka, *Modern Banking Law* (2nd edn., Oxford, 1995), 205–211.

[404] Although the five-point scale of knowledge adopted by Peter Gibson J in *Baden Delvaux* (n.363 above) may still have a function to play in this area. See the text to n.411 above.

[405] *Consul Developments Pty Ltd* v. *DPC Estates Pty Ltd*, n.389 above, 412; *Farah Construction Pty Ltd* v. *Say-Dee Pty Ltd*, n.388 above, [159]–[164].

[406] See, for example, *3464920 Canada Inc.* v. *Strother*, n.390 above, [25] leaving open the question of whether '"knowingly" should give way to "dishonesty" as the "defining ingredient" of accessory liability'.

[407] N.3 above.

man' that the breach in question was being committed or would put him on inquiry). Brightman J reached the same conclusion in *Karak Rubber Co. Ltd* v. *Burden (No. 2)*.[408] Banks were aghast.[409] These cases implied that a bank could be held liable as an accessory to a fraudulent breach of trust by merely being negligent. Despite the doubts cast on the correctness of this approach by Buckley and Goff LJJ in *Belmont Finance Corporation Ltd* v. *Williams*,[410] it was followed by Peter Gibson J in 1983 in *Baden,* Delvaux and Lecuit v. *Société Générale pour Favoriser le Développement du Commerce et de l'Industrie en France SA*.[411] In that case, the judge divided 'knowledge' into five categories: (i) actual knowledge; (ii) wilfully shutting one's eyes to the truth; (iii) wilfully and recklessly failing to make such enquiries as a reasonable and honest man would make; (iv) knowledge of circumstances that would indicate the facts to an honest and reasonable man; and (v) knowledge of circumstances that would put a reasonable man on enquiry. Categories (i) to (iii) represent 'dishonesty'; categories (iv) and (v) denote 'negligence'. Peter Gibson J inclined to the view that 'knowledge' of any of the five types listed, including the last two categories, could form an adequate basis for imposing liability on an accessory to a breach of trust or other fiduciary duty.

However, by the time the issue came before the Privy Council in *Tan,* there was an increasing body of case law, and also of academic opinion, in favour of the test being one of dishonesty.[412] This was confirmed in *Tan* itself, where Lord Nicholls, by way of *obiter dicta*, confirmed that 'dishonesty is a necessary ingredient of accessory liability. It is also a sufficient ingredient'.[413] Furthermore, according to his Lordship, 'knowingly' was better avoided in the future as a defining ingredient of this form of accessory liability and that the five-point scale of knowledge set out in *Baden* was 'best forgotten' in this context.[414] Lord Nicholls clarified the meaning of dishonesty in this context. Dishonesty

---

[408] N.400 above.

[409] *Barclays Bank plc* v. *Quincecare Ltd* [1992] 4 All ER 363, 375, where Steyn J indicated that 'those decisions apparently caused consternation in banking circles'.

[410] N.380 above, 267, 275. See also *D.P.C. Estates Pty. Ltd* v. *Grey and Consul Development Pty. Ltd* [1974] 1 NSWLR 443, 459 (NSWCA), affd. on this point: (1975) 132 CLR 373, 376, 398, 412 (HCA).

[411] N.363 above.

[412] See, for example, *Re Montagu's S.T.*, n.344 above, 285; *Agip (Africa) Ltd* v. *Jackson,* n.353 above, 293; *Barclays Bank plc* v. *Quincecare Ltd,* n.409 above, 375; *Lipkin Gorman* v. *Karpnale Ltd* [1989] 1 WLR 1340, 1355 (CA); *Eagle Trust plc* v. *S.B.C. Securities Ltd* [1993] 1 WLR 484, 495; *Polly Peck International plc* v. *Nadir (No. 2)* [1994] 4 All ER 769, 777 (CA). For supporting academic comment, see, for example, P. Birks, 'Misdirected Funds: Restitution from the Recipient' [1989] *LMCLQ* 296; C. Harpum, 'The Stranger as Constructive Trustee' (1986) 102 *LQR* 114, 267; C. Harpum, 'The Basis of Equitable Liability' in P. Birks (ed.), *The Frontiers of Liability* (Oxford, 1994), i, 9. The standard of dishonesty established in *Tan* has been followed in Hong Kong: *Dougguan City Long Lian Trading Co Ltd* v. *So Kit* [2002] HKCU 222, [10]; *PBM (Hong Kong) Ltd* v. *Allan,* n.393 above, [17]; *High Fashion Garments Co. Ltd* v. *Tong* [2005] 4 HKC 8, [18]; *Akai Holdings Ltd* v. *Kasikornbank Public Co Ltd* [2008] HKCU 810, [478]–[479], aff'd without reference to this issue: [2010] HKCU 2362 (HKCFA). Compare, however, the Australian position where *Tan* has not yet been adopted: *Consul Developments Pty Ltd* v. *DPC Estates Pty Ltd,* n.389 above, 412 ('If a defendant knows of facts which themselves would, to a reasonable man, tell of fraud or breach of trust the case may well be different, as it clearly will be if the defendant who has consciously refrained from inquiry for fear lest he learn of fraud'); *Farah Construction Pty Ltd* v. *Say-Dee Pty Ltd* , n.388 above, [159]-[164], [177]; *Chameleon Mining NL* v. *Murchison Metals Ltd*, n.388 above, [129]–[132]. The Canadian courts have similarly yet to endorse *Tan*: *Air Canada* v. *M&L Travel Ltd*, n.390 above, 811 ('The knowledge requirement for this type of liability is actual knowledge; recklessness or willful blindness will also suffice'); *Citadel General Assurance Co* v. *Lloyds Bank Canada*, n.346 above, [21]–[23]; *3464920 Canada Inc.* v. *Strother*, n.390 above, [25] (leaving open the question of whether ' "knowingly" should give way to "dishonesty" as the "defining ingredient" of accessory liability').

[413] N.342 above, 392.   [414] Ibid.

is to be assessed objectively not subjectively. The key passage from his judgment reads as follows:[415]

> Whatever may be the position in some criminal or other contexts (see, for instance, *Reg.* v. *Ghosh* [1982] Q.B. 1053), in the context of the accessory liability principle acting dishonestly, or with a lack of probity, which is synonymous, means simply not acting as an honest person would in the circumstances. This is an objective standard. At first sight this may seem surprising. Honesty has a connotation of subjectivity, as distinct from the objectivity of negligence. Honesty, indeed, does have a strong subjective element in that it is a description of a type of conduct assessed in the light of what a person actually knew at the time, as distinct from what a reasonable person would have known or appreciated. Further, honesty and its counterpart dishonesty are mostly concerned with advertent conduct, not inadvertent conduct. Carelessness is not dishonesty. Thus for the most part dishonesty is to be equated with a conscious impropriety. However, these subjective characteristics of honesty do not mean that individuals are free to set their own standards of honesty in particular circumstances. The standard of what constitutes honest conduct is not subjective. Honesty is not an optional scale, with higher or lower values according to the moral standards of each individual. If a person knowingly appropriates another's property, he will not escape a finding of dishonesty simply because he sees nothing wrong in such behaviour.
>
> In most situations there is little difficulty in identifying how an honest person would behave. Honest people do not intentionally deceive others to their detriment. Honest people do not knowingly take others' property. Unless there is a very good and compelling reason, an honest person does not participate in a transaction if he knows it involves a misapplication of trust assets to the detriment of the beneficiaries. Nor does an honest person in such a case deliberately close his eyes and ears, or deliberately not ask questions, lest he learns something he would rather not know, and then proceed regardless.

Asking what honesty required, Lord Nicholls continued:[416]

> The only answer to these questions lies in keeping in mind that honesty is an objective standard. The individual is expected to attain the standard which would be observed by an honest person placed in those circumstances. It is impossible to be more specific. Knox J. captured the flavour of this, in a case with a commercial setting, when he referred to a person who is 'guilty of commercially unacceptable conduct in the particular context involved': see *Cowan de Groot Properties Ltd* v. *Eagle Trust plc* [1992] 4 All E.R. 700, 761. Acting in reckless disregard of others' rights or possible rights can be a tell-tale sign of dishonesty.

Lord Nicholls expressly referred to an 'objective standard' of dishonesty, but he also spoke of honesty having 'a strong subjective element' and that, for the most part, 'dishonesty is to be equated with a conscious impropriety'. This has left room for doubt and uncertainty as to the precise test to be adopted when assessing whether or not an accessory has been dishonest. There are three possible standards that could be applied to determine whether a person has acted dishonestly:

(1) a purely subjective standard, whereby a person is only regarded as dishonest if he transgresses his own standards of honesty, even if that standard is contrary to that of reasonable and honest people;

---

[415] Ibid., 389. In *Twinsectra Ltd* v. *Yardley*, n.271 above, [113], Lord Millett described Lord Nicholls' opinion in *Tan* as 'magisterial ... every word of which merits close attention'.

[416] Ibid., 390. In *Governor & Company of the Bank of Scotland* v. *A Ltd*, n.353 above, [29], Lord Woolf said this passage, though referring to a solicitor, can equally apply to a banker.

(2) a purely objective standard, whereby a person acts dishonestly if his conduct is dishonest by the ordinary standards of reasonable and honest people, even if he does not realize this; or

(3) a standard combining an objective and a subjective test, and requiring that before there can be a finding of dishonesty it must be established that the defendant's conduct was dishonest by the ordinary standards of reasonable and honest people and that the defendant realized that by those standards his conduct was dishonest ('the combined test').

In *Twinsectra Ltd* v. *Yardley*,[417] a majority of the House of Lords held that the 'combined test' was the correct test to be applied in a case of dishonest assistance.[418] T granted Y a loan of £1 million, the application for which was processed by Y's solicitor, L, who in turn utilized the services of another solicitor, S. T disbursed the loan to S against his undertaking that the proceeds would be used solely for the acquisition of property by Y and that the funds would be retained by S until then. In breach of this undertaking, S paid the proceeds over to L who, knowing of the undertaking given by S, did not take steps to ensure that the funds were used for the acquisition of property by Y. Instead, L simply paid away the funds on Y's instructions and about £358,000 was used by Y for other purposes. Their Lordships affirmed the Court of Appeal's decision that S held the funds on trust and that, in the instant case, the wording of the undertaking demonstrated that the beneficial ownership of those funds remained vested in T. Accordingly, the payment to L, in breach of S's undertaking, constituted a breach of trust by S. However, the House of Lords restored the trial judge's decision that L was not to be held liable to account as a constructive trustee.[419] Although L was aware of the terms of the trust, he did not appreciate that, by paying the funds away without acquiring the assurance that it would be utilized only for the prescribed purpose, he acted in a manner that would be regarded as dishonest by the standards of honest and reasonable people. Accordingly, L had not been consciously dishonest as required to render him liable as an accessory.

Lord Hutton delivered the principal majority judgment on the dishonesty issue. His Lordship held that dishonesty meant both that 'the defendant's conduct was dishonest by the ordinary standards of reasonable and honest people' and that the defendant 'himself realized that by those standards his conduct was dishonest'.[420] Lord Millett delivered a powerful dissent rejecting the second element and stating that 'it is not necessary that [the defendant] should actually have appreciated that he was acting dishonestly; it is sufficient that he was'.[421] Nevertheless, Lord Hutton emphasized three points in favour of the 'combined test' of dishonesty.[422] First, a finding by a court that a defendant had been dishonest was a grave finding, and it was particularly grave against a professional man, such as a solicitor. Secondly, notwithstanding that the issue did not arise in a criminal context, it would be less than just for the law to permit a finding that a defendant had been 'dishonest' in assisting a breach of trust where he knew of the trust's existence and its breach, but had not been aware that what he was doing would be regarded by honest men as being dishonest. Thirdly, requiring a defendant to know that what he is doing would be regarded

---

[417] N.271 above (noted by R. Thornton, 'Dishonest Assistance: Guilty Conduct or a Guilty Mind?' [2002] *CLJ* 524; T. Yeo & H. Tijo, 'Knowing What Is Dishonesty' (2002) 118 *LQR* 502).

[418] This test was adopted by Lords Slynn, Steyn, Hoffmann, and Hutton; Lord Millett dissented, preferring a test of dishonesty based on a purely objective standard. See also *Abbey National plc* v. *Solicitors' Indemnity Fund Ltd* [1997] PNLR 306, 310.

[419] This was the issue upon which Lord Millett dissented. [420] N.271 above, [27].

[421] Ibid., [121]. [422] Ibid., [35]–[36].

as dishonest by honest people does not involve a defendant setting his own standards of honesty because he does not regard as dishonest what he knows would offend the normally accepted standards of honest conduct. On the facts, Lords Hoffmann, Hutton, and Millett all stated that there were no facts of which L was unaware.[423] In other words, *Twinsectra* was not a case where the defendant deliberately closed his eyes and ears, or deliberately refrained from asking questions, for fear that he might learn something he would rather not know. Accordingly, *Twinsectra* left open the possibility that 'in a different case' a defendant who had deliberately closed his eyes and ears might nevertheless lead a court to conclude that he had been dishonest.

A little over three years after *Twinsectra*, just such a case came before the Privy Council in *Barlow Clowes International Ltd* v. *Eurotrust International Ltd*.[424] Barlow Clowes International ('Barlow Clowes') operated a fraudulent offshore investment scheme in Gibraltar offering high returns to the investing public from investments in United Kingdom gilt-edged securities. The defendant company, ITC, was based in the Isle of Man and provided offshore financial services. These involved forming and administering offshore companies, providing offshore directors who would act on the instructions of beneficiaries, opening bank accounts, and moving money, sometimes through its own client account. Before the collapse of the Barlow Clowes scheme in 1988, ITC dealt with a number of payments from Barlow Clowes to offshore companies that it administered. Some of the monies from the impugned transactions passed through ITC's client account and other sums passed through the accounts of the companies administered by ITC. The liquidator of Barlow Clowes brought proceedings against ITC and its directors alleging that they had dishonestly assisted in defrauding the investors in the Barlow Clowes scheme. The appeal to the Privy Council concerned the liability of only one of ITC's directors, Mr Henwood.[425] The judge at first instance had held that Mr Henwood was fully aware of the nature of Barlow Clowes' business and of the dishonest nature of those running the investment scheme.[426] Furthermore, the judge held that Mr Henwood 'strongly suspected that the funds passing through his hands were moneys which Barlow Clowes had received from members of the public', but that he 'consciously decided not to make inquiries because he preferred in his own interest not to run the risk of discovering the truth'.[427] The judge concluded that deliberately shutting one's eyes in this way was dishonest. On appeal, Lord Hoffmann agreed that Mr Henwood's deliberate failure to inquire was dishonest 'by ordinary standards'.[428] There are two important points in *Barlow Clowes*.

The first (and most significant) point relates to the meaning now to be attributed to 'dishonesty' for the purposes of dishonest assistance liability. Following *Twinsectra*, there had been a good deal of disquiet about the 'combined test' adopted in that case.[429] The Privy

---

[423] Ibid., [22], [49], [141].   [424] [2006] 1 All ER 333 (PC).

[425] Ibid., [4].   [426] Ibid., [21]–[23].   [427] Ibid., [11].   [428] Ibid, [12].

[429] The test formulated in *Twinsectra* appears to go well beyond what Lord Nicholls had actually said in *Tan* and comes close to the criminal law standard of dishonesty laid down in *R* v. *Ghosh* [1982] QB 1053—a test specifically rejected by Lord Nicholls: R. Thornton, n.417, 525–526; C. Rickett, '*Quistclose* Trusts and Dishonest Assistance' [2002] *RLR* 112, 117–120; T.M. Yeo & H. Yijo, n.417, 508; C. Mitchell, 'Banks, Dishonesty and Negligence' in Meredith Lectures 2002, *Dirty Money: Civil and Criminal Aspects* (Quebec, 2003), ch. 4. For the rejection of *Ghosh* in Australia, see *Peters* v. *R* (1998) 192 CLR 493, [17] (HCA). Lord Walker (who subsequently heard the appeal in *Barlow Clowes*) doubted extrajudicially 'whether the law as stated in *Royal Brunei* [was] clear after *Twinsectra*': R. Walker, 'Dishonesty and Unconscionable Conduct in Commercial Life' (2005) 27 *Sydney L Rev* 187, 197. Moreover, the New Zealand Court of Appeal in *US International Marketing Ltd* v. *National Bank of New Zealand Ltd*, n.325 above, [7], [62], [78]–[79] (noted by T.M. Yeo, '*Twinsectra*: New Zealand's "reasonable banker" response' (2004) 120 *LQR* 208) expressed reservations about

Council in *Barlow Clowes* performed something of a *volte-face* on this issue, although their Lordships would never admit as much.[430] Applying *Tan*, Lord Hoffmann in *Barlow Clowes* stated that '[a]lthough a dishonest state of mind is a subjective mental state, the standard by which the law determines whether it is dishonest is objective'.[431] The judge at first instance had concluded, however, that Mr Henwood 'may well have lived by different standards and seen nothing wrong in what he was doing'.[432] This finding raised squarely the issue of whether the notion of 'dishonesty' in this context involved a further subjective requirement, as appeared to be recognized in *Twinsectra*, that a defendant must also be aware that his conduct was dishonest by ordinary objective standards. Roundly rejecting any such additional requirement, Lord Hoffmann stated that '[i]f by ordinary standards a defendant's mental state would be characterized as dishonest, it is irrelevant that the defendant judges by different standards'.[433] His Lordship considered that this approach was consistent with *Twinsectra*, as the principles laid down by the House of Lords in that case were in fact no different from those originally established in *Tan*.[434] In this regard, Lord Hoffmann accepted that Lord Hutton's judgment in *Twinsectra* may have contained 'an element of ambiguity', but that Lord Hutton had never intended to introduce a second subjective element into the test for dishonesty.[435] This is hardly convincing given that Lord Hutton in *Twinsectra* expressly referred more than once to the 'combined test' as being the correct test.[436] Furthermore, Lord Hoffmann in *Barlow Clowes* reinterpreted his own words from *Twinsectra*—his earlier statement that dishonesty involves 'consciousness that one is transgressing ordinary standards of honest behaviour' was subsequently revised to mean that there should be 'consciousness of those elements of the transaction which make participation transgress ordinary standards of honest behaviour'.[437] With respect, these are not the same thing.[438] As decisions following *Barlow Clowes* have stressed, however, even accepting that the test is an objective one, it is nevertheless

---

the subjective element of the 'combined test' in *Twinsectra*. See also *King's Wharf Coldstore Ltd* v. *Wilson* (2005) 2 NZCCLR 1042, [120] where Miller J indicated that the additional subjective element, doubted in *US International*, 'can be discounted now' in New Zealand following *Barlow Clowes*. In *Westpac New Zealand Ltd* v. *MAP & Associates Ltd*, n.325 above, [45]–[47], the New Zealand Court of Appeal confirmed its earlier (more tentative) view that 'a bank will be liable for dishonest assistance where it has actual knowledge of the circumstances of the transactions (the subjective element) such as to render its participation contrary to normally acceptable standards of honest conduct (the objective element)'.

[430] See, however, A. Hudson, n.402 above, 150, indicating that '[a] point missed by many commentators is that in *Dubai Aluminium* v. *Salaam* the majority of their Lordships expressed a clear preference for the objectivity of the approach in *Royal Brunei Airlines* v. *Tan*'.

[431] N.424 above.   [432] Ibid., [12].

[433] Ibid., [10]. In judging whether a defendant has met 'the ordinary standard of honest behaviour', it is irrelevant that 'there may be a body of opinion which regards the ordinary standard of honest behaviour as being set too high': *Starglade Properties Ltd* v. *Nash* [2010] EWCA Civ 1314, [32].

[434] Ibid., [18].   [435] Ibid., [15].

[436] N.271 above, [38], [50]. This was similarly Lord Steyn's understanding of Lord Hutton's judgment: ibid., [7].

[437] N.424 above, [16]. See also Lord Hoffmann's doubts about a purely objective test of dishonesty in *Aktieselskabet Dansk Skibsfinansiering* v. *Wheelock Marden & Co Ltd* [2000] 1 HKC 511, 523 (HKCFA), although Lord Millett has agreed with this approach when liability is based upon 'intent to defraud': *Twinsectra* v. *Yardley*, n.271 above, [116].

[438] *Barlow Clowes* has been described as a decision that 'takes the notion of judicial re-interpretation to new heights': G. Virgo, 'The Role of Fault in the Law of Restitution' in A. Burrows & A. Rodger, *Mapping the Law: Essays in Memory of Peter Birks* (Oxford, 2006), 86.

'an objective [test] which takes account of the individual's in question characteristics'.[439] In other words, the test is now 'predominantly objective'.[440]

The second point relates to the type of knowledge that a defendant must be shown to possess before he will be held to have transgressed the ordinary standards of honesty required for dishonest assistance liability. In particular, there had in the past been some uncertainty over whether the accessory had to be aware of the breach of trust or whether awareness of some other wrongdoing (for example, breach of contract, breach of foreign exchange controls, or evasion of tax) was enough. In *Royal Brunei Airlines* v. *Tan*,[441] Lord Nicholls observed that the law had in the past required the accessory to have knowledge of the breach of trust, but he did not deal with the issue in the light of the new test of dishonesty that he had adopted. Dicta in subsequent cases, however, in particular *Brinks Ltd* v. *Abu-Saleh (No. 3)*,[442] suggested that it was essential for the accessory to have knowledge of the facts giving rise to the breach of trust. In *Twinsectra* v. *Yardley*,[443] however, Lord Millett rejected this view indicating that it is 'obviously not necessary that he should know the details of the trust or the identity of the beneficiary', but that it is sufficient 'that [the accessory] knows that the money is not at the free disposal of the principal', 'that he knows that he is assisting in a dishonest scheme' or that he has 'knowledge of the arrangements which constitute the trust'. As Lord Millett had said many years earlier in *Agip (Africa) Ltd* v. *Jackson*, '[a] man who consciously assists others by making arrangements which he knows are calculated to conceal what is happening from a third party, takes the risk that they are part of a fraud practised on that party'.[444] Such a person similarly takes the risk that his actions provide assistance in breaching a trust.[445] The position has now been clarified in *Barlow Clowes*, where Lord Hoffmann, specifically rejecting the view in *Brinks*, held that it was not necessary that the accessory know about the existence of the trust, the facts giving rise to the trust, or even what a trust actually involves in legal terms.[446] According to his Lordship, it would be sufficient that the defendant 'entertained a clear suspicion' that the funds in question were held on trust or that the primary wrongdoers were not 'entitled to make free with [the funds] as they pleased'.[447] If accessory liability is indeed now a species of equitable

---

[439] A. Clarke, 'Claims Against Professionals: Negligence, Dishonesty and Fraud' (2006) 22 PN 70, applied in *AG of Zambia* v. *Meer Care & Desai*, n.344 above, [346], [357] ('…taking account of the individual's experience, his knowledge and his reasons for so acting'); *Merkel International Insurance Co. Ltd* v. *Surety Guarantee Consultants Ltd* [2008] EWHC 1135 (Comm.), [191]. See also *Fresh 'N' Clean (Wales) Ltd* v. *Miah* [2006] EWHC 903 (Ch), [18]; *Abou-Rahmah* v. *Abacha*, n.361 above, [66], [94]. See further *High Fashion Garments Co. Ltd* v. *Tong*, n.412 above, [61]; *Peconic Industrial Development Ltd* v. *Chio Ho Cheong* [2006] HKCU 865, [177].

[440] *Abou-Rahmah* v. *Abacha*, n.361 above, [66], [94].   [441] N.342 above, 387.

[442] N.394 above, 151. See also *Grupo Torras SA* v. *Al-Sabah*, n.347 above, 59.

[443] N.271 above, [135]–[136]. Lord Hoffmann appears to have adopted a similar stance (at [24]) when he said that '[a] person may dishonestly assist in the commission of a breach of trust without any idea of what a trust means'. See also *Abou-Rahmah* v. *Abacha*, n.361 above, [20]–[21].

[444] N.353 above, 295, approved in *Abou-Rahmah* v. *Abacha*, n.361 above, [38]–[39].

[445] *Twinsectra Ltd* v. *Yardley*, n.271 above, [136]. See also *Banque Nationale de Paris* v. *Hew Keong Chan Gary*, n.199 above, 333–334.

[446] N.424 above, [28]. See also *Abou-Rahmah* v. *Abacha*, n.361 above, [15]–[16]. Support for this position already existed in Hong Kong: *PBM (Hong Kong) Ltd* v. *Allan*, n.393 above, [29]–[31]. Compare *Air Canada* v. *M&L Travel Ltd*, n.390 above, [38]; *Commercial Union Life Assurance Co of Canada* v. *John Ingle Insurance Group Inc.*, n.390 above, [2]; *Glenko Enterprises Ltd* v. *Keller*, n.390 above, [23]–[25].

[447] Id. See also *Ultraframe (UK) Ltd* v. *Fielding*, n.343 above, [1504]; *Abou-Rahmah* v. *Abacha*, n.361 above, [23]. For practitioner support for this position, see M. Tugendhat, 'Assisting in Breach of Duty by a Fiduciary, the Common Law and Money-Laundering' in F. Rose (ed.), *Restitution and Banking Law* (Oxford, 1998), 140–143.

wrongdoing, and if it is to make a clean break from its 'constructive trust' origins,[448] then this broader approach to knowledge is the correct one.

Although the clarification provided by *Barlow Clowes* is to be welcomed, it is hardly an ideal state of affairs for lower courts,[449] which, in strict precedential terms, are bound to follow the actual words used by their Lordships in *Twinsectra*.[450] Nevertheless, no matter how unconvincing the sleight of hand in *Barlow Clowes*,[451] the lower courts appear to be playing the game and applying what their Lordships 'intended' to say in *Twinsectra* rather than what they actually said.[452] The principal effect of *Barlow Clowes* on corporate defendants, including banks, is that they will be more likely to be held liable for dishonest assistance than under the *Twinsectra* approach. Not only is there now one less requirement to satisfy in order to make a bank liable, but that requirement also involved the particularly difficult task of demonstrating that the bank had acted with conscious dishonesty. This second element was particularly difficult to satisfy in a corporate context, as it required the identification of an individual within the bank who acted with knowledge of the relevant facts and with conscious dishonesty and who could be identified as the bank's 'mind' (or, at the very least, an agent or employee whose dishonesty could be attributed to the bank) under the relevant principles of company law.[453] The English courts are unlikely simply to aggregate knowledge within the bank when assessing whether a corporate defendant has acted with knowledge of the relevant facts and with conscious dishonesty.[454]

---

[448] *Dubai Aluminium Co. Ltd* v. *Salaam*, n.150 above, [141]–[142].

[449] *AG of Zambia* v. *Meer Care & Desai*, n.344 above, [351], where Peter Smith J said that '[t]hese decisions present a nightmare for a first instance judge', but concluded that the issue of dishonesty is essentially a 'jury question' to be assessed in the light of all the material: ibid., [368]. See also *Law Society of England & Wales* v. *Habitable Concepts Ltd* [2010] EWHC 1449 (Ch), [24]–[26]. Compare M. Halliwell & E. Prochaska, 'Assistance and Dishonesty: Ring-A-Ring O'Roses' [2006] *Conv* 465, 466–467 with D. Ryan, 'Royal Brunei Dishonesty: Clarity at Last' [2006] *Conv* 188, 195–196; D. Ryan, 'Royal Brunei Dishonesty: A Clear Welcome for *Barlow Clowes*' [2007] *Conv* 168, 169, 174–175.

[450] See, however, *R* v. *James* [2006] EWCA Crim 14 for an example of the Court of Appeal applying a Privy Council decision in preference to a House of Lords decision.

[451] T. Yeo, 'Dishonest Assistance: A Restatement from the Privy Council' (2006) 122 *LQR* 171, 173–174; M. Conaglen & A. Goymour, 'Dishonesty in the Context of Assistance—Again' [2006] *CLJ* 18, 19–20.

[452] *Fresh 'N' Clean (Wales) Ltd* v. *Miah*, n.439 above, [18]; *Abou-Rahmah* v. *Abacha* [2006] 1 Lloyd's Rep.484, [43], affd. on the precedent point: [2007] 1 Lloyd's Rep. 115, [64]–[69] (CA), (although Rix LJ (at [23]–[24]) and Pill LJ (at [91]–[94]) preferred to leave this point more open); *Hanco ATM Systems Ltd* v. *Cashbox ATM Systems Ltd* [2007] EWHC 1599 (Ch), [68]; *Al Khudairi* v. *Abbey Brokers Ltd* [2010] EWHC 1486 (Ch), [134]; *Aerostar Maintenance International Ltd* v. *Wilson*, n.376 above, [183]–[184]; *Starglade Properties Ltd* v. *Nash*, n.433 above, [23]–[40]; but compare *AG of Zambia* v. *Meer Care & Desai*, n.344 above, [365] (dismissing Arden LJ's views in *Abou-Rahmah* as obiter); *Bryant* v. *Law Society* [2007] EWHC 3043 (Admin.), [153]–[155] (*Twinsectra* continues to apply in solicitor disciplinary proceedings). Jurisdictions that had adopted *Tan* have shown a preference for *Barlow Clowes* over *Twinsectra*: *Active Profit Ltd* v. *Nissho Iwai Hong Kong Corporation Ltd* [2003] HKCU 749, [170] (preferring Lord Millett in *Twinsectra*); *Peconic Industrial Development Ltd* v. *Chio Ho Cheong*, n.439 above, [179]–[184]; *Ho Lai Ming* v. *Chu Chik Leung* [2007] HKCU 1614, [20]–[24]; *Akai Holdings Ltd* v. *Kasikornbank Public Co Ltd*, n.412 above, [479]. Even before *Barlow Clowes* the Hong Kong courts had expressed a preference for Lord Millett's dissent in *Twinsectra*: *UBS AG* v. *Stand Ford International Enterprises Ltd* [2002] 3 HKC 621, 627–628.

[453] *Meridian Global Funds Management Asia Ltd* v. *Securities Commission* [1995] 2 AC 500, 507 (PC). See *Underhill and Hayton's Law of Trusts and Trustees* (18th edn., London, 2010), [98.66]. Even an objective approach to dishonesty, however, will usually require the identification of a particular bank officer whose conduct and knowledge can be measured against the relevant standard: *Abou-Rahmah* v. *Abacha*, n.361 above.

[454] *Galmerrow Securities Ltd* v. *National Westminster Bank plc* (Ch. D, 20 December 1993); *R.* v. *HM Coroner for East Kent, ex p Spooner* (1987) 88 Cr App. Rep. 10, 15–17; *A-G's Ref (No. 2 of 1999)* [2000] 3

That said, it is not anticipated that *Barlow Clowes* will produce a flood of successful dishonest assistance claims against banks, since the threshold for liability remains the high one of actual dishonesty, albeit determined now in a 'predominantly objective' manner.[455] Banks are not to be made detectives, and unless and until they are alerted to the possibility of wrongdoing they are entitled to proceed on the assumption that they are dealing with honest people.[456] Banks do not become constructive trustees merely because they entertain suspicions about the provenance of money deposited with them.[457] On the other hand, if the bank has strong grounds for doubting its customer's honesty, it may itself be held to be dishonest if it turns a blind eye to its doubts.[458] This is a difficult line to draw,[459] however, as demonstrated by the recent Court of Appeal decision in *Abou-Rahmah* v. *Abacha*,[460] in which the defendant, a Nigerian bank, had the proceeds of a fraudulent scheme paid into its account with HSBC, from where the funds were transferred by the defendant bank to the account of a corporate customer that was controlled by accomplices to the fraud. By the time the fraud was discovered, the customer's account had been cleared and proceedings were brought against the bank on the grounds of its dishonest assistance. The principal issue on appeal was whether the judge had been correct in finding that the bank had not been dishonest. Rix LJ clearly thought that the conduct of the bank came very close (and possibly even crossed) the line, since the judge had found that the bank officer in question 'probably suspected in a general way' that his customer's directors were involved in money-laundering transactions;[461] the bank had been lax in following anti-money laundering guidelines when opening the account;[462] the few transactions that had been conducted on the relevant account were suspicious in nature;[463] and the bank had failed to report transactions above a certain value in accordance with the anti-money laundering guidelines.[464] Rix LJ considered that there was a difference between 'failing to spot a possible money-launderer' and having 'good grounds for suspecting money laundering and then [proceeding] as though one did not'.[465] On this basis, his Lordship could not see why a bank, which through its managers has 'clear suspicion that a prospective client indulges in money laundering', should escape liability for dishonest assistance.[466] Nevertheless, Rix LJ did not consider it appropriate to interfere with the judge's discretion on this issue with the result that the bank escaped liability on this ground.[467] In contrast, Arden LJ, although agreeing that the exercise of the judge's

WLR 195, 211–212. Cf. *Macquarie Bank Ltd* v. *Sixty-Fourth Throne Pty Ltd* [1998] 3 VR 133, 161; *Equiticorp Industries Group Ltd* v. *R (No. 47)* [1998] 2 NZLR 481, 627–629.

[455] See, for example, *Abou-Rahmah* v. *Abacha*, n.361 above, [40], [73], [98], where a less than scrupulous bank escaped liability for dishonest assistance. In assessing dishonesty, the courts will examine the regulatory environment in which the accessory operates: *Manolakaki* v. *Constantinides* [2004] EWHC 749; *Tayeb* v. *HSBC Bank plc* [2004] 4 All ER 1024, [75]–[77].

[456] *Macmillan* v. *Bishopsgate Trust (No. 3)* [1995] 1 WLR 978, 1014; *Box* v. *Barclays Bank* [1998] Lloyds Rep. Bank. 185, 205, col. 2. Cf. S. Gardner, n.335 above.

[457] *The Bank* v. *A Ltd* [2000] Lloyd's Rep. Bank. 271, 283, col. 1, affd. [2001] 1 WLR 751 (CA).

[458] *Governor & Company of the Bank of Scotland* v. *A Ltd (sub nom. The Bank* v. *A Ltd)*, n.353 above, [37] (CA).

[459] *AG of Zambia* v. *Meer Care & Desai*, n.344 above, [371].

[460] N.361 above (noted by G. Virgo, 'Assisting the victims of fraud: the significance of dishonesty and bad faith' [2007] *CLJ* 22).

[461] Ibid., [29].

[462] Ibid., [31], [36]. For the relevance of account-opening procedures, see also *Bardissy* v. *D'Souza* [1999] HKCU 119.

[463] Ibid., [34].   [464] Ibid., [31], [35], but compare [72].   [465] Ibid., [37].   [466] Id.

[467] Ibid., [40], although the bank was held liable on the basis that the payments it received were made as a result of a mistake and that the bank was not entitled to raise a change of position defence: Ch. 12, Sect. 3(iii) below.

decision should stand, seemed far more reluctant than Rix LJ to attribute dishonesty to a bank that only had general suspicions about its customer's possible money-laundering activities, and that did not have knowledge of 'any specific act of dishonesty' or any particular suspicions about the transactions in question.[468] Although Pill LJ similarly agreed that the Court of Appeal should not interfere with the judge's decision,[469] he did not indicate his position on the specificity of the knowledge required on the part of the defendant bank, but did indicate that where a bank manager's conduct had 'fallen below normally acceptable standards, it can readily be inferred that he knew it did, so that his conduct would have amounted to dishonest assistance'.[470]

After *Abou-Rahmah*, which is probably a fairly unusual case given how solicitous United Kingdom banks are nowadays about complying with the anti-money laundering legislation,[471] it may be wondered how much of a risk dishonest assistance liability really poses for banks, irrespective of how one defines the elements of that wrong. In practice, a bank that has been used for the diversion of trust assets or as part of some other fraudulent or criminal scheme may well have other more pressing concerns. Two examples suffice. The first example arises when a bank has received information from the authorities conducting a criminal investigation that a customer's account may be involved in money-laundering or other criminal or fraudulent activity. As *Governor & Company of the Bank of Scotland* v. *A Ltd* demonstrates,[472] a bank with such information runs the risk of criminal liability and is placed in a real dilemma. The claimant bank opened an account for A Ltd, a new customer, and received a deposit of US $1.2 m into the account from B (an individual) and C Ltd. Following receipt of the money, the bank became suspicious that B and C Ltd were the victims of a prime bank instrument fraud. The bank was then informed by the Serious Fraud Office (SFO), in confidence, that it was investigating the activities of A Ltd.[473] The bank considered itself in a dilemma. It was concerned that, if it allowed A Ltd to continue operating the account, the balance would be withdrawn and the bank would be held liable for dishonest assistance and made to compensate those beneficially entitled to the account funds. On the other hand, if the bank raised the issue with A Ltd, it risked falling foul of section 93D of the Criminal Justice Act 1988 (now repealed and replaced),[474] which made it an offence to 'tip off' a person that he is the subject of investigation.

The bank applied (without notice to A Ltd) to the court for directions. Lightman J ordered the account to be frozen, but that A Ltd was not to be informed of the order or given any indication of why the account was frozen. Not surprisingly, A Ltd started proceedings against the bank when it was unable to access the money in its account. Following further hearings, most of the money in the account was released to A Ltd and

---

[468] Ibid., [72]. Arden LJ's approach is consistent with *R* v. *Da Silva* [2006] 2 Cr App. Rep. 517, [15] (CA), where Longmore LJ indicated that in the context of dishonest assistance 'a vague feeling of unease was not sufficient', and that there could only be liability if '[t]he suspicion [was] firmly grounded and targeted on specific facts' (citing *Manifest Shipping Co. Ltd* v. *Uni-Polaris Insurance Co. Ltd* [2003] 1 AC 469, [116] (HL)). See also *Akai Holdings Ltd* v. *Kasikornbank Public Co Ltd*, n.412 above, [480] ('…this suspicion must be firmly grounded/targeted in terms of specific facts…'), [484] ('…the court must not infer a person's dishonesty unless it is satisfied by cogent evidence that it is the *only possible* inference that can be drawn in the circumstances'). See also N. Kiri, 'Dishonest Assistance: the Latest Perspective from the Court of Appeal' (2007) 22 *JIBLR* 305, 312.

[469] Ibid., [98].

[470] Ibid., [90]. For suggested factors in determining bank liability in this context, see R. Lee, 'Dishonesty and Bad Faith After *Barlow Clowes: Abou-Rahmah* v. *Abacha*' [2007] *JBL* 209, 210–211.

[471] Ch.4, Sect. 3 above.

[472] N.353 above, [37]. See further Ch. 4, Sect. 4 & Ch. 5, Sect. 5(iii) above.

[473] The SFO investigations were later dropped.

[474] See now Proceeds of Crime Act 2002, s.333A. See further Ch. 4, Sect. 3(ii)(c) above.

only a small sum remained frozen to cover the bank's costs. The matter then came before Laddie J on an application to strike out or stay the proceedings commenced against A Ltd and to discharge the original order freezing the account. Laddie J discharged the injunction on the ground that it did not contain the usual provisions providing protection to the defendant.[475] The Court of Appeal agreed with his decision, but for different reasons. Lord Woolf CJ, delivering the judgment of the court, held that the appropriate defendant to any application for directions was not A Ltd but the SFO.[476] The hearing could have been held in private and there would have been no question of serving proceedings on A Ltd as it would not have been a party. The court would then have made an interim declaration setting out what information it would be proper for the bank to rely on. Once the issue of what information could be disclosed had been resolved, the bank could then decide what course it wished to adopt *vis-à-vis* A Ltd.[477] Lord Woolf CJ concluded:[478]

> The use of the court's power to grant interim declarations in proceedings involving the SFO will protect a bank from criminal proceedings but it will not automatically provide protection for the bank against actions by customers or third parties. However, it seems almost inconceivable that a bank which takes the initiative in seeking the court's guidance should subsequently be held to have acted dishonestly so as to incur accessory liability. The involvement of the court should however enable, in the great majority of cases, a practical solution to be determined which protects the interests of the public but allows the interests of a bank to be safeguarded.

The second example arises where the victim of the fraud also happens to be a customer of the bank, and is exemplified by *Lipkin Gorman* v. *Karpnale*.[479] A junior partner misappropriated large amounts of money standing to the credit of his firm's clients' account. The firm's actions against the bank, with which both the firm and the fraudster maintained their accounts, was based not only on the second branch of *Barnes* v. *Addy*, but also on the bank's alleged failure to observe its duty of care to its customer. Although it is unlikely that a court would impose a duty of care on a bank to the victim of a fraud when that person is not one of the bank's customers,[480] as considered previously,[481] the Court of Appeal in *Lipkin Gorman* recognized that a bank does owe a duty of care to its customers not to obey any payment instructions that it has reason to believe may involve a fraud being perpetrated on that customer. Although the bank escaped liability in *Lipkin Gorman*, the case demonstrates that, despite the general move away from a negligence-based standard of fault when it comes to assessing the liability of banks towards third party victims of fraud, negligence-based standards can still have a role to play in fixing a bank with liability when its customer happens to be the victim of the fraud. Even when the victim is a non-customer, there are other forms of liability, with a lower knowledge

---

[475] N.457 above.   [476] N.353 above, [40].

[477] Ibid., [41]. However, in *Amalgamated Metal Trading Ltd* v. *City of London Police Financial Investigation Unit* [2003] 1 All ER (Comm.) 900, Tomlinson J subsequently held that, where tipping off is not in issue, a bank that suspects it is holding funds that are the proceeds of crime should not seek declaratory relief from the court, but must make a commercial decision whether or not to contest proceedings if they are brought by the accountholder.

[478] Ibid., [47], applied in *Tayeb* v. *HSBC Bank plc*, n.455 above, [75]–[77].

[479] N.412 above, appealed on different grounds: [1991] 2 AC 548 (HL).

[480] *Royal Brunei Airlines* v. *Tan*, n.342 above, 391; *Box* v. *Barclays Bank plc*, n.456 above, 205. Where the bank has received a negotiable instrument, then the defrauded third party may be able to use the tort of conversion against the bank (Ch. 15, Sect. 2 below), although the existence of a defence for the collecting bank under Cheques Act 1957, s.4 means that the enquiry will focus largely upon the negligence or otherwise of the bank (Ch. 15, Sect. 4(iii) below).

[481] Ch. 5, Sect. 4(iii) above. For a further example, see *Abou-Rahmah* v. *Abacha*, n.361 above.

requirement than for dishonest assistance liability, that may nevertheless be imposed on the bank. As was made clear when *Lipkin Gorman* reached the House of Lords,[482] a victim of fraud will have a restitutionary claim against any third parties, including banks, by virtue of an action for money had and received.[483] Furthermore, where such a victim can demonstrate that the bank has beneficially received the funds in question, he may have a claim against the bank based upon their knowing receipt. This form of liability will be considered in the next section.

(iv) Knowing receipt

The liability of a recipient of property disposed of in breach of trust is generally known as liability for knowing receipt. It does not matter that the recipient no longer retains the property in question, for he remains liable personally to compensate the claimant for the loss caused by the breach of trust.[484] There are three requirements, all of which must be met, for liability to arise under this head of constructive trusteeship. In *El Ajou* v. *Dollar Land Holdings plc*,[485] Hoffmann LJ stated that the claimant must show:

> first, a disposal of his assets in breach of fiduciary duty; secondly, the beneficial receipt by the defendant of assets which are traceable as representing the assets of the [claimant]; and thirdly, knowledge on the part of the defendant that the assets he received are traceable to a breach of fiduciary duty.

Where there is no property capable of being the subject-matter of a trust, then no liability for knowing receipt can arise.[486] The two main types of 'knowing receipt, were identified by Millett J in *Agip (Africa) Ltd* v. *Jackson*,[487] as follows:

> The first is concerned with that of the person who receives for his own benefit trust property transferred to him in breach of trust. He is liable as a constructive trustee if he receives with notice, actual or constructive, that it was trust property and that the transfer to him was a breach of trust; or if he received it without notice but subsequently discovered the facts. In either case he is liable to account for the property, in the first case as from the time he received the property, and in the second as from the time he acquired notice....The second and...distinct class of case is that of a person, usually an agent of the trustees, who receives the property lawfully and not for his own benefit but who then either misappropriates it or otherwise deals with it in a manner inconsistent with the trust. He is liable to account as constructive trustee if he received the trust property knowing it to be such, though he will not necessarily be required in all circumstances to have known the exact terms of the trust...In either class of case it is immaterial whether the breach of trust was fraudulent or not. The essential feature of the first class is that the recipient must have received the property for his own use and benefit.

---

[482] N.328 above.

[483] Depending upon how one conceptualizes such a claim, a defendant may be able to raise a change of position defence: Ch. 12, Sects. 3(iii) & 6 below.

[484] See, for example, *Goose* v. *Wilson Sandiford & Co. (No. 2)*, n.373 above, [88].

[485] [1994] 2 All ER 685, 700 (CA), approved in *Brown* v. *Bennett* [1999] BCC 525, 530 (CA); *Niru Battery Manufacturing Co.* v. *Milestone Trading Ltd* [2004] 1 Lloyd's Rep. 344, [154] (CA); *Ultraframe (UK) Ltd* v. *Fielding*, n.343 above, [1478]–[1479]; *Charter plc* v. *City Index Ltd*, n.344 above, [7]; *Yugraneft* v. *Abramovich*, n.344 above, [248]; *Hollis* v. *Rolfe* [2008] EWHC 1747 (Ch), [172]; *Law Society of England & Wales* v. *Habitable Concepts Ltd*, n.449 above, [6]. See also *Bankgesellschaft Berlin AG* v. *Makris*, n.363 above. For the importance of establishing a breach of fiduciary obligation, see *Robb Evans* v. *European Bank Ltd*, n.3 above, [160].

[486] *Commonwealth Oil & Gas Ltd* v. *Baxter* [2009] CSIH 75, [93]–[95].

[487] N.353 above, 291–292, affd. [1991] Ch. 547 (CA).

The second class is sometimes referred to as 'liability for inconsistent dealing'.[488] But where the inconsistent dealing is not for the benefit of the agent—an essential require-ment of the 'knowing receipt' form of liability—there seems to be a strong case for saying that liability arises only if the requirements for dishonest assistance have been met.[489]

For knowing receipt liability, it must be possible to show a sufficient nexus between the original trust property and the property in the recipient's hands. The issue arose in *Satnam Investments Ltd* v. *Dunlop Heywood & Co. Ltd*.[490] S, who were property develop-ers, wished to purchase a site. However, their surveyors, in breach of fiduciary duty, told other developers (M) that the site was a bargain and that S's right to buy it had lapsed. M duly bought the site. S claimed that M held the site as constructive trustees as a result of its knowing receipt or dishonest assistance. The Court of Appeal held that M were not liable. Nourse LJ pointed out that the trust property received by M was confidential infor-mation and that there was not a sufficient nexus between this and the site to justify the imposition of a constructive trust over the site (the notion of a remedial constructive trust being firmly rejected). The assistance claim also failed as dishonesty on the part of M had not been proved. In addition, the receipt must be the direct consequence of the breach of trust. This can be illustrated by *Brown* v. *Bennett*,[491] the facts of which are set out in section (iii) above. The allegation of knowing receipt against O Ltd was that it purchased P Ltd's business with knowledge of all the dishonest breaches of fiduciary duty alleged against the defendant directors. The Court of Appeal held that the receipt had to be the direct consequence of the alleged breach of trust or fiduciary duty of which the recipient was said to have notice. In this case, O Ltd acquired the property *bona fide* under a purchase from independent fiduciary sellers, namely the administrative receivers. Accordingly, O Ltd did not receive any trust property as a result of a breach of trust.

(a) Beneficial receipt

Liability depends on *beneficial* receipt of the property disposed of in breach of trust or of its traceable product. Agents who receive trust money in a ministerial capacity (in other words, for the benefit of their principal and not for their own use and benefit) are not to be made liable for 'knowing receipt'.[492] In *Agip (Africa) Ltd* v. *Jackson*,[493] Millett J expressed the

---

[488] See, for example, A.J. Oakley (ed.), *Parker and Mellows: The Modern Law of Trusts* (9th edn., London, 2008) 440–442.

[489] W. Blair QC, n.335 above, 82.

[490] N.372 above. See also *Ultraframe (UK) Ltd* v. *Fielding* , n.343 above, [1465]–[1466]; *Yugraneft* v. *Abramovich*, n.344 above, [343]–[378], [1465]–[1466].

[491] N.369 above.

[492] *Twinsectra* v. *Yardley*, n.271 above, where Lord Millett accepted obiter that any knowing receipt claim in that case would fail 'for want of the necessary receipt'. This was because the accessory 'never regarded himself as beneficially entitled to the money', as he held the funds to his principal's order and paid it out to his principal or his companies. See also *AG of Zambia* v. *Meer Care & Desai* , n.344 above, [683], [900]; *Thanakharn* v. Akai Holdings Ltd [2010] HKCU 2362, [138]–[144]; Law Society of England & Wales v. Habitable Concepts Ltd, n.449 above, [14]; Law Society of England & Wales v. Isaac, n.350 above, [52]; Fiona Trust & Holding Corporation v. Privalov [2010] EWHC 3199 (Comm), [60]; Horler v. Rubin [2011] All ER (D) 149 (Feb), [140]., [900]. Cf. *Trustor AB* v. *Smallbone (No. 2)* [2001] 1 WLR 1177, [23], where Morritt V-C held a court entitled to 'pierce the corporate veil' and recognize receipt of a company (as principal) as that of the individual(s) in control of it if the company was used as a device or façade to conceal the true facts, thereby avoiding or concealing any liability of that individual(s).

[493] N.353 above, 292, implicitly approved on appeal: [1991] Ch. 547 (CA). The distinction between beneficial and agency receipt has also become established in Australia (*Adams* v. *Bank of New South Wales* [1984] 1 NSWLR 285; *Stephens Travel Services International* v. *Quantas Airways* (1988) 13 NSWLR 33; *Spangaro* v. *Corporate Investment Australia Funds Management Ltd* [2003] FCA 1025, [56]), New Zealand (*Lankshear* v. *ANZ Banking Group (New Zealand) Ltd* [1993] 1 NZLR 481; *Nimmo* v. *Westpac Banking Corp.*

clear view (obiter) that paying and collecting banks could not normally be brought within the 'knowing receipt' category since they do not generally receive money for their own benefit, acting only as their customer's agent. His Lordship indicated, however, that the position would be otherwise if the collecting bank used the money to reduce or discharge the customer's overdraft, as the bank would then be using the money for its own benefit.[494] A bank account may fluctuate between credit and debit and so it may not be easy to ascertain whether money received into the account was received beneficially or not. Writing extrajudicially, Lord Millett (as he now is) has emphasized that the mere continuation of a running account should not be sufficient to render the bank liable as a recipient: there must probably be some conscious appropriation of the sum paid into the account in reduction of the overdraft.[495] Moreover, the bank would be considered to have *beneficially* received trust property where it debited its commission, fees or other charges against the trust funds credited to its customer's account,[496] or where it has exercised a right of set-off against that account.

Support can be found in Canada for the view in *Agip* that discharging a customer's overdraft can involve the beneficial receipt of trust property by a bank. In *Citadel General Assurance Co.* v. *Lloyd's Bank Canada*,[497] Drive On, an insurance agent, negotiated insurance policies on behalf of Citadel, the insurer. Drive On collected insurance premiums from customers that it was deemed to hold on trust for Citadel.[498] The premiums were paid into Drive On's bank account at the respondent bank. Drive On's parent company also held an account at the bank. Following the receipt of instructions from Drive On's signing officers, each day the bank transferred the balance from Drive On's account into the parent company's account to reduce the latter's overdraft. On the insolvency of Drive On, Citadel brought an action against the bank for knowing receipt. The Supreme Court of Canada held that although the bank had been instructed by Drive On's officers to make the transfers, the bank did not act as mere agent in the circumstances. The bank, by using the insurance premiums to discharge the parent company's overdraft, received a benefit. The court went on to hold that, as the bank was aware of the nature of the funds transferred into and out of Drive On's account, and knew about the daily emptying of the account, a reasonable man would have been put on enquiry as to the possible misapplication of the trust funds. By failing to make the appropriate enquiries, the bank had constructive knowledge of Drive On's breach of trust and was liable for knowing receipt.

Beneficial receipt may also arise from currency exchange. In *Polly Peck International* v. *Nadir (No. 2)*,[499] following an alleged fraud, the Central Bank of Northern Cyprus exchanged £45 million received from another bank, IBK, for an equivalent sum of Turkish lire. Nine sterling transfers were also credited to IBK's account held at the Central Bank. At first instance, Millett J held that neither transaction involved beneficial receipt by the Central Bank. The Court of Appeal agreed that the nine sterling transfers had not

---

[1993] 3 NZLR 218), and Canada (*Gold* v. *Rosenberg*, n.390 above; *Citadel General Assurance Co.* v. *Lloyds Bank Canada*, n.346 above).

[494] This distinction has been criticized by Moore-Bick LJ in *Uzinterimpex JSC* v. *Standard Bank plc* [2008] EWCA Civ. 819, [39]–[40]. *Quaere* whether the reduction of an overdraft is of benefit to a bank that charges interest and fees for the use of that facility.

[495] P.J. Millett, 'Tracing the Proceeds of Fraud' (1991) 107 *LQR* 71, 83, n.46.

[496] *Twinsectra Ltd* v. *Yardley* [1999] Lloyd's Rep. Bank. 438, 466–467 (CA).

[497] N.346 above.

[498] By virtue of the operation of s.124(1) of the Insurance Act, RSA 1980.

[499] N.412 above. For criticism, see *Nimmo* v. *Westpac Banking Corp.*, n.493 above, 225, cited with approval in *Cigna Life Insurance New Zealand Ltd* v. *Westpac Securities Ltd* [1996] 1 NZLR 80, 86.

been beneficially received by the Central Bank, but held that the bank's exchange of sterling for Turkish lire constituted a beneficial receipt. Scott LJ said:[500]

> In respect of the nine sterling transfers I think that is right. The Central Bank received the funds transferred not in its own right but as banker, and, as banker, credited the funds to IBK in Northern Cyprus. But in respect of the bulk of the transfers the case is...one of 'receipt' rather than of 'assistance'. The Central Bank was exchanging Turkish lire for sterling and became entitled to the sterling not as banker for IBK but in its own right. IBK became entitled to the Turkish lire.

On Millett J's reasoning in *Agip*, if a bank receives trust property into an account in credit, knowing that it has been paid in breach of trust, the bank cannot be held liable for knowing receipt: the bank may, however, be held liable for 'dishonest assistance' if the necessary elements of that head of liability are all present. Yet it has been convincingly argued by several distinguished commentators that a bank receives beneficially *all* money deposited, unless otherwise specified in the contract governing the deposit, even if acting as agent and irrespective of the state of the account.[501] This follows from the fundamental principle of banking law that a bank is entitled to do as it pleases with money received to the credit of a customer's account provided it pays the customer an equivalent sum on demand.[502] In other words, a bank receives funds beneficially even if they are deposited into an account in credit.

It is believed that the better view is that the bank may be liable for 'knowing receipt' even if it has received the amount as an agent. It is clear that in his celebrated dictum, Lord Selborne in *Barnes* v. *Addy* envisaged that responsibility could be incurred by 'strangers' dealing with a fraudulent trustee in respect of transactions undertaken by the stranger, such as a bank, in the ordinary course of business. Lord Selborne's specific reference to banks and agents demonstrates that he contemplated that an action under the first limb of *Barnes* (for knowing receipt) could lie, even if the funds were received by such a stranger in its capacity as agent. Some support for this view is to be found in the decision of the Court of Appeal in *Carl–Zeiss Stiftung* v. *Herbert Smith & Co.*[503] In that case, an East German foundation, which was claiming to be entitled to the entire property of a West German foundation, alleged that funds received by the West German foundation's solicitors on account of fees and disbursements were recoverable under the first limb of *Barnes*. In summarizing the different headings of this doctrine, Edmund Davies LJ[504] listed, as one possible situation giving rise to liability, the case in which an agent received or dealt with money, knowing that his principal had no right to pay it over or to instruct him to deal with it.

---

[500] Ibid., 777.

[501] S. Gleeson, 'The Involuntary Launderer' in P.B.H. Birks (ed.), *Laundering and Tracing* (Oxford, 1995), 126–127; M. Bryan, 'Recovering Misdirected Money from Banks: Ministerial Receipt at Law and in Equity' in F. Rose, (ed.), *Restitution and Banking Law* (Oxford, 1998), 180–187; cf. C. Mitchell, n.429 above, citing the arguments of J.P. Moore, *Restitution from Banks* (unpublished D.Phil dissertation, University of Oxford, 2000), that banks receive money beneficially when deposited by the account holder, but only ministerially when deposited by someone else. In *Uzinterimpex JSC* v. *Standard Bank plc*, n.494 above, [37]–[40], the Court of Appeal recognised that there was a 'good deal of force' in the argument expressed in the text.

[502] *Foley* v. *Hill*, n.3 above, discussed in Ch. 5, Sect. 3 above.

[503] [1969] 2 Ch. 276 (CA). See also *Uzinterimpex JSC* v. *Standard Bank plc*, n.494 above, [37]–[42], where the Court of Appeal considered that a bank (described in the relevant documentation as the trustee and agent for a syndicate of banks) had 'sufficient interest' in the funds received into a bank account on behalf of the syndicate to make the agent bank liable for knowing receipt. In any event, funds paid into a bank account are received beneficially by the accountholder: *Law Society of England & Wales* v. *Habitable Concepts Ltd*, n.449 above, [14].   [504] Ibid., 303.

That said, distinguishing between beneficial and ministerial receipt does at least offer a bank some important protection. The speed of operation of modern payment systems leaves the bank with little time to make inquiries of its customers before receiving funds on their behalf. Accordingly, the current position may be justified on the basis that it gives the bank security of receipt. Indeed, if banks are to be held to accept beneficially all money deposited, even when acting as agents for their customers, then they must arguably be protected by other means. This may be through the required level of knowledge of the breach of trust necessary to impose liability, the burden of proof being on the claimant, or, if this head of liability goes down the road of strict liability (as remains possible), through reliance on the defences of change of position and *bona fide* purchaser, when the burden of proof is shifted to the bank.

(b) Level of knowledge required

The final requirement for receipt-based liability relates to the knowledge of the recipient. Liability depends on the recipient's knowledge of the breach of trust. Traditionally, 'knowledge' in this context has been assessed by reference to the five categories of knowledge identified by Peter Gibson J in *Baden, Delvaux and Lecuit v. Société Générale pour Favoriser le Développement du Commerce et de l'Industrie en France SA*, set out previously.[505] But the authorities have been unclear about what level of knowledge is required. Some cases have supported the view that liability arises only if the recipient has knowledge falling within the first three *Baden* categories, i.e., only in cases of dishonesty or want of probity.[506] This approach has the superficial attraction of putting the level of knowledge necessary for the receipt category of liability on a par with the need for dishonesty under the assistance category. However, it ignores the fact that a recipient *beneficially* receives trust property, whereas the accessory may only have assisted another's breach of trust without necessarily being personally enriched. This fact alone seems to argue in favour of some difference in measure between them. Other cases have suggested that knowledge within the first three categories is required in commercial transactions, but that knowledge falling within any of the five categories (so as to include constructive notice) is enough in non-commercial transactions.[507] Yet a third line of cases supports the view that liability arises whenever the recipient has knowledge falling within any of the five *Baden* categories, so that even negligence is enough to give rise to receipt-based liability.[508]

In reality, the line between the tests of 'dishonesty' and 'constructive notice' may be very fine. For many years, the courts voiced their reluctance to import the doctrine of constructive notice, as it had developed in relation to land, into commercial transactions. The concern, as famously expressed by Lindley LJ in *Manchester Trust v. Furness*,[509] was

---

[505] N.363 above, 575–576. For the five categories of knowledge, see text to n.411 above.

[506] See, for example, *Nelson v. Larholt* [1948] 1 KB 339 (as interpreted in *Carl-Zeiss-Stiftung v. Herbert Smith & Co. (No. 2)*, n.503 above); *Re Montagu's Settlement Trusts*, n.344 above; *Dubai Aluminium Co. Ltd v. Salaam* [1999] 1 Lloyd's Rep. 415; *Twinsectra Ltd v. Yardley*, n.496 above; *Bank of America v. Arnell* [1999] Lloyd's Rep. Bank. 399.

[507] See, for example, *Eagle Trust plc v. SBC Securities Ltd*, n.3 above (although Vinelott J clouded the issue by relying on the concept of 'inferred knowledge'); *Eagle Trust plc v. SBC Securities Ltd (No. 2)* [1996] 1 BCLC 121; *Cowan de Groot Properties Ltd v. Eagle Trust plc*, n.3 above.

[508] See, for example, *Nelson v. Larholt*, n.506 above, as interpreted in *Cowan de Groot Properties v. Eagle Trust plc*, n.3 above; *Belmont Finance Corp. Ltd v. Williams Furniture Ltd (No. 2)* [1980] 1 All ER 393 (CA); *International Sales and Agencies Ltd v. Marcus* [1982] 3 All ER 551; *Houghton v. Fayers* [2000] Lloyd's Rep. Bank. 145, 148, col. 2 (CA); *Westpac Banking Corp. v. Savin* [1985] 2 NZLR 41 (NZCA); *Powell v. Thompson* [1991] 1 NZLR 597, 607–610; *Citadel General Assurance Co. v. Lloyds Bank Canada*, n.346 above, 429; *Eden Refuge Trust v. Hohepa* [2011] 1 NZLR 197, [212]–[220]..

[509] [1895] 2 QB 539, 545 (CA).

that the prolonged investigation of title required for land transactions was incompatible with the fast moving world of commerce. However, recent authority has recognized
that constructive notice is sensitive to the customs and practices of the arena in which it
is to be applied and does not require the necessary importation of a standard of notice
in its conveyancing sense.[510] In other words, notice can take account of the demands of
commercial dealings where speed and security of transaction are essential.[511] Thus, the
conduct of a bank receiving a deposit of misappropriated trust money should be measured against the standard of enquiry that could reasonably be expected of a banker.[512]
The standard of enquiry for a banker was described by Millett J in *Macmillan Inc.* v.
Bishopsgate Investment Trust plc (No. 3) in the following terms:[513]

> Account officers are not detectives. Unless and until they are alerted to the possibility of
> wrongdoing, they proceed, and are entitled to proceed, on the assumption that they are
> dealing with honest men. In order to establish constructive notice it is necessary to prove
> that the facts known to the defendant made it imperative for him to seek an explanation,
> because in the absence of an explanation it was obvious that the transaction was probably
> improper.

This is tantamount to saying that the bank's duty to inquire arises only where the facts
point so strongly to impropriety that failure to make reasonable inquiries verges on dishonesty. Established practice in a similar field provides a useful yardstick against which
the recipient's conduct can be measured. The exigencies of a particular trade or business can be taken into account, and the recipient does not run the risk of being held
to a standard of behaviour that is unrealistic within the particular commercial context
in which he has to operate. There will always be exceptional cases. In *Westpac Banking
Corp.* v. *Savin*,[514] Richardson J in the New Zealand Court of Appeal, having expressed a
provisional preference for the view that constructive knowledge was enough to establish
liability for knowing receipt, said:[515]

> Clearly Courts would not readily import a duty to enquire in the case of commercial trans-
> actions where they must be conscious of the seriously inhibiting effects of a wide appli-
> cation of the doctrine. Nevertheless, there must be cases where there is no commercial
> justification on the known facts for allowing a commercial man who has received funds
> paid to him in breach of trust to plead the shelter of the exigencies of commercial life.

A similar approach has recently been taken by the English Court of Appeal in *Bank
of Credit and Commerce International (Overseas) Ltd* v. *Akindele*.[516] BCCI's liquidators
claimed that A, a Nigerian businessman, was liable to repay the proceeds of an investment
agreement that had been executed by BCCI's directors in breach of trust. The liquidators
brought claims for both 'knowing receipt' and 'dishonest assistance'. At first instance,
both claims failed.[517] There was no appeal on the assistance claim, as the liquidators could
not prove that A had been dishonest. Only the receipt claim reached the Court of Appeal,
where the key questions addressed by the court were related to the state of knowledge
required of the recipient and, in particular, whether the recipient had to be dishonest. The
answers to these questions provided by the Court of Appeal, as expressed in the judgment

---

[510] *El Ajou* v. *Dollar Land Holdings* [1993] 3 All ER 717, 739; *Macmillan* v. *Bishopsgate Investment Trust (No. 3)* [1995] 1 WLR 978, 1000.

[511] D. Fox, 'Constructive Notice and Knowing Receipt: An Economic Analysis' [1998] *CLJ* 391, 395.

[512] Id.

[513] N.456 above, 1014. See also *Box* v. *Barclays Bank plc* [1998] Lloyd's Rep. Bank. 185, 205–6.

[514] N.508 above.   [515] Ibid., 53.

[516] [2001] Ch. 437 (CA).   [517] [1999] BCC 669.

of Nourse LJ, can be summarized as follows. First, dishonesty is not a necessary ingredient of liability for knowing receipt.[518] Secondly, just as there was a single test of dishonesty for dishonest assistance, there should be a single test of knowledge for knowing receipt.[519] Thirdly, and crucially, all that is necessary is that the recipient's state of knowledge be such as to make it unconscionable for him to retain the benefit of the receipt.[520] Fourthly, this test, while it could not avoid difficulties of application, ought to avoid the difficulties of definition that have bedevilled other categorizations of the requisite degree of knowledge, such as the *Baden* five-point scale—Nourse LJ expressed 'grave doubts about its utility in cases of knowing receipt'.[521] Fifthly, applying that test to the facts of the case, A's state of knowledge was not such as to have made him liable under the head of knowing receipt.[522]

It is submitted that the rejection of dishonesty as the appropriate fault element for knowing receipt is welcome. Dishonesty is more appropriate to a cause of action founded on culpable acts, for example, procuring or assisting a breach of trust, than it is to passive receipt.[523] There are, however, two criticisms that may be levelled at the approach in *Akindele*. First, a test based on unconscionability may be criticized for lacking objectivity and being open to subjective interpretation, leading to greater uncertainty as to its application.[524] In *Royal Brunei Airlines Ltd* v. *Tan*,[525] Lord Nicholls was particularly critical of the use of unconscionability as the test of liability for assistance: '[i]f it means no more than dishonesty, then dishonesty is the preferable label. If it means something different, it must be said that it is not clear what that something different is. Either way, the term is best avoided in this context.'[526] Secondly, in *Criterion Properties plc* v. *Stratford UK Properties LLC*,[527] the House of Lords criticized the lower courts in that case for conflating issues of knowing receipt on the one hand with issues relating to the enforceability of an unauthorized agreement on the other—'[t]he question whether an executory contract is enforceable is quite different from the question whether assets of which there has been a "knowing receipt" are recoverable from the recipient'.[528] According to Lord Nicholls, the Court of Appeal in *Akindele* also 'fell into error on this point'.[529] On this basis, it has been suggested that *Akindele* was not in reality a knowing receipt case at all, and that '[a]s the claim in *Akindele* was incorrectly characterized by the court as one for "knowing receipt", it is submitted that it is weak authority as to the appropriate standard of liability applicable in such a case'.[530] Despite these criticisms, however, the approach to knowing receipt in *Akindele* has subsequently been applied by the Court of Appeal in *Charter plc* v. *City Index Ltd*.[531] Indeed, as against those criticisms, the Court of Appeal's express recognition in Akindele of the need to give common sense decisions in the commercial context, 'paying equal regard to the wisdom of Lindley LJ [in *Manchester Trust* v. *Furness*]

---

[518] N.516 above, 450, applying *Belmont Finance Corp.* v. *Williams Furniture Ltd (No. 2)*, n.508 above.

[519] Ibid., 455.

[520] Id. See also *Niru Battery Manufacturing Co.* v. *Milestone Trading Ltd*, n.485 above, [156]–[157]; *Charter plc* v. *City Index Ltd*, n.344 above. See also *Peconic Industrial Development Ltd* v. *Chio Ho Cheong*, n.439 above, [240].

[521] Id.   [522] Ibid., 302–303.   [523] R. Nolan, 'How Knowing is Knowing Receipt?' [2000] *CLJ* 447.

[524] J. Stevens, 'No New Landmark—An Unconscionable Mess in Knowing Receipt' [2001] *RLR* 99; S. Barkehall Thomas, '"Goodbye" Knowing Receipt. "Hello" Unconscientious Receipt' (2001) 21 *OJLS* 239.

[525] N.342 above, 392.   [526] Ibid., 392.   [527] [2004] 1 WLR 1846, [3]–[4] (HL).

[528] Ibid., [27].   [529] Ibid., [4].   [530] R. Stevens, n.376 above, 424.

[531] N.344 above, [8]. See also Uzinterimpex JSC v. Standard Bank plc, n.494 above, [43]; Hollis v. Rolfe [2008] EWHC 1747 (Ch), [172]–[174]; Independent Trustee Service Ltd v. GP Noble Trustees Ltd [2010] EWHC 1653 (Ch), [51]; Thanakharn v. Akai Holdings Ltd [2010] HKCU 2362, [125]–[128], [134]–[137]; Horler v. Rubin [2011] All ER (D) 149 (Feb), [141]–[148].

on the one hand and of Richardson J [in *Westpac Banking Corp.* v. *Savin*] on the other', is to be welcomed.[532] Subsequently, in *Criterion Properties plc* v. *Stratford UK Properties LLC*,[533] the Court of Appeal held that an assessment of unconscionability based merely on whether the recipient had actual knowledge of the circumstances giving rise to the breach of duty 'was too narrow and one-sided a view of the matter'.[534] The court should have regard to the recipient's actions and knowledge in the context of the commercial relationship as a whole to determine whether the test of unconscionability was satisfied.[535]

It was pointed out in Section (ii) above that some English courts have suggested that 'knowing receipt' should be regarded as restitution-based. Certain distinguished judges and scholars have argued in favour of a standard of strict liability subject only to the defences of *bona fide* purchaser without notice and change of position.[536] Writing extrajudicially, Lord Nicholls has put the case as follows:[537]

> …personal liability should be based on the combination of two separate principles of liability. First, recipient liability should cover all third party recipients. This would be a principle of strict liability in that it would apply to every recipient with an impeachable title irrespective of fault, but it would be restitutionary in nature. It would be confined to restoring an unjust gain. Change of position would be available as a defence accordingly. Secondly, dishonest recipients should be personally liable to make good losses as well as accounting for all benefits.

Nourse LJ touched on the issue in *BCCI* v. *Akindele*.[538] His Lordship doubted whether strict liability coupled with a change of position defence would be preferable to fault-based liability in many commercial transactions. Nourse LJ thought it was commercially unworkable, and also contrary to the internal management rule of company law,[539] that simply on proof of an internal misapplication of the company's funds, the burden should shift to the recipient to defend the receipt either by change of position or in some other way. There is clearly cause for concern. The way of a change of position defence is still developing and banks that innocently receive misapplied funds may feel insufficiently protected if they are left to rely on it.[540] Although the approach in *Akindele* has now been confirmed, at least at Court of Appeal level, in *Charter plc* v. *City Index Ltd*,[541] there remain scattered dicta in the House of Lords supporting the strict liability/restitutionary explanation of

---

[532] N.516 above, 455.

[533] [2003] 1 WLR 2108, [38] (CA), affd on different grounds: n.527 above. The House of Lords held that the critical question was whether the claimant's directors had actual or apparent authority to sign the agreement on its behalf and not whether the other party to the agreement was guilty of unconscionable receipt.

[534] In *Papamichael* v. *National Westminster Bank plc*, n.400 above, [247], Judge Chambers QC treated actual knowledge as a necessary condition for liability. More recently, in *Crown Dilmun* v. *Sutton* [2004] 1 BCLC 468, [200], Peter Smith J, (reluctantly) applying the Court of Appeal in *Criterion Properties*, held that 'attribution of knowledge is not enough. It must be unconscionable for the second defendant to retain the benefit'.

[535] N.533 above, [40]. There must be at least 'a clear suspicion' on the defendant's part: *Uzinterimpex JSC* v. *Standard Bank plc*, n.494 above, [44].

[536] See, for example, Lord Nicholls, writing extrajudicially, n.335 above, 231; P. Birks, 'Receipt' in P. Birks and A. Pretto (eds.), *Breach of Trust* (Oxford, 2002), 213; A.S. Burrows, *The Law of Restitution* (2nd edn., London, 2002), ch. 4; cf. L. Smith, 'Unjust Enrichment, Property and the Structure of Trusts, (2000) 116 *LQR* 412, 428–436.

[537] Lord Nicholls, n.335 above, 244.   [538] N.516 above, 455–456.

[539] *Royal British Bank* v. *Turquand* (1856) 6 El. & Bl. 327. Cf. R. Nolan, n.523 above, 448–449.

[540] Ch. 12, Sect. 3(iii)(a) below.   [541] N.344 above, [8].

knowing receipt.[542] It may not be too long, however, before the United Kingdom Supreme Court gets the opportunity to provide an authoritative judicial determination on this issue, although the planned appeal in *City Index* ultimately proved to be abortive.[543] When the Supreme Court finally has to deal with the issue squarely, their Lordships will have the choice between following their earlier dicta adopting strict liability or adopting the recent approach in *Farah Construction Pty Ltd* v. *Say-Dee Pty Ltd*[544] where the High Court of Australia indicated that it was a 'grave error' to view knowing receipt as involving strict liability 'for restitution based on the unjust enrichment of [the defendant]'. This accordingly lends further support to the fault-based position adopted in *Akindele*.

(v) Tracing money

In the past, it was common practice to refer to a person who had been defrauded of a sum of money as pursuing a 'tracing claim' or exercising a 'tracing remedy'. This was to misunderstand the nature of tracing. Through a series of illuminating judgments,[545] culminating in *Foskett* v. *McKeown*,[546] Lord Millett has authoritatively revealed that tracing is neither a claim nor a remedy:[547]

> It is merely the process by which a claimant demonstrates what has happened to his property, identifies its proceeds and the persons who have handled or received them, and justifies his claim that the proceeds can properly be regarded as representing his property.

'Tracing' must be distinguished from 'following'.[548] 'Following' is the process of following the same asset as it moves from hand to hand. 'Tracing' is the process of identifying a new asset as the substitute for the old. The defrauded party can 'follow' his money into the hands of the fraudster, but once the fraudster pays it into his bank account it is not possible to 'follow' the money any further because it loses its identity in the hands of the bank, which in any case obtains an unassailable title as a *bona fide* purchaser for value without notice of the claimant's beneficial interest. The defrauded party must instead trace the money into its proceeds, namely the debt due from the bank to the accountholder. In a strict sense, the claimant is not tracing one asset into another, but tracing the *value* inherent in the original asset into its substitute. In *Foskett* v. *McKeown*, Lord Millett

---

[542] *Twinsectra Ltd* v. *Yardley*, n.271 above, [105]; *Dubai Aluminium Co. Ltd* v. *Salaam* [2003] 2 AC 366, [87]; *Criterion Properties plc* v. *Stratford UK Properties LLC*, n.527 above, [4] (noted by R. Stevens, n.390 above).

[543] S. Gardner, 'Moment of Truth for Knowing Receipt' (2009) 125 *LQR* 20.

[544] (2007) 236 ALR 209, [130]–[131] (HCA).

[545] *Agip (Africa) Ltd* v. *Jackson*, n.353 above, 285; *Boscawen* v. *Bajwa* [1996] 1 WLR 328, 334 (CA); *Trustees of the Property of F.C. Jones & Sons (a firm)* v. *Jones* [1997] Ch. 159, 169–170 (CA).

[546] N.333 above. The facts of this case appear below. See also *Commonwealth Bank of Australia* v. *Saleh* [2007] NSWSC 903, [27]–[28].

[547] Ibid., 109, 113, 128. See also *Papamichael* v. *National Westminster Bank*, n.400 above, [227]; *Ultraframe (UK) Ltd* v. *Fielding*, n.343 above, [1461]–[1464]; *Yugraneft* v. *Abramovich* , n.344 above, [347]–[348], [372]. This analysis of tracing has been accepted in Australia (*Evans* v. *European Bank Ltd*, n.3 above, [133]), Hong Kong (*Terkildsen* v. *Barber Asia Ltd* [2007] HKCU 399, [113]–[115]; *Hang Seng Bank Ltd* v. *Lau Ching Che* [2008] 1 HKC 385, [32]–[35]), Singapore (*Caltong (Australia) Pty Ltd* v. *Tong Tien See Construction Pty Ltd* [2002] 3 SLR 241, [53] (SGCA)), and Canada (*BMP Global Distribution Inc* v. *Bank of Nova Scotia* [2009] 1 SCR 504, [75] (SCC)).

[548] Ibid., 127. See also L. Smith, *The Law of Tracing* (Oxford, 1997), 6–14. For further judicial acceptance of the concept of 'following', see *Evans* v. *European Bank Ltd*, n.3 above, [137]; *Ultraframe (UK) Ltd* v. *Fielding*, n.343 above, [1461], [1472]; *Grant* v. *Sainte Marie Estate* [2005] ABQB 35, [18]; *Darkinjung Pty Ltd* v. *Darkinjung Local Aboriginal Land Council* [2006] NSWSC 1217, [11], [21]; *Pacific Electric Wire & Cable Co Ltd* v. *Texan Management Ltd* [2008] HKCU 102, [221]; *Yugraneft* v. *Abramovich*, n.344 above, [347].

summarized the position with regard to money paid into and out of a bank account as follows:[549]

> We speak of money at the bank, and of money passing into and out of a bank account. But of course the account holder has no money at the bank. Money paid into a bank account belongs legally and beneficially to the bank and not to the account holder. The bank gives value for it, and it is accordingly not usually possible to make the money itself the subject of an adverse claim. Instead a claimant normally sues the account holder rather than the bank and lays claim to the proceeds of the money in his hands. These consist of the debt or part of the debt due to him from the bank. We speak of tracing money into and out of the account, but there is no money in the account. There is merely a single debt of an amount equal to the final balance standing to the credit of the account holder. No money passes from paying bank to receiving bank or through the clearing system (where the money flows may be in the opposite direction). There is simply a series of debits and credits which are causally and transactionally linked. We also speak of tracing one asset into another, but this too is inaccurate. The original asset still exists in the hands of the new owner, or it may have become untraceable. The claimant claims the new asset because it was acquired in whole or in part with the original asset. What he traces, therefore, is not the physical asset itself but the value inherent in it.

Tracing must also be distinguished from claiming.[550] Tracing does not affect or establish a claim. However, the successful completion of a tracing exercise may be preliminary to a personal claim or a proprietary one, involving the enforcement of either a legal right or an equitable one.[551]

   Tracing is available both at common law and in equity. The orthodox position is that the rules for each are different. This may soon change. There is a strong body of judicial and academic opinion arguing persuasively that 'there is no merit in having different tracing rules at law and in equity, given that tracing is neither a right nor a remedy but merely the process by which the [claimant] establishes what has happened to his property and makes good his claim that the asset which he claims can properly be regarded as representing his property'.[552]

---

[549] Ibid., 127–128.

[550] Ibid., 128. See also *Bracken Partners Ltd* v. *Gutteridge* [2004] 1 BCLC 377, [29] (CA); *Ultraframe (UK) Ltd* v. *Fielding*, n.343 above, [1461]–[1464]; *Commonwealth Bank of Australia* v. *Saleh*, n.546 above, [133]; *Hang Seng Bank Ltd* v. *Lau Ching Che*, n.547 above, [33], [35]; *Yugraneft* v. *Abramovich*, n.344 above, [347].

[551] Id. See also *Boscawen* v. *Bajwa*, n.333 above, 334. There appears to be some dispute over the precise nature of the claim that may be made to a substitute asset following a successful tracing exercise, and in particular whether such a claim is based upon property law principles (*Foskett* v. *McKeown*, n.333 above, 108–109, 115, 126–129) or restitutionary principles (*McIntosh* v. *Lord Advocate* [2003] 1 AC 1078, [43] (PC); *R* v. *Briggs-Price* [2009] UKHL 19, [27], [87]). For the principal claims that may be made to substitute assets following a successful tracing exercise, see R. Chambers, 'Tracing and Unjust Enrichment' in J. Neyers, M. McInnes, & S. Pitel, *Understanding Unjust Enrichment* (Oxford, 2004), ch. 11.

[552] *Trustees of the Property of F.C. Jones & Sons (a firm)* v. *Jones*, n.545 above, 169–170; *Foskett* v. *McKeown*, n.333 above, 113, 115, 128–129. There appears to be some confusion over whether *Foskett* has unified the legal and equitable tracing rules: compare *Shalson* v. *Russo* [2005] Ch 281, [103]–[104] ('...it cannot be said that *Foskett* has swept away the long recognized difference between common law and equitable tracing') and *Dick* v. *Harper* [2006] BPIR 20, [43] ('...there is now one set of tracing rules at law and in equity'). The rules remain distinct in Australia (*Commonwealth Bank of Australia* v. *Saleh*, n.546 above, [22]). This was also traditionally the position in Canada (Grant v. Sainte Marie Estate, n.548 above, [19]), although the Supreme Court in BMP Global Distribution Inc v. Bank of Nova Scotia, n.547 above, has now effectively paved the way for a unitary law of tracing in Canada by removing the traditional limitations upon common law tracing. See also P.B.H. Birks, 'The Necessity of a Unitary Law of Tracing' in R. Cranston (ed.), *Making Commercial Law* (Oxford, 1997), ch. 9; Smith, n.548 above, 120–130, 277–279, 342–347.

(a) Tracing at common law[553]

At common law, tracing was available in respect of chattels from at least the end of the eighteenth century.[554] In *Taylor* v. *Plumer*,[555] P, whose money was misappropriated by his broker, repossessed bullion and American securities purchased by the broker with those funds. Dismissing an action in conversion brought against P by the rogue's assignee in bankruptcy, Lord Ellenborough said:[556]

> The [claimant] ... is not entitled to recover if the defendant [P] has succeeded in maintaining these propositions in point of law—viz., that the property of a principal entrusted by him to his factor for any special purpose belongs to the principal, notwithstanding any change which that property may have undergone in point of form, so long as such property is capable of being identified and distinguished from all other property.

Where chattels can be traced in such a manner, the original proprietor will, in so far as he is entitled to the immediate possession, be able to bring an action in conversion against any person who has interfered with his property. This, for instance, is the basis for the action brought by the true owner of a cheque against the thief's collecting bank. But where the fraud has been perpetrated by the remission of amounts of money, the need for the identification of the 'property' presents serious problems to tracing at common law. In essence, the difficulty stems from the nature of money or currency. Whilst a chattel is capable of being owned, money is of a generic or non-specific nature. Although the owner of currency notes may, possibly, recover them whilst they are still in the possession of a thief or a donee,[557] such as a beggar to whom the thief handed them on his flight, the money cannot traditionally be recovered, at common law, from a third party who obtained the money after it had been commingled with other funds. This is so, first, because the common law does not recognize an action in conversion for money and, secondly, because the action for money had and received is not available against a 'subsequent' or 'second transferee' once the money has passed through a mixed fund.[558] In any event, the currency of money means that a transferee of money, who acts in good faith and for valuable consideration, acquires a fresh legal title to the money that is good against the whole world, including the original owner.[559]

The effect of this principle is that, in a modern economy, money is only rarely traceable at common law. When an amount is remitted from an account kept by one bank to an account maintained with another, the orthodox position is that it becomes commingled

---

[553] For the suggestion that common law tracing principles may have been overtaken by the identification principles in the Proceeds of Crime Act 2002 and may be inconsistent with the Human Rights Act 1998, see J. Ulph, 'Tracing Money at Common Law and the Significance of Possession' [2007] *RLR* 76, 84, 89.

[554] There remains a difficult question surrounding whether tracing is possible through 'assets' such as confidential information: D. Sheehan, 'Information, Tracing Remedies and the Remedial Constructive Trust' [2005] *RLR* 82.

[555] (1815) 3 M & S 562. See generally R. Goode, 'Right to Trace and its Impact in Commercial Transactions' (1978) 92 *LQR* 360; P. Millett, n.495 above. For the suggestion that *Plumer* has been misunderstood as a decision about common law tracing, see L. Smith, 'Tracing in *Taylor* v. *Plumer*: Equity in the Court of King's Bench' [1995] *LMCLQ* 240.

[556] Ibid., 574. [557] *Banque Belge pour l'Etranger* v. *Hambrouck*, n.328 above, 327.

[558] *London Allied Holdings Ltd* v. *Lee* [2007] EWHC 2061 (Ch), [256]. See also *Commissioner for Inland Revenue* v. *Singh* [2002] DCR 345, [15]–[16]; *Commonwealth Bank of Australia* v. *Saleh*, n.546 above, [24]. Liability for money had and received is receipt-based rather than retention-based: ibid., [23].

[559] *Miller* v. *Race*, n.328 above. See generally D. Fox, 'Bona Fide Purchaser and the Currency of Money' [1996] *CLJ* 547; D. Fox, *Property Rights in Money* (Oxford, 2008).

with other amounts cleared on the same day,[560] although this view has been questioned recently by the Canadian Supreme Court in *BMP Global Distribution Inc* v. *Bank of Nova Scotia*.[561] According to the traditional view, however, regardless of whether the funds are remitted by giro or by means of a cheque, settlement is effected through the clearing system involving the settlement at the Bank of England of the daily balance accrued between the banks involved. The only exception to this rule is where the transfer takes place over a real-time gross settlement system as each payment is settled individually on a pay-as-you-go basis.[562] However, even a real-time gross settlement payment must pass through the paying bank's settlement account held at the Bank of England, where it will probably end up being mixed with other funds credited to the account.[563] Moreover, even if, conceptually, it were possible to treat the funds as identified by means of the respective debit and credit entries in the accounts involved, they are bound to become part of—or mixed with—the other funds standing to the credit of the recipient's account. In this way, the funds end up in a mixed fund and lose their identity.

The problems arising in cases of this type are best illustrated through an early twentieth-century authority, *Banque Belge pour l'Etranger* v. *Hambrouck*.[564] A dishonest clerk paid crossed cheques drawn on his employer's account with the claimants, the B Bank, to the credit of his personal account with the F Bank, which was utilized only for the clearing of the cheques so converted. The clerk drew out the proceeds and paid part thereof to his mistress, who spent some of the money and paid the balance to the credit of her own account with the L-M Bank. Finding against the mistress, each member of the Court of Appeal provided different reasons for their conclusion. Bankes LJ emphasized that the mistress paid no money to the credit of her account 'except money which was part of the proceeds of the [clerk's] frauds'.[565] On this basis, his Lordship concluded that the money was traceable at common law. As the mistress had given no value for the money she had no defence to the action. Notably, Bankes LJ appears to have treated as insignificant the fact that, at the time the mistress had paid the relevant amount into her account, there had been a small credit balance. By contrast, Scrutton LJ thought that the funds had been mixed with the clerk's remaining funds when the money was received for the credit of his account with the B Bank. But whilst the money could, accordingly, not be traced at common law to the mistress' account, it remained traceable in equity. Atkin LJ agreed with Scrutton LJ's conclusion that the funds could be readily traced in equity and that, accordingly, an order should be made for the payment of the balance to the B Bank. His Lordship considered, however, that the funds could also be recovered as money had and received, as they remained traceable at common law. That said, his Lordship conceded that not every amount traceable in equity could also be traced at common law.

---

[560] *Agip (Africa) Ltd* v. *Jackson*, n.353 above, affd. on this point: [1991] Ch. 547, 566 (CA); *El Ajou* v. *Dollar Land Holdings plc*, n.485 above, 733; *Bank Tejaret* v. *Hong Kong and Shanghai Banking Corp. (CI) Ltd* [1995] 1 Lloyd's Rep. 239, 245; *Bank of America* v. *Arnell*, n.506 above, 405; *London Allied Holdings Ltd* v. *Lee*, n.558 above, [89], [256] (tracing at common law failed when monies passed through a clearing system, even when the recipient's account had a zero balance before receiving the payment in question).

[561] N.547 above, [67]–[80].   [562] See generally Ch. 13, Sect. 1(iv) below.

[563] For example, by funds having been earlier received into the account from another bank making a real time transfer to the bank that is now the paying bank, but was then the receiving bank. In *Bank of America* v. *Arnell*, n.506 above, 405, Aikens J held that there was mixing when funds were transmitted using CHAPS, which is a real-time gross settlement payment system. See further Ch. 13. Sect. 1(v) below.

[564] N.328 above. See also *Hong Kong & Shanghai Banking Corporation Ltd* v. *United Overseas Bank Ltd* [1992] 2 SLR 495, 502–503; *Kwai Hung Realty Co Ltd* v. *Kung Mo Ng* [1998] 1 HKC 145, 151–153; *BMP Global Distribution Inc* v. *Bank of Nova Scotia*, n.547 above, [62], [80], [80].

[565] Ibid., 328. See also *Commonwealth Bank of Australia* v. *Saleh*, n.546 above, [24]; *BMP Global Distribution Inc* v. *Bank of Nova Scotia*, n.547 above, [62], [77] -[80].

Referring to *Taylor* v. *Plumer*, discussed above, he doubted, at the same time, that the common law 'ever so restricted the right as to hold that the money became incapable of being traced, merely because paid into the broker's general account with his banker'.[566] He thought that, in the instant case, 'less difficulty than usual was experienced in tracing the descent of the money, for substantially no other money had ever been mixed with the proceeds of the fraud'.[567]

A modern example of the problems caused by the commingling of funds in a payment clearing system is *Agip (Africa) Ltd* v. *Jackson*.[568] An authorized signatory of the claimant (Agip) signed a payment order instructing Agip's Tunisian bankers, Banque du Sud, to transfer US$518,000 to a named payee. Zdiri, Agip's chief accountant, fraudulently altered the name of the payee to Baker Oil Services Ltd, a company controlled by the defendant chartered accountants who held a US dollar account at Lloyds Bank in London. On receipt of the altered payment order, Banque du Sud debited Agip's account and telexed Lloyds Bank in London to credit Baker Oil's account. Banque du Sud also telexed its correspondent bank, Citibank, in New York and instructed it to credit Lloyds Bank through the New York clearing system. As New York is five hours behind London, Lloyds Bank took a delivery risk and credited Baker Oil's account before being placed in funds through the New York clearing system. Later, the money was debited from Baker Oil's account and transferred to an account in the name of the defendants. Acting on their clients' instructions, the defendants transferred all but US$45,000 to unknown parties. When the fraud was discovered, the claimant brought an action against the defendants for, *inter alia*, money had and received. Millett J, at first instance, rejected the claim. He held that it was not possible for the claimant to trace its funds at law through the New York clearing system where they would have been mixed with other funds during this process.[569] The Court of Appeal expressly approved of Millett J's reasoning on this point.[570] Millett J also held that it was not possible to trace at law where money was transferred using electronic means. His Lordship held that a distinction was to be drawn between tracing the proceeds of a cheque, where there was a physical item that could be followed by common law tracing rules, and tracing an electronic transfer, where all that passed between the parties was a 'stream of electrons'.[571] This distinction was rejected by the Court of Appeal, albeit by way of *obiter dicta*, where Fox LJ stated that it did not matter that the payment order was not a cheque.[572] Both Millett J and the Court of Appeal upheld the claimant's right to trace in equity.

---

[566] Ibid., 335.   [567] Ibid., 336.

[568] N.353 above, affd. [1991] Ch. 547 (CA). It has been suggested that 'it is at least open to argument that [*Agip*] conflicts with *Banque Belge* and that arguably it was wrongly decided': *Kwai Hung Realty Co Ltd* v. *Kung Mo Ng*, n.564 above, 153. Although *Kwai Hung* can be distinguished from *Agip* on the ground that it involved the clearing of *cheque payments* rather than an *electronic funds transfer*, as indicated below, it is unclear why the payment method should matter given that tracing deals with locating *value* rather than physical assets. In *BMP Global Distribution Inc* v. *Bank of Nova Scotia*, n.547 above, [62], [81]–[83], Deschamps J distinguished *Agip* and *Banque Belge* on the basis that in the former case Lloyds Bank 'having assumed the delivery risk, paid with its own money', thereby breaking the link between the funds that it received and paid out.

[569] Ibid., 286. See also P.J. Millett, n.495 above, 73.   [570] [1991] Ch. 547, 566 (CA).

[571] N.353 above, 286. See also *El Ajou* v. *Dollar Land Holdings plc*, n.485 above, 733. See also P.J. Millett, n.495 above, 73–74. See generally L. Smith, 'Tracing and Electronic Funds Transfers' in F. Rose (ed.), *Restitution and Banking Law* (Oxford, 1998), ch. 8.

[572] N.570 above, 565, approved in *Australian Securities Commission* v. *Buckley* (NSWSC, 20 December 1996). Millett J was later followed on this point by Tuckey J in *Bank Tejarat* v. *Hong Kong and Shanghai Banking Corp. (CI) Ltd* [1995] 1 Lloyd's Rep. 239, 245–246 (Tuckey J does not appear to have been directed to the dismissal of the 'stream of electrons' point by the Court of Appeal in *Agip*). The New Zealand courts

The orthodox position, as reflected in the judgments of Bankes and Scrutton LJJ in the *Hambrouck* case, and in the reasoning of Millett J, as approved by the Court of Appeal, in *Agip*, is that money cannot be traced at common law once it gets mixed or commingled with other funds, as, for instance, when it becomes part of the general balance of a current account or is transferred through the clearing system to a subsequent holder. This appears to stymie common law tracing where funds are transferred using an electronic funds transfer system, which almost inevitably involves the mixing of funds in the payment clearing process.[573] Cheques, however, seem to be treated differently.[574] In *Trustees of the Property of F.C. Jones & Sons (a firm)* v. *Jones*,[575] the Court of Appeal had to consider a trustee in bankruptcy's proprietary claim to funds that had been paid into a third party's account by means of a cheque. The firm of F.C. Jones & Sons had gone bankrupt. After its act of bankruptcy, but before it was adjudicated bankrupt, one of the partners in the firm drew three cheques totalling £11,700 on the partnership account and gave them to his wife, Mrs Jones, the defendant in the action. She paid the cheques into her account with commodity brokers who invested the proceeds on the London potato futures market. The investments proved successful and Mrs Jones received two cheques totalling £50,000 from the commodity brokers and paid these into a deposit account that she had just opened at Raphaels. However, under the insolvency law as it then stood, the partnership account had already vested in the firm's trustee in bankruptcy by the time that the £11,700 was withdrawn from it. The trustee now claimed the £50,000 standing to the credit of Mrs Jones' account at Raphaels as his property. Raphaels interpleaded and the £50,000 was paid into court. So far as the original £11,700 was concerned, Mrs Jones conceded that the trustee could successfully trace his money at common law into her account, but she denied that he was also entitled to the profit made from her successful investment of that sum. The trial judge held in favour of the trustee in bankruptcy on the ground that Mrs Jones had made herself a constructive trustee for him. The Court of Appeal held that she was not a constructive trustee. Mrs Jones had no title to the money at all. The trustee was held entitled at law to the debt payable by Raphaels and hence to the £50,000 paid into court, which represented that debt. Millett LJ considered whether Mrs Jones' concession had been rightly made. He held that it had.[576] His Lordship distinguished the facts of the case before him from those in *Agip*. It was not necessary in this case to trace the passage of the money through the clearing system or the London potato market. The money in the partnership account could be traced into the cheques drawn by Mr Jones. It was then possible to by-pass the clearing system by following the cheques themselves 'from hand to hand' until they reached Mrs Jones and then to trace their proceeds into her account, where they had not been mixed with any other funds.[577] The account with the commodity brokers represented a chose in action, not in terms of the original amount paid in, but in

have followed Millett J's analysis: *Nimmo* v. *Westpac Banking Corporation*, n.493 above, 238; *Equiticorp industries Group Ltd* v. *The Crown (No. 47)*, n.454 above, 697–700. In *Hong Kong and Shanghai Banking Corp. Ltd* v. *United Overseas Bank Ltd*, n.564 above, 503–504, the Singaporean High Court suggested tentatively that, whilst common law tracing may fail in the case of a telegraphic transfer between two different banks (as in *Agip*), the situation may be different when the electronic transfer is between different branches of the same bank.

[573] *Agip (Africa) Ltd* v. *Jackson*, n.353 above, 286, affd. on this point [1991] Ch. 547, 566 (CA); *El Ajou* v. *Dollar Land Holdings plc*, n.485 above, 733; *Bank Tejarat* v. *Hong Kong and Shanghai Banking Corp. (CI) Ltd*, n.560 above, 245; *Bank of America* v. *Arnell*, n.506 above, 405; *London Allied Holdings Ltd* v. *Lee*, n.558 above, [89], [256]. For a possible distinction between end-of-day net settlement systems and real-time gross settlement systems in this context, see the text to n.562 above.

[574] *Kwai Hung Realty Co Ltd* v. *Kung Mo Ng*, n.564 above, 151–156.   [575] N.545 above.

[576] Ibid., 168.   [577] Ibid., 169.

terms of a right to claim whatever amount might be standing in the account at any given time. Thus, though the amount in the account might fluctuate, it represented the trustee's money and there was no need to trace the original money through the futures market.[578]

It is submitted that a series of misunderstandings lies at the heart of these cases. First, it has been convincingly demonstrated by Professor Lionel Smith that the rule preventing the common law tracing through mixtures of value or mixed substitutes is based on a misunderstanding of *Taylor* v. *Plumer*, which actually turned on tracing in equity and not common law tracing at all.[579] This was expressly recognized by Millett LJ in *Trustee of the Property of F.C. Jones* v. *Jones*, but his Lordship still affirmed the orthodox rule that common law tracing is barred if the property is mixed with other property.[580] More recently, the view that mixing funds in a bank account does not necessarily defeat common law tracing has been accepted by the Supreme Court of Canada in *BMP Global Distribution Inc* v. *Bank of Nova Scotia*.[581] Secondly, even if we must live with the orthodox rule for the present, the idea that there is inevitably 'mixing' in a clearing system misconstrues what happens in the clearing process, where transactions are accounted for individually and the only mixing is in the settlements, which are generally irrelevant.[582] Indeed, in *BMP Global Distribution*,[583] Deschamps J accepted that when tracing funds 'the clearing system should be a neutral factor' and that in assessing the traceability of an asset one should examine the position 'after the clearing process and not see that process as a systematic break in the chain of possession of the funds'. If the English courts were to adopt this approach, the passage of funds through a clearing system would no longer be fatal to a claimant's tracing exercise. Thirdly, distinctions that are made between the electronic transfer of funds and payment by a tangible asset, such as a cheque, fail to appreciate that what is traced is not the physical asset but the value inherent in it.[584] Even if payment is made by cheque, it is necessary to connect that cheque, probably through a payment clearing system, to the value with which it is paid.[585] The common law has traditionally never found a problem with this, even where the cheque has passed through the cheque clearing system,[586] and there should be no reason why payment by electronic funds transfer should be treated any differently. Modern banking requires fast and efficient money transmission systems to transfer funds between bank accounts both domestically and internationally. In terms of the value of payments, electronic funds transfer systems are the dominant systems in use. It is unacceptable that the English common law is incapable of operating in this modern environment. The only people to gain from this unsatisfactory state of affairs are criminals and other money launderers who use electronic funds transfer systems to shift their ill-gotten gains around the globe.

---

[578] Ibid., 170. For the dispute over the nature of the claim in *Jones*, compare P. Birks, 'At the Expense of the Claimant: Direct and Indirect Enrichment in English Law' in D. Johnston & R. Zimmerman (eds.), *Unjustified Enrichment: Key Issues in Comparative Perspective* (Cambridge, 2001) 493, 509 with M. McInnes, 'Interceptive Subtraction, Unjust Enrichment and Wrongs—A Reply to Professor Birks' [2003] *CLJ* 697, 700–702. See also P. Millett, '*Jones* v. *Jones*: Property or Unjust Enrichment?' in A. Burrows & A. Rodger, *Mapping the Law: Essays in Memory of Peter Birks* (Oxford, 2006), ch. 14.

[579] L. Smith, n.555 above; L. Smith, n.548 above, 162–174.

[580] [1997] Ch. 169 (CA).

[581] N.547 above, [81]–[86] (noted by D. Fox, 'Identification of Money at Common Law' (2010) 69 *CLJ* 28). See also *Cuthbert* v. *TD Canada Trust* [2010] OJ No 630, [17].

[582] L. Smith, n.548 above 252–255.   [583] N.547 above, [83].

[584] *Foskett* v. *McKeown*, n.333 above, 128.   [585] L. Smith, n.548 above, 257.

[586] *Marsh* v. *Keating* (1834) 2 Cl. & Fin. 250; *Banque Belge pour l'Etranger* v. *Hambrouck*, n.328 above; cf. *Bank of America* v. *Arnell*, n.506 above, 405. See also *Kwai Hung Realty Co Ltd* v. *Kung Mo Ng*, n.564 above, 151–156.

(b) Tracing in equity

As seen in *Hambrouck* and *Agip*, a claimant who is unable to trace at common law may, nevertheless, be able to trace in equity. It may benefit a claimant to trace his property in equity and seek a proprietary remedy against the recipient, provided they are not a *bona fide* purchaser.[587] This will be of real value to the claimant where the recipient is insolvent, as priority may be obtained over his general creditors.[588] The proprietary remedy may come in the form of an equitable charge, lien, constructive trust, or subrogation.[589] In *Boscawen* v. *Bajwa*,[590] for example, monies paid by a prospective purchaser under a contract for the sale of a house were used to obtain a premature discharge of the vendor's mortgage over the house before completion. Completion did not take place and the house was later sold under a charging order obtained by a judgment creditor. Through a combination of tracing and subrogation, the claimant was given a proprietary remedy against the proceeds of sale of the house in priority to the claims of the vendor's other creditors. On the other hand, equitable tracing may also be invoked with the aim of seeking a personal equitable remedy based on the 'knowing receipt' of trust property.[591] The personal claim, unlike the proprietary one, does not depend upon continued retention of the property by the recipient.

The main advantage of equitable tracing (although common law tracing may be in the process of neutralizing this advantage, at least in Canada) is that it is not defeated by the irretrievable mixing of property.[592] This makes equitable tracing of particular use where money has passed through different bank accounts. The basic principle emerges from *Re Hallett's Estate, Knatchbull* v. *Hallett*.[593] A solicitor instructed his bankers to sell certain

---

[587] *Compagnie Noga d'Importation et d'Exportation SA* v. *ANZ Banking Group Ltd* [2005] EWHC 225 (Comm.), [16]; *Sinclair Investments (UK) Ltd* v. *Versailles Trade Finance Ltd* [2010] EWHC 1614 (Ch), [153], aff'd [2011] EWCA Civ 347. There is a similar position in Canada (*HSBC Bank Canada* v. *Dillon Holdings Ltd* [2005] OJ No. 2331, [328]) and Australia (*Darkinjung Pty Ltd* v. *Darkinjung Local Aboriginal Land Council*, n.548 above, [16]; *Commonwealth Bank of Australia* v. *Saleh*, n.546 above, [40]–[41], which also suggests that change of position may operate as a defence to a proprietary claim to a substitute asset). Although the operation of the change of position defence in this context has been described as 'controversial' by Hart J in *Campden Hill Ltd* v. *Chakrani* [2005] EWHC 911 (Ch), [84], his Lordship nevertheless applied the defence: ibid., [84]–[88].

[588] It may also allow the beneficial owner of trust assets to claim interest accumulated when the funds are paid into an interest-bearing account: *Banton* v. *CIBC Trust Corp.* (2000) 182 DLR (4th) 486 (OSC), affd. (2001) 197 DLR (4th) 212 (OCA).

[589] Where the defendant has acquired an asset with a mixed fund, the claimant is entitled 'to claim a proportionate share of the asset or to enforce a lien upon it to secure his personal claim...for the amount of the misapplied money': *Foskett* v. *McKeown*, n.333 above, 131. See also *Ruwenzori Enterprises Ltd* v. *Walji*, n.376 above, [213]–[215]; *Ultraframe (UK) Ltd* v. *Fielding*, n.343 above, [1468]–[1469]; *British Columbia* v. *Egli* [2005] BCSC 654, [18]. For a recent example of the imposition of an equitable charge over two bank accounts in connection with a confiscation order under the Proceeds of Crime Act 2002, see *Serious Fraud Office* v. *Lexi Holdings plc* [2008] EWCA Crim 1443, [57]–[58]. See also *Denis Hanger Pty Ltd* v. *Brown* [2007] VSC 495, [36].

[590] N.333 above. On subrogation following tracing, see *Banque Financière de la Cité* v. *Parc (Battersea) Ltd* [1999] 1 AC 221 (HL); *Filby* v. *Mortgage Express (No. 2) Ltd* [2004] EWCA Civ 759, [11]–[13], [30]; *London Allied Holdings Ltd* v. *Lee*, n.558 above, [286].

[591] Ibid., 334. See also *Yugraneft* v. *Abramovich*, n.344 above, [372]. See further Sect. 5(iv) above.

[592] See, for example, *Commonwealth Bank of Australia* v. *Saleh*, n.546 above, [25]. Even with equitable tracing, however, the more mixing that takes place the more difficult the exercise is likely to prove: *Test Claimants in the FII Group Litigation* v. *Revenue and Customs Commissioners* [2008] EWHC 2893 (Ch), [36].

[593] (1879) 13 Ch. D 696. A second claim in the case, respecting bonds purchased with funds held by the solicitor under his own marriage settlement and held by him without express appropriation, was decided in favour of the *cestui* as, on the facts, the bonds could be identified. This principle is best explained by the classic statement of Viscount Haldane LC in *Sinclair* v. *Brougham* [1914] AC 398, 419: '[s]o long as the money

Russian bonds, held by him on behalf of a client. The proceeds were paid to the credit of his personal account. The solicitor drew cheques on this account reducing the balance from time to time to an amount smaller than the trust moneys; but he also regularly paid in cheques due to him. In his bankruptcy, the client claimed to be entitled to trace the proceeds of the bonds into the bank account. The trustee in bankruptcy contested this claim, arguing that the funds held by the solicitor as fiduciary had been exhausted. Under the rule in *Clayton's Case*,[594] amounts paid out were to be appropriated against the earliest credit entries in the account. It was claimed that, as a result, the trust moneys had effectively been withdrawn. The Court of Appeal affirmed Fry J's decision against the trustee in bankruptcy. It was held that the rule in *Clayton's Case* was inapplicable, as the solicitor was deemed to have utilized his own funds for his running payments.[595] Accordingly, the client's funds, which had been held by the solicitor in a fiduciary capacity, were to be treated as still standing to the credit of the account. Jessell MR was not disturbed by the fact that the money was commingled with the solicitor's own funds and, in this manner, became part of a mixed fund. Whilst the passing of the trust property into a mixed fund precluded the *cestui* from claiming the money back *in specie*, he was 'still entitled to a charge on the property purchased for the amount of the trust-money laid out in the purchase'.[596] On the same basis, the *cestui* would have a charge over a mixed fund of money. His Lordship explained:[597]

> Supposing the trust money was 1000 sovereigns, and the trustee put them into a bag, and by mistake, or accident, or otherwise, dropped a sovereign of his own into the bag. Could anybody suppose that a judge in Equity would find any difficulty in saying that the *cestui que trust* has a right to take 1000 sovereigns out of that bag? I do not like to call it a charge of 1000 sovereigns on 1001 sovereigns, but that is the effect of it.

Jessell MR added that it made no difference that, in the instant case, the solicitor was not a trustee in the strict sense of the word. The equitable principles involved were applicable whenever the funds were abstracted by a person who was the victim's fiduciary.

which the principal has handed to his agent to be applied specifically, and not on a debtor and creditor account, can be traced into what has been procured with it, the principal can waive his right of action for damages for tort, and, affirming the proceeding of the [agent], claim that his money is invested in a specific thing, which is his'.

[594] *Devaynes* v. *Noble* (*Clayton's Case*) (1816) 1 Mer. 529, 35 ER 767, 781. Recent case law in England has tended to disapply *Clayton's Case*: *Barlow Clowes International Ltd* v. *Vaughan* [1992] 4 All ER 22 (CA); *Russell-Cooke Trust Co* v. *Prentis* [2003] 2 All ER 478; *Commerzbank AG* v. *IMG Morgan plc*, n.331 above, [47]–[48]; *Re Ahmed & Co* [2006] EWHC 480 (Ch), [131]–[138]. The rule in *Clayton's Case* cannot apply when there is no evidence as to the order in which payments were made into and out of a current account: *Cooper* v. *PRG Powerhouse Ltd*, n.271 above, [27]. The Australian courts have refused to apply *Clayton's Case* to the allocation of losses between beneficiaries who have contributed to a mixed fund (*Re French Caledonia Travel Service Pty Ltd* [2003] 204 ALR 353, [31]–[34] (NSWSC); *Westpac Banking Corporation* v. *Earthwise International Ltd* [2005] NSWSC 1037, [10]–[11]; *ASIC* v. *Tasman Investment Management* [2006] NSWSC 943, [55]), but may continue to apply the presumption when a wrongdoer has mixed a claimant's funds with his own (*Commonwealth Bank of Australia* v. *Saleh*, n.546 above, [36]). See further Ch. 17, Sect. 2(iv) below.

[595] There are two rebuttable presumptions that operate when the fiduciary mixes trust money with his own money. The first presumption is that the fiduciary spends his own money first, so that the beneficiary can trace into the sum remaining in the fund: *Re Hallett's Estate*, n.593 above; *Dick* v. *Harper*, n.552 above, [54]; *Turner* v. *Jacob* [2006] EWHC 1317 (Ch), [100]. The alternative presumption is that the fiduciary spent the beneficiary's money first, so that where the fiduciary has used money from the fund to purchase an asset and dissipated the remaining amount, the beneficiary can trace into the purchased asset (*Re Oatway* [1903] 2 Ch. 356). See also *Serious Fraud Office* v. *Lexi Holdings plc*, n.589 above, [52]–[55]. See further Ch. 17, Sect. 2(iv) below.

[596] N.593 above, 709.   [597] Ibid., 711.

In *Re Hallett Estate*, the money was traced to a fund under the control of the fiduciary. In appropriate cases money can also be traced into the hands of a third party, such as a donee.[598] But this right is lost where the third party receives the money in good faith and for a valuable consideration.[599] This may prevent the victim of a fraud seeking a proprietary remedy against a bank where money has been deposited into a bank account. The bank could certainly raise the defence of *bona fide* purchaser for value without notice when it receives the money in discharge of an overdraft or other debt. What about the case where the account is in credit? Can the bank argue that it gave value in the form of a promise to pay at a future time? In *Lipkin Gorman* v. *Karpnale Ltd*,[600] Lords Templeman and Goff both suggested that if a thief steals money and gives it to a donee, and the donee deposits it at a bank, the bank is not a *bona fide* purchaser. In other words, 'value' requires not just a promise to pay but actual payment.[601] However, more recently, in *Foskett* v. *McKeown*,[602] Lord Millett has held that, where a fraudster pays money into a bank account, the bank usually obtains an unassailable title to the money as a *bona fide* purchaser without notice of the victim's beneficial interest. The victim is left to trace the money into its proceeds, *viz.* the debt presently due from the bank to the accountholder.[603] This may still allow the victim to claim against the bank, but instead of being able to seek a proprietary remedy the victim would only be left with a personal one, which would be vulnerable to the insolvency of the bank.[604]

Nevertheless, there are important restrictions on the right to trace in equity. The position has been authoritatively summarized in *Re Diplock*.[605] First, the claimant must be able to show that the property in which he had an equitable proprietary interest passed to the defendant through the hands of a fiduciary in breach of their duty. Secondly, tracing will fail where the claimant's property has ceased to exist and no specific asset deriving from it can be identified. This means, for example, that where the claimant's money has been paid into an overdrawn bank account there will be no asset representing the claimant's property.

---

[598] *Banque Belge pour l'Etranger* v. *Hambrouck*, n.328 above; *Ministry of Health* v. *Simpson* [1951] AC 251 (HL) (where trustees of a will distributed the trust property in good faith to the donees).

[599] N.559 above.

[600] N.328 above, 562, 577. See also P.B.H. Birks, 'The Burden on the Bank' in F. Rose (ed.), *Restitution and Banking Law* (Oxford, 1998), 215; D. Fox, 'The Transfer of Legal Title to Money' (1996) 4 *RLR* 60, 63.

[601] *Hong Kong & Shanghai Banking Corp.* v. *United Overseas Bank* Ltd, n.564 above, 504.

[602] N.333 above, 127. Lionel Smith has argued that Lords Templeman and Goff are incorrect in *Lipkin Gorman* on the ground that they focused on the equitable defence of *bona fide* purchaser, whereas there is also a common law version of the defence that is applicable to money, including negotiable instruments. For the purposes of the common law defence, 'value' includes an unconditional promise to pay money, and so a bank that gives value in this way gets an unimpeachable legal title to cash deposits and to value received in settlement for funds transfer instructions: L. Smith, n.548 above, 389; L. Smith, n.536 above, 434, n.90.

[603] Ibid., 132.

[604] In the case of trust property, it possible to bring a claim based upon the bank's 'knowing receipt' of that property: Sect. 5(iv) above. Alternatively (depending upon one's view of 'knowing receipt': Sects. 5(ii) & (iv) above), it may be possible to bring a claim against the bank based upon its unjust enrichment. Establishing that claim does not require tracing or following, but simply that the defendant has been enriched at the claimant's expense: *Foskett* v. *McKeown*, n.333 above, 129. The claim is a personal one, subject to the defence of ministerial receipt. It is irrelevant to a claim based on unjust enrichment whether the bank is a *bona fide* purchaser or not: *Papamichael* v. *National Westminster Bank plc*, n.400 above, [253]. But a claim for unjust enrichment is available only against someone who was directly enriched by a subtraction of wealth from the claimant. It would not assist the owner of the stolen money in the scenario outlined by Lords Templeman and Goff in *Lipkin Gorman*.

[605] [1948] Ch. 465 (CA), affd. *sub nom. Ministry of Health* v. *Simpson*[1951] AC 251 (HL) (which, however, turned mainly on other points).

(vi) A fiduciary relationship

The right to trace in equity is dependent on the establishment of a fiduciary relationship between the claimant and the defendant, or between the claimant and a third party through whose hands the property has passed.[606] This requirement has been widely criticized and seems irrational given that tracing is merely a process of identification and not a right or remedy.[607] Recent dicta from the House of Lords indicate that it is likely to be jettisoned when their Lordships next have to address the issue head on.[608] For now, the requirement stands, but it may not be a particularly onerous one to meet. In *Re Hallett's Estate*,[609] the requirement was satisfied because the rogue solicitor held both the funds credited to his client account and those from his own marriage settlement in a fiduciary capacity. In *Agip (Africa) Ltd v. Jackson*,[610] the rogue chief accountant was deemed to owe fiduciary duties to his employer, the claimant company. Moreover, Millett J observed that the requirement of a fiduciary relationship 'is...readily satisfied in most cases of commercial fraud, since the embezzlement of a company's funds almost inevitably involves a breach of fiduciary duty on the part of one of the company's employees or agents'.[611] Where money is paid away in breach of fiduciary

[606] Ibid. See also *Agip (Africa) Ltd* v. *Jackson*, n.353 above, 290, affd. [1991] Ch. 547, 566 (CA); *Boscawen* v. *Bajwa*, n.333 above, 335. Misapplied funds do not become traceable in equity merely because they happen to pass through the hands of a fiduciary somewhere along the chain of the recipients. The claimant must be the *beneficiary* of the relationship that entitles him to trace. Thus, in *Bank of America* v. *Arnell*, n.506 above, where the claimant bank paid away funds following presentation of a forged cheque drawn on its customer's account, Aikens J held that the fact that there might have been a fiduciary relationship between the forger and the customer did not assist the bank to trace its funds in equity as it was not privy to this relationship.

[607] See, for example, G. Virgo, *The Principles of the Law of Restitution* (2nd edn., Oxford, 2006), 629 ('Since the fiduciary relationship is so artificial it follows that the time has come to conclude that it should be rejected as no longer serving any useful purpose'); R. Goff and G. Jones, *The Law of Restitution* (7th edn., London, 2007), [2-031]–[2-033]. In *Elders Pastoral Ltd* v. *Bank of New Zealand* [1989] 2 NZLR 180, 193 (NZCA), Somers J suggested that the fusion of law and equity cast doubt upon the need for a 'fiduciary relationship' as a prerequisite to tracing.

[608] *Foskett* v. *McKeown*, n.333 above, 128–129, although there was no need for Lord Millett to decide the issue as there was a clear fiduciary relationship on the facts (the case involved a trustee wrongfully misappropriating trust money). These dicta have given rise to a degree of confusion in lower courts as to whether a fiduciary relationship is a precondition to tracing in equity: *Compagnie Noga d'Importation et d'Exportation SA* v. *ANZ Banking Group Ltd*, n.587 above, [16]. In *Shalson* v. *Russo*, n.552 above, Rimer J stated that 'it cannot be said that *Foskett* has swept away the long recognized difference between common law and equitable tracing'. In *Campden Hill Ltd* v. *Chakrani*, n.587 above, [74], Hart J stated that '[a]ccording to authority which is binding on me the Claimant must first establish a fiduciary relationship arising either from a division of the legal and beneficial ownership in monies sought to be traced or from the very nature of the relationship'. In *London Allied Holdings Ltd* v. *Lee*, n.558 above, [257], Etherton J clearly accepted that 'it is a prerequisite of the right to trace in equity that there must be a fiduciary relationship which calls the equitable jurisdiction into being'. The need for a fiduciary relationship was also assumed, without considering the point, in *Cooper* v. *PRG Powerhouse Ltd*, n.271 above, [25] (tracing property initially held on *Quistclose* trust). See also *Solomons* v. *Williams* (Ch. D, 23 May 2001); *Sinclair Investments (UK) Ltd* v. *Versailles Trade Finance Ltd* , n.587 above, [144], aff'd [2011] EWCA Civ 347. In contrast, in *Bracken Partners Ltd* v. *Gutteridge* [2003] 2 BCLC 84, 91, Peter Leaver QC considered that *Foskett* had removed the need to show a fiduciary relationship (the point was not considered on appeal: [2004] 1 BCLC 377 (CA)). For the suggestion that this is the 'better view', see *Commonwealth Bank of Australia* v. *Saleh*, n.546 above, [29]–[30].

[609] N.593 above.   [610] N.353 above, affd. [1991] Ch. 547 (CA).

[611] Ibid., 290. See also *Heinl* v. *Jyske Bank (Gibraltar) Ltd* [1999] Lloyd's Rep. Bank 511 (CA) (fraudulent misappropriation of bank's funds by managing director of bank); *Hong Kong & Shanghai Banking Corp.* v. *United Overseas Bank Ltd*, n.564 above (bank employee wrongfully transferred bank's funds to own account).

duty the courts will readily hold that there is a separation between its legal ownership, which passes to the payee or transferee, and its beneficial ownership, which remains with the claimant.[612]

The willingness of the courts to find the necessary fiduciary relationship is clear. In *El Ajou* v. *Dollar Land Holdings plc*,[613] Millett J held that the victim of a fraud is entitled to rescind the transaction thereby revesting his equitable title 'at least to the extent necessary to support an equitable tracing claim', and later acknowledged in *Bristol & West Building Society* v. *Mothew*[614] that, in doing so, he 'was concerned to circumvent the supposed rule that there must be a fiduciary relationship or retained beneficial interest before resort may be had to the equitable tracing remedy'. Moreover, in *Westdeutsche Landesbank Girozentrale* v. *Islington London Borough Council*,[615] where money was paid under a contract that was subsequently held void as being *ultra vires*, Lord Browne-Wilkinson stated (obiter) that when property is obtained by fraud, whether or not in breach of fiduciary duty, equity imposes a constructive trust on the fraudulent recipient so that the property is recoverable and traceable in equity. Thus, his Lordship continued, money stolen from a bank account can be traced in equity.[616] There is a certain degree of ambiguity, however, in Lord Browne-Wilkinson's statement as he makes no attempt to draw a clear line between 'theft' and 'fraud'. This led counsel for the claimant in *Twinsectra Ltd* v. *Yardley*,[617] the facts of which appear above,[618] to argue that, in a case of fraud, a constructive trust should be imposed upon the recipient of misappropriated property at the moment of receipt. Potter LJ, delivering the judgment of the Court of Appeal, rejected this interpretation of Lord Browne-Wilkinson's dicta.[619] According to Potter LJ, in a case of theft, where the transfer of property is non-consensual, a constructive trust arises at the moment of transfer. By contrast, in a case of fraud, where a transfer is made pursuant to a contract rendered voidable for misrepresentation, the transferor may elect whether to avoid or affirm the transaction and, until he elects to avoid it, there is no constructive (or resulting) trust. Before rescission the transferor has a 'mere equity' to rescind but he does

---

[612] Id., as applied in *Heinl* v. *Jyske Bank (Gibraltar) Ltd.*, n.611 above, 521, col. 1; *Collings* v. *Lee* [2001] 2 All ER 332, 357 (CA). This assumes the payee or transferee is not a *bona fide* purchaser for value without notice.

[613] N.485 above, 734. See also *Daly* v. *Sydney Stock Exchange* (1986) 160 CLR 371, 388–390 (HCA); *Lonrho plc* v. *Fayed (No. 2)* [1992] WLR 1, 11–12; *Bank Tejerat* v. *Hong Kong and Shanghai Banking Corporation* [1995] 1 Lloyd's Rep 239, 248; *Shalson* v. *Russo*, n.552 above, [111], [120]–[127]; *London Allied Holdings Ltd* v. *Lee*, n.558 above, [276]–[280].

[614] [1998] Ch. 1, 23 (CA).   [615] N.331 above, 716.

[616] Ibid. See also *Halley* v. *The Law Society* [2003] EWCA Civ. 97, [45]; *Commerzbank AG* v. *IMG Morgan plc*, n.331 above, [36]; *Campden Hill Ltd* v. *Chakrani*, n.587 above, [74]; cf. *Shalson* v. *Russo*, n.552 above, [110]; *Sinclair Investment Holdings SA* v. *Versailles Trade Finance Ltd* [2005] EWCA Civ 722, [31]–[43], [52]–[54]; *London Allied Holdings Ltd* v. *Lee*, n.558 above, [266]–[268]. For support for Lord Browne-Wilkinson's suggestion that stolen money is held on constructive trust by the thief and can be traced in equity, see A. Hudson, n.402 above, 151–152.

[617] N.496 above, 461, col. 2.   [618] Sect. 5(iii)(d) above.

[619] Id., following Millett J in *Lonrho plc* v. *Fayed (No. 2)*, n.613 above, 11–12, and in *El Ajou* v. *Dollar Land Holdings* [1993] 3 All ER 717. *Twinsectra* went on appeal to the House of Lords, but this issue was not considered further: [2002] 2 AC 164. See also *Box* v. *Barclays Bank plc*, n.456 above, 201, col. 1; *Papamichael* v. *National Westminster Bank plc*, n.400 above, 374; *Halley* v. *The Law Society*, n.616 above (where the Court of Appeal held that the 'contract' itself was an instrument of fraud, not merely induced by fraud, and hence void); *Shalson* v. *Russo*, n.552 above, [111], [119] ('[the authorities] do not in my view support the proposition that property transferred under a voidable contract induced by fraud will immediately (and prior to rescission) be held on trust for the transferor').

not have a vested proprietary interest.[620] Nevertheless, the equity to rescind binds donees and those who take with notice of the fraud, but it does not bind a *bona fide* purchaser for value without notice. The recognition by Lord Browne-Wilkinson that a thief may be treated as a fiduciary, since the thief's conscience will have been affected so that the stolen property is held on constructive trust for the victim, makes it even easier to meet the fiduciary relationship requirement for the purposes of equitable tracing. In effect, anyone can be treated as a fiduciary so long as he or she can be considered to have been acting unconscionably.[621] It may be possible to go further and interpret Lord Browne-Wilkinson's somewhat ambiguous dicta as removing the requirement for a fiduciary relationship altogether.[622] However, it is likely that he would have done so explicitly if that had been his intention.[623]

The more difficult case is where money is paid as a result of a mistake that has not been induced by fraud. In *Chase Manhattan Bank NA* v. *Israel British Bank (London) Ltd*,[624] the claimant bank instructed its correspondent, the M Bank, to credit the account of the defendant bank with an amount of some US$2m. Later on the same day, the claimant bank, by error, made a further payment of the same amount to the M Bank for the defendant bank's account. Both payments in question were effected through the New York clearing system. Subsequently, the defendant bank became insolvent and was wound up. The question was whether the claimant bank's only right was to prove for the amount paid in error or whether it was, in addition, entitled to trace in equity and recover the second payment *in specie*. The funds having gone through a mixed fund, there was, of course, no room for tracing at common law. The liquidators argued that equitable tracing was, likewise, unavailable because the case did not involve a breach of trust or breach of a fiduciary duty. Goulding J held that the law on the point was the same in the United States and in England. On the basis of a detailed review of the authorities, his Lordship held that the fiduciary relationship—required as a prerequisite to equitable tracing—did not have to arise on the basis of a consensual transaction. Following *Sinclair* v. *Brougham*,[625] his Lordship concluded that 'a person who pays money to another under a factual mistake retains an equitable property in it and the conscience of the other is subjected to a fiduciary duty to respect his proprietary right'.[626] The fact that the defendant bank was unaware of the mistake at the time it received the second payment was irrelevant as it was deemed to hold the mistaken payment on trust from that moment.

In *Westdeutsche Landesbank Girozentrale* v. *Islington London Borough Council*,[627] the House of Lords departed from its decision in *Sinclair* v. *Brougham*, and Lord Browne-Wilkinson disapproved of the reasoning of Goulding J in *Chase Manhattan*. Lord Browne-Wilkinson said (obiter):[628]

> I cannot agree with this reasoning. First, it is based on a concept of retaining an equitable property in money where, prior to the payment to the recipient bank, there was

---

[620] But if a fraudulent fiduciary misappropriates property in breach of duty there is a separation between its legal ownership which passes to the payee or transferee and its beneficial ownership which remains with the claimant: *Collings* v. *Lee*, n.612 above. See also *Clark* v. *Cutland* [2003] 4 All ER 733 (CA).

[621] G. Virgo, n.607 above, 629. See also cases cited in n.616 above.

[622] P.B.H. Birks, 'Trusts Raised to Reverse Unjust Enrichment: The *Westdeutsche* Case' [1996] *RLR* 1, 10.

[623] Elsewhere in his judgment in *Westdeutsche*, Lord Browne-Wilkinson stressed (at 714) that 'your Lordships should not be taken to be casting any doubt on the principles of tracing as established in *Re Diplock*'. See also A.J. Oakley, 'The Availability of Property Remedies' [1997] *Conv.* 1, 4.

[624] [1981] Ch. 105.

[625] N.593 above, overruled in *Westdeutsche Landesbank Girozentrale* v. *Islington London Borough Council*, n.331 above.

[626] N.624 above, 119.   [627] N.331 above.   [628] Ibid., 714.

no existing equitable interest. Further, I cannot understand how the recipient's conscience can be affected at a time when he is not aware of any mistake. Finally, the judge
found that the law of England and that of New York were in substance the same. I find
this a surprising conclusion since the New York law of constructive trust has for a long
time been influenced by the concept of a *remedial* constructive trust, whereas hitherto
English law has for the most part only recognised an institutional constructive trust.

Despite rejecting the reasoning of Goulding J, Lord Browne-Wilkinson considered that
Chase Manhattan may well have been rightly decided. Earlier in his judgment, Lord
Browne-Wilkinson held that the imposition of liability as a trustee 'depends upon the
conscience of the holder of the legal interest being affected' so that 'he cannot be a trustee
of the property if and so long as he is ignorant of the facts alleged to affect his conscience'.[629]
But, in *Chase Manhattan*, the defendant bank had known of the mistake within two days
of the receipt of the money. Lord Browne-Wilkinson concluded:[630]

> Although the mere receipt of the money, in ignorance of the mistake, gives rise to no trust,
> the retention of the monies after the recipient bank learned of the mistake may well have
> given rise to a constructive trust.

The reasoning of Goulding J in *Chase Manhattan* has also been criticized by Lord Millett,
writing extrajudicially:[631]

> It is easy to agree with Lord Browne-Wilkinson that [*Chase Manhattan*] was wrongly
> decided. But it was wrongly decided not because [the transferee] had no notice of the
> [transferor's] claim before it mixed the money with its own, but because the [claimant] had
> no proprietary interest for it to have notice of. The [claimant] had intentionally though
> mistakenly parted with all beneficial interest in the money. To this extent the case is on all
> fours with [*Westdeutsche Landesbank*]. The fact that the transferor intended to part with
> the beneficial interest was inconsistent with the existence of a resulting trust. The fact
> that the money was paid by mistake affords a ground for restitution. By itself notice of the
> existence of a ground of restitution is obviously insufficient to found a proprietary rem-
> edy; it is merely notice of a personal right to an account and payment. It cannot constitute
> notice [of] an adverse proprietary interest if there is none.

On the other hand, Lord Millett recognized that the position would be different if the
property transfer represented the traceable proceeds of fraud or trust property embezzled
by an absconding express trustee. *Chase Manhattan* has been as good as overruled.[632]

---

[629] Ibid., 705.

[630] Ibid., 715, applied in *Papamichael* v. *National Westminster Bank plc*, n.400 above, 372; *Clark* v. *Cutland*,
n.620 above, 743; *Commerzbank AG* v. *IMG Morgan plc*, n.331 above, [36]; *Re Farepak Foods and Gifts Ltd*,
n.271 above, [39]–[40]. See also *Ching Mun Fong (executrix of the estate of Tan Geok Tee, deceased)* v. *Liu Cho
Chit* [2000] 1 SLR 517, 528 (SGCA). The proper relationship between *Westdeutsche* and *Chase Manhattan*
was left open by Etherton J in *London Allied Holdings Ltd* v. *Lee*, n.558 above, [268]–[272].

[631] P.J. Millett, 'Restitution and Constructive Trusts' (1998) 114 *LQR* 399, 412–413. See also D. Hayton,
'Fiduciaries in Context: An Overview' in P. Birks (ed.), *Privacy and Loyalty* (Oxford, 1997), 301–304.

[632] In *Bank of America* v. *Arnell*, n.506 above, 406, col. 1, Aikens J declined to follow *Chase Manhattan*
for the reasons set out by Lord Browne-Wilkinson in *Westdeutsche Landesbank*. See also *Cashflow Finance*
v. *Westpac COD Factors* [1999] NSWSC 671; *Commerzbank AG* v. *IMG Morgan plc*, n.331 above, [36]; *Re
Farepak Foods and Gifts Ltd*, n.271 above, [39]–[40]; *London Allied Holdings Ltd* v. *Lee*, n.558 above, [268]–
[272]. Contrast P. Watts, 'Subrogation: a Step Too Far?' (1998) 114 *LQR* 341, 343, assuming *Chase Manhattan*
no longer represents good law, with D. Friedmann, 'Payment under Mistake—Tracing and Subrogation'
(1999) 115 *LQR* 195, arguing, somewhat optimistically, that *Chase Manhattan* has been indirectly vindicated
by *Banque Financière de la Cité* v. *Parc (Battersea) Ltd*, n.590 above.

(vii) **Overdrawn accounts**

Equity does not generally permit tracing through an overdrawn account, whether overdrawn at the time the money was paid into the account or subsequently.[633] The issue was decided in *Bishopsgate Investment Management Ltd* v. *Homan*.[634] The claimant company (BIM) was the trustee of the assets of various pension schemes for employees of companies with which the late Robert Maxwell was associated. On the death of Maxwell in 1991, it was discovered that very large amounts of pension fund moneys of BIM had been improperly paid, during his lifetime, into various bank accounts of Maxwell Communication Corporation plc (MCC) held at the National Westminster Bank. At the time of each wrongful payment of BIM's pension fund moneys into MCC's accounts those accounts were overdrawn, or later became so. It was also found that MCC was hopelessly insolvent. MCC was placed into administration. BIM went into liquidation. BIM's liquidators claimed that BIM was entitled to an equitable charge, in priority to all other unsecured creditors of MCC, on all the assets of MCC for the full amount of the pension moneys of BIM wrongly paid to MCC. The claim was based on certain observations of Lord Templeman in giving the advice of the Privy Council in *Space Investments Ltd* v. *Canadian Imperial Bank of Commerce Trust Co.*[635] In that case, Lord Templeman had said:[636]

> In these circumstances it is impossible for the beneficiaries interested in trust money misappropriated from their trust to trace their money to any particular asset belonging to the trustee bank. But equity allows the beneficiaries, or a new trustee appointed in place of an insolvent bank trustee... to trace the trust money to all the assets of the bank and to recover the trust money by the exercise of an equitable charge over all the assets of

---

[633] See, for example, *Style Financial Services Ltd* v. *Bank of Scotland* [1995] BCC 785, 790 (IH); *Australian Securities Commission* v. *Buckley*, n.572 above; *MacIntosh* v. *Fortex Group Ltd* [1997] 1 NZLR 711, 719; *Box* v. *Barclays Bank plc*, n.456 above, 203, col. 2; *Sinclair Investment Holdings SA* v. *Versailles Trade Finance Ltd* [2004] All ER (D) 158, [36]; *Shalson* v. *Russo*, n.552 above, [140]; *Ultraframe (UK) Ltd* v. *Fielding*, n.343 above, [1472]; *Campden Hill Ltd* v. *Chakrani*, n.587 above, [79]; *Re Ahmed & Co.*, n.594 above, [A94]; *Re BA Peters plc*, n.332 above, [18], affd. [2008] EWCA Civ 1604, [15], [20]; *Serious Fraud Office* v. *Lexi Holdings plc*, n.589 above, [50].

[634] [1995] Ch. 211 (CA).   [635] [1986] 1 WLR 1072 (PC).

[636] Ibid., 1074. For a recent approach reminiscent of Lord Templeman's 'swollen assets theory' in *Space Investments*, see *Cooper* v. *PRG Powerhouse Ltd*, n.271 above, [31]–[33]. Although the application of 'conventional principles' in *Cooper* would have led to the recovery of £31,218.82 as the 'lowest intermediate balance' of the current account in question, Evans-Lombe J nevertheless allowed recovery of the full amount of £34,239.00 on 'alternative grounds'. This was on the basis that, rather than limiting the tracing exercise to the lowest intermediate credit balance of the current account into which the payment was made, the asset into which the claimant could trace was the 'net balance due from Barclays Bank to the company' across all its accounts: ibid., [32]. Although the alternative approach in *Cooper* is a more limited approach than that in *Space Investments*, which treated *all* the company's assets as being the traceable proceeds of a payment, it nevertheless represents a significant expansion of the approach adopted in *Bishopsgate Investment Management Ltd* v. *Homan*, n.634 above. It may be doubted whether the 'alternative ground' in *Cooper* is likely to be accepted by subsequent courts in the light of the Court of Appeal decision in *Re BA Peters plc* [2008] EWCA Civ 1604, [13]–[24], where the claimants sought to assert a proprietary claim to the credit balance of a client account on the basis that the misappropriated funds should have been paid into that account rather than the overdrawn current account into which they were in fact paid. Lord Neuberger rejected the contention on the ground that the misappropriated monies 'never formed part of the fund against which a claim is now sought to be made, namely the money in the client account' (ibid., [23]). His Lordship simply refused to amalgamate the client and current accounts, so as to treat them as an 'aggregate fund', since 'the court should not be too ready to extend the circumstances in which proprietary or other equitable claims can be made in insolvent situations' (ibid., [21]). This is entirely consistent with the position in *Homan* (ibid., [15], [20]).

the bank...that equitable charge secures for the beneficiaries and the trust priority over the claims of the customers...and...all other unsecured creditors.

Upholding Vinelott J at first instance, the Court of Appeal unanimously rejected BIM's claim to an equitable charge over all the assets of MCC. In the context of the case before them, the remarks of Lord Templeman could be dismissed for two reasons. First, they were strictly obiter. On the facts, the Privy Council held that the bank trustee was authorized by the trust instruments to deposit trust money with itself as banker and so there had been no misappropriation. Secondly, following observations made by Lord Mustill in *Re Goldcorp Exchange Ltd*,[637] *Space Investments* could be distinguished as concerning a mixed, not a non-existent, fund. Instead, the Court of Appeal applied the recognized principle that property cannot be traced in equity when it has ceases to exist.[638] Money paid into an overdrawn account ceased to exist, or ceases to exist when the account later becomes overdrawn.[639] Consequently, equitable tracing could not be pursued through an overdrawn, and therefore non-existent, fund.[640] This basic position has been re-affirmed recently by Lord Neuberger in *Re BA Peters plc*,[641] where the claimants were unable to trace their misappropriated payments into a current account that had been overdrawn at all relevant times. This is not an absolute rule, however, but appears to be subject to one (admittedly narrow) exception: if the reason for the overdraft on the account in question is a payment that may be reversed or is otherwise provisional in nature, then the overdrawn nature of the account will not effect the claimant's ability to trace into or through that account. In *Cooper* v. *PRG Powerhouse Ltd*,[642] the claimant sought to trace his payment into a company's current account that had become overdrawn on 2 August. The following day, however, the payment that had caused the account to become overdrawn was re-credited as a result of the administrators, who had been appointed on 1 August, avoiding that payment. Evans-Lombe J allowed the claimant to trace into the account as if it had never become overdrawn. A similar principle would apply if a cheque that would have rendered an account overdrawn is subsequently dishonoured so that no payment in fact ever leaves the account.[643]

The Court of Appeal also confirmed that the same principle lay behind the longstanding first instance decision in *James Roscoe (Bolton) Ltd* v. *Winder*,[644] where trust funds had been mixed with private moneys in a bank account and the credit balance reduced at one point to £25 18s 0d. before being replenished. Sargant J held that the beneficiary's charge extended only to that sum. Unless it could be shown that by replenishing the account the trustee had intended to replace the trust funds wrongfully mixed and paid away, the beneficiary's claim would be restricted to the lowest intermediate balance on the account.[645] Despite the fact that there was a credit balance on an MCC account

---

[637] [1995] 1 AC 74, 105 (PC). For further rejection of *Space Investments*, see *Re Scutts* [1999] FCA 147; *The Bell Group Ltd* v. *Westpac Banking Corporation (No. 9)* (2008) 70 ACSR 1, [9683]–[9684] (WASC); *Serious Fraud Office* v. *Lexi Holdings plc*, n.589 above, [49]–[50]; *Re Lehman Brothers International (Europe) (No. 2)* [2010] 2 BCLC 301, [184]–[193]; but contrast *Re MW Lee & Sons Enterprises Ltd* [1999] 2 HKC 686, 697. See also D. Fox, *Property Rights in Money* (Oxford, 2008), [7.46].

[638] Following *Re Diplock*, n.605 above, 521, as endorsed in *Re Goldcorp Exchange Ltd* n.637 above, 105.

[639] *Re Goldcorp Exchange Ltd*, n.637 above, 105.   [640] N.634 above.

[641] N.636 above, [15], [20]. See also *Re Global Trader Europe Ltd* [2009] EWHC 602 (Ch), [66]–[68].

[642] N.271 above, [28].

[643] Ibid., [29]. See also *Australian Securities Commission* v. *Buckley*, n.572 above. See further L. Smith, n.548 above, 266.

[644] [1915] 1 Ch. 62.

[645] See also *Cooper* v. *PRG Powerhouse Ltd*, n.271 above, [26]–[30], where Evans-Lombe J, applying 'conventional principles', limited the claim to £31,218.82, as this was the 'lowest intermediate balance' of the

held at the National Westminster Bank when administrators were appointed, the Court of Appeal held there was no evidence that Maxwell had 'intended to make good the misappropriation of the B.I.M. pension moneys by the cryptic expedient of arranging to put M.C.C.'s account…into credit'.[646]

Vinelott J, at first instance, had reserved his position in relation to what he described as 'backward tracing' so as to allow certain factual investigations to be carried out. According to his Lordship, 'backward tracing' would be available to BIM where an asset was acquired by MCC with moneys borrowed from an overdrawn or loan account and there was an inference that when the borrowing was incurred it was intended to be repaid by misappropriations of BIM's money. Vinelott J also considered that tracing might be available where moneys misappropriated from BIM were paid into an overdrawn account of MCC in order to reduce the overdraft and so make finance available within the overdraft limits for MCC to purchase some particular asset. In either case, Vinelott J thought that BIM would have an equitable charge on the assets purchased. In the Court of Appeal, there was some difference of opinion between Dillon and Leggatt LJJ as to the availability of 'backward tracing'.[647] Dillon LJ thought backward tracing was 'arguable', although whether it applied in the case before him would depend on the facts as they emerged after further investigation.[648] Leggatt LJ took a more conventional approach to the issue: it was not possible to trace into an asset that had been acquired *before* misappropriation of the money takes place.[649] On the other hand, Leggatt LJ thought that if an asset were used as security for an overdraft, which was then discharged by means of misappropriated money, the beneficiary might obtain priority by subrogation.[650]

The Court of Appeal revisited 'backward tracing' in *Foskett* v. *McKeown*.[651] A trustee misappropriated trust money and used it to pay some of the annual premiums on a life insurance policy. The issue before the court was whether the claimants—beneficiaries of the trust—could claim a proportionate share of the £1 million that was paid on the death of the trustee. Reversing the Court of Appeal,[652] which had restricted the claimants to repayment of the premiums that could be identified as the proceeds of the trust money, the House of Lords[653] held that the proceeds of the insurance policy could be regarded as the traceable product of the trust money and allowed the claimants to claim a proportionate share of

---

sums standing to the credit of the company's payroll account. See also *Dick* v. *Harper*, n.552 above, [54]; *Re BA Peters plc*, n.332 above, [18], [48]–[50], affd. [2008] EWCA Civ 1604; *Re Global Trader Europe Ltd*, n.641 above, [69]. Although *Homan* has reaffirmed the lowest intermediate balance rule in England, the status of the rule is much less certain in Canada. On the one hand, the rule was reaffirmed in *British Columbia* v. *National Bank of Canada* (1994) 119 DLR (4th) 669 (BCCA); *Kolody* v. *Neil* (AQB, 11 December 1998), [14]; *Re Elliott* [2002] ABQB 1122, [17], [22]; *Re O'Dwyer* [2006] BCSC 328, [27]. On the other hand, the rule was rejected in *Law Society of Upper Canada* v. *Toronto-Dominion Bank* (1998) 169 DLR (4th) 353 (OCA); *Re Graphicshoppe Ltd* (2004) 74 OR (3d) 121, [23]–[35] (OSC), affd. (2005) 78 OR (3d) 401 (OCA). *Toronto-Dominion Bank* seems, however, to be based on a misunderstanding of *Re Ontario Securities Commission and Greymac Credit Corp.* (1986) 55 OR (2d) 673 (OCA), affd. [1988] 2 SCR 172 (SCC). See L. Smith, 'Tracing in Bank Accounts: The Lowest Intermediate Balance Rule on Trial' (2000) 33 *CBLJ* 75. The Australian courts have accepted the 'lowest intermediate balance' rule (*Re French Caledonia Travel Service Pty Ltd*, n.594 above, [173]–[174]; *Commonwealth Bank of Australia* v. *Saleh*, n.546 above, [34], [36]), as have the New Zealand courts (*Re Goldcorp Exchange Ltd*, n.637 above, 107–110; *Re International Unit Investment Trust* [2005] 1 NZLR 270, [43]).

[646] N.634 above, 220. See also *Campden Hill Ltd* v. *Chakrani*, n.587 above, [79]; *Dick* v. *Harper*, n.552 above, [54]; *Re BA Peters plc*, n.332 above, [18], [42]–[47], affd. [2008] EWCA Civ 1604.

[647] Henry LJ agreed with both judgments.   [648] N.634 above, 217.   [649] Ibid., 221.

[650] Ibid.   [651] [1998] Ch. 265 (CA).

[652] Sir Richard Scott V-C and Hobhouse LJ; Morritt LJ dissenting.

[653] N.333 above (Lords Browne-Wilkinson, Hoffmann, and Millett; Lords Steyn and Hope dissenting).

those proceeds. The principle of 'backward tracing' arose before the Court of Appeal, but not the House of Lords.[654] One of the annual premiums of £10,220 had been paid out of an account that was in credit only to the extent of £596.74. Shortly after the premium was paid there was a transfer into the overdrawn account of a sum of money sufficient to put it back in credit. Sir Richard Scott V-C was prepared to accept that, if the claimants could show that this was their money and also that it was the trustee's intention throughout to use the trust money to pay the premium, then the fact that the money was paid into the bank account shortly after the payment of the premium would not prevent the claimants from tracing their money into the premium that was paid. As Scott V-C said:[655]

> The availability of equitable remedies ought…to depend upon the substance of the transaction in question and not upon the strict order in which associated events happened.

Hobhouse LJ and Morritt LJ took a different, and more orthodox, view of this issue.[656] Both Lords Justice rejected the submission that tracing could be used to follow value into a previously acquired asset. Similar doubt appears to have been expressed obiter by Keene LJ in *Serious Fraud Office* v. *Lexi Holdings plc*.[657]

Despite the doubts expressed by these various Lords Justice, it is nevertheless submitted that Scott V-C's tentative endorsement of 'backward tracing' in *Foskett* is to be commended.[658] Whenever value is used to discharge a debt, it should be traceable into what was acquired in exchange for incurring that debt, as long as it is possible to establish a sufficiently strong evidential link between the initial payment and the acquisition or retention of the substitute asset. The substance of the transaction is what matters, not the precise order of exchange. There is some authority to support this. In *Re Diplock*,[659] money paid by mistake to the Heritage Craft Schools was used to pay a debt incurred to make improvements to a building. The Court of Appeal held that in substance the money had been used to pay for the improvements, and so it was possible to trace the value of the money into those improvements.

(viii) **Banks as agents**

The defrauded party may be able to trace in equity and seek a proprietary remedy against a third party who has not acquired the funds in good faith and for value and also against such a party's agent. It follows that, where money finds its way into a bank account, a proprietary remedy may be available both against the recipient and against the bank. But the proprietary remedy is available against an agent only until such time as he repays the money to the recipient.[660] It follows that if the money has been paid over by the bank to its customer—the recipient—the bank is not responsible to the defrauded party unless it

---

[654] This was because all three members of the Court of Appeal agreed that the claimants had not established a case justifying summary judgment on this issue.

[655] N.651 above, 283.   [656] Ibid., 289, 296.   [657] N.589 above, [51].

[658] In *Shalson* v. *Russo*, n.552 above, [141], without hearing argument on the point, Rimer J expressed his preference for the approach taken by Dillon LJ in *Homan*. See also L. Smith, 'Tracing into the Payment of a Debt' [1995] *CLJ* 290.

[659] N.605 above, 548–549, affd. on other grounds [1951] AC 251 (HL). See also *Agricultural Credit Corp. of Saskatchewan* v. *Pettyjohn* (1991) 79 DLR (4th) 22 (SCA).

[660] *Transvaal and Delagoa Bay Investment Co. Ltd* v. *Atkinson* [1944] 1 All ER 579. See also *Gowers* v. *Lloyds and National Provincial Foreign Bank Ltd* [1938] 1 All ER 766; *OEM plc* v. *The Estate of Brian Schneider* [2005] EWHC 1072 (Ch), [37]–[46]. The relationship between this defence and that of change of position is explored in Ch. 12, Sect. 4 below.

is liable as constructive trustee. The position was summarized by Millet J in *Agip (Africa) Ltd* v. *Jackson* as follows:[661]

> The tracing remedy in equity gives rise to a proprietary remedy which depends on the continued existence of the trust property in the hands of the defendant. Unless he is a bona fide purchaser for value without notice, he must restore the trust property to its rightful owner if he still has it. But even a volunteer who has received trust property cannot be made subject to a personal liability to account for it as a constructive trustee if he has parted with it without having acquired some knowledge of the existence of the trust.

What constitutes payment over by the bank to its customer is a vital, and somewhat controversial, issue. It is considered in detail subsequently.[662] Allowing the customer to withdraw the funds from his account is certainly enough,[663] but merely crediting funds (even if cleared)[664] to an account already in credit is apparently not enough.[665] Whether the mere crediting of the funds to the customer's overdrawn account constitutes payment over is unclear.[666] If the bank goes on to allow the customer further credit in reliance on the payment, it will be entitled to rely on the defence.[667]

6 **Closure of the current account**

Although the general principles applicable to the termination of the bank–customer relationship have already been considered,[668] the 'BPS regime' now contains express provisions that apply to the closure of a current account. In this regard, unless the account contract stipulates a longer period of time, BCOBS provides a customer with an initial period of 14 calendar days in which to cancel a contract for an account without incurring any penalty and without having to give any reasons.[669] The cancellation period runs from the conclusion of the account contract, or the day when the customer receives notice of the contractual terms if this is later.[670] A bank is required to accept 'any indication' that the customer wishes to cancel the current account and where the customer uses a remote form of communication to do so, the notice of cancellation is effective from the moment of dispatch.[671] In the event of a dispute over whether the account contract was cancelled in time, a bank is required to give the customer the benefit of the doubt as to the date upon which the cancellation notice was dispatched.[672] Although a customer can be required to pay for any services provided by the bank before the cancellation of the account, this is

---

[661] N.353 above, 290.   [662] Ch. 12, Sect. 4 below.

[663] *Gowers* v. *Lloyds & National Provincial Foreign Bank Ltd*, n.660 above; *Australia & New Zealand Banking Group Ltd* v. *Westpac Banking Corporation* (1988) 164 CLR 662 (HCA).

[664] *Jones* v. *Churcher* [2009] 2 Lloyd's Rep 94, [66]–[78].

[665] See, for example, *Bavins Junr. & Sims* v. *London & South Western Bank Ltd* [1900] 1 QB 270; *Standard Bank London Ltd* v. *Canara Bank* [2002] All ER (D) 340, [91]. Cf. M. Bryan, n.501 above. The issue probably turns on whether the credit entry is reversible: Ch. 12, Sect. 4 below.

[666] Contrast *Continental Caoutchouc & Gutta Percha Co.* v. *Kleinwort Sons & Co.* (1904) 90 LT 474 (CA) (payment over), with *Kleinwort & Sons & Co.* v. *Dunlop Rubber Co. Ltd* (1907) 97 LT 263 (HL) (no payment over). See also Ch. 12, Sect. 4 below.

[667] *Buller* v. *Harrison* (1777) 2 Cowp 565; *Australia & New Zealand Banking Group Ltd* v. *Westpac Banking Corp.*, n.663 above.

[668] Ch. 5, Sect. 6 above.   [669] BCOBS 6.1.1, 6.3.1.   [670] Ibid., 6.1.4.

[671] Ibid., 6.2.1–6.2.2. A bank is required to keep records concerning the exercise of the cancellation right for at least three years: ibid., 6.2.3.

[672] Ibid., 6.2.1.

only the case if the payment properly reflects the service actually provided by the bank[673] and if the customer 'was duly informed about the amount payable'.[674] Where the current account is in credit, the bank must return any sums deposited by the customer 'without undue delay' and within 30 days of it receiving notification of the cancellation of the account contract;[675] where the current account is overdrawn, the customer must repay any sums to the bank 'without undue delay' and within 30 days of dispatching the notice of cancellation.[676]

In addition to this relatively restricted right of cancellation, the parties to the current account contract are entitled to close the account during its currency. As a current account will usually constitute a 'framework contract',[677] its closure will nowadays be governed by the PSR 2009. These permit a customer to close a current account at any time without notice.[678] If the customer exercises this right, he is entitled to a proportionate refund of any charges that the bank has imposed for the services that it has undertaken to provide in connection with the account.[679] Although it is possible for the bank to insert a requirement that the customer must give notice before closing the current account, the contractual notice-period cannot exceed one month.[680] A bank may impose a charge on a customer who closes his current account, but that charge must reasonably correspond to the actual costs incurred by the bank as a result of the closure.[681] No such charge may be imposed, however, if the current account has been open for 12 months before the customer chooses to close it.[682] Where the customer chooses to move his current account to another bank, BCOBS requires the customer's existing bank to provide 'a prompt and efficient service' with respect to the closure of the customer's existing account, the transfer of any account balance, and the arrangements for transferring direct debits and standing orders.[683] When the bank wishes to close the account, the common law requirement that the bank need only give the customer reasonable notice[684] has now been replaced by a requirement in the PSR 2009 that the bank must give the customer at least two months' notice, provided that the current account was opened for an indefinite period and the account contract contains a provision to that effect.[685]

---

[673] Ibid., 6.3.2(2). If the bank has charged a fee for a range of services, the customer is only required to pay a proportionate share (ibid., 6.3.2(2)(a)) and under no circumstances must the payment constitute a penalty (ibid., 6.3.2(2)(b)).

[674] Ibid., 6.3.2(3).

[675] Ibid., 6.4.1. Any sums owed between the bank and the customer in relation to a current account may be set off against each other: ibid., 6.4.3.

[676] Ibid., 6.4.2.

[677] PSR 2009, reg. 2(1), which defines a 'framework contract' as '…a contract for payment services which governs the future execution of individual and successive payment transactions and which may contain the obligation and conditions for setting up a payment account': Ch. 2, Sect. 6(iii) above & Ch. 13, Sect. 5 (iv)–(vi) below.

[678] Ibid., reg. 43(1). This right is without prejudice to any other rights that the customer might have to treat the 'framework contract' as unenforceable or void: ibid., reg. 43(7).

[679] Ibid., reg. 43(6).   [680] Ibid., reg. 43(1).   [681] Ibid., reg. 43(2).   [682] Ibid., reg. 43(3).

[683] BCOBS 5.1.5–5.1.8. For a common approach to 'bank account switching', see European Banking Industry Committee, *Common Principles on Bank Account Switching* (1 December 2008).

[684] *National Commercial Bank of Jamaica Ltd* v. *Olint Corporation Ltd* [2009] UKPC 16, [1], discussed in Ch. 5, Sect. 6 above.

[685] PSR 2009, reg. 43(4). Notice of termination must be made available in an easily accessible manner, in easily understandable language, in a clear and comprehensible form, and in English or other agreed language: ibid., reg. 43(5).

8

Special Types of Account

1 Type of problem

It has already been shown that the banker-customer relationship is primarily a debtor–creditor relationship,[1] and that the foundation of this relationship is the current account operated by the bank.[2] As the sums deposited by the customer become part of the bank's own funds, the customer only has a chose in action against the bank and may reclaim the debt from the bank by demanding repayment or issuing payment instructions. When the customer instructs his bank to make payment, an agency relationship is superimposed on the debtor–creditor contract.[3] Thus, when the bank pays the customer's cheque it performs the two complementary functions of discharging its customer's debt to the payee and obeying its customer's mandate. Although neither of these functions gives rise to difficulties in the ordinary banker-customer relationship, there are special types of account that present problems with respect to one or other of these functions: in some cases, it is not always clear to whom the current account balance is due; in other cases, there is uncertainty over who may issue the bank with instructions. For example, in a joint account, it may be unclear who is entitled to draw cheques, and whether the debt is due to the various account holders jointly, or jointly and severally. Equally, in a corporate account, whilst there may no longer be issues concerning corporate capacity, the bank may still need to concern itself with the power of the board or the authority of individual directors to issue instructions on behalf of the company. Indeed, similar issues of capacity and/or power to issue instructions regarding an account arise in respect of executor and trust accounts and accounts held by minors or the mentally incapacitated. The bank's difficulties are not, however, limited to the honouring of payment instructions, but may also arise when a customer holding a special type of account applies for a loan or overdraft. Once again, the banks may need to adopt special procedures or exercise extra caution before granting such facilities. It is because of these extra steps that the bank may have to take that special types of account require separate consideration.

In this chapter, the first two sections deal with the joint account and the somewhat similar partnership account. As already indicated, the bank's concern in respect of these accounts is the identity of the person who can issue instructions and claim the balance of the account. The next five sections deal in turn with executors' accounts, trust accounts, solicitors' accounts, estate agents' accounts, and investment businesses' accounts, all of which involve a trust element arising from the fact that the ostensible customer is another's fiduciary. Accordingly, the bank has to take account of the fact that whilst the legal title to the chose in action representing the account might be vested in its ostensible customer, there is another person with equitable title to that chose. The subsequent sections then

---

[1] Ch. 5, Sect. 3 & Ch. 7, Sect. 1 above.   [2] Ch. 5, Sect. 2 & Ch. 7, Sect. 1 above.
[3] Ch. 7, Sect. 1 above & Ch. 11, Sect. 2 below.

deal with accounts held by legal persons and other organizations, such as local authorities, companies, and unincorporated associations. In relation to these accounts, the bank's prime concern relates to the capacity of the account holder (except in the case of corporate accounts), the powers of its organs, and the authority of its agents. Finally, the chapter will end by considering accounts of individuals who have limited capacity, such as minors and the mentally incapacitated. Whilst an account opened in a married woman's name would formerly have been included in this last category, married women (like everyone else) nowadays have full capacity to engage in account transactions.[4] The principal remaining problems that may arise from a bank's dealings with a married woman are considered elsewhere: a bank may need to exercise caution when a married woman stands surety for her husband's debts to ensure that she has not been subjected to any undue influence;[5] and when taking security over the matrimonial home, a bank needs to carry out relevant checks to ensure that a wife's informal unregistered interest in the matrimonial home[6] does not take priority over its mortgage, if she happens to be in 'actual occupation'.[7]

2 Joint accounts

(i) Nature of the account

A 'joint account' is opened in the name of two or more customers. It is distinguishable from accounts, such as corporate or administrator's accounts, on the ground that, although more than one person might be required to sign cheques drawn upon the latter types of account, they do so in a representative or fiduciary capacity. In contrast, joint account holders sign as principals, whether jointly or severally.

(ii) Right to draw

When a joint account is opened, the customers will instruct the bank as to whether cheques must be signed by all of the account holders acting jointly, by several of them, or by any one of them acting individually.[8] Where the account mandate requires multiple signatures, disputes can arise when one of the account holder's signatures on the cheque is forged or missing. In *Jackson* v. *White and Midland Bank Ltd,*[9] the claimant, who was negotiating with the first defendant to become a partner in his business, paid funds into an account at the defendant bank that he had opened jointly with the first defendant. The account mandate stipulated that cheques had to be signed by both parties. The defendant bank honoured a number of cheques drawn on the joint account that bore the claimant's forged signature. When his negotiations with the first defendant broke

---

[4] Married Women's Property Act 1882, s.6.   [5] Ch. 5, Sect. 4(ii) above & Ch. 22, Sect. 4 below.
[6] *Stack* v. *Dowden* [2007] 2 AC 432, [65]–[66], [86] (HL); *Hameed* v. *Qayyum* [2009] EWCA Civ. 352, [41]; *Kernott* v. *Jones* [2010] 2 FCR 372, [24]–[63], [65]–[85] (CA). See also C. Harpum, S. Bridge & M. Dixon, *The Law of Real Property* (7th edn., London, 2008), [11-009]–[11-032].
[7] Land Registration Act 2002, Sched. 3, para. 2. See also *HSBC Bank plc* v. *Dyche* [2010] BPIR 138, [47]. See further Ch. 19, Sect. 2(ii) below. The wife may be estopped from disputing the bank's mortgage if she knew of the arrangement: *Yeoman's Row Management Ltd* v. *Cobbe* [2008] 4 All ER 713 (HL). See generally *Governer & Co of the Bank of Scotland* v. *Hussain* [2010] EWHC 2812 (Ch), [88]–[111].
[8] The conversion of an existing account into joint names involves a variation of the original account contract by the addition of a party, rather than its extinction and replacement by a new contract: *Damayanti Kantilal Doshi* v. *Indian Bank* [1999] 4 SLR 1, [49]–[50] (SGCA).
[9] [1967] 2 Lloyd's Rep. 68.

down, the claimant applied for an injunction ordering the bank to reverse the debits from the joint account representing the forged cheques, and for an injunction ordering the first defendant to authorize the bank in future to honour cheques drawn by the claimant alone. Giving judgment for the claimant, Park J said:[10]

> ... the Bank made an agreement with the [claimant] and the first defendant jointly that it would honour any cheques signed by them jointly, and also a separate agreement with the [claimant] and the first defendant severally that it would not honour any cheques unless he had signed them. It follows, therefore, as the Bank has honoured cheques not signed by the [claimant], the [claimant] is entitled to sue for breach of that separate agreement.

A similar view was expressed by Bingham J in *Catlin* v. *Cyprus Finance Corporation (London) Ltd*[11] in which a bank again honoured a cheque that did not bear all the signatures required by the joint account mandate. Although his Lordship regarded the bank's mandate as being given jointly by all the account holders, he held that the bank owed a duty to each account holder *individually* to obey that mandate. According to his Lordship, 'the only purpose of requiring two signatures was to obviate the possibility of independent action by one account holder to the detriment of the other'.[12] As the evidence in both *Jackson* and *Catlin* established that the funds in the joint account were originally the claimant's property alone, the respective claimants were entitled to recover the *full* amount paid out against the invalid cheques. Where there is no such evidence, however, the innocent joint account holder is only entitled to recover an equal share of the amounts wrongfully paid out against cheques that did not bear his signature.[13] Indeed, in *Vella* v. *Permanent Mortgages Pty Ltd*,[14] Young CJ recently held that 'the weight of authority is in favour of the proposition that... where one joint holder sues the bank for breach of compliance with its mandate, it is only the [claimant's] proportional interest that is to be compensated for in damages'.

The innocent joint account holder is not entitled, however, to recover sums wrongfully paid out against a cheque with a forged or missing signature if the sums were paid in discharge of the innocent account holder's liabilities. Thus, as it was conceded in *Jackson* that one of the cheques had been drawn to pay the price of goods supplied to

---

[10] Ibid., 79. See also *Twibell* v. *London Suburban Bank* [1869] WN 127; *Welch* v. *Bank of England* [1955] Ch. 508 (CA); *Baker* v. *Barclays Bank Ltd* [1955] 1 WLR 822; cf. *Hirschorn* v. *Evans (Barclays Bank Ltd, Garnishee)* [1938] 2 KB 801, 812 (CA) (discussed in Ch. 11, Sect. 1(iii) below); *Brewer* v. *Westminster Bank* [1952] 2 All ER 650. This 'dual-contract analysis' has been accepted in Australia (*Ardern* v. *Bank of New South Wales* [1956] VLR 569, 573; *Simos* v. *National Bank of Australasia Ltd* (1976) 10 ACTR 4; *Commonwealth Director of Public Prosecutions* v. *Ly* [2007] NSWSC 805, [68]–[72]; *Vella* v. *Permanent Mortgages Pty Ltd* [2008] NSWSC 505, [424]–[434]) and New Zealand (*Vivar* v. *National Bank of New Zealand Ltd* (NZHC, 20 October 1998)). See also *Chartered Bank* v. *Yong Chan* [1974] 1 MLJ 157, 159–160 (MFCA); *Sinnatamby Seahomes Sdn Bhd* v. *Perwira Habib Bank Malaysia Bhd* [2001] 2 MLJ 450, 456. A bank may honour a cheque bearing only one joint account holder's signature, even though the account mandate requires two signatures, if there is evidence that the signatory has the other account holder's authority to sign on his behalf: *London Intercontinental Trust Ltd* v. *Barclays Bank Ltd* [1980] 1 Lloyd's Rep 241. This is, however, an 'exceptional case': A. Tyree & P. Weaver, *Weerasooria's Banking Law and the Financial System in Australia* (6th edn., 2006), [25.23]. See further *Belfast Telegraph Newspapers Ltd* v. *Blunden* [1995] NI 351 (NICA).

[11] [1983] QB 759.

[12] Ibid., 771, approved in *Dar International FEF Co* v. *Aon Ltd* [2004] EWCA Civ 921, [30]–[32].

[13] *Twibell* v. *London Suburban Bank*, n.10 above. See also *Ardern* v. *Bank of New South Wales*, n.10 above; *Official Trustee in Bankruptcy* v. *Alvaro* (1996) 138 ALR 341 (FCA). The report in *Twibell* is unsatisfactory: *Vella* v. *Permanent Mortgages Pty Ltd*, n.10 above, [439].

[14] N.10 above, [442].

the claimant, Park J thought that the bank was entitled to rely on counsel's concession in that regard so as 'to take advantage of the equitable doctrine by which a person who had in fact paid the debts of another without authority was allowed the advantage of his payments'.[15] It has been suggested[16] that this doctrine, which is based on *B. Liggett (Liverpool) Ltd* v. *Barclays Bank Ltd*,[17] may also explain why an innocent joint account holder may only recover an equal share of sums wrongfully paid out by a bank against a cheque missing a signature (as stated in *Vella* v. *Permanent Mortgages Pty Ltd*),[18] rather than the full amount of the instrument. A strict application of agency principles would lead to the opposite conclusion, since, at common law, a bank acting on an invalid mandate is not generally entitled to debit the account with any part of the amount paid out.[19] However, the equitable *Liggett* doctrine referred to in *Jackson* mitigates this harsh result. According to that doctrine, a customer, on whose mandate the bank has purported to act, cannot recover an amount exceeding the loss incurred by him due to the bank's unauthorized payment. Thus, where the owner of a joint account is the owner of one half only of the balance, he is not entitled to recover more than 50 per cent of sums paid by the bank without authority. In light of the decision in *Crantrave Ltd* v. *Lloyds Bank plc*,[20] however, it may be increasingly difficult to rely on *Liggett* as providing a secure basis for either the conclusion in *Jackson* or the general rule in *Vella*, as *Crantrave* has now virtually eliminated any role for the *Liggett* doctrine.

In contrast, the problems just considered do not arise where the joint account mandate allows the bank to honour cheques drawn by any one account holder acting individually. Unless there is evidence that the account has been opened for a specific object, each party is entitled to draw on the joint account for his own purposes. In *Re Bishop decd., National Provincial Bank Ltd* v. *Bishop*,[21] a husband purchased shares in his own name by drawing cheques upon a joint account that authorized either spouse to sign cheques. The bank duly honoured the cheques, and it was subsequently held that the shares were beneficially owned by the husband, and not held on trust for himself and his wife. This basic position may alter, however, if there is evidence that an asset purchased by one party with funds from the joint account was intended to be acquired jointly for both parties or the funds in the account were only intended to be joint funds,[22] or if the evidence indicates that the funds in the joint account had been contributed solely by the account holder who had not made the purchase in question.[23] Whilst the principle in *Bishop* has since been applied in

---

[15] N.9 above, 80.

[16] E.P Ellinger, E. Lomnicka, & R.J.A. Hooley, *Ellinger's Modern Banking Law* (Oxford, 2005), 292–293.

[17] [1928] 1 KB 48; cf. *Crantrave Ltd* v. *Lloyds Bank plc* [2000] QB 917 (CA). See further Ch. 11, Sect. 3(v) below.

[18] N.10 above, [442].

[19] *Barclays Bank Ltd* v. *W. J. Simms Son & Cooke (Southern) Ltd* [1980] QB 677, 695. A bank can only debit its customer's account if its payment is authorized or made as a result of necessity or legal compulsion: *Crantrave Ltd* v. *Lloyds Bank plc*, n.17 above. See further Ch. 11, Sect. 3(v) & Ch. 12, Sect. 3(iii)(b) below.

[20] N.17 above.

[21] [1965] Ch. 450, followed in *Pettitt* v. *Pettitt* [1970] AC 777, 815 (HL); *Taylor* v. *Mazorriaga* (CA, 12 May 1999); *West* v. *Mead* [2003] NSWSC 161. See also *Wong* v. *Chuan* [1992] 2 SLR 360, 373; *Daly* v. *Gilbert* [1993] 3 NZLR 731, 743; *Phua Beng Hong* v. *Ho Shik Ho* [2000] 2 MLJ 289, 308–309 (MCA); *Chan Sik Chi* v. *Wing Hang Cotton Drapers Co Ltd* [2004] HKCU 524, [29].

[22] *Jones* v. *Maynard* [1951] 1 Ch. 572, 575.

[23] *Heseltine* v. *Heseltine* [1971] 1 WLR 342, 347–348 (CA). See also *Ferris* v. *McCreedy* [1971] NIJB (April 15).

Australia[24] and Canada,[25] more recent decisions in these jurisdictions[26] and Scotland[27] have tended to cast doubt upon its standing.

Given that *Bishop* still remains authoritative in England, the basic position remains that a bank need not concern itself about the operation of a joint account when each account holder is entitled to operate it individually.[28] This principle has recently been reaffirmed in *Fielding* v. *Royal Bank of Scotland plc*,[29] in which the mandate for a joint account permitted cheques to be drawn by either spouse and provided that each account holder would be jointly and severally liable for any overdrafts incurred on the account. When the bank sought to recover from both account holders the significant overdraft that the husband had incurred on the joint account, the wife denied liability on the ground that she had neither known of, nor authorized, her husband's withdrawals from the account. The Court of Appeal gave the argument short shrift, holding that 'the mandate means what it says', namely that each account holder was jointly and severally liable for 'all borrowings on the joint account...without limit'.[30] Nor was Jonathan Parker LJ prepared to imply any limitation into the account mandate, thereby restricting the way it could be operated or limiting the purposes for which the funds might be used. His Lordship stated the general position to be that 'in the case of a joint account as between husband and wife there is no necessary limit on the purposes for which the joint account may be used; it is for the account holders themselves to decide what, if any, limitation to impose' and he considered that, absent such a self-imposed limitation, it is 'no concern of the bank how a husband and wife choose to operate the joint account provided that such operation is in accordance with the express terms of the mandate'.[31] Nevertheless, his Lordship suggested that there might potentially be one important limit to the general principle that banks need not concern themselves with the actions of account holders when each is entitled to operate the account. Jonathan Parker LJ suggested (without finally deciding the point) that a bank might breach its duty of care to one joint account holder if it continued to operate the account even though it 'had some reason to suppose the mandate was being abused' by the other account holder,[32] or had 'notice that a fraud is being committed'.[33] His Lordship did, however, indicate that it would be 'difficult to envisage a situation' where a bank would owe a duty of care to a joint account holder 'simply by operating an account in accordance with its (subsisting) mandate'.[34] This is entirely consistent with the duty of care owed generally to a customer to ignore payment instructions that the bank has strong grounds to suspect are an attempt to defraud that customer.[35] As was considered previously,[36] a duty of care to ignore an otherwise valid payment instruction is only owed

---

[24] *Re Marriage of Fogarty* (1976) 27 FLR 257; *Pickard* v. *Pickard* (1981) 7 Fam LR 636; *Re Reid* (1998) 85 FCR 452; *West* v. *Mead*, n.21 above.

[25] *Re Cameron* (1967) 62 DLR (2d) 389, 405; *Feaver* v. *Feaver* [1977] 5 WWR 271.

[26] For Australia, see *Re Ebner* (2003) 196 ALR 533, [27]–[28] (FCA) (referring to *Bishop* as 'doubtful authority'); *Waring* v. *Ellis* [2005] NSWSC 467, [54]–[55]. For Canada, see *Re Daly* (1907) 39 SCR 122, 148 (SCC); *Rathwell* v. *Rathwell* [1978] 2 SCR 436, 439 (SCC), (indicating a 'difficulty in understanding the basis upon which' *Bishop* was decided). Consider also *Kan Sabnani* v. *Ramesh Lachmandas* [1994] 3 SLR 712 (SGCA) (loan by joint account holders made as joint tenants).

[27] *Watson's Executors* v. *Watson* 2006 SCLR 121, [54], [58], [74] (*Bishop* to be 'approached with care').

[28] *Damayanti Kantilal Doshi* v. *Indian Bank*, n.8 above, [51].

[29] [2004] EWCA Civ. 64. A joint account holder may be liable to defrauded third parties whose funds have passed through the joint account: *OEM plc* v. *The Estate of Brian Schneider* [2005] EWHC 1072 (Ch), [33]–[46].

[30] Ibid., [103].   [31] Ibid., [101].   [32] Ibid., [108].

[33] Ibid., [101]. See also *Sansom* v. *Westpac Banking Corporation* (NSWSC, 1 March 1996).

[34] Ibid., [107].

[35] *Lipkin Gorman* v. *Karpnale & Co.* [1989] 1 WLR 1340, 1378 (CA), revsd. on another point: [1991] 2 AC 548 (HL).   [36] Ch. 5, Sect. 4(iii) above.

in the most exceptional of circumstances. *Fielding* suggests that the position is no different in the case of a joint account.

(iii) Survivorship

Where one of the holders of a joint account dies, the question arises as to whether it is the surviving account holder or the deceased account holder's estate that is entitled to claim the deceased account holder's share of any balance standing to the credit of the joint account at his death.[37] This issue tends to arise in three distinct contexts: first, when there is a dispute between the surviving account holder(s) and the deceased account holder's heir; secondly, when there is a dispute between the surviving account holder and the revenue authorities, usually as to whether inheritance tax is payable on the deceased account holder's share of the joint account balance;[38] and, thirdly, where there is a dispute between the bank and either the surviving account holder or the deceased account holder's estate, usually as to whether the bank is obliged to honour a particular person's demand for payment. In each of these cases, however, the issue is not whether the surviving account holder(s) or the deceased's estate obtains a *direct interest in the funds standing to the credit of the account* (since the bank has the legal and beneficial interest in the funds themselves from the time of their deposit),[39] but instead what rights they obtain (if any) to the chose in action that entitled the deceased account holder to draw upon the credit balance or instruct the bank to make payments from the joint account.[40] According to the case law, it is necessary to distinguish between the legal and equitable title to this chose in action. The former is important mainly as regards disputes between the bank and its customer; the latter is relevant to the remaining types of dispute that might arise between the surviving account holder(s), on the one hand, and either the tax authorities or the deceased's estate, on the other.

(a) Legal entitlement to the chose in action representing the credit balance

Following the death of a joint account holder, the bank's position is largely unaffected by questions concerning the identity of those beneficially entitled to the chose in action representing the account. The bank's main concern is to identify its legal owner and to meet that person's demands.[41] As the legal title to a chose in action cannot be held in common,[42] a joint account must create joint legal co-ownership of the debt owed by the bank.[43] Accordingly, it is well established that, upon a joint account holder's death, the legal title to the chose in action representing the joint account vests entirely in the remaining account holder(s) by virtue of a right of survivorship. In *Russell* v. *Scott*,[44] Dixon and

---

[37] An attempt to open a joint account that is not finalized before the death of one of the account holders may constitute an equitable assignment of the account funds: *Shahan* v. *Lloyds TSB Offshore Treasury Ltd* [2008] GRC 11 (Guernsey Royal Ct.).

[38] *O'Neill* v. *Inland Revenue Commissioners* [1998] STC 110.   [39] Ch. 5, Sect. 3 above.

[40] *Russell* v. *Scott* (1936) 55 CLR 440, 450 (HCA); *Edgar* v. *Commissioner of Inland Revenue* [1978] 1 NZLR 590, 607; *Lynch* v. *Burke & Allied Irish Banks plc* [1995] 2 IR 159 (IESC). See also D. Fox, *Property Rights in Money* (Oxford, 2008), [1.39].

[41] *Latifah Bte Mat Zin* v. *Rosmawati Bte Sharibun* [2006] 4 MLJ 705, [18] (MCA).

[42] *Re McKerrell* [1912] 2 Ch 648, 653 (joint insurance policy).

[43] *Re Bishop decd., National Provincial Bank Ltd* v. *Bishop*, n.21 above, 456; *Steele* v. *Steele* (Ch.D, 4 October 2001), [51]–[59]. See also D. Fox, n.40 above, [7.52]. The obligation owed by the bank to joint account holders is joint and several: Sect. 2(ii) above.

[44] N.40 above, 451, followed in *Goldin* v. *Hands, Golding & Boldt* [1969] WAR 121; *Haythorpe* v. *Rae* [1972] VR 633, 638–639; *Palmer* v. *Bank of New South Wales* (1975) 7 ALR 671, 675–677 (HCA); *Public Trustee* v.

Evatt JJ observed that '[t]he right at law to the balance standing at the credit of the account on the death of [the deceased party] was thus vested in the [survivor]'. The same principle has been reiterated more recently by the Supreme Court of Canada in *Pecore* v. *Pecore*,[45] which involved a dispute over the balance of a joint account that a father had opened for himself and his adult daughter before he died. Rothstein J indicated that it was 'not disputed that the daughter took legal ownership of the balance in the accounts through the right of survivorship'. This legal consequence is particularly important from the bank's perspective. Although most modern standard-form joint account mandates contain a clause requiring the bank to honour cheques drawn, and other payment instructions given, by the surviving account holder(s),[46] the accepted view is that, even without such a clause, the bank is entitled to meet the demand of the surviving account holder(s), and thereby obtain a good discharge.[47]

The leading English decision is *McEvoy* v. *Belfast Banking Co.*,[48] in which a customer deposited funds in an account in the joint names of himself and his minor son, and specifically ordered that the amount be payable to either of them or to the survivor. The father's aim was to save the death duties that would be payable on the relevant amount if it formed part of his estate. His remaining assets were left to his executors to hold in trust for his son until his majority. Following the father's death, and with the son's knowledge, the executors used the sums in the joint account to back, and even to repay part of, an overdraft granted to the deceased father's business. Only when the business failed, did the son, who had now reached the age of majority, make demand of the bank for the repayment of the joint account funds. The bank resisted repayment on the ground that the funds had been validly paid to the father's executors. Although the House of Lords held unanimously for the bank, their reasoning differed.[49] Lords Warrington and Macmillan considered that, as against the bank, the executors were entitled to the funds in the joint account, as the father had not manifested an intention to give it to his son. Lord Thankerton reached the same conclusion via a contractual route, holding that the account contract was solely between the bank and the father, as the initial customer, for the benefit of the son, as the other party to the joint account. On this approach, the surviving account holder would not be a party to the account contract, and would be nothing more than a third party to an agreement between the bank and the initial customer.[50] Lord Atkin disagreed with both these analyses. As regards the first, his Lordship observed that, on the facts, the father had manifested an intention of advancement, as he had clearly expressed his wish that the joint account balance be available to

---

Gray-Masters [1977] VR 154, 157–159; *Deputy Commissioner of Taxation* v. *Westpac Bank Ltd* (1987) 72 ALR 634, 638–641; *Maertin* v. *Klaus Maertin Pty Ltd* [2006] NSWSC 588, [25]; *Logan* v. *Gardiner* [2006] NSWSC 1069, [21]–[26]. See also *Chow Yee Wah* v. *Choo Ah Pat* [1978] 2 MLJ 41, 44 (PC); *Re Brownlee* [1990] 3 NZLR 243, 247–248.

[45] [2007] 1 SCR 795, [4] (SCC).

[46] *Niles* v. *Lake* [1947] SCR 291, 304 (SCC); *Aroso* v. *Coutts & Co* [2002] 1 All ER (Comm.) 241, [13]; *Pecore* v. *Pecore*, n.45 above, [10], [60]–[61]; *Madsen Estate* v. *Saylor* [2007] 1 SCR 838, [20]–[22] (SCC). See also Ogilvie, 'Banker and Customer: The Five-Year Review 2000–2005' (2007) 23 *BFLR* 107, 112.

[47] M. Hapgood, *Paget's Law of Banking* (13th edn., London, 2007), [11.26].

[48] [1935] AC 24 (HL).

[49] One line of reasoning that finds no echo in *McEvoy* would be to regard the joint account in that case as involving an instruction to the bank by the father, as the initial customer, to pay the joint account's credit balance to the survivor. This would not have altered the result in *McEvoy*, however, as the bank's mandate from the initial customer would have determined upon his death: Ch. 11, Sect. 1(vi) below.

[50] Depending upon the construction of the joint account mandate, a joint account holder might nowadays enforce the terms of the current account by virtue of the Contracts (Rights of Third Parties) Act 1999, s.1(1)(b): *Chitty on Contracts* (30th edn., London, 2008), [18-088]–[18-092].

his son after his death. As regards the second, his Lordship considered that the contract was between the bank and *both* the father and the son in whose names the amount was deposited. According to his Lordship, if this had been an ordinary case, the son would simply have had legal title to the chose in action representing the account by virtue of being a party to the banking contract. This basic proposition of Lord Atkin is preferable to the approaches of their other Lordships, as it *prima facie* gives effect to what the father intended, especially as he could have just as easily achieved his purpose by way of a power of attorney, trust, or testamentary disposition. *McEvoy* was not, however, an ordinary case, but was complicated by the account having been opened in the son's name whilst he was a minor, and upon the father's own initiative without the son's express consent. Lord Atkin emphasized that the son would, therefore, have to ratify the account contract before being able to enforce it, but that this had not occurred. On the contrary, the son's active participation in his deceased father's business, and his knowledge that the joint account balance had been used to support that business, indicated that he agreed with the executors' course of conduct. Accordingly, agreeing with their other Lordships, Lord Atkin concluded that the son was precluded from contesting the bank's right to pay the account funds to the executors. The real significance of *McEvoy* lies, however, in Lord Atkin's statement of general principle:[51]

> The suggestion is that where A deposits a sum of money with his bank in the names of A and B, payable to A or B, if B comes to the bank with the deposit receipt he has no right to demand the money from the bank or to sue them if his demand is refused. The bank is entitled to demand proof that the money was in fact partly B's, or possibly that A had acted with B's actual authority. For the contract, it is said, is between the bank and A alone. My Lords, to say this is to ignore the vital difference between a contract purporting to be made by A with the bank to pay A or B and a contract purporting to be made by A and B with the bank to pay A or B. In both cases of course payment to B would discharge the bank whether the bank contracted with A alone or with A and B. But the question is whether in the case put B has any rights against the bank if payment to him is refused. I have myself no doubt that in such a case B can sue the bank. The contract on the face of it purports to be made with A and B, and I think with them jointly and severally.

This suggests that ordinarily the bank is both entitled and obliged to meet the demands of the surviving joint account holder. Indeed, provided the surviving account holder has reached the age of majority when the account is opened, and accordingly has the capacity to contract, the ratification issue in *McEvoy* will not normally arise, as the surviving account holder's agreement with the bank will usually be manifested when he initially signs the joint account mandate. This was made clear by the Irish Supreme Court in *Lynch* v. *Burke & Allied Irish Banks plc*,[52] where the deceased had opened a joint account with her niece, who was seeking a declaration of entitlement to the joint account balance. As the niece had signed the joint mandate form when the account was first opened, no issue of ratification arose. Hamilton CJ held that the niece 'was a party to the [banking] contract from the outset'[53] and accordingly 'had a legal interest in the monies on deposit'.[54] Applying the above passage from *McEvoy*, his Lordship held that the niece had 'the right to demand from the bank so much of the money as was due on the deposit account'.[55] More recently, in *Aroso* v. *Coutts & Co.*,[56] Lawrence Collins J followed *McEvoy* and suggested that, irrespective of any dispute that existed between the surviving account holder and the deceased's executors, '[t]he bank was bound contractually to comply with

---

⁵¹ *McEvoy* v. *Belfast Banking Co*, n.48 above.
⁵² N.40 above, applied in *Prendergast* v. *Joyce* [2009] IEHC 199, [35]–[38].   ⁵³ Id.   ⁵⁴ Id.
⁵⁵ Id.   ⁵⁶ N.46 above.

instructions given by the surviving joint holder in accordance with the mandate'.[57] As his Lordship indicated, and as previously discussed,[58] a bank that has acted in accordance with its mandate will only be liable to a third party claiming to have an interest in the account if that third party can demonstrate that the bank was sufficiently at fault to be liable as a recipient of trust funds or as an accessory to a breach of trust or fiduciary duty.[59]

(b) Beneficial entitlement to the chose in action representing the credit balance

As the equitable or beneficial title to the chose in action representing the joint credit balance is quite separate from the legal title, it does not necessarily vest in the same way, and may accordingly vest in the deceased account holder's estate, rather than in the surviving account holder(s) by virtue of a right of survivorship. As pointed out above, the location of the beneficial entitlement will usually be relevant when resolving disputes between the surviving account holder(s), on the one hand, and either the deceased's heirs or the revenue authorities,[60] on the other. Identifying the person who is beneficially entitled to the rights over the account depends very much on the particular circumstances of each case.[61] If the joint account credit balance results from payments made by *each* of the account holders, then the right to those funds will be regarded as accruing beneficially to each of them during their lifetime, either as tenants in common, and in proportion to their contributions to the original fund,[62] or as joint tenants.[63] Like the common law position considered in the preceding section, joint equitable ownership of the right to the account funds carries with it a right of survivorship, so that, upon the death of one account holder, the entire beneficial interest will vest in the surviving account holder(s), leaving the deceased account holder's estate without any equivalent claim. In other words, in this situation, the beneficial title follows legal title.[64] In contrast, where the beneficial entitlement to the chose in action representing the account is held in common, the remaining account holder has no automatic right of survivorship.[65] Accordingly, as considered in the following paragraphs, the surviving account holder will have to demonstrate that the deceased intended either to make a gift of his beneficial entitlement during his lifetime or to confer an express right of survivorship upon his death.

A more complicated situation arises if the joint account balance is entirely or predominantly the result of deposits by the deceased account holder. In such a case, the beneficial interests over the joint account during the account holders' lifetime (and accordingly the respective entitlements of the surviving account holder(s) and the deceased account

---

[57] Ibid., [40].   [58] Ch. 7, Sect. 5 above.   [59] *Aroso* v. *Coutts & Co.*, n.46 above, [37]–[41].

[60] *O'Neill* v. *Inland Revenue Commissioners*, n.38 above; *Sillars* v. *Inland Revenue Commissioners* [2004] SpC 401; *Taylor* v. *Commissioners for Her Majesty's Revenue and Customs* (Special Commissioner, 5 August 2008). Cf. *Thomson* v. *Federal Commissioner of Taxation* (1949) 80 CLR 344 (HCA).

[61] M.H Ogilvie, n.46 above, 113.

[62] It is possible to have a tenancy in common over the equitable interest in a chose in action: D. Fox, n.40 above, [7.52].

[63] A joint tenancy can arise where the parties regard the joint account as a genuine common pool or 'common purse': *Jones* v. *Maynard*, n.22 above, 575; *Gage* v. *King* [1961] 1 QB 188, 192–193; *Heseltine* v. *Heseltine*, n.23 above, 347; *In re EH & K Pickard* (1981) 7 Fam LR 636; *Steele* v. *Steele*, n.43 above, [51]–[59]. See also *Trojan* v. *Corporation of Town of Hindmarsh* (1987) 82 ALR 255 (FCA). For the Canadian position, see *Plater* v. *Brealey* [1938] 4 DLR 765, affd. [1939] 2 DLR 767n; *Rathwell* v. *Rathwell*, n.26 above, 459–460; *Re Roberts* (1998) 58 OTC 378, [17]; *Hall Estate* v. *Marshall* [2000] BCTC Uned 529, [39]–[41]. An account that is joint merely as a matter of convenience is unlikely to be considered a 'common purse': *Yung Ki Fong* v. *Mark Oi Lin* [1959] HKCU 82; *Re Berry* [1978] 2 NZLR 373, 378–381 (NZCA).

[64] A transfer of funds from a joint account to a single-name account will sever any joint tenancy; cf. *Kogler* v. *Schabernig Estate* [2004] BCSC 522, [58]–[62]. See also Ogilvie, n.46 above, 114.

[65] *Koh Siew Keng* v. *Koh Heng Jin* [2008] 3 MLJ 822, [15] (MCA).

holder's estate upon his death) depend on the deceased account holder's intention in maintaining the funds in the joint account. In particular, the court will enquire as to whether the deceased established the joint account purely out of considerations of convenience, or whether the deceased intended to gift the equitable interest in the right to the joint account monies during his lifetime, which would continue after his death. As the deceased's intention is not usually on record, its determination depends largely upon the operation of presumptions.[66] In most relationships, including such proximate ones as siblings,[67] grandparent and grandchild,[68] cousins,[69] or aunt/uncles and nephews/nieces,[70] it is presumed that the deceased account holder intended to retain the entire beneficial interest in the right over the joint account during his lifetime, with the result that the surviving account holder(s) has no automatic beneficial entitlement to the funds upon his death. Accordingly, the surviving account holder holds the chose representing the joint account as trustee for the deceased account holder's estate ('the presumption of resulting trust').[71] The position is *a fortiori* when the joint account holders are not related.[72] In contrast, where the relationship is that of husband and wife[73] or parent and child,[74] the presumption is that the deceased account holder intended during his lifetime to make a gift to, or advance, the surviving account holder(s), who will accordingly be entitled beneficially to the right over the account after his death[75] ('the presumption of advancement').[76]

Although the presumption of advancement has in recent years been viewed somewhat less favourably in certain contexts, such as when determining rights over the matrimonial

---

[66] *Madsen Estate* v. *Saylor,* n.46 above, [2].

[67] *Niles* v. *Lake,* n.46 above, 300–302; *Frosch* v. *Dadd* (1960) 24 DLR (2d) 610; *Re Power Estate* (2001) 615 APR 163, [30]–[32] (NSC); *Re Harvey Estate* [2006] NSSC 118, [62]; *Tiedeman* v. *Tiedeman* [2008] OJ No. 1647, [30] (OSC).

[68] *Re Vinogradoff* [1935] WN 68; *Oolup* v. *R* [2003] TCC 947 (CTC).

[69] *Davies* v. *Donnell* (1973) 39 DLR (3d) 105; *Shkuratoff* v. *Carter Estate* [2007] BCSC 1061, [20].

[70] *Lynch* v. *Burke & Allied Irish Banks plc,* n.40 above; *Berbaum Estate* v. *Silver* (2001) NSR (2d) 120, [28] (NSSC); *Aroso* v. *Coutts & Co.,* n.46 above, [25]; *Stadnyk Estate* v. *Hrycan* [2006] SKQB 452, [8]–[18]; *Marshall* v. *Cole* [2008] NJ No. 340 (NSC); *Guerin* v. *Shoultz* [2010] OJ No. 2743, [9]–[13] (OSC).

[71] *Aroso* v. *Coutts & Co.,* n.46 above, [25].

[72] *Saarnok Estate* v. *Neufeld* [2002] BCTC 202, [95]–[100] (BCSC); *Strickland* v. *Thames Valley District School Board* [2007] OJ No. 3758, [76]; *Sillett* v. *Meek* [2007] EWHC 1169 (Ch), [32].

[73] *Re Pattison* (1885) 1 TLR 216; *Re Figgis* [1969] 1 Ch. 123, 144; *Juresic* v. *Juresic* (1977) 81 DLR (3d) 446; *West* v. *Mead,* n.21 above; *Kogler* v. *Schabernig Estate,* n.64 above, [41]–[44]; *Prendergast* v. *Joyce,* n.52 above, [38]; cf. *Re Ebner,* n.26 above. The presumption of advancement has no application between co-habitees: *Chow Yee Wah* v. *Choo Ah Pat,* n.44 above, 44; *Waring* v. *Ellis,* n.26 above, [54]; *Stack* v. *Dowden,* n.6 above, [111]–[112]; *Lim Chen Yeow Kelvin* v. *Goh Chin Peng* [2008] 4 SLR 783, [123] (SGHC). See also *Soar* v. *Foster* (1858) 4 K & J 152; cf *Hayward* v. *Giordani* [1983] NZLR 140, 148; *Green* v. *Snyder* (1989) 17 NSWLR 343. See further *Napier* v. *Public Trustee* (1980) 32 ALR 153 (HCA).

[74] *Fadden* v. *Deputy Federal Commissioner of Taxation* (1943) 68 CLR 76, 81 (HCA); *Re Brownlee,* n.44 above; *Re Kong Chee Mong* (1969) 7 DLR (3rd) 78; *Cohen* v. *Cohen* (1985) 60 OR 234 (QB); *Re Dagle* (1990) 70 DLR (4th) 201, 209; *O'Neill* v. *Inland Revenue Commissioners,* n.38 above; *Pang Siu Hing* v. *Tsang Kwok Man* [2004] HKCU 30, [8]–[10]. In Canada, the presumption of advancement applies as much between a mother and her minor child as between a father and his child: *Pecore* v. *Pecore,* n.45 above, [33], doubting *Edwards* v. *Bradley* [1957] SCR 599 (SCC). See also *Re Brownlee,* n.44 above, 248; *Nelson* v. *Nelson* (1995) 184 CLR 538 (HCA); *McLear* v. *Crowder* [2000] OTC 505, [39] (OSC); *Logan* v. *Gardiner,* n.44 above, [31]. The position appears different in England (M. McInnes, 'Presumption of Advancement Retained and Refined' (2007) 123 LQR 528) and Hong Kong (*Cheung Cho Kam Sindy* v. *Cheung Yuet Ying Rose* [2007] HKCU 1184, [15]).

[75] *McLean* v. *Vessey* [1935] 4 DLR 170, 178. Where the presumption of advancement applies, issues concerning the deceased account holder's mental capacity when opening the joint account (*Legg* v. *Nicholson* [2002] NSSC 217) or subjection to undue influence (*Hood Estate* v. *Young* [2008] NSSC 146) frequently arise. Consider also *Prendergast* v. *Joyce,* n.52 above; *Gorjat* v. *Gorjat* [2010] EWHC 1537 (Ch), [129]–[160].

[76] *Lau Siew Kim* v. *Yeo Guan Chye Terence* [2008] 2 SLR 108, [108] (SGCA).

home,[77] and although the presumption of resulting trust is seen as formally quite weak,[78] the Supreme Court of Canada in *Pecore* v. *Pecore*[79] has nevertheless recently confirmed that the presumptions of resulting trust and advancement 'continue to have a role to play in disputes over gratuitous transfers' in the context of joint accounts. According to Rothstein J, the presumptions provide courts with a guide when evidence of the transferor's intention is unavailable or unpersuasive, particularly when the transferor is deceased.[80] Whilst recognizing the continued utility of presumptions in this context, Rothstein J reduced the scope of the presumption of advancement in one important respect—it would not apply between a parent and an adult child, even if the child were still a dependant.[81] As *Pecore* itself involved a joint account opened by a father in the names of himself and his adult daughter, Rothstein J applied the presumption of resulting trust, but ultimately concluded that there was sufficient evidence to rebut that presumption. His Honour reiterated these principles, and in particular the limitation on the presumption of advancement operating in favour of adult children, in *Madsen Estate* v. *Saylor*.[82] Although *Madsen Estate* also involved a joint account between a father and his adult daughter, and was accordingly similarly governed by the presumption of resulting trust, unlike *Pecore*, Rothstein J concluded that there was insufficient evidence to rebut that presumption.[83] It is accordingly clear from *Pecore* and *Madsen Estate*, that neither presumption is conclusive and that they can be rebutted by contrary evidence.[84] In *Pecore*, Rothstein J considered the types of evidence that might be adduced to rebut the presumptions, such as 'evidence of intention that arises subsequent to a transfer' provided that it is 'relevant to the intention of the transferor at the time of transfer';[85] bank documents relating to the opening or operation of the joint account;[86] evidence relating to the control and use of the funds in the

---

[77] *Pettitt* v. *Pettitt*, n.21 above, 811, 814; *Gissing* v. *Gissing* [1971] AC 886, 907 (HL); *Stack* v. *Dowden*, n.6 above, [16], [101], & [112]; *Laskar* v. *Laskar* [2008] 2 FLR 589, [20] (CA); *Gibson* v. *Revenue & Customs Prosecution Office* [2008] EWCA Civ 645, [26]–[27] & [31]; *Ben Hashem* v. *Al Shayif* [2009] 1 FLR 115, [117]. See also *Edgar* v. *Commissioner of Inland Revenue*, n.40 above, 606–607.

[78] *Aroso* v. *Coutts & Co.*, n.46 above, [22]; *Sillett* v. *Meek*, n.72 above, [32]–[35].

[79] N.45 above, [23] (noted by M. McInnes, n.74 above). See also *Sillett* v. *Meek*, n.72 above, [33], [54].

[80] Id. See also *Siah* v. *Low Geok Khim* [2007] 1 SLR 795, [44] (SGCA) (noted by K. Low, (2007) 123 *LQR* 347). These presumptions are also applicable to jointly-held bank safety deposit boxes: *Albreght Estate* v. *Joris* [2008] OJ No. 524, [32]–[34].

[81] Ibid., [34]–[41]. See also *Erickson Estate* v. *Erickson* [2005] ABQB 334, [50]–[51]; *Hood Estate* v. *Young*, n.75 above, [19]–[20]; *Tarling* v. *Tarling* [2008] OJ No. 3009, [112]–[113]; *Inch* v. *Stead Estate* [2007] BCSC 1249, [57]; *Doucette* v. *Doucette Estate* [2007] BCSC 1021, [8]–[10]; *DLM* v. *JAM* [2008] NBCA 2, [17]–[18]; *Baker* v. *Bourque* [2008] NBQB 164, [78]–[80]; *Albreght Estate* v. *Joris*, n.80 above, [36]; *Kosterewa* v. *Kosterewa* [2008] OJ No. 3950, [28] (OSC); *Harrington* v. *Harrington* [2009] OJ No. 177, [31] (OCA). In England, the presumption of advancement still operates in favour of a non-dependent, adult child, albeit it is 'weaker' than in other contexts: *Laskar* v. *Laskar*, n.77 above, [20]. See also *Re Brownlee*, n.44 above, 248; *Low Geok Khim* v. *Low Geok Bian* [2006] 2 SLR 444, [41]–[47].

[82] N.46 above, [17].   [83] Ibid., [29].

[84] *Pecore* v. *Pecore*, n.45 above, [42]–[44]. See also *Lohia* v. *Lohia* (CA, 25 October 2001), [20]–[21]. There are suggestions that the presumptions have no role if evidence of intention actually exists: *Lim Chen Yeow Kelvin* v. *Goh Chin Peng*, n.73 above, [129].

[85] Ibid., [56]–[59]. In England, the admissibility of subsequent declarations is far more restrictive: *Shephard* v. *Cartwright* [1955] AC 431, 445 (HL); *Lavelle* v. *Lavelle* [2004] EWCA Civ 223, [19]; *Pang Siu Hing* v. *Tsang Kwok Man*, n.74 above, [12]–[15]; *Antoni* v. *Antoni* [2007] UKPC 10, [20]; *Ben Hashem* v. *Al Shayif*, n.77 above, [114]. See also *Standing* v. *Bowring* (1885) 31 Ch. D 282; *Aroso* v. *Coutts & Co.*, n.46 above, [35].

[86] Ibid., [60]–[61]. See also *Re Walker Estate* [2005] PESCTD 63, [25]; *Doucette* v. *Doucette Estate*, n.81 above, [16]–[17]. English decisions have indicated that these documents may only be useful in determining the parties to, and terms of, the bank-joint account holder relationship, but may be of limited assistance in determining the rights of the joint account holders *inter se*: *Aroso* v. *Coutts & Co.*, n.46 above, [33]; *Sillett* v.

joint account, although this will rarely be determinative;[87] any power of attorney granted by the transferor to the transferee, although 'the courts should use caution in relying upon it';[88] and evidence of the joint account's tax treatment.[89] Accordingly, the deceased account holder's intention in depositing funds into a joint account ultimately depends upon a careful assessment of the facts.[90]

An important example of the presumption of advancement being rebutted is *Marshal v. Crutwell*,[91] in which a terminally-ill husband transferred his personal account balance to a new account opened in the joint names of himself and his wife, which entitled either party to draw cheques on the account. Before the husband's death, the cheques drawn by the wife were done so at the husband's direction and related primarily to household expenses. Following his death, a dispute arose between the widow, as the surviving account holder, and the husband's remaining heirs over the joint account's credit balance. Although the presumption of advancement operated in favour of the widow, Jessel MR held that this was rebutted by evidence that the purpose behind the joint account was simply to provide a convenient method for managing the husband's affairs during his illness. Accordingly, the husband did not intend a gift to his wife during his lifetime, so that the husband's estate was beneficially entitled to the account. A similar result, although without the assistance of presumptions, was reached more recently in *Sillett v. Meek*,[92] in which the deceased had opened a joint account in the names of herself and her lifelong friend. Michael Furness QC concluded that on the evidence 'the joint account was a matter of administrative convenience' and that no gift was intended.[93] On the other side of the line are those cases where the deceased account holder intended to make a gift. This conclusion might result from there being sufficient evidence to rebut the presumption of resulting trust, as in *Aroso v. Coutts & Co.*,[94] which involved a joint account between an uncle and his nephew, or there being insufficient evidence to rebut the presumption of advancement, as in *Re Harrison*.[95] In this last case, a husband opened an account jointly with his wife, but did not inform her about the account or her entitlement to draw upon it. Only when the husband became ill did the branch manager provide the wife with details of the account. Following the husband's death, the wife discovered an envelope endorsed with her initials that contained the joint account deposit receipts. Moreover, the bank's ledger stated that the account was 'repayable to either or to survivor.' Russell J concluded that the husband's only possible motivation for opening the account was to gift the funds

---

Meek, n.72 above, [40]. The Singaporean position appears somewhat stronger: *Lim Chen Yeow Kelvin v. Goh Chin Peng*, n.73 above, [117]–[121]; *Lau Siew Kim v. Yeo Guan Chye Terence*, n.76 above, [108].

[87] Ibid., [62]–[66]. See also *Madsen Estate v. Saylor*, n.46 above, [19].   [88] Ibid., [67]–[68].

[89] Ibid, [69]–[70]. See also *Madsen Estate v. Saylor*, n.46 above, [19]; *Tarling v. Tarling*, n.81 above , [117].

[90] It may be significant that either party is entitled to draw on the account: *Palmer v. Bank of New South Wales*, n.44 above, 675.

[91] (1875) LR 20 Eq. 328. See also *Husband v. Davis* (1851) 10 CB 645; *Williams v. Davies* (1864) 3 Sw. & Tr. 547; *Re Potter* (1926) 39 OWN 327, 328; *McLean v. Vessey*, n.75 above; *Saarnok Estate v. Neufeld*, n.72 above, [100]; *Legg v. Nicholson*, n.75 above, [19]–[20]; *Sillett v. Meek*, n.72 above; *St. Onge Estate v. Breau* [2008] NBQB 117, [53]; *Tiedeman v. Tiedeman*, n.67 above, [23].

[92] N.72 above, [33], [54].

[93] Ibid., [53]. See also *Cheung Cho Kam Sindy v. Cheung Yuet Ying Rose*, n.74 above, [68].

[94] N.46 above, [35]. See also *Re Harvey Estate*, n.67 above, [74]; *Stadnyk Estate v. Hrycan*, n.70 above, [18]; *Hood Estate v. Young*, n.75 above, [20]; *Tarling v. Tarling*, n.81 above, [119]; *Lim Chen Yeow Kelvin v. Goh Chin Peng*, n.73 above, [106]; *Down Estate v. Racz-Down* [2009] OJ No. 5537, [79]–[110].

[95] (1920) 90 LJ Ch. 186. See also *Young v. Sealey* [1949] Ch. 278, 295; *Re Bishop decd., National Provincial Bank Ltd v. Bishop*, n.21 above; *Re Figgis*, n.73 above. See further *Re Reid* (1921) 50 Ont. LR 595; *Re Potter*, n.91 above; *Niles v. Lake*, n.46 above; *Re Cameron*, n.25 above, 405; *Kogler v. Schabernig Estate*, n.64 above, [51]; *Cooke v. Cooke Estate* [2005] BCCA 263, [14]; *Low Geok Khim v. Low Geok Bian*, n.81 above, [60].

to his wife during his lifetime, with her taking on his death by survivorship. Accordingly, she was legally and beneficially entitled to the joint account funds.

(c) Bare right of survivorship[96]

In the preceding paragraphs, it has been assumed that the beneficial entitlement of the surviving account holder(s) depends upon the deceased account holder's intention to make a gift *during his lifetime* of the *chose in action* representing the right to demand the joint account balance. Even if the evidence, or the presumption of resulting trust, points against such an intention, and instead supports the conclusion that the deceased account holder intended to retain the full control of, and beneficial interest in, the right to the funds *during his lifetime*, it is nevertheless possible for the surviving account holder(s) to acquire the beneficial interest in the account *upon the deceased's death*.[97] This is achieved by one account holder conferring a *bare right of survivorship* upon the other account holder, whilst retaining the entire beneficial interest to the chose in action representing the funds during his lifetime.[98] Usually a standard-form clause to this effect is inserted into the joint account mandate form, but this may equally be inferred from the deceased account holder's intentions. The Supreme Court of Canada in *Pecore* v. *Pecore*[99] recognized that this type of arrangement is frequently made to avoid fees or taxes upon death or 'to make after-death disposition to the transferee less cumbersome and time consuming'. The difficulty with such a bare right of survivorship, however, is that it appears to involve a transfer of property upon death to the surviving account holder(s) that is not in proper testamentary form.[100] This difficulty was, however, rejected in *Pecore* by Rothstein J, who considered that 'the rights of survivorship, both legal and equitable, vest when the joint account is opened and the gift of those rights is therefore *inter vivos* in nature'.[101] Interestingly, his Honour expressed the view that the transfer of a bare right of survivorship underlay the decision in *Russell* v. *Scott*,[102] in which an old lady opened an account jointly with her favourite nephew. During the aunt's lifetime, the joint account was utilized solely for her own purposes, although she informed her solicitors that the nephew was to take the account as survivor. The High Court of Australia held that the nephew acquired both the legal and the beneficial entitlement to the joint account balance upon his aunt's death.

There are also English examples of a deceased account holder retaining the legal and beneficial entitlement to a joint account during his lifetime, whilst conferring a bare right of survivorship on the other account holder(s). In *O'Neill* v. *Inland Revenue Commissioners*,[103] the issue concerned the inheritance tax chargeable on an account that the deceased account holder had opened jointly with his minor daughter. The tax liability depended upon whether the daughter had any beneficial interest in the rights over the joint account during her father's lifetime. The Special Commissioner concluded that the

---

[96] The principle under consideration is distinct from the *donatio mortis causa*, as it does not depend upon any transfer of the 'indicia of title': *Young* v. *Sealey*, n.95 above. See further Ch. 9, Sect. 4(iv) below.

[97] *Edgar* v. *Commissioner of Inland Revenue*, n.40 above, 607. In cases like *Edgar*, the surviving account holder would be accountable to the deceased account holder's estate for withdrawals made before his death: *New Zealand Guardian Trust Co. Ltd* v. *Jury* [1998] DCR 190.

[98] *Standing* v. *Bowring*, n.85 above, 287; *Edwards* v. *Bradley* [1956] OR 225, 234 (OCA); *Trustees of Cho Ki Tau Trust* v. *Yau Estate* (1999) 29 ETR (2d) 204, [25].

[99] N.45 above, [47].   [100] Ibid., [48].

[101] Id. See also *Re Reid*, n.95 above, 608; *Edwards* v. *Bradley*, n.98 above, 234; *Reber* v. *Reber* (1988) 48 DLR (4th) 376 (BCSC); *Shaw* v. *MacKenzie Estate* (1994) 4 ETR (2d) 306, [49] (NSSC); *Mordo* v. *Nitting* [2006] BCSC 1761, [233]–[238].

[102] N.40 above.   [103] N.38 above.

presumption of advancement was 'rebutted so far as the beneficial interest in the joint accounts during the deceased's lifetime is concerned', and that the father's real intention in opening the account was to evade the tax authorities and hide the account funds from his estranged wife. Indeed, as the daughter had never been informed of the account's existence, there was no indication that the father had intended to confer any rights on his daughter during his lifetime. Nevertheless, the Special Commissioner concluded that the deceased account holder 'intended the earlier provision by way of the joint accounts to operate as a "legacy" only, through survivorship'. As authority for 'the proposition that a joint tenancy not carrying a beneficial entitlement during the joint lives may nevertheless be succeeded by sole beneficial entitlement in the survivor by survivorship' he cited *Russell* v. *Scott*,[104] considered above, and *Young* v. *Sealey*.[105] More recently, this proposition has received further support from dicta in *Aroso* v. *Coutts & Co.*,[106] where Lawrence Collins J (as he then was) indicated that he would have applied the reasoning in *Russell* and *Sealey* had the case before him been argued on that basis.

3 Partnership accounts

(i) Opening and operating a partnership account

In formal terms, a partnership account is distinguishable from a joint account as it is opened in the single name of the firm, rather than in multiple names,[107] although the distinction cannot always be so neatly drawn in every case.[108] In *Fried* v. *National Australia Bank Ltd*,[109] Gray J explained that distinction as follows:

> It is true that joint and several liability of the partners is at the heart of the concept of partnership. It is also true that a partnership does not have its own legal personality, as does a natural person or a corporation.... Despite the absence of legal personality, a partnership is often regarded as a trading entity. The notion of the firm as a trading entity is not at all foreign to the law. The widespread use of a firm name as the name in which a partnership trades reinforces the notion that it is trading as a single entity. From the bank's point of view, when it deals with a firm of solicitors, it deals with a single entity.... the ordinary meaning of the phrase 'joint account' does not include an account opened in the name of a firm, or of an unincorporated association. An account opened in a single name, whether a firm name or the name of an unincorporated association is to be regarded as something other than a joint account. A joint account is one opened in a combination of names, whether of natural persons, corporate persons, firms or unincorporated associations. The essence of such an account is that the entitlement to the debt constituted by the account is held jointly by the combination of entities in whose name the account is opened. In the case of a firm, from the bank's point of view, there is only one entity entitled to the debt constituted by the account. The entity so entitled is the firm. How the entitlement would be adjusted as between the partners is a matter that does not concern the bank.

From the bank's perspective, this formal difference has practical consequences. In relation to a partnership account, the bank will only ever receive instructions from persons acting in a representative capacity, so banks should take steps to verify the scope of that

---

[104] N.40 above.   [105] N.95 above, 284, 295.   [106] N.46 above, [29]–[31], [36].
[107] *Belfast Telegraph Newspapers Ltd* v. *Blunden*, n.10 above.
[108] *Rees* v. *Dartnell* [2009] All ER (D) 244 (account held in partners' joint names).
[109] [2001] FCA 907.

person's authority to act. In relation to a joint account, a bank may only act upon instructions from the designated account holder(s) and accordingly need only verify the identity of the instructing party, rather than their authority to act. In substance, however, partnership and joint accounts resemble one another in that more than one person is ultimately entitled to the credit balance.[110] This is a consequence of the partnership not having a separate legal personality like a company. In contrast, a limited liability partnership will hold an account in its own name and will be entitled to the credit balance in its own right, as it has a separate legal personality from its members.[111] As partnership law only applies to limited liability partnerships to the extent that express statutory provision is made for this,[112] these entities probably have more in common with companies and will accordingly be considered further in the context of corporate accounts.[113]

In traditional partnerships, each partner is his firm's agent[114] and is therefore entitled to open an account on its behalf. Moreover, a partner is generally entitled to operate the partnership's account in his own right,[115] to draw cheques in the firm's name,[116] and to close the account if desired.[117] A partner's actual authority to bind the firm is, however, limited to acts 'for the purpose of the business of the partnership'.[118] Accordingly, a partner has no actual authority to withdraw funds from the account for his personal use or as part of a fraud perpetrated on the firm,[119] although the partner may potentially have ostensible authority to act in this way if the partnership has held the partner out to the bank as being so authorized.[120] A bank that permits such unauthorized withdrawals will be required to re-credit the partnership account. Nor does a partner have actual authority to deposit cheques into the partnership account to which the partnership has no entitlement,[121] with the result that the bank cannot generally seek an indemnity or contribution from the partnership if found liable for converting the cheque.[122] Similarly, in *Alliance Bank Ltd* v. *Kearsley*,[123] as the partner did not have authority to maintain a firm account in his *personal* name, the other partners were not liable to reimburse the bank for losses in respect of that account, even though it was used solely for the partnership's purposes. It may be wondered whether *Kearsley* is entirely supportable, however, given that the partnership would have been liable on an account opened in the *firm*'s name. The distinction seems incredibly fine. Either way, it is frequently the case that the partnership agreement abrogates the rights conferred upon partners by the Partnership Act 1890 to operate the firm's account. Nowadays, partnership agreements usually provide that a firm's account must be opened and operated by all the partners jointly or by two or more

---

[110] Partnership Act 1890 (PA 1890), s.24(1). The partners' rights over the account balance in a partnership account are joint and several: *Chartered Bank* v. *Yong Chan*, n.10 above, 159–160. Compare Sect. 2(ii) above. The *Hirschorn* principle (n.10 above) is applicable to partnership accounts: *Belfast Telegraph Newspapers Ltd* v. *Blunden*, n.10 above; cf. Civil Procedure Rules 1998 (CPR 1998), Part 72 Practice Direction, [3A.1–3A.3].

[111] Limited Liability Partnerships Act 2000 (LLPA 2000), s.1(2).   [112] Ibid., s.1(5).

[113] Limited Liability Partnerships (Application of Companies Act 2006) Regulations 2009, S.I. 2009/1804. See further Sect. 10 below.

[114] PA 1890, ss. 5–6.

[115] Id. There may be disputes as to whether funds deposited into the partnership account constitute a loan or a capital contribution: *Tannu* v. *Moosajee* [2003] EWCA Civ 815.

[116] *Laws* v. *Rand* (1857) 3 CB (NS) 442; *Backhouse* v. *Charlton* (1878) 8 Ch D 444.

[117] PA 1890, s. 5.   [118] Id.   [119] *Fried* v. *National Australia Bank Ltd*, n.109 above.   [120] Id.

[121] *National Commercial Banking Corporation of Australia Ltd* v. *Batty* (1986) 65 ALR 385, 390–391 (HCA).

[122] Ch. 15, Sect. 7 below.

[123] (1871) LR 6 CP 433, approved in *Pembinaan Thin Chai Sdn Bhd* v. *Citra Muda Sdn Bhd* [2002] 3 MLJ 107 [23] (MHC).

partners together.[124] As such provisions are commonplace, a bank that is asked to open an account in a partnership's name should probably consult the partnership agreement[125] and ideally require an authority executed by all the partners.

An example of how important it is for banks to verify the scope of a partner's authority is provided by *Forster* v. *Mackreth*,[126] in which a partner indorsed bills of exchange on behalf of the firm and drew post-dated cheques in the firm's name. The Court of Exchequer held that the other partners were not liable on the instruments. According to Martin B, as dealing in bills of exchange was not a type of business in which a legal partnership would be expected to engage, the indorsements were not within the partner's authority. Similarly, although the partner had authority to draw cheques on the partnership account, this did not extend to issuing post-dated cheques, even though these were drawn with the aim of raising finance for the firm by means of the cheques being discounted. It is doubtful whether Martin B's decision concerning the post-dated cheques would be followed today, since his Lordship's conclusion (together with that of Kelly CB)[127] was based in part upon treating a post-dated cheque as a term bill of exchange, which accordingly fell outside the partnership's business.[128] Nowadays, post-dated cheques are treated as being valid and regular cheques on their face.[129] Indeed, in *Guildford Trust Ltd* v. *Goss*,[130] cheques drawn by one partner and indorsed by another were valid cheques in the hands of the 'holder', despite their having been post-dated when he took them. Putting this narrow issue to one side, however, the general principle that emerges from *Mackreth* is likely to stand the test of time—a partner's ability to bind his firm and his co-partners depends upon the scope of his authority, which will vary from firm to firm. Accordingly, if the partnership in *Mackreth* had carried on the business of banking, it may have been held bound by the partner's indorsement of the bills of exchange.[131]

(ii) Borrowing through a partnership's account

A partner of a commercial or 'trading firm'[132] has the authority to raise credit and make arrangements for an overdraft.[133] As a necessary incident of this authority, the partner has

---

[124] Where the account mandate requires two signatures, it is inadequate for just one partner to sign on behalf of himself and the other partners, even if authorized: *Laws* v. *Rand*, n.116 above. As regards a cheque payable to a partnership being deposited in a partner's personal account, see *Souhrada* v. *Bank of New South Wales* [1976] 2 Lloyd's Rep. 444 (NSWSC).

[125] Australian banking practice is to the contrary, so as to avoid being fixed with notice of the partnership agreement's content: A. Tyree & P. Weaver, n.10 above, [21.101].

[126] (1867) LR 2 Ex. 163. See also *Bank of Baroda Ltd* v. *Punjab National Bank Ltd* [1944] AC 176 (PC).

[127] Ibid., 167.   [128] Ibid., 166.

[129] *Hodgson & Lee Pty Ltd* v. *Mardonius Pty Ltd* (1986) 78 ALR 573, 577. See also *Canadian Bank of Commerce* v. *Brash* (1957) 10 DLR (2d) 555, 556–557; *Canadian Imperial Bank of Commerce* v. *Burman* (1979) 38 NSR (2d) 262, 268, citing *Canadian Bank of Commerce* v. *Brash*, above, 556–557. See further Ch. 10, Sect. 3(iv) below.

[130] (1927) 136 LT 725. See also *Hodgson & Lee Pty Ltd* v. *Mardonius Pty Ltd*, n.129 above, 575.

[131] Cf. *Bank of Baroda Ltd* v. *Punjab National Bank Ltd*, n.126 above, 192–193.

[132] *Higgins* v. *Beauchamp* [1914] 3 KB 1192, 1195 (partnership operating cinema was not a 'trading firm'), approved in *R* v. *Trade Practices Tribunal, ex p St. George County Council* (1973–1974) 2 ALR 371, 399 (HCA). For a solicitor's authority to bind his firm to a transaction involving the granting of a security, see *United Bank of Kuwait Ltd* v. *Hammoud* [1988] 1 WLR 1051 (CA). See also *Hirst* v. *Etherington*, The Times, 21 July 1999 (CA); *Ruparell* v. *Anwan* [2001] 3 Lloyd's Rep PN 258, 262, 264–266; *Antonelli* v. *Allen* [2001] Lloyd's Rep PN 487, [75]–[76]; *Twinsectra Ltd* v. *Yardley* [2002] 2 AC 164, [15], [56] (HL); *JJ Coughlan Ltd* v. *Ruparelia* [2003] EWCA Civ 1057, [20].

[133] *Bank of Australasia* v. *Breillat* (1847) 6 Moore PC 152, 193 (PC); *Brown* v. *Kidger* (1858) 28 LJ Ex 66; *Goldberg* v. *Jenkins* (1889) 15 VLR 36; *Chop Cheong Tuck* v. *Chop Tack Loong* [1934] 1 MLJ 176, 177–178.

authority to grant security for any relevant loan.[134] In contrast, a partner in a 'professional firm', such as a law firm or medical practice, is unlikely to be authorized to borrow on the firm's behalf.[135] Usually, such a partnership will only enter a loan transaction when all the partners agree.

(iii) Dissolution of a partnership by death

The doctrine of survivorship, considered above in relation to joint accounts, is inapplicable to partnership accounts. Unless the partnership agreement provides otherwise, the firm is dissolved upon the death of any partner,[136] although the surviving partners have authority to continue the firm in order to wind up its affairs.[137] It would appear that a bank is not obliged to scrutinize the surviving partners' actions particularly carefully, but may assume that they are acting within their statutory authority. In *Backhouse v. Charlton*,[138] a father-and-son partnership instructed its bank that each partner was entitled to draw on the partnership account, both during and after the father's lifetime. After his father's death, the son, as surviving partner, continued to draw cheques on the partnership account and pay the proceeds into his personal account with the same bank. Malins V-C concluded that the bank was not liable to the father's estate and that the bank was entitled to honour cheques drawn by the son as surviving partner. His Lordship held that a bank was not required to make any enquiry concerning the payment of the cheques drawn by the surviving partner on the partnership account. Indeed, far from being under a duty to investigate, the bank was bound to honour the relevant cheques.[139] Similarly, in *Re Bourne*,[140] after a partnership was dissolved by a partner's death, the remaining partner continued the firm's bank account as part of winding up its affairs. As the partnership account was overdrawn, and a further increase in the overdraft was required, the surviving partner deposited with the bank some title deeds as security. The principal issue concerned whether the bank or the deceased partner's executors had priority over these deeds. Giving judgment for the bank, Romer LJ observed that the surviving partner had the power to give a good title to purchasers and mortgagees, and that third parties dealing with the surviving partner were entitled to assume that he was acting in good faith and within the scope of his authority to liquidate the partnership. His Lordship said:[141]

> When you find an account of that kind continued—and here it is only continued for something like nine months before the charge is given—the bankers...are entitled, in the absence of evidence shewing the contrary, to assume and to be credited with the belief that the surviving partner is continuing it for the purpose of realization, and that sums paid

---

An agreement that a partner will only pay his 'share' of overdraft borrowings can be binding: *Collier v. P&MJ Wright (Holdings) Ltd* [2007] BPIR 1452 (CA).

[134]   *Bank of Scotland* v. *Henry Butcher & Co.* [2003] 1 BCLC 575, [38]–[46], [90]–[93] (CA).
[135]   *Higgins* v. *Beauchamp*, n.132 above.
[136]   PA 1890, s.33(1). See further *Patel* v. *Patel* [2007] EWCA Civ 1520, [3]. This principle is inapplicable to limited liability partnerships: LLPA 2000, s.7.
[137]   Ibid., s.38. See also *Sandhu* v. *Gill* [2005] EWHC 43 (Ch), [11]–[15]; *Duncan* v. *The MFV Marigold PD145* 2007 SCLR 155, [19]–[21] (OH); *HLB Kidsons* v. *Lloyd's Underwriters Subscribing Policy* [2008] EWHC 2415 (Comm.).
[138]   N.116 above.
[139]   A bank may breach its duty of care to the surviving partners or the deceased partner's estate if it honours cheques with notice of a fraud being perpetrated on the partnership account: Ch. 5, Sect. 4(iii) above. A similar principle operates between joint account holders: *Fielding* v. *Royal Bank of Scotland plc*, n.29 above. See also *Consul Development Pty Ltd* v. *DPC Estates Pty Ltd* (1974–1975) 5 ALR 231 (HCA).
[140]   [1906] 2 Ch. 427 (CA). See *Newcombe* v. *Chapple* (NSWSC, 27 February 1985).   [141]   Ibid., 433.

into that account and sums drawn out of that account in the name of the partnership are paid in and drawn out for the purpose of the partnership.

(iv) Problems of insolvency

A partnership is dissolved by the firm's insolvency or the bankruptcy of a partner.[142] If, prior to the bankruptcy's commencement, the partner in question has incurred any debts in the partnership's name, the other partners are jointly and severally liable.[143] After his adjudication, the insolvent partner cannot bind the partnership. An interesting issue arose in *Watts* v. *Christie*,[144] in which a partnership's account was overdrawn, whilst the personal account of one of the partners with the same bank was in credit. When the bank failed, the partner assigned his personal credit balance to the partnership so as to facilitate a set-off of this credit balance against the partnership's debit balance on its account. The advantage of such a set-off was that the firm would be able to prove for the net credit balance in the bank's liquidation, and would avoid having to repay its overdraft to the trustee in bankruptcy. Lord Langdale MR held that the partner's purported assignment was ineffective. The bank did not have a valid lien on the personal account of the partner in respect of debts incurred by the firm. Thus, the two accounts had to be kept apart; the bank could not have combined the two.[145] It followed that it was too late by the time of the bank's liquidation for the individual partner to effect a set-off by means of an assignment. Effectively, the two account balances had crystallized at the time of the liquidation's commencement.

4 Executors' accounts

An account opened by executors or administrators constitutes an account of the estate. The executors are the estate's representatives and, unlike partners, have no personal interest in the estate's account or its property. As each executor is the estate's agent, he is not only entitled to open accounts in the estate's name, but is also entitled to countermand cheques drawn on that account, whether drawn by himself or another executor.[146] Banks will usually insist that the mandate for the operation of the estate's account is spelt out in indisputable terms, particularly with respect to the drawing of cheques. Ordinarily, each cheque should be signed by at least two executors to minimize the possibility of funds being misappropriated.

As with partnership accounts, one difficulty that arises with executors' accounts relates to whether or not the deceased's business can be carried on. In some cases, the will confers on the executors the power to continue the deceased's business, either for a specified period or for such period as they consider advisable. In such circumstances, the executors have both the power to conduct the business and the required incidental or complementary powers, such as borrowing for the purposes of the business and giving security over the estate's assets in respect of such loans.[147] Even with such express powers, however, the

---

[142] PA 1890, ss.33, 38. Insolvency Act 1986 governs the insolvency procedures involving limited liability partnerships: LLPA 2000, s.14(1). See also Limited Liability Partnerships Regulations 2001, S.I. 2001/1090, reg. 5(1) & Sched. 3 (as amended by S.I. 2005/1989, 2007/2073, and 2009/1833).

[143] Usually, this is expressly provided in the partnership account mandate forms.

[144] (1849) 11 Beav. 546.   [145] Ch. 7, Sect. 4 above.   [146] *Gaunt* v. *Taylor* (1843) 2 Hare 413.

[147] *Devitt* v. *Kearney* (1883) 13 LR Ir. 45, applied in *Commissioner of Inland Revenue* v. *Smith's Executors* [1950–1951] NI 88, 94–95. See also *Southwell* v. *Martin* (1901) 1 SR (NSW) Eq. 32; *Re Hammond* (1903) 3

bank would nevertheless be well advised to examine carefully any request on the part of the estate for an overdraft or loan. Indeed, if the bank decides to make such facilities available, it should ensure that the deceased's creditors have already been paid, or have given their approval to the transaction, otherwise the existing creditors may have priority over the bank as regards the estate's assets.[148] Such steps may be easier to state in theory than to adopt in practice, however, as banks will not wish to become involved in the details of the estate's administration. An alternative solution for the bank may, therefore, be to obtain the executors' personal assurance regarding the purpose of any overdraft or loan facility, so that the bank may recover against the executors personally in defined circumstances. Should the executors be unwilling or unable to give the required undertaking, the bank may nevertheless recover against the estate's creditors if it can rely on a possessory security. In *Berry* v. *Gibbons*,[149] an executrix pledged to the bank a picture belonging to the estate to secure a bank overdraft. At the time that the bank granted the overdraft, it was unaware that administration proceedings had already been successfully instituted against the executrix shortly before the transaction, thereby determining the executrix's appointment. As no receiver had been appointed when the pledge was granted, the bank was entitled to enforce its security. It is questionable, however, whether the bank could have enforced a non-possessory security, such as a floating charge or a bill of sale, in such circumstances.

If no provision is made in the will for the continuation of the testator's business, the basic statutory rule is that the executors can carry on the business for the purpose of winding up the estate, but they are not entitled to maintain it as a going concern.[150] The executors are additionally given the required incidental powers to perform their duties,[151] including the power to borrow and furnish security. If the executor exceeds his powers, he is answerable in his personal capacity;[152] but if he acts within his authority, he is not liable even if his decision eventually causes loss to the estate.[153] The resulting position will be largely the same as discussed in the previous paragraph.

5 Trust accounts

(i) General principles

Trust accounts are opened mainly by executors under a will, and by persons, such as solicitors or trust companies, who administer family or charitable trusts.[154] A trust is not a separate legal entity from its trustees. Broadly, the trustees have the legal title to the

SR (NSW) 270. A grant of security is effective provided the executor remained within his general authority: *Attenborough* v. *Solomon* [1913] AC 76 (HL), applied *In re Cunliffe-Owen* [1953] Ch 545, 558–559 (CA); *Booty* v. *Hutton* (1999) 140 Man R (2d) 186, [19]–[21]; *White* v. *Shortall* [2006] NSWSC 1379, [172]. See also the Trustee Act 2000, ss.17–18.

[148] *Berry* v. *Gibbons* (1873) LR 8 Ch. App. 747 (CA).

[149] Ibid. See also *In re Viscount Furness* [1943] Ch 415, 420–421.

[150] Administration of Estates Act 1925, ss.25, 39–40 (as amended by the Trusts of Land and Appointment of Trustees Act 1996 (TLATA 1996), s.25(1)). See also *Marshall* v. *Broadhurst* (1831) 1 C & J 403; *Edwards* v. *Grace* (1826) 2 M & W 190; *Kirkman* v. *Booth* (1848) 11 Beav. 273; *Travis* v. *Milne* (1851) 9 Hare 141, 151–152; *Farhall* v. *Farhall* (1871) LR 7 Ch. App. 123; *Flower* v. *Pretchel* [1934] All ER Rep 810, 812 (CA); *Re Rooke, Rooke* v. *Rooke* [1953] Ch. 176, 723. For the Australian position, see *Re Kerrigan* [1916] VLR 516.

[151] Ibid., ss.39–40. See also TLATA 1996, s.6(1) (as amended).

[152] Cf. *Farhall* v. *Farhall*, n.150 above.   [153] *Garret* v. *Noble* (1834) 6 Sim. 504.

[154] Consider *Brazill* v. *Willoughby* [2009] EWHC 1633 (Ch).

trust property—a chose in action in the case of a trust account—whilst the beneficiary of the trust has an equitable interest.[155] As the trustees have only legal title to the trust property, there are no difficulties with the issue of survivorship when a trustee dies. Section 18 of the Trustee Act 1925 authorizes the surviving trustee(s) (or their personal representative) to carry on the business of the trust for the time being, until another person is appointed trustee whether under the provisions of a will or by the court. This would probably entitle the surviving trustee(s) (or their personal representative) to draw cheques on the trust's account.

The trustees' function is to administer the trust assets in accordance with the trust deed appointing them. In addition to the powers conferred by the trust deed, the trustees also have the powers conferred by the Trustee Acts 1925 and 2000. Usually a trust deed requires the appointment of two or more trustees, so as to ensure that the trust property is under the control of more than one person. Consequently, trustees were not previously permitted to delegate their authority,[156] so that, unless the trust deed provided to the contrary, a cheque drawn on a trust account required all the trustees to sign it.[157] Nowadays, however, trustees can delegate, even to a sole trustee,[158] all but a few non-delegable functions, namely the power to appoint trustees, the power to decide whether a particular payment should be made out of income or capital, and 'any function relating to whether or in what way any assets of the trust should be distributed'.[159] It is unclear whether the last of these non-delegable functions includes the mechanics by which payment is effected. If so, then a trustee may still not be able to delegate the task of signing cheques on behalf of the trust, even under the Trustee Act 2000, although this result could probably be achieved by the relevant trustee executing a power of attorney.[160]

(ii) Borrowings by trustees

A trustee is entitled to 'make any kind of investment',[161] which includes depositing trust money in a bank account. Their right to borrow for the trust's purposes is, however, restricted. Under section 16 of the Trustee Act 1925, where the trustees are authorized either by law or under the trust deed to 'pay or apply capital money subject to the trust for any purpose or in any manner', they are deemed to have the power to raise the required amount by 'sale, conversion, calling in or mortgage of all or any part of the trust property'. Where the trustees have the power to mortgage, they also have the complementary power to borrow. There are specific statutory provisions entitling the trustees to borrow money in given cases;[162] and, in certain situations, the power is spelt out in the trust deed. In addition, there is support for the view that trustees have the power to borrow for the purpose of the trust's business.[163] Under section 17 of the Trustee Act 1925, a purchaser or mortgagee who pays or advances money to the trust in reliance on the powers vested in the trustees by law or under the trust deed, is not 'concerned to see that such money is wanted, or that no more than is wanted is raised, or [concerned] otherwise as to the application thereof'. Creditors and *bona fide* purchasers are, therefore, protected provided that they

---

[155] See generally P.H. Pettit, *Equity and the Law of Trusts* (11th edn., Oxford, 2009), ch. 2.

[156] *Re Flower and Metropolitan Board of Works* (1884) 27 Ch. D 592; *Green* v. *Whitehead* [1930] 1 Ch. 38 (CA), affd. on different grounds: [1930] 1 Ch 38; *McLellan Properties Ltd* v. *Roberge* [1946] OR 379, 384 (OCA); *Hotung* v. *Ho Yuen Ki* [2002] 4 HKC 233, [11] (HKCA).

[157] *Green* v. *Whitehead*, n.156 above.   [158] Trustee Act 2000, s.25.   [159] Ibid., s.11.

[160] Trustee Act 1925, s.25, as substituted by the Trustee Delegation Act 1999, s.5, which contains a wider power of delegation by means of a power of attorney than contained in the Trustee Act 2000.

[161] Trustee Act 2000, s.3(1).   [162] Trustee Act 1925, ss.16, 28.

[163] *Dowse* v. *Gorton* [1891] AC 190 (HL); *Re Elijah Murphy Estate* (1930) 4 LDAB 328.

ensure that the transaction falls within the scope of the trustee's formal authority. One might question, however, the extent to which this same provision can provide the trust's own bank with a general immunity,[164] since the bank may in certain circumstances be subject to fiduciary duties owed to its customer,[165] or may be liable for knowingly receiving trust property or dishonestly assisting in a breach of trust.[166] The bank's position in this regard is considered in the next section.

(iii) **Position of banks operating trust accounts**

The fact that a bank holds funds in a trust account for its customer can create two difficulties for the bank. First, as considered previously,[167] a bank cannot in general exercise its right of combination in respect of a trust account. In *Re Gross, ex p. Kingston*,[168] an official maintained two accounts with his bank: his personal account and another account marked 'Police Account'. The official absconded whilst his personal account was overdrawn and the 'Police Account' was in credit. The Court of Appeal held that the bank could not combine the two accounts. Mellish LJ said that 'if an account is in plain terms headed in such a way that a banker cannot fail to know it to be a trust account, the balance standing to the credit of that account will, on the bankruptcy of the person who kept it, belong to the trust'.[169] Even an account that is not expressly marked or headed in a manner that proclaims its purpose may be treated as a trust account if there are specific circumstances alerting the bank to that fact, such as the bank's familiarity with the will under which the trustees have opened the account.[170] The governing principle was recently stated by Lord Clarke in *Devron Potatoes Ltd* v. *Gordon & Innes Ltd*:[171] '...as from the point in time when a bank becomes aware that the funds paid into the client's account...are only held by the [payer] in a fiduciary capacity, they have no right to set off funds against sums due to them by their customer under other accounts'. In this regard, the knowledge of a bank officer acquired within the scope of his employment will be imputed to the bank. Conversely, in *Saudi Arabian Monetary Agency* v. *Dresdner Bank AG*,[172] the Court of Appeal stressed that a bank could exercise a right of combination against a trust account's credit balance when it had clear and indisputable evidence that the beneficiary of that account was a customer who was overdrawn on their personal account with the bank.

Secondly, by agreeing to lend to trustees or to honour a cheque on a trust account, the bank runs the risk that, even unwittingly, it may have assisted a trustee in carrying out an inappropriate transaction. In this regard, it is important to distinguish between claims brought by the estate's or trust's creditors and claims by the trust's beneficiaries. The necessity for the bank to have regard to creditor interests only generally arises where the trustee is acting as an executor, although given the narrow line of demarcation between executors, trustees, and administrators, it would be unwise for the bank to limit its checks to executor accounts alone. In such circumstances, as considered previously,[173] the bank should ensure that the estate's creditors have been paid or have given their approval to any subsequent bank loan to the executors. A bank need only concern itself, however, with the deceased's initial creditors, as debts incurred by the executors/trustees in winding up the estate are not entitled to preference. The bank's liability to the trust's beneficiaries rests on a different basis, however, as these are specifically protected by equity. Frequently, this is

---

[164] Trustee Act 1925, s.17. See also *City of London Building Society* v. *Flegg* [1988] AC 54, 71, 78–79 (HL).

[165] Ch. 5, Sect. 4(i), above.   [166] Ch. 7, Sect. 5 above.   [167] Ch. 7, Sect. 4(iii) above.

[168] (1871) LR 6 Ch. App. 632. See also *Royal Bank of Scotland plc* v. *Wallace International Ltd* [2000] All ER (D) 78 (CA).

[169] Ibid., 640. Cf. *Re Wall* (1885) 1 TLR 522.   [170] *Clark* v. *Ulster Bank Ltd* [1950] NI 132.

[171] 2003 SCLR 103, [27] (OH).   [172] [2005] 1 Lloyd's Rep 12, [23] (CA).   [173] Sect. 4 above.

done at the expense of innocent third parties who deal in good faith with a trustee acting fraudulently or *ultra vires*. In such circumstances, the bank is primarily at risk of being held liable to account as if a constructive trustee, where it has knowingly received trust property or dishonestly assisted in its dissipation. As considered previously,[174] a bank will only be liable on one or other of these grounds if the requisite fault element is established: unconscionability in the case of knowing receipt; and dishonesty in the case of dishonest assistance. The bank will rarely have the necessary level of fault when the proceeds of a trust, with which the bank had no particular connection, just happen to be paid into one of its customer's accounts without there being any particular indication of the funds' origin. In *Thomson v. Clydesdale Bank Ltd.*,[175] shareholders ordered their stockbroker to sell their shares. The broker paid the cheque representing the price paid for the shares into his overdrawn personal bank account. When the broker became insolvent, the bank claimed priority in respect of the cheque's proceeds. According to the evidence, the bank knew that the cheque represented the proceeds of selling shares, but did not know whether the stockbroker held the funds as agent or in his own right. Finding for the bank, the House of Lords held that the bank did not have sufficient notice of the transaction's wrongful nature to be imputed with knowledge of the stockbroker's breach of trust.

In contrast, the bank is more likely to be found liable, when the source of the misappropriated funds is a trustee or other fiduciary's account held with the bank itself. Indeed, *Thomson* may well have been decided differently if the stockbroker had initially paid the cheque into his 'clients' account' and then transferred the funds to his personal account. That said, even where funds have been misappropriated from a trust account with a particular bank, that bank is unlikely to be liable to the trust's beneficiaries unless it was aware of the nature of the account in question.[176] Such knowledge will clearly exist if the account is expressly opened and designated as a trust account. The absence of any designation that an account is a 'trust' account, does not necessarily mean, however, that the bank cannot have the requisite knowledge, since a bank may in fact know that a particular account is being used as a trust account, irrespective of its designation.[177] It would be wrong, however, to suggest that whenever a customer maintains more than one account with his bank there is a presumption that one of them must be a trust account.[178] The customer may open several accounts for the sake of convenience, such as segregating his personal transactions from those of a business carried on in his own name. Mere knowledge of the account's trust status is unlikely of itself to be sufficient, however, as the bank's primary concern when operating a trust account will be ensuring that the trustees act within their apparent powers. Thus, the bank's attention will be focused upon whether cheques drawn on the trust account bear all the requisite signatures. Accordingly, banks will not usually be liable for the trustee's misconduct unless they have sufficiently clear knowledge of the trustee's improper or fraudulent design.[179] A bank is not required to act as an amateur detective.

The most difficult type of case, however, is where a trustee pays a cheque drawn on a trust account into his personal account with the same bank. Naturally, there will be situations where a trustee acting in this way will be acting perfectly lawfully, such as

---

[174] Ch. 7, Sect. 5(iii)–(iv) above.

[175] [1893] AC 282 (HL). See also *Sinclair Investments (UK) Ltd* v. *Versailles Trade Finance Ltd* [2010] EWHC 1614 (Ch), [85]–[98], aff'd [2011] EWCA Civ 347, [109]–[122]. See further Ch. 7, Sects. 1 & 5(iv) above.

[176] *Thomson v. Clydesdale Bank Ltd*, n.175 above; *Union Bank of Australia Ltd* v. *Murray-Aynsley* [1898] AC 693 (PC); *Bank of New South Wales* v. *Goulburn Valley Butter Co. Pty. Ltd* [1902] AC 543 (PC).

[177] *New South Wales* v. *Commonwealth (No. 3)* (1932) 46 CLR 246, 265 (HCA).

[178] Ch. 7, Sect. 4(iii) above.

[179] *Re Gross, ex p. Kingston*, n.168 above, 639; *Greenwood Teale* v. *William, Williams, Brown & Co.* (1894) 11 TLR 56.

when the trust account cheque constitutes reimbursement for expenses incurred by the trustees or represents their remuneration. Equally, there are situations in which a bank is not allowed to ignore a 'red flag'. In *Gray* v. *Johnston*,[180] Lord Cairns observed that where a bank stands to benefit from the trustee's breach of trust, 'that circumstance, above all others, will most readily establish the fact that the bankers are in privity with the breach of trust'.[181] The position will be *a fortiori* when the cheque (or other type of payment) is for a large amount or the payment is made in unusual circumstances.[182] In *Foxton* v. *Manchester and Liverpool District Banking Co.*,[183] where a cheque was drawn by a trustee in order to reduce his personal overdraft, Fry J held that the bank would be liable to the trust's beneficiaries unless it could demonstrate that the relevant payment was legitimate and proper.[184] Some authorities have, however, questioned this view,[185] suggesting that the bank should only bear the onus of proof if, before the collection of the relevant cheque, the bank had struck a balance and became aware of the overdraft and pressed for payment. Nevertheless, Fry J's approach in *Foxton*, which is less generous to banks, has been followed subsequently[186] and is likely to prevail. Indeed, this appears to be the approach in *Rowlandson* v. *National Westminster Bank Ltd*,[187] where a bank was held liable to trust beneficiaries when it permitted a trustee to draw cheques on the trust account for his personal purposes. Arguably, *Rowlandson* constitutes something of an extension to *Foxton*, given that in the former case the cheque was not used to discharge an overdraft or other personal liability of the trustee to the bank.

6 Solicitors' accounts

(i) Operation of the account

The term 'clients' account' or 'solicitors' account' describes an account opened by a solicitor in order to deposit clients' money, which is held by the solicitor on trust.[188] In *Brazzill* v. *Willoughby*,[189] Peter Smith J recently identified the following features of a solicitor's clients' account:[190]

> A solicitor's client account is not a series of accounts but is one account in respect of which all clients' monies are deposited but each client's share is determined according to the amount set out in his ledger. The accounts are credited and withdrawn by reference to each individual client and there is no question (for example) of any part of the client account deposits being used for anything other than distribution as that client might nominate or decide. On that basis of course no client obtains an interest in the client account until he has sums credited in respect of it.

---

[180] (1868) LR 3 HL 1 (HL). See also *Bodeham* v. *Hoskins* (1852) 21 LJ Ch 864.   [181] Ibid., 11.

[182] Ch. 7, Sect. 5(iii) above.

[183] (1881) 44 LT 406. See also *John* v. *Dodwell & Co. Ltd* [1918] AC 563 (PC) (stockbrokers liable when cheques drawn on employer's account used to purchase shares in employee's name).

[184] Ibid., 408.

[185] *Gray* v. *Johnston*, n.180 above; *Coleman* v. *Bucks and Oxon Union Bank* [1897] 2 Ch. 243.

[186] *Attorney-General* v. *De Winton* [1906] 2 Ch. 106, 116; cf *Fulsang* v. *English Scottish and Australian Bank Ltd* [1959] Tas. SR 155 (bank only liable when it has actual knowledge of the fraudulent trustee's design).

[187] [1978] 1 WLR 798.

[188] *Twinsectra* v. *Yardley*, n.132 above, [12]; *Re Ahmed & Co.* [2006] EWHC 480 (Ch), [27]. For a picturesque description of a 'clients' account', see *Re H, a Solicitor* [1940] QWN 8.

[189] N.154 above.   [190] Ibid., [104].

Clients' accounts must be maintained as a separate fund and not commingled with the solicitors' own funds. This is the consequence of the Solicitors' Accounts Rules 1998, which are promulgated by the Law Society pursuant to its statutory powers.[191] These rules apply to all clients' accounts regardless of whether they are opened in the name of a single solicitor or in the joint names of several practitioners.[192] Although a detailed consideration of these rules is beyond this work, the broad effect of the rules are to 'require client money to be held in separate client bank accounts, prescribe the records which must be kept and the circumstances in which the solicitor is permitted to draw on client money and guard against the mixing of client money and office money'.[193] These procedures are designed to combat fraud and carelessness in the handling of the solicitors' trust funds.

From a bank's perspective, however, the most important provision relating to solicitors' accounts is section 85 of the Solicitors Act 1974, which provides that a bank is not under a duty to enquire into, and is not deemed to have any knowledge of, any right of a person to any money paid or credited to the clients' account 'which it would not incur or be under or be deemed to have in the case of an account kept by a person entitled absolutely to all the money paid or credited to it'. This may be narrower than at first sight appears, as the bank is only protected against any *additional* liability that might arise from the fact that the account is a solicitor's account, but not against any liability that would *ordinarily* arise, regardless of the nature of the account. Accordingly, section 85 does not protect banks against claims for knowing receipt or dishonest assistance.[194] Moreover, on its face, that provision deals solely with the rights of persons to money paid or credited to the account, but is silent on the bank's duties regarding amounts drawn on the account by a solicitor. One can safely presume, however, that a bank owes no general duty to the solicitor's client as regards drawings on the account.[195] Indeed, under the Solicitors Rules 1998, a solicitor is entitled to draw cheques on his clients' account. Accordingly, unless a cheque is drawn in clearly suspicious or extraordinary circumstances, the bank is not liable to the solicitor's client for a misappropriation of the funds.[196]

(ii) Third party debt orders and related problems: who owns the balance?

Occasionally, a solicitor's creditor may seek a third party debt order (formerly, a garnishee order) in respect of the credit balance of both a solicitor's personal account and his clients' account. In *Plunkett* v. *Barclays Bank Ltd*,[197] a bank froze a clients' account when a garnishee order nisi/interim third party debt order was served on it and accordingly dishonoured a cheque drawn on the account by returning it to the holder marked with the words 'refer to drawer'. In dismissing the solicitor's claims against the bank for defamation and breach of contract, Du Parcq J rejected the suggestion that 'money paid into a client account kept with a bank in the name of a solicitor is not a debt owing from the

---

[191] Solicitors Act 1974, s.32 (as amended by the Access to Justice Act 1999, Sched. 15; Legal Services Act 2007, ss. 177, 210 & Sched. 16).

[192] Ibid., s.87.   [193] *Re Ahmed & Co.*, n.188 above, [28].

[194] *Lipkin Gorman* v. *Karpnale Ltd* [1987] 1 WLR 987, 997.

[195] A bank is under a less stringent duty to heed a 'red signal' than other agents: *Penmount Estates Ltd* v. *National Provincial Bank Ltd* (1945) 173 LT 344. See also *Selangor United Rubber Estates Ltd* v. *Cradock (No. 3)* [1968] 1 WLR 1555, 1608.

[196] Ch. 5, Sect. 4(iii) above. A solicitor is accountable to his client for interest on sums deposited in the clients' account: *Brown* v. *IRC* [1965] AC 244 (HL). A bank, however, need not concern itself with this. See also Solicitors Act 1974, s.32; Solicitors' Accounts (Deposit Interest) Rules 1988.

[197] [1936] 2 KB 107. See also *Arab Bank Ltd* v. *Barclays Bank (DCO)* [1954] AC 495, 532 (HL).

banker to the solicitor'.[198] On this basis, a clients' account may be subject to a third party debt order issued by the solicitor's personal creditors. There are a number of reasons why this conclusion is questionable, and why the better view would simply be to treat the clients' account as a debt due to a third party that is unattachable by the solicitor's creditors. First, as stated above,[199] the credit balance of a clients' account constitutes trust funds that should not be available to satisfy the solicitor's personal liabilities. Secondly, as a bank is prohibited by statute from combining the credit balance on a clients' account with a debit balance on the solicitor's personal account,[200] it is unclear why other third party creditors should be given greater rights. Thirdly, allowing the clients' account to be attached in respect of a solicitor's personal liabilities is premised upon an assumption that the clients' account constitutes the solicitor's own property, yet this premise must be false if the solicitor can exercise a lien over the account in respect of amounts due for professional services.[201] Fourthly, in the context of a solicitor's bankruptcy, only the bankrupt's 'estate' vests in his trustee in bankruptcy,[202] and accordingly the 'estate' does not include property held by the bankrupt as a fiduciary or in trust for another.[203] As the credit balance of a clients' account does not vest in the solicitor's trustee in bankruptcy for the purpose of distribution to the solicitor's creditors,[204] it is difficult to justify those same creditors having greater rights pre-bankruptcy by being able to attach the clients' account. Fifthly, as the solicitor must account to his clients for the interest accrued on the clients' account,[205] the funds cannot be viewed as owned beneficially by the solicitor. Finally, once the order nisi/interim order has been served, the solicitor and bank are required to notify the court that the clients' account credit balance does not comprise his own funds.[206] Ordinarily, the court will then simply make an order protecting the clients' interest, which usually renders the account unattachable. Accordingly, the credit balance of a clients' account is best viewed as being unattachable by the solicitor's personal creditors.

7 Estate agents' accounts

Like solicitors, estate agents handle large amounts of client money. As a result, estate agents are required to maintain clients' accounts,[207] the credit balance of which constitutes trust funds.[208] For these purposes, clients' money includes money received by an estate agent in respect of the acquisition of an interest in land in the United Kingdom, regardless of whether that money is held as agent, bailee, stakeholder, or in any other

---

[198] Ibid., 118. A garnishee/third party debt order could only be made absolute over a clients' account to the extent of the solicitor's lien over the funds: *Loescher* v. *Dean* [1950] Ch. 491; *Re a Solicitor* [1952] Ch. 328.

[199] Sect. 6(i) above.   [200] Solicitors Act 1974, s.85(b).

[201] *Loescher* v. *Dean*, n.198 above, approved in *Revenue and Customs Prosecutions Office* v. *Allad* [2008] EWCA Crim 1741, [22], [37]–[39]. See also *Prekookeanska Plovidba* v. *LNT Lines Srl* [1989] 1 WLR 753, 756; *Euro Commercial Leasing Ltd* v. *Cartwright & Lewis* [1995] 2 BCLC 618, 621–622.

[202] Insolvency Act 1986, s.306(1).   [203] Ibid., s.283(3)(a).

[204] *Re a Solicitor*, n.198 above; *Re Ahmed & Co.*, n.188 above, [27].

[205] *Brown* v. *IRC*, n.196 above. See generally n.196 above.   [206] CPR 1998, r.72.8(2).

[207] Estate Agents Act 1979, s.14(1). Banks are amongst the institutions with which an estate agent's clients' account may be opened: Estate Agents (Accounts) Regulations 1981, S.I. 1981/1520, reg. 2. Although these regulations still refer to institutions covered by the Banking Act 1979, these might need to be understood nowadays as covering authorized institutions within the meaning of the Financial Services and Markets Act 2000 (FSMA 2000). The fact that these regulations were subsequently amended by S.I. 2001/1149 (without altering the reference to the Banking Act 1987) might, however, be an indication to the contrary.

[208] Ibid., s.13.

capacity.[209] To a significant extent, therefore, estate agent clients' accounts resemble solicitor clients' accounts, and the same basic legal problems arise and their solutions are broadly the same. Accordingly, if an estate agent opens an account and designates it a 'clients' account', he manifests the intention of using it to hold funds received from customers. The bank, therefore, has notice that the funds are impressed with a trust.

8 Investment businesses' accounts

As with solicitors and estate agents, investment businesses handle large amounts of clients' money that requires safeguarding. The Financial Services Authority (FSA) has the power to make rules applicable to clients' money held by authorized persons that may (a) impose a trust on clients' money (b) 'pool' accounts for the purposes of distributing the fund of clients' money equitably on the firm's insolvency, and (c) make provision for the entitlement to interest on client money.[210] The relevant rules—the 'Client Money Rules'[211]—may be found in the *FSA Handbook*. The stated purpose of the Client Money Rules is 'to protect money that customers place with a regulated firm by seeking as far as practicable to protect it from the claims of creditors in the event of a firm's insolvency and to prevent firms using client funds to finance their business'.[212] They generally[213] require the firm to keep client money in a separate bank account,[214] which must be held with a central bank, a credit institution within the Banking Consolidation Directive, a bank authorized in a third country or a 'qualifying money market fund'.[215] The Client Money Rules subject to a statutory trust any funds that are received directly from a client or a third party and deposited into a clients' money account.[216] According to Briggs J in *Re Lehman Brothers International (Europe) (No. 2)*, this statutory trust arises from the moment of the property's receipt.[217] In contrast, where a firm is required by the Client Money Rules to appropriate its own money towards the satisfaction of a client money entitlement then the firm must segregate money for its client and place this in its clients' account, in which case the statutory trust arises from the moment that funds are appropriated to the particular customer.[218] As stressed recently by Sir Andrew Park in *Re Global Trader Europe Ltd*,[219] the statutory trust is not required to comply with all the requirements for an enforceable private trust, but at the very least the clients' money in question must have been segregated so as to identify the relevant trust property.[220] Accordingly, where the firm fails to segregate funds and place them into a client account, no statutory trust can exist,[221]

---

[209] Ibid., s.12.

[210] FSMA 2000, s.139(1)–(3), replacing Financial Services Act 1986, s.55. See further Ch. 2, Sect. 4 above.

[211] Financial Services Authority (FSA) Handbook, *Business Standards*, 'Client Assets', Ch. 7 ('CASS7'). See also *Re Global Trader Europe Ltd* [2009] EWHC 602 (Ch), [34]–[41]. For the background to CASS7, see FSA, 'Protecting Client Money on the Failure of an Authorised Firm' (CP38, January 2000); FSA, 'The Conduct of Business Sourcebook Supplement' (CP58, July 2000), ch. 5. See further Ch. 2, Sect. 4(vi) above.

[212] FSA, 'Protecting Client Money on the Failure of an Authorised Firm' (CP38, January 2000). See also CASS, 7.1.16.

[213] Certain business clients may 'opt out' of the protection: CASS, 7.1.7.   [214] CASS, 7.4.1.

[215] Id. The term 'qualifying money market fund' is defined in the *Glossary* to the *FSA Handbook*.

[216] Ibid., 7.7.1–7.7.2.

[217] [2010] 2 BCLC 301, [144], [165]. See also *Re Lehman Brothers International (Europe)*; *Pearson* v. *Lehman Brothers Finance SA* [2010] EWHC 2914 (Ch), [225]–[264].

[218] Ibid., [143]–[148].   [219] N.211 above.

[220] Ibid., [91]. See also *Re Ahmed & Co.*, n.188 above, [110]–[114]. See further *Moriarty* v. *Atkinson* [2008] EWCA Civ 1604, [13]–[21]; *Brazill* v. *Willoughby*, n.154 above, [160]–[164].

[221] Ibid., [92]–[93].

although the clients may have a claim for breach of statutory duty against the firm.[222] Where the firm is insolvent, however, the client will remain an unsecured creditor in respect of such a claim.

Whatever the precise moment at which the statutory trust arises, the Client Money Rules require an authorized person to notify its bank that the clients' accounts contain trust money.[223] Accordingly, the bank is put on notice of the trust, is precluded from claiming the money, and may potentially be liable for dishonest assistance if the money is misused. That said, section 139(2) of the FSMA 2000 contains an express statutory protection for banks and provides that a bank 'does not incur any liability as constructive trustee if money is wrongfully paid from [a clients' account]' unless it permits the payment 'with knowledge that it is wrongful or having deliberately failed to make enquiries in circumstances in which a reasonable and honest person would have done so'. This may not, however, exempt a bank from liability for dishonest assistance for two reasons. First, as liability for assisting in a breach of trust is based upon dishonesty,[224] such a bank is likely to fall within the exception from statutory protection for those who know that their actions are wrongful. Secondly, liability for dishonest assistance is increasingly viewed as a form of personal, accessory liability, and not as based upon the imposition of a constructive trust at all.[225] The notion of constructive trusteeship is far more apt when the claim is based upon the bank's knowing receipt of trust property,[226] in respect of which section 139(2) of the FSMA 2000 may provide the bank with some protection. However, this provision affords protection only in respect of liability 'as constructive trustee', and therefore the bank might still be liable in contract or tort according to general principles.[227]

9 Local authorities

(i) General principles

A local authority is a corporate body with legal personality subject to the control, direction, and supervision of public officials who, together with the authority's employees, are effectively in a position of trust.[228] Generally, the local authority's functions will be discharged by a Council, Committee, or some other body of persons authorized to act on its behalf. As with an ordinary corporate customer,[229] a local authority's bank should bear in mind that, when the local authority's officers or employees enter into transactions on its behalf, their actions must fall within the authority's capacity and powers. The general position with respect to a local authority's powers can be found in section 111(1) of the Local Government Act 1972 (LGA 1972), which provides that 'a local authority shall have the power to do anything (whether or not involving the expenditure, borrowing or lending of money or the acquisition or disposal of any property rights) which is calculated to facilitate, or is conducive or incidental to, the discharge of any of their functions'. Although this provision reduces significantly the need for banks to concern themselves

---

[222] FSMA 2000, s.150(1).

[223] CASS, 7.8.1. The notice must require the bank to acknowledge in writing that the funds are held by the firm as trustee, so that it will not combine that account with another or exercise any right of set off against it (Ch. 7 Sect. 4 above), and that the title of the account distinguishes it sufficiently from accounts containing the firm's own funds.

[224] Ch. 7, Sect. 5(iii)(d) above.

[225] *Dubai Aluminium Co. Ltd* v. *Salaam* [2003] 2 AC 366, [141]–[142] (HL). See further Ch. 7, Sect. 5(iii) above.

[226] Ch. 7, Sect. 5(iv) above.   [227] Ch. 5, Sect. 4(iii) above.

[228] For a history of local authority law, see Chorley, *Gilbart Lectures* (1968).   [229] Sect. 10 below.

with a local authority's lack of capacity,[230] the bank must also ensure that any person acting on behalf of the authority remains within their individual mandate.

(ii) Operation of accounts and the power to borrow

The power of a local authority to open and operate an account and to draw cheques probably falls within its general powers contained in section 111(1) of the LGA 1972 and section 2 of the Local Government Act 2000. The bank account itself can now be maintained in the authority's own name, rather than having to be opened in the treasurer's name, as was the nineteenth century practice. The bank's duty to honour cheques drawn by a local authority depends on the instructions given in the account mandate. As regards account overdrafts and other loans, section 111(1) of the LGA 1972 expressly confers on local authorities the capacity to borrow, but this provision is expressly made subject to 'any other enactment passed before or after this Act'. Accordingly, the position is now specifically governed by section 1 of the Local Government Act 2003 (LGA 2003), which provides that a local authority may borrow money 'for any purpose relevant to its functions under any enactment' or 'for the purposes of the prudent management of its financial affairs'.[231] Although these borrowing powers appear broad enough to cover both term loans and overdraft financing, they are not unlimited and a particular exercise of the authority's borrowing power must bear some relation to the proper discharge of its functions. Furthermore, there are specific statutory limitations upon a local authority's borrowing powers, including the inability to borrow in a foreign currency without Treasury consent,[232] the inability to borrow beyond a self-imposed 'affordable borrowing limit'[233] or any borrowing limit imposed by the Secretary of State,[234] and the inability to 'mortgage or charge any of its property as security for money which it has borrowed or which it otherwise owes'.[235]

A bank that grants a local authority a loan or an overdraft facility falling within the purposes indentified in section 1 of the LGA 2003, and not falling within one of the statutory limits just discussed, is reasonably secure. If there is any doubt over the local authority's capacity or powers, it is possible for the bank to protect itself by requiring the relevant contract to be 'certified' under sections 2, 3, and 4 of the Local Government Contracts Act 1997. Where this is done, the contract has effect 'as if the local authority had had power to enter into it'.[236] Even if the bank fails to follow this procedure and makes a mistake as to a local authority's powers, it is not necessarily deprived of all protection. Under section 6 of the LGA 2003, a person lending money to a local authority 'shall not be bound to enquire whether the authority has power to borrow the money and shall not be prejudiced by the

---

[230] See further the Local Government (Contracts) Act 1997, ss.1 & 2, defining a local authority's powers to enter into contracts and deeming 'certified contracts' *intra vires* once executed.

[231] Ibid., s.1(1), conferring power on a local authority to enter into a contract for the provision of services (including banking services). For the power to make investments, see Local Government Act 2003 (LGA 2003), s.12. The power to borrow falls outside the Local Government Act 2000, s.2: *Risk Management Partners Ltd* v. *Brent London Borough Council* [2009] EWCA Civ. 490, [179].

[232] LGA 2003, s.2(3).

[233] Ibid., s.2(1)(a). A local authority is obliged to determine and review the maximum amount it can afford to borrow: ibid., s.3(1).

[234] Ibid., ss.2(1)(b), 4(1)–(2). There are also limits upon a local authority entering into a 'credit arrangement' beyond these limits: ibid., ss.7–8.

[235] Ibid, s.13(1). Any such security is unenforceable: ibid., s.13(2). All money borrowed and any interest will, however, 'be charged indifferently on all the revenues of the authority': ibid., s.13(3).

[236] Local Government (Contracts) Act 1997, s.2(1).

absence of any such power'. This provision is of major importance when local authorities borrow in the short-term money market. As dealings in that market need to be conducted promptly, the careful perusal of a transaction, which is generally advisable when a bank considers extending a medium- or long-term loan to a customer, is out of place. Unlike its predecessors, however, which were of an all-embracing nature,[237] there appear potentially to be three important limits on the protection afforded by section 6 of the LGA 2003. First, as indicated by *Haugesund Kommune* v. *Depfa ACS Bank*,[238] which involved an Irish bank entering into a swaps transaction with a Norwegian municipality, where the local authority is located in a foreign jurisdiction the issue of its capacity may be governed by foreign legislation rather than section 6 of the LGA 2003. Secondly, the bank is only protected against an argument that a local authority lacks the power, in the sense of capacity, to borrow the particular funds; it does not appear to afford protection when the Council or the committee or the individual officer, with whom the bank has dealt, lacks the necessary authority. Accordingly, a bank should still satisfy itself that the loan application is made by a duly authorized body of the local authority[239] and is within the mandate of the officers with whom it deals. The bank further has to satisfy itself that the mandate has been duly issued by the Council or by the appropriate committee. Thirdly, section 6 of the LGA 2003 removes the need for a bank to investigate the local authority's borrowing powers and protects the bank when its enquiries would have revealed the authority's lack of capacity in the particular circumstances. Undoubtedly, this will be useful for casual lenders, such as money market operators, who are now relieved of any obligation to enquire into the authority's borrowing powers or to examine whether the loan's object is within those powers. Section 6 does not, however, protect a bank that is aware of the authority's limited borrowing powers or that has been put on enquiry in that regard. Accordingly, section 6 of the LGA 2003 may in reality afford little protection to the local authority's own bank,[240] which might have been put on enquiry as to possible limits on the local authority's power to borrow through its prior dealings with that customer. Moreover, the position between a bank and a local authority customer is complicated by the fact that, as discussed previously,[241] the bank owes certain duties to its customer, such as a duty of care and (possibly even) fiduciary duties, which may require a bank to take certain minimum precautions to ensure that the authority's representatives do not commit it to transactions that it has no power to make. Accordingly, there remain a number of situations in which banks would still be well advised to scrutinize carefully a loan application made by a local authority customer.

Furthermore, a bank is likely to be put on enquiry, and potentially deprived of the protection afforded by section 6 of the LGA 2003, when the particular loan transaction is of an unusual nature, such as the transaction in *Hazell* v. *Hammersmith and Fulham London Borough Council*.[242] A local authority entered into interest rate swap agreements,

---

[237] M. Hapgood, n.47 above, [10.32].

[238] [2010] EWCA Civ 579, [42]–[62]. See also *Merrill Lynch Capital Services Inc* v. *The Municipality of the Piraeus* (QBD, 18 June 1997).

[239] *Southend-on-Sea Corporation* v. *Hodgson (Hickford) Ltd* [1962] 1 QB 416.

[240] For a similar view in relation to the predecessors of LGA 2003, s.6, see E.P. Ellinger, E. Lomnicka, & R.J.A. Hooley, n.16 above, 312.

[241] Ch. 5, Sects. 4(i) & (iii) above.

[242] [1992] AC 1 (HL). See also *Morgan Grenfell & Co Ltd* v. *The Mayor and Burgess of the London Borough of Sutton*, The Times, 23 March 1995 (*ultra vires* guarantee and indemnity), affd. (1996) 29 HLR 608 (CA); *Crédit Suisse* v. *Allerdale Borough Council* [1997] QB 306 (CA) (*ultra vires* guarantee); *Crédit Suisse* v. *Waltham Forest LBC* [1997] QB 362 (CA) (*ultra vires* guarantee). See also *Stretch* v. *United Kingdom* [2004] 1 EGLR 11, [24]–[25] (ECtHR); *Risk Management Partners Ltd* v. *Brent London Borough Council*, n.231 above, [117].

which involved speculating as to the rise and fall of interest rates, with a number of banks. The district auditor challenged these transactions as falling outside the authority's statutory powers. Granting a declaration that the transactions were void, the House of Lords held that they could not be regarded as ancillary to any of the local authority's functions. Moreover, their Lordships did not consider that the swaps transactions were sanctioned under either section 111 of the LGA 1972, as being calculated to facilitate any business incidental to the local authority's borrowing powers, or under the predecessor to section 1 of the LGA 2003.[243] As regards whether the banks could rely upon the protection afforded by the predecessor to section 6 of the LGA 2003,[244] the banks conceded that the provision could not 'be construed so as to afford protection to persons who enter into swaps transactions with local authorities'.[245] Where a bank is not protected by section 6 of the LGA 2003, as in the case of an interest rate swap agreement with a local authority, the bank may nevertheless be able to obtain restitution of any sums paid pursuant to the void transaction on the basis that they were paid under a mistake of law[246] or that there has been a total failure of consideration.[247] The local authority will have the usual restitutionary defences, such as change of position, although the mere fact that the borrowing contract is void does not *per se* provide a defence.[248] After a period of some uncertainty,[249] it is now clear that the bank would be entitled to compound interest representing the time-value of the funds paid by mistake.[250] Accordingly, a bank may be able to avoid suffering substantial losses in the event that a local authority's borrowing transaction turns out to be void.

10 Companies' accounts

(i) General principles

Like a local authority, a company, whether public or private, has a legal personality separate from its members and directors.[251] Accordingly, companies can enter into contracts in their own name and can sue and be sued. Whilst this feature traditionally distinguished companies from partnerships, which are identifiable with the partners themselves, limited liability partnerships blur this distinction somewhat by their advent, since (like a company) they have a separate legal personality.[252] Accordingly, similar concerns arise in respect of both types of entity.

Until 1972, a bank dealing with a corporate customer had to satisfy itself of the company's capacity by verifying the 'objects clause' in its memorandum of association.[253] Thus, a loan secured by the company's assets was *ultra vires*, and accordingly void, if it

---

[243] Local Government Act 1972, Sched. 13, Part 1.   [244] Ibid., [20].

[245] *Hazell* v. *Hammersmith and Fulham London Borough Council*, n.242 above, 33.

[246] *Kleinwort Benson Ltd* v. *Lincoln City Council* [1999] 2 AC 349 (HL). See also *Westdeutsche Landesbank Girozentrale* v. *Islington London Borough Council* [1996] AC 669 (HL); *Kleinwort Benson Ltd* v. *Sandwell Borough Council* [1994] 1 WLR 938 (CA), revsd. on a different point: [1996] AC 669 (HL).

[247] *Haugesund Kommune* v. *Depfa ACS Bank*, n.238 above, [62]. See further G. Virgo, 'Restitution of Void Loans' (2010) 69 *CLJ* 447.   [248] Ibid., [89]–[105].

[249] *Westdeutsche Landesbank Girozentrale* v. *Islington London Borough Council*, n.246 above.

[250] *Sempra Metals Ltd* v. *Inland Revenue Commissioners* [2008] 1 AC 561, [26], [33]–[35], [111]–[114], [132], [178], [184], [240] (HL).

[251] An English court will recognize corporate bodies created by a treaty: *Arab Monetary Fund* v. *Hashim (No. 3)* [1991] 2 AC 114 (HL). See also *Westland Helicopters Ltd* v. *Arab Organisation for Industrialisation* [1995] QB 282.   [252] LLPA 2000, s.1(2).

[253] A company's objects (if any) will nowadays be contained in the articles of association: Companies Act 2006 (CA 2006), s.31(1).

did not fall within the corporate objects or powers sanctioned by the memorandum.[254] The doctrine of *ultra vires* was, however, first modified in 1972,[255] and then effectively abolished in 1989 as far as third parties dealing with a company were concerned.[256] Since 1 October 2009, the position has been governed by section 39 of the Companies Act 2006 (CA 2006), which (like its predecessor) provides that 'the validity of an act done by a company shall not be called into question on the ground of lack of capacity by reason of anything in the company's constitution'. Similarly, section 1(3) of the Limited Liability Partnerships Act 2000 provides that a 'limited liability partnership has unlimited capacity'. Although banks need no longer concern themselves with issues of capacity for either type of entity, they will probably continue their previous practice of requiring companies to furnish copies of their constitutional documents before opening an account or receiving a loan.[257] This is due to the fact that a bank will still need to ensure that the board of directors has the power under the corporate constitution to enter the relevant transaction or the power to delegate to others in that regard.[258] According to section 40(1) of the CA 2006, 'the power of the directors to bind the company, or authorize others to do so, is deemed to be free of any limitation under the company's constitution'. This protection encompasses not only limitations deriving from the company's articles of association, but also limitations imposed by resolution of the general meeting or a shareholder class or imposed by a shareholders' agreement.[259]

The protection afforded to banks by section 40(1) of the CA 2006 may, however, be subject to several limitations.[260] First, protection is only afforded to third parties who 'deal with' the company, although this is satisfied by being 'a party to any transaction or other act to which the company is party', so banks are unlikely to fall foul of this requirement.[261] Secondly, the statutory protection only operates in favour of a person dealing with a company 'in good faith'. This requirement should, however, rarely present a problem for banks—not only is there a statutory presumption of good faith,[262] but a person dealing with a company is also not bound to enquire as to any limitation on the board's powers.[263] Indeed, since a person is not regarded as acting in bad faith 'by reason only' of his knowledge that an act is outside the powers of the board,[264] a bank that has had sight, or possession, of the corporate constitution without appreciating its limitations is still likely to be regarded as acting in 'good faith'. Thirdly, despite a significant change of wording when compared to its predecessor,[265] section 40(1) of the CA 2006 has been interpreted as

---

[254] *Re Introductions Ltd* [1970] Ch. 199; *Rolled Steel Products (Holdings) Ltd* v. *British Steel Corp.* [1986] Ch. 246 (CA). See generally E. Peel, *Treitel's The Law of Contract* (12th edn. London, 2007), [12-068].

[255] European Communities Act 1972, s.9(1).

[256] Companies Act 1985, s.35, as substituted by Companies Act 1989, s.108. Consider *Franks* v. *Midland Bank plc* (CA, 31 October 1995); *Financial Services Compensation Scheme Ltd* v. *Abbey National Treasury Services plc* [2008] EWHC 1897 (Ch), [61]–[62].

[257] A. Tyree & P. Weaver, n.10 above, [21.119].

[258] *Haugesund Kommune* v. *Depfa ACS Bank*, n.238 above, [139]–[141].

[259] CA 2006, s.40(3). See also *Youlton* v. *Charles Russell (a firm)* [2010] EWHC 1032 (Ch), [285].

[260] There is a further limitation when the company deals with its own directors: CA 2006, s.41.

[261] For a rare example where this requirement was not satisfied, see *EIC Services Ltd* v. *Phipps* [2005] 1 All ER 338 (CA) (issue of bonus shares to shareholder). See also *Cottrell* v. *King* [2004] EWHC 397 (Ch), [29].

[262] CA 2006, s.40(2)(b)(ii).

[263] Ibid., s.40(2)(b)(i). It may constitute bad faith not to investigate a matter further, once put on enquiry: *Wrexham Association Football Club Ltd* v. *Crucialmove Ltd* [2008] 1 BCLC 508, [47] (CA).

[264] Ibid., s.40(2)(b)(iii). See *Ford* v. *Polymer Vision Ltd* [2009] EWHC 945 (Ch), [73].

[265] CA 2006, s.40(1) refers only to 'the power of the *directors* to bind the company' and no longer 'the power of the *board of directors* to bind the company' as under the Companies Act 1985, s.35A(1).

providing a bank with no protection when it deals with an inquorate board,[266] although in such circumstances a bank may be protected by the common law 'indoor management rule' depending upon the nature of the limitation.[267] Fourthly, banks are only afforded protection by section 40(1) to the extent that they deal directly with the board of directors.[268] Where a third party deals with an individual director, section 40(1) only protects third parties from limitations on the board's *power to delegate*, but this does not mean that the board has *actually delegated* in the particular case. That can only be determined by applying ordinary common-law agency principles.[269] In determining whether a director has ostensible authority to bind the company, the absence of any requirement to enquire as to the company's capacity or the board's powers will be a relevant consideration.[270]

(ii) Lending to a company

Previously, a company's memorandum of association conferred a wide capacity to transact business and to borrow money and, even when not spelt out in the company's memorandum, a trading company was treated as having capacity to borrow as an incident of its carrying on business.[271] Nowadays, a company's objects are 'unrestricted', unless the company's articles of association expressly limit them. Invariably, therefore, a company will have capacity to borrow and grant security.[272] Under the Model Articles applicable under the CA 2006, the directors 'are responsible for the management of the company's business, for which purpose they may exercise all the powers of the company'.[273] Even where limitations exist upon either the company's capacity or the board's power to act, banks can usually rely on the statutory protections considered in the previous section.

(iii) Dealings in negotiable instruments and current account operations

Where a company appears to lack capacity, or its board appears to lack power, to draw or otherwise deal with a negotiable instrument, the position is governed by the provisions of the CA 2006 discussed in the preceding sections. These provisions do not, however, cover the situation where an individual director, a company secretary, or some other agent draws or otherwise deals with a negotiable instrument on the company's behalf without having the authority to do so or by abusing the powers conferred upon him to defraud the

---

[266] *Ford* v. *Polymer Vision Ltd*, n.264 above, [75]–[78], applying *Smith* v. *Henniker-Major & Co.* [2003] Ch. 182 (CA), [106]–[107]. As limited liability partnerships have nothing akin to corporate 'organs', these problems do not arise.

[267] *Royal British Bank* v. *Turquand* (1856) 6 E & B 327. See also *Northside Developments Pty Ltd* v. *Registrar-General* (1990) 170 CLR 146 (HCA).

[268] This is the preferable construction, despite the reference in section 40(1) of the CA 2006 to 'directors' and not 'the board of directors'. See generally *Criterion Properties plc* v. *Stratford UK Properties LLC* [2006] 1 BCLC 729 (HL).

[269] *Freeman & Lockyer* v. *Buckhurst Park Properties (Mangal) Ltd* [1964] 1 All ER 630 (CA), largely replacing the approach in *Royal British Bank* v. *Turquand*, n.267 above. The same issue arises in relation to limited liability partnerships: LLPA 2000, s.6.

[270] *Palmers' Company Law* (25th edn., London and Edinburgh, 1992 (loose-leaf)), [3.310] ff. See also *Rolled Steel Products (Holdings) Ltd* v. *British Steel Corp.*, n.254 above.

[271] *General Auction Estate and Monetary Co.* v. *Smith* [1891] 3 Ch. 432; cf. *Re Jon Beauforte (London) Ltd* [1953] Ch. 131.

[272] CA 2006, s.31(1).

[273] Companies (Model Articles) Regulations 2008, S.I. 2008/3229, Sched. 1, reg. 3, Sched. 2, reg. 3, and Sched. 3, reg. 3. For the position before 1 October 2009, see Companies (Tables A to F) Regulations 1985, S.I. 1985/805, Table A, art. 70.

company. According to section 52 of the CA 2006,[274] '[a] bill of exchange or promissory note is deemed to have been made, accepted or endorsed on behalf of the company if made, accepted or endorsed in the name of, or by or on behalf or on account of, the company by a person acting under its authority'. The company's 'name' in this context is probably its registered name.[275] At first sight, this provision apparently has two major shortcomings, but these are both explicable on historical grounds and are unlikely to prove significant. First, section 52 of the CA 2006 makes no mention of cheques. The current provision originated as section 47 of the Companies Act 1862, at a time when the terminology applicable to negotiable instruments was considerably less uniform than it became by the time of the Bills of Exchange Act 1882 (BEA 1882). Accordingly, the reference to 'bills of exchange' in section 52 of the CA 2006 is probably wide enough to cover cheques, which are after all bills of exchange drawn on a banker and payable on demand.[276] Secondly, reference is made to the making, acceptance, and indorsement of negotiable instruments, but not to their drawing. The word 'make', which in BEA 1882 is used only in respect of promissory notes, must, in the present context, include the notion of 'drawing', which is used to describe the issuing of bills of exchange, including cheques.

That said, there is possibly a more significant limitation upon the reach of section 52 of the CA 2006. To appreciate this limitation, one must distinguish between the two ways in which banks can deal in negotiable instruments. First, a bank may discount or negotiate bills of exchange (other than cheques) and promissory notes by purchasing from his customer a bill of exchange, either drawn on another or payable to himself. Alternatively, the bank may sometimes simply add its indorsement on the back of the instrument. Whichever method is adopted, the aim is to enable the customer to obtain funds immediately against an instrument maturing at a future date: in the case of a discount or negotiation, the customer obtains funds from the bank itself; in the case of the bank's accommodation indorsement, the customer can discount the bill in the money market and obtain funds from a third party in reliance on the bank's promise. The same object is served by discounting, negotiating, or indorsing a promissory note, or by discounting a post-dated cheque. In all of these situations, it seems clear that section 52 will operate to protect the bank, whether as discounter, negotiating bank, or indorser. Secondly, a bank may honour a cheque drawn on it by a corporate customer. It is much less certain whether section 52 of the CA 2006 protects banks in relation to this type of dealing. Clearly, a cheque falls within the scope of section 52 when it is 'made' (or drawn) on behalf of a corporate customer, with the result that a payee or an indorsee thereof can rely on section 52 in order to preclude the company from pleading lack or abuse of authority. The position of the drawee bank is different, however, since the bank does not pay the instrument because of its negotiable character—the bank would honour a 'payment instruction' even if it were a non-negotiable instrument, such as a conditional order or a non-transferable cheque, provided that the customer's account was in credit. A drawee bank's object when honouring a cheque is completely different from when a bank negotiates, discounts, or indorses bills or notes. When a bank honours its customer's cheque, it obeys its mandate and repays the debt represented by the account's credit balance. Thus, a bank honouring its customer's cheques acts as an agent and debtor;[277] but when a bank negotiates, discounts, or indorses the customer's bills or notes, it acts as a credit provider or dealer

---

[274] This provision is identical to its predecessor in Companies Act 1985, s.37.

[275] *Maxform SpA* v. *Mariani and Goodville Ltd* [1979] 2 Lloyd's Rep. 385, 389.

[276] Bills of Exchange Act 1882 (BEA 1882), s.73. See also N. Elliot, J. Odgers, & M. Phillips, *Byles on Bills of Exchange and Cheques* (28th edn., London, 2007), [6-003]; M. Hapgood, n.47 above, [10.8].

[277] Ch. 7, Sect. 1 above.

in negotiable instruments. This difference probably means that the drawee bank's protection from a corporate agent's lack or abuse of authority in drawing a cheque probably still depends on common law agency principles, rather than on section 52 of the CA 2006.

Those common law agency principles can provide the drawee bank with some protection against an agent lacking express authority. Some authorities treat a corporate agent, such as a director or company secretary, as having implied actual authority to draw cheques,[278] thereby protecting the bank despite the abuse of the agent's powers. The rationale for this approach is that, once a bank has received a document conferring the necessary authority on the director or secretary, it is not required to verify the authorizing document's validity or the agent's proper use of his powers. Other decisions have, however, restricted this wide and generally accepted principle. First, there have been suggestions that a bank cannot rely on a director's or secretary's implied authority, unless it has good reason to believe that such authority exists. In *Rama Corporation Ltd* v. *Proved Tin and General Investment Ltd.*,[279] Slade J held that a person could not plead an agent's implied authority unless he relied on it when he entered into the contract with the principal. Secondly, there are suggestions that a bank's ability to rely on an agent's implied authority depends on what is being held out in respect of that agent's position within the company.[280] The bank is not entitled to assume[281] that the agent's authority is wider than what can be inferred from the agent's position or the principal's representations in respect of him. Thirdly, a bank must exercise caution when it deals with a person other than a director. In *British Bank of the Middle East* v. *Sun Life Assurance Co. of Canada*,[282] an undertaking given by an insurance company's senior officers to repay amounts advanced to a property developer by a bank was held invalid as those corporate officers had neither express nor implied authority. Fourthly, suspicious circumstances may put a bank on enquiry, and accordingly prevent it from relying upon an agent's implied authority, if it fails to investigate matters further.[283] At first sight, this proposition may seem inconsistent with *London Joint Stock Bank* v. *Simmons*,[284] where Lord Herschell observed that

---

[278] *Biggerstaff* v. *Rowatt's Wharf Ltd* [1896] 2 Ch. 93, 102; *Hambro* v. *Burnand* [1904] 2 KB 10, 23; *Dey* v. *Pullinger Engineering Co.* [1921] 1 KB 77; *British Thomson-Houston Co. Ltd* v. *Federated European Bank Ltd* [1932] 2 KB 176. See also *Re Land Credit Co. of Ireland, ex p. Overend, Gurney & Co.* (1869) LR 4 Ch. App. 460. A bill of exchange or cheque that is a forgery will be ineffective in the holder's hands: *Kreditbank Cassel GmbH* v. *Schenkers Ltd* [1927] 1 KB 826.

[279] [1952] 2 QB 147; cf *Freeman & Lockyer* v. *Buckhurst Park Properties (Mangal) Ltd*, n.269 above, 493, 500, 507.

[280] *A. L. Underwood Ltd* v. *Bank of Liverpool and Martins* [1924] 1 KB 775, 786, 791–792 (CA). See also *Pharmed Medicare Private Ltd* v. *Univar Ltd* [2003] 1 All ER (Comm.) 321, [13]–[14] (CA). Consider also *Groves-Raffin Construction Ltd* v. *Bank of Nova Scotia* [1976] 1 Lloyd's Rep 373 (BCSC); *Bank of Montreal* v. *Royal Bank of Canada* (1981) 31 OR (2d) 177, 182–183; *Northside Developments Pty Ltd* v. *The Registrar-General*, n.267 above, 429; *Pekan Nenas Industries Sdn Bhd* v. *Chang Ching Chuen* [1998] 1 MLJ 465 (MFC); *Oris Funds Management Ltd* v. *National Australia Bank Ltd* [2005] VSCA 148, [17]; *NIML Ltd* v. *Man Financial Australia Ltd* [2006] VSCA 128, [32].

[281] *Houghton & Co.* v. *Nothard, Lowe & Wills Ltd* [1927] 1 KB 246 (CA), affd. on a different ground: [1928] AC 1 (HL).

[282] [1983] 2 Lloyd's Rep. 9 (HL). See also *Armagas Ltd* v. *Mundogas SA* [1986] AC 717, 748 (CA); *Hong Kong and Shanghai Banking Corporation Ltd* v. *Jurong Engineering Ltd* [2000] 2 SLR 54, [63]; *Criterion Properties plc* v. *Stratford UK Properties LLC*, n.268 above, [30]; *ING Re (UK) Ltd* v. *R&V Versicherung AG* [2007] 1 BCLC 108, [99]–[101].

[283] *Alexander Stewart & Son of Dundee Ltd* v. *Westminster Bank Ltd* [1926] WN 126, revsd., ibid. 271. See also *B. Liggett (Liverpool) Ltd* v. *Barclays Bank Ltd*, n.17 above; *Woodland Development Sdn Bhd* v. *Chartered Bank* [1986] 1 MLJ 84, 89.

[284] [1892] AC 201 (HL). See also *Bank of Bengal* v. *Fagan* (1849) 7 Moo. PC 61, 72 (PC); *Hambro* v. *Burnand*, n.278 above; *Dey* v. *Pullinger Engineering Co.*, n.278 above.

the doctrine of constructive notice has no application to negotiable instruments. On this basis, it might be suggested that a bank is under no obligation to make further enquiries when it encounters suspicious circumstances relating to cheques, bills of exchange, and promissory notes. It is submitted that, where the bank simply discounts these instruments, *Simmons* should apply, but that the position is different when the bank is deciding whether or not to honour a cheque drawn on a corporate customer's account. Indeed, the bank may owe its corporate customer a duty of care not to simply take a payment instruction at face value.[285]

The absence of express or implied actual authority on the part of the corporate agent is not, however, fatal to the bank's position. In *Freeman and Lockyer* v. *Buckhurst Park Properties (Mangal) Ltd.*,[286] the Court of Appeal held that a person dealing with an unauthorized agent may nevertheless be protected by an agent's 'apparent authority' if he can establish three points: first, that he relied upon a representation from the purported agent's principal as to the agent's authority; secondly, the person making the representation had actual authority to do so; and, thirdly, the transaction must be *intra vires*. As considered above, however, this last requirement will always be satisfied by virtue of section 39(1) of the CA 2006. Given the uncertainty at common law as to the extent of a corporate agent's implied authority, and the relationship between the doctrines relating to implied and apparent authority, the bank's most sensible course is to exercise care over cheques drawn on a corporate customer's account. Usually, the bank will safeguard its position (and also discharge its obligations to its corporate customer) by taking steps to verify that the persons drawing the instrument have been duly authorized. To a degree, the instrument can be taken at face value when executed as the company's constitution requires, but more may be expected of the bank when a 'red signal' manifests itself, such as a substantial corporate cheque being deposited into a corporate agent's overdrawn account.

The above principles relate to trading companies. As regards non-trading companies, it is again useful to distinguish between a bank's dealings in negotiable instruments and cheques drawn on the company's account. Dealings in negotiable instruments are associated with financial institutions and commercial enterprises, with the result that it would be unusual for a non-trading company to draw or indorse a bill of exchange or make a promissory note, despite generally having 'unrestricted' capacity to do so.[287] Opening a current account and issuing payment instructions stand on a different footing. Nowadays, any company, whether trading or non-trading, would have difficulty operating without a current account that could be used to receive and make payments, such as by receiving and drawing cheques. Accordingly, at least as regards the maintenance of a current account and issuing of payment instructions, there is no distinction between trading and non-trading companies.

---

[285] Ch. 5, Sect. 4(iii) above. The bank's duty to a corporate customer does not extend to its shareholders: *George Hudson Pty Ltd* v. *Bank of New South Wales* (1978) 3 ACLR 366 (NSWSC); *Pollnow* v. *Garden Mews-St. Leonards Pty Ltd* (1984) 9 ACLR 82 (NSWSC).

[286] N.269 above. See also *Hely-Hutchinson* v. *Brayhead Ltd* [1968] 1 QB 549 (CA); *British Bank of the Middle East* v. *Sun Life Assurance Co. of Canada*, n.282 above; *Armagas Ltd* v. *Mundogas SA*, n.282 above; *Ricci Burns Ltd* v. *Toole* [1989] 3 All ER 478 (CA); *Village Cay Marine Ltd* v. *Acland* [1998] 2 BCLC 327 (PC); *Hopkins* v. *TL Dallas Group Ltd* [2005] 1 BCLC 543, [92]–[94]; *ING Re (UK) Ltd* v. *R&V Versicherung AG*, n.282 above, [103]–[104]; *Magical Marking Ltd* v. *Holly* [2008] EWHC 2428 (Ch), [54].

[287] CA 2006, ss.31(1), 39(1).

11 Unincorporated associations' accounts

Unincorporated associations include bodies such as clubs, literary societies, and charitable institutions, whose objects are primarily non-commercial and whose activities are usually funded by subscriptions and donations. Such associations usually require a bank account to allow for the collection and payment of cheques and to effect payment by electronic means. Moreover, an unincorporated association may need to borrow money to further its objectives. An unincorporated association has no separate legal personality and is operated by a governing or management committee. This committee must remain within the powers conferred by its constitution,[288] but, within those powers, may delegate to agents whose acts will bind the association.[289] Such delegation may include dealing with the association's banking or other financial operations, such as drawing and indorsing bills of exchange.[290] Nowadays, it is common to include in an unincorporated association's constitution an express power authorizing the committee to delegate such powers as it sees fit, including the power to operate its current account. When an association applies to open a current account, the bank should obtain a copy of the association's constitution, or at least a copy of a resolution concerning the opening of, and drawing upon, the association's account. A bank should also ensure that it has clear instructions regarding who is entitled to operate the association's account. Even greater caution is required when making a loan or overdraft facility available to the association. Given that it may be difficult to recover anything from the persons forming the association, as considered next, the best advice to a bank wishing to lend to such an entity is to obtain adequate security.

An unincorporated association can neither sue nor be sued in its own name.[291] This last feature raises the issue, therefore, of who can be made liable for the unincorporated association's liabilities. As the liability of members to third parties is usually expressly limited to the amount of their subscriptions or membership fee, there is little point pursuing them, unless they have expressed their individual consent to the transaction.[292] A more fruitful target is likely to be the assets of the unincorporated association itself, for which claims must be brought in a representative capacity against the members of the committee that acts on behalf of the body.[293] It may be possible, however, to hold the members of the association's governing committee personally liable as well.[294] In *Coutts & Co.* v. *Irish Exhibition in London*,[295] a bank granted an overdraft to an association that was being

---

[288] For the similar position of local authorities, see *William Bean & Sons* v. *Flaxton Rural District Council* [1929] 1 KB 450 (CA). See further Sect. 9 above.

[289] *Bradley Egg Farm Ltd* v. *Clifford* [1943] 2 All ER 378 (CA). See also *Carlton Cricket and Football Social Club* v. *Joseph* [1970] VR 487, 498–499 (VSC); *Kelly* v. *Greene* (1979) 104 APR 196, 203–205 (NSC); *Rochfort* v. *Trade Practices Commission* (1981) 37 ALR 439 (FCA); *Jacobi* v. *Griffiths* [1999] 2 SCR 570, 615 (SCC); *Seven Network (Operations) Ltd* v. *TCN Channel Nine Pty Ltd* [2005] FCAFC 144, [23]–[32]; *Hostick* v. *New Zealand Railway and Locomotive Society* [2006] 3 NZLR 842, [25]–[26]; *Trustees of the Roman Catholic Church* v. *Ellis* [2007] NSWCA 117, [49]–[50].

[290] *Fleming* v. *Hector* (1836) 2 M & W 172.

[291] For the difficulties with unregistered trade unions, see *Taff Vale Railway Co.* v. *Amalgamated Society of Railway Servants* [1901] AC 426 (HL); *Willis* v. *Association of Universities of the British Commonwealth* [1965] 1 QB 140 (CA); *Oxford University* v. *Webb* [2006] EWHC 2490 (QB), [42]–[47]; *R* v. *L* [2009] 1 All ER 786, [15] (CA).

[292] *Howells* v. *Dominion Insurance Co. Ltd* [2005] EWHC 552 (QB), [30]–[36].

[293] CPR 1998, r.19.6(1).

[294] *English, Scottish & Australian Chartered Bank* v. *Adcock* (1881) 7 VLR (L) 157.

[295] (1891) 7 TLR 313. See also *Westpac Banking Corporation* v. *Smith* (VSC, 4 September 1991). For the committee members' right of indemnification, see *Wise* v. *Perpetual Trustee Co. Ltd* [1903] AC 139, 149 (PC);

formed as a result of a personal assurance given by one of the future association's committee members. Although the association was eventually formed, it subsequently failed. The bank sought to recover the overdraft from the association's committee members. As the account had not been officially transferred into the association's name, and as the bank had not released the committee members from their liability, the committee members remained the bank's customers, and accordingly were obliged to reimburse the amount involved.

12 Minors' accounts[296]

(i) General principles relevant in the context of banking

The age of majority in the United Kingdom is 18 years of age.[297] At common law, a contract made by a minor was voidable at his option, so that the contract could only generally be enforced by a minor, but not against him. Under section 1 of the Minors' Contracts Act 1987 (MCA 1987), the previous statutory regimes governing minors' contracts were repealed[298] and the old common law was substantially reinstated,[299] so that, subject to certain exceptions, contracts made by a minor are voidable at his option. Where a party is unable to enforce a contract by virtue of the other party's minority, a court may nevertheless require the defendant minor to transfer to the claimant any property acquired under the contract 'or any property representing it'.[300] There are certain types of contract that bound a minor at common law and that continue to bind minors under the MCA 1987—most significantly, a contract under which a minor is supplied with goods or services that constitute 'necessaries',[301] such as accommodation, food, and books. Loans to a minor for the acquisition of 'necessaries' are recoverable from the minor by the bank being subrogated to the supplier's rights.[302] Outside of such contracts, however, the bank should exercise caution before lending to a minor. In *R. Leslie Ltd* v. *Sheill*,[303] in which a minor obtained a loan by misrepresenting his age, the lender was precluded from recouping his losses, whether directly via a contractual route or indirectly in the tort of deceit or on the basis of the minor's unjust enrichment at the lender's expense. Possibly the only consolation for banks that have lent to a minor is that the minor cannot reclaim instalments under the void loan contract, unless there has been a total failure of consideration.[304] A bank may only seek

---

Howells v. *Dominion Insurance Co. Ltd*, n.292 above, [30]–[36]. See also *Bradley Egg Farm Ltd* v. *Clifford*, n.289 above; *Re Witney Town Football and Social Club* [1994] 2 BCLC 487.

[296] E. Peel, n.254 above, 566 ff; *Chitty On Contracts*, n.50 above, [8-002] ff.

[297] Family Law Reform Act 1969, s.1.

[298] Minors' Contracts Act 1987 (MCA 1987), s.1(a)–(b) (in force 9 June 1987) repealed the Infants Relief Act 1974 and the Betting and Loans (Infants) Act 1892, s.5. See also *Fisher* v. *Brook* [2009] UKHL 41, [21]–[27].

[299] *Chitty on Contracts*, n.50 above, [8-002] ff.   [300] MCA 1987, s.3.

[301] *Nash* v. *Inman* [1908] 2 KB 1 (CA). Opening a bank account may itself be a 'necessary' for a minor nowadays: A. Tyree & P. Weaver, n.10 above, [21.76]. See also *Steinberg* v. *Scala (Leeds) Ltd* [1923] 2 Ch 452.

[302] *Re National Permanent Benefit Building Society* (1869) LR 5 Ch. App. 309, 313; *Lewis* v. *Alleyne* (1888) 4 TLR 560. A negotiable instrument is void even if issued for 'necessaries': *Re Soltykoff, ex p. Margrett* [1891] 1 QB 413 (CA). See also *Star Cruise Services Ltd* v. *Overseas Union Bank Ltd* [1999] 2 SLR 412, [61]; *Jupiters Ltd* v. *Gan Kok Beng* [2007] 7 MLJ 228, [30].

[303] [1914] 3 KB 607 (CA), decided both under common law principles and the Infants Relief Act 1874. See also *Westdeutsche Landesbank Girozentrale* v. *Islington London Borough Council*, n.246 above, 716; *Papamichael* v. *National Westminster Bank plc* [2003] 1 Lloyd's Rep 341, [231].

[304] *Valentini* v. *Canali* (1890) 24 QBD 166; *Hamilton* v. *Vaughan Sherrin Electrical Engineering Co.* [1894] 3 Ch. 589; *Pearce* v. *Brain* [1929] 2 KB 310.

to recoup its losses by means of a set-off to the extent that the claim against the minor is legally enforceable.[305]

(ii) Specific problems faced by the bank: current account questions and lending

Three problems arise regularly when a minor wishes to have dealings with a bank: first, whether a current account can be opened in the minor's name;[306] secondly, whether the bank may honour cheques drawn on the account by a minor; and, thirdly, whether the bank can safely extend credit to a minor. Whilst the third of these problems will be considered further below, the first two are related to the basic question of whether a minor can draw cheques on a current account. Under section 22(1) of the BEA 1882, a person's capacity to issue a negotiable instrument is the same as his capacity to enter into a simple contract. A minor does not, therefore, have the required capacity to bind himself by issuing bills of exchange, cheques, and promissory notes.[307] A minor's signature does not, however, invalidate the instrument as a whole. According to section 22(2) of the BEA 1882, '[w]here a bill is drawn or indorsed by an infant [or] minor . . . the drawing or indorsement entitles the holder to receive payment on the bill, and to enforce it against any other party thereto'. Although it was previously suggested that this provision discharged a bank from its liability to pay the minor, once it had paid the cheque,[308] section 22(2) does not actually refer to the bank. That provision entitles the holder to receive payment and to enforce the instrument against the parties liable on it, but the bank (as mere drawee) is not liable on the cheque. Accordingly, it is incorrect to suggest that section 22(2) of the BEA 1882 protects a bank that has paid a minor's cheque. At the same time, common law principles enable a minor to give a valid discharge of a debt.[309] This view is supported by suggestions that, when a bank honours the minor's cheque, it cannot be compelled to pay the amount over again when the minor comes of age.[310] Arguably, as between the bank and the minor customer, a cheque performs a specific function—it constitutes not merely a receipt, but also a discharge of the bank's indebtedness to the minor.

Accordingly, a bank can safely open an account in a minor's name, and safely honour a minor's cheques provided the account is in credit, as with any ordinary account. As a matter of caution, however, banks tend to open accounts either in the name of the minor's guardians or in the minor's name, but on the understanding that it will be operated by

---

[305] *Rawley* v. *Rawley* (1876) 1 QBD 460 (CA).

[306] *Rowlandson* v. *National Westminster Bank Ltd*, n.187 above, discussed in Ch. 5, Sect. 2 above.

[307] *Williams* v. *Harrison* (1691) 3 Salk 197; *Re Soltykoff*, n.302 above; *Levene* v. *Brougham* (1909) 25 TLR 265. See also *Star Cruise Services Ltd* v. *Overseas Union Bank Ltd*, n.302 above, [61]; *Jupiters Ltd* v. *Gan Kok Beng*, n.302 above, [30]. A minor is not liable on a cheque post-dated to the date of his majority: *Hutley* v. *Peacock* (1913) 30 TLR 42; *Coutts & Co.* v. *Browne-Lecky* [1947] 1 KB 104; cf A.G. Guest, *Chalmers and Guest on Bills of Exchange and Cheques* (17th edn., London, 2009), [3-014], fn. 63. If a person of full age accepts a bill drawn on him whilst he is a minor, he will be liable: *Stevens* v. *Jackson* (1815) 4 Camp 164. Cf. *Belfast Banking Co.* v. *Doherty* (1879) 4 Ir. LR 124.

[308] *Paget's Law of Banking* (10th edn., London, 1989), 148 (cf. M. Hapgood, n.47 above). See generally A.G. Guest, n.307 above, [3-016].

[309] *Re Brocklebank* (1877) 6 Ch. D 358, 360 (CA). Cf. *Ledward* v. *Hansells* (1856) 2 K & J 370.

[310] J. Grant, *Law Relating to Bankers* (7th edn., London, 1924), 29. See also *Wilson* v. *Kearse* (1800) Peake Add. Cas. 196; *Valentini* v. *Canali*, n.304 above; *Pearce* v. *Brain*, n.304 above; *R.* v. *Inhabitants of Longnor* (1833) 4 B & Ad. 647; *Ewer* v. *Jones* (1846) 9 QB 623.

the guardians.[311] In both cases, the bank's customer is the minor.[312] In view of the trust element present in an account of this type, a bank may become subject to fiduciary duties to the minor,[313] particularly where the drawings by a guardian are out of the ordinary.[314] Generally, however, the bank is safe in observing the instructions given to it by the guardians, and is entitled to pay cheques drawn by them on the account.

The third problem mentioned above arises in the case where the bank wishes to grant a minor an overdraft or loan facility. In general, this is not a sensible course. In *Nottingham Permanent Benefit Building Society* v. *Thurstan*,[315] a minor applied to a building society for a loan to enable her to purchase some land and to erect buildings on it. The building society purchased the land from the owners and granted the minor the loan needed to complete the buildings. The society retained the title deeds over the land and obtained a mortgage over the property from the minor. Following her majority, the minor sought a declaration that the mortgage was void and an order for the delivery of the title deeds. Ultimately, the House of Lords granted the declaration in relation to the mortgage, as it had been granted in respect of a loan transaction that was avoided by the Infants Relief Act 1874. The contract for the purchase of the land between the land's original owners and the building society was a distinct and valid transaction and the bank had a lien over the documents of title for the amount paid by it for the land. Accordingly, the bank was entitled to retain those documents. If such a transaction had been executed under the MCA 1987, the mortgage would have been voidable at the minor's option,[316] but the bank would still have had a lien over the documents. One way in which the bank could have sought to improve its position would have been by seeking a guarantee from an adult in relation to the loan to the minor. Previously, such a technique would have been ineffective, as the secondary guarantee would have been as void as the primary obligation that it purported to secure.[317] This conclusion could have been avoided in the past in one of two ways: first, by insisting that the adult agree to indemnify the bank against any losses caused by its dealings with the minor, rather than providing a secondary guarantee, as a primary obligation to indemnify would be unaffected by the invalidity of any underlying loan and would not give rise to any rights of subrogation against the minor, which would otherwise be objectionable as being tantamount to enforcing the invalid loan transactions;[318] or, secondly, by insisting that an adult enter into a joint promise with the minor to pay the relevant amount (whether embodied in a negotiable instrument, such as a joint promissory note, or not), as the adult's undertaking as joint promisor will not be discharged despite the minor's obligation being unenforceable.[319] Whilst these two techniques may remain

---

[311] Appointing a minor's agent is fraught with difficulties: *Re Shephard, Shephard* v. *Cartwright* [1953] Ch. 728, 755. See also *Oliver* v. *Woodroffe* (1839) 4 M & W 650; *Calland* v. *Lloyd* (1840) 6 M & W 26, 31–32; *Doe d. Thomas* v. *Robert* (1847) 16 M & W 778. Exceptionally, an agent may be validly appointed by a minor who runs a business: *Denmark Productions Ltd* v. *Boscobel Productions Ltd* (1967) 111 So. J 715.

[312] *Rowlandson* v. *National Westminster Bank Ltd.*, n.187 above. See further Ch. 5, Sect. 2 above.

[313] Ch. 5, Sect. 4(i) above.

[314] *Rowlandson* v. *National Westminster Bank Ltd*, n.187 above. Cf. *McEvoy* v. *Belfast Banking Co. Ltd.*, n.48 above.

[315] [1903] AC 6 (HL).   [316] *Chitty on Contracts*, n.50 above, [8-030]–[8-031].

[317] *Coutts & Co.* v. *Brown-Lecky* [1947] KB 104. See also *Swan* v. *Bank of Scotland* (1836) 10 Bligh NS 627; *Heald* v. *O'Connor* [1971] 1 WLR 497, 505–506.

[318] *Yeoman Credit Ltd* v. *Latter* [1961] 1 WLR 828, 834 (CA). See also *Scottish & Newcastle plc* v. *Raguz* [2003] EWCA Civ 1070, [8], revsd. on a different point: [2008] UKHL 65; *Conister Trust Ltd* v. *John Hardman & Co.* [2008] EWCA Civ 841, [76]–[77]. See also *Walker Crips Stockbrokers Ltd* v. *Savill* [2007] EWHC 2598 (QB), [72]–[75]; *Pitts* v. *Jones* [2008] QB 706, [23]–[33] (CA); *Associated British Ports* v. *Ferryways NV* [2009] EWCA Civ 206, [9]–[15]. See generally E. Peel, n.254 above, [5-011]. See further Ch. 22, Sect. 1 below.

[319] *Wauthier* v. *Wilson* (1912) 28 TLR 239 (CA), affg. (1927) 27 TLR 582. See also *Lovell and Christmas* v. *Beauchamp* [1894] AC 607 (HL).

important in some jurisdictions when seeking to enforce guarantees of loans to minors, they are no longer required in the United Kingdom. Under section 2 of the MCA 1987, a guarantee given in respect of a minor's liabilities 'shall not for that reason alone be unenforceable against the guarantor', and accordingly such a guarantee is just as valid as any other type of guarantee taken by a bank.

13 Mentally incapacitated persons' accounts[320]

As a person who becomes mentally incapacitated loses the legal ability to manage his own financial affairs, at common law, he obtains a degree of protection from the consequences of any contractual liabilities incurred during that period. Accordingly, where a bank's customer becomes mentally incapacitated, the bank may encounter difficulties enforcing any loan agreements or seeking reimbursement for any transactions carried out on the customer's current account pursuant to the basic banker–customer contract. At common law, the notion of mental incapacity clearly covers mental illness, whether temporary or permanent, but in extreme circumstances may even cover cases of drunkenness.[321] Whatever the exact cause, whether a person is treated as mentally incapacitated depends upon whether he is able to 'understand the nature of the transaction when it is explained', and in that regard 'the degree or extent of understanding required...is relative to the particular transaction which it is to effect'.[322] This contextual approach was adopted recently in *Gorjat* v. *Gorjat*,[323] which involved a challenge by the deceased's children to the validity of instructions given by the deceased to his bank to transfer funds from an account in his sole name to a joint account with his second wife. In concluding that there was no relevant incapacity at common law, Sarah Asplin QC considered that the relevant factors when considering whether a customer had capacity to make a bank transfer included the period of time over which the challenged bank transfers took place, the value of the transfers when compared to the customer's overall assets, and the fact that every adult is presumed to have mental capacity until the contrary is proved.[324] Whilst this common law position will continue to govern for some time, for events occurring after 2007 the issue of whether a person lacks capacity will be decided by reference to the Mental Capacity Act 2005,[325] which provides that a person lacks capacity if he 'is unable to make a decision for himself in relation to the matter because of an impairment of, or disturbance in the functioning of, the mind or brain'.[326]

Where the customer is shown to be incapable of managing his affairs, it is not entirely settled at common law whether a bank must also have knowledge of that incapacity before it can affect its dealings with its customer. If the rule in *Yonge* v. *Toynbee*[327] applies to all agency relationships, including the banker–customer relationship, then the

---

[320] See generally British Bankers' Association, *Banking for People who Lack Capacity to Make Decisions* (November 2010).

[321] *Chitty on Contracts*, n.50 above, [8-080]–[8-081]. See also *Blomley* v. *Ryan* (1956) 99 CLR 362 (HCA); *Kurth* v. *McGavin* [2007] 3 NZLR 614, [94].

[322] *Manches* v. *Trimborn* (1946) 115 LJKB 305; *Re Beaney* [1978] 1 WLR 770, 774. See also *Chitty on Contracts*, n.50 above, [8-068]–[8-069].

[323] N.75 above, [129], [136]–[140].   [324] Ibid., [136]–[140].   [325] Ibid., [132].

[326] Mental Capacity Act 2005, s.2(1). For the meaning of 'inability to make decisions', see ibid., s.3.

[327] [1910] 1 KB 215. See also *Nelson* v. *Nelson* [1997] BPIR 702, 708–710 (CA); *Donsland Ltd* v. *Van Hoogstraten* [2002] EWCA Civ 253, [24]; *Tan King Hiang* v. *United Engineers (Singapore) Pte Ltd* [2005] 3 SLR 529, [28] (SGCA); *SEB Trygg Liv Holdings Aktiebolag* v. *Manches* [2006] 1 All ER 437, [60]–[63] (CA).

bank's mandate as agent would be terminated by the insanity of the customer as principal, even if the bank had no notice of that fact. As considered previously, however, the banker–customer contract is not purely an agent-principal relationship, but primarily a debtor–creditor relationship pursuant to which the bank is under a duty to discharge any indebtedness to his customer (represented by an account credit balance) by honouring its customer's instructions.[328] By analogy with the situation where the customer dies[329] or becomes bankrupt,[330] the better view is that the bank's mandate terminates only upon the bank receiving notice of the customer's mental incapacity. Moreover, in the situation where the bank has entered into a contract with the customer, such as a loan agreement, the bank appears able still to enforce that agreement as long as it has no notice of its customer's mental incapacity. In *Imperial Loan Co.* v. *Stone*,[331] which involved a mentally incapacitated person signing a promissory note as surety, the Court of Appeal held that the note's payee could enforce the instrument against the surety, as there was insufficient evidence to establish that the payee was aware of the surety's incapacity. Lord Esher MR observed:[332]

> When a person enters into a contract, and afterwards alleges that he was so insane at the time that he did not know what he was doing, and proves the allegation, the contract is as binding on him in every respect, whether it is executory or executed, as if he had been sane when he made it, unless he can prove further that the person with whom he contracted knew him to be so insane as not to be capable of understanding what he was about.

It is unclear why this principle should not equally govern the bank's mandate in relation to the customer's current account. Where a bank does know of its customer's mental incapacity, as its mandate will have come to an end, it should refuse to honour the customer's cheques and decline any request for an overdraft facility unless it has an order from a judge of the Court of Protection[333] authorizing the transaction. Alternatively, where a 'deputy' has been appointed under the Mental Capacity Act 2005 to make decisions on behalf of the incapacitated customer,[334] banks can safely transact business concerning the customer with his deputy, provided he remains within the scope of his appointment.[335]

If the rule in *Yonge* v. *Toynbee*[336] does apply in the banking context, however, there are three situations where a bank or a third party dealing with the customer may nevertheless be protected. First, mental incapacity does not affect transactions that involve the supply of 'necessaries'. In *Re Beavan, Davies, Banks & Co.* v. *Beavan*,[337] a bank that knew of its customer's mental incapacity subsequently sought to recover the amount of an overdraft that resulted from the customer's son drawing cheques on his father's account to pay for his father's 'necessaries'. Neville J concluded that as the overdraft on the father's account effectively resulted from sums loaned to the son, the father's administrator was *prima facie* entitled to repudiate liability on the facility as being incurred without authority. As the loans were used to pay for the father's 'necessaries',

---

[328] Ch. 5, Sect. 3 above.   [329] BEA 1882, s.75.   [330] Ch. 5, Sect. 6 above.

[331] [1892] 1 QB 599 (CA). See also *Hart* v. *O'Connor* [1985] 1 AC 1000 (PC); *Masterman-Lister* v. *Brutton & Co.* [2003] 3 All ER 162, [57] (CA); *Bailey* v. *Warren* [2006] EWCA Civ 51, [109], [155].

[332] Ibid., 601.   [333] Mental Capacity Act 2005, s.45(1).

[334] Ibid., s.16(2). Under the Mental Capacity Act 2005, s.48, the judge may make an order declaring the customer to be incapable of entering into any contractual liability, in which case contracts made by him thereafter are probably void: *Chitty on Contracts*, n.50 above, [8-070].

[335] The statutory powers of a deputy are extensive and include carrying on a profession, trade, or business on behalf of the incapacitated person and the carrying out of any contract entered into by that person: Mental Capacity Act 2005, s.18(1).

[336] N.327 above.   [337] [1912] 1 Ch. 196.

however, the son was entitled to be reimbursed by his father; but, as it was the bank that had reimbursed the son, the bank was entitled to be subrogated to the son's rights against his father and was accordingly entitled to recover the amount of the overdraft on its customer's account, but not any interest or bank charges. A broadly similar (albeit less circuitous and less generous) result would probably be achieved nowadays under section 7 of the Mental Capacity Act 2005, which provides that '[i]f necessary[338] goods or services are supplied to a person who lacks capacity to contract for the supply he must pay a reasonable price for them'.[339] This provision probably remains subject to the common law limitation that a mentally incapacitated person is not bound, even for necessaries, if the counterparty is aware of that incapacity.[340] Secondly, a bank can overcome problems arising out of withdrawals made by a mentally incapacitated customer from his account when these are used to discharge the customer's valid debts. In *Scarth* v. *National Provincial Bank Ltd*,[341] a bank that had frozen the account of a mentally incapacitated customer was persuaded by the customer's wife to transfer the credit balance of her husband's account to her own account, so that she might pay her husband's outstanding debts. When the husband was well again, he sought to recover the relevant sums, but was met with the equitable defence that the money had been used to discharge the husband's debts.[342] Humphreys J accepted that the wife could rely upon the defence as she had a legitimate interest in protecting her husband's standing, and accordingly should not be treated as a volunteer. It seems clear that the bank was also entitled to reap the benefit of this equitable defence, as it had provided the funds used to discharge its customer's debts. Given that the *Liggett* doctrine has very much fallen out of favour in recent years,[343] it is unclear whether *Scarth* would be decided in the same way in future. Thirdly, a third party dealing with the bank may be protected *vis-à-vis* the customer if the bank has acted within its apparent or ostensible authority. In *Drew* v. *Nunn*,[344] the claimant, who was completely ignorant of the defendant's mental incapacity, sought to enforce a contract of sale entered into by the defendant's wife acting as agent on the ground that, before becoming mentally incapable, the defendant had represented to the claimant that his wife was entitled to pledge his credit. Concluding that the defendant was not entitled to repudiate the sale contract on account of his insanity, and that the claimant could accordingly enforce it, Brett LJ held that, whilst in general a principal's mental incapacity automatically terminated an agent's authority, this principle was abrogated (and any contract entered into was accordingly enforceable against the principal) where a third party acted on the principal's representation by words or conduct that the agent was duly authorized to act for him, unless the third party knew of the principal's mental incapacity. This principle could potentially operate to protect a third party to whom a mentally incapacitated person has transferred funds from his account. Although the Mental Capacity Act 2005 contains no reference to any requirement of knowledge on the part of the person dealing with a mentally incapacitated person, it is not clear that this does away with the common law knowledge requirements considered above, as the legislation does not purport to deal comprehensively with the issue of the enforceability of transactions concluded by the mentally incapable.

---

[338] Mental Capacity Act 2005, s.7(2).   [339] Ibid., s.7(1).

[340] *Chitty on Contracts*, n.50 above, [8-075].   [341] (1930) 4 LDAB 241.

[342] *B. Liggett (Liverpool) Ltd* v. *Barclays Bank Ltd*, n.17 above. See further Ch. 11, Sect. 3(v) below.

[343] *Crantrave Ltd* v. *Lloyds Bank plc*, n.17 above. See further Ch. 11, Sect. 3(v) below.

[344] (1879) 4 QBD 661 (CA). See also *Daily Telegraph Newspaper Co. Ltd* v. *McLaughlin* [1904] AC 776 (PC).

9

Interest-bearing Accounts

1 Classification and comparison with current accounts

Traditionally, there has been a clear distinction between 'current' accounts and 'interest-bearing' accounts (although this latter term does not necessarily accord with technical banking terminology). This distinction was articulated by Lopes LJ in *Re Head, Head v. Head (No. 2)*,[1] in respect of the particular account in that case, as follows: 'While the money was on a current account it was payable on presentation of a cheque, and it carried no interest; when it was placed on deposit it bore interest, and was no longer payable on a cheque, but it was only payable after twenty-one days' notice'. Traditionally, there were three main distinctions between interest-bearing and current accounts. First, as the name suggests, all interest-bearing accounts earn a return for the customer. Whilst current accounts may not have earned interest in the past, most of the larger banks nowadays pay interest even on modest current account balances, although this is not always the case. Similarly, whilst it may have been advantageous in the past to maintain a minimum balance in order to avoid account charges, such charges are nowadays rare other than for unauthorized overdrafts.[2] Secondly, a current account balance can usually be withdrawn by cheque, whilst this was not traditionally the case with interest-bearing accounts, despite some old authorities to the contrary.[3] As a matter of general banking practice, cheque-books have simply not been furnished in respect of interest-bearing accounts. Moreover, since the automation of the clearing system, it is not now possible to use a cheque issued in respect of a current account to withdraw funds from a savings account, as each pre-printed cheque nowadays sets out the personalized details of the customer, and the account upon which it is drawn, in the magnetic ink strip on each cheque. Accordingly, cheques can only be used in relation to the account for which it is provided.[4] Nevertheless, whilst cheques are not generally drawn on interest-bearing accounts, it is not unusual for cheques to be collected for the benefit of such accounts, and the '2-6-6' commitments will apply in that regard.[5] Thirdly, current accounts may be either in credit or, with the bank's consent, overdrawn. In the former case, the customer is the creditor; in the latter, he is the debtor. Interest-bearing accounts are, however, opened on a different understanding and the law does not recognize an overdrawn interest-bearing account.[6] As a general rule, a customer who maintains such an account

---

[1] [1894] 2 Ch. 236, 238 (CA).

[2] *Office of Fair Trading* v. *Abbey National plc* [2010] 1 All ER 667 (UKSC).

[3] *Stein* v. *Ritherdon* (1868) 38 LJ Ch. 369; *Hopkins* v. *Abbott* (1875) LR 19 Eq. 222. See also *Dixon* v. *Bank of New South Wales* (1896) 12 WN (NSW) 101.

[4] Ch. 10, Sect. 2 below.

[5] Cheque and Credit Clearing Company, *Cheques and Cheque Clearing—The Facts* (November 2007), 7. See further Ch. 10, Sect. 2 below.

[6] *Barclays Bank Ltd* v. *Okenarhe* [1966] 2 Lloyd's Rep. 87, 94.

must apply for a personal loan if he requires additional funds. Occasionally, the principle is departed from in practice, when a cheque is collected for the credit of an interest-bearing account and the customer is allowed to withdraw the cheque's proceeds before it is cleared, but the cheque is returned unpaid. In such a case, the account must by necessity show a temporary debit balance.

There is also an economic distinction between current and interest-bearing accounts. The object of the former is to provide customers with access to the nationwide system of money transfers provided by the banks, such as cheque[7] and giro clearing, the BACS and CHAPS Sterling systems, and the 'Faster Payments Service'.[8] From the banks' perspective, furnishing customers with current accounts provides banks with access to funds on a short-term basis for which they have to pay no (or little) interest. In contrast, the interest-bearing account enables the customer to earn a return on his money and provides the bank with funds that it can invest for a period of time. Although all bank deposits are maintained as a commingled fund,[9] current accounts represent liquid funds for customers' everyday use, whilst interest-bearing accounts are best regarded as investment deposits. Whilst this economic distinction still has validity, the legal distinctions considered above have been eroded somewhat and are increasingly difficult to maintain in light of modern banking practice—banks nowadays usually pay interest on current account balances and even occasionally allow customers to draw cheques on accounts opened for savings purposes. Nevertheless, the traditional conceptual distinction remains importance particularly as most foreign-currency accounts opened in the United Kingdom fall squarely within the definition of an interest-bearing account.

Traditionally, there are different types of 'interest-bearing' account. Although the nomenclature of the different accounts varies from bank to bank, and some banks offer unique accounts that have no traditional counterpart, most accounts fall into one of several classic types or constitute a variation on those archetypes. One of the most common types of account is the savings account, into which the customer can deposit any amount he chooses and from which he can withdraw sums without notice. Interest is usually paid on the lowest balance in each calendar month, although some banks calculate interest daily. Depending upon whether the terms of the savings account allow the customer to use the account to make electronic payments, the account may constitute a 'framework contract' within the Payment Services Regulations 2009 (PSR 2009).[10] As discussed previously in relation to current accounts,[11] the PSR 2009 contain special provisions governing the opening and closure of certain types of savings account, such as flexible savings accounts, and impose restrictions on the manner in which the account terms can be varied. Other types of interest-bearing account impose greater restrictions on withdrawals and accordingly may not be used as a transactional account. These include the investment account and the 'extra interest' account, where the customer deposits certain minimum amounts and withdrawal is subject to an agreed period of notice. Furthermore, there is the fixed deposit, whereby 'the customer deposits an amount for a specified period of time at an agreed rate of interest'.[12] In practice, a fixed deposit can be withdrawn before the agreed maturity date, provided the customer is prepared to forego part of the interest. If the deposit is renewed (or 'rolled over') at maturity, a new rate of interest will be determined according to the prevailing market.[13] These other non-transactional types of interest-bearing account will generally fall within the scope of the Financial Services

---

[7] Ch. 10, Sect. 2 below.   [8] Ch. 13, Sect. 1 below.   [9] Ch. 6, Sect. 1 above.
[10] Payment Services Regulations 2009, S.I. 2009/209, reg. 2(1).   [11] Ch. 7, Sects. 2–3 & 6 above.
[12] *Bank of America National Trust and Savings Association* v. *Iskandar* [1998] 2 SLR 265, [30] (SGCA).
[13] Ibid., [30], [33].

Authority's *Banking: Conduct of Business Sourcebook* (BCOBS), which, as considered previously,[14] regulates the opening, cancellation and closure of such accounts and certain operational matters, such as account statements and changes to the account terms.

2 Legal nature of the arrangement

(i) Creditor–debtor relationship

Interest-bearing accounts share three principal similarities with current accounts. First, any funds in an interest-bearing account represent a debt due from the bank to its customer.[15] Such an account involves neither a trust relationship,[16] nor one involving a secured debt.[17] In *Akbar Khan* v. *Attar Singh*,[18] Lord Atkin expressed the point as follows:[19]

> A deposit of money is not confined to a bailment of specific currency to be returned in specie. As in the case of a deposit with a banker it does not necessarily involve the creation of a trust, but may involve only the creation of the relation of debtor and creditor, a loan under conditions.

In most types of interest-bearing account, only one contract arises between the customer and bank at the time that the account is opened, and any subsequent withdrawals or deposits are made pursuant to that contract. At one time, doubts were expressed as to whether this analysis applied to fixed deposits, as it was thought that each deposit was the subject of a separate arrangement subject to its own distinct terms. The prevailing view, however, is that fixed deposits by a customer (like other interest-bearing accounts) are the subject of only one contract with the bank.[20] In *Bank of America National Trust and Savings Association* v. *Iskandar*,[21] the Singaporean Court of Appeal expressly endorsed this analysis[22] and considered that it was a term of this 'one continuing contract' that, upon agreeing to accept one fixed deposit from its customer, it would 'accept further deposits into the account on the instructions of the customer, if they were above a prescribed minimum, as long as the banker–customer contract existed between the parties'.[23] Karthigesu JA held that, if the bank decides that it does not wish to accept new funds, it should at the very least give the customer reasonable notice before terminating the deposit account.[24] From a commercial perspective, banks will not often refuse customers who wish to deposit funds. Secondly, an interest-bearing account may be repayable on demand, in which case the account balance will be considered 'ready money'[25] in the same way as a current account. Unlike a current account, however, an interest-bearing account may also be payable at an agreed future time or upon the

---

[14] Ch. 7, Sects. 2–3 & 6 above.   [15] N.12 above [30]. See further Ch. 5, Sect. 3 above.

[16] Ibid., [32]. See also *DFC New Zealand* v. *Goddard* [1992] 2 NZLR 445, 447. See further Ch. 5, Sect. 3 above.

[17] *Hopkins* v. *Abbott*, n.3 above. A customer who opens the proposed 'safety deposit current account' would be a secured creditor in the bank's insolvency: Safety Deposit Current Accounts Bill 2008, cls. 1(2) & 1(5).

[18] [1936] 2 All ER 545, 548 (PC).   [19] Ibid., 548.

[20] *Hart* v. *Sangster* [1957] 1 Ch. 329, 337 (CA); *Barclays Bank Ltd* v. *Okenarhe*, n.6 above, 93; *Walker* v. *Centaur Clothes Group Ltd* [1997] STC 72, 83–84, revsd. on a different point: [2000] 2 All ER 589 (HL). See further *Ashton Mining Ltd* v. *Commissioner of Taxation* [2000] FCA 590; *Y-LL* v. *W-HC* [2008] NZFLR 432, [34].

[21] N.12 above, [34].   [22] Ibid., [32].   [23] Ibid., [34].

[24] Id. The duty was alternatively expressed as 'an implied duty of care' duly to notify the customer 'clearly, unequivocally, and promptly': ibid., [39]. See also Ch. 5, Sect. 6 above.

[25] *Stein* v. *Ritherdon*, n.3 above; *Hopkins* v. *Abbott*, n.3 above.

customer giving the required notice. In this last case, notice is a condition precedent to the bank's duty to pay.[26] At one time, the production of a pass-book or deposit receipt also used to be a condition precedent to repayment in some cases. Although, as discussed subsequently,[27] most banks have discontinued this practice, it remains a feature of building society accounts. Thirdly, as every interest-bearing account is maintained at a particular branch, the account balance is a debt situated at that place.[28] The traditional rule is that a customer has to make demand at the branch where the account is maintained,[29] although in light of technological developments, such as ATMs and internet banking, there are strong indications that the courts may abandon this position both generally[30] and, more specifically, in respect of fixed deposit accounts.[31] Assuming that the traditional rule remains good law, banks have tended to insist that demand be made at the relevant branch, at least where there is no deposit receipt or pass-book covering the account, but have been willing to make repayment at other branches when such documents are required, provided suitable identification is supplied.

(ii) **Payment to the wrong person**

The basic principle is that a bank should generally pay the accountholder alone and, if it pays anyone else, it does so at its peril.[32] When the account is simply held in the name of a particular person, then there can be little doubt as to who should be paid. The risk of paying the wrong person is heightened, however, when the interest-bearing account's terms make withdrawals or repayment conditional upon the production of a pass-book or a deposit receipt.[33] These documents are not negotiable instruments,[34] as they simply evidence the debt due from the bank. Nevertheless, customers have sometimes misunderstood their legal nature and have written a transfer instruction, addressed to the bank, at the foot of the document and then delivered it to the intended transferee. As considered subsequently,[35] such a transfer instruction may constitute a valid legal or equitable assignment of the account balance. It does, however, raise the spectre of payment being made to the wrong person, if the pass-book or deposit certificate falls into the wrong hands, although the same risk could presumably result from a fraudster extracting from the accountholder a letter of instruction directing the bank to transfer the balance to the person named therein. In *Wood* v. *Clydesdale Bank Ltd*,[36] the claimant indorsed a deposit receipt for £100, sent it to his brother, and separately instructed the bank to pay £60 of the accrued balance to his brother against the production of the receipt. The deposit receipt, with a copy of the claimant's letter attached, was stolen and was used by the thief

---

[26] *Bagley* v. *Winsome and National Provincial Bank Ltd* [1952] 2 QB 236, 243 (CA). Although *Bagley* is no longer good law in light of s.40 of the Senior Courts Act 1981 (as amended by S.I. 2001/3649) and the Civil Procedure Rules 1998 (CPR 1998), r.72.2(3), the Court of Appeal's analysis of the bank's duties in relation to interest-bearing accounts remains valid. See also *Root* v. *Nanyang Commercial Bank Ltd* [1982] 1 HKC 417, 421; *Borg-Warner Acceptance* v. *Janzen Builders* (1983) 24 Man R (2d) 48, [11]; *Commissioner of Police for the Metropolis* v. *Ewing* (CA, 4 November 1987).

[27] Sect. 4(ii) below.

[28] *R* v. *Lovitt* [1912] AC 212 (PC). See also *Workers' Compensation Board* v. *Enoch Indian Band* (1993) 141 AR 204, [25] (ACA); *McNamara* v. *Canadian Imperial Bank of Commerce* [2005] NBQB 209, [22].

[29] *Joachimson* v. *Swiss Bank Corporation* [1921] 3 KB 110, 127 (CA). See further Ch. 5, Sect. 3 above.

[30] Ch. 5, Sect. 3 above.

[31] *Damayanti Kantilal Doshi* v. *Indian Bank* [1999] 4 SLR 1, [24], [28] (SGCA).

[32] *Public Bank Bhd* v. *Ng Yoon Lin* [2001] 5 MLJ 70, [10] (MCA).

[33] *Voo Foot Yiu* v. *Overseas Chinese Banking Corporation Ltd* [1936] 1 MLJ 169, 171; *Bank of America National Trust and Savings Association* v. *Iskandar*, n.12 above, [36].

[34] Sect. 4(ii) below.   [35] Sect. 3(ii) & Ch. 21, Sect. 1 below.   [36] 1914 SC 397.

to obtain payment from the bank, which had failed to satisfy itself of the payee's identity. Concluding that payment to the thief did not discharge the bank's repayment obligation to the accountholder, Lord Mackenzie said:[37]

> If a deposit-receipt bearing a genuine endorsement is presented to the bank, say by a stranger, there is no absolute rule in regard to the liability of the bank to pay over again if it be ascertained that the person asking for the payment had not the authority of the true holder.

As the bank in *Wood* had been instructed to pay funds over to a specific person, it must be correct that the bank could not have discharged its obligations by paying a different, unauthorized person. If the transfer instruction had required the bank to pay the funds to whomever presented the deposit receipt, the conclusion in *Wood* might have been different, as the bank could have argued that it had acted within its mandate; that the customer was estopped from denying the generality of the transfer instruction; or that the bank had at the very least acted upon a reasonable interpretation of ambiguous instructions.[38]

(iii) **Terms of contract**

An interest-bearing account is usually governed by a set of standard terms and conditions that often impose on the customer a duty to exercise a certain degree of care and that ordinarily require the customer to abide by certain conditions relating to the repayment of the amount deposited. Occasionally, additional conditions may be printed at the foot of a deposit receipt or in a pass-book. In *Re Australia and New Zealand Savings Bank Ltd, Mellas* v. *Evriniadis*,[39] Pape J recognized the validity of such terms and stated that 'the provisions set out in the passbooks are part of the terms of the contract between the bank and its customers and do constitute conditions precedent to any obligation by the bank to repay the moneys at credit...' This view is sustainable when the customer's attention has been drawn to the relevant terms at the time that the account was opened, regardless of whether those terms are contained in a deposit receipt, a pass-book, a statement of account or a standard-form contract. Unless the customer objected to the terms involved, he is treated as having contracted on their basis. Where such terms are only provided at some point in time after the interest-bearing account is opened, then they will simply not be incorporated into the account contract, unless the customer thereafter consents to them.[40] Such problems should hopefully not arise in future, however, as BCOBS nowadays requires that banks, *inter alia*, 'provide the terms and conditions of the [account] contract... on paper or in another durable medium in good time before a banking customer is bound by them'.[41] Furthermore, a bank must nowadays give a customer reasonable notice of changes to the terms on which an interest-bearing account is provided.[42]

An interest-bearing account's standard terms and conditions will cover a broad range of issues, including the date upon which a fixed deposit matures and how it should be dealt with thereafter. There has, however, been some controversy as to how a bank should deal with such a matured fixed deposit in the absence of express terms to that effect. In *Bank of America National Trust and Savings Association* v. *Iskandar*,[43] the Singaporean

---

[37] Ibid., 402–403.   [38] Ch. 11, Sect. 3(iv) below.   [39] [1972] VR 690, 693 (VSC).
[40] *Burnett* v. *Westminster Bank Ltd* [1966] 1 QB 742 (clause in cheque-book folder not incorporated). See also *Covercraft Ltd* v. *Commissioners of Customs & Excise* (VAT Trib, 25 April 1989). See further Ch. 11, Sect. 1(i) below.
[41] Financial Services Authority, *Banking: Conduct of Business Sourcebook* (BCOBS) 4.1.2(2), 4.1.4(3).
[42] Ibid., 4.1.2(3)–(4).   [43] N.12 above.

Court of Appeal suggested that a bank should not simply 'roll over' a fixed deposit of its own accord, but rather should contact the customer to obtain instructions about how to deal with the matured deposit,[44] as the bank is 'under an implied duty of care to take reasonable steps to inform the account-holders on the maturity of their fixed deposits'.[45] This does not impose an absolute duty on the bank to seek out its customer, but one that can be discharged by simply writing to the customer once at the address provided upon opening the account.[46] This is hardly onerous given that reminders to customers are likely to be computer-generated and distributed automatically.[47] Where the customer renews the deposit, but fails to specify the precise terms of the renewed deposit, the customer's instruction is taken as a request to renew 'on the banker's usual terms and interest rates for the amount given (presumably at the then prevailing interest rate)'.[48] If the customer does not respond to the bank's enquiries, however, the bank should place the funds in the customer's current account or in a suspense or holding account.[49] Failure to do this will mean that the bank risks having to pay the accountholder interest on the deposit as if he had chosen to renew it.[50] An English court, however, may well refuse to follow exactly the same approach as in *Iskandar*. In *Suriya & Douglas* v. *Midland Bank plc*,[51] the claimant solicitors' firm held two client accounts with the defendant bank—a non-interest-bearing account with a cheque-book facility and a non-transactional interest-bearing account. In 1984, the bank introduced an interest-bearing operating account for professional clients, but only informed the claimant of this in 1988. Claiming the loss of interest between 1984 and 1988, the claimant contended that the bank had an implied contractual duty to inform it of relevant new banking facilities. Rejecting this claim, Schiemann LJ stated that '[a] bank's relationship with a client is not without more one in which duties of disclosure are imposed upon the bank as a matter of general law', and that, even if the bank had 'a policy of informing solicitor clients of the introduction of the special account', such customers did not thereby obtain any rights against the bank for failure to abide by that policy. In contrast, if a bank contracts to inform customers of any account changes or the introduction of new accounts, and has advertised that contractual commitment, then this might impose a duty of disclosure on the bank in that regard, but there was no evidence to support such a claim in *Suriya & Douglas*. In the present context, *Suriya & Douglas* suggests that, unlike Singaporean banks, English banks are unlikely to owe a positive duty to inform a customer of their deposit's maturity or to seek the customer's instructions regarding the matured deposit. In the absence of such instructions, an English bank would be best advised to transfer the funds, together with interest, to the customer's current account or a separate suspense account. In practical terms, the principal difference between the English and Singaporean positions concerns the requirement that a customer be approached for new instructions and that notice be given of the deposit's maturity.

---

[44] Ibid., [29]–[41], where it is indicated that the bank had in fact received express instructions to renew one of the deposits on maturity.

[45] Ibid., [48], [59].   [46] Ibid., [48].   [47] Ibid., [52].   [48] Ibid., [33].   [49] Ibid., [61].

[50] Id. See also Ch. 5, Sect. 3 above.

[51] [1999] 1 All ER (Comm.) 612 (CA). See also *Bournemouth & Boscombe Athletic Football Club Ltd* v. *Lloyds TSB Bank plc* [2003] EWHC 834 (Ch), [28]. It is unclear whether *Suriya & Douglas* could be decided in the same way nowadays in light of BCOBS 4.1.4(2), which imposes on banks a continuing obligation to inform a 'banking customer' of 'the different retail banking services offered by the [bank] which share the main features of the retail banking service the banking customer has enquired about'. That said, BCOBS 4.1.4(2) does not necessarily undermine the view expressed in the text that English banks are unlikely to be subjected to a positive duty to inform customers of their deposits' maturity, as that provision does not purport to impose any disclosure obligation of that nature.

(iv) **Joint deposits**

The legal difficulties arising out of joint deposits are largely the same as those arising in respect of joint current accounts.[52] Two of these difficulties have been specifically considered in the context of deposit accounts. First, in *Innes* v. *Stephenson*,[53] the parties to a joint savings account that (somewhat unusually) was operable by cheque, failed to specify who was entitled to withdraw the funds. Lord Tenterden CJ held that, as the accountholders were not partners, they were unable to act on each other's behalf, so that all the accountholders' signatures were required to withdraw funds. Accordingly, just as in the situation where the account mandate *expressly* stipulates that all signatures are required,[54] a bank that honours an instrument bearing only one signature, or bearing a forged signature, must compensate the innocent accountholder for any losses.[55] Secondly, in *Husband* v. *Davis*,[56] the issue concerned whether a matured deposit could be paid to any one of the joint accountholders or whether it was necessary to obtain their joint discharge. Maule J observed:[57]

> ...there can be no doubt that a man may pay a debt to one of several to whom he is indebted jointly. The case of bankers stands upon special grounds. Where trustees of others have a joint account with them as bankers, it is usual to require the authority of the whole to pay the money. But that arises from the peculiar contract and relation between bankers and their customers.

Provided the account mandate does not expressly permit the account to be operated by only one of several accountholders, this conclusion is probably correct in respect of accounts requiring all accountholders to consent to withdrawals, otherwise there would be an illogical distinction between the bank's mandate during the currency of the deposit and its mandate upon maturity.[58]

3 **Dispositions over balance**

(i) **Problems concerned**

A current account balance is repayable on demand,[59] and may be assigned like any other debt. Interest-bearing accounts give rise to greater complexity as regards dispositions over the account balance, as some such accounts will be repayable on demand, such as savings accounts and deposits repayable at call, whilst others will mature on a different basis. For example, some interest-bearing accounts, such as 'extra interest accounts' and 'investment accounts', require the customer to give notice before repayment, whilst others, such as fixed deposits, mature at an agreed future time. This distinction between different types of account should be borne in mind when considering the effect of an attempted disposition of an interest-bearing account's balance. Such dispositions can occur as a result of an assignment, the bank's right of set-off, or an application for a third party debt order. Each of these will be considered in turn before addressing the issue of limitation.

---

[52] Ch. 8, Sect. 2 above.   [53] (1831) 1 M & Rob. 145.
[54] *Jackson* v. *White and Midland Bank Ltd* [1967] 2 Lloyd's Rep. 68, 79; *Catlin* v. *Cyprus Finance Corporation (London) Ltd* [1983] QB 759, 771.
[55] Ch. 8, Sect. 2(ii) above.
[56] (1851) 10 CB 645; cf. *Sabnani* v. *Lachmandas* [1994] 3 SLR 712, 717 (SGCA).   [57] Ibid., 650.
[58] *Brewer* v. *Westminster Bank* [1952] 2 All ER 650.   [59] Ch. 5, Sect. 3 above.

(ii) Assignment of balance or of part thereof

The credit balance of any interest-bearing account is a debt and hence a legal chose in action[60] that arises upon the deposit of funds and ceases to exist at maturity or on demand as the case may be. As a legal chose in action, the credit balance may be assigned, even if the pass-book or deposit receipt describes the account as non-transferable,[61] by one of two methods: a statutory assignment under section 136 of the Law of Property Act 1925; or an equitable assignment.[62] Whichever method is adopted, the consequence of an effective assignment is the same—the customer is no longer entitled to be paid the account's credit balance[63] and the bank must pay the assignee. That said, given that the statutory method of assignment requires the parties to follow certain procedures and satisfy several conditions,[64] bank balances are commonly transferred by the less formal equitable means.[65] Indeed, where the account holder wishes to transfer only *part* of the account balance, this cannot be achieved by statutory means, but only in equity.[66]

Particular difficulties have arisen in circumstances where the interest-bearing account requires the presentation of a pass-book or deposit certificate. Although it was once considered that the mere delivery of one of these documents could effect a valid assignment of the account balance,[67] quite correctly, this view was subsequently repudiated.[68] Neither a deposit receipt nor a pass-book constitutes a negotiable instrument transferable by delivery[69] and, even though an equitable assignment requires nothing more than an intention to assign the chose in action and 'some outward expression by the assignor of his intention to make an immediate disposition of the subject matter of the assignment',[70] it is submitted that the mere delivery of a pass-book is too equivocal to satisfy this requirement. Support for this conclusion can be found in *Evans* v. *National Provincial Bank of England*,[71] where the claimant simply delivered a deposit receipt to a third party, so as to enable him to collect the interest due on the relevant account, without writing on the face of the receipt any words manifesting an intention to assign the account balance. When the third party claimed the account's *entire* balance, and not just the interest, the issue arose as to whether the bank was discharged of its obligation to pay the balance to its customer by paying the third party. Collins J held that, as the claimant had not intended to transfer the balance, the bank was not discharged. In contrast, if the customer had written words on the deposit receipt (or pass-book) that evidenced an intention to assign the account balance, then payment to that third party would have discharged the bank. Accordingly, in *Re Griffin, Griffin* v. *Griffin*,[72] the testator left his

---

[60] Ch. 8, Sect. 2(iii) above.

[61] *Re Griffin, Griffin* v. *Griffin* [1899] 1 Ch. 408; *Elliott* v. *Elliott* (1899) 15 WN (NSW) 186. See also *Pennington* v. *Waine* [2002] 1 WLR 2075, [113].

[62] This practice has not caused significant legal difficulties: Ch. 21, Sect. 1 below.

[63] *Partridge* v. *Bank of England* (1846) 9 QB 396.

[64] *In re Westerton* [1919] 2 Ch 104, 111–112. See also *Republica de Guatemala* v. *Nuñez* [1927] 1 KB 669, 694–695 (CA); *McEvoy* v. *Belfast Banking Co. Ltd* [1935] AC 24, 34 (HL); *Kolden Holdings Ltd* v. *Rodette Commerce Ltd* [2008] 1 BCLC 481, [86].

[65] Ch. 21, Sect. 1 below.   [66] Id.

[67] *Woodhams* v. *Anglo-Australian and Universal Family Assurance Co.* (1861) 3 Giff. 234, approved in *In re Hurcules Insurance Company* (1874) 19 LR Eq 302, 315.

[68] *Moore* v. *Ulster Banking Co.* (1877) 11 IR Cl 512; *Re Griffin, Griffin* v. *Griffin*, n.61 above.

[69] Sect. 4(ii) below.

[70] *Finlan* v. *Eyton Morris Winfield* [2007] 4 All ER 143, [33]; *Daleri Ltd* v. *Woolworths plc* [2008] EWHC 2891 (Ch), [18].

[71] (1897) 13 TLR 429.

[72] N.61 above. See also *Re Pinto Leite, ex p. Olivaes* [1929] 1 Ch. 221; *Elliott* v. *Elliott*, n.61 above; *Anning* v. *Anning* (1907) 4 CLR 1049 (HCA); *Haythorpe* v. *Rae* [1972] VR 633 (VSC).

residual estate to his two sons in equal shares, but gave to one of them a deposit receipt on which he had written, 'pay my son'. When the other son contested the gift's validity, Byrne J concluded that the testator had done everything required for a complete and effective *donatio mortis causa* (a gift to mature on the assignor's demise) by delivering the receipt with words of assignment written upon it. His Lordship said:[73] '[The testator] gave an order to pay, indorsed on the document without the production of which the bank would not pay, and he handed over the document itself to his son, thereby putting it out of his own power to claim the money.'[74]

(iii) **Set-off by bank**

Whilst the bank can generally exercise a right of combination against its customers' accounts,[75] an issue also arises as to whether such a right may be exercised against the assignee of an interest-bearing account. Essentially, the issue concerns which of two conflicting claims has priority to the funds in the account. In *Jeffryes* v. *Agra and Masterman's Bank*,[76] an English merchant sold goods to an Indian purchaser and negotiated the shipping documents to the AM Bank, which credited the merchant's account with a substantial part of the purchase price for the goods, but issued the merchant with a 'memorandum of receipt' in respect of the balance of the purchase price, which the bank decided to 'retain' as security. As the merchant required immediate access to the *entire* purchase price, he indorsed the 'receipt' to the R Bank as security for an advance. Subsequently, the R Bank notified the AM Bank about this transaction and asked to be advised when the AM Bank received the purchase price from the Indian purchaser, but the AM Bank refused to do so and simply notified the R Bank of its own rights over the balance. When the merchant suspended his payments, both banks asserted a competing right to the sums in the merchant's account—the AM Bank claimed pursuant to its right of combination and the R Bank claimed as assignee. Wood V-C suggested that the AM Bank's rights were subject to two important limitations as regards assignees of the account balance. First, the right of combination could only be exercised in respect of an accrued liability, but was not available in respect of future or contingent liabilities,[77] so that if the assigned debt was still subject to a contingency or otherwise payable in the future at the time that the right of combination was exercised, then the assignee would have priority. Secondly, as the bank's rights against the assignee are generally the same as its rights were against the assignor at the moment of the assignment, the assignee takes subject to certain equities, including potentially the bank's right of combination. Only the customer/assignor's liabilities to the bank that were 'actually accrued before [the bank] had notice of the assignment' can be raised as an equity *vis-à-vis* the assignee. Accordingly, on the facts of *Jeffryes*, as the payment of the receipt was subject to a contingency, namely payment of the price by the Indian purchaser, AM Bank's right of combination could not be exercised and the R Bank was entitled to the payment of the amount covered by the receipt. R Bank's rights as assignee were subject, however, to any liabilities of the merchant to the AM Bank that had been incurred and were accrued before notice of the assignment was given to AM Bank. A similar view was expressed by Clauson J in *Re Pinto Leite, ex p. Olivaes*:[78]

> …when the debt assigned is at the date of notice of the assignment payable in futuro, the debtor can set off against the assignee a debt which becomes payable by the assignor to the

---

[73] Ibid., 412.   [74] Id.   [75] Ch. 7, Sect. 4 above.   [76] (1866) LR 2 Eq. 674.
[77] Ch. 7, Sect. 4(ii) above. See also *Liverpool Freeport Electronics Ltd* v. *Habib Bank Ltd* [2007] EWHC 1149 (QB), [136].   [78] N.72 above, 236.

debtor after notice of assignment, but before the assigned debt became payable, but only if, the debt so to be set off was *debitum in praesenti* at the date of the notice of assignment.

His Lordship emphasized that the debt to be set off against the assignee must have accrued before the date of the notification of the assignment to the debtor. The fact that the debt had matured after the date of the notification was irrelevant. The crucial point was that it did not remain contingent at the time payment was claimed by the assignee, as a conditional debt at that stage could not be the subject of the bank's right of combination.

(iv) Third party debt proceedings

A debt can be the subject of third party debt proceedings (formerly called garnishee proceedings) if it is 'due or accruing due' at the time the interim order is made.[79] Accounts repayable on demand can be attached by virtue of such proceedings and the service of the third party debt order on the bank constitutes the requisite demand.[80] Until 1956, however, there were doubts as to whether fixed deposits and deposits repayable at a minimum notice could be attached in this way.[81] These doubts were subsequently removed by section 38 of the Administration of Justice Act 1958, which, as discussed subsequently,[82] has been replaced and extended by section 40 of the Senior Courts Act 1981.[83]

(v) Limitation of action

Contractual debts become statute-barred after a lapse of six years,[84] after which time the creditor cannot enforce payment. The six-year period runs from the date on which the cause of action accrues,[85] which in the case of an interest-bearing account is the date on which the debt becomes payable. Obviously, this date depends upon whether the funds are due at a fixed future date,[86] upon giving the requisite period of notice, or on demand.[87] Whilst this technical defence is available to banks in the same way as any other type of defendant, out of concern for their reputation, banks are disinclined to plead limitation, even in cases where the debt is clearly time-barred.[88] A bank may, however, plead limitation as a last resort where it suspects collusion or dishonesty on the customer's part. A rare example of a bank raising a limitation point is *Atkinson* v. *Bradford Third Equitable Benefit Building Society*,[89] which concerned a deposit account with a building society that was repayable subject to notice and the production of a pass-book. Two days after the customer's death, an unidentified person obtained payment of the account's balance

---

[79] CPR 1998, r.72.2(1).   [80] *Joachimson* v. *Swiss Bank Corporation*, n.29 above.

[81] *Bagley* v. *Winsome and National Provincial Bank Ltd*, n.26 above, 243.

[82] Ch. 11, Sect. 1(iii) below.   [83] As subsequently amended by S. I. 2001/3649.

[84] The same limitation period applies to actions based upon a wrongful account debit: *Das* v. *Barclays Bank plc* [2006] EWHC 817 (QB), [37].

[85] Limitation Act 1980, s.5.

[86] Ch. 5, Sects. 3 & 6 above. Where funds on fixed deposit have matured and the bank, in the absence of customer instructions to the contrary, has allowed the money 'to continue to lie in the fixed deposit account', the limitation period runs from the date of the customer's demand: *Bank of America National Trust and Savings Association* v. *Iskandar*, n.12 above, [67].

[87] For the effect of a customer's successive demands on the limitation period, see *Bank of Baroda* v. *Mahomed* [1999] 1 Lloyd's Rep. 14 (CA), discussed in Ch. 5, Sect. 6 above.

[88] *Bank of Baroda* v. *Mahomed*, n.87 above, 19.

[89] (1890) 25 QBD 377. See also *Ungku Sulaiman Bin Abdul Majid* v. *Director of Lands and Mines* [2001] 6 MLJ 75, [71]. For other examples of banks raising limitation defences, see *Bank of Baroda* v. *Mahomed*, n.87 above; *Das* v. *Barclays Bank plc*, n.84 above. See further Ch. 5, Sects. 3 & 6 above.

against the production of the pass-book and a withdrawal form on which he had forged the customer's signature. When the customer's administrators brought an action for the recovery of the deposit some ten years later, the bank pleaded that the claim was statute-barred. Rejecting this defence, the Court of Appeal held that the limitation period ran from the grant of the letters of administration, as the estate could not have made a valid demand for repayment of the balance before that date. Although the conclusion that the debt was not statute-barred appears unexceptional, the court's choice of date for the start of the limitation period is more questionable. This date is only really explicable on the basis that the action was treated as one for breach of the banker–customer contract resulting from payment being made to the wrong person, for which the limitation period would have started to run against the *deceased customer himself* as from the date of the wrongful payment, but, as against *his estate*, as from the first date on which the estate could have pursued the matter. The better view, however, is that the estate's claim was a simple debt action and that the limitation period ran from an even later date, namely the date of the administrators' demand for repayment of the balance.[90]

In the case of interest-bearing accounts repayable on demand, the conclusion that the limitation period runs from the date of demand gives rise, as recognized in *Joachimson* v. *Swiss Bank Corporation*,[91] to the risk that 'bankers may have to face legal claims for balances on accounts that have remained dormant for more than six years'. One of the ways in which a court might sidestep this problem was considered in *Douglass* v. *Lloyds Bank Ltd*,[92] where the original depositor's heirs brought proceedings in 1929 for the repayment of a deposit that was repayable on demand and evidenced by a deposit receipt issued in 1866. Although Roche J held that the limitation period would only start running upon the demand for repayment, he dismissed the action, since the bank's records, going back to 1873, disclosed no evidence of the existence of the deposit. As no trace of the deposit account could be discovered in later ledgers, his Lordship inferred that the money must have been repaid. In reaching his conclusion, Roche J gave weight to the consideration that banks could not be expected to keep bank records indefinitely. Obviously, in cases of this type, the extent to which a court can draw an inference of repayment from the absence of bank records relating to a particular deposit depends upon the prevailing banking practice concerning the length of time for which banks keep account records. In future, however, courts dealing with the type of problem that arose in *Douglass* may have to have regard to the Dormant Bank and Building Society Accounts Act 2008, which introduces a regime whereby monies standing to the credit of an account that has remained dormant for 15 years or more must be transferred to charities or other entities 'for social or environmental purposes'. If there is evidence to show that the bank dealt with the funds in accordance with the 2008 Act, then the bank is no longer liable;[93] if there is no evidence as to what happened to the funds, however, then a court may have to fall back on the type of factual inference drawn in *Douglass* and assume that, in the absence of relevant bank records, the account funds in question were either repaid or dealt with in accordance with the 2008 Act.

---

[90] Limitation Act 1980, ss.5, 6. See also *National Bank of Commerce* v. *National Westminster Bank* [1990] 2 Lloyd's Rep. 514.

[91] N.29 above.

[92] (1929) 34 Com. Cas. 263. See also *Standard Chartered Bank* v. *Tiong Ngit Ting* [1998] 5 MLJ 220, 230–232.

[93] Dormant Bank and Building Society Accounts Act 2008, s.1(2)(a).

4 Deposit receipts and pass-books

(i) Problems involved

In modern practice, most banks, including all the main retail banks, have abandoned the use of pass-books and deposit receipts, although some banks still use deposit receipts in respect of deposits denominated in foreign currencies and pass-books are still very much a feature of building society savings accounts. The move away from the use of such documents by banks was dictated by three considerations. First, banks had expressed concerns about their customers' tendency to treat pass-books and deposit receipts as a convenient way of effecting an informal assignment of an account balance. Frequently, banks were faced with the difficulty of determining whether to pay the pass-book's 'holder' or not,[94] given that he could either have no entitlement whatsoever to receive payment or could be a valid equitable assignee of the account balance.[95] Indeed, the bank's dilemma was exacerbated by the fact that many of the defences available to banks that have wrongfully paid a cheque[96] are not applicable to the wrongful payment of interest-bearing account balances. Secondly, the customer's loss of a pass-book or deposit receipt was a common occurrence that often went undetected for a period of time, since (unlike a current account) the relevant interest-bearing account would not have been accessed all that frequently, which accordingly gave rise to the risk that the documents might fall into the wrong hands. Thirdly, the need to supply deposit receipts, and to replace them whenever a deposit was renewed, entailed considerable clerical work, as did the need to update the pass-book. The computer-produced periodic statement, which has replaced the deposit receipt and the pass-book, is a time-saving device and is generally understood not to constitute a negotiable instrument that might transfer an entitlement to the account balance.[97] As some banks and building societies continue to use deposit receipts and pass-books, it remains necessary to consider the salient features of these documents.

(ii) Legal nature of deposit receipt and pass-book

Despite suggestions to the contrary,[98] it is now well established that neither deposit receipts nor pass-books are negotiable instruments and accordingly that neither document is ordinarily transferable by delivery[99] so as to confer rights of ownership on the transferee.[100] In *Akbar Khan* v. *Attar Singh*,[101] Lord Atkin pointed out that, unlike a

---

[94] Sect. 2(ii) above.   [95] Sect. 3(ii) above.   [96] Ch. 11, Sects. 3 & 4 below.

[97] A bank is not obliged to provide its customer with a periodic account statement if the account is covered by a pass-book: BCOBS 4.2.1(a).

[98] *Woodhams* v. *Anglo-Australian and Universal Family Assurance Co.*, n.67 above; *In re Hurcules Insurance Company*, n.67 above, 315. See also G.A. Weaver & C.R. Craigie, *Banker and Customer in Australia* (loose-leaf, 2nd edn., Sydney, 1990), [3.650].

[99] *Re Wee Cheow Keng* [1953] MLJ 206, 207; *Bank of America National Trust and Savings Association* v. *Iskandar*, n.12 above, [37]–[38].

[100] *Gray's Trustee* v. *Murray*, 1970 SC 1, 4 (IH, 1st Div). For the conclusiveness of entries in a pass-book, see Ch. 7, Sect. 3 above.

[101] N.18 above, 548. See also *Hopkins* v. *Abbott*, n.3 above; *Moore* v. *Ulster Banking Co.*, n.68 above; *Provincial Treasurer of Manitoba* v. *Hunt* [1937] SCR 138 (SCC); *Claydon* v. *Bradley* [1987] 1 WLR 521, 525–526 (CA); *Cheung Pui Yuen* v. *Worldcup Investments Inc.* [2008] HKCU 1669, [13] (HKCFA). See further Grant, *Law Relating to Bankers* (7th edn., London, 1924), 219; H.L. Hart, *Law of Banking* (4th edn., London, 1931), 268.

promissory note, a deposit receipt did not include an express promise by the bank to pay the amount involved, as its sole object was to record the relevant transaction. According to his Lordship, a deposit receipt simply evidences the existence of a debt.[102] A savings pass-book performs an identical function.[103] As a general rule, a bank cannot avoid this state of affairs by simply issuing a deposit receipt that is expressly stated to be 'negotiable' or by writing 'negotiable' on a pass-book, as parties cannot create at will new forms of negotiable instrument.[104] Accordingly, if the parties want a negotiable instrument, they should employ one of the generally recognized forms, namely a bill of exchange, cheque, or promissory note. That said, some banks do issue 'negotiable certificates of deposit' (NCDs),[105] which, as discussed subsequently,[106] have probably become negotiable instruments as a result of a commercial usage[107] that is sufficiently long standing,[108] certain,[109] notorious,[110] and generally recognized by the City.[111] NCDs aside, there can be no argument that ordinary deposit receipts have become negotiable by commercial usage given that their use has rapidly declined in recent years. This means that the only way in which a transferee of a deposit receipt or pass-book can establish a right to funds in an interest-bearing account is by showing, as considered previously,[112] that there has been a valid assignment as a result of the original accountholder writing appropriate words to that effect on the document and delivering the document to the intended transferee.

One of the consequences of deposit receipts and pass-books not constituting negotiable instruments is that depositing such documents with a creditor does not generally provide him with any form of security,[113] as the documents do not confer any rights to the account balance upon the 'holder'. As discussed above, a bank that pays the account balance to such a 'holder' remains liable to pay the customer.[114] Nevertheless, the custody of a debtor's deposit receipt or pass-book can give some protection to a creditor in circumstances where the production of the document is a condition precedent to the bank's obligation to repay the amount deposited, as the creditor may then be able to block access

---

[102] *Pearce* v. *Creswick* (1843) 2 Hare 286; *Jeffryes* v. *Agra and Masterman's Bank*, n.76 above, 680; *Hopkins* v. *Abbott*, n.3 above; *Birch* v. *Treasury Solicitor* [1951] 1 Ch. 298, 313 (CA).

[103] *Birch* v. *Treasury Solicitor*, n.102 above.

[104] *Crouch* v. *Crédit Foncier of England Ltd* (1873) LR 8 QB 374. See also *Ung Eng Huat* v. *Arab Malaysian Bank* [2003] 6 MLJ 1, [11]–[13].

[105] *National Bank of Australasia Ltd* v. *Scottish Union and National Insurance Co.* (1951) 84 CLR 177 (HCA). [106] Sect. 4(v) & Ch. 10, Sect. 9 below.

[107] *Goodwin* v. *Robarts* (1875) LR 10 Ex. 337, affd. (1876) 1 App. Cas. 476 (HL); *Bechuanaland Exploration Co.* v. *London Trading Bank Ltd* [1898] 2 QB 658; *London Joint Stock Bank* v. *Simmons* [1892] AC 201 (HL); *Edelstein* v. *Schuler & Co.* [1902] 2 KB 144, 154–155; *Clayton* v. *Le Roy* [1911] 2 KB 1031, 1042; *Bank of Baroda Ltd* v. *Punjab National Bank Ltd* [1944] AC 176, 183 (PC); *Wah Tat Bank Ltd* v. *Chan Cheng Kum* [1967] 2 Lloyd's Rep. 437, 442–443 (MFC).

[108] *Bechuanaland Exploration Co.* v. *London Trading Bank Ltd*, n.107 above; *Edelstein* v. *Schuler & Co.*, n.107 above.

[109] *Sewell* v. *Corp* (1824) 1 Car. & P 392, 393; *Devonald* v. *Rosser & Sons* [1906] 2 KB 728, 743; *Sagar* v. *H Ridehalgh & Son Ltd* [1931] 1 Ch 310, 338–339 (CA); *Glengate-KG Properties Ltd* v. *Norwich Union Fire Insurance Society* [1995] 1 Lloyd's Rep 278, 284; *Henry* v. *London General Transport Services Ltd* [2002] IRLR 472 (CA); *Solectron Scotland Ltd* v. *Roper* [2004] IRLR 4, [22]; *London Underground Ltd* v. *Fisher* (EAT, 13 September 2004), [19]. See also *Resene Paints Ltd* v. *Orica New Zealand Ltd* [2003] 3 NZLR 709, [36].

[110] 'Notorious' in this context means that it is clearly understood by those affected by it: *Tucker* v. *Linger* (1883) 8 App. Cas. 508, 511 (HL); *Danowski* v. *Henry Moore Foundation*, The Times, 19 March 1996 (CA); *Resene Paints Ltd* v. *Orica New Zealand Ltd*, n.109 above, [36].

[111] *Picker* v. *London and County Banking Co. Ltd* (1887) 18 QBD 515 (CA). [112] Sect. 3(ii) above.

[113] *Hopkins* v. *Abbott*, n.3 above. The mere deposit of a pass-book or deposit certificate as security for a debt probably does not amount to an assignment of the account balance by way of security, unless there is some further indication of the accountholder's intention: *In re Westerton*, n.64 above.

[114] Sect. 2(ii) above.

to his debtor's interest-bearing account until he is paid. The validity of clauses making the pass-book a precondition of payment was confirmed by the High Court of Australia in *Kauter* v. *Hilton*, where Dixon CJ stated:[115]

> The passbooks contain a notice that withdrawals may be made by the depositor personally on production of the passbook and the necessary completed withdrawal form or to the bearer of a completed withdrawal form signed by the depositor and presented with the passbook. The presentation of the passbook is therefore required before any moneys can be withdrawn from an account.

It is important, however, not to overestimate the benefit to a creditor from having custody of his debtor's pass-book or deposit receipt, since not only does he have no right to demand payment of the account's credit balance, but his debtor (the accountholder) may also be able to obtain payment of the funds without the deposit receipt or pass-book by convincing the bank that the relevant document has been lost.[116] Moreover, a creditor has no claim against the bank when it issues a replacement deposit receipt or pass-book to the customer and pays against that document. Accordingly, the best advice to a creditor holding a pass-book for security purposes would be to notify the bank of its claim and hope that the bank refuses to deliver the funds except against presentation of the relevant document, which may give the creditor sufficient time to obtain summary judgment against the accountholder and obtain a third party debt order against the account.

(iii) **Loss of deposit receipt or pass-book**

The customer's loss of his deposit receipt or pass-book does not free the bank from its obligation to pay. The bank will usually replace the lost document, provided the customer has agreed to indemnify it against any potential third party claims.[117] The commercial utility of this indemnity is unclear, given that possession of the deposit receipt does not usually entitle a third party to claim the account balance. Indeed, the customer is entitled to payment even if the bank has made payment to an unauthorized person against the wrongfully acquired receipt.[118] In such circumstances, the production of the deposit receipt or pass-book ceases to be a condition precedent to the customer receiving payment,[119] so that the customer can claim the balance at maturity without needing to have the deposit receipt or pass-book replaced.

---

[115] (1953) 90 CLR 86, 101 (HCA). See also *Atkinson* v. *Bradford Third Equitable Benefit Building Society*, n.89 above; *Re Dillon, Duffin* v. *Duffin* (1890) 44 Ch. D 76; *Re Tidd, Tidd* v. *Overell* [1893] 3 Ch. 154; *Re Griffin, Griffin* v. *Griffin*, n.61 above; *Anning* v. *Anning*, n.72 above; *Commissioners of State Savings Bank of Victoria* v. *Permewan, Wright & Co Ltd* (1914) 19 CLR 457, 471 (HCA); *Neitzke* v. *Wiehmayer* (1921) 62 SCR 262 (SCC); *Voo Foot Yiu* v. *Overseas Chinese Banking Corp. Ltd*, n.33 above, 170; *C&E Lewis Ltd* v. *Gribben* [1955] NI 51; *Re Australia and New Zealand Savings Bank Ltd, Mellas* v. *Evriniadis*, n.39 above, 693–694; *Haythorpe* v. *Rae*, n.72 above, 637–638; *Paleopoulos* v. *Paleopoulos* (1979) 5 Fam. LR 461, 463–464; *Root* v. *Nanyang Commercial Bank Ltd*, n.26 above, 420–422; *Brooker* v. *Pridham* (1986) 10 ACLR 428, 436–437 (SASC).

[116] Sect. 4(iii) below.

[117] *Pearce* v. *Creswick*, n.102 above; *Atkinson* v. *Bradford Third Equitable Building Society*, n.89 above; *Re Dillon, Duffin* v. *Duffin*, n.115 above. See also *Conflans Stone Quarry Co. Ltd* v. *Parker* (1867) LR 3 CP 1 (circular note lost in the mail).

[118] *Public Bank Bhd* v. *Ng Yoon Lin*, n.32 above, [10].

[119] *Wood* v. *Clydesdale Bank Ltd*, n.36 above, discussed in Sect. 2(ii) above.

(iv) **The deposit receipt and the pass-book as the subject of a _donatio mortis causa_**

As a general rule, gifts intended to take effect upon a person's death must be contained in a will that complies with the formal requirements of the Wills Act 1837. The common law has, however, given effect to some gifts made in anticipation of the donor's death and that are intended to take effect upon his death—termed a _donatio mortis causa_—even if the gift is not made in writing. An accountholder may wish to make such a gift of the balance of his interest-bearing account as his health fails. Sometimes this may simply be because the accountholder does not have sufficient time to make the requisite changes to his will, or because the accountholder may consider that it is possible to avoid inheritance tax by making a gift before his death. The law seeks to deal with the first problem by recognizing the validity of the _donatio mortis causa_. Just as in the case of an accountholder who transfers funds to a joint account with his heirs to avoid inheritance tax,[120] so too an accountholder who makes a _donatio mortis causa_ solely for the purpose of avoiding tax may find that purpose frustrated, as a gift occurring within the seven years preceding the donor's death will nevertheless by treated as a taxable part of the deceased's estate.[121] Accordingly, a gift, effected by the handing over of a deposit receipt or a pass-book with an instruction that the donee receive the funds upon the donor's demise will probably incur inheritance tax under section 4 of the Inheritance Tax Act 1984.

Whatever the ultimate aim behind making the gift, an accountholder may only make a valid _donatio mortis causa_ if two requirements are satisfied: first, the accountholder must transfer the 'indicia of title' to the relevant account; and, secondly, the transfer must have been made with the requisite donative intent. As regards the first of these requirements, the courts have had to consider what types of document constitute the relevant 'indicia of title' on a surprising number of occasions. Whilst the delivery of a deposit receipt or pass-book to a third party will not generally transfer rights to the account balance, unless it can take effect by way of an assignment,[122] the courts have accepted that in particular circumstances the transfer of a pass-book[123] or deposit receipt[124] is capable of constituting a valid _donatio mortis causa_.[125] The courts have, however, declined to attach the same significance to other bank account documents. In _Re Heathcote_,[126] one of the issues was whether there had been a valid _donatio mortis causa_ of the funds standing to the credit of a current account as a result of the deceased having transferred the cheque-book, paying-in book, and bank statements relating to that account. Rejecting the existence of a gift, Mummery J stated that '[t]here has been no case … in which it has been held that money in a current account at a bank is capable of being the subject of a valid _donatio mortis causa_ by delivery to a donee of a paying-in book or a cheque-book or of bank statements, or other account documents relating to the operation of the account'.[127] According

---

[120] _McEvoy_ v. _Belfast Banking Co._, n.64 above, discussed in Ch. 8, Sect. 2(iii) above.

[121] Finance Act 1986, s.102(1). See also _Ingram_ v. _Inland Revenue Commissioners_ [1997] 4 All ER 395, 410–411 (CA).

[122] Sect. 3(ii) above.

[123] _Bagley_ v. _Winsome and National Provincial Bank Ltd_, n.26 above, 241. See also _Re Andrews_ [1902] 2 Ch 394, 396–397; _Re Weston_ [1902] 1 Ch 680, 685; _Kendrick_ v. _Dominion Bank_ (1920) 48 OLR 539, 546 (OCA); _Birch_ v. _Treasury Solicitor_, n.102 above, 313; _Lord Advocate_ v. _R_ [1953] TR 119 (Ct. Sess.); _Re Heathcote_ (Ch. D, 2 March 1990).

[124] _McDonald_ v. _McDonald_ (1903) 33 SCR 145 (SCC); _M'Intyre_ v. _Gillies_ 1956 SC 437, 449 (IH, 1st Div.).

[125] _Re Kuyat_ (1962) 33 DLR (2d) 153, 156 (BCSC); _Randell's Estate_ v. _Randell_ (1972) 2 Nfld & PEIR 523, 533–534 (NSC); _Saulnier_ v. _Anderson_ (1987) NBR (2d) 1, [71]–[72] (NBQBD).

[126] N.123 above.

[127] Ibid. See also _Tawil_ v. _Public Trustee of New South Wales_ (NSWSC, 24 June 1998).

to his Lordship, as none of these documents were 'indicia of title' to the money in the account, nor represented the money in the account, their delivery could not be relied on as constituting a gift of the account balance. The same is also generally true of a cheque drawn by the donor on the account in question[128] and an ATM card without the PIN.[129] Even where the document in question is a pass-book or deposit certificate, however, there will only be a valid *donatio mortis causa* if the document reaches the donee's hands.[130] If it is retained by the donor or by his agent for delivery, the gift remains incomplete.[131] The gift is not, however, destroyed if the donor regains possession of the receipt from time to time following its initial delivery, provided the receipt is delivered back to the donee before the donor's death.[132]

Even when the pass-book or deposit receipt is handed over to, and retained by, the donee, it has long been accepted that this alone does not necessarily constitute a valid *donatio mortis causa* unless a second requirement is satisfied, namely that the donor has the requisite intention in handing over the document. It is necessary to show that the donor's intention was to make a gift that was conditional on his death, but that would otherwise lapse if the donor did not die, and that the intention to give had been formed 'in contemplation of death', in the sense that the donor believed death to be 'within the near future' or 'impending'.[133] Whether the requisite intention exists depends on the exact words uttered or written by the donor at the time that he delivered the pass-book or deposit receipt. Where the accountholder makes his intention clear by using such words as, 'this is yours when I go',[134] then there should be little difficulty. In other cases, the courts will have to determine the accountholder's intention by reference to surrounding circumstances and will seek to give effect to his wishes. This principle is easier to state in theory, however, than to apply in practice, and the case law is not easily reconcileable. This confusion probably stems in no small part from the need to draw the difficult distinction between two particular states of mind: on the one hand, an intention to relinquish immediate control over the subject-matter of the gift, albeit subject to a condition that the property revest if the donor does not die; and, on the other hand, an intention to retain an immediate interest that will ultimately vest in the donee upon the donor's death. The former intention is consistent with a *donatio mortis causa*; the latter is not. An example of the former intention can be found in *Re Dillon, Duffin* v. *Duffin*,[135] where the donor,

---

[128] *In re Leaper* [1916] 1 Ch 579, 582; *Re Heathcote*, n.123 above; *Curnock* v. *Inland Revenue Commissioners* [2003] STC 283, [6]–[7]; *Blackett* v. *Darcy* [2005] NSWSC 65, [24]–[26]. A cheque drawn in favour of the donor and endorsed in favour of the donee may be a valid *donatio mortis causa*: *Wilson* v. *Paniani* [1996] 3 NZLR 378, 382, citing *Clement* v. *Cheeseman* (1884) 27 Ch. D. 631. There might be a valid *donatio mortis causa* where the donor's cheque has been cashed and the proceeds paid into the recipient's account shortly before the donor's death: *Campbell* v. *Fenwick* [1934] OR 692, 695–696 (OCA). For other examples where there might be a valid *donatio mortis causa* of a cheque, see *In re Beaumont* [1902] 1 Ch 889, 893–894. See also Ch. 11, Sect. 1(vi) below.

[129] *Re Smith Estate* (1995) 410 APR 316, [26]–[27] (NSC), [26]–[27], although the ATM card had also been cut in half by the donor. There can be an effective *donatio mortis causa* by converting an individual account into a joint account: *Shaw* v. *MacKenzie Estate* (1994) 131 NSR (2d) 118, [51]–[53] (NSSC). See also *Re Fenton Estate* (1977) 26 NSR (2d) 662, [63] (NSSC).

[130] *Woodard* v. *Woodard* [1985] 3 All ER 980 (CA).

[131] *Moore* v. *Ulster Banking Co.*, n.68 above; cf. *In re Griffin*, n.61 above.

[132] *Watts* v. *Public Trustee* (1949) 50 SR (NSW) 130.

[133] *Re Craven's Estate* [1937] Ch 423, 426; *Re Heathcote*, n.123 above; *Sen* v. *Headley* [1991] Ch. 425, 431–432 (CA).

[134] *In re Estate of Hannah Mailman* [1941] SCR 368, 373–374 (SCC).

[135] N.115 above. See also *Re Griffin, Griffin* v. *Griffin*, n.61 above; *Re Weston* [1900–1903] All ER Rep 283, 284–285; *Delgoffe* v. *Fader* [1939] 3 All ER 682, 685–687; *Re Ward, Ward* v. *Warwick* [1946] 2 All ER 206; *Sen* v. *Headley*, n.133 above, 437–439.

who was seriously ill, completed a cheque form printed at the foot of a deposit receipt and delivered it to a relative. The donee was to retain the document if the donor died, but was asked to return it if he survived his illness. Upholding the validity of the gift, Cotton LJ held that the accountholder had lost his control over the account's funds by completing the cheque form and delivering the deposit receipt, since, even though the transfer did not necessarily constitute an irrevocable assignment of funds, the production of the receipt was a condition precedent to the bank's duty to pay. Accordingly, upon the accountholder's death, there was a valid *donatio mortis causa*. On the other side of the line is the decision in *Re Heathcote*,[136] in which, as discussed above, the documents that were transferred by the donor (namely a cheque-book, paying-in book, and bank statements) gave no control over the funds in the current account. The donor's retention of an interest in the account was inconsistent with any intention to relinquish absolute control over the funds; instead, the gift remained revocable and, therefore, invalid. Accordingly, in ascertaining the accountholder's intention, the modern case law emphasizes the significance of the relinquishment of control—the gift is effective only if the donee acquires the absolute right to dispose of the funds, subject only to the condition that the donor becomes entitled to the funds once again should he not die.[137]

(v) Negotiable certificates of deposit

In an attempt to facilitate the ready transfer of deposits, banks have developed a new type of document termed a 'negotiable certificate of deposit' or 'NCD'. Usually, such a document is issued to the customer in respect of each amount placed with the bank and the deposit's repayment is made conditional upon the NCD's production. Although NCDs describe themselves as being 'negotiable', this is not necessarily determinative of whether they constitute negotiable instruments in legal terms. It is clear that, as NCDs issued in London do not incorporate either an order to pay or the issuer's express undertaking to repay the amount deposited to the payee's order or to the bearer, but rather simply acknowledge the deposit of funds, such documents do not fall within the statutory definitions of either a bill of exchange[138] or a promissory note.[139] A conclusion to the contrary has been expressed by the Texan Court of Appeal in *Southview Corp.* v. *Kleberg First National Bank*,[140] but there are two reasons why this decision would probably not be followed in England. First, unlike their English counterparts, the certificate of deposit in *Kleberg* included the issuer's express promise to repay. Secondly, the definition of 'negotiable instruments' in Article 3 of the Uniform Commercial Code[141] is not *in pari materia* with section 3 of the Bills of Exchange Act 1882. That said, the English Court of Appeal did recognize in *Customs and Excise Commissioners* v. *Guy Butler (Int.) Ltd*[142] that the NCD constitutes a *novel* form of negotiable instrument as a result of mercantile usage. The fact that most NCDs contain a clause making withdrawal of the account funds conditional upon the production of the document itself probably supports this legal conclusion. It is not certain, however, that *Guy Butler* conclusively settles the issue of whether NCDs

---

[136] N.123 above.

[137] *Birch* v. *Treasury Solicitor*, n.102 above; *Kauter* v. *Hilton*, n.115 above; *Haythorpe* v. *Rae*, n.72 above.

[138] Bills of Exchange Act 1882 (BEA 1882), s.3(1).

[139] Ibid., s.83. An ordinary deposit receipt is not a promissory note: *Akbar Khan* v. *Attar Singh*, n.18 above, 548. See also *Claydon* v. *Bradley*, n.101 above, 525–526.

[140] 512 SW 2d 817 (Tex. CA, 1974). See also *Worden* v. *Thornburg*, 564 SW 2d 480, 483 (Tex. CA, 1978); *Wrightman* v. *American National Bank of Riverton* 610 P.2d 1001, 1004 (Wy. SC, 1980); *Dallas Fort Worth Airport Bank* v. *Dallas Bank and Trust Co.*, 667 SW 2d 572, 575 (Tex. CA, 1984).

[141] UCC, s.3–104(2)(a), (j).   [142] [1977] QB 377, 382 (CA).

are negotiable instruments. Not only was the issue dealt with obiter in *Guy Butler*, but it is also possible that, when a court finally faces the issue squarely, it remains unpersuaded that the mercantile usage recognizing NCDs as negotiable instruments is sufficiently certain, reasonable, 'notorious', and of general standing.[143] Indeed, persuading a court to recognize a whole new type of negotiable instrument involves the discharge of a relatively heavy burden and all it would take is for an expert banking witness in the relevant case to demonstrate some misunderstanding about the meaning of 'negotiability' in relation to NCDs, or to express some doubt about the certainty or uniformity of the practice relating to NCDs, for the court to reject the suggestions that they are negotiable instruments. Whilst banks may be perfectly conversant with NCDs and their usage, it is less certain whether other types of institution are as familiar with them.

If NCDs do not constitute negotiable instruments, then conceptually they are the same as traditional deposit receipts, which, as shown previously,[144] simply evidence a debt owed by the bank to his customer. Accordingly, as with ordinary deposit receipts, NCDs will not confer on the document's 'holder' any entitlement to the funds to which it relates, unless it can be shown that the 'holder' also happens to be an assignee of the account balance.[145] A further consequence would be that, if transferred to a bank as security for advances, an NCD would constitute a poor form of security. As an NCD simply evidences a debt, nothing can be pledged to the lending bank, as a chose in action cannot be the subject of a pledge.[146] It may be possible, however, for the transfer of an NCD as security for advances to create a charge over the account balance to which it relates. The mere delivery of the NCD may be too equivocal to create a charge, however, unless there is some further indication of the accountholder's intention in that regard. Provided the requisite intention can be shown, there are no difficulties with creating a charge in favour of a bank other than the one that issued the NCD. At one time, however, it would have been considered 'conceptually impossible' to charge the relevant account balance to the bank that issued the NCD.[147] Such impossibility was overcome in *Bank of Credit and Commerce International SA (No. 8)*,[148] where the House of Lords held that a bank could obtain a charge over a sum of money deposited with itself. In the final analysis, the bank's effective claim over the funds would probably be anchored in its statutory right of set-off under section 323 of the Insolvency Act 1986, but this right would be available regardless of whether the deposit was covered by an NCD or a simple deposit receipt.

Even if an NCD is treated as a negotiable instrument, so that there is little difficulty in transferring rights over the account balance to third parties, this does not necessarily mean that the 'holder' of the NCD will have priority over the account balance as against other potential claimants. This potential priority problem arises from the fact that the account balance, to which the NCD relates, appears in the issuing bank's books as a debt due to the customer, with the result that it can be subject to attachment by way of a freezing injunction or a third party debt order.[149] Furthermore, the debt due to the customer,

---

[143] Sect. 4(ii) above.   [144] Ibid.   [145] Sect. 3(ii) above.

[146] A pledge depends upon possession of the subject matter: *Alcom Ltd* v. *Republic of Columbia* [1984] 2 All ER 6; *Swiss Bank Corporation* v. *Lloyds Bank Ltd* [1982] AC 584 (HL). See also Ch. 20, Sect. 1 below.

[147] *Re Charge Card Services Ltd* [1987] Ch. 150, affd. [1989] Ch. 497 (CA).

[148] [1998] AC 214 (HL). See also *Broad* v. *Commissioner of Stamp Duties* [1980] 2 NSWLR 40, 46, 48; *Estate Planning Associates (Aust.) Pty. Ltd* v. *Commissioner of Stamp Duties* (1985) 2 NSWLR 495, 498–500; *Esanda Finance Corporation Ltd* v. *Jackson* (1992) 59 SASR 416, 418; *Welsh Development Agency* v. *Export Finance Co. Ltd* [1992] BCLC 148 (CA); *Griffiths* v. *Commonwealth Bank of Australia* (1994) 123 ALR 120, 120 (FCA); *Wily* v. *Rothschild* [1999] NSWSC 915; cf *Cinema Plus Ltd* v. *ANZ Banking Group Ltd* (NSWCA, 28 July 2000). See further Ch. 21, Sect. 3(iv) below.

[149] Senior Courts Act 1981, s.40 (amended by S. I. 2001/3649). See also Sect. 3(iv) above.

or depositor, passes to his liquidator or trustee in bankruptcy if the customer becomes insolvent. The 'holder' of the NCD does not necessarily have priority over these other claimants. The same is true where the NCD is deposited with the bank that issued the document as security for an advance. Whilst the NCD would undoubtedly confer on the issuing bank the right to refuse repayment of the amount involved to the customer, such a right would not necessarily confer any priority in a bankruptcy or winding up. A right to refuse payment could of course be effected just as neatly by a set-off agreement incorporating a 'retention' or 'flawed asset' clause.[150] A bank will, however, have the right to apply the account proceeds in satisfaction of a debt due under section 323 of the Insolvency Act 1986. This potential lack of priority on the part of an NCD's 'holder', even if it constitutes a negotiable instrument, can be usefully compared with the situation where a traditional negotiable instrument is to be retired or discharged out of the funds deposited.[151] Thus, where a post-dated cheque, handed by the customer to the payee as a security for payment, is meant to be paid out of the proceeds of the current account upon which it is drawn, the custody of the cheque gives the payee no priority over those account funds. The same is true as regards a bill of exchange accepted by the customer and domiciled by him at his bank. The holder of such a bill has the right to enforce it against the customer, but he does not acquire any priority over the funds available for its discharge.[152]

5 Foreign-currency deposits

Following the abolition of exchange control in the United Kingdom, banks have been able to make provision for deposits denominated in foreign currencies. The customer's object in placing part of his funds in such a foreign-currency deposit account is usually to make a profit in the event that the currency, in which the account is denominated, appreciates against sterling. Sometimes, the accountholder may also wish to profit from the higher rate of interest available for deposits in the relevant foreign currency. A foreign-currency deposit will be renewed in the relevant currency from time to time, but usually converted into sterling when the customer demands payment.[153] From a legal point of view, however, there is no fundamental difference between deposits denominated in sterling and foreign-currency deposits, as both constitute a debt due from the bank to the customer. Accordingly, foreign-currency deposits have not generally given rise to particular problems. The principal exception to this proposition arises in the case of foreign-currency deposits placed with banks whose head offices are overseas, as occasionally the government of that bank's home country may seek to exercise control over deposits denominated in the bank's home currency, irrespective of where the deposit was actually made. A notable recent example of such extraterritorial governmental action over foreign accounts

---

[150] Ch. 21, Sect. 3(iii) below.

[151] *Federal Deposit Insurance Corp.* v. *Pioneer State Bank*, 382 A. 2d 1958 (1977).

[152] BEA 1882, s.53.

[153] A customer has the option of demanding repayment of a foreign-currency deposit in notes of his chosen currency: *Libyan Arab Foreign Bank* v. *Bankers' Trust Co.* [1988] 1 Lloyd's Rep. 259. See also C. Proctor, *Goode on Payment Obligations in Commercial and Financial Transactions* (2nd edn., London, 2009), [5-19]. The standard terms and conditions of most foreign-currency accounts exclude this right. It may also be abrogated legislatively: G. Gomez Giglio, 'Argentine Supreme Court of Justice Confirmed the Pesification of Bank Deposits' (2007) 22 *JIBLR* 224.

can be found in the 'USA Patriot Act 2001',[154] which was passed shortly after the events of 9/11 in order to combat terrorist financing. In relation to unlawful activity falling within the scope of the legislation, the relevant United States authorities not only have 'long-arm' jurisdiction over foreign financial institutions that maintain a correspondent account at a financial institution in the United States,[155] but are also entitled to forfeit funds related to terrorist activity that are held in a bank account outside the United States by debiting funds from the foreign bank's correspondent account located within the jurisdiction.[156]

The more usual type of case involves a foreign court issuing an order, or a foreign government issuing an executive order, to freeze or attach the balance standing to the credit of a customer's account in another jurisdiction.[157] Such a situation arose recently in *European Bank Ltd* v. *Citibank Ltd*,[158] in which the claimant, a bank in Vanuatu, brought proceedings to recover a United States dollar deposit with the defendant, Citibank Ltd, in Sydney. The deposit in question was effected by the claimant's correspondent bank in New York transferring funds to the defendant's New York correspondent, which in turn credited the defendant's account with it. The funds were, however, maintained on the defendant's books in Sydney. By way of defence to the claim for the return of the deposit, the defendant relied upon a *force majeure* clause in the account contract with the claimant and the fact that the New York courts had issued a warrant directed against the defendant purporting to seize the claimant's deposit. The New South Wales Court of Appeal rejected the defence on the basis that the New York order could not affect a deposit governed by the law of New South Wales and situated there: '... [i]n the absence of some explicit provision it would be fanciful to think that the debt owed by Citibank to European Bank in Sydney could be discharged by a payment made in New York by someone other than the debtor, pursuant to a warrant issued under a foreign penal law which is not enforceable internationally'.[159] The approach in *European Bank* largely reflects the position adopted by the English courts when asked to give effect to similar extraterritorial orders issued by foreign governments—effect will only be given to a foreign order when the law of that foreign jurisdiction governs the issue before the English courts. The choice of law rule to be used depends upon the precise issue before the court: if the issue relates to whether the governmental order is effective to transfer the property in the account funds by means of an act of governmental expropriation, then the courts will apply the *lex situs*;[160] if, however, the issue concerns whether the governmental act affects the contractual obligations between the bank and its customer, then that is a matter for the law applicable to the banking contract.[161] Fortunately, despite this important conceptual difference, in practice both the *lex situs* of the bank balance—the debt due from the bank to its customer—and the law applicable to the contractual obligations arising from the banking contract are determined by reference to the law of the place of the branch at which the relevant account is kept.[162] The fact that the account is denominated in a foreign currency is irrelevant to

---

[154] Uniting and Strengthening America by Providing Appropriate Tools Required to Intercept and Obstruct Terrorism (USA Patriot Act) Act 2001, 115 Stat. 272 (26 October 2001). See also C. Proctor, n.153 above, [4-30]–[4-31].

[155] Ibid., s.317.   [156] Ibid., s.319.

[157] *China Mutual Trading Co. Ltd* v. *Banque Belge Pour l'Étranger (Extreme Orient) SA* (1954) 39 HKLR 144 (executive order penalizing firms trading with the People's Republic of China).

[158] [2004] NSWCA 76.

[159] Ibid., [51]. An application for special leave to appeal to the High Court of Australia has been refused: [2005] HCATrans 142. For subsequent proceedings, see *European Bank Ltd* v. *Evans* [2010] HCA 6.

[160] Dicey, Morris & Collins, *The Conflict of Laws* (14th edn., London, 2006), rule 128.

[161] Ibid., paras. [33-304]–[33-306].

[162] *Joachimson* v. *Swiss Bank Corp.*, n.29 above; *Arab Bank Ltd* v. *Barclays Bank (DCO)* [1954] AC 495, 529, 534, & 537 (HL); *The Chartered Bank of India, Australia & China* v. *The Public Trustee* [1957] 1 MLJ

determining the applicable law—a deposit denominated in United States dollars that is held with the London branch of a bank, and repayable there, is governed by English law.

The approach of the English courts to foreign expropriatory orders was expounded in two decisions arising from the freeze imposed by President Reagan on balances of Libyan Government institutions. In *Libyan Arab Foreign Bank* v. *Bankers Trust Co.*,[163] the claimant maintained two accounts with the defendant bank: a Eurodollars account with the defendant's London branch; and an account used predominantly for transfers and settlements with the defendant's head office in New York. The defendant had authority to transfer funds between the two accounts if the balances fell below, or rose above, a particular account balance. Shortly after President Reagan made his order, the claimant demanded payment in London of sums deposited in its London account, but the defendant bank refused on two grounds: first, that the defendant's entire banking relationship with the claimant was governed by New York law; and, secondly that, even if the banking relationship was governed by English law, the court should not order payment as it would involve the performance of an act in New York that was illegal by the law of that place. To substantiate this second argument, the defendant called expert evidence to establish that sums of the magnitude in question could only be cleared and settled in New York. Staughton J held that, although there was only one contract between the two banks, it was governed by two separate systems of law:[164] New York law governed the deposit there and English law governed the London deposit.[165] Accordingly, President Reagan's order did not affect the London deposit. That said, Staughton J accepted that, even applying English law, a court should not order the defendant bank to perform an act in the United States, such as the settlement or repayment of a debt through the United States clearing system, if that would involve performing an act that was illegal by the law of that place.[166]

211, 212–214 (SGCA); *X, Y & Z* v. *B* [1983] 2 Lloyd's Rep. 535; *MacKinnon* v. *Donaldson, Lufkin & Jenrette Securities Corp.* [1986] Ch. 482, 493 (CA); *Libyan Arab Foreign Bank* v. *Bankers' Trust Co.*, n.153 above, 270; *Libyan Arab Foreign Bank* v. *Manufacturers Hanover Trust Co.* [1988] 2 Lloyd's Rep. 494, 498–499; *Attock Cement Co. Ltd* v. *Romanian Bank for Foreign Trade* [1989] 1 WLR 1147, 1159 (CA); *Libyan Arab Foreign Bank* v. *Manufacturers Hanover Trust Co. (No. 2)* [1989] 1 Lloyd's Rep. 608, 616–617; *Irish Shipping Ltd* v. *Commercial Union Assurance* [1991] 2 QB 206, 221 (CA); *Zebrarise Ltd* v. *de Nieffe* [2005] 2 All ER (Comm.) 816, [30]–[31]. The common law principle that the banker–customer contract and the account contract are governed by the law of the branch at which the account is maintained still applied under the Rome Convention on the Law Applicable to Contractual Obligations 1980: *Sierra Leone Telecommunications Co. Ltd* v. *Barclays Bank plc* [1998] 2 All ER 821, 827. This was despite the fact that bank records are nowadays kept on centralized computers: *Walsh* v. *National Irish Bank Ltd* [2007] IEHC 325, [26]–[37]. This position has not changed under Regulation (EC) 593/2008 on the Law Applicable to Contractual Obligations (in force 17 December 2009), Arts. 4(1)(b), 19(2), as the law applicable to banking operations is *prima facie* 'the place where the branch…is located', although the applicable law may be that of the jurisdiction where the bank has its head office when two or more accounts are held in different jurisdictions (ibid., Art. 4(2)).

[163] N.153 above. See also *Sierra Leone Telecommunications Co. Ltd* v. *Barclays Bank plc*, n.162 above, 826–827; *Attorney-General of Zambia* v. *Meer, Care & Desai* [2007] EWHC 952 (Ch), [160].

[164] Ch. 5, Sect. 3 above.

[165] N.153 above, 271. See also Dicey, Morris & Collins, n.160 above, [32-005] ff; *Chitty on Contracts* (30th edn., London, 2008), [30-015]. See further *Hamlyn* v. *Talisker Distillery* [1894] AC 202 (HL); *Kahler* v. *Midland Bank* [1950] AC 24 (HL); *Re United Railways of the Havana and Regla Warehouse Ltd* [1960] Ch. 52, 92; *Attock Cement Co. Ltd* v. *Romanian Bank for Foreign Trade*, n.162 above.

[166] In determining illegality by the place of performance, relevant considerations include the motivation of the parties and whether the illegality was initial or supervening: *Regazzoni* v. *K. C. Sethia Ltd* [1958] AC 301; *Mackender* v. *Feldia AG* [1967] 2 QB 590, 601; *Toprak Mahsulleri Ofisi* v. *Finagrain Compagnie Commerciale Agricole et Financière SA* [1979] 2 Lloyd's Rep. 98; *Euro-Diam Ltd* v. *Bathurst* [1990] 1 QB 1, 20–21; *Ispahani* v. *Bank Melli Iran* [1998] Lloyd's Rep. Bank 133, 136; *Soleimany* v. *Soleimany* [1999] QB 785, 793–794 (CA); *Omnium de Traitement et de Valorisation SA* v. *Hilmarton Ltd* [1999] 2 Lloyd's Rep 222, 224–225; *Mahonia Ltd* v. *JP Morgan Chase Bank* [2003] 2 Lloyd's Rep 911, [13]–[19]; *JSC Zestafoni G Nikoladze*

Performance in the United States was not, however, the only way the defendant bank could have paid the claimant, as payment could have been made in cash in London in either United States currency, which could have been imported from the United States without infringing its laws,[167] or in sterling, with the currency conversion taking place in London. Accordingly, in respect of the account governed by English law, Staughton J refused to give effect to President Reagan's order.

Hirst J adopted a similar approach in *Libyan Arab Foreign Bank* v. *Manufacturers Hanover Trust Co. (No. 2)*,[168] which involved virtually identical facts to the *Banker's Trust* case just discussed, with two exceptions. First, in *Manufacturers Hanover Trust*, rather than demanding payment, the claimant had instructed the defendant bank to transfer the relevant amount to the account of one of the defendant bank's other customers. Such an in-house transfer did not give rise, therefore, to issues concerning the need for clearing and settlement through the New York clearing system. Secondly, the relevant deposit advices and confirmations that were issued by the defendant bank incorporated a provision stating that '[t]his deposit or placement is payable at [the defendant bank's counters in] London, and shall be governed by the laws of England.' It is hardly surprising, therefore, that Hirst J reached a similar conclusion to that of Staughton J in *Banker's Trust*. There was, however, one point of disagreement: unlike Staughton J, Hirst J regarded the relationship between the claimant and the defendant bank as involving two separate account contracts, governed respectively by the law of New York and England. Whilst different banking operations between a bank and its customer at a single branch are best viewed as being subject to a single contract,[169] Hirst J's view is at least consistent with the view that, for many purposes, a bank's different branches are actually treated as separate entities.[170] Having treated the two accounts as involving separate contracts between the same parties, however, Hirst J failed to determine which contract should govern the regular automatic transfers effected by the defendant bank between the London and New York accounts. As these transfers were the subject of a standing arrangement, it is difficult to regard them as facets of either one of the two separate contracts, or accounts, in question. In contrast, some support for Staughton J's analysis is provided by the cases recognizing that a bank can still combine accounts that are held at different branches.[171] These cases are premised on the view that, although the customer's accounts are maintained at different branches, the customer's contractual relationship is with the bank itself and not with the individual branch. Accordingly, in the final analysis, Staughton J's approach is conceptually preferable, so that where two accounts of a given customer are closely interrelated, though ostensibly kept at two separate branches, they should be regarded as two limbs of a single contract rather than two distinct contracts.[172]

This disagreement aside, however, both *Banker's Trust* and *Manufacturers Hanover Trust* highlight the two fundamental principles underlying how English courts deal with attempts by foreign governments to expropriate English bank deposits: first, the effect of

---

Ferroalloy Plant v. *Ronly Holdings Ltd* [2004] 2 Lloyd's Rep 335, [75]; *Mahonia Ltd* v. *JP Morgan Chase Bank* [2004] EWHC 1938 (Comm.), [425]–[426]; *Tamil Nadu Electricity Board* v. *ST-CMS Electric Company Private Ltd* [2008] 1 Lloyd's Rep 93, [46]–[48]. See generally *Chitty on Contracts*, n.165 above, [23-027]–[23-029].

[167] Cf. H.S. Scott, 'Where are the Dollars?—Offshore Funds Transfers' (1988–1989) 3 *BFLR* 243.

[168] N.162 above. For the earlier summary judgment proceedings in the case, see n.162 above. See also *Turkiye Is Bankasi AS* v. *Bank of China* [1993] 1 Lloyd's Rep 132, 135; *Sierra Leone Telecommunications Co. Ltd* v. *Barclays Bank plc*, n.162 above, 826–827; *Walsh* v. *National Irish Bank Ltd*, n.162 above.

[169] Ch. 5, Sect. 3 above.

[170] *R.* v. *Grossman* (1981) 73 Crim. App. Rep. 302, 307. See further Ch. 5, Sect. 5(vii) above.

[171] Ch. 7, Sect. 4(iii) above.   [172] Ch. 5, Sect. 3 above.

the foreign order will be determined by reference to the law governing the account contract, which will be English law in the case of deposits with English branches of English and foreign banks; and, secondly, the English courts will not compel a party to perform an act that is illegal by its place of performance. It follows that, in the converse situation, English courts will not generally seek to exercise control over deposits maintained with a foreign branch of a United Kingdom bank, as it will be governed by the foreign applicable law, and the courts will generally recognize foreign acts involving the attachment, confiscation, or freezing of such a 'foreign' account.[173] This basic position is subject, however, to one exception when the foreign branch of an English bank closes down prior to the foreign government's appropriation or attachment of funds held by that foreign branch, since in such circumstances the bank's debt to its customer 'reverts' to its head office in the United Kingdom and becomes repayable there.[174]

The English and Australian approach of treating deposits as governed by the law of the branch where the relevant account is held has similarly found acceptance in the United States.[175] Moreover, under the 'act of state' doctrine, United States courts usually recognize the validity of a confiscation order made by a foreign government in respect of funds deposited at a branch or office within its own jurisdiction.[176] Nevertheless, customers have sometimes been permitted to recover funds deposited with an overseas office from a bank's United States head office. In *Vishipco Line* v. *Chase Manhattan Bank*,[177] Vietnamese nationals were allowed to recover from the bank's head office in New York amounts deposited with its Saigon office. The Court of Appeals for the Second Circuit largely based its decision on the fact that the bank had closed its Saigon office prior to the fall of South Vietnam and before the publication of the new government's subsequent

[173] *Arab Bank Ltd* v. *Barclays Bank* (*DCO*), n.162 above; *Kahler* v. *Midland Bank Ltd* [1950] AC 24 (HL). For the origin of the doctrine, see *Luther* v. *Sagor* [1921] 3 KB 532, 543–546 (CA); *Princess Paley Olga* v. *Weisz* [1929] 1 KB 718; *Williams and Humbert* v. *W. and H. Trade Marks* [1986] 1 AC 368, 431 (HL); *Rafidain Bank* v. *Agom Universal Sugar Trading Co Ltd*, The Times, 23 December 1986 (CA); *Jeyaretnam* v. *Mahmood*, The Times, 21 May 1992; *Jones* v. *Ministry of the Interior of the Kingdom of Saudi Arabia* [2005] QB 699, [10] (CA), revsd. in part: [2007] 1 AC 270 (HL); *R (on the application of Yukos Oil Co)* v. *Financial Services Authority* [2006] EWHC 2044 (Admin.), [86]–[89]; *Islamic Republic of Iran* v. *Barakat Galleries Ltd* [2008] 1 All ER 1177, [143]–[149] (CA).

[174] *R.* v. *Lovitt* [1912] AC 212, 219 (HL); *Sokoloff* v. *National City Bank*, 224 NYS 102 (1927), affd. 227 NYS 907, affd. 164 NE 745 (1928); *United Commercial Bank Ltd* v. *Okara Grain Buyers Syndicate Ltd*, AIR 1968 SC 1115 (Ind. SC); cf. *Leader, Plunkett & Leader* v. *Direction der Disconto-Gesellschaft* (1914) 31 TLR 83, revsd. [1915] 3 KB 154 (CA) (German bank was held liable to repay in England a deposit placed with its Berlin office, which was subsequently affected by the outbreak of war). *Leader* has subsequently been explained on the ground that a claim in England for the repayment of a foreign deposit is not a debt claim, but a damages claim for failure to pay: *Lloyd Royal Belge Société Anonyme* v. *L Dreyfus & Co.* (1927) Lloyd LR 288 (CA); *Richardson* v. *Richardson (National Bank of India Ltd, Garnishees)* [1927] All ER Rep 92. See generally W. Blair, 'Liability for Foreign Branch Deposits in English Law' in R. Cranston (ed.), *Making Commercial Law: Essays in Honour of Roy Goode* (Oxford, 1997), ch. 13.

[175] *Sokoloff* v. *National City Bank*, n.174 above, affd. 227 NYS 907, affd. 164 NE 745 (1928); *United States* v. *First National City Bank*, (1965) 379 US 378, 380–381; *United States* v. *BCCI Holdings (Luxembourg) SA*, 833 F.Supp 32 (DDC, 1993). See further *Wells Fargo Asia Ltd* v. *Citibank NA* 495 US 660 (1990), remitted: 936 F.2d 723 (2nd Cir., 1991) (discussed in W. Blair, n.174 above, 322, 333–335).

[176] *Underhill* v. *Fernandez*, 92 US 520 (1876); *Banco Nacional de Cuba* v. *Sabbationo*, 376 US 398 (1964). The United States courts, like the English courts, will not recognize an act of state seeking to operate extraterritorially: *Allied Bank International* v. *Banco Credito Agricola*, 757 F. 2d 516 (2nd Cir., 1985), cert. denied 473 US 934 (1985); *Republic of the Philippines* v. *Marcos*, 806 F.2d 344, 352–354 (2nd Cir., 1986).

[177] 660 F. 2nd 854 (2nd Cir., 1981), cert. denied 459 US 976 (1982). See also *Edelmann* v. *Chase Manhattan Bank NZ*, 861 F.2d 1291, 1303–1304 (1st Cir., 1988); *Huynh* v. *Chase Manhattan Bank*, 465 F.3d 992, 1002 (9th Cir., 2006).

confiscation order.[178] In accordance with the 'exception' referred to above, the debts were, accordingly, treated as having reverted to New York prior to their confiscation—'[w]hen a branch is closed, the depositor has a claim against the parent bank; the *situs* of the debt represented by the deposit "springs back" to the home office'.[179] On this basis, at least, an English court would probably have reached the same conclusion as in *Vishipco*.[180] More doubtful, however, is the soundness of the second line of reasoning in *Vishipco* that, by operating through branches abroad rather than through subsidiaries, United States banks had assured Vietnamese customers that their deposits would be safer than with a locally incorporated bank.[181] By making the debt repayable at the bank's head office, this suggestion would tend to the gut of any application the principle that deposits are generally repayable at the branch where they are situated. Nevertheless, this principle was subsequently extended in *Garcia* v. *Chase Manhattan Bank*,[182] where a New York bank was ordered to repay in New York sums deposited with its Cuban branch, which remained in operation until nationalized by Cuba's revolutionary Government. The Court of Appeals for the Second Circuit held that bank officers had given customers verbal assurances that their money was safe when deposited with the Cuban branch and that, in addition, they had asserted that payment was guaranteed by the head office. Yet a further extension, shorn of any limitation, was made in *Wells Fargo Asia Ltd* v. *Citibank NA*,[183] where customers were allowed to recover in the United States deposits that had been placed with the bank's Manila office and effectively frozen by order of the Phillipine Government. The Court of Appeals for the Second Circuit emphasized that ultimately a parent bank was liable for obligations assumed by its foreign branches and that, in the absence of agreement to the contrary, a creditor was entitled to claim a debt at the place where it was made payable. As the parties had not ruled out payment in New York, the Court, somewhat surprisingly, concluded that the deposit was recoverable in New York.

It is clear that, whilst an English court would follow the more conservative ground of decision in *Vishipco*, they would be unlikely to follow its more radical suggestion, and its subsequent extensions, to the effect that foreign deposits are always recoverable from the bank's head office as it effectively stands guarantor for foreign branch deposits. This is simply inconsistent with the position in *Banker's Trust* and *Manufacturers Hanover Trust* that, subject to contrary agreement, deposits are repayable at the branch with which they are placed and subject to the law applicable there. Nevertheless, to avoid their head office being liable to repay foreign deposits, English banks can in practice take two precautionary steps. The first step should be taken once it is decided that a branch has to close down or cease operations, and is neatly set out in *Vishipco*:[184]

> A bank which accepts deposits at a foreign branch becomes a debtor, not a bailee, with respect to its depositors. In the event that unsettled local conditions require it to cease operations, it should inform its depositors of the date when its branch will close and give

---

[178] Ibid., 862–863. The act of state doctrine depends upon whether the *situs* of a debt is the foreign country at the time of the confiscation order: *Manas y Pineiro* v. *Chase Manhattan Bank*, 434 NYS 2d 868 (1980).

[179] *Edelmann* v. *Chase Manhattan Bank NZ*, n.177 above, 1303–1304. See also *Trinh* v. *Citibank NA*, 850 F.2d 1164, 1168–1169 (6th Cir., 1987).

[180] *Leader, Plunkett & Leader* v. *Direction der Disconto-Gesellschaft*, n.174 above.

[181] N.177 above, 863. See also *Trinh* v. *Citibank NA*, n.179 above, 1169–1170.

[182] 735 F. 2nd 645 (2nd Circ., 1984), approved in *Edelmann* v. *Chase Manhattan Bank NZ*, n.177 above, 1302–1305; *Wells Fargo Asia Ltd* v. *Citibank NA*, n.175 above, 669–670.

[183] 936 F. 2nd 723 (2nd Circ., 1991).

[184] *Vishipco Line* v. *Chase Manhattan Bank* n.177 above, 864. *Wells Fargo Asia Ltd* v. *Citibank NA*, n.175.

them the opportunity to withdraw their deposits or, if conditions prevent such steps, enable them to obtain payment at an alternative location.

As the bank may not always have time to wind up the affairs of a foreign branch when a foreign government passes emergency expropriatory legislation, it should take the second step of incorporating into the deposit receipt (or deposit confirmation) a clause making payment available solely at the relevant foreign branch. As demonstrated in *Libyan Arab Foreign Bank* v. *Manufacturers Hanover Trust Co. (No. 2)*,[185] such a clause can be effective.

6 Assessment

The main development respecting interest-bearing accounts in recent years has been the replacement of pass-books and deposit receipts by periodic statements similar to those used for current accounts. This modern practice is consistent with the tendency to regard the banker-customer contract as a continuous relationship that does not require separate records or memoranda of individual entries. This replacement of deposit receipts and pass-books with periodic statements is a welcome development for three reasons: first, banks have been able to achieve greater efficiency in their day-to-day business; secondly, as deposit receipts and pass-books simply evidence a debt, they serve no legal function that cannot equally well be served by the provision of periodic statements, which are probably also more easily understood by customers; and, thirdly, deposit receipts and pass-books carry with them far more risks for the bank, in legal terms, than periodic statements, particularly when the former are transferred to a third party with the intention of transferring the account balance. That said, deposit receipts and pass-books have not entirely disappeared, but continue to have relevance for foreign-currency bank deposits and building society accounts. Moreover, the development of NCDs demonstrates that there is a need for readily transferable deposits, albeit predominantly in the context of large deposits by commercial entities. The needs of the general public, however, are adequately served by the periodic statement.

---

[185] N.162 above.

10

The Bank as Paymaster: Negotiable Instruments (Including Cheques)

1 Negotiable instruments and the development of non-transferable payment orders

Negotiable instruments have been used since the thirteenth or fourteenth century. Their oldest form—the bill of exchange—was initially used to transfer money: the drawer gives the drawee an unconditional order to pay a given amount of money to the payee;[1] and the drawee's acceptance signifies his consent to the order.[2] Another type of negotiable instrument from approximately the same period is the promissory note, in which the maker promises to pay a given sum to the payee.[3] Over the years, negotiable instruments acquired three special features. First, a negotiable instrument confers a right of action[4] on the person who has its lawful possession. Such a person (known as the 'holder')[5] may be the payee of the instrument, an 'indorsee' to whom the instrument has been transferred by indorsement and delivery, or the bearer.[6] In other types of contract, the physical

---

[1] The Bills of Exchange Act 1882 (BEA 1882), s.3. The definition can be traced back to the sixteenth century.

[2] The mere drawing of the cheque does not bind the drawee and does not constitute an assignment to the payee of the funds owed by the drawee to the drawer: BEA 1882, s.53(1). See also *Schroeder* v. *Central Bank of London Ltd* (1876) 34 LT 735, 736; *Shand* v. *Du Buisson* (1874) LR 18 Eq. 283, 288–289; *Hopkinson* v. *Forster* (1874) LR 19 Eq. 74; *In re Beaumont* [1902] 1 Ch 889, 894; *Joachimson* v. *Swiss Bank Corporation* [1921] 3 KB 110, 120–121 (CA); *Auchteroni & Co.* v. *Midland Bank Ltd* [1928] 2 KB 294, 299–300; *Plein & Co. Ltd* v. *Inland Revenue Commissioners* (1946) 175 LT 453, 456. See also *McDonald* v. *McDonald* (1903) 33 SCR 145, 170–171 (SCC); *Ritchie* v. *Jeffrey* (1915) 52 SCR 243, 249–250 (SCC); *Geo. Thompson (Aust.) Pty Ltd* v. *Vittadello* [1978] VR 199 (VSC); *Blackett* v. *Darcy* [2005] NSWSC 65, [26]. Under the French *provision* doctrine, the payee acquires a right to be paid the amount against which the instrument is drawn: E.P. Ellinger, 'Negotiable Instruments' in U. Drobnig *et al.* (eds.), *International Encyclopedia of Comparative Law* (Hamburg, 2001), vol. IX, ch. 4, [195]. For Scotland, see BEA 1882, s.53(2). See also *Thompson* v. *Jolly Carters Inn Ltd* 1972 SC 215 (OH); *Williams* v. *Williams* 1980 SLT 25 (Sheriff Ct.); *Sutherland* v. *Royal Bank of Scotland plc* 1997 SLT 329 (OH).

[3] E.P. Ellinger, n.2 above, vol. IX, ch. 4, [57] et seq. For the English position, see J.M. Holden, *History of Negotiable Instruments in English Law* (London, 1955); A.G. Guest, *Chalmers and Guest on Bills of Exchange and Cheques* (17th edn., London, 2009), Pt. IV.

[4] BEA 1882, s.38(1). The battle for the recognition of promissory notes as valid negotiable instruments took place around the turn of the eighteenth century: *Williams* v. *Williams* (1693) Carth. 269; *Potter* v. *Pearson* (1702) 2 Ld. Raym. 759; *Clerke* v. *Martin* (1702) 2 Ld. Raym. 757; *Buller* v. *Crips* (1703) 6 Mod. 29. Their validity was settled by the passing of the Bills of Exchange Act 1704. On this historical background, see *Goodwin* v. *Robarts* (1874–1875) LR 10 Ex. 337, 348–350, affd. (1875–1876) LR 1 App Cas 476 (HL).

[5] BEA 1882, s.2. See, for example, *Barclays Bank plc* v. *Tackport Ltd* (CA, 25 April 1991); *Clifford Chance* v. *Silver* [1992] 2 Bank. LR 11 (CA); *Surrey Asset Finance Ltd* v. *National Westminster Bank plc*, The Times, 8 September 2000; *Dextra Bank & Trust Co. Ltd* v. *Bank of Jamaica* [2002] 1 All ER (Comm.) 193, [18] (PC); *Abbey National plc* v. *JSF Finance & Currency Exchange Co. Ltd* [2006] EWCA Civ 328, [12]–[13].

[6] For the distinction between 'bearer' and 'order' instruments, see Sect. 8(iv) below.

possession of the document evidencing its terms does not in itself confer a right of action. Thus, a simple contract is enforceable only by the parties to it and, in certain cases, by an assignee[7] or a 'third party' for whose benefit the contract is made and on whom it is intended to confer the right to enforce the contract.[8] Secondly, negotiable instruments are transferable. If the instrument is payable to the bearer, it can be transferred (or 'negotiated') by mere delivery.[9] If the instrument is payable to order, negotiation is effected by its payee's indorsement, followed by its delivery.[10] Contracts other than negotiable instruments may also be assigned, but the procedure involved can be cumbersome.[11] Thirdly, negotiable instruments are 'negotiable', which means that a transferee of an instrument may acquire a title superior to that of the transferor. This occurs when an instrument that is complete and regular on its face is delivered to a person (known as a 'holder in due course'), who acquires it in good faith and for valuable consideration.[12] In contrast, the assignee of a mere contractual right acquires no better title than the assignor can give— the assignee's rights against the debtor are subject to the 'equities' available to the debtor against the assignor.[13]

The effect of these three features is that a negotiable instrument constitutes a specific item of property. Accordingly, the right to the possession of the instrument confers further rights on the 'true owner', such as the right to bring an action for its conversion, that are unavailable in the case of simple contracts.[14] In addition, a negotiable instrument confers on its holder a contractual right, or a chose in action, which is basically the right to enforce the undertaking given by the maker of a promissory note or by a party liable on a bill of exchange, such as the acceptor. In that regard, negotiable instruments resemble simple contracts.[15] The time at which the chose in action matures depends on the tenor (or 'usance') of the instrument. Both bills of exchange and promissory notes can be payable 'at sight' (or in other words upon a demand for payment being made by the presentment of the instrument) or at a designated future time, for instance, 90 days after sight.

Nowadays, promissory notes continue to serve their original purpose; the main advantage of obtaining such an instrument in respect of payments due under an underlying contract is to be found in the first feature of negotiable instruments. Indeed, the possession of a promissory note enables the payee to enforce payment of an amount due to

---

[7] *Chitty on Contracts* (30th edn., London, 2008), ch. 19. See further Ch. 21, Sect. 1 below.

[8] Ibid., [18-043] et seq. See also Contracts (Rights of Third Parties) Act 1999, s.1. See generally *Nisshin Shipping Co. Ltd* v. *Cleaves & Co. Ltd* [2003] EWHC 2602 (Comm.); *Laemthong International Lines Co. Ltd* v. *Artis* [2005] EWCA Civ. 519; *Avraamides* v. *Colwill* [2006] EWCA Civ 1533; *Prudential Assurance Co. Ltd* v. *Ayres* [2008] EWCA Civ. 52.

[9] BEA 1882, s.31(2).   [10] Ibid., s.31(3).

[11] Ch. 21, Sects. 1–2 below. See further *Chitty on Contracts*, n.7 above, ch. 19.

[12] BEA 1882, s.29. See also *Banco Santander SA* v. *Banque Paribas* (CA, 25 February 2000); *Credit Agricole Indosuez* v. *Ecumet (UK) Ltd* (QBD, 29 March 2001); *Abbey National plc* v. *JSF Finance & Currency Exchange Co. Ltd*, n.5 above, [12]–[13].

[13] *Chitty on Contracts*, n.7 above, [19-070] et seq. See further Ch. 21, Sect. 1 below.

[14] *OBG Ltd* v. *Allan* [2008] AC 1, [100], [106], [210], [224], [271], [308], [321] (HL), although Lord Nicholls of Birkenhead expressed the view that 'the time has surely come to recognize . . . that the tort of conversion applies to contractual rights irrespective of whether they are embodied or recorded in writing' (ibid., [233], [238]). Baroness Hale of Richmond agreed with the possibility of taking a more expansive view of conversion (ibid., [302], [310], [317]). Despite not being able to sue in conversion, a contracting party or assignee may sometimes be able to assert a claim to property acquired with the contract's proceeds following a successful tracing exercise.

[15] Cf. *R* v. *Duru* [1974] 1 WLR 2, 8 (CA) (overruled in relation to the Theft Act 1968, s.15(1) by *R* v. *Preddy* [1996] AC 815 (HL)); *Pollway* v. *Abdullah* [1974] 1 WLR 493, 496 (CA); *R* v. *Mitchell* [2008] EWCA Crim 850, [17]. This applies to all forms of negotiable instrument: *R.* v. *Kohn* [1979] Crim. L.R. 675 (CA). See also *R* v. *Hilton* [1997] Cr. App. R. 445 (CA); *R* v. *Forsyth* [1997] Cr. App. R. 299 (CA); *R* v. *Williams* [2001] 1 Cr. App. R. 362 (CA).

him, such as a loan instalment, by bringing an action on the note made in respect of it. Such an action has the advantage of being available quite separately from any cause of action arising out of the underlying transaction. Moreover, the promissory note remains transferable, and accordingly can be discounted prior to its maturity. Unlike promissory notes, however, bills of exchange are no longer used for their original purpose, as nowadays they are used mainly in the context of international trade. Usually, a bill of exchange is drawn by the seller on the buyer for the price of the goods. Its transferability facilitates discount. Furthermore, bills of exchange are used in the context of credit lines (also known as 'acceptance credits') granted by banks to their customers. The customer is authorized to draw on the bank bills of exchange up to a total designated amount. The bank's acceptance of such a bill or bills—known as a bank's acceptance—is again readily discountable.

In the United Kingdom, the cheque developed in the seventeenth century as a special form of bill of exchange.[16] The chief characteristics of cheques are their being drawn on a bank and their being payable on demand (or 'at sight').[17] Cheques were not meant to be accepted, as the drawee bank either paid the designated amount or dishonoured the instrument by non-payment. Traditionally, cheques were used for two purposes. One was to enable the customer to withdraw funds standing to the credit of his current account.[18] In such a case, the cheque was made payable either to the customer's own order or to 'cash', and presented for payment at the branch where the account was kept. The use of cheques for this purpose was fortuitous. In continental Europe, the same object was achieved by means of a 'withdrawal voucher', which is similar to the form used in the United Kingdom for the withdrawal of funds from a savings account. In modern practice, customers usually withdraw funds by means of ATM cards.[19] The second function of a cheque is to pay sums due from the drawer to a third party, such as a supplier of goods or services, by posting the cheque to that third party or handing it to him personally. In essence, the cheque constitutes the drawer's order to the bank to pay the amount due to the payee.[20]

Where a cheque is uncrossed, the payee can utilize it to obtain payment in one of three ways. First, he can present it for payment at the branch on which it is drawn. The drawee bank must then decide promptly whether to pay or dishonour the instrument after having verified that the signature on the cheque is genuine and valid and that the account has an adequate credit balance available to cover the cheque.[21] Secondly, the payee can deposit the cheque for collection into his own bank account. The payee's bank (also known as the 'collecting bank') then presents the cheque to the drawee bank through the clearing system.[22] Thirdly, the payee can transfer (or 'negotiate') the cheque to another person. This method is often utilized for tax reasons or where the ostensible payee does not have a bank account. Where a cheque is negotiated, the transferee has himself these

---

[16] The earliest known handwritten cheque was known to be in existence on 16 February 1659: Cheque and Credit Clearing Company, *Cheques and Cheque Clearing—The Facts* (November 2007), 4.

[17] *West* v. *Revenue & Customs Commissioners* [2010] UKFTT 442, [25].

[18] *Foley* v. *Hill* (1848) 2 HLC. 28 (HL). See also Chap. 5, Sect.3 above.   [19] Ch. 14, Sect. 6 below.

[20] *London Joint Stock Bank* v. *Macmillan* [1918] AC 777 (HL), which treats the cheque as an instruction given by a principal (the customer) to his agent (the bank). See also *Hollicourt (Contracts) Ltd* v. *Bank of Ireland* [2001] Ch 555, [23], [31], [33] (CA); *Re Spectrum Plus Ltd* [2005] 2 AC 680, [59] (HL). This principle can be traced back to *Young* v. *Grote* (1827) 4 Bing. 253. If the customer countermands this order, the bank must dishonour the cheque: BEA 1882, s.75(1).

[21] Ch. 11, Sect. 1(ii) below.   [22] Sect. 2 below.

three options for obtaining payment under the instrument. Where a cheque is crossed,[23] however, the payee does not have the first option of presenting the instrument for payment directly to the drawee bank,[24] but must pursue the second option and arrange for the cheque's collection through the clearing system. In addition, prior to 1992, a payee could obtain payment by negotiating the cheque to a third party, as all cheques used to be pre-printed with the words 'or order' at the end of the line intended for the insertion of the payee's name. These words no longer appear on cheques and nowadays, since the enactment of the Cheques Act 1992, all cheques are pre-printed with the words 'a/c payee only' added to the instrument's crossing.[25] Such a crossing effectively renders modern cheques non-transferable by proscribing transfer and negotiation. Accordingly, unless the customer takes the unusual step of 'opening the crossing', by deleting it and adding the words 'pay cash', a payee cannot transfer title to the modern, standard-form cheque by indorsing and delivering the instrument to a third party. Given that modern 'cheques' are little more than 'non-transferable payment orders' used to effect payment between the drawer's and payee's accounts, it is little surprise that these instruments have been eclipsed by more efficient means of carrying out direct transfers between accounts.[26] Indeed, although customers remain familiar with cheques and continue to use them, the UK Payments Council has described cheque use as being 'in long-term decline'[27] and, more recently, 'in terminal decline'.[28]

In summary, all three forms of negotiable instrument are issued in respect of payments. Bills of exchange (other than cheques) are used predominantly in the context of international trade to facilitate the payment of the price for goods supplied by the drawer to the drawee. Furthermore, bills of exchange can be used in connection with lines of credit or 'acceptance credits' that enable a payee to obtain funds by discounting bills drawn upon, and accepted by, a bank. Promissory notes are used to crystallize the maker's promise to pay a given amount (often a specific instalment payable under a facility) to the payee. They are widely used in respect of all types of lending contract, including syndicated loans. As a result of most cheques being rendered non-transferable by virtue of a pre-printed 'a/c payee only' crossing, cheques are nowadays used mainly to facilitate the payment of the amount for which they are drawn from the drawer's account to that of the payee. Despite their rapidly declining use, however, cheques (whether in the usual form of a non-transferable payment order or in the unusual form of a negotiable cheque) still remain vastly more popular than the other types of negotiable instrument and are accordingly discussed separately in the following sections.[29] This is then followed by a review of other forms of bill of exchange, including bills drawn under acceptance credits, and promissory notes.

---

[23] This is the case regardless of whether the crossing is general or special and even where 'not negotiable' is added as a crossing.

[24] BEA 1882, s.79. See also *Ringham* v. *Hackett & Walmsley* (1980) 10 LDAB 206 (CA).

[25] Sect. 4(iv) below.   [26] Ch. 13, Sect. 1 below.

[27] UK Payments Council, *National Payments Plan—Setting the Strategic Vision for UK Payments* (14 May 2008), 6. See also UK Payments Administration, *The Way We Pay 2009: UK Cheques* (London, 2009).

[28] UK Payments Council, *Progress Report: Delivering the National Payments Plan* (June 2010), 1.

[29] R. Cranston, *Principles of Banking Law* (2nd edn., Oxford, 2003), 258.

2 The clearing of cheques and non-transferable payment orders

Conceptually, there is a clear distinction between negotiable cheques and non-transferable payment orders—the former are a category of bill of exchange and hence constitute negotiable instruments; the latter are mere payment instructions given by the drawer to the drawee bank. This distinction is immaterial, however, to the way banks use the clearing system to fulfil the requirement that a cheque must be physically presented for payment at the branch of the bank upon which it is drawn.[30] In this context, the two types of instrument are treated as a payment instruction.

The current process for the clearing of cheques is based on a procedure developed in the eighteenth century, when the use of cheques became common.[31] Initially, when customers deposited cheques for collection, each bank obtained payment by presenting them by messenger to the drawee bank. To save time, the bank messengers gathered in a single meeting-place each morning to exchange their respective cheques. They reconvened in the afternoon, when dishonoured cheques were returned to the messengers who had brought them, and a balance was struck between the messengers of the different banks in respect of 'cleared effects', namely cheques that had been honoured. This system, originally confined to cheques drawn and payable within the boundaries of the City of London, was modified from time to time to meet the demands of the constantly developing banking network. Between 1833 and the late 1980s, clearing took place at 10 Lombard Street—premises that were originally leased by the clearing banks and subsequently acquired by a company owned by the banks. Originally, the clearing system was divided into the 'town clearing' and the 'general clearing'. 'Town clearing' was used for the exchange of cheques and bankers' payments for less than £500,000 that were drawn on, and collected by, bank branches within the City of London. All other effects, including paper-originated giro transfers,[32] were collected through the 'general clearing'. 'Town clearing' was abolished in 1995, so that, apart from some direct delivery of cheques as between certain banks, only one system remained for the clearing of paper-generated money transfers. After a period located at the National Westminster Bank, Goodman's Fields, the clearing house moved to its current location in Milton Keynes in October 2003. The items passing through the clearing system are in the millions, although the volume and overall value of items cleared has been in constant decline since their peak in 1997,[33] no doubt occasioned by the steady increase in the use of electronic transfers, debit cards,

[30] Under BEA 1882, s.45(3), a cheque must be presented for payment 'at the proper place', which requires the physical delivery of the instrument to the branch of the paying bank on which it is drawn (*Barclays Bank plc* v. *Bank of England* [1985] 1 All ER 385, 392–394) and similarly, at common law, the general principle is that demand for payment must be made at the branch where the relevant account is held (*Joachimson* v. *Swiss Bank Corporation*, n.2 above, 127). See further Ch. 11, Sect. 1(ii) below. See also A.G. Guest, n.3 above, [6-062], [13-022].

[31] For an overview of the cheque's history, see Cheque and Credit Clearing Company, n.16 above, 4; Cheque and Credit Clearing Company, *The Great British Cheque Report* (London, February 2009), 4–12.

[32] Ch. 13, Sect. 1(iv) below.

[33] Cheque and Credit Clearing Company, *The Great British Cheque Report* (London, February 2009) 18–27. In 1990 cheques accounted for 57.7 per cent of the annual APACS (now UKPA) clearings volumes (APACS, *Annual Review 2000* (London, 2001) App. II), but only accounted for 26.4 per cent of those volumes by 2003 (APACS, *Annual Review 2003* (London, 2004) App.II). The rate of decrease in cheque use appears to have accelerated in recent years, with cheque volumes dropping by around 10 per cent during 2008 (UK Payments Council, *Annual Summary of Payment Clearing Statistics 2008* (London, 2009)) and by around 12 per cent per annum during 2009 and 2010 (UK Payments Council, *Statistical Release—9 September 2010* (London, 2010), 6).

and direct debits.[34] Such has been the decline in the use of cheques that the payments industry has been compelled to publish guidance reminding customers about how to draw and handle cheques in order to minimize the risk of fraud.[35]

During the twentieth century, there have been two key developments to the clearing process. First, non-clearing banks—banks that are not members of the clearing house—were granted access to the clearing facilities. Originally, the non-clearing banks had to present cheques for payment through messengers, but the modern system allows non-clearing banks to engage the services of a 'clearer' to exchange their cheques at the clearing house. Nowadays, most banks in the United Kingdom have such an arrangement. Secondly, there has been the gradual introduction of a computerized process. The initial development was the signing of the 'Golden Memorandum' in 1967,[36] which was primarily designed to publicize the bank giro system, but pursuant to which all the United Kingdom clearing banks agreed, *inter alia*, to act as each other's agent for the clearing of cheques. This meant that a cheque no longer had to be deposited by its payee or holder at the branch where he held the relevant account that was to be credited with the cheque's proceeds, but could instead deposit the cheque for collection at any branch of a participating bank. The 'Golden Memorandum' was eventually replaced by individual agreements to similar effect made between the clearing banks. Computerization has now further enhanced the degree to which banks can co-operate in clearing cheques, as has the development of umbrella bodies to oversee the clearing process. In 1985, the entire clearing system came to be regulated by the Association for Payment Clearing Services (APACS), which has now been replaced by the UK Payments Administration since 6 July 2009.[37] Despite these changes, the actual clearing process has for all practical purposes remained largely unchanged.

Traditionally, the general clearing process has been based on the use of two separate documents handed by the payee (or, more rarely nowadays, the holder) of a cheque to their collecting bank: the cheque that is completed by the drawer; and a 'credit slip' that is completed by the payee (or holder) and that is usually found in the payee's 'paying-in book'. Most cheque forms in United Kingdom cheque-books are already pre-printed with the drawer's name and an 'a/c payee only' crossing.[38] They also have a number of blank lines or spaces so that the drawer can insert the date of the cheque's issue,[39] the payee's name,[40] and the amount for which the cheque is drawn, both in figures and in words. The drawer will execute his signature just above his pre-printed name. An additional line, printed in magnetic ink at the foot of the cheque form, sets out the bank's clearing number and identifies the particular branch on which the cheque is drawn, the drawer's account number, and the number of the relevant cheque. This magnetic line is readable by the banks' reader-sorter machines. Like a cheque, a credit slip contains blank spaces for the date of the cheque's deposit, the details of any cheques and cash that the payee is depositing into his account, including the total amount of the deposit, and the name of the person actually depositing the instrument with the bank. In the majority of cases, the

---

[34] Ch. 13, Sect. 1 below.

[35] Cheque and Credit Clearing Company, *Advice When Writing and Receiving Cheques* (16 September 2009).

[36] Reprinted from time to time under the title of *Bank Money Transfer Services*.

[37] Ch. 1, Sect. 2(i) above.

[38] Cheques Act 1992, s.1, inserting BEA 1882, s.81A. To use such a form for the drawing of a negotiable cheque, the customer would have 'to open the crossing'. The cheque can then be paid over the counter.

[39] For post-dated cheques, see Sect. 3(iv) below.

[40] Whilst the line for the insertion of the payee's name originally read 'pay to . . . or order' (or 'or bearer'), since the enactment of the Cheques Act 1992, banks provide customers with cheque-books containing forms in which the words 'or order' are omitted.

person depositing the cheque will be the customer whose account is to be credited, but sometimes it may be an agent who is asked to arrange for the clearance of cheques payable to the customer. A line printed in magnetic ink at the foot of the credit slip sets out the bank's clearing number and identifies the particular branch that holds the account to be credited, the number of that account, and the credit slip's number.[41] The back of the credit slip includes a schedule in which the customer lists details of the individual cheques deposited. The cheque and the credit slip serve different functions in the clearing process: the credit slip is used to effect the credit entry in the payee's account; the cheque is used to arrange for the debiting of the drawer's account. That said, computerization is increasingly doing away with the need for credit slips. Nevertheless, as such credit slips do remain in use, the following discussion is premised upon a credit slip being used in the particular circumstances.

Originally, the clearing of cheques drawn on a different bank or branch took three days,[42] but, since 1994, the major clearing banks have operated a two-day clearing cycle.[43] In November 2007, however, the then subscribers to the *Banking Code*[44] have given a commitment to abide by standardized maximum time-limits for the clearing of their customers' cheques.[45] These are termed the '2-4-6' commitments for current accounts and the '2-6-6' commitments for savings accounts.[46] Pursuant to the '2-4-6' commitments, collecting banks undertake to credit the proceeds of a cheque to the customer's account for the purposes of earning interest on the second working day following the cheque being deposited into that account; to permit the customer to withdraw funds from the account on the fourth working day following the cheque's deposit; and to assure the customer that the cheque will not be dishonoured by the drawee bank from the end of the sixth working day following its deposit. The '2-6-6' commitments, which are applicable to savings accounts, are broadly similar, except that banks only commit to allowing customers to withdraw funds from the account on the sixth day following the cheque's deposit. Obviously, individual banks are free to apply shorter time-limits than those contained in these standard commitments. The changes introduced by the '2-4-6' and '2-6-6' commitments only purport to alter the position between collecting banks and their customers and do not directly alter the mechanics of the clearing process or the relationship between clearing banks.[47] It is possible, however, that the commitments may indirectly have such an effect, as the clearing banks will now have a common set of expectations regarding the timeliness of the clearing process, the mechanics of which are considered in the following paragraphs.

The actual clearing process, and the procedures adopted, are subject to variations. The most common situation occurs when the drawer and payee maintain their accounts with different banks and the cheque and credit slip are paid into the branch where the payee maintains his account. To illustrate the mechanics of the ordinary clearing procedure,[48] assume that the payee maintains his account with the L Bank's Piccadilly branch and the drawer's account is with the B Bank's Oxford Street branch. On the day that the credit slip and cheque are deposited ('Day 0'), they will be processed by the Piccadilly branch.[49] The

---

[41] Since the mid-1980s, customers have been supplied with deposit books containing such personalized slips.

[42] *Barclays Bank plc* v. *Bank of England*, n.30 above, 387.

[43] *Emerald Meats (London) Ltd* v. *AIB Group (UK) plc* [2002] EWCA Civ. 460, [15], [26].

[44] See generally *Banking Code* (March 2008) and *Business Banking Code* (March 2008), although these have now been replaced by a mix of the Banking Conduct of Business Sourcebook (BCOBS) and the *Lending Code* since 1 November 2009: Ch. 2, Sect. 6(i) above.

[45] Cheque and Credit Clearing Company, n.16 above, 7.   [46] UK Payments Council, n.27 above, 23.

[47] Cheque and Credit Clearing Company, n.16 above, 4.   [48] Ibid., 10–13.

[49] Some banks have introduced changes in this procedure. One major retail bank performs the entire encoding at its London clearing centre, which means that the bundles of cheques are sent to the clearing

cheque's amount is encoded in magnetic ink on the cheque and a computerized credit entry is made on the customer's account. If the credit slip is accompanied by a number of items, the payee's addition is verified. A special crossing to the Piccadilly branch is also inserted on the cheque. At present, the main object of this crossing,[50] which is added even where the drawer has executed a general crossing, is to identify on the cheque itself the branch that has arranged for its clearing. The credit slip remains at the branch, whilst the cheque itself is bundled with other cheques drawn on the B Bank. That evening, all the bundles of cheques deposited with the Piccadilly branch that day for collection are forwarded to the L Bank's clearing department in London. These arrive at the clearing department on the same evening or early the next day ('Day 1'). On the morning of Day 1, the L Bank's clearing department verifies that the bundles are not physically damaged and that each cheque contains all the required encoded details. The bundle containing the cheque in question is then placed in a box labelled with the name of the B Bank, which is either delivered at the clearing house to employees of that bank or placed on racks allocated to it. The box is then taken to the B Bank's clearing department.

At the B Bank's clearing department, the cheques are again fed into an electronic reader-sorter machine, which performs three functions. First, it places the cheque in question in a box of items drawn on customers of the Oxford Street branch. Secondly, the machine reads the magnetic ink line on the cheque. This information is passed on to the B Bank's computer, which will accordingly calculate the balance in the drawer's account at the close of the subsequent day, unless an advice to the contrary is received on that day from the Oxford Street branch. Obviously, the decision as to whether to pay or to dishonour the cheque is not taken at the clearing department. If the balance in the drawer's account is inadequate for meeting the cheque, however, the computer will place the cheque on an 'out of order list', comprising items specifically drawn to the manager's attention at the Oxford Street branch. The third function performed by the reader-sorter machine relates to the settlement between the L Bank and the B Bank. The B Bank's clearing department verifies the total amount of cheques presented each day for the customers of every clearer. The cheque in question will constitute part of the amount due from the B Bank to the L Bank. The actual settlement between the two banks takes place at the end of each trading day. The figure, which is based on setting off the balances of all items exchanged in the clearing house on that day, is confirmed the following morning. The settlement though is based on the provisional, or uncleared, balances. Any adjustment required as a result of the dishonour of individual items is effected subsequently. It is realistic to strike a balance on the assumption that all cheques cleared on a given day will be honoured, as in practice dishonoured items are minimal.

The cheque in the illustration is then forwarded by B Bank's clearing department to the Oxford Street branch at the end of Day 1—the day after its receipt by the L Bank's Piccadilly Branch. The cheque is processed at the Oxford Street branch the next day ('Day 2'). Theoretically, the branch is supposed to verify both the adequacy of the account's funds and the cheque's 'regularity', which, in this context, means checking the authenticity of the drawer's signature, the proper dating of the cheque, and the agreement between the amount in words and figures. In practice, the need to verify the balance arises only where a cheque is placed on the 'out of order list'. The relevant branch officer must then decide

centre in the state in which they are received by the branch. Moreover, some major customers, such as certain department stores, have direct access to that bank's clearing department. Such customers are given a sorting number as if they were a branch and, in processing the cheques received from consumers, they bypass the branch with which they maintain their account.

[50] Sect. 4(ii) below.

whether to grant the customer an overdraft or dishonour the cheque. The branch officer faces a practical problem in this regard, however, as the balance communicated to the branch officer by the computer terminal is not that day's balance, but the balance struck at the previous day's close. The officer's decision will accordingly be based on information known to be marginally out of date. In practice, this should not present a significant problem if the relevant account manager has been monitoring the account sufficiently closely and is aware of the dates when funds are regularly credited to the account, such as salary payments. Such a person will be well placed to assess the situation and decide whether to honour the instrument or not. The verification of the cheque's 'regularity' is only usually carried out if it exceeds a certain figure, which varies from bank to bank.[51] On the morning of Day 2, the '2-4-6' commitments require that the L Bank's Piccadilly branch have credited the cheque's proceeds to the payee's account at least for interest purposes, even though the payee may not yet be able to withdraw the funds.

If the Oxford Street branch resolves to dishonour the cheque in question, it must perform two tasks: first, it must key the information into its computer terminal; and, secondly, it must return the cheque by first-class mail to the L Bank's Piccadilly branch. The Oxford Street branch identifies the bank and branch to which the cheque should be returned by means of the crossing executed by the L Bank's Piccadilly branch before it transmitted the cheque. The cheque has to be sent out before the close of Day 2. A notation explaining the reason for the dishonour is frequently executed on the cheque.[52] The 'Cheque Clearing Rules', which are discussed further below, make provision for the return of cheques after the close of Day 2 of the cycle, under a clause known as the 'inadvertence rule'. If the cheque is honoured, the Oxford Street branch retains it. Some business customers, however, require their banks to return 'cancelled' cheques, as these can serve as receipts,[53] whether for auditing or tax purposes. In this type of arrangement, cheques paid by the customer's bank will be returned to the customer periodically. Where the Oxford Street branch has resolved to honour the cheque, it need not supply any information to the clearing department's computer centre, even if the cheque was originally included in the 'out of order list'. If the computer centre does not receive an advice of dishonour by the end of Day 2, it will carry out the necessary entries. According to the '2-4-6' commitments, the L Bank's Piccadilly branch must permit the cheque's payee to withdraw its proceeds by no later than the fourth working day following the cheque's initial deposit ('Day 4') and must guarantee the customer that they are absolutely entitled to the funds by the sixth working day following the cheque's initial deposit ('Day 6').

The above clearing procedure applies equally when the drawer and the payee maintain their respective accounts at separate branches of the same bank, and the '2-4-6' commitments are similarly applicable. In such a case, the cheque is processed initially by the collecting branch and then remitted, through the bank's clearing department, to the drawee branch. Although there is no need for the exchange of the cheque at the clearing house, the processing of the cheque in the bank's own clearing department can take just as long as the clearing of cheques involving two banks. The clearing procedure is modified, however, if the cheque is paid into a branch or bank, other than the branch

---

[51] As checking the 'regularity' of every cheque would be onerous, the paying bank has certain common law and statutory protections should it pay a cheque other than in accordance with its tenor: Ch. 11, Sects. 2–3 below.

[52] Most common is a notation indicating inadequate funds in the drawer's account, such as 'refer to drawer'.

[53] Cheques Act 1957, s.3 (as amended by the Deregulation (Bills of Exchange) Order 1996, S. I. 1996/2993, Art. 5).

where the payee holds his account. Assume, for the purposes of the above illustration, that the cheque is deposited for collection with the N Bank's Leicester Square branch. In such a case, the Leicester Square branch executes on the cheque a special crossing to itself and then sends the cheque and credit slip to the N Bank's own clearing department, which in turn delivers the credit slip through the clearing house to the L Bank's clearing department and the cheque to that of the B Bank. The respective clearing departments execute the required computer entries and the credit slip is then forwarded to the Piccadilly branch and the cheque to the Oxford Street branch of the respective banks. If the latter branch decides to dishonour the cheque, it returns it to the N Bank's Leicester Square branch, which in turn advises the L Bank's Piccadilly branch.[54] One result of this more involved procedure is that any notification of the cheque's dishonour[55] to the Piccadilly branch may take an extra day. As such delay accords with prevailing banking practice, the payee has no real ground for complaint. Moreover, if the cheque was paid in by a transferee, he retains the right to give notice of dishonour to previous parties.[56] Another variation in the clearing process takes place where the cheque's payee maintains his account with a bank that is not a member of the clearing house. In such circumstances, the payee's bank will engage a particular clearing bank to act as its agent for the clearance of its customers' cheques.[57] The payee's bank will then process the cheque as if it were a branch of the clearing bank that it uses as agent, save that most non-clearing banks keep their own records of their customers' accounts, and do not convey these to the agent bank's computer centre. The customer's credit slip is accordingly retained by his own bank and the cheque bundles alone are forwarded by the payee's bank to the agent bank's clearing department. The same department receives, through the clearing house, the cheques drawn on customers of the relevant non-clearing bank, and forwards these in the same way as it would a cheque drawn on one of its branches. In the case of non-clearing banks with a network of branches, each branch sends its cheques directly to its agent's clearing department and receives back cheques drawn on it. In contrast, the clearing procedure is simplified considerably in the case of an 'in-house' payment—where both the drawer and payee maintain their accounts with the same branch of a given bank. In such a case, both the crediting of the payee's account and the debiting of

---

[54] A similar procedure is basically followed where the cheque is paid into the L Bank's Leicester Square branch—the cheque and credit slip are sent directly to the L Bank's clearing department. The procedure is modified, however, where a bank has centralized all the steps of the clearing process at its clearing department.

[55] Sect. 5(iii) below.   [56] BEA 1882, s.49(13).

[57] Although there is a contractual relationship between a non-clearing bank and its agent, there is no privity of contract between the cheque's payee and the clearing/correspondent bank: *Calico Printers' Association v. Barclays Bank Ltd* (1931) 36 Com. Cas. 71, affd. (1931) 36 Com. Cas. 197 (CA); *Grosvenor Casinos Ltd* v. *National Bank of Abu Dhabi* [2006] EWHC 784 (Comm.), [34]; [2008] EWHC 511 (Comm.), [146]–[149]. As a general principle, there is no privity between an agent's principal and a sub-agent: *Henderson* v. *Merrett Syndicates Ltd* [1995] AC 145 (HL). The position appears to be no different when an international collection is subject to the Uniform Rules for Collection 522: *Grosvenor Casinos Ltd* v. *National Bank of Abu Dhabi*, above, [157]; cf. *Bastone & Firminger Ltd* v. *Nasima Enterprises (Nigeria) Ltd* [1996] CLC 1902, 1908 (considering the earlier Uniform Rules for Collection 322). See further Ch. 13, Sect. 5(v) below. Even after *Grosvenor Casinos*, a cheque's payee may still acquire contractual rights against a collecting/correspondent bank by virtue of the Contracts (Rights of Third Parties) Act 1999, but this will depend upon the precise wording of the collection instruction. Where such a direct claim is unavailable, however, the remitting bank may be able to claim damages from the collecting/correspondent bank on behalf of the cheque's payee: H. Bennett, 'Bank Collections, Privity of Contract, and Third Party Losses' (2008) 124 *LQR* 532, 535–538. Alternatively, a cheque's payee may sue its own bank, as remitting bank, for the clearing/correspondent bank's negligent actions: *AA Valibhoy & Sons (1907) Pte Ltd* v. *Habib Bank Ltd* [1982–1983] 1 SLR 379, 391; *AA Valibhoy & Sons (1907) Pte Ltd* v. *Banque Nationale de Paris* [1994] 2 SLR 772, 781. See further Ch. 15, Sect. 9 below.

the drawer's account are effected at the computer terminal of the relevant branch and this occurs on the same day as the cheque's deposit.[58]

At present, the Cheque and Credit Clearing Co. Ltd[59] is responsible for the clearing of cheques and paper-based giro credits. It is one of the three clearing companies operating under the umbrella of the UK Payments Administration Ltd (UKPA) (formerly APACS).[60] Clearing of electronic payments is effected either by BACS Payment Services Ltd or CHAPS Clearing Co. Ltd.[61] Cheque clearing is carried out subject to the 'Cheque Clearing House Rules',[62] which succeeded the 'General Clearing House Rules' and were adopted by the members of the cheque clearing house. The original version can be traced back to the early nineteenth century, although they have been amended from time-to-time as banking practice has changed. The legal nature of the cheque clearing rules has been considered in *Royal Bank of Ireland Ltd* v. *O'Rourke*,[63] which raised the question of whether the presentment of a cheque by the collecting bank to the paying bank took place when the instrument was first delivered to the clearing house, or alternatively when the cheque actually reached the branch on which it was drawn. Murnaghan J opted for the later time on the ground that presentment had to be made to a person who could decide whether to pay or dishonour the instrument, but this view was subsequently reversed by the Supreme Court of Ireland, where Lavery J held that presentment took place when the cheque was delivered to the drawee bank's employees at the clearing house. In *Barclays Bank plc* v. *Bank of England*,[64] however, Bingham J adopted Murnaghan J's view. His Lordship regarded the paying bank 'as being, from the time of receiving the cheque [in the clearing house] until the time of presenting it, a sub-agent of the [collecting] bank, which is itself the agent of the payee'.[65] In reaching this conclusion, Bingham J relied on the fact that 'the delivery of the cheque to the branch was the physical presentment to the banker for his decision whether to honour the cheque or not'.[66] Of paramount importance to his Lordship's analysis was the standing of the General Clearing House Rules:[67]

> If it is to be said that the drawer loses that right [i.e. to have the cheque duly presented] as the result of a private agreement made between the banks for their own convenience, the very strongest proof of his knowledge and assent would be needed, not only because of the general rule that an individual's rights are not to be cut down by an agreement made between others but also because, in this particular case, the rights of additional parties (such as indorsers) could be affected.

Bingham J clearly refused to treat the 'General Clearing House Rules' as constituting an independent customary source of law binding on all persons transacting business with banks. The contracts of adhesion, signed by customers when opening their ordinary accounts with banks, do not make express reference to these rules.[68] Despite

---

[58] Ch. 15, Sect. 8 below.

[59] Ch. 1, Sect. 2 above. In addition to the clearing of sterling-denominated cheques, the Cheque and Credit Clearing Co. Ltd also operates a clearing service for Euro-denominated cheques used in connection with a United Kingdom bank account. Volumes are comparatively low and declining: UK Payments Council, n.27 above, 20. These mechanisms are unaffected by the developing 'Single European Payment Area' and the advent of the Payment Services Directive and implementing regulations: Ch. 2, Sect. 6(iii) above & Ch. 13, Sects. 1(iv) & 5 below.

[60] Ch. 1, Sect. 2 above.   [61] Ch. 13, Sects. 1(v) & 3(iii)–(iv) below.

[62] The clearing of paper-based credit transfers, such as giro credits, are governed by the Credit Clearing Rules.   [63] [1962] Ir. R. 159 (IESC).

[64] N.30 above. See also *Sutherland* v. *Royal Bank of Scotland*, n.2 above; *Turner* v. *Royal Bank of Scotland plc* (1999) 143 SJLB 23 (CA); *Marlin UK LLC* v. *RFH Ltd* [2005] EWHC 235 (Ch), [27].

[65] Ibid., 392.   [66] Ibid., 394.   [67] Ibid.

[68] For a similar conclusion regarding the bank's duty of confidentiality, see Ch. 5, Sect. 5(vi) above.

the structural changes in the clearing system, the position probably remains the same nowadays.

The cumbersome nature of cheque clearing would be simplified by the introduction of 'cheque truncation', which avoids having to transfer cheques and other paper-based payment instructions physically from the collecting bank to the drawee bank. Under such a system, the exchange of paper in the clearing house is replaced by the collecting bank communicating to the drawee bank the essential data respecting the cheque, such as the details encoded on the cheque's magnetic ink line and its amount. The cheque is physically retained by the collecting bank. Alternatively, an electronic image of the cheque may be transmitted to the drawee bank. The Deregulation (Bills of Exchange) Order 1996[69] made provision for cheque truncation by amending the Bills of Exchange Act 1882 (BEA 1882). According to the new section 74A of the BEA 1882, a bank may by a notice published in the London, Edinburgh, and Belfast Gazettes specify an address at which cheques drawn on it may be presented for payment. A cheque presented at such an address—for instance a particular bank's own data-processing centre—is deemed to have been presented at the 'proper address'. Similarly, section 74B of the BEA 1882 sanctions the presentation of a cheque by means of an electronic or similar message setting out the 'fundamental features' of the instrument, including the cheque's serial number; the 'sorting code' identifying the drawee bank; the number of the account on which the cheque is drawn; and the cheque's amount. The first three details are set out in magnetic ink at the foot of the cheque and the last detail would be encrypted on the cheque by the collecting bank. Sections 74A–74B of the BEA 1882 apply only to cheques, however, but not to analogous instruments, such as non-negotiable bankers' drafts and other instruments listed in section 4(2) of the Cheques Act 1957. Moreover, even where cheque truncation is sanctioned, section 74B(3) of the BEA 1882 permits the drawee bank to demand the cheque's physical presentment. Under section 74B(4), such a demand does not constitute a dishonour of the cheque by non-payment.[70] Still, when no such demand is made, section 74C of the BEA 1882 provides that the cheque's presentment by the means sanctioned in section 74B disposes of the requirements that the bill of exchange (and hence a cheque) be exhibited to the drawee upon presentation for payment and delivered up when paid.[71] Accordingly, a truncated cheque can be retained at the presenting bank's gazetted address. Despite the existence nowadays of the necessary legal and technological framework for banks to adopt a system of cheque truncation, the old paper-based clearing system remains largely in operation, although some banks now operate a system of 'partial truncation', whereby cheques drawn on them are retained in their clearing centre, saving the need to forward cheques to branches and dispensing with the verification of the drawer's signature. Given the UK Payment Council's decision to close the cheque guarantee card scheme by 30 June 2011,[72] and its decision to set 31 October 2018 as the target closure date for cheque clearing in the United Kingdom,[73] it is highly unlikely that United Kingdom banks would now consider it worthwhile to invest the time and resources into developing a fully-fledged system of cheque truncation.

---

[69] S. I. 1996/2993. For the initial recommendation, see Review Committee on Banking Services Law and Practice (Cm. 622, HMSO, London, 1989), rec. 7(8), which was accepted by the Government (Cm. 1026, TSO, London, 1999), Annex 5, [5-11]–[5-13]. See also Vroegop, 'Legal Implications of Cheque Truncation' [1990] *LMCLQ* 244; A.G. Guest, n.3 above, [13-023]–[13-030].

[70] BEA 1882, ss.45, 74B(2); Cheques Act 1957, s.3(2) (concerning the effect of a cheque as a receipt), as amended by Deregulation (Bills of Exchange) Order 1996, S. I. 1996/2993, Art. 5.

[71] Ibid., s.54(2).   [72] UK Payments Council, n.28 above, 4.

[73] Ibid., 1. See also UK Payments Council, *Progress Report—Delivering the National Payments Plan* (London, March 2009), 1–3.

The above discussion of the clearing system shows that, throughout the process, the cheque is treated as a mere instrument issued to effect payment. As already mentioned, the cheque's role as a negotiable instrument remains of limited importance where it is cleared through the banking system. That role is relevant only in the rare cases in which a cheque is remitted for the collection of an account maintained by a person other than the ostensible payee. Moreover, even in these cases, only one attribute of negotiability is significant, namely the instrument's transferability by indorsement and delivery. The most important aspect of negotiability is that the transferee may acquire a better title to the instrument than the transferor, yet this remains irrelevant as regards the clearing process. The cheque's role as a negotiable instrument is, however, important in the relationship between drawer and payee, and as regards the rights of a holder.

3 The cheque as negotiable instrument

(i) Introductory

As discussed already, a cheque serves two functions. In the relationship between the bank and its customer, it constitutes an instruction to pay a certain amount of money to the payee's order or to the bearer. The mutual rights and obligations arising from the cheque as between the bank and its customer, the drawer, are discussed in Chapter 11. Certain elements of the cheque's negotiability that are relevant to that relationship are, of course, referred to in that context. As between the drawer of the cheque, who is the bank's customer, and the payee or a subsequent holder, the cheque constitutes a negotiable instrument. Unless issued as a non-transferable payment order, therefore, the payee or indorser is entitled to enforce a cheque against the drawer.[74] The bank, as drawee, is not a party to the cheque, and the instrument is unenforceable against it by the holder.[75] The position of a bank that collects the cheque for the holder is discussed in Chapter 15. In the present section, however, the discussion centres on the cheque as a negotiable instrument that is enforceable by the holder. In this context, it is necessary to consider the legal nature of a cheque and its form, its negotiability and restrictions imposed thereon, the special problems arising out of the post-dating of cheques, and the marking and crossing of cheques. A brief analysis of the dishonour of a cheque and of the holder's duties arising thereafter is also required.

(ii) Definition and attributes of a cheque

A cheque is defined in section 73 of the BEA 1882, as 'a bill of exchange drawn on a "banker"[76] payable on demand'.[77] On reading this definition together with that of a bill of exchange in section 3(1) of the BEA 1882, the following composite definition emerges: a

---

[74] BEA 1882, s.38(1). See *Banco Santander SA* v. *Banque Paribas*, n.12 above. See further Sect. 3(iii) below.

[75] Ibid., s.53(1). See also *Fiorentino Comm Giuseppe Srl* v. *Farnesi* [2005] 2 All ER 737, [39].

[76] Ch. 3, Sects. 1(ii)–(iii) above. A 'credit card cheque' is a cheque, whether or not drawn on a banker, that will result in the provision of credit under a credit-token agreement: Financial Services Act 2010, s.15(7). It is a criminal offence to send unsolicited 'credit card cheques': ibid, s.15(1).

[77] There is no requirement that a valid cheque bear a date: *Aspinall's Club Ltd* v. *Al-Zayat* [2007] EWHC 362 (Comm.), [10]. A 'bank cheque' does not fall within the definition of a cheque (*Yan* v. *Post Office Bank Ltd* [1994] 1 NZLR 154, 158–159 (NZCA)), nor does a payment bond (*Euro-National Corporation Ltd* v. *NZI Bank Ltd* [1992] 2 NZLR 739, 763). A 'credit card cheque' differs from a cheque drawn on a current account: Financial Services Act 2010, s.15(8).

cheque is an unconditional order in writing, drawn by one person upon another person who is a bank, signed by the drawer, requiring the bank to pay on demand a sum certain in money to or to the order of a specified person or to bearer. The cheque need not use the words 'on demand', but may use instead the synonymous expressions 'on sight' or 'on presentation', or simply may not specify a time for payment. In all three cases, the instrument is deemed to be payable on demand under section 10(1) of the BEA 1882.[78] Cheques issued in the United Kingdom follow the last pattern.

Three features that are common to cheques are not spelt out in the above composite definition. First, the definition does not explicitly require that a cheque be drawn on the bank by a customer. In practice, however, cheques are drawn against balances maintained in current accounts. As a general rule, a person who maintains such an account becomes the bank's 'customer'.[79] The only cases in which a cheque is drawn on a bank by a person other than a customer is where there is fraud in the transaction, such as in the case where the signature of the drawer is executed by a forger or by a person without authority to draw on behalf of the owner of the account. Such an instrument constitutes a cheque, and may confer rights against the indorsers or on a holder who takes the cheque without knowledge of the fraud.[80] But the instrument is not a valid mandate given by the customer, so that the bank is under a duty to dishonour it.[81]

Secondly, although the usual form of cheque sets out a space in which the drawer is expected to fill in the date of its issue, the legal definition of a cheque does not specifically require the cheque to disclose the date on which it was drawn.[82] Nor does it affect the cheque's validity if its issue date is added at a later date,[83] or is added in breach of a collateral agreement.[84] That said, the date is considered to be 'material'[85] in the sense that an unauthorized alteration to the existing date appearing on the cheque has the effect of discharging the instrument,[86] although this will only be the case if the altered date is later than the original date.[87] The cheque's date can also be important from the perspective that a cheque that has been outstanding for a prolonged period of time is considered 'stale' and should be dishonoured by the drawee bank as being 'out of date'.[88]

---

[78] *Commissioner of Inland Revenue* v. *Thomas Cook (NZ) Ltd* [2003] 2 NZLR 296, [16] (NZCA), affd. on a different ground: [2005] 2 NZLR 722 (PC). See also *Barsdell* v. *Kerr* [1979] 2 NZLR 731, 734–735.

[79] Ch. 5, Sect. 2 above.   [80] BEA 1882, s.55(2).

[81] Ibid., s.24. A cheque bearing a forged drawer's signature is 'a mere sham piece of paper': *National Westminster Bank Ltd* v. *Barclays Bank International Ltd* [1975] QB 654, 656–657; *First Sport Ltd* v. *Barclays Bank plc* [1993] 1 WLR 1229, 1233 (CA). See also *Vella* v. *Permanent Mortgages Pty Ltd* [2008] NSWSC 505, [250]–[255].

[82] *Aspinall's Club Ltd* v. *Al-Zayat*, n.77 above, [10]. The drawee bank is, however, entitled to refuse to pay an undated cheque: *Griffiths* v. *Dalton* [1940] 2 KB 264.

[83] *Aspinall's Club Ltd* v. *Al-Zayat* [2007] EWCA Civ 1001, [17].

[84] *Roberts & Co.* v. *Marsh* [1915] 1 KB 42.

[85] BEA 1882, s.64(2). See also *Vance* v. *Lowther* (1876) 1 Ex. D 176; *Griffiths* v. *Dalton*, n.82 above; *Ung Ent Huat* v. *Arab Malaysian Bank Bhd* [2003] 6 MLJ 1, [43].

[86] Ibid., s.64(1). See also *Smith* v. *Lloyds TSB Group plc* [2001] QB 541 (CA).

[87] *Rees* v. *Commissioners of Customs & Excise* (1989, London VAT Tribunal).

[88] Although the Cheque Clearing House Rules have no specific provision determining when a cheque becomes stale, an analogy can be drawn from BEA 1882, s.36(3), which provides that a bill payable on demand is to be regarded as overdue when it has been outstanding for an unreasonable time. This is a matter of banking custom: *Ullrich* v. *Commissioner of Inland Revenue* [1964] NZLR 386, 388–389. Eight days appears too short a period to render a cheque stale: *London and County Banking Co.* v. *Groome* (1881) 8 QBD 288. Nowadays, there appears to be a banking custom that cheques will not be honoured once a period of six months from their date of issue has elapsed: *Edmonton Motors Ltd* v. *Edmonton Savings & Credit Union Ltd* (1988) 85 AR 29, [81]–[82] (AQB); *Kashi* v. *Eshragi* (CA, 17 July 2000); *Commissioner of Inland Revenue* v. *Thomas Cook (NZ) Ltd*, n.78 above, [38], affd. on a different ground: [2005] 2 NZLR 722 (PC). See also *Lau Kwok Fai* v. *Renren Holdings Ltd* [2004] 3 HKC 288, [18].

Thirdly, the definition does not make clear that a cheque (as a type of bill of exchange)[89] must be supported by consideration moving from the promisee if it is to be enforceable by the payee. In the absence of such consideration, the document is nothing more than a revocable instruction by a customer to his bank to make payment.[90] Such consideration will generally be presumed[91] and, as well as including any consideration that would suffice to support a simple contract at common law, consideration for these purposes includes the discharge of an antecedent debt or liability.[92] The weight of authority appears to indicate, however, that this does not include the antecedent debt or liability of a third party debtor who is not the drawer of the cheque.[93] In *Lomax Leisure Ltd* v. *Miller*,[94] this principle was applied recently to deny recovery on a cheque drawn by liquidators on an insolvent company's account for the purpose of making a dividend payment to that company's creditors. Given the identity of interest between the liquidator and the corporate debtor in *Lomax Leisure*, and given the commercial consequence that creditors would not be able to rely with any confidence upon a liquidator's cheque, it may be questioned whether *Lomax Leisure* represents a step too far. This is particularly so when one remembers that a cheque will be supported by consideration when it can be shown that the payee has promised to forebear (or has actually foreborn) from suing the third party debtor.[95] Moreover, there are suggestions both in the United Kingdom[96] and other jurisdictions[97] that there may be consideration in support of a cheque drawn in respect of a third party's debt when there exists a close commercial or familial relationship between the drawer of the cheque and the debtor in question.

In all other regards, the form of a cheque must comply with the detailed requirements contained in the definition in the BEA 1882. Thus, the cheque forms issued in the United Kingdom include the imperative instruction 'pay', rather than a less direct command. Accordingly, the cheque constitutes an 'order'. This order can be couched in more polite language, such as 'please pay', as long as the request remains imperative rather than precative.[98] In addition, the order has to be 'unconditional'. The demarcation between a conditional and an unconditional order, however, is not always clear. An illustration is furnished by section 3(3) of the BEA 1882. According to this provision, an order to pay out of a particular fund is conditional; but if the order itself is unqualified it remains unconditional, even though it is coupled with an indication of a particular fund out of which the drawee is to reimburse himself, with an indication of a particular account to be debited with the amount, or with a statement of the transaction that gives rise to the drawing of

---

[89] Sect. 8(iii) below.   [90] *Lomax Leisure Ltd* v. *Miller* [2008] 1 BCLC 262, [50].

[91] Ibid., [22]. See also BEA 1882, s.30. For the burden of proving absence of consideration, see *Vecta Software Corp. Ltd* v. *Despec Supplies Ltd* [2004] EWHC 3151 (Ch), [20].

[92] Ibid., [23], [47]. See also BEA 1882, s.27 (discussed in Sect. 8(iii) below).

[93] *Oliver* v. *Davis* [1949] 2 KB 727 (CA); *Hasan* v. *Willson* [1977] 1 Lloyd's Rep. 431; *MK International Development Co. Ltd* v. *Housing Bank* [1991] 1 Bank. LR 74 (CA); *Wheeler* v. *Roberts* (CA, 11 July 1994). See also *Yan* v. *Post Office Bank Ltd*, n.77 above, 161–162. See further A.G. Guest, n.3 above, [4-023]; N. Elliott, J. Odgers, & M. Phillips, *Byles on Bills of Exchange and Cheques* (28th edn., London, 2007), [19-011].

[94] N.90 above, [47]–[50].   [95] A.G. Guest, n.3 above, [4-023].

[96] *Autobiography Ltd* v. *Byrne* [2005] EWHC 213, as explained in *Lomax Leisure Ltd* v. *Miller*, n.90 above, [49]. See also *Oliver* v. *Davis*, n.93 above, 735–736, 738.

[97] For Australia, see *Walsh, Spriggs, Nolan & Finney* v. *Hoag & Bosch Pty Ltd* [1977] VR 178 (VSC); *Dventures Pty Ltd* v. *Wily* [2001] NSWSC 641. For Canada, see *Albert Pearl (Management) Ltd* v. *JDF Builders Ltd* [1975] 2 SCR 846, 879 (SCC); *Toronto-Dominion Bank* v. *Cordi* (1997) 27 OTC 76, [8]–[11]. For New Zealand, see *Bonior* v. *Siery Ltd* [1968] NZLR 254, 258; *Electrical Technologies Ltd* v. *Auckland Electrical Services Ltd* [1995] 3 NZLR 726, 728–729; *Wrightson Farmers Finance Ltd* v. *Alan Hiscox Ltd* (NZHC, 22 September 1995); *Garratt Enterprises Ltd* v. *Lynds* (NZHC, 27 May 1997).

[98] *Little* v. *Slackford* (1828) 1 M & M 171; cf. *Hamilton* v. *Spottiswoode* (1849) 4 Exch. 200, 210.

the instrument. This rule is of practical importance, as it will be recalled that an ordinary cheque contained in a personalized cheque-book sets out certain details, including the drawer's account number, in magnetic ink. As this information is inserted solely for the purpose of identifying the account against which the cheque is drawn, however, it does not qualify the drawer's demand that the bank pay the cheque. Accordingly, the instrument remains unconditional.

Certain cheques, such as those issued by some social-security authorities,[99] contain a receipt form printed either on the front or at the back of the cheque. If the request for the signing of the receipt qualifies the drawer's order, then the instrument ceases to be an 'unconditional' order. Thus, in *Bavins Jnr. & Sims* v. *London and South Western Bank*,[100] it was held that a cheque was conditional when it read, 'Pay to B. Bavins the sum of sixty-nine pounds; provided the receipt at the foot hereof is duly signed, stamped and dated'. The instruction for the signature of the receipt was in *Bavins* directed to the drawee. If the instruction is not directed to the drawee, however, but to the payee, it does not necessarily qualify the order to pay. Thus, in *Nathan* v. *Ogdens Ltd*,[101] a cheque was issued to effect payment of a debt. It was in the ordinary form, but at the foot were printed the words, 'the receipt at the back hereof must be signed, which signature will be taken as an indorsement . . .'. The court held that this instrument remained unconditional despite the clause at its foot. The request for the receipt was directed to the payee and, therefore, did not qualify the order issued by the drawer to the drawee. The distinction between *Bavins* and *Nathan* is based on the nature of the request for the receipt. To determine which of these two cases applies to a particular request for a receipt, it is important to examine whether it is inserted or printed above or beneath the space meant for the drawer's signature. Any words appearing in front of the signature constitute part and parcel of the instruction given to the bank. Accordingly, they qualify the order. Words that appear beneath the signature are more likely to be regarded as auxiliary to the order part of the cheque. They are, therefore, directed to the payee and not to the drawee. An exception to this general statement is found in cheques that bear on their face the letter 'R'. This letter serves as an indication to the bank that its customer, the drawer, requires the bank to satisfy itself that the receipt form, provided either at the front or at the back of the cheque, is completed. This suggests that if such a signature on the receipt is missing, the bank is expected to dishonour the cheque. Thus, the execution of the payee's signature is a prerequisite to the payment of the instrument by the bank. Accordingly, the order is conditional.[102]

The condition that qualifies the order to pay is not always a request for the execution of a receipt. For example, there may be a note on the face of the instrument to the effect that the cheque will not be honoured if presented later than, say, the lapse of six months from the date of issue. It is a question of fact whether such an instruction qualifies the order to the bank or is merely directed to the payee. It is arguable that the very inclusion of a note to this effect is an implicit request to the bank not to pay the instrument if it is presented at a later date. In *Thairlwall* v. *Great Northern Ry.*,[103] however, it was held

---

[99] This is only likely to be the case for payees without a bank account, as most social security payments are now made by electronic means: see generally Ch. 13 below.

[100] [1900] 1 QB 270 (CA). See also *Lecomte* v. *O'Grady* (1918) 57 SCR 563, 569 (SCC).

[101] [1905] 93 LT 553, affd. (1905) 94 LT 126. See also *Thairlwall* v. *Great Western Ry. Co.* [1910] 2 KB 509; *Roberts & Co.* v. *Marsh*, n.84 above.

[102] Clearing banks regard such an instrument as conditional: Ch. 11, Sect. 4(v) below.

[103] N.101 above.

that where such a note appeared at the foot of a dividend warrant, which constituted a cheque, the instrument was unconditional.

Two further requirements arising from the definition of a cheque need to be emphasized. The first is that a cheque has to be in writing. For the purposes of the BEA 1882, the term 'written' includes 'printed' and the term 'writing' includes 'print'.[104] Although it is unclear whether 'writing' would include an electronic communication,[105] there is at least authority for the view that 'written' in this context includes writing in pencil.[106] A cheque written in pencil is so unusual in terms of modern banking practice, however, that banks would probably still honour a cheque written in pencil, but would likely request the customer to abandon this practice. In contrast, it is not clear whether the above definitions apply to the signature on the cheque,[107] and whether a signature may accordingly be executed by means of a rubber stamp. This issue arose in *Goodman* v. *J. Eban Ltd*,[108] where a majority of the Court of Appeal thought that a signature affixed by a solicitor on his bill of costs by means of a rubber stamp was an adequate signature within the meaning of section 65(2) of the Solicitors Act 1932. In his dissenting judgment, Denning LJ expressed the view that a document could not be signed by means of a rubber stamp,[109] although a mark executed by an illiterate person would be adequate. This distinction between a valid mark and a mere facsimile signature is not easy to discern.[110] Denning LJ expressed the view that a facsimile signature, unlike a valid mark, was a 'thoughtless impress of an automaton, in contrast to the reasoned attention of a sensible person'.[111] It may be wondered how valid this distinction is, given that a facsimile signature imprinted by means of a rubber stamp can be just as thoughtfully executed by a person as any other type of mark. In reality, the main distinction between a written signature and a valid mark, on the one hand, and a facsimile signature, on the other, is that the rubber stamp can be readily utilized by an unauthorized person, whilst a signature, or even a mark, is more difficult to forge. It is submitted, however, that this in itself is not a good ground for doubting the general validity of a facsimile signature or for departing from the majority view in *Goodman*. Indeed, that majority view may nowadays gain some support from Schedule 1 of the Interpretation Act 1978, which defines 'writing' as including 'other modes of representing or reproducing words in a visible form'.

The second point emphasized in the definition of a cheque is that the instrument has to be drawn by one person on another person who qualifies as a 'bank'.[112] This means that if one branch of a bank draws a cheque on another branch or on the head office of the same bank, the instrument is not within the definition, as it has been drawn by the bank on itself. It will, however, be seen that certain defences conferred on the collecting bank and the paying bank in respect of cheques are specifically extended to encompass dealings

---

[104] BEA 1882, s.2.

[105] No order has yet been made in respect of the BEA 1882 under the Electronic Communications Act 2000, s.8, which gives the Secretary of State the power to modify legislation 'in such manner as he may think fit for the purpose of authorizing or facilitating the use of electronic communications or electronic storage'.

[106] *Geary* v. *Physic* (1826) 5 B & C 234; cf. *Importers Co. Ltd* v. *Westminster Bank Ltd* [1927] 1 KB 869, 874, affd. [1927] 2 KB 297 (CA).

[107] The term 'signature' is not defined in the BEA 1882.

[108] [1954] 1 QB 550 (CA). See also *Bartletts de Reya* v. *Byrne*, The Times, 14 January 1983; *Re A Debtor* [1996] 1 BCLC 538; *Re Horne*, The Times, 14 June 2000 (CA).

[109] Ibid., 561. See also *Firstpost Homes Ltd* v. *Johnson* [1995] 1 WLR 1567, 1575 (CA); *Newell* v. *Tarrant* [2004] EWHC 772 (Ch), [45]–[47].

[110] *Edgell* v. *Glover* [2003] EWHC 2566 (QB), [43]–[47].

[111] *Goodman* v. *J. Eban Ltd*, n.108 above, 561. See also *Lazarus Estates Ltd* v. *Beasley* [1956] 1 QB 702 (CA). Denning LJ's view is supported by the decision of the Supreme Court of Ceylon in *Meyappan* v. *Manchanayake* (1961) 62 NLR 529.   [112] Ch. 1, Sects. 1(ii)–(iii) above.

in such 'bankers' drafts'.[113] In addition, the holder of a banker's draft is in as good a position as the holder of a negotiable instrument. This is so as, under section 5(2) of the BEA 1882, where the drawer and the drawee of an instrument are one and the same person, the holder has the option of treating the instrument either as a bill of exchange or a promissory note.[114] In both cases, the holder is entitled to enforce the instrument.[115]

(iii) **The transferability of a cheque**

The method for the transfer of a cheque depends on whether it is payable to a specific person's order or to bearer. A bill is payable to bearer either if it is expressed to be so payable or if the last indorsement on it is executed in blank.[116] A bill is payable to order either if it is expressed to be so payable or if it is expressed to be payable to a particular person and does not include words that prohibit transfer or that indicate an intention that it should not be transferable.[117] Where a negotiable cheque is payable to order, it is transferable by indorsement and delivery, and where it is payable to bearer, it is transferable by mere delivery. As negotiation is rare in the case of cheques and common in the case of other types of bill of exchange, it will be convenient to discuss details of the form of an indorsement and the distinction between a special indorsement and an indorsement in blank subsequently.[118] Two points need, however, to be made at this stage. The first point is that, in the case of cheques, an indorsement frequently serves the function of a receipt. This aspect of the law of cheques is illustrated by cases in which the ostensible payee of an uncrossed cheque cashes it over the drawee bank's counter. The bank has the intention of honouring, and hence of discharging, the instrument, rather than the intention of becoming a transferee, so that an indorsement for transfer or negotiation purposes is unnecessary. Nevertheless, under current banking practice, the payee is asked to sign his name on the back of the cheque.[119] The signature, which assumes the form of an indorsement in blank, simply evidences payment of the cheque by the bank to a person who claims to be the payee. The second point is that, where a cheque is transferred, the transferee is well advised to demand the payee's indorsement even if the cheque is payable to bearer. The reason for this is that, by executing an indorsement, the 'indorser' warrants that the cheque will be paid on presentment.[120]

Can a cheque, initially drawn as payable to bearer, be converted into an order cheque by means of a special indorsement, in which the indorser specifies the name of a designated indorsee? In Australia, there is authority suggesting that a cheque remains payable to bearer despite the execution of the special indorsement,[121] but this view is questionable in the United Kingdom. Under section 34(4) of the BEA 1882, 'any holder may convert [a] blank indorsement into a special indorsement by writing above the indorser's signature a direction to pay the bill to or to the order of himself or some other person'. Although this provision does not formally apply to a bill of exchange or cheque that was

---

[113] Ch. 11, Sect. 4(v) below.

[114] For the application of this provision to a 'counter cheque', see *Abbey National plc* v. *JSF Finance & Currency Exchange Co. Ltd*, n.5 above, [12]–[14].

[115] *Williams* v. *Ayers* (1877) 3 App. Cas. 133, 142–143; *Re Commercial Bank of South Australia* (1887) 36 Ch. D 522, 525; *Capital and Counties Bank Ltd* v. *Gordon* [1903] AC 240, 250 (HL). Cf. *Commercial Banking Co. of Sydney Ltd* v. *Mann* [1961] AC 1, 7 (PC), where Viscount Simonds described bankers' drafts as promissory notes issued by banks.

[116] BEA 1882, s.8(3). See *Sutters* v. *Briggs* [1922] 1 AC 1, 15–16 (HL).

[117] Ibid., s.8(4). A bill is payable to a specified person's order even if made payable to him without the addition of words indicating that it is payable to his order: ibid., s.8(5).

[118] Sect. 8(iv) below.   [119] Ch. 11, Sect. 4(v) below.   [120] BEA 1882, s.55(2).

[121] *Miller Associated (Australia) Pty. Ltd* v. *Bennington Pty. Ltd* (1975) 7 ALR 144.

drawn initially as payable to bearer, but instead applies only where the instrument has subsequently been indorsed in blank, it reflects the policy of the BEA 1882. As a cheque that has become payable to bearer by reason of its blank indorsement can be converted into an order instrument, it is difficult to see why a cheque that was drawn originally as payable to bearer may not equally be converted into an order cheque by the execution of a special indorsement. Some support for this view can be derived from section 8(5) of the BEA 1882, under which a cheque that 'either originally *or by indorsement*, is expressed to be payable to the order of a specified person, and not to him or his order, is nevertheless payable to him or his order at his option'. This provision envisages that the eventual tenor of an instrument depends either on the manner in which it was originally drawn or, following its negotiation, on its last indorsement. Section 8(5) of the BEA 1882 does not assume that, if in its original tenor the cheque is payable to bearer, it cannot be changed to an order instrument by a special indorsement.

Where a cheque or bill of exchange is payable to order, it must specify the identity of the payee with reasonable certainty.[122] A cheque that is made out for a specific purpose, such as 'cash or order', is not a bill of exchange, as it is not payable to a specific payee and is therefore also not a cheque.[123] Difficulties arise when the drawer leaves the payee's name in blank. It has been suggested that such an instrument should be treated as payable to bearer 'because that is the natural legal effect',[124] but the authorities remain divided on this point.[125] It is unlikely, however, that a cheque where the space between the printed words 'pay… *or order*' is left blank can similarly be construed as a bearer instrument.[126] The words 'or order' militate against such an interpretation. The fact remains, however, that the drawer of such an instrument intends to create a valid bill of exchange or cheque. One manner of giving effect to this intention is to treat the instrument as payable to the drawer himself. Thus, in *Chamberlain* v. *Young and Tower*,[127] it was held that an instrument reading 'pay to… order' should be construed as meaning 'pay my order' and, thus, considered a valid bill of exchange. In *R.* v. *Randall*,[128] however, an instrument reading 'pay… or order' was held not to be a bill of exchange. An attempt has been made to distinguish the two cases on the basis that the addition of the word 'my' to the phrase 'pay… or order' would be meaningless,[129] but the line could easily be construed as 'pay myself or order', which formula is commonly used in personal cheques cashed over the counter. Some support for this can be derived from a Scottish decision, in which such an instrument was treated as a promissory note and which accordingly provides an acceptable solution by giving effect to the drawer's intention of issuing a negotiable instrument.[130]

---

[122] BEA 1882, s.7(1).

[123] *North & South Insurance Corporation Ltd* v. *National Provincial Bank Ltd* [1936] 1 KB 328, 333–336; *Orbit Mining & Trading Co. Ltd* v. *Westminster Bank Ltd* [1963] 1 QB 794, 811, 820–821 (CA). See also A.G. Guest, n.3 above, [2-018]. Under s.3–109(a)(3) of the Uniform Commercial Code, a bill payable to 'cash or order' is deemed a valid bearer bill. A bill of exchange that is drawn payable to 'cash or bearer' is a valid bearer bill: *Grant* v. *Vaughan* (1764) 3 Burr. 1516.

[124] *Daun and Vallentin* v. *Sherwood* (1895) 11 TLR 211, 212. Some support for this may be derived from BEA 1882, s.20(1), which provides that an instrument without any indication as to the payee is an inchoate instrument that may be completed by the person who has possession of it. See also *Lipa* v. *Metabolic* [2006] NSWSC 997, [23]–[26].

[125] A.G. Guest, n.3 above, [2-049]–[2-050].

[126] *R* v. *Richards* (1811) Russ. & Ry. 193; *R* v. *Randall* (1811) Russ. & Ry. 195. Where the instrument is drawn 'pay to order', this can be a valid cheque: *Chamberlain* v. *Young and Tower* [1893] QB 206, 209–211 (CA).

[127] N.126 above, 209–211.   [128] N.126 above.

[129] *North & South Insurance Corporation Ltd* v. *National Provincial Bank Ltd*, n.123 above, 333–336.

[130] *Laurence Henderson, Sons & Co. Ltd* v. *Wallace and Pennell* 1902, 40 SLR 70, 71. The Lord Justice-Clerk, Lord Macdonald, treated the instrument as a bill. See also A.G. Guest, n.3 above, [2-049]–[2-050].

Under section 7(3) of the BEA 1882, where a bill of exchange or cheque is made payable to a fictitious or non-existing person, it may be treated as payable to bearer, which means that it will be transferable by delivery alone. It also means that the bank has the mandate to pay such a cheque to bearer. A difficulty arises, however, because the terms 'fictitious' and 'non-existing' are not defined in the BEA 1882. A 'fictitious' or 'non-existing' person may be not only the creation of fiction, such as 'Ivanhoe', or a person who has ceased to exist at the time that the bill of exchange is drawn, such as a deregistered company, a company that is never ultimately incorporated,[131] or a deceased individual,[132] but also a real payee whose name is put on the bill as a mere pretence. In the leading case of *Bank of England* v. *Vagliano Bros.*,[133] the claimants were in the habit of accepting bills of exchange drawn on them by X and payable to the order of P & Co. One of the claimants' clerks, G, forged just such a bill of exchange. The claimants, who were not aware of G forging X's signature as the purported drawer, accepted the bill of exchange and made it payable at the defendant bank. G then added a forged indorsement in P & Co.'s name, presented the bill of exchange to the defendant bank, and obtained payment. The claimants' action for a declaration that the defendant bank was not entitled to debit their account with the amount of the bill of exchange was dismissed. The House of Lords held that, as the bill of exchange was payable to a fictitious person, the defendant bank was entitled to pay it when presented by a bearer. In reaching this conclusion, their Lordships adopted a subjective approach, so that the question of whether a payee was 'fictitious' or not depended upon the intention of the person who actually drew the bill of exchange.[134] In *Vagliano*, although a firm known as P & Co. was actually in existence, when G drew the bill of exchange by forging X's signature, he had no intention that that firm should actually receive payment pursuant to the terms of the bill of exchange. A somewhat different approach was adopted subsequently in *Clutton* v. *Attenborough & Son.*[135] A clerk induced his employers to draw a cheque payable to 'John Brett' by falsely representing that a person of that name was entitled to remuneration for certain work done for the employer. Even though the employer, when drawing the cheque, intended to make it payable to a 'John Brett' who had completed some work for him, as there was in reality no such person as 'John Brett' in existence, it was held that the payee was a non-existing person. Lord Halsbury refused to give effect to the drawer's intention as had been done in *Vagliano*, but instead preferred to determine the question objectively by simply asking whether the payee referred to on the face of the instrument

---

[131] *Oates* v. *Parkland Savings & Credit Union Ltd* (1982) 46 AR 30, [5] (AQB).

[132] *Canada Trust Co.* v. *The Queen* [1982] 2 FC 722, 732–736 (CFC).

[133] [1891] AC 107 (HL). See also *Bank of Toronto* v. *Smith* [1950] OR 457, 460–461 (OCA); *Canada Trust Co.* v. *The Queen*, n.132 above, 732–736; *Fok Cheong Shing Investments Co.* v. *Bank of Nova Scotia* [1982] 2 SCR 488, 490 (SCC); *Boma Manufacturing Ltd* v. *Canadian Imperial Bank of Commerce* [1996] 3 SCR 277, [50], [54]–[57] (SCC); *Bank of Nova Scotia* v. *Toronto-Dominion Bank* (2001) 145 OAC 106, [16]–[21] (OCA); cf. *Paul* v. *Western Canada Lottery Foundation* (1981) 127 DLR (3d.) 502.

[134] Whilst this view is supportable in the case of cheques in which the drawer determines the tenor of the instrument and is, in effect, the main party to be charged in the event of its dishonour, it is difficult to see that the principle in *Vagliano* is appropriate in the case of bills of exchange. In such an instrument, the main obligor is the acceptor rather than the drawer: BEA 1882, s.54. If an acceptor, such as the claimants in *Vagliano*, intends the instrument to be payable to a designated payee, such as P & Co. in *Vagliano*, why should the court be guided by the intention of a person whose name does not even appear on the bill of exchange, as was the case with the forger, G, in *Vagliano*? This argument is reinforced in the case of a bill of exchange because the order to pay the bill is given to the designated bank, such as the defendants in *Vagliano*, by the acceptor!

[135] [1897] AC 90 (HL). See also *Royal Bank of Canada* v. *Concrete Column Clamps* [1977] 2 SCR 456, 464–465 (SCC); *Canada Trust Co.* v. *The Queen*, n.132 above, 732–736.

existed or not.[136] Accordingly, it appears that *Vagliano* will govern the situation where the payee exists, but is nevertheless 'fictitious', whereas *Clutton* will govern the situation where the payee is 'non-existing'.

The approach in *Vagliano* also appears not to govern the situation in which the drawer's intention to make a cheque payable to a particular designated real person is induced by another person's fraudulent misrepresentation. The reason for this is that, although the motive that induces the drawer to draw the instrument is the misrepresentation concerning his liability to a third party, he has nevertheless the intention of making the cheque payable to the very person concerned.[137] Accordingly, such a cheque would not be payable to a 'fictitious' person and hence would not be payable to bearer.[138] This situation has been considered most recently by the Canadian courts. In *Royal Bank of Canada* v. *Concrete Column Clamps (1961) Ltd*,[139] a payroll clerk perpetrated a fraud by including among the cheques presented to the authorized signing officer of the company, *inter alia*, a number of cheques payable to former employees of the company who were not in fact owed any wages. A majority of the Supreme Court of Canada held that the cheques were not payable to 'fictitious' payees, even though the drawer's intention to pay those persons was induced by fraudulent means. In doing so, their Honours adopted the following situation as exemplifying the case before them:[140]

> If Martin Chuzzlewit is the name of a real person, intended by Bede to receive payment, the payee is neither fictitious nor non-existing, notwithstanding that Bede has been induced to draw the bill by the fraud of some other person who has falsely represented to Bede that there is a transaction in respect of which Chuzzlewit is entitled to the sum mentioned in the bill.

Accordingly, the cheques did not have a fictitious or non-existing payee. In a forceful dissenting judgment, Laskin CJ agreed with the majority's general proposition that in the instant type of case 'the discovery of the real or imaginary character of the payee is post facto: and ordinarily the drawer, induced by the fraud, would intend that the cheque take its effect in favour of the named payee'.[141] His Honour considered, however, that this general position required some further refinement depending upon whether the drawee bank or the drawer were at fault in any way, including whether it was possible to attribute the acts of the fraudster to the drawer on the ground that the fraudster was acting as its agent or employee.[142] According to Laskin CJ, therefore, this type of case cannot be solved by reference to a general rule, but depends upon the facts of the particular case. More recently, however, in *Boma Manufacturing Ltd* v. *Canadian Imperial Bank of Commerce*,[143] the Supreme Court of Canada preferred the majority view in *Concrete Column Clamps*

---

[136] *Boma Manufacturing Ltd* v. *Canadian Imperial Bank of Commerce*, n.133 above, [105], where La Forest J referred to *Clutton* as authority for the proposition that the determination of whether a payee is 'non-existing' depends upon an objective test of whether the stated payee is a matter of pure invention and that the issue does not depend upon the drawer's subjective intentions. See also *Oates* v. *Parkland Savings & Credit Union Ltd*, n.131 above, [5]; cf. *Westboro Flooring & Décor Inc.* v. *Bank of Nova Scotia* (2004) 71 OR (3d) 723, [23]–[25] (OCA).

[137] This doctrine does not apply to a cheque bearing a crossing accompanied by the words 'a/c payee only'. Under the Cheques Act 1992, s.1, such a cheque is not transferable and, hence, cannot be payable to bearer. Consider *Rhostar (Pvt.) Ltd* v. *Netherland Bank of Rhodesia Ltd* [1972] 2 SALR 703, 709–711.

[138] *Vinden* v. *Hughes* [1905] 1 KB 795; *North and South Wales Bank Ltd* v. *Macbeth* [1908] AC 137 (HL). See also *Harvey* v. *Bank of Toronto* (1938) OR 100, 103–105 (OCA).

[139] N.135 above, 480–481. Cf. *Paul* v. *Western Canada Lottery Foundation*, n.133 above.

[140] Ibid., 483–484, applying Falconbridge, *Banking and Bills of Exchange* (7th edn., 1969), 485–486. See also *Khosla* v. *Korea Exchange Bank of Canada* [2008] OJ No. 4344, [16]–[19].

[141] Ibid., 465.   [142] Ibid., 477–482.   [143] N.133 above, [50].

to that of Laskins CJ. In this regard, Iacobucci J stated that 'it is neither necessary nor desirable to import notions of agency and vicarious liability into the analysis' and that 'it is quite evident that it is the intention of the drawer…that is of relevance'.[144] On this basis, his Honour reasserted the general principle that 'where a drawer is fraudulently induced by another person into issuing a cheque for the benefit of a real person to whom no obligation is owed, the cheque is to be considered payable to the payee, and not to a fictitious person'.[145] The approach in *Boma* is certainly consistent with that in *Vagliano*, even though the conclusion might be different.

Under section 8(1) of the BEA 1882, the drawer can make a bill of exchange 'not negotiable' by inserting in the instrument words prohibiting transfer or indicating an intention that the instrument be not transferable. Unfortunately, the BEA 1882 does not define what the term 'negotiable' means in this context. As considered above,[146] the concept of negotiability generally has three attributes, one of which is transferability, but the BEA 1882 neither explicitly equates 'negotiability' with 'transferability' nor expressly distinguishes between the two concepts. Accordingly, it is unclear whether a bill of exchange that is rendered 'non-negotiable' under this provision means that the instrument is rendered 'non-transferable' or whether it means something less than this. Although the Court of Appeal in *National Bank* v. *Silke*[147] failed to throw light on whether a non-negotiable instrument is also non-transferable, the better view is that a restriction on the negotiability of a bill of exchange affects all three aspects of its character as a negotiable instrument. Support for this view is to be found in *Hibernian Bank Ltd* v. *Gysin and Hanson*,[148] where the Court of Appeal held that a bill of exchange bearing the words, 'not negotiable', on its face was rendered non-transferable, so that it could not be transferred to a holder, let alone a holder in due course, capable of enforcing the instrument.

It is submitted that these principles established in the context of bills of exchange should apply equally to cheques.[149] The main reason why a drawer would employ such a procedure in respect of a cheque would be to prevent the drawee bank from paying the cheque to a person other than the ostensible payee. According to section 8(1) of the BEA 1882, 'negotiability' (in the sense of transferability) is restricted only if the instrument contains words to this effect, which means that the mere cancellation of the words 'or bearer' or 'or order' on a printed cheque form does not have the effect of restricting the 'negotiability' of the instrument. Under section 8(4) of the BEA 1882, a bill that is payable to a particular person remains payable to that person's order and the cancellation of the words 'or order' is ineffective to change the tenor of the instrument. In contrast, the cancellation of the words 'or bearer' renders the bill payable to the order of the particular payee named therein. The most obvious way to achieve the result in section 8(1) of the BEA 1882 is by writing the words 'not transferable' on the face of the cheque, but the more usual way of restricting the cheque's transferability is by inserting the word 'only' after the payee's name. More difficulty arises in relation to the addition of the words, 'not negotiable'. Where such words are added to an uncrossed cheque, the better view is that their effect would be to render the cheque non-transferable in the same way as it

---

[144] Ibid., [58]. See also *Fok Cheong Shing Investments Co. Ltd* v. *Bank of Nova Scotia*, n.133 above, 490; *City of Charlottetown* v. *Bank of Montreal* [2006] PEIJ No. 64, [37]–[39] (PEISC).

[145] Ibid., [59]. See also *Metroland Printing, Publishing & Distribution Ltd* v. *Canadian Imperial Bank of Commerce* [2001] OTC 330, [34]–[43].

[146] Sect. 1 above.   [147] [1891] 1 QB 435 (CA).

[148] [1939] 1 KB 483 (CA), affg. [1938] 2 KB 384, where, in addition to the words, 'not negotiable', the bill of exchange bore the word 'only' after the name of the payee. See also A.G. Guest, n.3 above, [2-060]–[2-061].

[149] BEA 1882, s.73.

would a bill of exchange.[150] This is not the case when the words, 'not negotiable', are written on a cheque and accompanied by a crossing, however, as in such circumstances the words do not render the cheque non-transferable, but simply non-negotiable in the sense that a transferor with a defective title cannot pass a better title than he possesses to a holder in due course.[151] If the drawer wishes to render a crossed cheque non-transferable, then, since 1992, this can be achieved by a crossing accompanied by the words 'a/c payee only'.[152]

In the event that a cheque has been rendered non-negotiable, does the payee have to present it for payment in person at the counter of the drawee bank? In practice, such a cheque may be crossed and presented for payment through clearing channels by the payee's bankers. As the collecting bank acts as a mere agent of the payee and not as a transferee in his own right, this practice is unexceptional.[153] On the same basis, though, the payee should be entitled to present the cheque for payment at the drawee bank's counter through a personal agent, such as a relative or business associate. In the absence of case law in point, it is difficult to determine the construction likely to be given to the drawer's intention by a court.

(iv) Post-dated cheques[154]

A cheque is an instrument payable on demand. The blank line meant for the insertion of the date of issue at the top of the cheque form does not have the object of enabling the drawer to determine the date upon which the instrument is to be presented for payment. There are, however, cases in which the drawer wishes to ensure that a cheque is not presented for payment before a certain date, such as the day on which his monthly salary is due to be paid into his account by his employers. In such a case, the drawer can post-date the cheque, which then gives the impression of the cheque having been issued on the postponed date. After that date, the cheque appears on its face to be an ordinary instrument that is payable upon being presented to the drawee bank. At one time, it was preferable to use a post-dated cheque instead of a bill of exchange payable at a fixed future date, as the stamp duty payable on cheques was lower than that on bills of exchange.[155] The current position is that stamp duty is not payable upon any of these types of instrument.[156]

An initial issue that arises in relation to post-dated cheques is whether they fall within the definition of a 'cheque' in section 73 of the BEA 1882. Whilst it is possible that that definition will be satisfied once the date on the post-dated cheque has arrived,[157] it is

---

[150] *Hibernian Bank Ltd* v. *Gysin and Hanson*, n.148 above, 488, shows that the words, 'not negotiable', restrict negotiability (in the sense of making the instrument non-transferable) when written on an instrument other than a cheque. This is probably also the most natural construction of these words when written on an uncrossed cheque, rather than the special meaning that those words have when written on a crossed cheque: BEA 1882, s.81.

[151] Sect. 4(iii) below.

[152] BEA 1882, s.81A, inserted by the Cheques Act 1992, s.1. See further Sect. 4(iv) below.

[153] Ch. 15, Sect. 3 below.

[154] J.M. Holden, 81 *JIB* 253; 95 *JIB* 41. See also A.G. Guest, n.3 above, [2-095]–[2-099], [13-008]–[13-009].

[155] Until 1961, bills of exchange were subject to an *ad valorem* duty, whilst cheques were subject to a fixed duty of 2p, but the Finance Act 1961 equated the duty payable on bills with that payable on cheques. Bills of exchange and promissory notes were subsequently exempt from duty under the Finance Act 1970, s.32 & Sched. 7, which was itself repealed by Finance Act 1999, Sched. 20.

[156] Finance Act 2003, s.125.

[157] *Robinson* v. *Benkel* (1913) 29 TLR 475, 476. See also *Royal Bank of Scotland* v. *Tottenham* [1894] 2 QB 715 (CA).

potentially less clear what the status of the instrument is before that date. In *Brien* v. *Dwyer*,[158] Barwick CJ in the High Court of Australia suggested that a post-dated cheque constituted a bill of exchange payable at a future date, rather than a cheque, since the statutory definition of a 'cheque' requires the instrument to be payable on demand. On this basis, it was decided that the furnishing of a post-dated cheque did not comply with a contractual term in a contract of sale that required payment by cheque. This decision, however, is questionable,[159] as under section 10(1)(*b*) of the BEA 1882 an instrument is payable on demand if no time for *payment* is expressed in it. Although a post-dated cheque bears an incorrect date of *issue*, it does not designate any date for *payment* and so should be treated as an instrument payable on demand. This view was accepted by the New South Wales Court of Appeal in *Hodgson & Lee Pty. Ltd* v. *Mardonius Pty. Ltd*,[160] where Samuels JA declined to follow the earlier dicta in *Dwyer* referring instead to section 18(2) of the Bills of Exchange Act 1908 (Cth), which provides that a bill of exchange (including a cheque) 'is not invalid by reason only that it is ante-dated or post-dated'. The fact that post-dating does not affect the validity of an instrument as a cheque has now been made even more explicit in Australia in section 16(3) of the Cheques Act 1986 (Cth), which now governs cheques in Australia[161] and which provides that '[f]or the purpose of determining whether a post-dated instrument is a cheque, the fact that the instrument is post-dated shall be disregarded'.

Similarly, English law (like New Zealand[162] and Canadian law[163]) inclines to the view that a post-dated cheque is valid in all regards, as section 13(2) of the BEA 1882 contains a provision similar to the earlier Australian provision to the effect that a bill of exchange is not invalid by reason of its being post-dated, ante-dated or bearing a date that falls on a Sunday.[164] Although this provision does not refer specifically to the validity of instruments such as cheques, but only to bills of exchange, it has been held that this provision validates a post-dated cheque.[165] The English authorities also conclude that the holder of a post-dated cheque is entitled to enforce payment of it and that a transferee who obtains a cheque for value and in good faith becomes a holder in due course on the date on which he acquires the instrument, and not only as from the date on which it purports to be made. This is because in *Hitchcock* v. *Edwards*,[166] it was suggested that the post-dating of a cheque does not render the instrument incomplete or irregular on its face.

Certain disadvantages are, however, attached to a post-dated cheque. They stem from the fact that, as between the drawer (who is the customer) and the drawee bank, the post-dating of the instrument has the effect of instructing the bank to refuse payment

---

[158] (1979) 22 ALR 485, 491–492, 508 (HCA). See also *Forster* v. *Mackreth* (1867) LR 2 Ex 163, 167.

[159] A.G. Guest, n.3 above, [2-098].

[160] (1986) 5 NSWLR 496 (NSWCA). See also *Husky Oil Ltd* v. *R* (1998) 157 FTR 308, [14]–[15] (CFC).

[161] Bills of Exchange Amendment Act 1986, s.3.

[162] Bills of Exchange Act 1908 (NZ), s.13(2). See also *Pollock* v. *Bank of New Zealand* [1902] 20 NZLR 174, 180, 182–183 (NZCA); *Light* v. *The Great Northern Tavern (1992) Ltd* (NZHC, 18 February 2003), [12].

[163] *Keyes* v. *Royal Bank of Canada* [1947] 3 DLR 161 (SCC); *Michaud* v. *Caisse Populaire Notre-Dame de Lourdes* (2001) 245 NBR (2d) 63, [12]–[13] (NBQB); *Markham School for Human Development* v. *Ghods* (2002) 60 OR (3d) 624, [24] (OSC).

[164] Cf. *Lien Chung Credit & Leasing Sdn Bhd* v. *Change Chin Choi* [1994] 3 MLJ 488, 492–494 (MCA).

[165] *Hitchcock* v. *Edwards* (1889) 60 LT 636; *Royal Bank of Scotland* v. *Tottenham*, n.157 above, 719; *Robinson* v. *Benkel*, n.157 above, 476.

[166] N.165 above. See also *Carpenter* v. *Street* (1896) 6 TLR 410; *Royal Bank of Scotland* v. *Tottenham*, n.157 above, 719; *Robinson* v. *Benkel*, n.157 above, 476; *Guildford Trust Ltd* v. *Goss* (1927) 43 TLR 167; *The Chartered Bank* v. *Yeoh Bok Han* [1965] 2 MLJ 125, 127–128; *Michaud* v. *Caisse Populaire Notre-Dame de Lourdes*, n.163 above, [13]–[16].

if the cheque is presented before the purported date of its issue.[167] Accordingly, a bank will be acting outside its mandate if it honours a post-dated cheque before the date marked on its face and will not be entitled to debit its customer's account.[168] Similarly, the bank cannot refuse to honour other cheques drawn on the account as a result of its having honoured a post-dated cheque before it falls due for payment. If the customer countermands the post-dated cheque during the period before the date marked on its face,[169] the instrument will be dishonoured by the bank.[170] The holder's only remedy in such a case is to sue the drawer. In addition, the bank will be bound to dishonour the cheque if the drawer dies or becomes insane while the cheque is post-dated.[171] For these reasons, it is inadvisable for a payee to take a post-dated cheque in satisfaction of an outstanding debt.

From an analytical viewpoint, it is clear that there is a degree of inconsistency in the legal treatment of post-dated cheques. On the one hand, as between the holder and the drawer of a post-dated cheque, the instrument is regarded as valid and as regular from its genuine date of issue. On the other hand, as between the drawer and his bank, the very same cheque is treated as unissued, and as not containing a valid instruction, until the arrival of the fictitious day of drawing. It is believed that it would be preferable to treat a post-dated cheque in the same manner in relation to all the legal relationships that it might give rise to. This could be attained by a statutory provision to the effect that a cheque is deemed payable on demand irrespective of its purported date of issue or by a provision similar to the current Australian provision, as discussed above.[172]

(v) **Marking of cheques**

There used to be two types of situation in which a bank was asked to mark or 'certify' a cheque drawn upon it as being good for payment. The first situation was where such a request had been made by the drawer, holder, or payee of the cheque; the second situation arose where the cheque reached the hands of the collecting bank too late for presentment through the clearing house on the same day. In such a case, the collecting bank could request the drawee bank to mark the cheque as good for payment on the understanding that the cheque would be cleared the next day. In both types of case, the object of the request made to the drawee bank was based on the presentor's wish to ascertain the fate of the instrument. Furthermore, whilst only one basic formula was in use, namely that the cheque was 'marked good for payment',[173] the effect of the marking differed to a considerable degree in the two situations. Until recently, where a cheque was marked at the request of the collecting bank, the certification by the drawee bank was recognized under the custom of bankers as constituting a promise to pay by that bank. This view was initially

---

[167] *Pollock* v. *Bank of New Zealand*, n.162 above.

[168] Given that most cheques nowadays are pre-printed with the crossing 'a/c payee only', the drawee bank is unlikely to be able to argue that it has become a holder of the instrument: A.G. Guest, n.3 above, [2-098].

[169] *Michaud* v. *Caisse Populaire Notre-Dame de Lourdes*, n.163 above, [23]; *Encan Construction Ltd* v. *R* [2007] TCC 579, [11]–[12].

[170] *Morley* v. *Culverwell* (1840) 7 M & W 174, 178; *Pollock* v. *Bank of New Zealand*, n.162 above; *Keyes* v. *Royal Bank of Canada*, n.163 above; *Michaud* v. *Caisse Populaire Notre-Dame de Lourdes*, n.163 above, [23]. Contrast *Magill* v. *Bank of North Queensland* (1885) 6 QLJ 262.

[171] Ch. 11, Sect. 1(vi) below. Consider *Blackett* v. *Darcy*, n.2 above, [27].

[172] Cheques Act 1986 (Cth), s.16(3); cf Israeli Bills of Exchange Ordinance (New Version), 5717-1957, s.73(*b*) under which a post-dated cheque is payable or acceptable only after the purported date of issue.

[173] *Benley Ltd* v. *Win Wave Industrial Ltd* [2001] HKCU 863, [37].

settled at the beginning of the nineteenth century.[174] Subsequently, this view was taken to the next logical step that such a marking was actually equivalent to payment, and that a marked instrument could not be returned as dishonoured.[175] A marking of this kind was valid for one day only, however, which meant that the instrument had to be cleared by the collecting bank without delay. This particular practice has now ceased to be of effect. In contrast, a certification requested by the drawer or payee of a cheque is not a request for immediate payment. The drawer who requests his bank to certify the cheque wishes to give that instrument extra currency by the addition of the bank's name to his own. The payee or holder, who could get payment forthwith by presenting the cheque, may wish for his own reasons to defer payment, but at the very same time may want the cheque to be certified by the drawee bank to obtain assurance of subsequent payment. A specific case in which the payee or holder may wish to obtain the assurance of due payment that is provided by the bank's certification is when he holds a cheque while it is still post-dated.

Some legal systems make provision for the certification of a cheque at the request of the holder or the drawer.[176] An example in point from the United States is section 3-409(d) of the Uniform Commercial Code, which provides that the certification of a cheque is essentially an acceptance of the cheque by the drawee bank. The drawee bank is not obliged to give such a certification, and a refusal to certify a cheque does not constitute a dishonour of the instrument. A certification must be written on the cheque and this can be achieved by means of the drawee bank's signature alone.[177] If the drawee bank does add its certification to a cheque, the drawer of the cheque and any indorsers are discharged from liability.[178] A bank that has certified a cheque commonly earmarks the amount required for meeting the instrument out of the balance standing to the drawer's credit.[179] Obviously, this will mean that the balance available for meeting other cheques drawn by the drawer would be reduced accordingly. In the United Kingdom, however, a cheque is regarded as not being a proper instrument for the bank's acceptance under section 18 of the BEA 1882. Although it was at one time suggested that a bank could accept a cheque if it so desired,[180] there is not only clear authority for the view that such a course would be unusual,[181] but also that certification does not constitute an acceptance. In *Bank of Baroda Ltd* v. *Punjab National Bank Ltd*,[182] Lord Wright observed that 'the marking of a cheque has so far been only judicially recognized to import a promise or undertaking to pay as between banker and banker for the purpose of clearance'.[183] As between the other parties, the certification was a mere representation as to the genuineness of the cheque and the signature that it

---

[174] *Robson* v. *Bennett* (1810) 2 Taunt. 388. See also *Goodwin* v. *Robarts*, n.4 above, 351–352, affd (1875–1876) LR 1 App Cas 476 (HL).

[175] Initially, this was settled in a circular of the Bankers Clearing House (February 1927).

[176] E.P. Ellinger, n.2 above, vol. IX, ch. 4, [529].

[177] UCC, s.3-409(a), (d). Alternatively, the cheque must be certified 'by a writing on the [cheque] which indicates that the [cheque] is certified'. For the obligations of the certifying bank, see UCC, s.3-413(b).

[178] Ibid., ss.3-409(d), 3-414(c), 3-415(d).

[179] *Edmonton Motors Ltd* v. *Edmonton Savings & Credit Union Ltd*, n.88 above, [57].

[180] *Robson* v. *Bennett*, n.174 above, 396. The acceptance of a cheque payable to bearer would, in any event, be contrary to the Bank Charter Act 1844, s.11.

[181] *Bellamy* v. *Marjoribanks* (1852) 7 Exch. 389, 404; *Bank of Baroda Ltd* v. *Punjab National Bank* [1944] AC 176, 188 (PC). See also *Hodgson & Lee Pty. Ltd* v. *Mardonius Pty. Ltd*, n.160 above.

[182] N.181 above. See also *Gaden* v. *Newfoundland Savings Bank* [1899] AC 281 (PC); *Imperial Bank of Canada* v. *Bank of Hamilton* [1903] AC 49, 53–54 (PC); *Southland Savings Bank* v. *Anderson* [1974] 1 NZLR 118, 120–121. For the Canadian position, see *Swartz* v. *Toronto-Dominion Bank* [1972] 2 OR 863, 864–865; *Re Maubach & Bank of Nova Scotia* (1987) 60 OR (2d) 189, 196–197; *Edmonton Motors Ltd* v. *Edmonton Savings & Credit Union Ltd*, n.88 above, [43]–[64]; *Honeywell Ltd* v. *Sherwood Credit Union Ltd* (1989) 76 Sask R 228, [19]–[28] (SQB). [183] Ibid., 187.

bears. If the cheque in *Bank of Baroda* had not been post-dated, the certification might also have been held to include a representation as to the then sufficiency of the balance standing to the credit of the drawer's account.[184] Indeed, the limited effect of certifying a cheque is highlighted by the fact that the instrument can be countermanded by the customer at any time before it is paid. The bank is then bound to dishonour the cheque,[185] and the certification is thus without any binding effect.

Even if the addition of the certification involves the drawee bank making one or more representations at the time of its addition, it seems unlikely that the holder of a marked cheque could sue the drawee bank on this basis. The holder's difficulty would be to establish a valid cause of action. It will be recalled that the drawing of a cheque does not constitute an assignment by the drawer to the payee of any funds against which the cheque is drawn. The bank, as mere drawee, is not bound as against the holder to meet the cheque, even if it is drawn against an adequate balance. For this reason, although the bank might be estopped by virtue of the certification from denying the validity of the drawer's signature or even from denying that, at the time the cheque was certified, his account had a sufficient balance for meeting the instrument, an estoppel based on such a representation would not give rise to a valid cause of action.[186] Furthermore, it is unlikely that an action could be based on negligence imputable to the bank in respect of its representation on the basis of the principle initially laid down in *Hedley Byrne & Co. Ltd* v. *Heller and Partners Ltd*.[187] The reason for this is that the drawee bank's representation cannot be taken to imply that the instrument would be paid when presented. It is well understood that the decision as to whether or not a cheque is to be dishonoured must invariably depend on the circumstances existing at the time of its presentation for payment, and not on the position prevailing at any earlier point of time.

The practice of marking cheques at the request of the holder or the drawer is no longer used by the main retail banks. The usual procedure is that, instead of marking a cheque as being good for payment at the request of the drawer or the holder, the bank exchanges the cheque for a bankers' draft issued by itself. However, it is understood that the marking of cheques is still practised by some private banks in the United Kingdom.

4 Crossed cheques

(i) Background and types of crossings

The crossing of cheques is a feature of United Kingdom law and the law of other countries that have adopted its system. Crossing is unknown in the United States, and has a different effect in those Continental jurisdictions that have accepted the practice. In the United Kingdom, the practice of crossing cheques originated in the eighteenth or early nineteenth century in the context of the procedures of the clearing house. The employees of different banks, who brought to the clearing house cheques that had been remitted for collection by customers, wrote the name of their banks on each cheque so as to facilitate

---

[184] Ibid., 191.

[185] *Keyes* v. *Royal Bank of Canada*, n.163 above; *Southland Savings Bank* v. *Anderson*, n.182 above, 121; cf. *Gibson* v. *Minet* (1824) 2 Bing 7.

[186] A.G. Guest, n.3 above, [7-010]. It is also unlikely that there would be any claim under the Misrepresentation Act 1967, s.2.

[187] [1964] AC 465 (HL). See further Ch. 16, Sect. 2(ii) below.

the settlement of the accounts at the clearing house.[188] At this time, there is no suggestion that the name of the collecting bank was written between the presently common transverse parallel lines. The crossing of cheques by drawers is later in origin. It was certainly known by the middle of the nineteenth century.[189] Crossed cheques became the subject of legislation for the first time in the Crossed Cheques Act 1856,[190] which made it an offence to obliterate or alter a crossing in a fraudulent manner. The next step was taken in the Crossed Cheques Act 1876, which repealed and replaced the earlier legislation. The two main innovations of this legislation were, first, to render a bank that had paid a cheque in contravention of a crossing liable to compensate the 'true owner' of the instrument,[191] and, secondly, to give statutory recognition to crossings accompanied by the words, 'not negotiable'. The Crossed Cheques Act 1876 further provided a general defence for banks as regards the collection of crossed cheques. This defence was subsequently re-enacted in section 82 of the BEA 1882, and was then widened in section 4 of the Cheques Act 1957.[192] Other provisions of the Crossed Cheques Act 1876 are currently reproduced, subject to minor variations, in sections 76–81 of the BEA 1882.

The BEA 1882 recognizes two basic types of crossing. The first type, known as a general crossing,[193] consists of placing two parallel transverse lines across the cheque. These lines may stand on their own or may be accompanied by the words 'and company' or an abbreviation thereof, which usually assumes the form '& Co.' In modern practice, it is uncommon to add these words to a general crossing. Their origin can again be traced back to the early practice of the clearing house. Where the drawer crossed a cheque in this manner, the collecting bank could add its own name in front of the symbol '& Co.', and in this way identify itself for the purpose of the clearing process. At present, this specific function is served by the encoded crossing executed by the collecting bank. The second type of crossing, known as a special crossing,[194] is executed by placing on the front of the cheque the name of a specific bank. This bank is obviously not the drawee bank, but the bank that is expected to collect the cheque. This type of crossing was the one originally executed by banks for the purpose of the clearing procedure. As a crossing executed by either the drawer or the holder of the cheque, a special crossing has become obsolete. In addition, both a general and a special crossing may be accompanied by the words 'not negotiable'.[195] In practice, it is common to add to these words the phrase, 'account payee only', which assumed a new significance in 1992.[196]

(ii) **Execution of a crossing and its effect**

According to section 77 of the BEA 1882, a cheque may be crossed generally or specially by either the drawer or the holder. The holder is entitled to cross a cheque even if an original crossing, usually pre-printed on the cheque, has been 'opened' by the drawer. Furthermore, the holder may turn a general crossing into a special one by adding the name of a bank, and can also add the words, 'not negotiable'. In this context, the word

---

[188] *Bellamy* v. *Majoribanks*, n.181 above, 402; *Carlon* v. *Ireland* (1856) 25 LJQB 113.

[189] *Smith* v. *Union Bank of London* (1875) 1 QBD 31, 33–35 (CA).

[190] The Crossed Cheques Act 1856 was subsequently amended by the Crossed Cheques Act 1858. Apart from specific provisions, such as the Stamp Act 1853, s.19, the Crossed Cheques Act 1856 was the first legislation dealing specifically with legal aspects of cheques. See also *Simmonds* v. *Taylor* (1857) 27 LJCP 248.

[191] Consider *Smith* v. *Union Bank of London*, n.189 above, which was decided under the earlier legislation, but was inconclusive on this particular issue.

[192] Ch. 15, Sect. 4 below.   [193] BEA 1882, s.76(1).   [194] Ibid., s.76(2).

[195] Ibid, s.76. See also BEA 1882, s.81.   [196] Sect. 4(iv) below.

'holder' includes an agent for collection,[197] so that a collecting bank is entitled under the BEA 1882 to alter a general crossing in the same manner as a transferee who acquires the instrument in his own right. In this way, the BEA 1882 gives effect to the procedures of the clearing house. Section 77 further provides that where a cheque is specially crossed, the bank to whom it is so crossed may again add to the instrument a special crossing to another bank for collection. The object of this provision is to enable banks that are not members of a clearing house to remit cheques payable to their customers to one of the clearing banks. Where an uncrossed cheque, or a cheque crossed generally, is sent to a bank for collection, that bank may add a special crossing in favour of itself.

There are some misconceptions in the business world about the effect of a crossing. It is often asserted that a crossing restricts the transferability of a cheque. This is incorrect. The effect of a crossing is best understood when one recalls the two main methods for obtaining payment that are available to the holder of an uncrossed cheque. One possibility is that the holder can send the uncrossed cheque for collection to his own bank, which will then present it to the drawee bank through the clearing channels. The other possibility is that the holder may present the uncrossed cheque for payment at the drawee bank's counter. When a cheque bears either a general or a special crossing, this second mode of realization is unavailable to the holder.[198] If the cheque bears a general crossing, it must be presented for payment through a bank; if it bears a special crossing, it must be presented for payment through the designated bank.[199] The holder of a crossed cheque also has the option of negotiating it to a third party.

Under section 79(2) of the BEA 1882, if the drawee bank pays a cheque otherwise than in the manner authorized by the crossing, it is liable to compensate the 'true owner' of the instrument for any loss sustained by the latter due to the improper payment of the cheque. The proviso to section 79(2) of the BEA 1882, however, affords a defence to the drawee bank when a cheque is presented for payment and does not at that time appear to be crossed or appear to have had a crossing altered or obliterated. In such circumstances, the drawee bank does not incur any liability to the 'true owner', provided that it has paid the cheque in good faith and without negligence. This proviso should not give the impression, however, that it is legitimate for a party to obliterate a crossing. Under section 78 of the BEA 1882, a crossing is a material part of a cheque and, except where an addition is authorized by the BEA 1882 as explained above, it is unlawful for any person to alter a crossing or to tamper with it.[200] Thus, one of the declared objects of a crossing is to protect the rights of the cheque's 'true owner'. Another effect of a crossing is to protect the rights of the drawer, since a bank that pays a cheque in a manner prohibited by that cheque's crossing exceeds its authority and is not entitled to debit the drawer's account.[201] Payment without negligence in accordance with the tenor of a crossing does, on the other hand, confer on the drawee bank a defence against an action by the drawer or by the 'true owner' of the cheque.[202]

---

[197] *Akrokerri (Atlantic) Mines Ltd* v. *Economic Bank* [1904] 2 KB 465, 472; *Dey* v. *Mayo* [1920] 2 KB 346, 354, 362 (CA); *Sutters* v. *Briggs*, n.116 above, 16; *Baker* v. *Barclays Bank Ltd* [1955] 1 WLR 822, 833–834.

[198] *Wilson & Meeson* v. *Pickering* [1946] KB 422 (CA).

[199] BEA 1882, s.79(2). Under BEA 1882, s.79(1), if a cheque is crossed specially to more than one bank, the drawee bank has to refuse payment, but this does not apply where the second bank is the first bank's agent for collection. It is possible for the drawer to 'open' a crossing by striking it out and adding the words 'pay cash'.

[200] BEA 1882, s.64(1)–(2), which explains the consequences of their being a material alteration to a cheque.

[201] *Bobbett* v. *Pinkett* (1876) 1 Ex. D 368, 372–373.

[202] BEA 1882, s.80, discussed in Ch. 11, Sect. 4(iv) below.

(iii) **Crossing accompanied by the words 'not negotiable'**

Whilst the effect of marking the words 'not negotiable' on a bill of exchange or uncrossed cheque has already been considered,[203] the effect of these words when marked upon a crossed cheque is specifically dealt with by section 81 of the BEA 1882. According to this provision, a person who takes a cheque with such a crossing cannot obtain a better title than that of the transferor and cannot confer a better title than he possesses on a subsequent transferee. It follows that the third characteristic of negotiable instruments, discussed previously,[204] is inapplicable where a cheque is crossed 'not negotiable'. Accordingly, although such a cheque remains transferable, each transferee takes the instrument subject to the defects in title of all the previous parties.[205] A person cannot, therefore, become a holder in due course of such an instrument. In *Great Western Railway Co.* v. *London and County Banking Company Ltd*,[206] Lord Lindley said: 'Everyone who takes a cheque marked "not negotiable" takes it at his own risk, and his title to the money got by its means is as defective as his title to the cheque itself.'[207]

(iv) **Cheques crossed with the words 'account payee only' added**

The practice of adding to a general crossing the words 'a/c payee only' or 'a/c payee' has been in use at least since the third quarter of the nineteenth century. In some instances, these words alone accompanied the crossing, but in more modern times they usually appeared together with the words 'not negotiable'. Until 1992, the phrase 'a/c payee only' was not given any statutory definition. Although customers frequently added these words to a crossing in the belief that they rendered a cheque non-transferable, a series of cases established that the writing of this phrase on a cheque did not have this effect. It was held that the words in question constituted a warning to the collecting bank that the cheque should not be collected for a person other than the nominated payee,[208] but that the transferability of the cheque was not in itself affected.[209] In essence, the courts took the view that, on a strict reading, the phrase 'account payee only' or 'a/c payee only' did not comprise words prohibiting transfer or evidencing an intention that the instrument be non-transferable within the meaning of section 8(1) of the BEA 1882. The courts were also influenced by the practical consideration that a ruling to the contrary would place the drawee bank in a difficult situation. It will be recalled that the crossing that accompanies

---

[203] Sect. 3(iii) above.

[204] Sect. 1 above. A bank does not breach its duty of care to its customer by failing to warn him of the risks involved in cashing a cheque bearing a 'not negotiable' crossing: *Redmond* v. *Allied Irish Banks* [1987] FLR 307, [1987] 2 FTLR 264. See also *The Honourable Society of the Middle Temple* v. *Lloyds Bank plc* [1999] 1 All ER (Comm.) 193.

[205] *Algemene Bank Nederland NV* v. *Happy Valley Restaurant Pte Ltd* [1991] 1 SLR 708, 713–714.

[206] [1901] AC 414 (HL).

[207] Ibid., 424. See also *Universal Guarantee Pty. Ltd* v. *National Bank of Australasia Ltd* [1965] 1 Lloyd's Rep. 525, 531. Cf. *Miller Associates (Australia) Pty. Ltd* v. *Bennington Pty. Ltd*, n.121 above.

[208] *Akrokerri (Atlantic) Mines Ltd* v. *Economic Bank*, n.197 above, 472; *House Property Co. of London Ltd* v. *London County and Westminster Bank* (1915) 84 LJKB 1846; *Universal Guarantee Pty. Ltd* v. *National Bank of Australasia Ltd*, n.207 above; *New Zealand Law Society* v. *ANZ Banking Group Ltd* [1985] 1 NZLR 280, 287; *Algemene Bank Nederland NV* v. *Happy Valley Restaurant Pte Ltd*, n.205 above, 713. No negligence may be involved where a suitable explanation is given: *Souhrada* v. *Bank of New South Wales* [1976] 2 Lloyd's Rep. 444, 452.

[209] *National Bank* v. *Silke*, n.147 above; *Importers Co. Ltd* v. *Westminster Bank Ltd*, n.106 above, 297; *Universal Guarantee Pty. Ltd* v. *National Bank of Australasia Ltd*, n.207 above. See also *Standard Bank of South Africa Ltd* v. *Sham Magazine Centre* [1977] 1 SALR 484 (App. Div.); *Wayfoong Credit Ltd* v. *Remoco (HK) Ltd* [1983] 2 HKC 445, 449.

the phrase, 'account payee only', proscribes the presentment of the cheque for payment at the drawee bank's counter; the cheque has to be cleared. When a cheque is presented through the clearing system, however, the drawee bank is not informed whether the instrument is being collected for the ostensible payee or for some other person's account. It is true that, where a cheque is collected for the account of such other person, the collecting bank, as a matter of practice, usually obtains the ostensible payee's indorsement, but in many cases the payee indorses the cheque even if it is collected for his own account. The appearance of the payee's indorsement or signature on the back of the cheque is, therefore, not conclusive evidence that the instrument has been transferred, just as the absence of an indorsement does not establish conclusively that the cheque is being collected for the ostensible payee.

This practical consideration was actually one of the grounds that induced the Review Committee on Banking Services Law (the 'Jack Committee')[210] to recommend that cheques should indeed remain transferable even if they bore a crossing accompanied by the phrase 'account payee only' or 'a/c payee only'.[211] This recommendation was rejected, however, in the White Paper presented to Parliament by the Chancellor of the Exchequer in March 1990.[212] Seeking to give effect to what was considered to be the natural meaning and common understanding of the words 'account payee only', the White Paper recommended that the addition of these words (or certain similar words) to a crossed cheque should render the instrument non-transferable. This recommendation resulted in the Cheques Act 1992, which amends certain provisions of the BEA 1882 and the Cheques Act 1957. In particular, section 1 of the Cheques Act 1992 inserts a new section 81A into the BEA 1882, which reads:

(1) Where a cheque is crossed and bears across its face the words 'account payee' or 'a/c payee', either with or without the word 'only', the cheque shall not be transferable, but shall only be valid as between the parties thereto.

(2) A banker is not to be treated for the purposes of section 80 [of the BEA 1882] as having been negligent by reason only of his failure to concern himself with any purported indorsement of a cheque which under subsection (1) above or otherwise is not transferable.

Section 81A(1) effectively applies section 8(1) of the BEA 1882, which was considered above,[213] to cheques bearing a crossing accompanied by the words 'a/c payee only' (or their equivalent). Such a cheque now has the same legal effect as a cheque that has the words 'not transferable' on its face or that has the word 'only' added after the payee's name. Accordingly, under sections 8(1) and 81A of the BEA 1882, the title to an instrument bearing any of these formulae cannot be passed by negotiation and the original payee, to whom the instrument has been issued, remains its owner notwithstanding his attempt to transfer the instrument. The transferee, thus, does not obtain a title to the cheque and cannot bring an action to enforce it in his own name.[214] Section 81A(2) gives

---

[210] *Banking Services: Law and Practice*, Report by the Review Committee Chaired by Professor R.B. Jack CBE (1989, London, Cm. 622), [7.18]–[7.20].

[211] The Jack Committee adopted the approach in the Cheques and Payment Orders Act 1986 (Cth), s.39(2), which became the Cheques Act 1986 (Cth), s.39(2) following the passing of the Cheques and Payment Orders Amendment Act 1998 (Cth). See also A. Tyree & P. Weaver, *Weerasooria's Banking Law and the Financial System in Australia* (6th edn., Sydney, 2006), ch. 12.

[212] *White Paper on Banking Services: Law and Practice* (1990, London, Cm. 1026), Annex 5, [5.6].

[213] Sect. 3(iii) above.

[214] Banks functioning outside the United Kingdom cannot be expected to be familiar with the British banking practice and the law in point: *The Honorable Society of the Middle Temple* v. *Lloyd's Bank plc*, n.204 above, 198; *Linklaters* v. *HSBC Bank plc* [2003] 2 Lloyd's Rep. 545.

effect to another recommendation made in the White Paper, as it sets out to ensure that the drawee or paying bank that pays a crossed cheque bearing the words 'a/c payee only' retains the defence provided by section 80 of the BEA 1882 (as augmented by section 1 of the Cheques Act 1957).[215] A consequential amendment to section 80 itself, which was effected by section 2 of the Cheques Act 1992, has the object of putting the matter beyond doubt.[216]

A question that has not been settled by the Cheques Act 1992 concerns the effect of the words 'a/c payee only' on an uncrossed cheque. The answer is provided by the authorities decided prior to 1992, which treated the words 'a/c payee only' as falling outside the ambit of section 8(1) of the BEA 1882, with the result that the uncrossed cheque remained transferable. This problem is largely academic, however, since in practice the words 'a/c payee only' are either printed on the cheque as part of the crossing or are appended by means of a rubber stamp that includes the two transverse lines of the crossing. The only situation in which the problem identified is likely to arise is where the drawer 'opens' a crossing, but fails to cancel the words 'a/c payee only'. As already indicated, the cheque would, in all probability, remain transferable.

(v) Crossing of instruments similar to cheques

The provisions of the BEA 1882 concerning the crossing of cheques apply to four types of instrument that are not encompassed within the definition of a 'bill of exchange', even though they are similar to cheques. First, under section 95 of the BEA 1882, the relevant provisions apply to dividend warrants. Secondly, the provisions on crossings are extended by virtue of section 4(2)(*b*) of the Cheques Act 1957 to 'any document issued by a customer of a banker which, though not a bill of exchange, is intended to enable a person to obtain payment from that banker of the sum mentioned in the document'.[217] This provision was introduced to facilitate the crossing of cheques made payable to 'cash or order',[218] which are not bills of exchange in the strict sense of the word as they are not payable to a specific person or to bearer.[219] Thirdly, section 5 of the Cheques Act 1957 applies the provisions on crossings to 'any document issued by a public officer which is intended to enable a person to obtain payment from the Paymaster General or the Queen's and Lord Treasurer's Remembrancer of the sum mentioned in the document'.[220] Finally, a crossing may be executed on a draft drawn by a banker on himself and payable on demand.[221] Such drafts do not fall within the definition of a bill of exchange, as they are not drawn by one person on another.

---

[215] Ch. 11, Sect. 4(iv) below.

[216] Ibid. Under the Cheques Act 1992, s.3, cheques crossed 'a/c payee only' (or the recognized similar formulae) are specifically equated with other types of cheque in respect of the defence conferred on the collecting bank: *The Honourable Society of the Middle Temple* v. *Lloyd's Bank plc*, n.204 above, 198. See further Ch. 15, Sect. 4 below. The provisions of the BEA 1882 concerning crossings apply to 'a/c payee only' cheques in the same manner as they apply to negotiable cheques: Cheques Act 1957, s.5, read together with the Cheques Act 1957, s.4 (as amended by the Cheques Act 1992, s.3).

[217] Cheques Act 1957, s.5. As regards cheques crossed with the addition of the words 'a/c payee only', see Sect. 4(iv) above. As to the effect of an 'a/c payee only' crossing on a cheque payable to bearer, see A.G. Guest, n.3 above, [14-039].

[218] *Orbit Mining and Trading Co.* v. *Westminster Bank Ltd*, n.123 above, 812–813.

[219] Sect. 3(iii) above.   [220] Cheques Act 1957, ss.4(2)(*c*) & 5.   [221] Ibid., ss.4(2)(*d*) & 5.

5 The holder's duties in respect of cheques

(i) The meaning of 'duty' and to whom it is owed

It is inaccurate to speak of a holder's 'duties' as regards the handling of a cheque. If the holder retains the cheque for good, or decides to destroy it, he does not commit a breach of any duty owed to another person. In the context of this discussion, 'duty' means an act that the holder of the cheque has to perform if he wishes to enforce the instrument against the drawer and any indorser. As the drawee bank does not commit a breach of its contract with the holder by dishonouring the cheque, to which the drawee bank is not even a party,[222] it would be fallacious to suggest that the holder owes any 'duty' that is a condition precedent to the drawee bank's 'duty' to perform. This is so even as regards the due presentment of a cheque. Whilst it is true that a cheque presented for payment after the lapse of an unreasonable time from the date of its issue is considered 'stale',[223] and that the drawee bank will dishonour the instrument on this ground alone, the bank's decision in this regard is based on the fact that the mandate from its customer, who is also the drawer of the cheque, sanctions the payment of a cheque only if it is presented for payment within a reasonable time.

The 'duties' to be performed by the holder as a condition precedent to his right to enforce a dishonoured cheque against the drawer and the indorsers are defined in the BEA 1882 in respect of bills of exchange generally.[224] There are, however, some modifications that apply only in the case of cheques. In this section, emphasis is placed on the special problems arising in respect of cheques. The holder's three 'duties' are, first, to present the cheque for payment; secondly, to send timely notice of dishonour if the instrument is unpaid; and, thirdly, to note and protest the dishonoured cheque if it falls within the definition of a 'foreign bill'.[225]

(ii) Presentment for payment of a cheque

Presentment of a cheque is a necessary precondition of the drawer's liability to pay according to the terms of the instrument.[226] Such presentment must comply with a number of detailed requirements,[227] including the requirement that the cheque be physically presented (ordinarily through the clearing system)[228] for payment at the branch of the bank upon which it is drawn.[229] At common law, however, a failure to present a cheque

---

[222] BEA 1882, s.53(1). See also *Fiorentino Comm Giuseppe Srl* v. *Farnesi*, n.75 above, [39], [41]. See further Sect. 8(ii) below.

[223] This is a matter of banking custom: *Ullrich* v. *Commissioner of Inland Revenue*, n.88 above, 388–389. There appears nowadays to be a banking custom that cheques will not be honoured once a period of six months from their date of issue has elapsed: *Edmonton Motors Ltd* v. *Edmonton Savings & Credit Union Ltd*, n.88 above, [81]–[82]; *Kashi* v. *Eshragi*, n.88 above; *Commissioner of Inland Revenue* v. *Thomas Cook (NZ) Ltd*, n.78 above, [38], affd. on a different ground: [2005] 2 NZLR 722 (PC). In Canada, a certified cheque will not be considered 'stale': *Kayu Pro Services* v. *Royal Bank of Canada* [2003] OJ No. 4558, [4].

[224] Sect. 5(ii) below.

[225] Sect. 5(iv) below. Choice of law issues may arise in relation to cheques with an international element: BEA 1882, s.72. See generally *Karafarin Bank* v. *Dara* [2009] EWHC 3265 (Comm.) (Iranian law).

[226] *Commissioner of Inland Revenue* v. *Thomas Cook (NZ) Ltd*, n.78 above, [27], affd. on a different ground: [2005] 2 NZLR 722 (PC).

[227] BEA 1882, s.45.   [228] Sect. 2 above.

[229] Under BEA 1882, s.45(3), a cheque must be presented for payment 'at the proper place', which requires the physical delivery of the instrument to the branch of the paying bank on which the cheque is drawn (*Barclays Bank plc* v. *Bank of England*, n.30 above, 392–394) and similarly, at common law, the

for payment did not discharge the instrument's drawer until the six-year limitation period had elapsed.[230] This principle continues to apply.[231] In circumstances, however, where the drawer has suffered actual damage as a result of the payee's failure to present the cheque within a reasonable time, at common law, the drawer was absolutely discharged of any liability on the instrument, even if that liability exceeded the loss suffered. This last principle has been altered by section 74(1) of the BEA 1882,[232] which requires that a cheque (like other types of bill of exchange payable on demand)[233] be presented for payment within a reasonable time of its issue[234] and which provides that a failure to do so discharges the cheque's drawer of his liability on the instrument, but only to the extent that the delay has caused him actual loss:[235]

> Where a cheque is not presented for payment within a reasonable time, and the drawer or the person on whose account it is drawn had the right at the time of such presentment as between him and the banker to have the cheque paid and suffers actual damage through the delay, he is discharged to the extent of such damage, that is to say, to the extent to which such drawer or person is a creditor of such banker to a larger amount than he would have been had such cheque been paid.

An example of circumstances in which this section is likely to apply is when the drawer's account had the required credit balance for meeting the cheque, but the bank became insolvent while the cheque was outstanding. Under section 74(3) of the BEA 1882, the holder of the cheque is subrogated to the drawer's rights against the drawee bank. Thus, if the cheque were dishonoured because the bank became insolvent during the delay, and the bank paid a dividend of 30p in the pound to its creditors, the drawer would be discharged to the extent of 70 per cent of the amount of the cheque. The holder could then prove for the amount involved in the bank's winding-up.

In addition to the requirement that the cheque be presented within a reasonable time of issue, the cheque must also be presented within a reasonable time of any indorsement on the cheque.[236] There is an important difference, however, between the position of the drawer and the indorser, as a failure to present a cheque within a reasonable time of an indorsement discharges the indorser quite regardless of whether or not he sustains loss as a result of the delay.[237] This principle is equally applicable to bills of exchange and cheques, although this is less likely to be an issue nowadays in relation to cheques.[238]

---

general principle is that demand for payment must be made at the branch where the relevant account is held (*Joachimson* v. *Swiss Bank Corporation*, n.2 above, 127). See further Sect. 2 above & Ch. 11, Sect. 1(ii) below. See also A.G. Guest, n.3 above, [6-062], [13-022].

[230] A.G. Guest, n.3 above, [13-017]. Furthermore, at common law, where a creditor takes a third party's cheque from his debtor in satisfaction of a debt and fails to present the cheque without delay, the subsequent insolvency of the drawee bank discharges the debtor from further liability: ibid., [6-042], [13-018]. The creditor is treated as a person who has wasted a security given to him by the debtor: *Polak* v. *Everett* (1876) 1 QBD 669; *Hopkins* v. *Ware* (1869) LR 4 Ex. 268; *Sawyer* v. *Thomas* (1890) 18 OAR 129. It is unclear to what extent this common law principle still survives and the extent to which it might be affected by BEA 1882, s.74(1): A.G. Guest, n.3 above, [6-042], [13-018].

[231] Id.

[232] *Commissioner of Inland Revenue* v. *Thomas Cook (NZ) Ltd*, n.78 above, [34], affd. on a different ground: [2005] 2 NZLR 722 (PC)..

[233] BEA 1882, s.45(2).

[234] The rules of presentment in BEA 1882, s.74(1) apply 'to the exclusion of [BEA 1882, s.45] in the case of cheques': *Fiorentino Comm Giuseppe Srl* v. *Farnesi*, n.75 above, [34]. See also *King* v. *Porter* [1925] NI 107.

[235] BEA 1882, s.45(2). [236] Id. [237] Id.

[238] This is a consequence of cheques being pre-printed with an 'a/c payee only' crossing: Cheques Act 1992, s.1.

There are circumstances, however, where a delay in making presentation may be excused,[239] or where presentation may be dispensed with altogether.[240] For example, in *Fiorentino Comm Giuseppe Srl* v. *Farnesi*,[241] Nicholas Warren QC had to consider whether presentment of a cheque for payment was excused as regards the drawer on the ground that 'the drawee . . . [was] not bound as between himself and the drawer, to accept or pay the bill, and the drawer [had] no reason to believe that the bill would be paid if presented'.[242] The first of these requirements would clearly be satisfied by the fact that the drawer has insufficient funds in the account to cover the instrument in question.[243] As regards the second requirement, it is not necessary to show that the drawer knew that the cheque would not be paid when it was initially drawn; it is enough that the drawer had that knowledge at 'any time at which presentment could be made'.[244]

Where presentment is not excused by section 46(2) of the BEA 1882, however, there are two considerations that must be taken into account when determining what amounts to a 'reasonable time' for presentation of a cheque. The first consideration relates to the time within which the payee should present a cheque that he has received to his bank for collection. At common law, a distinction was drawn between cases in which the payee lived in the same place as the drawee bank and cases in which he resided in a different place. In the former case, the drawer was expected to present the cheque for payment by the end of the day following its receipt.[245] In the latter case, the drawer had one day to arrange for the dispatch of the cheque to his own bank for collection.[246] This practice is now obsolete and it is nowadays common for businessmen to remit cheques payable to them for collection just once or twice a week. Whether this practice would involve presenting the cheque within a 'reasonable time' nowadays depends upon the interpretation of section 74(2) of the BEA 1882, which provides that in 'determining what is a reasonable time regard shall be had to the nature of the instrument, the usage of trade and of bankers, and the facts of the particular case'. The emphasis in this provision on the usage of bankers and in particular the 'usage of trade' may be sufficiently wide to encompass the modern practice of banking cheques whenever it is convenient, but there is an absence of modern authority on the point. Nevertheless, it seems clear enough that the common law position that existed before the enactment of the BEA 1882 can now be regarded as out of date in determining what is a 'reasonable time'. The second consideration relates to the time that must be allowed for the actual collection of the instrument, as most cheques nowadays are crossed[247] and, under both the BEA 1882 and the practice of bankers, a crossed cheque has to be presented through clearing channels by a collecting bank employed for that purpose.[248] The ordinary clearing cycle for cheques was traditionally three days, although an extra day was sanctioned under the 'inadvertence rule' contained in the Clearing House Rules.[249] Since 1994, however, the major clearing banks have operated a two-day clearing cycle,[250] which is increasingly likely to become the norm in light of the clearing banks'

---

[239] BEA 1882, s.46(1).

[240] Ibid., s.46(2). See also *Commissioner of Inland Revenue* v. *Thomas Cook (NZ) Ltd*, n.78 above [43], affd. on a different ground: [2005] 2 NZLR 722 (PC).

[241] N.75 above.   [242] BEA 1882, s.46(2)(c).

[243] *Fiorentino Comm Giuseppe Srl* v. *Farnesi*, n.75 above, [41].   [244] Ibid., [47].

[245] *Alexander* v. *Burchfield* (1842) 7 Man. & G 1061.

[246] *Hare* v. *Henty* (1861) 10 CB (NS) 65. Dispatch by post to the drawee bank was contrary to practice.

[247] Even in the case of uncrossed cheques, the holder may decide to add a crossing so that the instrument is then treated as being crossed.

[248] The presentment of a cheque to the drawee bank through the post office is regarded as anomalous.

[249] Sect. 2 above. Presentment is effected when the cheque reaches the branch on which it is drawn.

[250] *Emerald Meats (London) Ltd* v. *AIB Group (UK) plc*, n.43 above, [15], [26].

commitment since November 2007 to abide by the '2-4-6' commitments for the clearing of cheques into their customers' current accounts.[251] Thus, although the clearing process will clearly take a number of days to complete, it is impossible to generalize as to how many days might be required and as to what might be considered 'reasonable' in particular circumstances.

(iii) Notice of dishonour

The rules concerning the dispatch of a notice of dishonour by the holder of a bill of exchange to prior parties apply equally in the case of a cheque.[252] Notice must be given within a reasonable time of the instrument's dishonour.[253] For the purposes of the dispatch of notice of dishonour, an agent is regarded as a party to the bill and, therefore, discharges his duty by sending it to the principal from whom he received the instrument.[254] A collecting bank is thus entitled to give notice of dishonour to its customer and is not required to inform previous parties to the bill of exchange. The mere return of the instrument with a notation indicating dishonour is adequate,[255] or notice may be given orally by means of a telephone call.[256] If the holder fails to send notice in the prescribed manner and within the time provided for in the BEA 1882, the indorser and drawer are discharged.[257]

In practice, however, notice of the dishonour of a cheque is not usually required in order to safeguard the holder's rights against the drawer. First, the drawer is not entitled to notice of dishonour if, as between the drawee and himself, the drawee is not obligated to meet the instrument.[258] Thus, if a cheque is dishonoured for want of funds, the drawer is not entitled to notice of dishonour.[259] Secondly, the drawer is not entitled to notice of dishonour where he has countermanded payment.[260] The indorser is in a different position from that of the drawer, however, as the indorser is not aware of the likely fate of the cheque. He is entitled to notice of dishonour from the holder and, if notice is not given to him in accordance with the provisions of section 49 of the BEA 1882, he is discharged.[261]

(iv) Noting and protest

Where the dishonoured cheque qualifies as a 'foreign bill', then it is obligatory to 'protest' the instrument, in addition to giving notice of dishonour.[262] A 'foreign bill' includes any instrument that is (or purports on its face to be) either drawn or payable outside the United Kingdom, or any instrument the payee of which resides abroad.[263] This would accordingly include a cheque drawn on a United Kingdom bank by a foreign correspondent or customer, or even a cheque drawn by a local customer while he is abroad. That said, unless there is some indication on the face of the cheque that it is a 'foreign bill' (such as

---

[251] Sect. 2 above. See also Cheque and Credit Clearing Company, n.16 above, 7.

[252] BEA 1882, s.49. See further Sect. 8(vi) below.   [253] Ibid., s.49(12).   [254] Ibid., s.49(13).

[255] Ibid., s.49(6).

[256] *Ladup Ltd* v. *Shaikh* [1983] QB 225, 232–233. Notice is effective once posted, if it is subsequently lost: BEA 1882, s.49(15). See also *Eaglehill Ltd* v. *J. Needham Builders Ltd* [1973] AC 992 (HL), considered in *Tyco Fire & Security* v. *Norfolk Mechanical* [2007] NSWSC 585, [48]–[53].

[257] BEA 1882, s.48.

[258] Ibid., s.50(2)(c). This would be the case if one of the parties was fictitious: *Aziz* v. *Mayfair Casinos Ltd*, The Times, 6 July 1982.

[259] N. Elliott, J. Odgers, & M. Phillips, n.93 above, [15-042]–[15-043]. Before the BEA 1882, the issue depended upon whether the drawer could expect the drawee to pay.

[260] BEA 1882, s.50(2)(c).   [261] Ibid., s.48.

[262] Ibid., s.51(2). See also *Koch* v. *Dicks* [1933] 1 KB 307, 313 (CA). See further Sect. 8(vi) below.

[263] Ibid., s.4(1).

an indication that it was drawn abroad), then the holder is entitled to treat the cheque as an 'inland bill'.[264] This has the advantage that 'protest' is optional in the case of an 'inland bill'.[265] In procedural terms, a 'protest' is 'a declaration, in solemn form, that a bill has been dishonoured',[266] which involves a notary public presenting the cheque for payment following its initial dishonour when first presented. If the cheque is dishonoured for a second time, the notary public makes a copy of the instrument in his register and 'notes' on it the date of its re-presentment, the answer given, and his fee. A copy of the 'protest' has then to be sent to the drawer and each indorser, otherwise they are discharged.[267] Protesting is excused whenever the need to provide notice of dishonour is dispensed with,[268] and any delay in protesting is excused if this results from 'circumstances beyond the control of the holder' and is not attributable to fault on the holder's part.[269] Where the services of a notary public are unavailable, 'protest' can occur by a resident of the place of dishonour issuing a certificate in the presence of two witnesses attesting the dishonour of the instrument.[270] In practice, however, the difficulties of 'noting' and 'protesting' a cheque should rarely arise as the vast majority of cheques are drawn by United Kingdom residents on United Kingdom banks and accordingly are 'inland bills', even if the payee happens to reside abroad.

6 Implications of the Consumer Credit Act 1974

The Consumer Credit Act 1974 (CCA 1974) does not restrict the use of cheques as instruments issued to effect payment. Assuming the transaction falls with the ambit of the CCA 1974,[271] section 123(3) prohibits the taking of any negotiable instrument, including a cheque, by way of security and section 123(2) prohibits the transfer of a cheque by a creditor to a third person other than a bank. The object of this latter provision is to preclude dealers and finance houses from defeating a valid claim asserted by a consumer by the transfer of the cheque issued by him to an associated company that would claim to be a holder in due course. The transfer of a cheque to a bank for clearing purposes is, however, unaffected.

7 Travellers' cheques

A travellers' cheque is a misnomer, as it does not constitute a cheque either in form or substance. In a travellers' cheque, the issuer undertakes to pay the specified amount of money to the order of the original holder ('the purchaser') of the instrument or to a transferee,[272] provided that the signature executed by the purchaser when he purchases the instrument tallies with the countersignature that he executes at the time that he cashes the instrument. This requirement of a matching signature constitutes the common feature of all travellers' cheques, although the actual form assumed by them differs from issuer to issuer. The promise or order that appears in the travellers' cheque is usually

---

[264] Ibid., s.4(2).   [265] Ibid., ss.4(1), 51(1)–(2).   [266] A.G. Guest, n.3 above, [6-144]–[6-145].
[267] Id.   [268] Ibid., s.51(9).   [269] Id.   [270] Ibid., s.94.   [271] Ch. 2, Sect. 5 above.
[272] When the purchaser negotiates a travellers' cheque by countersigning it, he impliedly represents that he has the right to transfer the instrument and that it will be good and valid in the hands of the person who cashes it: *R* v. *Griffiths* [1960] NZLR 850, 853–854 (NZCA); *R* v. *Holland-Kearins* [1999] DCR 535, 560.

conditional, as the issuer undertakes to pay the instrument only if there is correspond-ence between the two signatures executed by the purchaser. As the issuer's undertaking is conditional, travellers' cheques do not fall within the definition of one of the established forms of negotiable instrument, namely bills of exchange, cheques,[273] and promissory notes. They are, in all probability, a new species of negotiable instrument established by a general mercantile usage.[274]

The principles governing travellers' cheques are largely based on United States decisions,[275] which have tended to equate travellers' cheques with money in circulation. Accordingly, just as with the case of stolen money,[276] a third party who has obtained pos-session of a stolen travellers' cheque *bona fide* and for valuable consideration obtains a title to the instrument that is superior to that of the 'true owner' and, therefore, is entitled to enforce the instrument against the issuing bank.[277] The better view is that this principle will only apply, however, if the travellers' cheques have been dated and (at least appar-ently) validly signed and countersigned in the presence of the third party accepting the instrument as payment.[278] Whilst the principles established in the United States authori-ties have been accepted in Malaysia,[279] there is an absence of authority on this point in the United Kingdom. In contrast, the few modern United Kingdom cases dealing with travel-lers' cheques have tended to involve a different issue, namely the issuing bank's liability to replace such an instrument, when it has been lost by the purchaser prior to his hav-ing executed a countersignature. In essence, the courts have given effect to a clause that renders the customer liable if the travellers' cheques are lost as a result of his carelessness in handling them. Such a clause will not be considered unreasonable.[280] In the absence of such a clause, however, the bank is under a duty to replace the lost travellers' cheques even if their loss resulted from the purchaser's negligence.[281]

---

[273] *Oversea Chinese Banking Corporation Ltd* v. *Woo Hing Brothers Sdn Bhd* [1992] 2 MLJ 86, 92–93 (MCA), approving E.P. Ellinger, 'Travellers' Cheques and the Law' (1969) 19 *UTLJ* 132, 137.

[274] Compare *Commissioner of Inland Revenue* v. *Thomas Cook (NZ) Ltd*, n.78 above, [15], affd. on a different ground n.78 above.

[275] *Chitty On Contracts*, n.7 above, [34-173] *et seq.*

[276] D. Fox, *Property Rights in Money* (Oxford, 2008), [3.17]–[3.19].

[277] *American Express Co.* v. *Anadarko Bank & Trust Co.*, 179 Okla. 606, 608 (Okla. SC, 1937); *Transcontinental & Western Air Inc.* v. *Bank of America National Trust & Savings Association*, 46 Cal. App. 2d 708, 715–717 (Cali. CA, 1941) ;p[;m ykn *Emerson* v. *American Express Co.*, 90 A. 2d 236, 241 (CA DC, 1952); *Wilson* v. *First National Bank & Trust Co. of Oklahoma City*, 276 P. 2d 766, 770 (Okla. SC, 1954); *American Express Co.* v. *Rona Travel Service Inc.*, 187 A. 2d 206, 210–211 (NJ Ch., 1962); *Ashford* v. *Thomas Cook & Son (Bankers) Ltd*, 52 Haw. 113, 118–119 (Haw. SC, 1970).

[278] *Venable* v. *American Express Co. & Railway Express Agency Inc.*, 217 NC 548, 550–552 (Nth. Car. SC, 1940); *United States* v. *Petti*, 168 F. 2d 221, 223–224 (2d Cir., 1948); *Xanthopoulos* v. *Thomas Cook Inc.*, 629 F. Supp. 164, 173–174 (SDNY, 1985).

[279] *Oversea Chinese Banking Corporation Ltd* v. *Woo Hing Brothers Sdn Bhd*, n.273 above, 97–101.

[280] *Braithwaite* v. *Thomas Cook Travellers Cheques Ltd* [1989] QB 553; cf. *Fellus* v. *National Westminster Bank plc* (1983) 133 NLJ 766, which shows that negligence will not be found too readily. See also *Rosenfeld* v. *First National City Bank*, 319 NYS 2d 35, 39–40 (CCNY, 1971); *Thomas Cook Ltd* v. *Kumari* [2002] NSWCA 141.

[281] *El Awadi* v. *Bank of Credit and Commerce International SA* [1990] 1 QB 606, in which Hutchison J doubted the generality of the principle in *Braithwaite* v. *Thomas Cook Travellers Cheques Ltd*, n.280 above.

8 Bills of exchange other than cheques

(i) **Nature and use**

The law relating to bills of exchange is technical and complex and the substantial case law is reviewed in works of considerable length.[282] For the purposes of this section, it is adequate to provide a general discussion of the cardinal legal principles relating to bills of exchange and the function of these instruments; the role of the parties to these instruments; the rights of the holder; and the main principles governing negotiation and discharge, and the procedure applicable upon the dishonour of a bill of exchange.

As pointed out already,[283] bills of exchange other than cheques are used mainly in international sales and in circumstances where a customer is granted an acceptance credit (or a line of credit)[284] authorizing him to draw bills of exchange on a particular bank within a prescribed limit. A bill of exchange drawn in the context of such transactions may be discounted. As previously discussed,[285] the principal legislation applicable to these types of instrument is the BEA 1882.[286] Section 3(1) of the BEA 1882 defines a bill of exchange as 'an unconditional order in writing, addressed by one person to another, signed by the person giving it, requiring the person to whom it is addressed to pay on demand or at a fixed or determinable future time a sum certain in money to or to the order of a specified person, or to bearer'. Thus, as a bill of exchange has to be drawn by one person on another, an instrument drawn by a person on himself is not a bill of exchange.[287] By way of contrast, a bill of exchange may be made payable to the drawer's own order.[288] The order given by the drawer to the drawee has to be unconditional. This point has already been discussed in respect of cheques.[289] Of importance is the fact that an order requiring the drawee to pay the bill of exchange out of a specific fund is deemed conditional.[290] An order that is in itself unqualified, however, is not rendered conditional because it is coupled with an indication of a particular fund out of which the drawee is to reimburse himself (or an account that is to be debited) or with a statement of the transaction that gives rise to the bill of exchange.[291] Consequently, a bill of exchange remains unconditional even though it includes a statement that it is drawn under a given contract of sale or letter of credit.[292]

A bill of exchange may be payable in one of three ways:[293] payable on demand,[294] which means on its presentment to the drawee; payable at a fixed future time, such as a specific

---

[282] A.G. Guest, n.3 above; N. Elliott, J. Odgers, & M. Phillips, n.93 above. See also *Chitty on Contracts*, n.7 above, ch. 34.

[283] Sect. 1 above.   [284] Sect. 10 below.   [285] Sect. 3 above.

[286] BEA 1882 provided the model for the legislation introduced in other Commonwealth jurisdictions. Most other legal systems, such as those of Continental Europe, are based on the Convention Providing a Uniform Law for Bills of Exchange and Promissory Notes (Geneva, 7 June 1930) League of Nations Treaty Series, vol. 143, 259, No. 3313. In the United States, the law is to be found in Article 3 of the Uniform Commercial Code. See generally E.P. Ellinger, n.2 above, vol. IX, ch. 4.

[287] Under BEA 1882, s.5, however, the holder may treat such an instrument either as a bill of exchange or as a promissory note. Under BEA 1882, s.6(2), a bill of exchange may be addressed jointly to a number of drawees, but a written order addressed to two or more drawees in the alternative or in succession is not a bill of exchange.

[288] Under BEA 1882, s.7(2), it may be payable to joint payees or in the alternative to two payees or more. For fictitious payees, see Sect. 3(iii) above.

[289] Sect. 3(ii) above.   [290] BEA 1882, s.3(3).   [291] Id.

[292] *Guaranty Trust Co. of New York* v. *Hannay & Co.* [1918] 2 KB 623, 656 (CA). For 'claused' bills of exchange, see *Benjamin's Sale of Goods* (8th edn., London, 2010), [22-042].

[293] BEA 1882, s.3(1).   [294] Ibid., s.10.

date; or payable at a 'determinable future time',[295] such as 'ninety days after sight' (effectively ninety days after the instrument's presentment for acceptance). The 'determinable date' on which the bill of exchange is to fall due has to be definite,[296] and accordingly there has been some difficulty experienced in relation to instruments that confer upon the maker a discretion whether or not to make payment before the stipulated date. In *Williamson v. Rider*,[297] a majority of the Court of Appeal held that an instrument payable 'on or before' a specified date was not a valid promissory note, as a contingency as to the time of payment prevented the instrument being payable at 'at a fixed or determinable future time'. Ormerod LJ dissented, stating that 'if [the maker] chooses to pay—and it is purely a matter for him—at an earlier date...then the holder of the bill is under an obligation to accept that payment'.[298] Whilst the Court of Appeal confirmed this position somewhat reluctantly in *Claydon v. Bradley*,[299] this view has since been firmly rejected in Canada,[300] Australia,[301] Ireland,[302] New Zealand,[303] and Hong Kong.[304] Furthermore, the 'determinable' future time must be related to an event that is certain to happen though the time of its occurrence may be uncertain.[305] Section 11 of the BEA 1882 gives a clue as to what is meant by a 'certain event' in this context, as it provides that an instrument expressed to be payable on a contingency is not a bill of exchange. Although the relevant distinction appears to be between an event that is on its face contingent and one that is usually treated as a certainty, this is not always a straightforward distinction to apply in practice. On one side of the line, an instrument that was drawn payable at 30 days after the arrival of a specific ship in a named port was not a bill of exchange,[306] but was 'mere waste paper'.[307] On the other side of the line, in *Novaknit Hellas SA v. Kumar Brothers International Ltd*,[308] Waller LJ held that an instrument expressed to be payable 'on 60 days from first presentation of documents' was as certain as an instrument payable 'at sight' and that an instrument payable 'on 60 days from shipment' was valid as 'shipment is certain to have taken place prior to presentation of documents including the [bill of exchange]'.[309] Although the latter conclusion has been described as 'contentious',[310] *Novaknit Hellas* has subsequently been applied to the phrase '180 days from date of bill of lading' in *Crédit Agricole Indosuez v. Ecumet (UK) Ltd*.[311]

Finally, the bill of exchange must be for a sum certain in money. Pursuant to section 9(1) of the BEA 1882, a sum is considered 'certain' even though it is payable with

---

[295] Ibid., s.11. See generally *Crédit Agricole Indosuez v. Ecumet (UK) Ltd*, n.12 above.

[296] In the case of an ambiguity, the courts will endeavour to uphold the negotiability of an instrument: *Hong Kong & Shanghai Banking Corp. Ltd v. G. D. Trade Co. Ltd* [1998] CLC 238 (CA), qualifying *Korea Exchange Bank v. Debenhams (Central Buying) Ltd* [1979] 1 Lloyd's Rep. 100 (CA). See also *Novaknit Hellas SA v. Kumar Brothers International Ltd* [1998] Lloyd's Rep. Bank. 287 (CA).

[297] [1963] 1 QB 89, 97–98 (CA). For South Africa, see *Salot v. Naidoo*, 1981 (3) SA 959; *Standard Credit Corp. v. Kleyn*, 1988 (4) SA 441. Cf. *Korea Exchange Bank v. Debenhams (Central Buying) Ltd*, n.296 above.

[298] Ibid., 102. [299] [1987] 1 All ER 522, 524–525 (CA) (instrument payable 'by' a specified date).

[300] *John Burrows Ltd v. Subsurface Surveys Ltd* [1968] SCR 607, 614 (SCC).

[301] *ASIC v. Emu Brewery Mezzanine Ltd* (2004) 187 FLR 270, [43]–[72] (WASC); *Re York St Mezzanine Pty Ltd* (2007) 64 ACSR 1, [18]–[23] (FCA). See also A.G. Guest, n.3 above, [2-085].

[302] *Creative Press Ltd v. Harman* (1973) IR 313 (IEHC).

[303] *Club Securities Ltd v. Hurley* [2008] 1 NZLR 711, [28]–[48].

[304] *Chevalier (E&M Contracting) Ltd v. Rotegear Development Ltd* [1994] 3 HKC 457, 461–462.

[305] BEA 1882, s.11(2).

[306] *Palmer v. Pratt* (1824) 2 Bing. 185. Similarly, an instrument payable 'within two months after I should be lawfully married' was held to be invalid: A.G. Guest, n.3 above, [2-088]. Contrast *Maha Syndicate v. Cooperative Exportvereniging 'Vecofa' UA* [1970] 2 MLJ 221, 222 (MFC).

[307] A.G. Guest, n.3 above, [2-088]. [308] N.296 above. [309] Ibid., 291.

[310] A.G. Guest, n.3 above, [2-088]. [311] N.12 above.

interest,[312] payable by stated instalments (even if coupled with a provision that the total balance falls due upon default in any one of the instalments),[313] or payable at a specified rate of exchange.[314] However, the nature of the obligation has to be set out clearly. Thus, a statement that a bill of exchange is payable with 'lawful interest'[315] or at the rate applied to advances made to 'most creditworthy customers'[316] introduces uncertainty and invalidates the instrument. In contrast, a bill of exchange payable at a rate of interest that is determinable by reference to everyday practice, such as 'with interest at 4 per cent above base rate at date of discharge', ought to be valid as the rate in question is readily ascertainable. A bill of exchange for a given amount plus 'bank charges' has been held to be for an uncertain amount.[317]

(ii) The parties to a bill of exchange

There are at least two parties to every bill of exchange, namely the drawer and the drawee. The payee of the instrument may be either a third party or the drawer himself. When a bill of exchange is 'negotiated', which means that it is transferred by the payee or a subsequent 'holder', the transferor frequently adds currency to the instrument by adding his signature on the back. He thereupon becomes an 'indorser', whose position is similar to that of the drawer. The drawer of the bill of exchange performs a dual function: first, he instructs the drawee to honour the instrument; and, secondly, he undertakes that, on due presentment of the bill of exchange to the drawee, it will be duly 'accepted' (where acceptance is needed) and paid.[318] The drawer thus warrants that the bill of exchange will be honoured by the drawee. In the event that the bill of exchange is dishonoured and the requisite procedures on dishonour have been complied with, the drawer is obliged to compensate the holder of the instrument or any indorser who is compelled to pay it. The drawer's undertaking that the instrument will be honoured is similar to that of a surety who guarantees the payment of a loan extended to the debtor.[319] This explains the principle under which

---

[312] This will not be the case, however, if the interest is to commence running from a date that is not certain from the face of the instrument, such as the date of the making of an advance: *Macleod Savings & Credit Union Ltd* v. *Perrett* [1981] 1 SCR 78 (SCC); *Roynat Ltd* v. *Sommerville* (1981) 35 NBR (2d) 236, [22] (NBQB); *Royal Bank of Canada* v. *Bauman* (1986) 72 AR 89, [3] (AQB); *Zed* v. *National Bank of Canada* (1986) 72 NBR (2d) 34, [23]–[27] (NBCA); *Gravelbourg Savings & Credit Union Ltd* v. *Bissonnette* (1988) 66 Sask R. 81, [6]–[8] (SCA); *Canadian Imperial Bank of Commerce* v. *Morgan* (1993) 143 AR 36, [13]–[20] (AQB); *Toronto-Dominion Bank* v. *JF Fennell Enterprises Ltd* (2002) 200 NSR (2d) 78, [27]–[29] (NSSC).

[313] A.G. Guest, n.3 above, [2-073].

[314] The rate must clearly relate to the obligation to pay: *Tropic Plastic and Packaging Industry* v. *Standard Bank of South Africa Ltd*, 1969 (4) SA 108.

[315] *Smith* v. *Nightingale* (1818) 2 Stark. 375; *Bolton* v. *Dugdale* (1833) 4 B & Ad. 619; cf. A.G. Guest, n.3 above, [2-071]. The statement must be certain: *Temple Terrace Assets Co. Inc.* v. *Whynot* [1934] 1 DLR 124. Cf. *Rosenhain & Co.* v. *Commonwealth Bank of Australia* (1922) 31 CLR 46 (HCA), where a bill payable with 8 per cent p.a. 'until arrival of payment in London for cover' was held uncertain. As interest would have continued to run until the very arrival of the cover, the decision may be questionable.

[316] *Bank of Montreal* v. *Dezcam Industries Ltd* (1983) 5 WWR 83 (BCCA).

[317] *Dalgety Ltd* v. *John J. Hilton Pty. Ltd* [1981] 2 NSWLR 169.

[318] BEA 1882, s.55(1)(*a*). See *Conoco Ltd* v. *Everett* (QBD, 19 February 1986).

[319] Thus, the drawer as well as any indorser are entitled to the equities of a surety if they have to pay the bill of exchange: *Duncan, Fox & Co.* v. *North and South Wales Bank* (1880) 6 App. Cas. 1, 19–20 (HL). See also *Rouquette* v. *Overmann* (1875) LR 10 QB 525, 537; *Double Diamond Bowling Supply Ltd* v. *Eglinton Bowling Ltd* [1963] 2 OR 222, 224–226; *Re Securitibank Ltd* [1978] 1 NZLR 97, 212; *Guaranty Trust Co. of Canada* v. *Seller's Oil Field Service Ltd* (1984) 55 AR 348, [13]–[15] (AQB); *Scholefield Goodman & Sons Ltd* v. *Zyngier* [1984] VR 445, affd. [1986] AC 562 (PC). See further E.P. Ellinger, 'The Drawer's Right of Subrogation Revisited' [1986] *JBL* 399; A.G. Guest, n.3 above, [7-020] *et seq*. For the application of *Fox* in

the drawer's liability is discharged if the payee or holder does not follow the procedures prescribed for when a bill of exchange is dishonoured.

The drawee of a bill of exchange (or, in other words, the person charged with its payment) does not incur liability on the instrument by reason only of its being drawn on him. Under section 53(1) of the BEA 1882, a bill of exchange 'of itself, does not operate as an assignment of funds in the hands of the drawee available for the payment thereof, and the drawee of a bill who does not accept [it] as required by [the] Act is not liable on the instrument'.[320] The drawee's refusal to accept a bill of exchange may, however, constitute a breach of its separate contract with the drawer. Thus, a bank that dishonours by non-acceptance a bill of exchange, drawn in conformity with the provisions of an acceptance credit or line of credit that it has issued, commits a breach of its separate contract with the drawer.[321] When the drawee does accept a bill of exchange, he becomes its acceptor and incurs liability on the instrument by engaging that he will pay it according to the tenor of his acceptance.[322] A person other than the drawee of a bill of exchange cannot accept the instrument and, if he purports to do so, he probably incurs the liability of an indorser.[323] 'Acceptance' is defined as the 'signification by the drawee of his assent to the order of the drawer'.[324] The drawee's liability is that of a primary obligor or debtor and the defences available to him against the drawer cannot usually be raised against subsequent parties.[325] To be valid, the acceptance has to be written on the bill of exchange and be signed by the drawee.[326] Although the drawee's mere signature without additional words is adequate,[327] the common practice is to add the word 'accepted' and the date of its execution. A bill of exchange may be accepted before it has been signed by the drawer, or whilst it is otherwise incomplete.[328] This principle is of importance in respect of acceptance credits or lines of credit, as in some cases the bills of exchange are accepted by the issuing bank before their execution by the drawer.[329] A bill of exchange may also be accepted when it is overdue, or after its initial dishonour by the drawee.[330]

In practice, not all bills of exchange are presented to the drawee separately for acceptance and then for payment. Thus, a bill of exchange that is payable on demand is ordinarily presented simultaneously for acceptance and payment or simply for payment. Similarly, if a bill of exchange is payable on a fixed date, or at a given time after its date of issue, presentment for acceptance is not necessary to determine the instrument's maturity.[331] The drawer or holder may, however, wish to present the bill of exchange for acceptance in order to charge the acceptor and thus to increase the currency of the instrument. Presentment for acceptance is required, and constitutes a 'duty' imposed on the holder by the BEA 1882, where an instrument is payable at a fixed time after sight. It is clear that, unless such a bill of exchange is presented for acceptance, its date of maturity remains

---

the general surety context, see *Berghoff Trading Ltd* v. *Swinbrook Developments Ltd* [2009] EWCA Civ 413, [24]–[38].

[320] N.2 above.   [321] Sect. 10 below.   [322] BEA 1882, s.54(1).   [323] Ibid., s.56.

[324] Ibid., s.17(1). See *R* v. *Nanayakkara* [1987] 1 All ER 650 (CA). A drawee's simple assent without any qualification is a 'general acceptance': BEA 1882, s.19(2). A partial or conditional assent is a 'qualified acceptance': ibid. The holder of a bill of exchange may refuse to take a qualified acceptance and, if he chooses to take it, the drawer and indorsers are usually discharged: ibid., s.44.

[325] Sect. 8(iii) below.   [326] BEA 1882, s.17(2)(*a*).   [327] Id.   [328] Ibid., s.18(1).

[329] This can be the case where the issuing bank furnishes instruments of given amounts to be completed by the drawer. See further Sect. 10 below.

[330] BEA 1882, s.18(2).

[331] Ibid., s.39(3). See also *Fiorentino Comm Giuseppe Srl* v. *Farnesi*, n.75 above, [32].

undetermined.[332] Further, a bill of exchange has to be presented for acceptance if this is expressly required by the instrument or if the instrument is drawn as payable at a place other than the drawee's residence or place of business.[333]

As bills of exchange are meant to be discounted, they do not usually remain in the hands of the ostensible payee until their date of maturity. When the payee transfers or 'negotiates' a bill of exchange,[334] he is generally asked to indorse it. In the majority of cases, the indorsement serves two purposes. First, it is executed to transfer the bill.[335] Secondly, an indorsement gives extra currency to the bill of exchange, as the indorser undertakes that the instrument will be duly accepted and paid, and that 'if it be dishonoured he will compensate the holder or a subsequent indorser who is compelled to pay it'.[336] As the indorser is in a position akin to that of a surety, the indorser's liability is similar to that of the drawer, which was discussed previously. The liability of an indorser is, therefore, incurred towards every party who acquires the bill of exchange after him and who is compelled to pay it. The indorser is precluded from denying to any such 'subsequent indorsee' that the bill of exchange was, at the time of his indorsement, a valid and subsisting instrument and that he then had a good title to it.[337]

In some cases, a party may be asked to sign a bill of exchange even though he is neither the ostensible payee nor a subsequent transferee. Such a signature cannot be treated as an acceptance of the bill of exchange, as a stranger to the instrument cannot assent to an order that is specifically directed to the drawee. A signature of this type is considered to be *sui generis*,[338] but is recognized as having some legal effect by section 56 of the BEA 1882, which provides that '[w]here a person signs a bill otherwise than as drawer or acceptor, he thereby incurs the liabilities of an indorser to a holder in due course'.[339] The intention of a party to act as indorser is usually manifested by him signing the back of the bill of exchange, although a signature placed by a person other than the drawee on the front of the instrument is also treated as an indorsement.[340] Occasionally, an indorser's signature may be placed on the back of the bill of exchange above the drawer's signature, whereas the indorsement should properly be placed below that signature. If this is due to inadvertence, the order of the signatures is to be ignored.[341] Moreover, the fact that the indorsement is placed on the bill of exchange before its execution by the drawer is irrelevant as, under section 20 of the BEA 1882, the drawer is entitled to complete such a bill by treating the signature on the back as that of an indorser.[342] In the

---

[332] Ibid., s.39(1).   [333] Ibid., s.39(2).   [334] Sect. 8(iv) below.

[335] An indorsement is not required for this purpose when the bill of exchange is payable to bearer: Sect. 8(iv) below. Most bills of exchange currently issued in the United Kingdom are payable to the order of a designated payee, whose indorsement is accordingly required.   [336] BEA 1882, s.55(2).

[337] Ibid., s.55(2)(c). An indorser, as well as the drawer, can exclude a right of recourse under BEA 1882, s.16(1). Such a 'without recourse' transaction is known as an *à forfait* (or 'forfaiting') transaction. The indorser is then in a position similar to that of a transferor by delivery: Sect. 8(iv) below.

[338] Such a signature has been referred to as an 'anomalous indorsement' or 'quasi-indorsement': A.G. Guest, n.3 above, [7-031]. A person who signs an instrument in a representative capacity does not thereby incur the personal liability of an indorser, as it is only the principal who becomes liable on the instrument: *Muirhead* v. *Commonwealth Bank of Australia* (1996) 139 ALR 561; *Australian Securities and Investments Commission* v. *Whitlam* (2002) 42 ACSR 407 (NSWSC); *Valamios* v. *Demarco* [2005] NSWCA 98, [32]–[51].

[339] For an innovative construction of this provision, see *G. & H. Montage GmbH* v. *Irvani* [1988] 1 WLR 1285, affd. [1990] 1 WLR 667 (CA). See further Sect. 8(iii) below.

[340] *Young* v. *Glover* (1857) 3 Jur. (NS) 637; *Ex p. Yates* (1857) 2 De G & J 191.

[341] *National Sales Corporation Ltd* v. *Bernardi* [1931] 2 KB 188, 192–193; *Lombard Banking Ltd* v. *Central Garage & Engineering Co. Ltd* [1963] 1 QB 220, 228–229. See also *Yee Sang Metal Supplies Co.* v. *Devon & Co Ltd* [1964] HKCU 98.

[342] *McDonald (Gerald) & Co.* v. *Nash & Co.* [1924] AC 625, 636, 648 (HL); *National Sales Corporation Ltd* v. *Bernardi*, n.341 above, 191–196; *Yeoman Credit Ltd* v. *Gregory* [1963] 1 WLR 343, 349–353. See also *G&H Montage GmbH* v. *Irvani* [1990] 1 WLR 667 (CA).

most usual case where a non-party signs a bill of exchange as indorser in order to 'back' the instrument, however, section 56 of the BEA 1882 only renders the indorser liable to a holder of the instrument, but not ostensibly to the original payee of the instrument.[343] The indorser's signature was also unable to operate as a collateral undertaking outside the bill of exchange as there would be no note or memorandum in writing as required by section 4 of the Statute of Frauds 1677.[344] In *McDonald (Gerald) & Co.* v. *Nash & Co.*,[345] a bill of exchange was drawn to the order of the drawer, subsequently endorsed by a third party, and then returned to the drawer/payee who indorsed their name above that of the indorser. The House of Lords allowed the drawer/payee to sue the indorser on the instrument on the basis that the drawer/payee had authority to complete the instrument and chain of indorsements under section 20 of the BEA 1882.[346] Accordingly, the indorser will be liable to the payee if it is established that he intended to be so bound when he signed the instrument,[347] and to this end it will be necessary to investigate the facts of the case and the intention of the parties.[348] Furthermore, as the indorser's liability in *McDonald* was based on the bill of exchange itself and not on an ancillary surety contract there could be no objection that it was unenforceable under section 4 of the Statute of Frauds 1677.

Although the House of Lords in *McDonald* achieved an equivalent (although not identical) result by the 'ingenious use' of the BEA 1882,[349] English law does not formally recognize an 'aval' or guarantee written on the bill of exchange itself.[350] In this regard, English law differs from the Uniform Law of the Geneva Convention, which applies in most European countries,[351] and from the Uniform Commercial Code in the United States.[352] An 'aval' that is expressed to back the drawee's acceptance and payment of a bill of exchange (e.g. *bon pour aval pour le compte du tiré*) effectively binds the 'guarantor' as a joint obligor of the drawee, so that he is liable for the payment of the instrument to all those party to it, regardless of whether they become parties to the instrument before or after the execution of the 'aval'. In English law, an 'aval' is treated as an indorsement and the party executing it generally assumes liability to subsequent parties only and on the same footing as the drawer.[353]

---

[343] *Steele* v. *M'Kinlay* (1880) 5 App. Cas. 754, 768, 772, 782 (HL); *Jenkins & Sons* v. *Coomber* [1898] 2 QB 168 (doubted on some points by *McDonald (Gerald) & Co.* v. *Nash & Co.*, n.342 above); cf. *Mander* v. *Evans & Rose* (1888) 5 TLR 75.

[344] Ibid., 768. See also *Jenkins & Sons* v. *Coomber*, n.343 above.

[345] N.342 above. See also *G&H Montage GmbH* v. *Irvani*, n.342 above, 672–673, 679, 689.

[346] Ibid., 647–648.   [347] *McCall Bros. Ltd* v. *Hargreaves* [1932] 2 KB 423, 427–430.

[348] *Glenie* v. *Bruce Smith* [1908] 1 KB 263, 266–269 (CA); *Re Gooch* [1921] 2 KB 593, 601, 602–603 (CA); *National Sales Corporation Ltd* v. *Bernardi*, n.341 above, 191–196; *Rolfe Lubell & Co.* v. *Keith* [1979] 1 All ER 860; *G&H Montage GmbH* v. *Irvani*, n.342 above, 672–673. See also *Valamios* v. *Demarco*, n.338 above, [43]–[51].

[349] *G&H Montage GmbH* v. *Irvani*, n.342 above, 672, 679–680, 689. The approach in *McDonald* does not provide a complete solution, as it can have no application to the situation where the payee does not sign the instrument so as to complete the chain of indorsements: A.G. Guest, n.3 above, [7-033]. See also *Rowe & Co. Pty Ltd* v. *Pitts* [1973] 2 NSWLR 159; *Valamios* v. *Demarco*, n.338 above, [43]–[46].

[350] *Bank Lenmi Le-Israel* v. *Coniplan (UK) Ltd* (QBD, 31 July 1987). For the principle of 'aval' in Canada, see *Grant* v. *Scott* [1919] 59 SCR 227, 228–231 (SCC); *Gallagher* v. *Murphy* [1929] SCR 288, 295–296 (SCC); *Double Diamond Bowling Supply Ltd* v. *Eglinton Bowling Ltd*, n.319 above, 229.

[351] Convention Providing a Uniform Law for Bills of Exchange and Promissory Notes (Geneva, 7 June 1930) League of Nations Treaty Series, vol. 143, 259, No. 3313, Arts. 30–32. See also E.P. Ellinger, n.2 above, vol. IX, ch. 4, [119] *et seq.*

[352] UCC, s.3-419.

[353] *Jackson* v. *Hudson* (1810) 2 Camp. 447, 448; *Steele* v. *M'Kinlay*, n.343 above, 772. One of the traditional arguments against the validity of an 'aval' in English law, namely the absence of a memorandum in writing as required under section 4 of the Statute of Frauds 1677, has been questioned by the Court of Appeal in *G. &*

The drawer, the acceptor, and the indorsers are the parties against whom the bill of exchange is enforceable. Primarily, they incur liability to the 'holder' of the instrument. Under section 2 of the BEA 1882, the 'holder' is the payee, the indorsee, or the bearer of an instrument who has possession thereof. Ordinarily, the holder seeks to enforce the bill of exchange against prior parties, but there is authority for the view that, if an instrument is acquired back by the drawer from a subsequent transferee or holder, the drawer obtains that party's rights against all intermediary parties.[354] On another view, the drawer reverts to his original position because, on the face of the bill of exchange, he has initially warranted the payment of the instrument and this undertaking accrues in favour of all subsequent parties. Support for this last view can be derived from the plain construction of section 37 of the BEA 1882.

Payment of the bill of exchange is to be arranged by the acceptor. Where this role is assumed by a bank, as is the case with a bill of exchange drawn under an acceptance credit or line of credit, the instrument is made payable at the premises of that bank or one of its designated branches. Where a bill of exchange is drawn on a person other than a bank, as is the case where the instrument is drawn by a seller on a buyer under a c.i.f. sale contract, the drawee normally accepts the instrument as payable at his own bank. Such an acceptance is considered a general one,[355] although the holder is then obliged to present it at the designated 'domicile'.[356] The bank at whose premises the bill of exchange is domiciled does not become a party to the instrument. In effect, its position is similar to that of a bank on which a customer has drawn a cheque. When the acceptor designates a bank as the 'domicile' of a bill of exchange, he instructs it to effect payment.[357] The bank's duty to obey this order is owed to the customer alone.

(iii) **Position of the holder**

As considered already,[358] 'holder' means the payee or indorsee of the instrument with possession of it, or the bearer thereof.[359] An indorsee is a person who has acquired the bill of exchange under an indorsement. As a forged indorsement is a nullity, a person who claims to hold a bill of exchange thereunder is not a holder.[360] This particular problem does not arise in the case of a bearer, however, as his rights are acquired by mere delivery and are not based on the indorsement to him of the bill of exchange.[361] The rights of a holder depend, however, on whether he is a 'mere holder', a 'holder for value', or a 'holder in due course'. In certain cases, it is also relevant whether a particular dispute is between 'immediate parties' to the instrument or 'remote parties'. Immediate parties are those

---

H. Montage GmbH v. *Irvani*, n.342 above. The point was obiter, however. as the main issue determined was the recognition by an English court of an 'aval' executed on a bill of exchange in a foreign country, the law of which made provision for an 'aval'. For the validity of an 'aval' executed on a foreign bill, see *Banco Atlantico SA* v. *British Bank of the Middle East* [1990] 2 Lloyd's Rep. 504 (CA). See also *Textiles Confecciones Europeas SA* v. *Lois Clothing Co. (UK) Ltd* (CA, 31 October 1988).

[354] *Jade International Steel Stahl und Eisen GmbH & Co. KG* v. *Robert Nicholas (Steels) Ltd* [1978] QB 917, 924, 926 (CA). See *Provincial Bank of Canada* v. *Beneficial Finance Co. of Canada* (1978) 23 NBR (2d) 524, [14] (NBQB).

[355] BEA 1882, s.19(2)(c). An acceptance is 'local' and 'qualified' if the bill of exchange provides that it is payable solely at the particular place specified: id.

[356] Ibid., s.45(4)(a).   [357] *Bank of England* v. *Vagliano Bros.*, n.133 above.   [358] Sect. 8(ii) above.

[359] BEA 1882, s.2.

[360] *Lacave & Co.* v. *Crédit Lyonnais* [1897] 1 QB 148, 152–153; *Carpenters' Co.* v. *British Mutual Banking Co. Ltd* [1938] 1 KB 511, 524–525 (CA).

[361] Sect. 8(iv) below.

who, in addition to the privity created by the bill of exchange itself, have a direct legal relationship with each other. The drawer and the acceptor, the drawer and the initial payee, and an indorser and his indorsee are usually parties who have entered into a contract with one another, such as an agreement to extend credit, a contract for the sale of goods, or an arrangement for the discount of a bill of exchange. These parties are, therefore, predominantly immediate parties, but in some cases even these parties may be remote parties. Thus, the drawer may make a bill of exchange payable to the order of the payee at a third party's request. Similarly, the drawee of a bill of exchange may agree to accept it on the basis of his contract with a stranger to the instrument. Some commentators maintain that, generally, the defences that can be pleaded against a remote party are more restricted than those available against an immediate party.[362] The distinction between remote and immediate parties, however, is mainly relevant in respect of actions brought on a bill of exchange by a holder for value. The superior rights of a 'holder in due course' are defined in section 38 of the BEA 1882, which does not draw a distinction between remote and immediate parties.[363] At the other end of the scale, a mere holder who does not furnish value appears to hold the bill of exchange subject to virtually all equities available against prior parties, including immediate ones.

The most clearly defined rights are those conferred on a 'holder in due course', a phrase that needs to be clarified. Under section 29 of the BEA 1882, four requirements must be fulfilled before a person is considered a 'holder in due course'. First, he must take the bill of exchange when it is 'complete and regular on the face of it'. Essentially, this means that the bill of exchange must not include on its front or back any detail that is out of the ordinary, such as there being a discrepancy between the words and the figures denoting the amount of the instrument,[364] or there being a material difference between the name in which the bill of exchange appears to be indorsed by the payee and the name inserted by the drawer on the front of the instrument. Thus, an indorsement by 'John Williams' of a bill of exchange drawn payable to 'J. Williams' is regular, but an indorsement in such a case by the payee as 'Walter Williams' would be irregular.[365] Equally irregular is the indorsement of a firm described by the drawer as a company if the word 'Ltd' or 'plc' is missing.[366] Secondly, a person is a 'holder in due course' only if he has taken the bill of exchange

[362] D.V. Cowen & L. Gering, *The Law of Negotiable Instruments in South Africa* (5th edn., Cape Town, 1985), 103–109; B. Crawford, *Payment, Clearing and Settlement in Canada* (Ontario, 2002), vol. 2, [23.01] *et seq*. See also *Ashley Colter Ltd* v. *Scott* [1942] 3 DLR 538, 541 (SCC); *Williams & Glyn's Bank Ltd* v. *Belkin Packaging Ltd* [1983] 1 SCR 661, 674–677 (SCC); *Bremner* v. *Patterson* [2001] BCTC Lexis 429, [7]–[8] (BCSC). This distinction is not yet fully worked out in the case law: *Watson* v. *Russell* (1864) 5 B & S 968, 34 LJQB 93 (suggesting that the drawer and drawee of a bill of exchange are not always immediate parties). See also *Oscar Harris, Son & Co.* v. *Vallarman & Co.* [1940] 1 All ER 185 (CA); *Bank Lenmi Le-Israel* v. *Coniplan (UK) Ltd*, n.350 above; *Solo Industries UK Ltd* v. *Canara Bank* [2001] 2 Lloyd's Rep. 578, [39] (CA). See further A.G. Guest, n.3 above, [4-005]–[4-009]. See also *The Chartered Bank* v. *Yeoh Bok Han*, n.166 above, 128. Consider *GMAC Commercial Finance Ltd* v. *Mint Apparel Ltd* [2010] EWHC 2452 (Comm.), [26].

[363] Only the transferee of an instrument can be a 'holder in due course' and only his transferor can be regarded as his immediate party. From a practical point of view, the circumstances under which a transferee has to take a bill of exchange in order to attain the status of a 'holder in due course' are such as to rule out the need to distinguish in his case between an action against an immediate and a remote party.

[364] *Banco di Roma SpA* v. *Orru* [1973] 2 Lloyd's Rep. 505, 507 (CA).

[365] *Arab Bank Ltd* v. *Ross* [1952] 2 QB 216, 222 (CA); *Bank of Cyprus (London) Ltd* v. *Jones* (CA, 13 July 1987). See also *All Terrain Forklift Hire Pty Ltd* v. *White* (NSWSC, 28 November 1994); *Lewko* v. *Peak Mechanical Ltd* [2005] SKQB 83, [16]. If genuine, the indorsement is effective to transfer title.

[366] Ibid., 223, 228–229, 234.

before it is overdue[367] and without notice of any act of dishonour that might have taken place. Thirdly, a 'holder in due course' must take the bill of exchange in good faith.[368] Under section 90 of the BEA 1882, a thing is deemed to be done in good faith where it is in fact done honestly, even it is also done negligently.[369] For these purposes, a holder does not act in good faith where he takes a bill of exchange despite his suspicion that something is wrong, although he may not have notice of the exact nature of the defect.[370] In addition to being in good faith, a 'holder in due course' must take the instrument without notice of any defect in the transferor's title.[371] In this regard, section 29(2) of the BEA 1882 provides a non-exhaustive list of what will constitute a 'defect of title' for these purposes, including duress, fraud, and any illegal means utilized by the transferor to obtain the acceptance of the instrument. In *Österreichische Länderbank* v. *S'Elite Ltd*,[372] the Court of Appeal held that 'fraud [within section 29(2)] means common law fraud'.[373] Canadian authorities have taken a broader view, suggesting that a firm, such as a finance company, cannot claim to be a holder in due course of bills of exchange transferred to it by another firm, such as a car dealer, if there is a very close business relationship between the two firms.[374] A United Kingdom court is unlikely, however, to agree with the view that a transferee of a bill of exchange, who does not have notice (within the meaning of section 29 of the BEA 1882) of any irregularity or suspicious circumstances concerning the transaction financed by means of a bill of exchange, loses its status as a holder in due course by reason only of its general business relationship with the transferor. Fourthly, a 'holder in due course' must take the bill of exchange for 'value', which means for a 'consideration'.[375] Apart from the

---

[367] A bill of exchange that is payable on demand is deemed overdue after it has been in circulation for an unreasonable length of time: BEA 1882, s.36(3).

[368] *Lipkin Gorman* v. *Karpnale Ltd* [1987] 1 WLR 987, 994–995, affd. on a different point: [1991] 2 AC 548 (HL). Where the alleged 'holder in due course' is a company, it will be necessary to identify the individual whose good faith or bad faith will be relevant for these purposes: *Bank of Credit and Commerce International SA* v. *Dawson* [1987] FLR 342.

[369] Under BEA 1882, s.90, 'want of good faith', 'dishonesty', and 'fraud' are synonyms: *Österreichische Länderbank* v. *S'Elite Ltd* [1981] QB 565, 569 (CA).

[370] *Jones* v. *Gordon* (1877) 2 App. Cas. 616, 625, 628 (HL); *Baker* v. *Barclays Bank Ltd*, n.197 above, 833–835; *Smith* v. *Morrison* [1974] 1 WLR 659, 672–673; *Bank of Cyprus (London) Ltd* v. *Jones* (1984) 134 NLJ 522; *Moscow Bank of the Savings Bank of the Russian Federation* v. *Amadeus Trading Ltd*, The Times, 1 April 1997. Under BEA 1882, s.30(2), a party is presumed to be a holder in due course and thus to have acted in good faith, but the burden of proof is shifted where there has been fraud or illegality in the transaction.

[371] *Ben Baron & Partners* v. *Henderson* (1959) 7 LDAB 219 (SASC). A holder that derives their title through a 'holder in due course' has all the rights of that holder provided he is 'not himself a party to any fraud or illegality' affecting the instrument: *Jade International Steel Stahl und Eisen GmbH & Co. KG* v. *Robert Nicholas (Steels) Ltd*, n.354 above, 924, 926; *First Discount Ltd* v. *Cranston* [2002] EWCA Civ 71, [4], [17].

[372] N.369 above.

[373] Ibid., 570, overruling *Banca Populare di Novara* v. *John Livanos & Sons Ltd* [1965] 2 Lloyd's Rep. 149. A transferee's knowledge that an indorsement has been effected for a restrictive purpose precludes him from being a 'holder in due course': *Williams & Glyn's Bank Ltd* v. *Belkin Packaging Ltd*, n.362 above, 678. See also *Bank of Credit and Commerce International SA* v. *Dawson*, n.368 above.

[374] *Federal Discount Corporation Ltd* v. *St. Pierre* [1962] OR 310, 321–322 (OCA); *Rand Investments Ltd* v. *Bertrand* (1966) 58 DLR (2d.) 372, 381 (BCSC); *Keelan* v. *Norray Distributing Ltd* (1967) 62 DLR (2d.) 466, 478, 483–484 (MBQB); *Range* v. *Corporation de Finance Belvedere* [1967] BR 932, 936 (Que. QB), affd. [1969] SCR 492 (SCC); *Beneficial Finance Co. of Canada* v. *Kulig* [1970] 3 OR 370, 380–384; *Bank of Montreal* v. *Kon* (1978) 8 AR 593, [46]–[61] (ASC). See also *Stenning* v. *Radio and Domestic Finance Ltd* [1961] NZLR 7. Contrast *Automobile Finance of Australia Ltd* v. *Henderson* (1928) 23 Tas. LR 9; *Scottish Loan and Finance Co. Ltd* v. *Payne* (1935) 52 WN (NSW) 175.

[375] *Mackenzie Mills* v. *Buono* [1986] BTLC 399 (CA); *Lipkin Gorman* v. *Karpnale Ltd* [1991] 2 AC 548, 583 (HL). For what counts as adequate value, see BEA 1882, s.27. A holder may be constituted a 'holder in due course' by reason of his having a lien over the instrument: BEA 1882, s.27(3). See also *Barclays Bank Ltd* v. *Astley Industrial Trust Ltd* [1970] 2 QB 527, 539; *Bank of Credit and Commerce International SA* v. *Dawson*,

four requirements stipulated in section 29, it is clear from the language of that provision that a 'holder in due course' can only include a person who has 'taken the bill'. It has been held that these words refer to a holder to whom the bill has been negotiated, and that the original payee of a bill cannot, therefore, be a holder in due course.[376]

Under section 38(2) of the BEA 1882,[377] a 'holder in due course' holds the bill of exchange free from any defects in the title of previous parties, as well as free from any equities available to prior parties among themselves, and may consequently enforce payment against all the parties liable on the instrument. In this way, the provision enables bankers and other financial institutions to discount bills of exchange without getting embroiled in disputes concerning the underlying business contracts. Thus, where the discounter is a holder in due course, he can enforce the bill of exchange against a drawee who has accepted it in the mistaken belief about the genuineness of a forged bill of lading that was attached to the instrument.[378] The position of a holder in due course is further safeguarded by the provisions of the BEA 1882 dealing with inchoate instruments;[379] the conclusive presumption that the bill of exchange has been delivered;[380] the preclusion of the acceptor, the drawer, or the indorsers from raising certain defences invalidating the bill of exchange;[381] and the preclusion of a party from relying upon alterations to the bill of exchange in certain cases.[382] In order to defeat an action by a holder in due course, it is necessary to establish a defect in his title to the bill of exchange (for example, that he holds the instrument under a forged indorsement) in which case he is not really a holder in due course.[383] The rights of a holder in due course accrue also to any holder (whether for value or not) who derives his title from a holder in due course.[384] Naturally, these rights cannot be pleaded by a transferee who is party to any fraud affecting the bill of exchange, but mere knowledge of fraud or illegality does not deprive such a transferee of his rights.[385] In *Jade International Steel Stahl und Eisen GmbH & Co. KG v. Robert*

---

n.368 above. See also *Silk Bros. Interstate Traders Pty Ltd* v. *Security Pacific National Bank* (1987) 72 ALR 535 (NSWSC). Under BEA 1882, s.30(1), a party is presumed to have acquired a bill for value, but this presumption can be displaced in the circumstances set out in BEA 1882, s.30(2): *Neigut* v. *Hannania*, The Times, 6 January 1983; *Bank of Cyprus (London) Ltd* v. *Jones*, n.365 above; *Vecta Software Corporation Ltd* v. *Despec Supplies Ltd*, n.91 above, [20]; *Lomax Leisure Ltd* v. *Miller*, n.90 above, [22]. In *Clifford Chance* v. *Silver*, n.5 above, the Court of Appeal held that a holder in due course could, equally, attain his status in reliance on value furnished by a previous party. For a critique, see L.P. Hitchens, 'Holders for Value and their Status: *Clifford Chance v Silver*' [1993] *JBL* 571.

[376] *R. E. Jones Ltd* v. *Waring & Gillow Ltd* [1926] AC 670, 680 (HL); *Lloyds Bank Ltd* v. *The Chartered Bank of India, Australia and China* [1929] 1 KB 40, 57, 75 (CA); *Abbey National plc* v. *JSF Finance & Currency Exchange Co. Ltd*, n.5 above, [13]; *DCD Factors plc* v. *Ramada Trading Ltd* [2007] EWHC 2820 (QB), [31]. The principle in *Waring & Gillow* has been adopted in Australia (*Inflatable Toy Company Pty Ltd* v. *State Bank of New South Wales Ltd* (1994) 34 NSWLR 243, 252–253 (NSWSC); *Lipa* v. *Metabolic* [2006] NSWSC 997, [26]), Malaysia (*Hon Chee Enterprise* v. *British Markitex Ltd* [1982] 1 MLJ 149, 150–151 (MFC)), New Zealand (*Yan* v. *Post Office Bank Ltd*, n.77 above, 161), Scotland (*Williams* v. *Williams*, n.2 above), Singapore (*Crédit Agricole Indosuez* v. *Banque Nationale de Paris* [2001] 2 SLR 1, [49] (SGCA)), and South Africa (*Ben Baron & Partners* v. *Henderson*, n.371 above). For the conflicting Canadian approaches, see *Coupar* v. *Cox* (1978) 42 NSR (2d) 461, [5]; cf *Ierullo* v. *Rovan* (2000) 46 OR (3d) 692, [18]–[20] (OSC).

[377] *Banco Santander SA* v. *Banque Paribas*, n.12 above.

[378] *Guaranty Trust Co. of New York* v. *Hannay & Co.*, n.292 above, 652.   [379] BEA 1882, s.20(2).

[380] Ibid., s.21(2).   [381] Ibid., ss.54(2), 55(2).   [382] Ibid., s.64(2).

[383] In such a case, the party would not be a holder, let alone a holder in due course.

[384] BEA 1882, s.29(3). See also *Jade International Steel Stahl und Eisen GmbH & Co. KG* v. *Robert Nicholas (Steels) Ltd*, n.354 above, 924, 926; *First Discount Ltd* v. *Cranston*, n.371 above, [4], [17].

[385] *May* v. *Chapman* (1834) 16 M & W 355; *Jones* v. *Gordon*, n.370 above, 625, 628; *Smith* v. *Morrison*, n.370 above, 672–673. See also *Bank of Montreal* v. *Tourangeau* (1980) 31 OR (2d) 177, 184–186.

Nicholas (Steels) Ltd,[386] the Court of Appeal held that, if a bill of exchange returns to the hands of the drawer who takes it for value, he may assume the status of a holder in due course,[387] but this proposition is questionable, as explained further below.[388]

The rights of a 'mere holder', who is a holder other than a 'holder in due course' or a 'holder for value', contrast sharply with those of a 'holder in due course'. Under section 38(1) of the BEA 1882, a 'mere holder' has the right to bring an action on the bill of exchange in his own name.[389] Under the former Rules of the Supreme Court,[390] the general rule was that a claimant on a bill of exchange, such as a holder of the instrument, was entitled to summary judgment save in exceptional circumstances.[391] The position is now governed by the Civil Procedure Rules 1998 (CPR 1998).[392] According to Waller LJ in *Safa Ltd* v. *Banque du Caire*,[393] '[t]here is no reason to think that the previous established principles [relating to summary judgment under the Rules of the Supreme Court] in relation to bills of exchange and of letters of credit or performance bonds were intended to be altered' by the introduction of the CPR 1998, so that the authorities decided under the former rules are likely to remain good law. Although the BEA 1882 does not indicate what type of defences have to be alleged in order to induce the court to refuse summary judgment,[394] a comparison of the language of subsections 38(1) and 38(2) of the BEA 1882 suggests that, as against a 'mere holder', a defendant is entitled to raise defences stemming from a defect in the title of prior parties and at least some of the personal defences available to those parties. Thus, the absence of consideration[395] and the total failure of consideration[396] are valid defences against a 'mere holder'. Partial failure of consideration

---

[386] N.354 above.

[387] Ibid., 924, 926. See *Provincial Bank of Canada* v. *Beneficial Finance Co. of Canada*, n.354 above, [14]. See further Sect. 8(v) below.

[388] Sect. 8(iv) below.   [389] *National Westminster Bank plc* v. *King* (CA, 7 October 1987).

[390] Rules of the Supreme Court (RSC), Order 14.

[391] *Brown Shipley & Co. Ltd* v. *Alicia Hosiery Ltd* [1966] 1 Lloyd's Rep. 668, 669 (CA); *Cebora SNC* v. *SIP (Industrial Products) Ltd* [1976] 1 Lloyd's Rep. 271, 274–280 (CA); *Nova (Jersey) Knit Ltd* v. *Kammgarn Spinnerei GmbH* [1977] 1 WLR 713, 720–722, 726–727, 732–733 (HL). Under the former RSC, a court would grant leave to defend, if the defendant established a *prima facie* defence that was arguably good in law. For examples of the type of defence that formerly induced a court to grant leave to defend under the RSC, see A.G. Guest, n.3 above, [4-010]. See also *Forestal Mimosa Ltd* v. *Oriental Credit Ltd* [1986] 1 WLR 631, 635–636 (CA).

[392] Civil Procedure Rules 1998 (CPR 1998), r.24.2.

[393] [2000] 2 Lloyd's Rep. 600, 605–606 (CA). See also *Central Bank of Yemen* v. *Cardinal Financial Investments Corporation* (CA, 23 October 2000), [7]; *Solo Industries UK Ltd* v. *Canara Bank*, n.362 above, [22]–[28]; *Isovel Contracts Ltd* v. *ABB Building Technologies* [2002] 1 BCLC 390, [15]–[22]; *Banque Saudi Fransi* v. *Lear Siegler Services Inc.* [2007] 2 Lloyd's Rep. 47, [14]–[16] (CA); *Enka Insaat Ve Sanayi AS* v. *Banca Popolare Dell'Alto Adige SpA* [2009] EWHC 2410 (Comm.), [19]–[25]. Under CPR 1998, r.24.2, summary judgment will be entered against a defendant if he has 'no real prospect of successfully defending the claim or issue' and 'there is no other compelling reason why the case or issue should be disposed of at a trial'.

[394] CPR 1998, Pt. 24, Practice Direction, rr.5.1–5.2.

[395] *Forman* v. *Wright* (1851) 11 CB 481, 492–494; *Thoni GmbH & Co. KG* v. *RTP Equipment Ltd* [1979] 2 Lloyd's Rep. 282, 284–285 (CA); *MK International Development Co. Ltd* v. *Housing Bank*, n.93 above; *Isovel Contracts Ltd* v. *ABB Building Technologies*, n.393 above, [17]–[18] cf. *Milnes* v. *Dawson* (1850) 5 Exch. 948, 950–951. See also A.G. Guest, n.3 above, [4-007].

[396] *Fielding & Platt Ltd* v. *Selim Najjas* [1969] 1 WLR 357, 361 (CA); *Nova (Jersey) Knit Ltd* v. *Kammgarn Spinnerei GmbH*, n.391 above, 721, 732–733; *Arneg SpA* v. *Arneg Refrigeration Ltd* (1983) 134 NLJ 61 (CA); *Case Poclain Corporation Ltd* v. *Jones*, The Times, 7 May 1986 (CA); *Isovel Contracts Ltd* v. *ABB Building Technologies*, n.393 above, [15]–[22]. See generally A.G. Guest, n.3 above, [4-008].

is a valid defence where a liquidated amount is involved,[397] but it cannot be raised where the amount involved is unascertained or unliquidated.[398] Thus, a claim for damages due under an underlying c.i.f. contract of sale cannot form the basis of a defence to an action on a bill of exchange drawn for the price. Neither can the claim involved be raised by way of a set-off or a counterclaim.[399] The position of a 'holder for value' who is not a 'holder in due course' is not expressly defined in the BEA 1882. Conceptually, such a holder is one who cannot, for some technical reason, be considered a holder in due course. Examples of persons who might constitute a 'holder for value' include a transferee who gives value for a bill of exchange that is irregularly indorsed and the ostensible payee of a bill of exchange, since as discussed above such a person cannot be a 'holder in due course'.[400]

The 'value' or consideration necessary to support a bill of exchange is defined in section 27(1) of the BEA 1882 as encompassing any consideration sufficient to support a simple contract, and also an antecedent debt or liability. Past consideration is, thus, good consideration for a bill of exchange.[401] Accordingly, if a customer negotiates to his bank a cheque payable to his order, so as to reduce an existing overdraft, the bank will become a holder for value of the instrument, as the preexisting debt or overdraft is sufficient consideration for the transfer of the cheque to the bank.[402] Although section 27(1) of the BEA 1882 abrogates the rule against past consideration, it does not modify the principle that consideration must move from the promisee. The better view is that an antecedent debt or liability of a third party does not without more constitute value for the negotiation of a bill of exchange.[403] There may be consideration for the bill of exchange, however, where there has been a promise to forbear or actual forbearance from suing a third party debtor[404] or there exists 'some relationship between the receipt of the bill and the antecedent debt or

---

[397] *Forman v. Wright*, n.395 above, 492–494; *Agra and Masterman's Bank Ltd v. Leighton* (1866) LR 2 Ex. 56, 64, 65; *Robinson v. Marsh* [1921] 2 KB 640, 646 (CA); *Nova (Jersey) Knit Ltd v. Kammgarn Spinnerei GmbH*, n.391 above, 720; *Thoni GmbH & Co. KG v. RTP Equipment Ltd*, n.395 above, 284–285; *Case Poclain Corporation Ltd v. Jones*, n.396 above; *MK International Development Co. Ltd v. Housing Bank*, n.93 above; *Hofer v. Strawson* [1999] 2 BCLC 336; *Safa Ltd v. Banque du Caire*, n.393 above, 605; *Solo Industries UK Ltd v. Canara Bank*, n.362 above, [22]; *Isovel Contracts Ltd v. ABB Building Technologies*, n.393 above, [15]–[21]. See generally A.G. Guest, n.3 above, [4-009].

[398] *Sully v. Frean* (1854) 10 Exch. 535; *Warwick v. Nairn* (1855) 10 Exch. 762; *Nova (Jersey) Knit Ltd v. Kammgarn Spinnerei GmbH*, n.391 above, 720; *Case Poclain Corporation Ltd v. Jones*, n.396 above; *Isovel Contracts Ltd v. ABB Building Technologies*, n.393 above, [20].

[399] *Nova (Jersey) Knit Ltd v. Kammgarn Spinnerei GmbH*, n.391 above, 720–722, 729–733.

[400] *R. E. Jones Ltd v. Waring & Gillow Ltd*, n.376 above, 680.

[401] E. Peel, *Treitel's Law of Contract* (12th edn., London, 2007), [3-018].

[402] *M'Lean v. Clydesdale Banking Co.* (1883) 9 App. Cas. 95, 111 (HL). See also *Ex p. Richdale* (1882) 19 Ch. D 409, 417 (CA); *Royal Bank of Scotland v. Tottenham*, n.157 above, 717; *Capital & Counties Bank v. Gordon*, n.115 above, 244–245; *Barclays Bank Ltd v. Astley Industrial Trust Ltd*, n.375 above, 539; *Edmonton Savings & Credit Union Ltd v. North East Flooring, Nova Real Estate Corporation Ltd* (1985) 60 AR 219, [43] (AQB); *National Australia Bank Ltd v. KDS Construction Service Pty Ltd* (1987) 76 ALR 27 (HCA); *Belarus Equipment of Canada Ltd v. C&M Equipment (Brooks) Ltd* (1994) 161 AR 246, [35]–[56] (AQB). As regards a consideration that fails *in toto*, see *Miller Associates (Australia) Pty. Ltd v. Bennington Pty. Ltd*, n.121 above, noted in (1981) 55 *ALJ* 135. As regards the effect of furnishing an illegal consideration, see *Ladup Ltd v. Shaikh*, n.256 above. See generally A.G. Guest, n.3 above, [4-011]–[4-023].

[403] *Crears v. Hunter* (1887) 19 QBD 341; *Pollway Ltd v. Abdullah*, n.15 above, 497; *Hasan v. Willson*, n.93 above, 441. See also *Oliver v. Davis*, n.93 above, 741–742; *MK International Development Co. Ltd v. Housing Bank*, n.93 above; *Wheeler v. Roberts*, n.93 above; *Lomax Leisure Ltd v. Miller*, n.90 above, [21]–[25], [47]–[50]. See further A.G. Guest, n.3 above, [4-023]; N. Elliott, J. Odgers, & M. Phillips, n.93 above, [19–011].

[404] A.G. Guest, n.3 above, [4-023].

liability'[405] or a commercial relationship between the drawer and the third party debtor.[406] There is a statutory modification to the principle that consideration must move from the promisee in section 27(2) of the BEA 1882, which provides that if value has at any time been given for the bill of exchange, the holder is deemed to be a holder for value as regards the acceptor and all persons who have become parties to the instrument prior to such time.[407] However, the holder who eventually furnishes consideration may be regarded as a promisee of all prior parties. He is within their contemplation when they assume liability on the bill of exchange. The principle that past consideration is adequate value for a bill of exchange is closely related to an additional rule. Where the holder of a bill of exchange has a lien on it arising either from contract or by implication of law, he is deemed to be a holder for value to the extent of the sum for which he has the lien.[408] In the majority of the cases, such a lien is based on a contract or implied by law in respect of a debt incurred before the issuing of the bill of exchange in question.

As already stated, the BEA 1882 does not define the rights of a 'holder for value'. For most practical purposes, he is in the same position as a mere holder.[409] Thus, his rights are defeated if the bill of exchange was obtained by means of fraud[410] or duress, or if there were any other defects of the type specified in section 29(2) of the BEA 1882. This proposition is based on the language of the legislation itself. Section 38(2) renders the rights of a 'holder in due course' effective, notwithstanding the defects in question, but the BEA 1882 fails to confer similar rights on a person who, though not a 'holder in due course', is a 'holder for value'. The latter's rights are, therefore, principally governed by section 38(1) of the BEA 1882, which is applicable to those who are not 'holders in due course'. At the same time, some defences cannot be raised against a 'holder for value' because he has furnished consideration for the bill of exchange. Thus, the absence of consideration between prior parties does not constitute a valid defence against him.[411] In respect of partial failure of consideration, it is necessary to recall the distinction between immediate parties and remote parties. An immediate party is entitled to plead partial failure of consideration as a defence to an action by a 'holder for value', provided the 'partial failure' involves an ascertained and liquidated amount.[412] For instance, if a seller supplies only one half of the

---

[405] *Oliver* v. *Davis*, n.93 above, 735.

[406] *Autobiography Ltd* v. *Byrne*, n.96 above, as explained in *Lomax Leisure Ltd* v. *Miller*, n.90 above, [49]. In *Oliver* v. *Davis*, n.93 above, 736, Lord Evershed MR stated that 'you must find something in the transaction sufficient at the very least to connect the receipt of the bill with the antecedent debt or liability'. Similar suggestions have been made in Australia (*Walsh, Spriggs, Nolan & Finney* v. *Hoag & Bosch Pty Ltd*, n.97 above; *Dventures Pty Ltd* v. *Wily*, n.97 above), Canada (*Albert Pearl (Management) Ltd* v. *JDF Builders Ltd*, n.97 above, 879; *Toronto-Dominion Bank* v. *Cordi*, n.97 above, [8]–[11]), and New Zealand (*Bonior* v. *Siery Ltd*, n.97 above, 258; *Electrical Technologies Ltd* v. *Auckland Electrical Services Ltd*, n.97 above, 728–729; *Wrightson Farmers Finance Ltd* v. *Alan Hiscox Ltd*, n.97 above; *Garratt Enterprises Ltd* v. *Lynds*, n.97 above).

[407] *Scott* v. *Lifford* (1808) 1 Camp. 246; *Diamond* v. *Graham* [1968] 1 WLR 1061, 1064; *Mackenzie Mills* v. *Buono*, n.375 above. See also *Yan* v. *Post Office Bank Ltd*, n.77 above, 163.

[408] BEA 1882, s.27(3). See also *Midland Bank Ltd* v. *Reckitt* [1933] AC 1, 18–19 (HL); *Barclays Bank Ltd* v. *Astley Industrial Trust Ltd*, n.375 above, 538–539; *Bank of Credit and Commerce International SA* v. *Dawson*, n.368 above.

[409] *Whistler* v. *Forster* (1863) 14 CB (NS) 248, 258, approved in *Bank of Cyprus (London) Ltd* v. *Jones*, n.370 above.

[410] *Österreichische Länderbank* v. *S'Elite Ltd*, n.369 above. See also *Universal Import Export* v. *Bank of Scotland*, 1994 SCLR 944 (OH).

[411] This follows from BEA 1882, s.27(2). See also *Mills* v. *Barber* (1836) 1 M & W 425, 430–431; *Barber* v. *Richards* (1851) 6 Ex. 63; *MK International Development Co. Ltd* v. *Housing Bank*, n.93 above; *Sum Wing Credits Ltd* v. *Shun Yip Textiles Ltd* [1988] 1 HKC 405, 410–411; cf. *Forman* v. *Wright*, n.395 above, 492–494.

[412] N.397 above. See also A.G. Guest, n.3 above, [4-009].

goods, he cannot recover more than one half of the amount of the bill of exchange drawn for the price and accepted by the buyer.[413] The same applies if the drawer's breach entitles the acceptor to a quantified or liquidated amount by way of compensation or damages.[414] If goods turn out to be of an inferior quality, however, whereupon the buyer becomes entitled to recover an amount of damages to be determined by the court, this claim cannot be raised as a defence to the seller's action on the bill of exchange.[415] Partial failure of consideration does not appear to afford a defence against a remote party who is a 'holder for value', even if the deficiency or loss is liquidated.[416] In *Watson* v. *Russell*,[417] it was suggested that total failure of consideration does not constitute a defence to an action brought by a 'holder for value' who is a remote party. This view deserves support. As a remote party who is a 'holder for value' has furnished consideration for the bill of exchange, it seems irrelevant that a consideration furnished by prior parties has failed.

Usually the holder of a bill of exchange is entitled to judgment for its full amount, but when he sues as an agent or trustee for another person, or when he sues wholly or in part for another person, any defence or set-off available against that person may be raised, *pro tanto*, against the holder.[418] A stay of execution may then be ordered in respect of that part of the instrument's amount that the holder seeks to recover on behalf, or for the benefit, of the third party.[419] The judgment itself will be for the full amount of the bill of exchange. The enforcement of the holder's right of action depends, however, on his performing certain duties imposed by the BEA 1882. Some, which arise only if the bill of exchange is dishonoured by the drawee, are discussed subsequently, but there are two basic duties with which the holder has to comply whilst the instrument is current. The first is to effect presentment for acceptance where the bill of exchange is of the type that needs to be so presented.[420] The rules as to what constitutes valid presentment for acceptance are technical.[421] Basically, presentment for acceptance has to be made to the drawee personally or to his authorized agent at a reasonable hour on a business day and before the bill of exchange is overdue. If the instrument is payable at a fixed time after sight, the holder has to present it for acceptance or negotiate it within a reasonable time.[422] Presentment for acceptance is excused in certain cases, including when such presentment cannot be effected despite the

---

[413] *Agra and Masterman's Bank* v. *Leighton*, n.397 above, 65, 66.

[414] *Thoni GmbH* v. *RTP Equipment Ltd*, n.395 above, 285. See also *Isovel Contracts Ltd* v. *ABB Building Technologies*, n.393 above, [17]–[18].

[415] *Fielding and Platt Ltd* v. *Najjar* [1969] 1 WLR 357, 361 (CA); *All Trades Distributors Ltd* v. *Agencies Kaufman* (1969) 113 SJ 995; *Montecchi* v. *Shimco (UK) Ltd* [1979] 1 WLR 1180; *Montebiano Industrie Tessili SpA* v. *Carlyle Mills (London) Ltd* [1981] 1 Lloyd's Rep. 509; *Re Mitrebrook Ltd* (Ch. Div., 18 October 1994). See also *Yeo Hiap Seng* v. *Australian Food Corp. Pte Ltd* [1991] 1 SLR 567, 575–576; *Wong Fook Heng* v. *Amixco Asia Pte Ltd* [1992] 2 SLR 342, 345–346 (SGCA); *Yuen Chak Construction Co. Ltd* v. *Tak Son Contractors Ltd* [1997] 3 HKC 294, 298–299; *Fu Tai Industrial Ltd* v. *Decapio International Industrial Ltd* [2000] 3 HKC 259, 261–262; *XChrx Townearn Industrial Ltd* v. *Golden Globe Holdings Ltd* [2002] HKCU 328, [13]; *Ted Ohya* v. *Abdo A Osman* [2006] HKCU 28, [84]; *Wesco China Ltd* v. *Liu Fu Tien* [2007] 1 HKC 576, [27]–[29]; *Li Hu* v. *Hui Yan Sui William* [2009] HKCU 1526, [21].

[416] *Archer* v. *Bamford* (1822) 3 Stark 175; cf. *Harris (Oscar) Son & Co.* v. *Vallarman & Co.* [1940] 1 All ER 185 (CA) (which regards the rule as insufficiently settled to justify the striking out of an action).

[417] N.362 above, approved in *Dextra Bank & Trust Co. Ltd* v. *Bank of Jamaica* n.5 above, [22]. See also *Currie* v. *Misa* (1876) 1 App. Cas. 554, 566 (HL).

[418] *De La Chaumette* v. *Bank of England* (1829) 9 B & C 208 (as explained in *Currie* v. *Misa*, n.417 above, 570); *Thornton* v. *Maynard* (1875) LR 10 CP 685.

[419] *Barclays Bank Ltd* v. *Aschaffenburger Zellstoffwerke AG* [1967] 1 Lloyd's Rep. 387, 389 (CA). See also *Re Bunyard, ex p. Newton* (1880) 16 Ch. D 330, 336; *Standard Chartered Bank* v. *Fook Choy Audio Sdn Bhd* [1988] 1 MLJ 443, 443–444. Cf. *Nova (Jersey) Knit Ltd* v. *Kammgarn Spinnerei GmbH*, n.391 above.

[420] BEA 1882, s.39. See further Sect. 8(ii) above.   [421] Ibid, s.41(1).   [422] Ibid., s.40(1).

exercise of due diligence by the holder.[423] The second 'duty' is that, every bill of exchange must be presented by its holder for payment.[424] Basically, the instrument must be presented when it is due, at a reasonable business hour, and at the proper place for payment. This place is usually either the drawee's place of business or an address specified for presentment in the bill of exchange. The instrument may, for example, be made payable by the acceptor at the premises of a given bank.[425] Unlike presentment for acceptance, presentment for payment is a localized rather than a personalized exercise. Delays in presentment for payment, or non-presentment of a bill of exchange, are excused, *inter alia*, where presentment cannot be effected despite the exercise of reasonable diligence,[426] such as where the premises of the domiciled bank are closed on the bill of exchange's maturity date. In addition, a party cannot complain of the holder's failure to present a bill of exchange for payment if, as between himself and the drawee, that party was not entitled to expect the discharge of the instrument.[427] Presentment for payment may also be waived by a party to the bill of exchange.[428]

If a bill of exchange is dishonoured by the drawee by non-acceptance or non-payment, the holder acquires an immediate right of recourse against the drawer and the indorsers.[429] The holder has to comply with certain formalities, however, before he is entitled to enforce this right.[430] Even then, the holder's right is exercisable only against parties who have signed the bill of exchange without excluding recourse.[431] If the holder fails to present a bill of exchange for payment, the drawer and indorsers are discharged.[432] They are equally discharged if a bill of exchange payable after sight is not presented for acceptance or negotiated by the holder within a reasonable time.[433] The drawer and any indorser may waive, however, as regard himself, some or all of the holder's duties.[434] The drawer and indorser may, thus, agree to remain bound even if the holder fails to present the bill of exchange.

(iv) Negotiation of a bill of exchange

A bill of exchange is 'negotiated' when it is transferred from one person to another in such a manner as to constitute the transferee the instrument's 'holder'.[435] How a bill of exchange is negotiated depends upon whether the instrument is payable to the order of a specified payee or to bearer. A bill of exchange is payable 'to bearer' if it is expressed to be so payable[436] and such an instrument can be transferred by the transferor simply deliver-

---

[423] Ibid., s.41(2).   [424] Sect. 5(ii) above.

[425] BEA 1882, s.45(4).

[426] Ibid., ss.46(1), 46(2)(*a*). See also *Cornelius* v. *Banque Franco-Serbe* [1942] 1 KB 29 (presentation rendered impossible by German invasion of Holland).

[427] Ibid., s.46(2)(*c*)–(*d*). Under BEA 1882, s.46(2)(*c*), presentment is dispensed with as against the drawer, if the drawee or acceptor is not bound as between himself and the drawer to accept or pay the bill of exchange, and the drawer had no reason to believe that the instrument would be paid if presented. In *Fiorentino Comm Giuseppe Srl* v. *Farnesi*, n.75 above, [47]–[58], Nicholas Warren QC held that the issue of the drawer's belief should be assessed at the time that the instrument would otherwise have been presented. See also *Aziz* v. *Mayfair Casinos Ltd*, n.258 above.

[428] Ibid., s.46(2)(*e*).

[429] Ibid., ss.43(2) (non-acceptance), 47(2) (non-payment). See *Fiorentino Comm Giuseppe Srl* v. *Farnesi*, n.75 above, [63].

[430] Sect. 8(vi) below.   [431] BEA 1882, s.16(1).   [432] Ibid., s.45.

[433] Ibid., s.40(2). In the case of other bills, the failure to present the bill for acceptance postpones the holder's right to present it for payment: BEA 1882, s.39(2).

[434] Ibid., s.16(2).   [435] Ibid., s.31(1).   [436] Ibid., s.8(3). See also *Sutters* v. *Briggs*, n.116 above.

ing it to the transferee, without the need for any indorsement.[437] Where a bearer bill is transferred without indorsement, the transferor is termed a 'transferor by delivery'.[438] Whilst such a party is not liable on the bearer bill of exchange,[439] when he negotiates the instrument he warrants 'to his immediate transferee being a holder for value that the bill is what it purports to be, that he has a right to transfer it, and that at the time of transfer he is not aware of any fact which renders it valueless'.[440] This warranty accordingly enables a 'holder for value'[441] to bring an action on the bearer instrument against his immediate transferor, and if the instrument turns out to be worthless, the transferee may seek restitution of the amount paid to the transferor.[442] In practice, however, the transferee of a 'bearer' bill of exchange may still request that the transferor indorse the instrument in order to ensure that the latter is liable on the instrument as indorser. The rights available to the transferee of a bearer instrument are not similarly available to its drawee when the instrument is presented for acceptance or payment, as such presentation does not involve the transfer of the instrument and accordingly does not trigger the statutory warranty relating to the authenticity or validity of the instrument.[443]

In contrast, an 'order' bill of exchange is negotiated by the indorsement of the payee, or of the indorsee to whom it has been specially indorsed, and by the delivery of the instrument.[444] An 'order' bill of exchange is an instrument drawn payable to a designated payee or to such a payee's order,[445] and it retains this status as long as the transferees execute 'special indorsements' on the instrument.[446] A 'special indorsement' occurs where the transferor of a bill of exchange signs the instrument and specifies the name of the indorsee or transferee.[447] In addition to being written on the instrument and signed by the indorser, the indorsement must purport to transfer 'the entire bill'.[448] A person will usually indorse a bill of exchange in his own name, although if a person is wrongly designated in a bill of exchange or their name misspelt, he may indorse the instrument according to the manner in which he is identified and add his ordinary signature.[449] This is, however, not mandatory, so that an indorsement by the payee of a bill of exchange in his own name will be valid even if he is misdescribed in the instrument.[450] Until the delivery of the instrument under the indorser's authority,[451] the latter's contract with other parties to the bill of exchange is incomplete and revocable,[452] although a valid and unconditional delivery by the indorser will be presumed, until the contrary is proved, where the instrument is no longer in his possession.[453] As against a holder in due course, however, valid delivery by the indorser is conclusively presumed.[454] Where an 'order' bill of exchange is delivered without indorsement, the transferee only acquires such title to the instrument

---

[437] Ibid., s.31(2). As regards delivery, see ibid., s.21.   [438] Ibid., s.58(1).   [439] Ibid., s.58(2).

[440] Ibid., s.58(3). There is no such liability to subsequent parties: *Miller Associates (Australia) Pty. Ltd* v. *Bennington Pty. Ltd*, n.121 above.

[441] Ibid., s. 27(1)–(3).

[442] *Gurney* v. *Womersley* (1854) 4 E & B 133; *Kennedy* v. *Panama, New Zealand & Australian Royal Mail Co.* (1867) LR 2 QB 580, 586.

[443] *Guaranty Trust Co. of New York* v. *Hannay & Co.*, n.292 above, 631–632.

[444] Ibid., s.31(3). For the position regarding cheques delivered to a bank for collection, see Cheques Act 1957, s.2. See further Ch. 15, Sect. 6 below.

[445] Ibid., s.8(4)–(5).

[446] Ibid., s.31(3). Where there are several indorsements on a bill of exchange, these are deemed to have been made in the order in which they appear on the instrument: ibid., s.32(5).

[447] Ibid., s.34(2).   [448] Ibid., s.32(1)–(2).   [449] Ibid., s.32(4).

[450] *Bird & Co. (London) Ltd* v. *Thomas. Cook & Son Ltd* [1937] 2 All ER 227; *Arab Bank Ltd* v. *Ross*, n.365 above. A material discrepancy between the payee's indorsement and his description in the instrument will prevent a transferee being a holder in due course: *Arab Bank Ltd* v. *Ross*, n.365 above.

[451] BEA 1882, s.21(2)(a).   [452] Ibid., s.21(1).   [453] Ibid., s.21(3).   [454] Ibid., s.21(2).

as the transferor,[455] although he does acquire the right to have the transferor's indorsement.[456] Without such an indorsement, the transferee remains a mere assignee of the chose in action embodied in the bill of exchange, and cannot acquire any rights superior to those of the transferor.[457] An 'order' instrument will be converted into a 'bearer' instrument where the last indorsement on the instrument is executed 'in blank'.[458] An indorser executes an 'indorsement in blank' by signing the instrument without designating a specific person as indorsee to whom it is payable.[459] Whilst the BEA 1882 does not explicitly indicate whether the execution of a special indorsement on a 'bearer' instrument converts it into an 'order' instrument, such a view was rejected by the New South Wales Supreme Court in *Miller Associates (Australia) Pty. Ltd* v. *Bennington Pty. Ltd*,[460] although as discussed previously this last view may be questionable.[461]

There are, however, two limitations to the general principle that the indorsement and delivery of an 'order' bill of exchange is primarily a mechanism for negotiating the instrument. The first limitation is that the indorser may not actually intend to negotiate the instrument when he indorses and delivers it, but may have some other purpose in mind. For example, a bill of exchange may be indorsed solely with the aim of making the indorser liable on the instrument, so that (as against a party other than a 'holder in due course') the indorser's delivery of the instrument back to the drawer will be 'for a special purpose only'.[462] In such a case, the indorser effectively acts as a surety,[463] thereby giving the instrument extra currency. A further example is where the bill of exchange is indorsed and delivered to a collecting bank simply to facilitate the instrument's collection.[464] Usually, the indorser will clarify that this is his intention by adding words such as 'pay Bank X for collection' to the instrument,[465] but it has also been suggested that the indorser's intention when indorsing an instrument can be inferred from the surrounding circumstances, including the nature of the instrument itself.[466] Such inferences should, however, be drawn with care, and the better view is probably that, in the absence of clear evidence to the contrary, an indorsement on a bill of exchange should be regarded as being for the purpose of negotiation.[467]

The second limitation is that the bill of exchange may no longer be negotiable. This may occur in a number of ways. First, according to section 8(1) of the BEA 1882, '[w]hen a bill contains words prohibiting transfer, or indicating an intention that it should not be transferable, it is valid as between the parties thereto, but is not negotiable'. Whatever words a drawer chooses to mark on the face of the instrument in order to restrict transferability, and hence negotiability, those words must clearly evince an intention to prohibit transfer and prevent third parties becoming a 'holder' of the instrument. A bill of

---

[455] Ibid., s.31(4).   [456] Id. See also *Walters* v. *Neary* (1904) 21 TLR 146.

[457] *Whistler* v. *Forster*, n.409 above; *Geo. Thompson (Aust.) Pty. Ltd* v. *Vittadello*, n.2 above, 208–212; *Bank of Cyprus (London) Ltd* v. *Jones*, n.370 above; *Re Neal* (1993) 114 ALR 659 (FCA).

[458] Ibid., s.8(3). As with a cheque, a bill of exchange may be treated as payable to bearer if the payee is a fictitious or non-existing person (BEA 1882, s.7(3)), but this will not be the case when the drawer is induced by a fraudulent misrepresentation to make a cheque payable to a designated real person. See further Sect. 3(iii) above.

[459] Ibid., s.34(1).   [460] N.121 above.   [461] Sect. 3(iii) above.   [462] BEA 1882, s.21(2)(b).

[463] Sect. 8(ii) above.

[464] Consider Cheques Act 1957, s.2 (delivery of 'order' cheque to bank for collection). See further Ch. 15, Sect. 6 below.

[465] *McDonald (Gerald) & Co.* v. *Nash & Co.*, n.342 above, 634.

[466] *Miller Associates (Australia) Pty. Ltd* v. *Bennington Pty. Ltd*, n.121 above, (payee's signature on a cheque payable to himself 'or bearer' was not an indorsement, since the instrument was transferable by mere delivery).

[467] BEA 1882, s.56 only defines the liability incurred by the execution of a security indorsement, but not its effect as regards the negotiation of a bill of exchange. See further Sect. 8(ii) above.

exchange drawn payable to 'X only' would satisfy this requirement,[468] but not an instrument that is simply drawn payable to a particular person without adding the words 'or order' or any words prohibiting transfer. Such an instrument remains payable to the particular person's order,[469] as does an instrument where the printed words 'or bearer' or 'or order' on the instrument's face have been deleted. Secondly, a 'restrictive indorsement' can render a bill of exchange non-negotiable. An indorsement is restrictive where it either 'prohibits the further negotiation of the bill' or states that it is not intended to effect a transfer of the instrument but to operate as 'a mere authority to deal with the bill as thereby directed'.[470] An indorsement will be restrictive if accompanied by words such as 'pay D only', 'Pay D for the account of D', or 'Pay D for collection',[471] but not if accompanied by a statement to the effect that consideration has been furnished by a third party[472] or if the indorsement is to a specific person without the addition of the words 'or order'.[473] Whilst an indorsee under a restrictive indorsement cannot generally qualify as a 'holder in due course' (given his knowledge of the defect in his transferor's title)[474] and cannot generally transfer the instrument, such an indorsee nevertheless retains the right to receive payment of the instrument and to sue any party that is liable to his transferor.[475] Where the indorsee misappropriates the amount paid to him against the bill of exchange, however, the drawee is not liable to the indorser who restricted transfer.[476] Even in the case of a restrictive indorsement, however, it is possible for the indorsee to be expressly authorized to effect *some* types of transfer.[477] Where such transfers are permitted, all subsequent indorsees have the same rights and liabilities under the bill of exchange as the initial 'restricted indorsee'.[478]

A bill of exchange may be negotiated multiple times following its discount. In this regard, bills of exchange differ from cheques, which in virtually every case nowadays are paid by payees to the credit of their accounts for collection. Where a bill of exchange is transferred back to a party already liable on the instrument, such as the drawer or an indorser, such a party may reissue the bill and negotiate it over again.[479] As a matter of practice, such a party will usually strike out all the indorsements executed by intermediary parties, but this does not discharge parties who were liable to him initially. In order to avoid circuity of action, however, a party who regains a bill of exchange may not enforce the instrument 'against any intervening party to whom he was previously liable'.[480] Accordingly, where the drawer of a bill of exchange negotiates that instrument to 'B' who in turn negotiates to 'C' and then back to the drawer, the drawer cannot sue 'B' or 'C'. Where a prior party regains possession of an instrument in this way, it has been suggested that the drawer or an indorser (as the case may be) is to be treated as a 'holder in due course' as against the acceptor, provided this status was enjoyed by the party from

---

[468] *Hibernian Bank Ltd* v. *Gysin and Hanson*, n.148 above. An acceptor may impose restrictions on an instrument's negotiability: *Meyer & Co.* v. *Decroix, Verley et Cie* [1891] AC 520 (HL).

[469] BEA 1882, s.8(4).   [470] Ibid., s.35(1).   [471] Id.

[472] *Buckley* v. *Jackson* (1868) LR 3 Ex. 135.

[473] Such an instrument is treated as if the words 'or order' are included and accordingly remains negotiable: BEA 1882, ss.8(4), 34(3).

[474] In contrast, a restrictive indorsement does not put the instrument's drawee or acceptor on enquiry.

[475] BEA 1882, s.35(2).   [476] *Williams Deacon & Co.* v. *Shadbolt* (1885) 1 TLR 417.

[477] 'Pay X or order for collection' would be a restrictive indorsement that still enables the indorsee to effect a transfer.

[478] BEA 1882, s.35(3).

[479] Ibid., s.37, although this is subject to the provisions concerning discharge of instruments: ibid., ss.59–64.

[480] Id. See also A.G. Guest, n.3 above, [5-051–5-052].

whom the drawer or indorser acquired the instrument back.[481] This reasoning may be questionable, however, as section 37 of the BEA 1882 does not purport to confer any right on a party who regains a bill of exchange, except the power to reissue the instrument.

(v) Discharge of a bill

When a bill of exchange is discharged, it ceases to be a negotiable instrument and all rights based upon it are extinguished.[482] To this absolute rule, there appears to be an exception where the discharged instrument purports to have been negotiated for valuable consideration to a party acting in good faith. Such an indorsee would probably have a claim against the person who purported to transfer the instrument for breach of the indorser's statutory warranties.[483] More controversial, however, is the suggestion that such an indorsee may enforce the discharged instrument according to its tenor against the acceptor by virtue of being a 'holder in due course'.[484] The principal difficulty with this suggestion stems from the fact that, where a bill of exchange is payable at a fixed future date, a person can no longer become a 'holder in due course' if he takes the instrument after it is overdue.[485] Nevertheless, where the discharged instrument is payable on demand, and the instrument does not appear on its face to have been in circulation for an unreasonable period of time,[486] it may be possible for a person to become a 'holder in due course'.[487] Given that such an instrument may no longer be negotiated after discharge, however, the better view is probably that a *bona fide* purchaser of a discharged instrument acquires no rights against the acceptor,[488] but only has such rights as the BEA 1882 confers upon him as against his immediate transferor.

There are five ways in which a bill of exchange may be discharged. First, this may occur by payment in due course to a 'holder'[489] by the drawee or acceptor at or after maturity, provided payment is made in good faith and without notice of any defect in the holder's title.[490] Payment does not necessarily have to be in cash.[491] Whilst payment to a person who holds an 'order' bill of exchange under a forged indorsement does not discharge the instrument,[492] payment to the thief of a bearer bill of exchange does discharge the instrument as the thief does not hold it pursuant to an indorsement.[493] Similarly, an instrument is discharged where a drawee in good faith pays an indorsee who has obtained a bill of exchange by fraud.[494] In contrast, payment by the drawer does not discharge a bill of exchange,[495] unless it is an accommodation bill.[496] That said, where a drawer pays a bill of exchange payable to a third party or to his order, the drawer may enforce payment against the instrument's acceptor, but may not re-issue it.[497] Alternatively, 'where a bill payable to drawer's order is paid by the drawer', the drawer is restored to his former rights against

[481] *Jade International Steel Stahl und Eisen GmbH & Co. KG* v. *Robert Nicholas (Steels) Ltd*, n.354 above. See also *Provincial Bank of Canada* v. *Beneficial Finance Co of Canada*, n.354 above.

[482] *Harmer* v. *Steele* (1849) 4 Exch. 1, 13; *Burchfield* v. *Moore* (1854) 23 LJQB 261.

[483] BEA 1882, ss.55(2)(c), 58(3).

[484] *Glassock* v. *Balls* (1889) 24 QBD 13, 15; cf. *Harmer* v. *Steele*, n.482 above, 13.

[485] BEA 1882, s.29(1)(a).   [486] Ibid., s.36(3).

[487] Indeed, there may be an argument that an acceptor who fails to indicate that the bill has been discharged is estopped from asserting this fact.

[488] A.G. Guest, n.3 above, [8-003].   [489] BEA 1882, s.2.   [490] Ibid., s.59(1).

[491] *Re York St Mezzanine Pty Ltd*, n.301 above, [24]–[26].

[492] Such a person does not qualify as a 'holder': Sects. 3(iii) & 8(iii) above.   [493] BEA 1882, s.31(2).

[494] *Robarts* v. *Tucker* (1851) 16 QB 560, 576–577, 579.

[495] BEA 1882, s.59(2). See also *Murray* v. *Morel & Co. Ltd* [2007] 3 NZLR 721, [135]–[138] (NZSC).

[496] Ibid., s.59(3).   [497] Ibid., s.59(2)(a).

the acceptor and any antecedent parties, may strike out his own indorsement, and may negotiate the instrument over again.[498] In addition, by making payment to a 'holder', a drawer is entitled to be subrogated *vis-à-vis* the acceptor to any securities that the acceptor has given to the holder.[499]

Secondly, a bill of exchange will be discharged if its acceptor becomes its holder at or after maturity.[500] This will only occur if the acceptor acquires the instrument 'in his own right',[501] which would not generally cover the situation where the acceptor acquires the instrument as agent or in some other representative capacity,[502] but may cover the situation where the acceptor becomes the holder's executor or administrator.[503] A bill of exchange is discharged if indorsed at maturity to one of several joint acceptors; the remaining acceptors will not be liable on the instrument, but may be liable to contribute as joint debtors.[504] Thirdly, where the holder of a bill of exchange 'absolutely and unconditionally' renounces his rights against the acceptor, the instrument is discharged.[505] Such renunciation can either be made in writing or by delivering the instrument to the acceptor[506] or his executor or administrator with the intention that it be discharged.[507] Whilst such a renunciation may release other parties to the bill of exchange from their liability, the rights of a subsequent 'holder in due course' are unaffected.[508] Fourthly, a bill of exchange is discharged if the holder or his agent intentionally cancels the instrument by making this obvious on the bill's face,[509] unless the holder can demonstrate that the purported cancellation was effected unintentionally, by mistake or without his authority.[510]

Finally, a bill of exchange is avoided where there is a 'material alteration' to the instrument itself, or to an acceptance executed upon it, without the assent of all the parties to it.[511] Indeed, the only parties who remain bound by a materially altered bill of exchange are the person(s) who made or assented to the alteration and those who have taken the instrument subsequently.[512] There is a non-exhaustive statutory list of alterations that will be treated as material,[513] namely alterations to the instrument's date,[514] sum payable, time of payment, or place of payment, and the addition of a place of payment without the acceptor's assent when the bill has been accepted generally. Beyond these

---

[498] Ibid., s.59(2)(b). The position is the same when an indorser makes payment: id.

[499] *Duncan, Fox & Co. v. North and South Wales Bank*, n.319 above, 10. See also *Commissioners of State Savings Bank of Victoria v. Patrick Intermarine Acceptances Ltd* [1981] 1 NSWLR 175, 180; *Scholefield Goodman & Sons Ltd v. Zyngier*, n.319 above (noted in [1986] *JBL* 399); *Becton Dickinson UK Ltd v. Zwebner* [1989] QB 208; *Niru Battery Manufacturing Co v. Milestone Trading Ltd (No. 2)* [2003] EWHC 1032 (Comm.), [30]–[31]; *Berghoff Trading Ltd v. Swinbrook Developments Ltd*, n.319 above, [26].

[500] BEA 1882, s.61.   [501] Id.   [502] *Nash v. De Freville* [1900] 2 QB 72, 89 (CA).

[503] A.G. Guest, n.3 above, [8-058]. See also *Jenkins v. Jenkins* [1928] 2 KB 501. See further Administration of Estates Act 1925, s.21A.

[504] *Harmer v. Steele*, n.482 above; cf. *Forster, Hight & Co. v. Ward* (1883) 1 Cab. & E 168.

[505] BEA 1882, s.62(1).

[506] Id. See also *Rimalt v. Cartwright* (1924) 40 TLR 803 (CA) (composition by acceptor with his creditors is not a renunciation).

[507] *Edwards v. Walters* [1896] 2 Ch. 157 (CA). Cf. *D. Gokal & Co. (HK) Ltd v. Rippleworth Ltd* [1998] 11 CL 370.   [508] BEA 1882, s.62(2).

[509] Ibid., s.63(1). See also *Bank of Scotland v. Dominion Bank* [1891] AC 592 (HL); *Royal Securities Corporation Ltd v. Montreal Trust Co.* [1967] 1 OR 137, 182–183 (OCJ). A holder in due course has occasionally been entitled to enforce a bill of exchange despite such cancellation: *Ingham v. Primrose* (1859) 7 CB (NS) 82 (bill of exchange that had been torn in two and discarded in the street by the acceptor was pasted together and successfully enforced by the innocent finder).   [510] Ibid., s.63(3).

[511] Ibid., s.64(1). This provision has been explained as an enactment of the rule in *Pigot's Case* (1614) 11 Co Rep 26b: *Habibsons Bank Ltd v. Standard Chartered Bank (Hong Kong) Ltd* [2010] EWCA Civ 1335, [28].

[512] Id. For the estoppels available, see Sect. 8(ii) above.

[513] Ibid., s.64(2).   [514] *Heller Factors Pty. Ltd v. Toy Corporation Pty. Ltd* [1984] 1 NSWLR 121.

examples, it is a question of fact whether a particular alteration is material or not.[515] For example, in *Smith* v. *Lloyds TSB Group plc*,[516] the Court of Appeal held that changing the payee on a cheque and banker's draft amounted to a material alteration. Where the relevant alteration to the bill of exchange is not deliberate, but merely accidental, the instrument is not avoided.[517] Similarly, an alteration to a bill of exchange is not material if it occurs before the instrument is completely issued, such as where an instrument accepted in blank by an acceptor is altered by the drawer,[518] although the position may be different if the same alteration occurred after the instrument has been issued.[519] Where a material alteration is 'not apparent', however, a 'holder in due course' may still enforce the instrument 'according to its original tenor',[520] so that where the amount payable is increased the instrument may still be enforced for the original amount.[521] According to Salter J in *Woollatt* v. *Stanley,* an alteration is 'apparent' if 'the intending holder on scrutinizing the document with reasonable care would observe that it had been altered'.[522]

(vi) **Procedure on dishonour**

A holder cannot bring an action on a bill of exchange against a drawee or acceptor unless it has been dishonoured when presented for acceptance or for payment. Following such dishonour, the holder must send a 'notice of dishonour' to the drawer and any indorsers advising them of the instrument's dishonour, otherwise the drawer and indorsers will be discharged of their liability to the holder on the instrument.[523] Such notice must be in writing or transmitted 'by personal communication',[524] must identify the instrument,[525] and must be given within a reasonable time of dishonour,[526] although delay in giving notice will be excused when this is attributable to 'circumstances beyond the control of the party giving notice'.[527] This can be achieved by simply returning the dishonoured instrument to the drawer or indorser.[528] As a holder may be unaware of the location of some prior indorsers, however, he may only be able to give notice to the immediate parties with whom he dealt. Accordingly, parties who receive notice of dishonour are similarly afforded a reasonable time to notify in turn the parties with whom they dealt.[529] Just as the acceptor is not discharged when the holder fails to present the bill of exchange for payment,[530] failure to give timely notice of dishonour does not discharge the acceptor's liability given that he is the party primarily obliged on the instrument. The holder's only duty to the bill of exchange's acceptor or drawee is to exhibit the instrument when he demands payment and to deliver it up when honoured.[531] As considered previously in relation to cheques,[532] where a dishonoured bill of exchange is, or purports on its face to be, a 'foreign bill',[533] then it is necessary for the instrument to be 'protested' in addition

---

[515]   *Gardner* v. *Walsh* (1855) E&B 83, 89; *Suffell* v. *Bank of England* (1882) 9 QBD 555, 565, 568, 574; *Slingsby* v. *District Bank Ltd* [1932] 1 KB 544 (CA). See generally A.G. Guest, n.3 above, [8-081]–[8-082].

[516]   N.86 above.   [517]   *Hong Kong and Shanghai Banking Corporation* v. *Lo* [1928] AC 181 (PC).

[518]   *Foster* v. *Driscoll* [1929] 1 KB 470, 494 (CA); *Koch* v. *Dicks,* n.262 above.

[519]   *Koch* v. *Dicks,* n.262 above. See also *Raiffeisen Zentralbank Österreich AG* v. *Crossseas Shipping Ltd* [2000] 1 WLR 1135, [19] (CA).

[520]   BEA 1882, s.64(1).   [521]   *Scholfield* v. *Londesborough* [1896] AC 514 (HL).

[522]   *Woollatt* v. *Stanley* (1928) 138 LT 620; *Automobile Finance Co. of Australia Ltd* v. *Law* (1933) 49 CLR 1, 10, 12 (HCA). See also Hudson, [1975] *JBL* 108.

[523]   BEA 1882, s.48. See further Sect. 5(iii) above.

[524]   Ibid., s.49(5); the notice has to identify the bill.   [525]   Id.   [526]   Ibid., s.49(12).

[527]   Ibid., s.50(1).   [528]   Ibid., s.49(6).   [529]   Ibid., s.49(14).   [530]   Ibid., s.52(1).

[531]   Ibid., s.52(4).   [532]   Sect. 5(iv) above.   [533]   BEA 1882, s.4(1).

to the holder sending a notice of dishonour.[534] Such a step is optional in the case of an 'inland bill'.[535]

9 Promissory notes

The other common type of negotiable instrument is the promissory note. These instruments serve an entirely different function to bills of exchange, as they are principally issued to secure the repayment of loan instalments or sums due under other types of commercial transaction. The principal advantage of a promissory note for the payee is that he may either receive early payment by discounting the instrument to a third party or sue for the face value of the instrument if dishonoured at maturity. In the latter case, the payee may obtain summary judgment for the amount of the instrument, as the defences that arise out of the underlying transaction are not necessarily available to an action on the note, even where the proceedings are between immediate parties.[536] As well as the differences in commercial use, promissory notes and bills of exchange differ in form— the latter involves the drawer giving the drawee an order to make payment, whilst the former involves the maker giving a promise to pay—so that an instrument taking the form of a bill of exchange may be reclassified as a promissory note and *vice versa*.[537] Since the maker of the promissory note effectively acts as both drawer and acceptor by both issuing the instrument and assuming the primary obligation to pay it, a note payable to the maker's own order does not become effective until indorsed by the maker.[538] Despite these differences, promissory notes and bills of exchange bear a close resemblance in conceptual terms. Accordingly, although some provisions of the BEA 1882 specifically have no application to promissory notes,[539] the BEA 1882 in general applies with the necessary modifications to promissory notes.[540] For the purpose of applying those provisions, the promissory note's maker is equated with a bill of exchange's acceptor and the note's first indorser is equated with the drawer of an accepted bill payable to his order.[541]

The legal requirements for a valid promissory note are the same as for bills of exchange: there must be an unconditional promise in writing signed by the maker to pay a sum certain at a fixed or determinable future time to the order of a specified payee or to bearer.[542] This definition can cover an 'IOU' embodying a promise to pay,[543] a bank cheque,[544] or any other document howsoever named that fulfils the statutory definition.[545] This definition may also encompass sterling commercial paper, which is generally issued by non-bank financial institutions and perform the same function as a 'negotiable certificate of deposit' (NCD). Whilst sterling commercial paper usually assumes the form of a promissory note payable to bearer,[546] NCDs usually just acknowledge the deposit of funds and accordingly

---

[534] Ibid., s.51(2).　　[535] Ibid., ss.4(1), 51(1)–(2).

[536] Sect. 8(iii) above. It has been held arguable that the terms of a promissory note could be contradicted by the terms of a contemporaneous oral agreement if the situation falls within one of the exceptions to the parole evidence rule: *Kazeminy* v. *Siddiqi* [2009] EWHC 3207 (Comm.), [50]–[54].

[537] BEA 1882, s.5(2). See also *Mason* v. *Lack* (1929) 45 TLR 363; *Haseldine* v. *Winstanley* [1939] 2 KB 101.

[538] Ibid., s.83(2).　　[539] Ibid., s.89(3).　　[540] Ibid., s.89(1).　　[541] Ibid., s.89(2).

[542] Ibid., s.83(1). See also *City Link Melbourne Ltd* v *Commissioner of Taxation* [2004] FCAFC 272, [33].

[543] *Brooks* v. *Elkins* (1836) 2 M&W 74; *Muir* v. *Muir*, 1912 1 SLT 304. A mere receipt for money is not a promissory note: *Akbar Khan* v. *Attar Singh* [1936] 2 All ER 545, 549–550 (PC).

[544] *Yan* v. *Post Office Bank Ltd*. n.77 above, 158–159; *Westpac Banking Corporation* v. *CIR* (2009) 24 NZTC 23,076, [34]–[41].

[545] *Klinac* v. *Lehmann* [2001] DCR 718, [33]–[35].

[546] R. MacVicar, 'Sterling Commercial Paper' (1986) 2 *BJIBFL* 40.

do not involve the payment promise necessary for a promissory note,[547] although they do probably constitute a novel form of negotiable instrument recognized by mercantile usage.[548] As regards the particular elements of the promissory note's statutory definition, the current view in the United Kingdom is that an instrument payable *before* or *not later than* a given day is not payable at a 'determinable future time' and accordingly not a valid promissory note,[549] although, as considered previously,[550] this view has been rejected in a number of other jurisdictions. As regards the requirement that a promissory note be for a 'sum certain', an instrument is still a valid note when it is payable by instalments, even where the instrument provides that the entire amount is payable upon failure to pay an instalment.[551] Although the definition of a promissory note refers to an unconditional promise 'made by *one* person to another',[552] it is clear that a note may refer to two or more makers who are either 'jointly' or 'jointly and severally' liable. In the case of joint liability, proceedings against, or a compromise with, one joint maker bars recourse against other joint makers, unlike the case of makers who are jointly and severally liable.[553] The mere fact that one joint maker is not liable on the note, such as where he is a minor, does not release the other joint maker.[554] Until its delivery, a promissory note remains 'inchoate and incomplete'.[555] As regards payment, there is no requirement to present a promissory note to the maker, unless it was made payable at a particular place,[556] although presentment is a precondition to the indorser's liability on the note.[557] Unlike cheques and bills of exchange, it is not necessary to protest a foreign note.[558]

10 Bills of exchange drawn under lines of credit and acceptance credits

An acceptance credit or a line of credit is a finance facility provided by a bank to its customer, whereby the bank undertakes to accept bills of exchange drawn by its customer payable to himself at a future date. By signing the bill of exchange as acceptor, the bank enables the customer to discount the instrument to a third party and thereby raise the necessary finance. Whilst the bank is primarily liable to the discounter as acceptor on the bill of exchange, as between itself and its customer the bank in reality acts in a role similar to that of a surety. This mismatch between the bank's formal role on the instrument and the role that it fulfils in reality gives rise to two particular difficulties.

The first difficulty is that any bills of exchange accepted by the bank under the 'acceptance credit' appear to have been so accepted for the customer's accommodation, which raises the issue of whether such instruments are 'accommodation bills'. According to the BEA 1882, '[a]n accommodation party to a bill is a person who has signed a bill as drawer,

---

[547] A.G. Guest, n.3 above, [15-018].

[548] *Customs and Excise Commissioners* v. *Guy Butler (International) Ltd* [1977] QB 377, 382.

[549] *Williamson* v. *Rider*, n.297 above, 97–98.   [550] Sect. 8(i) above.

[551] BEA 1882, s.9(1). See also *Kirkwood* v. *Carroll* [1903] 1 KB 531 (CA); *Gardiner* v. *Muir* (1917) 38 DLR 115, 117 (SCC); *Canadian Imperial Bank of Commerce* v. *Morgan*, n.312 above, [25].

[552] Ibid., s.83(1).

[553] *Kendall* v. *Hamilton* (1879) 4 App. Cas. 504 (HL); *Collier* v. *P&MJ Wright (Holdings) Ltd* [2007] BPIR 1452, [24] (CA); *Chelsea Building Society* v. *Nash* [2010] All ER (D) 180 (CA).

[554] *Wauthier* v. *Wilson* (1912) 28 TLR 239.   [555] BEA 1882, s.84.   [556] Ibid., s.87(1).

[557] Ibid., s.87(2). If the note is payable on demand, presentment must be effected within a reasonable time after its indorsement: BEA, s.86.

[558] Ibid., s.89(4).

acceptor, or indorser, without receiving value therefor, and for the purpose of lending his name to some other person'.[559] Whilst 'accommodation bills' are generally governed by the same principles as are applicable to other types of negotiable instrument, there are several important modifications that highlight the significance of determining whether a bill of exchange drawn under an acceptance credit is an accommodation bill. First, an accommodation party is liable to a holder for value of the bill of exchange, even if the holder knew at the time of taking the instrument that it had been accepted for accommodation purposes only.[560] This is consistent with the principle that absence or failure of consideration between prior parties is no defence, even if known to the holder for value.[561] That said, the accommodation party can raise as a defence any specific defect in the transferor's title of which the holder was aware when he took the 'accommodation bill'.[562] Secondly, the party accommodated is not necessarily discharged if the holder fails to present the 'accommodation bill' for payment[563] or fails to 'protest' the instrument or give notice of dishonour.[564] Thirdly, an 'accommodation bill' is discharged when the party accommodated pays the instrument in due course,[565] with the result that the instrument ceases to be a negotiable instrument and the accommodated party can no longer enforce the instrument against the acceptor[566] or re-issue it.[567]

Unfortunately, there is some confusion over whether a bill of exchange drawn under an acceptance credit is an 'accommodation bill' or not. In *Oriental Financial Corporation* v. *Overend, Gurney & Co.*,[568] Malins V-C considered that such instruments could not be 'accommodation bills', since the BEA 1882 required an accommodation party to act 'without receiving value therefor', and banks invariably charged a fee for issuing an acceptance credit. In contrast, in *Re Yglesias, ex p. Gomez*,[569] James LJ referred to the instruments before him as 'only accommodation acceptances for which [the drawee] charged commission', indicating that the charging of a fee under an acceptance credit is not necessarily inconsistent with their classification as 'accommodation bills'. This latter view finds some support in the High Court of Australia decision in *K.D. Morris & Sons Pty. Ltd* v. *Bank of Queensland Ltd*,[570] where bills issued under an acceptance facility were referred to obiter as 'accommodation bills', despite the issuing bank receiving an acceptance fee in return for its services. It is submitted that this second view is more consistent with the statutory requirement for an 'accommodation bill' that the accommodation party have accepted the instrument 'without receiving value therefor'.[571] The term 'therefor' makes clear that it is only when the bank receives the consideration in return for becoming party to the bills of exchange by accepting them that such instruments will fall outside the definition of 'accommodation bill'. In reality, however, a bank issuing an acceptance credit charges its fee for issuing that facility itself and in return for its promise to accept bills of exchange in

---

[559] Ibid., s.28(1). See also *Halloran* v. *Minister Administering National Parks and Wildlife Act 1974* [2006] HCA 3, [59]–[64].

[560] Ibid., s.28(2).   [561] A.G. Guest, n.3 above, [4-044].

[562] *Hornby* v. *McLaren* (1908) 24 TLR 494.   [563] BEA 1882, ss. 46(2)(*c*), 46(2)(*d*).

[564] Ibid., ss.50(2)(*c*), 50(2)(*d*), 51(9).   [565] Ibid., s.59(3).

[566] *Lazarus* v. *Cowrie* (1842) 3 QB 459; *Solomon* v. *Davis* (1883) 1 Cab. & E 83.

[567] Compare BEA, s.59(2)(*a*). See further Sect. 8(iii) above.

[568] (1871) LR 7 Ch. App. 142. Although the point was left open on appeal, Lord Hatherley's judgment (ibid., 161) is probably more consistent with the view that charging a commission does not preclude bills under an acceptance credit being 'accommodation bills'.

[569] (1875) LR 10 Ch. App. 639.

[570] [1980] 54 ALJR 424, 425, 429–430, 436 (HCA). See also *Brick & Pipe Industries* v. *Occidental Life Nominees Pty Ltd* (1990) 3 ACSR 649 (VSC); *Coles Myer Finance Ltd* v. *Commissioner of Taxation* (1993) 112 ALR 322 (HCA); *Silberman* v. *One Tel Ltd* [2001] NSWSC 895.

[571] BEA 1882, s.28(1).

the future, rather than in return for accepting any individual instrument.[572] This is supported by the fact that the bank's fee is not usually refundable even if the customer fails to utilize the facility at all. As the bank's fee is not directly related to the signing of each individual bill of exchange under the acceptance credit, each such instrument should be treated as an 'accommodation bill'. Indeed, any other conclusion would lead to commercially undesirable consequences, as it would leave open the possibility of the customer suing the bank on the instrument and of defeating an action brought by a third party on the instrument by reference to procedural technicalities, such as a failure to give notice of dishonour. If a bank has received some consideration beyond its acceptance fee, however, then bills of exchange drawn under the acceptance credit will not be 'accommodation bills'. For example, in *Re Securitibank Ltd*,[573] the bank received 'value' beyond a mere fee for issuing the acceptance credit, as the fee paid by the customer involved a 'clear mercantile arrangement' whereby the fee payable escalated sharply if the customer failed to remit to the bank the funds necessary to meet the acceptances. Accordingly, Barker J held that the bills drawn under the acceptance credit before the court were not 'accommodation bills'. It is possible to avoid this conclusion, however, by including a clause in the acceptance facility agreement to the effect that the bills of exchange are 'accommodation bills 'irrespective of whether the bank has received or will receive value from the customer for the acceptance'.[574]

The second difficulty arises when the bank (as is usual practice) has taken security from the customer in respect of the customer's obligation to reimburse it under the acceptance credit, such as by a deposit of commercial paper or a charge over assets or an account, but the bank subsequently fails and is unable to meet its acceptance of bills of exchange. In such circumstances, the customer (as drawer and possibly first indorser) is bound to pay any bills of exchange outstanding under the acceptance credit himself, as he is jointly and severally liable with the bank.[575] Even if the discounter of the bills drawn under the acceptance credit knows of the accommodation arrangement, he is still taken to have relied upon the credit of both the bank and its customer, so that the discounter is entitled to sue the customer on the bills, as well as under any underlying agreement between them.[576] Accordingly, if the customer has already remitted to the bank the funds needed to meet any bills of exchange before the bank's collapse, then the customer has no option but to pay again and then prove in the bank's liquidation as a general creditor. Nevertheless, in such circumstances, the customer is at least entitled to reclaim any security given to the bank. The customer is, however, in a much stronger position if the bank fails before he has remitted the funds needed to meet the bills, as the bank's inability to meet those instruments constitutes a 'total failure of consideration' discharging the customer of its duty to remit funds to the bank.[577] Accordingly, the customer can use those funds to discharge his liability to the holders of any outstanding bills of exchange. Whilst the obvious advice to the customer is to refrain from remitting

---

[572] The provision of funds by the party accommodated to meet bills drawn under the acceptance credit should not be treated as 'value' for the purposes of BEA 1882, s.28(1): *National Office Supplies* v. *Thazbhay*, 1975 (3) SA 977; *Sundelson* v. *Knuttel*, 2000 (3) SA 513, 518.

[573] N.319 above, 154, affd. [1978] 2 NZLR 136, 152–153 (NZCA).

[574] *Standard Chartered Bank of Australia Ltd* v. *Antico* (1995) 18 ACSR 1 (NSWSC).

[575] Sect. 8(ii) above.

[576] Consider *Saffron* v. *Société Minière Cafrika* (1958) 100 CLR 231, 244–245 (HCA); *Sale Continuation Ltd* v. *Austin Taylor & Co. Ltd* [1968] 2 QB 849; *W. J. Alan & Co. Ltd* v. *El Nasr Export & Import Co.* [1972] 2 QB 189 (CA); *Maran Road Saw Mill* v. *Austin Taylor & Co. Ltd* [1975] 1 Lloyd's Rep. 156, 159; *E. D. & F. Man Ltd* v. *Nigerian Sweets and Confectionery Co. Ltd* [1977] 2 Lloyd's Rep. 50.

[577] *Sale Continuation Ltd* v. *Austin Taylor & Co. Ltd*, n.576 above.

funds to a bank in connection with an acceptance credit, if there is any doubt as to the bank's solvency, this may not always be possible where the dealings between the customer and his bank are conducted on the basis of a current account from which the bank can deduct any sums owing.[578] Where neither the customer nor the bank is able to honour the outstanding bills of exchange,[579] a subsequent indorser may be compelled by their holders to honour the instruments. Such a party is, however, entitled to be subrogated to the holder's rights, including any securities held,[580] and should similarly have the right to be subrogated to any security provided by the customer to his bank, as the indorser will have discharged the debt in respect of which the customer provided the securities in the first place.

11 Negotiable instruments and the Consumer Credit Act 1974

Traditionally, negotiable instruments were used both in commercial transactions, such as international sales and acceptance credits, and in consumer transactions. Occasionally, they have been used to accommodate private individuals. The promissory note is also used in some commercial transactions, notably in the context of export credit guarantees, but was prevalent in consumer transactions such as hire-purchase agreements. In such transactions, the finance company usually relied upon its position as holder in due course of the promissory notes made by the hirer, so as to enforce its rights regardless of any justifiable claims that the hirer had against the dealer in respect of the goods covered. Abuses of this type led to section 123 of the CCA 1974 restricting the use of negotiable instruments in 'regulated' consumer credit and consumer hire agreements.[581] There is a prohibition on taking of negotiable instruments other than banknotes or cheques in discharge of amounts payable by the debtor or hirer or by a surety[582] and on the taking of any negotiable instrument (including a cheque) as a security for an amount payable under such an agreement.[583] A person who takes an instrument in contravention of these provisions cannot be a holder in due course and is unable to enforce it.[584]

Although the owner or creditor may take a cheque in payment of an amount due to him under a regulated agreement, he is not allowed to negotiate it except to a 'banker'.[585] This provision seeks to preclude the negotiation of a cheque to an assignee of a regulated agreement, or to the finance company's nominee, who may purport to enforce the cheque notwithstanding disputes related to the underlying contract. The object of the saving is to enable the finance company to remit the cheque for collection to a bank. Accordingly, the use of the word 'negotiation' in this context is puzzling, as the remittance of a cheque to a bank for collection does not involve the instrument being negotiated in the sense of its being transferred to a holder, who becomes its new owner and acquires the right to enforce it.[586] It would have been more consistent with the policy of the CCA 1974 to prohibit negotiation altogether, but to permit the transfer of a cheque to a bank for collection.

---

[578] Ch. 7, Sect. 1 above.

[579] *Re Securitibank Ltd*, n.319 above; *Re Standard Insurance Co. Ltd* [1970] 1 NSWLR 392.

[580] Id.

[581] Ch. 3, Sect. 4(ii) above. Under the Consumer Credit Act 1974 (CCA 1974), s.123(5), there is an exception for 'non-commercial' agreements (as defined in s.189(1)).

[582] CCA 1974, s.123(1).   [583] Ibid., s.123(3)–(4).   [584] Ibid., s.125(1).

[585] Ibid., s.123(2). See further Ch. 3, Sect. 1(ii) above.   [586] Sect. 8(iv) above.

In effect, the CCA 1974 has precluded the use of bills of exchange (other than cheques) and of promissory notes in regulated agreements.[587] Cheques may be used for the purpose of effecting payment, but not in lieu of bills or notes. Thus, the CCA 1974 prohibits the use of post-dated cheques appearing to be issued on the dates on which instalments fall due and serving the purpose of securing payment thereof. The CCA 1974 further protects consumers by prohibiting the transfer of cheques drawn by them except to a collecting bank.

---

[587] But note the exemption respecting certain consumer hire agreements which have a connection with external trade: Consumer Credit (Negotiable Instruments) (Exemption) Order 1984. Consumer *credit* agreements with such a connection are exempt agreements (and thus not regulated) by virtue of the Consumer Credit (Exempt Agreements) Order 1989, S. I. 1989/869, art. 5.

11

The Paying Bank

1 The bank's duty to pay cheques

(i) Form of cheques and scope of duty to pay

Despite the increasing popularity of electronic payments,[1] the payment of cheques drawn by customers on their current accounts remains an important (and currently the defining)[2] function of a bank. Although conceptually a cheque can be drawn on any piece of paper,[3] it is customary for banks to provide their customers with cheque-books and to insist that cheques be drawn on the forms contained therein. Moreover, where a customer has more than one current account with his bank, he is usually furnished with a separate cheque-book for every account and is advised to utilize the correct cheque-book for each account. This request is motivated by practical considerations. First, the name of the account and the address of the branch at which the account is kept are printed on the forms contained in each cheque-book. Any alteration to these forms requires extra checking by the bank. Secondly, the forms include a line with numbers printed in magnetic ink, which sets out the clearing number of the bank and the relevant branch, and the numbers of the account and the cheque itself. This data is automatically decoded in the computerized clearing process applicable since the 1960s, and facilitates the clearing of the cheque.[4] An alteration made to a particular form, such as a change effected in ordinary ink to the name and address of the branch on which the instrument is drawn, is bound to lead to confusion, as the computer will be unable to cope with it.

This point is illustrated by *Burnett* v. *Westminster Bank Ltd*,[5] where a customer had two current accounts with Westminster Bank: one with the X Branch and the other with the Y Branch. At the relevant time, the Y Branch had become linked to the computer network of Westminster Bank, which meant that cheques drawn on this branch were cleared by a process based on the decoding of the details imprinted on the cheque in magnetic ink. The X Branch had not been linked to the computer network and remained subject to the manual clearing process. Despite a request set out in the folder of the cheque-book issued by the Y Branch to the effect that forms contained in the book be used only for drawing cheques on the relevant account, the customer used one of the forms to draw a cheque on his account with the X Branch. To this end, he struck out the address of the Y Branch on the cheque and substituted that of the X Branch. On the following day, he gave notice of countermand to the X Branch. The cheque, however, was forwarded by means of the computerized clearing process to the Y Branch, where it was honoured. It was held that

---

[1] See generally Ch. 13 below.
[2] For the definition of a 'bank' at common law, see Ch. 3, Sect. 1(ii) above.
[3] *Roberts & Co.* v. *Marsh* [1915] 1 KB 42, 43–45 (CA).
[4] For the clearing procedure, see Ch. 10, Sect. 2 above.
[5] [1966] 1 QB 742. See also *Covercraft Ltd* v. *Commissioners of Customs & Excise* (VAT Trib, 25 April 1989).

the request set out in the cheque-book folder did not constitute a term of the contract between the bank and its customer, as the accounts in question had been opened before the computerization of the Y Branch. Accordingly, the notice printed in the cheque-book folder was given to the customer after the contract between himself and the bank had been concluded.[6] The defendant bank could not vary its contract with the customer by a unilateral act.[7] The cheque in question was, therefore, treated as drawn on the X Branch, and the countermand given to that branch was held to be effective.

Burnett shows that, as a general rule, the paying bank's contract with its customer cannot be abrogated unilaterally by the bank, even when there is a change in banking practice occasioned by such factors as technological developments. It is of course possible for the banker–customer contract to be varied by the express agreement of *both* parties, although such a variation would only be valid to the extent that it is supported by consideration.[8] In *Burnett*, the notice given in the cheque-book folder could have constituted a term of the contract if it had been made the subject of an agreement by means of a circular letter issued to customers and offering them some concession in consideration of their acceptance of the new practice. Furthermore, as was mentioned in *Burnett*,[9] the notice in the cheque-book folder could be made the basis of contracts with new customers. In modern banking practice, however, banks tends to deal with the kind of problem that arose in *Burnett* by including in the account contract a 'unilateral variation clause' that allows them to vary the account contract as required. Although the Payment Services Regulations 2009 (PSR 2009) now gives statutory recognition to a bank's right to include such a clause in its account contracts,[10] as discussed previously, there are an increasing number of common law and statutory controls on such clauses.[11]

A further point arises out of *Burnett*, namely that the bank's duty to pay a cheque, or to refuse its honour, is owed to the customer alone. In English law, the drawing of a cheque does not involve an assignment by the customer to the payee or holder of the instrument of a chose in action owed by the bank.[12] Furthermore, the bank does not accept the

---

[6] *Borhanuddin Bin Haji Jantara v. American International Assurance Co. Ltd* [1986] 1 MLJ 246, 248; *Trigg v. MI Movers International Transport Services Ltd* (1991) 4 OR (3d) 562, 569 (Ont. CA). Compare *US International Marketing Ltd v. National Bank of New Zealand Ltd* (2002) 7 NZBLC 103,738, [23], revsd. on a different point: N.17 below.

[7] *Hill v. National Bank of New Zealand Ltd* [1985] 1 NZLR 736, 742–744. Modern account contracts frequently contain a 'unilateral variation clause' that allows the bank to alter the terms of its relationship with its customer: see further Ch. 7, Sect. 2 above.

[8] *Re Williams Porter & Co. Ltd* [1937] 2 All ER 361. See also *Chitty on Contracts* (30th edn., London, 2008), para. 22-035. Following the liberalization of the doctrine of consideration in recent years, it will be more difficult to strike down a variation on the ground that it is unsupported by consideration: see, for example, *Williams v. Roffey Bros & Nicholls (Contractors) Ltd* [1991] 1 QB 1 (CA); *Joiner v. George* (Ch. D., 31 January 2000); *Compagnie Noga d'Importation et d'Exportation SA v. Abacha* [2003] 2 All ER (Comm.) 915, [43]–[61] (CA); *Adam Opel GmbH v. Mitras Automotive UK Ltd* [2007] EWHC 3252 (QB), [40]–[42]; *Forde v. Birmingham City Council* [2009] EWHC 12 (QB), [81]–[97]; but contrast *South Caribbean Trading Ltd v. Trafigura Beheer BV* [2005] 1 Lloyd's Rep 128, [107]–[108]. A similar approach is evident in New Zealand (see *Antons Trawling Co Ltd v. Smith* [2003] 2 NZLR 23 (NZCA)) and Singapore (see *Sunny Metal & Engineering Pte Ltd v. Ng Khim Ming Eric* [2006] SGHC 222, [28]–[30]).

[9] *Burnett v. Westminster Bank Ltd*, n.5 above, 763.

[10] Payment Services Regulations 2009, S.I. 2009/209 (PSR 2009), reg. 42(2).

[11] See further Ch. 7, Sect. 2 above.

[12] Bills of Exchange Act 1882 (BEA 1882), s.53(1). See also *Schroeder v. Central Bank of London Ltd* (1876) 34 LT 735, 736; *Shand v. Du Buisson* (1874) LR 18 Eq. 283, 288–9; *Hopkinson v. Forster* (1874) LR 19 Eq. 74; *In re Beaumont* [1902] 1 Ch 889, 894; *Joachimson v. Swiss Bank Corporation* [1921] 3 KB 110, 120–121 (CA); *Auchteroni & Co. v. Midland Bank Ltd* [1928] 2 KB 294, 299–300; *Plein & Co. Ltd v. Inland Revenue Commissioners* (1946) 175 LT 453, 456. See also *McDonald v. McDonald* (1903) 33 SCR 145, 170–171 (Can. Sup.

cheque, and hence does not engage to honour the instrument when presented.[13] Although the cheque itself is unenforceable against a bank, this does not mean that a bank can dishonour cheques drawn upon it with impunity, as the wrongful dishonour of a cheque constitutes a breach of the contract that arises between the bank and its customer upon the opening of an account.[14] The bank's duty to its customer to honour any cheques drawn on the account in a regular manner is, however, subject to certain limitations. First, the amount of the cheque must not exceed either the balance standing to the credit of the customer's account or the ceiling placed upon any agreed overdraft facilities, and the bank's duty to pay its customer's cheques continues to be restricted to circumstances where the instrument is presented at the branch at which the account is kept.[15] Secondly, the bank's duty to pay the customer's cheques may be abrogated by law. At common law, as discussed in other chapters, a bank is obliged to ignore a payment instruction where this would constitute a fraud on its customer,[16] or where it would assist in a breach of trust or other fiduciary duty owed to a third party.[17] The present discussion will accordingly focus on a number of common situations where the bank's obligation to honour its customer's payment instruction (such as payment by cheque) is abrogated by court order or statute. These include the situation where the bank holding the customer's account is served with a third party debt order, an injunction restraining payment, or a freezing injunction; the situation where, following the making of a disclosure under the Proceeds of Crime Act 2002 (POCA 2002), a bank freezes a customer's account pending the receipt of permission to release the funds; the situation where a customer dies, becomes mentally incapacitated, or is declared bankrupt (in the case of an individual customer) or wound up (in the case of a corporate customer); and the situation where the customer terminates the bank's mandate by countermanding payment.

The limitations to the bank's duty to pay assist in defining the scope of its actual mandate, and are considered in the remainder of this section. The formal requirements for a valid cheque and the actual process used by the banks for the clearance of cheques have already been discussed. The last two sections of the present chapter deal respectively

---

Ct.); *Ritchie v. Jeffrey* (1915) 52 SCR 243, 249–250 (Can. Sup. Ct.); *Geo. Thompson (Aust.) Pty Ltd v. Vittadello* [1978] VR 199 (Vic. Sup. Ct.). The position differs in Scotland: BEA 1882, s.53(2). See also *Thompson v. Jolly Carters Inn Ltd* 1972 SC 215 (OH); *Williams v. Williams* 1980 SLT 25 (Sheriff Ct.); *Sutherland v. Royal Bank of Scotland plc* 1997 Bank. LR 132 (OH).

[13] Id. See also *Fiorentino Comm Giuseppe Srl v. Farnesi* [2005] 2 All ER 737, [39]. In the United Kingdom, cheques are not generally 'certified': see further Ch. 10, Sect. 3(v) above. That cheques are not meant to be accepted has been established since the middle of the 19th century: *Bellamy v. Marjoribanks* (1852) 7 Exch. 389, 404; *Bank of Baroda Ltd v. Punjab National Bank Ltd* [1944] AC 176, 188 (PC). See also *Hodgson & Lee Pty. Ltd v. Mardonius Pty. Ltd* (1986) 5 NSWLR 496 (NSWCA).

[14] See Ch. 5, Sects. 2–3 & Ch. 7, Sect. 1 above.

[15] *Joachimson v. Swiss Bank Corporation*, n.12 above, 127. The necessity for the demand for payment to be made at the particular branch may often be overridden by contrary agreement (see *Bank of Scotland v. Seitz* 1990 SLT 584, 590 (Scot. 1st Div.)) and it has even been suggested that this is no longer a requirement '[i]n the light of modern technological and business development' (see *Damayanti Kantilal Doshi v. Indian Bank* [1999] 4 SLR 1, [28] (Sing. CA)). Under BEA 1882, s.45(3), however, a cheque must be presented for payment 'at the proper place', which requires the physical delivery of the instrument to the branch of the paying bank on which it is drawn: *Barclays Bank plc v. Bank of England* [1985] 1 All ER 385, 392–394. Some relaxation of this principle has been admitted, however, as BEA 1882, s.74A (inserted by the Deregulation (Bills of Exchange) Order 1996, S.I. 1996/2993) enables the paying bank by public notice to specify its clearing centre or head office as the proper place to present the cheque: see further Ch. 10, Sect. 2 above.

[16] *Lipkin Gorman v. Karpnale & Co.* [1989] 1 WLR 1340 (CA); *Barclays Bank plc v. Quincecare* [1992] 4 All ER 363, 376–377. See further Ch. 5, Sect. 4(iii) above.

[17] *US International Marketing Ltd v. National Bank of New Zealand Ltd* [2004] 1 NZLR 589, [4] (NZCA). See further Ch. 7, Sect. 5 above.

with the bank's liability for the wrongful payment of a cheque and with the converse situation, in which the bank wrongfully fails to honour its customer's cheque.

(ii) Availability of funds

As re-stated recently by Cresswell J in *Sierra Leone Telecommunications Co. Ltd* v. *Barclays Bank plc*,[18] the bank's duty to pay cheques depends on the availability of adequate funds on which the customer is entitled to draw. These may accrue either on the basis of an actual credit balance standing to the credit of the account,[19] or on the basis of an arrangement for an overdraft.[20] In some cases, it is difficult to assess at first glance whether or not a given cheque is covered by adequate funds when presented. This is because the issue of the funds that are available for immediate use by the customer is complicated by the mix of different payment methods that may be used to make withdrawals (such as ATM withdrawals or the use of a debit card)[21] and to deposit funds into the account, so that the account balance will depend upon the amount of the cheques processed at the close of the previous day,[22] plus any cash credited to the account that has been deposited during the course of the banking day, any direct debits that have cleared by that time through the three-day BACS clearing cycle,[23] any real-time funds transfers through CHAPS Sterling[24] and any payments or standing orders executed through the 'Faster Payments Service'.[25] Thus, an account might show a balance of, say, £500, although in reality cheques totalling an extra £1,000 were lodged at an hour that made it impossible to commence their processing on the same day. This fact is well known in the banking community. In practice, branch managers tend to be lenient in the exercise of their discretion to dishonour a cheque that appears uncovered when presented. Usually, the customer's banking record and creditworthiness are taken into account and, furthermore, banks maintain a list of questionable accounts that require extra caution. A cheque drawn on an account not mentioned in this list will frequently be met, even if it is for an amount exceeding the available balance, as banks always retain the option of affording the necessary overdraft facilities to a customer.[26]

From a purely legal perspective, however, the position is clear. The bank's duty to honour the customer's cheques depends on the actual state of the account at the time of presentment and the bank is at liberty to dishonour cheques that are not covered by

---

[18] [1998] 2 All ER 821. See also *Barclays Bank Ltd* v. *W.J. Simms & Cooke (Southern) Ltd* [1980] 1 QB 682, 699; *National Trust Co.* v. *Harold's Demolition Inc* (Ont. Sup. Ct., 8 August 2001). See generally M.H. Ogilvie, 'Banker and Customer: The Five-Year Review 2000–2005' (2007) 23 *BFLR* 107, 120–121.

[19] *Joachimson* v. *Swiss Bank Corporation*, n.12 above, 127; *Bank of New South Wales* v. *Laing* [1954] AC 135, 154 (PC). See also *Inglis* v. *Commonwealth Trading Bank of Australia* (1973) 46 ALJR 234 (Aust. HC).

[20] *Fleming* v. *Bank of New Zealand* [1900] AC 577 (PC); *Pyke* v. *Hibernian Bank Ltd* [1950] IR 195 (Ir. Sup. Ct.); *Bank of New South Wales* v. *Laing*, n.19 above, 154. There is no obligation to grant overdraft facilities to a customer to cover cheque payments: *Barclays Bank Ltd* v. *W.J. Simms & Cooke (Southern) Ltd*, n.18 above, 699; *Office of Fair Trading* v. *Abbey National plc* [2008] EWHC 875 (Comm.), [45].

[21] For debit cards, see Ch. 14, Sect. 5 below.   [22] For cheque clearing, see Ch. 10, Sect. 2 above.

[23] For BACS clearing, see Ch. 13, Sect. 3(iii) below. PSR 2009, regs.70(1)–(2) will require BACS to move to a one-day clearing cycle before 1 January 2012.

[24] PSR 2009, reg.73(1)–(2). See further Ch. 13, Sect. 3(iv)(a) below.

[25] Ibid. See further Ch. 13, Sect. 3(iv)(b) below.

[26] See, for example, *Barclays Bank Ltd* v. *W.J. Simms & Cooke (Southern) Ltd*, n.18 above, 699; *Office of Fair Trading* v. *Abbey National plc*, n.20 above, [45].

adequate funds.[27] At common law, the bank is given a reasonable time to credit to its customer's account any amounts paid in by way of cash, by means of a periodic payment (such as a standing order or direct debit), or by means of a cheque payable to the customer's order. Thus, in *Marzetti* v. *Williams*,[28] a customer's balance amounted to £69 19s 6d on the morning of 18 December 1828. At 11.00 a.m., the customer paid an amount of £40 in cash to the credit of his account, so that the actual available balance became £109 19s 6d. Despite this, a cheque drawn by the customer for £87 7s 6d was dishonoured when presented at the bank's counter at 3.00 p.m., as the amount of £40 had not been entered into the customer's ledger by then. The cheque was paid when presented again on the next day, but the customer brought an action for breach of contract based on the initial dishonour of the instrument. Lord Tenderden CJ said that a bank committed a breach of contract with its customer when it failed to pay a cheque when the customer's account had an adequate balance for meeting it, but that the bank was entitled to a reasonable time to credit funds paid in. The jury found that a delay of four hours was unreasonable.

It has been doubted[29] whether the conclusion in *Marzetti* v. *Williams*[30] that it is unreasonable for a bank to delay for four hours before crediting an account with a cash deposit would still represent the common law position nowadays. This was on the basis that modern banking practice was unlikely to treat such a short lapse of time between the moment at which the amount is paid in and that at which it is shown in the customer's ledger constitutes as an unreasonable delay. Such a view received some support from the apparent practice that, even in the case of an account being credited with an in-house payment, the amount may not necessarily be entered onto the account before the end of the banking day.[31] The amount is shown in the customer's balance in the statement of the subsequent day. This practice relating to in-house transfers may nowadays be more questionable[32] and, in the United Kingdom at least, the doubts as to the correctness of *Marzetti* may now need to be re-assessed in light of the PSR 2009, which apply to accounts that fall within the definition of a 'framework contract' (such as a current account or flexible savings account).[33] Nowadays, cash that is deposited by a customer who qualifies as a 'consumer, micro-enterprise or charity'[34] must be credited and made available to the customer immediately after the receipt of the funds by the bank.[35] In the case of other types of customer, the bank must credit the cash deposit to the customer's account and make it available to

---

[27] *Bank of New South Wales* v. *Laing*, n.19 above, 154; *Barclays Bank Ltd* v. *W.J. Simms & Cooke (Southern) Ltd*, n.18 above, 699; *Sierra Leone Telecommunications Co. Ltd* v. *Barclays Bank plc*, n.18 above.

[28] (1830) 1 B & Ad. 415.

[29] E.P. Ellinger, E. Lomnicka, & R.J.A. Hooley, *Ellinger's Modern Banking Law* (Oxford, 2005), 415.

[30] N.28 above.

[31] For a tacit recognition of the practice, see *Momm* v. *Barclays Bank International Ltd* [1977] QB 790, 799–800. See further Ch. 13, Sect. 6(ii) below.

[32] In *Sutherland* v. *Royal Bank of Scotland plc*, n.12 above, 144, Lord Penrose considered that, with the introduction of online and networked computer systems, 'the branch may well be able to review within a business day the whole transactions of a given client and adjust its position, precisely as it might have done under the manual accounting system'. Moreover, the practice referred to in *Momm* may no longer be followed in the light of the PSR 2009. Assuming they are applicable to in-house electronic transfers (see Ch. 13, Sect. 5(ii) below), the PSR 2009, regs. 71(1)–(2) & 73(2) require the transferred funds to be made immediately available to the payee upon their being credited to the account of the payee's bank, which may be interpreted as requiring the bank to give the payee same-day value.

[33] PSR 2009, reg. 2(1): '…a contract for payment services which governs the future execution of individual and successive payment transactions and which may contain the obligation and conditions for setting up a payment account'.

[34] Ibid., reg. 2(1).   [35] Ibid., reg. 72(a).

him 'no later than the end of the business day after the receipt of the funds'.[36] Accordingly, even under the PSR 2009, *Marzetti* v. *Williams*[37] might well be decided the same way nowadays in respect of the first type of customer, but not in respect of the second.

In *Marzetti*, the amount of £40 was deposited by the customer into his account in cash. Different problems arise when the customer's balance includes cheques payable to him that have been remitted to his bank for collection. As discussed previously,[38] a customer's account will be credited with the amount of a cheque before the cheque is actually cleared. Since November 2007, banks in general have undertaken to abide by standardized maximum time-limits in relation to the clearing of cheques for their customers, termed the '2-4-6' commitments for current accounts.[39] Pursuant to these commitments, collecting banks undertake to credit the proceeds of a cheque to the customer's account for the purposes of earning interest on the second working day following the cheque being paid into that account; to permit the customer to withdraw funds from the account on the fourth working day following the cheque being paid into the account; and to assure the customer that the cheque will not be dishonoured by the drawee bank from the end of the sixth working day following the cheque being paid into the account. If a cheque is dishonoured by the drawee bank, the payee's balance with his own bank will be reduced as the initial credit is reversed. Accordingly, an amount initially entered in the customer's account as a result of the deposit of a cheque is not necessarily available for the customer's use at the time of the crediting and does not necessarily accrue irreversibly to the customer until the completion of the clearing process. The problem that arises, therefore, is whether or not the customer is entitled to draw against funds that have been credited to his account subject to the possibility of the reversal of entries upon dishonour. Usually, banks inform their customers, in clauses printed on the credit slips or on the folder in which these forms are contained,[40] that the proceeds of cheques paid into the account cannot be withdrawn before clearance. On this basis, it is forcefully arguable that the bank is legally entitled to dishonour the customer's cheque if it is drawn against uncleared effects.[41] In practice, however, banks tend to honour a customer's cheque even if the available credit balance is based on such uncleared effects, and it may be arguable that such a practice could establish a course of dealings between a bank and its customer that defines the scope of their relationship.

In contrast to the view just expressed, the early case of *Rolin* v. *Steward*[42] decided that it is a question of fact whether or not the crediting of an account with the proceeds of an uncleared cheque demonstrates that the bank has permitted its customer to draw on the amount involved. The later decision in *Capital and Counties Bank Ltd* v. *Gordon*[43] suggested that usually the crediting of the customer's account with the amount of a cheque

---

[36] Ibid., reg. 72(b).   [37] N.28 above.

[38] For cheque clearing, see Ch. 10, Sect. 2 above.

[39] Cheque and Credit Clearing Company, *Cheques and Cheque Clearing—The Facts* (November 2007), 7.

[40] For the form and function of credit slips, see Ch. 10, Sect. 2 above.

[41] *A. L. Underwood Ltd* v. *Bank of Liverpool* [1924] 1 KB 775, 803–806 (CA) emphasizes that the mere crediting of the customer's account does not in itself indicate that he is permitted to draw against the uncleared component of the balance. See also *Westminster Bank Ltd* v. *Zang* [1966] AC 182 (HL). For the suggestion that the very crediting of the account evidences the bank's readiness to permit the customer to draw against the balance as shown, see *Capital and Counties Bank Ltd* v. *Gordon* [1903] AC 240, 249 (HL). See further Ch. 7, Sect. 1 above.

[42] (1854) 14 CB 595.

[43] N.41 above, 249. See also *Akrokerri (Atlantic) Mines Ltd* v. *Economic Bank* [1904–1907] All ER Rep 1054; *Bank of China* v. *Synn Lee & Co. Ltd* [1962] 1 MLJ 91.

gives him such a right, but this view has been doubted.[44] The better view is that the answer depends on the intention of the parties. This is discernible from both the express terms of the contract, as evidenced by a clause in the credit slip or cheque deposit slip, and from the prevailing banking practice, which is to be established by evidence. It is submitted that if the two are in conflict, the established banking practice should prevail.

Where the customer's balance is inadequate, the holder may be tempted to pay the difference between this balance and the amount of the cheque to the credit of the drawer's account so as to facilitate the payment of the cheque. In *Foster* v. *Bank of London*,[45] however, the court held that if the bank discloses the balance of the drawer's account to the holder of the cheque, it commits a breach of the duty of confidentiality owed to its customer.[46] In contrast, if the cheque's holder discovers the state of the account from other sources, modern banking practice enables him to cover the deficiency.[47] Under the 1967 'Golden Memorandum', which, though not in effect in its original form, remains, in certain areas, operative in spirit, the holder of a cheque is able to pay the necessary amount at a branch of any participating bank for the credit of the relevant account. Covering a deficiency in the drawer's account, however, involves a certain risk for the holder due to the fact that banks usually pay cheques in the order in which they are processed. If the holder makes up the deficiency in the account, but the cheque payable to him is accidentally processed after some other outstanding cheque drawn on the same account, his cheque may still be dishonoured. The amount paid by the holder into the drawer's account cannot be earmarked.

A fully automated, on-line clearing process would eliminate the problem of the simultaneous presentment of cheques totalling an amount exceeding the balance available in the customer's account. Under the old clearing procedure, where payment was effected by a fully manual process executed at each branch,[48] banks developed individual practices for dealing with situations of this type. Some banks paid the cheques in the order in which they were presented until the outstanding balance became inadequate for the payment of any remaining cheques. Other banks preferred to honour the cheques for the largest amounts, basing their practice on the assumption that the customer's reputation would be harmed to the greatest extent by the dishonour of a substantial cheque, whilst yet other banks prefer to honour the cheques for the least amounts first, on the assumption that this would be least injurious to its customer's reputation.[49] These practices have remained essentially the same under the current clearing system,[50] which involves an automated clearing process where balances are struck at the end of the day, but the introduction in the future of a fully computerized and 'online' clearing mechanism for cheques, where the entire process of debiting and crediting would be effected by a data-bank, would

[44] *A. L. Underwood Ltd* v. *Bank of Liverpool*, n.41 above, 803–806. See also *Fern* v. *Bishop, Burns & Co.* (1980) 130 NLJ 594. See further Ch. 15, Sect. 3 below.

[45] (1862) 3 F & F 214 (Assizes), approved in *Tournier* v. *National Provincial and Union Bank of England* [1924] 1 KB 461, 480 (CA).

[46] For the duty of confidentiality, see Ch. 5, Sect. 5 above.

[47] There has been much debate in the past over the question of the holder's right to cover any deficiency: Paget, *Law of Banking* (11th edn., London, 1996), 330 (although the issue is omitted from M. Hapgood, *Paget's Law of Banking* (13th edn., London, 2007), para. 18.8). See also Institute of Bankers, *Questions on Banking Practice* (10th edn.), quest. 417. Of course, the bank is precluded from communicating the balance to the presentor of the cheque.

[48] For the history of cheque clearing, see Ch. 10, Sect. 2 above.

[49] See A. Tyree, *Tyree's Banking Law in New Zealand* (2nd edn., Wellington, 2003), para. 9.3; A. Tyree & P. Weaver, *Weerasooria's Banking Law and the Financial System in Australia* (6th edn., Sydney, 2006), para. 21.62.

[50] For cheque clearing, see Ch. 10, Sect. 2 above.

introduce a change. Cheques would then be met strictly in the order in which the entries were made. The first cheque to be dishonoured would then be that drawn for an amount exceeding the balance available at the time of processing. This cheque would be forwarded to the branch on which it was drawn with a request for instructions. In the meantime, cheques for smaller amounts, drawn for a sum not exceeding the outstanding balance, would probably be met. The simultaneous presentment of cheques would cease to occur or be a problem.

Although a bank has a single legal personality, accounts are deemed to be domiciled at the branch where they are kept. This principle is explicable by banking practice in the nineteenth century. In the absence of expeditious means, such as the telephone, to enable a teller to verify the balance of an account maintained with a branch other than that at which the cheque was presented, and in the absence of facilities enabling the verification of a signature in any place other than at the drawee branch, it was impossible to develop a practice that would facilitate the payment of cheques at a place other than the branch on which they were drawn. Modern banking facilities have introduced new possibilities. A balance can be verified instantaneously by an enquiry made through the branch's computer facilities linked to the bank's central computer. A signature can be printed in invisible infra-red or ultra-violet ink when a document, such as a cheque form, is furnished to the customer, so that any signature executed can be compared with the 'hidden' one. At present, it is uncommon to print signatures in infra-red or ultra-violet ink on cheque forms, but such signatures are widely used in savings books and similar documents. Increasingly, banks in the United Kingdom and abroad store scanned copies of their customers' signatures on the central bank computer, which can be accessed and verified at each branch. The days in which cheques had to be regarded as payable solely at the drawee branch are over from a practical banking point of view.[51]

The legal position established in the 19th century has remained unaltered, however, and largely failed to keep pace with technological developments. In *Woodland* v. *Fear*,[52] a cheque was drawn on the G Branch of the S Bank. The holder of the instrument, whose place of residence was near the B Branch of the same bank, presented the cheque at this branch and received payment. When the B Branch forwarded the cheque to the G Branch, it turned out that the instrument had been drawn against an inadequate balance. The S Bank brought an action to recover the amount paid to the holder. The court held that the B Branch had not been under an obligation to honour the cheque as the instrument was not drawn on it and that presentment for payment could be made only at the G Branch. The B Branch was, accordingly, treated as having taken up the cheque for collection. When the cheque was dishonoured by the G Branch, the S Bank, as the collecting bank, had a right of recourse.

The principle that a cheque has to be presented for payment at the branch where the relevant account is kept has been approved in *Joachimson* v. *Swiss Bank Corporation*,[53]

---

[51] The introduction of cheque truncation will hasten this trend: see further Ch. 10, Sect. 2 above. See also BEA 1882, s.74A (inserted by the Deregulation (Bills of Exchange) Order 1996, S.I. 1996/2993), which enables the paying bank by public notice to specify its clearing centre or head office as the proper place to present the cheque.

[52] (1857) 7 E & B 519. See also *Henry Prince* v. *Oriental Bank Corporation* (1877–1878) LR 3 App. Cas. 325, 332 (PC); *King* v. *Irvine A Lovitt* [1912] AC 212, 219 (PC); *EB Savory & Co* v. *Lloyds Bank Ltd* [1932] 2 KB 122, 141 (CA); *Maude* v. *Commissioners of Inland Revenue* [1940] 1 KB 548, 552–3; *Arab Bank Ltd* v. *Barclays Bank (DCO)* [1954] AC 495; *Canada Life Assurance Co.* v. *Canadian Imperial Bank of Commerce* [1979] 2 SCR 669, 679 (Can. Sup. Ct.). See further *Clare & Co.* v. *Dresdner Bank* [1914–1915] All ER Rep 617; *Governor & Company of the Bank of Ireland* v. *Hussey* [1965] IR 46.

[53] N.12 above, 127. See further Ch. 5, Sect. 3 above.

which, further, lays down that a cheque need be honoured only in so far as it is presented during ordinary business hours. The bank, however, is not in breach of its duty to the customer if it pays a cheque within a reasonable time after its closing hours.[54] The confirmation in *Woodland* and *Joachimson* of the principle that a cheque needs to be presented for payment at the branch where the account is kept can, in certain cases, have far-reaching effects. Thus, in *Arab Bank Ltd* v. *Barclays Bank (DCO)*,[55] the A Bank maintained an account with the Jerusalem Branch of the B Bank. When hostilities broke out between the Jewish and Arab communities, that branch had to be provisionally closed. Shortly after the end of the Independence War, B Bank's Jerusalem branch, which by then fell within the Israeli part of Jerusalem, was reopened, but under Israeli law the funds standing to the credit of the A Bank's account became payable to the 'Custodian for Absentee Property'. As the A Bank was accordingly unable to make a valid demand at the Jerusalem branch, it claimed repayment of the amount involved from the B Bank's head office in London. The House of Lords held that the A Bank was not entitled to make a demand in London, as the amount standing to the credit of the customer's account was repayable only at the branch at which the account was kept. The debt was situated at this place. The A Bank's right to demand payment was, accordingly, governed by the laws of the State of Israel, which also formed the proper law of the contract.[56]

It follows that a cheque is to be regarded as payable by the branch on which it is drawn rather than by the bank as a whole. A customer who opens an account with a bank in a foreign country has to realize that payment is subject to the provisions of local laws.

(iii) **Third party debt proceedings**

The balance standing to the credit of a customer's account can be attached by way of a third party debt order issued under Part 72 of the Civil Procedure Rules 1998.[57] Proceedings of this type are usually instituted by a judgment creditor whose claim against the bank's

---

[54] *Baines* v. *National Provincial Bank Ltd* (1927) 96 LJKB 801.

[55] N.52 above, 529, 534 & 537. See also *Joachimson* v. *Swiss Bank Corporation*, n. 12 above, 127; *The Chartered Bank of India, Australia & China* v. *The Public Trustee* [1957] 1 MLJ 211, 212–214 (Sing. CA); *Canada Life Assurance Co.* v. *Canadian Imperial Bank of Commerce* (1975) 8 OR (2d) 210, 218–220 (Ont. Sup. Ct.); *X, Y & Z* v. *B* [1983] 2 Lloyd's Rep. 535; *MacKinnon* v. *Donaldson, Lufkin & Jenrette Securities Corp.* [1986] Ch. 482, 493 (CA); *Libyan Arab Foreign Bank* v. *Bankers' Trust Co.* [1988] 1 Lloyd's Rep. 259, 270; *Libyan Arab Foreign Bank* v. *Manufacturers Hanover Trust Co.* [1988] 2 Lloyd's Rep. 494, 498–499; *Attock Cement Co. Ltd* v. *Romanian Bank for Foreign Trade* [1989] 1 WLR 1147, 1159 (CA); *Libyan Arab Foreign Bank* v. *Manufacturers Hanover Trust Co. (No. 2)* [1989] 1 Lloyd's Rep. 608, 616–617; *Irish Shipping Ltd* v. *Commercial Union Assurance* [1991] 2 QB 206, 221 (CA); *Zebrarise Ltd* v. *de Nieffe* [2005] 2 All ER (Comm) 816, [30]–[31]; *Walsh* v. *National Irish Bank Ltd* [2007] IEHC 325, [26]–[34]. In *Vishipco Line* v. *Chase Manhattan Bank* (1981) 660 F. 2nd 854 (2nd Circ.), cert. denied (1982) 459 US 976 (USSC), the Court of Appeals for the Second Circuit held that a customer was entitled to claim repayment of a foreign deposit at the bank's head office where the foreign branch had closed down. See also *Leader, Plunkett & Leader* v. *Direction der Disconto-Gesellschaft* (1914) 31 TLR 83, revsd. [1915] 3 KB 154 (CA). For foreign deposits, see Ch. 9, Sect. 5 above. See also W. Blair, 'Liability for Foreign Branch Deposits in English Law' in R. Cranston (ed.), *Making Commercial Law: Essays in Honour of Roy Goode* (Oxford, 1997), ch. 13.

[56] See further Ch. 9, Sect. 5 above.

[57] These proceedings were formerly known as 'garnishee' proceedings, when orders were made 'nisi' and 'absolute'. When the Civil Procedure Rules 1998 (CPR) came into force in 1999, the existing rules (contained in Rules of the Supreme Court (RSC), Ord. 49 and County Court Rules (CCR), Ord. 30) were re-enacted in CPR, Scheds. 1 and 2. With effect from 25 March 2002, RSC, Ord. 49 and CCR, Ord. 30 were revoked and replaced by CPR Pt. 72.

customer has not been satisfied.[58] The creditor applies to the court for an order under which all debts 'due or accruing due' from the bank to the customer are to be attached for the purpose of satisfying the creditor's judgment against the customer. Initially, the court issues an interim third party debt order,[59] which becomes binding upon a bank when served upon it.[60] The service of an interim order gives rise to a number of disclosure obligations on the part of the bank,[61] operates to freeze a sum in the hands of the bank that is equivalent to the amount of the order,[62] and 'creates an equitable charge on the debt' in favour of the judgment creditor.[63] As the interim order does not constitute an order to the bank to pay the sum in question, any payment pursuant to such an order does not discharge the customer's debt to the judgment creditor (or the bank's debt to its customer) unless the customer specifically authorizes this.[64] After receiving the interim order, the bank may 'show cause' why it should not pay the amount owed by the customer to the creditor and the court will hold a further hearing to determine whether to issue a final third party debt order.[65] For example, in *Fraser* v. *Oystertec plc*,[66] the court refused to make a final order on the ground that the bank had an equitable charge over, or a 'flawed asset arrangement' in respect of, the account in question. If the bank does not 'show cause', the court is likely to exercise its discretion[67] in favour of issuing a final order that requires the bank to pay over an amount adequate to satisfy the customer's debt to

---

[58] As regards the issue of limitation arising in respect of the execution of judgment debts, see *Lowsley* v. *Forbes* [1999] AC 329 (HL), construing Limitation Act 1980, s.24(2). See also *Ezekiel* v. *Orakpo*, The Times, 16 September 1996 (CA); *Yorkshire Bank Finance Ltd* v. *Muhall* [2008] EWCA Civ 1156, [17]–[25].

[59] CPR, r.72.4(2)–(3).

[60] Ibid., r.72.4(4). For the procedure relating to the service of the interim order, see CPR, r.72.5.

[61] Pursuant to CPR, r.72.6(1), a bank served with an interim third party debt order must carry out a search and identify all accounts held with it by the judgment debtor. Within seven days of being served with an interim third party debt order, the bank must disclose to the court and the judgment creditor information relating to any account held by the judgment debtor, including whether the bank asserts any right to the money in the account (CPR, r.72.6(2)). Similarly, the bank has seven days from service of the interim order to declare that it does not hold any account of the judgment debtor or is otherwise unable to comply with the order (CPR, r.72.6(3)). However, a bank is not required to disclose information about accounts in the joint names of the judgment debtor and another person (Practice Direction 72PD.3.1–3.2).

[62] *Société Eram Shipping* v. *Compagnie Internationale de Navigation* [2004] 1 AC 260, [14] (HL). See also *Rogers* v. *Whiteley* [1892] AC 118, 121–123 (HL); *Galbraith* v. *Grimshaw* [1910] 1 KB 339, 343 (CA); *Joachimson* v. *Swiss Bank Corporation*, n.12 above, 131; *Choice Investments Ltd* v. *Jeromnimon* (*Midland Bank, Garnishee*) [1981] QB 149, 155 (CA); *Lexi Holdings plc* v. *Luqman* [2009] EWHC 496 (Ch), [209]–[210].

[63] *Joachimson* v. *Swiss Bank Corporation*, n.12 above, 131; *Société Eram Shipping* v. *Compagnie Internationale de Navigation*, n.62 above, [14], [95]; *Fraser* v. *Oystertec plc* [2006] 1 BCLC 491, [5]; *Masri* v. *Consolidated Contractors International UK Ltd (No. 2)* [2008] 1 All ER (Comm.) 305, [66].

[64] *Crantrave Ltd* v. *Lloyds Bank* [2000] QB 917, 921 (CA). See also *Filby* v. *Mortgage Express (No. 2) Ltd* [2004] EWCA Civ 759, [34]–[35]; *Liverpool Freeport Electronics Ltd* v. *Habib Bank Ltd* [2007] EWHC 1149 (QB), [141]; *Treasure & Son Ltd* v. *Martin Dawes* [2008] EWHC 2181 (TCC), [14]. There may be exceptional circumstances, however, where the bank's payment discharges its customer's debt even in the absence of authorization, although the nature of these circumstances remains unclear: *Gulf International Bank BSC* v. *Albaraka Islamic Bank* [2004] EWCA Civ 416, [36]; *Tayeb* v. *HSBC Bank plc* [2004] 4 All ER 1024, [97]–[99]; *Sweetman* v. *Shepherd* [2007] BPIR 455, [144]–[148].

[65] CPR, r.72.8.   [66] N.63 above.

[67] For the effect of delay on the court's discretion, see *Westacre Investments Inc.* v. *Yugoimport SDPR* [2008] EWHC 801 (Comm.), [25]–[26].

the creditor.[68] Payment to the judgment creditor or into court of the amount involved discharges the bank's debt to the customer.[69]

At one stage, there were some doubts regarding the applicability of the former garnishee procedure (now the third party debt procedure) to accounts maintained with banks. In the case of current accounts, the doubts were based on the fact that payment was due on demand. Accordingly, it was argued that before the customer made such a demand the debt was not 'due or accruing due' within the meaning of the provisions concerning garnishee/third party debt proceedings.[70] The point was resolved in *Joachimson* v. *Swiss Bank Corporation*,[71] where Bankes LJ observed that the service of an interim third party debt order on the bank operated as a demand.[72] *Joachimson* militates against a literal construction of rule 72.2(1) of the Civil Procedure Rules 1998 that would require the attached debt to be 'due or accruing due' at the very time the third party debt proceedings are instituted. From a commercial point of view, however, it is sound to enable a judgment creditor to levy execution against the balance standing to the credit of his debtor's current account, as in practice the funds serve the same function as cash.

Although *Joachimson* resolves the position with respect to current accounts, until 1956, the position was less clear in the case of deposit accounts. For the purpose of garnishee/third party debt proceedings, such accounts were traditionally divided into fixed deposits maturing at an agreed time, and deposit and savings accounts the balance of which was repayable subject to the giving of a minimum period of notice by the customer. Moreover, in both types of deposit, repayment was generally subject to the surrender by the customer of the deposit receipt or pass-book.[73] There was authority for the general view that a debt owed by a bank to a customer and maturing at a given future date was 'due or accruing due' and could be attached, but that the amount could not be claimed by the judgment creditor from the bank before the agreed maturity date.[74] At first glance, the debt represented by a deposit account would fall within the ambit of this principle, but the need to produce a deposit receipt or pass-book and the need, in the second type of deposit account mentioned above, to give minimum notice to determine

---

[68] For the process in relation to the former garnishee proceeding, see *Choice Investments Ltd* v. *Jeromnimon (Midland Bank, Garnishee)*, n.62 above, 155. See also *Z Ltd* v. *A-Z and AA-LL* [1982] QB 558, 593 (CA). The description of the garnishee process in *Jeromnimon* is equally apt to describe third party debt proceedings: *Société Eram Shipping* v. *Compagnie Internationale de Navigation*, n.62 above, [14], [96].

[69] CPR, r.72.9(2). It is an integral feature of the third party debt procedure that on compliance with the final order the third party is discharged from liability to the judgment debtor to the extent of his payment: *Société Eram Shipping Co. Ltd* v. *Compagnie Internationale de Navigation*, n.62 above, [25], [63], [97].

[70] Paget, *Law of Banking* (1st edn., London, 1906), 136. The view is not supported in the current edition: M. Hapgood, *Paget's Law of Banking* (13th edn., London, 2007), para. 25.9.

[71] N.12 above.

[72] Ibid., 115 & 131 (Warrington LJ). See also *Richardson* v. *Richardson* [1927] P 228, 236; *Rekstin* v. *Severo Sibirsko Gosudarstvennoe Akcionernoe Obschestvo Komseverputj* [1933] 1 KB 47, 53, 67 (CA); *Hirschorn* v. *Evans* [1938] 2 KB 801, 808–809 (CA); *Bagley* v. *Winsome and National Provincial Bank Ltd* [1952] 2 QB 236, 240–242 (CA); *Choice Investments Ltd* v. *Jeromnimon (Midland Bank, Garnishee)*, n.62 above, 154. If the third party gives the judgment debtor a cheque prior to the serving of the interim order, the account balance would not be attached unless the cheque was stopped: *Elwell* v. *Jackson* (1885) 1 TLR 454 (CA). See also *Cohen* v. *Hale* (1878) 3 QBD 371; *DPP* v. *Turner* [1974] AC 357, 369 (HL); cf. *ex p. Richdale* (1882) 19 Ch. D 409 (CA).

[73] For deposit receipts and pass-books, see Ch. 9, Sect. 4 above.

[74] *Webb* v. *Stenton* (1883) 11 QBD 518, 524, 527 (CA). Consider *Masri* v. *Consolidated Contractors International Co. SAL* [2008] EWCA Civ 303, [151], [162], [172].

the maturity of the debt were considered to pose obstacles.[75] The law was clarified by the passing of section 38 of the Administration of Justice Act 1956,[76] under which amounts standing to the credit of savings accounts, deposit accounts, and fixed deposits with banks may be attached. This provision was extended by section 40 of the Senior Courts Act 1981 to any deposit account with a bank or other deposit-taking institution, and so is wide enough to encompass modern deposit accounts which often do not fall fairly and squarely into one of the categories outlined above.[77] Accordingly, at present, any amounts deposited by a customer with his bank are subject to third party debt proceedings and the interim third party debt order attaches all the accounts opened by the relevant customer with his bank, including accounts opened for special purposes such as solicitors' 'clients accounts'.[78]

An interim third party debt order can attach a foreign-currency deposit maintained by the debtor with a bank in the United Kingdom.[79] The position is more complicated where the deposit is maintained with an overseas branch or bank. Rule 72.1(1) of the Civil Procedure Rules 1998 requires that the third party to be served with the proceedings must be within the jurisdiction, but there is no express requirement that the debt to be attached must also be within the jurisdiction. This raises the question whether a 'foreign debt'—one payable in a foreign jurisdiction and governed by a foreign law—can be the subject of a third party debt order. There is no reported case in which an English court has granted a final third party debt order in relation to a foreign debt.[80]

---

[75] *Bagley* v. *Winsome and National Bank Ltd*, n.72 above, 241. There is support for *Bagley* in Australia (see *Music Masters Pty. Ltd* v. *Minelle* (1968) Qd. R 326; *Haythorpe* v. *Rae* [1972] VR 633 (Vic. Sup. Ct.); *Re Australia and New Zealand Savings Bank Ltd*; *Mellas* v. *Evriniadis* [1972] VR 690, 696–697 (Vic. Sup. Ct.); *Bank of New South Wales Savings Bank* v. *Freemantle Auto Centre Pty. Ltd* [1973] WAR 161; *Paleopoulos* v. *Paleopoulos* (1979) 5 Fam. LR 461 (Aust. Fam. Ct.)), Hong Kong (see *Yik Keung* v. *Hong Kong & China Gas Co. Ltd* [1959] HKCU 17), and Ireland (see *C&E Lewis Ltd* v. *Gribben* [1955] NI 51). Although there is authority in Alberta refusing attachment of a deposit account where the presentation of a pass-book is required (see *Alberta (Provincial Treasurer)* v. *Minister of National Revenue* (1980) 22 AR 317, [13]–[28] (Alta. CA)), the courts in British Colombia, Saskatchewan, and Manitoba have held that deposit accounts may be readily attached (see *Bel-Fran Investments Ltd* v. *Pantuity Holdings Ltd* [1975] 6 WWR 374, 382 (BC Sup. Ct.); *Melville District Credit Union Ltd* v. *Jeffers* (1981) 16 Sask. R 254 (Sask. QB); *Farmstart* v. *Dagenais* (1983) 31 Sask. R 81 (Sask. QB); *Borg-Warner Acceptance* v. *Janzen Builders* (1983) 24 Man. R (2d) 48, [11]–[12] (Man. QB); *Spiritwood Credit Union* v. *Dagenais* (1985) 40 Sask. R 205 (Sask. CA); *Bank of Montreal* v. *Krisp (IM) Foods Ltd* (1996) 148 Sask R. 135, [28]–[34] (Sask. CA)). For the statutory reversal of *Bagley* in Singapore, see *Sincere Watch Ltd* v. *Bakery Mart Pte Ltd* [2003] 3 SLR 345, [18]–[19].

[76] *Ministry of Pensions and National Insurance* v. *Jones* [1966] 1 QB 484, 504–505; *Choice Investments Ltd* v. *Jeromnimon (Midland Bank, Garnishee)*, n.62 above, 154–156; *Commissioner of Police for the Metropolis* v. *Ewing* (CA, 4 November 1987).

[77] Senior Courts Act 1981, s.40 (as amended by S.I. 2001/3649) also extends to 'any withdrawable share account with any deposit-taking institution'. See also CPR, r.72.2(3).

[78] *Plunkett* v. *Barclays Bank Ltd* [1936] 2 KB 107, criticized in Ch. 8, Sect. 6(ii) above. See also *Arab Bank Ltd* v. *Barclays Bank (DCO)*, n.52 above, 532. This remains the view taken by Australian courts: *Melville Island Ltd* v. *Richards* (1933) 50 WN (NSW) 41. Furthermore, an interim third party debt order could attach an account maintained by the customer as a trustee, although the nature of the account is a fact to be considered in respect of the application for a final order: *Deutsche Schachtbau und Tiefbohrgesellschaft* v. *R'As al Khaima International Oil Co.* [1990] 1 AC 295, 351 (HL). In *AIG Capital Partners Inc.* v. *Republic of Kazakhstan* [2006] 1 All ER 284, [30]–[32], [95], Aikens J discharged an interim third party debt order on the basis that judgment debtor was not the account holder, even though it was entitled to a beneficial interest in the debt representing the account balance.

[79] *Choice Investments Ltd* v. *Jeromnimon (Midland Bank, Garnishee)*, n.62 above, 155–156; *Z Ltd* v. *A-Z and AA-LL*, n.68 above, 593; *Camdex International Ltd* v. *Bank of Zambia (No. 3)* (1997) 6 Bank. LR 44 (CA).

[80] *Société Eram Shipping* v. *Compagnie Internationale de Navigation* , n.62 above, [17].

In *Richardson* v. *Richardson*,[81] the matter was dealt with as one of jurisdiction. Hill J held that a garnishee/third party debt order did not attach to a deposit denominated in foreign currency and maintained with a foreign branch of a British bank. The debt had to be one that was recoverable within the jurisdiction. According to Hill J, it was not a question of the court exercising its discretion to refuse to make the order in question; there was simply no jurisdiction to make the order with regard to a foreign debt. By contrast, in *Martin* v. *Nadel*,[82] the Court of Appeal refused to make an interim garnishee order final on grounds of its discretion and not lack of jurisdiction.[83] In *Martin*, the judgment debtor had an account with the Berlin branch of the Dresdner Bank. It was clear that the German courts would not recognize payment under the third party debt order as discharging the bank's debt to its customer. Both Vaughan Williams LJ and Stirling LJ held that it would be inequitable to make an order that left the bank still liable to an action in Berlin.[84]

Lack of jurisdiction was the explanation recently adopted by Lords Bingham and Hobhouse in *Société Eram Shipping* v. *Compagnie Internationale de Navigation*,[85] when refusing to make a final third party debt order over a foreign debt. The judgment creditor had obtained a judgment in a French court against the judgment debtors, who held accounts with the Hong Kong branch of the Hong Kong and Shanghai Banking Corporation (HSBC), a bank that also maintained a branch in London and, hence, had a presence within the jurisdiction. The judgment creditor obtained an interim third party debt order against the Hong Kong accounts, but the House of Lords refused to make the order final. The undisputed evidence before their Lordships was that, under Hong Kong law, a third party debt order granted by an English court would not have the effect of extinguishing HSBC's debt to its customer in Hong Kong.

---

[81] N.72 above. *Richardson* was described as 'no longer good law' in *Interpool Ltd* v. *Galani* [1988] QB 738, 741 (CA), but this view was criticized in *Société Eram Shipping* v. *Compagnie Internationale de Navigation*, n.62 above, [26], [75]. A third party debt order will not attach the balance of a bank account maintained by a foreign embassy within the jurisdiction to finance its usual operations, unless 'the bank account was earmarked by the foreign state solely (save for *de minimis* exceptions) for being drawn upon to settle liabilities incurred in commercial transactions': *Alcom Ltd* v. *Republic of Colombia* [1984] AC 580, 601–606 (HL); cf. *Philipp Bros.* v. *Republic of Sierra Leone* [1995] 1 Lloyd's Rep. 289 (sum paid by the European Commission to a foreign state). See also *Orascom Telecom Holding SAE* v. *Republic of Chad* [2009] 1 All ER (Comm.) 315, [20]–[25], [51]. Under the State Immunity Act 1978, s.14(4), a court will not issue a third party debt order attaching the balance of an account maintained by a foreign central bank within the jurisdiction, irrespective of the source of the funds in the account, the use of the account, or the purpose for which the account was maintained: *AIC Ltd* v. *Federal Government of Nigeria* [2003] EWHC 1357 (QB); *AIG Capital Partners Inc.* v. *Republic of Kazakhstan*, n.78 above, [45], [56]–[58], [61], [89]–[91], [95]. For other types of claim against a central bank, see *Grovit* v. *De Nederlandsche Bank* [2006] 1 Lloyd's Rep 636, [81]–[84], aff'd [2008] 1 All ER (Comm.) 106, [16]–[17] (CA); *Koo Golden East Mongolia* v. *Bank of Nova Scotia* [2008] QB 717, [40]–[42], [47]–[48], [52]–[54] (CA).

[82] [1906] 2 KB 26 (CA).

[83] There are a number of cases that involved debts situated within the jurisdiction and not foreign debts where the court considered that there was jurisdiction to make a garnishee/third party debt order over a foreign debt, but stated that as a matter of discretion it would not do so where the final order would not discharge the liability of the third party in the foreign jurisdiction: *Swiss Bank Corpn* v. *Boehmische Industrial Bank* [1923] 1 KB 673, 678–679, 680–681 (CA); *SCF Finance Co. Ltd* v. *Masri (No. 3)* [1987] QB 1028, 1044 (CA); *Interpool Ltd* v. *Galani*, n.81 above, 743 (an Ord. 48 case); *Deutsche Schachtbau-und Tiefbohrgesellschaft mbH* v. *R'As al-Khaimah National Oil Co.*, n.78 above, 350, 355; *Zoneheath Associates Ltd* v. *China Tianjin International and Technical Cooperative Corp* [1994] CLC 348. See also *Re A Judgment Debtor* (QBD, 22 January 1987); *Crescent Oil and Shipping Services Ltd* v. *Banco Nacional de Angola* (QBD, 28 May 1999).

[84] N.82 above, 30, 31. See also *Swiss Bank Corp.* v. *Boehmische Industrial Park*, n.83 above, 681.

[85] N.62 above. See also *European Bank Ltd* v. *Citibank Ltd* [2004] NSWCA 76, [66]–[69].

Lord Bingham emphasized that it was an integral feature of third party debt proceedings that compliance with a third party debt order would have the effect of discharging the third party from its liability to the judgment debtor.[86] Where this could not be achieved, such as where the debt was situated outside the jurisdiction and was subject to a foreign law that did not recognize the English procedure, the court had no jurisdiction to make the order. As regards the competing approaches in *Richardson* v. *Richardson*[87] and *Martin* v. *Nadel*,[88] considered above, Lord Bingham said that '[i]n practical terms, it does not matter very much whether the House rules that the court has no jurisdiction to make an order in such a case or that the court has a discretion which should always be exercised against the making of an order'.[89] Nevertheless, his Lordship found himself 'in close agreement'[90] with the opinion of Hill J in *Richardson*, and Lord Hobhouse stated that Hill J's view—that the debt, not just the third party, must be properly recoverable within the jurisdiction—had been mistakenly criticized.[91] Lord Bingham, however, left the door open for an English court to make an order over a debt situated outside the jurisdiction where the debt was governed by a law that gave effect to the English order.[92] In contrast, Lords Hoffmann and Millett took a different approach, regarding the matter as one of legal principle and not just one relating to jurisdiction.[93] According to Lord Hoffmann, it was a general principle of international law that one sovereign state should not trespass upon the authority of another by attempting to seize the assets within that other state's jurisdiction.[94] Lord Millett relied upon the principle that the English courts ought not to exercise an exorbitant jurisdiction, contrary to generally accepted norms of international law, and expect a foreign court to sort out the consequences.[95]

In the subsequent Court of Appeal decision in *Masri* v. *Consolidated Contractors International Co. SAL*,[96] which in fact concerned the jurisdiction of the English courts to appoint a receiver by way of equitable execution or to grant a freezing order over foreign debts, counsel sought to argue that *Société Eram* had two ratios—a broader ratio that 'there is no subject matter jurisdiction over foreign debts' and a narrower ratio that 'it is not open to the court to make a third party debt order where the making of the order will not discharge the debt of the third party or garnishee to the judgment debtor according to the law which governs the debt'.[97] Lawrence Collins LJ considered that 'deciding whether there is one ratio or two is a sterile and unnecessary exercise',[98] and extracted the following key proposition from the judgments in *Société Eram*: '…a third party debt order cannot be made where it will not discharge the debt of the third party or garnishee to the judgment debtor according to the law which governs that debt, even if the order is directed *in personam* to a bank with a branch in London, because the order in respect of a foreign debt was an attempt to levy execution on an asset in the foreign jurisdiction'.[99] Whatever the differences between their Lordships in *Société Eram*, it is clear at least that, in practical terms, a judgment creditor will no longer be able to use the third party debt

---

[86] Ibid., [25].   [87] N.72 above.   [88] N.82 above.

[89] *Société Eram Shipping* v. *Compagnie Internationale de Navigation*, n.62 above, [26].

[90] Ibid.

[91] Ibid., [75]. For criticism of *Richardson* v. *Richardson*, n.72 above, see *SCF Finance Co. Ltd* v. *Masri (No. 3)*, n.83 above, 1044; *Interpool Ltd* v. *Galani*, n.81 above, 741.

[92] Ibid. [26].

[93] Lord Nicholls simply expressed agreement with the reasoning of both Lord Bingham and Lord Hoffmann: *Société Eram Shipping* v. *Compagnie Internationale de Navigation*, n.62 above, [31].

[94] *Société Eram Shipping* v. *Compagnie Internationale de Navigation*, n.62 above, [54]–[59]. See also *Gerling Australia Insurance Co. Pty Ltd* v. *Ludgater Holdings Ltd* [2009] NZCA 397, [61]–[66].

[95] Ibid., [109].   [96] N.74 above.   [97] Ibid., [41].   [98] Ibid., [42].

[99] Ibid., [47].

order procedure to obtain execution against a foreign debt because it is most unlikely that he will be able to show that a foreign court will regard the liability as automatically discharged by an order of the English court.[100] The judgment creditor would be better advised to seek enforcement in the jurisdiction where the debt is located.

In the past, an interim garnishee order would often be drafted in such a way as to attach 'all debts' and accordingly would attach the full amount standing to the credit of the customer's account. The bank was then unable to honour cheques drawn by the customer, even if their payment would not reduce the balance in the account beneath the figure required to discharge the debt due to the judgment creditor.[101] However, it is now general practice for an interim third party debt order to be framed in such a way as to attach debts only up to a specified sum.[102] In such a case, the bank earmarks the prescribed amount plus an additional sum to cover estimated costs, and permits the customer to draw on the remaining balance.[103] A difficulty may arise when there is an ambiguity in the third party debt order as to the accounts or the amount of money that is to be attached. In such circumstances it may be unwise for the bank simply to freeze all its customer's accounts and to refuse to honour any payment instructions.[104] Rather, the bank should as a matter of urgency communicate with its customer and the judgment creditor and, if necessary, seek further guidance from the court as to how to deal with its dilemma.

The interim third party debt order does not attach amounts paid to the credit of the customer's account after the date on which the order is made and served on the bank. This rule, decided in *Heppenstall* v. *Jackson (Barclays Bank, Garnishee)*,[105] might be clear in theory, but poses practical problems as regards the attachment by an interim order of the balance credited to the customer's current account. Does the interim third party debt order attach the value of cheques credited to the account before they are cleared? In *Jones & Co.* v. *Coventry*,[106] Darling J held that the interim order attached the account balance as it stood, including the amount of cheques remitted, but not as yet cleared. His Lordship thought, however, that this principle applied only in respect of fully negotiable cheques

---

[100] *Société Eram Shipping* v. *Compagnie Internationale de Navigation*, n.62 above, [16], [111]. In *Kuwait Oil Tanker Co SAK* v. *Qabazard* [2004] 1 AC 300 (HL), decided on the same day as *Société Eram*, the House of Lords again refused to make a final third party debt order over a foreign debt. Enforcement was sought in Switzerland, where the judgment creditor held his bank account, and so the Lugano Convention on Jurisdiction and the Enforcement of Judgments in Civil and Commercial Matters 1988, Art. 16(5) (as incorporated into English law by the Civil Jurisdiction and Judgments Act 1982) conferred exclusive jurisdiction on the Swiss court. Their Lordships added that, even without Art. 16(5), they would not have made the final order for the reasons set out in *Société Eram: Kuwait Oil Tanker Co SAK* v. *Qabazard*, above, [2], [17], [21].

[101] *Rogers* v. *Whiteley*, n.62 above, 121–123. See also *Edmunds* v. *Edmunds* [1904] P 362, 376–377; *Richardson* v. *Richardson*, n.72 above, 236; *Rekstin* v. *Severo Sibirsko Gosudarstvennoe Akcionernoe Obschestro Komseverputj*, n.72 above, 66–67; *Plunkett* v. *Barclays Bank Ltd*, n.78 above, 117–118; *Société Eram Shipping* v. *Compagnie Internationale de Navigation*, n.62 above, [14], [92].

[102] Lord Millett referred to this in *Société Eram Shipping* v. *Compagnie Internationale de Navigation*, n.62 above, [92] as the 'modern form of order'.

[103] As regards the bank's right to deduct its expenses from the amount attached when served with a third party debt order, see *Webb (Gerry) Transport* v. *Brenner* [1985] CL 152. A court has the power under CPR, r.72.7 to allow a bank to make payments to the judgment debtor where the interim order is causing him or his family hardship in meeting ordinary living expenses.

[104] See *Bumiputra-Commerce Bank Bhd* v. *Top-A Plastic Sdn Bhd* [2008] 5 MLJ 34, [26]–[33] (Malay CA), where Heliliah JCA referred to this as 'an easy way of handling the matter'.

[105] [1939] 1 KB 585, 592 (CA). See also *Re Australia and New Zealand Savings Bank Ltd*; *Mellas* v. *Evriniadis*, n.75 above; *Public Prosecutor* v. *Wong Hong Toy* [1986] 1 MLJ 133, 142; *Bumiputra-Commerce Bank Bhd* v. *Top-A Plastic Sdn Bhd*, n.104 above, [26].

[106] [1909] 2 KB 1029. See also *Fern* v. *Bishop Burns & Co. Ltd*, n.44 above.

over which the bank acquired a lien when it received them for collection and credited the customer's account. In Australia, the opposite view has been taken and, in *Bank of New South Wales Ltd* v. *Barlex Investments Pty. Ltd*,[107] the court held that an interim order does not attach amounts based on uncleared cheques as these are only provisionally credited to the customer's account. This latter view is to be preferred. According to rule 72.2(1) of the Civil Procedure Rules 1998, an interim third party debt order attaches only to debts 'due or accruing due' to the judgment debtor in the hands of a third party, such as a bank. The amount of a cheque paid into a customer's account does not become a debt 'due or accruing due' to him from the bank until the instrument is cleared. The proceeds of an uncleared cheque are, therefore, not attached by the third party debt order unless the customer is able to draw against them.[108]

Whilst *Heppenstall* makes clear that a third party debt order attaches 'no debts which do not exist at the moment when the order is *made and served*',[109] the Supreme Court of Victoria, in *Universal Guarantee Pty. Ltd* v. *Derefink*,[110] has suggested that the date on which the balance is attached is not the date of the service of the interim order, but the date on which the order is actually made. Accordingly, the interim order attaches the balance available at the time that it is made, less the amount of cheques paid by the bank after that time but before the service of the order. The difficulty with this test is that the balance standing to the credit of the customer's account at any given moment is not easily ascertainable at a later point of time. Balances are struck at the closing hour of the relevant day. The better view is that the interim order attaches the balance available at the time that the order is served. Indeed, adopting this approach enables the bank to freeze the customer's account as soon as it becomes aware of the order and open a new account for the customer's running operations. Interestingly, the Supreme Court of New South Wales in *Blacktown Concrete Services Pty Ltd* v. *Ultra Refurbishing & Construction Pty Ltd*[111] has recently distanced itself from *Derefink*, holding that '[f]or the purpose of determining when attachment occurs and thus priorities, service is the critical time'.[112] According to Santow J in *Blacktown*, *Derefink* was decided by reference to the particular language of the statutory provisions in that case and 'ignored the weight of decided authority on the point'.[113]

As indicated already, the interim third party debt order affords a bank the opportunity of raising objections to the making of a final order for the payment over of the funds into court or to the judgment creditor. There are several situations in which the bank may wish to raise such an objection, or may be compelled to do so by the Civil Procedure Rules 1998. First and foremost is the case in which there is a clash of priorities between the third party debt order and an assignment by the customer of the balance standing to the credit of his account.[114] In *Rekstin* v. *Severo Sibirsko Gosudarstvennoe Akcionernoe Obschestro Komseverputj*,[115] which involved money-transfer orders, the Court of Appeal held that an instruction by a customer to his bank to transfer the balance of his account

---

[107] (1964) 64 SR (NSW) 274.

[108] Contrast the position in relation to freezing injunctions and uncleared cheques: CPR Pt. 25, Practice Direction (Interim Injunctions), Annex (Freezing Injunction), para. 7.

[109] *Heppenstall* v. *Jackson (Barclays Bank, Garnishee)*, n.105 above, 592.

[110] [1958] VR 51 (Vic. Sup. Ct.). See also *Re Australia and New Zealand Savings Bank Ltd*; *Mellas* v. *Evriniadis*, n.75 above.

[111] (1998) 26 ACSR 759 (NSW Sup. Ct.).	[112] Ibid.	[113] Ibid.

[114] Under CPR, r.72.8(2), the bank 'must file and serve written evidence stating his knowledge' that a third party has a claim to the sums standing to the credit of the relevant account.

[115] N.72 above, 64–65, 69–70. See also *Curran* v. *Newpark Cinemas Ltd* [1951] 1 All ER 295 (CA); *Z Ltd* v. *A-Z and AA-LL*, n.68 above, 586; *ED&F Man (Coffee) Ltd* v. *Miyazaki SA* [1991] 1 Lloyd's Rep. 154; *Lewis &*

to a third party would not preclude a court from making a final order in favour of a judgment creditor when the transfer instruction remained revocable at the time that the order was served on the bank. It must follow that when an amount due to the customer from his bank is effectively and irrevocably assigned, the customer is no longer entitled to dispose of the chose in action involved. Thus, when an assignment of the amount standing to the credit of the account has been completed before the service of the interim third party debt order, the assignee's claim will prevail over that of the judgment creditor. A statutory assignment, made under section 136(1) of the Law of Property Act 1925, is complete when notice of it is served on the 'debtor', who, in the type of case considered here, is the bank.[116] Accordingly, where the clash is between a statutory assignment of an account balance and an interim third party debt order served on the bank's customer, priority is determined by the date of notification to the bank. The position differs in the case of an equitable assignment, which becomes effective when it is executed and quite irrespective of the notification to the debtor.[117] Accordingly, an equitable assignment would take priority over an interim third party debt order provided the customer acted in good faith and could prove his intention to assign the chose in action by 'some outward expression... of his intention to make an immediate disposition of the subject matter of the assignment'[118] before the order was served on the bank. Even if notification of the equitable assignment were given to the bank after the service of the interim order, the assignee would retain his priority.

The second situation in which the bank may wish to apply for a discharge of an interim third party debt order is when it claims some entitlement to the funds in the account. In such circumstances, the bank must disclose details of its entitlement to the court and the judgment creditor within seven days of being served with the interim third party debt order.[119] In this regard, the bank's interest in its customer's account may take the form of an equitable charge over the balance,[120] a 'flawed asset arrangement',[121] or a right to set off or combine the credit balance in the attached account with a debit balance accrued in another account maintained by the same customer.[122] Where the debit balance is accrued by way of an overdraft on a current account, the bank is entitled to exercise its right of set-off, as the amount is either known or readily ascertainable,[123] and an overdraft is in essence repayable on demand. As indicated recently in *Fraser* v. *Oystertec plc*,[124] the position usually differs in the case of loans repayable at a future date, as the amount is not due and claimable at the time the order is served. In that case, the bank sought to resist a final third party debt order on the basis that it had the right to set off against the credit balance in the account the sums owed by the customer under a loan facility. Although the loan agreement gave the bank the right to demand repayment of the loan

---

Peat (Produce) Ltd v. *Almatu Properties Ltd*, The Financial Times, 15 May 1992. For the Australian position, see *Cossill* v. *Strangman* (1962) 80 WN (NSW) 628.

[116] See, for example, *Mulkerrins* v. *PricewaterhouseCoopers* [2003] 4 All ER 1, [13] (HL); *Winterthur Swiss Insurance Co* v. *AG (Manchester) Ltd* [2006] EWHC 839 (Comm.), [59]; *Finlan* v. *Eyton Morris Winfield* [2007] 4 All ER 143, [5]. See further Ch. 21, Sects. 1& 3 below. See also Ch. 13, Sect. 5(iii) below.

[117] See further Ch. 21, Sects. 1& 3 below. See also Ch. 13, Sect. 5(iii) below.

[118] *Finlan* v. *Eyton Morris Winfield*, n.116 above, [33]. See also *Allied Carpets Group plc* v. *Macfarlane* [2002] EWHC 1155, [30]–[33]; *Scribes West Ltd* v. *Relsa Anstalt* [2005] 2 All ER 690, [9] (CA); *Daleri Ltd* v. *Woolworths plc* [2008] EWHC 2891 (Ch), [18].

[119] CPR, r.72.6(2)(c)(iii).

[120] *Fraser* v. *Oystertec plc*, n.63 above, [11]. See further Ch. 21, Sect. 3 below.   [121] Ibid., [12].

[122] See further Ch. 21, Sect. 3(iii) below. For the bank's right of combination, see Ch. 7, Sect. 4 above.

[123] *Tapp* v. *Jones* (1875) LR 10 QB 591, 593. See also *Fraser* v. *Oystertec plc*, n.63 above, [6].

[124] N.63 above, [13]–[19].

and a contractual right of set-off,[125] the bank did not make such a demand until after it had been served with the interim third party debt order and accordingly the judgment creditor took priority over the bank. Terence Mowschenson QC recognized, however, that 'if the bank wanted to obtain a right to set off amounts due on the facility prior to demanding repayment on the facility it should have used clearer language to achieve its objective'.[126] This highlights the fact that, whilst most modern lending agreements confer on the bank a right to demand repayment in full if an interim third party debt order is issued against the customer, to be fully effective the agreement must be carefully drafted to indicate that the right of set-off accrues immediately without the need for the bank to make prior demand of its customer.

The third situation in which a bank is required to raise objections to third party debt proceedings and file evidence in relation to its objections is where the balance in question is standing to the credit of a trust account.[127] The bank's duty to raise the matter with the court only arises where it 'knows or believes'[128] that its customer, the judgment debtor, is not beneficially entitled to the money in question. Although the interim order attaches the balance initially and precludes the bank from paying cheques drawn on the account,[129] it will be discharged when it is established that the accrued balance comprises amounts deposited with the customer as a trustee,[130] such as in the case of clients' funds standing to the credit of a stockbroker's trust account.[131] The converse situation arose recently in *AIG Capital Partners Inc.* v. *Republic of Kazakhstan*,[132] in which the claimants sought a third party debt order to enforce an arbitral award against the Republic of Kazakhstan by attaching cash and securities held in London by a third party pursuant to a global custody agreement with the National Bank of Kazakhstan. Aikens J refused to make the order final on the ground that there was no 'debt due or accruing due' to the judgment debtor, the Republic of Kazakhstan, but only to a separate entity, the National Bank of Kazakhstan.[133] Accordingly, there was no jurisdiction to grant a final third party debt order. Nor did Aikens J consider that this conclusion was altered by the fact that the judgment debtor held the ultimate beneficial interest in the relevant property.[134] After *AIG Capital Partners*, therefore, it appears that a court may refuse to make a final third party debt order in respect of any type of trust account, regardless of whether the judgment debtor is the trustee or the beneficiary of that account.

The fourth case in which the interim order may be discharged is where the balance standing to the credit of the customer's account is owned jointly by himself and by other parties.[135] The general rule in *Hirschorn* v. *Evans (Barclays Bank Ltd, Garnishee)*[136] is that moneys standing to the credit of a joint account are not attachable by means of a third party debt order issued against one of the owners of the account. Although *Hirschorn*

---

[125] Ibid., [16]–[17].   [126] Ibid., [18].

[127] CPR, r.72.8(2). Where a third party may have an interest in an account, the court will serve the notice of the application on that party: CPR, r.72.8(5). For trust accounts, see Ch. 8, Sect. 5 above.

[128] Ibid.

[129] *Plunkett* v. *Barclays Bank Ltd*, n.78 above. criticized in Ch. 8, Sect. 6(ii) above. See also *Arab Bank Ltd* v. *Barclays Bank (DCO)*, n.52 above, 532. This remains the view taken by Australian courts: *Melville Island Ltd* v. *Richards*, n.78 above.

[130] The nature of the account is a fact to be considered in respect of the application for a final order: *Deutsche Schachtbau und Tiefbohrgesellschaft* v. *R'As al Khaima International Oil Co.*, n.78 above, 351.

[131] *Hancock* v. *Smith* (1889) 41 Ch. D 456 (CA). See also *Harrods Ltd* v. *Tester* [1937] 2 All ER 236 (CA).

[132] N.78 above.   [133] Ibid., [30]–[32].   [134] Ibid., [31].   [135] CPR, r.72.8(2), (5).

[136] N.72 above, applying *Macdonald* v. *Tacquah Gold Mines Co.* (1884) 13 QBD 535 (CA). See also *Hoon* v. *Maloff (Jarvis Construction Co. Ltd, Garnishee)* (1964) 42 DLR (2nd) 770, showing that a partnership account cannot be attached to satisfy the debts of one of the partners.

was based on the somewhat outmoded view that a bank's obligations to joint account holders are owed jointly alone and not jointly and severally,[137] and although the decision has recently been criticized by the Nova Scotia Supreme Court for allowing 'judgment debtors to hide monies from execution creditors in an inequitable, unfair, and illogical manner' by the simple expedient of placing those funds in a joint account,[138] it nevertheless continues to represent the English position.[139] It is likely that if the judgment creditor could demonstrate convincingly that the moneys in the joint account in reality belonged to the judgment debtor and that he had secreted the funds away to avoid his creditors, the court might decline to apply *Hirschorn*.[140] However, where there is a judgment debt due jointly and severally from a number of debtors, it is possible to attach a balance standing to the credit of an account maintained by only some of them.[141]

The fifth case in which it is in the bank's interest to raise an objection is where the judgment debtor is described in the interim order by a name that differs from that under which he has opened the account. If the judgment debtor and the customer are not one and the same person, and the bank overlooks this fact and dishonours a cheque in reliance on the interim order, the bank may be liable for the wrongful dishonour of the cheque. Accordingly, there is authority for the view that, in the case of a discrepancy in the names, the bank is entitled to disregard the interim order.[142]

Finally, a bank is generally entitled to oppose the granting of a final third party debt order in cases where there is a real danger that the payment of the debt to the judgment creditor will not be recognized as a discharge of that debt in other jurisdictions, with the result that the bank may have to pay over the same amount again. Cases of this type arise mainly out of disputes litigated in more than one jurisdiction and banks are more likely to be vulnerable in such cases if they have offices or branches in the different jurisdictions involved.[143] Notably, an interim order would be discharged on the ground of the double jeopardy arising in cases of this type even if a foreign court's refusal to treat payment to the judgment creditor as a discharge would involve a lack of comity or, possibly, an exorbitant exercise of jurisdiction. Accordingly, an English court exercises its discretion in these cases by assessing the risk of double jeopardy and not by examining the propriety of the possible intervention by the foreign court. This is clear in *Deutsche Schachtbau und Tiefbohrgesellschaft* v. *R'As al Khaima International Oil Co,*[144] where Lord Goff considered

---

[137] *Hirschorn* v. *Evans (Barclays Bank Ltd, Garnishee)*, n.72 above, 812; but compare *Jackson* v. *White and Midland Bank Ltd* [1967] 2 Lloyd's Rep. 68, 79; *Catlin* v. *Cyprus Finance Corporation (London) Ltd* [1983] QB 759, 771. See further Ch. 8, Sect. 2(ii) above.

[138] *Smith* v. *Schaffner* [2007] NSSC 210, [15]. Alberta, Ontario, and Newfoundland have enacted legislation allowing for the garnishment of joint accounts: ibid., [15]–[18].

[139] *Pletchy* v. *Marrow* (CA, 21 May 1998). See also *D. J. Colburt & Sons Pty. Ltd* v. *Ansen* (*Commercial Banking Co. of Sydney Ltd, Garnishee*) (1966) 85 WN (NSW) (Pt. 1) 64, 66 (NSWCA) ('...the correctness of [*Hirschorn*] is, if I may respectfully say so, so obvious as not to require further attention...'); *Deputy Commissioner of Taxation* v. *Westpac Savings Bank Ltd* (1987) 72 ALR 634, 638–639 (NSW Sup. Ct.); *Belfast Telegraph Newspapers Ltd* v. *Blunden* [1995] NI 351 (NICA) (where *Hirshcorn* was applied in the context of a partnership account); cf *Cohen* v. *Cohen* (1983) 4 FLR 451.

[140] Consider *Harrods Ltd* v. *Tester*, n.131 above.

[141] *D. J. Colburt & Sons Pty. Ltd* v. *Ansen* (*Commercial Banking Co. of Sydney Ltd, Garnishee*), n.139 above.

[142] *Moore* v. *Peachey* (1842) 8 TLR 406; *Koch* v. *Mineral Ore Syndicate* (*London and South Western Bank Ltd, Garnishee*) (1910) 54 Sol. Jo. 600.

[143] The risk of 'double jeopardy' is the principal reason why a third party debt order will not be made against a third party debtor overseas: *Masri* v. *Consolidated Contractors International UK Ltd (No. 2)*, n.63 above, [116], affd. on other grounds: N.74 above.

[144] N.78 above. See also *Zoneheath Associates Ltd* v. *China Tianjin International and Technical Co-operative Corp*, n.83 above; *Camdex International Ltd* v. *Bank of Zambia*, The Times, 28 January 1997; *Soinco Saci* v.

that it would be 'inequitable' to make an absolute order 'where the payment by the [garnishee/third party debtor] under the order absolute will not necessarily discharge his liability under the attached debt, there being a real risk that he may be held liable in some foreign court to pay a second time'.[145] An English court can only exercise this type of discretion in cases where the judgment debtor's account or the debt to be attached is situate in England, as was the case in *Deutsche Schachtbau* itself. As considered above, where the account or other debt is situate abroad, the court does not have a discretion as to whether to make the order final or not, but simply does not have any jurisdiction to do so, or will refuse do so as a matter of principle.[146]

(iv) Freezing injunctions

In the course of the last three decades, a bank's duty to obey its customer's instructions for the payment of money and for the transfer of funds has frequently been abrogated by freezing injunctions. This modern type of order, formerly called a *Mareva* injunction after the first case that attempted to define it,[147] has been given statutory recognition in section 37 of the Senior Courts Act 1981.[148] Under this provision, the High Court's power to grant an interim injunction restraining any party from removing from the jurisdiction, or otherwise dealing with, assets located within the jurisdiction, is exercisable regardless of whether or not the party in question is domiciled, resident, or present within the jurisdiction.[149] Although the freezing injunction is accordingly available in disputes arising out of both international and domestic transactions, its main domain remains the former type of case. In the context of domestic banking transactions, it merits a general rather than a detailed discussion.

A freezing injunction does not act as a remedy *in rem*.[150] It constitutes a form of personal relief and hence acts *in personam*.[151] This basic principle reflects the freezing

---

Novokuznetsk Aluminium Plant [1998] 2 Lloyd's Rep. 346, 352–354 (CA); *Crescent Oil and Shipping Services Ltd* v. *Banco Nacional de Angola*, n.83 above.

[145] Ibid., 350, 355. See also *Société Eram Shipping* v. *Compagnie Internationale de Navigation*, n.62 above, [21], [105].

[146] *Société Eram Shipping* v. *Compagnie Internationale de Navigation*, n.62 above, [105], where Lord Millett stated: 'There is no doubt, of course, that the court's power to make an order in the case of an English debt is discretionary. The present question is different.' Lord Bingham expressed a similar view: ibid., [26].

[147] *Mareva Compania Naviera SA* v. *International Bulk Carriers SA (The 'Mareva')* [1975] 2 Lloyd's Rep. 509 (CA). For an earlier decision, see *Nippon Yusen Kaisha* v. *Marageorgis* [1975] 1 WLR 1093 (CA). The name change from '*Mareva* injunction' to 'freezing injunction' came with the introduction of CPR, r.25.1(1)(f).

[148] Despite controversy over the origin of the freezing order jurisdiction, the principal effect of the Senior Courts Act 1981, s.37 is that '[a]n all-out challenge to the entire concept…seems a rather unlikely event, at least in the courts of England and Hong Kong': see *Mercedes-Benz AG* v. *Leiduck* [1996] AC 284, 299, 306 (PC).

[149] For the form of a freezing injunction, see CPR Pt. 25, Practice Direction (Interim Injunctions), Annex (Freezing Injunction). The example may be adapted either to freeze assets within England and Wales or to freeze assets worldwide.

[150] *Customs and Excise Commissioners* v. *Barclays Bank plc* [2007] 1 AC 181, [10] (HL) ('The purpose [of the freezing injunction] is not to give a claimant security for his claim or give him any proprietary interest in the assets restrained'); *Fourie* v. *Le Roux* [2007] 1 All ER 1087, [2] (HL) ('[Freezing injunctions] are not a proprietary remedy').

[151] *Cretanor Maritime Co. Ltd* v. *Irish Marine Management Ltd* [1978] 1 WLR 966, 976–977 (CA); *Iraqi Ministry of Defence* v. *Arcepey Shipping Co SA ('The Angel Bell')* [1981] QB 65, 71–72; *AJ Bekhor & Co. Ltd* v. *Bilton* [1981] QB 923, 942 (CA); *K/S A/S Admiral Shipping* v. *Portlink Ferries Ltd* [1984] 2 Lloyd's

injunction's object, which is neither to attach the defendant's assets, nor to confer some priority on the claimant. The object of the order is, rather, to prevent the defendant from defeating a judgment that may be given against him by dissipating his assets.[152] Accordingly, an order is usually granted only if the claimant is able to establish four points. First, as was recently highlighted by the House of Lords in *Fourie* v. *Le Roux*,[153] the applicant for the freezing injunction must either have commenced proceedings (whether in the United Kingdom or abroad) relating to his substantive claim against the person to be enjoined or have undertaken to commence such proceedings. Whilst the absence of such proceedings or undertaking does not mean that the court has no jurisdiction at all to grant a freezing injunction, according to Lord Scott in *Fourie* 'without the issue of substantive proceedings or an undertaking to do so, the propriety of the grant of an interlocutory injunction would be difficult to defend'.[154] Secondly, the claimant must be able to show that he has a good arguable case on the merits, so that he is likely to obtain judgment against the defendant.[155] Thirdly, the claimant

Rep. 166, 168 (CA); *Felixstowe Dock & Railway Co.* v. *United States Lines Inc.* [1989] QB 360, 372; *Bank Mellat* v. *Kazmi* [1989] QB 541, 549 (CA); *Derby & Co.* v. *Weldon* [1990] Ch. 48, 57 (CA); *Derby & Co.* v. *Weldon (Nos. 3 and 4)* [1990] Ch. 65, 82–83, 95–96 (CA); *Christie Owen & Davies plc* v. *Tray* (CA, 23 November 1992); *Re Mordant* [1996] BPIR 302, 308 (CA); *Mercedes-Benz AG* v. *Leiduck*, n.148 above, 300; *Flightline Ltd* v. *Edwards* [2003] 1 WLR 1200, [43]–[47] (CA); *Kastner* v. *Jason* [2004] EWCA Civ 1599, [27]; *Technocrats International Inc* v. *Fredic Ltd* [2005] 1 BCLC 467, [9]–[13]; *Masri* v. *Consolidated Contractors International UK Ltd (No. 2)*, n.63 above, [67]–[69], affd. on other grounds: N.74 above. Lord Denning's dictum in *Z Ltd* v. *A-Z and AA-LL*, n.68 above, 573, comparing the freezing injunction with the attachment of a ship and treating it as a remedy *in rem*, has been criticized, rejected as incorrect, and treated as *per incuriam*: *Attorney-General* v. *Newspaper Publishing plc* [1988] Ch. 333, 343–344 (CA); *Babanaft International Co. SA* v. *Bassatne* [1990] Ch. 13 (CA); *Attorney-General* v. *Times Newspapers Ltd* [1992] 1 AC 191, 215 (HL).

[152] The interim order may contain an order requiring the defendant to provide information about his assets: CPR, r.25.1(1)(g). It is clear that a disclosure order is considered a very important part of the jurisdiction to make worldwide freezing orders: *Motorola Credit Corp* v. *Uzan* [2002] 2 All ER (Comm.) 945, [27]–[30] (CA); *Raja* v. *van Hoogstraten* [2004] 4 All ER 793, [101]–[105] (CA); *Congentra AG* v. *Sixteen Thirteen Marine SA* [2009] 1 All ER (Comm) 479, [59]. The defendant may be cross-examined on the disclosure that he makes: *Motorola Credit Corp* v. *Uzan (No. 2)* [2004] 1 WLR 113, [24]–[27] (CA); *West London Pipeline & Storage Ltd* v. *Total UK Ltd* [2008] EWHC 1729 (Comm.), [78]. A defendant who is in contempt of court by refusing to disclose assets or making inadequate disclosure may be precluded from applying to the court to discharge the freezing injunction, but such a situation 'will be rare indeed': ibid., [50]–[53], [58]. For the discretion to exclude a comtemnor from a hearing, see *Polanski* v. *Condé Nast Publications Ltd* [2005] 1 All ER 945, [18]–[19] (HL); *Konkola Copper Mines plc* v. *Coromin Ltd (No. 2)* [2006] 2 Lloyd's Rep 446, [11]; *Mubarak* v. *Mubarak* [2007] 1 FLR 722, [50].

[153] N.150 above. A freezing injunction may also be made where there are no existing proceedings, but the order is sought in aid of execution of a judgment: *Frances* v. *Al Assad* [2007] BPIR 1233, [80].

[154] Ibid., [32]–[37]. According to Lord Bingham, the claimant 'must at least point to proceedings already brought or proceedings about to be brought, so as to show where and on what basis he expects to recover judgment against the defendant': ibid., [3].

[155] *Z Ltd* v. *A-Z and AA-LL*, n.68 above, 585; *Ninemia Maritime Corp.* v. *Trave Schiffahrtsgesellschaft (The 'Niedersachsen')* [1984] 1 All ER 398, 402, 415–417 (CA). See also *Rasu Maritima SA* v. *Perusahaan Pertambangan Minyak Dan Gas Bumi Negara (Pertamina)* [1978] QB 644 (CA); *AJ Dunning & Sons (Weyhill) Ltd* v. *Miles* (CA, 13 May 1985); *Ashtiani* v. *Kashi* [1987] QB 888, 900 (CA); *Prekookedska Plovidba* v. *LNT Lines SRL* [1989] 1 WLR 753; *Derby & Co. Ltd* v. *Weldon (Nos 3 and 4)*, n.151 above, 92–93; *X* v. *Y* [1990] 1 QB 220, 231; *Polly Peck International plc* v. *Nadir (No. 2)* [1992] 4 All ER 782 (CA); *ALG Inc.* v. *Uganda Airlines Corporation*, The Times, 31 July 1992; *Grupo Torras SA* v. *Al-Sabah*, The Times, 17 March 1997 (CA); *Walsh* v. *Deloitte & Touche* (2001) 146 SJLB 13, [10] (PC); *Laemthong International Lines Co. Ltd* v. *Artis* [2004] 2 All ER (Comm.) 797, [33], [43], [53]; *Fourie* v. *Le Roux*, n.150 above, [7]; *Mobil Cerro Negro Ltd* v. *Petroleos De Venezuela SA* [2008] EWHC 532, [37]; *Guerrero* v. *Monterrico Metals plc* [2009] EWHC 2475 (QB), [24]–[26]. The cause of action must exist at the time the order is to be granted: *Veracruz Transportation Inc.* v. *VC Shipping Co. Inc.* [1992] 1 Lloyd's Rep.

must show that there is a 'sufficient risk of dissipation' in the sense that there is a 'real risk that, unless restrained by injunction, the defendant will dissipate or dispose of his assets other than in the ordinary course of business' or that 'unless the defendant is restrained by injunction, assets are likely to be dealt with in such a way as to make enforcement of any award or judgment more difficult'.[156] It is clear that this requirement confers on the court a wide discretion. Essentially, as stated in section 37(1) of the Senior Courts Act 1981, the court is considering whether it is 'just and convenient' to grant the freezing order.[157] One of the many potential considerations taken into account is the defendant's record and standing. Thus, in the context of a substantial international dispute, the Court of Appeal refused to grant a freezing injunction against a bank where there seemed to be no danger that the bank would remove its

353 (CA); *Zucker* v. *Tyndall Holdings plc* [1992] 1 WLR 1127, 1136 (CA); *Department of Social Security* v. *Butler* [1995] 1 WLR 1528, 1540 (CA); *C Inc. plc* v. *L*, [2001] 2 Lloyd's Rep. 459; *Petroleum Investment Co. Ltd* v. *Kantupan Holdings Co. Ltd* [2002] 1 All ER (Comm.) 124, [29]; but consider *Mercedes-Benz AG* v. *Leiduck*, n.148 above, 312.

156 *Congentra AG* v. *Sixteen Thirteen Marine SA*, n.152 above, [49]. See also, for example, *Rahman (Prince Abdul)* v. *Abu-Taha* [1980] 1 WLR 1268, 1272 (CA); *Searose Ltd* v. *Seatrain (UK) Ltd* [1981] 1 All ER 806, 808; *Ninemia Maritime Corp.* v. *Trave Schiffahrtsgesellschaft (The 'Niedersachsen')*, n.155 above, 406, 419; *Ashtiani* v. *Kashi*, n.155 above; *Babanaft International Co. SA* v. *Bassatne*, n.151 above; *Derby & Co. Ltd* v. *Weldon*, n.151 above; *Derby & Co. Ltd* v. *Weldon (No.6)* [1990] 3 All ER 263 (CA); *ALG Inc.* v. *Uganda Airlines Corporation*, n.155 above; *TSB Private Bank International SA* v. *Chabra* [1992] 2 All ER 245; *Polly Peck International plc* v. *Nadir (No. 2)*, n.155 above; *Gidrxslme Shipping Co. Ltd* v. *Tantomar-Transportes Maritimos Lda* [1994] 4 All ER 507; *Grupo Torras SA* v. *Al-Sabah*, n.155 above; *Federal Bank of the Middle East Ltd* v. *Hadkinson* [2000] 2 All ER 395 (CA); *Re Industrial Services Group Ltd* [2003] BPIR 392; *Laemthong International Lines Co. Ltd* v. *Artis*, n.155 above, [54]; *Frances* v. *Al Assad*, n.153 above, [63]; *Swift-Fortune Ltd* v. *Magnifica Marine SA* [2008] 1 Lloyd's Rep. 54, [17]–[18]; *Mobil Cerro Negro Ltd* v. *Petroleos De Venezuela SA*, n.155 above, [35]–[44]; *Ministry of Trade of the Republic of Iraq* v. *Tsavliris Salvage (International) Ltd* [2008] EWHC 612 (Comm.), [94]; *Guerrero* v. *Monterrico Metals plc*, n.155 above, [28].

157 *Ninemia Maritime Corp.* v. *Trave Schiffahrtsgesellschaft (The 'Niedersachsen')*, n.155 above, 418. See also *TRACS (Engineering) Ltd* v. *Sampson* [2001] EWCA Civ 1388, [42]–[53]; *Nigeria International Bank* v. *Assamull* [2002] EWHC 2133 (QB), [16]; *Thane Investments Ltd* v. *Tomlinson* [2003] EWCA Civ 1272, [21]; *Laemthong International Lines Co.* v. *Artis*, n.155 above, [54]; *Regalway Care Ltd* v. *Shillingford* [2005] EWHC 261 (Ch), [24]; *Celtic Resources Holdings plc* v. *Arduina Holdings BV* [2006] EWHC 2553 (Comm.), [20]; *Fourie* v. *Le Roux*, n.150 above, [33]; *Swift-Fortune Ltd* v. *Magnifica Marine SA*, n.156 above [19]–[35]; *United States Securities and Exchange Commission* v. *Manterfield* [2008] EWHC 1349 (QB), [30]; *Guerrero* v. *Monterrico Metals plc*, n.155 above, [29]–[33]. This point reflects the equitable nature of the freezing injunction. A related aspect thereof is the claimant's duty to make full disclosure of all material facts known to him and his duty to make a proper investigation of facts asserted by him. A failure to make such disclosure gives the court the discretion to discharge the injunction that has been made without notice: *Brink's-Mat Ltd* v. *Elcombe* [1988] 1 WLR 1350, 1358, 1359 (CA); *Behbehani* v. *Salem* [1989] 1 WLR 723, 729 (CA); *Tate Access Floors Ltd* v. *Boswell* [1991] Ch 512; *Gadget Shop Ltd* v. *Bug Com Ltd*, The Times, 28 March 2000; *Walsh* v. *Deloitte & Touche*, n.155 above, [19]; *Memory Corporation* v. *Sidhu (No.2)* [2000] 1 WLR 1443, 1455, 1459–1460 (CA); *Re Industrial Services Group Ltd*, n.156 above; *Arena Corporation Ltd* v. *Schroeder* [2003] EWHC 1089 (Ch), [113]–[118]; *Laemthong International Lines Co. Ltd* v. *Artis*, n.155 above, [64]; *Trade Credit Finance No 1 Ltd* v. *Bilgin* [2004] EWHC 2732, [23]–[25]; *Hakendorf* v. *Countess of Rosenborg* [2004] EWHC 2821 (QB), [83]–[101]; *FFSB Ltd* v. *Seward & Kissel LLP* [2007] UKPC 16, [40]; *Amedeo Hotels Ltd* v. *Zaman* [2007] EWHC 295 (Comm.), [30]; *Frances* v. *Al Assad*, n.153 above, [102]–[106]; *Congentra AG* v. *Sixteen Thirteen Marine SA*, n.152 above, [61]–[65]; *Dadourian Group International Inc* v. *Simms* [2009] EWCA Civ 169, [172]; cf. *Dormeuil Frères SA* v. *Nicolian International Textiles Ltd* [1988] 1 WLR 1362; *Adi and Fahd Shobokshi Group Ltd* v. *Moneim* [1989] 1 WLR 710.

assets from the jurisdiction.[158] Whilst at one stage the freezing injunction was regarded purely as an interim order, available principally before the giving of the final judgment in the relevant case, it is now established that the court also has the power to grant it between final judgment and execution.[159] Finally, in cases involving an international element, such as is likely to arise in the case of a 'worldwide' freezing injunction, the claimant may need to establish not only the court's power to make such an order,[160] but also its personal jurisdiction over the defendant. Where the English courts have jurisdiction over the substantive proceedings that have been or will be commenced against the defendant, there is no issue concerning its power to issue a freezing injunction, but the court will still have to consider whether to grant permission to serve the injunction out of the jurisdiction where the defendant is located abroad.[161] Where the substantive proceedings have been or will be commenced abroad, section 25 of the Civil Jurisdiction and Judgment Act 1982 now gives the English courts the power to grant a freezing injunction in support of those foreign proceedings.[162] The exercise of this power remains discretionary, however, and the court may refuse to grant a freezing injunction in such circumstances where it is 'inexpedient' for the court to do so[163] or where it is unwilling to give permission to serve out of the jurisdiction a defendant who is located abroad.[164]

Originally, the freezing injunction was granted only in respect of assets within the jurisdiction, but it is now established that, in respect of a dispute instituted before it, an English court may, in exceptional circumstances,[165] grant a freezing injunction

---

[158] *Etablissement Esefka International Anstalt* v. *Central Bank of Nigeria* [1979] 1 Lloyd's Rep. 455. See also *Polly Peck International plc* v. *Nadir (No. 2)*, n.155 above; *Camdex International Ltd* v. *Bank of Zambia (No. 2)* [1997] 1 All ER 728.

[159] *Orwell Steel (Erection and Fabrication) Ltd* v. *Asphalt and Tarmac (UK) Ltd* [1985] 3 All ER 747; *Gidrxslme Shipping Co. Ltd* v. *Tantomar-Transportes Maritimos Lda*, n.156 above; *Mercantile Group (Europe) AG* v. *Aiyela* [1994] QB 366, 377 (CA); *B* v. *B* [1998] 1 WLR 329; *Frances* v. *Al Assad*, n.153 above, [80]. The defendant may, further, be enjoined from leaving the jurisdiction: *Bayer AG* v. *Winter* [1986] 1 All ER 733, 737 (CA); *Arab Monetary Fund* v. *Hashim* [1989] 1 WLR 565; *Re M* [2006] 1 FLR 1031, [29].

[160] *Fourie* v. *Le Roux*, n.150 above, [31].

[161] CPR Pt. 6, Practice Direction (Service Out of the Jurisdiction), para. 3.1(1)–(2).

[162] Originally, s.25 of the Civil Jurisdiction and Judgments Act 1982 only applied in circumstances where the substantive proceedings were pending or contemplated in a 'Brussels or Lugano contracting state' (now 'Regulation state') and the subject matter of the proceedings was within the scope of the Brussels or Lugano Conventions (since replaced by Council Regulation 44/2001, [2001] OJ L12/1, Art. 31). Subsequently, the scope of s. 25 was extended to non-Convention/Regulation countries and to proceedings outside the scope of the Conventions/Regulation by the Civil Jurisdiction and Judgments Act 1982 (Interim Relief) Order 1997, S.I. 1997/302, which came into force on 1 April 1997: *Fourie* v. *Le Roux*, n.150 above, [31].

[163] Civil Jurisdiction and Judgments Act 1982, s.25(2). Although there are no statutory guidelines as to the test to be applied by the court in considering whether granting an order would be 'inexpedient', the courts have developed their own guidelines in this regard: *Republic of Haiti* v. *Duvalier* [1990] 1 QB 202 (CA); *Crédit Suisse Fides Trust SA* v. *Cuoghi* [1998] QB 818, 825–829, 831 (CA); *Refco Inc* v. *Eastern Trading Co.* [1999] 1 Lloyd's Rep. 159, 170–172, 174–175 (CA); *Motorola Credit Corp* v. *Uzan (No. 2)*, n.152 above, [114]–[128]; *Rhode* v. *Rhode* [2007] 2 FLR 971, [25]–[26]; *Amedeo Hotels Ltd* v. *Zaman*, n.157 above, [72]; *Banco Nacional de Comercio Exteriro SNC* v. *Empresa de Telecomunicaciones de Cuba SA* [2007] 2 Lloyd's Rep 484, [27]–[31] (CA); *United States Securities and Exchange Commission* v. *Manterfield*, n.157 above, [30]–[32]; *ETI Euro Telecom International NV* v. *Republic of Bolivia* [2008] EWCA Civ 880, [99]–[109]; *Belletti* v. *Morici* [2009] EWHC 2316 (Comm.), [38]–[59].

[164] CPR Pt. 6, Practice Direction (Service Out of the Jurisdiction), para. 3.1(5).

[165] *Derby & Co.* v. *Weldon*, n.151 above, 55, 62, suggesting that a 'worldwide' order would be granted only if the amount claimed could not be recovered from the defendant's assets within the jurisdiction. See also *Rosseel NV* v. *Oriental Commercial Shipping (UK)* [1990] 1 WLR 1387, 1388–1389 (CA); *Sociedade Nacional de Combustiveis de Angola UEE* v. *Lundquist* [1991] 2 QB 310 (CA); *Gidrxslme Shipping Co.*

encompassing not only such assets, but also assets located overseas, such as a deposit with a bank's branch abroad.[166] Such a 'worldwide' injunction may be granted even if the defendant does not have assets within the jurisdiction.[167] The order is granted despite the fact that the court does not have the machinery for its specific enforcement abroad, as the contempt proceedings, in the context of which the court can strike out the defence filed in the proceedings before it, are considered an adequate sanction.[168] Moreover, a 'worldwide' freezing injunction may be granted both prior to the trial and after judgment, but, in order to avoid the assertion of an exorbitant jurisdiction, the courts have tended, especially in the case of a post-trial freezing injunction, to incorporate a clause known as the *Babanaft* proviso'.[169] Essentially, the effect of such a clause is to clarify that the observance of the injunction is expected from the defendant alone and that there is no attempt to extend its effect to third parties residing outside the jurisdiction unless the order is declared enforceable or is enforced by the foreign court.[170] The importance of the *Babanaft* proviso' to foreign banks with branches in the United Kingdom and to local banks in respect of the operations of their foreign branches is self-evident. In addition, there is a further clause that may be included in the freezing injunction so as to protect the interests of banks operating in overseas countries against the risk of their being a clash between the freezing injunction issued in England and a foreign court order. Pursuant to this clause, the injunction does not preclude the bank from complying, in respect of assets located outside England, with the requirements of the foreign jurisdiction's banking law and practice and any orders given in respect of these assets by a court in the relevant foreign country.[171] Such a clause would usually be added to a worldwide freezing order unless the court considered on the particular facts of the case that this was inappropriate.[172]

Subject to the *Babanaft* proviso', considered already, the freezing injunction is usually addressed not only to the defendant but also to third parties who are believed to hold any of his assets. Accordingly, such an order usually instructs the defendant's bank to freeze his account or to ensure that the balance is not reduced beneath a given figure.[173] Usually, the order is not made in respect of a single specified account, but rather extends to the

---

Ltd v. *Tantomar-Transportes Maritimos Lda*, n.156 above; *S&T Bautrading* v. *Nordling* [1997] 3 All ER 718(CA); *Crédit Suisse Fides Trust SA* v. *Cuoghi*, n.163 above; *Belair LLC* v. *Basel LLC* [2009] EWHC 725 (Comm.), [26].

[166] *Republic of Haiti* v. *Duvalier*, n.163 above; *Babanaft International Co. SA* v. *Bassatne*, n.151 above; *Derby & Co.* v. *Weldon*, n.151 above; *Derby & Co.* v. *Weldon* (Nos. 3 and 4), n.151 above; *Derby & Co.* v. *Weldon* (No. 6), n.156 above (indicating that, in appropriate cases, the court may exercise its jurisdiction in order to preclude the transfer of assets from one jurisdiction to another or to order the transfer of assets from one foreign jurisdiction to another).

[167] *Derby & Co.* v. *Weldon* (Nos. 3 and 4), n.151 above, 77 ff; *Derby & Co.* v. *Weldon* (No.6), n.156 above; *Bank of China* v. *NBM LLC* [2002] 1 All ER 717, [15] (CA).

[168] Ibid., 80 ff.

[169] *Babanaft International Co. SA* v. *Bassatne*, n.151 above, 37, 44. See also *Derby & Co.* v. *Weldon* (Nos. 3 and 4), n.151 above, 83–84; *Crédit Suisse Fides Trust SA* v. *Cuoghi*, n.163 above; *Bank of China* v. *NBM LLC*, n.167 above, [9]; *Dadourian Group International Inc.* v. *Simms* [2005] 2 All ER 651, [46]–[47]; *Masri* v. *Consolidated Contractors International Co. SAL*, n.74 above, [37]–[39].

[170] As would be readily done in a Member State to which Council Regulation 44/2001 ([2001] OJ L12/1) applies: see, for example, *Derby & Co.* v. *Weldon* (Nos. 3 and 4), n.151 above, 83–84, in which a court in Luxembourg gave effect to the respective worldwide freezing injunction.

[171] *Baltic Shipping Co.* v. *Translink Shipping* [1995] 1 Lloyd's Rep. 673, 678–679. See also *Bank of China* v. *NBM LLC*, n.167 above, [12]–[22]; *Société Eram Shipping* v. *Compagnie Internationale de Navigation*, n.62 above, [23]; *Masri* v. *Consolidated Contractors International Co. SAL*, n.74 above, [39].

[172] *Bank of China* v. *NBM LLC*, n.167 above, [12]–[22].

[173] See, for example, *Nelson* v. *Halifax plc* [2008] EWCA Civ 1016, [4]–[5].

global balance due to the relevant customer from the bank,[174] although the standard-form freezing injunction anticipates that the claimant will state a maximum amount of funds to be frozen.[175] In this regard, the bank may be ordered to search its records so as to ascertain all the defendant's accounts,[176] and the claimant will ordinarily be asked to give security to cover the costs incurred by the bank in this regard.[177] Although a bank that has been served with a freezing injunction directed at its customer's assets can be guilty of contempt of court if it deliberately or knowingly disobeys the court's order by refusing to freeze the account,[178] according to the House of Lords in *Customs & Excise Commissioners* v. *Barclays Bank plc*,[179] a bank with notice of the freezing injunction does not owe the holder of that order a duty to take care to prevent the disposal of its customer's funds in breach of that order. According to their Lordships, there would be no voluntary assumption of responsibility by the bank to the holder of the order in such circumstances, as the bank had no choice but to comply with the freezing injunction and the holder of the order could not in any meaningful sense be said to have relied upon the bank.[180] Nor did a majority of their Lordships consider that it was 'fair, just and reasonable' to impose a duty of care on banks in such circumstances.[181] This is a particularly sensible conclusion, given that the bank cannot usually adopt the straightforward course of ruling off the customer's old account and permitting him to open a new account to be freely utilized for new operations (as might be the case with other types of order), since the freezing injunction attaches both existing assets and property acquired by the defendant after the date on which the order is made.[182] As funds paid to the credit of the customer's account after the service of the freezing injunction are caught by the order, the bank has to remain vigilant as regards all the dealings of the customer from the time that the order is served. Given the number of accounts operated by the clearing banks, it is sensible that they should not incur onerous liability for their non-deliberate failures to abide by the terms of a freezing injunction served on a customer.

---

[174] For the desirability of their being some specificity in the freezing injunction as to the accounts to be frozen, see *Federal Bank of the Middle East Ltd* v. *Hadkinson*, n.156 above.

[175] CPR Pt. 25, Practice Direction (Interim Injunctions), Annex (Freezing Injunction), para. 8. See also *Z Ltd* v. *A-Z and AA-LL*, n.68 above, 585; *McDonald* v. *Graham* [1994] RPC 407 (CA).

[176] Where the order restrains the defendant's use of his credit tokens or cheque card, the court will usually sanction debits arising from transactions concluded prior to the date on which the order is served on the bank: *Z Ltd* v. *A-Z and AA-LL*, n.68 above, 576–577.

[177] *Searose Ltd* v. *Seatrain (UK) Ltd*, n.156 above, 808; *Z Ltd* v. *A-Z and AA-LL*, n.68 above, 575, 584, 586; *Federal Bank of the Middle East Ltd* v. *Hadkinson*, n.156 above; *SmithKline Beecham plc* v. *Apotex Europe Ltd* [2007] Ch 71, [28] (CA).

[178] CPR Pt. 25, Practice Direction (Interim Injunctions), Annex (Freezing Injunction), para. 16. See also *Z Ltd* v. *A-Z and AA-LL*, n.68 above, 572, 578; *Attorney-General* v. *Times Newspapers Ltd*, n.151 above; *Steen* v. *Attorney-General* [2001] EWCA Civ 403, [60]–[61]; *C* v. *C* [2006] 1 FLR 936, [15]; *Crystalmews Ltd* v. *Metterick* [2006] EWHC 2653 (Ch), [43]; *Customs & Excise Commissioners* v. *Barclays Bank plc*, n.150 above, [11], [56]–[59]. Where the freezing injunction is obtained wrongfully, the customer whose account has been frozen may be able to recover his losses from the party that applied for the injunction: *Al-Rawas* v. *Pegasus Energy* [2008] EWHC 617 (QB), [34]–[39].

[179] N.150 above. See further Ch. 5, Sect. 4(iii) above.

[180] Ibid., [4], [14], [38]–[39], [65], [74], [109], [112].

[181] Ibid., [17]–[23], [64], [102]. Lord Walker (at [75] & [77]) did consider it 'just, fair, and reasonable' to impose liability on banks for negligently breaching the terms of a freezing injunction, but declined to impose a duty of care as such a result could not realistically be confined to the banking context.

[182] *TDK Tape Distributor (UK) Ltd* v. *Videochoice Ltd* [1985] 3 All ER 345. 349; *Soinco Saci* v. *Novokuznetsk Aluminium Plant*, n.144 above.

When granting a freezing injunction, the court will be as careful as possible not to interfere with the rights of third parties.[183] Unless the order is sufficiently clearly drafted so as to apply to all accounts to which the defendant is a party, a freezing injunction served on a bank does not automatically attach a joint account,[184] except where all its owners are defendants. This a principle that is probably honoured more in the breach than the observance, however, as the standard-form freezing injunction nowadays applies to all the defendant's assets 'whether they are solely or jointly owned'.[185] Similarly, as the standard-form order extends to 'any asset which [the defendant] has the power, directly or indirectly, to dispose of or deal with as if it were his own',[186] it would similarly cover the situation where the account is maintained in the defendant's sole name, but a third party steps forward claiming that he is beneficially entitled to the funds in question, such as where the account contains trust funds. The third party who is beneficially entitled to the funds in question could apply to the court to discharge or vary the injunction to the extent necessary.[187] The court is not, however, bound to discharge or vary the injunction simply on the basis of the third party's allegation that he owns the funds in question, but may instead require the third party to establish his claim to the funds.[188] If he succeeds, the court will set the order aside as regards the relevant funds. In this type of situation, the court once again exercises its jurisdiction on the basis of what appears 'just and convenient', since, if the court refuses to set the injunction aside in respect of the property claimed by the third party, it may nevertheless require the claimant to furnish security as a condition of the injunction's continuation and in order to protect the third party against loss.[189] The claimant's offer to furnish such security does not, however, necessarily preclude the court from setting the order aside in respect of the property involved. A freezing injunction is set aside if

[183] See, for example, *Miller Brewing Company* v. *Mersey Docks & Harbour Co.* [2003] EWHC 1606 (Ch), [40]; *Banco Nacional de Comercio Exterior SNC* v. *Empresa de Telecommunicaciones de Cuba SA*, n.163 above, [40].

[184] *Z Ltd* v. *A-Z and AA-LL*, n.68 above, 565, 591. See also *Nelson* v. *Halifax plc*, n.173 above, [4]–[5]. A court may issue a freezing injunction attaching an account maintained in a third party's name, if the court has 'good reason for supposing that the assets are in truth the assets of the defendant': *SCF Finance Co. Ltd* v. *Masri* [1985] 1 WLR 876, 884 (CA); *Allied Arab Bank Ltd* v. *Hajjar* [1989] Fam. Law 68 (CA); *TSB Private Bank International SA* v. *Chabra*, n.156 above, 241–242; *Mercantile Group (Europe) AG* v. *Aiyela*, n.159 above, 376; *Dadourian Group International Inc* v. *Simms* [2006] 3 All ER 48, [29] (CA).

[185] CPR Pt. 25, Practice Direction (Interim Injunctions), Annex (Freezing Injunction), para. 6.

[186] Ibid. According to *Raja* v. *van Hoogstraten*, n.152 above, [15], this provision was in response to the decision in *Federal Bank of the Middle East Ltd* v. *Hadkinson*, n.156 above, 406, where Mummery LJ held that the words 'his assets' in then standard-form injunction referred 'to assets belonging to that person, not to assets belonging to another person'. This would exclude assets held by the defendant as a bare trustee: *C Inc plc* v. *L* , n.155 above, [36].

[187] CPR Pt. 25, Practice Direction (Interim Injunctions), Annex (Freezing Injunction), para. 13.

[188] *SCF Finance Co. Ltd* v. *Masri*, n.184 above, 884. For approval of the *Masri* guidelines, see *Allied Arab Bank Ltd* v. *Hajjar*, n.184 above; *Federal Bank of the Middle East Ltd* v. *Hadkinson*, n.156 above; *TSB Private Bank International SA* v. *Chabra*, n.156 above; *Dadourian Group International Inc* v. *Simms*, n.184 above, [29]. The third party, or a bank that makes the claim on behalf of the trust, is entitled to costs: *Project Development Co. Ltd* v. *KMK Securities Ltd* [1982] 1 WLR 1470, 1471–1472. According to *Westminster City Council* v. *Citroen Wells* [2003] EWHC 2373 (Ch), [6]–[10], costs would be awarded 'on a solicitor and client, in effect an indemnity basis, but with a direction that it should be for the third party to establish that the costs have been reasonably incurred and were reasonable in amount'.

[189] *Clipper Maritime Co. Ltd* v. *Mineralimportexport* (*The 'Marie Leonhardt'*) [1981] 3 All ER 664; *Z Ltd* v. *A-Z and AA-LL*, n.68 above.

its maintenance would involve hardship, such as unwarranted interference with the third party's freedom to transact his business.[190]

The courts' policy of refraining from affecting third parties' rights when granting a freezing injunction is a reflection of the nature of this order. It is a procedural device that aims to protect the claimant against sharp practices employed by the defendant. As pointed out earlier, a freezing injunction acts *in personam*. The order does not confer new rights *in rem* on the claimant at whose request it is granted,[191] so that the satisfaction of debts owing to other creditors is not precluded by the granting of such an order. If their claims are established, the court usually allows the discharge of the debts out of the assets attached by the freezing injunction. The order, thus, does not confer any priority on the claimant and is not aimed at constituting him a secured creditor.[192] This principle is of considerable importance to banks, whose right of set-off against a customer will be upheld by a court that has issued a freezing injunction.[193]

It is clear that there are some similarities as well as distinctions between the freezing injunction and an interim third party debt order. From the bank's point of view, both preclude the payment of the customer's cheques and electronic funds transfers and the account is frozen to the extent prescribed by the court. There are three major distinctions between a freezing injunction and third party debt order. The first distinction is a substantive one: a freezing injunction only operates *in personam* and accordingly does not confer any new proprietary rights on the claimant, whereas a third party debt order operates *in rem* and has 'the proprietary effect of charging the debt owed to the judgment debtor in favour of the judgment creditor'.[194] Accordingly, as discussed above, the freezing injunction cannot have the effect of defeating the bank's own rights against its customer, such as its right of combination, whereas an interim third party debt order may defeat the bank's right of set-off pursuant to a loan facility,[195] but not the set-off of an overdraft facility. The second and third distinctions are essentially procedural: an interim third party debt order is available only to a judgment creditor, whereas a freezing injunction is generally used to freeze the defendant's account whilst the proceedings are pending; and an interim third party debt order is available to a judgment creditor as a matter of right, whilst the freezing injunction is a discretionary remedy.

(v) Terrorism Act 2000 and Proceeds of Crime Act 2002

As discussed already in detail,[196] the POCA 2002 can lead to the imposition of criminal liability on banks and other financial institutions that perform acts involving a 'money

---

[190] *Galaxia Maritime SA* v. *Mineralimportexport* [1982] 1 WLR 539 (CA); *Polly Peck International plc* v. *Nadir (No. 2)*, n.155 above; *Banco Nacional de Comercio Exterior SNC* v. *Empresa de Telecommunicaciones de Cuba SA*, n.163 above, [40].

[191] *Fourie* v. *Le Roux*, n.150 above, [2].

[192] *Iraqi Ministry of Defence* v. *Arcepey Shipping Co. SA*, n.151 above, 71–72; *PCW (Underwriting Agencies) Ltd* v. *Dixson* [1983] 2 All ER 158, 162; *Ninemia Maritime Corp.* v. *Trave Schiffahrtsgesellschaft (The 'Niedersachsen')*, n.155 above, 402; *Admiral Shipping* v. *Portlink Ferries Ltd*, n.151 above, 168; *Investment and Pensions Advisory Service Ltd* v. *Gray* [1990] BCLC 38; *Themehelp Ltd* v. *West* [1996] QB 84 (CA); *Mercedes-Benz AG* v. *Leiduck*, n.148 above, 300; *Technocrats International Inc.* v. *Fredic Ltd*, n.151 above, [11].

[193] *Oceania Castelana Armadora SA* v. *Mineralimportexport (The 'Theotokos')* [1983] 2 All ER 65; *Gangway Ltd* v. *Caledonian Park Investments (Jersey) Ltd* [2001] 2 Lloyd's Rep. 715, [14]; *Customs and Excise Commissioners* v. *Barclays Bank plc*, n.150 above, [10].

[194] *Masri* v. *Consolidated Contractors International UK Ltd (No. 2)*, n.63 above, [66]–[67].

[195] *Fraser* v. *Oystertec plc*, n.63 above, [13]–[19].   [196] See generally Ch. 4, Sects. 3–4 above.

laundering offence'[197] (which includes converting or transferring criminal property, possessing criminal property, or becoming concerned in an arrangement that the bank knows or suspects facilitates the acquisition, retention, use, or control of criminal property),[198] unless the bank makes an 'authorised disclosure' to the relevant authority[199] and obtains the 'appropriate consent' to the act in question from the relevant authority.[200] Moreover, banks and other financial institutions are particularly encouraged to make appropriate disclosures and accordingly are guilty of the 'failure to report offence'[201] if they know, suspect, or have reasonable grounds to know or suspect that another person is involved in money laundering and fail to disclose this fact as soon as practicable after acquiring the information.[202] As discussed previously,[203] a broadly similar regime exists under the Terrorism Act 2000 in order to combat the financing of terrorist activity.

In circumstances where a bank has made an 'authorised disclosure' under the POCA 2002 of its suspicions relating to a particular customer's account, good banking practice requires the bank to freeze that account until the 'appropriate consent' is received or the relevant time-limits expire if it is to avoid liability for money laundering.[204] As Laddie J stated in *Squirrell Ltd v. National Westminster Bank plc*,[205] '[t]he combined effect of these provisions is to force a [bank] to report its suspicions to the relevant authorities and not to move suspect funds or property either for seven working days or, if a notice of refusal is sent by the relevant authority, for a maximum of seven working plus 31 calendar days'.[206] In *Squirrell*, the claimant applied to unfreeze its account with the defendant bank, which had made an 'authorised disclosure' of its suspicions about the claimant to Customs and Excise and frozen the account without any explanation to its customer. Laddie J held that, as the defendant bank had a 'relevant suspicion'[207] within the POCA 2002, the course adopted by the bank in freezing its customer's account was 'unimpeachable'[208] and as a result the bank was 'obliged not to carry out any transaction in relation to that account'.[209] Whilst Laddie J expressed some misgivings about the fact that the POCA 2002 entitled a bank to ignore its customer's payment instructions upon the mere suspicion of relevant wrongdoing, his Lordship recognized that this was the clear result to which the legislation drove him.[210] The same basic issue arose, and similar concerns about the effect of the POCA 2002 on the bank–customer relationship were expressed, in *K v. National Westminster Bank plc*,[211] where a customer instructed the defendant bank by fax to make a payment out of its account to a third party, but the bank refused to do so on the (unstated) ground that it had made an 'authorised disclosure' under the POCA 2002. In refusing the claimant's application for an injunction ordering the bank to honour its customer's instructions, the Court of Appeal held that in the period between the bank making an 'authorised disclosure' and its receiving an 'appropriate consent' (or the relevant time period expiring),[212] the POCA 2002 had the effect of making it temporarily illegal to perform the bank–customer contract, so that the obligations under that contract were suspended until the illegality was removed.[213] Accordingly, during the period of

---

[197] For the 'money laundering offences', see Ch. 4, Sect. 3(ii)(a) above.
[198] Proceeds of Crime Act 2002 (POCA 2002), ss.327–329.   [199] Ibid., ss.338–339.
[200] Ibid., ss.335–336.   [201] For the 'failure to report offence', see Ch. 4, Sect. 3(ii)(b) above.
[202] POCA 2002, ss.330–332.   [203] See further Ch. 4, Sect. 3(iii) above.   [204] POCA 2002, s.335.
[205] [2005] 2 All ER 784.   [206] Ibid., [18].   [207] Ibid., [13].   [208] Ibid., [21].
[209] Ibid., [19].   [210] Ibid., [7].
[211] [2006] 2 All ER (Comm.) 655, [23] (CA). In *UMBS Online Ltd* v. *Serious and Organised Crime Agency* [2008] 1 All ER 465, [8] (CA), Ward LJ described the POCA 2002 as a 'raft of legislation of which Dracon, the Athenian legislator, would have been proud'.
[212] POCA 2002, s.335.
[213] *K v. National Westminster Bank plc*, n.211 above, [11].

suspension, 'no legal rights exist on which any claim to an injunction must depend'.[214] In this regard, Longmore LJ stated:[215]

> If the law of the land makes it a criminal offence to honour the customer's mandate in these circumstances there can, in my judgment, be no breach of contract for the bank to refuse to honour its mandate and there can, equally, be no invasion (or threat of an invasion) of a legal right on the part of the bank such as is required before a claimant can apply for an injunction.... Even if, for any reason, the above analysis is open to objection, the fact still remains that during the seven-working-day or 31-day period, as the case may be, the bank would be acting illegally by processing the cheque. It would be entirely inappropriate for the court, interlocutorily or otherwise, to require the performance of an act which would render the performer of the act criminally liable. As a matter of discretion any injunction should be refused.

These principles have been confirmed most recently in *Shah* v. *HSBC Private Bank (UK) Ltd*,[216] which has been discussed previously in the context of the bank's duty of care to its customer.[217] The customers' primary argument, however, was based on the fact that the bank had failed to carry out their payment instructions on the ground that it suspected the account funds to be criminal property, and had accordingly made an 'authorised disclosure' in accordance with the POCA 2002. In refusing the customer's damages claim, Hamblen J preferred to explain the bank's obligation to ignore its customer's instructions when it has made an 'authorised disclosure' under the POCA 2002 by reference to 'an obvious and/or necessarily implied restriction on or qualification of the bank's duties rather than on grounds of illegality [as in *K*], but the end result is the same'.[218] In that regard, his Lordship stated:[219]

> In circumstances where a banker is effectively compelled to make an authorized disclosure under POCA he cannot be in breach of contract in doing so. He is doing what the law forces him to do. Under POCA the mere fact of suspicion is the trigger for an authorized disclosure to be made. If so, the implied restriction on the banker's duty must equally be triggered by the mere fact of suspicion. To impose a superadded requirement of reasonableness would put a banker in an impossible position and mean that he could be in breach of duty even though he was acting as the law compelled him to. That would be neither sensible nor principled.

Accordingly, the only course realistically available to a customer who has had his instructions ignored as a result of an 'authorised disclosure' under the POCA 2002 is to 'impugn the decision to make an authorized disclosure...and challenge the good faith of the [bank's] suspicion'.[220] On appeal, Longmore LJ approved of the principles established by Hamblen J, although disagreed with the availability of summary judgment on the particular facts of *Shah*.[221]

(vi) **Customer's death or insanity**

Under section 75(2) of the Bills of Exchange Act 1882 (BEA 1882), the bank's duty and authority to pay cheques is terminated when it obtains notice of the customer's death. This section overrides in the case of cheques the principle that the mandate of an agent

---

[214] Id.   [215] Ibid., [10]–[12].
[216] N.401 above, affd. n.221 below.   [217] See Ch. 5, Sect. 4(iii) above.
[218] Ibid., [39].   [219] Ibid., [47].   [220] Ibid., [53].
[221] *Shah* v. *HSBC Private Bank (UK) Ltd* [2010] EWCA Civ. 31, [20]–[33].

is automatically determined by the principal's death, and that the agent is liable to the estate for any acts performed thereafter.[222] Section 75(2) is applicable only in the case of cheques, however, so that the issue of whether a bank should honour direct debit instructions or standing orders on a deceased's account is governed by the common law principle whereby the bank's authority terminates automatically upon the customer's death and not simply from the time when the bank has notice of that fact.[223] Nevertheless, section 75(2) of the BEA 1882 remains an important provision, as banks do not have any means of obtaining immediate notice of a customer's death. Interestingly, even before the BEA 1882 was passed, the Court of Common Pleas in *Rogerson* v. *Ladbroke*[224] applied a similar principle in a case where the bank paid a bill of exchange that the customer, who was the acceptor of the instrument, had domiciled at the bank's premises. As the bank paid the bill of exchange after the customer's death, but before obtaining notice thereof, the court held that the bank was entitled to debit the account.

When the bank obtains notice of its customer's death, it has to stop acting on his behalf. The bank is no longer entitled to pay cheques drawn by the customer before his death,[225] even if their amounts are trivial and it is clear that they were drawn for essential services rendered to the customer during his lifetime, such as the supply of electricity or gas. It is clear that, in practice, this principle leads to hardships, as payments due to tradesmen, professional men, and suppliers of services have to be deferred until the completion of the necessary probate or administration procedures. In some countries, such as the United States and New Zealand, the law has been amended to authorize the bank to pay cheques presented within ten days after it receives notice of a customer's death.[226] A person who claims to be entitled to a grant of letters of administration, or to be an executor of the deceased's will, is entitled to order the bank to refrain from paying cheques presented within this period. It is believed that this reform was well conceived.[227]

A question on which there appears to be no authority is whether or not the bank is obliged to refuse to accept any payments received for the credit of an account after the customer's death. As the bank accepts such payments as the customer's agent, it would appear that the bank's mandate is terminated either when the customer dies or, by analogy with section 75(2) of the BEA 1882, when the bank receives notice thereof. Payments made into the customer's account by tenants, business associates, and financial houses managing his portfolio investments have, therefore, to be rejected! A particularly acute problem relates to cheques paid by the customer to the credit of his account, but which have not been cleared by the time the bank receives notice of his death. On a strict common law analysis, the bank's mandate to receive the funds is terminated upon the customer's death (or, if an analogy is again to be drawn with section 75(2), when the bank obtains notice of the customer's death)! It is, however, to be doubted if in practice banks would apply the law quite so strictly in such cases.

Although there is no direct English authority regarding the effect of insanity on the bank's duty to pay its customer's cheques, as a matter of general principle an agent's

---

[222] *Campanari* v. *Woodburn* (1854) 15 CB 400.

[223] P. Watts (ed.), *Bowstead & Reynolds on Agency* (19th edn., London, 2010), para. 10-016.

[224] (1822) 1 Bing. 94.

[225] A cheque cannot constitute a *donatio mortis causa*, even when it is given by the customer to the payee with knowledge of impending death: see Ch. 9, Sect. 4(iv) above.

[226] For the United States position, see Uniform Commercial Code, s.4-405(b). For the New Zealand position, see Bills of Exchange Act 1908, s.75(2), inserted by the Bills of Exchange (Amendment) Act 1971, s.2. This provision will not apply to cheques bearing a date later than the ten-day grace period: ibid., s.75(2)(a).

[227] For executor's accounts, see Ch. 8, Sect. 4 above.

authority is automatically determined by the insanity of his principal.[228] As indicated previously,[229] however, the better view is that the bank–customer relationship is not governed by this general principle, as it is not purely a principal–agent relationship, but that, by analogy with section 75(2) of the BEA 1882, the bank's authority to pay only terminates upon receiving notice of the customer's insanity.[230] The uncertainty of the common law position may, however, be alleviated by the fact that it is possible to apply to the court under the Mental Capacity Act 2005 for the appointment of a deputy to take charge of the customer's affairs when he 'is unable to make a decision for himself in relation to the matter because of an impairment of, or disturbance in the functioning of, the mind or brain'.[231] A bank may safely follow the instructions of a duly appointed deputy.[232]

(vii) Bankruptcy and winding-up

The general effect of an individual customer's bankruptcy or a corporate customer's winding-up on the bank–customer relationship has been discussed previously.[233] The present discussion focuses on the effect of such an event on the bank's duty to pay customer's cheques. In this regard, the basic effect of a customer's bankruptcy is to vest his property in his trustee in bankruptcy.[234] For bankruptcy purposes, the customer's estate includes all property belonging to or vested in him at the commencement of the bankruptcy[235] or acquired by him before his discharge.[236] As the credit balance of the customer's account constitutes a debt owed to him by the bank, for bankruptcy purposes, such a debt is deemed to be an asset due to the customer. The bank is, however, entitled to set off (or exercise its right of combination) against the amount due to the customer any amount that the customer owes the bank, such as a sum accrued on an overdraft.[237] The bank has to pay over to the customer's trustee any balance that remains payable to the customer.[238]

Under the previous bankruptcy regime, the net account balance that the bank was required to pay over to its customer's trustee in bankruptcy was determined as at the 'commencement of the bankruptcy'. According to the 'relation back doctrine', this was not the date of the bankruptcy order, but the earlier date of the customer's first act of bankruptcy.[239] This placed banks in a somewhat difficult position, as the customer's trustee could subsequently challenge any account transactions made after the 'commencement of the bankruptcy' even though there were no grounds to question the validity of the particular transaction at the time that it was made.[240] The 'relation back' doctrine no longer creates

---

[228] *Young* v. *Toynbee* [1910] 1 KB 215. Although a third party dealing with the agent of an insane principal may nevertheless be protected if the agent has acted within its apparent or ostensible authority: *Drew* v. *Nunn* (1879) 4 QBD 661 (CA); *Daily Telegraph Newspaper Co. Ltd* v. *McLaughlin* [1904] AC 776 (PC).

[229] See Ch. 8, Sect. 14(ii) above.

[230] *Governor & Company of the Bank of Ireland* v. *Hussey*, n.52 above. See also Hart, *Law of Banking* (4th edn. London, 1932), 302; M. Megrah, *The Banker's Customer* (2nd edn., London, 1938), 76. See further F.H. Ryder, 'Bankers and the Law Relating to Lunacy' (1934) 55 *JIB* 14.

[231] Mental Capacity Act 2005, ss.2(1), 16(2). See further Ch. 8, Sect. 14 above.   [232] Ibid., s.18(1).

[233] See Ch. 5, Sect. 6 above.   [234] Insolvency Act 1986, s.306.

[235] Ibid., s.283(1), although certain property necessary for the bankrupt's trade or to satisfy his family's basic domestic needs are excluded (ibid., s.283(2)).

[236] Ibid., s.307(1).   [237] See Ch. 7, Sect. 4(v) above.

[238] Insolvency Act 1986, s.312(1). See *Smedley* v. *Brittain* [2008] BPIR 219, [45]: 'The burden on the debtor to deliver up is a heavy burden.'

[239] Bankruptcy Act 1914, s.37.

[240] There existed some protection for banks that dealt with the bankrupt during the 'relation-back' period without notice of the bankruptcy petition: Bankruptcy Act 1914, ss.45–46. See *Re Dalton, ex p. Herrington and Carmichael* [1963] Ch. 336; *Pettit* v. *Novakovic* [2007] BPIR 1643, [14].

such difficulties, as section 278 of the Insolvency Act 1986 now provides that an individual's bankruptcy 'commences with the day on which the bankruptcy order is made'. Nevertheless, there remains the practical problem that the court will not necessarily make an adjudication order at the very beginning of the relevant day and that a bank may honour a cheque or other payment instruction before the order is actually made later that day. The difficulty arises out of the fact that section 278 of the Insolvency Act 1986 appears to adopt the same principle as under the previous bankruptcy regime, namely that the adjudication order is to be treated as having been made at the start of the relevant day.[241] In such circumstances, the bank is treated as honouring the customer's cheque after the date of the order.[242] Under the previous bankruptcy regime, banks were held liable for all payments made from an account after the issuing of the bankruptcy order,[243] and were not entitled to set off against that liability the amount of any cheques paid into the customer's account after the date of the order, as any combination of accounts had to be based on the state of the account as at the time of the adjudication. Nowadays, section 284(5) of the Insolvency Act 1986[244] may protect a bank that pays one of its customer's cheques in the course of the day, but before it receives notice of the adjudication order. According to this provision, where a bank honours its customer's cheque or other payment instruction so that 'after the commencement of his bankruptcy the bankrupt has incurred a debt to a banker' the debit is maintainable, except in two cases: where the bank had notice of the bankruptcy before it honoured the cheque or other payment instruction; and where it is not reasonably practicable to recover the amount involved from the payee.

Furthermore, despite the disappearance of the 'relation back doctrine' under the Insolvency Act 1986, there remain two situations where a bank may still face difficulties due to the customer's trustee challenging his pre-bankruptcy account operations may be challenged by his trustee: first, where the transaction in question is voidable as an undervalue transaction or an undue preference given by the customer;[245] secondly, where a customer makes 'any disposition of property' or a 'payment' out of his account before the date of the adjudication order, but after the presentation of the adjudication petition. According to section 284(1)–(3) of the Insolvency Act 1986, unless it is made with the consent of the court or ratified by it subsequently, such a disposition or payment is void. In such circumstances, the Insolvency Act 1986 appears expressly to contemplate that the customer's trustee will have a remedy against the recipient or payee of a cheque, who will accordingly hold 'the sum paid for the bankrupt as part of his estate', unless the property or payment was received in good faith, for value, and without knowledge of the petition's presentation.[246] The legislation is silent, however, as to whether a remedy is also available against the bank that collects or honours a cheque on behalf of its bankrupt customer after the date of the petition's presentation. Although such account operations will not generally involve 'dispositions' of the customer's property in favour of the bank, since the latter generally acts as the former's

---

[241] *Re Pollard* [1903] 2 KB 41, 45; but note *Smith* v. *Braintree District Council* [1990] 2 AC 215, 237 (HL).

[242] A similar problem might arise where a bank honours a cheque that is presented for payment after the date of the adjudication order, but before the gazetted order is noted by the bank.

[243] *Re Wigzell, ex p. Hart* [1921] 2 KB 835 (CA); although consider the observation of Lord Sterndale MR: ibid., 850. Contrast *Re Wilson, ex p. Salaman* [1926] 1 Ch. 21.

[244] See formerly Bankruptcy (Amendment) Act 1926, s.4.

[245] See Ch. 7, Sect. 4(v) above. See further B. Hannigan, *Company Law* (2nd edn., Oxford, 2009), paras. 25-48–25-81.

[246] Insolvency Act 1986, s.284(4).

agent in this context,[247] *Pettit* v. *Novakovic*[248] recently left open the possibility that collecting and honouring a cheque might nevertheless involve a 'payment'[249] for which the bank is liable to account. Accordingly, once a bank has notice of an adjudication petition against a customer, its correct course is to defer payment until steps have been taken to validate the payment. Similarly, where one of the owners of a joint account is adjudicated a bankrupt, the bank is best advised to dishonour any further cheques drawn on the account, regardless of whether they are drawn by both owners jointly or by one of them entitled to sign on his own. As the bank's mandate to honour cheques emanates jointly and severally from all the owners,[250] the notice of one owner's bankruptcy may be regarded as terminating the bank's authority to pay.

Just as in the case of an individual customer's adjudication, a bank is not under any duty to honour cheques drawn on a corporate customer once it has notice of the presentation of a winding-up petition.[251] According to section 129 of the Insolvency Act 1986, the commencement date of a winding-up by the court depends on whether the proceedings were preceded by a company resolution to wind up or started with the presentation of the petition. In the former case, the winding-up commences on the date of the resolution; in the latter case, the relevant date is that of the petition's presentation. What is the bank's position, however, if it honours a cheque after the date of the petition whether due to oversight or its ignorance of the petition? Like section 284(1) of the Insolvency Act 1986, discussed above, section 127 renders void 'any disposition of the company's property' after the commencement of the winding-up.[252] At one time, it was thought that this provision required a bank to reimburse a customer's liquidator for any amounts paid out of an account when honouring that customer's cheques, unless those payments, which were regarded as 'dispositions', were validated by a court order.[253] The Court of Appeal took a different view in *Hollicourt (Contracts) Ltd (in liq.)* v. *Bank of Ireland*,[254] where the bank failed to freeze the company's account although a petition for its winding up had been presented and advertised. As the account was in credit, the bank continued to honour its customer's cheques until it became aware of the true position some three months later. Blackburne J refused to validate the payments out of the account and ordered the bank to reimburse them. The Court of Appeal disagreed and concluded that, whilst the honouring of a cheque by a bank might constitute a 'disposition' in favour of that cheque's payee, there was no 'disposition' in favour of the bank.[255] Two related reasons were given: first, as section 127 does not automatically 'avoid, revoke, or countermand the company's mandate to the bank', the bank paid the cheques as an agent, acting on its customer's mandate;[256] and secondly, the beneficial ownership of the property represented by the

[247] *Hollicourt (Contracts) Ltd (in liq.)* v. *Bank of Ireland* [2001] Ch. 555 (CA), discussed further below.

[248] N.240 above, [6]–[16].

[249] Insolvency Act 1986, s.284(2).   [250] See Ch. 8, Sect. 2 above.

[251] *Pettit* v. *Novakovic*, n.240 above, [7]. The presentation of such a petition does not *automatically* terminate the bank's mandate: *Hollicourt (Contracts) Ltd (in liq.)* v. *Bank of Ireland*, n.247 above.

[252] Ibid., [12], where HHJ Norris held that the term 'disposition' should be given the same meaning in the two provisions, but highlighted the fact that, as Insolvency Act 1986, s.284(2) only applies in the bankruptcy context and has no equivalent in the winding-up context, banks might find themselves in a very different position depending upon whether the customer in question was incorporated or not: ibid, [6]–[7].

[253] *Re Gray's Inn Construction Co. Ltd* [1980] 1 WLR 711 (CA); *Re Tramway Building and Construction Co. Ltd* [1988] Ch. 293.

[254] N.247 above. See also C. Hare, 'Banker's Liability for Post-petition Dispositions' (2001) 60 *CLJ* 468.

[255] Ibid., [31]. For the opposite view in Ireland, see *Re Industrial Services Company (Dublin) Ltd* [2001] 2 IR 118; *Re Worldport Ireland Ltd* [2005] IEHC 189.

[256] Ibid., [33]. It has been doubted whether this conclusion would have been open to the court if the bank had had notice of the winding-up petition: *Pettit* v. *Novakovic*, n.240 above, [7].

cheque was never transferred to the bank.[257] Moreover, according to Mummery LJ, it is irrelevant whether the insolvent customer's account is in credit or overdrawn when the bank honours the cheque.[258] Accordingly, in such circumstances, a customer's liquidator can only ever claim reimbursement from a cheque's payee, unless the court validates the 'disposition' of the money to him.

Whilst banks after *Hollicourt* might not need to be as vigilant as previously in checking for winding-up petitions against their customers, once notice of such a petition terminates its authority to honour its customer's cheques,[259] it would be well advised to seek a validation order from the court before continuing to operate the account. In exercising their discretion to validate payments under section 127, the courts will seek to do what is fair and equitable in the circumstances and do its best to ensure that the interests of unsecured creditors are not prejudiced.[260] A court will also be guided by the points set out in section 284(4)–(5) of the Insolvency Act 1986, with the result that, if a 'disposition' is made in good faith in the ordinary course of business when the parties are unaware of the presentation of the petition to wind up the company, and it is completed before the winding-up order is made, the court is likely to validate it, unless it can be challenged as a preference.[261] *Re T. W. Construction Ltd*[262] illustrates when a court might validate a payment. A bank agreed to extend overdraft facilities to a company after the presentation of a winding-up petition to enable the company to pay wages, on the understanding that sums, due to the company under certain letters of credit would be paid into the company's account with the bank. Wynn-Parry J validated the arrangement on that ground that it would have been unconscionable to permit the liquidator to rescind it.

(viii) **Countermand of payment**

Under section 75(1) of the BEA 1882, a bank's mandate to pay a cheque drawn on it by its customer is determined by countermand of payment. If a bank disregards such a countermand, it is unable to debit its customer's account with the amount of any cheques that it pays.[263] In the case of a joint account, the countermand may be validly issued by any account holder, regardless of whether the relevant cheque was drawn by himself or another account holder.[264] To be effective, however, the customer's countermand must

---

[257] Ibid., [23].

[258] Ibid., [32]. See also *Coutts & Co* v. *Stock* [2000] 1 WLR 906 (payment out of overdrawn account). As a cheque *paid into* an insolvent company's account, *when it is already in credit*, simply increases the credit balance of that account, there is similarly no 'disposition' in favour of the bank: *Re Barn Crown Ltd* [1994] 4 All ER 42; *Re Tain Construction Ltd* [2003] BPIR 1188, [11]. For criticism, see R.M. Goode, *Principles of Corporate Insolvency Law* (3rd edn., London, 2005), 495–498. Unless validated by the court, however, there is such a 'disposition' when a cheque is *paid into* an insolvent company's *overdrawn* account: *Re Gray's Inn Construction Ltd* [1980] 1 WLR 711 (CA); *Re Tain Construction Ltd*, above, [11]. As an alternative to a validation order, a bank may raise a change of position defence: *Re Tain Construction Ltd*, above, [41].

[259] *Pettit* v. *Novakovic*, n.240 above, [7].

[260] For the general principles governing the validation of a 'disposition', either prospectively or retrospectively, see *Re Gray's Inn Construction Ltd*, n.253 above, 717–719; *Denney* v. *John Hudson & Co Ltd* [1992] BCLC 901, 904–905 (CA); *Re Tain Construction Ltd*, n.258 above, [11]; *Re Airfreight Express (UK) Ltd* [2005] BPIR 250, [14]–[15].

[261] In *Re Tain Construction Ltd*, n.258 above, [21], it was held that this does not mean 'prefer' in the technical sense of a 'voidable preference' under the Insolvency Act 1986, but rather it meant circumvention of the *pari passu* distribution of assets, which it was the policy of s.127 to achieve.

[262] [1954] 1 WLR 540.   [263] This is subject to the equitable '*Liggett* defence': see Sect. 3(v) below.

[264] *Gaunt* v. *Taylor* (1843) 2 Hare 413; *Husband* v. *Davis* (1851) 20 LJCP 118, 120. For an equivalent rule in relation to executors' and administrators' accounts, see Ch. 8, Sect. 4 above.

comply with a number of requirements. First, the countermand must be communicated or delivered to the branch on which the cheque is drawn.[265] This rule is simply a reflection of the basic principle that the credit balance of a current account is repayable at the branch where the account is maintained and, like that principle, may be open to criticism in the light of technological developments in banking practice.[266]

Secondly, the countermand should be as clear as possible and free of ambiguity. From the bank's perspective, the principal difficulty arises where it honours a countermanded cheque in consequence of some ambiguity or the inclusion of some incorrect details in the stop order. The general rule applicable to such cases is that, as long as the bank acted in accordance with what it honestly believed to be the customer's intentions, it is entitled to debit his account with the amount of the cheque.[267] Thus, in *Westminster Bank* v. *Hilton*,[268] the customer drew a cheque on 31 July 1924 that bore the serial number 117285 and was post-dated to 2 August 1924. On 1 August, the customer cabled his bank, ordering it to stop 'cheque 1172823', but setting out the amount and payee of cheque 117285. When cheque 117285 was presented for payment on 6 August, the bank paid it in the belief that it was issued to replace cheque 117283, which it believed the customer had countermanded. Subsequently, the bank dishonoured another cheque drawn by the customer for an amount of £7, as the payment of cheque 117285 had exhausted the credit balance on the customer's account. The House of Lords dismissed the customer's claim for damages following the wrongful dishonour of the £7 cheque. Their Lordships held that the customer's countermand instruction was ambiguous because it made reference to the wrong serial number, but that the bank had made a reasonable inference from the facts available to it. The position differs, however, if 'the ambiguity is patent on the face' of the countermand',[269] in which case the bank should verify its instructions with the relevant customer, or if the countermand is sufficiently clear despite the customer failing to include full details in his instruction. An example of this second situation is *Reade* v. *Royal Bank of Scotland*,[270] where the customer's telegram countermanding a cheque set out the number of the cheque and the payee's name, but failed to indicate on which of his two accounts with the bank the cheque had been drawn.[271] The bank's clerk, who processed the instruction, made a note of the stop order against one account only. Shortly thereafter, the cheque was paid when presented and the amount was debited against the other account. As the countermand was held to be effective, the bank was not entitled to debit its customer with the amount thereof.[272]

---

[265] *London Provincial and South Western Bank* v. *Buszard* (1918) 35 TLR 142; *Burnett* v. *Westminster Bank Ltd*, n.5 above.

[266] See Ch. 7, Sect. 1 above.

[267] This is an application of the principle in *Ireland* v. *Livingston* (1872) LR 5 HL 395 (HL): see further Sect. 2 below.

[268] (1926) 43 TLR 124 (HL). See also *London Joint Stock Bank Ltd* v. *Macmillan and Arthur* [1918] AC 777 (HL); *Midland Bank Ltd* v. *Seymour* [1955] 2 Lloyd's Rep. 147, 148; *Cooper* v. *National Westminster Bank plc* [2009] EWHC 3035 (QB), [58]–[60].

[269] *European Asian Bank AG* v. *Punjab and Sind Bank (No. 2)* [1983] 1 WLR 642, 656 (CA); *Patel* v. *Standard Chartered Bank* [2001] Lloyds Rep. (Bank.) 229, [35]–[36]; *Cooper* v. *National Westminster Bank*, n.268 above, [61]–[63]. See further Sect. 3(iv) below.

[270] [1922] 2 IR 22.

[271] In modern banking practice, however, the reference to the cheque number would also identify the account.

[272] In *Remfor Industries Ltd* v. *Bank of Montreal* (1978) 90 DLR (3rd.) 316 (Ont. CA), the Ontario Court of Appeal held that if the details set out in a countermand notice were adequate to identify the cheque, the bank was under a duty to stop it, even if the notice was inaccurate in respect of one detail; where the cheque was described with reasonable accuracy, the bank had, in case of doubt, to enquire whether the cheque presented

Thirdly, the customer must communicate the countermand in the proper form and manner. Difficulties normally only arise in connection with this requirement in circumstances where the customer has sought to countermand payment by informal means, such as a telephone conversation (usually conducted with an unidentified bank employee) and has failed to confirm the stop order subsequently in writing. If the cheque is paid, the bank may deny that the conversation took place or that the employee in question had the authority to implement the countermand instruction, or alternatively may insist that a countermand is only effective if communicated in writing and authenticated by the customer's signature. Such a plea is likely to receive short shrift, however, since the basic common law rule is that a countermand need not be in any specific form, so that an oral countermand is basically effective.[273] Whilst a bank can always seek to reverse the common law position by means of a term to the effect that it will only act upon written instructions,[274] in *Morrell* v. *Workers Savings & Loan Bank*,[275] Lord Mance recognized that a bank remained entitled to act upon any oral instructions given by the customer and to debit that customer's account accordingly. Even though *Morrell* did not specifically involve a countermand, there is no logical reason why the reasoning in that case would not apply equally in the countermand context.

Whilst a bank at common law may not directly refuse to obey its customer's countermand on the ostensible ground of that countermand's *form*, a bank employee may nevertheless refuse to follow such an instruction if the customer is unable to identify himself to the satisfaction of the employee whether as a result of the form of the countermand or by not being able to provide the specific details provided to the bank on opening the account. As an alternative to refusing to follow the countermand outright, the bank may agree to suspend payment of the cheque for a period of time until it receives written confirmation of the caller's identity as one of its customers. In the absence of such written confirmation, the bank is probably entitled to disregard the oral countermand.[276] The fact that the form of a countermand might give rise to difficulties in identifying the relevant customer and authenticating his communications was recognized in *Curtice* v. *London City and Midland Bank*.[277] The customer attempted to countermand payment of a cheque by delivering a telegram to the bank's letterbox at 6.15 p.m. on the same day that the cheque was drawn. Due to an oversight, the bank did not clear the telegram from its letterbox on the next morning and accordingly paid the cheque when presented by the payee. One of the grounds that the Court of Appeal gave for rejecting the customer's claim that the bank had paid the cheque without mandate was that the countermand instruction, contained in the telegram, had not been authenticated. According to the Court of Appeal, whilst a bank that receives a countermand by telegram might defer honouring a cheque pending further enquiries, it was not 'bound as a matter of law to accept an unauthenticated telegram as sufficient authority for the serious step of refusing to pay a cheque'.[278] It may be wondered, however, whether a modern court would take so

---

was the one the customer sought to stop: *Giordano* v. *Royal Bank of Canada* [1973] 3 OR 771, 775–776 (Ont. CA); *Solomon* v. *Royal Bank of Canada* (1982) 20 Man. R. (2d.) 371, [17]–[22] (Man. QB).

[273] *Chua Neoh Kow* v. *Malayan Banking Bhd* [1986] 2 MLJ 396, 399 (Malay. CA); *Bank Bumiputra Bhd* v. *Hashbudin Bin Hashim* [1998] 3 MLJ 262, 270.

[274] For an express term allowing oral instructions, see *Earles* v. *Barclays Bank plc* [2009] EWHC 2500 (QB), [17].

[275] [2007] UKPC 3, [10]. See also *Hill Street Services Co. Ltd* v. *National Westminster Bank plc* [2007] EWHC 2379 (Ch), [14]–[17].

[276] *Commonwealth Trading Bank* v. *Reno Auto Sales Pty Ltd* [1967] VR 790 (Vic. Sup. Ct.).

[277] [1908] 2 KB 293 (CA).   [278] Ibid., 298–299.

stringent a view of the need for further verification in a case such as *Curtice*, given that technological developments since 1908 frequently require modern banks to act upon instructions that may not be capable of authentication by face-to-face contact or signature executed by hand. Nowadays, banks may need to be more pragmatic. It is arguable that, where a modern countermand accurately cites the correct number of the account and full details of the countermanded cheque, these details (read together with any other identifying information) should be sufficient authentication.

Fourthly, a countermand will not become effective until the bank has received actual notice thereof. This principle provided a second ground for concluding that the cheque in *Curtice* had not been effectively countermanded prior to payment, since the cheque in that case had been honoured before the telegram containing the countermand had actually been read by the bank's staff. The Court of Appeal held that there was no room for a 'constructive countermand' and that, to be effective, a countermand had to come to the notice of a bank employee with authority to act upon the instruction prior to the payment of the cheque.[279] This principle probably remains sound even in respect of modern banking practice, so that the communication of an oral countermand to a call-centre operator or the delivery of a written order to the bank's receptionist cannot have the desired effect until the message is passed on to the accounts section or other authorized employee.[280] Furthermore, if the cheque is presented for payment before the bank has had the time necessary to complete the internal procedures required to stop the cheque, such as issuing an appropriate notice to the tellers, the bank cannot be held responsible for paying the instrument. If a bank takes an unreasonably long time to stop a cheque, a customer may be entitled to dispute any debit to his account on the ground that the bank's negligence constitutes a breach of its duty of care to the customer.[281] Indeed, this may be a reason to exercise some caution over the actual conclusion of the Court of Appeal in *Curtice*, since the bank's failure in that case to clear its letterbox expeditiously probably constituted a breach of the duty of care owed to its customer. Whilst this point was actually emphasized in Cozens-Hardy MR's judgment, it could not form the basis of the decision in *Curtice* as the customer had failed formally raise any plea relating to the bank's negligence.

The issue of determining whether the countermand is issued in sufficient time to stop the cheque before it is 'paid' arises in a particularly acute form when the instrument passes through the cheque clearing system. In general terms, a cheque will only be considered 'paid' when its proceeds are unconditionally available to the payee, in the sense that the payee is able to draw on those proceeds and the branch on which the cheque is drawn is no longer free to dishonour it—in the absence of a special agreement with the payee, this will be at the end of the cheque's clearing cycle.[282] Accordingly, a countermand will be effective, even if it reaches the drawee branch after the cheque has been exchanged at the clearing house, provided the notice is received at the branch in time for the return of the cheque as a dishonoured instrument. In *Capital Associates Ltd* v. *Royal Bank of Canada*,[283] where the drawer and payee of a cheque maintained their accounts

---

[279] *Giordano* v. *Royal Bank of Canada*, n.272 above, 775.

[280] In *Commonwealth Trading Bank* v. *Reno Auto Sales Pty. Ltd*, n.276 above, a countermand notice was held ineffective when given over the telephone to an employee who lacked the authority to handle such messages and who failed to communicate the instruction to the teller in the belief that the message would be confirmed forthwith in writing.

[281] *Giordano* v. *Royal Bank of Canada*, n.272 above, 776. For a bank's right to restitution of a countermanded payment from the payee, see Ch. 12, Sects. 3(ii) & 5(ii) below. As regards the rights of the holder, where no consideration was received for the cheque, see *AEG (UK) Ltd* v. *Lewis* [1993] 2 Bank. LR 119.

[282] See Sect. 1(ii) above.   [283] (1970) 15 DLR (3d) 234 (Queb. Sup. Ct.).

with the same branch, the Quebec Supreme Court held that the bank was entitled to reverse the credit entry and treat the cheque as countermanded, even though the cheque had been credited to the payee's account before the countermand was received by the branch. Mackay J pointed out that when the cheque was accepted from the payee, the branch credited his account in the same way it would have done if the cheque had been drawn on some other bank. As the drawer's countermand was received before the bank took the ordinary steps involved in the honour of a cheque, such as verifying the signature and the adequacy of the account balance, the countermand was received prior to payment.[284]

The principles considered above represent the common law default position. Some banks, however, seek to escape liability for their failure to observe a countermand by including an exemption clause in the standard terms and conditions executed by the customer when opening the account. Whilst a narrow clause, such as a term restricting the bank's duty to the observance of a countermand given in writing, might be reasonable and hence binding, an unduly wide clause, such as a term that frees the bank from *all* relevant liability, might run foul of the Unfair Contract Terms Act 1977 or, where the customer is a 'consumer', the Unfair Terms in Consumer Contracts Regulations 1999.[285]

2 The bank's liability for wrongful payment: nature of the problem

As discussed previously,[286] a cheque has traditionally served two functions: first, as a negotiable instrument that can be utilized to effect the payment of a sum due from the drawer and that can circulate freely instead of cash; and, secondly, as a payment order or instruction issued by the customer to his bank directing the latter to pay the amount of a cheque to a named payee. Nowadays, however, cheques do not generally perform the first of these functions, as they are invariably pre-printed with an 'a/c payee' crossing that renders the cheque non-transferable and accordingly not a negotiable instrument.[287] A modern cheque continues to perform the second of the above functions and is, therefore, an instrument in which a customer, acting as principal, instructs the bank—as his agent—to perform a specific act, namely the payment of a definite sum of money to the payee's order or to the bearer.[288] As the contractual relationship between the bank and its customer arising from the drawing of the cheque is primarily governed by the principles of the law of agency, the bank's duty is to adhere strictly to the terms of its mandate. If the bank deviates therefrom, it does so at its peril. The point has been explained most clearly by Devlin J in *Midland Bank Ltd* v. *Seymour*,[289] which concerned the liability of

---

[284] Mckay J's other ground—that the bank acquired the cheque as a holder in due course—is to be doubted: see Ch. 15, Sect. 8 below.

[285] S.I. 1999/2083.   [286] See Ch. 10, Sect. 1 above.

[287] Cheques Act 1992, s.1 introducing BEA 1882, s.81A. See Ch. 10, Sect. 4(iv) above.

[288] *London Joint Stock Bank Ltd* v. *Macmillan and Arthur*, n.268 above; *Westminster Bank Ltd* v. *Hilton*, n.268 above, 126; *Re Spectrum Plus Ltd* [2005] 2 AC 680, [59] (HL).

[289] N.268 above, 168. Following *Ireland* v. *Livingston*, n.267 above, Devlin J suggested (at 153) that a bank could safely rely upon a reasonable interpretation of its customer's ambiguous instructions, even if that interpretation was not intended by the customer. This principle will have no application, however, if the bank's interpretation is not a reasonable one or if the 'ambiguity is patent on the face of the document': *European Asian Bank AG* v. *Punjab and Sind Bank (No. 2)*, n.269 above, 656; *Patel* v. *Standard Chartered Bank*, n.269 above, [35]–[36]; *Cooper* v. *National Westminster Bank*, n.268 above, [61]–[63]. A bank is not

a bank that departed from its customer's instructions regarding the opening of a letter of credit:

> It is a hard law sometimes which deprives an agent of the right to reimbursement if he has exceeded his authority, even though the excess does not damage his principal's interests. The corollary…is that the instruction to the agent must be clear and unambiguous.

When this statement is applied to the unauthorized payment of a cheque, it means that a bank is not entitled to debit its customer's account with the amount involved unless it can plead one of the recognized defences.[290] In this regard, the bank may rely upon the common law defences that can be raised by an agent who disobeys his principal, such as estoppel, ratification, and the ambiguity of the mandate. Furthermore, the bank is entitled to rely on a specific equitable defence that applies where its unauthorized payment of a cheque (such as when the bank honours a countermanded cheque) has benefited its customer (such as when payment of a cheque has the effect of discharging a valid debt due by the customer to the payee). In such circumstances, it would be inequitable to allow the customer to reap the benefit of the payment and at the same time to refuse to permit the bank to debit his account. This equitable defence is discussed below in conjunction with the bank's common law defences.[291]

Neither the common law defences nor the equitable defence, however, provide the bank with a comprehensive defence in all instances of a cheque being wrongfully paid. This can be illustrated by contrasting the different situations in which a bank pays a cheque without a valid mandate. On the one hand, where a cheque bears a forged drawer's signature, is signed in excess of an agent's authority, or is invalidated by a third party (such as a holder) altering the instrument without authorization (such as by raising the cheque's face amount),[292] the bank has a common law defence provided the customer has either facilitated the fraud or has led the bank to believe that all is well. On the other hand, on those occasions when a bank pays a cheque despite a countermand order, the common law protects a bank if the stop order was ambiguous or issued too late to be acted upon by the bank. In contrast to these two situations, where the payee's endorsement on the cheque is forged by a third party, the bank has no defence at common law even though the bank is unable to verify the genuineness of the payee's signature, particularly when the cheque is presented through a clearing house. In such circumstances, as the cheque is not paid to the genuine payee or to a person holding under that payee's indorsement, the cheque is not paid to the order of the designated person and hence is not discharged in accordance with the terms of the bank's mandate. Nevertheless, a bank may have a statutory defence in such circumstances by virtue of the BEA 1882 and the Cheques Act 1957.[293]

Where a bank is unable to avail itself of any such defence, however, its wrongful payment of a cheque entitles the drawer to claim damages for breach of contract resulting from the bank's breach of mandate. This, however, is not necessarily the only hazard faced by the paying bank. Where a cheque has been paid for the credit of a person who is not entitled to the proceeds, the 'true owner' of the instrument—in other words, the person entitled to the cheque's proceeds—may bring an action in conversion against the paying

---

entitled to give its own construction to the customer's instruction: *Thavorn v. Bank of Credit and Commerce International SA* [1985] 1 Lloyd's Rep. 259.

[290] A customer's cause of action based on an unauthorized debit does not accrue until the bank wrongfully dishonours a cheque in reliance on the balance struck in consequence of the debits involved. Accordingly, the limitation period does not start running upon the entry of the wrong debits in the account: *National Bank of Commerce v. National Westminster Bank plc* [1990] 2 Lloyd's Rep. 514. See further Ch. 5, Sect. 3 above.

[291] See Sect. 3 below.   [292] BEA 1882, s.64.   [293] See Sect. 4 below.

bank. This is a consequence of the fact that, as confirmed recently by the House of Lords in *OBG Ltd* v. *Allan*,[294] a cheque is considered an item of property with a value equal to the amount shown on its face.[295] Accordingly, provided the 'true owner' can show that he is entitled to the 'immediate possession' of the instrument and that the cheque has been misappropriated or destroyed then, he may be able to bring a claim for its conversion. As regards this last requirement, however, the paying bank does not appropriate the chattel either in its own name or on behalf of a principal. It simply purports to obey an instruction for payment, embodied in the cheque and issued by the customer. It is, however, arguable that the payment of the cheque discharges the instrument and hence has the effect of destroying the value of the cheque as a negotiable instrument. The purported conversion is, thus, the destruction of the instrument as an item of property. There is, indeed, a specific situation in which such an action, based on the payment of the cheque, is conferred on the true owner by the BEA 1882. It arises where the bank pays a cheque in a manner that contravenes a crossing executed on it.[296]

The existence of a general action in conversion by the true owner against a paying bank that has paid any type of cheque to the wrong person derives support from *Smith* v. *Union Bank of London*.[297] The payee of a cheque, drawn on the defendant bank, crossed it specially to the C Bank with which he maintained his account and indorsed the instrument in blank. The cheque was stolen thereafter and was remitted by an innocent third party, who became its holder in due course, to the credit of his account with the L Bank. The defendant bank, the drawee, paid the cheque when presented by the L Bank, despite the special crossing.[298] It was held that, as the crossing did not restrict the negotiability of the cheque, the payee had ceased to be its true owner when the instrument came into the hands of a holder in due course. Accordingly, the payee was not entitled to the immediate possession of the cheque and his action in conversion failed. But Blackburn J, whose decision was affirmed by the Court of Appeal, observed that if the bank had paid the cheque to a person other than the holder in due course, it would have laid itself open to an action in conversion by the true owner.[299]

On closer examination, the dictum in *Smith* v. *Union Bank of London* requires a narrow construction. The paying bank's act of conversion is supposed to be the destruction of the negotiable character of the cheque resulting from its discharge. But under section 59 of the BEA 1882, a bill, including a cheque, is discharged only upon its 'payment in due course'. This occurs where the instrument is paid by the drawee in good faith to a holder of whose defect in title the drawee has no knowledge. It follows that payment in due course does not occur where a cheque is paid to a person who has acquired it under a forged indorsement, as such a person is not a holder. It further follows that payment to such a person does not discharge the cheque or destroy its negotiability. The paying bank is therefore not subject to an action in conversion by the true owner.

In reality, the literal construction of the BEA 1882 leads to a paradox. To succeed in an action in conversion, the claimant has to establish both that he himself is the true owner of

---

[294] [2008] AC 1, [97]–[106], [225]–[238], [321] (HL). Their Lordships confirmed the traditional position somewhat reluctantly. Lord Hoffmann referred to it as 'an anomaly created by the judges to solve a particular problem' (ibid., [103]) and 'an insecure base on which to erect a comprehensive system of strict liability for interference with choses in action (ibid., [106]). Lord Nicholls referred to the traditional position as a 'legal fiction' (ibid., [227]).

[295] See Ch. 15, Sect. 2 below. The 'material alteration' of a cheque (such as the unauthorized alteration of its face amount) avoids the instrument: BEA 1882, s.64(1). As the cheque then becomes a 'worthless piece of paper', the measure of damages is no longer the face value, but merely nominal damages: *Smith* v. *Lloyd's TSB plc* [2001] QB 541 (CA).

[296] BEA 1882, s.79(2).   [297] (1875) LR 10 QB 291, affd. (1875) 1 QBD 31.

[298] Such payment was prohibited under s.2 of Act 21 & 22 Vict. c. 79.   [299] N.297 above.

the instrument, and that payment was made in due course; he has, therefore, to establish that the instrument was paid to a holder! If the claimant establishes this second fact, he runs the risk that the paying bank, the defendant in the action, may take the matter one step further and establish that the person to whom the payment was made was the holder in due course of the instrument and hence acquired its title. Alternatively, the paying bank can avoid liability in conversion to the true owner by pleading the forgery of the initial payee's indorsement, in which case the payment of the cheque does not constitute an act of conversion. In effect, the true owner's action in conversion is available only where payment of the cheque is made to a holder who, for some technical reasons,[300] cannot be regarded as a holder in due course!

Doubts concerning the availability of the action in conversion whenever a cheque has been improperly paid are to be found in the decision of the Court of Appeal in *Charles v. Blackwell*.[301] This case, which was heard before the enactment of the 1882 Act, decided that where a cheque was properly paid no action in conversion was maintainable against the bank. Cockburn CJ observed:[302]

> A cheque taken in payment remains the property of the payee only so long as it remains unpaid. When paid the banker is entitled to keep it as a voucher till his account with his customer is settled... If the cheque was duly paid, so as to deprive the payees of a right of action... they no longer have any property in it.

These words suggest that the payee, or true owner, loses his property in the cheque when it is paid. Notably, his Lordship referred specifically to a situation in which a cheque was 'duly paid'. In terms of the 1882 Act, these words are to be understood as referring to the proper mode of payment, which is payment in due course. This, as has been pointed out, is the only situation in which the action would arise at all. It is with respect suggested that the observation that the true owner loses his right when the cheque is paid is unfounded. The very discharge of the cheque is the basis of his complaint. If the argument were correct, it could be pleaded in any action in which a collecting bank was sued in conversion where a cheque had been paid to it by the paying bank.

Does the true owner have against the paying bank an alternative action for restitution? There is no doubt that, where the true owner is entitled to sue in conversion, he can waive this tort and sue for money had and received. This point has been well established since the decision of the House of Lords in *United Australia Ltd* v. *Barclays Bank Ltd*.[303] But this type of restitutionary action does not lie if the claimant, the true owner, does not have a tort to waive.

The more pertinent question is whether the true owner has an action for money had and received, such as an action based on payment made under a mistake of fact, or on total failure of consideration, which can be brought against the paying bank independently of the purported action in conversion.[304] The point is a difficult one, and does not appear to be covered by direct authority. Some indirect support for the availability of such an action can be derived from a dictum of Vaughan Williams LJ in the decision of the Court of Appeal in *Bavins Junr. and Sims* v. *London and South Western Bank Ltd*.[305]

But analysis suggests that the true owner of a cheque is not entitled to bring an action in money had and received against the paying bank where the cheque has been paid to a

---

[300] For example, if the cheque is irregular on its face.   [301] (1877) 2 CPD 151.   [302] Ibid., 162–3.
[303] [1941] AC 1. See *Morison* v. *London County and Westminster Bank Ltd* [1914] 3 KB 356.
[304] The nature of which is explained in detail in *Fibrosa Spolka Akcyjna* v. *Fairbairn Lawson Combe Barbour Ltd* [1943] AC 32, 62 (HL). See generally Ch. 12 below, considering also the implications of the House of Lords' decision in *Lipkin Gorman* v. *Karpnale & Co.* [1991] 2 AC 518 (HL).
[305] [1900] 1 QB 270, 278.

person without a title. The main reason for this becomes apparent when one recalls that the relationship between the paying bank and its own customer, the drawer of the cheque, is one of debtor and creditor. The bank does not hold its customer's money *in specie*. It follows that when a bank pays a cheque it utilizes its own funds and seeks reimbursement from the customer by debiting his account. It is therefore inaccurate to suggest that the paying bank discharges the cheque by paying upon its presentment any specific funds earmarked for the true owner's use by the customer. Moreover, even if the paying bank were regarded as discharging the cheque by paying the customer's money, it would not incur the risk of a restitutionary action by the true owner if it remitted the funds to the wrong party. The drawing of a cheque does not involve an assignment to the payee of the funds against which it is drawn.[306] Indeed, if the drawee dishonours the cheque the true owner has no action against him. How then can the payee, who claims to be the true owner of the cheque, be heard to complain that the money paid by the bank is either received or standing to his credit?

In conclusion, it is clear that the paying bank's main risk in cases of wrongful dishonour is the customer's action for breach of mandate. The true owner appears to have an action only in cases involving payment in violation of a crossing, and in cases in which any cheque payable to his order has been paid to a holder other than a holder in due course. This would usually occur where the cheque came into the hands of a holder after it was stolen from the true owner who had indorsed it in blank. The true owner's action would be brought in conversion and, concurrently, in waiver of tort. An independent action in money had and received is, it is submitted, unavailable to the true owner.

3 The paying bank's defences for wrongful payment at common law and in equity

(i) Outline

Common law and equity confer on the bank certain defences applicable where the customer disputes the validity of the payment of a cheque. Cases of this type occur where the bank has paid a cheque in a manner that contravened the customer's instructions. The situations involved can be classified into three groups.

The first group involves cases in which the cheque has been altered by an unauthorized party who may, for example, have raised the amount of the cheque or changed the name of the payee. If the bank pays the altered instrument, it exceeds the authority conferred on it by the customer. In addition, the unauthorized alteration avoids the cheque if it affects a material part of it.[307] The amount of the cheque, the name of the payee, the date on which the cheque is purported to be drawn, and any crossing are such material details.[308] When a bank honours a materially altered cheque, it not only fails to observe its mandate but also pays a void instrument. The customer is entitled to object to the debiting of his account with such unauthorized payment unless the bank has a specific defence. Common law confers such a defence on the bank either where the customer facilitated the alteration by his carelessness or where his conduct was such as to induce the bank to believe that all was well. Basically the customer's conduct gives rise to an estoppel.

The second type of case in which the bank obtains a defence for the wrongful payment of a cheque is where the customer ratifies an unauthorized signature or alteration of a cheque.

---

[306] BEA 1882, s.53(1).   [307] BEA 1882, s.64.
[308] For cheque crossings, see Ch. 10, Sect. 4(ii) above.

The third type of case in which common law confers on the bank a defence is where the customer's ambiguous instruction misleads the bank. A typical case is where the customer countermands payment of a cheque without supplying the necessary details or describes the instrument wrongly and as a result the bank fails to identify the cheque to be stopped.

Apart from the defences conferred on the bank at common law, there is the equitable defence based on the bank's discharge of a valid debt. This partial and extremely limited defence, already mentioned earlier on, is discussed after the three common law defences.

(ii) **Customer's carelessness and cases giving rise to estoppel**

This type of defence may be based either on the customer's conduct before the cheque is forged or altered, or on his behaviour after he has obtained knowledge thereof. The basic principle is best illustrated by *Brown* v. *Westminster Bank Ltd.*[309] The servants of an aged woman forged her signature on cheques drawn on her current account. The branch manager called on the woman on several occasions to enquire about the genuineness of the cheques but was assured by her that all was well. Although the branch manager had doubts about her mental capacity, it was held that her conduct precluded her from asserting, subsequently, that some of these cheques had been forged.

In *Brown* v. *Westminster Bank Ltd* the bank was able to plead an estoppel on the basis of the customer's explicit representation. A mode of conduct which lulls the bank into safety has a similar consequence. This principle applies where the customer fails promptly to inform the bank about forgeries of his cheques.[310] In *Greenwood* v. *Martins Bank Ltd*[311] a wife forged her husband's signature on cheques drawn on his account with the defendant bank. Initially, the husband accepted his wife's explanation for her conduct and, at her request, agreed not to disclose the forgeries to the bank. Some time thereafter he discovered that the wife's explanation had been false. When he threatened her with exposure, she committed suicide. The husband's action, disputing the bank's right to debit his account with the forged cheques, failed. It was held that he was under a duty to make full disclosure to the bank as soon as he discovered the initial forgeries.[312] His silence had lulled the bank into the belief that the signatures executed by the wife were genuine. The husband's silence further precluded the bank from instituting proceedings during the wife's life. Upon her death, the husband's liability for her frauds terminated. In effect, the bank lost a right of action as a result of the husband's silence.

---

[309] [1964] 2 Lloyd's Rep. 187. See also *Leach* v. *Buchanan* (1802) 4 Esp. 226; *Brook* v. *Hook* (1871) LR 6 Ex. 89; *Ontario Woodsworth Memorial Foundation* v. *Grozbord* (1964) 48 DLR (2d.) 385; *Mutual Mortgage Corporation Ltd* v. *Bank of Montreal* (1965) 55 DLR (2d.) 164; *Tina Motors Pty. Ltd* v. *Australia and New Zealand Banking Group Ltd* [1977] VR 205. Cf. *M'Kenzie* v. *British Linen Co.* (1881) 6 App. Cas. 82 (a Scottish appeal).

[310] The estoppel only operates against a person who qualifies as the bank's customer: *Royal Bank of Scotland plc* v. *Wallace International Ltd* (CA, 27 January 2000), [42].

[311] [1933] AC 51. See also *Geniki Investments International Ltd* v. *Ellis Stockbrokers Ltd* [2008] 1 BCLC 662, [44]–[46], where the *Greenwood* principle was extended to the context of a client failing to inform its stockbroker that one of the brokers was conducting unauthorized share trading upon its account. See further *Ewing & Co.* v. *Dominion Bank* (1904) 35 Can. SCR 133 (leave to appeal denied: [1904] AC 806); *Ontario Woodsworth Memorial Foundation* v. *Grozbord*, above, in which the customer's silence prevented the bank from bringing an action before the date on which the forger absconded.

[312] It is not necessary that the customer knows about the possible fraudulent nature of the transactions behind the erroneous entry, but simply that the entry relates to a transaction that was never authorized: *Geniki Investments International Ltd* v. *Ellis Stockbrokers Ltd*, n.311 above, [45].

This last element, in *Greenwood* v. *Martins Bank Ltd*, was based on the law applicable in the 1930s.[313] The case suggests that, if the customer's silence does not cause any loss to the bank, he is entitled to dispute the debits based on the forgeries. Moreover, the customer is entitled to dispute the genuineness of signatures on his cheques even if forgeries, executed without his knowledge, were perpetrated over a long period of time. In *National Bank of New Zealand Ltd* v. *Walpole and Patterson Ltd*,[314] it was held that a customer was not under an obligation to keep a vigilant eye on his business with a view to detecting forgeries expeditiously. This view has been approved by the Judicial Committee in *Tai Hing Cotton Mill Ltd* v. *Liu Chong Hing Bank Ltd*.[315]

The type of estoppel pleaded in cases like *Greenwood* v. *Martins Bank Ltd*, or in *Brown* v. *Westminster Bank Ltd*, can be asserted only in so far as the customer's representation or silence is not induced by pressure emanating from the bank. In *Brook* v. *Hook*,[316] a person, whose signature as joint maker had been forged on a promissory note, stated that it was genuine so as to avoid the forger's prosecution. As the holder was aware of the true facts, he was not allowed to plead an estoppel when the forgery was raised as a defence to his action on the note.

A specific mode of conduct by the customer that defeats his action against the bank is carelessness related to the drawing of the cheque. Where he signs a cheque in blank, the position is covered by statute. Under section 20(1) of the BEA 1882, a person in possession of a blank cheque has 'prima facie authority to fill up the omission in any way he thinks fit'.[317] The main object of this provision is to protect a subsequent holder who takes the completed cheque. Furthermore, it has been held that where the paying bank pays such a cheque in good faith, the customer is estopped from disputing payment, notwithstanding that the cheque has been completed in an unauthorized manner.[318]

A more complex principle applies where the customer does not sign the cheque in blank but draws it in a manner that enables a rogue to perpetrate a fraud. Basically the customer is liable if his conduct involved negligence. This principle can be traced back to *Young* v. *Grote*,[319] in which the amount of a cheque was written out in a manner that enabled the payee to raise it. The bank was held entitled to debit the customer's account with the altered amount. The principle of this case remained confined to the careless drawing of cheques. In *Scholfield* v. *Earl of Londesborough*,[320] it was held to be inapplicable where the acceptor of a bill of exchange, who had made it payable at his bank, contested the bank's right to debit him with the amount that had been fraudulently raised by the holder. The basis of this rule is to be found in a significant difference between the issuing of a cheque and the acceptance of a bill of exchange. When a bill of exchange is accepted, the blank spaces left by the drawer already appear in it. It is therefore difficult to impute negligence to the acceptor.

Scholfield's case induced the Privy Council in *Colonial Bank of Australasia Ltd* v. *Marshall*[321] to depart from the ruling in *Young* v. *Grote*. That principle was vindicated, however, in the leading case of *London Joint Stock Bank* v. *Macmillan and Arthur*.[322] A clerk prepared a cheque for £2 payable to bearer. There was no sum in words then written on the cheque, but after it had been signed by the employer, the clerk altered the figure to £120 and

---

[313] N.311 above. A husband is no longer liable for the wife's tort: Law Reform (Married Women and Tortfeasors) Act 1935.

[314] [1975] 2 NZLR 7.   [315] [1986] AC 80.   [316] N.309 above.

[317] See further Ch. 10, Sect. 8(ii) above.

[318] *London Joint Stock Bank Ltd* v. *Macmillan and Arthur*, n.268 above, 881. See also *Lloyds Bank Ltd* v. *Cooke* [1907] 1 KB 794; *Smith* v. *Prosser* [1907] 2 KB 735; *Wilson and Meeson* v. *Pickering* [1946] KB 422.

[319] (1827) 4 Bing. 253.   [320] N.268 above [1896] AC 514.

[321] [1906] AC 559.   [322] N.268 above.

inserted the words 'one hundred and twenty pounds' in the space provided. The bank was held entitled to debit the customer's account with that amount. Lord Finlay LC said:[323]

> A cheque drawn by a customer is in point of law a mandate to the banker to pay the amount according to the tenor of the cheque. It is beyond dispute that the customer is bound to exercise reasonable care in drawing the cheque to prevent the banker being misled. If he draws a cheque in a manner which facilitates fraud, he is guilty of a breach of duty as between himself and the banker and he will be responsible to the banker for any loss sustained by the banker as a natural and direct consequence of this breach of duty.

The principle of *Macmillan*'s case was irreconcilable with the approach adopted in *Marshall*, but even in Australia, where the Privy Council's decision remained binding, the High Court eventually adopted the principle in *Macmillan*. In *Sydney Wide Stores Pty. Ltd v. Commonwealth Trading Bank*,[324] a cheque, prepared by the customer's clerk for the alleged purpose of discharging a debt owed to a company known as 'Computer Accounting Services', was made payable to this firm under its initials 'CAS'. After the cheque was signed by the authorized persons, the clerk added the letter 'H' to the payee's name so that the cheque became payable to 'cash or bearer'. The employee then obtained payment for himself. Relying on *Marshall*, the Supreme Court of New South Wales struck out the bank's defence, alleging the customer's negligence in drawing the cheque, as being bad in law. An appeal from this order was allowed by the High Court, which decided to adopt the approach in *Macmillan*. Murphy J pointed out the policy considerations that induced the High Court to depart from the principle in *Marshall*. His Honour said:[325]

> …there is a real question whether it would be better to let the loss continue to fall on the banking industry. Although the standard of care habitually observed by cheque drawers may fairly be described as low, I am not satisfied that any considerable burden has been imposed on banks by the application of the *Marshall*…decision. If in practice the losses, which to individual bank customers would be onerous, are cumulatively only slight for the banking system in comparison with the vast amount of business done by cheque, a sensible system of loss spreading would be to continue as before. Further, if the cumulative losses are now slight, it would be absurd to impose a standard of care such that every drawer of cheques would have to regard employees and associates as potential forgers.

In *Sydney Wide Stores*, the High Court did not decide that the customer was negligent. This question was left for determination by the trial court, to whom the case was remitted. The question undoubtedly is one of mixed fact and law. The answer depends on whether or not the feasibility of the alteration involved would have been foreseen by a reasonable man. The decision of the Court of Appeal in *Slingsby* v. *District Bank Ltd*[326] suggests that not every blank space or incomplete detail left in a cheque when drawn involves negligence on the customer's part. In this case the customer left a blank space between the name of the payee and the printed words 'or order'. A fraudulent third party utilized this space and made the cheque payable to the payee '*per pro*' himself. He then negotiated the cheque by indorsing it in his own name. It was held that the customer had not been negligent and that, although the alteration was not apparent, the customer was entitled to dispute the debiting of his account with the amount of the cheque.

It is clear that the customer's duty of care, based on the principle in *Macmillan*, is a narrow one. Negligence that is not connected with the actual drawing of a cheque does not usually afford a defence to a bank that has wrongfully honoured a cheque. In *Bank of Ireland* v. *Evans'*

---

[323] Ibid., 789.   [324] (1981) 55 ALJR 574.   [325] N.324 above, 579.
[326] [1932] 1 KB 544, affg. [1931] 2 KB 588.

Trustees,[327] which related to the negligent keeping of a seal, Parke B expressed to the House of Lords the unanimous opinion of the judges: 'If there was negligence in the keeping of the seal it was very remotely connected with the act of transfer.' His Lordship went on to explain:[328]

> If such negligence could disentitle the plaintiffs, to what extent is it to go? If a man should lose his cheque book, or neglect to lock the desk in which it is kept, and a servant or stranger should take it up, it is impossible in our opinion to contend that a banker paying his forged cheque would be entitled to charge his customer with that payment.

It would appear that, while a customer must be careful not to facilitate fraud when drawing cheques, he is not under a duty to his banker to exercise care in organizing his business so as to prevent opportunities for others to forge his cheques.

This view derives support from *Lewes Sanitary Steam Co. Ltd v. Barclay & Co. Ltd.*[329] A company's secretary, who to the knowledge of the chairman of the board of directors had been convicted of forgery, was made a joint signatory and was entrusted with keeping the company's cheque-book and pass-book. It was held that the company's bank was not entitled to debit its account with the amount of a cheque on which the secretary had forged the signature of one of the directors, and that the company was not estopped by its conduct from alleging the forgery.

This principle was adopted in *Tai Hing Cotton Mill Ltd v. Liu Chong Hing Bank Ltd.*[330] The claimants maintained current accounts with three different banks in Hong Kong. An employee, L, who was in a position of trust, committed a series of frauds. Initially, he tricked one of the claimants' directors into signing cheques, which L converted. Subsequently, L resorted to the cruder method of forging the director's signature on cheques. During the entire period of six years in which L perpetrated the frauds, the claimants failed to make any security checks, and did not properly peruse the periodic statements furnished by the banks. When the frauds were detected the claimants did not contest the banks' right to maintain the debits based on the cheques signed by the director; but they demanded that their accounts be recredited with the amounts of the forged cheques. The banks disputed this claim, alleging that the claimants were in breach of a duty of care owed both in contract and in tort, and that they were estopped from contesting the entries.

The decision of the Hong Kong Court of Appeal vindicating the banks' stand was reversed by the Judicial Committee. Lord Scarman pointed out that, on the facts, none of the contracts between the claimants and the three banks included an express term imposing on the claimants a duty to conduct their business in a manner that would obviate the type of fraud that had taken place or precluding them from contesting entries based on forged items. The customer's duties that were implied into the contract of banker and customer by *Macmillan* and *Greenwood*, were confined to what could 'be seen to be plainly

---

[327] (1855) 5 HLC 389.   [328] Ibid., 410–411. See also *Welch v. Bank of England* [1955] Ch. 508.
[329] (1906) 95 LT 444. See also *Kepitigalla Rubber Estates Ltd v. National Bank of India Ltd* [1909] 2 KB 1010.
[330] N.315 above. Whilst it remains true, on the basis of *Tai Hing*, that a customer only bears the loss of facilitating a fraud when this results from his negligent drawing of a cheque, but not when this results from other types of dealing with a cheque, statutory developments have resulted in a potentially greater risk of liability for customers who pay by card or electronic funds transfers: Ch. 13, Sect. 5(iv) below & Ch. 14, Sects. 8(ii) & 9(ii) below. In particular, PSR 2009, reg. 62(2)(a) makes a payor liable for all losses resulting from his fraud, which presumably could include the fraud of employees and agents that is properly attributable to the payor. Furthermore, PSR 2009, reg. 57(2) imposes on customers an obligation to 'take all reasonable steps to keep [safe the] personalised safety features' of a payment card or device for making electronic funds transfers. The extent of the customer's liability depends upon whether he acted negligently, with gross negligence, or intentionally in failing to safeguard the personalised safety features associated with his payment cards or with the mechanisms for making electronic funds transfers.

necessary incidents of the relationship. Offered such a service, a customer must obviously take care in the way he draws his cheque, and must obviously warn his bank as soon as he knows that a forger is operating the account.'[331]

Lord Scarman rejected the view that a wider duty than that could be owed in tort. He thought that it would be confusing to formulate a tortious duty, imposed on the customer, when the parties were free to define their mutual obligations on a contractual basis. Obviously, the banks could have imposed more onerous duties on their customers, the claimants, in the contracts governing the current accounts. Thus, the banks could have stipulated that, if entries were not queried within a given period of time, the statements in which they were included would be deemed correct. The clauses incorporated in the three contracts between the claimants and the bank fell short of this. Lord Scarman concluded that as the claimants had not been in breach of a duty of care they were not precluded from pleading the forgeries. The banks were ordered to reverse the debit entries and, further, to pay interest on the amounts involved, as the claimants could have placed these sums in interest-bearing accounts.

The principle of *Tai Hing*, which redefines and clarifies the principle in *Macmillan* and *Greenwood*,[332] has a narrow scope of application. In many cases it is difficult for the bank to bring itself within its ambit. In some cases, however, the bank may be able to plead a third and related defence based on the specific relationship between the customer and the person who has committed the fraud. Thus, in *Greenwood*, the customer was estopped from pleading the forgery because his silence had deprived the bank of its right of action. Under the law as then applicable, if the forgeries had been notified to the bank before the wife's death, the bank could have sued the wife in deceit and joined the husband. The husband's liability would have been similar to the vicarious liability borne by an employer for the act of his employees.

Can a payee bank, on occasions, escape liability by invoking the customer's vicarious liability for the acts of the fraudster? This issue has been considered by the House of Lords in *Crédit Lyonnais Bank Nederland NV* v. *Export Credit Guarantee Department*.[333] In this case one C, acting in collusion with an employee of the ECGD, one P, perpetrated a fraudulent scheme under which the ECGD issued guarantees that induced the L Bank to finance transactions that turned out to be shams. The scam used by the rogues involved the application for ECGD guarantees by C and their ready approval by his accomplice P. When the truth came to light, C absconded. The ECGD refused to make payment under the guarantees whereupon the L Bank sued. Longmore J dismissed the L Bank's action, holding *inter alia* that, under a clause common to the guarantees, the count in contract failed as the L Bank had been reckless in granting C the finance he applied for. The Court of Appeal and the House of Lords concurred, holding also that the ECGD was not vicariously liable for P's deceit. On this issue, Lord Woolf MR's decision breaks new ground.

The action in the instant case was based on the fact that the deceit on the ECGD was perpetrated jointly by P, who was its employee, and by C, who had no nexus with it. The issue was whether, in these circumstances, the ECGD was vicariously liable. His Lordship's answer was that:[334] '[f]or vicarious liability what is critical, as long as one of the

---

[331] Ibid., 106.

[332] N.311 above, discussed above. See also *Price Meats Ltd* v. *Barclays Bank plc* [2002] 2 All ER (Comm.) 346; *Patel* v. *Standard Chartered Bank*, n.269 above (holding that such an estoppel does not arise if the customer has constructive as opposed to express notice).

[333] [2000] 1 AC 486. The vicarious liability point was first raised in *National Bank of New Zealand Ltd* v. *Walpole and Patterson Ltd*, n.314 above, 14. It was pleaded but not pursued in *Tai Hing Cotton Mill Ltd* v. *Liu Chong Hing Bank Ltd*, n.315 above. See also La Forest J (dissenting) in *Boma Manufacturing Ltd* v. *Canadian Imperial Bank of Commerce* (1996) 140 DLR (4th) 463, 499.

[334] N.333 above, 495, as explained in *Dubai Aluminium Co Ltd* v. *Salaam* [2003] 2 AC 366, [39], [114] (HL).

joint tortfeasors is an employee, is that the combined conduct of both tortfeasors is sufficient to constitute a tort in the course of the employee's employment'.

On this basis, Lord Woolf concluded that the ECGD would be liable only if the tortious act of both C and P occurred, conceptually, in the course of P's employment. 'You cannot therefore combine the actions of [P] in the course of his employment with actions of [C], which if done by [P] would be outside the course of [P's] employment'.[335] Lord Woolf then considered the L Bank's second argument, which was that the assistance rendered by P to C was, in itself, a primary 'wrong' and hence imposed vicarious liability on the ECGD. An examination of the authorities led him to the conclusion that there was no separate tort of 'procuring' or assisting a third person to commit a tort. Accordingly, P was not liable on a primary count in tort that would invoke the ECGD's vicarious liability.

Where the fraud is perpetrated by an employee in the course of his employment *Lloyd* v. *Grace Smith & Co.*[336] supports the argument that vicarious liability applies. An employer may, thus, be liable where a clerk raises the amount of a cheque entrusted to him for completion.

(iii) **Ratification**

Where an agent exceeds his authority in drawing a cheque, his act may be ratified, or adopted, by the principal. Ratification precludes the principal from disputing the paying bank's right to debit his account with the proceeds of the cheque. Cases of this type occur mainly where the bank honours a cheque drawn by the agent for an amount exceeding his authority, or where the instrument is paid although a director, who is authorized to draw on a company's account jointly with other officers, draws a cheque without obtaining an additional signature.

The latter type of case arose in *London Intercontinental Trust Ltd* v. *Barclays Bank Ltd.*[337] Here the cheques, which were honoured by the bank although they bore the signature of one director instead of the required two signatures, were drawn principally in order to transfer funds from one of the company's accounts into another. Initially, when the board of directors discovered the irregularity, it resolved to take no action. Subsequently, the company ran into financial difficulties and a new board was appointed. It was then decided to bring an action against the bank, alleging that the cheques in question had been paid in breach of mandate.

Slynn J gave judgment for the bank on three grounds. First, he held that the director in question had had the actual authority to transfer the relevant amounts, which meant that he could have issued an oral or written instruction to this effect on his own. The bank was, accordingly, entitled to act on the director's specific instructions although he gave them by means of cheques signed by him alone. His Lordship observed:[338] 'The bank as a result of its failure to observe the discrepancy took a risk in honouring the cheque that [the director] was not in fact authorized. In the case of both these cheques...he was so authorized.' Secondly, Slynn J concluded on the facts that the original board of directors had adopted the director's act with the full knowledge that the cheques had been improperly drawn. The company had, in this way, ratified the payment of these cheques by the bank. Thirdly, his Lordship noted that before the company brought its action against the bank it had pursued a claim in liquidation before the Stock Exchange on the basis that the transactions, the subject of the transfer of the funds by cheques, were valid. The company had thereby made its election and was bound by it.

---

[335] Ibid.   [336] [1912] AC 716.
[337] [1980] 1 Lloyd's Rep. 241, applied in *HJ Symons & Co* v. *Barclays Bank plc* [2003] EWHC 1249 (Comm.).
[338] Ibid., 249.

Ratification can thus be pleaded either where the principal expressly ratifies the unauthorized drawing or where his conduct indicates that he has adopted the agent's act. An interesting Australian authority concerning the latter type of case is *West* v. *Commercial Bank of Australia Ltd.*[339] A customer opened an account with a bank for the purposes of a business managed by his son, and instructed the bank to pay cheques only if these were signed jointly by the son and by the customer's wife. After a few months the son arranged with one of the bank's tellers to draw cheques signed solely by himself. The customer became aware of the arrangement but took no steps to preclude the honouring of such cheques. Moreover, on one occasion, when a promissory note was executed for the purposes of the business and made payable at the bank, the customer indorsed it although it was not signed by the wife. The High Court of Australia held that, under these circumstances, the customer was estopped from denying the bank's authority to honour cheques signed by the son alone. The customer could not acquiesce in the practice and then elect to repudiate the son's authority to the detriment of the bank. Although the High Court based its decision on an estoppel, the case manifests all the elements needed for ratification. In essence, the customer could not at one and the same time adopt and repudiate the act of the son.

Ratification, however, applies only in the relationship of principal and agent. It does not apply where a person who signs the cheque belonging to another has no authority at all. The prevailing view is that a forgery cannot be ratified.[340] This principle gives rise to a difficulty. Under section 9(1)(*d*) of the Forgery and Counterfeiting Act 1981, a document is false, and hence counterfeit, 'it it purports to have been made...on the authority of a person who did not in fact authorize its making in those terms'. This language suggests that a signature placed on a cheque by an agent who intends to misuse the instrument, rather than to utilize it in the course of his employment, constitutes a forgery. The decision in *Kreditbank Cassel GmbH* v. *Schenkers Ltd*,[341] decided under section 1(1) of the Forgery Act 1913, which used similar language, lends support to this view. In this case a manager fraudulently drew and indorsed bills on his company's behalf for his own purposes. It was held that his signatures on the bills were, therefore, forgeries within the meaning of the 1913 Act. This led the court to conclude that the bills were void as the agent's 'forged' signatures were inoperative under section 24 of the BEA 1882.

The question of ratification did not arise in *Kreditbank*, but it could be concluded that, as the signatures constitute forgeries, they could not be ratified. Section 24 of the BEA 1882, however, distinguishes between a forged signature and an unauthorized signature. This suggests that, for the purposes of the BEA 1882 which governs the law of bills of exchange and of cheques, an agent's unauthorized signature differs from a mere forgery. The proposed distinction accords with the law as it stood when the BEA 1882 Act was passed. Under section 22 of the Forgery Act 1861, which was then in force, an unauthorized signature of a bill or of a note was outside the definition of 'forgery'.[342]

---

[339] (1935) 55 CLR 315.

[340] *Brook* v. *Hook*, n.309 above. See also *Williams* v. *Bayley* (1866) LR 1 HL 200; *Imperial Bank of Canada* v. *Begley* [1936] 2 All ER 367, 374; *Stoney Stanton Supplies (Coventry) Ltd* v. *Midland Bank Ltd* [1966] 2 Lloyd's Rep. 373. Contrast *M'Kenzie* v. *British Linen Co.*, n.309 above, 99 (a Scottish case in which the earlier English authorities were not mentioned); and see, generally, *Bedford Insurance Co.* v. *Instituto de Resseguros do Brasil* [1985] QB 966, 986–989.

[341] [1927] 1 KB 826.

[342] See also *Morison* v. *London County and Westminster Bank Ltd*, n.303 above, 366. Although the Court of Appeal's decision was delivered after the 1913 Act came into effect, this Act was not relied upon as it had not been in force at the time of the trial. On the basis of the 1861 Act, cheques drawn in excess of the agent's authority were held not to be forgeries.

It is believed that, for the purposes of litigation between banker and customer, it is preferable to give effect to the distinction, made in section 24 of the BEA 1882, between forged and unauthorized signatures, rather than to conclude that the Forgery Act 1913, followed on this point in the 1981 Act, introduced an implicit reform equating the two. It is unrealistic to render the bank liable for the agent's abuse of his authority where the principal, the customer, is prepared to adopt the agent's act!

(iv) Customer's ambiguous instructions

It is a general principle of agency law that an agent is not liable for disobeying the customer's intended instruction if this was so ambiguous as to mislead a reasonable man. The agent is entitled to reimbursement as long as he acted on what he honestly considered to have been the principal's intention.[343] This principle applies only where the ambiguity is not apparent. In *Cunliffe, Brooks & Co.* v. *Blackburn and District Benefit Building Society*,[344] it was held that a banker was under a duty to obey his customer's instructions given in the cheque only if these were clearly expressed. In practice, banks dishonour cheques that are written in an illegible manner or that manifest an irregularity in the mandate, such as a difference between the words and the figures denoting the amount to be paid. This practice is doctrinally sound, as it is well established that if the instruction, given by a principal to his agent, is patently capable of more than one interpretation, or is patently unclear, the principal is under a duty to seek better particulars or simply to disobey the order.[345]

(v) The equitable doctrine

Usually, a person who decides to pay the debts of another cannot claim any remuneration. He is a mere volunteer and has no cause of action. A bank that pays a cheque in the mistaken belief that it does so under a mandate is, however, in a position different from that of a volunteer. It does not act on its own resolve, but on the basis of a mistake made by it. It has been suggested that, in cases of this type, the bank should be able to rely on the equitable principle of subrogation, which would entitle it to step into the shoes of the customer to the extent that he has derived some benefit from the payment made.[346] It has been further suggested that this principle should apply where the bank has paid an instrument that bears a forged signature, or less than the required number of signatures, to the extent that the customer has derived benefit as a result of the payment involved. The payment of a countermanded cheque is another illustration if its payment confers a benefit on the customer such as the discharge of a debt.

The doctrine was explained by Wright J in *B. Liggett (Liverpool) Ltd* v. *Barclays Bank Ltd*.[347] Here the bank paid a cheque drawn on the account of a company although the instrument bore only one instead of the required two signatures. The cheque had been drawn for the payment of amounts due to tradesmen for the supply of goods to the

---

[343] *Ireland* v. *Livingston*, n.267 above. For application of this principle in the banker–customer context, see *London Joint Stock Bank Ltd* v. *Macmillan and Arthur*, n.268 above; *Midland Bank Ltd* v. *Seymour*, n.268 above, 148; *Cooper* v. *National Westminster Bank plc*, n.268 above, [58]–[60]. See further Sects. 1(viii) & 2 above.

[344] (1884) 9 App. Cas. 857, 864.

[345] *European Asian Bank AG* v. *Punjab and Sind Bank (No. 2)*, n.269 above, 656; *Patel* v. *Standard Chartered Bank*, n.269 above, [35]–[36]; *Cooper* v. *National Westminster Bank*, n.268 above, [61]–[63].

[346] F.R. Ryder, 'Forgery on a Drawer's Cheque,' *Gilbert Lectures* (1972), 23–4.

[347] [1928] 1 KB 48. See further Ch. 12, Sect. 3(iii)(b) below.

company. His Lordship emphasized that the payment of the cheque had discharged the company's debt to the tradesmen. At common law this would, of course, be irrelevant. The bank would be treated as a mere volunteer. But the position differed in equity. Wright J applied:[348]

> ...the general principle of equity, that those who pay legitimate demands which they are in some way or other bound to meet, and have had the benefit of other people's money advanced to them for that purpose, shall not retain that benefit so as, in substance, to make those other people pay their debts.

His Lordship was of the view that this principle applied not only where the advance was made by means of actual payment but also where it involved a series of credits and debits. This principle was subsequently referred to in *Lloyds Bank Ltd* v. *Chartered Bank of India, Australia and China*,[349] and in *Re Cleadon Trust Ltd*,[350] where it was, however, held that it would apply only to the extent that the payment discharged the debt of the customer.[351] It would not apply where it discharged the debts of a connected business, such as a subsidiary company.

A restrictive approach is discernible also in the latest Court of Appeal decision in point. In *Crantrave Ltd* v. *Lloyds Bank plc*[352] the bank paid out funds standing to the credit of a corporate customer's account upon the service of an interim third party debt order. Before the interim order was made final, the corporate customer was wound up. The Court of Appeal held that the bank was not entitled to rely on the equitable doctrine. In the absence of evidence that the bank's payment had been made on the customer's behalf or was subsequently ratified by him, the payment to the creditor would not of itself protect the bank. It would, in addition, be necessary to show that the voluntary payment made by the bank discharged the customer's liability to the creditor. In the instant case, the bank simply made a mistake. Of particular interest are the words of May LJ, who thought that 'there might conceivably be circumstances not amounting to ratification in which it would nevertheless be unconscionable to allow the customer to recover from the bank the balance of his account without deduction of a payment which the bank had made gratuitously'.[353] As no such circumstances had been established in the instant case, May LJ did not have to give any further indication of what those circumstances might be.[354] Notably, where the equitable doctrine applies, it may be invoked as a partial defence to an action in conversion if part of the proceeds of the instrument were applied to reduce the true owner's indebtedness.[355]

---

[348] Ibid., 61. See also *Jackson* v. *White and Midland Bank Ltd*, n.137 above; *Majesty Restaurant Ltd* v. *Commonwealth Bank of Australia* (1998) 47 NSWLR 593. For a detailed analysis, see E.P. Ellinger and C.Y. Lee, 'The Liggett Defence' [1984] *LMCLQ* 459.

[349] [1929] 1 KB 40.   [350] [1939] Ch. 286, 302–5, 316.

[351] Attempts have been made to justify *Liggett* on the ground that the payment in that case was in reality authorized, but the Court of Appeal in *Filby* v. *Mortgage Express (No. 2) Ltd*, n.64 above, [39] clearly referred to the payment in *Liggett* as being unauthorized.

[352] N.64 above. See also *HJ Symons & Co* v. *Barclays Bank plc*, n.337 above; *Filby* v. *Mortgage Express (No. 2) Ltd*, n.64 above, [34]–[35]; *Liverpool Freeport Electronics Ltd* v. *Habib Bank Ltd*, n.64 above, [141]; *Treasure & Son Ltd* v. *Martin Dawes*, n.64 above, [14].

[353] Ibid., 884.

[354] The nature of these circumstances continues to remain unclear: *Gulf International Bank BSC* v. *Albaraka Islamic Bank*, n.64 above, [36]; *Tayeb* v. *HSBC Bank plc*, n.64 above, [97]–[99]; *Sweetman* v. *Shepherd*, n.64 above, [144]–[148].

[355] *Associated Midland Corporation* v. *Bank of New South Wales* [1980] 1 NSWLR 533.

4 The paying bank's defences for wrongful payment: statutory protections

(i) Outline

As considered above, the common law protects the paying bank from the consequences of an unauthorized payment in circumstances where the customer is estopped by virtue of his conduct, usually by facilitating a fraud on his account, from denying the bank's authority to pay against a forged signature, inadequate signature, or materially altered instrument. Alternatively, a bank may have a common law defence as a result of its customer's ratification or by virtue of having acted reasonably upon ambiguous instructions. In addition to these, a bank may have certain statutory defences that can operate regardless of the customer's fault. The cases involved are primarily those of payments made despite the forgery of the payee's indorsement, and certain cases of material alterations such as the skilful obliteration of a crossing. Usually, the bank's protection depends on its having acted either in the ordinary course of business or 'without negligence'. In certain other cases the bank obtains a valid defence if it has paid a cheque 'in due course'. The different defences require detailed consideration. Payment in due course is the basic principle involved, although such payment does not necessarily confer on the bank a defence against its customer.

(ii) Payment in due course

Under section 59 of the BEA 1882, 'payment in due course' means payment made at or after the maturity of the bill of exchange to the holder thereof in good faith and without notice that his title to the instrument is defective. The effect of such payment is to discharge the bill. As a cheque is a bill of exchange payable on demand, the question of its 'maturity' does not arise.

In most cases, payment in due course entitles the bank to debit its customer's account with the amount of the cheque. The reason is obvious. The customer instructs the bank to pay the instrument to A's order, or to 'A or bearer'. This is what the bank usually does when it pays a cheque to the holder. But not every person who obtains the possession of a cheque is a holder. In this respect, it is important to recall the distinction between a cheque payable to order and one payable to bearer. A cheque payable to bearer, which includes a cheque payable to a specified person or to bearer, is transferable by the mere delivery thereof.[356] Any person who obtains its possession by delivery is a bearer and hence the holder of the instrument. It follows that when the drawee bank pays such a cheque to a person who has its possession, it acts in accordance with the terms of its mandate.[357]

The position differs in the case of a cheque payable to the order of a specific payee. Such an instrument is deliverable by the payee's indorsement completed by the delivery of the instrument.[358] If the payee's indorsement is forged on the cheque, a subsequent party is not the holder of the instrument. The reason for this is that the holder of a bill of exchange or a cheque is defined as 'the payee or indorsee of a bill...who is in possession of it, or

---

[356] BEA 1882, s.31(2).　　[357] *Charles* v. *Blackwell*, n.301 above, 158.

[358] BEA 1882, s.31(3). A cheque that is rendered non-transferable by words prohibiting transfer or manifesting an intention that it be not transferred, and a cheque crossed and bearing the words 'a/c payee only' cannot be transferred at all and a person to whom it is delivered is not a 'holder': see Ch. 10, Sect. 4(iv) above.

the bearer thereof'.[359] A person who takes a cheque under the forged indorsement of the payee does not fall within any one of these categories and, therefore, is not a holder of the instrument.[360] Payment to him is not made in due course and does not constitute a discharge. The cheque is not paid in accordance with the drawer's instruction, as it is not paid to the payee or to his order. Moreover, even where a cheque is paid to the holder thereof—be he the payee, the indorsee, or a bearer—the bank does not necessarily honour the instrument in accordance with the drawer's instruction. Thus, the transferee of a stopped bearer cheque and the indorsee of a countermanded order cheque are 'holders' within the meaning of the BEA 1882, but the bank's duty is to obey the stop order given by the drawer and to dishonour the instrument!

(iii) Payment in the ordinary course of business

The BEA 1882 does not confer a defence on a bank that disobeys a stop order. But the problem of payment against a forged indorsement had to be tackled when the use of cheques became popular. A bank has no means of verifying the genuineness of the payee's indorsement. The payee is a stranger and the bank is not familiar with his signature. Furthermore, as a cheque may be negotiated several times before it is presented for payment, the task of verifying the genuineness of an indorsement is beyond the powers of the paying bank.

The first defence conferred on banks in cases of this type was to be found in section 19 of the Stamp Act 1853. This Act abolished the *ad valorem* duty on cheques, replacing it by a fixed amount. It was envisaged that this would lead to an increase in the use of cheques, and the need for the bank's protection in cases of payment against forged indorsements became paramount. Section 19 provides that, where a bank pays any draft or order drawn on it for a sum of money and payable to order on demand and the instrument purports to be indorsed by the payee, it is not incumbent on the paying bank to show that the indorsement of the payee, or any subsequent indorsement, was made by or under the authority of the person whose indorsement it purports to be, and the bank obtains a valid discharge. This provision is still in effect in respect of bankers' drafts and other instruments that are not encompassed by the definition of a 'bill of exchange'.[361] In the case of cheques, this provision has been superseded by section 60 of the BEA 1882, which adopts the pattern of section 19.

Section 60 applies, and deems the payment to have been made in due course, if the bank is able to show that it has acted in good faith and in the ordinary course of business. In an Australian authority, *Australian Mutual Provident Society* v. *Derham*,[362] it was decided that the last phrase means the mode of transacting business that is adopted by the banking community at large. It has been held that, where the bank pays a crossed cheque over the counter, or where it honours a cheque bearing an irregular indorsement, it is not acting within the ordinary course of business.

A question of some difficulty is whether a bank that acts with negligence may nevertheless be considered as paying a cheque in the ordinary course of business. In *Carpenters' Co.* v. *British Mutual Banking Co. Ltd*,[363] Greer LJ expressed the view that when a bank acts negligently it deviates from the ordinary course of business. Slesser LJ, who concurred with Greer LJ on other grounds, thought that a bank may be acting in the ordinary course of business despite its negligence. This view was supported by

---

[359] Ibid., s.2.   [360] *Lacave & Co.* v. *Crédit Lyonnais* [1897] 1 QB 148.
[361] See Ch. 10, Sect. 3(ii) above. See also *Benjamin's Sale of Goods* (8th edn., London, 2010), para. 22–027.
[362] (1979) 39 FLR 165, 173.   [363] [1938] 1 KB 511.

Mackinnon LJ, who delivered a dissenting judgment. The question thus remains open. In practice, the question is not likely to arise again. The ordinary course of business is determined on the basis of the business methods of a reasonably careful banker. A departure from this standard establishes negligence.

A question of some doubt is whether section 60 of the BEA 1882 protects the bank only in cases in which the forged indorsement was placed on the cheque before its presentment for payment, or even where it was executed when the cheque was tendered to the bank. The section does not expressly distinguish between the two cases. All it says is that, where payment is made by a bank in the ordinary course of business and in good faith, the bank need not show that an indorsement placed on the cheque is genuine. Obviously, if the indorsement is not required, as in the case of a cheque payable to bearer, the question is irrelevant. Furthermore, an indorsement is really not necessary where a cheque is presented to the bank by the ostensible payee. The paying bank does not wish to obtain a transfer to itself of the instrument, and hence a negotiation to it is not necessary. The bank's function is simply to pay the cheque. However, it is customary for banks to request the payee to sign a cheque presented over the counter, as his indorsement serves as a receipt.

South African cases suggest that, where payment is made to the payee over the counter, section 60 of the BEA 1882 has no application.[364] A similar view was taken by an Australian authority, *Smith* v. *Commercial Banking Co. of Sydney Ltd*,[365] where a thief signed his name twice on the back of a bankers' draft in the presence of the teller. It was held that the forged signature did not absolve the bank from liability, and that the Australian counterpart of section 60 (which applies also to drafts) conferred no defence. At first glance, it may appear that the case of *Brighton Empire and Eden Syndicate* v. *London and County Banking Co. Ltd*,[366] decided by the English High Court, went in the opposite direction. Here a director forged his company's indorsement on a cheque and thereafter negotiated it to another employee who presented it to the bank for payment. It was held that, as the bank had acted in good faith, it was entitled to plead the defence of section 60. This case is, however, distinguishable from *Smith*, as in the present case the indorsement was utilized for the transfer of the cheque and not merely as a receipt of its payment by the bank.

It is submitted that the South African and Australian authorities are good law. The object of section 60, as that of section 19 of the Stamp Act 1853, is to protect the bank where it has paid a cheque to a person holding it under a forged indorsement. Where the person who presents the instrument purports himself to be the payee of the instrument, the bank is able to verify his identity.

The main requirement in section 60 is that the cheque be paid in the ordinary course of business. In this regard, the words of Lord Halsbury in *Bank of England* v. *Vagliano Bros.*[367] are significant. His Lordship doubted that 'it would be possible to affirm that any particular course was either usual or unusual in the sense that there [was] some particular course to be pursued'.[368] The question is, basically, one of fact. Thus, the payment of a large cheque presented by a scruffy-looking individual may dictate a different 'ordinary course' than the payment of a cheque for an ordinary amount presented by a person with a usual appearance. As regards other circumstances, the bank is not at fault if it pays a cheque slightly after the official closing time.[369] An indorsement executed in a

---

[364] *National Bank of South Africa Ltd* v. *Paterson* [1909] 2 LDAB 214; *Stapleberg* v. *Barclays Bank (DCO)* [1963] 3 SALR 120.

[365] (1910) 11 CLR 667.   [366] The Times, 24 March 1904.   [367] [1891] AC 107.

[368] Ibid., 117. See also *Auchteroni & Co.* v. *Midland Bank Ltd*, n.12 above.

[369] *Baines* v. *National Provincial Bank*, n.54 above.

foreign language, unreadable by the average Englishman, is in all probability irregular; if a cheque with such an indorsement were honoured, this would be outside the ordinary course of business.[370]

Section 60 only applies to a cheque 'payable to order'. Section 60 does not apply to cheques crossed 'account payee' or 'a/c payee' as such cheques are non-transferable and are not payable to order.[371]

(iv) **Complementary defence of payment without negligence**

In addition to section 60 of the BEA 1882, there is a specific provision confined to crossed cheques.[372] Under section 80, where the cheque has been paid in accordance with the tenor of its crossing, in good faith, and without negligence, the paying bank is placed in the same position as if the cheque had been paid to the true owner thereof. Furthermore, the protection is also conferred on the drawer, provided the cheque was indorsed by a forger after it had reached the hands of the payee. For all practical purposes, the phrase 'without negligence' in section 80 replaces the phrase 'in the ordinary course of business' of section 60.

The existence side by side of sections 60 and 80 is explainable by historical reasons. As already pointed out, section 60 can be traced back to section 19 of the Cheques Act 1853. Section 80 stems from section 9 of the Crossed Cheques Act 1876, which explains why it is applicable only to cheques of such a type. In the United Kingdom, the need to have two provisions has been questioned by Holden.[373] Undoubtedly, unlike section 60, section 80 confers a protection not only on the paying bank but also on the drawer whose cheque was received by the payee. But the two provisions could have been amalgamated. However, an Australian authority suggests that section 80 is useful in its own right. In *Australian Mutual Provident Society* v. *Derham*,[374] an assured, who had decided to surrender his policy, lodged a form requesting the company to remit the proceeds to an agent. This agent completed the surrender form by inserting his own post-office box as the assured's address. When the agent received the company's crossed cheque payable to the assured, he forged on it the latter's indorsement and paid the cheque to the credit of his own bank account. McGregor J held, *inter alia*, that the paying bank was protected by the Australian equivalent of section 80. As the bank was not concerned with the regularity of the indorsement, it had paid the cheque in question 'without negligence'. That the bank was not concerned with the regularity of the indorsement followed from the Australian counterpart of section 1 of the Cheques Act 1957, discussed subsequently. His Honour, in effect, read section 80 together with the Australian equivalent of section 1. The decision in *Derham* could have been reached even if payment were not made 'in the ordinary course of business', provided it had been made without negligence.

---

[370] *Carlisle and Cumberland Banking Co.* v. *Bragg* [1911] 1 KB 489, 4906 (unaffected as regards this point by *Saunders* v. *Anglia Building Society (Gallie* v. *Lee)* [1971] AC 1004); *Arab Bank Ltd* v. *Ross* [1952] 2 QB 216.

[371] BEA 1882, s.81A(1).

[372] Under the Cheques Act 1992, s.2, the defence applies also to cheques bearing a crossing accompanied by the words 'a/c payee only'. Under Cheques Act 1957, s.5, the protection offered by BEA 1882, s.80 extends to certain other crossed instruments, analogous to cheques, referred to in s.4(2)(b), (c), and (d) of the 1957 Act.

[373] J.M. Holden, *History of Negotiable Instruments* (London, 1955), 268. See also A.G. Guest, *Chalmers and Guest on Bills of Exchange and Cheques* (17th edn., London, 2009), para. 14-027.

[374] N.362 above.

Although section 80 of the BEA 1882 is limited in its application to crossed cheques paid to a banker,[375] it is not limited to cheques payable to order.[376] Section 80 will apply if the cheque bears a forged or unauthorized indorsement, but it will not protect the paying bank if the drawer's signature has been forged or made without his authority as the instrument is not then a cheque at all, for the signature is wholly inoperative,[377] so that the instrument does not meet the requirements of a bill of exchange.[378] Neither will the section protect the paying bank where the cheque has been 'materially altered' so as to be caught by s.64(1) of the BEA 1882. The effect of the material alteration is to render the instrument void with the result that it is no longer a cheque but a 'worthless piece of paper'.[379] A banker is not to be treated for the purposes of section 80 of the BEA 1882 as having been negligent *by reason only* of his failure to concern himself with any purported indorsement of a cheque, which under s. 81A(1) of the 1882 Act or otherwise is not transferable.[380] In other words, the paying bank can normally ignore any purported indorsement on the cheque, as it is the responsibility of the collecting bank to ensure that a non-transferable cheque is collected only for the account of the named payee. However, there may be additional circumstances, for example, where the paying bank is reliably informed that the cheque has been stolen from the payee (assuming the drawer has not, or has not yet, countermanded payment), in which case it might be negligent for a bank to pay a non-transferable cheque bearing a purported indorsement without first satisfying itself that it was in fact being paid to the person entitled to receive it.[381]

(v) Irregularity in or absence of indorsement

Section 60 of the BEA 1882 and the complementary section 80 protect the paying bank only where the indorsement of an order cheque that appears regular on its face turns out to be forged. Payment against an absent or irregular indorsement is both outside the ordinary course of business and, on the same reasoning, negligent. The indorsement of the payee is irregular whenever it differs materially from the name by which he is described by the drawer. If a cheque is payable to 'John Williams', an indorsement by 'J. Williams' is regular. But if the payee is described on the face of the instrument under a misnomer (for example, W. Williams) and then indorses it in his correct name (for example, John Williams), the discrepancy between the front and the back of the instrument renders the indorsement irregular, although it may be effective for the purpose of negotiation.[382] Similarly, if a company indorses a cheque without adding the word 'company' or 'Ltd', which forms part of its description, as the payee of the cheque, the indorsement is irregular.[383]

A special problem concerning the regularity of an indorsement arises where it is executed by an agent. Where A is B's agent, usually he will indorse a cheque as 'A on behalf of B', or 'A *per pro* B' (*per pro* meaning *per procuratorem*, or by procuration). The drawer himself may make the cheque payable to 'A *per pro* B', which often occurs in cases such as settlements of claims, in which a cheque is made payable to the creditor through his solicitor. There is a view that the agent must indicate that he is signing on behalf of the

---

[375] BEA 1882, s.60 is not.   [376] Ibid., s.60 is so limited.   [377] Ibid., s.24.   [378] Ibid., s.3(1).
[379] *Smith* v. *Lloyds TSB Bank plc* [2001] QB 541, 556–557; cf. M. Hapgood, *Paget's Law of Banking* (13th edn., London, 2007), paras. 24.38 *et seq*).
[380] BEA 1882, s.81A(2).
[381] See A.G. Guest, n.373 above, para. 14–28.
[382] *Arab Bank Ltd* v. *Ross*, n.370 above.   [383] Ibid., 234.

principal and not merely that he is assuming the role of an agent. Thus, it has been suggested that where a cheque payable to 'John Brown' is indorsed 'John Brown, W. Robinson (agent)', the indorsement is irregular as the word 'agent' contextually signifies the signer's business rather than status.[384] But this view is pedantic. Banks accept such indorsements as valid.

The agent has to show that he is signing in representative capacity even if the cheque is made payable to him as an agent. In *Slingsby* v. *District Bank Ltd*,[385] an executor of a will instructed his solicitors, Messrs C & P, to draw a cheque payable to stockbrokers. One of the partners of the firm of solicitors initially made the cheque payable to the stockbrokers, obtained the required signatures, and then utilized a gap left after the stockbrokers' name as payee in order to make the cheque payable to these payees '*per pro* C & P'. The partner then indorsed the cheque merely as 'C & P', and paid it into an account of a company in which he had a personal interest. It was held that the indorsement was irregular, and hence the paying bank could not plead the protection of sections 60 and 80 of the BEA 1882.

In the case of a company, section 52 of the Companies Act 2006 provides that a negotiable instrument is deemed to be made, accepted or indorsed in the firm's name 'if…[signed] in the name of, or by or on behalf or on account of, the company by any person acting under its authority'. It follows that a company's indorsement is regular if its name is written out, or impressed with a rubber stamp. However, banks insist that the person who executes the indorsement should identify himself. In practice, therefore, a regular indorsement in the company's name should read 'X Ltd *per* A B, director', 'A B on behalf of X Ltd', or words to a similar effect.

It is obvious that cheques are frequently indorsed in an irregular manner. This stems from the misnomer of the payee's name on the front of the cheque, or from inaccuracies in the description of corporate bodies. The best advice that could be given to the payee was to indorse the cheque in the name in which he was described and then to add his genuine signature. The extent of the problem, in particular in the case of corporate bodies with a large clientele, can be best appreciated if one bears in mind that, at one stage, the firm of 'Thomas Cook & Sons' had several rubber stamps with different names to be employed for the indorsement of cheques payable to them under different variations of their proper corporate name![386]

Until 1957, the paying bank's correct legal course was to dishonour any cheque that was irregularly indorsed or on which the indorsement was missing. This was the case also where the cheque was presented for payment through the clearing system, as the collecting bank was expected to demand the payee's indorsement even where the cheque was not negotiated to a third party. Undoubtedly, such an indorsement served as a mere receipt rather than for the proper function of an indorsement, namely for the negotiation of the instrument. But an irregularity was considered to render the cheque as being paid with negligence and outside the ordinary course of business. This meant that, unless the paying bank was prepared to forego the protection of sections 60 and 80 of the BEA

---

[384] Chorley, *Law of Banking* (6th edn., London, 1974), 85. See also the dictum of Piggott CB in *O'Reilly* v. *Richardson* (1865) 7 ICLR 74; Scrutton LJ in *McDonald (Gerald) & Co.* v. *Nash & Co.* [1922] WN 272 (CA), revsd. on a different point: [1924] AC 625 (HL).

[385] N.326 above, affd. n.326 above.

[386] This procedure is described in *Bird & Co.* v. *Thomas Cook & Son Ltd* [1937] 2 All ER 227. Formerly, under Companies Act 1985, s.349(4), a director who signed a cheque or accepted a bill of exchange that described the company incorrectly was personally liable on the instrument: see *Chitty on Contracts*, n.8 above, para. 34-046. See also *Fiorentino Comm Giuseppe Srl* v. *Farnesi*, n.13 above, [24]–[26]. This provision was repealed on 1 October 2008 by Companies Act 2006, s.1295 & Sched. 16.

1882, it had to reject a substantial number of cheques. This situation was undesirable and, eventually, led the Committee on Cheque Indorsements ('the Mocatta Committee'), in its report of November 1956,[387] to recommend that indorsements no longer be required as a precondition for the payment of cheques other than those presented over the counter. The Cheques Act 1957, enacted in the wake of this report, went further than that. Under section 1(1), where a banker in good faith and in the ordinary course of business pays a cheque drawn on him and the cheque is not indorsed or is irregularly indorsed, the bank does not, in doing so, incur any liability by reason only of the absence of or the irregularity in the indorsement. The bank is, further, deemed to have paid the instrument in due course. Section 1(2) extends the application of this provision to documents that, although not bills of exchange, are intended to enable a person to obtain payment from the bank of the sum mentioned in the instrument. Instruments of this type include 'cheques' payable to 'cash or order' that, as has been pointed out,[388] do not constitute bills of exchange. Section 1(2) further extends the provision of section 1(1) to bankers' drafts that, likewise, are not bills of exchange within the definition of the BEA 1882.[389]

Section 1 had the effect of eliminating the need for an indorsement of a cheque as a prerequisite to the bank's right to invoke the protection of sections 60 and 80 of the BEA 1882, but the Committee of London Clearing Banks took the view that the public interest would be best served by retaining the need for indorsements in certain circumstances. These circumstances are stated in a circular of 23 September 1957, sent by the Committee to clearing bank managers. Despite the lapse of time, the practice laid down in the circular has remained unaltered. The procedure prescribed in the circular can thus be taken to establish the 'ordinary course of business' to be observed by banks when paying cheques. If this procedure is disregarded, the bank is deprived of the protection conferred on it by section 1. This follows from the language of the section, which states that a bank does not incur liability 'by reason only' of a missing or of an irregular indorsement. When a bank pays an irregularly indorsed cheque, although the practice based on the circular regards it as one on which a regular indorsement is required, the paying bank honours it not only despite the relevant defect but also in disregard of standard banking practice.

The situations in which the circular requires the paying bank to insist on an indorsement are: (a) where cheques are presented for payment over the counter; (b) in respect of combined cheques and receipt forms marked 'R'; and (c) where cheques payable to joint payees are paid into an account which is not maintained in the name of all of them. It is understood that, in this last type of case, the indorsement of one payee is sufficient if the cheque is payable to them in the alternative. Otherwise, the indorsement of all of them is required.

It is important to note that in most of the cases an indorsement, which is required under the circular, serves the function of a receipt rather than the negotiation of the cheque. This is the case in all combined cheques marked 'R', and whenever the person who presents any cheque for payment over the counter is the ostensible payee. If the cheque is presented by a subsequent holder, however, the bank will insist on having indorsements of both the holder and of the ostensible payee. The object is to ensure the apparent regularity in the line of indorsements. In reality, though, the usefulness of the practice is questionable.

---

[387] Cmnd. 3.   [388] See Ch. 10, Sect. 3(iii) above.

[389] The defence is extended to crossed cheques bearing the words 'a/c payee only'. Under the Cheques Act 1992, s.1 (inserting a new s.81A(2) in the BEA 1882), the paying bank is not to be treated for the purposes of s.80 as having been negligent by reason only of its failure to concern itself with any purported indorsement of such a cheque or of any cheque otherwise rendered non-transferable (for example, a cheque payable to 'X only'): see Ch. 10, Sect. 4(iv) above.

If a cheque, payable to X's order, is stolen by Y and presented by Y for payment over the counter, Y can easily forge X's indorsement before he goes to the bank; he can then add an indorsement in his own name! Under section 60 of the BEA 1882, the paying bank will be protected in such a case if the forged indorsement is regular. *Smith* v. *Commercial Banking Co. of Sydney Ltd*,[390] discussed above, does not deprive it of its defence, as the forged signature is that of X and not of Y, to whom the cheque is paid. Under the terms of the circular, however, the protection would be lost if X's indorsement were not only forged but also irregular.[391]

5 The customer's remedies for wrongful dishonour of his cheques

(i) Scope of problem

It will be recalled that the bank's duty to honour a cheque is owed to the customer alone.[392] A wrongful dishonour of a cheque constitutes a breach of contract on the bank's part. In certain cases the customer may have an additional action in defamation. This action is usually based on the reply that the bank writes on the cheque when it returns it unpaid. In certain cases, the reason stated is meant to save the customer's reputation. Thus, the bank may explain its dishonour of a cheque by the words 'amount in words and in figures differ'. Another instance, which occurs in the case of companies, is an indication by the bank that the cheque does not bear all the required signatures. The situation which leads to actions in defamation arises where a cheque is dishonoured due to a supposed inadequacy of funds standing to the credit of the customer's account. Where the bank's answer on the cheque gives the impression that this is the case, the customer's reputation may be harmed. He is then tempted to sue both for breach of contract and defamation.

(ii) Action in breach of contract

Under the basic principles governing actions for breach of contract, the innocent party is entitled to recover damages from the party in breach, but unless the innocent party has sustained a loss, he is confined to recovering nominal damages.[393] This general rule is applicable where the bank dishonours a cheque without a justifiable reason. A distinction used to be drawn in this context between a person who is in business and other members of the public. In the case of the latter group, the amount of damages recoverable for wrongful dishonour was nominal, unless special loss could be proved. This basic principle was best illustrated by *Evans* v. *London and Provincial Bank*.[394] The customer was the wife of a naval officer. When her cheque for groceries was wrongfully dishonoured

---

[390] N.365 above.

[391] As to whether the defences in BEA 1882, ss.60 and 80 are available where a cheque is avoided by a material alteration, see *Slingsby* v. *District Bank Ltd* [1932] 1 KB 544; *Kulatilleke* v. *Bank of Ceylon* (1958) 59 NLR (Ceylon) 188; *Kulatilleke* v. *Mercantile Bank of India* (1958) 59 NLR (Ceylon) 190. The avoidance of the instrument poses problems as regards its value: see *Smith* v. *Lloyds TSB Group plc*, n.379 above. See further Ch. 15, Sect. 2 below.

[392] See Ch. 10, Sect. 3(i) above.

[393] See, generally, *Chitty on Contracts*, n.8 above, para. 26-008.

[394] *The Times*, 1 March 1917.

by the bank, she sued in breach of contract. It was held that she had suffered no loss and she was, therefore, awarded one shilling by the jury. Similarly, in *Gibbons* v. *Westminster Bank Ltd*,[395] where the bank dishonoured a cheque drawn by a tenant in favour of a landlord, it was held that the customer had to prove loss in order to recover substantial damages. Lawrence J observed that such loss would have to be pleaded and proved as special damage.

The converse applied in the case of people engaged in trade. From the beginning of the 19th century a stigma attached to the reputation of a merchant whose bills of exchange (including cheques) were not met by the bank at which they were domiciled. This damage to reputation was recognized as early as 1830 in *Marzetti* v. *Williams*.[396] The principle involved was most clearly stated in *Rolin* v. *Steward*, where a merchant's cheque was wrongfully dishonoured by his bank, by Williams J in the Court of Common Pleas:[397]

> ...when...the [customer] is a trader...the jury, in estimating the damages, may take into their consideration the natural and necessary consequences which must result to the [customer] from the [bank's] breach of contract: just as in the case of an action for slander of a person in the way of his trade, or in the case of an imputation of insolvency on a trader, the action lies without proof of special damage.

The distinction between the position of tradesmen and other persons was postulated even in recent years.[398] It was based on the view that a tradesman's reputation suffered from the dishonour of a cheque as it implied that his bank had no trust in his financial position. The amount of damages to be awarded was, accordingly, a matter for the assessment of the judge or, where he was not sitting alone, for the jury.[399] No such assumption of the occurrence of such a loss could be made, automatically, in the case of other persons.

The ensuing distinction between a tradesman and other persons as regards the loss sustained in consequence of the dishonour of a cheque was, undoubtedly, suitable in days in which the significance of credit to traders was distinguishable from its meaning to other members of the public. In modern times this distinction has been eroded. To start with, professional men, such as solicitors and accountants, are in a position akin to that of businessmen.[400] So are, to an extent, persons such as physicians and dentists, whose financial reputation is of considerable significance as regards their ability to obtain supplies for their surgeries. In addition, even members of the public other than tradesmen, such as civil servants and employees in general, have credit ratings with credit card issuers and other financial institutions. A bounced cheque can cause as much harm to their reputation as to a tradesman's.

---

[395] [1939] 2 KB 882. See also *Rae* v. *Yorkshire Bank* [1988] 1 FLR 1; *Great Ore Coconut Products Industries (M.) Sdn Bhd.* v. *Malaysian Banking Berhad* [1985] 2 MLJ 469 (Malay. Sup. Ct.) (emphasizing the loss of reputation incurred by a trader in cases of this type).

[396] N.28 above.

[397] N.41 above, 607. See also *Bank of New South Wales* v. *Milvain* (1884) 10 VLR (Law) 3.

[398] See, for example, *Jayson* v. *Midland Bank Ltd* [1968] 1 Lloyd's Rep. 409.

[399] 'Reasonable damages' are to be awarded: see *Wilson* v. *United Counties Bank Ltd* [1920] AC 102, 112 (HL). See also *Szek* v. *Lloyds Bank* (1908) 2 LDAB 159. A bank's prompt apology can be taken into account in mitigation: *Davidson* v. *Barclays Bank* [1940] 1 All ER 316, 324; *Baker* v. *ANZ Bank Ltd* [1958] NZLR 907, 911.

[400] Thus, in *Davidson* v. *Barclays Bank Ltd*, n.399 above, a bookmaker was treated as a tradesman. In contrast, a firm engaged in kite-flying was treated as a non-trader in *Ellow Co. Ltd* v. *Lloyds Bank Ltd* (1934) 4 LDAB 455, although the court also took into consideration the poor record of the firm, which frequently drew uncovered cheques.

The appreciation of this social development explains the decision of the Court of Appeal in *Kpohraror* v. *Woolwich Building Society*.[401] The customer, who had described himself in the account opening form as a self-employed exporter/importer with an annual income of below £5,000, drew a cheque in favour of a supplier. Initially, the cheque was dishonoured by the bank in the mistaken belief that it had been reported lost. When the mistake was discovered, before the close of the very day of dishonour, the payee was informed there were adequate funds in the account. In the event, he agreed to accept the bank's cashier cheque in payment of the amount due. The Master awarded the customer general damages based on the loss to his reputation. The bank appealed, claiming the customer was entitled only to nominal damages. The customer cross-appealed, claiming special damages by reason of the loss of future orders and the loss caused by the delay in the shipment.[402] The Court of Appeal held that even a person other than a tradesman could recover substantial rather than nominal damages for loss of credit or business reputation resulting from a cheque being wrongly dishonoured by his bank. The Master's award of general damages was, accordingly, upheld. However, the special damages which the customer sought to recover were too remote, since there was no evidence to indicate that a one-day delay in payment would in itself cause a substantial loss to the customer's business.

The hazard of the wrongful dishonour of a cheque has not been eliminated by the introduction of the semi-automated clearing process of cheques, and by the system used in respect of money transfers.[403] Although a cheque sets out in magnetic ink the number of the account to be debited, and although the deposit slip used by the payee identifies his own account in the same manner, mistakes can occur when the amount of a cheque, initially written in ordinary ink by the drawer, is encoded in magnetic ink by the clerks who effect the respective debit or credit. As a result the balance in a specific account, against which a further cheque is drawn, may be shown inaccurately. Furthermore, the computerized process itself is fallible: the encoded details can be misinterpreted by the computer if the cheque has been folded or otherwise handled carelessly. In the past, the risk of error was even greater in the case of individual money-transfer orders. Such individual orders were written out by hand and did not always include the identifying details set out on cheques in magnetic ink. Nowadays, however, the risk of error is much reduced, though not eliminated, for since January 1988 inter-bank giro credits must be made using pre-printed credit forms, such as those found at the back of cheque-books or provided with utility bills.

This danger means that the bank has to compose with care its grounds for the dishonour of what appears to be an uncovered cheque. If it gave an answer such as 'insufficient funds' and it then turned out that the balance in the customer's account was adequate, the bank would face the hazards of an action, especially where the customer was a trader or a professional man.[404] The difficulty, however, is that standard formulas that may appear innocent have acquired a certain notoriety and indicate that the cheque is drawn without cover. Thus, in New Zealand, the words 'present again' have been held to indicate an inadequacy of funds simply because that was the meaning attributed to the phrase

---

[401] [1996] 4 All ER 119. See *Bumiputra-Commerce Bank Bhd* v. *Top-A Plastic Sdn Bhd*, n.104 above, [44]. For the application of *Kpohraror* to breach of confidence, see *Shah* v. *HSBC Private Bank (UK) Ltd* [2009] EWHC 79 (QB), [105]. See also *Nicholson* v. *Knox Ukiwa* [2007] EWHC 2430 (QB), [78]–[80]; *Al-Rawas* v. *Pegasus Energy*, n.178 above, [34]–[39].

[402] As a matter of caution, presumably.

[403] For discussion of the clearing of cheques, see Ch. 10, Sect. 2 above. For discussion of money transfers, see Ch. 13, Sect. 3 below.

[404] *Davidson* v. *Barclays Bank Ltd*, n,399 above. See also *Miles* v. *Commercial Banking Co. of Sydney* (1904) 1 CLR 470.

generally.[405] The formula 'refer to drawer' is another one which, at this stage, has become associated with uncovered cheques.[406] It is believed that almost any phrase that became associated with uncovered cheques would, in due course, acquire such an ulterior meaning. The safest course that can be adopted by the bank is the return of the unpaid cheque, accompanied by a note which confirms its dishonour but does not give any specific reason therefore.[407]

(iii) Action in defamation

Any carelessly composed answer written on a dishonoured cheque is capable of being construed as defamatory provided it is susceptible to such an interpretation by a reasonable man.[408] The question is one of mixed fact and law. The legal question is whether the words are at all open to such a construction.[409] If they are, it is a question of fact whether or not the words have conveyed such a meaning in the case in question. The innocent appearance of the words is irrelevant, as they may convey an innuendo. Thus, in *Baker* v. *Australia and New Zealand Bank Ltd*,[410] Shorland J, in the (former) Supreme Court of New Zealand, held that the words, 'present again' were both legally capable of such a meaning and that, in fact, they had conveyed that effect in the case before him. In *Pyke* v. *Hibernian Bank Ltd*,[411] Black J reached a similar conclusion as regards the words 'refer to drawer', and his decision was upheld by the Irish Court of Appeal. In *Jayson* v. *Midland Bank Ltd*,[412] an English jury, which found that the dishonour of a cheque was justified on the facts, found nevertheless that the last-quoted words could lower a person's reputation and were defamatory if untrue. Most recently, the Malaysian Court of Appeal, in *Bumpitra-Commerce Bank Bhd* v. *Top-A Plastic Sdn Bhd*,[413] held that the marking of the words 'frozen account' and 'refer to drawer' on a cheque were 'highly libelous and tantamount to mean that the [claimant] had been locked up or gone into liquidation'.

In practice, therefore, it is possible to bring an action for the wrongful dishonour of a cheque under the complementary causes of action of breach of contract and of defamation. The customer is, however, unlikely to be awarded a separate amount of damages in respect of each plea.[414] Indeed, in some cases juries awarded substantial damages for the one cause and nominal damages for the additional second cause of action.[415] There are, however, advantages to the bringing of the action in the alternative under

---

[405] *Baker* v. *Australia and New Zealand Bank*, n.399 above.

[406] This was not so initially: see *Szek* v. *Lloyds Bank Ltd*, n.399 above; *Flach* v. *London and South Western Bank Ltd* (1915) 31 TLR 334; *Plunkett* v. *Barclays Bank Ltd*, n.78 above. It is believed that the position differs today, as cheques are not 'referred to drawer' in other types of cases, and this fact is common knowledge. In a more recent Irish case, *Pyke* v. *Hibernian Bank Ltd*, n.20 above, the words were held defamatory by a jury. See also *Jayson* v. *Midland Bank Ltd*, n.398 above.

[407] *Frost* v. *London Joint Stock Bank Ltd* (1906) 22 TLR 760.

[408] The defence of qualified privilege has been rejected in this context in England (*Davidson* v. *Barclays Bank Ltd*, n.399 above, 322) and Australia (*Aktas* v. *Westpac Banking Corporation Ltd* [2010] HCA 25, [31]–[42]).

[409] The mere dishonour of the cheque, without the giving of a reason, is probably not the basis for an action in defamation: *Bank of New South Wales* v. *Milvain*, n.397 above; *Kinlan* v. *Ulster Bank Ltd* [1928] IR 171.

[410] N.399 above.   [411] N.20 above.

[412] N.398 above. See also *Aktas* v. *Westpac Banking Corporation Ltd* [2009] NSWCA 9, [17].

[413] [2008] 5 MLJ 34, [22] (Malay CA).

[414] See, for example, *Bumpitra-Commerce Bank Bhd* v. *Top-A Plastic Sdn Bhd*, n.413 above, [42].

[415] Thus, in *Szek* v. *Lloyds Bank Ltd*, n.399 above, the jury awarded £250 for breach of contract and nil for defamation. Grantham J, indeed suggested to the jury that one sum should be awarded for both claims. In

both causes. If the action in defamation fails but the action for breach for contract succeeds, the claimant has, in the very least, vindicated his right to have drawn the cheque. This may be important as regards his financial standing. It is, therefore, inadvisable to abandon the action in breach of contract. If, on the other hand, the action is confined to one in breach of contract, the action is to be heard by a judge sitting alone. If the action is brought in defamation, the claimant, subject to the court's discretion, is entitled to trial by jury.[416] Tactically, the claimant may see an advantage in having an action tried in this way.

Baker v. *Australia and New Zealand Bank Ltd*, n.399 above, a nominal amount was awarded for the breach of contract involved, but £100 for defamation.

[416] Moreover, judges under the Civil Procedure Rules 1998 have enhanced powers to dismiss all or part of a claim without the need for a trial: see CPR, Pt. 24, CPR, Pt. 53PD4 and CPR, r.3.4. See also the Defamation Act 1996, s.8. Overall, in recent years there has been a diminished role for the jury in the determination of defamation claims. See generally D. Price, K. Duodo, & N. Cain, *Defamation Law, Procedure and Practice* (4th edn., London, 2009).

12

Recovery of Money Paid by Mistake

1 The problem in practice and the basic principle

As discussed previously,[1] there are circumstances where banks that pay out their customer's money without a valid mandate may nevertheless debit their account. This may be due to the existence of some limitation on the bank's mandate in the particular circumstances or the relevance of some common law or statutory defence, such as the defences conferred by the Bills of Exchange Act 1882 (BEA 1882).[2] A bank cannot, however, always avail itself of such defences, such as where a computer error leads to an automated payment being made twice, or a bank error leads to a cheque being honoured despite the customer's valid countermand.[3] In such circumstances, the bank's only course is to reclaim the money from the payee. Moreover, even where the bank is entitled to debit its customer's account with a wrongful payment, it may make the commercial decision to pursue the payee rather than its customer.[4] In this context, however, the word 'payee' must be understood in a wide sense. Usually, the amount involved is paid by the paying bank to the collecting bank engaged by the ultimate payee, and restitution may be sought from either the ultimate payee or his bank. In many cases, the two may be sued jointly. The action against the collecting bank is, however, subject to certain limitations that are inapplicable to actions brought against the ultimate payee. The distinction stems from the fact that the collecting bank receives payment in a representative capacity, whilst the payee obtains payment for himself.[5] When the collecting bank acts for itself, for example where it discounts an instrument, its position is similar to that of the ultimate payee.

---

[1] Ch. 11, Sect. 1 above.   [2] Ch. 11, Sects. 3–4 above.

[3] Ch. 11, Sect. 1(viii) above. See, for example, *Lomax Leisure Ltd* v. *Miller* [2007] BPIR 1615, [52]–[54]. For useful historical background, see H. Luntz, 'Bank's Right to Recover on Cheques Paid by Mistake' (1968) 6 *Melb. Univ. L. Rev.* 308. A claim for restitution is not usually brought by a collecting bank, which can generally rely on the right of recourse conferred on it by the Bills of Exchange Act 1882 (BEA 1882); cf. *Deutsche Bank (London Agency)* v. *Beriro & Co.* (1895) 1 Com. Cas. 255.

[4] Where the bank recovers from the payee before debiting its customer's account, the bank's right to recover its loss from the customer is extinguished. Where the bank debits the customer's account before suing the payee, the bank will be treated as the customer's agent and must account to its customer for the fruits of recovery should its action be successful: C. Mitchell, 'Banks, Agency, and Unjust Enrichment' in J. Lowry and L. Mistelis (eds.), *Commercial Law: Dimensions and Practice* (London, 2005). See also *Niru Battery Manufacturing Co.* v. *Milestone Trading Ltd (No. 1)* [2002] 2 All ER (Comm.) 705, [145] (not considered on appeal: [2004] 4 All ER (Comm.) 193 (CA); *Bracken Partners Ltd* v. *Gutteridge* [2004] 1 BCLC 377 (CA).

[5] Sect. 4 below.

Where a bank pays money as a result of a mistake of fact or law it may bring a common law action for money had and received against the payee.[6] Nowadays, this is generally referred to as 'a personal claim in restitution at common law'.[7] The claim is founded on the unjust enrichment of the payee at the bank's expense. The bank's mistake renders the enrichment of the payee unjust because it vitiates the bank's intention to transfer the benefit to him. Reversal of that unjust enrichment lies at the heart of the claim.[8] The cause of action is complete upon receipt of the money by the payee and does not depend upon continued retention of the mistaken payment.[9] Accordingly, as the payee's liability crystallizes at the moment of receipt, as a general principle, the quantum of the payor's claim is unaffected by subsequent events. There are, however, two broad exceptions to this general principle. First, subsequent events may provide the payee with a defence: the fact that the payee has paid away the money without knowledge of the bank's mistake may give him a defence of change of position, or a defence of payment away as agent, which is the reason why a collecting bank usually escapes liability for money had and received.[10] Secondly, a majority of the House of Lords recognized recently, in *Sempra Metals Ltd v. Inland Revenue Commissioner*,[11] that a mistaken payor should be entitled to recover compound interest as a matter of right from the payee for the period between the payee's receipt of the payment and the payor's recovery of those funds. Such interest represented the 'time value' of the mistaken payment and the full benefit that the payee had derived from its use of the funds.[12]

To succeed with its personal restitutionary claim founded on the recipient's unjust enrichment, the bank must show that it once owned the money mistakenly paid away.

---

[6] Until recently, English law allowed a common law action to recover money paid by mistake only where there was a mistake of fact, but not of law. The mistake of law bar was much criticized: *Woolwich Equitable Building Society* v. *IRC* [1993] AC 70, 164, 199 (HL). See also Law Commission Report No. 227, Restitution: Mistakes of Law and *Utra Vires* Public Authority Receipts and Payments (1994). The bar on recovering for mistakes of law was abandoned in other common law jurisdictions (*Air Canada* v. *British Columbia* (1989) 59 DLR (4th) 161 (SCC); *David Securities Pty. Ltd* v. *Commonwealth Bank of Australia* (1992) 175 CLR 353 (HCA); New Zealand's Judicature Act 1908, s.94A, inserted by the Judicature Amendment Act 1958, s.2), nor was it the law in Scotland (*Morgan Guaranty Trust Co. of NY* v. *Lothian Regional Council*, 1995 SLT 299) or South Africa (*Willis Faber Enthoven (Pty.) Ltd* v. *Receiver of Revenue* 1992 (4) SA 202(A), (App. Div. Sup. C.). In *Kleinwort Benson Ltd* v. *Lincoln City Council*, n.6 above, the House of Lords held (by a 3–2 majority) that the mistake of law bar no longer formed part of English law, so that money was *prima facie* recoverable whether paid under a mistake of fact or law on the ground that its receipt would otherwise be unjustly enriched. See also *Deutsche Morgan Grenfell Group Inc.* v. *Inland Revenue Commissioner* [2007] 1 AC 558, [9]–[17], [38]–[62], [119]–[123] (HL); *Sempra Metals Ltd* v. *Inland Revenue Commissioner* [2007] 3 WLR 354, [19], [22]–[26], [70], [101], [137], [142]–[143], [149], [162], [192], [200], [229]–[240] (HL); *Monro* v. *Commissioners for HM Revenue & Customs* [2008] EWCA Civ. 306, [2]; *Haugesund Kommune* v. *Depfa ACS Bank* [2010] EWCA Civ. 579, [87]–[88].

[7] *Westdeutsche Landesbank Girozentrale* v. *Islington LBC* [1986] AC 669, 683 (HL).

[8] *Lipkin Gorman (a firm)* v. *Karpnale Ltd* [1991] 2 AC 548. See also *Westdeutsche Landesbank Girozentrale* v. *Islington LBC*, n.7 above, 710; *Kleinwort Benson Ltd* v. *Glasgow CC* [1997] 3 WLR 923, 931, 947; *Banque Financière de la Cité* v. *Parc (Battersea) Ltd* [1999] 1 AC 221, 237; and *Kleinwort Benson Ltd* v. *Lincoln City Council*, 373, 406; *Deutsche Morgan Grenfell Group Inc.* v. *Inland Revenue Commissioner*, n.6 above, [21]–[23], [37]–[41], [59]–[75], [132]–[137], [150]–[158]; *Sempra Metals Ltd* v. *Inland Revenue Commissioner*, n.6 above, [2], [8], [22], [25], [29]–[36], [107], [116], [132], [146], [174]–[183], [231]–[235]; *Barclays Bank plc* v. *Kalamohan* [2010] EWHC 1383 (Ch), [73]–[74].

[9] *Agip (Africa) Ltd* v. *Jackson* [1991] Ch. 547, 563 (CA).   [10] Sect. 4 below.

[11] N.6 above. See, for example, *NEC Semi-Conductors* v. *Revenue and Customs Commissioner* [2006] EWCA Civ. 25, [163]–[175]; *John Wilkins (Motor Engineers)* v. *Revenue & Customs Commissioners* [2010] STC 2418 (CA). For the Canadian position, see *Bank of America Canada* v. *Mutual Trust Co.* [2002] SCC 43 (SCC).

[12] D. Hayton, 'Developing the Common Law where Statute has Spoken' (2008) 29 *Co. Lawyer* 2.

Although ownership of the money mistakenly paid away usually passes to the payee, this does not affect the bank's claim. Moreover, as there is a *direct* relationship between the bank and payee, following or tracing is not required to show that the payee received his enrichment at the expense of the bank.[13] In contrast, where the bank seeks to recover the mistaken payment from an *indirect* recipient, who has received it via a third party, the bank must be able to assert a legal title to the money, or its substitute, that has reached the hands of the indirect recipient. This requires the bank to follow or trace its money at common law into the remote recipient's hands. In such circumstances, the bank's claim against the remote recipient does not rest on unjust enrichment, but on the vindication of the bank's property rights.[14] Until recently, the prevailing view was that a restitutionary action to recover a mistaken payment could not be brought by the customer, but only by the paying bank. This view was based upon *Foley* v. *Hill*,[15] which held that the banker-customer contract constituted a debtor-creditor relationship, so that funds paid into an account become the bank's money. How then could the customer, who had no title to the money in question, bring an action based on its having been paid out under a mistake? This reasoning has, however, been challenged in two important cases, which establish that, notwithstanding *Foley*, the customer has the right to bring an action for the recovery of funds that the bank pays out by mistake.

First, in *Agip (Africa) Ltd* v. *Jackson*,[16] the claimant company, Agip, brought a restitutionary claim to recover large sums fraudulently transferred by its chief accountant to accounts maintained by the defendant. The defendant argued that, as the funds remitted were conceptually the paying bank's money, Agip had no right to sue. Rejecting this argument, Millett J said that 'by honouring the customer's cheque in favour of a third party and debiting his account, the bank acts as principal in repaying part of the debt to its customer and as agent of the customer in paying his money to the third party'.[17] On appeal, Fox LJ accepted the principle under which money, paid by a customer to the credit of his account with a bank, became that bank's money, but considered that to 'say that the payment is made out of [the paying bank's] own funds, while true as far as it goes, only tells half the story. The banker's instruction is to pay from the customer's account. He does so by a payment from his own funds and a corresponding debit. The reality is a payment by the customer, at any rate in a case where the customer has no right to require a re-crediting of his account. Nothing passes *in specie*. The whole matter is dealt with by accounting transactions partly in the paying bank and partly in the clearing process.'[18] His Lordship further agreed with Millett J's conclusion that the position was not altered by the fact that in *Agip* the paying bank had paid the money in reliance on a fraudulent instruction and hence without a genuine mandate. His Lordship concluded that if the bank 'paid away Agip's money, Agip itself must be entitled to pursue such remedies as there may be for its recovery. The money was certainly paid under a mistake of fact.'[19]

---

[13] Ch. 7, Sect. 5(v) above.   [14] Sect. 6 below.

[15] (1848) 2 HLC 28, discussed in Ch. 5, Sect. 3 above.

[16] N.9 above, affirming Millett J: N.276 below (discussed in detail in Ch. 7, Sect. 5(v)(a) above).

[17] N.276 below, 283, applied in *Coutts & Co.* v. *Stock* [2000] 2 All ER 56, 60.

[18] N.9 above, 561.

[19] Ibid., 561–562. Fox LJ further agreed with Millett J's conclusions that, on the facts, the bank had paid out whilst acting within the ambit of Agip's general authorization. His Lordship seems to have been influenced in this respect by the fact that Agip had unsuccessfully brought proceedings against the bank in Tunisia to have its account re-credited, Tunisian law being the proper law of the banking relationship. Cf. E. McKendrick, 'Tracing Misdirected Funds' [1991] *LMCLQ* 378, 379–381.

Secondly, in *Lipkin Gorman (a firm)* v. *Karpnale Ltd*,[20] C, a partner in a firm of solicitors, used money obtained by fraud from the firm's client account in order to gamble at the defendants' club. Out of an amount of £323,222.14 that C had misappropriated, he lost a total of £154,695. Reversing the Court of Appeal, the House of Lords held that the solicitors were entitled to recover from the defendants the net amount lost at their tables by C. Rejecting the argument that the solicitors had no title to sue for the recovery of the misappropriated funds, Lord Goff said:[21]

> Before [C] drew upon the solicitors' client account at the bank, there was of course no question of the solicitors having any legal property in any cash lying at the bank. The relationship of the bank with the solicitors was essentially that of debtor and creditor; and since the client account was at all material times in credit, the bank was the debtor and the solicitors the creditors. Such a debt constitutes a chose in action, which is a species of property; and since the debt was enforceable at common law, the chose in action was legal property belonging to the solicitors at common law.... There is in my opinion no reason why the solicitors should not be able to trace their property at common law in that chose in action, or any part of it, into its product, i.e. cash drawn by [C] from their client account at the bank. Such a claim is consistent with their assertion that the money so obtained by [C] was their property at common law.

Lord Goff's conclusion as regards the firm's title to the money stolen by C is in accord with the Court of Appeal's view in *Agip*. It is true that Lord Goff based his conclusion on the solicitors' right to trace their property in the debt,[22] whilst *Agip* emphasized the right that a bank's customer has in the funds paid out at his request. Ultimately, however, both decisions recognize that a bank's *customer* is entitled to bring a restitutionary action for money wrongfully paid out of his account. Their Lordships simply reached the same conclusion by different routes. As the very object of a restitutionary claim is to enable one person to recover money from another, who has been unjustly enriched at his expense, the conclusion is readily supportable, regardless of whether it is based on the reasoning of Lord Goff or Fox LJ. From a practical point of view, however, the approach in *Agip* is preferable. Lord Goff's reasoning in *Lipkin Gorman* is, when strictly construed, applicable only where there is room for common law tracing. By contrast, Fox LJ's judgment, like Millett J's, recognizes the customer's general property right to, or title in, the money wrongfully paid out of his bank account. Commercially, this analysis accords with the general understanding of businessmen. It is, actually, most clearly explained by Millett J who, as mentioned, took the view that by the time the money was paid out to the third party, the property in it had reverted to the customer.

The cases just considered suggest that an action for the recovery of money paid by a bank under a mistake may be brought either by the bank itself or by the customer whose money had been paid out. The customer is unlikely to bring such an action against the third party recipient if he can have the relevant debit entry to his account reversed.

---

[20] N.8 above, varying: [1989] 1 WLR 1340 (CA).   [21] Ibid., 573–574.

[22] Lord Goff's decision respecting the right to trace is based on a distinction between the facts of the two cases. Whilst in *Agip* the funds were transmitted by the use of a clearing system, which meant that they went through a mixed fund, the funds in *Lipkin Gorman,* which were paid to the club in cash, had not lost their identity by becoming part of a mixed fund. The position was, therefore, different from what it would have been if C had paid the stolen money into his own account and thereafter drawn cheques payable to the club. The stolen money would have become mixed with the other funds in C's account and would also have lost its identity as it went through the clearing. Consider, however, *BMP Global Distribution Inc* v. *Bank of Nova Scotia* [2009] 1 SCR 504, [81]–[86] (SCC).

Indeed, where the bank is obliged to reverse the debit entry, such as when it has paid a countermanded cheque, the payee clearly cannot have been enriched at the customer's expense.[23] An action for the recovery from a third party of money paid by the bank under a mistake is generally only brought by a customer when he is precluded from denying the bank's right to debit his account with the wrongful payment.[24] Indeed, as considered in the remainder of the chapter, most reported cases involving restitutionary claims for recovery of mistaken payments have been instituted by banks that are unable or unwilling to debit their customers' accounts. The legal principles applicable to bank claims are equally applicable to claims by customers, although any special issues that arise in respect of the latter type of action are discussed where relevant.

The practical situations in which a restitutionary claim may be brought to recover a mistaken payment from its recipient fall into two main groups. First, there are cases in which the paying instruction is sent electronically or set out in a document other than a negotiable instrument. This group, in which reported decisions are still scarce, covers all cases involving the wrongful discharge of giro orders and other instructions for payments, such as CHAPS Sterling, BACS payments, and SWIFT transfers. Such instances might arise because the relevant payment was erroneously effected twice (usually as a result of computer error), or was carried out despite the customer revoking its instruction or in circumstances where the payee has became insolvent before receiving payment. There may also be instances of forged or fraudulent giro or electronic transfers. Secondly, there are cases involving the wrongful discharge of negotiable instruments, usually a cheque. This second group is well covered by the authorities and generally falls into the following categories: (a) the wrongful payment of a countermanded cheque; (b) the payment of a cheque bearing a forged signature of the payor or the signature of an agent executed in excess of his authority as conveyed to the bank; and (c) the payment of cheques bearing a false indorsement of the ostensible payee. In addition, the bank may pay a cheque although its amount has been fraudulently raised or may make a mistake about the identity of the payee. The same issues can arise in respect of bills of exchange. Thus, the bank may erroneously pay a bill of exchange that is on its face domiciled at its premises but which the bank has been ordered to dishonour or on which the instruction to pay has been forged by the acceptor's unscrupulous employee. The bank may, further, pay an instrument due to a mistake as to its customer's available balance. Whilst both groups of claim generally involve the bank seeking to make the payee personally liable to make restitution, there are some cases where the paying bank's aim is to obtain an advantage over the payee's general creditors. This will be the case where the paying bank has remitted an amount twice over. Normally, the amount would of course be refunded by the collecting bank without demur, but if the collecting bank becomes insolvent before the error is discovered, the paying bank is in the position of having to compete with the collecting bank's general creditors for a pool of assets that is unlikely to satisfy all claims. Is the bank that made the erroneous payment entitled to recover the amount *in specie* or is it confined to a person claims for the amount received by the recipient, in which case the bank would rank as general creditor in respect of it? As discussed below,

---

[23] In *Agip (Africa) Ltd* v. *Jackson*, n.9 above, Fox LJ observed that the customer's action in restitution may be available only where he is not entitled to demand that the bank reverse the debit entry in his account.

[24] Ch. 11, Sect. 3 above. In *Agip*, the action was brought against the defendant only after Agip failed in its claim against the bank under the applicable Tunisian law.

banks can sometimes recover a mistaken payment *in specie* by means of an equitable proprietary claim.[25]

2 Recovery where the mistake is known to the payee

Even where the bank's only object is to recover from the recipient a mistaken payment, it is necessary to distinguish between two situations: first, where the payee is aware of the bank's error in making payment; and, secondly, where the payee is ignorant of the bank's error, and is accordingly also acting under a mistake. As will be considered subsequently, cases of the second type—involving mistakes common to the bank and payee—require a careful analysis, as the authorities are not altogether conclusive. In contrast, cases in which the payee is aware of the bank's error are clear-cut. Frequently, the payee's conduct will amount to fraud, in which case the bank might claim damages for deceit or seek repayment of the money paid in error by means of an action for money had and received.[26] Alternatively, the claimant may bring a restitutionary claim founded on unjust enrichment, the ground of restitution being the bank's induced mistake. In each case, the action would be based on the fraudulent representation made by the payee. The argument is that the payee tacitly represents that he is entitled to the money. It is, however, questionable whether he is rightly regarded as making any statement, be it express or tacit. When he presents an instrument for payment, he is merely seeking an answer. Where payment is by giro or by some other money transfer order, all he does is to receive payment.

The payor's right to reclaim payment where the payee is guilty of fraud can be traced back to nineteenth-century authority. In *Martin* v. *Morgan*,[27] the payee of a cheque, who presented it to the drawee when he found out that the drawer was facing insolvency, failed to mention that the instrument had been post-dated at its inception. Dallas CJ ordered the payee to refund the amount paid, as there had been an 'inequality of knowledge' of the relevant facts.[28] In *Holt* v. *Ely*,[29] a solicitor who had been charged with the payment of certain bills of exchange by the drawer thereof was allowed to recover the amount paid to bill brokers who had misstated the nature of a bill of exchange held by them. Lord Campbell CJ said that the solicitor was entitled to recover, as the bill brokers had induced an error pertaining to their mandate. Erle J thought that the misrepresentation formed the basis for a valid action for money had and received. Alternatively, the payee may be aware of the mistake and yet innocent of fraud. In such circumstances, he would still be obliged to restore the mistaken payment to the claimant. Thus, in *Kendal* v. *Wood*,[30] the payees knew that partnership funds were used to discharge a personal debt of one of the partners. Allowing the partnership to recover the amount involved, Cockburn CJ in the Court of Exchequer Chamber observed that the payee had received the partnership's money at his peril. To be able to retain the funds, he would have needed to establish the payor's

---

[25] Sect. 6(ii) below.

[26] The alternative is sometimes described as part of the doctrine of 'waiver of tort' but this is misleading. All the claimant is doing is waiving the right to obtain remedies assessed by reference to the loss suffered, and instead he elects remedies which are assessed by reference to the benefit gained by the defendant as a result of committing the tort. In either case, the tort constitutes the claimant's cause of action: G. Virgo, *The Principles of the Law of Restitution* (2nd edn., Oxford, 2006), 454–458.

[27] (1819) 1 Broad. & B 290.

[28] The decision was influenced by the fact that a post-dated cheque was illegal under Stamp Act 1815, s.12 (now BEA 1882, s.13).

[29] (1853) 1 El. & Bl. 795.   [30] (1871) LR 6 Ex. 243, 248.

authority. In *John* v. *Dodwell & Co.*,[31] stockbrokers were ordered to repay the amount of a cheque drawn by a company manager on his employers' account for the payment of shares purchased in his own name. Lord Haldane held that it was sufficient that the brokers knew that the funds involved were owned by the company and it was not necessary to show that the brokers were aware of the fraud. In *Reckitt* v. *Barnett, Pembroke and Slater Ltd*,[32] where the facts were basically the same, Lord Hailsham LC emphasized that the action was based on the payee's receipt of funds known to him to be paid without proper authorization.

In the first two editions of the present work, there are suggestions that the payee's knowledge of the payor's error forms the basis for an action in restitution.[33] The claim to recover a mistaken payment from its immediate recipient is now understood to rest firmly on the principle of unjust enrichment.[34] Unless the payee can establish a relevant defence that defeats the restitutionary claim, liability will follow where the payor can establish that (a) the payee has received an enrichment, (b) the enrichment was received at the payor's expense, and (c) the enrichment was 'unjust', in the sense that the claim falls within one of the recognized grounds of restitution, such as mistake, duress, or total failure of consideration[35]—although increasingly there is discussion of whether recovery should be permitted on some more general ground, such as there being an 'absence of basis' or lack of juristic reason for the transfer of wealth.[36] In other words, it is the fact that the payment is made by mistake, and not the presence or absence of any knowledge on the part of the payee, that renders the payee's enrichment unjust. Whilst the payee's knowledge may not form the basis of a restitutionary claim founded on unjust enrichment, the existence of an equitable proprietary claim based on the fact that the payee holds a mistaken payment on constructive trust may turn on the payee's awareness of the payor's mistake.[37] Similarly, personal liability for dishonest assistance in a breach of trust or knowing receipt of trust property will turn respectively on whether the payee has acted dishonestly or unconscionably.[38] In contrast, the state of the payee's knowledge may impact on the availability of the payee's defences to the payor's restitutionary claim, but does not impact on the cause of action itself.[39] A recent illustration of the point can be found in *Jones* v. *Churcher*,[40] where the payee's knowledge of the circumstances sur-

---

[31] [1918] AC 563.   [32] [1929] AC 176.

[33] E.P. Ellinger, *Modern Banking Law* (Oxford, 1987), 318–319; E.P. Ellinger & E. Lomnicka, *Modern Banking Law* (2nd edn., Oxford, 1994), 395–396 (citing, *inter alia*, *Larner* v. *London CC* [1949] 2 KB 683 (CA)). See also H. Luntz, n.3 above, 309–310.

[34] Sect. 1 above.

[35] According to Henderson J in *FJ Chalke Ltd* v. *Revenue & Customs Commissioners* [2009] EWHC 952 (Ch), [127], 'English law has not yet recognized a single unifying principle in the law of restitution for unjust enrichment, and a number of different causes of action exist, each with their own separate requirements'. See also *Test Claimants in the FII Group Litigation* v. *Revenue & Customs Commissioners* [2008] EWHC 2893 (Ch), [245].

[36] *Deutsche Morgan Grenfell Group Inc.* v. *Inland Revenue Commissioner*, n.6 above, [150]–[158] (HL); *Sempra Metals Ltd* v. *Inland Revenue Commissioner*, n.6 above, [192]; *Test Claimants in the FII Group Litigation* v. *Revenue & Customs Commissioners* [2010] EWCA Civ 103, [156]. For rejection of 'absence of basis' in light of Lord Hoffmann's view in *Morgan Grenfell*, see *Marine Trade SA* v. *Pioneer Freight Futures Co Ltd BVI* [2009] EWHC 2656 (Comm.), [62]–[64]. See further R. Grantham, 'Absence of Juristic Reason in the Supreme Court of Canada' (2005) 13 *RLR* 102; A. Goymour, 'Premature Tax Payments and Unjust Enrichment' (2007) 66 *CLJ* 24; B. Hacker, 'Still at the Crossroads' (2007) *LQR* 177; C. Mitchell, 'Mistaken Tax Payments' [2007] RLR 123.

[37] *Westdeutsche Landesbank Girozentrale* v. *Islington London Borough Council*, n.7 above, 715 (criticized by P.J. Millett, 'Restitution and Constructive Trusts' (1998) 114 *LQR* 399, 412–413); *Deutsche Bank AG* v. *Vik* [2010] EWHC 551 (Comm.), [4]. See also Ch. 7, Sect. 4(v)(b)(i), above.

[38] Ch. 7, Sect. 4 above.   [39] Sect. 3(iii) below.   [40] [2009] 2 Lloyd's Rep 94, [56]–[62].

rounding the mistaken payment was considered in the context of whether the payee could raise a change of position defence, rather than in the context of whether there was restitutionary liability in the first place. The distinction is important since the claimant bears the burden of establishing the cause of action, and the defendant the burden of establishing defences.

3 Recovery in cases of payments not involving negotiable instruments

(i) Payor's liability and payee's entitlement

The basic principle was stated in *Kelly* v. *Solari*,[41] in which an insurance company paid out the sum due under a life policy overlooking that the policy had been cancelled before the assured's death. The Court of Exchequer held that, unless the directors had paid out without caring whether the policy was valid or rescinded, the company was entitled to recover. There was a new trial to determine whether or not the payment had been voluntary. According to Parke B:[42]

> ... where money is paid to another under the influence of a mistake, that is, upon the supposition that a specific fact is true, which would entitle the other to the money, but which fact is untrue, and the money would not have been paid if it had been known to the payer that the fact was untrue, an action will lie to recover it back, and it is against conscience to retain it; though a demand may be necessary in those cases in which the party receiving may have been ignorant of the mistake.

This passage is regarded as defining the nature of an action for the recovery of money paid under a mistake of fact.[43] It has, however, given rise to problems. The main one is that Parke B refers to a mistake that induces the payor to believe that he is legally liable to satisfy the payee's demand. If these words were to be taken literally, a bank would not usually be able to recover money paid under a mistake of fact. This is because a bank's duty to make payment is rarely owed to the payee. This is well understood in the case of cheques and is equally correct in respect of giro payments. However, Luntz[44] has pointed out that the relevant words are not included in the report of the case in the *Law Journal*. Whilst they derive support from some later cases[45] the better view is that they are unduly restrictive.[46]

---

[41] (1841) 9 M&W 54.

[42] Ibid., 58. The wording of the passage differs in the report of the case in (1841) 11 LJ (NS) Ex. 10. See H. Luntz, n.3 above, 312.

[43] It has withstood attacks by Lord Shaw of Dunfermline in *Jones (R. E.) Ltd* v. *Waring & Gillow Ltd* [1926] AC 670, 689 (HL). Similar principles ought reasonably to apply where an action is brought to recover money paid under a mistake of law.

[44] H. Luntz, n.3 above, 311–312.

[45] *Aiken* v. *Short* (1856) 25 LJ Ex. 321, 324 (but note that in the report of the same case in (1856) 1 H & N 210, the ratio emphasizes the payee's entitlement to receive payment); *Morgan* v. *Ashcroft* [1938] 1 KB 49; *Commonwealth Trading Bank* v. *Reno Auto Sales Pty. Ltd* [1967] VR 790. Cf. *South Australian Cold Stores Ltd* v. *Electricity Trust of South Australia* (1957) 98 CLR 65, 75, cited by H. Luntz, n.3 above, 311.

[46] R. Goff & G. Jones, *The Law of Restitution* (7th edn., London, 2007), paras. 4-003–4-007. Rolfe B in *Kelly* v. *Solari*, n.41 above, 58–9 does not restrict recovery to mistaken beliefs as to liability.

Thus, in *Kerrison* v. *Glyn, Mills, Currie & Co.*,[47] a Mexican mining company drew bills of exchange on a New York bank. To facilitate payment, the claimants, who had an interest in the Mexican company, remitted an amount of £500 to the defendant bankers, who were the London agents of the New York bank. The defendant bankers credited the New York bank's overdrawn account with the amount involved. Both the claimants and the defendant bankers were, at that time, unaware that the New York bank had just failed and, accordingly, was unable to meet the bills of exchange. The claimants demanded the repayment of the amount as money paid under a mistake of fact. Restoring Hamilton J's decision,[48] the House of Lords held that the claimants were entitled to recover the amount paid, although they would not have been under an obligation to remit it even if the New York bank had remained solvent. The mistake was operative as the claimants had made the payment involved in anticipation of the proper winding up of a transaction in which they had a commercial interest. The insolvency of the New York bank meant that this object was unattainable.[49] Similarly, in *R.E. Jones Ltd* v. *Waring & Gillow Ltd*,[50] B, who falsely introduced himself as an agent of a firm of car manufacturers, purported to arrange on their behalf for the claimants' appointment as franchise holders, provided the claimants agreed to pay a deposit of £5,000 for the purchase of 500 cars. B asked that the cheque be made payable to the defendants who, he claimed, were financing the manufacturers. In reality, B's story was a fabrication. He delivered the cheque to the defendants in order to obtain the release of chattels that they had seized when he defaulted under a hire-purchase agreement. Restoring Darling J's decision in favour of the claimants, the majority of the House of Lords held that the £5,000 was recoverable as money paid under a mistake of fact. No reference was made to the fact that, when the claimants drew the cheque, they were not under the mistaken belief that they had a relationship of contract with the defendants, who were the payees. The claimants' mistake related to their supposed contractual relationship with the car manufacturers or with the fraudster, B.[51]

Where a transaction is confined to two parties, the payor's liability is a reflection of the payee's right. Luntz,[52] though, rightly points out that the two are not necessarily concurrent. In certain cases, the payee may be entitled to demand the money not from the payor but from a third party, who instructs the payor to make payment. The payee does not, then, have any rights against the payor. This is invariably the case where debts are paid through banking channels. The payee of a bank giro credit or of a cheque may have rights against the issuer or drawer but none against the bank. The payee may, thus, be entitled to the money although the payor is not liable to him.

An argument that comes to mind is that under *Kelly* v. *Solari* the payee has the right to retain the money whenever he is entitled to it at all, be it as against the payor or as

---

[47] (1911) 17 Com. Cas. 41. See also *Colonial Bank* v. *Exchange Bank of Yarmouth* (1885) 11 App. Cas. 84; *Kleinwort, Sons & Co.* v. *Dunlop Rubber Co.* (1907) 97 LT 263; *Morgan* v. *Ashcroft*, n.45 above, 72–3.

[48] (1910) 15 Com. Cas. 1, reversed by the Court of Appeal, ibid., 241.

[49] G. Virgo, n.26 above, 157 argues convincingly that '*Kerrison* v. *Glyn, Mills, Currie and Co.* is a highly dubious authority…since the claimant's mistake related to a liability to pay in the future, so the case involved a misprediction rather than a mistake. The result of the case can, however, be justified on the basis that, but for the mistake, the claimant would not have paid the money to the bank'. A misprediction will not ground recovery: *Dextra Bank & Trust Co. Ltd* v. *Bank of Jamaica* [2002] 1 All ER (Comm.) 193, 202 (PC). See also *Deutsche Morgan Grenfell Group Inc.* v. *Inland Revenue Commissioner*, n.6 above. See further W. Seah, 'Mispredictions, Mistakes of Law and the Law of Unjust Enrichment' [2007] *RLR* 93.

[50] N.43 above. See also H. Luntz, n.3 above, 316. See also *Imperial Bank of Canada* v. *Bank of Hamilton* [1903] AC 49 (PC).

[51] *Barclays Bank Ltd* v. *W. J. Simms, Son & Cooke (Southern) Ltd* [1980] QB 677, 693–694. Cf. *Commercial Bank of Australia* v. *Younis* [1979] 1 NSWLR 444.

[52] H. Luntz, n.3 above, 314.

against a third party such as the payor's principal. This view derives support from Parke B's reference to the unconscionability of a payee who purports to retain money to which he has no entitlement. This element is missing where he can establish some valid claim. Most authorities, though, take a view contrary to this argument. Thus, in *Imperial Bank of Canada* v. *Bank of Hamilton*,[53] the amount of a cheque, which had been 'marked' by the drawee bank at the drawer's request, was fraudulently raised by him thereafter from $5 to $500. The bank was allowed to recover the excess from the holder in due course, to the credit of whose account the cheque had been paid. It was held that the 'marking' or 'certification' did not bind the bank. The Privy Council did not consider whether the holder was 'entitled' to receive the full amount from a party other than the bank, such as the drawer. The bank's mistake about the validity of the cheque formed the basis of its action in restitution against the holder. The mistake was operative even though the bank had not made a mistake about its liability, and despite the fact that the holder in due course might have been entitled to obtain the amount from the drawer. Similarly, in *Colonial Bank* v. *Exchange Bank of Yarmouth, Nova Scotia*,[54] the claimant bank, which had been instructed by a customer to pay an amount of money to the X Bank, paid it by mistake to the defendant bank. As the customer in question had a heavily overdrawn account with the defendant bank, it purported to retain the money to reduce his overdraft. The claimant bank clearly did not believe that it was under any liability to the defendant bank, but it could have thought that the defendant bank was entitled to the money. In the outcome, the claimant bank made no mistake about its own liability or about the defendant bank's rights because the customer was, indeed, indebted to this bank. Nevertheless, the claimant bank was allowed to recover the amount paid. Luntz concludes that this case shows 'that mistake as to the recipient's "entitlement"...is not a necessary condition for the recovery of money paid in such circumstances'.[55] Likewise, in *R. E. Jones Ltd* v. *Waring & Gillow Ltd*,[56] the claimants, who made a mistake concerning their liability to pay B or the car manufacturers, did not make a mistake about the payee's entitlement to receive the money.

The conclusion is that the payor's mistake, which forms the basis of his action in restitution, need concern neither his own liability to pay the amount involved nor the payee's entitlement to the money.[57] His right to recover the amount is unaffected by a claim that the payee may have against a third party. It is adequate that the payor is under an operative mistake concerning his own motive or reasons for making payment. A mistake made by a paying bank is operative whenever it causes the relevant payment. Only one authority runs counter to this view. In *Barclay & Co. Ltd* v. *Malcolm & Co. Ltd*,[58] a bank erroneously paid twice an amount that it had been ordered to transfer. The payee, however, was in effect entitled to obtain from the payor a substantial part of the amount overpaid. He, therefore, repaid the balance that had not been owing to him and purported to retain the amount due. The bank's action in restitution was dismissed on the ground that the payee, who was entitled to the amount involved, should not be regarded as acting unconscionably in purporting to retain the amount due to him. This decision has, however, been questioned by Robert Goff J in *Barclays Bank Ltd* v. *W.J. Simms Son & Cooke (Southern) Ltd*[59] on the basis that the bank's mistake about the existence of a valid mandate for the payor's extra payment was an adequate cause for ordering restitution. His Lordship further pointed out

---

[53] N.50 above.   [54] N.47 above.   [55] H. Luntz, n.3 above, 315.   [56] N.43 above.

[57] In *Kleinwort Benson Ltd* v. *Lincoln City Council*, the House of Lords did not address the question whether a restitutionary claim will succeed only if the mistake of law was such that it would make the payor liable to pay the money.

[58] (1925) 133 LT 512.   [59] N.51 above.

that *Malcolm* conflicted with the House of Lords' decision in *R.E. Jones Ltd* v. *Waring & Gillow Ltd*,[60] where recovery was allowed although the payee was entitled to be paid by B, from whom he had acquired the cheque. It is clear that the prevailing view is as stated by Goff J. The attraction of the principle in *Malcolm* is that it enables the payee to retain an amount to which he has a claim.[61] It remains to be seen which view will prevail.

(ii) **Nature of operative mistake**

Not every mistake made by the payor is operative. Some authorities suggest that the mistake must relate to some misconception affecting the payor's relationship with the payee. In *Kleinwort, Sons & Co.* v. *Dunlop Rubber Co.*,[62] the vendor of rubber assigned the price due to him to M1. Due to an error, the buyers paid the amount involved to M2, who had been the assignees in the other transactions. M2 actually received the amount involved in the belief that it was due to them. After the purchasers were ordered to pay the amount over again to M1, who was entitled to the amount as equitable assignee,[63] they brought an action to recover the amount paid by them to M2. The House of Lords held that the purchasers were entitled to succeed as the mistake, which concerned the relationship of payor and payee, was the sole cause of the payment involved. Doubts about the conclusiveness of this analysis were, however, raised in *Porter* v. *Latec Finance (Qld.) Pty. Ltd*,[64] where Barwick CJ pointed out that if an operative mistake had to be between the payor and payee, recovery would be ruled out unless the mistake was common to both parties. The inadequacy of the test is further highlighted by the fact that, if strictly applied, it precludes a bank from recovering the amount of a stopped cheque, as the bank's mistake is its oversight of the customer's instruction[65]—a mistake between the bank and its customer, not between bank and payee. In effect, the proposed test is supportable only if it is conceded that the mistake has to relate to the mutual rights and duties of the payor and payee: it would then follow that it must be 'between them'. It has already been shown, however, that the former test, based on Parke B's words in *Kelly* v. *Solari*, is too narrow. If the mistake need not concern the liability of the payor to the payee, it is difficult to see why, to be operative, the mistake has to be 'between them'. It is thus not surprising that in both *Kerrison* v. *Glyn, Mills, Currie & Co.*[66] and *R. E. Jones & Co. Ltd* v. *Waring & Gillow Ltd*[67] recovery was allowed, although the mistake was between the payor and a third party.

Robert Goff J settled any doubts on this issue, however, in *Barclays Bank Ltd* v. *W. J. Simms, Son & Cooke (Southern) Ltd*,[68] in which the drawer countermanded payment of his cheque when he discovered that a receiver had been appointed over the payee's undertaking. Due to a clerical error, the bank paid the cheque to the receiver on the day following the issuing of the stop order. When the bank discovered its mistake, it recredited the drawer's account and demanded repayment from the payee. Giving

---

[60] N.43 above.
[61] Roche J's judgment on this point in *Malcolm* is very briefly reported and the case was also decided on the grounds of ratification: R. Goff & G. Jones, n.46 above, para. 4–012, n.63.
[62] N.47 above. See also *Colonial Bank* v. *Exchange Bank of Yarmouth, Nova Scotia*, n.47 above; *Commonwealth Trading Bank of Australia* v. *Kerr* [1919] SASR 201; *Commonwealth Trading Bank* v. *Reno Auto Sales Pty. Ltd*, n.45 above. Cf. *Bank of New South Wales* v. *Deri* (1963) 80 WN (NSW) 1499; *Southland Savings Bank* v. *Anderson* [1974] NZLR 118.
[63] *William Brandt's Sons & Co.* v. *Dunlop Rubber Co. Ltd* [1905] AC 454 (HL).
[64] (1964) 111 CLR 177–178.
[65] *Commonwealth Trading Bank* v. *Reno Auto Sales Pty. Ltd*, n.45 above; cf. *Bank of New South Wales* v. *Deri*, n.62 above; *Southland Savings Bank* v. *Anderson*, n.62 above.
[66] N.47 above.   [67] N.43 above.   [68] N.51 above

judgment for the bank, Goff J emphasized that, if the mistake had caused the payment to be made, it did not have to be 'between' the bank, as payor, and the payee.[69] Subsequently, the English courts have consistently followed *Simms* and applied a causation test when determining whether a payor's mistake renders the defendant's enrichment unjust.[70] Indeed, in *Kleinwort Benson Ltd* v. *Lincoln City Council*,[71] Lord Hope said:[72]

> Subject to any defences that may arise from the circumstances, a claim for restitution for money paid under a mistake raises three questions: (1) Was there a mistake? (2) Did the mistake cause the payment? And (3) did the payee have a right to receive the sum which was paid to him?

The force of this dictum is somewhat weakened, however, by the claimant's mistake in *Kleinwort Benson* being a liability mistake. The claimant bank had thought it was liable to make payments to the defendant local authority under an interest rate swap agreement that was later held to be void *ab initio* as *ultra vires* the local authority. Nevertheless, Lord Hope made no reference to the mistake concerning a liability to pay the defendant, stressing only that the mistake must have caused the payment to be made.

Where the payee has induced the payor's mistake, such as by misrepresentation, the payor need only demonstrate that the mistake contributed to his decision to make the payment.[73] The payee's conduct dictates that a flexible test of causation should be applied. Where the payor makes a spontaneous mistake of fact, a 'but for' test of causation applies,[74] so that there will be no restitution unless the payor can establish that he would not have made the payment 'but for' the mistake. If the payor would still have made the payment, even if he had not been mistaken, the mistake cannot be taken to have caused the payee's enrichment. Similarly, where the payor takes the risk that the payment may not be due, he will be precluded from recovering his payment,[75] but the mere fact that the payor had some doubt as to his liability to pay does not necessarily make him a 'risk-taker' who is

---

[69] Ibid., 696. M. Hapgood, *Paget's Law of Banking* (13th edn., London, 2007), para. 19.18, endorses Goff J's rejection of the proposition that to ground recovery the mistake must have been 'as between' the payor and the payee, but does not think the issue settled as none of the authorities in support of the 'supposed rule' have been overruled.

[70] *Rover International Ltd* v. *Cannon Film Sales Ltd* [1989] 1 WLR 913, 933; *Nurdin and Peacock plc* v. *D. B. Ramsden and Co. Ltd* [1999] 1 All ER 941, 964; *Dextra Bank & Trust Co. Ltd* v. *Bank of Jamaica*, n.49 above, 202; *Deutsche Morgan Grenfell Group Inc.* v. *Inland Revenue Commissioner*, n.6 above, [60], [84], [143]; *Test Claimants in the FII Group Litigation* v. *Revenue & Customs Commissioners*, n.35 above, [247]–[252], [264]–[265]; *Jones* v. *Churcher*, n.40 above [41]; *FJ Chalke Ltd* v. *Revenue & Customs Commissioners*, n.35 above, [138]; *Marine Trade SA* v. *Pioneer Freight Futures Co Ltd BVI*, n.36 above, [78]. See also *Banque Financière de la Cité* v. *Parc (Battersea) Ltd*, n.8 above, 227, 234. A basic test of causation has also been adopted in Australia (*David Securities Pty. Ltd* v. *Commonwealth Bank of Australia*, n.6 above, 378), Canada (*Toronto-Dominion Bank* v. *Pella/Hunt Corp.* [1992] 10 O.R. (3d) 634, 635–637 (OSC); *BMP Global Distribution Inc* v. *Bank of Nova Scotia*, n.22 above, [21]–[24]; *Cuthbert* v. *TD Canada Trust* [2010] OJ No 630, [20]), and New Zealand (*University of Canterbury* v. *Attorney-General* [1995] 1 NZLR 78; *ASB Securities Ltd* v. *Geurts* [2005] 1 NZLR 484, [42]–[50]).

[71] N.6 above, 358, 371, 398.

[72] Ibid., 407. See also *Jones* v. *Churcher*, n.40 above, [42]; *Marine Trade SA* v. *Pioneer Freight Futures Co Ltd BVI*, n.36 above, [65]; *Deutsche Bank AG* v. *Vik*, n.37 above, [3].

[73] *Edginton* v. *Fitzmaurice* (1980) 25 Ch. D 459; *Barton* v. *Armstrong* [1976] AC 104.

[74] *Barclays Bank Ltd* v. *W.J. Simms (Southern) Ltd*, n.51 above; *David Securities Pty. Ltd* v. *Commonwealth Bank of Australia*, n.6 above.

[75] *Deutsche Morgan Grenfell Group Inc.* v. *Inland Revenue Commissioner*, n.6 above, [26]–[27], [31]–[32], [64]–[65].

precluded from recovering his payment.[76] It depends upon the payor's degree of doubt. The 'but for' test of causation was applied to a mistake of law by Neuberger J in *Nurdin and Peacock plc* v. *D. B. Ramsden and Co. Ltd*,[77] where rent was overpaid as a result of a misconstruction of a lease. The question arose whether the claimant could recover some of the overpayments that had been made when the claimant suspected that it was not liable to pay the defendant under the lease, but had paid nevertheless because it thought it would be able to recover the money if the defendant's construction of the lease proved wrong. Neuberger J held that the claimant could recover its overpayments, since they had been made under a mistake of law. His Lordship thought it clear that in order to found a claim for repayment of money paid under a mistake of law, it was necessary for the payor to establish that but for the mistake he would not have paid the money.[78] In addition, Neuberger J continued:[79]

> It may be that the payer must go further and establish, for instance, that the mistake was directly connected to the overpayment and/or was connected to the relationship between payer and payee.

These additional comments seem designed to control those mistakes that will give rise to a restitutionary claim. They do not, however, sit easily with Neuberger J's express endorsement of the causation test propounded by Robert Goff J in *Simms*.[80]

It is sometimes said that the mistake must be 'fundamental' to ground recovery. This means no more than that the mistake must be 'vital' or 'material', in the sense that the mistake caused the payor to pay the money to the payee.[81] There are, however, occasions where the courts have described a fundamental mistake as one 'in respect of the underlying assumption of the contract or transaction or as being fundamental or basic'.[82] This interpretation is unduly restrictive.[83] It should not be necessary, for the purposes of a claim founded on the reversal of unjust enrichment, that the mistake should be fundamental in the sense that it would have negatived the intention to contract.[84] As Virgo submits:[85]

> …a test which is appropriate in the context of vitiation of contracts is not necessarily appropriate where the claimant wishes to recover benefits without needing to set a transaction aside. Where a contract is set aside for mistake what needs to be shown is that the intention to contract was vitiated by the mistake. Where the claimant simply wishes to recover benefits from the defendant all we are concerned with is whether the claimant's intention to transfer the benefit was vitiated by the mistake. The policy of the law is very different in the two contexts as well. For there is a clear reluctance to set contracts aside for mistake because of the principle of law that parties should be held to their bargains wherever possible. There is no similar policy in operation where the claimant wishes to recover the value of a benefit from the defendant.

---

[76] *Marine Trade SA* v. *Pioneer Freight Futures Co Ltd BVI*, n.36 above, [69]–[77]; cf *Kleinwort Benson Ltd* v. *Lincoln City Council*, 410.

[77] N.70 above.   [78] Ibid., 963.   [79] Ibid., 964.   [80] Id.

[81] *Barclays Bank Ltd* v. *W. J. Simms, Son & Cooke (Southern) Ltd.*

[82] *Norwich Union Fire Insurance Society* v. *Price* [1934] AC 455 (PC), 463, applied in *Morgan* v. *Ashcroft*, n.45 above, 66, 74. See also *Aspinall's Club Ltd* v. *Al-Zayat* [2008] EWHC 2101 (Comm.), [66]–[67].

[83] It has been rejected in Australia in favour of the test of causation: *David Securities Pty. Ltd* v. *Commonwealth Bank of Australia*, n.6 above, 378.

[84] R. Goff & G. Jones, n.46 above, para. 4-005. See also *Citibank NA* v. *Brown Shipley and Co. Ltd* [1991] 2 All ER. 690, 700–701. Cf. P.B.H. Birks, *An Introduction to the Law of Restitution* (Oxford, 1985), 159.

[85] G. Virgo, n.26 above, 152–153 (footnotes omitted).

By contrast, where the restitutionary claim is to vindicate proprietary rights, and not to reverse unjust enrichment, it is entirely appropriate that the mistake should be fundamental in the sense that it prevents title to the property from passing to the defendant. The restrictive test is appropriate because it is only where the effect of the mistake is to negate the claimant's intention completely that it is proper to conclude that title did not pass to the defendant, so that the claimant can rely on his continuing title to recover property from the direct or indirect recipient.[86]

(iii) Defences

Restitutionary claims based on mistake are subject to the general defences which apply to all restitutionary claims: change of position, estoppel, and the agent's defence of payment over. The defence of 'good consideration' is particularly applicable to a restitutionary claim based on unjust enrichment arising from a mistaken payment, but it should not be confused with the entirely separate defence of *bona fide* purchaser for value, which applies only where the claimant's restitutionary claim is based on the vindication of property rights. How far any or all of these defences will be swallowed up in the continued development of the 'central' restitutionary defence of change of position remains to be seen. In *Kleinwort Benson* v. *Lincoln City Council*,[87] Lord Goff recognized that 'the law must evolve appropriate defences which can, together with the defence of change of position, provide protection where appropriate for recipients of money paid under a mistake of law in those cases in which justice or policy does not require them to refund the money'. Nevertheless, the House of Lords was generally reluctant to recognize any special defences to claims founded on mistake of law. Honest belief by the payee that he was entitled to a mistaken payment did not provide a defence,[88] nor did the fact that the transaction had been fully performed.[89] Moreover, a change in a settled view of law did not provide a defence to a restitutionary claim based on a mistake of law as the change constituted a mistake of law in itself.[90]

The defences of change of position, good consideration, estoppel, 'payment over', and *bona fide* purchaser defence are considered in this and following sections.

(a) Change of position

The defence based upon the payee's change of position is based on considerations of common justice. It appears inequitable to demand that a person repay money where he has, in reliance on its receipt, incurred a liability or given up an advantage. The argument, though, is not clear-cut. When taken to its extreme, a payee can always plead that a windfall, which he thought was due to him, has encouraged him to incur a liability. Thus, a person who believes himself to be the donee of a valid gift may on that basis enter into a contract for the purchase of a house. It is well recognized that the instant defence is not applicable in cases of this type.[91] In its more limited sense, the defence is applicable

---

[86] Ibid., 151. See also D. Fox, *Property Rights in Money* (Oxford, 2008), paras. 3.100–3.102, 4.116–4.119.

[87] N.6 above. [88] Ibid., 385.

[89] Ibid., 387, Cf. P.B.H. Birks, 'No Consideration: Restitution after Void Contracts' (1993) 23 *UWALR* 195, 230, n.137.

[90] Ibid., 383. See also *Deutsche Morgan Grenfell Group Inc.* v. *Inland Revenue Commissioner*, n.6 above, [16]–[18].

[91] *Standing* v. *Ross* (1849) 3 Exch. 527; *United Overseas Bank* v. *Jiwani* [1976] 1 WLR 964. See also Luntz, n.3 above, 323.

to a detriment incurred directly as a result of the payment. The release of a security is the classic example. Even in this restricted sense, however, the defence was not generally available until recent times. On the basis of nineteenth-century authorities, it was, actually, held inapplicable in English law in *R.E. Jones Ltd* v. *Waring & Gillow Ltd*.[92] However, in *Barclays Bank Ltd* v. *W.J. Simms, Sons & Cooke (Southern) Ltd*,[93] Robert Goff J pointed out that, in certain cases, the recipient of funds, paid to him under a mistake of fact, was entitled to retain them provided that he 'has changed his position in good faith, or is deemed in law to have done so'.

The general availability of a change of position defence to restitutionary claims was finally recognized by the House of Lords in *Lipkin Gorman (a firm)* v. *Karpnale Ltd*,[94] which concerned a junior partner ('C') in a firm of solicitors, who misappropriated money from the firm's client account and used those funds to purchase gaming chips at the defendant's premises. Occasionally, C won and paid part of his gains back into the firm's client account; but in most instances he lost. All in all, C lost £154,695.00 out of the total amount of £323,222.14 stolen by him from the firm. The firm brought a restitutionary action to recover the money from the club. The House of Lords held that the supply of the chips by the club's cashier to C did not constitute the furnishing of a separate lawful consideration by the club. C's transactions with the club involved gambling and, as the contracts so made were void, the club had not furnished value for the funds. The firm was, accordingly, entitled to recover. This finding gave rise to the question whether the firm was entitled to recover the total amount stolen and placed by C on the betting table or only the net amount lost by him. Finding that the club had changed its position to the extent of the amounts paid out to C, their Lordships held that only the net amount won by the club was recoverable. In reaching this conclusion, their Lordships expressly gave effect to the doctrine under which an action in restitution would not lie against a person who had in good faith changed his position in reliance on the funds received. According to Lord Goff of Chieveley:[95]

> ...where an innocent defendant's position is so changed that he will suffer an injustice if called upon to repay or to repay in full, the injustice of requiring him so to repay outweighs the injustice of denying the [claimant] restitution. If the [claimant] pays money to the defendant under a mistake of fact, and the defendant then, acting in good faith, pays the money or part of it to charity, it is unjust to require the defendant to make restitution to the extent that he has so changed his position. Likewise, on facts such as those in the present case, if a thief steals my money and pays it to a third party, who gives it away to charity, that party should have a good defence to an action for money had and received. In other words, bona fide change of position should of itself be a good defence in cases such as these.

---

[92] N.43 above, 695–696. See also *Commonwealth Trading Bank of Australia* v. *Kerr*, n.62 above; *Transvaal & Delagoa Bay Investment Co. Ltd* v. *Atkinson* [1944] 1 All ER 579. The defence was recognized in specific instances, such as in cases involving negotiable instruments (Sect. 5 below). The defence of an agent who has paid over funds received on behalf of his principal should be treated as a separate defence from that of change of position: Sect. 4 below.

[93] N.51 above, 695.

[94] N.8 above. See also *Jones* v. *Churcher*, n.40 above, [41]–[47]; *Haugesund Kommune* v. *Depfa ACS Bank*, n.6 above, [106]–[131].

[95] Ibid., 579.

The House of Lords has, thus, introduced a general defence of change of position to restitutionary claims.[96] Whether the defence extends to *all* restitutionary claims remains uncertain.[97] In *Foskett* v. *McKeown*,[98] Lord Millett distinguished between a restitution-ary claim founded on the reversal of unjust enrichment and one that seeks to vindicate property rights. Lord Millett considered that these two causes of action attracted different defences:[99]

> ...a claim in unjust enrichment is subject to a change of position defence, which usu-ally operates by reducing or extinguishing the element of enrichment. An action like the present is subject to the bona fide purchaser for value defence, which operates to clear the defendant's title.

Although it is clear that the change of position defence is available to most claims founded on the reversal of unjust enrichment,[100] Lord Millett's apparent assertion that it has no place when the claim is to vindicate property rights demands closer scrutiny. Significantly, the defence of change of position was applied in *Lipkin Gorman*, which can probably be better explained on grounds of vindication of property rights than unjust enrichment.[101] In *Lipkin Gorman*, the claimant's remedy was personal, whereas in *Foskett* v. *McKeown* it was proprietary. Is it necessary to distinguish between cases where the claimant seeks personal remedies (the defence applies) from cases where proprietary remedies are sought (the defence does not apply)? The preferable view is that the defence should apply even where the claimant seeks a proprietary remedy.[102] This approach emphasizes the restitu-tionary nature of the claim, which requires consideration of whether it is equitable that the defendant should make restitution where the defendant's position has changed in reliance on the validity of the receipt.

In *Lipkin Gorman*, Lord Goff emphasized that not every change in a payee's position would, as a matter of course, entitle him to plead the defence in question. His Lordship said:[103]

> I am most anxious that, in recognising this defence to actions of restitution, nothing should be said at this stage to inhibit the development of the defence on a case to case basis, in the usual way. It is, of course, plain that the defence is not open to one who has changed his position in bad faith, as where the defendant has paid away the money with

---

[96] *Rural Municipality of Storthoaks* v. *Mobil Oil Canada Ltd* (1975) 55 DLR (3d.) 1, 13 (SCC); *BMP Global Distribution Inc.* v. *Bank of Nova Scotia*, n.22 above, [62]–[65]. *David Securities Pty. Ltd* v. *Commonwealth Bank of Australia*, n.6 above, 385; New Zealand (Judicature) Act 1908, s.94B, as inserted by s.2 of the Judicature (Amendment) Act 1958.

[97] Change of position has no application to 'restitution for wrongdoing' (n.8 above, 580) or to '*Woolwich* claims' (*Littlewoods Ltd* v. *Revenue & Customs Commissioners* [2010] EWHC 1071 (CH), [109]).

[98] [2001] 1 AC 102 (HL).

[99] Ibid., 129. See also *Papamichael* v. *National Westminster Bank plc* [2003] 1 Lloyd's Rep. 341, 376.

[100] *South Tyneside Metropolitan Borough Council* v. *Svenska International plc* [1995] 1 All ER 545, where the availability of the defence was assumed although not established on the facts. Lord Millett's statement that the defence goes to the enrichment is less convincing (although supported by P.B.H. Birks, n.84 above, 441). It is submitted that the real function of the defence is to identify those cases in which the justice of the defendant not making restitution is greater that the justice of the claimant obtaining restitution: G. Virgo, n.26 above, 692.

[101] Sect. 6 below.

[102] *Westdeutsche Landesbank Girozentrale* v. *Islington London Borough Council*, n.7 above, 716. See also R. Goff & G. Jones, n.46 above, paras. 40-016–40-020; D. Fox, n.86 above, paras. 9.43–9.45, 9.73; but consider G. Virgo, n.26 above, 708–711.

[103] Ibid., 580.

knowledge of the facts entitling the [claimant] to restitution; and it is commonly accepted that the defence should not be open to a wrongdoer.

Lord Goff emphasized, further, that the mere fact that the payee had spent the money did not, of itself, involve a change in his position that would bring the new doctrine into operation. The 'expenditure might in any event have been incurred by him in the ordinary course of things'.[104] If the payee is to succeed with a defence of change of position he must have incurred expenditure that he would not otherwise have incurred or have otherwise acted in such a way as to render it unjust that he should now be compelled to refund the payment.[105] Where the payee has purchased goods or services, the benefit of which he still retains, he may still be held to have been unjustly enriched to their value as a result of the payment.

Cases decided since *Lipkin Gorman* have started to show how the defence operates. In *Scottish Equitable plc* v. *Derby*,[106] for example, the defendant invested a sum of money in an individual pension policy with the claimant life assurance company. He later exercised an option to take an early retirement benefit, but that was not recorded in the company's computer records due to an administrative error. When the defendant was aged 65 the claimant sent him a statement showing a fund of £201,000. The statement failed to take account of the defendant's exercise of the early retirement benefit, and of the fact that the fund actually stood at approximately £29,500. After receiving confirmation from the claimant that the statement was correct, the defendant took £51,300 as a lump sum cash payment, whilst reinvesting £150,600 with another pension company, NU. This meant that the defendant was overpaid approximately £172,500, including an overpayment of £121,100 on the amount reinvested with NU. Thanks to the latter overpayment, the defendant received an annual pension some £11,000 higher than he would have otherwise received. Of the lump sum payment, the defendant spent approximately £41,700 reducing his mortgage, while the balance of approximately £9,600 was spent on making modest improvements to his lifestyle. Upon discovering the error the claimant sought to recover the overpayment from the defendant on the ground that he had been unjustly enriched by the amount overpaid. Harrison J, the trial judge, held that the claimant was entitled to recover the overpayments, save for the change of position of £9,600.[107] At trial, the defendant, who was in the process of divorcing from his wife and facing severe financial difficulties, relied on the defence of change of position, emphasizing in particular that because of the claimant's error and his receipt of the overpayment, he had not tried to seek alternative sources of income or make savings which he would otherwise have made. Harrison J rejected any such general application of the change of position defence, emphasizing that 'there must be some causal link between the receipt of the payment and the change of position such that it would be inequitable to require the recipient to return the money to its owner'.[108] His Lordship held that the defendant's general financial difficulties arising from the separation from his wife were not causally linked in any way with the mistaken payment. Furthermore, the defendant had been in no position to make any savings and there was no realistic prospect of the defendant obtaining increased

---

[104] Ibid. See also *United Overseas Bank* v. *Jiwani*, n.91 above.

[105] In *Commerzbank AG* v. *Gareth Price-Jones* [2003] EWCA Civ. 1663, [39]–[40], [65]–[70], the Court of Appeal left open the possibility that the defence could apply to non-financial change of position. See further, P. Birks, 'Change of Position: The Two Central Questions' (2004) 120 *LQR* 373.

[106] [2000] 3 All ER 793, affd. n.111 below.

[107] Harrison J rejected a defence of estoppel: Sect. 3(iii)(c) below.

[108] Ibid., 802. Harrison J seems to have adopted the 'but for' test of causation in the case before him.

employment, given his age and health.[109] Nor had the defendant incurred a change of position in respect of the overpaid sum of £121,000 invested in the NU, as the NU had agreed to unwind the policy and put him in the same position he would have been in had the overpayment not been made. Finally, Harrison J considered that the defendant had not changed his position in relation to the sum of £41,700 used to reduce his mortgage.[110] First, the money was used to pay an existing debt that would have had to be paid in any event. Secondly, he had had the benefit of the increased equity of that amount in the house, and he could realize the asset of the increased equity to repay the claimant. The Court of Appeal adopted the reasoning of Harrison J,[111] but stressed two points regarding the change of position defence: first, that for the defence to apply there must be a causal link between the recipient's change of position and the mistaken payment which makes it inequitable for the recipient to be required to make restitution.[112] Moreover, the defence was to be available not only to those who had detrimentally relied on the mistaken payment (the 'narrow view') but also to those who had suffered some other misfortune, for example, the innocent recipient of a payment which is later stolen from him, so long as the misfortune could be causally linked to the mistaken receipt (the 'wide view').[113] Secondly, it was held that a court should not apply too demanding a standard of proof when an honest recipient says that he has spent an overpayment by improving his lifestyle, but cannot produce any detailed accounting. The defence was not to be limited, as it is in Canada and some of the states of the United States,[114] to specific identifiable items of expenditure. The more flexible approach taken by Jonathan Parker J in *Philip Collins Ltd* v. *Davis*[115] was expressly approved.[116]

In *Philip Collins Ltd* v. *Davis*, the defendants were musicians who played on five out of the 15 tracks on an album released by the claimant in 1990. In 1997 the claimant informed the defendants that it had wrongly overpaid them because they were only contractually entitled to royalties *pro rata* to the number of tracks they had played on whereas they had in fact been paid royalties on all 15 tracks. The claimant sought to set off the royalties allegedly overpaid against future royalties. Jonathan Parker J allowed the claim as to one half of the overpayment, but subject to a defence of change of position as to the other half. Stressing that the defence was to be applied according to legal principle and not as

---

[109] Cf. *Gertsch* v. *Atsas, Fidirrikos and Hamilton* [1999] NSWSC 898, where the beneficiary of a legacy under a forged will was held to have a defence of change of position to the extent that she had stopped work and had forgone earnings in excess of the legacy.

[110] *RBC Dominion Securities Inc.* v. *Dawson* (1994) 11 DLR (4th) 230 (NCA) (no detriment caused to payee who used mistaken overpayment to pay off a Visa debt earlier than otherwise would have been the case). See also *Gertsch* v. *Atsas, Fidirrikos and Hamilton*, n.109 above.

[111] [2001] 3 All ER 818 (CA). Whilst Robert Walker LJ agreed with Harrison J that it is not a detriment to pay off a debt that will have to be paid off sooner or later, his Lordship went on to observe that 'it might be if there were a long-term loan on advantageous terms': ibid., [35]. See also *National Bank of Egypt International Ltd* v. *Oman Housing Bank SAOC* [2003] 1 All ER (Comm.) 246.

[112] In *Philip Collins Ltd* v. *Davis* [2000] 3 All ER 808, 827, Jonathan Parker J said that the change of position must in some way be 'referable to' the mistaken payment. See also *Papamichael* v. *National Westminster Bank plc*, n.99 above, 366; *Commerzbank AG* v. *Gareth Price-Jones*, n.105 above, [43], [59]; *Crédit Suisse (Monaco) SA* v. *Attar* [2004] EWHC 374 (Comm.), [98].

[113] Ibid., [30]–[31]. His Lordship appears to give tacit approval to a 'but for' test of causation. Contrast the position in Australia, where change of position can be established only where the recipient has acted 'on the faith of the receipt': *David Securities Pty. Ltd* v. *Commonwealth Bank of Australia*, n.6 above, 385. See also *State Bank of New South Wales* v. *Swiss Bank Corp.* (1995) 39 NSWLR 350 (NSWCA).

[114] *David Securities Pty. Ltd* v. *Commonwealth Bank of Australia*, n.6 above, 385, noted by R. Goff & G. Jones, n.46 above, para. 40-001.

[115] N.112 above.   [116] N.111 above, [33].

a matter of fairness, Jonathan Parker J went on to identify four such principles which he regarded as relevant to the application of the defence in the case before him:[117]

> In the first place, the evidential burden is on the defendant to make good the defence of change of position. However, in applying this principle it seems to me that the court should beware of applying too strict a standard. Depending on the circumstances, it may well be unrealistic to expect a defendant to produce conclusive evidence of change of position, given that when he changed his position he can have had no expectation that he might thereafter have to prove that he did so, and the reason why he did so, in a court of law[118]...In the second place, as Lord Goff stressed...in the *Lipkin Gorman* case...to amount to a change of position there must be something more than mere expenditure of the money sought to be recovered, 'because the expenditure might in any event have been incurred...in the ordinary course of things'. In the third place, there must be a causal link between the change of position and the overpayment...in other words it must, on the evidence, be referable in some way to the payment of that money. In the fourth place, as Lord Goff also made clear...in the *Lipkin Gorman* case, in contrast to the defence of estoppel the defence of change of position is not an 'all or nothing' defence: it is available only to the extent that the change of position renders recovery unjust.

Applying these basic principles to the facts of the case before him, Jonathan Parker J held that, although the defendants' evidence did not show that any particular item of expenditure was referable to the overpayment of royalties, the overpayments caused a general change of position by the defendants in that they increased their level of outgoings by reference to the sums so paid. In his Lordship's opinion, it was significant that the overpayments took the form of a series of periodical payments over an extended period, for this placed the defendants in a stronger position to establish a general change of position consequent upon the overpayments. The defendants' financial affairs did not lend themselves to detailed analysis, but the judge was prepared to adopt a broad approach to the question and held, on a conservative assessment, that the defence of change of position extended to one half of the overpayments.

It was held by Clarke J in *South Tyneside Metropolitan Borough Council* v. *Svenska International plc*[119] that the defence of change of position was only available where the defendant had changed his position after receipt of the enrichment. In other words, anticipatory change of position was not sufficient to raise the defence. This restrictive interpretation of the defence has been heavily criticized.[120] The requirement that the change of position must follow receipt of the enrichment seems unnecessary. It should be enough that the two are causally linked or referable to each other in some way.[121] It is not surprising, therefore, to find that the Privy Council has recently indicated that the defence should extend to anticipatory change of position. In *Dextra Bank & Trust Co Ltd* v. *Bank*

---

[117] Ibid., 827. See also *Test Claimants in the FII Group Litigation* v. *Revenue & Customs Commissioners*, n.35 above, [343]–[347]; *Bloomsbury International Ltd* v. *Sea Fish Industry Authority* [2009] EWHC 1721(QB), [135].

[118] *RBC Dominion Securities Inc.* v. *Dawson*, n.110 above; *Gertsch* v. *Atsas, Fidirrikos and Hamilton*, n.109 above.

[119] N.100 above.   [120] A. Jones, 'It's a Fair Swap' [1995] *Conv.* 490.

[121] N.112 above. Jonathan Parker J left the issue of anticipatory change of position open in *Philip Collins Ltd* v. *Davis*, n.112 above, 827, but noted that if it was to be allowed 'it must, on the evidence, be referable in some way' to the receipt of the enrichment.

of Jamaica,[122] Lords Bingham and Goff, stated by way of *obiter dictum* that anticipatory expenditure was enough to raise the defence. Their Lordships reasoned that by the time a claim in unjust enrichment was brought to trial, the defendant would merely want to retain the benefit that *ex hypothesi* he already had received. Moreover, so long as there was a sufficient causal connection between receipt of the enrichment and the expenditure, the injustice of requiring the defendant to make restitution was the same whether the defendant incurred an exceptional expenditure before or after receiving the enrichment. In *Commerzbank AG* v. *Gareth Price-Jones*,[123] the Court of Appeal followed *Dextra* and held that a change of position in anticipation of an enrichment was to be treated in the same way as one that came afterwards.

For the defence of change of position to apply, not only must there be a causative link between the receipt of the payment by the defendant and his change of position or at least the two events be referable to each other, but the defendant's position must also have changed in circumstances which make it inequitable for him to make restitution to the claimant. Lord Goff expressly recognized in *Lipkin Gorman* that a defendant will not be able to rely on the defence where he acted in bad faith.[124] Lord Goff also stressed that the defence would not be available to someone who was a wrongdoer.[125] Bad faith includes dishonesty which, since *Twinsectra Ltd* v. *Yardley*,[126] is defined subjectively, i.e. the defendant must realize that his conduct would be regarded as dishonest by the standards of reasonable and honest people. However, bad faith goes further than subjective dishonesty. In *Niru Battery Manufacturing Co* v. *Milestone Trading Ltd*,[127] Moore-Bick J held that lack of good faith was a concept 'capable of embracing a failure to act in a commercially acceptable way and sharp practice of a kind that falls short of outright dishonesty as well as dishonesty itself'.[128] The judge was upheld on appeal, where Clarke LJ stressed that the key question was whether it would be equitable or unconscionable to deny restitution.[129] Bad faith does not include negligence.[130] Similarly, the defendant cannot rely on the defence where he changed his position knowing that the claimant was entitled to restitution, for example, where the defendant was aware that the claimant had paid over money by mistake,[131] or where he knew that there was a risk that he was not

---

[122] N.49 above. Their Lordships (at [39]) confined cases of reliance on void payments, where the defence failed, as in *South Tyneside Metropolitan Borough Council* v. *Svenska International plc*, n.100 above, above, to their exceptional facts.

[123] N.105 above, [38], [64].   [124] N.8 above, 580.

[125] Ibid. In *Kuwait Airways Corp.* v. *Iraqi Airways Co. (Nos. 5 & 6)* [2002] 2 AC 883, [79] (HL), Lord Nicholls indicated (obiter) that the defence might be available to a claim based on the tort of conversion.

[126] [2002] 2 AC 164.

[127] N.4 above, 741, approved n.4 above. See also *McDonald* v. *Coys of Kensington* [2004] EWCA Civ. 47, [41].

[128] Mere suspicion of possible money laundering that does not extend to the relevant transactions does not constitute bad faith for the change of position defence: *Abou-Rahmah* v. *Abacha* [2007] 1 Lloyd's Rep 115, [82]–[84], [87], [99]–[103] (CA).

[129] [2004] 1 All ER (Comm.) 193, [152], [183], [192] (CA). Cf. P. Birks, n.105 above, 377, who supports Moore-Bick J's analysis but feels that the references to 'inequitable' and 'unconscionable' merely 'muddy the water'.

[130] *Dextra Bank & Trust Company Ltd* v. *Bank of Jamaica*, n.49 above; *Niru Battery Manufacturing Co* v. *Milestone Trading Ltd*, [2002] 2 All ER (Comm.) 705, 738; *Maersk Air Ltd* v. *Expeditors International (UK) Ltd* [2003] 1 Lloyd's Rep. 491, 499.

[131] *RBC Dominion Securities Inc.* v. *Dawson*, n.110 above, 238. But for an exceptional case where the mistaken payor virtually forced the payment on a reluctant payee who was held entitled to the defence despite his knowledge, see *National Bank of New Zealand Ltd* v. *Waitaki International Processing (NI) Ltd* (1996) 6 NZLBC 102,646 (NZCA).

entitled to the money[132] or where he took a risk that no claim would be brought against him to recover it.[133]

But what if the defendant was merely careless? It has been suggested that the change of position defence is not open to the careless recipient,[134] although the better view is that as the careless payor can claim restitution for a mistaken payment,[135] the careless payee should be treated no differently.[136] The issue was addressed by Lords Bingham and Goff in *Dextra Bank & Trust Co. Ltd* v. *Bank of Jamaica*,[137] where their Lordships stated (obiter) that a judge should not 'balance the equities' and apportion loss according to the parties' relative merits. In their Lordships' opinion, any attempt to apply the defence of change of position to reflect relative fault would render it 'hopelessly unstable'.[138] Good faith on the part of the recipient was held to be a sufficient requirement for the defence of change of position.[139] Thus, *Dextra* is good authority for the proposition that mere negligence on the part of the recipient is not sufficient to deprive him of the defence of change of position.[140]

Finally, it should be noted that the defence of change of position is not available where the recipient's change of position involved the commission of an illegal act, unless the illegality was so minor that it would be ignored by the court on the *de minimis* principle.[141]

(b) Good consideration

A claim to recover money on the ground of mistake will fail if the defendant has provided 'good consideration' for the payment.[142] The consideration which is provided must be 'good' consideration and so excludes consideration that is illegal or contrary to public policy.[143] The defence must be distinguished from both the *bona fide* purchaser defence and that of change of position.[144] The *bona fide* purchaser defence is concerned with making good defects in the defendant's title to property. But whether or not the defendant has title to property is irrelevant where a restitutionary claim is based on unjust enrichment.

---

[132] *South Tyneside Metropolitan Borough Council* v. *Svenska International plc*, n.100 above, 569, Clarke J. See also *Goss* v. *Chilcott* [1996] AC 788, where the Privy Council rejected a defence of change of position when borrowers, who knew that they were liable to repay a loan to the claimant on the ground of total failure of consideration, deliberately took a risk and lent the money to a third party from whom it proved to be irrecoverable.

[133] *Re Tain Construction Ltd, Rose* v. *AIB Group (UK) plc* [2003] BPIR 1188, [55]–[56].

[134] *South Tyneside Metropolitan Borough Council* v. *Svenska International plc*, n.100 above, 569.

[135] *Banque Financière de la Cité* v. *Parc (Battersea) Ltd*, n.8 above, 227, 235, 242–243; *Scottish Equitable plc* v. *Derby*, n.106 above, 800, affd. n.111 above, [25].

[136] As recommended by the Law Commission in its report 'Restitution: Mistakes of Law and Utra Vires Public Authority Receipts and Payments' (Law. Com. No. 227, London, 1994), para. 2.23.

[137] N.49 above, [45]; applied in *Niru Battery Manufacturing Co.* v. *Milestone Trading Ltd* (No. 2) [2004] EWCA Civ. 487, [33].

[138] Ibid.   [139] Ibid.

[140] *Papamichael* v. *National Westminster Bank plc* [2003] 1 Lloyd's Rep. 341, 368.

[141] *Barros Mattos Junior* v. *MacDaniels Ltd* [2004] 3 All ER 299 (innocent recipient of stolen US dollars converted them into Nigerian naira in breach of Nigerian exchange control regulations).

[142] *Barclays Bank Ltd* v. *W. J. Simms Son & Cooke (Southern) Ltd*, n.51 above, 695. See also *Bank of New South Wales* v. *Murphett* [1983] VR 489 and *Lloyds Bank plc* v. *Independent Insurance Co. Ltd* [2000] QB 110 (CA).

[143] *Lipkin Gorman (a firm)* v. *Karpnale Ltd*, n.8 above, 575 (no valuable consideration provided where money paid to the defendant casino under a void gaming contract).

[144] Cf. *Lloyds Bank plc* v. *Independent Insurance Co. Ltd*, n.142 above, 125–126, 132, where Waller LJ assumed that the defence of good consideration was a form of change of position and Peter Gibson LJ, although separating good consideration from change of position, characterized the former as a form of the defence of *bona fide* purchaser for value.

On the other hand, the defendant's enrichment will not be unjust where he has given good consideration for it.[145] For this reason, it could even be said that 'good consideration' is not really a defence at all, but operates as a bar to the claimant's action. On this basis, the burden would be on the claimant to show that the defendant's enrichment was unjust, i.e. that he had not given good consideration for it.[146] The provision of good consideration can also be distinguished from change of position.[147] First, the change of position defence requires the defendant to have changed his position in an unusual way, for example by incurring extraordinary expenditure in reliance on the validity of a payment received from the claimant. On the other hand, the consideration given for the payment need not be unusual. Secondly, it follows from the definition of 'consideration' that the consideration provided by the defendant must have been expected by the claimant. By contrast, the defendant may change his position in a way that is unexpected, so long as it is extraordinary in some way.[148]

The good consideration defence operates where the claimant mistakenly pays the defendant and this has the effect of discharging a debt owed to the defendant.[149] As Robert Goff J said in *Barclays Bank Ltd* v. *W. J. Simms Son & Cooke (Southern) Ltd*,[150] good consideration is given for the mistaken payment where:

> the money is paid to discharge, and does discharge, a debt owed to the payee (or a principal on whose behalf he is authorised to receive the payment) by the payer or by a third party by whom he is authorised to discharge the debt.

In this case the claimant bank overlooked its customer's stop order and mistakenly paid a cheque drawn by the customer in favour of the defendant payee. The bank's claim for repayment of the money mistakenly paid away was resisted by the payee on the ground that the payment had gone to discharge a debt owed to the payee by the customer. Robert Goff J dismissed this line of defence on the ground that the payment was made outside the bank's mandate and without its customer's authority: after all, payment of the cheque had been countermanded by the customer. A payment made without the customer's authority could not discharge that customer's debt owed to the payee. However, his Lordship went on to note that:[151]

> even if the payee has given consideration for the payment, for example by accepting the payment in discharge of a debt owed to him by a third party on whose behalf the payer is authorised to discharge it, that transaction may itself be set aside (and provide no defence to the claim) if the payer's mistake was induced by the payee, or possibly where the payee, being aware of the payer's mistake, did not receive the money in good faith.

Robert Goff J distinguished between payments made within the bank's mandate and those made outside it. He held that where a bank makes a payment within its mandate it is entitled to debit the customer's account with the amount of the payment, and further the payment is effective to discharge the obligations of the customer to the payee, because the bank has paid the cheque with the authority of the customer. By contrast, where a payment is made outside the bank's mandate, for example, where the bank overlooks notice of the customer's death, pays a cheque bearing the forged signature of

---

[145] Ibid., at 132.

[146] G. Virgo, 'Recent Developments in Restitution of Mistaken Payments' [1999] *CLJ* 478, 481.

[147] Note that Robert Goff J dealt with them separately in *Barclays Bank Ltd* v. *W. J. Simms, Son & Cooke (Southern) Ltd*, n.51 above, 695.

[148] G. Virgo, n.26 above, 173–174.   [149] *Jones* v. *Churcher*, n.40 above, [48]–[55].

[150] N.51 above, 695.

[151] Ibid. See also *Lloyds Bank plc* v. *Independent Insurance Co. Ltd*, n.142 above, 130.

its customer as drawer, or overlooks notice of countermand of the customer, the bank cannot debit the customer's account, and the payment will not effectively discharge the obligation (if any) of the customer to the payee (unless the customer is able to and does ratify the payment).

Significantly, his Lordship placed one type of mistaken payment into the category of payments that falls within the bank's mandate. This is where the bank honours the customer's payment instruction in the mistaken belief that there are sufficient funds or overdraft facilities to meet the payment. In this case the effect of the bank's payment is to accept the customer's request for overdraft facilities. The payment is therefore within the bank's mandate, with the result that not only is the bank entitled to have recourse to its customer but the customer's obligation to the payee is discharged. It follows that the payee has given consideration for the payment with the consequence that, although the payment has been caused by the bank's mistake, the money is irrecoverable from the payee unless the transaction of payment is itself set aside.[152]

Lloyds Bank plc v. *Independent Insurance Co. Ltd*[153] provides a good example of the defence in operation. A customer paid a cheque into the claimant bank and, because he owed a similar sum to the defendant, instructed the bank to transfer that sum to the defendant as soon as possible. The bank agreed to do this but only on condition that the cheque had first cleared as there were insufficient funds in the account to cover the transfer otherwise. However, before the cheque cleared the money was transferred by CHAPS inter-bank electronic transfer into the defendant's bank account by mistake. On discovering its error, the bank tried to recover the payment from the defendant as money paid under a mistake of fact. Applying the dicta of Robert Goff J in n.46 above *Simms*, the Court of Appeal held that the bank was not entitled to restitution of a transfer of funds which had been made with its customer's authority to discharge a debt owed by that customer to the defendant. The payment had been made with the customer's actual authority and, because it discharged his debt to the defendant, had been made for good consideration. It was the bank, not its customer, which had imposed the qualification that the transfer was not to be made before the cheque cleared.

By contrast, in *Simms*, Robert Goff J held that payment of a countermanded cheque fell outside the bank's mandate, and did not discharge the drawer's debt to the payee, thereby enabling the drawee bank to recover the payment from the payee as money had and received. Professor Goode has been particularly critical of Robert Goff J's reasoning.[154] First, Goode argues that whilst the countermand terminated the bank's *actual* authority to pay the cheque, the payee was entitled to rely on the bank's continued *apparent* authority to make payment, so that this was effective to discharge the drawer's liability to the payee on the cheque. This criticism appears misplaced. Such an argument was firmly rejected by the Court of Appeal in *Lloyds Bank plc* v. *Independent Insurance Co. Ltd*,[155] on the grounds that, first, there was no holding out that the bank had authority to make the payment, and, secondly, there was no reliance by the payee on the bank having authority to pay.[156] Goode's second criticism is that a payee who gives up a cheque on which he has a valid claim in exchange for payment inevitably suffers a change of position, for he no longer has the instrument in his hands, and any claim he wishes to pursue against the drawer will have to be on the original consideration, not on the cheque, so that he loses valuable rights. Again, this criticism may not be fair. Under section 63(3)

---

[152] The nature of the bank's mistake is considered further in Sect. 6 below.   [153] N.142 above.
[154] R.M. Goode, 'The Bank's Right to Recover Money Paid on a Stopped Cheque' (1981) 97 *LQR* 254, 255–6.
[155] N.142 above, 123.   [156] R. Goff & G. Jones, n.46 above, ch. 41.

of the BEA 1882 a cancellation of a negotiable instrument under a mistake is inoperative, in which event it may be possible for the bank to restore the cheque to the payee to enable him to take proceedings upon it against the drawer. Further, in so far as there is any detriment from the mistaken payment of the cheque, there must be some doubt that it outweighs the injustice of denying the bank's claim to recover the monies.

In *B. & H. Engineering* v. *First National Bank of SA Ltd*,[157] the Appellate Division (now the Supreme Court of Appeal) in South Africa has recently held that payment of a countermanded cheque by the drawee bank discharges the underlying debt between drawer and payee, so that the drawee bank has no claim against the payee for mistaken payment but is left with a restitutionary claim against the drawer based on his unjust enrichment at the bank's expense. The problem with this approach is that it is based on the faulty premise that the unauthorized payment discharged the drawer's indebtedness to the payee.[158] Yet one (in)famous English case also reflects this approach. It is *B. Liggett (Liverpool) Ltd* v. *Barclays Bank Ltd*,[159] a decision that is popular with bankers but which, *prima facie*, does not sit easily with *Simms*.

Liggett was a breach of mandate case. Barclays' mandate was to honour cheques signed by two directors of its customer, Liggett (Liverpool) Ltd. In breach of mandate, Barclays honoured cheques payable to Liggett's trade creditors but signed by only one its directors (the other director claiming that this was all going on behind his back). The claimant company then tried to recover the amounts debited to its account from the defendant bank through an action for money had and received. Wright J held that the bank had a good defence to the claim on the ground that the defendant bank was entitled to take over the former creditor's remedies against the claimant. Although Wright J avoided using the language of subrogation (because he wrongly thought that subrogation could only be used to transfer secured rights), *Liggett* is generally regarded as a subrogation case. It stands as authority for the proposition that when a bank (P) pays its customer's (D's) creditor (X) in the mistaken belief that D has authorized it to do so, D's liability should be treated as *automatically discharged*, leaving the bank (P) unable to recover from the payee (X), but entitled to recover from its customer (D) by taking over (being subrogated to) X's former remedies against D (i.e. the discharged liability). *Liggett* can be explained on restitutionary reasoning as subrogation is used to reverse the unjust enrichment of the customer (D) at the expense of the bank (P), the unjust factor being the bank's mistake.

How can *Liggett* be reconciled with the established rule that the unrequested payment of another's debt discharges that debt automatically only where it was paid under legal compulsion or by necessity? In other cases, prior authorization, subsequent ratification, or some other form of acceptance of the payment by the debtor is required for a good discharge.[160] In *Re Cleadon Trust Ltd*,[161] the majority of the Court of Appeal considered that the decision in *Liggett* could be upheld only on the basis that the bank had been expressly authorized to pay by one of the company's directors, and that the director himself had the company's authority to do this, even though the director was not authorized to draw a cheque on the company's account for that purpose on his

---

[157] 1995 (2) SA 279 (A).

[158] The decision is strongly criticized by Justice van Zyl, 'Unauthorised Payment and Unjustified Enrichment in Banking Law' in F.D. Rose (ed.), *Restitution and Banking Law* (Oxford, 1998), 22–26.

[159] [1928] 1 KB 48.

[160] *Belshaw* v. *Bush* (1851) 11 CB 191; P.B.H. Birks and J. Beatson, 'Unrequested Payment of Another's Debt' (1976) 92 *LQR* 188; cf. A. Burrows, *The Law of Restitution* (2nd edn., London, 2002), 293–302.

[161] [1939] Ch. 286, 316–318, 326–327.

signature alone.[162] The majority's reasoning has recently been applied by the Court of Appeal in *Crantrave Ltd* v. *Lloyds Bank plc*,[163] where it was held that the *Liggett* defence arises only where the payment from the account is applied to reduce the customer's debt with the customer's authority, or if the customer has ratified the payment.[164] This reasoning helps distinguish *Liggett* from *Simms*. In *Simms* there was no authority to discharge the debt, whereas in *Liggett*, according to the majority in *Re Cleadon Trust*, there was authority to do so.

Although the effect of the majority's reasoning in *Re Cleadon Trust*, and the recent decision in *Crantrave*, is to limit the effect of *Liggett*, it is submitted that this is the right approach. The line taken by the Supreme Court of Appeal in South Africa, and by Wright J in *Liggett* itself,[165] has the superficial attraction of leaving the mistaken bank with a claim for unjust enrichment against its own customer, the drawer of the cheque, when it is denied recovery against the payee. However, the bank will not necessarily recover all of its mistaken payment from the drawer as the bank is merely subrogated to the payee's claim against him and the drawer may have a defence to some or all of that claim, for example, where the drawer stops the cheque because the payee has delivered defective goods. It is submitted that the bank should not be drawn into that dispute but should be allowed to recover its mistaken payment from the payee and withdraw from the scene, leaving the drawer and payee to fight it out amongst themselves.[166]

(c) Estoppel

The paying bank may be estopped by representation from recovering money paid under a mistake. Several requirements must be met for this to happen. First, there must be a representation by the paying bank leading the recipient to believe that he was entitled to treat the money as his own. In cases involving banker and customer, such an estoppel arises, for instance, where the crediting of the funds to the customer's account and the consequent entry in the periodic statement have led the customer to believe that he is entitled to the money involved and has acted accordingly. The mere payment of money cannot in itself constitute a representation which will estop the payor from recovering payment.[167] Secondly, the recipient must have relied on the representation to his detriment. Often a

---

[162] *H.J. Symons & Co.* v. *Barclays Bank plc* [2003] EWHC 1249 (Comm.), where Cook J held, when rejecting an application for summary judgment against the bank, that it was arguable that the sole director who gave the payment order—when the mandate required two signatures—was the directing mind and will of the company; cf. C. Mitchell, *The Law of Subrogation* (Oxford, 1994), 128–129. See generally C. Mitchell & S. Watterson, *Subrogation: Law & Practice* (Oxford, 2007), paras. 2.06–2.07.

[163] [2000] QB 917. See also *HJ Symons & Co* v. *Barclays Bank plc*, n.162 above; *Filby* v. *Mortgage Express (No.2) Ltd* [2004] EWCA Civ 759, [34]–[35]; *Liverpool Freeport Electronics Ltd* v. *Habib Bank Ltd* [2007] EWHC 1149 (QB), [141]; *Treasure & Son Ltd* v. *Martin Dawes* [2008] EWHC 2181 (TCC), [14].

[164] Pill and May LJJ (at 924 and 925 respectively) considered that the bank might also have a defence to a claim for breach of mandate where it can be established on the evidence that the customer has been 'unjustly enriched' by the unauthorized payment. The nature of these circumstances continues to remain unclear: *Gulf International Bank BSC* v. *Albaraka Islamic Bank* [2004] EWCA Civ 416, [36]; *Tayeb* v. *HSBC Bank plc* [2004] 4 All ER 1024, [97]–[99]; *Sweetman* v. *Shepherd* [2007] BPIR 455, [144]–[148]. For a case that might fall into this exceptional category, see *Majesty Restaurant Pty. Ltd* v. *Commonwealth Bank of Australia Ltd* (1999) 47 NSWLR 593.

[165] Note also that the American Uniform Commercial Code, s.4-407, denies direct recovery by a bank which made a mistaken payment against a payee who took a cheque in good faith and for value: the bank is subrogated to the rights of the payee or holder in due course of the cheque against the drawer, or those of the drawer against the payee, so as to prevent unjust enrichment.

[166] P.B.H. Birks, 'The Burden on the Bank' in Rose (ed.), n.158 above, 217.

[167] *R. E. Jones Ltd* v. *Waring and Gillow Ltd*, n.43 above; *Philip Collins Ltd* v. *Davis* n.112 above, 825.

correspondent bank can raise the defence because it has paid away the funds to the payee's order.[168] Thirdly, the recipient must not be at fault. There will be fault, for example, if the recipient realized the mistake and did nothing about it, or somehow induced it, or knows of material facts which would have made the payor recognize his mistake.[169]

The estoppel defence is said to differ from the change of position defence in two respects. First, it depends on a representation by the person making the payment whereas the change of position defence does not.[170] Secondly, because it is a rule of evidence, estoppel gives a total defence to the claim whereas the change of position defence provides only a *pro tanto* defence.[171] The second point of distinction must be treated with caution. There may well be cases where it would be inequitable or unconscionable for the recipient to rely on the fact that he has spent part of the mistaken payment to resist a claim for the balance.[172] Thus, in *Scottish Equitable plc* v. *Derby*,[173] the Court of Appeal upheld the trial judge's decision that it was unconscionable, or clearly inequitable, to allow the recipient to keep the whole of a mistaken overpayment of £172,451 when his resultant irrecoverable expenditure was limited to £9,662. The Court of Appeal adopted a similar approach in *National Westminster Bank plc* v. *Somer International (UK) Ltd*,[174] where it held that it would have been unconscionable for the defendant to have retained the balance of a mistaken payment of US$76,700 when the defendant's detrimental reliance was limited to US$21,600. However, the Court of Appeal did stress that in cases of this nature the burden on the defendant of proving the precise extent of his detriment should be a light one.[175] The inappropriateness of estoppel as an 'all or nothing' defence where it is clearly inequitable or unconscionable to retain the whole of the mistaken payment leaves the future of the defence uncertain. In *Philip Collins Ltd* v. *Davis*,[176] Jonathan Parker J has even gone so far as to suggest (obiter) that: 'the law has now developed to the point where a defence of estoppel by representation is no longer apt in restitutionary claims where the more flexible defence of change of position is in principle available'.[177]

4 Action against a collecting bank

The payment made by the bank under a mistake of fact or law may, in certain cases, be made directly to the payee. This occurs where a cheque is presented by the payee over the counter, or where the bank pays him in cash an amount remitted from overseas. In the majority of cases, though, the amount is credited to the payee's account with his own bank, that is, the 'collecting bank'. If the paying bank acted under a mistake, it may then

---

[168]   *Deutsche Bank* v. *Beriro & Co.*, n.3 above.
[169]   *George Whitechurch Ltd* v. *Cavanagh* [1902] AC 117, 145 (HL).
[170]   *Lipkin Gorman (a firm)* v. *Karpnale Ltd*, n.8 above, 579.
[171]   *Avon CC* v. *Howlett* [1983] 1 All ER 1073 (CA) (claimant could not recover mistaken overpayment of £1,000 when recipient has suffered detriment only in the sum of £550).
[172]   Ibid., 1075–1076, 1078, 1089.
[173]   N.106 above, affd. n.111 above. See also *Bloomsbury International Ltd* v. *Sea Fish Industry Authority*, n.117 above, [135].
[174]   [2002] QB 1286 (CA).   [175]   Ibid., [46], [68].   [176]   N.112 above, 826.
[177]   Citing dicta of Lord Goff in the *Lipkin Gorman* case, n.8 above, 580. See also *RBC Dominion Securities* v. *Dawson*, n.110 above, 237. Cf. E. Fung & L. Ho, 'Change of Position and Estoppel' (2001) 117 *LQR* 14. In *Scottish Equitable plc* v. *Derby*, n.111 above, [45]–[47], Robert Walker LJ (obiter) expressed tentative agreement with the 'novel and ingenious argument' of the claimant that, since *Lipkin Gorman*, the defence of change of position pre-empts and disables the defence of estoppel by negativing detriment.

wish to sue both parties or, where the payee is impecunious or has absconded, may have no option but to concentrate its efforts on an action against the collecting bank alone.

Even prior to the House of Lords' decision in *Lipkin Gorman*, it was established that, where a bank paid out to a customer a sum of money that had been remitted to it as the customer's agent, the money could not be recovered from the bank. Three requirements must be met for this defence to operate in the bank's favour. First, the bank must have received the money as agent and not as principal. Secondly, the bank must have acted in good faith and without notice of the true owner's claim before it disposed of the money. Thirdly, the bank, as agent, must have 'paid over' the money received to its customer, as principal. Although *Lipkin Gorman* introduces a comparable defence, namely change of position, available irrespective of whether a payee receives money as principal or as agent, the older authorities remain relevant as regards the collecting bank's position as a pure agent. In fact, the two defences should be kept separate. Whilst the basis of the agent's payment over defence may have originally been change of position,[178] this no longer seems to be the case. Payment over has developed into a separate, well-established defence with its own rules. It is based on the fact that the agent recipient is a conduit-pipe for the money, which is treated as paid to the principal, not to the agent, so that the principal, not the agent, is the proper party to be sued.[179] The point was recently expressed by HHJ Havelock-Allan QC in *Jones* v. *Churcher*[180] as follows:

> Ministerial receipt is a different defence to change of position. It is available only where a collecting bank has received funds as agent for the customer and has paid away the funds to the customer. Once the collecting bank has dealt with the funds in such a way that the credit to the customer is irreversible, the bank is entitled to plead a defence of ministerial receipt to any restitutionary claim by the payer to get the funds back. The defence complements the defence of change of position which may additionally be available to the collecting bank depending on the circumstances.

In this section, the discussion of the cases in point is followed by a consideration of the effect of the general defence, as formulated in *Lipkin Gorman*, on the position of a bank which receives the funds as principal.

The basic principle governing the position of a bank which receives funds as its customer's agent can be traced back to Lord Mansfield's decision in *Buller* v. *Harrison*.[181] It was succinctly restated in a modern case, *Gowers* v. *Lloyds and National Provincial Bank Ltd*.[182] A retired army officer's widow fraudulently continued to receive his pension by representing that he was still alive. The relevant payments were obtained by means of certificates, presented through the defendant bank, which included an attestation by an alleged medical practitioner to the effect that the army officer was well. The sums involved were remitted directly to the bank, which paid them out to the widow. Affirming the decision of the trial judge, the Court of Appeal held that the amounts were not recoverable from the bank. Sir Wilfred Greene MR said that money paid to an agent under a mistake of fact could be recovered from him as long as he had it in his hands. He went on: '[i]f, on the other hand, he had paid it away to his principal, then it cannot be recovered from the

---

[178] *Lipkin Gorman (a firm)* v. *Karpnale Ltd*, 578. See also W.J. Swadling, 'Ministerial Receipt' in P.B.H. Birks (ed.), *Laundering and Tracing* (Oxford, 1995), 243–260.

[179] *Portman Building Society* v. *Hamilton Taylor Neck (a firm)* [1998] 4 All ER 202, 207. See also *Niru Battery Manufacturing Co.* v. *Milestone Trading Ltd*, n.130 above, [133]. See also M. Bryan, 'Recovering Misdirected Money from Banks: Ministerial Receipt at Law and in Equity' in Rose (ed.), n.158 above, 168.

[180] N.40 above. See generally R. Stevens, 'Why Do Agents Drop Out?' [2005] *LMCLQ* 101; E. Bant, 'Payment Over and Change of Position: Lessons from Agency Law' [2007] *LMCLQ* 225.

[181] (1777) 2 Cowp. 565.   [182] [1938] 1 All ER 766.

agent, and the only remedy is to go against the principal'.[183] It was held irrelevant that the bank had believed that its principal was the army officer whilst, in reality, it was acting for the widow.[184]

It is interesting to note that in one respect the doctrine involved has led to an inconsistency respecting the general question of the collecting bank's liability where it acts for a fraudulent customer. If the customer requests it to collect a stolen cheque, or some other negotiable instrument, the bank will initially be liable to the true owner in conversion and, in the alternative, in a restitutionary action based on waiver of tort.[185] From a practical point of view, it is thereupon liable to damages equal to the amount of the instrument.[186] The bank's only effective defence is that provided by section 4 of the Cheques Act 1957, under which, *inter alia*, it has to establish that it had acted without negligence.[187] The fact that the bank has paid the proceeds of the converted instrument to the customer is no defence! But where payment is received by the collecting bank in a transaction, such as a money transfer or giro credit, which does not involve a negotiable instrument (or some other item that may be the subject of an action in conversion), its liability in a restitutionary action expires when it pays the amount over to the fraudulent customer. The bank's negligence is quite immaterial in such a case.

Practically, though, the difference between the principles governing cases involving negotiable instruments and cases involving money transfers is not as wide as might be expected. The defence of ministerial receipt, as applied to a collecting bank in *Gowers'* case, operates in a narrow area. Unlike the wider defence of change of position, it does not apply where the bank receives the money as principal, or in its own right, and not as an agent. Thus, in *Continental Caoutchouc & Gutta Percha Co. v. Kleinwort Sons & Co.*[188] K, a firm of rubber merchants, was regularly financed by two banks: the defendants and B & Co. The purchasers of some of K's rubber, who were ordered to remit part of the price to the defendants and the balance to B & Co., erroneously paid the full amount to the defendants, who received the money in good faith and credited K's account therewith. Affirming Bingham J's decision, the Court of Appeal held that the amount was recoverable by the payors, the purchasers. Collins MR distinguished two types of case. The first was where a bank received payment as a mere agent. Here the amount could not be recovered from the bank once it was paid out to the principal. The other was where the bank received payment for itself. It would then be in the same position as any other party to whom money was paid under a mistake. In the instant case, the defendants were generally entitled, under the financial agreement made with K, to the proceeds of rubber sales financed by them. They, thus, received the money in the belief that it was due to them in their own right. In reality it was received under mistake, as the proceeds related to a transaction financed by the second bank, B & Co. The money was therefore recoverable.[189] Support for this view is to be found in the decision of the New Zealand Court of

---

[183] Ibid., 773. See also *Jones* v. *Churcher*, n.40 above, [69].

[184] Funds may be deemed to have been paid out to the principal even where, at his request, the agent purchases items meant for his own use: *Transvaal & Delagoa Bay Investment Co. Ltd* v. *Atkinson*, n.92 above. Here the agent purchased household effects and settled bills which her husband, the payee, was bound to pay.

[185] Ch. 15, Sect. 2 below. See also n.21 above.

[186] Cf. *Smith* v. *Lloyds TSB plc* [2001] QB 541 (CA) (considering the effect of BEA, s.64(1) on a cheque that has been materially altered).

[187] Ch. 15, Sect. 4 below.   [188] (1904) 90 LT 474.

[189] (1904) 9 Com. Cas. 248–249, (1904) 90 LT 476. See also *Holland* v. *Russell* (1863) 4 B & S 14, 8 LT 468; *Newall* v. *Tomlinson* (1871) LR 6 CP 405.

Appeal in *Thomas* v. *Houston Corbett & Co.*[190] It was there held that whether an amount of money is received by the payee as agent or as principal depends on his understanding of the transaction and the capacity in which he purports to act.[191]

In some cases it may not be easy to determine whether the bank receives payment as principal or as agent. Undoubtedly, if the bank pays the customer cash or allows him an overdraft against an uncleared cheque, it is considered to act as a discounting bank. When the cheque is cleared, the funds are received by the bank for itself or as principal.[192] In such a case, the bank is just as open to an action in restitution by a payor as any other payee[193] although, in the wake of *Lipkin Gorman*, the bank ought to be able to plead a related change in its position within the principles governing the availability of that defence. But what is the position where the bank sanctions an insignificant overdrawing against an uncleared cheque, for example £10 (required to meet a cheque drawn by the customer) against an uncleared balance of £100? In such a case the bank is deemed to act concurrently as collecting bank and as discounting bank.[194] It is therefore difficult to decide in which capacity it receives the funds involved.

Another borderline type of case was considered in *Continental Caoutchouc*, discussed above. Here Collins MR referred to a difficulty that arose where an amount of money was received by the bank as an agent but applied in reduction of an existing overdraft extended to the principal. In such a case the money is effectively used to discharge a debt due from the principal to the agent. His Lordship observed:[195]

> [Such agent] has no doubt benefited by getting his debt paid, but he has done so in discharging his primary duty of passing the money on to his principal. He has constructively sent it on and received it back, and has done nothing incompatible with his position as a conduit-pipe or intermediary. He was entitled to be paid, and has been paid by his debtor, who was no doubt put in funds to do so by the receipt of the money, and who therefore, and not the intermediary, has had the benefit of the windfall. Hence the care with which the courts have considered whether the sum has in fact been effectually passed out of the hands of the agent into those of the principal, no entry by the agent in his books sufficing until the assent of the principal has completed the transaction.[196]

His Lordship's reference to the principal's assent is, unfortunately, unhelpful where the funds are used to reduce an existing overdraft.[197] It is in the nature of a current account

---

[190] [1969] NZLR 151. See also *Transvaal & Delagoa Bay Investment Co. Ltd* v. *Atkinson*, n.92 above, where a wife was held to have received as an agent amounts paid into her account by her husband in fraud of his employers and for his own use.

[191] *National Bank of Egypt International Ltd* v. *Oman Housing Bank SAOC*, n.111 above (*ultra vires* inter-bank loan recoverable by lender where borrower acting as principal and not as agent).

[192] Ch. 15, Sect. 3 below.   [193] *Dominion Bank* v. *Union Bank of Canada* (1908) 40 SCR 366 (SCC).

[194] Ch. 15, Sect. 3 below.

[195] N.188 above, 476. See also *Jones* v. *Churcher*, n.40 above, [69].

[196] His Lordship referred to *Buller* v. *Harrison*, n.181 above, which, however, is weak authority in point.

[197] In *Standard Bank London Ltd* v. *Canara Bank* [2002] All ER (D) 340, Moore-Bick J (obiter) acknowledged (at [91]) that a bank will often be able to rely on the agent's payment over defence when receiving payment into its customer's overdrawn account but added (at [99]) that 'in order for the payee to have given good consideration it is necessary that the payment operates in discharge of the debt and for that to occur the payment must have been made and received with the necessary authority'. The learned judge (at [98]) seems to have regarded the agent's payment over defence as merely an example of the operation of the 'good consideration' defence (Sect. 3(iii)(b) above). It is submitted that he was wrong to do so. They should be considered as entirely separate defences, the payment over defence going to the question of who is the proper defendant (*Portman Building Society* v. *Hamilton Taylor Neck (a firm)*, n.179 above, 207; *Niru Battery Manufacturing Co.* v. *Milestone Trading Ltd*, n.130 above, [133]).

that an amount paid to the credit of an overdrawn account is automatically set off against the existing debit balance. The customer's assent is given when an account of this type is opened. It is noteworthy that in *Kleinwort, Sons & Co.* v. *Dunlop Rubber Co.*, which involved another transaction of the same merchant and a similar type of mistake, Lord Loreburn LC expressed the view that an amount received by the bank in reduction of the customer's overdraft had not been paid over.[198] It was further held, on the facts, that it was immaterial that the payment involved induced the bank to extend the customer's overdraft. This finding, though, was based on the verdict of the jury, which concluded that the bank would have extended the facility in any event. Generally, the conclusion is questionable. Where the bank increases the customer's overdraft ceiling in reliance on the payment made, it gives him, in effect, a new facility.

A related problem arises in all cases in which the customer's current account is used for a considerable time before the payor demands repayment. It is in the nature of a current account that amounts are paid in and out on a running basis. What is the position if, subsequent to the erroneous payment, the customer withdraws funds in excess of the amount involved but also pays in money to the credit of his current account? Is it then possible to say that the bank has paid the erroneously received sum over to the customer? A positive answer is supported by a strict application of the rule in *Clayton's Case*,[199] under which debit items are to be set off against credit items on the basis of first in first out. The erroneous payment would, therefore, be exhausted before any items were set off against amounts paid into the account later on. But if the credit balance in the customer's account is not exhausted or reduced to an amount lower than that of the erroneous payment, it is difficult to see why the payor should be prevented from seeking recovery from the bank. The bank is a reservoir of money,[200] and the accrued balance is a debt owed by it to the customer. Moreover, it holds the funds as an agent. As the money is still available to the customer—who benefited from the windfall—why should it not be reclaimable from the bank—the customer's agent and debtor?[201]

Support for the last argument is to be found in two cases that suggest that the bank, or agent, should be answerable to the payor as long as the credit entry remains reversible.[202] It is true that in one of the cases, *Holland* v. *Russell*,[203] Cockburn CJ, who delivered the decision of the Court of Queen's Bench, suggested that the amount was to be regarded as paid

---

[198] N.47 above, 264; the dictum, though, is based on the finding of the jury. See further Sect. 3(ii) above. See also *Admiralty Commissioners* v. *National Provincial and Union Bank of England* (1922) 127 LT 452.

[199] *Devaynes* v. *Noble; Clayton's Case* (1816) 1 Mer. 529, 572.   [200] Ch. 6, Sect. 1 above.

[201] *Australia and New Zealand Banking Group* v. *Westpac Banking Corp.* (1988) 164 CLR 662 (HCA) suggesting that an order for restitution can be made notwithstanding that the money is no longer identifiable *in specie*. Cf. M. Bryan, 'Recovering Misdirected Money from Banks: Ministerial Receipt in Law and Equity' in Rose (ed.), n.158 above, 176, who submits that the argument in the text runs counter to recent decisions on tracing, namely *Re Goldcorp Exchange Ltd* [1995] 1 AC 74, 109–10 and *Bishopsgate Investment Management Ltd* v. *Homan* [1995] Ch. 211, which suggest that a bank is not to be regarded as an undifferentiated 'reservoir of money', at least for the purpose of identifying wealth in customer accounts. In reply it can be said that tracing is irrelevant to an action based on unjust enrichment between direct parties, any intermediate bank merely acting as an agent in the process (Sect. 6 below). The action in question is personal and not proprietary. There is no question of the mistaken payor taking priority over the bank's other creditors, which would be a matter of concern with any proprietary claim.

[202] *Holland* v. *Russell* (1861) 30 LJ (NS) QB 308, affd. (1863) 4 B & S 14; *Admiralty Commissioners* v. *National Provincial and Union Bank of England*, n.198 above. See also *Standard Bank London Ltd* v. *Canara Bank*, n.197 above.

[203] N.202 above, 313.

over when it had been made the subject of a 'settled account' or an account stated. But it will be recalled that a bank's periodic statement does not constitute a settled account. The bank is precluded from reversing payment only where the customer is able to invoke an estoppel based on the change in his position.[204] As long as the credit entry remains subject to reversal by the bank, payment ought to be recoverable from it. It should, therefore, be possible to join it as a party in an action in restitution brought against the customer by the payor. In *Jones* v. *Churcher*,[205] Judge Havelock-Allan QC recently emphasized that, for the purposes of the ministerial receipt defence, '[t]he critical point is the point at which the crediting of funds to the customer's account can no longer be reversed'. The issue for his Honour, however, was to identify the point at which a CHAPS payment mistakenly credited by the collecting bank to its customer's account could still be reversed. It was argued for the collecting bank that a CHAPS payment represented cleared funds in the customer's account and accordingly could not be recalled,[206] so that the bank should have a defence from the moment the funds were credited to the customer's account. In making this contention, the collecting bank relied upon an untested argument from the previous edition of this work[207] to the effect that, on a strict analysis of the banker–customer relationship, it is theoretically inaccurate to presuppose that the funds standing to the credit of the customer's account are held by the bank on his behalf. Whilst any amounts drawn by the customer are paid out by the bank as his agent, until the customer makes a demand, the funds standing to his credit are commingled with the bank's other funds and hence are its own money. The customer's only asset is a debt, or chose in action, due to him from the bank. Accordingly, a collecting bank ceases to hold any funds as the customer's agent from the moment at which these are credited to his account, and not from the time at which the customer withdraws them. The money may therefore be regarded as paid over by the bank when the amount becomes available to the customer on clearance. The bank would not be at risk of being liable to its customer if restitution is made to the claimant, and of being held liable to the claimant if it pays the money received to, or to the direction of, the customer. Moreover, the defence would operate whether the customer's account was already in credit or overdrawn. Security of receipt would be paramount.[208] Whilst his Honour in *Churcher* accepted that this argument had the advantage of placing the collecting bank in a more certain position, and of obviating the need to examine the history of drawings on the account,[209] he nevertheless rejected it. The chief reason was that acceptance of the collecting bank's argument would be tantamount to giving such banks immunity in relation to CHAPS transfers.[210] Accordingly, even in respect of a CHAPS transfer, a collecting bank can only avail itself of the ministerial receipt defence to the extent that the customer has drawn on the relevant funds before the bank has notice that those funds are being reclaimed.[211]

The agent's defence and that of change of position are compatible so that a bank could rely on both as defences to one restitutionary claim. As pointed out earlier, the exact scope of the change of position defence, recognized in *Lipkin Gorman*, remains to be determined, as does its precise relationship with the principle in *Gowers*. Whilst it may be arguable that a collecting bank changes its position in reliance on the receipt of the funds received when it pays those funds over to its customer, this suggestion was recently rejected by the Canadian Supreme Court in *BMP Global Distribution Inc.* v. *Bank of*

---

[204] Ch. 7, Sect. 2(iv) above.   [205] N.40 above, [69].   [206] Ibid., [70].

[207] Ibid., [73]. See also E.P. Ellinger, E. Lomnicka, & R. Hooley, *Modern Banking Law* (4th edn., Oxford, 2005), 498–499.

[208] Bryan, n.179 above, 188.   [209] N.40 above, [77].   [210] Ibid., [76].

[211] Ibid., [78].

Nova Scotia.[212] The *Lipkin Gorman* doctrine would probably protect the bank where it was able to establish that, in direct reliance on the receipt of the funds, it released a security furnished by the customer or approved his application for a facility such as a letter of credit or a line of credit. In each case, however, the bank would have to establish, as a point of fact, that the money was paid to the customer or that a facility or some other financial accommodation was granted to him in direct reliance on the funds received by the bank.

A more difficult issue is whether a change in the bank's position could be pleaded even where the bank was negligent. This issue could, for instance, arise where, due to an error, the message requesting the recipient bank to credit its customer's account was communicated twice by the remitting bank. If, in consequence, the recipient bank made two credit entries in the account and allowed the customer to withdraw the total amount, could the bank plead the change in its position resulting from the extra payment as a defence to action in restitution instituted by the remitting bank? Under *Gowers'* case, the payment over of the funds appears to have been treated as a defence *per se*, provided only the payment to the customer was made in good faith. Similarly, it seems that the recipient bank will not be precluded from raising a change of position defence merely because it was negligent, for instance, in failing to notice the patent error made by the remitting bank.[213] The mistaken payor can recover no matter how negligent it has been,[214] and so the recipient bank should be treated no differently. Good faith on the part of the recipient is considered to be a sufficient requirement.[215]

5 Recovery problems in cases of negotiable instruments

(i) **Special problems**

As pointed out at the outset, some special problems arise where money is paid by a bank under a mistake pertaining to the discharge of a negotiable instrument.[216] In the first place, it is necessary to define the meaning of 'operative mistake' in cases of this type. Secondly, there is a controversy concerning the effect of a change in the payee's position on the bank's right to demand repayment. As the House of Lords did not decide in *Lipkin Gorman*[217] that this type of case would, in the future, be governed by the general defence, it is, at this stage, best to regard the authorities involved as not having been superseded. It is, at the same time, necessary to consider the likely effect of *Lipkin Gorman* on the principles derived from them. This is particularly so as there is an inconsistency in the existing case law as regards the result of a delay in the bank's demand for repayment. It is,

---

[212] N.22 above, [62]–[65].

[213] *Dextra Bank & Trust Co. Ltd* v. *Bank of Jamaica*, n.49 above, [45] (any attempt to apportion loss according to the parties' relative fault would make the defence 'hopelessly unstable'). See also *Niru Battery Manufacturing Co.* v. *Milestone Trading Ltd*, n.130 above, 738, affd. on appeal n.137 above; *Niru Battery Manufacturing Co.* v. *Milestone Trading Ltd (No. 2)* [2004] EWCA Civ 487, [33]; cf. *Commerzbank AG* v. *Gareth Price-Jones*, n.105 above (defendant changed his position as a result of his own negligence so not equitable to allow him to rely on the defence).

[214] *Banque Financière de la Cité* v. *Parc (Battersea) Ltd*, n.8 above, 227, 235, 242–243; *Scottish Equitable plc* v. *Derby*, n.111 above, [25].

[215] *Dextra*, n.49 above, [45]; *Niru (No. 2)*, n.213 above, [33]. See also Sect. 3(iii)(a) above.

[216] *Lomax Leisure Ltd* v. *Miller*, n.3 above, [53].

[217] *Lipkin Gorman (a firm)* v. *Karpnale Ltd*, n.8 above, 578–579.

occasionally, said that the payee's position is automatically affected, as the delay precludes him from giving notice of dishonour to his transferee.

The two questions require separate treatment. It is, however, important to define the scope of the relevant doctrines. It can now be regarded as well established that the principles involved apply only to genuine negotiable instruments. Where an instrument is avoided as a result of forgery,[218] or of material alterations made to it,[219] or is non-negotiable due to a technicality,[220] the position is governed by the general principles of the law of restitution discussed earlier.[221] The cases, however, are not altogether consistent, as in a number of instances the point was not raised.

(ii) Nature of operative mistake

Basically, two types of mistakes may induce a bank to pay a negotiable instrument. The first relates to the bank's mandate. The second relates to its liability to pay. Different circumstances may mislead a bank as regards its mandate. First, it may fail to recognize the forgery of its customer's signature.[222] Secondly, its mandate may be vitiated by a fraudulent alteration of a material detail, such as the raising of the cheque's amount.[223] Thirdly, the bank may pay the cheque to a person who holds it under a forged indorsement of the ostensible payee's signature.[224] Fourthly, it may pay a cheque because it overlooks the customer's countermand. Here, too, the bank pays in the belief that it has the authority to do so whilst, in reality, its mandate has been revoked. There can be no doubt that a mistake involving the bank's failure to recognize a forgery or material alteration is fundamental. Accordingly, such a mistake is operative.[225] Moreover, the bank is not under a general duty to 'recognize its customer's signature'.[226] There is therefore nothing to prevent the bank from pleading the mistake. The only questions that arise relate to the payee's change of position.[227]

At one time it was uncertain whether the bank could recover payment where it overlooked its customer's countermand. In *Commonwealth Trading Bank* v. *Reno Auto Sales Ltd*,[228] Gillard J thought that recovery would be disallowed, as such a mistake was between

---

[218]   BEA 1882, s.24; *Bank of England* v. *Vagliano Bros.* [1891] AC 107.   [219]   Ibid., s.64.

[220]   For example, if a conditional order is included instead of an unconditional order, in which case it may, however, be valid between the parties.

[221]   *Imperial Bank of Canada* v. *Bank of Hamilton*, n.50 above; *National Westminster Bank Ltd* v. *Barclays Bank International Ltd* [1975] QB 654.

[222]   *Price* v. *Neal* (1762) 3 Burr. 1354; *Smith* v. *Mercer* (1815) 6 Taunt. 76; *Cocks* v. *Masterman* (1829) 9 B & C 902; *Imperial Bank of India* v. *Abeyesinghe* (1927) 29 NLR (Ceylon) 257; *National Westminster Bank Ltd* v. *Barclays Bank International Ltd*, n.211 above.

[223]   *Imperial Bank of Canada* v. *Bank of Hamilton*, n.50 above. The bank here claimed back the difference between the genuine amount of the cheque and the amount to which it had been raised. As the instrument was, however, avoided, the bank appears to have paid without any mandate; it should therefore have been allowed to recover the full amount. See also *Smith* v. *Lloyds TSB Bank plc*, n.186 above.

[224]   *London and River Plate Bank Ltd* v. *Bank of Liverpool Ltd* [1896] 1 QB 7.

[225]   Cf. *Hart* v. *Frontino and Bolivia South American Gold Mining Co. Ltd* (1870) LR 5 Ex. 623, 1652; *Simm* v. *Anglo-American Telegraph Co.* (1879) 5 QBD 188, 196 (where Lindley LJ restricted his dictum to the impossibility of recovering the money from a *bona fide* holder for value); *Dominion Bank* v. *Jacobs* [1951] 3 DLR 233 (mistake as to forgery held not to be between payor and payee). Cf. *Royal Bank of Canada* v. *R.* [1931] 2 DLR 685.

[226]   *London and River Plate Bank Ltd* v. *Bank of Liverpool Ltd*, n.224 above; *National Westminster Bank Ltd* v. *Barclays Bank International Ltd*, n.211 above.

[227]   Sect. 5(iii) below.

[228]   N.45 above; on the facts, his Honour decided that the countermand had been ineffective and that, accordingly, no mistake had been made by the bank. But he thought that, even if the countermand had

the bank and the drawer and not, as required, between the bank (payor) and the payee. It has been pointed out above that this analysis is wrong.[229] The better view is that the bank's mistake is operative as it concerns the very motive of its payment, namely its belief in the existence of the customer's mandate. Recent authorities have consistently held that such a mistake entitles the bank to recover the amount paid in an action in restitution.[230] Again, the payee may resist the action where he has changed his position.

It may be argued that the principle in point is decidedly slanted in the bank's favour. Why should the bank be allowed to recover an amount paid by it owing to a mistake incurred as a result of its own carelessness? Despite the convincing thrust of this rhetorical question, there are three strong arguments in favour of the bank's right of recovery. First, the payee gains a windfall. If the bank obeys the countermand order and dishonours the cheque, the payee is without any remedy against it. He has to settle his dispute with the drawer. It follows that, when he is required to refund the amount paid due to the bank's oversight, he is in no worse a position than he would have been in if the bank had followed the drawer's instructions. Secondly, except where the *Liggett* doctrine is applicable,[231] the bank may be unable to debit the drawer's account. It is unreasonable to expect the bank to bear a loss occasioned as a result of the dispute that has induced the drawer to stop the cheque delivered by him to the payee. Thirdly, the very notion of an action in restitution is that money paid due to a mistake of fact is recoverable despite the payor's negligence.[232]

There is an uncertainty as regards the bank's right to recover an amount paid due to an error concerning the drawer's balance. In *Chambers* v. *Miller*,[233] the payee was in the process of counting the money paid to him against a cheque he had just presented to the bank, when the teller discovered that the drawer's account had an inadequate balance. The teller attempted to take the money back from the payee by force. The payee's action in assault was successful. Furthermore, all the judges in the Court of Common Pleas held that the bank was not entitled to recover the money. Byles and Williams JJ expressed the view that the bank's mistake about the customer's balance was immaterial.[234] Erle CJ rested his decision on the fact that the error was not between the payor and the payee.[235] The ratio of the case, however, concerned the action in assault.

---

been effective, the action would fail. See also *Royal Bank of Canada* v. *Boyce* (1966) 57 DLR (2d) 683. *Barclays & Co. Ltd* v. *Malcolm & Co.*, n.58 above, discussed in the text to n.58 above, supports the same view but, undoubtedly, turned on its special facts.

[229] Sect. 3(ii) above.

[230] *Southland Savings Bank* v. *Anderson*, n.62 above; *Barclays Bank Ltd* v. *W. J. Simms, Son & Cooke (Southern) Ltd*, n.51 above; *Commonwealth Bank of Australia Ltd* v. *Younis*, n.51 above; *Bank of New South Wales* v. *Murphett*, n.142 above; *Toronto-Dominion Bank* v. *Pella/Hunt Corp.*, n.70 above, 635–637. See also *Commonwealth Trading Bank of Australia* v. *Kerr*, n.62 above; *Bank of New South Wales* v. *Deri* , n.62 above. Luntz, n.3 above, 310, refers also to a South African case: *Natal Bank Ltd* v. *Roorda*, 1903 TH 298.

[231] Sect. 3(iii)(b) above. Where it is argued that the *Liggett* doctrine is inapplicable in cases of countermand, unless there is subsequent ratification of the bank's actions.

[232] *Kelly* v. *Solari*, n.41 above, 59; *Banque Financière de la Cité* v. *Parc (Battersea) Ltd*, n.8 above, 227, 235, 242–3; *Kleinwort Benson Ltd* v. *Lincoln City Council*, n.6 above; *Scottish Equitable plc* v. *Derby*, n.106 above, 800, affd. n.111 above, [25]; *Dextra Bank & Trust Co. Ltd* v. *Bank of Jamaica*, n.49 above, [45]; *National Bank of Egypt International Ltd* v. *Oman Housing Bank SAOC*, n.111 above, [26]; *Abou-Rahmah* v. *Abacha*, n.128 above, [47]; *Test Claimants in the FII Group Litigation* v. *Revenue and Customs Commissioners*, n.35 above, [328].

[233] (1862) 13 CB (NS) 125.   [234] Ibid., 136.   [235] Ibid., 134.

In *Pollard* v. *Bank of England*,[236] a bank paid a bill of exchange domiciled at its premises because it overlooked that the acceptor's account had insufficient funds and, further, that he had countermanded payment.[237] It was held that under these circumstances the mistake was inoperative. This decision is no longer good law as regards the mistake relating to the stop order. The finding that the mistake concerning the insufficiency of funds was likewise inoperative was based on the fact that it was not an error between the payor and the payee. This argument has been shown to run counter to modern authority.

A different reason for the principle suggested in *Pollard*'s case is to be found in *Barclays Bank Ltd* v. *W. J. Simms, Son & Cooke (Southern) Ltd*.[238] Here, Robert Goff J pointed out that where the bank pays a cheque due to a mistake about the available balance, it still acts within the scope of its mandate. It therefore remains entitled to debit the customer's account and the bank's payment discharges the customer's obligation to the payee on the cheque. The bank may, presumably, be regarded as having assented to a request made by the customer for the extension of overdraft facilities.[239]

There are, however, two difficulties with this reasoning. One is that the bank's right to debit its customer's account is of very little value where he becomes insolvent.[240] This, of course, is the very case in which the bank seeks to recover the money from the payee. The other is that it is unrealistic to regard a bank that pays a cheque, or executes some other form of payment instruction, because of a mistake relating to the customer's balance as assenting to a request for an overdraft.[241] Undoubtedly, the bank does not make a mistake concerning its mandate. But it makes a mistake concerning its duty to pay. Thus, the customer's balance may be incorrectly stated due to his account having been credited twice with a single payment received by the bank. Alternatively, the balance may be based on the proceeds of forged or converted cheques which are reclaimable from the bank. In all these cases, the bank is under the genuine impression that the customer has adequate funds for meeting his cheques. The bank therefore erroneously believes that it is bound to honour them.

It is difficult to see why such a mistake is to be regarded as inoperative. The mistake is fundamental in that it is the sole cause of the bank's decision to make payment. In effect, it is as compelling as a mistake concerning the bank's mandate. Both types of mistake mislead the bank as regards its proper course of business or its legal obligations. It has to be conceded that the position differs where the 'swelled up' balance is based on uncleared effects remitted to the bank by the customer. The bank takes a calculated risk when it obeys his orders and pays cheques drawn by him against uncleared funds. It is certainly not bound to do so.[242] On the basis of Robert Goff J's dictum, the bank cannot, thereafter, be heard to plead a mistake. But where the bank does not act as a volunteer, its mistake about the customer's balance appears a fundamental one.

It is, therefore, believed that the proposition that a bank's error about the sufficiency of the customer's balance is inoperative is too sweeping. Where the mistake misleads the

---

[236] (1871) LR 6 QB 623. See also *Woodland* v. *Fear* (1857) 7 El. & Bl. 519, which has been generally doubted in *Prince* v. *Oriental Banking Corporation* (1878) 3 App. Cas. 325.

[237] The domicile bank was, thus, in the same position as if a customer had stopped a cheque drawn on it for which, further, his account had inadequate funds.

[238] N.51 above.

[239] Ibid. 699–700. See also *Lloyds Bank plc* v. *Independent Insurance Co. Ltd*, n.142 above, 118. (considered in Sect. 3(iii)(b) above).

[240] Cf. Luntz, n.3 above, 330.

[241] This reasoning is sound, however, where the bank is fully aware that it is extending overdraft facilities to its customer: *Lloyds Bank plc* v. *Voller* [2000] 2 All ER (Comm.) 982 (CA).

[242] Ch. 11, Sect. 1(ii) above.

bank about its duty to obey the customer's instruction, the amount paid ought, in principle, to be recoverable.[243]

(iii) **Payee's change of position**

As discussed previously,[244] the House of Lords in *Lipkin Gorman a firm)* v. *Karpnale Ltd*[245] accepted as a general principle that a payee, who has changed his position in good faith relying upon a payment made to him, would have a valid *pro tanto* defence to any claim against him for restitution of the monies that he received. Long before *Lipkin Gorman*, however, at a time when a generalized change of position defence was persistently rejected by the courts in respect of mainstream restitutionary actions, a related defence was recognized in respect of actions for the recovery of money paid in discharge of negotiable instruments. The early recognition of such a defence was linked to the need for dealings in negotiable instruments to be handled promptly. Accordingly, the drawee of a bill of exchange or cheque must decide forthwith whether to honour or to dishonour the instrument when the holder or payee makes presentment. Furthermore, where the relevant instrument is dishonoured, the holder is required to give notice of dishonour within a reasonable time,[246] as well as carry out any required noting or protest.[247] As a result, a holder or payee who presents a bill of exchange or cheque for payment expects to have the drawee's prompt advice of its fate and will generally expect the answer given to him to be the final one.[248] The legal principles, developed in the light of this universal expectation of merchants, require a careful analysis. The implications of *Lipkin Gorman* are considered after the discussion of the earlier case law in point.

At one stage, the courts took the view that, because of the nature of dealings in negotiable instruments, it would not usually be possible to bring a restitutionary action to recover any payments made according to the tenor of a negotiable instrument, even when the drawee could demonstrate that he was mistaken in making payment. This was certainly the view of Lord Mansfield in *Price* v. *Neal*.[249] Subsequently, in *Cocks* v. *Masterman*,[250] the position was explained in a different manner. In *Cocks*, a bank paid a bill of exchange that had been domiciled at its premises by the acceptor. Although the acceptor was a customer, the bank did not recognize that his purported signature was a forgery and honoured the instrument. Bayley J held that recovery was barred, since the holder was entitled to give notice of dishonour on the very day on which a bill was not met. According to his Lordship, as the parties 'who pay the bill ought not by their negligence to deprive the holder of any right or privilege',[251] the holder is entitled to know the bill's fate on the day of presentment. Once this day was over, the potential prejudice caused to the holder by not being able to give notice of dishonour to prior parties meant that the

---

[243] But subject to any available defences (Sect. 3(iii) above).   [244] Sect. 3(iii)(a) above.

[245] N.8 above.   [246] BEA 1882, s.49(12). See further Ch. 10, Sect. 5(iii) above.

[247] Ibid., s.51(9). See further Ch. 10, Sect. 5(iv) above.

[248] In *National Westminster Bank Ltd* v. *Barclays Bank International Ltd*, n.211 above, Kerr J thought that the special presentment of the cheque involved a tacit enquiry about cover, but not about the authenticity of the instrument. Accordingly, a bank would not expect such a presentment to be related to the holder's doubts about the drawer's signature. There is force in this view given that cheques drawn on United Kingdom banks are rarely negotiated in practice—most cheques will nowadays be crossed 'account payee' or 'account payee only' and accordingly will be non-transferable under the Cheques Act 1992.

[249] N.222 above. In *BMP Global Distribution Inc* v. *Bank of Nova Scotia*, n.22 above, [31], [71], Deschamps J refused to 'accept that [Price] provides a basis for an unqualified rule that a drawee will never have any recourse against either the collecting bank or the payee where payment has been made on the forged signature of the drawer'.

[250] N.222 above.   [251] Ibid., 908–9.

payment should be treated as final and irrecoverable.[252] Jervis CJ expressed a similar view in *Mather* v. *Maidstone*,[253] the bank ought to be deprived of the right to recover where it had had the means of satisfying itself of its liability to pay the instrument. Obviously, this would have been a narrower principle than that suggested either in *Price* or *Cocks*, but in *London and River Plate Bank Ltd* v. *Bank of Liverpool Ltd*,[254] in which a bank attempted to recover the amount of a bill bearing forged indorsements several months after payment, Mathew J reverted to the reasoning of the earlier cases. His Lordship thought that, if a mistake was discovered promptly, the money paid under it could possibly be recovered; but if 'the money is paid in good faith, and is received in good faith, and there is an interval of time in which the position of the holder may be altered, the principle seems to apply that money once paid cannot be recovered back'.[255] Mathew J thought that such a change in position was bound to take place due to the lapse of time.[256]

This principle came before the Privy Council in *Imperial Bank of Canada* v. *Bank of Hamilton*,[257] in which a cheque for $5 was presented by its drawer to the drawee bank, who agreed to 'mark' it. In Canada, this procedure was akin to an acceptance. The drawer then fraudulently raised the amount of the cheque to $500 and remitted it for collection to another bank. Initially, the drawee bank honoured the cheque, but when the fraud was uncovered the next morning, the drawee bank served a demand for repayment of the excessive amount forthwith on the collecting bank. Lord Lindley observed that, under the circumstances, the collecting bank was not adversely affected by the delay in notice; that, in any event, the instrument in question was a total forgery and hence not a negotiable instrument; and that the drawer who had committed the forgery was not entitled to notice of dishonour. Accordingly, the rule propounded in cases such as *Price* was inapplicable. Lord Lindley's point concerning notice of dishonour is unexceptional. In virtually all the cases in which the bank reclaims money paid in respect of a negotiable instrument, the payee is not required to give notice of dishonour to the party from whom he obtained it. Thus, if the instrument is a cheque that has been countermanded, the payee need not give notice of dishonour to the drawer.[258] As against a previous indorser, notice of dishonour may be given when repayment is claimed. The delay occasioned by circumstances beyond the payee's control is excused.[259] This is also the case where repayment is demanded on the basis of a forgery which is not noticed when the instrument is presented for payment, or because of any other operative mistake made by the bank. Moreover, it is questionable whether the instrument may be regarded as having been dishonoured at the time of payment when, in reality, the bank purported to discharge it! It is true that in *Barclays Bank Ltd* v. *W.J. Simms, Son & Cooke (Southern) Ltd*, Robert Goff J thought that, where the money is recovered, the bill is to be regarded as not having been paid at all so that it would have to be treated as dishonoured on presentment. It is, however, hard to see how a subsequent development can change what has taken place at the time of the presentment of the bill.[260]

It has to be conceded that the above argument based on *Bank of Hamilton*—that in cases involving mistaken payments made pursuant to the terms of a negotiable

---

[252] Cf. *Wilkinson* v. *Johnson* (1823) 3 B & C 428, where repayment was demanded on the very day of dishonour.   [253] (1856) 18 CB 273, 295.

[254] N.224 above. See also *Morison* v. *London County and Westminster Bank Ltd* [1914] 3 KB 356.

[255] N.224 above, 11.

[256] Mathew J thought that the change in position could take place even where the mistake was drawn to the payee's attention on the same day.   [257] N.50 above.

[258] BEA, s.50(2)(c) (case 5). See also *Barclays Bank Ltd* v. *W. J. Simms, Son & Cooke (Southern) Ltd*, n.51 above.   [259] Ibid., s.50(1).

[260] N.51 above, 702. See also *Bank of New South Wales* v. *Murphett*, n.142 above.

instrument the payee does not lose his right of recourse against prior parties by reason of his failure to give notice and extend protest—awaits decision. If it were accepted, however, the result would be that a mere delay in the drawee's claim for repayment would not cause detriment to the payee.[261] Support for the view that there is no absolute defence available to the payee as a result of the drawee's delay in pursuing his claim can be found in the Canadian Supreme Court's decision in *BMP Global Distribution Inc* v. *Bank of Nova Scotia*.[262] Deschamps J, who was unable to find a satisfactory interpretation for the rule in *Price* v. *Neal*,[263] did not accept that *Price* 'provides a basis for an unqualified rule that a drawee will never have any recourse against either the collecting bank or the payee where payment has been made on the forged signature of the drawer'.[264] Whilst it remains open to the English courts to follow the older authorities, given that these are built on the reasonable expectations of commercial men, it is submitted that the approach in *BMP Global* is preferable—as soon as one recognizes that there is no absolute defence available to payees of negotiable instruments, but that the defence depends upon the effect of delay or other factors upon the payee's *particular circumstances*, the rule in *Price* becomes difficult to distinguish from the general change of position defence.[265] Indeed, in *Lipkin Gorman (a firm)* v. *Karpnale Ltd*,[266] Lord Goff suggested that the defence in *Price* and *Cocks* might be species of change of position. Accordingly, were the scope of that defence to be considered again, a court might simply subsume *Price* into the more generalized change of position defence. The focus would then be upon whether the payee had in good faith changed his position in a relevant way. Despite the more generous approach to the change of position defence recently,[267] it would not cover expenditure that would have been incurred in any event, regardless of the mistaken payment or mere delay on the part of the drawee in asserting their claims, unless this was also accompanied by a valid change of position.[268]

6 Proprietary restitutionary claims

(i) At common law

So far we have considered the payor's personal restitutionary claim at common law against the *direct* recipient of a mistaken payment. To establish such a claim it is unnecessary for the payor to show that he retained legal title to the money mistakenly paid away. All that the mistaken payor need establish is that he had legal title to the money before payment was made so that he can claim that the direct recipient has been unjustly

---

[261] Cf. *Barclays Bank Ltd* v. *W.J. Simms, Son & Cooke (Southern) Ltd*, n.51 above, in which Robert Goff J took the view that a change in the payee's position constituted a defence to an action for the recovery of the money paid against a countermanded cheque, but did not indicate whether a mere delay would suffice. The point was left open in *Bank of New South Wales* v. *Murphett*, n.142 above. Kerr J's decision in *National Westminster Bank Ltd* v. *Barclays Bank International Ltd*, n.211 above, to the effect that a change in the payee's position furnished no defence, has to be distinguished. In that case, his Lordship considered the action for the recovery of money paid against a forged cheque to be governed by the general law of restitution and not by the cases respecting the discharge of genuine and valid negotiable instruments. The fundamental legal principle in point has since been drastically changed in *Lipkin Gorman*.

[262] N.22 above; cf *Bank of Montreal* v. *R* (1907) 38 SCR 258.   [263] N.222 above.

[264] N.22 above, [31], [35], [71].

[265] The generalized change of position defence applies to mistaken payments made on forged cheques: *BMP Global Distribution Inc* v. *Bank of Nova Scotia*, n.22 above, [62].

[266] N.8 above, 578.   [267] *Commerzbank AG* v. *Gareth Price-Jones*, n.105 above, [39].

[268] Uniform Commercial Code, s.3–418.

enriched at the payor's expense.[269] As there is a direct relationship between payor and payee, following or tracing is not required to show that the payee received his enrichment at the expense of the payor.[270] This would explain, for example, why neither following nor tracing was in issue in *Simms*.[271]

The position is different where the mistaken payment reaches the recipient via a third party, for the *indirect* recipient's enrichment will not be at the payor's expense but at that of the third party.[272] In such circumstances, the payor must assert a proprietary claim based on the fact that he has retained, or has been revested with, legal title to the money paid by mistake. If the mistaken payor is able to follow or trace *his* money at law[273] into the hands of the indirect recipient he will be able to hold the recipient personally liable for money had and received.[274] Vindication of the claimant's property rights, and not unjust enrichment, lies at the heart of the claim.[275] Being a personal action, the recipient is liable at the moment of receipt; it does not matter for the purposes of the cause of action that he may not have retained the property.[276]

Lipkin Gorman (a firm) v. *Karpnale Ltd*[277] provides a good example of an action for money had and received against an indirect recipient. Money was stolen from the claimant firm of solicitors by one of its partners who had gambled with it at the defendant's casino. The House of Lords held that the defendant was liable to make restitution to the claimant. The defendant was the indirect recipient of the claimant's money, it having reached the casino via the rogue partner, and so it was necessary for the claimant 'to establish a basis on which he is entitled to the money. This (at least, as a general rule) he does by showing that the money is his legal property'.[278] However, Lord Goff emphasized that the claimant's claim 'is not a proprietary claim, advanced on the basis that money remaining in the hands of the club is their property'.[279] The claim was for the personal remedy of money had and received. One of the difficulties with the case is that Lord Goff's emphasis on the money remaining the claimant's legal property is not easy to reconcile

---

[269] L. Smith, 'Tracing and Electronic Funds Transfers' in Rose (ed.), n.158 above, 129–30.

[270] Ibid., 130–1. Tracing is necessary when making a claim to a substituted asset against a direct recipient.

[271] N.51 above. Contrast *Bank Tejarat* v. *Hong Kong and Shanghai Banking Corp. (CI) Ltd* [1995] 1 Lloyd's Rep. 239, at 245, col. 2, where Tuckey J rejected an argument that tracing was not required when a claim was made in money had and received based on a transfer of funds which was induced by fraud. Smith argues that the *Tejarat* case should be seen as one of direct transfer from claimant to recipient with all intermediate banks that participated in the funds transfer process acting as agents for one side or the other: n.269 above, 131–2.

[272] A. Tettenborn, 'Lawful Receipt—A Justifying Factor?' (1997) 5 *RLR* 1.

[273] The orthodox view is that it is not possible to trace at law where money has passed through a clearing system and, in the process, been mixed with other funds. See Ch. 7, Sect. 4(v)(a) above.

[274] As a general rule, the common law has no proprietary remedies, so that the claimant is left to claim the value of his property rather than the property itself: *Trustee of the Property of F. C. Jones and Sons (a firm)* v. *Jones* [1997] Ch. 159, 168 (CA).

[275] But contrast, P.B.H. Birks, 'Property and Unjust Enrichment: Categorical Truths' [1997] *NZ Law Rev.* 623; A. Burrows, 'Proprietary Restitution: Unmasking Unjust Enrichment' (2001) 117 *LQR* 412. For the view presented in the text, see R. Grantham and C. Rickett, 'Property and Unjust Enrichment: Categorical Truths or Unnecessary Complexity?' [1997] *NZ Law Rev.* 668; *Enrichment and Restitution in New Zealand* (Oxford, 2000), ch. 3; and 'Tracing and Property Right: the Categorical Truth' (2000) 63 *MLR* 905; and also G. Virgo, n.26 above, ch. 1. The speeches of Lords Browne-Wilkinson, Hoffmann, and Millett in *Foskett* v. *McKeown*, n.98 above, 108, 115, 127, 129, draw a clear line between claims to vindicate property rights and those to reverse unjust enrichment.

[276] *Agip (Africa) Ltd* v. *Jackson* [1990] Ch. 265, 285, Millett J. Payment away may give the recipient a defence of ministerial receipt or change of position.

[277] N.8 above.   [278] Ibid., at 572, *per* Lord Goff.   [279] Ibid.

with his conclusion that the solicitors' claim 'is founded upon the unjust enrichment of the club, and can only succeed if, in accordance with the principles of the law of restitution, the club was indeed unjustly enriched at the expense of the solicitors'.[280]

Some commentators have argued that the claim in *Lipkin Gorman* was founded on the reversal of the defendant's unjust enrichment, with the ground of restitution or the 'unjust factor' being that the claimant was ignorant that the money had been stolen.[281] Alternatively, it has been argued that the claim was simply concerned with the vindication of the claimant's property rights in the money, those rights having been retained because the money had been stolen.[282] We are persuaded that this alternative analysis is the correct one for the following reasons. First, it is consistent with the fact that Lord Goff, delivering the leading judgment, emphasized the fact that the claimant had a persisting legal interest in the money. Secondly, none of the judges identified the particular ground of restitution, or 'unjust factor' upon which a claim based on unjust enrichment would depend. Thirdly, it reflects the important division between the law of property and the law of unjust enrichment, a division highlighted by the House of Lords in *Foskett* v. *McKeown*.[283] In that case, where trust money was used by a trustee in breach of trust to pay certain premiums on his own life assurance policy, the beneficiaries' claim was based on their continuing beneficial interest in the insurance money paid out on the trustee's death. Allowing the beneficiaries' claim, Lord Millett stated:[284]

> The transmission of a claimant's property rights from one asset to its traceable proceeds is part of our law of property, not the law of unjust enrichment. There is no 'unjust factor' to justify restitution (unless 'want of title' be one, which makes the point). The claimant succeeds if at all by virtue of his own title, not to reverse unjust enrichment.

As the proprietary claim was to vindicate the beneficiaries' equitable rights, and the property was still in the defendant's hands, a proprietary remedy was granted.[285]

The problem for the mistaken payor is that he must establish that he still has legal title to the money paid by mistake. He must show either that he has retained a continuing proprietary interest because the mistake was so fundamental that title to the money did not pass to the recipient, or that the mistake was induced by a fraudulent representation enabling the payor to elect to rescind the transaction at law and revest title in himself. As a general rule, the fact the claimant is mistaken does not prevent legal title to money passing to the recipient.[286] The payment was made intentionally despite the fact that it was based on a mistaken motive.[287] On the other hand, a mistake will be fundamental, and title will not pass, where the payor intends to pay X, but transfers funds to Y, there being

---

[280] Ibid., at 578.

[281] P.B.H. Birks, 'The English Recognition of Unjust Enrichment' [1991] *LMCLQ* 473, and E. McKendrick, 'Restitution, Misdirected Funds and Change of Position' (1992) 55 *MLR* 377.

[282] G. Virgo, 'What is the Law of Restitution About?' in W. Cornish *et al.* (eds.), *Restitution: Past, Present and Future* (Oxford, 1998), 314–16; D. Fox, n.86 above, paras. 9.19–9.29. This analysis was adopted by Ferris J in *Box* v. *Barclays Bank plc* [1998] Lloyd's Rep. Bank. 185, 201, col. 2, where he recognized that the claimant's claim in *Lipkin Gorman* was based on the fact that the money in which they had legal title could be traced into the defendant's hands. In fact, the claimant's money had probably become mixed with other funds so that it could no longer be traced in law, but the defendant conceded the point.

[283] N.98 above.   [284] Ibid., at 127.   [285] Ch. 7, Sect. 4(v) above.

[286] *Barclays Bank Ltd* v. *W. J. Simms, Son & Cooke (Southern) Ltd*, 689, where Robert Goff J said that legal title will 'almost invariably' pass where a mistaken payment is made.

[287] Even though legal title has passed the mistake still vitiates the payor's intention to benefit the *direct* recipient of the payment so that that payor will be able to recover the amount of the mistaken payment from the direct recipient under the principle of unjust enrichment.

a fundamental mistake of identity.[288] Moreover, it is arguable that mistakenly making a double payment is also fundamental. In *Chase Manhattan Bank NA* v. *Israel-British Bank (London) Ltd*,[289] where the claimant bank mistakenly made a second payment of US$2 million to the defendant, Goulding J assumed the payee took legal title to the payment and dealt with the claim in equity. This suggests that the mistake was not fundamental and should be treated as a case of overpayment resulting from a mistake about the transferor's liability to pay the recipient, where property in the excess would usually be deemed to pass to the recipient.[290] However, the better interpretation of the case is that legal title to the second payment of US$2 million was considered to have passed because the money became mixed in the defendant's bank account so that it was no longer possible to identify the claimant's property at law.[291] Mistakes about the essential identity of the property transferred are also fundamental so that legal title does not pass. Mistakes about the essential identity of money paid will be rare.[292]

In any event, even where the payor can establish that he retained legal title to the mistaken payment he will often be met by the defence of *bona fide* purchaser.[293] This defence applies at law where money that has passed into circulation as currency is received by the defendant in good faith and for value.[294] The *bona fide* purchaser is given a fresh title to the money and the original owner's title is destroyed.[295] The common law version of the defence is restricted to the *bona fide* purchase of money, including negotiable instruments. For this purpose 'money' has traditionally meant physical money, i.e., coins and notes. There is some doubt whether the defence also extends to the *bona fide* purchase of a bank deposit or other intangible money. It is arguable that the defence cannot apply to intangible money because it is not currency, legal title to which passes by delivery. However, the case for extending the defence to the *bona fide* purchase of a bank deposit or other intangible money is a strong one.[296] First, it does not matter that legal title to intangible money does not pass between the payor and the payee. The defence allows the *bona fide* purchaser to assert a fresh title to the asset, it does not give him a derivative title. Secondly, payment through the transfer of funds between bank accounts is now commonplace. It is part of modern commercial practice. The defence should reflect that practice just as in the past the courts have been willing to develop the defence to reflect commercial practice. There is a modern precedent in a related area. In *Esso Petroleum Co.*

---

[288] *R* v. *Hudson* [1943] KB 458; *R* v. *Middleton* (1873) LR 2 CCR 38; cf. *Citibank NA* v. *Brown Shipley and Co. Ltd*, n.84 above, 699 (Waller J emphasizing that identity must be 'a matter of crucial importance').

[289] [1981] Ch. 105. See Ch. 7, Sect. 4(v)(b)(i) above.

[290] D. Fox, 'The Transfer of Legal Title to Money' (1996) 4 *RLR* 60 at 66–7.

[291] G. Virgo, n.26 above, 586–588.

[292] Fox, n.290 above, at 66. Cf. *R.* v. *Ashwell* (1885) 16 QBD 190, 201, a criminal case, in which the victim gave the defendant a sovereign when he thought he was lending him a shilling. The mistake was as to the type of coin handed over. Cf. *R* v. *Potisk* (1973) 6 SASR 389.

[293] Revesting of legal title in the claimant through rescission will also be barred where property has already reached the hands of a *bona fide* purchaser for value. But the *bona fide* purchaser defence is not available where the claim is a personal one for unjust enrichment: *Papamichael* v. *National Westminster Bank plc*, n.99 above, [253].

[294] *Miller* v. *Race* (1758) 1 Burr. 452, 457–8. See also D. Fox, '*Bona Fide* Purchase and the Currency of Money' [1996] *CLJ* 547.

[295] The common law defence of *bona fide* purchase for value should not be confused with the separate equitable defence of *bona fide* purchase for value without notice: D. Fox, n.86 above, paras. 8.20–8.26.

[296] Some commentators simply take it for granted that the defence extends to intangible money. See, for example, Fox, n.294 above, 564, and L. Smith, 'Unjust Enrichment, Property and the Structure of Trusts' (2000) 116 *LQR* 412, 434, n.90; D. Fox, n.86 above, paras. 8.02–8.05, 8.36. See further R. Hooley, 'Payment in a Cashless Society' in B.A.K. Rider (ed.), *The Realm of Company Law* (London, 1998), at 256.

Ltd v. *Milton*,[297] the Court of Appeal was prepared to extend the no set-off rule, tradition-ally applied to payment by cheque, to payment by direct debit, on the ground that this reflected modern commercial practice.

What constitutes valuable consideration under the common law version of the *bona fide* purchaser defence is also a matter of controversy. The *bona fide* purchaser defence could not be established in the *Lipkin Gorman* case because the claimant's money had been transferred pursuant to an unlawful gambling transaction, and so the defendant casino could not be considered to have given value. Lords Templeman and Goff also suggested that a bank receiving a deposit of stolen money from a customer could not get title to it as *bona fide* purchaser.[298] The bank's obligation to repay its own deposi-tor would not constitute valuable consideration as against the true owner of the sto-len money. However, it is arguable that Lords Templeman and Goff were wrong on this issue.[299] They focused on the *equitable* defence of *bona fide* purchaser, which requires consideration to be *executed*, whereas with the *common law* version of the defence con-sideration need only be *executory*. If this is correct, then a bank which provides its cus-tomer with an unconditional promise to pay money does give value at law and gets an unimpeachable legal title to cash deposits and to value received in settlement for funds transfer instructions.[300]

(ii) In equity

Bringing an equitable proprietary claim and seeking a proprietary remedy can be advantageous from the claimant's point of view. Where the payee of an amount paid under a mistake of fact is insolvent, a proprietary remedy following on from the payor establishing an equitable interest in the money paid will enable him to recover the amount *in specie* and, effectively, in priority to the general creditors.

The general principles governing tracing in equity were discussed in Chapter 6. It will, however, be useful to demonstrate, at this point, the advantage which equitable trac-ing, and the availability of an equitable proprietary remedy, confers on a bank that seeks to recover an amount of money paid by it under a mistake of fact. *Chase Manhattan Bank NA* v. *Israel-British Bank (London) Ltd*[301] provides a good illustration. In this case, the claimant, a New York bank, was asked by one of its correspondents to pay a given amount to the M Bank, another New York bank, for the account of the defendant, an English bank. Due to an error, the claimant paid the amount twice. The claimant's personal claim for money had and received was not enough as the defendant bank was insolvent; the claimant's only hope of recovering the mistaken payment was to trace it in equity and assert a proprietary claim.[302] To do this, the claimant had to establish an equitable proprietary base upon which its proprietary claim could be built. Goulding J allowed the claim. He observed that such relief would be available under both the law of New York and that of England. His Lordship rejected the argument that equitable tracing would be

---

[297] [1997] 1 WLR 938.

[298] N.8 above, 562, 577. See also P.B.H. Birks, 'The Burden on the Bank' in Rose (ed.), n.158 above, 215; D. Fox, n.290 above, 63.

[299] D. Fox, n.86 above, paras. 8.37–8.38.

[300] L. Smith, *The Law of Tracing* (Oxford, 1997), 389; L. Smith, n.296 above, 434, n.90.

[301] N.289 above. See also *London Allied Holdings Ltd* v. *Lee* [2007] EWHC 2061 (Ch), [68]–[74]; *Duke of Norfolk* v. *Hibbert* [2009] EWHC 2855 (QB), [49]–[50]; *Governor & Company of the Bank of Ireland* v. *Pexxnet Ltd* [2010] EWHC 1872 (Comm.), [55]–[57].

[302] Goulding J assumed that the defendant bank took legal title to the payment and dealt with the claim in equity. See also Sect. 6(i) above.

available only where a fiduciary relationship existed between the payor and the payee at the time of payment. It was 'enough that...the payment into the wrong hands itself gave rise to a fiduciary relationship'.[303] According to Goulding J, such a relationship eventuated because a person who paid money to another under a factual mistake retained an equitable property in it, and the payee's conscience would be subjected to a fiduciary duty to respect this property right. The effect of the order so granted was that the claimant bank was allowed to recover the amount involved in full; it did not have to lodge a proof entitling it to a mere dividend.

In *Chase Manhattan* the claimant's equitable interest was generated by the law's response to the mistake. However, the reasoning of Goulding J has been subjected to sustained, authoritative criticism and the precise mechanism for generating that response remains uncertain.[304] It may be that the payor acquires an equitable interest in money paid by mistake by virtue of a constructive trust imposed on the payee from the moment the payee becomes aware of the mistake.[305] Alternatively, it has been argued that where the mistake is fundamental, as the mistake in *Chase Manhattan* might arguably have been,[306] but it is no longer possible to identify the claimant's money at law because it has been mixed in the payee's bank, the payor's intention to benefit the payee has been vitiated so that the money is held on resulting trust for the payor.[307]

---

[303] Ibid., at 119.

[304] See *Westdeutsche Landesbank Girozentrale* v. *Islington London Borough Council*, n.7 above, 715; P.J. Millett, n.37 above, 412–413. See also Ch. 7, Sect. 4(v)(b)(i) above. See generally D. Fox, n.86 above, paras. 4.149–4.157, 5.141–5.146.

[305] *Westdeutsche Landesbank*, n.7 above, at 715; *Papamichael* v. *National Westminster Bank plc*, n.99 above, 372; *Clark* v. *Cutland* [2003] 4 All ER 733, 743 (CA).

[306] Sect. 6(i) above.   [307] G. Virgo, n.26 above, 604.

13

The Giro System and Electronic Transfer of Funds

1 Introduction and basic concepts[1]

The word 'giro', which is used to describe money transfer operations, is derived from the Greek word for circle. Giro denotes the cyclical operation involved in the transfer of credit balances from one bank account into another. On the Continent, such systems have been used successfully for a considerable period of time as an alternative to the payment of accounts by cheque. Even in the United Kingdom, where payment by cheque was predominant for a considerable period of time,[2] the money transfer system is no novelty. In an elementary form, it has been operable for a long time by means of individual letters in which customers instructed their banks to pay given amounts of money to the credit of designated payees. As a fully operative system, providing an alternative to the settlement of accounts by cheque, the bank giro came into operation in the 1960s, in the wake of the introduction of the national giro, originally operated by the Post Office.[3] In the early

---

[1] For detailed coverage of the subject, see M. Hapgood (ed.), *Paget's Law of Banking* (13th edn., London, 2007), ch. 17; M. Brindle and R. Cox (eds.), *Law of Bank Payments* (4th edn., London, 2010), ch. 3; P. Cresswell *et al.* (eds.), *Encyclopaedia of Banking Law* (London, 1982, loose leaf), Division D1. For an outstanding treatment from an international perspective, see B. Geva, *The Law of Electronic Funds Transfers* (New York, 1992, updated with annual revisions); B. Geva, *Bank Collections and Payment Transactions—Comparative Study of Legal Aspects* (Oxford, 2001).

[2] Cheques are no longer the predominant means of non-cash payment in the United Kingdom. In 1990, cheques accounted for 57.7 per cent of the annual APACS (now UKPA) clearings volumes, whereas direct debits made up 19.9 per cent of those volumes (APACS, *Annual Review 2000* (London, 2001), App. II). By 2003, those figures were 26.4 per cent and 42.2 per cent respectively (APACS, *Annual Review 2003* (London, 2004), App. II). The volume of cheques cleared in 2008 dropped by over 10 per cent when compared to the previous year and the value of those clearings dropped by just under 7 per cent over the same period (UK Payments Council, *Annual Summary of Payment Clearing Statistics 2008* (London, 2009)). In the period between May 2008 and May 2009, cheque use dropped 12 per cent by volume and 13 per cent by value (UK Payments Council & APACS, *Clearing Statistics May 2009* (London, 2009)). The UK Payments Council has now recognized that cheques are 'in long-term decline' and initially canvassed 2018 as a possible closure date for cheque clearing in the United Kingdom: UK Payments Council, *National Payments Plan—Setting the Strategic Vision for UK Payments* (London, 14 May 2008), 6. By this time, the UK Payments Council has predicted that cheques will account for only two per cent of personal non-cash payments: *Annual Review 2008—Driving Change in UK Payments* (London, 2008), 11. Following an independent survey of cheque-users, however, the UK Payments Council appears to have softened its position somewhat and simply committed to developing 'a roadmap for the managed decline of cheques, including an agreed end date for the cheque clearing', and has made clear that 'the closure will not go ahead until alternatives are in place': *Progress Report—Delivering the National Payments Plan* (London, March 2009), 1–3. As part of this process, the UK Payments Council's aim is to close the cheque guarantee card scheme (discussed in Ch. 14, Sect. 4) by 30 June 2011 and cheque clearing by 31 October 2018: UK Payments Council, *Progress Report: Delivering the National Payments Plan* (June 2010), 1–3.

[3] Operations commenced in the 1960s. Subsequently, the Post Office (Banking Services) Act 1976 (widening the scope of the Post Office Act 1969, s.7(1)(b), which, basically, conferred only the power to engage in

1980s, the bank giro and the national giro became linked so that an amount could be transferred from an account maintained with a clearing bank to an account maintained with the National Girobank. Subsequently, in 1985, the National Girobank became a member of the clearing house. Later still, it was acquired by the Alliance and Leicester Building Society.[4] At present, Santander UK plc (which currently owns the business originally operated by (the National) Girobank) is a member of a number of the clearing companies operating under the umbrella of the UK Payments Administration Ltd (UKPA),[5] and the national giro has become amalgamated with the bank giro.

The bank giro system is a paper-based funds transfer system whereby the payer's money transfer order is conveyed manually from his own bank to that of the payee. In 2003, the bank giro accounted for only 2.4 per cent of the volume, and 0.1 per cent of the value, of clearings by the Association for Payment Clearing Services (APACS) (now UKPA).[6] Even when the paper-based bank giro and cheque clearing systems are taken together, they still only constituted 28.8 per cent of the volume, and 1.4 per cent of the value, of transactions that passed through the APACS (now UKPA) clearings in 2003.[7] Since then, the popularity of the paper-based bank giro has continued to decrease with the volume of inter-bank and inter-branch credits dropping by approximately 11 per cent during 2007, when compared to the previous year,[8] and by approximately 10 per cent and 14 per cent respectively during 2008.[9] By contrast, BACS and CHAPS, the main electronic funds transfer systems operating in the United Kingdom, accounted for 71.1 per cent of the volume, and 98.6 per cent of the value, of APACS (now UKPA) clearings in 2003.[10] Of these two electronic funds transfer systems, CHAPS has been predominant in terms of value, as it has traditionally been used for higher-value transactions. For example, in 2003, CHAPS payments represented a staggering 95.8 per cent of the £92,470 billion that passed through the APACS (now UKPA) clearings.[11] Whilst BACS transfers increased by approximately 3.4 per cent by volume, and 7.8 per cent by value, during 2007 when compared to the previous year,[12] and by 2 per cent and 6.8 per cent respectively during 2008 when compared to the previous year,[13] there has recently been a fairly dramatic decline in the volume and value of traditional CHAPS

giro activities) conferred on the Post Office the power to provide full banking services for its clients. See also the British Telecommunications Act 1981, s.58(1). Post Office Act 1969, s.7(1)(b) was replaced by the British Telecommunications Act 1981, s.58(1), which in turn has since been repealed by the Postal Services Act 2000, s.127(6) & Sched. 9. Pursuant to the Postal Services Act 2000, s.62, all the property, rights, and liabilities of the Post Office were transferred to Consignia plc (now called Royal Mail Holdings plc) on 26 March 2001. See also the Post Office Company (Nomination and Appointed Day) Order 2001, S.I. 2001/8.

    [4] Alliance and Leicester Building Society subsequently became Alliance and Leicester plc and then Alliance & Leicester Commercial Bank plc, which in turn became part of Grupo Santander in October 2008. In May 2010, Alliance & Leicester Commercial Bank plc transferred its business to Santander UK plc and began operating under the 'Santander' brand name. See Ch. 1, Sect. 2(i) above.

    [5] UK Payments Administration Ltd replaced the Association for Payment Clearing Services (APACS) on 6 July 2009.

    [6] APACS, *Annual Review 2003* (London, 2004), App.II.   [7] Ibid.

    [8] APACS, *Annual Summary of Clearing Statistics 2007* (London, March 2008), 3.

    [9] UK Payments Council & APACS, *Annual Summary of Payment Clearing Statistics 2008* (London, 2009), 3. Between May 2008 and May 2009, the use of paper-based credits decreased 12 per cent by volume and 13 per cent by value: UK Payments Council & APACS, *Clearing Statistics May 2009* (London, 2009), 1.

    [10] APACS, *Annual Review 2003* (London, 2004), App. II.   [11] Ibid.

    [12] APACS, *Annual Summary of Clearing Statistics 2007* (London, March 2008), 3.

    [13] UK Payments Council & APACS, *Annual Summary of Payment Clearing Statistics 2008* (London, 2009), 3. Interestingly, in the year between May 2008 and May 2009, the overall volume of BACS transfers dropped by 1 per cent, although the value of those transfers increased by 2 per cent: UK Payments Council & APACS, *Clearing Statistics May 2009* (London, 2009), 1. This slight decrease is chiefly attributable to the CHAPS 'Faster Payments Service' assuming responsibility for the execution of standing orders from 27 May 2008. see further Sects. 2(ii) and 3(iv)(b) below.

transfers. During 2007, traditional CHAPS transfers increased in volume by 7 per cent and in value by 15.5 per cent,[14] whilst during 2008 such transfers dropped 17.8 per cent by volume and 34.5 per cent by value.[15] This reversal is probably attributable to two factors: the closure of the CHAPS Euro clearing service on 16 May 2008 upon the replacement of the TARGET[16] system with the TARGET2 system;[17] and the introduction of the alternative CHAPS 'Faster Payments Service', which was used almost 83 million times between its launch on 27 May 2008 and the end of that year.[18] The latter innovation is designed to extend the benefits of CHAPS' technology to lower-value transactions, namely internet and phone payments for less than £10,000 and standing orders for less than £100,000, so that transfers can henceforth occur within hours, rather than on the previous three-day cycle.[19] Moreover, such transfers can be made all day, every day. The 'Faster Payments Service' has arguably brought about the demise of the paper-based bank giro, since, following a review,[20] the UK Payments Council has indicated that paper-based credit clearing is unlikely to last beyond the proposed end to cheque clearing by 31 October 2018.[21]

(i) **The nature of a giro transfer**

The common thread that runs through all giro operations, paper-based or electronic, is that they involve the movement of a credit balance from one account to another brought about through the adjustment of the balances to both the payer's and the payee's accounts.[22] The payer's account is debited and the payee's account is credited. This results in the debt owed to the payer by his bank being extinguished or reduced *pro tanto* (or, where his account is overdrawn, his liability to his bank being increased) by the amount of the transfer to the payee, whilst the debt owed to the payee by his own bank is increased (or, where his account is overdrawn, his liability is reduced) by the same amount. It is important to stress that there is no transfer of property by this process, simply the adjustment of the separate property rights (i.e. choses in action) of the payer and the payee against their respective banks.[23] It is, therefore, something of a misnomer to speak of the 'transfer' of funds as there is no actual transfer of coins or banknotes from the payer to the

---

[14] APACS, *Annual Summary of Clearing Statistics 2007* (London, March 2008), 3.

[15] UK Payments Council & APACS, *Annual Summary of Payment Clearing Statistics 2008* (London, 2009), 3. This trend has continued in the year between June 2008 and June 2009 with traditional CHAPS transfers decreasing 20 per cent by volume and 37 per cent by value: UK Payments Administration, *Clearing Statistics June 2009* (London, 2009), 1. Volumes continue to decline at an annual rate of 2.6 per cent and values at an annual rate of 12 per cent: UK Payments Administration, *Statistical Release—9 September 2010* (London, 2010), 7.

[16] 'TARGET' is an acronym for 'Trans-European Automated Real-Time Gross Settlement Express Transfer System'.

[17] European Central Bank, *Target Annual Report 2008* (Frankfurt, April 2009), 13. For a discussion of the change from the TARGET to TARGET2 system, see Sects. 1(iv)–(v) below.

[18] UK Payments Council & APACS, n.15 above, 3.

[19] For a list of founding members, see APACS Press Release, *Phased Roll Out for New Faster Payments Service* (London, 28 April 2008).

[20] Payments Council, *National Payments Plan—Setting the Strategic Vision for UK Payments* (London, 14 May 2008), 27; Payments Council, *Progress Report—Delivering the National Payments Plan* (London, March 2009), 5.

[21] UK Payments Council, *Progress Report: Delivering the National Payments Plan* (June 2010), 3.

[22] Usually the payer instructs his bank to debit his account with the amount of the transfer, but it is possible for a non-customer to instruct a bank to make a giro transfer simply by paying cash over the counter. Much turns on the practice of individual banks as to whether they will accept giro transfer instructions from non-customers. Where the payee does not have a bank account, the funds are usually deposited into a general account at the receiving bank, and left at the payee's disposal.

[23] *R v. Preddy* [1996] AC 815, 834 (HL), discussed in detail in Sect. 5(iii) below.

payee.[24] Moreover, there is no assignment of any debt that may be owed to the payer by his own bank.[25] As Staughton J observed in *Libyan Arab Foreign Bank* v. *Bankers Trust Co.*:[26]

> 'Transfer' may be a somewhat misleading word, since the original obligation is not assigned (notwithstanding dicta in one American case which speaks of assignment);[27] a new obligation by a new debtor is created.

Transfer of *value*, rather than the transfer of funds, is probably a more accurate description of the giro process.

(ii) Terminology

There has been some attempt to standardize the terminology in this area. This has arisen from the influence of Article 4A of the United States Uniform Commercial Code (UCC), which was adopted in 1989, and the UNCITRAL Model Law on International Credit Transfers (1992).[28] This terminology is summarized in the Prefatory Note to Article 4A of the UCC as follows:[29]

> X, a debtor, wants to pay an obligation owed to Y. Instead of delivering to Y a negotiable instrument such as a check or some other writing such as a credit card slip that enables Y to obtain payment from a bank, X transmits an instruction to X's bank to credit a sum of money to the bank account of Y. In most cases, X's bank and Y's bank are different banks. X's bank may carry out X's instruction by instructing Y's bank to credit Y's account in the amount that X requested. The instruction that X issues to its bank is a 'payment order'. X is the 'sender' of the payment order and X's bank is the 'receiving bank' with respect to X's order. Y is the 'beneficiary' of X's order. When X's bank issues an instruction to Y's bank to carry out X's payment order, X's bank 'executes' X's order. The instruction of X's bank to Y's bank is also a payment order. With respect to that order, X's bank is the sender, Y's bank is the receiving bank, and Y is the beneficiary. The entire series of transactions by which X pays Y is known as the 'funds transfer'. With respect to the funds transfer, X is the 'originator', X's bank is the 'originator's bank', Y is the 'beneficiary' and Y's bank is the 'beneficiary's bank'. In more complex transactions there are one or more additional banks known as 'intermediary banks' between X's bank and Y's bank. In the funds transfer, the instruction contained in the payment order of X to its bank is carried out by a series

---

[24] See *Foskett* v. *McKeown* [2001] 1 AC 102, 128 (HL), *per* Lord Millett: '[n]o money passes from paying bank to receiving bank or through the clearing system (where the money flows may be in the opposite direction) there is simply a series of credits and debits which are causally and transactionally linked'. See also *Customs and Excise Comrs.* v. *FDR Ltd* [2000] STC 672, [36]–[37] (CA); *Dovey* v. *Bank of New Zealand* [2000] 3 NZLR 641, 648 (NZCA); *European Bank Ltd* v. *Citibank Ltd* [2004] NSWCA 76, [57]–[62]; *Darkinjung Pty Ltd* v. *Darkinjung Local Aboriginal Land Council* [2006] NSWSC 1217, [13]; *Scottish Exhibition Centre Ltd* v. *Commissioners for Her Majesty's Revenue and Customs* [2008] STC 967, [19] (IH). See also D. Fox, *Property Rights in Money* (Oxford, 2008), [5.23]–[5.29].

[25] *R* v. *Preddy*, n.23 above (credit transfer); *Mercedez-Benz Finance Ltd* v. *Clydesdale Bank plc* [1997] CLC 81 (OH)(debit transfer). See further Sect. 5(iii) below.

[26] [1989] QB 728, 750.

[27] Presumably, Staughton J was referring to *Delbrueck & Co.* v. *Manufacturers Hanover Trust Co.*, 609 F 2d. 1047, 1051 (2nd Cir., 1979). See further Sect. 5(iii) below.

[28] On 25 November 1992, by Resolution 47/34, the United Nations General Assembly approved the UNCITRAL Report and Model Law on International Credit Transfers finalized at UNCITRAL's 25th Session of 4–22 May 1992: UN General Assembly, Official Records, 4th Session, Supp. No. 17, A/47/17.

[29] It should be noted, however, that Article 4A restricts the term 'funds transfer' to credit transfers and excludes debit transfers from its scope. In this chapter, the same terminology is used for both credit and debit transfers. For the idea of citing the Prefatory Note for this purpose, see R.M. Goode, *Commercial Law* (3rd edn., London, 2004), 466 (although this view is not repeated in the latest edition: E McKendrick, *Goode on Commercial Law* (4th edn., London, 2010)).

of payment orders by each bank in the transmission chain to the next bank in the chain until Y's bank receives a payment order to make the credit to Y's account.

This same terminology was adopted in the 'Credit Transfer Directive',[30] and accordingly became part of English law with the implementation of that Directive through the Cross-Border Credit Transfer Regulations 1999.[31] These regulations were, however, somewhat limited in scope, applying only to 'cross-border credit transfers'[32] that did 'not exceed 50,000 euro or its equivalent in another EEA currency'.[33] The 'Credit Transfer Directive' has now been replaced by the much wider 'Payment Services Directive',[34] which was incorporated into English law by the Payment Services Regulations 2009 (PSR 2009) from 1 November 2009.[35] These regulations apply generally to 'payment services', which is broadly defined and includes, *inter alia*, credit transfers and direct debits.[36] The supervisory and regulatory regime established by the regulations has been considered previously.[37] As considered further below,[38] Parts 5 and 6 of the PSR 2009 contain detailed provisions concerning the information that must be provided by banks or any other 'payment service provider'[39] to their customers engaged in funds transfers falling within their scope and a regime clarifying the rights and obligations of the parties to such a transaction—these have now entirely replaced the earlier provisions in the Cross-Border Credit Transfer Regulations 1999.

More importantly, for present purposes, PSR 2009 also introduce new terminology that differs from the earlier regulations. Although the terminology in the Cross-Border Credit Transfer Regulations 1999 had the advantage of not only being consistent with international instruments and domestic legislation in other jurisdictions, but also being specific to the context of electronic funds transfers,[40] it is nevertheless now appropriate to adopt the terminology of the new regulations given that they are so much broader in scope than their predecessor (not only applying to a broader range of payment transactions, but also applying to domestic and cross-border transactions alike)[41] and, therefore, are likely to be applicable far more frequently. Accordingly, this chapter will use the term 'payer' (rather than 'originator') to refer to the person who 'initiates or consents to the initiation

---

[30] Directive 97/5/EC on Cross-Border Credit Transfers [1997] OJ L43/25.

[31] S.I. 1999/1876 (in force 14 August 1999).

[32] Ibid., reg. 2(1): '…a transaction or series of transactions carried out as a result of instructions given directly by an originator to an institution in one EEA State, the purpose of which is to make funds in an EEA currency available to a beneficiary at an institution in another EEA State'.

[33] Id.

[34] Directive 2007/64/EC on Payment Services in the Internal Market [2007] OJ L319, Art. 93, repealing the earlier Directive 97/5/EC from 1 November 2009.

[35] S.I. 2009/209, reg. 1(2).

[36] Ibid., Sched. 1, para. 1(c). It appears that the definition of 'payment services' is limited to the situation where the funds are transferred by electronic rather than paper-based means, since the definition does not include 'payment transactions based on [paper-based vouchers] drawn on the payment service provider with a view to placing funds at the disposal of the payee': ibid., Sched. 1, para. 2(g)(iii). For the distinction between electronic and paper-based funds transfer systems, see Sect. 1(iv) below. For further discussion of the concept of 'payment services', see Ch. 2, Sect. 6(iii) above.

[37] See further Ch. 2, Sect. 6(iii) above.

[38] For the rights and obligations of the parties to a payment transaction covered by the Payment Services Regulations 2009, S.I. 2009/209 (PSR 2009), see Sects. 5(i) & (iv)–(vi) below.

[39] PSR 2009, reg. 2(1). See further Ch. 2, Sects. 6(i) & (iii) above.

[40] For these reasons, therefore, the terminology was adopted in previous editions of this work.

[41] For the scope of Parts 5 and 6 of the PSR 2009, see Sect. 5(i) below.

of a payment order'[42] and the term 'payee' (rather than 'beneficiary') to refer to the 'person who is the intended recipient of funds which have been the subject of a payment transaction'.[43] Rather than using the generic term 'payment service provider' that is used in the PSR 2009 in order to refer to the financial intermediaries involved in a transfer of funds,[44] this chapter will use as a shorthand the terms 'payer's bank' (rather than 'originator's bank'), 'payee's bank' (rather than 'beneficiary's bank') and 'correspondent bank' or 'intermediary bank' to refer to any further intermediary institutions. These terms will be used consistently, even in relation to fund transfer mechanisms that do not fall within the scope of the PSR 2009.

(iii) Credit and debit transfers

Funds transfer operations can be classified as either credit transfers or debit transfers according to the way in which the payment order is communicated to the payer's bank. A credit transfer represents a 'push' of funds by the payer to the payee. The payer instructs his bank to cause the account of the payee, at the same or another bank, to be credited. The payer's payment order may be for an individual credit transfer, for example by bank giro credit or CHAPS payment, or for a recurring transfer of funds under a standing order, which is an instruction given by a customer to his bank to make regular payments of a fixed amount to a particular payee. On receipt of the payer's payment order, the payer's bank will debit his account, unless the payer has provided his bank with some other means of reimbursement, and credit the payee's account where it is held at the same bank, or, where the payee's account is held at another bank, forward a payment order to the payee's bank, which will then credit the payee's account.

A debit transfer represents a 'pull' of funds by the payee from the payer. The payee conveys instructions to his bank to collect funds from the payer. These instructions may be initiated by the payer himself and passed on to the payee, for example, as happens with the collection of cheques. Alternatively, they may be initiated by the payee himself pursuant to the payer's authority, as happens with direct debits where the payer signs a mandate authorizing his bank to pay amounts demanded by the payee. On receipt of instructions from the payee, the payee's bank usually provisionally credits the payee's account with the amount to be collected and then forwards instructions to the payer's bank, which will then in turn debit the payer's account. The credit to the payee's account becomes final when the debit to the payer's account becomes irreversible.[45]

(iv) Clearing and settlement

Payment effected through a funds transfer system is initiated by a payment order given by the payer, or someone else acting with his authority, to his own bank. In cases where the payment is not 'in-house' (a payment is 'in-house' where the payer and the payee hold accounts at the same bank), the payer's payment order will lead to a further payment order passing between the payer's bank and the payee's bank, sometimes through the intermediation of other banks. The process of exchanging payment orders between participating banks is known as *clearing*. Clearing may take place through a series of bilateral

---

[42] PSR 2009, reg. 2(1). Where the payer has no account, he is defined as 'the person who gives a payment order': id.

[43] Id.

[44] The definition of 'payment service provider' is wider than just banks: PSR 2009, reg. 2(1).

[45] See generally Sect. 6 below.

exchanges of payment orders between banks, but in the United Kingdom it is more common for clearing to take place multilaterally through a centralized clearing house.[46]

Funds transfer systems are classified as either paper-based or electronic depending on the medium used for inter-bank communication of payment instructions.[47] In a paper-based funds transfer system, the paper embodying the payment instruction is physically transferred from one bank to another, for example, by direct courier or at a centralized clearing house. The cheque and credit clearing operated by the Cheque and Credit Clearing Company is a paper-based funds transfer system.[48] By contrast, with an electronic funds transfer system the inter-bank communication of payment instructions is by electronic means, for example, by magnetic tape, disc or, more usually, telecommunication link. The major inter-bank electronic funds transfer systems in the United Kingdom are the payment system operated by VocaLink Ltd (formerly known as BACS Ltd and then Voca Ltd) and BACS Payment Schemes Ltd (BACS)[49] and the two payment systems run by the CHAPS Clearing Company Ltd, namely CHAPS Sterling[50] and the 'Faster Payments Service'. The last of these was launched in May 2008 and is designed to allow for the more rapid execution of lower-value transactions (namely internet and phone payments for less than £10,000 and standing orders for less than £100,000) than was hitherto available.[51] The technical platform for the 'Faster Payments Service' is provided by Immediate Payments Ltd, a subsidiary of VocaLink Ltd. Additionally, since January 2008, a number of United Kingdom banks have been registered participants in the SEPA Credit Transfer Scheme (SCT) and it has been possible to register for the SEPA Direct Debit Scheme (SDD) since 1 May 2009, although the SDD was not officially launched until November 2009. These schemes have been developed under the aegis of the European Payments Council and are part of the development of a Single European Payment Area (SEPA). In essence, the SCT and SDD are harmonized payment instruments for making domestic and cross-border transfers denominated in Euros within the SEPA and the intention is that these instruments will eventually replace national mechanisms for making Euro-denominated funds transfers.[52] The development of these instruments has been made possible by the harmonized legal framework for payment services in the Payment Services Directive.[53] As regards the settlement and clearing of SCTs and SDDs, the European Payments Council has produced a framework ('the PE-ACH/CSM Framework') defining the principles that domestic Clearing and Settlement Mechanisms (CSMs) must comply with to ensure that they can process the harmonized payment instruments.[54] The aim of the framework is to ensure that all CSMs use the same technical standards—the settlement process being

---

[46] For a description of cheque clearing, see Ch. 10, Sect. 2 above.

[47] Geva, *The Law of Electronic Funds Transfers* (New York, 1992), [1.03(4)].

[48] See further Ch. 10, Sect. 2 above.   [49] For a fuller discussion, see Sect. 3(iii) below.

[50] For a fuller discussion, see Sect. 3(iv)(a) below. Formerly, it was necessary to distinguish between CHAPS Sterling and CHAPS Euro, which were consolidated on 27–28 August 2001 into a new dual-currency RTGS system called NewCHAPS. The CHAPS Euro clearing service was, however, closed on 16 May 2008 upon the replacement of the TARGET system with the TARGET2 system (the gross settlement system operated by the European System of Central Banks) and following the Bank of England's decision not to participate in TARGET2: European Central Bank, n.17 above, 13. Accordingly, the term 'CHAPS Sterling' is used to distinguish the present system from the combined, dual-currency NewCHAPS system.

[51] For a fuller discussion, see Sect. 3(iv)(b) below.

[52] European Central Bank, *Single Euro Payments Area—Sixth Progress Report* (Frankfurt, November 2008), 19–20.

[53] Directive 2007/64/EC on Payment Services in the Internal Market [2007] OJ L319.

[54] European Payments Council, *Framework for the Clearing and Settlement of Payments in SEPA* (January 2007).

executed within the integrated TARGET2 platform[55] and inter-bank messaging using a uniform standard developed by the International Organization for Standardization operated by SWIFT[56]—and to ensure full transparency in terms of each CSM's pricing and services. Banks and other payment service providers will accordingly be free to use whichever CSM that they consider to be the most competitive, regardless of its location within the SEPA. A number of CSMs across Europe (including VocaLink Ltd in the United Kingdom) are now capable of processing SCTs and SDDs in compliance with the PE-ACH/CSM Framework.[57]

Where the payer and the payee hold accounts at the same bank, the transfer of funds between the two accounts will usually involve a simple internal accounting exercise at the bank, known as an 'in-house' transfer:[58] the payer's account is debited and the payee's account is credited. The position will be different where the payer's account and the payee's account are held at different banks—the transfer between the two accounts is then known as an 'inter-bank' transfer. In such cases, an inter-bank payment order will pass from bank to bank, sometimes from the payer's bank directly to the payee's bank, otherwise via intermediary banks that each issue their own payment orders to the next bank down the chain, until a payment order finally reaches the payee's bank. Each inter-bank payment order must be paid by the bank sending the instruction to the bank receiving it. It is this process whereby payment is made between the banks themselves of their obligations *inter se* that is known as *settlement*.

Settlement can occur on either a bilateral or multilateral basis. Bilateral settlement occurs where the bank sending the payment order and the bank receiving it are 'correspondents', meaning that each holds an account with the other. Settlement is effected through an adjustment of those accounts. Multilateral settlement involves the settlement of accounts of the sending bank and the receiving bank held at a third bank. The third bank could be a common correspondent of the two banks, i.e. one where they both have accounts; alternatively, and more typically, the third bank could be a central bank. Furthermore, settlement may be either gross or net. With gross settlement, the sending and receiving banks settle each payment order separately without regard to any other payment obligations arising between them. This is usually done on a real-time basis, with settlement across the accounts of participating banks held at the central bank taking place as each payment order is processed. With net settlement, the mutual payment obligations of the parties are set off against each other and only the net balance is paid. This process occurs periodically, with net balances being settled either at the end of the day ('same-day' funds) or on the following day ('next-day' funds).

As indicated above, net settlement may be either bilateral or multilateral.[59] In a bilateral net settlement system, a participant's exposure is measured by reference to its net

---

[55] For a discussion of the change from the TARGET to TARGET2 system, see further below. On 16 December 2010, the European Commission published a proposal to enact a Regulation establishing technical requirements for credit transfers and direct debits in Euros. The European Payments Council responded with amendments to the proposal in March 2011.

[56] The use of this standard is compulsory in the bank-to-bank domain, but only recommended in the customer-to-bank domain. For further details, see www.iso20022.org. SWIFT is the registration authority for this standard. For discussion of SWIFT, see Sect. 4(iv) below.

[57] For a current list of SCT Scheme-compliant CSMs, see www.europeanpaymentscouncil.eu.

[58] *Libyan Arab Foreign Bank* v. *Bankers Trust Co.*, n.26 above, 750–751. Although payment need not be 'in-house' where the payer and the payee have accounts at separate branches of the same bank located in different jurisdictions and the transfer is in the currency of a third country: R. Cranston, *Principles of Banking Law* (2nd edn., London, 2002), 236.

[59] The text that follows is concerned only with payment netting and not with the netting of contractual commitments, for example, as carried out in a variety of contracts such as foreign exchange contracts, repurchase agreements, securities trades, and derivatives.

position with regard to each individual counterparty, and not by reference to the system as a whole. In a multilateral net settlement system, a participant's position is measured by reference to its net position with regard to all other participants in the system as a whole. As a result, each participant will end up as a net net-debtor or a net net-creditor in relation to all other participants in the system. Multilateral netting may arise through direct determination of multilateral net positions or indirectly by netting the net bilateral positions and thereby obtaining net net-positions. In each case, settlement follows the multilateral netting process.

The principal advantage of net settlement is that it reduces the number and value of inter-bank settlement operations, which in turn leads to reduced transaction costs and improved liquidity. On the other hand, net settlement does result in exposure to receiver risk. A bank receiving a payment instruction from another bank participating in a payment system usually makes funds available to its own customer before it has itself been placed in funds on completion of the multilateral net settlement at the end of the day (assuming the receiving bank turns out to be a net net-creditor). Thus, the receiving bank carries the risk that it may never be placed in funds. Furthermore, acting on its customer's instruction, the receiving bank may itself pass on a payment instruction down a chain of banks. The failure of one bank to make payment may mean that the other banks in the chain cannot meet their own payment commitments. This is known as systemic risk.

Although there are various ways to reduce systemic risk in settlement systems,[60] concern about systemic risk in large-value transfer systems led the Working Group on EC Payment Systems to adopt the principle that Member States should each develop their own real-time gross settlement system for large-value payments.[61] With real-time gross settlement, receiver risk is significantly reduced as no intra-day credit is granted to participants in the system.[62] The United Kingdom made CHAPS a real-time gross settlement system in April 1996. In 1999, the various real-time gross settlement systems of the EU Member States became connected by TARGET,[63] which was a payment system arrangement allowing high-value payments denominated in Euros to be made in real time across borders within the European Union. Since November 2007, TARGET has gradually been replaced by TARGET2 in a number of countries and finally ceased to operate in May 2008.[64] In contrast to TARGET, which simply focused on linking existing national settlement systems, TARGET2 provides for a higher level of integration by establishing a single technical infrastructure for gross clearing of euro payments (i.e. the 'Single Shared Platform' using SWIFTNet messaging) and a greater level of harmonization by providing

---

[60] See generally M. Giovanoli, 'Legal Issues Regarding Payment and Netting Systems' in J. Norton, C. Reed, and I. Walden (eds.), *Cross-Border Electronic Banking* (1st edn., London, 1995), ch. 9; R. Dale, 'Controlling Risks in Large-value Interbank Payment Systems' (1997) 11 *JIBFL* 426; R. Sappideen, 'Cross-border Electronic Funds Transfers Through Large Value Transfer Systems and the Persistence of Risk' [2003] *JBL* 584.

[61] Working Group on EC Payment Systems, *Report to the Committee of Governors of the Central Banks of the Member States of the European Economic Community on Minimum Common Features for Domestic Payment Systems* (November 1993). See also the Council of Minister's Common Position on Cross-Border Retail Transfers: [1995] OJ C353/52.

[62] Foreign currency exchange settlement risk ('Herstatt' risk) remains, but for those banks that have joined the Continuous Linked Settlement (CLS) system, which became operational in September 2002, it has largely been eliminated for certain foreign exchange transactions: Brindle and Cox (eds.), n.1 above, [3-019], [3-045]–[3-047]. As at January 2011, there are 17 major currencies eligible for CLS settlement and 72 bank members: www.cls-group.com.

[63] 'TARGET' is an acronym for 'Trans-European Automated Real-Time Gross Settlement Express Transfer System'.

[64] European Central Bank, n.17 above, 10–14.

a uniform set of services to TARGET2 participants in the various European jurisdictions.[65] As the Bank of England has elected not to participate in TARGET2,[66] and as the CHAPS Euro service has been closed with the demise of TARGET, United Kingdom banks were left to make individual arrangements for effecting large cross-border euro payments.[67] The making of such arrangements has been facilitated to a large degree by the development of the SEPA harmonized payment instruments considered above (namely, the STC and the SDD) with their uniform standards and their use of the TARGET2 Single Shared Platform. A number of United Kingdom banks have already registered as participants in the SCT Scheme since it became operational in January 2008 and as participants in the SDD Scheme since it began in November 2009.[68] According to the expressed intention of the European Central Bank, participation in these schemes will in the near future become the only means of effecting funds transfers denominated in Euros, replacing alternative domestic arrangements.[69]

Even a gross settlement system, however, has some risks associated with it. With the lack of intra-day credit in such a system, participants must have funds available at the central bank to meet their payment obligations before they can send payment instructions. This reduces liquidity and can lead to gridlock (i.e. the system cannot get going until participants have received sufficient credits from other participants), although this can be avoided by the central bank offering secured overdraft facilities to participating banks or entering into repurchase arrangements. Nor is a gross settlement system immune from certain risks associated with the insolvency of a participant. Certain EC Member States have rules giving retroactive effect to the pronouncement of insolvency. The 'zero-hour rule', which applies in the Netherlands, Austria, and Italy, renders all transactions void from midnight before (i.e. 'zero hour') the actual opening of insolvency proceedings. As a result, payment instructions introduced into the settlement system after 'zero hour' of the day on which the insolvency proceedings are commenced against a participant in a payment system, but before the formal pronouncement of insolvency, could be challenged by the liquidator of an insolvent participant. Furthermore, under English law a multilateral netting arrangement can be challenged by a liquidator of a participant on the ground that it allows the setting off of claims in relation to which there is no mutuality and that such an arrangement accordingly infringes the *pari passu* principle.[70]

In order to reduce systemic risk in payment systems that operate on the basis of payment netting, and to minimize the disruption caused by insolvency proceedings against a participant in a payment or securities settlement system, the European

---

[65] See generally *Guideline of the European Central Bank of 26 April 2007 on TARGET2*, [2007] OJ L237; *Decision of the European Central Bank of 24 July 2007 concerning the terms and conditions of TARGET2*, [2007] OJ L237. For a legal analysis of TARGET2, see K. Laurinavicius, K. Lober, & H. Weenink, 'Legal Aspects of TARGET2' (2008) 23 *JIBLR* 15. Besides using the TARGET2 system, Euro-denominated cross-border transfers can be effected through the EURO1, STEP1 and STEP2 payment systems established and operated by the Euro Banking Association: M. Brindle and R. Cox (eds.), n.1 above, [3-063]–[3-068].

[66] European Central Bank, n.17 above, 13.

[67] Some United Kingdom banks chose to participate in TARGET2 through the central banks in other Member States. For example, Lloyds Banking Group, Standard Chartered Bank plc, and HSBC plc have accessed the scheme through the Dutch central bank.

[68] United Kingdom banks could register as participants in the SDD Scheme from 1 May 2009.

[69] European Central Bank, n.52 above, 19–20.

[70] *British Eagle International Airlines Ltd* v. *Compagnie Nationale Air France* [1975] 1 WLR 758 (HL). See also *Hague* v. *Nam Tai Electronics Inc.* [2007] 2 BCLC 194, [8] (PC). A netting arrangement does not *automatically* infringe the *pari passu* principle, but this depends upon its proper construction: *International Air Transport Association* v. *Ansett Australia Holdings Ltd* (2008) 242 ALR 47 (HCA) (revisions made to the IATA clearing house system following the *British Eagle* decision held no longer to infringe the *pari passu* principle). The modern tendency is to restrict the ambit of the *British Eagle* principle: *Perpetual Trustee Co Ltd* v. *BNY Corporate Trustee Services Ltd* [2009] EWCA Civ 1160, [43]–[58]; *Lomas* v. *JFB Firth Rixson Inc* [2010] EWHC 3372 (Ch), [94]–[96].

Parliament and Council adopted Directive 98/26 on settlement finality in payment and securities settlement systems.[71] The Directive provides, *inter alia*, that (i) transfer orders and netting are to be legally enforceable and binding on third parties, even in the event of insolvency proceedings, provided the transfer orders were entered into the system before the moment of the opening of the insolvency;[72] (ii) there is to be no unwinding of a netting because of the operation of national laws or practice that provide for the setting aside of contracts and transactions concluded before the moment of the opening of insolvency proceedings;[73] (iii) a transfer order is not to be revoked by a participant in a system, nor by a third party, from the moment defined by the rules of that system;[74] and (iv) insolvency proceedings are not to have retrospective effect on the rights and obligations of a participant arising from, or in connection with, its participation in a system earlier than the moment of the opening of such proceedings.[75] The moment of the opening of insolvency proceedings is the moment when the relevant judicial or administrative authority handed down its decision.[76] The United Kingdom has implemented the Directive through the Financial Markets and Insolvency (Settlement Finality) Regulations 1999.[77] The Regulations apply only to systems that are accorded designation by a 'designating authority'.[78] In its capacity as a designating authority, the Bank of England has granted *inter alia* the CHAPS Sterling clearing 'designated system' status.[79] Part III of the Regulations largely displaces the rules of insolvency law, giving precedence to the proceedings of the relevant designated system. This effectively reverses the effect of the ruling in *British Eagle* so far as those designated systems are concerned.

(v) Clearing systems and clearing rules

The very nature of giro operations anticipates the existence of a suitable clearing system. Geva has identified two senses in which the term 'clearing system' can be used.[80] First, in its narrow sense, the term refers to a mechanism for the calculation of mutual positions within a group of participants with a view to facilitating the settlement of their mutual obligations on a net basis. Secondly, in its broad sense, the term also extends to the actual settlement of those obligations.

The banks and building societies that are members of the various clearing systems operated under the auspices of the UK Payments Administration Ltd (UKPA)[81] must have settlement accounts at the Bank of England. Other banks and building societies may gain access to these systems through agency agreements with those members.

---

[71] [1998] OJ L166/45 (as amended by Directive 2009/44/EC ([2009] OJ L146) & Directive 2010/78/EU ([2010] OJ L331)).

[72] Ibid., Art. 3(1) (as amended by Directive 2009/44/EC, Art. 1(6)). A transfer order that enters the system after the commencement of insolvency proceedings against a participant may nevertheless be enforceable provided it is executed on the same business day and provided the system operator can demonstrate that it was unaware of the insolvency proceedings at the time that the transfer order became irrevocable.

[73] Ibid., Art. 3(2).   [74] Ibid., Art. 5 (as amended by Directive 2009/44/EC, Art. 1(8)).

[75] Ibid., Art. 7 (as amended by Directive 2009/44/EC, Art. 1(9)).   [76] Ibid., Art. 6(1).

[77] S.I. 1999/2979 (as amended). For an excellent summary, see L.S. Sealy, 'The Settlement Finality Directive—Points in Issue' [2000] *CifLR* 221.

[78] Ibid., regs. 3–12 & Sched. 1 (as amended).

[79] APACS, *Annual Review 2000* (London, 2001), 9; APACS, *Annual Review 2003* (London, 2004), 8. The CHAPS Euro clearing was similarly granted designated system status, although this service was discontinued on 16 May 2008.

[80] B. Geva, 'The Clearing House Arrangement' (1991) 19 *Can. BLJ* 138.

[81] UK Payments Administration Ltd replaced the Association for Payment Clearing Services (APACS) on 6 July 2009.

Members are bound by the rules of the clearing system through a multilateral contract.[82] The rules must be interpreted against the background of the manner and operation of the particular clearing system. Any interpretation of the rules must also be in accordance with the nature of the rules themselves.[83] A customer of a clearing bank by virtue of may be bound by, and able to rely on, the clearing system rules against his own bank by virtue of an implied term of the banker–customer contract.[84] The customer is taken to have contracted with reference to the reasonable usage of bankers, including those clearing system rules that represent such reasonable usage.[85] However, where clearing house rules derogate from the customer's existing rights, the usage codified in the rules will be deemed unreasonable and will not bind the customer without his full knowledge and consent.[86]

There are four major clearing systems for giro transfers in the United Kingdom,[87] responsibility for which is divided between three independent companies operating under the auspices of the UKPA.[88] First, there is the credit clearing system run by the Cheque and Credit Clearing Co. Ltd, which is a paper-based credit transfer system used for the physical exchange of high-volume, low-value, credit collections such as bank giro credits. Secondly, there is BACS, operated by VocaLink Ltd (formerly known as BACS Ltd and then Voca Ltd) and BACS Payment Schemes Ltd,[89] which provides a high-volume, low-value, bulk electronic clearing service for credit and debit transfers, including direct debits and direct credits where the payer sends his instructions directly to BACS rather than through a bank (such as might occur for wages and salaries, pensions, and other government benefits).[90] Thirdly, there is CHAPS Sterling,

---

[82] Probably on the same principle as applied in *Clarke* v. *Dunraven, The Satanita* [1897] AC 59 (HL). Consider *White* v. *Shortall* [2006] NSWSC 1379, [333].

[83] R. Cranston, n.58 above, 280–282.

[84] It is always open, but most unlikely, for the clearing system rules to be expressly incorporated into a bank's contract with its customer. Alternatively, the customer may possibly be able to rely on the Contracts (Rights of Third Parties) Act 1999. This will not be easy for, in most cases, the member banks will probably be able to show that they did not intend to confer an enforceable benefit on customers: ibid., s.1(2).

[85] *Hare* v. *Henty* (1861) 10 CBNS 65; *Re Farrow's Bank Ltd* [1923] 1 Ch. 41; *Parr's Bank Ltd* v. *Thomas Ashby & Co.* (1898) 14 TLR 563; *Barclays Bank plc* v. *Bank of England* [1985] 1 All ER 385, [17]; *Tayeb* v. *HSBC Bank plc* [2004] 4 All ER 1024, [57].

[86] *Barclays Bank plc* v. *Bank of England*, n.85 above, [26]. See also *Turner* v. *Royal Bank of Scotland plc* [1999] Lloyd's Rep. Bank. 231 (CA).

[87] There is also cheque clearing, but this is not classified as a giro system for the reasons set out in Sect. 2(iv) below. For discussion of the cheque clearing, see Ch. 10, Sect. 2 above.

[88] UK Payments Administration Ltd replaced the Association for Payment Clearing Services (APACS) on 6 July 2009 and is now the umbrella body for the companies responsible for money transactions and payment clearing activity generally in the United Kingdom: Ch. 1, Sect. 2(i) above. In addition to the four major clearings mentioned in the text above, and the cheque clearing, UKPA also oversees the Currency Clearing Committee, which clears paper-based payment orders drawn in United States dollars on United Kingdom banks. For a review of this mechanism, see UK Payments Council, *National Payments Plan—Setting the Strategic Vision for UK Payments* (London, 14 May 2008), 23. A major clearing system available to United Kingdom banks, but operating outside the UKPA umbrella, is the Euro Banking Association's 'Euro Priority Payments Scheme', which has been available since October 2007, and has been described as 'an open-standard, non-proprietary value-added service open to all banks located in the European Economic Area (EEA). Participation in the scheme guarantees the end-to-end processing of single credit transfers within four hours and thereby enables banks to offer urgent, intra-day credit transfers in euro to their customers': www.abe-eba.eu. Some United Kingdom banks have accessed the TARGET2 clearing system through the central banks of other EU Member States. There are also a number of other payment networks that are not serviced by UKPA, such as the SWITCH Maestro, Visa, MasterCard, and LINK networks, which handle various types of payment card.

[89] VocaLink Ltd is responsible for the physical processing of payments and the maintenance of the payment network. BACS Payment Schemes Ltd is membership-based and manages the scheme.

[90] BACS payments previously included standing orders, but these are now dealt with through the 'Faster Payments Service'.

a real-time gross settlement (RTGS) system, which is used for electronic high-value sterling-denominated credit transfers.[91] CHAPS is based on SWIFT messages and formats and can only be made during ordinary banking hours. Fourthly, from May 2008, there is the CHAPS-operated 'Faster Payments Service', which provides a clearing service for high-volume, low-value sterling credit transfers, namely internet and phone payments (both immediate and diarized) for less than £10,000 and standing orders for less than £100,000. The advantages of the 'Faster Payments Service' for the customer are the ability to make immediate payments 24 hours a day, seven days a week, and the fact that the payment will occur in near-real time or on the same day depending upon the payment type. Rather than using SWIFT formats, the 'Faster Payments Service' is based around the ATM/debit card messages (i.e. 'ISO 8523').[92] Save for CHAPS Sterling, which is a real-time gross settlement systems, the other clearing systems are multilateral net settlement system with settlement of balances across the participants' accounts held at the Bank of England taking place at the end of each day, or several times each day in the case of the 'Faster Payments Service'.

(vi) **International funds transfers**

An international funds transfer occurs when either the payer's bank or the payee's bank, or both banks, are located in a country other than that of the transfer's currency: where either the payer's bank or the payee's bank is located in the country of the transfer's currency, the transfer is termed 'onshore'; where neither bank is located in the country of the transfer's currency, the transfer is termed 'offshore'.[93] A cross-border or overseas branch is considered as a separate bank for these purposes. Most international funds transfers are credit transfers and operate in a similar way to domestic credit transfers, although international credit transfers generally involve greater use of correspondent or intermediary banks. Furthermore, an international funds transfer may be subject to more than one law.[94] Each account relationship in the transfer—for example, as between the payer and his bank, the payer's bank and

---

[91] Formerly, it was necessary to distinguish between CHAPS Sterling and CHAPS Euro, which were consolidated on 27–28 August 2001 into a new dual-currency RTGS system called New CHAPS, but the CHAPS Euro clearing service was closed on 16 May 2008 upon the replacement of the TARGET system with the TARGET2 system and following the Bank of England's decision not to participate in TARGET2: see European Central Bank, n.17 above, 13. For discussion of TARGET and TARGET2, see Sect. 1(iv) above. See also K. Laurinavicius, K. Lober, & H. Weenink, n.65 above.

[92] The technical platform for the 'Faster Payments Service' is provided by Immediate Payments Ltd, a subsidiary of VocaLink Ltd.

[93] For this classification, see B. Geva, n.47 above, [4.02] ff. Geva also identifies a third category, termed an 'offshore intermediated outside transfer', which involves offshore clearing with settlement (usually) in the country of the currency of the transfer (for example, as with the currency clearings in London): ibid., [4.02(3)(c)]. With the introduction of the Euro amongst certain Member States of the European Union on 1 Jan. 1999, the linkage between a particular currency and a particular country has been removed for Euro-denominated inter-bank payments. The United Kingdom has not joined the single European currency. With the development of the 'Single European Payment Area', the intention is that cross-border Euro-denominated transfers within the SEPA will be viewed more like domestic transfers than international transfers. See further Sect. 1(iv) above.

[94] Relatively little attention has been paid to the role of private international law in the context of international funds transfers. The UNCITRAL Model Law on International Credit Transfers (1992) and Article 4A of the US Uniform Commercial Code adopt the traditional common law approach, which views an international funds transfer as a connected set of independent transactions: R. Bollen, 'Harmonization of International Payment Law: A Survey of the UNCITRAL Model Law on Credit Transfers' (2008) *JIBLR* 44, 57–58. Some continental legal systems take a 'single transaction' approach to the issue. For a useful review of the issues, see Luca G. Radicati di Brozolo, 'International Payments and the Conflicts of Laws' (2000) 48 *Am. J of Comp. L* 307.

an intermediary bank, the intermediary bank and the payee's bank, and the payee's bank and the payee himself—may be subject to its own applicable law, which in each case may be different from the law governing the underlying obligation between the payer and the payee.[95] It is of paramount importance to identify the law applicable to the particular relationship in issue.

In international funds transfers, each payment message, whether between the payer and his bank, the payee and his bank, or the banks themselves, may be communicated orally, in writing, or by electronic means. In the past, overseas or cross-border inter-bank payment messages were sent by airmail, telegram, or telex, whereas now most banks communicate with their overseas, or cross-border, counterparts using the telecommunication network operated by SWIFT.[96] It is important to stress that SWIFT is merely a messaging system; it does not have a settlement component.[97]

Where the transfer is 'onshore', the payer's bank and the payee's bank may be correspondents (i.e. each maintains an account with the other), thereby allowing bilateral settlement between them. Where the payer's bank and the payee's bank are not correspondents, it will be necessary to employ the services of at least one correspondent or intermediary bank.[98] Where funds are transferred from the payer's bank located overseas to the payee's bank located in the country of the transfer's currency—for example, where the payer's bank in London wants to transfer United States dollars to the payee's bank in New York—the payer's bank will employ a correspondent or intermediary bank in the country of the transfer's currency to transfer funds to the payee's bank. Typically, the transfer between the local correspondent and the payee's bank will be through the local clearing system (probably through the Clearing House Interbank Payments System (CHIPS) in the example given above),[99] but, where the payer's bank and the payee's bank use the same local correspondent, the transfer will be effected by account adjustments on the local correspondent's books. Where funds are transferred from the payer's bank located in the country of the transfer's currency to the payee's bank located overseas—for example, where the payer's bank in London wants to transfer sterling to the payee's bank in New York—the payer's bank will transfer funds to the local correspondent of the payee's bank, typically through the local clearing system (probably using CHAPS in the example given above), and that correspondent will complete the transfer to the payee's bank.

Where the transfer is 'offshore', it will usually pass through the country of the transfer's currency, but this will not always be the case. The transfer will not pass through the country of its currency where the payer's bank has a foreign currency account with the payee's bank, and both banks are located outside the country of the transfer's currency, or where the payer's bank and the payee's bank hold foreign currency accounts with a common

---

[95] A similar approach is adopted when determining the law applicable to the relationships that constitute a letter of credit transaction: *Bank of Baroda* v. *Vysya Bank Ltd* [1994] 2 Lloyd's Rep 87; *Marconi Communications International Ltd* v. *PT Pan Indonesia Bank Ltd TBK* [2005] EWCA Civ 422. See C. Hare, 'The Rome Convention and Letters of Credit' [2005] *LMCLQ* 417.

[96] 'SWIFT' is an acronym for 'Society for Worldwide Interbank Financial Telecommunication'. For further consideration of SWIFT, see Sect. 4(iv) below.

[97] *Raffles Money Change Pte Ltd* v. *Skandinaviska Enskilda Banken AB* [2009] 3 SLR 1, [30].

[98] In *Libyan Arab Foreign Bank* v. *Bankers Trust Co.*, n.26 above, 750–751, Staughton J refers to a transfer involving the use of an intermediary or correspondent bank as a 'correspondent bank transfer'.

[99] In this situation, and those considered subsequently, a further intermediary bank may have to participate in the credit transfer if the correspondent or intermediary bank in question is not a member of the clearing system.

correspondent or intermediary bank that is located outside the country of the transfer's currency. However, an 'offshore' transfer will pass through the country of the transfer's currency where the payer's bank employs a correspondent or intermediary bank in the country of the transfer's currency to make the transfer to the payee's bank. The transfer from the correspondent or intermediary bank to the payee's bank will either be direct, where it is a mutual correspondent of the payer's bank and the payee's bank,[100] or indirect, where this is not the case. Where the transfer is indirect, the correspondent of the payer's bank will transfer funds to the correspondent of the payee's bank in the country of the transfer's currency by using the clearing system of that country.[101] In a Eurodollar transaction,[102] for example, where the payer's bank in London wants to transfer United States dollars to the payee's bank in Switzerland, the correspondent of the payer's bank in New York would use the CHIPS system to make the transfer to the New York correspondent of the payee's bank.

2 Domestic giro forms and their comparison with cheques

(i) Individual money transfer forms (bank giro credit transfers)

The bank giro credit, or the individual money transfer form, is the basic facility used by the banks in money transfer operations. Prior to 1 January 1998, bank giro credit transfers were made using standard credit forms that left blank spaces for the payer to insert details concerning the transfer, such as the name on the payee's account and the other details concerning it, and the amount involved. However, many of these forms were completed inaccurately, which led to unacceptable delays in payment being made. Thus, since January 1998 inter-bank bank giro credits must generally be made using pre-printed credit forms, such as those found at the back of cheque-books or in bank branches, or provided with utility bills. These credit forms must comply with the design, layout, and printing requirements stipulated by the Cheque and Credit Clearing Company. It is a matter for individual banks whether they will continue to accept blank credit forms completed in manuscript for intra-bank transfers. The launch of the 'Faster Payments Service' in May 2008, providing consumers with the ability to make rapid, low-value money transfers over the internet or phone payments at any time of the day or night, may well spell the end of the paper-based bank giro. This certainly appears to be the prediction of the UK Payments Council, which has undertaken to review the future of the bank giro credit and, if necessary, the options for closing the paper-based credit clearing mechanism.[103] It is unlikely that paper-based credit clearing will remain a viable, standalone operation following the proposed closure of cheque clearing in October 2018.

---

[100] For example, in *Zim Israel Navigation Co.* v. *Effy Shipping Corp., The Effy* [1972] 1 Lloyd's Rep. 18, a United States dollar transfer between the payer's bank in Israel and the payee's bank in London passed through their mutual correspondent located in the United States.

[101] In *Libyan Arab Foreign Bank* v. *Bankers Trust Co.*, n.26 above, 750–751, Staughton J would have probably classified this type of transaction as a 'complex account transfer'. Where the respective correspondents of the payer's bank and the payee's bank are not themselves members of the relevant clearing system, further correspondent or intermediary banks, who are members of that system, must be engaged.

[102] A 'Eurodollar' is a credit in United States dollars at a bank or financial institution outside the United States, whether in Europe or elsewhere: *Libyan Arab Foreign Bank* v. *Bankers Trust Co.*, n.26 above, 735.

[103] UK Payments Council, *National Payments Plan—Setting the Strategic Vision for UK Payments* (London, 14 May 2008), 27; UK Payments Council, *Progress Report—Delivering the National Payments Plan* (London, March 2009), 5.

For the moment, however, the bank giro credit remains. A notable feature of the current bank giro credit form is that it sets out neither the payer's express request that the bank execute the transfer nor his authorization for the debiting of his account. The payer is, however, required to sign the form; his mandate to the bank as regards the remittance of the funds is based on his executing, in this manner, a standard bank giro credit; but the bank giro credit does not, even by implication, confer on the bank the authority to reimburse itself. The payer has to remit to the bank the required cash, a personal cheque, or third party cheques payable to himself in order to cover the credit transfer. In this regard, the bank giro credit in the United Kingdom differs from the giro systems used on the Continent, where the giro docket performs the dual function of authorizing the bank both to transfer the amount involved and to debit the customer's account.

(ii) **Standing orders**

Standing orders are used to arrange for periodic payments of fixed amounts, such as monthly rents, instalments due under hire-purchase agreements, and annual subscriptions. The clearing banks have their own *pro forma* standing order forms, with the payer supplying the same information as he used to provide on blank inter-bank credit forms before pre-printed credit forms became the norm. The form also enables the payer to provide his bank with a direction concerning the frequency and dates of the relevant payments. At the time that it receives the instructions, the bank does not earmark any specific funds from which it can reimburse itself, but the current form used by banks includes a clause that authorizes the bank to debit the payer's account with the amount of each payment when it is made.[104] The standing order is thus a self-contained instruction that need not be accompanied by the customer's cheque or by cash. Obviously, it can be used only by persons who maintain an account with the transferring bank. Until recently, the execution of standing orders was carried out by BACS, but this function is now performed through the CHAPS 'Faster Payments Service'.[105]

In practice, organizations such as charitable bodies arrange for the printing of standard forms, which set out the details of their account. The payer completes this form by inserting the details of his bank account. The order is transmitted to the payer's bank by the payee. From a legal point of view, this practice does not involve a departure from the principles discussed already,[106] and to be discussed further subsequently,[107] as the payee transmits the form as the payer's agent. In other cases, the creditor might supply the debtor with a pre-printed book of encoded bank giro credits, which the debtor uses to effect payments. According to this procedure, used by some local authorities and finance companies, a series of bank giro credits performs the same function as a standing order.

---

[104] A bank is under no obligation to make the transfer if there are insufficient funds in the account to cover it, nor is it obliged to monitor the account subsequently to see whether sufficient funds have been credited to the account to cover the standing order: *Whitehead* v. *National Westminster Bank Ltd*, The Times, 9 June 1982.

[105] For a detailed analysis of the different payment types undertaken by the 'Faster Payments Service', see www.fastpayments.co.uk.

[106] Sect. 1(iii) above.

[107] For an analysis of the legal nature of the relationships arising out of a funds transfer, see further Sect. 5 below.

(iii) **Direct debiting**

The direct debit scheme was introduced in 1967.[108] It facilitates the prompt payment of amounts due under commercial and consumer contracts by enabling the supplier, dealer, or other creditor to obtain payment of amounts due to him by issuing a direct demand for payment to his debtor's bank. The procedure involves some extra paperwork in the initial stages, but saves time thereafter. The payee asks the payer to sign a mandate executed on a standard form.[109] The form is returned to the payee, who either then the form to the payer's bank or, where the Automated Direct Debit Instruction Service (AUDDIS) is used, keeps the form and transmits details of the mandate electronically to the payer's bank.[110] The form authorizes the payer's bank to pay amounts demanded by the payee; there is no need to require on each occasion the confirmation of the payer's indebtedness. Although intimation of the sum payable is in the hands of the payee, the mandate remains that of the payer, and the direct debit does not operate to assign or vest in the payee any of the payer's rights against his own bank.[111] Accordingly, the payer alone retains the ability to amend the terms of the direct debit or cancel it entirely.[112]

All mandate forms used under the direct debit scheme must be variable in terms of amount, date, and frequency; as such, neither the amount of the debit, its date, nor its frequency is specified on the form. However, as part of the BACS' Direct Debit Guarantee Scheme, the payee must give the payer at least 10 working days' notice (unless a shorter period of notice has been agreed) of the amount and date of the first direct debit and of any subsequent changes to the amount and date of the direct debit. The payee must then collect the direct debit payment on, or within three working days of, the specified due date as advised to the payer; failure to do so results in the payee having to give the payer further notice of the new collection date. Conceptually, direct debiting can be used for the settlement of any type of payment. In the majority of cases, however, direct debiting is used to arrange for the payment of varying amounts falling due at regular or irregular intervals, such as amounts payable in respect of electricity bills or for the supply of different quantities of a particular commodity ordered by a purchaser from a supplier from time to time as old stock is used up.

It is obvious that direct debiting is open to abuses. There are, however, control measures in operation that reduce this risk. First, a firm that wants to collect payment by direct

---

[108] The system is currently administered by BACS and is governed by its own set of rules: *The Originator's Guide and Rules to the Direct Debiting Scheme* (London, 1997, and updated at regular intervals).

[109] There is also a Paperless Direct Debit service, where the payee obtains the payer's bank account details and then lodges the direct debit instruction with the payer's bank via AUDDIS. It has been estimated that paperless direct debits that are set up over the telephone or via the internet account for 30 per cent of direct debits: see APACS, *Annual Report 2002* (London, 2003), 13.

[110] The payee's failure properly to implement a correctly completed direct debit mandate might constitute a breach of a term implied into the underlying contract between the payer and payee, or even a breach of a tortious duty of care owed by the payee to the payer: *Weldon* v. *GRE Linked Life Assurance Ltd* [2000] 2 All ER (Comm.) 914.

[111] *Mercedes-Benz Finance Ltd* v. *Clydesdale Bank plc*, n.25 above. Although rejecting the view that a direct debit operated as an assignment of rights, Lord Penrose refused to strike out the argument that there might be a *jus quaesitum tertio* (or contract for the benefit of a third party) in that case.

[112] This can be done up to and including the direct debit's due date, namely the third day of the clearing cycle: Sect. 3(iii) below. With respect to the alteration and cancellation of direct debits by a payer, BACS has developed the Automated Direct Debit Amendment and Cancellation Service (ADDACS), which allows paying banks to inform payees of any such changes via the BACS Service. As the payee receives notification electronically, ADDACS ensures that the information is received in a timely fashion and reduces the risk of error and resulting indemnity claims. The payer's right to cancel a direct debit is expressly recognized in the Direct Debit Guarantee offered by banks that participate in the BACS scheme: see further www.bacs.co.uk.

debit (whether as a 'direct' or 'indirect submitter') must be sponsored by one of the banks or building societies that operate the scheme. Sponsorship is dependent on the sponsor being satisfied about a number of factors, including the financial status and administrative capability of the firm in question. Secondly, before being accepted into the scheme, the firm must provide all banks and building societies operating the scheme with an indemnity against any direct or consequential losses that may be caused to them, unless the loss was due to the particular bank or building society's own fault. Under the terms of the Direct Debit Guarantee Scheme, the payer is guaranteed a full and immediate refund from his bank should there be an error in the direct debiting process by the payee's bank or the payer's own bank—for example, where a payment is made after the payer cancelled his authority, where more than the notified sum is debited from the account, or where the debit was made on the wrong date. Where the error is due to the fault of the payee, the payer's bank can claim a refund from the payee under the terms of its indemnity.

Where the payee and the payer have agreed that payment shall be by direct debit, subsequent cancellation of the direct debit mandate by the payer gives the payee a claim for breach of contract against him. In *Esso Petroleum Co. Ltd* v. *Milton*,[113] the Court of Appeal treated such a claim as similar to the claim that a payee would have on a dishonoured cheque. In *Milton*, the claimants owned two garages operated and managed by the defendant under licence. Under the terms of two licence agreements, one for each garage, the defendant was obliged to purchase all his petrol supplies from the claimants and pay for them on or before delivery by direct debit. The defendant was also forbidden from selling petrol at prices greater than those notified to him by the claimants. Towards the end of 1995, the claimants instructed the defendant to cut petrol prices in the face of stiff pricing competition and increased his site rentals. The defendant complained that this made his operations unprofitable and, in order to put pressure on the claimants, he cancelled his direct debit mandate when almost £170,000 was owing to the claimants for petrol supplied. The claimants applied for summary judgment against him. The defendant admitted the claim, but alleged that the increasingly stringent financial terms that the claimants had imposed amounted to a repudiatory breach of contract, and he counterclaimed damages that he sought to set off in equity in extinction of his debt to the claimants. The first instance judge dismissed the claimants' application for summary judgment, but the claimants successfully appealed on two grounds. The first was that the defendant's counterclaim, even if good, would not give rise to an equitable set-off. The second was that no set-off or counterclaim was available where payment was made, or agreed to be made, by direct debit. On the second issue, the Court of Appeal held, by a majority, that the parties' arrangements for payment by direct debit were to be treated as assimilated to those of payment by way of cheque, and accordingly applied the rule (well established in the case of cheques and bills of exchange)[114] that there can be no set-off or counterclaim arising from the underlying contract unless there is fraud or a failure of consideration. This was, according to Thorpe LJ,[115] 'a natural evolution' of the rule that applies to bills of exchange and cheques, and reflected, according to Sir John Balcombe,[116] the modern commercial practice of treating a direct debit in the same way as a payment by cheque. By contrast, Simon Brown LJ, dissenting, held that there were insufficient similarities between cheques and direct debit arrangements to treat the two as equivalent.

---

[113] [1997] 2 All ER 593 (CA), applied in *Gibbs Mew plc* v. *Gemmell* [1999] 1 EGLR 43 (CA); *Courage Ltd* v. *Crehan* [1999] 2 EGLR 145 (CA); *Esso Petroleum Co. Ltd* v. *Ilanchelian* (Ch. D, 19 March 2001); *Geldof Metaalconstructie NV* v. *Simon Carves Ltd* [2010] EWCA Civ 667, [43]. See also *Integral Home Loans Pty Ltd* v. *Interstar Wholesale Finance Pty Ltd (No. 2)* [2007] NSWSC 592, [42].

[114] See further Ch. 10, Sect. 8(iii) above.   [115] *Esso Petroleum Co. Ltd* v. *Milton*, n.113 above, 606.

[116] Ibid., 607.

It is respectfully submitted that Simon Brown LJ was right, and the majority were wrong, on this issue.[117] The analogy with a dishonoured cheque is flawed. Where a cheque is dishonoured, the payee obtains a cause of action through breach of the drawer's payment obligation embodied in the cheque itself.[118] There is no similar promise embodied in a direct debit mandate, revocation of which does not of itself create a separate cause of action.[119] Where a direct debit mandate is revoked, the payee is left only with his claim for the debt due on the underlying contract. Why should the payer lose his right of set-off when sued on the underlying contract? The mere fact that the payment was to be by direct debit should not of itself be enough to imply an exclusion clause into the contract. Such a term is neither obvious, nor necessary for business efficacy, nor likely to be reasonably understood from the terms of the contract in question when read as a whole against the relevant background. If the payer's right of set-off is to be excluded, this should be done through an express term of the underlying contract.[120] Furthermore, the best explanation for applying the no set-off rule to bills of exchange and cheques is that it facilitates the free negotiation of such instruments for cash.[121] However, direct debits are not transferable and do not require the same protection. It does not answer this point simply to assert, as the claimants did in *Milton*, that as most cheques are now non-transferable (being pre-printed with the crossing 'account payee only' or 'a/c payee only'),[122] no distinction should be drawn between such cheques and direct debits. Perhaps it would show greater consistency if non-transferable cheques were also kept outside the no set-off rule. There is, after all, a strong case to be made that 'account payee only' cheques fall outside the Bills of Exchange Act 1882 (BEA 1882).[123]

(iv) Comparison of giro forms with cheques

Both giro forms and cheques are used for the settlement of accounts by means of the issuing of a written instruction to the bank, but a cheque system is not a giro system. There are three essential differences between them. First, a cheque system facilitates the transfer of the right to payment from the payee to a third-party holder of the cheque (unless the cheque is non-transferable),[124] whereas a giro transfer can be made only to the specified payee. Secondly, a cheque system allows the payee (or other holder of the instrument) to collect payment from an account at any bank (unless the cheque is crossed specially),[125] whereas a giro transfer can be made only to the payee's account at the bank specified in the payment instruction. Thirdly, a cheque system enables the payee of a cheque to collect payment in cash over the counter of the drawee bank (so long

---

[117] For criticism of the majority's conclusion, see R. Hooley, 'Direct Debits and Set-off—The Tiger Roars!' [1997] *CLJ* 500; A. Tettenborn, '"Pay Now, Sue Later"—Direct Debits, Set-off and Commercial Practice' (1997) 113 *LQR* 374.

[118] Bills of Exchange Act 1882 (BEA 1882), s.55(1)(a).

[119] See, by analogy, *The Brimnes* [1975] 1 QB 929, 949, 964–965, 969 (CA); but consider *Scottish & Newcastle plc v. Bond* (QBD, 25 March 1997).

[120] In fact, the claimants in *Milton* did attempt to rely on an express term of the licence agreements that purported to exclude any right of set-off, but the Court of Appeal held the term to be unreasonable under the Unfair Contract Terms Act 1977 (applying *Stewart Gill Ltd v. Horatio Myer & Co. Ltd* [1992] QB 600 (CA)). See also *Gao Bin v. OCBC Securities Pte Ltd* [2009] 1 SLR 500, [12]–[13]. For unease about implying an exclusion of set-off in circumstances where an express exclusion clause has been struck down as unreasonable within the Unfair Contract Terms Act 1977, see *Star Rider Ltd v. Inntrepreneur Pub Co.* [1998] 16 EG 140.

[121] *Nova (Jersey) Knit Ltd v. Kammgarn Spinnerei GmbH* [1977] 1 WLR 713, 721 (HL).

[122] See further Ch. 10, Sect. 4(iv) above.

[123] J.K. MacLeod, 'The Plight of the Unbanked Payee' (1997) 113 *LQR* 133, 156.

[124] This distinction is maybe more theoretical than practical as most cheques are now pre-printed with the crossing 'account payee only' or 'a/c payee only': Ch. 10, Sect. 4(iv) above.

[125] Ch. 10, Sect. 4(i) above.

as the cheque is uncrossed), whereas the payee of a giro transfer must receive payment through a bank account.[126]

In addition to these technical differences, a comparison of the practice involved in the two types of system highlights the relative advantages and disadvantages inherent in each of them. There are two principal advantages associated with giro systems. The first advantage is the potential for fraud reduction. It has been shown in earlier chapters that cheques lend themselves to sharp practices. The main danger is that the payee, who obtains possession of a cheque, may alter it by raising the amount involved.[127] Frauds by agents, such as employees, who fraudulently complete cheque forms signed by their principals in blank, are equally common. Even if such a fraud does not cause financial loss to the bank, it may involve it in expensive litigation. The danger of fraud is increased if the drawer fails to cross the cheque or overlooks the practical need of adding the words 'a/c payee only' to a crossing.[128] It would be wrong to assert that the danger of fraud is altogether eliminated in the case of giro transactions. However, as bank giro forms are generally posted or delivered to the transferring bank, and not to the payee, the danger of fraud or conversion is reduced. A giro fraud will have to be perpetrated by one of the payer's clerks or agents.

The second advantage of giro payments over the payment of debts by cheque manifests itself when an instrument, presented for payment through a bank, is dishonoured by non-payment. Under the existing cheque clearing procedure, the payee's account is credited before the cheque is set into transmission for its presentment to the drawee bank.[129] If the cheque is dishonoured by the latter bank, due to an irregularity or the inadequacy of funds standing to the drawer's account, the cheque has to be returned to the collecting bank, which in turn returns it to the payee and reverses the credit entry made in his account. In giro credit operations (direct debit operations aside), the money transfer form is processed initially by the payer's bank. It is only when this bank has satisfied itself of the regularity of the form, and that payment is otherwise in order, that the payee's bank becomes involved in the transaction. The payer's account is debited before the crediting of the payee's account; the latter step usually completes the cycle and is final. It is important to emphasize that the giro credit clearing procedure does not rule out the need for occasional reversals of ledger entries, but the problem arises only where an amount is credited to a wrong account as a result of an error in decoding, or the insertion of inaccurate details into, the bank giro credit.

The giro system is not superior to payment by cheque in all regards. First, it will be recalled that errors made by customers when completing blank bank giro credit forms led to unacceptable delays in payments being made. The chances of a mistake being made by the payer when filling out the form have been reduced since January 1998 with the introduction of the requirement that pre-printed forms be used for inter-bank transfers.[130] Nevertheless, blank giro credit forms can still be used for intra-bank transfers, so that in addition to writing out the payee's name and the transfer amount—both of which appear also on a cheque—the payer has also to insert in the giro form all the

---

[126] B. Geva, n.47 above, [1.03(3)].   [127] BEA 1882, s.64.

[128] Ch. 10, Sect. 4(iv) above. This danger has, however, been reduced by the modern practice of issuing cheque-books that include forms bearing a crossing accompanied by the words 'a/c payee only', but not all cheque-books, especially those supplied to companies, contain forms of this type.

[129] Ch. 10, Sect. 2 above.

[130] In January 2003, APACS (now UKPA) implemented the Bank Giro Credit Certification Scheme in order to rationalize the design of giro credits and their code lines, and thereby reduce the number of mis-reads and rejections during the clearing process: see generally APACS, *Best Practice Guidelines for the Design and Use of Bank Giro Credit Vouchers* (August 2003).

details concerning the payee's bank account, and in some cases a reference explaining the object of the payment in question. Secondly, the use of giro forms in the place of cheques generates extra work for both the payer's bank and the payee's bank compared with their involvement with cheques. The payer's bank has to deliver a credit voucher to the payee's bank in the clearing house,[131] and some banks undertake the burden of advising the payer about the execution of his instruction. The payee's bank then has to notify the payee.[132] Thus, the giro system involves multiple notices. In comparison, a cheque serves in itself the purpose of notice and, except where it is dishonoured, its clearance involves a minimum of paperwork for all concerned.

3 The clearance of giro transfers

(i) Paper clearing and electronic clearing

As discussed already,[133] at present there are four main clearing methods for giro transfer operations in the United Kingdom. One of these methods is paper-based, involving the manual transmission of giro forms, and is similar to the clearing of cheques.[134] The other procedures—BACS, CHAPS Sterling, and CHAPS 'Faster Payments Service'—involve electronic clearing. Although the clearing techniques are basically a matter of practice rather than of law, certain aspects of the procedure involved are relevant for defining the legal roles assumed by the parties. Before embarking on a description of the practices involved, it is necessary to refer back to a fundamental distinction between the clearance of cheques and giro transfers.[135] In the case of cheques, the clearing process is initiated by the collecting bank, which sets into motion the machinery for obtaining the payment of an amount due to one of its customers. The process can, therefore, be described as the collection by an agent of a debt due to his principal. Direct debits aside, in giro operations the process is usually initiated by the payer's bank, which remits an amount payable by one of its customers. The object of this bank is, thus, to effect payment on behalf of its customer, not to demand it. Nonetheless, the notion of settling debts by means of the transfer of bank balances is essentially one and the same regardless of whether the transfer is by cheque or giro. In both cases, a series of ledger entries is substituted for the payment of cash.

(ii) The manual clearing procedure

The procedure involved in the clearing of bank giro credits is fundamentally the same as that used in the case of cheques.[136] The payer delivers to his bank a bank giro credit accompanied by a cheque or a withdrawal form. At the branch of the payer's bank with which the payer maintains his account, the relevant data is entered on the bank giro credit

---

[131] A correspondent or intermediary bank may be involved where one or both of the banks are not members of the clearing house.

[132] Some banks have discontinued the practice of advising the receipt of the funds to the payee.

[133] Sect. 1(v) above. The 'Town Clearing' system, which handled the same-day clearing of cheques drawn for more than £500,000 on a City of London branch of a participating bank by another such branch, was abolished in February 1995: see further Ch. 10, Sect. 2 above.

[134] The paper-based giro credit clearing is operated by the Cheque and Credit Clearing Co. Ltd, which is one of the clearing companies serviced by UKPA (Ch. 1, Sect. 2(i) above). For consideration of the company's role in cheque clearing, see Ch. 10, Sect. 2 above.

[135] Sect. 2(iv) above.   [136] For a description of cheque clearing, see Ch. 10, Sect. 2 above.

form in magnetic ink.[137] The figures printed set out the clearing numbers for the payer's bank and the relevant branch, the numbers for the payee's bank and his branch, the numbers for the accounts of the payer and the payee, and the amount to be transferred. The payer's account is debited by means of a message keyed into the computer terminal at his branch. The bank giro credit is then dispatched to the clearing office of the payer's bank. On the next day, the clearing office delivers this form through the clearing house to the clearing office of the payee's bank.[138] In the case of some banks, the amount involved is there credited to the payee's account and, on the same day, the form is thereafter forwarded to the branch of the payee's bank where his account is held. In the case of other banks, the crediting of the payee's account is carried out at the relevant branch and not at the head office of the payee's bank. The payee is informed by his own branch of the credit received.[139]

The procedure varies slightly if the bank giro credit is delivered at a bank other than that with which the payer maintains his account. Individual agreements between banks participating in the giro credit clearing system allow money to be paid into a bank by someone who does not hold an account with that bank in order for that money to be credited to an account held at that bank or at another bank.[140] Where a payer delivers a bank giro credit and accompanying cheque to a bank with which he does not maintain an account, the credit and the cheque will be transmitted through the respective clearing systems, so that the credit will reach the payee's bank and the cheque will reach the drawer's branch. A special procedure is used where a member of the public who is not a customer of the bank wishes to utilize the money transfer system in order to settle a debt due to a third party in cash. The money paid in cash by the payer to the respective branch becomes part of the funds of the 'pay-in bank'. A credit balance accrues, at the same time, for the benefit of the payee's account, the details of which are, of course, set out in the bank giro credit form tendered by the payer. Obviously, there is no need for the paying branch to debit any account. All it has to do is to send the form to the payee's bank through the clearing house.

The manual clearing system of money transfer orders is obviously cumbersome and slow. The ordinary cycle takes three banking days and, if the account to be credited is maintained in a remote part of the United Kingdom, it may take yet another day, even if the form is handed to the payer's own branch.[141] Despite this, the manual clearing system of money transfer orders continues to be used for individual bank giro credits, although the volume and value of such transfers is in decline.[142] The process outlined above applies, however, where the payer and payee hold accounts at different banks. Where the payer

---

[137] In the case of pre-printed credits, which are supplied to the payer by the payee, the payee's account details are already encoded on the credit and so the payer's bank need encode only the amount of the transfer on the credit. Encoding is usually done at branch level, though in some banks it is done at regional centres.

[138] Some banks and building societies exchange paper-based credits directly between themselves under bilateral arrangements.

[139] Some banks have discontinued the practice of sending an advice of payments received to their customers.

[140] This practice had previously been sanctioned by the 'Golden Memorandum', originally issued in 1967. Under this memorandum, participating banks gave notice that each one of them was authorized to act on behalf of all the others in giro transactions.

[141] Note the 'unavoidable delay' provision in the Clearing House Rules.

[142] During 2008, the volume of paper-based giro credits cleared in England and Wales dropped by 10.3 per cent and the volume of such transfers declined by 9.8 per cent: UK Payments Council & APACS, *Annual Summary of Payment Clearing Statistics 2008* (London, 2009), 3. Between May 2008 and May 2009, the use of paper-based credits decreased a further 12 per cent by volume and 13 per cent by value: UK Payments Council & APACS, *Clearing Statistics May 2009* (London, 2009), 1.

and payee hold accounts at the same branch of the same bank, the bank giro credit will not pass through the clearing system. The necessary account adjustments will be made at the branch. Similarly, where the payer and payee hold accounts at different branches of the same bank, the bank giro credit will not pass through the clearing system—either the payer's branch will send the credit to the bank's central clearing department for onward transmission to the payee's branch, or the payer's branch will itself send the credit directly to the payee's branch.[143]

(iii) Clearance through BACS

BACS provides an alternative to the manual transfer of funds and typically deals with high-volume, but low-value, credit and debit funds transfers. The main difference between this automated system and the manual clearance of cheques and of bank giro credits is one of method. There is no distinction as regards the element of time, as the cycle is spread over three days.[144] The procedure used by BACS involves electronic transfers that obviate the need for a great deal of paperwork and for the physical transmission of documents. As a substitute for the exchange of paper at the clearing house, the automated process utilizes an electronically effected transfer system executed with the aid of the central agency, BACS. The fact that the BACS clearing cycle is spread over three days is, however, the principal shortcoming of the system when compared to other electronic funds transfer systems.[145] Whilst the PSR 2009 will require BACS to move to a one-day clearing cycle before 1 January 2012,[146] a significant proportion of BACS' previous workload (principally the execution of standing orders)[147] has now been transferred to the recently developed CHAPS 'Faster Payments Service',[148] which provides a near-real time or same-day service. BACS does retain responsibility for the clearing of direct debit payments, however, and continues to operate a direct credit clearing system. Although BACS credit clearing is likely to remain popular with parties who submit their payment instructions directly to BACS ('direct submitters'), such as company payroll departments, the popularity of the system for parties who submit their payment instructions through a bank ('indirect submitter'), such as one-off consumer payments, may well decline as a result of the more efficient processes of the CHAPS 'Faster Payments Service'.[149]

BACS currently claims 16 member banks and building societies.[150] Each member has direct access to the BACS system and will supply BACS with credit and debit instructions as computer data ('input data') for processing. Members may also sponsor their non-personal customers (i.e. non-member banks and building societies, and corporate customers) to submit their own input data to BACS, either directly or through a computer bureau. Sponsored customers remain the responsibility of their sponsor, however, and any transfer that they initiate must still be processed with reference to the sponsoring

---

[143] As with inter-bank transfers, the volume and value of such inter-branch transfers are similarly in decline. During 2008, the volume of inter-branch paper-based giro credits dropped by 14.5 per cent: UK Payments Council & APACS, *Annual Summary of Payment Clearing Statistics 2008* (London, 2009), 3.

[144] For discussion of the cheque clearing cycle, see Ch. 10, Sect. 2 above.

[145] For a proposal that the BACS payment cycle be reduced from three to two days, see Office of Fair Trading, *UK Payment Systems* (London, May 2003), [7.27], [9.139].

[146] PSR 2009, regs. 70(1)–(2).   [147] Sect. 2(ii) above.   [148] See Sect. 3(iv)(b) below.

[149] The volume of BACS direct credits between May 2008 and May 2009 has remained at approximately the same level as the previous year (UK Payments Council & APACS, *Clearing Statistics May 2009* (London, 2009), 1), although one would usually expect to see an annual increase.

[150] For a list of current members, see www.bacs.co.uk (1 January 2011). For a detailed analysis of the mechanics of BACS transfers, see M. Brindle and R. Cox (eds.), n.1 above, [3-023]–[3-031]. .

member. The rules governing the operation of the system are set out in procedural manuals, called BACS Users' Manuals, and in various agreements reached between the BACS members themselves. Input data submitted by sponsored customers must be received by BACS at its main processing centre by 10.30 p.m. on the first day of the clearing cycle in respect of payments due on the third day. However, BACS has a data storage facility so that non-urgent credit and debit instructions can be dispatched to BACS by members and their sponsored customers up to 30 days in advance of the required payment date.

BACS users submit input data to BACS through BACSTEL-IP, a telecommunications service that offers direct communication to the BACS processing centre. BACSTEL-IP provides a secure online channel for the submission of input data to BACS by its members and enables members to track and view payment files at any time, from anywhere, and to receive and store reports electronically. In terms of connectivity, 'direct submitters' can access the service through one of five means: the internet, dial-up extranet, Broadband Direct, DSL Connect and Fixed Extranet Connect.[151] There are also two ways in which direct submitters can access BACSTEL-IP—either by using the BACS Approved Software Service (BASS) or by using a secure website called 'BACS Payment Services'.[152] The website can be used to view submission history, to access reports, and to maintain details of service users and contacts.

BACS processes the input data overnight between days one and two of the clearing cycle. Input data are validated and recorded by BACS and an input report is sent to the user. BACS then sorts the data and produces a series of credit and debit instructions ('output data') for each member bank and building society. BACS is a self-balancing system in that every instruction to credit an account must be accompanied by an instruction to make a corresponding debit to the account from which payment is to be made. Individual output files are produced by BACS for each member bank and building society. These record the output data relevant to the accounts of that member's customers. The practical importance of this process can be illustrated by referring to a university's payroll. Where the university is a 'direct submitter', it will prepare a file of payments setting out details of the amount of each salary payment, the identity of the payee, and his or her bank, branch, and account number. These data, together with instructions to credit the bank accounts of the listed employees and to debit the university's account, are then transmitted to BACS. Computers at the BACS processing centre sort the items and group them by recipient bank. BACS completes processing by 6 a.m. on the second day of the clearing cycle, by which time all the output data will have been dispatched to member banks and building societies. On the second day of the clearing cycle, the member banks and building societies process the output data received from BACS and ensure that credits and debits are made to customers' accounts by the opening of business at 9.30 a.m. on the third day. The inter-bank obligations that arise through BACS are settled at the Bank of England on a multilateral net basis on the third day of the payment cycle. This occurs at 9.30 a.m. each day by posting multilateral net amounts directly to settlement members' settlement accounts using the CHAPS real-time gross settlement processor.[153]

Payments made by BACS direct credit are initiated by instructions issued by the payer. An important exception occurs in the case of direct debits. It will be recalled that, in such

---

[151] For further details, see www.bacs.co.uk (1 January 2011).

[152] The website address is www.paymentservices.co.uk.

[153] Bank for International Settlements—Committee on Payments and Settlement Systems, *Payment and Settlement Systems in Selected Countries* (April 2003) (the 'Red Book'), 411.

an operation, a trading firm (the payee) is authorized by a client (the payer) to demand from the latter's bank payments of accounts posted to him from time to time.[154] In such a transaction, the payee acts as the payer's agent. If the demand is made through BACS, the payee's bank issues a demand for payment and not an order to transfer or to pay.[155] The procedure involved is, however, the same as in the case of a payment instruction. The only difference is that the 'recipient bank' is required to pay rather than to receive payment. Currently, this demand for payment can be refused before the close of the third day of the respective clearing cycle, but, from 1 January 2012, the PSR 2009 require that any refusal to execute a payment order must be notified before the end of the one-day clearing cycle.[156] Similarly, where Part 6 of the PSR 2009 applies,[157] the payer may not revoke the direct debit payment after the end of the business day preceding the day agreed for the debiting of the funds.[158]

Given the three-day clearing cycle, BACS is not a true immediate electronic funds transfer system as the order to pay, or collect, must be made at least two days before the payment date. By contrast, CHAPS allows for the near instantaneous transfer of funds.

(iv) **Clearance through CHAPS**

The Clearing House Automated Payment System, better known by the acronym CHAPS, started operation as a same-day value electronic sterling credit transfer system in February 1984.[159] It is run by the CHAPS Clearing Co. Ltd,[160] which operates under the umbrella of UKPA. The original CHAPS system, which dealt solely with sterling-denominated transfers, became known as CHAPS Sterling. This distinguished it from CHAPS Euro, which started operation on 4 January 1999 as a same-day value electronic credit transfer system for Euro-denominated payments. CHAPS Euro was connected to the various real-time gross settlement systems of other Member States by TARGET,[161] which was a payment system arrangement allowing high-value payments denominated in Euros to be made in real time across borders within the European Union. On 27–28 August 2001, CHAPS Sterling and CHAPS Euro were consolidated into a dual-currency RTGS system called NewCHAPS, so that the two clearing systems operated under the same generic SWIFT technical infrastructure and were governed by the same set of clearing rules, namely the CHAPS Rules.[162] All payments made through NewCHAPS were denominated in either sterling or Euro and settled on an individual basis in real time across the relevant members' settlement accounts in the respective currency. In May 2008, TARGET was replaced by TARGET2,[163] which provides for a higher level of integration by establishing a single

---

[154] See further Sect. 2(iii) above.

[155] If the payee is a 'direct submitter', it can issue the instruction directly to BACS.

[156] PSR 2009, regs. 66(2), 70(1).   [157] Sect. 5(iv) below.

[158] PSR 2009, reg. 67(3). In other cases where the payment transaction is initiated by or through the payee, the payer may not revoke the payment after transmitting the order or giving consent to the payee: ibid., reg. 67(2).

[159] CHAPS was introduced to replace the 'Town Clearing' system for cheques. The 'Town Clearing', which eventually closed on 24 February 1995, handled the same-day clearing of cheques drawn for more than £500,000 on a City of London branch of a participating bank and received for collection by another such branch: see further Ch. 10, Sect. 2 above.

[160] Formerly called the 'CHAPS and Town Clearing Company Limited' until the closure of the 'Town Clearing' system.

[161] Sect. 1(iv) above.   [162] Effective as from 27 August 2001, and amended from time to time.

[163] European Central Bank, n.17 above, 10–14. See also K. Laurinavicius, K. Lober, & H. Weenink, n.65 above.

technical infrastructure for gross clearing of Euro payments. As the Bank of England elected not to participate in TARGET2,[164] CHAPS Euro was decommissioned on 16 May 2008 and NewCHAPS became once again CHAPS Sterling.[165] On 27 May 2008, CHAPS launched the 'Faster Payments Service', which was a separate clearing system designed to extend the benefits of CHAPS technology to lower-value transactions made over the internet and phone.[166] Like BACS, the 'Faster Payments Service' is a net settlement system, although, unlike BACS, transfers under the 'Faster Payments Service' take place in near-real time or on the same day depending upon the precise nature of the payment made. The 'Faster Payments Service', therefore, differs in at least one important respect from CHAPS Sterling, which is a real-time gross settlement (RTGS) payment system.[167]

(a) CHAPS Sterling

There are currently 17 settlement members of CHAPS Sterling. They are all banks.[168] The CHAPS settlement members are bound by the CHAPS Rules. Unlike BACS, CHAPS Sterling does not operate a central clearing system. CHAPS Sterling settlement members use their SWIFT interfaces to communicate directly with other settlement members over the SWIFT network. The settlement member sends credit transfer messages to, and receives similar messages from, other settlement members via its SWIFT interface. The CHAPS Sterling system currently operates between 6.00 a.m. and 4.20 p.m., although the deadline for submitting customer payments is 4.00 p.m.[169] CHAPS Sterling settlement members may also enter into separate contractual agreements with their corporate or institutional customers (for example, a bank which is not a settlement member) allowing them to participate in the CHAPS Sterling system. Such agreements usually mirror the terms of the CHAPS Rules. These participants are treated like branches of the settlement member and may be linked, via a computer system or an existing SWIFT connection, to the settlement member's payment processing system. The participant cannot access the CHAPS Sterling system directly, but must always go through its settlement member. As with all CHAPS payment messages transmitted through its SWIFT interface, the settlement member remains responsible for the authenticity of any payment message transmitted by the participant. In all cases, payment must be guaranteed by the sending settlement member.

Each settlement member has its own internal computer system that enables the settlement member's branches to access its payment processing system. Customers may use a variety of means to instruct their branch to issue a CHAPS Sterling payment message, for example, by telephone, telex, or in writing. The customer will usually provide the bank with the names of the payer and payee, details of the banks and branches where

---

[164] Ibid., 13.

[165] For a detailed discussion of CHAPS Euro, see E.P. Ellinger, E. Lomnicka, & R.J.A. Hooley, *Ellinger's Modern Banking Law* (4th edn., Oxford, 2005), Ch. 13, Sect. 3(iv)(b). With the development of the 'Single European Payment Area', the European Payments Council has developed standardized payment instruments using the common technical framework of TARGET2 for making Euro-denominated payments in the SEPA. The stated intention is that these instruments replace alternative national mechanisms for making Euro-denominated payments: European Central Bank, n.52 above, 19–20.

[166] The 'Faster Payments Service' was used approximately 83 million times between its launch on 27 May 2008 and the end of that year: UK Payments Council & APACS, *Annual Summary of Payment Clearing Statistics 2008* (London, 2009), 3.

[167] CHAPS changed from being a same-day net settlement system to become a real-time gross settlement system on 22 April 1996.

[168] For a list of current members, see www.chapsco.co.uk (1 January 2011). For a detailed analysis of the mechanics of CHAPS Sterling transfers, see M. Brindle and R. Cox (eds.), n.1 above, [3-032]–[3-035].

[169] Bank for International Settlements, n.153 above, 408. There is, however, a 'Late Transfer Scheme' that operates until 5.00 p.m.: id.

the accounts to be debited and credited are held, the numbers of those accounts, and the amounts to be transferred. Incoming payment instructions given by overseas banks to their United Kingdom correspondent or intermediary banks will usually be transmitted over SWIFT, although airmail and telex may be used for this purpose. Where the United Kingdom correspondent or intermediary bank is a CHAPS settlement member, it will normally debit the account of the overseas sender and then use CHAPS in order to make payment to the payee's bank or its correspondent.

Each CHAPS Sterling payment message is settled across members' accounts at the Bank of England before full payment data is sent to the 'receiving bank'.[170] The SWIFT 'Y-Copy Service' ensures that a settlement request, derived from each payment message received by the CHAPS Sterling Closed User Group, is sent initially to the Bank of England. If there are sufficient funds in the account of the 'sending bank',[171] the Bank of England settles the transaction by debiting the account of the 'sending bank' and crediting the account of the 'receiving bank' in the same amount. Thereafter a form of confirmation is added to the full message stored by the SWIFT 'Y-Copy Service'. On receipt of this confirmation, the full payment message and confirmation are automatically released to the 'receiving bank'. The 'receiving bank' receives the full payment message and confirmation and, once authenticated, it immediately transmits a positive user acknowledgement (or 'UAK') back to the 'sending bank'. The UAK confirms safe receipt and acceptance of the output message. The 'receiving bank' has the assurance that, on receipt of the full payment message, plus the confirmation, the relevant funds have been credited to its settlement account.

For each payment message, settlement takes place in real time against sufficient funds in the sending bank's account. To avoid gridlock,[172] however, the Bank of England provides the CHAPS Sterling banks with intra-day liquidity, so that they can maintain an even flow of funds through the system, by purchasing from them certain high-quality assets under sale and repurchase agreements.[173] More recently, a circles processing facility has been developed that provides a central scheduling and queue management facility for CHAPS members at the Bank of England and allows the simultaneous settlement of payments queued on behalf of different banks.[174] Under this facility, a CHAPS Sterling settlement request is received by the central scheduler from a CHAPS Sterling member. The central scheduler enables members to prioritize payments, hold individual payments, or schedule payments by value and/or by counterparty, so long as that counterparty is also a CHAPS Sterling member. Payments are released from the central scheduler to the RTGS settlement process. At this point, payment requests are either queued awaiting funds or settled immediately if funds are available. Members are able to allocate a priority to a payment, which determines the queuing order once payments are forwarded to the RTGS processor. Nevertheless, the member may amend that priority or cancel the payment at any time up to settlement. Members are even able to reserve part of their liquidity to enable urgent payments to be settled without waiting for the arrival of funds from other CHAPS Sterling members. CHAPS Sterling members are able to track the status

---

[170] A 'receiving bank' may be the payee's bank itself or, where the payee's bank is not a CHAPS settlement member, the 'receiving bank' will be a CHAPS settlement member employed by the payee's bank to act as its agent.

[171] A 'sending bank' may be the payer's bank or some other bank acting as a correspondent or intermediary of the payer's bank.

[172] Gridlock risk is the risk in a gross settlement or payment system that one or more participants defer the performance of their settlements until such time as they have received sufficient credits from other participants, thereby preventing the system from starting work: M. Giovanoli, n.60 above, 224.

[173] Bank for International Settlements, n.153 above, 409.

[174] Ibid., 408–409 See also C Becher, M Galbiati and M Tudela, 'The Timing and Funding of CHAPS Sterling Payments' *Economic Policy Review* (Federal Reserve Bank of New York, 2008).

of individual payments as they progress through the scheduler and the RTGS settlement process through a computer-based enquiry service called 'Enquiry Link'.

The CHAPS Rules subject the 'sending bank' and the 'receiving bank' to various obligations. The rules provide that payments made through CHAPS Sterling must be unconditional.[175] This is certainly consistent with Part 6 of the PSR 2009,[176] which provide that as a general rule a payer cannot revoke his payment instruction once it has been received by his bank,[177] but these do not expressly deal with the revocability of the CHAPS Sterling payment as between the CHAPS members themselves. Pursuant to the CHAPS Rules, a payment message cannot be revoked by the sending settlement member, or any other party, from the point at which the relevant member's settlement account is debited.[178] The receiving settlement member 'must for the purposes of making payments through CHAPS...accept and give same day value to all payments denominated in sterling' received within a timetable set out by the CHAPS Clearing Co. Ltd.[179] It is arguable that the payee who is due to receive such a sterling payment may have a right of action against his own bank for breach of contract should it fail to give same-day value as provided by the CHAPS Rules.[180] Even if this argument were to be rejected, however, a payee might nowadays have an action for breach of statutory duty pursuant to the PSR 2009, if applicable,[181] if the payee's bank fails to give the payee same-day value in respect of any CHAPS Sterling transfers received.[182]

In *Tayeb* v. *HSBC Bank plc*,[183] Colman J recently held that when a customer opens an account with his bank, which is available for receiving incoming CHAPS transfers, the bank engages that it will accept into his account all CHAPS transfers that comply with the CHAPS Rules and that are otherwise in accordance with the terms of the account. In this case, the 'receiving bank' became suspicious of the origin of funds that had been transferred into its customer's account using CHAPS and, without its customer's consent, returned those funds to the 'sending bank'. Colman J held that the 'receiving bank' was indebted to its customer in the amount of the sum transferred. His Lordship held that a CHAPS transfer was ordinarily irreversible once the 'receiving bank' had authenticated the transfer, had sent an acknowledgement informing the 'sending bank' that the transfer had been received and had credited the funds to its customer's account.[184] All this had occurred in the instant case. In reaching this conclusion, Colman J took account of the CHAPS Rules. His Lordship noted that the transfer in question had taken place prior to

---

[175] CHAPS Rules (Version 2.0, 2009), r.3.2.1.   [176] See further Sect. 5(iv) below.

[177] PSR 2009, regs. 65(1) & 67(1).

[178] CHAPS Rules (Version 2.0, 2009), r.3.2.1. Whenever the Bank of England's systems are not capable of processing a CHAPS payment message, and so CHAPS is operating in RTGS By-Pass mode, the payment message is considered irrevocable from the point in time when the 'sending bank' is unconditionally and irrevocably liable to pay the 'receiving bank' the amount in the payment message: ibid., r.3.2.2.

[179] Ibid., r.2.2.3.

[180] This is based on the argument that CHAPS Rules (Version 2.0, 2009), r.2.2.3. represents the reasonable usage of bankers and as such constitutes an implied term of the payee's contract with his bank: see *Hare* v. *Henty*, n.85 above; *Re Farrow's Bank Ltd*, n.85 above; *Parr's Bank Ltd* v. *Thomas Ashby & Co.*, n.85 above; *Barclays Bank plc* v. *Bank of England*, n.85 above, [17]; *Tayeb* v. *HSBC Bank plc*, n.85 above, [57]. The payee could not rely on the Contracts (Rights of Third Parties) Act 1999 to enforce a term of the CHAPS Rules against his bank as this possibility is expressly excluded by the wording of the Rules themselves, although this exclusion is made 'without prejudice to any right or remedy of the third party which may exist or be available apart from the Act': CHAPS Rules (Version 2.0, 2009), r.11.1.1.

[181] See further Sect. 5(iv) below.   [182] PSR 2009, regs. 73(1)–(2), 120(1)(c).

[183] N.85 above, [83]. For the view that *Tayeb* is in line with market expectations, see E.P. Ellinger, 'Irrevocability of CHAPS Money Transfer' (2005) 121 *LQR* 48, 51.

[184] Ibid., [85].

2000 when changes to the CHAPS system had taken place, but observed that 'the questions raised by these proceedings are pertinent also to the present CHAPS system'.[185] According to his Lordship, given that the CHAPS Rules contain specific provisions for the return of unapplied transfers and for applied transfers made in error, and no other provision for the reversal of credit entries following authentication, there was a 'very strong implication that following application to the customer's account, in the absence of error, the banking practice relating to CHAPS transfers is that they are made ordinarily irreversible'.[186] Colman J added, however, that there was an appropriate analogy with the practice in relation to documentary letters of credit where, at the time of the presentation of documents, a bank with cogent evidence of fraud can decline to make payment.[187] His Lordship added that the same exception was likely to apply in respect of illegal transactions.[188] Nowadays, however, the vast majority of CHAPS Sterling transfers are likely to fall within the scope of Part 6 of the PSR 2009,[189] which provide that as a general rule a payer cannot revoke his payment instruction once this has been received by his bank.[190] Whilst the Payment Services Regulations will clearly govern the revocability of CHAPS Sterling transfers falling within their scope and when the issue arises between the payer and his bank, *Tayeb* may still provide guidance as to when a CHAPS Sterling transfer becomes irrevocable and complete as between the payee and his bank.

(b) CHAPS 'Faster Payments Service'

Following the Cruickshank Report,[191] responsibility for regulating and reforming the United Kingdom payments systems was conferred upon the Office of Fair Trading,[192] which in turn set up the Payment Systems Task Force in 2004. The Payments Task Force suggested the development of a system for the streamlining of low-value electronic payments,[193] a suggestion that was further developed by its successor, the UK Payments Council, following its establishment in 2007.[194] On May 2008, CHAPS launched the 'Faster Payments Service' to provide a service for same-day clearing of high-volume, low-value, sterling-denominated credit transfers.[195] The 13 founding members are principally

---

[185] Ibid., [10].   [186] Ibid., [60].

[187] Id., citing *United Trading Corporation* v. *Allied Arab Bank Ltd* [1985] 2 Lloyd's Rep. 554. For the leading statement on the 'fraud exception' in documentary letters of credit, see *United City Merchants (Investments) Ltd* v. *Royal Bank of Canada* [1983] 1 AC 168 (HL).

[188] Ibid., [61], citing *Mahonia Ltd* v. *JP Morgan Chase Bank* [2003] 2 Lloyd's Rep 911. For tentative support for the existence of an 'illegality exception' in documentary letters of credit, see *Oliver* v. *Dubai Bank Kenya Ltd* [2007] EWHC 2165 (Comm.), [12].

[189] See further Sect. 5(iv) below.   [190] PSR 2009, regs. 65(1) & 67(1).

[191] D. Cruickshank, *Competition in UK Banking—A Report to the Chancellor of the Exchequer* (London, March 2000) (available at www.bankreview.org.uk). See further Ch. 1, Sect. 2(iii) above.

[192] HM Treasury Consultation Document (London, December 2000); HM Treasury Press Release, 21 December 2000. In May 2003, the OFT published a report containing a market study covering the UK's money transmission clearing systems and a review of its work on debit, credit, and ATM card networks since 2000: see *UK Payment Systems* (London, 2003).

[193] Payment Systems Task Force, *Final Report of the Payment Systems Task Force* (London, February 2007), Sect. 3.

[194] UK Payments Council, *Annual Review 2008—Driving Change in UK Payments* (London, 2008).

[195] The 'Faster Payments Service' was used approximately 83 million times between its launch on 27 May 2008 and the end of that year: UK Payments Council & APACS, *Annual Summary of Payment Clearing Statistics 2008* (London, 2009), 3. In addition to providing a more efficient clearing service, the 'Faster Payments Service' will allow CHAPS to compete for payment processing business as the 'Single European Payment Area' develops For a detailed analysis of the mechanics of the 'Faster Payments Service', see M. Brindle and R. Cox (eds.), n.1 above, [3-036] -[3-044].

banks, but also include one building society.[196] The 'Faster Payments Service' covers three types of payment instruction: 'immediate payments' for when the payer wishes to make a single credit transfer straightaway; 'diarized payments' for when the payer wishes to make a single credit transfer at some future date; and 'standing orders' for when the payer wishes to give its bank a mandate to make a series of credit transfers on a number of future dates or on a regular basis indefinitely.[197] There are currently monetary limits on the payments that can be cleared through the 'Faster Payments Service': the initial limit for internet and phone payments (both immediate and diarized) was £10,000 and the individual payment limit for standing orders is £100,000. From 6 September 2010, the maximum limit for all types of payment through the 'Faster Payments Service' will be £100,000.

There are a number of differences (mostly advantageous) that exist between the 'Faster Payments Service' and other clearing services for giro transfers. The most noticeable difference between the 'Faster Payments Service' and the BACS system is the speed of the processing. As considered above,[198] BACS has a three-day clearing cycle, whereas the 'Faster Payments Service' offers near-real-time or same-day clearing depending on the type of payment instruction involved. In contrast to BACS and CHAPS Sterling, the 'Faster Payments Service' is available for immediate and diarized payments, 24 hours a day, seven days a week, although the standing order service is only operated between midnight and 6.00 a.m. on banking days. Furthermore, unlike CHAPS Sterling, the 'Faster Payments Service' is a net settlement rather than RTGS system. The principal drawback of the 'Faster Payments Service', when compared to CHAPS Sterling, however, is likely to prove the ceiling on the monetary value of payments that the service is prepared to handle. The recent increase in that ceiling, however, reduces somewhat the significance of this particular disadvantage.

The 'Faster Payments Service' has two components: a messaging element, the technical platform for which is provided by Immediate Payments Ltd (IPL), a subsidiary of VocaLink Ltd; and a settlement element that takes place across members' accounts held with the Bank of England. When a payer wishes to make an immediate payment through the 'Faster Payments Service' (usually over the phone or via the internet), he should first use a 'Sort Code Checker Tool' to verify that the payee's account is set up to receive this type of payment. Once the payer has cleared his own bank's authentication procedures to verify that he is a genuine customer, he will instruct his bank to effect the payment by specifying the amount and the payee's account number and sort code. At least where Part 6 of the PSR 2009 applies,[199] the payer will not generally be able to revoke his payment instruction after this point.[200] After carrying out any necessary verification procedures and checking that the payer has sufficient funds to cover the payment, the payer's bank will generate a message (based upon the 'ISO 8523' format for ATM/debit card messages, rather than the SWIFT formats used for CHAPS Sterling) and forward this to the message switching system operated by IPL. The system will verify the identity of the payer's bank and will then forward the message to the payee's bank. At this point, the payer's account is debited by his bank. Upon receiving the message, the payee's bank will verify the payee's account details, carry out any other necessary checks and credit the payee's account. The payee's bank generates a return message confirming that the payee's account has been credited and this is sent to the message switching system, which in turn forwards the message to the payer's bank, which in turn sends confirmation of payment to the payer. This should be completed in a matter of minutes or seconds. As regards settlement between the banks, there are a number of

---

[196] For a list of founding members, see APACS Press Release, *Phased Roll Out for New Faster Payments Service* (London, 28 April 2008).

[197] See further Sect. 2(ii) above. Before the 'Faster Payments Service', standing orders were executed through BACS: Sect. 3(iii) above.

[198] Sect. 3(iii) above.   [199] See further Sect. 5(iv) below.   [200] PSR 2009, regs. 65(1) & 67(1).

settlement cycles per United Kingdom banking day. At the end of each cycle, IPL will calculate the multilateral position of each bank based on the messages transmitted. IPL then informs the Bank of England of the settlement position, which in turn alerts the members to the fact that settlement is about to occur before debiting or crediting the members' accounts as necessary. The member has to ensure that there are sufficient funds in their account at the Bank of England to allow this to happen. According to the CHAPS Rules, the transfer becomes irrevocable as between CHAPS members from the moment that the relevant member's settlement account is debited with the payment.

The same messaging and settlement processes are used for diarized payments and standing orders, the principal difference being the length of time between the payer's initial instruction to his bank and the sending of the message to the message switching service. Although no guarantees are given, most standing orders will be executed before 6.00 a.m. on the payment due date.

4 International money transfers

(i) Methods in use

The international transfer of money is an essential facet of free trade. In many countries, such transfers are restricted by exchange control legislation, the object of which is to safeguard the stability of the national currency and to prevent the undue outflow of local capital. In the United Kingdom, exchange control was abolished in 1980,[201] so that there are at present no restrictions on the amounts that may be transferred overseas or on the flow of funds into the United Kingdom.[202]

In practice, all international money transfers, except the very limited importation and exportation of currency notes, are effected through banking channels. Travellers' cheques[203] and travellers' letters of credit facilitate the provision of foreign currency to individuals who travel abroad, but even in the use of these facilities, settlement is effected by means of banking channels: travellers' cheques are cleared through banks; and travellers' letters of credit involve the drawing of cheques by the holder on the issuing bank. Traditionally, four main methods have been used to make international money transfers: the bankers' draft; the mail transfer; telegraphic transfers, effected mainly by means of telex messages; and SWIFT transfers. Nowadays, banks almost invariably use SWIFT to make international funds transfers.[204] Special considerations may, however, apply to international electronic transfers within the EEA that are denominated

---

[201] Exchange Control (Authorised Dealers and Depositaries) (Amendments) (No. 4) Order 1979, S.I. 1979/1338; Exchange Control (Revocation) Directions 1979, S.I. 1979/1339; Exchange Control (General Exemption) Order 1979, S.I. 1979/1660. These orders had the effect of suspending the operation of the Exchange Control Act 1947, which was eventually repealed *in toto* by the Finance Act 1987, s.68(1).

[202] An international transfer of funds may nevertheless be affected by foreign exchange control legislation that either forms part of the underlying contract's applicable law, forms part of the law of the place where the transfer is to be completed, or part of the law of the currency in which the transfer is expressed: L. Collins *et al.* (eds.), *Dicey, Morris & Collins on the Conflict of Laws* (14th edn., London, 2006), vol. II, [36R-061]–[36-077].

[203] See further Ch. 10, Sect. 7 above.

[204] See *Dovey* v. *Bank of New Zealand*, n.24 above, 645, where the New Zealand Court of Appeal endorsed the trial judge's findings that SWIFT constituted 'the almost universal system for transferring funds across international boundaries'. For a detailed consideration of the legal nature of SWIFT messages in the context of documentary letters of credit, see *Industrial & Commercial Bank Ltd* v. *Banco Ambrosiano Veneto SpA* [2003] 1 SLR 221, [254]–[261]. See also *Bank of China* v. *Jian Sing Bank Ltd* [2000] HKCU 243.

in Euros or the national currency of an EEA State that has not adopted the single currency. Not only does the Payment Services Directive[205] now provide a harmonized legal framework determining the rights and obligations of the parties to such a transfer, but, in the context of Euro-denominated payments, the European Payments Council has developed standardized payment instruments (the 'STC' and 'SDD') and a common framework for clearing and settlement mechanisms ('the PE-ACH/CSM Framework') using the integrated TARGET2 platform and standard ISO messaging formats operated by SWIFT.[206] As the Single European Payment Area is completed, payments of this nature will have to be made according to increasingly standardized legal, technical, and formal requirements. This section will discuss the various means of effecting an international funds transfer in general, without further specific reference to these particular European developments.

(ii) **The use of bankers' drafts**

As regards the legal nature of a banker's draft,[207] it constitutes a negotiable instrument only if it is drawn by one bank on another. This applies regardless of whether the draft is issued to effect payment in the United Kingdom or overseas. The legal distinction between drafts that are negotiable instruments and those that fall outside the definition is, however, irrelevant as regards the applicable clearing or collection procedure.

Bankers' drafts are used in two main situations. One is where a person who travels overseas wishes to transfer a large amount to the credit of a bank account that he intends to open on arrival. The expense involved in the acquisition of travellers' cheques makes the use of a banker's draft attractive. The other case is where a person wishes to remit money to someone residing overseas, but does not know the identity of the payee's bank. The banker's draft, in which the payer's bank orders its correspondent, as drawee bank, (or its own overseas office) to pay a specified amount to the payee's order, is remitted by the payee to his own bank for collection. That bank presents the banker's draft for payment to the drawee bank through the usual clearing channels available for cheques.[208] The drawee bank obtains reimbursement either by debiting the drawing bank's account with itself or, if this account is overdrawn, by drawing for the required amount.

The main risks associated with the use of a banker's draft are its theft, or, if sent by mail, its loss in transmission. The payee is, however, protected. In the United Kingdom, a collecting bank that acts for the thief of a draft exposes itself to an action in conversion, and may frequently be without any defence.[209] Furthermore, the payee, as holder, is entitled to have the draft replaced by his bank against an indemnity. As that indemnity can be enforced by the issuing bank only if the draft comes into the hands of a holder in due course,[210] the payee is usually protected. The reason for this is that bankers' drafts are made payable to the payee's order, which means that transfer can be effected only by means of the payee's genuine indorsement.[211] A person acquiring the instrument under a forged indorsement is not a holder.[212] However, this rule is applicable only under United

---

[205] Directive 2007/64/EC on Payment Services in the Internal Market [2007] OJ L319, implemented by the PSR 2009.

[206] See further Sect. 1(iv) above.   [207] Ch. 10, Sect. 3(ii) above.

[208] This is the practice in the United Kingdom, but it is applicable in other countries as well.

[209] See further Ch. 15, Sect. 4 below.

[210] This is the case where the draft is a negotiable instrument: BEA 1882, s.69.

[211] BEA 1882, s.31(3). This section applies only to drafts that are negotiable instruments. As regards 'in-house' bankers' drafts, see Ch. 10, Sect. 3(ii) above.

[212] Ibid., s.24. See further Ch. 11, Sect.4(iii) below.

Kingdom and United States law. In other jurisdictions, an indorsement that is regular on its face is, in certain cases, effective to transfer title even if the signature is forged.[213] The risk of the loss or of the theft of a banker's draft dispatched overseas is, therefore, not to be dismissed lightly in such cases.

(iii) **Mail and telegraphic transfers**

Mail transfers and telegraphic transfers can be discussed together, as the procedure used is the same in both cases, except that in the former the customer's instruction is executed by letter whilst in the latter it is carried out by a telegram or telex. In both types of transaction, the customer (the payer) requires his own bank to remit a specified amount to a designated person or firm overseas (the payee). Ideally, the payer should be able to provide his bank with details of the payee's bank account. Where these details are furnished, the payer's bank instructs its correspondent bank in the payee's jurisdiction to arrange the crediting of the relevant account with the amount involved. If the correspondent or intermediary bank happens to be the payee's bank, the procedure is straightforward. The payee's account is credited, and the account of the payer's bank held with its correspondent is debited with the amount in question. If the payee's account is maintained with a bank other than the correspondent of the payer's bank, the transfer can be executed in either of two ways. In most cases, the payer's bank still uses the services of its correspondent bank, which will then remit the amount involved through local clearing channels to the credit of the payee's account with the payee's own bank. Alternatively, the payer's bank may send a message directly to the payee's bank, requesting it to credit the payee's account with the amount involved and authorizing it to reimburse itself by drawing either on the payer's bank itself or more frequently on its local correspondent bank. In some cases the payee's bank is asked to draw on an overseas bank. By way of illustration, take a case in which an amount expressed in United States dollars is remitted from London to a bank in Kuwait, which is asked to reimburse itself by drawing on the London bank's account with its correspondents in New York. The procedure differs where the payer is unable to furnish his bank with the details concerning the payee's account. In such a case, the payer's bank engages its correspondent bank overseas, which then informs the payee about the receipt of the funds and asks for his instructions. Usually, the payee will thereupon request that the amount involved be paid to the credit of his account with a specific bank. This instruction is, again, carried out through the local clearing channels.

It is clear that international money transfers usually involve at least two currencies— that of the country from which the funds are remitted and that of the country to which the money is being transferred. By way of illustration, take a telegraphic transfer of funds from the United Kingdom to Australia. The amount involved may be transferred as a sum expressed in either pounds sterling or Australian dollars. In the former case, the conversion of the amount from one currency into the other takes place when the amount transferred is received in Australia. It will then be converted into Australian dollars on the basis of the banks' buying rate for telegraphic transfers ('the Foreign Currency T/T Exchange Rates'). In the latter case, the conversion takes place in London. In other words,

---

[213] See generally Geneva Convention Providing a Uniform Law for Bills of Exchange and Promissory Notes, No. 3313 of 7 June 1930, 143 LNTS 257, Art. 16; UNCITRAL Convention on International Bills of Exchange and International Promissory Notes 1988, Art. 25 (adopted by the General Assembly, Forty-third Session, A/43/165). For a penetrating analysis, see E.P. Ellinger, 'Negotiable Instruments' in U. Drobnig *et al.* (eds.), *International Encyclopedia of Comparative Law* (Hamburg, 2001), vol. IX, ch. 4, esp. [413].

the payer's account is debited with the amount in pounds sterling required to issue the telegraphic order in question. In some cases, a telegraphic transfer involves three rather than two currencies. This takes place where a contract stipulates payment on the basis of a currency other than that of the seller's or buyer's country.[214] Thus, in a sale of oil by an exporter in Kuwait to an importer in Brazil, the price is usually expressed in United States dollars. Here, the purchaser will have to arrange for a telegraphic transfer of the amount expressed in United States currency.[215]

The difference between the selling rate and the buying rate for a specific type of transaction in a given currency is maintained by banks for two main reasons. First, there is a need to maintain a margin of profit for dealings in foreign currency. For this reason, the selling rate of a currency is invariably higher than the banks' buying rate thereof. Secondly, the difference involved is meant to act as a partial hedge against currency fluctuations. As banks are unable to match completely their purchases and sales of a specific currency during every trading day, the difference between the selling and buying rates is meant to cover them against daily fluctuations. Consequently, the difference between the selling and buying rates for a particular currency increases as its stability declines. The currency fluctuations that may occur where payment is made in a foreign currency are not unique to settlements arranged by telegraphic transfer. Such fluctuations manifest themselves also if the payment is to be made by a banker's draft or by the drawing of a bill of exchange accompanied by documents of title. This practical problem has been considered at this stage, however, because it is most readily explainable in the context of telegraphic transfers, which are inter-bank transactions.

In general terms, telegraphic transfers constitute a satisfactory method for rendering payment of amounts due overseas or for transferring funds abroad. The main risk is that the funds might erroneously be credited to an account other than that specified by the payer. The mistake is usually rectified within a few days, but the delay involved can have serious consequences. Thus, where the initial error in transfer leads to a delay in the payment of an amount due under a charterparty, the shipowner may be entitled to withdraw the vessel.[216] This type of loss is incurred not only in the case of a transmission error, but also in cases where the transfer is delayed as a result of faults in the telecommunication system used. Regardless of whether a transfer is made by telegram or telex message, breakdowns and technical problems are known to have taken place. These problems have encouraged the development of the banks' own network for international money transfers. Transfers using this network are termed 'SWIFT transfers'.[217]

(iv) **SWIFT transfers**

The Society for Worldwide Interbank Financial Telecommunication (SWIFT) is a co-operative society governed by the law of Belgium, where its headquarters are

---

[214] On the question of whether a particular currency is the 'currency of account', which is merely used to calculate the amount payable, or the 'currency of payment', which is the legal tender in which payment is to be rendered, see L. Collins *et al.* (eds.), n.202 above, vol. II, [36R-017]–[36-022], [36R-051]–[36-059].

[215] Where a price expressed in foreign currency is due at a future date, the seller can protect himself against currency fluctuations by a forward exchange contract for the purchase of the currency. The buyer too can protect himself by selling the foreign currency due to him on a 'forward' basis.

[216] For further consideration of this type of situation, see further Sect. 6(iii) below.

[217] *Industrial & Commercial Bank Ltd* v. *Banco Ambrosiano Veneto SpA*, n.204 above, [255]: 'The SWIFT system is a more advanced means of communication than tested telexes. Clearly the system was meant to be an improvement over tested telexes in terms of speed and security.'

located, and is maintained by banks and financial institutions throughout the world with primary oversight resting with the National Bank of Belgium.[218] It operates a network of communications that can be used by banks and other financial institutions for money transfers, for the opening of letters of credit, and generally for the transmission of messages from institution to institution.[219] It is important to stress that SWIFT is merely a messaging system; it does not have a settlement component.[220]

Originally, the system operated through three main operating centres, located respectively in Brussels, Amsterdam, and Culpepper, Virginia in the United States. These centres constituted the link between the remitting bank and the recipient bank. Subsequently, the Brussels centre was decommissioned. In 1990, the entire system was restructured and renamed SWIFT II, and in 2001 access was improved with the launch of SWIFTNet. The SWIFT system now comprises a number of 'slices', each of which is effectively a network that receives messages, forwards them, and stores them. Each slice is composed of modular elements capable of functioning independently, and its operations are carried out by a 'slice processor'. At present there are two such slice processors, located in the Netherlands and the United States. SWIFT II, thus, comprises a network of networks, supervised by the system control processors located in the two main centres.

Individual banks have access to the SWIFT system through their regional centres, known as SWIFT Access Points (SAP).[221] Each country is assigned to such a centre.[222] Banks in the United Kingdom, for instance, are linked to a SAP situated at BACS' headquarters. When a customer instructs his local bank to carry out a money transfer or some other SWIFT operation, his instruction is conveyed by the bank's terminal to the regional SAP. This can be done by a special SWIFT link or by means of a telex message. The SAP encodes the message and dispatches it to the slice processor. The message has to set out all the relevant details concerning the transfer, including the name of the correspondent bank that the transferring bank wishes to use overseas in order to complete the transfer. This latter bank is not necessarily the payee's bank, which may not have a SWIFT link.[223] The slice processor transmits the message, after verifying some encoded security numbers, to the appropriate SAP in the country of destination, where the message is decoded and transmitted to the transferring bank's chosen correspondent or intermediary bank. If the correspondent or intermediary bank is not the payee's bank, it completes the transaction by using the facilities available for domestic transfers. Reimbursement of amounts

---

[218] The relations between SWIFT and its users are governed by SWIFT bylaws and its user handbook, but these do not govern the relationships among users as participants in a funds transfer. The applicable law between SWIFT and each user is Belgian law. For further details, see H.F. Lingl, 'Risk Allocation in International Interbank Electronic Fund Transfers: CHIPS & SWIFT' (1981) 22 *Harv. Int'l. LJ* 621; E.U. Byler and J.L. Baker, 'SWIFT: A Fast Method to Facilitate International Financial Transactions' (1983) 17 *J. World Trade Law* 458; J. Etzklorn, 'The SWIFT Rules' in W. Hadding and U.H. Schneider (eds.), *Legal Issues in International Credit Transfers* (Berlin, 1993), 421 ff. For the most detailed and lucid account, see B. Geva, 'International Fund Transfers: Performance by Wire Payment' (1990) 4 *BFLR* 111; B. Geva, n.47 above, [4.03]. For further information, see www.swift.com.

[219] SWIFT UK is a membership organization that falls under the umbrella of the UK Payments Administration Ltd and that represents the United Kingdom community of SWIFT users by co-ordinating views and forming a common United Kingdom policy on SWIFT issues.

[220] *Raffles Money Change Pte Ltd* v. *Skandinaviska Enskilda Banken AB*, n.97 above, [30].

[221] For expert evidence on the security and other features of the SWIFT messaging system, see *Industrial & Commercial Bank Ltd* v. *Banco Ambrosiano Veneto SpA*, n.204 above.

[222] Most countries are allotted a single SAP, but some major countries have a number of such terminals. In some countries, where usage is relatively low, there is a Remote Access Point (RAP) that is connected to a SAP in another country.

[223] In SWIFT terminology, the payee's bank is called the 'account with' bank.

transferred is obtained in the same way as in telegraphic transfers. Just as SWIFT I, SWIFT II is a communications network; it is not a clearing or settlement centre. In legal terms, the importance of SWIFT messaging is that it eliminates the need for the recipient to authenticate the identity of the sender or the genuineness of the message, since 'the external security measures coupled with the technical inviolability of the system ensure that only authentic and authorized communication enters the system and that such communication can be accessed or copied by only authorized persons at the destination'.[224] Accordingly, it is not generally open to a sending bank to argue that a particular message was unauthorized,[225] so that 'SWIFT messages have the legal effect of binding the sender bank according to the contents'.[226]

SWIFT operations are transmitted by the payer's bank on the day that instructions are received from the customer, and are expected to reach their destination on the same date. However, the time zone differential has to be taken into account in this regard. Obviously, a message dispatched from London to Melbourne will reach its destination after business hours, even if it is executed immediately. To cope with this problem, messages are stored at the SAP if they arrive after it has closed for the day. They are processed on the next day in the order in which they were received, except that 'priority' messages, which involve extra cost, are placed at the head of the queue.

SWIFT transfers have four advantages over telegraphic transfers.[227] First, a telegram or telex may be garbled as a result of a failure in operations. As the banks have no control over the transmission agency, the hazard is a serious one. By contrast, SWIFT is attuned to the special needs of banks and other financial institutions, which are in a position to control operations. Secondly, in telex or telegraphic transfers there is no standard formula or text used to convey a message. As a result, there is room for confusion. In SWIFT operations, however, the banks use standard forms. This harmonization obviates ambiguities and misconstructions. Thirdly, there is no universal language for telegraphic transfers. In the case of SWIFT, English has been adopted as the language for SWIFT operations. Finally, a telegraphic or telex message is not recorded, except by the sending and recipient banks. Accordingly, there is no certainty that a message that appears as transmitted on the sending bank's telex terminal has in fact reached its destination.[228] This danger is avoided in SWIFT operations, as each SAP stores all messages received by it. Furthermore, each message received on a SWIFT terminal is automatically acknowledged.

---

[224] *Industrial & Commercial Bank Ltd* v. *Banco Ambrosiano Veneto SpA*, n.204 above, [255].

[225] This is a feature that SWIFT messages share with 'tested' telexes: *Standard Bank London Ltd* v. *The Bank of Tokyo Ltd* [1995] 2 Lloyd's Rep. 169, 173.

[226] *Industrial & Commercial Bank Ltd* v. *Banco Ambrosiano Veneto SpA*, n.204 above, [257]. Tay Yong Kwang JC does, however, recognize two exceptions to the absolutely binding nature of SWIFT messages, namely where the recipient has knowledge or notice of the unauthorized nature of the message, and where the message is introduced into the system by a 'hacker' so that the message does not emanate from within the sending bank: ibid., [258]. Both exceptions are likely to prove difficult to establish in practice.

[227] In *Dovey* v. *Bank of New Zealand*, n.24 above, 651–652, the New Zealand Court of Appeal held that the payer's bank had not breached its contract with the payer when it used the SWIFT system to make an international funds transfer, rather than a tested telex as instructed by the payer. Such a conclusion is hardly surprising given that 'the SWIFT system is a more advanced means of communication than tested telexes [and] ... an improvement over tested telexes in terms of speed and security': *Industrial & Commercial Bank Ltd* v. *Banco Ambrosiano Veneto SpA*, n.204 above, [255].

[228] For judicial recognition of the difficulties posed by telex communications, see *Entores Ltd* v. *Miles Far East Corporation* [1955] 2 QB 327 (CA); *Brinkibon Ltd* v. *Stahag Stahl Und Stahlwarenhandels-gesellschaft GmbH* [1983] 2 AC 34 (HL).

At present, there is a growing conviction in the banking world that the safest and fastest way to effect transfers is by means of SWIFT.[229] The popularity of the system has increased enormously during the last decades and this trend is likely to continue.

5 The legal nature of money transfer orders

(i) The problem area

It is difficult to define the legal nature of money transfer orders. Despite the popularity that operations of this type have attained in the course of the last 30 years, there remains a relative dearth of case law in point.[230] Moreover, the discussion in the foregoing pages demonstrates that it is erroneous to regard money transfer orders as comprising a single type of transaction. There is a marked difference between the methods used in domestic and international money transfers, and even these two types of transfer have to be divided into different categories. The divergence in the transactions covered under the umbrella of 'money transfer orders' contrasts with the system built around cheques and their clearance through banking channels. Although the rights of the parties to a cheque may vary from case to case, on account of the different types of crossing or of other words appearing in the instrument,[231] the nature of the cheque itself is clearly defined. To date, no certainty of this type prevails in respect of 'money transfer orders'. Only three points can be asserted with confidence. The first is that the documents used in money transfer transactions are not negotiable instruments. The second is that the law of assignment is inapplicable. The third, and only positive, rule is that for most purposes the relationships of the parties to money transfer orders are governed by the law of agency. Whilst it is clear that the banks involved in the transaction act in a representative capacity, it is frequently difficult to determine on whose behalf a given bank is acting at any particular moment. Thus, if an amount is transferred by means of a telex, does the payee's bank receive the message as the agent of the payer's bank or as agent for the payee? This question may be of considerable importance for determining the point in time at which the payer loses the right to countermand the payment order issued by him—the answer applicable in the case of telegraphic transfers may not necessarily be applicable to a transfer executed through SWIFT or CHAPS Sterling.

Much of the uncertainty surrounding money transfer operations probably stems from the absence of a comprehensive statutory regime within the United Kingdom.[232] As considered further below,[233] neither the law of negotiable instruments nor the principles of assignment are applicable to such operations with the result that the statutory regimes

---

[229] *Industrial & Commercial Bank Ltd* v. *Banco Ambrosiano Veneto SpA*, n.204 above, [254]–[261].

[230] For the same view expressed in relation to the lack of Canadian jurisprudence, see M.H. Ogilvie, 'Banker and Customer: The Five Year Review, 2000–05' (2007–2008) 23 *BFLR* 107, 109. See generally D. Fox, n.24 above, [5.23]–[5.29].

[231] See further Ch. 10, Sect. 4 above.

[232] On 25 November 1992, by Resolution 47/34, the United Nations General Assembly approved the UNCITRAL Report and Model Law on International Credit Transfers finalized at UNCITRAL's 25th Session of 4–22 May 1992: UN General Assembly, Official Records, 4th Session, Supp. No. 17, A/47/17. The General Assembly recommended the enactment of national legislation based on the Model Law. There is presently no indication of any such forthcoming legislation in the United Kingdom. References to the provisions of the Model Law are, therefore, made in a few instances only.

[233] See further Sect. 5(ii) & (iii) below.

governing those areas can provide little assistance.[234] The legal landscape is somewhat different in the United States where two statutory regimes are in force. The first regime, which is applicable to consumer transactions, is contained in federal legislation—the Electronic Fund Transfer Act 1978 (EFTA).[235] The second regime, governed by Article 4A of the Uniform Commercial Code and introduced as state law,[236] applies to fund transfers that are outside the ambit of EFTA.[237] Both enactments, however, reflect common law principles so that some of the cases decided thereunder may be of marginal persuasive authority in the United Kingdom.

The absence of a statutory framework in the United Kingdom was rectified to an extent by the implementation of the 'Credit Transfer Directive'[238] by the Cross-Border Credit Transfer Regulations 1999.[239] These regulations were, however, far from comprehensive, applying only to 'cross-border credit transfers'[240] between parties in different European Economic Area (EEA) states in Euros or an EEA currency, provided that the transfer did 'not exceed 50,000 euro or its equivalent in another EEA currency'.[241] This regime has now been replaced from 1 November 2009 by the PSR 2009,[242] which implement the 'Payment Services Directive'[243] and apply generally to 'payment services' (broadly defined to include, *inter alia*, credit transfers and direct debits).[244] The supervisory and regulatory regime introduced by these regulations has been considered previously.[245] Of importance for the present discussion are Parts 5 and 6 of the PSR 2009, which contain detailed rules governing the information that banks must provide to their customers involved with a funds transfer and which establish a regime setting out the rights and

---

[234] See generally BEA 1882; Law of Property Act 1925, s.136.

[235] Financial Institutions Regulatory Controls Act of 1978 (FIRA), Title XX, Pub. L. No. 95-630, 92 Stat. 3741, 3728 (1978), 15 USCA, s.1693a. See generally B. Geva, n.47 above, [6.03] ff.

[236] B. Geva, n.47 above, [2.02] ff. See also McLaughlin and Cohen, 'Electronic Transfer of Funds' (1991) 203 *NYLJ* 3; C. Felsenfeld, 'Comparability of the UNCITRAL Model Law on International Credit Transfers with Article 4A of the UCC' (1991–1992) 60 *Fordham LR* 553.

[237] As regards the exclusion of transactions subject to EFTA from the ambit of Article 4A, see UCC, s.4A-108.

[238] Directive 97/5/EC on Cross-Border Credit Transfers [1997] OJ L43/25. The 'Credit Transfer Directive' was extended to European Economic Area (EEA) states that were not EC Member States, and to cross-border credit transfers in the currencies of those states, by virtue of Decision 1/98 of the EEA Joint Committee (30 January 1998). Thus, the 'Credit Transfer Directive' covered transfers between EC Member States, as well as Norway, Iceland, and Liechtenstein.

[239] S.I. 1999/1876 (in force 14 August 1999). For detailed analysis, see R. Hooley, 'EU Cross-Border Credit Transfers—The New Regime' (1999) 9 *JIBFL* 387. On 19 December 2001, the EU also adopted Regulation 2560/2001/EC on Cross-Border Payments in Euro ([2001] OJ L344/130), requiring that bank charges for cross-border payments in Euro be the same as for similar national payments. The Regulation was implemented in the United Kingdom through the Cross-Border Payments in Euro Regulations 2003, S.I. 2003/488 On 11 February 2008, a report by the European Commission identified a number of practical difficulties regarding the implementation of Regulation 2560/2001. This has resulted in Regulation 924/2009/EC replacing the earlier regime from 1 November 2009. On 16 December 2010, the European Commission published its proposal to amend Regulation 924/2009 further and to enact a Regulation establishing technical requirements for credit transfers and direct debits in Euros.

[240] Ibid, reg. 2(1): '…a transaction or series of transactions carried out as a result of instructions given directly by an originator to an institution in one EEA State, the purpose of which is to make funds in an EEA currency available to a beneficiary at an institution in another EEA State'.

[241] Id.   [242] S.I. 2009/209, reg. 1(2).

[243] Directive 2007/64/EC on Payment Services in the Internal Market [2007] OJ L319, Art. 93, repealing the 'Credit Transfer Directive' from 1 November 2009.

[244] PSR 2009, Sched. 1, para. 1(c). It appears that the definition of 'payment services' may be limited to the situation where the funds are transferred by electronic rather than paper-based means, since the definition does not include 'payment transactions based on [paper-based vouchers] drawn on the payment service provider with a view to placing funds at the disposal of the payee': ibid., Sched. 1, para. 2(g)(iii). For the distinction between electronic and paper-based funds transfer systems, see Sect. 1(iv) below.

[245] For detailed consideration, see Ch. 2, Sect. 6(iii) above.

responsibilities of those participating in such transactions.[246] Although there are still limits upon the operation of Parts 5 and 6, so that they still fall short of establishing a comprehensive statutory regime, they are nevertheless significantly wider than the regime they replace under the Cross-Border Credit Transfer Regulations 1999. Parts 5 and 6 apply to any 'payment services' (including electronic funds transfers) that are provided from an establishment maintained by a bank, other 'payment service provider', or their agent in the United Kingdom, provided also that the payer's and payee's banks are located within the EEA, and that the payment service is carried out in Euros or the currency of an EEA State that has not adopted the single currency.[247] Accordingly, not only do Parts 5 and 6 apply to a broader range of transactions than their predecessor, but more importantly they can also apply to entirely domestic payment transactions in the United Kingdom (arguably, even entirely 'in-house' transfers) and not just 'cross-border' payments.

(ii) Are money transfer orders negotiable instruments?

The question of whether a money transfer order is a negotiable instrument has been raised in the United States, where the definition of a negotiable instrument is wider than the relevant definition in the United Kingdom. Under section 4–104(a)(7) of the Uniform Commercial Code, some of the principles of the law of negotiable instruments apply for certain purposes to an 'item'. An 'item' was originally defined as 'any instrument for the payment of money' and the term encompassed a money transfer order.[248] Nowadays, the term is defined more restrictively. The 1990 official UCC text defines 'item' in section 4–104(a)(9) as 'an instrument or a promise or order to pay money handled by a bank for collection or payment. The term does not include a payment order governed by Article 4A or a credit or debit card slip'. By contrast, the position in the United Kingdom is not so clearly stated. Section 3 of the BEA 1882 provides that a document is a bill of exchange only if it meets the following requirements: it has to be an 'unconditional order' in writing, addressed by one person to another, instructing the addressee to pay a certain sum in money to the order of a specified payee or to the bearer. Payment may be due on demand or at a fixed or determinable future time. Clearly, the requirement that there be 'writing' makes it difficult to apply the definition of a 'negotiable instrument' to the situation where the payer conveys his payment instructions to his bank electronically and the transfer is executed electronically without ever being incorporated in a written or typed instrument.[249] Transfers executed through the 'Faster Payments Service', CHAPS Sterling, or SWIFT would therefore be unlikely to be regarded as involving a negotiable instrument.[250] The need for 'writing' may be overcome where the payer issues his instructions in a written form, as is the

---

[246] For the operation of these Parts in the context of card payments, see Ch. 14, Sect. below.

[247] PSR 2009, regs. 33(1), 51(1). The rules relating to value date and availability of funds in reg. 73 apply regardless of whether both payer and payee are located within the EEA: ibid., reg. 51(2).

[248] D.I. Baker, *Law of Electronic Funds Transfers* (2nd edn., New York, 1988), [12.02(1)].

[249] In the United States, the term 'writing' is defined in UCC, s.1-201(b)(43) as including 'printing, typewriting or any other intentional reduction to tangible form'. This may include an electronic message. In the United Kingdom, although the Interpretation Act 1978, Sched. 1 defines 'writing' as including 'other modes of representing or reproducing words in a visible form', no order has yet been made in respect of the BEA 1882 under the Electronic Communications Act 2000, s.8, which gives the Secretary of State the power to modify legislation 'in such manner as he may think fit for the purpose of authorizing or facilitating the use of electronic communications or electronic storage'.

[250] Sects. 3(iv) & 4(iv) above. Even if the electronic instruction were held to be 'writing' for the purposes of the BEA 1882, or a written order were given to the payer's bank to effect a transfer by means of an electronic

case in bank giro credits, direct debits, and telegraphic transfers.[251] There are, however, three grounds for concluding that the orders issued in these types of transaction do not constitute negotiable instruments. These are best explained by examining the form of a bank giro credit in the light of the definition of a 'bill of exchange'.

The first distinction between a negotiable instrument and a bank giro credit is that the giro form is not payable at a determinable future time or on demand. The words 'payable on demand' in section 3 of the BEA 1882 refer to payment at sight or on presentment,[252] which means that the payment is to be effected when demanded by the payee or holder. The bank giro credit, which is delivered to the drawee bank and not to the payee, is payable as soon as the drawee, *viz.* the payer's bank, can make payment. It might be argued that a bill of exchange is deemed to be payable on demand if no time for payment is expressed in it,[253] and that this is the case in a bank giro credit. The answer, as regards the bank giro credit, is that an instrument can be treated as payable on demand only if the payee is afforded the opportunity to claim payment. The same argument is applicable to all giro forms, such as direct debits, and to telegraphic transfers, which do not stipulate a payment date.[254]

The second ground for regarding a bank giro credit as being outside the definition of a negotiable instrument is that the giro form is not payable to the order of a specified person or to bearer. Instead, the form nominates a specific payee to whom, or to whose account, the money is to be paid. It may be argued that a bank giro credit may nevertheless be an order instrument because a bill is payable 'to the order of a specified payee', even if it is made payable to him alone without the addition of the words in question.[255] However, this rule applies only where it is clear from the nature of the instrument that the payee is to be given the opportunity of deciding that the bill be paid to the order of a person other than himself. To this end, he must be able to transfer the bill in the appropriate manner. Any other construction of the words 'or order' in section 3 of the BEA 1882 would render them meaningless. In a bank giro credit, the payee is not given the opportunity of transferring the instrument or, in other words, of determining to whose order it is to be paid.

The third, and most important, ground for treating a bank giro credit as falling outside the definition of a negotiable instrument is that the giro form does not include any words that can be construed as a formal instruction given by the payer to his bank. Accordingly, the form is not an 'order'. This point is true in respect of all giro forms used in the United Kingdom, and it must follow that these forms do not constitute negotiable instruments.[256] The conclusion that giro forms do not constitute negotiable instruments is of considerable practical importance in instances of fraud. Where a giro form is fraudulently issued or altered, the rights of the parties depend on the principles of the law of contract and of agency alone; the law of negotiable instruments is inapplicable.[257]

(rather than paper-based) transfer system, the order should still not be considered a 'negotiable instrument' for the reasons given hereafter in the main text in relation to the bank giro credit.

[251] Since 27 May 2008, standing orders have been executed through the 'Faster Payments Service', so that the payer's instructions are nowadays more likely to be given electronically.

[252] BEA 1882, s.10(1)(a).   [253] Ibid., s.10(1)(b).

[254] Note the notion of 'value date' in SWIFT transfers.   [255] BEA 1882, s.8(4).

[256] *Tenax Steamship Co. Ltd* v. *Brimnes (Owners of), The Brimnes,* n.119 above, 949, 969, holding that a telexed transfer order is not a negotiable instrument. See also *Min Hong Auto Supply Pte Ltd* v. *Loh Chun Seng* [1993] 3 SLR 498, 516.

[257] See, for example, BEA 1882, s.64.

(iii) **Is a money transfer order an assignment?**[258]

The answer to this question is of considerable practical importance. If a money transfer order constitutes an assignment, it would be irrevocable once it is complete. For the purposes of the law of assignment, the payer would be the 'assignor', the payee would be the 'assignee', and the payer's bank would be the 'debtor'.[259] Assuming the payer's account was in credit, the balance of the account owed to the payer by his bank would constitute the chose in action to be assigned in whole or in part.[260] In the case of a statutory assignment under section 136 of the Law of Property Act 1925, notification to the payer's bank as debtor completes the assignment.[261] In the case of an equitable assignment of a present chose in action, all that is required is an intention to assign the chose in action and 'some outward expression by the assignor of his intention to make an immediate disposition of the subject matter of the assignment',[262] and the transaction is complete when the debt is assigned, without there being any need for writing or consideration.[263] Notification to the debtor is advisable but not a prerequisite to validity.[264] On the other hand, notice to, or prior agreement of, the assignee is necessary for the assignment to be irrevocable.[265]

---

[258] For a discussion of the general principles of assignment, see Ch. 21, Sect. 1 below.

[259] The various roles of the parties to a money transfer operation are explained by Lord Chorley, an advocate of the assignment theory: Chorley, *Law of Banking* (6th edn., London, 1974), 268–269.

[260] For the nature of the bank–customer relationship, see Ch. 5, Sect. 3 above.

[261] Law of Property Act 1925, s.136. See *Hockley* v. *Goldstein* (1922) 90 LJKB 111; *Flightline Ltd* v. *Edwards* [2003] 1 BCLC 427, [43] (CA); *Mulkerrins* v. *PricewaterhouseCoopers* [2003] 4 All ER 1, [13] (HL); *Winterthur Swiss Insurance Co* v. *AG (Manchester) Ltd* [2006] EWHC 839 (Comm.), [59]; *Finlan* v. *Eyton Morris Winfield* [2007] 4 All ER 143, [5]. See also *W.H. Coole* v. *B. Pasco* [1911] HKCU 16. An assignment may only be perfected in equity once notice has been given to the debtor: *Three Rivers District Council* v. *Governor & Company of the Bank of England* [1996] QB 292, 313–315 (CA); *Harrison Logistics Ltd* v. *Global Freight International Ltd* [2002] EWHC 1098 (Ch), [14]; *Freund* v. *Charles Scott Developments (South Devon) Ltd* [2002] EWCA Civ 106, [30]; *Paragon Finance plc* v. *Pender* [2003] EWHC 2834 (Ch), [137]. See also *R.L. Polk & Co (Great Britain) Ltd* v. *Edwin Hill & Partners* [1988] 18 EG 71. There is no requirement that the notice to the debtor refer to the date of the assignment, and the requirement of notice may be satisfied by sending the debtor a copy of the written assignment: *Van Lynn Developments Ltd* v. *Pelias Construction Co. Ltd* [1969] 1 QB 607, 612–615 (CA); *Firstdale Ltd* v. *Quinton* [2005] 1 All ER 639, [59]. On the question of priorities between competing assignments, see *E. Pfeiffer Weinkellerei-Weineinkauf GmbH & Co.* v. *Arbuthnot Factors Ltd* [1988] 1 WLR 150.

[262] *Finlan* v. *Eyton Morris Winfield*, n.261 above, [33]. See also *Allied Carpets Group plc* v. *Macfarlane* [2002] EWHC 1155, [30]–[33]; *Scribes West Ltd* v. *Relsa Anstalt* [2005] 2 All ER 690, [9] (CA); *Daleri Ltd* v. *Woolworths plc* [2008] EWHC 2891 (Ch), [18].

[263] Ibid., [31]–[33]. See also *Daleri Ltd* v. *Woolworths plc*, n.262 above, [18]. For the distinction between an equitable assignment and a declaration of trust, see *Barbados Trust Co. Ltd* v. *Bank of Zambia* [2007] 1 Lloyd's Rep 495, [43] (CA).

[264] *Brandt's Sons & Co.* v. *Dunlop Rubber Co. Ltd* [1905] AC 454, 462. See also *Mountain Road (No. 9) Ltd* v. *Michael Edgley Corporation Pty Ltd* [1999] 1 NZLR 335, 343 (NZCA); *Thomas* v. *National Australia Bank Ltd* [2000] 2 Qd R 448 (QCA); *Phelps* v. *Spon-Smith & Co.* [2001] BPIR 326, [34]; *Coulter* v. *Chief of Dorset Police* [2004] BPIR 462, [12]–[13]; *Scribes West Ltd* v. *Relsa Anstalt*, n.262 above, [9]; *Jewson Ltd* v. *Batey* [2008] EWCA Civ 18, [3].

[265] This is the case whether the assignment be at law (*Curran* v. *Newpark Cinemas Ltd* [1951] 1 All ER 295 (CA); cf. *Grey* v. *Australian Motorists & General Insurance Co. Pty. Ltd* [1976] 1 NSWLR 669 (NSWCA)) or in equity (*Morrell* v. *Wooten* (1852) 16 Beav. 197; *Re Hamilton* (1921) 124 LT 737; *Re Margaretta Ltd* [2005] STC 610, [24]). See also *General Communications Ltd* v. *Development Finance Corporation of New Zealand Ltd* [1990] 3 NZLR 406, 434; *Lee* v. *K-Leigh Holdings Ltd* (15 December 1997, BCSC), [14]–[15]; *Bank of Commerce Bhd* v. *Mahajaya Property Sdn Bhd* [1997] 3 MLJ 620, 630. For the rejection of the requirement of giving notice to an equitable assignee for a valid equitable assignment, see *Tsu Soo Sin* v. *Oei Tjiong Bin* [2009] 1 SLR 529, [33]–[57] (SGCA).

It has been argued that a money transfer operation constitutes an assignment of debt. In *Delbrueck* v. *Manufacturers Hanover Trust Co.*,[266] the Court of Appeals for the Second Circuit observed that the amounts deposited by the payer with his bank constituted a chose in action and were therefore assignable. Moore J added[267] that, under the law of the United States:

> In order for there to be a valid assignment of a chose in action, there must be a specific direction to transfer by the assignor and notice to the assignee.

The order to transfer was given by the payer to his bank, and the credit slip, delivered to the payee's bank, was adequate notice. The court treated the payee's bank as an assignee that received the amount transferred as the payee's agent.

It is submitted that, despite the persuasive character of the authority in question, the better view is that in the United Kingdom a giro operation does not involve an assignment.[268] English law differs from United States law in that it distinguishes between statutory and equitable assignments. Two arguments demonstrate that a money transfer operation does not constitute a statutory assignment. In the first place, a money transfer order does not usually involve the transfer of the total debt due to the payer from his bank, as debtor. The assignment of part of a debt is, of course, not sanctioned by the Law of Property Act 1925, s.136.[269] Secondly, a money transfer order does not always relate to funds standing to the credit of the payer's account with his bank at the time that the instruction is issued. A standing order is a typical example in point. Undoubtedly, the payer assumes that the required funds will be available at the time the transfer is to be effected. It is, nevertheless, unrealistic to regard the debt to be owed by the payer's bank to the payer at a future time as anything but an expectancy. As such it is not assignable under the Law of Property Act 1925, s.136.[270]

The points raised above do not, however, rule out the classification of a money transfer operation as an equitable assignment of a legal chose in action. However, to attribute to the payer an intention to effect an assignment militates against the nature of the transaction. The one and only object of all the different types of money transfer operation is to instruct the payer's bank to perform a service on behalf of the payer, who is that bank's customer and principal. This instruction need not relate to a debt due to the payer from his bank, but may involve a request for the extension of an overdraft. In other words, the bank is not always the payer's debtor. Moreover, it is frequently difficult to decide whether any instruction given to a bank for the transfer of an amount of money constitutes an assignment or is a mere order issued by the customer as a principal.[271] In most money transfer orders it is assumed by the parties that the instruction may be revoked at least until the time it reaches the recipient bank. This emerges from the explanation of the giro system originally included in the Golden Memorandum 1967[272] and in most

---

[266] N.27 above, 1051. See also *Richards* v. *Platte Valley Bank*, 866 F.2d 1576, 1580 (10th Cir., 1989); *State of Ohio* v. *Warner*, 55 Ohio St. 3d 31, 45–46 (Ohio Sup. Ct., 1990).

[267] Ibid.   [268] D. Fox, n.24 above, [5.25]–[5.29].

[269] *Williams* v. *Atlantic Assurance Co. Ltd* [1933] 1 KB 81, 100; *Walter and Sullivan Ltd* v. *Murphy & Sons Ltd* [1955] 2 QB 584, 588 (CA); *Ramsey* v. *Hartley* [1977] 2 All ER 673, 681–682 (CA); *National Westminster Bank plc* v. *Kapoor* [2011] EWHC 255 (Ch), [97]. See also *Federal Commissioner of Taxation* v. *Everett* (1980) 28 ALR 179, 182–183 (HCA); *Bitz, Szemenyei, Ferguson & MacKenzie* v. *Cami Automotive Inc.* (1997) 34 OR (3d) 566, 570–571 (OGD). Contrast Property Law Act 2007 (NZ), s.48, which permits the statutory assignment of part of a debt.

[270] *Durham Bros.* v. *Robertson* [1898] 1 QB 765 (CA); cf. *Walker* v. *Bradford Old Bank Ltd* (1884) 12 QBD 511.

[271] See, for example, *Morrell* v. *Wooten*, n.265 above, 204; cf. *Williams* v. *Everett* (1811) 14 East. 582.

[272] Ch. 10, Sect. 2 above.

modern brochures issued by banks, from the language of the forms used in standing orders and, above all, from the phraseology of the forms signed by the payer in direct debiting arrangements. None of the forms used in money transfer orders, be they domestic or international, discloses an intention to confer on the payee the right to claim payment of the amount involved from the payer's bank, as would result in the case of an assignment.[273] The parties, accordingly, do not manifest any intention that part of the balance constituting a debt payable by the payer's bank to the payer be made over to the payee as a chose in action claimable by him. It is submitted that, on the facts, money transfer operations are inconsistent with the machinery and with the objectives pertaining to the assignment of debts.

On this analysis, money transfer orders involve a string of operations carried out by the different banks acting in a representative capacity. This view derives support from Webster J's decision in *Royal Products Ltd* v. *Midland Bank Ltd*. His Lordship said:[274]

> [Money transfers] are to be regarded simply as an authority and instruction, from a customer to its bank, to transfer an amount standing to the credit of that customer with that bank to the credit of its account with another bank, that other bank being impliedly authorized by the customer to accept that credit by virtue of the fact that the customer has a current account with it, no consent to the receipt of the credit being expected from or required of that other bank, by virtue of the same fact. It is, in other words, a banking operation, of a kind which is often carried out internally, that is to say, within the same bank or between two branches of the same bank and which, at least from the point of view of the customer, is no different in nature or quality when, as in the present case, it is carried out between different banks.

That these operations do not involve the assignment of a debt has since been confirmed by the reasoning of the House of Lords in *R.* v. *Preddy*.[275] In that case, the defendants were charged with obtaining or attempting to obtain mortgage advances from lending institutions by deception, contrary to section 15(1) of the Theft Act 1968.[276] In making their applications for mortgage advances, the defendants had deliberately given false information to the lending institutions. In cases where the advances were approved, they were paid, not in cash, but by the CHAPS electronic transfer of funds from the bank account of the lending institution to the account of the defendant (or his solicitor).[277] The key question for the House of Lords was whether this process meant that the defendants had 'obtain[ed] property belonging to another' as required by section 15(1) of the Theft Act 1968. Reversing the Court of Appeal,[278] the House of Lords held that it did not.

---

[273] Lack of such an intention also appears to defeat any direct right of action by the payee against the payer's bank under the Contracts (Rights of Third Parties) Act 1999.

[274] [1981] 2 Lloyd's Rep. 194, 198. For a similar conceptual analysis of the bank as its customers' paymaster, see *Barclays Bank plc* v. *Quincecare Ltd* [1992] 4 All ER 363, 375. See also *Morrell* v. *Wooten*, n.265 above, 203–204; *Comptroller of Stamps* v. *Howard Smith* (1936) 54 CLR 614 (HCA) (distinguishing a mandate from an assignment with emphasis on the element of revocation); *Houston Contracting Corp.* v. *Chase Manhattan Bank*, 539 F Supp. 247 (1982); *FDIC* v. *European American Bank and Trust Co.*, 576 F Supp. 950, 957 (1983).

[275] N.23 above. *Preddy* involved a credit transfer, but see also *Mercedes-Benz Finance Ltd* v. *Clydesdale Bank plc*, n.25 above, where Lord Penrose held that a direct debit does not operate to vest in the payee any right of the payer against his own bank.

[276] For the current offences, see Fraud Act 2006, ss. 2 & 11.

[277] Some advances were paid by telegraphic transfer, but the House of Lords held (n.23 above, 833) that no distinction need be drawn for present purposes between the CHAPS system and telegraphic transfers. In some cases, the sums were paid by cheque, but the House of Lords was not asked to consider such payments. However, Lord Goff did make some obiter statements on payment by cheque (ibid., 835–837).

[278] [1995] Crim. LR 564 (CA).

Lord Goff, delivering the main speech, dealt first with the position where the account of the lending institution was in credit.[279] In such a case, the credit balance standing in the account represented property (i.e. a chose in action) of the lender. When funds were 'transferred' to the account of the defendant (or his solicitor) that chose in action was reduced or extinguished, and the defendant's (or his solicitor's) chose in action against his own bank was created or increased. However, as Lord Goff emphasized, the defendant's (or his solicitor's) chose in action against his own bank had never belonged to the lender—it was a newly created proprietary right quite distinct from the lender's chose in action against its own bank. Where the lender's account was overdrawn, his Lordship recognized that it might have to be argued that it was the bank's property, and not the lender's property, that had been 'obtained' by the defendant, but again he concluded that, as a result of the transfer, the defendant (or his solicitor) would be given a new chose in action against his own bank, a chose in action that had never belonged to the lender's bank.[280] However, where the account of the defendant (or his solicitor) was overdrawn, he would not acquire a chose in action against his own bank, but rather the bank's chose in action against him would be reduced.

The importance of *Preddy* extends far beyond the criminal law.[281] *Preddy* confirms that it is something of a misnomer to speak of the 'transfer' of funds in a funds transfer operation, as cash (i.e. coins and banknotes) is not transferred from one account to another and the debt owed to the payer by his bank, assuming his account is in credit, is not assigned to the payee.[282] *Preddy* highlights the important distinction between the transfer of property rights and the extinction and creation of property rights. The point was emphasized by Lord Jauncey in *Preddy* itself: 'In applying these words ["belonging to another"] to circumstances such as the present there falls to be drawn a crucial distinction between the creation and extinction of rights on the one hand and the transfer of rights on the other. It is only in the latter situation that the words apply.'[283]

---

[279] N.23 above, 834.

[280] Ibid., 834–835. See also *R* v. *Shabir* [2008] EWCA Crim 1809, [10].

[281] *Preddy* made a considerable impact on the criminal law as it exposed an important lacuna. Only three months after *Preddy* was decided, the Law Commission of England & Wales published its report, *Offences of Dishonesty: Money Transfers* (Law Com. No. 243, 10 October 1996), proposing, *inter alia*, a new s.15A of the Theft Act 1968, introducing a specific offence of 'obtaining a money transfer by deception'. Lord Goff introduced the Law Commission's draft Bill into the House of Lords on 24 October 1996, and it was enacted as the Theft (Amendment) Act 1996 on 18 December 1996. For the scope of the Theft Act 1968, s.15A, see *Re Holmes* [2005] 1 Cr. App. Rep. 229, [14], [16] (CA) (offence not committed until account unconditionally credited and may be committed without specifically identifying the debited account). For the application of *Preddy* to the Theft Act 1978, s.1, see *Sofroniou* v. *R* [2004] QB 1218, [32]–[33] (CA). *Preddy* has frequently been distinguished when the property offence involves a cheque rather than a funds transfer: see, for example, *Parsons* v. *R* (1999) 160 ALR 531 (HCA); *R* v. *Adams* [2003] EWCA Crim 3620, [17]–[20]; *HKSAR* v. *Lim Jackson Lung Hin* [2006] HKCU 1043, [35]–[38] (HKCA). Nowadays, *Preddy* would be covered by the offences of fraud by false representation (see Fraud Act 2006, s.2) and obtaining services dishonestly (see Fraud Act 2006, s.11), which have replaced the offences in Theft Act 1968, ss. 15 & 15A.

[282] See also *Libyan Arab Foreign Bank* v. *Bankers Trust Co.*, n.26 above, 750; *Customs and Excise Comrs* v. *FDR Ltd.*, n.24 above, [36]–[37]; *Dovey* v. *Bank of New Zealand*, n.24 above, 648; *European Bank Ltd* v. *Citibank Ltd*, n.24 above, [57]–[62]; *Darkinjung Pty Ltd* v. *Darkinjung Local Aboriginal Land Council*, n.24 above, [13]; *Scottish Exhibition Centre Ltd* v. *Commissioners for Her Majesty's Revenue and Customs*, n.24 above, [19]. *Preddy* also undermines *R* v. *King* [1992] 1 QB 20 (CA), where the Court of Appeal (Criminal Division) held that a CHAPS payment order was a 'valuable security', for the purposes of the Theft Act 1968, s.20(2)–(3), on the ground that it created or transferred a right over property. In *R* v. *Manjdadria* [1993] Crim. LR 73, however, it was held that a telegraphic transfer of funds was not a 'valuable security'. See also *R* v. *Graham* [1997] 1 Cr. App. Rep. 302.

[283] N.23 above, 841, applied in *R* v. *Wilkinson* [1999] 1 NZLR 403, 407–409 (NZCA).

(iv) Position of the payer's bank

In assessing the position of the payer's bank *vis-à-vis* the other parties to a money transfer operation, it is necessary first to identify the relevant applicable principles. The obligations and liabilities of the payer's bank will be determined according to Parts 5 and 6 of the PSR 2009,[284] where the 'payment service' in question (defined to include, *inter alia*, credit transfers and direct debits)[285] is provided from an establishment maintained by a bank or its agent in the United Kingdom, the payer's and payee's banks are located within the EEA, and the transfer is carried out in Euros or the currency of an EEA State that has not adopted the single currency.[286] Any breach of the requirements of Parts 5 or 6 is actionable by an individual who suffers loss as a breach of statutory duty and the claim is subject to the defences and other incidents applicable to that tort.[287] For these purposes, there is nothing to suggest that the PSR 2009 would not apply to a payment transaction between two branches of the same bank located within the United Kingdom or in different EEA states,[288] nor that they would not apply to the situation where the payer and payee are one and the same person. Where the payer or the payee (as the case may be) is a 'consumer, micro-enterprise or charity',[289] Parts 5 and 6 have mandatory application, but may be displaced in other cases by contrary agreement to the extent allowed by the regulations.[290] In effect, these regulations will now apply to the vast majority of domestic transfers in the United Kingdom (unless these happen to be in a currency falling outside their scope, such as United States dollars), and to a large proportion of international transfers sent to other European Union States from the United Kingdom (again depending upon the currency of the transfer). Accordingly, the impact of the PSR 2009 will be considered first. Where the money transfer operation falls outside the scope of these regulations, the common law will continue to determine the obligations imposed upon the payer's bank and the payer must rely on his common law remedies in contract and tort. Given the now subsidiary role of these principles, they will be considered second.

(a) Position of the payer's bank under the Payment Services Regulations 2009

Part 5 of the PSR 2009 establishes certain minimum requirements in respect of the information that the payer's bank must provide to his customer.[291] Where the payer is

---

[284] S.I. 2009/209, reg. 1(2) (in force 1 November 2009). For further discussion of the scope of these provisions, see Sect. 5(i) above.

[285] PSR 2009, Sched. 1, para. 1(c).

[286] Ibid., regs. 33(1), 51(1). The rules relating to value date and availability of funds in reg. 73 apply regardless of whether both payer and payee are located within the EEA: ibid., reg. 51(2).

[287] Ibid., reg. 120(1). For the elements of the tort of breach of statutory duty, see W.V.H. Rogers, *Winfield and Jolowicz's Tort* (18th edn., London, 2010), 398–404.

[288] Some support for the proposition in the text may be derived from the statement that '...all places of business set up in the same EEA State other than the United Kingdom by an authorized payment institution are to be regarded as a single branch': PSR 2009, reg. 2(1).

[289] Ibid., reg. 2(1), where a 'consumer' is defined as 'an individual who, in contracts for payment services to which these regulations apply, is acting for purposes other than a trade, business or profession'. A 'charity' in England and Wales is defined as a body with an annual income of less than £1 million that falls within the Charities Act 2006, s.1(1): PSR 2009, reg. 2(1).

[290] Ibid., regs. 33(4), 51(3).

[291] The requirements relating to the information that must be supplied during the course of a 'framework contract' (see PSR 2009, reg. 41), or when there is a change to such a contract (ibid., reg. 42), are disapplied in relation to regulated contracts falling within the scope of the Consumer Credit Act 1974, s.189(1): ibid., reg. 34(1)(a). Similarly, there are amendments to the initial disclosure requirements in respect of both 'framework contracts' and 'single payment service contracts': ibid., reg. 34(1)(b)–(c). Furthermore, the provisions relating to the termination of 'framework contracts' (ibid., reg. 43) are also disapplied: ibid., reg. 34(1)(a).

a consumer, micro-enterprise, or charity, these information provisions are mandatory, but may be displaced in their entirety by contrary agreement outside those contexts.[292] The precise nature of the information depends upon whether the payer makes a one-off request for the transfer of funds from a bank with which there will not necessarily be a continuing commercial relationship (a 'single payment service contract'),[293] or whether the payment request is made within the context of an ongoing contractual or account relationship (a 'framework contract').[294] It is likely that most 'single payment service contracts' will involve business-to-business transfers, as most consumer transfers will usually be made from a current or (flexible) savings account that will likely constitute a 'framework contract' for these purposes. As the information that must be provided to the customer when the payment service is provided pursuant to a 'framework contract' has been discussed already,[295] the present discussion will focus on the case of a one-off payment involving a 'single payment service contract'.[296]

Under a 'single payment service contract', the payer's bank has to make certain information available to the payer either before the contract is concluded or 'immediately' after if the payer's transfer request is made by a 'means of distance communication', such as the phone or internet.[297] This includes details concerning, *inter alia*,[298] the information that the payer needs to provide to his bank in order to ensure the proper execution of his payment order; the maximum time that it will take for the transfer to be effected; the charges for the service provided by the payer's bank and a breakdown of those charges; and any exchange rate that will be applied by the payer's bank to the payment transaction.[299] In addition, the payer's bank must provide the information in Schedule 4 of the PSR 2009 that is relevant to a 'single payment service contract'.[300] Following receipt of the payment order from the payer, the payer's bank must immediately provide further information to the payer,[301] including a reference enabling the payer to identify the payment transaction and, where appropriate, the payee's details; the amount and currency of the payment transaction; the amount and breakdown of the charges payable by the payer; where the actual exchange rate differs from that originally advertised by the payer's bank, details of the rate and amount of the payment after conversion; and the date when the payer's bank received the payment instruction.[302] Whatever the information to be disclosed, there are certain minimum

---

[292] Ibid., reg. 33(4).

[293] Ibid., reg. 2(1): '...a contract for a single payment transaction not covered by a framework contract'.

[294] Id.: '...a contract for payment services which governs the future execution of individual and successive payment transactions and which may contain the obligation and conditions for setting up a payment account'. Where the payer requests a single payment to be made pursuant to the terms of a 'framework contract', the payer's bank is permitted to avoid the duplication of information: ibid., reg. 39.

[295] Ch. 7, Sect. 2 above. Where a customer makes payment by means of a payment card that has been issued in connection with an account, a bank need only comply with the information requirements applicable to a 'single payment service contract' (see PSR 2009, reg. 2(1)) to the extent that these are not duplicated by the information already required to be provided under the 'framework contract' (ibid., reg. 2(1)): ibid, reg. 39. For detailed consideration of the application of the PSR 2009 to payment cards, see Ch. 14, Sect. 9 below.

[296] Although the provision of individual payment services is not generally covered by the FSA's *Banking: Conduct of Business Sourcebook*, BCOBS 2, 5, and 6 will nevertheless continue to apply: see further Ch. 7, Sect. 2 above.

[297] PSR 2009, reg. 36(1).   [298] Ibid., reg. 36(2)(e) & Sched. 4.

[299] Ibid., reg. 36(2). Additional information may be required when payment is to be effected not by funds transfer but by means of a payment card, such as information concerning additional charges: ibid., reg. 50(1). For the application of the PSR 2009 to payment cards, see further Ch. 14, Sect. 9 below.

[300] Ibid., reg. 36(2)(e). For discussion of the information required by Sched. 4, see further Ch. 7, Sect. 2 above.

[301] Ibid., reg. 37(1).   [302] Ibid., reg. 37(2).

standards regarding the manner in which that disclosure must take place—the relevant information must be made available in an easily accessible manner, in easily understandable language, in a clear and comprehensible form, and in English or other agreed language.[303] The payer has the right to request a hard copy of any information that his bank is required to disclose[304] and to receive that information free of charge,[305] unless the information in question is not strictly required by the PSR 2009 or is provided more frequently than required.[306]

Part 6 of the PSR 2009 governs the authorization and execution of a payment instruction and establishes a regime governing the rights and obligations of the parties to a payment transaction. Although Part 6 (unlike Part 5) does not expressly establish distinct regimes for 'framework contracts' on the one hand and 'single payment service contracts' on the other hand, this distinction may still operate to a degree in practice. Where a payer has an account with his bank that he may use to give instructions for a payment transaction (namely, a 'framework contract'), the payer's bank may provide the payer with a device that must be used to initiate a payment transaction on the account,[307] or with a special password, or additional procedures that must be followed in order to initiate a payment transaction online. These additional security features are most likely to occur in the context of an ongoing account relationship (or 'framework contract') and are much less likely to be required in the context of a one-off request for a payment transaction (or a 'single payment service contract'). The reason why this is significant is because such a device, procedure, or password may well constitute a 'payment instrument' for the purpose of the PSR 2009.[308] The use of a 'payment instrument' in order to initiate a payment transaction may well lead to the payer and his bank incurring additional legal responsibilities[309] or may lead to different legal results in comparison to the situations when no 'payment instrument' is used.[310] Although the following paragraphs will focus primarily upon the application of Part 6 of the PSR 2009 to 'single payment service contracts', the same principles will normally also govern the situation where the payment is made pursuant to the terms of a 'framework contract'. Reference will also be made, however, to those situations in which the existence of a 'framework contract' or 'payment instrument' may affect the legal position.[311]

---

[303] Ibid, reg. 47(1).   [304] Id.   [305] Ibid., 48(1).

[306] Ibid., reg. 48(2). Any charges imposed must reasonably correspond to the bank's actual costs: ibid., reg. 48(3).

[307] For example, the device might generate a random code that must be entered into the bank's website to authenticate all internet transactions or transactions above a certain threshold.

[308] See PSR 2009, reg. 2(1), which defines a 'payment instrument' as 'any (a) personalized device; or (b) personalized set of procedures agreed between the payment service user and the payment service provider, used by the payment service user in order to initiate a payment order'. For discussion of the concept of 'payment instrument' in the context of payment cards, see Ch. 14, Sect. 9 below.

[309] There are a number of obligations imposed upon the payer's bank with respect to the issuing of a 'payment instrument', namely to ensure that the personalized security features of the 'payment instrument' are not accessible to persons other than the payer; to refrain from sending the payer an unsolicited 'payment instrument' unless it is a replacement for an instrument previously issued; to ensure that the payer has appropriate means available for notifying his bank of the loss or misuse of a 'payment instrument'; to provide the payer with the means to prove that he duly notified his bank; and to prevent the use of the 'payment instrument' once the payer has notified his bank of the loss, theft, misappropriation or unauthorized use of the 'payment instrument': PSR 2009, reg. 59(1).

[310] In particular, as discussed further below, the use of a 'payment instrument' in connection with a payment transaction may alter the allocation of losses between the payer and his bank when an unauthorized transaction results from the misuse of that instrument: PSR 2009, reg. 62.

[311] Ibid., reg. 53, which enables the payer and his bank to agree that certain provisions of the PSR 2009 will not apply when the payment transaction in question is initiated by means of a 'payment instrument'

As regards the authorization of the payment instruction, the payer's bank will only execute a payment transaction to which the payer has given his consent.[312] As a general rule, such consent must be given before the execution of the payment transfer, but may be given after execution if agreed between the parties,[313] and must be given in the form and according to the procedure agreed between the payer and his bank.[314] Where the payer is required to use a 'payment instrument' (whether a security device or a particular procedure)[315] in order to initiate the payment transaction, the payer must only use the 'payment instrument' in accordance with its terms and conditions of issue,[316] and must comply with any monetary limits that the payer and his bank agree should apply to any transaction initiated with the 'payment instrument' in question.[317] The payer's bank may not refuse to comply with instructions from the payer that comply with any relevant 'framework contract', unless it would be unlawful for the bank to execute the payment transaction.[318] Where the payer's bank does refuse to execute the payer's instructions, it must generally notify the payer of the fact of that refusal, the reasons for the refusal, and the procedure that the payer might follow to rectify any factual errors that led to the refusal.[319] Such notification must be given in the agreed manner and 'at the earliest opportunity',[320] but generally no later than the end of the business day following the bank's receipt of the payer's instructions.[321] The payer's bank may reserve the right pursuant to the terms of a 'framework contract' to charge the payer for notifying him about its refusal to comply with his payment instruction, provided the bank's refusal is reasonably justified.[322] In the specific situation where the payment transaction must be initiated using a 'payment instrument', the payer's bank can reserve the right to refuse payment where it has concerns on reasonable grounds about the security of the 'payment instrument', about the suspected unauthorized or fraudulent use of the 'payment instrument' or about the payer's ability to repay when use of the 'payment instrument' has caused him to exceed his credit limit.[323] In such circumstances, the payer's bank must inform the payer beforehand of its intention to stop the 'payment instrument' and give its reasons for doing so.[324] Where it is not possible to do so beforehand, the payer's bank must inform the payer that the 'payment instrument' has been stopped 'immediately after' this occurs,[325] and must allow the payer to resume using the 'payment instrument' as soon as practicable afterwards.[326] The payer's bank need not comply with any of the aforementioned notification requirements, however, when such notification would be unlawful.[327]

---

that limits the amount that the payer may transfer below certain defined thresholds. See further Ch. 14, Sect. 9 below.

[312] Ibid., reg. 55(1).   [313] Ibid., reg. 55(2)(a).   [314] Ibid., reg. 55(2)(b).   [315] Ibid., reg. 2(1).
[316] Ibid., reg. 57(1)(a).
[317] Ibid., reg. 56(1). The imposition of a credit-limit occurs most frequently in the context of a 'payment instrument' that is a payment card: see further Ch. 14, Sect. 9 below.
[318] Ibid., reg. 66(5). For discussion of the circumstances in which it may be unlawful for a bank to pay in accordance with a customer's instructions, see Ch. 4, Sects. 3–4 above & Ch. 11, Sect. 1 above.
[319] Ibid., reg. 66(1). Where the payer's bank has refused to execute a payment instruction, the payment order is deemed never to have been received: ibid., reg. 66(6).
[320] Ibid., 66(2).
[321] Ibid., reg. 70(1). There are different time-limits applicable *inter alia* to payment transactions made before 1 January 2012 and where the payment transaction is initiated by way of a paper payment order: ibid, reg. 70(2)–(4).
[322] Ibid., reg. 66(3). Such a charge must have been agreed in advance between the payer and his bank and must reasonably correspond to the actual costs incurred by the payer's bank: ibid., reg. 54(1).
[323] Ibid., reg. 56(2). For the application of this provision to payments cards, see Ch. 14, Sect. 9 below.
[324] Ibid. reg. 56(3).   [325] Ibid., reg. 56(4).   [326] Ibid., reg. 56(6).
[327] Ibid., regs. 56(5), 66(4). For discussion of 'tipping off' liability, see Ch. 4, Sects. 3–4 above.

In the more usual case where the bank elects to follow the payer's payment instruction, the charges imposed by the payer's bank for that service will be for the payer's account,[328] provided the charges have been agreed with the payer and reflect the actual costs incurred by the payer's bank.[329] The payer's bank must impose any such charges separately and is not entitled to deduct them from the sum to be transferred, but must ensure that the full amount of the payment transaction is transferred to the payee's bank.[330] The payment transfer must also be executed in the currency agreed between the payer and his bank.[331] In that regard, where the payer's bank offers a currency conversion service before the initiation of the payment transaction, it must disclose to the payer all charges together with the exchange rate to be used in relation to the payment.[332] In the situation where the payer has provided his bank with a 'unique identifier',[333] such as the payee's account number and sort code or the SWIFT code for the payee's bank, a payment order executed in accordance with that identifier is deemed to have been correctly executed by the payer's bank in relation to the payee to whom the identifier relates.[334] Where the payer has provided his bank with an incorrect 'unique identifier', that bank is not liable for the non-execution or defective execution of the payment transaction, but must nevertheless make reasonable efforts to recover the funds involved in the payment transaction and may charge the payer for those efforts if the account contract provides for this.[335]

In addition to the aforementioned requirements, the PSR 2009 establish certain time-limits within which the payer's bank must comply with the payer's instructions. The various time-limits are generally calculated from the 'time of receipt', which is defined as the time at which the payer's bank receives the instruction to make the payment transfer either directly from the payer (in the case of a credit transfer) or indirectly by or through the payee (in the case of a direct debit).[336] In the case of a standing order, where the payer and his bank have agreed that the execution of the payment order is to take place on a certain date, the 'time of receipt' will be taken as the agreed date.[337] In both these cases, the 'time of receipt' will be the next business day if the instruction is received by the payer's bank on a non-business day.[338] It is also possible for the payer's bank to set a deadline so that the 'time of receipt' is the next business day for instructions received after that time.[339] It is mandatory that the payer's bank comply with the various time-limits in the PSR 2009 where the payment transaction is in Euro or sterling or where the payment transaction involves a single conversion between those currencies that is carried out in the United Kingdom and, in the case of cross-border payment, takes place in Euro.[340] In such cases, the general

---

[328] Ibid., reg. 54(2). Only certain charges may be imposed by the payer's bank: ibid., regs. 66(3), 67(6), 74(2)(b).

[329] Ibid., reg. 54(1)(b)–(c).

[330] Ibid., reg. 68(1). The payer's bank will be liable to reimburse any deductions when the payment transaction is initiated by the payer: ibid., reg. 68(3).

[331] Ibid., reg. 49(1). [332] Ibid., reg. 49(2).

[333] Ibid., reg. 2(1): '"unique identifier" means a combination of letters, numbers or symbols…to be provided by the payment service user in relation to a payment transaction in order to identify unambiguously one or both of—(a) the other payment service user who is a party to the payment transaction; (b) the other payment service user's payment account'.

[334] Ibid., reg. 74(1). This appears to remain the case even where the payer has provided his bank with other information: ibid., reg. 74(3).

[335] Ibid., reg. 74(2). Such charges must have been agreed in advance between the payer and his bank and must reasonably correspond to the actual costs incurred by the payer's bank: ibid., reg. 54(1).

[336] Ibid., reg. 65(1).

[337] Ibid., reg. 65(4). [338] Ibid., regs. 65(2), 65(5). [339] Ibid., reg. 65(3). [340] Ibid., reg. 69(1).

rule is that the payer's bank must ensure that the amount of the payment transaction is credited to the account at the payee's bank by the end of the business day following the 'time of receipt' of the payment instruction by the payer's bank.[341] A different rule applies where the payer's instructions are initially given by paper-based means, rather than over the telephone or internet, as the payer's bank must then ensure that the account of the payee's bank is credited by the end of the second business day following the 'time of receipt' of the payer's instruction.[342] Even where these various time-limits just described do not have mandatory application, the payer and his bank may nevertheless agree that they shall apply.[343] Although the payer and his bank are free in certain circumstances to agree that some other time-limit should apply to their payment transaction, there is one limit upon that freedom: where a payment transaction is to be wholly executed within the EEA, the payer's bank must ensure that the amount of the payment transaction is credited to the account at the the payee's bank by the end of the fourth business day following the 'time of receipt' of the payment instruction.[344] The payer's bank may not treat the payer's account as being debited for the purpose of calculating interest until the funds are actually debited from that account.[345]

With respect to the potential liability of the payer's bank for the non-execution or defective execution of the payer's instructions, the PSR 2009 alter the common law position quite dramatically. Under the former, the payer's bank is effectively subject to strict liability, whilst at common law the bank's liability turns on its failure to exercise reasonable skill and care in and about the execution of the payer's payment instruction.[346] Under the PSR 2009, where the payment transaction is initiated by the payer (as in the case of a CHAPS Sterling transfer or a standing order),[347] the payer's bank will be liable to the payer for the non-execution or defective execution of the payment transaction, unless it can demonstrate that the payee's bank received the full amount of the payment transaction within the time-limits considered above.[348] To this end, the payer's bank must, if the payer so requests, make immediate efforts to trace the whereabouts of the payment and inform the payer of the outcome of its investigations.[349] If those investigations do not reveal that the payment transaction was correctly executed, then the payer's bank must refund the amount in question to the payer 'without undue delay' and, if necessary, re-credit the payer's account.[350] Where the payment transaction is initiated by the payee (as in the case of a direct debit),[351] the payer's bank will be liable to refund the payer the amount of the direct debit payment, and if necessary re-credit the payer's account, if the payee's bank has been able to demonstrate that it correctly transmitted the direct debit payment request to the payer's bank within the time-limits agreed with the payee.[352] In addition to being entitled to claim a refund of any payment, the payer can also seek compensation for any interest

---

[341] Ibid., reg. 70(1). Until 1 January 2012, this period may be extended to the end of the third business day following receipt of the payment order: ibid., reg. 70(2).

[342] Ibid., reg. 70(3)(a). Until 1 January 2012, this period may be extended to the end of the fourth business day following receipt of the payment order: ibid., reg. 70(3)(b).

[343] Ibid., reg. 69(2).   [344] Ibid., reg. 70(4).   [345] Ibid., reg. 73(3).

[346] See further Sect. 5(iv)(b) below.   [347] PSR 2009, reg. 75(1).

[348] Ibid., reg. 75(2). Where the payer's bank can prove that the payment reached the payee's bank within the relevant time-limits, then the payee's bank may incur liability to the payee: ibid., reg. 75(5). For further consideration, see Sect. 5(vi) below.

[349] Ibid., reg. 75(3). A breach of the bank's obligation to make immediate efforts to trace the whereabouts of the funds may be enforced by way of an action for breach of statutory duty if the payer suffers further losses as a result of the failure to carry out the necessary investigations at all or in a timely manner: ibid., reg. 120(1).

[350] Ibid., reg. 75(4).   [351] Ibid., reg. 76(1).   [352] Ibid., regs. 70(6), 76(2), 76(5).

or other charges (such as a financial penalty for late payment pursuant to the terms of the underlying contract with the payee) that he has incurred as a result of the non-execution or defective execution of the payment transaction.[353] A payer is only entitled to the redress just described if he notifies his bank without undue delay, and no later than 13 months after the debit date, upon becoming aware that the transaction in question has not been executed at all or incorrectly executed.[354] The payer is relieved of this obligation, however, if his bank has failed to comply with the various information requirements in Part 5 of the PSR 2009, considered above.[355] The payer's bank may escape its ordinary liability for failing to execute the payment instruction, however, where the failure to perform its part of the transfer was due to its compliance with a provisions of United Kingdom or European Union law (such as relevant anti-money laundering legislation),[356] or was due to 'abnormal and unforeseeable circumstances' beyond the bank's control, the consequences of which would have been unavoidable despite all efforts to the contrary.[357] Alternatively, as considered further below,[358] the payer's bank may seek to pass any liability on to the payee's bank or a correspondent or intermediary bank, if it can be shown that the liability of the payer's bank is 'attributable' to one of those banks.[359] As considered further below,[360] this provision potentially alters the common law position whereby the payer's bank is required to claim against the correspondent or intermediary bank that it has actually instructed, leaving that bank in turn to pass any losses on to its own correspondent and so on down the chain until the losses are passed on to the negligent party ultimately responsible for them. It is arguable that the PSR 2009 would allow the payer's bank to short-circuit the contractual chain of banks and claim against a remote correspondent to whom the liability in question is 'attributable'.

The payer is entitled to withdraw his consent to the transaction,[361] but as a general rule cannot revoke the payment instruction once it has been received by his bank.[362] If receipt does not occur on a business day, then it is deemed to occur on the next business day.[363] The payer's bank is entitled to set a time before which it must receive the payer's instructions if the payment instruction is to be treated as received on that day. A different rule for the revocation of instructions applies for direct debits, as the payer may not revoke his payment instruction after the end of the business day preceding the day agreed for the debiting of the funds.[364] Where the payer and his bank have agreed that the payment transaction is to be executed on a particular day (such as the day when the payer places funds at his bank's disposal) or on the last day of a certain period (as in the case of a standing order) the payer may not revoke the payment after the end of the business day preceding the agreed day of payment.[365] It is possible for the payer to revoke a payment instruction outside the various time-limits imposed by the PSR 2009 provided that he obtains his bank's consent to such revocation.[366] In the case of direct debits or other payee-initiated payments, the payer must also obtain the payee's consent before the payment instruction

---

[353] Ibid., reg. 77. The losses that may be recovered are subject to the same defences and limitations as would be applicable to an action for breach of statutory duty: ibid., reg. 120(1). See further W.V.H Rogers, n.287 above, 398–404.

[354] Ibid., reg. 59(1).   [355] Ibid., reg. 59(2).   [356] Ibid., reg. 79(1).   [357] Ibid., reg. 79(2).

[358] See further Sect. 5(v) below.   [359] PSR 2009, reg. 78.   [360] See further Sect. 5(v) below.

[361] Ibid., reg. 55(3).   [362] Ibid., regs. 65(1), 67(1).   [363] Ibid., reg. 65(2).

[364] Ibid., reg. 67(3). In other cases where the payment transaction is initiated by or through the payee, the payer may not revoke the payment after transmitting the order or giving consent to the payee: ibid., reg. 67(2).

[365] Ibid., reg. 67(4). At any time, the payer may withdraw consent to future transactions executed as part of a series of payment transactions: ibid., 55(4).

[366] Ibid., reg. 67(5)(a).

can be revoked out of time.[367] Where the payer revokes a payment instruction that is issued pursuant to the terms of a 'framework contract' (such as a current account contract),[368] the payer's bank is entitled to impose a charge for complying with the payer's revocation.[369]

Where the payer's bank has executed a payment transaction that the payer has never authorized in the first place[370] or that the payer has revoked before it becomes irrevocable,[371] then the bank must refund the amount of the unauthorized transaction to the payer.[372] If the unauthorized transaction is debited from the payer's account then, as part of the process of refunding the payment, the payer's bank must restore the debit to that account.[373] As considered above in the context of the defective execution of payment instructions, in order to claim a refund of an unauthorised transfer, the payer must notify his bank 'without undue delay' upon becoming aware of the unauthorized nature of the transaction, and this can never exceed 13 months from the date when the payer was debited with the payment.[374] The payer is relieved of this obligation to notify his bank, however, if it can be shown that the bank failed to comply with the information requirements contained in Part 5 of the PSR 2009,[375] which were discussed above. In determining whether to make a refund to the payer, his bank will no doubt be mindful of the fact that it bears the burden of proving that the payment was in fact authorized.[376] Accordingly, unless the payer's bank has convincing evidence that the payer authorized the payment transaction, it should refund the amount of the payment. The mere fact that the payer's bank can produce records to show that the relevant 'payment instrument' (whether a security device or a particular procedure)[377] was used to initiate the payment transaction is not in itself necessarily sufficient to prove that it was authorized by the payer himself.[378]

There are extremely limited grounds upon which the payer's bank can pass some of the losses resulting from an unauthorized credit transfer or a direct debit back to the payer. As a general rule, the payer will only bear the loss for such a transaction when it can be shown that he has acted fraudulently.[379] The position appears to be different, however, when the payer is required to use a 'payment instrument' (whether a security device or a particular procedure)[380] in order to initiate the payment transaction. In addition to cases of fraud,[381] the payer will be liable for all the losses resulting from an unauthorized payment transaction if he has intentionally or with 'gross negligence' failed to comply with his statutory obligations regarding the 'payment instrument',[382] namely to use

---

[367] Ibid., reg. 67(5)(b).

[368] Id.: '…a contract for payment services which governs the future execution of individual and successive payment transactions and which may contain the obligation and conditions for setting up a payment account'. Where the payer requests a single payment to be made pursuant to the terms of a 'framework contract', the payer's bank is permitted to avoid the duplication of information: ibid., reg. 39.

[369] Ibid., reg. 67(6). Such a charge must have been agreed in advance between the payer and his bank and must reasonably correspond to the actual costs incurred by the payer's bank: ibid., reg. 54(1).

[370] Ibid., reg. 55(1)–(2).   [371] Ibid., reg. 67.   [372] Ibid., reg. 61(a).   [373] Ibid., reg. 61(b).

[374] Ibid., reg. 59(1). There is a related requirement upon a payer to inform his bank 'without undue delay' upon becoming aware of 'the loss, theft, misaapropriation or unauthorised use of the payment instrument': ibid., reg. 57(1)(b). For the suggested relationship between the requirement that notification occur 'without undue delay' and the maximum 13-month notification period in reg. 59(1), consider *Bankers Trust Co* v. *State Bank of India* [1991] 2 Lloyds Rep 443.

[375] Ibid., reg. 59(2).   [376] Ibid., reg. 60(1).   [377] Ibid., reg. 2(1).   [378] Ibid., reg. 60(3)(a).

[379] Ibid., reg. 62(2)(a).

[380] Ibid., reg. 2(1). For the application of these provisions to the unauthorized use of a payment card, see Ch. 14, Sect. 9 below.

[381] Ibid., reg. 62(2)(a).

[382] Ibid., reg. 62(2)(b). The payer's bank must produce something more than records that reveal simply that the correct 'payment instrument' was used to initiate the payment transaction: ibid., reg. 60(3)(b).

the 'payment instrument' according to the terms and conditions governing its use;[383] to notify his bank 'without undue delay' upon becoming aware of the loss, theft, misappropriation, or unauthorized use of the 'payment instrument';[384] and to take all reasonable steps to keep the personalized security features of the 'payment instrument' safe.[385] In the absence of fraudulent, intentional or grossly negligent conduct on the part of the payer, he will only be liable up to a maximum of £50 for any losses resulting from an unauthorized payment transaction that has been caused by the loss or theft of the 'payment instrument', or by its use when the payer has failed to take proper care of its security details.[386] Apart from cases of fraud, however, the payer will not be liable at all for any losses incurred after he has informed his bank of the loss, theft, misappropriation, or unauthorized use of the 'payment instrument' nor will the payer be liable where his bank has failed to provide him with appropriate means for notifying it.[387] The payer will also bear no responsibility for losses resulting from a 'payment instrument' that has been lost in the post.[388]

In addition to being entitled to a refund when the transaction is unauthorized, a payer may in certain circumstances also be entitled to a refund from his bank in respect of a payment transaction initiated by or through the payee (such as a direct debit), even when such a transaction is authorized.[389] Although a bank may agree to more generous terms,[390] such a refund is usually available when the payer did not specify the exact amount of the payments when initially authorizing the direct debit and the amount of a particular payment 'exceeded the amount that the payer could reasonably have expected taking into account the payer's previous spending pattern, the conditions of the framework contract and the circumstances of the case'.[391] The aim of this provision appears to be to protect a payer against the possible abuse of a direct debit instruction by a payee and even to protect the payer from the payee suddenly increasing the amount that it intends to claim under the direct debit.[392] In determining whether the direct debit payment exceeds the amount that the payer could reasonably have expected to pay, a court should generally ignore currency exchange fluctuations.[393] It is also possible for an account contract to limit the payer's right to a refund in such circumstances by stipulating that there shall be no refund when the payer has specifically authorized the direct debit payment in question,[394] or when the payer has been provided with the necessary information about the particular direct debit payment at least four weeks before payment is made.[395] Before the payer is entitled to such a refund, he must make the necessary request of his bank within eight weeks of the disputed debit,[396] and may be required to provide his bank with 'such information as is reasonably necessary to ascertain' that the payer is in fact entitled to the refund.[397] Within 10 business days of the payer's bank receiving the payer's request for the refund of a payment made under a direct debit instruction,[398] the payer's bank

---

[383] Ibid., reg. 57(1)(a).   [384] Ibid., reg. 57(1)(b).   [385] Ibid., reg. 57(2).   [386] Ibid., reg. 62(1).

[387] Ibid., reg. 62(3). The payer will also not be liable when the 'payment instrument' is used in connection with a 'distance contract' within the Consumer Protection (Distance Selling) Regulations 2000, S.I. 2000/2334, other than an 'excepted contract': ibid., reg. 62(3)(c).

[388] Ibid., reg. 58(2).   [389] Ibid., reg. 63(1).

[390] Ibid., reg. 63(3). The payer's bank must provide the payer with a full refund of the amount of the payment transaction in such circumstances: ibid., reg. 64(4).

[391] Ibid., reg. 63(2).

[392] See Directive 2007/64/EC on Payment Services in the Internal Market [2007] OJ L319, Preamble, [36]: 'This Directive should lay down rules for a refund to protect the consumer when the executed payment transaction exceeds the amount which could reasonably have been expected'.

[393] PSR 2009, reg. 63(4).

[394] Ibid., reg. 63(5)(a).   [395] Ibid., reg. 63(5)(b).   [396] Ibid., reg. 64(1).   [397] Ibid., reg. 64(2).

[398] Ibid., reg. 64(5).

must either refund the full amount of the payment transaction or provide a justification for refusing to do so, together with details of the bodies to which the payer can refer the matter if he disagrees with his bank's decision.[399]

(b) Position of the payer's bank at common law

The payer's bank is engaged in giro transactions in a representative capacity. In the majority of cases, it is employed by a customer (the payer) who orders the transfer of a given amount of money, usually to a third party but occasionally to the credit of the payer's own account with an overseas bank. As an agent, the payer's bank is obliged to carry out the instructions given to it with reasonable skill and care.[400] The main duty of the payer's bank, however, is to adhere strictly to the instruction given to it. This principle is forcefully stated in the context of a different type of transaction (i.e. a documentary letter of credit transaction) by Devlin J in *Midland Bank Ltd* v. *Seymour*:[401]

> It is a hard law sometimes which deprives an agent of the right to reimbursement if he has exceeded his authority, even though the excess does not damage his principal's interests. The corollary…is that the instruction to the agent must be clear and unambiguous.

The harshness of this doctrine has been mitigated in respect of money transfer orders by Webster J in *Royal Products Ltd* v. *Midland Bank Ltd*,[402] where it was argued that the doctrine of strict compliance, pertaining to documentary credit transactions, applied equally to the duty of the payer's bank to carry out its customer's instruction to transfer money.[403] His Lordship disagreed:[404]

> I reject the submission…that in construing those instructions [for the transfer of money] I should, as a matter of law or banking practice, give a legal implication to each detail of them, for it seems to me that the doctrine which would lead to that result has little application to the facts of the present case, having received its first authoritative cognition…in the context of confirmed credits.

Webster J concluded that the doctrine of strict compliance had no application in the case of money transfer orders. This meant that the payer's bank was not in breach of its mandate as long as it carried out its instruction with skill and in a manner sanctioned by current banking practice.[405]

---

[399] Ibid., reg. 64(3).

[400] *Royal Products Ltd* v. *Midland Bank Ltd.*, n.274 above, 198. See also *Tayeb* v. *HSBC Bank plc*, n.85 above, [81].

[401] [1955] 2 Lloyd's Rep. 147, 168. Cf. *European Asian Bank AG* v. *Punjab and Sind Bank (No. 2)* [1983] 1 WLR 642, 656 (CA), where Goff LJ observed that an agent could rely on an ambiguity to justify the reasonable construction given by him to the mandate only if the ambiguity was not patent. See also *AIB Group (UK) plc* v. *Henelly Properties Ltd* (CA, 1 December 2000), [62]–[64]; *Crédit Agricole Indosuez* v. *Muslim Commercial Bank Ltd* [2000] 1 Lloyd's Rep. 275, 279–280 (CA); *Patel* v. *Standard Chartered Bank* [2001] Lloyd's Rep. Bank 229, [37] (ambiguity apparent on face of customer's mandate form).

[402] N.274 above.

[403] For the leading authority on the doctrine of 'strict compliance', see *Equitable Trust Co. of New York* v. *Dawson Partners Ltd* (1926) 27 Ll. LR 49 (HL).

[404] Ibid., 199. See also *FDIC* v. *European American Bank and Trust Co.*, n.274 above.

[405] But the payer's bank must, of course, adhere to the terms of its mandate. A United States authority, *Walker* v. *Texas Commerce Bank NA*, 635 F Supp. 678 (SD Tex., 1986), held that the payer's bank was not entitled to debit the payer's account with an amount exceeding the sum he had ordered the bank to remit. See also *Avila* v. *Bank of America National Trust & Savings Association*, 826 F. Supp. 92, 98 (SDNY, 1993). Nevertheless, problems over mandate arise where the payer's bank receives funds transfer instructions through the use of an electronic access device, for example, via a computer terminal, where the customer uses a password or access code. What if a third party has assumed control of the access device or bypassed it

There are three specific aspects of the duty of care and skill imposed on the payer's bank that require consideration. First, the duty obliges the payer's bank to transfer the amount in question on time.[406] Thus, if a specific time for transfer is expressly specified in the order, the payer's bank has to comply with the deadline prescribed if it accepts the instruction to transfer. Where there is no express stipulation as to time, the time of transfer is usually discernible from the circumstances of the transaction. If the payer orders that the money be transmitted by a telegraphic transfer or by telex, it is to be assumed that he requires the transaction to be carried out on the same day.[407] The same applies, *a fortiori*, if the bank is asked to effect the transfer by the use of SWIFT. The need for a speedy execution of the order may, further, be conveyed to the bank by familiarizing it with the object of the transfer involved. Thus, where the amount to be transferred is known to be a rental due on a given day under a charterparty, the payer's bank has to exercise all the means at its disposal to ensure that the amount reaches its destination on time.

The duty of the payer's bank to act promptly and with skill applies not only to the execution of the payer's payment instruction but also to the handling of a stop order issued by him. In a United States case, *Mellon Bank* v. *Securities Settlement Corp.*,[408] SSC, at the request of its client K, instructed the M Bank to transfer the amount of US$113,080.50 to the account of one B with the F Bank. An appropriate message was dispatched forthwith by the M Bank to the F Bank through the intermediary of the M Bank's correspondents, MHT. A few hours after the M Bank had dispatched its instruction to MHT, SSC discovered that K did not have the means to reimburse it. Accordingly, SSC instructed the M Bank to stop payment, whereupon the M Bank dispatched another message to MHT, with the object of countermanding the previous order. However, as the M Bank failed to set out the correct details in its second message, MHT remitted the funds to the F Bank. By the time the error was discovered, B had withdrawn the funds credited to his account by the F Bank. The United States District Court dismissed the M Bank's action against SSC.

altogether? From the bank's point of view, any technologically effective entry of the access code appears to be a valid authorization. The situation may be dealt with in the express terms of any contract between a bank and its customer, at least insofar as those terms are not rendered ineffective by relevant legislation. On the other hand, it has been argued by Geva that in an electronic environment the bank's liability should not be strict—as in the case of the drawer's signature being forged on a cheque—but instead premised on whether it has exhibited 'systemic negligence', with a correspondent duty on the customer to exercise reasonable care and diligence to prevent unauthorized electronic funds transfers: B. Geva, 'Unauthorised Electronic Funds Transfers—Comparative Aspects' in J.S. Ziegel (ed.), *New Developments in International Commercial and Consumer Law* (Oxford, 1998), especially, 110–112; B. Geva, *Bank Collections and Payment Transactions— Comparative Study & Legal Aspects* (Oxford, 2001), Pt. 4C. See also *Standard Bank London Ltd* v. *Bank of Tokyo Ltd.*, n.225 above (estoppel against defendant bank where fraudsters sent tested telex from its premises); *Industrial & Commercial Bank Ltd* v. *Banco Ambrosiano Veneto SpA*, n.204 above, [254]–[261] (estoppel against defendant bank where fraudsters sent SWIFT message from its premises).

[406] *Central Coordinates Inc.* v. *Morgan Guaranty Trust Co.*, 494 NYS 2d 602 (NY Sup. Ct., 1985), which, at the same time, held that the bank would be liable for consequential loss only if it had been apprised of the special circumstances respecting the remittance in question.

[407] Note that in *Dovey* v. *Bank of New Zealand*, n.24 above, 651–652, the New Zealand Court of Appeal held that, where the payer's bank had been instructed to make a transfer of funds by tested telex, the bank was not in breach of contract by using the even faster SWIFT method of transfer. Similarly, an obligation due to be settled by means of a bank cheque may be settled by means of an electronic funds transfer, which is arguably a swifter means of transferring money: *Rick Dees Ltd* v. *Larsen* [2006] 2 NZLR 765, [64]–[66] (NZCA), affd. on this point: [2007] 3 NZLR 577, [3], [30]–[31], [36] (NZSC). See also *Otago Station Estates Ltd* v. *Parker* [2005] 2 NZLR 734, [27] (NZSC), where Blanchard J stated that '...a contractual requirement for the making of a payment must, as a matter of law, be performed by means of legal tender, bank cheque or other cleared funds...'. See further *Redoute Securities Ltd* v. *Thomson* (2007) 9 NZCPR 212, [26]–[32].

[408] 710 F. Supp. 991 (D. NJ, 1989).

Observing that 'no reasonable fact finder could conclude that [the M Bank] acted with ordinary care'[409] in executing the countermand order, Fisher DJ held that the M Bank was not entitled to claim reimbursement of the money paid to B. The M Bank had owed SSC a duty to exercise care and skill in the execution of the stop order given to it. By setting out the wrong details in its message to MHT, the M Bank committed a breach of this contractual duty of care. Having caused the loss resulting from the payment of the funds to B, the M Bank was not entitled to reimbursement of the amount involved.

Secondly, the duty of skill and care requires the payer's bank to engage a reliable correspondent or intermediary bank in the payee's jurisdiction. Obviously, the problem does not arise in every transfer of funds. If the payee maintains his account with one of the overseas correspondents of the payer's bank, a direct transfer is possible. In many cases, however, there is a need for a correspondent or intermediary bank. This problem is not confined to international transfers, although it is most likely to arise in that context. It may also arise in domestic money transfer operations if the payee maintains his account with a bank that does not participate in the giro system.

At common law, the payer's bank is vicariously liable for the negligence or default of its correspondent. The point was settled by the House of Lords in *Equitable Trust Co. of New York* v. *Dawson Partners Ltd*,[410] in respect of the engagement of a correspondent or intermediary bank by a bank issuing a letter of credit. The principle is applicable also to the engagement of a correspondent or intermediary bank by a bank charged by its customer with the collection of a bill of exchange drawn on a merchant overseas.[411] In modern practice, banks engaged in transactions requiring the assistance of a correspondent or intermediary bank usually stipulate in the contract with their customer that the correspondent is employed at the customer's expense and risk. Exemption clauses of this type are frequently included in the contract in which the customer instructs his bank to transfer an amount of money by means of a giro operation. They have been upheld by courts in the past.[412] Nowadays, such an exemption clause would be open to scrutiny under the Unfair Contract Terms Act 1977 (UCTA 1977) and also, where the payer is a consumer, the Unfair Terms in Consumer Contracts Regulations 1999.[413] Where the payer is acting in a business capacity, a clause disclaiming liability for the correspondent or intermediary bank's negligence is likely to be upheld as reasonable under Schedule 2 of UCTA 1977 on the ground that the payer's bank has no direct control over its correspondent. On the

---

[409] Ibid., 996. The court based its judgment on both common law principle and the UCC.

[410] N.403 above. For a similar view in the letter of credit context, see *Bank Melli Iran* v. *Barclays Bank (DCO)* [1951] 2 Lloyd's Rep 367; but contrast *European Asian Bank AG* v. *Punjab and Sind Bank*, n.401 above; *Crédit Agricole Indosuez* v. *Muslim Commercial Bank Ltd*, n.401 above. For criticism of the view in *Bank Melli Iran*, see Wright & Ward, 'The Advising Bank in Letter of Credit Transactions and the Assumption of Agency' [1993] *JIBL* 432.

[411] *Mackersy* v. *Ramsays, Bonars & Co.* (1843) 9 Cl. & F 818, 846, 851 (HL). See also *Henry Prince* v. *Oriental Bank Corporation* [1878] 3 App. Cas. 325 (PC); *Calico Printers' Association* v. *Barclays Bank Ltd* (1931) 36 Com. Cas. 71, 78–79, affd. (1931) 36 Com. Cas. 197 (CA)). For acceptance of this principle in Singapore, see *AA Valibhoy & Sons (1907) Pte Ltd* v. *Habib Bank Ltd* [1982–1983] 1 SLR 379, 391; *AA Valibhoy & Sons (1907) Pte Ltd* v. *Banque Nationale de Paris* [1994] 2 SLR 772, 781.

[412] *Calico Printers' Association Ltd* v. *Barclays Bank Ltd*, n.411 above.

[413] S.I. 1999/2083. See Ch. 5, Sect. 3 & Ch. 7, Sect. 2 above. An exclusion or limitation clause is also likely to be ineffective to the extent that it seeks to limit the payer's bank liability pursuant to Part 6 of the PSR 2009 when the payer is 'a consumer, a micro-enterprise or a charity': PSR 2009, reg. 51(3). Similarly, the payer's bank cannot contract out of the information requirements in Part 5: ibid., reg. 33(4). It is possible for the payer's bank to contract out of these provisions to the extent permitted in relation to other types of customer.

other hand, where the payer is a consumer, there must be a greater chance that the clause will be considered both unreasonable under UCTA 1977 and/or unfair under the Unfair Terms in Consumer Contracts Regulations 1999.[414] In both cases, a limitation of liability is likely to be treated more favourably than an outright exclusion.[415] The contract will also usually include a clause reserving the right of the payer's bank to act through a correspondent or intermediary bank, although the bank's right to use a correspondent has been recognized by the courts even in the absence of such a clause.[416] Where the payer's bank selects a reputable bank to act as its correspondent, any claim that the bank failed to exercise reasonable care and skill in choosing its correspondent is unlikely to succeed. It is important to note, however, that the problems relating to the liability of the payer's bank for its correspondent arise only if the bank engages an entity other than its own overseas branch or office. The bank is, of course, liable to the payer for the negligence of any of its own branches and offices. The reason for this is obvious. Although the customer, the payer, is expected to make his demand at the branch with which he maintains his account,[417] his contractual relationship is with the bank, which, despite its numerous branches, has only one legal personality.[418]

Thirdly, at common law, the payer's bank only generally owes a duty to exercise reasonable skill and care to a payer or transferor who is also its customer.[419] In such a case, the duty will be implied as an aspect of the bank–customer contract and owed concurrently in tort.[420] Whilst it is undoubtedly most commonly the case that the payer will be a customer of the paying bank, in certain cases, a bank may carry out a giro operation at the request of a member of the public who is not its customer. In acceding to this request, which normally involves the transfer of an amount paid in cash to the credit of a third party's account, the transferring bank acts in accordance with modern practice as influenced, originally, by the spirit of the Golden Memorandum.[421] If the amount that the payer wishes to transfer is paid to the credit of a customer of the bank that he approaches, the sum in question is received by the bank on behalf of the payee. Accordingly, whilst the bank clearly owes a contractual duty to the payee to exercise care in executing the payment instruction, it is less clear whether any tortious duty may also be owed to the payer. Some guidance may be derived from *Abou-Rahmah* v. *Abacha*,[422] where the claimants, who were the victims

---

[414] See, in particular, Unfair Terms in Consumer Contracts Regulations 1999, S.I. 1999/2083, Sched. 2, para. 1(b).

[415] For the different treatment of limitation and exclusion clauses at common law, see *Ailsa Craig Fishing Co. Ltd* v. *Malvern Fishing Co. Ltd* [1983] 1 WLR 964, 966, 970 (HL); *Bovis Construction (Scotland) Ltd* v. *Whatlings Construction Ltd* (1995) 75 BLR 1 (HL); *Price Waterhouse* v. *The University of Keele* [2004] EWCA Civ 583, [35]; *Frans Maas (UK) Ltd* v. *Samsung Electronics (UK) Ltd* [2004] 2 Lloyd's Rep. 251, [131]; *Biffa Waste Services Ltd* v. *Maschinenfabrik Ernst Hese GmbH* [2008] EWHC 6 (TCC), [184]–[188]; *Regus (UK) Ltd* v. *Epcot Solutions Ltd* [2008] EWCA Civ 361, [46]; but consider *HIH Casualty & General Insurance Ltd* v. *Chase Manhattan Bank* [2003] 2 Lloyd's Rep. 61, [63] (HL). For the approach to limitation clauses in the context of UCTA 1977, consider *George Mitchell (Chesterhall) Ltd* v. *Finney Lock Seeds Ltd* [1983] 2 AC 803 (HL). See E. Peel, *Treitel's Law of Contract* (12th edn., London, 2007), [7-017].

[416] *Royal Products Ltd* v. *Barclays Bank Ltd*, n.274 above, 197.

[417] *Joachimson* v. *Swiss Bank Corporation* [1921] 3 KB 110, 127 (CA). For discussion of this principle in the context of technological advances in banking practice, see Ch. 5, Sect. 3 & Ch. 7, Sect. 1 above.

[418] Ch. 5, Sect. 3 above.

[419] Obviously, where the PSR 2009 are applicable, the paying bank's potential liability to the payer will be the same regardless of whether the payer is a customer of the paying bank or not. For the definition of who qualifies as a 'customer', see Ch. 5, Sect. 2 above.

[420] For detailed consideration, see further Ch. 5, Sect. 4(iii) above.   [421] Ch. 10, Sect. 2 above.

[422] [2005] EWHC 2662 (QB), affd. on a different point: [2007] 1 Lloyd's Rep 115 (CA). Consider also *London Borough of Bromley* v. *Ellis* [1971] 1 Lloyd's Rep. 97; *The Zephyr* [1984] 1 Lloyd's Rep. 58, revd. [1985] 2 Lloyd's Rep. 529.

of an international fraud, instructed Gulf Bank to transfer funds to the payee (Trust International) by crediting the account of the defendant (City Express Bank of Lagos) that was held with HSBC in London. Following the defendant's release of the funds to 'Trusty International' rather than 'Trust International', as was indicated in the SWIFT message,[423] the payer argued that the defendant had breached its common law duty of care. Applying the 'threefold test',[424] Treacy J gave a number of reasons for rejecting the existence of a duty of care: the claimants were not the defendant's customers; there had been no contact between the parties prior to the defendant bank's receipt of the funds and the bank had not undertaken any 'special responsibility' to the claimant; the defendant bank received the funds as agent for its customer to whom it already owed a contractual duty of care; banks in general have 'a huge number of potential payers who can remit money without significant control by the bank'; and, in the absence of special circumstances, the recognition of a duty of care would 'impose very heavy burdens on banks and significantly hamper their efficiency'.[425] Although these factors were considered in the different context of whether the payee's bank owes a duty of care to a payer, a number of them would similarly point against the existence of a common law duty of care owed by a paying bank to a non-customer who instructs it to make a giro transfer.[426] There is potentially one important point of difference, however, between this last situation and that in *Abou-Rahmah*, namely that the paying bank will generally have some form of direct contact with the payer before the transfer is made and as a result of that contact undertakes to perform a service at that party's request. Whilst the factors identified in *Abou-Rahmah* should continue to preclude the general existence of a duty to the non-customer payer when the payee is a customer of the paying bank, it may be open in appropriate circumstances to base a common law duty of care upon a voluntary assumption of responsibility by the paying bank to the non-customer instructing party.[427]

The position is even less clear, however, if the non-customer instructs a paying bank to transfer funds to the account of a payee who is the customer of another bank. It is likely that the question of whether the paying bank owes the non-customer a common law duty of care in this type of case will generally be decided in the same way as where the payee is the paying bank's customer.[428] The additional difficulty that arises, however, when the payee is the customer of another bank is that of determining with whom the paying bank

---

[423] For consideration of SWIFT messages, see Sect. 4(iv) above.

[424] See, for example, *Caparo Industries plc* v. *Dickman* [1990] 2 AC 605, 618, 628 (HL); *Customs & Excise Commissioners* v. *Barclays Bank plc* [2007] 1 AC 181, [6] (HL).

[425] *Abou-Rahmah* v. *Abacha*, n.422 above, [68], affd. on a different point: [2007] 1 Lloyd's Rep 115 (CA). See also *So* v. *HSBC Bank plc* [2009] EWCA Civ 296, [95]–[102]. In *Abou-Rahmah*, Treacy J relied upon a number of Canadian authorities in support of his conclusion that no duty of care existed: *Groves-Raffin Construction Ltd* v. *Bank of Nova Scotia* (1975) 64 DLR (3d) 78 (BCCA); *Toor* v. *Bank of Montreal* (1992) 2 Bank LR 8; *Dennison* v. *Cronin* (1994) 45 ACWS (3d) 1279; *Kyser* v. *Bank of Montreal* (1999) 88 ACWS (3d) 1156 (OCA); but compare *Royal Bank of Canada* v. *Stangl* (1992) 32 ACNS (3d) 17 (OGD). See also *Dupont Heating & Air Conditioning Ltd* v. *Bank of Montreal* [2009] OJ No. 386, [31]–[40].

[426] In a different context, a paying bank has been held not to owe a duty of care to a non-customer payee when acting on behalf of a customer in carrying out a payment instruction: *Wells* v. *First National Commercial Bank* [1998] PNLR 552, 557–560 (CA). For the converse situation and the refusal to impose a duty of care on a payee to a paying bank, see *Yorkshire Bank plc* v. *Lloyds Bank plc* (QBD, 16 March 1999), [6.11]–[6.12].

[427] See generally *Hedley Byrne & Co. Ltd* v. *Heller & Partners* [1964] AC 465 (HL); *Customs & Excise Commissioners* v. *Barclays Bank plc*, n.424 above, [5]. In considering whether a paying bank owed a duty of care to the intended recipient of the funds, Evans LJ in *Wells* v. *First National Commercial Bank*, n.426 above, 563, considered that it might be arguable that the bank owed the payee a duty of care on *Hedley Byrne* principles if there had been direct contact between the parties. For the refusal to impose a duty of care upon a payee towards a paying bank, see *Yorkshire Bank plc* v. *Lloyds Bank plc*, n.426 above, [6.11]–[6.12].

[428] *Abou-Rahmah* v. *Abacha*, n.422 above, [53]–[77], affd. on a different point: [2007] 1 Lloyd's Rep 115 (CA).

is in a contractual relationship—does the paying bank act, for this specific transaction, as the agent of the payer or as the agent of the payee's bank? If the paying bank acts on behalf of the payer, it will be subject to the usual duty of care owed by an agent to his principal.[429] If the paying bank effects the transfer on behalf of the payee's bank, then it owes no duty to the payer except that of acting honestly. The better view in such a case is that the paying bank has no contractual relationship with the payer.[430] The bank has not accepted him as a customer, may receive no consideration for effecting the transfer,[431] and, above all, has no intention of entering into a contract with the payer. The paying bank accepts the money for transmission solely in reliance on an established banking practice, and accordingly it is believed that in cases of this type there is no privity of contract between the payer and the paying bank.

In the usual case where the payer is a customer of the bank effecting the funds transfer, the duty of care that the payer's bank owes to the payer does not extend to the payee. As regards contractual liability, the payer's bank will generally not owe a contractual duty of care to the payee because the latter will not be a customer of the former,[432] although the position will be different where the payee holds an account at the payer's bank. In this last situation, however, the contractual duty of care imposed upon the payer's bank results solely from its additional status as the payee's banker and does not in any way suggest that such a duty is owed by the payer's bank when acting in that particular role. As regards tortious liability, in the normal course of events, the payer's bank will not owe the payee a common law duty of care.[433] The point arose in *Wells* v. *First National Commercial Bank*,[434]

---

[429] See generally E. Peel, n.415 above, [16-094].

[430] This conclusion derives support from *Great Western Railway Co.* v. *London and County Banking Co. Ltd* [1901] AC 414 (HL), in which it was held that the mere payment of cash against cheques handed over by X, did not constitute X the bank's customer and did not, therefore, lead to the creation of a contract between them. Despite X cashing cheques with the bank on a regular basis, in the absence of an account, he was not a 'customer' of the bank: see further Ch. 5, Sect. 2 above. See also *Federal Deposit Insurance Corp.* v. *Imperial Bank*, 859 F.2d 101 (9th Cir., 1988) where it was held that the mere channelling of a money transfer through a correspondent bank did not in itself establish a contractual relationship between it and the payer or owner of the funds.

[431] Obviously, it remains open to the bank to change this position by charging the payer for the payment service that it provides.

[432] Even a named payee of a funds transfer would find it difficult to bring himself within the Contracts (Rights of Third Parties) Act 1999, s.1(1): see generally *Nisshin Shipping Co. Ltd* v. *Cleaves & Co. Ltd* [2003] EWHC 2602 (Comm.); *Laemthong International Lines Co. Ltd* v. *Artis* [2005] EWCA Civ. 519; *Avraamides* v. *Colwill* [2006] EWCA Civ 1533; *Prudential Assurance Co. Ltd* v. *Ayres* [2008] EWCA Civ. 52. There must be grave doubt that, within the context of the transaction as a whole, the payer and his bank intended to confer an enforceable benefit on the payee. For more detailed reasoning along similar lines, see R. Hooley (ed.), 'Payment and Payment Systems' in P. Cresswell *et al.*, n.1 above, Division D1, [855.1].

[433] *National Westminster Bank Ltd* v. *Barclays Bank International Ltd* [1975] QB 654, 662 (drawee bank did not owe duty of care to payee when deciding whether to honour cheque); *Dublin Port & Docks Board* v. *Governor & Company of the Bank of Ireland* [1976] IR 118, 139, 141 (IESC) ('...a bank owes no duty of care to a payee') ('...the general principle is that a payee named in a cheque has no right of action against the bank on which the cheque is drawn if the cheque is dishonoured'). Cf. *T. E. Potterton Ltd* v. *Northern Bank Ltd* [1995] 4 Bank. LR 179, (IEHC) (drawee bank owes duty to act carefully and honestly when advising payee of cheque of reasons for its dishonour), criticized by E.P. Ellinger, 'Bank's Liability for Information, Respecting Dishonour of Cheque' [1995] *JBL* 583–585. Subsequent decisions appear to have limited *Potterton* to the situation where the payer's bank has clearly voluntarily assumed responsibility to the payee, so that the decision does not undermine the general principle that no duty of care is owed: *Kennedy* v. *Allied Irish Banks plc* [1998] 2 IR 48, 56 (IESC); *Carrickowen Ltd* v. *Bank of Ireland* [2006] 1 IR 570, [67] (IESC). For broadly similar reasons, the courts have also refused to impose a duty of care upon the payee towards the paying bank: *Yorkshire Bank plc* v. *Lloyds Bank plc*, n.426 above, [6.11]–[6.12].

[434] N.426 above, approved in a different context in *Jeffers* v. *Northern Bank Ltd* [2004] NIQB 81, [28], [39]. See further Ch. 5, Sect. 4(iii) above.

in which the claimant lent money to a Spanish company, secured by a charge on property held by that company in Spain, and secured by four post-dated bills of exchange issued personally in favour of the claimant by U and W, who were owners of the company. The bills of exchange were subsequently dishonoured. The claimant commenced proceedings on the bills, those proceedings reaching the stage where either judgment was entered or the claimant was entitled to enter judgment. Meanwhile, the defendant bank agreed to provide new finance to the company, in return for a first charge on the Spanish property. In order to persuade the claimant to release the charge on the property, and in consideration for not entering judgment and/or enforcing judgment in the proceedings on the bills of exchange, the company issued irrevocable instructions to the defendant bank to pay one million pesetas to discharge the charge on the property, and to pay a further £275,000 to the claimant's solicitors in respect of the sums owing on the bills of exchange. The bank acknowledged receipt of those instructions, knowing that the claimant was the intended payee, although there was no direct communication between the bank and the claimant. The bank failed to make the transfer and the claimant started proceedings against the bank for breach of a tortious duty of care. The claimant argued that the bank owed him a duty of care because of the irrevocable nature of the payment instructions and the fact that the bank knew that the claimant was the intended payee. On the bank's application, the judge struck out the claim as disclosing no cause of action. The Court of Appeal dismissed the claimant's appeal against that decision.

Evans LJ, delivering a judgment with which Hutchison and Mantell LJJ agreed, rejected the claimant's submission that the case was analogous to *White* v. *Jones*.[435] In that case, the House of Lords held, by a three-to-two majority, that a solicitor who accepts instructions to draft a will owes a duty of care to the intended beneficiary and may be liable to the intended beneficiary in the tort of negligence if he fails to implement his client's instructions within a reasonable time period. However, Evans LJ held that *White* v. *Jones* was an exceptional case that turned on two factors. First, there was the critical point that there was no effective remedy either for the beneficiary or the testator's estate if a duty of care was not imposed.[436] Secondly, there was the fact that a solicitor has something of a peculiar status when preparing a will. Neither of these factors was present in *Wells*; on the contrary, the relationships between the various parties were governed by contracts that gave the claimant a right of action against the payer for non-payment. So far as Evans LJ was concerned, the case before him was not exceptional. According to his Lordship, this was a straightforward commercial situation where a duty of care had never been held to exist and where there were no grounds for creating an exception to the orthodox principles in *Hedley Byrne & Co. Ltd* v. *Heller & Partners*[437] that there must be a special relationship ('equivalent to contract' according to Lord Devlin) between the parties for a duty of care to exist. As Evans LJ said, 'the [claimant] contends for a duty of care which, if it arises here, would arise in the course of an everyday commercial transaction and would go a long way to revolutionise English banking law'.[438] Yet Evans LJ did concede, albeit by way of *obiter dicta*, that 'if the [payee] had communicated with the bank then it could be, I say no more, a situation which was in Lord Devlin's words "equivalent to contract". It may be

---

[435] [1995] 2 AC 207 (HL).

[436] This point has subsequently been identified as vital to the majority's reasoning in *White* v. *Jones*, n.435 above: see *Carr-Glynn* v. *Frearsons* [1999] Ch. 326, 335 (CA); *Gorham* v. *British Telecommunications plc* [2000] 1 WLR 2129, 2140, 2144, 2146 (CA); *Corbett* v. *Bond Pearce* [2001] 3 All ER 769, [26] (CA); *Hughes* v. *Richards* [2004] EWCA Civ 266, [24]; *Rind* v. *Theodore Goddard* [2008] EWHC 459 (Ch), [36]–[37].

[437] N.427 above.   [438] *Wells* v. *First National Commercial Bank*, n.426 above, 562.

that in such a situation it would be arguable that a *Hedley Byrne* duty would arise. It would arise from the relationship which in fact was established between them'.[439]

(v) Position of the correspondent or intermediary bank

It will be recalled that a correspondent or intermediary bank is employed only where the payer's bank is unable to transmit the funds directly to the payee's bank. A correspondent or intermediary bank that is appointed by the payer's bank acts as that bank's agent,[440] and accordingly where it incurs liability as a result of carrying out the instructions of the payer's bank, it will usually be entitled to an indemnity or contribution from its instructing party.[441] In terms of the correspondent or intermediary bank's liability, at common law, such a bank owes the payer's bank an implied contractual duty of care and skill.[442] A concurrent duty of care may also arise in tort.[443] Accordingly, the payer's bank may recoup any losses resulting from the execution of the payment transaction from its correspondent or intermediary bank, not only when those losses are caused by the negligence of the correspondent itself, but also when they are caused by a bank that the correspondent has instructed to act on its own behalf.[444] In this last situation, however, the payer's bank may only claim against the correspondent or intermediary bank that it actually instructed, leaving it to this bank in turn to recoup its losses from its own correspondent, and so on down the chain until the losses are ultimately passed on to the negligent party responsible for them. As a general principle, the payer's bank will not be permitted to 'short-circuit' the contractual chain of correspondent banks in order to claim directly against a remote party.[445]

The potential liability of a correspondent or intermediary bank to its instructing party differs where the funds transfer in question falls within the scope of the PSR 2009.[446] Where there has been a failure to execute a payment order (whether at all or in a timely

---

[439] Ibid., 563. For the importance of there being contact or communication between parties before a 'special relationship' will be recognized, see *Customs & Excise Commissioners* v. *Barclays Bank plc*, n.424 above, [14], [65], [74], [94], [109].

[440] For discussion of the relationship between the payer's bank and its correspondent, see Sect. 5(iv)(b) above.

[441] *Honourable Society of the Middle Temple* v. *Lloyds Bank plc* [1999] 1 All ER (Comm.) 193; *Linklaters (a firm)* v. *HSBC Bank plc* [2003] 1 Lloyd's Rep. 545.

[442] The same duty also applies between the payee's bank and any correspondent or intermediary bank that it appoints. For a statement of this duty in the context of collecting a bill of exchange, see *AA Valibhoy & Sons (1907) Pte Ltd* v. *Habib Bank Ltd*, n.411 above, 391–392.

[443] In either case, an exclusion clause may purport to exclude the duty. For an example of such a clause in a different context, see *Calico Printers' Association* v. *Barclays Bank Ltd*, n.411 above. Such a clause may nowadays be subject to judicial control pursuant to the Unfair Contract Terms Act 1977.

[444] Consider *Equitable Trust Co. of New York* v. *Dawson Partners Ltd*, n.403 above, discussed in Sect. 5(iv) above.

[445] *Henderson* v. *Merrett Syndicates Ltd* [1995] 2 AC 145, 195 (HL), where Lord Goff considered that it would be 'most unusual' for the courts to 'short-circuit' a contractual chain by imposing a duty of care on remote parties. See also *Simaan General Contracting Co.* v. *Pilkington Glass Ltd (No. 2)* [1988] QB 758 (CA); *Pacific Associates Inc.* v. *Baxter* [1990] 1 QB 993 (CA); but contrast *Riyad Bank* v. *Ahli United Bank (UK) plc* [2006] 2 Lloyd's Rep. 292, [32], [36]–[48] ('There cannot be a general proposition that, just because a chain exists, no responsibility for advice is ever assumed to a non-contractual party'); *Galliford Try Infrastructure Ltd* v. *Mott MacDonald Ltd* [2008] EWHC 1570 (TCC), [189].

[446] Parts 5 and 6 of the PSR 2009 apply when the 'payment service' in question (defined to include, *inter alia*, credit transfers and direct debits: ibid., Sched. 1, para. 1(c)) is provided from an establishment maintained by a bank or its agent in the United Kingdom, the payer's and payee's banks are located within the EEA, and the transfer is carried out in Euros or in the currency of an EEA State that has not adopted the single currency (ibid., regs. 33(1), 51(1)): see further Sect. 5(iv) above. The PSR 2009 have replaced

manner)[447] and this is 'attributable' to the actions of a correspondent or intermediary bank,[448] that bank must compensate the payer's bank (or potentially, in the case of debit transfers, the payee's bank)[449] for any losses incurred as a result of the defective execution or non-execution of a payment order.[450] The correspondent or intermediary bank may avoid liability, however, where the payer has originally provided an incorrect unique identifier[451] or in cases of *force majeure*.[452] The statutory position appears to differ from the common law position in two important respects. First, a correspondent or intermediary bank may be liable under the PSR 2009 if the losses in question are 'attributable' to it.[453] Whilst this term clearly imposes a requirement that the actions of the correspondent or intermediary bank must have caused or contributed to the losses of the payer's bank, it does not on its face require any type of fault on the part of the correspondent. Unlike the common law position, therefore, where a correspondent bank must be shown to have acted negligently, such a bank appears to be strictly liable under the PSR 2009. Secondly, the position under the PSR 2009 appears to differ from the common law in circumstances where the execution of the payment instruction involves a chain of correspondents or intermediary banks. Whilst the common law, as discussed previously, generally limits the payer's bank to recouping its losses from the bank that it actually instructed to act as its correspondent, the PSR 2009 seem to enable the payer's bank to bring a claim directly against the correspondent bank that is responsible for the losses (or to which the losses are 'attributable'),[454] even where that bank is a remote party without any direct contractual relationship with the payer's bank.

What is less clear is whether this is intended to be the only claim available to the payer's bank or whether the payer's bank may still seek to recoup its losses from the bank that it has instructed directly. Given that this latter type of claim was formerly permitted by the express terms of the Cross-Border Credit Transfer Regulations 1999[455] and is permitted by the 'Payment Services Directive',[456] it may be telling that the PSR 2009 make no reference to the ability of the payer's bank to claim against the correspondent that it has instructed. Moreover, in respect of funds transfers falling within their scope, the

the previous regime under the Cross-Border Credit Transfer Regulations 1999, S.I. 1999/1876 from 1 November 2009: ibid., reg. 1(2)(c) & Sched. 6. See further Sect. 1(ii) above.

[447] PSR 2009, regs. 75–76. As a general rule, in the case of a credit transfer, the payer's bank must ensure that the amount of the payment transaction is credited to the account of the payee's bank by the end of the business day following receipt of the payment instruction (ibid., reg. 70(1)), and, in the case of a direct debit, the payee's bank must transmit the relevant payment order within the time-limits agreed between the payee and his bank (ibid., reg. 70(6)). For further consideration of the time-limits, see Sect. 5(iv) above & Sect. 5(vi) below.

[448] In strict terms, PSR 2009 reg. 78 refers to 'another payment service provider or intermediary', rather than a 'correspondent or intermediary bank'.

[449] This may be the case where the payment order is initiated by the payee, as in the case of a direct debit: PSR 2009, reg. 76.

[450] PSR 2009, reg. 78. The losses that may be recovered from the correspondent or intermediary bank include any sums that the payer's bank has been required to pay to the payer pursuant to the terms of the PSR 2009. For the potential liability of the payer's bank to the payer, see Sect. 5(iv) above. For the position of the payee's bank, see Sect. 5(vi) below.

[451] Ibid., reg. 74. See further Sect. 5(iv) above.   [452] Ibid., reg. 79. See further Sect. 5(iv) above.

[453] Ibid., reg. 78.

[454] The payer's bank may seek to pass on its liability to refund the payer for a failed transfer under the 'money-back guarantee' (PSR 2009, reg. 75(4)) or its liability for interest or charges incurred by the payer as a result of the failure (ibid., reg. 77). See further Sect. 5(iv) above.

[455] S.I. 1999/1876, reg. 10(1)–(2), repealed on 1 November 2009 by the PSR 2009.

[456] Directive 2007/64/EC on Payment Services in the Internal Market [2007] OJ L319, art. 77(2) (implementation required by 1 November 2009).

PSR 2009 do not expressly preserve the remedies that the parties might otherwise have had at common law and accordingly appear to establish an exclusive remedial regime when applicable. Whilst this appears to be the most likely construction, this must await confirmation from the courts. If the PSR 2009 are construed in this way, however, it is likely to have two important practical consequences. First, the payer's bank may find it more difficult to recoup its losses from a remote party with which it may not have an ongoing commercial relationship and, more importantly, for which it may not hold an account. Secondly, the risk of the 'wrongdoing' correspondent or intermediary bank becoming insolvent is effectively shifted away from the party that instructed that bank to the payer's bank.

In addition to the liability of the correspondent or intermediary bank to the payer's bank, a further issue that arises concerns the extent of that bank's liability to the payer himself. Where applicable, the PSR 2009 do not appear to recognize any such liability.[457] At common law, as the correspondent or intermediary bank is engaged by the payer's bank, there is no privity of contract between the correspondent and the payer. In *Calico Printers' Association* v. *Barclays Bank Ltd*,[458] the claimant engaged Barclays as its agent for the presentment to the buyer of a bill of exchange, accompanied by commercial paper for goods. Barclays, in turn, engaged its correspondent, the AP Bank. As the bill was dishonoured, the claimant ordered Barclays to arrange for the storage and insurance of the goods. This instruction was transmitted by Barclays to the AP Bank, which stored the goods but failed to insure them. When the goods were destroyed by fire, the claimant sued the two banks for breach of contract and in negligence for their failure to adhere to their mandate. It was held that Barclays was not liable, as an exemption clause included in the contract between it and the claimant exonerated it from liability for the negligence of its correspondents. The AP Bank was also held not to be liable to the claimant as there was no privity between them. Wright J observed that as a general rule there was no privity of contract between a principal and his agent's sub-agent.[459] The principle in *Calico Printers' Association* has been confirmed recently in the international cheque collection context by Flaux J in *Grosvenor Casinos Ltd* v. *National Bank of Abu Dhabi*,[460] and has been adopted by Webster J in *Royal Products Ltd* v. *Midland*

---

[457] PSR 2009, regs. 75–77, which refer only to the liability of the payer's bank to his customer and that of the payee's bank to his customer.

[458] N.411 above. See also *SS Steamship Co Ltd* v. *Ship 'Alchatby'* (1986) 5 FTR 253, [18] (CFC); *Ram Realty Ltd* v. *Sicherman* (1991) 119 AR 69, [12] (AQB). For an argument to the contrary, see J. Vroegop, 'Role of Correspondent Banks in Money Transfers' [1990] *LMCLQ* 540, especially 550 ff. See also *Bastone & Firminger Ltd* v. *Nasima Enterprises (Nigeria) Ltd* [1996] CLC 1902, 1908, where Rix J held it arguable that the ICC's Uniform Rules for Collections introduced privity of contract between a seller and collecting bank. It may now be doubted, however, whether the view expressed in *Bastone & Firminger* remains good law in the light of *Grosvenor Casinos Ltd* v. *National Bank of Abu Dhabi* [2008] EWHC 511 (Comm.), [153], [157]. In this case, Flaux J distinguished *Bastone & Firminger* as a case dealing with the earlier Uniform Rules for Collection 322, which are materially different from the current Uniform Rules for Collection 522. His Lordship also made the point (ibid., [153]) that *Bastone & Firminger* 'was only concerned with whether the point was sufficiently arguable at an interlocutory stage' and, therefore, was 'of limited assistance in determining after a full trial whether URC 522 does indeed alter the common law position'. Furthermore, Flaux J appears to have suggested (ibid., [157]) that the Uniform Rules for Collection 522 do not provide a distinct basis for the imposition of a common law duty of care.

[459] For an application of *Calico* as authority for this general principle, see *United States of America* v. *Shearn Delamore & Co.* [2007] 8 MLJ 654, [27].

[460] N.458 above, [146]–[149]. Even after *Grosvenor Casinos* it may be possible for the payee of a cheque to acquire contractual rights against a collecting/correspondent bank by virtue of the Contracts (Rights of Third Parties) Act 1999, but this will depend upon the precise wording of the collection instruction. Where such a direct claim is unavailable, however, the remitting bank may be able to claim damages from the

Bank Ltd[461] as governing the question of the relationship between the issuer of a money transfer order ('the payer') and his bank's correspondent.

The fact that under English law there is no privity between the payer and his bank's correspondent should not, however, lull British banks that have offices abroad into a false false sense of security.[462] The point is illustrated by two United States authorities. In the first, *Silverstein* v. *Chartered Bank*,[463] it was held that there was privity of contract between the payer and his bank's correspondent, as the latter had been expressly selected by the payer. In the second case, *Evra Corporation* v. *Swiss Bank Corporation*,[464] a rental was due under a charterparty at the Banque de Paris in Geneva at a predetermined time. The charterer ordered his bank in Chicago to effect the transfer. A telex message was duly transmitted by the London branch of the Chicago bank to its correspondent in Geneva, the defendant. Owing to the fact that the defendant's telex terminal in Geneva had run out of paper, the message was not received, although the terminal automatically acknowledged the message to the sending bank's branch in London. When the breakdown was

collecting/correspondent bank on behalf of the cheque payee (see H. Bennett, 'Bank Collections, Privity of Contract, and Third Party Losses' (2008) 124 *LQR* 532, 535–538) or the payee may be able to sue its own bank, as remitting bank, for the negligent actions of the collecting/correspondent bank (see *Mackersy* v. *Ramsays, Bonars & Co.*, n.411 above, 846, 851; *Henry Prince* v. *Oriental Bank Corporation*, n.411 above; *Calico Printers' Association* v. *Barclays Bank Ltd*, n.411 above). For acceptance of this last principle in Singapore, see *AA Valibhoy & Sons (1907) Pte Ltd* v. *Habib Bank Ltd*, n.411 above, 391; *AA Valibhoy & Sons (1907) Pte Ltd* v. *Banque Nationale de Paris*, n.411 above, 781. For further discussion, see Sect. 5(iv)(b) above.

[461] N.274 above, 198. Webster J also appears to have ruled out the existence of any direct tortious or fiduciary duties between the payer and his bank's correspondent: ibid. See also *Balsamo* v. *Medici* [1984] 1 WLR 951; *BP plc* v. *Aon Ltd* [2006] EWHC 424 (Comm.), [89]; *Grosvenor Casinos Ltd* v. *National Bank of Abu Dhabi*, n.458 above, [157]. Cf. *Henderson* v. *Merrett Syndicates Ltd.*, n.445 above, 195, where a sub-agent was held to owe a tortious duty of care to the principal in what Lord Goff considered to be a 'most unusual situation'. Consider also *Nicholls* v. *Peers* (NZCA, 22 September 2003).

[462] The position would change if domestic legislation were to be enacted in the United Kingdom that was based on the UNCITRAL Model Law on International Credit Transfers (1992). According to Art. 8(2) of the Model Law, a correspondent bank is under a duty to issue a 'payment order' to either the payee's bank or a correspondent or intermediary bank within the prescribed period contained in Art. 11. The 'sender' (defined in Art. 2(e) as 'including the [payer] and any sending bank') may recover from the correspondent or intermediary bank any interest that he has had to pay to the payee as a result of the failure to make the transfer (Art. 17(3)). In the event that the instructions received by the correspondent or intermediary bank do not contain sufficient information to enable the payment order to be executed (Art. 8(4)), or where there is some inconsistency over the amount of money to be transferred (Art. 8(5)), the correspondent bank is obliged to give the 'sender' notice of that fact within the time-frame in Art. 11. A failure to give the requisite notice renders the correspondent or intermediary bank liable to pay the 'sender' interest for the period that it retains the funds (Art. 17(4)). No matter what the circumstances, claims for consequential loss over and above any interest payments are excluded (Art. 18). As considered already above, the correspondent or intermediary bank has no direct liability to the payer under the PSR 2009.

[463] 392 NYS 2d. 296 (NY Sup. Ct., 1977). See also *AA Valibhoy & Sons (1907) Pte Ltd* v. *Habib Bank Ltd*, n.411 above, 391, where the Singapore High Court has suggested that privity might exist between a principal and sub-agent 'where the principal was party to the appointment of the sub-agent'. In contrast, in *Calico Printers' Association* v. *Barclays Bank Ltd*, n.411 above, the claimant also specifically nominated the correspondent bank, but Wright J held that this nomination did not create privity of contract between the claimant and the correspondent bank. More recently, in *Grosvenor Casinos Ltd* v. *National Bank of Abu Dhabi*, n.458 above, [149], Flaux J indicated that privity could only exist between a customer and his bank's correspondent if the customer not only contemplated the involvement of the particular correspondent bank, but also authorized his bank to create privity between himself and the correspondent.

[464] 522 F Supp. 820 (ND. Ill., 1981), revd. on another ground: 673 F 2d. 951 (7th Cir., 1982), cert. denied 459 US 1017 (1982). The decision of the District Court was followed in *Securities Fund Services Inc.* v. *American National Bank & Trust Co.*, 542 F. Supp. 323 (ND. Ill., 1982); *Mellon Bank* v. *Securities Settlement Corporation*, n.408 above.

discovered, the time for the payment of the amount to the shipowners' bank, the Banque de Paris in Geneva, had passed. The shipowner accordingly withdrew the ship. The charterer then brought an action against the correspondent bank, the defendant, in Illinois. The United States District Court held that bank liable in damages for breach of contract and negligence. It concluded, by an analogy with Article 4 of the Uniform Commercial Code, that under the common law of the United States there was privity of contract between the charterer, as payer, and the defendant, his bank's Swiss correspondent. The same conclusion would undoubtedly have been reached if the correspondent had been a British bank. This decision was reversed by the Court of Appeals for the Seventh Circuit, on the ground that the defendant bank, which had not been familiarized with the special circumstances of the case, was not liable for the consequential loss.[465] The loss sustained by the charterer as a result of the withdrawal of the ship was too remote, but the appellate court did not question the existence of privity between the charterer, as payer, and the correspondent bank.

Although *Evra Corporation* may be questioned on the basis of considerations of private international law,[466] the recognition that a correspondent bank might potentially be liable at common law to the payer has now received confirmation in the United States in Article 4A of the Uniform Commercial Code.[467] What is maybe a cause for particular alarm for United Kingdom banks operating abroad, however, is that the United States is not the only country in which there is deemed to be privity of contract between the correspondent or intermediary bank and the customer of the bank by which it is engaged.

(vi) Position of the payee's bank

Unlike the position of the payer's bank and the correspondent or intermediary bank, whose legal functions are conceptually well defined, the common law position of the payee's bank in a money transfer operation has been subject to a number of uncertainties. Whilst these will persist in fund transfers governed by the common law principles, which are considered further below, the vast majority of domestic funds transfers and a significant number of international ones will now fall within the scope of the PSR 2009,[468] which serve to clarify the legal position of the payee's bank somewhat. Just like the payer's bank,[469] the payee's bank is subject to certain information disclosure requirements. Where the payee's bank operates an account for its customer that may be used to make and receive funds transfers, the bank will have to satisfy the information requirements

---

[465] See also *Lloyds Bank plc* v. *Lynch*, 702 F. Supp. 157 (ND. Ohio, 1988).

[466] There may be a question as to whether the alleged contract between the charterer and the correspondent was governed by Swiss or by United States law, although the District Court accepted the application of United States law with impunity. For the current choice of law rules, see UCC, Art. 4A–507. See also *Shawmut Worcester County* v. *First American Bank and Trust Co.*, 731 F Supp. 57 (D. Mass., 1990).

[467] UCC, Art. 4A–305. See also UNCITRAL Model Law on International Credit Transfers (1992), Arts. 17–18.

[468] Parts 5 and 6 of the PSR 2009 apply when the 'payment service' in question (defined to include, *inter alia*, credit transfers and direct debits: ibid., Sched. 1, para. 1(c)) is provided from an establishment maintained by a bank or its agent in the United Kingdom, the payer's and payee's banks are located within the European Economic Area ('EEA'), and the transfer is carried out in Euros or in the currency of an EEA State that has not adopted the single currency (ibid., regs. 33(1), 51(1)): see further Sect. 5(iv) above. The PSR 2009 have replaced the previous regime under the Cross-Border Credit Transfer Regulations 1999, S.I. 1999/1876 from 1 November 2009: ibid., reg. 1(2)(c) & Sched. 6. See further Sect. 1(ii) above.

[469] See further Sect. 5(iv) above.

for 'framework contracts'[470] that have been discussed previously.[471] Most standing order and direct debit payments are likely to be covered by these information requirements. The present focus is upon the information requirements imposed upon the payee's bank in connection with the execution of a 'single payment service contract'.[472] Where the payment transaction is initiated by the payee who approaches a bank to act and receive the funds on his behalf (in other words, a debit transfer),[473] the payee's bank will be required to make certain information available to the payee either before the payment contract is concluded or 'immediately' after, if the payee's approach is made by a 'means of distance communication', such as the phone or internet.[474] This includes details concerning, *inter alia*,[475] the information that the payee needs to provide for the proper execution of the order; the maximum time that it will take for the transfer to be effected; the charges for the service that the payee's bank will provide and a breakdown of those charges; and any exchange rate that will be applied by the payee's bank in respect of the payment transaction.[476] In addition, the payee's bank must provide such of the information in Schedule 4 of the PSR 2009 as is relevant to a 'single payment service contract'.[477]

Once the relevant information has been provided to the payee, regardless of whether the payment is made pursuant to a 'framework contract' or 'single payment service contract', the payee's bank will transmit the payment order to the payer's bank unless it notifies the payee of its reasons for refusing to do so.[478] In the case of a direct debit instruction, the payee's bank must transmit the payment order within the time-limits that have been agreed with the payee.[479] Following its receipt of funds from the payer's bank, the payee's bank must credit the payee's account with the amount in question.[480] Regardless of whether the payee has an account with the bank that receives the funds on his behalf, those funds must be made immediately available to the payee upon their being credited to the account of the payee's bank.[481] When being credited to the payee's account, the transferred funds must start to earn interest by the end of the business day upon which the payee's bank received those funds.[482] In this regard, the payee's bank must ensure that the full amount is transferred to the payee,[483] and it may not deduct any charges from the amount transferred before crediting it to the payee's account, unless the payee has previously agreed to this happening and the payee's bank subsequently informs the payee of what deductions

---

[470] PSR 2009, reg. 2(1): '...a contract for payment services which governs the future execution of individual and successive payment transactions and which may contain the obligation and conditions for setting up a payment account'.

[471] Ch. 7, Sect. 2 above.

[472] PSR 2009, reg. 2(1): '...a contract for a single payment transaction not covered by a framework contract'. For the distinction between a 'framework contract' and a 'single payment service contract', see Sect. 5(iv) above.

[473] Ibid., reg. 71. For the distinction between credit and debit transfers, see Sect. 1(iii) above.

[474] Ibid., reg. 36(1).   [475] Ibid., reg. 36(2)(e) & Sched. 4.

[476] Ibid., reg. 36(2). Additional information may be required when payment is to be effected not by funds transfer but by means of a payment card, such as information concerning additional charges: ibid., reg. 50(1). For the application of the PSR 2009 to payment cards, see further Ch. 14, Sect. 9 below.

[477] Ibid., reg. 36(2)(e). For discussion of the information required by Schedule 4, see further Ch. 7, Sect. 2 above.

[478] Ibid., reg. 66(1). The payee's bank must also inform the payee of anything he can do to rectify any factual errors that led to the refusal: ibid., reg. 66(1)(c). The notification must be given at the earliest opportunity and in the agreed manner (ibid., reg. 66(2)) and may be subject to charges if this is permitted by the payee's account contract (ibid., reg. 66(3)). No notification need be given where this would be illegal (ibid., reg. 66(5)), such as where it might give rise to liability for 'tipping off' (Ch. 4, Sects. 3–4 above).

[479] Ibid., reg. 70(6).   [480] Ibid., reg. 70(5).   [481] Ibid., regs. 71(1)–(2), 73(2).

[482] Ibid., reg. 73(1).   [483] Ibid., reg. 68(1).

have been made.[484] The payee's bank will be liable to reimburse the payee for any unauthorized deductions, irrespective of who makes the deduction, when the payment transaction is of a type that was initiated by the payee.[485] In contrast, the payer's bank will bear responsibility for reimbursing the payee in respect of any unauthorized deductions in circumstances where the payer initiates the payment transaction.[486] Following the execution of the payment transaction, howsoever it is initiated, the payee's bank is required to provide the payee with certain additional information:[487] some form of reference that will enable the payee to identify the payment transaction and, where appropriate, the payer and any information transferred as part of the payment transaction; the amount of the payment transfer stated in the currency in which the funds are placed at the payee's disposal; the amount and breakdown of any charges payable by the payee; the exchange rate applied by the payee's bank to the payment transaction and the amount of the payment before the currency conversion; and the date upon which the funds will be credited to the payee's account for the purpose of earning interest.[488]

The allocation of responsibility between the payer's bank and the payee's bank for the non-execution or defective execution of a payment instruction depends upon which party initiated the funds transfer. Where the payer is the initiating party,[489] as in the case of a CHAPS Sterling transfer or a standing order, the payer's bank bears primary responsibility for executing the payment instruction and is generally liable for the defective execution or non-execution of the payment transfer, unless that bank can show that the funds were in fact received by the payee's bank in a timely manner.[490] In circumstances where the payer's bank is able to demonstrate that the funds had been transferred to the payee's bank within the relevant time-limits, responsibility for the defective execution or non-execution of the payment transfer passes to the payee's bank, which must then immediately make available to the payee a sum equivalent to the amount of the transfer and must credit the payee's account where possible.[491] In the case of payment transactions initiated by the payee,[492] such as direct debits, the payee's bank is primarily responsible for effecting the transfer and is liable to the payee for the correct transmission of the payment order.[493] If a payee-initiated payment order is not transmitted correctly or at all, the payee's bank must immediately re-transmit the payment order to the payer's bank,[494] and, if requested to do so by the payee, must make immediate efforts to trace the payment and inform the payee of the outcome.[495] Where the payee's bank can demonstrate that it has correctly transmitted the payment order to the payer's bank in a timely manner, responsibility for the defective execution or non-execution of the payment transaction shifts to the payer's bank, which must then refund the amount of the payment transaction to the payer and, if necessary, re-credit the payer's account.[496] If the payee incurs any interest or other charges as a result of a breach by the payee's bank of its obligations under the PSR 2009, he may recover these from his bank by way of an action for breach of statutory duty.[497]

---

[484] Ibid., reg. 68(2). Any charges imposed must reasonably correspond to the actual costs of the payee's bank (ibid., reg. 54(1)(c)) and must be levied upon the payee (ibid., reg. 54(2)).

[485] Ibid., reg. 68(3).   [486] Id.   [487] Ibid., reg. 38(1).   [488] Ibid., reg. 38(2).

[489] Ibid., reg. 75(1).   [490] Ibid., regs. 70(1), 75(4), 75(2). See further Sect. 5(iv) above.

[491] Ibid., reg. 75(5).   [492] Ibid., reg. 76(1).   [493] Ibid., reg. 76(2).

[494] Ibid., reg. 76(3).   [495] Ibid., reg. 76(4).

[496] Ibid., reg. 76(5). The payer's bank may also be liable in respect of a direct debit payment when a particular request exceeds what might be reasonably expected, having regard to the payer's previous spending patterns: ibid., regs. 63–64.

[497] Ibid., regs. 77, 120(1).

Whilst the payee's bank will generally bear the onus of proving that it correctly transmitted the payment order in question if it is to avoid liability,[498] there are also a number of specific defences that the bank can rely upon. First, the payee's bank may escape liability if the payee has failed to inform it without undue delay (and no later than 13 months after the debit from the payer's account) that the payment transaction had not been executed correctly.[499] This defence will not be available to the payee's bank, however, if it has itself failed to comply with any of the information requirements contained in Part 5 of the PSR 2009 that were considered previously.[500] Secondly, where the payee provides his bank with a 'unique identifier' in connection with a payment transaction,[501] such as the payer's account number, sort code, or bank details, the payee's bank will not be liable for the failure to execute the payment order correctly if the 'unique identifier' in question is incorrect.[502] Even so, the payee's bank remains under an obligation to make reasonable efforts to obtain the funds in question.[503] Thirdly, the payee's bank will escape liability in cases of *force majeure*, such as when its breach of the PSR 2009 is due to the need to comply with statutory obligations[504] or due to 'abnormal and unforeseeable circumstances' producing consequences that the bank could not have avoided despite all efforts to the contrary.[505] Finally, the payee's bank may be able to recoup any losses that it has suffered, as a result of the incorrect execution of a payment transaction, from the payer's bank or any correspondent or intermediary bank to which those losses are 'attributable'.[506]

As indicated previously, the position of the payee's bank at common law is far less clear than the position under the PSR 2009. Essentially, the difficulty lies in determining for whom the payee's bank is acting at any particular point in time during the funds transfer. The answer to this question may be important in determining to whom the payee's bank may be liable for the defective execution of a payment transaction, the point in time before which a funds transfer may be countermanded, and whether the funds transfer is effective to discharge the payer's obligations pursuant to the underlying contract.[507] Fortunately, in some types of money transfer, guidance is provided by the contracts made between the banks involved in the transaction.[508] For example, in SWIFT transfers, the master agreement between the banks participating in the SWIFT network makes detailed provision for the allocation of losses in cases of breakdown and of improperly executed instructions. In the absence of such contractual provisions, the question has to be decided by reference to basic common law principles. The problem of determining the legal position of the payee's bank according to these principles is, however, exacerbated by the fact that the bank's position can vary from one giro operation to another and according to the facts of the particular case. In direct debit operations, the payee's bank acts as the payee's agent. It is true that when the payee initiates the direct debit operation he acts as the payer's agent, but when he selects his bank and nominates the account into which payment is to be made, the payee

---

[498] Ibid., reg. 60(1).

[499] Ibid., reg. 59(1). For the potential relationship between the requirement that the payee notify his bank 'without undue delay', but not outside the 13-month time-limit, consider *Bankers Trust Co* v. *State Bank of India*, n.374 above.

[500] Ibid., reg. 59(2).   [501] Ibid., reg. 2(1).   [502] Ibid., reg. 74(2).   [503] Id.

[504] Ibid., reg. 79(2). An example would be the bank's need to comply with anti-money laundering legislation: see further Ch. 4, Sect. 3 above.

[505] Ibid., reg. 79(1).   [506] Ibid., reg. 78. See further Sect. 5(v) above.

[507] See further Sect. 6(iii) below.

[508] See, for example, *State Bank of New South Wales Ltd* v. *Swiss Bank Corporation* [1997] Bank. LR 34 (NSWCA) (CHIPS rules).

consciously designates the receiving station at which he expects to receive the payment due to him. Whilst the order to the payer's bank is executed by the payee of the direct debit in a representative capacity, the payee proposes to accept the payment involved in his own right. The better view is, therefore, that the payee's bank is, therefore, designated as the payee's agent for that purpose.

The position is less certain in the case of a credit transfer. The problem in such cases stems from the fact that the payee's bank credits the payee's account in reliance upon an instruction given to it by the payer's bank (or its correspondent),[509] but, once this instruction is carried out, the payee's bank holds the funds to its customer's order.[510] It follows that, when the payee's bank credits the payee's account with the sum involved, its legal position changes, in that its principal is no longer the payer's bank but its own customer who becomes entitled to draw on the funds. The exact moment at which this legal metamorphosis takes place has, however, given rise to disputes. Where funds are transferred to the payee's bank in accordance with the terms of the underlying contract between the payer and payee, or with the express consent of the payee, the payee's bank is deemed to have authority to accept funds into the account and so will receive the funds and execute the payment transaction as the payee's agent.[511] Accordingly, there will be a change in the principal for whom the payee's bank acts at the point when the payee's bank accepts the funds or takes steps to execute the funds transfer. Presumably, the payee's bank should be deemed to have accepted the funds, and accordingly become the payee's agent, where there is an error in transmitting the payment instruction that is caused by a fault or breakdown at the premises of the payee's bank.[512] Although it has been argued that the relationship of the payee and his bank is that of banker and customer and not that of agent and principal at all,[513] the better view is that the agency relationship is only temporary[514] and is transformed into the traditional debtor–creditor relationship once the funds are deposited into the account upon their being unconditionally credited to that account.[515] The position is

---

[509] *Shawmut Worcester County* v. *First American Bank and Trust Co.*, n.466 above, holding that the payee's bank was the agent of the payer's bank for this purpose alone.

[510] Ibid., holding further that, as the payee's bank accepted payment as the payee's agent, it was not entitled to obey the subsequent instruction of the payer's bank to reverse the credit entry in the payee's account and refund the money. On the same point and to the same effect, see *Middle East Banking* v. *State Street Bank International*, 821 F 2d. 897 (2d Cir., 1987).

[511] *Mardorf Peach & Co. Ltd* v. *Attica Sea Carriers Corp. of Liberia, The Laconia* [1977] AC 850 (HL); *TSB Bank of Scotland plc* v. *Welwyn Hatfield District Council* [1993] Bank. LR 267, 271–272; *Customs & Excise Commissioners* v. *National Westminster Bank plc* [2003] 1 All ER (Comm.) 327, [7]–[9]; *PT Berlian Laju Tanker TBK* v. *Nuse Shipping Ltd* [2008] EWHC 1330 (Comm.), [67]. For further discussion of these cases, see Sect. 6(iii) below. For the suggestion that the payee's bank acts as the payee's agent for the purpose of receiving payment pursuant to a standing order, see *Whitbread Group plc* v. *Goldapple Ltd* 2005 SCLR 263, [27] (OH). See also *Dovey* v. *Bank of New Zealand*, n.24 above, where the New Zealand Court of Appeal held that the payee's bank held the transferred funds for the payee despite the fact that no account had been opened for him. The mere fact that a payee has an account with the receiving bank does not make that bank the payee's agent to receive the funds: *Customs & Excise Commissioners* v. *National Westminster Bank plc*, above, [7]–[10]; *PT Berlian Laju Tanker TBK* v. *Nuse Shipping Ltd*, above, [67].

[512] *Entores Ltd* v. *Miles Far East Corporation*, n.228 above; *Brinkibon Ltd* v. *Stahag Stahl Und Stahlwarenhandels-gesellschaft GmbH*, n.228 above. For a case involving such a breakdown at the premises of the correspondent or intermediary bank, see *Evra Corporation* v. *Swiss Bank Corporation*, 522 F Supp. 820 (ND. Ill., 1981), revd. on another ground 673 F 2d. 951 (7th Cir., 1982), cert. denied 459 US 1017 (1982).

[513] R. King, 'The Receiving Bank's Role in Credit Transfer Transactions' (1982) 45 *MLR* 369.

[514] For the recognition of an equivalent agency relationship in relation to the collection of cheques, see Ch. 15, Sect. 3 below.

[515] *Balmoral Supermarkets Ltd* v. *Bank of New Zealand* [1974] 2 NZLR 155, 157, where McMullin J appears to suggest that funds become subject to the traditional debtor–creditor relationship between bank and customer at the moment that they are deposited into an account with the bank. See further Ch. 5, Sect. 2 above.

different again, however, where the credit transfer is initiated by the payer without the express consent of the payee, such as where a tenant pays rent due under a lease to a bank with which he happens to know that his landlord maintains an account. In such a case, the payee's bank acts solely at the request of the payer or his bank and not as the payee's agent. Accordingly, the payee's bank can only be said to act on the payee's behalf, when the payee decides not to reject the credit entry[516] and adopts the bank's act in accepting payment.[517] A similar result may arguably follow where the means by which the payee's alleged consent to the payer making the transfer is a forgery.[518] It follows that, when the payee's bank has no authority at the outset of the payment transaction to accept the funds, the change in its principal occurs at a later stage of the transfer process than when it is so authorized.

A more complex problem arises in the situation where the payee's bank has authority to receive and accept the funds on the payee's behalf (such as where an account with the payee's bank is designated for payment in the underlying contract), but there is some limit upon that authority. An interesting example of such a situation can be found in a series of cases in which an attempt was made to pay an amount due to the payee after the date stipulated in the underlying contract for that payment.[519] Thus, a charterparty or a commercial lease frequently requires payment by a definite date to the credit of a designated account that the payee holds with a designated bank. The payee, who may wish to use a delay in payment as an excuse to withdraw the ship or terminate the lease, may instruct his bank to reject any payment tendered after the stipulated date. Despite this clear instruction, the banking practice prevailing at the payee's bank may lead to a situation in which the late payment is nevertheless credited to the unwilling payee's account. In such circumstances, the question arises as to whether the payee's bank can still be said to receive and accept the funds as the payee's agent despite its limited authority, or whether the amount accepted by the payee's bank is received by it as an agent of the payer's bank, or its correspondent or intermediary bank, until the payment is expressly adopted by the payee. Article 10 of the UNCITRAL Model Law on International Credit Transfers (1992)[520] treats the payee's

---

[516] *PT Berlian Laju Tanker TBK* v. *Nuse Shipping Ltd*, n.511 above, [67]: 'Payment under a contract cannot be made without the consent of the creditor. Even if payment is to be in cash, i.e. legal tender, the creditor may not necessarily accept it'. Payment must be distinguished from tender, as the former discharges the debtor's liability whilst the latter does not: *TSB Bank of Scotland plc* v. *Welwyn Hatfield District Council*, n.511 above. A valid tender does, however, protect the debtor from having to pay interest on the debt and may have certain costs implications: ibid. On the issue of whether a funds transfer amounts to a valid tender when the contract requires payment 'in cash', see *The Brimnes*, n.119 above. This would certainly appear to be the position in New Zealand: *Dovey* v. *Bank of New Zealand*, n.24 above, 651–652; *Otago Station Estates Ltd* v. *Parker*, n.407 above, [27] ('…a contractual requirement for the making of a payment must, as a matter of law, be performed by means of legal tender, bank cheque or other cleared funds…'); *Rick Dees Ltd* v. *Larsen*, n.407 above, [64]–[66], affd. on this point: [2007] 3 NZLR 577, [3], [30]–[31], [36]; *Redoute Securities Ltd* v. *Thomson*, n.407 above, [26]–[32]; *Southbourne Investments Ltd* v. *Greenmount Manufacturing Ltd* [2008] 1 NZLR 30, [19]–[23] (NZSC).

[517] *TSB Bank of Scotland plc* v. *Welwyn Hatfield District Council*, n.511 above; cf. *HMV Fields Properties Ltd* v. *Bracken Self Selection Fabrics Ltd*, 1991 SLT 31. In *Customs & Excise Commissioners* v. *National Westminster Bank plc*, n.511 above, [7]–[10], it was held that a bank was not authorized to receive a payment on its customer's behalf simply because the customer held a current account with the bank. See also *PT Berlian Laju Tanker TBK* v. *Nuse Shipping Ltd*, n.511 above, [67]. For further discussion of these cases, see Sect. 6(iii) below.

[518] *Securities Fund Services Inc.* v. *American National Bank & Trust Company of Chicago*, n.464 above, affd. 718 F.2d 1104 (7th Cir., 1983). It is even less clear how the position of the payee's bank would be altered if the payee's consent to the funds transfer was vitiated by a mistake or misrepresentation: *TSB Bank of Scotland plc* v. *Welwyn Hatfield District Council*, n.511 above.

[519] See further Sect. 6(iii) below.

[520] On 25 November 1992, by Resolution 47/34, the United Nations General Assembly approved the UNCITRAL Report and Model Law on International Credit Transfers finalized at UNCITRAL's 25th Session of 4–22 May 1992: UN General Assembly, Official Records, 4th Session, Supp. No. 17, A/47/17.

bank as the agent of the payer's bank (or the agent of its correspondent or intermediary bank) until the payee's bank accepts the funds for the credit of the payee's account. It is submitted that, at common law, the answer generally depends on the payer's knowledge of the payee's attitude to the late payment. If the payer is unaware of the payee's intention to refuse payment, he is able to argue that the payee's bank has accepted payment with the ostensible or apparent authority apparently conferred upon it by the payee. If the payer is aware of the payee's order to his bank to reject late payment, then this contention becomes untenable. This issue will be discussed more fully subsequently.[521]

In the more common situation where the payee's bank is acting as the payee's agent, the payer may nevertheless wish to hold the payee's bank liable. As there will be no privity of contract between the two parties,[522] the payer will have to argue that the payee's bank owes it a common law duty of care. As considered previously,[523] the existence of such a duty was considered in *Abou-Rahmah* v. *Abacha*,[524] where the claimants, who were the victims of an international fraud, instructed Gulf Bank to transfer funds to the payee (Trust International) by crediting the account of the defendant (City Express Bank of Lagos) that was held with HSBC in London. Following the defendant's release of the funds to 'Trusty International' rather than 'Trust International', as was indicated in the SWIFT message,[525] the payer argued that the defendant had breached its common law duty of care. Treacy J rejected this contention, indicating that 'no special responsibility had been undertaken by the defendant to the claimants'.[526] This conclusion that there had been no voluntary assumption of responsibility was based primarily on the fact that the payer was not a customer of the payee's bank and the fact that there had been no contact between the parties at any point before the payee's bank received the funds.[527] Treacy J also rejected the existence of a duty of care applying the 'threefold test'.[528] The main reasons why it was not 'fair, just, and reasonable' to impose a duty upon the payee's bank included the fact that it received the funds as agent for the payee, to whom it already owed a contractual duty of care; the fact that banks in general have 'a huge number of potential [payers] who can remit money without significant control by the bank'; and the fact that, in the absence of special circumstances, the recognition of a duty of care would 'impose very heavy burdens on banks and significantly hamper their efficiency'.[529] His Lordship indicated, however,

---

[521] See further Sect. 6(iii) below.

[522] Furthermore, the payer is most unlikely to have a contractual claim based on the Contracts (Rights of Third Parties) Act 1999, s.1(1)(b), as no term of the contract between the payee and his bank will generally purport to confer any benefit on the payer: see generally *Nisshin Shipping Co. Ltd* v. *Cleaves & Co. Ltd*, n.432 above; *Laemthong International Lines Co. Ltd* v. *Artis*, n.432 above; *Avraamides* v. *Colwill*, n.432 above; *Prudential Assurance Co. Ltd* v. *Ayres*, n.432 above.

[523] See further Sect. 5(iv) above.

[524] N.422 above, affd. on a different point: [2007] 1 Lloyd's Rep 115.

[525] For consideration of SWIFT messages, see Sect. 4(iv) above.

[526] *Abou-Rahmah* v. *Abacha*, n.422 above, [68], affd. on a different point: [2007] 1 Lloyd's Rep 115. See generally *Hedley Byrne & Co. Ltd* v. *Heller & Partners*, n.427 above; *Customs & Excise Commissioners* v. *Barclays Bank plc*, n.424 above, [5].

[527] Id. In *Wells* v. *First National Commercial Bank*, n.426 above, 563, Evans LJ denied the existence of a duty of care owed by the payer's bank to the payee, but considered that such a duty might arguably be owed on *Hedley Byrne* principles if there had been direct contact between the parties.

[528] Id. See, for example n.424 above.

[529] Id. See also *So* v. *HSBC Bank plc*, n.425 above, [95]–[102]. In *Abou-Rahmah*, Treacy J relied upon a number of Canadian authorities in support of his conclusion that no duty of care existed: *Groves-Raffin Construction Ltd* v. *Bank of Nova Scotia*, n.425 above; *Toor* v. *Bank of Montreal*, n.425 above; *Dennison* v. *Cronin*, n.425 above; *Kyser* v. *Bank of Montreal*, n.425 above; but compare *Royal Bank of Canada* v. *Stangl*, n.425 above. See also *Dupont Heating & Air Conditioning Ltd* v. *Bank of Montreal*, n.425 above, [31]–[40].

that had he recognized the existence of a duty of care on the facts before him, he would not have reduced the damages on the grounds of the claimants' contributory negligence.[530]

Although some limited support for the conclusion in *Abou-Rahmah* can be found in *So v. HSBC Bank plc*,[531] there remains Canadian[532] and United States authority to the contrary. In *Securities Fund Services Inc.* v. *American National Bank and Trust Co. of Chicago*,[533] an unknown person forged an instrument that misled the claimant into selling shares deposited with it by John Bushman and that instructed the claimant to remit the proceeds of the sale to the account of 'John Bushman, Trustee // 204471, which was described as being maintained with the defendant bank. The claimant instructed the New England Merchants National Bank to transfer the amount in question and the defendant bank accepted the payment for the credit of account number 204471, even though this was in fact held in the name of 'Gerald S. Haberkorn Inc'. Giving judgment for the claimant, as payer, Leighton DJ stated that for Illinois law to impose a duty of care the occurrence in question had to be reasonably foreseeable and that in the case before him 'the loss of the transferred funds is the reasonably foreseeable result of a deposit made where the name on the transfer instructions differs from the name on the account into which the funds are deposited'.[534] Given that this conclusion was based at least in part upon a finding that the payer was a customer of the payee's bank, however, it is not clear that *Securities Fund Services* would provide any general basis for an English court in the future to depart from *Abou-Rahmah*.[535] Even if *Securities Fund Services* were to be applied, the payer may still face the difficulty of overcoming the issue of remoteness if he is seeking to recover damages resulting from consequential losses.

As an alternative to the argument that the payee's bank had breached its common law duty of care to the payer by crediting funds to the wrong account,[536] the payer in

---

[530] Ibid., [77].

[531] N.425 above, [95]–[102]. See further C. Witting, 'Banks, Dangerous Documents and Other People's Money' (2010) 126 *LQR* 39.

[532] See *Royal Bank of Canada* v. *Stangl*, n.425 above, where the payee's bank was held to have been negligent when it credited funds to a specified account number, without seeking clarification from the payer's bank, when the payment order, as well as giving the account number, identified a differently named payee. In *Abou-Rahmah* v. *Abacha*, n.422 above, [60]–[69], affd. on a different point: [2007] 1 Lloyd's Rep 115, Treacy J expressly refused to follow this decision.

[533] N.464 above, affd. 718 F.2d 1104 (7th Cir., 1983).

[534] Ibid., 327. Cf. *Bradford Trust Co. of Boston* v. *Texas American Bank*, 790 F 2d. 407 (5th Cir. 1986), where the loss resulting from a forged instruction was held to fall on the payer's bank, which had failed to detect the forgery, and not on the payee's bank, which overlooked the difference between the name of the account holder and the name of the payee nominated in the payment order. English law might reach a similar result, not by imposing any duty of care upon the payer's bank to the payee's bank, but by accepting that, by allowing the payee to withdraw funds from its account, the payee's bank would have a change of position or payment over defence to any restitutionary defence brought by the payer's bank: see further Ch. 12, Sect. 3(iii) above. See also *Shawmut Worcester County* v. *First American Bank and Trust Co.*, n.466 above, where the payee's bank was held not to have been negligent when, instead of crediting the funds to an account maintained solely by the payee, it received them for a joint account in the name of the payee and of a third party; but contrast *Royal Bank of Canada* v. *Stangl*, n.425 above.

[535] See also *Wells* v. *First National Commercial Bank*, n.426 above, for the refusal to impose a duty of care upon the payer's bank towards the payee. See further Sect. 5(iv) above.

[536] Under Illinois law, a payer is not entitled to bring a conversion claim against the payee's bank as the property in question is intangible (see *Securities Fund Services Inc.* v. *American National Bank and Trust Co. of Chicago*, n.464 above, affd. 718 F.2d 1104 (7th Cir., 1983); *Bachmeier* v. *Bank of Ravenswood*, 663 F.Supp. 1207, 1225 (ND. Ill, 1987)), although New York law appears to allow such a claim 'where there is a specific, identifiable fund' (see *Manufacturers Hanover Trust Co.* v. *Chemical Bank*, 559 NYS 2d 704, 712 (NY Sup. Ct. App. Div., 1990)). The English courts have adopted the same stance as the courts of Illinois: *OBG Ltd* v. *Allan* [2008] AC 1, [100], [106], [210], [224], [271], [308], [321] (HL).

Abou-Rahmah v. *Abacha*[537] also sought to recover the funds transfer from the payee's bank on the ground that it had dishonestly assisted in a breach of trust,[538] that the funds were held on a *Quistclose* trust by the payee's bank for the claimants,[539] and that the payee's bank was liable for money had and received due to the mistaken nature of the funds transfer.[540] Although Treacy J rejected the first two claims, his Lordship held that, as the claimants had made the payment under an operative mistake, they had a *prima facie* entitlement to recover the sums credited by the payee's bank to the wrong account.[541] This conclusion is consistent with the recognition in *Agip (Africa) Ltd* v. *Jackson*[542] and *Lipkin Gorman* v. *Karpnale Ltd*[543] that the payer (as well as his bank) may bring an action to recover a mistaken payment.[544] In cases involving a mistaken payment, however, the payee's bank may be able to establish a defence based on a change in its position resulting from the withdrawal of the funds by the payee.[545] In *Abou-Rahmah* v. *Abacha*,[546] Treacy J confirmed that the change of position defence would similarly apply when the funds transfer was credited to the wrong account and the holder of that account withdrew the funds in question, provided the payee's bank changed its position *in good faith*—a concept that is 'capable of embracing a failure to act in a commercially acceptable way and sharp practice that falls short of outright dishonesty as well as dishonesty itself'.[547] Whilst his Lordship made clear that bad faith for these purposes required something more than mere negligence,[548] the level of culpability that is required to preclude the payee's bank from relying on the defence (such as where it is grossly negligent in failing to make proper enquiries before crediting the wrong account with the funds transfer in question) depends upon the circumstances of the individual case.[549] Where the payee's bank is shown to have acted in bad faith it will also be precluded from relying upon the 'payment over' defence that would otherwise be available to a bank collecting funds on behalf of its customer.[550]

The scope of the possible restitutionary claim against the payee's bank and the defences that that bank may raise in order to mitigate its exposure have also been considered in *Manufacturers Hanover Trust Co.* v. *Chemical Bank*.[551] A Saudi bank instructed its correspondent, MHT, to remit a specified amount of money to the C Bank for the credit of the nine-digit account held with C Bank in the name of the investment bank, Merrill Lynch, which in turn held an eight-digit account in the name of the ultimate beneficiary, AH. In its CHIPS message to the C Bank,[552] MHT by mistake provided only the name of AH as payee and AH's eight-digit account number, but failed to mention Merrill Lynch as recipient of the funds or its nine-digit account number. As a result of this error, the C Bank credited the sum in question to AH's nine-digit account held with itself, which

---

[537] N.422 above, affd. [2007] 1 Lloyd's Rep 115.

[538] Ibid., [34]–[52]. For a detailed discussion of dishonest assistance, see Ch. 7, Sect. 5(iii) above.

[539] Ibid., [78]–[80]. See *Barclays Bank Ltd* v. *Quistclose Investments Ltd* [1970] AC 567 (HL); *Twinsectra Ltd* v. *Yardley* [2002] 2 AC 164 (HL). See further Ch. 7, Sect. 4(iii) above. [540] Ibid., [81]–[82].

[541] Ibid., [83]. For recovery of mistaken payments, see further Ch. 12, Sect. 3. above.

[542] [1991] Ch 547, 561 (CA), aff'g [1990] Ch 265, 283. [543] [1991] 2 AC 548 (HL).

[544] See further Ch. 12, Sect. 1 above.

[545] For detailed discussion of the change of position defence, see further Ch. 12, Sect. 3(iii)(a) above.

[546] N.422 above, [84]–[92] affd. on a different point: [2007] 1 Lloyd's Rep 115. Consider also *Jones* v. *Churcher* [2009] EWHC 722 (QB).

[547] Ibid., [87], applying *Niru Battery Manufacturing Co.* v. *Milestone Trading Ltd* [2004] QB 985, [164] (CA).

[548] Ibid., [88]. [549] Ibid., [87].

[550] For detailed discussion of the 'payment over' defence, see further Ch. 12, Sect. 4 above.

[551] N.536 above. For the liability of the payee's bank under the Uniform Commercial Code for the improper execution or failure to execute a funds transfer, see UCC, s.4A-305.

[552] CHIPS is an acronym for 'Clearing House Interbank Payments System', an electronic clearing system in the United States that is similar to CHAPS, discussed in Sect. 3(iv)(a) above.

was overdrawn at the relevant time. Later on the same day, when MHT realized that a line had been omitted from its original CHIPS message, it dispatched forthwith a second transfer order including all the relevant details, with the result that a similar amount was credited to Merrill Lynch's nine-digit account with the C Bank in favour of AH's eight-digit Merrill Lynch account. Subsequently, AH was adjudicated a bankrupt. The trial judge ordered the C Bank to refund the amount credited to AH's account with itself. The Appellate Division of the Supreme Court of New York affirmed the trial judge and, during the course of his judgment, Sullivan J highlighted three particular aspects of the restitutionary claim against the C Bank. First, Sullivan J held that MHT's negligence in the formulation of its original remittance instruction did not defeat its action for restitution of the funds transfer.[553] The same approach to this issue would likely be adopted by an English court.[554] Secondly, as MHT's original message contained clear indications that the instruction was incomplete or garbled, his Honour concluded that the funds transfer was largely due to C's failure to ask for better particulars of the intended payee before crediting the funds to AH's account with itself.[555] This was particularly so given that MHT's message did not include any reference to the account that the C Bank in fact credited. In contrast, any negligence on the part of the payee's bank is unlikely to carry much weight with the English courts given their rejection of notions of relative fault in the context of recovering mistaken payments.[556] Thirdly, Sullivan J held that, on the facts, the C Bank had failed to establish that it had changed its position to its detriment in reliance on the payment involved. Although Sullivan J did not consider the issue of whether the C Bank's own carelessness in acting on the patently incomplete or garbled original message prevented it from asserting a change in its position (as considered above, a view rejected by Treacy J in *Abou-Rahmah*), his Honour considered that the C Bank had not proved that AH had been allowed to continue to operate his overdraft facility in reliance on the amount credited to his account with the C Bank.[557] In the absence of any causal link between the mistaken payment and the alleged change of position, the English courts would reach the same result, even though they have expressly adopted a liberal and non-technical approach to the issue of causation.[558] In rejecting the argu-

---

[553] *Manufacturers Hanover Trust Co.* v. *Chemical Bank*, n.536 above, 708. See also *Bank of America National Trust and Savings Association* v. *Santi*, 14 Cal. Rptr. 2d 615 (Cal. App. 1992); *First Wall St. Settlement Corp.* v. *Hart*, 187 AD 2d 352, 353 (NY Sup. Ct. App. Div., 1992); *AI Trade Finance* v. *Petra Bank*, 89 Civ. 7987 (JFK) (SDNY, 1997); *Bank of New York* v. *Spiro*, 267 AD 2d 339, 340 (NY Sup. Ct. App. Div., 1999); *Allstate Insurance Co.* v. *Halima*, 2009 US Dist Lexis 22443 (EDNY).

[554] See, for example, *Kelly* v. *Solari* (1841) 9 M&W 54, 59; *Banque Financière de la Cité* v. *Parc (Battersea) Ltd* [1999] AC 221, 227, 235, 242–243 (HL); *Kleinwort Benson Ltd* v. *Lincoln City Council* [1999] 2 AC 349 (HL); *Scottish Equitable plc* v. *Derby* [2000] 3 All ER 793, 800, affd. [2001] EWCA 369, [25]; *Dextra Bank & Trust Co. Ltd* v. *Bank of Jamaica* [2002] 1 All ER (Comm.) 193, [45] (PC); *National Bank of Egypt International Ltd* v. *Oman Housing Bank SAOC* [2003] 1 All ER (Comm.) 246, [26]; *Abou-Rahmah* v. *Abacha* [2007] 1 Lloyd's Rep. 115, [47] (CA); *Test Claimants in the FII Group Litigation* v. *Revenue and Customs Commissioners* [2009] STC 254, [328]. See further Ch. 12, Sect. 5(ii) above.

[555] *Manufacturers Hanover Trust Co.* v. *Chemical Bank*, n.536 above, 708–709. See also *Security Pacific International Bank* v. *National Bank of Western Pennsylvania*, 772 F Supp. 874 (1991).

[556] *Dextra Bank & Trust Co. Ltd* v. *Bank of Jamaica*, n.554 above, [45]; *National Bank of Egypt International Ltd* v. *Oman Housing Bank SAOC*, n.554 above, [26]; *Re Tain Construction Ltd* [2003] BCLC 374, [44], [47], [60]; *Abou-Rahmah* v. *Abacha*, n.554 above, [47], [79]; *Test Claimants in the FII Group Litigation* v. *Revenue and Customs Commissioners*, n.554 above, [328]; but contrast *Thomas* v. *Houston Corbett & Co.* [1969] NZLR 151 (NZCA); *National Bank of New Zealand Ltd* v. *Waitaki International Processing (NI) Ltd* [1999] 2 NZLR 211 (NZCA).

[557] *Manufacturers Hanover Trust Co.* v. *Chemical Bank*, n.536 above, 709–711.

[558] *Philip Collins Ltd* v. *Davis* [2000] 3 All ER 808, 827; *Commerzbank AG* v. *Jones* [2003] EWCA Civ 1663, [43]. See further Ch. 12, Sect. 3(iii)(a) above.

ments of the C Bank, it is clear that the Appellate Division was out of sympathy with that bank's desire to derive a benefit from MHT's patent error. The C Bank's unmeritorious arguments in an attempt to retain a windfall were readily thwarted.

6　Time of payment and countermand

(i)　Complexity of the problem

The analysis of the legal relationships between the parties to a money transfer does not furnish a decisive answer to the question as to when the payment order is executed. An attractive argument is that the payment order is executed when the payment is complete in the sense that there is no longer room for a countermand. Unfortunately, this answer leads to circularity, as, on the same basis, payment is complete and a countermand precluded when the order is executed upon the receipt of the funds by the payee or the payee's bank, acting as his agent. Accordingly, the object is to find a test for determining the moment at which the funds are so received. The difficulty is that, as shown in the previous section, the position of the payee's bank varies from transaction to transaction. This uncertainty means that it is impossible to give a general answer to the question of when a money transfer is complete and accordingly when payment occurs. In each situation, a number of factors have to be taken into account. First and foremost, it is essential to have regard to the nature of the money transfer operation involved. Thus, the moment at which a SWIFT transfer is complete may differ from the moment at which a telegraphic transfer is deemed to have been executed. Similarly, a transfer executed through BACS becomes irreversible at a time different from that at which a bank giro credit is completed. In some of these cases, the master agreement between the banks determines the time at which an instruction to transfer becomes irrevocable.[559] This moment could, therefore, be regarded as the time at which the money transfer is complete and accordingly the time of payment. In others cases, where the payment system in question does not expressly deal with this issue, the analysis has to proceed on the basis of common law principles.

Secondly, the time of payment may depend on the number of parties involved in the transaction and on the role assumed by each of them. At one end of the scale, there is the in-house transfer, in which the payer and the payee maintain their accounts with the same branch of a given bank.[560] At the other end of the scale, there is the international transfer, which can involve up to five parties—the payer, the payer's bank, the correspondent or intermediary bank, the payee's bank, and the payee. To these parties may be added the transmission network run by a third party, such as SWIFT.[561] It is conceivable that,

---

[559] The importance of the role played by the particular rules of the payment transfer system has recently been reinforced by Directive 98/26/EC on Settlement Finality in Payment and Securities Settlement Systems [1998] OJ L166/45 (as amended by Directive 2009/44/EC and Directive 2010/78/EU). Art. 5 of the Directive provides that a transfer order may not be revoked by a participant in a system covered by the Directive, or by a third party, from the moment defined by the rules of that system. Directive 98/26/EC has been implemented in the United Kingdom through the Financial Markets and Insolvency (Settlement Finality) Regulations 1999, S.I. 1999/2979 (as amended by the Financial Markets and Insolvency (Settlement Finality) (Amendment) Regulations 2006, S.I. 2006/50, the Financial Markets and Insolvency (Settlement Finality) (Amendment) Regulations 2007, S.I. 2007/832, and the Financial Markets and Insolvency (Settlement Finality) (Amendment) Regulations 2009, S.I. 2009/1972).

[560] If the transfer involves two branches of the same bank, it usually involves transmission through that bank's computer centre.

[561] See further Sect. 4(iv) above.

although a specific instruction may be 'executed' as between two parties in the chain, it remains executory as regards some other party.[562] An example is furnished by a telex dispatched by the payer's bank to its correspondent with a request that the funds be credited to the payee's account with his bank. As between the payer's bank and the correspondent or intermediary bank, the transaction may arguably be complete and executed when the correspondent dispatches its own message to the payee's bank. The payee, however, may not be regarded as having been 'paid' until the amount is credited to his account by the payee's bank.[563]

Thirdly, it is important to note that the answer to a problem of the type under discussion is influenced by the practical context in which it arises.[564] Thus, in cases in which the payer's bank wishes to stop payment, or to reverse a credit entry, the payee is likely to maintain that payment has been completed before the attempted countermand is made.[565] In such a case, if any question were to arise as to the authority of the payee's bank to receive payment on behalf of the payee, the latter would proffer arguments supporting the validity of his bank's mandate to do so, including the plea that he had given his consent in advance to the bank's receipt of the amount involved. In contrast, the payee would be likely to take a different stand where a contract entitled him to invoke an attractive forfeiture clause if payment were made out of time. In such a case, the payee has an interest in disputing the authority of his bank to obtain or receive payment on his behalf, and in raising arguments to the effect that the payment was late. The payee may even attempt to establish that, although payment was complete as between the payer's bank and his own bank, it was nevertheless revocable or reversible as between himself and the payer.

The courts are unlikely to succeed in developing a uniform rule for determining the time at which a money transfer is complete. In every case coming up for decision, there are potentially six points in time at which a particular payment may be regarded as executed.[566] The first is the time at which the payer's instruction is transmitted by his bank. The second is the time at which the instruction reaches the payee's bank or its agent. The third is the time at which the payee's bank sets into motion the internal machinery for crediting the payee's account. The fourth is the time at which the payee's account is credited with the amount involved. The fifth is the time at which the payee is notified of the receipt of the funds. The sixth is the time at which the payee agrees to receive the amount involved, either expressly or by implication.

The case law in point, comprising mainly United States and English authorities involving international transfers, is not easy to reconcile. This is not surprising, as the cases arose in respect of different methods of transfer and in different practical situations. It will be convenient to divide the cases into two groups: those dealing with attempts to countermand money transfer orders or to reverse payment, and those concerning the completion of payment before a specified deadline.[567] As discussed previously, the PSR 2009 may have an impact on both of these issues, since they provide guidance not only as to the point in time up to which a payer can countermand a funds transfer, but also as to

---

[562] See, for example, Sects. 3(iii)–(iv) above. See also *Libyan Arab Foreign Bank* v. *Bankers Trust Co.*, n.26 above, 750.

[563] For elaboration, see Sect. 6(iii) below.

[564] See, for example, *Raffles Money Change Ltd* v. *Skandinaviska Enskilda Banken AB*, n.97 above, [29]–[30].

[565] Consider, for example, cases in which the payer dies or becomes bankrupt after the issuing of the payment order, whereupon the mandate to pay is determined: *Pool* v. *Pool* (1889) 58 LJ P 67 (death); *Drew* v. *Nunn* (1879) 4 QBD 661, 665–666 (bankruptcy); *Governor and Company of the Bank of Ireland* v. *Hussey* [1965] IR 46 (mental illness). See also *Salton* v. *New Beeston Cycle Co.* [1900] 1 Ch. 43 (knowledge of revocation).

[566] For a suggestion as to six similar points in time, see D.I. Baker, n.248 above, [29.03(3)], [29.21]–[29.27].

[567] For discussion of the proprietary aspects of a funds transfer, see D. Fox, n.24 above, [5.50]–[5.73].

the point in time at which a payee will be considered to have received the relevant funds. The PSR 2009 have already been considered in detail above. As those Regulations may not always be applicable, however, the following analysis will focus on the common law principles applicable to the two issues just identified and will consider each in turn.

(ii) Cases involving countermand of payment and reversals of credit entries

Attempts to countermand money transfers, or to question their execution, arise in different circumstances. The earliest English decision in point is *Rekstin v. Severo Sibirsko Gosudarstvennoe Akcionernoe Obschestvo Komseverputj*.[568] A customer instructed his bank to transfer the total credit balance of his account to an account maintained with the same branch by another customer. After the bank had effected the transfer by making the required ledger entries, but before notification was given to the payee, a judgment creditor served a garnishee order nisi (now known as an interim third party debt order) attaching the payer's account balance.[569] It was held by both Acton and Talbot JJ in the Divisional Court and Lord Hanworth MR, Slesser, and Romer LJJ in the Court of Appeal that, at the time the order nisi was served, the amount transferred was still accruing to the payer. In reaching this decision, however, Talbot J,[570] at first instance, and Lord Hanworth MR,[571] in the Court of Appeal, emphasized that the payer did not owe any debt to the payee, and that there was nothing to indicate that the payee had anticipated payment. As there was no evidence to establish the payee's assent to the transfer of the amount involved, the bank could not be regarded as having the authority to hold the amount involved as a debt accrued to the payee. It is submitted that this decision, which favours the view that payment is incomplete until the payee manifests his consent to the transfer of the funds, has a narrow scope of application.[572] In most modern money transfers, where an amount is transmitted to the payee's account at his own request, the payee's bank is given implied authority to credit the payee's account.

That the payee's readiness to accept payment can be inferred from the circumstances preceding the execution of the money transfer can be demonstrated by two United States authorities concerning remittances of funds from Japan made on the eve of the attack on Pearl Harbor. In *Singer v. Yokohama Specie Bank Ltd*,[573] the claimant, who was owed an amount of approximately US\$557,561 by the Tokyo office of the YS Bank, instructed that that amount be remitted to him in the United States. The Tokyo office thereupon ordered its agency in New York to make such an amount available to the claimant. The agency notified the claimant and requested him to obtain the Treasury licence required to authorize the payment over of the funds. Before this was granted, however, the agency was put into liquidation by the Alien Property Custodian. The Supreme Court of New York held that the amount involved had not accrued to the claimant at the time the agency was taken over—the payee's bank would be liable to the payee only 'upon its making an

---

[568] [1933] 1 KB 47 (CA). See also *TSB Bank of Scotland plc* v. *Welwyn Hatfield District Council*, n.511 above, where Hobhouse J described *Rekstin* as 'concerned with what acts by a banker are required to complete a payment so that it ceases to be revocable by the [payer]'.

[569] Ch. 11, Sect. 1(iii) above.

[570] *Rekstin* v. *Severo Sibirsko Gosudarstvennoe Akcionernoe Obschestvo Komseverputj*, n.568 above, 57.

[571] Ibid., 62–63.

[572] *Momm* v. *Barclays Bank International Ltd* [1977] QB 790, where Kerr J suggested that *Rekstin* 'should be treated as confined to its special facts'.

[573] 47 NYS 2d 881 (NY Sup. Ct., 1944), affd. 48 NYS 2d 799 (NY Sup. Ct. App. Div., 1944), but revd. 58 NE 2d 726 (NY CA, 1946), cert. denied *Lyon* v. *Singer*, 339 US 841 (1950). For further proceedings in the case, see *Singer* v. *Tokohama Specie Bank Ltd*, 85 NE 2d 894 (NY CA, 1949).

enforcible [*sic*] promise to pay the sum' involved.[574] A mere representation that funds were held at the payee's disposal was inconclusive, even if it was complemented by permission to draw against the funds. The Appellate Division affirmed this judgment, but it was over-ruled, on the point in question, by the New York Court of Appeals. It was held that the notification of the transfer to the claimant 'served to create an enforceable legal obligation by the New York Agency to make such payment'.[575] This decision was followed by the New York Supreme Court in *Guaranty Trust Co. of New York* v. *Lyon*,[576] in which the facts were similar, except that the funds were remitted to the payee at the order of a third party. It was held that the New York agency of a Japanese bank—acting as the recipient of funds transferred from Tokyo—obtained the amount involved on behalf of the payee. When the payee was informed of the amount standing to his credit, the funds were available to him and payment was regarded as irreversible.

These two decisions of the New York courts suggest that the transfer of the amount involved to the payee's bank, acting as the payee's agent, is tantamount to the receipt of the funds by the payee himself.[577] The basic principles of the law of agency sup-port this conclusion, provided the agent has acted within the scope of his authority in accepting the payment. It can thus be argued that payment becomes complete and irrevocable at the moment it reaches the hand of the payee's bank, acting as agent. Unfortunately, it is not always clear at which point in time the payee's bank makes its decision to accept the amount involved on the payee's behalf. The importance of determining the moment at which payment has accrued to the payee is demonstrated by the leading English decision in point, *Momm* v. *Barclays Bank International Ltd*.[578] On 26 June 1974, the defendant bank received a telex instruction from one of its cus-tomers, the Herstatt Bank of Frankfurt, to credit the account of the claimant, another customer of the same branch, with an amount of £120,000. The transfer was part of a currency exchange transaction between Herstatt Bank and the claimant. Despite Herstatt Bank's account not having an adequate credit balance, the assistant man-ager of the defendant bank decided nevertheless to credit the claimant's account. The necessary forms were accordingly prepared and processed by the defendant bank's computer operators. Later in the day, Herstatt Bank suspended payment. On the next day, the defendant bank reversed the credit entry that had appeared in the claimant's account. The claimant, who was notified neither of the credit entry nor of its reversal, discovered the facts through a perusal of the defendant bank's books. He thereupon brought an action for a declaration that his account had been wrongfully debited on 27 June. Giving judgment for the claimant, Kerr J observed:[579]

> The issue is whether or not a completed payment had been made by the defendants to the [claimants] on June 26. This is a question of law. If the answer is 'Yes,' it is not contested that the [claimants] have a good cause of action. If there were no authorities on this point, I think that the reaction, both of a lawyer and a banker, would be to answer this question in the affirmative. I think that both would say two things. First, that in such circumstances

---

[574] Ibid., 882.   [575] *Singer* v. *Yokohama Specie Bank Ltd*, n.573 above 728.

[576] 124 NYS 2d 680 (NY Sup. Ct., 1953).

[577] See also *Manufacturas International Ltd* v. *Manufacturers Hanover Trust Co.*, 79 F Supp. 180 (EDNY, 1992): 'The funds transfer is considered completed at the moment the receiving bank receives the credit message not when the [payee] acquires the funds.' See further *In re Pioneer Commercial Funding Corporation*, 140 BR 951, 958 (SDNY, 1992).

[578] N.572 above, *sub nom. Delbrueck* v. *Barclays Bank International Ltd* [1976] 2 Lloyd's Rep. 341.

[579] Ibid., 799–800. See also *Customs & Excise Commissioners* v. *FDR Ltd*, n.24 above, [36]; *Scottish Exhibition Centre Ltd* v. *Commissioners for Her Majesty's Revenue and Customs*, n.24 above, [19].

a payment has been made if the payee's account is credited with the payment at the close of business on the value date, at any rate if it was credited intentionally and in good faith and not by error or fraud. Secondly, I think that they would say that if a payment requires to be made on a certain day by debiting a [payer] customer's account and crediting a payee customer's account, then the position at the end of that day in fact and in law must be that this has either happened or not happened, but that the position cannot be left in the air. In my view both these propositions are correct in law.

His Lordship distinguished *Rekstin* v. *Severo Sibirsko Gosudarstvennoe Akcionernoe Obschestvo Komseverputj*[580] as having been decided on its special facts. Kerr J stressed that what was important in *Rekstin* was the fact that the payee knew nothing of the proposed transfer, that there was no underlying transaction between the payer and the payee, and that the payee had accordingly never assented to its account being credited with the funds that were purportedly transferred to it. By contrast, in *Momm*, the claimant had specifically designated that payment of sums due under the currency exchange contract should be made into his account held at the defendant bank.[581] Accordingly, in *Momm*, the bank clearly had the claimant's authority to accept the transfer on his behalf.[582] Kerr J emphasized that the question of whether payment had been completed on a particular date should be assessed at the end of the 'value date', which is the date on which funds are to be made available to the payee.[583] Although the end of the 'value date' was chosen to reflect the fact that banking practice relating to in-house transfers allowed the bank to reverse erroneous entries during the course of the banking day, in *Tayeb* v. *HSBC Bank plc*,[584] Colman J recently stressed that *Momm* is not to be taken as authority for the general proposition that 'once an account has been credited on the value date with an incoming transfer, the entry can be reversed at any time up to the end of business on that day'.[585]

Herstatt Bank's collapse also led to litigation concerning money transfers in the United States. In *Delbrueck & Co.* v. *Manufacturers Hanover Trust Co.*,[586] the claimant, a German bank that maintained an account with the defendant bank in the United States, entered into exchange contracts with Herstatt. An amount of US$12.5 million was payable by the claimant to Herstatt Bank under these contracts on 26 June. On 25 June, the claimant sent a telex message to the defendant bank requesting it to credit Herstatt Bank's account with the Chase Manhattan Bank with the amount involved. At 10.30 a.m. on 26 June (at Eastern Standard Time prevailing in New York), Herstatt Bank was closed down by the German Reserve Bank. At approximately 11.40 a.m., the defendant bank transferred to Chase Manhattan Bank the amount of $12.5 million, by using the

---

[580] N.568 above.

[581] See also *Customs & Excise Commissioners* v. *National Westminster Bank plc*, n.511 above, [13].

[582] See also *Dovey* v. *Bank of New Zealand*, n.24 above, 650 (by nominating the bank to which funds were to be transferred, the claimant gave that bank authority to accept funds on his behalf, even though the bank had yet to open an account for him).

[583] See also *Tayeb* v. *HSBC Bank plc*, n.85 above [91], where Colman J emphasized that *Momm* is 'authority for the proposition that the question whether the payment had been made on the value date was to be tested by reference to an account entry at the close of business on that date'. Cf. *Libyan Arab Foreign Bank* v. *Bankers Trust Co.* [1988] 1 Lloyd's Rep. 259, 273–274, where Staughton J (obiter) inclined to the view that payment in an in-house transfer was complete when the bank set the transferring procedure into motion. See also B. Geva, 'Payment into a Bank Account' [1990] *JIBL* 108, 112–115, who submits that, at least in those cases where funds are available to the payee's bank, a 'hypothetical positive response test' works better. This test is objective: if the payee had contacted his bank, at what point would he have been informed that the bank had made an unconditional decision to credit his account? Geva himself prefers a 'receiver finality' test (at 115–117), but this does not represent English law (see R. Cranston, 'Law of International Funds Transfers in England' in W. Hadding & U. H. Schneider (eds.), n.218 above, 228–231).

[584] N.85 above.   [585] Ibid., [91].   [586] N.27 above, affirming 464 F Supp. 989 (SDNY, 1979).

United States CHIPS system. Within the following 30 minutes, the claimant called the defendant bank in order to stop this payment, and immediately thereafter confirmed the countermand by telex. At 9.00 p.m. on the same day, Herstatt Bank's account with Chase Manhattan Bank was formally credited with the amount involved. The claimant based its action on negligence. It claimed that the defendant bank committed a breach of its duty of care when it failed to act on the countermand order, given to it at 11.40 a.m., in the course of the remaining business hours of 26 June. The District Court dismissed this action and its decision was upheld by the Court of Appeals for the Second Circuit. Moore J reviewed the technology involved in CHIPS transfers, pointing out that a transfer executed through this autonomous network invariably reached the payee's bank almost as soon as it was released or executed by the computer terminal of the payer's bank.[587] It was the understanding of all the banks participating in the system that funds transferred by means of CHIPS could be drawn upon by the payee as soon as the electronic message was received by the payee's bank. Accordingly, his Honour concluded that the transfer of funds to the credit of Herstatt Bank's account was complete as from the time it was effected by the defendant bank. The fact that the credit was not entered in Herstatt Bank's account until 9.00 p.m. on 26 June was merely a matter of bookkeeping and hence irrelevant. Moore J observed:[588]

> Based on the nature of the CHIPS system, and the fact that the member banks viewed the transactions as irrevocable…we hold that the CHIPS transfers were irrevocable when made.

For this reason, the defendant bank had not acted negligently when it failed to revoke the transfer of the funds to Chase Manhattan Bank. Moore J, therefore, held that a money transfer executed by means of CHIPS could not be revoked or stopped once it was set into transmission by an electronic message executed on the 'value date'. His Honour further concluded that Herstatt Bank's bankruptcy did not revoke Chase Manhattan Bank's mandate to receive funds on its behalf.[589]

At first glance, there appears to be an inconsistency between the English decision in *Momm* and its United States counterpart in *Delbrueck*. In the former case, Kerr J held that payment became irrevocable at the close of the 'value date'. In the latter case, Moore J thought that payment was complete, and hence irreversible, when executed by means of a CHIPS transfer. The distinction between the two conclusions, however, is explainable by the difference in the respective methods of transfer employed in the two cases and by the banking practices related thereto. In *Momm*, Kerr J based his decision on the finding that banking practice relating to in-house transfers made provision for a reversal of entries on the day of execution.[590] Moore J gave effect to the practice

---

[587] Assuming that the payer's bank and the payee's bank are the 'sending bank' and 'receiving bank' for the purposes of the transfer without the intervention of any correspondent or intermediary bank.

[588] *Delbrueck & Co.* v. *Manufacturers Hanover Trust Co.*, n.27 above, 1051. See also *Evra Corporation* v. *Swiss Bank Corporation*, 522 F.Supp 820, 827–828 (ND Ill., 1981); *Banque Worms* v. *Bank America International*, 726 F Supp. 940, 942 (SDNY, 1989), affd. 928 F. 2d 538 (2nd Cir., 1991); *Banque Worms* v. *Bank America International*, 77 NY 2d 362, 372 (NY CA, 1991). For a full description of CHIPS, see *Delbrueck & Co.* v. *Manufacturers Hanover Trust Co.*, 464 F Supp. 989, 992 (SDNY, 1979).

[589] Moore J also found support for his decision by invoking the law of assignment of debt: see further Sect. 5(iii) above.

[590] This part of Kerr J's reasoning was highlighted by Lord Penrose in *Sutherland* v. *Royal Bank of Scotland plc* [1997] Bank. LR 132, 144 (OH). Lord Penrose also noted that the bank's ability to reverse debit and credit entries before close of business on the same day had been a characteristic of manual book-keeping practices that pre-dated those 'cumbersome' computerized procedures applicable at the time of *Momm*, and further

developed in respect of CHIPS transfers, which precluded revocation once the transfer was 'released' by the computer terminal of the payer's bank.[591] It is arguable that as regards the question of countermand, therefore, both cases support the view that the position is governed by banking practice rather than by an abstract application of legal principles.[592] The suggestion that the method of transfer and the technology used from transaction to transaction will affect the question of when the payment becomes irrevocable has now received further support from *Tayeb* v. *HSBC Bank plc*,[593] where Colman J concluded that *Momm* 'has no application to payments by CHAPS transfer to a customer's account'[594] since CHAPS Sterling transfers involve not only the provision of same-day value, but also the real-time transfer of funds.[595] This is consistent with the approach to CHIPS transfers in *Delbrueck*.

The importance of banking practice in respect of money transfers is further illustrated by Webster J's decision in *Royal Products Ltd* v. *Midland Bank Ltd*.[596] The claimants, Maltese merchants, maintained their account in the United Kingdom with the defendant bank. In Malta, they had two current accounts, one with the B Bank and the other with the N Bank. The claimants, who wished to transfer £13,000 from their account with the defendant bank in the United Kingdom to the credit of their account with the N Bank in Malta, were deterred from ordering a direct transfer by the N Bank's high banking charges. The claimants, therefore, ordered the defendant bank to remit the amount involved to the credit of their account with the B Bank in Malta, intending to complete the cycle by eventually remitting the amount involved from the B Bank to the N Bank. The claimants issued their instruction to the defendant bank on 23 November 1972. On the same day, the defendant bank sent a telex message instructing its correspondent in Malta, which by sheer coincidence happened to be the N Bank, to credit the amount in question to the claimants' account with the B Bank. The N Bank received the telex on 24 November 1972. Usually, the N Bank would have completed the transfer by delivering a banker's payment to the B Bank, but as there were rumours on the morning of the day in question that the B Bank was facing liquidity problems, the N Bank departed from this procedure and credited the amount involved to a suspense account opened by it in the B Bank's name. The N Bank, which recognized that the claimants were its own customers and was aware that the ultimate destination of the funds was the claimants' account with the N Bank itself, contacted the claimants and suggested that the funds be diverted directly to the credit of this account. As the N Bank did not disclose its reasons for making this suggestion, however, the claimants mistook that bank's motives, and insisted that the amount be transferred as instructed. On the evening of 24 November 1972, it was thought that the B Bank had overcome its financial crisis. On the same evening, or possibly on the morning of 25 November 1972, the N Bank notified the B Bank, by means of a credit note,

---

noted that, with the introduction of online and networked computer systems, 'the branch may well be able to review within a business day the whole transactions of a given client and adjust its position, precisely as it might have done under the manual accounting system'. In the absence of a banking practice permitting the bank to reverse credit entries (such as is the case with in-house transfers), *Momm* is not authority for the general proposition that 'once an account has been credited on the value date with an incoming transfer, the entry can be reversed at any time up to the end of business on that day': *Tayeb* v. *HSBC Bank plc*, n.85 above, [91].

[591] See also *Mellon Bank* v. *Securities Settlement Corp.*, n.408 above (discussed in Sect. 5(iv)(b) above), in which it was held that the payer's bank was under a duty to exercise skill in the execution of a stop order. As the system there used, BankWire, did not preclude a countermand, payment was treated as complete when the funds were credited to the payee's account.

[592] *Middle East Banking Co.* v. *State Street Bank International*, n.510 above, 903.

[593] N.85 above.   [594] Ibid., [92].   [595] Sect. 3(iv)(a) above.   [596] N.274 above.

that it had transferred a remittance for the amount involved to the credit of the claimants' account. On the morning of 25 November 1972, the B Bank was forced to suspend operations and, in due course, was put into liquidation. As general creditors, the claimants were unable to recover any part of the amount involved. Initially, they instituted proceedings against the N Bank in Malta, based on breach of contract and negligence. When this action failed, the claimants attempted to recover their loss from the defendant bank in the United Kingdom.

The claimants based their action on two main contentions. The first contention was that their instruction for the transfer of funds to the credit of their account with the B Bank had not been carried out. The defendant bank in the United Kingdom was, therefore, bound to reimburse the amount involved and, if necessary, had to do so by revoking its instruction to the B Bank. In support of this point, the claimants argued that on 28 November 1972—which was well after the dispatch of the N Bank's order to the B Bank—they had instructed the N Bank to divert the funds to the credit of the claimants' account with it. The claimants' second contention was that the N Bank had been negligent in effecting payment to the credit of their account with the B Bank. To start with, the N Bank should have warned the claimants, as its customers, of the rumours concerning the B Bank's shaky financial position. In addition, it was argued that the N Bank's knowledge of the true circumstances surrounding the transaction imposed on it a fiduciary duty. The defendant bank, it was argued, was vicariously liable for these breaches. Webster J gave judgment for the defendant bank. His Lordship held that the defendant bank was entitled to use the services of a correspondent to effect the transfer ordered by the claimants. His Lordship conceded that the defendant bank owed the claimants a duty of care and skill in choosing the correspondent involved,[597] and that the defendant bank was vicariously liable for any negligent acts committed by its correspondent. As sub-agent, the N Bank had no privity of contract, however, in respect of the instant transaction with the claimants, as payers. His Lordship then examined the transfer. Explaining its legal nature and the manner in which it was carried out, his Lordship observed that a payee's bank, such as the B Bank, was:[598]

> ...impliedly authorized by the customer to accept that credit by virtue of the fact that the customer [had] a current account with it, no consent to the receipt of the credit being expected from or required of the same bank, by virtue of the same fact.

Webster J concluded on this basis that there was no need for an express consent by the B Bank to the transfer ordered by the claimants.[599]

Having made these preliminary findings, Webster J turned to the main issues of the case: the time of payment and the bank's duty of care. His Lordship concluded that three events had to take place before payment was complete. First, the B Bank had to be put in a position where it was entitled to draw on the funds made available for transmission to the claimants' account. Secondly, the B Bank had to be informed that the funds were to be made available to the claimants. Thirdly, the transfer was complete even before the claimants, as payees, were notified that the funds had been credited to their account. On the facts before Webster J, the B Bank had obtained definite notice that the funds

---

[597] See further Sect. 5(iv)(b) above.

[598] *Royal Products Ltd* v. *Midland Bank Ltd*, n.274 above, 198. See also *Customs & Excise Commissioners* v. *National Westminster Bank plc*, n.511 above, [14].

[599] See also *Dovey* v. *Bank of New Zealand*, n.24 above, 650 (by nominating the bank to which funds were to be transferred, the claimant gave that bank authority to accept funds on his behalf, even though the bank had yet to open an account for him).

were available to it for drawing when it obtained the payment order on the evening of 24 November 1972 (or early on the morning of 25 November 1972). The transfer was then complete. In determining the time at which the B Bank was deemed to have received the necessary notification, his Lordship relied on the course of dealings used by reputable banks.

On the other issue, Webster J held that the N Bank had not been in breach of a duty of care in carrying out the instruction to transfer the amount in question to the credit of the claimants' account with the B Bank. The N Bank was precluded, by a duty of secrecy owed to the B Bank, from disclosing to the claimants the disturbing information that it had received. Moreover, there was, in his Lordship's opinion, no evidence to show that the transfer should have been delayed or refused. The claimants 'called no evidence to the effect that a reasonably competent bank in the position of [the N Bank], with the information that it had received... would or should, as a result of any such doubts, have refrained from passing the credit to [the B Bank] or, indeed, that it would have been entitled to have done so'.[600] The instruction to transfer had to be completed on the day following its receipt, and the N Bank was entitled to act accordingly. His Lordship further mentioned that, in carrying out the instruction to transfer, the N Bank was acting upon the instruction of the defendant bank. Being thus the agent of the defendant bank for the purposes of this specific transaction, the N Bank was not acting in breach of a duty, arising under its general banker–customer contract with the claimants, by executing the transfer in question. Webster J thus concluded that the claimants' order to reverse the payment was issued after the transfer of the funds had been completed. As the execution of the order in question did not involve any negligence on the part of the N Bank, the question of the defendant bank's vicarious liability did not, therefore, arise. In this regard, it is clear that Webster J reached his conclusion by relying on the banking practice prevailing in respect of the type of money transfers involved.

As the payer and payee in *Royal Products* was one and the same person,[601] it is not surprising that Webster J held that the B Bank had implied authority from its customer (Royal Products) to accept the credit by virtue of the fact that the customer had an account with the bank. It should not be thought, however, that a bank necessarily has its customer's implied authority to accept a transfer of funds from a third party into that customer's account simply by virtue of holding that account. This point arose in *Customs and Excise Commissioners* v. *National Westminster Bank plc*,[602] where the claimants, the Customs and Excise, were under a statutory obligation to repay overpaid value added tax (VAT) to the taxpayer Car Disposals Ltd (CDL). CDL wrote to the Customs and Excise informing them that 'the cheque be paid direct to our solicitors... for them to bank into their client account. The reason [we] make this request is that we are experiencing difficulties with our bank.' Despite this request, the Customs and Excise paid in error a sum representing the amount of overpaid VAT into CDL's account with the defendant bank, National Westminster Bank (NatWest), which duly credited CDL's account with the money and thereby reduced CDL's existing overdraft. On discovering this, CDL complained to the Customs and Excise, which paid CDL a second time by transfer to their solicitors as originally requested. Meanwhile, the Customs and Excise asked NatWest to repay the sum that had been transferred to it by mistake. When NatWest refused to do so, the Customs and Excise commenced proceedings. NatWest's defence was that the payment had been

---

[600] *Royal Products Ltd* v. *Midland Bank Ltd*, n.274 above, 205.

[601] For a similar situation, where the payer and payee were the same person, see *Dovey* v. *Bank of New Zealand*, n.24 above, 650.

[602] N.511 above.

made for good consideration, which was a recognized defence to a claim for recovery of a mistaken payment.[603] In this regard, NatWest claimed that it was authorized to accept payment on behalf of CDL and that the payment accordingly discharged the Customs and Excise's debt to CDL. The Customs and Excise denied that a payment made in a manner that was contrary to CDL's instructions could discharge the debt in question.

Judge Rich QC, sitting as a judge of the High Court, held that the payment had not discharged the Customs and Excise's debt to CDL and that the Customs and Excise were entitled to recover the mistaken payment from NatWest. The judge held that an unsolicited payment to a creditor's bank account did not constitute payment of a debt unless it was accepted as such, and there had been no indication of the payment being accepted by CDL.[604] His Lordship then turned to *Royal Products*, where Webster J had stated that a bank was impliedly authorized by its customer to accept a credit 'by virtue of the fact that the customer had a current account with it'.[605] Judge Rich QC observed that this was said in the context of an instruction to one bank, of which the claimant was a customer, to transfer funds to another bank, of which he was also a customer.[606] The same did not apply when the credit came from a third party as payment to the bank's customer. His Lordship concluded that there was no general rule to the effect that NatWest was, merely by virtue of holding a current account for CDL, authorized to receive payment from the Customs and Excise on CDL's behalf so as to discharge their debt to CDL.[607] This conclusion has recently been confirmed in *PT Berlian Laju Tanker TBK* v. *Nuse Shipping Ltd*,[608] where Clarke J stated: 'Payment under a contract cannot be made without the consent of the creditor. Even if payment is to be in cash, i.e. legal tender, the creditor may not necessarily accept it. If payment is made through the banking system, a bank may have authority to receive payment; but it will not be able to accept payment in discharge of the debt without the authority of the creditor'.[609]

The conclusion to be drawn from *Momm*, *Delbrueck* and *Royal Products* is that a money transfer is complete when the funds are made available to the payee's bank and accepted by it, intentionally, on behalf of the payee. This view derives further support from an observation made by Hirst J in *Libyan Arab Foreign Bank* v. *Manufacturers Hanover Trust Co. (No. 2)*[610] in respect of a money transfer effected between accounts maintained by two separate branches of the same bank. His Lordship concluded that the transfer was complete when the transferring branch debited the recipient branch's account with it and the receiving branch effected a matching 'intentional and *bona fide*' credit entry in the payee's account.[611] Effectively, this meant that the funds transfer was complete, and hence irreversible, when the funds were made available to the payee. Notably, this decision, just like the earlier decisions in point, took into account the respective banking practice. As the question of countermand is primarily one that arises either between the payer and his bank or between the payee and his bank, the

---

[603] For detailed consideration of this defence, see Ch. 12, Sect. 3(iii)(b) above.

[604] *Customs & Excise Commissioners* v. *National Westminster Bank plc*, n.511 above, [10], applying *TSB Bank of Scotland plc* v. *Welwyn Hatfield District Council*, n.511 above, which is discussed in Sect. 6(iii) below.

[605] *Royal Products Ltd* v. *Midland Bank Ltd*, n.274 above, 198.

[606] *Customs & Excise Commissioners* v. *National Westminster Bank plc*, n.511 above, [14].

[607] Ibid., [15].   [608] N.511 above.

[609] Ibid., [67]. See also *University of the Arts London* v. *Rule* UKEAT/0245/10/CEA (5 November 2010), [27]–[28].

[610] [1989] 1 Lloyd's Rep. 608, 631–632.

[611] Ibid., 631. See also *Sutherland* v. *Royal Bank of Scotland plc*, n.590 above.

emphasis on banking practice is understandable.[612] In this regard, the decision of the Court of Appeals for the Second Circuit in *Delbrueck* remains one of the most important authorities in point.

(iii) Cases involving payments out of time

Cases involving payments out of time arise under different types of contract. A good example is an agreement under which a forfeiture clause can be invoked if payment is not rendered by a given date. Generally speaking, such clauses are included in contracts in which time is made of the essence.[613] To date, most of the relevant United Kingdom cases have concerned withdrawals by shipowners of vessels on the ground that a rental due from a charterer was paid out of time. In cases of this type, the question relates, in essence, to the contract between the payer and payee. As pointed out previously,[614] different considerations may be applicable in determining what constitutes due or timely payment in this type of case from the relevant considerations in respect of disputes concerning the banker-customer contract. The basic rule was formulated in *The Brimnes*,[615] where the Court of Appeal held that, in order to determine whether an amount due under a charterparty was paid on time, an analogy had to be drawn with cases concerning the question of when payment was complete if made in cash. Edmund-Davies LJ concluded:[616]

> The owners' contention, however, that the tendering of the commercial equivalent of cash would suffice found favour with Brandon J [the trial judge]. In particular, he concluded that any transfer of funds to [the payee's bank] for the credit of the owners' account so as to give them the unconditional right to the immediate use of the funds transferred was good payment. In my judgment, that was clearly right.[617]

Megaw LJ, who delivered a concurring judgment, said that payment by means of a credit entry was complete when the creditor was bound to treat it as the equivalent of cash, in the sense that he was able to draw on the balance accrued.

Where the underlying contract between the payer and payee contains some express or implied condition that must be satisfied before the payee can use the funds, it is clear that this must be satisfied before the payment can be effective.[618] Beyond this situation, however, it is not always easy to determine the time at which the credit balance, entered in the payee's account, becomes the equivalent of cash. Thus, in *Mardorf Peach & Co. Ltd*

---

[612] See also *Libyan Arab Foreign Bank* v. *Bankers Trust Co.*, n.26 above, where emphasis was placed on clearing practices.

[613] For a recent example where the time of payment was made of the essence in the context of a land purchase transaction, see *Rick Dees Ltd* v. *Larsen*, n.407 above, affd. on this point: [2007] 3 NZLR 577.

[614] See Sect. 6(i) above.

[615] *Tenax Steamship Co. Ltd* v. *Brimnes (Owners of)*, '*The Brimnes*', n.119 above.

[616] Ibid., 948. See also *Libyan Arab Foreign Bank* v. *Bankers Trust Co.*, n.26 above, 749; *PT Berlian Laju Tanker TBK* v. *Nuse Shipping Ltd*, n.511 above, [21].

[617] The word 'unconditional' was later interpreted by Lord Bridge in *The Chikuma* [1981] 1 WLR 314, 319 (HL) to mean 'unfettered and unrestricted', and not merely 'that the transferee's right to use the funds transferred is neither subject to the fulfilment of a condition precedent nor defeasible on failure to fulfil a condition subsequent'.

[618] See, for example, *Rick Dees Ltd* v. *Larsen*, [2007] 3 NZLR 577, [33] (NZSC), where Blanchard J held that the underlying contract required not only the payee to be provided with cleared funds, but also to be notified of that fact.

v. *Attica Sea Carriers Corporation of Liberia ('The Laconia')*,[619] the payee's bank received a telex message requiring it to credit the shipowners' account with an amount due under a charterparty. This telex was received at the payee's bank after the date appointed in the charterparty, but shortly before the bank had been given an instruction by the shipowners to refuse late payment. The bank began taking the steps required for the crediting of the shipowners' account with the amount remitted, but, on receiving the instruction to refuse payment, it refunded the amount to the payer's bank before executing the actual entry. One of the questions in the case was whether the transfer of funds to the payee's bank had had the effect of completing the payment due from the charterer. Giving judgment for the shipowners, the House of Lords held that the transfer had not been completed before the amount was refunded, as the payee's bank had not manifested a conscious decision to accept payment. The steps taken by it for processing the telegraphic transfer were purely provisional and procedural.

The Laconia illustrates that payment as between payer and payee will be complete only where the payee's bank has the payee's actual or apparent authority both to receive and accept the transfer of funds on the payee's behalf.[620] Their Lordships held in *The Laconia* that the shipowners' bank had only limited authority to receive payment and obtain instructions from the owners, as it did not have authority to accept late payments on behalf of the owners:[621]

> In most cases where funds are transferred to the [payee's] bank in accordance with the terms of an underlying contract between the [payer] and the [payee], the bank will have the [payee's] actual authority to receive and accept the payment on the [payee's] behalf. In the more unusual case of the payee, having instructed his bank not to accept such a payment, the [payer] could still claim that the [payee's] bank had apparent authority to receive and accept the payment. To succeed with such an argument, the [payer] must establish that he relied on the bank's appearance of authority, something he cannot do where he knew of the limit placed on the bank's authority or where he ought reasonably to have known that there was such a limit.[622] The [payee] may give the [payer] actual notice by telling him not to make further payments. Furthermore, it is submitted that the [payer] may also be put on notice where he makes a payment outside the terms of his underlying contract with the [payee] (for example, a late payment) on the ground that he ought then to be put on enquiry regarding the extent of the authority of the [payee's] bank to accept such payment so as to bind the payee. Of course, when the [payee] becomes aware that payment has been received and accepted by his bank without authority, he may decide to ratify the bank's actions.

In *The Laconia*, Lord Salmon observed that the shipowners could have been deemed to have accepted the payment if their bank had kept it for an unreasonable time.[623] More

---

[619] N.511 above, questioning on this point, *Astro Amo Compania Naviera SA* v. *Elf Union SA, 'The Zographia M'* [1976] 2 Lloyd's Rep. 382; and overruling *Empresa Cubana de Fletes* v. *Lagonisi Shipping Co. Ltd, 'The Georgios C'* [1971] 1 QB 488. For the basic rule, see *Tankexpress AIS* v. *Compagnie Financiére Belge de Petroles SA* [1949] AC 76 (HL).

[620] For the same principle in the context of payment by cheque, see *Whitbread Group plc* v. *Goldapple Ltd*, n.511 above, [27]; *Southbourne Investments Ltd* v. *Greenmount Manufacturing Ltd*, n.516 above, [19]–[23].

[621] *Mardorf Peach & Co. Ltd* v. *Attica Sea Carriers Corp. of Liberia, The Laconia*, n.511 above, 871–872. A bank that does not have the payee's authority to receive the payment has been described as receiving the funds 'in a ministerial capacity': *Dovey* v. *Bank of New Zealand*, n.24 above, [27].

[622] *Overbrooke Estates Ltd* v. *Glencombe Properties Ltd* [1974] 1 WLR 1335; *Heinl* v. *Jyske Bank (Gibralter) Ltd* [1999] Lloyds Rep. Bank. 511, 521, 533 (CA); *Sphere Drake Insurance Ltd* v. *Euro International Underwriting Ltd* [2003] EWHC 1636 (Comm.), [58].

[623] N.511 above, 880.

recently, in *TSB Bank of Scotland plc* v. *Welwyn Hatfield District Council and Council of the London Borough of Brent*,[624] Hobhouse J held that a payee would be deemed to have accepted an unauthorized payment made into his account where he dealt with the transferred funds as his own. The issue before the court was whether an inter-bank transfer of funds by one local authority into the account of another local authority amounted to payment of an underlying restitutionary liability. Hobhouse J held that, despite its initial protestations, retention of the money for three weeks, use of the money, and its eventual return without interest amounted to acceptance of tender by the payee local authority and, therefore, payment. By contrast, in *HMV Fields Properties Ltd* v. *Bracken Self Selection Fabrics Ltd*,[625] a tenant continued to pay rent through the bank giro system for several weeks after being served with a notice of forfeiture for breach of a covenant in the lease. When the rent payments eventually came to the landlord's attention, it returned them to the tenant, again using the bank giro system. The First Division of the Court of Session held that the landlord was not barred from forfeiture by reason of having received rent. It was held that 'acceptance' was a question of fact and, despite the landlord's initial delay of several weeks before returning the rent, there had been no acceptance here. In this case, the payee had no knowledge of the payment being made into the account, whereas in *Welwyn Hatfield* the payee was fully aware of the payment.

A giro transfer will be considered conditional, and therefore not an effective payment, where it fails to provide the payee with the same availability as cash. The point was made authoritatively by the House of Lords in *The Chikuma*,[626] which involved a rental that was due in Rome, on 22 January 1976. On the preceding day, the charterers instructed their bank to remit the funds. By a telex message, dispatched on the due date, the payer's bank remitted the funds to the payee's bank. The amount was received on the same day, but it was noted that the 'value date' was shown as Monday 26 January. Under Italian law, the funds became available to the shipowners on 22 January 1976, although interest was to accrue only as from the 'value date' of 26 January 1976. Thus, if the shipowners had withdrawn the amount on the day of transfer they would probably have incurred interest to the bank for the period of four days ending on 26 January 1976. On 23 January 1976, the shipowners, who decided to treat this remittance as being out of date, instructed their Italian bank to reject payment. Giving judgment for the shipowners, Lord Bridge conceded that 'payment' in the context of money transfers encompassed settlement not only by legal tender but also by means of final credit entries. Broadly speaking, payment was effected when the payee had the unconditional use of the amount settled by means of the ledger entry. His Lordship stressed that, although payment by legal tender was not expected in cases of this type, the payee was entitled to expect the full equivalent of it. Transferred funds that could not yet be used for investment purposes, for example, by earning interest on the funds, was not the equivalent of cash. His Lordship said:[627]

> The book entry made by the owners' bank on January 22 in the owners' account was clearly not the equivalent of cash, nor was there any reason why the owners should have

---

[624] N.511 above.   [625] N.517 above.
[626] *A/S Awilco of Oslo* v. *Fulvia SpA di Navigazione of Cagliari, 'The Chikuma'*, n.617 above. See also *PT Berlian Laju Tanker TBK* v. *Nuse Shipping Ltd*, n.511 above, [21].
[627] Ibid., 320.

been prepared to treat it as the equivalent of cash. It could not be used to earn interest, e.g. by immediate transfer to a deposit account. It could only be drawn subject to a (probable) liability to pay interest. In substance it was the equivalent of an overdraft facility which the bank was bound to make available.

On this basis, the amount remitted could not be regarded as the equivalent of cash as the shipowners, as payees, did not have the unconditional use of it on the due date.

Lord Bridge's judgment was forcefully criticized[628] on the ground that the case should have been regarded as governed by English law, under which the funds would have accrued to the shipowners unconditionally when credited to their account, regardless of the stipulated 'value date'. It is believed that this criticism is unfounded. Even if the case were decided on the basis of English law, the payment should not have been regarded as equal to cash. The reason for this is that the majority of English banks would regard the stipulation of a 'value date' in a money transfer order as an indication that the payee's account ought not to be credited before that date. Thus, it is believed that, under the prevailing English banking practice, the amount in question would not have been entered in the shipowners' account until 26 January 1976. This would, without a shred of doubt, have been payment out of time. Any earlier crediting of the amount involved to the credit of the shipowners would have been coupled, in English banking practice, with an indication that the amount might not be drawn upon before the date in question, although most banks would have followed the simpler practice of entering the amount in a suspense account until 26 January 1976.

In summary, it is arguable that the cases decided on the point in question emphasize the need to make the funds available to the payee by the stipulated date. Funds are so available only if the payee can utilize them without any restrictions as if they constituted amounts in cash.

(iv) **Comparison of the two types of cases**

The cases concerning a payee's attempt to countermand a money transfer order have to be regarded as distinct from the cases concerning the payment of money by a due date stipulated in a contract between a payer and payee. In the former type of case, the authorities suggest that there is no room for countermand of payment, or for reversal of entries, once the funds have been made available to the payee's bank and the bank has agreed, expressly or impliedly, to receive payment thereof for the payee. A key to the determination of the issue involved is to be found in prevailing banking practice. This is understandable as the litigation invariably involves one of the banks participating in the money transfer operation. On this basis, it is realistic to suggest that the practice developed over the years in the banking community furnishes the necessary clues regarding the payer's right to countermand payment or to demand a reversal of entries. Undoubtedly, the courts use as an analogy the completion of the clearing cycle of cheques, which, as discussed previously,[629] is determined exclusively by banking practice. In contrast, in the second type of case, the parties are the payer and payee, and the issue concerns the performance by a commercial firm of a contractual obligation. The analogy must, therefore, be taken from cases determining the time at which payment by cash or by legal tender is complete between the payer and payee.

---

[628] F.A. Mann, 'Uncertain Certainty' (1981) 97 *LQR* 379.   [629] Ch. 10, Sect. 2 above.

This demarcation has led to an interesting difference in the basic principles applicable in the two types of case. Between the banks, or between a bank and one of its customers, the transfer is complete when the credit balance is irrevocably available to. and accepted by, the payee's bank as the payee's agent. Between payer and payee, payment is complete when it stands to the unconditional order of the payee. It remains to be seen whether the House of Lords will eventually be able to find a general principle applicable to all the cases in point.

7 **Confidentiality of information**

Computer centres, such as BACS or SWIFT, acquire in the course of their operations a great deal of information respecting the customers of the participating banks. This is so regardless of whether the information is obtained directly from the customers themselves, as is the case in some BACS transactions, or from data transmitted by the banks. The data or computer department of the bank also has access to information recorded about each customer. In the United Kingdom, information or data about individuals is generally protected by the Data Protection Act 1998 (DPA 1998), passed to implement EC Directive 95/46 on the Protection of Individuals with regard to the Processing of Personal Data and on the Free Movement of Such Data.[630] The DPA 1998 repeals and replaces the Data Protection Act 1984.[631] The two enactments have a number of similar features. Both contain registration requirements. The DPA 1998 continues with the office of the Data Protection Registrar, which was originally set up under the 1984 Act, but has renamed the office as the Data Protection Commissioner. The DPA 1998 has itself been amended by the Freedom of Information Act 2000, so that, with effect from 30 January 2001, the Data Protection Commissioner is now known as the Information Commissioner.[632] The DPA 1998 provides that a 'data controller' intending to process personal data must be registered with the Information Commissioner.[633] The DPA 1998, like its predecessor, is also based on a set of Data Protection Principles. Unlike the 1984 Act, however, those failing to register or exempt from registration will still be liable if they fail to comply with the Data Protection Principles. Perhaps the most significant difference between the two pieces of legislation is that the 1984 Act extended only to information about individuals processed by computer, whereas the DPA 1998 covers personal data processed by computer and also manual records held within a 'relevant filing system'.

---

[630] [1995] OJ L281/31. For an overview of the Data Protection Act 1998 (DPA 1998), see S v. *United Kingdom* [2008] 25 BHRC 557, [30]–[32] (ECtHR).

[631] For commencement, see DPA 1998, s.75; Data Protection Act 1998 (Commencement) Order 2000, S.I. 2000/183.

[632] DPA 1998, s.6(1), as substituted by the Freedom of Information Act 2000, s.18(4), Sched. 2, Pt. 1, para. 13(1), (2). For commencement, see Freedom of Information Act 2000, s.87(2)(c).

[633] Ibid., s.17(1). There are certain exemptions set out in the DPA 1998, Pt. IV, including the processing of information held by law enforcement and security services, and exemptions for 'special purposes' relating to the use of personal data for journalism, literary purposes, and artistic purposes.

This is not the place for anything more than a few general observations concerning the DPA 1998 and its effect.[634] 'Personal data' is defined in s.1(1) of the DPA 1998 as data relating to a living individual who can be identified from those data, or from those data and other information in the possession of the data controller. The reference to a living individual means that information about a limited liability company or limited liability partnership falls outside the definition. The scope of the definition of 'personal data' was recently considered by the Court of Appeal in *Durant* v. *Financial Services Authority*.[635] The case is authority for the following propositions:[636] (a) that the concept of 'personal data' in the DPA 1998 should be given a narrow interpretation, and accordingly does not include all information retrieved from a search against an individual's name or unique identifier; (b) that mere mention of an individual in a document held by a data controller does not mean that the document contains personal data in relation to that individual; (c) that whether information is capable of constituting personal data depends on where it falls in a continuum of relevance or proximity to the data subject; (d) that in answering that question it is relevant to consider whether the information is biographical in a significant sense, and whether it has the putative data subject as its focus; and (e) that personal data is information that affects the privacy of the data subject. According to the House of Lords recently in *Common Services Agency* v. *Scottish Information Commissioner*, information derived from 'personal data' may not itself qualify as such, if steps have been taken to anonymize it fully.[637]

The definition of 'data' in s.1(1) of the DPA 1998 goes beyond information held in computerized databases and includes information 'recorded as part of a relevant filing system or with the intention that it should form part of a relevant filing system'.[638] A 'relevant filing system' is defined as 'any set of information relating to individuals to the extent that, although the information is not processed by means of equipment operating automatically in response to instructions given for that purpose, the set is structured, either by reference to individuals or by reference to criteria relating to individuals, in such a way that specific information relating to a particular individual is readily accessible'.[639] It has been held that information kept in a non-computerized manual system is only to be treated as 'data' if the filing system is sufficiently structured to allow easy access to information specific to the data subject.[640] Unstructured bundles of documents kept in boxes do not fall within the scope of a 'relevant filing system',[641] and have been held not to constitute 'data' even if they could be easily scanned and turned into digital information.[642] The question of whether information is data within the meaning of the DPA 1998 is to be determined at the time when the data subject makes his request to the data controller as to whether (and what) personal data is held on him.[643]

---

[634] But see Ch. 5, Sect. 5(i) above, for further analysis of the DPA 1998, and also consideration of the impact of the Human Rights Act 1998 on the bank's duty of confidentiality. The Freedom of Information Act 2000 has only marginal relevance for banks and for computer centres such as BACS or SWIFT, as it only covers information held by 'public authorities' (defined in s.3), not information held by private institutions.

[635] [2004] FSR 28 (CA).

[636] *Smith* v. *Lloyds TSB Bank plc* [2005] EWHC 246 (Ch), [31]. See also *Ezsias* v. *Welsh Ministers* [2007] All ER (D) 65, [59]–[66], [72], [75], [80], [88], [104] (information concerning complaints made by the data subject are not 'personal data', unless they involve an opinion expressed about the data subject personally).

[637] [2008] 4 All ER 851, [26]–[27], [79]–[83], [92] (HL).

[638] DPA 1998, s.1(1)(c).   [639] Ibid., s.1(1).

[640] *Durant* v. *Financial Services Authority*, n.636 above, [45]–[50].

[641] *Smith* v. *Lloyds TSB Bank plc*, n.635 above, [10]–[11], [13].

[642] Ibid., [20]–[23].   [643] Ibid., [12], [17].

A 'data controller' is defined as someone who, either alone or with others, determines the purposes for which, and the manner in which, any personal data are, or are to be, processed.[644] The bank's computer centre, and hence the bank itself, is a 'data controller'. By contrast, the DPA 1998 defines a 'data processor', as someone (other than an employee of the data controller) who processes the data on behalf of the data controller.[645] BACS, which simply processes data and does not determine the purpose for which the data are processed, seems to fall within this definition. Liability for failing to register with the Information Commissioner, and liability for failing to comply with the Data Protection Principles, rest with the data controller and not the data processor.[646]

The DPA 1998 reinforces the bank's duty of confidentiality in several ways. First, personal data may be treated as processed fairly—as required by the first Data Protection Principle—only where disclosure of the personal data does not infringe the disclosure requirements contained in Schedules 2 and 3.[647] Secondly, any disclosure of personal data must take place in conformity with the second to fifth Data Protection Principles: personal data must be obtained for specified purposes and used only in ways compatible with those purposes; personal data must be adequate, relevant, and not excessive in relation to the purpose for which the data are processed; personal data must be accurate and, where necessary, kept up to date; and personal data must not be kept longer than is necessary for the specified purpose or purposes for which they are required.[648] Thirdly, any disclosure of personal data must take account of the right of the 'data subject'—the individual who is the subject of personal data—to object to processing likely to cause damage or distress,[649] and the right of the data subject to have inaccurate personal data relating to him rectified, blocked, erased, or destroyed, and to have third parties, to whom the data have been disclosed, notified of that rectification, blocking, erasing, or destruction.[650] Fourthly, the sixth Data Protection Principle requires appropriate security measures to be taken against unauthorized or unlawful processing and against accidental loss, destruction, or damage to personal data, which includes an obligation placed on the data controller to ensure that any data processor employed by him has similarly effective security measures in place.[651] Finally, the data processor, or other third party, commits an offence if he knowingly or recklessly obtains, procures, or discloses personal data without the consent of the data controller.[652]

In view of the detailed rules concerning bank confidentiality, discussed in Chapter 5, the DPA 1998 is unlikely to affect the duties of a bank towards its customers. Furthermore, the conditions relevant to the fair and lawful processing of personal data, as set out in Schedule 2 to the DPA 1998, are broadly similar to the qualifications to bank confidentiality. Thus, disclosure of data may be sanctioned under the DPA 1998 by a court order or legislation, may be justified when it is in the public interest or in the legitimate interests

---

[644] DPA 1998, s.1(1).   [645] Id.   [646] Ibid., ss.4(1), 17(1), 21(1).

[647] For these requirements, see Ch. 5, Sect. 5(i) above. The definition of 'processing' contained in s.1(1) of the DPA 1998 is wide-ranging and includes 'disclosure of the information or data by transmission, dissemination or otherwise making available'. For the limits of the concept of 'processing', see *Johnson* v. *Medical Defence Union* [2007] EWCA Civ 262, [23]–[25], [48].

[648] Ch. 5, Sect. 5(i) above.   [649] DPA 1998, s.10.

[650] Ibid., s.14.   [651] Ibid., Sched. 1. Pt. II, paras. 11 & 12.

[652] Ibid., s.55(1). Section 55(4) also provides for an offence of selling personal data obtained or to be obtained in contravention of s.55(1). See *Attorney-General's Reference (No. 140 of 2004)* [2004] EWCA Crim 3525; *R* v. *Rooney* [2006] All ER (D) 158 (CA).

of the data controller, and may be allowed where the data subject has consented to it.[653] The importance of the DPA 1998 as regards banking law is that it precludes organizations, such as BACS, with whom an individual bank's customer does not have privity of contract, from disclosing information concerning him without the data controller's consent.

---

[653] Ibid., Sched. 2, paras. 1, 3, 5, & 6(1). See also s.55(2)(a), which provides that s.55(1) does not apply to a person who shows that the obtaining, disclosing, or procuring (i) was necessary for the purpose of preventing or detecting crime, or (ii) was required or authorized by or under any enactment, by any rule of law, or by the order of a court. See further Ch. 5, Sect. 5(i) above.

14

Payment Cards

1 Available cards reviewed and classified

Payment cards—small pieces of plastic that may be used to obtain goods or services—are widely used in various types of transaction. The oldest form[1] was the 'store card' which a department store or chain of petrol stations supplied to its clients to enable them to obtain goods or services against its production. In such a bipartite arrangement, the card was used to charge the client's account with the issuer, which the customer settled later. These cards were largely replaced by store cards issued by a financial institution with which the store had an arrangement and now more universally useable cards with a variety of functions. The newest form is the digital cashcard or 'electronic purse'. Digital technology has been introduced more generally into payment cards to improve security and enable the development of multifunction cards that include the electronic purse facility. Payment cards—or rather the functions they perform—fall into six main groups.

This section will consider how these cards operate in practice. The following sections will examine the legal position of each, which varies between the different types of card. This is governed not only by the general law but also, to some extent, by the Consumer Credit Act 1974[2] and the Payment Services Regulations 2009 (PSR 2009).[3] In practice the 'Lending Code' is also relevant.[4]

The first type of card is the credit card issued by a bank or other financial institution.[5] As explained below, these are either 'three-party' or 'four-party' and the issuers are members of one of the credit card networks—for example American Express or Visa. The cardholder can utilize the card to obtain goods or services from dealers who have entered into a 'merchant agreement' with a member of the network[6] and display the network's insignia. The dealer supplies the relevant items when the cardholder produces the card and gives his signature or keys in his 4-digit 'personal identification number' (his 'PIN'), which authorizes the card issuer to debit the cardholder's account. In the past, the cardholder's signature was obtained on a paper voucher produced by the dealer, but now the card is generally inserted into (and 'read' by) a machine attached to the dealer's point-of-sale terminal and the amount of the transaction is entered by the salesperson.

Any invalid card—such as a card reported lost and, in consequence, placed on the stop list—is rejected at this stage. If the transaction is for an amount above the dealer's

---

[1] For an excellent historical review, see E.E. Bergsten, 'Credit Cards—A Prelude to a Cashless Society' (1967) 8 *BC Ind. & Com. L Rev.* 485. See also D.N. Chorafas, *Electronic Funds Transfer* (London, 1988), ch. 21–22; G. Stephenson, *Credit, Debit and Cheque Cards* (Birmingham, 1993); M. Smith & P. Robertson, 'Plastic Money' in M. Brindle & R. Cox (eds.), *Law of Bank Payments* (3rd edn., London, 2004).

[2] See further Sect. 8 below.   [3] See further Sect. 9 below.

[4] Esp. Sect. 6 thereof. See Chap. 2, Sect. 6(ii).

[5] See further Sect. 2 below. The first credit card to be introduced in the UK was Barclaycard in 1966.

[6] With the issuer of the card in 'three-party' cards or a 'merchant acquirer' in the case of 'four-party' cards, see Sect. 2 below.

'floor limit' (the maximum amount at which goods or services can be supplied without verification of the amount available), the salesperson has to obtain authorization from the card issuer. If the transaction is accepted, a till receipt is usually issued; it identifies the terminal and sets out the date, the time, and the amount of the transaction. Originally, the cardholder was required to sign the receipt (or a pad on the machine) but increasingly he is required to type his PIN on a machine keyboard. The salesperson verifies his signature by comparing it with the one on the card or, if a PIN has been used, waits for the transaction to be accepted. One copy of the receipt is retained by the retailer and the other is handed to the customer. With the increasing popularity of mail order and internet shopping, this procedure has been replaced in those contexts by the cardholder giving his card number over the telephone or electronically (as the case may be), with additional security checks usually being used. Even more recently, 'contactless' cards enable purchases for small amounts to be effected merely by touching the card against an 'electronic pad'. However the card is used, the dealer then receives payment directly or indirectly[7] from the issuer, (minus a fee) who obtains reimbursement from the cardholder. Settlement by the cardholder may be made either in full when the issuer submits the account (in which case the cardholder does not incur a finance charge), or by instalments, each of which must be not less than a given percentage of the balance outstanding at the time of payment. Where payment is made by instalments, interest is charged on the balance due (interest being charged at the end of each billing cycle, which is usually a calendar month). As well as using the credit card to obtain goods or services, the cardholder may obtain cash by the use of the card and is then charged interest from the date the amount is debited from the account with the issuer.

The second type of payment card—a 'charge card' or T & E (travelling and entertainment) card—is a variant of the credit card.[8] The procedure for its use is the same as that described, except that cash withdrawals are not available and the cardholder is expected to settle promptly and in full when the account is periodically submitted to him by the issuer.

The third type of card is the 'cheque card' or the 'cheque guarantee card'.[9] Here the issuer undertakes to pay cheques drawn by the customer up to an amount specified on the card,[10] provided certain conditions are complied with.[11] Cheque cards differ from credit cards in that the issuer undertakes to honour a negotiable instrument drawn by its customer whatever the state of his bank account, rather than to pay for his purchases or to reimburse advances made to him. As the use of these cards (and cheques) is declining, it has been announced that they will be withdrawn in June 2011.

The fourth type of card is the 'debit' card, which the cardholder uses in designated retail stores to obtain goods or services.[12] The main difference between such a card and

---

[7] Depending on whether it is a 'three-party' or 'four-party' card, see Sect. 2 below.

[8] See further Sect. 3 below. In the UK, Diners' Club and American Express issue such 'three party' charge cards.

[9] See further Sect. 4 below. The most common card of this type is the Eurocheque card, issued by most clearers, which guarantees the payment of special 'eurocheques' drawn within Europe. R.M. Goode, *Consumer Credit Law and Practice* (London, loose-leaf), para. 1A[2.61] does not classify these as 'payment cards' (as they need to be used in conjunction with a cheque-book).

[10] Typically, £100.

[11] 'Guarantee' is a misnomer as they do not give rise to a true 'guarantee' in the sense of the bank agreeing to pay on the customer's default, as was confirmed by Evans LJ in *First Sport Ltd* v. *Barclays Bank plc* [1993] 3 All ER 789, 795, noted further Sect. 4 below.

[12] See further Sect. 5 below. Most debit cards are currently issued by networks, or schemes, shared by a number of banks and building societies.

a credit or charge card is that, when the cardholder uses a debit card, the amount due is remitted to the retailer by an electronic funds transfer involving a debit of the sum concerned to the cardholder's bank account. The transfer is either instantaneous (an 'online system'[13]) or occurs in batches some time after the transaction (an 'off-line' system). Again, a cardholder may also obtain cash (this time directly from his bank account) with a debit card. In some ways, debit cards are the modern equivalent of cheques in giving the customer direct access to his bank account.

The fifth type of card is the 'cashcard' or 'ATM' card,[14] which is used by the cardholder in order to obtain cash from an automatic teller machine (hence ATM) by typing in his PIN on the keyboard of the ATM terminal. The customer's bank account is debited by the amount of the cash issued. Most institutions issuing cashcards are members of networks[15] using shared ATMs.

The sixth—and newest—type of card is the 'electronic purse' or 'digital cashcard'.[16] Monetary value in the form of digital information ('digital cash') is loaded onto a 'smart card'—a piece of plastic with a microchip—and a corresponding deduction made from the customer's bank or credit card account.[17] The card can then be used to pay for goods and services by the electronic transfer of the digital information (in the form of an encrypted[18] digital payment message) from the microchip on the card to the retailer's microchip. The retailer may then transfer that value electronically either to his creditors or to his bank account.

Despite the differences between the types of card, they basically serve one general purpose: to enable the cardholder to obtain goods or services or cash by the use of a card, saving the cardholder the inconvenience of carrying cash. Functionally, the different types of card are complementary. The cardholder may, on a given day, withdraw cash from a shared ATM by the use of his cashcard and 'recharge' his electronic purse, pay a bill for services by means of a cheque backed by his cheque card, use his credit card to order goods over the telephone and his debit card or electronic purse to pay for groceries purchased at a supermarket. It is, accordingly, not surprising that some cards serve a number of purposes, for instance, that of a debit card, of a cheque card, and of a cashcard. Conceptually, however, such a multi-function, (here three-purpose) card is to be regarded as comprising three card types incorporated in a single card. Each of these is, of course, governed by the principles applying to cards of its type. But although each type of card differs in certain ways from the others, there is a similarity in the practical problems arising in all of them. Disputes may arise as to liability for the misuse of the card by unauthorized persons, especially where the cardholder fails to notify the issuer of its loss or conversion. Another problem that sometimes arises concerns the dealer's right to enforce his claim against the issuer of one of the first four types of card in cases of its misuse by the cardholder. In the case of cashcards, which involve bipartite agreements, and of electronic purses that are treated like cash, the last problem does not arise.

---

[13] Visa Electron and Solo are online debit cards.   [14] See Sect. 6 below.

[15] LINK is the main one in the UK, joining most banks and building societies.

[16] See Sect. 7 below. In the UK, the Mondex digital cash system was piloted in 1995. It is run by Mondex International Ltd (now a subsidiary of Mastercard), described in J. Finlayson-Brown, 'Mondex: Structure of a New Payment Scheme' (1997) 9 *JIBL* 362. Visa Cash is a newer version. Both are 'open' systems that can be used at a wide variety of third-party suppliers. Hence they are distinguishable from 'closed' pre-payment cards, which is the term generally used for cards issued by suppliers to customers, enabling customers to 'spend' the digital cash only with that supplier.

[17] Some cards may be loaded by a machine which converts cash into digital money.

[18] This enables the 'message' to be sent securely via the internet.

Two further problems arise in respect of payment cards. The first (which does not apply to the electronic purse) is the cardholder's criminal liability for his misuse of the card by excessive drawings or purchases. In credit, charge, cheque cards, and debit cards, this type of problem arises where an extravagant cardholder embarks on a shopping spree. With cashcards, such a case manifests itself only in extreme situations, where a cardholder who is aware of the delay in the sifting of information by the computer centre, withdraws excessive amounts by relying on a recorded credit balance which he knows to be out of date. The second, and particularly complex, problem is the application to all types of card of the consumer credit and payment services legislation. A discussion of these two issues follows that of the analysis of the six types of card.[19]

2 Credit cards

Credit card transactions may be 'three-party' or 'four-party'. In the former case, the issuer enters into 'merchant agreements' directly with the dealers who agree to accept the issuer's cards as payment.[20] In the latter case, dealers are recruited by 'merchant acquirers' who agree to reimburse the dealer (less a 'merchant service fee') and who obtain reimbursement (less an 'interchange fee') from the issuer.[21] The dealers are subject to extensive obligations and usually undertake to honour, without discrimination, all cards they have agreed to accept.[22]

A credit card transaction therefore involves three or four distinct contracts involving three or four parties: the cardholder, the card issuer, the dealer and (in the case of a four-party card), the merchant acquirer. First is the contract between the issuer and the cardholder. Basically, the issuer undertakes to pay for the purchases made by the cardholder within a specified credit limit. The issuer further agrees to the settlement of the amounts outstanding from time to time by minimum payments to be made upon the presentation to the cardholder of each periodic (usually monthly) statement. The cardholder agrees to reimburse the issuer in the prescribed manner, and undertakes to pay the applicable credit charge and (if applicable) annual and other fees. The contract is concluded in standard form, drafted by the issuer. In the past, it typically contained many terms which were disadvantageous to the cardholder[23] but the contracts have now been

---

[19] See Sect. 8 (Consumer Credit Act 1974), Sect. 9 (Payment Services Regulations 2009 (PSR 2009), S.I. 2009/209), and Sect. 11 (criminal liability).

[20] It is understood that American Express operates on this basis (see *OFT* v. *Lloyds TSB Bank plc* [2008] 1 Lloyd's Rep. 30, see per Lord Mance, [23]). Moreover, many store cards are 'three-party', with a financial institution agreeing to issue cards to the store's customers.

[21] Visa and Mastercard operate on this basis: see *OFT* v. *Lloyds TSB Bank plc*, n.20 above. For a detailed description, see: *Lancore Services Ltd* v. *Barclays Bank plc* [2008] EWHC 1264 (Ch).

[22] For further details, see Goode, n.9 above, para. 1A[2.62], who refers to two additional rules which were used: the first was a prohibition on price discrimination in the sense of granting discounts for cash purchases and the second was a minimum volume commitment. These two rules were described as contrary to the public interest in the Monopolies and Mergers Commission report entitled *Credit Card Services: A Report on the Supply of Credit Card Services in the UK* (Cmnd. 718, London, 1989). Visa's application for judicial review was dismissed in *R* v. *Monopolies and Mergers Commission, ex p. Visa International Service Association* [1991] CCLR 13, affg. [1990] CCLR 72 (Hodgson J). They were rendered unlawful by the Credit Cards (Merchant Acquisition) Order 1990, S.I. 1990/2158 and the Credit Cards (Price Discrimination) Order 1990, S.I. 1990/2159, made under the Fair Trading Act 1973.

[23] Such as a term enabling the issuer to alter the terms at will—a provision invoked when issuers unilaterally imposed 'annual fees'.

redrafted in the light of consumer protection legislation, especially the Unfair Terms in Consumer Contracts Regulations.[24]

It will be shown[25] that the agreement between the issuer and the cardholder often constitutes a regulated credit agreement within the meaning of the Consumer Credit Act 1974. The card itself is a 'credit token' and the agreement, if 'regulated', a 'credit-token agreement'. In addition, the PSR 2009 also apply to most payment card agreements,[26] but in so far as there is duplication, the 1974 Act applies instead of the Regulations if the agreement is a 'regulated agreement'.[27] In terms of general common law principles, the contract resembles that made between a bank and an applicant for a traveller's letter of credit. In such a transaction, the customer requests the bank to issue to him a letter of credit in which correspondents are invited to provide him with cash on the strength of the bank's promise to reimburse them. The contract involves the extension of credit by the bank (issuer); the customer undertakes to reimburse it and to pay the agreed charge.[28]

The second contract (the 'merchant services agreement') is between the dealer and either the issuer or (in the case of a four-party card) the merchant acquirer.[29] It is a master agreement in which the issuer or merchant acquirer agrees to pay to the dealer amounts due from cardholders, provided the goods or services are supplied on the agreed terms.[30] For example, the dealer cannot supply goods or services without making a credit enquiry if the price exceeds a given ('floor') figure. If the cardholder's signature is still used as the means of authenticating the transaction, the dealer is, further, expected to compare the signature the cardholder gives with the signature on the card. The issuer obtains an agreed percentage of each amount paid under the card as a consideration for the service rendered to the dealer.

Initially there was some dispute as to the nature of this transaction, it being suggested that it was to be regarded as an assignment by the dealer to the issuer of the amount due from the cardholder. However, it seems clear that this is incorrect as the dealer supplies the goods or services to the cardholder with a view to obtaining payment from the issuer (or merchant acquirer). That person makes a direct promise of reimbursement to the dealer in the master agreement[31] and hence the debt is due from him and not from the cardholder.[32] The issuer's (or merchant acquirer's) promise to the dealer is thus similar to that made by a bank in a traveller's letter of credit.

---

[24] S.I. 1999/2083. See the OFT's statement on credit card default charges of April 5, 2006 whereby it threatened to take action against credit card issuers that imposed default charges in excess of £12 on the basis that (in its view) higher charges were in breach of those Regulations. The Consumer Credit Act 1974 (see Sect. 8) and the PSR 2009 (see Sect. 9) also contain provisions protecting the cardholder as does the Lending Code (see Ch. 2, Sect. 6(ii)).

[25] See Sect. 8 below.   [26] See Sect. 9 below.

[27] PSR 2009, regs. 38 and 52, considered further in Sect. 9.

[28] As regards travellers' letters of credit, see M. Bridge (ed.), *Benjamin's Sale of Goods* (7th edn., London, 2010), paras. 23-01 ff. And see Goode, n.9 above, para. 1C[39.62] who compares the transaction with a documentary credit. As regards the background of such cards, see Chorafas, n.1 above, ch. 22.

[29] See R. Brownsword & J. MacGowan, 'Credit Card Fraud' [1997] *NLJ* 1806.

[30] For a case concerning a breach of these terms, see: *Lancore Services Ltd* v. *Barclays Bank plc* [2008] EWHC 1264 (Ch).

[31] And see the analysis of Lord Diplock in *Metropolitan Police Commissioner* v. *Charles* [1977] AC 177, 182 (which, though concerning a cheque card, appears applicable to credit cards) and *Lancore Services Ltd* v. *Barclays Bank plc* [2008] EWHC 1264 (Ch). See also P. Dobson, 'Credit Cards' [1979] *JBL* 331.

[32] Bergsten, n.1 above, 511 ff.; W.B. Davenport, 'Bank Credit Cards and the Uniform Commercial Code' (1968) 85 *Banking LJ* 941, 961; R.E. Brandel & C.A. Leonard, 'Bank Charge Cards: New Cash or New Credit' (1971) 69 *Mich. L Rev.* 1033, 1047–9; R.A. Reiter, 'Bank Credit Cards and Enterprise Liability' (1973)

The third agreement is between the dealer and the cardholder. This agreement remains a contract of sale or a contract for the provision of a service, although payment is expected from the issuer.[33] A difficult question arises in respect of this contract where the issuer or merchant acquirer becomes insolvent. Is the dealer able only to lodge a proof for the amounts outstanding or can he demand payment from the cardholder? The answer depends on whether the use of the card by the cardholder constitutes absolute or conditional payment of the goods or services.

An analogy with letters of credit suggest that the use of the card constitutes a conditional discharge and that the cardholder remains liable to pay the price of the goods to the dealer upon the issuer's insolvency.[34] But this analogy was rejected by the Court of Appeal in *Re Charge Card Services Ltd.*[35] Affirming Millett J's decision, it was held that the contract between a cardholder and a dealer was distinguishable from the contract of sale stipulating for the furnishing of a banker's documentary credit covering the price of the goods. The buyer, who furnishes the documentary credit, has the right to select the issuing bank. He can therefore be expected to bear the loss if the bank chosen by him becomes insolvent and, consequently, defaults. In contrast, in cases involving credit cards, the dealer is already in a relationship with the issuer.[36] Moreover, the parties agree that a procedure, namely payment by the specified issuer, is the means for the discharge of the debt incurred by the cardholder. When the card is used to effect payment, the dealer agrees to accept this in lieu of the cardholder's personal payment obligation.

The contract between the cardholder and the dealer does not require further consideration; nor is the fourth contract (in the case of a four-party card) discussed here. The rights of the cardholder and the issuer are, if the agreement between them is regulated by the Consumer Credit Act 1974, predominantly governed by that Act, and are otherwise governed by the PSR 2009. It will be shown[37] that this legislation contains provisions concerning the vexed question of liability for the misuse of the card by a stranger.

There is a dearth of authority concerning the contract between the issuer and the dealer.[38] It is clear that, in the master agreement, the issuer undertakes to pay the amount accrued by the use of the card less a given percentage.[39] The issuer is under a duty to perform this promise even if the cardholder absconds or fails. Indeed, the object of the transaction is to enable the cardholder to obtain goods and services on the issuer's credit.

21 *UCLA L Rev.* 278; Goode, n.9 above. And see S.A. Jones, 'Credit Cards, Card Users and Account Holders' [1988] *JBL* 457.

[33] S.A. Jones, 'Credit Cards, Card Users and Account Holders' [1988] *JBL* 457, 463–5.

[34] See for example, the following case law on letters of credit: *Sale Continuation Ltd* v. *Austin Taylor & Co. Ltd* [1968] 2 QB 849; *W. J. Alan & Co. Ltd* v. *El Nasr Export and Import Co.* [1972] 2 QB 189, 212; *Maran Road Saw Mill* v. *Austin Taylor & Co. Ltd* [1975] 1 Lloyd's Rep. 156, 159, noted in (1977) 40 *MLR* 91.

[35] [1989] Ch. 497, [1988] 3 All ER 702, affg. [1987] Ch. 150. See also *Customs and Excise* v. *Diners Club Ltd* [1989] 2 All ER 385, *per* Woolf J at 394.

[36] Directly in the case of three-party cards and indirectly in four-party cards and both have dealings with the corporation running the Visa or MasterCard Scheme.

[37] See Sects. 8 and 9 below.

[38] It is thought that the situation is the same whether the dealer has a contract with the issuer (in 'three-party' cards) or with a merchant acquirer (in 'four-party' cards).

[39] See *Debenhams Retail plc* v. *Customs and Excise Commissioners* [2004] EWHC 1540: where a percentage of the total price is payable to a card-handling company, the amount on which the retailer is liable for VAT is the total price minus the card-handling fee.

3 Charge cards

As in the case of credit cards, the rights of the charge cardholder and the issuer are, if the agreement between them is now[40] regulated by the Consumer Credit Act 1974, predominantly governed by that Act and are otherwise governed by the PSR 2009.[41] Until the enactment of the Regulations, there were many unresolved issues with little English case law to draw on.[42] American decisions that pre-dated the introduction of legislation there[43] had grappled with the problem of who was responsible for any misuse of the card. An early American authority suggested that, where there is no relevant express term in the contract between the parties, the risk of loss is borne by the issuer. The reason is simple: the issuer can seek reimbursement only if a transaction has been sanctioned by the genuine cardholder.[44] However, there was no uniformity in the approach of the courts when the contract in question absolved the issuer from liability where the cardholder failed to give prompt notice of the loss of the card. Some decisions took the view that the cardholder was bound by his contractual undertaking.[45] In one case, on the other hand, it was held that, despite the clause, the issuer owed a duty of care to the cardholder. It was incumbent on the issuer to prove that its duty was discharged before it could invoke the clause.[46] In another case, where the thief went on a shopping spree with the converted card, the court refused to give effect to the clause. The issuer should have been alerted by the obvious pattern of the frauds. However, in that case the dealers were clearly at fault, as they supplied to the thief items that were not within the legitimate purpose of the card[47] and therefore presumably the issuer could have recovered an indemnity from them. As will be considered below, the PSR 2009 now contain detailed provisions dealing with the issue.[48]

The other main problem concerning the contract between the issuer and the cardholder was that of countermand of payment. It will be recalled that a drawer has the right to instruct his bank to dishonour a cheque even if the payee is entitled to its payment.[49] The reason for this is that, as against the bank, which acts as an agent, the drawer is entitled to cancel his instruction. Could the same reasoning be applied when the cardholder uses his charge card? It is believed that such an analogy would be misconceived. A cheque can be countermanded, as the bank does not make a promise to the payee. The position of the issuer of a card is different. Under his contract with the dealer, the issuer is bound to pay the amounts incurred by the use of the card by the cardholder. Moreover,

---

[40] Since the implementation of the Consumer Credit Directive, see Ch. 2, Sect. 5(i); previously they were generally issued under 'exempt agreements'. See Sect. 8(i), below.

[41] See Sect. 9, below.

[42] But see *Customs and Excise* v. *Diners Club Ltd* [1989] 2 All ER 385, a VAT case which analyses the legal position.

[43] The Uniform Commercial Code, the Uniform Consumer Credit Code, and the federal legislation in point. See, generally, Davenport, n.32 above, 941; A.G. Cleveland, 'Bank Credit Cards' (1973) 90 *Banking LJ* 719, especially 725–727 (discussing the Uniform Consumer Credit Code); L.B. Orr & J.H. Tedards, 'Bank Credit Cards and the Right of Setoff' (1975) 26 *SC L Rev.* 89.

[44] *Thomas* v. *Central Charge Service Inc.*, 212 A 2d. 533 (DC Cir. 1965).

[45] *Magnolia Petroleum Co.* v. *McMillan*, 168 SW 2d. 881 (Tex. Civ. App. 1943); *Texaco Inc.* v. *Goldstein*, 229 NYS 2d. 51 (Mun. Ct. 1962), affd. 241 NYS 2d. 495 (Sup. Ct. 1963) (clause held fair).

[46] *Union Oil Co. of California* v. *Lull*, 349 P 2d. 243 (Ore. 1960).

[47] *Gulf Refining Co.* v. *Williams Roofing Co.*, 186 SW 2d. 790 (Ark. 1945).   [48] See Sect. 9(ii), below.

[49] Ch. 10, Sect. 1 above.

the cardholder enters into his contract with the issuer on the basis of this understanding. He knows that his use of the card involves the creation of a binding payment obligation on the issuer's part. For this reason, it is thought that at common law the cardholder is not entitled to countermand his instruction any more than the applicant for a documentary credit is entitled to demand that the bank revoke its binding promise to the beneficiary of the facility.[50] However, again the PSR 2009 provide the answer: consent to (any) payment transaction may be withdrawn at any time before the point at which the payment order can no longer be revoked in accordance with those Regulations.[51] Revocation is generally possible until the payment order has been received by the card issuer[52] but in the case of a transaction 'initiated by the payee', the payor may not revoke after transmitting the payment order or giving consent to execute the transaction to the payee.[53] Although it is unclear how these general provisions apply to a charge card, it seems that the payment transaction would be regarded as 'initiated' by the payee and hence once the cardholder uses the card, he is not entitled to countermand his instruction. It remains to consider whether, at common law, the issuer may be liable for the dealer's default or misrepresentation. One American authority sought to achieve such a result by subjecting the issuer to product liability, on the ground that the display of its insignia conferred an aura of respectability on the dealer.[54] As will be discussed below,[55] the Consumer Credit Act 1974 imposes a similar 'connected lender liability' in certain cases and this express statutory provision suggests that otherwise such liability does not arise under English law.

The contract between the issuer and the dealer is carefully defined in the master agreement. If the cardholder's signature is used as the means of authenticating the transaction, usually the dealer is granted the right to be paid provided the cardholder's signature matches that on the card. The dealer is therefore entitled to recover against a skilful forgery.[56] There are, however, two exceptions. First, the dealer may not recover payment if he has rendered services or provided goods under a card, which has been put on a stop list communicated to him. Secondly, the card has to be used for the purposes for which it is issued. Thus, if a card is issued with an endorsement to the effect that it can be used only for 'travelling and entertainment', the dealer cannot seek reimbursement from the issuer for the price of a radio sold to the cardholder.[57]

---

[50] But note that, in the case of cards governed by the Consumer Credit Act 1974, the cardholder can make effective against the issuer most of the claims that he has against the dealer (Sect. 8(v) below). This is an even more effective remedy than the power to countermand payment.

[51] Reg. 55(3). This is a mandatory provision applicable in all cases.

[52] Reg. 67(1)—applicable in the case of agreements regulated by the Consumer Credit Act 1974 but contracting out by non-consumers is possible (reg. 51(3)(a)).

[53] Reg. 67(2)—again, applicable in the case of agreements regulated by the Consumer Credit Act 1974 but contracting out by non-consumers is possible (reg. 51(3)(a)).

[54] *Connor* v. *Great Western Savings & Loan Association*, 447 P 2d. 609 (1969); contrast *Bradler* v. *Craig*, 79 Cal. Reptr. 401 (2d. Dis. 1969); *Sherlec* v. *Wells Fargo Bank*, 96 Cal. Reptr. 434 (1st Dis. 1971). And see Reiter, n.32 above.

[55] See Sect. 8, below.

[56] So held in respect of cheque cards in *First Sport Ltd* v. *Barclays Bank plc* [1993] 3 All ER 789, discussed in Sect. 4, below.

[57] *Gulf Refining Co.* v. *Williams Roofing Co.*, 186 SW 2d. 790 (Ark. 1945).

4 Cheque 'guarantee'[58] cards

In a card of this type, the issuer warrants to the payee that a cheque, drawn by the card-holder for not more than a stated maximum amount, will be paid on presentment, as long as a number of conditions,[59] including that the signature on the cheque corresponds to that on the card, are met.

There are two significant differences between a cheque card and a credit or charge card. The first, as mentioned above, is that in a cheque card the bank undertakes to honour its customer's cheque rather than to make payment for goods or services obtained. Secondly, the bank's undertaking in a cheque card is addressed to the world at large. Any bank, merchant, or private person is entitled to act on it. In the case of credit and charge cards, the bank's promise is directed only to the appointed merchants and financial institutions with which the issuer or merchant acquirer has a merchant agreement and who display its insignia. The reimbursement promise is therefore addressed to specified persons, and is not a unilateral offer to enter into a contract with anybody who accepts it.

A bank's promise in a cheque card is comparable to the undertaking given in a traveller's letter of credit.[60] In such a facility, the issuer undertakes to reimburse advances made to the holder (beneficiary) against cheques drawn by him for up to a specified maximum amount.[61] The beneficiary's signature is usually set out in a separate letter of introduction, which the traveller is required to keep apart from the letter of credit. The letter itself may be addressed either to the world at large, in which case it is a general letter of credit, or to a given person or persons, such as the issuer's correspondents, in which case it is 'specially advised'.[62] A person who acts on the bank's promise in such a letter of credit can enforce it provided he is a promisee within the contemplation of the instrument and provided further that he complies with the conditions set out in it.[63]

The cheque card clearly resembles the general variety of a traveller's letter of credit. The bank's undertaking in a cheque card was described by Lord Diplock in *Metropolitan Police Commissioner* v. *Charles*[64] as one that: gives the payee a direct contractual right against the bank itself to payment on presentment, provided that the use of the card by the drawer to bind the bank to pay the cheque is within the actual or ostensible authority conferred upon him by the bank. Thus the relationship between the bank and the dealer is a unilateral contract: the bank's offer is accepted by the dealer when the dealer accepts payment by the cheque supported by the card.[65]

A cheque card is considered not to fall within the ambit of the Consumer Credit Act 1974.[66] Nor is it a 'payment instrument' issued under a 'payment services' contract within

---

[58] See n.11 above to the effect that 'guarantee' is a misnomer and note that cheque guarantee cards will no longer be in use after 30 June 2011.

[59] In particular: (1) the cheque must be signed in the presence of the payee; (2) the cheque must bear the code number shown on the card; (3) the card must not have expired; (4) the card number must be written on the back of the cheque by the payee.

[60] Brandel & Leonard, n.32 above, 1047.

[61] E.P. Ellinger, *Documentary Letters of Credit—A Comparative Study in Law* (Singapore, 1970), 5–7; *Benjamin's Sale of Goods*, n.28 above, paras. 23-01 ff.

[62] *Birckhead and Carlisle* v. *Brown*, 5 Hill (NY) 634, 642–3 (1843), affd. 2 Den. (NY) 375 (1845); *Evansville National Bank* v. *Kaufman*, 93 NY 273, 280 (1993), both of which include an interesting analysis.

[63] *Northumberland County Bank* v. *Eyer*, 58 Pa. St. 97, 103 (1868).

[64] [1977] AC 177, 182, considered further in Sect. 10, below.

[65] *First Sport Ltd* v. *Barclays Bank plc* [1993] 3 All ER 789, *per* Evans LJ.   [66] Sect. 8(i) below.

the PSR 2009.[67] The rights of the parties to the transaction depend, therefore, on common law principles. The problems arising in respect of the contract between the banker and the cardholder are mainly the cardholder's right to countermand payment and the question of liability for the misuse of the card by an impostor. Cases of the misuse of the card by the cardholder also give rise to problems regarding the contract between the bank and the issuer.

The terms and conditions on which the bank agrees to furnish the cheque card usually include a provision withdrawing the cardholder's right of countermand. But is such a term effective? When the customer draws a cheque on his account, he instructs the bank, which is his agent, to make payment thereof.[68] The bank's mandate to pay is terminated if the customer countermands his order.[69] Is a provision in a contract between principal and agent effective to restrict the principal's right to cancel an instruction?

It is believed that the answer is to be gleaned from the law pertaining to letters of credit. Where the customer instructs his bank to open an irrevocable credit, he forgoes his right to order the bank to refuse to perform its promise to the beneficiary.[70] Conceptually, the explanation is that, when a principal orders his agent to give an independent undertaking to a third party, the relationship ceases to be one of pure agency. The agent, who binds himself to the third party, becomes in effect an independent contractor. Courts will not make orders that preclude banks from performing irrevocable undertakings given at a customer's request.[71] In a cheque card transaction, the customer—the cardholder—is aware of the fact that, when he uses his cheque card, he confers on the payee an irrevocable right to seek payment directly from the bank.

Questions concerning liability for the misuse of cheque cards by the cardholder are governed by the common law principles discussed above in respect of charge cards. There is, however, one additional consideration where the misused card is a cheque card. The underlying relationship between the bank and its customer, the cardholder, is more closely grounded on agency principles than is the relationship between the issuer of a charge card and its cardholder. It is therefore arguable that, quite regardless of the terms on which the card is issued, the bank is not entitled to debit its customer's account with a cheque, or order, which has not emanated from him. The bank has no genuine mandate in such cases.[72] The answer, probably, is that the question here is not one of the determination of the scope of the bank's authority but that of the allocation of risks connected with the use of cheque cards and consumer protection considerations. If the parties agree that in a given situation the risk is to be borne by the cardholder, subject to such a term being regarded as 'unfair' under the Unfair Terms in Consumer Contracts Regulations 1999,[73] the arrangement ought to be binding on him.

As a matter of practice, banks do not impose absolute liability on the cardholder of a cheque card, no doubt partly due to the Unfair Terms in Consumer Contracts Regulations. The cardholder bears the loss only if he fails to give notice to the bank of the loss or misappropriation of the card. Further, customers are asked not to carry

---

[67] See Sect. 9(i), below.   [68] Ch. 10, Sect. 1 above.

[69] Bills of Exchange Act 1882, s.75.

[70] See, for example, *Sovereign Bank of Canada* v. *Bellhouse, Dillon & Co. Ltd* (1911) 23 Que. KB 413. The principle is essential, as otherwise the bank would be in a quandary where its own undertaking was binding *vis-à-vis* the beneficiary but subject to objections by the customer.

[71] See, especially, *Harbottle (RD) (Mercantile) Ltd* v. *National Westminster Bank Ltd* [1978] 1 QB 146, 155–6, *per* Kerr LJ; *Edward Owen Engineering Ltd* v. *Barclays Bank International Ltd* [1978] 1 Lloyd's Rep. 166, 171, *per* Lord Denning MR, both applied in *Banque Saudi Fransi* v. *Lear Siegler Services Inc.* [2006] EWCA Civ 1130, [2007] 1 All ER (Comm.) 67.

[72] Ch. 11, Sect. 2 above.   [73] S.I. 1999/2083.

the card and the cheque-book together. Obviously, if only one of those items is stolen, the thief does not have the immediate means for perpetrating a fraud.[74] Customers are well advised to observe these requirements which, it is submitted, are reasonable and fair and in line with obligations imposed in relation to other payment cards by the PSR 2009.[75]

The contract between the bank and the payee of the cheque can give rise to problems only where the drawer's signature is a forgery. Where it is genuine, the bank has to pay the cheque provided the terms and conditions set out in the card are met. Thus, the cheque and card have to tally, the amount must not exceed the prescribed maximum, the cheque has to be drawn before the expiry date of the card and the payee has to write the number of the card on the back of the cheque. If all these requirements are complied with, the bank has to pay the cheque regardless of the availability of adequate funds standing to the drawer's account.

The problems that arise in cases of cheques bearing a forgery of the cardholder's signature were considered by the Court of Appeal in *First Sport Ltd* v. *Barclays Bank plc*.[76] A retailer took a cheque delivered to him by a fraudster, who pretended to be the rightful owner of the cheque-book and of the cheque card and who executed on the cheque a signature corresponding, in its appearance, to the signature written on the card. The issue was whether the retailer, whose good faith was not disputed, was entitled to enforce the promise given by the bank on the cheque card although the signature on the cheque was a skilfully executed forgery. It was held by a majority that, as the retailer had accepted the cheque in good faith, and had met all the conditions he had to comply with if he wished to enforce the bank's undertaking in the cheque card,[77] (including the requirement respecting the correspondence between the specimen signature on the card and the one executed on the cheque) he was entitled to payment. In consequence, the bank had to honour the cheque, notwithstanding a clause, printed just beneath the space used for the 'authorised signature', which read: '[t]his card may only be used by the authorised signatory ...'. It was accepted that these words put the retailer on notice that he should deal only with that person for the purposes of entering into a transaction with the bank; but the clause did not provide that the retailer was unable to recover where he dealt with another person whom he believed, reasonably and in good faith, to be the authorized signatory. The card had the effect of conveying to the retailer the bank's unilateral offer to enter into a contract. The genuine cardholder had the bank's actual authority to communicate the offer. Some other bearer of the card, even a thief, had the ostensible authority so to do.[78] As this decision turned on the precise wording of that clause, it is understood that the defendant and

---

[74] Although it is understood that professional criminals are frequently able to fake cheque forms so as to match the card and the cheque!

[75] See Sect. 9, below and the reference to S.I. 2009/209, reg. 57.

[76] [1993] 3 All ER 789, noted by L.P. Hitchens, 'Forgery and Cheque Cards' (1994) 57 *MLR* 811. And see *R* v. *Beck* [1985] 1 WLR 22 and *R* v. *Kassim* [1992] AC 9, both of which considered appeals against convictions respecting credit obtained by the misuse of stolen cards. In both it was assumed that banks would make payment against a docket or cheque with a forgery of the cardholder's signature, provided that retailers had acted in good faith and the forgery corresponded on its face with the specimen signature.

[77] See above.

[78] The dissenting judgment of Kennedy LJ gave more weight to the warning that the card could be used only by the authorized signatory and further thought that a bearer other than that person could be held to have had ostensible authority only where the bank had conducted itself in such a manner as to be estopped from denying it (which, in his view, was not established in the instant case).

other banks[79] have since changed their conditions to make it clear that they will honour cheques only if they are signed by the actual account holder.[80]

5 Debit cards

From a legal point of view, the contractual relationships established by the use of a debit card are similar to those described in respect of charge cards. The only substantive difference is that, in the case of charge cards, the issuer obtains reimbursement of amounts charged by the cardholder to his charge card upon the presentation of the periodic statements whilst, in the case of debit cards, each amount is debited to the cardholder's bank account at about the time at which the transaction takes place.[81] Thus the cardholder obtains credit from the issuer only where the amount is charged to an overdrawn account.[82]

It may be asked whether this process which involves the direct remittance of funds by the issuer to the retailers, means that payment by such a card constitutes an assignment to the retailer of a debt owed by the issuer to the cardholder. The discussion of this problem in respect of electronic funds transfers[83] suggests that this is not so, especially as amounts charged to the cardholder's account in respect of transactions executed by the use of the debit card are often covered by an overdraft extended by the issuer. The transaction is, rather, to be regarded as involving an instruction, or a mandate, for the payment of the sum involved given by the cardholder to the issuer. The position respecting countermands would, of course, be basically the same as in respect of charge cards and is now governed by the Payment Service Regulations 2009.[84]

At the time of writing, debit cards have not been judicially considered in the United Kingdom.[85] However, it can be safely assumed that, in so far as the contract between the issuer and the retailer is concerned, the parties are in the same position as in the case of charge cards. This is also the position as regards the contract between the dealer and cardholder. As the use of the card by the cardholder does not constitute an assignment, the analysis applied in *Re Charge Card Services*[86] ought to apply. Accordingly, if the card issuer becomes insolvent, the dealer is not entitled to demand payment from the cardholder.[87]

---

[79] Fellow members of APACS (Association for Payment Clearing Services).

[80] The APACS Conditions now state that the cheque must be signed 'in the presence of the payee by the person whose signature appears on the card'.

[81] Switch, for instance, leaves the arrangement respecting the date of charging to the agreement between the issuer and the cardholder. The clearing cycle, basically, involves three days. At the evening of the first day the retailer gathers the Switch-backed transactions executed through all its terminals; on the second day these are transmitted to the issuer; settlement by the issuer is effected on the third day. Since 1992, the Switch system has enabled participating issuers to link cards issued by them with an international electronic scheme, which enables cardholders to use their cards at terminals of certain firms abroad.

[82] As regards the question whether a debit card is subject to the provisions of the Consumer Credit Act 1974, see below Sect. 8(i).

[83] Ch. 13, Sect. 5(iii) above.

[84] See Sect. 3, above. Historically, the card agreement often precluded countermand once the cardholder had given his signature or PIN.

[85] Although the judge in *Lancore Services Ltd* v. *Barclays Bank plc* [2008] EWHC 1264 (Ch) refers to 'debit cards' and 'credit cards' interchangeably, the case concerned credit cards, not debit cards.

[86] [1989] Ch. 497, discussed in Sect. 2 above.

[87] Although in practice, as there is such a short time lag between transaction and electronic transfer, the risk to the dealer is small.

6 Cashcards

There are two types of cashcard: off-line and on-line. Off-line cards operate by means of an identification of the PIN, which is encoded on the card itself, by the automatic teller machine (ATM). The transaction is thus scrutinized by the program used by the terminal and there is no direct link, for individual transactions, with the central computer of the bank. The danger, of course, is that a person who misappropriates the card may succeed in decoding the PIN from the card. In contrast, an on-line card does not have any record of the PIN. Instead, the number is retained by the central computer to which the terminal is linked (or 'online'). When the customer keys the PIN into the terminal and requests to withdraw cash, the computer verifies the correctness of the number and the availability of an adequate balance. In on-line cards the PIN remains safe. The disadvantage is that the 'line' between terminals and the computer centre is, of course, subject to mechanical disturbances and breakdowns.

Although originally some banks used the off-line type of card, there has been a general shift to on-line cards.[88] Moreover, most banks and building societies enter into a master agreement and become members of networks[89] that enable their cards to be used in the terminals of each other. Terminals servicing more than one card issuer are known as 'shared ATMs'. The precise contractual relationships between the cardholder, his bank, and the other bank whose machine he uses, awaits judicial determination. The use of the card at another bank's ATM gives rise to a unilateral contract between the cardholder and that bank,[90] although it may be—depending on the master agreement between the banks—that the other bank is merely an agent of the cardholder's bank when dispensing the cash.[91]

If the cardholder memorizes his PIN, the danger of misuse is minimal. Unfortunately, many cardholders find it difficult to remember their PINs and carry a record with them. If this falls into the hands of a thief together with the card itself, misuse becomes easy. It is likewise facilitated where the cardholder 'lends' his card to a friend, even if the main object is to obtain funds for himself through that person's use thereof. Liability for misuse has to be considered both in the light of the Consumer Credit Act 1974[92] (for cashcards issued under 'regulated agreements') and the PSR 2009[93] (for other cashcards). However, as certain non-consumer cardholders may contract out of most of the relevant provisions in the 2009 Regulations,[94] the common law will be relevant in such cases.

The common law approach is best illustrated by an American authority, *Judd* v. *Citibank*.[95] The cardholder disputed the debiting of her account with an amount of $800, which was shown on her statement as having been withdrawn by the use of her cashcard. The ATM involved was programmed to effect a withdrawal only if the card was verified and the numbers on it were matched with the PIN keyed in. The cardholder testified that at the time of the withdrawals she had been at work, that she had not entrusted her card

---

[88] See n.13 above.   [89] Such as LINK (see n.15 above).

[90] In a similar way to the use of a cheque card (between the bank and the retailer), see Sect. 4, above and Smith and Robertson, n.1 above, ch. 4; M. Brindle & R. Cox (eds.), *Law of Bank Payments* (3rd edn., London, 2004), para. 4-64.

[91] For the consequences in the context of the definition of 'credit token' for the purposes of the Consumer Credit Act 1974, see further, Sect. 8(i), below.

[92] Sect. 8(ii) below.   [93] Sect. 9(ii), below

[94] See S.I. 2009/209, reg. 51(3)—but some (esp. regs. 57 & 58, imposing obligations on cardholder and issuer) are mandatory.

[95] 435 NYS 2d. 210 (1980).

to anybody, and that she had kept her PIN to herself. Bearing in mind that machines can malfunction, the Civil Court of the City of New York preferred the testimony of the cardholder and gave judgment for her.

A similar conclusion was reached by the same court in *Porter* v. *Citibank*,[96] where the cardholder made three unsuccessful attempts to withdraw money from an ATM on two separate days. Although the cardholder reported the matter promptly on both occasions, the bank allowed the debits recorded by the terminal to stand. At the trial, the bank admitted that the terminal was on average out of balance once or twice a week and conceded that, due to a defect in the machine, the money could have been dispensed to the next customer. On these facts, judgment was entered for the cardholder. The cardholder, however, did not always succeed. This is illustrated by *Feldman* v. *Citibank*,[97] where the same court dealt with two separate cases. One was decided in favour of the cardholder, whose testimony was accepted by the court. In the other case, the cardholder's testimony was rejected. The court concluded that he had been fraudulently induced to make an extra withdrawal by the use of the card by a person standing next to him at the ATM. Judgment was given for the bank, although the cardholder testified that nobody had stood next to him at the terminal.

The courts in New York have based their decisions on their assessment of the cardholder's credibility. English courts will need to do the same in cases outside the 2009 Regulations, although for cashcards covered by the Regulations the burden of proof is on the issuer to establish that their systems operated properly.[98] A further issue that may arise for consideration by the English courts in the case of cashcards not covered by the 2009 Regulations is the effectiveness of the hitherto standard clause in the master agreement between the bank and the cardholder under which the bank's record is deemed conclusive proof of transactions effected through the use of the ATM. Clauses of this type have been held valid in the context of performance bonds and first-demand guarantees, where the term usually states that a demand made by the beneficiary of the facility constitutes conclusive proof of the happening of the event on which payment is due.[99] There is, however, a difference between the object of a conclusive evidence clause in a performance bond agreement and the corresponding clause in a cashcard agreement. In the former case, the object is to enable the bank to honour its undertaking without getting embroiled in disputes between the beneficiary of the performance bond and the 'account party' at whose request the facility was furnished. In the latter case, the object of the clause is to preclude the bank's customer—the cardholder—from disputing inaccuracies in his statement. The cases are, therefore, distinguishable.

The risk inherent in the misuse of cashcards is further demonstrated by another American authority. In *Ognibene* v. *Citibank NA*,[100] a rogue, who was standing near the bank's terminals, memorized the PIN of a cardholder who was using a machine. The rogue, who pretended to be engaged in the servicing of the terminals, used an adjacent telephone to conduct a fictitious conversation with his employers, after which he asked

---

[96] 472 NYS 2d. 582 (1984). See also *Gaffney* v. *Community Federal Savings and Loan Association*, 706 SW 2d. 530 (Mo. Ct. App. 1986).

[97] 443 NYS 2d. 43 (1981).

[98] See S.I. 2009/209, reg. 60(1) and (3). This provision also applies to cards issued under agreements regulated by the Consumer Credit Act 1974.

[99] See, for example, *Bache & Co. (London) Ltd* v. *Banque Vernes et Commerciale de Paris SA* [1973] 2 Lloyd's Rep. 437, 440; *Van Der Merwe* v. *IIG Capital LLC* [2008] EWCA Civ 542; Benjamin's *Sale of Goods*, n.28 above, para. 24–003.

[100] 446 NYS 2d. 845 (1981). And see *Feldman* v. *Citibank*, 443 NYS 2d. 43 at 45 (Cit. Ct. 1981); *State* v. *Citibank*, 537 F Supp. 1192, 1194 (SDNY 1982).

the cardholder to let him have the use of the card so as to ensure that the terminal was in order. After withdrawing money by keying in the number, the rogue returned the card to the cardholder saying all was well. The cardholder contested the bank's right to debit his account with the amount extracted by the rogue, claiming that the bank had failed to introduce a safe method for the use of the card. Giving judgment in his favour, the Civil Court of the City of New York held that the bank had been negligent in not taking measures, for example alerting cardholders, to combat a ruse of which it had been aware. Again, it is difficult to predict whether an English court would adopt a similar approach.[101] The cardholder may be regarded as having committed a breach of his contract with the issuer by allowing an unknown person to use his card. But in the instant case the cardholder did not disclose his PIN to the rogue. Is he to be held liable for his failure to prevent a person from looking over his shoulder?

7 Electronic purses or digital cashcards

The nature of 'electronic purses' has been described briefly above.[102] They resemble physical cash in that they are 'loaded' with monetary value in the form of digital information ('digital cash') which may be instantaneously transferred from the cardholder to the retailer, in satisfaction of a payment obligation. Indeed, the old Banking Code[103] advised customers to 'treat your electronic purse like cash in a wallet' so that if the card is lost, 'you will lose any money in it, in just the same way as if you lost your wallet'.[104] Thus, although they physically resemble other payment cards and enable goods and services to be obtained by the production of the card, legally they are very different from such cards.[105] The digital cash is issued by an 'originator'[106] to participating banks (which pay for it by transferring real funds to the originator) and the banks re-issue it to customers in electronic purses (who pay for it from their accounts). The customers may then use the digital cash as described above. There is a contractual relationship between the originator and the participating banks and between the bank and its customer, but in order for the system to work the obligations to redeem the digital cash (by converting it into real value) undertaken by the originator and the participating banks should enforceable not only by the contracting parties but also by anyone who has acquired the digital cash. A number of possible analyses enable this result to be achieved[107] but the simplest is to regard the originator and participating banks as making, by displaying the relevant logo, a standing offer to redeem digital cash that is accepted by anyone who tenders the digital cash for conversion into real value.[108] Consideration could either be (exceptionally) dispensed

---

[101] But note the obligations imposed on cardholders and issuers by the PSR 2009, regs. 57 and 58 (which are mandatory, see n.94). However, it is not thought that they would be helpful in a case like *Ognibene*.

[102] See Sect. 1, above. 'Open' digital cashcards are considered here, not the 'closed' pre-payment cards issued by retailers to their customers. As noted below (see Sect. 9(i), n.221), such 'closed' pre-payment cards are also outside the scope of the PSR 2009.

[103] See Sect. 11(ii), below.   [104] See Chap. 2, Sect. 6(i).

[105] For discussions of the legal issues, see (on the Mondex system): C. Reed & L. Davies, *Digital Cash—The Legal Implications* (London, 1995), 7–9 and 'Electronic Cash and Payment Systems: Digitising the Future' (1997) 3 *JIBFL* 103; Cresswell *et al.* (eds.), *Encyclopedia of Banking Law* (London, 1998, loose-leaf), Div. D1 (ed. Hooley), paras. 3011 ff.; R. Hooley, 'Payment in a Cashless Society' in B. Rider (ed.), *The Realm of Company Law—A Collection of Papers in Honour of Professor Leonard Sealy* (London, 1998), 245.

[106] A private body—digital cash systems are privately run and have no endorsement from the State.

[107] See literature cited at n.105 above.

[108] Reed & Davies, n.105 above, 14–14; Hooley, n.105 above.

with—as in the case of a bank's promise in a letter of credit[109]—or could be found in the form of the digital cash.[110] More drastic—but commercially more attractive—solutions are legislative intervention or the recognition of digital cash as currency.[111]

As will be noted below, electronic purses are outside the Consumer Credit Act 1974[112] but they are 'payment instruments' issued under 'payment services' contracts for the purposes of the PSR 2009.[113]

8 The provisions of the Consumer Credit Act 1974[114]

(i) Cards affected: meaning of 'credit token' and 'credit-token agreement'

The Consumer Credit Act 1974 contains special provisions on credit tokens[115] and credit-token agreements.[116] Section 14(1) defines the term 'credit token'. The token may be a card, a check,[117] a voucher, or some other 'thing'. It must be issued to an individual, i.e. not to a company or a partnership of more than three members.[118] The issuer must be someone who carries on 'a consumer credit business', that is, he must be in the business of making regulated credit agreements.[119] Moreover, the issuer must give one or other of the following undertakings. The first alternative is that, on production of the token, he will supply cash, goods, or services 'on credit'.[120] The second alternative is that, where a third party supplies cash, goods, or services against the production of the token, the issuer will pay the third party for them.[121] The first alternative covers bipartite credit tokens. These fall within the definition only if the issuer himself undertakes to supply cash, goods, or services 'on credit'. But there is no express credit requirement in the case of the second alternative. Moreover, under section 14(3), it is stated that the issuer is taken to provide credit when the cash, goods, or services are supplied by the third party. Views differ on whether a credit requirement is implicit in the second alternative—section 14(3) merely identifying *when and by whom* the credit is provided—or whether there is no requirement for an undertaking as to credit, with section 14(3) 'deeming' it to arise.[122] If a credit requirement is not implicit, a tripartite credit token arises under the second alternative even if there is no undertaking to provide on credit. However, the preponderance of academic opinion is that an undertaking to provide 'on credit' is implicitly required in this

---

[109] Suggested by Hooley, ibid.   [110] Ibid.   [111] Ibid.   [112] See Sect. 8(i), below

[113] See Sect. 9(i), below – as long as they are not the 'closed' variety (see n.221 below). Note the special provision as to liability for misuse in reg. 53(3) for 'low value' electronic purses.

[114] For fuller discussions, see R.M. Goode, *Consumer Credit Law and Practice* (London, loose-leaf) and A.G. Guest & M. Lloyd, *Encyclopaedia of Consumer Credit Law* (London, 1974, loose-leaf). And see, generally, Ch. 2, Sect. 5, above.

[115] See especially ss.14, 51, discussed below.

[116] See especially ss.66, 84–85, discussed at Sect. 8(iv) below.

[117] *Sic*, not to be confused with 'cheques'. 'Checks' are documents entitling the holder to acquire goods at designated shops and that are issued on terms that the holder will pay the issuer their face value, plus interest, by instalments.

[118] See the definition of 'individual' in Consumer Credit Act 1974, s.189(1), substituted by the Consumer Credit Act 2006, s.1.

[119] Consumer Credit Act 1974, s.189(1). See Ch. 2, Sect. 5(ii), above.

[120] Consumer Credit Act 1974, s.14(1)(a).   [121] Ibid., s.14(1)(b).

[122] See Goode, n.114 above, and Guest and Lloyd, n.114 above, para. 2-015. For the argument that s.14(3) may resolve doubts as to who (the dealer or the issuer) is providing the 'credit': see S.A. Jones, 'Credit Cards, Card Users and Account Holders' [1988] *JBL* 457, 472.

second alternative.[123] The omission of an express reference to 'credit' may be explained on the basis that when the 1974 Act was passed, the only form of tripartite card was the credit card, which inevitably resulted in a deferment of payment and hence credit being provided. Thus those types of tripartite cards that were subsequently devised and that do not give rise to credit (for example, those cashcards and debit cards that cannot cause the bank account to be overdrawn) are probably not credit tokens.[124]

It is irrelevant whether or not the issuer deducts a discount or commission from the amount paid to the supplier. It is, further, irrelevant whether the cash, goods, or services are to be supplied against the mere production of the token or whether 'some other action is also required'.[125] These words were presumably added to cover the added requirements of a signature or PIN when the token is used, but they also cover other steps to be taken. Thus in *Elliott* v. *Director General of Fair Trading*,[126] a token was held to fall within section 14 although all that had been furnished was a provisional card, to be exchanged for the final card when the cardholder supplied some financial details about himself and entered into a written credit agreement. These requirements were held to constitute 'some other [required] action', which did not take the provisional card outside the ambit of section 14. It was further held immaterial that the undertaking given in the provisional card was not contractually binding.

The definition of a 'credit token' is a wide one: it may take any (tangible)[127] form and need not be the traditional piece of plastic. It encompasses a book of vouchers that the debtor may use under a credit agreement in order to draw on his account, provided the issuer undertakes to meet these. But ordinary cheque forms, supplied by a bank to its customer, are not covered. The reason for this is that the bank's undertaking to the customer is for the payment of the instruments, not for the supply of cash, goods, or services.[128] Cheques are outside the definition, even if the customer's name and account number are written on them, and regardless of whether they are 'open' cheques or include a printed crossing.

It is clear that credit cards fall within the ambit of section 14. They involve tripartite arrangements[129] for the supply of cash, goods, or services to the cardholder by appointed dealers, with the cardholder eventually reimbursing the card issuer. Before the implementation of the Consumer Credit Directive,[130] charge cards generally gave rise to 'exempt agreements'[131] and hence the cards were not credit tokens[132] and a credit-token agreement did not arise[133] However, as such an exemption was incompatible with the Directive, it is no longer available and therefore charge cards now fall within the ambit of section 14 and

---

[123] See Goode, n.114 above, and Guest & Lloyd, n.114 above.

[124] In relation to these cards, see further, below. In any event, as credit is not provided, there is no 'credit-token agreement', see below.

[125] Consumer Credit Act 1974, ss.14(1)(a) and 14(1)(b).

[126] [1980] 1 WLR 977. And see generally Guest & Lloyd, n.114 above, paras. 2-015 ff.

[127] It must be a 'thing'.   [128] Guest & Lloyd, n.114 above, para. 2-015.

[129] Whether 'three-party' or 'four-party', see above, Sect. 2. As there explained, in four-party transactions, the dealer reimburses his 'merchant acquirer' who reimburses the card issuer.

[130] Directive 2008/48/EC, see Ch. 2, Sect. 7(vi).

[131] See the previous version of the Consumer Credit (Exempt Agreements) Order 1989, S.I. 1989/869, art. 3(1)(a)(ii)—exempting such debtor–creditor–supplier agreements where the amount outstanding was repayable in one installment (see on exempt agreements, Ch. 2, Sect. 5(ii)).

[132] If the issuer did not otherwise carry on a 'consumer credit business', unless the requirement of carrying on a consumer credit business in s.14 is to be read narrowly as applying only *in relation to* the issue of the card.

[133] Which must be a 'regulated' (and not exempt) agreement.

give rise to credit-token agreements. Nevertheless, as will be noted below,[134] charge cards are now exempted from section 75: the 'connected lender liability' section.

Section 14 does not cover cheque guarantee cards. Here, the issuer promises to honour cheques drawn by his customer for up to a specified amount and provided certain conditions are met. The issuer does not promise to reimburse third parties who deal with the cardholder.[135] The distinction is a technical one, as the cardholder invariably acquires cash, goods, or services against the production of the card and cheque.

Cashcards normally constitute credit tokens[136] unless the bank account from which withdrawals are made cannot go into debit. Because of the two alternative 'undertakings' required by section 14 noted above, a distinction may need to be made between cards that are used to withdraw cash from the issuer's own ATMs on the one hand, and those that may be used at 'shared' ATMs as a result of mutual arrangements between various issuers of cards on the other. It will be recalled that in the two-party situation, there must be an undertaking to supply cash 'on credit'.[137] Thus, such cards will be credit tokens only if there is an agreement, or at least an understanding, that the ATM will supply cash to the customer even if the withdrawals involve an overdraft of the account. Thus if the machine is 'online' and so programmed that an overdraft cannot arise, then the card is not a credit token. On the other hand, some machines function on the basis of the balance at the close of the day preceding the transaction and so a customer may, in certain circumstances, become overdrawn although he has no agreement for an overdraft. Normally this system would give rise to an implied undertaking to supply cash on credit but it seems that this would not arise—and the card not be a credit token—if the cardholder is expressly prohibited from incurring an overdraft.[138]

More difficult questions arise in respect of cashcards used at shared ATMs. Unless the cash-dispensing bank can be regarded as acting as the agent of the issuer in dispensing the cash,[139] the situation falls within the second alternative of the definition of 'credit token' (i.e. the token is produced to a *third party*). As noted above, it is unclear whether this alternative (implicitly) requires an undertaking by the issuer to supply 'on credit'. If it does, then the situation is the same as that just discussed in relation to the two-party situation. So, if the account cannot go into overdraft, the card is not a credit token. On the other hand, if credit is not required, then all cashcards that may be used at shared ATMs are credit tokens even if the cardholder's account cannot go into overdraft. Such a distinction between two-party and three-party cards cannot be justified on any rational grounds and this reinforces the view taken above that 'credit' is implicitly required in this second situation.

Debit cards also pose problems, largely stemming from the fact that they were devised after the 1974 Act was passed and therefore how the Act applies to them is uncertain.[140]

---

[134] See Sect. (v).   [135] See Consumer Credit Act 1974, Sched. 2, Pt. 2, Example 21.

[136] And see ibid., s.14(4), under which the use of an object to operate a machine provided by the issuer or a third party is deemed the production of the object to such a person.

[137] Ibid., s.14(1)(a).

[138] Guest & Lloyd, n.114 above. See also P. Dobson, 'The Cheque Card as a Consumer Credit Agreement' [1977] *JBL* 126 where it is argued that similar prohibitions in current account agreements—where cheque guarantee cards are issued which can, in fact, cause the account to go into overdraft—preclude the agreement being a credit agreement.

[139] In which case the issuer (as principal) undertakes to issue cash through the agency of the other bank's machine, within s.14(1)(a).

[140] Goode, n.114 above, paras. 1A[3.50], 1C[25.83], 1C[25.84] takes the view that debit cards are not credit tokens, on the basis, *inter alia*, that they are merely a modern payment mechanism, equivalent to a cheque. *Sed quaere.*

As a third-party supplier provides the cardholder with goods or services and is then reimbursed by the issuer of the card by way of debit from the cardholder's account, they will be credit tokens if they fall within the second alternative of the definition.[141] The same problem, discussed above, of whether there is an implicit requirement that the issuer undertakes to provide 'on credit' arises. As noted in that discussion, although the issue is not free from doubt, it seems that if the account cannot go into overdraft then the card is not a credit token. A second difficulty arises as a result of the requirement that the issuer must carry on a 'consumer credit business'. Like debit cards, electronic purses were devised long after the passing of the 1974 Act. On a literal reading of section 14, they fall within the definition of a tripartite credit token:[142] the issuer undertakes to pay the supplier (by redeeming the digital cash transferred to him) in return for payment to him by the cardholder (through the debiting of his account when the card is loaded with digital cash).[143] But it may be argued that the cardholder 'pays' for the goods or services by digital cash (in the same way as a customer 'pays' by ordinary cash or cheque) and therefore that there is no 'payment' of the supplier for the goods or services by the issuer, merely the redemption of the digital cash. If digital cash is regarded as the modern equivalent to ordinary cash, then such an interpretation would seem appropriate. Secondly, if an undertaking to give the cardholder credit is implicitly required[144] then, in any event, electronic purses will be credit tokens only if the issuer provides credit facilities to the cardholder when issuing the digital cash.[145]

Not every agreement involving a credit token is a credit-token agreement. Under section 14(2) a 'credit-token agreement' is a regulated agreement[146] for the provision of credit in connection with the use of a credit token. Thus, even if a card is a credit token within the meaning of the Act, there is no credit-token agreement unless the card is issued under a regulated agreement for the provision of credit in connection with the credit token involved.[147] If the credit-token agreement permits the cardholder to overdraw only his current account, it need not comply with some of the formalities prescribed in Part V of the Act.[148] But not all cashcards are confined to such arrangements. If the issuing of such cards involves an agreement to provide to the cardholder other forms of credit, such as loans, then the exemption from Part V would probably be inapplicable.[149] As noted above, section 14(3) of the Act clarifies the nature of tripartite credit tokens. The issuer of such a token is deemed to provide the cardholder 'with credit drawn on whenever a third party [*viz.* dealer] supplies him with cash, goods or services'. Such an agreement is, therefore, a credit-token agreement, unless it is not a 'regulated agreement' in being an exempt agreement under section 16.[150]

The agreement leading to the issuing of a token may be within the ambit of the Act even if the card itself is not a credit token. An example is an account with a cheque card. Thus,

---

[141] Consumer Credit Act 1974, s.14(1)(b) and see n.122 and accompanying text.

[142] Within Consumer Credit Act 1974, s.14(1)(b).

[143] Nothing is said about the timing of this reimbursement.   [144] See above.

[145] Even if an electronic purse is regarded as a 'credit token' (despite no credit being provided), then there will be no 'credit-token agreement': see below. The provisions of the Act which apply only to 'credit tokens' without the need for a credit-token agreement (ss.51 (see Sect. (iii), below) & 66 (see Sect. (ii), below—concerning the unsolicited sending and the acceptance of tokens), will not cause problems as the customer will have to take steps to 'charge' his card before he can use it.

[146] For the meaning of 'regulated agreement' see the Consumer Credit Act 1974, s.8(3), & Ch. 2, Sect. 5(ii) above.

[147] See Guest & Lloyd, n.114 above, para. 2-015.

[148] Consumer Credit Act 1974, s.74; Ch. 17, Sect. 2(v) below.

[149] See Guest & Lloyd, n.114 above, para. 2-015.   [150] See Ch. 2, Sect. 5(ii) above.

the 1974 Act suggests that the contract under which a bank supplies a cheque card to its customer is a credit agreement because the cardholder can draw cheques that the bank is bound to honour at the payee's demand even if the cardholder's account is overdrawn.[151] The agreement is therefore an unrestricted-use debtor–creditor agreement within the meaning of section 13(c) of the Act.[152]

In conclusion, it has been seen that a token may be a credit token and yet not be issued under a credit-token agreement, assuming that an undertaking as to the provision of credit is always required.[153] Examples are charge cards, cashcards and debit cards that may not cause the account to go into overdraft, in all cases if the issuer otherwise carries on a consumer credit business. Here the token falls within section 14(1)(b) and yet, because there is no provision of credit under a regulated agreement,[154] no credit-token agreement arises. In such a case the provisions of the Act on credit tokens apply[155] but not those on credit-token or regulated agreements. On the other hand, the token may not be a credit token and yet it may be issued under a regulated agreement. An example is a cheque guarantee card, as discussed above. Here, as there is no credit token, there cannot be a credit-token agreement and thus neither the provisions on credit tokens nor those on credit-token agreements apply. However, if the agreement is a 'regulated agreement', the general provisions of the Act on regulated agreements will apply. Finally, the token may qualify as a credit token and, because it involves the provision of credit under a regulated agreement, there may also be a credit-token agreement. An example is the credit card and the cash or debit card that may be used to incur an overdraft. Here, as well as the provisions on regulated agreements, those relating both to credit tokens and credit-token agreements apply.

(ii) **Misuse of cards**

The general rule applicable to regulated agreements[156] is stated in section 83(1) of the Act: the debtor is not liable to the creditor for any loss arising from the use of the credit facility by an unauthorized person. The provision is wide enough to cover facilities other than 'credit tokens' as defined, although cases concerning the misuse of cheques and other instruments covered under section 4 of the Cheques Act 1957 are expressly excluded.[157]

Section 84 makes an exception to the general rule in the case of credit-token agreements.[158] It allows the issuer to include a clause,[159] which makes the cardholder liable for loss by unauthorized persons to a certain extent. Its provisions may be summarized as follows. First, the cardholder may be liable to the extent of £50 for loss arising from the

---

[151] Consumer Credit Act 1974, Sched. 2, Example 21. Dobson argues (see n.138 above—relying, *inter alia*, on the Consumer Credit Act 1974, s.188(2), which renders the examples in Sched. 2 subordinate to other provisions of the Act) that this conclusion can be avoided by the bank including an express provision prohibiting the customer from incurring an overdraft.

[152] For the meaning of these terms, see Ch. 3, Sect. 5(ii).   [153] See n.123 above.

[154] Because there is no provision of credit: see above.

[155] *Viz.*, s.51 (see Sect. (iii), below) & s.66 (see Sect. (ii), below).

[156] For the meaning of this term, see Ch. 2, Sect. 5(ii).

[157] Consumer Credit Act 1974, s.83(2); and see, as regards s.4, Ch. 15, Sects. 4 ff below.

[158] See Sect. 8(i) above.

[159] Compare the position under the PSR 2009, noted in Sect. 9(ii), below, where the position is similar but not dependent on contractual provision being made.

use of the card when the card was not in his possession.[160] Secondly, the cardholder may be made liable for *any* loss caused by the misuse of the card by a person who acquires possession of it with his consent.[161] Thirdly, the cardholder cannot be so rendered liable unless the credit-token agreement sets out details of a person or body to be contacted in the case of the loss or theft of the card.[162] Fourthly, the cardholder's liability terminates (even for the first £50) when he gives notice of the loss to the issuer.[163] The notice may be given orally or in writing and takes effect when received; but the agreement may require an oral notice to be confirmed in writing. In such a case the cardholder has to write within seven days.[164] Fifthly, any sum paid by the cardholder for the issuing of the card is to be treated as paid towards his liability for loss, unless it has previously been set off against amounts due for the use of the token.[165] Where more than one token is issued under one agreement, the applicable provisions apply to each token separately.[166]

The cardholder's liability under section 84 is confined to cases in which the agreement between the parties includes appropriate clauses. If the agreement is silent, the position is governed by the general principle of section 83, which frees the cardholder from liability for loss in cases of misuse. But section 83 is subject to one important limitation. It applies only to the unauthorized use of the credit facility. It has, accordingly, been argued that if 'the debtor maintains an account with the creditor and there is a credit balance on the account in favour of the debtor, nothing in section 83 would prevent the debtor being made liable to the creditor for any loss arising from unauthorised withdrawals of that credit balance'.[167] The words 'credit facility', however, are not defined. It is arguable that an account that may be overdrawn by the use of a credit token constitutes a credit facility even where, at a given moment, it is in funds. It seems disturbing that a 'facility' may be governed by the Act at one time but outside its operation a few minutes thereafter. Indeed, occasionally, it may be difficult to determine with certainty whether, at a given moment, an account is overdrawn or in credit.[168] The theoretical importance of this problem in respect of cashcards issued by banks is obvious, although in practice, the standard form agreements of banks are not onerous and generally imposes a limit of £50 in the event of the misuse of a card before notification of its loss.

As a result of the implementation of the first EU 'distance marketing' Directive,[169] section 84 does not apply[170] when a credit token is used to effect certain[171] distance contracts, such as contracts concluded over the internet, e-mail, or telephone. As noted below,[172] such contracts, if made through 'fraudulent use' of a 'payment card' are cancellable, with the cardholder being entitled to have his account re-credited. To give full effect to this protection, section 84 does not apply to enable the creditor to impose any liability

---

[160] Consumer Credit Act 1974, s.84(1), as modified by the Consumer Credit (Further Increase of Monetary Amounts) Order 1983, S.I. 1983/1571 (replaced, with no change, by S.I. 1998/997).

[161] Ibid., s.84(2). See s.84(7).

[162] Ibid., s.84(3)–(4); and see for the relevant details the Consumer Credit (Credit-Token Agreements) Regulations 1983, S.I. 1983/1555.

[163] Consumer Credit Act 1974, s.84(3).   [164] Ibid., s.84(5).   [165] Ibid., s.84(6).

[166] Ibid., s.84(8). Note that under the Consumer Credit (Agreements) Regulations 1983, S.I. 1983/1553, Sched. 2, Pt. 1, Form 15 (but not under the Consumer Credit (Agreements) Regulations 2010, S.I. 2010/1014) the consumer has to be informed of the position in cases of loss or misuse.

[167] Guest & Lloyd, n.114 above, para. 2-084. Goode, n.114 above, para. 1C[39.9] agrees and says common law principles will determine liability.

[168] As cheques may have been in the clearing process at the relevant time.   [169] See Sect. 10 below.

[170] See s.84(3A)–(3C) and added by the Consumer Protection (Distance Selling) Regulations 2001, S.I. 2001/2334.

[171] Certain 'excepted contracts' are excluded.   [172] See Sect. 10.

on a debtor when he uses a credit token to make such a distance contract. Hence in such circumstances the general principle in section 83 will apply.[173]

There is one further limitation on the liability of the cardholder under a credit-token agreement governed by the Act. Under section 66, the cardholder can be made liable for loss resulting from the use of the token only where he has previously 'accepted' it. Acceptance takes place when the token or a receipt for it is signed by the cardholder, or by a person authorized by him, or when the token is validly used for the first time.[174] The onus of proving both the receipt and the acceptance of the card rests on the creditor.[175] Where the creditor does not have a receipt signed by the cardholder in person, it is of course difficult for him to prove delivery. It is thought that even a valid receipt given for a parcel containing the card is inadequate, as it fails to signify the acceptance of the card itself.[176] Where the Act (or the PSR 2009[177]) is inapplicable, the cardholder's liability for loss occasioned by the misuse of the card is governed by the terms of his agreement with the issuer and by the common law principles discussed earlier on.

(iii) **Unsolicited credit tokens and credit card cheques**

The Act forbids the 'giving'[178] of unsolicited credit tokens.[179] Hence the unsolicited dispatch or delivery of such a token constitutes an offence. The object of the prohibition is to preclude consumers being tempted to incur debts beyond their means by the provision of easily available finance. But the prohibition on the supply of unsolicited credit tokens does not apply in two cases. First, the issuer may send an unsolicited credit token under a credit-token agreement already made. Secondly, the provision is inapplicable in respect of replacement tokens under credit-token agreements, even if the agreement under which they are sent is varied.[180]

Unless these exceptions apply, creditors must be sure to have received a request for the card before they give it. The cardholder's request for a credit token must usually be expressed in a document signed by him.[181] It is noteworthy that the Act does not free the cardholder from the duty to reimburse where he has used an unsolicited credit token. Such a provision would have been a more effective deterrent for breaches of the provision.[182]

In the wake of disquiet about credit cardholders overcommitting themselves by the use of 'cheques' enabling them to draw on credit card accounts, the Financial Services Act 2010 added a new prohibition with a criminal sanction: the provision of unsolicited credit card cheques.[183] These are defined as cheques (not necessarily drawn on a banker)

---

[173] Indeed, if s.83 applies (as it does as a result of the disapplication of s.84), then the 'distance contract' protections in the regulations (which are slightly narrower in expressly requiring the 'fraudulent use' of the card) are stated not to apply: S.I. 2001/2334, reg. 21(4). See further, Sect. 10.

[174] Consumer Credit Act 1974, s.66(2).   [175] Ibid., s.177(4)(*a*).

[176] Goode, n.114 above, para. 1C[39.6].   [177] See Sect. 9.

[178] Defined in s.189(1) as 'deliver or send by post to'.

[179] Consumer Credit Act 1974, s.51(1). Note that this applies even to a provisional token: *Elliott* v. *Director General of Fair Trading* [1980] 1 WLR 977, discussed in Sect. (i) above.

[180] Ibid., s.51(3). Note that these two exceptions apply only to credit tokens issued under 'credit-token agreements', see Sect. 8(i) above. For difficulties raised by these provisions, see Guest & Lloyd, n.114 above, para. 2-052.

[181] Ibid., s.51(2). But note that exceptions apply where the credit-token agreement is a 'small, debtor–creditor–supplier' agreement.

[182] See the similar provision in the PSR 2009, reg. 59(1)(b), considered in Sect. 9(ii), below and the different sanction for breach.

[183] Ss.51A–B, added by s.15 of the 2010 Act.

that result in the provision of credit under a credit-token agreement.[184] This time the 'request', although it can only cover a batch of up to three cheques, does not need to be in a written, signed document and the prohibition does not apply to 'business' credit-token agreements.[185]

(iv) The credit-token agreement

The credit-token agreement, made between the issuer and the cardholder, is necessarily a regulated consumer credit agreement.[186] Hence the creditor must comply with the pre-contracting information obligations, the form of agreement requirements and the copy requirements.[187] If the issuer fails to comply with these requirements, the agreement is not properly executed.[188] Further, the issuer must supply a copy of the credit agreement and of documents mentioned in it when he furnishes to the cardholder a replacement credit token.[189] If the issuer fails to comply with this requirement he is not entitled, during the period of default, to enforce the agreement.[190]

Details of the debtor's right to withdraw from the agreement within 14 days[191] and how it is to be exercised, need to be given in the agreement itself. For agreements where this right is not available[192] and where the agreement is 'cancellable',[193] another document that has to be supplied by the issuer to the cardholder is a notice that sets out the cardholder's right to cancel the agreement.[194] This document must be supplied within the time-limit applicable for the dispatch of the copy of the agreement and, in practice, is furnished together with it.[195] There are detailed provisions that govern the consequences of withdrawal[196] or cancellation.[197]

(v) Nexus with underlying transaction

In a credit card transaction, there is a connection between the agreement between the issuer and cardholder and the acquisition of the goods or services from the dealer or supplier. This stems from the fact that the cardholder is able to use his card only when the issuer has entered into contracts with the 'appointed dealers', who have either been recruited by the issuer (in the case of 'three-party' transactions) or by a 'merchant acquirer' (in the case

---

[184] S.51A(7). Hence it seems that the term covers any bill of exchange payable on demand. Subs.(8) confirms that the term does not include a cheque to be used *only* in connection with a current account.

[185] S.51B. Of course, 'business' agreements for credit above £25,000 are exempt (and hence do not give rise to credit-token agreements): see s.16B, Ch. 2, Sect. 5(ii).

[186] See ibid., s14(2) & Sect. 8(i) above.

[187] See Ch. 2, Sect. 5(iv). These requirements vary depending on whether the agreement is covered by the regime derived from the Consumer Credit Directive (as will usually be the case) or by the previous, non-Directive regime.

[188] Ibid., ss.55(2); 61(1); s.61A(5), 62(3), 63(5). For the consequences, see s.65 (court order required for enforcement) & Ch. 2, Sect. 5(xiii).

[189] Ibid., s.85(1). See s.171(4)(a): in proceedings by creditor, onus of proof on creditor that credit token 'lawfully supplied' i.e. that supplied with copy of the agreement.

[190] Ibid., s.85(2)(a). Originally, the issuer also committed an offence but the relevant provision (s.85(2)(b)) was repealed by the Consumer Protection from Unfair Trading Regulations 2008, S.I. 2008/1277.

[191] S.66A, see Ch. 2, Sect. 5(iv).

[192] Essentially, agreements where credit over £60,620 is provided where the creditor has not opted into the 'Directive' regime: see Ch. 2, Sect. 5(iv).

[193] See below and Ch. 2, Sect. 5(iv) above.   [194] Consumer Credit Act 1974, s.64(1).

[195] Ibid., s.64(2).   [196] Under s.66A, see s.66A.   [197] Under s.69, see ss.70–73.

of 'four-party' transactions). After some doubts in relation to four-party transactions,[198] it is now clear that a credit card transaction is a 'debtor–creditor–supplier' agreement.[199] In such a case, the Consumer Credit Act 1974, section 75 provides that if the cardholder (debtor) has a claim based on a misrepresentation[200] or on breach of contract against the dealer (supplier), he has 'a like claim' against the issuer (creditor).[201] These two parties may be sued by the cardholder jointly and severally, although the dealer will have to indemnify the issuer.[202] The cardholder has this claim even if, in entering into an agreement with the dealer, he has exceeded a credit limit set by the issuer.[203]

With the increased use of credit cards abroad, the question arises whether this (joint and several) liability of credit card issuers for misrepresentations or breaches of contract by the supplier extends beyond purely domestic situations. In *Office of Fair Trading* v. *Lloyds TSB Bank plc*[204] the House of Lords held that the liability does apply in relation to domestically issued cards financing transactions with a foreign supplier,[205] although they left open the difficult questions of the applicability of section 75 if the credit card agreement (as opposed to the underlying supply contract) had foreign connections.[206] Section 75 applies only to 'regulated agreements'.[207] It will be recalled that previously charge-card agreements were generally not regulated.[208] Moreover these provisions apply only to 'debtor–creditor–supplier' agreements, that is, agreements where there are 'arrangements'[209] between the issuer and the dealer. Transactions involving cheque cards are not debtor–creditor–supplier agreements, as the bank's 'guarantee' in the card is directed to the world at large. The cardholder, thus, is not bound to seek out an 'appointed dealer'. Similarly, cashcards are not issued under debtor–creditor–supplier agreements as the cash obtained is available for use with any dealer. On the other hand, debit card agreements, which enable the use of the card at designated dealers only, were arguably debtor–creditor–supplier agreements on the basis that the arrangements between the dealers and the issuer for the transfer of funds constitute pre-existing arrangements between them. However under the Banking Act 1987, debit card issuers gained an exemption from

---

[198] The issue was resolved in *OFT v Lloyds TSB Bank plc* [2007] QB 1 (no appeal, on this point, when the case went to the House of Lords). It primarily turned on whether there are 'arrangements' (as defined in CCA 1974, s.187) between the issuer and the dealer, given the lack of direct contractual nexus in a four-party case. For unresolved difficulties, see C. Hare, 'Credit cards and connected lender liability' [2008] *LMCLQ* 338. See also *The Governor and Company of The Bank of Scotland v Alfred Truman* [2005] EWHC 583 (QB) (five parties involved; s.75 applied).

[199] Ibid., s.12(*b*)–12(*c*). See Guest & Lloyd, n.114 above, para. 2-013.

[200] As well as the liability under s.75 at issue, it should also be noted that s.56(1)(c), (2), provides that negotiations by the supplier (but only 'in relation to' the supply contract) with the debtor are deemed conducted by him as agent of the creditor. The card issuer may therefore also be liable for any misrepresentations made by the supplier under this provision.

[201] See Ch. 3, Sect. 5(xii), above. But note that agreements for the acquisition of items for a price of less than £100 or of more than £30,000 are excluded, as, indeed, are 'non-commercial agreements' (which, under s.189(1), are defined as those made by the non-consumer party outside the scope of his business): s.75(3) and see Guest & Lloyd, n.114 above, para. 2-076.

[202] Ibid., s.75(2).   [203] Ibid., s.75(4).   [204] [2008] 1 AC 316.

[205] Although the statutory indemnity provision in s.75(2) does not apply in relation to a foreign supplier—but the creditor may negotiate a contractual indemnity under the terms of the merchant or (in the case of four-party cases) related agreements or may have a restitutionary indemnity claim.

[206] For a discussion of the possibilities, see Hare, n.198 above.

[207] For the meaning of this term, see Ch. 2, Sect. 5(ii), above.

[208] They were exempt if the card may be used only to acquire goods or services: see Sect. 8(i), n.131 above. But they are now just exempted from s. 75: see s. 75(3)(c).

[209] See Consumer Credit Act 1974, s.12(b) and s.187 (definition of 'arrangements').

these provisions in that arrangements for the electronic transfer of funds from a current account at a bank are deemed not to be relevant 'arrangements'.[210] The close connection between the two contracts in a credit card transaction leads to a further result. The supply of the goods or services is a transaction 'linked' with the regulated credit agreement.[211] It is therefore 'automatically rescinded if the debtor [cardholder] exercises a right to withdraw from or cancel the credit card agreement, and may be affected by various other events vitiating that agreement'.[212]

9 The provisions of the Payment Services Regulations 2009

(i) Cards affected: 'payment instrument' and 'payment services' contract

The PSR 2009[213] are of relevance to payment cards in that most cards considered in this chapter fall within the definition in those Regulations of a 'payment instrument' issued under a 'payment services' contract. Hence such cards are subject to the consumer protection provisions in those Regulations concerning information provision[214] and the rights and liabilities of the parties.[215] Contracting-out of most of these protections[216] is permitted, unless the 'payment services user' is a 'consumer', a 'micro-enterprise' or a 'charity', terms that are all defined in the Regulations.[217]

The PSR 2009[218] define 'payment instrument' widely as, broadly speaking, any personalized device or set of procedures used to initiate a payment transaction by a payment service provider.[219] This covers all payment cards discussed in this chapter apart from cheque guarantee cards.[220] There is an exclusion for store cards issued by a retailer for use in his store and for electronic purses that can only be used in a limited number of outlets.[221] In addition, the contract under which those 'payment instrument' cards are issued

---

[210] See ibid., s.187(3A), inserted by the Banking Act 1987, s.89. The 'bank' must be such within the meaning of the Bankers' Books Evidence Act 1879 (see Ch. 3, Sect. 2(iii) above). The argument that the use of paper vouchers (as a preliminary to the electronic funds transfer) precludes the EFTPOS exemption applying is, it seems, erroneous: see Guest & Lloyd, n.114 above, para. 2-188.

[211] Within the meaning of s.19(1)(*b*) of the Consumer Credit Act 1974. See Ch. 2, Sect. 5(xii), above.

[212] Goode, n.114 above, paras. 1C[43.01] ff. See also Guest & Lloyd, n.114 above, para. 2-020. The provisions in the Act concerning 'linked transactions' are ss.57(1), 69(1)(i).

[213] S.I. 2009/209, in force on 1 November 2009. See the more detailed discussion in Ch. 13, Sect. 5.

[214] Ibid., Pt. 5.   [215] Ibid., Pt. 6.

[216] Contracting-out is permitted in relation to all of Pt. 5 (information provisions) but some provisions in Pt. 6 are mandatory (see esp. regs. 56 (limits on use of cards), 57 (obligations of cardholder), 58 (obligations of card issuer), 59 (notification of errors), 61 (liability of issuer)).

[217] PSR 2009, reg. 2(1). A 'consumer' is 'an individual...acting for purposes other that a trade, business or profession'.

[218] Reg. 2(1).

[219] The definition of 'payment instrument' refers to initiating a 'payment order', which is in turn defined as an instruction to a 'payment service provider' requesting the execution of a 'payment instruction', defined as an act of placing, transferring, or withdrawing funds.

[220] Moreover, paper cheque-based transfers are not 'payment services' (see PSR 2009, reg. 2(1), Sched. 1, Pt. 2, para. 2(g) and FSA Handbook, PERG 15, para. 15.1).

[221] See PSR 2009, Sched. 2, para. 2(k) which excludes 'services based on instruments than can be used to acquire goods or services only (i) in or on the issuer's premises; or (ii) under a commercial agreement with the issuer, either within a limited network of service providers or for a limited range of goods or services'. It is clear that 'limited' is to be interpreted narrowly so as not to catch ordinary credit, charge, debit,

falls within the definition of a 'framework' 'payment services' contract.[222] Finally, the cardholder falls within the definition of 'payment service user'[223] whilst the card issuer is the 'payment services provider'.[224]

It is important to note that, for payment cards issued under 'regulated agreements' within the meaning of the Consumer Credit Act 1974, the PSR 2009 consumer protection provisions are generally excluded in so far as (but only in so far as) they would otherwise duplicate the provisions of the 1974 Act.[225] So where the PSR 2009 impose obligations over and above those in the 1974 Act, then these obligations are also imposed in relation to Consumer Credit Act 1974 'regulated agreements'.[226] In addition, the PSR provisions are significantly modified in relation to certain 'low-value payment instruments', that is cards that can be used only to execute individual payment transactions of 60 euro or less,[227] or have a spending limit of 300 euros or less[228] or (in the case of electronic purses) that store funds that do not exceed 500 euros.[229] Broadly speaking, only minimal information need be provided[230] and contracting-out of some of the provisions is permitted.[231]

For ease of comparison, the same issues as those considered in relation to the application of the Consumer Credit Act 1974 to payment cards[232] will be discussed in this section, in so far as corresponding provision is made in the PSR 2009. The PSR 2009 are considered in greater detail elsewhere,[233] but it is useful to provide a general outline of the relevant PSR 2009 provisions. Part 5 of the Regulations imposes a number of 'information' obligations[234] in relation to payment services provided under a 'framework contract' and so is applicable to the contract between the cardholder and the card issuer and will be noted further below.[235] Part 6 of the Regulations regulates the rights and obligations of the parties and hence the legal relationship between the cardholder and the issuer. For example, there are elaborate, general provisions concerning the imposition of charges,[236] consent, and withdrawal of consent by the cardholder to a payment transaction,[237]

---

cashcards, and electronic purses. See the guidance on the PSR 2009, issued by the FSA in the PERG15 part of its Handbook, paras. 40 & 41.

[222] See the definitions of 'payment services' and 'framework contract' in PSR 2009, reg. 2(1).

[223] And the definition of 'payer'—a term used in the 'liability' regs. 60–62, considered in Sect. 9(ii) below.

[224] PSR 2009, reg. 2(1).   [225] PSR 2009, regs. 34 and 52.

[226] Thus some 'extra' information requirements are imposed (see reg. 38(b) and (c)) as are some consumer protection obligations (see especially reg. 54 (charges), 55 (consent and withdrawal of consent), 57 (obligations of cardholder), 58 (apart from 58(1)(c)—obligations of card issuer) and 60 (evidence)).

[227] If the payment transaction is executed wholly in the UK, otherwise the limit is 30 euros.

[228] If the payment transaction is executed wholly in the UK, otherwise the limit is 150 euros.

[229] PSR 2009, regs. 35 and 53. See the special provisions made for liability for misuse in relation to electronic purses by reg. 53(3).

[230] Ibid., reg. 35(2)(a).

[231] Ibid., reg. 35(2)(b), (c) and reg. 53(2). Note also reg. 53(3) (electronic money).

[232] See Sect. 8, above.   [233] See Ch. 13, Sect. 5. See also Ch. 2, Sect. 6(iii).

[234] Such statutorily required information must be provided free of charge: PSR 2009, reg. 48(1).

[235] See Sect. 9(iv). For the detail, see Ch. 13, Sect. 5(iv)(d).

[236] PSR 2009, reg. 54. This applies to both CCA regulated agreements and 'low value payment instruments'. But see reg. 51(3)(a) (contracting out).

[237] PSR 2009, reg. 55, considered in detail in Ch. 13, Sect. 5(iv)(c). This also applies to both CCA regulated agreements and 'low value payment instruments'. But see reg. 51(3)(a) (contracting out). Reg. 61 requires the card issuer to refund unauthorized transactions, but this does not apply to CCA regulated agreements, which have their own provisions (ss.83 and 84), see Sect. 9(ii) below.

incorrectly executed payment transactions,[238] unauthorized payment transactions,[239] and the execution of payment transactions.[240]

Of particular relevance to payment cards covered by the PSR 2009 are the special provisions concerning 'payment instruments'. First, the right of the card issuer to place cards on a 'stop' list is regulated, with the cardholder generally[241] being entitled to be given reasons and to have the stop removed as soon as practicable after the reasons for the stop cease to exist.[242] Secondly, there are detailed provisions concerning the misuse and the unsolicited sending of cards, which will now be considered in turn.

(ii) Misuse of cards

The PSR 2009 provide a comprehensive liability framework in relation to the misuse of those payment cards within their scope.[243] First, express obligations are imposed on the cardholder both to 'take all reasonable steps' to keep his personalized security features (for example, his PIN) safe[244] and to notify the issuer 'in the agreed manner and without undue delay' once he becomes aware of the loss, theft, misappropriation, or unauthorized use of the card.[245] These obligations apply even in relation to credit tokens covered by the Consumer Credit Act 1974.[246] Except in the case of agreements that are regulated by the Consumer Credit Act 1974 (which has other detailed provisions concerning credit token misuse[247]), failure to comply with these obligations 'with intent or gross negligence' renders the cardholder liable for all losses incurred in respect of an authorized transaction.[248] Corresponding obligations are imposed on the card issuer to ensure that 'appropriate means are available at all times' to so notify of possible misuse[249] and to prevent any use once notification has been made.[250] The card issuer is also obliged to ensure that personalized security features 'are not accessible' to persons other than the cardholder[251] and the issuer bears the risk of sending the card or any personalized security features.[252] If the cardholder disputes a transaction, the onus is on the card issuer to prove that the transaction was 'authenticated',[253] accurately recorded, and 'not affected by a technical breakdown or some other deficiency'.[254] And the mere use of the card as recorded by the

---

[238] PSR 2009, reg. 59. This is disapplied in relation to CCA regulated agreements (in the light of CCA, ss.66, 83, and 84), but it applies to 'low value payment instruments'. Contracting out is generally (but see reg. 51(3)(b)) not permitted.

[239] PSR 2009, regs. 60–64, considered further under Sect. 9(ii) below.

[240] PSR 2009, regs. 65–79, applicable also to both CCA regulated agreements and 'low value payment instruments'. But see reg. 51(3)(a) (contracting out permitted to some extent).

[241] Unless this would 'compromise reasonable security measures or is otherwise unlawful': PSR 2009, reg. 56(5).

[242] PSR 2009, reg. 56(3)–(6). These 'stopping' provisions do not apply to CCA regulated agreements, to which the corresponding CCA provisions apply (ss.76 and 87). But they do apply to 'low value payment instruments' and cannot be contracted out of (reg. 51(3)).

[243] Other than cheque cards, which are not 'payment instruments' within the PSR 2009, see Sect. 9(i), above.

[244] PSR 2009, reg. 57(2).   [245] PSR 2009, reg. 57(1).

[246] Moreover, contracting-out (in the case of non-consumers) is not permitted (see reg. 51(3)) but as regards 'low value instruments', contracting out of the second obligation (in reg. 57(1)(b)) is permitted.

[247] See Sect. 8(ii) above.   [248] PSR 2009, reg. 62(2), see below.

[249] Ibid., reg. 58(1)(c), and, on request, to provide the cardholder with the means to prove that such notification was made (reg. 58(1)(d)).

[250] Ibid., reg. 58(1)(e).   [251] Ibid., reg. 58(1)(a).   [252] Ibid., reg. 58(2).

[253] Defined to mean the use of any procedure to verify the use of the card, including its personalized security features: reg. 60(2).

[254] PSR 2009, reg. 60(1).

card issuer 'is not in itself necessarily sufficient' to prove either that the transaction was authorized by the payor or that the payor acted fraudulently or failed with intent or gross negligence to comply with his notification obligation[255] so as to make him liable to an unlimited extent.[256] Again, all these card issuer obligations also apply in relation to regulated agreements covered by the Consumer Credit Act 1974.[257]

The PSR liability provisions for misuse of the card are similar, but by no means identical, to those applicable to credit tokens issued under credit-token agreements in the Consumer Credit Act 1974.[258] To avoid duplication, the 1974 Act provisions applies 'in place of' those in the PSR 2009 to cards is issued under an agreement regulated by that Act.[259] As will be seen, the overall result under both liability regimes is similar but there are significant differences in the detail. First, there is a general provision in the PSR 2009[260] requiring the issuer immediately to refund transactions that are 'not authorized' in accordance with the PSR 2009 provision as to the giving (and withdrawal) of consent to payment transactions by the cardholder.[261] This corresponds to the general provision in section 83 of the 1974 Act[262] but there are clear differences in that section 83 only applies to the use of a credit facility[263] and says nothing about *immediate* refunds.

Second, as is the case under the 1974 Act, the PSR 2009 provide derogations from this general principle so as to impose a degree of liability on the cardholder. However, these PSR derogations apply as a matter of law and so, unlike the position under the 1974 Act, do not need to be contractually imposed. Moreover, although they are similar in effect to those under the 1974 Act, there are differences in the detail. Thus the cardholder is generally liable up to a maximum of £50 for loss arising from the use of a lost, stolen or misappropriated[264] card.[265] However, the cardholder is liable for *all* loss in two cases. The first case is where he has acted 'fraudulently', a term that is not defined but that clearly connotes knowing that misuse is occurring. The second case is where the cardholder has 'with intent or gross negligence' failed to comply with his obligations[266] to 'take all reasonable steps' to keep his personalized security features safe and to notify the issuer 'in the agreed manner and without undue delay' once he becomes aware of the possible misuse of the card.[267] Where the issuer has not complied with his obligation to ensure that 'appropriate means are available at all times' to so notify of possible misuse,[268] then, unless the cardholder has acted fraudulently, he is not liable for any loss (not even for the first £50).[269] And again, unless the cardholder has acted fraudulently, his liability terminates (even for the first £50) when he gives the issuer notice 'in the agreed manner'[270] of possible misuse.

---

[255] i.e. his obligation to notify on becoming aware of possible misuse imposed by reg. 57(1)(b), see above.

[256] Under PSR 2009, reg. 62(2), see below.

[257] Moreover, contracting-out (in the case of non-consumers) is not permitted in relation to obligations in reg. 58 (although it is allowed for those in reg. 60) and, as regards 'low value instruments', some contracting out is permitted. See PSR 2009, reg. 51(3) and reg. 53(2), respectively.

[258] See Sect. 8(ii) above.   [259] PSR 2009, reg. 52.   [260] PSR 2009. reg. 61.

[261] See PSR 2009, reg. 55, noted in Sect. 9(i) above.   [262] See Sect. 8(ii) above.

[263] This supports the argument suggested at Sect. 8(ii) that 'credit facility' should be interrupted broadly at least to cover an account (whatever its existing state) that may provide credit.

[264] 'where the [cardholder] has failed to keep the personalized security features safe'.

[265] PSR 2009, reg. 62(1). The corresponding provision in the 1974 Act refers to the card not being in the cardholder's 'possession'.

[266] Under PSR 2009, reg. 57, see above.

[267] PSR 2009, reg. 62(2). The corresponding provision in the 1974 Act refers to losses caused by misuse of the card by a person who acquires possession with the cardholder's consent.

[268] Imposed by PSR 2009, reg. 58(1)(c), see n.249 above.   [269] PSR 2009, reg. 62(3)(b).

[270] 'under' PSR 2009, reg. 57(1)(b) which refers to notice 'in the agreed manner and without due delay'.

There is no provision in the PSR 2009 that corresponds directly with section 66 of the 1974 Act, which only imposes liability on a cardholder once he has 'accepted' the card.[271] The PSR 2009 state[272] that the provisions as to misuse considered above[273] apply in place of section 66 when it comes to payment cards not issued under agreements regulated by the 1974 Act. However, other PSR provisions that are not disapplied in relation to agreements regulated by the 1974 Act will also be relevant in the case of a card that has not reached the cardholder. Thus, it will be recalled, the PSR 2009 state that the issuer is to bear the risk of sending the card or any personalized security features[274] and the burden is on him to prove that the transaction was 'authenticated'.[275]

(iii) Unsolicited payment cards

There is a similar prohibition to section 51 of the Consumer Credit Act 1974[276] in the PSR 2009: they forbid the sending of an unsolicited 'payment instrument'[277] except by way of replacement of one already issued.[278] Again, to avoid duplication, this prohibition is disapplied in the case of agreements regulated by the 1974 Act, which will therefore continue to be subject to the 1974 provision. However, the terms of the disapplication[279] refer to 'contracts...which are regulated agreements' and thus (in terms) do not apply if such an agreement is not in place. It follows that the PSR 2009 provision is *not* disapplied in relation to unsolicited credit tokens that are sent *before* any regulated credit agreement is made with the cardholder[280] and hence both the prohibitions in the 1974 Act and the PSR 2009 apply in such a case.

A comparison of the two provisions reveals that not only is the PSR 2009 provision less elaborate than section 51 of the 1974 Act, but the sanctions for breach of the respective provisions differ. Both may give rise to regulatory sanctions, although it is the FSA that is the regulator (with the corresponding disciplinary powers under the PSR 2009[281]) for the purposes of breach of the PSR 2009 whilst it is the Office of Fair Trading that is the regulator (with the slightly different powers under the 1974 Act[282]) for the purposes of breach of section 51. In addition, whilst breach of section 51 is a criminal offence, breach of the PSR 2009 provision is actionable as a breach of statutory duty by a private person suffering loss.[283] It remains to be seen if a court will take the view that a cardholder receiving and using an unsolicited card will be able to resist liability for his spending in reliance on such a claim or whether the decision to use the card will be regarded as breaking the chain of causation.

(iv) The card agreement

As card agreements are 'framework contracts' for the purposes of the PSR 2009, the relevant 'information' provisions in Part 5 of those regulations will apply. However, again

---

[271] See Sect. 8(ii), above.   [272] PSR, reg. 52(b).   [273] i.e. PSR 2009, regs. 59, 61, and 62.

[274] PSR 2009, reg. 58(2).

[275] PSR 2009, reg. 60(1), 'authenticated' being defined to mean the use of any procedure to verify the use of the card, including its personalized security features: reg. 60(2).

[276] See Sect. 8(iii), above: criminal offence to send unsolicited 'credit tokens'.

[277] See Sect. 9(i) above.   [278] PSR 2009, reg. 58(1)(b).   [279] PSR 2009, reg. 52.

[280] Moreover, on one interpretation of CCA, s.14(1)(b), there can be a 'credit token' issued under an agreement that is not a regulated 'credit-token agreement', see Sect. 8(ii). In such a case also, the PSR 2009 are not (in terms) disapplied.

[281] As to which, see Ch. 2, Sect. 6(iii).   [282] As to which, see Ch. 2, Sect. 5(iii).

[283] PSR 2009, reg. 120(1)(b).

to avoid duplication, these PSR provisions are generally excluded in relation to agreements that are 'regulated agreements' under the Consumer Credit Act 1974.[284] But the exclusion is not total and there are a few 'extra' items of information that are required under the Regulations, which must also be given in the case of regulated agreements.[285]

In outline, the PSR 2009 'information' requirements are as follows. First, pre-contracting information (which may take the form of the draft contract) must usually be provided 'in good time' to the cardholder before he is bound by the contract.[286] Second, the cardholder is given the right, during the contract and free of charge,[287] to obtain certain information and the terms of the contract.[288] Third, there are elaborate provisions concerning the notification of variations in the contractual information and terms.[289] Finally, there are provisions concerning information to be provided in relation to each payment transaction[290] and provisions governing the termination of the contract by either party.[291]

The two regimes—that under the 1974 Act and that under the PSR 2009—differ significantly. In general, the 1974 Act (and the regulations made thereunder) imposes very detailed 'information' requirements whereas the PSR 2009 merely list what needs to be disclosed without prescribing form and detailed content. Moreover, as discussed above in relation to unsolicited cards,[292] the sanctions for breach are again different. This time, agreements not complying with the 1974 Act (and the regulations made thereunder) are generally unenforceable whilst the cardholder relying on a breach of the PSR 2009 has a breach of statutory duty action. The 1974 Act gives the court a discretion whether to enforce the agreement[293] whereas, if the PSR 2009 have not been complied with, the cardholder will have to raise his breach of statutory duty claim and establish loss in order to resist liability.

10 Distance marketing

So-called 'distance contracting' is subject to special consumer protection measures, largely as a result of two EU Directives, the first extending to 'distance contracts' other than those for 'financial services'[294] and the second extending to distance contracts for

---

[284] PSR 2009, reg. 34.

[285] In particular: (i) information as to interest and currency exchange rates: reg. 34(b) and (c) and (ii) information prior to individual transactions, if requested.

[286] PSR 2009, reg. 40 (the requisite information is set out in Sched. 4)—unless this cannot be done in the case of a 'distance' contract concluded at the user's request, in which case it must be provided immediately after the contract is made. See also reg. 47 (communication of information). Reg. 40 does not generally apply to CCA regulated agreements (which have their own requirements as to pre-contract information (see Ch. 2, Sect. 5(iv)), but information as to details of interest and exchange rates must be applied (reg. 38(b)).

[287] PSR 2009, reg. 48(1).

[288] Ibid., reg. 41(the requisite information is set out in Sched. 4). Further information may be charged for, at cost: reg. 48(2). See also reg. 47 (communication of information). Reg. 41 does not apply to CCA regulated agreements (reg. 34(a)), which have their own as to information requirements (see Ch. 2, Sect. 5(iv)).

[289] PSR 2009, reg. 42. Reg. 42 does not apply to CCA regulated agreements (reg. 34(a)) which have their own provisions as to variation (CCA, s.82). See further, Ch. 13, Sect. 5(iv)(b).

[290] PSR 2009, regs. 44–46. These apply, to some extent, to CCA regulated agreements (see reg. 34(c)). See also reg. 47 (communication of information).

[291] PSR 2009, reg. 43. Reg. 43 does not apply to CCA regulated agreements (reg. 34(a)) which have their own provisions as to termination (CCA, s.87, 98)).

[292] Sect. 9(iii).   [293] See Ch. 2, Sect. 5(xiii).

[294] Directive 97/7/EC, implemented by the Consumer Protection (Distance Selling) Regulations 2001, S.I. 2001/2334.

'financial services'.[295] Originally, both Directives accorded protections to consumers where their 'payment cards' were used 'fraudulently' by another[296] to make a payment in connection with a distance contract. However, the protection in relation to 'financial services' distance contracts has been repealed and replaced by the more general provisions in the Payment Services Directive.[297]

In relation to distance contracts other than those for financial services, the consumer is entitled to cancel the payment and to have all sums paid, re-credited or returned by the card issuer.[298] The scope of the protection should be noted. First, it only applies to the use of cards in relation to a 'distance contract', a term that covers a contract made in the context of an 'organized distance sales or service-provision scheme' operated by the supplier where there has been no face-to-face contact between the supplier and consumer up to and including the time of the conclusion of the contract.[299] Thus contracts made exclusively over the internet or by E-mail or by telephone, as a result of an organized marketing campaign, are the only ones covered. Secondly, only 'consumers' are protected, a term that excludes persons acting in their trade, business, or profession.[300] Thirdly, the protection only applies to the use of a 'payment card', a term which is stated to include 'a credit card, a charge card, a debit card and a store card'[301] and which therefore presumably excludes an 'electronic purse' (or 'digital cashcard').

It will be recalled that the Consumer Credit Act 1974 also contains a provision covering the misuse of credit tokens,[302] enabling the card issuer to impose a degree of liability on the cardholder.[303] In the light of the 'distance marketing' protection for distance contracts other than those for financial services, this provision is inapplicable in the case of the use of credit tokens when making such distance contracts.[304] Therefore the general provision in Consumer Credit Act 1974, section 83, which renders a debtor under an agreement regulated by that Act not liable for loss arising from the use of the credit facility by another, becomes operative.[305] If section 83 is applicable, then the distance marketing protection for fraudulent use of the card is stated not to apply.[306] Presumably it was felt that section 83 already provided sufficient protection; indeed it is, in terms, wider in not requiring the fraudulent use of the card—although in practice most unauthorized uses of a payment card are likely to be regarded as 'fraudulent'.[307] Where a situation falls outside section 83—for example, the payment card is not issued under a 'regulated agreement',[308] then the distance marketing provisions will apply to enable the cardholder to obtain reimbursement from the card issuer.

---

[295] Directive 2002/65/EC (as amended by the Payment Services Directive, Directive 2007/64/EC), implemented by the Financial Services (Distance Marketing) Regulations 2004, S.I. 2004/2095. See also Ch. 2, Sect. 5(vi).

[296] 'not acting, or to be treated as acting, as [the consumer's] agent'.

[297] Directive 2007/64/EC. See Ch. 2, Sect. 6(iii), implemented by the PSR 2009, see Sect. 9(ii) above.

[298] S.I. 2001/2334, reg. 21.

[299] S.I. 2001/2334, reg. 2(1): the definition in the regulations is a 'copy out' of the Directive's definition. Some contracts are 'excepted' from the provisions.

[300] Ibid.   [301] S.I. 2001/2334, reg. 21(6).

[302] For the meaning of this term, see Consumer Credit Act 1974, s.14(1), considered in Sect. 8(i), above.

[303] Consumer Credit Act 1974, s.84, considered in Sect. 8(ii), above.

[304] S.84(3A)–(3D) and added by S.I. 2001/2334, reg. 21 and S.I. 2004/2095, reg. 14.

[305] See Sect. 8(ii) above.   [306] S.I. 2001/2334, reg. 21(4).   [307] The term is not defined.

[308] See Ch. 2, Sect. 5(ii).

11 Criminal liability for misuse of cards

When the cardholder violates the terms on which the card is provided to him, the issuer is entitled to its return and will usually take steps to try and prevent the card being misused. Thus in the case of a card supported by electronic systems, these are programmed to refuse acceptance of cards that have been placed on such a notional 'stop list'. However, this does not cut off all opportunities for the misuse of the cards. Moreover, cheque cards present more problems. It will be recalled that the bank's promise to pay is directed to the world at large. It is difficult to find a way to recall such a promise effectively.

The misuse of cards can give rise to criminal liability. Before the enactment of the Fraud Act 2006, the 'deception' offences in the Theft Acts 1968 (as amended) and 1978 were largely relied on.[309] However, not only did their technicalities present difficulties,[310] but their application to automated transactions was problematic in that it has been held that a machine cannot be 'deceived'.[311] The Fraud Act 2006 replaced these 'deception' offences with a more general 'fraud' offence in section 1, which catches a person who 'dishonestly makes a false representation' and thereby intends to make a gain or cause a loss.[312] Hence the requisite *actus reus* is now the making of a false representation, with no need for any 'deception'.

In *Metropolitan Police Commissioner* v. *Charles*,[313] a case under the old 'obtaining a pecuniary advantage by deception' provision in the Theft Act 1968, s.16, the House of Lords held that a cardholder who used his cheque card in order to exceed his overdraft limit represented to the payee that he had the required funds with the bank for meeting the cheques and not just that the cheques would be paid by the bank.[314] Under the new 'fraud' offence the former representation (as it is false) can secure a conviction whilst the latter representation (as it is true), cannot. *R* v. *Lambie*,[315] concerned a credit cardholder who exceeded her credit limit on a number of occasions and so the bank demanded the card's return. The House of Lords noted that a merchant would not accept a credit card

---

[309] Esp. Theft Act 1968, s.16 (see the cases of *Charles* and *Lambie*, below) and later s.15A (added by the Theft (Amendment) Act 1996) as well as Theft Act 1978, s.1 (see *R* v. *Sofroniou* [2003] EWCA Crim 3681, n.317 below). In addition, the narrowly drafted Theft Act 1968, s.20(2) ('procuring the execution of valuable securities'), also repealed, was sometimes used: see *R* v. *Kassim* [1992] AC 9 and *R*. v. *King* [1992] QB 20 (CA).

[310] Many prosecutions under s.20(2) (see previous footnote) failed as it required a 'valuable security' to be 'executed'. Hence it was held that a telegraphic transfer was not a 'valuable security' (*R* v. *Johl* [1994] Crim. LR 522 (CA Crim)) and that 'execution' had a narrow meaning (*R* v. *Kassim* [1992] AC 9; *Nolan* v. *Governor of Holloway Prison* [2003] EWHC 2709).

[311] See *Holmes* v. *Governor of Brixton Prison* [2004] EWHC 2020; [2005] 1 All ER 490 (QBD (Admin.)) noted [2005] Crim. LR 229. See now Fraud Act 2006, s.2(5), criticized as unnecessary in D. Ormerod, 'The Fraud Act 2006—criminalising lying?' [2007] Crim. LR 193, 200.

[312] Fraud Act 2006, ss.1, 2. The Theft Act 1978, s.1 (obtaining services by deception) has been replaced by Fraud Act 2006, s.11. For a discussion of the 2006 Act, see Ormerod, n.311 above.

[313] [1977] AC 177. See also *R* v. *Kovacs* [1974] 1 WLR 370 and *R* v. *Waites* [1982] Crim. LR 369. For cases where the customer draws a cheque which he knows to be uncovered and which he has no reason to believe will be met, see *DPP* v. *Turner* [1974] AC 357. Note also *R* v. *Gilmartin* [1983] 1 All ER 829 (post-dated cheque) and *R* v. *Hamilton* (1991) 92 Cr. App. R. 54 (withdrawal slips). And note that a prosecution could be brought under (the now repealed) Theft Act 1968, s.16 in the UK even in respect of a misuse of the card overseas: *R* v. *Bevan* (1987) 84 Crim. App. R 143. As regards an electronic fraud involving money transfers executed overseas, see *R* v. *Thompson* [1984] 3 All ER 565.

[314] [1977] AC 182 (Lord Diplock) and 191 (Lord Edmund-Davies). See also *R* v. *Kovacs* [1974] 1 WLR 370, 373, *per* Lawton LJ.

[315] [1982] AC 449, especially 460.

if he knew that the cardholder was utilizing it in breach of their contract with the issuer and therefore held that the cardholder obtained credit by tacitly representing that she was using the card in compliance with this contract. Thus the use of a card, whether a charge card or credit card, which the holder is no longer entitled to use,[316] would clearly involve a false representation and hence fall within the new 'fraud' offence. Moreover, obtaining a card itself by false representations will also clearly now be covered.[317]

Finally, since the introduction by the Theft (Amendment) Act 1996 of a new Theft Act 1968, section 24A[318] it has been an offence dishonestly to retain a 'wrongful credit'[319] made to a bank account (including an account with an issuer of electronic money) with the knowledge or belief that it is wrongful. Using payment cards to transfer funds, to which the cardholder is not entitled, into his bank account could be caught by this provision, although it is primarily aimed at persons who 'retain' (that is, who fail to take such steps as are reasonable to secure the cancellation of) an amount erroneously credited to their account.

---

[316] A. Kewley, 'The Dishonest Cheque and Credit Card User' (1983) 127 *Sol. Jo.* 719: when the cardholder presents his card to a merchant or to a bank, he effectively warrants his right to utilize it.

[317] Although, a charge under Fraud Act 2006, s.11 (replacing the 'obtaining services' deception offence in the Theft Act 1978, s.1) will still fail if the 'services' provided by the card may be gratuitous: *R* v. *Sofroniou* [2003] EWCA Crim. 3681.

[318] As amended by the Fraud Act 2006, s.14(1) and Sched. 1, para. 7.

[319] Defined to include an amount of money (s.24A(2)) derived from a contravention of the Fraud Act 2006, s.1 (as well as from theft, blackmail, or stolen goods). Whether the account is overdrawn before or after the credit is made is irrelevant: s.24A(5).

15

The Bank's Role in Collecting Cheques

1 The bank's role in the transaction

When a customer asks a bank to present a cheque for payment to the drawee bank, it assumes the role of either a collecting bank or discounting bank. Whatever the role adopted by the bank, where its customer's title to the cheque in question is defective, the bank may be sued by the cheque's 'true owner'. Although the causes of action available to the true owner are identical regardless of whether the bank has collected or discounted the cheque,[1] there is a difference between the defences available to the two types of bank. For this reason, the distinction between the role of a collecting bank and of a discounting bank is of considerable importance. This question is discussed in section 3.

Sections 4 and 5 of this chapter deal, respectively, with the defences available to the collecting bank and those available to a discounting bank. Section 6 considers the plea of contributory negligence and section 7 deals with a problem which arises where the holder remits a cheque for collection not to his own bank but to another bank, which he requests to arrange for the collection of the instrument to the credit of his usual account.[2] The position of a bank that receives the cheque for such processing (termed the 'processing bank') in situations in which the payee does not have a good title to the cheque is uncertain, and requires separate analysis. The last section considers the issues arising where the drawer of the cheque and its holder maintain their accounts with the same bank.

2 The true owner's cause of action

A bank that collects a cheque for a person who has no title to it, or whose title is defective, faces the hazard of an action by the true owner of the instrument. Two causes of action are available to substantiate such an action. The first is an action in conversion. In *OBG Ltd* v. *Allan*,[3] where the issue concerned the extent to which the tort of conversion could protect interference with intangible property, their Lordships confirmed that a cheque is to be treated as a chattel for these purposes. Although their Lordships considered that the availability of a conversion claim in relation to a cheque was 'an anomaly' and a 'legal fiction',[4] they nevertheless confirmed the position that, where a bank converts a cheque

---

[1] See Sect. 2 below.   [2] And see above, Ch. 11, Sect. 2.
[3] [2008] AC 1, [97]–[106], [225]–[238], [321] (HL).
[4] Ibid., [106], [227]. For the historical development of the 'legal fiction', see S. Green & J. Randall, *The Tort of Conversion* (Oxford, 2009), 33–38.

by receiving it for collection and presenting it for payment,[5] the bank is liable for the face value of the instrument.[6] The second cause of action is based on restitution for wrongdoing. Traditionally, in this type of action the true owner is said to 'waive the tort'. Thus, in *Morison* v. *London County and Westminster Bank Ltd*, in which an agent misused his authority by drawing on his principal's account cheques payable to his own order and by arranging for their collection for the credit of his personal account, Lord Reading CJ explained the basis of this second cause of action as follows: 'The claimant is entitled to waive the tort and sue for the same amount as money had and received to his use'.[7]

Following the decision of the House of Lords in *Lipkin Gorman* v. *Karpnale & Co.*[8] the true owner can, in appropriate cases, also base his restitutionary action on a general cause of action based on the fact that the defendant has been unjustly enriched at the claimant's expense, such as where payment had been made under a mistake of fact, or on the vindication of his property rights. Such an action is certainly feasible where the true owner is also the drawer of the cheque and, hence, the person whose money is misappropriated by the payment of the instrument.

From a practical point of view, the cause of action in conversion is to be preferred to the restitutionary action based on waiver of tort. The reason for this is that the collecting bank receives the funds as its customer's agent. It is established that an agent who in good faith has paid over to his principal money to which the principal has no right cannot be required to return the money to the payor.[9] This doctrine applies to a collecting bank that has received the proceeds of cheques collected by it on behalf of a customer. Once the money is paid to the customer, the bank has changed its position and, being a mere agent, is no longer answerable in an action in money had and received.[10] However, the doctrine in question applies only where the action is brought under this heading and is thus based on the wrongful receipt of the funds. The defence cannot be raised in the context of an action in trover, which is based on the misappropriation of a chattel.

As indicated above, for the purposes of the action in conversion, the cheque is deemed to have a value equal to the amount for which it is drawn.[11] This principle is based on equating the chose in action, or the debt, incurred when the cheque is issued with the value of the instrument itself. In *International Factors Ltd* v. *Rodriguez*,[12] a company

---

[5] *Morison* v. *London County and Westminster Bank Ltd* [1914] 3 KB 356; *A. L. Underwood Ltd* v. *Bank of Liverpool* [1924] 1 QB 775; *Lloyds Bank Ltd* v. *Savory & Co.* [1933] AC 201; *Bute (Marquess of)* v. *Barclays Bank Ltd* [1955] 1 QB 202. The history of the action is traced in *Arrow Transfer Co. Ltd* v. *Royal Bank of Canada* [1971] 3 WWR 241, affd. [1972] SCR 845. See also Green & Randall, n.4 above, 184–185.

[6] *OBG Ltd* v. *Allan*, n.3 above, [102]–[104].

[7] N.5 above, 365. *See also Bavins Jnr. and Sims* v. *London and South-Western Bank* [1900] 1 QB 270, 277–278 (CA); *United Australia Ltd* v. *Barclays Bank Ltd* [1941] AC 1, 19 (HL). See W. Swadling, 'Ignorance and Unjust Enrichment: the Problem of Title' (2008) 28 *OJLS* 627, 627; Green & Randall, n.4 above, 211–212.

[8] [1991] 2 AC 548. See further Ch. 11, Sect. 1 above.

[9] See *Admiralty Commissioners* v. *National Provincial and Union Bank of England Ltd* (1922) 127 LT 452; *Gowers* v. *Lloyds and National Provincial Bank Ltd* [1937] 3 All ER 55; *Koster's Premier Pottery Pty. Ltd* v. *Bank of Adelaide* (1981) 28 SASR 335 (Aust.). See also Ch. 12, Sects. 3–4 above.

[10] As to when the money is so paid over, see Ch. 12, Sect. 4 above.

[11] *Bobbett* v. *Pinkett* (1876) 1 Ex. D 368; *Fine Art Society Ltd* v. *Union Bank of London Ltd* (1866) 17 QBD 705; *Macbeth* v. *North and South Wales Bank* [1908] 1 KB 13, affd. [1908] AC 137; *Orbit Mining and Trading Co. Ltd* v. *Westminster Bank Ltd* [1963] 1 QB 794; *Stoney Stanton Supplies (Coventry) Ltd* v. *Midland Bank Ltd* [1966] 2 Lloyd's Rep. 373, 385; *OBG Ltd* v. *Allan*, n.3 above, [102]–[104]. This principle holds even if the instrument is not negotiable: see *Morison* v. *London County and Westminster Bank Ltd*, n.5 above; *Lloyds Bank Ltd* v. *Chartered Bank of India, Australia and China* [1929] 1 KB 40.

[12] [1979] QB 351. See also *MCC Proceeds Inc.* v. *Lehman Bros. International (Europe)* [1998] 4 All ER 675 (CA); *London Borough of Hounslow* v. *Jenkins* [2004] EWHC 315 (QB), [9]–[12]; *Cofacredit SA* v. *Clive*

assigned all its book debts to a firm of factors. This meant that any debts paid to the company by its clients had to be remitted to the factors. In breach of this agreement, a director of the company arranged for the collection of cheques, sent to the company in discharge of book debts due to it, for the credit of the company's current account. The factors sued the director in conversion. Two defences were pleaded. The first was that the factors did not have a property in the instruments but merely a right in contract to the proceeds. The second was that, even if the factors had an action in conversion, they could recover nominal damages only. The Court of Appeal held that the factors had an equitable interest in the cheques that conferred on them the right to sue in conversion. As regards the measure of damages, Sir David Cairns observed:[13]

> ...the general position in relation to the conversion of a cheque is that the conversion gives the person entitled to the cheque a right to damages measured by the face value of the cheque. That...has been established by a whole series of cases in some of which the defendants were banks. The damages may, of course, be mitigated by special circumstances; for example...if the cheque were stopped before payment into his bank by the wrongdoer and a fresh cheque given in substitution for it which was duly met.

His Lordship added that such special circumstances had to be established by the defendant to the action in conversion. In the instant case, it was argued that the factors had not suffered any loss because they still had a right of action against the debtors, who had drawn the cheques. This, however, was irrelevant as the factors, who might have had a cause of action against more than one party, were entitled to make their election.

It is clear that the Court of Appeal equated the value of the cheques in question with the amounts for which they were drawn. On this basis, a countermanded cheque ought to retain its face value even if a substituted instrument is issued by the drawer. The reason for this is that the stop order does not vitiate the cheque. The drawer remains liable to an action brought by a holder in due course.[14]

The true object of treating a converted cheque as having its face value is to enable the 'true owner' to sue for the proceeds under the guise of an action brought in tort. The fictive element in the conclusive presumption that a cheque has a value equal to the amount for which it is drawn becomes apparent when one reflects on the true value of a cheque issued by an impecunious customer whose account is heavily overdrawn.[15] The instrument is bound to be dishonoured by the drawee bank, and an action against the penniless customer is hopeless. The real value of the cheque involved is, therefore, nil. Why, then, should it be regarded at law as having its face value?

The same question can be raised in respect of a cheque bearing a forged signature of the drawer or a cheque which has been materially altered by an unauthorized person.[16] Such an instrument is a nullity. It is therefore unrealistic to plead that it has a value based on the amount for which it is drawn. This inconsistency was recognized in *Mathew and Cousins v. Sherwell*[17] by Sir James Mansfield, who observed that, even if an action for a forged cheque was successful, the most that the true owner could recover would be the value of the piece of paper on which the instrument was written. A similar reasoning has been

---

Morris & Mora UK Ltd [2006] EWHC 353 (Ch), [103]; *Islamic Republic of Iran v. Barakat Galleries Ltd* [2008] 1 All ER 1177, [28]–[30] (CA).

[13] Ibid., 358.   [14] See Ch. 10, Sect. 1 above.   [15] See *OBG Ltd v. Allan*, n.3 above, [227].

[16] See, respectively, the Bills of Exchange Act 1882 (BEA 1882), ss.24 and 64.

[17] (1810) 2 Taunt. 439.

adopted in modern Canadian and Australian authorities[18] and, recently, by the Court of Appeal in *Smith* v. *Lloyds TSB Group plc*.[19] In this case, a fraudster erased the name of the ostensible payee and arranged for the collection of the instrument for the credit of an account opened by him in the substituted name inserted by him on the cheque. Affirming Blofeld J's decision, their Lordships held that the 'true owner' could not recover the face value of the instrument from the collecting bank. When the cheque was avoided upon the execution of the unauthorized alteration of the payee's name, it became worthless.

The collecting bank's liability in conversion and under the related action based on the waiver of this tort is founded on its having handled the cheque on behalf of the tortfeasor, its customer, who has misappropriated the instrument. The true owner of such a cheque is able to recover the amount of the instrument from the collecting bank. The action involved has to be based on the cheque and not on the proceeds thereof, as the law does not recognize an action in conversion for the misappropriation of money or of a mere chose in action. This point is demonstrated by the decision in *Bavins Jnr. and Sims* v. *London and South Western Bank*.[20] An instrument that was in the form of a cheque, but payment of which was conditional on the execution of a receipt, was converted after reaching the payee's hands. It was collected on behalf of the rogue by his bank. Before the proceeds were paid out to the rogue, the true payee informed the collecting bank that the instrument had been issued to him. His action against the collecting bank was successful under the heading of money had and received, but the Court of Appeal was divided in respect of the action in conversion. A. L. Smith LJ thought that both causes of action ought to succeed. The action in money had and received was to be allowed, as the collecting bank had been informed before it changed its position that the proceeds of the instrument were in reality for the initial payee's use. His Lordship would have further allowed the action in trover, as the collecting bank had converted a document belonging to the payee. He attached no importance to the non-negotiable character of the document. Collins LJ preferred not to resolve the question of the availability of an action in conversion. His Lordship observed:[21]

> ...the money...received by [the collecting bank] by reason of [the] wrongful user of the [payee's] document can be treated as money received by them to the use of the true owners of the document.

Vaughan Williams LJ was likewise inclined to base his judgment on the count of money had and received:[22]

> Having received the money by presenting the document which belonged to the [payees] [the collecting bank] cannot...if the [payees] choose to waive the tort, say that they did not receive the money on account of the [payees]. They certainly could not say so after they obtained knowledge of the payee's title.

---

[18] In Canada, see *Arrow Transfer Ltd* v. *Royal Bank of Canada*, n.5 above, 256–7, affd. n.5 above; *Number 10 Management Ltd* v. *Royal Bank of Canada* (1976) 69 DLR (3d.) 99, 105, where it was also held that an action would not lie in money had and received. In Australia, see *Koster's Premier Pottery Pty. Ltd* v. *Bank of Adelaide*, n.9 above.

[19] [2001] QB 541 (CA). See also *OBG Ltd* v. *Allan*, n.3 above, [227]. Contrast the earlier cases of *Orbit Mining and Trading Co. Ltd* v. *Westminster Bank*, n.11 above; *Building and Civil Engineering Holidays Scheme Management Ltd* v. *Post Office* [1964] 2 QB 430, 444–7; *Stoney Stanton Supplies (Coventry) Ltd* v. *Midland Bank Ltd*, n.11 above, 385. A cheque avoided by a material alteration was described as a nullity in *Slingsby* v. *District Bank Ltd* [1932] 1 KB 544. See also *Kulatilleke* v. *Bank of Ceylon* (1958) 59 NLR (Ceylon) 188; *Kulatilleke* v. *Mercantile Bank of India* (1958) 59 NLR (Ceylon) 190.

[20] N.7 above.   [21] Ibid., 277.   [22] Ibid., 278.

The reasoning in *Bavin* is perplexing. Why should a person recover in waiver of tort an amount exceeding that recoverable in respect of the tort that he waived?[23] The case, however, clarifies the policy involved in treating cheques as items of property for the purposes of the tort of conversion. The object is to enable the true owner of a cheque to recover the amount that he loses when the instrument is paid through the clearing house to the wrong party.

Under both causes of action—conversion and waiver of tort—the claimant has to establish that he is the true owner of the cheque. The phrase 'true owner' is mentioned,[24] but is not defined in the Bills of Exchange Act 1882 (BEA 1882). It follows that whether or not a person is the 'true owner' of a cheque is determined by common law principles, which in turn take into account the special features of negotiable instruments.

Fundamentally, the 'true owner' is the person entitled to the immediate possession of the instrument. In *Bute (Marquess of)* v. *Barclays Bank Ltd*,[25] three warrants, which bore crossings accompanied by the words 'not negotiable', were dispatched by the drawers to M, who was the employee of the Marquess of Bute. M arranged for the collection of these warrants, which were payable to '[M] for the Marquess of Bute', to the credit of an account opened in his own name. The Marquess brought an action for the conversion of these warrants, which (legally) constituted cheques, against the collecting bank. An argument to the effect that, to bring such an action, the Marquess had to establish that he was the owner of the warrants was rejected by McNair J. His Lordship held that, in order to bring an action in conversion, all the claimant had to establish was his entitlement to the immediate possession of the instrument at the time the tort took place. He did not have to show that he had the property in the converted chattel.

In *Marquess of Bute*, the right to the possession of the warrants remained vested in the Marquess as he had never evinced the intention of parting with it. The position might have differed had the warrants been sent to the Marquess and delivered by him to M. *Citibank NA* v. *Brown Shipley & Co. Ltd*[26] illustrates this point. Fraudsters, who managed to get access to an account maintained with the claimant bank, induced this bank to issue certain bankers' drafts payable to the defendant bank. On obtaining the claimant bank's assurance about the regularity of these drafts, the instruments were taken up by the defendant bank and the amount received on clearance was duly placed to the credit of the fraudsters' account. Dismissing the claimant bank's action in conversion, Waller J held that, as the drafts in question had been delivered to the defendant bank by a person authorized to do so by the claimant bank, the title in them and the right to their possession had passed to the defendant bank.[27]

---

[23] In the light of the House of Lords' decision in *Lipkin Gorman* v. *Karpnale & Co.*, n.8 above (discussed in Ch. 12, Sect. 1 above) the claimant in *Bavin* could, in all probability, have succeeded also in an action based on the cause of action based upon the defendant's unjust enrichment. He would not have been confined to a waiver of tort action.

[24] BEA 1882, ss.79(2), 80.

[25] N.5 above, followed in *International Factors Ltd* v. *Rodriguez*, n.12 above.

[26] [1991] 2 Lloyd's Rep. 576. See also *Surrey Asset Finance Ltd* v. *National Westminster Bank plc* [2000] TLR 852; *Dextra Bank & Trust Co. Ltd* v. *Bank of Jamaica* [2002] 1 All ER (Comm.) 193, [23]–[25] (PC); *Abbey National plc* v. *JSF Finance & Currency Exchange Co. Ltd* [2006] EWCA Civ 328, [15]–[21]; cf. *Australian Guarantee Corporation* v. *State Bank of Victoria* [1989] VR 617 (Sup. Ct. Vic., Aus.).

[27] His Lordship further found, on the facts, that the representations made by the claimant bank in reply to the defendant bank's enquiries would preclude the defendant bank from denying the valid transfer and delivery of the instruments. As the funds had been paid out by the defendant bank to the fraudsters, an action in money had and received would have failed due to the change in that bank's position: see Ch. 12, Sects. 3–4 above.

Where an instrument has been forged, the true owner is the proprietor of the cheque-book from which the form has been extracted by the rogue.[28] Where a cheque payable to the order of a specific person is removed from that person's custody before he has negotiated the instrument, the title to it cannot pass to a third party and the ostensible payee remains the true owner.[29] The position differs if such a cheque is abstracted by the rogue after the ostensible payee has indorsed it in blank.[30] The cheque thereupon becomes a bearer instrument that is transferable by mere delivery. A person who takes such a cheque for value and in good faith becomes a holder in due course, provided the cheque is complete and regular on its face at the time of its negotiation to the person concerned. A holder in due course acquires a good title to the instrument and hence becomes its true owner.[31] As a general principle, the true owner of the cheque is the last person to whom the instrument has been validly transferred. If the instrument has not been validly issued or negotiated, or if the issuing of the instrument is vitiated by forgery, then the original owner of the piece of paper remains the owner of the cheque.[32]

In certain cases the true ownership of a cheque may be determined only by reference to agency principles. In *Channon* v. *English Scottish and Australian Bank*,[33] a cheque posted by a debtor to his creditor was stolen from the mail by a thief, who successfully presented it for payment to the drawee bank. The Supreme Court of New South Wales held that the drawer's right to sue his own bankers in conversion[34] depended on his being the true owner of the instrument. If the drawer, the debtor, was asked by the creditor to post the cheque, then the Post Office was the creditor's agent for delivery and the creditor would therefore become the cheque's true owner as soon as it was put in transmission. The converse would be the case if the debtor mailed the cheque on his own initiative. In the absence of direct evidence in point, a new trial was ordered.[35]

3 Collection and discount distinguished

The distinction between a collecting bank and a discounting bank is fundamental. A bank that presents a cheque for payment on its customer's behalf acts as an agent.[36] It is a collecting bank that does not purport to acquire the property in the cheque and does not become its holder. The position differs where the bank discounts the cheque. In such a

---

[28] *Morison* v. *London County and Westminster Bank*, n.5 above; *Bute (Marquess of)* v. *Barclays Bank Ltd*, n.5 above.

[29] *Lacave & Co.* v. *Crédit Lyonnais* [1897] 1 QB 148, which shows that a person who holds a cheque payable to order under a forged indorsement is not a holder and has no title to it.

[30] This assumes the cheque is transferable and not crossed 'account payee' which, following the Cheques Act 1992, would make the cheque non-transferable.

[31] *Smith* v. *Union Bank of London* (1875) 1 QBD 31. See generally Lord Chorley, *Gilbart Lectures* (1953).

[32] *Ladbroke & Co.* v. *Todd* (1914) 30 TLR 433. See also *Commercial Banking Co. of Sydney Ltd* v. *Mann* [1961] AC 1.

[33] (1918) 18 SR (NSW) 30. See also *London Bank of Australia Ltd* v. *Kendall* (1920) 28 CLR 401, 409.

[34] The action could, of course, have been brought in breach of mandate, in which case the question of the true ownership would not have arisen.

[35] If it is uncertain whether a cheque was misappropriated whilst in the hands of the drawer or the payee, under s.21(3) of the BEA 1882, the payee will be deemed to have received a valid and unconditional delivery of the cheque, and hence be the true owner, until the contrary is proved: *Surrey Asset Finance Ltd* v. *National Westminster Bank plc*, n.26 above.

[36] The collecting bank does not hold the proceeds of the cheque on trust for the customer, but the bank merely incurs a commitment to credit the customer's account with an equivalent amount: *Emerald Meats (London) Ltd* v. *AIB Group (UK) Ltd* [2002] EWCA Civ. 460.

case the bank furnishes consideration to the customer by permitting him to draw against the proceeds of the cheque before its clearance. When the cheque is paid, the discounting bank receives payment of the amount involved for itself.[37] However, cheque forms issued by United Kingdom banks are now almost invariably crossed and pre-printed with the words 'account payee', which makes the cheques non- transferable.[38] This means that it is now very rare for a collecting bank to become the holder of a cheque drawn on a United Kingdom bank and to present the cheque for payment on its own behalf.[39]

Whether in a specific case the bank acts as a discounting bank or as a collecting bank depends on the facts. At one time it was thought that the bank became a discounting bank whenever it credited its customer's account with the amount of the cheque before clearance.[40] On this view, however, every collection of a cheque would have involved a discount because the amount of cheques remitted to a bank for collection has always been credited to the customer's account before clearance. This procedure is utilized as a matter of accounting practice with the aim of obviating the need for short entries of items pending clearance. It is traditionally employed even where the customer is not allowed to draw against the amount so credited until the cheque is cleared. It is now well established that a cheque is discounted only if, apart from crediting its amount to the customer's account before clearance, the bank agrees to grant the customer an overdraft against the proceeds or actually permits him to draw against them.[41]

Thus, in *Re Farrow's Bank Ltd*[42] a customer's account with the F Bank was credited forthwith with the amount of the cheque payable to him. The pay-in slip, however, contained a note to the effect that the bank reserved to itself the right 'to defer payment of cheques against uncleared effects which may have been credited to the account'. As the F Bank was not a member of the clearing house, it remitted the cheque to the B Bank, where the cheque was forthwith credited to the F Bank's account subject to recourse. The cheque was duly honoured upon its presentment by the B Bank to the drawee bank, but the F Bank suspended payment before it received advice thereof, and before the proceeds were actually credited to the B Bank's account with the drawee bank. Two issues arose in the case. The first was whether the F Bank had acted as a discounting bank or as a collecting bank. The second was whether, in so far as the F Bank had acted as a collecting bank, it had received the proceeds solely as its customer's agent or in the context of the banker-customer relationship between them, in which case the amount would become a debt due to the customer from his bank. In this latter case, the customer would have had to prove in the F Bank's liquidation as a general creditor. This would also have been the position if the F Bank had assumed the role of a discounting banker. But if the amount involved had been received by the F Bank as a mere agent, the customer would be entitled to have the amount remitted to him *in specie*.

Astbury J held that the mere crediting of the customer's account did not involve the furnishing of a consideration by the F Bank.[43] This conclusion was supported by the language of the credit slip. To assume the role of a discounting bank, the F Bank would have had to permit its customer to draw against the proceeds. It was further held that

---

[37] *Capital and Counties Bank Ltd* v. *Gordon* [1903] AC 240, which, on this point, remains good law.

[38] BEA 1882, s.81A(1).

[39] R. Hooley, 'Prevention of Fraud by Non-Transferable Cheques' [1992] *CLJ* 432, 433.

[40] See *Capital and Counties Bank Ltd* v. *Gordon*, n.37 above.

[41] This was specifically clarified by the Bills of Exchange (Crossed Cheques) Act 1906, now replaced by s.4(1)(b) of the Cheques Act 1957.

[42] [1923] 1 Ch. 41.

[43] See also *A. L. Underwood Ltd* v. *Bank of Liverpool*, n.5 above; *Westminster Bank Ltd* v. *Zang* [1966] AC 182; *Barclays Bank Ltd* v. *Astley Industrial Trust Ltd* [1970] 2 QB 527, 539.

the amount of the cheque was received by the F Bank as its customer's agent, and not in circumstances where these proceeds would be credited to his account as a debt owed to him by the F Bank. This regular relationship of debtor and creditor, prevailing between banker and customer under ordinary circumstances, was suspended when the F Bank closed its doors. Amounts received by that bank after that date were received purely on the customer's behalf.[44]

Re Farrow's Bank Ltd establishes that a cheque is discounted where the bank agrees to grant its customer an overdraft against the proceeds, or actually allows the customer to draw against them before the instrument is cleared. Another instance in which the bank assumes the role of a discounter is where it reduces the customer's existing overdraft by the amount of a cheque before its clearance, with the effect that the proceeds are taken into account in the calculation of the balance, or ceiling, available for drawings.[45]

It follows that there is a clear conceptual demarcation between the collection and the discount of a cheque. In practice, though, the specific role assumed by a bank in a given transaction is not necessarily based on a conscious decision as to whether the cheque is to be collected or discounted. By way of illustration, take a customer's account that has a credit balance adequate for meeting all outstanding cheques drawn by him as they are presented for payment. The question of the discount of any of the cheques paid in by this customer, with a view to granting him an overdraft against their uncleared proceeds, does not even arise. The absence of such a need may, however, be due to a coincidence rather than to a restraint by the customer as regards the drawing of cheques against uncleared effects, as the time at which the cheques drawn by the customer are presented is out of his control. Indeed, although the customer may have arranged for an overdraft against uncleared proceeds, a delay in the presentment of cheques drawn by him may result in a situation where his bank collects rather than discounts effects payable to him!

Where the customer's balance is inadequate for meeting cheques drawn by him, the bank's decision to allow him to draw against uncleared effects payable to him may again be a matter of chance. If the customer is of good standing, then the bank will permit him to draw against uncleared proceeds within a given ceiling and usually without prior approval. But here, too, the extent of the required overdraft depends on the speed of the presentment for payment of cheques drawn by him. Moreover, if the customer has paid to the credit of his account cheques totalling more than the amount of the required overdraft, the bank will not resolve which of these uncleared items is to be regarded as the one against which a new cheque of the customer is to be debited.[46]

In the case of some banks, the position has been further complicated by the computer programs currently employed by them in respect of the collection and the payment of cheques. Where a customer's balance, based on cleared effects, is marginally short of the amount required for meeting cheques drawn by him, the bank's computer automatically sanctions the payment of the cheques drawn. The computer does so quite regardless of whether or not there are any uncleared effects deposited for the credit of the customer's

---

[44] The case suggests that the ordinary relationship of banker and customer is determined by the bank's insolvency. See Ch. 5, Sect. 6 & Ch. 11, Sect. 1(iv) above, regarding the bank's insolvency.

[45] *M'Lean* v. *Clydesdale Banking Corporation* (1883) 9 App. Cas. 95. For a detailed analysis, see *National Australia Bank Ltd* v. *KDS Construction Services Pty. Ltd* (1988) 76 ALR 27 (Aust.). See also *Taylor* v. *Australia and New Zealand Banking Corporation* (Sup. Ct. Vic., 26 May 1988, unreported). Both Australian authorities consider also whether the transaction constituted an undue preference. A Canadian authority suggests that the bank becomes a discounter even if the overdraft is granted by error: see *Bank of Nova Scotia* v. *Taylor* (1979) 60 APR 14.

[46] The answer probably depends on the 'rule of appropriation of payments', discussed in Ch. 17, Sect. 2(iv) below.

account.[47] In reality, the bank is prepared to grant its customer an unsecured overdraft within a given limit and, to this effect, a certain tolerance as regards 'cover' is programmed by the computer. The effect in law is, however, very different. When the bank grants in this manner an overdraft to its customer, it acquires a lien, which is a form of security, over all uncleared effects deposited to the credit of his account.[48] In this way the bank, unwittingly, becomes the holder for value of such effects to the extent of the overdraft or advance involved.[49] As the bank becomes the 'holder' of the uncleared effects, it cannot possibly be regarded a mere collecting agent. It receives payment of the uncleared effects in part for itself and in part for the customer.

This analysis suggests that, from a practical point of view, it is not easy to draw a clear-cut distinction between a collecting bank and a discounting bank. In effect, the two roles are not mutually exclusive of one another. A bank may be acting at one and the same time as its customer's collecting agent and as a discounting bank. This point has been recognized in *Barclays Bank Ltd* v. *Astley Industrial Trust Ltd*,[50] where it was observed that a bank that grants its customer an overdraft of £5 against an uncleared cheque for £100 has given value for it, but it cannot be said that, as a result of this, the bank ceases to be the customer's agent for collection.

4 The collecting bank's protection

(i) Background: section 82 and section 4

Conversion is a strict tort.[51] The tortfeasor's good faith is not a valid defence.[52] Banks, however, are not in a position to verify that each of their customers has a good title to every cheque paid to the credit of his account. To save banks from having to collect cheques at their peril, it was felt necessary to introduce a statutory defence. The original provision in point, in the Crossed Cheques Act 1876,[53] was reproduced without substantial alterations in section 82 of the BEA 1882. Under this provision, a bank was not liable to the 'true owner' of the cheque where it received payment of the instrument for a customer, and provided the bank was able to establish that it had acted in good faith and without negligence. The two main limitations of this provision were that it applied, first, only to crossed cheques and, secondly, only where the payment involved was received for the customer. The first limitation was introduced by inadvertence—the draftsman of the BEA 1882, who was guided by the provision taken from the 1876 Act, did not consider the need to protect banks in respect of the collection of uncrossed cheques. The significance of the second limitation became apparent in the wake of the House of Lords' decision in *Capital and Counties Bank Ltd* v. *Gordon*.[54] It was there held that section 82 did not protect a bank that had credited the customer's account before the clearance of the cheque because, in such a case, the bank received payment for itself. This decision would have destroyed the effect of section 82 since, even under the prevailing banking practice found in the

---

[47] A suitably programmed software package distinguishes between the accrued balance and an amount available against uncleared effects.

[48] BEA 1882, s.27(3). See also Ch. 20, Sect. 2 below. 　　[49] Ibid. 　　[50] N.43 above, 538.

[51] See Green & Randall, n.4 above, 67–74. For the historical development, see D. Ibbetson, *A Historical Introduction to the Law of Obligations* (Oxford, 1999), 107–112.

[52] See, for example, *Hollins* v. *Fowler* (1875) LR 7 HL 757.

[53] Crossed Cheques Act 1876, s.12, interpreted in *Matthiessen* v. *London and County Bank* (1879) 5 CPD 7.

[54] N.37 above.

'2-4-6' commitments,[55] cheques will invariably be credited to the customer's account when deposited by him and not after their clearance. An amendment was, accordingly, passed in 1906,[56] under which a bank was deemed to have received payment of a cheque for a customer notwithstanding that the amount had been credited to his account before clearance.

Section 82 of the BEA 1882 was repealed and replaced by section 4(1) of the Cheques Act 1957,[57] which reads:

(1) Where a banker, in good faith and without negligence,—

    (a) receives payment for a customer of an instrument to which this section applies; or

    (b) having credited a customer's account with the amount of such an instrument, receives payment thereof for himself;

(2) and the customer has no title, or a defective title, to the instrument, the banker does not incur any liability to the true owner of the instrument by reason only of having received payment thereof.

This provision, which is still in force, is wider than section 82 of the BEA 1882. In the first place, section 4 confers the defence involved not only on a collecting bank but also on a discounting bank. This aspect of section 4 is discussed subsequently. Secondly, section 4 of the Cheques Act 1957 is not confined to crossed cheques. Under section 4(2), the legislation applies to all cheques, including cheques which under section 81A of the BEA 1882 or otherwise are not transferable,[58] as well as to three types of instruments that, although not cheques within the orthodox definition of the term, serve a similar function. The first type comprises documents that though not bills of exchange (and hence not cheques) are issued by a bank's customer in order to enable a person to obtain payment from that bank of the amount of the instrument. The draftsman's object was to extend the protection of section 4 of the Cheques Act 1957 to instruments payable to 'cash or order', which do not constitute bills of exchange within the definition of section 3 of the BEA 1882.[59] The second type of instrument to which section 4 is made applicable comprises documents issued by public officers with the intention of enabling a person to obtain payment of the sum involved from the Postmaster-General or from the Queen's or Lord Treasurer's Remembrancer. The documents involved are usually outside the definition of a bill of exchange, as they are specifically made payable to the designated person subject to his identifying himself and, furthermore, are issued as non-transferable. The third type of instrument comprises drafts payable on demand drawn by a banker on himself, whether payable at the head office or at some other branch. Such bankers' drafts fall outside the definition of a bill of exchange, as they are not drawn by one person on another.[60]

(ii) Analysis of section 4(1)

Section 4(1) applies a well defined test for the collecting bank's protection. To invoke it successfully the bank has to satisfy four requisites. First, it must establish that it has acted for a customer. Secondly, it must have 'received payment' either for that customer or, if

---

[55] See Ch. 10, Sect. 2 above.   [56] Bills of Exchange (Crossed Cheques) Act 1906.

[57] For the purpose underlying this provision, see *OBG Ltd* v. *Allan*, n.3 above [97].

[58] Cheques Act 1992, s.3. See further Ch. 10, Sect. 4(iv) above.

[59] *Orbit Mining and Trading Co. Ltd* v. *Westminster Bank Ltd*, n.9 above. For the Scottish position, see *Nimmo* v. *Bank of Scotland* [2005] SLT 133.

[60] *Commercial Banking Co. of Sydney Ltd* v. *Mann*, n.32 above 7.

it has credited the customer's account forthwith, for itself. Thirdly, the bank must act in good faith and, finally, it must act without negligence.[61]

The first requisite has not led to significant litigation in modern times. Indeed, the fact that section 4(1) of the Cheques Act 1957 applies only where the bank has acted for a customer gives effect to modern banking practice, which discourages banks from acting for strangers. However, the construction of the word 'customer' in modern case law has given rise to an element of circularity in the test laid down in section 4(1). It has been shown that 'customer' means a person in whose name the bank has either opened or has agreed to open some type of an account.[62] It follows that, in so far as the other three requisites of section 4(1) are established, the provision applies whenever the bank has credited the amount of the cheque to the account of any person who maintains an account with that bank. The section does not require that the proceeds of the cheque be credited to an account maintained by the payee or by the holder. Section 4(1) would have achieved the same object by requiring that the proceeds be credited to an account other than one maintained in the bank's own name for internal accounting purposes, such as a hold or a suspense account.

The reference in section 4(1) to the word 'customer' in addition to the word 'account' is, in effect, redundant. The use of the word 'customer' in the section is based on historical reasons. During the nineteenth century it was thought that a person became a customer not upon the opening of his account, but after the lapse of some time whereupon the relationship became one of 'habit'.[63] The test aimed at by the draftsman of the 1876 Act was, thus, considerably narrower than that prevailing at present. His object was to confine the application of the protection conferred by the Act to cases in which the bank collected a cheque for an established customer.

The second requisite of section 4(1), to the effect that the proceeds must have been 'received', caused some apprehension when the original provision, section 82, was introduced in the BEA 1882. It was argued that the section applied only as from the time at which the proceeds were properly *received* by the collecting bank. It was, indeed, arguable that the receipt of the funds took place when the amount was credited to the collecting bank's account, namely when settlement took place at the Bank of England.[64] This settlement was, of course, preceded by certain steps, taken by the collecting bank in respect of the cheque, which could in themselves amount to conversion. As these steps took place before the time at which the bank acquired its protection under section 4(1) of the Cheques Act 1957, the provision was at one time described as a trap.[65] The apprehensions in point were, however, allayed in *Lloyds Bank Ltd* v. *Savory & Co.*,[66] in which the defence of section 82—the predecessor of section 4—was described as accruing as from the time at which the cheque was handed to the collecting bank.

There is a dearth of authority as regards the third requisite of section 4(1) of the Cheques Act 1957, concerning the collecting bank's good faith. This is not surprising,

---

[61] As regards the application of Cheques Act 1957, s.4 to cheques avoided by a material alteration, see *Slingsby* v. *District Bank Ltd*, n.19 above; *Kulatilleke* v. *Bank of Ceylon*, n.19 above. See also Sect. 2 above, as regards the true value of such an instrument.

[62] See Ch. 5, Sect. 2 above.

[63] See *Mathews* v. *Brown & Co.* (*sub nom. Matthews* v. *Williams, Brown & Co.*) (1894) 63 LJQB 494, which is still echoed in *Great Western Railway Co.* v. *London and County Banking Co. Ltd* [1901] AC 414. The view was exploded in *Commissioners of Taxation* v. *English, Scottish and Australian Bank Ltd* [1920] AC 683.

[64] For the procedure involved, see Ch. 10, Sect. 2 above.

[65] *Capital and Counties Bank Ltd* v. *Gordon*, n.37 above, 244. See also *Morison* v. *London County and Westminster Bank Ltd*, n.5 above.

[66] N.5 above.

as the bank's good faith is readily established by a denial of actual knowledge and of any suspicion of the existence of a defect in the customer's title. There is only one reported case in which the collecting bank's good faith was questioned, and even in this instance the bank was successful.[67]

(iii) **Negligence: general standard**

Most of the actions against collecting banks concern the fourth requisite of section 4(1) of the Cheques Act 1957, which is that the collecting bank must have acted without negligence. Section 4(1) does not establish a direct duty of care owed by the bank to the 'true owner'. Instead, it prescribes a standard with which the bank has to comply in order to be able to invoke the defence conferred upon it. The distinction between a duty of care and a general observable standard is of practical importance: the bank loses the protection of section 4(1) whenever it fails to act 'without negligence', and there is no need to establish that the departure from the standard involved had any direct bearing on the true owner's position or, indeed, that it was the cause of the loss involved.[68] This is so although the standard of 'reasonable care' is prescribed in the interests of the true owner.[69]

The standard of care imposed under section 4(1) of the Cheques Act 1957 depends, fundamentally, on what is considered expedient and reasonable in terms of general banking practice.[70] This is clear from the recent decision in *Architects of Wine Ltd* v. *Barclays Bank plc*,[71] in which the claimant, Architects of Wine Ltd, was the payee of around 400 cheques, but was unable to deposit these into its own account as these had been frozen. Accordingly, the cheques were paid into an account held with the defendant bank in the name of an indirect subsidiary, Architects of Wine (UK) Ltd. When the claimant brought a claim for conversion against the defendant bank for collecting the cheques for the wrong company, the bank relied upon section 4(1) of the Cheques Act 1957 by way of defence. In determining whether a bank had acted 'without negligence', Rix LJ preferred a test of negligence as to 'whether the transaction of paying any given cheque was so out of the ordinary course that is ought to have aroused doubts in the banker's mind, and caused them to make inquiry'.[72] In applying this test, there are a number of general factors that a court should bear in mind. First, the court should not make an assumption of negligence on the part of the bank, even though the bank bears the onus of demonstrating that it has acted 'without negligence'.[73] Secondly, the court should be wary of hindsight, but should seek to place itself in the bank's position when the cheque was presented for payment.[74] Thirdly, the court should not expect the bank to have acted as an 'amateur detective' and consideration must be given to the 'vastness of the modern bank's enterprise' and the number of cheques passing across their counters.[75] Fourthly, negligence must be examined by reference to the type of employees

---

[67] *Lawrie* v. *Commonwealth Trading Bank of Australia* [1970] Qd. R. 373.

[68] See *Savory & Co.* v. *Lloyds Bank Ltd* [1932] 2 KB 122, 148 (CA), affd. N.5 above, 216. See also *Bissell & Co.* v. *Fox Bros. & Co.* (1884) 51 LT 663, varied on a different point: (1885) 53 LT 193. Cf. *Commissioners of Taxation* v. *English, Scottish and Australian Bank*, n.63 above, 688, 691.

[69] See *Hannan's Lake View Central Ltd* v. *Armstrong* (1900) 5 Com. Cas. 188, 191.

[70] See *Ross* v. *London County Westminster and Parr's Bank Ltd* [1919] 1 KB 678, 685; *Commissioners of Taxation* v. *English, Scottish and Australian Bank Ltd*, n.63 above, 689; *A. L. Underwood Ltd* v. *Bank of Liverpool*, n.5 above; *Lloyds Bank Ltd* v. *Savory & Co.*, n.5 above 221; *Orbit Mining and Trading Co. Ltd* v. *Westminster Bank Ltd*, n.9 above; *Marfani & Co. Ltd* v. *Midland Bank Ltd* [1968] 1 WLR 956, 973; *Architects of Wine Ltd* v. *Barclays Bank plc* [2007] 2 Lloyd's Rep. 471, [7]–[9], [12], [56] (CA).

[71] N.70 above.   [72] Ibid., [6], [12].   [73] Ibid., [12].   [74] Ibid.

[75] Ibid., [9], [12].

or bank officials that would deal with the matters at hand and by reference to what would be expected of that particular type of employee.[76] In *Architects of Wine* itself, the defendant bank led evidence of the fact that it was unaware that there were two companies with similar names and led evidence that the current banking practice only required cashiers to establish a 'sufficient match' between the cheque payee and name on the account.[77] In this regard, the Court of Appeal indicated that '[c]urrent banking practice is highly relevant to the issue of negligence'.[78] Such practice will usually be established by expert evidence and, where the bank's evidence on this is unchallenged the court 'is not bound by such evidence, but it will be hesitant to reject it'.[79] As this practice is subject to change over time, however, the standard prescribed by section 4(1) is equally subject to periodic variations. The point is illustrated by two cases.

In the first case, *Lloyds Bank Ltd* v. *Savory & Co.*,[80] two stockbrokers' clerks misappropriated crossed bearer cheques drawn by their employers. The clerks paid the cheques in at the head office of the defendant bank for the credit of two accounts maintained with branches. One account was maintained in the name of the first clerk and the other account in the name of the second clerk's wife. When opening these accounts, the bank had not asked for the name of the first clerk's employers nor, in the case of the wife, for the name of her husband's employers. It was established that these oversights were contrary to the practice prescribed in the defendant bank's own manual. The House of Lords held that the bank had failed to discharge its duty to act without negligence. Lord Warrington of Clyffe observed that the standard by which the absence or presence of negligence is to be determined must be ascertained by reference to the practice of reasonable men carrying on the business of bankers and endeavouring to do so in such a manner as may be calculated to protect themselves and others against fraud.[81] To this end, the defendant bank should have ascertained the identity of the employers of the male customer when it agreed to open his account and, in the case of the married woman, the relevant details about her husband's occupation.

In the second, and more recent, case of *Marfani & Co. Ltd* v. *Midland Bank Ltd*,[82] the claimants, a firm of importers, had a substantial client called Eliaszade. A clerk of the claimants, K, introduced himself as 'Eliaszade' to A, a respectable customer of the defendant bank. A in turn introduced K as 'Eliaszade' to this bank, and furnished in good faith a favourable reference. Initially, K paid a small amount in cash to the credit of his new account. He then stole a cheque, drawn by his employers in favour of the real Eliaszade, and arranged for its collection by the defendant bank for the credit of his 'Eliaszade' account. K then withdrew the proceeds. The Court of Appeal held that the defendant bank had acted without negligence. Diplock LJ observed that the standard of care imposed on a collecting bank has to be interpreted with regard to current banking practice. The fact that a bank's mode of conduct might be regarded as negligent under authorities decided in a previous era was not conclusive. Banking facilities were considerably less widespread in the past than in recent years, and the required standard of care had changed accordingly. His Lordship thought that whether or not a banker acted 'without negligence' depended on the following test:[83]

---

[76] Ibid., [8]–[9]. [77] Ibid., [56]–[57]. [78] Ibid., [12]. [79] Ibid.
[80] N.5 above. [81] Ibid., 221.
[82] N.70 above. See also *Architects of Wine Ltd* v. *Barclays Bank plc*, n.70 above [4]–[5].
[83] Ibid., 973.

[W]ere those circumstances such as would cause a reasonable banker possessed of such information about his customer as a reasonable banker would possess, to suspect that his customer was not the true owner of the cheque?

If the answer was negative, the banker had acted in accordance with existing banking practice. A court ought in such a case to be hesitant before it condemned as negligent a practice generally adopted by the banking world. One important rider was added to this observation in the concurring judgment of Cairns J. His Lordship warned bankers against an attempt to rely on this decision in order to relax the practice applying to the collection of cheques. Whilst 'the defendant bank here exercised sufficient care, it was...only just sufficient'.[84]

Savory, and *Marfani* demonstrate the importance of banking practice for the determination of the bank's standard of care under section 4(1) of the Cheques Act 1957.[85] In *Savory*, the bank was held liable because it had departed from the very stringent practice prescribed in its own manual. In *Marfani*, the bank succeeded because it had adhered to the standard practice of the day. That this new practice would have been regarded as negligent in 1933, when *Savory* was decided, was considered inconclusive in 1968 when *Marfani* came before the Court of Appeal. The lesson to be derived from the two cases is that older authorities concerning the collecting bank's standard of care have to be constantly reviewed in the light of changing circumstances. The validity of modern banking practice is, however, subject to the warning in Cairns J's judgment. A dramatic relaxation of the standard of care may induce a court to conclude that banks have manifested an intention to bear the risk of losses resulting from frauds related to cheques. Such a stand would be explainable either by the banking world's realization that it was better equipped to absorb such losses than individual firms or by its tendency to yield to expediencies motivated by the ever-increasing competition for custom.[86]

Although the standard of care expected from a collecting bank is subject to change, there are some well-defined situations in which negligence may take place. Basically, these can be divided into cases in which the bank is careless at the time it opens the customer's account and cases in which the carelessness is directly connected with the cheque received for collection.

(iv) Negligence in opening an account

The notion that the collecting bank's negligence may occur at the time of the opening of the customer's account has its background in the banking practice of the nineteenth century. Banking facilities were at that period extended primarily to the business community, to members of the professions, and to the landed classes. Banks were particular as regards the acceptance of customers. In the past, it was customary for banks to demand a reference from a person who wished to open an account. Today, banks are less likely to require references when a new account is opened as they can be easily fabricated.

---

[84] Ibid., 982. See also *Thackwell* v. *Barclays Bank plc* [1986] 1 All ER 676, which also supports the view that a failure to make an enquiry is not excused by the fact that an answer would have allayed fears of fraud. See also *Crumplin* v. *London Joint Stock Bank Ltd* (1913) 19 Com. Cas. 69, 109 LT 856, where Pickford J observed that pressure of business does not excuse the bank's carelessness.

[85] For its potentially determinative nature, see *Architects of Wine Ltd* v. *Barclays Bank plc*, n.70 above, [12].

[86] On the dangers of such a course, see also *A. L. Underwood Ltd* v. *Bank of Liverpool*, n.5 above, 793.

As discussed already,[87] a bank must nowadays satisfy certain 'customer due diligence' contained in the Money Laundering Regulations 2007 before it 'establishes a business relationship' with its customer,[88] such as opening an account. In this regard, the bank is required to take steps to establish and verify the customer's identity 'on the basis of documents, date or information obtained from a reliable and independent source'[89] and obtain information from the customer concerning 'the purpose and intended nature of the business relationship'.[90] Current banking practice will require the prospective customer to produce as a minimum some form of identification, such as a passport or driving licence, together with proofs of residence at the given address, such as public utility or local authority bill. The Money Laundering Regulations 2007, therefore, are likely to provide the standard against which the reasonableness of the bank's actions will be measured.

It may be asked whether the bank's duty to make enquiries about new customers has any bearing on the type of case that gives rise to litigation involving the defence conferred under section 4(1) of the Cheques Act 1957. In many of the cases in point, the fraud and conversion perpetrated by the collecting bank's customer takes place well after the opening of the account involved, but even in these cases the account is frequently opened by the customer to facilitate the fraud. The connection between the bank's carelessness in making due enquiries concerning a new customer and frauds related to cheques collected on his behalf was discussed for the first time at the turn of the century in *Turner* v. *London and Provincial Bank Ltd*,[91] but the point was left open. The bank's duty to make enquiries was established in *Ladbroke* v. *Todd*.[92] A letter containing a cheque payable to one R. H. Jobson, an undergraduate at Oxford University, was abstracted by a rogue who forged the payee's indorsement on the cheque, and then took it to the defendant, a London banker, asking to open an account for the credit of which he proposed to remit the cheque. The rogue, who pretended to be the true payee, explained that he wished to open this new account as the cheque was in payment of a gambling debt due to him from a bookmaker, and that, if he arranged for its clearing through his usual banking account at Oxford, the college authorities might come to know of his involvement in betting activities. The rogue gave the master of the college as referee, but in view of his story, the bank opened the account and collected the cheque without making enquiries. The bank was held liable to the drawer of the cheque, who sued as the true owner. It was held that the bank's failure to take up the reference constituted negligence.

In this specific instance, an enquiry by the bank would have been effective, as the rogue was not familiar with the correct proper names of the payee, 'R. H. Jobson', and hence opened the account in the name of 'Richard Henry Jobson' instead of 'Robert Howard Jobson'. An enquiry would have revealed that the man who opened the account was not the person he purported to be. There is, however, authority for the view that the failure to make an enquiry is not excused even if it is unlikely to elucidate the truth.[93] Furthermore, the enquiry made by the bank has to solicit specific details about its prospective new customer. In theory, the object of the enquiry is to satisfy the bank that it does not undertake

---

[87] See Ch. 4, Sect. 3(iv) & Ch. 7, Sect. 2 above.

[88] Money Laundering Regulations 2007, S.I. 2007/2157 (as amended by S.I.s 2007/3299 & 2009/209), regs. 7(1)(a) & 9(2).

[89] Ibid., reg. 5(a).   [90] Ibid., reg. 5(c).

[91] (1903) 2 LDAB 33. Paget (in 24 *JIB* 220) thought that the failure to make an enquiry was too remote to have a bearing on the fraud.

[92] N.32 above.

[93] A. L. Underwood Ltd v. Bank of Liverpool, n.5 above; Thackwell v. Barclays Bank plc, n.84 above. As regards the need for references, see also *Hampstead Guardians* v. *Barclays Bank Ltd* (1923) 39 TLR 229. Cf. *Commissioners of Taxation* v. *English, Scottish and Australian Bank Ltd*, n.63 above, 688, 691.

an unusual risk when it opens the new account. The reply should provide the necessary information about the customer.

In the past, it was common practice for a bank to obtain a report about its prospective customer from a referee. The referee's report had to supply certain minimal details. To start with, the referee had to be asked about the customer's character and creditworthiness and, generally, about his circumstances in life. The customer's employment and occupation were also relevant details, as they might alert the banker's attention if at some future time the customer attempted to convert cheques of his employer.[94] At one time, when employment used to be steady, this type of enquiry was of paramount importance. It will be recalled that in *Lloyds Bank Ltd* v. *Savory & Co.*[95] it was held that the bank had to go so far as to make an enquiry about the employment of the customer's husband. In the present era, when changes in employment have become both common and acceptable, this point is likely to be given less emphasis by the courts. Thus, in *Orbit Mining and Trading Co. Ltd* v. *Westminster Bank Ltd*[96] it was held that the bank was not under a duty to keep an eye on changes in its customer's employment.

The ruling in *Orbit* is to be explained by the phenomenal increase in the number of persons who utilize banking facilities. At present, it has become impossible for banks to be familiar with the position of each of their customers. The courts have taken notice of this change of circumstances. Thus, in 1929 it was suggested in *Lloyds Bank Ltd* v. *Chartered Bank of India, Australia and China*[97] that, in addition to the enquiries made when the customer's account is opened, the bank is under a duty to scrutinize the account from time to time so as to assure itself that everything appears regular. *Orbit* shows that this suggestion is no longer in accord with modern banking practice.

In point of fact, there is good reason for doubting the entire usefulness of the request for a reference in the present era. Fundamentally, the prospective customer's referee may be either a person who is well known to the bank, such as an existing customer, or a stranger. In the former case, the bank is deemed to be entitled to rely on the referee's judgement. In the latter case, the manuals of most banks prescribe that a referee who is unknown to the bank be asked to give the name of his own bankers when he replies to the enquiry. *Marfani & Co. Ltd* v. *Midland Bank Ltd*[98] shows the ease with which even a respectable customer of a bank can be misled by an imaginative rogue who wishes to use him as a referee. In the case of a referee who is a stranger, the hazard of a misleading reference is demonstrated by *Lumsden & Co.* v. *London Trustee Savings Bank*,[99] in which a firm of accountants used to make cheques payable to their clients in an abbreviated manner. Thus, cheques payable to a firm by the name of Brown & Co. were made payable to 'Brown'. A clerk used this procedure to his own advantage. He opened an account with the defendant bank in the name of 'Brown' and gave himself as referee. Unsurprisingly, he wrote a glowing reference about 'Brown' but failed to comply with the defendant bank's request to mention the name of his own bankers. He then converted cheques drawn by his employers to the order of 'Brown', added his assumed initials, and paid the cheques into his 'Brown' account. The bank was held to have acted with negligence, as it had not followed up the referee's reply by further enquiries as to his bankers. In failing to do so, the bank had deviated from the procedure laid down in its own manual. On this basis the decision is unexceptional—an enquiry as to the rogue's bankers would have disclosed that the 'referee' was employed by the very firm whose cheques were being paid into the bogus account!

---

[94] *Lloyds Bank Ltd* v. *Savory & Co.*, n.5 above.   [95] Ibid.
[96] N.9 above, 825.   [97] N.11 above, 70.   [98] N.70 above.
[99] [1971] 1 Lloyd's Rep. 114. And see *Nu-Stilo Footwear Ltd* v. *Lloyds Bank Ltd* (1956) 7 LDAB 121, 77 JIB 239.

In reality, though, a determined rogue usually finds means of defeating a system based on communications such as references. In a society in which a large segment of the population has free access to banking facilities, the reference supplied by a person, who is able to establish that he himself is a bank's customer, loses a great deal of its significance. It is no longer what it used to be at the time that *Savory* was decided,[100] namely a document issued by a person whose status as the customer of a bank evidenced his standing and reputation. It is thus not surprising that most banks have effectively discontinued the practice of demanding references as a prerequisite to the opening of a new account.

(v) **Negligence in collection: frauds by employees, trustees, and agents**

The conversion by employees of cheques owned by their employers is a well-known source of litigation. In some cases the employee pays to the credit of his personal account a cheque payable to the employer. A forged indorsement of the employer's name is usually executed in such cases. In other cases, the employee either abuses his authority to draw cheques on the employer's account or resorts to forgery of the employer's signature or to the making of material alterations in cheques handed to him by the employer in a semi-complete state.[101] Here again, the employee arranges for the collection of the cheques for his own credit. The same practices are occasionally employed by agents who abuse their principals' trust[102] and by directors or other officers of a company.

The basic rule is that whenever a bank is aware that an employer or a principal has an interest in a cheque paid to the credit of the account of an employee, an agent, or a director, the bank is put on enquiry.[103] But this is only a general rule. There are circumstances in which the bank has no reason to become suspicious. Thus, the monthly wage cheque drawn by a firm's treasurer or secretary for his salary can be collected for the credit of his personal account without the need for an enquiry. The same applies to cheques for small amounts that can be taken to involve the reimbursement of expenses. The fact that cheques payable to the employers are paid regularly into the employee's account, however, bearing a 'per pro' indorsement, does not exonerate the bank if it had failed to make an enquiry at the initial stages. The words 'per pro' may, in effect, constitute a red flag, as they indicate to the bank that the employee acts by procuration and that there is, therefore, a possibility of an abuse of authority.[104]

Two cases illustrate the ramifications of the bank's duty of care in cases of this type. In *Lloyds Bank Ltd* v. *Chartered Bank of India, Australia and China*,[105] the chief accountant of the claimant bank had the authority to draw cheques on an account that his principals had with another bank. In abuse of this authority, he drew cheques on this account, made them payable to yet a third bank, and had them collected for a personal account that he kept without his principals' knowledge with that third bank. The cheques were collected

---

[100] *Lloyds Bank Ltd* v. *Savory & Co*, n.5 above.

[101] For an illustration, see *London Joint Stock Bank Ltd* v. *Macmillan and Arthur* [1918] AC 777, discussed in Ch. 11, Sect. 3(ii) above.

[102] See *Slingsby* v. *District Bank Ltd*, n.19 above, discussed in Ch. 11, Sect. 2(ii) above.

[103] See *Souchette* v. *London County Westminster and Parr's Bank Ltd* (1920) 36 TLR 195; *Lloyds Bank Ltd* v. *Savory & Co.*, n.5 above; *Bute (Marquess of)* v. *Barclays Bank Ltd*, n.5 above. See also *A. L. Underwood Ltd* v. *Bank of Liverpool*, n.5 above; Cf. *Moser* v. *Commercial Banking Co. of Sydney Ltd* (1974) 22 FLR 123 (Aust.).

[104] See *Morison* v. *London County and Westminster Bank Ltd*, n.5 above, which on this point is actually supported by *Midland Bank Ltd* v. *Reckitt* [1933] AC 1.

[105] N.11 above. See also *United Australia Ltd* v. *Barclays Bank Ltd*, n.7 above, 23–4; *Bute (Marquess of)* v. *Barclays Bank Ltd*, n.5 above.

without enquiries although the collecting bank was aware of the accountant's employment. It was assumed that the drawing and the collection of the cheques in question had some taxation purposes. The collecting bank was held liable in conversion, as the defence of section 82 of the BEA 1882 (now section 4(1) of the Cheques Act 1957) failed. The bank was negligent in collecting without enquiries for the accountant's personal account cheques drawn on his principals. The bank's suspicions should have been aroused by a set of circumstances. First, the cheques were drawn, without any discernible reason, by the accountant, who was an employee or agent, on the account maintained by his employers with another bank. Secondly, the amounts involved were substantial. Thirdly, as soon as the cheques were cleared, the accountant drew large sums against the proceeds in favour of persons who, to the collecting bank's knowledge, were his stockbrokers. Foul play should therefore have been suspected. An enquiry would have readily disclosed the truth.

In *Australia and New Zealand Bank Ltd* v. *Ateliers de Constructions Electriques de Charleroi*,[106] the collecting bank was in a position that lulled it into safety. A foreign company carried on business in Australia through an agent. Amounts due to the firm were usually settled by cheques made payable to it. These cheques were sent to the agent, who indorsed them and arranged for the collection for the credit of his personal account. Amounts received were regularly remitted by the agent to the foreign principals but, in the end, he became heavily indebted to them, as he had used substantial sums for his own purposes. The foreign firm's action in conversion against the collecting bank was unsuccessful. It was established that the cheques in question had been payable in Australian currency and that it would have been unreasonable to dispatch them overseas for the principal's indorsement. It was further proved that the agent had the authority to receive payments made to the principals in cash, and that the principals had never raised any objection to the clearance of cheques payable to themselves through the agent's account. The principals, thus, had been content to leave the settlement of all Australian accounts in the agent's hands. On these facts it was held that the course of business so established conferred on the agent an authority to indorse the cheques, and that the collecting bank was therefore not negligent in crediting them to his personal account. The bank, furthermore, was under no duty to supervise the drawing out of amounts received by the agent. Unlike the bank in the previously discussed case, the bank in *Ateliers de Constructions Electriques* was not expected to keep a watchful eye. It may be that, to a certain extent, the apparent difference in standard is explainable on the basis of the change in banking practice that took place during the thirty-six years that had elapsed between the two decisions.

Employers and corporations are not the only targets of frauds committed by persons in positions of trust. Public authorities are occasionally defrauded by high-ranking officials, such as rate-collectors or officers employed in a paymaster's office. Banks have to exercise caution where cheques drawn on such bodies are paid into an officer's personal account.[107] The same applies where a cheque, collected for the credit of the personal account of a trustee, is drawn on a trust account.[108] Obviously, it is important for the bank to exercise common sense.[109] A trustee will, undoubtedly, be entitled to periodic payments for

---

[106] [1967] AC 86.   [107] See *Ross* v. *London County Westminster and Parr's Bank Ltd*, n.70 above.

[108] See *House Property Co. of London Ltd* v. *London County and Westminster Bank Ltd* (1915) 31 TLR 479.

[109] Thus, the bank need not scrutinize every cheque paid into a stockbroker's account even though it is known that, in practice, he deals in trust money: *Thomson* v. *Clydesdale Bank* [1893] AC 282. See also *London and Montrose Shipbuilding and Repairing Co. Ltd* v. *Barclays Bank Ltd* (1925) 31 Com. Cas. 67, where Mackinnon J refused to accept that the bank was automatically put on enquiry where a cheque payable to

services rendered to the trust, just as a civil servant is entitled to his salary, but when the cheque, paid into a personal account out of a trust or a public fund, is of a particularly large amount, the bank ought to make an enquiry.[110]

(vi) **Negligence related to crossings**

Negligence on the collecting bank's part may take place at the time at which the cheque is handed to it. This occurs where the bank pays inadequate attention to specific details of the cheque such as a crossing and indorsements, or ignores specific aspects which question the regularity of the instrument. In *Architects of Wine Ltd* v. *Barclays Bank plc*,[111] for example, the claimant argued that the defendant collecting bank had acted negligently not only because the payee's name on the cheque differed from the name on the relevant account, but also because the cheques in question were in dollars, were mostly for large amounts, and payable to an entity whose address was abroad.[112] According to Rix LJ, these matters were insufficient to deprive the bank of its defence under section 4(1) of the Cheques Act 1957 when viewed in the light of the relevant banking practice.[113]

A particular feature of a cheque, to which a bank must pay special regard, is its crossing. As considered previously,[114] crossings are divided into special and general crossings. The former type is now obsolete and it is, in any event, unlikely that a bank will collect a cheque that is specially crossed to some other bank. An ordinary or general crossing does not impose any particular duty to take care on the bank to whom a cheque is remitted for collection. At one time, it was thought that the collecting bank had to exercise extra care when a crossing was accompanied by the words 'not negotiable', as these words could possibly hint at a defect in the payee's title,[115] but this view is no longer supported.[116] The words 'not negotiable' have the object of precluding a transferee of a cheque from becoming a holder in due course. They do not suggest that a cheque has to be collected for the account of the ostensible payee.[117] Such a cheque remains transferable and may, therefore, be collected for an account other than the ostensible payee's.[118] It will be shown that if a cheque is collected for an account other than that of the ostensible payee, however, the bank needs to satisfy itself that it bears an indorsement appearing to be in that payee's name.

Extreme caution is needed where cheques are crossed and marked 'account payee only'. This was the position even before the enactment in 1992 of section 81A(1) of the BEA 1882, which rendered such cheques non-transferable.[119] A series of cases established

---

a company was collected for an indorsee's account. This finding appears unaffected by the decision of the Court of Appeal, ibid. 182, which reversed the decision on the facts.

[110] See *Lloyds Bank Ltd* v. *Chartered Bank of India, Australia and China*, n.11 above; *Motor Traders Guarantee Corporation Ltd* v. *Midland Bank Ltd* [1937] 4 All ER 90; *Baker* v. *Barclays Bank Ltd* [1955] 1 WLR 822; *Day* v. *Bank of New South Wales* (1978) 19 ALR 32 (Aust.).

[111] N.70 above.   [112] Ibid., [58].   [113] Ibid.

[114] See Ch. 10, Sect. 4(i) above.

[115] See *Great Western Railway Co.* v. *London and County Banking Co. Ltd*, n.63 above, 422, echoed in *Morison* v. *London County and Westminster Bank Ltd*, n.5 above, 373. See also *Turner* v. *London and Provincial Bank Ltd*, n.91 above.

[116] See M. Hapgood, *Paget's Law of Banking* (13th edn., London, 2007), para. 24.31.

[117] See Ch. 10, Sect. 4(iii) above.

[118] See *Crumplin* v. *London Joint Stock Bank Ltd*, n.84 above. This applies also where the crossing is opened by the use of the words 'pay cash': *Smith and Baldwin* v. *Barclays Bank Ltd* (1944) 5 LDAB 370, 375, 65 JIB 171; *Day* v. *Bank of NSW* (1978) 19 ALR 32 (Aust.).

[119] Inserted by the Cheques Act 1992, discussed in Ch. 10, Sect. 4(iv) above.

that the words 'a/c payee only' on a crossed cheque constituted a warning to the collecting bank that the cheque might be collected for an account other than the ostensible payee's only subject to an acceptable explanation.[120] This was so, even if the words in question were added to a crossed cheque payable to 'X' or 'bearer'.[121] With the introduction in 1992 of section 81A(1) into the BEA 1882, the standards demanded of a collecting bank have, if anything, increased. The collecting bank will now have to show exceptional circumstances to come within the protection of section 4 of the Cheques Act 1957 if it collects a cheque crossed 'account payee only' for someone other than the named payee. On the other hand, if the bank collects such a cheque for the account of someone who has the same name as the named payee, but who is a different person, the bank will not be negligent on that ground alone.[122]

The cases concerning the collecting bank's duty to make enquiries in respect of crossed cheques bearing the words 'a/c payee only' dealt with instances in which the instrument was remitted for collection by a customer other than a bank, such as a private individual or a firm. The position differs where a cheque is sent for collection by a bank. Thus, in *Importers Co. Ltd* v. *Westminster Bank Ltd*,[123] a cheque bearing the crossing in question was remitted by a foreign bank to an English bank for collection for the credit of a person other than the ostensible payee. It was held that the English bank was not negligent, although it had failed to make enquiries as regards the identity of the person for whom the cheque was collected.

Does the fact that a cheque crossed 'account payee only' is now non-transferable alter the situation in any way? In *Honourable Society of the Middle Temple* v. *Lloyds Bank plc*,[124] an English clearing bank collected a stolen 'account payee' (in other words, non-transferable) cheque as collecting agent for a foreign bank located in Turkey. Rix J held the English bank to have been negligent and unable to rely on section 4 of the Cheques Act 1957 against the true owner's action for conversion of the cheque. His Lordship distinguished between a bank acting as collecting agent for a domestic bank and one acting on behalf of a foreign bank. Rix J held that a bank acting as collecting agent for a domestic bank was entitled to assume that the domestic bank knew of its responsibilities under the Cheques Act 1992, so that the agent would not be negligent in leaving it to that bank to ensure that the cheque was being collected for the named payee, unless there was something exceptional that brought the cheque to the agent's notice. By contrast, Rix J held that a bank acting as a collecting agent for a foreign bank was not entitled to make the same assumption, so that the agent would be negligent if it had failed to inform the foreign bank of its responsibilities under the Cheques Act 1992, as Lloyds had failed to do in this case. Rix J also held, however, that whilst the negligence of the English bank deprived it of the defence under section 4 of the Cheques Act 1957, it did not constitute a breach of duty to the foreign bank: 'an English clearing bank has no duty to its foreign correspondent

---

[120] *Bevan* v. *National Bank Ltd* (1906) 23 TLR 65; *Morison* v. *London County and Westminster Bank Ltd*, n.5 above, 373–4 (*obiter dictum*); *Ross* v. *London County Westminster and Parr's Bank Ltd*, n.70 above, 687; *Rhostar (Pvt.) Ltd* v. *Netherlands Bank of Rhodesia Ltd* [1972] 2 SALR 703, 705; *Standard Bank of South Africa Ltd* v. *Sham Magazine Centre* [1977] 1 SALR 48 (App. Div.); *Algemene Bank Nederland NV* v. *Happy Valley Restaurant Pte. Ltd* [1991] 2 MLJ 289 (S'pore Sup. Ct.). And see *National Commercial Banking Corp.* v. *Robert Bushby Ltd* (1984) 1 NSWLR 559, affd. *sub nom. National Commercial Banking Corp.* v. *Batty* (1986) 65 ALR 385 (Aust.).

[121] *House Property Co. of London Ltd* v. *London County and Westminster Bank Ltd*, n.108 above.

[122] Support for this proposition may be derived from *Architects of Wine Ltd* v. *Barclays Bank plc*, n.70 above, although the report does not indicate whether the cheque in that case bore any crossing.

[123] [1927] 2 KB 297.   [124] [1999] 1 All ER (Comm.) 193.

banks to advise them of every aspect of English banking law'.[125] The English collecting agent was held to be entitled to a full indemnity from its Turkish principal.[126]

Even where the bank is put on guard by the words in question, it is not obligated to refuse to collect the cheque. The collecting bank's duty is restricted to the making of due enquiries. It would be absurd to regard the bank as negligent if, at the request of the person for whose 'account only' the cheque was payable, it collected the instrument for the credit of some other account.[127] Such cases are common if the ostensible payee does not have a banking account of his own, or if some business consideration induces him to arrange that the cheque be credited to the account of some other person, such as his spouse or son.

(vii) **Negligence related to indorsements**

Until 1957, one of the traps encountered by collecting banks concerned the regularity of the payee's indorsement. There was authority for the view that, if the bank collected a cheque on which the payee's indorsement was absent or irregular, the bank forfeited its defence under section 82 of the BEA 1882 (the predecessor to section 4 of the Cheques Act 1957).[128] The seriousness of the problem is readily appreciated when one reflects on the general unfamiliarity of members of the public with the exact initials of individuals to whom they send cheques in payment of accounts, and with the exact style of the names of commercial firms.[129] Misnomers of the payee are common. Until 1957, bankers asked to collect cheques for their customers were therefore in a precarious position. To start with, it was cumbersome and time-consuming to verify the material correspondence of each indorsement of the payee of a cheque with the name by which he was described by the drawer.[130] In addition, it would have brought the entire clearing system to a standstill if, on perusal, banks had to return to their customers every cheque which was irregularly indorsed.

In some Commonwealth jurisdictions, the banking community solved its problem by supplying customers with cheque-books including forms reading 'pay—or bearer'. As such an instrument, when completed, constitutes a bearer cheque,[131] an indorsement is not needed for its transfer and the collecting bank is thus not negligent by collecting it for any customer or 'bearer'. In the United Kingdom, in which cheque forms tradition-ally assumed the style of 'pay—or order',[132] there was a need for reform. The problem was considered by the Mocatta Committee,[133] which concluded that, in view of the volume of banking business, the need to verify the regularity of indorsements ought to be abolished.

This recommendation was given effect by the enactment of section 4(3) of the Cheques Act 1957, which provides that a banker is not negligent *by reason only* of his failure to concern himself with the absence of or the irregularity in an indorsement.[134]

---

[125] Ibid., 225.   [126] See further Sect. 7 below.

[127] *Souhrada* v. *Bank of New South Wales* [1976] 2 Lloyd's Rep. 444, 452 (where the payee requested that the cheque be collected for the account of another person).

[128] *Bavins Jnr. & Sims* v. *London and South Western Bank Ltd*, n.7 above. See also *Bissell & Co.* v. *Fox Bros. & Co.*, n.68 above varied, on a different point, n.68 above.

[129] *Architects of Wine Ltd* v. *Barclays Bank plc*, n.70 above, [56].   [130] Ibid., [9].

[131] See Ch. 10, Sect. 3(iii) above.

[132] Oddly enough, bearer forms were common during the second half of the nineteenth century, but order forms took precedence from the beginning of this century.

[133] See Ch. 11, Sect. 4(v) above.

[134] The bank is therefore discharged from liability: *Westminster Bank* v. *Zang*, n.43 above, 218.

This provision was, however, considered too sweeping by the CLCB, which thought that it was in the interest of the public that, in certain cases, collecting banks should continue to require regular indorsements of cheques. A circular in point, issued on 23 September 1957, prescribed that indorsements be required in three cases. The first was where a cheque was tendered for an account other than that of the ostensible payee. In such cases, the bank had to verify the regularity of the indorsements of the original payee and of any subsequent party to whom the cheque had been specially indorsed, except the customer for whose account the instrument was collected. The second type of case was where the payee's name was misspelt on the cheque, or where he was incorrectly designated and the surrounding circumstances were suspicious. Thirdly, the indorsement of each payee continued to be needed where the cheque was payable jointly to more than one person, but was collected for an account to which not all payees were parties.[135]

Although the circular in question did not have the force of law, the practice established by it has remained in effect. A bank that ignores it does so at its peril. This is due to the wording of section 4(3) of the Cheques Act 1957, under which a bank is not to be considered negligent 'by reason only' of the defect related to the indorsement. If the bank disregards the procedures consecrated by the circular, it is negligent not by reason of the irregular or absent indorsement, but because it has departed from the guidelines concerning indorsements formulated by the CLCB, which can currently be taken to represent prevailing banking practice. It can, further, be assumed that where the circular requires the collecting bank to demand an indorsement, it is essential that this indorsement be regular.

(viii) **Negligence: summary**

The instances outlined above are by no means an exhaustive list of the situations in which a bank may be held to have acted negligently within the meaning of section 4(1) of the Cheques Act 1957. The constant changes in banking practice may lead to the development of new case law in point, and, as indicated already, procedures that were considered to involve negligence in days gone by may currently be sanctioned by modern practice.[136] There may also be one factor that has not been given adequate emphasis to date, namely the amount of the cheque. Although the amount of the cheque is only likely to be in itself a ground for suspicion in the most extreme cases,[137] the amount of money at stake may well alter the level of enquiry that a bank is expected to undertake. It is arguable that, where an oddity or red flag appears in a cheque for a relatively small amount, the collecting bank is entitled to dismiss any concerns it might have on the basis of a cursory enquiry of the instrument itself. The same enquiry may not suffice where the amount of the cheque is out of proportion to the known position in life of the customer.[138] Such a consideration is

---

[135] Indorsements also remained necessary under the circular in the case of the collection of the following documents: bills of exchange other than cheques; promissory notes; drafts and other instruments drawn on the General Post Office; internal revenue warrants; drafts drawn on the Paymaster-General or the Queen's and Lord Treasurer's Remembrancer; drafts drawn on the Crown Agents and other specified agents; travellers' cheques and instruments payable by banks abroad.

[136] For example, the failure to enquire at the time of the opening of the account about the occupation of the customer's spouse, which was held to involve negligence in *Lloyds Bank Ltd* v. *Savory & Co.*, n.5 above.

[137] See *Architects of Wine Ltd* v. *Barclays Bank plc*, n.70 above, [58].

[138] The collection without enquiry of a cheque the sum of which is out of proportion to the customer's station in life has been held to involve negligence: see *Lloyds Bank Ltd* v. *Chartered Bank of India, Australia and China Ltd*, n.11 above; *Motor Traders Guarantee Corporation Ltd* v. *Midland Bank Ltd*, n.110 above; *Nu-Stilo Footwear* v. *Lloyds Bank Ltd*, n.99 above; *Day* v. *Bank of New South Wales*, n.110 above.

likely to be much more relevant in relation to personal customers rather than corporate customers.

In all cases of conversion, the bank's duty to act without negligence is given a reasonable construction. As indicated previously, the Court of Appeal in *Architects of Wine Ltd* v. *Barclays Bank plc*[139] stressed that a bank is not expected to assume the role of an amateur detective, and need not be unduly suspicious.[140] Thus, in *Orbit Mining and Trading Co. Ltd* v. *Westminster Bank Ltd*[141] a rogue perpetrated a series of frauds by utilizing a cheque-book of the company left in his sole custody by a fellow director. In some instances, cheques had been signed by the fellow director in blank so that the rogue was able to complete them by adding his signature. In other cases he forged his fellow director's signature and added his own. He made all these cheques out either to 'cash or order' or to himself, and paid them for the credit of his personal account with the defendant bank. To camouflage his dual role as signatory and payee, he indorsed the cheques with a signature differing from that executed by him on the front of the cheque. The bank was unaware of the rogue's current occupation because he had changed his post and entered the service of the company after the opening of his account. The bank, therefore, collected the cheques without making enquiries. The company's action in conversion failed as the bank was held entitled to the protection of section 4 of the Cheques Act 1957. The bank had not acted negligently by failing to compare the signature with the indorsement, although, consequently, it did not discover that the customer was both the payee and the actual drawer of the cheque. The fact that some of the cheques were payable to 'cash or order' was likewise no cause for extra concern.

5 The defence of contributory negligence

In certain situations, the conversion of a cheque is facilitated by the true owner's carelessness. This is the case where a cheque is handed to an employee in an incomplete form, or where an employee is left in charge of the affairs of his employers without any attempt at supervision. In *Morison* v. *London County and Westminster Bank Ltd*,[142] it was suggested that, on common law principles, the true owner of a series of cheques converted by his employee and collected by the latter's bank, ought not to succeed if his actions had lulled the bank into safety or alleviated its suspicions. The weakness in this argument is that, if the bank's own negligence had facilitated the conversion of the initial instrument, the bank should not be heard to argue that it was misled by the true owner's lack of vigilance on later occasions.

An alternative defence is the plea of contributory negligence, under which the loss is to be apportioned between the bank and the true owner on the basis of their respective negligent acts. At one stage the availability of this defence was doubted because the true owner's action against the bank was brought in conversion or based on waiver of tort. It was, thus, not an action in negligence. It was thought that, as the true owner was not attempting to recover damages for a loss resulting from the bank's breach of a duty of care

---

[139] N.70 above [11]–[12].

[140] See *Penmount Estates Ltd* v. *National Provincial Bank Ltd* (1945) 173 LT 344, 346. See also *Smith and Baldwin* v. *Barclays Bank Ltd*, n.118 above.

[141] N.9 above.   [142] N.5 above.

owed to him, he could equally not be regarded as being in breach of a duty of care owed by him to the bank.[143]

The thrust of this analysis was to assert that contributory negligence could not be maintained as a defence in an action brought for a tort other than negligence. This view was refuted in 1950 by the New Zealand Court of Appeal in *Helson* v. *McKenzies (Cuba Street) Ltd.*[144] A handbag that a customer had forgotten at a counter of a department store was innocently delivered by a shop assistant to an impostor. A plea of contributory negligence raised as a partial defence to the customer's action in conversion was allowed on the basis of a local provision *in pari materia* with section 1 of the Law Reform (Contributory Negligence) Act 1945. The Court held that it was not necessary to establish that the claimant, the customer, had committed a breach of duty of care owed by her to the store-owners. Contributory negligence was established once it was shown that the claimant had acted in a careless manner that facilitated the conversion of the chattel.

The reasoning in *Helson*'s case was adopted by Donaldson J in *Lumsden & Co.* v. *London Trustee Savings Bank*,[145] in which the employers' lack of vigilance and careless mode of drawing cheques enabled an employee to appropriate them to his own use. It was held that the employers' carelessness, which had facilitated the fraud, involved contributory negligence on their part, and could be raised as a partial defence to their action in conversion against the collecting bank. A series of Australian decisions[146] has, however, questioned the correctness of this decision on the ground that, under section 1, the defence of contributory negligence is available only in situations in which it could have been pleaded as an absolute defence at common law. At common law, it is asserted, the plea was available only in respect of actions in negligence. The point is debatable from an historical point of view. In the United Kingdom it has been settled by section 47 of the Banking Act 1979, under which the defence is available to a banker 'in any circumstances in which proof of absence of negligence on the part of the banker would be a defence in proceedings by reason of section 4 of the Cheques Act 1957'.[147]

It is believed that the plea of contributory negligence provides an equitable solution. There is no justification for forcing banks to carry the burden of the full loss incurred in a fraud facilitated by the carelessness of the drawer of a cheque. The argument that, commercially, losses of this type can be more readily absorbed by banks than by individual firms is without merit. In the first place, a means test constitutes an arbitrary method for the distribution of losses. Secondly, if such losses have to be absorbed by the banks they are bound to be passed on to the general body of customers by means of eventual increases in bank charges. There is no reason for apportioning losses incurred due to the carelessness of specific individuals or firms among the general body of the collecting bank's customers.

---

[143] This view is echoed in *Savory & Co.* v. *Lloyds Bank Ltd* [1932] 2 KB 122, 137 (CA), affd. n.5 above.

[144] [1950] NZLR 878.   [145] N.99 above. See Sect. 4(iv) above.

[146] *Wilton* v. *Commonwealth Trading Bank of Australia* [1973] 2 NSWLR 644; *Tina Motors Pty. Ltd* v. *Australia and New Zealand Banking Group Ltd* [1977] VR 205, 208–9; *Day* v. *Bank of New South Wales*, n.110 above, 42 ff; *Grantham Homes Pty. Ltd* v. *Interstate Permanent Building Society Ltd* (1979) 37 FLR 191; *Oxland Enterprises Pty. Ltd* v. *Gierke* (1980) 91 LSJS 276. Cf. *Varker* v. *Commercial Banking Co. of Sydney Ltd* [1972] 2 NSWLR 967.

[147] The object of this provision (not repealed by the 1987 Act) was to resolve any doubts that could have arisen on this point under s.11(1) of the Torts (Interference with Goods) Act 1977 (see *Uzinterimpex JSC* v. *Standard Bank plc* [2008] EWCA Civ 819, [57]).

6 The discounting bank's protection

On occasions a discounting bank is entitled to plead two defences against an action for the conversion of a cheque. The first is the defence based on section 4 of the Cheques Act 1957. The second defence is that, by discounting the cheque, the bank became its holder in due course and consequently acquired an indefeasible title to the instrument. However, as United Kingdom banks now almost invariably issue their customers with cheque forms which are crossed and pre-printed with the words 'account payee' or 'account payee only', thereby making the cheque non-transferable, the holder in due course defence will rarely be available to a collecting bank in this country.

For a considerable period of time some authorities continued to maintain that, even after the enactment of the Cheques Act in 1957, the defence of section 4 was not available to a discounting bank.[148] Support for this view was found in the marginal note of the section, which reads: 'Protection of bankers collecting payment of cheques etc.' A discounting bank was, accordingly, alleged to be outside the ambit of this provision. However, the language of the section itself supports the very opposite view, as the provision explicitly protects a banker, who 'having credited a customer's account with the amount of such an instrument receives payment thereof for himself'.

The view that section 4 of the Cheques Act 1957 is wide enough to protect a discounting bank is further supported by a consideration of the historical background of this provision. It will be recalled that, originally, section 82 of the BEA 1882 applied only where a bank 'received payment for a customer'. This phraseology induced the House of Lords to conclude, in *Capital and Counties Bank Ltd* v. *Gordon*,[149] that the section was inapplicable where the bank credited the customer's account before clearance as, in such a case, the bank received payment for itself. Under the ensuing amending Act of 1906,[150] a bank was deemed to have received payment for a customer notwithstanding that it credited his account before receiving payment of the cheque. Obviously, this specific amendment did not purport to extend the protection of section 82 to a banker who, in addition to the crediting of the customer's account before clearance, agreed to grant him overdraft facilities against the cheque. In such a situation, the crediting of the customer's account was not a mere matter of accounting procedure, and the bank became a holder of the cheque.[151] It followed that, in such cases, the bank received payment of the instrument for itself. Thus, between 1906 and 1957 the defence in section 82 of the BEA 1882 remained available only to a collecting bank, but it could not be pleaded by a discounting bank.

The position has been altered by section 4 of the Cheques Act 1957, as its language is patently wider than that of the 1906 amendment. As pointed out above, subsection 1(*b*) extends the defence to a bank that receives payment for itself after having credited the customer's account. This formula encompasses the discounting bank's activity. Obviously, to succeed under section 4 the discounting bank has to satisfy the requirements prescribed in this provision. The bank must have acted in good faith and 'without negligence' for a customer. Furthermore, the discounting bank can invoke the defence in section 4 of the Cheques Act 1957 only if the amount of the cheque has been credited to the customer's account. If the discount was arranged by means of payment of cash

---

[148] See, for example, M. Megrah, *Paget's Law of Banking* (7th edn., London, 1966); but see now M. Hapgood, n.116 above, paras. 24.32–24.35.

[149] N.37 above.   [150] The Bills of Exchange (Crossed Cheques Act) 1906, s.1.

[151] See *Re Farrow's Bank Ltd*, n.42 above; *A. L. Underwood Ltd* v. *Bank of Liverpool*, n.5 above.

against the instrument or by the crediting of some third party's account, the section is inapplicable.[152]

Where a discounting bank is unable to invoke the defence of section 4, it may still resist a claim by establishing that it received payment as the holder in due course of the instrument. The holder in due course of a negotiable instrument becomes its true owner and cannot be sued in conversion.[153] To be considered the holder in due course of a cheque, the bank has to prove that it took it in good faith and for value, and that the cheque was, at that time, complete and regular on its face.[154]

The last requirement can frequently constitute a pitfall. A cheque is considered incomplete if any material detail, such as the name of the payee or the amount payable, is missing. A cheque is considered irregular whenever anything in it ought to give rise to doubts or suspicion, as is the case where the words denoting the amount differ from the figures, or where the cheque is pasted together after having been torn.[155] Moreover, the word 'face' in section 29 of the BEA 1882 includes the back of the cheque. Under this section, a cheque payable to order is, therefore, considered irregular if it is unindorsed or if it is irregularly indorsed by the payee.[156] But the requisite concerning the indorsements has been mitigated by the Cheques Act 1957. Section 2 confers on a bank which gives value for a cheque payable to order, which the holder delivers to it for collection without indorsing it, such rights as the bank would have had if the cheque had been indorsed in blank.

Two cases show that a discounting bank may rely on section 2 in order to establish that it is a holder in due course of an unindorsed cheque. In *Midland Bank Ltd* v. *R.V. Harris Ltd*,[157] a customer paid into his personal account with the claimant bank two cheques drawn by the defendant on Lloyds Bank and payable to the customer's firm. The cheques were dishonoured by Lloyds Bank, and the claimant bank brought an action claiming to be a holder in due course of the cheques. It was proved that the customer was allowed to draw against the cheques before their clearance. Although the cheques did not bear an indorsement, it was held that, under section 2, the claimant bank was to be treated as a holder in due course of the cheques despite the absence of an indorsement.[158]

In *Westminster Bank* v. *Zang*,[159] a customer of the claimant bank paid into the account of a company of which he was a director, and which maintained its account with the same bank, an unindorsed cheque, drawn by the defendant and payable to the customer's order. The defendant stopped the cheque, which was accordingly dishonoured by the drawee bank. The claimant bank brought an action to enforce payment, claiming to be a holder in due course. As it was proved that the claimant bank had not given value for the cheque, it was held that it was not a holder in due course or for value, and could not enforce payment. The House of Lords held, however, that if the claimant bank had given value for the cheque, it would have been a holder in due course despite the missing indorsement. It was further held that the fact that the cheque was not collected for the original payee's account was irrelevant.

These two cases demonstrate that a bank may be considered a holder in due course in circumstances in which an ordinary member of the public—who is less familiar with

---

[152] In this regard the position has remained the same as under s.82 of the BEA 1882, which was discussed in this regard in *Capital and Counties Bank Ltd* v. *Gordon*, n.37 above. See also *Great Western Railways* v. *London and County Banking Co. Ltd*, n.63 above; *Commissioners of Taxation* v. *English, Scottish and Australian Bank Ltd*, n.63 above.

[153] See Ch. 11, Sect. 2 above. [154] BEA 1882, s.29, discussed in Ch. 10, Sect. 5(iii) below.

[155] Ibid. [156] *Arab Bank Ltd* v. *Ross* [1952] 2 QB 216. [157] [1963] 1 WLR 1021.

[158] The circular of 11 September 1957, mentioned in Ch. 10, Sect. 2 above, was not discussed. Probably no reliance was put on it, as the claimant bank had discounted rather than collected the cheques.

[159] N.43 above.

negotiable instruments than a bank—would not be so regarded. It should be noted that a person may be a holder in due course although he has acted with negligence. Accordingly, a discounting bank may find it useful to rely on its being a holder in due course of a cheque if it is unable to prove that it had acted without negligence. If the bank cannot show that it is a holder in due course, for example, where it has discounted an order cheque bearing a forged indorsement,[160] it may still escape liability for conversion by relying on section 4, provided the cheque has been credited to the account of a customer.

7 The processing bank's position

In certain cases the holder of a cheque delivers it to a branch other than that with which he maintains his account. This appears to have been possible as from the turn of the century if both branches were of the same bank. The Golden Memorandum[161] of 1967 went further than that. It enabled a person to remit a cheque to any branch of one of the participating banks for the credit of any account maintained with one of the banks within the system. Although the memorandum is no longer in effect, there are specific arrangements—known as agency agreements—between some of the clearing banks which give effect to the system on a bank to bank basis.

Where a customer remits a cheque to his bank account through any branch of his own bank, the position is simple. As a bank constitutes one single legal entity regardless of the number of its branches, the branch to which the holder remits his cheque and the branch of the same bank at which he maintains the account credited with the proceeds constitute two arms of the collecting bank. The fact that the cheque is collected through a branch other than that with which the account is maintained does not in itself involve negligence, and does not deprive the collecting bank of the defence of section 4. The bank would, however, be considered negligent if knowledge possessed by the branch at which the account was maintained would have put that branch on enquiry.[162]

The position differs altogether where the cheque is remitted by the holder to one bank with a request that its proceeds be credited to an account which he maintains with a different bank. By way of illustration, take a cheque drawn on the West End Branch of the L Bank, which the payee remits to the Piccadilly Branch of the B Bank with a request that the proceeds be credited to his account with the Holborn Branch of the M Bank. What is the position of the B Bank and of the M Bank if it turns out that the cheque has been converted by the payee? For the sake of convenience the M Bank will be called the collecting bank and the B Bank the processing bank.

It would appear that both the collecting bank and the processing bank can be sued in conversion. This analysis is based on the fact that in a transaction of this sort the processing bank acts as the collecting bank's agent. As the payee of the cheque does not maintain an account with the processing bank and has no other relationship of contract with it, it is inconceivable that the bank agrees to act on his behalf without obtaining any direct or indirect remuneration. As the processing bank arranges for the presentation of the cheque to the drawee bank, it performs a proprietary act affecting the instrument. The fact that it

---

[160] See Ch. 10, Sect. 8(iii) below.   [161] See Ch. 10, Sect. 2 above.

[162] See *Ross* v. *London County Westminster and Parr's Bank Ltd*, n.70 above; *Lloyds Bank Ltd* v. *Savory & Co.*, n.5 above, 235 (note that in the Court of Appeal it was thought that the collection through another branch involved negligence: [1932] 2 KB 122, 141); *Orbit Mining and Trading Co. Ltd* v. *Westminster Bank Ltd*, n.9 above, 814.

performs this act on behalf of the collecting bank does not exonerate the processing bank from liability in conversion any more than the collecting bank, in an ordinary transaction, can be heard to say that it is discharged from liability as it acts as the customer's agent. The collecting bank, in the type of transaction here analysed, is also liable. It is answerable to the true owner as it is vicariously liable for the conversion of the cheque by its agent, the processing bank. If the collecting bank has not paid out the proceeds to the customer, it can, further, be sued in an action in restitution for wrongdoing based on the true owner's waiver of the tort.[163]

When an action is brought by the true owner, are the processing bank and the collecting bank entitled to plead the defence of section 4? This question gives rise to two problems. The first is whether either one of the two banks, or perhaps both of them, are encompassed by the language of section 4 in a transaction of the type here described. The second problem involves the consideration of the ability of each of the two banks to satisfy the most difficult requirement of the section, namely the absence of negligence. It will be convenient to discuss the position of the two banks separately.

The processing bank appears to be altogether outside the scope of section 4. It collects the cheque for the credit of an account maintained by the payee with another bank. The payee, therefore, is usually not a customer of the processing bank. Undoubtedly, there are cases in which the payee may be a customer of both the processing bank and the collecting bank, and may request for reasons of his own that the account to be credited be that of the collecting bank.[164] But even in such a case the processing bank does not receive the proceeds for the payee's account with itself. It arranges for the clearance of the cheque for the payee's account with the collecting bank and hence, in the specific transaction involved, is not acting for the payee qua customer. It may be asked whether the difficulty is to be overcome by treating the collecting bank as the processing bank's customer. The argument, however, is futile, as the processing bank does not receive the proceeds and does not itself credit the collecting bank's account. It simply remits the cheque to the drawee bank through the clearing house, and transmits an advice of the receipt of the cheque to the collecting bank. It is submitted that the better view is that the processing bank cannot claim the defence of section 4. Moreover, even if it were able to rely on it, the processing bank would in all probability be unable to establish that it had acted without negligence: in practice a processing bank accepts such cheques without making any enquiries.

The position of the collecting bank is less hazardous. When the customer's account is credited by the clearing department and the customer is not permitted to withdraw the funds before the cheque is cleared, the collecting bank receives payment on the customer's behalf. The collecting bank then falls within the ambit of section 4(1) of the Cheques Act 1957. If the customer is granted an overdraft before clearance, his bank assumes the role of a discounting bank.[165] It is therefore engaged in a transaction covered by section 4(1)(b). The difficulty that is likely to arise relates, however, to the question of negligence. In the type of case here discussed, the collecting bank does not make a conscious decision to accept the cheque for collection. It usually receives the proceeds without demur. How, then, can it be heard to claim that it has acted without negligence?

The collecting bank's main hope in such cases is to establish that under current banking practice it is not obliged to exercise any discretion where a cheque is being collected through a processing bank. The importance of banking practice which is found to be too lax or too risky as regards the care in the collection of cheques is, of course, well

---

[163] See Sect. 2 above, discussing also the feasibility of a general count in money had and received.
[164] For example, if he has drawn cheques on his account with the collecting bank.
[165] See Sect. 3 above.

established.[166] But it would be an error to ignore the warning in *Marfani*'s case, where Cairns J indicated that the courts may decide to condemn as negligent a general banking practice which is found to be too lax or too risky as regards the public interest.[167] It is believed that the practice originally introduced by the 1967 memorandum, and currently consecrated in specific agreements between some clearing banks, may become a source of litigation.

Issues arising from the processing of a cheque by two banks arise also where the holder maintains his account with a bank that does not have direct access to the clearing system. It will be recalled that, in such a case, the collecting bank delivers the cheque to the clearing department of the clearer, whom it uses as its agent.[168] Undoubtedly, both banks are liable in conversion if the holder of the cheque does not have a title to it. It is, at the same time, believed that both banks are entitled to plead the defence of section 4 of the Cheques Act 1957. As the holder maintains an account with the non-clearing bank, he is that bank's customer. Accordingly, the non-clearing bank has the usual defence conferred on a collecting bank under section 4. The non-clearing bank, in turn, is its agent's customer. It may be argued that, as the amount of the cheque is credited directly to the holder's account with the non-clearing bank and not to that bank's account with its agent, the clearer cannot invoke the defence of section 4(1)(*b*). However, when the amount of the cheque is paid as part of the global settlement at the Bank of England, the clearing bank receives the amount of the cheque for the non-clearing bank, which is its customer. As between these two banks the transaction falls, accordingly, within the ambit of section 4(1)(*a*).

In the event that a clearing bank is held liable in conversion to the true owner of a cheque when collecting the cheque as agent of another bank, the clearing bank, as collecting agent, will usually seek to recover against that other bank as its principal. The collecting agent may have the benefit of an indemnity from the principal bank to cover any liabilities incurred by the agent whilst acting for the principal. Alternatively, the principal may have warranted to the collecting agent that, for example, the customer for whom the principal is collecting the cheque was entitled to do so.

In *Honourable Society of the Middle Temple* v. *Lloyds Bank plc*,[169] an English clearing bank (Lloyds) collected a stolen English cheque marked 'account payee only' as agent for a foreign collecting bank (Sekerbank) whose customer was not the named payee. The true owner (Middle Temple) sued both banks for converting the cheque. Rix J held that both Lloyds and Sekerbank were unable to bring themselves within the 'no negligence' defence provided by section 4 of the Cheques Act 1957 and that each was liable to Middle Temple. Lloyds then claimed an indemnity from Sekerbank. The claim was put in two ways. First, that as an agent requested to collect a cheque, Lloyds did precisely what it was asked to do and was entitled to an implied indemnity from Sekerbank against any liability incurred in the course of carrying out its instructions. Secondly, that Sekerbank had impliedly warranted to Lloyds that Sekerbank's customer was entitled to have the proceeds of the cheque paid to him. Rix J held that Lloyds was entitled to a complete indemnity from Sekerbank on both these grounds.

Rix J's decision was subsequently followed by Gross J in *Linklaters* v. *HSBC Bank plc*,[170] which only differed on its facts from the *Middle Temple* decision in one material respect. In this case HSBC was both the bank upon which the stolen cheque had been drawn and also the collecting agent for the foreign bank into which it had been paid. In the

---

[166] See Sect. 4(iii) above.   [167] Ibid.   [168] See Ch. 10, Sect. 2 above.
[169] N.124 above.   [170] [2003] 2 Lloyd's Rep. 545.

Middle Temple case the paying bank and the collecting agent had been different banks. However, Gross J held that this was a distinction without a difference and that, in the interests of certainty, the result should be the same in both cases.[171]

8 The collecting bank which is also the paying bank

Up to now the discussion has related to situations in which two or more banks participate in clearing a cheque. In some cases, though, only one bank is involved in the process. This occurs in two types of situation. The first is where one branch of a given bank acts as the collecting agent of the payee and the cheque is drawn on another branch of the same bank. The second case is where both the drawer and the payee maintain their accounts with one and the same branch. Cases of the latter type are uncommon. Cases of the former type are numerous, as each of the five big clearing banks has a substantial share of current accounts opened in England and Wales. Two branches of one of these giant chains often act respectively for the payee and for the drawer.

From a legal point of view, both types of case lead to complex problems. A bank has a single legal personality, which encompasses all its branches.[172] It is true that the owner of an account has to demand payment at the branch at which the account is kept.[173] But this rule is based on a term of the contract of banker and customer, and does not imply that, for the purpose of the clearance of cheques, each branch is to be treated as if it had a separate legal personality.[174] It follows that where two branches of the same bank act, respectively, as the collecting agent and as the paying station, the bank itself performs both the function of a collecting bank and of a paying bank. What is such a bank's position? The specific protections which are given to banks under the BEA 1882 and the Cheques Act 1957 confer separate defences on the bank as payor of cheques drawn on it and as collector of cheques remitted by customers. This clear-cut separation is based on historical reasons. In the nineteenth century the English banking world comprised a network of small and independent banks, many of which had one office only. It comes, therefore, as no surprise that the 1882 Act and the 1957 Act, which amended it, fail to deal with the type of situation discussed presently. Sections 60 and 80 of the 1882 Act, as augmented by section 1 of the 1957 Act, deal exclusively with the protection of a bank that wrongfully honours a cheque drawn on it; section 4 of the 1957 Act (which has replaced section 82 of the original Act) confers a protection on a bank that collects a cheque for a customer. Which defence is available to a bank that acts for both the drawer and the payee?

Three basic solutions to the problem are possible. The first is to confer a right of election on the bank that acts, at one and the same time, as paying and as collecting bank. Under this solution, a bank that was sued for the wrongful payment of a cheque could still plead the defence of section 4, provided it had also acted as a collecting bank, and provided further that it was able to establish the absence of negligence in its having done so. The second approach is to expect the bank to carry out all duties imposed on it as regards both the collection and the payment of cheques.

The third possibility is to expect the bank to meet the standard prescribed in respect of the function or functions consciously performed by it in respect of a given cheque. Thus,

---

[171] See E.P. Ellinger, 'Liabilities of Bank when Crossed Cheque Collected Overseas' (2004) 120 *LQR* 226.

[172] But not subsidiary companies, such as an affiliated merchant bank.   [173] See Ch. 7, Sect. 1 above.

[174] The same applies to cases in which the branches are situated in different countries. For an example, see *Power Curber International Ltd* v. *National Bank of Kuwait* [1981] 1 WLR 1233.

if a cheque is collected and paid through two separate branches, the bank consciously performs the roles of both a collecting and a paying bank. The bank may therefore be expected to act with the degree of care required by a bank in both capacities. Accordingly, it could plead the defences available to it in both roles. If a cheque is paid to the credit of a customer whose account is maintained with the branch on which it is drawn, the cheque is, in effect, paid rather than collected. The bank is, therefore, to be regarded as a paying bank rather than as a collecting bank. Its liability should not exceed that to which it is subjected when a cheque is presented for payment over the counter.

The courts appear to favour the third, functional, solution. Thus, where a cheque is handled by two separate branches of the same bank, the courts treat the holder's branch as if it were a collecting bank and the drawer's branch as a paying bank. This approach is evident already in the nineteenth-century decision in *Woodland* v. *Fear*.[175] Here the B Branch of the S bank, which, at the holder's request, had cashed a cheque drawn on the G Branch, was allowed to recover the amount paid to the holder when the cheque, for which there was no adequate cover, was dishonoured by the G Branch. As the B Branch had, functionally, agreed to negotiate or collect the cheque, it had a collecting bank's right of recourse when the cheque was dishonoured. Similarly, in *London Provincial and South-Western Bank* v. *Buszard*[176] the drawer countermanded a cheque by giving notice to the branch with which he maintained his account. Lawrence J held that another branch of the same bank, which had paid the payee part of the proceeds of the cheque in cash and credited the balance to her account, became the holder of the instrument. The bank was, accordingly, entitled to reimbursement when the cheque was dishonoured when presented to the drawer's branch.

A modern Canadian authority suggests that in the type of situation under consideration the bank may be in a position to enforce the cheque against the drawer. In *William Cuirliani Ltd* v. *Royal Bank of Canada*,[177] the claimant, who was a car dealer, gave one J—from whom he had purchased a car—a cheque drawn on the defendant bank's B Branch. J asked the C Branch to pay him $2,900 against the cheque and to credit the balance to the account maintained by him with that branch. On obtaining an assurance of the availability of cover from the B Branch, the manager of the C Branch approved the advance. Later in the day the claimant discovered that the car was subject to an encumbrance and, thereupon, countermanded payment. The defendant bank refused to reverse the debit entry made in the claimant's account. Although Parker J accepted that the countermand given to the B Branch was valid, he concluded that, when the C Branch gave value for the cheque by the payment of the $2,900, the defendant bank became a holder in due course. It was, therefore, entitled to enforce payment.

In the cases just considered, the courts regarded the collecting branch and the paying branch as performing separate functions. The bank was, effectively, treated as if each branch had been a separate legal entity. By the same token, if, in a different type of case, a bank were sued in conversion by a true owner, whose cheque had been paid by a fraudster to the credit of an account maintained with the C Branch, the bank would be entitled to rely on the defence of section 4 although the cheque was drawn upon and honoured by that bank's P Branch. If the action were instead brought by the drawer for the wrongful

---

[175] (1857) 7 E & B 519, discussed in Ch. 11, Sect. 1(ii) above.   [176] (1918) 35 TLR 142.

[177] (1972) 26 DLR (3d.) 552 (Ont. HC). See also *Bank of NSW* v. *Ross, Stuckey and Morowa* [1974] 2 Lloyd's Rep. 110 (W. Aust. Sup. Ct.); cf. *Capital Associates Ltd* v. *Royal Bank of Canada* (1970) 15 DLR (3d) 234 (Queb. Sup. Ct.), where a similar principle was applied where collection and payment were effected by the same branch. Mackay J held that the countermand became effective only by the end of the time needed by a single branch to set the necessary procedures into motion and to act on it.

honour of the cheque, the bank would, it is believed, be entitled to rely on the common law and statutory defences available to it in respect of the payment effected by the P Branch.

The principles governing cases in which a cheque is collected and paid by two separate branches of a single bank appear, accordingly, to be clear-cut. No such certainty prevails where the cheque is collected and paid by a single branch. Some authorities treat the bank as assuming, in this type of case, the function of honouring the cheque. Thus, in *Bissell & Co.* v. *Fox Bros. & Co.*,[178] a mercantile firm had a travelling salesman, whose personal account was maintained with the same single office bank as his employers' account. This salesman indorsed a number of cheques payable to the firm by executing a 'per pro' indorsement, and arranged for their payment to the credit of his personal account. One of the cheques in question was actually drawn by the client on the bank with which the travelling salesman and the firm kept their respective accounts. At the trial, Denman J held that the bank was liable in conversion as a collecting bank in respect of the cheques drawn on other banks, but that it was protected in the case of the cheque drawn on itself under section 60 of the 1882 Act. The Court of Appeal affirmed this decision, treating the bank as having paid rather than collected the cheque drawn on itself. The court reached this decision notwithstanding that the cheque in question was credited by the bank to the travelling salesman's account and not paid to him over the counter. A similar approach was adopted by the Court of Appeal in *Gordon* v. *London, City and Midland Bank Ltd.*[179] Collins MR held that, where the bank was able to satisfy the requirements set out in section 60, it was not liable as a collecting bank. In this case the cheque was collected by a branch other than that on which it was drawn; but the court regarded itself as bound by its previous decision. On the facts, however, the bank was held not to have been negligent. It is noteworthy that the exact role of a bank that assumes the dual capacity of paying and of collecting a cheque was not discussed by the House of Lords.[180]

A different view was taken by the Court of Appeal in *Carpenters' Co.* v. *British Mutual Banking Co. Ltd.*[181] In this case both the claimant company and one of its clerks maintained accounts with the defendant bank, which had only one office. By means of different types of frauds the clerk obtained cheques drawn by the company in favour of tradesmen and, having forged the required indorsements, paid these cheques for the credit of his personal account with the defendant bank. When the frauds were discovered, the company sought to recover its losses from the bank in an action based alternatively on the wrongful payment of the cheques and on their conversion. The bank relied on the defences available to it both as paying bank and as collecting bank. Branson J followed the decision of the Court of Appeal in the *Gordon* case but was reversed by the Court of Appeal. Greer LJ, who delivered one of the majority judgments, thought that section 60 'only protects a bank when that bank is merely a paying bank, and is not a bank which receives the cheque for collection'.[182] He thought that the trial judge had erred in treating the defendant bank as if it had merely paid the cheque. On the facts, the case involved an action in conversion and the only defence available to the defendant bank, qua collecting

[178] (1885) 53 LT 19. See also *Backhouse* v. *Charlton* (1878) 8 Ch. D 444. See further Ch. 8, Sect. 3(iii) above.

[179] N.37 above, 274–5. See also *Universal Guarantee Pty. Ltd* v. *National Bank of Australasia Ltd* [1965] 1 WLR 691, 696 (PC).

[180] [1903] AC 240 sub nom. *Capital and Counties Bank Ltd* v. *Gordon*, affirming the decision of the Court of Appeal; the ratio related to the fact that the amount had been received before clearance and hence not for a customer.

[181] [1938] 1 KB 511.   [182] Ibid, 529.

bank, was that of section 82 of the 1882 Act (now section 4 of the 1957 Act). Greer LJ was not convinced by the argument that the defendant bank should not be in a position more onerous than if it had paid the cheques over the counter. His Lordship observed:[183]

> [The defendant bank] did not in this case cash the cheques over the counter, and it is unnecessary to consider what would have been the result if instead of passing them to [the clerk's] credit the bank had paid him the cash over the counter. In my opinion, though it is unnecessary to decide this in the present case, it would still as receiving bank be liable for conversion. Be this as it may, on the facts proved in the present case...when the bank received the cheques and passed them to the credit of [the clerk's] private account it converted the cheques by dealing with them as if they were [the clerk's] property and immediately crediting him with the amount thereof.

Greer LJ disagreed with the view expressed in *Gordon*'s case, in which the cheques were drawn on one branch and collected for the credit of an account maintained with another branch. He thought that in such a case, even more forcefully than in the case before him, the bank 'was no less a collecting bank because it was collecting from one of its branches for the customer and paying the money so collected'.[184] His Lordship thought that, in situations of the type considered in *Gordon*'s case, the bank would have to claim the defence of section 60 if sued as paying bank and the defence of section 82 if sued as collecting bank. Obviously, if the bank was sued in both capacities it would have to succeed under both sections to escape liability. Slesser LJ agreed with Greer LJ on the points under consideration. MacKinnon LJ, in a dissenting judgment, thought that, under *Gordon*'s case, he was bound to hold that the bank discharged its liability by successfully pleading the defence of section 60, although he thought that the decision reached by Greer and Slesser LJJ was preferable.

It is believed that the view of the majority of the Court of Appeal in *Carpenters Co.*'s case is to be preferred to the solution propounded in *Bissell & Co.*'s case. In the first place, the doctrine of *Carpenters' Co.*'s case applies to cases in which the cheque is collected and paid by a single branch, the principle governing cases in which the two functions are performed by separate branches of the bank. Accordingly, the doctrine leads to uniformity. Secondly, the effect of the *Carpenters' Co.* solution is to avoid a situation in which a bank, which collects and pays a cheque through a single branch, is absolved from liability although it has failed to exercise the duties expected of it in the performance of one of its two roles. Thirdly, the solution of *Bissell & Co.*'s case, which would exonerate a bank that can plead the defence of section 60 from liability for neglect in collection, overlooks the historical background of this section. Undoubtedly, if the claimant is the drawer of the cheque, he can sue the bank both in conversion for the wrongful collection of the instrument and for breach of mandate based on its wrongful payment.[185] But if the claimant is a person other than the drawer, such as the ostensible payee of the instrument from whose possession it has been stolen, the action has to be based on conversion.[186] In such a case the bank is primarily sued as a collecting bank and not as a paying bank.[187] Section 60 was not meant to protect the bank against actions of this type. This much is clear from the history of the provision, derived, it will be recalled, from section 19 of the Stamp Act 1853 which aimed at protecting the bank in its role as payor of its customers' cheques.[188] It would be fortuitous to extend this defence to a bank which opened itself to an action

---

[183] Ibid., 531.   [184] Ibid., 532.   [185] See Ch. 11, Sect. 2 above.
[186] Or on the complementary action in restitution.
[187] Although the 'true owner' can sue also the paying bank in conversion: see Ch. 11, Sect. 2 above.
[188] See Ch. 11, Sect. 3(iii) above.

in conversion based on the wrongful collection of the cheque, simply because that bank happened to have acted for both the drawer and the payee of the instrument through a single branch. The solution based on *Carpenters' Co.*'s case is, thus, preferable analytically and also on grounds of policy. It expects the bank to exercise the standard of professional skill imposed on it in respect of each of its roles.

It may be claimed that this argument is more appropriate where the cheque is collected by a branch other than that on which it is drawn than in situations in which the cheque is drawn on the very branch with which the payee maintains his account. In practice, though, the point is doubtful. If a cheque is processed in a single branch, the bank is still in a position to evaluate both the request for the collection of the cheque and the question of paying it. The only difference between this type of case, and that in which two separate branches of the bank are involved, is that the decisions concerning the collection and the payment of the cheque are made by one employee of the bank, and not by two separate tellers or branch managers.

9 The collecting bank's duty to its own customer

(i) The nature of problems arising

The majority of the decided cases defining the position of a collecting bank concerned litigation in conversion instituted by the true owner of the instrument. It is important to bear in mind that, in the usual circumstances in which a validly acquired cheque is remitted to a bank for collection, the bank's main duty is owed to its own customer. The bank's obligations are to process the cheque speedily, to take the necessary steps for crediting the customer's account, and to notify the customer, without delay, if the cheque is dishonoured by the drawee bank.

The collecting bank's duties arise in part as a result of the provisions of the BEA 1882 and in part under the contract of agency which it has with the customer. But although this contract constitutes the bank its customer's agent—or collection agent—the bank is not regarded as owing him a general duty of care[189] or a duty to advise him on risks involved in the handling of specific items. Thus, in *Redmond* v. *Allied Irish Bank*[190] one G, who had obtained a number of cheques payable to other persons and bearing crossings accompanied by the words 'Not negotiable—a/c payee only', asked R to arrange for the collection of these cheques through R's bank account. G explained that these cheques had been issued in respect of the sale of certain cars and that their collection through some other person's bank account was dictated by taxation problems. R, who believed this story, asked the A Bank to collect the cheques for the credit of his account and to allow him to withdraw the proceeds forthwith. R then paid the money over to G.

When it turned out that the cheques in question had been acquired by fraud, the A Bank settled the true owners' action in conversion and debited R's account. Saville J dismissed R's action seeking to hold the bank liable in negligence for its failure to advise him of the risks in the transaction. To start with, his Lordship found that the A Bank's personnel had warned R of the dangers involved in the collection for his account of cheques payable to

---

[189] A remitting bank may, however, be liable to its customer for failing to exercise adequate care in selecting a suitable collecting/correspondent bank or for the negligent acts or omissions of that bank: see *AA Valibhoy & Sons (1907) Pte Ltd* v. *Habib Bank Ltd* [1982–1983] 1 SLR 379, 391; *AA Valibhoy & Sons (1907) Pte Ltd* v. *Banque Nationale de Paris* [1994] 2 SLR 772, 781.

[190] [1987] FLR 307.

third parties and crossed in the manner here used. But Saville J further concluded that a bank did not owe its customer the type of duty of care pleaded. His Lordship said: 'I can see no basis for a duty to advise or warn a customer that there are risks attendant upon something which the customer wishes to do. Such a duty...is not required in order to give efficacy to the contractual relationship between the parties.'[191] Saville J added that the circumstances of the case were not such as to give rise to a duty of care owed by the A Bank in tort.

(ii) **The collecting bank's duty to effect presentment**

Under section 45(2) of the BEA 1882, a bill has to be presented within a reasonable time after its issue in order to charge the drawer and within a reasonable time after its transfer to charge the indorser. This section, however, defines the duties which the holder has to discharge if he wishes to recover the amount of the instrument from the drawer or from the indorsers. As the relationship of the collecting bank with its customer is based on the contract between them rather than on the bill, section 45(2) provides, at best, a guideline indicating that presentment needs usually to be effected within a reasonable time. The nature of the 'reasonable time' involved depends, under sections 45 and 74, on the practice of bankers which at present is contained in the Clearing Rules of the Cheque and Credit Clearing Co. Ltd. These, however, tend to give effect to established case law, which in turn supports the need for speedy presentment and has defined the available 'reasonable time'. If the cheque is collected by a branch operating at the same place as the branch on which the cheque is drawn, the collecting bank has to present the cheque, at the latest, on the day following its receipt.[192] If the cheque is drawn on a branch in another place, be it a branch of the same bank or of another bank, the bank may either present the cheque or forward it for clearing on the next day.[193] The Clearing Rules are to the same effect.

As presentment needs to be effected through the clearing system, it is customary for non-clearing banks, such as foreign banks who are not members of a clearing house, to remit their cheques to a clearing bank.[194] Such a remittance, which may involve extra time in the process of presentment, is sanctioned by the usages of merchants,[195] which also approve, where convenient, the remittance of cheques for presentment by one branch of a collecting bank to another branch of the same bank.[196]

A special type of case arises where the drawer of the cheque and the payee maintain their accounts with the same bank. Naturally, if the two parties bank, respectively, with different branches, then the payee's branch receives the cheque on a collection basis and sets it into motion in about the same way as if the cheque were drawn on a branch of some other bank.[197] But if the two parties bank with the same branch of a chain bank, or maintain their accounts with the same single-office bank, it is a question of fact whether the

---

[191] Ibid., at 311.

[192] *Forman* v. *Bank of England* (1902) 18 TLR 339; *Hamilton Finance Co. Ltd* v. *Coverley, Westray, Walbaum and Tosetti Ltd* [1969] 1 Lloyd's Rep. 53 (the case law in point can be traced back to the beginning of the nineteenth century: *Rickford* v. *Ridge* (1810) 2 Camp. 537).

[193] *Prideaux* v. *Criddle* (1869) LR 4 QB 455; *Heywood* v. *Pickering* (1874) LR 9 QB 428. See further, Ch. 10, Sect. 5 above.

[194] See, for instance, *Honourable Society of the Middle Temple* v. *Lloyds Bank plc*, n.124 above; *Linklaters* v. *HSBC Bank plc*, n.170 above. Presentment through the Post Office as between banks was at one time permissible: *Prideaux* v. *Criddle*, n.193 above, but is no longer practised at present.

[195] Ibid.

[196] Ibid. But note that currently they will be forwarded to the bank's clearing department in London.

[197] But it will not of course be exchanged at the clearing house.

cheque is presented by the payee for payment or handed to the relevant branch or bank on a collection basis.[198] In the former case, the question of the bank's duty as a collecting bank does not arise. In the latter case the bank has the usual time for returning the cheque to the payee if, in its capacity as the drawer's bank, it resolves to dishonour it.[199] Basically, this means that the bank has one extra day for making its decision concerning the fate of the cheque. Presentment of the cheque to itself through the clearing system would be an absurdity!

It may be justifiably pointed out that in cases of this type the bank does not take a conscious decision whether to handle the cheque on a collection basis or as an instrument presented for payment. In some cases, the decision is made by the payee. If he presents the cheque over the counter for payment in cash, then it is clear that the bank is requested to pay the instrument; the question of collection does not arise. If the cheque is handed to the teller, accompanied by a deposit slip, the payee requests the bank to collect the cheque for the credit of his account. By accepting the two documents as presented by the payee, the bank in reality agrees to collect the instrument and, in this type of case, to act in the dual role of payor and of collecting agent. In other cases, though, the fate of the cheque and the role of the bank in regard to it is determined by the drawer! Where the cheque is a crossed cheque, the bank is not allowed to pay it over the counter.[200] This means that the payee, or transferee, has to remit the cheque for collection. If he banks with the very branch, or single-office bank, on which the instrument is drawn, he is practically bound to ask this bank to act as his collecting agent.

Where the collecting bank fails to present a cheque speedily, it is liable to its customer for the loss sustained as a result of the delay. This liability is based on the contract of banker and customer. By presenting the cheque after an undue delay, the bank fails to comply with the instructions given to it by its principal, the customer.[201] The loss that may be incurred by the customer arises in three types of case. First, the drawer of the cheque may have either closed his account or become insolvent during the period of the delay. The effect of the delay is that the cheque will, thereupon, be dishonoured by the drawee bank. Secondly, the delay in presentment discharges any indorser. The collecting bank's client thus loses his action on the bill against the indorser. This is particularly significant where the drawer is insolvent. Thirdly, if the cheque is not duly presented and the drawee bank becomes insolvent in the meantime, the drawer suffers loss, as he is no longer able to dispose over the funds. In effect, the delay results in the non-payment of the cheque by the drawee bank. Under section 74(1) of the 1882 Act, the holder loses his right of action against the drawer if a delay in presentment has led to such a loss. If the holder has employed a collecting bank for presenting the cheque, this bank has to compensate the holder for the loss sustained by him due to its failure to present the cheque in time.

The collecting bank's liability to its customer is, however, incurred only if the customer is able to establish that the cheque would have been paid if presented on time. Thus, the collecting bank does not have to compensate the customer if the cheque was drawn against inadequate funds and did not bear the signature of an indorser. In such a case, the delay

---

[198] This point did not arise directly in *Carpenters' Co.* v. *British Mutual Banking Co. Ltd*, n.181 above, discussed in Sect. 8 above, but the treatment of one branch bank as a distinct entity for collection and for payment suggests that it is entitled not only to the duties but also to the rights of a collecting bank.

[199] This point emerges from an early nineteenth-century case: *Boyd* v. *Emmerson* (1834) 2 Ad. & El. 184.

[200] See Ch. 10, Sect. 4(ii) above.

[201] *Lubbock* v. *Tribe* (1838) 3 M & W 607; *Yeoman Credit Ltd* v. *Gregory* [1963] 1 WLR 343.

does not result in a loss. Where a loss is incurred, and the collecting bank compensates its customer, it is subrogated to the rights which he has as holder of the cheque.[202]

In the majority of cases, the customer's loss will be restricted to the amount of the cheque dishonoured by the drawee bank as a result of the delay in its presentment by the collecting bank. In some cases, though, there is room for additional loss incurred where the customer's balance with the collecting bank is inadequate, owing to that bank's failure duly to clear the cheque in question, for meeting the customer's own cheques. In such a case the bank is liable to its customer for the damage done to his creditworthiness.[203] Its liability is, then, that of a paying bank that has wrongfully dishonoured its customer's cheques.[204]

(iii) **Notice of dishonour**

When the drawee bank dishonours a cheque, it returns it to the collecting bank.[205] Under section 48 of the 1882 Act, notice of dishonour has to be given to the drawer and indorsers. Failure to do so discharges their liability on the instrument. However, the giving of such notice is excused in certain situations.[206] One of them is where the drawee is not bound, as between the drawer and himself, to honour the instrument. In such cases, which cover situations in which a cheque is drawn against an inadequate balance or on an account which has been closed,[207] it would be futile to make notice to the drawer a condition precedent to his liability on the instrument.

The rules as to the method of giving notice of dishonour are set out in detail in section 49 of the Act. From the collecting bank's point of view, the only relevant provision is subsection (13), under which an agent may either himself give notice to the parties liable on the instrument or may give notice to his principal. The standard banking practice is to return a dishonoured cheque to the customer with a note indicating that it has not been paid. It is believed that this practice is adequate under the Act, and, equally, all that can be expected from the bank as an agent.

---

[202] See, generally, Ch. 10, Sect. 10(iii) below.

[203] *Kilsby* v. *Williams* (1822) 5 B & Ald. 815.   [204] See Ch. 11, Sect. 5 above.

[205] This is the practice prescribed by the Clearing House Rules. The cheque is returned to the branch that received it from the payee or holder.

[206] BEA 1882, s.50(2).

[207] The rule is based on an eighteenth-century authority, *Bickerdike* v. *Bollman* (1786) 1 TR 405. If the balance is fluctuating the drawer may be unaware of the inadequacy of funds and hence may be entitled to notice: see *Orr* v. *Maginnis* (1806) 7 East. 359; *Blackham* v. *Doren* (1810) 2 Camp. 503.

16
Incidental Services Performed by Banks

1 The common thread

Modern banks provide their customers with a range of services that are incidental to any core account services, such as insurance services, share-trading facilities, and financial services generally. Given the diverse nature of such services, there is no obvious commonality between them: some services will only be provided for a charge, whilst others will be free of charge; some services are automatically provided to customers without the need for any special arrangement, such as cheque clearing services, whilst others must be the subject of specific contractual arrangements, such as the provision of insurance; and some services are provided primarily to customers, whilst others are rendered in order to encourage the public to use their general banking facilities. Where services of this kind are made available to, and utilized by, the general public, they do so on the basis of the implicit trust in the bank's integrity, judgement, and skill. Where such services are provided to a customer, it would appear that the common thread between them is that they are largely 'incidental' to the principal services that a bank provides to its customers as part of the business of banking. These features have been emphasized by the courts in the case law concerning the bank's 'incidental' services.

There are, in particular, three types of 'incidental' service that banks have traditionally provided to their customers. First, since at least the middle of the nineteenth century, accepting houses[1] regularly engaged in the practice of providing references to third parties about their clients' creditworthiness, but this practice was traditionally outside the accepted activities of the clearing banks,[2] for which it remained an exceptional activity until after the Second World War.[3] A banker's reference usually involves two banks: a person ('the enquirer'), who wishes to contract or enter into some other business dealing with another ('the person investigated'), will ask his bank ('the enquiring bank') to approach the bank of the person investigated ('the referee bank') in order to obtain a confidential report about that person's financial standing, credit history, and creditworthiness. Ordinarily, the enquiring bank itself will make its request of the referee bank directly and will receive the requested information in return. When the enquirer and the person investigated are large businesses, however, this procedure may sometimes differ, as the enquirer may approach the referee bank directly and request it to supply his bank with the relevant financial details of the person investigated. Regardless of the procedure used, the referee usually furnishes its report without a charge, but usually stipulates that the information is provided 'in confidence' and 'without responsibility' on its part. Secondly, banks may provide customers with financial advice in relation to a range of business

---

[1] Ch. 1, Sect. 3 above.   [2] *Banbury* v. *Bank of Montreal* [1918] AC 626 (HL).
[3] *Woods* v. *Martins Bank Ltd* [1959] 1 QB 55.

transactions, whether the acquisition of shares or a business or the exporting of goods. Often, the advice may be tendered in an informal manner and without charge, although, in more complex cases, the customer may request his bank to investigate a particular venture's feasibility, and may authorize it to commission any necessary experts' reports. Indeed, a situation in which a bank is particularly likely to tender financial advice to a customer (whether deliberately or inadvertently) is where a customer requests his bank to invest funds on his behalf and manage his securities portfolio. In these types of case, a bank is likely to charge, whether a flat fee or a commission. As considered previously, however, banks risk attracting significant liability by acting as an adviser and they frequently take steps to exclude or prevent such liability from arising.[4] Thirdly, banks may provide customers with safe-deposit services. This usually takes one of two forms,[5] both of which are best explained as involving a bailment.[6] On the one hand, a bank may undertake the safe custody of their customers' documents or items of value by placing them in its own vault. Banks usually provide this service gratuitously and may even extend it to non-customers who wish to deposit a sealed envelope or locked small box. On the other hand, banks may provide customers with their own safe-deposit boxes that can only be opened by using a key provided to the customer in conjunction with a key retained by the bank. Banks usually charge a rental for such safe-deposit boxes. If the proposal for 'safety deposit current accounts' were ever to become law,[7] however, then a third type of bailment relationship between a bank and its customer may be possible.

2 Bankers' references

(i) The rights of the person investigated

A customer may suffer loss as a result of his bank responding to a status request from another bank by providing a banker's reference and, depending upon the circumstances, may raise one of a number of causes of action against his bank. First, a customer may complain about the fact that his bank responded to the status enquiry at all and that, by disclosing information concerning the customer's bank account or his banking relationship more generally, the bank has breached its implied contractual duty of confidentiality.[8] Although a customer can raise such a claim in respect of any response, he is most likely to complain when the bank's reference is unfavourable, albeit perfectly accurate, or discloses inaccurate information.[9] Whilst disclosure in response to a status enquiry

---

[4] Ch. 5, Sect. 4(iii) above.

[5] Large banking groups, securities houses, and investment banks provide global custody services for their customers' securities, frequently including settlement services in respect of the purchase and sale of securities. Physical custody of security certificates giving rise to a bailment relationship must be distinguished from arrangements whereby the custodian holds securities in its own name, but as its customer's fiduciary, recording their interests in its books. Global custody of securities raises complex legal issues, especially when those securities are immobilized (centrally deposited) or dematerialized (no tangible certificate or instrument issued). See generally M. Yates, & G. Montagu, *The Law of Global Custody* (3rd edn., London, 2009); A.O. Austen-Peters, *Custody of Investments: Law and Practice* (Oxford, 2000); R. Goode & L. Gullifer, *Legal Problems of Credit and Security* (4th edn., London, 2008), ch. VI.

[6] Although it may be relevant in tax cases whether there is also a contract of hire in relation to the safe-deposit box.

[7] Safety Deposit Current Accounts Bill 2008, cls. 1(2) & 1(5), which requires banks to segregate funds in such an account from its general assets, since the 'legal and equitable title to any money deposited in the account is fully vested in the customer'.   [8] Ch. 5, Sect. 5 above.

[9] A claim for breach of confidence can cover the provision of inaccurate information: R.G. Toulson & C.M. Phipps, *Confidentiality* (2nd edn., London, 2006), [3-092]–[3-097].

prima facie constitutes a breach of the duty of confidentiality, as discussed previously,[10] banks have long justified this practice on the grounds that disclosure was made with the customer's consent. The position is straightforward when the customer has expressly consented to disclosure, subject to the bank being able to establish the existence and scope of that consent adequately, but, even in the absence of such express consent, banks have traditionally justified their responses to status enquiries on the ground that the customer had impliedly consented. Whilst this stance previously had some judicial and academic support,[11] the Younger Committee on Privacy[12] considered that at least personal customers (who are generally unaware of the banking custom relating to bankers' references) should be asked to give their express consent before a bank responds to a particular status enquiry (as under the German model) and the Jack Committee recommended legislative reform along similar lines.[13] The need for express customer consent before a bank could respond to a reference request was similarly the position under the *Banking Code* from March 1994 until its replacement in November 2009.[14] That this also now represents the common law position was confirmed by the Court of Appeal in *Turner* v. *Royal Bank of Scotland plc*,[15] which involved a claim by a personal customer against his bank for breaching its duty of confidentiality by responding in unfavourable terms to reference requests from another bank, without first seeking the customer's express consent to disclosure. By way of defence, the bank relied upon a banking usage and custom permitting banks to respond to reference requests on their customers' behalf. It was argued that customers generally should be treated as having knowledge of the relevant banking practice, and accordingly should be treated as impliedly consenting to any necessary disclosures, regardless of whether the particular customer *actually* knew of the practice or not. Sir Richard Scott V-C rejected this argument, concluding that a bank could not hold a customer to a banking practice of which he was unaware unless that practice was sufficiently 'notorious' amongst customers generally to constitute a banking usage or custom that could form the basis of an implied term in the banker–customer contract. Although the banking practice in *Turner* was certainly notorious amongst banks, this was not the case amongst customers generally. Whilst the clarification provided by *Turner* is welcome, as considered previously,[16] there remains uncertainty as to whether that decision applies to business (as well as personal) customers, whether a customer's consent to a banker's reference may be general or must be specific, and whether the customer will have suffered any special damage in the event that the bank gives a reference without its customer's consent.

Secondly, even where the person investigated has consented to the referee bank providing the reference, the former may have a contractual claim against the latter for breach

---

[10] Ch. 5, Sect. 5(vi) above.

[11] *Tournier* v. *National Provincial and Union Bank of England* [1924] 1 KB 461, 473, 486 (CA). See also M. Hapgood, *Paget's Law of Banking* (11th edn., London, 1996), 124, although this view is not repeated in recent editions: M. Hapgood, *Paget's Law of Banking* (13th edn., London, 2007), [8.11]–[8.16].

[12] (Cmnd. 5012, London, 1972).

[13] *Banking Services: Law and Practice*, Report by the Review Committee Chaired by Professor R.B. Jack CBE (1989, London, Cm. 622), [6.39].

[14] *Banking Code* (March 2008), [11.2]; *Business Banking Code* (March 2008), [11.2]. Although the *Lending Code* (November 2009), [36], [39], requires express customer consent to be given in the related context of bank disclosures to credit reference agencies, it makes no explicit reference to any equivalent requirement in the banker's reference context. The position is the same under the *Lending Code* (March 2011), [40]–[41], [48]. See further Ch. 2, Sect. 6 above.

[15] [1999] 2 All ER (Comm.) 664 (CA), discussed in detail in Ch. 5, Sect. 5(vi) above.

[16] Ch. 5, Sect. 5(vi) above.

of its mandate. For such a claim to succeed, however, it will be necessary to show that the person investigated provided his bank with the necessary instructions, which may be difficult when the bank responds directly to a request from the enquirer or the enquiring bank. Thirdly, where the referee bank either fails to provide a reference at all or furnishes an inaccurate (and most likely unfavourable) reference, the person investigated may seek to recover any losses suffered by alleging that the bank has breached its duty to act with reasonable skill and care. Not only could such a claim be based upon a breach of the bank's implied duty of care in the banker–customer contract,[17] but according to the House of Lords in *Spring* v. *Guardian Assurance plc*,[18] which involved a claim by an employee against his former employer in respect of a negative reference provided to a potential future employer, a person providing a reference for another also owes that person a common law duty to exercise reasonable care in the preparation of the reference.[19] In *Spring*, both Lords Goff and Lowry based the existence of that duty of care upon the reference-giver voluntarily undertaking responsibility to the subject of the reference,[20] whilst Lords Slynn and Woolf considered that such a duty would be 'fair, just and reasonable', provided that economic loss was also reasonably foreseeable and that there was a proximate relationship between the parties.[21] There is no reason why a similar common law duty would not be recognized in the context of a banker's reference. In terms of establishing the breach of such a duty, the courts should not necessarily adopt the same restrictive approach as has been adopted in relation to the provision of ordinary banking services,[22] since, just as with the situation where a bank provides financial advice to a customer,[23] a bank that undertakes to provide a reference for its customer should be treated as having stepped outside its usual role of banker.[24] Where the person investigated suffers loss as a result of the negligent actions of both the referee and enquiring banks, the banks will be jointly and severally liable to the claimant.

Finally, the person investigated may bring an action in the tort of libel or slander, depending upon the form that the reference takes. The difficulty with such a claim, however, is that the bank can raise the defence of justification, where the reference is accurate, and the defence of qualified privilege, where it is not. Whilst this latter defence is not available when the bank has acted maliciously, this is not relevant in the vast majority of cases. In *Robshaw* v. *Smith*,[25] where the enquirer and the person investigated were customers of the same bank and that bank showed the enquirer an unfavourable anonymous letter concerning the person investigated, Grove J concluded that the bank's communication was privileged, as the bank had acted in reply to a request for information. Whilst there may be an argument that the bank's response to a reference request should not be privileged because it is not supplied in pursuance of a *duty*,[26] in *Reynolds* v. *Times Newspapers Ltd*,[27] Lord Nicholls indicated that the essence of qualified privilege

---

[17] *Selangor United Rubber Estates Ltd* v. *Cradock (No. 3)* [1968] 1 WLR 1555, 1608. See also Supply of Goods and Services Act 1982, s.13. See generally Ch. 5, Sect. 4(iii) above.

[18] [1995] 2 AC 296 (HL). See also *Customs & Excise Commissioners* v. *Barclays Bank plc* [2007] 1 AC 181, [90] (HL).

[19] *Punjab National Bank* v. *de Boinville* [1992] 1 Lloyd's Rep. 7, 35–36. See also *Henderson* v. *Merrett Syndicates Ltd* [1995] 2 AC 145 (HL). See further Ch. 5, Sect. 4(iii) above. It seems futile to investigate the feasibility of an action for breach of a fiduciary duty: Ch. 5, Sect. 4(i) above.

[20] N.18 above, 316, 325.   [21] Ibid., 329–335, 342–345.   [22] Ch. 5, Sect. 4(iii) above.

[23] Sect. 3 below.

[24] A. Tyree, *Tyree's Banking Law in New Zealand* (2nd edn., Wellington, 2003), [4.6.1]; A. Tyree & P. Weaver, *Weerasooria's Banking Law and the Financial System in Australia* (6th edn., Sydney, 2006), [30.7].

[25] (1878) 38 LT 423.   [26] *Gatley on Libel and Slander* (11th edn., London, 2008), [14.29].

[27] [2001] 2 AC 127 (HL).

lay in 'the need, in the public interest, for a particular recipient to receive frank and uninhibited communication of particular information from a particular source' and that the defence would operate on 'an occasion where the person who makes a communication has an interest or a duty, legal, social, or moral, to make it to the person to whom it is made, and the person to whom it is so made has a corresponding interest or duty to receive it'.[28] In making this determination, a court should examine 'every circumstance associated with the origin and publication of the defamatory matter'.[29] Applying Lord Nicholls' broad approach to the banker's reference context, it is clear that the enquirer has an interest in receiving the information that he has requested, and that the referee bank has at the very least an interest, even if not a duty, of a 'legal, social, or moral' nature in making disclosure, as there is a general public interest in promoting responsible lending.[30] There is also a clear expectation amongst banks that they will respond to each other's reference requests and that this practice is so widespread that it may even amount to a banking custom or usage. Indeed, in *Reynolds*, Lord Nicholls expressly recognized that qualified privilege would operate to afford a reference-giver protection in respect of statements given in the context of an employment reference.[31] A banker's reference is analogous. It may be, however, that the defence of qualified privilege, as it applies to references in general, may nowadays need to be reassessed in the light of the Human Rights Act 1998 and the Data Protection Act 1998.[32]

Whilst the most likely claim of the person investigated will be against the referee bank, there may also be circumstances where that person has a claim against the enquiring bank. This may occur when the enquiring bank is negligent in conveying the contents of the reference to the enquirer, such as where the reference contains positive information about the person investigated, but the enquiring bank reports the information in such a way as to give it a negative hue. In such circumstances, the enquirer may terminate negotiations with the person investigated for a particularly lucrative contract, with the result that the latter loses the opportunity to make a significant profit. As there is no contractual relationship between the person investigated and the enquiring bank, the latter's liability will depend upon the existence of a common law duty of care. Just as with the issue of the referee bank's liability to the enquirer, which is considered in the following section, the enquiring bank is likely to be treated as having voluntarily assumed responsibility to the person investigated to exercise care in conveying the reference's contents. The person investigated will certainly be relying upon the enquiring bank to carry out this task properly. The fact that the enquiring bank can also be liable to the enquirer for failing to convey the terms of the reference accurately should not preclude the enquiring bank's liability to the person investigated. This is because the enquiring bank is unlikely ever to be liable to both parties concurrently, but will only be liable to the person investigated when it conveys a positive reference in negative terms and will only be liable to the enquirer when it conveys a negative reference in positive terms.

---

[28] Ibid., 194–195, citing *Adam* v. *Ward* [1917] AC 309, 334 (HL). Lords Hope and Hobhouse adopted a similar approach: ibid., 228–235, 238–240.

[29] Id. See also *London Association for Protection of Trade* v. *Greenlands Ltd* [1916] 2 AC 15, 23 (HL).

[30] Consider *McGuffick* v. *Royal Bank of Scotland plc* [2009] EWHC 2386 (Comm.), [36].

[31] N.27 above, 194. See also *Spring* v. *Guardian Assurance plc*, n.18 above, 308–309, 322–325, 329–330, 346.

[32] *Clift* v. *Slough Borough Council* [2009] 4 All ER 756, [110]–[125].

(ii) **Position of the enquirer**

As indicated in the preceding paragraph, where the enquiring bank inaccurately conveys the negative information contained in the reference to the enquirer so that he contracts with the person investigated and thereby suffers loss, the enquirer will wish to sue the enquiring bank. Given that there will ordinarily be a banker–customer relationship between the enquirer and the enquiring bank, the former will be entitled to rely upon the implied term in that contract that the bank will provide any services with reasonable skill and care.[33] It would appear to be a breach of this contractual duty for a bank to fail to take reasonable steps to ensure that the information requested by his customer is conveyed to him in a full and accurate manner.[34] The enquiring bank should not, however, be required to institute its own independent investigation into the accuracy of the reference,[35] but is entitled to trust to the reliability of the views expressed by the referee bank. Indeed, where the referee bank's views result from a failure on its part to exercise reasonable care or involve deliberate misstatements, the enquirer may bring a claim against the referee bank in the tort of either negligence or deceit, but not for breach of contract as there is no contractual relationship between these parties.

Where the referee bank's misstatements are deliberately made, the enquirer may bring a claim in the tort of deceit if he can show that the referee bank made a false statement of fact with the relevant mental state, namely that the 'misrepresentation has been made knowingly, without belief in its truth, or recklessly, careless whether it be true or false',[36] and the relevant statement was intended to be relied upon and was in fact relied upon.[37] If the enquirer can establish these elements on a balance of probabilities,[38] not only does he insulate himself from any attempt by the referee bank to minimize the damages payable by pointing to the enquirer's own contributory negligence,[39] but the courts have also adopted a more generous approach to the measure of damages.[40] That said, given that bankers' references by their very nature involve a statement as to another's creditworthiness, the enquirer may fail in his deceit claim unless he can satisfy section 6 of the Statute of Frauds Amendment Act 1828 ('Lord Tenterden's Act'), which is available as a defence to both individual and corporate misrepresentors,[41] including banks. According to section 6 of Lord Tenterden's Act, a claim can only be based upon a 'representation or assurance

---

[33] Ch. 5, Sect. 4(iii) above.

[34] *Midland Bank Ltd* v. *Seymour* [1955] 2 Lloyd's Rep. 147, 157–158; *Commercial Banking Co. of Sydney Ltd* v. *R. H. Brown & Co.* [1972] 2 Lloyd's Rep. 360 (HCA).

[35] Ibid.

[36] *Derry* v. *Peek* (1889) 14 App. Cas. 337, 374 (HL). See also *Club Travel 2000 Holdings Ltd* v. *Murfin* [2008] EWHC 2729 (Ch), [49].

[37] *The Kriti Palm* [2007] 1 All ER (Comm.) 667, [252]–[258] (CA); *Cheshire Building Society* v. *Dunlop Haywards (DHL) Ltd* [2008] EWHC 51 (Comm.), [46]; *Grosvenor Casinos Ltd* v. *National Bank of Abu Dhabi* [2008] EWHC 511 (Comm.), [100]; *Harris* v. *Society of Lloyd's* [2008] EWHC 1433 (Comm.), [64]–[65]; *BSkyB Ltd* v. *HP Enterprise Services UK Ltd* [2010] EWHC 86 (TCC), [304]–[327]; *Lindsay* v. *O'Loughnane* [2010] EWHC 529 (QB), [86]; *Cassa di Risparmio della Repubblica di San Marino SpA* v. *Barclays Bank Ltd* [2011] EWHC 484 (Comm.), [210]–[233]. See also *Dadourian Group International Inc.* v. *Simms* [2009] 1 Lloyd's Rep. 601, [99]–[101] (CA).

[38] As to the applicable standard of proof, compare *Dadourian Group International Inc.* v. *Simms*, n.37 above, [30]–[32] with *Lindsay* v. *O'Loughnane*, n.37 above, [89].

[39] *Standard Chartered Bank* v. *Pakistan National Shipping Corp. (No.2)* [2003] 1 AC 959, [9]–[18], [25]–[28], [42]; *Moore Stephens* v. *Stone Rolls Ltd* [2010] 1 All ER (Comm.) 125, [62] (HL); *Barclays Bank plc* v. *Kalamohan* [2010] EWHC 1383 (Ch), [77].

[40] *Smith New Court Securities* v. *Citibank NA* [1997] AC 254, 266–268, 282–284 (HL); *Parabola Investments Ltd* v. *Browallia Cal Ltd* [2010] EWCA Civ 486, [22]–[60].

[41] *Hirst* v. *West Riding Union Banking Co. Ltd* [1901] 2 KB 560, 562–564; *UBAF Securities Ltd* v. *European American Banking Corp.* [1984] QB 713, 719 (CA).

made or given concerning or relating to the character, conduct, credit, ability, trade, or dealings of any other person, to the intent or purpose that such other person may obtain credit, money, or goods', if the statement involved was 'made in writing, signed by the party to be charged therewith'. The mischief at which this provision was aimed was the practice of a creditor bringing a misrepresentation claim against a person who had given an oral assurance or casual comment concerning a debtor's solvency or creditworthiness, thereby circumventing the requirement that a guarantee of another's liabilities is only enforceable if it complies with the formality requirements of the Statute of Frauds.[42] The particular difficulty that section 6 of Lord Tenterden's Act gives rise to in the bankers' reference context stems from the fact that such references are usually unsigned.

There are a number of requirements that must be satisfied before the bank can avail itself of this defence. First, there must be an actionable misrepresentation. Although the literal terms of Lord Tenterden's Act suggest that the legislation is capable of applying to *any* type of misrepresentation, in *Banbury* v. *Bank of Montreal*,[43] the House of Lords limited the legislation's scope to fraudulent misrepresentations. Accordingly, negligent or innocent misrepresentations are actionable without needing to comply with the legislation's formal requirements. This limitation is certainly consistent with the historical aims of Lord Tenterden's Act, since damages for non-fraudulent misrepresentation were not available in 1828. This restriction may lead to slightly strange litigation incentives, however, since an enquirer may be well advised to sue the referee's bank in negligence, and thereby forego the remedial and procedural advantages of a successful deceit claim, even where he is able to establish the bank's fraud. Secondly, the representation must relate to another person's 'character, conduct, credit, ability, trade, or dealings'. The courts have tended to adopt a restrictive interpretation of this requirement, with the result that it covers neither a fraudulent misrepresentation that goods for sale were in existence,[44] nor a fraudulent misrepresentation that a delay in payment had been due to the inefficiency of the misrepresentor's bank.[45] In the context of bankers' references, however, this requirement should not pose much difficulty given that the reference will usually refer to the creditworthiness or financial standing of the person investigated. Thirdly, the misrepresentation must be 'made in writing'. Whilst this requirement will clearly be satisfied if an *express* representation of the relevant type is contained in a written document,[46] it will also be satisfied in the case of a representation contained, *inter alia*, in an e-mail message or a document attached to an e-mail.[47] Whatever the concept of 'writing' includes, however, it appears that a misrepresentation may still be actionable under Lord Tenterden's Act provided that at least some part of the relevant fraudulent statement is 'in writing', even if some of the words in question are uttered orally.[48] Moreover, it is not always necessary

---

[42] *Lyde* v. *Barnard* (1836) 1 M&W 101, 103; *Williams* v. *Mason* (1873) 28 LT 232, 233; *Contex Drouzhba Ltd* v. *Wiseman* [2007] EWCA Civ 1201, [15]–[16]; *Lindsay* v. *O'Loughnane*, n.37 above, [93]–[95].

[43] N.2 above, 693, 707–708, 713. See also *Swift* v. *Jewsbury* (1874) LR 9 QB 301, 316; *W. B. Anderson & Sons Ltd* v. *Rhodes (Liverpool) Ltd* [1967] 2 All ER 850, 856; *Diamond* v. *Bank of London & Montreal Ltd* [1979] QB 333, 347 (CA); *Australia & New Zealand Banking Group Ltd* v. *Commonwealth of Australia*, The Financial Times, 28 February 1989. Lord Tenterden's Act may also apply, however, to actions under s.2(1) of the Misrepresentation Act 1967 as the representor is liable only if he 'would be liable to damage in respect thereof had the misrepresentation been made fraudulently': *UBAF Securities Ltd* v. *European American Banking Corp.*, n.41 above, 718–719.

[44] *Diamond* v. *Bank of London and Montreal Ltd*, n.43 above. Lord Denning MR did indicate, however, that Lord Tenterden's Act might furnish a defence in respect of the other fraudulent misrepresentation made in *Diamond* concerning the supplier being of good standing.

[45] *Lindsay* v. *O'Loughnane*, n.37 above, [113].   [46] *Contex Drouzhba Ltd* v. *Wiseman*, n.42 above, [9].

[47] *Lindsay* v. *O'Loughnane*, n.37 above, [95]. See also Interpretation Act 1978, Sched. 1, which defines 'writing' as including 'other modes of representing or reproducing words in a visible form'.

[48] *Tatton* v. *Wade* (1856) CB 371.

that the fraudulent misrepresentation in question actually be 'in writing' to be actionable: where a fraudulent misrepresentation of the relevant type is *implied* from the terms
of a document or other writing that complies with the requirements of Lord Tenterden's
Act, that misrepresentation will be actionable even though the representation itself has
not been reduced to writing.[49] This does not, however, mean that *all* implied fraudulent
misrepresentations are automatically actionable under Lord Tenterden's Act: a misrepresentation implied from the representor's oral statement or conduct, or from a document
that does not otherwise comply with the legislation, will not be actionable.[50]

Finally, the relevant writing must be 'signed by the party to be charged therewith'. As
well as a handwritten signature, a document (such as an e-mail) will be 'signed' where it
'includes a written indication of who is sending the email', such as where the e-mail contains an electronic signature or the typed name of the sender.[51] It is not enough to satisfy
the requirement of a signature, however, that the e-mail was simply sent from a particular person's e-mail address.[52] In *Swift* v. *Jewsbury*,[53] however, which involved a branch
manager intentionally giving a false favourable reference about a customer during the
course of his employment with a banking partnership, Lord Coleridge CJ and Bramwell
B held that it was only the person who had *personally* signed the document containing
the fraudulent misrepresentation that could be sued in respect of that misrepresentation
pursuant to Lord Tenterden's Act. As a person could not be sued under Lord Tenterden's
Act by virtue of their agent's signature, the Court of Exchequer Chamber held that the
branch manager was personally liable to the enquirer for the misrepresentation, but that
the banking partnership was not,[54] even though the giving of the bank reference was
within the branch manager's authority. It has been stressed subsequently, however, that
the principle established in *Jewsbury*—that a misrepresentation does not become actionable against a person as a result of his agent's signature—is limited to the context of an
agent signing on behalf of an individual or partnership.[55] The position appears to be
different, therefore, in the case of a company, as this has a separate legal personality and
is unable to sign a document containing a fraudulent misrepresentation personally, but
must instead always act through its agents or employees. This was recognized in *UBAF
Securities Ltd* v. *European American Banking Corporation*,[56] where Ackner LJ stated that
'the signature on behalf of a company of its duly authorized agent acting within the
scope of his authority is, for the purposes of section 6 of Lord Tenterden's Act, the signature of the company'.[57] Accordingly, where a bank director or other bank representative, acting within the scope of his authority, signs a document containing a fraudulent
misrepresentation, that statement will be attributable to his bank. In this regard, some
fine distinctions have arisen in the context of section 26 of the Bills of Exchange Act 1882
between the various ways in which a director or agent might sign a bill of exchange: some
forms of signature have been taken as representing the signature of the company itself
executed by the director (such as where the director signs, 'X Ltd per A, Director'), whilst
other forms of signature have been taken as being the personal signature of the director

---

[49] *Contex Drouzhba Ltd* v. *Wiseman*, n.42 above, [10]–[11]. See also *Lindsay* v. *O'Loughnane*, n.37 above,
[87], [107]–[108].

[50] Ibid., [10]–[12]. See also *John Hudson & Co Ltd* v. *Oaten* (CA, 19 June 1980).

[51] *Lindsay* v. *O'Loughnane*, n.37 above, [95].   [52] Id.

[53] N.43 above. See also *Hyde* v. *Johnson* (1836) 2 Bing NC 776; *Re Whitley Partners Ltd* (1886) LR 32 Ch D
337, 339; *Hirst* v. *West Riding Union Banking Co. Ltd*, n.41 above, 562–564; *Banbury* v. *Bank of Montreal*, n.2
above, 693, 713; *St Ermins Property Co.* v. *Tingay* [2002] EWHC 1673 (Ch), [22]–[26]; *General Legal Council,
ex parte Whitter* v. *Frankson* [2006] UKPC 42, [5]–[6].

[54] The banking partnership did not have any knowledge of the branch manager's fraudulent behaviour.

[55] *UBAF Securities Ltd* v. *European American Banking Corp.*, n.41 above, 723–725.   [56] Ibid.

[57] Ibid., 724–725. In *UBAF* itself, the agent in question was the defendant bank's assistant secretary.

executed in a representative capacity (such as where he signs, 'A, Director of X').[58] It is submitted that these subtle and outmoded[59] distinctions that are designed to determine the capacity in which an agent signs a negotiable instrument are ill-suited to determining a bank's, or other company's, right to rely on Lord Tenterden's Act. Recently, in *Contex Drouzhba Ltd* v. *Wiseman*,[60] Waller LJ indicated that Lord Tenterden's Act is 'concerned with proving by evidence the existence of a representation', but is 'not concerned with excusing fraudulent behaviour or with differentiating between capacities in which persons put their names to documents'.[61] Accordingly, rather than focusing on the form of his signature, a court should simply examine whether the bank director or other bank representative purported to act on behalf of the bank, and whether he had authority to do so. Where such authority exists, the signature will be attributable to the bank for the purposes of Lord Tenterden's Act. That does not mean, however, that the bank director or other bank representative can escape his personal liability for making a fraudulent misrepresentation by arguing that his signature is that of the bank alone. For the purposes of Lord Tenterden's Act, a bank representative's authorized signature will have the dual effect of rendering the fraudulent misrepresentation actionable against the bank's agent *personally* as well as against the bank itself.[62]

Where the enquirer chooses to seek damages from the referee bank in the tort of negligence, rather than the tort of deceit, the enquirer must establish that the bank owed him a duty of care in respect (usually) of the pure economic loss suffered. This was considered in *Hedley, Byrne & Co. Ltd* v. *Heller & Partners Ltd*,[63] where the enquirer was an advertising agency that had been asked by a client to obtain advertising time on television and advertising space in newspapers. As the advertising agency was to contract personally with the various television and newspaper companies, and thereby become personally liable for the significant sums due to those companies, the agency requested its bank to obtain a reference from their client's bank so as to verify the client's creditworthiness. The referee bank supplied a confidential reference for the enquiring bank's 'private use'. The reference was given 'without responsibility on the part of [the] bank'. The referee bank indicated that the sums involved in the advertising campaign were 'larger than [it was] accustomed to see' on the client's account, but that otherwise the client was a 'respectably constituted company, considered good for its ordinary business engagements'. The referee bank failed, however, to disclose its concerns about the fact that the client was heavily indebted to the bank itself. The House of Lords unanimously held that the referee bank had breached a duty of care owed to the enquirer, but ultimately absolved the referee bank of liability because of its disclaimer of responsibility. Lord Reid described the scope of that duty:[64]

> I can see no logical stopping place short of all those relationships where it is plain that the party seeking information or advice was trusting the other party to exercise such a degree of care as the circumstances required, where it was reasonable for him to do that, and where the other gave the information or advice when he knew or ought to have known that the inquirer was relying on him.

Despite some differences in reasoning, in general their Lordships in *Hedley Byrne* all based their judgments on the fact that, despite the reference being provided to the enquiring bank

---

[58] *Chitty on Contracts* (30th edn., London, 2008), [34–057]. [59] Companies Act 2006, s.52.
[60] N.42 above.   [61] Ibid., [16].   [62] Ibid., [12]–[16].
[63] [1964] AC 465, applying *Nocton* v. *Ashburton* [1914] AC 932 (HL); *Robinson* v. *National Bank of Scotland*, 1916 SC (HL) 154, 157. Cf. A.M. Honoré, '*Hedley Byrne & Co. Ltd* v. *Heller and Partners Ltd*' (1965) 8 J. Soc. *Pub. Teach. of Law* 284. See generally *Chitty on Contracts*, n.58 above, [6–081] ff.
[64] Ibid., 486, 503, 511.

for its 'private use', the referee bank 'voluntarily assumed responsibility' to the enquirer for the task of supplying the reference, which accordingly gave rise to a relationship of proximity between the parties when the enquirer relied upon that assumption of responsibility, and imposed upon the referee bank a duty to exercise care when completing the reference. The approach first adopted in *Hedley Byrne* has since become arguably the leading general test for determining the existence of a duty of care in relation to pure economic loss,[65] and is likely to remain the approach adopted in future when determining the existence of a duty of care between enquirer and referee bank in the specific context of bankers' references. Accordingly, for such a common law duty of care to arise, two elements must be present: a 'voluntary assumption of responsibility' by the referee bank and reasonable reliance by the enquirer.[66] Each of these requirements will be discussed in turn.

As originally perceived in *Hedley Byrne*, the concept of a 'voluntary assumption of responsibility' was not 'a responsibility imposed by law upon certain types of persons or in certain sorts of situations', but rather as 'a responsibility that is voluntarily accepted or undertaken, either generally where a general relationship, such as that of solicitor and client or banker and customer, is created, or specifically in relation to a particular transaction'. Subsequent authority has, however, emphasized the objective nature of the concept,[67] and Lord Bingham in *Customs & Excise Commissioners* v. *Barclays Bank plc*[68] stressed that whether there is an 'assumption of responsibility' in particular circumstances 'is not answered by consideration of what the defendant thought or intended'.[69] Applying this objective approach, there will usually exist a relationship of proximity between a referee bank and an enquirer, even where the information is supplied to the enquiring bank, since the referee bank ought to be aware that the information in the reference is likely to have been requested, and is likely to be required, by a person other than the enquiring bank; ought to be aware of the likely identity of that person (namely, that the enquirer will be a customer of the enquiring bank); and ought to have foreseen that that person would be likely to rely on the reference in the conduct of their business dealings.[70] The position

[65] *Mutual Life and Citizens' Assurance Co. Ltd* v. *Evatt* [1971] AC 793 (PC); *Henderson* v. *Merrett Syndicates Ltd*, n.19 above, 180; *White* v. *Jones* [1995] 2 AC 207 (HL); *Williams* v. *Natural Life Health Foods Ltd* [1998] 2 All ER 577, 583 (HL); *Customs & Excise Commissioners* v. *Barclays Bank plc*, n.18 above, [4], [52], [83] (assumption of responsibility is 'a sufficient but not necessary condition of liability'). See also *Commercial Banking Co. of Sydney Ltd* v. *R. H. Brown & Co.*, n.34 above; *Perre* v. *Apand Pty. Ltd* (1999) 164 ALR 606 (HCA). Contrast *Smith* v. *Eric S. Bush* [1990] 1 AC 831, 862 (HL); *Phelps* v. *Hillingdon LBC* [2001] 2 AC 619, 654 (HL); *Van Colle* v. *Chief Constable of Hertfordshire Police* [2008] 3 All ER 977, [42] (HL).

[66] *Henderson* v. *Merrett Syndicates Ltd*, n.19 above, 180.

[67] *Smith* v. *Eric S. Bush*, n.65 above, 862; *Caparo Industries plc* v. *Dickman* [1990] 2 AC 605, 637 (HL); *Henderson* v. *Merrett Syndicates Ltd*, n.19 above, 181; *White* v. *Jones*, n.65 above, 273; *Williams* v. *Natural Life Health Foods Ltd*, n.65 above, 582 ('[t]he touchstone of liability is not the state of mind of the defendant. An objective test means that the primary focus must be on things said or done by the defendant or on his behalf in dealings with the [claimant]'); *Phelps* v. *Hillingdon LBC*, n.65 above, 654 ('[assumption of responsibility means] simply that the law recognizes that there is a duty of care. It is not so much that responsibility is assumed as that it is recognized or imposed by law'). See also *Merrett* v. *Babb* [2001] QB 1174, [37] (CA).

[68] N.18 above, [5].

[69] See also *Royal Bank of Scotland plc* v. *Bannerman Johnstone Maclay* 2005 1 SC 437, [48]–[53] (IH).

[70] *Hedley, Byrne & Co. Ltd* v. *Heller & Partners Ltd*, n.63 above, 486–487, 502–503, 511, 529–530, 539. In *Caparo Industries plc* v. *Dickman*, n.67 above, 621, Lord Bridge similarly indicated that a defendant, who had provided information, would be liable to a particular claimant, who had relied upon that information, only if there was sufficient proximity between the parties in that the defendant knew that his statement would be communicated to the claimant, either as an individual or as a member of an identifiable class, specifically in connection with a particular transaction or transactions of a particular kind, and that the claimant would be very likely to rely on the information for the purpose of deciding whether or not to enter upon that transaction or upon a transaction of that kind. See also *Royal Bank of Scotland plc* v. *Bannerman Johnstone Maclay*, n.69 above, [45].

will be *a fortiori* where the referee bank is aware of the enquirer's identity or the reference request comes directly from the enquirer. It is not, however, sufficient simply to adduce evidence showing that the referee bank was aware that the enquirer might rely on its words. First, it is necessary to show that the statement was uttered in circumstances demonstrating the bank's willingness to assume responsibility for its accuracy.[71] Ordinarily, this requirement should be relatively straightforward to establish in the banker's reference context, unless it can be shown (as in *Hedley Byrne* itself) that the terms of the reference itself negate any assumption of responsibility.

Secondly, the existence of a duty of care owed by a referee bank (or other supplier of information) to a particular person, and the extent of that duty, will depend upon the scope of the bank's assumption of responsibility.[72] In the context of bankers' references, this issue will largely turn upon whether or not the bank provided the information for the purposes for which it was used.[73] Although not decided in the bankers' references context, the point can be illustrated by referring to *Caparo Industries plc* v. *Dickman*,[74] which concerned the extent to which a target firm's auditors owed a duty of care to a company that had formulated its successful take-over bid for the target company's shares by relying on the accounts prepared by the auditors for the target company's annual general meeting and that had accordingly paid an excessive amount for the target company's shares. Although it was common ground that the auditors had been negligent in preparing the accounts, the House of Lords rejected the claim against the auditor. According to their Lordships, an auditor would not generally owe a duty to a person who purchased shares in a company,[75] or lent money to a company,[76] on the strength of its audited accounts because such persons would not be relying upon the information in the accounts for the purpose for which it was prepared and disseminated, namely to provide the annual general meeting with accurate financial information about the company.[77] As Lord Oliver indicated in *Caparo*,[78] '[t]o widen the scope of the duty to include loss caused to an individual by reliance upon the accounts for purposes for which they were not supplied and were not intended would be to extend it beyond the limits which are so far deducible from the decisions of this House'. Provided the enquirer uses the referee bank's information for the particular transaction or type of transaction in relation to which the reference was initially sought, this requirement should not pose much difficulty for an enquirer in its claim against the referee bank.

Thirdly, a duty of care is only owed to those persons to whom the relevant information is supplied or to those for whose benefit the information was provided. This will usually limit an information-provider's duty of care to the immediate recipient of the relevant

---

[71] *Chaudhry* v. *Prabhakar* [1989] 1 WLR 29 (CA).

[72] *Banque Bruxelles Lambert SA* v. *Eagle Star Insurance Co Ltd* [1997] AC 191, 211 (HL); *Sasea Finance Ltd* v. *KPMG* [2000] 1 BCLC 236, 242–243 (CA); *Kuwait Airways Corporation* v. *Iraqi Airways Co.* (*Nos. 4&5*) [2002] 2 AC 883, [71] (HL); *Moore Stephens* v. *Stone Rolls Ltd*, n.39 above, [81]–[82]. See also *The Achilleas* [2009] AC 61 (HL).

[73] *Al-Nakib Investments (Jersey) Ltd* v. *Longcroft* [1990] 1 WLR 1390; *Possfund Custodian Trustee Ltd* v. *Diamond* [1996] 1 WLR 1351; *Customs & Excise Commissioners* v. *Barclays Bank plc*, n.18 above, [35]; *Man Nutzfahrzeuge AG* v. *Freightliner Ltd* [2008] 2 BCLC 22, [47]–[50] (CA).

[74] N.67 above.

[75] Ibid., 624–625. See also *Moore Stephens* v. *Stone Rolls Ltd*, n.39 above, [19], [72]–[76], [85], [119], [168], [191], [211]–[215].

[76] Id. See also *Al Saudi Banque* v. *Clarke Pixley* [1990] Ch. 313.

[77] *Berg, Sons & Co. Ltd* v. *Mervyn Hampton Adams* [1993] BCLC 1045; *Equitable Life Assurance Society* v. *Ernst & Young* [2003] 2 BCLC 603, [122]–[123] (CA).

[78] N.67 above, 654.

information. In *James McNaughton Paper Group Ltd* v. *Hicks Anderson & Co.*[79] which involved a negligence claim by a purchaser of a company against that company's account-ant as a result of the purchaser having relied upon a set of draft accounts that had been prepared by the accountant for the use of the company and its then members in relation to the sale, Neill LJ observed that 'in England a restrictive approach is now adopted to any extension of the scope of the duty of care beyond the person directly intended by the maker of the statement to act upon it'.[80] Applying this approach, Neill LJ rejected any duty of care owed by the accountant to the purchaser, as the accounts had not been prepared with a view to their being used by potential purchasers of the business and, as the accounts were still in draft form and had not been certified, the accountant could not foresee that the purchasers, as experienced businessmen, would rely on the accounts.[81] At first sight, the approach in *James McNaughton* would tend to negate any duty of care owed by the referee bank to the enquirer when a bank reference is supplied directly to the enquiring bank. Neill LJ, however, highlighted a number of general considerations that might be used to identify the circumstances in which an information-provider would owe a duty of care to someone other than the information's immediate recipient: the purpose for which the statement is made, namely whether the information was intended to be communicated to, and was for the benefit of, its direct recipient only, or whether it was made for the benefit of another;[82] the purpose for which the statement was communi-cated, namely whether the statement was communicated for information only or with the expectation that it would be acted upon by someone other than the immediate recipient of the information; the relationship between the information-provider, the person to whom the information was provided, and the third party; the size of the class to which the third party recipient belonged; and the state of the information-provider's knowledge, namely whether he was aware that the information would be communicated to a third party and was aware of the purpose for which the information would be communicated. Applying these considerations to the banker's reference context, it is probably the case that a ref-eree bank will ordinarily owe a duty of care to an enquirer, even where the enquiring bank solicits the reference, since it will usually be the express understanding of all the parties that the referee bank is supplying the information for the ultimate benefit of the enquirer.[83] It follows from the considerations in *James McNaughton*, however, that the

---

[79] [1991] 2 QB 113 (CA). See also *Machin* v. *Adams* (1997) 84 Build LR 83, 99 (CA); *Payne* v. *John Setchell Ltd* [2002] BLR 489, [47]–[48]; *Mirant-Asia Pacific Ltd* v. *Oapil* [2004] EWHC 1750 (TCC), [372]–[376]; *So* v. *HSBC Bank plc* [2009] EWCA Civ. 296, [44]–[49].

[80] Id. See also *BDG Roof-Bond Ltd* v. *Douglas* [2000] 1 BCLC 401.

[81] Contrast *Morgan Crucible Co. plc* v. *Hill Samuel & Co. Ltd* [1991] Ch. 295 (CA). In *Galoo Ltd (in liq.)* v. *Bright Grahame Murray* [1994] 1 WLR 1360 (CA), the auditor of the target company's accounts was held to owe a duty of care to the bidder in a take-over bid, where he had been informed that an identified bidder would be relying on the accounts and the auditor intended that that bidder should so rely. See also *Barings plc* v. *Coopers & Lybrand (a firm)* [1997] BCC 498; *Bank of Credit and Commerce International (Overseas) Ltd* v. *Price Waterhouse (No. 2)* [1998] PNLR 564 (CA); *Andrew* v. *Kounnis Freeman* [1999] 2 BCLC 641 (CA); *Electra Private Equity Partners* v. *KPMG (a firm)* [2000] PNLR 247 (CA); *Barings plc* v. *Coopers & Lybrand* [2002] 2 BCLC 364.

[82] Mere foresight or knowledge that particular third parties are likely to place reliance upon the informa-tion does not, without more, give rise to a duty of care on the part of the information-provider, but 'there must be some positive permission expressed or implied for that advice to be passed on, in the sense that it is aimed at the eventual recipient who relies upon it': *A. & J. Fabrications (Batley) Ltd* v. *Grant Thornton* [2000] BPIR 1, 7 (solicitors' knowledge that a liquidator was passing on their advice to the creditor, who was funding the liquidation, did not involve the solicitors assuming responsibility to that creditor). See also *BDG Roof-Bond Ltd* v. *Douglas*, n.80 above, 420–421.

[83] *Rise Home Loans Pty Ltd* v. *Dickinson* [2010] VSC 29, [36].

referee bank's duty of care in relation to the information supplied will be limited to the enquirer for whose use the information was solicited. A person to whom the enquirer might have shown the reference will be unlikely to establish that the referee bank had assumed responsibility towards him for the contents of the reference. Nevertheless, as discussed further below, it is usual for the referee bank to protect itself from claims by such remote parties by including an express statement in the reference to the effect that it 'is intended for and made available to the named recipient only on a confidential basis, and is not to be passed on to third parties'.

As indicated above, it is not enough that the referee bank have assumed responsibility to the enquirer; the enquirer must also have relied in some way upon the relevant information.[84] Ultimately, the existence or otherwise of reliance is a factual question.[85] In the context of a banker's reference, the element of reliance can usually be established by showing that the enquirer solicited the information for his use and entered (or declined to enter) into the transaction(s) with the person investigated for which the information was initially sought. The basic principle that reliance is essentially a factual enquiry is subject to three provisos. First, whilst the fact that the enquirer is an experienced businessman does not preclude a finding that he relied upon the information supplied by the referee bank in contracting with the person investigated,[86] a court may be reluctant to find such reliance when the enquirer has his own means of assessing the creditworthiness or otherwise of the person investigated, and is in fact in a better position than the referee bank to make this determination.[87] Secondly, it is necessary to demonstrate that the information-

---

[84] Lord Steyn stressed the element of reliance in *Williams* v. *Natural Life Health Foods Ltd*, n.65 above, 583. See also *Henderson* v. *Merrett Syndicates Ltd*, n.19 above, 180. Most recently, in *Customs & Excise Commissioners* v. *Barclays Bank plc*, n.18 above, [14], [65], [112], one of the grounds for refusing to impose liability upon a bank that had overlooked an injunction freezing a customer's account was the absence of any reliance by the claimant, who held the injunction, on the defendant bank's actions. In exceptional circumstances, there may be no need for reliance, provided that the defendant's act or omission caused the loss to the claimant: *White* v. *Jones*, n.65 above (solicitor who accepted instructions to draft a will owed a duty of care to the intended beneficiary, even though the latter was unaware that the solicitor had been engaged on such a task). See also *Carr-Glynn* v. *Frearsons* [1998] 4 All ER 225 (CA); *Gorham* v. *British Telecommunications plc* [2000] 4 All ER 867 (CA); *Richards* v. *Hughes* [2004] EWCA Civ. 266, [22]–[28]. The principle in *White* would be unlikely to apply in the banker's reference context, where liability will continue to be governed by orthodox *Hedley Byrne* principles: *Commercial Banking Co. of Sydney Ltd* v. *R. H. Brown & Co.* n.34 above, 364, 367.

[85] *Royal Bank and Trust Company (Trinidad) Ltd* v. *Pampellonne* [1987] 1 Lloyd's Rep. 218, [1987] 1 FTLR 90, 98 (PC); *JEB Fasteners Ltd* v. *Marks Bloom & Co.* [1983] 1 All ER 583 (CA). See also *Mohr and Mohr* v. *Cleaver and Cleaver* [1986] WAR 67 (WASC); *Cypress-Batt Enterprises Ltd* v. *Bank of British Columbia* [1994] 9 WWR 438 (BCSC).

[86] *Rust* v. *Abbey Life Insurance Co. Ltd* [1978] 2 Lloyd's Rep. 386.

[87] *James McNaughton Paper Group Ltd* v. *Hicks Anderson & Co.*, n.79 above. In *Mutual Mortgage Corporation Ltd* v. *Bank of Montreal* (1965) 55 DLR (2nd) 164, Sheppard JA held that a bank owed no duty of care to a mortgage company in relation to losses suffered by the mortgage company as a result of the bank's introduction of a customer whom the mortgage company knew had exceeded its credit-limit with the bank. Although the bank had not disclosed to the mortgage company its internal correspondence concerning the customer, the mortgage company was not treated as having relied on the bank's advice, since it specialized in dealing with high-risk loans and there was no evidence that it would have refused to grant the relevant loan if it had been familiarized with the customer's record. According to his Honour, the particular loan in *Mutual Mortgage* fell more within the mortgage company's area of expertise than that of the bank. See also *Cypress-Batt Enterprises Ltd* v. *Bank of British Columbia*, n.85 above. Although the Canadian courts have held that a referee bank might owe a fiduciary duty to an enquirer when giving a reference, at least where the enquirer is also a customer of the referee bank and the bank has a clear financial interest in the enquirer continuing to deal with the person investigated (*Vita Health (Co.) (1985) Ltd* v. *Toronto Dominion Bank* (1994) 118 DLR (4th) 289 (MBCA)), such a conclusion is unusual (*Kuruyo Trading Ltd* v. *Acme Garment Co. (1975) Ltd* [1988] 3 WWR 644 (MBQB), revsd. (1988) 51 DLR (4th) 334 (MBCA); *Royal Bank* v. *Aleman* [1988] 3 WWR 461

provider could have foreseen that reliance would be placed on the information given by him in the manner that had eventuated, and that he assumed liability. Thirdly, the enquirer must be shown to have acted in a reasonable manner in relying upon the relevant information in the way that he did. The reasonableness of the enquirer's actions will depend upon the proper interpretation of the information provided in its commercial context, the clarity and importance of that information, and the enquirer's skill and comprehension. Accordingly, an enquirer may not be considered to have acted reasonably when he has simply relied on a patently ambiguous reference, rather than seeking clarification from the referee bank.[88] Once such reliance is established, however, there is no further requirement that the enquirer's reliance upon the relevant information be the *sole* cause of his losses.[89] It appears to be enough that the information played 'a real and substantial part, though not by itself a decisive part' in inducing the enquirer to act in the way that he did,[90] that the information was a 'real and effective' cause of the enquirer's decision,[91] or that the information 'substantially contributed' to the enquirer's decision.[92]

Having established the existence of a duty of care on the part of the referee bank, the enquirer must also establish the content or scope of that duty in order to determine whether it has been breached. The referee bank's duty of care is limited to providing a fair report about the person investigated based upon the knowledge that it possesses and any other information readily available to it, but its duty does not extend to conducting a thorough investigation of its own records before composing the reference or to making enquiries from outside sources available to it.[93] Moreover, by providing a reference to the enquirer, the referee bank does not thereby assume any duty of care to the enquirer to verify that the person investigated is in fact the person with whom the enquirer is proposing to deal.[94] This legal duty to provide a fair report only extends to the provision of the formal reference or any advice given by the referee bank in a proper business context, and does not extend to subsequent comments or clarifications about a customer's standing that may be made on an informal or social occasion.[95] There also appears to be a general principle that, in providing a reference, a referee is only required to exercise reasonable skill and due care in relation to matters about which the referee has sufficient expertise to

(AQB); *Weitzman v. Hendin* (1989) 69 OR (2d) 678 (OCA); *Coral-Reef Holdings Ltd v. Canadian Imperial Bank of Commerce* [1995] 5 WWR 1 (MBCA); *Accord Business Credit Inc. v. The Bank of Nova Scotia* (1997) 33 OTC 362, [47]–[60] (OCJ); *Valentine v. Toronto-Dominion Bank* [2000] OTC 531, [123]–[140] (OSC)). In *Barrett v. Reynolds* (1998) 170 NSR (2d) 201, [201] (NSCA), *Vita Health* was explained as a case involving the provision of financial advice, rather than simply the provision of information.

[88]   *McInerny v. Lloyds Bank Ltd* [1974] 1 Lloyd's Rep. 246.

[89]   *Mann v. Coutts & Co.* [2003] EWHC 2138 (Comm.), [197]–[214]; *Dadourian Group International Inc. v. Simms*, n.37 above, [99]–[100].

[90]   *JEB Fasteners Ltd v. Marks Bloom & Co.*, n.85 above, 589. See also *Compafina Bank v. Australia and New Zealand Banking Group Ltd* (1984) Aust. Tort Reports 80–546; *Avon Insurance plc v. Swire Fraser Ltd* [2000] 1 All ER (Comm.) 573, 589; *Mayor & Burgess of The London Borough of Waltham Forest v. Roberts* [2004] EWCA Civ. 940, [41]; *Street v. Coombes* [2005] EWHC 2290 (Ch), [93]; *Raiffeisen Zentralbank Österreich AG v. Royal Bank of Scotland plc* [2010] EWHC 1392 (Comm.), [154]–[191].

[91]   *Assicurazioni Generali SpA v. Arab Insurance Group* [2002] EWCA Civ. 1642, [59]; *So v. HSBC Bank plc*, n.79 above, [66].

[92]   *BSkyB Ltd v. HP Enterprise Services UK Ltd*, n.37 above, [325].

[93]   *Parsons v. Barclay & Co. Ltd* (1910) 103 LT 196; *Mutual Life and Citizens' Assurance Co. Ltd v. Evatt*, n.65 above.

[94]   *Gold Coin Joailliers SA v. United Bank of Kuwait plc* [1997] PNLR 217, 225 (CA) (bank gave a reference about the person investigated, when the enquirer was in fact dealing with an imposter pretending to be the person investigated). See also *Gooden v. Northamptonshire County Council* [2001] EWCA Civ. 1744, [68].

[95]   *Hedley, Byrne & Co. Ltd v. Heller & Partners Ltd*, n.63 above.

render the enquirer's reliance on his judgement justifiable. In *Mutual Life and Citizens' Assurance Co. Ltd* v. *Evatt*,[96] where a policy-holder in the defendant insurance company sought to recover the losses on his investment in one of the defendant's subsidiaries after relying on the defendant's advice concerning that subsidiary's standing, a majority of the Privy Council held that the defendant was not liable, as the giving of financial advice was not within the province of the insurance company's business[97] and as there were no particular facts suggesting that the company had voluntarily assumed responsibility for that advice. This particular principle will not be applied too stringently,[98] however, and will not ordinarily present much of an obstacle in the case of a banker's reference—as Lord Goff stated obiter in *Spring* v. *Guardian Assurance plc*,[99] 'the skill of preparing a reference in respect of an employee falls as much within the expertise of an employer as the skill of preparing a bank reference fell within the expertise of the defendant bank in *Hedley Byrne* itself'. That said, the referee bank will only be liable for losses resulting from the inaccuracy of its advice, but not losses resulting from defects in the goods ultimately supplied by the person investigated provided the general commercial standing of the person investigated is accurately reflected by the reference's positive terms.

Despite the above legal principles operating to limit banks' exposure, the task of providing references for customers retains a number of inherent risks for banks, since banks cannot afford to spend a great deal of time composing a reference that is gratuitously provided and their familiarity with the intimate details of a particular customer's business activities is by necessity limited. Moreover, given the pace of modern business and trade, information contained in a reference may quickly become out-of-date. To minimize such risks, banks invariably include a disclaimer of responsibility in their references. As indicated above, such a disclaimer was held to be effective in *Hedley Byrne*, where the reference indicated that it was provided 'without responsibility on the part of [the] bank'.[100] Similarly, in *Commercial Banking Co. of Sydney Ltd* v. *R. H. Brown & Co.*,[101] where the claimant asked its bank to obtain a bank reference in respect of a purchaser that was rumoured to be facing financial difficulties and the referee bank supplied a favourable reference without believing in its truth, Menzies and Gibbs JJ agreed that, where a bank had disclaimed liability in its reference, there could be no negligence liability as the referee bank had made it clear that it refused to assume a duty of care.

---

[96] N.65 above. *Evatt* has not been followed in Australia: *L. Shaddock & Associates Pty. Ltd* v. *Council of the City of Parramatta* (1981) 150 CLR 225 (HCA); *Re Sebastian Pty. Ltd* (1986) 68 AJR 161 (HCA).

[97] A different conclusion might follow where the adviser has a financial interest in the transaction upon which he has given advice: *W. B. Anderson & Sons Ltd* v. *Rhodes (Liverpool) Ltd*, n.43 above.

[98] *Kellogg Brown & Root Inc.* v. *Concordia Maritime AG* [2006] EWHC 3358 (Comm.), [8-105]–[8-107].

[99] N.18 above.

[100] *Totem Building Supplies Ltd* v. *Toronto-Dominion Bank* (1999) 248 AR 241, [17]–[18] (AQB). Contrast *Keith Plumbing & Heating Co.* v. *Newport City Club Ltd* [2000] 6 WWR 65 (BCCA), where the British Columbia Court of Appeal, by a majority, held that a referee bank was liable to the enquirer for negligently providing an inaccurate reference, despite the presence of a disclaimer in similar terms to the disclaimer in *Hedley Byrne*. *Hedley Byrne* was distinguished on the basis that: (i) the referee bank had been approached directly by the enquirer rather than through an enquiring bank, as in *Hedley Byrne*; (ii) the initial request in *Hedley Byrne* indicated clearly that the information sought was 'without responsibility' on the part of the bank, whereas there was no such stipulation in *Keith Plumbing*; and (iii) the basis of liability in *Hedley Byrne* was a 'voluntary assumption of responsibility', whereas in *Keith Plumbing* the action was based on negligence. This third point was of vital importance, as, in *Hercules Management Ltd* v. *Ernst & Young* [1997] 2 SCR 165 (SCC), the Supreme Court of Canada had rejected the *Hedley Byrne* assumption of responsibility test for liability for negligent misstatement, preferring instead to impose a duty of care in circumstances where the defendant ought reasonably to have foreseen that the claimant would rely on the representation and that the claimant's reliance was reasonable in the circumstances.

[101] N.34 above.

Nevertheless, the Australian High Court held the referee bank liable in the tort of deceit, as it had provided the reference with the requisite degree of fault,[102] and the disclaimer of liability could not protect the bank from the consequences of its own fraud or intentional wrongdoing.[103]

Whilst *Hedley Byrne* and *Brown* demonstrate that a disclaimer of liability may be effective at common law, they do not deal with the issue of whether such a disclaimer might nowadays be subject to control pursuant to the Unfair Contract Terms Act 1977 (UCTA 1977).[104] It is clear that a term or notice that purports to *exclude* or *limit* liability for economic loss caused by negligence will fall within the scope of UCTA 1977,[105] and will only be effective to the extent that it satisfies the test of reasonableness.[106] As the duty owed by a referee bank to an enquirer depends upon the former's voluntary assumption of responsibility to the latter, rather than resulting from a general relationship of proximity (such as exists between neighbours or drivers), the effect of a disclaimer in a banker's reference is not so much to *exclude* or *limit* the bank's liability, but rather to *prevent any duty of care arising in the first place* by narrowing the scope of the bank's assumption of responsibility. Whilst recent authority has tended to conclude that clauses defining the scope of the parties' contractual undertakings (particularly in a commercial context) fall outside UCTA 1977,[107] in *Smith* v. *Eric S. Bush*,[108] the House of Lords has held that a disclaimer in a mortgage valuation fell within section 13(1) of UCTA 1977, which extends the general scope of UCTA 1977 beyond terms or notices that seek to exclude or limit *liability* to also include terms or notices that 'exclude or restrict' the relevant *duty of care*. Accordingly, courts are likely to apply *Smith* to the specific context of disclaimers of responsibility contained in bankers' references, so that such disclaimers are likely to be subjected to the reasonableness test in UCTA 1977.[109] Although the point awaits final judicial determination, it is likely that standard-form disclaimers contained in bankers' references will be held reasonable, since bankers' references are usually provided gratuitously; disclaimers are used universally by banks when providing references;[110] there is usually a relative equality of bargaining strength between enquirer and referee bank given that most bankers' references are given in the commercial sphere;[111] and the courts should be wary of taking steps that might undermine the commercially important practice of

---

[102] *Derry* v. *Peek*, n.36 above.

[103] *HIH Casualty & General Insurance Ltd* v. *Chase Manhattan Bank* [2003] 2 Lloyd's Rep. 61 (HL).

[104] As a general rule, the Unfair Terms in Consumer Contracts Regulations 1999, S.I. 1999/2083 (UTCCR 1999) will have no application to a disclaimer in a non-contractual document, such as a banker's reference, as they only apply to contractual terms (ibid. reg. 3), but (as considered further below) there may occasionally be a contractual relationship between the enquirer and the referee bank.

[105] Unfair Contract Terms Act 1977 (UCTA 1977), s.2(2). UCTA 1977, s.3, which deals with the exclusion or limitation of contractual liability where the parties either deal with each other on one party's 'written standard terms of business' or one of the parties 'deals as consumer'.

[106] Ibid., s.11 & Sched. 2.

[107] *IFE* v. *Goldman Sachs* [2007] 1 Lloyd's Rep. 264, [71]; *JP Morgan Chase Morgan* v. *Springwell Navigation Corporation* [2008] EWHC 1186 (Comm.), [597]–[605], aff'd [2010] EWCA Civ 1221; *Titan Steel Wheels Ltd* v. *Royal Bank of Scotland plc* [2010] EWHC 211 (Comm.), [98]–[104]; *Raiffeisen Zentralbank Osterreich AG* v. *Royal Bank of Scotland plc* [2010] EWHC 1392 (Comm.), [313]–[315].

[108] N.65 above. See also *Halloway* v. *Cuozzo* (CA, 9 February 1999); *Customs & Excise Commissioners* v. *Barclays Bank plc*, n.18 above, [88]; *Scullion* v. *Bank of Scotland plc* [2010] EWHC 572 (Ch), [94]–[99].

[109] UCTA 1977, ss.2(2), 11(3) & 11(5).

[110] *Titan Steel Wheels Ltd* v. *Royal Bank of Scotland plc*, n.107 above, [105], although widespread use of a standard-form disclaimer within a particular industry does not necessarily make it reasonable under UCTA 1977 in every case (*First National Commercial Bank plc* v. *Loxleys (a firm)* [1997] PNLR 211 (CA)).

[111] Id.

providing bankers' references.[112] Accordingly, despite UCTA 1977, the form of disclaimer employed in *Hedley Byrne* and *Brown* will probably remain effective to relieve the referee bank of responsibility. Whether the disclaimer also operates to protect the branch manager or other bank employee who prepares the reference from personal liability for negligent misstatement[113] will depend upon the disclaimer's precise wording. Most disclaimers currently in use resolve this difficulty by stating that any reference or opinion 'is given without responsibility on the part of the bank and its officers and employees'.[114]

There may be one exceptional situation that has received little judicial attention, however, where a disclaimer in a banker's reference may be more susceptible to statutory control, namely when the same bank acts as both enquiring bank and referee bank.[115] Whilst it may be rare for the enquirer and the person investigated to maintain their accounts at exactly the same branch,[116] it is far from inconceivable that they would hold accounts at different branches of a clearing bank.[117] In circumstances where the enquiring bank and referee bank are the same, that bank will owe an implied contractual duty of care to both the person investigated and the enquirer, at least where the enquirer is also a customer of the bank,[118] or (somewhat more unusually) may owe such a duty as a result of the reference being provided to the enquirer pursuant to the terms of a specific contract to that effect between the parties. Where the referee bank's disclaimer takes effect by way of a term in the contract between that bank and the enquirer, not only might section 2(2) of UCTA 1977 subject the disclaimer to control (as considered above), but section 3 of UCTA 1977 might also operate to control the disclaimer as an attempt to exclude liability for breach of contract, at least where one of the parties 'deals as a consumer or on the other's written standard terms of business.'[119] Whichever of these provisions applies, however, the disclaimer will only be effective if it satisfies the legislation's test of reasonableness. In addition, where an enquirer can be classified as a 'consumer' for the purposes of the Unfair Terms in Consumer Contracts Regulations 1999 (UTCCR 1999),[120] any disclaimer contained in his contract with the referee bank may be rendered non-binding on the consumer if deemed 'unfair' pursuant to the UTCCR 1999.[121] An 'unfair term' is any contractual term (but not a 'core term')[122] that 'has not been individually negotiated' and that,

---

[112] *Banking Services: Law and Practice*, n.13 above, [6.35], where the Jack Committee recommended that, given the risk that banks might discontinue the practice of supplying references if disclaimers in bankers' references were rendered ineffective, such clauses should be allowed to stand.

[113] Such liability is most likely to be based upon the bank manager or employee voluntarily assuming responsibility to the enquirer: *Williams* v. *Natural Life Health Foods Ltd*, n.65 above.

[114] Although such a disclaimer will not operate to protect either the referee bank itself, its managers, or its employees from the consequences of a fraudulent statement contained in a bank reference, as considered above, section 6 of Lord Tenterden's Act will prevent a deceit claim being actionable against the referee bank or its agents in the usual case where the bank reference is unsigned. Where a bank manager or employee with authority to sign the reference has done so, both the referee bank itself, and the individual who actually signed the reference, could potentially be liable in deceit for the fraudulent statements contained in the reference: *UBAF Securities Ltd* v. *European American Banking Corp.*, n.41 above, 724–725; *Contex Drouzhba Ltd* v. *Wiseman*, n.42 above, [12]–[16].

[115] The practice is for the referee bank's manager to formulate his response to the reference request in exactly the same manner as if the request had come from another bank.

[116] *Robshaw* v. *Smith*, n.25 above.

[117] The courts might decide for these purposes to treat separate branches as if they were distinct banks, as occurs in relation to the collection of cheques: Ch. 15, Sect. 8 above.

[118] Ch. 5, Sect. 4(iii) above.   [119] Nn.104–105 above.

[120] UTCCR 1999, reg. 3 defines a 'consumer' as a 'natural person … acting for purposes which are outside his trade, business or profession'.

[121] Ibid., regs. 4 & 8.

[122] Ibid., reg. 6(2). See also *Office of Fair Trading* v. *Abbey National plc* [2010] 1 All ER 667 (UKSC).

'contrary to the requirement of good faith ... causes a significant imbalance in the parties' rights and obligations arising under the contract, to the detriment of the consumer'.[123] In assessing the unfairness of a particular term, a court must consider the nature of the services provided to the enquirer, all the circumstances surrounding the conclusion of the contract, and any other relevant contractual terms.[124] Moreover, in reaching a conclusion on this issue, a court is also likely to consider the factors discussed above in relation to whether a standard bank disclaimer in a reference is reasonable for the purposes of the UCTA 1977. Although there is not the same relative equality of bargaining strength between an enquirer, who is a 'consumer', and a referee bank as there is in a commercial setting, the factors that render disclaimers in general reasonable under the UCTA 1977 are also likely to support the conclusion that such disclaimers are not 'unfair' under the UTCCR 1999, at least where the disclaimer is clearly worded and unambiguous, and has been brought to the consumer's attention.

Whether the enquirer succeeds in the tort of negligence or deceit, issues concerning the remoteness and quantification of damages are likely to arise.[125] The referee bank may also raise questions relating to whether the enquirer's loss was caused by the errors in the bank's reference. In *Commercial Banking Co. of Sydney Ltd* v. *R. H. Brown & Co.*,[126] for example, the referee bank argued that the misrepresentation in the reference had not caused the enquirer's loss, as the enquirer had concluded its contract with the person investigated before requesting the reference. In response, the enquirer contended that, if the reference had revealed the true situation, it would have refrained from performing its contract with the purchaser. The High Court of Australia accepted the latter argument and the enquirer was allowed to recover the full loss, since if it had been forewarned about the status of the person investigated, and thereupon terminated the sale of the wool to that person, its liability to the purchaser would have been restricted to nominal damages.

3 Giving advice on financial investments

The potential liability of a bank to its customer when providing traditional or core banking services has already been considered previously.[127] In providing such services, whether they be of an ordinary or an unusual and complex nature, it seems relatively well established that a bank will not generally be held liable for breach of a common law or contractual duty to exercise reasonable care, unless it can be taken to have 'crossed the line' and *impliedly* assumed the duties of an adviser, rather than those of a mere banker.[128] As an incidental service to its core banking activities, a bank may also *expressly* undertake to provide financial advice to its customer. In *Woods* v. *Martins Bank Ltd*,[129] which involved the provision of financial advice by a bank manager to a financially inexperienced investor, Salmon J held that a bank owed a customer an implied contractual duty to exercise reasonable skill and care in tendering such financial advice.[130] Although

---

[123] Ibid., reg. 5(1). See also *Director General of Fair Trading* v. *First National Bank plc* [2002] 1 AC 481 (HL).

[124] Ibid., reg. 6(1). There is an indicative and non-exhaustive list of terms that may be regarded as unfair: ibid., Sched. 2.

[125] N.40 above.   [126] N.34 above.   [127] Ch. 5, Sect. 4 4(iii) above.

[128] Id.   [129] N.3 above, discussed in Ch. 5, Sects. 2 & 4(i) above.

[130] Ibid., 63. Salmon J achieved the result in *Woods* by holding that the banker–customer relationship could potentially arise from an earlier time than the opening of an account for a person, namely from the time that the bank accepted a person's instructions to open an account on his behalf: Ch. 5, Sect. 2 above.

his Lordship in *Woods* also explained the bank's potential liability for providing neg-ligent financial advice in terms of a breach of a fiduciary duty owed to the recipient of that advice[131]—a type of claim that could be brought by either a customer or a non-customer—it is likely that a modern court would reconceptualize the liability in *Woods* as being based upon either a common law duty of care owed concurrently with a contrac-tual duty (in the case of a customer) or a freestanding common law duty of care (in the case of a non-customer).[132] In either case, as recognized in *Hedley Byrne*,[133] the existence of such a common law duty is likely to result from the bank's voluntary assumption of responsibility for the task of providing accurate financial advice to the person seeking it. The fact that the bank has accepted and responded to a request for advice is usually strong evidence of such an assumption of responsibility,[134] although, where the advice provided by the bank falls within the scope of its business, a court may be prepared to find that the bank voluntarily assumed responsibility for that advice without there being any need to demonstrate an antecedent request by the recipient of that advice.[135] Moreover, where the financial advice in question falls within the scope of banks' ordi-nary business, a bank cannot usually escape the consequences of its negligent advice by pleading its employees' lack of authority to advise. In this regard, it was recognized in *Woods* that nowadays the provision of financial advice generally forms part of a bank's business.[136] Nevertheless, it always remains possible for a bank to establish by evidence that a certain type of advice is outside the scope of its business, or is of a type on which the customer cannot reasonably expect to rely.[137]

For an extreme example of a court striving to establish contractual liability to enable a person to recover losses resulting from his reliance on a bank's advice, see *De la Bere* v. *Pearson Ltd* [1907] 1 KB 483.

[131] Ch. 5, Sect. 4(i) above.

[132] *Hedley, Byrne & Co. Ltd* v. *Heller & Partners Ltd*, n.63 above, 495. See also L.S. Sealy, 'Fiduciary Obligations, Forty Years On' (1995) 9 *JCL* 37, 42, fn.45.

[133] Ibid. See also *Henderson* v. *Merrett Syndicates Ltd*, n.19 above; *White* v. *Jones*, n.65 above; *Williams* v. *Natural Life Health Foods Ltd*, n.65 above; *Customs & Excise Commissioners* v. *Barclays Bank plc*, n.18 above.

[134] A bank's failure to provide advice would not usually involve liability in negligence, unless such advice was solicited by the customer and the bank agreed to furnish it in circumstances giving rise to a duty of care: *Williams & Glyn's Bank Ltd* v. *Barnes* [1981] Com. LR 205, 207 (considered in Ch. 17, Sect. 5(i) below); *Investor's Compensation Scheme Ltd* v. *West Bromwich Building Society* [1999] Lloyd's Rep. PN 496 (edited report), where the defendant building society was held not to owe a common law duty of care to borrowers not to market defective mortgage packages or to advise them on the financial and other risks to which they would be exposed. Evans-Lombe J held (ibid., 519–527) that there had been no assumption of responsibility by the society, stressing that the borrowers had at all times dealt through an independent financial adviser and had had no direct contact with the society. See also *Wells* v. *First National Commercial Bank* [1998] PNLR 552 (CA), where there was no direct contact between a paying bank and the transferee of a funds transfer. See further Ch. 13, Sect. 5(iv).

[135] *Morgan* v. *Lloyds Bank plc* [1998] Lloyd's Rep. Bank. 73, 80 (CA).

[136] For a similar view in Australia, see *Barrow* v. *Bank of New South Wales* [1931] VLR 323 (advice to customer A to invest funds in customer B, both of whom held accounts with the same branch, was within the scope of the branch manager's authority). See also *Holmes* v. *Walton* [1961] WAR 96. Originally, the Canadian courts regarded the giving of financial advice as being outside the scope of a bank's business (*Banbury* v. *Bank of Montreal*, n.2 above; *Royal Bank* v. *Mack* [1932] 1 DLR 753; *Bank of Montreal* v. *Young* (1966) 60 DLR (2d.) 220), but they have since reversed their view on this point (*Goad* v. *Canadian Imperial Bank of Commerce* [1968] 1 OR 579, 592–596; *Royal Bank of Canada* v. *Nowosad* [1972] 6 WWR 705 (MBQB), affd. (1974) DLR (3d) 159 (MBCA)).

[137] *Thornett* v. *Barclays Bank (France) Ltd* [1939] 1 KB 675, 684 (CA). See also *Mutual Life and Citizens' Assurance Co. Ltd* v. *Evatt*, n.65 above (insurance company not liable for advice given on corporate finance).

Not every communication, however, between a bank and its customer, nor every piece of information provided by a bank, nor every opinion expressed by a bank will necessarily involve the provision of 'financial advice' to a customer. Accordingly, it should be possible for a bank to offer informal support or encouragement to a customer, or set out the range of options open to him, without leaving itself open to potential liability on the ground that it proffered advice on the course of action that the customer should take. Thus, in *Morgan* v. *Lloyds Bank plc*,[138] the defendant bank's branch manager wrote to the claimant stating that his nursing home business should be sold quickly as a going concern, otherwise the bank would make a formal demand and exercise its power of sale as mortgagee. The branch manager also expressed the view that the claimant had overvalued the property. The Court of Appeal agreed that the claimant's claim for negligent advice should be struck out on the ground that it disclosed no reasonable cause of action, since the bank's communications had been made 'in its capacity as mortgagee to give a choice', not 'in its capacity as banker to its customer'.[139] The limits of what qualifies as 'financial advice' was similarly highlighted in *Royal Bank Trust Company* v. *Pampellonne*,[140] where the claimants, who maintained an account with the defendant bank's Nassau branch, asked the bank's manager of the Trinidad branch to recommend a United Kingdom-based deposit-taking company. Relying on a contemporary credit information report, the branch manager recommended a particular deposit-taking firm to the claimants as being trustworthy for its ordinary business engagements. Acting upon this recommendation, the claimants instructed the branch manager to transfer funds from its account with the Nassau branch to the United Kingdom deposit-taking firm. The claimants renewed the deposit with the United Kingdom firm on a number of occasions over several years, but the firm eventually failed. The trial judge dismissed the claimants' negligence and deceit claims,[141] a judgment that was subsequently reversed by the Trinidad Court of Appeal. On further appeal to the Privy Council, Lord Templeman and Sir Robin Cooke, in their dissenting opinion, were prepared to uphold the Court of Appeal's judgment. In their Lordships' view, the bank owed the claimants a duty of care, since the latter had sought information from the bank in the context of a business transaction, trusting that the bank would exercise care in providing the information necessary to make an informed business decision.[142] It followed that the bank could have fulfilled its duty by undertaking to conduct further enquiries on the claimants' behalf, by recommending that the claimants seek professional advice, or at least by informing the claimants that the information available was inadequate to make a fully informed investment decision.[143] Delivering the majority opinion, however, Lord Goff held that 'whether the furnishing of information is in any particular case to be treated as equivalent to advice must depend upon the facts of the case, and in particular upon the precise circumstances in which the relevant information has been given'.[144] On that basis, his Lordship concluded that the Court of Appeal should not have interfered with the trial judge's factual findings to the effect that the defendant bank had not given any recommendation that it was safe to invest in the United Kingdom deposit-taking firm, but had instead only agreed to provide the claimants with the information available to it about the firm.[145] Moreover, as regards the placing of the original deposits and their subsequent renewal, Lord Goff also stressed that

---

[138] N.135 above. See also *Bale* v. *HSBC Bank plc* [2003] EWHC 1268 (QB), [120]–[125].

[139] Ibid., 80.   [140] N.85 above.

[141] Some additional counts relating to the branch manager's advice respecting another investment firm, on which the Court of Appeal had affirmed the trial judge's decision in favour of the bank, were not appealed to the Privy Council.

[142] *Royal Bank Trust Company* v. *Pampellonne*, n.85 above, [29].

[143] Ibid., [30]–[31].   [144] Ibid., [19], [23].   [145] Id.

the claimants had effectively made their investment decisions 'on their own initiative independently of any advice which might have been given by the bank'.[146] Not only did this negate the existence of a duty of care, but also the causative potency of any breach. Accordingly, his Lordship upheld the trial judge's legal conclusion that the bank owed the claimants no duty of care with respect to the information provided.[147] It is implicit in this holding, however, that Lord Goff would have similarly upheld the trial judge's conclusion that the bank *did* owe the claimants a duty of care, if the factual finding at first instance had happened to have been that the branch manager *had undertaken to advise the claimants*.[148]

As the nature of the bank's communication—whether it involves the mere furnishing of information, on the one hand, or the provision of financial or other advice, on the other[149]—is critical in determining the content and scope of its duty to the customer, it is necessary to identify those factors that might point to a particular communication being classified in one way or the other. Arguably, the most important factor is likely to be the source of the information provided to the customer. Where the source is a third party, and the bank simply acts as a conduit in passing the relevant information on to its customer,[150] or even tenders an opinion on an informal basis about the particular investment on the basis of that information, the situation is likely to be classified as one that involves the mere furnishing of information. As indicated in *Pampellonne*, considered above, a bank in such circumstances will not be under any obligation to investigate that information thoroughly or research its accuracy. In contrast, where the information or other communication is generated by the bank itself, such as where a bank provides a feasibility report upon a particular investment at its customer's request or gives a customer an express assurance that a particular result will eventuate,[151] the situation is more likely to be classified as one involving the provision of advice and consequently result in the imposition of greater liability on the bank. This is analogous to the situation that arose in *South Australia Asset Management Corporation* v. *York Montague Ltd*,[152] which concerned the level of damages recoverable from a surveyor, who had negligently overvalued a property that was provided as security for a mortgage loan advanced by the claimant lender. Given that the surveyor itself conducted the valuation of the property, it was not unreasonable for the surveyor to be held responsible for the losses resulting from the inaccuracy of its own valuation when the lender subsequently relied upon the surveyor's report. The source of the relevant information is not, however, the sole criterion that may be relevant. A further factor that may influence a court in its classification of a particular communication, and accordingly its decision to impose liability on a bank, is whether the bank's interests conflict with those of the person receiving the communication, in the sense that the bank has a direct interest in how the recipient acts upon it.[153] Although a bank will not generally owe any fiduciary obligation to its customer, or to a third party recipient of information,

---

[146] Ibid., [21]–[22].   [147] Ibid., [19].

[148] This might have been the case if expert evidence established that the bank should have formed its own views about the proposed investment before it forwarded the information available to it to the claimants.

[149] For endorsement of this distinction, see *McEvoy* v. *Australia and New Zealand Banking Group Ltd* (NSWCA, 16 February 1990).

[150] A person acting as a mere conduit for information will not generally be liable under the Fair Trading Act 1986 (NZ): *Red Eagle Corporation Ltd* v. *Ellis* [2010] 2 NZLR 492, [38] (NZSC).

[151] *Box* v. *Midland Bank Ltd* [1979] 2 Lloyd's Rep. 391 (bank liable to customer for losses resulting from the refusal of a bank loan following the customer entering into a concluded transaction as a result of the branch manager giving the impression that approval of the customer's loan application would be a mere formality).

[152] [1997] AC 191 (HL).

[153] *Esso Petroleum Co. Ltd* v. *Mardon* [1976] QB 801 (CA) (petrol company liable for misrepresentation made in its own interests concerning the likely profits from a station it was negotiating to let to a prospective

that would oblige the bank to disclose such a conflict,[154] the bank is still best advised to provide the other party with full details concerning the transaction.[155] Additionally, as considered previously,[156] there are other factors that may influence the classification of a particular communication as 'financial advice', including the particular status and role within the bank of the person with whom the customer has dealt (so that a bank employee who acted purely in their capacity as a salesperson of certain bank products will not generally be taken to have advised a customer when communicating with him in that capacity);[157] the customer's financial acumen[158] (and accordingly the reasonableness in the particular circumstances of his treating the bank's communication as 'advice' upon which he was entitled to rely and act);[159] the existence of any prior course of dealings or relationship or any promotional literature or contractual documentation that might indicate that the bank undertook to advise the customer;[160] the nature of any account;[161] and the terms of the parties' relationship.[162]

Where the bank is held simply to have furnished information to its customer, then the bank probably owes two limited duties to the recipient. First, a bank will owe a duty to take reasonable care when selecting the source from which the relevant information is to be obtained—a duty satisfied in *Pampellonne* by the credit information report in that case coming from a known and reputable agency. Secondly, a bank will owe a duty to ensure that whatever information has been received from third parties is passed on to its customer accurately—a duty similarly satisfied in *Pampellonne*. Beyond these two duties, however, it is submitted that the majority view in *Pampellonne* should be preferred to that of the minority, and that a bank should not be expected to conduct a detailed analysis or assessment of the available information, including any information received from third party sources. The position is *a fortiori* when, as in *Pampellonne*, the source of the information (or the basis of the bank's opinion) is reports prepared by reputable credit information agencies. In contrast, where the bank has undertaken to provide the customer with financial advice, such as in the case of a feasibility report, there is an expectation that the bank will analyse and provide a detailed assessment of all the available information, including verifying the accuracy or reliability of information received from third

---

franchise-holder, when the representor knew that the statement was bound to influence the other party's decision-making).

[154] Ch. 5, Sect. 4(i) above.

[155] *Rust* v. *Abbey Life Assurance Co.*, n.86 above.   [156] Ch. 5, Sect. 4(iii) above.

[157] *JP Morgan Chase Bank* v. *Springwell Navigation Corporation*, n.107 above, [101]–[105], [373]–[374], [445]–[459]; *Titan Steel Wheels Ltd* v. *Royal Bank of Scotland plc*, n.107 above, [93]–[94]. Where the claimant has a personal relationship with the defendant bank's representative, with the result that the relevant discussions take place informally, the courts will be more reluctant to impose an advisory duty on the bank: *Camarata Property Inc* v. *Credit Suisse Securities (Europe) Ltd* [2011] EWHC 479 (Comm.), [143]–[150].

[158] *Bankers Trust International plc* v. *P. T. Dharmala Sakti Sejahtera* [1995] Bank. LR 381, 419; *JP Morgan Chase Bank* v. *Springwell Navigation Corporation*, n.107 above, [264], [432], [448], [455]; *Titan Steel Wheels Ltd* v. *Royal Bank of Scotland plc*, n.107 above, [94]–[96].

[159] *Mutual Life and Citizens' Assurance Co. Ltd* v. *Evatt*, n.65 above.

[160] *Bankers Trust International plc* v. *P. T. Dharmala Sakti Sejahtera*, n.158 above, 408; *JP Morgan Chase Bank* v. *Springwell Navigation Corporation*, n.107 above, [434]–[444]; *Titan Steel Wheels Ltd* v. *Royal Bank of Scotland plc*, n.107 above, [30], [94].

[161] *Valse Holdings SA* v. *Merrill Lynch International Bank Ltd* [2004] EWHC 2471 (Comm.), [22], [69].

[162] *Peekay Intermark Ltd* v. *Australia & New Zealand Banking Group Ltd* [2006] 2 Lloyd's Rep. 511, [60] (CA); *JP Morgan Chase Bank* v. *Springwell Navigation Corporation*, n.107 above, [475]; *Titan Steel Wheels Ltd* v. *Royal Bank of Scotland plc*, n.107 above, [30], [98]; *Raiffeisen Zentralbank Osterreich AG* v. *Royal Bank of Scotland plc*, n.107 above, [97], [230]–[256]; *Cassa di Risparmio della Repubblica di San Marino SpA* v. *Barclays Bank Ltd*, n.37 above, [505]–[509]; *Camarata Property Inc* v. *Credit Suisse Securities (Europe) Ltd*, n.157 above, [151]–[187]; *Bank Leumi (UK) plc* v. *Wachner* [2011] EWHC 656 (Comm.), [185]–[210].

party sources. The bank's duty to its customer in this regard will be limited to exercising reasonable care so as to ensure that the advice tendered is accurate and reliable *at the time that it is furnished.* In the absence of a specific undertaking to that effect, the bank does not assume a further continuing obligation to keep its advice under review and, if necessary, to correct it in the light of supervening events.[163] Similarly, neither the bank nor its employees are expected to guarantee the strength of a particular investment,[164] but it is usually sufficient for them to show that they had reasonable grounds for believing in the accuracy or general reliability of the advice tendered,[165] even if there were in fact further steps that might have been taken by the bank to verify or evaluate that advice.[166]

Where the evidence establishes that the bank has breached its duty to exercise reasonable care in tendering advice, the damages that may be recovered depend upon the nature of that advice. In *South Australia Asset Management*, Lord Hoffmann drew a distinction between the situation where a person furnishes advice, or generates information for the purpose of enabling someone else to decide upon a course of action, and the situation where a person advises another on what course of action they should take. According to his Lordship, in the former situation (into which fell the valuation report in *South Australia Asset Management*), the duty is to take reasonable care to ensure that the information or advice is correct and, if the defendant has been negligent, it will be responsible for all reasonably foreseeable consequences of that information or advice being wrong.[167] In the latter situation, however, the duty is to take all reasonable care to consider all potential consequences of the proposed course of action and, if negligent, the defendant will be responsible for all foreseeable loss that is a consequence of that course of action being taken.[168] In either situation, a customer's claim will usually include the actual amount lost as a result of him relying upon the bank's inapt advice,[169] together with damages for reasonably foreseeable consequential losses,[170] and compound interest on these amounts[171] (whether representing interest paid or foregone).[172] Whilst the case law demonstrates that such losses are most frequently claimed in circumstances where a customer or other person has relied upon a representation made by a bank employee in the course of his occupation, damages would also be available in other circumstances, such as where the customer's losses are caused by the bank's negligent management of a fund entrusted to it or the mismanagement of a customer's portfolio investments.[173]

---

[163] *Fennoscandia Ltd* v. *Clarke* [1999] 1 All ER (Comm.) 365 (CA); *Dancorp Developers Ltd* v. *Auckland City Council* [1991] 3 NZLR 337, 352–353.

[164] *Nestlé* v. *National Westminster Bank (No. 2)* [1993] 1 WLR 1260, which shows that, even in the case of trust funds, a trustee is not liable for a decline in value except where he is in default. The Trustee Act 2000 introduces a new standard of care in relation to, *inter alia*, investing trust property, and section 1 now provides that a trustee must 'exercise such skill and care as is reasonable in the circumstances', although allowance is made for any 'special knowledge or experience', or for the situation where the defendant 'acts as trustee in the course of a business or profession'.

[165] *Howard Marine and Dredging Co. Ltd* v. *A. Ogden & Son (Excavations) Ltd* [1978] QB 574 (CA).

[166] *Byrne* v. *Nickel* [1950] QSR 57, 71.

[167] *South Australia Asset Management Corporation* v. *York Montague Ltd*, n.152 above, 214.

[168] Id.   [169] *Woods* v. *Martins Bank Ltd*, n.3 above.

[170] *South Australia Asset Management Corporation* v. *York Montague Ltd*, n.152 above.

[171] *Hungerfords* v. *Walker* (1989) 171 CLR 125, 142–144 (HCA); *Bank of America Canada* v. *Mutual Trust Co.* [2002] 2 SCR 601, [44]–[46] (SCC); *Sempra Metals Ltd* v. *Inland Revenue Commissioners* [2008] 1 AC 561, [132] (HL); *Clarkson* v. *Whangamata Metal Supplies Ltd* [2008] 3 NZLR 31, [22]–[36] (NZCA). See also *Holmes* v. *Walton*, n.136 above.

[172] For example, in *Woods* v. *Martins Bank Ltd*, n.3 above, the claimant lost approximately £5,000, which he could have invested in an interest-bearing account.

[173] *Wilson* v. *United Counties Bank Ltd* [1920] AC 102 (HL) (bank breached its duty of care by negligently carrying on the business of a customer who had entrusted it to the bank when he joined the army).

There will be rare circumstances where a customer or other person can bring a deceit claim if he can establish, on a balance of probabilities,[174] that he relied upon the bank's inaccurate financial advice, that the advice was provided 'knowingly, without belief in its truth, or recklessly, careless whether it be true or false',[175] and that it was intended by the bank to be relied upon.[176] The principal advantages to the customer of bringing a deceit claim are threefold: the customer can recover damages for all losses directly flowing from the inaccuracy of the bank's advice, regardless of whether these are reasonably foreseeable or not;[177] the advising bank loses the ability to reduce the damages payable by pointing to the customer's own contributory negligence;[178] and the advising bank may not rely upon any disclaimer of liability to negate its liability for deceit.[179] Nevertheless, where it is possible to establish the existence of a duty of care, a negligence action may remain more attractive in certain circumstances. First, it is notoriously difficult to establish the mental element necessary for a deceit claim, particularly when neither the bank nor its employees have derived any pecuniary advantage from providing the inaccurate advice.[180] Secondly, as discussed above,[181] if the customer's claim concerns negligent financial advice that involves the making of a misrepresentation of the relevant type, Lord Tenterden's Act may prove an obstacle in the absence of writing.

4 The banker as bailee and custodian

(i) Safe deposit services

As indicated previously, a common incidental service rendered by banks to their customers, and frequently to the public in general, is the acceptance of valuables for safe custody in the bank's own safe or strongroom. These goods will be returned to the owner or his authorized agent against the production of a receipt or appropriate identification. In such circumstances, the bank clearly becomes a bailee of the deposited goods. The position is maybe less clear, however, with respect to one of the more recent incarnations of the safe-deposit services offered by banks, namely the night safe, which enables customers to deposit cash, cheques, or documents with a bank outside normal banking hours. Where the bank enters into an agreement with the customer for the provision of night-safe services and provides the customer with exclusive means of accessing the night safe, such as a key or code,[182] there is little difficulty in concluding that the bank has agreed to enter into a bailment relationship with the customer from the moment of deposit. Where the night-safe services are provided to customers or even to the public more generally (such as occurs in the modern practice of allowing persons to deposit funds in an ATM machine by using the designated envelopes), it may be more difficult to find any particular acceptance on the part of the bank to act as bailee in relation to any particular deposit. Nevertheless,

---

[174] As to the applicable standard of proof, compare *Dadourian Group International Inc.* v. *Simms*, n.37 above, [30]–[32] with *Lindsay* v. *O'Loughnane*, n.37 above, [89].

[175] *Derry* v. *Peek*, n.36 above, 374. See also *Club Travel 2000 Holdings Ltd* v. *Murfin*, n.36 above, [49].

[176] N.37 above.   [177] N.40 above.   [178] N.39 above.

[179] *HIH Casualty & General Insurance Ltd* v. *Chase Manhattan Bank*, n.103 above. For the effectiveness of such disclaimers in the context of negligent advice, see *Peekay Intermark Ltd* v. *Australia & New Zealand Banking Group Ltd*, n.162 above, [60]; *JP Morgan Chase Bank* v. *Springwell Navigation* Corporation, n.107 above, [475]; *Titan Steel Wheels Ltd* v. *Royal Bank of Scotland plc*, n.107 above, [30], [98].

[180] *Woods* v. *Martins Bank Ltd*, n.3 above.   [181] Sect. 2(ii) above.

[182] *Bernstein* v. *Northwestern National Bank of Philadelphia*, 41 A 2d 440, 441–442 (1945); *Kolt* v. *Cleveland Trust Co.*, 89 Ohio App. 347, 352 (Ohio App., 1950).

it is submitted that the relationship should still be classified as one of bailment on the basis that the bank is either an involuntary bailee,[183] or a voluntary bailee that signified its implied acceptance of the bailment relationship by making night-safe facilities available in the first place.[184] Unlike the situation where goods are deposited for safe custody in the bank's own safe or strongroom, in which case the bailment relationship is usually ongoing, cash deposited in a night safe only gives rise to a bailment relationship[185] of a temporary nature.[186] By analogy with the situation where cash is deposited over the counter, the initial bailment relationship will be converted into the usual debtor-creditor relationship once the bank has had the opportunity to check the amount of the deposit and signify its acceptance of the amount, for example, by crediting the customer's account.[187]

Where a bank charges a specific fee for its safe-custody or night-box services, as occasionally occurs, the bank will be considered a bailee for reward.[188] More commonly, however, banks do not charge specific fees for such services, but provide them as part of their general relationship with customers. In *Giblin* v. *McMullen*,[189] the Privy Council initially treated such a bank as a gratuitous bailee of the deposited goods, with the liability that such a classification entails. This case was distinguished, however, in *Re United Service Co.*,[190] where a customer deposited shares for safekeeping with his bank and gave the bank conditional access to the share certificates so that it could collect any dividends payable thereon. In an action for the conversion of the shares by a bank employee, the Court of Appeal treated the bank as a bailee for reward and distinguished *Giblin* on the ground that the bank in *United Service* had some (albeit conditional) access to the relevant share certificates and had received consideration in the form of its banker's lien attaching to the documents.[191] As this last line of reasoning was potentially of wide application, given that the banker's lien attaches to most items deposited with a bank for safekeeping,[192] it is not surprising that the Privy Council, in *Port Swettenham Authority* v. *T.W. Wu & Co. (M.) Sdn. Bbd.*,[193] eventually recanted its earlier views in *Giblin*. According to their Lordships, 'a bank, which offers its customers, in the ordinary course of business, the service of looking after goods deposited with it, can hardly be described as a gratuitous bailee'.[194] This classification of a bank as a bailee for reward (at least when the deposited goods belong to a customer) was justified on the basis that, as a bank has a pre-existing contractual relationship with its customers, the customer in question will provide consideration for the safe-deposit services (despite not paying a specific fee for the items' safe custody) by agreeing to continue his general banking relationship with that bank.[195] It is arguable, however, on the basis of *Port Swettenham* that, even where a non-customer deposits valuables with a bank without charge, the bank receives consideration as it only takes on the responsibility of acting as bailee in the hope of inducing the bailor to utilize the bank's other services. It

---

[183] *Robot Arenas Ltd* v. *Waterfield* [2010] EWHC 115 (QB), [8]–[23].

[184] *Bernstein* v. *Northwestern National Bank of Philadelphia*, n.182 above, 442.

[185] *Balmoral Supermarket Ltd* v. *Bank of New Zealand* [1974] 2 NZLR 155, 158–159; *R* v. *Allpress* [2009] EWCA Crim. 8, [48]. See also C. Proctor, *Mann on the Legal Aspects of Money* (6th edn., Oxford, 2005), [1.28]–[1.31], [1.54]–[1.59].

[186] *Bernstein* v. *Northwestern National Bank of Philadelphia*, n.182 above, 442.

[187] *Balmoral Supermarket Ltd* v. *Bank of New Zealand*, n.185 above, 157.

[188] *Bernstein* v. *Northwestern National Bank of Philadelphia*, n.182 above (customer charged nominal fee for night safe key).

[189] (1868) LR 2 PC 317. See also *Kahler* v. *Midland Bank Ltd* [1948] 1 All ER 811, 819–820 (CA), affd. [1950] AC 24 (HL).

[190] (1871) LR 6 Ch. App. 212.   [191] Cf. *Leese* v. *Martin* (1873) LR 17 Eq 224.

[192] Ch. 20, Sect. 2 below.

[193] [1979] AC 580, 589 (PC) (doubting *Giblin* v. *McMullen* , n.189 above.

[194] Ibid. See also *Morris* v. *C.W. Martin & Sons Ltd* [1966] 1 QB 716 (CA).   [195] Ibid.

has been held in a different context that a person who provides a service, in the expectation of receiving future custom from the recipient, in fact receives a valuable benefit that counts as sufficient consideration.[196] Indeed, the very fact that banks continue to advertise their safe-custody facilities suggests that they must in practice derive some pecuniary or commercial benefit from offering such services for free.[197]

It may be wondered, however, whether the dichotomy between gratuitous bailees and bailees for reward has not become a rather sterile exercise in classification following *Houghland* v. *R. R. Low (Luxury Coaches) Ltd*,[198] where Ormerod LJ considered that the standard of care to be expected of a bailee 'is the standard demanded by the circumstances of [the] particular case' and that 'to try to put a bailment, for instance, into watertight compartments—such as gratuitous bailments on the one hand, and bailment for reward on the other—is to overlook the fact that there might well be an infinite variety of cases which might come into one or the other category'.[199] Although the Privy Council in *Port Swettenham* accepted that the line between gratuitous bailments and bailments for reward 'is a very fine line, difficult to discern and impossible to define',[200] it nevertheless accepted that the standard expected of gratuitous bailees 'although high, may be a less exacting standard than that which the common law requires of a bailee for reward'.[201] Lord Denning expressed a similar view in *Morris* v. *C. W. Martin & Sons Ltd*.[202] Accordingly, as indicated by the House of Lords recently in a different context,[203] it may still be important to draw the distinction between the different types of bailment relationship.

As a bailee, a bank may be held liable to its customer in respect of deposited goods on a number of grounds that may be raised as alternatives or concurrently. First, where the bank charges a fee for keeping goods safe, so that consideration is provided for the bank's safe-custody services, the bank may be (usually strictly) liable for breaching the express or implied terms of the contract with its customer. One such implied term would be to exercise 'reasonable skill and care' in the provision of its safe-custody services.[204] Secondly, whether classified as a gratuitous bailee or a bailee for reward, a bank may be liable in the tort of negligence for any failure to exercise reasonable care in the custody of the customer's goods and will be vicariously liable for the negligent actions of its agents or employees that contribute to the customer's losses. Thirdly, where the bank is a gratuitous bailee, it will certainly be liable for breach of its duty *as bailee* if it has failed to exercise the ordinary care to be expected in the safeguarding of another's property,[205] but, where the bank is a bailee for reward, its duty *as bailee* may require it to meet a heightened standard of care in relation to the deposited goods, since '[a]ccording to orthodox theory, the measure of a bailee's responsibility for a chattel is governed by the existence and location

---

[196] *De la Bere* v. *Pearson Ltd*, n.130 above; cf. *Williams* v. *Roffey Bros & Nicholls (Contractors) Ltd* [1991] 1 QB 1 (CA).

[197] N.E. Palmer, *Bailment* (2nd edn., London, 1991), 513.   [198] [1962] 1 QB 694 (CA).

[199] Ibid., 698. See also *AVX Ltd* v. *EGM Solders Ltd* (1982) The Times, 7 July; *Chaudhry* v. *Prabhakar*, n.71 above; *Sutcliffe* v. *The Chief Constable of West Yorkshire* [1996] RTR 86 (CA).

[200] *Port Swettenham Authority* v. *T.W. Wu & Co. (M.) Sdn. Bbd.*, n.193 above. See also *R* v. *Ngan* [2008] 2 NZLR 48, [17] (NZSC).

[201] Id. See also *Yearworth* v. *North Bristol NHS Trust* [2009] EWCA Civ. 37, [48(f)]. See further Herbert Jacobs (ed.), *Grant on the Law Relating to Bankers and Banking Companies* (7th edn., London, 1923), 282–283.

[202] N.194 above, 725–726. See also *China Pacific SA* v. *Food Corporation of India, The Winson* [1982] AC 939, 960 (HL). Cf. *Garlick* v. *W&H Rycroft Ltd* (CA, 30 June 1982); *Sutcliffe* v. *Chief Constable of West Yorkshire*, n.199 above, 90.

[203] *TRM Copy Centres (UK) Ltd* v. *Lanwall Services Ltd* [2009] UKHL 35, [10]–[11].

[204] Supply of Goods and Services Act 1982, s.13.   [205] *Banbury* v. *Bank of Montreal*, n.2 above, 657.

of any benefit received'.[206] There may be some situations, however, where the bank's liability *as bailee* is strict: if the bank specifically agrees to store an item in one place, but stores it elsewhere, it may be liable for any losses, unless it can be shown that the change of location had no causative effect so that the relevant loss would inevitably have resulted even if the bailment terms had been strictly observed.[207] Outside such circumstances, however, the burden is on the bank[208] to prove that it exercised the requisite degree of care, skill, diligence, and judgement not only in the safe custody of those goods,[209] but also in appointing those charged with their safekeeping.[210] In addition to being *directly* liable for selecting an inappropriate employee to look after the customer's goods, the bank may be *vicariously* liable for its employees' wrongdoing. The bank is not, however, vicariously liable for the negligent or deliberate wrongdoing of an employee whose employment merely provided the opportunity to damage, lose, or steal the goods,[211] but only for the wrongdoing of employees to whom the safekeeping of the goods was entrusted as part of their employment.[212] Accordingly, a bank will only likely be vicariously liable for the wrongdoing of senior management and other employees who can access the safe or strongroom where the relevant goods are stored.[213] Fourthly, whether a gratuitous bailee or bailee for reward, a bank may be strictly liable in the tort of conversion where it engages in deliberate conduct that interferes with the customer's immediate right to possession of the deposited goods, and thereby excludes the customer from use and possession of the goods.[214] This would occur where the goods are delivered to a person without a right to the goods' immediate possession.[215] Formerly, a customer would have had a detinue claim against the bank where the deposited goods had been lost or destroyed.[216] Nowadays, however, a customer will have a 'statutory conversion' claim against the bank 'for loss or destruction of goods which a bailee has allowed to happen in breach of his duty to his bailor'.[217] This statutory liability is not strict, but depends upon whether the loss or

---

[206] N.E. Palmer, n.197 above, 53–54, 504–505. See also *Houghland* v. *R.R. Low (Luxury Coaches) Ltd*, n.198 above, 698.

[207] *Lilley* v. *Doubleday* (1881) 7 QBD 510; *London & North Western Railway Company* v. *Neilson* [1922] 2 AC 263 (HL); *A/S Rendal* v. *Arcos Ltd* (1937) 43 Com. Cas. 1, 14 (HL); *Yearworth* v. *North Bristol NHS Trust*, n.201 above, [48(i)].

[208] *Port Swettenham Authority* v. *T.W. Wu & Co. (M.) Sdn. Bbd.*, n.193 above; *Morris* v. *CW Martin & Sons Ltd*, n.194 above; *Matrix Europe Ltd* v. *Uniserve Holdings Ltd* [2009] EWHC 919 (Comm.), [47].

[209] An important factor in determining the bank's liability as bailee will be the security systems that the bank has adopted to protect depositors' goods: *Shelton* v. *ANZ Banking Group* (VSC, 9 October 1984).

[210] *Williams* v. *Curzon Syndicate Ltd* (1919) 35 TLR 475 (CA) (club liable for carelessness in the appointment of a night porter).

[211] *Lister* v. *Hesley Hall Ltd* [2001] 2 All ER 769, [45]–[46], [59]–[60] (HL).

[212] *Morris* v. *CW Martin & Sons Ltd*, n.194 above, 722–723, 737, 740–741 (CA); *Heasmans* v. *Clarity Cleaning Co. Ltd* [1987] ICR 949, 950 (CA); *Frans Maas* v. *Samsung Electronics (UK) Ltd* [2004] 2 Lloyd's Rep. 251, [104]–[121].

[213] *Frans Maas* v. *Samsung Electronics (UK) Ltd*, n.212 above, [112] (vicarious liability may arise where a wrongdoing employee has been entrusted with the keys and alarm code of the premises where goods are located).

[214] *Caxton Publishing Co. Ltd* v. *Sutherland Publishing Co. Ltd* [1939] AC 178 (HL); *Kuwait Airways Corporation* v. *Iraqi Airways Co. (Nos. 4&5)*, n.72 above, [39]. Contributory negligence is not available as a defence to a conversion claim: Torts (Interference with Goods) Act 1977, s.11(1). Contributory negligence is available in particular circumstances to an action for the conversion of a cheque: Banking Act 1979, s.47.

[215] *Stephenson* v. *Hart* (1828) 4 Bing. 476, 482–483; *Hiort* v. *London and North Western Railway Co.* (1879) 4 Ex. D 188, 194; *Glyn, Mills, Currie & Co.* v. *East and West India Dock Co.* (1880) 6 QBD 475, 493, affd. (1882) 7 App. Cas. 591; *Marcq* v. *Christie Manson & Woods Ltd* [2004] QB 286, [23] (CA). Misdelivery no longer gives rise to liability in detinue: Torts (Interference with Goods) Act 1977, s.2(1).

[216] Detinue has been abolished: Torts (Interference with Goods) Act 1977, s.2(1).

[217] Torts (Interference with Goods) Act 1977, s.2(2).

destruction 'was caused by an event which occurred without any default on [the bank's] part' and upon whether the bank 'had exercised all reasonable care during the period of the bailment'.[218] Moreover, it is an element of the 'statutory conversion' claim that there must be an 'unequivocal demand' for the goods by the customer and an 'unequivocal refusal' to do so by the bank.[219]

Where a bank is faced with such an unequivocal demand, it can sometimes find itself in a difficult position, as it may harbour doubts as to the genuineness of a letter making demand or as to the identity or rights of the person doing so.[220] In such circumstances, the bank is not required to make an immediate decision, but is entitled to retain the deposited goods for such time as is reasonably necessary to confirm the validity of the depositor's demand. In *Clayton* v. *Le Roy*,[221] which involved a demand by a solicitor, representing the original owner of a stolen antique watch, for its return from a shopkeeper who had subsequently purchased the watch, Fletcher-Moulton LJ stated that '[t]he cases show clearly, as one would expect, that it is not unlawful refusal for a man to decline to give up property at once and without taking time to inquire as to the title of the claimant'.[222] As a bank is generally estopped from denying the original depositor's title,[223] a bank that wrongfully refuses to return the goods to the original depositor after making such enquiries, or delivers them to a third person who is not so entitled, will be liable in damages.[224] Should the bank's enquiries reveal that a third party has a better title to the goods than the original depositor, the bank has a defence to any claim subsequently brought by the original depositor.[225] Where it is a party other than the original depositor who has demanded the return of the goods, the bank similarly has time to verify the title of the claimant and is able to retain the goods for as long as it has 'a bona fide doubt as to the title to the goods'.[226]

---

[218] *Kuwait Airways Corporation* v. *Iraqi Airways Co. (Nos. 4&5)*, n.72 above, [438]. See also *Schwarzschild* v. *Harrods Ltd* [2008] EWHC 521 (QB), [18]–[24].

[219] *Schwarzschild* v. *Harrods Ltd*, n.218 above, [20]–[25].

[220] A particularly complex situation arises where a person deposits items, such as shares, with the foreign correspondent of an English bank and that correspondent (at the depositor's request) in turn deposits the goods with one of the bank's English branches in order to avoid the political, legal, or economic regime applicable in the foreign jurisdiction. Where the goods are deposited with the English bank in the depositor's name, then there will be a bailment relationship between the depositor and the English bank that is governed by English law and the depositor will be entitled *as bailor* to the return of his property. Where the deposit by the correspondent bank with the English bank makes no reference to the original depositor's name, the bailment relationship remains between the original depositor and the foreign correspondent bank and continues to be governed by the foreign law: *Kahler* v. *Midland Bank Ltd*, n.189 above, 33, 37. As there is no bailment or privity of contract between the depositor and the English bank, the depositor is not usually entitled to the return of the goods from that bank, even with proof of ownership, unless the foreign correspondent bank gives the appropriate instruction. In the absence of such an instruction, the English bank cannot act unless the depositor establishes that he is not only beneficially entitled to the deposited goods, but also has the right to their immediate possession: *Gorden* v. *Harper* (1976) 7 Term Rep. 9, 101 ER 828; *Bradley* v. *Copley* (1845) 1 CB 685, 135 ER 711; *Kahler* v. *Midland Bank Ltd* [1948] 1 All ER 811, 818 (CA), affd. n.189 above; *Zivnostenska Banka National Corporation* v. *Frankman* [1950] AC 57 (HL); cf. *Isaacs* v. *Barclays Bank Ltd* [1943] 2 All ER 682.

[221] [1911] 2 KB 1031 (CA).   [222] Ibid.

[223] *Cheesman* v. *Exall* (1851) 6 Exch. 341, 346; *Biddle* v. *Bond* [1861–1873] All ER Rep. 477.

[224] The effect of a damages award against the bank is to extinguish the depositor's interest in the goods: Torts (Interference with Goods) Act 1977, s.5(1). See also *United States of America and Republic of France* v. *Dollfuss Mieg et Cie SA and Bank of England* [1952] AC 582.

[225] Torts (Interference with Goods) Act 1977, s.8(1). This defence is probably inapplicable where the deposit is made by co-owners jointly, as the bank is not entitled to return the goods to only one joint bailor: *Brandon* v. *Scott* (1857) 7 E&B 234.

[226] *Hollins* v. *Fowler* (1875) LR 7 HL 757, 766 (HL).

This type of situation commonly arises where executors,[227] divorcing spouses,[228] the revenue authorities,[229] prosecution authorities,[230] or other third parties claim the deposited goods. Should the bank still have substantial doubts about the claimant's rights to the goods once a reasonable time has elapsed and its investigations have been completed, its best course is then to interplead, which involves the court resolving the dispute as to title and providing directions as to how the dispute is to be resolved.[231]

It is always open to the bank to exclude or limit the above forms of liability by inserting a clause into either the deposit contract (if any) or the general banker–customer contract signed upon the opening of the customer's account. In that regard, it is not unusual for banks to include a disclaimer that goods deposited in a sealed envelope or locked box are done so at the customer's risk. Where the issue is whether such a clause is effective to exclude or limit the bank's liability for breaching its contract with respect to the custody of the goods, or where the clause purports to allow the bank to perform its contractual obligations in a substantially different manner or not at all[232] (and the customer is either a consumer[233] or deals 'on the [bank's] written standard terms of business'), the clause will only be effective if it satisfies the statutory test of reasonableness.[234] Similarly, where the issue is whether a disclaimer is effective to exclude liability for 'negligence', which includes not only the bank's general duty of care in negligence to the depositor, but also its duty as bailee to exercise requisite care,[235] the clause must also satisfy the reasonableness test.[236] This is an intensely factual question that depends upon weighing up various factors in the particular case. Factors that have been considered in assessing whether such a disclaimer is reasonable or not include whether the person depositing the goods is a commercial party rather than a consumer;[237] whether the relevant clause is in common use amongst banks;[238] whether insurance is available and been taken out or not;[239] whether the clause is fairly brought to the customer's attention;[240] whether the clause is an exclusion or limitation clause;[241] and the size of the monetary amount to which liability is limited.[242] Where the exclusion or limitation clause is considered reasonable, it can protect the bank against direct liability for its own negligent (but not fraudulent)[243] acts, and even against vicarious liability for the deliberate wrongdoing of bank employees.[244] Such protection is, however, subject to the clause not otherwise being ineffective as 'unfair' pursuant to the UTCCR 1999,[245] which applies when the person depositing the goods is a 'consumer'.[246]

---

[227] *Albreght Estate* v. *Joris* [2008] OJ No. 524; *Re Balanyk* [2010] OJ No. 2722, [21]–[24] (OSC).

[228] *Bindra* v. *Bindra* [2009] OJ No. 2919, [30]–[45] (OSC).

[229] *Re Boyce* [1993] 1 FC 280 (CFC).

[230] *Director of the Assets Recovery Agency* v. *Jackson* [2007] EWHC 2553 (QB); *Capper* v. *Chaney* [2010] EWHC 1704 (Ch).

[231] Civil Procedure Rules 1998, Sched. 1, RSC, Ord. 17. See also *Halsbury's Laws of England* (4th edn., reissue, London, 2001), vol. 37, [1425].

[232] UCTA 1977, s.3(1)–(2).   [233] Ibid., s.12.   [234] Ibid., s.11(1).

[235] Ibid., s.1(1). This does not include circumstances where the bank's liability as bailee is strict: id.

[236] Ibid., s.2(2).

[237] *Frans Maas* v. *Samsung Electronics (UK) Ltd*, n.212 above, [158]–[160]. See also *Sonicare International Ltd* v. *East Anglia Freight Terminal Ltd* [1997] 2 Lloyd's Rep. 48.   [238] Id.

[239] Id. See also *Singer Co. (UK)* v. *Tees and Hartlepool Port Authority* [1988] 2 Lloyd's Rep. 164, 169.

[240] *Scheps* v. *Fine Art Logistic Ltd* [2007] EWHC 541 (QB), [30]–[32].

[241] Id. See also *Singer Co. (UK)* v. *Tees and Hartlepool Port Authority*, n.239 above, 168.   [242] Id.

[243] *HIH Casualty & General Insurance Ltd* v. *Chase Manhattan Bank*, n.103 above.

[244] *Frans Maas* v. *Samsung Electronics (UK) Ltd*, n.212 above, [158]–[160].

[245] UTCCR 1999, regs. 5(1), 8(1). An exclusion or limitation clause is indicatively unfair: ibid., Sched. 2, para. 1(a). See further Ch. 17, Sects. 2(ii) & 3(ii) below.

[246] Ibid., reg. 3(1).

(ii) **Safe deposit boxes**

Rather than storing goods in the bank's own vaults, an increasingly common means of providing safe-custody services to customers and non-customers alike involves the provision of safe deposit boxes. Ordinarily, the terms upon which the bank is prepared to provide the depositor with a safe deposit box are set out in a written agreement, so that the parties' respective rights will depend upon the precise terms of that agreement. Additionally, as with the case of a deposit in the bank's own vaults, the parties' relationship may also be governed by the law of bailment.[247] Whether this is the case depends upon the degree of the bank's access to, and control over, the items contained in the safe deposit box, since a principal requirement of a bailment is that the bailee be given the (exclusive)[248] possession or custody of the relevant subject matter.[249] Certainly where the bank retains a right to inspect the contents of the safe deposit box at periodic intervals,[250] possesses a key for emergency access to a particular box,[251] has a master key for all its boxes, or possesses one of the keys required to access the box,[252] it is likely to be treated as a bailee,[253] even where the bank has contractually undertaken not to open the box.[254] Where the bank has no right of access to the deposited goods, the relationship between the parties is not one of bailment, but one for the hire of the safe deposit box.

As banks generally charge for the hire of safe deposit boxes, a bank with the requisite degree of control or access will be a bailee for reward[255] and will accordingly be liable in the same way as a bank that stores goods in its vault, as considered in the previous section. As well as potential liability in contract and tort, therefore, the bank may also be liable for breach of its duty as bailee where goods have disappeared from the safe deposit box and the bank is unable to prove that the loss did not result from any negligent or wrongful act on its part. In *Cuvelier* v. *Bank of Montreal*,[256] for example, a bank was held liable for the shortfall in the deposited goods where it had failed to keep adequate records of the contents of the claimants' safe deposit box and had 'drilled' the box in the mistaken belief that the rental had not been paid.[257] Alternatively, the bank may be liable for conversion. In *Schwarzschild* v. *Harrods Ltd*,[258] for example, the claimant's mother hired a safe deposit box for the safe custody of her jewellery with the defendant and when she died this passed

---

[247] *Federal Commissioner of Taxation* v. *Harmer* (1990) 94 ALR 541 (FCA).

[248] No reference to 'exclusivity' can be found in Lord Hope's definition of 'bailment' in *TRM Copy Centres (UK) Ltd* v. *Lanwall Services Ltd*, n.203 above, [10].

[249] *Fairline Shipping Corporation* v. *Adamson* [1975] QB 180, 189–190; *Yearworth* v. *North Bristol NHS Trust*, n.201 above, [48(d)]. See also *Chitty on Contracts*, n.58 above, [33–001].

[250] *Schwarzschild* v. *Harrods Ltd*, n.218 above, [5].

[251] *Commissioner of Taxation* v. *Australia and New Zealand Banking Group Ltd* (1979) 143 CLR 499 (HCA), which involved an application for production of documents in a bank safe deposit box pursuant to the Income Tax Assessment Act 1936, s.264 on the ground that the documents were in the bank's 'custody' or 'control'. Although their Honours left open the issue of whether there was a bailment relationship, they held that the bank had 'actual custody or physical control of the contents of the locker': ibid., 521. Consider *Revenue and Customs Commissioners* v. *Principal and Fellows of Newnham College in the University of Cambridge* [2008] UKHL 23, [12].

[252] *Cuvelier* v. *Bank of Montreal* (2000) 189 NSR (2d) 26, [10], [22], [29] (NSSC).

[253] *Federal Commissioner of Taxation* v. *Smorgon* (1977) 16 ALR 721 (HCA). See also *Smorgon* v. *Australia and New Zealand Banking Group Ltd* (1976) 134 CLR 475, 478 (HCA).

[254] *Commissioner of Taxation* v. *Australia and New Zealand Banking Group Ltd*, n.251 above, 521.

[255] *Federal Commissioner of Taxation* v. *Smorgon*, n.253 above.

[256] N.252 above. See also *Kedia International Inc.* v. *Royal Bank of Canada* [2006] BCJ No. 2729 (BCSC).

[257] Punitive damages have been awarded against banks in Canada: *Mohtadi* v. *Canada Trust* [2002] BCCA 562, [17]–[18]. Contrast *Jefferson* v. *Toronto-Dominion Bank* [2004] BCPC 152, [18].

[258] N.218 above.

to the claimant, who eventually ceased payment of the rentals for the box. Following five years of unpaid rentals, the defendant opened the safe deposit box, as permitted by the hire contract, and mixed the contents with other goods. As a result of the defendant's failure to return the goods following investigations by the claimant's agents, the claimant brought a claim for 'statutory conversion'.[259] According to Eady J, it was an essential element of the claimant's cause of action that there had been an unequivocal demand for the return of the goods and an unequivocal refusal to do so,[260] and that, as these had not yet occurred, the limitation period had not yet started to run against the claimant.[261]

---

[259] Torts (Interference with Goods) Act 1977, s.2(2).
[260] *Schwarzschild* v. *Harrods Ltd*, n.218 above, [25].   [261] Ibid., [35].

PART III

The Bank as Financier and Lender in Domestic Transactions

17

Current Account Financing and Loans

1 Overdrafts and loans compared

Conceptually, an overdraft involves the extension of credit to a customer for a relatively short period of time. Although it is common for a customer to make specific arrangements for an overdraft and specifically to agree to its particular conditions, overdrafts are often granted on an *ad hoc* basis without any prior arrangement, although a fee is usually charged for such a facility.[1] Where such agreement exists, the customer is given a ceiling defining the maximum amount he is allowed to overdraw on his account at any given time. Interest is calculated on the daily balance, but is debited to the account periodically, usually monthly in arrears. The customer's best course is to have a respectable margin available for drawings. Further, he should attempt to keep the amount utilized by him to a minimum. It is obvious that, in this way, he saves interest. However, he may have to pay a commitment fee if the bank grants him an overdraft which he does not use. Even if it is possible for the customer to obtain an overdraft on more attractive financing terms than a loan, as considered further below, from the customer's perspective an overdraft has one significant disadvantage when compared to loans—an overdraft is repayable at call or on demand, whereas a loan is granted for a fixed period of time.[2]

With a loan, the bank is committed to providing finance when the borrower wishes to draw on it. In the case of most loans to consumers, and for smaller commercial loans, the advance is usually credited forthwith to the borrower's current account and stands at his disposal at any time. In some industrial and construction loans the amount lent may be drawn down by the borrower in instalments within an agreed period.[3] The amount so lent is debited to a loan account opened in the borrower's name. Interest is charged on the debit balance entered in the loan account. Repayments have to be made according to a fixed repayment schedule; a right to make early repayments is usually available to the borrower. Absent an express provision allowing for early repayment, there is some uncertainty whether a borrower can make early repayment.[4] In the case of ordinary loans, amounts that are repaid may not be re-borrowed, but some commercial loans offer

---

[1] *Office of Fair Trading* v. *Abbey National plc* [2010] 1 All ER 667 (UKSC), discussed in Sect. 2(ii) below.

[2] Clearly, the loan's express terms may make it repayable on demand, although this can lead to difficult questions of contractual interpretation when the loan agreement also states that it extends for a fixed period. See Sect. 2(ii) below.

[3] The borrower will have to pay a larger commitment fee for this facility.

[4] *Hyde Management Services (Pty.) Ltd* v. *FAI Insurances* (1979–80) 144 CLR 541 (HCA); *Airberg Ltd* v. *National Mutual Royal Bank Ltd* (NSWCA, 6 February 1996); *Myross (NSW) Pty Ltd* v. *Kahlefeldt Securities Pty Ltd* [2003] NSWSC 138. See also *Hooper* v. *Western Counties and South Wales Telephone Co. Ltd* (1892) 68 LT 78.

a revolving credit facility where the borrower is allowed to repay and re-borrow through-out the life of the facility, so long as the maximum limit of the facility is not exceeded.[5] Loans for a specified period are known as term loans. Term loans may be granted for a short or a medium period (up to one year and between one and five years respectively), and, in some cases, even for a longer period of time (usually between five and 10 years, although sometimes even longer).

There is considerable variation in the rates of interest charged on overdrafts by banks and building societies.[6] In some cases, it may be possible to borrow on overdraft at a lower rate of interest than that charged on a loan, but personal customers usually find that lower rates are charged as the amount of the loan increases.[7] In all cases, the amount of interest on unauthorized overdrafts is considerably higher than for authorized ones. By contrast, research shows that the rate of interest charged on loans to small business customers is generally higher than that charged on overdrafts.[8] However, even in the case of loans, interest is frequently charged on a variable (or 'floating') basis. The rate of interest may be calculated in various ways and will be the subject of agreement between the lender and borrower at the time the loan is negotiated. For personal loans, and smaller commercial loans, interest is usually expressed in terms of a margin over base rate, which is the rate at which United Kingdom banks are prepared to lend sterling to its customers with the best credit rating. It usually tracks the Bank of England's lending rate. For larger commercial loans, particularly those involving syndication, because the lender funds the loan by bor-rowing funds from other banks on the inter-bank market, the interest rate will usually be expressed in terms of a margin over LIBOR (the London Inter-Bank Offered Rate).[9]

Apart from these practical considerations, there is a conceptual distinction between an overdraft and a loan. An overdraft constitutes current account financing, which pro-vides a flexible means of obtaining financial accommodation, and which is frequently granted for a general object or for multiple purposes. Its principal aim is to enable the customer to continue his running account operations. A loan is effectively the converse of an interest-bearing account. The bank extends the loan as part of its investment of the funds deposited with it, although for larger commercial loans the bank may borrow matching funds from the inter-bank market to finance the particular loan. Ordinarily, the customer seeks the loan in order to fund a specific project or investment. Despite this conceptual difference, the distinction between loans and overdrafts is being eroded. Nevertheless, for some purposes, such as the consumer credit legislation, bank loans and overdrafts continue to be treated differently. As discussed subsequently,[10] overdrafts are less affected by the Consumer Credit Act 1974 (CCA 1974), and the regulations made thereunder, than bank loans, which fall squarely within the ambit of the CCA 1974, unless secured by a mortgage over land.

---

[5] Revolving loans differ from current account financing, as they are not repayable on demand.

[6] D. Cruickshank, *Competition in UK Banking—A Report to the Chancellor of the Exchequer* (London, March 2000), [4.17].

[7] *Lloyds Bank plc v. Voller* [2000] 2 All ER (Comm.) 978 (CA), which shows the claimant bank's annual rate for an authorized overdraft to be 17.4 per cent, whereas its annual rate for a loan of £50,000 was only 9.25 per cent.

[8] N. Clay & M. Cowling, 'Small Firms and Bank Relationships: A Study of Cultural Differences between English and Scottish Banks' 24(1) *OMEGA* 115, February 1996; M.R. Binks & C.T. Ennew, 'The Relationship between UK Banks and their Small Business Customers' (1997) 9 *Small Business Economics* 167.

[9] Others bases used for calculating floating interest rates in a loan agreement include LIBID (the London Inter-Bank Bid Rate) and LIMEAN (the London Inter-Bank Mean Rate).

[10] Sects. 2(v) & 3(iii) below.

2 Overdrafts

(i) Prevailing practice

A customer who maintains a current account with his bank may seek an overdraft facility on his account if he requires short-term financial accommodation.[11] As a matter of practice, the letter from the bank that informs the customer of the overdraft having been granted should also specify the ceiling of the overdraft facility and the period for which the overdraft is available. As a matter of lending practice, a bank is required to inform a customer that the overdraft is repayable on demand.[12] Whilst the customer can expect to utilize the overdraft for the nominated period, the bank can, under the standard formulation, demand immediate repayment if there are unfavourable developments.[13] In essence, pursuant to the overdraft facility, the bank authorizes the customer to draw cheques on his account, or to make withdrawals or payments from the account by debit card or electronic funds transfer, up to a ceiling that may not be exceeded at any one time, unless the customer is prepared to have his payment instructions dishonoured or to pay unauthorized overdraft charges. As amounts are paid to the credit of the account, the available balance of the overdraft increases. As the bank honours its customer's payment instructions, whether given by cheque or other authorized means, the available portion of the overdraft facility decreases. An overdraft may be either secured over assets of the customer, guaranteed by a third party, or completely unsecured.[14]

The method of charging interest on an overdraft is considered in detail subsequently. When the accrued interest is debited to the customer's account, it is capitalized, becoming part of the outstanding balance for future calculations.[15] The bank thus earns compound interest on the amount overdrawn, although this aspect is eliminated if the customer, forthwith, pays to the credit of his account an amount equal to the interest charged.[16] The rate of interest charged on overdrafts varies from customer to customer, and from transaction to transaction. The lowest rate at which accommodation is granted to particularly sound customers in respect of low risk ventures is known as the 'base rate'. A customer is usually notified whether he is charged on this basis or at a higher rate calculated by reference to the base rate.[17] As the base rate is subject to variations depending, *inter alia*, on the minimum rate quoted by the Bank of England, the interest rate charged on bank overdrafts is reviewed from time to time. Lending at a fixed rate is not a practice used widely by banks in the United Kingdom.

---

[11] If the customer's application for an overdraft is declined he should be told the reasons: *Lending Code* (November 2009), [56]; *Lending Code* (March 2011), [88].

[12] *Lending Code* (November 2009), [55]; *Lending Code* (March 2011), [88].   [13] Sect. 2(ii) below.

[14] See generally Ch. 18 below.

[15] Capitalization of interest does not alter its quality as interest or convert the interest into capital. See *Re Morris, Mayhew* v. *Halton* [1922] 1 Ch. 126, 133 (CA); *IRC* v. *Oswald* [1945] AC 360 (HL); *Bank of New South Wales* v. *Brown* (1983) 151 CLR 514 (HCA); *United Malayan Banking Corp Bhd* v. *Pekeliling Triangle Sdn Bhd* [1991] 2 MLJ 559; *Whitbread plc* v. *UCB Corporate Services Ltd* [2000] 3 EGLR 60 (CA).

[16] For the legality of this method of charging interest, see Sect. 2(iii) below.

[17] Current account customers must, in relation to overdrafts, be provided 'with details of the interest rate to be applied or, if reference interest rates are to be used, the method for calculating the actual interest rate' before the account is opened: *Lending Code* (November 2009), [53]. Information about interest rates should be easily accessible: ibid., [58]. Banks should give customers 14 days' notice of how much interest will be collected: ibid., [60]. Notice of interest rate changes must be given at branches and in newspapers within three days of the change: ibid., [62]. On these requirements, see now *Lending Code* (March 2011), [76]–[98]. For other notice requirements relating to changes in interest rate, see Ch. 7, Sect. 2 above.

(ii) **The legal nature of an overdraft**

From a legal point of view, an overdraft is a loan granted by the bank to the customer, so that the bank is the creditor and the customer is the debtor.[18] A bank is not obliged to allow its customer to overdraw an account unless it is contractually committed to doing so.[19] Accordingly, a customer, who gave his bank a document of title as a security for an advance he was promised, provided sufficient consideration for the undertaking of the bank, which was accordingly obliged to provide the overdraft.[20] The bank's contractual undertaking to extend an overdraft facility is a chose in action belonging to the customer. Accordingly, whilst the money in an account remains the bank's money, rather than the customer's money, until payment,[21] the customer's contractual right to an overdraft is a valuable form of 'property' that can be stolen from him through the presentation of forged cheques.[22] Unless the bank has undertaken to grant an overdraft, where there are insufficient funds credited to the customer's account to cover the full amount of the customer's payment order, the bank may ignore the order completely. In such circumstances, the customer's payment order, for example, a cheque drawn by him on his account, stands as an offer to the bank to extend credit to him on the bank's usual terms as to interest and other charges.[23] The bank has the option of accepting or rejecting its customer's offer, but will be deemed to have accepted it where it executes the customer's payment order, for example, by honouring the customer's cheque.[24] Allowing the customer to run up or increase an overdraft in this *ad hoc* manner may create a course of dealing that binds the bank so that it must give the customer reasonable notice of any change of practice.[25]

Where the customer's account becomes overdrawn, or exceeds its overdraft limit without the bank's prior consent, the bank may charge the customer a higher rate of interest and potentially additional bank charges.[26] Recently, such practices have been

---

[18] Ch. 5, Sect. 3 above.

[19] *Cunliffe Brooks & Co.* v. *Blackburn and District Benefit Building Society* (1884) 9 App. Cas. 857, 864 (HL); *Bank of New South Wales* v. *Laing* [1954] AC 135 (PC); *Barclays Bank Ltd* v. *W. J. Simms Son & Cooke (Southern) Ltd* [1980] QB 677, 699; *Office of Fair Trading* v. *Abbey National plc* [2008] EWHC 875 (Comm.), [45], [55].

[20] *Fleming* v. *Bank of New Zealand* [1990] AC 577.   [21] Ch. 5, Sect. 3 above.

[22] *R* v. *Kohn* (1979) 69 Cr. App. R. 395 (CA); *R* v. *Williams* [2001] 1 Cr. App. R. 362, [17]–[19] (CA).

[23] *Lloyds Bank plc* v. *Voller*, n.7 above, 978, 982; *Barclays Bank Ltd* v. *W. J. Simms Son & Cooke (Southern) Ltd.*, n.19 above, 699; *Cuthbert* v. *Robarts Lubbock & Co.* [1909] 2 Ch. 226, 233; *Office of Fair Trading* v. *Abbey National plc*, n.19 above, [64]–[66]. Where the customer exceeds the limit on a previously agreed overdraft facility governed by special terms agreed with the bank that differ from the bank's standard terms, the customer's offer would be deemed to be on the same terms as the existing facility: *Barclays Bank Ltd* v. *Simms*, n.19 above, 699. Equally, where express representations have been made by the bank, or agreement reached with the bank, then these would supersede the terms that would otherwise be implied by law: *Lloyds Bank* v. *Voller*, n.17 above, 983. The bank's standard terms as to interest will not be implied into the overdraft agreement where they are deemed to be 'extortionate or contrary to all approved banking practice': *Emerald Meats (London) Ltd* v. *AIB Group (UK) Ltd* [2002] EWCA Civ. 460, [14]; *Office of Fair Trading* v. *Abbey National plc*, n.19 above, [65]. However, a reference in the bank's standard-form account opening agreement to its 'usual rate of interest' or 'usual terms' is not necessarily insufficiently certain to be enforceable as a contract term, but depends on the totality of the evidence: *Financial Institutions Services Ltd* v. *Negril Negril Holdings Ltd* [2004] UKPC 40, [27].

[24] Ibid. See also *Verjee* v. *CIBC Bank and Trust Co (Channel Islands) Ltd* [2001] Lloyd's Rep. Bank. 279 (bank not put on enquiry by cheque drawn against an inadequate balance, so no breach of duty of care to customer by honouring instrument).

[25] *Cumming* v. *Shand* (1860) 5 H & N 95. The bank receives consideration for this accommodation by way of the receipt of interest and other charges. Cf. *Narni Pty. Ltd* v. *National Australia Bank Ltd* [2001] VSCA 31 (but note the criticisms of J. Sheahan, 'Bank Overdrafts: Inferences and Implications' (2001) 12 *JBFLP* 122).

[26] *Lloyds Bank plc* v. *Voller*, n.7 above, 978, 982 (bank entitled to apply its higher standard rates for unauthorized overdrafts if desired). Details of banks charging structures for overdrafts should be publicly

challenged, but the courts have not shown themselves overly eager to control them. As regards the increased rates of interest, even in the commercial context, the courts have expressed a willingness to strike down clauses imposing punitive rates of interest as unlawful penalties.[27] In *Office of Fair Trading* v. *Abbey National plc*,[28] the penalty jurisdiction was similarly relied upon to challenge standard-form provisions in current account agreements that permitted the major United Kingdom banks to impose additional charges upon customers simply for incurring an unauthorized overdraft on their account.[29] The Office of Fair Trading (OFT) argued that the charges were penalties as they were imposed for breaches of the banks' standard terms and conditions, which generally required customers to ensure that their accounts had sufficient funds to cover any payment instructions and sometimes prohibited customers from drafting cheques in excess of the amount shown on the cheque guarantee card. Andrew Smith J rejected this argument.[30] His Lordship recognized that it is not every contractual provision that is subject to the penalty clause jurisdiction, but only those provisions that condition the customer's obligation to make further payments, or to assume more onerous obligations, upon the breach of its contract with the bank.[31] Provided the relevant provision is at least sometimes triggered by a breach of contract, it does not matter that it can also be triggered by circumstances that do not constitute a breach[32] or only triggered by some types of breach, but not others.[33] According to Andrew Smith J, the banks' standard terms and conditions did not impose a contractual prohibition on the customer becoming overdrawn without authorization, but rather merely advised the customer of his rights and how his account would be operated in such a situation and defined the bank's obligation to honour the customer's instruction in such circumstances.[34] Even in those cases where the unauthorized overdraft did amount to a breach of the customer's contract with the bank, his Lordship concluded that the bank charges were not in fact imposed as a result of that breach.[35] These conclusions were not challenged as part of the appeal to the United Kingdom Supreme Court, although Lord

available and 30 days' notice must be given before increasing or introducing new overdraft charges: *Lending Code* (November 2009), [64]–[65]; *Lending Code* (March 2011), [96]–[97].

[27] *Financial Institutions Services Ltd* v. *Negril Negril Holdings Ltd*, n.23 above, [34]–[36]. See further Sect. 3(ii) below.

[28] N.19 above.

[29] Ibid, [295]–[324]. The charging structures for unauthorized overdrafts varied significantly between the different United Kingdom banks. The various types of unauthorized overdraft charge that were challenged in *Abbey National* include charges imposed when (a) the customer gives a payment instruction that is declined or tries to make a cash withdrawal that is refused on the ground that the account contains insufficient funds, (b) the bank honours a payment instruction or allows a customer to withdraw cash with the result that the account becomes overdrawn without any agreement to this effect, (c) the customer exceeds their overdraft facility or becomes overdrawn without any authorization regardless of how this happens, and (d) the bank honours a cheque supported by a cheque guarantee card, which causes the customer's account to become overdrawn without any agreement to this effect: Ibid., [6].

[30] Although the position was left open in respect of the Royal Bank of Scotland plc: n.32 below, [120]–[130].

[31] *Office of Fair Trading* v. *Abbey National plc*, n.19 above, [295]–[299], applying *Jervis* v. *Harris* [1996] Ch 195, 206.

[32] *Office of Fair Trading* v. *Abbey National plc* [2008] EWHC 2325 (Comm.), [20].   [33] Ibid., [19].

[34] For bank charges falling into this category in the first *Abbey National* judgment: n.19 above, [300]–[307] (Abbey National plc); ibid., [313]–[314] (Clydesdale Bank plc); ibid., [315] (Lloyds TSB plc); ibid., [316]–[318] (Nationwide Building Society); and ibid., [319]–[322] (Royal Bank of Scotland Group plc). For the bank charges falling into this category in the second *Abbey National* judgment: n.32 above, [42]–[45] (Barclays Bank plc), [61]–[62] (Clydesdale Bank plc), [71], [80] (HBOS plc), & [85]–[89] (HSBC plc).

[35] For bank charges falling into this category in the first *Abbey National* judgment: n.19 above, [308]–[312] (Barclays Bank plc). For the bank charges falling into this category in the second *Abbey National* judgment: n.32 above, [28] (Abbey National plc), [46] (Barclays Bank plc), [71], [79] (HBOS plc) & [117]–[118] (Lloyds TSB plc).

Mance lent some support to them.[36] Given that so much turns upon the exact wording of the relevant provisions, however, *Abbey National* should not be taken as completely closing the door to customers challenging bank charges as penalties in appropriate future cases, although banks are in future likely to be particularly careful about drafting such clauses. This possibility may prove to be particularly important for commercial customers, as clauses imposing bank charges would not generally come within the ambit of the Unfair Contract Terms Act 1977 (UCTA 1977), as such clauses do not purport to exclude or limit liability[37] or entitle the bank or customer to render substantially different contractual performance (or no performance at all).[38]

Besides the penalty jurisdiction, the OFT in *Abbey National* also sought to challenge the charges for unauthorized overdrafts by reference to the Unfair Terms in Consumer Contracts Regulations 1999 (UTCCR 1999),[39] which enable 'consumers' to challenge 'unfair' contractual terms.[40] For these purposes, an 'unfair' term is one that 'has not been individually negotiated' and that 'contrary to the requirement of good faith' causes 'a significant imbalance in the parties' rights and obligations arising under the contract'.[41] This narrow issue was the subject of the appeal to the United Kingdom Supreme Court,[42] where their Lordships were posed the question whether such charges could be subjected to the court's scrutiny under the UTCCR 1999 or whether they escaped scrutiny entirely (assuming they were written in 'plain intelligible language')[43] as being related 'to the adequacy of price or remuneration, as against the goods or services supplied in exchange'.[44] Avoiding the label 'core terms' entirely to describe this concept,[45] Lord Walker considered that charges for an unauthorized overdrafts were exempt from control under the UTCCR 1999 as they 'constitute part of the price or remuneration for the banking services provided'.[46] According to his Lordship, the services offered by banks to current account customers formed a 'package' that included the provision of overdraft facilities on the account. Similarly, the consideration provided by customers in return for those services had to be seen as a package and included charges that were payable in the event that a customer incurred an unauthorized overdraft on the account and any interest forgone on the current account.[47] Accordingly, unauthorized overdraft charges were part of the overall price paid for the package of banking services. Lord Phillips agreed that the overdraft charges did not represent a distinct price paid for the overdraft facility,[48] but that they represented part of the overall price charged by banks for providing the package of current accounts and other banking services to customers—'[i]f [banks] did not receive the relevant charges they [would] not be able profitably to provide current account services to their customers in credit without making a charge to augment the value of the use of their funds'.[49] Accordingly, like Lord Walker, Lord Phillips considered that the charges escaped control under the UTCCR 1999. Lady Hale[50] and Lords Mance[51] and Neuberger[52] similarly agreed with these conclusions.[53]

---

[36] N.1 above, [114].   [37] UCTA 1977, ss.2(2) & 3(2)(a).   [38] Ibid., s.3(2)(b).

[39] S.I. 1999/2083, revoking and replacing S.I. 1994/3159 from 1 October 1999.   [40] Ibid., reg. 3(1).

[41] Ibid., reg. 5(1).   [42] N.1 above, [57].

[43] See also *Office of Fair Trading* v. *Foxtons Ltd* [2009] EWHC 1681 (Ch), [58]–[75].

[44] Unfair Terms in Consumer Contracts Regulations 1999, S.I. 1999/2083 (UTCCR 1999), reg. 6(1).

[45] N.1 above, [38], [46].   [46] Ibid., [51].   [47] Ibid., [42].   [48] Ibid., [75].

[49] Ibid., [88]–[89]. In the absence of judicial control of bank charges for unauthorized current account overdrafts, the issue may fall to Parliament to devise an appropriate solution: P. Davies, 'Bank Charges in the Supreme Court' (2010) 69 *CLJ* 21.

[50] Ibid., [92]–[93].   [51] Ibid., [103]–[105].

[52] Ibid., [119]–[120].   [53] Ibid., [103]–[105].

When the bank honours a customer's payment order, causing his account to go into overdraft or further into overdraft, it acts as the customer's agent in making payment.[54] Thus, in *Re Hone, ex p. The Trustee* v. *Kensington Borough Council*,[55] a customer drew a cheque under an agreed overdraft facility and sent it to the cheque's payee, who paid the cheque into its own bank account. The customer was adjudicated bankrupt before funds were cleared. The actual decision by the drawee bank to honour the cheque took place after the adjudication of bankruptcy and it was only then that the payee was able to draw on the funds. The Trustee in Bankruptcy claimed the cheque proceeds back from the payee under section 45 of the Bankruptcy Act 1914, as it had been paid without his approval after the bankruptcy's commencement.[56] Finding for the Trustee, Harman J held that the payment took place when the drawee bank resolved to honour the cheque. Until then, any credit entry in the payee's account was reversible and constituted conditional payment alone. According to his Lordship, the cheque proceeds were recoverable by the Trustee, as the money paid was that of the customer. Harman J observed:[57]

> ...a payment by a bank, under an arrangement by which the customer has an overdraft, is a lending by the bank to the customer of the money. It is the customer who pays the money and not the bank. Otherwise, the bank might be able to sue the payees of the cheque for the money, which they clearly cannot do. They have only paid it as agent for the customer just as if [he] had money there.

Similarly, in *Coutts & Co.* v. *Stock*,[58] Lightman J had to decide whether the acts of the bank in honouring cheques drawn on a company's overdrawn account involved a 'disposition' of the company's property within section 127 of the Insolvency Act 1986.[59] The defendant, who was a company director, had guaranteed the company's overdraft with the bank. Following the presentation of a winding-up petition against the company, the bank continue to honour the cheques, thereby increasing the company's overdraft. When sued on his guarantee, the defendant argued that the bank could not debit the company's account with the post-petition cheques as these constituted void 'dispositions' of the company's property within section 127. Concluding that section 127 had no effect on the state of the account between the company and the bank, Lightman J distinguished between '(i) loans of the sums in question by the bank to the company and (ii) payment by the bank as agent of the company of sums loaned as moneys of the company to the party in whose favour the cheques are drawn'.[60] On this analysis, loans by the bank to the company were not dispositions of the *company*'s money to the bank, but dispositions of the *bank*'s money to the company, and accordingly outside section 127. On the other hand, there were 'dispositions' of the company's money between the company and the cheques' payees. These 'dispositions' were avoided by section 127, but Lightman J held that this did not

---

[54] The text which follows deals with payment by cheque (a debit transfer), but an agency relationship also arises when the bank executes its customer's order to make a credit transfer to the payee: *Royal Products Ltd* v. *Midland Bank Ltd* [1981] 2 Lloyd's Rep. 194, 198; *Barclays Bank plc* v. *Quincecare Ltd* [1992] 4 All ER 363, 375.

[55] [1951] Ch. 85.   [56] Ch. 11, Sect. 1(vii) above.

[57] *Re Hone, ex p. The Trustee* v. *Kensington Borough Council*, n.55 above, 89.

[58] [2000] 1 WLR 906. See also *Hollicourt (Contracts) Ltd* v. *Bank of Ireland* [2001] Ch. 555, [21], [32] (CA), where Mummery LJ (holding that there was no 'disposition' *vis-à-vis* the bank within the Insovency Act 1986, s.127 when a bank honoured post-petition cheques on an account in credit) commended Lightman J's 'valuable summary of the relevant principles' in *Coutts* and indicated that he would have reached the same conclusion had the account in *Hollicourt* been overdrawn. *Hollicourt* was similarly based upon the notion that the bank acted as its customer's agent in paying third parties.

[59] Ch. 11, Sect. 1(vii) above.   [60] N.58 above, 909.

retrospectively countermand the instructions given to the bank as the company's agent to make payments of the company's money to the third parties.[61]

As an overdraft is essentially a loan, there may be issues that arise concerning repayment, such as whether a bank can demand repayment at any time, without regard to the customer's interests. In *Rouse* v. *Bradford Banking Co.*,[62] following the reorganization of a partnership, the new partnership was allowed to increase an existing overdraft granted to the original firm. This raised the question of whether a surety for the partnership's overdraft was discharged by the bank giving extra time to the partnership, as principal debtor, without the surety's consent. The argument was that the increase of the overdraft ceiling, coupled with the mention of a new date, effectively gave the partnership the entitlement to have the overdraft available for the relevant period. Rejecting this argument, Lord Herschell LC said:[63]

> It may be that an overdraft does not prevent the bank who have agreed to give it from at any time giving notice that it is no longer to continue, and that they must be paid their money. This I think at least it does; if they have agreed to give an overdraft they cannot refuse to honour cheques or drafts, within the limit of that overdraft, which have been drawn and put into circulation before any notice to the person to whom they have agreed to give the overdraft that the limit is to be withdrawn.

His Lordship added that although an overdraft arrangement may not in itself grant the customer a period in which he will be able to utilize the facility, neither of the parties would contemplate a withdrawal of the overdraft without notice shortly after the time of its extension. Giving notice before the withdrawal of an overdraft would probably also be the ordinary commercial expectation in normal circumstances where a trusted customer carrying on a sound business retained the confidence of its bankers.[64] In both cases, however, notice would be given as a matter of good business practice, so as not to alienate customers, rather than as a matter of legal obligation.[65]

The bank's right to claim repayment of an overdraft at its pleasure may be abrogated by the bank's express or implied agreement.[66] In *Williams & Glyn's Bank* v. *Barnes*[67] the bank granted its customer an overdraft to assist him in financing some transactions of a company in financial difficulty that he controlled. When that company's affairs deteriorated further, the bank demanded repayment of the overdraft facility. The customer argued that the bank had abrogated its right to demand payment at call, as the circumstances surrounding the transaction clearly indicated that the overdraft was required for a specific purpose, and that demanding repayment of the overdraft was accordingly contrary to the object of the agreement between the bank and customer. Gibson J rejected this defence, as the documentation in the particular case established that the bank had expressly retained

---

[61] Ibid.   [62] [1894] AC 586.

[63] Ibid., 596. No time need be given to the debtor when the demand is made: Sect. 5(ii) below.

[64] *Socomex Ltd* v. *Banque Bruxelles Lambert SA* [1996] 1 Lloyd's Rep. 156, 189.

[65] Ibid., 189. See also *Bank of Ireland* v. *AMCD (Property Holdings) Ltd* [2001] 2 All ER (Comm.) 894, [17]. Lord Herschell is more equivocal in *Rouse* v. *Bradford Banking Co.*, n.62 above, 580, but places greater emphasis on commercial factors, rather than legal obligation, as the source of the practice.

[66] A bank will breach its contract with the customer if it withdraws an overdraft facility prematurely, unless the borrower has committed a repudiatory breach of contract or there has been some other event of default triggering the right to withdraw according to the facility letter's terms: *Crimpfil Ltd* v. *Barclays Bank plc*, Independent, 21 April 1994 (interim award affd. [1995] CLC 385 (CA)). In the absence of agreement, a bank may nevertheless be estopped from demanding repayment of the overdraft without notice if it has made a representation to that effect to the borrower: *Emory* v. *UCB Bank plc*, unreported, 15 May 1997 (CA).

[67] [1981] Com. LR 205 (abridged report).

the right to withdraw the overdraft at any time. His Lordship further held that the bank's mere knowledge of the nature of the transaction to be financed would not in itself suggest that the overdraft was available for a fixed time.[68] In *Williams*, however, the bank had had more than mere knowledge of the transaction's purpose, but had actually granted the overdraft for a specific purpose that entailed its being available for a suitable period of time. Accordingly, if the bank had not expressly reserved its right of withdrawal, his Lordship would have treated it as impliedly abrogated by the parties' arrangement. This view derives support from *Titford Property Co. Ltd* v. *Cannon Street Acceptances Ltd*,[69] in which the document granting a customer an overdraft facility described it as being available for 12 months, but included a printed clause providing for repayment at call. Goff J held that the overdraft was not repayable at call, as such an interpretation would have frustrated the object of the transaction and left the borrower in a disastrous position. His Lordship cited *Photo Production Ltd* v. *Securicor Transport Ltd*[70] in which the House of Lords held that, if one party to a contract proffered one of its standard forms for signature to the other, then any printed clause would be construed as subordinate to the main object of the transaction.

Whether an express right providing for repayment at call is repugnant to the lending agreement as a whole is obviously a matter of contractual interpretation. *Titford* can be contrasted with *Lloyds Bank plc* v. *Lampert*,[71] in which the facility letter provided that the amounts owing under the overdraft facility were repayable on demand, but also that it was the bank's 'present intention' to make the facility available until a specified date. The Court of Appeal did not see these two provisions as inconsistent. According to Kennedy LJ, delivering the judgment of the court:[72] '[i]t is in no way inconsistent for a bank, or any other lender to grant a facility which it and the borrower both envisage will last for some time, but with the caveat that the lender retains the right to call for repayment at any time on demand'. It is significant that in *Titford* the overdraft facility was expressed to be available for a specified period, whereas there was no similar commitment in *Lloyds Bank plc* v. *Lampert*. Similarly, in *Bank of Ireland* v. *AMCD (Property Holdings) Ltd*,[73] as the facility letter only referred to 'a maximum intended total exposure period of 12 months' and that in the ordinary course the facility would be 'repaid from the sale of the development within 12 months, the cautious nature of these phrases was not enough to abrogate the clear statement in the facility letter that repayment was 'on demand'.

(iii) **The right to charge interest**

Until recently, the position was that a creditor was not entitled to claim interest (before judgment), unless there was an express or implied agreement to that effect.[74] In *Sempra Metals Ltd* v. *IRC*,[75] the House of Lords appears to have altered the position significantly, as Lord Nicholls recognized that there is nowadays 'a common law jurisdiction to award interest, simple and compound, as damages in claims for non-payment of debts'.[76] Albeit that this suggestion was obiter in *Sempra Metals*, it appears to have commanded the

---

[68] *Barclays Bank plc* v. *Green & Challis* (QBD, 17 November 1995) (noted [1996] JIBL N–82).

[69] (QBD, 22 May 1975). See also *Malayan Banking Bhd* v. *Fleur Chem Sdn Bhd* [2009] 9 MLJ 844, [40].

[70] [1980] AC 827 (HL).   [71] [1999] 1 All ER (Comm.) 161 (CA).   [72] Ibid., 167–168.

[73] N.65 above, [17]. See also *Commonwealth Bank of Australia* v. *Renstel Nominees Pty Ltd* (VSC, 8 June 2001).

[74] *President of India* v. *La Pintada Compania Navigacion SA* [1985] AC 104. An equitable charge carried equitable interest despite the absence of any words in the charge allowing interest: *Al-Wazir* v. *Islamic Press Agency Inc.* [2001] EWCA Civ. 1276, [2002] 1 Lloyd's Rep. 410 (CA).

[75] [2008] 1 AC 561 (HL), [15]–[17].   [76] Ibid., [74]–[100].

approval of a majority of the House of Lords.[77] Whilst it remains the case that a creditor, who has not been paid, will not be able to recover unproven and unparticularized interest losses,[78] nevertheless *Sempra Metals* at least recognizes that 'subject to the ordinary rules of remoteness...the [proven and pleaded] loss suffered as a result of the late payment of money is recoverable'.[79] Whether such an award of interest is simple or compound, and the rate that is used, will depend upon the precise losses that the creditor can show that he suffered in the circumstances. The practical impact of *Sempra Metals* on banks is likely to be fairly limited, however, as most overdraft or loan agreements will contain a provision relating to the accrual of interest. The significance of *Sempra Metals* for banks is likely to be that, in those rare cases where the bank has not included any stipulation as to interest, they are more likely to be able to recover any loss of interest following a customer's default.

Assuming that the overdraft facility document stipulates for interest to be payable, this is usually based upon variable market rates. Despite the dearth of authority on the bank's right to charge such variable rates,[80] if this right were ever disputed, banks would probably be able to show a sufficiently well established banking custom in that regard.[81] There have, however, been attempts to question the bank's right to add the half yearly (or yearly) interest to the outstanding balance, and to charge interest for the next six months (or one year) on a balance comprising the capitalized interest. The validity of the practice has been affirmed in *Yourell* v. *Hibernian Bank Ltd*,[82] where the House of Lords recognized that this method of charging interest was legitimate as between banker and customer despite the compounding involved.[83] Despite the judicial recognition of this practice for at least 80 years, until recently, the accepted view was that the bank's right to compound interest in this way applied only to current account operations and not generally to all types of borrowing from banks. This view was largely based upon *Deutsche Bank und Disconto Gesellschaft* v. *Banque des Marchands de Moscou*,[84] where Greer LJ explained that '[f]irst, there can be no title to compound interest without a contract express or implied; and, secondly, that it is never implied except as to mercantile accounts current for mutual transactions'.[85]

The House of Lords reached a different conclusion, however, in *National Bank of Greece S-A* v. *Pinios Shipping Co. (No. 1)*,[86] in which shipbuilders demanded payment under a guarantee opened in their favour by the claimant bank at the request of the purchasers of the vessel. The claimant, in turn, exercised its right of reimbursement against the purchasers and a third party who had executed a counter guarantee in its favour. Whilst the claimant's right of reimbursement was not disputed, both defendants contested its right to charge compound interest on the amount outstanding, pleading that all that the claimant was entitled to claim was simple interest for arrears in payment. This

---

[77] Ibid., [15]–[17], [164]–[165]. Lord Mance was more cautious: ibid, [215]–[224]. Lord Scott did not consider such a step should be taken in light of the Senior Courts Act 1981, s.35A: ibid., [152].

[78] Ibid., [95]–[97].   [79] Ibid., [16].

[80] *Re City and County Property Bank* (1895) 21 VLR 405, 410–411 (VSC).

[81] A term under which a supplier of financial services reserves the right to alter the rate of interest payable by a consumer falls outside the scope of UTCCR 1999, Sched. 1, para. 1(i), which would otherwise have deemed the term *prima facie* 'unfair' and unenforceable: UTCCR 1999, Sched. 2, para. 2(b).

[82] [1918] AC 372 (HL). See also *Ex p. Bevan* (1803) 9 Ves. 223; *Fergusson* v. *Fyffe* (1841) 8 Cl. & Fin. 121; *National Bank of Australasia* v. *United Hand-in-Hand and Band of Hope Co.* (1879) 4 App. Cas. 391, 409.

[83] Ibid., 385, 393. Their Lordships regarded the debt accrued on the basis of the interest charge as accrued on the day it was debited to the account.

[84] (1931) 4 LDAB 293.

[85] Ibid., 296. See also *Fergusson* v. *Fyffe*, n.82 above (bank not entitled to charge periodic interest on deceased customer's account).

[86] [1990] 1 AC 637 (HL).

argument succeeded in the Court of Appeal, where, after tracing the history of the usage entitling banks to charge compound interest, Lloyd LJ limited such compounding to the case of 'mercantile accounts current [opened] for mutual transactions'.[87] Furthermore, his Lordship concluded that a bank's right to charge compound interest, which was based on the fiction of the capital and interest being simultaneously repaid and re-lent at each half yearly or yearly rest, was abrogated when the account ceased to be current upon being closed or frozen by the bank. Reversing the Court of Appeal, Lord Goff of Chieveley held that the usage in question prevailed generally as 'between bankers and customers who borrow from them and do not pay the interest as it accrues',[88] and doubted that the usage was restricted to 'accounts current for mutual transactions'. Accordingly, his Lordship regarded the usage in question, although developed in the context of the usury laws, as having a general application to borrowings by customers from bankers.[89] His Lordship also concluded that a bank could continue to compound interest, even after a bank had demanded repayment. His Lordship said:[90]

> ... if it be equitable that a banker should be entitled to capitalize interest at, for example, yearly or half year rests because his customer has failed to pay interest on the due date, there appears to be no basis in justice or logic for terminating that right simply because the bank has demanded payment of the sum outstanding in the customer's account.

This conclusion was, however, reached without argument for the defendants, who had abandoned the case at that stage.[91] There are potentially two criticisms of *Pinios*. First, *Pinios* might produce harsh results in the situation where a customer defaults in making repayment following the bank calling in a loan and the loan agreement permits the rate of interest charged on the defaulting facility to be increased substantially. In such circumstances, *Pinios* might permit compounding at the penalty rate chargeable upon the customer's default. Any such concerns can probably be addressed by the penalty jurisdiction and statutory controls in UCTA 1977, UTCCR 1994, and CCA 1974.[92] Secondly, as was accepted recently by Underhill J in *Halliday* v. *HBOS plc*,[93] there is no reciprocity as regards the charging of compound interest, so that, where sums are wrongfully debited from a customer's account, there is no implied term in the account contract that the *customer* is entitled to recover compound interest. This criticism may have been addressed, however, by the subsequent decision of the House of Lords in *Sempra Metals Ltd* v. *IRC*,[94] which may allow a customer to recover compound interest as sought in *Halliday*, provided he can prove that this was his actual foreseeable loss.

---

[87] N.86 above, 658.

[88] *Paton* v. *IRC* [1938] AC 341, 357 (HL); *Parr's Banking Co. Ltd* v. *Yates* [1898] 2 QB 460.

[89] Two points should be noted. First, Lord Goff pointed out that the cases reviewed by him dealt with the application of the usage to loans involving yearly and half-yearly rests, apparently leaving open the question whether the usage similarly applied where the loan involved quarterly rests: [1990] 1 AC 637, 685. In *Pinios*, the right to capitalize at quarterly rests was conceded. In *Kitchen* v. *HSBC Bank plc* [2000] 1 All ER (Comm.) 787, 791, Brooke LJ referred to the use of quarterly rests as being 'in accordance with modern banking practice'. Secondly, in *Pinios* the usage was relied on by the bank to imply a term into its contract with a business customer. Nowadays, a court may be more reluctant to allow the bank to rely on such usage against a personal or small business customer, where the bank did not disclose at the start of the relationship that compounding would or might occur: *Lending Code* (November 2009), [52]–[63]; *Lending Code* (March 2011), [76]–[79].

[90] N.86 above, 684.

[91] Nevertheless, it was applied in *Bank of Credit and Commerce International SA* v. *Malik* [1996] BCC 15 (contractual right to charge compound interest not terminated by the appointment of a provisional liquidator over the bank's affairs).

[92] Sect. 3(ii)–(iii) below.   [93] [2007] EWHC 1780 (QB), [7]–[10].   [94] N.75 above.

There are several issues that remained unresolved after *Pinios*. First, that decision is based on the principle that a bank's demand ought not to affect the method in which the account is maintained. Accordingly, one uncertainty that remained was whether the same method of calculation can be equally applied to situations in which the original loan does not involve periodic repayments leading to the compounding of interest, but is repayable in full, with interest accrued, at a designated time or on demand.[95] Secondly, doubts also remained as regards the charging of interest on sums due to a bank under a guarantee from a non-customer. In such a case, there will generally be no account that can be debited with the interest accrued on the sum demanded.[96] Furthermore, the guarantor's liability, as defined in the facility, may not encompass an undertaking to pay, on his own default, interest to be charged at any given intervals. Thirdly, and linked to the previous point, it was also unclear what the bank's rights to interest might be in relation to a guarantee given by a customer. The bank's right to charge compound interest is based on a usage related to the original fiction under which a loan was considered repaid and readvanced at each agreed rest or instalment. It appears far-fetched to apply it in a situation in which the customer's initial undertaking in his guarantee is to pay to the bank a given maximum amount on demand. Obviously, the bank's right to charge compound interest could, in such a case, be set out in the guarantee executed by the customer. Additionally, the bank may achieve its object by debiting the amount involved to the guarantor's current account, which the bank may be entitled to do under a letter of set-off or pursuant to its general right of combination. It remains to be seen whether the guarantor (who is a customer) can defeat the bank's right by instructing it to close his account as soon as he realizes that a call on the guarantee is imminent.[97] It may be that in future, however, even if *Pinios* itself cannot technically provide a solution in these three situations, the liberalization of claims for compound interest in *Sempra Metals* may provide banks with an alternative means of achieving a similar result.

In *Pinios* the purchasers also provided the bank with security for their indebtedness by executing a mortgage over the relevant vessel. The relationship between the bank and the purchasers was, therefore, that of mortgagee and mortgagor, but this did not affect the bank's right to charge compound interest that was to be implied into their underlying banker–customer relationship. In different circumstances, however, such as where the bank provides a home loan secured by a residential mortgage, the bank's right to claim compound interest as a matter of usage may be more doubtful. It is an established rule that only simple interest can be charged on a mortgage account unless there had been express agreement to charge compound interest.[98] The usage sanctioned in *Pinios* related to the banker–customer relationship in respect of an overdrawn account and not the somewhat different relationship that arises between the bank as home-loan provider and the customer as borrower. Not only is there a reluctance to bind customers to bank

---

[95] This point has been regarded as raising a triable issue: *Minories Finance Ltd* v. *Daryanani* (CA, 13 April 1989). See also *Habib Bank Ltd* v. *Central Bank of Sudan* [2006] 2 Lloyd's Rep. 412, [70]–[71].

[96] *Habib Bank Ltd* v. *Central Bank of Sudan*, n.95 above, [70]–[71].

[97] Cf. *Crosskill* v. *Bower* (1863) 32 Beav. 86, which was considered by Lord Goff (at 678–679) in *Pinios*. The bank's ability to charge compound interest can be taken into account in assessing the damages to be awarded against the bank in cases involving a breach of a fiduciary duty: *The 'Golden Med'* [1992] 2 Lloyd's Rep. 193, revs'd. on other grounds [1994] 2 Lloyd's Rep. 152 (CA). See further Ch. 5, Sect. 4(iv) above.

[98] *Daniell* v. *Sinclair* (1881) 6 App. Cas. 181 (PC); *Bank of Credit and Commerce International SA* v. *Blattner* (CA, 20 November 1986); *Kitchen* v. *HSBC Bank plc.*, n.89 above 787, 892. See also M. Hapgood, *Paget's Law of Banking* (13th edn., London, 2007), [13.6].

usages of which they may have no awareness or understanding,[99] but, in light of the prevailing culture of consumer protection and the desire to make interest-charging practices of banks more transparent to their customers,[100] a court would be unlikely to imply a right to compound interest into a residential mortgage where the bank had not informed the customer at the start of their relationship that compound interest would or might be charged.[101] For the bank to be sure of its position, the right to charge compound interest should be stated expressly in the mortgage documentation.

In practice, the bank charges the interest due at the designated half yearly or yearly rests by debiting the respective amount to the customer's account, but this raises the issue of whether such debiting discharges the customer's liability for interest or simply converts the nature of the debt. Essentially, the question is one of fact. If the customer's account has a credit balance at the relevant time, and the balance is reduced by debiting the interest, then the interest is paid. In this regard, a mere debit entry can constitute payment.[102] If the customer's account is overdrawn, however, simply increasing the amount of the overdraft by the relevant interest does not, in reality, discharge a liability. Although the decision of Lord Cowan in *Reddie* v. *Williamson*[103] appears inconsistent with this last statement, and suggests that the debiting of the interest to the balance of an overdrawn account constitutes payment of the amount due, subsequent authority has taken the opposite view,[104] suggesting that, even for tax purposes, the periodic debiting of interest does not constitute payment. Where interest is debited from the customer's account without his express agreement, such as where the account becomes overdrawn without prior arrangement, the customer's failure to object to the respective entry is considered acquiescence in the charge so made.[105] In modern banking practice, the bank's right to charge interest on an occasional overdraft is usually contained in the current account opening forms.

(iv) **Appropriation of payments**

A particular feature of overdrawn accounts is that the debit balance changes from day to day as a result of the current nature of the account and the mutual dealings between bank and customer transacted through it. For most purposes it is adequate to determine the account's net credit or debit balance at the end of each banking day. Occasionally, it is important to ascertain precisely which debit items in the statement of account are to be regarded as discharged by particular incoming credit entries. This issue tends to be particularly relevant in two types of case: first, where a bank is seeking to enforce a security covering a revolving amount; and, secondly, in respect of a partnership account following the firm's dissolution.

A situation of the first type can arise when a guarantee is given to secure a customer's overdraft facility. Assume that the guarantor is liable for the principal debtor's liabilities

---

[99] *Turner* v. *Royal Bank of Scotland* [1999] 2 All ER (Comm.) 664, 671 (CA); *Kitchen* v. *HSBC Bank plc*, n.89 above, 795 ('[t]he law's assumption that people know what bankers know about the latter's practices has, I would respectfully think, only limited reality').

[100] *Kitchen* v. *HSBC Bank plc.*, n.89 above, 792 ('this desirable philosophy').

[101] *Lending Code* (November 2009), [52]–[63]; *Lending Code* (March 2011), [76]–[79].

[102] Ch. 13 Sect. 6(iii) above.

[103] (1863) 1 Macph. 228 (Ct Sess.). Inglis LJC took a different view: ibid., 237.

[104] *Re Jauncey, Bird* v. *Arnold* [1926] Ch. 471, 476; *Paton* v. *IRC*, n.88 above, 349–351. See also *IRC* v. *Oswald*, n.15 above, 373, 379; *Bank of New South Wales* v. *Brown*, n.15 above, 522–3; *Whitbread plc* v. *UCB Corporate Ltd*, n.15 above.

[105] *Fergusson* v. *Fyffe*, n.82 above; *Crosskill* v. *Bower*, n.97 above; *Yorell* v. *Hibernian Bank Ltd* [1918] AC 372. Nicholls LJ summarized this point in the Court of Appeal in *Pinios*, and this point remains unaffected by the House of Lords.

incurred on an overdraft up to a specified date. If the bank decides not to freeze the debtor's account on that date, but allows him to continue operating it, so that the bank honours further cheques on the account after that date and continues to collect certain effects for the credit of the account, then a dispute may subsequently arise as to the amount covered by the guarantee when the bank seeks to enforce it.[106] Obviously the bank and guarantor will be at odds over this question: the bank will argue that the guarantee covers the account balance shown on its final validity day; the guarantor in contrast will argue that, just as payments into the account reduced the overdraft, so too they reduce the liability on the guarantee. The second type of case arises in the partnership context.[107] Each partner is answerable for the partnership's debts,[108] but his liability terminates when the partnership is dissolved and notice thereof is publicized.[109] Thus, if a partnership account continues to be used despite the partnership's dissolution, or despite the withdrawal of the partner sought to be charged, the question that arises is the extent of his liability. Both of these types of problem are solved by using 'the rule of appropriation of payments', which treats each item paid to the credit of the account as discharging the account's earliest debit items. Generally, where applicable, this principle works against the creditor's interests.[110]

The principle of 'appropriation of payments', which may be described as 'first incurred, first discharged', constitutes a rule of convenience.[111] It was established at the beginning of the nineteenth century in *Devaynes v. Noble; Clayton's Case*.[112] One of the partners in a bank died. Although the partnership was thereupon dissolved, the remaining partners continued to trade as a going concern. When the bank became insolvent, a customer sought to recover from the deceased partner's estate the substantial credit balance that he held with the banking partnership at the time of the partner's death. During the period following the relevant partner's death, the customer had drawn cheques for an amount exceeding his credit balance; but he also paid numerous items into his account during this period, so that the balance due to him when the bank became insolvent was actually larger than the original balance when the partner died. The partner's estate argued that its liability to the customer was discharged when the banking partnership honoured the customer's cheques during the period following the partner's death. Giving judgment for the estate, Sir William Grant MR emphasized that in practice neither the customer nor the bank contemplated that any specific debit item would be set off against any given credit entered in the account. Indeed, the parties' sole concern had been the existence of

---

[106] Assuming that the guarantor's liability is not also discharged on the day in question.

[107] This issue does not arise in a limited liability partnership created under the Limited Liability Partnerships Act 2000, as its members are not liable to third parties.

[108] Partnership Act 1890, s.5. See also R.C. I'Anson, *Lindley and Banks On Partnership* (19th edn., London, 2010), Pt. 3. Cf. Limited Liability Partnerships Act 2000, s.6.

[109] Ibid, s.37. As regards a partner's death, see Partnership Act 1890, s.36(3).

[110] Occasionally, the principle may work in the creditor's favour, such as where a floating charge is taken to secure a pre-existing overdraft. The principle of 'appropriation of payments' means that sums paid to the credit of the account are applied to the pre-existing indebtedness and any new drawings constitute 'new value', insulating the security from attack under the Insolvency Act 1986, s.245 to the extent of that new value: *Re Yeovil Glove Co. Ltd* [1965] 1 Ch. 148. See further Ch. 19, Sect. 4(v) below.

[111] *Re Diplock* [1948] Ch. 465, 554 (CA); *Barlow Clowes International Ltd v. Vaughan* [1992] 4 All ER 22, 42, 46 (CA). See also *Campden Hill Ltd v. Chakrani* [2005] EWHC 911 (Ch), [65] & [75]; *Re Ahmed & Co.* [2006] EWHC 480 (Ch), [A93]. The rule in *Clayton's Case* cannot apply when there is no evidence as to the order in which payments were made into and out of a current account: *Cooper v. PRG Powerhouse Ltd* [2008] EWHC 498 (Ch), [27].

[112] (1816) 1 Mer. 572.

an adequate fund, or balance, for meeting cheques drawn on the account. His Lordship explained:[113]

> In such a case, there is no room for any other appropriation than that which arises from the order in which the receipts and payments take place, and are carried into the account. Presumably, it is the first sum paid in, that is first drawn out. It is the first item on the debit side of the account, that is discharged, or reduced, by the first item on the credit side. The appropriation is made by the very act of setting the two items against each other. Upon that principle, all accounts current are settled, and particularly cash accounts.

If the creditor wished to depart from this arrangement, he had to make his intention clear to the debtor. In *Clayton's Case* itself, there was no evidence to this effect. The amounts paid out by the bank had, therefore, discharged the initial balance due to the customer at the day of the relevant partner's death. Accordingly, the estate was not liable for debts incurred by the bank in respect of money deposited with it thereafter.

Although the rule in *Clayton's Case* is based on a presumption as to the probable intention of the parties, it is not easily displaced as between banker and customer.[114] In *Deely* v. *Lloyds Bank Ltd*,[115] the bank obtained a first mortgage to secure its customer's overdraft. When the bank received notice that the customer had been granted a second mortgage over the property, it failed to freeze the account balance as it stood when the bank received notice, allowing the customer to continue operating the account in the ordinary manner. The amounts paid in by the customer were greater than the overdraft as it stood at the date of the notification, although subsequent fresh drawings on the account had left it in debit. The second mortgagee argued that his title had become superior to that of the bank, as applying *Clayton's Case* the amounts paid by the customer had discharged the earlier indebtedness under the first mortgage. Although the Court of Appeal took the view that the rule in *Clayton's Case* had been displaced by the parties' intention, the House of Lords held that primarily the right to appropriate a payment made to the credit of a current account rested with the debtor. If he did not evince such an intention, the creditor had the opportunity to do so.[116] In the absence of a specific appropriation, the rule in *Clayton's Case* applies. If the bank, or creditor, had intended to appropriate the payments made to it after it received the second mortgagee's notification, it could resort to the simple device of striking a balance in the account and then opening a fresh account in the customer's name.[117] In *Siebe Gorman & Co. Ltd* v. *Barclays Bank Ltd*,[118] Slade J reiterated the view that the opening of a fresh account displaces the rule of appropriation of payments.[119] His Lordship further pointed out that the rule in *Clayton's Case* was subject to two exceptions. First, the rule would not apply in respect of secured transactions where the second

---

[113] Ibid., 608.

[114] By contrast, *Clayton's Case* is readily displaced when beneficiaries seek to assert competing claims for money mixed in a bank account: *Russell-Cooke Trust Co.* v. *Prentis*.[2003] 2 All ER 478.

[115] [1912] AC 756, 783 (HL).

[116] *West Bromwich Building Society* v. *Crammer* [2002] EWHC 2618 (Ch), [13]–[18]. See also *Wannan* v. *R* [2004] 3 FCR D 20, [27]–[28]; *Walters* v. *Meiner* [2004] BCSC 393, [19]; *Sydney Concrete & Contracting Pty Ltd* v. *BNP Paribas Equities (Australia) Ltd* [2005] NSWSC 408, [25]–[30]; *Siebert* v. *JWS International Trade Corporation* [2007] BCSC 1633, [55]–[56]; *Advocate-General for Scotland* v. *Montgomery* 2008 SCLR 1, [58] (OH).

[117] *Royal Bank of Canada* v. *Bank of Montreal* (1976) 67 DLR (3d.) 755. For an interesting modification of the rule, see the Consumer Credit Act 1974 (CCA 1974), s.81. Where the debtor has incurred a number of debts, he is entitled to appropriate a payment made by him to any one of them; if he fails to do so, the amount paid in is to be credited to the different outstanding debts on a *pro rata* basis.

[118] [1979] 2 Lloyd's Rep. 142, 164.

[119] *Re Sherry; London and County Banking Co.* v. *Terry* (1883) 25 Ch. D 692.

mortgagee agreed to the making of fresh advances by the first mortgagee. Secondly, the rule would be equally displaced where the fresh advances were made in pursuance of the terms of the initial agreement between the debtor and the first mortgagee. It is believed that, in addition, the rule would be inapplicable if a clause respecting further advances to be made by the first mortgagee was brought to the second mortgagee's attention.[120]

In modern banking practice, banks include clauses in their contracts with customers excluding the rule in *Clayton's Case*. One such clause provides that the security furnished by the customer is to apply in respect of his indebtedness as standing from time to time.[121] A complementary clause—termed a 'negative pledge' clause—prohibits the granting of any fresh security by the customer without the bank's consent, and provides that an arrangement made in violation of this term is to be void against it.[122] Moreover, banks frequently exercise their right to appropriate payments by making their own decisions, in the absence of the customer's instruction, concerning the account to be debited with the credit made.[123] Furthermore, the rule is displaced if the bank makes it clear that, although it does not seek to exercise its right immediately, it reserves the right to do so in due course.[124]

The rule in *Clayton's Case* applies only to current accounts. In *'The Mecca'*,[125] the House of Lords held it inapplicable to accounts that were not of a running nature.[126] Even in a current account, however, the 'appropriation of payments' rule does not apply in respect of a number of payments made on a single day, as the order in which these are settled is purely fortuitous. Additionally, the rule in *Clayton's Case* does not apply where a person who holds money as a trustee or in a fiduciary capacity pays it into his bank account, where it is mixed with his own money, and afterwards draws out funds for his own purposes.[127] In such circumstances, the trustee or other fiduciary is presumed to be acting honestly and to draw out his own money from the account in priority to the money that he held as a trustee or in a fiduciary capacity.[128] The rule in *Clayton's Case* may, however, be used to resolve conflicting claims between beneficiaries.[129] In *Barlow Clowes International Ltd* v. *Vaughan*,[130] the Court of Appeal confirmed that the rule provided a convenient method of determining competing claims where the funds of several beneficiaries had been mixed in one account and there was a deficiency, or where there had been a wrongful mixing of different sums of trust money in a single account. The Court held, however, that, even in such cases, *Clayton's Case* would not be applied where it was impractical or unjust as between the competing beneficiaries to do so, or where it would be contrary to the beneficiaries' express, implied, or presumed intention. The Court of Appeal held that there had been such a presumed intention as between the various investors in a collective investment scheme by which their money would be mixed together and invested through a

---

[120] Ch. 19, Sect. 4(iii) below.   [121] Ch. 19, Sects. 2 & 4(iv) below.   [122] Ch. 19, Sect. 4(iv) below.

[123] *Simson* v. *Ingham* (1823) 2 B & C 65; *London and Westminster Bank* v. *Button* (1907) 51 Sol. Jo. 466; *Customs & Excise Commissioners* v. *British Telecommunications plc* [1996] 1 WLR 1309 (CA).

[124] *'The Mecca'* [1897] AC 286, 294; *Seymour* v. *Pickett* [1905] 1 KB 715.   [125] Ibid.

[126] The 'appropriation of payments' rule is not restricted to banking accounts, but also applies 'to the appropriation of payments between any trader and his customer where there is an account current or running account': *Barlow Clowes International Ltd* v. *Vaughan*, n.111 above, 28. See also *Re Footman Bower & Co. Ltd* [1961] 1 Ch. 443; *Yarra Capital Group Pty Ltd* v. *Sklash Pty Ltd* [2006] VSCA 109, [25]–[27]; *Tsapepas* v. *Rhino Strategic Communications* [2008] VSC 55, [36]; cf. *Re Diplock*, n.111 above, 555.

[127] *Re Hallett's Estate* (1880) 13 Ch. D 696 (CA).   [128] Ibid.

[129] *Pennell* v. *Deffell* (1853) 4 De GM & G 372 (CA). See also *Hancock* v. *Smith* (1889) 41 Ch. D 456, 461; *Re Diplock*, n.111 above, 554.

[130] N.111 above. See also *Australian Securities Commission* v. *Buckley* (NSWSC, 20 December 1996) (*Clayton's Case* inappropriate in case of collective investment scheme).

common fund. Consequently, the assets that remained available for distribution would be distributed rateably between the investors and not according to the rule in *Clayton's Case* which, had it applied, would have significantly preferred later investors at the expense of earlier ones.[131]

Similarly, in *Russell-Cooke Trust Co.* v. *Prentis*,[132] when determining the ownership of funds in a solicitor's account received from a number of investors for use in an investment scheme, Lindsay J preferred to distribute the various contributions to the scheme rateably amongst the respective investors. Lindsay J suggested that 'in terms of its actual application between beneficiaries who have in any sense met a shared misfortune, it might be more accurate to refer to the exception that is, rather than the rule in, *Clayton's* case' and that the rule could be displaced 'even by a slight counterweight'.[133] Lindsay J held that the available counterweight in the case before him was that payments out of the account over the period of its operation showed a pattern of allocation that did not reflect a sequence whereby a payment out should be allocated to an earlier payment into the account.[134] The expectations and intentions of the investors were inconsistent with the application of the rule in *Clayton's* case and so the rule was held not to apply.[135] In other cases, the impracticality or injustice of applying the rule in *Clayton's* case might provide the available counterweight.[136] A similar approach can be found in New Zealand[137] and Ireland.[138] The Canadian[139] and Australian courts appear to have gone even further, however, by limiting the rule in *Clayton's Case* to the question of the appropriation of payments between a bank and its customer[140] and denying it any role whatsoever when the issue concerns the allocation of losses between beneficiaries who have contributed to a mixed fund (such as in a bank account) and who are seeking to locate the value of their

---

[131] In the United States and Canada, the preferred solution is to treat each withdrawal from the blended account as attributable to all depositors so as to reduce all their deposits *pro rata*: *Ontario (Securities Commission)* v. *Greymac Credit Corporation* (1986) 55 OR (2d.) 673 (OCA), affd. [1988] 2 SCR 172 (SCC). The Court of Appeal in *Barlow Clowes* rejected this approach as being too complex and expensive to administer in a case where there are many depositors.

[132] N.114 above (noted by M. Pawlowski, 'The Demise of the Rule in *Clayton's* Case' [2003] Conv. 339; M. Conaglen, 'Contests Between Rival Trust Beneficiaries' [2005] *CLJ* 45). See also *Stevens* v. *Long* [2009] All ER (D) 188.

[133] Ibid., [55].   [134] Ibid., [56].   [135] Ibid.

[136] In *Commerzbank AG* v. *IMG Morgan plc* [2005] 1 Lloyd's Rep. 298, [47]–[48], where numerous victims of an 'advance fee fraud' had proprietary claims to the funds in a bank account, but the funds were insufficient to meet all the claims, it was held that the funds were to be shared rateably between the victims in accordance with the amount of their contributions. See also *Re Ahmed & Co.*, n.111 above, [131]–[138] (deficiency in solicitor's client account to be borne by clients rateably to their contributions to the account); cf. *Campden Hill Ltd* v. *Chakrani*, n.111 above. In *Q & M Enterprises Sdn Bhd* v. *Poh Kiat* [2005] 4 SLR 494, [53]–[59] Andrew Phang Boon Leong JC referred to the 'apparent judicial limitation of the rule in *Clayton's Case*' in other jurisdictions, but preferred to leave the point open on an interlocutory application.

[137] *Re Registered Securities Ltd* [1991] 1 NZLR 545 (NZCA); *Re International Unit Investment Trust* [2005] 1 NZLR 270, [50]–[57].

[138] *Re W&R Murrogh* [2003] IEHC 95, [20.3], [20.6]. See also *Hess* v. *Kavanagh* [1999] 4 IR 267. For the Jersey position, see *In re Esteem Settlement* [2002] Jersey LR 53.

[139] *Ontario (Securities Commission)* v. *Greymac Credit Corporation*, n.131 above. See also *Re Elliott* [2002] ABQB 1122, [46]–[47]; *Re Graphicshoppe Ltd* (2005) 78 OR (3D) 401, [72]–[81] (OCA); *Grant* v. *Sainte Marie Estate* [2005] ABQB 35, [22]; *Barnett* v. *Barnett* [2006] ABQB 920, [16]–[19]; *Re O'Dwyer* [2006] BCSC 328, [19]–[26] (rejecting *Clayton's Case* 'as a discredited methodology if the issue involved the distribution of the proceeds of a mingled trust fund'); *Mycyk* v. *University of Saskatchewan* [2006] SKQB 450, [219]–[223].

[140] *Re French Caledonia Travel Service Pty Ltd* [2003] 204 ALR 353, [31]–[34] (NSWSC), following *ANZ Banking Group Ltd* v. *Westpac Banking Corporation* (1988)164 CLR 662, 676 (HCA).

payments in that fund.[141] There is recent authority, however, suggesting that *Clayton's Case* may apply when the wrongdoer has mixed a claimant's funds with his own.[142]

(v) Consumer credit aspects

It will be recalled that the CCA 1974 applies certain protective measures to regulated credit agreements.[143] Basically, the relevant provisions apply if the credit is extended to an 'individual'.[144] A bank overdraft falls within the definition of a regulated consumer credit agreement for unrestricted-use running account credit,[145] even if it is extended by the bank without prior arrangements with the customer.[146] The Act applies where the bank has agreed to grant the customer an overdraft but has not finalized details of the arrangement. A case in point is where the bank informs the customer that no bank charges are incurred when the account is in credit, but that such charges will be levied if the account is overdrawn. However, often a maximum limit for an available overdraft is set at this time. It has been pointed out that such an arrangement involves a multiple agreement within the meaning of section 18(1)(*a*), and that, under section 18(2), each part is treated as a separate agreement for the purposes of the Act.[147]

Originally, many of the Act's stringent requirements were relaxed in respect of most overdrafts. In particular, most overdrafts were excluded from all of the documentation and cancellation provisions in Part V.[148] But the implementation of the Consumer Credit Directive[149] has resulted in the imposition of more requirements, although overdrafts are still given special treatment in some instances. An example of new requirements are those that arise in the case of 'overrunning', the term used in the Directive to mean incurring an overdraft where none has been pre-arranged or exceeding an arranged overdraft.[150] If there is a possibility of this being allowed by the bank, detailed information about the rate(s) of interest and any other charges must be included in the current account agreement and re-issued annually.[151] Moreover, if there is actual significant[152] overrunning, then details about the rate of interest and any other charges need to be given 'without delay'.[153]

---

[141] Ibid., [169]. See also *ASIC* v. *Nelson* (2003) 44 ACSR 719 (NSWSC); *Westpac Banking Corporation* v. *Earthwise International Ltd* [2005] NSWSC 1037, [10]–[11]; *ASIC* v. *Tasman Investment Management* [2006] NSWSC 943, [55].

[142] *Commonwealth Bank of Australia* v. *Saleh* [2007] NSWSC 903, [36].   [143] Ch. 2, Sect. 5 above.

[144] CCA 1974, s.8. See further Ch. 2, Sect. 5(ii) above.

[145] Ibid., s.10(1). See also CCA 1974, s.9, under which credit includes a 'loan and any other form of financial accommodation'.

[146] Ibid., Sched. 2, Example 17. But note CCA 1974, ss.74A–74B on 'over-running', considered below.

[147] Ibid., Sched. 2, Example 18; A.G. Guest & M. Lloyd, *Encyclopaedia of Consumer Credit Law* (London, 1974, loose-leaf), [2-019]; cf. R.M. Goode (ed.), *Consumer Credit Law and Practice* (London, 2000), [IC(25.107)].

[148] If they fell within a 'Determination' made by the OFT under CCA 1974, ss.74(3)–(3A), which merely required the notification of certain information (especially as regards charges).

[149] Directive 2008/48/EC. See further Ch. 2, Sect. 7(vi) above.

[150] Ibid, Art. 3(e), as reworded in CCA 1974, ss.74A–74B.

[151] CCA 1974, s.74A, added by S.I. 2010/1010, reg. 21 (as amended by S.I. 2010/1969) from 1 February 2011. This does not apply to an overdraft secured on land (as this is outside the scope of the Directive): CCA 1974, s.74A(5).

[152] i.e. for a 'significant' amount (e.g. (see CCA 1974, s.74B(3)) if an extra charge is payable or if the overrunning will have an adverse effect on the customer's ability to access more credit) for a period of one month (or three months if the overdraft is secured on land).

[153] Unless such written information has already been given during that period: CCA 1974, s.74B, added by S.I. 2010/1010, reg. 22 (as amended by S.I. 2010/1969) from 1 February 2011. See also CCA 1974, s.82(1E): s.82(1) (notice needed for unilateral variation by creditor) does not apply.

The Act otherwise makes a distinction between so-called 'authorised business over-drafts' and 'authorised non-business overdrafts' and it essentially maintains the previous concessions in relation to the former,[154] as business credit is outside the scope of the Directive. However, the new duty to assess the creditworthiness of the debtor[155] and a new special 'copy' duty to supply a document containing the terms of the overdraft agreement[156] have been extended to all such overdrafts. Moreover, the new more onerous duty to notify changes of interest rate is modified in the case of all overdrafts so that it only applies to increases in rate.[157] 'Authorised non-business overdrafts' are now generally subject to pre-contract disclosure requirements and the form and content of agreement requirements,[158] although the precise requirements are specific to overdrafts.[159] One concession that has been retained for most overdrafts[160] is that they are not subject to the right of withdrawal (or cancellation).[161]

Current accounts opened 'at a distance' (i.e. as a result of an 'organized distance service-provision scheme' where there has been no face-to-face interaction[162])—as is the case in some internet accounts, are subject to protections deriving from the Distance Marketing Directive.[163] In such 'distance' contracts, the customer must receive 'pre-contract' information and has a right of cancellation which is exercisable for 14 days after the account is opened. However, these protections will not apply if the customer has to visit a branch with proof of identification in compliance with the bank's prevention of money laundering procedure,[164] as then the account will not be regarded as a 'distance' account.[165] Advertising is another area in which there are concessions in the consumer credit legislation pertaining to overdrafts.[166] Thus advertisements for overdrafts need not state the 'representative APR'[167] nor disclose any compulsory contracts for 'ancillary services'.[168] Moreover, only advertisements that allow overdrawing on a current account may use the term 'overdraft'.[169]

---

[154] CCA 1974, s.74(1)(b), (1B).

[155] Ibid., s.55B, added by S.I. 2010/1010, reg. 5 from 1 February 2011. See further Ch. 2, Sect. 5(iv) above.

[156] Ibid, s.61B added by S.I. 2010/1010, reg. 9 from 1 February 2011. See further Ch. 2, Sect. 5(iv) above. Non-business overdrafts that would fall within the definition of 'authorised non-business overdraft' (in CCA 1974, s.187(1)) but for the fact that the credit is not repayable on demand or within three months are subject to the usual s.61A 'copy' requirements: CCA 1974, s.74(1D)(h).

[157] Ibid., s.78A, added by S.I. 2010/1010, reg. 27 from 1 February 2011. See also CCA 1974, s.78A(4), (5). See further Ch. 2, Sect. 5(iv) above.

[158] Ch. 2, Sect. 5(iv) above. The new duty to give a copy of the draft agreement on request under CCA 1974, s.55C also applies.

[159] Consumer Credit (Disclosure of Information) Regulations 2010, S.I. 2010/2013 (made under s.55), reg. 10 and the Consumer Credit (Agreements) Regulations 2010, S.I. 2010/2014 (made under s.60), reg. 8.

[160] But non-business overdrafts that would fall within the definition of 'authorised non-business overdraft' (in CCA 1974, s.187(1)) but for the fact that the credit is not repayable on demand or within three months have the s.66A right of withdrawal: CCA 1974, s.74(1)(b) & (1D)(i).

[161] CCA 1974, s.74(1)(b) and (1B) and (1C). For these rights, see Ch. 2, Sect. 5(iv) above.

[162] Financial Services (Distance Marketing) Regulations 2004, S.I. 2004/2095 ('the DMD Regs').

[163] Directive 2002/65/EC. See further Ch. 2, Sect. 7(vi) above.   [164] Ch. 4 above.

[165] As the definition of 'distance contract' in the DMD Regs, reg. 2(1) requires the 'exclusive use of... distance communication up to and including the time at which the contract is concluded'.

[166] The old, pre-Directive provisions, the Consumer Credit (Advertisements) Regulations 2004, S.I. 2004/1484, are now only applicable to agreements secured on land and, in the case of overdrafts secured on land, do not require the citation of the APR but only the interest rate and any charges: reg. 8(6).

[167] The Consumer Credit (Advertisements) Regulations 2010, S.I. 2010/1012, reg. 5(5). For consumer credit advertising, see Ch. 2, Sect. 5(vi) above.

[168] Ibid., reg. 8.

[169] Ibid., reg. 11(1)(a); the Consumer Credit (Advertisements) Regulations 2004, S.I. 2004/1484, reg. 9(1)(a).

Another important modification of the general provisions of the CCA 1974 in respect of overdrafts concerns canvassing, which means the soliciting of business off trade premises.[170] Generally, the Act prohibits the canvassing of persons to enter into debtor–creditor agreements.[171] But section 49(3) exempts the canvassing of entry into overdraft agreements where two conditions are fulfilled. First, the exemption applies only to accounts covered by a Determination of the OFT. Current accounts operable by cheques or similar orders have been the subject of such a Determination.[172] Secondly, the person canvassed has to be the holder of an account. It is irrelevant whether or not his account is interest-bearing.

The Act and the Directive preserve the bank's right to demand repayment of an overdraft without notice. Although the creditor is normally required to give seven days' notice before he can enforce his agreement,[173] this requirement applies only if the loan is extended for a given period.[174] As overdrafts are repayable on demand, the bank need not give such notice where it considers it advisable to demand immediate repayment, unless the overdraft has been granted for a specified period and is called up within that time. And although the Directive introduced new provisions for the termination of agreements of no fixed duration (whether by the debtor or the creditor),[175] these do not apply to overdrafts.[176] However, if repayment is demanded because of default, then a default notice under section 87 is needed.[177]

The last relevant provision concerns the giving by the bank of information regarding the state of an existing account. The bank is obliged to give its customer, at his request, information on the state of his account, and, further, is required automatically to send him periodic statements.[178]

3 Bank loans

(i) Scope

Bank loans may be granted for business or consumer purposes—a distinction that must be maintained for exposition purposes as a result of the CCA 1974. The application of industry guidelines setting out the best lending practice also differs according to whether the lending is to a consumer, small business, or large enterprise.[179] That said,

---

[170] As regards the meaning of 'canvassing', see Guest & Lloyd, n.147 above, [2-049 ff]. See also Ch. 2, Sect. 5(vii).

[171] As regards the prohibition of canvassing, see CCA 1974, s.49. See also Guest & Lloyd, n.147 above, [2-049 ff]. As regards the meaning of 'canvassing', see Ch. 2, Sect. 5(vii) above.

[172] Determination of 1 June 1977; Goode (ed.), n.147 above, [IVB(2.1)]; Guest & Lloyd, n.147 above, [4-4800].

[173] CCA1974, s.76 (enforcement without termination of agreement), s.98 (termination of agreement).

[174] Ibid., s.76(2); s.98(2).

[175] Ibid., s.98A added by S.I. 2010/1010, reg. 38 on 1 February 2011. See further Ch. 2, Sect. 5(v) above.

[176] Ibid., s.98A(8).   [177] Ch. 2, Sect. 5(v) below.

[178] Required under CCA 1974, s.78(4) and the Consumer Credit (Running-Account Credit Information) Regulations 1983, S.I. 1983/1570. Banks must provide customers with 'regular statements of account', subject to certain exceptions, such as where an account is operable by passbook: Financial Services Authority, *Banking Conduct of Business Sourcebook*, 4.2.1(1).

[179] Formerly, the *Business Banking Code* (March 2008) set out principles of best practice in relation to banks' dealings with their business customers. Best practice when lending to 'micro-enterprises' is now governed by the *Lending Code* (November 2009), replaced by the *Lending Code* (March 2011). See also British Bankers' Association (BBA), *A Statement of Principles: Banks and Micro-enterprises—Working*

the basic concepts of a loan apply to both types of transaction. Initially, the bank has to satisfy itself of the viability of the loan application made by the proposed borrower. If the bank agrees to lend, the agreements tend to follow a standard form, except that in consumer transactions the form has to be adapted to comply with the CCA 1974 and its regulations. Many doctrines applying to loans fall within the domain of general contract law, and accordingly a detailed discussion is outside the scope of this work. It is, however, necessary to review the banks' approach to loans, which is basically the same in both commercial and consumer transactions. The provision of security in relation to bank loan transactions is discussed in Chapters 18–21.

(ii) Review of the transaction by the bank

Where a bank reviews a loan application, it aims to avoid speculative transactions by considering the financial soundness of both the venture and the borrower, the profitability of the transaction, its legality, and its regularity. Thus, a bank will not lend if it has any doubt about the mandate or the *bona fides* of the corporate officers applying for a loan on the company's behalf, or even doubts about the company's capacity to borrow. One of the bank's main concerns, particularly for business loans, is the borrower's cash-flow and source of repayments. Where a loan is needed for setting-up purposes, the bank will appreciate that the borrower may be unable to repay capital at the initial stages. Accordingly, the bank may agree to charge him interest only for a given period of time. The bank must also consider whether the loan is to be repaid by way of equal instalments (commonly known as 'amortized repayment'), whether repayments are to increase in amount over the period of the loan (known as 'balloon repayment'), or whether repayment is to come in one shot at the end of the term (known as 'bullet repayment'). Generally, the bank attempts to identify the fund that will enable the borrower to make repayments, although there is no provision in the contract that these are to come exclusively from that fund.[180] In general, banks will attempt to avoid 'accommodation banking',[181] This phrase denotes transactions in which a party guarantees or grants accommodation without a financial interest in the business venture, be it direct or indirect.

The detailed terms of different loan agreements vary, but each contains similar core provisions. There has been some attempt to standardize loan documentation. In October 1999, the Loan Market Association, working with the British Bankers' Association, the Association of Corporate Treasurers, and major City law firms, introduced recommended forms of facility agreements for use in the syndicated lending market.[182] Early anecdotal evidence indicated that the recommended forms were being widely used.[183] Commercial loan agreements usually contain conditions precedent to the availability of the loan; representations, warranties, and covenants made and given by the borrower; and extensive events of default.[184] The conditions precedent must be satisfied before the

---

Together (November 2009). From March 2011, the *Principles* are incorporated in the *Lending Code* (March 2011).

[180] A bank may obtain an assignment by way of security or charge for security purposes: Ch. 21 below.

[181] Ch. 17, Sect. 3(ii) below.

[182] These are recommended forms of primary loan agreements; different documentation is used in secondary debt trading.

[183] M. Campbell, 'The LMA Recommended Form of Primary Documents' [2000] *JIBFL* 53, at 55.

[184] E. Ferran, n.354 below, 462–481; E. Ferran, n.195 below, 325–339.

borrower can draw down the funds. Usually, the borrower is required to supply the lender with specified documentation, such as a corporate borrower's constitutional documents, a resolution of its board approving the facility, and, in the case of cross-border loans, legal opinions of relevant foreign lawyers on its validity.[185] Another common condition precedent is that the borrower must confirm that there have been no events of default and the representations and warranties remain accurate.[186] Representations and warranties usually fall into two basic categories: (a) those relating to legal aspects, such as the legal status, powers, and authority of the borrower and validity of the documents, and (b) those relating to commercial aspects covering the credit standing and financial condition of the borrower.[187] Representation and warranties perform an investigative function.[188] They are used, in conjunction with a due diligence exercise, to investigate and obtain information on both the borrower and the project being financed. Representations and warranties are usually drafted on an 'evergreen' basis, which means that they are deemed to be repeated on each draw down of funds by the borrower and/or at other specified intervals.[189] The loan agreement will usually specify that it is an event of default to make a representation or warranty that is incorrect or, in some cases, that is incorrect in any material respect.[190] The function of the covenants in a loan agreement is to give the lender some control over the borrower and restrict the borrower in the conduct of its business so as to ensure the borrower's credit rating does not decline. Precisely which covenants appear in a loan agreement depends on a variety of factors such as the size and duration of the loan, the financial position of the borrower, the negotiating strength of the borrower, and the presence of competition from other banks.[191] Covenants are the most negotiated areas of the loan agreement. The key covenants that will usually be demanded of a corporate borrower relate to (a) provision of information (financial statements, management accounts, etc.),[192] (b) maintenance of certain financial ratios (for example, requiring the borrower to maintain a minimum net worth),[193] (c) restrictions on disposals of assets (including prohibitions on quasi-security transactions that are not included in the negative pledge),[194] (d) restrictions on the grant of security to other creditors (a negative pledge clause),[195] and (e) assurances that obligations under the loan agreement will rank at least equally (a *pari passu* clause) with other unsecured obligations.[196] Failure to comply with a covenant is usually an event of default that entitles the lender to terminate the loan.[197]

---

[185] Loan Market Association, *Multicurrency Term and Revolving Facility Agreement* ('LMA.MTR.03') (May 2004), cl. 4.1 & Sched. 2, Pt. 1.

[186] LMA.MTR.03, cl. 4.2. Sometimes, it is also specified as a condition precedent to draw down that there has been no material adverse change in the borrower's financial position: R. Hooley, 'Material Adverse Change Clauses After 9/11' in S. Worthington (ed.), *Commercial Law and Commercial Practice* (Oxford, 2003), ch. 11.

[187] Ibid.   [188] P.R. Wood, *International Loans, Bonds and Securities Regulation* (London, 1995), 29.

[189] LMA.MTR.03, cl. 19.14.   [190] Ibid., cl. 23.4.

[191] J. Day & P. Taylor, 'Evidence on the Practice of U.K. Bankers in Contracting for Medium-Term Debt' [1995] 9 *JIBL* 394; J. Day & P. Taylor, 'Bankers' Perspectives on the Role of Covenants in Debt Contracts' [1996] 5 *JIBL* 201.

[192] LMA.MTR.03, cl. 20.

[193] Ibid., cl. 21 (it was recognized that this was too complex an area to be dealt with in the Recommended Forms and so a blank space has been left to be filled in by the parties and/or their legal advisers).

[194] Ibid., cl. 22.4.

[195] Ibid., cl. 22.3. The literature on the subject of the negative pledge is vast, especially with regard to its effect on third parties who take security from the borrower in breach of the covenant: E. Ferran, *Principles of Corporate Finance Law* (Oxford, 2008), 334–339. For the effectiveness of a negative pledge in the context of secured lending, see Ch. 19, Sect. 4(iv) below.

[196] LMA.MTR.03, cl. 19.12.   [197] Ibid., cls. 23.2 and 23.3.

The conditions in the loan agreement concerning security, interest, and repayments vary to a considerable extent. The arrangement for security depends on whether the borrower is a public corporation, a private company, an unincorporated trader, or a person borrowing for private purposes. A great deal depends on the object of the loan. In many cases the loan is, in any event, unsecured. This is particularly so where it is extended to an individual. The interest rate charged depends largely on the bank's assessment of the risk, on the period for which the loan is extended, and on the security furnished. The rate is usually variable, being quoted at a given percentage above the bank's base (or prime) lending rate or, in the case of many commercial loans, at an agreed margin over the market rate, such as the cost of funds on the London inter-bank market (known as 'LIBOR' or the 'London Inter-Bank Offered Rate'). But even a loan with a variable interest rate may contain provision for a fixed rate period. In some (rare) cases, the loan may even provide for the rate of interest to be variable entirely at the lender's discretion.[198]

It is clear that the object of a loan may vary from that of a personal loan for such purposes as travelling and housing loans to a syndicated loan extended to enable a corporation to finance a capital project. The loan agreement will usually specify the purpose of the loan.[199] Failure to use the loan for the specified purpose will constitute a repudiatory breach of the loan agreement,[200] and it may even be that money lent for a specified purpose is held by the borrower on trust for the lender.[201] The mere fact that the lender knows the purpose for which the loan was to be used is not enough to create a trust: once the money was lent it would be at the free disposal of the borrower.[202] The borrower's freedom to dispose of the money is 'necessarily excluded by an arrangement that the money shall be used *exclusively* for the stated purpose'.[203] Between these two extremes, it is ultimately an issue of determining whether the parties intended the loan to be at the recipient's free disposal or not.[204]

---

[198] The lender's discretion is not totally unfettered. In *Paragon Finance plc* v. *Staunton* [2001] EWCA Civ. 1466, [2001] 2 All ER (Comm.) 1025, where a residential mortgage agreement contained a variable interest clause at the lender's discretion, the Court of Appeal held that a term could be implied into the agreement that the discretion to vary interest rates should not be exercised dishonestly, for an improper purpose, capriciously or arbitrarily. It also held that there was an implied term that the lender's power should not be exercised unreasonably. The Court of Appeal accepted that a lender could not exercise its discretion in a way that no reasonable lender acting reasonably would do, but it did not accept an implied term that the lender would not impose unreasonable rates. In *Sterling Credit Ltd* v. *Rahman* [2002] EWHC 3008 (Ch), Park J held that *Paragon Finance* did not require a lender to reduce interest rates from time to time as prevailing market rates fell: this would have imposed a positive obligation on the lender whereas *Paragon Finance* only imposed a negative obligation. See also *Office of Fair Trading* v. *Abbey National plc*, n.19 above, [79].

[199] Ibid., cl. 3.1.   [200] *Reid* v. *National Westminster Bank plc* (CA, 22 October 1999).

[201] *Barclays Bank Ltd* v. *Quistclose Investments Ltd* [1970] AC 567 (HL), where the House of Lords held that money lent for a specified purpose was held by the borrower subject to a primary purpose trust and, in the event of the primary trust's failure, on a secondary resulting trust in favour of the lender. In most cases, the claimant is concerned to invoke the secondary trust when the primary purpose has become impossible, so as to avoid the loan monies becoming part of the insolvent borrower's estate. See also *Re Crown Forestry Rental Trust* [2004] UKPC 13, [41].

[202] *Twinsectra Ltd* v. *Yardley* [2002] UKHL 12, [2002] 2 AC 164, [73].

[203] Ibid., [74] (emphasis added). LMA.MTR.03, Cl. 3.1 falls short of this.

[204] Id. A *Quistclose* trust may be inconsistent with the company's business model: *Re Farepak Food & Gifts Ltd* [2006] EWHC 3272 (Ch), [33]–[35]. For the recognition of a *Quistclose* trust over loan proceeds, see *Templeton Insurance Ltd* v. *Penningtons Solicitors LLP* [2006] EWHC 685 (Ch), [15]–[18]; *Cooper* v. *PRG Powerhouse Ltd*, n.111 above, [15]–[24]. For the rejection of such a trust on the facts, see *Shalson* v. *Russo* [2005] Ch. 281, [128]–[130]; *Re Margaretta Ltd* [2005] STC 610, [15]–[30]; *Abou-Rahmah* v. *Abacha* [2005] EWHC 2662 (QB), [78]–[80]; *Blackburn* v. *Revenue & Customs Commissioners* [2008] EWHC 266 (Ch), [54]–[60]; *Soutzos* v. *Asombang* [2010] BPIR 960, [142]–[148].

Virtually all lending agreements specify certain 'events of default' that give the lender the option of accelerating repayment of the loan and any other sums due, and terminating its commitment to make further advances.[205] Unless the relevant event of default is expressly specified in the loan agreement, it is unlikely to be implied.[206] These rights are additional to any other rights the lender may have at common law in respect of the borrower's breach of the loan agreement.[207] Typical 'events of default' include the borrower's failure to pay principal or interest when due, or his bankruptcy (or, in the case of a corporate borrower, the appointment of a receiver or the company being wound up). Any materially adverse change in the borrower's financial condition or operation may also be specified as an event of default.[208] The occurrence of any of the events listed in the 'events of default' clause may not *automatically* constitute default under the loan agreement, as the borrower may be allowed a grace period to rectify the position, or a materiality test may have to be satisfied, before the lender calls in the loan. Perhaps the most important 'event of default' in commercial loan agreements is the cross-default clause,[209] which provides that any default by the borrower in relation to other indebtedness to the same or another lender will equally constitute a default under the particular loan agreement. A lender will not want to be 'left behind' if the borrower has already defaulted on other loan agreements and those other lenders have started enforcement or renegotiation of terms. Where one of the borrower's loan agreements contains particularly strict 'events of default'—with no grace periods or 'materiality' requirement—there is a danger of a 'domino' effect whereby a single default triggers defaults on all other loan agreements.

In the case of corporate borrowers, there is no statutory control on the lender's exercise of its discretion to invoke its remedies under the 'events of default' clause.[210] A consumer borrower may be able to rely on the UTCCR 1999, which invalidates certain contract terms that are deemed 'unfair'.[211] Thus, in *Director General of Fair Trading* v. *First National Bank plc*,[212] a term of the bank's standard loan agreement provided that,

---

[205] LMA.MTR.03, cl. 23. See also R. Youard, 'Default in International Loan Agreements I and II' [1986] *JBL* 276, 378. A borrower may challenge the basis of a notice of acceleration: *BNP Paribas SA* v. *Yukos Oil Co.* [2005] EWHC 1321 (Ch), [19]. Mere service of a notice of acceleration, at a time when no event of default has occurred, does not constitute a breach of contract by a lender acting in good faith, although enforcing security or withdrawing a contractually agreed facility on the basis of an invalid demand is clearly a different matter: *Concord Trust* v. *Debenture Trust Corporation plc* [2005] WLR 1591 (HL) (trustee of bond issue held to have given ineffective notice and not to be in breach of contract). See also *Jafari-Fini* v. *Skillglass Ltd* [2007] EWCA Civ. 261, [112]–[118]; *Verizon UK Ltd* v. *Swiftnet Ltd* [2008] EWHC 551 (Comm.), [55].

[206] *Cryne* v. *Barclays Bank plc* [1987] BCLC 548 (CA) (no implied term entitling the bank to require repayment and/or to appoint a receiver if its security was in jeopardy).

[207] At common law, non-payment or other breach of a loan agreement entitles the lender to treat the agreement as at an end only where this amounts to the breach of a condition, or amounts to a repudiation of the borrower's obligations under the agreement, and this may not always be the case: R. Salter, 'Remedies for Banks: An Outline of English Law', ch. 3 in W. Blair QC (ed.), *Banks and Remedies* (2nd edn., London, 1999).

[208] Material adverse change clauses (MACs) may even be more broadly worded than this: R. Hooley, n.186 above, ch. 11. LMA.MTR.03, cl. 23.12 leaves the wording of the MAC blank for the parties to agree upon.

[209] LMA.MTR.03, cl. 23.5.

[210] The Unfair Contract Terms Act 1977 (UCTA 1977) has no obvious application to 'events of default' clauses, as these do not constitute an exemption or limitation clause. There may be an argument that as an 'events of default' clause permits a bank to terminate the loan agreement that it permits the bank to render no contractual performance, or one substantially different from that reasonably expected (UCTA 1977, s.3(2)(b)(i)–(ii)). Even so, such a clause is unlikely to fail the statutory test of 'reasonableness'.

[211] Sect. 2(ii) above.

[212] [2002] 1 AC 481 (HL). For the litigation under UTCCR 1999 in relation to 'shared appreciation mortgages', see *Tew* v. *BoS (Shared Appreciation Mortgages) No. 1 plc* [2010] EWHC 203 (Ch).

should the borrower default on his repayments, interest would continue to be payable at the contractual rate until any judgment obtained by the bank was discharged. The House of Lords held that the term was susceptible to control under the UTCCR 1999, as it did not fall within the exclusion for clearly drafted terms that relate (a) to the definition of the main subject matter of the contract, or (b) to the adequacy of the price or remuneration as against the goods or services supplied in exchange.[213] On that basis, it was open to their Lordships to assess whether the relevant term was 'unfair' or not. Their Lordships concluded that it was not, as the term did not cause 'a significant imbalance in the parties' rights and obligations arising under the contract to the detriment of the consumer',[214] but instead operated to prevent an imbalance the other way. Its purpose was 'to ensure that the borrower does not enjoy the benefit of the outstanding balance after judgment without fulfilling the corresponding obligation which he has undertaken to pay interest on it as provided for in the contract'.[215] In addition to the UTCCR 1999, an individual borrower or an unincorporated firm will generally be able to rely upon the protections in the CCA 1974,[216] and both consumer and commercial borrowers may rely upon the range of common law doctrines that are used by the courts to police contractual bargains. That said, the traditional reluctance of the common law to impose obligations of good faith or fair dealing on contracting parties means that these common law principles will only rarely assist the borrower, at least where the loan agreement is reasonably well drafted.[217] For example, the borrower cannot obtain relief against forfeiture where the lender simply relies on an 'events of default' clause.[218] nor invoke the penalty clause jurisdiction to void a clause enabling a lender to accelerate loan repayments.[219] If the relevant clause additionally provides that interest is payable immediately for the full unexpired period of the loan this may constitute a penalty.[220] That said, as money is more expensive for a less good credit risk than for a good credit risk, there are good commercial reasons, as held in *Lordsvale Finance plc* v. *Bank of Zambia*,[221] why the penalty clause jurisdiction should

---

[213] This conclusion has recently received some endorsement in *Office of Fair Trading* v. *Abbey National plc*, n.1 above, [43], [101], where Lord Walker emphasized that the type of 'default provision' in issue in *First National Bank* should not be allowed to escape control under the UTCCR 1999.

[214] UTCCR 1999, reg. 5(1).

[215] N.212 above, [46]. See also *UK Housing Alliance (North West) Ltd* v. *Francis* [2010] EWCA Civ. 117, [17]–[29].

[216] Sect. 3(iii) below.

[217] The *contra proferentem* principle can only operate in the borrower's favour when the loan agreement is ambiguous: *Bank of Scotland* v. *Ladjadj* [2000] 2 All ER (Comm.) 583, 589 (CA) ('the *contra proferentem* rule possesses special force' where the bank's mortgage documentation was 'disgracefully sloppy and well capable of creating confusion'). See also *Financial Institutions Services Ltd* v. *Negril Negril Holdings Ltd*, n.23 above, [43]; *Morrell* v. *Workers Savings & Loan Bank* [2007] UKPC 3, [33]; *Office of Fair Trading* v. *Abbey National plc*, n.19 above, [323], revsd. on a different point: n.1 above.

[218] *T.C. Trustees Ltd* v. *J.S. Darwen (Successors) Ltd* [1969] 2 QB 295, 301–302 (CA). Moreover, any general doctrine of unconscionability is unlikely to apply in this situation.

[219] *Protector Endowment Loan and Annuity Co.* v. *Grice* (1880) 5 QBD 592, 596; *Wallingford* v. *Mutual Society* (1880) 5 App. Cas. 685, 696; *Oresundsvarvet Aktiebolag* v. *Marcos Diamantis Lemos, The 'Angelic Star'* [1988] 2 Lloyd's Rep. 122, 125; *Cine Bes Filmcilik VE Yapimcilik* v. *United International Pictures* [2003] EWCA Civ. 1669, [16]; *Maple Leaf Macro Volatility Master Fund* v. *Rouvroy* [2009] EWHC 257 (Comm.), [264]; *BNP Paribas* v. *Wockhardt EU Operations (Swiss) AG* [2009] EWHC 3116 (Comm.), [38]. An acceleration clause may be 'unfair' under the UTCCR 1999: E. Macdonald, *Exemption Clauses and Unfair Terms* (2nd edn., London, 2006), 264.

[220] *Oresundsvarvet Aktiebolag* v. *Marcos Diamantis Lemos, The 'Angelic Star'* [1988] 2 Lloyd's Rep. 122, 125 (CA).

[221] [1996] QB 752, 763–764 (increase of 1 per cent). See also *Petromec Inc.* v. *Petroleo Brasileiro SA Petrobas* [2004] EWHC 127 (Comm.), [184]; *North Shore Ventures Ltd* v. *Anstead Holdings Inc.* [2010] EWHC 1485 (Ch), [234]–[239] (increase from 15 per cent to 20 per cent not penalty). English law appears to have been

not cover a small rateable increase in interest charged *prospectively* from default until repayment. In contrast, if default interest is applied retrospectively (even if the increase is modest),[222] involves a significant increase when compared to the pre-default interest rate,[223] or involves a change from charging simple interest to compound interest,[224] then the clause is more likely to constitute a penalty. To avoid any argument that an increase in the default interest rate constitutes a penalty, mortgages may provide for a reduction in a specified rate upon punctual payment.[225]

(iii) Consumer credit implications

There is one fundamental distinction between overdrafts and bank loans in so far as the application of the CCA 1974 is concerned. None of the special provisions and concessions applicable to overdrafts[226] apply to bank loans. Naturally, the transaction has to be of one of the types covered by the Act, in particular, a loan to an 'individual'.[227]

Part V of the Act introduces some far-reaching measures for the protection of consumers. The rights of cancellation or withdrawal (which, however, do not apply to loans secured on land), have been considered elsewhere.[228] Moreover, if a loan is a 'distance' contract (that is, made as a result of an 'organized distance service-provision scheme' where there has been no face-to-face interaction,[229]) then the cancellation rights conferred on such a contract will apply. However, this right will not arise if, before concluding the loan contract, the customer visits a branch and talks to a bank employee, as then the loan will not be regarded as a 'distance' contract.[230] Problems are, moreover, presented by section 58(1), which requires the bank to follow a stringent procedure where a loan is secured by a mortgage over land. The problem is discussed in Chapter 19.

In practice, very few loans are cancelled by a borrower against the bank's will as bank loans are usually made on terms more favourable than those available to the borrower from other sources. It is far more common for a borrower to ask for an extension of the time of repayment than to offer to discharge the debt prematurely.

A more onerous provision of the Act affecting bank loans is section 60, which empowers the Secretary of State to make regulations prescribing, *inter alia*, the form of regulated consumer credit agreements. The highly technical Consumer Credit (Agreements) Regulations,[231] made in pursuance of this provision, must be strictly complied with;

---

brought into line with US, Canadian, and Australian law on this point: ibid., 765–767. Even a term establishing prospective default interest may be 'unfair' under the UTCCR 1999, Sched. 2, para. 1(e). Under CCA 1974, s.93, the rate of interest cannot be varied for regulated agreements.

[222] Id.

[223] *Jeancharm Ltd* v. *Barnet Football Club Ltd* [2003] EWCA Civ. 58, [15]–[18]; *White* v. *Davenham Trust Ltd* [2010] EWHC 2748 (Ch), [51]–[60].

[224] *Donegal International Ltd* v. *Zambia* [2007] EWHC 197 (Comm.), [519]–[523].

[225] *Wallingford* v. *Mutual Society*, n.219 above, 702. But a 'discount' provision may be held to be unfair under the UTCCR 1999, Sched. 2, para. 1(e): *Falco Finance Ltd* v. *Gough* [1998] Tr. L Rep. 526; *Bairstow Eves London Central* v. *Smith* [2004] EWHC 263.

[226] Sect. 2(v) above.   [227] Ch. 2, Sect. 5(ii) above.   [228] Ch. 2, Sect. 5(iv) above.

[229] Financial Services (Distance Marketing) Regulations 2004, S.I. 2004/ 2095 (DMD Regs.), Sect. 5(iv).

[230] As the definition of 'distance contract' in the DMD Regs., reg. 2(1) requires the 'exclusive use of … distance communication up to and including the time at which the contract is concluded'.

[231] Ch. 2, Sect. 5(iv) above for the two sets of regulations: (i) the Consumer Credit (Agreements) Regulations 1983, S.I. 1983/1553, as amended (especially by S.I. 2004/1482) (applicable to agreements secured on land unless the creditor has 'opted into' the newer regime) and (ii) the Consumer Credit (Agreements) Regulations 2010, S.I. 2010/1014. As regards exempt agreements: Ch. 2, Sect. 5(ii) above.

otherwise the loan is unenforceable by the bank without an order of the court.[232] Moreover, the Consumer Credit (Disclosure of Information) Regulations require 'pre-contract' information to be given in the prescribed form before the loan contract is concluded.[233] Again, the agreement is unenforceable without a court order if such 'pre-contract' information is not given.

The Agreement Regulations require certain information to be contained in the agreement. They also prescribe that the agreement bears a heading stating that it is an agreement regulated by the CCA 1974, that it contains statutory notices advising the debtor of his rights under the Act, and that the signature of the debtor be executed in a prescribed form.[234] Historically, loan agreements by banks were often constituted by an informal 'letter of offer' setting out the basic terms of the arrangement, which was signed and returned by the customer. Such informal agreements have now disappeared and are replaced by formal agreements complying with the Act. The Act itself also requires all the terms of the agreement (other than implied terms) to be embodied in the document.[235]

The Agreement Regulations make elaborate provision as to the 'information' that must be disclosed in the document signed by the debtor and as to how it must be disclosed.[236] The information is extensive and covers all the essential aspects of the agreement, in particular, the amount of credit or credit limit, the contract's duration, the total amount payable, the timing and amount of repayments, information about the APR, detailed information about the total charge for credit (with a list of its constituents), the annual rate of interest, how interest is calculated and, if the APR is variable, the circumstances in which variation occurs. In addition, any security must be described, any default charges must be listed, and information as to rebates on early settlement given. These requirements are onerous and easy to get wrong. Moreover, if the loan also finances an optional credit insurance premium and hence a 'multiple agreement' arises,[237] there is much dispute as to how the agreement should be documented.[238]

Further difficulties arise under the Act and Regulations where the agreement is varied by agreement between the bank and the customer.[239] For example, a further advance may be made under an existing agreement, or the security for the loan may be varied (as is the case where a customer sells a home charged to the bank and buys a new one, or where stocks and shares lodged as security are sold and replaced by others). In such cases a modifying agreement will arise, and it will need to comply with the Regulations

---

[232] Ch. 2 Sect. 5(xiii) above.

[233] Ch. 2, Sect. 5(iv) above for the two sets of regulations: (i) the Consumer Credit (Disclosure of Information) Regulations 2004, S.I. 2004/1481 (in the case of 'distance' contracts', these regulations do not apply as a similar requirement is imposed by the Financial Services (Distance Marketing) Regulations 2004, S.I. 2004/2095) and (ii) the Consumer Credit (Disclosure of Information) Regulations 2010, S.I. 2010/1013 as amended by S.I. 2010/1969. For 'distance' contracts, the requirements are imposed by the DMD Regs., see above.

[234] The Agreements Regulations 1983, reg. 6 (as amended by the Consumer Credit Act 1974 (Electronic Communications) Order 2004, S.I. 2004/3236, reg. 4 in order to facilitate the electronic contracting) and the Agreements Regulations 2010, reg. 4.

[235] Consumer Credit Act 1974, s.61(1)(b).

[236] S.I. 1983/1553, Sched. 1, as amended by S.I. 2004/1482; S.I. 2010/1014, Sched. 1 as amended by S.I. 2010/1969.

[237] Under the Consumer Credit Act 1974, s.18, the effect of which is unclear. See the discussions in the works referred to in Sect. 2(v) above, n. 147.

[238] See also S.I. 1983/1553, reg. 2(8), (9); S.I. 2010/1014, reg. 3(6), (7).

[239] Consumer Credit Act 1974, s.82(2).

applicable to such an agreement.[240] Questions may arise whether there is a modifying agreement when the bank grants indulgence to the customer by allowing him to defer payment of one or more instalments or reduces the amount of the instalment and extends his time to pay. Such acts of indulgence probably do not constitute modifying agreements. But they do so, for example, where the customer furnishes consideration by agreeing to pay a higher rate of interest on the overdue amount.

Where the loan agreement is secured on land (other than section 58(2) cases) the Act contains special provisions which require the bank to send the customer an advance copy of the agreement and legal charge. The bank must then allow him at least seven days to consider whether he wishes to withdraw from the transaction. At the end of this period (if he has not withdrawn), the bank must send him the agreement and legal charge for signature. There then must follow a further seven-day 'consideration period' during which the bank must not approach the customer in any way except at the customer's own request. The object of these elaborate provisions is to ensure that the customer has a chance to peruse the agreement and make up his mind without any pressure from the bank. But they also have the effect of preventing the customer from getting the loan quickly, especially since the charge document has to be complete in all respects before the advance copy is sent.[241]

The bank also has to take care to comply with the requirements as to the provision of copies. Unless the simpler provisions enacted in compliance with the Consumer Credit Directive apply,[242] where the bank has pre-signed the loan agreement, or it is signed by the bank and the customer at the same time, only one copy of the executed agreement has to be given to the customer.[243] Otherwise, two copies must be provided. The first copy (of the unexecuted agreement) must be supplied when the agreement is delivered or sent to him for signature. The second copy, of the executed agreement, has to be given to him within seven days following the making of the agreement.[244] If there are joint borrowers, each of them has to receive these copies.[245] As a result, where there are joint borrowers and the agreement is secured on land, up to 14 documents may be required. The Directive provisions[246] are much simpler and merely require one copy of the agreement to be given to the customer.[247]

As has been noted elsewhere,[248] the creditor's duties of disclosure under the Act do not end when the contract is executed and he is obliged to give periodic statements of account.[249] Moreover, the creditor must provide the debtor, at his request, with a copy

---

[240] S.I. 1983/1553, reg. 7 & Sched. 8 (extremely complex) & S.I. 2010/1014, reg. 5 as amended by S.I. 2010/1969 (much simpler).

[241] Ch. 18, Sect. 4 below.

[242] The older provisions apply to (i) agreements that are 'cancellable' within the meaning of CCA 1974, s.67 (Ch. 2, Sect. 5(iv) above) and (ii) agreements outside the scope of the Directive (secured on land and/or for credit in excess of £60,620 and/or business credit under £25,000) unless the creditor has 'opted into' the Directive regime: CCA 1974, s.61A(6) & ss.62–63.

[243] But note Consumer Credit Act 1974, s.64(1)(b), concerning notice of cancellation rights.

[244] Consumer Credit Act 1974, ss.62–63   [245] Ibid., s.185.

[246] Ibid., s.61A, added by S.I. 2010/1010, reg. 8 from 1 February 2011.

[247] Either a copy of the executed agreement or a copy of the unexecuted agreement if it is in identical terms to the executed agreement (but then the creditor has to inform the debtor in writing that the agreement has been made, that it is in identical terms and that the debtor may request a copy).

[248] Ch. 2, Sect. 5(iv) above.

[249] For fixed-sum credit, see Consumer Credit Act, s.77A (added by CCA 2006, s.6 and amended by the Legislative Reform (Consumer Credit) Order 2008, S.I. 2008/2826. For running-account credit see ibid., s.78(4)–(7) (as amended by the CCA 2006, s.7). It seems no charge may be made: s.77A(3) makes this clear whilst s.78(4)–(7) makes no mention of a fee.

of the agreement and with details about the financial state of the transaction.[250] Notice must generally be given of unilateral variations of the agreement by the creditor[251] and there are now special provisions generally requiring written notification of variations in interest rate.[252]

The Act regulates certain aspects of the transaction during its currency. Whilst a detailed analysis is outside the scope of this work, it is important to mention that, if the customer defaults in payment, the bank must give him at least 14 days' notice before it calls in the loan or enforces any security (including any guarantee).[253] The notice must be in a statutory form which advises the customer that, if he pays off the arrears, no further action will be taken against him or any surety.[254] It also informs him that if he has difficulties in making the payments he can apply to the court, which may make an order giving him time to pay. Similar (but different) notices have to be served in non-default cases where the bank wishes to call in a loan[255] or terminate the agreement, for example, on bankruptcy.[256] There is a further provision governing the termination of agreements without a fixed duration, for reasons other than breach, both by debtors (they may terminate, free of charge, by notice of not more than one month) and by creditors (they must give at least two months' notice).[257]

4 Syndicated loans

(i) Distinguishing between syndicated loans and loan participations[258]

A syndicated loan involves two or more banks each making separate loans to a borrower on common terms governed by a single loan agreement. Each bank in the syndicate contributes a proportion of the loan. Large commercial loans are syndicated when a single bank may be unwilling or unable to advance the whole amount itself or when there are likely to be savings in terms of time and money in dealing with a single agent bank

---

[250] For fixed-sum credit, see Consumer Credit Act 1974, s.77 and (for instalment agreements of fixed duration within the scope of the Directive) note the more onerous obligations in s.77B. For running-account credit, see Consumer Credit Act 1974, s.78(1)–(3).

[251] Consumer Credit Act 1974, s.82(1). See further Ch. 2, Sect. 5(iv) above.

[252] Consumer Credit Act 1974, s.78A, added by S.I. 2010/1010, reg. 27 on 1 February 2011. This provision is inapplicable to agreements secured on land.

[253] Consumer Credit Act 1974, s.87. See further Ch. 2, Sect. 5(v) above.

[254] Consumer Credit Act 1974, ss.87–88, as amended by the Consumer Credit Act 2006, s.14. Default notices have to be in paper form: Consumer Credit (Enforcement, Default and Termination Notices) (Amendment) Regulations 2004, S.I. 2004/3237. This is also the case for non-breach enforcement and termination notices given under ss.76 and 98.

[255] Consumer Credit Act 1974, s.76(1). Such notices have to be in paper form: Consumer Credit (Enforcement, Default and Termination Notices) (Amendment) Regulations 2004, S.I. 2004/3237. This is also the case for default and non-breach termination notices given under ss.87 and 98.

[256] Consumer Credit Act 1974, s.98. Such notices have to be in paper form: Consumer Credit (Enforcement, Default and Termination Notices) (Amendment) Regulations 2004, S.I. 2004/3237. This is also the case for default and non-breach enforcement notices given under ss.87 and 76.

[257] Consumer Credit Act 1974, s.98A added by S.I. 2010/1010, reg. 38 on 1 February 2011. There are also controls on the creditor's ability to exercise a contractual power to terminate or suspend the right to draw on credit, whether for breach or not: s.98A(4)–(6) and see s.87(5) (s.98A(4) applies). Overdrafts are excluded from this provision (s.98A(8)(a)–(c)) as are agreements secured on land (s.98A(8)(d)).

[258] A. Mugasha, *The Law of Multi-Bank Financing* (Oxford, 2007), [1.14]–[1.53]. See also P. Wood, n.188 above, ch. 6; R. Tennekoon, *The Law and Regulation of International Finance* (London, 2006 reprint), Pt. II; D. Warne & N. Elliott QC (eds.), *Banking Litigation* (2nd edn., London, 2005), ch. 4.

pursuant to a single set of documentation. The amount of the loan and its purpose will usually determine the size of the lending syndicate.[259] A syndicated loan must, however, be distinguished from a loan participation.[260] In a loan participation, only one bank ('the lead bank'), enters into the loan agreement with the borrower and then sells part of its interest in that loan to other banks (the 'participants'). There are many good commercial reasons why the lead bank may wish to sell part of its interest in the loan subsequently, including there being no time to syndicate; avoiding too much exposure to a single borrower; or diversifying the bank's loan portfolio.[261] The various methods by which a participant can take an interest in a loan are considered subsequently.[262]

(ii) **Mechanics of syndication**[263]

The borrower grants a mandate to a single bank or group of banks (the 'arranging bank') to arrange the syndicated loan. The arranging bank's main function is to put together the loan, although it may also agree to 'underwrite' the loan—in other words, the arranging bank agrees to lend the whole amount itself if it is unable to form a bank syndicate. The arranging bank may initially send out a 'term sheet', which includes brief, but essential, details in order to gauge lender interest. At the same time, the arranging bank will work with the borrower to prepare a more detailed information memorandum about the borrower and the loan that will then be used to market the loan to other banks that have expressed an interest.[264] The arranging bank may also be one of the banks advancing funds to the borrower and so it will assess the extent of its own credit risk, as well as negotiating the terms of the loan facility and security with the borrower. Execution of the loan agreement brings about direct contractual relations between the borrower and the syndicate banks, and, upon advancing funds, each bank enters a debtor–creditor relationship with the borrower. At this point (or upon the completion of the syndicate, if later), the arranging bank's role is complete. The loan agreement will, however, provide for the appointment of a bank that will act as the agent of the syndicate (the 'agent bank') in dealing with the borrower and administering the loan facility. The agent bank's functions commence with its appointment. Whilst this role may often be assumed by the arranging bank, it is not uncommon for a different bank to perform the role of agent bank.

---

[259] For example, the financing for the construction of Eurotunnel involved more than 200 lenders.

[260] P. Wood, n.188 above, ch. 7; R. Rendell, 'Current Issues in Participation and Other Co-lending Arrangements' in J. Norton, C.-J. Cheng, & I. Fletcher (eds.), *International Banking Operations and Practices* (Dordrecht, 1994); R. Tennekoon, n.258 above, ch. 6; A. Mugasha, n.258 above, ch. 6.

[261] Wood, n.188 above, 104.   [262] Sect. 4(v) below.

[263] A. Mugasha, n.258 above, [3.01]–[3.141].

[264] Should the information memorandum subsequently prove to be inaccurate, the syndicate banks that loaned money to the borrower on the strength of that document. The arranging bank's liability will depend upon whether it acted as a mere conduit for the information between the borrower and the syndicate or whether it produced and/or actively markets the loan on the basis of the information memorandum: *Re Colocotronis Tanker Securities Litigation*, 420 F. Supp. 998 (1976); *Royal Bank Trust Co. (Trinidad) Ltd* v. *Pampellonne* [1987] 1 Lloyd's Rep. 218 (PC)). If the arranging bank has marketed the loan, it may be liable for negligence or for misrepresentation (*Sumitomo Bank* v. *Banque Bruxelles Lambert* [1997] 1 Lloyd's Rep. 487), although the courts have expressed a reluctance to impose such liability between sophisticated commercial parties: *IFE Fund SA* v. *Goldman Sachs International* [2007] EWCA Civ. 811; *Raiffeisen Zentralbank Österreich AG* v. *Royal Bank of Scotland plc* [2010] EWHC 1392 (Comm.). Moreover, the information memorandum itself, and subsequent loan agreement, usually state that the arranger bank takes no responsibility for the accuracy of the information provided and that each bank should make its own assessment (LMA. MTR.03, cl. 26.8). Such clauses are usually upheld between commercial parties, unless the arranger bank has acted fraudulently. For the same reason, UCTA 1977 is unlikely to invalidate such clauses.

(iii) **Terms of a syndicated loan agreement**[265]

Recent attempts to standardize the documentation used in syndicated loan agreements has met with some success. In October 1999, the Loan Market Association, the Association of Corporate Treasurers, and major City law firms, introduced recommended forms of primary loan documentation.[266] Some of the core provisions of the LMA's recommended forms for a multicurrency term and revolving facilities agreement have been considered previously,[267] in particular those terms relating to the bank lender-borrower relationship. This section focuses upon those provisions dealing with the syndicated nature of the facility.[268] Syndicated loan agreements provide that (a) each bank will make loans up to its specified commitment during the commitment period; (b) each bank's obligations are several; and (c) each bank's rights are divided.[269] These provisions reflect the severability of each lender's rights and obligations *vis-à-vis* the borrower, as each bank agrees to make a separate loan to the borrower. Accordingly, one bank's failure to perform its lending obligations does not absolve the other banks of their respective obligations and normally the syndicate banks do not underwrite each other.[270] The divided nature of each bank's rights reinforces that each separate loan is owed to each bank individually. Furthermore, each bank may enforce its own rights separately, unless the particular bank has agreed to refrain from so doing under its loan agreement. Whilst the bank's rights are legally separate, with respect to the administration of the loan—in particular, such matters as waivers of breaches of covenant or consents to relaxation of covenants, or the right to accelerate the loan on an event of default—the syndicate banks usually agree to abide by a decision of a majority of the syndicate.[271] Majorities require either more than half or two-thirds of the relevant votes, and votes are measured according to the amount of the bank's participation.[272]

A syndicated loan agreement will also contain a *pro rata* sharing clause,[273] by which each bank agrees to share with the other banks any recovery from the borrower (whether by way of set-off, litigation proceeds, or discriminatory repayment by the borrower) that is in excess of what the other banks have recovered, taking into account the proportion that each bank has contributed overall. In short, the clause is designed to share sums received by one bank amongst the others. The clause may expressly entitle the bank that shares sums to be subrogated to the receiving banks to the extent that the bank pays them and, in cases of set-off, this can allow the sharing bank to 'double dip'.[274] Unless litigation proceeds are exempted from its ambit, the sharing clause may discourage an individual bank from exercising its direct rights against a borrower.[275] In practice, the principle embodied in the sharing clause is more honoured in the breach than in its observance.[276]

A syndicated loan agreement provides for the appointment of the agent bank as agent of the syndicate members,[277] and specifies the duties of such a bank.[278] The main

---

[265] A. Mugasha, n.258 above, [5.16]–[5.124].

[266] 'Primary' documentation must be distinguished from documentation used in secondary debt trading.

[267] Sect. 3(ii) above.   [268] These are mainly, but not exclusively, found in LMA.MTR.03, cl. 10.

[269] LMA.MTR.03, cl. 2.   [270] Ibid., cl. 2.2(a).   [271] Ibid., cl. 26.7.

[272] For the definition of 'majority lenders', see LMA.MTR.03, cl. 1.1. The majority lenders must act in good faith, but need not exercise the power for the benefit of the lenders as a whole (*Redwood Master Fund Ltd* v. *TD Bank Europe Ltd* [2002] EWHC 2703 (Ch) (noted by P. Wood, 'Syndicated Credit Agreement: Majority Voting' [2003] *CLJ* 261)).

[273] LMA.MTR.03, cl. 28.   [274] Ibid., cl. 28.3.

[275] Ibid., cl. 28.5(b), which contains an exemption for recoveries from legal or arbitration proceedings.

[276] M. Hughes, 'Loans Agreements—Single Bank and Syndicated' [2000] *JIBFL* 115, 119.

[277] LMA.MTR.03, cl. 26.1.   [278] Ibid., cl. 26.2.

functions of the agent bank are mechanical and administrative in nature, such as acting as a conduit for payment and repayment; receiving and forwarding documents required to satisfy the loan's conditions precedent; calculating the interest rate in the case of floating rate loans; and forwarding financial and other information received from the borrower. Many syndicated loan agreements also confer some discretionary powers on the agent bank, such as the power to call for compliance certificates and financial information from the borrower and the power to accelerate the loan on default without first ascertaining the views of the banks in certain emergency situations. Although it is arguable that the power of the agent bank to call for compliance certificates and other information from the borrower obliges that bank to monitor the borrower's compliance, many loan agreements expressly state that the agent bank is not subject to any such duty and further provide that the agent bank need not act unless directed by the majority banks.[279] Moreover, the granting of discretionary powers to the agent bank could subject it to fiduciary duties in favour of the syndicate members under normal agency principles.[280] Usually, it is expressly provided that nothing in the loan agreement constitutes the agent bank a trustee or fiduciary of another person.[281] Similarly, the agent bank would ordinarily be expected to act with care, skill, and diligence with the other banks' interests in mind, but the loan agreement will usually exempt the agent bank from liability to the syndicate banks, unless it has acted with gross negligence or wilful misconduct.[282] Unless the loan agreement otherwise provides, an agent bank generally owes no duties to anyone other than its principal, the syndicate members.

(iv) Legal nature of a loan syndicate[283]

There has been some uncertainty as to the juridical nature of a loan syndicate. One possible explanation is that a syndicate of banks constitutes a partnership between those banks. A partnership is defined as 'the relation which subsists between persons carrying on a business in common with a view of profit'.[284] The better view is probably that loan syndicates are not partnerships because there is no sharing of net profit between the syndicate members. The opposite conclusion would lead to the imposition of fiduciary duties between the member banks, as well as other consequences such as the banks having joint liability for each other's actions and each bank being able to bind the rest. Nevertheless, there is support for the notion that a bank syndicate does create fiduciary relationships, in particular between the arranging bank and the other banks. In *UBAF Ltd* v. *European American Banking Corporation*,[285] the defendant-arranging bank invited the claimant bank to participate in two loans that the defendant bank intended to make to two shipping companies. The claimant bank asserted that the defendant bank had represented that the loans were 'attractive financing to two companies in a sound and profitable group' and that, in reliance upon these representations, the claimant bank participated in the loan. When the borrowers later defaulted on the loans, the claimant bank alleged that the defendant was liable for deceit, misrepresentation under section 2(1) of the Misrepresentation Act 1967, and negligence. As the issue before the Court of Appeal

---

[279] Ibid., cl. 26.7. If the agent bank has actual knowledge of the borrower's default it must pass this on to the syndicate members and await instructions: ibid., cl. 26.2).

[280] L. Clarke & S.F. Farrar, 'Rights and Duties of Managing and Agent Banks in Syndicated Loans to Government Borrowers' (1982) *U. Ill. L. Rev.* 229, 244–245.

[281] LMA.MTR.03, cl. 26.4.   [282] Ibid., cl. 26.9.

[283] A. Mugasha, n.258 above, [5.01]–[5.15], [5.106]–[5.124].   [284] Partnership Act 1890, s.1.

[285] [1984] 1 QB 713 (CA).

concerned whether to set aside service of the writ (claim form) outside the jurisdiction, it was not necessary to consider the specific question of the arranging bank's relationship with the syndicate banks. Nevertheless, Ackner LJ stated obiter that:[286]

> The transaction into which [the claimant bank] was invited to enter, and did enter, was that of contributing to a syndicate loan where, as seems to us, quite clearly [the defendant bank] were acting in a fiduciary capacity for all the other participants. It was [the defendant bank] who received [the claimant bank's] money and it was [the defendant bank] who arranged for and held, on behalf of all the participants, the collateral security for the loan. If, therefore, it was within [the defendant bank's] knowledge at any time whilst they were carrying out their fiduciary duties that the security was as [the claimant bank] allege, inadequate, it must we think, clearly have been their duty to inform the participants of that fact and their continued failure to do so would constitute a continuing breach of their fiduciary duty.

This dictum must, however, be treated with caution.[287] There were several distinguishing factors in *UBAF*: first, it was merely an interlocutory appeal on a jurisdictional point where the court did not hear full arguments on the fiduciary issue; secondly, the fact that the defendant bank in *UBAF* had had a longstanding relationship with the borrowers may have influenced Ackner LJ in finding a fiduciary relationship; and, thirdly, as the defendant bank was also the trustee of the security for the benefit of the syndicate banks, the imposition of fiduciary obligations was more justifiable in *UBAF* than in other cases. Given these unusual features of *UBAF*, courts should not in future see that decision as giving them *carte blanche* to impose fiduciary duties on arranging banks. Something more than the standard relationship between an arranging bank and the syndicate banks should be required before fiduciary obligations are recognized. This approach is mirrored in the United States where the courts have generally been reluctant to impose fiduciary duties on the arranging bank without 'unequivocal contractual language' to that effect in the loan agreement.[288] The United States courts recognize that the relationship between the arranging bank and the lenders is, like the relationship between the lenders themselves, one of arm's-length contractual agreements between sophisticated commercial parties and that it should be governed by the terms of those contracts.[289] Indeed, most loan agreements nowadays expressly provide that 'nothing in this agreement constitutes the agent or the arranger as a trustee or fiduciary of any other person'.[290] This is a legitimate and effective technique for controlling the intervention of fiduciary obligations into a contractual relationship.[291]

---

[286] Ibid., 728. See also *NZI Securities Ltd* v. *Unity Group Ltd* (NZHC, 11 February 1992).

[287] R. Cranston, *Principles of Banking Law* (2nd edn. Oxford, 2002), 59.

[288] *Banque Arabe et Internationale d'Investissement* v. *Maryland National Bank*, 819 F. Supp. 1282 (SDNY 1993); *Banco Espanol de Credito* v. *Security Pacific National Bank*, 763 F. Supp. 36 (SDNY 1991), affd. 973 F.2d 51 (2d Cir. NY 1992), cert. denied, 113 S. Ct. 2992 (1993); *New Bank of New England NA* v. *Toronto-Dominion Bank*, 768 F. Supp. 1017 (SDNY 1991); *Women's Federal Savings & Loan Association* v. *Nevada National Bank*, 811 F.2d 1255 (9th Cir., 1987); *First Citizens Federal Savings and Loan Association* v. *Worthen Bank & Trust Co. NA*, 919 F 2d 510 (9th Cir. Ariz. 1990); *Koken* v. *First Hawaiian Bank*, (9th Cir, 5 September 2000). Cf. *Chemical Bank* v. *Security Pacific National Bank*, 20 F 3d 375 (9th Cir. Cal. 1994); *Banque Arabe et Internationale d'Invesissetment* v. *Maryland National Bank*, 850 F. Supp. 1199 (SDNY 1994).

[289] J.N. Brooks, 'Participation and Syndicated Loans: Intercreditor Fiduciary Duties for Lead and Agent Banks Under US Law' [1995] *JIBFL* 275.

[290] LMA.MTR.03, cl. 26.4.

[291] *Kelly* v. *Cooper* [1993] AC 205, 213–215 (PC); *Henderson* v. *Merrett Syndicates Ltd* [1995] AC 145, 206 (HL). See further Ch. 5, Sect. 4(i) above.

The search for a fiduciary relationship between the arranging bank and the syndicate members is often driven by the members' desire to enforce the duty of disclosure that fiduciaries traditionally owe. The syndicate members may wish to argue that the arranging bank failed to disclose information that would have materially affected their decision to join the syndicate. In the absence of a fiduciary relationship, non-disclosure by the arranging bank does not generally constitute a misrepresentation or breach of a common law duty of care. Indeed, in *IFE Fund SA* v. *Goldman Sachs*,[292] in which it was alleged that, between the date of the information memorandum and the claimant's investment, the arranging bank had received further negative reports from the accountants who had prepared the report attached to the information memorandum, but that the arranging bank has failed to disclose that information. The Court of Appeal held that the existence of any duty of care was inconsistent with the terms upon which the arranging bank provided the information memorandum in that case[293] and that there was no implied representation on its part that the information contained in the information memorandum was, or continued to be, accurate.[294] According to Gage LJ, the only representation made by the arranging bank when sending the information memorandum to potential syndicate members was a representation of good faith, so that the arranging bank would only be liable if it 'actually knew that it has in its possession information which made the information in the [memorandum] misleading...this would amount to an allegation of dishonesty'.[295] Support for this approach can also be found in *Raiffeisen Zentralbank Österreich AG* v. *Royal Bank of Scotland plc*,[296] which similarly involved a syndicate member seeking to convert an arranging bank's failure to disclosure certain matters into positive 'implied' representations in that regard. In rejecting the claims, Clarke J highlighted a number of features indicating that such implied representations would not generally be found, including the fact that the arranging and syndicate banks were 'sophisticated participants in the syndicated loans market'[297] and that 'whilst a bank could reasonably expect that the principal credit issues were addressed, it could not reasonably assume that the [information memorandum] contained everything that anyone might think relevant (even on credit issues)'.[298] These two factors would tend to close the door upon the arranging banks' liability for any failing to disclose particular details in the information memorandum, unless there was deliberate concealment, some positive misrepresentation, or an assumption of responsibility to the particular bank to disclose certain matters.

Indeed, the 'assumption of responsibility' principle may provide, the most satisfactory explanation for the imposition of liability in *NatWest Australia Bank Ltd* v. *Tricontinental Corporation Ltd*[299] in which the arranging bank prepared and distributed an information memorandum to prospective participants that did not disclose that the borrower had given third party guarantees supporting related company obligations, including one guarantee in favour of the arranging bank itself. The borrower's most recent accounts did not disclose these contingent liabilities. When the borrower later went into receivership, a participant claimed that the arranging bank had been negligent in failing to disclose the existence of the borrower's liabilities. Indeed, the participant had enquired specifically about contingent liabilities before agreeing to participate and claimed that it would not have participated in the syndicate loan had the related-party guarantees been disclosed beforehand. The Supreme Court of Victoria held that the arranging bank was liable to the participant for breach of its common law duty of care and under the Trade Practices Act 1974. It was held that specific enquiries made by the participant placed the

---

[292] N.264 above. See further Ch. 5, Sect. 4(iii) above.   [293] Ibid., [29].   [294] Ibid., [74]–[76].
[295] Ibid., [74]–[75].   [296] N.264 above.   [297] Ibid., [92].   [298] Ibid., [93].
[299] [1993] ATPR (Digest) 46–109.

arranging bank under a duty to disclose the existence of the guarantees. Unlike *IFE Fund* and *Raiffeisen Zentralbank*, which deal with the general position of the arranging bank in the absence of 'something more', *Tricontinental* deals with the situation where the arranging bank has gone beyond its usual role of preparing and sending out the information memorandum and specifically assumed responsibility to a particular syndicate member for the accuracy of information. Whilst the arm's length commercial contracts between the arranging and syndicate banks may well make such an argument more difficult, the fact that the parties' contractual relationship does not entirely preclude the possibility of imposing liability on the basis that there has been a voluntary assumption of responsibility was recognized in *Sumitomo Bank Ltd* v. *Banque Bruxelles Lambert S.A.*[300] Langley J held that contractual provisions as to the arranging bank's duties, rights, and exonerations under the loan agreement did not prevent, and were not inconsistent with the existence of a common law duty of care, and the fact that the arranging bank owed duties of a limited scope as agent under the terms of the loan agreement did not mean that other and wider duties might not have arisen from the relationship of the parties.[301] Accordingly, Langley J held that the arranging bank owed a duty of care to the members of the lending syndicate when disclosing information to the insurers that were to issue policies as part of the security package for the loan.

(v) **Loan participations**[302]

In a loan participation, the lead bank enters into the loan agreement with the borrower and then sells part of its interest in the loan to other banks (the 'participants'). The main methods for granting a participation are by assignment, novation, sub-participation, and risk participation.[303] Although only an assignment can be said to involve a 'sale' of an asset in the strict legal sense of the term, the lead bank and participant are commonly termed 'seller' and 'buyer' whatever method of participation is used.

Assignment involves the outright transfer of the lead bank's rights to all or part of its interest in the loan to the participant. The participant acquires a proprietary interest in the chose in action representing the loan. An assignment may either be statutory[304] or equitable,[305] but as loan participations usually only involve the transfer of part of the loan to any one participant, the assignment will usually fall outside the statutory requirements and take effect in equity. An equitable assignee of a legal chose in action, such as a debt or contractual rights under a loan agreement, must join the assignor to any action he may bring to enforce the assigned chose against the debtor/obligor. A statutory assignee may bring an action in his own name and does not have to join the assignor to the action. Two factors may limit the advantages of using an assignment for a loan participation. First, there may be a term in the loan agreement prohibiting its assignment by the lead bank or making an assignment subject to certain preconditions. Such clauses will render the purported assignment ineffective as against the borrower,[306] but, depending upon the construction of the particular clause, it may be possible to avoid the restrictions on assignability by transferring the interest in the loan by other means, such as a

---

[300] N.264 above.   [301] Ibid., 493.   [302] A. Mugasha, n.258 above, ch. 6.

[303] An alternative form of loan sale involves securitization: P. Wood, *Title Finance, Derivatives, Securitisations, Set-off and Netting* (London, 1995), chs. 4 & 5.

[304] Law of Property Act 1925, s.136(1).   [305] Ch. 21, Sects. 1–2 below.

[306] *Linden Gardens Trust Ltd* v. *Lenesta Sludge Disposals Ltd* [1994] 1 AC 85 (HL); *Ruttle Plant Ltd* v. *Secretary of State for the Environment, Food & Rural Affairs* [2007] EWHC 2870 (TCC), [71]–[75].

declaration of trust.[307] Secondly, an assignment will transfer only the lead bank's rights, but not its obligations, to the participant.[308] Accordingly, where the original loan facility is a revolving one, or there are further funds to be advanced to the borrower under the loan agreement, the lead bank remains responsible to the borrower for performing these obligations, despite the fact that the right to repayment has been assigned to the participant. In such circumstances, the lead bank will want to transfer both its rights and obligations to the participant, but this may only be achieved by a novation.

Novation involves the substituting of a new contract for an existing one. In the case of a loan participation, novation involves an agreement between the borrower and the lead bank releasing the lead bank of its obligations and agreeing that the participant shall take the lead bank's place as the other party to the contract for all purposes. The participant's agreement to provide further finance to the borrower constitutes the consideration necessary to support the new contract. Unlike an assignment, which does not usually require the borrower's consent,[309] novation requires the consent of all the parties. Indeed, it is possible for the parties to provide for 'novation in advance' by establishing a contractual mechanism whereby novation takes place automatically on the happening of a specified act or event.[310] Novation is the technique most widely used to transfer the lead bank's rights and obligations in a loan participation. Essentially, the loan agreement constitutes a standing offer to novate made by all the parties to the loan agreement; an offer that must be accepted in accordance with its terms.[311] The loan agreement may, however, restrict the entities that are capable of accepting that offer, such restricting novation to entities that qualify as a 'bank or other financial institution'.[312] The commercial rationale for such restrictions is that, as a novation transfers the lead bank's obligations, the borrower may have to look to the new entity for any further advances. The borrower accordingly has an interest in ensuring that the new entity is in a position to fulfil its obligations.[313] In addition, the loan agreement may require the parties to follow particular procedures before a novation is treated as effective.[314] Usually this involves serving a prescribed form of 'transfer certificate', signed by the lead bank and the participant, upon the agent bank. The agent, on receipt of the certificate, executes it and the novation takes effect from that point. One advantage of this procedure is that the commercial terms of the transfer between the lead bank and the participant are recorded separately from the transfer certificate and remain confidential as between them.[315]

---

[307] *Barbados Trust Co. Ltd* v. *Bank of Zambia* [2007] 1 Lloyd's Rep. 495, [29]–[47], [74]–[89] (CA); *Masri* v. *Contractors International UK Ltd* [2007] EWHC 3010 (Comm.), [126].

[308] *Tolhurst* v. *Associated Portland Cement Manufacturers Ltd* [1902] 2 KB 660, 668 (CA); *Linden Gardens Trust Ltd* v. *Lenesta Sludge Disposals Ltd*, n.306 above, 103.

[309] A loan agreement may provide that the borrower's consent is required even for a valid assignment: *Barbados Trust Co. Ltd* v. *Bank of Zambia*, n.307 above. In such circumstances, the loan agreement will also usually provide that the borrower's consent must not be unreasonably withheld or delayed: LMA.MTR.03, cl. 24.2(a)–(b). If the borrower's consent is not required there is always the danger that an assignment that materially increases the borrower's liability, such as under a tax grossing-up or an increased cost clause, may be implicitly prohibited: *Tolhurst* v. *Associated Portland Cement Manufacturers Ltd.*, n.308 above. See further Wood, n.188 above, [7-7]; Cranston, n.287 above, 362.

[310] E. McKendrick, *Goode on Commercial Law* (4th edn., London, 2010), 117.

[311] M. Hughes, 'Contracts, Consideration and Third Parties' [2000] *JIBFL* 79, 81. See also M. Hughes, 'Transferability of Loans and Loan Participations' [1987] *JIBL* 5.

[312] *Argo Fund Ltd* v. *Essar Steel Ltd* [2006] EWCA Civ. 241, [51], [68]; *Barbados Trust Co. Ltd* v. *Bank of Zambia*, n.307 above, [110]; *British Energy Power & Trading Ltd* v. *Crédit Suisse* [2008] EWCA Civ. 53, [19]–[24].

[313] *Barbados Trust Co. Ltd* v. *Bank of Zambia*, n.307 above, [68].   [314] LMA.MTR.03, cl. 24.5.

[315] M. Hughes, n.276 above, 119.

Sub-participations and risk participations can be distinguished from assignments and novations in that, unlike the latter, they have no effect whatsoever on the underlying loan agreement between the lead bank and borrower.[316] Sub-participations and risk participations are no more than separate contracts made between the lead bank and the participant. In the case of a sub-participation, the participant places a deposit with the lead bank for the amount of its participation and the lead bank agrees to pay to the participant a share of the payments received by the lead bank from the borrower.[317] The participant has no claim against the borrower and is exposed to the double risk of default by the borrower and by the lead bank. In the case of a risk participation, the participant, in return for payment of a fee, gives the lead bank a guarantee to pay under the terms of the loan agreement in the event of the borrower's failure. Accordingly, the 'risk participant' does not provide any funding to the lead bank, but simply assumes part of the risk of the borrower's default.[318]

Whatever the method of loan participation employed, there are several key issues that the parties should address.[319] Two issues deserve special mention. First, the lead bank owes a duty of confidentiality to the borrower that could inhibit the transfer of information about the loan to potential participants. This difficulty is usually addressed, however, by a provision in the loan agreement whereby the borrower consents to the disclosure of information about the loan that would otherwise breach its confidence.[320] The lead bank usually disclaims liability to the participant for the accuracy of such borrower information, leaving the participant to satisfy itself as to such matters.[321] Secondly, it may be necessary to transfer to the participant the benefit of any security given by the borrower, particularly in cases of assignment and novation, where the participant is given direct rights against the borrower and may have to resort to its security interest in order to realize those rights. The problem is especially acute in cases of novation, as this involves the cancellation of the borrower's original debt to the lead bank, thereby threatening any security given to that bank. Novation of the security should be avoided[322] as the new security agreement will probably require registration, may not have the same priority as the old agreement, and could be exposed afresh to being set aside as a 'preference'.[323] The solution is for a 'security trustee', which may be the lead bank itself, to hold the security on trust for all participants from time to time. If the security is not held in trust, it should be assigned rather than novated.[324]

---

[316] There may be restrictions in the loan agreement upon the lead bank's ability to enter into sub-participation agreements: *British Energy Power & Trading Ltd* v. *Crédit Suisse*, n.312 above.

[317] Wood, n.188 above, [7-18].

[318] *Lloyds TSB Bank plc* v. *Clarke* [2002] 2 All ER (Comm.) 992. See also Wood, n.188 above, [7-35].

[319] Wood, n.188 above, ch. 7. See also L. Stuart & G. Old, 'The FSA Rules for Securitisation and Loan Transfers—A User's Guide' [2000] *JIBL* 211.

[320] LMA.MTR.03, cl. 24.7.

[321] Ibid., cl. 24.4. Where the parties are 'sophisticated and of equal bargaining power', such a disclaimer will usually satisfy the statutory test of reasonableness in UCTA 1977: *National Westminster Bank* v. *Utrecht-America Finance Company* [2001] 3 All ER 733, [58]–[59] (CA); *Raiffeisen Zentralbank Österreich AG* v. *Royal Bank of Scotland plc*, n.264 above, [319]–[327].

[322] Cf. Cranston, n.287 above, 361.   [323] Insolvency Act 1986, ss.239–240.

[324] Although the assignment of security may have to be registered, for example, as for ships and land.

5 Lender liability

'Lender liability' has been described as a 'chameleon-like catch-word with several meanings',[325] and 'an elastic term, which can cover a range of liabilities, based on a variety of legal doctrines'.[326] It is a descriptive term that brings together a variety of separate claims that may be made against the lender by the borrower or third parties, but it does not represent a single unitary concept of liability. Lender liability may arise because a bank has made a misrepresentation, has given negligent advice to the borrower, has not exercised reasonable care and skill, or has become liable as a constructive trustee. These may be described as 'orthodox' claims, the legal basis of which are well-established and the risks of which are well-recognized by banks. The present focus is, however, on some of the more novel claims that have been made, or could be made in future, against commercial lenders, namely claims that may arise out of pre-contractual negotiations; the management and termination of the loan facility; the insolvency of the borrower; or harm to the environment.

(i) Pre-contractual negotiations

When a bank gives investment advice it owes a contractual duty to customers, and potentially a tortious duty to third parties if there has been an assumption of responsibility,[327] to take reasonable care in the provision of that advice. In other words, once the bank has assumed the role of financial adviser, it must exercise reasonable care and skill in performing that role. One issue that arises, however, is whether a bank or other commercial lender owes a duty to give investment advice to a prospective borrower. As a general rule, a bank owes no duty to its customer to advise on the soundness of the transaction for which the customer requires the loan or overdraft. In *Williams & Glyn's Bank Ltd* v. *Barnes*,[328] the claimant, was an experienced businessman and a customer of the defendant bank, as was his company. The claimant personally borrowed money to invest in his company, which was heavily indebted to the bank. When the company collapsed, the bank called in the personal loan. The claimant argued that the bank owed a duty to have warned him that his proposed investment was unsound. Rejecting this argument, Ralph Gibson J said:[329]

> ... no duty in law arises upon the bank either to consider the prudence of the lending from the customer's point of view, or to advise with reference to it. Such a duty could arise only by contract, express or implied, or upon the principle of the assumption of responsibility and reliance stated in *Hedley Byrne* or in cases of fiduciary duty. The same answer is to be given to the question even if the bank knows that the borrowing and application of the loan, as intended by the customer, are imprudent.

In the absence of an express contractual undertaking to advise the borrower, such a duty is unlikely to be implied into a loan contract, as it is neither obvious nor necessary to give business efficacy to the agreement. Moreover, the simple act of granting a loan to a customer does not in itself involve any assumption of responsibility sufficient to generate

---

[325] W. Park, 'Arbitration in Banking and Finance', ch. 9 in W. Blair (ed.), n.207 above.
[326] R. Cranston, n.287 above, 221.
[327] *Hedley Byrne & Co. Ltd* v. *Heller and Partners Ltd* [1964] AC 465 (HL).   [328] N.67 above.
[329] Ibid., 207. See also *Murphy* v. *HSBC Bank plc* [2004] EWHC 467 (Ch), [87], [96]. For the similar position in Canada, see *Pierce* v. *Canada Trustco Mortgage Company* (2005) 254 DLR (4th) 79, 85 (OCA); *Canada Trustco Mortgage Co.* v. *Renard* [2006] BCSC 1609, [84]–[85], revsd. on other grounds: [2008] BCCA 343.

a duty of care by the bank,[330] nor the imposition of any fiduciary duty.[331] The reasoning in *Barnes* was later echoed by Scott LJ in *Lloyds Bank plc v. Cobb*:[332]

> ...in order to place the bank under a duty of care to the borrower the borrower must, in my opinion, make clear to the bank that its advice is being sought. The mere request for a loan, coupled with the supply to the bank of the details of the commercial project...does not suffice to make clear to the bank that its advice is being sought.

More recently, in *National Commercial Bank (Jamaica) Ltd v. Hew*, Lord Millett stated that:[333]

> ...the viability of a transaction may depend on the vantage point from which it is viewed; what is a viable loan may not be a viable borrowing. This is one reason why a borrower is not entitled to rely on the fact that the lender has chosen to lend him money as evidence, still less as advice, that the lender thinks that the purpose for which the borrower intends to use it is sound.

It follows from this that, when it examines a borrowing proposal to decide whether or not to lend, the bank does this for its own purposes as lender and not for the borrower's benefit. There are sound policy and commercial reasons for this. Given the potential conflict between the bank's responsibility to its shareholders as a commercial lender and the borrower's interests in securing the loan, no general duty of care should be imposed on a lender *vis-à-vis* either the customer or a third party known by the bank to have a financial interest in the borrower's affairs.[334] Similarly, the bank owes no duty to assess the borrower's capacity to repay.[335] Moreover, where the bank requires the borrower to act in a certain way as a condition of granting the loan facility, the lender does not owe the borrower a duty of care to consider whether it is in fact a prudent course for the borrower to fulfil that particular condition precedent.[336] The position is no different if the borrower is

---

[330] Ch. 16, Sect. 2(ii) above.

[331] *Governor and Company of the Bank of Scotland v. A Ltd* [2001] Lloyd's Rep. Bank. 73, [25] (CA); *Murphy v. HSBC Bank plc*, n.329 above, [101]; *Wright v. HSBC plc* [2006] EWHC 930 (QB), [61]; *Tamimi v. Khodari* [2009] EWCA Civ. 1042, [42]; *Kotonou v. National Westminster Bank plc* [2010] EWHC 1659 (Ch), [136]. See further Ch. 5, Sect. 4(i) above.

[332] (CA, 18 December 1991).   [333] [2003] UKPC 51, [22].

[334] *Goldsworthy v. Brickell* [1987] 1 Ch. 378, 405 (CA); *Chapman v. Barclays Bank plc* [1997] Bank. LR, 315, 318 (CA); *Jeffers v. Northern Bank Ltd* [2004] NIQB 81 [29]–[43]; *Diamantides v. JP Morgan Chase Bank* [2005] EWCA Civ. 1612, [42]; cf. *Weir v. National Westminster Bank* [1995] Bank. LR 249, 256 (IH). See also *Toronto Dominion Bank v. Forsythe* (2000) 47 OR (3d) 321, 327 (OCA). Where the third party is a surety for the borrower there may, in special cases, be a duty to advise on the nature and effect of the security and to advise the surety to take independent legal advice: *Barclays Bank plc v. Khaira* [1992] 1 WLR 623; *Union Bank of Finland v. Lelakis* [1995] CLC 27; *Bank of New Zealand v. Geddes* (NZHC, 28 May 2009), [25]–[26]; cf. *Cornish v. Midland Bank plc* [1985] 3 All ER 513, 522–523 (CA) (general duty to advise surety who is customer). See further Ch. 5, Sect. 4(iii) above. Sometimes, equity requires lenders to take special measures with regard to certain types of surety (especially wives) when the lender is on notice of the principal debtor's undue influence: *Barclays Bank plc v. O'Brien* [1994] 1 AC 180; *Royal Bank of Scotland plc v. Etridge (No. 2)* [2002] 2 AC 773. See further Ch. 5, Sect. 4(ii), above.

[335] This general principle remains unaffected even though banks have been held to be contributorily negligent—because they did not make adequate enquiries of borrowers, or they lent on too high a proportion of the value of the property—in actions they have brought against surveyors for negligently valuing property which the banks took as security for loans: *Platform Home Loans Ltd v. Oyston Shipways Ltd* [2000] 2 AC 190 (HL). This case says nothing about the bank's duty to the borrower, as 'the essence of contributory negligence is a failure to take reasonable care of one's own interests and does not necessarily connote any failure to take reasonable care in relation to others': Cranston, n.287 above, 222: cf. J. Wadsley, 'Bank lending and the family home: prudence and protection' [2003] *LMCLQ* 341, 351.

[336] *Frost v. James Finlay Bank Ltd* [2002] Lloyd's Rep. IR 503 (CA).

in fact mistaken, albeit on reasonable grounds, about whether such a condition precedent has in fact been imposed.

Accordingly, the broad effect of *Barnes* is to insulate lenders from claims that they did not take sufficient steps to warn or advise borrowers about the wisdom of particular transaction or course of conduct. Nevertheless, lenders can be liable for failing to advise borrowers properly when they have voluntarily assumed responsibility to do so and the borrower had relied upon this.[337] A rare example of a lender having crossed this particular line is *Verity and Spindler* v. *Lloyd's Bank plc*[338] in which the claimants, a teacher and an acupuncturist who wished to renovate a property, approached the defendant bank to take advantage of its advertised financial advisory service.[339] The branch manager of the defendant bank encouraged the claimants to buy one of the two properties that they were considering as it was the better investment and accordingly granted them the loan needed to buy that property. The investment failed when the property market slumped. When the bank demanded repayment of the loan, the claimants resisted on the ground that the bank had breached its contractual and tortious duties to them by tendering them negligent advice. Judge Taylor held that, on the particular facts, the bank had voluntarily assumed responsibility to the borrowers to advise them with reasonable care. The key factors that appear to have influenced the conclusion in *Verity* were the borrowers' financial inexperience; the manager's inspection of the properties (contrary to usual practice) and encouragement to purchase a particular property; and the terms of the bank's advertisements. As considered previously,[340] even outside the lending context, the borrower's or customer's financial inexperience (or otherwise) has become one of the principal factors considered by the courts when deciding whether or not to impose a duty to advise on a bank.[341] Indeed, in *Barnes* itself,[342] Ralph Gibson J laid particular stress on the fact that the borrower was 'a businessman of full age and competence' when rejecting a duty to consider the prudence of the transaction from the borrower's point of view. In contrast, in *Woods* v. *Martins Bank Ltd*,[343] Salmon J was clearly influenced, when imposing a fiduciary duty of care on the bank regarding its investment advice, by the fact that the claimant was

---

[337] *Hedley Byrne & Co. Ltd* v. *Heller and Partners Ltd*, n.327 above. See generally *Henderson* v. *Merrett Syndicates Ltd*, n.291 above; *White* v. *Jones* [1995] 2 AC 145 (HL); *Williams* v. *Natural Life Health Foods Ltd* [1998] 2 All ER 577 (HL); *Phelps* v. *Hillingdon LBC* [2001] 2 AC 619 (HL); *Customs & Excise Commissioners* v. *Barclays Bank plc*, [2007] 1 AC 181, [19] (HL). See further Ch. 5, Sect. 4(iii) above.

[338] [1995] CLC 1557, discussed in Ch. 5, Sect. 4(iii) above. Cf. *Murphy* v. *HSBC Bank plc*, n.329 above, where Silber J held that the bank had not assumed any responsibility to borrowers who (a) following the bank's initial recommendation, had appointed their own solicitors and accountants to advise them; (b) had not paid the bank for advice; (c) had greater knowledge than the bank of the project to be financed by the loan; (d) knew other people from whom they could seek relevant advice; (e) saw their role at the start of the negotiations as that of selling themselves and their project to the bank; and (f) had not asked the bank for advice.

[339] The bank's brochure indicated that borrowers could expect to receive 'tailor-made' advice for business ventures and that 'your bank manager will help you to decide how much you can readily afford to invest'. Cf. *Wilkins* v. *Bank of New Zealand* [1998] DCR 520.

[340] Ch. 5, Sect. 4(iii) above.

[341] *Foti* v. *Banque Nationale de Paris* (1989) 54 SASR 354, 423–427, affd. [1990] Aust. Torts Rep. 81,025 (SASC). See also *Bankers Trust International plc* v. *P. T. Dharmala Sakti Sejahtera* [1995] Bank. LR 381, 394; *JP Morgan Chase Bank* v. *Springwell Navigation Corp.* [2008] EWHC 1186 (Comm.), [264], [432], [448], [455]; *Titan Steel Wheels Ltd* v. *Royal Bank of Scotland plc* [2010] EWHC 211 (Comm.), [94]–[96]. See further P. Nankivell, 'The Liability of Australian Banks for Swiss Franc Loans' in W. Blair (ed.), *Banks, Liability and Risk* (3rd edn., London, 2001).

[342] *Williams & Glyn's Bank Ltd* v. *Barnes*, n.67 above.   [343] [1959] 1 QB 55.

a gullible young man (albeit a 30-year-old!) with no business experience.[344] Accordingly, in practice, banks should exercise care when dealing with financially inexperienced borrowers, and should probably inform them that the lender is primarily concerned with its own interests and not those of the borrower—'the difficulty may be to reconcile that relatively unhelpful businesslike approach with the sentiments expressed in the bank's publicity'.[345]

(ii) **Management and termination of the facility**

In the United States defaulting borrowers have sometimes claimed damages for a lender's alleged failure to meet its implied obligation of 'good faith' when dealing with a customer.[346] Such claims are typically made upon the termination of a line of credit, upon acceleration of payment under a note, or at foreclosure on collateral.[347] Bankers have been held liable even when exercising an express contractual power under a loan agreement. The duty of good faith can arise under common law[348] or commercial statute.[349] In contrast, English law knows no general doctrine of good faith,[350] but has instead 'developed piecemeal solutions in response to demonstrated problems of unfairness',[351] including such concepts as election, estoppel, waiver, and relief against forfeiture.

Under English law, the loan facility's terms are paramount. The courts will construe those terms to give effect to the parties' intention, but only rarely will the courts imply additional duties into loan contracts, such as a duty to increase the facility, or to give adequate notice of its refusal to do so.[352] Nevertheless, the lender must be careful to act consistently with the loan agreement's terms, otherwise the borrower may be able to raise a case of estoppel or waiver.[353] The courts have no general power to review the fairness of terms imposed on corporate borrowers and, although there are specific areas where relief from harsh bargains may be available—such as in relation to penalties—a general doctrine of 'unconscionability' is not yet a clearly recognized part

---

[344] Nowadays, *Woods* would probably be decided on the basis of the *Hedley Byrne* principle: L.S. Sealy, 'Fiduciary Obligations, Forty Years On' (1995) 9 *JCL* 37, 42.

[345] J. Wadsley (ed.), *Penn & Shea's Law Relating to Domestic Banking* (2nd edn., London, 2000), [5-073]. See also J. Wadsley, n.335 above, 354–355, who calls for the imposition of a 'duty on the act of lending' when the bank's statements or conduct lead to the customer's justified reliance on the bank.

[346] J.J. Norton, 'Lender Liability in the United States' in W. Blair (ed.), n.341 above. See also D.R. Fischel, 'The Economics of Lender Liability' (1989) 99 *Yale Law Journal* 131.

[347] *Reid* v. *Key Bank*, 821 F 2d 9 (1st Cir. 1987); *KMC* v. *Irving Trust*, 757 F 2d. 752 (6th Cir. 1985); *Martin Speciality Vehicles* v. *Bank of Boston*, 87 Bankruptcy Reporter 752 (Bankruptcy Ct. D Mass. 1988), revsd. on other grounds, 97 Bankruptcy Reporter 721 (D Mass. 1989); *Duffield* v. *First Interstate Bank of Denver*, 13 F 3d 1403 (10th Cir. 1993), cert. denied, 13 June 1994; *Reger Development LLC* v. *National City Bank*, 592 F.3d 759 (7th Cir., 2010).

[348] The duty usually arises under state law rather than federal law: *Restatement (Second) of Contract* (St. Paul, Minn.), s.205.

[349] Uniform Commercial Code, s.1-203. The UCC governs security agreements under Art. 9 (Secured Transactions), but there is uncertainty whether the UCC also covers other aspects of secured loans themselves.

[350] *Walford* v. *Miles* [1992] 2 AC 128, 138 (HL).

[351] *Interfoto Picture Library Ltd* v. *Stiletto Visual Programmes Ltd* [1988] 1 All ER 348, 353 (CA).

[352] *Williams & Glyn's Bank Ltd* v. *Barnes*, n.67 above; *Socomex Ltd* v. *Banque Bruxelles Lambert SA*, n.64 above.

[353] *Emery* v. *UCB Bank plc* (CA, 15 May 1997) (bank estopped from enforcing its security without further notice to the borrower following interim agreement to reschedule payments); *Bank of Ireland* v. *AMCD (Property Holdings) Ltd.*, n.65 above (waiver of condition precedents).

of English law.[354] Consumer borrowers fare somewhat better. The UTCCR 1999 allow the courts to set aside a term in a consumer contract that has not been individually negotiated 'if, contrary to the requirement of good faith, it causes a significant imbalance in the parties' rights and obligations arising under the contract, to the detriment of the consumer'.[355] As considered previously,[356] in *Director General of Fair Trading* v. *First National Bank plc*,[357] a term in the bank's standard loan agreement provided that, should the borrower default on his repayments, interest would continue to be payable at the contractual rate until any judgment obtained by the bank was discharged. The House of Lords held that the term was not unfair, as it did not cause a significant imbalance to the detriment of the consumer, but instead operated to prevent an imbalance the other way. Lord Hope stated that the purpose of the term was 'to ensure that the borrower does not enjoy the benefit of the outstanding balance after judgment without fulfilling the corresponding obligation which he has undertaken to pay interest on it as provided for in the contract'.[358]

English law takes a strict approach to the lender's right to terminate a loan facility. Where the lender has such a right to terminate under the facility agreement, the courts will not readily interfere with the exercise of that right. Exceptional cases arise where the lender has acted in such a way that it may be estopped from withdrawing the facility without reasonable notice, or may be deemed to have waived his right to do so, or if the language of the facility is unclear so that on a *contra proferentem* interpretation the court may impose an obligation to give reasonable notice.[359] This issue has arisen in particular with regard to overdraft or on demand facilities. The English courts are reluctant to imply a term to give reasonable notice before a bank refuses further finance under an overdraft or on demand facility.[360] Moreover, an express term calling for repayment of an overdraft or loan on demand will be upheld by the courts, unless the facility agreement, when construed as a whole, shows the term to be repugnant to its main provisions.[361] There are good commercial reasons for this. As Ralph Gibson J said in *Williams & Glyn's Bank* v. *Barnes*:[362]

> A bank which lent on overdraft might find urgent need for funds so lent because of commercial misfortunes or other demands and had to be free to call for repayment as and when the terms of the loan permitted it to do so.

---

[354] E. Ferran, *Company Law and Corporate Finance* (Oxford, 1999), 481.

[355] UTCCR 1999, reg. 5(1). So far as it is in plain intelligible language, no assessment of fairness is to be made of a term relating either to the definition of the subject-matter of the contract or to the adequacy of the price or remuneration (reg. 6(2)).

[356] Sect. 3(ii) above.   [357] N.212 above.   [358] Ibid., [46].

[359] *Crimpfil Ltd* v. *Barclays Bank plc* [1995] CLC 385 (CA). Cf. *Raypath Resources Ltd* v. *Toronto Dominion Bank* (1996) 135 DLR (4th) 261 (ACA) (customer's claim for negligent misrepresentation).

[360] *Socomex Ltd* v. *Banque Bruxelles Lambert SA*, n.64 above. Cf *KMC Co. Ltd* v. *Irving Trust Co.*, n.347 above, where the US Court of Appeals for the Sixth Circuit held that the implied obligation of good faith imposed a duty on the bank to give notice before withdrawing a line of credit from its borrower, at least in the absence of a valid business reason. The Sixth Circuit's conclusion that there was no business reason for terminating the facility without notice was influenced by the fact that the lender was adequately secured at the time (at 762). Not all courts in the United States have accepted this approach to the implied duty of good faith, especially where the terms give the lender a wide discretion to terminate or renew a facility: J.M. Paterson, 'Limits on a Lender's Right to Repayment on Demand: Construction, Implication and Good Faith?' (1998) 26 *ABLR* 258, 269–270; Norton, n.346 above, 365–6, 390–391. See also *Pavco Industries Inc.* v. *First National Bank of Mobile*, 534 So.2d 572 (1988); *Van Arnem Co* v. *Manufacturers Hanover Leasing Corporation*, 776 F. Supp. 1220 (EDM, 1991).

[361] Sect. 2(ii) above.   [362] N.67 above, 209.

It could be argued that a contract term entitling the bank to demand repayment at its discretion is either unenforceable under section 3(2)(b) of the UCTA 1977,[363] or not binding on the consumer under the UTCCR 1999.[364] In the former case the term would be exposed to a test of reasonableness, and in the latter to a test of unfairness. Ordinarily, however, where the term is reasonably transparent and the bank has not led the borrower reasonably to expect that it would not be relied on, the term should survive both tests and allow the bank to call in the overdraft or loan on demand. Even accepting that some borrowers are less commercially experienced than their lenders, borrowers may be expected to appreciate the scope of the term, leaving them with a choice to enter into a loan repayable on demand as opposed to some other type of arrangement. Furthermore, borrowers may benefit from such terms because credit costs (interest and other charges) are reduced, and borrowers who are confident about their prospects are able to signal their beliefs to lenders, and thus borrow on more attractive terms.[365]

The most the borrower will be given with an 'on demand' facility is a 'reasonable time' to repay, and a reasonable time is not the time it takes to refinance from another lender, but the short time it takes to set the mechanics of repayment into operation. In *Bank of Baroda* v. *Panessar*,[366] where the bank was held to be entitled to appoint a receiver within one hour of demanding repayment of an unspecified sum,[367] Walton J set out the test as follows:

> Money payable 'on demand' is repayable immediately on demand being made... Nevertheless, it is physically impossible in most cases for a person to keep the money required to discharge the debt about his person. He may in a simple case keep it in a box under his bed; it may be at the bank or with a bailee. The debtor is therefore not in default in making the payment demanded unless and until he has had a reasonable opportunity of implementing whatever reasonable mechanics of payment he may need to employ to discharge the debt. Of course, this is limited to the time necessary for the mechanics of payment. It does not extend to any time to raise the money if it is not there to be paid.

In *Sheppard & Cooper Ltd* v. *TSB Bank plc*,[368] Blackburne J held that the bank had been entitled to send in the receivers within 30 minutes after demanding repayment of over £600,000 from the debtor and provided further guidance on the 'mechanics of payment' test. First, the time available to the debtor to implement the mechanics of payment depends on the circumstances of the case. Secondly, if the sum demanded is an amount that the debtor will likely have in a bank account, the debtor must be given whatever time is reasonable in all the circumstances for the debtor to contact his bank and make the necessary arrangements for the relevant sum to be transferred from his bank to the creditor. Thirdly, if the demand is made outside banking hours, the time period is likely to

---

[363] As the borrower will invariably deal on the bank's written standard terms of business, the borrower might be able to argue that, by relying on such a term, the bank was 'claim[ing] to be entitled to render a contractual performance substantially different from that which was reasonably expected'. In *Paragon Finance plc* v. *Staunton* [2001] 2 All ER (Comm.) 1025, [75]–[77] (CA), the Court of Appeal held that varying the interest rate on a loan was not a change in 'contractual performance' falling within UCTA 1977, s.3(2)(b).

[364] R. Salter, n.207 above, 44–45.   [365] Fischel, n.346 above, 136–7; Paterson, n.360 above, 263.

[366] [1987] Ch. 335, 348. See also *Brighty* v. *Norton* (1862) 3 B & S 305; *R. A. Cripps & Son Ltd* v. *Wickenden* [1973] 1 WLR 944; *Sullivan* v. *Samuel Montagu & Co Ltd* [1999] BPIR 316; *Silven Properties Ltd* v. *Royal Bank of Scotland* [2002] EWHC 1976 (Ch), [108]; *Sucden Financial Ltd* v. *Fluxo-Cane Overseas Ltd* [2010] EWHC 2133 (Comm.), [33]; *Marex Financial Ltd* v. *Fluxo-Cane Overseas Ltd* [2010] EWHC 2690 (Comm.), [73]–[74] (seven hours is ample time to arrange payment).

[367] There is no need to specify the amount of the debt in the demand: *County Leasing Ltd* v. *East* [2007] EWHC 2907 (QB), [121]; *Bank of New York Mellon* v. *GV Films Ltd* [2009] EWHC 3315 (Comm.), [20].

[368] [1996] 2 All ER 654.

be longer than if the demand is made during banking hours and is likely to involve waiting until banks reopen. Fourthly, where proper demand has been made, and the debtor makes it clear to the creditor that the necessary moneys are unavailable, the creditor need not give the debtor any further time before treating him as in default—*Sheppard & Cooper* fell into this final category. Subsequently, in *Lloyds Bank plc v. Lampert*,[369] counsel argued before the Court of Appeal that the 'mechanics of payment' test should now give way to the more liberal approach prevailing in Canada and Australia where the borrower is given reasonable time to raise money elsewhere.[370] Kennedy LJ noted, however, that the liberality of the Commonwealth approach should not be overstated. His Honour referred to *Whonnock Industries Ltd v. National Bank of Canada*,[371] where the British Columbia Court of Appeal reviewed the authorities, and concluded that where the amount is very large Canadian law requires that lenders should give 'at least a few days' in which to meet the demand, but that reasonable notice may otherwise range from a few days to no time at all. It was unnecessary for Kennedy LJ to decide the issue finally, as the evidence suggested that, even with a few more days, the borrower in *Lampert* would have not found the £600,000 necessary to repay the overdraft. In any event, the suggestion that a borrower should be given a reasonable time, however short, to find an alternative financing has little to commend it—it simply does not provide the same level of commercial certainty as the 'mechanics of payment' test. A 'reasonable time' test would place the bank in the uncertain position of having to decide just how long to wait before enforcing its security: on the one hand, there is a real risk that the lender will underestimate the required period, particularly when it is unaware of the borrower's circumstances; on the other, the bank's security may become impaired if it waits too long.

(iii) Insolvency of the borrower[372]

When a borrower faces financial difficulties it may be in the bank's interests to provide the borrower with some assistance by entering into some sort of 'workout' arrangement, rather than exercising its formal rights under the loan agreement and enforcing any security it has.[373] Indeed, taking such steps may be premature if the problems are short-term and the borrower is able to trade out of them. As part of the modern 'rescue culture', banks are encouraged to explore the possibility of saving businesses rather than withdrawing

---

[369] N.71 above.

[370] The liberal approach seems more prevalent in Canada than Australia: *Ronald Elwyn Lister Ltd* v. *Dunlop Canada Ltd* (1982) 135 DLR (3d.) 1 (SCC); *Mister Broadloom (1968) Ltd* v. *Bank of Montreal* (1979) 101 DLR (3d.) 713, 723, revsd. on other grounds (1984) 4 DLR (4th) 74 (OCA); *Whonnock Industries Ltd* v. *National Bank of Canada* (1987) 42 DLR (4th) 1 (BCCA); *Kavcar Investments Ltd* v. *Aetna Financial Services Ltd* (1989) 62 DLR (4th) 277 (OCA); *National Bank of Canada* v. *Houle* [1990] 3 SCR 122 (SCC); *Royal Bank of Canada* v. *W. Got & Associates Electric Ltd* (2000) 178 DLR (4th) 385 (SCC); *Leby Properties Ltd* v. *Manufacturers Life Insurance Co* [2006] NBCA 14, [26]–[27]; *Royal Bank of Canada* v. *Profor Kedgwick Ltd* [2008] NBQB 78, [26]–[27]. See also M.H. Ogilvie, 'Canadian Bank Lender Liability: Semper Caveat Lendor' in W. Blair (ed.), n.207 above. For the Australian position, see *Bunbury Foods Pty. Ltd* v. *National Bank of Australasia Ltd* (1984) 153 CLR 491 (HCA); *Pioneer Park Pty Ltd* v. *ANZ Banking Group Ltd* [2002] NSWSC 883, [345]–[352]; *Iaconis* v. *Pynt* [2008] NSWSC 781, [9]–[13] (although some later cases have favoured a more narrow 'mechanics of payment' test: *Bond* v. *Hong Kong Bank of Australia Ltd* (1991) 25 NSWLR 286 (NSWCA); *Parras Holdings Pty. Ltd* v. *Commonwealth Bank of Australia* [1998] FCA 682, affd. [1999] FCA 391; *Commonwealth Bank of Australia* v. *Renstel Nominees Pty Ltd*, n.73 above).

[371] N.370 above. See also *Degelder Construction Co.* v. *Dancorp Developments Ltd* (1996) 73 BCAC 45, [24]–[27] (BCCA).

[372] R. Goode & A. Hockaday, 'Liabilities on Insolvency' in W. Blair (ed.), n.207 above.

[373] For the lender's duties when enforcing security, see Ch. 19, Sect. 2(viii) below.

their financial support prematurely.[374] A bank must take care, however, that its actions do not operate to the detriment of the borrower's other creditors and that it does not take undue advantage of the borrower's financial position to improve its position over the borrower's other creditors. The Insolvency Act 1986 contains provisions that reverse any such benefit derived by a bank from its dealings with a corporate customer by enabling a liquidator to unwind transactions at an undervalue,[375] voidable preferences,[376] and certain floating charges.[377] These provisions operate more harshly in relation to 'connected persons', which term includes the company's 'shadow directors'.[378] This raises the issue of whether a bank could ever be treated as a 'shadow director' of a corporate customer. Not only is this important for determining the bank's liability under the avoidance provisions just mentioned, but also for determining whether it can be liable for wrongful trading.[379] Such liability arises when a company's 'director', who knew or ought to have concluded that there was no reasonable prospect of the company avoiding insolvent liquidation fails to take every step to minimize loss to creditors that he ought to have taken, having regard to his general knowledge, skill, and experience and that could reasonably be expected of someone carrying out the same functions. In such circumstances, upon the company going into insolvent liquidation, the director may be liable personally to contribute to the insolvent company's assets. For these purposes, 'director' includes 'shadow director'.[380]

The standard definition of the term 'shadow director' is found in sections 251(1)–(2) of the Companies Act 2006 and section 22(5) of the Company Directors Disqualification Act 1986. For the purposes of 'wrongful trading' liability, the relevant definition is contained in section 251 of the Insolvency Act 1986:

> 'shadow director', in relation to a company, means a person in accordance with whose directions or instructions the directors of the company are accustomed to act (but so that a person is not deemed a shadow director by reason only that the directors act on advice given by him in a professional capacity).

In *Re a Company (No. 005009 of 1987)*,[381] Knox J held that there was a triable issue as to whether a bank had become a 'shadow director' of an insolvent company for the purposes of wrongful trading liability, but his Lordship declined to give reasons for this conclusion, and at trial this contention was 'rightly abandoned'.[382] As a result of these decisions, some concern was expressed about banks withdrawing support from their corporate borrowers at the first sign of financial trouble, rather than assist them through their financial difficulties, so as to avoid any risk of becoming a 'shadow director'. Millett J, writing extrajudicially, eased those concerns by stating that a bank would have to step outside the ordinary bank–customer relationship before being treated as a 'shadow director'.[383] Subsequently, in *Re Hydrodan (Corby) Ltd*,[384] Millett J held that, for a particular defendant to become a 'shadow director', it was necessary to allege and prove: (i) who the company's directors are, whether *de facto* or *de iure*; (ii) that the defendant directed those

---

[374] Banks will generally follow the voluntary code setting out best banking practice when dealing with small and medium-sized businesses in financial difficulties: BBA, n.179 above, 9–13. From March 2011, the *Principles* are incorporated in the *Lending Code* (March 2011).

[375] Insolvency Act 1986, s.238. See generally *Phillips* v. *Brewin Dolphin Bell Lawrie Ltd* [2001] 1 WLR 153 (HL).

[376] Ibid., s.239.   [377] Ibid., s.245.   [378] Ibid., s.249.   [379] Ibid., s.214.

[380] Ibid., s.214(7).   [381] [1989] BCLC 13.

[382] *Re M. C. Bacon Ltd* [1990] BCLC 324, 326. See also *Ultraframe (UK) Ltd* v. *Fielding* [2005] EWHC 1638 (Ch), [1264].

[383] Sir Peter Millett, 'Shadow Directorships—A Real or Imagined Threat to the Banks' [1991] *Insolvency Practitioner* 14.

[384] [1994] 2 BCLC 181, 183.

directors how to act in relation to the company or that he was one of the persons who did so; (iii) that those directors acted in accordance with such directions; and (iv) they were accustomed so to act. In *Re Unisoft Group Ltd (No. 2)*,[385] Harman J stressed that a shadow director is someone who controls the whole, or at least a majority, of the board. His Lordship added that the directors must act on that person's instructions or directions as a matter of regular practice and not just on isolated occasions.[386] Subservience or surrender of discretion by the board is not, however, required. As Morritt LJ stated in *Secretary of State for Trade and Industry* v. *Deverell*:[387]

> What is needed is that the board is accustomed to act on the directions or instructions of the shadow director...such directions and instructions do not have to extend over all or most of the corporate activities of the company; nor is it necessary to demonstrate a degree of compulsion in excess of that implicit in the fact that the board are accustomed to act in accordance with them.

Applying these principles, it is submitted that a typical lending relationship does not constitute the lender a 'shadow director' of the borrower. When negotiating the loan initially, the lender will usually require certain warranties and covenants from the borrower and impose conditions precedent to the borrower obtaining the funds. By these measures, the lender is not seeking to give directions or instructions, but is simply attaching terms and conditions to the provision and continuation of financial support that the company is free to accept or reject.[388] The bank has a greater dilemma, however, when there has been an event of default and it seeks to renegotiate the terms upon which it is prepared to continue supporting the borrower, as it must balance its own interests in recovering repayment against the risk of being treated as a 'shadow director' if it becomes too closely involved in the borrower's rescue package.[389] Nevertheless, the same result should follow as when the bank seeks to impose conditions at the very start of the relationship. In *Re PTZFM Ltd*,[390] Judge Baker QC rejected the allegation that the lenders had become 'shadow directors' of their borrower simply by 'trying to rescue what they could out of the company using their undoubted rights as secured creditors'. It was held that 'where the creditor made terms for the continuation of credit in the light of threatened default', the borrower was not accustomed to act in accordance with the lenders' instructions, as '[t]he directors of the company were quite free to take the offer or leave it'. In *Ultraframe (UK) Ltd* v. *Fielding*,[391] Lewison J accepted the broad proposition that a 'lender is entitled to keep a close eye on what is done with his money, and to impose conditions on his support for the company'. Indeed, where there was 'doubt whether the acts of a person were referable to an assumed directorship or to some other capacity...the person in question must be entitled to the benefit of the doubt'.[392]

There are other circumstances, however, where it may be more difficult to draw the line between simply 'advising' the borrower how to act, which will probably bring the lender within the 'professional adviser' safe harbour, and giving the kind of 'directions' or 'instructions' to the borrower that might make the lender a 'shadow director'. When assessing whether any particular communication between the alleged 'shadow director'

---

[385] [1994] BCC 766, 775. See also *Lord* v. *Sinai Securities Ltd* [2005] 1 BCLC 295; *Ultraframe (UK) Ltd* v. *Fielding*, n.382 above, [1270]–[1272].

[386] Ibid. See also *Ultraframe (UK) Ltd* v. *Fielding*, n.382 above, [1273]–[1278].

[387] [2001] Ch. 340, 355 (CA). See also *Ultraframe (UK) Ltd* v. *Fielding*, n.382 above, [1258]–[1263].

[388] E. Ferran, n.354 above, 483; E. Ferran, n.195 above, 41, 344–345.   [389] Ibid.

[390] [1995] 2 BCLC 354.   [391] N.382 above, [1268].

[392] *Re Mea Corporation Ltd* [2007] 1 BCLC 618, [86]–[90].

and the board constitutes a 'direction' or an 'instruction', the courts assess the matter objectively.[393] One problematic circumstance might be where the lender commissions a report on the borrower's affairs that the borrower implements.[394] In such a case, the safest course for the lender may well be to express the report's proposals for the company's rehabilitation as conditions for the lender's continued financial support. Whilst the borrower may in reality have little choice but to accept the lender's conditions, in legal terms the borrower has a choice between accepting the lender's proposals or having its liabilities accelerated—the existence of such a choice should generally negate any suggestion that the lender is a 'shadow director'.[395] The other problematic circumstance arises when the lender seeks to appoint a representative on the borrower's board. This should not prove particularly problematic,[396] as nominating one or more board representatives will not provide the lender with control of the whole, or a majority of the, board as required for a shadow directorship.[397]

(iv) Environmental liability

One might question why a commercial lender should be liable for environmental damage caused by a borrower. As Jarvis and Fordham have observed:[398]

> Banks do not pollute rivers. Why should they be responsible for the activities of their borrowers? If someone buys a car and kills a pedestrian the bank which provided the loan is not held responsible.

The reasons suggested for such liability[399] include political, economic, and legal considerations:[400] first, lenders provide the funds to enable the polluting activity to continue and may have made considerable profits from that activity; secondly, lenders have sufficiently 'deep pockets' to meet clean-up costs; and, thirdly, lenders are in a good position to investigate and require environmental compliance from their borrowers. Indeed, one need only examine the United States experience in implementing the 'Superfund' legislation to demonstrate how seriously lenders should take the risk of environmental liability. The Comprehensive Environmental Response Compensation and Liability Act 1980 (CERCLA), as amended, set up the 'Superfund' to be used by the Environmental Protection Agency to clean up contaminated sites. Those costs are then recoverable from 'potentially responsible parties', which includes the current 'owner or operator' of the site. Lenders will not be troubled by the risk of liability where they can rely on the 'secured creditor' exception which defines 'owner or occupier' to exclude 'a person, who, without participating in the management of a vessel or facility, holds indicia of ownership primarily to protect his security interest in the vessel or facility'.[401] This exemption gives rise to the issue of when a lender would be taken to have 'participated in the management'

---

[393] *Secretary of State for Trade and Industry* v. *Deverell*, n.387 above.

[394] *Re a Company*, n.381 above.

[395] *Re PFTZM Ltd*, n.390 above; *Ultraframe (UK) Ltd* v. *Fielding*, n.382 above, [1254]. See also Financial Law Panel, *Shadow Directorships* (London, 1994). There is always the risk that the arrangement may be struck down as a sham: Ferran, n. 354 above, 484.

[396] *Lord* v. *Sinai Securities Ltd*, n.385 above.

[397] *Kuwait Asia Bank EC* v. *National Mutual Life Nominees Ltd* [1991] 1 AC 187 (PC).

[398] J. Jarvis QC & M. Fordham, *Lender Liability: Environmental Risk and Debt* (London, 1993), 2.

[399] Ibid., 2; M. Fordham, 'A Rude Awakening' (1993) 143 *NLJ* 750.

[400] R.M. Auerback, 'Environmental Law, Practice and Liability: Background' in J.J. Norton, R.M. Auerback, & J.M. Gaba (eds.), *Environmental Liability for Banks* (London, 1995).

[401] 42 USC s.9601 (20)(A).

of a facility so as to lose its protection. In *United States* v. *Fleet Factors Corporation*,[402] the Eleventh Circuit Court of Appeals proposed a test based upon the lender's 'capacity to influence' the borrower's treatment of waste. It was not necessary for a creditor to be involved in day-to-day operational decisions, nor to participate in management decisions concerning hazardous waste. The court held that '[a] secured creditor will be liable if its involvement with the management of the facility is sufficiently broad to support the inference that it could affect hazardous waste disposal decisions if it so chose'.[403] Interestingly, the court observed that nothing prevented a secured creditor from monitoring any aspect of the borrower's business, nor did it prevent the secured creditor from becoming involved in 'occasional and discrete' financial decisions relating to the protection of its security interest.[404] *Fleet Factors* prompted the federal Environmental Protection Agency to promulgate a regulation that provided, *inter alia*, that the lender's ability to influence the borrower's activities would not be enough in future to impose liability.[405] In *Kelley* v. *Environmental Protection Agency*,[406] the DC Circuit declared the rule invalid on the ground that it was *ultra vires* the Environmental Protection Agency. This necessitated the passing, in September 1996, of the Asset Conservation, Lender Liability and Deposit Insurance Protection Act. Section 2502 (amending section 107 of CERCLA) provides that a lender is not liable for clean-up costs under CERCLA as long as: (a) pre-foreclosure, it does not take over control of environmental compliance at the borrower's facility, or substantially all its operational function; and (b) post-foreclosure, it seeks to sell or otherwise dispose of the facility within a reasonable time and on commercial terms.[407]

Turning to the position in the United Kingdom, there are potentially direct and indirect consequences of environmental liability for lenders. The most important *direct* consequence is the possibility that the lender itself may be held liable to pay a fine, clean-up costs, or compensation to affected persons (liability risks). The *indirect* consequences can be just as serious. Environmental compliance costs may affect the borrower's ability to service its debt (credit risks), and clean-up costs may reduce the value of an asset over which the lender has taken security (security risks).

(a) Indirect consequences

The cost of environmental compliance may affect the borrower's profitability and hence its ability to service its debt. Strict licensing regimes control various areas of commercial activity where there is a recognized risk of pollution. The compliance costs of meeting the conditions attached to such licences can be high. Failure to obtain a licence or a breach of licensing conditions can attract heavy fines.[408] Regulatory authorities have powers

---

[402] 901 F 2d. 1550 (11th Cir., 1990); cert. denied, 111 S Ct. 752 (1991).

[403] Ibid., 1557–1558. In *Re Bergsoe Metal Corporation*, 910 F 2d. 668 (9th Cir., 1990), the Ninth Circuit Court of Appeals held that the lender does not lose exemption merely by having the *power* to become involved in the borrower's management; the lender, but must exercise *actual* management authority before liability attaches.

[404] Ibid., 1558.

[405] *Fleet Factors* was remitted to the District Court which held that, even under the standards laid down by the Environmental Protection Agency, the lender was liable as the sale of the borrower's assets by the lender's agent, following foreclosure by the lender on its security interest on some of the borrower's inventory and equipment, had led to the release of toxic chemicals and asbestos and had been conducted 'with all the finesse of a Viking raiding party': 819 F. Supp. 1079 (SD 1993) and 821 F. Supp. 707 (SD Ga. 1993).

[406] 1994 WL 27881 (DC Cir. 1994).

[407] *Canadyne-Georgia Corporation* v. *Bank of America*, 174 F.Supp. 2d 1360 (2001).

[408] *Criminal* liability can arise from the 'integrated pollution control' (IPC) regime under the Environmental Protection Act 1990 (EPA 1990), Pt. 1, and its replacement, the 'pollution prevention and control' (PPC) regime under the Pollution Prevention and Control Act 1999. See also Pollution Prevention

under assorted legislation to require the polluter or the owner or occupier of land to clean up pollution.[409] Again, the costs may be high and insurance cover may be difficult, if not impossible, to obtain. At common law, the borrower may be held liable for polluting activity in the tort of nuisance, under the rule in *Rylands* v. *Fletcher*,[410] for negligence, or for breach of statutory duty. Moreover, a borrower can incur liability abroad as a result of operations there, or because of products exported there, or because of operations in the United Kingdom causing damage there (for example, the potential for claims against United Kingdom electricity generators for damage caused by acid rain in Germany and Scandinavia).[411] Most Member States have implemented strict liability regimes for environmental damage.[412]

The lender's security over land may prove worthless because of contamination. The threat of contamination can undermine property values as much as actual contamination. For example, on 1 April 2000 a new, and potentially far-reaching, contaminated land regime came into operation in England under Part IIA of the Environmental Protection Act 1990 (EPA 1990), as amended by the Environment Act 1995.[413] The regime's main objective is to provide an improved system for the identification and remediation (clean-up) of contaminated land, where the contamination is causing unacceptable risks to human health or the wider environment. This regime enables local authorities in England, or the Environment Agency in the case of certain 'special sites'—referred to as the 'enforcing authority' in Part IIA of the EPA 1990—to serve a remediation (clean-up) notice on an 'appropriate person' specifying what the recipient must do to clean up the site.[414] Every 'enforcing authority' must keep a public register recording designations of contaminated land, specified clean-up works, voluntary works undertaken, and any

and Control (England) Regulations 2000, S.I. 2000/1973. It is an offence to carry out heavily polluting industrial processes (for example, chemical and metal manufacture) without or in breach of a licence to do so. EPA 1990, s.33 makes it a criminal offence to dispose of controlled waste on a site without or in breach of a licence. In relation to contaminated land, it is a criminal offence to fail to remediate when instructed to do so: EPA 1990, Pt. IIA. EPA 1990, s.79 lists certain statutory nuisances, failure to abate which when required to do so is a criminal offence under EPA 1990, s.80. Ss. Water Resources Act 1991, ss. 85 & 161A provide for the offences of polluting controlled water without or in breach of a licence, and failing to clean up water when instructed to do so. Discharge of trade effluent into sewers is covered by the Water Industry Act 1991, s.118.

[409] Clean-up liabilities include those for IPC (EPA 1990, s.27) or PPC (Pollution Prevention and Control Act 1999, Pollution Prevention and Control (England) Regulations 2000, S.I. 2000/1973); controlled waste (EPA 1990, s.59); contaminated land (EPA 1990, Pt. IIA); statutory nuisance (EPA 1990, s.81); and water pollution (Water Resources Act 1991, s.161A).

[410] (1868) LR 3 HL 330. Foreseeability of harm by the defendant is a prerequisite to recovery of damages: *Cambridge Water Co.* v. *Eastern Counties Leather plc* [1994] 2 AC 264 (HL). See also *Transco plc* v. *Stockport Metropolitan Borough Council* [2004] 2 AC 1 (HL); *Colour Quest Ltd* v. *Total Downstream UK plc* [2009] EWHC 540 (Comm.).

[411] S. Cromie, 'Contaminated Land. The Risks for Lenders' (1997) 8(1) *PLC* 33, 37.

[412] P. Thieffry & D. McKenney, 'Lender's Liability in the European Union' in Norton, Auerback, & Gaba (eds.), n.400 above, 83–88; N.S.J. Koeman (ed.), *Environmental Law in Europe* (The Hague, 1999). See also Directive 2004/35 of the European Parliament and of the Council of 21 April 2004 on environmental liability with regard to the prevention and remedying of environmental damage ([2004] OJ L143/56), amended by Directive 2006/21 ([2006] OJ L102). For some of the voluminous literature on EC environmental law, see J. Scott, *EC Environmental Law* (London, 1998); L. Kramer, *EC Environmental Law* (6th edn., London, 2006).

[413] EPA 1990 is supplemented by the Contaminated Land (England) Regulations 2000, S.I. 2000/227. See also Department for Environment, Food & Rural Affairs, Circular 01/2006 on Contaminated Land (hereafter 'Guidance Notes'). See also Contaminated Land (Scotland) Regulations 2000, S.I. 2000/178; Contaminated Land (Wales) Regulations 2001, S.I. 2001/2197.

[414] EPA 1990, s.78F provides that the 'appropriate person' is, in the first instance, the person who caused or knowingly permitted the contamination ('Class A person') or, if such a person cannot be found after reasonable enquiry, the land's current owner or occupier ('Class B person').

appeals lodged.[415] There is no statutory mechanism for removing land from the register, even after the clean-up operations, although the Department of Environment, Food and Rural Affairs has issued Circular 01/2006 on Contaminated Land (hereafter 'Guidance Notes'), indicating how the regulator may 'sign off' a site on an informal basis.[416] Where the 'enforcing authority' itself incurred the costs of cleaning up contaminated land, it could always prove in the landowner's liquidation for those costs,[417] but under the EPA 1990 regime the 'enforcing authority' may now serve a charging notice on the owner that will constitute a charge on the premises consisting of or including the relevant contaminated land. The 'enforcing authority' will have the powers and remedies available under the Law of Property Act 1925 to enforce the charge,[418] including the power to appoint a receiver and sell the property. The enforcing authority's charge is likely to have priority over all other interests in the land[419] and over an insolvent polluter's other creditors. Similarly, where pollution clean-up costs are incurred by the bank's receiver during the course of its receivership over a borrower's property, it has been suggested that those costs reduce the assets of the polluter available for distribution to its creditors, as those assets are to be used for the clean-up rather than being paid to secured creditors.[420]

(b) Direct liability

There are a number of legislative provisions under which a lender could potentially incur environmental liability and could even incur overlapping liability under several provisions—for example, the new contaminated land regime overlaps with other statutory provisions dealing with waste,[421] and a lender may be liable under a number of environmental protection statutes if it has 'caused or knowingly permitted' damage to the environment.[422] Other statutory provisions and common law principles impose liability on the 'owner or occupier' of land, usually where the original polluter cannot be found.[423] These are the 'triggers' of liability. Pollution is 'caused' on proof of some connection, however direct or indirect, between the polluter's activities and the pollution in question. Simply carrying on the activity that caused the pollution is enough. There is no

---

[415] Ibid., s.78R.   [416] Guidance Notes, n.413 above, Annex 2, [15.6].

[417] *Re Shirley* (1996) 129 DLR 105 (OGD).   [418] EPA 1990, s.78P.

[419] *Westminster City Council* v. *Haymarket Publishing Ltd* [1981] 1 WLR 677 (CA) (land charge representing unpaid rating surcharge under the General Rate Act 1967 took priority over all other interests in the land).

[420] *Panamericana de Bienes y Servicos* v. *Northern Badger Oil & Gas* (1991) 81 DLR (4th) 280, 291 (ACA). See also *Bank of Montreal* v. *Lundigrans Ltd* (1992) 318 APR 36, [25]–[33]; *Harbert Distressed Investment Fund* v. *General Chemical Canada Ltd* [2006] OJ No. 3087.

[421] EPA 1990, Pt. IIA contains provisions dealing with overlap.

[422] Water Resources Act 1991, s.85 (offence of causing or knowingly permitting any polluting matter to enter 'controlled waters'); EPA 1990, s.33 (offence to knowingly cause or knowingly permit controlled waste to be deposited without a licence or in a manner likely to cause pollution of the environment or harm to human health); EPA 1990, s.78F(2) (clean up of contaminated land by person who caused or knowingly permitted the contaminating substances to be present in, on or under the land).

[423] EPA 1990, s.59 (owner or occupier of land upon which controlled waste has been deposited without a licence is liable for the cost of removing it, unless he can show that he did not knowingly cause or knowingly permit the deposit of the offending waste); EPA 1990, s.78F(4) (where, after reasonable enquiry, the original polluter cannot be 'found' the owner or occupier for the time being becomes the 'appropriate person'); EPA 1990, ss.80–81 (the owner or occupier of land can be ordered to abate a statutory nuisance if the person responsible for it cannot be found, or to pay the local authority's costs in abating it). At common law, the owner or occupier can be held liable for nuisance or under *Rylands* v. *Fletcher*, n.410 above, even if he did not create the nuisance or bring the damaging substance onto his land.

requirement of knowledge, negligence, or fault.[424] The chain of causation may be broken by intervening factors such as a third party act or an Act of God,[425] but more than one person may be held to have caused the same pollution, even though they act quite independently of each other.[426]

A person may 'permit' pollution to take place by allowing it to occur or continue; in other words, not taking those steps that might possibly have avoided the pollution altogether or prevented it from continuing. This covers allowing pollution to remain on a site, even though it was already there when the site was acquired. A person can 'permit' pollution to take place, however, only when he has sufficient power to prevent it. Thus, in *Berton* v. *Alliance Economics Investment Co. Ltd*,[427] the phrase 'to permit' was defined to include 'abstain[ing] from taking reasonable steps to prevent [an] act where it is within a man's power to prevent it'.[428] There must also be knowledge of the circumstances bringing about the pollution. In the context of the new contaminated land regime, this probably means that liability flows from mere knowledge that substances are present on the land, even though one does not realize that those substances render the land contaminated within the meaning of Part IIA of the EPA 1990.[429] A person's knowledge may be actual or constructive, so that turning a blind eye or deliberately refraining from inquiry may attract liability,[430] and a person is deemed to know that which a person could in all the circumstances be expected to know.[431]

The theme linking the phrases 'cause' and 'knowingly permit' is that of 'control'. Either the defendant has control of the activity that causes pollution or such control that he could have prevented it. This raises the issue of whether merely lending money to a borrower who operates a polluting facility gives the lender such control over the borrower's affairs as to make it vulnerable to direct environmental liability under these 'triggers' of liability. The greater danger probably lies under the 'knowingly permitting' trigger. The mere act of lending is probably not sufficient to trigger liability, as the act of lending money by itself does not involve the necessary element of control over the borrower's business. That said, loan agreements commonly contain provisions requiring compliance with relevant legislation and a lender is usually entitled to declare an event of default and demand repayment if it discovers that the borrower is breaching environmental legislation. If such a demand would close down the business and thus prevent further pollution, then it may be arguable that the lender had the power to prevent the contamination and failed to use it. The Guidance Notes indicate, however, that the better view is probably that no such liability attaches, since 'the lender, irrespective of any covenants it may have required from the polluter as to its environmental behavior, would have no permissive rights over the land in question to prevent contamination occurring or continuing'.[432] Moreover, the new contaminated land regime does contain

---

[424] *Alphacell Ltd* v. *Woodward* [1972] AC 824 (HL); *Environment Agency* v. *Empress Car Co. (Abertillery) Ltd* [1999] 2 AC 22, 29 (HL); *Express Ltd* v. *The Environment Agency* [2004] EWHC 1710 (Admin), [22].

[425] Whether a third party act breaks the chain of causation is a matter 'of degree and depends on a proper attribution of responsibility': *Alphacell Ltd* v. *Woodward*, n.424 above, 835; *Environment Agency* v. *Empress Car Co. (Abertillery) Ltd*, n.424 above, 25, 35–36.

[426] *Att.-Gen.'s Reference (No. 1 of 1994)* [1995] 1 WLR 599 (CA).   [427] [1922] 1 KB 742 (CA).

[428] Ibid., 759. See also *Test Valley Investments* v. *Tanner* [1964] Crim. LR 62 (DC). 'Permit' has been defined as having 'the possession of the power to prevent' the relevant contamination: Guidance Notes, n.413 above, Annex 2, [9.8]–[9.15].

[429] *Current Law Annotated Statutes 1995* (London, 1996), iii, 25–154.

[430] *Westminster City Council* v. *Croyalgrange Ltd* [1986] 1 WLR 674, 684 (HL).

[431] *Schulmans Incorporated Ltd* v. *National Rivers Authority* [1993] *Env. LR* D.1.

[432] Guidance Notes, n.413 above, Annex 2, [9.11]. See also J. Marks, 'Domestic Environmental Liability', ch. 5 in W. Blair (ed.), n.341 above, [5.18].

a special exemption for lenders,[433] which excludes from the category of Class A 'appropriate persons'—namely, those who are responsible for remediation costs by reason of having 'caused or knowingly permitted' contaminating substances to be in, on, or under the land—a person who provides or withholds 'financial assistance to another person'. The provision of financial assistance includes making loans or providing any other form of credit, as well as investing in the undertaking of a company by acquiring share capital or loan capital of that company (as long as a holding company/subsidiary relationship is not thereby created).[434] This exemption only applies, however, if there are others who will be left in the 'Class A' category after its operation.[435] It is important to note though that the Guidance Notes specifically provide that the existence of this exemption should not be read as undermining its initial statement that lenders are not caught by the phrase 'knowingly permit' in the first place.[436]

Whilst the simple act of lending may not put the lender at risk of environmental liability, the risks increase the more closely the lender becomes involved with its borrower's affairs, particularly if it crosses the line to become a 'shadow director',[437] and knowingly fails to use its powers to stop the borrower breaching environmental law. As considered previously,[438] however, a bank will not readily be treated as a 'shadow director', even if it appoints a nominee to the board[439] and provided any rescue package is framed in terms of a condition for the continuation of the bank's support.[440] The risk of liability becomes particularly acute, however, where the borrower has defaulted and the lender forecloses or goes into possession of the property.[441] By taking over the borrower's business and continuing its activities after it has foreclosed or gone into possession, a lender may itself incur liabilities under the 'causing' or 'knowingly permitting' triggers. For the purposes of the new contaminated land regime, an 'owner' is a person, other than a mortgagee not in possession, who is or would be entitled to receive the rent for the property.[442] It has been suggested that the exclusion of a mortgagee who is not in possession from this category hardly seems necessary as 'there seems no reason why the existence of a mortgage should increase the chances of a lender being found liable under any of the provisions under consideration, until the lender attempts to enforce its rights under it'.[443] The position of the mortgagee in possession seems much less secure. Indeed, a mortgagee in possession was held liable for local authority work,[444] and liable to pay a rating surcharge as it was he 'who has control of the letting'.[445] Essentially, by going into possession, the mortgagor is deemed to have taken the necessary degree of control of the mortgagor's affairs to warrant liability. In contrast, in *Midland Bank* v. *Conway*,[446] where the bank collected rents paid by its customer's tenants, it was held not to be an 'owner', for the purpose of being served with a noise abatement notice under section 343 of the Public

---

[433] Guidance Notes, n. 413 above, Annex 3, D.48(a).   [434] Companies Act 2006, s.1159.

[435] Guidance Notes, n.413 above, Annex 3, D.41(c).   [436] Ibid., Annex 3, D.47.

[437] Text to n.380 above.   [438] Sect. 5(iii) above.

[439] *Kuwait Asia Bank EC* v. *National Mutual Life Nominees Ltd*, n.397 above; *Lord* v. *Sinai Securities Ltd*, n.385 above.

[440] *Secretary of State for Trade and Industry* v. *Deverell*, n.387 above; *Re PFTZM Ltd.*, n.390 above.

[441] Cf. Asset Conservation, Lender Liability and Deposit Insurance Protection Act 1996, s. 2502.

[442] EPA 1990, s.78A(9).   [443] Cromie, n.411 above, 36.

[444] *Maguire* v. *Leigh-on-Sea UDC* (1906) 95 LT 319.

[445] *Westminster City Council* v. *Haymarket Publishing Ltd*, n.419 above, 680; cf *Re Sobam BV* [1996] 1 BCLC 446.

[446] [1965] 1 WLR 1165 (CA).

Health Act 1936,[447] but a mere 'conduit-pipe' or 'office boy'—the element of control was missing.[448] Nevertheless, there can be little doubt that by receiving rents lenders run an increased risk of liability.[449]

In contrast, there is no statutory definition of the term 'occupier' in the EPA 1990. Accordingly, 'occupation' should probably be defined as involving some form of possession and control over premises.[450] In *Meigh* v. *Wickenden*,[451] a receiver and manager was held liable under sections 130 and 133 of the Factories Act 1937 for failure to ensure adequate guards on machinery in a factory that the receiver was continuing to run. The legislation made the 'occupier' liable and this was held to include the receiver because of his potential power of management and control, rather than any need for the actual exercise of control.[452] It has been suggested that this approach resembles the 'capacity to influence' test in *Fleet Factors*.[453] Perhaps the case is best read, however, in the particular context of the statute in issue, which imposed strict liability for breaches of workplace safety.[454] Indeed, some degree of caution must be exercised when seeking to define a term used in one statute for the purposes of defining the same term in another statute. 'No useful progress can be made... by inquiring what meaning the courts have given [the word "occupier"] in reported cases, for they draw their meaning entirely from the purpose for which and the context in which they are used'.[455] What is clear, however, is that in the context of the new contaminated land regime both foreclosure and possession render the lender the 'owner or occupier' of contaminated land (a Class B 'appropriate person'), and liable for clean-up costs if no Class A person can be found.[456] During the parliamentary debates, banks and other institutions, such as the Council of Mortgage Lenders, expressed concern that the Environment Act 1995, which introduced Part IIA into the EPA 1990, would expose lenders to liability in situations that they could not readily control. What if the lender is in possession by default where the borrower abandoned the property and sent the keys to the lender? What if the lender took possession to a limited extent to secure the property or deal with obvious hazards? The Government proved unsympathetic to these concerns and refused to give lenders special treatment in these circumstances.[457]

Where the borrower defaults the safer option for the secured lender may be to appoint a receiver under the terms of its debenture.[458] The mere appointment of a receiver over the borrower's assets will not *per se* bring home to the lender any environmental liability

---

[447] An owner of property was defined as 'the person for the time being receiving the rackrent of premises... whether on his own account or as agent or trustee for any other person'.

[448] In *Midland Bank* v. *Conway*, n.446 above, 1170, 1172–1173, the Court of Appeal unanimously emphasized that the case concerned only the ordinary banker-customer relationship, but that if there were 'special circumstances' the bank might be liable.

[449] Jarvis & Fordham, n.398 above, 131–134; G. Beringer & E. Thomas, 'Lenders and Environmental Liability' (1991) 2 (11) *PLC* 3, 8.

[450] *Wheat* v. *E. Lacon & Co.* [1966] AC 552 (HL). See also R. Lee, 'Lending and the Environment in the UK: Environmental Risks for Bankers' in Norton, Auerback, & Gaba (eds.), n.400 above, 60–61.

[451] [1942] 2 KB 160.   [452] Ibid., 164–165.

[453] J. Jarvis QC, M. Fordham & D. Wolfson, 'Domestic Environmental Liability' in R. Cranston (ed.), *Banks, Liability and Risk* (2nd edn., London, 1995), 162.

[454] Lee, n.450 above, 60.

[455] *Southern Water Authority* v. *Nature Conservancy Council* [1992] 1 WLR 775, 781 (HL) (quoting *Madrassa Anjuman Islamia* v. *Municipal Council of Johannesburg* [1922] 1 AC 500, 504 (HL)); *Revenue & Customs Commissioners* v. *Principal and Fellows of Newnham College in the University of Cambridge* [2008] UKHL 23, [9].

[456] EPA 1990, s.78F(4)–(5). This would include a dissolved company: Guidance Notes, n.413 above.

[457] HL Debs., vol. 560, col. 1445, HL Debs., vol. 562, cols. 165, 1040, 1042–1043.

[458] The Enterprise Act 2002 severely curtailed a lender's power to appoint an administrative receiver under a floating charge (subject to exceptions), but as the new law is not retrospective, there is likely to

of the receiver. At least until the point of liquidation, the receiver acts as the company's agent, not that of the charge-holder.[459] However, a lender will be held liable for the defaults of a receiver if it 'gives him directions or interferes with his conduct of the realisation'.[460] Following liquidation it will be a question of fact whether the receiver acts on his own behalf or as agent for the mortgagee.[461] The lender cannot completely ignore, however, the risk of paying for environmental liability incurred by the receiver—as 'owner or occupier' or for 'causing or knowingly permitting' pollution—as a receiver will usually require an indemnity from the lender thereby indirectly imposing environmental liability upon the lender. The lender would be well advised to limit the extent of the indemnity by excluding liability for contamination or other pollution caused or knowingly permitted by the receiver or, if that is unacceptable to the receiver, for contamination or other pollution resulting from his unreasonable acts or omissions. The contaminated land regime does, however, provide some protection to receivers, which will accordingly indirectly benefit lenders who have given the receiver an indemnity. Neither a receiver nor administrator is personally liable for the cost of any remedial work, unless it is referable to his own unreasonable acts or omissions.[462] Although it has been suggested that 'ordinary receivers appointed under a debenture or other security who are not licensed insolvency practitioners would not be covered by this exemption',[463] this view is incorrect as it ignores the express wording of section 78X(4)(f)(ii) of the EPA 1990 extending the exemption to 'a person acting as receiver or receiver and manager . . . by virtue of his appointment as such by an order of a court *or by any other instrument*'.

(c) Conclusion

The banking industry has been quick to point out the dangers of too readily imposing liability on lenders for environmental damage.[464] Uncertainty as to the extent of the lender's potential liability, together with the risk of being held liable for huge uninsurable losses that could affect a bank's capital adequacy requirements, could inhibit lending to environmentally sensitive industries. There is evidence from the United States that, following *Fleet Factors*, businesses in environmentally sensitive industries found it more difficult to raise money from banks and that insurance companies have limited environmental cover.[465] Hopefully, English courts will not adopt the 'capacity to influence' approach that has been subsequently rejected in the United States. Lenders not exercising operational control should not incur liability.[466] Nevertheless, lenders cannot ignore the risks of direct or indirect environmental liability entirely, even though some such risks

be a long period of overlap between the old and new regimes: Insolvency Act 1986, s.72A, inserted by the Enterprise Act 2002, s.250.

[459] *Gaskell* v. *Gosling* [1897] AC 575 (HL); *Dolphin Quays Developments Ltd* v. *Mills* [2008] EWCA Civ. 385, [23]–[27]. An administrative receiver is deemed to be the company's agent unless and until the company goes into liquidation: Insolvency Act 1986, s.44(1)(a).

[460] *Standard Chartered Bank* v. *Walker* [1982] 1 WLR 1410, 1416 (CA); *National Bank of Greece S-A* v. *Pinios Shipping Co. (No. 1)*, n.86 above.

[461] *American Express International Banking Corp.* v. *Hurley* [1985] 3 All ER 564; *TSB Bank plc* v. *Platts (No.2)* [1997] BPIR 302.

[462] EPA 1990, s.78X(3)–(4).   [463] T. Hellawell, *Contaminated Land* (London, 2000), 24.

[464] BBA, 'Position Paper on Banks and the Environment' (London, July 1993); E. Welch & T. Parker, 'A Bank's View of Lender Liability in Environmental Legislation' [1993] *JIBL* 217.

[465] P. Blackman, 'Lender Liability and Deep Pockets; Managing Environmental Risks in Financing Businesses in Europe' in H. Enmarch-Williams (ed.), *Environmental Risks and Rewards for Business* (London, 1996).

[466] European Commission, *White Paper on Environmental Liability*, COM(2000)66 final. See now Directive 2004/35 of the European Parliament and of the Council of 21 April 2004 on environmental

may be reasonably remote. In any event, the risk of environmental liability can be considerably reduced by following safe lending practices. Those practices attempt to tread the (sometimes fine) line between the lender being fully aware of all risks in respect of the lending and avoiding conduct that might be characterized as participation in or control of the borrower's business. The following points are offered as general guidance to banks and other lenders:[467] (i) ensure that relevant staff are properly trained; (ii) carry out environmental audits prior to lending and before enforcing security; (iii) ensure adequate warranties, covenants, and events of default are contained in contractual documentation, including a requirement that the borrower comply with environmental laws and allowing the lender to declare an event of default, if he does not; (iv) take an assignment of any environmental insurance policy that the borrower may have;[468] (v) consider taking security over assets other than land; and (vi) when enforcing security, seek methods of obtaining the benefit of that security which do not involve 'ownership' or 'occupation' of secured property.

liability with regard to the prevention and remedying of environmental damage ([2004] OJ L143/56), amended by Directive 2006/21 ([2006] OJ L102).

[467] Jarvis & Fordham, n.398 above, 168–174; Cromie, n.411 above, 38–40; Beringer & Thomas, n.449 above, 8; J. Marks, n.432 above, [5.41]–[5.57].

[468] Insurance cover for gradually occurring pollution damage, as opposed to that caused by a catastrophe, is increasingly difficult to find: Blackman, n.465 above, 99; Cromie, n.411 above, 38.

18

Securities for Bankers' Advances: The General Part

1 Nature, purpose, and classification of securities

(i) The nature of 'security'

When lending to customers, banks often require the customer to provide 'security' for the loan to improve the bank's chances of repayment. In commerce, the word 'security' is used in more than one sense. Thus shares or debentures issued by a company, which are often furnished by a shareholder or debenture-holder to their lender to secure a loan, are loosely called (company) 'securities',[1] hence the term 'asset securitization'.[2] Moreover, the term 'security' is sometimes also used to describe negotiable instruments issued by debtors to secure instalments due under a credit facility.

In the context of bank lending, a bank is said to have 'security' where it has proprietary or possessory rights in its customer's—or a third party's—property that it may exercise in order to enforce repayment of the loan.[3] The essence of 'security' is that the creditor's rights in the property (the 'collateral') generally bind third parties.[4] Other rights, which may also 'secure' the payment of the debt, are not generally regarded as 'security' in this sense. Thus guarantees and indemnities, which are also sometimes described as 'securities',[5] are distinct arrangements under which a third party—the surety—agrees to assume personal liability[6] if the debtor defaults or causes loss to the creditor. The former arrangement is a guarantee; the latter involves an indemnity.[7] Certain contractual arrangements, such as contractual set-offs,[8] subordination agreements, flawed asset arrangements,[9] and negative pledge clauses,[10] are also not true 'security' as they only confer personal rights on

---

[1] Shares are, equally confusingly, sometimes called 'equities'.   [2] See further, Ch. 21, Sect. 2(vii).

[3] See the discussion of the meaning of 'security' (in the Insolvency Act 1986) in *Bristol Airport plc* v. *Powdrill* [1990] Ch. 744, 760 (for the purposes of the Insolvency Act 1986, s.248(b)(i)) and in *Razzaq* v. *Pala* [1997] 1 WLR 1336 (for the purposes of ibid. s.383(2)). For a general discussion, see R. Goode, *Legal Problems of Credit and Security* (4th edn., London, 2009), ch. 1 and H. Beale, M. Bridge, L. Gullifer, & E. Lomnicka, *The Law of Personal Property Security* (Oxford, 2007), chs. 1 & 2.

[4] A further source of confusion is that the term 'security' is sometimes used to refer to property that is the subject of the security interest and not to the security interest itself. The US term 'collateral' is useful to denote the property itself, reserving 'security' for the creditor's rights over it.

[5] These come within the definition of 'security' in the Consumer Credit Act 1974, s.189(1): see Sect. 4 below.

[6] Although this personal liability may itself be 'secured' by rights over the surety's (or another's) property.

[7] Because of the importance of guarantees in bank lending, they are considered in Ch. 22 below.

[8] See Ch. 21, Sect. 3(iii).   [9] See ibid.   [10] See Ch. 19, Sect. 4(iv).

the creditor against the debtor and do not necessarily affect other parties (in particular, competing creditors).[11]

More problematic is the question whether retention of title arrangements, such as hire-purchase agreements, conditional sales,[12] and long-term leases, are 'security'. Conceptually, such arrangements differ from other contracts for security because the finance company or supplier, which lets or sells the property, *retains* ownership. It does not rely on the debtor conferring on it an interest in property initially owned by him.[13] Accordingly, where the relevant context confines the meaning of 'security' to rights granted by the debtor,[14] retention of title is not 'security'. Economically, though, the finance company or supplier reserves title in the property in order to secure payment of the instalments or rentals and when all the rentals or instalments are paid the debtor usually acquires title to the property. This is expressly provided in a hire-purchase agreement and conditional sale.[15] In practice, this is contemplated in some leases where the lessee is simply given the opportunity of acquiring the chattel concerned for its (usually small) residual value. Hence it is becoming increasingly common to term such arrangements 'quasi-security'.[16]

Some financing transactions are documented as sales rather than as secured transactions: instead of creating rights in property as security for a loan, the trader may 'sell' the property to the financier. Thus, in block discounting and factoring[17] the trader 'sells' the debts due to him from his customers to a financier at a discount. The financier eventually receives the proceeds of the debts, the trader usually agreeing to repurchase any bad debts. So-called 'repos' are transactions whereby transferable investments, such as shares or bonds, are sold to a financier on terms that they will be repurchased (hence 'repo') by the seller at a price reflecting the fact that the seller will have had the use of the funds representing the original price until then. Another example, of less relevance to banks, is where the financier purchases goods from the trader at a discount and allows the trader to retain possession and either to resell them as its agent[18] or to repurchase them.[19] Are these genuine 'sales' to the financier conferring an absolute interest or are these disguised secured loans with any discount being disguised interest and any rights to repurchase being disguised rights of redemption? The question may be important for a number of reasons. Transactions secured by way of a 'charge' in the case of corporate debtors are

---

[11] But the competing creditor may be affected by such contractual arrangements. For example, an assignee of a debt may be affected by rights of set-off. See the discussions by R.M. Goode in (1989) 15 *Mon. LR* 361, 362.

[12] Including sales with 'Romalpa' clauses. See Ch. 19, Sect. 2(vi).

[13] See the basic analysis in *Helby* v. *Matthews* [1895] AC 471 and note *Armour* v. *Thyssen Edelstahlwerke AG* [1991] 2 AC 339: 'security' connotes a grant by the debtor of rights over his property.

[14] As noted below (Sect. 4), the Consumer Credit Act 1974 defines 'security' in s.189 (for the purposes of the Act) to mean a right *provided by the debtor*. Hence hire-purchase or conditional sale (or hire) is not 'security' for the purposes of that Act. Similarly, the Companies Act 2006, s.860 (see Ch. 19, Sect. 4(iii)) only renders charges granted *by* a company registrable.

[15] Where the agreement is a genuine hire-purchase agreement the hirer is given an option to purchase the goods, whilst in a conditional sale the property passes automatically when all instalments have been paid: *Forthright Finance Ltd* v. *Carlyle Finance Ltd* [1997] 4 All ER 90 (CA).

[16] See the Law Commission Report, *Company Security Interests*, Law Com. No. 296 (2005) and Beale, Bridge, Gullifer & Lomnicka, n.3 above, ch. 5.

[17] See Ch. 21, Sect. 2(ii) and *Re George Englefield* [1933] Ch. 1 (CA); *Lloyd's and Scottish Finance Co. Ltd* v. *Cyril Lord Carpets Sales Ltd* [1992] BCLC 609 (but decided in 1979), discussed by Giddins (1980) 130 *NLJ* 207.

[18] *Welsh Development Agency* v. *Export Finance Co. Ltd* [1992] BCLC 148 (CA).

[19] *Curtain Dream plc* v. *Churchill Merchandising* [1990] BCLC 925.

registrable whilst 'sales' are not.[20] A 'sale' will not breach a prohibition in a contract, constitution, or statute against 'borrowing' or creating 'security'. A 'sale' does not confer any right of redemption on the seller[21] nor create any obligation on the purchaser to account for any profit on resale or confer a right on the purchaser to recover any shortfall on resale.[22] Special statutory provisions, for example, transaction avoidance provisions on insolvency[23] and consumer protection provisions,[24] may be applicable in the case of 'security' but not outright sale. Finally, the taxation[25] and accounting[26] consequences differ between a sale and security transactions.

The leading case on the question of characterizing such transactions is now *Welsh Development Agency* v. *Export Finance Co. Ltd.*[27] Also of relevance is Lord Millett's two-stage analysis of characterization in general in *Agnew* v. *Commissioners of Inland Revenue:*[28] first, determine (as a matter of fact) what obligations the parties have agreed to undertake and second, determine (as a matter of law) what the legal effect is. In the former case the Court of Appeal also acknowledged that it must look at the 'substance' of the transaction and not be bound by the 'labels' used by the parties. Moreover, 'substance' means its legal and not economic effect. Therefore, after a full review of appellate authorities in other contexts,[29] the court accepted that the contract at issue, which was documented and operated as a sale and agency agreement, was indeed a sale and not a (registrable) charge. The advice of Lord Devlin in *Chou Yoong Hong* v. *Choong Fah Rubber Manufactory Ltd*[30] was cited: 'if in form it is not a loan, it is not to the point to say that its object was to raise money for one of them or that the parties could have produced the same

---

[20] Companies Act 2006, s.860. See generally, Ch. 19, Sect. 4(iii) and *Re George Inglefield Ltd* [1933] Ch. 1; *Welsh Development Agency* v. *Export Finance Co. Ltd* [1992] BCLC 148 (CA); *Orion Finance Ltd* v. *Crown Financial Management Ltd* [1996] BCC 621. But *any* general assignment (whether outright or by way of charge) of book debts by an individual is registrable under the Insolvency Act 1986, s.344, see Ch. 21, Sect. 2(v) below.

[21] See Sect. 3 below.   [22] See *Re George Inglefield Ltd* [1933] Ch. 1, 27–28.

[23] Insolvency Act 1986, s.239, as amended. During administration, the permission of the administrator or court is needed to take any steps to enforce a 'security' (or repossess goods under a hire-purchase agreement) whilst this is only needed to begin or continue 'legal process' in any other case.

[24] See Consumer Credit Act 1974, considered in Sect. 4. See also *Olds Discount Co. Ltd* v. *John Playfair Ltd* [1938] 3 All ER 275 (purchase of book debts not moneylending) and *Chou Yoong Hong* v. *Choong Fah Rubber Manufactory Ltd* [1962] AC 209 (PC), noted below.

[25] For example, sales are liable to stamp duty and VAT whilst security transactions are not. When a debt is sold any profit is taxable. When a loan is obtained on the security of a debt the interest may be tax deductible.

[26] Security transactions appear as loans on the balance sheet, a consequence sought to be avoided in *Welsh Development Agency* v. *Export Finance Co. Ltd* [1992] BCLC 148 (CA). Debts used as security remain on the balance sheet as assets whilst 'sold' debts do not.

[27] [1992] BCLC 148 (CA), noted by E. Ferran, 'Form and Substance in Financing Transactions' [1992] *CLJ* 434; F. Oditah, 'Financing Trade Credit: Welsh Development Agency v Exfinco' [1992] *JBL* 541. See now, A. Berg, 'Recharacterisation after Enron' [2003] *JBL* 205. See also *Orion Finance Ltd* v. *Crown Financial Management Ltd* [1996] BCC 621 (CA). Compare *Re Curtain Dream plc* [1990] BCLC 925 (sale and repurchase held to be a disguised loan, the repurchase being an equity of redemption) with *Orion Finance Ltd* v. *Crown Financial Management Ltd* [1996] 2 BCLC 78, 84 (option to repurchase not necessarily disguised equity of redemption). See the extensive discussion in Beale, Bridge, Gullifer & Lomnicka, n.3 above, ch. 2.

[28] [2001] 2 AC 710. The issue was whether the charge was fixed or floating (see further Ch. 21, Sect. 2(ii) below), but his approach was applied to the more general context of whether security or absolute interests are created by Lord Scott in *Smith* v. *Bridgend BCB* [2001] UKHL 58, [53]; [2002] 1 AC 336, 355.

[29] Including cases on the licence/lease distinction (*Street* v. *Mountford* [1985] AC 809) and tax evasion/avoidance (*Ramsay* v. *IRC* [1982] AC 300).

[30] [1962] AC 209, 216 (PC) a case holding that buying bills of exchange at a discount was distinct from moneylending.

result more conveniently by borrowing and lending money'. In particular, the amount of the discount, although dependent on when the financier eventually received payment, was held not to be disguised interest. A similar conclusion had previously been reached in cases concerning factoring and block discounting where it was further held that obligations to repurchase bad debts were not disguised rights of redemption.[31] Whether a transaction creates a registrable charge has also arisen in the context of reservation of title provisions and here the rights of the supplier over the proceeds of sale of the goods have generally been characterized as rights by way of charge.[32]

(ii) **The purpose of security**

Security provides the creditor with a means—through the exercise of proprietary or possessory rights—of obtaining payment, in addition to mere reliance on the debtor's personal liability. Accordingly, the main object of security is to protect the creditor should the debtor be unable or unwilling to repay. Inability to pay through insolvency is the most important situation where security is particularly valuable. Instead of joining the other unsecured creditors who will at best receive only a fraction of what they are owed, a secured creditor can look to their security for the satisfaction of their debt.[33] Moreover, a secured creditor may generally pursue their security rights without regard to the constraints on dealings with the debtor's property on insolvency. In addition, the creditor's proprietary rights enable the creditor to assert their claim to the property against other claimants such as execution creditors or distraining landlords and sometimes to 'trace' the security rights into any proceeds resulting from the disposal of the property. If the debtor is unwilling to pay, a threat to enforce the security is often enough to encourage a debtor to find a means to fulfil the secured obligation.

(iii) **Classification of securities**

Securities can be classified in a number of ways. One classification is based on the rights that the arrangement confers on the creditor. Another looks at the manner in which the security is created: consensually or by operation of law. Another looks to the extent of the property covered by the security.

The first classification divides securities into proprietary securities and possessory securities. The former type encompasses all arrangements whereby the debtor confers on the creditor proprietary rights in the relevant property. Such rights enable the creditor to seize the goods if the debtor defaults or becomes insolvent and to satisfy the debt from the proceeds of their sale. But during the currency of the arrangement—whilst the debtor complies with the agreement—the property is left in the debtor's possession. The debtor is, therefore, able to utilize it. The mortgage, both over chattels and over real property, as well as a fixed and a floating charge granted by a corporation, fall into this group.

Possessory securities, as indicated by their name, are based on the acquisition by the creditor of possession of the property that serves as the collateral. The classic example

---

[31] *Re George Englefield* [1933] Ch. 1 (CA); *Olds Discount Co. Ltd* v. *John Playfair Ltd* [1938] 3 All ER 275; *Lloyd's and Scottish Finance Co. Ltd* v. *Cyril Lord Carpets Sales Ltd* [1992] BCLC 609 (but decided in 1979), discussed by Giddins, n.17 above. See Ch. 21, Sect. 2(ii).

[32] *Pfeiffer (E.) Weinkellerei-Weinkauf GmbH* v. *Arbuthnot Factors Ltd* [1988] 1 WLR 150; *Tatung (UK) Ltd* v. *Galex Telesure Ltd* (1989) 5 BCC 325; *Compaq Computers Ltd* v. *Abercorn Group Ltd* [1993] BCLC 603. See further Ch. 21, Sect. 2(vi).

[33] See further Sect. 2 below.

is the pledge, in which the creditor is given custody of a chattel until the discharge of the debt by the debtor. Bills of exchange, some marketable securities, and documents of title, such as bills of lading, can also be the subject of a pledge. The pledge confers on the creditor a right to sell the chattel involved and to satisfy the debt from the proceeds.[34] The creditor's rights are therefore identical to those acquired under a proprietary security. However, custody of the chattel gives the creditor extra protection, as the debtor is unable to whisk the chattels away in breach of the arrangement. Another possessory security is the lien, which is of particular importance to bankers.[35] From the debtor's point of view, a possessory security carries a patent disadvantage. The debtor does not enjoy exclusive possession and hence the unrestricted right to use the chattel. However, it will be shown that, to some extent, this difficulty may be avoided by the release of the item covered by the possessory security to a third party or custodian, who holds it on behalf of the creditor but has the power to grant access to the debtor.[36]

The division of security devices into proprietary and possessory securities is not appropriate in the case of securities over money or choses in action, such as contractual rights. The very concept of possession is inapplicable, and that of property is subject to substantial modification. There is thus no room for a pledge or a lien over a contractual right. A security over such an item is effected by means of an assignment, which may be an absolute one or by way of charge.[37] The assignment of book debts, of an amount standing to the credit of a customer's bank account, and of an insurance policy are examples that are considered further below.[38]

The second classification of securities divides them into consensual securities (created by agreement between the parties) and securities created by operation of law. There are only four categories of consensual securities:[39] the pledge, the contractual lien, the mortgage, and the charge. Various types of liens (other than the contractual lien) are created by operation of law, for example, the unpaid vendor's lien, bankers' liens,[40] and various statutory liens.

The third classification of securities divides them into open-ended and closed-ended securities. An open-ended security is one that covers all or some of the property of the debtor for the time being. The classic example is the floating charge.[41] It 'hovers over' the corporate debtor's property without precluding the disposal of that property in the ordinary course of trade. Items so disposed of cease to be covered by the security, but the charge applies to property acquired after its creation. When the charge 'attaches' or 'crystallizes'—usually upon the debtor's default—it becomes, in effect, a fixed charge covering the debtor's property as at that time. A banker's lien is similar in nature.[42] It attaches to items, such as shares acquired by the customer, whilst the share certificates are in the bank's custody. Such securities are open-ended, as the chattels or assets covered by them continue to change and, basically, are unaffected by the security interest unless the debtor is in default.

A closed-ended security attaches to a given chattel or item of property. Examples are a mortgage over land,[43] a fixed charge given by a body corporate over a specific piece of

---

[34] See Ch. 20, Sect. 1(ii) below.   [35] See Ch. 20, Sect. 2 below.   [36] See Ch. 20, Sect. 1(v) below.

[37] Note that an absolute assignment may be either equitable or statutory; an assignment by way of charge is necessarily an equitable assignment: Ch. 21, Sect. 1 below.

[38] See Ch. 21.   [39] See *Re Cosslett (Contractors) Ltd* [1998] Ch. 495, 508, *per* Millett LJ.

[40] Considered in Ch. 20, Sect. 2.

[41] See generally, Ch. 19, Sect. 4(ii) where it is noted that it is the freedom that the debtor has to dispose of the collateral, rather than the nature of the collateral, that is the hallmark of a floating charge.

[42] See generally, Ch. 20, Sect. 2.   [43] See generally, Ch. 19, Sect. 2.

machinery,[44] and a pledge of given documents of title.[45] An assignment of a specific chose in action, such as a life policy, is also a closed-ended security.[46] But an assignment by way of charge of a company's book debts resembles an open-ended security if it covers the debts outstanding from time to time. On the other hand, an absolute assignment of book debts, stipulating for their discharge to the assignee is, of course, a closed-ended security.[47]

Of the classifications of securities, their division into proprietary and possessory securities is more closely related to the legal nature of the arrangement involved. The classification of securities into the open-ended and the closed-ended types is based on economic factors. It is, therefore, preferable to adopt the former classification in a work like this. Accordingly, Chapter 19 deals with proprietary securities and Chapter 20 with possessory securities. Securities over choses in action are discussed in Chapter 21. A final chapter on guarantees, Chapter 22, has also been included. Although not regarded as 'security' in the strict sense of rights in relation to property, guarantees are so important in the context of bank lending that some discussion is necessary.

There are, however, three problems that are of importance in respect of all security arrangements. The first is the effect of a valid security in the debtor's insolvency,[48] the second is the nature of the equity of redemption,[49] and the third concerns the relevant provisions in the Consumer Credit Act 1974.[50]

2 The effect of valid security in insolvency

When a private individual or an unincorporated business, such as a partnership, becomes insolvent, the position is governed by the Insolvency Act 1986.[51] The bankrupt's estate, or property, is vested in the trustee in bankruptcy,[52] who realizes it for the purpose of dividing the proceeds among the unsecured creditors. The bankrupt's debts are, for this purpose, divided into three groups: preferential claims, claims of general creditors, and deferred claims. The preferential claims, which include wages payable to employees for the four months immediately preceding the receiving order, are paid in priority to all other claims.[53] The balance of the amount recovered by the trustee from the realization of the bankrupt's assets is divided on a *pro rata* basis among the debtor's general creditors.[54] Obviously, not all the assets are necessarily utilized at one and the same time. Once the preferential claims have been settled, a dividend payable to the general creditors is declared whenever the trustee acquires sufficient funds for making significant payments.[55]

---

[44] See generally, Ch. 19, Sect. 4.　　[45] See generally, Ch. 20, Sect. 1(iv).
[46] See generally, Ch. 21, Sect. 4.　　[47] See further, Ch. 21, Sect. 2(iii).　　[48] Sect. 2 below.
[49] Sect. 3 below.　　　[50] Sect. 4 below.

[51] Until 1985, the position was governed by the Bankruptcy Act 1914. This Act was repealed and replaced by the Insolvency Act 1985 which, in turn, was repealed and replaced by the 1986 Act. For the sake of clarity, and to assist readers consulting older authorities, reference is made in some cases not only to the current provision but also to the sections of the 1914 Act replaced by the 1986 Act.

[52] Insolvency Act 1986, s.306, derived from the Bankruptcy Act 1914, s.18.

[53] Insolvency Act 1986, ss.328, 386, and Sched. 6, as amended by the Enterprise Act 2002 (and see the Bankruptcy Act 1914, s.33). As regards corporations, see the 1986 Act, s.40 (receivership) and s.175 (winding up). Liability to the Inland Revenue and Customs and Excise in respect of certain 'withholding' taxes such as income tax deducted at source and VAT used to give rise to 'preferential debts' until the Enterprise Act 2002.

[54] Insolvency Act 1986, s.328(3) (and see the Bankruptcy Act 1914, s.62(1)).

[55] Insolvency Act 1986, s.324; and see, as regards winding-up, ibid., s.168(4).

Any balance left after the general creditors have been satisfied is used to satisfy certain deferred claims.

Most trade creditors are general creditors. So are an insolvent bank's customers, in respect of money standing to the credit of their accounts.[56] Similarly, a bank is a general creditor in respect of any unsecured overdraft or loan granted to a defaulting customer. It is obvious that any creditor who falls within the group of a bankrupt's general creditors stands to incur substantial loss; if the debtor were able to discharge his running debts, he would not be forced into bankruptcy.

The main purpose of a security is to enable the creditor to recover the debt due to him in priority to the general creditors.[57] The object of the security is to arrange that some property—be it real property, chattels, or choses in action—be utilized in the debtor's insolvency to satisfy the secured creditor's claim in priority to those of the general creditors. If the proceeds of the collateral exceed the amount of the debt, the balance is paid over to the trustee in bankruptcy and forms part of the general assets or 'the estate' of the bankrupt. If the proceeds are less than the amount due, the secured creditor can prove for the deficiency as a general creditor.[58] The secured creditor's position depends, therefore, both on the validity of his security and on the adequacy of the value of the property covered by it. Frequently, the validity of a security is subject to the observance of certain formalities. Thus, a security over book debts effected as a 'general assignment' is void against the trustee in bankruptcy unless registered under the Bills of Sale Act 1878.[59]

The principles of the law of bankruptcy concerning the rights of creditors, which have just been discussed, apply with certain modifications to the winding-up of companies.[60] However, it will be shown that in some respects securities furnished by bodies corporate are governed by principles differing to a certain extent from those applicable to securities provided by individuals and by unincorporated business firms. For example, a body corporate can grant a security over after-acquired property, whilst other debtors' securities in practice attach only to property which is in existence at the time of the arrangement.[61]

Both proprietary securities and possessory securities generally give adequate protection to the creditor against the debtor's insolvency. Possessory securities, though, have the added advantage of generally protecting the creditor against any unauthorized dispositions by the debtor. This result is due to practical rather than conceptual reasons. Thus, if the creditor acquires a security by way of pledge, the debtor is no longer able to dispose of the property, as it is no longer in his possession. The debtor regains the ability to make dispositions of the pledged property if the creditor relinquishes his possession. But in such a case the pledge is usually destroyed.[62]

---

[56] The point has been clear since the decision of the House of Lords in *Foley* v. *Hill* (1848) 2 HLC 28, where the relationship of banker and customer was defined as one of creditor and debtor. See Ch. 5, Sect. 3.

[57] The security cannot constitute the claim a preferential one, as the list of such claims is exhaustively set out in Sched. 6 to the Insolvency Act 1986, as amended by the Enterprise Act 2002, Sched. 26.

[58] Insolvency Act 1986, s.269 (cf. Bankruptcy Act 1914, s.7(2), Sched. 2, r.10).

[59] Insolvency Act 1986, s.344. See Ch. 21, Sect. 2(v).

[60] Under the earlier regime, the relevant provisions of the Bankruptcy Act 1914 were applied to the winding-up of corporations by the Companies Act 1948, s.317 (which was replaced by the Companies Act 1985, s.612). The Insolvency Act 1986 repealed this provision; at present the similarity in the provisions of the winding-up of companies and the bankruptcy of individuals results from the fact that both procedures have been brought under the umbrella of the Insolvency Act 1986; and see the Insolvency Rules 1986, S.I. 1986/1925, as (extensively) amended.

[61] Ch. 19, Sect. 3(ii) below.   [62] Ch. 20, Sect. 1 below.

The position is less certain in the case of proprietary securities. Some of them do not aim at protecting the creditor against dispositions of the debtor's property to third parties. Thus the floating charge, which 'hovers over' all the company's assets, envisages that dealings in the company's ordinary business will continue as before. Accordingly, the company may sell property subject to the floating charge, and the purchaser acquires a good title although aware of the existence of the charge.[63] The assumption is that the charge will 'hover over' the proceeds and will cover replacement property within its terms. The question is discussed separately in respect of the various proprietary securities covered in Chapter 19.

3 The right of redemption

The right of redemption is a principle developed in the context of mortgages over land.[64] Its basic tenet is simple. The debtor (mortgagor) is entitled to redeem or free his property from the mortgage by repaying the amount due at the time of discharge.[65] The right is available even where the date of repayment has passed[66] and despite the fact that valid steps have been taken to put the mortgaged property up for sale.[67] The right of redemption cannot be excluded by agreement. A provision to this effect is considered a 'clog' on the equity of redemption and is void.[68] The parties may, however, agree that the right should not be exercisable for a given period during the currency of the agreement.[69] The right is effectively lost only when the mortgaged property has been sold by the mortgagee upon the debtor's default.[70]

The person primarily entitled to exercise the right of redemption is the debtor (mortgagor), but so are other parties who have an interest in the property mortgaged. Persons encompassed in this group are a second mortgagee[71] who, on exercising the right, steps into the first mortgagee's shoes, a surety or guarantor of the debt,[72] or even the mortgagor's tenant who wishes to remain in occupation.[73] Any attempt to restrict the right

---

[63] Ch. 19, Sect. 4(ii) and (iv) below.   [64] See further, Ch. 19, Sect. 2(ix).

[65] *Fairclough* v. *Swan Brewery Co. Ltd* [1912] AC 565 (PC); *Krelinger* v. *New Patagonia Meat and Cold Storage Co. Ltd* [1914] AC 25, 48. At common law a mortgagor had no right to redeem *before* the redemption date in the contract (*Brown* v. *Cole* (1845) 14 Sim 427; 60 ER 424), unless this was unduly postponed (and hence a 'clog', see below) but a debtor under an agreement regulated by the Consumer Credit Act 1974 (see Ch. 3, Sect. 5(ii), above) has an indefeasible right to repay early: CCA 1974, s.94.

[66] *Re Moss; Levy* v. *Sewill* (1887) 31 Ch. D 90; *Cromwell Property Investment Co. Ltd* v. *Western & Toovey* [1934] Ch. 322.

[67] See, for a general analysis, *Duke* v. *Robson* [1973] 1 WLR 267.

[68] *Noakes & Co. Ltd* v. *Rice* [1902] AC 24, 30. See Ch. 20, Sect. 2(ix) for the case law on a mortgagee's right to purchase the collateral (held to be a 'clog' in *Samuel* v. *Jarrah Timber and Wood Paving Corporation* [1904] AC 323 (HL) and *Jones* v. *Morgan* [2002] EWCA Civ 995, but upheld as part of a separate contract in *Reeve* v. *Lisle* [1902] AC 461 (HL)). But debentures issued by a company may be irredeemable: Companies Act 2006, s.738.

[69] *Teevan* v. *Smith* (1882) 20 Ch. D 724, 729; *Williams* v. *Morgan* [1906] 1 Ch. 804 (postponement for 14 years held valid); *Knightsbridge Estates Trust Ltd* v. *Byrne* [1939] Ch. 441; *Re Rudd and Son Ltd* [1986] BCC 98 (CA). But in certain cases, a postponement for a long time, such as 28 years, may be regarded as unreasonable: *Morgan* v. *Jeffreys* [1910] 1 Ch. 620. See also *Fairclough* v. *Swan Brewery Co* [1912] AC 565 (PC); *Davis* v. *Symons* [1934] Ch. 442.

[70] *Waring (Lord)* v. *London and Manchester Assurance Company Ltd* [1935] Ch. 310. See, generally, *Halsbury's Laws of England* (4th edn., reissue, London, 2005) vol. 32, paras. 307, 502–535.

[71] *Smith* v. *Green* (1844) 1 Coll. 555, 563; *Pearce* v. *Morris* (1869) LR 5 Ch. App. 227.

[72] By operation of the doctrine of subrogation.   [73] *Tarn* v. *Turner* (1888) 39 Ch. D 456.

of redemption of the mortgagor or other given parties is void as a 'clog' on the equity.[74] A party that exercises the right must, however, redeem the property in full.[75]

Redemption is effected by means of a notice served on the mortgagee. Where the mortgage is for a fixed term, the mortgagee must, if the contract so provides, be given adequate time to make alternative arrangements for the investment of his money.[76] If the mortgagee is not given adequate notice, the debtor may have to pay interest for the period involved. Notice is not required where the mortgagee has taken possession of the property, has made a demand for payment in full, or has instituted proceedings to realize the security.[77] Similarly, the debtor can of course repay without notice any debt payable on demand— such as an overdraft—and thereupon redeem any security.[78]

Traditionally, the right of redemption has been applicable in the case of mortgages and charges over land and chattels. However, it is equally available in respect of other types of proprietary securities.[79] It has also been applied in the case of some possessory securities, such as the classic pledge.[80] In the case of other security arrangements, such as those in relation to agreements regulated by the Consumer Credit Act 1974, similar rights are conferred by that statute.[81] These rights are of major importance, as they mitigate the harshness that can otherwise manifest itself in agreements providing for security.

4 Effect of the Consumer Credit Act 1974 on securities

(i) Basic terms and structure of Part VIII of the Act

Part VIII of the Consumer Credit Act 1974[82] makes provision concerning securities that secure agreements regulated by that Act.[83] The relevant sections are not drafted specifically with a view to affecting the relationship of banker and customer, but they have a considerable impact on securities taken by banks with respect to regulated credit agreements. The main object of the Act is to confer certain protections on a person providing security. It is necessary to review the relevant basic definitions of the Act and the provisions, and to consider the impact of Part VIII on banking practice.

The fundamental term 'security' is broadly defined in the Act and encompasses a mortgage, a charge, a pledge, a bond, a debenture, an indemnity and a guarantee, a bill or note, and 'any other right provided by the debtor, or at his express or implied request by another person, to secure the performance of the agreement involved'.[84] The Act therefore applies both to securities furnished by the debtor and to those provided at his request by another. It thus affects the traditional forms of securities taken by banks such as charges over land, shares, insurance policies, and bank balances. It also extends to guarantees

---

[74] *Salt* v. *Marquess of Northampton* [1892] AC 1.   [75] *Hall* v. *Heward* (1886) 32 Ch. D 430.

[76] *Cromwell Property Investment Co. Ltd* v. *Western & Toovey* [1934] Ch. 322 (six months usually).

[77] *Bovill* v. *Endle* [1896] 1 Ch. 648.

[78] See, as regards a temporary loan, *Fitzgerald's Trustee* v. *Mellersh* [1892] 1 Ch. 385.

[79] See, for example, *Salt* v. *Marquess of Northampton* [1829] 1 AC 1, where an assured was allowed to redeem a life policy assigned by him for security. See also *Davis* v. *Symons* [1934] Ch. 442: collateral included endowment policies maturing just before redemption date.

[80] See Ch. 20, Sect. 1(ii) below.   [81] Ch. 2, Sect. 5(v) above.

[82] Ss.105–126. See A.G. Guest & M. Lloyd, *Encyclopaedia of Consumer Credit Law* (loose-leaf, London, 1974), paras. 2-106–2-114 and R.M. Goode, *Consumer Credit Law and Practice* (loose-leaf, London, 1977), vol. 1C, ch. 37.

[83] For the definition of 'regulated agreement', see Ch. 2, Sect. 5(ii) above.

[84] Consumer Credit Act 1974, s.189(1).

and indemnities. However, as the security has to be *provided by* the debtor or another (at his request), retention of title transactions do not give rise to 'security' within the Act.[85] Moreover, it is thought that the common term in bank loan contracts where a bank reserves the right to take missed repayments from other accounts kept by the debtor with the bank, in so far as this confers rights on the bank *beyond* its common law right to combine current accounts,[86] constitutes 'security'.

The provisions of the Act apply not only to securities given in respect of concluded regulated agreements but also to securities in relation to prospective regulated agreements.[87] In the latter case, the security becomes subject to the main provisions of Part VIII only at the time the agreement is concluded.[88] Until then, the security is unenforceable. Furthermore, up to that time the person who agrees to furnish the security may, by serving notice on the creditor, invalidate the security under section 106.[89] In practice, these provisions do not pose serious problems to banks. If the main agreement, such as the contract for a loan, is not executed, the bank does not require the security. If the surety exercises his right of withdrawal before the conclusion of the underlying contract, the bank in turn is entitled to refuse to extend credit.

The Act defines two other basic terms. First, the term 'surety' is defined so as to include the debtor if he furnishes security, any third party who provides security, and any 'person to whom his rights and duties in relation to the security have passed by operation of law'.[90] The last branch of the definition is of importance where a third party is subrogated to the original surety's rights. A bank that pays a customer's debts may occasionally be in such a position. Secondly, a 'security instrument' is a document whereby a third party provides security.[91] The Act distinguishes between a security granted by the debtor and a security effected by a third party. The latter security must be in writing—the document being a 'security instrument'—and must comply with regulations made under section 105.[92] It will be shown that, in some respects, the Act applies different regimes to the two types of arrangement. Banks, of course, take securities of both types.

The Act introduces four measures aimed at regulating the taking of securities in respect of regulated agreements. First, section 105 regulates the form and contents of securities.[93] A security which is not properly executed is enforceable only on a court order.[94] If such an order is not granted, the security is avoided by section 106 and the surety is entitled to be repaid any amount realized from the security. It will be shown that these provisions have an impact on banking practice. Secondly, it is provided that specified information be furnished to sureties.[95] These provisions impose certain cumbersome duties on banks but, in reality, do not pose serious obstacles to the ordinary functioning of the banking

---

[85] See Sect. 1(i) above. In more complex financing arrangements it may be a moot point whether a creditor's rights are provided at the debtor's request (and hence are 'security' within s.189(1)): see *Governor and the Company of the Bank of Scotland* v. *Euclidian (No. 1) Ltd* I [2007] EWHC 1732 (Comm.).

[86] See Ch. 7, Sect. 3 and see *Bradford Old Bank Ltd* v. *Sutcliffe* [1918] 2 KB 833 (CA).

[87] Consumer Credit Act 1974, s.189(1).   [88] Ibid., s.113(6).   [89] Considered further below.

[90] Consumer Credit Act 1974, s.189(1).

[91] Ibid., s.105(2). By s.105(6), subs. (1) (and hence subs. (2)) does not apply to a security provided by the debtor.

[92] See ibid., s.105(1) (writing requirement) and s.105(2) (regulations on 'security instruments'). For the regulations, see Sect. (ii) below.

[93] See subss. (1)–(5) ('security instruments', i.e. security provided by a third party) and subs. (9) (security provided by debtor).

[94] Consumer Credit Act 1974, s.105(7) ('security instruments'), s.65 (security provided by debtor).

[95] In relation to third party sureties, see ibid., ss.107–108, 111. In relation to the debtor providing security see ss.77–78, 110. These provisions were amended by the Consumer Credit Act 2006: see Ch. 2, Sect. 5(i) above.

world. Thirdly, regulations may be made under section 112 of the Act for the purpose of governing the realization of securities. No such regulations have been made to date and none are presently intended.[96] Fourthly, section 113(1) precludes the use of security for the purpose of evading any provision of the Act applicable to regulated agreements. To this end, a security may not be enforced so as to benefit the creditor to an extent greater than would be the case if the security were not provided. Furthermore, if the agreement itself is enforceable only on the order of a court or of the Office of Fair Trading, the security is also subject thereto.[97] This provision has a considerable impact on certain types of guarantees and indemnities furnished to banks, which characteristically include clauses to the effect that the security remains valid even if the main agreement is avoided.

All the provisions that have just been mentioned, and that are applicable to all securities, are discussed in the following sections. Special provisions in the 1974 Act applicable to pledges (replacing the Pawnbrokers Acts 1872–1960) are noted in Chapter 20.

(ii) **Form of security**

Under section 105(2)–(3), regulations may be made in order to prescribe the form and content of 'security instruments'.[98] But the only regulations made so far under this provision affect guarantees and indemnities,[99] and no further regulations are expected. In the case of security provided by the debtor himself, the position is governed by the regulations governing the regulated agreement.[100] These provide that a description of the security needs to be stated in the document signed by the debtor.[101] Sometimes the security itself needs to be part of that documentation.[102]

Section 105(4) lays down a number of requisites concerning the 'proper execution' of a 'security instrument'. To start with, the document, which needs to embody[103] all the express terms of the security, has to be signed by or on behalf of the surety. When presented for signature, the document must be 'in such a state that its terms are readily legible'. Furthermore, when the document is presented to the surety for execution, or sent to him for this purpose, he must be furnished with a copy.[104] Similar requirements apply to securities provided by the debtor.[105] These provisions have an impact on banking practice. They militate against some of the informal arrangements developed by banks,

---

[96] Ministerial announcement on 20 July 1982: A.G. Guest & M. Lloyd, *Encyclopedia of Consumer Credit Law* (London, 1974, loose-leaf), para. 2-113.

[97] Consumer Credit Act 1974, s.113(2). A security is avoided under s.106 if the main agreement is declared unenforceable by the court or OFT (except on technical grounds only) and the cancellation or termination of the main agreement renders the security ineffective: s.113(3). But note the exceptions in subss. (4)–(5) and the special provision in relation to indemnities: subs. (7).

[98] As was noted in Sect. 4(i), this term covers only securities provided by third parties, see n.91.

[99] Consumer Credit (Guarantees and Indemnities) Regulations 1983, S.I. 1983/1556. However, all security instruments have to be in writing: Consumer Credit Act 1974, s.105(1).

[100] The Consumer Credit (Agreements) Regulations 1983, S.I. 1983/1553, as amended, esp. by S.I. 2004/1482 and the Consumer Credit (Agreements) Regulations 2010, S.I. 2010/1014 (as amended by S.I. 2010/1969), made under Consumer Credit Act 1974, s.60, discussed above, Ch. 2, Sect. 5(iv).

[101] S.I. 1983/1553, Sched. 1, para. 21; S.I. 2010/1014, Sched. 1, para. 23.

[102] For agreements covered by S.I. 1983/1553, reg. 2(10) provides that the agreement must 'embody' (see n.103, below) the security.

[103] Under Consumer Credit Act 1974, s.189(4) a document 'embodies' a provision either if this provision is set out in it, or if it is set out in a document referred to in the main document.

[104] And he must also receive a copy of the regulated agreement itself: ibid., s.105(5).

[105] The requirements are in Consumer Credit Act 1974, s.61 and in the Agreements Regulations made under s.60 (see n.100).

such as securities affected by means of the mere deposit of title deeds or of commercial paper.

If these formal requirements are not complied with, the security is enforceable only on order of the court[106] and if the application for an order is dismissed, the security is treated as having never been effected.[107] Property lodged with the creditor has, thereupon, to be returned by him forthwith. He is, further, required to repay any amounts received in the realization of the security.[108] However, these consequences only follow if the application for enforcement of the credit agreement is dismissed. Thus unless or until this occurs, the security is effective.

(iii) Information to be supplied by the creditor

As in the case of regulated agreements covered by the 1974 Act,[109] a creditor is required to supply information to a surety on request. The Act draws a distinction in this regard between securities provided for the different types of credit agreements—namely, agreements for fixed-sum credit[110] and agreements for running-account credit.[111] Basically, the creditor is required to supply to the surety a copy of the regulated agreement and the security instrument, and a financial statement which, *inter alia*, has to disclose the amounts payable under the regulated agreement.[112] If the creditor fails to comply with a request for information, he is unable to enforce the security during the period of his default.[113] The information required by the surety has to be supplied by the creditor within 12 working days.[114]

The creditor is also under a duty to serve on a third party surety a copy of any default or similar notice served on the debtor.[115] If the creditor fails to comply with this requirement, the security is enforceable on a court order only.[116] Although the requirement is phrased in terms of serving a copy 'when' the relevant notice is served on the debtor, it is not clear whether this requires the contemporaneous serving of a copy or whether the creditor may serve the copy at any time before seeking to enforce the security.

The requirements of providing information related to securities and of providing copies and of serving copies of notices generate a great deal of work for the banks. But the provisions in point do not appear to have made a major impact on any substantive aspect of banking practice.

---

[106] Consumer Credit Act 1974, s.105(7) ('security instruments') and see s.65 (security provided by debtor).

[107] Ibid., s.106. But see the savings in s.177 for registered charges over land.

[108] He is also required to remove or cancel from the relevant register any entries of the charge or mortgage: ibid. In *Wilson* v. *Howard (t/as Howard Pawnbrokers)* [2005] EWCA 147 (distinguished in *Wilson* v. *Robertsons (London) Ltd (No. 2)* [2006] EWCA 1088) 'realisation of the security' was held to cover not only the sale of the collateral but also repayment by the debtor. *Sed quaere*: A. Guest & M. Lloyd, *Encyclopedia of Consumer Credit Law* (London, 1974, loose-leaf), para. 2–107.

[109] Ch. 2, Sect. 5 above.

[110] See Consumer Credit Act 1974, s.107 (third party sureties) and ss.77, 77A, 110 (debtor surety).

[111] See ibid., s.108 (third party sureties) & ss.78, 110 (debtor surety).

[112] See ibid., ss.107(1)(*c*), 108(1)(*c*) (third party sureties) & ss.77(1)(*c*); 78(1)(*c*), 110 (debtor sureties).

[113] Ibid., ss.107(4), 108(4) (third party sureties) & ss.77(4), 78(4), 110(3) (debtor sureties).

[114] Consumer Credit (Prescribed Periods for Giving Information) Regulations 1983, S.I. 1983/1569, reg. 2. And see some special provisions applicable in the case of a variation of a security: Consumer Credit (Cancellation Notices and Copies of Documents) Regulations 1983, S.I. 1983/1557, reg. 7.

[115] i.e. default notices served under Consumer Credit Act 1974, s.87 and notices services under ss.76(1) & 98(1): s.111(1). For these notices see further, Ch. 2, Sect. 5(v) above.

[116] Ibid., s.111(2).

(iv) **Realization of security**

As no regulations have been made under section 112,[117] there are no special provisions relating to the realization of security provided in relation to regulated agreements. In this regard, it should be noted that, in relation to bills of sale, the Bills of Sale (1878) Amendment Act 1882, has been amended by the Consumer Credit Act 1974.[118] Banks, however, are strongly disinclined to take securities by way of bills of sale. The problems concerning the realization of the typical securities used by banks, such as charges or mortgages over land, are discussed where relevant.

(v) **Anti-evasion provision**

Section 113 of the 1974 Act seeks to combat the evasion of the provisions of the Act by the use of security devices. The basic rule is that 'the security shall not be enforced so as to benefit the creditor...directly or indirectly, to an extent greater (whether as respects the amount of any payment or the time or manner of its being made) than would be the case if the security were not provided'.[119] Specific applications of this principle are that, where the regulated agreement is improperly executed, the security is also enforceable on a court order only[120] and that, where the contract itself is cancelled, the security is rendered ineffective.[121] It is clear that banks have to be wary of this provision: obviously security arrangements cannot be utilized to escape the mandatory provisions of the Act seeking to protect the debtor and his backers. Moreover, it is arguable that the remedy of foreclosure,[122] which a mortgagee normally has, is not available in the case of a mortgage securing a regulated agreement as such a remedy would benefit the mortgagee to a greater extent than would be the case if the security were not provided in enabling him to acquire the property used as collateral.

---

[117] See n.96 to this Section. [118] Sched. 4, Pt. 1 para. 1, which inserts a new s.7A in the 1882 Act.
[119] Consumer Credit Act 1974, s.113(1). [120] Ibid., s.113(2); and see s.113(3)(c).
[121] Ibid., s.113(3). [122] See further, Ch. 19, Sect. 2(viii).

19

Proprietary Securities

1 Scope

The present chapter deals with proprietary securities over both land and other corporeal property. Banks, of course, make use of all security devices available to financiers generally. Thus, the mortgage over land is used by banks just as it is employed by other financiers. Similarly, the floating charge and fixed charge over chattels and book debts are in general use by financial institutions. The object of the discussion of these arrangements in this book is to review their salient points and to highlight elements relevant to banking law. Specialist texts should be consulted for fuller treatments.

A specific problem that arises from the classification of securities in this book is that different arrangements concerning a given type of property occasionally have to be covered in separate chapters. Thus, the hypothecation of goods and the chattel mortgage, which are proprietary securities, are discussed in this chapter. The pledge over goods and over documents of title falls within the scope of Chapter 20, devoted to possessory securities. Security arrangements over choses in action, such as debts, bank balances and life policies, fall into yet a different class, and are discussed in Chapter 21.

It will be recalled that, in practical terms, the common thread of proprietary securities is that the debtor or surety retains the possession and use of the collateral. Conceptually, all securities of this class are arranged on the basis of conferring on the creditor some specific rights in the land or the goods. Although the exact nature of the rights so acquired may differ from arrangement to arrangement, in all cases the creditor will be able to satisfy the debt from the proceeds of the sale of the collateral in priority to other creditors.

The security arrangements covered in this chapter are the mortgage over land, chattel mortgages, hypothecation of goods, and fixed and floating charges granted by corporate borrowers.

2 Mortgages over land

(i) Introduction

This subject is a complex one, reflecting the complexity of English land law. Its proper understanding requires an appreciation of the history of the subject, as its present state is explicable only in terms of its historical development.[1] There is clearly no

---

[1] For its history see C. Harpum (ed.), *Megarry and Wade on The Law of Real Property* (7th edn., London, 2008) ch. 19; W. Holdsworth, *History of English Law*, iii; A.W.B. Simpson, *Historical Introduction to Land Law*; F. Pollock & F.W. Maitland, *The History of English Law* (2nd edn.), ii.

place for this here and only a brief outline of the present state of the subject will be attempted.[2]

The terminology needs some explanation. The borrower who grants the mortgage over his land is known as the 'mortgagor'. The lender is known as the 'mortgagee'. When the loan is repaid and the land becomes free of the mortgage again, the mortgagor is said to 'redeem' the land. During the currency of the mortgage, the mortgagor's residual rights in the land are known as his 'equity of redemption' or his 'equity'.[3] Its value is the value of his unencumbered collateral minus the value of the secured loan(s). Strictly speaking the terms 'mortgage' and 'charge' connote conceptually different interests. A mortgage connotes the transfer of the mortgagor's interest in the property as security, with a proviso for retransfer on satisfaction of the obligation. A charge connotes a mere right to look to the chargor's property to satisfy an obligation without such transfer.[4] Confusingly the term 'charge' is often used in the context of land to cover a mortgage and vice versa.[5] However, in this discussion the technical meanings will be adhered to.

In common with all problems relating to security, two distinct issues need to be considered. First, it must be asked: what is the nature of the interest in the land (or the collateral) that is the subject matter of the security? This is particularly important here because the nature of the mortgage and consequent priority questions depend on this issue. Thus, the mortgagor may have a freehold or leasehold estate in the land and his interest may be legal or equitable. Moreover, his land may be registered or (increasingly rarely, see below) still unregistered. Secondly, the nature of the security interest created (or to be created) must be ascertained. Thus, it may be a legal or equitable mortgage or an equitable charge.

Most of England and Wales now comprise registered land[6] and the Land Registration Act 2002[7] contains some special rules as to mortgages of registered land. Moreover, once electronic conveyancing is introduced, this will simplify the position considerably.[8] Nevertheless, the 2002 Act operates primarily by modifying the rules applicable to unregistered land and hence some discussion of this is still necessary.

---

[2] The leading work is Fisher and Lightwood, *Law of Mortgage* (12th edn., London, 2006). See also Megarry and Wade, n.1 above, ch. 19. Wide-ranging proposals for reform were made by the Law Commission's Report, *Land Mortgages*, Law Com. No. 204 (London, 1991) (and see its working paper: *Land Mortgages*, WP No. 99 (London, 1986)) but these have not been implemented and have, to some extent, been overtaken by the Land Registration Act 2002 (itself preceded by a Law Commission Report (with H.M. Land Registry): *Land Registration for the 21st Century: A Conveyancing Revolution*, Law Com. No. 271 (London, 2001)).

[3] The reason is historical. Equity developed many principles to protect the mortgagor, including the right to redeem after the legal date for redemption (i.e. the date by which the parties agreed the loan would be repaid and the mortgage extinguished). Hence his 'equitable right to redeem' and, more generally (see *Kreglinger* v. *New Patagonia Meat and Cold Storage Co. Ltd* [1914] AC 25, 47–8), his 'equity of redemption' in the land.

[4] *Re Bond Worth Ltd* [1980] Ch. 228, 250.

[5] See, for example, Law of Property Act 1925 (hereafter LPA 1925), s.205(1)(xiv).

[6] The creation of a first legal mortgage protected by deposit of deeds (see Sect. (iii)) over unregistered land triggers compulsory registration of the mortgagor's title (unless he only has a leasehold interest with less than seven years to run): Land Registration Act 2002, s.4(1)(g); (8).

[7] In force on 13 Oct. 2003, replacing Land Registration Act 1925. See n.2 above.

[8] See Land Registration Act 2002, Part 8. E-conveyancing is being introduced in stages and is expected to be fully operational in 2010. Once in operation, rights will only arise on entry on the register (see s.93) therefore the distinction between legal and equitable rights will reduce in significance.

(ii) **The subject-matter of the security (the collateral)**

In its technical sense, the word 'land' means the ground itself, any buildings erected on it, and any chattels affixed to it. A mortgage over land attaches to everything that forms part of the land in this sense. The mortgagor may have a freehold or a leasehold estate in the land. This distinction can be traced back to the land tenure system of feudal times. Today, the holder of a freehold has a perpetual interest in the land, while the holder of a leasehold has rights of occupation which technically are for a period of time, though that time may be very long, for instance 999 years.

Rights in freehold and in leasehold may exist in law and in equity. A legal estate in fee simple gives the owner full rights to deal with the property. An equitable interest will give lesser rights, for instance for life only. In some cases the equitable interest may be created by a contract in which the owner undertakes to convey his title or to mortgage it.[9] An equitable interest is generally as enforceable as a legal estate, although compliance with some statutory requirements for protection may be necessary.

The distinction between legal estates and equitable interests is based on the Law of Property Act 1925. As a result of section 1, only two estates may exist at law: the fee simple and a lease. But some other rights may also exist at law. The one here relevant is the 'charge' over land 'by way of legal mortgage'.

When a bank decides to grant a secured loan to a customer, it has to satisfy itself that the customer is legally in a position to grant a mortgage over the relevant property. To this end, the bank conducts a search into the title. The procedure depends on whether the land involved is in an area covered by the land registration system or by (increasing rarely, see below) the older system, based on deeds.

In the case of unregistered land, the bank first arranges for a search of the deeds concerning the property. These are usually held by the freeholder or leaseholder, except that, if the land is already subject to a mortgage, the deeds may be in the mortgagee's custody. In addition to the deeds, the bank has to arrange for a search of the register kept under the Land Charges Act 1972, which will bring to light details about interests and rights adverse to those of the owner and not disclosed by the deeds. In this way question marks may be raised for the bank. If the customer is a body corporate, the bank will further search in the register kept under the Companies Act 2006.[10] It is also important to search the register of local land charges, kept under the Local Land Charges Act 1975, in which local authorities record certain liabilities, for instance in respect of road charges.

To simplify conveyancing, a system of registered land was introduced under the Land Registration Act 1925, now replaced by the Land Registration Act 2002. This substitutes the protection of title through deeds by the making of entries in the Land Register of titles to land. These entries obviate the need to trace the history of the title, but the existence of some unregistrable rights means that it is still sometimes necessary to look beyond the register itself. As noted above, the registration system now covers most of England and Wales.

Banks need to take particular care to ensure that they are not adversely affected by the rights of persons (other than the mortgagor) in occupation of the land. In the case of registered land such rights may be 'overriding interests'[11] binding on the mortgagee. In a

---

[9] Under the principle of *Walsh* v. *Lonsdale* (1882) 21 Ch. 9, see Sect. (iii) below.

[10] See Sect. 4(iii) below.

[11] Land Registration Act 2002 (hereafter LRA 2002), ss.11, 12 and Sched. 1, previously Land Registration Act 1925 (hereafter LRA 1925), s.70(1)(g). See *Abbey National Building Society* v. *Cann* [1991] 1 AC

series of cases,[12] banks have found themselves bound by the rights of the spouse or other relative of the mortgagor who has contributed to the purchase price and thus acquired rights in the land. In consequence banks need to make sure that they also investigate the rights of persons in actual occupation.

(iii) Legal and equitable mortgages and equitable charges

A distinction needs to be drawn between three types of security over land. First, there is the legal mortgage. This confers a legal interest on the mortgagee and thus may be granted only by a mortgagor who has a legal estate in the land: either the fee simple or a lease. Secondly, there is the equitable mortgage. This confers an equitable interest on the mortgagee. It may also be granted by a mortgagor who has a legal estate, but if the mortgagor has only an equitable interest (for example, he is a beneficiary under a trust), then he may grant only an equitable mortgage of it. Lastly, there is the equitable charge. This also confers an equitable interest on the chargee but with more limited rights than the equitable mortgage.[13] Each of these types of security needs to be considered in turn.

Since the Law of Property Act 1925, a legal mortgage may be created only[14] by either granting the mortgagee a lease in the legal estate (a 'mortgage by demise') or conferring a charge by deed 'expressed to be by way of legal mortgage' over the legal estate (a 'mortgage by charge').[15] The latter, in being called a 'charge', may cause confusion. Although called a 'charge', the lender is deemed to be in the same position as if he had been granted a mortgage by demise.[16] In practice, the second method of creating legal mortgages—the mortgage by charge—is by far the most common.[17] If the mortgagor has the freehold, the mortgagee is placed in the position of a lessee of the land.[18] If the mortgagor is himself a leaseholder then the mortgagee becomes a sub-lessee.[19] But, as noted below, in the case of registered land, legal mortgages may only be created by way of charge (and not 'by demise').[20]

The creation of equitable mortgages was unaffected by the 1925 Act. Again a distinction has to be drawn, but this time between the mortgagor who himself has only an equitable

56: occupation must exist at time of creation of mortgage and continue until date of registration (and see *Barclays Bank plc* v. *Zaroovabli* [1997] Ch. 321).

[12] Applying *Williams and Glyn's Bank* v. *Boland* [1981] AC 487. But see *City of London Building Society* v. *Flegg* [1988] AC 54; *Equity and Law Ltd* v. *Prestidge* [1992] 1 WLR 137 (CA).

[13] See Sect. 2(viii) below.

[14] An attempt to convey the interest outright by way of security operates as if the correct statutory method had been adopted: LPA 1925, s.85(2) (freeholds); s.85(2) (leaseholds). See, on the outright assignment of leaseholds by way of security, *Grangeside Properties Ltd* v. *Collingwood Securities Ltd* [1964] 1 WLR 139.

[15] LPA 1925, s.85(1) (freeholds); s.86(1) (leaseholds).

[16] Ibid., s.87. See *Grand Junction Co. Ltd* v. *Bates* [1954] 2 QB 160 (mortgage by charge of a lease treated as a sub-lessee for the purposes of relief against forfeiture).

[17] The document is more intelligible; the mortgagor can mortgage a mixed portfolio of properties, whether leasehold or freehold, in one document; in the case of a mortgage of leasehold, such a mortgage (as opposed to one by demise) is less likely to be in breach of any covenant against sub-leasing.

[18] LPA 1925, s.85(1). Usually a term of 3,000 years is granted, with a proviso for its cesser on redemption. The mortgagee has the right to the title deeds (see the proviso to s.85(1)).

[19] Ibid., s.86(1). The mortgagee's lease is usually 10 days shorter than the mortgagor's lease so as to make room for any subsequent mortgages. These are made for a day longer than the previous mortgage lease so as to facilitate realization if required. Again the mortgagee has the right to the title deeds (see the proviso to s.86(1)).

[20] See below and s.51: however, the mortgage is created, once registered, it takes effect as a charge by deed by way of legal mortgage under LPA 1925, s.87.

interest in the land and the mortgagor who has a legal interest. In the former case, as noted above, the mortgagor may create only an equitable mortgage. He does so in the traditional manner of assigning his interest[21] to the mortgagee as security, with a proviso for reassignment on redemption. In the latter case, the equitable mortgage is used where less formality than that required for legal mortgages is preferred.[22] The equitable principle that a specifically enforceable contract gives rise to an equitable right[23] is invoked. Thus an informal (but specifically enforceable) agreement to create a mortgage is made and this, without more, gives rise to an equitable mortgage.[24] Usually the deeds or (in the case of registered land) the land certificate are deposited with the mortgagee. Whilst this used to constitute a sufficient act of part performance so as to dispense with the requirement of writing for the purposes of section 40 of the Law of Property Act 1925,[25] as a result of the Law of Property (Miscellaneous Provisions) Act 1989, section 2,[26] such an agreement must now be in writing. Thus equitable mortgages by mere deposit of deeds, unaccompanied by a written contract, are no longer effective.[27] In practice, equitable mortgages obtained by banks are executed on a standard written form and under seal to ensure that the bank has adequate remedies on default.[28] Equitable mortgages are used mainly to secure short-term loans.

An equitable charge over an interest in land may be created by agreement between the borrower and his bank whereby the interest is appropriated to the discharge of some debt or obligation. These are rarely deliberately created by banks as mortgages give banks more attractive rights and remedies.[29]

The fact that the land is registered does not in principle affect the way that the land may be mortgaged. The only difference is that the Land Registration Act 2002 contains a new provision whereby legal mortgages may only be created by way of charge and not demise.[30] However, the position is more complex because of the provisions on the protection of a mortgagee of registered land considered in Section 2(iv) below.

(iv) Protection of mortgagees

A mortgagee needs to be sure that his security rights are secure and will not be defeated by third parties, such as subsequent mortgagees or outright purchasers of the land, acquiring rights in the land that override his. The method of protection depends on whether the land is registered or not.

In the case of unregistered land, the mortgagee may either take possession of the deeds[31] or register his interest under the Land Charges Act 1972.[32] If he has possession

---

[21] By ibid., s.53(1)(c) such a disposition of an equitable interest is void unless in writing. Notice to the trustees should be given, to preserve priority: *Dearle* v. *Hall* (1828) 3 Russ. 1 and see n.59 below.

[22] See *McCarthy and Stone Ltd* v. *Hodge Ltd* [1971] 1 WLR 154. But note the requirement of writing introduced by the Law of Property (Miscellaneous Provisions) Act 1989, noted below.

[23] See *Walsh* v. *Lonsdale* (1882) 21 Ch. 9.

[24] *Cradock* v. *Scottish Provident Institution* (1893) 69 LT 380.   [25] LPA 1925, s.40(2).

[26] Repealing LPA 1925, s.40. See *Newell* v. *Tarrant* [2004] EWHC 772.

[27] *United Bank of Kuwait plc* v. *Sahib* [1997] Ch. 107 (CA); *Newell* v. *Tarrant* [2004] EWHC 772.

[28] See Sect. (viii) below.   [29] See ibid.

[30] LRA 2002, s.23(1) and see s.51 (however the mortgage is created, once registered, it takes effect as a charge by deed by way of legal mortgage). LPA 1925, ss.86 & 87 are consequently amended by LRA 2002, s.113 & Sched. 1, paras. 2(7) and 8.

[31] The provisos to LPA 1925, ss.85(1) & 86(1) give the mortgagee the right to take possession of the title deeds.

[32] Equitable mortgages that are estate contracts may need registration even if the deeds are taken by the mortgagee: see below.

of the deeds, persons subsequently dealing with the land will be put on notice, by virtue of the absence of the deeds, that someone may have a prior interest in the land. If he does not take possession of the deeds, the Land Charges Act 1972 renders the mortgage registrable.[33] Registration gives notice to everyone that the registered rights exist in relation to the land.[34] Moreover, registered mortgages rank according to their dates of registration.[35] If rights are registrable but not actually registered then they are void against certain purchasers[36] (including subsequent mortgagees[37]). Legal mortgages that are not protected by deposit of deeds are registrable as 'puisne mortgages'.[38] It used to be thought that all equitable mortgages or charges not protected by deposit of deeds were registrable as 'general equitable charges'[39] but it now seems that if they take the form of agreements to create legal mortgages, even if they are protected by deposit of deeds, they are registrable as 'estate contracts'.[40]

In the case of registered land the position is as follows. Legal mortgages can only be created by substantive registration in the 'charges' part of the Land Register[41] and such an entry protects a legal mortgagee against subsequent dealings.[42] A mortgagee of registered land obtains a legal mortgage and is able to exercise his powers as mortgagee only if he obtains such substantive registration.[43] Thus banks generally insist on substantively registering their mortgages. In other situations, the mortgage is necessarily equitable and may be protected by 'notice',[44] an 'agreed notice' if the registered proprietor consents and a 'unilateral notice' if he does not.[45]

(v) Second or subsequent mortgages

If the value of the collateral, the interest in the land, used to secure the first mortgage exceeds the extent of the loan secured by it, a second mortgagee may be willing to lend on the security of the mortgagor's 'equity'.[46] As noted at Section 2(vi) below, second (and subsequent) mortgages usually rank in priority behind mortgages previously effected over the land. For this reason, banks prefer to lend on first mortgage and will take a second mortgage only provided it is clear that the value of the land substantially exceeds the amount covered by the first mortgage.

A second mortgage does not differ in form from a first mortgage. If the first mortgage is a legal mortgage, the lease of a second legal mortgagee will be slightly shorter than the lease of the first mortgagee. In the case of unregistered land the first mortgagee is likely to

---

[33] See previous note.   [34] LPA 1925, s.98.

[35] Ibid., s.97 (as amended by the Land Charges Act 1972).   [36] Land Charges Act 1972, s.4(5).

[37] Ibid., s.17(1).

[38] Ibid., s.2(4)(i). The definition of 'puisne mortgage' ('a legal mortgage which is not protected by a deposit of documents relating to the legal estate affected') causes some difficulty. See the texts cited at n.2 and R. Megarry (1940) 7 *CLJ* 243.

[39] Ibid., s.2(4)(iii). Again the definition ('any equitable charge which [does not fall within a statutory list]') is not free from difficulty.

[40] Ibid., s.2(4)(iv), see *United Bank of Kuwait plc* v. *Sahib* [1997] Ch. 107 (CA). This possibility was discussed in the texts cited at n.2, but most commentators supported the view that registration was only required as an alternative to taking the deeds.

[41] LRA 2002, s.27(1), (3).   [42] LRA 2002, s.30(2).

[43] LRA 2002, s.51: the charge 'has effect … as a charge by deed by way of legal mortgage'. And see s.52: proprietor of registered charge has 'the powers of disposition conferred by law on the owner of a legal mortgage'. See also *Lever Finance* v. *Needleman's Trustee* [1956] Ch. 375.

[44] LRA 2002, s.32. The old 'cautions' under the LRA 1925 have been abolished and replaced by 'unilateral notices', see next note.

[45] LRA 2002, s.34.   [46] See Sect. 2(i) above.

hold the deeds and therefore the second mortgagee must take care to register his interest under the Land Charges Act 1972. In the case of registered land, if the first mortgagee has substantively registered his charge then the second mortgagee can similarly register his.[47] If the first mortgagee has taken a deposit of the land certificate then the second mortgagee cannot register his charge substantively[48] and must protect his mortgage by the entry of a notice.[49]

When the second mortgage is created, the second mortgagee should notify the first mortgagee. The first mortgagee is then under an obligation to hand the title deeds over to the second mortgagee when the first mortgage is discharged.[50] The second mortgagee should also ask the first mortgagee to state the amount due to him, and to confirm that he is not under a duty to make further advances to the mortgagor. If such further advances are called for under the first mortgage, they will rank in priority to the second mortgage.[51] If it is confirmed that no such obligation is imposed on the first mortgagee, then the debt covered by the second mortgage ranks above advances made by the first mortgagee after he receives the second mortgagee's notification.[52]

The remedies of the second mortgagee are similar to those of the first mortgagee.[53] In particular, he is entitled to arrange for the sale of the property upon the mortgagor's default.[54] He can resort to this remedy without obtaining the consent of the first mortgagee. However, the property is then sold subject to the first mortgage. Usually, therefore, the second mortgagee persuades the first mortgagee to obtain repayment on the same occasion. If the first mortgagee withholds his consent, he may be compelled to join in.[55] In effect, the second mortgagee has the power to redeem the property from the first mortgage.

A second mortgage has to be distinguished from a sub-mortgage, which is a mortgage of a mortgage.[56] Usually, the sub-mortgage assumes the form of an equitable assignment by way of charge of the mortgagee's rights under the main mortgage to another financier. There are also cases in which a company, engaged in lending on mortgages, gives a bank a floating charge over its assets. If this charge crystallizes, it attaches also to the mortgages held by the company.[57]

(vi) Priorities

If there is more than one mortgage over the borrower's interest in the land and the value of the interest is insufficient to satisfy all the mortgagees then the issue of priority becomes crucial. This is because there is no principle (as there is in relation to unsecured creditors on insolvency) of *pro rata* satisfaction of the debts secured on the land. The debts are satisfied in full in order of the priority of their security.

Again this is a complex subject.[58] In principle,[59] the mortgages take priority in the order in which they have been created unless there is something to disturb this order.[60]

---

[47] And the charges will rank according to order of registration: LRA 2002, s. 48.
[48] As he needs the land certificate to do this.   [49] See Sect. 2(iv) above.   [50] LPA 1925, s.96(2).
[51] Ibid., s.94(1)(c); LRA 2002, s.49.
[52] Ibid. See further the discussion of 'tacking' below in Sect. 2(vii).
[53] For remedies, see Sect. 2(viii) below.   [54] LPA 1925, s.101(1), (4).   [55] Ibid., s.50.
[56] Megarry & Wade, n.1 above, paras. 19-185 ff.   [57] For company charges, see Sect. 4 below.
[58] See the texts cited at n.2 above, especially Megarry & Wade, paras. 19-194 ff.
[59] However, priority issues in relation to mortgages of equitable interests are governed by the rule in *Dearle* v. *Hall* (1828) 3 Russ. 1, as altered by LPA 1925, s. 137.
[60] See, in relation to registered land, *Barclays Bank Ltd* v. *Taylor* [1974] Ch. 137, decided under the old Land Registration Act 1925. The general approach adopted is, it seems, still appropriate.

Mortgages that are prior in time may be postponed by reason of either: (a) statutory provisions as to registration which render mortgages ineffective against certain persons if the mortgages have not been adequately protected by registration[61] or which rank mortgages according to their order of registration rather than creation;[62] and (b) general land-law principles, especially that which renders equitable interests ineffective against *bona fide* purchasers of the legal interest without notice of those equitable interests or that which postpones a mortgagee that has not acted appropriately, for example, in relation to the title deeds.[63] Moreover, the doctrine of 'tacking', considered at Section 2(vii) below, may disturb the usual priority.

The position in relation to unregistered land is in essence[64] as follows. If a bank takes a legal mortgage and protects itself either by taking and retaining[65] the deeds (if available) or registering its interest under the Land Charges Act 1972,[66] it will generally be safe against subsequent mortgagees. An equitable mortgagee or chargee is in the same position, except that such a creditor taking a deposit of deeds may also need to register his interest.[67] Moreover, in taking a mortgage, if the deeds are produced and there is no entry on the Land Charges Register, that mortgage will generally[68] take priority over any previous one. Such a previous mortgagee will lose his priority, as he has not protected himself either by deposit of deeds or registration.

The position in relation to registered land has been clarified somewhat by the Land Registration Act 2002.[69] It provides that substantively registered charges[70] rank in order of their registration (and not creation).[71] Moreover, a legal mortgage takes free of any unprotected interests (such as equitable mortgages that have been protected by notice).[72] As for equitable mortgages and charges, once protected by notice, they bind subsequent purchasers and mortgagees (even legal mortgagees).[73] However, apart from protecting the equitable mortgagee protected by a notice as against *subsequent* purchasers and legal mortgagees, no further statutory effect is given to the notice. Indeed, there is a provision that appears to preserve the order of creation priority in all such cases.[74] Thus, as

---

[61] See Land Charges Act 1972, s.4(5) and LRA 2002, s.48, cited in Sect. 2(iv) above.

[62] See LRA 2002, s.48, (see below), and LPA 1925, s. 97.   [63] See n.65 below.

[64] For more detailed consideration of some of the intractable problems that can arise, see the texts cited at n.2 above.

[65] If the bank parts with the deeds, it may be postponed to a subsequent mortgagee who lends on the faith of those deeds if the bank is regarded as being guilty of 'fraud, misrepresentation or gross negligence' with respect to the deeds: *Northern Counties of England Fire Insurance Co.* v. *Whipp* (1884) 26 Ch. D 482.

[66] See Sect. 2(iv) above. The relevant provision is s.2(4)(i) (puisne mortgages).

[67] See Sect. 2(iv) above. The relevant provisions are s.2(4)(iv) (for equitable mortgages which are estate contracts) and s.2(4)(iii) (for other equitable mortgages and charges).

[68] Unless the previous mortgagee sought to protect himself by a deposit of deeds and was tricked into parting with them, thus enabling the mortgagor to show them to the bank. Then, unless the first mortgagee is regarded as within the *Whipp* principle (see n.65 above) he will not lose priority.

[69] For the position under the old LRA 1925, see R.J. Smith, 'The Priority of Competing Minor Interests in Registered Land' (1977) 93 *LQR* 541; D.J. Hayton, *Registered Land* (3rd edn., London, 1981), 141.

[70] See Sect. 2(iv) above.

[71] LRA 2002, s.48—although a prospective lender who (as is likely in the case of a bank) has 'priority protection' under s.72 whilst searching the register, will take priority over a mortgage registered during the priority period.

[72] LRA 2002, s.30   [73] LRA 2002, s.32(3) & see ss.29 & 30.

[74] LRA 2002, s.28. Previous case law had reached this conclusion where the 'equities' were equal: *Re White Rose Cottage* [1965] Ch. 940; *Barclays Bank* v. *Taylor* [1974] Ch. 137. However, it now seems the rule is absolute, irrespective of 'equities': see the Law Commission Report, see n.2, para. 5.5.

between two equitable mortgages, if the subsequent mortgagee enters a notice, this does not gain him priority over a prior equitable mortgagee that has not entered a notice.[75]

(vii) **Tacking**

Despite these general rules as to priorities, in some circumstances a first mortgagee may 'tack' advances made by him after a subsequent mortgage has been created, onto his original loan and thus secure those advances by the first mortgage. Such a process, which gives priority to such advances over an intervening mortgagee, is known as 'tacking'. This is of particular relevance to banks as they often secure overdrafts by land mortgages and continue to meet cheques after the borrower may have created subsequent mortgages in favour of other lenders. The bank is obviously anxious to have all the advances on the overdraft secured by its first mortgage in priority to any intervening mortgagees. The circumstances in which it can 'tack' depend on whether the land is registered or not.

In relation to unregistered land, the position is governed by section 94 of the Law of Property Act 1925. This enables further advances to be tacked onto a first mortgage if (a) the intervening mortgagee consents, or (b) the bank had no notice of the intervening mortgage at the time of the further advance, or (c) the original mortgage actually obliged the bank to make further advances. In relation to (b), if the first mortgage 'was made expressly for securing a current account or further advance', then mere registration of the intervening mortgage does not constitute notice.[76] This exception to the general principle that registration constitutes notice[77] is regarded as desirable as it would be impractical to expect banks to check the register every time they met a cheque from an overdraft secured by a land mortgage. Thus, in practice, situation (b) is of particular relevance to banks. They can rarely invoke (c) as they rarely undertake to make further advances. However, if neither (b) nor (c) is of assistance they may often rely on (a) and obtain the consent of the intervening mortgagee to their obtaining priority. This is because the threat of refusing to make further advances unless such priority is forthcoming usually induces the intervening mortgagee to agree to postpone his mortgage, as the whole business of the borrower (and thus the value of his intervening security) is likely to be prejudiced by the withdrawal of banking finance.

As regards registered land, section 94 of the Law of Property Act 1925 is excluded in relation to substantively registered charges[78] and the position is governed by section 49 of the Land Registration Act 2002. This slightly alters the position as it was under the Land Registration Act 1925[79] and approximates the position to that in relation to unregistered land. Thus a bank may tack if (a) the intervening mortgagee consents[80] or (b) the bank had no notice of the intervening mortgage from the subsequent mortgagee,[81] or (c) the original mortgage actually obliged the bank to make further advances and this obligation

---

[75] See a decision to this effect under the old law: *Mortgage Corporation Ltd* v. *Nationwide Credit Corporation* [1994] Ch. 49.

[76] LPA 1925, s.94(2). However, actual notice does. Hence the desirability of a subsequent mortgagee actually notifying a prior mortgagee of his mortgage, referred to in Sect. 2(v) above.

[77] Ibid., s.198.   [78] Ibid., s.94(4), as amended by the LRA 2002, s.133 & Sched. 1, para. 2(9).

[79] Where the Registrar was obliged to notify of any proposed subsequent mortgage if the registered mortgage contemplated further advances.

[80] LRA 2002, s.49(6): the general rule.

[81] Ibid., s.49(1)—making it clear that it is the subsequent chargee (and not the Registrar, see n.79) that must give notice. The Land Registration Rules 2003, S.I. 2003/1417, make provision as to when such notice is received.

is entered on the register,[82] or (d) the first mortgage contained a maximum amount of advance to be secured and this was entered on the register.[83] The fourth alternative is new and allows a mortgage to be drawn down in tranches—up to a maximum—in priority to subsequent mortgages.

If tacking is not possible, the bank risks being prejudiced by the rule in *Clayton's Case*.[84] This provides that, unless there is an express agreement to the contrary, payments to the credit of a current account are impliedly appropriated in discharge of the earliest debits that are not statute-barred. In this context, this has the consequence that the debt secured by the bank's mortgage is reduced by payments in, whilst the security for further advances ranks after the intervening mortgage.[85] In this way, any credit entry made thereafter in the current account dissipates the value of the bank's security. The best advice that can be given to the bank is to 'rule off' the mortgagor's account at the time it grants the mortgage and open a new account for his current operations.

The problem of priorities as between the bank and a second mortgagee does not usually arise where the security is granted to the bank in respect of a loan extended to the customer. In the ordinary course, such an arrangement does not contemplate the making of future advances. But is the bank entitled to refuse to honour cheques drawn on the customer's current account, which has an adequate credit balance, if, without the bank's consent, he has granted a second mortgage over the land securing his borrowings from the bank? Most loan and mortgage agreements, executed on standard forms current in banking, prohibit the execution of a second mortgage without the bank's consent. It has been argued that a breach of this condition entitles the bank to combine the loan account with the credit balance of the current account.[86] But if the value of the mortgaged property is adequate to cover the debt due to the bank, it is unlikely that such a course will be adopted.

(viii) Remedies of mortgagee

As a lender, a bank will have the usual right to bring a personal action against the debtor on his promise to repay. However, its rights as holder of a security interest are more extensive and of particular importance should the debtor become insolvent.[87] The remedies of a bank depend to some extent on the nature of its security: whether it is a legal or equitable mortgage or an equitable charge and whether the security was effected by deed.[88] The remedies of a bank with a legal mortgage effected by deed will be considered first as this is the security most favoured by banks. The less extensive remedies of an equitable mortgagee and chargee will then be noted.

---

[82] LRA 2002, s.49(3). This continues the position under the 1925 Act.   [83] S.49(4).

[84] *Devaynes v. Noble, Clayton's Case* (1816) 1 Mer. 572; see Ch. 17, Sect. 2(iv).

[85] *Clayton's Case* was applied in this context in *Deeley v. Lloyd's Bank* [1912] AC 756 (HL) and *Siebe Gorman & Co. Ltd v. Barclays Bank Ltd* [1979] 2 Lloyd's Rep. 142.

[86] J.M. Holden, *Securities for Bankers' Advances* (8th edn., London, 1993), 69–71.

[87] See Ch. 18, Sect. 2.

[88] The statutory powers of sale and appointing a receiver are only available to mortgages effected by deed: LPA 1925, s.101(1): see below. But this will change when electronic conveyancing (see Sect. (i) above) becomes possible.

First, the bank has in principle[89] the right to take possession of the land.[90] This right stems from its status as lessee of the mortgagor[91] and thus is theoretically not dependent on the debtor being in default[92] although in practice a bank will only contemplate possession in such circumstances. In fact the taking of possession is rarely an attractive proposition for banks[93] (who are interested only in receiving repayment of their loan), except in order to ensure vacant possession or preservation of the property as a preliminary step to the sale of the property. It is usual to proceed by way of court order so as not to fall foul of legislation creating criminal offences in the context of eviction.[94] There are a number of restrictions on the bank being able to enter into possession. First, if the mortgaged property is a dwelling-house then the court has a discretion to adjourn the action if the mortgagor is likely to be able, within a reasonable period, to pay the sums due.[95] Secondly, if the mortgagee secures a loan regulated by the Consumer Credit Act 1974,[96] a similar protection is accorded to the mortgagor.[97] Thirdly, the case of *Quennell* v. *Maltby*[98] suggests there may be a general discretion in the court to refuse possession to a mortgagee if possession is not sought *bona fide* for the purposes of enforcing the security but for some ulterior purpose such as the avoidance of the Rent Acts. A similar principle applies to the exercise of the power of sale, considered below.[99]

Secondly, section 101(1)(iii) of the Law of Property Act 1925 provides for a statutory power to appoint a receiver in order to collect any income the land is producing. This will be an attractive remedy only if the bank wishes to continue with the mortgage[100] and the land is income-producing. The Act specifies the circumstances in which the power 'arises'[101] (i.e. when the mortgage is by deed, when the money is due, and if there is no contrary

---

[89] But note the restrictions mentioned below.

[90] But the mortgagor is 'in possession' for the purposes of the Limitation Act 1980 and hence the mortgagee's rights may eventually become statute-barred: *Ashe* v. *National Westminster Bank plc* [2008] EWCA Civ. 55.

[91] See Sect. 2(iii) above.

[92] In *Four-Maids Ltd* v. *Dudley Marshall Properties Ltd* [1957] Ch. 317 Harman J said at 320 that the mortgagee is entitled to possession 'before the ink is dry on the mortgage'. This may be altered by agreement between the parties although an implied term that possession requires default is not to be lightly implied (*Western Bank Ltd* v. *Schindler* [1977] Ch. 1). The right to possession is not defeated by a cross-claim by the mortgagor: *Ashley Guarantee* v. *Zacaria* [1993] 1 WLR 62 (CA) and *Midland Bank plc* v. *McGrath* [1996] EGCS 61 (CA).

[93] Mortgagees in possession are under a strict duty to account: *White* v. *City London Brewery* (1889) 42 Ch. D 237.

[94] See Criminal Law Act 1977, s.6, and note Protection from Eviction Act 1977.

[95] Administration of Justice Act 1970, s.36; Administration of Justice Act 1973, s.8. See also the Mortgage Repossessions (Protection of Tenants) Act 2010 (protection of tenants with leases not binding on mortgagee).

[96] The Administration of Justice Act 1970, s.36 does not apply to mortgages securing a regulated agreement within the Consumer Credit Act: ibid., s.38A, added by Consumer Credit Act 1974, Sched. 4, para. 30.

[97] See Sect. (xi) below and ss.126, 129 of that Act (time orders). See also *First National Bank plc* v. *Syed* [1991] 2 All ER 250.

[98] [1979] 1 WLR 318 (CA), applied in *Albany Home Loans* v. *Massey* [1997] 2 All ER 609 (CA) but distinguished in *Sadiq* v. *Hussain* (1997) 73 P&CR D44. See also *Palk* v. *Mortgage Services Funding plc* [1993] Ch. 330 where the court ordered the sale sought by the mortgagor, refusing to let the mortgagee retain the property and let it out. The value of the property was insufficient to cover the loan and the rent would not cover the interest payable, with the result that the mortgagor's liability would increase if the mortgagee remained in possession unless property values rose sharply.

[99] *Downside Nominees Ltd* v. *First City Corp. Ltd* [1993] AC 295.

[100] For example, if the terms (such as the rate of interest) are particularly advantageous.

[101] LPA 1925, s.101(1).

intention) and thus is available to the mortgagee. The power is 'exercisable' only when further conditions are fulfilled.[102] The Act lays down how a receiver must deal with the income he receives[103] and there is extensive case law setting out the duties of a receiver.[104] Essentially, although they are designated agents of the mortgagor[105] and must take steps to protect and preserve the mortgaged property, when it comes to selling the property they owe the same duties to the mortgagor and others interested in the equity of redemption as does the mortgagee. As noted below, this means that although they must obtain the best price reasonably obtainable, they are not obliged to take steps to enhance the value of the property or to delay a sale in order to achieve a higher price.

The remedies of entry into possession and the appointment of a receiver do not bring the mortgage to an end but are generally interim remedies used primarily to protect the security. The next two remedies are more drastic and result in the termination of the mortgage.

Thirdly, section 101(1)(i) of the Law of Property Act 1925 gives a mortgagee a statutory power of sale. This power 'arises' and is 'exercisable'[106] in the same circumstances as the power to appoint a receiver noted above. Once it becomes clear that the mortgagor is likely to remain in default of his obligations, this is the remedy most often sought by banks (in conjunction with obtaining vacant possession beforehand). The proceeds of sale are held by the mortgagee in trust, the surplus after satisfying the mortgagees being due to the mortgagor.[107] However, it has repeatedly been emphasized that a mortgagee 'is not a trustee of the power of sale for the mortgagor'[108] and he has 'an unfettered discretion to sell when he likes to achieve repayment of the debt which he is owed'.[109] In particular, he need only have regard to his own interests and thus need not postpone the sale in the hope of obtaining a higher price[110] or take other steps to achieve a higher price. His only duty is preserve (rather than increase) the value of the security and to obtain the best price that can reasonably be obtained.[111] However, the power of sale must be

---

[102] Ibid., s.109(1). As noted above at Sect. 2(iv), in the case of registered land, only a mortgagee who has obtained substantive registration of his mortgage may exercise this power.

[103] Ibid., s.109(8).

[104] Most recently reviewed in *Silven Properties Ltd* v. *Royal Bank of Scotland* [2003] EWCA 1409; [2004] 4 All ER 484. See *Downsview Nominees Ltd* v. *First City Corp. Ltd* [1993] AC 295 (PC); *Medforth* v. *Blake* [2000] Ch. 96 (CA). See also *Shamfi* v. *Johnson Matthey* [1991] BCLC 36 (CA) (a bank owed no duty of care to mortgagors in deciding to appoint receivers but could do so to protect its own interests).

[105] The mortgage deed traditionally provided for this in order to render the mortgagor liable for the acts of the receiver. However, this agency has 'some peculiar incidents' and hence the ordinary principles of agency are of 'limited assistance in identifying the duties owed by the receiver to the mortgagor': see *Silven Properties Ltd* v. *Royal Bank of Scotland*, n.104 above.

[106] See *Bishop* v. *Blake* [2006] EWHC 831 (Ch) (example of breach by mortgagor within LPA 1925, s.103(iii)).

[107] LPA 1925, s.105.   [108] *Nash* v. *Eads* (1880) 25 Sol. Jo. 95, *per* Jessel MR.

[109] *Silven Properties Ltd* v. *Royal Bank of Scotland* [2003] EWCA 1409; [2004] 4 All ER 484, containing a review and comparison of the duties of a mortgagee and receiver (which, in relation to sale of the mortgaged property, are the same). For a case where the duty was breached, see *Bishop* v. *Blake* [2006] EWHC 831 (Ch).

[110] *Tse Kwong Lam* v. *Wong Chit Sen* [1983] 3 All ER 54, 59; [1983] 1 WLR 1349, 1355; *Raja (administratrix of the estate of Raja (decd)* v. *Austin Gray (a firm)* [2002] EWCA Civ. 1965, [55]. A statement to the contrary by Denning MR in *Standard Chartered Bank Ltd* v. *Walker* [1982] 1 WLR 1410, 1415–1416 was disapproved in *Silven Properties Ltd* v. *Royal Bank of Scotland*, n.104 above.

[111] *Cuckmere Brick Co. Ltd* v. *Mutual Finance* [1971] Ch. 948; *Downsview Nominees* v. *First City Corp. Ltd*, noted at n.104 above.

exercised in good faith for the purpose of obtaining repayment and not purely for some ulterior motive.[112]

Finally, the right to foreclose the mortgage—a right inherent in all mortgages—is available to the bank. This requires a court order[113] whereby the court extinguishes the right of the mortgagor to redeem the land and conveys the land to the mortgagee. It is rarely used and only if the value of the outstanding debt is equal to (or less than) the value of the interest in the land. Otherwise the court will order a sale.[114]

An equitable mortgagee probably[115] has no inherent right to possession but often reserves such a right expressly under the mortgage contract. If the mortgage is under seal, he has a statutory right to appoint a receiver or sell the land.[116] Otherwise such rights must be reserved by the contract creating the mortgage. As regards the appointment of a receiver, in default of the statutory power being available, the equitable mortgagee may invoke the court's discretion to appoint a receiver 'when just or convenient to do so'.[117] As regards sale, it is again unclear whether the equitable mortgagee has the power to convey the legal estate.[118] Again the problem is avoided in well-drafted mortgage contracts which either give the mortgagee a power of attorney to convey the legal estate or declare him beneficiary (under a trust) of the legal estate so as to enable the mortgagee to effect the transfer of it. Foreclosure is in principle available to an equitable mortgagee, the court order directing the mortgagor to convey the legal estate to the mortgagee.

An equitable chargee has the right neither to possession nor to foreclose. If the charge is made by deed then the statutory powers of sale and appointment of receiver are probably available.[119] Otherwise the chargee is obliged to apply to court for an order for sale or for the appointment of a receiver.

As noted above, in exercising his powers as mortgagee, a mortgagee (and any receiver he appoints) owes a duty to the mortgagor and subsequent encumbrancers to act 'in good faith' for the purposes of protecting his security interest.[120] Additional equitable obligations arise, depending on the particular case, but no general duty of care in negligence is imposed as this would be inconsistent with those equitable duties.[121]

---

[112] *Downsview Nominees Ltd* v. *First City Corp. Ltd*, noted at n.104, above, applied in *Meretz Investments NV* v. *ACP Ltd* [2006] EWHC 74 (Ch) (affirmed, on a different point: [2007] EWCA Civ. 1303) where it was held that 'mixed motives' were not enough to impugn the sale.

[113] The procedure is cumbersome. First a decree nisi is obtained and then a decree absolute. A decree absolute may be reopened: *Campbell* v. *Holyland* (1877) 7 Ch. D 166.

[114] Under LPA 1925, s.91(2). It has an unfettered discretion to order a sale, even if the price does not cover the loan and against the wishes of the lender, if it would be unfair to the borrower to postpone a sale: *Palk* v. *Mortgage Services Funding*, n.98 above.

[115] There is some doubt: see the texts cited at n.2.   [116] LPA 1925, s.101(1)(i), (iii).

[117] Supreme Court Act 1981, s.37.

[118] All turns on the interpretation of the power. As far as the statutory power is concerned, it depends on whether the statutory words 'the mortgaged property' in LPA 1925, s.101(1)(i) cover the legal interest.

[119] LPA 1925, s.101 applies to a 'mortgagee' under a 'mortgage' and LPA 1925, s.205(1)(xvi) extends the definition of 'mortgage' to 'any charge'. However, the definition of the term 'mortgagee' is stated to 'include a chargee by way of legal mortgage' and therefore may be limited to such a legal mortgagee.

[120] *Downsview Nominees* v. *First City Corp. Ltd* [1993] AC 295 (PC), a duty not breached as long as this is one of his purposes in acting: *Meretz Investments NV* v. *ACP Ltd* [2006] EWHC 74 (Ch) (affirmed, on a different point: [2007] EWCA Civ. 1303).

[121] *Downsview Nominees* v. *First City Corp. Ltd* [1993] AC 295 (PC) and see *AIB Finance Ltd* v. *Alsop* [1998] 2 All ER 929 (CA).

(ix) **Protection of mortgagor**

A mortgage differs from other transactions in one important respect. The courts have always been astute to ensure that the mortgagee does not take undue advantage of the mortgagor and have consequently interfered in the contractual terms to protect the mortgagor.[122] This interference manifests itself in two related ways. First, if a transaction is in essence a loan on security, it will be treated as a mortgage whatever its form[123] with the result that the borrower may redeem his property no matter what the contract says. Secondly, once a transaction is identified as a mortgage, the courts ensure that there are no 'clogs or fetters on the equity of redemption' unduly prejudicing the mortgagor. This interventionist approach is at variance with the traditional principle of freedom of contract[124] which generally enables the parties, in particular the lender, to determine the terms on which they deal without any interference from the courts. Thus banks may find that terms they have inserted into a mortgage transaction are particularly vulnerable to attack.

Examples of terms in mortgage agreements that have been declared void by the courts are a term that the mortgagee can purchase the mortgaged property at his option,[125] a term postponing redemption unduly,[126] a term conferring a collateral advantage on the mortgagee, especially beyond the duration of the mortgage,[127] and a term that is 'oppressive'.[128] Many of the older cases are examples of crude consumer protection by the courts in the days when Parliament had not yet conferred intervention powers on the courts in the consumer context. Thus, more recently the courts have been more reluctant to upset properly negotiated commercial mortgage transactions,[129] although the possibility of mortgage terms prejudicing the mortgagor being overturned at common law should not be ignored.[130]

There are two statutory powers of intervention in particular that banks should be aware of. First, consumer credit legislation contains general provisions enabling the courts to

[122] 'For necessitous men are not, truly speaking, free men, but, to answer a present exigency will submit to any terms the crafty may impose on them': *per* Lord Northington in *Vernon* v. *Bethell* (1761) 2 Eden 110 at 113.

[123] *Re Watson* (1890) 25 QBD 27 (CA); *Grangeside Properties Ltd* v. *Collingwood Securities Ltd* [1964] 1 WLR 139. On the characterization of transactions as creating secured loans rather than absolute interests, see Ch. 18, Sect. 1.

[124] Which is in any event now modified by statute, see below. The 'clogs' doctrine has been criticized judicially (e.g. see *Jones* v. *Morgan* [2002] EWCA Civ. 995 per Phillips MR that it 'no longer serves a useful purpose') and by commentators (e.g. A. Berg, 'Clogs on the Equity of Redemption or Chaining an Unruly Dog' [2002] *JBL* 335).

[125] *Samuel* v. *Jarrah Timber and Wood Paving Corporation* [1904] AC 323 (HL); *Jones* v. *Morgan* [2002] EWCA Civ. 995 (but cf. *Warnborough* v. *Garmite Ltd* [2006] EWHC 10 (Ch)). But such an option granted in a separate and independent agreement after the mortgage has been granted has been upheld: *Reeve* v. *Lisle* [1902] AC 461 (HL).

[126] *Morgan* v. *Jeffreys* [1910] 1 Ch. 620 (postponement for 28 years); *Fairclough* v. *Swan Brewery Co. Ltd* [1912] AC 565 (PC) (mortgage of lease postponed redemption until the lease had almost expired). Cf. *Williams* v. *Morgan* [1906] 1 Ch. 804 (postponement for 14 years held valid); *Knightsbridge Estates Trust Ltd* v. *Byrne* [1939] Ch. 441; *Re Rudd and Son Ltd* [1986] BCC 98 (CA). But note that debentures may be irredeemable: Companies Act 2006, s.738.

[127] In *Biggs* v. *Hoddinott* [1898] 2 Ch. 307 and *Noakes* v. *Rice* [1902] AC 24: 'brewer's ties' which ended on redemption were upheld, but today they would have to satisfy the restraint of trade rules: *Esso Petroleum Co. Ltd* v. *Harper's Garage (Stourport) Ltd* [1965] AC 269.

[128] *Cityland and Property (Holdings) Ltd* v. *Debrah* [1968] Ch. 166.

[129] *Multiservice Bookbinding Ltd* v. *Marden* [1979] Ch. 84 (indexation of capital repayable upheld).

[130] See *Jones* v. *Morgan* [2002] EWCA Civ. 995, where, despite criticism of the 'clogs' doctrine, it was applied to invalidate a contractual right of the mortgagee to purchase the mortgaged property.

re-open credit agreements and adjust the rights of the parties—irrespective of the size of the loan as long as the debtor is not corporate or a large partnership—if the credit relationship is judged 'unfair' to the debtor.[131] Secondly, the Unfair Terms in Consumer Contracts Regulations 1999[132] enable the court to declare 'void' certain terms in standard term contracts made with consumers if those terms are 'unfair'. A mortgagee operating in the secondary 'non-status' sector found that various terms in its mortgage (as to dual interest rates and as to rebate on early settlement) were successfully challenged under the consumer credit legislation[133] and the 1999 Regulations in *Falco Finance* v. *Gough*.[134]

(x) Common clauses

To give themselves maximum protection, banks include a number of provisions in their standard contracts for land mortgages. The ones concerning priorities have already been mentioned. Other terms attempt to safeguard the bank's interest during the currency of the mortgage. Foremost among these is a term that requires the mortgagor to keep the property in good repair.

Another term requires him to keep the property fully insured against fire and other natural disasters. The mortgagor is further required to pay the premium regularly and, on his failure to do so, the bank is given the power to pay the premium at his expense. To protect itself fully, the bank further notifies the insurance company of its interest in the property. If the property is subsequently destroyed by fire, the company will not pay the amount insured to the owner without consulting the bank.

Another clause common in bank mortgages prohibits the leasing of the property during the currency of the mortgage.[135] The object of this clause is to ensure that the bank is able to obtain vacant possession of the property on the mortgagor's default.[136] A lease made in contravention of such a clause is invalid as against the mortgagee.[137]

(xi) Effect of the Consumer Credit Act 1974

The provisions of the Consumer Credit Act 1974 governing securities, discussed in Chapter 18, apply to regulated agreements secured by mortgages over land. However, a number of agreements secured by land mortgages are 'exempt agreements' and hence generally[138] outside the protection of the Act. Section 16 exempts certain agreements secured

---

[131] See Consumer Credit Act 1974, ss.140A–140D (added by the Consumer Credit Act 2006) and generally, Ch. 2, Sect. 5(xiii).

[132] S.I. 1999/2083 (replacing S.I. 1994/3159), implementing EC Council Directive 93/13/EC [1993] OJ L95/29.

[133] In fact under the (harder to invoke) old 'extortionate credit bargain' provisions (Consumer Credit Act 1974, ss.137–140, replaced by the 'unfair credit relationship' provisions, n.131 above).

[134] Only a county court decision, but noted in (1999) 111 *LQR* 360.

[135] In the absence of such a clause, the mortgagor is entitled to lease the property for a term not exceeding 50 years under s.99 of the Law of Property Act 1925.

[136] The clause is valid under s.99(13) of the Law of Property Act 1925.

[137] *Dudley and District Benefit Building Society* v. *Emerson* [1949] 1 Ch. 707. Cf. *Universal Permanent Building Society* v. *Cooke* [1952] Ch. 95, where the lease was granted fractionally before the creation of the mortgage. But see the Mortgage Repossessions (Protection of Tenants) Act 2010, n.95 above.

[138] However, the following provisions apply to exempt agreement (except mortgages regulated under the Financial Services and Markets Act 2000): (i) the 'unfair credit relationships' provisions (see Ch. 2, Sect. 5(xiii) above): ss.16(7A), 140A(5) & (ii) s.126 (see below, requiring a court order to enforce an agreement secured by a land mortgage): s.16(6D).

on land if the creditor falls within a defined class of lender. As noted above,[139] these lenders include institutions authorized under the Financial Services and Markets Act 2000 and their subsidiaries. In consequence many bank and finance house loans secured by land mortgages are exempt from the controls of the Act. Moreover, as discussed below,[140] those mortgages (and 'home purchase plans') that are regulated under the Financial Services and Markets Act 2000 are exempt from regulation under the 1974 Act. Finally, there is now an exemption for certain 'buy-to-let' mortgages.[141]

The Act contains two special provisions concerning regulated agreements secured by land mortgages. First, section 67—which confers on the debtor a right of cancellation in certain circumstances[142]—does not apply to a regulated agreement secured on land, to a restricted-use credit agreement[143] to finance the purchase of land, or to a bridging loan granted for such a purchase.[144] The Financial Services (Distance Marketing) Regulations 2004[145] similarly exclude 'restricted use' land mortgages and bridging loans from the right of cancellation conferred by those Regulations on certain 'distance' contracts.[146] Section 58 provides a different withdrawal procedure for regulated agreements secured by land mortgages, essentially giving the mortgagor a cooling-off period before he concludes the mortgage.

The other special provision applicable to land mortgages securing a regulated agreement concerns the question of enforcement. Under section 126, such a mortgage is enforceable (so far as provided in relation to the agreement) on the order of a court only. A shortcoming of this section is its failure to confer on the mortgagor any remedy for the breach of this provision.[147] A mortgagee who, in violation of this provision, takes possession of the land or puts it up for sale is not subject to any civil sanction,[148] although he will risk disciplinary action (and ultimately loss of his consumer credit licence) by the OFT.[149] Moreover, the purchaser of the mortgaged land is expressly protected.[150] There are, of course, cases in which the mortgagor is prepared to allow the mortgagee, or bank, to realize the security without a court order and hence the expense of such an order may be avoided by securing the mortgagor's express consent to enforcement.[151]

As the Consumer Credit Directive[152] does not apply to agreements secured on land, the provisions of the Act that have been introduced in order to implement that Directive do not apply to such agreements, although creditors may 'opt into' some of them.[153]

---

[139] See Ch. 2, Sect. 5(ii) and Consumer Credit (Exempt Agreements) Order 1989, S.I. 1989/869 (as amended).

[140] See Sect. (xii).

[141] Consumer Credit Act 1974, s.16C, added by the Legislative Reform (Consumer Credit) Order 2008, S.I. 2008/2826 (and see S.I. 2008/831).

[142] See Ch. 2, Sect. 5(iv).

[143] If the credit is provided in such a way that in practice (even if this is in contravention of the loan agreement) it leaves the debtor free to use it as he chooses, this is not a 'restricted-use' agreement: Consumer Credit Act 1974, s.11(3).

[144] Consumer Credit Act 1974, s.67(a). But note that s.57, governing the effect of the withdrawal from a prospective agreement (Ch. 2, Sect. 5(xii) above), is applicable to regulated agreements secured on land: s.57(4).

[145] S.I. 2004/2095, considered further in Ch. 2, Sect. 5(iv).   [146] Reg. 11(1)(g).

[147] Although an injunction is available under the Consumer Credit Act 1974, s.170(3).

[148] Ibid., s.170(1).   [149] See further, Ch. 2 Sect. 5(iii) above.

[150] Consumer Credit Act 1974, s.177(2).

[151] Ibid., s.173(2). The consent can only be given at the time the mortgagee wishes to act and so cannot be obtained from the mortgagor in the original agreement.

[152] Directive 2008/48/EC, see Ch. 2, Sect. 7(vi).

[153] By opting to comply with the Consumer Credit (Disclosure of Information) Regulations 2010, S.I. 2010/1012, mortgagees become subject to the Consumer Credit (Total Charge for Credit) Regulations 2010,

(xii) **Effect of the Financial Services and Markets Act 2000**

An outline of the Financial Services and Markets Act 2000 (FSMA 2000), as it applies to banks, was given in Chapter 2, Section 4. Since 31 October 2004 this Act has regulated certain mortgage lending, administration, arranging, and advising,[154] as well as certain mortgage advertising.[155] On 6 April 2007 regulation was extended to cover so-called 'Islamic mortgages'.[156] Some UK banks are beginning to offer these, especially 'home purchase plans'.[157] The intention is[158] that there is no overlap with the Consumer Credit Act 1974,[159] as those mortgages (and 'home purchase plans') and their financial promotions that are covered by the FSMA 2000 are removed from regulation under the 1974 Act.[160]

FSMA 2000 applies where the mortgage[161] satisfies the following conditions:[162] the borrower must be an individual or trustee, the mortgage must be secured by a first legal charge over UK property and the property must be at least 40 per cent occupied by the borrower (or his immediate family). The purpose and length of the loan is immaterial. However, the definition excludes mortgages securing loans to corporations (unless a trustee for individuals), second or subsequent mortgages[163] and mortgages of land where 60 per cent of it or more is used for non-residential purposes.[164] Further, the promotion of 'qualifying credit' is also regulated—'qualifying credit' being defined to include all secured lending (not only lending secured by mortgages satisfying the conditions listed above) by firms that are authorized by the Financial Services Authority (FSA) for mortgage lending purposes.[165] Thus a bank that is authorized to effect mortgages (and 'home purchase plans') satisfying the conditions noted above will find that the promotion of all

---

S.I. 2010/1010 (reg. 3) and the Consumer Credit (Agreements) Regulations 2010, S.I. 2010/1014 (see reg. 2(2), (3)(a)). However, it is not possible to 'opt into' the Consumer Credit (Advertisements) Regulations 2010, S.I. 2010/1970.

[154] See the FSMA 2000 (Regulated Activities) Order 2001, S.I. 2001/544 (as extensively amended), the 'RAO', arts. 61 (lending and administration), 25A (arranging mortgages), 53A (advising on mortgages). Initially, the RAO only covered lending and administration, but after consultation, it was decided to extend regulation to arranging and advising.

[155] See the FSMA 2000 (Financial Promotion) Order 2005, S.I. 2005/1529, the 'FPO', Sched. 1, paras. 10–12 (providing, arranging, and advising on 'qualifying credit'), and para. 28 (rights under agreement for 'qualifying credit'). See below.

[156] That fall within the definition of 'home purchase plan' or 'home reversion plan': see the RAO, arts. 63B–63I (corresponding to art. 61), arts. 25C & 25D (corresponding to art. 25B) and arts. 53B & 53C (corresponding to art. 53A), added by S.I. 2006/2383.

[157] As defined in RAO, art. 63F(3) which reflects the ordinary mortgage definition in RAO, art. 61.

[158] There is a small degree of overlap in that some mortgage brokers and advertisers (see below) need to comply with both regimes.

[159] See previous Sect.

[160] By the RAO (see Ch. 2, Sect. 4(ii)), arts. 90 & 91, adding s.16(6)(C)–(E) to the Consumer Credit Act 1974 as amended (to add 'home purchase plans') by S.I. 2006/2383. In fact most bank mortgages are exempt under the 1974 Act (see previous Sect.), so the only effect is that they will no longer be subject to that Act's Advertising Regulations (see Ch. 2, Sect. 5(vi)) but are subject to corresponding provisions under FSMA 2000.

[161] Termed a 'regulated mortgage' by the RAO, art. 61. And see RAO, art. 63F for the corresponding definition of a 'home purchase plan' (see n.156).

[162] See RAO, art. 61. In addition, the mortgage must be made after these provisions are brought into force. See the corresponding definition of 'regulated home purchase plan' in RAO, art. 63F(3).

[163] Some of these may be regulated under the Consumer Credit Act 1974, unless 'exempted' (as most bank mortgages usually are): see Ch. 2, Sect. 5(ii).

[164] Although, of course, some (but not lending on mortgage to a corporation or large partnership) may be regulated by the Consumer Credit Act 1974, see previous section and Ch. 2, Sect. 5(i) above.

[165] See FPO (see Ch. 2, Sect. 4(vii)), art. 2(1) & Sched. 1, para. 10.

its secured lending (for example, lending on second mortgages) is subject to FSMA 2000 regulation. As explained above,[166] financial promotion covered by the FSMA 2000 may only be effected, or if not so effected must be approved, by an authorized person.

Most of the detailed rules applicable to the regulation of mortgage lending and the promotion of 'qualifying credit' are in the 'MCOB' Module—part of the FSA Handbook.[167] The MCOB Module is a long and detailed part of the Handbook and it has had a major impact on banks who lend on first, legal, residential mortgages and (for banks offering them) 'home purchase plans'. It requires the provision of detailed information[168] to borrowers at all stages of the borrowing process: from promotion through to entry into the agreement and during the life time of the agreement. A cooling-off period is given for certain (but not conventional house-purchase) mortgages and an obligation to be a 'responsible lender' is also imposed. Certain charges payable under the mortgage are regulated, in particular, charges arising on arrears and 'exorbitant credit charges' are controlled. Finally, there are rules in relation to the protection of debtors who are in arrears.

3 Proprietary securities over goods

(i) General considerations

The making of banks' advances against chattels or goods is best known in international transactions involving the financing of exports and imports. The security used in such transactions is mainly the pledge, which is discussed in the next chapter. In domestic transactions, banks provide finance for the acquisition of goods mainly in respect of plant and equipment, although banks also finance the operations of finance companies active in the consumer market. In this last type of financial operation, the banks normally acquire a security over the finance companies' book debts or obtain a security by way of a floating charge.[169] The financing of transactions involving specific chattels is usually effected by means of letters of hypothecation. Chattel mortgages or bills of sale are not ordinarily used by banks.[170]

From an economic point of view a security over chattels or goods is less satisfactory than a land mortgage. Experience has shown that the price of land generally tends to rise steadily over the long term. As long as a bank ensures that its lending against land is within safe margins, and that the borrower has a residual interest in the property that encourages him to maintain it properly, the bank holds a sound security. Moreover, registration of the mortgage or the retention of the deeds gives the bank excellent protection against sharp practices.

By way of contrast, the value of goods or chattels is generally subject to substantial fluctuations, depending on the supply and demand in the market, which may be dictated by seasonal and other factors. Furthermore, some goods depreciate quickly or, in the light of modern technology, are rendered obsolete. Another hurdle is that goods are not

---

[166] Ch. 2, Sect. 4(vii).   [167] For the FSA Handbook see Ch. 2, Sect. 4(vi).

[168] The rules as to the calculation of the APR (see Ch. 2, Sect. 5(iv)) in MCOB 10 are almost identical to the pre-Directive rules (in S.I. 1980/51) for regulated consumer credit agreements (which still apply to mortgages regulated by the CCA 1974.

[169] As regards the transfer of book debts, see Ch. 21, Sect. 2 below; as regards floating charges, see Sect. 4 & Ch. 21, Sect. 2(iii) below.

[170] Leverage leasing, which is one of the methods for arranging transactions of this sort, is also not widely used by banks.

easily traceable if spirited away by an unscrupulous debtor. At the same time, transactions involving the acquisition of goods have the advantage of usually being for a shorter term than transactions involving the acquisition of land.

(ii) Chattel mortgages

A chattel mortgage is a security based on the transfer to the mortgagee of the legal or equitable property in the goods. Such an instrument falls within the definition of a bill of sale that has to be registered within seven days of its execution, otherwise it is void against the debtor's trustee in bankruptcy.[171] Furthermore, if the bill is given by way of security,[172] it is void unless issued in a prescribed form.[173] Yet a further hurdle is that a bill of sale cannot attach to chattels acquired by the mortgagee after the execution of the instrument.[174] This provision renders a chattel mortgage an unsuitable security where the goods may be replaced from time to time.[175]

The cumbersome provisions for registration and the need to follow the prescribed form applicable to bills of sale render the chattel mortgage an unattractive security. Furthermore, for historical reasons the granting of a bill of sale tends to cast doubts on the credit standing of the trader who effects it. The tendency in modern trade is to avoid it whenever possible. Thus, a trader who wishes to raise credit against a security over his plant or equipment is frequently asked to incorporate his business, whereupon the bank is able to provide the required finance against a floating charge.[176]

In practice, chattel mortgages are only used in the case of farming stock and agricultural assets generally. Such mortgages can be given under the Agricultural Credits Act 1928, and do not require registration as bills of sale.[177]

(iii) Hypothecation

When a customer hypothecates goods to his bank, he purports to create a security, which constitutes neither a legal mortgage nor a pledge. The goods are made available to the bank as a security without the bank obtaining either the possession of the goods or a legal title to them.[178] Instead, the debtor agrees to hold the goods in trust for the creditor. It has been held that such an arrangement confers on the creditor an equitable charge or interest in the goods.[179] This arrangement is distinguishable from the *hypothec* of Roman Law and of modern civil law, which is comparable to a mortgage.

British banks use the hypothecation of goods where the customer is unable or unwilling to give the bank actual or constructive possession of the goods by way of pledge and, as is common, the parties wish to avoid a chattel mortgage and hence a bill of sale. It

---

[171] Bills of Sale Act 1878, ss.8, 10; Bills of Sale Act (1878) Amendment Act 1882, s.8. The December 2009, BIS Consultation on, *inter alia*, whether the Bills of Sale Acts 1878 and 1882 should be repealed concluded they should stay.

[172] Since the Amendment Act of 1882, there are certain distinctions between the law applicable to absolute bills of sale and to those given by way of charge. Naturally, a bank seeks to obtain a security by way of charge.

[173] Bills of Sale Act (1878) Amendment Act 1882, s.9.

[174] Ibid., s.5. But note the different position in the case of companies: Sect. 4(ii) below.

[175] For example, a dealer's stock in trade.   [176] See Sect. 4(ii) & (v) below.

[177] Agricultural Credits Act 1928, s.8(1). But they are mortgages within the meaning of the Law of Property Act 1925, s.205(1)(xvi). On a bank's power to provide such finance, see Ch. 3, Sect. 2(ii) above.

[178] M. Holden, *Securities for Bankers' Advances* (8th edn., London, 1993), 307.

[179] *Re Slee, ex p. North Western Bank* (1872) LR 5 Eq. 69; *Re Hamilton Young & Co.* [1905] 2 KB 722; *Official Assignee of Madras* v. *Mercantile Bank of India Ltd* [1935] AC 53, *per* Lord Wright at 64.

should be noted that the word 'hypothecation' is used loosely in practice. Thus, when a bank acquires a pledge over documents of title, it may require the customer to execute a 'letter of hypothecation'.[180] The use of the phrase in this context, however, is a misnomer. A genuine hypothecation is effected where the goods are not in the debtor's immediate possession or control. An example is where they are in a warehouse together with other goods of the customer. A pledge is then feasible only if it is practical to separate the goods in question from the rest.[181] If such a separation of the goods that are to serve as collateral from the bulk is impractical, the debtor's best course is to grant the bank a hypothecation over them. Hypothecation is also used in respect of goods that are not in existence at the time the security is given, or goods that are in the manufacturing process.[182]

Although the hypothecation of goods is a valid transaction,[183] it constitutes a poor security. As the creditor acquires no control over the goods, the debtor has no difficulty in dealing with them in disregard of the hypothecation. Moreover, the creditor merely has an equitable interest in the goods that may easily be defeated. Thus, an innocent purchaser[184] and a pledgee who obtains possession in good faith[185] are unaffected by the hypothecation. Another weakness inherent in the hypothecation of goods arises from the provisions of the Bills of Sale Acts. The essence of the letter of hypothecation is the debtor's undertaking to hold the goods for the account or as a trustee of the creditor. The document constitutes, therefore, a declaration of trust over the goods without effecting a transfer. As such it *prima facie* falls within the definition of a bill of sale in section 4 of the 1878 Act. Under section 8 of the same Act, a bill of sale is void against the debtor's trustee in bankruptcy unless registered. Thus, in *National Provincial Bank and Union Bank of England* v. *Lindsell*,[186] a letter in which a car-owner instructed a repairer to hold the car and the proceeds thereof on behalf of a bank was held void for want of registration.

The position is further complicated by the fact that the 1878 Act expressly excludes from the definition of a bill of sale any transfers in the ordinary course of business[187] or 'any other document used in the ordinary course of business as proof of the possession or control of goods'.[188] The relevance of this saving to letters of hypothecation was considered in *Re Hamilton, Young & Co.*,[189] which concerned a security by way of a 'letter of lien' over wool which was being processed into cloth. The document in question, which had all the attributes of a hypothecation, was held to confer on the creditor a valid equitable charge. However, as the document was found to be of a type used in the ordinary course

---

[180] The term was used in this way by H.C. Gutteridge & M. Megrah, in earlier editions of *Law of Bankers' Commercial Credits*. See now the 8th edition (London, 2001) by R. King, paras. 8.19–8.30.

[181] For the need to identify goods to execute a pledge by means of constructive possession, see Ch. 20, Sect. 1 below.

[182] See, for example, *Re Hamilton Young & Co.* [1905] 2 KB 772 below.

[183] *Re Slee, ex p. North Western Bank Ltd* (1872) LR 15 Eq. 69; *Re Hamilton, Young & Co.* [1905] 2 KB 772; *Re David Allester Ltd* [1922] 2 Ch. 211.

[184] *Re Slee, ex p. North Western Bank Ltd*, n.183 above.

[185] *Lloyds Bank Ltd* v. *Bank of America National Trust and Savings Association* [1938] 2 KB 147, 165; *Mercantile Bank of India Ltd* v. *Central Bank of India Ltd* [1938] AC 287. Both cases concerned 'letters of trust'. The basis of letters of trust and of letters of hypothecation is conceptually the same.

[186] [1922] 1 KB 21.Cf *Re Slee, ex p. North Western Bank* (1872) LR 15 Eq. 69, decided under the Bills of Sale Act 1854, which contained a narrower definition of 'bill of sale' than the later Act of 1878.

[187] See *Stephenson* v. *Thompson* [1924] 2 KB 240 (CA)   [188] Bills of Sale Act 1878, s.4.

[189] [1905] 2 KB 772.

of business as proof of the possession or control of goods, it did not require registration as a bill of sale.

It is arguable that the decision in *Re Hamilton, Young & Co.* cannot withstand close analysis. It is unrealistic to regard a letter of hypothecation as constituting 'proof of the possession or control of goods by the creditor'. In reality, its words import a message to the contrary. The person who has possession and control declares that he holds the goods for the account of another person. But there is no attempt to confer the actual possession or control on that beneficiary.[190] Hence, it may be that some letters of hypothecation would not be regarded as documents used 'in the ordinary course of business'.[191] In *R v. Townshend*[192] it was held that a letter of hypothecation, in terms similar to those used in the previous case, constituted a declaration of trust without transfer, and there was no finding to the effect that it was made in the ordinary course of business. The transaction would have been avoided for want of registration, except that it fell within the scope of another exemption applicable to goods on board a ship.

Thus, it would seem wrong to regard a hypothecation as anything but a declaration of trust without transfer and hence as a bill of sale. It is typical that, in *Ladenburg v. Goodwin Ferreira & Co. Ltd*,[193] a letter of hypothecation, which attached to the proceeds of sale of goods which had been sold at the time of its execution, was held registrable as a charge over a company's book debts. The case suggests that the true object of a letter of hypothecation is to create a charge or chattel mortgage, and not to constitute proof of the possession of goods. This supports the view that a hypothecation granted by an unincorporated trader constitutes a bill of sale.

A letter of hypothecation is thus a questionable security. This applies not only to hypothecations effected by individuals but also to those effected by companies. The reason for this is that any charge which would require registration as a bill of sale if effected by an individual has to be registered as a charge under the Companies Act 2006 if effected by a company.[194]

An important exception is made in respect of letters of hypothecation made over imported goods prior to their being warehoused, stored, reshipped for export, or delivered to a person other than the debtor who executes the document. In the interests of commercial practice, such letters have been expressly excluded from the scope of the Bills of Sale Acts.[195]

(iv) **Effect of the Consumer Credit Act 1974**

Both a chattel mortgage and a letter of hypothecation issued in the context of a regulated agreement fall within the definition of a security for the purposes of the Consumer Credit Act 1974.[196]

---

[190] See ibid. *per* Stirling LJ at 789.

[191] See *Halsbury's Laws of England* (4th edn., London, 2002), vol. 4(1), para. 641, which doubts whether a general letter of hypothecation, as opposed to one over identified goods (as in *Re Hamilton*), n.189 above, would fall within the exception.

[192] (1884) 15 Cox CC 466.

[193] [1912] 3 KB 275.

[194] S.870(7)(b), see Sect. 4(iii) below; and see *Dublin City Distillery Ltd* v. *Doherty* [1914] AC 823.

[195] Bills of Sale Amendment Act 1891, s.1.   [196] See Ch. 18, Sect. 4(i) above.

4 Securities granted by companies[197]

(i) Nature and flexibility of companies' charges

The security used most widely to secure advances made to a company is the charge. It will be recalled that such a security differs from both a mortgage, which transfers the property to the creditor, and a pledge, which confers on the creditor actual or constructive possession. Basically, a charge gives the creditor the right to apply to court[198] to realize the security upon the debtor's default and to recover his debt from the proceeds in priority to other claims. Conceptually, therefore, a charge may be identified with a hypothecation.

Although at law a charge is regarded as a mere agreement to confer some security interest, equity treats the security as being effected at the time of the execution of the agreement.[199] Three conditions have to be fulfilled for equity to intervene. First, it has to be shown that the advance has been made.[200] Secondly, it has to be established that the parties intend to confer on the creditor an equitable interest in the property and not a mere contractual right.[201] Thirdly, the parties must have manifested an intention that the interest attach immediately or, if the property is to be acquired by the debtor at a later date, as soon as he acquires the title thereto. A charge, which is to attach on a contingency, constitutes a mere contract to furnish security and is ineffective as a charge.[202] In *Holroyd* v. *Marshall*,[203] Lord Westbury proposed, as a general rule, that a charge is effective if the agreement under which it is created would be specifically enforced in equity.[204]

The charge is not commonly used by banks for the financing of individual traders or of unincorporated business firms as it falls within the definition of section 4 of the Bills of Sale Act 1878.[205] The practical problems posed by the Bills of Sale Acts, in particular in relation to after-acquired property, have been noted above in relation to chattel mortgages.[206]

Those drawbacks do not apply in the case of charges granted by companies. Such charges are outside the ambit of the Bills of Sale Acts[207] and are instead registrable under the more flexible provisions of the Companies Act 2006.[208] Consequently, the onerous requirements of form and the restriction on covering after-acquired property are inapplicable.

It may be asked whether, quite regardless of the Bills of Sale Acts, equity recognizes the validity of a charge over after-acquired property.[209] In the landmark case of *Holroyd*

---

[197] We should like to acknowledge our debt to the contributions on the subject by W.J. Gough, *Company Charges* (2nd edn., London, 1996), and R.M. Goode, *Legal Problems of Credit and Security* (4th edn., London, 2009).

[198] Powers to realize the security without recourse to the courts may be conferred on the chargee by contract or by statute (e.g. LPA 1925, s.101: charges by deed).

[199] See generally Gough, n.197 above, 18; Goode, n.197 above, paras. 1–51–1–52.

[200] *Rogers* v. *Challis* (1859) 27 Beav. 175.   [201] *Tailby* v. *Official Receiver* (1888) 13 App. Cas. 523, 547.

[202] *Re Jackson & Bassford Ltd* [1906] 2 Ch. 467; *Re Gregory Love & Co. Ltd* [1916] 1 Ch. 203; *Williams* v. *Burlington Investments Ltd* (1977) 12 SJ 424. And see Goode, n.197 above, para. 2-15. But a charge on an interest which is bound to materialize at a future date, such as an expectancy, is valid: *Re Lind* [1915] 2 Ch. 345.

[203] (1862) 10 HLC 191.   [204] Cf. Goode, n.197 above, para. 2-11.

[205] Sect. 3(ii) above; most charges, given in lieu of mortgages, would not fall within any of the exceptions.

[206] See ibid.

[207] *Re Standard Manufacturing Co.* [1891] 1 Ch. 627; *Richards* v. *Kidderminster Overseers* [1896] 2 Ch. 212.

[208] See Sect. (iii) below.   [209] For a detailed analysis, see Gough, n.197 above, 25 ff.

v. *Marshall*,[210] the owner of a mill granted a financier a mortgage covering the existing plant of his enterprise and any machinery acquired by way of replacement. It was held that the mortgage attached to the after-acquired property from the date of its acquisition by the mill-owner, notwithstanding that his interest in it was acquired at a date later than the execution of the mortgage. It was enough that the parties to the transaction contemplated the substitution of the existing plant during the currency of the mortgage. Moreover, the charge retains its priority even if competing charges are given in the period preceding the acquisition of the property by the debtor, and although the debtor becomes insolvent in the meantime.[211]

The resulting flexibility of charges created by companies renders them attractive to banks that finance the ongoing commercial activities of their customers. Frequently, individual traders and partnerships are asked to incorporate their business so that they may secure an overdraft obtained from the bank by a floating charge or by a fixed charge attaching to after-acquired property.

(ii) Fixed and floating charges

The availability of companies' charges covering after-acquired property has facilitated the development of two separate categories of company charge: the fixed charge and the floating charge. A fixed charge gives the chargee, from its inception, an immediate proprietary interest in a specific asset (hence it is sometimes called a 'specific charge'), which precludes the asset from being dealt with by the chargor without the chargee's consent. A floating charge notionally 'hovers over' the company's assets for the time being, enabling the company to deal with the assets in the ordinary course of business[212] and attaches to them only when the charge crystallizes.[213]

The floating charge is unique to English law, which has recognized its validity for well over 100 years,[214] and to systems derived from it. American law has refused to recognize the validity of such a security, as it fails to give the chargee adequate control over the charged assets.[215] The concept was also not recognized by Scottish law until it was introduced by statute.[216]

---

[210] (1862) 10 HLC 191.

[211] *Re Reis* [1904] 2 KB 769; *Re Lind* [1915] 2 Ch. 345 discussed in detail by Goode, n.197 above, para. 2-14. For a forceful criticism of the case law, see P. Matthews, 'Effect of Bankruptcy on Mortgages of Future Property' [1981] *LMCLQ* 40. And note that, under the Insolvency Act 1986, s.127 a disposition is void only if made after the commencement of the winding-up; the charge, though, is notionally regarded as attached when the agreement is made.

[212] *Ashborder BV* v. *Green Gas Power Ltd* [2004] EWHC 1517 (Ch): wide meaning given to the term 'ordinary course of business' (although transfers in that case held to be outside the term).

[213] For crystallization, see Sect. 4 (vi) below.

[214] *Re Panama, New Zealand and Australia Royal Mail Co.* (1870) LR 5 Ch. App. 318; followed by the House of Lords in *Illingsworth* v. *Houldsworth* [1904] AC 355, affg. *Re Yorkshire Woolcombers Association Ltd* [1903] 2 Ch. 284. The history of the floating charge is described in *Agnew* v. *CIR* [2001] 2 AC 710; [2001] 3 WLR 454 (PC). See also R. Gregory & P. Walton, 'Fixed and Floating Charges—a revelation' [2000] *LMCLQ* 123 who argue that floating charges have a much longer provenance.

[215] G. Gilmore, *Security Interests in Personal Property* (Boston and Toronto, 1965), para. 11.7. See also P.F. Coogan & J. Bak, 'The Import of Article 9 of the UCC and the Corporate Indenture' (1959) 69 *Yale LJ* 203, 251 ff.; R. Pennington, 'The Genesis of the Floating Charge' (1960) 23 *MLR* 630.

[216] By the Companies (Floating Charges) (Scotland) Act 1962. See now Companies Act 2006, Pt. 25, Ch. 2 and Bankruptcy and Diligence etc (Scotland) Act 2007. It is expected that the power under Companies Act 2006, s.893 will be used to recognize registration under the 2007 Act (when brought into force) as satisfying the registration requirement under the 2006 Act.

The conceptual distinction between a floating charge and a fixed charge is compli-cated by the fact that a fixed charge may cover future assets and attach as soon as the debtor acquires those assets. It follows that not every charge that attaches to a class of future assets is floating. Historically, the classic description of a floating charge was found in Romer LJ's judgment in *Re Yorkshire Woolcombers Association Ltd*,[217] which stressed three characteristics: the charge covers a class of assets, the assets are of a type that, in the ordinary course of the business of the company, change from time to time and, until some future step is taken by or on behalf of the chargee, the company is permitted to carry on its dealings in this class of assets in its ordinary course of business. Recent case law has established that it is the third characteristic that is the hallmark of a floating charge,[218] the first two merely being 'typical of a floating charge'.[219] Thus it is the degree of control that the chargee obtains over the revolving property, or its corollary, the freedom the chargor retains to deal with the property and remove it from the charge, that is the main determinant whether the charge is fixed or floating. But as both types of charge are the result of the contract between the chargor and chargee, it is possible for the chargee of a fixed charge to give some permission to the chargor to dispose of the property[220] and it is possible for the chargee of a floating charge to impose some restrictions—for example, by means of 'negative pledge clauses'—on the chargor's power to deal with the proper-ty.[221] Such contractual provisions on freedom to deal with the charged property make the drawing of the line between fixed and floating charges problematic. This is particularly so in relation to charges over book debts, as is discussed in Chapter 21.[222] The process has two stages: the nature of the rights and obligations created by the contract are ascertained (as a matter of fact) and then these are used to characterize the charge (as a matter of law) as either fixed or floating.[223]

Thus, the mere fact that a charge is granted over a class of future assets does not neces-sarily establish that it is a floating charge. By way of illustration, take a charge over all existing and future book debts of a company coupled with a stipulation that the proceeds be paid directly into the account maintained by the company with the bank that acquires the security on terms that the bank must consent to all withdrawals.[224] As is noted in Chapter 21, it has been held that such an arrangement usually involves the creation of a fixed charge because the company is deprived of the freedom to release the book debts from the charge and deal with them in the ordinary course of business.[225] Similarly, an arrangement between a bank and a customer for the financing of stock-in-trade, stored in the bank's name and replaced from time to time with its consent, has all the ingredients

---

[217] Above, n.214, at 295; and see Goode, n.197, para. 4-04, who compares a floating charge to a river that is in existence although the water in it changes constantly. For more recent judicial examinations of the nature of a floating charge, see Hoffmann J's judgment in *Re Brightlife* [1987] Ch. 200 and Lord Millett's in *Agnew* v. *CIR* [2001] 2 AC 710; [2001] 3 WLR 454 (PC).

[218] *Re Spectrum Plus Ltd* [2005] 2 AC 680.

[219] And not necessarily inconsistent with a fixed charge: see *Agnew* v. *CIR* [2001] 2 AC 710; [2001] 3 WLR 454 (PC).

[220] *Re Cimex Tissues Ltd* [1995] BCLC 409; *Re Atlantic Computer Systems plc* [1992] Ch. 505.

[221] *Re Brightlife* [1987] Ch. 200. For 'negative pledge clauses', see Sect. (iv) below.

[222] See Ch. 21, Sect. 2(iii).

[223] Per Lord Millett in *Agnew* v. *CIR* [2001] 2 AC 710; [2001] 3 WLR 454 and see Ch. 18, Sect. 1(ii).

[224] *Re Keenan Bros Ltd* [1986] BCLC 242.

[225] *Re Spectrum Plus Ltd* [2005] 2 AC 680, disapproving *Siebe Gorman & Co. Ltd* v. *Barclays Bank Ltd* [1979] 2 Lloyd's Rep. 142 where the bank account was not 'blocked' in this way. See further Ch. 21, Sect. 2(iii) below.

of a fixed rather than a floating charge.[226] However, in practice it is usually more convenient to leave access to the funds or the management of the stock-in-trade to the company, which means that the charge will be floating.

It has been pointed out long ago by Buckley LJ that a floating charge is not a specific mortgage of the assets involved, coupled with a licence to the mortgagor to continue trading in them; it is a 'floating mortgage applying to every item comprised in the security, but not specifically affecting any item until some event occurs or some act on the part of the mortgagee is done which causes it to crystallise into a fixed security'.[227] Nevertheless, the true conceptual nature of the floating charge continues to divide commentators.[228]

It may be asked why it matters whether a charge is fixed or floating. The answer lies in the special rules that apply to floating charges, which are noted below.[229] Thus the priority of a chargee, both as against other secured creditors and preferential creditors, depends on whether the charge is fixed or floating, the floating charge being more likely to be postponed to subsequent charges and being postponed to preferential creditors. Moreover, floating charges are particularly susceptible to being avoided in administration or liquidation. Yet, despite these drawbacks, there are distinct practical advantages to a floating charge stemming primarily from the freedom it gives the chargor to carry on business by dealing with the charged property. Thus where a bank has confidence in its corporate customer's standing and creditworthiness, the floating charge is considered an adequate protection.

(iii) **Registration of company charges**

Certain company charges require registration in the Companies Register under Part 25 of the Companies Act 2006.[230] The registration system was first introduced in 1900 to enable those dealing with a company to establish how much of its property was already charged to creditors. It has been the subject of much criticism and many proposals for reform over the years.[231] The Companies Act 2006 essentially re-enacts the existing provisions but the Act now enables those provisions to be amended by secondary legislation.[232] At the time of writing a consultation process is in progress on the use of this power.[233]

Non-registration of a registrable charge within 21 days of its creation, gives rise to the 'invalidity sanction': the charge becomes void against the liquidator, administrator,

---

[226] *Re Bond Worth* [1980] Ch. 228. See *Re Brightlife Ltd* [1987] Ch. 200 where the (non-bank) chargee had no control over the bank account into which the proceeds of the debts were paid.

[227] *Evans* v. *Rival Granite Quarries Ltd* [1901] KB 979, 999.

[228] See, for example, R. Pennington, 'The Genesis of the Floating Charge' (1960) 23 *MLR* 630; E. Ferran, 'Floating Charges—the Nature of the Security' (1988) 47 *CLJ* 213; S. Worthington, 'Floating Charges—an Alternative Theory' (1994) 53 *CLJ* 213; Nolan, 'Property in a Fund' (2004) 120 *LQR* 108. See also J. Getzler & J. Payne, *Company Charges: Spectrum and Beyond* (Oxford, 2006), and H. Beale, M. Bridge, L. Gullifer, & E. Lomnicka, *The Law of Personal Property Security* (Oxford, 2007), paras. 4.45–4.51.

[229] See Sect. (v) below.   [230] In force on 1 October 2009, replacing Companies Act 1985, Pt. XII.

[231] The Companies Act 1989, Pt. IV contained provisions on the registration of company charges but they were never brought into force and were repealed by the 2006 Act (Sched. 16). The issue was considered as part of the DTI's Company Law Review in 1997 (which led to the Companies Act 2006) and then the Law Commission took over the project, see its Report, *Company Security Interests*, Law Com. No. 296 (London, 2005), preceded by its Consultation Paper No. 164, *Registration of Security Interests: Company Charges and Property other than Land* (London, 2002) and Consultation Paper No. 176, *Company Security Interests: A Consultative Report* (2004). For a discussion of those proposals for reform, see Beale, Bridge, Gullifer, & Lomnicka, n.228 above, ch. 22.

[232] Companies Act 2006, s.894.   [233] See BIS's Consultation Paper, March 2010.

and 'a creditor of the company'.[234] When this occurs, any money secured by the charge immediately becomes payable, but the charge and the obligation secured by it remain valid as between the company and the chargee.[235] The chargee may therefore still exercise enforcement and other rights under the charge against the company, but is treated as an unsecured creditor as against other creditors and on liquidation and during administration. The Companies Register presently operates alongside specialist registers relating to specific types of property such as land, aircraft, ships, and intellectual property.[236] Whilst registration under those systems is usually required in order to create the security, registration under the Companies Act 2006 is required merely to preserve the validity of the security against other creditors and on liquidation or administration.

The obligation to register under the Companies Act 2006 applies to charges created by the company.[237] Therefore, charges arising by operation of law are not covered,[238] nor are true retentions of title.[239] Moreover, the Act makes it clear that the term 'charge' includes a mortgage for these purposes.[240] But, of course, the term does not cover genuine outright assignments that are not made by way of charge.[241] Nor does it cover other forms of security that are not 'charges' such as contractual liens.[242]

Section 860(7) of the Act contains a specific and comprehensive list of charges that require registration. The list comprises charges on land wherever situate,[243] charges which, if executed by an individual, would require registration as a bill of sale,[244] charges on ships or aircraft,[245] charges on certain intangibles, namely goodwill, intellectual property,[246] book debts[247] and uncalled share capital,[248] charges for securing an issue of debentures,[249]

---

[234] Companies Act 2006, s. 874 (previously the 1985 Act, s.395(1)). See *Smith (Administrator of Cosslett (Contractors) Ltd)* v. *Bridgend BC* [2002] 1 AC 336; [2002] 1 All ER 292 (HL). But purchasers of the collateral take subject to the (unregistered) charge.

[235] Ibid., s.874(2) (previously, Companies Act 1985, s.395(2)).

[236] The need for dual registration and the 'tension' between the two systems, especially as to priority, cause difficulties in practice and hence the Companies Act 2006, s.893 confers power on the Secretary of State to deal with this problem (and see n.232 above).

[237] Companies Act 2006, s.860 (previously, Companies Act 1985, s.395(1)).

[238] *Bruton* v. *Electrical Engineering Corp.* [1892] 1 Ch. 434 (solicitor's lien); *London and Cheshire Insurance Co.* v. *Laplagrene Property Co.* [1971] Ch. 499 (unpaid vendor's lien).

[239] For example, under a hire-purchase agreement or a 'Romalpa' clause (see Ch. 21, Sect. 2(vi)). But claims to proceeds under *Romalpa* clauses are generally regarded as by way of charge, see Ch. 18, Sect. 1(i).

[240] Companies Act 2006, s.861(5) (previously Companies Act 1985, s.396(4)).

[241] *Re George Inglefield* [1933] Ch. 1 and see Ch. 18, Sect. 1(i).

[242] *Re Hamlet International plc* [1998] 2 BCLC 164: power of sale in contractual lien did not render it a 'charge'.

[243] Including charges on interests in land other than rent charges: ss.860(7)(a), 861(2) (previously Companies Act 2006, s.396(1)(d)). And note s.861(1) (previously, Companies Act 1985, s.396(3)): debentures entitling holder to charge on land not covered.

[244] S.860(7)(b) (previously, Companies Act 1985, s.396(1)(c)). For bills of sale, see Sect. 3(ii) above.

[245] S.860(7)(h) (previously, Companies Act 1985, s.396(1)(h)).

[246] S.860(7)(i) (previously, Companies Act 1985, s.396(1)(j)). See also s.861(4) (previously, Companies Act 1985, s.396(3A)): meaning of 'intellectual property'.

[247] S.860(f) (previously, Companies Act 1985, s.396(1)(e)). For 'book debts', see Ch. 21, Sect. 2(i) and, for example, *Independent Automatic Sales Ltd* v. *Knowles & Foster* [1962] 1 WLR 974; *Paul & Frank Ltd* v. *Discount Bank (Overseas) Ltd* [1967] Ch. 348. Note also s.861(3) (previously Companies Act 1985, s.396(2)): deposit of negotiable instrument to secure payment of book debts not treated as charge over those book debts (so as to preserve its negotiability). For registration of assignments of book debts, see Ch. 21, Sect. 2(v).

[248] S.860(7)(d) (previously, Companies Act 1985, s.396(1)(b)). Charges on called but unpaid capital are also covered: s.870(7)(e) (previously, Companies Act 1985, s.396(1)(g)).

[249] S.870(7)(c) (previously, Companies Act 1985, s.396(1)(a)).

and floating charges on the whole or part of the company's undertaking.[250] Registration is also required if a company acquires property that is subject to an existing charge that would, if created by the company, have been registrable, although non-registration does not incur the 'invalidity sanction'.[251] Although most charges given by companies are covered, there are conspicuous omissions from the list of registrable charges: fixed charges over receivables that are not 'book debts',[252] and fixed charges over insurance policies.[253] Moreover, as a security financial collateral arrangement (or a charge created or arising thereunder) is not registrable,[254] fixed charges over various company securities are also not registrable.

Special mention needs to be made of land securities that may also be registrable either in the Land Charges Register in the case of unregistered land or in the Land Registry in the case of registered land.[255] It should be noted that although all land securities are registrable in the Companies Register, a narrower category of land securities are also registrable in the Land Charges Registry. As regards unregistered land, only legal mortgages not protected by deposit of deeds and certain equitable mortgages need to be registered in the Land Charges Register.[256] Moreover, there is a special provision rendering registration of a floating charge with the Companies Register equivalent to registration in the Land Charges Register.[257] As regards registered land, the usual provisions apply.[258]

The Companies Act 2006 requires the Companies Registrar to maintain a register of company charges, open to public inspection.[259] The company is obliged to deliver to the Registrar within 21 days of creating the charge both prescribed particulars of the charge and the charge instrument.[260] The obligation to take these steps is on the company, and it has an incentive to do so due to the 'invalidity sanction' mentioned above which renders the money advanced immediately repayable if the charge is not registered. However, non-registration also prejudices the chargee and therefore 'any person interested' in the charge may also effect the registration.[261] The Registrar enters certain details of the charge in the register,[262] returns the charge instrument to the presenter, and issues a certificate of registration setting out the amount secured.[263] The certificate is conclusive evidence that registration has been effected[264] and therefore gives assurance that the charge cannot be void for non-registration.[265] Provision is made for applications to be made to court to rectify the register by allowing late registration or the amendment of particulars. The court

---

[250] S.870(7)(g) (previously, Companies Act 1985, s.396(1)(f)).

[251] Companies Act 2006, s.862 (previously, Companies Act 1985, s.400). For the invalidity sanction, see above. But it is a criminal offence not to register the existing charge.

[252] See further, Ch. 21, Sect. 2(i).

[253] The BIS March 2010 Consultation (see n.233, above) is likely to result in a more comprehensive approach.

[254] The Financial Collateral Arrangements (No. 2) Regulations 2003, S.I. 2003/3226 (implementing the Financial Collateral Arrangements Directive, 2002/47/EC), reg. 4.

[255] See further Sect. 2(iv) above.   [256] See further ibid.   [257] Land Charges Act 1972, s.3(7).

[258] See further, Sect. 2(iv) above.

[259] Companies Act 2006, s.869 (previously, Companies Act 1985, s.401).

[260] S.869(1) (previously, Companies Act 1985, s.399(1)) (charges it creates), s.862 (previously, Companies Act 1985, s.400) (existing charges on property acquired). The 21-day period is imposed by s.870. There is a criminal sanction (as well as the 'invalidity sanction') for breach of s.860: s.860(4), (5) & s.862(4), (5).

[261] S.860(2) (previously, Companies Act 1985, s.395(1)).

[262] Listed in s.869(4): date of charge, amount secured, 'short particulars' of the collateral and the chargee(s).

[263] S.869(5).   [264] S.869(6)(b).

[265] The certificate is conclusive even if there were errors in the particulars delivered: *Re CL Nye* [1971] Ch. 442 (CA).

has a wide discretion which in practice it exercises in such a way so as not to prejudice third parties (in particular, intervening creditors).[266]

As noted above, registration preserves the validity of the charge from the date of its creation. However, during the 21-day period when registration may be effected, it is not obvious to persons dealing with the company that such a (potentially valid) charge has been created. This gives rise to the so-called '21 day invisibility problem' and may result in a chargee being bound by a duly registered prior charge it had no means of knowing about. However, although this situation does not appear to arise significantly in practice, chargees need to be aware of this slight risk and protect themselves by obtaining undertakings from the company and not releasing the funds until their charge has been duly registered (and hence the prior charge also revealed).

In addition to being obliged to register certain charges at the central Companies Register, companies are also obliged to make available at their registered office information about *all* charges over their property.[267] Thus they must keep copies of every instrument creating or evidencing such a charge[268] and a register containing details of those charges.[269] This obligation extends to all charges, whether or not they are registrable at the Companies Registry under section 860. The only sanction provided for failure to comply with these obligations is criminal;[270] the charge remains valid.[271] Clearly this domestic register at the registered office—if properly maintained—provides a more accurate picture of the securities created by a company than the central Companies Register. However, the fact that creditors may—if it is not properly maintained—be prejudiced by it led to the enactment of the provisions requiring registration at the central Companies Registry and the 'invalidity sanction'.

(iv) **Priorities**

The position here is rather complex and not altogether settled.[272] In principle, company charges take priority in the order in which they have been created unless there is something to disturb this order. This natural chronological order may be disturbed by a number of factors.

First, by their very nature, floating charges are in principle postponed to any subsequent charge that is created by the company in the ordinary course of business. This is because the essence of a floating charge is that the chargee permits the company to carry on dealing with (including charging) its assets.[273] Thus a subsequent fixed charge generally takes priority over a prior (uncrystallized) floating charge[274] as does a subsequent floating charge over part of the charged property.[275] However the situation is complicated

---

[266] S.873 (previously, Companies Act 1985, s.404).

[267] Ss.875–877. But note the (new) relaxations in s.877 allowing the documents to be kept elsewhere (as specified by regulations).

[268] S.875 (registrable charges), s.877 (other charges).

[269] S.876. The copies and register are open to inspection and to the taking of copies by anyone: s.876(1) (register) and ss.875 & 877 (instruments creating charges).

[270] S.876 (register), s.877 (instruments).

[271] *Wright* v. *Horton* (1887) 12 App. Cas. 371 (HL); *Re General South American Company Co.* (1876) 2 Ch. D 337 (CA) (errors on register).

[272] See Beale, Bridge, Gullifer & Lomnicka, n.228 above, Pt. III; Gough, n.197 above, Pt. 8.

[273] *Robson* v. *Smith* [1895] 2 Ch. 118, 124.

[274] *Wheatley* v. *Silkstone and Haigh Moor Coal Co.* (1885) 29 Ch. D 715; *Re Hamilton's Windsor Ironworks, ex p. Pitman and Edwards* (1879) 12 Ch. 707; *Re Castell and Brown Ltd* [1898] 1 Ch. 315.

[275] At least if the first floating charge contains an express power permitting this: *Re Automatic Bottle Makers Ltd* [1926] Ch. 412 (CA). However, two floating charges, both over the whole undertaking, rank

by 'negative pledge' clauses in floating charges which stipulate that the chargor may not create subsequent security interests in priority to or *pari passu* with the floating charge. Such clauses clearly do not affect subsequent chargees if they do not have notice of them.[276] Registration of the charge itself probably[277] does not give constructive notice of any restrictive clauses in it[278] nor does the placing of the restrictions themselves on the register.[279] Other special rules that apply to floating charges and that may affect priority are considered further below.[280]

Secondly, the registration provisions noted above may have some impact on priority in other cases. This impact is again not altogether clear, as the provisions were not intended to regulate priority but merely to publicize charges.[281] However it will be remembered that a registrable but unregistered charge is void against a liquidator, administrator, and 'a creditor'.[282] Thus such a charge will lose its priority to a subsequent chargee and will be completely ineffective in liquidation or administration. As nothing is said about 'notice', it seems clear that a subsequent chargee obtains priority even if he knew of the prior, unregistered charge.[283]

Thirdly, there is the general principle that an equitable interest is overridden by the *bona fide* purchaser of the legal estate. Thus equitable chargees are liable to be postponed to subsequent legal chargees if the latter are *bona fide*. However it should be noted that a person is generally deemed to have notice of any matter requiring registration and disclosed on the register[284] and thus once an equitable charge is registered, its priority against subsequent charges is secure.

One problem that arises in respect of all charges concerns the amount for which a given charge attains priority. Does it cover any amount outstanding at the time of the dispute, or only the amount that was due under the first ranking charge when the subordinate

---

according to date of creation even if the second purports to be prior to or *pari passu* with the first: *Re Benjamin Cope & Sons Ltd* [1914] 1 Ch. 800.

[276] *English and Scottish Mercantile Investment Co. v. Bruton* [1892] 2 QB 700 (legal assignment of chose in action); *Re Castell & Brown Ltd* [1898] 1 Ch. 315 (equitable charge by deposit of title deeds); *Re Valletort Sanitary Steam Laundry* [1903] 2 Ch 654 (charge by deposit of deeds).

[277] But for a view that such clauses are so ubiquitous that there may be 'inferred knowledge' of them, see J.H. Farrar, 'Floating Charges and Priorities' (1974) 38 *Conv.* 315 and note also Goode, n.197 above, paras. 2-23–2-29. See also the discussion in Beale, Bridge, Gullifer & Lomnicka, n.228 above, paras. 11.15–11.17.

[278] *G. and T. Earle Ltd v. Hemsworth RDC* [1928] TLR 605; *Re Standard Rotary Machine Co. Ltd* (1906) 95 LT 829; *Wilson v. Kelland* [1910] 2 Ch. 6; *ABN AMRO Bank NV v. Chiyu Banking Corp. Ltd* [2003] 3 HKC 381. The dictum of Morritt J in *Griffiths v. Yorkshire Bank plc* [1994] 1 WLR 1427, 1435 that such clauses have *no* effect as a matter of property law is generally regarded as too absolute: see *Siebe Gorman & Co. Ltd v. Barclays Bank* [1979] 2 Lloyd's Rep. 142 (*actual* notice would bind third party).

[279] On the basis that there could be no constructive notice of matters, which were not *required* to be registered: Gough, n.197 above, ch. 10 and *ABN AMRO Bank NV v. Chiyu Banking Corp. Ltd* [2003] 3 HKC 381. Hence the untested practice of requiring the company to pass a special resolution approving the floating charge and incorporating such a clause in the hope that the doctrine of constructive notice would come into play in that a special resolution has to be registered (Companies Act 2006, s.30).

[280] See Sect. (v) below.

[281] Cf. the position in Scotland under the Bankruptcy and Diligence (Scotland) Act 2007, ss.40, 41 where floating charges rank according to the date of registration. It seems that the power in Companies Act 2006, s.894 to amend the registration regime (see n.232 above) cannot be used to determine priority.

[282] Companies Act 2006, s.874. See further Sect. (iii) above.

[283] *Re Monolithic Building Co.* [1915] 1 Ch. 643 (CA).

[284] *G. and T. Earle Ltd v. Hemsworth Rural District Council* (1928) 44 TLR 605, 608 (affirmed on other grounds, (1928) 44 TLR 758). This is not uncontroversial, see the detailed discussion in J de Lacy (ed.), *The Reform of UK Company Law* (London, 2002) ch. 15 and Beale, Bridge, Gullifer & Lomnicka, n.228 above, paras. 11.04–11.17.

charge was registered or communicated to the superior chargee? The problem, thus, is whether 'future advances' made under the preferred charge are entitled to priority. The solution, which is of major importance in the case of bankers' running accounts, is in all probability the same as that discussed in respect of land mortgages.[285]

(v) Special rules governing floating charges

The fact that a floating charge enables the chargor to continue to deal with the charged assets in the ordinary course of business has been noted.[286] But a price has to be paid by the chargee for giving the chargor such freedom of action. First, as noted above, this freedom gives the chargor the opportunity to create subsequent charges with priority over the floating charge.[287] Secondly, if the business of the chargor does not prosper, the charged assets will be depleted in the course of trading.

In addition to these inherent practical disadvantages of the floating charge there are three important statutory provisions that apply to floating (but not fixed) charges and further reduce the attractiveness of the floating charge as a security. First, section 245 of the Insolvency Act 1986 enables the liquidator or administrator of a company to avoid a floating charge created within 12 months[288] of insolvency or administration (as the case may be) except to the extent of new consideration provided at the time of or subsequent to the creation of the charge.[289] In *Re Yeovil Glove Co. Ltd*,[290] the meeting of cheques from an overdraft facility by a bank was held to be the provision of consideration. The application of *Clayton's Case*[291] in that case meant that payments into the account after the creation of a floating charge securing the overdraft discharged pre-charge (i.e. unsecured) indebtedness, and thus post-charge debits became secured by the floating charge. If it can be shown that the company could pay its debts at the time of creation of the charge[292] then the charge cannot be so impeached.[293] The rationale of section 245 seems to be to avoid the temptation of existing unsecured creditors of a company in difficulties obtaining floating charges which would then attach to subsequently acquired property at others' expense.[294]

---

[285] Sect. 2(vii) above; Gough, n.197 above, 906 ff.   [286] See Sect. (ii) above.

[287] See Sect. (iv) above. If the collateral comprises debts, then rights of set-off may arise: *Rother Iron Works Ltd* v. *Canterbury Precision Engineers Ltd* [1974] QB 1 (CA). And any levy of execution will bind the chargee: *Evans* v. *Rival Granite Quarries* [1910] 2 KB 112 (CA).

[288] The period is two years if the chargee is 'connected with' (as defined in s.249) the company as such person will often be the first to realize that the company's finances are deteriorating and so tempted to secure any loans they have made to it.

[289] A payment made a short period before the execution of the charge and in anticipation of it was held valid under the predecessor of s.245: *Re Columbian Fireproofing Co. Ltd* [1910] 2 Ch. 120; *Re F. & D. Stanton Ltd* [1929] 1 Ch. 180. But see *Re Shoe Lace Ltd* [1992] BLCL 636 and *Power* v. *Sharpe Investments Ltd* [1994] 1 BCLC 111. The new value must be genuinely 'new' and hence merely to repay old unsecured debts and thus convert such debts into debts secured by the floating charge, does not qualify: *Re Destone Fabrics Ltd* [1941] Ch. 319; *Re G. T. Whyte & Co. Ltd* [1983] BCLC 311.

[290] [1965] Ch. 148 (CA). The Committee to Review Insolvency Law and Practice (the Cork Committee) Report (Cmnd. 8558, London, 1982), paras. 1561–1562, recommended the reversal of this case by statute.

[291] (1816) 1 Mer. 572.

[292] And that the transaction creating the charge did not deprive it of this ability.

[293] S.245(4). This exception applies only in favour of a chargee who is not 'connected with' (see n.288, above) the company.

[294] See the Committee to Review Insolvency Law and Practice (the Cork Committee) Report, n.290 above. Although it is possible to create *fixed* charges over future assets, see Sect. (i) and *Holroyd* v. *Marshall* (1862) 10 HLC 191 above.

Secondly, floating charges are postponed to the claims of so-called 'preferential creditors' that have accrued up to the date the company is either put into receivership or into liquidation.[295] The list of preferential creditors now only comprises[296] employees in respect of four months' wages, accrued holiday pay, and certain pension contributions.[297] This provision now applies to all charges that are floating at their inception and thus crystallization does not improve the position of the chargee *vis-à-vis* such creditors.[298]

Thirdly, once a company is in liquidation, administration, or a receiver has been appointed, a prescribed (by statutory instrument) part of the property secured by charges that are floating at their inception, is generally made available ('ring-fenced') for unsecured creditors.[299]

There have been two recent changes to the status of a floating chargee. First, when administration was first introduced by the Insolvency Act 1986, Part II, the floating chargee with a charge over all (or substantially all) of the company's property could veto the making of an administration order.[300] However, this veto power has now been withdrawn and instead, such a floating chargee has the power (without going to court) to appoint the administrator.[301] Secondly, the Insolvency Act 1986 now provides that the costs of liquidation are payable out of the assets which were subject to a floating charge.[302]

(vi) **Crystallization of floating charges**

The floating charge becomes a far more effective security when it crystallizes or attaches to the company's assets upon the occurrence of a given event.[303] At that stage, the floating charge is effectively transformed into a fixed equitable charge.[304] When that takes place, the company ceases to have the power to carry on business transactions affecting the property covered. In terms of agency law, the company loses its creditor's permission

---

[295] Insolvency Act 1986, s.40 (receivership); s.175 (winding up). Preferential creditors do not have preference in administration.

[296] Since the Enterprise Act 2002, s.251 removed the Inland Revenue and Customs and Excise from the list, see Ch. 18, Sect. 2. Employees have been preferential creditors since the Preferential Payments in Bankruptcy Amendment Act 1897, s.107.

[297] See ibid., s.386 & Sched. 6, as amended by the Enterprise Act 2002.

[298] See the definition of 'floating charge' in ibid. s.251, noted further in Sect. (vi) below. Before this provision, crystallization before the appointment of a receiver or liquidator rendered the chargee unaffected by preferential creditors: *Re Griffin Hotel Co. Ltd* [1941] Ch. 129; *Re Woodroffes (Musical Instruments) Ltd* [1986] Ch. 366; *Re Brightlife Ltd* [1987] Ch. 200. Hence the popularity of 'automatic crystallization' clauses, see Sect. 4(vi) below.

[299] Insolvency Act 1986, s.176A, added by the Enterprise Act 2002, s.252. See the Insolvency Act 1986 (Prescribed Part) Order 2003, S.I. 2003/2097: in principle, 50 per cent of the first £10,000 plus 20 per cent of the remainder up to £600,000.

[300] Insolvency Act 1986, s.9(3). Thus 'lightweight' floating charges became popular so as to give a creditor this veto power.

[301] Insolvency Act 1986, Sched. B1, para. 14 (added by Enterprise Act 2002, s.251).

[302] S.176ZA (added by the Companies Act 2006, s.1282). It had been so held in *Re Barleycorn Enterprises Ltd* [1970] Ch. 465, but this was overruled by the House of Lords in *Buchler v. Talbot* [2004] 2 AC 298 (now itself reversed by s.176ZA). A floating (but not a fixed) charge is also subordinate to the costs of administration: Insolvency Act 1986, Sched. B1, para. 99.

[303] *Governments Stock and Other Securities Investment Co. Ltd* v. *Manila Ry. Co. Ltd* [1897] AC 81, 86. See Beale, Bridge, Gullifer & Lomnicka, n.228 above, paras. 4.52–4.67.

[304] *Re Griffin Hotel Co Ltd* [1941] Ch 129. In *George Barker (Transport) Ltd* v. *Eynon* [1974] 1 WLR 462 the Court of Appeal regarded crystallization as effecting an equitable assignment by way of charge. See also Gough, n.197 above, ch. 8; Goode, n.197 above, paras 4-28–4-56; and Sect. (ii) above.

to make dispositions over the collateral that is the subject of the charge.[305] However, the Insolvency Act 1986 defines 'floating charge' as 'a charge which, as created, was a floating charge'[306] and therefore crystallization does not improve the position of the floating chargee for the purposes of the Insolvency Act provisions. In particular, crystallization does not affect preferential creditors whose claims remain prior to claims secured by a charge that was floating when created nor does it protect that part of the assets that are made available for liquidation expenses and unsecured creditors. It also seems clear that although on crystallization a floating charge becomes a fixed charge, this does not mean it acquires priority over an existing floating charge to which it was subordinate.[307]

Nevertheless, it is sometimes crucial to determine when a floating charge crystallizes. In principle, this depends on the terms, express or implied, of the floating charge. The case law establishes that it is an implied term of a floating charge that it crystallizes in various circumstances. In particular, it does so upon the making of a winding-up order[308] or when the company ceases its business operations[309] or when the creditor seeks to enforce his security usually by appointing a receiver under a power in the charge to do so (in certain circumstances).[310] An express provision in the floating charge may also determine when a charge crystallizes, for example, it may provide for crystallization on notice[311] when a specified event occurs or even automatically. Such 'semi-automatic' (on notice) or 'automatic' (on the occurrence of the specified event) crystallization clauses are considered further below. In the absence of such express terms, events such as default in making repayments do not cause crystallization.[312] When a floating charge crystallizes, its

---

[305] *Re Florence Land and Rubber Works Co., ex p. Moor* (1878) 10 Ch. D 530, 541, *per* Jessell MR; *N. W. Robbie & Co. Ltd* v. *Witney Warehouses Co. Ltd* [1963] 3 All ER 613.

[306] S.251(a).

[307] Thus, the view of Morritt J in *Griffiths* v. *Yorkshire Bank plc* [1994] 1 WLR 1427 that crystallization affects priority as between existing charges is generally regarded as wrong. See A. Walters, 'Priority of Floating Charges in Corporate Insolvency' (1995) 16 *Co. Lawyer* 291 citing an Ontario case to the contrary: *Re Household Products Co. Ltd and Federal Business Development Bank* (1981) 124 DLR (3d.) 325.

[308] *Re Colonial Trusts Corporation* (1879) 15 Ch. D 465; *Re Panama, New Zealand & Australian Royal Mail Co.* (1870) LR 5 Ch. App. 318; *Edward Nelson & Co. Ltd* v. *Faber & Co.* [1903] 2 KB 367, 376; *Evans* v. *Rival Granite Quarries Ltd*, n.227 above. Where the winding-up is compulsory, crystallization takes place upon the presentation of the petition (*Stein* v. *Saywell* [1969] ALR 481) otherwise it occurs at the time the court order is made (*Re Victoria Steamboats Ltd* [1897] 1 Ch. 158). Being an implied term, it can be excluded by express provision to the contrary: *Re Brightlife* [1987] Ch. 200, 212.

[309] *Edward Nelson & Co. Ltd* v. *Faber & Co.* [1903] 2 KB 367, 376. In *Re Woodroffes (Musical Instruments) Ltd* [1986] Ch. 366 it was held that, as crystallization of another subsequent floating charge (by notice) did not cause cesser of business, this did not in itself crystallize the prior charge in question. See also *National Australian Bank Ltd* v. *Composite Buyers Ltd* (1991) 6 ACSR 94 where the appointment of an administrative receiver under one charge did not cause cesser of business and hence did not crystallize another floating charge and *Federal Business Development Bank* v. *Prince Albert Fashion Bin Ltd* [1983] 3 WWR 464, where business *did* cease on the appointment of an administrative receiver under a second charge and thus crystallized a prior one. Cf. *Northland Bank* v. *GIC Industries Ltd* (1985) 36 Alta. LR (2d) 200: mere fact of crystallization of one charge was held to cause crystallization of another.

[310] *Evans* v. *Rival Granite Quarries Ltd* [1910] 2 KB 979, especially 986. Crystallization takes place when the receiver accepts his appointment: *Windsor Refrigerator Co. Ltd* v. *Branch Nominees Ltd* [1961] Ch. 375; *Cripps (Pharmaceuticals) Ltd* v. *Wickenden* [1973] 2 All ER 606. Gough, n.197 above, 165–6 argues that crystallization takes place when the receiver takes possession of the assets, but the cases are inconclusive. As the management of a company by a receiver is conducted for the benefit of the creditor and not the shareholders, the company can no longer be seen as operating independently in its own interest.

[311] *Re Brightlife Ltd* [1987] Ch. 200.

[312] *Governments Stock and Other Securities Investment Co. Ltd* v. *Manila Ry. Co. Ltd* [1897] AC 81. Although the chargee will have the usual remedies for default (*Re Woodroffes (Musical Instruments) Ltd* [1986] Ch 366, 378), including the appointment of a receiver which will then crystallize the charge. It is unclear if (after the Enterprise Act 2002) the appointment of an administrator crystallizes the charge (in

priority in relation to subsequent dealings depends on the application of the usual principles and it will generally take priority over all charges created after crystallization.[313] However, being a fixed equitable charge, it will be postponed to a subsequent *bona fide* legal mortgagee without notice of its crystallization. It has been argued that a subsequent equitable chargee's position is similarly unaffected if, at the time he took his fixed charge, he had neither knowledge nor the means of knowing of the crystallization.[314] Such a creditor is entitled to rely on the company's apparent authority to deal with its assets. However, this cannot arise when the crystallization takes place upon the appointment of a receiver or the company's winding-up, which will be evident to those dealing with the company.

Usually crystallization takes place too late from the point of view of the floating chargee. By the time any of these crystallizing events occurs, the floating chargee has usually already been irrevocably prejudiced by the activities of his debtor: other charges with priority over him have been created and the assets depleted. Thus banks have sought to strengthen their position by introducing an 'automatic' or 'semi-automatic' crystallization clause. This clause usually specifies that a charge is to crystallize automatically or on notice if any one of a number of given events takes place. Included are usually the grant of a security to another creditor, the levy of distress or execution against the debtor's assets, the failure of the company to meet any of its debts, and the failure to keep a stated minimal ratio of assets *vis-à-vis* liabilities.

There is some controversy about the validity of such clauses. Moreover, the word 'validity' needs to be clarified in this context. Does it refer to validity as between the creditor secured by the charge and the company, or does it refer to validity as against third parties, such as *bona fide* purchasers and competing secured creditors? The effect of the clause on the position of a liquidator of the company (which effect determines its validity against the general creditors) depends on the validity of the clause between the parties to it.[315] As between these parties, the automatic or semi-automatic crystallization clause has the effect of terminating the company's actual authority to deal in its assets. As against third parties, the clause is relevant only if it terminates the company's apparent authority to trade. Then different considerations apply. As between the contracting parties, there is good reason to uphold the clause. There appears to be no contractual principle, which militates against it.[316] Equally, the clause ought to be valid as against unsecured creditors levying execution after crystallization. Such creditors have no cause for complaining about the effect of the clause.

The position differs in the case of third parties such as subsequent equitable chargees who are subordinate to a prior fixed equitable charge.[317] Their complaint is bound

---

that the business may well continue): see Beale, Bridge, Gullifer & Lomnicka, n.228 above, para. 4.55 and references cited therein.

[313] *Business Computers Ltd* v. *Anglo-African Leasing Ltd* [1977] 2 All ER 741 and cases there cited. As noted above (see n.307), it seems clear that crystallization itself does not give the chargee priority (as fixed chargee) over *prior* charges, despite the view of Morritt J to the contrary in *Griffiths* v. *Yorkshire Bank plc*, n.307 above.

[314] Goode, n.197 above, 5-37–5-40.; Gough, n.197 above, 255, who also discusses exceptions.

[315] For a full analysis, see Gough, n.197 above, ch. 11; Goode, n.197 above, para, 4-53. And see Speight J's judgment in *Re Manurewa Transport Ltd* [1971] NZLR 909.

[316] Dicta in some older cases disclose a tendency in the opposite direction: *Re Horne & Hellard* (1885) 29 Ch. D 736; *Davey & Co.* v. *Williamson & Sons Ltd* [1898] 2 QB 194; *Governments Stock and Other Securities Investment Co. Ltd* v. *Manila Ry. Co. Ltd* [1897] AC 81; *Illingworth* v. *Houldsworth* [1904] AC 355. But see the explanation of the cases by A.J. Boyle, 'Validity of Automatic Crystallisation Clauses' [1979] *JBL* 231.

[317] See W.J. Gough, 'The Floating Charge: Traditional Themes and New Directions' in P.D. Finn (ed.), *Equity and Commercial Relationship* (Sydney, 1987), 262.

to be that they have no means of ascertaining that the crystallization clause has come into effect. A modern New Zealand authority (but now overtaken by legislative intervention[318]), *Re Manurewa Transport Ltd*,[319] illustrates the point. A debenture included a clause under which the floating charge was to crystallize automatically if the company gave, or attempted to create, a fixed charge without the debenture holder's prior consent. In breach of this clause, the company executed a chattel mortgage to a garage-owner over a truck. Speight J held, *inter alia*, that under section 4 of the Chattels Transfer Act 1924 the garage owner had constructive notice of the restrictive covenant of the floating charge.[320] The mortgage was, therefore, subordinate to the charge. His Honour further held that the automatic crystallization clause was valid and that it had the effect of deferring the mortgage to the crystallized charge. However, in a subsequent Canadian case, *R v. Consolidated Churchill Copper Corporation*,[321] as a matter of policy such a clause was not upheld on the basis that it unduly prejudiced preferential creditors.[322]

English authority at first instance[323] tends to favour the New Zealand approach, the view being taken that the courts (as opposed to Parliament) should not limit the freedom of the parties to create floating charges on whatever terms they wish.[324] In any event, many third parties are likely to be able to take advantage of the apparent authority that the company still has, despite the automatic crystallisation of which they have no notice, to deal with the collateral and hence create effective third party rights.[325]

(vii) **Assessment**

The floating charge is a security favoured by banks. The explanation is to be found in economic rather than in legal factors. Such a charge leaves the corporate customer the desired freedom of action and has some of the practical advantages of being a security.[326] It enables the customer to carry on business without the need constantly to seek the bank's consent to dispositions over property covered by the security. If the customer's credit is good and its trading methods fair, the bank need have no worries. It can acquire additional protection, which overcomes some of the inherent weaknesses of the floating charge, by obtaining a fixed charge over the customer's permanent assets, such as land or plant.

---

[318] Property Securities Act 1999.

[319] [1971] NZLR 909 and, more recently, *Covacich v. Riordan* [1994] 2 NZLR 502. See also *Stein v. Saywell* [1969] ALR 481 (Aust.); *Re Permanent Houses (Holdings) Ltd* [1988] BCLC 563; *Fire Nymph Products Ltd v. The Heating Centre Pty. Ltd* (1988) 14 ACLR 274 (NSW). Cf. *R. v. Consolidated Churchill Copper Corporation Ltd* [1978] 5 WWR 652; *Norgard v. Deputy Federal Commissioner of Taxation* (1986) 86 ATC 494.

[320] But note that registration under the UK Companies Act 2006 (probably) does not give notice of the contents of the charge, see Sect. (iv) above and n.324 below.

[321] [1978] 5 WWR 652.

[322] But under English law the crystallization of a floating charge does not prejudice preferential creditors: see the text to n.298 above.

[323] *Re Brightlife Ltd* [1986] Ch. 200. The case concerned a 'semi-automatic' crystallization clause (see Sect. (vi), above. See also *Covacich v. Riordan* [1994] 2 NZLR 502.

[324] The Committee to Review Insolvency Law and Practice (the Cork Committee) Report, n.290 above, recommended (a recommendation not implemented by the Insolvency Act 1986) at para. 1580 that statute stipulates when crystallization was to occur and that automatic crystallization not be permitted. The Companies Act 1989, s.102 opened the way for such control in enabling regulations to be made precluding automatic crystallization unless notice of the occurrence of events leading to the crystallization is entered on the Companies Register. However, these reforms were never implemented (although they theoretically could be under the new general power to amend the Companies Act 2006, Pt. 25 conferred by s.894).

[325] See Sect. (iv) above.   [326] Ch. 18, Sect. 1(ii).

The floating charge has one further conceptual attraction from a bank's point of view. In its monetary dealings with the customer, the bank operates on the basis of a current account, which has been shown to resemble a reservoir of money available to the customer. The same type of flexibility is attained in respect of security by means of the floating charge. Naturally, the floating charge does not mirror the movement of funds through the customer's account. The company's assets may actually increase and the security replenish itself quite regardless of the balance of the customer's account. Notionally, though, the revolving nature of a current account and of a floating charge is in harmony with a bank's way of transacting business. It is believed that this element explains the banks' preference for a floating charge over more effective securities.

20

Possessory Securities

1 The pledge[1]

(i) Utilization of pledges by banks

'A pawn or pledge involves a transfer of the possession of personal property from the pawnor to the pawnee by way of security; the ownership in the property remains in the pawnor subject only to the "special interest" to which the pawnee is entitled for the purpose of protecting and realising his security.'[2] The pledge is by its nature a contract of bailment for security purposes, with the pledgee acquiring both possession of the items covered and some special right or interest in them, in particular a power of sale.[3] It is common to describe this right as a 'special property',[4] although in *The Odessa*[5] the Judicial Committee of the Privy Council pointed out that the pledgee's only power was to sell the goods upon the pledgor's default and concluded that, analytically, this was not a right of property at all but a 'special interest'. The point is well taken, as the pledgee does not have the power to acquire full ownership of the subject matter by means of foreclosure.[6] One thing is clear: the general property or ownership in the items pledged remains vested in the pledgor.[7] It has been said that the pledge ranks between a mortgage, which confers on the mortgagee a definite property right, and a lien, which is purely possessory in nature.[8] On the view taken by the Judicial Committee, the pledge is much closer to the latter than to the former. The main distinction between a pledge and a lien is that a lienee's only right

---

[1] For more detailed consideration of the law on pledges, see, *Halsbury's Laws of England* (4th edn., reissue, London, 2007), vol. 36(1); N.E. Palmer, *Bailment* (3rd edn., London, 2009); N. Palmer & E. McKendrick (eds.), *Interests in Goods* (2nd edn., London, 1998), ch. 24; H. Beale, M. Bridge, L. Gullifer, & E. Lomnicka, *The Law of Personal Property Security* (Oxford, 2007), paras. 3.01–3.48.

[2] *Per* Chadwick J in *Mathew* v. *T. M. Sutton Ltd* [1994] 4 All ER 793. As this excerpt shows, the cases use the terms 'pawn' and 'pledge' interchangeably. However, the Consumer Credit Act 1974 (see Sect. 1(vi) below) uses 'pawn' to denoted the collateral and 'pledge' to denote the pledgee's rights.

[3] *Re Hardwick, ex p. Hubbard* (1886) 17 QBD 690 (CA), and see Sect. 1(ii) below. *Marcq* v. *Christie Manson & Woods Ltd (t/a Christie's)* [2003] EWCA 980; [2003] 3 All ER 561. The pledgee also has the power to subpledge: *Donald* v. *Suckling* (1866) LR 1 QB 585.

[4] *Coggs* v. *Barnard* (1703) 2 Ld. Raym. 909, 916; *Donald* v. *Suckling* (1866) LR 1 QB 585, 606, 614; *Burdick* v. *Sewell* (1883) 10 QBD 363, 376, affd. (1884) 10 App. Cas. 74; *Re Morritt, ex p. Official Receiver* (1886) 18 QBD 222, 234.

[5] [1916] 1 AC 154, 158–159.

[6] *Carter* v. *Wake* (1877) 4 Ch. D 605, 606. But see Consumer Credit Act 1974, s.120(1)(a): pledgee under a regulated agreement may acquire ownership of unredeemed pawns securing small advances.

[7] *Re Morritt, ex p. Official Receiver*, n.4 above; *Attenborough* v. *Solomon* [1913] AC 76, 84. In *Mathew* v. *T. M. Sutton Ltd*, n.2 above, Chadwick J characterized the pledgor's interest, during the pledge, as beneficial.

[8] *Halliday* v. *Holgate* (1868) LR 3 Ex. 299, 302.

is to detain the subject matter pending satisfaction of the debt. He does not have a right of sale.[9]

It will be recalled that a pledge, as it involves the transfer of possession, does not require registration under the Bills of Sale Acts 1878–1891[10] nor, in the case of a corporate pledgor, under the Companies Act 2006, section 860.[11]

Ordinarily, the pledge is effective only whilst the pledgee retains possession.[12] There is, however, authority for the view that the release of the goods to the pledgor, or to his nominee, for a restricted purpose such as the making of arrangements for their storage, does not destroy the pledge.[13] From a bank's point of view the general principle that possession is essential[14] is cumbersome. Banks do not wish to keep in custody goods, plant, or machinery belonging to a customer. First, they do not have the necessary facilities. Secondly, such a genuinely possessory transaction is not banking business. Thirdly, such an arrangement defeats the object of the typical transaction financed by a bank. Quite regardless of whether credit is extended to the customer to finance the acquisition of plant, of equipment, or of stock-in-trade, the customer requires the custody or use of the items involved. The giving of actual possession thereof to the bank is thus out of the question.

There is one category of case, involving certain documents, where banks do effect traditional pledges by taking actual possession: the case of negotiable instruments[15] and all types of marketable securities transferable by delivery.[16] Otherwise, the solution in the case of a transaction involving goods is to confer on the bank *constructive* instead of actual possession of goods.[17] This can be achieved in two ways, both of which are effective to create a pledge. One method is to deliver to the bank possession of documents of title which symbolize the goods. Possession of documents of title to goods constitutes constructive possession of the goods.[18] Such a transaction is effective where the goods are on board a ship, when the transfer of the bill of lading transfers the property in the goods,[19]

---

[9] See Sect. 2 below. It is not always easy to distinguish a contractual lien (with an express power of sale) from a pledge: see Beale, Bridge, Gullifer, Lomnicka, n.1 above, paras. 3.53–3.54.

[10] *Re Hardwick, ex p. Hubbard* (1886) 17 QBD 690, see Ch. 19, Sect. 3(ii). However, if the pledge is created by a document providing for attornment, that document may be a bill of sale: *Re Far East Structural Steelwork Engineering Ltd* [2006] HKEC 1067, per Le Pichon JA at para. [30].

[11] *Wrightson* v. *McArthur and Hutchinsons (1919) Ltd* [1921] 2 KB 807; see Ch. 19, Sect. 4(iii).

[12] *Singer Manufacturing Co.* v. *Clark* (1879) 5 Ex. D 37; *Babcock* v. *Lawson* (1880) 5 QBD 284.

[13] *Reeves* v. *Capper* (1838) 5 Bing. NC 136; *North Western Bank Ltd* v. *John, Poynter, Son and Macdonalds* [1895] AC 56, 64–8; *Official Assignee of Madras* v. *Mercantile Bank of India Ltd* [1935] AC 53; *Lloyds Bank Ltd* v. *Bank of America National Trust and Savings Association* [1938] 2 KB 147. And see *Re David Allester Ltd* [1922] 2 Ch. 211, in which the practice of releasing pledged goods to the pledgor to facilitate a sale was not regarded as defeating the pledge. But both the *David Allester* and *Bank of America* cases clarify that the pledgor can, in such cases, confer a good title on an innocent purchaser or mortgagee: see Sect. 1(iv) below.

[14] *Martin* v. *Reid* (1862) 11 CB (NS) 730, 734; *Ayers* v. *South Australian Banking Co.* (1871) LR 3 PC 548, 554.

[15] As these constitute choses in possession; Ch. 10, Sect. 8(i) above.

[16] *Gorgier* v. *Mieville* (1824) 3 B & C 45 (pledge of Prussian bonds); *Donald* v. *Suckling* (1866) LR 1 QB 585 (debentures); *Langton* v. *Waite* (1868) LR 6 Eq. 165 (railway stock); *Halliday* v. *Holgate* (1869) LR 3 Ex. 299 (scrip).

[17] The basic principle can be traced back to *Reeves* v. *Capper* (1838) 5 Bing. NC 136. And see the analysis in *Young* v. *Lambert* (1870) LR 3 PC 142; *Hilton* v. *Tucker* (1888) 39 Ch. D 669; *Wrightson* v. *McArthur and Hutchinsons (1919) Ltd* [1921] 2 KB 807.

[18] *Lickbarrow* v. *Mason* (1787) 2 TR 63; revsd. (1790) 1 H Bl. 357 but restored (1793) 2 H Bl. 211.

[19] *Sewell* v. *Burdick* (1884) 10 App. Cas. 74; *Bristol and West of England Bank* v. *Midland Ry. Co.* [1891] 2 QB 653.

or when they are stored in a warehouse pending their resale.[20] A sophisticated system involving the use of 'trust receipts' has developed for the release of such documents of title or the goods themselves to the customer to enable him to continue dealing in them. This method, which is utilized mainly in respect of overseas transactions and constitutes an important facet of banking business, is considered further below.[21] The other method involves the storing of the goods in a warehouse in the bank's name or in a part of the pledgor's own warehouse, the key to which is then given to the bank.[22] This method, often described as 'field warehousing', is used to finance a dealer's stock-in-trade and is also considered below.[23]

(ii) Standard conditions in pledges and rights conferred on banks

When a customer creates a pledge in favour of his bank, he is usually required to sign a 'letter of pledge' or 'letter of lien'. Some banks prefer to execute such a document in respect of every transaction, whilst others request the customer to sign a master agreement. Quite regardless of the form, the tendency is to stipulate that the pledge be extended to all of the customer's property that is given into the bank's possession or custody. This provision is of special importance in the case of a pledge to the bank of marketable securities which the customer purchases and delivers to the bank from time to time. Another common provision is that the pledge is to secure all amounts advanced by the bank to the customer.

Where the pledge covers goods, the customer undertakes to keep them fully insured and promises to pay all charges due for their storage. Usually, it is provided that if he fails to comply with this condition, the bank can make suitable arrangements and demand reimbursement of the expenses incurred. The document further confers on the bank the right to dispose of the goods in a public or private sale if the customer fails to comply with the provisions of the underlying credit transaction. The last provision does not, in principle, confer on the bank any powers beyond its common law power of sale. The power of sale is inherent in the security arrangement created by the pledge.[24] The pledgor, however, has a right to redeem the pledge, notwithstanding his default and quite regardless of the terms of the contract, at any time preceding the sale of the property pledged.[25] Where the pledgee sells the goods, he does so by virtue of an implied authority from the pledgor for the benefit of both the pledgor and himself.[26] Accordingly, the pledgee has to arrange for

---

[20] Provided it has the power to issue warehouse receipts of a negotiable character. Such a power is conferred on given warehouses by local Acts: M. Bridge (ed.), *Benjamin's Sale of Goods* (8th edn., London, 2010) para. 18-233. Otherwise, the same object is achieved by requiring the warehouseman to attorn to (i.e. to declare that he holds the goods for) the bank. See further Sect. 1(v) below and generally, *Official Assignee of Madras* v. *Mercantile Bank of India Ltd* [1935] AC 53; *Alicia Hosiery Ltd* v. *Brown, Shipley & Co. Ltd* [1970] 1 QB 195.

[21] See Sect. 1(iv) below.

[22] *Meyerstein* v. *Barber* (1866) LR 2 CP 38, 52; *Young* v. *Lambert* (1870) LR 3 PC 142; *Hilton* v. *Tucker* (1888) 39 Ch. D 669; *Wrightson* v. *McArthur and Hutchinsons (1919) Ltd* [1921] 2 KB 807.

[23] See Sect. 1(v) below.

[24] *Martin* v. *Reid* (1862) 11 CB (NS) 730; *Pigot* v. *Cubley* (1864) 15 CB (NS) 701; *France* v. *Clark* (1883) 22 Ch. D 830; *Re Morritt, ex p. Official Receiver* (1886) 18 QBD 222, 235.

[25] *France* v. *Clark*, n.24 above; *Re Morritt, ex p. Official Receiver*, n.24 above; 'The Ningchow' [1916] P 221, 224.

[26] *The Odessa* [1916] 1 AC 145.

a prudent sale[27] and account to the pledgor for any surplus[28] which he holds as fiduciary.[29] Any shortfall is recoverable from the pledgor.[30]

The pledgee ranks as a secured creditor in respect of all items pledged before the commencement of the pledgor's bankruptcy or winding-up. If the proceeds of the sale of the pledge are insufficient to settle the debt, the pledgee can prove for the balance, but ranks in this respect as a general creditor.[31] However, such a claim is unavailable if the goods have perished or were destroyed due to the pledgee's fault.[32]

These general principles apply to all pledges. Special problems arise in respect of the three special arrangements used by banks mentioned earlier: the pledge of negotiable instruments and marketable securities, the pledge of documents of title, and 'field warehousing', which will now be considered in turn.

(iii) Pledge of negotiable instruments and marketable securities

Negotiable instruments[33] and marketable securities transferable by delivery[34] can be the subject of a pledge.[35] They qualify because they are not only choses in action, in that they confer a right to their proceeds on the holder, but also choses in possession, and hence a special category of property.[36] A pledge over negotiable instruments or marketable securities is usually accompanied by a written document in which the instruments or securities are constituted a continuing security granted in respect of all advances made by the bank to the customer.[37] For all practical purposes, the effect of such a pledge is similar to that of a pledge of goods.

A pledge is not possible in the case of other documents, such as share certificates, which are not negotiable in character.[38] Such documents are not choses in possession and their retention does not in itself create a possessory security. Thus, in *Harrold* v. *Plenty*,[39] Cozens-Hardy MR held that the deposit of share certificates involved the creation of an equitable charge on the shares or an agreement to execute a transfer of the shares by way of mortgage and not a pledge of the shares.

(iv) Pledge by means of documents of title

Lickbarrow v. *Mason*[40] established that a document of title to goods has the effect of conferring on its holder constructive possession of and the right to the delivery of the

---

[27] Ibid., 159.

[28] *Jay's the Jewellers Ltd* v. *IRC* [1947] 2 All ER 762. See also Consumer Credit Act 1974, s.121(3), n.82 below.

[29] *Mathew* v. *T. M. Sutton Ltd* [1994] 4 All ER 793. But see *Re E Dibbens & Sons Ltd* [1990] BCLC 577 (proceeds not held on trust).

[30] *Jones* v. *Marshall* (1889) 24 QBD 269.   [31] Ch. 18, Sect. 2 above.

[32] *Polak* v. *Everett* (1876) 1 QBD 669; *Ellis & Co.'s Trustees* v. *Dixon-Johnson* [1925] AC 489, 493.

[33] See n.15 above.   [34] See n.16 above.   [35] Ch. 18, Sect. 1(iii) above.

[36] See Ch. 10, Sect. 8(i) above. The discussion of negotiable instruments there undertaken applies also to marketable securities, such as stock, share warrants, and bonds which are transferable.

[37] *Carter* v. *Wake* (1877) 4 Ch. D 605; *Harrold* v. *Plenty* [1901] 2 Ch. 314 (the latter case may have been a mortgage).

[38] *Longman* v. *Bath Electric Tramway Ltd* [1905] 1 Ch. 646, 665.

[39] [1901] 2 Ch. 314, 316. See further, Ch. 21, Sect. 5(i). See also Beale, Bridge, Gullifer, Lomnicka, n.1 above, para. 3.32.

[40] (1787) 2 TR 63, revsd. (1790) 1 H Bl. 357 but restored (1793) 2 H Bl. 211. And see *Sanders Bros.* v. *Maclean & Co.* (1883) 11 QBD 327, 341.

goods. An indorsee of the document of title obtains a special property in the goods, regardless of whether the transfer is effected by way of sale or of pledge.[41]

The only document of title recognized at common law is the bill of lading.[42] A pledge of a bill of lading accordingly constitutes a pledge of the goods[43] and gives the bank, or pledgee, a power of sale. The bank's right has been described as 'a right of property...to secure the amount...advanced'.[44] Special or local Acts confer a similar status on warehouse receipts issued by designated bodies.[45] Although the Factors Act 1889 recognizes other documents as falling within its own definition of a 'document of title',[46] such documents do not acquire the common law attribute of becoming symbols of the goods covered by them.[47] New forms of documents of title may, of course, be recognized by reason of a mercantile usage.[48]

When the bill of lading, or some other effective document of title, is transferred to the bank by way of pledge, the bank acquires the necessary control over or special rights in the goods.[49] If the carriers deliver the goods to some other person, without demanding the production of the bill of lading, they are liable to compensate the bank.[50]

Whilst the bank retains the bill of lading, it has an effective security. It could, further, arrange for the delivery of the goods, and for their storage, by using an agent. In practice, banks release the documents to the customer for this purpose under a 'trust receipt' or 'letter of trust'. Such a document usually stipulates that the customer will hold the documents and the goods as the bank's trustee or agent. He is authorized to sell the goods, but the proceeds are impressed with a trust in the bank's favour and usually are to be paid into the customer's account with it. It is clear that in his handling of the documents and the goods, the customer acts as the bank's agent. In *Re David Allester Ltd*[51] his position was described as that of a 'trust agent'.

The trust receipt enables the bank to retain an adequate security in the event of the customer's insolvency. The release of the bill of lading to the customer for the special purpose of storing the goods does not destroy the pledge.[52] If the customer becomes insolvent

---

[41] *Sewell* v. *Burdick* (1884) 10 App. Cas. 74, 86; *Brandt* v. *Liverpool, Brazil and River Plate Steam Navigation Co. Ltd* [1924] 1 KB S75.

[42] See generally, Palmer & McKendrick (eds.), n.1 above, ch. 22 and Beale, Bridge, Gullifer, Lomnicka, n.1 above, para. 3.26.

[43] *Official Assignee of Madras* v. *Mercantile Bank of India Ltd* [1935] AC 53, 60.

[44] *Rosenberg* v. *International Banking Corporation* (1923) 14 Ll. LR 344, 347, but note the discussion of *The Odessa* [1916] 1 AC 154, in Sect. 1(i) above.

[45] Such as a dock warrant covered by the Port of London Act 1968, s.146. And see *Benjamin's Sale of Goods*, n.20 above, para. 18-238.

[46] S.1(4), applied by reference to the Sale of Goods Act 1979 by its s.61(1). Included are, *inter alia*, delivery orders.

[47] They are operative merely for the purposes of certain provisions in the Act concerning mercantile agents. See, generally, *Benjamin's Sale of Goods*, n.20 above, para. 18-236.

[48] *Merchant Banking Co. of London* v. *Phoenix Bessemer Steel Co.* (1877) 5 Ch. D 205 (warrants used in iron trade); *Kum* v. *Wah Tat Bank Ltd* [1971] 1 Lloyd's Rep. 439 (mate's receipt in trade between Singapore and Sarawak). See also *Official Assignee of Madras* v. *Mercantile Bank of India Ltd*, n.43 above, where the Privy Council accepted that the relevant Indian legislation rendered railway receipts documents of title.

[49] *Sewell* v. *Burdick* (1884) 10 App. Cas. 74; *Guaranty Trust Co. of New York* v. *Hannay & Co.* [1918] 2 KB 623, 651, 653.

[50] *Bristol and West of England Bank* v. *Midland Ry. Co.* [1891] 2 QB 653; *Sze Hai Tong Bank Ltd* v. *Rambler Cycle Co. Ltd* [1959] AC 576. For authority that the carrier's duty to deliver is subject to his being tendered the bill of lading see *Barclays Bank Ltd* v. *Commissioners of Customs and Excise* [1963] 1 Lloyd's Rep. 81, 89.

[51] [1922] 2 Ch. 211, 219.

[52] *North Western Bank Ltd* v. *John Poynter, Son, and Macdonalds* [1895] AC 56, 68.

before he has disposed of the goods, the bank is therefore able to claim the documents and the goods.[53] Moreover, even before 1986 the customer was not normally considered the 'reputed owner' of the goods under section 38(c) of the Bankruptcy Act 1914.[54] This was important because, if the customer had been so considered, the documents and goods would have been deemed to form part of his estate for bankruptcy purposes. The Insolvency Act 1986 has, of course, abolished the doctrine of reputed ownership. It can be safely concluded that the trust receipt furnishes an effective security over the goods. Further, the bank is protected in respect of the proceeds. If the customer becomes insolvent after the sale of the goods, the bank is likely to gain priority over the proceeds[55] as it has an equitable proprietary interest in them.

The trust receipt is, however, a far less effective security against sharp practices perpetrated by the customer. When a bill of lading is returned to the customer to enable him to sell the goods, the customer is considered the bank's mercantile agent within the meaning of section 2 of the Factors Act 1889. A sale or pledge of the goods to an innocent third party is accordingly valid against the bank.[56] To protect itself against such abuses, the bank should require the customer to store the goods in its name. And if they have been stored in the customer's name, the warehouseman should be required to attorn to the bank. This means that he is required to confirm to the bank that he is holding the goods on its behalf. Thereafter any release of the goods from the warehouse requires the bank's approval, and an attempt to create a pledge ranking in priority will be abortive.[57]

The trust receipt does not appear to require registration as a 'bill of sale' as it potentially falls within one or more of the exclusions in the definition of bill of sale.[58] Thus it is likely to be regarded as a transfer of goods 'in the ordinary course of business' or a document used 'in the ordinary course of business as proof of the possession or control of the goods'.[59] Moreover, in relation to imported goods, there is a more specific exception for instruments given or executed at any time before the goods are deposited in the warehouse or reshipped.[60] It is further arguable that the trust receipt does not create a charge but simply extends the bank's existing rights as pledgee over the documents and the goods. On this basis it is altogether outside the scope of the relevant definition of the

---

[53] Ibid.

[54] *Re Hamilton, Young & Co.* [1905] 2 KB 381, 389–390, affd. ibid., 772. The reputed ownership doctrine in any event was inapplicable to companies in liquidation: Bankruptcy Act 1914, s.126.

[55] *North Western Bank Ltd* v. *John Poynter, Son, and Macdonalds*, n.52 above; *Re David Allester Ltd* [1922] 2 Ch. 211. But such a 'tracing' claim failed in *Re Far East Structural Steelwork Engineering Ltd* [2006] HKEC 1067.

[56] *Lloyds Bank Ltd* v. *Bank of America National Trust and Savings Association* [1938] 2 KB 147. Cf. *Mercantile Bank of India Ltd* v. *Central Bank of India Ltd* [1938] AC 287, which is distinguishable in that the bank's position under the Factors Act 1889 was not raised on the facts.

[57] See, generally, H. Beale (ed.), *Chitty on Contracts* (30th edn., London, 2008), ii, para. 33-125. For a discussion of a pledge created by attornment, see *Re Far East Structural Steelwork Engineering Ltd* [2006] HKEC 1067.

[58] Bills of Sale Act 1878, s.4.

[59] *Re Hamilton, Young & Co.* [1905] 2 KB 772 (a letter of hypothecation case), considered in Ch. 19, Sect. 3(iii). See also *Re Far East Structural Steelwork Engineering Ltd* [2006] HKEC 1067, (Le Pichon JA dissenting on this point).

[60] Bills of Sale Act 1890, s.1 (substituted by Bills of Sale Act 1891, s.1), but see *NV Slavenburg's Bank* v. *Intercontinental Natural Resources Ltd* [1980] 1 WLR 1076 where Lloyd J stated, obiter, that this exemption applied only to existing consignments and not to documents covering future goods.

Bills of Sale Act 1878.[61] On the same basis, the trust receipt does not require registration as a charge under section 860 of the Companies Act 2006.[62]

(v) Field warehousing

Trust receipts and the hypothecation of goods are used mainly when the bank finances an import of goods right from the early stages of the transaction. In some cases, a bank is asked for accommodation at a later stage, when the goods have arrived and have been stored, either at an independent warehouse or at the customer's own premises. In both cases, a pledge of the goods can be used as a security by conferring on the bank constructive possession of the goods.

Where the goods are in an independent warehouse, constructive possession is given to the bank by means of appropriate documentation. If the warehouse has the power of issuing negotiable warehouse receipts or warrants,[63] which are documents of title, the delivery of the document to the bank has the same effect as the delivery of a bill of lading and thus effects a pledge of the goods. If the document is not of this type, it is necessary to ensure that the warehouseman will not deliver the goods without the bank's authority. To this end, the warehouse is notified of the bank's interest and is requested to attorn to the bank.[64] The warehouseman then enters the bank's name as the party entitled to delivery of the goods and issues a new receipt or warrant in its name. The goods are thus held at the bank's disposal.[65] One risk borne by the bank in such an arrangement is that the goods are subject to the warehouseman's lien for the storage charges. To safeguard the bank's position, the customer may be required to execute a letter of pledge, which includes the usual conditions rendering him liable for all expenses.[66]

Where the goods are stored on the customer's own premises or in a warehouse owned by him, constructive possession is conferred on the bank by delivering the key to the warehouse or to the room in which the goods are stored.[67] The pledge is not destroyed if the customer, or pledgor, is given the key to enable him to have access to the goods for limited purposes, such as their maintenance, or in order to enable potential purchasers to inspect them.[68] To avoid any suggestion that the customer has been given general access to the goods and in this way has destroyed the pledge, it is preferable to appoint one of his

---

[61] *Re David Allester Ltd* [1922] 2 Ch. 211. But see Beale, Bridge, Gullifer, Lomnicka, n.1 above, paras. 3.22–3.23 (arguing it creates a charge) and *Re Far East Structural Steelwork Engineering Ltd* [2006] HKEC 1067.

[62] See Ch. 19, Sect. 4(iii) above. But note that if the goods have been sold before the execution of the trust receipt, in which case the security is to attach to the proceeds, the instrument may constitute a charge on book debts, which is registrable under s.860(7)(f): *Ladenburg & Co.* v. *Goodwin, Ferreira & Co. Ltd* [1912] 3 KB 375.

[63] Sect. 1(iv) above.　　　[64] On the meaning of the phrase, see Sect. 1(iv) above.

[65] *Official Assignee of Madras* v. *Mercantile Bank of India Ltd* [1935] AC 53; cf. *Alicia Hosiery Ltd* v. *Brown, Shipley & Co. Ltd* [1970] 1 QB 195.

[66] See Sect. 1(ii) above.

[67] The method has a long pedigree: *Meyerstein* v. *Barber* (1866) LR 2 CP 38, 52; *Young* v. *Lambert* (1870) LR 3 PC 142; *Hilton* v. *Tucker* (1888) 39 Ch. D 669; *Wrightson* v. *McArthur and Hutchinsons (1919) Ltd* [1921] 2 KB 807. However, recent opinion questions its effectiveness: see Beale, Bridge, Gullifer, Lomnicka, n.1 above, paras. 3.20, 9.15 (bill of sale and hence registrable company charge) and note *Dublin City Distillery* v. *Doherty* [1914] AC 823, 854 (pledge can give rise to charge within predecessor to Companies Act 2006, s.860(7)(b)).

[68] *Reeves* v. *Capper* (1838) 5 Bing. NC 136; *Hilton* v. *Tucker*, n.67 above; cf. *Dublin City Distillery Ltd* v. *Doherty* [1914] AC 823. For the position in the USA, see G. Gilmore, *Security Interests in Personal Property* (Botson and Toronto, 1965, reprint, 1999), ch. 6.

employees as a 'custodian', who is empowered to give the customer occasional and limited access to the goods only when required.

Due to the artificiality involved in the arrangement,[69] banks now tend to avoid field warehousing. It is utilized mainly by finance companies and by some investment banks. The clearers and most investment banks prefer to secure their advances by floating charges.[70]

(vi) **Effect of the Consumer Credit Act 1974[71]**

Sections 114–122 of the Consumer Credit Act 1974[72] make provision governing 'pawns' or pledges taken under a regulated agreement.[73] Banks therefore have to be wary of that Act whenever they take a pledge which secures a regulated agreement. However, pledges of documents of title and of bearer bonds are excluded from most of the statutory requirements.[74] Many of the pledges obtained by banks fall within the ambit of these exclusions. This is so despite the fact that the exclusions involved are narrower than may appear at first glance. To start with, as 'document of title' is not defined, the phrase is presumably confined to documents of title in the strict (or common law) sense of the word.[75] Accordingly, whilst a pledge of a bill of lading is unaffected by the 1974 Act, a pledge of documents such as delivery orders and non-negotiable warehouse receipts is regulated by the Act. Similarly, whilst a pledge of bearer bonds is excluded, a pledge of share warrants is covered. A pawn created by a field warehousing agreement, where it secures a regulated agreement, is also covered.

It is believed that even if the provisions apply, they are not so onerous as to dissuade banks from using the pledge. First, there is a procedural requisite. When the pledge is effected, the pledgee must give the pledgor a 'pawn receipt' in the prescribed form.[76] Secondly, the pledged property remains effectively redeemable until the very moment it is realized by the pledgee.[77] An unreasonable refusal by the pledgee to consent to the redemption of the property constitutes an offence.[78]

---

[69] Especially where the pledgor attorns to the pledgee, see above.

[70] See further, Ch. 19, Sect. 4(ii) above.

[71] See generally J.K. Macleod, 'Pawnbroking: A Regulatory Issue' [1995] *JBL* 155; A.G. Guest & M. Lloyd, *Encyclopedia of Consumer Credit* (London, 1974, loose-leaf), paras. 2.115–2.123.

[72] Replacing and repealing the Pawnbrokers Act 1872.

[73] See generally Ch. 2, Sect. 5(ii) above, noting that there is now (since the Consumer Credit Act 2006) no financial limit, although the debtor must be an 'individual' (i.e. non-corporate or small partnership).

[74] Consumer Credit Act 1974, s.114(3)(*a*) as amended by s.38(2) of the Banking Act 1979. However, the Consumer Credit (Conduct of Business) (Pawn Records) Regulations 1983, S.I. 1983/1565 (which apply to all licensees under the 1974 Act irrespective of the exclusions in s.112(3)) require a pawnee under a regulated agreement to maintain certain records (including the issue of some form of pawn receipt).

[75] See Sect. (iii) above.

[76] Consumer Credit Act 1974, s.114(1); as regards the form of such a receipt see (i) the Consumer Credit (Agreements) Regulations 1983, S.I. 1983/1553, reg. 4 and the Consumer Credit (Agreement) Regulations 2010, S.I. 2010/1014, reg.6 (where the pawn receipt and agreement are combined); (ii) the Consumer Credit (Pawn-Receipts) Regulations 1983, S.I. 1983/1566, reg. 2 (where the pawn receipt and agreement are separate). Failure to comply with the documentation and copy requirements of the Act, as well as failure to issue the requisite pawn receipt, constitutes an offence: s.115.

[77] This is the outcome of s.116(1)–(3) of the Act. On the redemption procedure, based on the surrender of the pawn receipt, see s.117.

[78] Consumer Credit Act 1974, s.119(1).

If the property has not been redeemed by the end of the prescribed redemption period (which is usually six months[79]), the pledgee is entitled to realize the security.[80] The Act prescribes a procedure,[81] based on giving the pledgor a last notice to enable him to make a final effort to redeem. Naturally, where the proceeds of the sale exceed the debt, the pledgee has to account to the pledgor for the balance.[82] The pledgee must use reasonable care to ensure that the sale realizes the true market value. If the pledgor disputes that this has been done, the onus of proof rests on the pledgee.[83]

Although the Consumer Credit Directive[84] does not apply to pawn agreements, to maintain a coherent regime the implementing provisions have generally been extended to such agreements.[85]

2 The banker's lien[86]

By mercantile usage, a bank has a lien over commercial paper coming into its possession in the ordinary course of banking business.[87] Accordingly, there is no need for an express agreement between the parties to bring the lien into existence. It attaches in the absence of an express agreement or of circumstances evincing an intention to the contrary.[88] A special feature is that, unlike other types of common law liens, a banker's lien carries with it the right to sell the security.[89] In this respect, the banker's lien resembles a pledge.[90]

Usually the lien secures the customer's total indebtedness to the bank at any one time and is therefore a so-called 'general lien'.[91] But the extent of the lien can be limited by an agreement, express or implied. Thus, in *Re Bowes*[92] a policy of insurance was deposited with the bank, accompanied by a memorandum to the effect that it was to constitute a security for all sums up to £4,000. North J held that the lien did not secure any amounts exceeding the agreed overdraft. The generality of the lien may also be abrogated by the circumstances of the transaction. The most common example is a deposit made to

---

[79] The period runs from the date of the agreement or (if later) the date when the pawnee obtains possession: *Wilson* v. *Robertson (London) Ltd* [2005] EWHC 1425 (Ch).

[80] Ibid., s.120.

[81] Ibid., s.121. As regards the length of the period of notice and whether a default notice under s.87 is also necessary, see Guest & Lloyd, n.7 above, paras. 2-121 & 2-122.

[82] Consumer Credit Act 1974, s.121(3), confirming the common law position: see Sect. (ii) above.

[83] Ibid., s.121(6).   [84] Directive 2008/48/EC, see Ch. 2, Sect. 7(vi).

[85] The exceptions are: s.55B (assessment of creditworthiness), s.55C (copy of draft agreement) and s.77B (statement of account to be provided on request). Moreover, s.55A (pre-contractual explanation) is modified (see s.55A(7)).

[86] See *Halsbury's Laws of England* (4th edn., reissue, London, 2005), vol. 3(1), paras. 170–174.

[87] *Brandao* v. *Barnett* (1846) 12 Cl. & F 787.

[88] Ibid., 806. And see *Davis* v. *Bowsher* (1794) 5 Term Rep.488; *Jones* v. *Peppercorne* (1858) John. 430; *Re London and Globe Finance Corporation* [1902] 2 Ch. 416; *General Produce Co.* v. *United Bank Ltd* [1979] 2 Lloyd's Rep. 255 (suggesting that the terms of an express letter of lien displaces the banker's common law lien).

[89] *Rosenberg* v. *International Banking Corporation* (1923) 14 Ll. LR 344, 347.

[90] Indeed it was called an 'implied pledge' in *Brandao* v. *Barnett* (1846) 12 Cl. & F 787.

[91] Rather than a so-called 'particular lien'. *Re London and Globe Finance Corporation* [1902] 2 Ch. 416, 420; *Re Keever* [1967] Ch. 82, 189; *Bank of New South Wales* v. *Ross, Stuckey and Morawa* [1974] 2 Lloyd's Rep. 110, 112.

[92] (1886) 33 Ch. D 586.

cover an advance arranged for a specific purpose.[93] But the customer's conduct in such a situation may, in the end, result in the creation of a general lien. A case in point is where the customer permits the bank to retain the securities after the discharge of the debt. The securities then become the subject of a general lien securing all future advances.[94]

The banker's lien extends to all classes of negotiable and semi-negotiable instruments deposited by the customer and belonging to him.[95] Included are the traditional bills of exchange, cheques, promissory notes, bonds, and share warrants,[96] as well as share certificates,[97] money transfer orders,[98] and deposit receipts.[99] The lien, accordingly, has a wider scope of application than a pledge of securities which, it will be recalled, attaches to negotiable securities alone.[100] As both the pledge and the lien are possessory securities, this distinction is fortuitous. However, even a lien is not all-embracing in its application. It does not attach to documents that evidence mere choses in action. Thus, in *Wylde v. Radford*,[101] it was held that a deed respecting the conveyance of land was not covered by the banker's lien. But this rule is not absolute. In *Re Bowes*,[102] for instance, an insurance policy was assumed to be subject to the lien. It has been suggested that where title deeds to land are deposited with a bank, the effect is to create a special type of charge akin to a lien, though not to be confused with the bank's general lien.[103] In practice, the deposit of the deeds is normally made in the context of a mortgage and hence is the subject of an express contractual arrangement.[104]

The lien attaches to all securities remitted by the customer to the bank for collection, although these are delivered to the bank for a specific purpose.[105] This is so because the transaction as a whole involves the delivery of the documents to the bank in the ordinary course of its business.[106] Moreover, a bank that receives negotiable instruments for collection from a correspondent retains a lien over them to secure the correspondent's indebtedness.[107] The lien is not defeated by the bank's knowledge that the instruments are the property of the correspondent's customer. It attaches to all cheques paid to the credit of his account, and to any bill of exchange or promissory note remitted by him to his bank. When the instruments have been paid by the drawee, the bank is entitled to apply the proceeds in reduction of the customer's overdraft or other debit balance unless the amount received has been earmarked for a different purpose.[108]

---

[93] *Wilkinson v. London and County Banking Co.* [1884] 1 TLR 63.

[94] *Re London and Globe Finance Corporation* [1902] 2 Ch. 416 (a case on the similar stockbroker's lien).

[95] Instruments belonging to a third party are probably not covered: *Cuthbert v. Robarts, Lubbock & Co.* [1909] 2 Ch. 226, 233. But see *Siebe Gorman & Co. Ltd v. Barclays Bank Ltd* [1979] 2 Lloyd's Rep. 142, 166 (reversed on another point by *Re Spectrum Plus* [2005] UKHL 41) suggesting that this rule applies only where the bank was aware that the securities were not the customer's property at the time it granted the advance.

[96] *Wylde v. Radford* (1863) 33 LJ Ch. 51, 53.

[97] *Re United Service Co., Johnston's Claim* (1870) LR 6 Ch. App. 212, 217.

[98] *Misa v. Currie* (1876) 1 App. Cas. 554, 567, 573.   [99] Ch. 9, Sect. 4 above.

[100] *Jeffreyes v. Agra and Masterman's Bank* (1866) LR 2 Eq. 674. See Sect. (1)(i) & (iii) above.

[101] (1863) 33 LJ Ch. 51. Cf. the explanation of the case in *Re London and Globe Finance Corporation* [1902] 2 Ch. 416, 420.

[102] (1886) 33 Ch. D 586.

[103] M. Hapgood (ed.), *Paget's Law of Banking* (13th edn., London, 2007), para. 29.4.

[104] Ch. 19, Sect. 2 above.

[105] *Akrokerri (Atlantic) Mines Ltd v. Economic Bank* [1904] 2 KB 465. And see *Sutters v. Briggs* [1922] 1 AC 1, 18, where doubts were expressed about the application of the Bills of Exchange Act 1882, s.27(3) to a collecting bank on the ground of its probably not being a holder in its own right. But the case does not cast any doubt on the existence of the lien.

[106] *Misa v. Currie* (1876) 1 App. Cas. 554, 565, 569, 573.

[107] *Johnson v. Roberts* (1875) LR 10 Ch. App. 505; cf. *Re Dilworth, ex p. Armistead* (1828) 2 Gl. & J 371.

[108] *Re Keever* [1967] Ch. 182.

The lien does not attach to securities remitted to the bank for safe custody. In such a case the securities are retained by the bank as a bailee, and not in the ordinary course of its banking business.[109] Occasionally, it is not easy to determine in what capacity the bank has received some instruments. Thus bonds may be deposited with the instruction that the bank cut off the coupons and use them to collect interest payments. It has been suggested that, in such a case, the bonds and coupons are subject to the bank's lien.[110] If the customer requires the bank to keep the securities but retrieves them periodically in order to collect the interest due, the arrangement is said to involve safe custody. In terms of commercial reality, the principle is questionable. A customer may deposit his securities with a bank purely for safe custody, but may instruct the bank to collect the interest as his agent. In other instances, he may intend to deposit the instruments for security purposes but, for reasons of his own, may wish to collect the interest due by presenting the coupons himself. It is believed that the lien attaches whenever the bank and its customer regard the instruments as creating a security interest. The matter thus depends on their intention.

A lien does not attach to the balance standing to the credit of the customer's account with his bank. The reason is clear: the funds in question represent a debt due from the bank to the customer, and not tangible 'money' or cash owned by him. The bank's right in such a case is to effect a set-off against the credit balance involved in respect of debts due to it from the customer.[111]

It is more difficult to define the rights that the bank has in a balance in foreign currency maintained at the customer's request. Such a balance may be credited to an account opened in the customer's name by his bank's overseas correspondent. In such a case the contract is between the foreign bank and the customer, and his local bank cannot have any lien or right of set-off against the funds involved. But in many cases the amount involved is remitted to the credit of the local bank's own account with its correspondent, and the balance is shown as standing to the credit of the customer's account with his local bank. It is then a debt in foreign currency due to the customer from his own bank, and payable either *in specie* in the foreign country concerned or in local currency at the rate of exchange prevailing at the time of payment. Until payment, though, it remains a debt. In *Choice Investments Ltd* v. *Jeromnimon (Midland Bank, Garnishee)*,[112] it was held that such a balance was a debt attachable by means of a garnishee order.[113] By the same token, it should be the subject of a valid set-off and, being a mere chose in action, unaffected by the bank's lien.

The banker's lien is not registrable either under the Bills of Sale Act 1878 in the case of an unincorporated customer or under the Companies Act 2006 in the case of a corporate customer.[114] It gives the bank an effective security against the interests of competing creditors. There are, however, some restrictions on its effect. First, the lien is ineffective in respect of property which is not owned by the customer,[115] although this point may be doubted in respect of negotiable instruments.[116] In this last case, the bank has the benefit

---

[109] *Leese* v. *Martin* (1873) LR 17 Eq. 224, 235.

[110] *Re United Service Co., Johnston's Claim* (1870) LR 6 Ch. App. 212; *Paget*, n.103 above, 527.

[111] Ch. 6, Sect. 3 above. In *Re BCCI SA (No. 8)* [1996] 2 All ER 121, although Lord Hoffmann suggested that a 'charge-back' of a credit bank balance was effective (see Ch. 21, Sect. 3(iv)), he confirmed that a lien was not possible.

[112] [1981] 1 All ER 225, 228.   [113] Now a third party debt order, see Ch. 11, Sect. 1(iii).

[114] And see *Re Hamlet International plc* [1998] BCLC 164 (contractual lien not registrable).

[115] *Cuthbert* v. *Robarts, Lubbock & Co.* [1909] 2 Ch. 226, 233 but see n.95 above.

[116] *Brandao* v. *Barnett* (1846) 12 Cl. & F 787, 805–06.

of the lien if it obtained the instruments in good faith and for valuable consideration. The second limitation to the effect of the lien is that it fails to protect the bank in respect of advances made after notice that the instruments have been mortgaged or assigned in equity to a third party.[117]

---

[117] *Jeffreyes* v. *Agra and Masterman's Bank* (1866) LR 2 Eq. 674; *Siebe Gorman & Co. Ltd* v. *Barclays Bank Ltd* [1979] 2 Lloyd's Rep. 142.

21

Security Interests in Choses in Action

1 General principles

Choses in action, such as contractual rights to sums of money, differ from choses in possession in that they are rights enforceable by court action and not by taking physical possession.[1] Examples are a balance standing to the credit of a customer's bank account, an amount owed to a supplier by a trader for goods delivered on credit, and a debt due to a finance company under a hire-purchase agreement. From a legal point of view, the amounts involved constitute debts enforceable at their maturity.[2] Economically, they are shown as assets in the creditor's balance sheet and so they can be utilized for the creditor's business transactions. First, they can be converted into cash, for example by the drawing of a cheque on a bank. Alternatively, a supplier may 'sell' all the amounts receivable from his customers at a discount. In such a 'factoring' transaction,[3] the purchaser of the 'receivables' acquires the rights to be paid by the traders. Secondly, choses in action can be utilized as collateral to secure the 'owner's' transactions with third parties. Thus a finance company may grant its bank a charge over amounts due under all its hire-purchase agreements to secure its overdraft.[4]

The value of a chose in action as collateral depends on a number of factors. One is the debtor's creditworthiness: obviously, an (unsecured) amount due from an insolvent trader is worthless. Another is the nature of the debt in question. Amounts due under a long-term transaction, such as the financing of a capital project, may be less attractive than debts due within a short term. At the same time, choses in action generally have one attractive feature. Unlike land and goods, which have to be sold in the process of realization and the value of which may fluctuate considerably, choses in action have a fixed value and realization is relatively simple. Choses in action are therefore considered good collateral. In view of their liquidity, they are particularly appropriate in the context of a transaction involving bank finance.

A security interest over choses in action has to be effected in a form recognized as valid at law or in equity. A pledge over a chose in action is ruled out by the fact that the

---

[1] See *Torkington* v. *Magee* [1902] 2 KB 427, *per* Channel J at 430 (revsd. [1903] 1 KB 644).
[2] The creditor will usually be able to obtain summary judgment under the Civil Procedure Rules (CPR), Pt. 24.
[3] Discussed in Sect. 2(ii) below.   [4] Discussed in Sect. 2(iii) below.

concept of possession is inapplicable to mere rights.[5] Usually,[6] transactions over choses in action are effected by means of either a statutory or an equitable assignment.[7] The former enables the assignee to sue in his own name;[8] in the case of an equitable assignment he usually has to join the assignor as a party.[9]

A statutory assignment, which has to be effected in the manner prescribed by section 136 of the Law of Property Act 1925, involves an outright transfer of the debt to the assignee. Such an assignment has to be absolute[10] and not by way of charge.[11] However an assignment by way of mortgage—where there is an outright transfer to the assignee/mortgagee with the assignor/mortgagor having the right to have the debts reassigned to him on redemption—is within the section.[12] Section 136 requires express notice of the assignment to be given to the debtor in writing.[13]

Alternatively, an equitable assignment may be effected which merely requires an intention to assign and does not need to satisfy the requirements of section 136.[14] Thus an assignment by way of charge may be effected in equity and notice of the assignment need not be given to the debtor.[15] In some situations the assignor may not wish his debtors to know that he has assigned the debts, but the giving of notice is generally advisable from the point of view of the equitable assignee. First, after receiving notice, the debtor is only discharged by paying the assignee,[16] whilst if he has no notice of the assignment he is discharged by paying the assignor.[17] Secondly, after notice has been given, the agreement between the debtor and the assignor cannot be modified without the assignee's consent in any manner that affects the amount due.[18] Thirdly, certain 'equities' or defences of the

---

[5] A pledge of negotiable instruments and marketable securities is effective, as these instruments constitute both choses in action and choses in possession: Ch. 10, Sect. 8(i), Ch. 20, Sect. 1(iii) above. For the same reason they may be subject to a lien.

[6] But note also the special form for legal mortgages of insurance policies provided for by the Policies of Assurance Act 1867 considered in Sect. 4 below.

[7] See G. Tolhurst, *The Assignment of Choses in Action* (Oxford, 2006); M. Smith, *The Law of Assignment* (Oxford, 2007).

[8] Law of Property Act 1925, s.136(a).

[9] *Durham Bros.* v. *Robertson* [1898] 1 QB 765; *Performing Right Society Ltd* v. *London Theatre of Varieties Ltd* [1924] AC 1. But an equitable assignee of an equitable chose in action (for example, in interest in a trust fund) can sue in his own name.

[10] And not conditional: *Durham Bros.* v. *Robertson*, n.9 above. And note that an assignment of part of a debt is not within s.136: *Forster* v. *Baker* [1910] 2 KB 636; *Re Steel Wing Co. Ltd* [1921] 1 Ch. 349, 354; *Williams* v. *Atlantic Assurance Co. Ltd* [1933] 1 KB 81, 100; *Deposit Protection Board* v. *Dalia* [1994] 2 AC 367, 392.

[11] This is clear from the language of s.136 and see *Jones* v. *Humphreys* [1902] 1 KB 10.

[12] *Tancred* v. *Delagoa Bay & East Africa Rly. Co.* (1889) 23 QBD 239; *Hughes* v. *Pump House Hotel Co. Ltd* [1902] 2 KB 190; *Bovis International Inc.* v. *Circle Ltd Partnership* (1995) 49 Con LR 12 (*per* Millett LJ at 29). See also *Burlinson* v. *Hall* (1884) 12 QBD 347 (debts assigned on trust for assignee and assignor).

[13] And see *Holt* v. *Heatherfield Trust Co. Ltd* [1942] 2 KB 1. The assignment itself must be in writing and it seems the written notice may also constitute the written assignment: *Curran* v. *Newpark Cinemas Ltd* [1951] 1 All ER 295 (CA); *Cossill* v. *Strangman* [1963] NSWR 1695 (Sup. Ct. NSW). For case law on what constitutes an effective notice see *W. F. Harrison & Co. Ltd* v. *Burke* [1956] 1 WLR 419 (CA) and *Van Lynn Developments Ltd* v. *Pelias Construction Co. Ltd* [1969] 1 QB 607 (CA).

[14] *William Brandt's Sons & Co.* v. *Dunlop Rubber Co. Ltd* [1905] AC 454 (HL).

[15] *Gorringe* v. *Irwell India Rubber and Gutta Percha Works* (1886) 34 Ch. D 128 (CA).

[16] Thus if the debtor pays the assignor, he remains liable to pay the assignee: *Brice* v. *Bannister* (1878) 3 QBD 569. The notice must unambiguously indicate that there has been an assignment for the debtor to remain liable after paying the assignor: *James Talcott Ltd* v. *John Lewis & Co. Ltd* [1940] 3 All ER 592 (CA).

[17] *Stocks* v. *Dobson* (1853) 4 De G M & G 11; *Warner Bros. Records Inc.* v. *Rollgrenn Ltd* [1976] QB 430, 442; *Bence* v. *Shearman* [1898] 2 Ch. 582.

[18] *Brice* v. *Bannister*, n.16 above, especially *per* Bramwell LJ at 581.

debtor against the assignor no longer bind the assignee after notice of the assignment.[19] In particular, any right of set-off or equity arising from transactions undertaken between the debtor and the assignor after this date cannot be pleaded against the assignee.[20] Finally, if there are competing assignments, the first to give notice generally has priority under the rule in *Dearle* v. *Hall*.[21]

The main advantage of a statutory assignment is that it enables the assignee to sue in his own name without the need to join the assignor as a party.[22] There are dicta in the cases that the section confers more than this procedural advantage and renders the assignment 'legal' as opposed to merely equitable.[23] This has led to suggestions that the statutory assignee without notice of a prior equitable assignment can take advantage of the *bona fide* legal purchaser rule and take priority over such assignees.[24] However, as section 136 provides that the statutory assignment is 'subject to equities having priority over the right of the assignee', it seems clear that a statutory assignee takes subject to prior equitable assignments and does not, at least to this extent, enjoy the usual status of a legal purchaser.[25]

An assignment of choses in action is often expressed to cover 'future' choses in action if their creation is predictable. A business's dealings over time give a good indication of receivables likely to stand to its credit from time to time. Commercially, it is therefore possible to assess their value for the purposes of security. However, such 'future' choses in action pose legal problems. Historically, the common law did not recognize assignments of 'future' property, although equity regarded a purported assignment for value of future or 'after-acquired' property as a contract to assign which equity would enforce when the property came into being.[26] Thus assignments of future choses in action are possible only for value.[27] A further problem is that the meaning of 'future' as opposed to 'existing' has caused difficulties in the case of contingent debts.[28] Whilst debts that have accrued and are payable are clearly 'existing' and debts under contracts that have not yet been entered into are clearly 'future', the status of potential debts under existing contracts is more problematic.[29] Thus it has been held that debts that have accrued but are not yet payable

---

[19] For a detailed discussion, see F. Oditah, *Legal Aspects of Receivables Financing* (London, 1991), ch. 8; S. R. Derham, *Set-Off* (4th edn., London, 2010), ch. 13 and S.R. Derham, 'Set-off against an Assignee: The Relevance of Marshalling, Contribution, and Subrogation' (1991) *LQR* 126. For a case summarizing the authorities, see *Business Computers Ltd* v. *Anglo-African Leasing Ltd* [1977] 1 WLR 578.

[20] *Roxburgh & Co.* v. *Cox* (1881) 17 Ch. D 520; *Pinto Leite, ex p. Olivaes, Re* [1929] 1 Ch. 221; *N. W. Robbie & Co. Ltd* v. *Witney Warehouse Co. Ltd* [1963] 3 All ER 613; *Business Computers Ltd* v. *Anglo-African Leasing Ltd*, n.19 above.

[21] (1823) 3 Russ. 1. See Sect. 2(vi) below.   [22] Law of Property Act 1925, s.136(a).

[23] See, for example, *Read* v. *Brown* (1888) 22 QBD 128, *per* Esher MR at 131–2.

[24] *Ellerman Lines Ltd* v. *Lancaster Maritime Co. Ltd* [1980] 2 Lloyd's Rep. 497, *per* Goff LJ at 503 and *Performing Right Society Ltd* v. *London Theatre of Varieties Ltd* [1924] AC 1, *per* Viscount Finlay at 19. And see F. Oditah, 'Priorities: Equitable versus Legal Assignments of Book Debts' (1989) 9 *OJLS* 511.

[25] See Channell J in *Marchant* v. *Morton, Down & Co.* [1901] 2 KB 829, 832 and, more recently, Phillips J in *Pfeiffer (E.) Weinkellerei-Weinkauf GmbH* v. *Arbuthnot Factors Ltd* [1988] 1 WLR 150 and (after a full review of the authorities) Mummery J in *Compaq Computers Ltd* v. *Abercorn Group Ltd* [1993] BCLC 603.

[26] *Holroyd* v. *Marshall* (1862) 10 HL Cas. 191 applied to debts in *Tailby* v. *Official Receiver* (1888) 13 App. Cas. 523; *Norman* v. *Federal Commissioner of Taxation* (1963) 109 CLR 9; *Independent Automatic Sales Ltd* v. *Knowles & Foster* [1962] 1 WLR 974, as explained in *Paul and Frank Ltd* v. *Discount Bank (Overseas) Ltd* [1967] 1 Ch. 348.

[27] *Norman* v. *Federal Commissioner of Taxation* (1963) 109 CLR 9, following *Re Ellenborough* [1903] 1 Ch. 697: a voluntary assignment by deed of future choses in action was ineffective.

[28] Smith, n.7 above, paras. 2-38–2.51, 3.13–3.14, 3.21.

[29] See the discussion by Oditah, n.19 above, 28–29. Cf. the New Zealand Law of Property Act 2007, s.53: 'an assignment of an amount that will or may be payable in the future under a right already possessed by the assignor . . . treated as an assignment of a thing in action'.

pending the fulfilment of some condition are nevertheless 'existing',[30] but other types of debt that may or may not become payable under existing contracts have been regarded as 'future'.[31] However, as a bank invariably provides value for an assignment of choses in action, these problems will rarely be of concern except to the extent that the bank wishes to challenge a competing voluntary assignment.

2 Security interests over book debts and other receivables[32]

(i) Meaning of 'book debts' and 'receivables'

A book debt is an amount of money due to a company or to an unincorporated firm in the course of its business.[33] It has been described as a debt that would ordinarily be entered in a trader's books regardless of whether or not it is so entered in a given case.[34] The price of goods sold on credit, rentals due under a hire-purchase agreement or equipment lease, and amounts due from clients for services rendered by traders or by professionals such as accountants, are all covered by the definition. Generally, the balance standing to the credit of an account with a bank is probably not a 'book debt'.[35] Although the amount involved constitutes a debt due from the bank, it is not usually one due to the bank customer in the course of his trading operations or ordinary course of business.[36] Rather, it is a deposit made for investment purposes or to maintain a balance for regular drawings. It has also been held that rights under insurance contracts are not 'book debts'.[37]

Whether a chose in action is a 'book debt' is primarily important for the purposes of deciding whether a charge on it is registrable[38] under the Companies Act 2006[39] or the

---

[30] The condition may be the passing of time (for example, under an instalment sale) or the happening of some event (for example, the issue of a certificate: *G. & T. Earle (1925) Ltd* v. *Hemsworth RDC* (1928) 140 LT 69 (CA)).

[31] *Norman* v. *Federal Commissioner of Taxation* (1963) 109 CLR 9: interest payable in the future on a deposit repayable without notice and future dividends on shares were held to be 'future' debts. Windeyer J dissented in relation to the interest. But future royalties have been held to be 'existing' choses in action: *Sheperd* v. *Federal Taxation Comr.* (1965) 113 CLR 385, *per* Owen J, dissenting.

[32] See R.M. Goode, *Commercial Law* (3rd edn., London, 2004), 744–752. Smith, n.7 above, ch. 11. For a comprehensive text see Oditah, n.19 above. On factoring, see F. Salinger, *Factoring: The Law and Practice of Invoice Finance* (4th edn., London, 2005).

[33] *Shipley* v. *Marshall* (1863) 14 CB (NS) 566, 571; *Dawson* v. *Isle* [1906] 1 Ch. 633.

[34] *Independent Automatic Sales Ltd* v. *Knowles & Foster* [1962] 1 WLR 974 (applying the *Shipley* v. *Marshall* (see previous note) definition); *Obaray* v. *Gateway (London) Ltd* [2004] 1 BCLC 555 (rent deposit in separate account not 'book debt').

[35] *Re Stevens, Stevens* v. *Keily* [1888] WN 110; *Watson* v. *Parapara Coal Co. Ltd* (1951) 17 GLR 791 (NZ); *Re Brightlife Ltd* [1987] Ch. 200; *Re Permanent Houses (Holdings) Ltd* [1988] BCC 151, 154 (point left open); *Northern Bank Ltd* v. *Ross* [1990] BCC 883 (NICA). In *Re BCCI SA (No. 8)* [1998] AC 214, 227 Lord Hoffmann expressly refused to express an opinion but noted Lord Hutton's view in *Northern Bank Ltd* v. *Ross* that a bank balance was not a book debt. See further Sect. 3(iv). See also Oditah, n.19 above, 23.

[36] But in the case of those institutions specializing in placing amounts borrowed by them on the money market, the balances accrued by such placings may possibly constitute 'book debts', as the institutions involved are in the business of borrowing for re-lending to the banks participating in the money market.

[37] *Paul and Frank Ltd* v. *Discount Bank (Overseas) Ltd* [1967] Ch. 348.

[38] Hence the controversy over bank balances. Note Prof. A. Diamond's comments in his *Review of Security Interests in Property* (London, 1989), para. 23.4.12, that the sizes of such bank balances are not known to creditors and thus an unregistered charge over them is unlikely to prejudice them. Nevertheless, a number of commentators advise registration as a precaution: see further Sect. 3 (iv).

[39] S.860(7)(f) (previously, Companies Act 2006, s.396(1)(e)); see Ch. 19, Sect. 4(iii) above and Sect. 2(v) below.

Bills of Sale Act 1878.[40] Otherwise, the term 'receivable' is now[41] usually used to describe debts owed to (and 'receivable' by) a business. This term does not have a precise legal definition but is wider than 'book debt' and connotes all monetary obligations owed to a business underpinning its cash flow. A negotiable instrument is sometimes referred to as a 'documentary receivable'.[42]

(ii) **'Receivables financing'**

The value of a receivable as collateral is based on the debtor's payment obligation. Although every business acquires some bad debts, a global security interest over all its 'receivables' provides a safe yield if realization becomes necessary. Banks take such a security interest where they finance either the entire business operations of their customer or some well-defined facet of it. Frequently, the security is additional to a charge over some goods. Thus, the bank may demand a charge over goods acquired by means of the credit extended to the customer and also over the proceeds of their sale. A fixed charge is preferable to a floating charge, available in the case of a corporate customer, for reasons discussed earlier.[43]

There are a number of well-established financing techniques involving receivables.[44] Conceptually they may be divided into techniques involving the outright sale of the receivables at a discount and those involving the raising of money on the security of receivables. Examples of the former are factoring and block discounting. In factoring,[45] the financier or 'factor' and the 'client' enter into a master factoring agreement covering the terms on which the former will buy the receivables of the latter prior to their maturity. The purchase is at a discount, which takes into account the time between the payment of the purchase price by the factor and the receipt by him of the proceeds of the receivables, as well as the risks the factor undertakes. The client will usually provide a right of recourse in the case of bad debts, often agreeing to repurchase them. Usually notice is given to the account-debtor and the debts are collected directly from him by the factor. If payment is made to the client by the account-debtor by mistake, the client holds any cheques and money on trust for the factor.[46] However in 'non-notification factoring' (sometimes called 'invoice discounting')—used where the client is unwilling to reveal that he has factored his debts—notice is not given to the account-debtor and the client collects the debts on the factor's behalf. 'Block discounting'[47] is a similar arrangement where rights under 'blocks' of agreements under which debts will mature—such as instalment sales—are assigned at a discount to a financier under a master block discounting agreement. This time, it is usual not to give notice to the account-debtors under the agreements, who continue to pay

---

[40] By virtue of the Insolvency Act 1986, s.344; see Sect. 2(v) below.

[41] Diamond, n.38 above, para. 23.9.22 regarded the term 'book debt' as having 'a slightly antique air' and recommended its replacement with 'receivables'.

[42] See Oditah, n.19 above, 26.   [43] Ch. 19, Sect. 4(ii) above. See also Sect. 2(iii) below.

[44] See H. Beale, M. Bridge, L. Gullifer, & E. Lomnicka, *The Law of Personal Property Security* (Oxford, 2007), paras. 5.70 *et seq*, 18.42 *et seq*. See also UNCITRAL's (the UN Commission on International Trade Law) Convention on the Assignment of Receivables in International Trade (New York, 2004) which aims to facilitate such transactions internationally by harmonizing the legal principles underpinning them.

[45] See Beale, Bridge, Gullifer, & Lomnicka, n.44 above, paras. 5.105 *et seq*. For more detail, see Salinger, n.32 above. For an example see *Re Charge Card Services Ltd* [1987] Ch. 150, affd. [1989] Ch. 497. UNIDROIT (the International Institute for the Unification of Private Law) in 1988 produced a Convention on International Factoring. And see also previous note on the work of UNCITRAL.

[46] *International Factors Ltd* v. *Rodriguez* [1979] QB 351.

[47] See Beale, Bridge, Gullifer, & Lomnicka, n.44 above, paras. 5.118–5.121. For an early case see *Re George Inglefield Ltd* [1933] Ch. 1 (CA).

their creditor. For the reasons noted above,[48] both non-notification factoring and block discounting present greater risks to the financier.

As an alternative to being sold outright to raise money, receivables may be used as collateral for loans. A financier may take a mortgage or charge over receivables as security for a loan or for revolving credit such as an overdraft. The important consequences of the distinction between a 'true sale' and a secured transaction have been noted above.[49] Yet, as Professor Goode has commented: 'in economic terms, a sale of receivables with recourse is virtually indistinguishable from a loan on the security of the receivables, for in both cases the trader receives money now and has to repay it himself, or ensure payments by debtors later'.[50] Nevertheless, the courts have consistently upheld this distinction and accepted as a 'sale' a factoring or block discounting or other transaction that is documented and operated as a 'sale'. Thus the discount is generally not regarded as disguised interest[51] and the obligations to repurchase bad debts are generally not viewed as disguised rights of redemption.[52]

(iii) **Fixed or floating charge?**

The special features of a 'floating charge' are considered above.[53] The nature of charges over the receivables of a company—whether those charges are fixed or floating—has posed special problems in the past. However, in *Re Spectrum Plus Ltd*,[54] the House of Lords laid at least two controversies to rest and confirmed that, in general, a charge over present and future book debts will be a floating charge as the intention will be that the proceeds will be used by the chargor in its business.[55]

First, *Spectrum Plus* overruled *Siebe Gorman & Co. Ltd* v. *Barclays Bank Ltd*,[56] a case that concerned a charge in favour of a bank over its customer's existing and future book debts where the proceeds were paid into the customer's ordinary bank account. In that case, the only restriction imposed on the customer was a 'negative pledge clause'[57] prohibiting the creation of any subsequent charges and the effecting of any assignment without the bank's prior consent. Slade J had held the bank's argument that the charge was 'fixed' rather than 'floating' on the basis that the requirement that the amounts received be paid into a designated account with the bank[58] meant that the customer did not have an

---

[48] See the reasons the giving of notice is advisable, set out in Sect. 1.   [49] Ch. 18, Sect. 1(i).

[50] Goode, n.32 above, 744.

[51] *Lloyd's and Scottish Finance Co. Ltd* v. *Cyril Lord Carpets Sales Ltd* [1992] BCLC 609 (but decided in 1979), discussed by Giddins (1980) *NLJ* 207, *per* Lord Wilberforce.

[52] *Re George Inglefield Ltd*, n.47 above; *Olds Discount Co. Ltd* v. *John Playfair Ltd* [1938] 3 All ER 275; *Lloyd's and Scottish Finance Co. Ltd* v. *Cyril Lord Carpets Sales Ltd*, n.51 above. But arrangements with absolute obligations to repurchase (rather than limited obligations in relation to bad debts) might be treated differently: see Oditah, n.19 above, 38–39.

[53] Ch. 19, Sect. 4(ii), (v).   [54] [2005] 2 AC 680.

[55] The early leading case on floating charges, *Illingworth* v. *Houldsworth* [1904] AC 355, concerned a charge over book debts.

[56] [1979] 2 Lloyd's Rep. 142, 159, citing *Evans, Coleman & Evans Ltd* v. *R. A. Nelson Construction Ltd* (1958) 16 DLR 123. *Siebe Gorman* had been criticized on the basis that the chargor was in fact free to use the proceeds in its business (see A. Berg, 'Charges over Book Debts: a Reply' [1995] *JBIL* 433, 442–9) and, for this reason, was not followed in New Zealand (see *Supercool Refrigeration and Air Conditioning* v. *Hoverd Industries* [1994] 3 NZLR 300). The Review Committee on Insolvency Law and Practice (Cmnd. 8558, 1982) para. 1586 (the Cork Report) recommended its reversal by statute on the basis that preferential creditors (see Ch. 19, Sect. 4(v)) were unduly prejudiced.

[57] See Ch. 19, Sect. 4(iv).

[58] Hence the decision did not help a chargee who was not a banker and who required the proceeds to be paid into the customer's current bank account: *Re Brightlife Ltd* [1987] Ch. 200.

unrestricted right to deal with the proceeds in the ordinary course of business; the bank had sufficient 'control' over the proceeds of the book debts. *Spectrum Plus*, concerned an almost identically drafted charge but the House of Lords held that, in not sufficiently restricting the use by the chargor of the proceeds of the book debts in the normal course of business, the charge was a floating and not a fixed charge. It was not enough that the bank could, in the future, intervene and preclude further drawings.[59] Indeed, such an act would constitute the crystallization of the floating charge.[60]

The second controversy was whether the Court of Appeal decision in *Re New Bullas Trading Ltd*[61] would be upheld, despite being regarded as wrongly decided by the Judicial Committee of the Privy Council in *Agnew* v. *CIR*.[62] Both cases concerned a contest between a creditor secured by a charge over book debts and preferential creditors.[63] The creditor took a general floating charge over the company's assets and a charge stated to be a 'fixed charge' over its uncollected book debts. The proceeds of the book debts were to be paid into the company's bank account whereupon they were released from the fixed charge but caught by the general floating charge. The agreement gave the chargee a power (which was never exercised) to direct that the proceeds be paid into a separate account to be nominated by him. The Court of Appeal took the view that, as the parties were in principle free to agree on the terms of the charge, they could stipulate for a charge that was fixed as to the outstanding book debts but became a floating charge if, at the time the book debts were realized, no instruction had been given for their payment into a designated account over which the chargee exercised control. In this manner, a distinction was drawn between the nature of the charge as it applied to the book debts prior to their collection and its nature on the proceeds realized on their payment. In *Agnew*, this distinction was not accepted; the charge over uncollected book debts was a floating charge on the basis that the company's freedom to deal with the proceeds was inconsistent with a fixed charge over the uncollected debts. Although agreeing that the parties were free to draw up whatever agreement they liked, the court held that the categorization of the agreement as fixed or floating was a matter of law for the court, to be determined on the basis of the factual position as agreed by the parties. And although agreeing that a debt and its proceeds were different assets, the court declined to consider each in isolation: the nature of the charge on the uncollected debts depended on the freedom the chargor had to deal with the proceeds. *Spectrum Plus* agreed with the reasoning in *Agnew* and hence *Re Bullas* can be regarded as wrongly decided.

The impact of two further controversies—both considered below—on the rights of a bank taking a charge over book debts and their proceeds has not yet been judicially considered or determined.[64] The first is whether a negative pledge clause in the instrument of charge, which stipulates that the customer may not assign any credit balances with his bank resulting from the realization of the book debts, renders those balances non-assignable. The case law on 'non-assignment clauses', considered below,[65] suggests that a purported assignment will not defeat the bank's rights in the balance and thus the bank

---

[59] Although it would be enough if, as in *Re Keenan Bros Ltd* [1986] BCLC 242, every drawing had to be counter-signed by the bank.

[60] For crystallization of floating charges, see Ch. 19, Sect. 4(vi).

[61] [1994] BCC 36, reversing [1993] BCC 251 (Knox J). For criticisms, see, R.M. Goode, 'Charges over Book Debts: a Missed Opportunity' (1994) 110 *LQR* 592; M.G. Bridge, 'Fixed Charges and Freedom of Contract' (1994) 110 *LQR* 340 and Millett LJ in *Royal Trust Bank* v. *National Westminster Bank plc* [1996] 2 BCLC 682 (CA). For support, see Berg, n.56 above, 451–463

[62] [2001] 3 WLR 454 (PC), on appeal from New Zealand.

[63] On the vulnerability of floating (but not fixed) charges to preferential creditors see Ch. 19, Sect. 4(v).

[64] They are discussed by Goode, n.61 above, and Berg, n.56 above.   [65] See Sect. 2(iv) below.

can in this way preserve its priority over subsequent claimants. On the other hand, case law on negative pledge clauses suggests that they are ineffective—at least against those with no notice of them.[66] It is suggested that the latter principle should prevail and that the case law upholding the effectiveness of non-assignment clauses should not be extended to prejudice receivables financiers taking assignments of debts—such as book debts—which are assumed to be freely assignable. The second controversy is whether it is possible for a bank to have a charge—be it fixed or floating—over the proceeds of book debts which have resulted in its customer's account being in credit (a 'charge-back').[67] If it is not, the bank has, at most, a right of set-off which has different consequences to a charge.[68] As it now seems that 'charge-backs' are possible, there is no objection on this score to a bank having a fixed or floating charge over the proceeds of its customer's book debts which have resulted in a credit balance in the customer's account—although in certain circumstances a right of set-off may be preferable.[69]

(iv) Restrictions on assignment

Debtors often include 'non-assignment' clauses in their contracts restricting or abso-lutely prohibiting the assignment of their debts.[70] The reasons are various. The debtor may wish to deal only with his creditor and not anyone else either because he values the personal qualities of the other contracting party[71] or because he wishes to retain, up to the very date of the discharge of the debt, rights of set-off and the right of rais-ing counterclaims based on different liabilities.[72] He may also wish to avoid the risk of making the error of paying twice owing to an oversight of a notice of assignment[73] or having to pay more than one creditor if there is an assignment of part of his debt.[74] Whilst these considerations favour the validity of non-assignment clauses, there are countervailing arguments that support the principle of free assignability of debts. Once it is accepted that debts are *prima facie* assignable, the interests of third par-ties—the assignees—become relevant,[75] although the courts have not gone so far as to regard debts as 'property' for the purposes of insisting that they are freely alienable.[76]

---

[66] See Ch. 19, Sect. 4(iv).   [67] See Sect. 3(iv) below.   [68] See Sect. 3(iii) below.

[69] See Berg, n.56 above 433, 465–7.

[70] See G. McCormack, 'Debts and Non-assignment Clauses' [2000] *JBL* 422; McMeel, 'The Modern Law of Assignment: Public Policy and Contractual Restrictions on Transferability' [2004] *LMCLQ* 483; Smith, n.7 above, ch. 12, Sect. F.

[71] See *Don King Productions Inc.* v. *Warren* [1999] 3 WLR 276 (concerning boxing promotion where the identity of the promoter was crucial) and building contract cases where the identity of the contractor is important to the employer (e.g. *Linden Garden Trust Ltd* v. *Lenesta Sludge Disposal Ltd* [1994] AC 85; *Yeandle* v. *Wynn Realisations Ltd* (1995) 47 Con. LR 1; *R* v. *Chester and Northern Wales Legal Aid Area Office (No. 12), ex p. Floods of Queensferry Ltd* [1998] BCC 685). The identity of the creditors (and their attitude to default) is also of importance in syndicated loans: *Barbados Trust Company Ltd* v. *Bank of Zambia* [2007] EWCA Civ. 148.

[72] See Sect. 1 above: certain new 'equities' may not be invoked after notice of assignment.

[73] R.M. Goode, *Legal Problems of Credit and Security* (4th edn., 2009), para. 3-40; and see Oditah, n.19 above, 259 ff.

[74] See Salinger, n.32 above, chs. 7 and 8. There is also the greater practical inconvenience of dealing with an unfamiliar assignee.

[75] Such non-assignment clauses resemble negative pledge clauses (see Ch. 19, Sect. 4(iv)), except that they are inserted by the debtor in the contract creating the debt rather than by a previous chargee of the debt. Analogies with negative pledge clauses suggest that non-assignment clauses should not affect assignees without notice of them. See also Sect. 2(iii) above.

[76] Thus, authorities on the (limited) validity of non-assignment clauses in leases of land have been regarded as irrelevant: *Helstan Securities Ltd* v. *Hertfordshire County Council* [1978] 3 All ER 262; *Linden*

Moreover, from a commercial point of view, non-assignment clauses affect the marketability of debts and therefore the attractiveness of receivables financing. Such considerations have prevailed in the USA where the Uniform Commercial Code renders non-assignment clauses ineffective[77] and this approach has influenced the drafting of international conventions.[78]

English law has adopted a compromise position in relation to this 'tension between the [debtor's] contractual autonomy and the [assignee's] proprietary rights'.[79] *Prima facie* it upholds non-assignment clauses as against the debtor and regards it as legitimate for the contracting parties, as between themselves, to insist that they deal only with each other.[80] However, it is now settled that an assignment in breach of such a clause is an effective contract as between the assignor and assignee. The leading case is the House of Lords' decision in *Linden Garden Trust Ltd* v. *Leneseta Sludge Disposal Ltd*,[81] where it was held that a non-assignment clause was not contrary to public policy and that an assignment in breach of it was therefore ineffective as against the debtor. However, Lord Browne-Wilkinson observed that a prohibition of assignment normally invalidated the assignment only as against the other party to the contract, *viz.* the debtor, but 'in the absence of the clearest words, it [could not] operate to invalidate the contract as between the assignor and the assignee and even then it [might] be ineffective on the ground of public policy'. Moreover, an assignment in breach of such a clause could give rise to an obligation on the part of the assignor to account to the assignee for whatever he receives from the debtor.[82] This is because the debtor cannot have any legitimate objection to the fate of his payment once it has reached the hands of his creditor, *viz.* the assignor.[83] This suggestion is of considerable practical importance in the case of the assignor's insolvency. If the assignment is valid as between the assignor and assignee, with the assignor having an obligation to account, it would confer on the assignee priority over the sum involved in the assignor's insolvency.[84] The subsequent first instance decision of *Don King Productions Inc.* v. *Warren*[85] went further and suggested that a non-assignment clause would not normally preclude

Garden Trust Ltd v. Lenesta Sludge Disposal Ltd, n.71 above; *Hendry* v. *Chartsearch Ltd* [1998] CLC 1382 (CA).

[77] See Art. 9-318(4) of the UCC. The revised Art. 9-406(d) is to similar effect. See McCormack, n.70 above, 426–7.

[78] See the UNIDROIT Factoring Convention (Sect. 2(ii), n.45), Art. 6 and the UNCITRAL Convention (Sect. 2(ii), n.44). Both render non-assignment clauses *prima facie* ineffective but Member States may derogate from these provisions in relation to domestic debtors.

[79] McCormack, n.70 above, 438.

[80] *Linden Garden Trust Ltd* v. *Lenesta Sludge Disposal Ltd*, n.71 above; *Hendry* v. *Chartsearch Ltd* [1998] CLC 1382 (CA); *Stansell Ltd* v. *Co-operative Group (CWS) Ltd* [2005] EWHC 1601. But a non-assignment clause may be construed as merely extending to the assignment of 'personal' rights to performance and not to the debts arising: *Re Bewejem Ltd* [1999] 1 All ER (Comm.) 371, [1999] BCC 157 (CA), *per* Robert Walker LJ. This construction was rejected in *Helstan Securities Ltd* v. *Hertfordshire County Council*, n.76 above and *Linden Garden Trust Ltd* v. *Lenesta Sludge Disposal Ltd*, n.71 above. However, in *R.* v. *Chester and Northern Wales Legal Aid Area Office (No. 12), ex p. Floods of Queensferry Ltd*, n.71 above, the clause expressly so provided.

[81] [1994] AC 85 and see the categorical statement that the assignment contract is valid despite the non-assignment clause, by Millett LJ in *Hendry* v. *Chartsearch Ltd* [1998] CLC 1382. For some previous decisions see: *Re Turcan* (1889) 40 Ch. D 5; *Tom Shaw & Co.* v. *Moss Empires Ltd and Bastow* (1908) 25 TLR 190; *Spellman* v. *Spellman* [1961] 1 WLR 921; *Helstan Securities Ltd* v. *Hertfordshire County Council*, n.80 above.

[82] See *Re Turcan* (1889) 40 Ch. D 5.

[83] See Goode, n.73 above, para. 3-40 and, by the same author, 'Inalienable Rights?' (1979) 42 *MLR* 553; and note Oditah, n.19 above, 259–260.

[84] See McCormack, n.70 above, 442.

[85] [1999] 3 WLR 276, [1998] 2 All ER 608 (Lightman J); [1999] 2 All ER 218 (CA). Lightman J made the suggestion (at length) but the Court of Appeal decided the case on another ground.

a declaration of trust by the assignor of the benefit of contractual rights in favour of the assignee. Although this view has been criticized on the basis that such a declaration of trust is indistinguishable from an equitable assignment and would undermine the non-assignment clause,[86] the majority of the Court of Appeal in *Barbados Trust Co. Ltd* v. *Bank of Zambia*[87] allowed an assignee of rights under a syndicated loan with restrictions on its assignment, who became the beneficiary of an express declaration of trust, to recover against the original debtor. It may be that this decision will be regarded as an exceptional one, decided on its special facts, and that generally if the assignor is a trustee of his rights against the debtor, the debtor is only liable to pay that trustee-assignor.

The effect of non-assignment clauses on the creation of security interests in receivables—rather than on outright assignments—has not been the subject of litigation. As a matter of construction, a non-assignment clause may not extend to the creation of a charge,[88] especially if the purpose of the clause is to preserve the relationship between the original parties to the contract. But should the clause purport to extend to the creation of security interests, it would seem that similar principles would apply as they do to outright assignments.[89] These principles may also govern the effect of 'flawed asset arrangements' which are contractual terms between a bank and its customer that restrict the extent to which the customer can deal with credit balances.[90]

(v) Registration, and the effect of failure to do so

Registration is required in the case of charges on the 'book debts' both of an incorporated and of an unincorporated business. Although the provisions for registration and the machinery provided therefor differ as between the two types of enterprise, the failure to comply with the applicable procedure has a similar effect in both cases. It renders the charge ineffective in the assignor's insolvency. However, if the assignor is incorporated, an unregistered charge is also void against its creditors and therefore the unregistered chargee may be postponed to a subsequent competing secured creditor. The difficult question whether registration constitutes constructive notice, which may be of relevance to questions of priorities, may also be resolved differently depending on the status of the assignor.

A charge[91] on the book debts of a company requires registration under section 860(7)(f) of the Companies Act 2006. This provision applies to charges over future book debts[92]

---

[86] A. Tettenborn, 'Trusts of Unassignable Agreements' [1998] *LMCLQ* 498, [1999] *LMCLQ* 353 and see McCormack, n.70 above.

[87] [2007] EWCA 148, reversing Langley J [2006] EWHC 222. The declaration of trust was made for the sole purpose of enabling the assignee (who fell within the prohibition against assignment) to recover directly against the debtor, the assignor/trustee being joined as defendant on the *Vandepitte* principle (see the case of that name: [1933] AC 70).

[88] But a mortgage (which takes effect as an outright assignment (subject to reassignment): see Sect. (1)) would *prima facie* be covered.

[89] See McCormack, n.70 above, 439–442.

[90] See Sect. 3(iii) below. In *Re BCCI SA (No. 8)* [1998] AC 214, such 'flawed asset arrangements' were upheld.

[91] A term which includes a mortgage: Companies Act 2006, s.861(5). Therefore a statutory assignment by way of mortgage (see Sect. 1, n.12 above) is registrable. For the registration of company charges generally, see Ch. 19, Sect. 4(iii).

[92] *Independent Automatic Sales Ltd* v. *Knowles & Foster* [1962] 1 WLR 974, decided under the predecessor s.95(1)(e) of the Companies Act 1948, which was identical. But the decision in *Paul and Frank Ltd* v. *Discount Bank (Overseas) Ltd* [1967] Ch. 348, that rights under insurance and other 'contingency' contracts are not 'book debts', gives rise to doubts about the applicability of s.860(7)(f) to debts arising on contingencies: see

and to any transaction which effectively creates a charge, however the transaction is described. Thus in *Re Kent and Sussex Sawmills Ltd*[93] a supplier ordered his purchaser to remit all amounts due under the contract to a designated bank, and stipulated that the instruction could be revoked only with the bank's written consent. It was held that the arrangement constituted a registrable charge on book debts created by the supplier in favour of the bank. But if the transaction is a true 'sale' of book debts (albeit at a discount and with rights of recourse), for example a factoring or block discounting transaction, rather than a loan secured on the book debts, this does not create a registrable charge[94] nor does a true retention of title under a *'Romalpa'* clause.[95] Moreover, section 860(7)(f) applies only to charges created by agreement; it has no application to encumbrances created by operation of law.[96] It is also inapplicable to charges effected over book debts by the pledge of negotiable instruments representing them.[97] In addition to this specific provision in the Companies Act 2006 as to the registration of charges over 'book debts', it should not be forgotten that some charges over book debts may be regarded as 'floating charges',[98] in which case they will be registrable as such under Companies Act.[99]

The effect of non-registration of a company registrable charge is to avoid the charge against the liquidator, administrator, and other creditors.[100] But this is not the case as regards any book debts which are paid over to the assignee or become the subject of a set-off between the assignor and the assignee,[101] as the charge remains valid as between assignor and assignee until administration or liquidation.[102] As well as preserving the validity of the charge, registration has a further impact on persons dealing with the company. It probably constitutes constructive notice of the charge itself,[103] although probably not of its detailed terms other than the 'prescribed particulars' entered on the Register.[104] Dicta suggest that everyone—whether likely to search the register or not—has constructive notice of a company registered charge.[105]

The registration of the assignment of the book debts of an unincorporated firm is outside the immediate scope of the Bills of Sale Acts[106] and is governed by section 344 of the Insolvency Act 1986, which replaced section 43(1) of the Bankruptcy Act 1914. Under section 344(1), a general assignment by a trader of his existing or future book debts or any class thereof is void against his trustee in bankruptcy unless it has been registered under

---

Contemporary Cottages (NZ) Ltd v. *Margin Traders Ltd* [1981] 2 NZLR 114, *per* Thorp J at 126. For problems with 'future' choses in action, see Sect. 1 above.

[93] [1947] 1 Ch. 177.

[94] See Sect. 2(ii) above (and, in relation to asset securitization, Sect. 2(vii) below) and, on the distinction between a sale and secured loan, Ch. 18, Sect. 2(i).

[95] See Sect. 2(vi) below. But claims to *proceeds* are usually characterized as charges: see Ch. 18, Sect. 1(i).

[96] *Bruton* v. *Electrical Engineering Corp.* [1892] 1 Ch. 434 (solicitor's lien); *London and Cheshire Insurance Co.* v. *Laplagrene Property Co.* [1971] Ch. 499 (unpaid vendor's lien).

[97] Companies Act 2006, s.861(3). And see *Dawson* v. *Isle* [1906] 1 Ch. 633, illustrating when a negotiable instrument falls within the definition of a book debt. *Chase Manhattan Asia* v. *First Bangkok Finance (OA and Liquidators of)* [1990] 1 WLR 1181 (PC), shows that the exception does not apply if the negotiable instruments covering the book debts are retained by the chargor; delivery thereof to the chargee is, thus, essential.

[98] See Sect. (iii) above.   [99] Under s.860(7)(g).

[100] Companies Act 2006, s.874. See Ch. 19, Sect. 4(iii) above.

[101] Before the commencement of the winding-up: *Re Row Dal Construction Pty. Ltd* [1966] VR 249.

[102] Companies Act 2006, s.874(3).   [103] See Ch. 19, Sect. 4(iv) above.   [104] See ibid.

[105] *G. and T. Earle Ltd* v. *Hemsworth RDC* (1928) TLR 605, 608 (affirmed on other grounds, (1928) 44 TLR 758). This is not uncontroversial, see Ch. 19, n.284.

[106] As book debts are excluded from the definition of a chattel in s.4 of the Bills of Sale Act 1878.

the Bills of Sale Act 1878.[107] Under subsection (4) such an assignment is treated as if it were a bill of sale given otherwise than by way of security. 'Assignment', in this context, includes any assignment by way of security or charge on book debts.[108] The use of the word 'includes' suggests that other assignments, such as outright assignments or sales, are also included. This is in contrast to the position in relation to assignments by corporations where it is clear that only charges on, and not sales of, book debts are registrable.

Under section 344(4), the provisions of the Bills of Sale Act 1878 are applied to a registrable assignment of book debts with the necessary modifications. Significantly, the section makes no reference to the Bills of Sale Act 1882, which means that a charge covering future book debts is valid. Section 344(3)(b) excludes four types of assignment of book debts from the registration requirement: they do not constitute 'general assignments' within the meaning of section 344. The first is an assignment of the debts due at the date of the assignment from persons specified in the instrument. The second is an assignment of debts 'becoming due under specified contracts'. The third is any assignment made in the course of the bona fide transfer of a business, and the fourth is any assignment of assets for the benefit of the general creditors.

Section 43(1) of the 1914 Act, which preceded the current section 344, had not been the subject of a great deal of litigation in the United Kingdom.[109] Canadian authorities hold that registration under an analogous provision does not have the effect of conferring constructive notice on the debtor who is not expected to search the register before paying the debt.[110] And recent New Zealand legislation provides that registration 'does not, of itself, give actual notice of the assignment'.[111] It is unclear if this approach will be followed in the United Kingdom.

(vi) Priorities

The problem of ranking competing claims to receivables is complicated by the fact that the adverse rights often accrue under different types of transaction. First, there are cases in which the owner of the receivables, the assignor, creates two conflicting assignments over them. In some cases his motives are fraudulent; in others he may not be fully aware that the assignments cover the same receivables. Secondly, the competing claims may arise from entirely separate arrangements. Two types of situation are common. One involves a conflict between the claims of a supplier, who has a security interest over goods supplied to the assignor and their proceeds under a so-called 'retention of title' or 'Romalpa'[112] clause, and of a bank, which has a charge on existing and future book debts to secure a

---

[107] Hill v. Alex Lawrie Factors Ltd, The Times, 17 August 2000.

[108] Insolvency Act 1986, s.344(3)(a).

[109] For a discussion of its background see Re Lovegrove [1935] Ch. 464.

[110] Snyder's Ltd v. Furniture Finance Corporation Ltd [1931] 1 DLR 398; Re Royal Bank of Canada (1979) 94 DLR (3d.) 692, the importance of which is pointed out by Goode, n.73 above, para. 3-31. Cf. the probable position in relation to non-registration of company charges, that registration confers constructive notice to 'the whole world' noted above, n.105.

[111] Law of Property Act 2007 (New Zealand), s.52(1).

[112] First recognized in Aluminium Industrie Vaassen BV v. Romalpa Aluminium Ltd [1976] 1 WLR 676. See generally R.M. Goode, 'The Right to Trace and its Impact in Commercial Transactions' (1976) 92 LQR 360, 528; A.G. Guest, 'Romalpa Clauses' (1979) 95 LQR 477 and [1980] CLJ 48; M. Bridge (ed.) Benjamin's Sale of Goods, (8th edn., London, 2010), para. 5-141 ff.; Beale, Bridge, Gullifer, Lomnicka, n.44 above, paras. 5.07–5.25. As regards the attachment of the clause to proceeds, see in particular Re Bond Worth Ltd [1980] Ch. 228; Pfeiffer (E.) Weinkellerei-Weinkauf GmbH v. Arbuthnot Factors Ltd [1988] 1 WLR 150; Tatung (UK) Ltd v. Galex Telesure Ltd (1989) 5 BCC 325; Compaq Computers Ltd v. Abercorn Group Ltd [1993] BCLC 603.

general overdraft. Is the supplier or the bank entitled to the proceeds of sale of the goods? The other case involves competing types of security, such as a fixed charge over book debts granted to a clearing bank and a floating charge granted to an investment bank.[113] In addition, there may be a clash between the holder of a charge over the assignor's book debts and an absolute assignment thereof to a factor.

The basic principle for determining priorities of competing assignments is known as the rule in *Dearle* v. *Hall*.[114] The assignee who is the first to give notice of the assignment to the debtor takes precedence. If neither of the competing assignees gives notice, the assignments take priority in the order of their execution. The priority conferred on a subsequent assignee by the rule in *Dearle* v. *Hall* is defeated if he knew or ought to have known, at the time he took the assignment, of the existence of an earlier one.[115] In principle, it seems that if the assignor is a company, registration of an earlier charge constitutes constructive notice of the charge.[116] If the assignor is unincorporated, it may be that registration constitutes only constructive notice to those who would be expected to search the register.[117] This would cover subsequent assignees but not suppliers under 'Romalpa' clauses.

This basic principle is modified by the registration provisions in so far as they invalidate registrable charges which are unregistered. As noted above,[118] an unregistered company charge is void as against both subsequent creditors and the liquidator and administrator. An unregistered assignment in the case of an unincorporated assignor is void as against his trustee in bankruptcy. Thus, before applying *Dearle* v. *Hall*, it must be asked whether the registration requirements invalidate the assignment in the circumstances.

The rule in *Dearle* v. *Hall* is not easy to support on policy grounds.[119] Although it was established in the context of competing *equitable* assignments of an *equitable* chose in action,[120] it has been applied both to statutory assignments[121] and to assignments of legal choses in action.[122] It has even been held to apply as between competing absolute assignments and assignments by way of charge.[123] The rule is therefore applicable in cases involving a conflict between the claims of a bank, which is an assignee by way of charge of a firm's book debts, and a factor who has purchased them. The rule is equally applicable where the competing assignments cover future book debts. However, there is some doubt whether the rule in *Dearle* v. *Hall* applies as between a supplier of goods claiming the

---

[113] See Sect. 2(iii) above on when charges over book debts are fixed or floating.

[114] (1828) 3 Russ. 1. See also, Beale, Bridge, Gullifer & Lomnicka, n.44 above, paras. 13.09–13.20. But see Sect. 5(v) below: priorities in relation to shares are determined by rules applicable to mortgages.

[115] *Re Holmes* (1885) 29 Ch. D 786. For a criticism of this proviso, see J. de Lacey, 'Reflections on the Ambit of the Rule in Dearle v. Hall and the Priority of Personal and Property Assignments' (1999) 28 *Anglo-Am. LR* and 197. Constructive notice (resulting from being put on enquiry) suffices: *Spencer* v. *Clarke* (1878) 9 Ch. D 137.

[116] See Sect. 2(v) above.   [117] Ibid.   [118] Ibid.

[119] See *Ward* v. *Duncombe* [1893] AC 369, *per* Lord MacNaghten at 391. See Beale, Bridge, Gullifer & Lomnicka, n.44 above, para. 13.10.

[120] And note the Law of Property Act 1925, s.137(3) which now requires notice of the assignment of an 'equitable interest' to be in writing to preserve priority.

[121] Under ibid., s.136: see Sect. 1 above. In particular, as a statutory assignee takes 'subject to equities having priority' over him, he cannot argue that he defeats a prior equitable assignment as a *bona fide* legal purchaser: *Pfeiffer (E.) Weinkellerei-Weinkauf GmbH* v. *Arbuthnot Factors Ltd* [1988] 1 WLR 150; *Compaq Computers Ltd* v. *Abercorn Group Ltd* [1993] BCLC 603.

[122] Such as debts: *Marchant* v. *Morton, Down & Co.* [1901] 2 KB 829; *Pfeiffer (E.) Weinkellerei-Weinkauf GmbH* v. *Arbuthnot Factors Ltd*, n.121 above; *Compaq Computers Ltd* v. *Abercorn Group Ltd*, n.121 above.

[123] *Harding Corp. Ltd* v. *Royal Bank of Canada* [1980] 4 WWR 149, cited by Goode, n.73 above, para. 5-09. See now *Pfeiffer (E.) Weinkellerei-Weinkauf GmbH* v. *Arbuthnot Factors Ltd*, n.121 above and *Compaq Computers Ltd* v. *Abercorn Group Ltd*, n.121 above.

proceeds of their sale under a '*Romalpa*' clause and an assignee who takes an assignment of those proceeds,[124] as will now be discussed.

A difficult priority problem arises where there is competition between the claims of a supplier under a '*Romalpa*' clause and of an assignee of a customer's book debts. By way of illustration, take the case of a supplier who contracts for a reservation of title over both the goods delivered by him on credit and the proceeds arising from their sale. If the purchaser resells the goods involved on credit terms, the supplier will regard the debt arising as subject to his security interest. A competing right will be asserted by a bank that has granted the purchaser a general overdraft, or other credit facility, secured on all exist-ing and future book debts. Which claim takes precedence in the purchaser's insolvency? The commentators are divided[125] and the cases provide no clear answer.[126] In particular, it is unclear whether the rule in *Dearle* v. *Hall* applies only to competing *assignments* or whether it extends to a contest between a supplier who is not an assignee of a debt but has an equitable interest based on the assignor's duty to hold the proceeds of the goods as trustee or fiduciary.

If the supplier's claim is by way of true retention of title and not by way of charge or assignment, it is not registrable.[127] On the other hand, the assignee's claim may be regis-trable, depending on the circumstances.[128] Assuming the assignee's claim is registrable, the supplier may be regarded as having constructive notice, for the purposes of the rule in *Dearle* v. *Hall* (if applicable), of any prior registered assignment.[129] Who obtains priority probably depends on whether the supplier's rights over the proceeds attach before they become subject to the assignment. If they do, the supplier acquires priority, as the assign-ee's rights are subject to the equities prevailing between the assignor and the supplier.[130] If they do not, the assignee obtains priority although he may lose it in two circumstances. The first is on insolvency if his assignment is registrable but unregistered.[131] The second is if the rule in *Dearle* v. *Hall* applies and he is not the first to give notice.[132]

The position differs altogether if, despite its label, the reservation of title clause con-stitutes a charge over the proceeds. Recent case law has construed claims to proceeds as constituting claims by way of charge. For example, in *Pfeiffer (E.) Weinkellerei-Weinkauf*

---

[124] See further below.

[125] D.W. McLauchlan, 'Priorities—Equitable Tracing Rights and Assignment of Book Debts' (1980) 96 *LQR* 90; Oditah, n.19 above, 149–54; Goode, n.73 above para. 5-36 (and Goode, n.32 above, 750–751); G. McCormack, *Reservation of Title* (2nd edn., 1995), ch. 9.

[126] The issue was raised but not decided (as the supplier's claim was held to be by way of equitable assign-ment not true retention of equitable interest) in *Pfeiffer (E.) Weinkellerei-Weinkauf GmbH* v. *Arbuthnot Factors Ltd*, n.121 above and *Compaq Computers Ltd* v. *Abercorn Group Ltd*, n.121 above.

[127] See Sect. 2(v) above. It is not a 'charge' for the purposes of the Companies Act 2006, s.860, nor is it an 'assignment' for the purposes of the Insolvency Act 1986, s.344.

[128] Ibid. If the assignor is unincorporated, it will be registrable if it is a 'general assignment'. If the assignor is a company, it will be registrable if it is by way of 'charge' rather than outright sale.

[129] Ibid. It seems it will in the case of a corporate assignor, but perhaps not in the case of an unincorpo-rated assignor as a supplier would not be expected to search the register of charges. See Sect.(v) above.

[130] This is the view of Goode, relying on *Harding Carpets Ltd* v. *Royal Bank of Canada* [1980] 4 WWR 149. Note that under s.9-312 of the Uniform Commercial Code, the trade creditor, who has a purchase money security, would also take priority.

[131] See Sect. (v) above. If the supplier is regarded as 'any creditor' of a corporate assignor, then even before insolvency or administration, the unregistered charge is void as against him.

[132] See below. But, if the assignee has registered his charge, it may be that the supplier will be taken to have constructive notice of his charge and thus cannot take advantage of this rule: see Sect. (v) above. In practice, only the assignee is likely to give notice.

GmbH & Co. v. *Arbuthnot Factors Ltd*,[133] German exporters sold wine to an English importer on terms which included a curiously worded clause entitled 'property reservation clause'.[134] The importer sub-sold the wine on credit terms and, subsequently, entered into a factoring agreement under which the debts accruing under the sub-sales were assigned by him absolutely[135] to a financier. Notice of this assignment was given by the financier to the sub-purchasers. The exporters, who were not paid by the importer, brought an action in which they claimed to be the beneficial owners of the proceeds of each sub-sale and asserted that the financier's claim was subordinate to their equitable title. The financier defended the action on two grounds. First, it argued that the exporters' interest in the proceeds was in the nature of a charge that was avoided as it had not been registered.[136] Secondly, the financier pleaded that, quite regardless of the nature of the exporters' interest, the assignment effected by the factoring agreement created a title superior to it.

Phillips J decided both issues in favour of the financier. As regards the first issue, his Lordship concluded that the language of the clause indicated that the exporters obtained an assignment by way of charge of the amounts to be received by the importer from the sub-sales on credit terms of the wine. In consequence, the assignment was void against the importer's creditors (including the financier) for want of registration. As regards the second issue, Phillips J held that the question of priorities was to be determined by the rule in *Dearle* v. *Hall*. In consequence, the financier, which was the first to notify, ranked above the exporters.

The *Pfeiffer Weinkeleri-Weinkauf* case shows that, where there is competition between a party asserting a right over the book debts of an insolvent company on the basis of a reservation of title clause and another party who relies on an assignment, the first issue to be considered is the true nature of the reservation. If, as is likely, the reservation of title clause creates a charge over proceeds, to be assured of priority the supplier must both register the charge and give notice for the purposes of the rule in *Dearle* v. *Hall*.[137]

(vii) Asset securitization

Finally, because it involves using choses in action as collateral for raising funds, mention should be made of 'asset securitization',[138] although it is used by banks to raise

---

[133] [1988] 1 WLR 150. See also *Tatung (UK) Ltd* v. *Galex Telesure Ltd* (1989) 5 BCC 325 (Phillips J) and the similar subsequent case *Compaq Computers Ltd* v. *Abercorn Group Ltd* [1993] BCLC 603 (Mummery J). But see the elaborate 'retention of title' clause in *Associated Alloys Pty Ltd* v. *CAN 001452106 Pty Ltd* [2000] HCA 25; [2000] ALJR 862 that provided for a beneficial interest under a trust (held not to be a 'charge') in the proceeds of sale.

[134] Under this clause, the exporters retained the title in the wine until it was paid for but granted the importer the right to effect sub-sales. If such sales were effected on credit terms, the importer was required, upon the exporters' demand, to notify his sub-purchasers that the 'claims' were assigned to the exporters. In the case of cash sales, the amounts received were to vest immediately in the exporters and had to be 'booked correspondingly' and be administered by the importer 'until called for'.

[135] Within the meaning of the Law of Property Act 1925, s.136.

[136] Under what is now Companies Act 2006, s.860(7)(f) and hence avoided under what is now s.874. See further, Ch. 19, Sect. 4(iii).

[137] Although registration may constitute constructive notice: see Sect. 2(v) above.

[138] See S.L. Schwarcz, *The Alchemy of Asset Securitisation* (1994) *Stan. JL Bus & Fin*, 133. There is also so-called 'future-flow' or 'project-backed' securitization that 'securitizes' the future choses in action expected from a project, for example, the building of toll roads or bridges. For a (now dated) consideration, see D. Bonsall, *Securitisation* (London, 1990), esp. chs. 1 & 7; J. Borrows (ed.) *Current Issues in Securitisation* (London, 2002).

funds in the basis of *their* portfolios of credit agreements. 'Asset securitisation' is the name given to a method of raising finance on the security of a portfolio of credit trans-actions such as mortgages,[139] personal loans or credit card agreements (the 'assets'). It has been noted above[140] that the term 'security' is sometimes used to mean company shares, bonds and similar 'instruments' or rights, and it is this use of the word that gives 'asset securitisation' its name. Asset securitization takes many forms[141] but the most common in the UK involves creating a company—a 'special purpose vehicle' (an 'SPV')[142]—and causing it to purchase the choses in action arising under a portfolio of credit agreements and to issue debt-instruments such as bonds ('securities') for the pur-pose of raising funds. The debt-instruments are 'asset backed' in the sense that the SPV has underlying assets—the choses in action it has purchased—so that income payable on the instruments is paid out of[143] the income received on the loans, whilst the capital payable on redemption is paid out of the capital received on repayment of the loans. Banks often 'securitize' portfolios of their debts for a number of reasons. As well as raising funds and increasing liquidity, there are commercial,[144] tax and balance-sheet advantages[145] to securitizing their debts.

The choses in action under the credit agreements are transferred outright[146] to the SPV by way of equitable assignment. Notice is not given to the borrowers and the bank may continue to service the loans but pays the money received into a trust account to protect the SPV (that is, the purchasers of the SPV's 'securities') should the bank become insolvent. If the choses in action are themselves secured (as will be the case if the credit agreements are mortgages) then the SPV will take a power of attorney to obtain trans-fer of the collateral which it will exercise if it needs to enforce the security. The attrac-tiveness of the SPV's 'securities' and therefore the success of the securitization depends primarily on the value of the choses in action. There will be the usual inherent risks of non-payment, unenforceability in the case of agreements regulated by the Consumer Credit Act 1974,[147] and diminution in value due to claims from borrowers accruing before notice is given.[148] The usual commercial devices—buying the debts at a discount and with recourse, ensuring that there is a large margin between the rights bought and the obligations undertaken to the SVP's investors, obtaining a guarantee or insurance from a third party—are used to meet these risks. Absence of proper management of these risks when US 'sub-prime' mortgages were securitized, was largely to blame for the banking crisis of 2007–2008.

---

[139] For more detail, see E. Ferran, *Mortgage Securitisation: Legal Aspects* (London, Butterworths, 1992).

[140] See Ch. 18, Sect. 1.

[141] The trust device may be (as is common in the US) used instead of an SPV, funds being raised by giving beneficial interests in a trust fund comprising a portfolio of loans.

[142] Often incorporated in a tax haven and deliberately not a subsidiary of the original creditor to make it 'insolvency remote'. There may be a chain of SPVs. The FSA capital adequacy requirements set out in its Handbook and noted in Ch. 2, Sect. 4(vi), require a clear separation between the bank and the SPV.

[143] But there may be a disparity between the interest rates under the credit agreements and those payable in respect of the debt instruments.

[144] It is usually cheaper to raise money by securitization as the SPV's securities are deliberately made attractive (by ensuring that the SPV is 'insolvency remote' and utilizes other 'credit enhancements').

[145] The amount of outstanding debt is relevant to capital adequacy requirements imposed by banking regulators so there is an incentive to 'sell' debt.

[146] It is essential that the transfer be characterized as a 'sale' (and not a loan on security), primarily so as to ensure that the SVP is 'insolvency remote' (i.e. not affected—as it would be if it were merely a secured creditor of the bank—by the insolvency of the bank).

[147] See Ch. 2, Sect. 5(xiii).   [148] See Sect. 1 above.

3 Security interests over bank balances

(i) Basic problems

A balance standing to the credit of a customer's account constitutes a debt owed to him by the bank.[149] This is the position regardless of whether the balance accrues on a current account, a savings account, a fixed deposit, or any other interest-bearing account. From the customer's point of view, such a debt is an asset.[150] He may, therefore, wish to utilize it as collateral either in respect of a transaction financed by the bank itself or in respect of one backed by another financial institution. By way of illustration, the customer may request the bank, or other institution, to issue a letter of credit or guarantee to back his purchase of goods. He may wish to use his deposits with the bank, which may be earmarked for some other specific purpose, as collateral securing the bank's or other institution's promise to the supplier under the letter of credit or guarantee.

The creation of a security interest over a bank balance is fraught with practical difficulties. First, the balance may be depleted by the customer by withdrawals. Although this hurdle can be overcome by the arrangement of a suitable date of maturity, this solution is unattractive. The customer's object in depositing funds with his bank is to maintain his liquidity. Even in the case of a fixed deposit, the agreed date of maturity can normally be altered to accommodate the customer, provided he is prepared to forgo the interest. To render a deposit unclaimable until the completion of the transaction secured by it may induce the customer simply to make immediate payment to the secured party. Secondly, a bank balance standing to the credit of a current or an interest-bearing account is subject to third party debt (previously known as a 'garnishee') proceedings by a judgment creditor,[151] which undermines the attractiveness of a security interest over a bank balance. The techniques used to overcome it will be shown to place impediments on the customer's freedom of action. Thirdly, the security interest is valueless unless it affords protection in the customer's insolvency. It will be shown that this outcome is not always attainable. Finally, in the case of a non-corporate customer, the security has to be drafted so as to be effective against his estate in the event of his death.

Different techniques are used for the granting of a security interest over a bank balance. Basically, the form used depends on whether it is to be given to the bank with which the funds are deposited or to a third party.

(ii) Security interest to a bank with which funds are deposited: set-off in equity and insolvency

The right of a bank to effect a set-off by combining a customer's different accounts has been discussed in Chapter 7.[152] The right is based on the principle of equity which allows a debtor to reduce the amount claimed by his creditor, by any liquidated sum due from the creditor to himself.[153] It is, accordingly, a procedural right[154] and does not confer on the party entitled to exercise it a property right.[155] The subject of the set-off need not be an amount standing to the customer's credit in a specific bank account. It is sufficient if

---

[149] Ch. 5, Sect. 3 above.

[150] But it is, usually, not a 'book debt', see Sect. 2(i) above.   [151] Ch. 11, Sect. 1(iii) above.

[152] Ch. 7, Sect. 4 above. Generally on set-off see Derham, n.19 above; P.R. Wood, *English and International Set-Off* (London, 1989); D. Pollard, 'Credit Balances as Security' [1988] *JBL* 127, 219.

[153] And see Derham, n.19 above, 266–8, who regards it as an accounting procedure; and see Goode, n.73 above, para. 7–02.

[154] *Stein* v. *Blake* [1996] AC 243 (HL).   [155] Goode, n.73 above, paras. 1-19, 7-14.

it is a definite and liquidated claim.[156] A contingent claim and, possibly, one maturing at a future date cannot, in equity, be set off against an immediate right.[157] An important requisite of an equitable set-off is that the claims must be mutual, in the sense of arising between the same parties and in their own respective rights.[158] If the set-off involves a liquidated demand, that demand need not be based on the same transaction as the right in respect of which it is exercised or a transaction closely linked with it. If the claim arises from such a transaction, it may be set off even if it is unliquidated.[159]

Equitable set-off is of considerable assistance to banks. Thus, a bank that is required to make payment under a bank guarantee issued by it can reimburse itself by exercising a set-off against balances standing to the credit of the customer's accounts. But two limitations of this right of set-off pose problems. First, up to the time its own claim is due, the bank cannot effect a set-off in order to preclude the customer from drawing on the balances in question. Secondly, its right is subordinate to those of a judgment creditor who has served a third party debt (previously known as a 'garnishee') order before the exercise of the set-off, except in respect of a claim of the bank that is due at the very time the order nisi is served on it.[160]

When an unincorporated customer is adjudicated a bankrupt, the bank's right of set-off is no longer governed by the equitable principles set out above, but by the mandatory provisions of section 323 of the Insolvency Act 1986. A corresponding provision has been applied to the winding up of companies in Rule 4.90 of the Insolvency Rules 1986.[161]

Section 323 has been discussed in some detail earlier,[162] but it will be convenient to mention here its salient features.[163] First, the application of the section cannot be excluded by agreement.[164] Secondly, the claims that are the subject of the set-off must be based on 'mutual dealings', a phrase that has the same meaning as in respect of the equitable set-off. Claims arising in the course of transactions involving the financing of a customer by his bank are within the ambit of the definition.[165] Thirdly, 'bankruptcy set-off...affects the substantive rights of the parties by enabling the bankrupt's creditor to use his indebtedness to the bankrupt as a form of security'[166] as the bank will recover the full amount of its claim—up to the amount its insolvent customer owes it—instead of having to prove in his insolvency.[167] Fourthly, bankruptcy set-off applies to any claim provable as a 'bankruptcy

---

[156] *Hanak* v. *Green* [1958] 2 QB 9, 17.

[157] *Jeffryes* v. *Agra and Masterman's Bank* (1866) LR 2 Eq. 674; *Bower* v. *Foreign and Colonial Gas Co. Ltd, Metropolitan Bank (Garnishees)* (1874) 22 WR 740; cf. *Business Computers Ltd* v. *Anglo-African Leasing Co. Ltd* [1977] 1 WLR 578.

[158] *Middleton* v. *Pollock* (1875) LR 20 Eq. 515; *Re Pennington and Owen Ltd* [1925] Ch. 825; *N. V. Robbie & Co. Ltd* v. *Witney Warehouse Co. Ltd* [1963] 3 All ER 613; *Re Whitehouse & Co.* (1878) 9 Ch. D 595.

[159] *Aries Tanker Corporation* v. *Total Transport Ltd* [1977] 1 All ER 398, 406–7.

[160] *Tapp* v. *Jones* (1875) LR 10 QB 591, 593; and see Ch. 11, Sect. 1(iii) above.

[161] S.I. 1986/1925 as substituted by S.I. 2005/537, r.23. Note that the predecessor of s.323, which the Bankruptcy Act 1914, s.31, applied to the winding-up of companies under s.317 of the Companies Act 1948 (which was replaced by the Companies Act 1985, s.612, and repealed by the Insolvency Act 1986, s.438). And note that, where a debt has to be set off against a number of liabilities, the appropriation has to be carried out in an equitable manner as between the liabilities involved: *Re Unit 2 Windows (in liq.)* [1985] 1 WLR 1383.

[162] Ch. 7, Sect. 4(v) above.   [163] And see *Stein* v. *Blake* [1996] AC 243 (HL).

[164] S.323(2), confirming the majority decision in *National Westminster Bank Ltd* v. *Halesowen Presswork and Assemblies Ltd* [1972] AC 785 (on its predecessor, the Bankruptcy Act 1914, s.31). But see Ch. 7, Sect. 4(v) where this is questioned.

[165] *National Westminster Bank Ltd* v. *Halesowen Presswork and Assemblies Ltd*, n.164 above.

[166] *Per* Lord Hoffmann in *Stein* v. *Blake*, n.163 above.

[167] Ibid. But if the bank becomes insolvent, note that a director is entitled to set off his deposit with it as against that bank's call on an indemnity guarantee executed by him: *M. S. Fashions* v. *Bank of Credit and Commerce International (in liq.) (No. 2)* [1993] Ch. 425.

debt'. This term is defined widely[168] and extends to contingent and unliquidated claims. If the liability is not yet quantifiable because it is contingent, its value has to be estimated by the trustee in bankruptcy.[169] Thus it follows that, if the customer becomes insolvent, the bank can exercise in his bankruptcy a set-off based on the customer's duty to reimburse the bank for payments that it may be forced to make under a performance bond granted at his instruction.

(iii) Security interests to a bank with which funds are deposited: contractual set-off and flawed asset arrangements

In view of the restricted scope of application of the equitable right of set-off, it has become the practice for a bank that finances its customer to reserve a contractual right of set-off. The right may be the subject of a special agreement, known as a letter of set-off, or may be created by means of specific clauses incorporated in the underlying financial agreement between the bank and its customer. The object of the set-off clause is to confer on the bank a right to set off against balances maintained with it by the customer *any* claim that it has against him, be it contingent, unconditional, liquidated, unliquidated, future, or existing.

In practical terms, the clause aims to confer two rights on the bank. The first is to suspend the customer's right to make withdrawals as long as he is subject to any liability to the bank. The second is to enable the bank to debit against the balance accrued any amount due to itself. By way of illustration, the customer may be under an obligation to reimburse to the bank any amount that may be demanded by the beneficiary of a performance bond. The set-off clause precludes the withdrawals of amounts standing to the customer's credit as long as this liability is contingent. It further entitles the bank to debit against the balance any amount falling due once this liability crystallizes.[170] In the majority of cases, the bank is loath to shackle its customer's business operations in this way and so the clause may be drafted so as to preclude withdrawals only if their effect is to reduce the balance beneath an agreed figure.

A variant of the set-off clause is the 'flawed asset arrangement'.[171] As indicated by its name, the arrangement imposes a 'flaw' on the customer's 'asset' or, in plain language, restricts his rights to utilize his balance with the bank. Thus the arrangement is based on the first element found in the classic set-off agreement. The second element—a right to exercise the set-off—is not conferred on the bank. It is believed that, as a result, the agreement does not require to be registered as a charge.[172] In practical terms, the flawed asset arrangement has the same basic effect as a contractual set-off. Under both types of agreement the bank is entitled to freeze the bank balance until such time as the customer's liability to it is discharged. Four legal problems arise in respect of a set-off agreement, and some apply equally to a flawed asset arrangement. They concern the validity of the agreement in the customer's insolvency and the question of priorities.

The first problem concerns conflicts between the right of the bank to effect its set-off and the rights of an assignee of the bank balance. Being a chose in action, a bank balance may be assigned under section 136 of the Law of Property Act 1925 or in equity.[173] But regardless of the form of the assignment, the assignee's rights are subject to the equities

---

[168] In the Insolvency Act 1986, s.382.   [169] Ibid., s.322(3) and see *Stein* v. *Blake*, n.163 above.

[170] Goode, n.73 above, para. 7-22; Wood, n.152 above, 162 ff.

[171] F.W. Neate, 'Set-off' (1981) 9 *Int. Business Lawyer* 247. For a judicial consideration of a 'flawed asset arrangement' see now *Re Bank of Credit and Commerce International SA (No. 8)* [1998] AC 214.

[172] Sect. 3(iv) below.   [173] Sect. 1(i) above.

available to the bank (the 'debtor') against the customer (the 'assignor'). To this rule there is one important limitation. Such an equity must have accrued before the debtor was given notice of the assignment.[174] The set-off agreement between the bank and the customer constitutes an equity which is accordingly available against the assignee if it has 'accrued' before the serving of notice on the bank. 'Accrued' in this context probably means 'effected' under the set-off agreement. Thus it appears to follow that a set-off agreement takes priority over an assignment notified to the bank after the execution of the set-off agreement.[175]

Does the flawed asset arrangement constitute a similar equity, which can be pleaded against an assignee of the bank balance? On the one hand, it is arguable that the restriction on the customer's right to draw on the funds is effective as against an assignee.[176] On the other hand, the arrangement does not confer property rights on the bank but simply restricts the customer's freedom to dispose of his assets and therefore should not affect an assignee. It may be that the answer is to be found in a consideration of the fundamental effect of the arrangement, which is to postpone the bank's duty to repay the debt represented by the bank balance in question. It seems clear that the assignee of the balance cannot enforce its repayment where the assignor (customer) is unable to do so. Nevertheless, the assignee can enforce payment if the terms of the deposit are varied by means of the flawed asset arrangement after the serving of notice of assignment on the bank. This approach was endorsed in *Re Bank of Credit and Commerce International SA (No. 8)*.[177]

The second problem respecting a contractual set-off arises where a judgment creditor serves on the bank a third party debt (previously known as a 'garnishee') order nisi.[178] Is the bank entitled to reap the benefit of the set-off or is the entire balance to be 'garnisheed'? Two principles are here in conflict. One is that contingent liabilities cannot be set off against the claim of a judgment creditor.[179] The other is that the judgment creditor cannot obtain by means of the third party debt order rights superior to those held by the debtor.[180] It is believed that, again, the correct answer is to be found in a basic principle. A third party debt order does not attach to a debt unless the debt is due at the time the order is served.[181] It is true that this principle has been abrogated in respect of balances standing to the credit of a deposit account.[182] But where the debt is suspended indefinitely, as is the case in a set-off agreement, it is possible to regard it as not having accrued at the time the third party debt order is served. The order therefore ought not to attach to it. The same solution appears to apply in cases where third party debt proceedings are instituted in respect of a customer who has effected a flawed asset arrangement in favour of his bank.

The third problem is whether the set-off agreement requires registration as a charge or, if effected by an individual, as a bill of sale. It has been shown that a bank balance is usually not a 'book debt'.[183] Ordinarily the question should therefore not arise.[184] In the case of an unincorporated customer, the answer would remain the same even if the balance did constitute a 'book debt', as registration is not required where the debtor is specified

---

[174] Sect. 1(i) above.

[175] For the same view, see P. Cresswell *et al.*, *Encyclopedia of Banking Law* (London, loose-leaf), i, para. E2466. And see *Business Computers Ltd* v. *Anglo-African Leasing Ltd* [1977] 1 WLR 578, 585.

[176] Sect. 2(iv) above.   [177] [1998] AC 214.   [178] See Ch. 11, Sect. 1(iii).

[179] Ch. 11, Sect. 1(iii) above and *Tapp* v. *Jones* (1875) LR 10 QB 591, 593.

[180] *Re General Horticultural Co., ex p. Whitehouse* (1886) 32 Ch. D 512, 516.   [181] Ibid.

[182] Ibid. For an interesting analysis see *Evans Coleman & Evans* v. *R. A. Nelson Construction Ltd* (1958) 16 DLR 123.

[183] Sect. 2(i) above.   [184] Goode, n.73 above, para. 3-26 and see below n.209.

in the instrument creating the assignment.[185] The position would differ in the case of an incorporated customer, as any charge on 'book debts' requires registration under section 860(7)(f) of the Companies Act 2006. But is a set-off agreement a charge? Its effect is to postpone payment and to enable the bank to strike a balance when the debt matures. It is therefore incorrect to regard the bank balance as an asset set aside to enable the bank to recover its claim to set-off.[186] The same argument applies, *a fortiori*, to the flawed asset arrangement.

The fourth problem arises only where an incorporated customer, who has entered into a set-off agreement with his bank, is in liquidation. The basic principle, originally set out in section 302 of the Companies Act 1948, which has been replaced by sections 107 and 143 of the Insolvency Act 1986, is that all claims which are not given a special status (such as preferential claims or claims of secured creditors) are to rank *pari passu*. In *British Eagle International Airlines Ltd* v. *Compagnie Nationale Air France*,[187] an agreement between certain airlines and the International Airlines Transport Association (IATA) made arrangements under which credit facilities extended by individual member airlines to others were to be settled, not directly between the airlines involved, but through a clearing system run by IATA, which provided for monthly settlements. When British Eagle (BE) went into voluntary liquidation, the question arose whether other airlines could set off, through the clearing system, amounts due to it against debts due to such airlines from BE. The House of Lords, by a majority, held that the liquidator was not bound by the clearing arrangement, which meant that there was no room for such set-offs. In consequence, the liquidator was entitled to demand the payment of amounts due from other airlines in full, the airlines having to prove in the liquidation for the amounts due to them from BE. Lord Cross of Chelsea pointed out that the agreement between the airlines, and the ensuing clearing arrangement, purported to confer on the parties a position similar to that of a secured creditor but in a manner that avoided the need for registering a charge. On this basis, his Lordship concluded that the agreement was contrary to public policy, in that it defeated the principle enshrined in section 302. The fact that the offending clearing agreement was not made with a view to defeating that provision, but constituted an acceptable commercial arrangement, was held irrelevant.

It is significant that the agreement used in the *British Eagle* case sought to achieve its object by set-off. It has been argued that, on the same reasoning, the courts would invalidate a contractual set-off and a flawed asset arrangement.[188] It is, however, possible to distinguish the agreement in *British Eagle* from the type of agreements used by banks. In the former, the set-off was to be executed by a third party, with whom both the creditor and the insolvent debtor maintained their accounts. In the latter type of agreement, the set-off is to be effected directly in respect of cross-claims of the creditor and the debtor. It is, accordingly, unrealistic to regard these agreements as seeking merely to create priorities in winding-up. Both the contractual set-off and the flawed asset arrangement provide effective machinery for treating a number of transactions between the same two parties as comprising one basic relationship. Moreover, both the set-off agreement and the flawed asset arrangement postpone the bank's duty to repay the debt owed by it to the customer

---

[185] Insolvency Act 1986, s.344(3)(b); and see Sect. 2(v) above.

[186] For the same view, see Goode, n.73 above, para. 1-19. See also Wood, n.152 above, 210; Cresswell *et al.*, n.175 above, i, E2476, relying on *Swiss Bank Corporation* v. *Lloyds Bank Ltd* [1982] AC 584; Derham, n.19 above, 298 ff. But cf. Neate, n.171 above.

[187] [1975] 1 WLR 758.

[188] Cresswell *et al.*, n.175 above, i, para. E2478. This appears also to have been the view of the Committee to Review Insolvency Law and Practice (the Cork Committee) (Cmnd. 8558, London, 1982) para.1350.

up to the time the latter has discharged his liability to the bank. The clause ought to be effective up to the time that condition is met.[189]

(iv) Charges over bank balances

A balance standing to the credit of a customer's bank account is a chose in action.[190] It can accordingly be the subject of a charge or mortgage, effected by means of an assignment. Some firms tend to utilize section 136 of the Law of Property Act 1925, in order to effect an absolute assignment of a bank balance,[191] coupled with a right of redemption.[192] Whilst the existence of the equity of redemption does not in itself convert the absolute assignment into a charge,[193] care needs be taken to avoid the use of language suggesting that the assignment is made solely for the purpose of providing a secure source of payment for the assignee. Thus, in *Durham Bros.* v. *Robertson*,[194] an assignment to a financier of the proceeds of a building contract was held to be outside the scope of section 136, as it was expressly stated to lapse upon the repayment of the amounts advanced to the builder.[195]

In practice, an assignment by way of charge, which is of course an equitable assignment, is adequate security.[196] Where such security is given to a third party, such as a financier or a supplier of goods on credit, it is essential to include provisions precluding the depletion of the bank balance by drawings. This is easily achieved in the case of a balance standing to the credit of a fixed deposit or other interest-bearing account. It is more difficult to achieve this result in the case of a current account, as any attempt to freeze it is bound to interfere with the customer's ability to carry on his ordinary trading transactions.

Can security over a bank balance be given to the very bank with which it is maintained? It will be recalled that the amount standing to the credit of the customer's account is considered the bank's own money, the bank being mere debtor to the customer.[197] Can the bank, then, have a charge over funds which are its property and be chargee of a debt where it is the debtor? The conceptual problem involved was considered by Millett J in *Re Charge Card Services Ltd.*[198] The case concerned a factoring agreement which provided that the debts involved would be collected by the factor, Commercial Credit, and paid (less certain disbursements) to the credit of an account maintained by it in Charge Card's name. Commercial Credit had the absolute discretion to retain money standing to the credit of the account in question as security for any amount required to meet Charge Card's liabilities. One of the issues which arose upon Charge Card's insolvency was whether this right of retention was void as against the liquidator by reason of its being an

---

[189] In *Re Charge Card Services Ltd* [1987] Ch. 150 at 156, affd. [1989] Ch. 497, Millett J held that a retention clause in a factoring agreement, which resembled a flawed asset arrangement, was not avoided by reason of its purporting to confer on the factor a set-off overriding the provisions applying on insolvency; the clause conferred a right to effect debits rather than a set-off. The point was not considered by the Court of Appeal. Note that, if the agreements were considered invalid, the bank would still have its right of set-off under the Insolvency Act 1986, s.323, see Sect. (ii) above.

[190] Ch. 5, Sect. 3 above.   [191] Cresswell *et al.*, n.175 above, i, para. E2486.

[192] *Tancred* v. *Delagoa Bay and East Africa Ry. Co.* (1889) 23 QBD 239; *Durham Bros.* v. *Robertson* [1898] 1 QB 765; *Hughes* v. *Pump House Hotel Co. Ltd* [1902] 2 KB 190.

[193] *Tancred* v. *Delagoa Bay and East Africa Ry. Co.*, n.192 above.

[194] Above at n.192; and see *Jones* v. *Humphreys* [1902] 1 KB 10.

[195] But note that the assignment could still be valid in equity: *Palmer* v. *Carey* [1926] AC 703; *Rother Iron Works Ltd* v. *Canterbury Precision Engineers Ltd* [1974] QB 1; *Swiss Bank Corporation* v. *Lloyds Bank Ltd* [1982] AC 584.

[196] Especially if notice is given to the bank: see Sect. 1 above.   [197] Ch. 5, Sect. 3 above.

[198] [1987] Ch. 150, affd. [1989] Ch. 497. The issue was not considered by the Court of Appeal.

unregistered charge over book debts. Giving judgment for Commercial Credit, Millett J held that it did not constitute a charge. Conceptually, the credit balance in Charge Card's account, which constituted an indebtedness of Commercial Credit to Charge Card, could not be mortgaged or charged to Commercial Credit itself. The real effect was to grant Commercial Credit a contractual set-off, which was effective in so far as it did not go beyond the provisions of section 31 of the Bankruptcy Act 1914 (now section 323 of the Insolvency Act 1986).[199]

The view that a bank cannot have a charge over its customer's bank balance (a 'charge-back') but must rely on contractual arrangements such as contractual set-off and flawed asset arrangements has its supporters.[200] Professor Goode points out that a bank balance is a mere chose in action due from the bank to the customer and the essence of an assignment is to enable the assignee to recover the debt. Yet the bank, which would be both the debtor and the assignee after assignment, cannot sue itself to recover the debt. Moreover, the view that the purported security agreement does not create a charge or a mortgage is supported by two Australian authorities.[201]

However, *Re Charge Card Services Ltd* generally had a hostile reception, especially from the banking community where such 'charge-backs'—usually as part of a 'triple cocktail' also including a flawed asset arrangement and a contractual right of set-off—are common.[202] The argument in favour of 'charge-backs' relies on looking at the nature of the bank balance from the customer's viewpoint.[203] It is undeniable that, for the purposes of his dealings and his balance sheet, a bank balance constitutes an asset. In effect, this argument purports to treat the balance as an item of property by reason of its being one of the customer's assets.[204] The argument derives some support from authorities that have recognized the customer's right to bring an action in restitution where funds standing to the credit of his account are paid out by the bank under a mistake of fact.[205] For the purposes of such an action the customer is treated as having an adequate interest, or some property right, in the funds. It is, therefore, arguable that the same type of right may be the subject of a charge.

It seems that, although the issue has not yet been authoritatively settled, charge-backs will be recognized as effective charges by the English courts. Thus in *Re Bank of Credit and Commerce International SA (No. 8)*,[206] Lord Hoffmann went out of his way

---

[199] See Sect. 3(ii) above.

[200] See D. Pollard, 'Credit Balances as Security' [1988] *JBL* 127; R.M. Goode, 'Charge-backs and legal fictions' (1998) 114 LQR 178; n.73 above, para. 3-12. See also G. Weaver & C. Craigie, *Banker and Customer in Australia* (2nd edn., Perth, 1990), paras. 20.850 ff.

[201] *Broad* v. *Commissioner of Stamp Duties* [1980] 2 NSWLR 40; *Estate Planning Associates (Australia) Pty. Ltd* v. *Commissioner of Stamp Duties* (1985) 16 ATR 862.

[202] See the Financial Law Panel's Papers: *Practice Recommendation on Security over Cash Deposits* (London, July 1994); *Security over Cash Deposits: A Supplementary Practice Recommendation* (London, March 1996).

[203] W. Blair, 'Charges over Cash Deposits' *Int. Financial Law Rev.*, Nov. 1983, 14; Hapgood, ibid., 34; Wood, n.152 above, paras. 5-179–5-181 (and (1987) 8 *Co. Lawyer* 262); Derham, n.19 above, 303; Oditah, n.19 above, 103–5 (and n.24 above); but note that *Re Hart, ex p. Caldicott* (1884) 25 Ch. D 716 and *Re Jearons, ex p. Mackay* (1873) LR 8 Ch. App. 643 are only marginally in point. Note also *Swiss Bank Corporation* v. *Lloyds Bank Ltd* [1982] AC 584, in which it was assumed (although the point was not fully argued) that a bank could have a charge over proceeds of shares deposited with it.

[204] *Re Jeavons, ex p. MacKay, ex p. Brown* (1873) 8 Ch. App. 643: a debtor can have a charge over royalties due from him. And see *Alcom Ltd* v. *Republic of Columbia* [1984] AC 580.

[205] Ch. 12, Sect. 1 above.

[206] [1998] AC 214. Judicial support for charge-backs can also be found in the dicta in *Welsh Development Agency* v. *Export Finance Co. Ltd* [1991] BCLC 936, [1992] BCLC 148 (CA) although doubts were expressed in the Court of Appeal judgments in *Re BCCI (No. 8)* itself (see [1996] Ch. 245).

to disagree—albeit in an *obiter dictum*—that it was 'conceptually impossible' for a bank to take a charge over an amount standing to the credit of its customer. His answer to the impossibility of realizing the security by action was that 'instead of the [chargee] having to claim payment from the debtor, realisation would take the form of a book entry'. Otherwise the bank, as equitable chargee, would have a 'proprietary interest...binding upon assignees and a liquidator or trustee in bankruptcy'. This endorsement of 'charge-backs' has generated further criticism[207] but it should be noted that a number of jurisdictions have placed the matter beyond doubt by enacting legislation permitting 'charge backs'.[208]

It remains to be considered whether a 'charge-back' requires registration. It has been noted that the prevailing view is that, usually, a bank balance does not constitute a 'book debt'[209] and therefore a fixed charge on it is not registrable whether the customer is incorporated[210] or not.[211] In the case of an unincorporated customer, the answer would remain the same even if the balance constituted a 'book debt', as registration is not required where the debtor is specified in the instrument creating the assignment.[212] In the case of incorporated customers, it may be prudent to register charge-backs in case the balance is subsequently held to be a 'book debt'[213] and, in any event, charges over a fluctuating current balance ought also to be registered in case the charge is regarded as a floating charge.[214]

4 Security interests over life policies

Life assurance policies can provide protection against two events: loss that the creditor may incur upon the debtor's death and loss from the debtor's insolvency or default. As against the former risk, the policy is good security for the amount insured. As against the latter, the policy is security only for the amount that it yields at the time of the default or insolvency. For this purpose it is necessary to distinguish between two arrangements that may take place if a policy is relinquished before its maturity. One involves the immediate conversion of the insurer's payment obligation into cash. The assured is then paid

---

[207] See Lipton (1998) 9 *JBFLP* 101, 109; G. McCormack, 'Charge Back and Commercial Certainty in the House of Lords' [1998] *CfiLR* 111; S. McCracken, *The Banker's Remedy of Set-off* (2nd edn., 1998), 205–206; R. Goode, 'Charge Backs and Legal Fictions' (1998) 114 *LQR* 178. But support was forthcoming from the Financial Law Panel ('*Security over Cash Deposits: A Valedictory*' (April 1998)) and see also R. Calnan, 'Fashioning the Law to Suit the Practicalities of Life' (1998) 114 *LQR* 174.

[208] Hong Kong, Singapore, Bermuda, the Cayman Islands. If 'charge-backs' are not possible, this suggests that banks cannot take charges—fixed or floating—over proceeds of book debts paid into their customers' bank accounts if they are in credit: see Sect. 2(iii) and R. Goode, 'Charges over book debts: A missed opportunity' (1994) 111 *LQR* 592; A. Berg, 'Charges over book debts: a reply' [1995] *JBL* 465.

[209] Sect. 2(i) above. In *Re BCCI (No. 8)* Lord Hoffmann expressly refused to take a view but cited the judgment of Lord Hutton in *Northern Bank Ltd* v. *Ross* [1990] BCC 883 that, 'in the case of deposits with banks, an obligation to register is unlikely to arise'.

[210] Only fixed charges 'on book debts' are registrable: Companies Act 2006, s.860(7)(f) (previously, Companies Act 1985, s.396(1)(e)), Ch. 19, Sect. 4(iii) above & Sect. 2(v) above.

[211] Insolvency Act 1986, s.344 & Sect. 2(v) above.

[212] Insolvency Act 1986, s.344(3)(b); and see Sect. 2(v) above.

[213] Cresswell, n.175 above, para. 2489 states registration is advisable and in accordance with current practice. Cork, n.188 above, para. 1920 was of the same view. This was the view of the Registrar in 1985: (1985) 82 LS Gaz 2868.

[214] And therefore registrable under the Companies Act 2006, s.860(7)(h) (previously, Companies Act 1985, s.396(1)(f)). And see Sect. 2(iii) above & Ch. 19, Sect. 4(iii).

the 'surrender value' of the policy, which is calculated by an actuary on the basis of the amounts paid to date. Generally, the surrender value of a policy is negligible during its first three years and increases proportionately to the premiums paid thereafter. The other arrangement for the discontinuation of a policy involves its conversion into a 'paid-up policy'. The amount accrued at the relevant time from the premiums paid by the assured (plus a bonus) is retained by the company as a fund payable at the original maturity date. Naturally, the value of a paid-up policy is considerably higher than its surrender value. In the context of commercial transactions, banks look to the surrender value of policies and are disinclined to treat a policy as collateral for an amount considerably higher than its surrender value at the time the loan is extended to the customer.

From a bank's point of view, life policies can broadly be divided into two types: 'whole life' policies and 'endowment' policies. In a whole life policy, the assured's main object is to protect those surviving him against his own death. The amount of the policy is therefore payable only on his death. In an endowment policy, the amount involved plus profits is payable either on the assured's death or when he reaches an agreed age, whichever occurs sooner. The policy is therefore a savings vehicle with a life assurance element. Generally, the amount yielded by an endowment policy is smaller than the amount for which the policy would give cover, on payment of the same premiums, in a whole life policy. But the surrender value of an endowment policy is usually higher than that of a whole life policy for a similar amount. An endowment policy is therefore superior collateral in the hands of a bank.

An insurance policy is a chose in action.[215] A security interest over it may be effected[216] by means either of an equitable charge[217] or of a section 136 statutory mortgage[218] or under the Policies of Assurance Act 1867. An equitable charge is created by the deposit of the insurance policy document with the bank. Normally, a memorandum of charge is executed setting out the terms of the loan and security and the bank serves notice of its interest on the insurance company to protect itself under the rule in *Dearle* v. *Hall*.[219] Although both writing and notice are desirable, they are not essential. Even if no notice is given, where the assured attempts to give a security interest over the same policy to another financier, the latter is probably put on notice by the assured's inability to produce the policy document and so takes subject to the first assignee's rights.[220]

A mortgage under the Policies of Assurance Act 1867 may be executed by means either of an endorsement on the policy or of a separate deed of assignment as provided in the Schedule to that Act.[221] The assignee is given the statutory right to recover the amount of the policy by instituting proceedings in his own name once he gives written notice of the assignment to the insurer.[222] The assignee takes subject to equities[223] and, as from the date of the notice, any payment by the company to the assured is made at its peril. The

---

[215] *Re Moore* (1878) 8 Ch. D 519 (CA), 520.

[216] But some policies—for example retirement policies qualifying for tax relief—are not assignable.

[217] *Chowne* v. *Baylis* (1862) 31 Beav. 351, 360; *Re Turcan* (1888) 40 Ch. D 5 (CA); Re *Griffin, Griffin* v. *Griffin* [1902] 1 Ch. 135 (CA). For a more recent case concerning an equitable charge on a fire policy, where it was confirmed that the charge operated by way of equitable assignment and was subject to the rule in *Dearle* v. *Hall*, see *Colonial Mutual* v. *ANZ Banking* [1995] 1 WLR 1140 (PC).

[218] See Sect. 1 above.   [219] See Sect. 1 & Sect. 2(vi) above.

[220] *Spencer* v. *Clarke* (1878) 9 Ch. D 137: a policy was deposited with a creditor who did not give notice; the second equitable assignee gave notice but was held to have been put on inquiry by the absence of the policy. See also *Re Weniger's Policy* [1910] 2 Ch. 291 in which Parker J confirmed that, although, in principle, the giving of notice determined priority (under the rule in *Dearle* v. *Hall*, see Sect. 2(vi)), this applied only if the second creditor giving notice was not put on inquiry.

[221] Polices of Assurance Act 1867, s.5.   [222] Ibid., ss.1, 3.   [223] Ibid., s.2.

date of the receipt of the notice is also used for determining the ranking of competing assignments.[224] The assignment contract itself will usually confer on the bank the right to debit the customer's account in order to pay premiums that the customer (in breach of his agreement) has not paid and the right to sell, surrender, or convert the policy into a paid-up policy on behalf of the assured.[225] Although an insurance policy is valuable collateral, the bank has to be aware of a number of risks. First, an insurance policy is an *uberrimae fidei* contract. This means that the assured owes a duty of full disclosure to the insurance company. If he fails to disclose any material fact, or gives any inaccurate answer to the questions put to him in the 'proposal form' (completed when he applies for cover), the policy may be avoided by the insurance company.[226] Although many policies include a clause waiving the insurance company's right of cancellation if the policy has been in operation for three years, the policy can still be avoided if the assured has fraudulently given an untruthful answer. Insurance companies are usually unwilling to avoid a policy which has been assigned by way of security, at least where the non-disclosure is not deliberate. They do, however, have the right to do so as the bank—the assignee—takes subject to equities.[227]

Secondly, the amount of a life policy is not recoverable by the assured's estate if he commits suicide whilst of sound mind.[228] It is not certain that an assignee, too, is unable to recover in such a case.[229] In principle, it seems that its position cannot be superior to the estate's. A bank that takes a life policy as collateral does therefore take subject to this risk. It is true that suicide is no longer a crime in English law.[230] But the assured's estate should not be allowed to recover from the insurance company a loss occasioned intentionally by the assured's own hand.

Thirdly, if a bank is asked to take a security over a policy taken out by its holder on the life of another person, the bank has to satisfy itself that the holder has an 'insurable interest' in the 'life assured'. Under the Life Assurance Act 1774,[231] a policy is void where the policyholder does not have such an interest. A person is deemed to have an insurable interest in his own life and in that of his spouse.[232] The common law further recognizes that a person has an insurable interest in the life of another by reason of a valid pecuniary interest.[233]

Finally, the bank obtains a good security against the assured's bankruptcy or death. On his death or on the maturity of the policy, the bank can give a good discharge to the insurance company for the amount of the policy.[234] If the amount received exceeds the debt due from the assured, the bank holds the surplus as trustee for the estate.[235] Where the bank has a statutory assignment it is, of course, able to enforce its assignment against the trustee in bankruptcy. Moreover, it has been held that even an equitable charge, which

---

[224] Policies of Assurance Act 1867, s.3. On what constitutes proof of notice, see ibid., s.6.

[225] Most assignments exclude the operation of the Law of Property Act 1925, s.103 so as to exclude any restrictions on the bank's power to realize the security.

[226] See, generally, H. Beale (ed.), *Chitty on Contracts* (30th edn., London, 2008), ii, para. 41-030.

[227] And see the Policies of Assurance Act 1867, s.2.

[228] *Beresford* v. *Royal Insurance Co. Ltd* [1938] AC 586.   [229] Ibid., *per* Lord Atkin at 607.

[230] The Suicide Act 1961, s.1.

[231] S.1.   [232] Ibid.

[233] Such as debtors or partners to the extent of their financial interest; see, generally, *Chitty on Contracts*, n.226 above, ii, para. 41-006.

[234] Law of Property Act 1925, s.107. If the bank has only an equitable charge, the assured or his personal representatives have to join in the receipt.

[235] This was confirmed by Lord Hoffmann in *Colonial Mutual* v. *ANZ Banking* [1995] 1 WLR 1140 (PC).

has not been perfected by notice, is valid against the trustee.[236] But such a charge would in principle[237] be ineffective against subsequent equitable mortgagees who gave notice to the company and against *bona fide* legal mortgagees.

5 Security interests over shares etc.

(i) General principles

Investments such as shares in a company, bonds and debentures issued by companies, governments, or public authorities, warrants and convertibles, all confer on the investor rights against the issuer. They are therefore 'choses in action'. A company share[238] has been famously described[239] as 'the interest of a shareholder in the company measured by a sum of money for the purposes of liability in the first place, and of interest in the second'. The shareholder's rights and liabilities are primarily set out in the company's constitution.[240] This normally confers rights on shareholders to dividends declared to vote at the shareholders' general meetings and to a share of any surplus capital when the company is wound up. Bonds and debentures represent loans by the investor to the company; warrants give the investor the right to acquire shares in the future and convertibles enable the investor to 'convert' one type of investment (usually loan stock) into another (usually shares). To be good collateral, these choses in action need to be readily realizable—preferably listed or at least traded on a stock market. Thus shares in a private company—where there are usually[241] restrictions on transfer and in any event problems in finding a purchaser—are generally not attractive collateral.

In everyday business practice it is common to refer to 'pledges' of shares, effected by the deposit with the bank of a borrower's share certificates together with a Memorandum of Deposit and a blank transfer form. Conceptually, the description of this arrangement as a pledge is incorrect. A share certificate merely constitutes *prima facie* evidence that the person in whose name it is issued owns the stated number of shares in the company.[242] The certificate is not a document of title and its delivery does not transfer any property in the shares covered by it.[243] To effect a transfer of ownership, the company has to be given an instruction, executed by the shareholder on the 'transfer form',[244] to register the shares into the name of the transferee.[245] The transfer of the legal title is incomplete until the transferee is entered on the register.[246]

---

[236] *Re Wallis, ex p. Jenks* [1902] 1 KB 719.

[237] Unless the equitable chargee had custody of the policy and this put subsequent assignees on enquiry: see the text to n.220 above.

[238] For judicial confirmation that it is a chose in action see *Colonial Bank* v. *Whinney* (1886) 1 App. Cas. 426 (HL); *Harrold* v. *Plenty* [1901] 2 Ch. 314, considered further below.

[239] By Farwell J in *Borland's Trustee* v. *Steel Brothers & Co. Ltd* [1901] 1 Ch. 279 at 288.

[240] Since the Companies Act 2006, the articles of association in the case of a registered company: see ibid., s.33 (effect of articles). The terms of issue may also confer special rights on the holder.

[241] But not necessarily, since the repeal of the Companies Act 1948, s.28 (in 1980).

[242] Companies Act 2006, s.768.

[243] *Longman* v. *Bath Electric Tramways Ltd* [1905] 1 Ch. 646, 667, *per* Stirling LJ.

[244] See Stock Transfer Act 1963. But see below as to 'dematerialised' securities.

[245] *Colonial Bank* v. *Cady and Williams* (1890) 15 App. Cas. 267, especially *per* Lord Herschell at 285.

[246] *Société Générale de Paris* v. *Walker* (1885) 11 App. Cas. 20; *Shropshire Union Railways and Canal Co.* v. *R* (1875) LR 7 HL 496; *Macmillan Inc.* v. *Bishopsgate Investment Trust (No. 3) plc* [1995] 1 WLR 978.

The position differs where the collateral given by the debtor comprises marketable (*viz.* negotiable) securities, such as bearer bonds,[247] share warrants,[248] scrip,[249] or exchequer bills.[250] Such securities are transferable by delivery (and, if necessary, indorsement) and, in consequence, constitute choses in possession. As pointed out in Chapter 20, they can, accordingly, be pledged in the same way as bills of exchange or promissory notes.

By contrast, a deposit of share certificates, in the manner described, effects an equitable charge or mortgage over a chose in action. In *Harrold* v. *Plenty*,[251] H, as a security for a loan granted by him to P, obtained a deposit of 10 share certificates, which, however, were not accompanied by a transfer form. Upon P's default, H applied for a foreclosure order or, in the alternative, for an order empowering him to sell the shares. Allowing foreclosure, Cozens-Hardy J drew the classic distinction between a pledge and a mortgage. In his Lordship's words:[252]

> Now, it is plain that a pledgee is in a very different position from an ordinary mortgagee. He has only a special property in the thing pledged. He may obtain a sale, but he cannot obtain a foreclosure. I do not think that this is properly a case of pledge. A share is a chose in action. The certificate is merely evidence of title, and whatever may be the result of the deposit of a bearer bond…I cannot treat [H] as a mere pledgee. The deposit of the certificate by way of security for the debt…seems to me to amount to an equitable mortgage or, in other words, to an agreement to execute a transfer of the shares by way of mortgage.

On this basis, his Lordship concluded that H was entitled to the type of foreclosure order that would have been available if the collateral had been a title-deed of real estate or an insurance policy.

It follows that a holder can create a pledge over his securities only if they are negotiable. Where he holds ordinary share certificates, the only security interest he may grant is a legal mortgage or an equitable mortgage or charge. Although a 'charge' is strictly

---

[247] *Gorgier* v. *Mieville* (1824) 3 B & C 45 (foreign government bonds); *Carter* v. *Wake* (1877) 4 Ch. D 605 (English bearer bonds, where Jessell MR refused to grant an order for the foreclosure of the bonds, based on his finding that the arrangement involved a pledge thereof); *London Joint Stock Bank* v. *Simmons* [1892] AC 201 (local bonds: pledge by fraudulent stockbroker held effective); *Eckstein* v. *Midland Bank Ltd* (1926) 4 LDAB 91 (foreign bonds pledged by stockbroker).

[248] *Webb Hale & Co.* v. *Alexandria Water Co. Ltd* (1905) 93 LT 339.

[249] *Goodwin* v. *Robarts* (1875) LR 10 Ex. 337, affd. (1876) 1 App. Cas. 476 (foreign government scrip; and note that this leading case indicates that the negotiability of a security can be established by the proof of a general mercantile usage); *Rumball* v. *Metropolitan Bank* (1877) 2 QBD 194 (scrip issued by an English company); *Bechuanaland Exploration Co.* v. *London Trading Bank* [1898] 2 QB 658 (bearer debentures). But note that a security will not be recognized as negotiable in English law if it cannot be sued upon by the holder: *London and County Banking Co. Ltd* v. *London and River Plate Bank Ltd* (1887) 20 QBD 239 (American share certificate). The owner may, however, be estopped from disputing the title of the bank which received such a foreign certificate from the broker with whom the owner deposited it: *Fuller* v. *Glyn, Mills, Currie & Co.* [1914] 2 KB 168.

[250] *Wookey* v. *Pole* (1820) 4 B & Ald. 1.

[251] [1901] 2 Ch. 314; see also *London and Midland Bank* v. *Mitchell* [1899] 2 Ch. 161; *Stubbs* v. *Slater* [1910] 1 Ch. 632, 638 (CA, *per* Cozens-Hardy V-C).

[252] Ibid. at 316. Earlier cases, distinguished by Cozens-Hardy J, include *Halliday* v. *Holgate* (1868) LR 3 Ex. 299; *Donald* v. *Suckling* (1866) LR I QB 585; *Ex p. Sargent* (1874) LR 17 Eq. 273; and *Colonial Bank* v. *Cady* (1890) 15 App. Cas. 267. In all of them the word 'pledge' was loosely used to describe a security constituted by the deposit of share certificates.

speaking an equitable concept,[253] the cases often talk of 'legal charges' when they are, in fact, referring to legal mortgages.

The Uncertificated Securities Regulations 2001[254] make provision for company securities to be evidenced and transferred electronically and this is now possible under the 'CREST' system.[255] Thus securities within the CREST system are said to be 'dematerialised' in not being evidenced by share certificates and in not being transferred by paper transfer. However, it is thought that the principles developed in the case law in relation to share certificates and share transfers are likely to be the starting point in resolving any legal problem arising in relation to 'dematerialised' shares, especially as it is made explicit that the CREST register is only 'prima facie evidence…unless the contrary is shown, of any matters' which are in it.[256]

(ii) Types of security interest: legal mortgage and equitable mortgage or charge

Harrold v. *Plenty*[257] shows that the deposit of share certificates, without a transfer form, constitutes an equitable mortgage or charge. This is also the security created where the bank obtains the transfer form.[258] In addition to handing over a transfer form executed in blank, the chargor is usually required, to execute a document called either a Memorandum of Charge or a Memorandum of Deposit, which explicitly grants the bank a charge over the shares, entitles it to retain the share certificates 'as a continuing security' until the discharge in full of the debts secured by the charge, and confers on the bank the power to sell the shares, or to have them transferred into its name, in the event of a default. The security created by the execution of such a document is, again, an equitable mortgage or charge.

However, in accordance with general principles, it is possible to create an equitable charge by agreement without even depositing the share certificates. This is appropriate where the chargor wishes to continue dealing in the shares—although the charge, if given by a company, is then likely to be regarded as a (registrable) floating charge.[259] Moreover, even if the charge is fixed, it is likely to be defeated by subsequent dealings by the chargor.[260]

To create a legal mortgage the shares have to be registered in the name of the bank or of its nominee company. Such a legal mortgage may be executed either *ab initio* or later, where considerations respecting the chargor's solvency convince the bank that it is advisable to convert a charge that was originally equitable into a legal mortgage. To carry out the required registration of the shares, the bank utilizes the transfer form executed by the chargor in blank, filling in the missing details, including the date and the transferee's name, and sending the form to the company for registration.

A different procedure is necessary where the transfer must be under seal. Here the bank requires, in addition to the blank transfer form, a power of attorney conferring on it the authority to complete the transfer form on behalf of, or as a deed executed by, the chargor. Usually, a clause to this effect is included in the Memorandum of Charge or of

---

[253] But, since the Law of Property Act 1925, it is now possible to have a legal charge over land. See further Ch. 19, Sect. 2(iii) above.

[254] S.I. 2001/3755, as amended, made under Companies Act 1989, s.270 and replacing S.I. 1995/3272.

[255] For a description, see Smith, n.7 above, ch. 19C. See also, Cresswell *et al.*, n.175 above, i, paras. E2259, E2271–2273, E2314.1.

[256] S.I. 2001/3755, reg. 24(1). This view is shared by Smith, n.9 above, para. 19.88.

[257] See n.251 above.   [258] *Stubbs* v. *Slater* [1910] 1 Ch. 632, 638 (*per* Cozens-Hardy V-C).

[259] See n.293 below & Ch. 19, Sect. 4(ii) above.   [260] See Sect. 5(iii) below.

Deposit. In the absence of such a clause, the completed form does not constitute a deed executed by the chargor and, in consequence, no legal title passes under it to the bank even if the shares are registered in its name.[261]

It may be asked why banks are content to rely on equitable charges over shares. The reasons emerge when one considers the advantages and the disadvantages of each security device.

(iii) **Advantages and disadvantages of an equitable mortgage or charge**

The main advantage of an equitable charge over shares is its flexibility. If the borrower wishes to redeem the security, the share certificates can be returned to him. There is no need to transfer the shares back into his name or that of his purchaser. Custody of the share certificates makes it difficult[262] for the borrower to deal with the shares and create interests which take priority over the bank's charge. In addition, the equitable charge confers on the bank the power to sell the shares upon the chargor's default.[263] If, as is usual, the bank has a blank transfer form, a sale can easily be effected,[264] although if no transfer form has been deposited with the bank it will have to apply for a court order if the chargor is unwilling to co-operate with the sale. The bank will also have to go to court if it wishes to apply for foreclosure.

But there are, of course, some serious disadvantages associated with an equitable charge stemming from its vulnerability in priority disputes. First, the equitable chargee's rights will be defeated by a prior equitable interest, for example, the company's lien under its articles of association over the shares.[265] In *Ireland* v. *Hart*[266] a trustee executed a blank transfer of trust shares registered in his name as security for a loan. After the transfer form and the certificates had been lodged with the lender, but prior to the actual registration of the shares in the lender's name, the beneficiary discovered her trustee's fraud and instituted proceedings. Joyce J concluded that the lender had the authority to complete the form and to lodge it for registration. But, despite this finding, he gave judgment for the beneficiary. A legal title was not effective as against an equitable owner until the purchaser or legal mortgagee had acquired a 'present absolute and unconditional right' to the shares. As such a title could be acquired only upon registration, the lender's equitable interest remained subordinate to the beneficiary's prior beneficial title. But had the lender actually obtained registration, his then legal interest would have prevailed.[267]

Secondly, an equitable charge is subordinate to a subsequent *bona fide* legal purchaser. Notably, the creation of a legal mortgage, or the sale of shares to a *bona fide* purchaser, is not ruled out by the deposit of the share certificates with the equitable chargee, as the chargor can usually acquire a fresh certificate by declaring that he has lost the original. As

---

[261] *Powell* v. *London and Provincial Bank* [1893] 2 Ch. 555 (CA). The statutory provisions requiring the deed were in the Companies Clauses Consolidation Act 1845, ss.14, 15.

[262] But not impossible, see below.

[263] *Deverges* v. *Sandeman, Clark & Co.* [1902] Ch. 579 (reasonable notice must, however, be given to the chargor so as to give him the opportunity to repay); *Stubbs* v. *Slater* [1910] 1 Ch. 632 at 646, *per* Buckley LJ.

[264] *Re Tahiti Cotton Co., ex p. Sargent* (1873) LR 17 Eq. 273.

[265] *Champagne Perrier SA* v. *HH Finch Ltd* [1982] 1 WLR 1359, [1982] 3 All ER 713. But see *Bradford Banking Co. Ltd* v. *Henry Briggs, Son & Co. Ltd* (1886) 12 App. Cas. 29.

[266] [1902] 1 Ch. 522. See also *Kelly* v. *Munster and Leinster Bank* (1891) 29 ILR 19, 42–44 (holding, at the same time, that the first equitable mortgagee's failure to acquire custody of the certificate involved negligence and, accordingly, precluded him from asserting his prior equitable interest).

[267] *Per* Millett J in *Macmillan Inc.* v. *Bishopsgate Investment Trust plc* [1996] 1 WLR 387, [1996] 1 All ER 585. See further Sect. 5(v) below.

long as the legal mortgagee, or purchaser, acquires his interest in good faith and for value, his title is not defeated by the chargor's fraud.

In an attempt to prevent this type of fraud, an equitable chargee may consider notifying the company of the existence of his charge and asking to be advised whether the company has received notice of any prior charge or whether the company itself has a lien over the shares. In the standard reply to notices of this type, the company advises that, under section 126 of the Companies Act 2006,[268] it cannot enter in its register a notice of a trust over, or an encumbrance upon, shares. It follows that the service of the notice cannot have the effect of conferring constructive notice of the existence of the charge on third parties. Nevertheless, the notice may, in practice, preclude the type of fraud mentioned above, as the company's secretary is most unlikely to issue, without enquiry, a substitute certificate in respect of the shares covered by the charge. In addition, a lien conferred on the company in respect of these shares under the articles of association does not extend to indebtedness incurred by the shareholder after the date of the notice.[269] In the past, a chargee could invoke the procedure of serving on the company a copy of a 'stop notice' issued under the Civil Procedure Rules[270] requiring the company to give the chargee 14 days' notice before registering a subsequent transfer of the shares involved. However, as this procedure was rarely used in practice, it has ceased to be available.

(iv) **Advantages and disadvantages of a legal mortgage**

The main advantage of a legal mortgage is that it confers on the mortgagee a title that takes precedence over any prior equitable interest of which he had no notice. In addition, the legal mortgagee's security is effective against all subsequent interests, including those of a purchaser.

But even a legal mortgage falls short of constituting iron-clad security. Where the mortgagor, who tenders the certificates to the mortgagee, has a defective or a void title, the mortgagee may not acquire a better title. Moreover, the legal mortgagee may lose out even if the defect is discovered after the shares have been registered in his name. Thus, in *Sheffield Corporation* v. *Barclay*[271] a legal mortgage over S Corporation stock, registered in the joint names of two trustees called T and H, was given as security to the B Bank. H was unaware of the arrangement and the transfer of the shares into the name of the B Bank's nominee was effected under a transfer form on which T had forged H's signature. When the fraud was discovered, H obtained judgment against the S Corporation based on the wrongful transfer of the stock. The S Corporation, in turn, brought an action to recover its loss from the B Bank. The House of Lords held that, by presenting the transfer form for registration, the B Bank had warranted that it had a good title to the stock and that the transfer form was genuine. The B Bank was, accordingly, ordered to compensate the S Corporation.

Sheffield Corporation v. *Barclay* rests on two complementary principles. The first is that a forged transfer does not confer a good title on the transferee even if his name is entered in the company's register as the owner of the shares. Secondly, the decision establishes that a person who presents a share certificate for registration warrants its genuineness.

---

[268] Previously, the Companies Act 1985, s.360. And note that, although the provision applies only to shares, most debenture deeds include a similar provision.

[269] *Bradford Banking Co. Ltd* v. *Henry Briggs, Son & Co. Ltd* (1886) 12 App. Cas. 29.

[270] See the old CPR, Sched. 1, RSC, O 50, r. 11, now revoked by S.I. 2001/2792.

[271] [1905] AC 392. And see, to the same effect, *Ortigosa* v. *Brown* (1878) 47 LJ Ch. 168; *Colonial Bank* v. *Cady and Williams* (1890) LR 15 HL 267.

Where the legal mortgagee acquires such a defective title under an improperly completed transfer form, his best chance of defeating the true owner's action is to prove facts establishing an estoppel. Such a plea is, for instance, available where a transfer form signed by the shareholder in blank is utilized by a stockbroker, with whom it is deposited, in order to misappropriate the relevant shares. The rationale is that, by leaving the transfer form and the share certificates with a stockbroker, the shareholder confers on the stockbroker the apparent authority to make dispositions over them.[272] However, the estoppel plea fails where some specific facts pertaining to the transaction ought to have put the chargee or purchaser on notice. Thus, in *Earl of Sheffield* v. *London Joint Stock Bank*[273] S gave E certificates of railway stock accompanied by transfer forms signed in blank and, in addition, some foreign bonds alleged to be negotiable. E deposited these stock and bonds as security for an advance made to E by M, who was a professional moneylender. M, in turn, deposited the securities in question together with similar securities obtained by him from other clients as security for substantial running account loans granted to him by several banks. When M became bankrupt, the banks sold some of the securities and claimed to hold the proceeds thereof and the remaining securities as security for M's total indebtedness to them. S contested their right so to do and demanded the return of the securities against his repayment of the loan.

Reversing the decision of the Court of Appeal in favour of the banks, the House of Lords emphasized that the banks were familiar with the nature of M's business and, accordingly, knew that he held stocks and shares as security for loans granted by him to borrowers. The banks were, therefore, put on enquiry. Having failed to make proper enquiries, the banks could not defeat S's title by relying on their bare assumption that M had been granted the authority to deal with the securities deposited with him in the manner he did.[274]

Similarly, in *Colonial Bank* v. *Cady*[275] the executors of W's estate, who wished to transfer into their names shares which W had owned in certain American railway companies, dispatched the respective share certificates to their stockbrokers in London and signed in blank the transfer forms printed on the backs thereof. Instead of carrying out the instructions given to them, the stockbrokers delivered the certificates, together with some other property, as a security for a loan granted to them by a number of banks. When the executors discovered the fraud, they brought an action challenging the banks' title to the shares.

Affirming the Court of Appeal's decision in favour of the executors, the House of Lords emphasized that, in the instant case, the transfer forms printed on the backs of the certificates were not signed by the registered owner but by the executors of his estate. Lord Watson observed that, if the transfer forms had been signed by the registered owner, an innocent purchaser might have been able to plead an estoppel as against an action based on the stockbroker's unauthorized act. The reason for this was that the execution of the blank transfer form by the registered owner would have manifested his intention 'of passing his rights on to a transferee'. But this was not the case where the transfer form was

---

[272] *Fuller* v. *Glyn, Mills Currie & Co.* [1914] 2 KB 168; *Eckstein* v. *Midland Bank Ltd* (1926) 4 LADB 91, 94–5, *per* Greer J, who also points out, at 97, that the estoppel would operate even where the transfer form was signed by the customer without the intention of authorizing the stockbroker to make any disposition over the shares. *A fortiori*, a stockbroker can confer a good title to negotiable securities left in his custody by the owners: *London Joint Stock Bank* v. *Simmons* [1892] AC 201, at 213, *per* Lord Watson, and at 220, *per* Lord Herschell.

[273] (1888) LR 13 HL 333, revg. (1887) 34 Ch. D 95 *sub. nom. Easton* v. *London Joint Stock Bank.*

[274] And see, in particular, Lord Bramwell's judgment, ibid. at 345, emphasizing that the banks' notice would preclude them from acquiring a good title even over fully negotiable securities.

[275] (1890) 15 App. Cas. 267.

executed by persons acting as executors because their object could, equally, be to arrange for the registration of the shares in their names as trustees.[276]

It may be argued that *Colonial Bank* v. *Cady* involved a clash between the executors' legal title and the bank's equitable charge. However, as a share certificate constitutes only *prima facie* evidence of share ownership,[277] the decision would have been to the same effect even if the banks had perfected their charge by registering the shares in their names. Further support for this argument is to be found in the *Earl of Sheffield's case*, discussed above.

Thus, it can be concluded that neither an equitable charge nor a legal mortgage gives the bank an iron-clad security over shares. Naturally, a legal mortgage is, generally, a security superior to a mere equitable charge. But, where there are any doubts whatsoever respecting the validity of the borrower's title, the bank should investigate. If the bank is satisfied that its customer has a good title to the relevant shares and, in addition, the bank has no reason to doubt his integrity, it ought, usually, to be satisfied with the more flexible equitable charge. As mentioned earlier, the registration of the shares in the bank's name so as to perfect a legal mortgage involves some expense and is cumbersome. In addition, the bank needs to consider how to deal with any dividends and rights issues as well as voting and other rights which it acquires as registered owner.[278]

(v) **Priorities**[279]

Although shares constitute choses in action, determining priorities respecting competing claims to them on the basis of the rule in *Dearle* v. *Hall*[280] would cause difficulties as the company cannot enter any notice of any trust on the share register.[281] Hence priorities are determined on the basis of the general principles of *nemo dat* applicable to mortgages.[282] Accordingly, no priority is conferred on a party by his serving on the company an informal notice of an equitable interest created in his favour.

Some of the authorities have already been considered above. Thus priorities between charges of the same standing are governed by the order of their creation. Naturally, a legal mortgage takes priority over an earlier equitable charge of which the legal mortgagee had no notice when he acquired the security.[283] In *Macmillan Inc.* v. *Bishopsgate Investment Trust (No. 3) plc*,[284] Millett J was of the view that, whatever the position was in relation to land, in relation to shares the equitable chargee who has a blank transfer form and may obtain registration without recourse to the legal owner, 'may gain priority over an earlier equitable interest of which he had no notice when he advanced the money if he

---

[276] Ibid., 280, and see Lord Herschell at 286. For another instance of a fraud by a trustee, see *Shropshire Union Railways and Canal Co.* v. *R* (1875) LR 7 HL, 496.

[277] Companies Act 2006, s.768, see Sect. 5(i) above.

[278] And, should the shares (exceptionally) only be partly paid, the bank will be liable for calls made.

[279] For more detail see A. Boyle, *Gore-Browne on Companies* (44th edn., Bristol, 1986, loose-leaf), paras. 16-5 ff. For a case on priorities where other legal systems potentially applied see *Macmillan Inc.* v. *Bishopsgate Investment Trust (No. 3) plc* [1996] 1 WLR 387, [1996] 1 All ER 585.

[280] (1828) 3 Russ. 1, discussed in Sect. 2(vi) above.

[281] Companies Act 2006, s.126, see Sect. 5(iii) above.

[282] *Société Générale de Paris* v. *Walker* (1885) 11 App. Cas. 20, 30; *Re Holmes* (1885) 29 Ch. D 786, 789 (CA).

[283] For the basic statement see *Shropshire Union Railways and Canal Co.* v. *R* (1875) LR 7 HL 496 at 506–507, *per* Lord Cairns LC.

[284] [1995] 1 WLR 978; [1995] 3 All ER 747 (affirmed on a narrower point: [1996] 1 WLR 387, [1996] 1 All ER 585).

perfects his security by registration *even if he had actual notice of the prior interest before registration*.[285]

A related question concerns the exercise of a set-off as between the claim of the customer for the value of shares deposited by him and amounts due from him to the bank or other lender. In *Ellis & Co. (Trustee of)* v. *Dixon Johnson*[286] a firm of stockbrokers wrongfully sold shares deposited with it by a client as security for his dealings on the market. When the stockbrokers became bankrupt, their trustee brought an action in which he sought to recover from the client the debt due from him less the value of the shares as at the date of the receiving order. The client resisted the action, pointing out, *inter alia*, that the value of the shares had kept rising with the effect that their market price eventually exceeded the amount owed by him to the brokers. Affirming the Court of Appeal's judgment in favour of the client, the House of Lords held that, usually, a mortgagee who had wrongfully parted with the collateral given to him could not enforce the mortgagor's debt. The principle, though, was flexible. In the instant case, where shares identical to those wrongfully sold by the stockbrokers could be purchased on the open market, the stockbrokers could recover the debt due from the client upon the tender of such shares or the value thereof as at the day on which the Master certified the market value of the shares. Viscount Cave LC[287] emphasized, however, that this exercise involved a redemption of the security and not a set-off under section 31 of the Bankruptcy Act 1914.[288] Such a statutory set-off was unavailable as the dealings between the stockbrokers and the client did not involve mutual credits.

(vi) **Registration**

A charge over shares granted by an individual falls outside the ambit of the Bills of Sale Act 1878 and, in consequence, does not require registration as a bill of sale. The reason for this is that the Act does not apply to shares and other choses in action.[289] Section 344 of the Insolvency Act 1986, which renders certain charges over 'book debts' registrable as if the security covered chattels,[290] is equally inapplicable as shares are not 'book debts'.

The position differs in the case of charges over shares granted by a corporation. Basically, a fixed charge over shares requires registration only where it is granted on 'uncalled share capital of the company'[291] or 'calls made but not paid'.[292] However, a charge granted by a company over shares requires registration if it is floating.[293] As discussed above, whether a given charge is fixed or floating depends, basically, on the issue of how much control the chargee has over the property.[294] Thus, where the borrower grants a charge over a changing pool of shares, the share certificates of which are left in his custody so as to enable

---

[285] Emphasis in the original, relying on *Dodds* v. *Hill* (1865) 2 H & M 424, 71 ER 528. *Coleman* v. *London County and Westminster Bank Ltd* [1916] 2 Ch. 353, where a lender who had no notice at the time of the advance but who, on acquiring notice at the time of registration, was held unable to defeated a prior equitable interest, was not cited and appears no longer to be good law.

[286] [1925] AC 489, affg. [1924] 2 Ch. 451.   [287] Ibid., at 491–492; and see Lord Buckmaster at 494.

[288] Currently the Insolvency Act 1986, s.323: see Sect. 3(ii) above.

[289] Bills of Sale Act 1878, s.4 (definition of 'chattel').   [290] See, Sect. 2(v) above.

[291] Companies Act 2006, s.860(7)(d) (previously, Companies Act 1985, s.396(1)(b)). For registration of company charges generally, see Ch. 19, Sect. 4(iii) above.

[292] Ibid., s.870(7)(e) (previously, Companies Act 1985, s.396(1)(g)); and note that s.870(7)(c) requires the registration of a charge securing an issue of debentures.

[293] Companies Act 2006, s.860(7)(g) (previously, Companies Act 1985, s.396(1)(f)), which applies regardless of whether the floating charge extends to the whole or only to part of the company's 'property'.

[294] See Sect. 2(iii) above.

him to continue trading with them, the charge is, undoubtedly, a floating charge. This is so even if the charge, granted, for instance, by a stockbroker to a bank, includes a clause under which the bank is given the right to demand the delivery up of the share certificates at will.[295]

[295] For three interesting illustrations see *Re Lin Securities Pte. Ltd* [1988] 2 MLJ 137 (Sup. Ct. Singapore); *City Securities Ltd* [1990] 2 MLJ 257, affd. *sub. nom. Dresdner Bank AG v. Ho Mun-Tuke Don* [1993] 1 SLR 114 (CA, Singapore); *Chase Manhattan Bank NA v. Wong Tui Sun* [1993] 1 SLR 1 (CA, Singapore).

22

Guarantees*

1 Definitions and distinctions

The essential feature of a guarantee is that it is a contract whereby one person (the guarantor or surety) promises to be answerable for a liability of another (the principal debtor) to a third person (the creditor or lender). The guarantor therefore assumes a secondary liability. A guarantee may simply be a personal undertaking by the guarantor, but such promise is often secured by a further charge on property owned by the guarantor. Guarantees are a common form of security taken by lenders from directors (and members of families) of smaller private companies.

In the banking context a guarantee is usually constituted by all three parties (the creditor, guarantor, and principal debtor) all agreeing that the guarantor's liability is secondary. Sometimes, however, the written document on its face may show that there are two joint debtors, but those debtors have agreed either orally or by a separate written instrument that one is to be secondarily liable. Once the creditor has notice or becomes aware of this fact, even if this occurs subsequent to the execution of the guarantee, he will have to treat that party as a guarantor.[1] The consequence is that the guarantor will be discharged by certain types of conduct of the creditor, for example, if the creditor agrees to extend the date for the repayment of the loan without the guarantor's consent or improperly releases a security held for its enforcement.[2] This is a somewhat odd result since the creditor has never specifically agreed to the co-debtor assuming the status of a surety, but it is illustrative of the law's general protective attitude towards guarantors.

A guarantee is distinct from an indemnity, which is an undertaking by 'one party to keep the other party harmless against loss'[3] arising from particular transactions, or events, and is not dependent on the continuing liability and default of the principal debtor. An indemnity is thus in the nature of a primary rather than a secondary obligation. Unlike a guarantee, it is not required to be in writing, or evidenced in writing, and is usually unaffected by the fact that the obligation indemnified is void or enforceable. Additionally, certain types of conduct of the creditor will discharge a guarantor but not an indemnifier.

Despite these distinctions between a guarantee and an indemnity, the categorization is not always an easy one. Clauses in the agreement preserving the liability of the guarantor in the event of the principal debtor's release or permitting the creditor 'to act for all purposes as though the guarantor were a principal debtor' will not in themselves be

---

* This chapter is by Professor John Phillips of King's College London.

[1] *Oakeley* v. *Pasheller* (1836) 4 Cl. & Fin. 207; *Goldfarb* v. *Bartlett* [1920] 1 KB 639. Similarly, if they have originally agreed as joint debtors, but subsequently agree between themselves that one is to be a guarantor: *Rouse* v. *Bradford Banking Co. Ltd* [1894] AC 586.

[2] See below, Sect. 6.   [3] *Yeoman Credit Ltd* v. *Latter* [1961] 1 WLR 828, at 830–831.

sufficient to convert what would otherwise be interpreted as a guarantee into a contract of guarantee.[4] Indeed, even if the agreement contains a separate express promise of indemnity, as well as a promise of guarantee, it may still be construed as a guarantee, especially if there are other clauses in the agreement which are commonly included in a simple guarantee.[5]

Sometimes the term 'guarantee' is used within the banking industry even though it is not a guarantee in the sense of being predicated upon the default of another party. A common form of security is an unconditional performance 'guarantee'—more properly described as a performance bond—given by a bank in favour of a beneficiary to secure the obligations under a contract, often to be performed overseas. Examples include a bond given to an owner to secure the performance of the contractor pursuant to a building contract or given to a vendor of goods to secure payment of the purchase price by the buyer. The usual unconditional performance bond makes it clear that the bank is liable to pay simply upon a demand being made by the beneficiary, as in a bond which states 'the bank unconditionally undertakes and covenants to pay on demand any sum or sums which may from time to time be demanded'. The beneficiary is entitled to demand the sums without proving any default by the other party to the underlying transaction and the bank must pay unless it knows the claim is fraudulent.[6] Unconditional performance bonds are analogous to letters of credit[7] or promissory notes payable on demand.[8] No element of suretyship is involved[9] so that the bank will not be discharged by circumstances (discussed below) which normally discharge a guarantor.

Whether or not a particular instrument is characterized as predicated on default or as an unconditional bond is often a difficult question of construction.[9A] When the document is not issued by a bank there is a presumption against construing the words 'on demand' in themselves as creating an unconditional obligation,[9B] but such presumption does not apply in the banking context.[9C]

Arrangements having similar characteristics to a guarantee may arise in the context of bills of exchange and, in particular, (as discussed in section 8) through the mechanism of acceptance credits.

---

[4] This is the dominant view of the effect of a principal debtor clause: *Heald* v. *O'Connor* [1971] 1 WLR 497; *Clipper Maritime Ltd* v. *Shirlstar Container Transport Ltd* [1987] 1 Lloyd's Rep. 546.

[5] *Stadium Finance Co Ltd* v. *Helm* (1965) 109 SJ 471.

[6] *Edward Owen Engineering Ltd* v. *Barclays Bank International Ltd* [1978] QB 159; *Turkiye Is Bankasi AS* v. *Bank of China* [1996] 2 Lloyd's Rep. 611 and, on appeal, [1998] 1 Lloyd's Rep. 250. For a detailed discussion of performance bonds see J. O'Donovan & J. Phillips, *The Modern Contract of Guarantee* (English edn., London, 2003), ch. 13.

[7] *R.D. Harbottle (Mercantile) Ltd* v. *National Westminster Bank Ltd* [1978] QB 146; *Solo Industries UK Ltd* v. *Canara Bank* [2001] 1 WLR 1800 at 1804.

[8] *Edward Owen Engineering Ltd* v. *Barclays Bank International Ltd* [1978] 1 QB 159 at 170–171.

[9] *Wood Hall Pty Ltd* v. *Pipeline Authority* (1979) 141 CLR 443 at 445; *State Trading Corp of India Ltd* v. *E.D & F. Man (Sugar) Ltd* [1981] Com. LR 235.

[9A] *Marubeni Hong Kong Ltd* v. *Mongolian Government* [2005] 1 WLR 2497; *IIG Capital Llc* v. *Van Der Merwe* [2008] EWCA 542 at para. 8.

[9B] *Marubeni Hong Kong Ltd* v. *Mongolian Government*, ibid.

[9C] In fact, the presumption appears to be the reverse. See *IE Contractors Ltd* v. *Lloyd's Bank plc* [1990] 51 BLR 1.

2 Formation

Unless the contract of guarantee is under seal, the guarantor's promise must be supported by consideration, which is often constituted by the creditor's action in entering into the principal transaction (e.g. by supplying goods to the principal or by the provision of financial accommodation). The guarantee will not be properly constituted, however, if it is stated to be given for a past consideration (such as 'an advance *having been made*') or if the expressed consideration has occurred prior to the execution of the guarantee. Thus, in *Astley Industrial Trust Ltd* v. *Grimston Electric Tools*[10] the guarantee was stated to be in consideration of the creditor entering into a hiring agreement, but the guarantee was executed four days after the hiring agreement was concluded. The approach of the courts, however, has generally been to construe the circumstances as supporting the existence of consideration if this is at all possible.[10A]

The existence of the guarantee will also be dependent on conditions precedent to the operation of the guarantee being satisfied. In particular, a guarantee expressed to be 'joint and several' with other guarantors will not come into operation unless all those nominated execute the agreement.[11]

The language of the undertaking must also be sufficiently promissory. Thus, letters of comfort whereby a parent company indicates that its subsidiaries will be able to pay their debts will usually not amount to enforceable guarantees. In *Kleinwort Benson Ltd* v. *Malaysia Mining Corp Bhd*[12] the Court of Appeal held that a letter of comfort imposed no contractual obligation when the wording of the relevant part of the letter ('it is our policy to ensure that the business of [our subsidiary] is at all times in a position to meet its liabilities to you') was consistent with a statement amounting only to a representation of fact. This interpretation was supported by the fact that the letter of comfort was only entered into after the parent company had refused to assume joint and several liability with the borrower or to give a guarantee.

Guarantees are required to be in writing, or evidenced in writing, pursuant to section 4 of the Statute of Frauds 1677, which imposes this requirement in respect of 'any special promise to answer for the debt default or miscarriage of *another person*'.[13] This wording therefore only encompasses those who are secondarily liable so that (as has been seen) writing is not required when the contract is one of indemnity or where the alleged surety in reality has assumed a primary liability (e.g. if he orders goods and instructs them to be

---

[10] (1965) 109 SJ 149.

[10A] See generally, O'Donovan & Phillips, n.6 above, paras. 2.54–2.83. See also *Pitts* v. *Jones* [2007] EWCA Civ 1301 at paras. 14–18 where the alleged consideration for the guarantee was the signing of documents waiving certain rights at pre-emption. The Court of Appeal held that this constituted good consideration despite the fact that the beneficiary of the guarantee had 'never given any thought to the possibility of refusing to sign the document' [at 17]. Arguably this diminishes (ignores?) the usual requirement that the consideration should be incurred at the promisor's express and implied request.

[11] *National Provincial Bank of England* v. *Brackenbury* (1906) 22 TLR 797; *Evans* v. *Bremridge* (1855) 25 LJ Ch. 102.

[12] [1989] 1 All ER 785.

[13] Note also the requirements of the Consumer Credit Act 1974 s. 105. As to the forms and contents of the required memorandum see G. Andrews & R. Millett, *Law of Guarantees* (5th edn., London, 2008) paras. 3-023–3-028, and as to e-mail communications see *Mehta* v. *J Pereira Fernandes* [2006] 1 WLR at 1543 (typing of name in e-mail may constitute signature for the purposes of s.4, but not the automatic insertion of the e-mail address in the message by the internet service provider). Note the additional requirements of the Consumer Credit Act 1974 (as amended by the Consumer Credit Act 2006), ss.105, 107–109 in relation to the contracts governed by that legislation.

delivered to a third party, and it is clear that he, rather than the third party, is alone to be liable for the price).[14]

The question of whether or not a person agrees 'to answer for the debt . . . of another person' is to be determined as a matter of substance rather than form. In *Actionstrength Ltd v. International Glass Engineering INGLEN SpA*[15] a building employer promised a subcontractor that he 'would ensure that the [sub-contractor] would receive any amount due to it from the [main contractor]. . . . if necessary by re-directing to the [sub-contractor] amounts due by the [employer] to the [main contractor]'. The Court of Appeal held that in substance the employer's undertaking was a guarantee and failed to comply with section 4 of the Statute of Frauds. As the main contractor had not agreed that the money owing to it should be paid directly to the sub-contractor, it could not be said that there had been 'something tantamount' to a novation or assignment of its liability to the employer, thereby imposing a primary liability on the employer to pay the sub-contractor. The main contractor's primary obligation to pay the sub-contractor remained and the employer's undertaking, despite its ambiguity, was in substance a promise to 'answer for the debt . . . of another person' (that is the main contractor) from the employer's own funds.

On appeal to the House of Lords[16] the sub-contractor did not seek to challenge the Court of Appeal's ruling, but argued that the employer was estopped from going back on its promise and relying on the statute. The House of Lords rejected this argument, since the only assurance given by the employer to the sub-contractor was the promise of guarantee itself and, as Lord Hoffmann put it, '[t]o admit an estoppel on these grounds would be to repeal the Statute'.[17]

Nevertheless, it is significant that two of their Lordships pointed to situations where an estoppel might arise preventing a guarantor relying on the statute. Lord Walker considered this might be the case if there was 'some unambiguous representation that there was an enforceable contract or that [the employer] would not take any point on section 4 of the Statute of Frauds,[18] in addition to the bare promise of guarantee. And Lord Clyde thought that an estoppel could have arisen on the facts if there had been 'some additional encouragement, inducement, or assurance' and 'some influence exerted by [the employer] on [the sub-contractor] to lead it to assume that the promise would be honoured'.[19] The possibility of guarantees being enforceable on the basis of estoppel, despite non-compliance with section 4 of the Statute of Frauds, cannot therefore be dismissed.

Aside from issues of estoppels, certain promises, although in form guarantees, will not fall within the ambit of section 4.[19A] In particular, this is so if the object of the promise is not simply to guarantee the liability of another, but rather the promise arises as an incident of a broader agreement having a different object. Thus, in *Sutton & Co v. Grey*[19B] a firm of stockbrockers agreed with the defendant that he would introduce business to them which they would conduct on the stock exchange. If any profit were made it would be shared equally, but the defendant also promised as part of the agreement to be liable for half of any losses made on such business. But the principle is a limited one, being confined to where there is a single larger contract; it is not sufficient if the promise is merely 'linked' to other separate transactions.[19C]

---

[14] *Birkmyr* v. *Darnell* (1704) 1 Salk. 27.   [15] [2002] 1 WLR 566.   [16] [2003] AC 541.
[17] Ibid., at [26].   [18] Ibid., at [51].
[19] Ibid., at [35].
[19A] See generally, Andrews & Millett, n.[13] above, paras. 3–007–3–016.
[19B] [1894] 1 QB 285. See, similarly, *Walker Crips Ltd* v. *Robert Savill* [2007] EWHC 2598.
[19C] See *Pitts* v. *Jones* [2007] EWCA Civ. 1301 esp. at paras. 32–37. Note the emphasis in paras. 36–37 that there must be one larger transaction. This requirement was probably met in *Sutton & Co* v. *Grey* [1894] 1 QB 285. Cf. *Harburg India Rubber Co* v. *Martin* [1902] 1 KB 778 and *Pitts* v. *Jones* itself.

3 Co-extensiveness

As guarantees are secondary obligations the general principle is that the guarantor's liability is co-extensive with that of the principal debtor. As Lord Selbourne said in *Lakeman* v. *Mountstephen* 'until there is a principal debtor there can be no suretyship. Nor can a man guarantee anyone else's debt unless there is a debt of some other person to be guaranteed'.[20] Thus, if the principal contract is void or is voidable (and has been rescinded by the principal) no liability will attach to the guarantor.[21] In some cases, (e.g. minors' contracts and consumer credit transactions) the guarantor's liability is preserved by statute.[22] The guarantor will also be discharged if the principal is released,[23] even if this occurs pursuant to a voluntary arrangement in bankruptcy,[24] or there is a novation of the principal obligation.[25]

The notion of co-extensiveness also means that if the creditor repudiates the principal contract or is in breach of a condition of that contract, and the principal accepts the repudiation or breach as terminating the principal contract, the guarantor is discharged in respect of obligations arising subsequent to the termination.[26] But what is the position if the principal repudiates or is in breach of a condition of the principal contract and the creditor elects to terminate? It might reasonably be supposed that the guarantor remains liable since the reason for the creditor obtaining a guarantee in the first place is to provide security against the contingency of the principal's breach. In *Moschi* v. *Lep Air Services Ltd*,[27] in the context of a guarantee of a debt payable by instalments, it was, however, submitted to the contrary on the basis that, since the principal contract had come to an end by the creditor's acceptance of the principal's breach, the obligation of the principal and, therefore, the guarantor to make any future payments ceased. Although the principal would be liable in damages to the creditor, the guarantor argued that he had 'personally guaranteed the performance by the debtor of the obligation to make the payments' and not any damages payable by the principal. The House of Lords rejected this argument since *prima facie* the nature of the surety's obligation is to undertake to see that the principal carries out his contract, not simply to pay if the principal fails to make a payment. Thus, the guarantor was liable in damages, with the breach of the principal contract by the debtor putting the guarantor in breach of his contract of guarantee.

Whilst this analysis of the general nature of the guarantor's obligation may lack historical foundation,[28] its application in this context usually means that the guarantor remains liable, a result that is both just and commercially sensible. But in some cases

---

[20] (1874) LR 7 HL 17 at 24–25.

[21] *Heald* v. *O'Connor* [1971] 1 WLR 497. As to unenforceable contracts, where the position is less clear, see O'Donovan & Phillips, n.6 above, para. 5.123.

[22] Minors' Contracts Act 1987, s.2; Consumer Credit Act 1974, s.113.

[23] *Cragoe* v. *Jones* (1873) LR 8 Exch. 81.

[24] *Johnson* v. *Davies* [1999] Ch. 117. As to the rights of creditors voting against a company voluntary arrangement which released the guarantors, see *Prudential Assurance Co. Ltd* v. *Luctor Ltd* [2007] EWHC 2002.

[25] *Commercial Bank of Tasmania* v. *Jones* [1893] AC 313. Note that in all these cases the guarantor's liability may be preserved by a clause in the guarantee: see O'Donovan & Phillips, n.6 above, paras. 6.74, 6.101.

[26] *National Westminster Bank plc* v. *Riley* [1986] FLR 213.   [27] [1973] AC 331.

[28] See R. Goode, *Commercial Law* (3rd edn., London, 2004), 814–815.

the guarantor may still be discharged. In *Moschi* v. *Lep Air Services Ltd*[29] the guarantor specifically 'guaranteed the performance' of the principal contract, thus contemplating a liability in damages. As Lord Reid acknowledged,[30] however, if the guarantor only promises to make payments if the principal does not ('in case the debtor is in default of payment, I will forthwith make the payment on behalf of the debtor'), the guarantee will only encompass a liability for the instalments, which have ceased to be payable when the principal contract comes to an end upon termination. The guarantor will therefore be no longer liable for their payment.

4 Vitiating factors

According to usual contractual principles, the guarantee may be vitiated on the grounds of misrepresentation (e.g. as to the transactions embraced by the guarantee, or the principal's financial position), *non est factum*, illegality, a unilateral mistake as to the terms of the guarantee, or common mistake. The essential elements of these doctrines are well known, but there have been some surprising applications of the principles to guarantees.[31] In respect of common mistake, for example, in *Associated Japanese Bank (International) Ltd* v. *Crédit du Nord SA*[32] it was held that a guarantee of the performance of a lease was void for common mistake when the creditor and the co-guarantors both erroneously believed that the goods which were leased existed at the date of the execution of the guarantee. Steyn J was of the view that the 'subject matter of the guarantee...was essentially different from what it was reasonably believed to be' since the creditor and the guarantors (who had an interest in the goods through their contingent right of subrogation) regarded the existence of the goods as of fundamental importance as a security. It is perhaps to be doubted that the mistake here was sufficiently fundamental (since the lease itself was in existence).[33] Certainly it is thought that this would not be the case if the creditor and guarantor have simply made a mistake as to the value of the security.

Undue influence, especially presumptive undue influence, is the most usual ground for setting aside a guarantee. In particular, a wife can avoid a guarantee as against the creditor who knows of her marital status if it has been induced by the undue influence of her husband.[34] As has been seen earlier in this text[35] presumptive undue influence requires not only that there is a relationship of trust and confidence, but also that the transaction is not readily explicable between the parties and calls for an explanation, that is, the transaction must be 'manifestly disadvantageous' to the party seeking to set it aside.

In *Royal Bank of Scotland plc* v. *Etridge*[36] the House of Lords addressed the question of whether or not a wife's guarantee of her husband's bank overdraft, together with a charge on her share of the matrimonial home, was a transaction manifestly to her disadvantage. Lord Nicholls considered that 'in the ordinary case' a guarantee of this nature is not to be

---

[29] [1973] AC 331.   [30] Ibid., at 344–345.

[31] See generally as to the operation of the doctrines, Andrews & Millett, n.13 above, ch. 5, O'Donovan & Phillips, n.6 above, ch. 4.

[32] [1989] 1 WLR 255.

[33] For criticism, see J.W. Carter, 'An Uncommon Mistake' (1991) 3(3) *JCL* 237.

[34] *Royal Bank of Scotland plc* v. *Etridge* [2002] 2 AC 773.   [35] See above, Ch. 5, Sect. 5(ii).

[36] [2002] 2 AC 773.

regarded as a transaction which is explicable only on the basis that it has been procured by the exercise of the undue influence of her husband.[37] His Lordship said that:[38]

> In a narrow sense, such a transaction plainly ('manifestly') is disadvantageous to the wife. She undertakes a serious financial obligation, and in return she personally receives nothing. But that would be to take an unrealistically blinkered view of such a transaction. Unlike the relationship of solicitor and client or medical advisor and patient, in the case of husband and wife there are inherent reasons why such a transaction may well be for her benefit. Ordinarily, the fortunes of husband and wife are bound up together. If the husband's business is the source of the family income, the wife has a lively interest in doing what she can to support the business. A wife's affection and self-interest run hand-in-hand in inclining her to join with her husband in charging the matrimonial home, usually a jointly-owned asset, to obtain the financial facilities needed by the business. The finance may be needed to start a new business, or expand a promising business, or rescue an ailing business.

This is perhaps an uncontroversial analysis, but more difficulty arises in identifying the extraordinary guarantee to which Lord Nicholls alludes. Even though most guarantees have broadly similar standard terms, Lord Hobhouse in *Etridge* considered that no lender who had proper regard to the wife's interests would ask her to sign an unlimited guarantee,[39] so this may indicate the guarantee is manifestly disadvantageous. And in *Dunbar plc* v. *Nadeem*[40] a decisive factor in arriving at the same view was that the guarantee was an 'all monies' guarantee securing the husband's business debts.

Another circumstance where a wife's guarantee may not be 'ordinary' and may constitute a manifestly disadvantageous transaction is where the husband's borrowings are made for a speculative purpose, especially if it is for a commercial enterprise beyond the scope usually undertaken by the family business. An example is *Bank of Scotland* v. *Bennett*[41] in which the husband had a total lack of experience in a speculative venture and the loan had been rejected by a number of other financial institutions. Furthermore, the wife received no salary or dividends and took no part in the management of the company.

If the presumption of undue influence does apply, it will be rebutted if the creditor shows that it was entered into as the result of a free exercise of independent will.[42] The most usual way of doing this is to show that the wife had received independent legal advice before entering into the transaction.[43] Indeed, generally,[44] the creditor can rely upon a certification from a solicitor that the transaction has been explained to the wife. This is so even though the solicitor acts for the lender or the husband, or both, even where the husband is the principal borrower.[45] We place, it seems, great faith in the integrity of our solicitors, even where there is an apparent conflict of interest.

---

[37] Ibid., at 800, para. 30.   [38] Ibid., at 799, para. 28.

[39] Ibid., at 824, para. 112.   [40] [1997] 2 All ER 253 at 265.

[41] See the analysis of facts by the trial judge [1997] 3 FCR 193. The case was eventually decided on different grounds by the House of Lords. See *Royal Bank of Scotland plc* v. *Bennett* [2002] 2 AC 773 at 871–878, paras. 310–351.

[42] *Royal Bank of Scotland plc* v. *Etridge* [2002] AC 773 at 798, para. 20.

[43] Ibid., *Allcard* v. *Skinner* (1887) 36 Ch. D 145 at 190.

[44] Although not in all cases. See in detail O'Donovan & Phillips, n.6 above, paras. 4.199–4.216. See especially *National Westminster Bank plc* v. *Amin* [2002] UKHL 9.

[45] *Royal Bank of Scotland plc* v. *Etridge*, n.42 above, 809–810, paras. 73–74, *per* Lord Nicholls; at 817 para. 96, *per* Lord Clyde, confirming previous Court of Appeal authority.

In addition to the application of normal contractual principles to guarantees, a guarantee may set aside on the basis of the creditor's failure to disclose unusual facts to the guarantor. Lord Nicholls in *Royal Bank of Scotland plc* v. *Etridge*[46] stated the principle in this way:

> stated shortly, a creditor is obliged to disclose to a guarantor any unusual feature of the contract between the creditor and the debtor which makes it materially different in a potentially disadvantageous respect from what the guarantor might naturally expect.

The emphasis here is upon any 'unusual feature of *the contract*' between creditor and debtor, which is in accordance with earlier authority to the effect that the unusual feature must amount to a 'contractual condition or obligation'[47] of the principal obligation.

This limitation means there are few examples, but in *Royal Bank of Scotland* v. *Bennett*[48] the Royal Bank of Scotland increased the borrowing company's overdraft facility, taking as security a guarantee from the wife of the major shareholder of the company as well as a fixed and floating charge over the company's new factory and business. An additional loan was made by another lender supported also by a fixed charge over the factory, and the Royal Bank of Scotland agreed that this charge was to rank ahead of its own fixed and floating charge. It was held that this 'unusual feature' of the overdraft facility should have been disclosed. The guarantor was disadvantaged in a material respect because the ranking agreement reduced the amount of company assets that would be available for payment of the company's debt to the Royal Bank of Scotland, thereby increasing the likelihood that the bank would have recourse to the guarantee. It also diminished the value of the securities to which the guarantor would be entitled to be subrogated on payment of the debt to the bank.

The fact that the usual formulation of the rule of disclosure requires only the disclosure of unusual features amounting to a term of the principal transaction leads to the odd result that other crucial matters relevant to the guarantor's risk (including suspicions by the creditor of the principal's fraudulent conduct)[49] need not. But some recent case law now suggests that the rule of disclosure should extend to matters amounting to 'equitable impropriety'.[50]

5 Interpretation of guarantees

Historically, the judicial approach to the construction of contracts of guarantee has been characterized by inconsistency. A number of different methods of construction have been suggested, but principally the cases have vacillated between two views.[51]

---

[46] [2002] 2 AC 773 at 812, para. 81. See generally O'Donovan & Phillips, n.6 above, paras, 4.06–4.35.

[47] See this expression used in *Levett* v. *Barclays Bank plc* [1995] 2 All ER 615 at 632(j).

[48] One of the appeals decided in *Royal Bank of Scotland plc* v. *Etridge*, n.42 above, 871–878.

[49] *National Provincial Bank of England Ltd* v. *Glanusk* [1913] 3 KB 335.

[50] *Bank of Scotland* v. *Henry Butcher* [2001] 2 All ER (Comm.) 691 at 715, para. 80(7) but the allegation that the creditor knew the borrower was using the account for purposes other than his business was not proved on the facts. (On appeal [2003] 2 All ER (Comm.) 557 this statement was not challenged.) See also *Scales Trading Ltd* v. *Far Eastern Shipping Co Public Ltd* [2001] Lloyd's Rep. Bank 29 (fraudulent collusion between principal and creditor designed to avoid foreign exchange restrictions) and generally O'Donovan & Phillips, n.6 above, para. 4.13.

[51] A third view was that the guarantee should be construed against the guarantor. See *Mayer* v. *Isaac* (1840) 6 M&W 557. See generally, Andrews & Millett, The Law of Guarantees, paras. 4-001–4-003, O'Donovan & Phillips, n.6 above, paras. 5-001–5-007.

First, the courts have often stated that in cases of ambiguity the guarantee should be construed in favour of the guarantor, sometimes referring to it as a 'rule of construction'. For example, in *Eastern Counties Building Society* v. *Russell*,[52] Hilbery J said:

> Rather will the court in case of doubt lean in [the surety's] favour. Neither equity nor law will put a construction on the document which results in imposing on the surety any more than, on the strictest construction of the instrument, he must be said expressly to have undertaken.

Sometimes this rule of construction is expressed in more liberal terms than laid down by Hilbery J, with an emphasis on a 'fair but strict reading of the language of the guarantee'[53] rather than restricting the guarantor's obligation to that which 'on the strictest construction of the instrument, he must be said to have expressly undertaken'.

The second approach treats a guarantee like any other mercantile document or commercial contract, having regard to the surrounding circumstances and the factual matrix.[54] Thus, the guarantee should be given a reasonable business meaning and should not be construed so as to render the guarantee ineffective or illusory. This broader view probably represents the trend of modern authority.[54A]

These two approaches are, of course, not alternatives (since the former only applies in cases of ambiguity) and recent statements of principle articulate both views, but with an emphasis on treating the guarantee as a commercial document. Thus, in *Estates Gazette Ltd* v. *Benjamin Restaurants Ltd*[55] the Court of Appeal put it this way:

> Lastly it was submitted on behalf of the defendants that if there is an ambiguity or doubt upon the meaning of the suretyship covenant I should construe it in favour of the defendants and against the plaintiffs. Certainly it is true that neither equity nor law will put a construction on a contract of guarantee which results in imposing on the surety any greater obligation than that which on the strictest construction of the instrument he must be said expressly to have undertaken: see *Eastern Counties Building Society* v. *Russell* [1947] 1 All ER 500. On the other hand, the words have to be fairly construed in their context and in accordance with their proper meaning without in any way favouring the guarantor, who is not placed in any more favourable position in this regard than any other contracting party. The so-called rule of construction is very much a matter of last resort.

It is not clear, however, why the strict 'so-called rule of construction' should be described as 'a last resort'. A preferable formulation would be to state simply that guarantees are to be construed according to usual contractual principles,[56] but cases of doubt and ambiguity are to be resolved in favour of the guarantor.[57] It is considered that this represents a sensible approach to the interpretation of guarantees. They should be construed as any other commercial documents, but ambiguities which cannot be resolved by reference to

---

[52] [1947] 1 All ER 500 at 503.

[53] *First National Finance Corp. Ltd* v. *Goodman* [1983] BCLC 203 at 213.

[54] *Bacon* v. *Chesney* (1816) 1 Stark. 192. For these principles see Lord Hoffmann in *Investors Compensation Scheme Ltd* v. *West Bromwich Building Society* [1998] 1 All ER 98 at 114–115.

[54A] *Static Contral Components (Europe) Ltd* v. *Egan* [2004] 2 Lloyd's Rep. 429; *Vodaphone Ltd* v. *GNT Holdings (UK) Ltd* [2004] 1 All ER (D) 194; *Tam Wing Chuen* v. *Bank of Credit and Commerce Hong Kong Ltd* [1996] 2 BCLC 69.

[55] [1994] 1 WLR 1528 at 1533, adopting the view of Millett J in *Johnsey Estates Ltd* v. *Webb* [1990] 19 EGLR 80 at 82. See also *Melvin International S.A.* v. *Poseidon Schiffahrt GmBH (The Kalma)* [1999] 2 Lloyd's Rep. 374.

[56] For these principles see Lord Hoffmann in *Investors Compensation Scheme Ltd* v. *West Bromwich Building Society*, n.54 above, at 114–115.

[57] See this approach in *Melvin International S.A.* v. *Poseidon Schiffahrt GmBH (The Kalma)*, n.55 above.

the surrounding circumstances or the factual matrix should be resolved in favour of the guarantor.

Guarantees, however construed, are usually drafted so that they are very wide in scope, often encompassing all moneys owed by the principal to the creditor 'on any account whatsoever'. Such clauses may embrace obligations of the debtor other than those arising from loans made directly to it. Thus, in *Bank of Scotland* v. *Wright*[58] a guarantee which related to 'sums due or to become due to you by your customer...on any account, manner or way whatsoever' was interpreted as including within its scope liabilities which had been incurred in the principal debtor's capacity as a guarantor of a loan made by the creditor to another company in the same group. This conclusion was influenced by the fact that at the date of the execution of the guarantee the guarantor knew it was to be part of an 'interlinked mesh of securities' involving a cross guarantee given by the company whose debt he had guaranteed.[59]

6 Discharge of the guarantor

The guarantor may be discharged by certain types of conduct by the creditor towards the principal. Such is the case if the creditor without the guarantor's consent agrees with the principal to vary the principal contract, unless 'it is evident without inquiry that the alteration is unsubstantial, or that it can otherwise be beneficial to the surety'.[60] It is unlikely that the variation needs to be a variation in the strict contractual sense, but can be constituted by a waiver or estoppel, provided that there is a consensual agreement between creditor and principal.[61] The rationale of the principle is clear: the guarantor should only be responsible for the precise obligations which are guaranteed.

This expansive formulation of the rule, whereby only obviously unsubstantial (or alternatively, beneficial) variations are excluded from its ambit, means that it is not unduly difficult for the guarantor to establish that a particular variation discharges him from liability. In *Crédit Suisse* v. *Borough Council of Allerdale*[62] a variation of a loan facility was agreed, which consolidated previous drawdowns to provide for a common interest period for all drawdowns. Depending upon the subsequent movement of interest rates, this variation might have been beneficial to the borrower, but it might also have resulted in increased liability for interest. The variation had the consequence of discharging the guarantor since it would therefore not have been 'inevitably' beneficial to the guarantor. Similarly, in the context of a guarantee of a lease, a variation involving a change of use of,[63] or modification[64] to the demised premises will discharge the guarantor if there is any 'argument'[65] that the potential burden on the tenant will be increased (e.g. by potentially increasing the rent payable pursuant to a future rent review or by increasing insurance payments).

---

[58] [1990] BCC 663.

[59] See as to other difficulties of construction, Andrews & Millett, n.13 above, ch. 4, O'Donovan & Phillips, n.6 above, ch. 5.

[60] *Holme* v. *Brunskill* (1878) 3 QBD 495 at 505.

[61] *Bank of Baroda* v. *Patel* [1966] 1 Lloyd's Rep. 391 at 396.   [62] [1995] 1 Lloyd's Rep. 315.

[63] *Howard de Walden Estates Ltd* v. *Pasta Place Ltd* [1995] 1 EGLR 79 (variation allowing wine to be served to diners and to use premises as an off-licence).

[64] *West Horndon Industrial Park Ltd* v. *Phoenix Timber Group plc* [1995] 1 EGLR 77.

[65] See this formulation in *Howard de Walden Estates Ltd* v. *Pasta Place Ltd*, n.64 above, at 78.

A special rule applies where the variation involves an extension of time for the performance of the principal's obligations, for example, an agreement permitting a loan to be repaid at a later date. Here any variation, even if it is obviously unsubstantial, will suffice to discharge the guarantor from liability.[66] The rationale upon which the discharge of the guarantee is based is that the giving of time would prejudice the guarantor in circumstances where he chose to pay off the creditor and sue the principal for an indemnity. If the guarantor were prevented from suing until the relevant period of time had expired, the guarantor's position would be altered. If, on the other hand, the law allowed the guarantor to proceed at once against the principal debtor, the agreement to give time would be effectively nullified from the principal's point of view, and a fraud on the principal would result. To avoid these results the guarantor is discharged, a bizarrely favourable outcome from his point of view. As one commentator put it 'the law has shaped its judgments upon the fictitious assumption that a surety, who has probably lain awake nights for fear that payment may some day be demanded, has in truth been smarting under a repressed desire to force an unwelcome payment on a reluctant or capricious creditor'.[67]

The strictness of the rule regarding variation sits uneasily with the position where there is no consensual agreement to vary the principal contract but simply a breach of that contract by the creditor. In these circumstances the dominant view is that the guarantor will not be discharged unless it is a repudiatory breach which is accepted by the principal debtor as terminating the principal contract,[68] or unless the terms of the principal contract have become 'embodied', that is, incorporated, as conditions of the guarantee.[69] The result is inconsistent. The guarantor is discharged by a very minor agreed variation of the principal contract, but not if the creditor is in serious breach of the principal contract, however prejudicial this might be to the guarantor.[70]

The guarantor may also be discharged by the creditor's conduct towards the guarantor himself. Although there is no overarching principle that prejudicial conduct in a general sense will discharge the guarantor,[71] certain categories of specified conduct have been identified by the courts which will do so.[72] Sometimes the creditor may breach a condition of the guarantee, for example, that the creditor must obtain a particular security from the principal. Such a condition may be inferred from the wording of the recital or the statement of consideration, as in *Greer* v. *Kettle*,[73] where the recital stated that the principal had requested an advance 'on the security of', a specified security. A guarantor will also be discharged if the creditor agrees to the release of co-guarantors.

The discharge is absolute where the continued existence of the guarantor is a condition of the guarantee (as in the case of 'joint and several' guarantors)[74] and otherwise to the extent that the right of contribution has been taken away or prejudiced by the release.[75]

---

[66] *Samuell* v. *Howarth* (1817) 3 Mer. 272 at 277–279; *Polak* v. *Everett* (1876) 1 QBD 669 at 673–674.

[67] B.N. Cardogo, 'The Nature of the Judicial Process' (Storrs Lecture 1934) at 153–154.

[68] *National Westminster Bank plc* v. *Riley* [1986] FLR 213.

[69] e.g. *Blest* v. *Brown* (1862) 4 De GF & J 367; 45 GR 1225, discussed in O'Donovan & Phillips, n.6 above, paras. 8.15–8.19.

[70] In *The Mystery of the Mercers of the City of London* v. *New Hampshire Insurance Co* [1992] 2 Lloyd's Rep. 365 at 376 Lord Scott seemed to recognize this inconsistency since he was of the opinion that in the case of a breach of the principal contract by the creditor (whether the breach is repudiatory or otherwise) the guarantor's discharge should depend 'on the importance of the breach in relation to the risk undertaken'.

[71] *Bank of India* v. *Trans Commodity Merchants Ltd & Patel* [1983] 2 Lloyd's Rep. 298 at 302, *per* Goff LJ See also O'Donovan & Phillips, n.6 above, paras. 8.106–8.114.

[72] See, generally, ibid., ch. 8.   [73] [1938] AC 156.

[74] *Smith* v. *Wood* [1929] 1 Ch. 14; *Bolton* v. *Salmon* [1891] 2 Ch. 48; *Ward* v. *National Bank of New Zealand* (1883) 8 App. Cas. 75J at 764.

[75] *Re Wolmershausen* (1890) 62 LT 541.

A creditor who is in possession of the guarantee and materially alters it in a way that is capable of prejudicing the rights of the guarantor will also discharge the guarantor.[76]

As the guarantor is entitled to be subrogated to securities held by the creditor for the enforcement of the principal obligation, the creditor is under an obligation to preserve these securities for the guarantor's benefit. Thus, if the creditor improperly releases or fails to perfect a security (e.g. by registration) the guarantor will be discharged to the extent of the loss.[77] There is, however, no general duty to enforce a security, even though it is shown that the security would have produced greater financial benefits if realized at an earlier point of time.[78] The basis for this view is that the guarantor has a remedy in this situation because he can pay off the principal debt and obtain the benefits of the security by subrogation, despite the fact that the guarantor is hardly likely to adopt such course of action.

Once the creditor does enforce the security, however, the creditor has a duty to take reasonable care to obtain a proper price, that is, the true market value.[79] This duty has been held to apply to the creditor exercising a power of sale as mortgagee[80] and logically it should also apply to a receiver exercising a power of sale appointed by the creditor acting under the powers of a debenture. As to the latter, however, some difficulty has been occasioned by the fact that the basis of the receiver's duty in managing mortgaged property has been said to arise only in respect of those with an interest in the equity of redemption. In *Burgess* v. *Auger*[81] Lightman J was of the view that a guarantor who has made no payment to the bank and has therefore presently acquired no right of subrogation to the security has insufficient standing to complain of the breach of duty. He 'has yet to acquire an interest in the equity of redemption'.[82] With respect, this is erroneous. There is clear authority[83] establishing a general equitable duty towards the guarantor, and it should be sufficient that the guarantor has a contingent entitlement to subrogation on payment of the debt. Indeed, the reasoning of Lightman J would mean that the guarantor could never assert a claim for breach of duty until the whole debt had been paid off since it is only then that the right of subrogation arises. Significantly, in *Cohen* v. *TSB plc*[84] the Court of Appeal, albeit without debate, accepted that a duty to take reasonable care to obtain a proper price is owed to a guarantor by a receiver exercising a power of sale.

Most standard form guarantees contain provisions designed to preserve the liability of the guarantor in circumstances (outlined in this section) which would otherwise lead to his discharge. Such clauses may not always be well drafted, and may have certain inherent limitations,[85] but will otherwise be effective for this purpose and they are probably

[76] *Raiffeisen Central Bank Österreich AG* v. *Crosseas Shipping Ltd* [2000] 1 WLR 1135 (where it was held, however, that the insertion of the name and address of an agent to accept service was not material).

[77] *Wulff* v. *Jay* (1882) LR 7QB 756 (failure to register a bill of sale); *Pledge* v. *Buss* (1860) John 663 (release of mortgage).

[78] *China & South Sea Bank Ltd* v. *Tan* [1990] 1 AC 536. Exceptionally, however, there is the possibility of a court order pursuant to s.91(2) of the Law of Property Act 1925. See *Palk* v. *Mortgage Services Funding plc* [1993] Ch. 330.

[79] *Skipton Building Society* v. *Stott* [2001] QB 261, esp. at 271; *Yorkshire Bank plc* v. *Hall* [1991] 1 All ER 879 at 892.

[80] Ibid.   [81] [1998] 2 BCLC 478.   [82] Ibid., at 483.

[83] Most recently *Skipton Building Society* v. *Stott* [2001] QB 261. See generally O'Donovan & Phillips, n.6 above, paras. 8.49–8.54.

[84] [2002] 2 BCLC 32.

[85] See, for example, *Tridos Bank NV* v. *Dobbs* [2005] 2 Lloyd's Rep. 588 (a clause stating that the guarantor was to remain liable notwithstanding a 'variation' of the principal agreement was not effective where the 'variations' were so extensive as to be in effect a replacement of the original principal agreement).

not subject to the Unfair Contract Terms Act 1977. This view derives from the wording of section 3 of the Act which states:

(3)(1) This section applies as between contracting parties where one of them deals as consumer or on the other's written standard terms of business.

(2) As against that party, the other cannot by reference to any contract term—

    (a) when himself in breach of contract, exclude or restrict any liability of his in respect of the breach; or

    (b) claim to be entitled—

        (i) to render a contractual performance substantially different from that which was reasonably expected of him or

        (ii) in respect of the whole or any part of his contractual obligation, to render no performance at all,

except in so far as (in any of the cases mentioned above in this subsection) the contract term satisfies the requirement of reasonableness.

In the context of guarantees, the guarantor will either be dealing as a consumer or, more commonly, on the other's (i.e. the creditor's) written standard terms of business within the meaning of section 3(1). Yet section 3(2) does not appear to embrace the present type of clause. Section 3(2)(a), translated into the language of guarantor and creditor, means that as against 'that party' (the guarantor) dealing on the other's (the creditor's) written standard terms of business the other (the creditor) cannot when *himself in breach of contract exclude or restrict any liability of his in respect of the breach*. Thus, to come within the ambit of section 3(2)(a) and be subject to the test of reasonableness, the relevant clause must restrict the creditor's liability in respect of the *creditor's* breach of contract. But clauses preventing the guarantor being discharged (e.g. in the event of a variation of the principal contract or a release of a security) by the creditor do not have this effect. They simply preserve the guarantor's liability in circumstances when otherwise under the general law the guarantor would be discharged, so that there is no exclusion of any liability of the creditor in respect of *his* breach of contract. Nor pursuant to section 3(2)(b)(i) is the creditor claiming to be entitled by such clauses 'to render a *contractual performance substantially different from that which was reasonably expected of him*' unless 'contractual performance' is interpreted in a (probably unrealistically) broad sense to include ancillary equitable duties, for example, to preserve and maintain securities for the benefit of the guarantor.[85A]

The impact of the Unfair Terms in Consumer Contracts Regulations 1999 upon clauses in a guarantee preserving the liability of the guarantor in circumstances which would otherwise discharge him is uncertain,[85B] but on one view such clauses in all guarantees made by consumers would be subject to the test of 'unfairness' in regulation 5(1). It has been held that the Regulations do not apply to a guarantee given by a company director.[86A]

[85A] Note, however, that clauses excluding the guarantor's right of set-off or excluding the creditor's liability for loss that he causes to the guarantor may be subject to the Act. See *The Governor & Co of the Bank of Scotland v. Singh* (QBD, unreported 7 June 2005) and O'Donovan & Phillips, n.6 above, para. 4-162.

[85B] See, generally ibid., paras 4.163–4.176. See, generally O'Donovan & Phillips, n.6 above, paras. 4.163–4.176; Andrews & Millett, n.13 above, paras. 3-037–3-038.

[86A] *The Governor of the Bank of Scotland v. Singh*, n.85A above.

7 Rights of the guarantor

The guarantor is entitled to have payments made by him, or the proceeds of any security given by him for the enforcement of the principal obligation, credited in reduction of the principal debt.[86] Sometimes the principal has a claim against the debtor for damages and where this amounts to an equitable set-off the guarantor may plead this as a defence,[87] at least where the principal debtor is joined as a party to the proceedings.[88] This is also the case where the principal has a liquidated claim amounting to a legal set-off[89] which (unlike an equitable set-off) may arise out of a transaction other than the guaranteed obligation.[90] Thus, the creditor may find that his rights against the guarantor are affected by reason of a debt owed by him to the principal which is quite unrelated to the guaranteed obligation.

Prior to satisfying the principal obligation the guarantor also has a right against the principal to bring a *quia timet* action for a declaration that he is entitled to be exonerated by the principal.[91] The court may order that the principal pay the money to the creditor so that the guarantor is discharged from liability.[92] This enables the guarantor to protect his position at an early stage, whilst the principal may still have sufficient assets to discharge his liability. The guarantor does not need to wait until a demand is made upon him before seeking relief,[93] but the principal must be in default and the debt due, so that the creditor is in a position to proceed against the guarantor immediately.[94] As it has been put, 'there must be a cloud that hangs over him'.[95]

Once the guarantor has paid the debt, or in some cases part of it, other rights arise. First, there is an equitable right of contribution from other guarantors of the same debt since they share a common secondary liability.[96] It may be invoked whether or not the guarantors are bound jointly, jointly or severally, or merely severally (by the same or different instruments),[97] or even if the guarantors were unaware of each other's existence. They must, however, share a common liability for the same debt,[98] so that no contribution will arise when A guarantees repayment of the principal's overdraft and B guarantees repayment of a separate advance by the lender to the same principal, or when A (called a

---

[86] Ibid. O'Donovan & Phillips, n.6 above, paras. 6.33–6.35.

[87] *Hyundai Shipbuilding & Heavy Industries Co. Ltd* v. *Pournaras* [1978] 2 Lloyd's Rep. 502 at 508; *BOC Group plc* v. *Centeon LLC* [1999] 1 All ER (Comm.) 53 at 64.

[88] See this limitation in *Cellulose Products* v. *Truda* (1970) 92 WN (NSW) 561. The reasoning in this case was described as 'impressive' by Slade J in *National Westminster Bank plc* v. *Skelton* [1993] 1 WLR 72.

[89] *Hyundai Shipbuilding & Heavy Industries Co. Ltd* v. *Pournaras*, n.88 above, at 508; *BOC Group plc* v. *Centeon LLC*, n.88 above, at 64.

[90] The scope of equitable set-off is somewhat imprecise but the counter-claim at the very least must be 'closely connected' to the transaction giving rise to the claim. See O'Donovan & Phillips, n.6 above, paras. 11.64–11.65.

[91] *Wolmershausen* v. *Gullick* [1893] 2 Ch. 514; *Ascherson* v. *Tredegar Dock Co. Ltd* [1909] 2 Ch. 401.

[92] Ibid.

[93] *Re Anderson-Berry* [1928] Ch. 290; *Papamichael* v. *National Westminster Bank plc* [2002] 1 Lloyd's Rep. Bank. 86.

[94] *Tate* v. *Crewdon* [1938] Ch. 869; *Morrison* v. *Barking Chemicals Co.* [1919] 2 Ch. 235.

[95] *Re Anderson-Berry* [1928] 1 Ch. 209 at 304, *per* Lord Hanworth.

[96] *Dering* v. *Earl of Winchelsea* (1787) 2 B&P 270. See, Andrews & Millett, n.13 above, ch. 12, O'Donovan & Phillips, n.6 above, ch. 12.

[97] *Re Ennis* [1893] 3 Ch. 238.

[98] *Stimpson* v. *Smith* [1999] Ch. 340; *Cooper* v. *Twynam* (1823) 1 T&R 426; *Ellis* v. *Emmanuel* (1876) 1 Ex. D 157 at 162.

'sub-surety') guarantees the obligation of another guarantor of the principal debt, rather than the principal debt itself.[99]

Claims for contribution between co-guarantors in respect of liability for *damage* as opposed to debt are now governed by the Civil Liability Contribution Act 1978. This means that when the creditor's claim against the guarantor is properly framed in damages (e.g. a guarantee of the performance of a building contractor when the contractor becomes liable to the owner because of his defective work) the claim for contribution must be made pursuant to the Act.[100] This has the potential disadvantage that the applicable limitation period is two years. It has been suggested that the claim must also be made under the Act[101] where the drafting of the guarantee is such that the guarantor may have a liability to the creditor in damages as well as debt,[102] even though in the particular circumstances the guarantor's liability to the creditor is in debt.[103] But it is difficult to see that the Act, which does not govern rights of contribution in respect of debt, should apply when the guarantor's liability to the creditor is on that basis.

As to the amount of contribution in equity, the general rule is that all must contribute in equal shares.[104] Yet only solvent guarantors at the time when contribution is sought are liable to contribute, so if there are three guarantors and one is insolvent at the time of the action each of the two solvent sureties are obliged to pay half the debt.[105] The principle of equal contribution can also be displaced by an express or implied agreement[106] or, possibly, by wider equitable considerations.[107]

The guarantor also has a right of indemnity against the principal if it has met and satisfied the principal liability, or part of it, although this is often more theoretical than real since it is the principal's impecuniosity that has resulted in the creditor taking action against the guarantor in the first place. Where the guarantee has been requested by the principal the claim to an indemnity if founded upon an implied contract between guarantor and principal.[108] Such a contract will usually be construed as an undertaking by the principal to indemnify the guarantor if he fails to pay, regardless of whether or not the principal could be compelled to pay.[109] The result is that the indemnity is enforceable even if the liability was not enforceable against the principal, for example, because of a failure to comply with the Statute of Frauds[110] or Money Lenders Acts.[111] In the absence of the guarantor undertaking his liability at the request of the debtor, his right to indemnity will

---

[99] *Craythorne* v. *Swinburne* (1807) 14 Ves. 160; *Re Denton's Estate* [1964] 2 Ch. 178.

[100] *Hampton* v. *Minns* [2002] 1 WLR 1.

[101] C. Mitchell, *The Law of Contribution and Re-imbursement* (Oxford, 2003), para. 4.42.

[102] Many guarantees are drafted in this way. See ibid., para. 4.41.

[103] This would be so where the guarantee is in respect of a debt and the guarantor has undertaken that 'in case the debtor is in default of payment I will forthwith make the payment on behalf of the debtor'.

[104] *Steel* v. *Dixon* (1881) 17 Ch. D 825. Pursuant to the Civil Liability (Contribution) Act 1978, s.2(1) the amount of the contribution is that which may be found by the court to be 'just and equitable' having regard to the extent of the 'person's responsibility for the damage in question'.

[105] *Peter* v. *Rich* (1830) 1 Ch. Cas. 19 at 34; *Lowe* v. *Dixon* (1885) 16 QBD 455. Cf. the former common law rule in *Browne* v. *Lee* (1827) 6 B&C 689.

[106] *Trotter* v. *Franklin* [1991] NZLR 92.

[107] See also *Official Trustee in Bankruptcy* v. *Citibank Ltd* (1995) 38 NSWLR 116, esp. at 127–128 (surety enjoying whole benefit of the guarantee as sole shareholder of borrowing company not allowed to claim contribution).

[108] *Re a Debtor* [1937] Ch. 156.

[109] *Argo Caribbean Group Ltd* v. *Lewis* [1976] 2 Lloyd's Rep. 288 at 295.

[110] *Alexander* v. *Vane* (1836) 1 M&W 511.

[111] *Re Chetwynd's Estate* [1938] Ch. 13. Cf. *Coneys* v. *Morris* [1922] 1 IrR 81, discussed in O'Donovan & Phillips, n.6 above, para. 12.41.

be restitutionary and, at least on one view, will only be available where he has incurred the obligation out of some practical necessity and where it is just and reasonable for him to be reimbursed.[112]

A guarantor who has satisfied the principal obligation in full is entitled to be subrogated to securities held by the creditor for the enforcement of the principal obligation. The rule was originally equitable, but is now encapsulated in section 5 of the Mercantile Law Amendment Act 1856, which states that the surety is entitled to have assigned to him 'every judgment, speciality or other security' held by the creditor in respect of the debt. In essence this gives the guarantor who has satisfied the principal debt the right to become the statutory assignee of the creditor in respect of securities held by the creditor for the enforcement of the principal obligation. They may then be utilized by the guarantor to enforce his right of indemnity against the principal. As regards co-guarantors, however, he cannot take the security, for his exclusive benefit. As all guarantors share a common burden for the principal obligation, the security, and its proceeds, must be shared *pro tanto* between them in accordance with their respective liabilities.[113]

8 Acceptance credits

In some cases a bank may not be prepared to grant its customer an advance or to extend him a loan but may be willing to back his arrangements with another credit provider. One way to achieve this purpose is for the bank to guarantee a loan obtained by the customer from another financial institution. Another method is to provide him with a line of credit or an acceptance credit.

In the letter of facility issued in respect of an acceptance credit, the customer is authorized to draw bills of exchange on the bank for an amount not exceeding a given ceiling at any one time. The bank's signature as acceptor enables the customer, who figures as drawer, to discount the instruments in the commercial bills market.[114] When any bill is due, the discounter, who acquires the bill through a bill broker, presents it for payment to the bank that issued the acceptance credit (the issuing bank). The customer may place the issuing bank in funds for meeting the acceptance, or may require that the bill be 'rolled over'. Under the latter arrangement, the customer draws a fresh bill for the amount required to discharge (*viz.* 'retire') the original bill. In many cases the roll-over is sanctioned by the acceptance credit. Thus, if the ceiling has not been reached at the time the initial instrument is due, the customer is entitled under the facility to draw a new bill. If the ceiling has been reached, or if the acceptance credit has expired, a new arrangement must be made between the customer and the issuing bank.

The bank's remuneration is a fee charged for the granting of the facility plus an acceptance fee for each bill drawn on it. In addition, the customer has to bear in mind that the amount paid to him when the bill is negotiated is its face value less the discount charge. Accordingly, he has to draw a bill for a gross amount that would assure him of obtaining the required net. It further follows that, whenever a roll-over is required, the new instrument is for an amount higher than that of the retired bill.

---

[112] See *Owen v. Tate* [1976] QB 402, discussed and criticized in R. Goff & G. Jones, *The Law of Restitution* (6th edn., Oxford, 2002), 430–432; A. Burrows, *The Law of Restitution* (2nd edn., Oxford, 2002), 280–286.

[113] *Steel v. Dixon* (1881) 17 Ch. D 825.

[114] For an excellent description, see Gillett Bros., The Bill on London, London, 1964.

The effect of an acceptance credit is to enable the customer to raise funds on the issuing bank's credit. In this respect, the arrangement is similar to one in which the customer obtains a loan granted by a financial institution in reliance on the bank's guarantee.[115] But there is a substantive distinction between the two arrangements. Where the bank guarantees a loan granted to its customer, it assumes secondary or ancillary liability.[116] The customer is the main debtor although, on his default, the creditor is usually entitled to enforce the guarantee forthwith.[117] The acceptance credit involves a more sophisticated arrangement. As against its customer, the bank functions as a surety. It has the right to obtain reimbursement from him for any amount paid out on bills drawn under the facility. As against the discounters of the customer's bills, the bank, which figures as an acceptor, assumes primary liability.[118]

One of the main advantages of an acceptance credit is that it leaves the customer considerable freedom as regards the sources from which he obtains each advance when needed. He can discount the bills accepted by the bank with the credit provider who offers the most favourable terms.

For most purposes, the customer's rights and liabilities depend on the terms of the acceptance credit and on the law of bills of exchange. A general discussion of the law of bills of exchange, to be followed by a discussion of the special problems pertaining to bills drawn under acceptance credits, is required.

---

[115] In the United States, acceptance credits issued by banks are valid under the Federal Reserve Act, 12 USC, para. 24, 7th power, as they are not considered to be guarantees. See generally, J.P. Benjamin, *Benjamin's Sale of Goods* (5th edn., London, 1997) para. 23–218.

[116] See, generally, H.G. Beale, *Chitty on Contracts* (28th edn., London, 1999), vol. 2, paras. 44–013 ff.

[117] *Belfast Banking Co.* v. *Santley* (1867) 15 WR 989; but note that a demand by the debtor may be made a condition precedent to the creditor's right to sue the guarantor: *Re Brown, Brown* v. *Brown* [1893] 2 Ch. 300.

[118] Bills of Exchange Act 1882 (BEA), s.54.

Index

Introductory Note

References such as "178–9" indicate (not necessarily continuous) discussion of a topic across a range of pages. Wherever possible in the case of topics with many references, these have either been divided into sub-topics or only the most significant discussions of the topic are listed. Because the entire work is about 'banking', the use of this term (and certain others which occur constantly throughout the book) as an entry point has been minimized. Information will be found under the corresponding detailed topics.